BASEBALL GUIDE

W9-DHN-046

1991 EDITION

Editor/Baseball Guide
DAVE SLOAN

Associate Editor/Baseball Guide
TOM DIENHART

Contributing Editors/Baseball Guide
CRAIG CARTER   JOE HOPPEL
BARRY SIEGEL   MIKE NAHRSTEDT
LARRY WIGGE   STEVE ZESCH

President-Chief Executive Officer
THOMAS G. OSENTON

Director, Specialized Publications
GARY LEVY

Published by

The Sporting News

1212 North Lindbergh Boulevard
P.O. Box 56 — St. Louis, MO 63166

Copyright © 1991
The Sporting News Publishing Company

A Times Mirror
Company

ISBN 0-89204-382-2   ISSN 0078-3838

TABLE OF CONTENTS

For Index to Contents See Page 536

(Index to Minor League Cities on Page 531)

ON THE COVER: Oakland's Bob Welch won 27 games in 1990 to win the American League Cy Young Award and help the Athletics capture their third consecutive A.L. pennant.

—Photo by Rich Pilling

Game Overcomes Early Unrest In an Ironic, Fateful Season

By CLIFFORD KACHLINE

A season that began on a decidedly negative note because of a lockout and subsequently produced many spectacular performances—climaxed by a stunning World Series upset—helped make 1990 a classic study of the unexpected and ironic. Seldom in baseball's long history has a single year witnessed as many unusual twists of fate.

The lockout by major league owners postponed the start of spring training and delayed the opening of the regular season, leaving a sour taste with the public. Still, once play began, the athletes delivered a phenomenal string of record or near-record achievements, including an incredible nine no-hitters, and the fans soon forgot the early inconveniences and unpleasantness and turned out in full force.

The array of no-hit gems, among them Nolan Ryan's sixth, set the tone for a season that yielded many memorable moments. Ryan also reached the coveted 300-victory plateau—only the 20th pitcher ever to do so. Some of the other notable accomplishments were tinged with irony. After a one-year "exile" in Japan, Detroit's Cecil Fielder celebrated his return to the majors by leading both leagues with 51 home runs. The 50-homer mark had been attained only 17 times previously. And Willie McGee captured his second National League batting title even while he was playing in the American League.

The ultimate irony, though, developed during the League Championship Series and World Series. Just a few months after Pete Rose began serving time in prison and George Steinbrenner was banned from bossing the New York Yankees, two men who left the latter's employ the previous winter—Manager Lou Piniella and General Manager Bob Quinn—joined forces to guide Rose's former team, the Cincinnati Reds, to a pennant and four-game World Series sweep over the highly favored Oakland Athletics. In the meantime, the Yankees had closed out the season with the year's second poorest record and their worst mark in 77 years.

A lengthy dispute between the owners and the players' union over terms of a new labor agreement precipitated the lockout. By the time the impasse ended, four weeks of spring drills had been lost. To compensate for the shortened training period, the two sides agreed to move back opening day a full week to Monday, April 9, and to extend the season three days. Many officials and observers felt the abbreviated three-week training session would take its toll, especially on pitchers. Although a few suffered the consequences, most rounded into top form quickly and, as a whole, pitchers more than held their own as evidenced by the nine no-hitters and the fact that six hurlers—a total last exceeded in 1980—attained the 20-victory mark.

The pennant races supplied their customary share of surprises. In the National League, the only two teams that failed to claim a division title in the 1980s—the Cincinnati Reds and Pittsburgh Pirates—emerged victorious in the first campaign of the '90s. Curiously, both had last won in 1979—and each had finished fifth just one year earlier. By contrast, the Oakland A's breezed to their third consecutive American League West crown, and the Boston Red Sox took A. L. East honors for the third time in five years.

Even before the World Series sweep, Piniella's debut season at the Cincinnati helm took several unusual turns. Traditionally the Reds begin the campaign at home, but because of the lockout they had to open on the road. They proceeded to reel off nine straight victories, six on the road, before absorbing their initial defeat. They went on to win 18 of their first 23 games. It marked the best getaway in franchise history and helped the Reds to become the first wire-to-wire leaders in the National League since the advent of the 162-game schedule in 1962.

By June 3, Cincinnati sported a 33-12 record and headed the N.L. West by 10 games. Although the Reds played at less than a .500 clip (58-59) the remainder of the way, they were never seriously threatened. The defending champion San Francisco Giants provided a brief scare when they swept a four-game set from the Reds at Candlestick Park on July 26-29 to climb within 5½ games of first place. The Los Angeles Dodgers were within 3½ games on three days in September. Cincinnati, however, held on to finish with a 91-71 record and a five-game bulge over the runner-up Dodgers as Piniella led the Reds out of the shadow of the 1989 Rose gambling scandal.

In the National League East, the Pirates faced considerably stiffer opposition. Like the Reds, Jim Leyland's crew established itself as a contender early on. Meantime, the favored New York Mets and defending champion Chicago Cubs faltered badly. The Mets began a turnaround shortly after Bud Harrelson succeeded Dave Johnson as manager on May 29. Still, when the Pirates won the opener of a series at Shea Stadium on June 7, New York found itself 9½ games back at 23-27. Sparked by Darryl Strawberry, who launched an 18-game hitting streak, the Mets then beat Pittsburgh three straight and won 15 of their next 17 games, including 11 in a row, to take over first place briefly on June 29.

Pittsburgh regained the top spot the following day, only to relinquish it to the Mets several times later on as the top teams remained closely bunched throughout July and August. Labor Day marked New York's last appearance in first place. The Pirates moved back into the lead the following night and then swept a three-game series from the visiting Mets on September 5-6. One day after Cincinnati clinched the N.L. West, Doug Drabek sewed up division honors for Pittsburgh with a three-hit, 2-0 victory in St. Louis on September 30. With a 95-67 record, the Pirates wound up four lengths ahead of the second-place Mets.

For the third year in a row, the Oakland A's, under the leadership of Tony La Russa, compiled the majors' best record, winning 103 games. This gave them a nine-game edge over their closest rivals, the Chicago White Sox. Pitching superiority proved the A's edge. Oakland hurlers posted a combined 3.18 earned-run average, nearly half a run better than any other A.L. staff. Bob Welch and Dave Stewart accounted for almost half of the club's victories, while relief ace Dennis Eckersley notched 48 saves in 50 opportunities. Welch led the pitchers of both leagues with a 27-6 record, and Stewart went 22-11 to become the first pitcher to notch four consecutive 20-win seasons since Jim Palmer with Baltimore in 1975-78.

Despite Oakland's hefty final margin, the upstart White Sox caused the A's some concern before tailing off slightly in the last two months. A streak of eight straight victories, including a three-game sweep in Oakland, enabled Jeff Torborg's club to move into first place ahead of the A's by percentage points several times during an 11-day period starting June 27. Overall, the White Sox, whose 94 victories were the majors' third highest total, defeated Oakland in eight of 13 meetings and earned the distinction of being the only team to win the season series from the A's.

The tightest and, in many ways, oddest race took place in the American League East. Five of the division's seven teams finished below .500. Meanwhile, Boston and Toronto battled down to the final day of the extended season, October 3, before the Red Sox emerged winners. A Blue Jay triumph that night combined with a Boston loss would have resulted in a first-place deadlock and necessitated a playoff the next afternoon in Toronto. Instead, Mike Boddicker pitched the Red Sox to a 3-1 victory over Chicago at Fenway Park while the Blue Jays were losing in Baltimore, 3-2. The outcome left the Red Sox with an 88-74 record, poorest of the four division leaders, and a two-game margin over Toronto.

The first two months of the campaign found all A.L. East teams except the Yankees closely bunched, but from early June on it was strictly a Boston-Toronto contest. A 10-game winning streak that began with 2-0, 1-0 and 1-0 victories at Toronto on August 24-26 propelled the Red Sox to the biggest lead (6½ games) enjoyed by either team. The spurt ended Labor Day. The following night, seeming disaster struck the Bosox when tendinitis in his pitching shoulder forced ace Roger Clemens to quit during a 6-2 loss to Oakland. In his absence, Manager Joe Morgan was left with a so-called "no-name" pitching staff, and the team's lead quickly evaporated.

While the Red Sox were dropping 12 of 17 decisions, Toronto reeled off a pair of six-game winning streaks and assumed sole possession of first place on September 19. Nine days later, the two rivals, deadlocked at 84-72, began a crucial three-game showdown at Fenway Park. Boston won the Friday night opener, 7-6. Clemens then returned to the mound following a 24-day absence and pitched six shutout innings to earn his 21st victory, 7-5. When Toronto won the Sunday finale, 10-5, the race boiled down to the closing series —Chicago at Boston, Toronto at Baltimore—and eventually to the final night of the season. Ironically, both of the closing series were makeups of opening-week bookings that had to be rescheduled because of the season's delayed start.

The lockout, together with baseball's television contract, also led to major changes in the format of the League Championship Series. The moves were made to accommodate CBS-TV, which was in the first season of a four-year, $1.06 billion deal for video rights. To avoid a conflict with the network's Friday evening programming and weekend football commitments, as well as the Monday night National Football League telecast on ABC, it was agreed to: (1) Begin the National League playoffs on Thursday, October 4—one day after the regular season ended—with a night game to be followed by an afternoon contest the next day; (2) Play the first two American League playoff games on Saturday and Sunday evenings while the N.L. teams took two days off instead of the customary one, and (3) Resume the National League series on Monday afternoon rather than at night.

The pennant-deciding matchups provided sharp contrasts. One developed into a heart-wrenching encounter; the other became a blowout marked by a blowup. Outscoring Boston by 20-4, Oakland breezed to a four-game sweep. The Red Sox's frustration was capped by the ejection of Roger Clemens by umpire Terry Cooney in Game 4. On the other hand, the Cincinnati-Pittsburgh series saw four games decided by a single run and the other two games decided by two and three runs as the Reds prevailed. The brilliance of the Reds' Nasty Boys bullpen trio of Rob Dibble, Randy Myers and Norm Charlton and the poor stickwork of the Pirates' 3-4-5 hitters—Andy Van Slyke, Bobby Bonilla and Barry Bonds—proved to be the difference.

In the American League's championship series, Clemens pitched six shutout innings and owned a 1-0 lead over Dave Stewart before being lifted because of his tender shoulder. Oakland promptly tied the score against reliever Larry Andersen in the seventh inning, added another run in the eighth and exploded for seven in the ninth to win, 9-1. Bob Welch then beat the Red Sox the next evening, 4-1.

When the series resumed in Oakland two days later, the A's made it three straight by winning 4-1 behind Mike Moore and a trio of relievers. Clemens faced off against his nemesis, Stewart, again in Game 4. However, with two out, one runner aboard and Oakland ahead by 1-0 in the second inning, the Red Sox ace became enraged by a ball-four call and unleashed invective at Cooney, who promptly thumbed him out. A dispute lasting nearly 15 minutes ensued. When play resumed, Mike Gallego tagged reliever Tom Bolton for a two-run double, and Stewart breezed to his second victory, 3-1, to complete the sweep.

Pittsburgh drew first blood in the National League's title series. Despite yielding three first-inning runs, Bob Walk pitched the Pirates to a 4-3 victory in the opener. Tom Browning squared accounts when he bested Pirate ace Doug Drabek the next afternoon, 2-1.

Outfielder Billy Hatcher, obtained from the Pirates shortly before the season began, celebrated his return to Three Rivers Stadium by smashing a homer, double and single to lead Cincinnati to a 6-3 victory in the third game. With Chris Sabo driving in three runs on a homer and sacrifice fly, the Reds won again the next night, 5-3. But Drabek kept Pittsburgh's hopes alive by winning the fifth game, 3-2, helped by a sensational game-ending double play. After another day off, the series returned to Cincinnati and the Reds wrapped up the flag with a 2-1 victory. A leaping catch by Glenn Braggs above the right-field wall in the ninth inning deprived Carmelo Martinez of a potential two-run homer and preserved the Cincinnati victory.

In sweeping the American League playoffs, Oakland became the first team in either league to capture three successive pennants since the New York Yankees of 1976-77-78. The sweep also gave the A's a string of 10 postseason victories in a row and 12 in their last 13 games. Amidst glowing conjecture of an Oakland dynasty, the Athletics entered the World Series as prohibitive favorites. Instead, the Cinderella Reds quickly and emphatically shattered the A's dream. In another bizarre twist, it was a pitcher acquired in a trade with Oakland—Jose Rijo—who figured prominently in Cincinnati's victory in the fall classic. To add to the irony, Rijo's father-in-law, Hall of Famer Juan Marichal, was employed by the A's as their Latin-American scouting director.

Rijo worked seven shutout innings before being relieved as the Reds routed the A's, 7-0, in the World Series opener at Riverfront Stadium. Eric Davis set the tone by shelling Stewart for a two-run homer in the first inning, and Hatcher enjoyed a perfect night at bat with two doubles, a single and a walk. Hatcher extended his streak to seven successive hits—a Series record—and 10 consecutive times on base with another pair of doubles, a bunt single, triple and intentional walk as the Reds won Game 2 in 10 innings, 5-4. Oakland relief ace Dennis Eckersley was the victim this time. Taking over in the 10th, he retired the first Cincinnati batter before yielding three successive singles for the winning run.

Two nights later in Oakland, Chris Sabo's bat and glove sparked the Reds to an 8-3 victory in the third game. The Reds' third baseman tagged Mike Moore for a homer in the second inning and connected again with one on to highlight a seven-run third inning. Early in Game 4, it appeared Cincinnati's luck was about to run out. A

Stewart fastball struck Hatcher on the left hand in the first inning, forcing the Reds' center fielder to leave the game an inning later with his Series-record .750 batting average. In the bottom half of the first, Davis suffered a bruised rib and kidney injury while attempting a diving catch of Willie McGee's liner, and he departed at the end of the inning for the hospital. McGee, credited with a double, eventually scored on Carney Lansford's single to give Oakland a 1-0 lead. Rijo held the A's hitless thereafter, and the Reds rallied for two runs off Stewart in the eighth inning to win, 2-1, and wrap up the championship.

The spate of no-hitters ranked with Cincinnati's World Series sweep as the year's biggest surprises. The nine gems established a modern-day record, exceeding the former standard of seven registered in both 1908 and 1917. The total also was only two shy of the all-time high of 11 no-hitters set in 1884, when there were three major leagues in operation.

Six of the no-hit performances consisted of route-going, nine-inning efforts. The season's first was a two-pitcher venture, while one came in an eight-inning losing appearance and another was a rain-shortened six-inning stint. Each of the masterpieces was against a different team. In addition to the nine gems, three other pitchers came within one out of a nine-inning no-hitter.

The parade of no-hitters, coming on the heels of a season that saw no such performance, defied explanation. Batting averages overall were slightly higher than the previous year. The National League composite actually soared 10 points to .256. Even though down two points, the American League enjoyed an even heftier average at .259.

Despite the shortened spring training, the season was only three days old when the first no-hitter was registered. Lefthander Mark Langston, signed by California to a five-year, $16 million free-agent contract, celebrated his debut as an Angel by teaming with Mike Witt to mesmerize his former team, Seattle, in a 1-0 squeaker at Anaheim Stadium on April 11. Langston was lifted after seven innings because he was tiring and Witt wrapped things up with two perfect innings. Langston walked four, including two of the first three batters he faced, and struck out three. Unfortunately, he later turned into a big disappointment for California, posting a 10-17 record and 4.40 ERA.

Lefthander Randy Johnson of Seattle, at 6-foot-10 the tallest pitcher in the majors, uncorked the year's second masterpiece.

He stopped Detroit, 2-0, at the Kingdome on June 2 for the first no-hitter in the Mariners' 14-year history. Ironically, Seattle acquired Johnson as part of a 1989 trade that sent Langston to Montreal.

The most talked-about of the year's no-hitters, of course, was by Nolan Ryan. The remarkable 43-year-old Texas right-hander became the oldest pitcher ever to throw a no-hitter when he turned the trick in a 5-0 victory at Oakland on June 11. It was the sixth of Ryan's career—two more than anyone else in history. By coincidence, his wife Ruth, son Reese and daughter Wendy flew to Oakland to attend the game. Reese, 14, even sat in the dugout with his dad throughout the contest. Ryan, who was making only his second start following a 15-day stretch on the disabled list with his lower back pain, struck out 14 A's and walked only two.

Even before Ryan's gem, the Seattle Mariners announced a "Guaranteed No-Hitter Night" promotion for Saturday, June 16. Jeff Smulyan, the team's new managing general partner, came up with the idea after Johnson threw his hitless effort and rookie Russ Swan tossed seven hitless innings against Detroit one week later before losing his no-hit bid. As coincidence would have it, the Texas Rangers were due to visit the Kingdome that weekend and Ryan, in fact, was slated to pitch that night. The crowd of 37,248 didn't get to witness a no-hitter, but did see Matt Young pitch a three-hitter to beat Ryan, 5-0. In the absence of a no-hitter, the fans were advised their ticket stubs would be good for a future game.

Dave Stewart of Oakland and Fernando Valenzuela of Los Angeles helped write history by unfurling no-hitters on the same night, June 29. Just hours after Stewart treated a crowd of 49,817 in the SkyDome to the first gem ever in Toronto, Valenzuela baffled St. Louis, 6-0, at Dodger Stadium. It was the first time there were no-hitters in both leagues on the same date. Stewart walked the first two Blue Jay batters he faced, then retired 26 in a row before issuing a two-out pass in the ninth as he won, 5-0. He struck out 12. Valenzuela also walked three while fanning seven.

Andy Hawkins of the New York Yankees authored the majors' third no-hitter within 48 hours, only to come up a 4-0 loser in Chicago on July 1. Three Yankee errors ruined his eight-inning performance. With two out in the eighth, the White Sox's Sammy Sosa was safe on a hard one-hopper that third baseman Mike Blowers backhanded, dropped, picked up and then threw to first base too late to nail Sosa. The Comiskey Park scoreboard quickly flashed "H" for hit, but the official scorer ruled the play an error. Hawkins subsequently walked the next two batters, filling the bases. Robin Ventura followed with a deep fly to left field, but the ball glanced off the glove of Jim Leyritz, normally a third baseman, for a two-base error that allowed all three runners to score. Ivan Calderon then hit a fly to right field that Jesse Barfield lost in the sun, and when the ball bounced off his glove for another error, the Sox's fourth run scored.

Eleven days later, Hawkins wound up the loser in another no-hitter. This time it was Melido Perez of the White Sox who achieved the feat during an 8-0 victory at Yankee Stadium on July 12. Rain halted the contest in the top of the seventh inning. Perez's six-inning no-hitter was the first rain-shortened gem since his brother, Pascual, pitched a five-inning no-hitter for Montreal in 1988. Pascual, on the Yankees' disabled list, watched Melido's effort from the New York dugout. The only other brothers ever to pitch no-hitters in the majors were Ken Forsch for Houston in 1979 and Bob Forsch with St. Louis in 1978 and 1983.

Philadelphia's Terry Mulholland faced the minimum 27 batters when he throttled San Francisco without a hit, 6-0, at Veterans Stadium on August 15. Only an error by third baseman Charlie Hayes kept him from a perfect game. Hayes' throwing error allowed Rick Parker to reach base in the seventh inning, but he was subsequently erased on a double play. Oddly, Mulholland, Hayes and Parker all were involved in a 1988 trade that sent Steve Bedrosian from the Phillies to the Giants.

The last of the year's no-hitters took place in Cleveland on September 2. Dave Stieb of Toronto, who had come within one out of a no-hitter on three occasions the previous two seasons, finally achieved the goal in a 3-0 victory over the Indians. He struck out nine and walked four.

The trio who came within one out of a no-hitter in 1990 consisted of Brian Holman of Seattle, Scott Garrelts of San Francisco and Doug Drabek of Pittsburgh. Holman had the most heartbreaking experience. On April 20 in Oakland, he retired 26 batters in a row before his bid for the 15th perfect game in major league history evaporated. Pinch-hitter Ken Phelps ended Holman's hopes by lining a 370-foot drive over the right-field fence, forcing the Mariner hurler to settle for a one-hit, 6-1 victory.

Garrelts' near-miss came during a 4-0 conquest of Cincinnati at Candlestick Park on July 29, and Drabek's came while he breezed to an 11-0 decision in Philadelphia on August 3.

Ryan chalked up his cherished 300th victory in Milwaukee on July 31. The game's all-time strikeout king achieved the milestone on his second attempt. Six nights earlier, a sellout crowd of 41,954, the Rangers' biggest of the season, packed Arlington Stadium to watch him try for No. 300. Unfortunately, the Yankees nailed the Texas ace for seven runs, including three homers, in eight innings. However, the Rangers rallied to knot the score in the ninth and went on to win, 9-7, in 11 innings.

Sensing an opportunity to witness a historic moment, 51,533 fans—the Brewers' best crowd of the year—showed up for Ryan's next start. Included were 15 of his friends and family members and one of the Rangers' general partners, George W. Bush, son of the U.S. President. Ryan proceeded to limit Milwaukee to six hits and one earned run over 7⅔ innings to earn the decision, 11-3. Entering the eighth, he led by a 5-1 score. Two errors by second baseman Julio Franco and a pair of singles accounted for two unearned runs before Brad Arnsberg relieved and preserved the victory—Ryan's sixth straight and No. 11 of the season. The partisan Milwaukee crowd game him a standing ovation both prior to the game and again when he was lifted. Franco later redeemed himself with a grand slam that keyed a six-run ninth inning.

Ryan finished the season with a 13-9 won-lost mark and led American League pitchers in strikeouts with 232. This boosted his career strikeout total to a record 5,308, nearly 1,200 ahead of runner-up Steve Carlton. It was the 14th time in 24 years that Ryan attained the 200-strikeout level and represented the 11th season that he was his league's strikeout king. David Cone of the New York Mets paced National League pitchers with 233 strikeouts.

Each league boasted a trio of 20-game winners. Bob Welch of Oakland, who never won more than 17 games in 12 previous seasons, set the pace with 27 victories, the majors' best total since Carlton won that many for Philadelphia in 1972. Teammate Dave Stewart won 22 games and Roger Clemens of Boston won 21. Doug Drabek of Pittsburgh headed National League pitchers with 22 victories, while Ramon Martinez of Los Angeles and Frank Viola of New York each had 20.

Clemens captured American League ERA honors with a sensational 1.93 mark and tied Stewart for most shutouts with four. Danny Darwin of Houston was the National League ERA leader at 2.21. Bobby Thigpen of the Chicago White Sox established a record for relievers with 57 saves, while John Franco of the Mets topped National League relief pitchers with 33 saves.

The season witnessed almost as many remarkable batting and fielding feats as pitching performances. Cecil Fielder's phenomenal slugging stood out among hitting accomplishments. Signed as a free agent by Detroit following an excellent season in Japan, the 26-year-old former Toronto Blue Jay became the year's biggest surprise with his 51 home runs. He finished 12 ahead of the American League runner-up, Mark McGwire of Oakland. Fielder also paced both leagues in RBIs with 132 and slugging percentage with .592.

For a few weeks in September it appeared Oakland might wind up with a major league first—having the batting champions of both leagues, Rickey Henderson and Willie McGee. As it turned out, McGee emerged with the National League crown while playing for the A's, but Henderson had to settle for second place behind George Brett of Kansas City in the American League batting race.

A serious injury suffered by center fielder Dave Henderson prompted Oakland to swing a trade with St. Louis for McGee on August 30. At the time, McGee trailed Philadelphia's Len Dykstra by five points, .340 to .335, in the battle for the N.L. batting title, and Rickey Henderson, at .323, was six points ahead of his closest A.L. challengers. During the ensuing weeks Dykstra, who had led the N.L. virtually all season, saw his average fade sharply and McGee ended up as N.L. batting champ, with Eddie Murray of Los Angeles finishing second. Meantime, Brett continued his sensational comeback from a dismal start (.256 average entering July) to edge Rickey Henderson, .329 to .325, in the American League. It was the 37-year-old Kansas City star's third batting title and made him the first player to win batting championships in three decades. Brett has won batting crowns in 1976, 1980 and 1990.

Although he missed the batting title, Rickey Henderson topped both leagues in on-base percentage, .439, and runs scored, 119, and paced the A.L. in stolen bases, 65. It marked the 10th time in 11 years that he led the American League in steals. The 65 steals hiked his career total to 936, breaking Ty Cobb's longtime A.L. record and leaving Rickey only two behind Lou Brock's all-time mark.

In the National League, Ryne Sandberg of the Chicago Cubs claimed top honors in home runs, 40; total bases, 344, and runs scored, 116. Dykstra boasted the best on-base percentage, .418. Barry Bonds of Pittsburgh led in slugging percentage, .565, and became the first major leaguer ever to have at least 30 homers, 100 RBIs, 100 runs scored and 50 stolen bases in the same season. Matt Williams' 122 RBIs made him the third different San Francisco Giant in as many years to head that department, while Vince Coleman of St. Louis led the N.L. in stolen bases for the sixth consecutive season with 77.

The year's most remarkable fielding performance was turned in by Cal Ripken Jr. of Baltimore. Appearing in all 161 of his team's games, he committed only three errors and compiled a .996 fielding average—both all-time records for a shortstop. The previous standard for fewest errors by a shortstop playing in at least 150 games was seven by Detroit's Eddie Brinkman in 1972. Ripken also established two other records for the position by playing 95 consecutive games and handling 431 chances without a miscue. Both streaks ended when he bobbled a grounder in the first game of a doubleheader in Kansas City on July 28.

A chronology of some other significant on-field incidents in 1990 follows:

● April 11—Snow wiped out Cleveland's home opener in the bottom of the fourth inning, with the Indians leading the Yankees, 2-1. Snow also forced postponement of the Chicago-at-Milwaukee and Philadelphia-at-Chicago games. Meantime, in the majors' first opening-day doubleheader since 1982, the Braves launched their 25th season in Atlanta by splitting a twi-night bill with San Francisco.

● April 26—Nolan Ryan posted the 12th one-hitter of his career in pitching Texas to a 1-0 victory over the White Sox at Arlington Stadium. Chicago's lone hit was a check-swing bloop by Ron Kittle in the second inning.

● April 27—Pitcher Orel Hershiser, after making only four starts, was lost to the Dodgers for the season when he underwent arthroscopic surgery to repair a damaged rotator cuff.

● April 27—Wally Backman became the first player since 1975 to collect at least six hits in a nine-inning game when he went 6-or-6 to spark a 9-4 Pittsburgh victory at San Diego.

● April 29—Greg Maddux of the Cubs established a record for pitchers with seven putouts, all while covering first base, during a 4-0 victory in Los Angeles.

● May 14—After Montreal pitcher Kevin Gross hit Fernando Valenzuela's first pitch in the third inning for a home run, Valenzuela led off the bottom of the inning with a first-pitch homer off Gross to lead the Dodgers to a 3-2 victory.

● May 18—The two-season errorless streak of Cubs second baseman Ryne Sandberg ended at 123 games—most ever for an infielder other than first basemen—in Chicago's 7-0 victory at Houston.

● May 22—Andre Dawson of the Cubs was walked intentionally a record five times as Cincinnati pitchers doled out a total of seven intentional passes, tying another record, as the Reds dropped a 16-inning, 2-1 decision at Chicago.

● May 26—Rickey Henderson equaled Ty Cobb's 62-year-old American League record of 892 stolen bases when he swiped third base in the fifth inning of a 6-3 victory over Cleveland in Oakland. Three nights later, Henderson added No. 893 during a 2-1 loss to visiting Toronto.

● May 29—For the first time ever, both Chicago teams played home night games on the same date, with 28,925 fans watching the Cubs bow to San Francisco, 6-2, at Wrigley Field while 15,353 saw the White Sox edge the Yankees, 5-4, at Comiskey Park.

● June 4—Ramon Martinez struck out the side in three of the first four innings and fanned 14 of 19 batters through six innings, but he had to settle for 18 strikeouts—one shy of the National League record—when he failed to fan anyone in the ninth inning while pitching Los Angeles to a three-hit, 6-0 victory over Atlanta at Dodger Stadium.

● June 9—Eddie Murray of the Dodgers equaled Mickey Mantle's record for hitting home runs from both sides of the plate in the same game when he did it for the 10th time in an 11-inning, 5-4 victory at San Diego.

● June 12—Cal Ripken Jr., appeared in Baltimore's starting lineup for the 1,308th consecutive game to move past Everett Scott into second place behind Lou Gehrig's 2,130 consecutive games played. (The 29-year-old Oriole shortstop's streak stood at 1,401 consecutive games at season's close.)

● June 19—Gary Carter of San Francisco broke Al Lopez's National League record for most games caught when he worked his 1,862nd contest behind the plate in a 4-3 loss to San Diego.

● June 23—Spike Owen of Montreal saw his streak of consecutive errorless games

at shortstop end at 63, a National League record, during a 6-1 victory over Pittsburgh.

● July 17—Minnesota became the first major league team to turn two triple plays in a game while dropping a 1-0 decision in Boston. Both three-way killings, in the fourth and eighth innings, came on grounders and went from third baseman Gary Gaetti to second baseman Al Newman to first baseman Kent Hrbek.

● July 18—One night after their triple-play feat, the Twins completed six double plays—one short of the record—and the Red Sox turned four for a two-team record of 10 as Boston won again, 5-4.

● July 25—George Brett of Kansas City connected for the cycle for the second time in his career during a 6-1 victory in Toronto.

● July 26—Toronto scored three runs on an apparent inning-ending strikeout and went on to beat Kansas City, 7-5, in the SkyDome. With the bases full and two out in the second inning, Mookie Wilson struck out, but when Royals catcher Mike Macfarlane, after permitting the third-strike pitch to roll a few feet away, threw wildly to first base, all three runners scored.

● August 5—A line shot off the bat of Minnesota's Gary Gaetti struck Seattle pitcher Bill Swift squarely on the forehead in the fourth inning and caromed into the third-base stands at the Kingdome for a ground-rule double. Felled by the drive, Swift lay sprawled for four minutes before walking off the field with assistance and later was found to have suffered only a concussion.

● August 12—Following a rain delay of almost 7½ hours, a Sunday game against Texas that was due to begin at 1:35—but never even started—was finally called off at 9 p.m. by the Chicago White Sox with about 200 fans still in the stands. The game marked the Rangers' last scheduled date in Comiskey Park and was made up later at Texas.

● August 15—Mark McGwire attained the distinction of being the only player to reach the 30-homer mark in each of his first four seasons in the majors when he greeted Boston reliever Rob Murphy with a grand slam in the bottom of the 10th inning to give Oakland a 6-2 victory.

● August 17—Carlton Fisk of the Chicago White Sox broke Johnny Bench's record for home runs by a catcher (328) when he drove a Charlie Hough pitch into the left-field stands in the second inning to spark a 4-2 victory in the second half of a doubleheader at Texas.

● August 19—Homerless in 454 at-bats

with Albuquerque (Pacific Coast), short-stop Jose Offerman celebrated his major league debut by homering off Dennis Martinez as Los Angeles' first batter of the game, but visiting Montreal went on to win, 2-1.

● August 20—Yankees rookie Kevin Maas smashed his 15th home run in his 133rd at-bat—the fastest anyone ever reached the 15-homer mark in the majors—as New York defeated Toronto, 6-5, in 11 innings at Yankee Stadium.

● August 25—Cecil Fielder became the first Detroit Tiger—and only the third player ever—to clear the left-field roof at Tiger Stadium with a fourth-inning shot off Dave Stewart to highlight a 14-4 victory over Oakland.

● August 26—Bo Jackson celebrated his return from the disabled list by walloping a 450-foot homer on the first pitch from Seattle's Randy Johnson to tie the record of four consecutive home runs and lead Kansas City to an 8-2 victory. The Royals' slugger had hit three successive homers at Yankee Stadium on July 17 before a shoulder injury suffered later in that game put him on the DL.

● August 27—Ellis Burks equaled the record of two home runs in an inning when he connected off both Tom Candiotti and Colby Ward in the fourth inning of Boston's 12-4 victory at Cleveland.

● August 27—Thousands of bugs descended on the playing field of Toronto's SkyDome, forcing a 35-minute delay in the fifth inning of the Brewers-Blue Jays game. Stadium engineers drove the bugs away by closing the retractable roof and turning up the air conditioning.

● August 31—Ken Griffey Sr., 40, and Ken Griffey Jr., 20, became the first father-son duo to play together in the majors and each singled and scored in the first inning as Seattle defeated Kansas City, 5-2, at the Kingdome. Ken Sr. had joined the Mariners following his release a few days earlier by Cincinnati.

● September 15—After making just one pitch the night before and gaining an 8-7 victory when Toronto rallied in the bottom of the ninth inning, reliever Willie Blair needed just two pitches to pick up another win over Baltimore, 4-3, when Kelly Gruber delivered a three-run, ninth-inning homer.

● September 25—The Yankees equaled two records by collecting eight successive hits—Roberto Kelly's leadoff homer, six singles and Randy Velarde's three-run homer—and scoring eight times in the first inning before Baltimore pitchers retired a batter in a 15-3 rout at Yankee Stadium.

Despite some negative fan reaction caused by the lockout, the majors enjoyed another banner year at the turnstiles. For the sixth season in succession, the American League set an attendance record with 30,332,260. The National League gate fell short of the circuit's 1989 record, but the 24,491,508 admissions represented the fourth-best total in league history. The combined total of 54,823,768 was less than 350,000 shy of the all-time record set a year earlier.

Led by the Toronto Blue Jays, five American League teams and one in the National established attendance records. The Blue Jays closed out their first full season in the SkyDome by attracting 3,885,284 fans, more than 275,000 better than the previous major league mark set by the Los Angeles Dodgers in 1982. Toronto fans purchased 26,000 season tickets during the winter before management cut off the sale with 9,000 still on the waiting list. The Blue Jays enjoyed sellouts on 67 occasions, including their last 50 home games.

The other clubs that boasted record gates were Oakland, which drew 2,900,217; Boston, with 2,528,986; Pittsburgh, 2,049,908; Texas, 2,057,911, and Seattle, 1,509,727. In addition to Toronto, the Dodgers also reached the three-million count, marking the eighth time they did so. Altogether, 15 teams had attendance exceeding two million. The only team that failed to draw a million fans was Atlanta, which missed for the third successive year, finishing with 980,129.

The Chicago White Sox registered the year's largest attendance increase. Playing in what was billed as their last season in 80-year-old Comiskey Park, the White Sox attracted 2,002,357—a gain of more than 950,000. The team's new stadium, located just across the street from Comiskey, was due to be ready for the start of the '91 season.

The startling improvement shown by Jeff Torborg's White Sox team, together with nostalgia and solid promotion, accounted for the big gate improvement. One innovative promotion occurred July 11. To commemorate the White Sox's last World Series championship of 1917, management decided to stage a re-creation of that season. The players were outfitted with replica uniforms similar to those worn by the 1917 champions, general admission was set at 50 cents and all other tickets were half price. A hand-operated scoreboard was installed and batters were announced by megaphone, popcorn sold for a nickel and an organ grinder and his monkey made the rounds of the park. The occasion attracted a crowd of 40,666.

Even with the Blue Jays' record crowds, the Toronto SkyDome experienced a sizable financial shortfall in its first full year in operation. The facility, owned by a public-private corporation that includes the Ontario and Toronto governments, hosted approximately 170 events during the year, including the 81 Blue Jays home games. Although receipts for the year totaled around $17 million, this was far short of the more than $30 million in interest due on an outstanding loan of $300 million. The SkyDome, opened in June 1989, cost an estimated $572 million to build.

Five teams—four of them in the National League—changed managers during the year. One switch saw a general manager come down from the front office to take charge in the dugout. Another found a manager stepping aside to concentrate on the front-office phase of his dual role. A third ended with the retiring skipper remaining with his team in an executive capacity.

The first two managerial firings involved New York teams. The Mets started it off by dismissing Dave Johnson on May 29 and naming third base coach Buddy Harrelson to succeed him. In Johnson's six previous years at the helm, the Mets averaged 96 victories, compiled the majors' best winning percentage (.593) and won one World Series and two N.L. East titles while finishing second on four occasions. At the time of the change, the team was stumbling along in fourth place with a 20-22 record, six games behind first-place Pittsburgh. After losing four of their first five contests under Harrelson, the Mets had an abrupt turnaround. But they could not sustain the momentum down the stretch and had to settle for another second-place finish.

Eight days after the Mets' change, the Yankees also shuffled managers. Bucky Dent, the majors' youngest pilot at 38, was dumped in favor of Carl (Stump) Merrill. Merrill had been manager of the Yankees' Columbus (International) farm team. Dent himself had been promoted from Columbus the previous August to replace Dallas Green. The June 6 switch came with the Yankees already entrenched in the cellar and having the worst record (18-31) in either league. It marked the 18th managerial change in the 18 seasons that George Steinbrenner served as principal owner of the Yankees. Fired along with Dent were batting coach Champ Summers, third base coach Joe Sparks and bullpen catcher Gary Tuck. They were replaced by Gene Michael, Buck Showalter and Marc Hill.

Russ Nixon of Atlanta was the next manager to lose his job. His third season as the Braves' field boss came to an end June 22 when, with the team in last place with a 25-40 record, he was replaced by General Manager Bobby Cox. Cox had previously managed the Braves in 1978-81 and the Toronto Blue Jays in 1982-85 before returning to Atlanta as general manager. in October 1985. In addition to serving as manager, he continued to handle the general-manager role through the remainder of the season.

Whitey Herzog observed his 10th anniversary as manager of the St. Louis Cardinals on June 9, but less than a month later he resigned, saying he couldn't stomach his team's losing ways.

"I don't think I have done a good job as manager this year," he said upon stepping down July 6. "I just couldn't get the guys to play."

The Cardinals were 33-47 at the time and in last place. Among active managers, only Tom Lasorda of Los Angeles and Sparky Anderson of Detroit had been with the same team longer than Herzog. In his 10-plus seasons in St. Louis, he led the Cardinals to three pennants and one World Series crown. Herzog, under contract through 1992 at an estimated $600,000 annual salary, remained with the team as a vice president and consultant.

While club officials conducted a search for a successor, coach Red Schoendienst assumed the Cardinals' helm on an interim basis and led the team to 13 victories in 24 games. From a list of seven final candidates, General Manager Dal Maxvill announced the appointment on August 1 of ex-teammate Joe Torre as the team's new manager. He formally took over the following night. Torre, who had been working as a California Angels broadcaster, managed the New York Mets from 1977-81 and the Atlanta Braves from 1982-84. During each stint Maxvill served as one of his coaches.

The other managerial change involved the San Diego Padres. Deciding that "two jobs were too much," Jack McKeon gave up his position as skipper on July 11 to concentrate on his role as vice president of baseball operations. Greg Riddoch, a coach with the Padres since 1987, was named the team's manager. The Padres had lost 10 of their last 12 games under McKeon and were in fourth place with a 37-43 ledger when he stepped down. They got off to a rocky 1-11 start under Riddoch, but then played at better than a .500 clip the remainder of the way.

For the second successive year, on-the-field activities were forced to share the headlines much of the season with a lengthy investigation that culminated in severe disciplinary action against another of the sport's most prominent figures. Less than a year after Pete Rose was bounced from baseball by Bart Giamatti, the late commissioner's successor, Francis (Fay) Vincent, found it necessary to mete out equally stiff punishment to George Steinbrenner. The decision effectively terminated Steinbrenner's nearly 18-year tenure as operational head of the Yankees. Ramifications of the episode still were being felt as 1990 came to a close.

A $40,000 payment to an admitted gambler—an offshoot of Steinbrenner's long, troubled relationship with Dave Winfield—proved to be Steinbrenner's downfall. Declaring the Yankee principal owner's relationship with the gambler constituted conduct "not in the best interests of baseball," Vincent permanently banned Steinbrenner from any further involvement in the management or day-to-day operations of the team.

Vincent's verdict represented one of the strongest sanctions ever against a team owner. In the 70-year history of the commissioner's office, the only major league club owner to be officially thrown out of the game was William D. Cox. Kenesaw M. Landis ended Cox's brief stewardship of the Philadelphia Phillies late in 1943 by barring him for life for betting on his team's games. Early in 1953, Ford Frick ordered Fred Saigh of the St. Louis Cardinals to remove himself from active participation in league affairs following his sentencing to a prison term for tax evasion, and a few weeks later Saigh sold the team to Anheuser-Busch, Inc.

Steinbrenner himself was suspended for two years by Bowie Kuhn in November 1974 after pleading guilty to a charge of making illegal contributions to the 1972 presidential campaign of Richard Nixon, but the Yankee owner was reinstated 15 months later. Kuhn also suspended Ted Turner of the Atlanta Braves for a year in December 1976 for tampering with potential free agent Gary Matthews of the San Francisco Giants.

A three-page expose by a New York newspaper provided the public—and the commissioner—with the first insight into the dealings that led to Steinbrenner's eventual downfall. In its March 18 edition, the Daily News published the content of correspondence and audio tapes of telephone calls between the Yankee owner and Howard Spira, a 30-year-old self-professed sports promoter and acknowledged gambler. The newspaper said the material had been made available by Spira, who lived in a Bronx apartment with his parents.

The article described what the Daily News characterized as "the bizarre and tangled relationship of two unlikely soulmates (Steinbrenner and Spira) sharing an obsession of making life miserable for (Dave) Winfield." It revealed that on January 8, 1990, Steinbrenner had paid Spira $40,000, supposedly for damaging information he provided the Yankee owner to use in his bitter 1989 legal attack against Winfield. Spira received the money after signing an agreement promising never to reveal the transaction. The payment was made by two checks for $9,500 and $30,500 drawn on a special account of Gold & Wachtel, a New York City law firm in which William Dowling, an attorney for Steinbrenner and the Yankees, was a partner.

The taped conversations disclosed that in the months following the payment, Spira dogged Steinbrenner and one of his key aides at American Ship Building Co. in Tampa, Philip McNiff, for more money. Spira asked for an additional $110,000 as well as a job in Tampa, which he contended the Yankee owner had promised. In a crucial March 2 conversation, he told Steinbrenner that he was "going to make everything that I've gone through public" unless he received another check.

Contacted the day before the story appeared and asked why he paid Spira in January, Steinbrenner was quoted by the Daily News writer as saying: "I did it absolutely out of the goodness of my heart. No other reason. I said, 'Howard, go and try to start your life over.'" As for the secrecy clause in the agreement, the Yankees boss told the writer that it was inserted by his attorneys and that he didn't care if the payment was publicized. "I have nothing to hide with this guy," he added. During the interview, Steinbrenner also revealed that McNiff, former head of the FBI office in Tampa, had turned the entire matter over to federal authorities because of the alleged extortion threats. Four FBI agents had, in fact, already raided Spira's apartment on March 8. Armed with a search warrant, they seized 11 audio tapes, telephone records and various documents, but the Daily News had 17 key tapes.

Spira's involvement in the complicated scenario dated back to 1981. He became associated with Al Frohman, Winfield's agent who died in 1987, shortly after the Yankees signed the free-agent outfielder to a 10-year, $20 million contract in December 1980. Spira, then 21, soon was working in a non-paying public relations capacity for the David M. Winfield Foundation, which was set up to help children. He also worked for Top Hat, a firm formed by Frohman in February 1981 to secure endorsements and other income-producing ventures. Under an agreement signed by Steinbrenner and Frohman, Top Hat and the Yankees were to share in the income. Spira's association with Winfield and Frohman ended when his relations with the outfielder soured. A $15,000 loan made by Winfield so Spira could pay off gambling debts—and the player's alleged demand for $18,500 in repayment two weeks later—reportedly led to the breakup. In 1986, Spira began dealing with Steinbrenner, supposedly in hopes of getting even with Winfield.

On March 23, a federal grand jury in Tampa returned an eight-count indictment against Spira. It charged him with making "extortionate demands" on Steinbrenner, threatening to release information that could damage the reputations of the Yankee owner and former Yankee employees, and illegally recording conversations with Steinbrenner in furtherance of his extortion scheme. Spira's attorney subsequently won a change of venue, and the case was shifted from Florida to the Southern District of New York. Because of legal maneuverings by both sides, the case still had not gone to trial as the year ended.

Two days after the Daily News expose appeared, Commissioner Vincent swung into action, appointing John M. Dowd to investigate the Steinbrenner-Spira relationship. It was Dowd, a Washington, D.C., attorney, who led the Pete Rose probe a year earlier. He immediately began conducting interviews and compiling a portfolio of tapes, letters and telephone and financial records.

Meantime, spring training had belatedly gotten under way, and Winfield was in the Yankees' camp at Fort Lauderdale. After missing the entire '89 season because of surgery for a herniated disk in his back, he appeared fully recovered as he prepared for the final season under his 10-year contract. The 38-year-old slugger began the season as New York's designated hitter, but following a zero-for-23 slump late in April he was reduced to platoon status by Manager Bucky Dent. On May 11, while the Yankees were in Seattle, General Manager Harding Peterson called Winfield away from the team's early batting practice and informed him that he had been traded to the California Angels for pitcher Mike Witt.

Winfield promptly announced he would not report to the Angels and flew home to New Jersey the next day. As a player with 10 years in the majors, including the last five with the same team, he insisted the 10-and-5 provision of the Basic Agreement precluded his being traded without his consent. The Yankees, on the other hand, pointed out that a clause in the contract Winfield signed in December 1980 stipulated that he would list seven teams each year to which his contract could be assigned without prior written approval. Besides California, the clubs Winfield had named earlier in the year were Kansas City, Oakland, Toronto, Chicago Cubs, Los Angeles and New York Mets.

The deal escalated the Winfield-Steinbrenner feud to new heights. In 1989 they had engaged in a legal battle that started when the outfielder sued his boss and Steinbrenner countersued. Each charged the other with failure to make payments—$450,000 by Steinbrenner, $380,000 by Winfield—to the Winfield Foundation as required in the player's contract. The two parties reached an out-of-court settlement late in the year. While the Yankee owner denied having a hand in the Winfield-Witt trade, saying his "baseball people" arranged it, some writers claimed he had repeatedly tried to trade the outfielder for the last three years. Several even suggested that Steinbrenner had hoped Spira could supply information that could be used to pressure Winfield into consenting to a deal.

Witt joined the Yankees the day after the swap was announced, but Winfield remained a player without a team for several days. In what was termed an "air-clearing" meeting, he talked with Steinbrenner for two hours on May 14. During the confab, the Yankee owner assured Winfield that he would be a full-time player with the Yankees if an arbitrator disallowed the trade. However, one day later Vincent declared the transaction completed when the Yankees gave the outfielder a check for $100,000, the sum of three bonus stipulations contained in his contract.

A grievance filed by the Players Association still had to be heard, however, and arbitrator George Nicolau scheduled a hearing for May 16. Representatives of Winfield, the Yankees, the players' union and management attended. Instead of an arbitration proceeding, the lengthy session saw the participants attempt to work out a negotiated settlement. Late in the day the issue was resolved when Winfield agreed to report to the Angels in return for a sweetened contract. Besides giving him a $100,000 signing bonus, the Angels extended his contract through '91 with options for 1992-93. The pact calls for a 1991 salary of $3.2 million.

Unfortunately, the ordeal still wasn't quite over. On May 18 the Angels revealed they were preparing to file a complaint with the commissioner seeking $2 million in damages from the Yankees. They charged Steinbrenner's meeting with Winfield earlier in the week damaged their bargaining position and represented "tampering in its grandest form." The Yankee owner's actions, California General Manager Mike Port contended, helped Winfield get more money from the Angels.

While Dowd was pursuing his investigation of the Steinbrenner-Spira relationship, he quietly interviewed witnesses as far away as Florida and Texas. After devoting 2½ months to the assignment, he delivered his report to Vincent on June 7. The commissioner steadfastly declined to reveal any contents of the Dowd report, but separate investigations by the media produced some interesting revelations. They included: (1) Telephone records showed Spira made nearly 500 calls, some approaching an hour in length, to Steinbrenner and McNiff from late 1986 through early 1990; (2) Spira flew to Florida at Steinbrenner's expense to meet at least once with the Yankee owner and on two other occasions with McNiff; (3) Steinbrenner told the New York Post that he paid Spira in hopes he would not release damaging information about two former Yankee employees—David Weidler and Pat Kelly—who were fired a few years earlier; (4) In seeking to damage Winfield's reputation, the Yankee owner may have played a behind-the-scenes role in assisting Sandra Renfro of Houston in her divorce suit against Winfield; (5) Under orders from Steinbrenner, Pat Kelly, who was the Yankees' director of stadium operations until 1987, and his successor, Bill Squires, reportedly checked the visitors' clubhouse late at night after games to see if the opponents' bats had been doctored with cork or other materials.

In anticipation of the upcoming hearings, both the commissioner and Steinbrenner engaged additional legal counsel. Vincent retained former Federal Judge Harold R. Tyler Jr., one of the country's most respected legal minds. The Yankee boss increased his legal staff by retaining two criminal lawyers, Stephen E. Kaufman and Dominick F. Amorosa, both former assistant U.S. attorneys. Kaufman was designed as Steinbrenner's lead coun-

sel, and Robert Gold of New York and Robert Banker of Tampa continued as co-counsel. Paul Curran, another former U.S. attorney, also served on the Yankee owner's legal team.

Vincent opened the Steinbrenner hearing on July 5. By coincidence, the previous day marked the Yankee principal owner's 60th birthday. The hearing took place in the offices of Judge Tyler in the Rockefeller Center building in midtown Manhattan. Ironically, Spira was arraigned in U.S. District Court in downtown Manhattan that very same morning. He pleaded innocent to the eight-count indictment of March 23 that charged him with attempting to extort $150,000 from Steinbrenner.

Even as the Steinbrenner hearing was proceeding, the commissioner's office distributed a release that disclosed Vincent had assessed the Yankees $225,000 for tampering in the Winfield trade. In addition to being fined $25,000, the club was ordered to pay the Angels $200,000 in compensation for the tampering. "Mr. Steinbrenner's statement that Mr. Winfield would be welcomed back to the Yankees if he won the arbitration and should play on a full-time basis was clearly improper," Vincent declared in the release. It marked the fifth time the Yankees had been fined by a commissioner for imprudent actions by Steinbrenner.

Three days before the hearing began, Steinbrenner's attorneys submitted to Vincent a list of 48 possible witnesses, starting with the Yankee owner himself. Others named included Dowd, Spira, Winfield, former commissioner Peter Ueberroth, Ed Durso (former executive vice president of the commissioner's office) and Kevin Hallinan, director of security for baseball.

Steinbrenner was the only witness to be heard, however. With his lawyers in attendance, he spent seven hours on July 5 providing explanations to questions raised by Vincent about issues detailed in the Dowd report. He returned the following morning and testified for an additional two hours. At the conclusion of the second session, Vincent gave the Yankee owner 10 days to submit any additional evidence or affidavits he wanted considered. Neither the commissioner nor Steinbrenner and his counsel would tell the media what was discussed during the nine hours of testimony.

In responding to queries by the media, Vincent said: "I do not wish to cross-examine other witnesses. The central witness, the person who knows the facts in the case the best, is Mr. Steinbrenner...His testimony is the essential testimony. . . and his cooperation was complete." He added that he would be studying the case and discussing it further with Judge Tyler, Dowd and Stephen Greenberg, deputy commissioner. When one writer asked whether the sport's image had been damaged during the unpleasant week, which also saw the two league presidents suspend nine players and a manager for brawls on the field, Vincent replied: "No. The thing the American public loves is the game on the field. This is not baseball; this is the business of baseball. We should never confuse the two."

While Vincent was pondering the case, the July 18 edition of the sports newspaper The National created a stir. It published excerpts of some testimony from a hearing transcript that it had somehow obtained. In the aftermath of one exchange, the paper revealed, Steinbrenner linked Lou Piniella with gambling. Upon learning of The National's disclosures, the commissioner's office promptly issued a statement in which Vincent cleared Piniella and said the Cincinnati manager was not under investigation. "I am satisfied that Lou Piniella did not engage in any activity warranting further attention from this office," the Vincent statement said. "I regret that public disclosure of this testimony has unfairly insinuated Mr. Piniella into this affair."

The transcript also quoted Steinbrenner as saying he felt his payment to Spira was "in the best interests of baseball" because it was intended to keep Spira from revealing details about Piniella's alleged sports betting habits and about two former Yankee executives—Weidler and Kelly—who were fired for allegedly stealing such giveaway items as helmets, bats and yearbooks. When Weidler, former club treasurer, heard about the comments, he responded: "I was a loyal employee of Mr. Steinbrenner for 18 years, and I am deeply hurt that he has used me as a scapegoat to exonerate himself."

The soap opera continued with Steinbrenner getting back in the act July 19. In a meeting with the media in his Park Avenue hotel suite, he denied he had leaked a 372-page transcript of the hearing. "The commissioner says our people did. No way did we release it," he insisted. He said he "never implicated Lou Piniella as a gambler, other than a guy betting on horses at the track, like I do and like a lot of other fine people do."

A bid by Steinbrenner's lawyers to call Ueberroth, Winfield and others as witnesses was rebuffed on July 20, when Vincent denied their request. He did agree, however, to grant the Yankee owner's legal team a few more days to submit "statements of affidavits of fact." Earlier in the week, with Vincent's approval, Steinbrenner and seven of his lawyers spent nearly four hours taking a deposition from Hallinan, presumably in an attempt to establish that the Yankee boss had informed the game's security director and Ueberroth of his contact with Spira.

Steinbrenner's fate was finally settled on Monday, July 30. Accompanied by his chief legal counsel, Kaufman, and another lawyer, the Yankee owner arrived at the commissioner's office at 9:15 a.m. to hear Vincent's decision. Sitting in with Vincent were deputy commissioner Greenberg, Dowd and Judge Tyler. The two sides spent approximately 11 hours discussing and finalizing the matter. Vincent then adjourned to the Helmsley Palace Hotel for a news conference at which his verdict was publicly announced.

In a three-page "Statement from the Commissioner" that was distributed to the media, Vincent said "Mr. Steinbrenner has accepted. . .my decision" and "has agreed to resign on or before August 20, 1990, as the general partner of the New York Yankees" and after that date "will have no further involvement in the management. . .or in the day-to-day operations of that club."

"For all purposes," the commissioner's statement further noted, "Mr. Steinbrenner agrees that he is to be treated as if he had been placed on the permanently ineligible list, subject to the following exceptions: (1) With my approval, he may consult upon and participate in major financial and business decisions of the New York Yankees solely in his capacity as a limited partner. (2) Commencing in this spring 1991, he may seek my approval in writing to attend a limited number of games in the major leagues on such terms and conditions as I may impose."

Other stipulations set forth in the commissioner's ruling included: (1) A new general partner was to be appointed pursuant to the Yankees' Partnership Agreement on or before August 20, 1990, with the designee being subject to approval of the commissioner and the other clubs in accordance with standard practice; (2) All officers of the Yankees and any member of Steinbrenner's family who may become involved in the club's operation "will be bound by the terms of the supplemental order governing conduct of New York Yankees officials and restricting the involvement of Mr. Steinbrenner," and (3) Violation of the agreement or of the supplemental order "may result in additional discipline up to and including permanent ineligibility."

The document also emphasized that "By accepting these sanctions, Mr. Steinbrenner has agreed he will not litigate or challenge the decision or these sanctions and that he will not institute litigation as a result of any decision I might make arising out of this agreement or these sanctions."

In a separate 11-page "Summary of Decision," Vincent explained he concluded Steinbrenner's $40,000 payment to Spira and his undisclosed working relationship with him "constitute conduct that is not in the best interests of Baseball" and a violation of Major League Rule 21(f). "The interests of Baseball," he noted, "are not served by permitting an owner to deal with an admitted gambler." The commissioner also pointed out that while Steinbrenner "now claims he was extorted and feared possible violence directed against him and his family, neither of his two principal advisers, (Philip) McNiff and William Dowling, testified there was extortion involved in the payment. McNiff is a former FBI agent. . .and Dowling is a former prosecutor. Presumably they know extortion when they see it." Vincent further stressed that in the Yankee owner's two days of testimony he was "able to discern an attempt to force explanations in hindsight onto discomforting facts. . .(and) to evaluate a pattern of behavior that borders on the bizarre." Despite what he termed "serious instances of misconduct," the commissioner said he did "not find the misconduct enough to warrant permanent explusion from Baseball."

Word of Vincent's verdict quickly reached Yankee Stadium, where the Yankees were playing Detroit, and the crowd of 24,037 greeted the news with a 90-second standing ovation.

Queried at the news conference about his decision, the commissioner explained: "There were alternatives, and this was an alternative I was willing to accept." The comment aroused media interest, and a followup story by Murray Chass in the August 1 edition of the New York Times revealed that Vincent originally intended to hand Steinbrenner a two-year suspension plus three years on probation. According to Chass, his sources indicated that when the Yankee owner asked about an alternative penalty during the July 30 meeting in the commissioner's office, Vincent proposed the permanent ban on his involvement in the team's management, and Steinbrenner chose the alternative. The assumption was, Chass wrote, that by avoiding the label of "suspended" Steinbrenner might be able to retain his coveted position of vice president of the U.S. Olympic Committee. Nevertheless, at the USOC meeting in Colorado Springs three weeks later, the organization's executive committee requested Steinbrenner to accept an inactive role for an indefinite period.

To address various other complexities, some posed by the Yankees' partnership setup, Vincent issued two additional documents on July 31. One titled "Agreement and Resolution" spelled out the following sanctions to which he said Steinbrenner agreed: (1) Prior to August 20, 1991, Steinbrenner will reduce his ownership in the Yankees from 55 percent to less than 50 percent; (2) The commissioner will approve the appointment of either of Steinbrenner's sons as general partner; (3) Steinbrenner shall not visit the clubhouse, offices, owner's box or press box at Yankee Stadium or the Yankees' spring-training facility, or any other area not generally open to the public at either location, without prior approval of the commissioner, or the clubhouse, offices or press box of any other major league club; (4) With advance approval of the commissioner, Steinbrenner can participate in such "material and extraordinary financial and business affairs" of the Yankees as television and radio contracts, concessions agreements, lease agreements and banking relationships.

In the document headed "Supplemental Order," Vincent decreed that, except as provided in the "Agreement and Resolution," no Yankee official or employee would be permitted to confer, consult, advise or communicate with Steinbrenner. Every six months a Yankee executive must certify in writing to the American League president that no such communications occurred or, if they did, disclose all details. In addition, for the next five years the Yankees may not hire, fire, promote, demote or reassign any officer of the club without prior approval of the league president.

Steinbrenner's original choice to succeed him as general partner of the Yankees was his eldest son, Hank, 33. Although he had never held an official position with the club, Hank worked in various capacities with the team in 1986. When he expressed a preference to continue running the family's Kinsman Stud Farm, a horse-breeding operation in Ocala, Fla., his father proposed naming Leonard Kleinman as general partner. Kleinman had joined the Yankees the previous winter as executive vice president and CEO. Vincent nixed the plan because of a pending hearing into Kleinman's involvement in the Spira affair.

At a meeting in Cleveland on August 15, Steinbrenner and his 18 limited partners elected Robert Nederlander as the Yankees' new general partner. Nederlander, 57, was president of the Nederlander Organization, a wide-reaching entertainment enterprise that owns 30 theaters and produces Broadway shows. He and his four older brothers all were original limited partners when Steinbrenner bought the team, although two of the brothers had since sold their interests in the team.

Under partnership law, one or more partners can be designated as general partners with the right to manage the group's assets. The limited partners share in the profits but do not make management decisions. Steinbrenner owned 55 percent of the Yankees. The Crown family—Lester and sons Daniel and James, industrialists from Chicago—owned between 10 and 12 percent. The holdings of the 15 other limited partners, who included the three Nederlander brothers and Steinbrenner's wife Joan, ranged from 0.5 percent to 6 percent. Vincent's ruling did not require Steinbrenner to sell any of his interest, but merely to reduce it below 50 percent and to become a limited partner. The Yankee owner's plan to give some of his stock to a family member, possibly his wife, who already owned 5 percent, was approved by the commissioner.

The day following Nederlander's election, two of the Yankees' minority owners—Daniel McCarthy and Harold Bowman, both of Cleveland—filed a lawsuit in federal court on behalf of all of the limited partners. It sought a temporary restraining order that would keep Steinbrenner in control. The suit termed the commissioner's investigation an "inquisition." At the same time, Steinbrenner's lawyers called for "a complete and thorough investigation of the commissioner's actions" and asked major league club owners to appoint an independent counsel to carry out the investigation of the commissioner.

Although the federal courts traditionally have upheld the broad powers of the commissioner, the suit touched off a flurry of activity. The commissioner's office sent letters to the other limited partners asking whether they were joining in the court challenge. They disavowed any involvement in the McCarthy-Bowman action, as did Steinbrenner himself. In a separate letter to the Yankee owner's chief counsel, deputy commissioner Greenberg warned: "Mr. Steinbrenner's failure to vigorously

oppose this lawsuit would raise serious questions as to (his) role in the initiation of this litigation. I hardly need remind you or Mr. Steinbrenner that his active or behind-the-scenes support of this (or any other) lawsuit against the commissioner would subject Mr. Steinbrenner to further disciplinary action, up to and including permanent placement on the ineligible list."

Steinbrenner's last day as head of the Yankees, August 20, went quietly even while producing several significant developments. In Cleveland, U.S. District Court Judge Alice M. Batchelder ruled against the McCarthy-Bowman suit. At Yankee Stadium the atmosphere resembled a reunion. Charging themselves and associates $20 apiece, Yankee employees put on a tribute luncheon of chateaubriand and fresh salmon for Steinbrenner at the Stadium Club and presented him with a plaque enscribed with a poem written by former commissioner Bart Giamatti.

Before and after the luncheon, it was business as usual for Steinbrenner as he completed the restructuring of the club's personnel. A few days earlier, he had announced that—pending the approval of Nederlander as general partner by the other major league owners—Jack Lawn would serve as the executive in charge of operating the club. Lawn, a former official of the Drug Enforcement Administration, had joined the Yankees in March as vice president and chief of operations shortly after concluding his 27-year government career. On August 19, Steinbrenner notified Stump Merrill that his contract as manager was being extended two years through 1992. And on the final day of his reign, the Yankee owner shuffled front-office personnel again. He signed Gene Michael to a three-year contract as vice president and general manager, demoted Harding Peterson from G.M. to special adviser and had George Bradley move from the club's minor league complex in Tampa to Yankee Stadium with the revised title of vice president of baseball operations. At 7 p.m., shortly before that night's Yankee-Toronto game was to begin, Steinbrenner departed Yankee Stadium after having forwarded his letter of resignation to the commissioner's office. In a final touch of irony, Toronto's starting pitcher that evening was Todd Stottlemyre, whose dad, Mel Sr., started on the mound for the Yankees in their first league game under Steinbrenner's ownership in 1973.

The fallout from the Steinbrenner-Spira dealings subsequently took several additional turns. Leonard Kleinman filed a $22 million suit in U.S. District Court in Manhattan on September 4, charging the commissioner with trying to run him out of baseball. Following a two-hour hearing, Judge Leonard B. Sand rejected the Yankee executive's request for a temporary restraining order. This paved the way for Vincent to hold his hearing into Kleinman's possible involvement in the Steinbrenner-Spira incident. Although a nine-page decision signed November 15 by Vincent cleared him of any wrongdoing, Kleinman said he intended to continue his suit.

Early in September two of the Yankees' minority owners—Jack Satter of Boston and Harvey Leighton of Cleveland—arranged for a Manhattan investment bank to seek buyers for their interests in the club. The pair, who became limited partners when Steinbrenner bought the team in 1973 for $10.2 million, owned a combined 9.6 percent and reportedly decided to sell for economic reasons. Although the investment bank's president declined to reveal the asking price, he said some analysts estimated the Yankees were worth between $300 million and $400 million.

In another development, it was disclosed that Steinbrenner twice requested permission to become involved in the Yankees' postseason negotiations with free agents and that Commissioner Vincent turned him down both times.

Like Steinbrenner, Pete Rose found the year to be a trying one. Less than 11 months after being permanently barred from baseball by Bart Giamatti, the game's all-time hits leader was sentenced to prison for cheating on his federal income-tax returns.

Rose's latest troubles stemmed from a federal investigation into his income from sources other than as a player or manager. His potential tax problems began to surface shortly after Giamatti hired John Dowd early in 1989 to look into reports of gambling activities by Cincinnati's then-manager. Faced with the prospect of an indictment by a federal grand jury, Rose and his lawyers signed a plea agreement with law enforcement officials on April 16 that ended the nearly year-long Internal Revenue Service investigation. Four days later, flanked by attorneys Robert Pitcairn Jr., and Roger Makley, Rose appeared before U.S. District Judge S. Arthur Spiegel in Cincinnati and pleaded guilty to two felony counts of filing false tax returns for the four-year period of 1984-87. By pleading guilty, he avoided the possibility of facing the more serious charge of tax evasion.

In addition, the agreement provided that the government would not press further tax charges. Each felony count carried a maximum penalty of three years in prison and a $250,000 fine.

A bill of information filed with the court revealed that Rose reported taxable income of $4,660,368 for the years 1984 through 1987 and paid taxes totaling $2,027,417.20. However, it also stated that Rose admitted he knew those figures were not correct.

The document, which Rose and his attorneys signed as part of the plea agreement, detailed the charges filed by U.S. Attorney D. Michael Crites. Noting that Rose was a "chronic gambler during the years 1984 through 1988, betting substantial amounts of money at horse and dog racetracks, as well as with illegal bookmakers," the document stated that Rose—without the knowledge of his advisers—began selling memorabilia and taking fees from card-show appearances to cover his gambling losses. On 10 occasions during the period 1984-87, according to the report, he entered into partnerships with other persons on Pik-Six horse track bets that produced winnings of $136,945.30, topped by $59,788 in 1984. Nevertheless, his gambling losses for the four years exceeded his winnings.

When his advisers learned in 1987 about the extra income from memorabilia and appearances, they filed amended tax returns, the court document disclosed. Despite the amendments, the IRS investigation showed that Rose's income exceeded the revised amounts by $51,800 in 1984, $95,168 in 1985, $30,659 in 1986 and $171,552.60 in 1987. Because of the shortfall, Rose was required to pay $366,042.86 to the IRS, including $169,342.97 in back taxes, $66,984.64 in interest and $129,715.25 in penalties.

Following the half-hour hearing, Judge Spiegel allowed Rose to go free on his own recognizance pending the customary pre-sentence investigation, which usually takes four to six weeks. Federal guidelines require a confidential pre-sentencing report detailing the defendant's criminal history, education, employment history and other facts. Once probation officers complete the report, both sides have 10 days to present objections to any factual statements in the report.

Prior to the April court appearance, Rose kept himself occupied with autograph sessions, golf tournaments, speaking engagements and a sports show on a Cincinnati radio station. For a talk on baseball at the University of Florida at Gainesville in February, his fee reportedly was $11,000. However, his hopes of taking part in the Phillies' 10th anniversary reunion of their 1980 World Series champions, set for August 3-4, were dashed early in the year when Commissioner Vincent rejected the idea. After Rose pleaded guilty to the tax charges, several charities dropped plans to use him in publicizing their causes, but Barbara Pinska, his publicist, said he still had a number of autograph appearances—he received $17 a pop for his signature—and charity golf events scheduled. He also continued to do his radio sports show.

Upon receipt July 2 of the pre-sentencing report, Judge Spiegel set July 19 as the date for sentencing Rose. By coincidence, it was Judge Spiegel who earlier sent two of Rose's former associates to prison. In 1989, he handed Ron Peters, Rose's onetime bookie, concurrent two-year sentences for tax evasion and cocaine possession, and on February 1, 1990, he ordered Tommy Gioiosa, once a close friend and housemate of Rose, to prison for five years for transporting cocaine and conspiring to hide some of Rose's racetrack winnings from the IRS.

Rose, 49, was known for his confident, cocky demeanor as a player, but he displayed a noticeably subdued mood as he entered U.S. District Court just three blocks from the Cincinnati street that bears his name. His wife Carol and his lawyers accompanied him into the filled-to-capacity courtroom. Given an opportunity to speak before the sentence was pronounced, Rose addressed Judge Spiegel: "Your Honor, I would like to say that I am very sorry. I am shameful to be here today in front of you. . .I hope no one has to go through what I went through the last year and a half. I lost my dignity. I lost my self-respect." Visibly shaken and his voice quivering, he thanked his wife for her moral support and added: "It had to be very tough on her when your 5-year-old son (Tyler) would come home from school and tell her that his daddy is a jailbird. . .I really have no excuses because it's all my fault. . . ."

Before pronouncing sentence, Judge Spiegel explained the reasoning behind the decision he had reached. "We must recognize that there are two people here: Pete Rose, the living legend. . .and the idol of millions; and Pete Rose, the individual, who appears today convicted of two counts of cheating on his taxes," the judge said. "Today we are not dealing with the legend. . . .With regard to Pete Rose the individual, he has broken the law. . .and stands ready to pay the penalty. . .I have at-

tempted to weigh all. . .considerations in determining Mr. Rose's sentence in an effort to be fair to the defendant and to fulfill the court's responsibility to society."

Judge Spiegel then handed Rose two five-month prison sentences to be served concurrently and with no possibility of parole. He also ruled that, after being released from prison, Rose would be required to serve three months in a community treatment center, or halfway house, as a condition of his supervised release. He said the supervised release would last one year. During that time, Rose must put in 1,000 hours of community service, including at least 20 hours per week in inner-city schools and boys' clubs in his native Cincinnati. In addition, the judge ordered Rose to continue psychiatric treatment for what Rose described as a gambling addiction until medical officials deem such therapy no longer necessary. He also fined him $50,000, charged him a total of $100 in special assessments and ordered him to pay the cost of his prosecution, confinement and supervision.

Because Rose was scheduled to undergo arthroscopic surgery the next day for a knee injury he suffered while playing stickball at his wife's family reunion in Indiana the previous weekend, Judge Spiegel gave him a stay of sentence and set August 10 as the date by which he must report to prison. He recommended that Rose be assigned to serve his time at the Federal Correctional Institution Camp in Ashland, Ky., about 160 miles southeast of Cincinnati. When it was learned that construction of the complex still was not complete, Rose was ordered to report instead to the minimum security federal prison camp in Marion, Ill. This produced another twist of irony because it was a Marion native and hero, former catcher Ray Fosse, whom Rose barreled over in the famous home-plate collision that ended the 1970 All-Star Game.

Rose checked in at the southern Illinois prison camp shortly after noon on August 8, two days before the deadline. The year-old, art deco style dormitory, which has no fence around it and houses about 200 prisoners, is adjacent to but separate from the federal penitentiary in Marion, where about 350 of the nation's toughest criminals are kept. Interviewed by the prison camp's staff soon after arrival to determine his work skills, Rose was assigned to the machine shop, where he helped weld and fabricate metal with 70 other prisoners. Despite rumors of preferential treatment, warden John Clark said Rose was being treated like any other inmate. This included sharing a dormitory cubicle with another prisoner and working eight hours a day for the customary prison wage of 11 cents per day. Prison officials said his release from the prison camp was scheduled for January 7, 1991.

Rose's lawyers decreed there would be no media interviews with Pete while he was incarcerated. However, a young couple from Mississippi, posing as musicians, schemed their way into the prison camp on August 25 in a bid to get a story for the National Enquirer. Rose was so impressed by their boldness and ingenuity that he gave them a 15-minute interview and posed for pictures that later appeared in the tabloid.

Although Rose no longer had any connection with baseball, one aspect of his legacy made its presence felt in '90. At the start of the season, league Presidents Bobby Brown and Bill White sent out directives ordering the clubs to have their switchboard operators keep complete records of all phone calls to and from the team clubhouses and the umpires' locker rooms. The new policy was prompted by concerns over attempts by gamblers to gain helpful information about injuries, etc., directly from the clubhouse.

Another protracted labor dispute triggered the spring lockout that fouled up 1990 scheduling arrangements. The episode continued a pattern that has marked relations between major league club owners and the players' union in recent years. Not since the 1960s have they concluded a collective bargaining agreement without a work stoppage.

The 32-day lockout, which wiped out much of spring training and delayed the start of the season for a week, marked the sixth time that major league baseball had been shut down in the last 19 years. In 1972, a player strike forced cancellation of the first 13 days of the season; a lockout by the owners in 1976 kept spring-training camps closed until Commissioner Bowie Kuhn intervened on March 17 and ordered them opened; a player strike in 1980 canceled the final eight days of spring-training games; a player walkout caused a 50-day shutdown in midseason of 1981, and another player strike halted action for two days in August 1985.

Both sides entered the latest negotiations with a call for an end to the hostility that raged in previous bargaining sessions. Early on, however, it became evident that reaching an agreement would once again be a lengthy, bitter process. Observers felt the major issues to be resolved involved the rules governing free agency and arbitration, which became more urgent as salaries soared past the $3 million level. But the owners' decision to press for an economic partnership with the players through a radically new concept of revenue sharing threw a monkey wrench into the deliberations for weeks and contributed to the delay in reaching a settlement.

Talks aimed at producing a new Basic Agreement began less than five weeks before the old five-year pact expired on December 31, 1989. Management's negotiating arm, the Player Relations Committee (PRC), consisted of Charles O'Connor, the group's newly appointed general counsel; Bud Selig of Milwaukee, committee chairman; Fred Wilpon, New York Mets; Jerry Reinsdorf, Chicago White Sox; John McMullen, Houston; Carl Pohlad, Minnesota, and Fred Kuhlmann, St. Louis. The Players Association representatives included Donald Fehr, executive director and general counsel; Gene Orza, associate counsel, and Mark Belanger, special assistant.

Soon after negotiations began, the PRC proposed what it called "an innovative Baseball Partnership" between the clubs and players. The concept represented a drastic change. The plan stipulated the clubs would make 48 percent of all gate receipts and all revenues from network and local broadcasting available for player salaries and benefits. Besides assuring the players of a guaranteed share of revenue, the proposal called for the establishment of a team payroll cap as well as a minimum team payroll. Once a team reached the salary ceiling, it would be prohibited from signing a free agent from another team until its payroll dropped below the cap.

Another component of the proposal provided for a pay-for-performance system to establish "a more direct relationship between the performance and pay for young players." Designed to replace salary arbitration, it would apply only to players with less than six seasons in the major leagues. Those players would be grouped into four categories, and their salaries would be determined by their length of service in the majors and their ranking within their group based on a statistical formula covering the last two seasons. The four categories consisted of (a) starting pitchers, (b) relief pitchers, (c) catchers, second basemen and shortstops, and (d) first basemen, third basemen, outfielders and designated hitters. When players reached the six-year level, they would become free agents as in the past.

Management contended the revenue-sharing partnership arrangement, together with the payroll cap and pay-for-performance system, would correct distortions in the salary structure of players and clubs, eliminate economic and competitive disparities among the clubs, and create a degree of cost certainty for the teams.

In demonstrating how the plan would work, O'Connor revealed that major league baseball had total revenues of $1.018 billion in 1988. This consisted of $412.6 million in gate receipts, $213.2 million from local broadcasting, $210.5 million from national broadcasting, $134.7 million from concessions, $20.8 million from licensing and $26.8 million from other sources. Proceeds from the gate together with local and network broadcasting amounted to $836.3 million—or 82 percent of the overall total. Under the Baseball Partnership setup, O'Connor noted, the players would have received 48 percent of that amount.

O'Connor also explained that the clubs anticipated a 7 percent yearly increase in revenue from ticket sales over the next four years and a 12 percent annual increase in money from local broadcasting contracts. In addition, the new four-year contracts with CBS-TV and ESPN boosted revenue from national broadcasting by approximately $185 million annually. With the Baseball Partnership proposal in place, O'Connor predicted the average player salary would be $611,000 in 1990 and $770,000 by 1993.

Discussions of the complex revenue-sharing idea dominated the negotiating sessions for several weeks. Although the players' union was not opposed philosophically to revenue sharing—a concept already in effect in the National Basketball Association—the proposal elicited little enthusiasm from Fehr. He said he felt the plan was another attempt by management to roll back the free-market system that was agreed to in 1976 when arbitrator Peter Seitz stripped away the reserve clause. The salary cap would severely restrict the mobility—and thus the bargaining power—of free agents, the players' union boss contended, while he claimed the pay-for-performance facet of the proposal would not only end salary arbitration, but also would eliminate multi-year contracts, guaranteed salaries, the 20 percent maximum salary cut rule and the need for agents for roughly two-thirds of the players. Salary arbitration and player agents were especially distasteful subjects with management.

"For the players to accept revenue sharing," Fehr commented on January 24, "they're going to have to be satisfied it presents a situation for players at least as good in all respects as some variant of the current system would. It's difficult to see how this arrangement produces something better."

Fehr said he was not aware of any short-term economic problem in baseball and saw "no immediate problem with respect to competitive imbalance," adding that if a "disparity in locally generated revenue is a problem among the clubs, they can not quantify it."

As the talks dragged on, evidence began mounting that management had been preparing for a possible lockout or strike, and fears grew that the start of spring training was in jeopardy. The owners' Player Relations Committee, it was disclosed, sent a letter to all clubs on January 9 advising that training camps "may not be opened until the PRC instructs you to do so." The letter further ordered that camps "shall remain closed during the duration of any labor dispute and the PRC will arrange for a security service to guard all spring training camps 24 hours a day during the labor dispute." It also noted that the PRC had "previously advised clubs that, to the extent possible, any spring-training contractual obligations (hotels, food services, etc.) that a club is normally required to enter into should contain cancellation clauses providing that the club has the right to cancel the contract 'in the event of a labor dispute, including a strike or lockout.'"

The two sides had held 19 bargaining sessions, with little progress to show for their efforts, when the 26 club owners gathered in suburban Chicago on February 9. Commissioner Vincent chaired the meeting, which was arranged so O'Connor and members of the Player Relations Committee could brief the owners on the negotiations. At the close of the meeting, PRC chairman Bud Selig announced to the press: "If there is no agreement, camps won't be opened." Originally the first groups of players—primarily batterymen plus others who were recuperating from injury or surgery—were due to report on February 15 and begin workouts the next day, but it was now obvious that spring training would not begin on schedule.

Following a weekend break, negotiations resumed February 12 and the commissioner sat in on the discussions for the first time. Demonstrating that he's an activist commissioner, Vincent offered a series of proposals that provided for: (1) Dropping the revenue-sharing and pay-for-performance plan; (2) A four-year agreement, with the clubs having the right to reopen after two years; (3) A joint committee to study revenue sharing and report on it by April 1, 1991; (4) The free agency system would remain as it has been; (5) Minimum salaries of $75,000, $125,000 and $200,000, respectively, for players in their first three years in the majors; (6) Salary arbitration would be retained for players with at least three but fewer than six years in the majors, with arbitration awards limited to a 75 percent increase over the player's salary of the previous year; (7) The owners' contribution to the players' benefit plan would remain at $39 million a year; (8) A settlement of the three collusion cases.

While Fehr found few of the ideas acceptable, Vincent's decision to step into the leadership void, presumably with the support of some of the more moderate owners, served to get the stalled talks moving by returning them to a more conventional bargaining level. Some observers felt Vincent had risked his standing with his employers, the owners, with his suggestions, but in an interview with Murray Chass of the New York Times, he commented: "I really believe it would be a terrible mistake for any commissioner, faced with the enterprise and the season being in real jeopardy, not to get involved."

The two sides began swapping proposals the following week and reached agreement on a number of issues. However, four of the union's primary concerns were still unresolved when Fehr departed New York City on February 26 to begin a series of meetings with the players. The pivotal issue was the union's demand that any player credited with two years of major league service should be eligible for salary arbitration. In a concession to management in the 1985 negotiations, the players agreed to raise the minimum requirement to three years, but now the union insisted on a return to the two-year eligibility standard. The other remaining issues involved minimum salary, size of rosters, and the owners' contribution to the players' pension/health care plan.

At a February 27 meeting in Phoenix, Fehr was authorized by the Players Association executive board to send checks for $5,000 on March 15 to each player who spent the '89 season in the majors. The money came from the work stoppage fund accumulated by the union from licensing money. The fund reportedly amounted to $80-$90 million. Meantime, Fehr himself had stopped drawing any of his $475,000 annual salary as of January 1. (The Players Association distributed the remainder of its strike fund in May. Each player, manager, coach and trainer who had been in the majors all four years—1986 through 1989—received $84,674.45, while those who were in the majors only in 1989 received $37,160.77.)

From Phoenix, Fehr flew to Los Angeles and then to Tampa to rally the players on the union's position. During his week-long absence, bargaining talks came to halt, and in an interview with the Associated Press the commissioner conceded: "The season is in very heavy jeopardy." He said both sides felt a minimum of three weeks of spring training was needed to prepare for the regular season and described the stalemated negotiations as "two giant organizations, overwhelmed with riches, fighting in circumstances where there's a national obligation or trust at stake. I find it tragic to the point of absurdity." So, too, did 14 of the nation's governors, who sent Vincent a letter terming the labor dispute "a national disgrace." The letter added: "Baseball is too important to our country—both economically and culturally—to allow this to drag on."

Following a nine-day layoff, negotiations resumed on March 6. Two days later the commissioner proposed the owners end the lockout in return for a no-strike pledge by the players. The Players Association rejected the idea. The talks broke down later that day over the salary arbitration eligibility issue, and for the ensuing week there were no meetings across the bargaining table.

In the absence of talks, Fehr tried a new tactic on March 14. He petitioned George Nicolau, an arbitrator in the collusion cases, to order the clubs to put $51.6 million in escrow. The figures represented the damages the owners acknowledged existed under Collusion II for salaries lost by the players in 1987 and 1988. The owners' contingency fund reportedly totaled $200 million. Nicolau brought the parties together the following day for a two-hour hearing and then took the matter under advisement.

Although major league training camps remained closed, most players were working out on their own in Florida and Arizona or in their hometowns. Farm system complexes, meanwhile, were in full swing, but the only players permitted to participate were those under contract to minor league teams. Even youngsters who were moved up to the 40-player big league rosters over the winter and were certain to be sent back to the minors were barred from the camps.

With the ire of the public rising, the negotiators finally returned to the bargaining table on March 16. They continued meeting throughout the weekend, working from noon to midnight on Sunday, March 18. At a 1:15 a.m. news conference, Commissioner Vincent announced that an agreement in principle had been reached on a four-year contract. He said it was agreed to open the season on April 9 and have each team play 158 games, with the possibility of 162 games to be studied, and that spring training would officially begin on March 20 and exhibition games on March 26. The laywers involved in drafting the language of the settlement completed the chore at 5:54 a.m., March 19, and signed a memorandum of understanding.

Terms of the new Basic Agreement included the following: (1) Either side may reopen the contract on major issues after three years; (2) The minimum major league salary was increased to $100,000 (up from $68,000) and the minimum for a player sent from the majors to the minors was set at $25,000 (up from $22,700); (3) The owners' annual contribution to the players' benefit fund was increased from an average of $34.2 million to an average of $55 million per year; (4) Minimum eligibility for salary arbitration will remain at three years, but the top 17 percent of players with at least two years but fewer than three in the majors—and who spent at least 86 days of the previous season in the majors—will also be eligible (it was estimated this would involve about 15 players each year); (5) The players' union will be awarded treble damages if the owners are found to conspire against the signing of free agents, and the affected players will return to free agency; (6) Continuation of 24-player rosters in 1990 was approved, but clubs must carry 25 players starting in 1991; (7) Within 90 days, the National League will announce a timetable for expansion; (8) A six-man study committee on revenue sharing and industry economic conditions will be set up; (9) A permanent committee on labor-management relations and also a committee to address player and family security issues will be named; (10) The deadline for clubs to decide whether to offer salary arbitration to former free agents covered by repeater rights restrictions was moved up from January to October; (11) Draft choice compensation for teams losing a player to free agency would apply only in those cases where the player was offered salary arbitration; (12) Waivers on players to be assigned to the minors cannot be withdrawn, and waivers are needed to bring back a player sent outright to the minors; (13) Players released before March 16 will receive 30 days' pay and those released after March 15 will receive 45 days' pay (instead of the former sliding scale of 33 to 43 days); (14) Injured pitchers can be placed on 30-day rehabilitation assignments in addition to 20-day assignments; (15) Meal money was increased to $54 per day (up from $51.50); (16) Spring training allowance was increased to $167.50 a week (up from $160); tip allowance to $30 (up from $28.50), and meal allowance to $47.50 a day (up from $45.50); (17) The Chicago Cubs will be permitted to reschedule a rained-out game as part of a split day-night bill once a season, a privilege previously given only to the Boston Red Sox.

Some 12 hours after the settlement was reached, representatives of both sides met again to clean up loose ends. They agreed to expand rosters to 27 players for the first 21 days of the season. In addition, with pitchers having barely three weeks to get ready, they decided that during the first two weeks of the season a starting pitcher would have to work only three innings—instead of the customary five—to be eligible for the victory. That proposal, however, was dropped before the season opened.

The players' union suggested that a week be added to the season so teams could play all 162 games. Because such a move would affect postseason schedules, management officials requested that a decision be delayed until they could confer with CBS. With the nation's concurrence, a compromise was reached on March 22 to extend the season three days. That made way for one of two series that was missed by the delayed start, and the other series would be made up on open dates or as parts of doubleheaders.

Just when things seemed ready to return to normal, the head of the Major League Umpires Association, Richie Phillips, announced on March 23 that the umpires would not work spring training games but would be ready to work on opening day. He said the decision resulted from differences with the owners over compensation for the canceled exhibition games and other factors—such as fewer off-days arising from the 32-day lockout and revised schedule. Minor league umpires filled in until an out-of-court settlement brought the major league arbiters back on April 1. Under the agreement the umpires were reimbursed for the canceled exhibitions and were given three more vacation days during the regular season.

The abbreviated spring drills proved especially costly to the cities where major league teams train. Spring training usually brings in more than $300 million in annual revenue to those communities in Florida and an estimated $165 million in Arizona. Merchants in Arizona figured they lost at least $100 million. A total of 362 exhibition games were canceled. One victim was a March 1 rematch of the 1989 World Series rivals, Oakland and San Francisco, in Phoenix that was expected to raise $50,000 for victims of the October 1989 earthquake. The Toronto Blue Jays lost an estimated $700,000 when they had to cancel two exhibitions against St. Louis on March 16-17 in the SkyDome.

Numerous clubs took steps to make amends with their fans or with organizations that support them in spring training. The Blue Jays made a $75,000 contribution to the city of Dunedin, Fla., to compensate it for the shortfall caused by the curtailed exhibition schedule. The Oakland A's donated $40,000 to four Phoenix charities as a gesture of goodwill. The Chicago Cubs gave $25,000 to the Ho-Ho-Kam organization of Mesa, Ariz., for distribution to local youth groups, and the Seattle Mariners donated $10,000 to the Diablos, their support group in Tempe, Ariz. Several other clubs, including Milwaukee, Philadelphia and Cleveland, offered their fans free tickets for specified regular-season games.

The players still active in the majors weren't the only ones to benefit from the new Basic Agreement. Retired players also shared in the improvements made possible by the huge hike in revenue designated for the Players Association benefit fund. In August, the union and the owners' Player Relations Committee agreed on a new schedule of pensions and other benefits to take effect immediately. Pensions for each class of retirees were boosted markedly, with the biggest percentage increase going to players who were active before 1959. Under the new schedule, a player with 10 years in the majors who began collecting his pension at age 50 prior to 1959 saw his pension rise from $650 a month to $1,394. The top pension for recent retirees was raised from $90,000 a year to the new federal maximum of $102,582. Other changes in the benefit plan provided for an increase in benefits to widows from about 50 percent to 100 percent, a boost in maximum lifetime health insurance from $2 million to $10 million, and elimination of health care deductibles.

The National League's plans for expanding to 14 teams were announced June 14 at the close of a two-day quarterly meeting of major league owners in Cleveland. League President Bill White said the timetable provides the four-member expansion committee will present its recommendations

for the two new franchises to the owners' meeting in June 1991 and the two expansion teams will begin play in April 1993. The price tag for each new franchise was set at $95 million.

The last time the majors expanded was in 1977 when the American League increased its membership to 14 teams by adding Toronto and Seattle. The franchise fees for those two were $7 million and $6.25 million, respectively. Although former commissioner Peter Ueberroth predicted several years ago that each league would have 16 teams by the year 2000, Commissioner Vincent said that was "a pace unlikely to be met" when he appeared before the U.S. Senate Task Force on Baseball Expansion on May 8. He reiterated that position following the National League announcement, declaring that before further expansion is considered "baseball should be permitted to see how these two (franchises) develop."

A total of 26 prospective ownership groups expressed interest in obtaining one of the National League expansion franchises. However, only 18 of them, representing 10 different metropolitan areas, returned the required questionnaire and $100,000 application fee by the September 4 deadline. Two of the groups later withdrew, leaving three from both Miami and St. Petersburg-Tampa, two each from Phoenix and Washington, D.C., and one apiece from Buffalo, Charlotte, Denver, Nashville, Orlando and Sacramento.

Representatives of each ownership group were invited to New York beginning September 18 to make a presentation to the league's four-member expansion committee. Douglas Danforth of Pittsburgh headed the committee, whose other members were White, John McMullen of Houston and Fred Wilpon of New York. The committee disclosed on December 18 that the list of expansion candidates had been narrowed to six ownership groups representing the cities of Buffalo, Denver, Miami, Orlando, St. Petersburg-Tampa and Washington. Committee members planned to conduct on-site visits early in 1991.

Once the two expansion franchises are formally awarded in September 1991, the new owners will be permitted to set up farm systems for the '92 season. An expansion draft to stock the two new teams will be held in November 1992, with each franchise selecting 36 players off the rosters of the 12 existing N.L. teams.

An unexpected offshoot of the National League's expansion plans was a heated dispute that developed when American

League club owners contended they should receive a share of the $190 million in expansion fees. Because money funneled into Baseball's Central Fund from the World Series, broadcasting revenue, etc., was divided 50-50 between the leagues, the 14 A.L. teams received smaller amounts than the 12 N.L. teams from 1977 until March 1989, when the formula was changed so that all teams shared equally. "What everybody has to realize is when the American League expanded in 1977, there was a financial adjustment made," Dr. Bobby Brown, American League president, told Hal Bodley of USA Today. "The National League was concerned in 1977 about the impact of expansion. We've got the same concerns now." The disagreement between the two leagues was still unresolved at year's end.

A dispute of another kind—the collusion cases brought by the players against the owners—was finally settled. A ruling by arbitrator George Nicolau on July 18 completed a clean sweep for the players and paved the way for the athletes to reap a huge financial bonanza. Under the settlement, reached late in the year, major league owners agreed to pay the players $280 million in damages to close out the three cases, which revolved around players who became free agents after the 1985, 1986 and 1987 seasons.

In his decision on Collusion III, Nicolau found the owners guilty because they shared salary offers through an information bank they had set up following the 1987 season. His ruling dealt with the 76 players who were free agents that winter. All three conspiracy cases stemmed from the owners' efforts under former commissioner Ueberroth to halt the escalation of salaries that began after free agency was created in 1976.

Arbitrator Thomas Roberts handled Collusion I, which involved 63 players who became free agents in the fall of 1985. On September 21, 1987 he ruled the owners had violated the Basic Agreement in their dealings with those athletes. He later ordered the owners to pay $10,528,086.71 to 139 players whose salaries were affected. In Collusion II dealing with 77 free agents of 1986, Nicolau issued a similar ruling on August 31, 1988. Following each of those two cases, certain players were granted "new look" free agency.

Nicolau's July 18 verdict in Collusion III charged that the owners' information bank served as a restraint on the free agent market. "It must be remembered that the bank was unilaterally established shortly after chairman Roberts' decision, follow-

ing two years in which bids for free agents desired by their former clubs were either nonexistent or virtually so," Nicolau wrote in his 34-page decision. "Against that backdrop, the bank's message was plain—if we MUST go into that market and bid, then let's quietly cooperate by telling each other what the bids are. If we all do that, prices won't get out of line and no club will be hurt too much."

After nearly three years of hearings, Nicolau announced on September 17 that he was ordering the owners to pay $102.5 million to the players affected by Collusion II. The award represented damages suffered by the players because of management's effort to suppress the free-agent market after the 1986-87 seasons in violation of the collective bargaining agreement. In arguments before Nicolau, the clubs had proposed damages totaling $55 million to $60 million, while the union had put the figure at around $125 million. Using complex mathematical formulas, the arbitrator decided the salary shortfall for players with six or more years of major league service was $25 million for 1987 and $39 million for 1988, and for players with at least three but fewer than six years of experience it was $13 million and $25.5 million, respectively—or an overall total of $102.5 million.

The subject of damages and possible "new look" free agency under Collusion III was next on Nicolau's agenda. Hearings got under way in October. The Players Association pressed for "new look" free agency for 21 of the 76 players who became free agents in 1987. With the hearings process still in its early stages, management and the players' union reached an agreement on October 26 that brought the conspiracy cases to a close. Under the accord, the owners agreed to pay the players a total of $280 million to settle all three collusion cases. This included the $115 million previously awarded by arbitrators Roberts and Nicolau as well as damages that had not yet been determined and interest. The $280 million, which amounted to $10,769,230 per club, was to be paid starting in 1991.

Besides the cash settlement, the agreement provided for "new look" free agency for 15 players. Six others were removed from the original list because their status had changed before the decision was officially ratified in December. Those lopped off were Joe Price of Baltimore, Greg Minton of California and John Candelaria of Toronto, who had already filed for free agency; Bill Gullickson of Houston, who had been released; Bob McClure of California, who waived his free-look rights upon signing a new contract, and Dennis Martinez of Montreal, who did likewise when he inked a three-year, $9.5 million contract with the Expos.

The 15 who were granted "new look" free agency effective December 7 were: American League—Larry Andersen, Boston; Chili Davis, California; Mike Heath and Jack Morris, Detroit; Juan Berenguer and Gary Gaetti, Minnesota; Dave LaPoint and Mike Witt, New York; Dave Henderson, Oakland. National League—Charlie Leibrandt, Atlanta; Danny Darwin and Dave Smith, Houston; Jack Clark, San Diego, and Brett Butler and Mike LaCoss, San Francisco.

Two clubs underwent major changes in ownership during the year. They were San Diego and Kansas City, although the Royals' transaction in effect merely restored the erstwhile sole owner to that position again. One other team—Montreal—appeared on the verge of being sold, while the Houston Astros also were put up for sale.

The biggest shift in owners involved San Diego. On April 2, approximately six months after Joan Kroc placed the Padres on the block, a group headed by Hollywood producer Tom Werner, 43. signed a letter of intent to buy the team. The price reportedly was $75 million. Werner, whose Los Angeles-based Carsey-Werner company produces such hit television series as "The Cosby Show" and "Roseanne," had nine partners, including eight from the San Diego area, at that point. The group expanded to 15 investors by the time the other major league owners unanimously approved the sale on June 13. Werner became chairman and managing general partner of the Padres.

Ewing Kauffman took a step toward regaining sole ownership of the Kansas City Royals on June 22 when he agreed to loan $34 million to co-owner Avron Fogelman. The loan was secured by Fogelman's 50 percent share of the team, with Kauffman having the option to buy out his partner on January 3, 1991. Fogelman, a Memphis real estate dealer, proposed the loan arrangement in an effort to save his floundering real-estate business. In 1983, when Kauffman was experiencing health problems, he sold a 49 percent interest in the Royals to Fogelman for $11 million. Fogelman became an equal partner in 1988 when he purchased another 1 percent as well as an option to buy Kauffman's share. Under terms of their latest transaction, Kauffman disclosed that he will not have to guarantee the lifetime contracts that his partner gave to George Brett, Willie Wilson and Dan Quisenberry. The contracts included real estate deals, and Fogelman will be required to meet any shortfall.

Shortly before the season opened, Charles Bronfman announced that he and his partners, Hugh Hallward and Lorne Webster, wanted to sell the Montreal Expos. The reported asking price was $100 million. Bronfman, majority owner and chairman of the board, and his group paid $10 million for the expansion franchise in 1968. Late in the year, the city of Montreal revealed it would invest $15 million in a consortium that was being set up to buy the club, and the province of Quebec offered an $18 million low-interest loan.

The San Francisco Giants' hopes of finding a new home to replace Candlestick Park suffered another jolt. A request by Bob Lurie, the Giants' owner, to move the team at some future date to Santa Clara, 35 miles south of San Francisco, received the approval of major league club owners at their June meeting. However, in November, residents of Santa Clara County voted down a measure that called for a 1 percent utility tax to build a new park for the Giants. It was the third successive year that Bay Area voters rejected a ballot proposal for a new stadium.

The top level of club management experienced its heaviest turnover in years. Nine teams underwent significant changes in front-office personnel. Next to the Yankees, the biggest involved San Diego and the Chicago White Sox. In addition to new ownership, the Padres found themselves with a new general manager and other staff personnel late in the year, as did the White Sox. Ten days after firing Jack McKeon, San Diego lured Joe McIlvaine away from the New York Mets on October 1 by giving him a five-year contract worth an estimated $1.6 million to become executive vice president and general manager. The White Sox dismissed Larry Himes as G.M. in mid-September and on November 3 named Ron Schueler, formerly of Oakland, as senior vice president and general manager. Two other clubs named new general managers. John Schuerholz resigned his position with Kansas City in October to succeed Bobby Cox as front-office boss in Atlanta. To replace Schuerholz, the Royals promoted Spencer (Herk) Robinson to general manager.

Five clubs witnessed changes in the role of president. The Detroit Tigers announced the appointment of Glenn (Bo) Schembechler, longtime University of Michigan football coach, as president and chief operating officer on January 8. Jim

Campbell, who had been president, became chairman and continued as the Tigers' chief executive officer. The Oakland A's promoted Walter J. Haas, son of the club's owner, to the position of president and chief executive officer on January 19. Eddie Einhorn relinquished his role as president of the Chicago White Sox in March to concentrate on his television involvement, and Mike Stone announced his resignation as president of the Texas Rangers late in September. Owner Gene Autry stepped down as president of the California Angels at season's close, and Richard M. Brown, the club's legal counsel, was named to succeed him.

Dr. Bobby Brown, whose term as American League president was due to expire December 31, received a new two-year contract to continue in that position at the league's September meetings. He will remain through December 1992, but a successor is to be named president-elect by January 1, 1992.

Several incidents of drug abuse again marred the year. Darryl Strawberry of the New York Mets was admitted to Smithers Center for Alcohol and Drug Treatment in New York on February 3 for a month of treatment for a drinking problem. In June outfielder Joey Belle, who began the season with Cleveland, was suspended by the Indians' Colorado Springs (Pacific Coast) farm team and subsequently spent two months in an alcoholism treatment program at Cleveland Clinic. Pitcher Bryan Harvey of the California Angels was fined $1,031 and placed on three years' probation in July after pleading guilty to driving under the influence of alcohol. Rick Leach, San Francisco Giants outfielder, was suspended for 60 days by Commissioner Vincent on August 6 after he tested positive for drugs. And in September outfielder Mark Carreon of the Mets entered Smithers Center for treatment.

Bob Engel, veteran National League umpire, encountered problems of a different nature. He was placed on indefinite suspension by the league April 25 after being arrested for allegedly stealing seven boxes of baseball cards—valued at $144—from a store in his hometown of Bakersfield, Calif. When he pleaded no-contest to the charges July 25, the judge placed him on three years' probation and ordered him to perform 40 hours of community service. Engel, who had umpired in the National League since 1965, then announced his retirement as an arbiter.

The year's regular class of free agents—players with six or more years of service in the majors whose contracts expired—turned out to be the biggest ever. A total of 96 players became free agents by filing by the November 4 deadline. This was five more than the record set a year earlier. In addition to the 96, Darren Daulton of Philadelphia filed, as did Terry Kennedy when San Francisco declined to exercise its option to renew his contract at $1 million, but both subsequently re-signed with their teams before the free-agency period began.

One player on the list of 96 also had a contract that gave his team an option to renew. He was Ron Kittle of Baltimore. Because the Orioles' right to renew ran to December 15, he decided to file for free agency as a precautionary measure.

The complete list of players who became free agents under the rules follows:

American League: Baltimore—Ron Kittle, Joe Price, Mickey Tettleton; Boston—Mike Boddicker, Tom Brunansky, Danny Heep; California—Brian Downing, Donnie Hill, Greg Minton, Max Venable; Chicago—Phil Bradley; Cleveland—Tom Brookens, Candy Maldonado, Ken Phelps; Detroit—Darnell Coles, Edwin Nunez, Dan Petry, Larry Sheets, John Shelby, Gary Ward; Kansas City—Bob Boone, Steve Crawford, Steve Farr, Steve Jeltz, Andy McGaffigan, Gerald Perry, Frank White, Willie Wilson; Milwaukee—Rob Deer, Ted Higuera, Bill Krueger, Paul Mirabella; Minnesota—Randy Bush, John Moses; New York—Tim Leary, Dave Righetti, Jeff Robinson; Oakland—Ron Hassey, Willie McGee, Jamie Quirk, Willie Randolph, Scott Sanderson, Bob Welch; Seattle—Ken Griffey Sr., Matt Young; Texas—Charlie Hough, Craig McMurtry; Toronto—George Bell, Bud Black, John Candelaria, Rance Mulliniks.

National League: Atlanta—Jim Presley; Chicago—Curtis Wilkerson; Cincinnati—Tom Browning, Bill Doran, Danny Jackson, Rick Mahler, Ron Oester; Houston—Juan Agosto, Rich Gedman, Terry Puhl, Franklin Stubbs, Glenn Wilson; Los Angeles—Rick Dempsey, Kirk Gibson, Mickey Hatcher, Juan Samuel, Fernando Valenzuela; Montreal—Kevin Gross, Dave Schmidt; New York—Dan Schatzeder, Darryl Strawberry, Pat Tabler; Philadelphia—Don Carman; Pittsburgh—Wally Backman, Doug Bair, Rafael Belliard, Sid Bream, Ted Power, Gary Redus, Jerry Reuss, R.J. Reynolds, Don Slaught, Zane Smith; St. Louis—Vince Coleman, Ken Dayley, Tom Niedenfuer, Terry Pendleton, John Tudor, Denny Walling; San Diego—Fred Lynn, Mike Pagliarulo, Dennis Rasmussen, Eric Show; San Francisco—Gary Carter, Mark

Thurmond.

In keeping with the trend of the two previous winters—after the clubs' collusive machinations ended—the bidding for free agents became furious and pushed salaries to higher levels. The first signing came on November 7, when the Los Angeles Dodgers signed outfielder Darryl Strawberry to a five-year, $20.25 million contract—a record for a free agent. A flurry of multi-year, megabucks signings followed. The San Francisco Giants quickly moved to the fore by inking lefthander Bud Black to a four-year, $10 million contract, signing outfielder Willie McGee to a four-year, $13 million deal and then handing reliever Dave Righetti a four-year, $10 million contract. Despite the disappointing seasons by Mark Davis and Storm Davis, two high-priced free agents signed the previous winter, Kansas City proffered a three-year, $9.25 million contract to pitcher Mike Boddicker. Cincinnati succeeded in retaining Tom Browning by offering him a four-year, $12.24 million pact, Milwaukee held on to Ted Higuera with a four-year, $13 million deal, the Chicago Cubs landed George Bell with a three-year, $13 million contract, the Dodgers added Brett Butler with a three-year, $10 million offer, and the Oakland A's held onto Bob Welch by giving him a four-year, $13.8 million pact.

The ever-escalating world of baseball economics saw the average salary of a major league player rise to $582,256.70 in 1990, according to figures compiled by USA Today. A total of 152 players were paid at least $1 million, with 28 of them drawing $2 million or more. Three teams—Boston, Kansas City and the New York Mets—each had 10 players with salaries of $1 million or better, while Baltimore ranked last in that department with one. Kansas City showed the highest player payroll at $21,978,745; Baltimore had the smallest with $7,985,584.

Outfielder Jose Canseco and the Oakland A's established a new salary plateau when they agreed on a five-year, $23.5 million contract extension on June 27. The pact included a $3.5 million signing bonus plus salaries of $2.8 million in 1991 followed by $3.6 million, $4.1 million, $4.4 million and finally $5.1 million in 1995. Counting the free-agent signings and several big-bucks contract extensions, at least 29 players boasted multi-year or 1991 contracts worth an average of $3 million or more per season. Besides Canseco and the free-agent group, the list included Don Mattingly, Will Clark, Kevin Mitchell, Dave Winfield, Andre Dawson, Dave Stewart, Nolan Ryan, Mark Davis, Mark Langston, Robin Yount, Eric Davis, Joe Carter, Paul Molitor, Rickey Henderson, Kirby Puckett, Dennis Eckersley, Dennis Martinez, Steve Sax, Tim Raines and Kevin McReynolds.

It appeared likely that another player or two from either the regular or "new look" group of free agents might also be joining the elite $3 million class.

While management voluntarily doled out huge contracts to star performers, salary arbitration continued to be a strong force behind rising payrolls. The owners, in fact, for years have charged that arbitration has been more responsible for escalating salaries than free agency.

A total of 162 players filed for salary arbitration early in the year. All but 24 reached agreement on contract terms with their teams without going to arbitration. Data compiled by Murray Chass of the New York Times revealed the aggregate salaries negotiated by or awarded to the 162 players for 1990 amounted to $138 million—an increase of approximately 102 percent over their '89 salaries.

Of the 24 whose cases went to an arbitrator, 14 were awarded the salaries they requested. The 10 others had to settle for the club's offer. Only one of the 24—Joe Hesketh of Montreal—wound up taking a cut. Paid $417,000 the previous season, he sought a raise to $485,000, but the arbitrator decided the club's offer of $375,000 was a more appropriate. Despite Hesketh's setback, the salaries of the 24 players involved in arbitration rose from $397,667 to $881,458.

The players who won their salary arbitration cases, with the team's offer in parentheses, were: Terry Pendleton, St. Louis, $1,850,000 ($1,000,000); Wally Joyner, California, $1,750,000 ($1,225,000); David Cone, New York Mets, $1,300,000 ($815,000); Benito Santiago, San Diego, $1,250,000 ($750,000); Shawon Dunston, Chicago Cubs, $1,250,000 ($925,000); Doug Drabek, Pittsburgh, $1,100,000 ($630,000); John Smiley, Pittsburgh, $840,000 ($630,000); Billy Hatcher, Pittsburgh, $690,000 ($525,000); Matt Nokes, Detroit, $650,000 ($400,000); Bob Kipper, Pittsburgh, $525,000 ($380,000); Andy Allanson, Cleveland, $410,000 ($250,000); Rafael Belliard, Pittsburgh, $380,000 ($235,000); Jeff Musselman, New York Mets, $315,000 ($220,000), and Wallace Johnson, Montreal, $295,000 ($215,000).

The salaries of the 10 who lost in arbitration, with the players' rejected figure in parentheses, follow: Lonnie Smith, Atlanta, $1,750,000 ($2,000,000); Bobby Bonilla, Pittsburgh, $1,250,000 ($1,700,000);

Bo Jackson, Kansas City, $1,000,000 ($1,900,001); Doug Jones, Cleveland, $950,000 ($1,150,000); Ivan Calderon, Chicago White Sox, $925,000 ($1,250,000); Randy Myers, Cincinnati, $875,000 ($1,100,000); Barry Bonds, Pittsburgh, $850,000 ($1,600,000); Devon White, California, $580,000 ($865,000); R. J. Reynolds, Pittsburgh, $535,000 ($785,000), and Joe Hesketh, Montreal, $375,000 ($485,000).

Despite the rapid escalation of player payrolls because of free agency and salary arbitration, most clubs still have fared handsomely in recent years judging by financial figures obtained by the Associated Press in November. The data revealed the 26 teams had record revenues of $1.241 billion in 1989, a 23 percent increase over the previous season, and enjoyed record pretax operating profits of $214.5 million—an average of $8.25 million per team. It was the sixth consecutive year the clubs increased operating profits. Only four franchises experienced a loss in '89, according to the figures, but Charles O'Connor of management's Player Relations Committee said the number of teams showing a loss for '89 would rise to nine when they included their share of the $280 million collusion settlement.

Winners of the Baseball Writers' Rookie of the Year voting were Sandy Alomar of Cleveland and Dave Justice of Atlanta. Alomar drew all 28 first-place votes in the American League to easily beat out runner-up Kevin Maas of the New York Yankees. Justice received all but one of the 24 first-place votes in the National League balloting to win handily over Delino DeShields of Montreal.

The disappointment suffered by Oakland's management, playing personnel and fans during the World Series—and earlier by their Pittsburgh counterparts in the League Championship Series—was eased somewhat when results of voting for the year's top player awards were announced in November. Two members of the A's and a pair of Pirates swept the major honors that are conferred annually by the Baseball Writers' Association of America.

Bob Welch captured the Cy Young Award in the American League and Rickey Henderson was voted the circuit's Most Valuable Player, while Doug Drabek emerged as the Cy Young winner in the National League and Barry Bonds was chosen as the senior loop's MVP.

With two BBWAA members from each city participating in the polls, Welch received 15 of 28 first-place votes to finish

with 107 points in the A.L. Cy Young balloting. Roger Clemens of Boston wound up second, gaining eight first-place votes and 77 points. Dave Stewart of Oakland ranked third with 43 points, followed by Bobby Thigpen of Chicago with 20. In the N.L. poll, Drabek missed being a unanimous selection by one vote. He was the top choice of 23 of the 24 voters and collected 118 of a possible 120 points. Ramon Martinez of Los Angeles received the other first-place vote and was runner-up with 70 points. Frank Viola and Dwight Gooden of the New York Mets wound up third and fourth with 19 and 8 points, respectively. A breakdown of the voting, with five points for a first-place vote, three for second and one for third, follows:

American League

Pitcher—Team	1	2	3	Pts.
Bob Welch, Oakland	15	10	2	107
Roger Clemens, Boston	8	10	7	77
Dave Stewart, Oakland	3	7	7	43
Bobby Thigpen, Chicago	2	1	7	20
Dennis Eckersley, Oakland	..	..	2	2
Dave Stieb, Toronto	..	..	2	2
Chuck Finley, California	..	..	1	1

National League

Pitcher—Team	1	2	3	Pts.
Doug Drabek, Pittsburgh	23	1	0	118
Ramon Martinez, L.A.	1	21	2	70
Frank Viola, New York	0	2	13	19
Dwight Gooden, New York	0	0	8	8
Randy Myers, Cincinnati	0	0	1	1

Like his teammate Drabek, Bonds was a near-unanimous selection in the National League MVP voting. He was listed No. 1 on 23 of the 24 ballots and collected 331 of a possible 336 points. Teammate Bobby Bonilla received the other first-place vote and finished second with 212 points, followed by Darryl Strawberry of New York with 167 and Ryne Sandberg of Chicago with 151. The Most Valuable Player balloting in the American League saw Henderson receive 14 of 28 first-place votes and 317 points to edge Cecil Fielder of Detroit, who was the top pick of 10 voters and collected 286 points. Roger Clemens finished third with 212 points, followed by Kelly Gruber of Toronto with 175. Results of the MVP balloting in the two leagues, with 14 points for a first-place vote, nine for second and on down to one for 10th, follow:

National League

Name, Club	1	2	3	4	5	6	7	8	9	10	Pts.
Barry Bonds, Pittsburgh	23	1	-	-	-	-	-	-	-	-	331
Bobby Bonilla, Pittsburgh	1	18	3	1	-	1	-	-	-	-	212
Darryl Strawberry, New York	-	3	12	4	-	1	2	-	1	1	167
Ryne Sandberg, Chicago	-	2	4	7	6	1	2	1	-	-	151
Eddie Murray, Los Angeles	-	-	2	6	5	4	1	3	1	-	123
Matt Williams, San Francisco	-	-	1	2	1	7	3	5	2	1	95
Barry Larkin, Cincinnati	-	-	-	-	7	5	1	3	1	-	82
Doug Drabek, Pittsburgh	-	-	-	2	1	2	2	4	4	1	59
Lenny Dykstra, Philadelphia	-	-	1	1	-	-	2	1	4	7	41
Tim Wallach, Montreal	-	-	-	-	-	1	6	-	3	1	36
Kevin Mitchell, San Francisco	-	-	-	-	1	-	1	2	1	2	20
Eric Davis, Cincinnati	-	-	1	-	-	-	1	-	-	-	12
Chris Sabo, Cincinnati	-	-	-	-	1	1	-	-	-	-	11
Ron Gant, Atlanta	-	-	-	-	-	-	-	-	4	2	10
Dwight Gooden, New York	-	-	-	-	-	1	1	-	-	1	10
Ramon Martinez, Los Angeles	-	-	-	1	-	-	-	-	-	2	9
Joe Carter, San Diego	-	-	-	-	-	-	1	-	1	1	7
Randy Myers, Cincinnati	-	-	-	-	-	-	1	1	-	-	7
Paul O'Neill, Cincinnati	-	-	-	-	1	-	-	-	-	-	6
Jose Rijo, Cincinnati	-	-	-	-	1	-	-	-	-	-	6
Andre Dawson, Chicago	-	-	-	-	-	-	-	2	-	-	6
Dave Magadan, New York	-	-	-	-	-	-	-	1	-	1	4
Benito Santiago, San Diego	-	-	-	-	-	-	-	1	-	-	3
Brett Butler, San Francisco	-	-	-	-	-	-	-	-	-	2	2
Dave Justice, Atlanta	-	-	-	-	-	-	-	-	1	-	2
Pedro Guerrero, St. Louis	-	-	-	-	-	-	-	-	1	-	2
Kal Daniels, Los Angeles	-	-	-	-	-	-	-	-	-	1	1
Andy Van Slyke, Pittsburgh	-	-	-	-	-	-	-	-	-	1	1

American League

Name, Club	1	2	3	4	5	6	7	8	9	10	Pts.
Rickey Henderson, Oakland	14	11	2	-	1	-	-	-	-	-	317
Cecil Fielder, Detroit	10	8	5	4	1	-	-	-	-	-	286
Roger Clemens, Boston	3	4	7	5	4	3	1	-	-	-	212
Kelly Gruber, Toronto	-	2	12	3	4	1	2	-	1	1	175
Bobby Thigpen, Chicago	-	3	-	12	4	4	3	1	-	-	170
Dennis Eckersley, Oakland	1	-	-	-	7	5	3	5	2	-	112
George Brett, Kansas City	-	-	-	1	2	1	4	4	2	4	60
Dave Stewart, Oakland	-	-	1	3	-	3	1	2	1	-	56
Bob Welch, Oakland	-	-	-	-	1	5	4	2	-	1	54
Fred McGriff, Toronto	-	-	-	-	2	-	1	3	2	1	30
Mark McGwire, Oakland	-	-	-	-	-	2	1	2	2	5	29
Jose Canseco, Oakland	-	-	-	-	-	-	4	2	2	-	26
Ellis Burks, Boston	-	-	-	-	1	1	2	-	3	-	25
Rafael Palmeiro, Texas	-	-	-	-	-	-	1	2	4	4	22
Carlton Fisk, Chicago	-	-	-	-	-	2	-	-	2	2	16
Dave Parker, Milwaukee	-	-	-	-	1	-	-	-	2	1	11
Ozzie Guillen, Chicago	-	-	-	-	-	-	-	2	1	2	10
Jody Reed, Boston	-	-	1	-	-	-	-	-	-	1	9
Ken Griffey Jr., Seattle	-	-	-	-	-	-	-	1	1	2	7
Alan Trammell, Detroit	-	-	-	-	-	1	-	-	1	-	7
Tony Pena, Boston	-	-	-	-	-	-	1	-	1	-	6
Wade Boggs, Boston	-	-	-	-	-	-	-	1	1	-	5
Doug Jones, Cleveland	-	-	-	-	-	-	-	1	-	-	3
Cal Ripken, Baltimore	-	-	-	-	-	-	-	-	-	2	2
Nolan Ryan, Texas	-	-	-	-	-	-	-	-	-	1	1
Dave Stieb, Toronto	-	-	-	-	-	-	-	-	-	1	1

NATIONAL LEAGUE

Including

Team Reviews of 1990 Season

Team Day-by-Day Scores

1990 Standings, Home-Away Records

1990 Pitching Against Each Club

1990 Official N.L. Batting Averages

1990 Official N.L. Fielding Averages

1990 Official N.L. Pitching Averages

Barry Larkin was a key cog in Cincinnati's drive to the World Series title, batting .301 with 30 steals while playing a spellbinding shortstop.

Reds Lead From Start to Finish

By JACK BRENNAN

Wire to wire.

It suggests a cakewalk, a cinch, child's play. But for the Cincinnati Reds, the 1990 regular season was none of those things.

Oh, the Reds won the National League pennant and then a World Series championship in four games, but they were a grim bunch during much of a regular season in which they led the N.L. West from Day One.

Only when it was over, when their 91-71 record edged second-place Los Angeles by five games, could the Reds savor the accomplishment of being the first N.L. team to reside in first place from start to finish in a 162-game season.

"It's a lot harder psychologically being in first place every day than it is when you're hanging back in second or third," Manager Lou Piniella said. "This team was scrutinized and criticized every day, and I think some of it was totally unfair."

The Reds caught everyone's attention with an exceptionally hot start, winning their first nine games en route to a 33-12 record on June 3. It was the best getaway in club history, yet it also set an artificially high standard for the rest of the season.

When the Reds were unable to maintain that torrid pace, they were pegged as possible chokers. Although their lead never fell below 3½ games from early May through season's end, they inspired grumbles from their fans by playing sub-.500 baseball (58-59) after June 3.

"When our gait slowed some, people started asking, 'What's wrong?'" said an exasperated Piniella. "But if we were supposed to be 10 or 12 games better than anybody else, why didn't anybody pick us to finish first?

"We carried an extra burden all year, getting compared to the Big Red Machine teams."

The Reds bolted ahead of the N.L. West pack with very little help from Eric Davis. Their star outfielder started the year slowly (.186), then went on the disabled list from April 24 through May 19 with a strained knee ligament. But there was no lack of performers ready to take up the slack. Outfielder Billy Hatcher, acquired from Pittsburgh just before opening day, filled in for Davis by hitting .333 in April and .313 in May.

At the same time, the hard-throwing bullpen trio of Randy Myers, Rob Dibble

Chris Sabo unexpectedly became a power hitter for the Reds in 1990, clubbing a team-high 25 homers.

and Norm Charlton became a force to fear as the so-called "Nasty Boys." Dibble did not allow an earned run in his first 15 outings, paving the way for a 1.74 earned-run average, an 8-3 record, 11 saves and 136 strikeouts in 98 innings. Myers, acquired from the Mets for 1989 closer John Franco, earned a victory and two saves within the first week and ranked second in the league with 31 saves (to Franco's 33) and 59 games finished.

Piniella, managing his first season in the league, wasn't necessarily astonished to see his team take an early lead.

"I knew when we left spring training that we had two advantages over everyone in the division," he said. "First, we were a young team that could get in shape quickly. Because of the shortened spring training, that was a big edge.

"Second, we had the best bullpen in

SCORES OF CINCINNATI REDS' 1990 GAMES

APRIL

Date		Score	Winner	Loser
9—At Hous.	W	8-4§	Myers	Kerfeld
10—At Hous.	W	3-2	Layana	Agosto
11—At Hous.	W	5-0	Armstrong	Portugal
13—At Atlanta	W	5-2	Browning	Lilliquist
15—At Atlanta	W	13-6	Birtsas	Glavine
16—At Atlanta	W	5-3	Armstrong	Smith
17—San Diego	W	2-1	Browning	Benes
18—San Diego	W	11-7	Layana	Valdez
21—Atlanta	W	8-1	Armstrong	Clary
22—Atlanta	L	1-3	Glavine	Browning
24—At Phila.	L	3-6	Howell	Rijo
25—At Phila.	W	12-7	Mahler	Ruffin
27—Montreal	W	3-2	Dibble	Hall
28—Montreal	W	6-4	Armstrong	Boyd
29—Montreal	L	3-6	Gross	Robinson
30—Phila.	W	6-2	Rijo	Howell

Won 13, Lost 3

MAY

Date		Score	Winner	Loser
1—Phila.	L	2-4	Ruffin	Birtsas
2—At N.Y.	L	0-5	Viola	Browning
3—At N.Y.	W	5-0	Armstrong	Fernandez
4—At St. L.	W	8-3	Robinson	Tudor
5—At St. L.	W	4-2	Rijo	Magrane
6—At St. L.	W	5-1	Scudder	B. Smith
7—At St. L.	W	3-0	Browning	DeLeon
9—At Pitts.	L	2-6	Smiley	Armstrong
10—At Pitts.	W	10-4	Charlton	Power
11—Chicago	W	7-5	Charlton	Williams
12—Chicago	L	2-4	Bielecki	Browning
13—Chicago	W	13-9	Dibble	Wilson
14—Pittsburgh	W	5-3	Armstrong	Terrell
15—Pittsburgh	W	5-4§	Layana	Patterson
17—St. Louis	L	0-3	DeLeon	Browning
18—St. Louis	W	1-0	Charlton	Dayley
19—St. Louis	W	4-0	Armstrong	Tudor
20—St. Louis	L	2-6	Magrane	Jackson
21—At Chicago	W	4-3	Rijo	Maddux
22—At Chicago	L	1-2z	Long	Scudder
24—At Mon.	W	7-1	Robinson	Gross
25—At Mon.	W	5-0	Armstrong	Martinez
26—At Mon.	W	5-3	Dibble	Burke
27—At Mon.	L	3-5	Hall	Birtsas
29—New York	W	2-1	Browning	Ojeda
31—At L.A.	L	1-2‡	Aase	Charlton

Won 17, Lost 9

JUNE

Date		Score	Winner	Loser
1—At L.A.	W	5-2	Jackson	Wetteland
2—At L.A.	W	8-3	Charlton	Crews
3—At L.A.	W	2-0	Browning	Valenzuela
4—At S.F.	L	1-10	Burkett	Robinson
5—At S.F.	L	1-6	Garrelts	Armstrong
6—At S.F.	L	2-3§	Brantley	Dibble
7—At Hous.	W	6-1	Rijo	Gullickson
8—At Hous.	L	1-3‡	Scott	Myers
9—At Hous.	L	1-4	Clancy	Mahler
10—At Hous.	L	2-4	Darwin	Armstrong
12—Atlanta	L	3-8	Glavine	Jackson
12—Atlanta	L	2-3	Greene	Rijo
13—Atlanta	W	13-4	Browning	Avery
14—Atlanta	W	4-3	Dibble	Boever
15—Houston	W	6-3	Armstrong	Clancy
16—Houston	W	6-2	Jackson	Deshaies
17—Houston	W	7-1	Rijo	Portugal
19—At Atlanta	W	4-2	Charlton	Luecken
19—At Atlanta	L	0-3	Leibrandt	Mahler
20—At Atlanta	W	9-8‡	Myers	Luecken
21—At Atlanta	L	3-4	Smoltz	Dibble
22—Los Ang.	L	6-7‡	Howell	Myers
23—Los Ang.	W	11-6	Browning	Belcher
24—Los Ang.	W	10-6	Mahler	Valenzuela
25—San Fran.	W	5-2	Armstrong	Burkett
26—San Fran.	W	3-2x	Myers	Thurmond
27—San Fran.	L	3-8	Robinson	Browning
28—At N.Y.	L	4-5	Gooden	Rijo
29—At N.Y.	L	2-4	Ojeda	Mahler
30—At N.Y.	W	7-4	Charlton	Musselman

Won 16, Lost 14

JULY

Date		Score	Winner	Loser
1—At N.Y.	L	2-3	Franco	Charlton
3—At Mon.	W	2-0	Browning	Smith
4—At Mon.	L	3-5	Martinez	Scudder
5—At Phila.	W	9-2	Armstrong	Howell
6—At Phila.	W	4-1	Jackson	DeJesus
7—At Phila.	W	5-0	Mahler	Ruffin
8—At Phila.	L	3-4	Akerfelds	Charlton
12—New York	L	3-10	Gooden	Charlton
12—New York	W	3-2	Jackson	Darling
13—New York	W	4-2	Browning	Viola
14—New York	L	3-6	Cone	Armstrong
15—New York	W	2-1	Charlton	Fernandez
16—Montreal	W	8-3	Layana	Smith
17—Montreal	W	6-2	Scudder	Gardner
18—Montreal	W	8-7§	Mahler	Schmidt
19—Phila.	L	2-5	Combs	Armstrong
20—Phila.	W	5-1	Charlton	Parrett
21—Phila.	W	6-1	Rijo	Mulholland
22—Phila.	L	2-6	DeJesus	Scudder
23—At S.D.	W	9-2	Browning	Rasmussen
24—At S.D.	L	0-10	Hurst	Armstrong
25—At S.D.	L	1-2	Whitson	Charlton
25—At S.D.	L	4-10	Schiraldi	Mahler
26—At S.F.	L	3-4	Thurmond	Rijo
27—At S.F.	L	3-4	Robinson	Scudder
28—At S.F.	L	2-3§	Bedrosian	Myers
29—At S.F.	L	0-4	Garrelts	Armstrong
30—At L.A.	L	1-4	Morgan	Charlton
31—At L.A.	W	5-2	Rijo	Belcher

Won 14, Lost 15

AUGUST

Date		Score	Winner	Loser
1—At S.D.	W	6-3	Scudder	Benes
2—San Diego	L	5-8	Rasmussen	Browning
3—San Diego	L	2-3	Harris	Dibble
4—San Diego	L	3-7§	Harris	Mahler
5—San Diego	W	6-2	Rijo	Schiraldi
7—Los Ang.	W	1-0	Browning	Neidlinger
8—Los Ang.	L	2-4	Valenzuela	Scudder
9—Los Ang.	L	3-10	Martinez	Armstrong
10—San Fran.	W	7-0	Charlton	Robinson
11—San Fran.	L	2-4	Burkett	Rijo
12—San Fran.	W	6-4	Browning	Garrelts
13—San Fran.	W	6-5	Layana	Wilson
14—At St. L.	W	9-4	Armstrong	DeLeon
15—At St. L.	W	3-1x	Dibble	Niedenfuer
17—Pittsburgh	L	1-7	York	Rijo
17—Pittsburgh	L	3-4	Smiley	Layana
18—Pittsburgh	L	1-3	Smith	Hammond
19—Pittsburgh	L	3-6	Drabek	Armstrong
20—Chicago	L	1-3†	Bielecki	Charlton
21—Chicago	W	8-1	Mahler	Harkey
22—Chicago	W	4-1	Rijo	Pico
23—At Pitts.	L	3-9	Smith	Hammond
24—At Pitts.	W	4-3	Dibble	Kipper
25—At Pitts.	W	6-1	Charlton	Belinda
26—At Pitts.	W	6-2	Mahler	Tomlin
28—St. Louis	W	2-1	Rijo	Magrane
29—St. Louis	L	1-9	Tewksbury	Browning
30—At Chicago	W	6-5	Jackson	Bielecki
31—At Chicago	L	3-4	Long	Myers

Won 15, Lost 14

SEPTEMBER

Date		Score	Winner	Loser
1—At Chicago	W	8-1	Mahler	Nunez
2—At Chicago	W	6-2	Rijo	Maddux
3—At Atlanta	L	6-8	Grant	Layana
4—At Atlanta	L	4-7	Glavine	Jackson
5—At S.F.	W	5-3	Charlton	Robinson
6—At S.F.	L	2-6	Garrelts	Mahler
7—At L.A.	L	1-3	Neidlinger	Rijo
8—At L.A.	W	8-4	Browning	Valenzuela
9—At L.A.	L	4-6	Martinez	Jackson
11—Houston	W	5-3	Charlton	Deshaies
12—Houston	L	1-3y	Agosto	Layana
13—Houston	W	7-5	Dibble	Meyer
14—Los Ang.	L	4-10	Valenzuela	Browning
15—Los Ang.	L	0-3	Martinez	Jackson
16—Los Ang.	W	9-5	Scudder	Morgan
17—San Fran.	W	4-0	Rijo	Garrelts
18—San Fran.	L	3-5	Burkett	Browning
19—At Hous.	L	2-5	Portugal	Jackson
20—At Hous.	L	2-3	Hernandez	Myers
21—At S.D.	W	10-1	Rijo	Rasmussen
22—At S.D.	W	6-4	Dibble	Harris
22—At S.D.	W	9-5	Browning	Hammaker
23—At S.D.	W	9-2	Jackson	Whitson
25—Atlanta	L	0-10	Glavine	Charlton
26—Atlanta	W	5-2	Rijo	Smoltz
27—Atlanta	W	4-2	Browning	Avery
28—San Diego	L	1-2	Hurst	Myers
29—San Diego	L	1-3*	Whitson	Charlton
30—San Diego	L	0-3	Lilliquist	Rijo

Won 14, Lost 15

OCTOBER

Date		Score	Winner	Loser
1—Houston	W	4-3	Myers	Meyer
2—Houston	W	3-2	Scudder	Hernandez
3—Houston	L	2-3	Smith	Birtsas

Won 2, Lost 1

*6½ innings. †8 innings. ‡10 innings. §11 innings. x12 innings. y13 innings. z16 innings.

Hard-throwing Norm Charlton formed one-third of Cincinnati's "Nasty Boys" bullpen trio.

baseball. And with starting pitchers going only five innings in the early games . . . once we got to the sixth with Dibble and Charlton and Myers—my gosh, it was almost an invincible situation."

The Reds, despite entering the All-Star break with a major league-low 3.04 ERA, had their share of pitching worries, particularly with a string of injuries to starters Jack Armstrong, Jose Rijo, Danny Jackson and Tom Browning. "We had problems with our pitching just like everyone," Piniella noted, "even though all the talk was about the problems the Dodgers and Giants had."

In the end, the Reds met the challenge with help from Charlton and veteran Rick Mahler. Charlton was outstanding in 14 starts from mid-July through late September, posting a 6-3 record and a 1.94 ERA. Mahler, despite early season shoulder troubles, won three straight starts down the stretch.

The Reds survived scares in early August and late September, when their lead over Los Angeles shrunk to 3½ games on both occasions. After Houston swept a two-game series that concluded September 20, the Reds won six of their next seven games to set up a September 29 title-clinching date (in the midst of losing a three-game series to San Diego).

The Reds won their first division title since 1979 with relatively few outstanding individual accomplishments.

No pitcher won more than 15 games. Browning was the top winner at 15-9 and tied for the league lead with 35 starts. Rijo was 14-8 and limited opponents to a .212 batting average, second lowest in the league. Armstrong, pitching in his first full season, was 11-3 through the All-Star break but won just once more, tying Charlton with 12 wins.

No batter hit more than 25 home runs. Third baseman Chris Sabo unexpectedly became a power hitter and rapped a team-leading 25 homers, topping Davis by one. Mariano Duncan, the second baseman until Bill Doran arrived from Houston on August 31 (and the regular again when Doran was injured after just 17 games), belted a career-high 10 homers and 11 triples to supply unforeseen extra-base power.

No batter came close to contending for the league RBI lead. Davis knocked in 86 runs, followed by right fielder Paul O'Neill's 78 and Sabo's 71 RBIs.

And the Reds had no strong contenders for the league batting title, with shortstop Barry Larkin, at .301, their top qualifier. Rookie Hal Morris took over first base from Todd Benzinger in the second half and batted .340. Duncan's .306 mark was a personal best, but Hatcher slipped to .276 after his hot start.

When the players were polled to determine the team's Most Valuable Player, nine declined to vote, saying it was too much a team effort. But the Reds who did respond strongly agreed upon Larkin. In addition to hitting .300 over a full season for the first time in his career, Larkin had a career-high 67 RBIs and played outstanding defense, leading N.L. shortstops in assists and double plays.

Davis and Rijo, two players who would help lead the Reds through the postseason, put the hammer down on the rest of the N.L. West with strong finishes.

Davis, hitting just .223 on August 19, batted .357 with nine homers and 29 RBIs the rest of the way. From August 22 through season's end, Rijo posted a 6-2 record and a 1.27 ERA.

"Anytime we had to be tested, we answered," Piniella said. "When we were most pressured, we responded. Finally, we were able to silence most of the critics."

Kal Daniels stayed healthy and became an offensive force in Los Angeles, hitting .296 with 27 homers and 94 RBIs.

Dodgers Pursue Reds, Pitchers

By GORDON VERRELL

You could have monitored the comings and goings of one John Wetteland to get a handle on what ailed the Los Angeles Dodgers in 1990.

Wetteland, a second-year pitcher who just missed landing a starting job in spring training, opened the season as a long reliever in the Dodger bullpen. By the end of April, Wetteland's role changed dramatically, to emergency starter, when the unthinkable happened: Dodger ace Orel Hershiser was lost for the year with a sore shoulder that required reconstructive surgery.

Within a month, however, Wetteland was on the move again, first back to the bullpen and by June 21 to the minor leagues. Unable to meet the Dodgers' needs as either a starter or reliever, Wetteland was farmed out to make room for other candidates. Mike Maddux tried and failed to win a job in the rotation, followed two weeks later by Terry Wells.

It took until August to find a capable replacement for Hershiser: rookie Jim Neidlinger, who was called up from Albuquerque (Pacific Coast) on July 31. But two weeks later, the Dodgers needed another starter when Tim Belcher was sidelined with a shoulder injury that necessitated surgery. Another rookie, Mike Hartley, was asked to take over.

In all, the Dodgers used 21 pitchers, the most since the team moved to Los Angeles in 1958. As if the search for starters wasn't work enough, Manager Tom Lasorda had to scrounge around a bullpen that saved a major league-low 29 games.

Four days before Hershiser went out, Lasorda lost stopper Jay Howell for a month to knee surgery. But the Dodgers were blowing big leads as late as September, when they were successful in only three of eight save opportunities. Welcome back John Wetteland. (He did, incidentally, fashion a 0.84 earned-run average after his recall on September 12.) For the year, the Dodgers lost seven games in which they had led by four or more runs.

And so, without Hershiser, without an effective bullpen for a good part of the season and without so much as one full big-league season between two starters, how did the Dodgers climb to within 3½ games of first-place Cincinnati in the National League West on September 20 after trailing by 13½ lengths on July 23?

Eddie Murray's offensive resurgence helped propel the Dodgers into second place in the N.L. West.

The most obvious reason was spindly second-year righthander Ramon Martinez, who at age 22, became the Dodgers' youngest 20-game winner since Ralph Branca (21 wins at age 21) in 1947. Lasorda's reasoning was typical rah-rah: "We didn't quit, that's how. This team just kept bouncing back."

Los Angeles was the National League's best team after the All-Star break (47-33) and finished second in the N.L. West, five games behind Cincinnati. The Dodgers' 86-76 record was just their second above .500 in five seasons.

"We were the best team in the division in the second half," said catcher Mike Scioscia, who reached career highs in homers (12) and runs batted in (66). "Obviously, we didn't get a chance to show it."

At the end of the season, the Dodgers had a distinctly different look. Opening-day third baseman Jeff Hamilton played only seven games before undergoing shoulder surgery. That left Lasorda with a third-base platoon of Lenny Harris and Mike Sharperson, yet they batted a combined .301, some 64 points better than Hamilton's career mark.

In May, the center fielder (Juan Samuel) became the second baseman when the second baseman (Willie Randolph) was

38

SCORES OF LOS ANGELES DODGERS' 1990 GAMES

APRIL

Date		Score	Winner	Loser
9—San Diego	W	4-2	Wetteland	Hurst
10—At S.D.	W	1-0	Belcher	Show
11—At S.D.	L	1-3	Benes	Valenzuela
12—At S.D.	L	6-8	Schiraldi	Aase
13—At Hous.	W	6-1	Morgan	Gullickson
14—At Hous.	L	3-7	Andersen	Wetteland
15—At Hous.	W	5-4*	Howell	Kerfeld
16—San Fran.	L	1-3	LaCoss	Valenzuela
17—At S.F.	W	10-5	Aase	Hammaker
18—At S.F.	W	6-2	Morgan	Gunderson
19—Houston	W	7-3	Hershiser	Scott
20—Houston	L	2-4	Deshaies	Belcher
21—Houston	L	5-6	Agosto	Howell
22—Houston	W	2-0	Martinez	Portugal
24—St. Louis	W	3-0	Morgan	Magrane
25—St. Louis	L	1-5	B. Smith	Hershiser
26—St. Louis	L	1-7	DeLeon	Belcher
27—Chicago	W	5-0	Valenzuela	Nunez
28—Chicago	W	5-4	Martinez	Williams
29—Chicago	L	0-4	Maddux	Morgan
30—San Fran.	L	4-8	Burkett	Wetteland

Won 11, Lost 10

MAY

Date		Score	Winner	Loser
1—Pittsburgh	W	4-1	Belcher	Terrell
2—Pittsburgh	W	6-2	Valenzuela	Smiley
4—At Phila.	L	3-8	Carman	Martinez
5—At Phila.	W	3-0	Morgan	Howell
6—At Phila.	L	5-9	Carman	Munoz
8—At Mon.	L	1-9	Sampen	Belcher
9—At Mon.	L	3-5	Gross	Valenzuela
10—At Mon.	L	2-8	De. Martinez	R. Martinez
11—At N.Y.	L	4-9	Gooden	Morgan
12—At N.Y.	L	0-7	Viola	Wetteland
14—Montreal	W	3-2	Valenzuela	Gross
15—Montreal	W	3-2	R. Martinez	De. Martinez
16—Montreal	W	3-2	Morgan	Hall
18—Phila.	W	4-2	Belcher	Ruffin
19—Phila.	L	12-15†	McDowell	Howell
20—Phila.	W	6-3	Martinez	Combs
21—New York	L	3-12	Gooden	Morgan
22—New York	L	3-8	Ojeda	Crews
23—At Chicago	W	4-3	Belcher	Assenmacher
24—At Chicago	W	15-6	Valenzuela	Lancaster
25—At St. L.	W	4-1	Martinez	Magrane
26—At St. L.	W	8-0	Morgan	B. Smith
27—At St. L.	W	14-7	Crews	DeLeon
28—At Pitts.	L	5-6	Landrum	Howell
29—At Pitts.	L	5-9	Patterson	Valenzuela
30—At Pitts.	L	3-5	Terrell	Martinez
31—Cincinnati	W	2-1*	Aase	Charlton

Won 14, Lost 13

JUNE

Date		Score	Winner	Loser
1—Cincinnati	L	2-5	Jackson	Wetteland
2—Cincinnati	L	3-8	Charlton	Crews
3—Cincinnati	L	0-2	Browning	Valenzuela
4—Atlanta	W	6-0	Martinez	Glavine
5—Atlanta	L	4-6	Smith	Morgan
6—Atlanta	W	7-5	Howell	Kerfeld
8—At S.D.	L	6-12	Lefferts	Gott
9—At S.D.	W	5-4†	Wetteland	Show
10—At S.D.	L	1-2*	Harris	Howell
11—At Hous.	L	3-5	Andersen	Morgan
12—At Hous.	L	4-5	Gullickson	Maddux
13—At Hous.	L	1-5	Scott	Belcher
15—San Diego	L	1-3§	Schiraldi	Hartley
16—San Diego	W	5-2	Martinez	Dunne
17—San Diego	W	6-3	Morgan	Rasmussen
18—Houston	W	5-2	Belcher	Gullickson
19—Houston	W	5-1	Valenzuela	Scott
20—Houston	W	3-2	Martinez	Clancy
22—At Cin.	W	7-6*	Howell	Myers
23—At Cin.	L	6-11	Browning	Belcher
24—At Cin.	L	6-10	Mahler	Valenzuela
25—At Atlanta	W	5-2	Martinez	Leibrandt
26—At Atlanta	L	2-4	Avery	Morgan
27—At Atlanta	L	0-4	Smoltz	Belcher
29—St. Louis	W	6-0	Valenzuela	DeLeon
30—St. Louis	L	5-6	Tudor	Gott

Won 11, Lost 15

JULY

Date		Score	Winner	Loser
1—St. Louis	L	5-6	DiPino	Crews
2—Chicago	W	3-1	Belcher	Pico
3—Chicago	W	7-6	Hartley	Assenmacher
4—Chicago	L	3-5	Harkey	Valenzuela
5—Pittsburgh	L	6-9	Reed	Martinez
6—Pittsburgh	L	3-6	Smiley	Morgan
7—Pittsburgh	W	4-2	Belcher	Terrell
8—Pittsburgh	L	2-7	Drabek	Wells

JULY

Date		Score	Winner	Loser
12—At Chicago	W	6-3	Valenzuela	Harkey
13—At Chicago	W	5-2	Martinez	Boskie
14—At Chicago	W	7-0	Morgan	Maddux
15—At Chicago	L	1-5	Wilson	Belcher
16—At St. L.	W	5-2	Wells	Tewksbury
17—At St. L.	L	0-3	B. Smith	Valenzuela
18—At St. L.	W	6-1	Martinez	DeLeon
20—At Pitts.	L	2-4	Walk	Morgan
21—At Pitts.	W	6-0	Belcher	Heaton
22—At Pitts.	L	6-11	Kipper	Wells
23—San Fran.	W	11-1	Valenzuela	Wilson
24—San Fran.	W	9-2	Martinez	Burkett
25—San Fran.	L	2-7	Garrelts	Morgan
26—Atlanta	W	8-1	Belcher	Clary
27—Atlanta	W	5-4‡	Searage	Luecken
28—Atlanta	W	8-7	Hartley	Grant
29—Atlanta	W	4-3	Martinez	Leibrandt
30—Cincinnati	W	4-1	Morgan	Charlton
31—Cincinnati	L	2-5	Rijo	Belcher

Won 16, Lost 11

AUGUST

Date		Score	Winner	Loser
1—San Fran.	L	1-2	Robinson	Howell
2—At S.F.	L	1-3	Burkett	Valenzuela
3—At S.F.	W	11-2	Martinez	Garrelts
4—At S.F.	L	1-2	Wilson	Morgan
5—At S.F.	W	12-6	Hartley	Novoa
7—At Cin.	L	0-1	Browning	Neidlinger
8—At Cin.	W	4-2	Valenzuela	Scudder
9—At Cin.	W	10-3	Martinez	Armstrong
10—At Atlanta	L	2-3	Avery	Morgan
11—At Atlanta	W	6-4*	Howell	Clary
12—At Atlanta	W	7-3	Neidlinger	Glavine
13—At Atlanta	L	5-9	Smoltz	Valenzuela
14—At N.Y.	L	8-9	Gooden	Martinez
14—At N.Y.	W	2-1	Hartley	Cone
15—At N.Y.	W	3-2	Morgan	Fernandez
16—At N.Y.	L	1-4	Darling	Belcher
17—Montreal	W	7-6	Neidlinger	Gardner
18—Montreal	W	3-2	Valenzuela	Rojas
19—Montreal	L	1-2	De. Martinez	R. Martinez
20—Phila.	W	2-1	Gott	Mulholland
21—Phila.	L	11-12	McDowell	Crews
22—Phila.	W	3-2	Gott	Boever
23—New York	W	4-2	Valenzuela	Cone
24—New York	L	2-3	Gooden	Gott
25—New York	W	3-2x	Aase	Darling
26—New York	W	2-1	Hartley	Viola
28—At Phila.	W	5-1	Neidlinger	DeJesus
29—At Phila.	W	12-2	Valenzuela	Greene
30—At Phila.	W	3-2	Martinez	Boever
31—At Mon.	L	2-5	Nabholz	Morgan

Won 18, Lost 12

SEPTEMBER

Date		Score	Winner	Loser
1—At Mon.	L	0-6	Boyd	Hartley
2—At Mon.	W	12-5	Crews	Gardner
3—Houston	L	3-7	Gullickson	Valenzuela
4—Houston	L	8-10	Meyer	Gott
5—Atlanta	L	2-6	Smoltz	Morgan
6—Atlanta	W	5-0	Hartley	Marak
7—Cincinnati	W	3-1	Neidlinger	Rijo
8—Cincinnati	L	4-8	Browning	Valenzuela
9—Cincinnati	W	6-4	Martinez	Jackson
10—At S.D.	L	2-5	Rasmussen	Crews
11—At S.D.	L	0-4	Hurst	Hartley
12—At S.D.	W	10-3	Crews	Hammaker
14—At Cin.	W	10-4	Valenzuela	Browning
15—At Cin.	W	3-0	Martinez	Jackson
16—At Cin.	L	5-2	Scudder	Morgan
17—At Atlanta	W	5-2	Crews	Leibrandt
18—At Atlanta	W	6-2	Neidlinger	Marak
19—San Diego	L	4-9	Lilliquist	Holmes
20—San Diego	W	7-2	Martinez	Benes
21—San Fran.	W	16-3	Morgan	Robinson
22—San Fran.	W	6-3	Cook	LaCoss
23—San Fran.	L	2-6	Burkett	Neidlinger
24—At Hous.	W	7-5†	Gott	Smith
25—At Hous.	W	3-1*	Howell	Agosto
26—At Hous.	L	1-10	Deshaies	Morgan
28—At S.F.	L	6-7	Oliveras	Gott
29—At S.F.	L	3-4	Downs	Neidlinger
30—At S.F.	L	2-8	Reuschel	Valenzuela

Won 14, Lost 14

OCTOBER

Date		Score	Winner	Loser
1—San Diego	W	2-1	Martinez	Benes
2—San Diego	W	8-7*	Walsh	Lefferts
3—San Diego	L	3-7	Show	Cook

Won 2, Lost 1

*10 innings. †11 innings. ‡12 innings. §13 innings. x14 innings.

The stopper role belonged to Jay Howell, who paced the Dodgers with 16 saves.

traded for a center fielder (Stan Javier). While playing center, Samuel batted .182 as the Dodgers' leadoff hitter. Moved back to his natural position at second base and dropped to seventh in the order, he batted .277 after the All-Star break and finished at .242 overall. Javier, obtained from Oakland, batted .304 in 104 games.

The prime catalysts of the Dodgers' vastly improved offense were first baseman Eddie Murray and left fielder Kal Daniels. Neither was without question marks entering the season: for Murray, it was his age, 34, coming off a career-low .247 season in 1989; for Daniels, it was the numerous operations on his knees. Murray, besides belting 26 homers with 95 RBIs, wound up with the best average in the majors (.330) but was second in the N.L. batting race to Willie McGee, whose .335 mark with St. Louis was frozen when he was traded to the American League in August (McGee batted .324 between both leagues). Daniels batted .296 and established career highs with 27 homers and 94 RBIs.

With right fielder Hubie Brooks, a free-agent signee, adding 20 homers and 91 RBIs, the Dodgers boasted their first 20-homer, 90-RBI trio since 1974.

The offense might have packed an even more intense punch had outfielder Kirk Gibson been activated before June. Coming off major surgery to repair his left hamstring, Gibson finished with eight homers and a .260 average due to a September slump (.159, no homers), but he stole 26 bases in 28 attempts.

Among the regulars, only shortstop Alfredo Griffin suffered a substantial dropoff, batting .210 (43 points below his career mark) and fanning a career-high 65 times. Backup outfielder Chris Gwynn was headed in the opposite direction, setting career bests with a .284 average, five homers and 22 RBIs. Backup catcher Rick Dempsey, meanwhile, appeared in his fourth decade in the big leagues.

Overall, the Dodgers scored 174 more runs than in 1989, raised their batting average 22 points to .262 and hit 40 more home runs. Trouble is, they also surrendered 149 more runs.

The loss of Hershiser after just four starts was staggering, made worse when Wetteland, Maddux and Wells failed to fill the void. Finally, Neidlinger came aboard, winning five of his first six decisions and finishing with a 3.28 ERA. Similarly, Hartley pitched well when Belcher (9-9) went down, posting a 6-3 record and 2.95 ERA in six starts and 26 relief spots.

But the undisputed pitching star was Martinez, who finished second in the league in wins (tied) and strikeouts (223), and led all N.L. pitchers with 12 complete games. And on June 4 against Atlanta, he fanned 18 batters to match Sandy Koufax's single-game club record.

The two other full-time starters were veterans Fernando Valenzuela and Mike Morgan. Valenzuela's 13 wins were second to Martinez on the staff, but he also lost 13 games and posted a career-high 4.59 ERA. On June 29 against St. Louis, he hurled the first no-hitter of his career. Morgan, after a 6-3 start (including three shutouts, matching his total through nine seasons), lost 12 of his last 17 decisions and finished 11-15.

In the bullpen, setup man Jim Gott pitched in 50 games after missing all but one game with Pittsburgh in 1989 due to elbow surgery. Crews picked up five saves in 66 games, and veteran Don Aase added three more. In October, Howell underwent his second knee surgery after managing a team-best 2.18 ERA and 16 saves.

While the Dodgers may have been slow to catch fire, they caught on with the faithful from the outset. They topped the 3 million mark in attendance for an unprecedented eighth season, leading the league with 3,002,396.

Matt Williams became the third different Giants' player in the last three years to lead the National League in RBIs, driving in 122 runs in 1990.

'Character' Year Satisfies Giants

By MARK NEWMAN

The World Series returned to the Bay Area in 1990, without any confusion about the local partisanship. There were no half-orange, half-green hats, no placards declaring "Go Giants" on one side, "Go A's" on the other.

There were no Giants, period.

So why did Roger Craig claim to be "more proud of this team than any I've managed?" How could the Giants slip from the World Series to a third-place finish in the National League West and tranquility? How could they call an 85-77 season "fulfilling" after dancing in Humm-Baby heaven?

Consider that San Francisco choked for two months on Cincinnati's exhaust fumes, using up so many relievers that Rollie and the Goose could have shown up at any minute. The Giants were 17-28 and 14½ games back on May 28, moving Will Clark to extricate a water fountain from the Wrigley Field dugout wall.

Then Craig opened his mail and found a vial of dirt, which some fan had scooped off the pitcher's mound on the Iowa field featured in the movie "Field of Dreams." Craig slipped the magic dust into his pocket for good luck, and the Giants won 16 of the first 17 games they played in June.

From that point until mid-September, the Giants had hopes of overtaking the Reds, who failed to play .500 baseball (58-59) after June 3. Those hopes weren't dashed until the Giants' final trip of the season, when they lost seven of 10 games and fell nine lengths behind.

"It wasn't a successful season, but it was a fulfilling one," center fielder Brett Butler said. "It was fulfilling in the fact that ability and talent weren't looked upon so much as. . .individuals collectively working together. Character was brought to the forefront by the situation of us being counted out four or five times throughout the course of the year. We still reached within ourselves to a place some people don't understand."

The Giants' only other choice would have been to pack it in and punch out water fountains. They had enough reason.

San Francisco used 26 pitchers, one shy of the major league record shared by three teams. In all, 51 players suited up, five more than the franchise record and five under the major league mark. The Giants also used the disabled list a club-record 15 times.

The late-season absence of relief stopper Jeff Brantley was the most damaging. The gutsy righthander rose from obscurity to the 1990 N.L. All-Star squad, posted the best earned-run average (1.54) among N.L. relievers and was just overcoming a post-All-Star Game slump when he was hospitalized four days because of back spasms. When he tried to throw too hard, too soon, in a simulated game immediately afterward, Brantley suffered a shoulder injury that ended his season on September 3. His absence was most noticeable during the final trip, when Houston won three one-run games, two of them in the ninth inning.

At his best, Brantley represented one of many individual highlights. Matt Williams, playing his first full big-league season, belted 33 homers, handled third base with a veteran's aplomb and led the league with 122 runs batted in. He followed first baseman Will Clark and left fielder Kevin Mitchell as the N.L. RBI kingpin, making the Giants the first team since the 1925-27 New York Yankees to have three different players win consecutive RBI titles.

Mitchell and Clark, though neither was satisfied with his own production after finishing first and second, respectively, in the 1989 N.L. MVP voting, nonetheless had seasons other players would use to set up million-dollar retirement funds in Miami. Clark, playing all year with a damaged nerve in his left foot, batted .295 with 19 homers and 95 RBIs; Mitchell, bothered by bone spurs in his right wrist, hit .290 with a team-leading 35 homers and 93 RBIs. Each underwent postseason surgery.

The San Francisco outfield was anchored by Butler, who again performed the necessary duties that make him one of the top leadoff hitters in baseball. He tied for the N.L. lead with 192 hits and ranked among the top 10 in batting, walks, triples, runs scored, stolen bases and on-base percentage. Butler also collected at least 20 bunt hits (22) for the seventh straight year.

The arrival of free agent Kevin Bass failed to solve the annual platoon dilemma in right field, however. Bass underwent knee surgery in May, but former Seattle Mariner Mike Kingery, signed to a minor league contract in April, came up to bat .295. Former American Leaguer Rick Leach batted .293 as part of the platoon un-

SCORES OF SAN FRANCISCO GIANTS' 1990 GAMES

APRIL

Date		Score	Winner	Loser
11—At Atlanta	W	8-0	Reuschel	Glavine
11—At Atlanta	L	3-4	Smith	Swan
12—At Atlanta	W	13-4	LaCoss	Smoltz
13—San Diego	L	3-8	Harris	Quisenberry
14—San Diego	L	3-5*	Lefferts	Brantley
15—San Diego	L	3-4	Harris	Bedrosian
16—At L.A.	W	3-1	LaCoss	Valenzuela
17—Los Ang.	L	5-10	Aase	Hammaker
18—Los Ang.	L	2-6	Morgan	Gunderson
20—At S.D.	L	2-9	Whitson	Reuschel
21—At S.D.	W	6-4	LaCoss	Hurst
22—At S.D.	W	3-1	Hammaker	Show
23—At S.D.	L	3-13	Benes	Gunderson
24—Pittsburgh	L	1-4	Drabek	Garrelts
25—Pittsburgh	L	4-7‡	Patterson	Bedrosian
26—Pittsburgh	L	1-2	Smiley	LaCoss
27—St. Louis	W	12-3	Hammaker	Mathews
28—St. Louis	L	0-5	Tudor	Garrelts
29—St. Louis	W	9-7	Reuschel	Magrane
30—At L.A.	W	8-4	Burkett	Wetteland
Won 8, Lost 12				

MAY

Date		Score	Winner	Loser
1—Chicago	L	4-7	Bielecki	Knepper
2—Chicago	L	6-9	Harkey	Garrelts
4—At Mon.	L	4-5	Gross	Reuschel
5—At Mon.	W	4-1	Burkett	Martinez
6—At Mon.	L	0-7	Gardner	Hammaker
7—At Mon.	L	6-7	Frey	Bedrosian
8—At N.Y.	L	1-4	Fernandez	Reuschel
9—At N.Y.	W	4-2	Knepper	Ojeda
11—At Phila.	L	6-10	Howell	Burkett
12—At Phila.	W	6-2	Garrelts	Ruffin
13—At Phila.	L	1-4	Cook	Reuschel
14—New York	W	4-2	Knepper	Fernandez
15—New York	W	6-5	Thurmond	Ojeda
16—New York	W	4-3*	Brantley	Pena
18—Montreal	W	7-2	Hammaker	Frey
19—Montreal	L	4-7	Gross	Knepper
20—Montreal	L	5-6†	Sampen	Hammaker
21—Phila.	L	2-5	Mulholland	Garrelts
22—Phila.	L	2-4	Howell	Reuschel
23—At St. L.	W	6-1	Knepper	Mathews
24—At St. L.	L	2-3‡	DiPino	Vosberg
25—At Pitts.	W	9-8	Burkett	Terrell
26—At Pitts.	L	4-10	Drabek	Garrelts
27—At Pitts.	L	2-5	Heaton	Reuschel
28—At Chicago	L	1-5	Harkey	Knepper
29—At Chicago	W	6-2	Robinson	Blankenship
30—At Chicago	W	4-1	Burkett	Boskie
31—Houston	L	3-5	Deshaies	Garrelts
Won 11, Lost 17				

JUNE

Date		Score	Winner	Loser
1—Houston	W	6-5†	Bedrosian	Clancy
2—Houston	W	5-4*	Bedrosian	Darwin
3—Houston	W	7-3	Hammaker	Scott
4—Cincinnati	W	10-1	Burkett	Robinson
5—Cincinnati	W	6-1	Garrelts	Armstrong
6—Cincinnati	W	3-2†	Brantley	Dibble
8—At Atlanta	W	23-8	Wilson	Lilliquist
9—At Atlanta	L	3-5	Leibrandt	Hammaker
10—At Atlanta	W	9-3	Burkett	Smith
11—At Atlanta	W	8-3	Garrelts	Smoltz
12—At S.D.	W	7-2	Robinson	Rasmussen
13—At S.D.	W	6-0	Wilson	Whitson
14—At S.D.	W	6-2	Vosberg	Hurst
15—Atlanta	W	8-2	Burkett	Smith
16—Atlanta	W	7-0	Garrelts	Smoltz
17—Atlanta	W	9-7	Bedrosian	Castillo
18—San Diego	W	2-1	Wilson	Whitson
19—San Diego	L	3-4	Hurst	Oliveras
20—San Diego	L	3-4†	Lefferts	Bedrosian
22—At Hous.	W	4-3	Garrelts	Deshaies
23—At Hous.	L	2-4	Portugal	Bedrosian
24—At Hous.	L	2-8	Gullickson	Robinson
25—At Cin.	L	2-5	Armstrong	Burkett
26—At Cin.	L	2-3‡	Myers	Thurmond
27—At Cin.	W	8-3	Robinson	Browning
29—Pittsburgh	W	7-3	Wilson	Heaton
30—Pittsburgh	L	3-4	Kipper	Thurmond
Won 19, Lost 8				

JULY

Date		Score	Winner	Loser
1—Pittsburgh	L	5-8	Tibbs	Oliveras
2—St. Louis	W	3-2	Robinson	Magrane
3—St. Louis	W	4-0	Wilson	Tewksbury
4—St. Louis	W	9-2	Burkett	DeLeon
6—Chicago	L	2-5	Boskie	Garrelts
7—Chicago	W	10-9	Brantley	Lancaster
8—Chicago	W	5-3	Wilson	Pico
8—Chicago	W	10-4	Burkett	Bielecki
12—At St. L.	W	4-2	Garrelts	B. Smith
13—At St. L.	W	6-1	Robinson	DeLeon
14—At St. L.	L	1-2	L. Smith	Wilson
15—At St. L.	W	5-3	Bedrosian	Niedenfuer
16—At Pitts.	W	6-1	Garrelts	Reed
17—At Pitts.	W	6-3	Robinson	Smiley
18—At Pitts.	L	2-11	Drabek	Wilson
20—At Chicago	L	4-5	Bielecki	Brantley
21—At Chicago	L	2-3	Harkey	Brantley
22—At Chicago	L	2-4	Assenmacher	Hammaker
23—At L.A.	L	1-11	Valenzuela	Wilson
24—At L.A.	L	2-9	Martinez	Burkett
25—At L.A.	W	7-2	Garrelts	Morgan
26—Cincinnati	W	4-3	Thurmond	Rijo
27—Cincinnati	W	4-3	Robinson	Scudder
28—Cincinnati	W	3-2†	Bedrosian	Myers
29—Cincinnati	W	4-0	Garrelts	Armstrong
30—Houston	L	1-6	Darwin	Bedrosian
31—Houston	W	3-2	Brantley	Agosto
Won 17, Lost 10				

AUGUST

Date		Score	Winner	Loser
1—At L.A.	W	2-1	Robinson	Howell
2—Los Ang.	W	3-1	Burkett	Valenzuela
3—Los Ang.	L	2-11	Martinez	Garrelts
4—Los Ang.	W	2-1	Wilson	Morgan
5—Los Ang.	L	6-12	Hartley	Novoa
6—At Hous.	L	1-4	Gullickson	Robinson
7—At Hous.	L	0-4	Portugal	Burkett
8—At Hous.	W	8-4	Wilson	Agosto
10—At Cin.	L	0-7	Charlton	Robinson
11—At Cin.	W	4-2	Burkett	Rijo
12—At Cin.	L	4-6	Browning	Garrelts
13—At Cin.	L	5-6	Layana	Wilson
14—At Phila.	L	3-4§	Cook	Bedrosian
15—At Phila.	L	0-6	Mulholland	Robinson
16—At Phila.	L	4-6	McDowell	Thurmond
17—New York	W	3-2	Garrelts	Viola
18—New York	L	2-9	Cone	Wilson
19—New York	L	9-10	Gooden	LaCoss
20—Montreal	W	4-2	Robinson	Gross
21—Montreal	L	5-10	Rojas	Wilson
22—Montreal	W	2-1	Bedrosian	Frey
23—Phila.	W	6-3	Oliveras	Cook
24—Phila.	W	13-2	LaCoss	Combs
25—Phila.	W	4-2	Robinson	Mulholland
26—Phila.	L	1-5	Grimsley	Burkett
28—At Mon.	L	2-5	Gardner	Garrelts
29—At Mon.	W	6-5	Brantley	Sampen
30—At N.Y.	L	2-12	Fernandez	LaCoss
31—At N.Y.	L	3-4	Viola	Bedrosian
Won 12, Lost 17				

SEPTEMBER

Date		Score	Winner	Loser
1—At N.Y.	L	5-6	Valera	Burkett
2—At N.Y.	L	6-10	Cone	McClellan
3—At S.D.	W	5-4	Downs	Schiraldi
4—At S.D.	W	6-4	LaCoss	Hammaker
5—Cincinnati	L	3-5	Charlton	Robinson
6—Cincinnati	W	6-2	Garrelts	Mahler
7—Houston	L	1-2	Darwin	Burkett
8—Houston	W	2-1*	Bedrosian	Meyer
9—Houston	W	5-1	LaCoss	Portugal
10—Atlanta	W	7-6*	Bedrosian	Mercker
11—Atlanta	W	2-0	Garrelts	Grant
12—Atlanta	W	8-3	Burkett	Leibrandt
14—At Hous.	L	1-2	Portugal	Downs
15—At Hous.	L	2-3*	Hernandez	Bedrosian
16—At Hous.	L	2-3	Agosto	Robinson
17—At Cin.	L	0-4	Rijo	Garrelts
18—At Cin.	W	5-3	Burkett	Browning
19—At Atlanta	L	1-5	Glavine	Downs
20—At Atlanta	W	5-3	Gunderson	Smoltz
21—At L.A.	L	3-16	Morgan	Robinson
22—At L.A.	L	3-6	Cook	LaCoss
23—At L.A.	W	6-2	Burkett	Neidlinger
24—San Diego	W	3-1	Downs	Lilliquist
25—San Diego	W	3-1	Dewey	Benes
26—San Diego	W	7-6	O'Neal	Rasmussen
28—Los Ang.	W	7-6	Oliveras	Gott
29—Los Ang.	W	4-3	Downs	Neidlinger
30—Los Ang.	W	8-2	Reuschel	Valenzuela
Won 17, Lost 11				

OCTOBER

Date		Score	Winner	Loser
1—Atlanta	L	3-5	Smoltz	Wilson
2—Atlanta	L	7-16	Freeman	Dewey
3—Atlanta	W	6-3	Bedrosian	Avery
Won 1, Lost 2				

*10 innings. †11 innings. ‡12 innings. §13 innings.

Brett Butler ranked as one of the top leadoff hitters in baseball in 1990, finishing among the league's top 10 in several offensive categories.

til suspended by the commissioner's office in August for a positive drug test.

Up the middle, the Giants had one of the league's best double-play combinations in second baseman Robby Thompson and shortstop Jose Uribe, but neither could bat .250. Backups Ernest Riles and Greg Litton (a sub at five positions) also found that mark out of reach, though Riles popped eight homers in just 155 at-bats.

The preseason concern over the catchers' bats was partly justified, what with Terry Kennedy driving in just 26 runs despite hitting .277, his best mark since 1983. Free-agent signee Gary Carter had nine homers but only 27 RBIs, though he broke Al Lopez's N.L. record when he caught game No. 1,862 in June. Steve Decker, the organization's top hitting prospect, batted .296 with three homers and eight RBIs in 15 games in September.

As anticipated, the often-injured starting pitchers held true to form, but youngsters such as rookie John Burkett and Trevor Wilson provided a spark of life. Burkett led all rookie hurlers with 14 victories and paced the Giants' staff with 32 starts, while Wilson tossed a one-hitter en route to an 8-7 season.

Among the veterans, Kelly Downs didn't pitch until August due to shoulder surgery. Knee injuries and subsequent surgeries befell Rick Reuschel, who was side-lined May 14 through September 16, and Mike LaCoss, who missed May, June and July. Don Robinson came back to win 10 games after starting the year on rehabilitation assignment (off-season knee surgery), and Scott Garrelts, who missed the last two weeks with tendinitis in his right shoulder, fired a one-hitter among his 12 victories.

In the bullpen, Francisco Oliveras (2.77 earned-run average) and Mark Thurmond, acquired from Houston in May to fill a lefthanded void, were the two steadiest bridges to the late innings. Rebounding from a tough start that coincided with his son's diagnosed case of leukemia, Steve Bedrosian tied for the N.L. lead with nine relief wins and posted seven saves in September. He finished with 17 saves, second on the staff to Brantley's 19.

Watching the end of the 1990 season was something of a paradox for Craig. He knew any repeat hopes were minuscule, yet he felt a sense of accomplishment. He told the troops as much in a meeting the day after former Giant Terry Mulholland no-hit the club on August 15.

"I told them I'm more proud of this team than any I've managed, and that includes the years we won," Craig related. "This team was counted out again and again, and it kept coming back. That says a lot about these people."

San Diego's 1990 woes could not be blamed on Bip Roberts, who played three infield positions and in the outfield while compiling career highs in most offensive categories.

Padres Split by Firings and Ice

By BARRY BLOOM

In 1990, there was a schism in the San Diego Padres' clubhouse as wide as the crack left at Loma Prieta, the epicenter of the great San Francisco Bay Area earthquake.

The situation came to a head in September when a prankster took an action figurine of right fielder Tony Gwynn, cut off its arms and feet and hung it in effigy in the Padres' home dugout. An infuriated Gwynn, at the center of clubhouse friction all season long, suspected one of his teammates had committed the crude act. (Later, a member of the grounds crew confessed he'd staged the prank alone.)

The incident was emblematic of a season that would end in mass executions, so to speak, a season in which a club secured the previous 16 years by the Kroc hamburger fortune would wind up gutted.

At the All-Star break, less than one month after a new ownership group headed by TV producer Tom Werner purchased the club from Joan Kroc, Jack McKeon resigned as manager and returned to the front office. Bench coach Greg Riddoch, who hadn't managed since 1981 (and then in the short-season Northwest League), took over and lost 11 of his first 12 games.

The wholesale housecleaning began in earnest when McKeon, the team's architect and general manager for nearly a decade, was fired on September 21. He was replaced by Joe McIlvaine, who left a similar position with the New York Mets. In short order, the new hierarchy handed some 30 members of the organization their walking papers.

"It was a tough, tough month," said club president Dick Freeman.

It was a tough year, considering the Padres had been tabbed a preseason favorite to win the National League West after finishing three games out of first in 1989. Instead, they slipped to a fourth-place tie, trailing by 16 lengths at 75-87.

It was a disturbing season of acrimony that was punctuated by injuries. First baseman Jack Clark, Gwynn's chief adversary, managed to lead the team with 25 homers but missed 47 games with assorted ailments. Gwynn missed the last 19 games when he broke a finger while crashing into the fence in pursuit of a fly ball in Atlanta. He was unable to win his fourth straight N.L. batting title, tying for sixth with a

Joe Carter, who collected 115 RBIs, was the only N.L. player to play in all 162 games in 1990.

.309 mark, but knocked in a career-high 72 runs and won his fourth Gold Glove.

But the most damaging blow came on June 14, when Gold Glove catcher Benito Santiago was nearly beaned in a pinch-hitting appearance against San Francisco's Jeff Brantley. Santiago, second on the club in homers and RBIs at the time, threw up his left hand to protect his face, but the pitch fractured his forearm in three places. The Padres, 30-27 and six lengths behind Cincinnati entering the game, fell to 51-59 and 12½ games back before Santiago returned on August 10.

The foundation had actually started cracking the previous October, when Kroc announced she was putting the club up for sale—the very same day the quake struck San Francisco. The aftershocks were felt when 1989 N.L. Cy Young winner Mark Davis was lost following careless free-agent negotiations, and when Gwynn was treated like a pariah after requesting a review of his contract when newcomer Joe Carter signed a three-year, $9.2 million deal.

With Davis and his 44 saves departed, the pitching staff was under considerable

SCORES OF SAN DIEGO PADRES' 1990 GAMES

APRIL

Date		Score	Winner	Loser
9—At L.A.	L	2-4	Wetteland	Hurst
10—Los Ang.	L	0-1	Belcher	Show
11—Los Ang.	W	3-1	Benes	Valenzuela
12—Los Ang.	W	8-6	Schiraldi	Aase
13—At S.F.	W	8-3	Harris	Quisenberry
14—At S.F.	W	5-3‡	Lefferts	Brantley
15—At S.F.	W	4-3	Harris	Bedrosian
17—At Cin.	L	1-2	Browning	Benes
18—At Cin.	L	7-11	Layana	Valdez
20—San Fran.	W	9-2	Whitson	Reuschel
21—San Fran.	L	4-6	LaCoss	Hurst
22—San Fran.	L	1-3	Hammaker	Show
23—San Fran.	W	13-3	Benes	Gunderson
24—Chicago	W	13-3	Rasmussen	Maddux
25—Chicago	W	3-0	Whitson	Bielecki
26—Chicago	L	1-3	Harkey	Hurst
27—Pittsburgh	L	4-9	Heaton	Show
28—Pittsburgh	L	3-4	Walk	Benes
29—Pittsburgh	L	1-10	Drabek	Rasmussen

Won 9, Lost 10

MAY

Date		Score	Winner	Loser
1—St. Louis	L	1-2	B. Smith	Whitson
2—St. Louis	W	4-3	Hurst	DeLeon
5—At Chicago	L	2-3	Maddux	Lefferts
5—At Chicago	W	6-5	Rasmussen	Nunez
6—At Chicago	W	8-3	Whitson	Bielecki
7—At Pitts.	L	1-4	Walk	Hurst
8—At Pitts.	L	2-10	Terrell	Show
9—At St. L.	L	5-11	Horton	Benes
10—At St. L.	W	9-1	Rasmussen	Magrane
11—Montreal	W	5-3	Lefferts	Hall
12—Montreal	W	5-2	Hurst	Smith
13—Montreal	L	0-15	Boyd	Show
14—Phila.	W	5-1	Benes	Combs
15—Phila.	L	1-2	Mulholland	Rasmussen
16—Phila.	L	5-6	Howell	Whitson
18—New York	W	6-3	Hurst	Viola
19—New York	L	4-6	Cone	Benes
20—New York	W	3-1	Harris	Darling
22—At Mon.	L	1-6	Gardner	Whitson
23—At Mon.	L	0-4	Boyd	Hurst
24—At N.Y.	W	5-4	Benes	Viola
25—At N.Y.	W	5-4	Rasmussen	Cone
26—At N.Y.	L	0-11	Fernandez	Dunne
27—At N.Y.	W	8-4	Whitson	Gooden
28—At Phila.	W	9-5	Grant	Parrett
30—At Phila.	W	8-3	Benes	Ruffin
31—Atlanta	W	2-1	Rasmussen	Smith

Won 15, Lost 12

JUNE

Date		Score	Winner	Loser
1—Atlanta	L	11-16	Castillo	Dunne
2—Atlanta	W	9-0	Whitson	Lilliquist
3—Atlanta	L	2-4‡	Kerfeld	Harris
4—Houston	W	10-2	Benes	Clancy
5—Houston	W	11-2	Rasmussen	Deshaies
6—Houston	W	3-2	Lefferts	Portugal
8—Los Ang.	W	12-6	Lefferts	Gott
9—Los Ang.	L	4-5§	Wetteland	Show
10—Los Ang.	W	2-1‡	Harris	Howell
12—San Fran.	L	2-7	Robinson	Rasmussen
13—San Fran.	L	0-6	Wilson	Whitson
14—San Fran.	L	2-6	Vosberg	Hurst
15—At L.A.	W	3-1y	Schiraldi	Hartley
16—At L.A.	L	2-5	Martinez	Dunne
17—At L.A.	L	3-6	Morgan	Rasmussen
18—At S.F.	L	1-2	Wilson	Whitson
19—At S.F.	W	4-3	Hurst	Oliveras
20—At S.F.	W	4-3§	Lefferts	Bedrosian
23—At Atlanta	W	7-5	Whitson	Glavine
24—At Atlanta	L	10-11x	Luecken	Lefferts
25—At Hous.	L	3-5	Scott	Benes
26—At Hous.	W	7-0	Rasmussen	Clancy
27—At Hous.	L	1-9	Deshaies	Hurst
28—At Hous.	L	1-2‡	Andersen	Grant
29—Chicago	L	2-3	Long	Harris
30—Chicago	L	3-7	Wilson	Benes

Won 11, Lost 15

JULY

Date		Score	Winner	Loser
1—Chicago	L	10-11	Lancaster	Lefferts
2—Pittsburgh	L	3-4z	Patterson	Schiraldi
3—Pittsburgh	L	3-5	Landrum	Lefferts
4—Pittsburgh	W	5-4	Show	Heaton
5—St. Louis	L	1-4	L. Smith	Harris
6—St. Louis	L	3-5	Tudor	Rasmussen
7—St. Louis	W	3-1	Hurst	Magrane
8—St. Louis	L	1-4	Tewksbury	Whitson
12—At Pitts.	L	3-4a	Patterson	Schiraldi
13—At Pitts.	L	1-4	Drabek	Rasmussen

JULY

Date		Score	Winner	Loser
14—At Pitts.	L	4-8	Power	Harris
15—At Pitts.	W	4-1	Whitson	Heaton
16—At Chicago	L	3-4	Harkey	Show
17—At Chicago	L	2-7	Boskie	Benes
18—At Chicago	L	2-4	Maddux	Rasmussen
19—At St. L.	L	3-8	Magrane	Hurst
20—At St. L.	L	2-4	Tudor	Whitson
21—At St. L.	L	2-4†	Tewksbury	Show
22—At St. L.	L	4-6	Dayley	Harris
23—Cincinnati	L	2-9	Browning	Rasmussen
24—Cincinnati	W	10-0	Hurst	Armstrong
25—Cincinnati	W	2-1	Whitson	Charlton
25—Cincinnati	W	10-4	Schiraldi	Mahler
26—Houston	W	8-2	Show	Portugal
27—Houston	W	6-2	Benes	Gullickson
28—Houston	L	3-5	Scott	Rasmussen
29—Houston	W	4-3	Harris	Smith
30—Atlanta	L	3-4§	Henry	Schiraldi
31—Atlanta	W	7-6	Lefferts	Luecken

Won 10, Lost 19

AUGUST

Date		Score	Winner	Loser
1—Cincinnati	L	3-6	Scudder	Benes
2—At Cin.	W	8-5	Rasmussen	Browning
3—At Cin.	W	3-2	Harris	Dibble
4—At Cin.	W	7-3§	Harris	Mahler
5—At Cin.	L	2-6	Rijo	Schiraldi
7—At Atlanta	W	7-2	Benes	Glavine
7—At Atlanta	W	11-9	Show	Clary
8—At Atlanta	L	1-7	Smoltz	Rasmussen
9—At Atlanta	W	7-0	Hurst	Leibrandt
10—At Hous.	W	2-0	Whitson	Deshaies
11—At Hous.	W	6-3‡	Show	Smith
12—At Hous.	W	9-0	Lilliquist	Gullickson
14—Montreal	L	3-8	Martinez	Rasmussen
15—Montreal	L	3-5b	Sampen	Davis
16—Montreal	W	3-2§	Rodriguez	Burke
17—Phila.	L	1-2	DeJesus	Schiraldi
18—Phila.	W	4-2	Benes	Greene
19—Phila.	L	2-3	Boever	Rasmussen
20—New York	W	3-1	Hurst	Fernandez
21—New York	W	7-0	Whitson	Darling
22—New York	L	1-4	Viola	Schiraldi
24—At Mon.	W	2-1	Benes	Martinez
25—At Mon.	L	1-2	Nabholz	Rasmussen
26—At Mon.	L	2-4	Frey	Hurst
27—At Mon.	W	4-1	Whitson	Boyd
28—At N.Y.	L	0-4	Cone	Schiraldi
29—At N.Y.	L	1-2	Ojeda	Harris
31—At Phila.	L	2-4	McDowell	Hammaker

Won 15, Lost 13

SEPTEMBER

Date		Score	Winner	Loser
1—At Phila.	L	2-3‡	Boever	Harris
1—At Phila.	L	1-2	Akerfelds	Rodriguez
2—At Phila.	W	9-1	Whitson	DeJesus
3—San Fran.	L	4-5	Downs	Schiraldi
4—San Fran.	L	4-6	LaCoss	Hammaker
5—Houston	W	5-2	Rasmussen	Scott
6—Houston	W	3-0‡	Harris	Meyer
7—Atlanta	L	1-4	Leibrandt	Whitson
8—Atlanta	L	5-11	Parrett	Lilliquist
9—Atlanta	W	5-4§	Show	Mercker
10—Los Ang.	W	5-2	Rasmussen	Crews
11—Los Ang.	W	4-0	Hurst	Hartley
12—Los Ang.	L	3-10	Crews	Hammaker
14—At Atlanta	L	3-7	Glavine	Lilliquist
15—At Atlanta	W	5-3§	Lefferts	Parrett
16—At Atlanta	W	9-4	Rasmussen	Avery
17—At Hous.	W	5-0	Hurst	Darwin
18—At Hous.	W	8-1	Whitson	Gullickson
19—At L.A.	W	9-4	Lilliquist	Holmes
20—At L.A.	L	2-7	Martinez	Benes
21—Cincinnati	L	1-10	Rijo	Rasmussen
22—Cincinnati	L	4-6	Dibble	Harris
22—Cincinnati	L	5-9	Browning	Hammaker
23—Cincinnati	L	2-9	Jackson	Whitson
24—At S.F.	L	1-3	Downs	Lilliquist
25—At S.F.	L	1-3	Dewey	Benes
26—At S.F.	L	6-7	O'Neal	Rasmussen
28—At Cin.	W	2-1	Hurst	Myers
29—At Cin.	W	3-1*	Whitson	Charlton
30—At Cin.	W	3-0	Lilliquist	Rijo

Won 14, Lost 16

OCTOBER

Date		Score	Winner	Loser
1—At L.A.	L	1-2	Martinez	Benes
2—At L.A.	L	7-8‡	Walsh	Lefferts
3—At L.A.	W	7-3	Show	Cook

Won 1, Lost 2

*6½ innings. †7 innings. ‡10 innings. §11 innings. x12 innings. y13 innings. z14 innings. a15 innings. b17 innings.

The shining star in the San Diego rotation was Ed Whitson, who ranked third in the league with a 2.60 ERA.

pressure. Craig Lefferts, signed as a free agent and made a full-time closer for the first time in his career, saved 23 games. Greg Harris made up nine more saves, led all Padre pitchers with a 2.30 earned-run average and pitched in 73 games, but he allowed 21 of 42 inherited runners to score.

Besides rookie Rich Rodriguez, who relieved in 32 games after being recalled from the minors in late June, the San Diego bullpen was staffed by a corps of part-time starters: Calvin Schiraldi, midseason acquisition Derek Lilliquist (from Atlanta for Mark Grant) and August pickup Atlee Hammaker (released by San Francisco). Eric Show, coming off 1989 back surgery, was relegated to the bullpen for two long periods, but he posted his club-record 100th career victory on the final day of the season.

The starting rotation was headed by Ed Whitson, who ranked third in the league with a 2.60 ERA and walked only 1.8 batters per nine innings, second best among N.L. pitchers. Whitson's 14 victories topped the 11 recorded by both Bruce Hurst and Dennis Rasmussen. Hurst hurled six complete games, including four shutouts, down the stretch, but Rasmussen won only four games after June 26 and surrendered a league-high 28 home runs. Andy Benes, who last won on August 24, finished 10-11 in his first full big-league season.

McKeon's blockbuster deal to acquire Carter from Cleveland was met with mixed reviews. Carter drove in 115 runs and was the only N.L. player to appear in 162 games, but he batted just .232. In the end, the consensus was that McKeon paid a high price (catcher Sandy Alomar Jr., outfielder Chris James and third baseman Carlos Baerga) for a negligible center fielder and not much of a take-charge player.

McKeon tried to replace James in left field with 38-year-old free agent Fred Lynn, who proved early that he was no longer an everyday player. Bip Roberts seized the opportunity to prove he was, establishing career bests in almost every offensive category. He tied Gwynn for the team batting lead (.309) and ranked among the league leaders in runs (104), doubles (36) and stolen bases (46).

Lynn was a valuable asset off the bench, however, leading the club with a .344 pinch-hitting average. Jerald Clark (.286 as a pinch-batter), Shawn Abner and Phil Stephenson also filled utility roles. Second baseman Roberto Alomar, meanwhile, ranked third on the team with a .287 average and knocked in a career-high 60 runs, the most ever by a Padre second sacker.

At third base, Mike Pagliarulo, playing next to gimpy-kneed shortstop Garry Templeton, helped give the Padres one of the weakest left sides in the league. But Pagliarulo, who produced only seven homers and 38 RBIs, left his mark in the clubhouse. He joined Clark to stir up the pot against Gwynn, carping to a reporter about a teammate who cared only about hitting for average.

The remark, coupled with the team's bad play, led to a players-only meeting that left Gwynn bitter for much of the season. After suffering his season-ending finger injury, Gwynn elected to spend the final two weeks at home.

In print, Gwynn criticized some of his teammates, but Clark returned the favor. "If this is a bad year and he rips his teammates, what would he do if he really had a bad year?" Clark wondered. ". . . What (was he) so stressed out about?"

Like everyone else who has been around San Diego for a few years, Gwynn was undone by another season that had gone over the brink.

The Astros received solid production from catcher Craig Biggio, who hit .276 and stole 25 bases.

Ill Winds Buffet Astros Outdoors

By NEIL HOHLFELD

Even in their best years, the Houston Astros have never embraced the concept of playing outdoor baseball. But in 1990, the Astros' abject failure outside the Astrodome doomed them to their worst season since 1978.

In a telltale stretch from June 1 through July 7, the Astros lost 20 of 21 road games. By season's end, they owned the worst road record in baseball (26-55) and suffered their poorest finish (75-87, 16 games back in the National League West) in a dozen seasons.

While the Astros' success at home (49-32, tied for second in the league) saved them from an even sorrier season, it did not mask their ongoing offensive problems and the steady decline of a once dominant pitching staff.

Inside the cavernous Astrodome, where pitchers aren't punished for mistakes, the Houston staff fashioned a 2.73 earned-run average. Outdoors, where mistakes became home runs (83 in 81 road games), that ERA jumped to 4.55.

The real root of Houston's problems, however, was an offense that ranked last or next to last in 13 N.L. offensive categories. Here, the home-road comparison hardly mattered—the Astros were equally inept both places.

For the first time in five seasons, Houston entered September already out of the running in the N.L. West. In the final weeks, several veterans were traded as the team committed to a rebuilding phase. Second baseman Bill Doran (who rebounded from his worst ever season in 1989 to bat a career-best .300) and relievers Larry Andersen and Dan Schatzeder were dealt to contending teams for six minor league players.

What figured to be a below-average attack was sent into shock when first baseman Glenn Davis was sidelined nine weeks in June, July and August with a rib-cage injury. Playing in just 93 games, Davis still managed 22 home runs and 64 runs batted in. Without him, however, the Astros had no hub in their lineup.

Manager Art Howe scrambled to come up with a lineup that would work. In all, he used 125 different combinations.

Franklin Stubbs, acquired from Los Angeles in spring training, proved to be a godsend with Davis out of the order. Given his first career chance to play regularly,

Given his first chance to play regularly, Franklin Stubbs responded with 23 homers and 71 RBIs.

Stubbs belted 23 home runs, a club record for lefthanded hitters, and drove home 71 runs, a personal best.

After Doran was traded, Casey Candaele, who had been the team's top spare part, took over at second base and finished with a career-high .286 average in 130 games. Outfielder Glenn Wilson, despite battling injuries that limited him to 368 at-bats, was the club's best clutch hitter, driving home 46 runs with men in scoring position. He also recorded his 100th career assist.

Beyond that, the offensive highlights were limited, at best. Rookie Eric Anthony, the opening-night starter in right field, spent seven weeks in the minors trying to regain his ability to make contact. Anthony had more strikeouts than hits (78 to 46), fanning once every three at-bats.

Three years after his rip-roaring 1987 rookie debut, center fielder Gerald Young continued his downward spin. The Astros

SCORES OF HOUSTON ASTROS' 1990 GAMES

APRIL

Date		Score	Winner	Loser
9—Cincinnati	L	4-8†	Myers	Kerfeld
10—Cincinnati	L	2-3	Layana	Agosto
11—Cincinnati	L	0-5	Armstrong	Portugal
13—Los Ang.	L	1-6	Morgan	Gullickson
14—Los Ang.	W	7-3	Andersen	Wetteland
15—Los Ang.	L	4-5*	Howell	Kerfeld
17—Atlanta	W	5-3	Portugal	Smoltz
18—Atlanta	W	10-5	Schatzeder	Lilliquist
19—At L.A.	L	3-7	Hershiser	Scott
20—At L.A.	W	4-2	Deshaies	Belcher
21—At L.A.	W	6-5	Agosto	Howell
22—At L.A.	L	0-2	Martinez	Portugal
24—Montreal	L	3-5	Gross	Scott
25—Montreal	L	0-1	Frey	Smith
26—At Atlanta	W	3-0	Clancy	Lilliquist
27—New York	L	0-1	Viola	Portugal
28—New York	W	8-4	Gullickson	Fernandez
29—New York	W	2-1*	Darwin	Machado
30—At Mon.	W	4-2	Andersen	Martinez

Won 9, Lost 10

MAY

Date		Score	Winner	Loser
1—At Mon.	L	1-2‡	Hall	Andersen
2—At Phila.	L	4-14	Cook	Clancy
3—At Phila.	W	10-3	Gullickson	Mulholland
5—At N.Y.	W	9-5	Scott	Gooden
6—At N.Y.	L	4-7†	Franco	Smith
6—At N.Y.	L	6-7	Pena	Schatzeder
7—At N.Y.	L	1-7	Viola	Clancy
8—Phila.	W	3-2*	Smith	Noles
9—Phila.	L	1-10	Combs	Scott
11—At Pitts.	L	3-4	Drabek	Deshaies
12—At Pitts.	L	1-3	Heaton	Portugal
13—At Pitts.	L	1-5	Walk	Gullickson
15—At St. L.	L	0-4	Magrane	Scott
16—At St. L.	L	6-10	B. Smith	Deshaies
17—Chicago	W	5-4†	Smith	Nunez
18—Chicago	L	0-7	Harkey	Gullickson
19—Chicago	L	1-4	Lancaster	Clancy
20—Chicago	L	1-5	Boskie	Scott
21—Pittsburgh	W	3-2†	Agosto	Power
22—Pittsburgh	W	4-8	Heaton	Schatzeder
23—Pittsburgh	W	7-3	Agosto	Ruskin
26—At Chicago	W	8-1	Scott	Boskie
26—At Chicago	W	12-3	Deshaies	Maddux
27—At Chicago	L	6-11	Bielecki	Portugal
28—St. Louis	W	5-1	Gullickson	Mathews
29—St. Louis	L	2-3	Tudor	Schatzeder
30—St. Louis	W	2-1	Agosto	Magrane
31—At S.F.	W	5-3	Deshaies	Garrelts

Won 11, Lost 17

JUNE

Date		Score	Winner	Loser
1—At S.F.	L	5-6†	Bedrosian	Clancy
2—At S.F.	L	4-5*	Bedrosian	Darwin
3—At S.F.	L	3-7	Hammaker	Scott
4—At S.D.	L	2-10	Benes	Clancy
5—At S.D.	L	2-11	Rasmussen	Deshaies
6—At S.D.	L	2-3	Lefferts	Portugal
7—Cincinnati	L	1-6	Rijo	Gullickson
8—Cincinnati	W	3-1*	Scott	Myers
9—Cincinnati	W	4-1	Clancy	Mahler
10—Cincinnati	W	4-2	Darwin	Armstrong
11—Los Ang.	W	5-3	Andersen	Morgan
12—Los Ang.	W	5-4	Gullickson	Maddux
13—Los Ang.	W	5-1	Scott	Belcher
15—At Cin.	L	3-6	Armstrong	Clancy
16—At Cin.	L	2-6	Jackson	Deshaies
17—At Cin.	L	1-7	Rijo	Portugal
18—At L.A.	L	2-5	Belcher	Gullickson
19—At L.A.	L	1-5	Valenzuela	Scott
20—At L.A.	L	2-3	Martinez	Clancy
22—San Fran.	L	3-4	Garrelts	Deshaies
23—San Fran.	W	4-2	Portugal	Bedrosian
24—San Fran.	W	8-2	Gullickson	Robinson
25—San Diego	W	5-3	Scott	Benes
26—San Diego	L	0-7	Rasmussen	Clancy
27—San Diego	W	9-1	Deshaies	Hurst
28—San Diego	W	2-1*	Andersen	Grant
29—At Phila.	L	0-2	Combs	Gullickson
30—At Phila.	W	8-3	Scott	Freeman

Won 12, Lost 16

JULY

Date		Score	Winner	Loser
1—At Phila.	L	4-8	McDowell	Andersen
2—At Phila.	L	1-5	Ruffin	Deshaies
3—At N.Y.	L	0-12	Viola	Portugal
4—At N.Y.	L	4-7	Gooden	Agosto
5—At Mon.	L	0-11	Gardner	Scott
6—At Mon.	L	2-3	Sampen	Agosto
7—At Mon.	L	1-3	Smith	Deshaies
8—At Mon.	W	5-3	Portugal	Martinez
12—Phila.	W	7-4	Gullickson	Ruffin
13—Phila.	L	2-4	DeJesus	Scott
14—Phila.	L	8-12	Combs	Deshaies
15—Phila.	W	6-1	Darwin	Parrett
16—New York	W	4-1	Portugal	Ojeda
17—New York	L	2-6	Gooden	Gullickson
18—New York	W	1-0	Scott	Pena
19—Montreal	W	4-3†	Andersen	Sampen
20—Montreal	W	12-6	Darwin	Gross
21—Montreal	L	2-3	Smith	Agosto
22—Montreal	W	3-2	Agosto	Schmidt
23—At Atlanta	L	1-3	Smoltz	Scott
24—At Atlanta	L	3-9	Leibrandt	Deshaies
24—At Atlanta	L	8-9*	Mercker	Agosto
25—At Atlanta	W	5-1	Darwin	Avery
26—At S.D.	L	2-8	Show	Portugal
27—At S.D.	L	2-6	Benes	Gullickson
28—At S.D.	W	5-3	Scott	Rasmussen
29—At S.D.	L	3-4	Harris	Smith
30—At S.F.	W	6-1	Darwin	Bedrosian
31—At S.F.	L	2-3	Brantley	Agosto

Won 11, Lost 18

AUGUST

Date		Score	Winner	Loser
2—Atlanta	W	3-1	Gullickson	Glavine
3—Atlanta	W	3-0	Scott	Smoltz
4—Atlanta	W	6-2	Deshaies	Leibrandt
5—Atlanta	W	6-2	Darwin	Avery
6—San Fran.	W	4-1	Gullickson	Robinson
7—San Fran.	W	4-0	Portugal	Burkett
8—San Fran.	L	4-8	Wilson	Agosto
10—San Diego	L	0-2	Whitson	Deshaies
11—San Diego	L	3-6*	Show	Smith
12—San Diego	L	0-9	Lilliquist	Gullickson
13—At Chicago	W	7-2	Portugal	Dickson
14—At Chicago	L	2-5	Maddux	Scott
15—At Chicago	W	8-4*	Smith	Pico
16—At St. L.	W	4-2	Darwin	Magrane
17—At St. L.	L	0-5	Tewksbury	Gullickson
18—At St. L.	W	3-2†	Smith	DiPino
19—At St. L.	L	3-7	DeLeon	Scott
20—At Pitts.	L	1-7	Heaton	Deshaies
21—At Pitts.	W	2-1	Darwin	Patterson
22—At Pitts.	L	2-4	Smiley	Gullickson
23—At Atlanta	W	8-3	Portugal	Leibrandt
24—St. Louis	L	2-3†	Terry	Smith
25—St. Louis	W	6-4	Deshaies	DeLeon
26—St. Louis	W	4-2	Darwin	Hill
28—Chicago	L	2-5	Maddux	Gullickson
29—Chicago	W	1-0	Portugal	Sutcliffe
31—Pittsburgh	W	3-2	Agosto	Patterson

Won 16, Lost 11

SEPTEMBER

Date		Score	Winner	Loser
1—Pittsburgh	W	2-1*	Smith	Power
2—Pittsburgh	L	6-7	Smiley	Darwin
3—At L.A.	W	7-3	Gullickson	Valenzuela
4—At L.A.	W	10-8	Meyer	Gott
5—At S.D.	L	2-5	Rasmussen	Scott
6—At S.D.	L	0-3*	Harris	Meyer
7—At S.F.	W	2-1	Darwin	Burkett
8—At S.F.	L	1-2*	Bedrosian	Meyer
9—At S.F.	L	1-5	LaCoss	Portugal
11—At Cin.	L	3-5	Charlton	Deshaies
12—At Cin.	W	3-1‡	Agosto	Layana
13—At Cin.	L	5-7	Dibble	Meyer
14—San Fran.	W	2-1	Portugal	Downs
15—San Fran.	W	3-2*	Hernandez	Bedrosian
16—San Fran.	W	3-2	Agosto	Robinson
17—San Diego	L	0-5	Hurst	Darwin
18—San Diego	L	1-8	Whitson	Gullickson
19—Cincinnati	W	5-2	Portugal	Jackson
20—Cincinnati	W	3-2	Hernandez	Myers
21—At Atlanta	W	4-3*	Agosto	Mercker
22—At Atlanta	L	1-3	Leibrandt	Darwin
23—At Atlanta	L	0-3	Marak	Gullickson
24—Los Ang.	L	5-7†	Gott	Smith
25—Los Ang.	L	1-3*	Howell	Agosto
26—Los Ang.	W	10-1	Deshaies	Morgan
28—Atlanta	W	2-1*	Osuna	Mercker
29—Atlanta	W	9-0	Gullickson	Leibrandt
30—Atlanta	W	6-2	Portugal	Glavine

Won 15, Lost 13

OCTOBER

Date		Score	Winner	Loser
1—At Cin.	L	3-4	Myers	Meyer
2—At Cin.	L	2-3	Scudder	Hernandez
3—At Cin.	W	3-2	Smith	Birtsas

Won 1, Lost 2

*10 innings. †11 innings. ‡13 innings.

Danny Darwin was Houston's best pitcher in 1990 with an 11-4 record and league-leading 2.21 ERA.

all but gave up on the speedy outfielder, keeping him in the minors from mid-May until late August. Without a legitimate leadoff hitter or center fielder, the Astros turned to Eric Yelding. He finished second in the league with 64 steals but his on-base percentage was barely over .300. He also brought an infielder's arm to the outfield.

Catcher Craig Biggio and third baseman Ken Caminiti, counted on to provide punch after big seasons in 1989, both dropped off significantly. They combined for eight home runs and 93 RBIs in more than 1,000 at-bats, down from 23-132 a year earlier. Biggio, however, became the first catcher in club history to lead the regulars in batting (.276) and hits (153).

Shortstop Rafael Ramirez's production sagged as well. His 37 RBIs were 17 fewer than he collected in 1989, and he had the poorest fielding percentage (.953, 25 errors) among regular N.L. shortstops.

On the Houston bench, outfielder Mark Davidson batted .327 against lefties and

.292 overall, easing the pain of veteran infielder Ken Oberkfell's career-low .207 season.

This distinct lack of offense was reflected in the won-lost records on the Houston staff. But there were other reasons for Mike Scott's plunge from a 20-win season in 1989 to a 9-13 mark in 1990. After the shortened spring training caused by the lockout, Scott couldn't throw his fastball past hitters and went 2-6 with a 5.53 ERA through June 3. He never really hit his stride, surrendering a career-high 27 home runs (second in the league) and striking out just 121 batters—the fourth straight year of decline after he fanned 306 in 1986.

In the past, the Astros were able to overcome their poor offense with a dominant pitching staff. In 1990, Mark Portugal led the club with just 136 strikeouts and the staff had 854, the fourth lowest total in club history.

The bright spot among pitchers was veteran Danny Darwin, who came out of the bullpen on July 1 and went 9-3 the rest of the way. Overall, Darwin was 11-4 and led the league with a 2.21 ERA, which set a club record.

Among the other starters, Bill Gullickson returned from two seasons in Japan to finish 10-14, but he was released five days after shutting out Atlanta in late September. Jim Deshaies didn't win a game on the road after May 31 and was 7-12, a career low.

In the bullpen, Juan Agosto broke his club record by pitching in 82 games, most in the major leagues. Long reliever Xavier Hernandez reduced his ERA to 4.62 by holding opponents scoreless in his last 10 appearances. Jim Clancy was hit hard (100 hits in 76 innings) as a starter/reliever and spent part of the season in the minor leagues.

Dave Smith had another solid season as the Astros' closer, but his 23 saves left him one short of the 200 mark for his career. Because the Astros rarely had the lead on the road, Smith went from May 4 through July 7 without a save away from home.

But Smith's road season only mirrored the Astros' frustrations in 1990. They started out slowly, never picked up the pace and were the most welcome guest in baseball.

During one of the Astros' eight consecutive winning home stands, Howe came upon a solution to his team's problems. "All we have to do is put the 'Dome on wheels and bring it around the country with us," he mused.

If only it were that easy.

Hard-throwing John Smoltz led the beleaguered Atlanta pitching staff with 14 wins and 170 strikeouts.

Braves Are Bad, Knowhutimean?

By BILL ZACK

The Atlanta Braves could have hired Stephen King instead of Ernest P. Worrell as the team's promotional pitchman in 1990. The season was more horror story than slapstick, with plenty of twists and turns along the way.

The Braves lost their first baseman to vertigo, traded their most popular player, fired a manager and began a search for a new general manager. They also posted the majors' worst record (65-97), ensuring their seventh consecutive losing season and third straight finish in the National League West basement.

"With the time we've given the young players in the last two years, it's time to start winning," Manager Russ Nixon had declared before the season. The Braves won two of their first 15 games and Nixon was replaced as manager by General Manager Bobby Cox on June 22.

There were some positives for the future. Center fielder Ron Gant and rookie right fielder Dave Justice formed the club's best power duo since Dale Murphy and Bob Horner, combining for 60 homers and 162 runs batted in. With the two youngsters leading the way, the Braves batted .252 as a team, 18 points better than in 1989, and belted 162 home runs, their most since 1973.

Yet the offense couldn't overcome mistakes committed on the mound and in the field. The Braves billed themselves as a team building around a solid foundation of young pitching, but they compiled a major league-high 4.58 earned-run average. Not to be outdone, the defense committed 158 errors, the most in both leagues.

John Smoltz paced the staff with 14 victories, but only one other starter broke into double figures: 10-game winner Tom Glavine. The only members of the rotation with ERAs below 4.00 were Smoltz and Charlie Leibrandt, who was sidelined until June 3 due to a partially torn rotator cuff. Leibrandt led the staff with a 3.16 ERA, helped by a sparkling 0.81 mark over a six-start stretch.

A sore shoulder ended Pete Smith's season in June, just about the time heralded 20-year-old Steve Avery was summoned from the minors. Avery finished 3-11 with a 5.64 ERA, but fellow rookie Paul Marak managed a 3.69 mark in seven September starts. Marty Clary, who pitched two seven-game stints as a starter, wound up 1-

After being recalled in mid-May, Dave Justice belted 28 homers and finished the year as the National League's Rookie of the Year.

10 as a swingman.

In the bullpen, rookie Mike Stanton was given the stopper's job but pitched just seven times before a shoulder injury halted his season. The Braves used 18 different relievers to compile 30 saves, the league's next-to-lowest total. Hard-throwing rookie Kent Mercker emerged from the crowd to notch a team-high seven saves, tying a club record for lefthanded relievers.

As the bullpen struggled, the Braves started shopping. At the All-Star break, they traded Derek Lilliquist to San Diego for Mark Grant. Three weeks later, they dealt the most successful hitter in the club's 25 years in Atlanta, Dale Murphy, to Philadelphia for righthanded reliever Jeff Parrett. Murphy, who departed as Atlanta's career leader in virtually every offensive category, collected 371 home runs

SCORES OF ATLANTA BRAVES' 1990 GAMES

APRIL

Date			Winner	Loser
11—San Fran.	L	0-8	Reuschel	Glavine
11—San Fran.	W	4-3	Smith	Swan
12—San Fran.	L	4-13	LaCoss	Smoltz
13—Cincinnati	L	2-5	Browning	Lilliquist
15—Cincinnati	L	6-13	Birtsas	Glavine
16—Cincinnati	L	3-5	Armstrong	Smith
17—At Hous.	L	3-5	Portugal	Smoltz
18—At Hous.	L	5-10	Schatzeder	Lilliquist
21—At Cin.	L	1-8	Armstrong	Clary
22—At Cin.	W	3-1	Glavine	Browning
24—At N.Y.	L	1-2	Machado	Stanton
25—At N.Y.	L	5-8	Darling	Stanton
26—Houston	L	0-3	Clancy	Lilliquist
27—Phila.	L	1-7	Cook	Stanton
28—Phila.	L	1-2	Parrett	Boever
29—Phila.	W	3-1	Smith	Combs
30—New York	W	7-4	Smoltz	Cone

Won 4, Lost 13

MAY

Date			Winner	Loser
1—New York	W	5-2	Lilliquist	Darling
2—At Mon.	W	8-1	Clary	Smith
3—At Mon.	W	4-1	Kerfeld	Hall
6—At Pitts.	L	4-6	Heaton	Smoltz
6—At Pitts.	L	2-4	Drabek	Lilliquist
7—At Chicago	W	9-8	Kerfeld	Williams
8—At Chicago	L	8-10§	Long	Henry
9—At Chicago	L	0-4*	Lancaster	Smith
11—At St. L.	L	2-5	B. Smith	Smoltz
12—At St. L.	L	3-4‡	L. Smith	Boever
13—At St. L.	W	3-1	Castillo	Terry
14—Chicago	W	3-2	Henry	Williams
15—Chicago	L	2-12	Pico	Smith
16—Chicago	W	4-0	Smoltz	Maddux
17—Pittsburgh	W	6-1	Lilliquist	Heaton
18—Pittsburgh	L	3-9	Walk	Clary
19—Pittsburgh	W	2-1	Glavine	Terrell
20—Pittsburgh	W	13-11	Smith	Kipper
21—St. Louis	W	6-5	Boever	Terry
22—St. Louis	L	3-4	DeLeon	Lilliquist
24—At Phila.	L	4-8	Ruffin	Clary
25—At Phila.	L	4-5	Parrett	Hesketh
26—At Phila.	W	12-3	Smith	Combs
27—At Phila.	W	6-1	Smoltz	Mulholland
28—Montreal	L	1-4	Gross	Lilliquist
30—Montreal	L	6-9	Schmidt	Glavine
31—At S.D.	L	1-2	Rasmussen	Smith

Won 13, Lost 14

JUNE

Date			Winner	Loser
1—At S.D.	W	16-11	Castillo	Dunne
2—At S.D.	L	0-9	Whitson	Lilliquist
3—At S.D.	W	4-2‡	Kerfeld	Harris
4—At L.A.	L	0-6	Martinez	Glavine
5—At L.A.	W	6-4	Smith	Morgan
6—At L.A.	L	5-7	Howell	Kerfeld
8—San Fran.	L	8-23	Wilson	Lilliquist
9—San Fran.	W	5-3	Leibrandt	Hammaker
10—San Fran.	L	3-9	Burkett	Smith
11—San Fran.	L	3-8	Garrelts	Smoltz
12—At Cin.	W	8-3	Glavine	Jackson
12—At Cin.	W	3-2	Greene	Rijo
13—At Cin.	L	4-13	Browning	Avery
14—At Cin.	L	3-4	Dibble	Boever
15—At S.F.	L	2-8	Burkett	Smith
16—At S.F.	L	0-7	Garrelts	Smoltz
17—At S.F.	L	7-9	Bedrosian	Castillo
19—Cincinnati	L	2-4	Charlton	Luecken
19—Cincinnati	W	3-0	Leibrandt	Mahler
20—Cincinnati	L	8-9‡	Myers	Luecken
21—Cincinnati	W	4-3	Smoltz	Dibble
23—San Diego	L	5-7	Whitson	Glavine
24—San Diego	W	11-10x	Luecken	Lefferts
25—Los Ang.	L	2-5	Martinez	Leibrandt
26—Los Ang.	W	4-2	Avery	Morgan
27—Los Ang.	W	4-0	Smoltz	Belcher
29—At Mon.	W	4-2	Glavine	Martinez
30—At Mon.	W	7-6	Leibrandt	Gardner

Won 13, Lost 15

JULY

Date			Winner	Loser
1—At Mon.	L	1-5	Boyd	Avery
2—At Mon.	W	6-3	Smoltz	Farmer
3—At Phila.	L	1-5	Parrett	Clary
4—At Phila.	W	4-1	Glavine	Combs
5—New York	L	8-9	Whitehurst	Hesketh
6—New York	L	7-10	Cone	Avery
7—New York	W	4-3	Mercker	Innis
8—New York	L	1-2	Viola	Clary
12—Montreal	L	0-3	Gardner	Glavine
14—Montreal	W	3-2	Mercker	Schmidt
14—Montreal	L	2-6	Boyd	Leibrandt
15—Montreal	L	14-16	Frey	Mercker
16—Phila.	L	2-7	Mulholland	Clary
17—Phila.	W	14-10	Glavine	Ruffin
18—Phila.	L	3-4	Cook	Smoltz
19—At N.Y.	L	2-6	Cone	Leibrandt
20—At N.Y.	L	1-6	Fernandez	Avery
21—At N.Y.	L	2-4	Darling	Clary
22—At N.Y.	W	3-2‡	Mercker	Innis
23—Houston	W	3-1	Smoltz	Scott
24—Houston	W	9-3	Leibrandt	Deshaies
24—Houston	W	9-8‡	Mercker	Agosto
25—Houston	L	1-5	Darwin	Avery
26—At L.A.	L	1-8	Belcher	Clary
27—At L.A.	L	4-5x	Searage	Luecken
28—At L.A.	L	7-8	Hartley	Grant
29—At L.A.	L	3-4	Martinez	Leibrandt
30—At S.D.	W	4-3§	Henry	Schiraldi
31—At S.D.	L	6-7	Lefferts	Luecken

Won 10, Lost 19

AUGUST

Date			Winner	Loser
2—At Hous.	L	1-3	Gullickson	Glavine
3—At Hous.	L	0-3	Scott	Smoltz
4—At Hous.	L	2-6	Deshaies	Leibrandt
5—At Hous.	L	2-6	Darwin	Avery
7—San Diego	L	2-7	Benes	Glavine
7—San Diego	L	9-11	Show	Clary
8—San Diego	W	7-1	Smoltz	Rasmussen
9—San Diego	L	0-7	Hurst	Leibrandt
10—Los Ang.	W	3-2	Avery	Morgan
11—Los Ang.	L	4-6‡	Howell	Clary
12—Los Ang.	L	3-7	Neidlinger	Glavine
13—Los Ang.	W	9-5	Smoltz	Valenzuela
14—At Pitts.	L	1-3	Drabek	Leibrandt
14—At Pitts.	L	4-6	Smith	Avery
15—At Pitts.	W	8-1	Castillo	Heaton
16—At Pitts.	L	3-4	Kipper	Mercker
17—At Chicago	L	0-7	Harkey	Smoltz
18—At Chicago	W	17-6	Leibrandt	Dickson
19—At Chicago	L	4-5	Maddux	Mercker
20—At St. L.	L	2-7	Hill	Glavine
21—At St. L.	W	7-2	Smoltz	Magrane
22—At St. L.	W	2-1	Castillo	Tewksbury
23—Houston	L	3-8	Portugal	Leibrandt
24—Chicago	W	3-0	Avery	Maddux
25—Chicago	L	3-6	Bielecki	Glavine
26—Chicago	W	4-3	Smoltz	Williams
28—Pittsburgh	W	9-0	Leibrandt	Smiley
29—Pittsburgh	L	0-10†	Drabek	Avery
30—St. Louis	L	3-5x	DiPino	Henry
31—St. Louis	W	4-1	Smoltz	DeLeon

Won 11, Lost 19

SEPTEMBER

Date			Winner	Loser
1—St. Louis	W	4-3	Castillo	Hill
2—St. Louis	W	5-0	Leibrandt	Tudor
3—Cincinnati	W	8-6	Grant	Layana
4—Cincinnati	W	7-4	Glavine	Jackson
5—At L.A.	W	6-2	Smoltz	Morgan
6—At L.A.	L	0-5	Hartley	Marak
7—At S.D.	W	4-1	Leibrandt	Whitson
8—At S.D.	W	11-5	Parrett	Lilliquist
9—At S.D.	L	4-5§	Show	Mercker
10—At S.F.	L	6-7‡	Bedrosian	Mercker
11—At S.F.	L	0-2	Garrelts	Grant
12—At S.F.	L	3-8	Burkett	Leibrandt
14—San Diego	W	7-3	Glavine	Lilliquist
15—San Diego	L	3-5§	Lefferts	Parrett
16—San Diego	L	4-9	Rasmussen	Avery
17—Los Ang.	L	2-5	Crews	Leibrandt
18—Los Ang.	L	2-6	Neidlinger	Marak
19—San Fran.	W	5-1	Glavine	Downs
20—San Fran.	L	3-5	Gunderson	Smoltz
21—Houston	L	3-4‡	Agosto	Mercker
22—Houston	W	3-1	Leibrandt	Darwin
23—Houston	W	3-0	Marak	Gullickson
25—At Cin.	W	10-0	Glavine	Charlton
26—At Cin.	L	2-5	Rijo	Smoltz
27—At Cin.	L	2-4	Browning	Avery
28—At Hous.	L	1-2‡	Osuna	Mercker
29—At Hous.	L	0-9	Gullickson	Leibrandt
30—At Hous.	L	2-6	Portugal	Glavine

Won 12, Lost 16

OCTOBER

Date			Winner	Loser
1—At S.F.	W	5-3	Smoltz	Wilson
2—At S.F.	W	16-7	Freeman	Dewey
3—At S.F.	L	3-6	Bedrosian	Avery

Won 2, Lost 1

*4½ innings. †6½ innings. ‡10 innings. §11 innings. x12 innings.

Greg Olson enjoyed a fairy tale first half of the season, but his production waned in the second half when he was platooned.

and 1,901 hits for the Braves dating back to 1976.

The offense in 1990 revolved around Gant and Justice. Gant, demoted to the minors for much of 1989, appeared destined for a similar fate by collecting just two homers, six RBIs and a .247 average through May 17. By season's end, he became the majors' 13th 30-30 member (32 homers, 33 steals), batted .303 and led the Braves with 84 RBIs.

Justice, voted the N.L. Rookie of the Year after being called up from the minors in mid-May, led all first-year players with 28 homers and 78 RBIs. It wasn't until Murphy was traded, however, that Justice got hot. Shifted from first base back to his natural position in right field, he tied Detroit's Cecil Fielder for the most home runs after the All-Star break, belting 23.

Nevertheless, the offense couldn't overcome the loss of first baseman Nick Esasky, who was signed as a free agent but played in just nine games because of vertigo. Without Esasky, counted on to provide lefthanded power in the heart of the order, the Braves rotated young first basemen, beginning with Tommy Gregg, then Justice, and finally with a platoon of Gregg and Francisco Cabrera.

Gregg was more valuable off the bench, slamming a club-record four pinch home runs and leading the major leagues with 18 pinch hits and 17 pinch RBIs. Cabrera showed a measure of power, popping seven home runs in 137 at-bats.

There was much more offense than defense in the infield. Second baseman Jeff Treadway, third baseman Jim Presley and shortstops Jeff Blauser and Andres Thomas combined for 43 home runs and 66 errors; at first base, seven different players totaled another 26 errors. The Atlanta infielder with the best glove, rookie backup Mark Lemke, was limited by a severely sprained ankle and a weak bat (.226).

Presley, connecting for 19 home runs and 72 RBIs, had the most productive year of any Braves third baseman since Horner, but he committed a league-high 25 errors at third base and had limited range. At second, Treadway posted career highs in homers (11), RBIs (59) and batting average (.283).

Left fielder Lonnie Smith started slowly after reporting to spring training 20 pounds overweight. Batting .235 on June 3, he was shifted to the leadoff slot and finished with a team-leading .305 mark, becoming only the second Atlanta regular (after Ralph Garr) to post back-to-back .300 seasons. Still, the power and speed he contributed in 1989 vanished: his home runs declined from 21 to nine, RBIs from 79 to 42 and stolen bases from 25 to 10. In center field, Oddibe McDowell drove in just 25 runs in 113 games.

Catcher Greg Olson, a 29-year-old rookie signed as a minor league free agent, was the Braves' lone representative at the All-Star Game following a fairy tale first half. Then, platooned with Ernie Whitt following the break, Olson played sporadically, hitting just .228 to drop his average to .262. Whitt, acquired from Toronto to bridge the club's present and future catching needs, missed June and July after suffering ligament damage in his left thumb. He batted just .172 with a pair of homers and 10 RBIs.

The Braves were saved from an ignominious triple failure by the Expos and Astros—only Houston's .242 team batting average and Montreal's .250 mark prevented Atlanta from ranking last in the league in pitching, hitting and fielding.

The 1990 season belonged to Doug Drabek, who pitched tremendously all year en route to earning the National League Cy Young Award.

'Career Years' Mark Bucs' Title

By JOHN MEHNO

When Pittsburgh Manager Jim Leyland assured his coaches in an April meeting that they'd be working for the 1990 National League East champion, a sapient few might have put that prediction into context.

After all, 25 other managers usually pay lip service to the obligatory optimism that resonates through Florida and Arizona every spring. And the Pirates were a team that had taken a significant step backward from 1988 to 1989, dropping from second to fifth place in a season ruined by injuries.

But the perceptive Leyland saw a team that was healthy and motivated, a club that was poised to gain the rewards of a rebuilding program that had begun quietly when Leyland was a rookie big-league manager in 1986.

"I liked our club in spring training," Leyland said. "We kind of low-keyed it, but I felt we had a good club."

Aside from the private confessions to his staff, Leyland kept his observations and lofty ambitions under wraps. True to his word, he guided the Pirates to their first division title since 1979, edging the New York Mets by four games, and was named The Sporting News' N.L. Manager of the Year.

"We didn't have very many major injuries and we had guys who had career years," observed center fielder Andy Van Slyke. "That's what it takes."

At the head of the list of major achievers were left fielder Barry Bonds, voted the N.L. Most Valuable Player, The Sporting News' Player of the Year and a Gold Glove winner, and pitcher Doug Drabek, the Cy Young recipient.

Bonds was the most interesting case. The Pirates shopped him during the winter but couldn't make what they considered an equitable deal for a career .256 hitter. Bonds went to work in the weight room and used a bitter loss in salary arbitration to further hone his focus. The final challenge was posed when Leyland designated Bonds his No. 5 hitter. Bonds had been the Bucs' leadoff man by default and chafed in that role, especially when the Pirates used his lack of run production (58, 58 and 59 runs batted in since 1987) to win their arbitration case.

Bonds answered with a performance of grandiose proportions: 33 home runs, 114 RBIs, a .301 average, 104 runs scored and

Barry Bonds headed the list of Pittsburgh's major achievers in 1990, capping his season by earning the N.L. Most Valuable Player award.

52 stolen bases. He thus became the first 30-30 player in the club's 104-year history.

Drabek's Cy Young season was a product of his steady improvement over the previous two years. Pitching coach Ray Miller harnessed Drabek's energy and curveball, a project that paid off in 1990 with a league-best 22-6 record and a 2.76 earned-run average. Drabek was at his best when the Pirates weren't, winning 12 times after Pittsburgh losses.

The other pitching story (short as it was) involved the August 8 acquisition of Zane Smith from Montreal. In an 11th-hour effort to shore up an unsettled rotation, the Pirates packaged three prospects to acquire Smith, a potential free agent with a 45-66 lifetime record. He proved to be the perfect lefthanded complement to the righthanded Drabek, fashioning a 6-2 record and 1.30 ERA in 11 games.

Leyland masterfully juggled a bullpen that lacked a dominant force, carefully picking the spots for his no-name crew.

Bill Landrum, who had come out of no-

SCORES OF PITTSBURGH PIRATES' 1990 GAMES

APRIL

Date		Score	Winner	Loser
9—At N.Y.	W	12-3	Drabek	Gooden
11—At N.Y.	L	0-3	Viola	Smiley
12—At N.Y.	W	6-2	Heaton	Fernandez
13—Chicago	L	0-2	Maddux	Walk
14—Chicago	L	1-4	Harkey	Drabek
15—Chicago	W	4-3†	Patterson	Lancaster
16—St. Louis	L	4-6	DeLeon	Smiley
17—St. Louis	W	7-2	Heaton	Mathews
18—St. Louis	L	0-3	Tudor	Walk
19—At St. L.	W	5-1	Drabek	Magrane
20—At Chicago	W	9-4*	Roesler	Bielecki
21—At Chicago	W	4-3	Smiley	Wilson
22—At Chicago	W	3-2	Heaton	Nunez
23—At St. L.	L	4-7	Tudor	Walk
24—At S.F.	W	4-1	Drabek	Garrelts
25—At S.F.	W	7-4§	Patterson	Bedrosian
26—At S.F.	W	2-1	Smiley	LaCoss
27—At S.D.	W	9-4	Heaton	Show
28—At S.D.	W	4-3	Walk	Benes
29—At S.D.	W	10-1	Drabek	Rasmussen

Won 14, Lost 6

MAY

Date		Score	Winner	Loser
1—At L.A.	L	1-4	Belcher	Terrell
2—At L.A.	L	2-6	Valenzuela	Smiley
6—Atlanta	W	6-4	Heaton	Smoltz
6—Atlanta	W	4-2	Drabek	Lilliquist
7—San Diego	W	4-1	Walk	Hurst
8—San Diego	W	10-2	Terrell	Show
9—Cincinnati	W	6-2	Smiley	Armstrong
10—Cincinnati	L	4-10	Charlton	Power
11—Houston	W	4-3	Drabek	Deshaies
12—Houston	W	3-1	Heaton	Portugal
13—Houston	W	5-1	Walk	Gullickson
14—At Cin.	L	3-5	Armstrong	Terrell
15—At Cin.	L	4-5‡	Layana	Patterson
17—At Atlanta	L	1-6	Lilliquist	Heaton
18—At Atlanta	W	9-3	Walk	Clary
19—At Atlanta	L	1-2	Glavine	Terrell
20—At Atlanta	W	11-13	Smith	Kipper
21—At Hous.	L	2-3‡	Agosto	Power
22—At Hous.	W	8-4	Heaton	Schatzeder
23—At Hous.	L	3-7	Agosto	Ruskin
25—San Fran.	L	8-9	Burkett	Terrell
26—San Fran.	W	10-4	Drabek	Garrelts
27—San Fran.	W	5-2	Heaton	Reuschel
28—Los Ang.	W	6-5	Landrum	Howell
29—Los Ang.	W	9-5	Patterson	Valenzuela
30—Los Ang.	W	5-3	Terrell	Martinez

Won 15, Lost 11

JUNE

Date		Score	Winner	Loser
1—Montreal	L	1-4	Gross	Drabek
2—Montreal	W	4-3†	Landrum	Hall
3—Montreal	L	3-4	Sampen	Belinda
4—Chicago	W	6-2	Patterson	Boskie
5—Chicago	W	6-5	Belinda	Williams
6—Chicago	W	6-1*	Drabek	Maddux
7—At N.Y.	W	5-4	Ruskin	Musselman
8—At N.Y.	L	1-7	Fernandez	Walk
9—At N.Y.	L	3-9	Cone	Patterson
10—At N.Y.	L	3-8	Ojeda	Terrell
11—At St. L.	W	8-7	Belinda	Niedenfuer
12—At St. L.	W	6-3	Heaton	DeLeon
13—At St. L.	W	6-5	Huismann	DiPino
15—New York	L	5-7	Ojeda	Terrell
16—New York	W	11-6	Kipper	Viola
17—New York	L	3-4	Gooden	Heaton
19—At Phila.	L	1-2†	Carman	Landrum
20—At Phila.	L	2-7	Ruffin	Patterson
22—At Mon.	L	3-4	Sampen	Belinda
23—At Mon.	L	1-6	Smith	Drabek
24—At Mon.	W	5-3	Heaton	Martinez
25—Phila.	W	5-0	Reed	DeJesus
26—Phila.	W	1-0	Ruskin	Ruffin
27—Phila.	W	5-3	Kipper	Howell
28—At St. L.	L	1-5	Tewksbury	Drabek
29—At S.F.	L	3-7	Wilson	Heaton
30—At S.F.	W	4-3	Kipper	Thurmond

Won 14, Lost 13

JULY

Date		Score	Winner	Loser
1—At S.F.	W	8-5	Tibbs	Oliveras
2—At S.D.	W	4-3x	Patterson	Schiraldi
3—At S.D.	W	5-3	Landrum	Lefferts
4—At S.D.	L	4-5	Show	Heaton
5—At L.A.	W	9-6	Reed	Martinez
6—At L.A.	W	6-3	Smiley	Morgan
7—At L.A.	L	2-4	Belcher	Terrell
8—At L.A.	W	7-2	Drabek	Wells
12—San Diego	W	4-3y	Patterson	Schiraldi
13—San Diego	W	4-1	Drabek	Rasmussen
14—San Diego	W	8-4	Power	Harris
15—San Diego	L	1-4	Whitson	Heaton
16—San Fran.	L	1-6	Garrelts	Reed
17—San Fran.	L	3-6	Robinson	Smiley
18—San Fran.	W	11-2	Drabek	Wilson
20—Los Ang.	W	4-2	Walk	Morgan
21—Los Ang.	L	0-6	Belcher	Heaton
22—Los Ang.	W	11-6	Kipper	Wells
23—At Mon.	L	0-5	Martinez	Smiley
24—At Mon.	W	5-3	Drabek	Gross
25—At Mon.	L	7-8†	Sampen	Belinda
26—Phila.	L	4-12	Mulholland	Heaton
27—Phila.	L	3-5	Cook	Reed
28—Phila.	L	3-4	Parrett	Landrum
29—Phila.	W	2-1	Drabek	Combs
31—At Chicago	W	9-1	Patterson	Boskie

Won 15, Lost 11

AUGUST

Date		Score	Winner	Loser
1—At Chicago	L	0-5	Maddux	Reed
2—At Chicago	W	8-5	Smiley	Wilson
3—At Phila.	W	11-0	Drabek	Ruffin
4—At Phila.	W	3-1†	Patterson	McDowell
5—At Phila.	L	6-8	Carman	Ruskin
6—At Phila.	W	10-1	Tomlin	Mulholland
6—At Phila.	W	4-3†	Landrum	McDowell
7—Montreal	W	4-3§	Ross	Mohorcic
8—Montreal	L	2-6	Martinez	Drabek
9—Montreal	L	6-7†	Frey	Landrum
10—St. Louis	L	3-8	Dayley	Kramer
11—St. Louis	L	2-3	Magrane	Tomlin
12—St. Louis	L	0-6	Tewksbury	Smiley
14—Atlanta	W	3-1	Drabek	Leibrandt
14—Atlanta	W	6-4	Smith	Avery
15—Atlanta	L	1-8	Castillo	Heaton
16—Atlanta	W	4-3	Kipper	Mercker
17—At Cin.	W	7-1	York	Rijo
17—At Cin.	W	4-3	Smiley	Layana
18—At Cin.	W	3-1	Smith	Hammond
19—At Cin.	W	6-3	Drabek	Armstrong
20—Houston	W	7-1	Heaton	Deshaies
21—Houston	L	1-2	Darwin	Patterson
22—Houston	W	4-2	Smiley	Gullickson
23—Cincinnati	W	9-3	Smith	Hammond
24—Cincinnati	L	3-4	Dibble	Kipper
25—Cincinnati	L	1-6	Charlton	Belinda
26—Cincinnati	L	2-6	Mahler	Tomlin
28—At Atlanta	L	0-9	Leibrandt	Smiley
29—At Atlanta	W	10-0*	Drabek	Avery
31—At Hous.	L	2-3	Agosto	Patterson

Won 17, Lost 14

SEPTEMBER

Date		Score	Winner	Loser
1—At Hous.	L	1-2†	Smith	Power
2—At Hous.	W	7-6	Smiley	Darwin
3—Phila.	W	4-1	Drabek	Ruffin
4—Phila.	W	11-7	Landrum	Akerfelds
5—New York	W	1-0	Smith	Franco
5—New York	W	3-1	Heaton	Ojeda
6—New York	W	7-1	Tomlin	Valera
7—Montreal	L	1-4	Boyd	Smiley
8—Montreal	W	6-1	Drabek	Farmer
9—Montreal	L	5-9	Rojas	Walk
10—At Phila.	W	3-2	Belinda	Boever
11—At Phila.	W	5-1	Tomlin	Grimsley
12—At N.Y.	L	1-2	Cone	Smiley
13—At N.Y.	L	3-6	Gooden	Drabek
14—At Mon.	L	2-4	Frey	Heaton
15—At Mon.	L	3-4	Sampen	Smith
16—At Mon.	L	1-4	Ruskin	Tomlin
18—At Chicago	L	5-8	Maddux	Smiley
19—At Chicago	W	8-7	Drabek	Sutcliffe
20—At Chicago	W	11-2	Walk	Kramer
21—St. Louis	W	1-0	Smith	DeLeon
22—St. Louis	L	2-3	Hill	Tomlin
23—St. Louis	W	7-2	Smiley	Tewksbury
25—Chicago	W	5-3	Drabek	Wilson
26—Chicago	W	4-3	Smith	Coffman
27—Chicago	W	3-2	Tomlin	Bielecki
28—At St. L.	W	6-4	Landrum	Hill
29—At St. L.	W	8-0	Walk	Tewksbury
30—At St. L.	W	2-0	Drabek	Magrane

Won 19, Lost 10

OCTOBER

Date		Score	Winner	Loser
1—New York	L	1-4	Cone	Smith
2—New York	W	9-4	Landrum	Gooden
3—New York	L	3-6	Viola	York

Won 1, Lost 2

*6½ innings. †10 innings. ‡11 innings. §12 innings. x14 innings. y15 innings.

Mike LaValliere formed half of a solid catching tandem that helped the Pirates to the N.L. East title.

where to save 26 games a year earlier, earned 12 saves before the All-Star break but only one in the second half. Ted Power was successful in all seven of his save opportunities, however, and rookie Stan Belinda notched eight more (a club rookie record) in the last three months. Bob Patterson's eight victories topped his career total, and Bob Kipper was effective when used against lefthanders. Down the stretch, minor league recall Vicente Palacios pitched 15 scoreless innings in seven games.

After Drabek, the starting rotation was punctuated by question marks. The Pirates signed well-traveled free agent Walt Terrell but released him in July after he was 2-7 in 16 starts. That done, they called Class AA Harrisburg (Eastern) for Randy Tomlin, who went 4-4 with a 2.55 ERA in 12 starts. Neal Heaton was 10-4 at midseason, thanks to a hybrid pitch he called the "screw-knuckle-change." In the second half, however, shoulder problems knocked him out of the rotation. Nonethe-

less, the two lefties compensated for John Smiley, who stumbled to a 9-10, 4.64 season after fracturing his hand in May. Bob Walk, bothered by groin injuries, was 7-5 in 24 starts.

The comeback story was provided by first baseman Sid Bream, who had undergone three operations on his right knee in 1989. After struggling with a .221 average through late May, Bream finished at .270 with 15 home runs—one short of his career high—and 67 RBIs. His smooth glove work at first saved innumerable throwing errors.

The offense's best supporting cast member was Bobby Bonilla, who teamed with Bonds to form an awesome power duo dubbed the "Killer Bs." Moved back to right field after playing third base in 1989, Bonilla belted a career-high 32 homers, drove home a team-leading 120 runs and finished second to Bonds in the MVP voting.

With the Killer Bs providing the pyrotechnics, Van Slyke's rebound season almost went unnoticed. Coming off a career-low .237 year, Van Slyke batted .284 with 17 home runs and 77 RBIs. He also played center field better than anyone in the league, winning his third straight Gold Glove.

On the infield, second baseman Jose Lind contributed nearly flawless defense and exceptional range. He also lifted his average to .261 after falling to .232 in 1989. Jay Bell solved the Pirates' decade-long search for a shortstop. Batting second, he set a team record for sacrifices, despite 109 strikeouts.

Wally Backman, a largely unwanted free agent, turned into a bargain find. He batted .292 as a part-time third baseman and gave Pittsburgh a leadoff hitter to facilitate Bonds' drop in the order. Backman's veteran presence also let Jeff King develop at his own pace. King finished with 14 home runs and 53 RBIs after a slow start.

The catching platoon of Mike LaValliere and Don Slaught was particularly solid, with Slaught batting .300 in his first N.L. season.

R.J. Reynolds hit .288 in a very limited role, backing up the league's best outfield. Veteran Gary Redus allowed the Bucs to rest Bream at first. Redus collected his six homers and 23 RBIs all against lefthanded pitching.

The Pirates' 95-67 record was a near reversal from their 64-98 mark in Leyland's first year. "This was not a one-year thing," Leyland said. "This was a five-year thing."

The Pirates kept to the schedule.

When John Franco entered a game, the Mets could count on him sealing the victory with one of his league-high 33 saves.

Mets Guilty of Underachieving

By JOHN HARPER

Not so long ago, they were the team everyone loved to hate. Anymore, the New York Mets have become the team no one can quite figure out.

The arrogance of the 1986 championship era has long since gone the way of the Backmans, Dykstras, Carters and Hernandez'. Color the Mets' new personality vanilla—they don't make people mad anymore, but they are indeed maddening.

In 1990, they finished a disappointing second in the National League East for the second straight year, getting Manager Davey Johnson fired along the way. What made it so exasperating—again—for New Yorkers was the Mets' tendency to be unbeatable at times, unbearable at others.

Their combination of power and pitching seemed to be a recipe for dominance. This was a team, after all, which led the National League in home runs for the third straight year and placed four pitchers among the top five N.L. strikeout leaders.

The numbers, however, didn't add up. The Mets were explosive enough to win 27 of 32 games in June and July under new Manager Bud Harrelson (who replaced Johnson on May 29), yet they struggled to play four games over .500 the rest of the season. They had the best home record in the major leagues, but with the division title on the line, they lost seven of their last nine games at Shea Stadium.

When the Mets finally were eliminated, Harrelson's analysis was indicting: "I think we underachieved for most of the season. We were all guilty of it."

In the end, it wasn't so hard to explain as it was hard to fathom. The Mets, a notoriously poor clutch-hitting team for the third straight year, didn't hit enough when it counted to overcome their fundamental weakness: an inability to do the little things, offensively and defensively, that win games.

A pair of late-season failures by closer John Franco, so reliable all year with a league-high and club-record 33 saves, were costly. But most glaring down the stretch, and most puzzling of all, was the Mets' continued failure to hit lefthanded pitching (.233 for the season). Against lefthanded starters, they had the league's worst record (27-33).

The most telling series of the season was a three-game sweep the first-place Pirates dealt New York on September 5 and 6. The

Kevin McReynolds enjoyed another strong statistical season, collecting 24 homers and 82 RBIs.

Mets managed a total of two runs and 11 hits in those three losses, falling from half a game back to 3½ behind.

Injuries also were a factor. In August, the Mets lost platoon center fielder Mark Carreon (knee surgery) and shortstop Kevin Elster (shoulder surgery), two of the club's better RBI bats against lefties.

But that didn't begin to explain the problem. Left fielder Kevin McReynolds had another nice statistical season, with 24 home runs and 82 runs batted in, but he went 0-for-17 in five games against Pittsburgh in September and hit only four homers with 15 RBIs against lefthanders all season.

Howard Johnson helped keep the Mets in the race by moving off third base and playing remarkably well at shortstop when

SCORES OF NEW YORK METS' 1990 GAMES

APRIL

Date		Score	Winner	Loser
9—Pittsburgh	L	3-12	Drabek	Gooden
11—Pittsburgh	W	3-0	Viola	Smiley
12—Pittsburgh	L	2-6	Heaton	Fernandez
13—At Mon.	W	4-1*	Machado	Hall
14—At Mon.	L	5-6	Martinez	Gooden
15—At Mon.	L	1-3	Smith	Darling
16—At Chicago	W	10-1	Viola	Wilson
17—Chicago	L	6-8§	Assenmacher	Innis
18—Chicago	L	5-8	Maddux	Cone
19—Chicago	W	4-1	Gooden	Harkey
20—Montreal	L	1-2	Smith	Darling
21—Montreal	W	5-4	Viola	Boyd
22—Montreal	W	5-0	Fernandez	Gardner
24—Atlanta	W	2-1	Machado	Stanton
25—Atlanta	W	8-5	Darling	Stanton
27—At Hous.	W	1-0	Viola	Portugal
28—At Hous.	L	4-8	Gullickson	Fernandez
29—At Hous.	L	1-2*	Darwin	Machado
30—At Atlanta	L	4-7	Smoltz	Cone

Won 9, Lost 10

MAY

Date		Score	Winner	Loser
1—At Atlanta	L	2-5	Lilliquist	Darling
2—Cincinnati	W	5-0	Viola	Browning
3—Cincinnati	L	0-5	Armstrong	Fernandez
5—Houston	L	5-9	Scott	Gooden
6—Houston	W	7-4†	Franco	Smith
6—Houston	W	7-6	Pena	Schatzeder
7—Houston	W	7-1	Viola	Clancy
8—San Fran.	W	4-1	Fernandez	Reuschel
9—San Fran.	L	2-4	Knepper	Ojeda
11—Los Ang.	W	9-4	Gooden	Morgan
12—Los Ang.	W	7-0	Viola	Wetteland
14—At S.F.	L	2-4	Knepper	Fernandez
15—At S.F.	L	5-6	Thurmond	Ojeda
16—At S.F.	L	3-4*	Brantley	Pena
18—At S.D.	L	3-6	Hurst	Viola
19—At S.D.	W	6-4	Cone	Benes
20—At S.D.	L	1-3	Harris	Darling
21—At L.A.	W	12-3	Gooden	Morgan
22—At L.A.	W	8-3	Ojeda	Crews
24—San Diego	L	4-5	Benes	Viola
25—San Diego	L	4-5	Rasmussen	Cone
26—San Diego	W	11-0	Fernandez	Dunne
27—San Diego	L	4-8	Whitson	Gooden
29—At Cin.	L	1-2	Browning	Ojeda

Won 11, Lost 13

JUNE

Date		Score	Winner	Loser
1—At Phila.	W	4-0	Viola	Cook
2—At Phila.	L	4-5	Howell	Gooden
3—At Phila.	L	3-8	Combs	Fernandez
4—Montreal	L	3-5	Sampen	Cone
5—Montreal	W	6-5†	Franco	Mohorcic
6—Montreal	W	4-3	Viola	Gross
7—Pittsburgh	L	4-5	Ruskin	Musselman
8—Pittsburgh	W	7-1	Fernandez	Walk
9—Pittsburgh	W	9-3	Cone	Patterson
10—Pittsburgh	W	8-3	Ojeda	Terrell
11—At Chicago	L	5-8	Williams	Pena
12—At Chicago	W	19-8	Gooden	Bielecki
13—At Chicago	W	15-10	Franco	Lancaster
13—At Chicago	W	9-6	Darling	Harkey
15—At Pitts.	W	7-5	Ojeda	Terrell
16—At Pitts.	L	6-11	Kipper	Viola
17—At Pitts.	W	4-3	Gooden	Heaton
19—St. Louis	W	6-0	Cone	Tudor
20—St. Louis	W	6-3	Fernandez	B. Smith
22—Phila.	W	5-1	Viola	Howell
23—Phila.	W	3-0	Gooden	Combs
24—Phila.	W	6-5	Innis	McDowell
25—At St. L.	W	3-2	Cone	L. Smith
26—At St. L.	W	8-6†	Pena	Dayley
27—At St. L.	W	5-2	Viola	Magrane
28—Cincinnati	W	5-4	Gooden	Rijo
29—Cincinnati	W	4-2	Ojeda	Mahler
30—Cincinnati	L	4-7	Charlton	Musselman

Won 21, Lost 7

JULY

Date		Score	Winner	Loser
1—Cincinnati	W	3-2	Franco	Charlton
3—Houston	W	12-0	Viola	Portugal
4—Houston	W	7-4	Gooden	Agosto
5—At Atlanta	W	9-8	Whitehurst	Hesketh
6—At Atlanta	W	10-7	Cone	Avery
7—At Atlanta	L	3-4	Mercker	Innis
8—At Atlanta	W	2-1	Viola	Clary
12—At Cin.	W	10-3	Gooden	Charlton
12—At Cin.	L	2-3	Jackson	Darling
13—At Cin.	L	2-4	Browning	Viola
14—At Cin.	W	6-3	Cone	Armstrong
15—At Cin.	L	1-2	Charlton	Fernandez
16—At Hous.	L	1-4	Portugal	Ojeda
17—At Hous.	W	6-2	Gooden	Gullickson
18—At Hous.	L	0-1	Scott	Pena
19—Atlanta	W	6-2	Cone	Leibrandt
20—Atlanta	W	6-1	Fernandez	Avery
21—Atlanta	W	4-2	Darling	Clary
22—Atlanta	L	2-3*	Mercker	Innis
23—At Phila.	L	4-7	Akerfelds	Viola
24—At Phila.	W	7-4	Machado	McDowell
25—At Phila.	W	10-9	Fernandez	Parrett
26—St. Louis	W	6-1	Darling	Tewksbury
26—St. Louis	L	1-3	Hill	Ojeda
27—St. Louis	W	10-1	Viola	B. Smith
28—St. Louis	L	0-1	Magrane	Cone
29—St. Louis	W	6-0	Gooden	DeLeon
31—At Mon.	L	4-7	Boyd	Fernandez

Won 17, Lost 11

AUGUST

Date		Score	Winner	Loser
1—At Mon.	W	6-4‡	Ojeda	Sampen
2—At Mon.	W	5-1	Viola	Martinez
3—At St. L.	W	5-4	Machado	L. Smith
4—At St. L.	L	5-7	Hill	Gooden
5—At St. L.	L	3-8	Tudor	Fernandez
6—At St. L.	L	1-5	Magrane	Darling
7—Phila.	L	0-9	DeJesus	Viola
8—Phila.	W	8-4	Cone	Carman
9—Phila.	W	5-4	Ojeda	Akerfelds
10—Chicago	W	5-1	Fernandez	Maddux
11—Chicago	L	3-6	Wilson	Darling
12—Chicago	L	2-10	Harkey	Viola
14—Los Ang.	W	9-8	Gooden	Martinez
14—Los Ang.	L	1-2	Hartley	Cone
15—Los Ang.	L	2-3	Morgan	Fernandez
16—Los Ang.	W	4-1	Darling	Belcher
17—At S.F.	L	2-3	Garrelts	Viola
18—At S.F.	W	9-2	Cone	Wilson
19—At S.F.	W	10-9	Gooden	LaCoss
20—At S.D.	L	1-3	Hurst	Fernandez
21—At S.D.	L	0-7	Whitson	Darling
22—At S.D.	W	4-1	Viola	Schiraldi
23—At L.A.	L	2-4	Valenzuela	Cone
24—At L.A.	W	3-2	Gooden	Gott
25—At L.A.	L	2-3x	Aase	Darling
26—At L.A.	L	1-2	Hartley	Viola
28—San Diego	W	4-0	Cone	Schiraldi
29—San Diego	W	2-1	Ojeda	Harris
30—San Fran.	W	12-2	Fernandez	LaCoss
31—San Fran.	W	4-3	Viola	Bedrosian

Won 16, Lost 14

SEPTEMBER

Date		Score	Winner	Loser
1—San Fran.	W	6-5	Valera	Burkett
2—San Fran.	W	10-6	Cone	McClellan
3—At St. L.	W	9-3	Gooden	Tewksbury
4—At St. L.	L	0-1	Magrane	Fernandez
5—At Pitts.	L	0-1	Smith	Franco
5—At Pitts.	L	1-3	Heaton	Ojeda
6—At Pitts.	L	1-7	Tomlin	Valera
7—At Phila.	L	1-4	DeJesus	Cone
8—At Phila.	W	12-2	Gooden	Ruffin
9—At Phila.	L	2-6	Combs	Fernandez
10—St. Louis	W	10-1	Viola	DeLeon
11—St. Louis	W	10-8	Franco	L. Smith
12—Pittsburgh	W	2-1	Cone	Smiley
13—Pittsburgh	W	6-3	Gooden	Drabek
14—Phila.	L	1-4	Combs	Fernandez
15—Phila.	W	4-2	Viola	Mulholland
16—Phila.	L	3-8	DeJesus	Cone
18—Montreal	L	3-4	Burke	Franco
20—Montreal	L	4-6	Rojas	Viola
20—Montreal	L	0-2	Nabholz	Fernandez
21—At Chicago	L	3-4	Assenmacher	Cone
22—At Chicago	W	11-5	Darling	Nunez
23—At Chicago	W	7-3	Gooden	Maddux
24—At Chicago	L	3-4	Assenmacher	Viola
25—At Mon.	W	3-1	Pena	Nabholz
26—At Mon.	W	4-0	Cone	Martinez
27—At Mon.	W	6-0	Darling	Gross
28—Chicago	W	7-1	Gooden	Maddux
29—Chicago	L	2-3	Lancaster	Viola
30—Chicago	L	5-6	Nunez	Franco

Won 15, Lost 15

OCTOBER

Date		Score	Winner	Loser
1—At Pitts.	W	4-1	Cone	Smith
2—At Pitts.	L	4-9	Landrum	Gooden
3—At Pitts.	W	6-3	Viola	York

Won 2, Lost 1

*10 innings. †11 innings. ‡12 innings. §13 innings. x14 innings.

In his first full season in the N.L., Frank Viola won 20 games and led the league in innings pitched.

One of the Mets' curiosities was how much change they underwent, particularly on the infield, while contending for the division title.

After starting the season on the bench behind Mike Marshall, first baseman Dave Magadan got a chance to play and never stopped hitting. He stamped himself as the Mets' first sacker of the future, giving chase in the N.L. batting race and finishing third at .328. On the road, his .372 average was the league's best.

Meanwhile, late-season trades brought veteran Tommy Herr, who became the everyday second baseman, and Charlie O'Brien, who did most of the catching in September after an ankle injury cut short a breakthrough season by Mackey Sasser. A .307 hitter in 100 games, Sasser matched his career total by knocking in 41 runs.

Another in-season addition, waiver pick-up Daryl Boston, filled a need in center field and hit better than anyone figured. Starting mostly against righthanders, Boston finished with a career-best 45 RBIs. Keith Miller, who made 42 starts in center, offered little production (12 RBIs) and twice visited the disabled list.

Reserve infielder Tim Teufel saw his playing time cut for the third straight year, although he belted 10 homers in 175 at-bats.

The constant for the Mets again was their starting pitching. Frank Viola won 20 games and led the league in innings pitched; Dwight Gooden won 16 of his last 18 decisions and was 19-7 overall; David Cone led the majors with 233 strikeouts and won 14 games for the second straight season, and Sid Fernandez, average-wise, was the toughest starting pitcher for N.L. opponents to hit (.200). Down the stretch, all four gave the Mets quality starts.

The bullpen, however, was another matter. Until he blew saves in his last two appearances (both Mets losses), Franco met all expectations in his first year with the club. But the Mets waited almost all year for a reliable setup man, and it wasn't until September that Alejandro Pena finally found his fastball. Bob Ojeda, pulled in and out of the rotation, pitched better in relief (3-1, 2.16 ERA in 26 appearances), but Ron Darling struggled in a similar role. Wally Whitehurst was a dependable middle reliever, walking just nine batters in 65⅔ innings.

All in all, it was a year that left the Mets shaking their heads and wondering about change. Harrelson made it clear he wanted more speed, better defense and less waiting for the three-run homers that didn't come at the right times in 1990.

Elster was sidelined. He also put up the numbers (23 homers, 90 RBIs), including his fourth straight 20-20 season (34 steals), but the switch-hitter batted only .208 against lefties, with six home runs.

Gregg Jefferies made the transition from second to third base (perhaps to stay, Harrelson said) and led the league with 40 doubles, but his .190 hitting in September took some of the stuffing out of a fat year at the plate (a career-high 15 homers, 68 RBIs and 96 runs scored).

Then there was right fielder Darryl Strawberry. He too was vulnerable to lefthanders, collecting only nine of his 37 homers and 29 of his club-record 108 RBIs against them. But he capped a big comeback year by carrying the club in September, slugging eight home runs with 23 RBIs.

Rookie Delino DeShields was the Expos' starting second baseman at the beginning of the 1990 season and a big reason for the team's surprising success last year.

Montreal Rookies Surprise Foes

By IAN MacDONALD

The Montreal Expos made the best of what could have been a bad situation in 1990, and they surprised a lot of people in the process. But in the end, the Expos' emphasis of speed, pitching and defense was not enough to earn the team the National League East title.

But that was no cause for sorrow, considering Montreal's situation. Using a rookie-loaded lineup, the Expos finished third in the East (10 games out of first place) with an 85-77 record which was remarkable considering the problems they faced entering the season. Three members of the starting rotation from 1989, Bryn Smith, Mark Langston and Pascual Perez, had signed lucrative free-agent contracts elsewhere. And for a team tailored around pitching efficiency, this could have been catastrophic. But for Manager Buck Rodgers and his staff, it wasn't.

History has dictated that Montreal can't count on luring superstar free agents with big bucks, so the decision was made to go with the club's home-grown talent in 1990.

Rodgers employed 15 rookies during the year. At least one rookie appeared in every game and at least two played in 150 of the first 162. Led by second baseman Delino DeShields and outfielders Larry Walker and Marquis Grissom, the Expos everyday first-year players combined for a .260 batting average.

Plus the rookies were in the thick of a running game which saw the team lead the major leagues in stolen bases (235) for the second straight year. In 1980, when they set their club record with 237 thefts, Ron LeFlore (97) and Rodney Scott (63) did the running. In 1990, it was a team project. Otis Nixon, a pinch-running specialist, led the way with 50, edging Tim Raines by one. Along with DeShields' 42 steals, the Expos had three different players swipe at least 40 bases. Grissom (22) and Walker (21) gave the team five men with over 20 steals.

With righthander Bill Sampen and lefthander Chris Nabholz leading the way, the Expos' rookie pitchers might have been an even bigger story. They combined to post a 30-24 record and 3.34 earned-run average. Sampen's contribution verged more on shocking than surprising. Drafted as a starter, he was converted to relief after showing a strong arm at spring camp. Sampen went on to lead the staff with 12

Veterans like Andres Galarraga helped steady the youthful Montreal attack.

wins.

After Zane Smith was traded to the Pittsburgh Pirates in August, Nabholz was recalled from Class AAA Indianapolis and proceeded to win six straight decisions and finished 6-2 in 11 starts.

Another rookie starter, Mark Gardner, battled for the league's ERA lead through July, but he became ineffective in August. His problem was diagnosed as a tired arm and he was sent home for exercise and rehabilitation in September.

Veterans Dennis Martinez and Dennis (Oil Can) Boyd stabilized the rotation, with each winning 10 games to pace the starters. Boyd was as effective as any starter. A gamble after experiencing shoulder problems for three years, Boyd paid big dividends with a 2.93 ERA in 31 starts.

Kevin Gross was also enjoying a strong season in the rotation until a mishap. With a shutout at Philadelphia June 11, he had eight wins. But while fielding a bunt at Chicago in late June, Gross fractured the middle finger on his pitching hand. He finished the year 9-12.

The overall pitching performance was one that pitching coach Larry Bearnarth deserves credit for. The staff captured the N.L. ERA title with a 3.37 mark. Only the Oakland Athletics were better in the major leagues with a 3.18 ERA. Plus a makeshift

SCORES OF MONTREAL EXPOS' 1990 GAMES

APRIL

			Winner	Loser
9—At St. L.	L	5-6†	Dayley	Gardner
10—At St. L.	L	2-4	B. Smith	Z. Smith
11—At St. L.	W	6-4	Boyd	Mathews
13—New York	L	1-4*	Machado	Hall
14—New York	W	6-5	Martinez	Gooden
15—New York	W	3-1	Smith	Darling
16—Phila.	W	5-4	Hesketh	Parrett
17—Phila.	W	2-1	Hall	Frohwirth
18—Phila.	L	3-4	Howell	Gross
19—At Phila.	W	5-0	Martinez	Ruffin
20—At N.Y.	W	2-1	Smith	Darling
21—At N.Y.	L	4-5	Viola	Boyd
22—At N.Y.	L	0-5	Fernandez	Gardner
24—At Hous.	W	5-3	Gross	Scott
25—At Hous.	W	1-0	Frey	Smith
27—At Cin.	L	2-3	Dibble	Hall
28—At Cin.	L	4-6	Armstrong	Boyd
29—At Cin.	W	6-3	Gross	Robinson
30—Houston	L	2-4	Andersen	Martinez

Won 10, Lost 9

MAY

			Winner	Loser
1—Houston	W	2-1§	Hall	Andersen
2—Atlanta	L	1-8	Clary	Smith
3—Atlanta	L	1-4	Kerfeld	Hall
4—San Fran.	W	5-4	Gross	Reuschel
5—San Fran.	L	1-4	Burkett	Martinez
6—San Fran.	W	7-0	Gardner	Hammaker
7—San Fran.	W	7-6	Frey	Bedrosian
8—Los Ang.	W	9-1	Sampen	Belcher
9—Los Ang.	W	5-3	Gross	Valenzuela
10—Los Ang.	W	8-2	De. Martinez	R. Martinez
11—At S.D.	L	3-5	Lefferts	Hall
12—At S.D.	L	2-5	Hurst	Smith
13—At S.D.	W	15-0	Boyd	Show
14—At L.A.	L	2-3	Valenzuela	Gross
15—At L.A.	L	2-3	R. Martinez	De. Martinez
16—At L.A.	L	2-3	Morgan	Hall
18—At S.F.	L	2-7	Hammaker	Frey
19—At S.F.	W	7-4	Gross	Knepper
20—At S.F.	W	6-5†	Sampen	Hammaker
22—San Diego	W	6-1	Gardner	Whitson
23—San Diego	W	4-0	Boyd	Hurst
24—Cincinnati	L	1-7	Robinson	Gross
25—Cincinnati	L	0-5	Armstrong	Martinez
26—Cincinnati	L	3-5	Dibble	Burke
27—Cincinnati	W	5-3	Hall	Birtsas
28—At Atlanta	W	4-1	Gross	Lilliquist
30—At Atlanta	W	9-6	Schmidt	Glavine

Won 15, Lost 12

JUNE

			Winner	Loser
1—At Pitts.	W	4-1	Gross	Drabek
2—At Pitts.	L	3-4*	Landrum	Hall
3—At Pitts.	W	4-3	Sampen	Belinda
4—At N.Y.	W	5-3	Sampen	Cone
5—At N.Y.	L	5-6†	Franco	Mohorcic
6—At N.Y.	L	3-4	Viola	Gross
7—St. Louis	W	3-2	Smith	DeLeon
8—St. Louis	W	18-2	Martinez	B. Smith
9—St. Louis	W	3-1	Gardner	Terry
10—St. Louis	L	3-5	Magrane	Boyd
11—At Phila.	W	5-0	Gross	Cook
11—At Phila.	W	3-2	Hall	Parrett
12—At Phila.	L	2-7	Howell	Smith
13—At Phila.	W	4-3*	Schmidt	McDowell
14—At St. L.	W	3-2	Sampen	Niedenfuer
15—At St. L.	W	7-4	Frey	Magrane
16—At St. L.	L	3-5	Tewksbury	Hall
17—At St. L.	L	1-7	DeLeon	Smith
18—Chicago	W	5-1	Martinez	Harkey
19—Chicago	L	1-2	Boskie	Gardner
20—Chicago	W	3-2	Mohorcic	Maddux
22—Pittsburgh	W	4-3	Sampen	Belinda
23—Pittsburgh	W	6-1	Smith	Drabek
24—Pittsburgh	L	3-5	Heaton	Martinez
25—At Chicago	W	7-3	Gardner	Boskie
26—At Chicago	W	6-5	Schmidt	Lancaster
27—At Chicago	L	3-5	Pico	Gross
28—At Chicago	L	2-3	Lancaster	Sampen
29—Atlanta	L	2-4	Glavine	Martinez
30—Atlanta	L	6-7	Leibrandt	Gardner

Won 17, Lost 13

JULY

			Winner	Loser
1—Atlanta	W	5-1	Boyd	Avery
2—Atlanta	L	3-6	Smoltz	Farmer
3—Cincinnati	L	0-2	Browning	Smith
4—Cincinnati	W	5-3	Martinez	Scudder
5—Houston	W	11-0	Gardner	Scott
6—Houston	W	3-2	Sampen	Agosto
7—Houston	W	3-1	Smith	Deshaies
8—Houston	L	3-5	Portugal	Martinez
12—At Atlanta	W	3-0	Gardner	Glavine
14—At Atlanta	L	2-3	Mercker	Schmidt
14—At Atlanta	W	6-2	Boyd	Leibrandt
15—At Atlanta	W	16-14	Frey	Mercker
16—At Cin.	L	3-8	Layana	Smith
17—At Cin.	L	2-6	Scudder	Gardner
18—At Cin.	L	7-8†	Mahler	Schmidt
19—At Hous.	L	3-4†	Andersen	Sampen
20—At Hous.	L	6-12	Darwin	Gross
21—At Hous.	W	3-2	Smith	Agosto
22—At Hous.	L	2-3	Agosto	Schmidt
23—Pittsburgh	W	5-0	Martinez	Smiley
24—Pittsburgh	L	3-5	Drabek	Gross
25—Pittsburgh	W	8-7*	Sampen	Belinda
26—Chicago	W	3-2*	Burke	Williams
27—Chicago	L	0-2*	Maddux	Sampen
28—Chicago	L	7-10	Long	Burke
29—Chicago	L	1-2	Harkey	Gross
31—New York	W	7-4	Boyd	Fernandez

Won 13, Lost 14

AUGUST

			Winner	Loser
1—New York	L	4-6‡	Ojeda	Sampen
2—New York	L	1-5	Viola	Martinez
3—At Chicago	L	4-10	Harkey	Gardner
4—At Chicago	L	2-10	Boskie	Gross
5—At Chicago	L	1-3	Maddux	Boyd
7—At Pitts.	L	3-4‡	Ross	Mohorcic
8—At Pitts.	W	6-2	Martinez	Drabek
9—At Pitts.	W	7-6*	Frey	Landrum
10—Phila.	W	4-3	Boyd	Mulholland
11—Phila.	W	5-4‡	Sampen	Carman
12—Phila.	W	6-3	Nabholz	DeJesus
14—At S.D.	W	8-3	Martinez	Rasmussen
15—At S.D.	W	5-3y	Sampen	Davis
16—At S.D.	L	2-3†	Rodriguez	Burke
17—At L.A.	L	6-7	Neidlinger	Gardner
18—At L.A.	L	2-3	Valenzuela	Rojas
19—At L.A.	W	2-1	De. Martinez	R. Martinez
20—At S.F.	L	2-4	Robinson	Gross
21—At S.F.	W	10-5	Rojas	Wilson
22—At S.F.	L	1-2	Bedrosian	Frey
24—San Diego	L	1-2	Benes	Martinez
25—San Diego	W	2-1	Nabholz	Rasmussen
26—San Diego	W	4-2	Frey	Hurst
27—San Diego	L	1-4	Whitson	Boyd
28—San Fran.	W	5-2	Gardner	Garrelts
29—San Fran.	L	5-6	Brantley	Sampen
31—Los Ang.	W	5-2	Nabholz	Morgan

Won 13, Lost 14

SEPTEMBER

			Winner	Loser
1—Los Ang.	W	6-0	Boyd	Hartley
2—Los Ang.	L	5-12	Crews	Gardner
3—Chicago	W	3-2‡	Frey	Kramer
4—Chicago	L	1-3	Bielecki	Martinez
5—At St. L.	W	6-2	Nabholz	DeLeon
6—At St. L.	L	2-4	Dayley	Gardner
7—At Pitts.	W	4-1	Boyd	Smiley
8—At Pitts.	L	1-6	Drabek	Farmer
9—At Pitts.	W	9-5	Rojas	Walk
10—At Chicago	W	7-4	Nabholz	Long
11—At Chicago	L	6-11	Pavlas	Gross
12—St. Louis	W	6-2	Boyd	Tewksbury
13—St. Louis	L	4-6	Olivares	Sampen
14—Pittsburgh	W	4-2	Frey	Heaton
15—Pittsburgh	W	4-3	Sampen	Smith
16—Pittsburgh	W	4-1	Ruskin	Tomlin
18—At N.Y.	W	4-3	Burke	Franco
20—At N.Y.	W	6-4	Rojas	Viola
20—At N.Y.	W	2-0	Nabholz	Fernandez
21—At Phila.	L	4-5‡	Malone	Sampen
22—At Phila.	L	2-3	Greene	Anderson
23—At Phila.	L	1-2x	Carman	Farmer
24—At Phila.	L	0-3	Combs	Barnes
25—New York	L	1-3	Pena	Nabholz
26—New York	L	0-4	Cone	Martinez
27—New York	L	0-6	Darling	Gross
28—Phila.	L	4-5	Grimsley	Boyd
29—Phila.	W	5-1	Barnes	Combs
30—Phila.	L	1-2	Mulholland	Nabholz

Won 14, Lost 15

OCTOBER

			Winner	Loser
1—St. Louis	W	15-9	Burke	Dayley
2—St. Louis	W	2-1	Gross	Olivares
3—St. Louis	W	9-2	Sampen	Hill

Won 3, Lost 0

*10 innings. †11 innings. ‡12 innings. §13 innings. x16 innings. y17 innings.

Tim Burke saved 20 games for Montreal despite spending six weeks on the disabled list.

bullpen tied for the N.L. lead in saves (50) with the more publicized "Nasty Boys" of the world champion Cincinnati Reds.

The main man from the bullpen was again Tim Burke, though veteran Dave Schmidt was brilliant when Burke went down with a hairline fracture of the right fibula in late May. Burke parlayed a sensational September into a team-leading 20-save season.

Schmidt notched 13 saves and two wins during the five weeks Burke was on the disabled list. Unfortunately, he hurt his shoulder and needed surgery in September. Steve Frey picked up nine saves and showed he can be a lefthanded complement to Burke as a closer. Plus rookies Scott Ruskin, acquired in the Smith deal, and Mel Rojas, along with Dale Mohorcic, all pitched well in relief. But Drew Hall struggled with a 5.09 ERA.

After making a dramatic major league debut with four hits on opening day at St. Louis, DeShields flirted with batting .300 through the first four months of the season. He finished at .289 and led the team with six triples. Alternating between first, second and third in the batting order, DeShields used his speed to tie third baseman Tim Wallach for the team lead in runs scored with 69.

Walker equalled Andre Dawson's team rookie record of 19 home runs, although he experienced several slumps during the season. But while Walker and DeShields, along with fellow rookie Grissom and his .257 average, played major roles, the keys to the offense were veterans Wallach, Andres Galarraga and Raines.

Wallach was the unanimous choice as team player of the year. While gaining that distinction for the third time in four years, he led the Expos in batting average (.296), hits (185), doubles (37), home runs (21) and runs batted in (98).

Galarraga made sound use of his .256 average by hitting 20 homers. But he continues to strike out far too much, pushing his own single-season Expos' record to 169.

After four years (1984-87) of hitting .309 or better, Raines had fallen to .270 in 1988. But the fleet outfielder made strides toward the .300 level again, batting .287 in 1990. His stolen base total was also an improvement on his 1988 and '89 totals.

Dave Martinez was also an exciting contributor for the offense, hitting .279. Given the chance to play when Grissom suffered a broken nose May 9, Martinez ended up platooning with Nixon in the outfield.

When catcher Nelson Santovenia started slowly and then had to undergo knee surgery in late July, Mike Fitzgerald took over and played well. Fitzgerald posted seven straight extra-base hits during an early-season stint. Plagued for years by a finger injury, Fitzgerald threw as well as he ever has. And for the seventh straight season, his teams have been winners when he starts behind the plate.

Besides hitting and pitching, the Expos played defense. With a .982 fielding percentage, they finished third in the league in fielding, just one point behind the Reds and San Francisco Giants, who tied at .983. Spike Owen set a season record for N.L. shortstops with 63 consecutive errorless games. Wallach and Galarraga each earned Gold Gloves.

The reserves also supplied help. A more comfortable Mike Aldrete contributed well as a backup, starting 35 games between the outfield and first base. Tom Foley struggled at the plate, but spelled Owen and DeShields in the middle infield. Jerry Goff supplied rest for Fitzgerald after Santovenia's surgery. Nixon was a valuable outfield reserve, batting .251, and Junior Noboa was the team's top pinch-hitter.

Prognosticators and even baseball insiders had every reason to believe the Expos would struggle. But the young bloods combined pitching, speed and defense to post an exciting season that left the Montreal brass optimistic about the future.

Lenny Dykstra sported a red-hot .360 batting average at the All-Star break, but he tapered off in the second half and finished at .325.

Phils Roadworthy in Title Chase

By BILL BROWN

They weren't cruising Easy Street, but the Philadelphia Phillies believe 1990 was the year they finally turned that infamous corner of Bored and Dying On The Vine.

After finishing last in the National League East the previous two seasons, the players viewed a fourth-place tie as an important milepost on the road back to respectability. The Phils' 77-85 record was 10 victories better than in 1989, an improvement topped only by division champions Cincinnati and Pittsburgh among N.L. teams.

For the fans, 1990 will be remembered for Lenny Dykstra's hitting .400 through June 10, and for Terry Mulholland's pitching the Phillies' first-ever modern-day no-hitter at home.

Dykstra, due to become a free agent at the end of 1991, was rewarded in August with a new three-year contract. "I wouldn't have signed here if I didn't think the Phillies were going to be contenders," said Dykstra, who rapped an N.L.-high 192 hits, had the league's best on-base average, its longest hitting streak (23 games) and ranked fourth with a .325 average. "I really think we're close to getting it all together."

Mulholland, who no-hit San Francisco at Veterans Stadium on August 15, closed the year with a 1.99 earned-run average and three complete games in his final 10 starts. Those numbers were more reflective of his pitching than his overall 9-10 record and 3.34 ERA.

The Phillies had entered the season with a starting rotation that was tenuous at best. That they led the league in relief appearances wasn't any surprise.

Ken Howell, a .500 pitcher in 1989 who was tabbed as the No. 1 starter out of spring training, started 8-3 and appeared headed for an All-Star invitation when a shoulder injury struck in June. A stint on the disabled list and four losses followed before Howell was sidelined for good in early August.

Philadelphia was counting heavily on rookie Pat Combs, who finished 10-10 only after winning four straight starts in September. He still led the staff in victories, innings and strikeouts, but failed to win a game from July 20 through September 8.

While Bruce Ruffin, a veteran of nearly five big-league seasons at age 26, might have pitched his way out of the Phils' plans

After leaving Atlanta, Dale Murphy hit seven homers for the Phillies over the last two months of the season.

with a 6-13 record and 5.38 ERA, rookie Jose DeJesus earned a spot in the rotation. Acquired from Kansas City in spring training, DeJesus (7-8, 3.74) was at his best against the Mets, beating them three times with a pair of complete games.

Two other rookies, Jason Grimsley (3-2, 3.30) and Tommy Greene (3-3, 5.08), played to mixed reviews as minor league call-ups.

The bullpen, despite plenty of practice, was not the force it was supposed to be. Closer Roger McDowell squandered half a dozen save opportunities in the first half before rounding into form. He led the league with 60 games finished and ranked sixth among N.L. relievers with 22 saves.

The bane of the Phils' bullpen was the lack of lefthanded relief. Don Carman had a cosmetic 6-2 record but a 4.15 ERA. Dennis Cook, who was 5-0 as a starter in April and May, was moved to the bullpen in June and to Los Angeles in September. And rookie Chuck McElroy did little to help his

SCORES OF PHILADELPHIA PHILLIES' 1990 GAMES

APRIL

Date		Score	Winner	Loser
10—At Chicago	L	1-2	Lancaster	Parrett
12—At Chicago	W	5-4	Mulholland	Wilson
12—At Chicago	L	3-6	Nunez	Combs
13—St. Louis	L	0-11	Tudor	Howell
14—St. Louis	W	6-2	Ruffin	Magrane
15—St. Louis	W	4-0	Cook	B. Smith
16—At Mon.	L	4-5	Hesketh	Parrett
17—At Mon.	L	1-2	Hall	Frohwirth
18—At Mon.	W	4-3	Howell	Gross
19—Montreal	L	0-5	Martinez	Ruffin
20—At St. L.	W	3-0	Cook	B. Smith
21—At St. L.	W	7-6*	McDowell	Terry
22—At St. L.	W	5-3	Combs	Horton
24—Cincinnati	W	6-3	Howell	Rijo
25—Cincinnati	L	7-12	Mahler	Ruffin
27—At Atlanta	W	7-1	Cook	Stanton
28—At Atlanta	W	2-1	Parrett	Boever
29—At Atlanta	L	1-3	Smith	Combs
30—At Cin.	L	2-6	Rijo	Howell

Won 10, Lost 9

MAY

Date		Score	Winner	Loser
1—At Cin.	W	4-2	Ruffin	Birtsas
2—Houston	W	14-4	Cook	Clancy
3—Houston	L	3-10	Gullickson	Mulholland
4—Los Ang.	W	8-3	Carman	Martinez
5—Los Ang.	L	0-3	Morgan	Howell
6—Los Ang.	W	9-5	Carman	Munoz
8—At Hous.	L	2-3*	Smith	Noles
9—At Hous.	W	10-1	Combs	Scott
11—San Fran.	W	10-6	Howell	Burkett
12—San Fran.	L	2-6	Garrelts	Ruffin
13—San Fran.	W	4-1	Cook	Reuschel
14—At S.D.	L	1-5	Benes	Combs
15—At S.D.	W	2-1	Mulholland	Rasmussen
16—At S.D.	W	6-5	Howell	Whitson
18—At L.A.	L	2-4	Belcher	Ruffin
19—At L.A.	W	15-12†	McDowell	Howell
20—At L.A.	L	3-6	Martinez	Combs
21—At S.F.	W	5-2	Mulholland	Garrelts
22—At S.F.	W	4-2	Howell	Reuschel
24—Atlanta	W	8-4	Ruffin	Clary
25—Atlanta	W	5-4	Parrett	Hesketh
26—Atlanta	L	3-12	Smith	Combs
27—Atlanta	L	1-6	Smoltz	Mulholland
28—San Diego	L	5-9	Grant	Parrett
30—San Diego	L	3-8	Benes	Ruffin

Won 14, Lost 11

JUNE

Date		Score	Winner	Loser
1—New York	L	0-4	Viola	Cook
2—New York	W	5-4	Howell	Gooden
3—New York	W	8-3	Combs	Fernandez
4—At St. L.	L	2-3†	DiPino	Freeman
5—At St. L.	W	9-6	Carman	Terry
6—At St. L.	L	11-12*	DiPino	McDowell
7—At Chicago	W	3-1	Howell	Bielecki
8—At Chicago	L	2-15	Pico	Mulholland
9—At Chicago	L	3-4†	Lancaster	Parrett
10—At Chicago	L	3-7	Wilson	Ruffin
11—Montreal	L	0-5	Gross	Cook
11—Montreal	L	2-3	Hall	Parrett
12—Montreal	W	7-2	Howell	Smith
13—Montreal	L	3-4*	Schmidt	McDowell
15—Chicago	W	6-5*	Akerfelds	Nunez
15—Chicago	W	7-0	Ruffin	Bielecki
16—Chicago	W	2-1	Akerfelds	Maddux
17—Chicago	L	3-5	Pico	Parrett
19—Pittsburgh	W	2-1*	Carman	Landrum
20—Pittsburgh	W	7-2	Ruffin	Patterson
22—At N.Y.	L	1-5	Viola	Howell
23—At N.Y.	L	0-3	Gooden	Combs
24—At N.Y.	L	5-6	Innis	McDowell
25—At Pitts.	L	0-5	Reed	DeJesus
26—At Pitts.	L	0-1	Ruskin	Ruffin
27—At Pitts.	L	3-5	Kipper	Howell
29—Houston	W	2-0	Combs	Gullickson
30—Houston	L	3-8	Scott	Freeman

Won 11, Lost 17

JULY

Date		Score	Winner	Loser
1—Houston	W	8-4	McDowell	Andersen
2—Houston	W	5-1	Ruffin	Deshaies
3—Atlanta	W	5-1	Parrett	Clary
4—Atlanta	L	1-4	Glavine	Combs
5—Cincinnati	L	2-9	Armstrong	Howell
6—Cincinnati	L	1-4	Jackson	DeJesus
7—Cincinnati	L	0-5	Mahler	Ruffin
8—Cincinnati	W	4-3	Akerfelds	Charlton
12—At Hous.	L	4-7	Gullickson	Ruffin
13—At Hous.	W	4-2	DeJesus	Scott
14—At Hous.	W	12-8	Combs	Deshaies
15—At Hous.	L	1-6	Darwin	Parrett
16—At Atlanta	W	7-2	Mulholland	Clary
17—At Atlanta	L	10-14	Glavine	Ruffin
18—At Atlanta	W	4-3	Cook	Smoltz
19—At Cin.	W	5-2	Combs	Armstrong
20—At Cin.	L	1-5	Charlton	Parrett
21—At Cin.	L	1-6	Rijo	Mulholland
22—At Cin.	W	6-2	DeJesus	Scudder
23—New York	W	7-4	Akerfelds	Viola
24—New York	L	4-7	Machado	McDowell
25—New York	W	9-10	Fernandez	Parrett
26—At Pitts.	W	12-4	Mulholland	Heaton
27—At Pitts.	W	5-3	Cook	Reed
28—At Pitts.	W	4-3	Parrett	Landrum
29—At Pitts.	L	1-2	Drabek	Combs
31—St. Louis	L	2-4	Tudor	Howell

Won 14, Lost 13

AUGUST

Date		Score	Winner	Loser
1—St. Louis	W	11-10	Mulholland	Hill
2—St. Louis	L	3-4	Tewksbury	DeJesus
3—Pittsburgh	L	0-11	Drabek	Ruffin
4—Pittsburgh	L	1-3*	Patterson	McDowell
5—Pittsburgh	W	8-6	Carman	Ruskin
6—Pittsburgh	L	1-10	Tomlin	Mulholland
6—Pittsburgh	L	3-4*	Landrum	McDowell
7—At N.Y.	W	9-0	DeJesus	Viola
8—At N.Y.	L	4-8	Cone	Carman
9—At N.Y.	L	4-5	Ojeda	Akerfelds
10—At Mon.	L	3-4	Boyd	Mulholland
11—At Mon.	L	4-5‡	Sampen	Carman
12—At Mon.	L	3-6	Nabholz	DeJesus
14—San Fran.	W	4-3§	Cook	Bedrosian
15—San Fran.	W	6-0	Mulholland	Robinson
16—San Fran.	W	6-4	McDowell	Thurmond
17—At S.D.	W	2-1	DeJesus	Schiraldi
18—At S.D.	L	2-4	Benes	Greene
19—At S.D.	W	3-2	Boever	Rasmussen
20—At L.A.	L	1-2	Gott	Mulholland
21—At L.A.	W	12-11	McDowell	Crews
22—At L.A.	L	2-3	Gott	Boever
23—At S.F.	L	3-6	Oliveras	Cook
24—At S.F.	L	2-13	LaCoss	Combs
25—At S.F.	L	2-4	Robinson	Mulholland
26—At S.F.	W	5-1	Grimsley	Burkett
28—Los Ang.	L	1-5	Neidlinger	DeJesus
29—Los Ang.	L	2-12	Valenzuela	Greene
30—Los Ang.	L	2-3	Martinez	Boever
31—San Diego	W	4-2	McDowell	Hammaker

Won 11, Lost 19

SEPTEMBER

Date		Score	Winner	Loser
1—San Diego	W	3-2*	Boever	Harris
1—San Diego	W	2-1	Akerfelds	Rodriguez
2—San Diego	L	1-9	Whitson	DeJesus
3—At Pitts.	L	1-4	Drabek	Ruffin
4—At Pitts.	L	7-11	Landrum	Akerfelds
5—Chicago	W	4-1	Mulholland	Wilson
6—Chicago	L	2-5	Nunez	Grimsley
7—New York	W	4-1	DeJesus	Cone
8—New York	L	2-12	Gooden	Ruffin
9—New York	W	6-2	Combs	Fernandez
10—Pittsburgh	L	2-3	Belinda	Boever
11—Pittsburgh	L	1-5	Tomlin	Grimsley
12—At Chicago	L	3-9	Maddux	DeJesus
13—At Chicago	L	5-6	Assenmacher	McDowell
14—At N.Y.	W	4-1	Combs	Fernandez
15—At N.Y.	L	2-4	Viola	Mulholland
16—At N.Y.	W	8-3	DeJesus	Cone
18—At St. L.	W	6-3	Grimsley	Tewksbury
19—At St. L.	W	8-4	Combs	Magrane
20—At St. L.	L	4-5	Perez	McDowell
21—Montreal	W	5-4‡	Malone	Sampen
22—Montreal	W	3-2	Greene	Anderson
23—Montreal	W	2-1x	Carman	Farmer
24—Montreal	W	3-0	Combs	Barnes
25—St. Louis	L	0-1	Magrane	Mulholland
26—St. Louis	L	1-8	B. Smith	DeJesus
27—St. Louis	W	4-3	Greene	DeLeon
28—At Mon.	W	5-4	Grimsley	Boyd
29—At Mon.	L	1-5	Barnes	Combs
30—At Mon.	W	2-1	Mulholland	Nabholz

Won 16, Lost 14

OCTOBER

Date		Score	Winner	Loser
1—Chicago	W	7-6	DeJesus	Coffman
2—Chicago	L	1-3	Bielecki	Greene
3—Chicago	L	3-4	Maddux	McElroy

Won 1, Lost 2

*10 innings. †11 innings. ‡12 innings. §13 innings. x16 innings.

Terry Mulholland provided the Phillies with one of their major highlights of 1990 when he no-hit San Francisco August 15.

cause with a 7.71 ERA in two stints with the club.

The most notable righthanded casualty was setup man Jeff Parrett, who was 3-6 with a ghastly 4.98 ERA at the All-Star recess and traded to Atlanta for veteran slugger Dale Murphy in August. Greene joined the Phils as part of that deal.

Among the bright spots were Joe Boever, who picked up six saves with a 2.15 ERA in late relief after coming from Atlanta in July for Marvin Freeman, and Darrel Akerfelds, who was purchased from Texas in March and pitched in 71 games, ranking fifth in the league.

After Dykstra, catcher Darren Daulton was the Phillie who opened the most eyes offensively. A career .206 hitter entering the season, Daulton batted .268 and set additional personal bests with 12 home runs and 57 RBIs. Steve Lake hit .250 in only 80 at-bats as Daulton's caddy but didn't play after July 21 due to a hand injury.

There was good and bad news at first base. John Kruk put together another solid season, batting .291, to wrench the job

from Ricky Jordan, who started the season as the everyday first baseman and cleanup hitter. Jordan slumped to .241 after batting a combined .293 in his first two seasons and was replaced in the No. 4 hole by Murphy.

Murphy, who signed a two-year contract after joining the Phils, batted .266 with seven home runs in the final two months for his new club. "He might not be the MVP guy he was a few years back with the Braves," Manager Nick Leyva observed, "but he's shown that he can do a job for us in the four spot and he's still a heck of an outfielder."

Neither Leyva nor General Manager Lee Thomas was 100 percent certain that rookie second baseman Mickey Morandini was completely ready to take over a regular job. Promoted from the minors on August 31 when the Phils traded Tom Herr to the Mets, Morandini batted .241 in 25 games. "I think he can do the job," Thomas said. "He's a gamer, we know that. Let's say it's his job to lose."

At shortstop, Dickie Thon slipped from 15 home runs in 1989 to eight in 1990, but he batted .255 to keep his job safe.

The Phils would rather have the Charlie Hayes who reported to spring training 20 pounds thinner than in 1989 and batted .280 before the All-Star break with just six errors at third base. But the pounds returned as the season wore on and Hayes finished with a .258 average and 20 errors.

Philadelphia's more famous Hayes, outfielder Von, paced the club with 17 homers and 73 RBIs, but those totals were short of his usual standards. He moved from right to left field upon Murphy's arrival.

On the bench, Dave Hollins (three pinch-hit homers) and Sil Campusano stayed in Philadelphia since they were acquired in the major league draft and couldn't be optioned to the minors. Randy Ready and Rod Booker were frequent contributors, with Ready collecting a team-high 12 pinch hits.

The Phils were looking toward the future when they sent veteran Carmelo Martinez to the Pirates in August for hot rookie prospect Wes Chamberlain and two other minor leaguers. Chamberlain hit safely in nine of his 10 starts and flashed plenty of extra-base power. "I'm not saying out of spring training, but Mr. Chamberlain could make our club at some point in 1991," Thomas predicted.

And so the Phils ended the season feeling they'd turned a corner of sorts. Are they headed in the right direction? "We'd better be," quipped Thomas. "I'd sure hate to find my name in the transactions."

Aside from a splendid year at the plate, Ryne Sandberg captured his eighth straight Gold Glove and established a major league record with 123 consecutive errorless games at second base.

Cubs Lack Arms to Defend East

By JOE GODDARD

Make no mistake, the Chicago Cubs have made an indelible impression as a team that elects to take care of business with bat in hand. In the last 45 years, however, that approach has produced tangible success (read first place) exactly twice: in 1984 and 1989. In each case, pitching helped push the slugging North Siders over the top. And in each successive season, a lack of pitching dropped the club from first to fourth place in the National League East.

Back in 1985, one season after Rick Sutcliffe finished 16-1 to win the N.L. Cy Young Award, the Cubs lost all five starting pitchers during one stretch and finished 77-84. Last season, year after they fashioned the club's best earned-run average since 1972, Cub pitchers were plagued by injuries and inconsistency, dropping Chicago to a 77-85 finish. In each post-championship season, the Cubs hung up the league's next-to-worst ERA.

In all, the 1990 Cubs used 15 starting pitchers, tying a club record. Sutcliffe didn't throw a pitch until August 29 due to a shoulder injury. Rookie Mike Harkey, after injuries postponed his 1989 arrival, was sidelined in early June and September with shoulder tendinitis. An elbow injury halted Shawn Boskie's rookie season on August 4. Then there was the off-and-on success of Greg Maddux, who was 0-8 over a two-month stretch, and Mike Bielecki.

The Chicago bullpen was nearly as unsettled. Ace reliever Mitch Williams stumbled before yielding to knee surgery, saving 16 games after a 36-save 1989 season. Bill Long spent most of June on the disabled list, and Jeff Pico was lost in September with a broken thumb. Les Lancaster, who pitched a string of 30⅔ scoreless innings in 1989, pitched in the minor leagues for part of 1990.

To a lesser extent, the same problem plagued the position players. A broken right hand and injured left wrist forced 1989 Rookie of the Year Jerome Walton to miss 81 games. The 1989 left-field platoon of Dwight Smith and Lloyd McClendon was a bust in '90, combining for just seven home runs and 37 runs batted in (compared with 21 homers and 92 RBIs a year earlier) until McClendon was traded to Pittsburgh in September.

"I never thought it was a lack of hitting," General Manager Jim Frey said. "I trace (the decline) back to a lack of consistent

Despite some shoulder problems, rookie Mike Harkey blossomed with a 12-6 record and 3.26 ERA.

pitching, starting and relieving. When Mitch went down, we had no one to save a game. We lost game after game after game in the bullpen. That coupled with our starting pitching being shaky hurt us."

While Cub hitters raised the team batting average to .263 from a league-high .261 in 1989, the pitchers' ERA skied almost a full run, from 3.43 to 4.34, with 40 more walks and 41 fewer strikeouts.

Three arms were critical to the Cubs' fortunes in 1989 . . . and their misfortunes of 1990. Maddux, Bielecki and Sutcliffe pitched the Cubs to a division title with a combined 53-30 record and 3.24 ERA; for a fourth-place team, they were 23-28 with a 4.16 ERA.

Maddux was the only starter to pitch more than 200 innings, but it was a season-long struggle to get to .500. Still, his 15-15 record increased his victory total to 52 over the last three years, the most for a Cub since Rick Reuschel's 52 wins from 1977-79. He also led N.L. pitchers in putouts, assists, double plays, chances and fielding

SCORES OF CHICAGO CUBS' 1990 GAMES

APRIL

Date	W/L	Score	Winner	Loser
10—Phila.	W	2-1	Lancaster	Parrett
12—Phila.	L	4-5	Mulholland	Wilson
12—Phila.	W	6-3	Nunez	Combs
13—At Pitts.	W	2-0	Maddux	Walk
14—At Pitts.	W	4-1	Harkey	Drabek
15—At Pitts.	L	3-4§	Patterson	Lancaster
16—New York	L	1-10	Viola	Wilson
17—At N.Y.	W	8-6z	Assenmacher	Innis
18—At N.Y.	W	8-5	Maddux	Cone
19—At N.Y.	L	1-4	Gooden	Harkey
20—Pittsburgh	L	4-9†	Roesler	Bielecki
21—Pittsburgh	L	3-4	Smiley	Wilson
22—Pittsburgh	L	2-3	Heaton	Nunez
24—At S.D.	L	3-13	Rasmussen	Maddux
25—At S.D.	L	0-3	Whitson	Bielecki
26—At S.D.	W	3-1	Harkey	Hurst
27—At L.A.	L	0-5	Valenzuela	Nunez
28—At L.A.	L	4-5	Martinez	Williams
29—At L.A.	W	4-0	Maddux	Morgan

Won 8, Lost 11

MAY

Date	W/L	Score	Winner	Loser
1—At S.F.	W	7-4	Bielecki	Knepper
2—At S.F.	W	9-6	Harkey	Garrelts
5—San Diego	W	3-2	Maddux	Lefferts
5—San Diego	L	5-6	Rasmussen	Nunez
6—San Diego	L	3-8	Whitson	Bielecki
7—Atlanta	L	8-9	Kerfeld	Williams
8—Atlanta	W	10-8x	Long	Henry
9—Atlanta	W	4-0*	Lancaster	Smith
11—At Cin.	L	5-7	Charlton	Williams
12—At Cin.	W	4-2	Bielecki	Browning
13—At Cin.	L	9-13	Dibble	Wilson
14—At Atlanta	L	2-3	Henry	Williams
15—At Atlanta	W	12-2	Pico	Smith
16—At Atlanta	L	0-4	Smoltz	Maddux
17—At Hous.	L	4-5x	Smith	Nunez
18—At Hous.	W	7-0	Harkey	Gullickson
19—At Hous.	W	4-1	Lancaster	Clancy
20—At Hous.	W	5-1	Boskie	Scott
21—Cincinnati	L	3-4	Rijo	Maddux
22—Cincinnati	W	2-1b	Long	Scudder
23—Los Ang.	L	3-4	Belcher	Assenmacher
24—Los Ang.	L	6-15	Valenzuela	Lancaster
26—Houston	L	1-8	Scott	Boskie
26—Houston	L	3-12	Deshaies	Maddux
27—Houston	W	11-6	Bielecki	Portugal
28—San Fran.	W	5-1	Harkey	Knepper
29—San Fran.	L	2-6	Robinson	Blankenship
30—San Fran.	L	1-4	Burkett	Boskie

Won 13, Lost 15

JUNE

Date	W/L	Score	Winner	Loser
1—At St. L.	L	4-6	DeLeon	Maddux
2—At St. L.	W	7-6	Lancaster	L. Smith
3—At St. L.	L	4-7	B. Smith	Blankenship
4—At Pitts.	L	2-6	Patterson	Boskie
5—At Pitts.	L	5-6	Belinda	Williams
6—At Pitts.	L	1-6†	Drabek	Maddux
7—Phila.	L	1-3	Howell	Bielecki
8—Phila.	W	15-2	Pico	Mulholland
9—Phila.	W	4-3x	Lancaster	Parrett
10—Phila.	W	7-3	Wilson	Ruffin
11—New York	W	8-5	Williams	Pena
12—New York	L	8-19	Gooden	Bielecki
13—New York	L	10-15	Franco	Lancaster
13—New York	L	6-9	Darling	Harkey
15—At Phila.	L	5-6§	Akerfelds	Nunez
15—At Phila.	L	0-7	Ruffin	Bielecki
16—At Phila.	L	1-2	Akerfelds	Maddux
17—At Phila.	W	5-3	Pico	Parrett
18—At Mon.	L	1-5	Martinez	Harkey
19—At Mon.	W	2-1	Boskie	Gardner
20—At Mon.	L	2-3	Mohorcic	Maddux
22—St. Louis	L	0-7	Magrane	Wilson
23—St. Louis	L	7-8	Tewksbury	Bielecki
24—St. Louis	W	3-2§	Assenmacher	Niedenfuer
25—Montreal	L	3-7	Gardner	Boskie
26—Montreal	L	5-6	Schmidt	Lancaster
27—Montreal	W	5-3	Pico	Gross
28—Montreal	W	3-2	Lancaster	Sampen
29—At S.D.	W	3-2	Long	Harris
30—At S.D.	W	7-3	Wilson	Benes

Won 12, Lost 18

JULY

Date	W/L	Score	Winner	Loser
1—At S.D.	W	11-10	Lancaster	Lefferts
2—At L.A.	L	1-3	Belcher	Pico
3—At L.A.	L	6-7	Hartley	Assenmacher
4—At L.A.	W	5-3	Harkey	Valenzuela
6—At S.F.	W	5-2	Boskie	Garrelts
7—At S.F.	L	9-10	Brantley	Lancaster
8—At S.F.	L	3-5	Wilson	Pico
8—At S.F.	L	4-10	Burkett	Bielecki
12—Los Ang.	L	3-6	Valenzuela	Harkey
13—Los Ang.	L	2-5	Martinez	Boskie
14—Los Ang.	L	0-7	Morgan	Maddux
15—Los Ang.	W	5-1	Wilson	Belcher
16—San Diego	W	4-3	Harkey	Show
17—San Diego	W	7-2	Boskie	Benes
18—San Diego	W	4-2	Maddux	Rasmussen
20—San Fran.	W	5-4	Bielecki	Brantley
21—San Fran.	W	3-2	Harkey	Brantley
22—San Fran.	W	4-2	Assenmacher	Hammaker
23—At St. L.	W	3-1	Maddux	DeLeon
24—At St. L.	L	4-9	Terry	Wilson
25—At St. L.	L	0-9	Tudor	Harkey
26—At Mon.	L	2-3§	Burke	Williams
27—At Mon.	W	2-0§	Maddux	Sampen
28—At Mon.	W	10-7	Long	Burke
29—At Mon.	W	2-1	Harkey	Gross
31—Pittsburgh	L	1-9	Patterson	Boskie

Won 14, Lost 12

AUGUST

Date	W/L	Score	Winner	Loser
1—Pittsburgh	W	5-0	Maddux	Reed
2—Pittsburgh	L	5-8	Smiley	Wilson
3—Montreal	W	10-4	Harkey	Gardner
4—Montreal	W	10-2	Boskie	Gross
5—Montreal	W	3-1	Maddux	Boyd
7—St. Louis	W	5-3	Assenmacher	Terry
8—St. Louis	W	4-3a	Long	Niedenfuer
9—St. Louis	L	1-3	Hill	Dickson
10—At N.Y.	L	1-5	Fernandez	Maddux
11—At N.Y.	W	6-3	Wilson	Darling
12—At N.Y.	W	10-2	Harkey	Viola
13—Houston	L	2-7	Portugal	Dickson
14—Houston	W	5-2	Maddux	Scott
15—Houston	L	4-8§	Smith	Pico
17—Atlanta	W	7-0	Harkey	Smoltz
18—Atlanta	L	6-17	Leibrandt	Dickson
19—Atlanta	W	5-4	Maddux	Mercker
20—At Cin.	W	3-1‡	Bielecki	Charlton
21—At Cin.	L	1-8	Mahler	Harkey
22—At Cin.	L	1-4	Rijo	Pico
24—At Atlanta	L	0-3	Avery	Maddux
25—At Atlanta	W	6-3	Bielecki	Glavine
26—At Atlanta	L	3-4	Smoltz	Williams
28—At Hous.	W	5-2	Maddux	Gullickson
29—At Hous.	L	0-1	Portugal	Sutcliffe
30—Cincinnati	L	5-6	Jackson	Bielecki
31—Cincinnati	W	4-3	Long	Myers

Won 15, Lost 12

SEPTEMBER

Date	W/L	Score	Winner	Loser
1—Cincinnati	L	1-8	Mahler	Nunez
2—Cincinnati	L	2-6	Rijo	Maddux
3—At Mon.	L	2-3y	Frey	Kramer
4—At Mon.	W	3-1	Bielecki	Martinez
5—At Phila.	L	1-4	Mulholland	Wilson
6—At Phila.	W	5-2	Nunez	Grimsley
7—St. Louis	L	3-4	Tewksbury	Maddux
8—St. Louis	W	5-4	Pavlas	Dayley
9—St. Louis	L	2-9	Tudor	Bielecki
10—Montreal	L	4-7	Nabholz	Long
11—Montreal	W	11-6	Pavlas	Gross
12—Phila.	W	9-3	Maddux	DeJesus
13—Phila.	W	6-5	Assenmacher	McDowell
14—At St. L.	L	2-4	B. Smith	Williams
15—At St. L.	W	6-2	Lancaster	DeLeon
16—At St. L.	W	8-4	Nunez	Hill
18—Pittsburgh	W	8-5	Maddux	Smiley
19—Pittsburgh	L	7-8	Drabek	Sutcliffe
20—Pittsburgh	L	2-11	Walk	Kramer
21—New York	W	4-3	Assenmacher	Cone
22—New York	L	5-11	Darling	Nunez
23—New York	L	3-7	Gooden	Maddux
24—New York	W	4-3	Assenmacher	Viola
25—At Pitts.	L	3-5	Drabek	Wilson
26—At Pitts.	L	3-4	Smith	Coffman
27—At Pitts.	L	2-3	Tomlin	Bielecki
28—At N.Y.	L	1-7	Gooden	Maddux
29—At N.Y.	W	3-2	Lancaster	Viola
30—At N.Y.	W	6-5	Nunez	Franco

Won 13, Lost 16

OCTOBER

Date	W/L	Score	Winner	Loser
1—At Phila.	L	6-7	DeJesus	Coffman
2—At Phila.	W	3-1	Bielecki	Greene
3—At Phila.	W	4-3	Maddux	McElroy

Won 2, Lost 1

*4½ innings. †6½ innings. ‡8 innings. §10 innings. x11 innings. y12 innings. z13 innings. a15 innings. b16 innings.

A slow start plagued Mark Grace, but in the second half of the season he hit .351 and finished with a career-high 82 RBIs.

average (a perfect 1.000) and received the first Gold Glove of his career.

Bielecki plummeted to an 8-11 season and 4.93 ERA after 18-7, 3.14 marks in '89. Harkey, despite his sore shoulder, blossomed with a 12-6 showing and 3.26 ERA, earning The Sporting News' N.L. Rookie Pitcher of the Year award. Boskie, despite losing his curveball, was 5-6 with a 3.69 ERA before yielding to elbow surgery.

As Williams faltered in the bullpen (the Cubs twice tried him as a starter in late September, but he was pounded both times and wound up 1-8), Paul Assenmacher finished in the closer's role with a career-high 10 saves and a 1.04 ERA in his last 13 appearances. Lancaster re-established himself in September (2-0, one save, 2.05 ERA in two starts and eight relief spots), and rookie Dave Pavlas helped his 1991 chances with a 2-0 record and 2.11 ERA in 13 appearances. Steve Wilson and Jose Nunez both pitched in middle relief and made frequent starts in the rotation's No. 5 hole.

Aside from the many frustrations, there was a brilliant season from second baseman Ryne Sandberg, a heroic comeback from major knee surgery by right fielder Andre Dawson and a blistering second half by first baseman Mark Grace.

Sandberg slugged 40 home runs and became the first N.L. second baseman to win a home run crown since Rogers Hornsby in 1925. The league leader in runs scored for the second straight year, Sandberg also drove home a career-high 100 runs and topped off his offense with 25 stolen bases. He won his eighth straight Gold Glove in the field, where his streak of consecutive errorless games ended at 123, a major league record for second basemen.

Dawson defied the skeptics who doubted he'd bounce back from an off-season operation on his creaky knees, batting a career-best .310, cracking 27 homers and matching Sandberg with 100 RBIs in the cleanup spot. Dawson also swiped his 300th career base on September 22, becoming just the second player in major league history (next to Willie Mays) to collect at least 2,000 hits, 300 home runs and 300 steals.

Grace, meanwhile, entered the All-Star break with a .270 average, but went on a .351 tear when the schedule resumed and closed the year at .309 with a career-high 82 RBIs.

Shortstop Shawon Dunston added long-ball power up the middle, blasting 17 home runs, but he lapsed into a .170 funk over the final six weeks. Joe Girardi also tailed off after a hot first half (.288). He nearly made the All-Star team as a catching reserve, but he slipped to .270 and ended up sharing the September catching chores with Damon Berryhill, who hadn't played in 12 months due to rotator-cuff surgery.

The remaining positions were, for the most part, missing in action. When healthy, Walton batted just .263 in center field. Often injured Luis Salazar knocked in only 47 runs at the Cubs' most troublesome position, third base. Left field ended up in the hands of Doug Dascenzo, who extended his career errorless streak to 172 games and batted .253.

Among the reserves, outfielder Dave Clark and infielder Domingo Ramos enjoyed second-half surges, hitting .310 and .319 after the break, respectively. Hector Villanueva, a rookie without a position, belted seven homers in just 114 at-bats. Gary Varsho tied Clark for the team lead with 11 pinch hits.

The final standings in the N.L. batting race were reflective of the Cubs' deep offense, listing Dawson (fifth), Grace (sixth) and Sandberg (10th) among the top 10. They were the Cubs' first trio of .300 hitters since Phil Cavarretta, Stan Hack and Roy Johnson in 1945. Those Cubs won a National League pennant, however; these weren't even close.

Tom Pagnozzi emerged as the Cardinals' No. 1 catcher in 1990, forcing Todd Zeile to third base.

Cards Fold Early, Herzog Resigns

By RICK HUMMEL

They made Whitey Herzog quit a baseball job for the first time in his life. Two days after the St. Louis Cardinals "totally embarrassed" him while losing a three-game series to San Francisco in early July, Herzog resigned as their manager with 2½ years remaining on his contract.

"I can't get the guys to play," Herzog lamented. "That's the first time that I've ever felt like that in 17 years of managing."

When Herzog stepped down on July 6, he conceded he'd "had some bad teams before. We were terrible in '86 and terrible in '88." But these Cardinals, picked by many to contend for the National League East title, dropped out of the race in mid-April. They finished in last place for the first time since 1918, rising higher than fifth place only once (on June 4) after May 1.

Amid the fallout, the Cardinals did have their first N.L. batting champion since 1985. Willie McGee, the winner that season with a .353 mark, won the title again—in absentia, in the American League. Batting .335 through August 29, McGee was traded the following day to Oakland for rookie outfielder Felix Jose and two minor leaguers. Some criticized the rule that allowed a "ghost" to remain eligible for the title, noting McGee's combined .324 average between both leagues (a mark topped by two other N.L. batters).

Once new Manager Joe Torre took over for interim skipper Red Schoendienst on August 2, the final two months amounted to extended camp. Torre conducted wholesale experiments, sending as many as seven rookies on the field at one time. That didn't help the final record (70-92) any, and the Cardinals closed the schedule with a season-high seven-game losing streak.

As a team, St. Louis scored fewer runs than every other N.L. club but one (Houston). Two of the few veterans who produced were left fielder Vince Coleman and first baseman Pedro Guerrero. Coleman batted a career-best .292 and led the league in stolen bases (77) for the sixth straight year. Guerrero paced the team with 80 runs batted in, but even that total was mildly disappointing. He was not exactly a stabilizer in the field, committing more errors (13) than any other N.L. first baseman.

One Cardinal who was a rampart was Jose Oquendo. He established a major league record for fewest errors (three) by

By the end of the season, former catching prospect Todd Zeile's future was at third base.

a second baseman playing 150-plus games, breaking the mark (five errors) he shared with three other players. His accomplishments were mainly on defense, however, for Oquendo drove in just 37 runs.

Incredibly, Oquendo was denied a Gold Glove, although shortstop Ozzie Smith was minted an award for the 11th straight season. The middle infield was the steadiest part of a St. Louis defense that turned the fewest double plays in franchise history and committed its most errors since 1983. Overall, the Cards ranked sixth in the league in fielding after leading the N.L. the previous six seasons.

One victim of Torre's maneuvering was third baseman Terry Pendleton, who batted just six times after September 4. Pendleton, a .230 hitter, was sent to the bench when the Cards' brain trust decided rookie catcher Todd Zeile's future was at third base. Zeile led the team in home runs (15) and collected 57 RBIs, but he batted just .151 (19-for-126) with runners in scoring position.

The Cardinals insisted Zeile was not a bad receiver, but they concluded he wasn't

SCORES OF ST. LOUIS CARDINALS' 1990 GAMES

APRIL

Date		Score	Winner	Loser
9—Montreal	W	6-5‡	Dayley	Gardner
10—Montreal	W	4-2	B. Smith	Z. Smith
11—Montreal	L	4-6	Boyd	Mathews
13—At Phila.	W	11-0	Tudor	Howell
14—At Phila.	L	2-6	Ruffin	Magrane
15—At Phila.	L	0-4	Cook	B. Smith
16—At Pitts.	W	6-4	DeLeon	Smiley
17—At Pitts.	L	2-7	Heaton	Mathews
18—At Pitts.	W	3-0	Tudor	Walk
19—Pittsburgh	L	1-5	Drabek	Magrane
20—Phila.	L	0-3	Cook	B. Smith
21—Phila.	L	6-7†	McDowell	Terry
22—Phila.	L	3-5	Combs	Horton
23—Pittsburgh	W	7-4	Tudor	Walk
24—At L.A.	L	0-3	Morgan	Magrane
25—At L.A.	W	5-1	B. Smith	Hershiser
26—At L.A.	W	7-1	DeLeon	Belcher
27—At S.F.	L	3-12	Hammaker	Mathews
28—At S.F.	W	5-0	Tudor	Garrelts
29—At S.F.	L	7-9	Reuschel	Magrane

Won 9, Lost 11

MAY

Date		Score	Winner	Loser
1—At S.D.	W	2-1	B. Smith	Whitson
2—At S.D.	L	3-4	Hurst	DeLeon
4—Cincinnati	L	3-8	Robinson	Tudor
5—Cincinnati	L	2-4	Rijo	Magrane
6—Cincinnati	L	1-5	Scudder	B. Smith
7—Cincinnati	L	0-3	Browning	DeLeon
9—San Diego	W	11-5	Horton	Benes
10—San Diego	L	1-9	Rasmussen	Magrane
11—Atlanta	W	5-2	B. Smith	Smoltz
12—Atlanta	W	4-3†	L. Smith	Boever
13—Atlanta	L	1-3	Castillo	Terry
15—Houston	W	4-0	Magrane	Scott
16—Houston	W	10-6	B. Smith	Deshaies
17—At Cin.	W	3-0	DeLeon	Browning
18—At Cin.	L	0-1	Charlton	Dayley
19—At Cin.	L	0-4	Armstrong	Tudor
20—At Cin.	W	6-2	Magrane	Jackson
21—At Atlanta	L	5-6	Boever	Terry
22—At Atlanta	W	4-3	DeLeon	Lilliquist
23—San Fran.	L	1-6	Knepper	Mathews
24—San Fran.	W	3-2§	DiPino	Vosberg
25—Los Ang.	L	1-4	Martinez	Magrane
26—Los Ang.	L	0-8	Morgan	B. Smith
27—Los Ang.	L	7-14	Crews	DeLeon
28—At Hous.	L	1-5	Gullickson	Mathews
29—At Hous.	W	3-2	Tudor	Schatzeder
30—At Hous.	L	1-2	Agosto	Magrane

Won 11, Lost 16

JUNE

Date		Score	Winner	Loser
1—Chicago	W	6-4	DeLeon	Maddux
2—Chicago	L	6-7	Lancaster	L. Smith
3—Chicago	W	7-4	B. Smith	Blankenship
4—Phila.	W	3-2‡	DiPino	Freeman
5—Phila.	L	6-9	Carman	Terry
6—Phila.	W	12-11†	DiPino	McDowell
7—At Mon.	L	2-3	Smith	DeLeon
8—At Mon.	L	2-18	Martinez	B. Smith
9—At Mon.	L	1-3	Gardner	Terry
10—At Mon.	W	5-3	Magrane	Boyd
11—Pittsburgh	L	7-8	Belinda	Niedenfuer
12—Pittsburgh	L	3-6	Heaton	DeLeon
13—Pittsburgh	L	5-6	Huismann	DiPino
14—Montreal	L	2-3	Sampen	Niedenfuer
15—Montreal	L	4-7	Frey	Magrane
16—Montreal	W	5-3	Tewksbury	Hall
17—Montreal	W	7-1	DeLeon	Smith
19—At N.Y.	L	0-6	Cone	Tudor
20—At N.Y.	L	3-6	Fernandez	B. Smith
22—At Chicago	W	7-0	Magrane	Wilson
23—At Chicago	W	8-7	Tewksbury	Bielecki
24—At Chicago	L	2-3†	Assenmacher	Niedenfuer
25—New York	L	2-3	Cone	L. Smith
26—New York	L	6-8‡	Pena	Dayley
27—New York	L	2-5	Viola	Magrane
28—Pittsburgh	W	5-1	Tewksbury	Drabek
29—At L.A.	L	0-6	Valenzuela	DeLeon
30—At L.A.	W	6-5	Tudor	Gott

Won 11, Lost 17

JULY

Date		Score	Winner	Loser
1—At L.A.	W	6-5	DiPino	Crews
2—At S.F.	L	2-3	Robinson	Magrane
3—At S.F.	L	0-4	Wilson	Tewksbury
4—At S.F.	L	2-9	Burkett	DeLeon
5—At S.D.	W	4-1	L. Smith	Harris
6—At S.D.	W	5-3	Tudor	Rasmussen
7—At S.D.	L	1-3	Hurst	Magrane
8—At S.D.	W	4-1	Tewksbury	Whitson
12—San Fran.	L	2-4	Garrelts	B. Smith
13—San Fran.	L	1-6	Robinson	DeLeon
14—San Fran.	W	2-1	L. Smith	Wilson
15—San Fran.	L	3-5	Bedrosian	Niedenfuer
16—Los Ang.	L	2-5	Wells	Tewksbury
17—Los Ang.	W	3-0	B. Smith	Valenzuela
18—Los Ang.	L	1-6	Martinez	DeLeon
19—San Diego	W	8-3	Magrane	Hurst
20—San Diego	W	4-2	Tudor	Whitson
21—San Diego	W	4-2*	Tewksbury	Show
22—San Diego	W	6-4	Dayley	Harris
23—Chicago	L	1-3	Maddux	DeLeon
24—Chicago	W	9-4	Terry	Wilson
25—Chicago	W	9-0	Tudor	Harkey
26—At N.Y.	L	1-6	Darling	Tewksbury
26—At N.Y.	W	3-1	Hill	Ojeda
27—At N.Y.	L	1-10	Viola	B. Smith
28—At N.Y.	W	1-0	Magrane	Cone
29—At N.Y.	L	0-6	Gooden	DeLeon
31—At Phila.	W	4-2	Tudor	Howell

Won 15, Lost 13

AUGUST

Date		Score	Winner	Loser
1—At Phila.	L	10-11	Mulholland	Hill
2—At Phila.	W	4-3	Tewksbury	DeJesus
3—New York	L	4-5	Machado	L. Smith
4—New York	W	7-5	Hill	Gooden
5—New York	W	8-3	Tudor	Fernandez
6—New York	W	5-1	Magrane	Darling
7—At Chicago	L	3-5	Assenmacher	Terry
8—At Chicago	L	3-4x	Long	Niedenfuer
9—At Chicago	W	3-1	Hill	Dickson
10—At Pitts.	W	8-3	Dayley	Kramer
11—At Pitts.	W	3-2	Magrane	Tomlin
12—At Pitts.	W	6-0	Tewksbury	Smiley
14—Cincinnati	L	4-9	Armstrong	DeLeon
15—Cincinnati	L	1-3§	Dibble	Niedenfuer
16—Houston	L	2-4	Darwin	Magrane
17—Houston	W	5-0	Tewksbury	Gullickson
18—Houston	L	2-3‡	Smith	DiPino
19—Houston	W	7-3	DeLeon	Scott
20—Atlanta	W	7-2	Hill	Glavine
21—Atlanta	L	2-7	Smoltz	Magrane
22—Atlanta	L	1-2	Castillo	Tewksbury
24—At Hous.	W	3-2‡	Terry	Smith
25—At Hous.	L	4-6	Deshaies	DeLeon
26—At Hous.	L	2-4	Darwin	Hill
28—At Cin.	L	1-2	Rijo	Magrane
29—At Cin.	W	9-1	Tewksbury	Browning
30—At Atlanta	W	5-3§	DiPino	Henry
31—At Atlanta	L	1-4	Smoltz	DeLeon

Won 14, Lost 14

SEPTEMBER

Date		Score	Winner	Loser
1—At Atlanta	L	3-4	Castillo	Hill
2—At Atlanta	L	0-5	Leibrandt	Tudor
3—New York	L	3-9	Gooden	Tewksbury
4—New York	W	1-0	Magrane	Fernandez
5—Montreal	L	2-6	Nabholz	DeLeon
6—Montreal	W	4-2	Dayley	Gardner
7—At Chicago	W	4-3	Tewksbury	Maddux
8—At Chicago	L	4-5	Pavlas	Dayley
9—At Chicago	W	9-2	Tudor	Bielecki
10—At N.Y.	L	1-10	Viola	DeLeon
11—At N.Y.	L	8-10	Franco	L. Smith
12—At Mon.	L	2-6	Boyd	Tewksbury
13—At Mon.	W	6-4	Olivares	Sampen
14—Chicago	W	4-2	B. Smith	Williams
15—Chicago	L	2-6	Lancaster	DeLeon
16—Chicago	L	4-8	Nunez	Hill
18—Phila.	L	3-6	Grimsley	Tewksbury
19—Phila.	L	4-8	Combs	Magrane
20—Phila.	W	5-4	Perez	McDowell
21—At Pitts.	L	0-1	Smith	DeLeon
22—At Pitts.	W	3-2	Hill	Tomlin
23—At Pitts.	L	2-7	Smiley	Tewksbury
25—At Phila.	W	1-0	Magrane	Mulholland
26—At Phila.	W	8-1	B. Smith	DeJesus
27—At Phila.	L	3-4	Greene	DeLeon
28—Pittsburgh	L	4-6	Landrum	Hill
29—Pittsburgh	L	0-8	Walk	Tewksbury
30—Pittsburgh	L	0-2	Drabek	Magrane

Won 10, Lost 18

OCTOBER

Date		Score	Winner	Loser
1—At Mon.	L	9-15	Burke	Dayley
2—At Mon.	L	1-2	Gross	Olivares
3—At Mon.	L	2-9	Sampen	Hill

Won 0, Lost 3

*7 innings. †10 innings. ‡11 innings. §12 innings. x15 innings.

Lee Smith was the saving grace of the St. Louis bullpen.

as good as Tom Pagnozzi, their backup the previous two seasons. Given the regular job in September, Pagnozzi batted .293 after the All-Star break and threw out 46 percent of would-be thiefs.

The acquisition of Jose settled the uncertainty in right field, where Tom Brunansky and Milt Thompson had opened the year as platoons. Brunansky was traded to Boston for reliever Lee Smith in May, and Thompson played himself out of the lineup by hitting .218. Jose made an indelible impression by crushing one of the longest home runs in Busch Stadium's history: a 463-foot drive into the left-field upper deck.

Jose wasn't the only young outfielder who stood up to be counted when Torre looked toward the future. Triple-A callups Ray Lankford and Bernard Gilkey impressed with their speed (14 steals combined) and batting stroke (Gilkey, .297; Lankford, .286) in September.

Another of Torre's many missions was to learn whether hellbent Rex Hudler could contribute. He answered in the affirmative by hitting .333 after Torre took over and ranking third on the team with seven hom-

ers. Rookie Craig Wilson (.391 as a pinch-hitter) and Denny Walling (a team-high 11 pinch-hits) were valuable bench players.

Pitching would have been a total letdown if not for John Tudor, Bob Tewksbury and Lee Smith. Despite that trio's best efforts, the Cardinals ranked among the league's bottom five in earned-run average, runs, hits, strikeouts and complete games.

Tudor, battling shoulder trouble all season, finished 12-4 in a remarkable comeback effort. On the disabled list for all but 14⅓ innings with Los Angeles in 1989, Tudor re-signed with St. Louis and led the rotation in victories and ERA (2.40). Tewksbury, outrighted to the minors in May, returned to post 10 victories and a 3.47 ERA, totals that ranked second among starters.

The downfall of the staff can be traced to lefthander Joe Magrane and righthander Jose DeLeon, who ranked one-two in the league in losses (DeLeon, 19; Magrane, 17). Between them, they won just 17 games, down 50 percent from their 34 victories in 1989.

Between the highs and lows were rookie Omar Olivares' 2.92 ERA following his August recall and Ken Hill's 4-1 start (but 1-5 finish) after being brought up in July. Free-agent signee Bryn Smith was a steady 9-8 but missed 5½ weeks with a sore shoulder.

The saving grace of the bullpen was Lee Smith, who won or saved 43 percent of the Cardinals' 60 victories after arriving from Boston in May. His 27 saves with St. Louis (he also had four for Boston) ranked third in the league. After Smith, righty Tom Niedenfuer was a strong arm in middle relief (52 appearances), while Ken Dayley led lefthanded relievers with a 3.56 ERA, mostly in a setup role.

The year was bittersweet for Frank DiPino, who led the staff with 62 appearances but allowed 54 percent (20 of 37) of inherited runners to score. His ERA ballooned from 2.45 in 1989 to 4.56 and he had a personal 12-game winning streak snapped in June. Then there was Scott Terry, a durable starter/reliever in 1989. Tabbed as the closer to replace injured Todd Worrell entering spring training, Terry tried to pitch through shoulder pain from the outset. He finished 2-6 with a 4.75 ERA, then underwent arthroscopic surgery at season's end.

"Murphy's Law," said General Manager Dal Maxvill, summing up the Cardinals' plight. "Everything that could go wrong, did go wrong."

National League Averages for 1990

CHAMPIONSHIP WINNERS IN PREVIOUS YEARS

1876—Chicago .788	1914—Boston .614	1952—Brooklyn .627
1877—Boston .646	1915—Philadelphia .592	1953—Brooklyn .682
1878—Boston .683	1916—Brooklyn .610	1954—New York .630
1879—Providence .705	1917—New York .636	1955—Brooklyn .641
1880—Chicago .798	1918—Chicago .651	1956—Brooklyn .604
1881—Chicago .667	1919—Cincinnati .686	1957—Milwaukee .617
1882—Chicago .655	1920—Brooklyn .604	1958—Milwaukee .597
1883—Boston .643	1921—New York .614	1959—Los Angeles‡ .564
1884—Providence .750	1922—New York .604	1960—Pittsburgh .617
1885—Chicago .777	1923—New York .621	1961—Cincinnati .604
1886—Chicago .726	1924—New York .608	1962—San Francisco§ .624
1887—Detroit .637	1925—Pittsburgh .621	1963—Los Angeles .611
1888—New York .641	1926—St. Louis .578	1964—St. Louis .574
1889—New York .659	1927—Pittsburgh .610	1965—Los Angeles .599
1890—Brooklyn .667	1928—St. Louis .617	1966—Los Angeles .586
1891—Boston .630	1929—Chicago .645	1967—St. Louis .627
1892—Boston .680	1930—St. Louis .597	1968—St. Louis .599
1893—Boston .662	1931—St. Louis .656	1969—New York (East) .617
1894—Baltimore .695	1932—Chicago .584	1970—Cincinnati (West) .630
1895—Baltimore .669	1933—New York .599	1971—Pittsburgh (East) .599
1896—Baltimore .698	1934—St. Louis .621	1972—Cincinnati (West) .617
1897—Boston .705	1935—Chicago .649	1973—New York (East) .509
1898—Boston .685	1936—New York .597	1974—Los Angeles (West) .630
1899—Brooklyn .677	1937—New York .625	1975—Cincinnati (West) .667
1900—Brooklyn .603	1938—Chicago .586	1976—Cincinnati (West) .630
1901—Pittsburgh .647	1939—Cincinnati .630	1977—Los Angeles (West) .605
1902—Pittsburgh .741	1940—Cincinnati .654	1978—Los Angeles (West) .586
1903—Pittsburgh .650	1941—Brooklyn .649	1979—Pittsburgh (East) .605
1904—New York .693	1942—St. Louis .688	1980—Philadelphia (East) .562
1905—New York .686	1943—St. Louis .682	1981—Los Angeles (West) .573
1906—Chicago .763	1944—St. Louis .682	1982—St. Louis (East) .568
1907—Chicago .704	1945—Chicago .636	1983—Philadelphia (East) .556
1908—Chicago .643	1946—St. Louis* .628	1984—San Diego (West) .568
1909—Pittsburgh .724	1947—Brooklyn .610	1985—St. Louis (East) .623
1910—Chicago .675	1948—Boston .595	1986—New York (East) .667
1911—New York .647	1949—Brooklyn .630	1987—St. Louis (East) .586
1912—New York .682	1950—Philadelphia .591	1988—Los Angeles (West) .584
1913—New York .664	1951—New York† .624	1989—San Francisco (West) .568

*Defeated Brooklyn, two games to none, in playoff for pennant. †Defeated Brooklyn, two games to one, in playoff for pennant. ‡Defeated Milwaukee, two games to none, in playoff for pennant. §Defeated Los Angeles, two games to one, in playoff for pennant.

STANDING OF CLUBS AT CLOSE OF SEASON

EAST DIVISION

Club	Pitt.	N.Y.	Mon.	Chi.	Phil.	St.L.	Cin.	L.A.	S.F.	Hou.	S.D.	Atl.	W.	L.	Pct.	G.B.
Pittsburgh	..	8	5	14	12	10	6	8	8	7	10	7	95	67	.586	....
New York	10	..	10	9	10	12	6	7	7	7	5	8	91	71	.562	4
Montreal	13	8	..	7	10	11	3	6	7	7	6	6	85	77	.525	10
Chicago	4	9	11	..	11	8	4	3	7	6	8	6	77	85	.475	18
Philadelphia	6	8	8	7	..	10	5	4	8	7	7	7	77	85	.475	18
St. Louis	8	6	7	10	8	..	3	5	3	6	9	5	70	92	.432	25

WEST DIVISION

Club	Cin.	L.A.	S.F.	Hou.	S.D.	Atl.	Pitt.	N.Y.	Mon.	Chi.	Phil.	St.L.	W.	L.	Pct.	G.B.
Cincinnati	..	9	7	11	9	10	6	6	9	8	7	9	91	71	.562	....
Los Angeles	9	..	8	9	9	12	4	5	6	9	8	7	86	76	.531	5
San Francisco	11	10	..	8	11	13	4	5	5	5	4	9	85	77	.525	6
Houston	7	9	10	..	4	13	5	5	5	6	5	6	75	87	.463	16
San Diego	9	9	7	14	..	10	2	7	5	4	5	3	75	87	.463	16
Atlanta	8	6	5	5	8	..	5	4	6	6	5	7	65	97	.401	26

Championship Series—Cincinnati defeated Pittsburgh, four games to two.

SHUTOUT GAMES

Club	S.D.	N.Y.	Mon.	Cin.	L.A.	Pitt.	S.F.	St.L.	Chi.	Phil.	Atl.	Hou.	W.	L.	Pct.
San Diego	..	1	0	2	1	0	0	0	1	0	0	2	12	6	.667
New York	2	..	3	1	1	1	0	2	0	2	0	2	14	8	.636
Montreal	2	1	..	0	1	1	1	0	0	2	1	2	11	7	.611
Cincinnati	0	1	2	..	2	0	2	3	0	1	0	1	12	8	.600
Los Angeles	1	0	0	1	..	1	0	3	2	1	2	1	12	8	.600
Pittsburgh	0	1	0	0	0	..	0	3	0	3	1	0	8	8	.500
San Francisco	1	0	0	1	0	0	..	1	0	0	3	0	6	6	.500
St. Louis	0	2	0	1	1	2	1	..	2	2	0	2	13	15	.464
Chicago	0	0	1	0	1	2	0	0	..	0	2	1	7	9	.438
Philadelphia	0	1	1	0	0	1	2	1	1	..	0	1	7	11	.389
Atlanta	0	0	0	2	1	1	0	1	2	0	..	1	8	14	.364
Houston	0	1	0	0	0	0	1	0	1	0	3	..	6	16	.273

RECORD AT HOME

EAST DIVISION

Club	N.Y.	Pitt.	Mon.	Phil.	Chi.	St.L.	Hou.	S.F.	L.A.	Cin.	Atl.	S.D.	W.	L.	Pct.
New York	....	6-3	4-5	6-3	3-6	7-2	5-1	5-1	4-2	4-2	5-1	3-3	52	29	.642
Pittsburgh	5-4	....	3-6	6-3	7-2	3-6	5-1	3-3	5-1	2-4	5-1	5-1	49	32	.605
Montreal	3-6	7-2	....	6-3	4-5	7-2	4-2	4-2	5-1	2-4	1-5	4-2	47	34	.580
Philadelphia	5-4	3-6	5-4	....	5-4	4-5	4-2	5-1	2-4	2-4	3-3	3-3	41	40	.506
Chicago	3-6	2-7	6-3	7-2	....	4-5	2-4	4-2	1-5	2-4	4-2	4-2	39	42	.481
St. Louis	4-5	2-7	5-4	3-6	5-4	....	4-2	2-4	1-5	0-6	3-3	5-1	34	47	.420

WEST DIVISION

Club	Hou.	S.F.	L.A.	Cin.	Atl.	S.D.	N.Y.	Pitt.	Mon.	Phil.	Chi.	St.L.	W.	L.	Pct.
Houston	....	7-2	5-4	5-4	9-0	3-6	4-2	4-2	3-3	3-3	2-4	4-2	49	32	.605
San Francisco	6-3	....	5-4	8-1	7-2	4-5	4-2	1-5	3-3	3-3	3-3	5-1	49	32	.605
Los Angeles	5-4	4-5	....	4-5	7-2	6-3	3-3	3-3	5-1	4-2	4-2	2-4	47	34	.580
Cincinnati	7-2	6-3	4-5	....	5-4	3-6	4-2	2-4	5-1	3-3	4-2	3-3	46	35	.568
Atlanta	5-4	3-6	4-5	4-5	....	3-6	3-3	4-2	1-5	2-4	4-2	4-2	37	44	.457
San Diego	8-1	2-7	6-3	3-6	4-5	....	4-2	1-5	3-3	2-4	2-4	2-4	37	44	.457

RECORD ABROAD

EAST DIVISION

Club	Pitt.	N.Y.	Chi.	Mon.	Phil.	St.L.	Cin.	L.A.	S.D.	S.F.	Atl.	Hou.	W.	L.	Pct.
Pittsburgh	....	3-6	7-2	2-7	6-3	7-2	4-2	3-3	5-1	5-1	2-4	2-4	46	35	.568
New York	4-5	....	6-3	6-3	4-5	5-4	2-4	3-3	2-4	3-3	2-4	39	42	.481	
Chicago	2-7	6-3	....	5-4	4-5	4-5	2-4	2-4	4-2	3-3	2-4	4-2	38	43	.469
Montreal	6-3	5-4	3-6	....	4-5	4-5	1-5	1-5	3-3	3-3	5-1	3-3	38	43	.469
Philadelphia	3-6	3-6	2-7	3-6	....	6-3	3-3	2-4	4-2	3-3	4-2	3-3	36	45	.444
St. Louis	6-3	2-7	5-4	2-7	5-4	....	3-3	4-2	4-2	1-5	2-4	2-4	36	45	.444

WEST DIVISION

Club	Cin.	L.A.	S.D.	S.F.	Atl.	Hou.	Pitt.	N.Y.	Chi.	Mon.	Phil.	St.L.	W.	L.	Pct.
Cincinnati	....	5-4	6-3	1-8	5-4	4-5	4-2	2-4	4-2	4-2	4-2	6-0	45	36	.556
Los Angeles	5-4	....	3-6	4-5	4-5	4-5	1-5	2-4	5-1	1-5	4-2	5-1	39	42	.481
San Diego	6-3	3-6	....	5-4	6-3	6-3	1-5	3-3	2-4	2-4	3-3	1-5	38	43	.469
San Francisco	3-6	5-4	7-2	....	6-3	2-7	3-3	1-5	2-4	2-4	1-5	4-2	36	45	.444
Atlanta	4-5	2-7	5-4	2-7	....	0-9	1-5	1-5	2-4	5-1	3-3	3-3	28	53	.346
Houston	2-7	4-5	1-8	3-6	4-5	....	1-5	1-5	4-2	2-4	2-4	2-4	26	55	.321

1990 N.L. Pitching Against Each Club

ATLANTA—65-97

Pitcher	Chi. W—L	Cin. W—L	Hou. W—L	L.A. W—L	Mont. W—L	N.Y. W—L	Phil. W—L	Pitt. W—L	St.L. W—L	S.D. W—L	S.F. W—L	Totals W—L
Avery	1—0	0—2	0—2	2—0	0—1	0—2	0—0	0—2	0—0	0—1	0—1	3—11
Boever	0—0	0—1	0—0	0—0	0—0	0—0	0—1	0—0	1—1	0—0	0—0	1—3
Castillo	0—0	0—0	0—0	0—0	0—0	0—0	0—0	1—0	3—0	1—0	0—1	5—1
Clary	0—0	0—1	0—0	0—2	1—0	0—2	0—3	0—1	0—0	0—1	0—0	1—10
Freeman	0—0	0—0	0—0	0—0	0—0	0—0	0—0	0—0	0—0	1—0	0—0	1—0
Glavine	0—1	4—1	0—2	0—2	1—2	0—0	2—0	1—0	0—1	1—2	1—1	10—12
Grant	0—0	1—0	0—0	0—1	0—0	0—0	0—0	0—0	0—0	0—0	0—1	1—2
Greene	0—0	1—0	0—0	0—0	0—0	0—0	0—0	0—0	0—0	0—0	0—0	1—0
Henry	1—1	0—0	0—0	0—0	0—0	0—0	0—0	0—0	1—0	0—0	0—0	2—2
Hesketh	0—0	0—0	0—0	0—0	0—0	0—1	0—1	0—0	0—0	0—0	0—0	0—2
Kerfeld	1—0	0—0	0—0	0—1	1—0	0—0	0—0	0—0	0—0	1—0	0—0	3—1
Leibrandt	1—0	1—0	2—3	0—3	1—1	0—1	0—0	1—1	1—0	1—1	1—1	9—11
Lilliquist	0—0	0—1	0—2	0—0	0—1	1—0	0—0	1—1	0—1	0—1	0—1	2—8
Luecken	0—0	0—2	0—0	0—1	0—0	0—0	0—0	0—0	0—0	1—1	0—0	1—4
Marak	0—0	0—0	1—0	0—2	0—0	0—0	0—0	0—0	0—0	0—0	0—0	1—2
Mercker	0—1	0—0	1—2	0—0	1—1	2—0	0—0	0—1	0—0	1—1	0—0	4—7
Parrett	0—0	0—0	0—0	0—0	0—0	0—0	0—0	0—1	0—0	0—0	1—0	1—1
Smith	0—2	0—1	0—0	1—0	0—0	0—0	2—0	1—0	0—0	0—1	1—2	5—6
Smoltz	2—1	1—1	1—2	3—0	1—1	1—0	1—1	0—1	2—1	1—0	1—4	14—11
Stanton	0—0	0—0	0—0	0—0	0—0	0—2	0—0	0—0	0—0	0—0	0—0	0—3
Totals	6—6	8—10	5—13	6—12	6—6	4—8	5—7	5—7	7—5	8—10	5—13	65—97

No Decisions—Richards, Sisk, Valdez.

CHICAGO—77-85

Pitcher	Atl. W—L	Cin. W—L	Hou. W—L	L.A. W—L	Mont. W—L	N.Y. W—L	Phil. W—L	Pitt. W—L	St.L. W—L	S.D. W—L	S.F. W—L	Totals W—L
Assenmacher	0—0	0—0	0—0	0—2	0—0	3—0	1—0	0—0	2—0	0—0	1—0	7—2
Bielecki	1—0	2—1	1—0	0—0	1—0	0—1	1—2	0—2	0—2	0—2	2—1	8—11
Blankenship	0—0	0—0	0—0	0—0	0—0	0—0	0—0	0—0	0—1	0—0	0—1	0—2
Boskie	0—0	0—0	1—1	0—1	2—1	0—0	0—0	0—2	0—0	1—0	1—1	5—6
Coffman	0—0	0—0	0—0	0—0	0—0	0—0	0—1	0—1	0—0	0—0	0—0	0—2
Dickson	0—1	0—0	0—1	0—0	0—0	0—0	0—0	0—0	0—1	0—0	0—0	0—3
Harkey	1—0	0—1	1—0	1—1	2—1	1—2	0—0	1—0	0—1	2—0	3—0	12—6
Kramer	0—0	0—0	0—0	0—0	0—1	0—0	0—0	0—1	0—0	0—0	0—0	0—2
Lancaster	1—0	0—0	1—0	0—1	1—1	1—1	2—0	0—1	2—0	1—0	0—1	9—5
Long	1—0	2—0	0—0	0—0	1—1	0—0	0—0	0—0	1—0	1—0	0—0	6—1
Maddux	1—2	0—2	2—1	1—1	2—1	1—3	2—1	3—1	1—2	2—1	0—0	15—15
Nunez	0—0	0—1	0—1	0—1	0—0	1—1	2—1	0—1	1—0	0—1	0—0	4—7
Pavlas	0—0	0—0	0—0	0—0	1—0	0—0	0—0	0—0	1—0	0—0	0—0	2—0
Pico	1—0	0—1	0—1	0—1	1—0	0—0	2—0	0—0	0—0	0—0	0—1	4—4
Sutcliffe	0—0	0—0	0—1	0—0	0—0	0—0	0—0	0—1	0—0	0—0	0—0	0—2
Williams	0—3	0—1	0—0	0—0	0—1	0—1	1—0	0—0	0—1	0—1	0—0	1—8
Wilson	0—0	0—1	0—0	1—0	0—0	1—1	1—2	0—3	0—2	1—0	0—0	4—9
Totals	6—6	4—8	6—6	3—9	11—7	9—9	11—7	4—14	8—10	8—4	7—5	77—85

No Decisions—Dascenzo, Kraemer, Wilkins.

CINCINNATI—91-71

Pitcher	Atl. W—L	Chi. W—L	Hou. W—L	L.A. W—L	Mont. W—L	N.Y. W—L	Phil. W—L	Pitt. W—L	St.L. W—L	S.D. W—L	S.F. W—L	Totals W—L
Armstrong	2—0	0—0	2—1	0—1	2—0	1—1	1—1	1—2	2—0	0—1	1—2	12—9
Birtsas	1—0	0—0	0—1	0—0	0—1	0—0	0—1	0—0	0—0	0—0	0—0	1—3
Browning	3—1	0—1	0—0	4—1	1—0	2—1	0—0	0—0	1—2	3—1	1—2	15—9
Charlton	1—1	1—1	1—0	1—2	0—0	2—2	1—1	2—0	1—0	0—2	2—0	12—9
Dibble	1—1	1—0	1—0	0—0	2—0	0—0	0—0	1—0	1—0	1—1	0—1	8—3
Hammond	0—0	0—0	0—0	0—0	0—0	0—0	0—0	0—2	0—0	0—0	0—0	0—2
Jackson	0—2	1—0	1—1	1—2	0—0	1—0	1—0	0—0	0—1	1—0	0—0	6—6
Layana	0—1	0—0	0—1	0—0	1—0	0—0	0—0	1—1	0—0	1—0	1—0	5—3
Mahler	0—1	2—0	0—1	1—0	1—0	0—1	2—0	1—0	0—0	0—2	0—1	7—6
Myers	1—0	0—1	2—2	0—1	0—0	0—0	0—0	0—0	0—0	0—1	1—1	4—6
Rijo	1—1	3—0	2—0	1—1	0—0	0—1	2—1	0—1	2—0	2—1	1—2	14—8
Robinson	0—0	0—0	0—0	0—0	1—1	0—0	0—0	0—0	1—0	0—0	0—1	2—2
Scudder	0—0	0—1	1—0	1—1	1—1	0—0	0—1	0—0	1—0	1—0	0—1	5—5
Totals	10—8	8—4	11—7	9—9	9—3	6—6	7—5	6—6	9—3	9—9	7—11	91—71

No Decisions—Brown, Gross, Minutelli, Rodriguez.

HOUSTON—75-87

Pitcher	Atl. W—L	Chi. W—L	Cin. W—L	L.A. W—L	Mont. W—L	N.Y. W—L	Phil. W—L	Pitt. W—L	St.L. W—L	S.D. W—L	S.F. W—L	Totals W—L
Agosto	1—1	0—0	1—1	1—1	1—2	0—1	0—0	3—0	1—0	0—0	1—2	9—8
Andersen	0—0	0—0	0—0	2—0	2—1	0—0	0—1	0—0	0—0	1—0	0—0	5—2
Clancy	1—0	0—1	1—1	0—1	0—0	0—1	0—1	0—0	0—0	0—2	0—1	2—8
Darwin	2—1	0—0	1—0	0—0	1—0	1—0	1—0	1—1	2—0	0—1	2—1	11—4
Deshaies	1—1	1—0	0—2	2—0	0—0	0—2	0—2	1—1	1—2	1—1	1—1	7—12
Gullickson	2—1	0—2	0—1	2—2	0—0	1—1	2—1	0—2	1—1	0—3	2—0	10—14
Hernandez	0—0	0—0	1—1	0—0	0—0	0—0	0—0	0—0	0—0	1—0	0—0	2—1
Kerfeld	0—0	0—0	0—1	0—1	0—0	0—0	0—0	0—0	0—0	0—0	0—0	0—2
Meyer	0—0	0—0	0—2	0—0	0—0	0—0	0—0	0—0	0—0	0—1	0—1	0—4
Osuna	1—0	0—0	0—0	1—0	0—0	0—0	0—0	0—0	0—0	0—0	0—0	2—0
Portugal	3—0	2—1	1—2	0—1	1—0	1—2	0—1	0—1	0—0	0—2	3—1	11—10
Schatzeder	1—0	0—0	0—0	0—0	0—0	0—1	0—0	0—1	0—1	0—0	0—0	1—3
Scott	1—1	1—2	1—0	1—2	0—2	2—0	1—2	0—0	0—2	2—1	0—1	9—13
Smith	0—0	2—0	1—0	0—1	0—1	0—1	1—0	1—0	1—1	0—2	0—0	6—6
Totals	13—5	6—6	7—11	9—9	5—7	5—7	5—7	5—7	6—6	4—14	10—8	75—87

No Decisions—Clark, Fisher, Hennis.

LOS ANGELES—86-76

Pitcher	Atl. W—L	Chi. W—L	Cin. W—L	Hou. W—L	Mont. W—L	N.Y. W—L	Phil. W—L	Pitt. W—L	St.L. W—L	S.D. W—L	S.F. W—L	Totals W—L
Aase	0—0	0—0	1—0	0—0	0—0	0—0	0—0	0—0	0—0	0—1	1—0	3—1
Belcher	1—1	2—1	0—2	1—2	0—1	0—1	1—0	3—0	0—1	1—0	0—0	9—9
Cook	0—0	0—0	0—0	0—0	0—0	0—0	0—0	0—0	0—0	0—1	1—0	1—1
Crews	1—0	0—0	0—1	0—0	1—0	0—1	0—1	0—0	1—1	1—1	0—0	4—5
Gott	0—0	0—0	0—0	1—1	0—0	0—1	2—0	0—0	0—1	0—1	0—1	3—5
Hartley	2—0	1—0	0—0	0—0	0—0	2—0	0—0	0—0	0—0	0—2	1—0	6—3
Hershiser	0—0	0—0	0—0	1—0	0—0	0—0	0—0	0—0	0—0	0—0	0—0	1—1
Holmes	0—0	0—0	0—0	0—0	0—0	0—0	0—0	0—0	0—0	0—1	0—0	0—1
Howell	2—0	0—0	1—0	2—1	0—0	0—0	0—0	0—1	0—0	0—1	0—1	5—5
Maddux	0—0	0—0	0—0	0—1	0—0	0—0	0—0	0—0	0—0	0—0	0—0	0—1
Martinez	3—0	2—0	3—0	2—0	1—2	0—1	2—1	0—2	2—0	3—0	2—0	20—6
Morgan	0—4	1—1	1—1	1—2	1—2	1—2	1—0	0—2	2—0	1—0	2—2	11—15
Munoz	0—0	0—0	0—0	0—0	0—0	0—0	0—0	0—0	0—0	0—0	0—0	0—1
Neidlinger	2—0	0—0	1—1	0—0	1—0	0—0	1—0	0—0	0—0	0—0	0—2	5—3

LOS ANGELES—Continued

Pitcher	Atl. W—L	Chi. W—L	Cin. W—L	Hou. W—L	Mont. W—L	N.Y. W—L	Phil. W—L	Pitt. W—L	St.L. W—L	S.D. W—L	S.F. W—L	Totals W—L
Searage	1—0	0—0	0—0	0—0	0—0	0—0	0—0	0—0	0—0	0—0	0—0	1—0
Valenzuela	0—1	3—1	2—3	1—1	2—1	1—0	1—0	1—1	1—1	0—1	1—3	13—13
Walsh	0—0	0—0	0—0	0—0	0—0	0—0	0—0	0—0	0—0	1—0	0—0	1—0
Wells	0—0	0—0	0—0	0—0	0—0	0—0	0—0	0—2	1—0	0—0	0—0	1—2
Wetteland	0—0	0—0	0—1	0—1	0—0	0—1	0—0	0—0	0—0	2—0	0—1	2—4
Totals	12—6	9—3	9—9	9—9	6—6	5—7	8—4	4—8	7—5	9—9	8—10	86—76

No Decisions—Perry, Poole.

MONTREAL—85-77

Pitcher	Atl. W—L	Chi. W—L	Cin. W—L	Hou. W—L	L.A. W—L	N.Y. W—L	Phil. W—L	Pitt. W—L	St.L. W—L	S.D. W—L	S.F. W—L	Totals W—L
Anderson	0—0	0—0	0—0	0—0	0—0	0—0	0—1	0—0	0—0	0—0	0—0	0—1
Barnes	0—0	0—0	0—0	0—0	0—0	0—0	1—1	0—0	0—0	0—0	0—0	1—1
Boyd	2—0	0—1	0—1	0—0	1—0	1—1	1—1	1—0	2—1	2—1	0—0	10—6
Burke	0—0	1—1	0—1	0—0	1—0	1—0	0—0	0—0	1—0	0—1	0—0	3—3
Farmer	0—1	0—0	0—0	0—0	0—0	0—0	0—1	0—1	0—0	0—0	0—0	0—3
Frey	1—0	1—0	0—0	1—0	0—0	0—0	0—0	2—0	1—0	1—0	1—2	8—2
Gardner	1—1	1—2	0—1	1—0	0—2	0—1	0—0	0—0	1—2	1—0	2—0	7—9
Gross	1—0	0—4	1—1	1—1	1—1	0—2	1—1	1—1	1—0	0—0	2—1	9—12
Hall	0—1	1—0	0—1	1—0	0—1	0—1	2—0	0—1	0—1	0—1	0—0	4—7
Hesketh	0—0	0—0	0—0	0—0	0—0	0—0	1—0	0—0	0—0	0—0	0—0	1—0
De. Martinez	0—1	1—1	1—1	0—2	2—1	1—2	1—0	2—1	1—0	1—1	0—1	10—11
Mohorcic	0—0	1—0	0—0	0—0	0—0	0—0	0—0	0—1	0—0	0—0	0—0	1—2
Nabholz	0—0	1—0	0—0	0—0	1—0	1—1	1—1	0—0	1—0	0—0	0—0	6—2
Rojas	0—0	0—0	0—0	0—0	0—1	1—0	0—0	1—0	0—0	0—0	1—0	3—1
Ruskin	0—0	0—0	0—0	0—0	0—0	0—0	0—0	1—0	0—0	0—0	0—0	1—0
Sampen	0—0	0—2	0—0	1—1	1—0	1—1	1—1	4—0	2—1	1—0	1—1	12—7
Schmidt	1—1	1—0	0—1	0—1	0—0	0—0	1—0	0—0	0—0	0—0	0—0	3—3
Smith	0—1	0—0	0—2	2—0	0—0	2—0	0—0	1—0	1—2	0—1	0—0	6—7
Totals	6—6	7—11	3—9	7—5	6—6	8—10	10—8	13—5	11—7	7—5	7—5	85—77

No Decisions—Costello, Gideon, Malloy, Da. Martinez, Noboa, Thompson.

NEW YORK—91-71

Pitcher	Atl. W—L	Chi. W—L	Cin. W—L	Hous. W—L	L.A. W—L	Mont. W—L	Phil. W—L	Pitt. W—L	St.L. W—L	S.D. W—L	S.F. W—L	Totals W—L
Cone	2—1	0—2	1—0	0—0	0—2	1—1	1—2	3—0	2—1	2—1	2—0	14—10
Darling	2—1	2—1	0—1	0—0	1—1	1—2	0—0	0—0	1—1	0—2	0—0	7—9
Fernandez	1—0	1—0	0—2	0—1	0—1	1—2	1—3	1—1	1—2	2—1	2—1	9—14
Franco	0—0	1—1	1—0	1—0	0—0	1—1	0—0	0—1	1—0	0—0	0—0	5—3
Gooden	0—0	4—0	2—0	2—1	4—0	0—1	2—1	2—2	2—1	0—1	1—0	19—7
Innis	0—2	0—1	0—0	0—0	0—0	0—0	1—0	0—0	0—0	0—0	0—0	1—3
Machado	1—0	0—0	0—0	0—1	0—0	1—0	1—0	0—0	1—0	0—0	0—0	4—1
Musselman	0—0	0—0	0—1	0—0	0—0	0—0	0—0	0—1	0—0	0—0	0—0	0—2
Ojeda	0—0	0—0	1—1	0—1	1—0	1—0	1—0	2—1	0—1	1—0	0—2	7—6
Pena	0—0	0—1	0—0	1—1	0—0	1—0	0—0	0—0	1—0	0—0	0—1	3—3
Valera	0—0	0—0	0—0	0—0	0—0	0—0	0—0	0—1	0—0	0—0	1—0	1—1
Viola	1—0	1—3	1—1	3—0	1—1	3—1	3—2	2—1	3—0	1—2	1—1	20—12
Whitehurst	1—0	0—0	0—0	0—0	0—0	0—0	0—0	0—0	0—0	0—0	0—0	1—0
Totals	8—4	9—9	6—6	7—5	7—5	10—8	10—8	10—8	12—6	5—7	7—5	91—71

No Decisions—Brown, Schatzeder.

PHILADELPHIA—77-85

Pitcher	Atl. W—L	Chi. W—L	Cin. W—L	Hous. W—L	L.A. W—L	Mont. W—L	N.Y. W—L	Pitt. W—L	St.L. W—L	S.D. W—L	S.F. W—L	Totals W—L
Akerfelds	0—0	2—0	1—0	0—0	0—0	0—0	1—1	0—1	0—0	1—0	0—0	5—2
Boever	0—0	0—0	0—0	0—0	0—2	0—0	0—0	0—1	0—0	2—0	0—0	2—3
Carman	0—0	0—0	0—0	0—0	2—0	1—1	0—0	2—0	1—0	0—0	0—0	6—2
Combs	0—3	0—1	1—0	3—0	0—1	1—1	3—1	0—1	2—0	0—1	0—1	10—10
Cook	2—0	0—0	0—0	1—0	0—0	0—1	0—1	1—0	2—0	0—0	2—1	8—3
DeJesus	0—0	1—1	1—1	1—0	0—0	0—1	3—0	0—1	0—2	1—1	0—0	7—8
Freeman	0—0	0—0	0—0	0—1	0—0	0—0	0—0	0—0	0—1	0—0	0—0	0—2
Frohwirth	0—0	0—0	0—0	0—0	0—0	0—1	0—0	0—0	0—0	0—0	0—0	0—1
Greene	0—0	0—1	0—0	0—0	0—1	1—0	0—0	0—0	1—0	0—1	0—0	2—3
Grimsley	0—0	0—1	0—0	0—0	0—0	1—0	0—0	0—1	1—0	0—0	1—0	3—2
Howell	0—0	1—0	1—2	0—0	0—1	2—0	1—1	0—1	0—2	1—0	2—0	8—7
Malone	0—0	0—0	0—0	0—0	0—0	0—0	0—0	0—0	0—0	1—0	0—0	1—0
McDowell	0—0	0—1	0—0	1—0	2—0	0—1	0—2	0—2	1—2	1—0	1—0	6—8
McElroy	0—0	0—1	0—0	0—0	0—0	0—0	0—0	0—0	0—0	0—0	0—0	0—1
Mulholland	1—1	2—1	0—1	0—1	0—1	1—1	0—1	1—1	1—0	1—0	2—1	9—10
Noles	0—0	0—0	0—0	0—1	0—0	0—0	0—0	0—0	0—0	0—0	0—0	0—1
Parrett	3—0	0—3	0—1	0—1	0—0	0—2	0—1	1—0	0—0	0—1	0—0	4—9
Ruffin	1—1	1—1	1—2	1—1	0—1	0—1	1—3	1—3	1—0	0—1	0—1	6—13
Totals	7—5	7—11	5—7	7—5	4—8	8—10	8—10	6—12	10—8	7—5	8—4	77—85

No Decisions—Moore, Ontiveros.

PITTSBURGH—95-67

Pitcher	Atl.	Chi.	Cin.	Hous.	L.A.	Mont.	N.Y.	Phil.	St.L.	S.D.	S.F.	Totals
	W—L	W—L	W—L	W—L	W—L	W—L	W—L	W—L	W—L	W—L	W—L	W—L
Belinda	0—0	1—0	0—1	0—0	0—0	0—3	0—0	1—0	1—0	0—0	0—0	3—4
Drabek	3—0	3—1	1—0	1—0	1—0	2—3	1—1	3—0	2—1	2—0	3—0	22—6
Heaton	1—2	1—0	0—0	3—0	0—1	1—1	2—1	0—1	2—0	1—2	1—1	12—9
Huismann	0—0	0—0	0—0	0—0	0—0	0—0	0—0	0—0	1—0	0—0	0—0	1—0
Kipper	1—1	0—0	0—1	0—0	1—0	0—0	1—0	1—0	0—0	0—0	1—0	5—2
Kramer	0—0	0—0	0—0	0—0	0—0	0—0	0—0	0—0	0—1	0—0	0—0	0—1
Landrum	0—0	0—0	0—0	0—0	1—0	1—1	1—0	2—2	1—0	1—0	0—0	7—3
Patterson	0—0	3—0	0—1	0—2	1—0	0—0	0—1	1—1	0—0	2—0	1—0	8—5
Power	0—0	0—0	0—1	0—2	0—0	0—0	0—0	0—0	0—0	1—0	0—0	1—3
Reed	0—0	0—1	0—0	0—0	1—0	0—0	0—0	1—1	0—0	0—0	0—1	2—3
Roesler	0—0	1—0	0—0	0—0	0—0	0—0	0—0	0—0	0—0	0—0	0—0	1—0
Ross	0—0	0—0	0—0	0—0	0—0	1—0	0—0	0—0	0—0	0—0	0—0	1—0
Ruskin	0—0	0—0	0—0	0—1	0—0	0—0	1—0	1—1	0—0	0—0	0—0	2—2
Smiley	0—1	2—1	2—0	2—0	1—1	0—2	0—2	0—0	1—2	0—0	1—1	9—10
Smith	1—0	1—0	2—0	0—0	0—0	0—1	1—1	0—0	1—0	0—0	0—0	6—2
Terrell	0—1	0—0	0—1	0—0	1—2	0—0	0—2	0—0	0—0	1—0	0—1	2—7
Tibbs	0—0	0—0	0—0	0—0	0—0	0—0	0—0	0—0	0—0	0—0	1—0	1—0
Tomlin	0—0	1—0	0—1	0—0	0—0	0—1	1—0	2—0	0—2	0—0	0—0	4—4
Walk	1—0	1—1	0—0	1—0	1—0	0—1	0—1	0—0	1—2	2—0	0—0	7—5
York	0—0	0—0	1—0	0—0	0—0	0—0	0—1	0—0	0—0	0—0	0—0	1—1
Totals	7—5	14—4	6—6	7—5	8—4	5—13	8—10	12—6	10—8	10—2	8—4	95—67

No Decisions—Bair, Palacios, Reuss.

ST. LOUIS—70-92

Pitcher	Atl.	Chi.	Cin.	Hous.	L.A.	Mont.	N.Y.	Phil.	Pitt.	S.D.	S.F.	Totals
	W—L	W—L	W—L	W—L	W—L	W—L	W—L	W—L	W—L	W—L	W—L	W—L
Dayley	0—0	0—1	0—1	0—0	0—0	2—1	0—1	0—0	1—0	1—0	0—0	4—4
DeLeon	1—1	1—2	1—2	1—1	1—3	1—2	0—2	0—1	1—2	0—1	0—2	7—19
DiPino	1—0	0—0	0—0	0—1	1—0	0—0	0—0	2—0	0—1	0—0	1—0	5—2
Hill	1—1	1—1	0—1	0—0	0—0	0—1	2—0	0—1	1—1	0—0	0—0	5—6
Horton	0—0	0—0	0—0	0—0	0—0	0—0	0—0	0—1	0—0	1—0	0—0	1—1
Magrane	0—1	1—0	1—2	1—2	0—2	1—1	3—1	1—2	1—2	1—2	0—2	10—17
Mathews	0—0	0—0	0—0	0—1	0—0	0—1	0—1	0—0	0—1	0—0	0—2	0—5
Niedenfuer	0—0	0—2	0—1	0—0	0—0	0—1	0—0	0—0	0—1	0—0	0—1	0—6
Olivares	0—0	0—0	0—0	0—0	0—0	1—0	0—0	0—0	0—0	0—0	0—1	1—1
Perez	0—0	0—0	0—0	0—0	0—0	0—0	0—0	1—0	0—0	0—0	0—0	1—0
B. Smith	1—0	2—0	0—1	1—0	2—1	1—1	0—2	1—2	0—0	1—0	0—1	9—8
L. Smith	1—0	0—1	0—0	0—0	0—0	0—0	0—3	0—0	0—0	1—0	1—0	3—4
Terry	0—2	1—1	0—0	1—0	0—0	0—1	0—0	0—2	0—0	0—0	0—0	2—6
Tewksbury	0—1	2—0	1—0	1—0	0—1	1—1	0—1	2—1	2—2	2—0	0—1	10—9
Tudor	0—1	2—0	0—2	1—0	1—0	0—0	1—1	2—0	2—0	2—0	1—0	12—4
Totals	5—7	10—8	3—9	6—6	5—7	7—11	6—12	8—10	8—10	9—3	3—9	70—92

No Decisions—Camacho, Carpenter, Clarke, Costello, Hilton, Jones, Sherrill.

SAN DIEGO—75-87

Pitcher	Atl.	Chi.	Cin.	Hous.	L.A.	Mont.	N.Y.	Phil.	Pitt.	St.L.	S.F.	Totals
	W—L	W—L	W—L	W—L	W—L	W—L	W—L	W—L	W—L	W—L	W—L	W—L
Benes	1—0	0—2	0—2	2—1	1—2	1—0	1—1	3—0	0—1	0—1	1—1	10—11
Davis	0—0	0—0	0—0	0—0	0—0	0—1	0—0	0—0	0—0	0—0	0—0	0—1
Dunne	0—1	0—0	0—0	0—0	0—1	0—0	0—1	0—0	0—0	0—0	0—0	0—3
Grant	0—0	0—0	0—0	0—1	0—0	0—0	0—0	1—0	0—0	0—0	0—0	1—1
Hammaker	0—0	0—0	0—1	0—0	0—1	0—0	0—0	0—1	0—0	0—0	0—0	0—4
Harris	0—1	0—1	2—0	2—0	1—0	0—0	1—1	0—1	0—1	0—2	2—0	8—8
Hurst	1—0	0—1	2—0	1—1	1—1	1—2	2—0	0—0	0—1	2—1	1—2	11—9
Lefferts	2—1	0—2	0—0	1—0	1—1	1—0	0—0	0—0	0—1	0—0	2—0	7—5
Lilliquist	0—2	0—0	1—0	1—0	1—0	0—0	0—0	0—0	0—0	0—0	0—1	3—3
Rasmussen	2—1	2—1	1—2	3—1	1—1	0—2	1—0	0—2	0—2	1—1	0—2	11—15
Rodriguez	0—0	0—0	0—0	0—0	0—0	1—0	0—0	0—1	0—0	0—0	0—0	1—1
Schiraldi	0—1	0—0	1—1	1—0	2—0	0—0	0—2	0—1	0—2	0—0	0—1	3—8
Show	2—0	0—1	0—0	2—0	1—2	0—1	0—0	0—0	1—2	0—1	0—1	6—8
Valdez	0—0	0—0	0—1	0—0	0—0	0—0	0—0	0—0	0—0	0—0	0—0	0—1
Whitson	2—1	2—0	2—1	2—0	0—0	1—1	2—0	0—1	1—0	0—3	1—2	14—9
Totals	10—8	4—8	9—9	14—4	9—9	5—7	7—5	5—7	2—10	3—9	7—11	75—87

No Decisions—Clements.

SAN FRANCISCO—85-77

Pitcher	Atl.	Chi.	Cin.	Hous.	L.A.	Mont.	N.Y.	Phil.	Pitt.	St.L.	S.D.	Totals
	W—L	W—L	W—L	W—L	W—L	W—L	W—L	W—L	W—L	W—L	W—L	W—L
Bedrosian	3—0	0—0	1—0	3—3	0—0	1—1	0—1	0—1	0—1	1—0	0—2	9—9
Brantley	0—0	1—2	1—0	1—0	0—0	1—0	1—0	0—0	0—0	0—0	0—1	5—3
Burkett	3—0	2—0	3—1	0—2	3—1	1—0	0—1	0—2	1—0	1—0	0—0	14—7
Dewey	0—1	0—0	0—0	0—0	0—0	0—0	0—0	0—0	0—0	0—0	1—0	1—1
Downs	0—1	0—0	0—0	0—1	1—0	0—0	0—0	0—0	0—0	0—0	2—0	3—2
Garrelts	3—0	0—2	3—2	1—1	1—1	0—1	1—0	1—1	1—2	1—1	0—0	12—11

Every National League club beat Jose DeLeon at least once last year as the St. Louis righthander lost a league-leading 19 games.

SAN FRANCISCO—Continued

Pitcher	Atl. W—L	Chi. W—L	Cin. W—L	Hou. W—L	L.A. W—L	Mont. W—L	N.Y. W—L	Phil. W—L	Pitt. W—L	St.L. W—L	S.D. W—L	Totals W—L
Gunderson	1—0	0—0	0—0	0—0	0—1	0—0	0—0	0—0	0—0	0—0	0—1	1—2
Hammaker	0—1	0—1	0—0	1—0	0—1	1—2	0—0	0—0	0—0	1—0	1—0	4—5
Knepper	0—0	0—2	0—0	0—0	0—0	0—1	2—0	0—0	0—0	1—0	0—0	3—3
LaCoss	1—0	0—0	0—0	1—0	1—1	0—0	0—2	1—0	0—1	0—0	2—0	6—4
McClellan	0—0	0—0	0—0	0—0	0—0	0—0	0—1	0—0	0—0	0—0	0—0	0—1
Novoa	0—0	0—0	0—0	0—0	0—1	0—0	0—0	0—0	0—0	0—0	0—0	0—1
Oliveras	0—0	0—0	0—0	0—0	1—0	0—0	0—0	1—0	0—1	0—0	0—1	2—2
O'Neal	0—0	0—0	0—0	0—0	0—0	0—0	0—0	0—0	0—0	1—0	0—0	1—0
Quisenberry	0—0	0—0	0—0	0—0	0—0	0—0	0—0	0—0	0—0	0—0	0—1	0—1
Reuschel	1—0	0—0	0—0	0—0	1—0	0—1	0—1	0—2	0—1	1—0	0—1	3—6
Robinson	0—0	1—0	2—2	0—0	0—3	1—1	1—0	0—0	1—1	2—0	1—0	10—7
Swan	0—1	0—0	0—0	0—0	0—0	0—0	0—0	0—0	0—0	0—0	0—0	0—1
Thurmond	0—0	0—0	1—1	0—0	0—0	0—0	1—0	0—1	0—1	0—0	0—0	2—3
Vosberg	0—0	0—0	0—0	0—0	0—0	0—0	0—0	0—0	0—0	0—1	1—0	1—1
Wilson	1—1	1—0	0—1	1—0	1—1	0—1	0—1	0—0	1—1	1—1	2—0	8—7
Totals	13—5	5—7	11—7	8—10	10—8	5—7	5—7	4—8	4—8	9—3	11—7	85—77

No Decisions—Booker, Camacho, McCament, McGaffigan, Rodriguez.

OFFICIAL NATIONAL LEAGUE BATTING AVERAGES

(Compiled by the MLB-IBM Baseball Information Service)

CLUB BATTING

CLUB	AVG	G	AB	R	H	TB	2B	3B	HR	RBI	SH	SF	HP	BB	IBB	SO	SB	CS	GI DP	LOB	SHO	SLG	OBP
Cincinnati	.265	162	5525	693	1466	2205	284	40	125	644	88	42	42	466	73	913	166	66	99	1137	8	.399	.325
Chicago	.263	162	5600	690	1474	2194	240	36	136	649	61	51	30	406	68	869	151	50	100	1124	9	.392	.314
San Francisco	.262	162	5573	719	1459	2206	221	35	152	681	76	45	33	488	61	973	109	56	83	1167	6	.396	.323
Los Angeles	.262	162	5491	728	1436	2099	222	27	129	669	71	48	31	538	78	952	141	65	110	1132	8	.382	.328
Pittsburgh	.259	162	5388	733	1395	2181	288	42	138	693	96	66	24	582	64	914	137	65	115	1121	8	.405	.330
San Diego	.257	162	5554	673	1429	2111	243	35	123	628	79	48	28	509	75	902	138	59	117	1139	6	.380	.320
New York	.256	162	5504	775	1410	2246	278	21	172	734	54	56	32	536	65	851	110	33	89	1114	8	.408	.323
St. Louis	.256	162	5462	599	1398	1954	255	41	73	554	77	50	21	517	54	844	221	55	101	1164	15	.358	.320
Philadelphia	.255	162	5535	646	1410	2010	237	27	103	619	59	39	30	582	92	915	108	35	115	1242	11	.363	.327
Atlanta	.252	162	5504	682	1376	2177	263	26	162	636	49	31	27	473	36	1010	92	55	101	1074	14	.396	.311
Montreal	.250	162	5453	662	1363	2018	227	43	114	607	87	47	26	576	67	1024	235	99	96	1126	7	.370	.322
Houston	.242	162	5379	573	1301	1856	209	32	94	536	79	41	28	548	64	997	179	83	107	1132	16	.345	.313
Totals	.256	972	65968	8173	16917	25257	2967	405	1521	7650	876	564	352	6221	797	11164	1787	727	1233	13672	116	.383	.321

INDIVIDUAL BATTING

(Top Fifteen Qualifiers for Batting Championship—502 or More Plate Appearances)

(* Lefthanded Batter   †Switch-Hitter)

Player, Club	AVG	G	AB	R	H	TB	2B	3B	HR	RBI	SH	SF	HP	BB	IBB	SO	SB	CS	GI DP	SLG	OBP
McGee, Willie, St. Louis†	.335	125	501	76	168	219	32	5	3	62	3	2	1	38	6	86	28	9	9	.437	.382
Murray, Eddie, Los Angeles†	.330	155	558	96	184	290	22	3	26	95	0	4	1	82	21	64	8	5	19	.520	.414
Magadan, David, New York*	.328	144	451	74	148	206	28	6	6	72	4	10	2	74	4	55	2	1	11	.457	.417
Dykstra, Lenny, Philadelphia*	.325	149	590	106	192	260	35	3	9	60	4	3	7	89	14	48	33	5	5	.441	.418
Dawson, Andre, Chicago	.310	147	529	72	164	283	28	5	27	100	0	3	2	42	21	65	16	2	12	.535	.358
Roberts, Leon, San Diego†	.309	149	556	104	172	241	36	3	9	44	8	4	2	55	1	54	46	12	8	.433	.375
Grace, Mark, Chicago*	.309	157	589	72	182	243	32	1	9	82	8	5	5	59	5	23	15	6	10	.413	.372
Gwynn, Anthony, San Diego*	.309	141	573	79	177	238	29	10	4	72	7	8	0	44	20	17	8	8	13	.415	.357
Butler, Brett, San Francisco*	.309	160	622	108	192	239	20	9	3	44	9	4	6	90	1	62	51	19	3	.384	.397
Sandberg, Ryne, Chicago	.306	155	615	116	188	344	30	3	40	100	0	9	6	50	8	84	25	7	8	.559	.354
Smith, Lonnie, Atlanta	.305	135	466	72	142	214	27	9	9	42	1	1	6	58	0	69	10	10	2	.459	.384
Gant, Ronald, Atlanta	.303	152	575	107	174	310	34	3	32	84	3	4	4	50	3	86	33	16	8	.539	.357
Larkin, Barry, Cincinnati	.301	158	614	85	185	243	25	6	7	67	7	7	4	49	3	49	30	5	14	.396	.358
Bonds, Barry, Pittsburgh*	.301	151	519	104	156	293	32	3	33	114	0	6	3	93	15	83	52	13	8	.565	.406
Daniels, Kalvoski, Los Angeles*	.296	130	450	81	133	239	23	1	27	94	1	3	3	68	3	104	4	3	9	.531	.389

DEPARTMENTAL LEADERS: G—Carter, S.D., 162; AB—Carter, S.D., 634; R—Sandberg, Chi., 116; H—Dykstra, Phil., Butler, S.F., 192; TB—Sandberg, Chi., 344; 2B—Jefferies, N.Y., 40; 3B—Duncan, Cin., 11; HR—Sandberg, Chi., 40; RBI—Williams, S.F., 122; SH—Bell, Pitt., 39; SF—Bonilla, Pitt., 15; HP—Davis, Hou., 8; BB—Ja. Clark, S.D., 104; IBB—Dawson, Chi., Murray, L.A., 21; SO—Galarraga, Mtl., 169; SB—Coleman, St. L., 77; CS—Yelding, Hou., 25; GIDP—Murphy, Atl.-Phil., 22; Slg. Pct.—Bonds, Pitt., .565; OB. Pct.—Dykstra, Phil., .418.

INDIVIDUAL BATTING
ALL PLAYERS LISTED ALPHABETICALLY
(*Lefthanded Batter †Switch-Hitter)

Player, Club	AVG	G	AB	R	H	TB	2B	3B	HR	RBI	SH	SF	HP	BB	IBB	SO	SB	CS	GI DP	SLG	OBP
Abner, Shawn, San Diego	.245	91	184	17	45	57	9	0	1	15	2	0	0	9	1	28	2	3	3	.310	.286
Agosto, Juan, Houston*	.000	82	2	0	0	0	0	0	0	0	0	0	0	0	0	3	0	0	0	.000	.000
Akerfelds, Darrel, Philadelphia	.167	71	6	1	1	1	0	0	0	0	2	0	0	0	0	3	0	0	0	.167	.167
Aldrete, Michael, Montreal*	.242	96	161	22	39	51	7	1	1	18	0	1	1	37	2	31	1	2	2	.317	.385
Alomar, Roberto, San Diego†	.287	147	586	80	168	223	27	5	6	60	5	5	2	48	1	72	24	7	16	.381	.340
Alou, Moises, Pitt.-Mont.	.200	16	20	4	4	6	0	1	0	0	0	0	0	0	0	3	0	0	1	.300	.200
Andersen, Larry, Houston	.000	50	3	0	0	0	0	0	0	0	0	0	0	0	0	0	0	0	0	.000	.000
Anderson, David, San Francisco.	.350	60	100	14	35	45	5	1	0	6	1	0	0	3	0	20	0	1	0	.450	.369
Anderson, Scott, Montreal	.000	4	4	0	0	0	0	0	0	0	1	0	0	0	0	3	0	0	2	.000	.000
Anthony, Eric, Houston*	.192	84	239	26	46	84	8	0	10	29	1	6	2	29	3	78	5	1	4	.351	.279
Armstrong, John, Cincinnati	.106	29	47	2	5	5	0	0	0	3	13	0	2	0	0	21	0	2	0	.106	.143
Assenmacher, Paul, Chicago*	.000	74	8	0	0	0	0	0	0	0	2	0	0	0	0	3	0	0	0	.000	.000
Avery, Steven, Atlanta*	.133	21	30	1	4	4	0	0	0	0	2	0	0	0	0	7	0	1	1	.133	.133
Backman, Walter, Pittsburgh†	.292	104	315	62	92	125	21	3	2	28	0	3	1	42	0	53	6	3	5	.397	.374
Baez, Kevin, New York.	.167	5	12	0	2	3	1	0	0	0	0	0	0	0	0	2	0	0	2	.250	.167
Bailey, Mark, San Francisco†	.143	5	7	1	1	4	0	0	1	3	0	0	0	0	0	1	0	0	0	.571	.143
Bair, C. Douglas, Pittsburgh	.000	22	1	0	0	0	0	0	0	0	0	0	0	0	0	2	0	0	0	.000	.000
Baldwin, Jeffrey, Houston*	.000	7	8	1	0	0	0	0	0	0	0	0	0	1	0	7	0	0	0	.000	.111
Barnes, Brian, Montreal*	.000	4	9	0	0	0	0	0	0	0	1	0	0	0	0	2	0	0	0	.000	.100
Bass, Kevin, San Francisco†	.252	61	214	25	54	86	9	1	7	32	0	2	1	14	3	26	2	2	5	.402	.303
Bates, William, Cincinnati†	.000	8	5	2	0	0	0	0	0	0	0	0	0	0	0	2	2	0	0	.000	.000
Bathe, William, San Francisco	.229	52	48	3	11	22	3	1	2	12	0	0	0	7	2	12	0	0	2	.458	.321
Bedrosian, Stephen, San Francisco.	.500	68	4	0	2	2	0	0	0	1	5	0	0	0	0	1	0	0	0	.500	.500
Belcher, Timothy, Los Angeles	.163	24	43	5	7	8	1	0	0	0	9	0	2	0	0	15	0	1	0	.186	.200
Belinda, Stanley, Pittsburgh.	.000	55	5	0	0	0	0	0	0	0	0	0	0	0	0	3	0	0	0	.000	.000
Bell, Jay, Pittsburgh	.254	159	583	93	148	211	28	7	7	52	39	6	3	65	0	109	10	6	14	.362	.329
Bell, Michael, Atlanta*	.244	36	45	8	11	21	5	1	0	5	0	0	1	2	0	9	0	1	4	.467	.292
Belliard, Rafael, Pittsburgh	.204	47	54	10	11	14	3	0	0	6	5	0	0	5	1	13	1	2	1	.259	.283
Benes, Andrew, San Diego.	.100	32	60	2	6	7	1	0	0	2	5	0	0	5	0	25	0	0	1	.117	.127
Benjamin, Michael, San Francisco.	.214	22	56	7	12	23	3	1	2	3	2	1	0	3	0	10	3	0	2	.411	.254
Benzinger, Todd, Cincinnati†	.253	118	376	35	95	128	14	2	5	46	2	7	4	19	4	69	3	4	3	.340	.291
Berroa, Geronimo, Atlanta	.000	7	4	0	0	0	0	0	0	0	0	0	0	0	0	1	0	0	0	.000	.000
Berryhill, Damon, Chicago†	.189	17	53	3	10	17	4	0	1	9	0	1	0	5	1	14	0	0	0	.321	.254
Bielecki, Michael, Chicago	.163	36	43	6	7	7	0	0	0	1	10	0	0	2	0	20	0	0	3	.163	.200
Biggio, Craig, Houston	.276	150	555	53	153	193	24	2	4	42	9	1	3	53	1	79	25	11	11	.348	.342
Bilardello, Dann, Pittsburgh.	.054	19	37	1	2	2	0	0	0	3	3	0	0	4	1	10	0	0	0	.054	.146
Birtsas, Timothy, Cincinnati*	.000	29	4	0	0	0	0	0	0	0	3	0	0	0	0	3	0	0	0	.000	.000
Blankenship, Kevin, Chicago	.000	3	4	0	0	0	0	0	0	0	0	0	0	0	0	3	0	0	4	.000	.000
Blauser, Jeffrey, Atlanta.	.269	115	386	46	104	158	24	3	8	39	3	3	5	35	0	70	3	5	4	.409	.338
Boever, Joseph, Atl.-Phil.	.000	67	3	0	0	0	0	0	0	0	0	0	0	0	0	0	0	0	0	.000	.000
Bonds, Barry, Pittsburgh*	.301	151	519	104	156	293	32	3	33	114	0	6	3	93	15	83	52	13	8	.565	.406
Bonilla, Roberto, Pittsburgh†	.280	160	625	112	175	324	39	7	32	120	0	15	3	45	9	103	4	3	7	.518	.322
Booker, Roderick, Philadelphia*	.221	73	131	19	29	38	5	2	0	10	2	0	1	15	7	26	3	1	1	.290	.301
Boskie, Shawn, Chicago.	.222	15	36	1	8	11	3	0	0	3	5	0	0	0	0	8	0	0	7	.306	.222
Boston, Daryl, New York*	.273	115	366	65	100	161	21	2	12	45	2	2	2	28	2	50	18	7	7	.440	.328
Boyd, Dennis, Montreal	.051	31	59	1	3	3	0	0	0	0	12	0	0	0	1	20	0	0	1	.051	.051
Braggs, Glenn, Cincinnati	.299	72	201	22	60	89	9	1	6	28	1	3	3	26	1	43	3	4	3	.443	.385

Player, Club	AVG	G	AB	R	H	TB	2B	3B	HR	RBI	SH	SF	HP	BB	GI IBB	SO	SB	CS	DP	SLG	OBP
Brantley, Jeffrey, San Francisco	.286	55	7	1	2	3	1	0	0	2	4	0	0	0	0	1	0	0	0	.429	.286
Bream, Sidney, Pittsburgh*	.270	147	389	39	105	177	23	2	15	67	4	5	2	48	5	65	8	4	6	.455	.349
Brewer, Rodney, St. Louis*	.240	14	25	4	6	7	1	0	0	2	0	0	0	0	0	4	0	0	1	.280	.240
Brooks, Hubert, Los Angeles	.266	153	568	74	151	241	28	1	20	91	0	11	6	33	10	108	2	5	13	.424	.307
Browning, Thomas, Cincinnati*	.093	38	75	7	7	9	2	0	0	4	9	0	0	2	0	29	0	0	1	.120	.117
Brunansky, Thomas, St. Louis*	.158	19	57	9	9	15	3	0	1	2	0	1	0	12	0	10	0	0	1	.263	.310
Bullock, Eric, Montreal*	.500	4	2	0	1	1	0	0	0	0	0	0	0	0	0	0	0	0	0	.500	.500
Burke, Timothy, Montreal	.167	58	6	1	1	1	0	0	0	0	0	0	0	1	0	3	0	0	0	.167	.286
Burkett, John, San Francisco	.048	33	63	1	3	3	0	0	0	3	8	0	0	5	1	35	0	0	0	.048	.118
Butler, Brett, San Francisco*	.309	160	622	108	192	239	20	9	3	44	7	7	6	90	1	62	51	19	3	.384	.397
Cabrera, Francisco, Atlanta	.277	63	137	14	38	66	5	1	7	25	0	7	6	5	0	21	0	0	4	.482	.301
Caminiti, Kenneth, Houston†	.242	153	541	52	131	167	20	2	4	51	3	4	0	48	7	97	9	4	15	.309	.302
Campusano, Silvestre, Philadelphia	.212	66	85	10	18	27	1	1	2	9	0	1	2	0	0	16	7	5	0	.318	.269
Candaele, Casey, Houston†	.286	130	262	30	75	104	8	6	3	22	4	0	0	31	5	42	7	1	4	.397	.364
Cangelosi, John, Pittsburgh†	.197	58	76	13	15	17	0	1	0	1	0	0	0	11	0	12	7	1	2	.224	.307
Carman, Donald, Philadelphia*	.273	59	11	3	3	3	0	0	0	0	0	0	0	0	0	4	0	0	0	.273	.273
Carpenter, Cris, St. Louis	.000	4	2	0	0	0	0	0	0	0	2	0	0	0	0	0	0	0	0	.000	.000
Carr, Charles, New York†	.000	4	2	0	0	0	0	0	0	0	0	0	0	0	0	2	1	0	0	.000	.000
Carreon, Mark, New York	.250	82	188	30	47	89	12	0	10	26	0	2	0	15	1	29	1	1	1	.473	.312
Carter, Gary, San Francisco	.254	92	244	24	62	99	10	0	9	27	2	0	2	25	1	31	1	1	2	.406	.324
Carter, Joseph, San Diego	.232	162	634	79	147	248	27	1	24	115	0	8	7	48	18	93	22	6	12	.391	.290
Carter, Steven, Pittsburgh*	.200	5	5	1	1	1	0	0	0	0	0	0	0	0	0	1	0	0	0	.200	.200
Castillo, Antonio, Atlanta*	.143	52	14	0	0	0	0	0	0	0	2	0	0	0	0	5	0	0	0	.143	.250
Cedeno, Andujar, Houston	.000	7	8	1	0	0	0	0	0	0	0	0	0	0	0	5	0	0	0	.000	.000
Chamberlain, Wesley, Philadelphia	.283	18	46	9	13	22	3	0	2	4	0	2	0	1	0	9	4	0	0	.478	.298
Charlton, Norman, Cincinnati†	.135	57	37	4	5	5	0	0	0	0	2	0	2	3	0	21	0	0	2	.135	.238
Clancy, James, Houston	.214	33	14	1	3	3	0	0	0	2	2	0	0	0	0	4	0	0	0	.214	.214
Clark, David, Chicago*	.275	84	171	22	47	70	4	2	5	20	0	2	2	8	1	40	7	1	4	.409	.304
Clark, Jack, San Diego	.266	115	334	59	89	178	12	1	25	62	0	2	0	104	11	91	4	3	12	.533	.441
Clark, Jerald, San Diego	.267	53	101	12	27	48	4	1	5	11	0	1	0	5	0	24	0	0	3	.475	.299
Clark, Terry, Houston	.500	1	2	0	1	1	0	0	0	0	0	0	0	0	0	0	0	0	0	.500	.500
Clark, William, San Francisco*	.295	154	600	91	177	269	25	5	19	95	2	13	3	62	9	97	8	2	7	.448	.357
Clary, Martin, Atlanta	.000	8	28	0	0	0	0	0	0	0	0	0	0	0	0	1	0	0	0	.000	.034
Coffman, Kevin, Chicago	.200	124	5	0	1	1	0	0	0	1	2	0	0	0	0	10	0	0	0	.200	.200
Coleman, Vincent, St. Louis†	.292	124	497	73	145	199	18	9	6	39	4	0	3	35	1	88	77	17	6	.400	.340
Collins, David, St. Louis†	.224	99	58	12	14	14	1	0	0	3	2	3	0	13	2	10	7	1	1	.241	.366
Combs, Patrick, Philadelphia*	.150	32	60	6	9	11	2	0	0	2	5	0	0	3	0	21	0	0	0	.183	.190
Cone, David, New York*	.200	32	70	7	14	15	1	0	0	5	4	0	0	5	0	24	0	1	0	.214	.253
Cook, Dennis, Phil.-L.A.*	.306	48	49	8	15	19	1	0	0	5	9	0	0	0	0	12	0	0	2	.388	.306
Cora, Jose, San Diego†	.270	51	100	12	27	30	3	0	0	2	3	1	0	6	2	4	8	0	3	.300	.311
Crews, S. Timothy, Los Angeles	.000	66	1	0	0	0	0	0	0	0	1	0	0	0	0	9	0	0	1	.000	.000
Daniels, Kalvoski, Los Angeles*	.296	130	450	81	133	239	23	1	27	94	0	3	3	68	9	104	4	3	9	.531	.389
Darling, Ronald, New York*	.129	34	31	2	4	4	0	0	0	3	4	0	0	0	0	12	0	0	0	.129	.206
Darwin, Danny, Houston	.132	52	38	5	5	8	1	1	0	2	2	3	1	3	1	18	0	0	3	.211	.175
Dascenzo, Douglas, Chicago†	.253	113	241	27	61	83	9	1	1	26	5	4	0	21	0	18	15	6	3	.214	.312
Daulton, Darren, Philadelphia*	.268	143	459	62	123	191	30	1	12	57	3	2	2	72	9	72	7	3	6	.388	.367
Davidson, J. Mark, Houston	.292	57	130	12	38	48	5	1	1	11	4	9	1	10	1	18	1	1	1	.369	.340
Davis, Eric, Cincinnati	.260	127	453	84	118	220	26	2	24	86	1	3	8	60	6	100	21	3	7	.486	.347
Davis, Glenn, Houston	.251	93	327	44	82	171	15	2	22	64	0	0	0	46	17	54	8	3	5	.523	.357

Player, Club	AVG	G	AB	R	H	TB	2B	3B	HR	RBI	SH	SF	HP	BB	IBB	SO	SB	CS	GI DP	SLG	OBP
Davis, Jody, Atlanta	.071	12	28	0	2	2	0	0	0	1	0	0	0	3	0	3	0	0	1	.071	.161
Davis, John, San Diego	.000	6	1	0	0	0	0	0	0	0	0	0	0	0	0	0	0	0	0	.000	.000
Dawson, Andre, Chicago	.310	147	529	72	164	283	28	5	27	100	0	8	2	42	21	65	16	2	12	.535	.358
Dayley, Kenneth, St. Louis*	.000	58	6	1	0	4	0	0	0	0	1	0	0	0	0	3	0	0	0	.000	.000
DeJesus, Jose, Philadelphia	.079	22	38	1	3	4	1	0	0	2	4	0	0	4	0	21	0	0	1	.105	.167
Decker, Steven, San Francisco	.296	15	54	5	16	27	2	0	3	8	1	0	0	1	0	10	0	0	1	.500	.309
DeLeon, Jose, St. Louis	.107	32	56	5	6	8	0	1	0	3	5	0	0	1	0	23	0	0	8	.143	.123
Dempsey, J. Rikard, Los Angeles	.195	62	128	13	25	36	5	0	2	15	0	0	0	23	0	29	1	0	8	.281	.318
Deshaies, James, Houston*	.063	34	63	1	4	4	0	0	0	3	7	0	0	2	0	33	0	0	0	.063	.092
Dewey, Mark, San Francisco	.000	14	1	0	0	0	0	0	0	0	0	0	0	0	0	0	0	0	0	.000	.500
DeShields, Delino, Montreal*	.289	129	499	69	144	196	28	6	4	45	1	2	4	66	3	96	42	22	10	.393	.375
Diaz, Mario, New York	.136	16	22	0	3	4	1	0	0	1	0	1	0	0	0	3	0	0	0	.182	.130
Dibble, Robert, Cincinnati*	.000	68	7	0	0	0	0	0	0	0	3	0	0	0	0	1	0	0	0	.000	.000
Dickson, Lance, Chicago	.000	3	3	0	0	0	0	0	0	0	1	0	0	0	0	0	0	0	0	.000	.000
DiPino, Frank, St. Louis*	.250	62	4	0	1	2	1	0	0	0	0	0	0	0	0	2	0	0	0	.500	.250
Doran, William, Hou.-Cin.†	.300	126	403	59	121	175	29	2	7	37	1	5	1	79	2	58	23	9	3	.434	.411
Downs, Kelly, San Francisco	.000	13	13	0	0	0	0	0	0	1	3	0	1	0	0	4	0	0	0	.000	.067
Drabek, Douglas, Pittsburgh.	.214	33	84	8	18	23	2	0	1	6	7	1	0	1	0	25	0	0	3	.274	.258
Duncan, Mariano, Cincinnati.	.306	125	435	67	133	207	22	11	10	55	6	4	4	24	4	67	13	7	10	.476	.345
Dunne, Michael, San Diego*	.000	10	6	0	0	0	0	0	0	0	0	2	0	0	0	2	0	0	0	.000	.000
Dunston, Shawon, Chicago	.262	146	545	73	143	232	22	8	17	66	4	6	3	15	11	87	25	5	9	.426	.283
Dykstra, Lenny, Philadelphia*	.325	149	590	106	192	260	35	3	9	60	2	3	7	89	14	48	33	5	5	.441	.418
Elster, Kevin, New York	.207	92	314	36	65	114	20	1	9	45	2	6	1	30	2	54	2	5	4	.363	.274
Esasky, Nicholas, Atlanta	.171	9	35	2	6	6	0	0	0	2	0	0	0	4	0	14	0	1	0	.171	.256
Faries, Paul, San Diego	.189	14	37	4	7	8	1	0	0	2	2	1	1	4	0	7	0	0	1	.216	.279
Farmer, Howard, Montreal	.400	6	5	0	2	2	0	0	0	0	1	0	0	0	0	1	0	0	0	.400	.400
Fernandez, C. Sid, New York*	.190	30	58	3	11	12	1	0	0	4	5	0	0	0	0	22	0	2	2	.207	.190
Fitzgerald, Michael R., Montreal	.243	111	313	36	76	123	18	0	9	41	5	3	2	60	2	60	8	1	5	.393	.365
Fletcher, Darrin, L.A.-Phil.*	.130	11	23	3	3	4	1	0	0	1	0	1	0	1	0	6	0	0	1	.174	.167
Foley, Thomas, Montreal*	.213	73	164	11	35	39	2	1	0	12	2	0	0	12	2	22	0	1	4	.238	.266
Ford, Curtis, Philadelphia*	.111	22	18	0	2	2	0	0	0	0	4	0	0	1	0	5	0	0	1	.111	.158
Franco, John, New York*	.000	55	5	0	0	0	0	0	0	0	7	0	0	0	0	1	0	0	0	.000	.000
Freeman, Marvin, Phil.-Atl.	.000	25	7	0	0	0	0	0	0	0	1	0	0	0	0	6	0	0	0	.000	.000
Frey, Steven, Montreal	.000	51	1	0	0	0	0	0	0	0	0	0	0	0	0	0	0	0	0	.000	.000
Galarraga, Andres, Montreal	.256	155	579	65	148	237	29	0	20	87	1	5	4	40	8	169	10	1	14	.409	.306
Gant, Ronald, Atlanta	.303	152	575	107	174	310	34	3	32	84	1	4	1	50	0	86	33	16	8	.539	.357
Garcia, Carlos, Pittsburgh	.500	4	4	1	2	2	0	0	0	0	0	0	0	0	0	2	0	0	0	.500	.500
Gardner, Mark, Montreal	.114	27	44	5	5	8	1	1	0	1	8	0	0	0	0	23	0	0	1	.182	.114
Garrelts, Scott, San Francisco.	.061	42	66	4	4	5	1	0	0	0	6	0	0	1	0	28	0	0	0	.076	.088
Gedman, Richard, Houston*	.202	40	104	4	21	31	7	0	1	10	2	1	1	15	6	24	0	0	2	.298	.300
Gibson, Kirk, Los Angeles*	.260	89	315	59	82	126	20	0	8	38	0	3	3	39	0	65	26	2	4	.400	.345
Gilkey, Bernard, St. Louis	.297	18	64	11	19	31	5	2	1	3	2	0	1	8	0	5	6	1	1	.484	.375
Girardi, Joseph, Chicago	.270	133	419	36	113	144	24	2	1	38	4	4	3	17	11	50	8	3	13	.344	.300
Glavine, Thomas, Atlanta*	.113	34	62	9	7	9	2	0	0	4	7	0	1	8	0	24	0	3	0	.145	.211
Goff, Jerry, Montreal*	.227	52	119	14	27	37	2	1	2	7	1	0	1	21	4	36	0	2	1	.311	.343
Gonzalez, Jose, Los Angeles	.232	106	99	15	23	40	5	0	1	8	0	0	0	6	1	27	3	1	0	.404	.280
Gonzalez, Luis, Houston*	.190	12	21	1	4	6	2	0	0	0	3	0	2	2	0	5	0	0	0	.286	.261
Gooden, Dwight, New York	.187	35	75	0	14	20	0	0	2	9	0	1	0	2	0	15	0	0	0	.267	.225
Gott, James, Los Angeles	.000	50	1	0	0	0	0	0	0	0	0	0	0	0	0	1	0	0	0	.000	.000

Player, Club	AVG	G	AB	R	H	TB	2B	3B	HR	RBI	SH	SF	HP	BB	IBB	SO	SB	CS	GI DP	SLG	OBP
Grace, Mark, Chicago*	.309	157	589	72	182	243	32	0	9	82	1	8	5	59	5	54	15	6	10	.413	.372
Grant, Mark, S.D.-Atl.	.333	59	6	2	2	2	0	0	0	0	1	0	1	1	0	2	0	0	0	.333	.500
Greene, I. Thomas, Atl.-Phil.	.167	15	12	2	2	3	1	0	0	0	3	0	1	0	0	1	0	0	0	.250	.167
Gregg, W. Thomas, Atlanta*	.264	124	239	18	63	93	13	1	5	32	0	1	1	20	4	39	4	3	2	.389	.322
Griffey, G. Kenneth, Cincinnati*	.206	46	63	6	13	18	2	0	1	8	6	2	1	2	1	5	2	1	0	.286	.235
Griffin, Alfredo, Los Angeles†	.210	141	461	38	97	117	11	3	0	35	3	4	2	29	1	65	6	3	5	.254	.258
Grimsley, Jason, Philadelphia	.188	12	16	3	3	3	0	0	0	2	1	0	0	1	0	2	0	0	0	.188	.235
Grissom, Marquis, Montreal	.257	98	288	42	74	101	14	2	3	29	4	4	2	27	2	40	22	2	3	.351	.320
Gross, Kevin, Montreal	.200	32	50	3	10	17	4	0	1	4	7	1	0	2	0	21	0	1	0	.340	.231
Guerrero, Pedro, St. Louis	.281	136	498	42	140	212	31	0	13	80	0	11	1	44	14	70	1	0	14	.426	.334
Gullickson, William, Houston	.158	32	57	2	9	12	0	0	0	5	7	1	0	4	0	14	0	1	2	.211	.210
Gunderson, Eric, San Francisco	.000	7	6	0	0	0	0	0	0	0	0	0	0	0	0	4	0	0	0	.000	.000
Gwynn, Chris, Los Angeles*	.284	101	141	19	40	59	2	1	5	22	0	3	0	7	0	28	0	1	2	.418	.311
Gwynn, Anthony, San Diego*	.309	141	573	79	177	238	29	10	4	72	7	4	1	44	20	23	17	8	13	.415	.357
Hall, Andrew, Montreal*	.000	42	4	1	0	0	0	0	0	1	1	0	0	0	0	4	0	0	1	.000	.000
Hamilton, Jeffrey, Los Angeles	.125	7	24	1	3	3	0	0	0	0	0	0	0	0	0	3	0	0	0	.125	.125
Hammaker, C. Atlee, S.F.-S.D.†	.105	34	19	2	2	2	0	0	0	0	1	0	0	0	0	6	0	0	1	.105	.150
Hammond, Christopher, Cincinnati*	.000	3	3	0	0	0	0	0	0	0	3	0	0	0	0	1	0	0	0	.000	.000
Hansen, David, Los Angeles*	.143	5	7	0	1	1	0	0	0	0	0	0	0	1	0	3	0	0	0	.143	.143
Harkey, Michael, Chicago	.250	27	56	4	14	18	4	0	0	4	8	0	0	0	0	16	0	0	3	.321	.276
Harris, Gregory W., San Diego	.083	73	12	1	1	3	0	1	0	0	1	0	0	1	0	8	0	0	0	.250	.083
Harris, Leonard, Los Angeles*	.304	137	431	61	131	161	16	4	2	29	8	3	0	29	2	31	15	10	8	.374	.348
Hartley, Michael, Los Angeles	.077	32	13	0	1	1	0	0	0	0	3	0	0	0	0	8	0	0	0	.077	.077
Hatcher, William, Cincinnati	.276	139	504	68	139	192	28	5	5	25	9	1	6	33	2	42	30	10	4	.381	.327
Hatcher, Michael, Los Angeles	.212	85	132	12	28	33	3	1	0	13	3	2	0	6	0	22	4	4	12	.250	.248
Hayes, Charles, Philadelphia	.258	152	561	56	145	195	20	0	10	57	1	6	2	28	3	91	4	7	10	.348	.293
Hayes, Von, Philadelphia*	.261	129	467	70	122	193	14	3	17	73	0	10	4	87	16	81	16	6	10	.413	.375
Heaton, Neal, Pittsburgh*	.047	32	43	3	2	2	0	0	0	0	3	0	0	4	0	13	0	0	3	.047	.128
Hennis, Randall, Houston	.000	3	2	0	0	0	0	0	0	0	1	0	0	0	0	1	0	0	0	.000	.000
Hernandez, Carlos, Los Angeles	.200	10	20	2	4	5	0	0	0	1	0	0	0	0	0	2	0	0	0	.250	.200
Hernandez, Xavier, Houston*	.333	35	3	1	1	1	0	0	0	0	2	0	0	0	0	1	0	0	0	.333	.333
Herr, Thomas, Phil.-N.Y.†	.261	146	547	48	143	190	26	3	5	60	6	2	2	50	5	58	7	1	11	.347	.324
Hershiser, Orel, Los Angeles	.000	4	7	0	0	0	0	0	0	0	1	0	0	0	0	1	0	0	0	.000	.000
Hesketh, Joseph, Mon.-Atl.*	.000	33	1	0	0	0	0	0	0	0	1	0	0	0	0	1	0	0	0	.000	.000
Hill, Kenneth, St. Louis	.211	17	19	0	4	4	0	0	0	0	5	0	0	1	0	5	1	0	0	.211	.286
Hollins, David, Philadelphia†	.184	72	114	14	21	36	0	0	5	15	1	1	0	10	0	28	0	0	1	.316	.252
Horton, Ricky, St. Louis*	.000	32	4	0	0	0	0	0	0	0	1	0	0	0	0	1	0	0	0	.000	.000
Howard, Thomas, San Diego†	.273	20	44	4	12	14	2	0	0	0	7	0	0	0	0	11	0	1	0	.318	.273
Howell, Jay, Los Angeles	.000	45	2	0	0	0	0	0	0	0	3	0	0	0	0	0	0	0	0	.000	.000
Howell, Kenneth, Philadelphia	.067	18	30	2	2	3	1	0	0	2	8	0	0	1	0	15	0	0	1	.100	.097
Hudler, Rex, Mon.-St.L.	.282	93	220	31	62	98	11	2	7	22	2	1	2	12	0	32	18	10	3	.445	.323
Hughes, Keith, New York*	.000	8	9	0	0	0	0	0	0	0	2	0	0	0	0	4	0	0	0	.000	.000
Hundley, Todd, New York†	.209	36	67	8	14	20	6	0	0	2	1	0	0	6	0	18	0	0	2	.299	.274
Hurst, Bruce, San Diego*	.090	33	67	2	6	6	0	0	0	0	7	0	0	4	0	43	1	0	1	.090	.141
Infante, Alexis, Atlanta	.036	20	28	3	1	2	1	0	0	0	3	0	0	0	0	7	0	0	0	.071	.069
Innis, Jeffrey, New York	.000	18	0	1	0	0	0	0	0	0	4	0	0	0	0	0	0	0	0	.000	.000
Jackson, Danny, Cincinnati	.054	23	37	1	2	4	1	0	0	0	6	1	0	0	1	21	0	0	2	.108	.054
Jackson, Darrin, San Diego	.257	58	113	12	29	41	3	0	3	9	0	0	0	5	0	24	3	0	3	.363	.286
Javier, Stanley, Los Angeles†	.304	104	276	56	84	110	9	4	3	24	6	2	0	37	2	44	15	7	6	.399	.384

Player, Club	AVG	G	AB	R	H	TB	2B	3B	HR	RBI	SH	SF	HP	BB	IBB	SO	SB	CS	GIDP	SLG	OBP
Jefferies, Gregory, New York†	.283	153	604	96	171	262	40	3	15	68	0	4	5	46	2	40	11	2	12	.434	.337
Jelic, Christopher, New York	.091	4	11	1	1	4	1	0	0	1	0	0	0	0	0	3	0	0	0	.364	.091
Johnson, Howard, New York†	.244	154	590	89	144	256	37	3	23	90	0	9	0	69	12	100	34	8	7	.434	.319
Johnson, Wallace, Montreal†	.163	47	49	6	8	12	1	0	1	5	0	0	1	7	2	6	1	0	1	.245	.281
Jones, Ronald, Philadelphia*	.276	24	58	5	16	27	2	0	3	5	0	0	1	9	0	9	0	1	1	.466	.373
Jones, W. Timothy, St. Louis*	.219	67	128	9	28	40	7	1	1	12	3	0	1	12	1	20	0	0	1	.313	.291
Jordan, Paul, Philadelphia	.241	92	324	32	78	114	21	4	5	44	4	4	5	13	6	39	3	4	9	.352	.277
Jose, Felix, St. Louis†	.271	25	85	12	23	38	4	1	3	13	0	0	0	8	0	16	2	4	1	.447	.333
Justice, David, Atlanta*	.282	127	439	76	124	235	23	2	28	78	0	1	0	64	4	92	11	6	2	.535	.373
Kennedy, Terrence, San Francisco*	.277	127	303	25	84	112	23	1	2	26	2	2	1	31	7	38	1	3	7	.370	.342
King, Jeffrey, Pittsburgh	.245	127	371	46	91	152	17	1	14	53	2	7	1	21	1	50	3	3	12	.410	.283
Kingery, Michael, San Francisco*	.295	105	207	24	61	70	7	1	0	24	5	1	1	12	0	19	6	1	1	.338	.335
Kipper, Robert, Pittsburgh*	.143	41	7	0	1	1	0	0	0	0	0	0	0	0	0	2	0	0	0	.143	.143
Knepper, Robert, San Francisco*	.231	12	13	1	3	4	1	0	0	4	1	0	0	0	0	7	0	0	0	.308	.231
Komminsk, Brad, San Francisco	.200	8	5	2	1	1	0	0	0	0	0	0	0	1	0	2	0	0	0	.200	.333
Kramer, Randall, Pitt.-Chi.	.000	22	6	0	0	0	0	0	0	0	0	0	0	0	0	2	0	0	0	.000	.000
Kremers, James, Atlanta*	.110	29	73	7	8	14	0	0	2	2	0	0	0	6	1	27	0	0	0	.192	.177
Kruk, John, Philadelphia*	.291	142	443	52	129	191	25	8	7	67	0	6	0	69	16	70	10	5	11	.431	.386
LaCoss, Michael, San Francisco	.043	23	23	2	1	2	1	0	0	0	2	1	0	0	0	10	0	0	0	.087	.043
Laga, Michael, San Francisco*	.185	23	27	4	5	12	1	0	2	4	8	0	1	1	0	7	0	0	1	.444	.241
Lake, Stephen, Philadelphia	.250	23	80	4	20	22	2	0	0	6	0	0	0	3	0	12	0	0	2	.275	.286
Lampkin, Thomas, San Diego*	.222	26	63	4	14	19	2	0	1	6	0	1	0	4	1	9	0	1	2	.302	.269
Lancaster, Lester, Chicago	.050	55	20	2	1	1	0	0	0	0	4	0	0	0	0	11	0	0	0	.050	.174
Landrum, T. William, Pittsburgh	.111	54	9	2	1	2	1	0	0	0	0	0	0	0	0	5	0	0	0	.222	.111
Lankford, Raymond, St. Louis**	.286	39	126	12	36	57	10	1	3	12	2	0	0	13	0	27	8	2	1	.452	.353
Larkin, Barry, Cincinnati	.301	158	614	85	185	243	25	6	7	67	7	4	7	49	3	49	30	5	14	.396	.358
LaValliere, Michael, Pittsburgh*	.258	96	279	27	72	96	15	0	3	31	7	1	2	44	8	20	0	3	6	.344	.362
Layana, Timothy, Cincinnati	.000	55	5	0	0	0	0	0	0	0	4	0	0	0	0	2	0	0	0	.000	.000
Leach, Richard, San Francisco*	.293	78	174	24	51	70	13	0	2	16	0	0	1	21	2	20	0	2	1	.402	.372
Lee, Terry, Cincinnati	.211	12	19	1	4	5	1	0	0	3	0	0	0	0	0	2	0	0	2	.263	.273
Lefferts, Craig, San Diego*	.250	56	4	1	1	1	0	0	0	1	2	0	0	0	0	2	0	0	1	.250	.250
Leibrandt, Charles, Atlanta	.180	24	50	4	9	9	0	0	0	3	5	0	0	3	0	11	0	0	0	.180	.226
Lemke, Mark, Atlanta†	.226	102	239	22	54	67	13	0	0	21	4	3	0	21	3	22	0	1	6	.280	.286
Leonard, Mark, San Francisco*	.176	11	17	3	3	7	1	0	1	2	0	0	0	3	0	8	0	0	0	.412	.300
Liddell, David, New York	1.000	1	1	0	1	1	0	0	0	0	0	0	0	0	0	0	0	0	0	1.000	1.000
Lilliquist, Derek, Atl.-S.D.*	.256	29	43	6	11	17	0	0	2	3	2	0	0	0	0	8	1	0	3	.395	.273
Lind, Jose, Pittsburgh	.261	152	514	46	134	175	28	5	1	48	4	7	1	35	0	52	8	2	20	.340	.305
Litton, J. Gregory, San Francisco	.245	93	204	17	50	64	9	1	1	24	2	0	1	11	1	45	1	0	5	.314	.284
Lombardozzi, Stephen, Houston	.000	42	9	0	0	0	0	0	0	0	0	0	0	1	0	4	0	0	0	.000	.167
Long, William, Chicago	.000	6	5	0	0	0	0	0	0	0	2	0	0	1	0	2	0	0	0	.000	.500
Lopez, Luis, Los Angeles	.000	36	6	0	0	0	0	0	0	0	0	0	0	0	0	1	0	0	0	.000	.000
Luecken, Richard, Atlanta	.333	36	3	0	1	2	1	0	0	0	0	0	0	0	0	1	0	0	1	.667	.333
Lynn, Frederic, San Diego*	.240	90	196	18	47	70	3	0	6	23	3	3	1	22	2	44	2	2	1	.357	.315
Lyons, Barry, N.Y.-L.A.	.235	27	85	9	20	29	3	0	3	9	1	0	0	2	0	10	0	0	2	.341	.261
Maddux, Gregory, Chicago	.145	35	83	1	12	12	0	0	0	3	4	0	1	2	0	25	0	0	1	.145	.165
Maddux, Michael, Los Angeles*	.000	11	2	0	0	0	0	0	0	0	0	0	0	0	0	0	0	0	0	.000	.000
Magadan, David, New York*	.328	144	451	74	148	206	28	6	6	72	9	10	2	74	4	55	2	1	11	.457	.417
Magrane, Joseph, St. Louis	.127	31	55	3	7	9	2	0	0	0	5	1	0	3	0	19	0	0	2	.164	.172
Mahler, Richard, Cincinnati	.114	35	35	1	4	5	1	0	0	2	0	1	0	1	0	4	0	0	3	.143	.135

Player, Club	AVG	G	AB	R	H	TB	2B	3B	HR	RBI	SH	SF	HP	BB	IBB	SO	SB	CS	GI DP	SLG	OBP
Mann, Kelly, Atlanta	.143	11	28	2	4	8	1	0	1	2	0	0	0	0	0	6	0	0	0	.286	.143
Manwaring, Kirt, San Francisco	.154	8	13	1	2	4	1	0	0	1	1	0	0	0	0	3	0	0	0	.308	.154
Marak, Paul, Atlanta	.091	7	11	1	1	1	0	0	0	0	0	0	0	1	0	4	0	0	0	.091	.167
Marshall, Michael, New York	.239	53	163	24	39	67	8	1	6	27	0	3	3	7	0	40	0	2	2	.411	.278
Martinez, Carmelo, Phil.-Pitt.	.240	83	217	26	52	91	9	1	10	35	0	2	1	30	2	42	0	1	3	.419	.332
Martinez, David, Montreal*	.279	118	391	60	109	165	13	5	11	39	3	2	1	24	2	48	13	11	8	.422	.321
Martinez, J. Dennis, Montreal	.103	32	68	7	7	8	1	0	0	6	12	0	0	1	0	25	0	0	3	.118	.129
Mathews, Gregory, St. Louis*	.125	33	80	2	10	10	0	0	0	6	9	1	1	2	0	32	0	0	1	.125	.145
May, Derrick, Chicago*	.214	12	14	2	3	4	1	0	0	0	0	0	0	0	0	5	0	0	0	.286	.313
McCament, L. Randall, San Francisco	.246	17	61	8	15	21	3	0	1	11	1	1	0	2	0	7	0	0	1	.344	.270
McClellan, Paul, San Francisco	.000	4	2	0	0	0	0	0	0	0	0	0	0	0	0	0	0	0	0	.000	.000
McClendon, Lloyd, Chi.-Pitt.	.164	53	110	6	18	27	3	0	2	12	0	0	0	14	0	22	1	2	3	.245	.256
McDowell, Oddibe, Atlanta*	.243	113	305	47	74	109	14	0	7	25	1	2	2	21	2	53	13	9	2	.357	.295
McDowell, Roger, Philadelphia	.000	72	2	1	0	0	0	0	0	0	1	0	0	0	0	1	0	0	0	.000	.000
McGee, Willie, St. Louis†	.335	125	501	76	168	219	32	5	3	62	1	8	1	38	6	86	28	9	9	.437	.382
McGriff, Terence, Cin.-Hou.	.000	6	9	0	0	0	0	0	0	0	1	0	1	1	0	1	0	0	0	.000	.000
McReynolds, W. Kevin, New York	.269	147	521	75	140	237	23	1	24	82	0	8	2	71	11	61	9	3	8	.455	.353
Meadows, Michael, Hou.-Phil.*	.107	30	28	4	3	3	0	0	0	0	2	0	2	3	0	6	0	0	0	.107	.194
Mercado, Orlando, N.Y.-Mon.	.214	50	98	10	21	31	3	1	3	7	0	0	1	8	3	12	0	0	4	.316	.287
Merced, Orlando, Pittsburgh†	.208	25	24	3	5	6	1	0	0	2	0	0	0	1	0	9	0	0	0	.250	.240
Mercker, Kent, Atlanta*	.000	36	3	0	0	0	0	0	0	0	0	0	0	0	0	1	0	0	0	.000	.000
Meyer, Brian, Houston	.000	14	1	0	0	0	0	0	0	0	0	0	0	0	0	1	0	0	0	.000	.000
Miller, Keith A., New York	.258	88	233	42	60	71	8	0	1	12	2	2	2	23	1	46	16	3	8	.305	.327
Mitchell, Kevin, San Francisco	.290	140	524	90	152	285	24	2	35	93	0	5	2	58	9	87	4	7	8	.544	.360
Mohorcic, Dale, Montreal	.125	34	8	1	1	1	0	0	0	0	5	0	0	0	0	1	0	0	0	.125	.125
Morandini, Michael, Philadelphia*	.241	25	79	9	19	26	4	0	1	3	2	0	0	6	0	19	3	0	1	.329	.294
Morgan, Michael, Los Angeles	.113	33	71	2	8	8	0	0	0	2	5	2	0	6	0	25	0	0	0	.113	.137
Morris, William, Cincinnati*	.340	107	309	50	105	154	22	3	7	36	3	2	1	21	4	32	9	3	12	.498	.381
Morris, John, St. Louis*	.111	18	18	2	2	2	0	0	0	2	2	0	0	3	0	6	0	0	2	.111	.238
Mulholland, Terence, Philadelphia	.097	33	62	6	6	7	1	0	0	2	4	0	0	0	0	30	0	0	1	.113	.111
Munoz, Michael, Los Angeles*	.000	8	1	0	0	0	0	0	0	0	0	0	0	0	0	1	0	0	2	.000	.000
Murphy, Dale, Atl.-Phil.	.245	154	563	60	138	235	23	1	24	83	0	4	1	61	14	130	9	3	22	.417	.318
Murray, Eddie, Los Angeles†	.330	155	558	96	184	290	22	3	26	95	0	4	1	82	21	64	8	5	19	.520	.414
Musselman, Jeffrey, New York*	.000	28	1	1	0	0	0	0	0	1	2	0	0	0	0	2	0	0	0	.000	.000
Myers, Randall, Cincinnati*	.250	66	4	1	1	1	0	0	0	2	0	0	0	0	0	9	0	0	0	.250	.250
Nabholz, Christopher, Montreal*	.000	11	21	1	0	0	0	0	0	0	3	0	1	0	0	8	0	0	0	.000	.045
Neidlinger, James, Los Angeles†	.120	12	25	1	3	3	0	0	0	0	3	0	0	2	0	4	0	0	0	.120	.185
Nelson, Robert, San Diego*	.000	5	5	1	0	0	0	0	0	0	1	0	0	0	0	11	0	0	0	.000	.000
Nichols, Carl, Houston	.204	32	49	7	10	13	3	0	0	11	2	2	1	8	1	11	0	0	2	.265	.317
Niedenfuer, Thomas, St. Louis	.000	52	3	1	0	0	0	0	0	0	0	0	0	0	0	2	0	0	0	.000	.000
Nieto, Thomas, Philadelphia	.167	17	30	1	5	5	0	0	0	4	3	1	0	3	0	11	0	0	2	.167	.265
Nixon, Otis, Montreal†	.251	119	231	46	58	71	6	2	1	20	3	1	1	28	0	33	50	13	0	.307	.331
Noboa, Milciades, Montreal	.266	81	158	15	42	53	7	2	0	14	4	1	0	7	0	14	4	1	2	.335	.294
Noce, Paul, Cincinnati	1.000	7	1	1	1	1	0	0	0	1	0	0	0	0	0	0	0	0	0	1.000	1.000
Novoa, Rafael, San Francisco*	.200	1	5	1	1	1	0	0	0	1	1	1	1	0	0	2	0	1	0	.200	.333
Nunez, Jose, Chicago	.000	21	11	0	0	0	0	0	0	0	2	0	0	1	0	5	1	0	2	.000	.083
Oberkfell, Kenneth, Houston*	.207	77	150	10	31	42	6	1	1	12	1	2	1	15	1	17	1	1	1	.280	.281
O'Brien, Charles, New York	.162	28	68	6	11	14	3	0	0	9	2	2	1	10	2	8	1	0	1	.206	.272

Player, Club	AVG	G	AB	R	H	TB	2B	3B	HR	RBI	SH	SF	HP	BB	IBB	SO	SB	CS	GI DP	SLG	OBP
Oester, Ronald, Cincinnati	.299	64	154	10	46	58	10	1	0	13	6	1	0	10	1	29	1	2	1	.377	.339
Offerman, Jose, Los Angeles†	.155	29	58	7	9	12	0	0	1	7	1	0	0	4	1	14	1	0	0	.207	.210
Ojeda, Robert, New York*	.133	38	30	2	4	5	1	0	0	0	1	0	0	0	0	11	0	0	0	.167	.133
Olivares, Omar, St. Louis	.176	9	17	2	3	7	1	0	1	4	0	0	0	0	0	4	0	0	0	.412	.167
Oliver, Joseph, Cincinnati	.231	121	364	34	84	131	23	0	8	52	1	1	2	37	15	75	1	1	6	.360	.304
Oliveras, Francisco, San Francisco	.000	33	5	0	0	0	0	0	0	0	5	0	0	0	0	4	0	0	0	.000	.000
Olson, Gregory, Atlanta	.262	100	298	36	78	113	12	1	7	36	1	1	2	30	4	51	1	1	8	.379	.332
O'Malley, Thomas, New York*	.223	82	121	14	27	43	7	0	3	14	0	1	0	11	0	20	0	0	1	.355	.286
O'Neal, Randall, San Francisco	.167	26	6	0	1	1	0	0	0	0	1	0	0	0	0	3	0	0	0	.167	.167
O'Neill, Paul, Cincinnati*	.270	145	503	59	136	212	28	5	16	78	1	5	2	53	13	103	13	11	12	.421	.339
Oquendo, Jose, St. Louis†	.252	156	469	38	118	148	17	1	1	37	5	5	0	74	8	46	1	1	7	.316	.350
Ortiz, Javier, Houston	.273	30	77	7	21	31	5	1	1	10	0	1	0	12	0	11	1	1	1	.403	.367
Owen, Spike, Montreal†	.234	149	453	55	106	155	24	5	5	35	5	5	3	70	12	60	8	6	6	.342	.333
Pagliarulo, Michael, San Diego*	.254	128	398	29	101	149	23	2	7	38	2	4	1	39	3	66	1	3	2	.374	.322
Pagnozzi, Thomas, St. Louis	.277	69	220	20	61	82	15	0	2	23	2	0	3	14	1	37	1	1	5	.373	.321
Palacios, Vicente, Pittsburgh	.000	3	4	0	0	0	0	0	0	0	0	0	0	1	0	2	0	0	0	.000	.200
Paredes, Johnny, Montreal	.333	3	6	0	2	3	1	0	0	1	0	0	0	1	0	0	0	0	0	.500	.429
Parent, Mark, San Diego	.222	65	189	13	42	62	11	0	3	16	3	1	0	16	3	29	0	0	2	.328	.283
Parker, Richard, San Francisco	.243	54	107	19	26	37	5	0	2	14	2	0	1	0	0	15	6	1	1	.346	.314
Parrett, Jeffrey, Phil-Atl	.091	67	11	0	1	1	0	0	0	1	2	0	0	0	0	4	0	0	0	.091	.091
Patterson, Robert, Pittsburgh	.053	55	19	0	1	1	0	0	0	0	1	0	0	0	0	6	0	0	0	.053	.053
Pavlas, David, Chicago	.000	13	1	0	0	0	0	0	0	0	0	0	0	0	0	1	0	0	0	.000	.000
Pena, Alejandro, New York†	.167	52	6	0	1	1	0	0	0	0	0	0	0	0	0	3	0	0	0	.167	.286
Pena, Antonio, St. Louis†	.244	18	45	5	11	13	2	0	0	2	1	0	0	4	0	14	0	0	0	.289	.314
Pendleton, Terry, St. Louis†	.230	121	447	46	103	145	20	2	6	58	0	6	1	30	8	58	7	5	12	.324	.277
Perez, Michael, St. Louis	.000	13	1	0	0	0	0	0	0	0	0	0	0	0	0	0	0	0	0	.000	.000
Perezchica, Antonio, San Francisco	.333	7	22	1	6	7	0	0	0	1	0	0	0	0	0	2	1	0	0	.333	.500
Perry, W. Patrick, Los Angeles*	.000	31	1	0	0	0	0	0	0	0	1	0	0	0	0	1	0	0	0	.000	.000
Pico, Jeffrey, Chicago	.273	32	22	2	6	7	1	0	0	1	5	0	0	3	0	5	0	0	0	.318	.360
Portugal, Mark, Houston	.136	32	66	2	9	9	0	0	0	5	3	0	0	1	0	8	0	0	0	.136	.149
Power, Ted, Pittsburgh	.125	40	8	0	1	2	1	0	0	0	1	0	0	0	0	5	0	0	0	.250	.125
Presley, James, Atlanta	.242	140	541	59	131	224	34	1	19	72	0	4	3	29	9	130	0	1	10	.414	.282
Prince, Thomas, Pittsburgh	.100	4	10	1	1	1	0	0	0	0	1	0	0	1	0	2	0	1	0	.100	.182
Puhl, Terrance, Houston*	.293	37	41	5	12	13	1	0	0	8	1	4	1	5	0	7	1	2	3	.317	.375
Quinones, Luis, Cincinnati	.241	83	145	10	35	48	7	0	2	17	3	1	0	13	3	29	0	0	3	.331	.301
Quisenberry, Daniel, San Francisco	.000	5	1	0	0	0	0	0	0	0	0	0	0	0	0	0	0	0	0	.000	.000
Raines, Timothy, Montreal†	.287	130	457	65	131	179	11	5	9	62	0	8	3	70	8	43	49	16	9	.392	.379
Ramirez, Rafael, Houston	.261	132	445	44	116	147	19	3	2	37	9	2	1	24	9	46	10	5	9	.330	.299
Ramos, Domingo, Chicago	.265	98	226	22	60	71	5	0	2	17	2	3	1	27	0	29	1	0	7	.314	.342
Randolph, William, Los Angeles	.271	26	96	15	26	33	4	1	1	9	3	1	0	13	0	9	9	2	3	.344	.364
Rasmussen, Dennis, San Diego*	.290	33	62	8	18	20	2	0	0	8	6	0	1	2	0	18	0	0	1	.323	.308
Ready, Randy, Philadelphia	.244	101	217	26	53	67	9	1	1	26	1	3	2	29	3	35	3	2	3	.309	.332
Redus, Gary, Pittsburgh	.247	96	227	32	56	95	15	3	6	23	1	1	2	33	3	38	11	5	1	.419	.341
Reed, Darren, New York	.205	26	39	5	8	17	1	1	2	2	0	0	0	3	0	11	1	1	1	.436	.262
Reed, Jeffrey, Cincinnati*	.251	72	175	12	44	63	8	1	3	16	5	1	1	24	5	26	0	0	4	.360	.340
Reed, Richard, Pittsburgh	.250	13	16	2	4	4	0	0	0	0	0	0	0	0	0	1	0	0	0	.250	.278
Reuschel, Ricky, San Francisco	.154	15	26	4	4	5	1	0	0	3	3	2	0	1	0	6	0	0	0	.192	.154
Reuss, Jerry, Pittsburgh*	.000	4	0	0	0	0	0	0	0	0	2	0	0	0	0	0	0	0	0	.000	.000
Reynolds, Robert J., Pittsburgh†	.288	95	215	25	62	74	10	1	0	19	0	2	0	23	1	35	12	2	12	.344	.354

Player, Club	AVG	G	AB	R	H	TB	2B	3B	HR	RBI	SH	SF	HP	BB	IBB	SO	SB	CS	GI DP	SLG	OBP
Reynolds, Ronn, San Diego	.067	8	15	1	1	1	—	—	0	1	0	1	0	—	0	6	0	0	0	.133	.125
Rhodes, Karl, Houston*	.244	38	86	12	21	32	6	1	1	3	1	0	0	13	3	12	4	1	1	.372	.340
Rijo, Jose, Cincinnati	.161	29	62	3	10	11	1	0	0	2	11	1	0	2	0	10	0	0	1	.177	.188
Riles, Ernest, San Francisco*	.200	92	155	22	31	59	11	1	5	21	2	1	0	26	3	26	0	0	2	.381	.313
Roberts, Leon, San Diego†	.309	149	556	104	172	241	36	3	8	44	8	4	6	55	1	65	46	12	8	.433	.375
Robinson, Don, San Francisco	.143	31	63	4	9	16	1	0	2	7	3	0	0	0	0	17	0	0	2	.254	.143
Robinson, Ronald, Cincinnati	.091	6	11	1	1	1	—	—	0	—	1	0	0	0	0	6	0	0	0	.091	.091
Rodriguez, Richard, San Diego*	.000	32	3	0	0	0	0	0	0	0	0	0	0	1	0	1	0	0	0	.000	.250
Roesler, Michael, Pittsburgh	.000	5	1	1	0	0	0	0	0	0	0	0	0	0	0	1	0	0	0	.000	.000
Rohde, David, Houston†	.184	59	98	8	18	22	4	0	0	5	4	1	0	9	2	20	0	0	3	.224	.283
Rojas, Melquides, Montreal	.000	23	3	0	0	0	0	0	0	0	3	0	0	0	0	1	0	0	0	.000	.000
Roomes, Rolando, Cin.-Mon.	.227	46	75	6	17	25	1	0	2	8	0	0	0	1	1	26	2	2	2	.333	.237
Rosario, Victor, Atlanta	.143	9	7	3	1	1	—	—	0	0	0	0	0	1	0	1	0	0	0	.143	.250
Ross, Mark, Pittsburgh	.000	9	1	0	0	0	—	—	0	—	1	0	0	0	0	1	0	0	0	.000	.000
Ruffin, Bruce, Philadelphia†	.068	32	44	3	3	3	—	—	0	1	5	0	0	0	0	9	0	0	0	.068	.128
Ruskin, Scott, Pitt.-Mon.	.250	67	8	1	2	5	1	1	0	1	3	0	0	3	0	5	0	0	0	.625	.250
Ryal, Mark, Pittsburgh*	.083	9	12	0	1	1	—	—	0	0	0	0	0	0	0	3	0	0	0	.083	.083
Sabo, Christopher, Cincinnati	.270	148	567	95	153	270	38	2	25	71	1	3	4	61	7	58	25	10	8	.476	.343
Salazar, Luis, Chicago	.254	115	410	44	104	159	13	3	12	47	0	1	4	19	3	59	3	1	4	.388	.293
Sampen, William, Montreal	.000	59	8	0	0	0	0	0	0	0	2	0	0	0	0	4	0	0	0	.000	.000
Samuel, Juan, Los Angeles	.242	143	492	62	119	188	24	3	13	52	5	5	5	51	5	126	38	20	8	.382	.316
Sandberg, Ryne, Chicago	.306	155	615	116	188	344	30	3	40	100	0	9	1	50	8	84	25	7	8	.559	.354
Santana, Andres, San Francisco†	.000	9	4	1	0	0	0	0	0	0	1	0	0	0	0	0	2	0	0	.000	.000
Santiago, Benito, San Diego	.270	100	344	42	93	144	8	5	11	53	1	7	3	27	2	55	5	4	5	.419	.323
Santovenia, Nelson, Montreal	.190	59	163	13	31	54	3	1	6	28	0	2	1	8	9	31	0	0	7	.331	.222
Sasser, Mackey, New York*	.307	100	270	31	83	115	14	0	6	41	0	5	2	15	9	19	0	3	7	.426	.344
Schatzeder, Daniel, Hou.-N.Y.*	.250	51	4	0	1	1	—	—	0	0	6	0	0	0	0	2	0	0	0	.250	.250
Schiraldi, Calvin, San Diego	.190	42	21	2	4	9	2	0	1	1	9	0	0	1	0	6	0	0	0	.429	.227
Schmidt, David, Montreal	.000	34	3	0	0	0	0	0	0	0	3	0	0	0	0	0	0	0	0	.000	.000
Scioscia, Michael, Los Angeles*	.264	135	435	46	115	176	25	0	12	66	1	4	3	55	14	31	4	1	11	.405	.348
Scott, Michael, Houston	.130	32	54	1	7	7	0	0	0	1	6	0	0	2	0	22	0	0	1	.130	.190
Scudder, W. Scott, Cincinnati	.056	21	18	1	1	1	0	0	0	0	6	0	0	2	0	6	0	0	0	.056	.150
Searage, Raymond, Los Angeles*	.000	29	2	0	0	0	0	0	0	0	1	0	0	0	0	2	0	0	0	.000	.000
Sharperson, Michael, Los Angeles	.297	129	357	42	106	133	14	2	3	36	8	3	1	46	6	39	15	6	5	.373	.376
Shelby, John, Los Angeles†	.250	25	24	2	6	7	1	0	0	2	0	0	0	0	0	7	0	0	0	.292	.250
Show, Eric, San Diego	.200	39	25	3	5	6	1	0	0	2	3	0	0	0	0	8	0	0	0	.240	.200
Simms, Michael, Houston	.308	12	13	3	4	8	1	0	1	2	0	0	0	1	0	4	0	0	0	.615	.308
Slaught, Donald, Pittsburgh	.300	84	230	27	69	105	18	3	4	29	3	4	3	27	2	27	0	1	2	.457	.375
Smiley, John, Pittsburgh*	.122	26	49	1	6	6	0	0	0	3	7	0	0	3	0	15	0	0	1	.122	.173
Smith, Bryn, St. Louis	.256	26	39	2	10	14	1	0	1	7	11	0	0	1	0	9	0	0	0	.359	.275
Smith, David, Houston	.000	49	2	0	0	0	0	0	0	0	0	0	0	0	0	0	0	0	0	.000	.000
Smith, J. Dwight, Chicago*	.262	117	290	34	76	109	15	3	6	27	1	2	0	28	2	46	11	6	7	.376	.329
Smith, Gregory, Chicago†	.205	18	44	9	9	13	2	1	0	5	0	1	0	3	0	5	1	1	0	.295	.234
Smith, Lee, St. Louis	.000	53	2	0	0	0	0	0	0	0	0	0	0	0	0	0	0	0	0	.000	.000
Smith, Lonnie, Atlanta	.305	135	466	72	142	214	27	2	9	42	1	6	6	58	3	69	10	10	8	.459	.384
Smith, Ozzie, St. Louis†	.254	143	512	61	130	156	21	1	1	50	7	10	2	61	4	33	32	6	1	.305	.330
Smith, Peter, Atlanta	.087	13	23	2	2	2	0	0	0	2	8	0	0	1	0	16	0	0	0	.087	.125
Smith, Zane, Mon.-Pitt.*	.162	34	68	7	11	12	1	0	0	4	7	0	0	1	0	16	0	0	1	.235	.174
Smoltz, John, Atlanta	.162	38	74	7	12	14	3	0	0	4	7	0	0	6	0	32	1	0	2	.189	.225

Player, Club	AVG	G	AB	R	H	TB	2B	3B	HR	RBI	SH	SF	HP	BB	IBB	SO	SB	CS	GI DP	SLG	OBP
Stephens, C. Ray, St. Louis*	.133	5	15	2	2	6	1	1	0	1	0	0	0	0	0	3	0	0	1	.400	.133
Stephenson, Phillip, San Diego*	.209	103	182	26	38	61	9	1	4	19	0	1	0	30	1	43	2	1	2	.335	.319
Strawberry, Darryl, New York*	.277	152	542	92	150	281	18	1	37	108	1	5	4	70	15	110	15	8	3	.518	.361
Stubbs, Franklin, Houston*	.261	146	448	59	117	213	23	0	23	71	1	0	2	48	3	114	19	6	5	.475	.334
Sutcliffe, Richard, Chicago*	.000	5	5	0	0	0	0	0	0	0	1	0	0	2	0	2	0	0	4	.000	.286
Swan, Russell, San Francisco*	.000	1	1	0	0	0	0	0	0	0	0	0	0	0	0	1	0	0	0	.000	.000
Tabler, Patrick, New York	.279	17	43	6	12	18	1	1	1	10	1	0	1	3	0	8	0	1	4	.419	.340
Templeton, Garry, San Diego†	.248	144	505	45	125	183	25	3	9	59	8	4	0	24	7	59	1	4	17	.362	.280
Terrell, C. Walter, Pittsburgh	.107	16	28	0	3	6	0	0	0	0	7	0	0	1	0	13	0	0	1	.107	.138
Terry, Scott, St. Louis	.455	50	11	1	5	6	1	0	0	0	5	0	0	0	0	3	0	0	0	.545	.455
Teufel, Timothy, New York	.246	80	175	28	43	84	11	0	10	24	1	1	0	28	1	33	0	0	5	.480	.304
Tewksbury, Robert, St. Louis	.171	28	41	2	7	8	1	0	0	2	9	0	0	0	0	18	0	0	1	.195	.244
Thomas, Andres, Atlanta	.219	84	278	26	61	84	8	1	5	30	1	1	5	4	1	43	2	1	10	.302	.248
Thompson, Milton, St. Louis*	.218	135	418	26	91	137	14	7	6	30	9	0	6	39	0	60	25	5	4	.328	.292
Thompson, Robert, San Francisco	.245	144	498	67	122	195	22	3	15	56	1	3	3	34	5	96	14	4	9	.392	.299
Thon, Richard, Philadelphia	.255	149	552	54	141	193	20	4	8	48	8	1	2	37	1	77	12	5	14	.350	.305
Thurmond, Mark, San Francisco*	.000	43	5	0	0	0	0	0	0	0	1	0	0	0	0	4	0	0	0	.000	.000
Tomlin, Randy, Pittsburgh*	.040	12	25	1	1	1	0	0	0	0	2	0	0	1	0	7	0	0	0	.080	.077
Torve, Kelvin, New York*	.289	20	38	0	11	15	4	0	0	2	0	0	2	4	0	9	0	0	1	.395	.386
Traxler, Brian, Los Angeles*	.091	9	11	0	1	2	1	0	0	2	0	0	0	0	0	4	0	0	0	.182	.091
Treadway, H. Jeffrey, Atlanta*	.283	128	474	56	134	191	20	2	11	59	5	4	3	25	1	42	3	4	10	.403	.320
Trevino, Alejandro, Hou.-N.Y.-Cin.	.221	58	86	3	19	27	2	0	2	13	1	3	3	7	0	11	0	0	2	.314	.293
Tudor, John, St. Louis*	.152	25	46	3	7	9	2	0	0	3	7	0	0	2	0	19	0	0	0	.196	.188
Uribe, Jose, San Francisco†	.248	138	415	35	103	126	8	6	0	24	4	0	2	29	13	49	5	9	8	.304	.297
Valdez, Rafael, San Diego	.000	3	1	0	0	0	0	0	0	0	0	0	0	0	0	0	0	0	0	.000	.000
Valenzuela, Fernando, Los Angeles*	.304	35	69	8	21	29	5	0	1	11	3	0	1	1	0	12	0	0	0	.420	.310
Van Slyke, Andrew, Pittsburgh*	.284	136	493	67	140	229	26	6	17	77	4	4	1	66	2	89	14	4	6	.465	.367
Varsho, Gary, Chicago*	.250	46	48	10	12	16	4	0	0	7	0	0	0	5	0	6	2	0	1	.333	.265
Vatcher, James, Phil.-Atl.	.260	57	73	7	19	26	2	1	1	7	1	0	2	4	1	15	0	0	3	.356	.308
Villanueva, Hector, Chicago	.272	52	114	14	31	58	5	1	7	18	0	0	0	4	2	27	1	0	1	.509	.308
Viola, Frank, New York*	.153	35	85	4	13	13	0	0	0	4	13	0	0	2	0	20	0	0	1	.153	.153
Vizcaino, Jose, Los Angeles†	.275	37	51	3	14	17	1	1	0	4	3	1	0	0	0	8	0	0	1	.333	.327
Walk, Robert, Pittsburgh	.162	26	37	3	6	7	1	0	0	2	10	0	0	1	0	13	0	0	0	.189	.205
Wallach, Timothy, Montreal*	.241	133	419	59	101	182	18	0	19	51	0	2	1	49	5	112	1	7	8	.434	.326
Walling, Dennis, St. Louis*	.296	161	626	69	185	295	37	5	21	98	3	7	0	42	11	80	6	9	12	.471	.339
Walton, Jerome, Chicago	.263	101	392	63	103	129	16	2	2	21	1	2	4	50	1	70	14	7	4	.329	.350
Wells, Terry, Los Angeles*	.000	5	7	0	0	0	0	0	0	0	1	0	0	0	0	4	0	0	0	.000	.000
Wetteland, John, Los Angeles	.143	22	7	2	1	4	0	0	1	3	1	0	0	0	0	1	0	0	0	.571	.143
Whitehurst, Walter, New York	.250	38	8	2	2	2	0	0	0	0	1	0	0	0	0	0	0	0	0	.250	.250
Whitson, Eddie, San Diego	.149	33	67	6	10	14	1	0	1	4	3	0	0	2	0	16	0	0	2	.209	.174
Whitt, L. Ernest, Atlanta*	.172	67	180	14	31	45	8	0	2	10	0	2	0	23	1	27	0	0	6	.250	.265
Wilkerson, Curtis, Chicago†	.220	77	186	21	41	48	5	1	0	16	3	1	0	7	0	36	2	1	2	.258	.249
Williams, Edward, San Diego	.286	14	42	5	12	24	3	0	3	9	0	0	0	5	0	6	0	2	0	.571	.362
Williams, Mitchell, Chicago*	.000	59	5	1	0	0	0	0	0	0	4	0	0	0	0	0	0	0	0	.000	.000
Williams, Matthew, San Francisco	.277	159	617	87	171	301	27	2	33	122	2	5	7	33	9	138	7	4	13	.488	.319
Wilson, Craig, St. Louis	.248	55	121	13	30	32	2	0	0	7	0	2	0	8	0	14	0	2	7	.264	.290

Player, Club	AVG	G	AB	R	H	TB	2B	3B	HR	RBI	SH	SF	HP	BB	IBB	SO	SB	CS	GI DP	SLG	OBP
Wilson, Glenn, Houston	.245	118	368	42	90	134	14	0	10	55	0	4	1	26	1	64	0	3	16	.364	.293
Wilson, Stephen, Chicago*	.162	45	37	3	6	7	1	0	0	0	5	0	0	3	0	11	0	0	0	.189	.225
Wilson, Trevor, San Francisco*	.138	27	29	2	4	4	0	0	0	0	5	0	0	2	0	10	0	0	0	.138	.194
Winningham, Herman, Cincinnati*	.256	84	160	20	41	68	8	5	3	17	2	1	0	14	2	31	6	4	0	.425	.314
Wrona, Rick, Chicago	.172	16	29	3	5	5	0	0	0	0	1	0	1	2	1	11	1	0	0	.172	.226
Wynne, Marvell, Chicago*	.204	92	186	21	38	62	8	2	4	19	1	0	0	14	3	25	3	2	4	.333	.264
Yelding, Eric, Houston	.254	142	511	69	130	152	9	5	1	28	4	5	0	39	1	87	64	25	11	.297	.305
York, Michael, Pittsburgh	.333	4	3	1	1	1	0	0	0	0	1	0	0	0	0	1	0	0	0	.333	.333
Young, Gerald, Houston†	.175	57	154	15	27	36	4	1	1	4	4	1	0	20	0	23	6	3	3	.234	.269
Zeile, Todd, St. Louis	.244	144	495	62	121	197	25	3	15	57	0	6	2	67	3	77	2	4	11	.398	.333

AWARDED FIRST BASE ON CATCHER'S INTERFERENCE—Reynolds, Pitt.3 (Daulton, Goff, O'Brien); Van Slyke, Pitt. 2 (Berryhill, Scioscia); Kingery, S.F. (Reed); Walton, Chi. (Fitzgerald); Wilson, Hou. (Zeile).

PLAYERS WITH TWO OR MORE CLUBS DURING 1990 SEASON

Player, Club	AVG	G	AB	R	H	TB	2B	3B	HR	RBI	SH	SF	HP	BB	IBB	SO	SB	CS	GI DP	SLG	OBP
Alou, Moises, Pittsburgh	.200	2	5	0	1	1	0	0	0	0	0	0	0	0	0	3	0	0	1	.200	.200
Alou, Moises, Montreal	.200	14	15	4	3	5	1	0	0	0	1	0	0	0	0	0	0	0	0	.333	.200
Boever, Joseph, Atlanta	.000	33	2	0	0	0	0	0	0	0	0	0	0	0	0	0	0	0	0	.000	.000
Boever, Joseph, Philadelphia	.000	34	1	0	0	0	0	0	0	0	4	0	0	0	0	0	0	0	0	.000	.000
Cook, Dennis, Philadelphia*	.310	43	42	6	13	16	0	0	1	4	4	0	0	0	0	4	0	0	2	.381	.310
Cook, Dennis, Los Angeles*	.286	5	7	2	2	3	1	0	0	0	0	0	0	0	0	0	0	0	1	.429	.286
Costello, John, St. Louis	.000	4	2	0	0	0	0	0	0	0	0	0	0	0	0	0	0	0	0	.000	.000
Costello, John, Montreal	.000	5	0	0	0	0	0	0	0	0	0	0	0	0	0	0	0	0	0	.000	.000
Doran, William, Houston†	.288	109	344	49	99	142	21	0	6	32	0	5	0	71	1	53	18	9	2	.413	.405
Doran, William, Cincinnati†	.373	17	59	10	22	33	8	0	1	5	1	0	0	8	1	5	5	0	1	.559	.448
Fletcher, Darren, Los Angeles*	.000	2	1	0	0	0	0	0	0	0	0	0	0	0	0	1	0	0	0	.000	.000
Fletcher, Darren, Philadelphia*	.136	9	22	3	3	4	1	0	0	5	0	0	0	0	0	5	0	0	0	.182	.174
Freeman, Marvin, Philadelphia	.000	16	7	0	0	0	0	0	0	0	0	2	0	0	1	0	6	0	0	.000	.000
Freeman, Marvin, Atlanta	.000	9	0	0	0	0	0	0	0	0	0	0	0	0	0	0	0	0	0	.000	.000
Grant, Mark, San Diego	.500	26	2	0	1	1	0	0	0	0	0	0	0	0	0	2	0	0	0	.500	.500
Grant, Mark, Atlanta	.250	33	4	1	1	1	0	0	0	0	1	0	0	0	0	0	0	0	0	.250	.500
Greene, I. Thomas, Atlanta	.000	5	1	0	0	0	0	0	0	0	0	0	0	0	0	1	0	0	0	.000	.500
Greene, I. Thomas, Philadelphia	.182	10	11	2	2	3	1	0	0	0	2	0	0	0	0	1	0	0	0	.273	.182
Hammaker, C. Atlee, San Francisco†	.059	25	17	2	1	1	0	0	0	0	1	0	0	1	0	5	0	0	0	.059	.111
Hammaker, C. Atlee, San Diego†	.500	9	2	0	1	1	0	0	0	0	0	0	0	0	0	0	0	0	0	.500	.500
Herr, Thomas, Philadelphia†	.264	119	447	39	118	157	21	3	4	50	6	2	2	36	4	47	7	1	10	.351	.320
Herr, Thomas, New York†	.250	27	100	9	25	33	5	0	1	10	2	2	2	14	0	11	0	0	1	.330	.342
Hesketh, Joseph, Montreal*	.000	2	1	0	0	0	0	0	0	0	0	0	0	0	0	1	0	0	0	.000	.000
Hesketh, Joseph, Atlanta*	.000	31	1	0	0	0	0	0	0	0	0	0	0	0	0	0	0	0	0	.000	.000
Hudler, Rex, Montreal	.333	4	3	1	1	1	0	0	0	0	0	0	0	0	0	1	0	0	0	.333	.333
Hudler, Rex, St. Louis	.281	89	217	30	61	97	11	2	7	22	2	0	1	12	0	31	18	10	3	.447	.323
Kramer, Randall, Pittsburgh	.000	12	5	0	0	0	0	0	0	0	2	0	0	0	0	2	0	0	0	.000	.000
Kramer, Randall, Chicago	.000	10	1	0	0	0	0	0	0	0	1	0	0	0	0	0	0	0	0	.000	.000
Lilliquist, Derek, Atlanta*	.348	13	23	3	8	14	0	0	2	3	0	0	0	0	0	4	0	0	2	.609	.348

Player, Club	AVG	G	AB	R	H	TB	2B	3B	HR	RBI	SH	SF	HP	BB	IBB	SO	SB	CS	GI DP	SLG	OBP
Lilliquist, Derek, San Diego*	.150	16	20	3	3	3	0	0	0	0	2	0	0	1	0	4	0	0	1	.150	.190
Lyons, Barry, New York	.238	24	80	8	19	25	0	0	2	7	0	0	1	2	0	9	0	0	2	.313	.265
Lyons, Barry, Los Angeles	.200	3	5	1	1	4	0	0	1	2	0	0	0	0	0	1	0	0	0	.800	.200
Martinez, Carmelo, Philadelphia	.242	71	198	23	48	80	8	0	8	31	0	0	0	29	0	37	2	1	3	.404	.339
Martinez, Carmelo, Pittsburgh	.211	12	19	3	4	11	1	0	2	4	0	0	0	1	0	5	0	0	0	.579	.250
McClendon, Lloyd, Chicago	.159	49	107	5	17	23	3	0	1	10	0	1	0	14	2	21	1	0	2	.215	.254
McClendon, Lloyd, Pittsburgh	.333	4	3	1	1	4	0	0	1	2	0	0	0	0	0	1	0	0	0	1.333	.333
McGriff, Terence, Cincinnati	.000	2	4	0	0	0	0	0	0	0	0	0	0	0	0	1	0	0	0	.000	.000
McGriff, Terence, Houston	.000	4	5	0	0	0	0	0	0	0	0	0	0	0	0	0	0	0	0	.000	.000
Meadows, Michael, Houston*	.143	15	14	1	2	2	0	0	0	0	0	0	0	2	0	4	0	0	0	.143	.250
Meadows, Michael, Philadelphia*	.071	15	14	1	1	1	0	0	0	0	0	0	0	1	0	2	0	0	0	.071	.133
Mercado, Orlando, New York	.211	42	90	10	19	29	1	0	3	7	0	0	2	8	3	11	0	0	4	.322	.290
Mercado, Orlando, Montreal	.250	8	8	0	2	2	1	0	0	0	0	0	0	0	0	1	0	0	0	.250	.250
Murphy, Dale, Atlanta	.232	97	349	38	81	146	14	0	17	55	0	3	1	41	11	84	9	2	11	.418	.312
Murphy, Dale, Philadelphia	.266	57	214	22	57	89	9	1	7	28	0	1	0	20	3	46	0	1	11	.416	.328
Parrett, Jeffrey, Philadelphia	.000	47	10	0	0	0	0	0	0	1	2	0	0	0	0	4	0	0	0	.000	.000
Parrett, Jeffrey, Atlanta	1.000	20	1	0	1	1	0	0	0	0	0	0	0	0	0	0	0	0	0	1.000	1.000
Roomes, Rolando, Cincinnati	.213	30	61	5	13	19	0	1	0	7	0	0	0	1	0	20	2	0	2	.311	.213
Roomes, Rolando, Montreal	.286	16	7	1	2	6	1	0	0	0	0	0	0	0	0	6	0	0	0	.429	.333
Ruskin, Scott, Pittsburgh	.333	44	6	1	2	5	0	1	0	1	0	0	0	0	0	4	0	0	0	.833	.333
Ruskin, Scott, Montreal	.000	23	2	0	0	0	0	0	0	0	0	0	0	1	0	1	0	0	0	.000	.000
Schatzeder, Daniel, Houston*	.250	45	4	0	1	1	0	0	0	0	0	0	0	0	0	2	0	0	0	.250	.250
Schatzeder, Daniel, New York*	.000	6	1	0	0	0	0	0	0	0	0	0	0	0	0	0	0	0	0	.000	.000
Smith, Zane, Montreal*	.175	23	40	1	7	10	2	0	0	2	7	0	2	0	0	9	0	0	0	.250	.175
Smith, Zane, Pittsburgh*	.143	11	28	1	4	6	2	0	0	0	1	0	0	1	0	7	0	0	1	.214	.172
Trevino, Alejandro, Houston	.188	42	69	3	13	19	3	0	1	10	1	1	2	6	1	11	0	1	2	.275	.266
Trevino, Alejandro, New York	.300	9	10	0	3	4	1	0	0	2	0	2	1	1	0	0	0	0	0	.400	.333
Trevino, Alejandro, Cincinnati	.429	7	7	0	3	4	1	0	0	1	0	0	0	0	0	0	0	0	0	.571	.500
Vatcher, James, Philadelphia	.261	36	46	5	12	16	1	0	1	4	0	1	0	4	0	6	0	0	1	.348	.320
Vatcher, James, Atlanta	.259	21	27	2	7	10	1	1	0	3	0	0	0	1	0	9	0	0	0	.370	.286

OFFICIAL NATIONAL LEAGUE FIELDING AVERAGES
CLUB FIELDING

Club	PCT	G	PO	A	E	TC	DP	TP	PB
Cincinnati	.983	162	4369	1690	102	6161	126	0	19
San Francisco	.983	162	4339	1825	107	6271	148	0	11
Montreal	.982	162	4420	1648	110	6178	134	0	21
Philadelphia	.981	162	4347	1739	117	6203	150	0	8
Chicago	.980	162	4328	1756	124	6208	136	0	24
St. Louis	.979	162	4330	1734	130	6194	114	0	11
Los Angeles	.979	162	4326	1612	130	6068	123	0	10
Pittsburgh	.979	162	4341	1777	134	6252	125	0	9
Houston	.978	162	4350	1602	131	6083	124	1	18
New York	.978	162	4320	1565	132	6017	107	0	20
San Diego	.977	162	4385	1668	141	6194	141	0	9
Atlanta	.974	162	4289	1735	158	6182	133	0	15
Totals	.980	972	52144	20351	1516	74011	1561	1	175

INDIVIDUAL FIELDING
(*Throws Lefthanded)
FIRST BASEMEN

Leader, Club	PCT	G	PO	A	E	TC	DP
MAGADAN, N.Y.	.998	113	830	71	2	903	52

Player, Club	PCT	G	PO	A	E	TC	DP
Aldrete, Mon.*	1.000	18	109	8	0	117	16
Anderson, S.F.	1.000	3	9	0	0	9	2
Bell, Atl.*	.981	24	97	9	2	108	6
Benzinger, Cin.	.992	95	707	52	6	765	58
Bonilla, Pit.	1.000	3	16	1	0	17	0
Bream, Pit.*	.993	142	971	104	8	1083	80
Brewer, St.L.*	.981	9	46	6	1	53	5
Cabrera, Atl.	.990	48	264	19	3	286	15
G. Carter, S.F.	1.000	3	25	0	0	25	3
J. Carter, S.D.	.948	14	107	3	6	116	15
Ja. Clark, S.D.	.994	109	855	69	6	930	72
Je. Clark, S.D.	1.000	15	76	6	0	82	3
W. Clark, S.F.*	.992	153	1456	119	12	1587	118
Collins, St.L.*	1.000	49	80	0	0	80	5
G. Davis, Hou.	.995	91	796	55	4	855	56
J. Davis, Atl.	1.000	6	45	5	0	50	4
Esasky, Atl.	.944	9	79	5	5	89	7
Foley, Mon.	.000	1	0	0	0	0	0
Galarraga, Mon.	.993	154	1300	94	10	1404	93
Goff, Mon.	1.000	3	19	0	0	19	1
Gonzalez, Hou.	1.000	2	17	0	0	17	0
Grace, Chi.*	.992	153	1324	180	12	1516	116
Gregg, Atl.*	.987	50	334	34	5	373	31
Griffey, Cin.*	.979	9	42	4	1	47	2
Guerrero, St.L.	.989	132	1083	73	13	1169	74
Hatcher, L.A.	1.000	25	73	7	0	80	9
Hayes, Phi.	1.000	4	28	2	0	30	0
Hollins, Phi.	1.000	1	8	1	0	9	0
Hudler, St.L.	1.000	6	54	4	0	58	6
Johnson, Mon.	1.000	7	39	0	0	39	7
Jordan, Phi.	.995	84	743	37	4	784	65
Justice, Atl.*	.981	69	488	38	10	536	43
King, Pit.	1.000	1	3	0	0	3	0
Kruk, Phi.*	.996	61	402	43	2	447	34
Laga, S.F.*	1.000	10	33	5	0	38	4

Player, Club	PCT	G	PO	A	E	TC	DP
Leach, S.F.*	1.000	7	37	2	0	39	4
Lee, Cin.	1.000	6	28	3	0	31	1
Lopez, L.A.	1.000	1	4	0	0	4	1
Magadan, N.Y.	.998	113	830	71	2	903	52
Marshall, N.Y.	.993	42	277	24	2	303	19
Martinez, Phi.-Pit.	.995	48	340	28	2	370	35
McClendon, Pit.	1.000	8	58	7	0	65	5
Morris, Cin.*	.995	80	589	53	3	645	50
Murray, L.A.	.992	150	1180	113	10	1303	88
Nichols, Hou.	.920	3	22	1	2	25	1
Oberkfell, Hou.	.987	11	69	7	1	77	7
O'Malley, N.Y.	.938	3	15	0	1	16	0
Pagnozzi, St.L.	1.000	2	11	0	0	11	0
Presley, Atl.	.989	17	77	11	1	89	10
Puhl, Hou.	1.000	1	1	0	0	1	0
Quinones, Cin.	1.000	1	2	0	0	2	0
Redus, Pit.	.988	72	447	35	6	488	29
Sasser, N.Y.	1.000	1	3	0	0	3	0
Sharperson, L.A.	.983	6	55	2	1	58	5
Simms, Hou.	1.000	6	20	1	0	21	2
Stephenson, S.D.*	.997	60	345	36	1	382	33
Stubbs, Hou.*	.991	72	497	42	5	544	42
Teufel, N.Y.	.991	24	106	9	1	116	11
Torve, N.Y.*	1.000	9	65	0	0	65	6
Traxler, L.A.*	1.000	3	6	2	0	8	0
Trevino, Cin.	.938	1	14	1	1	16	0
Villanueva, Chi.	.985	14	62	4	1	67	4
Walling, St.L.	1.000	15	86	6	0	92	4
C. Wilson, St.L.	1.000	1	1	0	0	1	0
G. Wilson, Hou.	1.000	1	2	0	0	2	0
Zeile, St.L.	.991	11	104	8	1	113	7

TRIPLE PLAY: Simms, Hou

FIRST BASEMEN WITH TWO OR MORE CLUBS

Player, Club	PCT	G	PO	A	E	TC	DP
Martinez, Phi.	.994	43	318	24	2	344	31
Martinez, Pit.	1.000	5	22	4	0	26	4

SECOND BASEMEN

Leader, Club	PCT	G	PO	A	E	TC	DP
OQUENDO, St.L.	.996	150	285	393	3	681	65

Player, Club	PCT	G	PO	A	E	TC	DP
Alomar, S.D.	.976	137	311	392	17	720	73
Anderson, S.F.	.964	13	7	20	1	28	3
Backman, Pit.	1.000	15	22	32	0	54	5
Bates, Cin.	1.000	1	0	1	0	1	0
Belliard, Pit.	1.000	21	23	16	0	39	5
Blauser, Atl.	1.000	14	23	25	0	48	6
Booker, Phi.	.975	23	17	22	1	40	4
Candaele, Hou.	.989	49	75	107	2	184	18
Cora, S.D.	.938	15	43	32	5	80	12
DeShields, Mon.	.981	128	236	371	12	619	65
Diaz, N.Y.	.000	1	0	0	0	0	0

Player, Club	PCT	G	PO	A	E	TC	DP
Doran, Hou.-Cin.	.988	111	198	302	6	506	49
Duncan, Cin.	.973	115	245	287	15	547	51
Faries, S.D.	1.000	7	20	18	0	38	3
Foley, Mon.	.940	20	18	29	3	50	4
Harris, L.A.	.985	44	62	70	2	134	13
Hayes, Phi.	1.000	1	2	3	0	5	1
Herr, Phi.-N.Y.	.989	140	275	349	7	631	94
Hudler, St.L.	.946	10	9	26	2	37	3
Infante, Atl.	.964	10	14	13	1	28	3
Jefferies, N.Y.	.976	118	219	278	12	509	49
Jones, St.L.	.977	19	15	28	1	44	3
Lemke, Atl.	.985	44	70	121	3	194	22
Lind, Pit.	.991	152	330	449	7	786	74
Litton, S.F.	1.000	18	19	25	0	44	7

SECOND BASEMEN—Continued

Player, Club	PCT	G	PO	A	E	TC	DP
Miller, N.Y.	.972	11	19	16	1	36	5
Morandini, Phi.	.990	25	37	61	1	99	10
Noboa, Mon.	1.000	31	31	45	0	76	9
Oberkfell, Hou.	1.000	11	12	14	0	26	6
Oester, Cin.	.982	50	80	88	3	171	14
Oquendo, St.L.	.996	150	285	393	3	681	65
Paredes, Mon.	.889	2	1	7	1	9	2
Parker, S.F.	.000	2	0	0	0	0	0
Pena, St.L.	.982	11	24	30	1	55	7
Perezchica, S.F.	1.000	2	2	0	0	2	0
Quinones, Cin.	.964	13	22	31	2	55	12
Ramos, Chi.	.000	1	0	0	0	0	0
Randolph, L.A.	.969	26	50	73	4	127	10
Ready, Phi.	.985	28	46	84	2	132	18
Riles, S.F.	.974	24	28	48	2	78	6
Roberts, S.D.	.921	8	10	25	3	38	6
Rohde, Hou.	1.000	32	27	63	0	90	11
Rosario, Atl.	.000	1	0	0	0	0	0
Samuel, L.A.	.972	108	194	258	13	465	47
Sandberg, Chi.	.989	154	278	469	8	755	81
Sharperson, L.A.	.957	9	10	12	1	23	1
Smith, Chi.	1.000	7	10	17	0	27	3
Teufel, N.Y.	.970	24	29	35	2	66	5
Thompson, S.F.	.989	142	287	441	8	736	94
Treadway, Atl.	.976	122	241	360	15	616	72
Vizcaino, L.A.	1.000	6	4	3	0	7	1
Wilkerson, Chi.	.946	14	24	29	3	56	3
Wilson, St.L.	1.000	9	5	8	0	13	3
Yelding, Hou.	.953	10	21	20	2	43	3

TRIPLE PLAY: Rohde, Hou.

SECOND BASEMEN WITH TWO OR MORE CLUBS

Player, Club	PCT	G	PO	A	E	TC	DP
Doran, Hou.	.989	99	170	265	5	440	43
Doran, Cin.	.985	12	28	37	1	66	6
Herr, Phi.	.991	114	240	290	5	535	79
Herr, N.Y.	.979	26	35	59	2	96	15

THIRD BASEMEN

Leader, Club	PCT	G	PO	A	E	TC	DP
SABO, Cin.	.966	146	70	273	12	355	17

Player, Club	PCT	G	PO	A	E	TC	DP
Anderson, SF	1.000	2	0	1	0	1	0
Backman, Pit.	.920	71	34	104	12	150	5
Belliard, Pit.	1.000	5	3	3	0	6	0
Blauser, Atl.	1.000	9	5	6	0	11	1
Bonilla, Pit.	.923	14	10	26	3	39	1
Booker, Phi.	.909	10	5	5	1	11	0
Caminiti, Hou.	.945	149	118	243	21	382	22
Candaele, Hou.	1.000	1	0	1	0	1	0
Doran, Cin.	.667	4	0	4	2	6	0
Faries, S.D.	.875	1	1	6	1	8	1
Foley, Mon.	1.000	7	0	5	0	5	0
Goff, Mon.	.833	3	1	4	1	6	0
Gonzalez, Hou.	1.000	4	5	10	0	15	1
Hamilton, L.A.	1.000	7	3	12	0	15	2
Hansen, L.A.	.500	2	0	1	1	2	0
Harris, L.A.	.959	94	77	133	9	219	11
Hatcher, L.A.	.813	10	3	10	3	16	0
Hayes, Phi.	.957	146	121	324	20	465	30
Hollins, Phi.	.932	30	19	36	4	59	0
Hudler, St.L.	.929	6	5	8	1	14	0
Infante, Atl.	1.000	4	0	3	0	3	0
Jefferies, N.Y.	.956	34	23	63	4	90	5
Johnson, N.Y.	.913	92	52	159	20	231	11
Jones, St.L.	1.000	6	0	3	0	3	0
King, Pit.	.938	115	58	215	18	291	15
Lemke, Atl.	.989	45	20	71	1	92	7
Litton, S.F.	1.000	5	2	3	0	5	0
Magadan, N.Y.	.972	19	7	28	1	36	1
Noboa, Mon.	.714	8	3	2	2	7	0
Oberkfell, Hou.	.935	24	12	31	3	46	3
Oester, Cin.	.667	3	0	2	1	3	0
Olson, Atl.	.000	1	0	0	0	0	0
O'Malley, N.Y.	.983	38	26	33	1	60	4
Pagliarulo, S.D.	.955	116	79	200	13	292	16
Parker, S.F.	.500	1	1	0	1	2	0
Pendleton, St.L.	.947	117	91	248	19	358	18
Presley, Atl.	.930	133	101	231	25	357	19
Quinones, Cin.	.981	22	12	41	1	54	0
Ramos, Chi.	.932	66	23	46	5	74	2
Riles, S.F.	1.000	10	4	8	0	12	0
Roberts, S.D.	.953	56	34	89	6	129	7
Rohde, Hou.	1.000	4	0	5	0	5	0
Sabo, Cin.	.966	146	70	273	12	355	17
Salazar, Chi.	.950	91	55	136	10	201	12
Sharperson, L.A.	.949	106	70	153	12	235	10
Teufel, N.Y.	.952	10	6	14	1	21	0
Thomas, Atl.	1.000	5	1	7	0	8	2
Wallach, Mon.	.954	161	128	309	21	458	23
Walling, St.L.	1.000	11	6	19	0	25	1
Wilkerson, Chi.	.888	52	25	62	11	98	4
E. Williams, S.D.	.897	13	5	21	3	29	2
M. Williams, S.F.	.959	159	140	306	19	465	33
Wilson, St.L.	.971	13	13	20	1	34	1
Yelding, Hou.	.667	3	0	2	1	3	0
Zeile, St.L.	.883	24	11	42	7	60	2

TRIPLE PLAY: Caminiti, Hou.

SHORTSTOPS

Leader, Club	PCT	G	PO	A	E	TC	DP
OWEN, Mon.	.989	148	216	340	6	562	52

Player, Club	PCT	G	PO	A	E	TC	DP
Alomar, S.D.	.895	5	5	12	2	19	4
Anderson, S.F.	1.000	29	17	38	0	55	5
Baez, N.Y.	1.000	4	5	7	0	12	1
Bell, Pit.	.970	159	260	459	22	741	85
Belliard, Pit.	.933	10	11	17	2	30	3
Benjamin, S.F.	.988	21	29	53	1	83	10
Blauser, Atl.	.961	93	141	257	16	414	47
Booker, Phi.	.976	27	35	47	2	84	11
Candaele, Hou.	.944	13	6	11	1	18	2
Cedeno, Hou.	.833	3	3	2	1	6	0
Cora, S.D.	.833	21	13	17	6	36	3
Diaz, N.Y.	.958	10	5	18	1	24	1
Duncan, Cin.	.914	12	16	16	3	35	4
Dunston, Chi.	.970	144	255	392	20	667	77
Elster, N.Y.	.960	92	159	251	17	427	42
Faries, S.D.	.909	4	0	10	1	11	4
Foley, Mon.	.987	45	62	89	2	153	22
Garcia, Pit.	1.000	3	0	4	0	4	1
Griffin, L.A.	.959	139	221	382	26	629	63
Harris, L.A.	1.000	1	0	2	0	2	0
Hudler, St.L.	1.000	1	1	1	0	2	0
Infante, Atl.	.941	3	8	8	1	17	1
Johnson, N.Y.	.972	73	98	176	8	282	28
Jones, St.L.	.944	29	28	74	6	108	12
Larkin, Cin.	.977	156	254	469	17	740	86
Lemke, Atl.	1.000	1	0	1	0	1	0
Litton, S.F.	1.000	7	9	9	0	18	2
Miller, N.Y.	1.000	4	3	4	0	7	2
Nixon, Mon.	1.000	1	0	1	0	1	1
Noboa, Mon.	1.000	7	4	4	0	8	1
Offerman, L.A.	.946	27	30	40	4	74	5
Oquendo, St.L.	.950	4	9	10	1	20	2
Owen, Mon.	.989	148	216	340	6	562	52
Parker, S.F.	1.000	1	0	2	0	2	0
Perezchica, S.F.	.000	2	0	0	0	0	0
Quinones, Cin.	.875	9	8	13	3	24	3
Ramirez, Hou.	.953	129	190	321	25	536	57

SHORTSTOPS —Continued

Player, Club	PCT	G	PO	A	E	TC	DP	Player, Club	PCT	G	PO	A	E	TC	DP
Ramos, Chi.	.949	21	39	54	5	98	17	O. Smith, St.L.	.980	140	212	378	12	602	66
Riles, S.F.	.986	26	21	49	1	71	8	Templeton, S.D.	.957	135	214	367	26	607	74
Roberts, S.D.	.984	18	23	38	1	62	8	Thomas, Atl.	.967	72	103	193	10	306	41
Rohde, Hou.	1.000	2	1	2	0	3	0	Thon, Phi.	.964	148	222	439	25	686	86
Rosario, Atl.	1.000	3	3	4	0	7	0	Uribe, S.F.	.965	134	182	373	20	575	73
Santana, S.F.	1.000	3	2	1	0	3	1	Vizcaino, L.A.	.956	11	19	24	2	45	5
Sharperson, L.A.	.977	15	17	26	1	44	7	Wilkerson, Chi.	1.000	1	0	2	0	2	0
G. Smith, Chi.	.912	7	10	21	3	34	5	Yelding, Hou.	.958	40	64	97	7	168	16

OUTFIELDERS

Leader, Club	PCT	G	PO	A	E	TC	DP	Player, Club	PCT	G	PO	A	E	TC	DP
B. HATCHER, Cin.	.997	131	308	10	1	319	2	Komminsk, S.F.	1.000	7	3	0	0	3	0
								Kruk, Phi.*	.986	87	141	2	2	145	0
Player, Club								Lancaster, Chi.	.000	1	0	0	0	0	0
Abner, S.D.	.991	62	108	1	1	110	0	Lankford, St.L.*	.989	35	92	1	1	94	0
Aldrete, Mon.*	.982	38	51	4	1	56	0	Leach, S.F.*	.989	52	86	3	1	90	0
Alou, Pit.-Mon.	1.000	7	9	1	0	10	0	Leonard, S.F.	1.000	7	10	0	0	10	0
Anthony, Hou.*	.970	71	124	5	4	133	0	Litton, S.F.	.985	56	60	6	1	67	1
Baldwin, Hou.*	1.000	3	1	0	0	1	0	Lynn, S.D.*	1.000	55	92	1	0	93	0
Bass, S.F.	.968	55	88	2	3	93	0	Marshall, N.Y.	.000	1	0	0	0	0	0
Benzinger, Cin.	1.000	10	26	0	0	26	0	C. M'tinez, Phi-Pit.	1.000	22	34	1	0	35	0
Berroa, Atl.	1.000	3	1	0	0	1	0	D. Martinez, Mon.*	.989	108	257	6	3	266	1
Biggio, Hou.	.967	50	111	6	4	121	0	May, Chi.	.972	17	34	1	1	36	0
Blauser, Atl.	.000	1	0	0	0	0	0	McCl'ndon, Chi-Pit.	.980	24	49	0	1	50	0
Bonds, Pit.*	.983	150	338	14	6	358	2	McDowell, Atl.*	.971	72	134	2	4	140	0
Bonilla, Pit.	.961	149	289	8	12	309	1	McGee, St.L.	.957	124	341	13	16	370	4
Boston, N.Y.*	.986	109	203	3	3	209	1	McReynolds, N.Y.	.988	144	237	14	3	254	2
Braggs, Cin.	.968	60	110	10	4	124	3	Meadows, Hou-Pit*	1.000	13	8	0	0	8	0
Brooks, L.A.	.964	150	255	9	10	274	2	Merced, Pit.	.000	1	0	0	0	0	0
Brunansky, St.L.	.950	17	37	1	2	40	1	Miller, N.Y.	.980	61	146	1	3	150	1
Butler, S.F.*	.986	159	420	4	6	430	0	Mitchell, S.F.	.971	138	295	9	9	313	3
Campusano, Phi.	.976	47	40	1	1	42	0	H. Morris, Cin.*	.857	6	6	0	1	7	0
Candaele, Hou.	1.000	58	66	1	0	67	0	J. Morris, St.L.*	1.000	6	4	0	0	4	0
Cangelosi, Pit.*	1.000	12	24	0	0	24	0	Murphy, Atl.-Phi.	.985	152	321	7	5	333	1
Carr, N.Y.	.000	1	0	0	0	0	0	Nichols, Hou.	.000	1	0	0	0	0	0
Carreon, N.Y.*	1.000	60	87	1	0	88	0	Nixon, Mon.	.994	88	149	5	1	155	0
J. Carter, S.D.	.988	150	385	13	5	403	4	Noboa, Mon.	1.000	9	9	1	0	10	0
S. Carter, Pit.	1.000	3	4	0	0	4	0	O'Neill, Cin.*	.993	141	271	12	2	285	0
Chamberlain, Phi.	.958	10	23	0	1	24	0	Ortiz, Hou.	.978	25	44	1	1	46	0
D. Clark, Chi.	1.000	39	60	2	0	62	0	Parker, S.F.	.978	35	44	1	1	46	0
Je. Clark, S.D.	.963	13	26	0	1	27	0	Puhl, Hou.	1.000	8	8	0	0	8	0
Coleman, St.L.	.981	120	244	12	5	261	2	Raines, Mon.	.976	123	239	3	6	248	1
Collins, St.L.*	.900	12	9	0	1	10	0	Ready, Phi.	1.000	30	32	2	0	34	0
Daniels, L.A.	.987	127	207	13	3	223	2	Redus, Pit.	.882	7	14	1	2	17	0
Dascenzo, Chi.*	1.000	107	174	2	0	176	1	Reed, N.Y.	.955	14	20	1	1	22	0
Davidson, Hou.	.981	51	103	1	2	106	0	Reynolds, Pit.	.972	59	102	3	3	108	0
Davis, Cin.	.993	122	257	11	2	270	1	Rhodes, Hou.*	.955	30	61	2	3	66	0
Dawson, Chi.	.981	139	250	10	5	265	4	Roberts, S.D.	.982	75	160	8	3	171	1
Duncan, Cin.	1.000	1	4	0	0	4	0	Roomes, Cin.-Mon.	1.000	25	39	1	0	40	0
Dykstra, Phi.*	.987	149	439	7	6	452	5	Ryal, Pit.*	1.000	4	4	0	0	4	0
Fitzgerald, Mon.	1.000	6	5	1	0	6	0	Salazar, Chi.	.955	28	41	1	2	44	0
Ford, Phi.	1.000	3	2	0	0	2	0	Samuel, L.A.	.965	31	79	4	3	86	0
Gant, Atl.	.978	146	357	7	8	372	2	Shelby, L.A.	1.000	12	8	0	0	8	0
Gibson, L.A.*	.995	81	191	4	1	196	1	D. Smith, Chi.	.986	81	139	4	2	145	2
Gilkey, St.L.	.961	18	47	2	2	51	0	L. Smith, Atl.	.956	122	254	6	12	272	2
Gonzalez, L.A.	1.000	81	62	1	0	63	0	Strawberry, N.Y.*	.989	149	268	10	3	281	4
Gregg, Atl.*	.957	20	22	0	1	23	0	Stubbs, Hou.*	.991	71	112	1	1	114	0
Griffey, Cin.*	1.000	6	12	0	0	12	0	Tabler, N.Y.	1.000	10	20	1	0	21	1
Grissom, Mon.	.988	87	165	5	2	172	0	Thompson, St.L.	.971	116	232	4	7	243	0
C. Gwynn, L.A.*	1.000	44	39	1	0	40	0	Thornton, N.Y.	1.000	2	1	0	0	1	0
T. Gwynn, S.D.*	.985	141	327	11	5	343	2	Torve, N.Y.*	.000	1	0	0	0	0	0
Harris, L.A.	1.000	2	1	0	0	1	0	Van Slyke, Pit.	.976	133	326	6	8	340	0
B. Hatcher, Cin.	.997	131	308	10	1	319	2	Varsho, Chi.	1.000	3	2	0	0	2	0
M. Hatcher, L.A.	1.000	10	10	0	0	10	0	Vatcher, Phi.-Atl.	1.000	30	27	0	0	27	0
Hayes, Phi.	.979	127	272	8	6	286	0	Walker, Mon.	.985	124	249	12	4	265	5
Howard, S.D.	.950	13	19	0	1	20	0	Walling, St.L.	1.000	8	11	1	0	12	0
Hudler, St.L.	.979	45	89	3	2	94	0	Walton, Chi.	.977	98	247	3	6	256	0
Hughes, N.Y.*	1.000	5	5	0	0	5	0	Wilkerson, Chi.	.000	1	0	0	0	0	0
Jackson, S.D.	.985	39	63	1	1	65	1	C. Wilson, St.L.	1.000	13	26	2	0	28	1
Javier, L.A.	1.000	87	204	2	0	206	1	G. Wilson, Hou.	.975	108	225	12	6	243	6
Jelic, N.Y.	1.000	4	1	0	0	1	0	Winningham, Cin.	1.000	64	89	3	0	92	0
Jones, Phi.	1.000	16	25	1	0	26	0	Wynne, Chi.*	.991	66	108	3	1	112	2
Jose, St.L.	1.000	23	42	0	0	42	0	Yelding, Hou.	.971	94	230	5	7	242	2
Justice, Atl.*	.968	61	116	4	4	124	1	Young, Hou.	.990	50	99	4	1	104	1
Kingery, S.F.*	.978	95	126	7	3	136	2	Zeile, St.L.	.000	1	0	0	0	0	0

OUTFIELDERS WITH TWO OR MORE CLUBS

Player, Club	PCT	G	PO	A	E	TC	DP	Player, Club	PCT	G	PO	A	E	TC	DP
Alou, Pit.	1.000	2	3	0	0	3	0	Meadows, Phi.*	1.000	4	1	0	0	1	0
Alou, Mon.	1.000	5	6	1	0	7	0	Murphy, Atl.	.981	97	208	3	4	215	0
Martinez, Phi.	1.000	20	32	1	0	33	0	Murphy, Phi.	.992	55	113	4	1	118	1
Martinez, Pit.	1.000	2	2	0	0	2	0	Roomes, Cin.	1.000	19	33	1	0	34	0
McClendon, Chi.	.980	23	49	0	1	50	0	Roomes, Mon.	1.000	6	6	0	0	6	0
McClendon, Pit.	.000	1	0	0	0	0	0	Vatcher, Phi.	1.000	24	20	0	0	20	0
Meadows, Hou.*	1.000	9	7	0	0	7	0	Vatcher, Atl.	1.000	6	7	0	0	7	0

CATCHERS

Leader, Club	PCT	G	PO	A	E	TC	DP	PB
OLIVER, Cin	.992	118	686	596	75	1	8	16

Player, Club	PCT	G	PO	A	E	TC	DP	PB
Bailey, S.F.	1.000	1	3	0	0	3	0	0
Bathe, S.F.	1.000	8	10	1	0	11	1	0
Berryhill, Chi.	.978	15	87	3	2	92	0	2
Biggio, Hou.	.985	113	546	54	9	609	4	7
Bilardello, Pit.	1.000	19	69	9	0	78	0	2
Cabrera, Atl.	1.000	3	5	0	0	5	0	0
Carter, S.F.	.992	80	323	31	3	357	2	4
Cora, S.D.	1.000	1	3	0	0	3	0	0
Daulton, Phi.	.989	139	683	70	8	761	10	6
Davis, Atl.	1.000	4	19	1	0	20	0	0
Decker, S.F.	.989	15	75	11	1	87	2	1
Dempsey, L.A.	.992	53	213	27	2	242	3	4
Fitzgerald, Mon	.990	98	560	41	6	607	10	3
Fletcher, L.A.	1.000	7	30	3	0	33	0	0
Gedman, Hou.	1.000	39	180	25	0	205	5	8
Girardi, Chi.	.985	133	653	61	11	725	5	16
Goff, Mon.	.963	38	196	13	8	217	2	12
Hernandez, LA	1.000	10	37	2	0	39	0	1
Hundley, N.Y.	.988	36	162	8	2	172	2	6
Kennedy, S.F.	.991	103	390	38	4	432	3	5
Kremers, Atl.	.992	27	107	10	1	118	2	2
Lake, Phi.	.993	28	115	19	1	135	1	2
Lampkin, S.D.	.971	20	91	10	3	104	1	2
LaValliere, Pit.	.990	95	478	36	5	519	6	3
Liddell, N.Y.	1.000	1	1	0	0	1	0	0
Lyons, NY-LA	.980	25	183	12	4	199	1	2

Player, Club	PCT	G	PO	A	E	TC	DP	PB
Mann, Atl.	1.000	10	40	3	0	43	1	3
Manwaring, SF	1.000	8	22	3	0	25	1	1
McClendon, Pit.	1.000	8	13	2	0	15	0	1
McGriff, Cin-Ho	.938	5	13	2	1	16	1	0
Mercado, N.Y.	.992	48	239	9	2	250	2	4
Merced, Pit.	.000	1	0	0	0	0	0	0
Nichols, Hou.	.986	15	64	9	1	74	3	2
Nieto, Phi.	.984	17	57	5	1	63	1	0
O'Brien, N.Y.	.986	28	191	21	3	215	1	1
Oliver, Cin.	.992	118	686	59	6	751	8	16
Olson, Atl.	.987	97	501	43	7	551	3	2
Pagnozzi, St.L.	.989	63	334	39	4	377	4	0
Parent, S.D.	.992	60	324	31	3	358	6	1
Prince, Pit.	1.000	3	16	1	0	17	0	0
Reed, Cin.	.987	70	358	26	5	389	1	3
Reynolds, S.D.	1.000	8	26	2	0	28	0	0
Santiago, S.D.	.980	98	538	51	12	601	6	6
Santovenia, Mn	.980	51	264	24	6	294	7	6
Sasser, N.Y.	.975	87	498	43	14	555	4	5
Scioscia, L.A.	.989	132	842	58	10	910	9	5
Slaught, Pit.	.979	78	345	36	8	389	4	4
Stephens, St.L.	1.000	5	31	2	0	33	0	1
Sutko, Cin.	1.000	1	3	0	0	3	0	0
Trevino, Hou.	.982	39	158	8	3	169	0	3
Villanueva, Chi.	.991	23	108	6	1	115	2	4
Whitt, Atl.	.991	59	296	42	3	341	1	8
Wrona, Chi.	.970	16	55	9	2	66	2	1
Zeile, St.L.	.988	105	533	56	7	596	3	10

CATCHERS WITH TWO OR MORE CLUBS

Player, Club	PCT	G	PO	A	E	TC	DP	PB	Player, Club	PCT	G	PO	A	E	TC	DP	PB
Fletcher, L.A.	.000	1	0	0	0	0	0	0	Mercado, N.Y.	.991	40	213	8	2	223	2	4
Fletcher, Phi.	1.000	6	30	3	0	33	0	0	Mercado, Mon.	1.000	8	26	1	0	27	0	0
Lyons, N.Y.	.980	23	180	12	4	196	1	2	Trevino, Hou.	.992	30	124	7	1	132	0	1
Lyons, L.A.	1.000	2	3	0	0	3	0	0	Trevino, N.Y.	.929	7	25	1	2	28	0	2
McGriff, Cin.	1.000	1	4	2	0	6	1	0	Trevino, Cin.	1.000	2	9	0	0	9	0	0
McGriff, Hou.	.900	4	9	0	1	10	0	0									

PITCHERS

Leader, Club	PCT	G	PO	A	E	TC	DP
Six pitchers tied at	1.000						

Player, Club	PCT	G	PO	A	E	TC	DP
Aase, L.A.	1.000	32	1	3	0	4	0
Agosto, Hou.*	1.000	82	11	18	0	29	1
Akerfelds, Phi.	.941	71	2	14	1	17	0
Andersen, Hou.	.958	50	11	12	1	24	1
Anderson, Mon.	1.000	4	0	2	0	2	0
Armstrong, Cin.	1.000	29	15	20	0	35	2
As'nmacher, Chi*	1.000	74	1	18	0	19	0
Avery, Atl.*	.929	21	4	22	2	28	0
Bair, Pit.	.857	22	2	4	1	7	1
Barnes, Mon.*	.875	4	4	3	1	8	0
Bedrosian, S.F.	.952	68	9	11	1	21	1
Belcher, L.A.	1.000	24	11	11	0	22	1
Belinda, Pit.	1.000	55	2	4	0	6	0
Benes, S.D.	.960	32	15	9	1	25	1
Bielecki, Chi.	.943	36	17	33	3	53	2
Birtsas, Cin.*	1.000	29	3	8	0	11	0
Blankenship, Chi.	.750	3	1	2	1	4	0
Boever, Atl.-Phi.	.867	67	6	7	2	15	1
Booker, S.F.	.000	2	0	0	0	0	0
Boskie, Chi.	1.000	15	12	12	0	24	2
Boyd, Mon.	.912	31	7	24	3	34	1
Brantley, S.F.	.944	55	6	11	1	18	1

Player, Club	PCT	G	PO	A	E	TC	DP
K.E. Brown, Cin.	1.000	8	1	2	0	3	0
K.D. Brown, N.Y.*	1.000	2	0	1	0	1	0
Browning, Cin.*	.921	35	8	27	3	38	1
Burke, Mon.	1.000	58	3	20	0	23	1
Burkett, S.F.	.973	33	11	25	1	37	4
Camacho, SF-StL	1.000	14	0	1	0	1	0
Carman, Phi.*	.944	59	5	12	1	18	1
Carpenter, St.L.	.000	4	0	0	1	1	0
Castillo, Atl.*	1.000	52	5	13	0	18	1
Charlton, Cin.*	.967	56	6	23	1	30	3
Clancy, Hou.	1.000	33	4	13	0	17	1
Clark, Hou.	.000	1	0	0	0	0	0
Clarke, St.L.*	.000	2	0	0	0	0	0
Clary, Atl.	.963	33	6	20	1	27	0
Clements, S.D.*	1.000	9	3	2	0	5	0
Coffman, Cin.	1.000	8	3	4	0	7	0
Combs, Phi.*	1.000	32	10	25	0	35	1
Cone, N.Y.	.925	31	17	20	3	40	1
Cook, Phi.-L.A.*	1.000	47	10	22	0	32	1
Costello, StL-Mon	.000	8	0	0	0	0	0
Crews, L.A.	.938	66	8	7	1	16	0
Darling, N.Y.	.935	33	7	22	2	31	0
Darwin, Hou.	.963	48	11	15	1	27	1
Dascenzo, Chi.*	.000	1	0	0	0	0	0
Davis, S.D.	1.000	6	0	1	0	1	0

PITCHERS—Continued

Leader, Club	PCT	G	PO	A	E	TC	DP
Dayley, St.L.*	.929	58	5	8	1	14	1
DeJesus, Phi.	.920	22	9	14	2	25	1
DeLeon, St.L.	.920	32	8	15	2	25	0
Deshaies, Hou.*	.946	34	3	32	2	37	1
Dewey, S.F.	1.000	14	2	2	0	4	1
Dibble, Cin.	1.000	68	5	8	0	13	0
Dickson, Chi.*	1.000	3	1	6	0	7	1
DiPino, St.L.*	1.000	62	2	15	0	17	1
Downs, S.F.	.947	13	6	12	1	19	0
Drabek, Pit.	.984	33	25	36	1	62	1
Dunne, S.D.	1.000	10	4	5	0	9	1
Farmer, Mon.	1.000	6	1	7	0	8	1
Fernandez, N.Y.*	.895	30	1	16	2	19	0
Fisher, Hou.	.000	4	0	0	0	0	0
Franco, N.Y.*	.944	55	4	13	1	18	0
Freeman, Phi.-Atl.	.875	25	1	6	1	8	1
Frey, Mon.*	.917	51	4	7	1	12	0
Frohwirth, Phi.	.500	5	0	1	1	2	0
Gardner, Mon.	1.000	27	9	25	0	34	4
Garrelts, S.F.	.912	31	5	26	3	34	0
Gideon, Mon.	1.000	1	0	1	0	1	0
Glavine, Atl.*	.981	33	19	33	1	53	1
Gooden, N.Y.	.926	34	15	35	4	54	5
Gott, L.A.	1.000	50	6	5	0	11	0
Grant, S.D.-Atl.	.952	59	6	14	1	21	1
Greene, Atl.-Phi.	.900	15	3	6	1	10	0
Grimsley, Phi.	.955	11	13	8	1	22	2
Ke. Gross, Mon.	.950	31	6	13	1	20	0
Ki. Gross, Cin.	.000	5	0	0	0	0	0
Gullickson, Hou.	1.000	32	11	13	0	24	1
Gunderson, S.F.*	1.000	7	0	4	0	4	0
Hall, Mon.*	.929	42	2	11	1	14	1
H'maker, SF-SD*	1.000	34	6	7	0	13	2
Hammond, Cin.*	.600	3	0	3	2	5	0
Harkey, Chi.	.972	27	19	16	1	36	0
Harris, S.D.	1.000	73	4	17	0	21	1
Hartley, L.A.	.917	32	3	8	1	12	1
Heaton, Pit.*	.931	30	5	22	2	29	1
Hennis, Hou.	1.000	3	2	0	0	2	0
Henry, Atl.	1.000	34	4	1	0	5	0
Hernandez, Mon.	1.000	34	3	5	0	8	0
Hershiser, L.A.	1.000	4	1	3	0	4	0
Hesketh, Mon.-At.*	.875	33	4	3	1	8	0
Hill, St.L.	.944	17	7	10	1	18	1
Hilton, St.L.	.000	2	0	0	0	0	0
Holmes, L.A.	1.000	14	1	1	0	2	0
Horton, St.L.*	1.000	32	2	14	0	16	2
J. Howell, L.A.	1.000	45	3	8	0	11	0
K. Howell, Phi.	.895	18	6	11	2	19	0
Huismann, Pit.	.000	2	0	0	0	0	0
Hurst, S.D.*	.976	33	7	34	1	42	3
Innis, N.Y.	1.000	18	4	3	0	7	0
Jackson, Cin.*	.944	22	4	13	1	18	0
Jones, St.L.	.000	1	0	0	0	0	0
Kerfeld, Hou.-Atl.	.571	30	2	2	3	7	0
Kipper, Pit.*	1.000	41	5	8	0	13	0
Knepper, S.F.*	1.000	12	1	8	0	9	0
Kraemer, Chi.*	.857	18	2	4	1	7	1
Kramer, Pit.-Chi.	1.000	22	9	5	0	14	1
LaCoss, S.F.	.929	13	5	8	1	14	1
Lancaster, Chi.	1.000	55	9	19	0	28	1
Landrum, Pit.	1.000	54	11	6	0	17	0
Layana, Cin.	1.000	55	10	9	0	19	1
Lefferts, S.D.*	1.000	56	6	10	0	16	2
Leibrandt, Atl.*	1.000	24	10	28	0	38	2
Lilliquist, Atl-SD*	1.000	28	4	7	0	11	0
Long, Chi.	.933	42	5	9	1	15	0
Luecken, Atl.	1.000	36	5	6	0	11	0
Machado, N.Y.	1.000	27	1	3	0	4	0
G. Maddux, Chi.	1.000	35	39	55	0	94	6
M. Maddux, L.A.	1.000	11	0	2	0	2	0
Magrane, St.L.*	.979	31	8	38	1	47	1
Mahler, Cin.	.966	35	11	17	1	29	1
Malloy, Mon.	.000	1	0	0	0	0	0
Malone, Phi.	.000	7	0	0	0	0	0
Marak, Atl.	1.000	7	6	9	0	15	1
Da. M'tinez, Mon*	.000	1	0	0	0	0	0
De. Martinez, Mon..	.981	32	16	35	1	52	2

Player, Club	PCT	G	PO	A	E	TC	DP
R. Martinez, L.A.	.977	33	16	27	1	44	0
Mathews, St.L.*	.944	11	2	15	1	18	1
McCament, S.F.	1.000	3	1	0	0	1	0
McClellan, S.F.	1.000	4	1	2	0	3	1
McDowell, Phi.	.828	72	1	23	5	29	2
McElroy, Phi.*	.500	16	1	0	1	2	0
McGaffigan, S.F.	.000	4	0	0	0	0	0
Mercker, Atl.*	.750	36	2	1	1	4	0
Meyer, Hou.	1.000	14	2	7	0	9	0
Minutelli, Cin.*	.000	2	0	0	0	0	0
Mohorcic, Mon.	1.000	34	2	9	0	11	2
Moore, Phi.	1.000	3	0	1	0	1	0
Morgan, L.A.	.985	33	25	39	1	65	3
Mulholland, Phi.*	.893	33	8	17	3	28	0
Munoz, L.A.*	.000	8	0	0	0	0	0
Musselman, N.Y.*	1.000	28	5	5	0	10	0
Myers, Cin.*	1.000	66	1	12	0	13	0
Nabholz, Mon.*	.929	11	3	10	1	14	0
Neidlinger, L.A.	1.000	12	8	5	0	13	0
Niedenfuer, St.L.	.833	52	3	7	2	12	0
Noboa, Mon.	.000	1	0	0	0	0	0
Noles, Phi.	.000	1	0	0	0	0	0
Novoa, S.F.*	.000	7	0	0	0	0	0
Nunez, Chi.	.900	21	11	7	2	20	1
Ojeda, N.Y.*	.951	38	8	31	2	41	1
Olivares, St.L.	1.000	9	7	8	0	15	0
Oliveras, S.F.	1.000	33	1	5	0	6	1
O'Neal, S.F.	1.000	26	1	8	0	9	1
Ontiveros, Phi.	1.000	5	2	3	0	5	0
Osuna, Hou.*	1.000	12	1	1	0	2	0
Palacios, Pit.	1.000	7	2	0	0	2	0
Parrett, Phi.-Atl.	.826	67	1	18	4	23	1
Patterson, Pit.*	1.000	55	9	10	0	19	0
Pavlas, Chi.	1.000	13	1	2	0	3	0
Pena, N.Y.	1.000	52	2	4	0	6	0
Perez, St.L.	1.000	13	3	2	0	5	0
Perry, L.A.*	.333	7	0	1	2	3	0
Pico, Chi.	.967	31	13	16	1	30	2
Poole, L.A.*	1.000	16	0	1	0	1	0
Portugal, Hou.	.977	32	23	19	1	43	2
Power, Pit.	1.000	40	3	4	0	7	0
Quisenberry, S.F.	1.000	5	0	1	0	1	0
Rasmussen, S.D.*	.929	32	8	31	3	42	2
Reed, Pit.	.909	13	6	4	1	11	0
Reuschel, S.F.	.947	15	2	16	1	19	1
Reuss, Pit.*	1.000	4	1	2	0	3	0
Richards, Atl.	.000	1	0	0	0	0	0
Rijo, Cin.	.958	29	19	27	2	48	0
D. Robinson, S.F.	1.000	26	4	18	0	22	0
R. Robinson, Cin.	1.000	6	2	4	0	6	0
Rica. R'riguez, SF	1.000	3	1	0	0	1	0
Ro. R'riguez, Cin*	1.000	9	0	3	0	3	0
Rich. R'riguez, SD*	1.000	32	1	10	0	11	1
Roesler, Pit.	.000	5	0	0	0	0	0
Rojas, Mon.	.857	23	2	4	1	7	0
Ross, Pit.	1.000	9	1	3	0	4	0
Ruffin, Phi.*	1.000	32	5	23	0	28	2
Ruskin, Pit.-Mon.*	.882	67	1	14	2	17	2
Sampen, Mon.	1.000	59	5	9	0	14	0
Schatz'r, H-NY*	.917	51	1	10	1	12	0
Schiraldi, S.D.	.842	42	5	11	3	19	0
Schmidt, Mon.	.857	34	2	10	2	14	0
Scott, Hou.	.968	32	10	20	1	31	0
Scudder, Cin.	.917	21	5	6	1	12	0
Searage, L.A.*	1.000	29	2	8	0	10	0
Sherrill, St.L.	1.000	8	1	0	0	1	0
Show, S.D.	.950	39	7	12	1	20	1
Sisk, St.L.	1.000	3	0	1	0	1	0
Smiley, Pit.*	.941	26	8	24	2	34	1
B. Smith, St.L.	.929	26	10	16	2	28	2
D. Smith, Hou.	.800	49	1	3	1	5	1
L. Smith, St.L.	1.000	53	2	1	0	3	0
P. Smith, Atl.*	1.000	13	5	5	0	10	0
Z. S'th, Mn-Pt*	.938	33	10	35	3	48	5
Smoltz, Atl.*	.946	34	26	27	3	56	4
Stanton, Atl.*	1.000	7	0	2	0	2	0
Sutcliffe, Chi.	1.000	5	2	5	0	7	0
Swan, S.F.*	1.000	2	0	1	0	1	0

PITCHERS—Continued

Player, Club	PCT	G	PO	A	E	TC	DP	Player, Club	PCT	G	PO	A	E	TC	DP
Terrell, Pit.	1.000	16	10	13	0	23	1	Vosberg, S.F.*	1.000	18	1	5	0	6	0
Terry, St.L.	.944	50	3	14	1	18	0	Walk, Pit.	.885	26	12	11	3	26	0
Tewksbury, St.L.	.963	28	6	20	1	27	2	Walsh, L.A.*	1.000	20	2	3	0	5	0
Thompson, Mon.	.000	1	0	0	0	0	0	Wells, L.A.*	.333	5	1	0	2	3	0
Thurmond, S.F.*	.950	43	4	15	1	20	2	Wetteland, L.A.	.800	22	1	3	1	5	0
Tibbs, Pit.	1.000	5	1	1	0	2	0	Whitehurst, N.Y.	1.000	38	4	9	0	13	1
Tomlin, Pit.*	1.000	12	1	19	0	20	0	Whitson, S.D.	1.000	32	18	42	0	60	3
Tudor, St.L.*	.975	25	10	29	1	40	2	Wilkins, Chi.	.000	7	0	0	0	0	0
R. Valdez, S.D.	.000	3	0	0	0	0	0	Williams, Chi.*	1.000	59	1	5	0	6	0
S. Valdez, Atl.	1.000	6	2	1	0	3	0	S. Wilson, Chi.*	.909	45	4	16	2	22	0
Valenzuela, LA*	.923	33	5	31	3	39	2	T. Wilson, S.F.*	1.000	27	9	22	0	31	1
Valera, N.Y.	.500	3	1	0	1	2	0	York, Pit.	1.000	4	1	3	0	4	0
Viola, N.Y.*	.978	35	11	34	1	46	1								

PITCHERS WITH TWO OR MORE CLUBS

Player, Club	PCT	G	PO	A	E	TC	DP	Player, Club	PCT	G	PO	A	E	TC	DP
Boever, Atl.	.600	33	1	2	2	5	1	Hesketh, Mon.*	1.000	2	1	0	0	1	0
Boever, Phi.	1.000	34	5	5	0	10	0	Hesketh, Atl.*	.857	31	3	3	1	7	0
Camacho, S.F.	1.000	8	0	0	0	0	0	Kerfeld, Hou.	.000	5	0	0	1	1	0
Camacho, St.L.	1.000	6	0	1	0	1	0	Kerfeld, Atl.	.667	25	2	2	2	6	0
Cook, Phi.*	1.000	42	7	20	0	27	1	Kramer, Pit.	1.000	12	5	4	0	9	1
Cook, L.A.*	1.000	5	3	2	0	5	0	Kramer, Chi.	1.000	10	4	1	0	5	0
Costello, St.L.	.000	4	0	0	0	0	0	Lilliquist, Atl.*	1.000	12	3	4	0	7	0
Costello, Mon.	.000	4	0	0	0	0	0	Lilliquist, S.D.*	1.000	16	1	3	0	4	0
Freeman, Phi.	1.000	16	1	4	0	5	1	Parrett, Phi.	.813	47	1	12	3	16	1
Freeman, Atl.	.667	9	0	2	1	3	0	Parrett, Atl.	.857	20	0	6	1	7	0
Grant, S.D.	1.000	26	1	10	0	11	1	Ruskin, Pit.*	.818	44	1	8	2	11	1
Grant, Atl.	.900	33	5	4	1	10	0	Ruskin, Mon.*	1.000	23	0	6	0	6	1
Greene, Atl.	1.000	5	0	1	0	1	0	Schatzeder, Hu*	.917	45	1	10	1	12	0
Greene, Phi.	.889	10	3	5	1	9	0	Schatzeder, NY*	.000	6	0	0	0	0	0
Hammaker, SF*	1.000	25	4	6	0	10	2	Smith, Mon.*	.912	22	4	27	3	34	3
Hammaker, SD*	1.000	9	2	1	0	3	0	Smith, Pit.*	1.000	11	6	8	0	14	2

OFFICIAL NATIONAL LEAGUE PITCHING AVERAGES

CLUB PITCHING

CLUB	W-L	ERA	G	CG	SHO	SV	IP	H	TBF	R	ER	HR	SH	SF	HB	TBB	IBB	SO	WP	BK
Montreal	85-77	3.37	162	18	11	50	1473.1	1349	6173	598	551	127	69	48	38	510	76	991	27	13
Cincinnati	91-71	3.39	162	14	12	50	1456.1	1338	6128	597	549	124	64	37	34	543	60	1029	48	26
Pittsburgh	95-67	3.40	162	18	8	43	1447.0	1367	5997	619	546	135	68	38	30	413	48	848	42	22
New York	91-71	3.43	162	18	14	41	1440.0	1339	6009	613	548	119	53	41	27	444	35	1217	51	14
Houston	75-87	3.61	162	12	6	37	1450.0	1396	6143	656	581	130	67	61	38	496	74	854	36	15
San Diego	75-87	3.68	162	21	12	35	1461.2	1437	6208	673	597	147	79	37	19	507	69	928	39	19
Los Angeles	86-76	3.72	162	29	12	29	1442.0	1364	6082	685	596	137	56	42	28	487	49	1021	63	10
St. Louis	70-92	3.87	162	8	13	39	1443.1	1432	6132	698	621	98	70	64	34	475	72	833	45	5
Philadelphia	77-85	4.07	162	18	7	35	1449.0	1381	6259	729	655	124	79	48	29	651	81	840	69	15
San Francisco	85-77	4.08	162	14	6	45	1446.1	1477	6235	710	655	131	70	50	21	553	84	788	37	19
Chicago	77-85	4.34	162	13	7	42	1442.2	1510	6320	774	695	121	107	44	28	572	85	877	62	14
Atlanta	65-97	4.58	162	17	8	30	1429.2	1527	6303	821	727	128	94	54	26	579	64	938	61	15
Totals	972-972	3.79	972	200	116	476	17381.1	16917	73989	8173	7321	1521	876	564	352	6221	797	11164	580	187

NOTE—Totals of earned runs for several clubs do not agree with the composite totals for all pitchers of each respective club due to instances in which provisions of Section 10.18(i) of the Scoring Rules were applied. The following differences are to be noted: Atlanta pitchers add to 728 earned runs, Houston pitchers add to 583, Los Angeles pitchers add to 599, Philadelphia pitchers add to 659, St. Louis pitchers add to 622, San Diego pitchers add to 598.

PITCHERS' RECORDS
(Top Fifteen Qualifiers for Earned-Run Average Leadership—162 or More Innings)
(*Lefthanded Pitcher)

Pitcher, Club	L	ERA	G	GS	CG	SHO	GF	SV	IP	H	TBF	R	ER	HR	SH	SF	HB	BB	IBB	SO	WP	BK	OPP AVG
Darwin, Danny, Houston	4	2.21	48	17	3	2	14	0	162.2	136	646	42	40	11	4	3	4	31	4	109	0	2	.225
Smith, Zane, Mon.-Pitt.*	9	2.55	33	31	4	2	0	0	215.1	196	860	77	61	15	3	3	3	50	4	130	2	0	.245
Whitson, Eddie, San Diego	9	2.60	32	32	6	3	0	0	228.2	215	918	73	66	13	9	6	1	47	8	127	2	0	.251
Viola, Frank, New York*	12	2.67	35	35	7	3	0	0	249.2	227	1016	83	74	15	13	3	2	60	1	182	11	0	.242
Rijo, Jose, Cincinnati	8	2.70	29	29	7	1	0	0	197.0	151	801	65	59	10	8	1	3	78	2	152	2	5	.212
Drabek, Douglas, Pittsburgh	6	2.76	33	33	9	3	0	0	231.1	190	918	78	71	15	10	3	3	56	2	131	6	0	.225
Martinez, Ramon, Los Angeles	6	2.92	33	33	12	3	0	0	234.1	191	950	89	76	22	7	5	4	67	5	223	3	3	.221
Boyd, Dennis, Montreal	6	2.93	31	31	7	3	0	0	190.2	164	774	64	62	19	12	4	1	52	10	113	3	3	.234
Martinez, Dennis, Montreal	11	2.95	32	32	7	2	0	0	226.0	191	908	80	74	16	11	3	6	49	9	156	1	1	.228
Hurst, Bruce, San Diego*	9	3.14	33	33	9	4	0	0	223.2	188	903	85	78	21	15	1	1	63	5	162	7	1	.228
Leibrandt, Charles, Atlanta*	11	3.16	24	24	5	2	0	0	162.1	164	680	72	57	9	7	6	1	35	1	76	4	3	.261
Cone, David, New York	10	3.23	31	30	6	2	1	0	211.2	177	860	84	76	21	4	6	7	65	1	233	10	4	.226
Harkey, Michael, Chicago	6	3.27	27	27	2	1	0	0	173.2	153	728	71	63	14	5	4	7	59	8	94	8	1	.234
Mulholland, Terence, Philadelphia*	10	3.34	33	26	6	2	1	0	180.2	172	746	78	67	15	7	12	5	42	7	75	7	7	.252
Armstrong, John, Cincinnati	9	3.42	27	27	1	1	2	0	166.0	151	704	72	63	9	8	5	6	59	7	110	7	5	.242

HR—Rasmussen, S.D., 28; SH—Glavine, Atl., 21; SF—Deshaies, Hou., Mulholland, Phil., 12; HB—Gardner, Mtl., 9; BB—Smoltz, Atl., 90; IBB—Gullickson, Hou., 14; SO—Cone, N.Y., 233; WP—Smoltz, Atl., 14; Bk.—Five pitchers tied with 5.

DEPARTMENTAL LEADERS: W—Drabek, Pitt., 22; L—DeLeon, St.L., 19; G—Agosto, Hou., 82; GS—Browning, Cin., Maddux, Chi., Viola, N.Y., 35; CG—Martinez, L.A., 12; SHO—Hurst, S.D., Morgan, L.A., 4; GF—McDowell, Phil., 60; Sv.—Franco, N.Y., 33; IP—Viola, N.Y., 249.2; H—Maddux, Chi., 242; TBF—Viola, N.Y., 1016; R—Maddux, Chi., 116; ER—Valenzuela, L.A., 104;

INDIVIDUAL PITCHING
(*Throws Lefthanded)

Pitcher, Club	W	L	ERA	G	GS	CG	SHO	GF	SV	IP	H	TBF	R	ER	HR	SH	SF	HB	BB	IBB	SO	WP	BK
Aase, Donald, Los Angeles	3	1	4.97	32	0	0	0	13	3	38.0	33	163	24	21	5	2	0	4	19	4	24	3	0
Agosto, Juan, Houston*	9	8	4.29	82	0	0	0	29	3	92.1	91	404	46	44	4	7	2	0	39	8	50	7	1
Akerfelds, Darrel, Philadelphia	5	2	3.77	71	0	0	0	18	6	93.0	65	395	45	39	10	9	5	3	54	8	42	1	1
Andersen, Larry, Houston	5	2	1.95	50	0	0	0	20	6	73.2	61	301	19	16	2	5	5	1	24	5	68	7	0
Andersen, Scott, Montreal	0	1	3.00	4	3	0	0	1	0	18.0	12	71	6	6	1	1	1	0	5	0	16	2	0
Armstrong, John, Cincinnati	12	9	3.42	29	27	2	1	1	0	166.0	151	704	72	63	9	8	5	6	59	5	110	7	5
Assenmacher, Paul, Chicago*	7	2	2.80	74	1	0	0	21	10	103.0	90	426	33	32	10	3	3	1	36	7	95	0	1
Avery, Steven, Atlanta*	3	11	5.64	21	20	1	0	0	0	99.0	121	466	79	62	7	0	4	2	45	2	75	5	1
Bair, C. Douglas, Pittsburgh	1	0	4.81	22	0	0	0	5	0	24.1	30	112	15	13	3	1	0	1	11	1	19	3	1
Barnes, Brian, Montreal*	0	1	2.89	4	4	0	0	0	0	28.0	25	115	10	9	2	3	0	0	7	0	23	3	0
Bedrosian, Stephen, San Francisco	9	9	4.20	68	0	0	0	53	17	79.1	72	349	40	37	6	3	1	2	44	9	43	3	1
Belcher, Timothy, Los Angeles	9	9	4.00	24	24	5	0	0	0	153.0	136	627	76	68	17	6	6	2	48	3	102	6	0
Belinda, Stanley, Pittsburgh	3	4	3.55	55	0	0	0	17	8	58.1	48	245	23	23	4	5	2	1	29	3	55	1	2
Benes, Andrew, San Diego	10	11	3.60	32	31	2	0	0	0	192.1	177	811	87	77	18	2	6	5	69	11	140	3	5
Bielecki, Michael, Chicago	8	11	4.93	36	29	0	0	6	0	168.0	188	749	101	92	13	5	4	0	70	6	103	11	0
Birtsas, Timothy, Cincinnati*	1	3	3.86	29	2	0	0	8	0	51.1	69	239	24	22	7	1	2	0	24	6	41	4	2
Blankenship, Kevin, Chicago	0	2	3.36	3	2	0	0	0	0	12.1	13	57	10	8	1	0	0	0	6	0	5	1	0
Boever, Joseph, Atl.-Phil.	3	6	3.36	67	0	0	0	34	14	88.1	77	388	35	33	6	4	4	0	51	12	75	0	0
Booker, Gregory, San Francisco	0	0	13.50	2	0	0	0	0	0	2.0	7	13	3	3	0	0	2	0	0	0	1	3	1
Boskie, Shawn, Chicago	5	6	3.69	15	15	1	0	0	0	97.2	99	415	42	40	8	8	2	4	31	0	49	3	2
Boyd, Dennis, Montreal	10	6	2.93	31	31	3	3	0	0	190.2	164	774	64	62	19	2	2	1	52	10	113	3	3
Brantley, Jeffrey, San Francisco	5	3	1.56	55	0	0	0	32	19	86.2	77	361	18	15	3	2	0	3	33	6	61	0	3
Brown, Keith, Cincinnati	0	0	4.76	8	0	0	0	2	0	11.1	12	46	6	6	2	1	0	0	3	0	8	0	0
Brown, Kevin, New York	0	0	0.00	2	0	0	0	1	0	2.0	4	9	0	0	0	0	0	0	1	0	0	0	0
Browning, Thomas, Cincinnati*	15	9	3.80	35	35	2	1	0	0	227.2	235	957	98	96	24	13	5	5	52	13	99	5	1
Burke, Timothy, Montreal	3	3	2.52	58	0	0	0	35	20	75.0	71	316	29	21	6	3	3	4	21	6	47	3	1
Burkett, John, San Francisco	14	7	3.79	33	32	2	0	1	0	204.0	201	857	92	86	18	8	5	1	61	7	118	3	3
Camacho, Ernie, S.F.-St.L.	0	0	5.17	14	0	0	0	6	1	15.2	17	72	10	9	3	6	2	0	9	1	15	2	0
Carman, Donald, Philadelphia*	6	2	4.15	59	0	0	0	11	0	86.2	69	368	43	40	13	0	4	0	38	9	58	6	1
Carpenter, Cris, St. Louis	0	1	4.50	4	0	0	0	1	0	8.0	6	32	4	4	0	0	1	0	2	1	6	0	0
Castillo, Antonio, Atlanta*	5	1	4.23	52	3	0	0	7	2	76.2	93	337	41	36	4	4	2	1	20	3	64	2	2
Charlton, Norman, Cincinnati*	12	9	2.74	56	16	1	1	13	2	154.1	131	650	53	47	10	7	4	4	70	9	117	9	1
Clancy, James, Houston	2	8	6.51	33	10	0	0	8	0	76.0	100	352	58	55	4	1	4	3	33	9	44	3	0
Clark, Terry, Houston	0	0	13.50	1	1	0	0	0	0	4.0	9	25	7	6	0	0	0	0	3	0	2	0	0
Clary, Stanley, St. Louis*	0	0	2.70	2	1	0	0	0	0	3.1	9	12	1	1	0	1	0	1	0	0	3	0	0
Clements, Patrick, San Diego*	1	0	5.67	33	14	0	0	5	0	101.2	128	466	72	64	9	5	5	1	39	4	44	5	1
Coffman, Kevin, Chicago	0	0	4.15	9	2	0	0	3	0	13.0	20	63	9	6	1	0	0	0	7	0	6	4	0
Combs, Patrick, Philadelphia*	10	10	4.07	32	31	3	0	0	0	183.1	179	800	90	83	12	2	7	4	86	7	108	9	1
Cone, David, New York	14	10	3.23	31	30	6	2	0	0	211.2	177	860	84	76	21	7	6	4	65	9	233	10	4
Cook, Dennis, Phil.-L.A.*	9	4	3.92	47	16	1	0	4	1	156.0	155	663	74	68	20	4	7	2	56	6	64	4	3
Costello, John, St.L.-Mon.	0	0	5.91	8	0	0	0	5	0	10.2	12	47	8	7	1	3	1	1	2	1	2	0	0
Crews, S. Timothy, Los Angeles	4	5	2.77	66	0	0	0	18	1	107.1	98	440	40	33	9	7	3	1	24	6	76	2	0
Darling, Ronald, New York	7	9	4.50	33	18	1	0	3	0	126.0	135	554	73	63	20	5	3	5	44	4	99	5	2
Darwin, Danny, Houston	11	4	2.21	48	17	3	0	14	2	162.2	136	646	42	40	11	4	2	4	31	4	109	0	0
Dascenzo, Douglas, Chicago*	0	0	0.00	1	0	0	0	0	0	1.0	1	3	0	0	0	0	0	0	0	0	0	0	0
Davis, John, San Diego	0	1	5.79	6	0	0	0	5	0	9.1	9	39	7	6	1	0	2	0	4	0	7	5	0
Dayley, Kenneth, St. Louis*	4	4	3.56	58	0	0	0	17	2	73.1	63	307	32	29	5	2	5	0	30	7	51	6	0

Pitcher, Club	W	L	ERA	G	GS	CG	SHO	GF	SV	IP	H	TBF	R	ER	HR	SH	SF	HB	BB	IBB	SO	WP	BK
DeJesus, Jose, Philadelphia	7	8	3.74	22	22	3	1	0	0	130.0	97	544	63	54	10	8	0	2	73	3	87	4	0
DeLeon, Jose, St. Louis	7	19	4.43	32	32	2	0	0	0	182.2	168	793	96	90	15	11	8	5	86	9	164	5	0
Deshaies, James, Houston*	7	12	3.78	34	34	2	0	0	0	209.1	186	881	93	88	21	17	12	8	84	9	119	3	3
Dewey, Mark, San Francisco	1	1	2.78	14	0	0	0	5	0	22.2	22	92	7	7	1	2	1	0	5	1	11	0	1
Dibble, Robert, Cincinnati	8	3	1.74	68	0	0	0	29	11	98.0	62	384	22	19	3	4	6	3	34	3	136	3	1
Dickson, Lance, Chicago*	0	3	7.24	3	3	0	0	0	0	13.2	20	61	12	11	2	1	1	0	4	0	11	1	0
DiPino, Frank, St. Louis*	5	2	4.56	62	0	0	0	24	0	81.0	92	360	45	41	8	8	7	1	31	12	49	2	1
Downs, Kelly, San Francisco	5	2	3.43	13	9	0	0	0	0	63.0	56	265	26	24	8	8	1	2	20	0	31	2	1
Drabek, Douglas, Pittsburgh	22	6	2.76	33	33	9	3	0	0	231.1	190	918	78	71	15	10	3	3	56	2	131	6	2
Dunne, Michael, San Diego	0	0	5.65	10	6	0	0	1	0	28.2	28	134	18	18	4	1	0	3	17	0	15	4	0
Farmer, Howard, Montreal	0	3	7.04	6	4	0	0	0	0	23.0	26	99	18	18	9	0	1	5	10	0	14	1	0
Fernandez, C. Sid, New York*	9	14	3.46	30	30	2	1	0	0	179.1	130	735	79	69	18	7	6	5	67	2	181	0	0
Fisher, Brian, Houston	0	0	7.20	4	0	0	0	3	0	5.0	9	24	5	4	1	0	2	0	0	0	1	0	2
Franco, John, New York*	5	3	2.53	55	0	0	0	48	33	67.2	66	287	24	19	5	2	1	0	21	6	56	7	0
Freeman, Marvin, Phil.-Atl	1	2	2.10	25	0	0	0	5	1	48.0	41	207	15	14	4	3	0	5	17	0	38	4	0
Frey, Steven, Montreal*	8	2	2.31	51	0	0	0	21	9	55.2	44	236	15	13	0	2	0	1	29	2	29	0	0
Frohwirth, Todd, Philadelphia	0	1	18.00	5	0	0	0	3	0	1.0	3	12	2	2	0	0	0	0	6	0	1	0	0
Gardner, Mark, Montreal	7	9	3.42	27	26	3	3	1	0	152.2	129	642	62	58	13	4	7	9	61	5	135	2	4
Garrelts, Scott, San Francisco	12	11	4.15	31	31	4	2	0	0	182.0	190	786	91	84	16	10	5	3	70	8	80	7	0
Gideon, B. Brett, Montreal	0	0	9.00	4	0	0	0	2	0	1.0	2	8	1	1	0	0	0	0	4	0	0	0	1
Glavine, Thomas, Atlanta*	10	12	4.28	33	33	1	0	0	0	214.1	232	929	111	102	18	21	2	2	78	10	129	8	1
Gooden, Dwight, New York	19	7	3.83	34	34	2	1	0	0	232.2	229	983	106	99	19	10	7	0	70	3	223	6	3
Gott, James, Los Angeles	3	5	2.90	50	0	0	0	24	3	62.0	59	270	27	20	5	2	7	4	34	11	44	4	0
Grant, Mark, S.D.-Atl.	2	3	4.73	59	1	0	0	21	3	91.1	108	411	53	48	9	6	4	2	37	7	69	2	1
Greene, I. Thomas, Atl.-Phil.	3	3	5.08	15	9	0	0	0	0	51.1	50	227	31	29	8	5	0	6	26	0	21	8	0
Grimsley, Jason, Philadelphia	3	2	3.30	11	11	0	0	0	0	57.1	47	255	21	21	1	5	1	3	43	0	41	6	1
Gross, Kevin, Montreal	9	12	4.57	31	26	2	1	0	0	163.1	171	712	86	83	7	9	9	4	65	7	111	4	1
Gross, Kip, Cincinnati	0	0	4.26	2	0	0	0	2	0	6.1	6	25	3	3	0	0	0	0	2	0	3	0	0
Gullickson, William, Houston	10	14	3.82	32	32	1	0	0	0	193.1	221	846	100	82	21	6	8	2	61	14	73	3	2
Gunderson, Eric, San Francisco*	0	1	5.49	7	4	0	0	1	0	19.2	24	94	14	12	6	6	0	2	11	1	14	0	0
Hall, Andrew, Montreal*	4	7	5.09	42	9	0	0	13	3	58.1	52	254	35	33	2	6	4	1	35	5	40	0	3
Hammaker, C. Atlee, S.F.-S.D.*	4	4	4.36	34	7	0	0	8	0	86.2	85	363	44	42	8	5	4	0	27	5	44	4	2
Hammond, Christopher, Cincinnati*	0	2	6.35	3	3	0	0	0	0	11.1	13	56	9	8	1	4	4	0	12	0	4	1	1
Harkey, Michael, Chicago	12	6	3.26	27	27	2	1	0	0	173.2	153	728	71	63	14	5	5	4	59	8	94	8	3
Harris, Gregory W., San Diego	8	8	2.30	73	0	0	0	33	9	117.1	92	488	35	30	6	9	7	4	49	13	97	2	0
Hartley, Michael, Los Angeles	6	3	2.95	32	6	0	0	8	1	79.1	58	325	32	26	9	2	6	1	30	1	76	3	1
Heaton, Neal, Pittsburgh*	12	9	3.45	30	24	0	0	2	0	146.0	143	599	66	56	17	10	6	2	38	1	68	0	0
Henry, Randall, Houston	0	0	0.00	3	1	0	0	1	0	9.2	1	34	0	0	0	0	0	0	3	0	4	0	0
Henry, Dwayne, Atlanta	2	2	5.63	34	0	0	0	14	0	38.1	41	176	26	24	3	8	1	2	25	5	34	2	0
Hernandez, Xavier, Houston	2	1	4.62	34	1	0	0	10	1	62.1	60	268	34	32	8	8	4	4	24	4	24	6	0
Hershiser, Orel, Los Angeles	1	1	4.26	4	4	0	0	0	0	25.1	26	106	12	12	1	1	2	1	4	0	16	0	1
Hesketh, Joseph, Mon.-Atl.*	1	2	5.29	33	4	0	0	15	5	34.0	32	147	20	20	5	5	0	0	14	1	24	5	0
Hill, Kenneth, St. Louis	5	6	5.49	17	14	0	0	1	0	78.2	79	343	49	48	7	9	5	0	33	1	58	5	0
Hilton, Howard, St. Louis	0	0	0.00	2	0	0	0	1	0	3.0	2	14	0	0	0	0	0	0	0	0	3	0	0
Holmes, Darren, Los Angeles	0	1	5.19	14	0	0	0	2	0	17.1	15	77	10	10	3	0	2	1	11	3	19	2	0
Horton, Ricky, St. Louis*	0	0	4.93	32	0	0	0	8	0	42.0	52	193	25	23	3	4	1	0	22	7	18	1	0
Howell, Jay, Los Angeles	5	5	2.18	45	0	0	0	35	16	66.0	59	271	16	16	5	5	6	6	20	3	59	4	1
Howell, Kenneth, Philadelphia	8	7	4.64	18	18	0	0	0	0	106.2	106	467	60	55	12	2	1	6	49	6	70	8	0
Huismann, Mark, Pittsburgh	0	0	9.00	2	0	0	0	1	0	3.0	6	15	5	3	2	0	0	1	1	0	2	0	1
Hurst, Bruce, San Diego*	11	9	3.14	33	33	9	4	0	0	223.2	188	903	85	78	21	15	0	1	63	5	162	7	1

Pitcher, Club	W	L	ERA	G	GS	CG	SHO	GF	SV	IP	H	TBF	R	ER	HR	SH	SF	HB	BB	IBB	SO	WP	BK
Innis, Jeffrey, New York	1	3	2.39	18	0	0	0	12	1	26.1	19	104	9	7	4	4	2	1	10	3	12	3	1
Jackson, Danny, Cincinnati*	6	6	3.61	22	21	0	0	1	0	117.1	119	499	54	47	11	0	5	2	40	4	76	3	1
Jones, W. Timothy, St. Louis	0	0	6.75	1	0	0	0	1	0	1.1	2	8	2	1	0	0	0	0	2	0	0	1	0
Kerfeld, Charles, Hou.-Atl.	3	3	6.62	30	0	0	0	11	2	34.0	40	168	28	25	2	5	2	3	29	4	31	1	0
Kipper, Robert, Pittsburgh*	5	3	3.02	41	1	0	0	7	3	62.2	44	260	24	21	7	2	3	1	26	4	35	1	5
Knepper, Robert, San Francisco*	3	3	5.68	12	7	0	0	0	0	44.1	56	202	28	28	7	3	3	2	19	4	24	2	3
Kraemer, Joseph, Chicago*	0	0	7.20	18	0	0	0	8	0	25.0	31	119	25	20	2	0	2	2	14	2	16	1	1
Kramer, Randall, Pitt.-Chi	0	4	4.50	22	12	1	0	0	0	46.0	47	207	25	23	6	1	0	1	21	6	27	2	0
LaCoss, Michael, San Francisco	6	4	3.94	13	6	1	0	6	0	77.2	75	337	37	34	5	5	4	0	39	2	39	1	0
Lancaster, Lester, Chicago	9	5	4.62	55	0	0	0	26	6	109.0	121	479	57	56	11	6	5	1	40	8	65	7	1
Landrum, T. William, Pittsburgh	7	3	2.13	54	0	0	0	41	13	71.2	69	292	22	17	4	4	4	2	21	5	39	1	0
Layana, Timothy, Cincinnati	5	3	3.49	55	0	0	0	17	0	80.0	71	344	33	21	4	4	3	4	44	5	53	5	4
Lefferts, Craig, San Diego*	7	5	2.52	56	0	0	0	44	23	78.2	68	327	26	22	10	5	1	3	22	3	60	4	0
Leibrandt, Charles, Atlanta*	9	11	3.16	24	24	5	2	1	0	162.1	164	680	72	57	9	3	6	4	35	3	76	4	3
Lilliquist, Derek, Atl.-S.D.*	5	5	5.31	28	18	1	0	0	0	122.0	136	537	74	72	16	9	5	3	42	5	63	2	3
Long, William, Chicago	6	1	4.37	42	0	0	0	21	5	55.2	66	244	29	27	8	8	3	1	21	4	32	1	0
Luecken, Richard, Atlanta	1	1	5.77	36	0	0	0	11	0	53.0	73	255	36	34	5	3	0	3	30	7	35	2	0
Machado, Julio, New York	4	1	3.15	27	0	0	0	14	0	34.1	32	151	13	12	4	4	1	2	17	4	27	3	3
Maddux, Gregory, Chicago	15	15	3.46	35	35	8	2	0	1	237.0	242	1011	116	91	11	1	2	5	71	10	144	2	3
Maddux, Michael, Los Angeles	0	0	6.53	11	2	0	0	0	0	20.2	24	88	15	15	3	1	0	1	4	0	11	1	1
Magrane, Joseph, St. Louis*	10	17	3.59	31	31	3	0	0	2	203.1	204	855	86	81	10	0	1	8	59	7	100	0	0
Mahler, Richard, Cincinnati	7	6	4.28	35	16	2	0	9	0	134.2	134	564	67	64	16	8	6	3	39	0	68	1	2
Malloy, Robert, Montreal	0	0	0.00	4	0	0	0	3	0	2.0	1	8	0	0	0	0	0	0	1	0	3	0	0
Malone, Charles, Philadelphia	1	0	3.68	7	0	0	0	3	0	7.1	6	34	4	3	0	0	3	0	6	0	7	1	1
Marak, Paul, Atlanta	1	2	3.69	7	7	1	0	0	0	39.0	39	172	16	16	2	0	3	6	19	0	15	1	0
Martinez, David, Montreal*	0	0	54.00	2	0	0	0	1	0	0.1	2	5	2	2	0	0	0	0	2	0	1	0	0
Martinez, Dennis, Montreal	10	11	2.95	32	32	7	2	0	0	226.0	191	908	80	74	16	11	3	4	49	5	156	3	1
Martinez, Ramon, Los Angeles	20	6	2.92	33	33	12	3	0	0	234.1	191	950	89	76	22	7	5	5	67	7	223	3	1
Mathews, Gregory, St. Louis*	0	5	5.33	11	10	0	0	0	0	50.2	53	229	34	30	9	4	2	1	30	2	18	2	0
McCament, L. Randall, San Francisco	0	1	3.00	3	1	0	0	2	0	6.0	8	30	2	2	0	1	0	1	5	0	5	0	0
McClellan, Paul, San Francisco	0	1	11.74	2	1	0	0	0	0	7.2	14	39	10	10	3	0	4	2	6	0	5	2	0
McDowell, Roger, Philadelphia	6	8	3.86	72	0	0	0	60	22	86.1	92	373	41	37	2	10	4	2	35	9	39	0	2
McElroy, Charles, Philadelphia*	0	1	7.71	16	0	0	0	8	0	14.0	24	76	13	12	2	0	1	0	10	0	16	1	0
McGaffigan, Andrew, San Francisco	0	1	17.36	4	0	0	0	0	0	4.2	10	27	9	9	2	1	0	2	4	0	4	1	0
Mercker, Kent, Atlanta*	4	7	3.17	36	0	0	0	7	7	48.1	43	211	22	17	6	1	2	2	24	3	39	4	1
Meyer, Brian, Houston	0	4	2.21	14	0	0	0	7	1	20.1	16	84	7	5	3	1	0	4	6	3	6	2	0
Minutelli, Gino, Cincinnati	0	0	9.00	3	0	0	0	0	0	1.0	1	5	1	1	0	0	0	0	2	0	1	0	0
Mohorcic, Dale, Montreal	1	2	3.23	34	0	0	0	12	0	53.0	56	226	21	19	2	11	2	5	18	5	29	1	0
Moore, Bradley, Philadelphia	0	0	3.38	3	0	0	0	2	0	2.2	2	13	1	1	0	0	0	0	2	0	1	0	0
Morgan, Michael, Los Angeles	11	15	3.75	33	33	6	4	0	0	211.0	216	891	100	88	19	11	12	5	60	8	106	4	1
Mulholland, Terence, Philadelphia*	9	10	3.34	33	26	6	1	0	0	180.2	172	746	78	67	15	7	2	5	42	1	75	2	0
Munoz, Michael, Los Angeles*	0	1	3.18	8	0	0	0	3	0	5.2	4	24	2	2	0	1	0	0	3	2	2	0	0
Musselman, Jeffrey, New York*	0	2	5.63	28	0	0	0	5	0	32.0	40	144	22	20	3	1	2	1	11	8	14	0	0
Myers, Randall, Cincinnati*	4	6	2.08	66	0	0	0	59	31	86.2	59	353	24	20	6	1	2	2	38	8	98	1	0
Nabholz, Christopher, Montreal*	6	2	2.83	11	11	0	0	0	0	70.0	43	282	23	22	4	4	2	2	32	2	53	3	1
Neidlinger, James, Los Angeles	5	3	3.28	12	12	1	1	0	0	74.0	67	302	30	27	3	4	3	2	15	0	46	1	1
Niedenfuer, Thomas, St. Louis	0	6	3.46	52	0	0	0	12	1	65.0	66	276	26	25	3	0	5	0	25	5	32	2	0
Noboa, Milciades, Montreal	0	0	0.00	1	0	0	0	1	0	0.2	0	2	0	0	0	0	0	0	0	0	0	0	0
Noles, Dickie, Philadelphia	0	1	27.00	1	0	0	0	2	0	0.1	2	3	1	1	0	0	1	0	0	0	0	0	0
Novoa, Rafael, San Francisco*	0	1	6.75	7	2	0	0	1	0	18.2	21	88	14	14	3	0	1	0	13	1	14	0	0

Pitcher, Club	W	L	ERA	G	GS	CG	SHO	GF	SV	IP	H	TBF	R	ER	HR	SH	SF	HB	BB	IBB	SO	WP	BK
Nunez, Jose, Chicago	4	7	6.53	21	10	0	0	4	0	60.2	61	274	47	44	5	11	3	3	34	4	40	2	2
Ojeda, Robert, New York*	7	6	3.66	38	12	0	0	9	0	118.0	123	500	53	48	10	3	3	0	40	4	62	2	3
Olivares, Omar, St. Louis	1	1	2.92	9	6	0	0	0	0	49.1	45	201	17	16	5	1	1	2	17	4	20	1	1
Oliveras, Francisco, San Francisco	2	2	2.77	33	2	0	0	9	2	55.1	47	231	22	17	5	1	3	1	21	6	41	1	1
O'Neal, Randall, San Francisco	1	0	3.83	26	0	0	0	4	0	47.0	58	208	23	20	3	3	2	1	18	4	30	4	1
Ontiveros, Steven, Philadelphia	0	0	2.70	5	0	0	0	1	0	10.0	9	43	8	3	1	0	0	0	3	0	6	3	0
Osuna, Alfonso, Houston*	2	0	4.76	12	0	0	0	2	0	11.1	10	48	6	6	1	0	2	0	6	1	6	2	0
Palacios, Vicente, Pittsburgh	5	0	4.64	7	5	0	0	0	0	15.0	4	50	8	6	0	1	3	0	2	3	8	2	2
Parrett, Jeffrey, Phil.-Atl.	8	5	2.95	67	5	0	0	19	3	108.2	119	479	62	56	11	7	5	3	55	10	86	5	1
Patterson, Robert, Pittsburgh	3	3	2.11	55	5	0	0	19	5	94.2	88	386	33	31	9	5	3	1	21	7	70	3	2
Pavlas, David, Chicago	1	0	3.20	13	0	0	0	3	0	21.1	23	93	7	5	4	0	2	1	6	0	12	3	0
Pena, Alejandro, New York	0	3	3.95	52	0	0	0	32	5	76.0	71	320	31	27	4	7	6	1	22	5	76	4	0
Perez, Michael, St. Louis	0	0	8.10	13	0	0	0	7	1	13.2	12	55	6	6	0	0	2	1	3	0	5	1	0
Perry, W. Patrick, Los Angeles*	4	4	4.79	7	0	0	0	2	0	6.2	9	36	5	5	0	0	1	1	3	10	2	1	0
Pico, Jeffrey, Chicago	0	0	4.22	31	8	0	0	8	2	92.0	120	421	53	49	7	7	2	0	37	4	37	6	0
Poole, James, Los Angeles*	1	0	3.62	16	0	0	0	4	2	10.2	7	46	5	5	1	0	0	2	8	4	6	1	0
Portugal, Mark, Houston	11	10	3.66	32	32	1	0	0	0	196.2	187	831	90	79	21	7	6	4	67	6	136	6	0
Power, Ted, Pittsburgh	1	3	13.50	40	5	0	0	25	7	51.2	50	218	23	21	5	3	2	1	17	2	42	0	1
Quisenberry, Daniel, San Francisco	1	1	4.51	5	0	0	0	2	0	6.2	13	37	12	10	1	0	0	1	0	1	2	0	0
Rasmussen, Dennis, San Diego*	11	15	4.36	32	32	0	0	0	0	187.2	217	825	110	94	28	14	4	3	62	8	86	9	0
Reed, Richard, Pittsburgh	2	3	3.93	13	8	0	0	2	1	53.2	62	238	32	26	6	1	1	3	12	4	27	0	0
Reuschel, Ricky, San Francisco	3	6	3.52	15	13	3	0	0	0	87.0	102	390	40	38	8	8	5	2	31	9	49	1	0
Reuss, Jerry, Pittsburgh*	0	0	3.52	4	1	0	0	1	0	7.2	8	36	3	3	1	0	0	0	1	0	1	0	0
Richards, Russell, Atlanta	0	0	27.00	1	0	0	0	0	0	1.0	2	6	3	3	1	0	0	0	1	1	0	0	0
Rijo, Jose, Cincinnati	14	8	2.70	29	29	7	1	0	0	197.0	151	801	65	59	10	8	3	1	78	1	152	2	0
Robinson, Don, San Francisco	10	7	4.57	25	25	4	0	0	0	157.2	173	667	84	80	18	4	1	1	41	8	78	1	2
Robinson, Ronald, Cincinnati	2	0	4.88	26	5	0	0	4	0	31.1	36	137	18	17	2	8	0	2	14	0	14	1	5
Rodriguez, Ricardo, San Francisco	0	1	8.10	6	0	0	0	4	0	3.1	5	16	8	3	0	0	0	0	0	0	2	0	0
Rodriguez, Rosario, Cincinnati*	0	0	6.10	9	0	0	0	4	1	10.1	15	47	7	7	3	1	1	0	2	4	8	1	0
Rodriguez, Richard, San Diego*	1	1	2.83	32	0	0	0	15	5	47.2	52	201	17	15	5	3	2	1	16	4	22	0	3
Roesler, Michael, Pittsburgh	0	0	3.00	5	0	0	0	1	0	6.0	5	25	2	2	1	0	0	0	0	2	4	0	0
Rojas, Melquides, Montreal	3	1	3.60	23	0	0	0	5	0	40.0	34	173	17	16	2	2	0	1	24	4	26	0	0
Ross, Mark, Pittsburgh	0	0	3.55	9	0	0	0	6	0	12.2	11	50	5	5	1	0	0	0	4	2	5	1	0
Ruffin, Bruce, Philadelphia*	6	13	5.38	32	25	0	0	0	0	149.0	178	678	99	89	14	10	6	2	62	7	79	3	3
Ruskin, Scott, Pitt.-Mon.*	3	2	2.75	67	4	0	0	12	2	75.1	75	336	34	23	4	5	2	2	38	6	57	3	1
Sampen, William, Montreal	12	3	2.99	59	4	0	0	26	2	90.1	94	394	34	30	7	5	2	2	33	6	69	4	0
Schatzeder, Daniel, Hou.-N.Y.*	1	3	2.20	51	2	0	0	16	0	69.2	66	283	34	17	2	5	5	1	23	4	39	2	1
Schiraldi, Calvin, San Diego	3	8	4.41	42	8	0	0	14	2	104.0	105	468	59	51	11	2	3	0	60	6	74	1	0
Schmidt, David, Montreal	3	3	4.31	34	0	0	0	20	1	48.0	58	213	26	23	5	7	1	0	13	5	22	1	1
Scott, Michael, Houston	9	13	3.81	32	32	2	0	0	0	205.2	194	871	82	87	27	4	8	1	66	6	121	1	3
Scudder, W. Scott, Cincinnati	5	5	4.90	21	10	0	0	3	0	71.2	74	316	102	39	12	7	1	0	30	6	42	5	3
Searage, Raymond, Los Angeles*	1	0	2.78	29	0	0	0	8	0	32.1	30	136	12	10	1	3	4	0	10	2	19	1	0
Sherrill, Timothy, St. Louis*	0	0	6.23	9	0	0	0	2	0	4.1	10	25	11	3	0	2	0	0	2	0	3	0	0
Show, Eric, San Diego	6	8	5.76	39	12	0	0	14	0	106.1	131	482	74	68	16	1	4	0	41	9	55	3	3
Sisk, Douglas, Atlanta	0	0	3.86	26	0	0	0	0	0	2.1	1	13	1	1	0	0	4	0	4	1	1	1	3
Smiley, John, Pittsburgh*	9	10	4.64	26	25	2	0	0	0	149.1	161	632	83	77	15	5	4	2	36	1	86	2	0
Smith, Bryn, St. Louis	9	9	4.27	26	25	2	0	0	0	141.1	160	605	81	67	11	7	5	4	30	1	78	2	2
Smith, David, Houston	6	6	2.39	49	0	0	0	42	23	60.1	45	239	18	16	4	4	1	0	20	4	50	5	0
Smith, Lee, St. Louis	3	6	2.10	53	0	0	0	45	27	68.2	58	280	22	16	3	2	0	0	20	5	70	1	5
Smith, Peter, Atlanta	5	6	4.79	13	13	3	0	0	0	77.0	77	327	45	41	11	4	3	0	24	2	56	2	1

Pitcher, Club	W	L	ERA	G	GS	CG	SHO	GF	SV	IP	H	TBF	R	ER	HR	SH	SF	HB	BB	IBB	SO	WP	BK
Smith, Zane, Mon.-Pitt. *	12	9	2.55	33	31	4	2	1	0	215.1	196	860	77	61	15	3	1	3	50	4	130	2	0
Smoltz, John, Atlanta	14	11	3.85	34	34	6	2	0	0	231.1	206	966	109	99	20	9	8	1	90	3	170	14	3
Stanton, Michael, Atlanta*	0	3	18.00	7	0	0	0	4	2	7.0	16	42	16	14	1	1	1	1	4	2	7	1	0
Sutcliffe, Richard, Chicago	0	2	5.91	5	5	0	0	0	0	21.1	25	97	14	14	2	1	0	0	12	0	7	4	0
Swan, Russell, San Francisco*	0	1	3.86	16	1	0	0	0	0	2.1	6	18	4	1	0	0	2	0	4	1	7	1	2
Terrell, C. Walter, Pittsburgh. *	2	7	5.88	16	16	0	0	0	0	82.2	98	377	59	54	13	6	2	4	33	1	34	1	2
Terry, Scott, St. Louis	2	6	4.75	50	2	0	0	26	2	72.0	75	323	45	38	7	3	5	3	27	5	35	7	0
Tewksbury, Robert, St. Louis	10	9	3.47	28	20	3	2	1	1	145.1	151	595	67	56	5	5	7	0	15	3	50	2	0
Thompson, Richard, Montreal	0	0	0.00	1	0	0	0	1	0	1.0	4		0	0	0	0	0	0	0	0	0	0	0
Thurmond, Mark, San Francisco	2	3	3.34	43	0	0	0	16	4	56.2	53	238	26	21	6	8	6	0	18	3	24	1	0
Tibbs, Jay, Pittsburgh	0	0	2.57	5	0	0	0	3	0	7.0	7	29	7	2	0	0	2	1	2	1	4	0	0
Tomlin, Randy, Pittsburgh*	4	4	2.55	12	12	2	0	0	0	77.2	62	297	24	22	5	2	2	1	12	1	42	1	3
Tudor, John, St. Louis*	12	4	2.40	25	22	1	1	0	0	146.1	120	575	48	39	10	8	1	2	30	4	63	0	0
Valdez, Rafael, San Diego	0	1	11.12	3	0	0	0	2	0	5.2	11	30	7	7	0	0	0	0	3	0	3	1	0
Valdez, Sergio, Atlanta	0	0	6.75	6	3	0	0	3	0	5.1	6	26	4	4	0	0	4	0	3	0	3	1	1
Valenzuela, Fernando, Los Angeles*	13	13	4.59	33	33	5	2	0	0	204.0	223	900	112	104	19	11	3	7	77	4	115	13	1
Valera, Julio, New York*	1	1	6.92	5	3	0	0	0	0	13.0	20	64	11	10	1	1	0	0	7	1	4	1	0
Viola, Frank, New York*	20	12	2.67	35	35	7	3	0	0	249.2	227	1016	83	74	15	13	3	0	60	2	182	11	0
Vosberg, Edward, San Francisco*	1	1	5.55	18	0	0	0	5	0	24.1	21	104	16	15	3	2	3	4	12	2	12	0	3
Walk, Robert, Pittsburgh	7	5	3.75	26	24	1	1	1	1	129.2	136	549	62	54	17	3	4	4	36	2	73	5	1
Walsh, David, Los Angeles*	1	0	3.86	20	0	0	0	7	1	16.1	15	70	12	7	0	1	1	0	6	1	15	1	0
Wells, Terry, Los Angeles*	1	0	7.84	5	5	0	0	0	0	20.2	25	102	23	18	6	4	0	4	14	1	18	8	0
Wetteland, John, Los Angeles	2	4	4.81	22	5	0	0	7	0	43.0	44	190	28	23	5	1	1	4	17	3	36	2	0
Whitehurst, Walter, New York	1	0	3.29	38	0	0	0	16	2	65.2	63	263	27	24	13	4	0	4	9	1	46	2	0
Whitson, Eddie, San Diego	14	9	2.60	32	32	6	3	0	0	228.2	215	918	73	66	13	3	6	1	47	8	127	2	0
Wilkins, Dean, Chicago	0	0	9.82	7	0	0	0	3	1	7.1	11	41	8	8	4	0	0	1	7	2	3	3	3
Williams, Mitchell, Chicago*	1	8	3.93	59	0	0	0	39	16	66.1	60	310	38	29	4	5	3	3	50	6	55	4	2
Wilson, Stephen, Chicago*	4	9	4.79	45	15	0	0	5	0	139.0	140	597	77	74	17	9	2	1	43	6	95	5	1
Wilson, Trevor, San Francisco*	8	7	4.00	27	17	3	2	3	1	110.1	87	457	52	49	11	6	1	1	49	3	66	0	2
York, Michael, Pittsburgh.	1	1	2.84	4	1	0	0	0	0	12.2	13	56	5	4	1	2	1	0	5	1	4	0	1

NOTE.—The following pitchers combined to pitch shutout games: Atlanta (2)—Leibrandt, Parrett and Grant; Glavine and Grant; Chicago (3)—Maddux and Williams; Harkey and Williams; Maddux and Long; Cincinnati (7)—Browning and Myers 3, Armstrong and Mahler; Robinson and Charlton; Houston (3)—Clancy, Agosto and Smith; Portugal, Agosto and Smith; Portugal and Andersen; Los Angeles—None. Montreal (1)—Martinez, Frey and Burke; New York (7)—Viola and Franco 2; Viola, Whitehurst and Franco; Fernandez and Pena; Gooden and Ojeda; Cone and Franco; Darling, Ojeda and Innis; Philadelphia (1)—Cook and McDowell; Pittsburgh (1)—Patterson, Ruskin and Belinda; St. Louis (8)—Tudor and Tewksbury; Tudor and Dayley; Tudor, Dayley and Terry; DeLeon, Dayley and L. Smith; B. Smith and L. Smith; Magrane and L. Smith; Magrane, Olivares and L. Smith; Magrane, Perez and Dayley; San Diego (3)—Whitson and Lefferts; Hurst and Harris; Lilliquist and Harris; San Francisco (2)—Reuschel, Brantley and Hammaker; Garrelts and Bedrosian.

PITCHERS WITH TWO OR MORE CLUBS IN 1990

Pitcher, Club	W	L	ERA	G	GS	CG	SHO	GF	SV	IP	H	TBF	R	ER	HR	SH	SF	HB	BB	IBB	SO	WP	BK
Boever, Joseph, Atlanta	1	3	4.68	33	0	0	0	21	8	42.1	40	198	23	22	6	2	2	0	35	10	35	2	0
Boever, Joseph, Philadelphia	2	3	2.15	34	0	0	0	13	6	46.0	37	190	12	11	4	2	0	0	16	2	40	1	2
Camacho, Ernie, San Francisco	0	0	3.60	8	0	0	0	3	0	10.0	10	42	6	4	1	0	0	0	3	0	8	1	2
Camacho, Ernie, St. Louis	0	3	7.94	6	0	0	0	3	0	5.2	7	30	6	5	0	1	0	0	6	1	7	1	0
Cook, Dennis, Philadelphia*	8	3	3.56	42	13	2	0	4	0	141.2	132	594	61	56	13	5	2	2	54	9	58	6	3
Cook, Dennis, Los Angeles*	1	0	7.53	5	3	0	0	0	0	14.1	23	69	13	12	7	2	5	1	2	0	6	0	0
Costello, John, St. Louis	0	0	6.23	4	0	0	0	3	0	4.1	7	21	3	3	1	0	2	0	1	1	1	0	0
Costello, John, Montreal	0	0	5.68	5	0	0	0	1	0	6.1	5	26	5	4	2	1	0	1	1	0	1	0	1
Freeman, Marvin, Philadelphia	0	1	5.57	16	3	0	0	4	1	32.1	34	147	21	20	5	1	1	0	14	2	26	4	1
Freeman, Marvin, Atlanta	1	0	1.72	9	0	0	0	1	0	15.2	7	60	3	3	0	4	3	1	9	1	12	0	1
Grant, Mark, San Diego	1	2	4.85	26	1	0	0	5	0	39.0	47	180	23	21	5	2	2	2	19	8	29	1	0
Grant, Mark, Atlanta	1	2	4.64	33	0	0	0	16	3	52.1	61	231	30	27	4	1	0	3	18	3	40	1	1
Greene, I. Thomas, Atlanta	1	0	8.03	5	1	0	0	0	0	12.1	14	61	11	11	3	2	1	1	9	3	4	0	0
Greene, I. Thomas, Philadelphia	2	3	4.15	10	7	0	0	1	0	39.0	36	166	20	18	5	3	0	0	17	1	17	3	1
Hammaker, C. Atlee, San Francisco*	4	5	4.28	25	6	0	0	5	0	67.1	69	282	33	32	7	3	4	0	21	4	28	3	1
Hammaker, C. Atlee, San Diego*	1	4	4.66	9	0	0	0	3	0	19.1	16	81	11	10	1	4	0	0	6	1	16	1	0
Hesketh, Joseph, Montreal*	1	0	0.00	2	0	0	0	0	0	3.0	2	12	0	0	0	0	0	0	1	0	3	0	0
Hesketh, Joseph, Atlanta*	0	2	5.81	31	0	0	0	15	5	31.0	30	135	23	20	5	0	2	0	12	2	21	5	0
Kerfeld, Charles, Houston	0	0	16.20	6	0	0	0	1	0	3.1	9	25	6	6	2	0	0	1	6	3	4	1	0
Kerfeld, Charles, Atlanta	3	1	5.58	25	2	0	0	10	2	30.2	31	143	22	19	3	3	2	0	23	4	27	1	0
Kramer, Randall, Pittsburgh	0	2	4.91	12	2	0	0	2	0	25.2	27	112	15	14	3	2	3	0	9	2	15	0	0
Kramer, Randall, Chicago	0	2	3.98	10	2	0	0	4	0	20.1	20	95	10	9	1	3	0	1	12	2	12	0	0
Lilliquist, Derek, Atlanta*	2	3	6.28	12	11	1	0	1	0	61.2	75	279	45	43	10	6	4	1	19	4	34	0	2
Lilliquist, Derek, San Diego*	2	8	4.33	16	7	0	1	2	1	60.1	61	258	29	29	6	3	1	1	23	0	29	2	1
Parrett, Jeffrey, Philadelphia	4	9	5.18	47	0	0	0	14	1	81.2	92	355	51	47	9	3	4	1	36	8	69	2	1
Parrett, Jeffrey, Atlanta	1	2	3.00	20	0	0	0	5	1	27.0	27	124	11	9	1	4	0	1	19	2	17	2	0
Ruskin, Scott, Pittsburgh*	1	2	3.02	44	0	0	0	8	2	47.2	50	221	21	16	2	3	2	0	28	3	34	3	1
Ruskin, Scott, Montreal*	1	0	2.28	23	0	0	0	4	0	27.0	25	115	7	7	2	2	0	0	10	3	23	3	0
Schatzeder, Daniel, Houston*	1	0	2.39	45	2	0	0	13	0	64.0	61	264	23	17	2	2	5	3	23	4	37	2	0
Schatzeder, Daniel, New York*	0	0	0.00	6	0	0	0	3	0	5.1	5	19	0	0	0	0	2	0	1	0	2	0	0
Smith, Zane, Montreal*	6	7	3.23	22	21	1	0	0	0	139.1	141	578	57	50	11	2	1	3	41	3	80	2	1
Smith, Zane, Pittsburgh*	6	2	1.30	11	10	3	2	1	0	76.0	55	282	20	11	4	1	1	0	9	1	50	1	0

AMERICAN LEAGUE

Including

Team Reviews of 1990 Season

Team Day-by-Day Scores

1990 Standings, Home-Away Records

1990 Pitching Against Each Club

1990 Official A.L. Batting Averages

1990 Official A.L. Fielding Averages

1990 Official A.L. Pitching Averages

Despite an injury, Dave Henderson still enjoyed an outstanding season, clubbing 20 home runs and driving in 63 runs.

Winning's Hard For Rugged A's

By KIT STIER

The Oakland Athletics have learned that winning isn't easy.

That's hard to imagine, considering the mighty A's rampage through the American League in recent years. After winning 103 games in 1990 and 306 over the past three seasons, Oakland became only the 11th team in history to lead all of baseball in victories three straight seasons. So how could winning be difficult for Oakland?

"Since you enjoy the winning you want it more," A's Manager Tony La Russa said after Oakland became the first team to win three straight division titles since the New York Yankees, Kansas City Royals and Philadelphia Phillies ruled their divisions between 1976-78. "You personally want it more and there are higher expectations from others. So it adds a certain pressure."

The A's theme in spring training was to "Stay Focused, Complacency Stinks," and third baseman Carney Lansford handed everyone in an A's uniform a T-shirt with those words that served as a reminder throughout the season.

Staying focused, it turned out, was easy. Playing through a rash of injuries and shaking the surprising Chicago White Sox, on the other hand, was not.

Oakland managed to win the A.L. West by nine games despite playing through a season in which key figures like Jose Canseco, Lansford, Walt Weiss, Willie Randolph, Dave Henderson and Terry Steinbach all spent time on the disabled list.

"We've been hunted all year, they looked to bump us off, they looked to beat us," said pitcher Dave Stewart. "They wanted to take it away from us. We've never complained about the injuries or anything all during the course of this year. We're a very strong ball club."

What carried the A's, as is most often the case with a team that wins, was their pitching and defense. The A's became the first team to win three straight earned-run average titles since the Baltimore Orioles won five consecutive (1969-73). Oakland's 3.18 ERA was the best in the majors last year.

And while position players hobbled into the trainer's room, the pitching staff was a beacon of health through the season.

The Oakland hurlers nearly became the first staff since the 1965 Los Angeles Dodgers to use just five starting pitchers during the course of the entire year. But an in-

Mark McGwire became the first player ever to hit at least 30 homers in each of his first four seasons.

jury to Mike Moore forced reliever Todd Burns to make a start on September 13, and later in the month rookie Reggie Harris became the team's seventh different starter as La Russa set up the rotation for the postseason.

The rotation, as it has been for four years, was anchored by Stewart. He hasn't missed a start since joining the A's rotation midway through 1986. Stewart won a career-high 22 games and became the first pitcher to win 20 games in four straight seasons since Baltimore's Jim Palmer turned the trick between 1975-78.

It was Stewart who set the tone for the season by winning on opening day. He was also on the mound in Cleveland when the A's took over first place in the A.L. West for good, plus he pitched the division-clincher in Kansas City and also tossed a no-hitter in Toronto.

Then there was Bob Welch, a 12-year veteran who'd never won more than 17 games in a season. He became the earliest 20-game winner in 17 years on August 17 in Baltimore. He finished with 27 victories, the most by anyone since Steve Carlton won 27 for the Phillies in 1972 and the most in the A.L. since Denny McLain won 31 for

SCORES OF OAKLAND ATHLETICS' 1990 GAMES

APRIL			Winner	Loser
9—Minnesota	W	8-3	Stewart	Anderson
10—Minnesota	W	5-3	Welch	Smith
11—Minnesota	L	0-3	Tapani	Moore
13—At Seattle	W	15-7	Sanderson	Bankhead
14—At Seattle	W	5-2	Stewart	Young
15—At Seattle	W	3-0	Welch	Holman
17—At Calif.	W	7-5‡	Norris	Eichhorn
18—At Calif.	W	3-1	Sanderson	Witt
19—Seattle	W	5-2	Stewart	Eave
20—Seattle	L	1-6	Holman	Welch
21—Seattle	W	7-6†	Eckersley	Reed
22—Seattle	L	2-5	Hanson	Sanderson
24—At Balt.	W	7-1	Stewart	Johnson
25—At Balt.	W	4-3‡	Nelson	Hickey
26—At Balt.	W	6-4	Moore	Tibbs
27—At Bos.	L	6-7	Reardon	Nelson
28—At Bos.	L	3-12	Harris	Young
29—At Bos.	W	1-0	Stewart	Clemens
30—At N.Y.	W	6-0	Welch	Parker
		Won 14, Lost 5		

MAY			Winner	Loser
1—At N.Y.	W	4-2	Moore	Hawkins
2—At N.Y.	W	2-0	Sanderson	Leary
4—Boston	W	8-3	Stewart	Clemens
5—Boston	L	1-5	Boddicker	Welch
6—Boston	W	4-2	Young	Hetzel
7—New York	W	5-1	Moore	Leary
8—New York	W	5-0	Sanderson	Cadaret
9—New York	W	2-1†	Honeycutt	Plunk
11—Baltimore	W	5-0	Welch	Milacki
12—Baltimore	L	2-3	Williamson	Nelson
13—Baltimore	L	1-4	Tibbs	Moore
14—At Minn.	L	2-6	Anderson	Stewart
15—At Cleve.	W	4-5	Guante	Honeycutt
16—At Cleve.	W	7-6	Eckersley	Jones
18—At Milw.	L	0-5	Wegman	Moore
19—At Milw.	W	9-1	Stewart	Filer
20—At Milw.	L	2-5	Bosio	Sanderson
21—At Tor.	W	4-1	Welch	Stottlemyre
22—At Tor.	W	5-4	Young	Wills
23—Milwaukee	W	12-5	Moore	Wegman
24—Milwaukee	W	13-1	Stewart	Filer
25—Cleveland	W	5-2	Sanderson	Swindell
26—Cleveland	W	6-3	Welch	S. Valdez
28—Toronto	L	0-1	Stieb	Moore
29—Toronto	L	1-2	Wells	Stewart
30—Toronto	W	8-5	Burns	Blair
31—At K.C.	W	6-4	Welch	Gordon
		Won 18, Lost 9		

JUNE			Winner	Loser
1—At K.C.	W	4-3	Sanderson	Appier
2—At K.C.	L	4-10	Saberhagen	Moore
3—At K.C.	L	2-8	Gubicza	Stewart
5—At Texas	W	7-4	Welch	Bohanon
6—At Texas	W	5-4	Sanderson	Ryan
7—At Texas	L	1-3	Witt	Moore
8—Kan. City	W	3-1	Young	Gubicza
9—Kan. City	W	5-0	Stewart	Appier
10—Kan. City	W	3-2	Welch	Farr
11—Texas	L	0-5	Ryan	Sanderson
12—Texas	L	5-6	Arnsberg	Eckersley
13—Texas	W	3-2†	Burns	Arnsberg
14—At Chicago	L	2-3	King	Stewart
15—At Chicago	W	5-4	Welch	Jones
16—At Chicago	W	12-3	Sanderson	Perez
17—At Chicago	W	5-2	Moore	Pall
18—At Detroit	L	2-7	Robinson	Young
19—At Detroit	L	6-7	Gibson	Stewart
20—At Detroit	W	12-7	Welch	Petry
22—Chicago	L	0-5	King	Sanderson
23—Chicago	L	3-5	McDowell	Moore
24—Chicago	L	2-3*	Thigpen	Stewart
25—Detroit	W	4-3	Welch	Petry
26—Detroit	W	3-2	Sanderson	Morris
27—Detroit	L	4-5	Henneman	Burns
29—At Toronto	W	5-0	Stewart	Cerutti
30—At Toronto	W	9-4	Welch	Stieb
		Won 15, Lost 12		

JULY			Winner	Loser
1—At Toronto	L	3-4	Blair	Burns
2—At Toronto	W	3-2	Moore	Key
3—At Milw.	W	5-0	Young	Krueger
4—At Milw.	L	1-7	Robinson	Stewart
5—At Milw.	L	3-4	Higuera	Welch
6—At Cleve.	L	1-6	Swindell	Sanderson
6—At Cleve.	W	12-1	Moore	S. Valdez
7—At Cleve.	L	0-1	Black	Young
8—At Cleve.	W	8-3	Stewart	Nipper

JULY			Winner	Loser
11—At Minn.	W	11-7	Sanderson	Anderson
12—Milwaukee	W	5-3	Moore	Higuera
13—Milwaukee	L	0-2	Knudson	Stewart
14—Milwaukee	W	3-1	Welch	Krueger
15—Milwaukee	W	4-1	Young	Bosio
16—Cleveland	W	3-0	Sanderson	Nipper
17—Cleveland	L	2-4	Swindell	Moore
18—Cleveland	W	4-1	Welch	Candiotti
18—Cleveland	W	5-2	Stewart	Nichols
20—Toronto	L	6-8	Cerutti	Young
21—Toronto	L	1-2	Stieb	Sanderson
22—Toronto	W	3-0	Moore	Key
23—California	W	7-6*	Nelson	Young
24—California	W	5-3	Welch	Abbott
25—California	W	13-3	Young	Blyleven
26—California	L	2-4†	Harvey	Eckersley
27—At Minn.	L	4-9	Smith	Moore
28—At Minn.	W	4-1	Stewart	Guthrie
28—At Minn.	L	4-9	Erickson	Welch
29—At Minn.	L	5-6*	Aguilera	Honeycutt
30—Seattle	W	6-2	Honeycutt	Johnson
31—Seattle	L	2-7	Swift	Moore
		Won 17, Lost 14		

AUGUST			Winner	Loser
1—Seattle	W	1-0†	Stewart	Schooler
2—At Calif.	W	7-5	Welch	McCaskill
3—At Calif.	W	8-6	Harris	Fraser
4—At Calif.	L	5-6‡	Eichhorn	Burns
5—At Calif.	W	4-1	Stewart	Finley
7—Baltimore	W	3-2	Welch	Mitchell
8—Baltimore	L	1-4	McDonald	Sanderson
9—Baltimore	W	5-2	Moore	Johnson
10—New York	W	3-0	Stewart	LaPoint
11—New York	W	10-1	Young	Hawkins
12—New York	W	6-1	Welch	Witt
13—Boston	W	4-0	Sanderson	Harris
14—Boston	L	0-2	Clemens	Moore
15—Boston	W	6-2*	Stewart	Irvine
17—At Balt.	W	8-3	Welch	Mitchell
18—At Balt.	W	3-1	Nelson	McDonald
19—At Balt.	L	2-3	Telford	Sanderson
20—At Chicago	L	1-11	McDowell	Stewart
21—At Chicago	L	1-4	Hibbard	Moore
22—At Chicago	W	7-1	Welch	Perez
24—At Detroit	W	6-4	Sanderson	Terrell
25—At Detroit	L	4-14	Tanana	Stewart
26—At Detroit	L	3-7	Robinson	Welch
28—Kan. City	W	3-2	Moore	Montgomery
29—Kan. City	L	0-6	Appier	Sanderson
30—Kan. City	W	6-5	Eckersley	Crawford
31—Texas	W	4-2	Welch	Moyer
		Won 18, Lost 9		

SEPTEMBER			Winner	Loser
1—Texas	L	2-3	Witt	Young
2—Texas	W	4-2	Moore	Hough
3—At Bos.	W	9-5	Sanderson	Kiecker
4—At Bos.	W	6-2	Stewart	Clemens
5—At Bos.	W	10-0	Welch	Harris
7—At N.Y.	W	7-1	Young	Hawkins
8—At N.Y.	W	5-2	Sanderson	Witt
9—At N.Y.	W	7-3	Stewart	Leary
10—At Seattle	L	2-5	Hanson	Welch
11—At Seattle	W	10-2	Young	Johnson
12—At Seattle	W	9-3	Sanderson	Gardiner
13—Minnesota	L	1-3*	Berenguer	Nelson
14—Minnesota	W	9-1	Stewart	Guthrie
15—Minnesota	W	4-1	Welch	Abbott
16—Minnesota	W	5-4†	Eckersley	Berenguer
17—Chicago	L	0-7	Perez	Sanderson
18—Chicago	L	2-8	Fernandez	Moore
19—Chicago	W	7-3	Stewart	McDowell
21—Detroit	W	6-5	Welch	Parker
22—Detroit	W	5-1	Sanderson	Searcy
23—Detroit	L	0-6	Morris	Moore
24—At K.C.	L	3-10	Gordon	Young
25—At K.C.	W	5-0	Stewart	Appier
26—At K.C.	W	3-2	Welch	Saberhagen
27—At Texas	L	6-8	Chiamparino	Sanderson
28—At Texas	W	4-1	Moore	Hough
29—At Texas	W	7-3	Burns	McMurtry
30—At Texas	W	4-3	Chitren	Ryan
		Won 20, Lost 8		

OCTOBER			Winner	Loser
1—California	L	0-2	Grahe	Stewart
2—California	W	6-4	Welch	Fraser
3—California	L	6-11	Young	Moore
		Won 1, Lost 2		

*10 innings. †11 innings. ‡12 innings.

Bob Welch's 27 wins were the most in the major leagues since Steve Carlton won 27 in 1972.

Detroit in 1968.

Stewart and Welch combined to win 49 games, the most by two teammates since Sandy Koufax and Don Drysdale rang up the same total for the 1965 Dodgers.

The rest of the rotation included Scott Sanderson, a free-agent acquisition who won a career-high 17 games, Moore, who struggled to finish 13-15 after winning 19 games in 1989, and Curt Young, who finshed 9-6.

Backing the rotation was a bullpen that saved 64 games in 71 opportunities and held opposing hitters to a .210 batting average. The amazing Dennis Eckersley saved 48 games in 50 attempts for a team that was 89-2 when it took a lead into the ninth inning. Eckersley topped the team with a microscopic 0.61 ERA, walking just four batters in 73⅓ innings.

Gene Nelson, Joe Klink and Rick Honeycutt all pitched effectively out of the bullpen. Aside from their spot starts late in the season, Burns and Harris also pitched well in relief.

Because A's starters were so successful, the relief corps pitched only 417⅓ innings, the third-lowest total in the league, and

yielded a league-low 24 homers.

So it was pitching much more than the well-publicized "Bash Brothers" that got the job done for the A's. Oakland's .254 team batting average ranked 12th in the league, but the team finished third in runs scored and homers.

This isn't to say the A's were total patsies at the plate. Leadoff-man Rickey Henderson earned A.L. Most Valuable Player honors. He barely missed winning his first batting crown.

Mark McGwire hit a paltry .235, but he became the first player in history to hit at least 30 homers (39 in 1990) in each of his first four seasons. He also led the club with 108 runs batted in and earned a Gold Glove at first base.

Before they got hurt, Canseco (37 homers, 101 RBIs) and Dave Henderson (20 homers, 63 RBIs) were enjoying strong seasons. Ditto for Weiss and Lansford. But the A's depth pulled them through the injuries. Players like Mike Gallego, Doug Jennings and Lance Blankenship filled the gaps, although their hitting left something to be desired.

The catching crew also did a fine job. Between Steinbach, Jamie Quirk and Ron Hassey, Oakland got steady performances from its receivers.

General Manager Sandy Alderson acquired veteran second baseman Randolph from the Dodgers on May 12 to give the infield a little more punch. Then on August 29, the A's added two more proven hitters. Harold Baines was acquired from Texas and Willie McGee, who would win his second National League batting crown, was obtained from St. Louis. The tandem brought experience to the club down the stretch and into the playoffs.

The A's reached the playoffs in workmanlike fashion. They got off to a fast start, ground through the middle months of the season and then finished with a burst.

They won a club-record 20 games in September, and over the last three years are 56-25 in September and 115-56 from August 1 to the end of the season.

"I don't feel amazed," La Russa said as the season drew to an end. "Impressed. There's a big difference. It's so hard to do once, then keep doing it."

But despite its regular-season success, Oakland stumbled in the postseason. The A's advanced to the A.L. Championship Series and swept Boston to reach their third straight World Series. But Cincinnati stunned the A's with a sweep of its own in the Series, proving that winning isn't so easy for the A's.

Robin Ventura was part of a youth movement in Chicago last year that saw the White Sox make a 25-game improvement over their 1989 record.

Comiskey Era Ends With a Bang

By DAVE VAN DYCK

As the lights dimmed for the last time on Comiskey Park, it ended a "Field of Dreams" era and season for the Chicago White Sox.

"It wasn't a dream season because we didn't finish first, but it certainly was a satisfying season," said Manager Jeff Torborg.

Despite posting the second-best record in the American League, the White Sox only finished second in the A.L. West. But they were first in the hearts of the more than two million fans who came to see the surprising team and to close Comiskey, the baseball icon that harbors a myriad of memories, including the 1919 "Black Sox" scandal.

Ironically, when the 1990 season ended the team wore black socks as part of a new uniform ensemble to signify the beginning of a new era in 1991 in a new park across the street. But there was no scandal in 1990, only a surprisingly exciting 94-68 season that closed the door on 80 years of tradition at Comiskey Park.

If there was any hint of scandal in 1990, it was the mysterious departure of former general manager Larry Himes late in the season. But Himes left his mark on the White Sox for years to come, as his last four No. 1 draft choices contributed heavily to the team's 1990 success and figure to blossom in future seasons. Himes also rebuilt a barren minor league system and brought an attitude of hope for the future.

"Larry said he thought we could be the franchise of the '90s," Torborg said.

The job of nurturing the White Sox into a habitual contender now belongs to former Oakland front-office executive Ron Schueler. He has cornerstone rookies to build around at third base (Robin Ventura), first base (Frank Thomas), right field (Sammy Sosa) and on the pitching mound (Alex Fernandez).

Fernandez, Thomas and Ventura, Himes' last three No. 1 picks, all arrived in the big leagues quickly, skipping Class AAA. Plus the team's best starting pitcher down the stretch in 1990, Himes' first No. 1 choice Jack McDowell, spent all of 1989 in the minor leagues.

Despite their youth, the White Sox pushed the eventual pennant-winning A's until the final two weeks of the season, even though they were the first second-

Ozzie Guillen's .279 batting average tied his career-high effort.

place team to be eliminated.

"It really was quite an accomplishment," Torborg said. "Especially when it's in what I consider the best division in baseball. We accomplished a lot, a whole lot. These guys did a heckuva job, more than anyone thought they could.

"To say I'm proud doesn't say enough. This club has never let down. Even when it hit a couple of flat spots, the attitude never changed. Every time someone counted us out, we responded."

Perhaps it was because of the team's innocent youthfulness, not knowing they should not challenge Oakland. But one definite key to the team's first-place push was pitching.

Eric King and Greg Hibbard led a pitching corps that finished with a 3.61 earned-run average, second best in the league and a marked improvement over its 4.23 ERA in 1989. The staff was led in victories by a different pitcher for the eighth straight season, as McDowell and Hibbard each

SCORES OF CHICAGO WHITE SOX' 1990 GAMES

APRIL

Date		Score	Winner	Loser
9—Milwaukee	W	2-1	Jones	Fossas
10—At Milw.	W	5-3	Radinsky	Filer
13—Cleveland	L	2-6	Farrell	Long
14—Cleveland	W	9-4	Perez	Swindell
15—Cleveland	W	4-1	Hibbard	Bearse
17—Boston	W	2-1	Jones	Smith
18—Boston	L	5-7	Clemens	McDowell
21—At Cleve.	L	4-8	Candiotti	Perez
22—At Cleve.	L	2-5	Black	Hibbard
24—At Texas	L	4-5	Rogers	Thigpen
25—At Texas	W	5-4	McDowell	Witt
26—At Texas	L	0-1	Ryan	Perez
27—Toronto	W	6-1	Hibbard	Cerutti
28—Toronto	W	5-4	Kutzler	Flanagan
29—Toronto	W	10-3	King	Key
30—Texas	W	5-4x	Thigpen	Moyer

Won 10, Lost 6

MAY

Date		Score	Winner	Loser
1—Texas	W	5-1	Perez	Ryan
2—Texas	L	3-6	Hough	Hibbard
4—At K.C.	W	5-4‡	Jones	Farr
5—At K.C.	W	6-0	King	Dotson
6—At K.C.	L	6-7†	Farr	Thigpen
7—At Toronto	L	1-6	Stieb	McDowell
8—At Toronto	W	4-1	Hibbard	Cerutti
9—At Toronto	L	3-4	Wills	Edwards
11—Kan. City	W	6-4	Jones	M. Davis
12—Kan. City	W	6-3	Perez	Dotson
13—Kan. City	W	4-3	Radinsky	Montgomery
15—Baltimore	W	3-2	Jones	Harnisch
16—Baltimore	W	4-2	Kutzler	Milacki
17—Baltimore	W	7-3	Jones	Holton
18—Detroit	L	2-8	DuBois	Perez
19—Detroit	L	4-6	Tanana	McDowell
20—Detroit	L	2-3†	Nunez	Edwards
21—At N.Y.	W	6-5	Radinsky	Guetterman
22—At N.Y.	L	2-5	LaPoint	Perez
23—At Balt.	W	6-3	King	Johnson
24—At Balt.	W	5-3	Radinsky	Tibbs
25—At Detroit	L	1-2	Gibson	Hibbard
26—At Detroit	W	10-4	Patterson	Robinson
27—At Detroit	W	2-1	Perez	Morris
28—New York	W	2-1	King	Leary
29—New York	W	5-4	Thigpen	Robinson
30—New York	W	5-2	Hibbard	Cary
31—Minnesota	L	2-3	Guthrie	Kutzler

Won 18, Lost 10

JUNE

Date		Score	Winner	Loser
1—Minnesota	W	2-1	Jones	Leach
2—Minnesota	L	1-2	Candelaria	King
3—Minnesota	W	5-2	McDowell	Anderson
5—Seattle	L	6-10	Holman	Hibbard
6—Seattle	W	5-0	Perez	Young
7—Seattle	L	1-2	Johnson	Pall
8—At Minn.	W	3-2	Radinsky	Berenguer
9—At Minn.	W	4-2	King	Anderson
10—At Minn.	W	5-3	Hibbard	Smith
11—At Seattle	W	3-1	Perez	Young
12—At Seattle	L	2-5	Johnson	Peterson
13—At Seattle	W	11-2	McDowell	Hanson
14—Oakland	W	3-2	King	Stewart
15—Oakland	L	4-5	Welch	Jones
16—Oakland	L	3-12	Sanderson	Perez
17—Oakland	L	2-5	Moore	Pall
18—California	L	1-4	Abbott	McDowell
19—California	L	3-5	McCaskill	Perez
20—California	W	2-1	Jones	Langston
22—At Oak.	W	5-0	King	Sanderson
23—At Oak.	W	5-3	McDowell	Moore
24—At Oak.	W	3-2†	Thigpen	Stewart
25—At Calif.	W	2-0	Hibbard	Langston
26—At Calif.	W	11-9	Jones	Eichhorn
27—At Calif.	W	5-2	King	Finley
29—New York	W	1-0	McDowell	Cary
30—New York	L	7-10	Robinson	Perez

Won 17, Lost 10

JULY

Date		Score	Winner	Loser
1—New York	W	4-0	Jones	Hawkins
2—Detroit	W	5-4	Thigpen	Henneman
3—Detroit	L	7-13	Nunez	King
4—Detroit	L	7-10§	McCullers	Patterson
6—Baltimore	W	4-2	Perez	Harnisch
7—Baltimore	L	1-4	Mitchell	Hibbard
8—Baltimore	L	6-8‡	Williamson	Thigpen
11—Milwaukee	L	9-12x	Plesac	Pall
12—At N.Y.	W	8-0*	Perez	Hawkins
13—At N.Y.	W	3-2	Hibbard	Cary
14—At N.Y.	W	8-7†	Pall	Guetterman
15—At N.Y.	W	8-5	Patterson	Mills
16—At Detroit	L	4-5	Henneman	Pall
17—At Detroit	W	7-3	Perez	Morris
18—At Detroit	W	7-5	Pall	Henneman
19—At Balt.	L	1-4	Mitchell	Peterson
20—At Balt.	L	2-3†	Williamson	Thigpen
21—At Balt.	L	0-2	McDonald	McDowell
22—At Balt.	L	3-9	Harnisch	Perez
23—Cleveland	W	3-1	Hibbard	Candiotti
24—Cleveland	W	8-3	Peterson	Nichols
25—Cleveland	L	1-6	Black	King
27—Milwaukee	W	7-4	McDowell	Robinson
28—Milwaukee	W	5-4	Radinsky	Plesac
29—Milwaukee	L	8-9‡	Mirabella	Radinsky
30—At Bos.	L	0-3	Clemens	Peterson
31—At Bos.	L	2-7	Kiecker	King

Won 13, Lost 14

AUGUST

Date		Score	Winner	Loser
1—At Bos.	L	5-9	Bolton	McDowell
2—At Milw.	W	4-3	Jones	Veres
2—At Milw.	W	4-2	Perez	Navarro
3—At Milw.	W	6-2	Hibbard	Knudson
4—At Milw.	W	9-6	Peterson	Krueger
5—At Milw.	W	6-1	McDowell	Powell
6—At K.C.	L	4-5	S. Davis	Perez
7—At K.C.	W	5-3	Fernandez	Filson
8—At K.C.	L	1-5	Gordon	Hibbard
9—At K.C.	L	3-5	Appier	Peterson
10—Texas	W	5-2	McDowell	McMurtry
10—Texas	W	5-1	Edwards	Ryan
11—Texas	L	5-7	Hough	Perez
13—Toronto	L	3-4	Ward	Thigpen
14—Toronto	L	4-12	Stottlemyre	Hibbard
15—Toronto	W	4-3	McDowell	Candelaria
17—At Texas	L	0-1x	Rogers	Pall
17—At Texas	W	4-2	Perez	Hough
18—At Texas	L	3-8	Barfield	Fernandez
19—At Texas	W	4-2	Edwards	Moyer
20—Oakland	W	11-1	McDowell	Stewart
21—Oakland	W	4-1	Hibbard	Moore
22—Oakland	L	1-7	Welch	Perez
23—California	W	4-2	Fernandez	McCaskill
24—California	W	5-2	Edwards	Abbott
25—California	L	2-3	Langston	Thigpen
26—California	L	1-4	Grahe	Hibbard
27—At Minn.	L	0-7	Anderson	Perez
28—At Minn.	L	6-12	Drummond	Peterson
29—At Minn.	L	1-6	Guthrie	Edwards
30—At Minn.	W	4-3	McDowell	West
31—At Calif.	W	6-5	King	Langston

Won 17, Lost 15

SEPTEMBER

Date		Score	Winner	Loser
1—At Calif.	W	9-5	Perez	Grahe
2—At Calif.	L	0-1	Finley	Fernandez
3—Kan. City	W	4-2	Edwards	Appier
4—Kan. City	W	6-3	McDowell	McGaffigan
5—Kan. City	W	3-0	Hibbard	Farr
7—At Toronto	L	1-3	Stottlemyre	Perez
8—At Toronto	L	0-3	Stieb	Fernandez
9—At Toronto	L	1-6	Key	McDowell
10—At Cleve.	L	2-3	D. Jones	B. Jones
10—At Cleve.	W	6-2	King	Nagy
11—At Cleve.	L	3-4	Orosco	Jones
12—At Cleve.	L	2-12	Black	Perez
13—Boston	W	9-6	Fernandez	Bolton
14—Boston	W	4-0	McDowell	Hesketh
15—Boston	W	7-4	Hibbard	Harris
16—Boston	W	4-2	King	Kiecker
17—At Oak.	W	7-0	Perez	Sanderson
18—At Oak.	W	8-2	Fernandez	Moore
19—At Oak.	L	3-7	Stewart	McDowell
20—At Seattle	L	3-7	Hanson	Hibbard
21—At Seattle	W	5-4	King	Johnson
22—At Seattle	W	14-5	Rosenberg	Knackert
23—At Seattle	W	2-1	Fernandez	Young
25—Minnesota	L	3-4	Guthrie	McDowell
26—Minnesota	W	3-1	Hibbard	Tapani
27—Milwaukee	W	6-4	Edwards	Edens
28—Seattle	L	4-13	Johnson	Fernandez
29—Seattle	W	5-2	King	Young
30—Seattle	W	2-1	McDowell	DeLucia

Won 18, Lost 11

OCTOBER

Date		Score	Winner	Loser
1—At Bos.	L	3-4	Reardon	Jones
2—At Bos.	W	3-2‡	Pall	Lamp
3—At Bos.	L	1-3	Boddicker	Fernandez

Won 1, Lost 2

*6 innings. †10 innings. ‡11 innings. §12 innings. x13 innings.

Alex Fernandez rounded out the Chicago rotation upon his recall from Class AA.

registered a team-leading 14 victories. Last year's leader, Melido Perez, struggled to win 13 games. King, who spent nearly a month on the disabled list with a sore shoulder, ended with a 12-4 record and Fernandez was 5-5.

But it was the bullpen that kept the White Sox in most games, making a league-high 367 relief appearances. It also preserved 52 of Chicago's 94 victories by one or two runs.

No one contributed more to Chicago's pitching renaissance than Bobby Thigpen, who set a major league record with 57 saves and was also involved in a record 64.9 percent of his team's 94 victories. Thigpen blew only eight save opportunities while recording a 1.83 ERA in a league-high 77 appearances.

The entire bullpen was nearly as good as Thigpen, with Barry Jones getting credit for setting up most of Thigpen's saves. Rookies Wayne Edwards, Scott Radinsky and Adam Peterson, along with Ken Patterson and Donn Pall, helped Chicago set a major league saves record (68).

The offense also did its share of work, winning 16 times in its final at-bat. That helped the White Sox post a winning record against every Western Division opponent.

Taking the team concept to extremes, the offense boasted eight players with 50 or more runs batted in for the first time since 1977, while featuring three players with 30 or more steals for the first time since 1902.

Torborg, the A.L. Manager of the Year, credits the team's improved play and positive attitude to Gold Glove shortstop Ozzie Guillen and catcher Carlton Fisk, who were both named co-captains in spring training.

"When they became captains it really helped," Torborg said. "Ozzie is so enthusiastic and Pudge (Fisk) is so respected with everything he says."

Fisk, at age 42, led the team in homers (18) and tied rejuvenated center fielder Lance Johnson for the team's top batting average. Guillen found his hitting stroke, along with backup catcher Ron Karkovice, teaming with fiery second baseman Scott Fletcher to form one of the best double-play combinations in baseball.

But the big offensive numbers belonged to left fielder Ivan Calderon, whose 44 doubles were one shy of the team record. Calderon also led the team in runs, hits, total bases and RBIs.

Despite left shoulder problems much of the season, Calderon also joined Johnson and the flashy Sosa with more than 30 steals. Sosa, in fact, was the only A.L. player to record double figures in doubles, triples, homers and stolen bases.

If there was one area in which the White Sox lacked, it was home run power. Without the 16 hit by Ron Kittle before his trade to Baltimore, Chicago would have hit the fewest homers in the league. Outfielder/designated hitter Dan Pasqua provided some punch, pacing the team in slugging percentage.

But even the lack of power couldn't hide an amazing and amusing season.

Not only did utilityman Steve Lyons inadvertently pull down his pants in front of television cameras in Detroit, but the White Sox and Rangers endured a 7½-hour delay to play a game, Perez threw a rain-shortened, six-inning no-hitter versus New York and Chicago was no-hit by the Yankees' Andy Hawkins and still won. Yes, it was a crazy final season at Comiskey Park.

"If someone would have said we would win that many games, I would have said, 'What, are you crazy, are you trying to make us feel good?'" Torborg said.

"This means so much to me because last year killed me, it was embarrassing."

Rafael Palmeiro set his sites on the 1990 American League batting title, but finished third with a .319 average.

Woeful Start Corrals Rangers

By PHIL ROGERS

Another season has passed and the Texas Rangers have again posted another middle-of-the-pack finish.

More than five years after Manager Bobby Valentine provided fresh hope for a struggling franchise, the Rangers can still resemble the franchise they once were—the pathetic Washington Senators. That was the case in April and May, anyway, when Texas fell out of the American League West picture.

A 21-32 start through early June sentenced the Rangers to a third-place finish in the West, 20 games behind first-place Oakland. The 83-79 record did, however, give them consecutive winning seasons for the first time since the club posted winning marks between 1977-79; no small blessing for a franchise that has never won a division title.

"The final record is what it is," Valentine said. "I'll take it. It's nothing to shoot for, but there were some good things. It was an extraordinary season and situation where the guys pulled together to play good ball after a bad May."

Starting pitching was the key for a team that never clicked offensively. Bobby Witt came of age as a consistently dominating starter, Nolan Ryan turned in his sixth no-hitter and another solid year and Kevin Brown flashed enough potential to whet the Rangers' appetite for the time when he contributes for a full season.

Witt had teased the Rangers in the past, but he put it together in 1990. He boasted a 17-10 record with a 3.36 earned-run average and finished behind only Ryan in the A.L. strikeout race with 221. More importantly, Witt reduced his walks to 4.46 per nine innings.

Ryan provided the two top moments in the season. He no-hit the Oakland Athletics June 11 at the Oakland Coliseum. Then he became the 20th 300-game winner in baseball history, reaching the milestone July 31 at Milwaukee. He pitched with a bad back much of the season, but still went 13-9 with a 3.44 ERA while leading the A.L. in strikeouts with 232.

Brown wore down in September, but won 12 games for the second consecutive year. Charlie Hough, the club's Pitcher of the Year six times between 1982 and 1988, showed his age as the fourth starter but still finished 12-12 with a 4.07 ERA. The fifth starter's spot was a black hole until

Jeff Huson solidified the shortstop position for Texas.

General Manager Tom Grieve traded Harold Baines to the A's for prospect Scott Chiamparino, who compiled a 2.63 ERA in six late starts.

There was trouble in the bullpen, as 1989 Fireman of the Year Jeff Russell struggled. He underwent elbow surgery in late May and saw his save total drop from 38 to 10.

Kenny Rogers, who paced the team with 15 saves, and Brad Arnsberg, who notched five saves, picked up some of the slack. Mike Jeffcoat, a solid fifth starter in 1989, was moved to middle relief but battled a bad back and saw his ERA jump from 3.58 to 4.47. His troubles allowed rookie John Barfield to earn a spot.

Gary Mielke and Craig McMurtry didn't impress in relief roles and Jamie Moyer ended the season as an unimpressive reliever after failing during two different stints in the rotation.

Brian Bohanon, a No. 1 draft choice in 1987, broke camp with the team but was ineffective and saw little action, perhaps because of arm troubles that were diagnosed later.

A big-bang offense was expected to be the club's calling card, but the Rangers produced only 676 runs, a drop from the previous year. The decrease would have been worse without an impressive season

SCORES OF TEXAS RANGERS' 1990 GAMES

APRIL

			Winner	Loser
9—Toronto	W	4-2	Ryan	Stottlemyre
10—At Toronto	L	1-2	Stieb	Hough
11—At Toronto	W	11-5	Brown	Cerutti
12—At Toronto	L	1-7	Flanagan	Moyer
13—At N.Y.	L	0-3	Perez	Witt
14—At N.Y.	W	8-4	Ryan	Hawkins
15—At N.Y.	L	1-3	Plunk	Russell
17—Milwaukee	W	6-2	Brown	Fossas
18—Milwaukee	L	6-11	Fossas	Moyer
19—Milwaukee	L	0-11	Bosio	Witt
20—New York	W	6-5	Ryan	Guetterman
21—New York	W	9-6	Hough	Cadaret
22—New York	W	10-4	Brown	Leary
24—Chicago	W	5-4	Rogers	Thigpen
25—Chicago	L	4-5	McDowell	Witt
26—Chicago	W	1-0	Ryan	Perez
27—At K.C.	W	7-6	Russell	M. Davis
28—At K.C.	W	9-2	Brown	S. Davis
29—At K.C.	L	2-5	Montgomery	Rogers
30—At Chicago	L	4-5‡	Thigpen	Moyer

Won 11, Lost 9

MAY

			Winner	Loser
1—At Chicago	L	1-5	Perez	Ryan
2—At Chicago	W	6-3	Hough	Hibbard
5—At Cleve.	W	9-5	Brown	Guante
6—At Cleve.	L	5-9	Candiotti	Bohanon
6—At Cleve.	L	0-3	Shaw	Witt
8—Kan. City	L	5-10	Gubicza	Ryan
9—Kan. City	W	9-3	Hough	S. Davis
10—Kan. City	L	2-6	Montgomery	Brown
11—Cleveland	L	4-5	Olin	Russell
12—Cleveland	W	2-1	Witt	Black
13—Cleveland	L	1-4	Farrell	Hough
15—Detroit	L	2-3	Petry	Brown
16—Detroit	L	0-12	Robinson	Bohanon
17—Detroit	L	5-7*	Henneman	Russell
18—At Balt.	L	1-13	Johnson	Witt
19—At Balt.	W	5-3	Hough	Tibbs
20—At Balt.	L	0-4	Harnisch	Brown
21—At Bos.	L	2-4	Boddicker	Mielke
22—At Bos.	W	5-4	Witt	Kiecker
23—At Detroit	L	1-5	DuBois	Jeffcoat
24—At Detroit	W	3-2	Hough	Tanana
25—Baltimore	L	2-12	Harnisch	Brown
26—Baltimore	L	5-7†	Olson	Russell
27—Baltimore	L	2-9	Ballard	Witt
28—Boston	L	3-4	Reed	Russell
29—Boston	L	1-2	Clemens	Hough
30—Boston	W	4-3*	Rogers	Gardner

Won 8, Lost 19

JUNE

			Winner	Loser
1—California	L	3-4	Blyleven	Witt
2—California	W	6-3	Jeffcoat	Finley
3—California	L	4-7	Abbott	Hough
4—California	W	1-0	Brown	McCaskill
5—Oakland	L	4-7	Welch	Bohanon
6—Oakland	L	4-5	Sanderson	Ryan
7—Oakland	W	3-1	Witt	Moore
8—At Calif.	W	10-6	Hough	Fetters
9—At Calif.	L	3-8	McCaskill	Jeffcoat
10—At Calif.	W	2-1	Brown	Langston
11—At Oak.	W	5-0	Ryan	Sanderson
12—At Oak.	W	6-5	Arnsberg	Eckersley
13—At Oak.	L	2-3†	Burns	Arnsberg
14—At Seattle	L	4-5	Comstock	Rogers
15—At Seattle	W	4-3	Brown	Holman
16—At Seattle	L	0-5	Young	Ryan
17—At Seattle	L	3-6	Johnson	Witt
18—Minnesota	W	7-1	Hough	West
19—Minnesota	W	5-4	Arnsberg	Candelaria
20—Minnesota	W	8-0	Brown	Drummond
22—Seattle	W	5-2	Ryan	Young
23—Seattle	L	6-8†	Jackson	Rogers
24—Seattle	L	5-11	Hanson	Hough
25—At Minn.	L	1-9	Erickson	Jeffcoat
26—At Minn.	L	4-5	Berenguer	Brown
27—At Minn.	W	9-2	Ryan	Tapani
28—At Minn.	W	8-6	Witt	West
29—At Bos.	W	4-3	Barfield	Gray
30—At Bos.	W	6-5	Jeffcoat	Reardon

Won 16, Lost 13

JULY

			Winner	Loser
1—At Bos.	L	4-15	Bolton	Brown
2—At Bos.	L	2-3	Boddicker	Rogers
3—Baltimore	W	7-2	Witt	Mitchell
4—Baltimore	L	4-9	Johnson	Hough
5—Baltimore	W	3-2	Jeffcoat	Milacki
6—Boston	W	4-0	Brown	Gardner
7—Boston	W	7-4	Ryan	Boddicker
8—Boston	W	4-3†	Rogers	Gray
12—At Detroit	W	11-1	Brown	Morris
13—At Detroit	W	7-6	Witt	Gleaton
14—At Detroit	W	5-3	Ryan	Robinson
15—At Detroit	L	2-3	Searcy	Jeffcoat
16—At Balt.	L	6-7	Olson	Rogers
17—At Balt.	L	3-5	Harnisch	Brown
18—At Balt.	W	7-1	Witt	Johnson
20—Detroit	W	5-3	Ryan	Searcy
21—Detroit	L	1-8	Petry	Jeffcoat
22—Detroit	W	5-3	Arnsberg	Morris
23—New York	W	3-2	Brown	Cary
24—New York	W	4-1	Witt	Leary
25—New York	W	9-7†	Rogers	Leiter
27—At Toronto	L	0-1	Stieb	Hough
28—At Toronto	W	3-2‡	Arnsberg	Wills
29—At Toronto	L	8-10	Acker	McMurtry
30—At Milw.	W	3-1	Witt	Krueger
31—At Milw.	W	11-3	Ryan	Bosio

Won 17, Lost 9

AUGUST

			Winner	Loser
1—At Milw.	W	8-2	Hough	Robinson
2—Toronto	W	5-4†	Arnsberg	Candelaria
3—Toronto	W	9-1	Moyer	Wells
4—Toronto	W	3-2	Witt	Stottlemyre
5—Toronto	L	4-6	Cerutti	Ryan
6—Toronto	W	4-3	Hough	Stieb
7—At Cleve.	L	4-8	Ward	Brown
8—At Cleve.	L	3-5	Shaw	Moyer
9—At Cleve.	W	13-5	Witt	Black
10—At Chicago	L	2-5	McDowell	McMurtry
10—At Chicago	L	1-5	Edwards	Ryan
11—At Chicago	W	7-5	Hough	Perez
13—At K.C.	L	3-5	Appier	Brown
14—At K.C.	L	0-1	Farr	Mielke
15—At K.C.	W	2-1	Witt	S. Davis
17—Chicago	W	1-0‡	Rogers	Pall
17—Chicago	L	2-4	Perez	Hough
18—Chicago	W	8-3	Barfield	Fernandez
19—Chicago	L	2-4	Edwards	Moyer
20—Seattle	W	6-5	Jeffcoat	Jackson
21—Seattle	L	3-4	Johnson	Hough
22—Seattle	W	5-4	Ryan	Swift
24—Minnesota	W	2-0	Barfield	Guthrie
25—Minnesota	L	5-8	West	Mielke
26—Minnesota	W	1-0	Witt	Leach
27—At Calif.	L	3-7	Fraser	Barfield
28—At Calif.	L	0-2	McCaskill	Ryan
29—At Calif.	L	2-9	Abbott	Barfield
31—At Oak.	L	2-4	Welch	Moyer

Won 14, Lost 15

SEPTEMBER

			Winner	Loser
1—At Oak.	W	3-2	Witt	Young
2—At Oak.	L	2-4	Moore	Hough
3—Cleveland	W	6-2	Ryan	Walker
4—Cleveland	L	5-7	S. Valdez	Brown
5—Cleveland	W	3-2	Rogers	Jones
6—Kan. City	W	12-1	Witt	Codiroli
7—Kan. City	W	9-4	Hough	Gordon
8—Kan. City	W	2-1	Rogers	Appier
9—Kan. City	W	6-5	Arnsberg	Farr
10—At N.Y.	W	1-0†	Rogers	Guetterman
11—At N.Y.	L	4-5	Guetterman	Witt
12—At N.Y.	W	5-4	Hough	Adkins
14—Milwaukee	W	2-1*	Rogers	Crim
15—Milwaukee	W	6-3	Moyer	Edens
16—Milwaukee	L	3-5	Robinson	Chiamparino
17—At Seattle	W	10-4	Witt	Gardiner
18—At Seattle	L	3-7	DeLucia	Jeffcoat
19—At Seattle	W	6-5	Barfield	Young
21—At Minn.	W	2-1	Witt	Berenguer
22—At Minn.	L	0-2	Casian	Chiamparino
23—At Minn.	L	4-6	Erickson	Hough
24—California	L	2-3	Langston	Ryan
25—California	L	2-8	Lewis	Witt
26—California	W	6-2	Rogers	McCaskill
27—Oakland	W	8-6	Chiamparino	Sanderson
28—Oakland	L	1-4	Moore	Hough
29—Oakland	L	3-7	Burns	McMurtry
30—Oakland	L	3-4	Chitren	Ryan

Won 16, Lost 12

OCTOBER

			Winner	Loser
1—At Milw.	W	4-2	Jeffcoat	Robinson
2—At Milw.	L	0-1	Brown	Rogers
3—At Milw.	L	3-6	Higuera	Barfield

Won 1, Lost 2

*10 innings. †11 innings. ‡13 innings.

Bobby Witt became a dominating starter in 1990, winning 17 games and finishing second in the league strikeout race to teammate Nolan Ryan.

from first baseman Rafael Palmeiro, who had 14 homers and 89 runs batted in and chased Kansas City's George Brett for the A.L. batting title until the final week of the season. Palmeiro finished with a .319 average and led A.L. players with 191 hits.

Second baseman Julio Franco was a steady All-Star for the second consecutive year, batting .296 and leading the team with 96 runs scored. He also stole 31 bases.

Shortstop Jeff Huson was a pleasant surprise. He came cheaply from Montreal in a spring trade and solidified one of the team's major weaknesses. His batting average slid to .240 as he played with a bad knee late in the year. Gary Green started the final 30 games at shortstop, but he never found his hitting stroke.

Catcher Geno Petralli and third baseman Steve Buechele added almost nothing to the offense, although there was an excuse for Buechele. He was off to a fast start before a pitch broke his wrist, finishing with a .215 average and only seven homers.

Backup catchers Mike Stanley and John Russell both provided steady bats. But Scott Coolbaugh and Jeff Kunkel did little to impress as reserve infielders.

Jack Daugherty was a pleasant surprise. He hit .300 in his first full major league season as a backup first baseman/designated hitter with a .435 slugging average.

Ruben Sierra felt he did not play up to his abilities, but he still led the team with 96 RBIs. His defense was shaky in right field, however, and he finished the year fighting Valentine's urge to make him a full-time DH.

The rest of the outfield played according to form. Left fielder Pete Incaviglia hit for power (24 homers, 85 RBIs), but not average (.233), and center fielder Gary Pettis earned a Gold Glove, but was a liability at the plate (.239). He did pace the club in steals, swiping 38 bases.

Backup outfielder/DH Kevin Reimer provided a solid bat off the bench, collecting 12 pinch-hits to tie the club single-season record.

Youngster Juan Gonzalez looked ready for the big leagues, hitting .289 with four homers and 12 RBIs in a 90 at-bat trial in September. He led the Class AAA American Association with 29 homers and 101 RBIs before his call-up.

But club accountants may have had the best season of all. Texas set a home attendance record for the fourth time in five years, surpassing the two-million mark for the second straight year. Management can only speculate what attendance might have been if the Rangers had shed their cloak of mediocrity and contended the entire season.

Lefthander Chuck Finley won 18 games, finished second in the American League with a 2.40 ERA and was voted by his teammates as the Angels' most valuable player.

Instability Clips Angels' Wings

By DAVE CUNNINGHAM

Baseball keeps track of many different records, but you won't find an entry for "most lineups used in a season" anywhere. Apparently, it's never been considered significant before.

But in 1990, the California Angels' never-ending succession of lineups became their most remarkable statistic. During the first 94 games of the season, Manager Doug Rader penciled out 93 different batting orders.

"God knows I would've loved to use a set lineup every day," he said. "I would love to have continuity and have everyone understand their roles, but the amount of juggling that was necessary, due to injury and a roster that wasn't balanced the way we hope to have it next year, made that impossible."

Rader began to have bad feelings about the season even before it began. During spring training, injuries cut down four key players—shortstop Dick Schofield, reliever Bob McClure, third baseman Jack Howell and catcher Bill Schroeder. By the end of the season, the Angels had tied a club record with 15 disabling injuries.

"It was like a dike leaking," Rader said. "You stick a finger in here, all of a sudden it's leaking over there, and pretty soon you feel like you've run out of fingers.

"I don't want to dwell on the injuries because it sounds like an alibi, but it was a strange year."

Expected to challenge the Oakland Athletics for the American League West title, the Angels stumbled to an 80-82 record that placed them fourth in the division, 23 games behind the first-place A's.

Injuries aside, the Angels' biggest problem was their inexplicable failure to field the ball with any consistency. They committed 46 more errors than the previous season when they set a club record for fewest miscues.

"Our defensive play was the most disappointing thing," Rader said, "and the pitching staff suffered because of it. It did more to affect us adversely than anything else, even more than the injuries.

"Offensively, we were no different than last year. Take last year's statistics and compare them to this year's, and you'll see."

In fact, almost all of the Angels' batting numbers were up. They hit .260, compared to .256 the year before, and also hit more

Outstanding play from Lance Parrish was one commodity the Angels could count on last year.

home runs (147-145), scored more runs (690-669) and totaled more runs batted in (646-624).

"And we did all that," Rader pointed out, "without having Wally Joyner a great deal of the year, without having Chili Davis for a while, without having Luis Polonia and Dave Winfield for a whole year and with subpar years from some of our people."

The Angels' offensive charge can be attributed to General Manager Mike Port's wheeling and dealing. He pulled off two productive trades in 1990, both with the Yankees. He got Polonia in exchange for Claudell Washington and pitcher Rich Monteleone on April 29, then just 11 days later acquired Winfield in a one-for-one deal for Mike Witt.

Witt (5-9 with a 4.00 ERA) and Washington (.167 batting average) had unproductive, injury-plagued seasons in New York, while Polonia and Winfield flourished under the California sun.

Polonia led the Angels in hitting at .335 and stole 21 bases, tying Devon White for the club lead. Winfield drove in a team-high 78 runs and hit 21 homers.

Several other Angels enjoyed strong seasons. Second baseman Johnny Ray, along with designated hitter Brian Downing and

SCORES OF CALIFORNIA ANGELS' 1990 GAMES

APRIL

Date	W/L	Score	Winner	Loser
9—Seattle	L	4-7	Holman	Blyleven
10—Seattle	W	7-0	Finley	Johnson
11—Seattle	W	1-0	Langston	Eave
12—Minnesota	W	3-1	McCaskill	West
13—Minnesota	L	4-7	Anderson	Witt
14—Minnesota	W	7-5‡	Harvey	Aguilera
15—Minnesota	W	4-1	Finley	Tapani
17—Oakland	L	5-7‡	Norris	Eichhorn
18—Oakland	L	1-3	Sanderson	Witt
20—At Minn.	L	1-13	Tapani	Abbott
21—At Minn.	L	0-8	West	Blyleven
22—At Minn.	W	5-2	Finley	Anderson
24—At Bos.	L	2-4	Clemens	Langston
25—At Bos.	W	3-1	McCaskill	Boddicker
26—At Bos.	L	4-5	Smith	Harvey
27—At N.Y.	L	4-5	Guetterman	Fraser
28—At N.Y.	L	2-3	Cadaret	Finley
29—At N.Y.	W	4-3	Langston	LaPoint
30—At Balt.	L	1-2‡	Holton	Witt

Won 8, Lost 11

MAY

Date	W/L	Score	Winner	Loser
1—At Balt.	W	7-1	Abbott	Tibbs
2—At Balt.	W	3-0	Blyleven	Ballard
3—At Seattle	L	8-10	Knackert	Finley
4—New York	L	2-5	LaPoint	Langston
5—New York	L	3-11	Parker	McCaskill
6—New York	L	2-4	Hawkins	Abbott
7—Baltimore	L	5-6	Tibbs	Eichhorn
8—Baltimore	W	6-0	Finley	Ballard
9—Baltimore	L	1-9	Harnisch	Langston
10—At Seattle	L	2-5	Holman	McCaskill
11—Boston	L	2-3	Boddicker	Eichhorn
12—Boston	L	1-7	Harris	Blyleven
13—Boston	W	8-4	Finley	Lamp
15—At Milw.	W	8-3	Langston	Bosio
16—At Milw.	L	5-13	Higuera	Abbott
17—At Milw.	L	3-6	Mirabella	Fraser
18—At Toronto	W	4-2	Abbott	Stieb
19—At Toronto	W	11-9	Fraser	Ward
20—At Toronto	L	1-5	Wills	Langston
21—At Cleve.	W	5-3	Blyleven	Shaw
22—At Cleve.	W	8-3	Finley	Candiotti
23—Toronto	W	5-4	Bailes	Ward
24—Toronto	W	4-3†	Harvey	Henke
25—Milwaukee	W	5-4§	Fraser	Fossas
26—Milwaukee	W	10-3	Blyleven	Knudson
27—Milwaukee	W	7-3	Finley	Wegman
28—Cleveland	L	0-3*	Guante	Abbott
29—Cleveland	W	2-1	McCaskill	Farrell
30—Cleveland	L	2-4	Candiotti	Langston

Won 15, Lost 14

JUNE

Date	W/L	Score	Winner	Loser
1—At Texas	W	4-3	Blyleven	Witt
2—At Texas	L	3-6	Jeffcoat	Finley
3—At Texas	W	7-4	Abbott	Hough
4—At Texas	L	0-1	Brown	McCaskill
5—At K.C.	W	6-4	Langston	Dotson
6—At K.C.	W	6-2	Blyleven	Gordon
7—At K.C.	W	2-1	Finley	Saberhagen
8—Texas	L	6-10	Hough	Fetters
9—Texas	W	8-3	McCaskill	Jeffcoat
10—Texas	L	1-2	Brown	Langston
11—Kan. City	W	3-2	Blyleven	M. Davis
12—Kan. City	W	3-0	Finley	Saberhagen
13—Kan. City	L	4-11	Aquino	Abbott
15—At Detroit	L	1-2*	Gleaton	Harvey
16—At Detroit	L	2-6	Morris	Blyleven
17—At Detroit	W	7-3	Finley	DuBois
18—At Chicago	W	4-1	Abbott	McDowell
19—At Chicago	W	5-3	McCaskill	Perez
20—At Chicago	L	1-2	Jones	Langston
21—Detroit	W	6-4	Blyleven	Morris
22—Detroit	W	1-0	Bailes	Gibson
23—Detroit	L	4-9	Robinson	Abbott
24—Detroit	W	10-2	McCaskill	Tanana
25—Chicago	L	0-2	Hibbard	Langston
26—Chicago	L	9-11	Jones	Eichhorn
27—Chicago	L	2-5	King	Finley
29—At Cleve.	W	7-2	Abbott	Nagy
30—At Cleve.	L	1-4	Candiotti	McCaskill

Won 15, Lost 13

JULY

Date	W/L	Score	Winner	Loser
1—At Cleve.	L	3-5	Swindell	Langston
2—At Cleve.	W	2-1	Finley	Orosco
3—At Toronto	L	2-5	Stottlemyre	Blyleven
4—At Toronto	L	2-4	Cerutti	Abbott
5—At Toronto	L	2-9	Stieb	McCaskill
6—At Milw.	W	9-8x	Minton	Edens
7—At Milw.	W	4-3†	Fetters	Veres
8—At Milw.	L	7-20	Edens	Minton
11—At Seattle	L	1-2	Hanson	Langston
12—Toronto	L	0-5	Wells	McCaskill
13—Toronto	W	2-0	Abbott	Stottlemyre
14—Toronto	W	8-7	Eichhorn	Ward
15—Toronto	W	3-2	Finley	Henke
16—Milwaukee	L	1-3	Robinson	Langston
17—Milwaukee	W	8-1	McCaskill	Higuera
18—Milwaukee	L	2-3	Knudson	Abbott
20—Cleveland	W	9-4	Blyleven	Black
21—Cleveland	W	5-2	Finley	Walker
22—Cleveland	L	1-8	Swindell	Langston
23—At Oak.	L	6-7*	Nelson	Young
24—At Oak.	L	3-5	Welch	Abbott
25—At Oak.	L	3-13	Young	Blyleven
26—At Oak.	W	4-2†	Harvey	Eckersley
27—At Seattle	L	1-8	Hanson	Langston
28—At Seattle	L	1-2	Holman	McCaskill
29—At Seattle	W	6-2	Abbott	Young
30—At Minn.	L	3-7	Tapani	Blyleven
31—At Minn.	W	13-2	Finley	Anderson

Won 12, Lost 16

AUGUST

Date	W/L	Score	Winner	Loser
1—At Minn.	W	11-5	Langston	Smith
2—Oakland	L	5-7	Welch	McCaskill
3—Oakland	L	6-8	Harris	Fraser
4—Oakland	W	6-5‡	Eichhorn	Burns
5—Oakland	L	1-4	Stewart	Finley
7—Boston	L	3-6	Bolton	Langston
8—Boston	W	8-6†	Fraser	Lamp
9—Boston	L	3-14	Clemens	Abbott
10—Baltimore	W	2-1*	Fraser	Olson
11—Baltimore	W	12-4	Finley	Weston
12—Baltimore	L	6-11	Mitchell	Langston
13—New York	W	4-2	McCaskill	Cary
14—New York	W	9-5	Abbott	Leary
15—New York	W	8-1	Langston	LaPoint
17—At Bos.	W	1-0	Finley	Boddicker
18—At Bos.	W	4-3	McCaskill	Bolton
19—At Bos.	L	1-4	Clemens	Abbott
20—At Detroit	W	5-3	Langston	Gibson
21—At Detroit	L	2-6	Petry	Grahe
22—At Detroit	L	4-7	Morris	Finley
23—At Chicago	L	2-4	Fernandez	McCaskill
24—At Chicago	L	2-5	Edwards	Abbott
25—At Chicago	W	3-2	Langston	Thigpen
26—At Chicago	W	4-1	Grahe	Hibbard
27—Texas	W	7-3	Fraser	Barfield
28—Texas	W	2-0	McCaskill	Ryan
29—Texas	W	9-2	Abbott	Barfield
31—Chicago	L	5-6	Hibbard	Langston

Won 16, Lost 12

SEPTEMBER

Date	W/L	Score	Winner	Loser
1—Chicago	L	5-9	Perez	Grahe
2—Chicago	W	1-0	Finley	Fernandez
3—At N.Y.	W	7-0	McCaskill	Leary
5—At N.Y.	L	1-2	LaPoint	Harvey
6—At N.Y.	W	12-6†	McClure	Guetterman
7—At Balt.	L	2-6	McDonald	Grahe
8—At Balt.	L	4-5	Price	Eichhorn
9—At Balt.	L	1-3	Telford	McCaskill
10—Minnesota	W	3-1	J. Abbott	P. Abbott
11—Minnesota	W	9-0	Langston	Tapani
12—Minnesota	W	8-6	Grahe	Drummond
13—Seattle	W	7-1	Finley	Comstock
14—Seattle	W	7-5	McClure	Young
15—Seattle	L	2-7	Hanson	Abbott
16—Seattle	L	3-5	Swift	Harvey
18—Detroit	L	2-3	Morris	Finley
19—Detroit	L	5-12	Terrell	Grahe
21—At K.C.	W	12-5	McCaskill	Saberhagen
22—At K.C.	L	3-4	M. Davis	Abbott
23—At K.C.	L	0-4	Farr	Finley
24—At Texas	W	3-2	Langston	Ryan
25—At Texas	W	8-2	Lewis	Witt
26—At Texas	L	2-6	Rogers	McCaskill
27—Kan. City	W	7-6	Harvey	Montgomery
28—Kan. City	L	1-2	Farr	Finley
29—Kan. City	L	6-9	McGaffigan	Langston
30—Kan. City	L	1-2	Appier	Lewis

Won 12, Lost 15

OCTOBER

Date	W/L	Score	Winner	Loser
1—At Oak.	W	2-0	Grahe	Stewart
2—At Oak.	L	4-6	Welch	Fraser
3—At Oak.	W	11-6	Young	Moore

Won 2, Lost 1

*10 innings. †11 innings. ‡12 innings. §13 innings. x16 innings.

Kirk McCaskill helped anchor a solid California rotation with 12 wins and a 3.25 ERA.

catcher Lance Parrish, provided steady offense. Ray's .277 average helped offset his defensive liabilities, while Downing (14 homers, 51 RBIs) and Parrish (a club-leading 24 homers and 70 RBIs) proved they still have a lot of pop in their aging bats.

Schofield rebounded from his injury to bat .255 after hitting .186 as late as August 1. The surge probably recaptured some job security for him in a season when several Angels were losing theirs.

But utilitymen Donnie Hill, Rick Schu and Kent Anderson helped their cause with surprising years at the plate. And even though they struggled in 1990, outfielder Dante Bichette and first baseman Lee Stevens, who filled in for an injured Joyner, figure to blossom into steady performers.

Third baseman Howell (.228) and center fielder White (.217), both of whom were temporarily demoted to the minor leagues in July, where two of the biggest disappointments. Reserve outfielder Max Venable also did little to distinguish himself.

But even with the strong campaigns registered by several individuals, the Angels couldn't advert a decline. The 1989 team won 11 more games than the '90 edition, finishing in third place just eight games

behind the eventual World Series champion A's. The 1990 Angels were never a factor in the race.

Chuck Finley was a bright spot on the pitching staff, emerging as one of the most dominating lefthanders in the A.L. Finley posted an 18-9 mark, ranked second in the league in earned-run average (2.40) and was voted by his teammates as the Angels' Most Valuable Player. But in two years, Finley will be eligible for free agency, a thought that obviously frightens the Angels.

"We need to make changes," Rader said. "We need to get things done quickly because we have a few players, especially on our pitching staff, who in a couple of years can opt for free agency. And if we don't start putting a ball club on the field that they can feel confident pitching for, they're going to go someplace else.

"I think that's the most pressing issue; that we do the best thing for the group, so we're able to keep all the components."

Kirk McCaskill (12-11, 3.25 ERA) is another pitching component California would like to keep. He is just one season away from free agency. A couple years behind will be Jim Abbott, who has posted double-figure win totals in each of his first two big-league seasons.

One player who figures to be in California a while is Mark Langston. But a lack of support badgered him after he signed a five-year, $16-million contract last year. He produced a 10-17 ledger and 4.40 ERA to become the Angels' losingest pitcher in 16 years. Aging Bert Blyleven rounded out the rotation, but he struggled with a 5.24 ERA.

The Angels got a glimpse of their future when Scott Lewis and Joe Grahe made late-season starts. Both flashed promise during their trials.

And for the most part, the Angels' bullpen performed admirably, paced by Bryan Harvey's team-high 25 saves. Mark Eichhorn (13 saves), Mike Fetters and Willie Fraser also pitched well, while Scott Bailes failed with a 6.37 ERA in relief.

"Sweeping changes are not practical, but there will be changes," Rader said. "I really believe we have the people here who can get things very solidly under way. We need more speed and more depth, but by adding just the right kind of people in the right roles, I think we can do some things.

"Starting pitching is our strength, and it has been for years. Finley's been terrific. Jimmy Abbott could easily have had 15 wins, and so could McCaskill. And I don't see any reason why Mark Langston can't have a big year next year."

Erik Hanson paced the Seattle pitching staff in 1990, setting a team-record for wins by a righthander with 18.

Mariner Milestones Lack Wins

By JIM STREET

The Seattle Mariners' 1990 season was full of firsts. Among other things, a Seattle pitcher tossed the first no-hitter in team history, a father and son played on the same team at the same time for the first time and for the first time the team drew more than 1.5 million fans. But the Mariners couldn't accomplish their most important first: achieving a winning season.

For the 14th consecutive year, Seattle posted a losing record. But in this season of firsts, it wasn't supposed to happen that way.

"Five teams in our division are capable of winning 90 games this season, and the Mariners are one of them," Oakland Athletics Manager Tony La Russa said during spring training in handicapping the American League West.

But as it turned out, only two A.L. West teams won as many as 90 games in 1990, and the Mariners weren't one of them. Their 77-85 record was the second-best in club history, but so much more was expected.

In sorting out the 1990 Mariners' season, two categories—runners left on base and the disabled list—address why they continued their losing ways.

Their uncanny inability to hit in the clutch was measured by the number of runners left on base, 1,227 (the third-highest total in the A.L.) That also helped cause Seattle to post a 20-28 mark in one-run games.

As Ken Griffey Sr., who spent the last month of the season with the Mariners playing alongside his son, Ken Griffey Jr., put it: "They play hard, but they don't know how to win. Sometimes, they don't know what to do. They don't have the killer instinct."

But they do know how to get hurt.

In his two seasons as manager of the Mariners, Jim Lefebvre has used more than 200 lineups. It's not that he can't make up his mind, but injuries have kept him from playing with a full deck.

The disabled list was used a club-record 15 times in '90. Jay Buhner was the Mariners' disabled list king with 108 games missed. But outfielder Tracy Jones had the strangest injury of all. As he stepped out of his car after driving home from a game, he suffered torn cartilage in his right knee and missed the last two months of the season.

Despite a drop in his batting average, second baseman Harold Reynolds earned a Gold Glove.

Position players were on the disabled list so often that they combined to miss 307 games. Add to that number the 29 missed starts by projected pitching ace Scott Bankhead and the month-long absence of closer Mike Schooler and starter Brian Holman and the picture becomes even more black and blue.

The development of Seattle's young pitchers was the most encouraging aspect of the season. When healthy, the Mariners' staff emerged as potentially one of the best in the league. Seattle set several club records, including best earned-run average (3.69, which ranked third in the A.L.). The staff also led the league in strikeouts (1,064) and ranked second in batting average against (.243), both team records.

The Seattle starters allowed a major league low .239 batting average. Erik Hanson (18-9) developed into the ace of the staff. He won 12 of his last 15 decisions, including seven in a row at the end of the season to become the first Seattle right-hander to win 18 games. He also paced the club in strikeouts (211) and had the best ERA among starters (3.24).

Lefthander Randy Johnson (14-11) pitched the first no-hitter in franchise history, beating Detroit at home June 2. His only problem was control.

Holman (11-11) came within one out of a

SCORES OF SEATTLE MARINERS' 1990 GAMES

APRIL

Date		Score	Winner	Loser
9—At Calif.	W	7-4	Holman	Blyleven
10—At Calif.	L	0-7	Finley	Johnson
11—At Calif.	L	0-1	Langston	Eave
13—Oakland	L	7-15	Sanderson	Bankhead
14—Oakland	L	2-5	Stewart	Young
15—Oakland	L	0-3	Welch	Holman
16—Minnesota	W	6-3	Johnson	West
17—Minnesota	L	5-6	Berenguer	Comstock
18—Minnesota	L	3-4	Leach	Young
19—At Oak.	L	2-5	Stewart	Eave
20—At Oak.	W	6-1	Holman	Welch
21—At Oak.	L	6-7†	Eckersley	Reed
22—At Oak.	W	5-2	Hanson	Sanderson
24—At N.Y.	L	2-6	LaPoint	Young
25—At N.Y.	W	5-2	Holman	Perez
26—At N.Y.	W	6-2	Johnson	Hawkins
27—At Balt.	W	4-3	Hanson	Ballard
28—At Balt.	W	4-3	Jackson	Hickey
29—At Balt.	L	4-5	Williamson	Jackson
30—At Bos.	L	0-11	Boddicker	Holman

Won 8, Lost 12

MAY

Date		Score	Winner	Loser
1—At Bos.	L	2-8	Hetzel	Johnson
2—At Bos.	W	9-2	Hanson	Harris
3—California	W	10-8	Knackert	Finley
4—Baltimore	L	8-9	Hickey	Jackson
5—Baltimore	W	5-2	Holman	Johnson
6—Baltimore	W	5-4	Swift	Williamson
7—Boston	L	4-5	Harris	Hanson
8—Boston	W	2-1	Swift	Gardner
9—Boston	L	1-4	Clemens	Eave
10—California	W	5-2	Holman	McCaskill
11—New York	L	5-8	Guetterman	Harris
12—New York	L	1-4	Leary	Hanson
13—New York	W	10-5	Young	Cadaret
15—At Toronto	W	4-3*	Comstock	Acker
16—At Toronto	W	4-2	Holman	Stottlemyre
17—At Toronto	W	14-6	Johnson	Key
18—At Cleve.	L	0-5	Black	Hanson
19—At Cleve.	L	3-4	Orosco	Young
20—At Cleve.	W	8-7*	Schooler	Orosco
21—At Milw.	W	9-4	Clark	Plesac
22—At Milw.	L	2-3	Knudson	Swift
23—Cleveland	W	4-1	Hanson	Black
24—Cleveland	L	3-5	Orosco	Young
25—Toronto	L	1-3†	Acker	Swift
26—Toronto	L	4-11	Wills	Holman
27—Toronto	L	1-5	Cerutti	Johnson
28—Milwaukee	W	4-3	Hanson	Navarro
29—Milwaukee	L	3-5	Crim	Jackson
30—Milwaukee	W	2-1	Clark	Bosio

Won 15, Lost 14

JUNE

Date		Score	Winner	Loser
1—Detroit	L	7-9	Morris	Bankhead
2—Detroit	W	2-0	Johnson	Robinson
3—Detroit	L	0-2	Tanana	Hanson
5—At Chicago	W	10-6	Holman	Hibbard
6—At Chicago	L	0-5	Perez	Young
7—At Chicago	W	2-1	Johnson	Pall
8—At Detroit	W	5-2	Hanson	Tanana
8—At Detroit	L	3-6	Henneman	Comstock
9—At Detroit	W	5-2	Swan	Petry
10—At Detroit	L	3-4	Morris	Holman
11—Chicago	L	1-3	Perez	Young
12—Chicago	W	5-2	Johnson	Peterson
13—Chicago	L	2-11	McDowell	Hanson
14—Texas	W	5-4	Comstock	Rogers
15—Texas	L	3-4	Brown	Holman
16—Texas	W	5-0	Young	Ryan
17—Texas	W	6-3	Johnson	Witt
18—At K.C.	L	2-6	Gubicza	Hanson
19—At K.C.	L	1-2	Farr	Swan
20—At K.C.	W	3-2	Holman	Appier
22—At Texas	L	2-5	Ryan	Young
23—At Texas	W	8-6†	Jackson	Rogers
24—At Texas	W	11-5	Hanson	Hough
26—Kan. City	L	1-4	Gordon	Holman
27—Kan. City	W	3-2	Jackson	M. Davis
28—Kan. City	W	6-4	Comstock	M. Davis
29—Milwaukee	W	4-2	Johnson	Crim
30—Milwaukee	W	6-2	Hanson	Higuera

Won 16, Lost 14

JULY

Date		Score	Winner	Loser
1—Milwaukee	W	6-5‡	Comstock	Mirabella
3—At Cleve.	L	4-9	Nipper	Young
4—At Cleve.	W	3-2	Johnson	Nagy
5—At Cleve.	W	4-1	Hanson	Candiotti
6—At Toronto	L	0-1	Wells	Holman
7—At Toronto	L	2-4	Key	Swan
8—At Toronto	W	6-3	Young	Stottlemyre
11—California	W	2-1	Hanson	Langston
12—Cleveland	L	4-5	Seanez	Schooler
13—Cleveland	L	7-13	Candiotti	Young
14—Cleveland	L	0-3	Black	Johnson
15—Cleveland	W	7-0	Swift	Nagy
16—Toronto	L	3-4	Key	Hanson
17—Toronto	W	7-5	Jackson	Ward
18—Toronto	W	5-2	Young	Stottlemyre
19—At Milw.	L	0-4	Krueger	Johnson
20—At Milw.	W	6-4	Comstock	Veres
21—At Milw.	L	3-10	Robinson	Hanson
22—At Milw.	W	4-3	Holman	Higuera
24—At Minn.	W	8-2	Young	West
25—At Minn.	L	0-6	Tapani	Johnson
26—At Minn.	W	6-4	Swift	Anderson
27—California	W	8-1	Hanson	Langston
28—California	W	2-1	Holman	McCaskill
29—California	L	2-6	Abbott	Young
30—At Oak.	L	2-6	Honeycutt	Johnson
31—At Oak.	W	7-2	Swift	Moore

Won 15, Lost 12

AUGUST

Date		Score	Winner	Loser
1—At Oak.	L	0-1†	Stewart	Schooler
2—Minnesota	W	7-2	Holman	Guthrie
3—Minnesota	L	2-6§	Aguilera	Schooler
4—Minnesota	W	4-3	Jackson	Savage
5—Minnesota	W	4-0	Harris	Anderson
7—New York	L	1-3	Witt	Hanson
8—New York	L	4-6	Plunk	Comstock
9—New York	L	0-1	Leary	Young
10—Boston	W	4-1	Johnson	Kiecker
11—Boston	L	2-4x	Irvine	Schooler
12—Boston	L	2-7	Bolton	Jackson
13—Baltimore	L	2-3	McDonald	Holman
14—Baltimore	W	7-1	Young	Johnson
15—Baltimore	W	2-0	Johnson	Harnisch
17—At N.Y.	L	2-3	Guetterman	Swift
18—At N.Y.	L	0-6	Witt	Holman
19—At N.Y.	L	1-3	Leary	Young
20—At Texas	L	5-6	Jeffcoat	Jackson
21—At Texas	W	4-3	Johnson	Hough
22—At Texas	L	4-5	Ryan	Swift
23—At K.C.	L	1-4	Appier	Holman
24—At K.C.	L	3-4	Farr	Harris
25—At K.C.	W	6-3	Hanson	S. Davis
26—At K.C.	L	2-8	Campbell	Johnson
28—Detroit	W	4-3	Comstock	Gibson
29—Detroit	L	2-4	Terrell	Young
30—Detroit	L	2-3	Henneman	Jackson
31—Kan. City	W	5-2	Johnson	S. Davis

Won 10, Lost 18

SEPTEMBER

Date		Score	Winner	Loser
1—Kan. City	W	3-0	Swan	Crawford
2—Kan. City	L	0-8	Gordon	Holman
3—At Balt.	W	6-2	Young	Telford
4—At Balt.	W	7-2	Hanson	Harnisch
5—At Balt.	W	9-5	Comstock	Hickey
7—At Bos.	L	4-5†	Gray	Jackson
8—At Bos.	L	2-10	Bolton	Medvin
9—At Bos.	W	3-1	Young	Hesketh
10—Oakland	W	5-2	Hanson	Welch
11—Oakland	L	2-10	Young	Johnson
12—Oakland	L	3-9	Sanderson	Gardiner
13—At Calif.	L	1-7	Finley	Comstock
14—At Calif.	L	5-7	McClure	Young
15—At Calif.	W	7-2	Hanson	Abbott
16—At Calif.	W	5-3	Swift	Harvey
17—Texas	L	4-10	Witt	Gardiner
18—Texas	W	7-3	DeLucia	Jeffcoat
19—Texas	L	5-6	Barfield	Young
20—Chicago	W	7-3	Hanson	Hibbard
21—Chicago	L	4-5	King	Johnson
22—Chicago	L	5-14	Rosenberg	Knackert
23—Chicago	L	1-2	Fernandez	Young
25—At Detroit	L	1-4	Henneman	DeLucia
26—At Detroit	W	8-4	Hanson	Tanana
28—At Chicago	W	13-4	Johnson	Fernandez
29—At Chicago	L	2-5	King	Young
30—At Chicago	L	1-2	McDowell	DeLucia

Won 12, Lost 15

OCTOBER

Date		Score	Winner	Loser
1—At Minn.	L	5-7	Tapani	Swan
2—At Minn.	W	3-0	Hanson	Abbott
3—At Minn.	L	4-7	Casian	Johnson

Won 1, Lost 2

*10 innings. †11 innings. ‡12 innings. §13 innings. x14 innings.

Ken Griffey Jr. became the first Mariner to be voted to a starting position in the All-Star Game.

perfect game at Oakland April 20, but was kayoed the final month because of elbow surgery.

The Mariners' prospects look even better if Bankhead comes back from shoulder surgery. He tossed just eight innings last year. Russ Swan, acquired from San Francisco in May for Gary Eave, who struggled with Seattle, filled in for Bankhead in the rotation until he got hurt in July.

Matt Young, the dean of the staff in terms of experience, weathered a nightmarish season in one aspect, but it was encouraging in another way. His 8-18 record wasn't indicative of the way he pitched coming off a career-threatening elbow injury that forced him to miss all of the 1988 season and half of 1989. But he showed his durability by pacing the staff with seven complete games.

Prospect Rich DeLucia looked good in a brief trial at the end of the year. He started the season at Class A and ended it with five strong starts with the Mariners, allowing two or less runs each outing.

Schooler, who had a club-record 33 saves a year ago, anchored the bullpen with a team-high 30 saves. But a shoulder injury sidelined him in late August. Bill Swift started and relieved and did a magnificent job in each role. Keith Comstock (2.89

ERA) also proved to be strong out of the bullpen. But Greg Harris, Mike Jackson, Brent Knackert and Jerry Reed all struggled in relief.

For the first time in a full season, Seattle boasted two hitters among the top 10 A.L. batters. Third baseman Edgar Martinez (.302) and Ken Griffey Jr. (.300) finished sixth and seventh, respectively. Ken Griffey Jr. has stardom stamped all over him and became the first Mariner in history to be voted to a starting position for the All-Star Game while earning a Gold Glove in center field.

"He can be as good as he wants to be, and better," said Ken Griffey Sr., who hit .377 with 18 runs batted in upon arriving from Cincinnati in late August. "He likes to play and that's an important asset. As time goes on, he'll be a more selective hitter and be more dangerous. He'll hit 30 or 40 homers."

Ken Griffey Sr.'s influence as an outfielder during the final month of the season helped not only his son, but the entire club, which has longed for a veteran leader.

Henry Cotto and Greg Briley rounded out the outfield, but neither impressed with their hitting. But Cotto (21 steals) and Briley (16) did flash speed on the basepaths.

The signing of free-agent first baseman Pete O'Brien ($7.6 million over four years) was supposed to help the defense and offense. His glove work was fine. His bat was a bust, posting career lows in virtually every offensive category.

The signing of O'Brien shoved Alvin Davis off first base and into the designated hitter slot, and he had a difficult time adjusting to his new role. Although the .290 career hitter batted a solid .283, his home runs (17) and RBIs (68) weren't Davis-caliber numbers.

Second baseman Harold Reynolds earned his third straight Gold Glove and scored more runs (100) than ever before, but his .252 averaged represented a 48-point drop from '89. And Seattle's hitting from the shortstop slot wasn't much better. Neither Omar Vizquel, Mike Brumley or Brian Giles distinguished themselves.

Dave Valle handled catching duties. No one questioned his defensive work, but his hitting was atrocious (.214 average). His backup, Scott Bradley, led the team in pinch-hitting and became Seattle's all-time pinch-hit leader.

With Bradley's pinch-hit record and the other notable firsts in Seattle history, the 1990 season was the best-ever for the franchise. But in the most important way—the number of wins—it wasn't.

In a season littered with free-agent flops and injuries, Kevin Appier compiled a 2.76 ERA to emerge as the Royals' pitching ace.

Royals Practice Murphy's Law

By STEVE CAMERON

Numbers can lie. But there are times when they almost scream the truth.

Consider this mixed bag of figures: The Kansas City Royals were forced to use a club-record 46 players in 1990, including a team-record 23 pitchers. No fewer than 21 of those players were wearing a Royals uniform for the first time. The Royals also used the disabled list 18 times for 15 different players.

And how did these ghoulish numbers add up for the Royals? Predictably, not very well. The Royals limped their way to a 75-86 mark, good for a sixth-place finish in the American League West, which was their worst finish in franchise history.

The Royals didn't hit, pitch or field efficiently when it mattered most. For instance, Kansas City's shaky bullpen posted a 3.93 earned-run average and allowed opponents a .256 batting average. Given that late-inning leakage, it's no surprise that the Royals were 32-42 in games decided by two runs or less.

The big stories for Kansas City were its two free-agent flops and injuries. Pitchers Mark Davis and Storm Davis inked huge contracts, but both failed miserably and were affected by injuries like many of their teammates.

But the Royals were struggling even before the wholesale rash of injuries. After a 4-4 start, they went 2-12 in a stretch which lasted through May 5 and left them 10½ games behind Oakland before the anticipated race had begun.

So what happened?

Former general manager John Schuerholz, who had such high hopes for the '90 Royals but left to work for the Atlanta Braves after the season, put it this way: "You've heard of Murphy's Law, that 'whatever can go wrong, will go wrong?' We turned out to be baseball's version of Murphy's Law."

Things certainly went awry in the rotation. By the time the season concluded, 16 different pitchers started a game. Opponents hit .268 against the starters, who compiled a 51-65 record and 3.93 ERA.

The team's top two starters, Bret Saberhagen and Mark Gubicza, both had endured surgery during the season. Saberhagen recovered from a relatively minor elbow operation and was pitching again in September, but Gubicza needed work done on his rotator cuff and was finished for the year in August. The Royals hope they'll see him again in 1991. Saberhagen and Gubicza combined to win nine games last season after winning 38 together in 1989.

Storm Davis made 20 starts en route to just seven wins after posting 35 the previous two years at Oakland. Free agent Richard Dotson was ran out of town after seven failed starts produced an 0-4 record and 8.48 ERA. Pete Filson was equally as unimpressive in seven starts before succumbing to an injury in September.

The good news is rookie Kevin Appier and Tom Gordon took regular turns in the rotation. Appier became the staff ace, compiling a 2.76 ERA. He and Gordon both registered 12 wins. Andy McGaffigan also pitched well in 11 starts.

The bullpen, which managed to post a 24-21 mark, also featured two unlikely heroes: Jeff Montgomery and Steve Farr. Montgomery paced the team with 24 saves, while Farr led in victories (13) and ERA (1.98).

Luis Aquino and Steve Crawford also pitched well in relief, despite spending time on the disabled list. After that, though, it went downhill.

Mark Davis was awful. After saving 44 games for San Diego and winning the National League Cy Young Award in 1989, he encountered mechanical problems, finger and elbow injuries and a total loss of confidence. He wound up 2-7 with a 5.11 ERA and just six saves. In fact, he lost his role as the team's stopper and saved only one game after May 11.

Rookies Mel Stottlemyre Jr. and Hector Wagner also took their lumps.

"You hate to use the injuries as an excuse," Manager John Wathan said, "but the fact is that we almost never had our full team on the field, or anything close to it. Our rotation never seemed to stay intact for more than a week."

The Royals offense was also pinched by injuries. Outfielder Danny Tartabull tore a leg muscle shagging flies before the second game of the year. He was injured once more and appeared in only 88 games. He did manage to hit 15 homers and drive in 60 runs.

Outfielder Bo Jackson, the other legitimate long-ball threat, suffered minor tissue damage in his left shoulder on July 17 in New York—after hitting three home runs in the game—and missed over a month. That didn't keep Jackson from hitting a career-high .272 with a team-

SCORES OF KANSAS CITY ROYALS' 1990 GAMES

APRIL

Date	W/L	Score	Winner	Loser
9—Baltimore	L	6-7†	Aldrich	Montgomery
11—Baltimore	W	2-1	Gubicza	Ballard
13—Toronto	L	1-3	Key	S. Davis
14—Toronto	W	3-1	Saberhagen	Stottlemyre
15—Toronto	L	4-5	Stieb	Crawford
16—Cleveland	L	3-6	Candiotti	Gubicza
17—Cleveland	W	4-2	Farr	Olin
18—Cleveland	W	7-0	S. Davis	Farrell
20—At Toronto	L	6-17	Stottlemyre	Saberhagen
21—At Toronto	L	1-5	Stieb	Gubicza
22—At Toronto	W	7-1	Gordon	Cerutti
23—At Balt.	L	5-8	Harnisch	S. Davis
24—At Milw.	L	3-7	Bosio	Dotson
25—At Milw.	L	0-1	Filer	Saberhagen
26—At Milw.	L	2-3	Knudson	Gubicza
27—Texas	L	6-7	Russell	M. Davis
28—Texas	L	2-9	Brown	S. Davis
29—Texas	W	5-2	Montgomery	Rogers

Won 6, Lost 12

MAY

Date	W/L	Score	Winner	Loser
1—Milwaukee	L	4-6	Higuera	Saberhagen
3—Milwaukee	L	5-9	Navarro	Gubicza
4—Chicago	L	4-5†	Jones	Farr
5—Chicago	L	0-6	King	Dotson
6—Chicago	W	7-6*	Farr	Thigpen
7—At Cleve.	W	4-2†	Montgomery	Guante
8—At Texas	W	10-5	Gubicza	Ryan
9—At Texas	L	3-9	Hough	S. Davis
10—At Texas	W	6-2	Montgomery	Brown
11—At Chicago	L	4-6	Jones	M. Davis
12—At Chicago	L	3-6	Perez	Dotson
13—At Chicago	W	3-4	Radinsky	Montgomery
14—Boston	W	9-5*	M. Davis	Reardon
16—Boston	L	1-7	Boddicker	Gordon
18—At N.Y.	W	4-1	Saberhagen	Leary
19—At N.Y.	L	4-5†	McCullers	Farr
20—At N.Y.	W	4-3*	Montgomery	Robinson
21—At Detroit	L	6-11	Robinson	Gordon
22—At Detroit	W	9-8	Farr	Morris
23—At Bos.	W	4-1	Saberhagen	Harris
24—At Bos.	L	1-4	Clemens	Gubicza
25—New York	L	3-6	Cary	S. Davis
26—New York	W	9-4	Gordon	Hawkins
27—New York	W	6-2	Appier	LaPoint
28—Detroit	W	3-2	Saberhagen	DuBois
29—Detroit	W	5-3	Farr	Henneman
30—Detroit	W	4-3	Aquino	Petry
31—Oakland	L	4-6	Welch	Gordon

Won 14, Lost 14

JUNE

Date	W/L	Score	Winner	Loser
1—Oakland	L	3-4	Sanderson	Appier
2—Oakland	W	10-4	Saberhagen	Moore
3—Oakland	W	8-2	Gubicza	Stewart
5—California	L	4-6	Langston	Dotson
6—California	L	2-6	Blyleven	Gordon
7—California	L	1-2	Finley	Saberhagen
8—At Oak.	L	1-3	Young	Gubicza
9—At Oak.	L	0-5	Stewart	Appier
10—At Oak.	L	2-3	Welch	Farr
11—At Calif.	L	2-3	Blyleven	M. Davis
12—At Calif.	L	0-3	Finley	Saberhagen
13—At Calif.	W	11-4	Aquino	Abbott
15—Minnesota	W	5-1	Appier	Drummond
16—Minnesota	W	5-3	Gordon	Guthrie
17—Minnesota	L	1-4	Tapani	Saberhagen
18—Seattle	W	6-2	Gubicza	Hanson
19—Seattle	W	2-1	Farr	Swan
20—Seattle	L	2-3	Holman	Appier
21—At Minn.	W	14-4	Gordon	Guthrie
22—At Minn.	L	2-3	Tapani	Saberhagen
23—At Minn.	L	1-5	West	Gubicza
24—At Minn.	W	11-2	S. Davis	Anderson
26—At Seattle	W	4-1	Gordon	Holman
27—At Seattle	L	2-3	Jackson	M. Davis
28—At Seattle	L	4-6	Comstock	M. Davis
29—Detroit	W	3-2	Crawford	Robinson
30—Detroit	L	3-5	Nunez	S. Davis

Won 11, Lost 16

JULY

Date	W/L	Score	Winner	Loser
1—Detroit	L	4-9	Morris	Gordon
2—New York	W	11-5	Appier	Jones
3—New York	W	6-1	Farr	Leary
4—New York	W	13-6	Crawford	Guetterman
5—At Detroit	W	15-3	Aquino	Petry
6—At Detroit	L	0-4	Morris	Gordon
7—At Detroit	W	4-0	Appier	Tanana
8—At Detroit	L	4-10	Petry	M. Davis
11—At Balt.	L	5-7	Schilling	Farr
13—At Bos.	W	5-3	Gordon	Boddicker
14—At Bos.	W	2-1	Aquino	Murphy
14—At Bos.	L	7-8	Bolton	Baller
15—At Bos.	W	13-4	Crawford	Kiecker
16—At N.Y.	L	2-3	Robinson	Filson
17—At N.Y.	W	10-7	S. Davis	Hawkins
18—At N.Y.	L	3-5	Plunk	Crawford
20—Boston	W	5-0	Appier	Clemens
20—Boston	L	1-3	Kiecker	Aquino
21—Boston	W	4-2	Farr	Reardon
22—Boston	W	2-1	S. Davis	Bolton
24—At Toronto	W	5-3‡	Farr	Ward
25—At Toronto	W	6-1	McGaffigan	Stottlemyre
26—At Toronto	L	5-7	Cerutti	Appier
27—Baltimore	L	2-9	McDonald	S. Davis
28—Baltimore	W	10-9	Crawford	Williamson
28—Baltimore	L	1-3	Johnson	Farr
29—Baltimore	L	1-4	Mitchell	Gordon
30—At Cleve.	W	7-6	McGaffigan	Shaw
31—At Cleve.	W	8-4	Appier	Walker

Won 17, Lost 12

AUGUST

Date	W/L	Score	Winner	Loser
1—At Cleve.	L	1-4	Swindell	M. Davis
2—At Balt.	L	1-5	Johnson	Filson
3—At Balt.	L	1-14	Mitchell	Gordon
4—At Balt.	W	9-1	McGaffigan	Harnisch
6—Chicago	W	5-4	S. Davis	Perez
7—Chicago	L	3-5	Fernandez	Filson
8—Chicago	W	5-1	Gordon	Hibbard
9—Chicago	W	5-3	Appier	Peterson
10—Milwaukee	W	6-5	Montgomery	Plesac
10—Milwaukee	W	9-4	S. Davis	Powell
11—Milwaukee	L	5-11	Robinson	Filson
12—Milwaukee	W	7-1	Gordon	Navarro
13—Texas	W	5-3	Appier	Brown
14—Texas	W	1-0	Farr	Mielke
15—Texas	L	1-2	Witt	S. Davis
17—At Milw.	L	1-2	Higuera	Gordon
18—At Milw.	W	10-1	Appier	Navarro
19—At Milw.	L	2-7	Knudson	McGaffigan
20—Minnesota	W	7-1	S. Davis	West
21—Minnesota	W	8-7	Crawford	Abbott
22—Minnesota	W	6-2	Gordon	Erickson
23—Seattle	W	4-1	Appier	Holman
24—Seattle	W	4-3	Farr	Harris
25—Seattle	L	3-6	Hanson	S. Davis
26—Seattle	W	8-2	Campbell	Johnson
28—At Oak.	L	2-3	Moore	Montgomery
29—At Oak.	W	6-0	Appier	Sanderson
30—At Oak.	L	5-6	Eckersley	Crawford
31—At Seattle	L	2-5	Johnson	S. Davis

Won 17, Lost 12

SEPTEMBER

Date	W/L	Score	Winner	Loser
1—At Seattle	L	0-3	Swan	Crawford
2—At Seattle	W	8-0	Gordon	Holman
3—At Chicago	L	2-4	Edwards	Appier
4—At Chicago	L	3-6	McDowell	McGaffigan
5—At Chicago	L	0-3	Hibbard	Farr
6—At Texas	L	1-12	Witt	Codiroli
7—At Texas	L	4-9	Hough	Gordon
8—At Texas	L	1-2	Rogers	Appier
9—At Texas	L	5-6	Arnsberg	Farr
10—Toronto	L	1-6	Wells	Wagner
11—Toronto	L	4-8	Wills	Stottlemyre
12—Toronto	W	7-5	Gordon	Stottlemyre
14—Cleveland	L	4-6	S. Valdez	Appier
15—Cleveland	L	6-14	Swindell	McGaffigan
16—Cleveland	W	9-6	Montgomery	E. Valdez
17—At Minn.	L	1-0	Farr	Casian
18—At Minn.	L	4-10	Erickson	Gordon
19—At Minn.	L	0-1†	Wayne	Montgomery
21—California	L	5-12	McCaskill	Saberhagen
22—California	W	4-3	M. Davis	Abbott
23—California	W	4-0	Farr	Finley
24—Oakland	W	10-3	Gordon	Young
25—Oakland	L	0-5	Stewart	Appier
26—Oakland	L	2-3	Welch	Saberhagen
27—At Calif.	L	6-7	Harvey	Montgomery
28—At Calif.	W	2-1	Farr	Finley
29—At Calif.	W	9-6	McGaffigan	Langston
30—At Calif.	W	2-1	Appier	Lewis

Won 10, Lost 18

OCTOBER

Date	W/L	Score	Winner	Loser
2—At Cleve.	L	3-13	Candiotti	Wagner
3—At Cleve.	L	2-5	S. Valdez	Smith

Won 0, Lost 2

*10 innings. †11 innings. ‡13 innings.

Rookie second baseman Terry Shumpert looked impressive until a thumb injury ended his season in June.

leading 28 home runs.

But the injuries to Jackson and Tartabull allowed rookie outfielder Brian McRae to emerge. The son of Royals' legend Hal, McRae exploded onto the scene to hit .286 in 46 games.

Jim Eisenreich turned in his second straight consistent season in the outfield. He matched his career high of 139 hits set in 1989. Veteran Willie Wilson was also productive as a fourth outfielder. He led the team with 24 stolen bases in 30 attempts en route to swiping his 600th career base in June. Even Pat Tabler produced, hitting .275 before his trade to the New York Mets in August.

First baseman George Brett, who made baseball history by hitting .329 to win his third batting title in three separate decades (1976, 1980, 1990), anchored the infield with a great offensive year. But he admitted he was part of the Royals' problem in their washout year. Kansas City's Most Valuable Player hit just .200 through May 7 as the Royals continually failed in close games.

"Where was I when it mattered early in the year?," Brett scolded himself on the day he clinched the batting championship. "I had good numbers (14 homers, 87 runs batted in) but I needed some of them early when the team had to have a key hit."

When a guy hits .329 (.388 after the All-Star break) and still thinks he didn't pull his load, well, you know it was a bizarre season.

Along with Brett, the rest of the Kansas City infield enjoyed a good year at the plate. Rookie Terry Shumpert unseeded veteran Frank White at second base and looked impressive until a thumb injury ended his season in June. White struggled with a .216 average.

Third baseman Kevin Seitzer hit a solid .275 and paced the team in runs (91) and walks (67) while batting leadoff most of the year.

Mike Macfarlane became the No. 1 catcher when veteran Bob Boone was limited to 40 games due to an injury. Macfarlane established career highs in nearly every offensive category.

Kurt Stillwell was again steady at shortstop, hitting .249. He drove in 50 or more runs for the third straight year.

Gerald Perry split time between serving as designated hitter and playing first base. His .254 average was 13 points below his career mark, but he still stole 17 bases.

Bill Pecota became the consummate utilityman, playing six different positions and batting .242 in 87 games. Fellow utilityman Steve Jeltz split time between second base and shortstop, but he failed to hit.

Summing it up for the 1990 Royals, statistics were accurate. The Royals, who bounced into the season brimming with optimism on the heels of a 92-win season, were pretty poor from start to finish.

"We just screwed it up from the beginning," Jackson said. "From beginning to end."

Kevin Tapani's staff-leading 12 wins offered a glimmer of hope in an otherwise disappointing season for the Twins.

Futile Offense Perplexes Twins

By JIM CAPLE

Minnesota Twins' fans must still be rubbing their eyes in disbelief of the crazy 1990 season they just witnessed. It was an odd year, a bad year and a year third baseman Gary Gaetti felt that the Twins weren't even consistently inconsistent.

It was a year the Twins turned two triple plays in one game. A year the Twins allowed 10 unearned runs in one game. A year outfielder John Moses pitched twice in relief of Allan Anderson. And a year Kirby Puckett played right field, shortstop, third base and second base in the same game. There was one constant among all of those zany events—the Twins lost on each occasion.

How consistently inconsistent were the Twins? The club compiled its best-ever record in May, finishing 21-7. But in a transformation that would make Dr. Hyde smile, the Twins posted a ghoulish 7-21 mark in June. They capped their season by posting the majors' worst record the final four months. Thrown in that fatal finish were two nine-game losing streaks. By August 6, Minnesota claimed last place in the American League West and never relinquished the dishonor.

Minnesota figured it would have ups and downs in 1990 while weaning a youthful rotation into the major leagues. It also figured its perennially robust offense would help keep the team afloat during rough times. But a funny thing happened by season's end. For the first time in years, there were more questions about the offense than about the pitching. The Twins did hit .265 as a team, but only two A.L. teams scored fewer runs.

The Twins' offensive woes can be attributed to the poor seasons Puckett, Kent Hrbek and Gaetti experienced. For years they were as dangerous as any trio in baseball. But in 1990 they hit fewer home runs combined (50) than Detroit's Cecil Fielder hit by himself (51). Other than those three, no other Twin reached double digits in home runs. Minnesota finished with 100 home runs, hitting only 57 over the final four months.

There were times Gaetti looked like a victim of a bad back and old age. And times when he resembled the awesome Gaetti of 1988. And times when he looked like both in the same game. "It's been elusive," said Gaetti, who hit a career-low .229 while leading the team in runs batted in (85).

Brian Harper punctuated his season with a 25-game hitting streak, the longest ever by an A.L. catcher.

Puckett registered two five-hit games and was hitting .345 with nine home runs by June 6. But he hit .270 with three home runs the rest of the year, collecting no homers after July 15. He missed games due to injury for the first time in his career. To top it off, Puckett was moved from center field in mid-August, the club said, to save his legs. But the veteran never admitted they were hurting.

Having signed a big contract in the off-season, Hrbek amassed fewer RBIs than in 1989 when he missed nearly two months. At times, the first baseman looked like an oversized slap hitter. He did manage to pace the Twins in homers (22).

There were middle-infield problems, too. Second base remained a black hole. Acquired on opening day, Fred Manrique showed no range, then no bat. Switch-

SCORES OF MINNESOTA TWINS' 1990 GAMES

APRIL

Date		Score	Winner	Loser
9—At Oak.	L	3-8	Stewart	Anderson
10—At Oak.	L	3-5	Welch	Smith
11—At Oak.	W	3-0	Tapani	Moore
12—At Calif.	L	1-3	McCaskill	West
13—At Calif.	W	7-4	Anderson	Witt
14—At Calif.	L	5-7‡	Harvey	Aguilera
15—At Calif.	L	1-4	Finley	Tapani
16—At Seattle	L	3-6	Johnson	West
17—At Seattle	W	6-5	Berenguer	Comstock
18—At Seattle	W	4-3	Leach	Young
20—California	W	13-1	Tapani	Abbott
21—California	W	8-0	West	Blyleven
22—California	L	2-5	Finley	Anderson
23—Detroit	L	3-6	Tanana	Smith
24—Detroit	W	16-4	Candelaria	Ritz
25—Detroit	L	4-6	Robinson	Tapani
27—At Cleve.	L	2-7	Black	West
28—At Cleve.	L	0-3	Farrell	Anderson
29—At Cleve.	L	4-6	Swindell	Smith

Won 7, Lost 12

MAY

Date		Score	Winner	Loser
1—At Detroit	W	9-5	Candelaria	Gibson
2—At Detroit	W	8-2	West	Morris
3—At Detroit	W	3-1*	Leach	Henneman
5—At Milw.	W	9-5	Candelaria	Crim
6—At Milw.	W	4-0	Tapani	Higuera
8—Cleveland	W	6-5	Berenguer	Olin
9—Cleveland	L	3-7	S. Valdez	Candelaria
10—Cleveland	W	3-2	Smith	Swindell
11—Milwaukee	L	3-6	Wegman	Anderson
12—Milwaukee	W	5-2	Tapani	Knudson
13—Milwaukee	W	8-6	Berenguer	Krueger
14—Oakland	W	6-2	Anderson	Stewart
15—At N.Y.	L	3-7	Cary	Smith
17—At N.Y.	W	4-1	Tapani	LaPoint
18—At Bos.	W	6-0	Candelaria	Harris
19—At Bos.	L	1-13	Clemens	Anderson
20—At Bos.	W	5-4	Smith	Hetzel
21—At Balt.	W	7-3	Guthrie	Milacki
22—At Balt.	L	2-10	Williamson	Tapani
23—New York	L	0-12	Leary	Drummond
24—New York	W	5-4	Aguilera	Cadaret
25—Boston	W	16-0	Smith	Hetzel
26—Boston	W	6-5	Candelaria	Murphy
27—Boston	W	3-1	Tapani	Kiecker
28—Baltimore	W	6-4	Berenguer	Price
29—Baltimore	L	1-5	Milacki	Anderson
30—Baltimore	W	12-3	Smith	Harnisch
31—At Chicago	W	3-2	Guthrie	Kutzler

Won 21, Lost 7

JUNE

Date		Score	Winner	Loser
1—At Chicago	L	1-2	Jones	Leach
2—At Chicago	W	2-1	Candelaria	King
3—At Chicago	L	2-5	McDowell	Anderson
5—At Toronto	L	3-7	Wells	Smith
6—At Toronto	W	12-5	Candelaria	Blair
7—At Toronto	L	3-10	Stottlemyre	Tapani
8—Chicago	L	2-3	Radinsky	Berenguer
9—Chicago	L	2-4	King	Anderson
10—Chicago	L	3-5	Hibbard	Smith
12—Toronto	L	4-5	Stottlemyre	Candelaria
13—Toronto	L	1-10	Cerutti	West
14—Toronto	L	1-7	Stieb	Anderson
15—At K.C.	L	1-5	Appier	Drummond
16—At K.C.	L	3-5	Gordon	Guthrie
17—At K.C.	W	4-1	Tapani	Saberhagen
18—At Texas	L	1-7	Hough	West
19—At Texas	L	4-5	Arnsberg	Candelaria
20—At Texas	L	0-8	Brown	Drummond
21—Kan. City	L	4-14	Gordon	Guthrie
22—Kan. City	W	3-2	Tapani	Saberhagen
23—Kan. City	L	5-1	West	Gubicza
24—Kan. City	L	2-11	S. Davis	Anderson
25—Texas	W	9-1	Erickson	Jeffcoat
26—Texas	W	5-4	Berenguer	Brown
27—Texas	L	2-9	Ryan	Tapani
28—Texas	L	6-8	Witt	West
29—Baltimore	L	2-6	Johnson	Anderson
30—Baltimore	L	0-6	Milacki	Erickson

Won 7, Lost 21

JULY

Date		Score	Winner	Loser
1—Baltimore	W	4-3	Aguilera	Olson
3—Boston	W	7-3	Tapani	Clemens
4—Boston	L	3-4	Lamp	Aguilera
5—Boston	W	7-4	Drummond	Murphy
6—At N.Y.	W	2-0‡	Berenguer	Hawkins
6—At N.Y.	L	3-5	LaPoint	Smith
7—At N.Y.	L	4-5‡	Guetterman	Leach
8—At N.Y.	W	6-3	West	Leary
11—Oakland	L	7-11	Sanderson	Anderson
13—At Balt.	L	5-8	Williamson	Berenguer
13—At Balt.	W	3-1	West	Johnson
14—At Balt.	L	2-3†	Williamson	Leach
15—At Balt.	W	10-3	Anderson	Milacki
16—At Bos.	W	3-2	Berenguer	Gray
17—At Bos.	L	0-1	Bolton	Erickson
18—At Bos.	L	4-5	Lamp	Berenguer
19—New York	L	1-2	Leary	Smith
20—New York	W	2-1	Anderson	LaPoint
21—New York	W	2-1	Guthrie	Robinson
22—New York	L	6-10	Cadaret	Aguilera
24—Seattle	L	2-8	Young	West
25—Seattle	W	6-0	Tapani	Johnson
26—Seattle	L	4-6	Swift	Anderson
27—Oakland	W	9-4	Smith	Moore
28—Oakland	L	1-4	Stewart	Guthrie
28—Oakland	W	9-4	Erickson	Welch
29—Oakland	W	6-5*	Aguilera	Honeycutt
30—California	W	7-3	Tapani	Blyleven
31—California	L	2-13	Finley	Anderson

Won 15, Lost 14

AUGUST

Date		Score	Winner	Loser
1—California	L	5-11	Langston	Smith
2—At Seattle	L	2-7	Holman	Guthrie
3—At Seattle	W	6-2§	Aguilera	Schooler
4—At Seattle	L	3-4	Jackson	Savage
5—At Seattle	L	0-4	Harris	Anderson
6—Milwaukee	L	0-6	Robinson	Smith
7—Milwaukee	L	3-5	Navarro	Guthrie
8—Milwaukee	W	4-2	Erickson	Knudson
10—At Toronto	W	7-3	West	Cerutti
11—At Toronto	L	4-7	Stieb	Leach
12—At Toronto	W	5-4	Anderson	Key
14—At Cleve.	W	5-4	Guthrie	Black
15—At Cleve.	L	4-5	Orosco	Drummond
16—At Cleve.	L	5-7	Swindell	Tapani
17—Toronto	L	1-5	Stieb	Erickson
18—Toronto	L	0-3	Key	Anderson
19—Toronto	L	1-9	Wells	Guthrie
20—At K.C.	L	1-7	S. Davis	West
21—At K.C.	L	7-8	Crawford	Abbott
22—At K.C.	L	2-6	Gordon	Erickson
24—At Texas	L	0-2	Barfield	Guthrie
25—At Texas	W	8-5	West	Mielke
26—At Texas	L	0-1	Witt	Leach
27—Chicago	W	7-0	Anderson	Perez
28—Chicago	W	12-6	Drummond	Peterson
29—Chicago	W	6-1	Guthrie	Edwards
30—Chicago	L	3-4	McDowell	West
31—Detroit	L	6-12	Parker	Abbott

Won 9, Lost 19

SEPTEMBER

Date		Score	Winner	Loser
1—Detroit	L	5-9	Nosek	Anderson
2—Detroit	W	4-3	Erickson	Morris
3—At Milw.	W	6-0	Guthrie	Knudson
3—At Milw.	W	9-5	Aguilera	Plesac
4—At Milw.	W	7-1	Drummond	Edens
5—At Milw.	L	4-7	Robinson	Wayne
7—Cleveland	W	2-0	Anderson	Black
8—Cleveland	W	6-1	Erickson	Walker
9—Cleveland	L	9-12	Olin	Savage
10—At Calif.	L	1-3	J. Abbott	P. Abbott
11—At Calif.	L	0-9	Langston	Tapani
12—At Calif.	L	6-8	Grahe	Drummond
13—At Oak.	W	3-1*	Berenguer	Nelson
14—At Oak.	L	1-9	Stewart	Guthrie
15—At Oak.	L	1-4	Welch	Abbott
16—At Oak.	L	4-5†	Eckersley	Berenguer
17—Kan. City	L	0-1	Farr	Casian
18—Kan. City	W	10-4	Erickson	Gordon
19—Kan. City	L	1-0†	Wayne	Montgomery
21—Texas	L	1-2	Witt	Berenguer
22—Texas	W	2-0	Casian	Chiamparino
23—Texas	W	6-4	Erickson	Hough
25—At Chicago	W	4-3	Guthrie	McDowell
26—At Chicago	L	1-3	Hibbard	Tapani
28—At Detroit	L	1-3	Morris	Anderson
29—At Detroit	W	2-0	Erickson	Aldred
30—At Detroit	L	0-1	Terrell	Guthrie

Won 13, Lost 14

OCTOBER

Date		Score	Winner	Loser
1—Seattle	W	7-5	Tapani	Swan
2—Seattle	L	0-3	Hanson	Abbott
3—Seattle	W	7-4	Casian	Johnson

Won 2, Lost 1

*10 innings. †11 innings. ‡12 innings. §13 innings.

Rick Aguilera shined in the bullpen for the Twins, saving 32 games in his first season as a closer.

hitting Nelson Liriano arrived from Toronto to fill the void. He swung well from the left side of the plate but was inconsistent most of the season.

Shortstop Greg Gagne also disappointed. He got off to a good start, but fell into his bad habit of swinging at poor pitches. He was on the bench occasionally the final few months and his confidence seemed to wane because of it. Even his underrated defense began to suffer.

The bad news continued in the outfield. Left fielder Dan Gladden got off to a good start, but tailed off and fell out of favor with Manager Tom Kelly. He still showed he has speed, leading the team in stolen bases with 25. The 1990 right-field platoon of Randy Bush and Carmen Castillo was either injured, on the bench or not hitting.

But there were bright spots. Brian

Harper and Junior Ortiz combined to hit .305 as the catching tandem. Harper flirted with hitting .300 most of the year and enjoyed a 25-game hitting streak, the longest by a catcher in league history. Ortiz sported a team-high .325 average.

Outfielder Shane Mack was drafted out of the San Diego organization and given his first real playing opportunity. He flourished as the season progressed, hitting a gaudy .326 and playing well enough defensively that the Twins felt comfortable putting him in center field so they could move Puckett.

With the offense's big bats sputtering, the last thing the Twins needed was a collapse by Anderson, their pitching ace in 1989. He was supposed to provide stability on the young staff. Instead, he came up flat, posting a 7-18 mark and 4.53 earned-run average. But he did pitch well late in the season.

Fellow starter David West's prospect label wore thin with his continued inconsistency and 5.10 ERA, while Roy Smith limped home with a 4.81 ERA and 5-10 record.

But by season's end, the starting pitching offered some hope for 1991. Rookie Kevin Tapani led the team in wins and was compared to Jim (Catfish) Hunter. Scott Erickson jumped from Class AA Orlando in late June, and with the help of a hard-breaking sinker, won eight games. He finished strong, compiling a 5-0 record with a 1.35 ERA in September.

After making two round trips between Minnesota and Class AAA Portland, Mark Guthrie finished the year by pitching into the seventh inning in his final 11 starts. No Twin had done that since Frank Viola.

In the bullpen Rick Aguilera saved 32 games in his first season as a closer, though his second-half problems with tendinitis may entice the Twins to get him back into the rotation in 1991.

Juan Berenguer provided steady relief. Even though his fastball lost some of its zing, he registered an 8-5 record and 3.41 ERA. Terry Leach also pitched adequately out of the bullpen, but Gary Wayne and Tim Drummond struggled.

The Twins suffered the pains of transition in 1990. They are in a race against time as they attempt to build a pitching staff before their position players start drawing from the pension plan. Perhaps Hrbek summed up the Twins' plight best during the team's second nine-game losing streak: "We're in a rebuilding year and we'll have to suffer through it. Hopefully we'll develop the young pitchers before (the veterans) start losing it."

Ellis Burks was a key cog on the division-winning Red Sox, leading the team in home runs and RBIs en route to earning a Gold Glove.

Improbable Boston Defies Logic

By JOE GIULIOTTI

The 1990 Boston Red Sox defied logic.

Boston was a team with a patchwork rotation and an inconsistent bullpen. A team devoid of power or speed. A team that lost it's ace starter for four weeks down the stretch and whose only legitimate closer had late-season back surgery. To the casual observer, it would seem the perfect anatomy of a loser. But in the case of the Red Sox, it was quite the contrary.

The Red Sox were the consummate over-achievers. They captured their second American League East title in three years with an 88-74 mark, two games ahead of Toronto.

For the record, Boston hit only 106 home runs (with no one collecting more than 21), failed to feature one player with more than 90 runs batted in and ranked last in the major leagues in steals (53).

They still advanced to the A.L. Championship Series, where the Oakland Athletics swept them in four straight, but that can't tarnish what was an amazing season.

What makes the season extraordinary is the starting rotation included Greg Harris, a reliever who had been released by the pitching poor Philadelphia Phillies in August 1989; Tom Bolton, a lefthander who was almost released in spring training and Dana Kiecker, a 29-year-old rookie who had never been on a major league roster.

Add to all the above the fact Roger Clemens came down with severe shoulder tendinitis and made only one start after September 4 and Jeff Reardon had a ruptured disk removed August 4 and it makes Boston's season even more incredible.

Among the starters, Clemens (21-6) and Mike Boddicker (17-8) almost single-handedly kept the Red Sox alive all season. Clemens won 11 times following a defeat, while Boddicker, a Gold Glove pitcher, was 6-0 with a 2.77 earned-run average in his last nine starts. Those two got ample help from the overachieving Harris, Bolton and Kiecker.

Harris, who had made only one start since 1987, was forced into the rotation and had a career-high 13 victories, 12 as a starter. But he ran out of gas in September and October, registering a 1-5 mark.

Bolton, who was largely unimpressive in the previous three seasons, got the call from Class AAA Pawtucket June 13 and had a dream year. He was 10-5, with eight wins coming as a starter, and he didn't get

Roger Clemens paced the major leagues with a 1.93 ERA.

his first victory until July 1.

Kiecker had bounced around the minors the previous seven seasons and had been in Class AAA the previous two, but he showed he belonged in the majors. He made 25 starts, the most for a Red Sox rookie since Mike Nagy had 28 in 1969.

But not all of the pitchers reached their potential. John Dopson made four starts without a decision before undergoing season-ending elbow surgery in June. Wes Gardner finished with three victories and wasn't even on the postseason roster. Mike Rochford made one start and had two appearances before being sent back to the minors and eventually leaving for Japan.

The bullpen also had its problems. It was believed to be the team's strength leaving spring training, but it turned out to be its Achilles' heel. If it hadn't been for Jeff Gray, released by Philadelphia in spring training, it would have been a complete disaster.

Used as the closer when Reardon was disabled, Gray notched seven saves in seven chances in August and September. In 18 appearances between July 29 and September 17, he was 1-0 with seven saves and a 2.05 ERA. But like most everyone in the bullpen, he was overworked and not as effective in the final three weeks.

The biggest disappointments were Rob

SCORES OF BOSTON RED SOX' 1990 GAMES

APRIL

Date	W/L	Score	Winner	Loser
9—Detroit	W	5-2	Clemens	Morris
10—Detroit	W	4-2	Boddicker	Ritz
11—Detroit	W	3-2*	Harris	Gleaton
12—At Detroit	L	7-11	Lugo	Rochford
13—Milwaukee	L	5-9	Crim	Murphy
14—Milwaukee	W	4-3	Clemens	August
16—Milwaukee	L	0-18	Higuera	Boddicker
17—At Chicago	L	1-2	Jones	Smith
18—At Chicago	W	7-5	Clemens	McDowell
20—At Milw.	L	0-5	Filer	Boddicker
21—At Milw.	L	0-2	Higuera	Hetzel
22—At Milw.	W	4-2†	Smith	Plesac
24—California	W	4-2	Clemens	Langston
25—California	L	1-3	McCaskill	Boddicker
26—California	W	5-4	Smith	Harvey
27—Oakland	W	7-6	Reardon	Nelson
28—Oakland	W	12-3	Harris	Young
29—Oakland	L	0-1	Stewart	Clemens
30—Seattle	W	11-0	Boddicker	Holman

Won 11, Lost 8

MAY

Date	W/L	Score	Winner	Loser
1—Seattle	W	8-2	Hetzel	Johnson
2—Seattle	L	2-9	Hanson	Harris
4—At Oak.	L	3-8	Stewart	Clemens
5—At Oak.	W	5-1	Boddicker	Welch
6—At Oak.	L	2-4	Young	Hetzel
7—At Seattle	W	5-4	Harris	Hanson
8—At Seattle	L	1-2	Swift	Gardner
9—At Seattle	W	4-1	Clemens	Eave
11—At Calif.	W	3-2	Boddicker	Eichhorn
12—At Calif.	W	7-1	Harris	Blyleven
13—At Calif.	L	4-8	Finley	Lamp
14—At K.C.	L	5-9*	M. Davis	Reardon
16—At K.C.	W	7-1	Boddicker	Gordon
18—Minnesota	L	0-6	Candelaria	Harris
19—Minnesota	W	13-1	Clemens	Anderson
20—Minnesota	L	4-5	Smith	Hetzel
21—Texas	W	4-2	Boddicker	Mielke
22—Texas	L	4-5	Witt	Kiecker
23—Kan. City	L	1-4	Saberhagen	Harris
24—Kan. City	W	4-1	Clemens	Gubicza
25—At Minn.	L	0-16	Smith	Hetzel
26—At Minn.	L	5-6	Candelaria	Murphy
27—At Minn.	L	1-3	Tapani	Kiecker
28—At Texas	W	4-3	Reed	Russell
29—At Texas	W	2-1	Clemens	Hough
30—At Texas	L	3-4*	Rogers	Gardner

Won 12, Lost 14

JUNE

Date	W/L	Score	Winner	Loser
1—At Cleve.	W	4-3	Reed	Jones
2—At Cleve.	L	5-7	S. Valdez	Murphy
3—At Cleve.	W	8-2	Clemens	Farrell
4—New York	W	5-3	Reardon	Robinson
5—New York	W	9-8	Reardon	Plunk
6—New York	W	4-1	Boddicker	LaPoint
7—New York	W	3-0	Harris	Leary
8—Cleveland	W	4-3	Clemens	Farrell
9—Cleveland	W	11-6	Kiecker	S. Valdez
10—Cleveland	L	0-4	Candiotti	Gardner
11—Cleveland	L	3-4‡	Seanez	Lamp
12—At N.Y.	L	4-5	Guetterman	Murphy
13—At N.Y.	W	4-1	Clemens	Leary
14—At N.Y.	L	1-3	Cary	Kiecker
15—At Balt.	W	4-3	Gardner	Harnisch
16—At Balt.	W	6-3	Boddicker	Mitchell
17—At Balt.	W	6-5	Harris	Ballard
18—At Balt.	L	2-7	Johnson	Clemens
19—At Toronto	W	4-2	Kiecker	Ward
20—At Toronto	L	0-11	Stieb	Gardner
22—Baltimore	W	4-3	Boddicker	Ballard
23—Baltimore	W	4-3*	Gray	Olson
24—Baltimore	W	2-0	Harris	Milacki
25—Toronto	W	10-8	Lamp	Blair
26—Toronto	W	3-0	Gardner	Wells
27—Toronto	W	9-5	Boddicker	Key
28—Toronto	W	4-3	Clemens	Stottlemyre
29—Texas	L	3-4	Barfield	Gray
30—Texas	L	5-6	Jeffcoat	Reardon

Won 20, Lost 9

JULY

Date	W/L	Score	Winner	Loser
1—Texas	W	15-4	Bolton	Brown
2—Texas	W	3-2	Boddicker	Rogers
3—At Minn.	L	3-7	Tapani	Clemens
4—At Minn.	W	4-3	Lamp	Aguilera
5—At Minn.	L	4-7	Drummond	Murphy
6—At Texas	L	0-4	Brown	Gardner
7—At Texas	L	4-7	Ryan	Boddicker
8—At Texas	L	3-4†	Rogers	Gray
13—Kan. City	L	3-5	Gordon	Boddicker
14—Kan. City	L	1-2	Aquino	Murphy
14—Kan. City	W	8-7	Bolton	Baller
15—Kan. City	L	4-13	Crawford	Kiecker
16—Minnesota	L	2-3	Berenguer	Gray
17—Minnesota	W	1-0	Bolton	Erickson
18—Minnesota	W	5-4	Lamp	Berenguer
19—At K.C.	L	0-1	Robinson	Harris
20—At K.C.	L	0-5	Appier	Clemens
20—At K.C.	W	3-1	Kiecker	Aquino
21—At K.C.	L	2-4	Farr	Reardon
22—At K.C.	L	1-2	S. Davis	Bolton
23—At Milw.	L	0-13	Knudson	Boddicker
24—At Milw.	W	5-6*	Plesac	Reed
25—At Milw.	W	2-0	Clemens	Bosio
26—At Detroit	L	4-10	Petry	Gardner
27—At Detroit	W	1-0	Bolton	Morris
28—At Detroit	L	9-17	Gibson	Lamp
29—At Detroit	W	13-3	Harris	Robinson
30—Chicago	W	3-0	Clemens	Peterson
31—Chicago	W	7-2	Kiecker	King

Won 12, Lost 17

AUGUST

Date	W/L	Score	Winner	Loser
1—Chicago	W	9-5	Bolton	McDowell
3—Detroit	W	14-5	Harris	Robinson
4—Detroit	W	3-1	Clemens	Searcy
5—Detroit	L	2-7	Petry	Boddicker
7—At Calif.	W	6-3	Bolton	Langston
8—At Calif.	L	6-8†	Fraser	Lamp
9—At Calif.	W	14-3	Clemens	Abbott
10—At Seattle	L	1-4	Johnson	Kiecker
11—At Seattle	W	4-2§	Irvine	Schooler
12—At Seattle	W	7-2	Bolton	Jackson
13—At Oak.	L	0-4	Sanderson	Harris
14—At Oak.	W	2-0	Clemens	Moore
15—At Oak.	L	2-6*	Stewart	Irvine
17—California	L	0-1	Finley	Boddicker
18—California	L	3-4	McCaskill	Bolton
19—California	W	4-1	Clemens	Abbott
20—Baltimore	W	2-1	Harris	Harnisch
21—Baltimore	L	5-9	Mitchell	Kiecker
22—Baltimore	W	13-2	Boddicker	McDonald
23—At Toronto	L	3-4	Henke	Hesketh
24—At Toronto	W	2-0	Kiecker	Ward
25—At Toronto	W	1-0	Clemens	Wells
26—At Toronto	W	1-0	Harris	Stottlemyre
27—At Cleve.	W	12-4	Boddicker	Candiotti
28—At Cleve.	W	6-5	Gardner	Jones
29—At Cleve.	W	7-1	Kiecker	Walker
30—At Cleve.	W	9-2	Clemens	Jones
31—New York	W	7-3	Harris	Cary

Won 19, Lost 9

SEPTEMBER

Date	W/L	Score	Winner	Loser
1—New York	W	15-1	Boddicker	Hawkins
2—New York	W	7-1	Bolton	Witt
3—Oakland	L	5-9	Sanderson	Kiecker
4—Oakland	L	2-6	Stewart	Clemens
5—Oakland	L	0-10	Welch	Harris
7—Seattle	W	5-4†	Gray	Jackson
8—Seattle	W	10-2	Bolton	Medvin
9—Seattle	L	1-3	Young	Hesketh
10—Milwaukee	W	5-4	Harris	Knudson
10—Milwaukee	L	1-6	Edens	Kiecker
11—Milwaukee	L	2-4	Robinson	Gardner
12—Milwaukee	W	6-1	Boddicker	Higuera
13—At Chicago	L	6-9	Fernandez	Bolton
14—At Chicago	L	0-4	McDowell	Hesketh
15—At Chicago	L	4-7	Hibbard	Harris
16—At Chicago	L	2-4	King	Kiecker
17—At Balt.	W	7-3	Boddicker	McDonald
18—At Balt.	L	1-4	Mesa	Bolton
19—At Balt.	L	4-8	Telford	Harris
21—At N.Y.	W	3-0	Kiecker	Cary
22—At N.Y.	L	2-5	Plunk	Gray
23—At N.Y.	L	4-5	Witt	Bolton
25—Cleveland	L	2-5	Swindell	Harris
26—Cleveland	W	7-2	Kiecker	Candiotti
27—At Detroit	W	3-2	Bolton	Searcy
28—At Detroit	W	7-6	Reardon	Henke
29—Toronto	W	7-5	Clemens	Stottlemyre
30—Toronto	L	5-10	Key	Hesketh

Won 12, Lost 16

OCTOBER

Date	W/L	Score	Winner	Loser
1—Chicago	W	4-3	Reardon	Jones
2—Chicago	L	2-3†	Pall	Lamp
3—Chicago	W	3-1	Boddicker	Fernandez

Won 2, Lost 1

*10 innings. †11 innings. ‡12 innings. §14 innings.

Carlos Quintana surprised the Red Sox with a .287 batting average.

Murphy and Dennis Lamp. Murphy had a nightmare of a season. He finished 0-6 with an astronomical 6.32 ERA and was only used in mop-up situations late in the season.

Lamp had a terrible time keeping games close. He allowed 26 of 60 inherited runners to score. First batters he faced coming into an inning hit .367 against him with two walks, two sacrifice flies, two sacrifices and 12 runs driven in.

But the biggest blow to the bullpen was the loss of Reardon, an off-season free-agent acquisition. He only made 47 appearances because of his bad back, but when he was healthy he was effective as his 5-3 record, 21 saves, 3.16 ERA and yeoman work in the stretch will attest.

The Boston offense didn't suffer any major injuries, but it had its own problems. It led the league in hitting with a .272 mark, but it also paced the league in leaving runners on base (1,233), while grounding into 154 double plays.

Third baseman Wade Boggs paced the infield. As usual, he led the team in hitting and was the only Red Sox who batted over .300. But his .302 average was 50 points below his career mark and he failed to record 200 hits for the first time since 1982.

Second baseman Jody Reed tied for the league lead in doubles (45) while batting .289. Luis Rivera accompanied Reed at shortstop. He was batting .300 through early June, but slumped the rest of the season and finished at .225.

Marty Barrett began the season as the starting second baseman, but after hitting .246 in April, he became a reserve the rest of the year.

Carlos Quintana was a big surprise. He became the regular first baseman in early May and delivered a .287 average with 67 RBIs.

Veteran Dwight Evans made 121 starts as a designated hitter. A nagging back injury kept him from the outfield and lineup occasionally. Evans hit just 13 homers, snapping his string of 20 or more home runs each season since 1981.

The Red Sox acquired Mike Marshall from the New York Mets in July. After overcoming gastrointestinal inflammation, he played in 30 games between DH, first base and the outfield and hit .286 with 12 RBIs.

One of the major reasons for the team's winning ways was catcher Tony Pena who, along with Reardon, was plucked out of the free-agent market. Pena took charge behind the plate and in the clubhouse and brought fun back to a team that had always seemed to walk around wearing a game face. His handling of pitchers and game-calling skills were credited with the turnarounds of Harris, Bolton, Gray and the emergence of Kiecker as a bonafide major leaguer.

The Boston outfield was solid. The Red Sox felt they had solved part of their power problem when they dealt reliever Lee Smith to the St. Louis Cardinals for Tom Brunansky early in the season. But while Brunansky hit 15 home runs, only two came on the road and he hit five in a three-game series against Toronto on the last weekend of the regular season.

Ellis Burks enjoyed a great year. He ranked among the top 10 in the A.L. in seven offensive categories and won a Gold Glove for his stellar fielding.

Mike Greenwell, plagued with a bad ankle, hit .238 through May. After a cortisone shot, Greenwell began using a brace and batted .345 over the final 72 games. He was the hottest Red Sox down the stretch, batting .423 with 13 RBIs with runners in scoring position from September 1 to the end of the season.

Kevin Romine opened the season as Boston's starting right fielder. He became a reserve and hit .272 in 136 at-bats.

Like Romine and the rest of his teammates, the Red Sox survived their gut check late in the season. And it turned out they had the anatomy of a winner.

Tom Henke's 32 saves and 2.17 ERA offered stability to a shaky bullpen, but the Blue Jays' bid to win the American League East fell short.

Fundamentals Make Jays Blue

By NEIL MacCARL

The Toronto Blue Jays are like a flower that for some reason fails to reach full blossom every season.

They have been everybody's favorite in recent years to win the weak American League East. And with their win totals in recent years, it's no wonder. Toronto has won more than 85 games eight years in a row, but only has two division titles to show (1985 and 1989).

This past season was yet another close call for the Blue Jays. After coming excruciatingly close in 1987 and 1988, Toronto again fell short of first place in 1990. The Blue Jays finished 86-76, two games behind A.L. East champ Boston. In '87 and '88, the Blue Jays also finished two games behind.

But the Blue Jays have only themselves to blame for their bridesmaid's status. Poor fundamentals, including missed cut-off men, failed sacrifices and blundered baserunning, caused Toronto to blow many games it should have won.

"The only thing consistent was our inconsistency," said General Manager Pat Gillick.

But the Blue Jays' hitting was consistent. Toronto batted .265 and collected 167 home runs, second only to Detroit. But if their big bats flopped, they couldn't manufacture runs, posting a 36-46 record in games decided by one or two runs.

Toronto's fundamentals were so bad that Gaston shunned the sacrifice bunt because the Blue Jays' execution was so poor. The team's 18 sacrifices were the fewest ever in a major league season.

Lost among the postseason cries of sorrow was a fantastic season registered by Kelly Gruber. He enjoyed a career year with 31 home runs and 118 runs batted in. The third baseman also earned a Gold Glove. But after hitting .296 with 20 homers before the All-Star break, Gruber slumped in the second half, batting just .247 with 11 homers.

First baseman Fred McGriff continued to shine. He finally achieved his goal of batting .300 by improving his average 35 points in the second half. He was among the league leaders in walks and on-base percentage, while pacing the team with 35 home runs.

Shortstop was another solid position in the Toronto infield. Tony Fernandez batted .276, thanks largely to a .308 mark at

John Olerud bolstered a powerful Toronto lineup with 14 homers and 48 RBIs in only 358 at-bats.

home. He led the league in triples (17) and had a career-high 71 walks, while leading the team in stolen bases (26).

The familiar catching platoon continues to work wonders for the Blue Jays. Pat Borders and rookie Greg Myers shared the position with Borders getting the biggest share of work (115 games behind the plate). They combined for 20 homers and 71 RBIs, and Borders threw out 41 percent of the runners attempting to steal on him. But both were poor at blocking the plate.

The only weak link in the infield was second base. Nelson Liriano and Manny Lee, both switch-hitters, were platooned until Liriano was traded in late July to Minnesota. But Lee did little to solidify his hold on the position with a .243 batting average and one strikeout every 4.3 at-bats. He did lead league second basemen in fielding percentage (.993). Rance Mulliniks was a steady reserve infielder and the team's best pinch-hitter.

The outfield wasn't quite as impressive as the infield. Left fielder George Bell, who had averaged 104 RBIs over the six previous seasons, tailed off dramatically after having an eye problem in late August. That relegated him to designated hitter duties (a role he despises) and he did not hit with his customary authority.

Center fielder Mookie Wilson provided

SCORES OF TORONTO BLUE JAYS' 1990 GAMES

APRIL

Date		Score	Winner	Loser
9—At Texas	L	2-4	Ryan	Stottlemyre
10—Texas	W	2-1	Stieb	Hough
11—Texas	L	5-11	Brown	Cerutti
12—Texas	W	7-1	Flanagan	Moyer
13—At K.C.	W	3-1	Key	S. Davis
14—At K.C.	L	1-3	Saberhagen	Stottlemyre
15—At K.C.	W	5-4	Stieb	Crawford
16—Baltimore	W	4-2	Cerutti	Tibbs
17—Baltimore	W	8-2	Flanagan	Ballard
18—Baltimore	L	5-8	Harnisch	Wills
20—Kan. City	W	17-6	Stottlemyre	Saberhagen
21—Kan. City	W	5-1	Stieb	Gubicza
22—Kan. City	L	1-7	Gordon	Cerutti
23—Cleveland	W	12-9	Wills	Wickander
24—Cleveland	W	4-3	Key	Swindell
25—Cleveland	W	5-3	Stottlemyre	Nichols
26—Cleveland	L	3-4	Candiotti	Stieb
27—At Chicago	L	1-6	Hibbard	Cerutti
28—At Chicago	L	4-5	Kutzler	Flanagan
29—At Chicago	L	3-10	King	Key
30—At Cleve.	W	10-4	Stottlemyre	Bearse

Won 12, Lost 9

MAY

Date		Score	Winner	Loser
1—At Cleve.	W	4-3	Stieb	Candiotti
2—At Cleve.	L	0-3	Black	Cerutti
4—Detroit	L	1-3	Petry	Flanagan
5—Detroit	W	5-1	Stottlemyre	Robinson
6—Detroit	W	11-7	Key	DuBois
7—Chicago	W	6-1	Stieb	McDowell
8—Chicago	L	1-4	Hibbard	Cerutti
9—Chicago	W	4-3	Wills	Edwards
10—At Detroit	L	5-10	Robinson	Stottlemyre
11—At Detroit	W	4-2	Key	DuBois
13—At Detroit	W	6-3	Wells	Morris
14—At Detroit	W	8-3*	Ward	Henneman
15—Seattle	L	3-4*	Comstock	Acker
16—Seattle	L	2-4	Holman	Stottlemyre
17—Seattle	L	6-14	Johnson	Key
18—California	L	2-4	Abbott	Stieb
19—California	L	9-11	Fraser	Ward
20—California	W	5-1	Wills	Langston
21—Oakland	L	1-4	Welch	Stottlemyre
22—Oakland	L	4-5	Young	Wills
23—At Calif.	L	4-5	Bailes	Ward
24—At Calif.	L	3-4†	Harvey	Henke
25—At Seattle	W	3-1†	Acker	Swift
26—At Seattle	W	11-4	Wills	Holman
27—At Seattle	W	5-1	Cerutti	Johnson
28—At Oak.	W	1-0	Stieb	Moore
29—At Oak.	W	2-1	Wells	Stewart
30—At Oak.	L	5-8	Burns	Blair

Won 14, Lost 14

JUNE

Date		Score	Winner	Loser
1—Milwaukee	L	1-7	Higuera	Stottlemyre
2—Milwaukee	L	6-7	Fossas	Wells
3—Milwaukee	W	7-4	Stieb	Knudson
5—Minnesota	W	7-3	Wells	Smith
6—Minnesota	L	5-12	Candelaria	Blair
7—Minnesota	W	10-3	Stottlemyre	Tapani
8—At Milw.	W	11-5	Gilles	Crim
9—At Milw.	W	7-3	Stieb	Bosio
10—At Milw.	W	13-5	Wells	Navarro
11—At Milw.	L	1-4	Krueger	Blair
12—At Minn.	W	5-4	Stottlemyre	Candelaria
13—At Minn.	W	10-1	Cerutti	West
14—At Minn.	W	7-1	Stieb	Anderson
15—At N.Y.	W	5-4	Wells	Robinson
16—At N.Y.	W	2-1†	Wills	Mills
17—At N.Y.	W	8-1	Stottlemyre	LaPoint
19—Boston	L	2-4	Kiecker	Ward
20—Boston	W	11-0	Stieb	Gardner
21—New York	L	6-7	Mills	Acker
22—New York	L	7-8§	Cadaret	Blair
23—New York	W	8-4	Stottlemyre	Leary
24—New York	W	8-3	Cerutti	Cary
25—At Bos.	L	8-10	Lamp	Blair
26—At Bos.	L	0-3	Gardner	Wells
27—At Bos.	L	5-9	Boddicker	Key
28—At Bos.	L	3-4	Clemens	Stottlemyre
29—Oakland	L	0-5	Stewart	Cerutti
30—Oakland	L	4-9	Welch	Stieb

Won 15, Lost 13

JULY

Date		Score	Winner	Loser
1—Oakland	W	4-3	Blair	Burns
2—Oakland	L	2-3	Moore	Key
3—California	W	5-2	Stottlemyre	Blyleven
4—California	W	4-2	Cerutti	Abbott
5—California	W	9-2	Stieb	McCaskill
6—Seattle	W	1-0	Wells	Holman
7—Seattle	W	4-2	Key	Swan
8—Seattle	L	3-6	Young	Stottlemyre
12—At Calif.	W	5-0	Wells	McCaskill
13—At Calif.	L	0-2	Abbott	Stottlemyre
14—At Calif.	L	7-8	Eichhorn	Ward
15—At Calif.	L	2-3	Finley	Henke
16—At Seattle	W	4-3	Key	Hanson
17—At Seattle	L	5-7	Jackson	Ward
18—At Seattle	L	2-5	Young	Stottlemyre
20—At Oak.	W	8-6	Cerutti	Young
21—At Oak.	W	2-1	Stieb	Sanderson
22—At Oak.	L	0-3	Moore	Key
24—Kan. City	L	3-5‡	Farr	Ward
25—Kan. City	L	1-6	McGaffigan	Stottlemyre
26—Kan. City	W	7-5	Cerutti	Appier
27—Texas	W	1-0	Stieb	Hough
28—Texas	L	2-3‡	Arnsberg	Wills
29—Texas	W	10-8	Acker	McMurtry
30—At Balt.	W	9-2	Stottlemyre	Milacki
31—At Balt.	L	4-6	McDonald	Cerutti

Won 14, Lost 12

AUGUST

Date		Score	Winner	Loser
1—At Balt.	W	7-4	Stieb	Ballard
2—At Texas	L	4-5†	Arnsberg	Candelaria
3—At Texas	L	1-9	Moyer	Wells
4—At Texas	L	2-3	Witt	Stottlemyre
5—At Texas	W	6-4	Cerutti	Ryan
6—At Texas	L	3-4	Hough	Stieb
7—Detroit	W	11-5	Key	Morris
8—Detroit	W	8-3	Wells	Terrell
9—Detroit	L	4-5	Robinson	Stottlemyre
10—Minnesota	L	3-7	West	Cerutti
11—Minnesota	W	7-4	Stieb	Leach
12—Minnesota	L	4-5	Anderson	Key
13—At Chicago	W	4-3	Ward	Thigpen
14—At Chicago	W	12-4	Stottlemyre	Hibbard
15—At Chicago	L	3-4	McDowell	Candelaria
17—At Minn.	W	5-1	Stieb	Erickson
18—At Minn.	W	3-0	Key	Anderson
19—At Minn.	W	9-1	Wells	Guthrie
20—At N.Y.	L	5-6†	Cadaret	Acker
21—At N.Y.	L	2-3	Cary	Candelaria
22—At N.Y.	L	2-4	Hawkins	Cerutti
23—Boston	W	4-3	Henke	Hesketh
24—Boston	L	0-2	Kiecker	Ward
25—Boston	L	0-1	Clemens	Wells
26—Boston	L	0-1	Harris	Stottlemyre
27—Milwaukee	L	2-4	Higuera	Acker
28—Milwaukee	L	2-6	Navarro	Stieb
29—Milwaukee	W	7-3	Key	Knudson
31—At Cleve.	W	12-8	Acker	Swindell

Won 13, Lost 16

SEPTEMBER

Date		Score	Winner	Loser
1—At Cleve.	W	8-0	Stottlemyre	Candiotti
2—At Cleve.	W	3-0	Stieb	Black
3—At Detroit	L	0-5	Terrell	Key
4—At Detroit	L	1-3	Gibson	Ward
5—At Detroit	W	7-3	Wells	Parker
7—Chicago	W	3-1	Stottlemyre	Perez
8—Chicago	W	3-0	Stieb	Fernandez
9—Chicago	W	6-1	Key	McDowell
10—At K.C.	W	4-3	Wells	Wagner
11—At K.C.	W	8-4	Wills	Stottlemyre
12—At K.C.	L	5-7	Gordon	Stottlemyre
13—Baltimore	L	3-5	Mesa	Stieb
14—Baltimore	W	8-7	Blair	Olson
15—Baltimore	W	4-3	Blair	Schilling
16—Baltimore	W	6-5	Henke	Price
17—New York	W	6-4	Cerutti	Plunk
18—New York	W	3-2	Black	Guetterman
19—New York	W	7-6	Key	Leary
21—Cleveland	L	1-2‡	E. Valdez	Wills
22—Cleveland	L	2-5	Shaw	Stottlemyre
23—Cleveland	W	5-4*	Acker	Ward
24—At Milw.	W	9-5	Key	Navarro
25—At Milw.	L	4-8	Krueger	Black
26—At Milw.	L	0-6	Robinson	Wells
28—At Bos.	L	6-7	Reardon	Henke
29—At Bos.	L	5-7	Clemens	Stottlemyre
30—At Bos.	W	10-5	Key	Hesketh

Won 17, Lost 10

OCTOBER

Date		Score	Winner	Loser
1—At Balt.	L	3-6	Mesa	Wells
2—At Balt.	W	2-1	Black	Johnson
3—At Balt.	L	2-3	Olson	Henke

Won 1, Lost 2

*10 innings. †11 innings. ‡13 innings. §15 innings.

Kelly Gruber could do no wrong in 1990, hitting 31 homers and collecting 118 RBIs and a Gold Glove.

Toronto with enthusiasm and an offensive spark. Despite hitting just .265, Wilson scored 81 runs and stole 23 bases. Plus he committed just three errors in the outfield.

Junior Felix was hitting .284 at the All-Star break. But the right fielder tore a calf muscle the first game after the break and had to go on the disabled list. He still enjoyed a strong season, hitting .295 with runners in scoring position.

Rookie Glenallen Hill hit a dozen homers as a part-time outfielder and DH. He spent time on the disabled list after suffering cuts and scrapes on his feet and knees when he had a nightmare about spiders, a childhood phobia. He finished the season in the hospital where he had an appendectomy.

Another bright spot in the outfield was Canadian Rob Ducey, who was a September call-up. He played extremely well defensively in left field while batting .302. Plus, prospect Mark Whiten (.273 average) impressed in two stints with the Blue Jays. But backup Kenny Williams struggled at the plate with a .161 average after being claimed on waivers from Detroit in June.

Toronto led the league in fielding, committing the fewest errors in the A.L. (86). But outfield defense was a major problem. Opposing teams repeatedly challenged the arms of Bell, Wilson and Felix.

But no one challenged John Olerud's potential. The rookie impressed everybody with a sweet swing that produced 14 home

runs and 48 RBIs, mostly as a DH. But overall, the Blue Jays' DH numbers ranked near the bottom of the A.L. in average, home runs and RBIs.

Pitching, which was regarded as a strong suit, was disappointing overall. Toronto icon Dave Stieb again anchored the rotation. He won a team-record 18 games, including a no-hit jewel against the Indians in Cleveland September 2, the first in team history. But Stieb, who won 11 games in the first half of the season and paced starters with a 2.93 ERA, failed to win his final three starts of the year.

Jimmy Key rebounded from off-season arthroscopic surgery on his shoulder. A hamstring injury slowed him in late May, but he became the Blue Jays' biggest winner in the second half of the season, going 8-3 to finish 13-7.

The big gamble in the rotation was shifting David Wells from the bullpen, but it paid off. He won 10 games in his new role, 11 overall, and pitched so well he figures to stay. Wells received his starting shot when John Cerutti never found his groove and was dropped from the rotation. He finished with a 9-9 record and 4.76 ERA.

Todd Stottlemyre received more offensive support than any other starter, but won only once when the Blue Jays failed to score at least five runs. He lost 17 games, one shy of the team record.

Veteran Mike Flanagan was released in early May and the Blue Jays were still looking for a steady fifth starter until they acquired Bud Black from Cleveland in September. Hoping to solidify its title aspirations, Toronto had to give up three pitching prospects, Mauro Gozzo, Alex Sanchez and Steve Cummings, to get Black. But Black's 2-1 record and 4.02 ERA with Toronto wasn't enough to earn a divisional crown.

As usual, Tom Henke headed the bullpen. He logged 32 saves in 38 opportunities. But as a unit, the relievers compiled a 20-24 mark with a 3.64 ERA. Part of the Blue Jays' problem was the failure of Duane Ward as a setup man. He finished 2-8 and never developed any consistency, saving only 11 games in 20 chances.

Jim Acker, Frank Wills and Paul Kilgus only exacerbated Toronto's bullpen woes by struggling all season. And John Candelaria provided little depth to the bullpen following his acquisition from Minnesota in late July.

But all of Toronto's problems can be traced back to an inability to execute fundamentals. And before that problem is addressed, the Blue Jays may never reach full bloom.

Detroit's fortunes changed dramatically when Cecil Fielder arrived from Japan to collect 51 home runs, the most by a major leaguer since 1977.

Fielder Restores Tigers' Roar

By TOM GAGE

Motor City natives are too familiar with Japan and its competitive exports, specifically its automobiles. But in 1990, Detroit welcomed a big Japanese import with open arms—Cecil Fielder.

The Tigers' 1990 improvement had its origins with the Hanshin Tigers, the Japanese Central League team that wouldn't give Fielder a contract extension following the 1989 season. And because they wouldn't, the former Toronto Blue Jay began to consider a return to America and the major leagues.

Spurned in their free-agent offers by Pete O'Brien and Kent Hrbek, the Tigers needed a home-run hitting first baseman. They were able to lure Fielder from "The Land of the Rising Sun" with a two-year, $3 million contract.

"We thought he would adjust back to the majors because he was only 26," said General Manager Bill Lajoie, "but he far exceeded our expectations."

Or as Manager Sparky Anderson put it, "I predicted 30 home runs because I knew he couldn't miss. Anything after that was above and beyond."

Fielder was more than one step beyond, however. Hitting two home runs in the final game of the season against the New York Yankees, Fielder finished with a major league-leading 51 homers and 132 runs batted in. That made him the first major leaguer to hit the 50-mark since George Foster collected 52 in 1977 for the Cincinnati Reds (who were managed by Anderson), the first American Leaguer since New York sluggers Roger Maris (61) and Mickey Mantle (54) in 1961 and the first Tiger since Hank Greenberg smashed 58 in 1938.

"It was the most exciting individual accomplishment I've seen since I've been with the Tigers," said Alan Trammell. "We all got caught up in the kind of year Cecil had. It gave a big lift to everyone."

Those who voted for Fielder as the A.L. Most Valuable Player reasoned, in addition to his outstanding season, that the Tigers would have been nowhere without him. Those who didn't vote for him reasoned that Fielder wasn't enough to make the Tigers a top team, and that the MVP must always play for a contender.

If the Tigers improve half as much in 1991, however, as they did in 1990, they will contend. They improved by 20 games,

Able to avoid injury, Alan Trammell raised his batting average from .243 in 1989 to .304 last year.

from 59 to 79 victories, and Fielder wasn't the only reason, just the biggest.

Another reason for the Tigers' turnaround was a rejuvenated bullpen, especially Jerry Don Gleaton. Gleaton entered the 1990 campaign with 11 career saves but finished with 13 for the Tigers, with all but two posted after the All-Star break.

"As far as I'm concerned," said Anderson, "he was the best lefthanded relief pitcher in the league. There were some with more saves, but none that pitched better."

Mike Henneman complemented Gleaton as a righthanded closer. Of Henneman's 22 saves, 17 were before the All-Star break, but Henneman didn't mind sharing the bullpen limelight.

"It was 'Joe Committee' for us in the bullpen this year," he said, "Whoever got the job done got the call, and a lot of people got it done."

There were other contributors in the bullpen, namely Paul Gibson and Edwin Nunez. Gibson wasn't called on in many save situations, but had his best year as a setup man. Nunez, who was Gibson's counterpart on the right side, posted the best earned-run average on the team (2.24). Lance McCullers and Clay Parker both

SCORES OF DETROIT TIGERS' 1990 GAMES

APRIL

			Winner	Loser
9—At Bos.	L	2-5	Clemens	Morris
10—At Bos.	L	2-4	Boddicker	Ritz
11—At Bos.	L	2-3‡	Harris	Gleaton
12—Boston	W	11-7	Lugo	Rochford
13—Baltimore	W	10-6	Morris	Price
14—Baltimore	L	4-7	Johnson	Ritz
15—Baltimore	W	6-4	Petry	Aldrich
17—New York	L	1-4	Leary	Tanana
18—New York	W	8-4	Morris	LaPoint
19—At Balt.	L	2-4	Johnson	Ritz
20—At Balt.	L	0-6	Milacki	Robinson
21—At Balt.	W	3-2	Lugo	Aldrich
22—At Balt.	L	2-3§	Olson	Henneman
23—At Minn.	W	6-3	Tanana	Smith
24—At Minn.	L	4-16	Candelaria	Ritz
25—At Minn.	W	6-4	Robinson	Tapani
27—Milwaukee	L	6-9	Krueger	Morris
28—Milwaukee	W	13-5	Tanana	August
29—Milwaukee	L	1-6	Bosio	Petry
30—Milwaukee	L	1-6	Knudson	Robinson

Won 8, Lost 12

MAY

			Winner	Loser
1—Minnesota	L	5-9	Candelaria	Gibson
2—Minnesota	L	2-8	West	Morris
3—Minnesota	L	1-3‡	Leach	Henneman
4—At Toronto	W	3-1	Petry	Flanagan
5—At Toronto	L	1-5	Stottlemyre	Robinson
6—At Toronto	L	7-11	Key	DuBois
7—At Milw.	L	4-5	Krueger	Morris
8—At Milw.	L	5-7	Mirabella	Tanana
9—At Milw.	W	2-1†	Petry	Bosio
10—Toronto	W	10-5	Robinson	Stottlemyre
11—Toronto	L	2-4	Key	DuBois
13—Toronto	L	3-6	Wells	Morris
14—Toronto	L	3-8‡	Ward	Henneman
15—At Texas	W	3-2	Petry	Brown
16—At Texas	W	12-0	Robinson	Bohanon
17—At Texas	W	7-5‡	Henneman	Russell
18—At Chicago	W	8-2	DuBois	Perez
19—At Chicago	W	6-4	Tanana	McDowell
20—At Chicago	W	3-2†	Nunez	Edwards
21—Kan. City	W	11-6	Robinson	Gordon
22—Kan. City	L	8-9	Farr	Morris
23—Texas	W	5-1	DuBois	Jeffcoat
24—Texas	L	2-3	Hough	Tanana
25—Chicago	W	2-1	Gibson	Hibbard
26—Chicago	L	4-10	Patterson	Robinson
27—Chicago	L	1-2	Perez	Morris
28—At K.C.	L	2-3	Saberhagen	DuBois
29—At K.C.	L	3-5	Farr	Henneman
30—At K.C.	L	3-4	Aquino	Petry

Won 12, Lost 17

JUNE

			Winner	Loser
1—At Seattle	W	9-7	Morris	Bankhead
2—At Seattle	L	0-2	Johnson	Robinson
3—At Seattle	W	2-0	Tanana	Hanson
5—At Cleve.	W	6-2	Petry	Candiotti
6—At Cleve.	W	6-4	Morris	Swindell
7—At Cleve.	W	8-0	DuBois	Black
8—Seattle	L	2-5	Hanson	Tanana
9—Seattle	W	6-3	Henneman	Comstock
9—Seattle	L	2-5	Swan	Petry
10—Seattle	W	4-3	Morris	Holman
12—Cleveland	L	3-7	Black	DuBois
13—Cleveland	W	5-4	Henneman	Seanez
14—Cleveland	W	7-3	Tanana	S. Valdez
15—California	W	2-1‡	Gleaton	Harvey
16—California	W	6-2	Morris	Blyleven
17—California	L	3-7	Finley	DuBois
18—Oakland	W	7-2	Robinson	Young
19—Oakland	W	7-6	Gibson	Stewart
20—Oakland	L	7-12	Welch	Petry
21—At Calif.	L	4-6	Blyleven	Morris
22—At Calif.	L	0-1	Bailes	Gibson
23—At Calif.	W	9-4	Robinson	Abbott
24—At Calif.	L	2-10	McCaskill	Tanana
25—At Oak.	L	3-4	Welch	Petry
26—At Oak.	L	2-3	Sanderson	Morris
27—At Oak.	W	5-4	Henneman	Burns
29—At K.C.	L	2-3	Crawford	Robinson
30—At K.C.	W	5-3	Nunez	S. Davis

Won 16, Lost 12

JULY

			Winner	Loser
1—At K.C.	W	9-4	Morris	Gordon
2—At Chicago	L	4-5	Thigpen	Henneman
3—At Chicago	W	13-7	Nunez	King
4—At Chicago	W	10-7§	McCullers	Patterson
5—Kan. City	L	3-15	Aquino	Petry
6—Kan. City	W	4-0	Morris	Gordon
7—Kan. City	L	0-4	Appier	Tanana
8—Kan. City	W	10-4	Petry	M. Davis
12—Texas	L	1-11	Brown	Morris
13—Texas	L	6-7	Witt	Gleaton
14—Texas	L	3-5	Ryan	Robinson
15—Texas	W	3-2	Searcy	Jeffcoat
16—Chicago	W	5-4	Henneman	Pall
17—Chicago	L	3-7	Perez	Morris
18—Chicago	L	5-7	Pall	Henneman
19—Boston	W	1-0	Robinson	Harris
20—At Texas	L	3-5	Ryan	Searcy
21—At Texas	W	8-1	Petry	Jeffcoat
22—At Texas	L	3-5	Arnsberg	Morris
23—Baltimore	L	3-13	Johnson	Tanana
24—Baltimore	W	8-2	Robinson	Mitchell
25—Baltimore	W	4-3	Henneman	Milacki
26—Boston	W	10-4	Petry	Gardner
27—Boston	L	0-1	Bolton	Morris
28—Boston	W	17-9	Gibson	Lamp
29—Boston	L	3-13	Harris	Robinson
30—At N.Y.	L	2-6	LaPoint	Searcy
31—At N.Y.	L	4-10	Leiter	Petry

Won 13, Lost 15

AUGUST

			Winner	Loser
1—At N.Y.	W	15-4	Morris	Hawkins
2—At N.Y.	W	6-5x	Parker	Mills
3—At Bos.	L	5-14	Harris	Robinson
4—At Bos.	L	1-3	Clemens	Searcy
5—At Bos.	W	7-2	Petry	Boddicker
7—At Toronto	L	5-11	Key	Morris
8—At Toronto	L	3-8	Wells	Terrell
9—At Toronto	W	5-4	Robinson	Stottlemyre
10—At Cleve.	L	2-5	Walker	Searcy
11—At Cleve.	L	4-13	Swindell	Petry
12—At Cleve.	L	5-9	Candiotti	Morris
13—At Cleve.	W	6-5	Terrell	Shaw
14—Milwaukee	L	6-7	Crim	Gleaton
15—Milwaukee	L	3-7	Mirabella	Searcy
16—Milwaukee	L	4-8	Robinson	Petry
17—Cleveland	W	3-0	Morris	Candiotti
18—Cleveland	W	6-3	Terrell	Shaw
20—California	L	3-5	Langston	Gibson
21—California	W	6-2	Petry	Grahe
22—California	W	7-4	Morris	Finley
24—Oakland	L	4-6	Sanderson	Terrell
25—Oakland	W	14-4	Tanana	Stewart
26—Oakland	W	7-3	Robinson	Welch
28—At Seattle	L	3-4	Comstock	Gibson
29—At Seattle	W	4-2	Terrell	Young
30—At Seattle	W	3-2	Henneman	Jackson
31—At Minn.	W	12-6	Parker	Abbott

Won 14, Lost 13

SEPTEMBER

			Winner	Loser
1—At Minn.	W	9-5	Nosek	Anderson
2—At Minn.	L	3-4	Erickson	Morris
3—Toronto	W	5-0	Terrell	Key
4—Toronto	W	3-1	Gibson	Ward
5—Toronto	L	3-7	Wells	Parker
6—Cleveland	L	0-6*	Candiotti	Nosek
7—At Milw.	L	5-6	Higuera	Morris
8—At Milw.	L	2-5	Navarro	Terrell
9—At Milw.	W	5-0	Aldred	Krueger
10—At Balt.	W	8-0	Tanana	Harnisch
11—At Balt.	W	2-1	Gibson	Schilling
12—At Balt.	L	1-2	McDonald	Morris
13—New York	L	3-7	Witt	Terrell
14—New York	L	2-5	Leary	Aldred
15—New York	W	4-3	Tanana	Eiland
16—New York	W	5-2	Searcy	Cary
18—At Calif.	W	3-2	Morris	Finley
19—At Calif.	W	12-5	Terrell	Grahe
21—At Oak.	L	5-6	Welch	Parker
22—At Oak.	L	1-5	Sanderson	Searcy
23—At Oak.	W	6-0	Morris	Moore
25—Seattle	W	4-1	Henneman	DeLucia
26—Seattle	L	4-8	Hanson	Tanana
27—Boston	L	2-3	Bolton	Searcy
28—Minnesota	W	3-1	Morris	Anderson
29—Minnesota	L	0-2	Erickson	Aldred
30—Minnesota	W	1-0	Terrell	Guthrie

Won 14, Lost 13

OCTOBER

			Winner	Loser
1—At N.Y.	W	2-0	Tanana	Cary
2—At N.Y.	L	1-4	Guetterman	Nunez
3—At N.Y.	W	10-3	Morris	Adkins

Won 2, Lost 1

*5 innings. †8 innings. ‡10 innings. §12 innings. x14 innings.

Mike Henneman excelled before the All-Star break, compiling 17 of his 22 saves.

pitched well in relief, too.

But there were no surprises in the rotation. The starters were the primary reason why Detroit posted the worst ERA in the A.L. (4.39). Veterans Dan Petry and Jack Morris headed the rotation, with Petry posting the best ERA (4.45) and Morris collecting the most wins (15).

Aging Frank Tanana and Jeff Robinson were the other two regular starters. Each registered winning records in spite of their woeful ERAs.

Walt Terrell, Steve Searcy and Brian DuBois also took turns starting, but none distinguished themselves.

Aside from Fielder, the infield was led by a healthy Trammell. Because he was able to dodge the back problems of the previous year, Trammell raised his batting average from .243 to .304. With Fielder on hand, Trammell wasn't forced to bat cleanup and reached the .300 level for the sixth time in his career.

"He's become a complete hitter," said Anderson, "because he's learned how to drive the ball to all fields."

Trammell's sidekick at second base for the last 13 years, Lou Whitaker, didn't have the best of seasons. Whitaker's batting average plunged to .237, his lowest since 1980. He didn't get it above .200 until June 24, but finished with 18 home runs and 60 RBIs, his second-best totals in the last four years.

Tony Phillips had trouble adjusting to third base early in the year, but finished strong both defensively and offensively. He hit .251, but because of 99 walks, his on-base percentage of .364 was higher than some hitters who contended for the batting title. He also paced the team in stolen bases (19).

"Some guys play the game but don't really know how to play," said Anderson. "Phillips knows. He was a great asset to this team."

The catchers did an admirable job. Mark Salas signed as a free agent, and while he hit only .232, he had nine home runs in just 164 at-bats. He was a particular threat at Tiger Stadium where he hit eight of his nine home runs.

Fellow catcher Mike Heath's batting average dropped from .300 to .270 in the last two months of the season, but he still finished as the team's third-highest hitter with more than 300 at-bats. He's had better defensive years, however.

And the Tigers' prospects began to rear their heads. Travis Fryman, who took over at third base late in the season, was the best prospect to emerge from the Tigers' farm system in several years. He hit .297 in 66 games, and along with Milt Cuyler, who's expected to play center field, provided a glimpse at a younger than usual future for the Tigers.

There were no individual stars in the outfield. Larry Sheets, who didn't embarrass himself defensively after a season of serving primarily as a designated hitter for the Baltimore Orioles, led the contingent with a .261 batting average and 52 RBIs. Lloyd Moseby paced the pack with 14 home runs. But other than that, as Anderson said, "we didn't have many bricks, but we had good mortar."

Gary Ward, for instance, hit a steady .256 and his 46 RBIs in just 309 at-bats were more than enough for the Tigers to feel that he did his role.

Injuries limited Chet Lemon to 322 at-bats. He only hit five home runs, giving him 12 over the last two seasons. John Shelby continued to strike out too often for his number of at-bats, hitting just .248.

Darnell Coles split time between the outfield, infield and DH role. But no matter where he played, he failed to hit (.209 batting average). On the other hand, Dave Bergman fared much better as a DH and pinch-hitter, batting .278.

Overall, it wasn't a spectacular season by any means. But there was one spectacular story for the Tigers in 1990, and Detroit has Japan to thank.

Cleveland's Sandy Alomar Jr. made a sudden impact last year, winning American League Rookie of the Year honors and earning a Gold Glove.

Pitching Collapse Dooms Tribe

By SHELDON OCKER

The Cleveland Indians spent last year combining precise parts of bad luck and poor performance to maintain their reputation as the American League East's most intractable losers.

Though the Indians have failed to win a pennant since 1954, hope continues to spring eternal. Last season, the basis for Cleveland's optimism rested with a starting rotation alleged to be the deepest and most dependable in the division.

But as usual, the Indians' hope sprung a leak. Last year, the bottom fell out in late July and early August when they lost 15 of 20 games to tumble from the division race for good.

On the other hand, Cleveland ended the season with a rush, posting an 18-13 record in September and October to finish in fourth place for the first time (excluding strike-marred 1981) since 1976.

Nevertheless, the promise of remaining in contention from start to finish had vanished before Cleveland's September surge, which included administering fatal or near fatal blows to the title chances of the Chicago White Sox and Toronto Blue Jays.

The primary reason for the Indians' 1990 swoon was the inability of the starting pitchers to live up to expectations.

What could go wrong with a rotation composed of Greg Swindell, Tom Candiotti, John Farrell, Bud Black and a host of touted minor leaguers waiting for their chance? Practically everything.

Though Swindell pitched effectively in the second half, he struggled the first 2½ months of the season. Manager John McNamara and pitching coach Mark Wiley attributed Swindell's problems to everything from the shortened spring training and Swindell's duties as player representative to one or more flaws in his mechanics.

Swindell finally hinted that a fear of reinjuring his fragile elbow might have preented him from cutting loose with his breaking pitches. Once he was convinced the arm was sound, Swindell became a winning pitcher with a 12-9 record.

Candiotti and Black were Cleveland's most consistent pitchers, but even they missed a combined six starts because of injuries.

Even so, Candiotti reached the 200-inning plateau for the fifth season in a row. In four of those years, he won at least 13 games, including a team-high 15 in 1990. His 3.65 earned-run average was tops among starters.

Club President Hank Peters faced a tough decision with Black, who was eligible for free agency in October. Peters had two choices: either trade Black during the season or take the chance on losing him and receiving only a draft pick as compensation.

Consequently, Black was dealt to Toronto in mid-September for pitchers Mauro Gozzo, Alex Sanchez and Steve Cummings.

The biggest blow to Cleveland's staff was the loss of John Farrell, who went on the disabled list June 25 and didn't pitch again until late September.

After seeking a cause for Farrell's elbow pain virtually all season, Dr. Paul Jacobs, the team physician of the Milwaukee Brewers, performed exploratory surgery on Farrell in October. The news was not good.

Jacobs repaired a torn ligament, removed a bone chip and relocated the ulnar nerve. The prognosis for a complete recovery was good, but Farrell is not expected to return to the rotation until late in the 1991 season.

Unfortunately for Cleveland, its minor league pitching prospects failed to fill the vacuum until it was too late. Nor did McNamara ever uncover a reliable fifth starter.

Kevin Bearse, Charles Nagy, Rod Nichols, Al Nipper, Jeff Shaw, Sergio Valdez and Mike Walker all were given the ball. Only Nagy and Valdez found success, and then only in the fading stages of the season.

Some observers suggested that in Cleveland's anxiety to remain in the race, some of these pitchers were rushed to the big leagues before they were ready. Others say their talent was lacking. But no one questions Doug Jones' talent.

The anchor of the bullpen, Jones erased his own franchise record for saves by ringing up 43 with a team-best 2.56 ERA. But the Indians struggled to find capable middle relievers who could get to Jones.

Jesse Orosco was unable to find the plate, 21-year-old Rudy Seanez failed to tame his 95-mph fastball, and Cecilio Guante and Colby Ward were just plain ineffective.

On the other hand, submarine-style righthander Steve Olin attracted McNamara's attention. Olin's difficulties in retiring lefthanded batters forced his demotion in June. When he returned from Class

SCORES OF CLEVELAND INDIANS' 1990 GAMES

APRIL

Date		Score	Winner	Loser
12—At N.Y.	L	4-6	Plunk	Orosco
13—At Chicago	W	6-2	Farrell	Long
14—At Chicago	L	4-9	Perez	Swindell
15—At Chicago	L	1-4	Hibbard	Bearse
16—At K.C.	W	6-3	Candiotti	Gubicza
17—At K.C.	L	2-4	Farr	Olin
18—At K.C.	L	0-7	S. Davis	Farrell
19—New York	W	1-0	Swindell	Perez
21—Chicago	W	8-4	Candiotti	Perez
22—Chicago	W	5-2	Black	Hibbard
23—At Toronto	L	9-12	Wills	Wickander
24—At Toronto	L	3-4	Key	Swindell
25—At Toronto	L	3-5	Stottlemyre	Nichols
26—At Toronto	W	4-3	Candiotti	Stieb
27—Minnesota	W	7-2	Black	West
28—Minnesota	W	3-0	Farrell	Anderson
29—Minnesota	W	6-4	Swindell	Smith
30—Toronto	L	4-10	Stottlemyre	Bearse

Won 9, Lost 9

MAY

Date		Score	Winner	Loser
1—Toronto	L	3-4	Stieb	Candiotti
2—Toronto	W	3-0	Black	Cerutti
3—At N.Y.	W	10-5	Orosco	Robinson
5—Texas	L	5-9	Brown	Guante
6—Texas	W	9-5	Candiotti	Bohanon
6—Texas	W	3-0	Shaw	Witt
7—Kan. City	L	2-4‡	Montgomery	Guante
8—At Minn.	L	5-6	Berenguer	Olin
9—At Minn.	W	7-3	S. Valdez	Candelaria
10—At Minn.	L	2-3	Smith	Swindell
11—At Texas	W	5-4	Olin	Russell
12—At Texas	L	1-2	Witt	Black
13—At Texas	W	4-1	Farrell	Hough
15—Oakland	W	5-4	Guante	Honeycutt
16—Oakland	L	6-7	Eckersley	Jones
18—Seattle	W	5-0	Black	Hanson
19—Seattle	W	4-3	Orosco	Young
20—Seattle	L	7-8†	Schooler	Orosco
21—California	L	3-5	Blyleven	Shaw
22—California	L	3-8	Finley	Candiotti
23—At Seattle	L	1-4	Hanson	Black
24—At Seattle	W	5-3	Orosco	Young
25—At Oak.	L	2-5	Sanderson	Swindell
26—At Oak.	L	3-6	Welch	S. Valdez
28—At Calif.	W	3-0†	Guante	Abbott
29—At Calif.	L	1-2	McCaskill	Farrell
30—At Calif.	W	4-2	Candiotti	Langston

Won 13, Lost 14

JUNE

Date		Score	Winner	Loser
1—Boston	L	3-4	Reed	Jones
2—Boston	W	7-5	S. Valdez	Murphy
3—Boston	L	2-8	Clemens	Farrell
5—Detroit	L	2-6	Petry	Candiotti
6—Detroit	L	4-6	Morris	Swindell
7—Detroit	L	0-8	DuBois	Black
8—At Bos.	L	3-4	Clemens	Farrell
9—At Bos.	L	6-11	Kiecker	S. Valdez
10—At Bos.	W	4-0	Candiotti	Gardner
11—At Bos.	W	4-3§	Seanez	Lamp
12—At Detroit	W	7-3	Black	DuBois
13—At Detroit	L	4-5	Henneman	Seanez
14—At Detroit	L	3-7	Tanana	S. Valdez
15—Milwaukee	W	5-3	Candiotti	Powell
16—Milwaukee	W	10-9	Jones	Sebra
17—Milwaukee	W	12-4	Black	Robinson
19—Baltimore	W	5-4	Jones	Olson
20—Baltimore	L	1-3	Harnisch	Orosco
21—Baltimore	W	4-3†	Jones	Holton
22—At Milw.	L	7-9	Edens	Black
23—At Milw.	L	1-11	Robinson	Nipper
24—At Milw.	W	9-5	Farrell	Knudson
25—At Milw.	W	10-5	Candiotti	Bosio
26—At Balt.	W	5-3	Jones	Harnisch
27—At Balt.	L	3-6†	Olson	S. Valdez
28—At Balt.	W	7-4	Nipper	Ballard
29—California	L	2-7	Abbott	Nagy
30—California	W	4-1	Candiotti	McCaskill

Won 14, Lost 14

JULY

Date		Score	Winner	Loser
1—California	W	5-3	Swindell	Langston
2—California	L	1-2	Finley	Orosco
3—Seattle	W	9-4	Nipper	Young
4—Seattle	L	2-3	Johnson	Nagy
5—Seattle	L	1-4	Hanson	Candiotti
6—Oakland	W	6-1	Swindell	Sanderson
6—Oakland	L	1-12	Moore	S. Valdez
7—Oakland	L	1-0	Black	Young
8—Oakland	L	3-8	Stewart	Nipper

JULY

Date		Score	Winner	Loser
12—At Seattle	W	5-4	Seanez	Schooler
13—At Seattle	W	13-7	Candiotti	Young
14—At Seattle	W	3-0	Black	Johnson
15—At Seattle	L	0-7	Swift	Nagy
16—At Oak.	L	0-3	Sanderson	Nipper
17—At Oak.	W	4-2	Swindell	Moore
18—At Oak.	L	1-4	Welch	Candiotti
18—At Oak.	L	2-5	Stewart	Nichols
20—At Calif.	L	4-9	Blyleven	Black
21—At Calif.	L	2-5	Finley	Walker
22—At Calif.	W	8-1	Swindell	Langston
23—At Chicago	L	1-3	Hibbard	Candiotti
24—At Chicago	L	3-8	Peterson	Nichols
25—At Chicago	W	6-1	Black	King
27—New York	L	0-3	Hawkins	Swindell
27—New York	L	1-4	Robinson	Walker
28—New York	W	2-1	Candiotti	Cary
29—New York	L	5-8	Leary	Black
29—New York	L	3-4	Plunk	Guante
30—Kan. City	L	6-7	McGaffigan	Shaw
31—Kan. City	L	4-8	Appier	Walker

Won 11, Lost 19

AUGUST

Date		Score	Winner	Loser
1—Kan. City	W	4-1	Swindell	M. Davis
3—At N.Y.	L	4-6	Guetterman	Candiotti
4—At N.Y.	W	17-3	Black	Leary
5—At N.Y.	L	3-5	Cadaret	Olin
6—At N.Y.	L	1-2	Hawkins	Swindell
7—Texas	W	8-4	Ward	Brown
8—Texas	W	5-3	Shaw	Moyer
9—Texas	L	5-13	Witt	Black
10—Detroit	W	5-2	Walker	Searcy
11—Detroit	W	13-4	Swindell	Petry
12—Detroit	W	9-5	Candiotti	Morris
13—Detroit	L	5-6	Terrell	Shaw
14—Minnesota	L	4-5	Guthrie	Black
15—Minnesota	W	5-4	Orosco	Drummond
16—Minnesota	W	7-5	Swindell	Tapani
17—At Detroit	L	0-3	Morris	Candiotti
18—At Detroit	L	3-6	Terrell	Shaw
20—At Milw.	L	3-4	Edens	Olin
21—At Milw.	L	5-6	Plesac	Ward
22—At Milw.	W	4-2	Candiotti	Higuera
24—At Balt.	L	4-5‡	Price	Ward
25—At Balt.	W	11-5	Olin	Harnisch
26—At Balt.	W	8-3	Swindell	Price
27—Boston	L	4-12	Boddicker	Candiotti
28—Boston	L	5-6	Gardner	Jones
29—Boston	L	1-7	Kiecker	Walker
30—Boston	L	2-9	Clemens	Jones
31—Toronto	L	8-12	Acker	Swindell

Won 12, Lost 16

SEPTEMBER

Date		Score	Winner	Loser
1—Toronto	L	0-8	Stottlemyre	Candiotti
2—Toronto	L	0-3	Stieb	Black
3—At Texas	L	2-6	Ryan	Walker
4—At Texas	W	7-5	S. Valdez	Brown
5—At Texas	L	2-3	Rogers	Jones
6—At Detroit	W	6-0*	Candiotti	Nosek
7—At Minn.	L	0-2	Anderson	Black
8—At Minn.	L	1-6	Erickson	Walker
9—At Minn.	W	12-9	Olin	Savage
10—Chicago	W	3-2	D. Jones	B. Jones
10—Chicago	L	2-6	King	Nagy
11—Chicago	W	4-3	Orosco	Jones
12—Chicago	W	12-2	Black	Perez
14—At K.C.	W	6-4	S. Valdez	Appier
15—At K.C.	W	14-6	Swindell	McGaffigan
16—At K.C.	L	6-9	Montgomery	E. Valdez
17—Milwaukee	W	4-2	Olin	Higuera
18—Milwaukee	W	8-3	Nagy	August
19—Milwaukee	W	6-3	S. Valdez	Navarro
20—At N.Y.	W	12-7	Walker	Monteleone
21—At Toronto	W	2-1x	E. Valdez	Wills
22—At Toronto	W	5-2	Shaw	Stottlemyre
23—At Toronto	L	4-5†	Acker	Ward
25—At Bos.	W	5-2	Swindell	Harris
26—At Bos.	L	2-7	Kiecker	Candiotti
27—Baltimore	L	3-5	Johnson	Farrell
28—Baltimore	L	0-2	McDonald	S. Valdez
30—Baltimore	L	3-6	Milacki	Swindell
30—Baltimore	W	7-3	Nagy	Taylor

Won 16, Lost 13

OCTOBER

Date		Score	Winner	Loser
2—Kan. City	W	13-3	Candiotti	Wagner
3—Kan. City	W	5-2	S. Valdez	Smith

Won 2, Lost 0

*5 innings. †10 innings. ‡11 innings. §12 innings. x13 innings.

Second baseman Jerry Browne led the Indians with 92 runs scored and 72 walks but had trouble turning the double play.

AAA five weeks later, he had overcome this weakness.

The Indians' expected offensive problems never materialized, despite Cory Snyder's second consecutive year-long slump. With 14 homers, 55 runs batted in and an average of one strikeout for every 3.71 at-bats, Snyder eventually found a permanent home on the bench. From September 5 on, Snyder came to the plate only once.

But outfielder Candy Maldonado revived a flagging career by leading the club in home runs (22) and RBIs (95), and center fielder Alex Cole's arrival from Class AAA gave Cleveland its most dangerous leadoff hitter since Brett Butler.

In 63 games, Cole finished fourth in the A.L. in stolen bases and posted an on-base percentage of .379.

Mitch Webster, Dion James and Stan Jefferson combined for 15 homers and 87 RBIs (most of them by Webster) to compensate for Snyder's poor season. Nevertheless, the Indians missed Snyder's strong arm and hell-bent-for-leather attitude in the outfield.

The off-season trade that brought catcher Sandy Alomar Jr., infielder Carlos Baerga and outfielder/designated hitter Chris James from San Diego in exchange for Joe Carter appears to one of Peters' best deals ever.

Alomar lived up to his press clippings with his play behind the plate and exceeded expectations offensively, batting .290 with nine homers and 66 RBIs. He earned A.L. Rookie of the Year honors, a Gold Glove and was elected to start in the All-Star Game.

Backup catcher Joel Skinner coupled his solid fielding with a sturdy .252 average.

Baerga played second base, third and shortstop before finally settling in at third, batting .260 with 47 RBIs in 108 games.

After an early-season slump as he adjusted to being the DH, Chris James became Cleveland's No. 3 run producer with 70 RBIs. His bid to bat .300 fell one point short on the last day of the season.

Brook Jacoby started the year at third, but circumstances forced him to become Cleveland's regular first baseman, a transition that was hardly noticed. Jacoby finished second to Maldonado in RBIs with 75 and batted a solid .293.

Keith Hernandez, who was given a two-year, $3.5 million guaranteed contract to play first base, batted .200 in 43 games. He spent most of the time on the disabled list with a strained calf muscle.

Though second baseman Jerry Browne had problems turning the double play, he remained an important contributor at the plate by scoring 92 runs. Shortstop Felix Fermin continued to shine defensively and made important strides at the plate. In addition to batting .256, Fermin struck out only 22 times in 414 at-bats.

Utilityman Tom Brookens enjoyed a strong season. The 12-year veteran batted .266 and finished the season by hitting .417 in September.

But despite some strong performances, the Indians were forced to take solace in yet another disappointing season.

Even though the Orioles' luck turned sour in 1990, Gregg Olson enjoyed a sweet season that featured 37 saves and a 2.42 ERA.

Orioles' Magic Vanishes in '90

By PETER SCHMUCK

The Baltimore Orioles were discussed in a lot of preseason pep talks last year. They almost went from last to first in 1989, and thus became the inspiration for divisional doormats everywhere.

Chicago White Sox Manager Jeff Torborg reasoned that if the Orioles could rise from the ashes, his team could, too. Detroit Manager Sparky Anderson also figured his Tigers could achieve a big turnaround in one season. But while the White Sox and the Tigers returned to respectability in 1990, the Orioles returned to the lower reaches of the American League East with a fifth-place 76-85 record.

What happened? Why did the Orioles' magic of a 32½-game turnaround in 1989 wear off so quickly and so completely?

Injuries were one major reason. It was hard to get lonely on the disabled list, where Ben McDonald, Mark Williamson and Tim Hulett began the season and were followed by a steady stream of replacements. Designated hitter Sam Horn was one of them. He was forced onto the disabled list after experiencing a fast start. He went on to compile 14 homers and 45 runs batted in with just 246 at-bats.

Next, the club lost two front-line players starting in early August, first baseman Randy Milligan (who finished with 20 homers and 60 RBIs) and second baseman Billy Ripken (who paced the team in hitting with a .291 average). Before the month was over, the Orioles would also lose Williamson, again, and their winningest starter, Dave Johnson (13-9).

Aside from the injuries, last year's wonder-kid pitchers also led to Baltimore's decline. Jeff Ballard, who led the '89 Orioles with 18 victories, lost nine of his first 10 decisions before he was lifted from the starting rotation, and Jay Tibbs went 2-7 before being designated for assignment in June.

The disappointment didn't end there. Bob Milacki, who was 14-12 in 1989, won just four games in the first half of 1990 en route to a 5-8 record.

A lack of depth also paralyzed the Orioles. General Manager Roland Hemond spent a lot of time calling up reinforcements from the minor leagues or pulling players off the waiver list, but his come-one-come-all concept—which worked so well the year before—did not produce the desired result.

Brad Komminsk came and went. So did

Joe Orsulak set career highs in homers and RBIs in 1990.

veterans Donell Nixon, Dave Gallagher and Greg Walker. Where the plug-ins of 1989 always seemed to contribute, their latter-day counterparts only seemed to contribute to the roster instability that became chronic in 1990.

"I said from the start that we did not have the depth to survive even one or two significant injuries," Manager Frank Robinson said. "I don't like to talk about injuries, but I had never seen anything like what happened to us in early August."

Still, the disappointing season was made more bearable by the emergence of young pitchers Pete Harnisch and McDonald.

Harnisch survived a 1-6 slump between August 4 and September 15 to post an 11-11 record and 4.34 earned-run average. But his arm tired in the final months of his first full season in the major leagues.

Injuries forced McDonald to spend the first half of the season in the minor leagues, but his long-awaited debut in the starting rotation did not disappoint anyone. He pitched a complete-game four-hitter over Chicago and went on to set a club record by winning his first five starts and first six decisions en route to compiling an 8-5 record and 2.43 ERA.

Jose Mesa became one of the Orioles' most dependable starters after his recall from Class AA, and fellow prospect Anthony Telford looked impressive in eight starts following his rise from Class A.

The tired-arm syndrome that affected

SCORES OF BALTIMORE ORIOLES' 1990 GAMES

APRIL

Date		Score	Winner	Loser
9—At K.C.	W	7-6†	Aldrich	Montgomery
11—At K.C.	L	1-2	Gubicza	Ballard
13—At Detroit	L	6-10	Morris	Price
14—At Detroit	W	7-4	Johnson	Ritz
15—At Detroit	L	4-6	Petry	Aldrich
16—At Toronto	L	2-4	Cerutti	Tibbs
17—At Toronto	L	2-8	Flanagan	Ballard
18—At Toronto	W	8-5	Harnisch	Wills
19—Detroit	W	4-2	Johnson	Ritz
20—Detroit	W	6-0	Milacki	Robinson
21—Detroit	L	2-3	Lugo	Aldrich
22—Detroit	W	3-2‡	Olson	Henneman
23—Kan. City	W	8-5	Harnisch	S. Davis
24—Oakland	L	1-7	Stewart	Johnson
25—Oakland	L	3-4‡	Nelson	Hickey
26—Oakland	L	4-6	Moore	Tibbs
27—Seattle	L	3-4	Hanson	Ballard
28—Seattle	L	3-4	Jackson	Hickey
29—Seattle	W	5-4	Williamson	Jackson
30—California	W	2-1‡	Holton	Witt
Won 9, Lost 11				

MAY

Date		Score	Winner	Loser
1—California	L	1-7	Abbott	Tibbs
2—California	L	0-3	Blyleven	Ballard
4—At Seattle	W	9-8	Hickey	Jackson
5—At Seattle	L	2-5	Holman	Johnson
6—At Seattle	L	4-5	Swift	Williamson
7—At Calif.	W	6-5	Tibbs	Eichhorn
8—At Calif.	L	0-6	Finley	Ballard
9—At Calif.	W	9-1	Harnisch	Langston
11—At Oak.	L	0-5	Welch	Milacki
12—At Oak.	W	3-2	Williamson	Nelson
13—At Oak.	W	4-1	Tibbs	Moore
15—At Chicago	L	2-3	Jones	Harnisch
16—At Chicago	L	2-4	Kutzler	Milacki
17—At Chicago	L	3-7	Jones	Holton
18—Texas	W	13-1	Johnson	Witt
19—Texas	L	3-5	Hough	Tibbs
20—Texas	W	4-0	Harnisch	Brown
21—Minnesota	L	3-7	Guthrie	Milacki
22—Minnesota	W	10-2	Williamson	Tapani
23—Chicago	L	3-6	King	Johnson
24—Chicago	L	3-5	Radinsky	Tibbs
25—At Texas	W	12-2	Harnisch	Brown
26—At Texas	W	7-5†	Olson	Russell
27—At Texas	W	9-2	Ballard	Witt
28—At Minn.	L	4-6	Berenguer	Price
29—At Minn.	W	5-1	Milacki	Anderson
30—At Minn.	L	3-12	Smith	Harnisch
Won 12, Lost 15				

JUNE

Date		Score	Winner	Loser
1—At N.Y.	L	3-4	LaPoint	Ballard
2—At N.Y.	W	4-2	Johnson	Leary
3—At N.Y.	W	4-3	Milacki	Witt
4—At Milw.	W	6-4	Price	Krueger
5—At Milw.	L	4-6	Navarro	Tibbs
6—At Milw.	W	8-7	Williamson	Krueger
7—At Milw.	W	5-2	Johnson	Mirabella
8—New York	W	5-4*	Holton	Mills
9—New York	W	10-1	Harnisch	Cary
10—New York	L	2-5	Jones	Tibbs
12—Milwaukee	W	4-3*	Olson	Plesac
13—Milwaukee	L	2-7	Knudson	Johnson
14—Milwaukee	L	5-8	Sebra	Holton
15—Boston	L	3-4	Gardner	Harnisch
16—Boston	L	3-6	Boddicker	Mitchell
17—Boston	L	5-6	Harris	Ballard
18—Boston	W	7-2	Johnson	Clemens
19—Cleveland	L	4-5	Jones	Olson
20—Cleveland	W	3-1	Harnisch	Orosco
21—Cleveland	L	3-4*	Jones	Holton
22—At Bos.	L	3-4	Boddicker	Ballard
23—At Bos.	L	3-4*	Gray	Olson
24—At Bos.	L	0-2	Harris	Milacki
26—Cleveland	L	3-5	Jones	Harnisch
27—Cleveland	W	6-3*	Olson	S. Valdez
28—Cleveland	L	4-7	Nipper	Ballard
29—At Minn.	W	6-2	Johnson	Anderson
30—At Minn.	W	6-0	Milacki	Erickson
Won 13, Lost 15				

JULY

Date		Score	Winner	Loser
1—At Minn.	L	3-4	Aguilera	Olson
3—At Texas	L	2-7	Witt	Mitchell
4—At Texas	W	9-4	Johnson	Hough
5—At Texas	L	2-3	Jeffcoat	Milacki
6—At Chicago	L	2-4	Perez	Harnisch
7—At Chicago	W	4-1	Mitchell	Hibbard
8—At Chicago	W	8-6†	Williamson	Thigpen
11—Kan. City	W	7-5	Schilling	Farr
13—Minnesota	W	8-5	Williamson	Berenguer
13—Minnesota	L	1-3	West	Johnson
14—Minnesota	W	3-2†	Williamson	Leach
15—Minnesota	L	3-10	Anderson	Milacki
16—Texas	W	7-6	Olson	Rogers
17—Texas	W	5-3	Harnisch	Brown
18—Texas	L	1-7	Witt	Johnson
19—Chicago	W	4-1	Mitchell	Peterson
20—Chicago	W	3-2*	Williamson	Thigpen
21—Chicago	W	2-0	McDonald	McDowell
22—Chicago	W	9-3	Harnisch	Perez
23—At Detroit	W	13-3	Johnson	Tanana
24—At Detroit	L	2-8	Robinson	Mitchell
25—At Detroit	L	3-4	Henneman	Milacki
27—At K.C.	W	9-2	McDonald	S. Davis
28—At K.C.	L	9-10	Crawford	Williamson
28—At K.C.	W	3-1	Johnson	Farr
29—At K.C.	W	4-1	Mitchell	Gordon
30—Toronto	L	2-9	Stottlemyre	Milacki
31—Toronto	W	6-4	McDonald	Cerutti
Won 17, Lost 11				

AUGUST

Date		Score	Winner	Loser
1—Toronto	L	4-7	Stieb	Ballard
2—Kan. City	W	5-1	Johnson	Filson
3—Kan. City	W	14-1	Mitchell	Gordon
4—Kan. City	L	1-9	McGaffigan	Harnisch
7—At Oak.	L	2-3	Welch	Mitchell
8—At Oak.	W	4-1	McDonald	Sanderson
9—At Oak.	L	2-5	Moore	Johnson
10—At Calif.	L	1-2*	Fraser	Olson
11—At Calif.	L	4-12	Finley	Weston
12—At Calif.	W	11-6	Mitchell	Langston
13—At Seattle	W	3-2	McDonald	Holman
14—At Seattle	L	1-7	Young	Johnson
15—At Seattle	L	0-2	Johnson	Harnisch
17—Oakland	L	3-8	Welch	Mitchell
18—Oakland	L	1-3	Nelson	McDonald
19—Oakland	W	3-2	Telford	Sanderson
20—At Bos.	L	1-2	Harris	Harnisch
21—At Bos.	W	9-5	Mitchell	Kiecker
22—At Bos.	L	2-13	Boddicker	McDonald
24—Cleveland	W	5-4†	Price	Ward
25—Cleveland	L	5-11	Olin	Harnisch
26—Cleveland	L	3-8	Swindell	Price
27—New York	L	0-4	Hawkins	McDonald
28—New York	L	3-11	Witt	Mesa
29—New York	L	2-3	Leary	Telford
30—New York	W	6-1	Harnisch	LaPoint
31—At Milw.	L	1-4	Robinson	Mitchell
Won 9, Lost 18				

SEPTEMBER

Date		Score	Winner	Loser
1—At Milw.	L	3-4	Higuera	McDonald
2—At Milw.	L	2-4	Navarro	Mesa
3—Seattle	L	2-6	Young	Telford
4—Seattle	L	2-7	Hanson	Harnisch
5—Seattle	L	5-9	Comstock	Hickey
7—California	W	6-2	McDonald	Grahe
8—California	W	5-4	Price	Eichhorn
9—California	W	3-1	Telford	McCaskill
10—Detroit	L	0-8	Tanana	Harnisch
11—Detroit	L	1-2	Gibson	Schilling
12—Detroit	W	2-1	McDonald	Morris
13—At Toronto	W	5-3	Mesa	Stieb
14—At Toronto	L	7-8	Blair	Olson
15—At Toronto	L	3-4	Blair	Schilling
16—At Toronto	L	5-6	Henke	Price
17—Boston	L	3-7	Boddicker	McDonald
18—Boston	W	4-1	Mesa	Bolton
19—Boston	W	8-4	Telford	Harris
21—Milwaukee	W	5-3	Harnisch	Robinson
22—Milwaukee	W	3-2	Johnson	Brown
23—Milwaukee	W	2-1*	Ballard	Higuera
24—At N.Y.	W	6-3*	Bautista	Mills
25—At N.Y.	L	3-15	Eiland	Telford
26—At N.Y.	L	2-4	Cary	Ballard
27—At Cleve.	W	5-3	Johnson	Farrell
28—At Cleve.	W	2-0	McDonald	S. Valdez
30—At Cleve.	W	6-3	Milacki	Swindell
30—At Cleve.	L	3-7	Nagy	Taylor
Won 14, Lost 14				

OCTOBER

Date		Score	Winner	Loser
1—Toronto	W	6-3	Mesa	Wells
2—Toronto	L	1-2	Black	Johnson
3—Toronto	W	3-2	Olson	Henke
Won 2, Lost 1				

*10 innings. †11 innings. ‡12 innings.

Ben McDonald set a Baltimore record last season by winning his first six decisions.

Harnisch also reached into the Orioles' bullpen, where Gregg Olson showed signs of wear in the final weeks of the season. But he still managed to save 37 games to further establish himself as one of baseball's most dependable stoppers. His save total might have been higher if Williamson had been around to set him up all season. Williamson topped the club with a 2.21 ERA while posting an 8-2 mark.

Joe Price and Curt Schilling received extensive work in relief. Price was second on the club in appearances (50), while Schilling sported a solid 2.54 ERA in 46 innings. But in three separate trials with Baltimore, Jose Bautista struggled in relief, along with Brian Holton (who was sent to the minors August 1).

If the season was something of a letdown for the Orioles, it did not keep veteran shortstop Cal Ripken from setting nine records. Among them, he moved into second place on baseball's consecutive games-played list when he played in his 1,308th successive contest. He also set records for consecutive errorless games (95) and errorless chances (431) by a shortstop, as well as fewest errors by a shortstop in a season (3). But curiously, that was not good enough to earn him his first Gold Glove.

Cal Ripken had a disappointing first half at the plate, but he was one of several everyday Orioles who did not live up to pre-season expectations. Third baseman Craig Worthington was hit hard by the sophomore jinx (.226 average). Catcher Mickey Tettleton set a major league record for switch-hitters when he struck out 160 times in 444 at-bats. Backup Bob Melvin didn't fare much better.

But they weren't the only players to struggle for the Orioles, whose .245 team batting average and 1,230 runners left on base were both second worst in the A.L. Outfielders Mike Devereaux (.240 average) and Steve Finley (.256) were among the disappointments, along with utility infielder Rene Gonzales. But Devereaux did hit 12 homers and Finley paced the team in stolen bases with 22.

Baltimore unloaded disgruntled outfielder Phil Bradley to the White Sox for Ron Kittle in late July. But Kittle did little to impress, along with Brady Anderson, who was limited to 89 games by several injuries. Outfielder Joe Orsulak did impress, setting personal highs in home runs (11) and RBIs (57). And hot prospect David Segui showed potential in two stints with Baltimore.

But not even a bevy of hot prospects could have salvaged the Orioles' 1990 season, a season in which their magic expired amidst a myriad of injuries and disappointments.

Dave Parker hammered opposing pitchers for 21 home runs and 92 RBIs to earn Designated Hitter of the Year honors for the second straight year.

Brewers' Skid Reaches 3 Years

By CLIFF CHRISTL

If the 1990 Milwaukee Brewers were an aging team coming off several years of success or a young team building for the future, their sixth-place finish in the American League East wouldn't seem so bad.

The problem is, they were neither.

Milwaukee was a team that overhauled its roster five years ago with the intent of being a pennant contender in 1990. They were a team that signed Dave Parker as a free agent last winter with the idea that he might be the missing link in their quest to win the division.

But for the third straight year, the Brewers continued to slide in the standings. After winning 91 games in 1987, they won 87 in 1988, 81 in 1989 and 74 last year.

Their .457 winning percentage was their fourth worst in the last 13 years and they finished the season in a state of disarray.

They had a severe pitching shortage among other talent deficiencies. And whatever team chemistry is, they didn't have it. A faction of the team felt isolated from Manager Tom Trebelhorn, whose non-confrontational style had contributed to a breakdown of communication within the clubhouse.

Pitching was the main component that ruined their chances after a 22-14 start. Teddy Higuera and Chris Bosio, their top two starters, didn't stay healthy. And Chuck Crim and Dan Plesac, the staples of their bullpen, had sub-par seasons.

Higuera was bothered by an assortment of injuries and Bosio had his season cut short by a knee injury. Together, they started only 47 games and won just 15 of 34 decisions.

Plesac's earned-run average was 4.43, the first time in his career it had been above 3.00. Opponents hit a healthy .257 off him and he blew 11 of 35 save opportunities. Crim finished strong, but his ERA still rose from 2.83 to 3.47.

They weren't the only disappointments, either. Jaime Navarro, counted on as the No. 3 starter, had to be sent to the minors twice before he finally found himself, posting a 5-2 mark in his last eight starts. Don August, a 13-game winner as a rookie in 1988, spent most of the year in Class AAA where he was nothing more than a mediocre pitcher. Occasional starter Bill Krueger didn't fare much better. And Juan Nieves and Bill Wegman, two valued young starters three years ago, vanished from the scene with more arm problems.

The lack of pitching depth in the organization became apparent when the Brewers needed to call up three pitchers over a 12-day span in late May and early June, and all three arrived with ERAs over 5.00 at Class AAA. And two of the three, Tom Edens and Randy Veres, wound up pitching in a combined 61 games for Milwaukee, uniting for a 4-8 record and 4.22 ERA.

Additionally, Paul Mirabella and Tony Fossas each saw extensive duty in middle relief, but neither impressed.

The only bright spot on the staff was starter Ron Robinson, who was acquired in a trade with Cincinnati on June 9. Robinson arrived too late to reverse the Brewers' skid, but he led the staff with 12 victories and had a 2.91 ERA.

Mark Knudson also pitched well in a starting role until shoulder tendinitis spoiled his last three starts. In his first 24, he was 10-6 with a 3.58 ERA. But in his last three, he was 0-3 with a 12.27 ERA.

On top of having a thin pitching staff, the Brewers also were the worst defensive team in the A.L. for the second straight year.

Catcher B.J. Surhoff has yet to gain the confidence of the team's pitching staff. The outfielders committed 28 errors, the second-highest total in the league. The pitchers committed 17 errors, the third-highest total in the league. The infield included two players who had limited or no major league experience at their positions: Gary Sheffield at third base and Paul Molitor at first.

In spite of their pitching and defensive woes, the Brewers scored more runs than all but three teams in the A.L., but had a better record than only the New York Yankees.

Still, upon closer inspection, they ranked high in run production largely because of their running game, not because a lot of players had big offensive years. The Brewers ranked 11th in hitting and seventh in homers, but led the league in stolen bases for the fourth consecutive season and ranked fourth in grounding into the fewest double plays.

Among the players who had disappointing years were the two biggest names in the franchise's history, Molitor and Robin Young. Molitor missed 59 games with injuries and failed to hit .300 for the first time since 1986.

Center fielder Yount had the worst year

SCORES OF MILWAUKEE BREWERS' 1990 GAMES

APRIL

Date		Score	Winner	Loser
9—At Chicago	L	1-2	Jones	Fossas
10—Chicago	L	3-5	Radinsky	Filer
13—At Bos.	W	9-5	Crim	Murphy
14—At Bos.	L	3-4	Clemens	August
16—At Bos.	W	18-0	Higuera	Boddicker
17—At Texas	L	2-6	Brown	Fossas
18—At Texas	W	11-6	Fossas	Moyer
19—At Texas	W	11-0	Bosio	Witt
20—Boston	W	5-0	Filer	Boddicker
21—Boston	W	2-0	Higuera	Hetzel
22—Boston	L	2-4‡	Smith	Plesac
24—Kan. City	W	7-3	Bosio	Dotson
25—Kan. City	W	1-0	Filer	Saberhagen
26—Kan. City	W	3-2	Knudson	Gubicza
27—At Detroit	W	9-6	Krueger	Morris
28—At Detroit	L	5-13	Tanana	August
29—At Detroit	W	6-1	Bosio	Petry
30—At Detroit	W	6-1	Knudson	Robinson

Won 12, Lost 6

MAY

Date		Score	Winner	Loser
1—At K.C.	W	6-4	Higuera	Saberhagen
3—At K.C.	W	9-5	Navarro	Gubicza
5—Minnesota	L	5-9	Candelaria	Crim
6—Minnesota	L	0-4	Tapani	Higuera
7—Detroit	W	5-4	Krueger	Morris
8—Detroit	W	7-5	Mirabella	Tanana
9—Detroit	L	1-2*	Petry	Bosio
11—At Minn.	W	6-3	Wegman	Anderson
12—At Minn.	L	2-5	Tapani	Knudson
13—At Minn.	L	6-8	Berenguer	Krueger
15—California	L	3-8	Langston	Bosio
16—California	W	13-5	Higuera	Abbott
17—California	W	6-3	Mirabella	Fraser
18—Oakland	W	5-0	Wegman	Moore
19—Oakland	L	1-9	Stewart	Filer
20—Oakland	W	5-2	Bosio	Sanderson
21—Seattle	L	4-9	Clark	Plesac
22—Seattle	W	3-2	Knudson	Swift
23—At Oak.	L	5-12	Moore	Wegman
24—At Oak.	L	1-13	Stewart	Filer
25—At Calif.	L	4-5x	Fraser	Fossas
26—At Calif.	L	3-10	Blyleven	Knudson
27—At Calif.	L	3-7	Finley	Wegman
28—At Seattle	L	3-4	Hanson	Navarro
29—At Seattle	W	5-3	Crim	Jackson
30—At Seattle	L	1-2	Clark	Bosio

Won 11, Lost 15

JUNE

Date		Score	Winner	Loser
1—At Toronto	W	7-1	Higuera	Stottlemyre
2—At Toronto	W	7-6	Fossas	Wells
3—At Toronto	L	4-7	Stieb	Knudson
4—Baltimore	L	4-6	Price	Krueger
5—Baltimore	W	6-4	Navarro	Tibbs
6—Baltimore	L	7-8	Williamson	Krueger
7—Baltimore	L	2-5	Johnson	Mirabella
8—Toronto	L	5-11	Gilles	Crim
9—Toronto	L	3-7	Stieb	Bosio
10—Toronto	L	5-13	Wells	Navarro
11—Toronto	W	4-1	Krueger	Blair
12—At Balt.	L	3-4†	Olson	Plesac
13—At Balt.	W	7-2	Knudson	Johnson
14—At Balt.	W	8-5	Sebra	Holton
15—At Cleve.	L	3-5	Candiotti	Powell
16—At Cleve.	L	9-10	Jones	Sebra
17—At Cleve.	L	4-12	Black	Robinson
18—New York	W	4-2	Knudson	Leary
19—New York	L	1-5	Cary	Bosio
20—New York	L	4-5	Guetterman	Crim
22—Cleveland	W	9-7	Edens	Black
23—Cleveland	W	11-1	Robinson	Nipper
24—Cleveland	L	5-9	Farrell	Knudson
25—Cleveland	L	5-10	Candiotti	Bosio
26—At N.Y.	L	2-8	Guetterman	Powell
27—At N.Y.	W	5-4	Krueger	Jones
28—At N.Y.	L	2-3	Righetti	Sebra
29—At Seattle	L	2-4	Johnson	Crim
30—At Seattle	L	2-6	Hanson	Higuera

Won 10, Lost 19

JULY

Date		Score	Winner	Loser
1—At Seattle	L	5-6§	Comstock	Mirabella
3—Oakland	L	0-5	Young	Krueger
4—Oakland	W	7-1	Robinson	Stewart
5—Oakland	W	4-3	Higuera	Welch
6—California	L	8-9y	Minton	Edens
7—California	L	3-4‡	Fetters	Veres
8—California	W	20-7	Edens	Minton
11—At Chicago	W	12-9x	Plesac	Pall
12—At Oak.	L	3-5	Moore	Higuera

JULY

Date		Score	Winner	Loser
13—At Oak.	W	2-0	Knudson	Stewart
14—At Oak.	L	1-3	Welch	Krueger
15—At Oak.	L	1-4	Young	Bosio
16—At Calif.	W	3-1	Robinson	Langston
17—At Calif.	L	1-8	McCaskill	Higuera
18—At Calif.	W	3-2	Knudson	Abbott
19—Seattle	W	4-0	Krueger	Johnson
20—Seattle	L	4-6	Comstock	Veres
21—Seattle	W	10-3	Robinson	Hanson
22—Seattle	L	3-4	Holman	Higuera
23—Boston	W	13-0	Knudson	Boddicker
24—Boston	W	6-5†	Plesac	Reed
25—Boston	L	0-2	Clemens	Bosio
27—At Chicago	L	4-7	McDowell	Robinson
28—At Chicago	L	4-5	Radinsky	Plesac
29—At Chicago	W	9-8‡	Mirabella	Radinsky
30—Texas	L	1-3	Witt	Krueger
31—Texas	L	3-11	Ryan	Bosio

Won 12, Lost 15

AUGUST

Date		Score	Winner	Loser
1—Texas	L	2-8	Hough	Robinson
2—Chicago	L	3-4	Jones	Veres
2—Chicago	L	2-4	Perez	Navarro
3—Chicago	L	2-6	Hibbard	Knudson
4—Chicago	L	6-9	Peterson	Krueger
5—Chicago	L	1-6	McDowell	Powell
6—At Minn.	W	6-0	Robinson	Smith
7—At Minn.	W	5-3	Navarro	Guthrie
8—At Minn.	L	2-4	Erickson	Knudson
10—At K.C.	L	5-6	Montgomery	Plesac
10—At K.C.	L	4-9	S. Davis	Powell
11—At K.C.	W	11-5	Robinson	Filson
12—At K.C.	L	1-7	Gordon	Navarro
14—At Detroit	W	7-6	Crim	Gleaton
15—At Detroit	W	7-3	Mirabella	Searcy
16—At Detroit	W	8-4	Robinson	Petry
17—Kan. City	W	2-1	Higuera	Gordon
18—Kan. City	L	1-10	Appier	Navarro
19—Kan. City	W	7-2	Knudson	McGaffigan
20—Cleveland	W	4-3	Edens	Olin
21—Cleveland	W	6-5	Plesac	Ward
22—Cleveland	L	2-4	Candiotti	Higuera
23—At N.Y.	W	8-2	Navarro	Witt
24—At N.Y.	W	1-0	Knudson	Leary
25—At N.Y.	W	5-3	Lee	Righetti
26—At N.Y.	L	3-4‡	Guetterman	Plesac
27—At Toronto	W	4-2	Higuera	Acker
28—At Toronto	W	6-2	Navarro	Stieb
29—At Toronto	L	3-7	Key	Knudson
31—Baltimore	W	4-1	Robinson	Mitchell

Won 16, Lost 14

SEPTEMBER

Date		Score	Winner	Loser
1—Baltimore	W	4-3	Higuera	McDonald
2—Baltimore	W	4-2	Navarro	Mesa
3—Minnesota	L	0-6	Guthrie	Knudson
3—Minnesota	L	5-9	Aguilera	Plesac
4—Minnesota	L	1-7	Drummond	Edens
5—Minnesota	W	7-4	Robinson	Wayne
7—Detroit	W	6-5	Higuera	Morris
8—Detroit	W	5-2	Navarro	Terrell
9—Detroit	L	0-5	Aldred	Krueger
10—At Bos.	L	4-5	Harris	Knudson
10—At Bos.	W	6-1	Edens	Kiecker
11—At Bos.	W	4-2	Robinson	Gardner
12—At Bos.	L	1-6	Boddicker	Higuera
14—At Texas	L	1-2†	Rogers	Crim
15—At Texas	L	3-6	Moyer	Edens
16—At Texas	W	5-3	Robinson	Chiamparino
17—At Cleve.	L	2-4	Olin	Higuera
18—At Cleve.	L	3-8	Nagy	August
19—At Cleve.	L	3-6	S. Valdez	Navarro
21—At Balt.	L	3-5	Harnisch	Robinson
22—At Balt.	L	2-3	Johnson	Brown
23—At Balt.	L	1-2†	Ballard	Higuera
24—At Toronto	L	5-9	Key	Navarro
25—Toronto	W	8-4	Krueger	Black
26—Toronto	W	6-0	Robinson	Wells
27—At Chicago	L	4-6	Edwards	Edens
28—New York	L	2-7	Adkins	Higuera
29—New York	W	8-1	Navarro	Witt
30—New York	L	2-7	Eiland	Edens

Won 11, Lost 18

OCTOBER

Date		Score	Winner	Loser
1—Texas	L	2-4	Jeffcoat	Robinson
2—Texas	W	1-0	Brown	Rogers
3—Texas	W	6-3	Higuera	Barfield

Won 2, Lost 1

*8 innings. †10 innings. ‡11 innings. §12 innings. x13 innings. y16 innings.

Greg Vaughn was solid in the field but his poor hitting helped doom Milwaukee to a sixth-place finish.

of his 17-year career. His average dropped 71 points from .318 in his 1989 Most Valuable Player year to a career-low .247. And he had just 39 extra-base hits. In 1989, he had 38 doubles.

Greg Vaughn and Rob Deer, who flanked Yount in left and right field, respectively, provided some power (44 combined homers). But they were even less consistent than Yount. Together, they hit .214 with 238 strikeouts.

But reserve outfielder Mike Felder enjoyed his best season in the big leagues. He hit a career-high .274 and swiped at least 20 bases for the third time in his career.

Darryl Hamilton also proved to be a pleasant surprise, pacing the team in hitting with a .295 average. He was used as an alternate in the outfield the second half of the season and finished with a team-high .357 average with runners in scoring position.

Glenn Braggs, a starter on opening day, was traded to Cincinnati along with Bill Bates for Robinson and Bob Sebra in early June following an undistinguished start with Milwaukee.

The infield was far from spectacular. Surhoff raised his average almost 30 points from the year before, but had only four more runs batted in. Charlie O'Brien backed up Surhoff until he was traded to the New York Mets in late August. He shined defensively but hit poorly.

Shortstop Bill Spiers also had a quiet year at the plate, along with utilityman Dale Sveum. But fellow reserve Edgar

Diaz excelled with a .271 average.

First baseman Greg Brock, who never has hit for power in the majors, lost his job when second baseman Jim Gantner and Molitor finally were both healthy for most of the last two months of the season.

Had it not been for Parker, there is no telling how many games out the Brewers might have finished. They easily could have found themselves in the cellar because he carried them for most of the season. Parker earned the Designated Hitter of the Year Award for the second straight season, finishing with 21 home runs and a club-high 92 RBIs.

Next to Parker, Sheffield probably had as good a year as anyone else on the team. After a contentious rookie season, Sheffield showed signs of realizing his offensive potential with 41 extra-base hits in 125 games, and he wasn't a cancer in the clubhouse the way he had been in 1989.

Still, his season was cut short by a mysterious ailment that he contacted in Arlington, Tex., and he was accused two weeks later of leaving the team without permission in the closing days of the season.

No player, however, put on a more inspiring performance than Gantner. At age 36, he recovered from a career-threatening knee injury to hit only 12 points below his career average and steal 18 bases in 21 attempts.

But other than Gantner, Parker, Sheffield and Robinson, the Brewers' season had few silver linings.

During a season filled with many lows in New York, Jesse Barfield led the
Yankees in home runs (25) and RBIs (78).

Bronx Bombers Bomb in 1990

By JACK O'CONNELL

The New York Yankees, baseball's winningest club of the 1980s, began the new decade as the American League's losingest club.

In fact, the Yankees (67-95) lost more games in 1990 than in any season since 1912. In pursuit of its ghastly record, New York lost every game it played at Boston's Fenway Park and Texas' Arlington Stadium, every game it played against Oakland (the first time the Yankees were swept in a season series) and two no-hitters to the Chicago White Sox (one thrown by a Yankee pitcher).

If the Yankees' on-field exploits didn't provide enough turmoil, their front-office shenanigans did. It started with general partner George Steinbrenner's dismissal of manager Bucky Dent in June and the promotion of Stump Merrill to the top post. Next he replaced general manager Pete Peterson with Gene Michael in August. But before the season concluded, Steinbrenner found himself on the outside looking in.

The Yankees played under a shroud most of the year while an investigation of Steinbrenner concerning payments to a known gambler was being conducted by Commissioner Fay Vincent. Finally, on July 30 Vincent ordered Steinbrenner to relinquish controlling interest in the Yankees as punishment.

Steinbrenner's reign officially ended August 20. His choice to succeed himself as general partner, theater magnate Robert Nederlander, was accepted by the club's limited partners and approved by the major leagues's ownership committee.

But Steinbrenner's quandary only punctuated the Yankees' pitiful plight in 1990. Their last-place finish was deserved. After all, the Yankees finished last in so many other categories, including batting average, runs, hits, doubles, triples, runs batted in, walks, on-base average, sacrifice flies and slugging percentage. The Yankees didn't have a regular hit .300 or drive in 100 runs for the first time in 11 years (except for the strike-shortened 1981 season).

Outfielder Roberto Kelly led the regulars with a .285 average. Kelly was one of the few bright spots in a dim season, playing in 162 games and stealing 42 bases with 61 RBIs.

Fellow outfielder Jesse Barfield paced the team in home runs (25) and RBIs (78),

Despite hitting 21 homers, Kevin Maas collected only 41 RBIs.

but his RBI total was the fewest by a club leader since 1969 (except for 1981).

New York could never establish a steady third outfielder. Mel Hall, Oscar Azocar, Claudell Washington and Deion Sanders all jockeyed for playing time at various junctures of the season. Hall, who also saw duty as a designated hitter, enjoyed the most success, batting .258 with 46 RBIs in 113 games. Azocar was marginally successful, while Washington (acquired from California in April and released at season's end) and Sanders (who was placed on waivers in late September so he could pursue his two-sport interest elsewhere) both flopped.

Any chance the Yankees had of rising from their offensive ashes was dashed when Don Mattingly missed most of the second half of the season with a chronic back ailment. He hit .256, well below his career .323 mark, and only produced five home runs and 42 RBIs in 102 games.

"Basically, it was a waste," Mattingly said of his 1990 season.

The only good that came out of Mattingly's injury was the emergence of Kevin Maas. The lefthanded slugger set big league records for the quickest to get 10, 13 and 15 home runs in a career. He tied the mark for quickest to reach 12. He recorded only 41 RBIs despite hitting 21 home runs,

SCORES OF NEW YORK YANKEES' 1990 GAMES

APRIL

Date	W/L	Score	Winner	Loser
12—Cleveland	W	6-4	Plunk	Orosco
13—Texas	W	3-0	Perez	Witt
14—Texas	L	4-8	Ryan	Hawkins
15—Texas	W	3-1	Plunk	Russell
17—At Detroit	W	4-1	Leary	Tanana
18—At Detroit	L	4-8	Morris	LaPoint
19—At Cleve.	L	0-1	Swindell	Perez
20—At Texas	L	5-6	Ryan	Guetterman
21—At Texas	L	6-9	Hough	Cadaret
22—At Texas	L	4-10	Brown	Leary
24—Seattle	W	6-2	LaPoint	Young
25—Seattle	L	2-5	Holman	Perez
26—Seattle	L	2-6	Johnson	Hawkins
27—California	W	5-4	Guetterman	Fraser
28—California	W	3-2	Cadaret	Finley
29—California	L	3-4	Langston	LaPoint
30—Oakland	L	0-6	Welch	Parker

Won 7, Lost 10

MAY

Date	W/L	Score	Winner	Loser
1—Oakland	L	2-4	Moore	Hawkins
2—Oakland	L	0-2	Sanderson	Leary
3—Cleveland	L	5-10	Orosco	Robinson
4—At Calif.	W	5-2	LaPoint	Langston
5—At Calif.	W	11-3	Parker	McCaskill
6—At Calif.	W	4-2	Hawkins	Abbott
7—At Oak.	L	1-5	Moore	Leary
8—At Oak.	L	0-5	Sanderson	Cadaret
9—At Oak.	L	1-2‡	Honeycutt	Plunk
11—At Seattle	W	8-5	Guetterman	Harris
12—At Seattle	W	4-1	Leary	Hanson
13—At Seattle	L	5-10	Young	Cadaret
15—Minnesota	W	7-3	Cary	Smith
17—Minnesota	L	1-4	Tapani	LaPoint
18—Kan. City	L	1-4	Saberhagen	Leary
19—Kan. City	W	5-4‡	McCullers	Farr
20—Kan. City	L	3-4†	Montgomery	Robinson
21—Chicago	L	5-6	Radinsky	Guetterman
22—Chicago	W	5-2	LaPoint	Perez
23—At Minn.	W	12-0	Leary	Drummond
24—At Minn.	L	4-5	Aguilera	Cadaret
25—At K.C.	W	6-3	Cary	S. Davis
26—At K.C.	L	4-9	Gordon	Hawkins
27—At K.C.	L	2-6	Appier	LaPoint
28—At Chicago	L	1-2	King	Leary
29—At Chicago	L	4-5	Thigpen	Robinson
30—At Chicago	L	2-5	Hibbard	Cary

Won 10, Lost 17

JUNE

Date	W/L	Score	Winner	Loser
1—Baltimore	W	4-3	LaPoint	Ballard
2—Baltimore	L	2-4	Johnson	Leary
3—Baltimore	L	3-4	Milacki	Witt
4—At Bos.	L	3-5	Reardon	Robinson
5—At Bos.	L	8-9	Reardon	Plunk
6—At Bos.	L	1-4	Boddicker	LaPoint
7—At Bos.	L	0-3	Harris	Leary
8—At Balt.	L	4-5†	Holton	Mills
9—At Balt.	L	1-10	Harnisch	Cary
10—At Balt.	W	5-2	Jones	Tibbs
12—Boston	W	5-4	Guetterman	Murphy
13—Boston	L	1-4	Clemens	Leary
14—Boston	W	3-1	Cary	Kiecker
15—Toronto	L	4-5	Wells	Robinson
16—Toronto	L	1-2‡	Wills	Mills
17—Toronto	L	1-8	Stottlemyre	LaPoint
18—At Milw.	L	2-4	Knudson	Leary
19—At Milw.	W	5-1	Cary	Bosio
20—At Milw.	W	5-4	Guetterman	Crim
21—At Toronto	W	7-6	Mills	Acker
22—At Toronto	W	8-7y	Cadaret	Blair
23—At Toronto	L	4-8	Stottlemyre	Leary
24—At Toronto	L	3-8	Cerutti	Cary
26—Milwaukee	W	8-2	Guetterman	Powell
27—Milwaukee	L	4-5	Krueger	Jones
28—Milwaukee	W	3-2	Righetti	Sebra
29—At Chicago	L	0-1	McDowell	Cary
30—At Chicago	W	10-7	Robinson	Perez

Won 11, Lost 17

JULY

Date	W/L	Score	Winner	Loser
1—At Chicago	L	0-4	Jones	Hawkins
2—At K.C.	L	5-11	Appier	Jones
3—At K.C.	L	1-6	Farr	Leary
4—At K.C.	L	6-13	Crawford	Guetterman
6—Minnesota	L	0-2§	Berenguer	Hawkins
6—Minnesota	W	5-3	LaPoint	Smith
7—Minnesota	W	5-4§	Guetterman	Leach
8—Minnesota	L	3-6	West	Leary
12—Chicago	L	0-8*	Perez	Hawkins
13—Chicago	L	2-3	Hibbard	Cary
14—Chicago	L	7-8†	Pall	Guetterman
15—Chicago	L	5-8	Patterson	Mills
16—Kan. City	W	3-2	Robinson	Filson
17—Kan. City	L	7-10	S. Davis	Hawkins
18—Kan. City	W	5-3	Plunk	Crawford
19—At Minn.	W	2-1	Leary	Smith
20—At Minn.	L	1-2	Anderson	LaPoint
21—At Minn.	L	1-2	Guthrie	Robinson
22—At Minn.	W	10-6	Cadaret	Aguilera
23—At Texas	L	2-3	Brown	Cary
24—At Texas	L	1-4	Witt	Leary
25—At Texas	L	7-9‡	Rogers	Leiter
27—At Cleve.	W	3-0	Hawkins	Swindell
27—At Cleve.	W	4-1	Robinson	Walker
28—At Cleve.	L	1-2	Candiotti	Cary
29—At Cleve.	W	8-5	Leary	Black
29—At Cleve.	W	4-3	Plunk	Guante
30—Detroit	W	6-2	LaPoint	Searcy
31—Detroit	W	10-4	Leiter	Petry

Won 12, Lost 17

AUGUST

Date	W/L	Score	Winner	Loser
1—Detroit	L	4-15	Morris	Hawkins
2—Detroit	L	5-6x	Parker	Mills
3—Cleveland	W	6-4	Guetterman	Candiotti
4—Cleveland	L	3-17	Black	Leary
5—Cleveland	W	5-3	Cadaret	Olin
6—Cleveland	W	2-1	Hawkins	Swindell
7—At Seattle	W	3-1	Witt	Hanson
8—At Seattle	W	6-4	Plunk	Comstock
9—At Seattle	W	1-0	Leary	Young
10—At Oak.	L	0-3	Stewart	LaPoint
11—At Oak.	L	1-10	Young	Hawkins
12—At Oak.	L	1-6	Welch	Witt
13—At Calif.	L	2-4	McCaskill	Cary
14—At Calif.	L	5-9	Abbott	Leary
15—At Calif.	L	1-8	Langston	LaPoint
17—Seattle	W	3-2	Guetterman	Swift
18—Seattle	W	6-0	Witt	Holman
19—Seattle	W	3-1	Leary	Young
20—Toronto	W	6-5‡	Cadaret	Acker
21—Toronto	W	3-2	Cary	Candelaria
22—Toronto	W	4-2	Hawkins	Cerutti
23—Milwaukee	L	2-8	Navarro	Witt
24—Milwaukee	L	0-1	Knudson	Leary
25—Milwaukee	L	3-5	Lee	Righetti
26—Milwaukee	W	4-3‡	Guetterman	Plesac
27—At Balt.	W	4-0	Hawkins	McDonald
28—At Balt.	W	11-3	Witt	Mesa
29—At Balt.	W	3-2	Leary	Telford
30—At Balt.	L	1-6	Harnisch	LaPoint
31—At Bos.	L	3-7	Harris	Cary

Won 16, Lost 14

SEPTEMBER

Date	W/L	Score	Winner	Loser
1—At Bos.	L	1-15	Boddicker	Hawkins
2—At Bos.	L	1-7	Bolton	Witt
3—California	L	0-7	McCaskill	Leary
5—California	W	2-1	LaPoint	Harvey
6—California	L	6-12‡	McClure	Guetterman
7—Oakland	L	1-7	Young	Hawkins
8—Oakland	L	2-5	Sanderson	Witt
9—Oakland	L	3-7	Stewart	Leary
10—Texas	L	0-1‡	Rogers	Guetterman
11—Texas	W	5-4	Guetterman	Witt
12—Texas	L	4-5	Hough	Adkins
13—At Detroit	W	7-3	Witt	Terrell
14—At Detroit	W	5-2	Leary	Aldred
15—At Detroit	L	3-4	Tanana	Eiland
16—At Detroit	L	2-5	Searcy	Cary
17—At Toronto	L	4-6	Cerutti	Plunk
18—At Toronto	L	2-3	Black	Guetterman
19—At Toronto	L	6-7	Key	Leary
20—Cleveland	L	7-12	Walker	Monteleone
21—Boston	L	0-3	Kiecker	Cary
22—Boston	W	5-2	Plunk	Gray
23—Boston	W	5-4	Witt	Bolton
24—Baltimore	L	3-6†	Bautista	Mills
25—Baltimore	W	15-3	Eiland	Telford
26—Baltimore	W	4-2	Cary	Ballard
28—At Milw.	W	7-2	Adkins	Higuera
29—At Milw.	L	1-8	Navarro	Witt
30—At Milw.	W	7-2	Eiland	Edens

Won 10, Lost 18

OCTOBER

Date	W/L	Score	Winner	Loser
1—Detroit	L	0-2	Tanana	Cary
2—Detroit	W	4-1	Guetterman	Nunez
3—Detroit	L	3-10	Morris	Adkins

Won 1, Lost 2

*6 innings. †10 innings. ‡11 innings. §12 innings. x14 innings. y15 innings.

Roberto Kelly was one of the few bright spots in a dim season for the Yankees.

but that was due in part to the Yankees' failure to get on base regularly. Of Maas' home runs, 15 were solo shots.

Alvaro Espinoza and Steve Sax were iron men at shortstop and second base, respectively, but both struggled at the plate. Espinoza hit a meager .224. Sax owned a .260 average after hitting .315 in 1989. But the scrappy veteran led New York in stolen bases (43).

Third base was an abyss most of the season. Randy Velarde, Jim Leyritz and Mike Blowers (who tied an A.L. record with four errors in a game against Cleveland) all took turns at the hot corner; none had much success.

Matt Nokes, acquired from Detroit in June, and Bob Geren shared catching duties. Nokes was the better hitter, but Geren enjoyed an exceptional defensive season. Plus, veteran catcher Rick Cerone posted great offensive numbers before succumbing to a knee injury in June.

Big Steve Balboni got his swings as a DH. He had a terrible batting average (.192), but still hit 17 homers in 266 at-bats.

The weak offense was chiefly the fault for the Yankees finishing in the cellar for the first time since 1966, but the pitching wasn't much better. The staff earned-run average (4.21) ranked 12th in the A.L.

Yankee pitchers allowed 1,430 hits in 1,444⅔ innings, while walking 618 batters.

Starters combined for a 42-71 record, a 4.47 ERA and 15 complete games. No starter reached double figures in victories. Tim Leary, who led the rotation with nine wins, did not pitch after September 19 by order of Michael, who didn't want to risk the chance the righthander would lose 20.

But New York should have known it was in for a long year from the start of the season. The year began with Pascual Perez, who signed a three-year, $5.7-million deal as a free agent, arriving eight days late to spring training, which already had been shortened because of the lockout. His season was over 12 games into the schedule because of a muscle strain in his shoulder that required surgery, which Perez delayed until August. For their investment, the Yankees received 14 innings from a pitcher whose future is now questionable.

The most bizarre event involving a pitcher occurred July 1 in the last game the Yankees would play at Chicago's Comiskey Park. Andy Hawkins pitched a no-hitter but lost the game as the White Sox scored four runs in the eighth inning due to errors by Blowers, Leyritz and Barfield.

Eleven days later, Hawkins was the losing pitcher in another no-hitter. Chicago's Melido Perez, Pascual's younger brother, tossed a rain-shortened, six-inning 8-0 victory against the Yankees. It was the first no-hitter versus New York since 1958 when Hoyt Wilhelm turned the trick for Baltimore.

Mike Witt (acquired from California for Dave Winfield in May), Dave LaPoint and Chuck Cary rounded out the rotation. All three struggled as opponents hit a sturdy .261 against Yankee pitchers. But New York got a glimpse of the future when Dave Eiland and Steve Adkins each made five starts at the end of the season. Prospect Mark Leiter struggled in two stints with the Yankees as both a starter and reliever.

The Yankees' bullpen was average at best. It posted a 25-24 mark with 41 saves and a 3.77 ERA, but had 233 walks and only 331 strikeouts in 498⅓ innings. It did feature the staff's top winner, Lee Guetterman, whose 11 wins tied the club record for fewest victories by a team leader.

Dave Righetti paced the bullpen with 36 saves. But his ERA has been rising in recent years. Eric Plunk pitched well in the second half of the season, but he walked a lot of batters. Jeff Robinson, Greg Cadaret, Alan Mills and Chuck Cary rounded out a bullpen that couldn't prevent the Yankees from opening the decade as the A.L.'s biggest loser.

American League Averages for 1990

CHAMPIONSHIP WINNERS IN PREVIOUS YEARS

1900—Chicago* .607	1930—Philadelphia .662	1960—New York .630
1901—Chicago .610	1931—Philadelphia .704	1961—New York .673
1902—Philadelphia .610	1932—New York .695	1962—New York .593
1903—Boston .659	1933—Washington .651	1963—New York .646
1904—Boston .617	1934—Detroit .656	1964—New York .611
1905—Philadelphia .622	1935—Detroit .616	1965—Minnesota .630
1906—Chicago .616	1936—New York .667	1966—Baltimore .606
1907—Detroit .613	1937—New York .662	1967—Boston .568
1908—Detroit .588	1938—New York .651	1968—Detroit .636
1909—Detroit .645	1939—New York .702	1969—Baltimore (East) .673
1910—Philadelphia .680	1940—Detroit .584	1970—Baltimore (East) .667
1911—Philadelphia .669	1941—New York .656	1971—Baltimore (East) .639
1912—Boston .691	1942—New York .669	1972—Oakland (West) .600
1913—Philadelphia .627	1943—New York .636	1973—Oakland (West) .580
1914—Philadelphia .651	1944—St. Louis .578	1974—Oakland (West) .556
1915—Boston .669	1945—Detroit .575	1975—Boston (East) .594
1916—Boston .591	1946—Boston .675	1976—New York (East) .610
1917—Chicago .649	1947—New York .630	1977—New York (East) .617
1918—Boston .595	1948—Cleveland† .626	1978—New York (East) .613
1919—Chicago .629	1949—New York .630	1979—Baltimore (East) .642
1920—Cleveland .636	1950—New York .636	1980—Kansas City (West) .599
1921—New York .641	1951—New York .636	1981—New York (East) .551
1922—New York .610	1952—New York .617	1982—Milwaukee (East) .586
1923—New York .645	1953—New York .656	1983—Baltimore (East) .605
1924—Washington .597	1954—Cleveland .721	1984—Detroit (East) .642
1925—Washington .636	1955—New York .623	1985—Kansas City (West) .562
1926—New York .591	1956—New York .630	1986—Boston (East) .590
1927—New York .714	1957—New York .636	1987—Minnesota (West) .525
1928—New York .656	1958—New York .597	1988—Oakland (West) .642
1929—Philadelphia .693	1959—Chicago .610	1989—Oakland (West) .611

*Not recognized as major league in 1900. †Defeated Boston in one-game playoff for pennant.

STANDING OF CLUBS AT CLOSE OF SEASON

EAST DIVISION

Club	Bos.	Tor.	Det.	Cle.	Bal.	Mil.	N.Y.	Oak.	Chi.	Tex.	Cal.	Sea.	K.C.	Min.	W.	L.	Pct.	G.B.
Boston	..	10	8	9	9	5	9	4	6	5	7	8	4	4	88	74	.543	....
Toronto	3	..	8	9	8	6	8	5	7	5	5	6	7	9	86	76	.531	2
Detroit	5	5	..	8	7	3	7	6	7	6	7	7	5	6	79	83	.488	9
Cleveland	4	4	5	..	7	9	5	4	7	7	5	7	6	7	77	85	.475	11
Baltimore	4	5	6	6	..	7	6	4	6	8	7	3	8	6	76	85	.472	11½
Milwaukee	8	7	10	4	6	..	6	5	2	5	5	4	8	4	74	88	.457	14
New York	4	5	6	8	7	7	..	0	2	3	6	9	4	6	67	95	.414	21

WEST DIVISION

Club	Oak.	Chi.	Tex.	Cal.	Sea.	K.C.	Min.	Bos.	Tor.	Det.	Cle.	Bal.	Mil.	N.Y.	W.	L.	Pct.	G.B.
Oakland	..	5	8	9	9	9	7	8	7	6	8	8	7	12	103	59	.636	....
Chicago	8	..	7	8	8	9	7	6	5	5	5	6	10	10	94	68	.580	9
Texas	5	6	..	5	6	8	8	7	7	6	5	4	7	9	83	79	.512	20
California	4	5	8	..	5	7	9	5	7	5	7	5	7	6	80	82	.494	23
Seattle	4	5	7	8	..	6	7	4	6	5	5	9	8	3	77	85	.475	26
Kansas City	4	4	5	6	7	..	8	8	5	7	6	3	4	8	75	86	.466	27½
Minnesota	6	6	5	4	6	5	..	8	3	6	5	6	8	6	74	88	.457	29

Championship Series—Oakland defeated Boston, four games to none.

SHUTOUT GAMES

Club	Mil.	Cal.	Det.	Chi.	Oak.	Cle.	Min.	Tor.	K.C.	Tex.	Bos.	Bal.	Sea.	N.Y.	W.	L.	Pct.
Milwaukee	..	0	0	0	2	0	1	1	1	2	4	0	1	1	13	5	.722
California	0	..	1	1	1	0	1	1	1	1	1	2	2	1	13	6	.684
Detroit	1	0	..	0	1	2	1	1	1	1	1	1	1	1	12	7	.632
Chicago	0	1	0	..	2	0	0	0	2	0	1	0	1	3	10	7	.588
Oakland	1	0	0	0	..	1	0	2	2	0	3	1	2	4	16	12	.571
Cleveland	0	1	1	0	1	..	1	1	0	1	1	0	2	1	10	10	.500
Minnesota	2	1	1	1	1	1	..	0	1	1	2	0	1	1	13	14	.481
Toronto	0	1	0	1	1	2	1	..	0	1	1	0	1	0	9	10	.474
Kansas City	0	1	1	0	1	1	1	0	..	1	1	0	1	0	8	9	.471
Texas	0	1	0	2	1	0	3	0	0	..	1	0	0	1	9	11	.450
Boston	1	0	1	1	1	0	1	4	0	0	..	1	1	2	13	16	.448
Baltimore	0	0	1	1	0	1	0	0	1	0	0	..	0	0	5	7	.417
Seattle	0	0	1	0	0	1	2	0	1	1	0	1	..	0	7	15	.318
New York	0	0	0	0	0	1	1	0	0	1	0	1	2	..	6	15	.286

RECORD AT HOME

EAST DIVISION

Club	Bos.	Tor.	Cle.	Bal.	Det.	Mil.	N.Y.	Oak.	Chi.	Tex.	K.C.	Cal.	Min.	Sea.	W.	L.	Pct.
Boston	....	6-1	3-3	5-1	5-1	3-4	7-0	2-4	5-1	3-3	2-4	3-3	3-3	4-2	51	30	.630
Toronto	2-4	....	4-3	5-2	4-2	2-4	5-2	1-5	5-1	4-2	3-3	4-2	3-3	2-4	44	37	.543
Cleveland	1-6	1-5	....	3-4	3-4	6-0	2-4	3-3	5-1	4-2	3-3	2-4	5-1	3-3	41	40	.506
Baltimore	3-4	3-3	2-4	....	4-3	4-2	3-4	1-5	4-2	4-2	4-1	4-2	3-3	1-5	40	40	.500
Detroit	4-3	3-4	4-2	4-2	....	1-6	3-3	4-2	2-4	2-4	3-3	4-2	2-4	3-3	39	42	.481
Milwaukee	4-2	3-4	4-3	4-3	4-2	....	2-4	4-2	0-6	2-4	5-1	3-3	1-5	3-3	39	42	.481
New York	4-2	3-3	4-3	3-3	3-4	3-4	....	0-6	1-5	3-3	3-3	3-3	3-3	4-2	37	44	.457

WEST DIVISION

Club	Oak.	Chi.	Tex.	K.C.	Cal.	Min.	Sea.	Bos.	Tor.	Cle.	Bal.	Det.	Mil.	N.Y.	W.	L.	Pct.
Oakland	....	1-5	3-3	5-1	4-3	5-2	4-3	4-2	2-4	5-1	3-3	4-2	5-1	6-0	51	30	.630
Chicago	3-4	....	4-2	6-0	3-4	3-3	3-3	5-1	4-2	4-2	4-2	1-5	4-2	5-1	49	31	.613
Texas	2-5	4-3	....	5-2	3-4	5-1	3-3	4-2	5-1	3-3	2-4	2-4	3-3	6-0	47	35	.573
Kansas City	3-4	4-3	3-3	....	2-4	5-1	5-2	4-2	2-4	4-2	3-3	3-3	5-1		45	36	.556
California	1-5	1-5	4-2	3-4	....	6-1	4-3	2-4	5-1	3-3	3-3	3-3	4-2	3-3	42	39	.519
Minnesota	4-2	3-4	4-3	4-3	3-3	....	3-3	5-1	0-6	4-2	3-3	2-4	3-3	3-3	41	40	.506
Seattle	1-5	2-5	4-3	4-2	5-1	4-3	....	2-4	2-4	2-4	4-2	2-4	5-1	1-5	38	43	.469

RECORD ABROAD

EAST DIVISION

Club	Tor.	Det.	Bos.	Bal.	Cle.	Mil.	N.Y.	Oak.	Chi.	Sea.	Cal.	Tex.	Min.	K.C.	W.	L.	Pct.
Toronto	....	4-3	1-6	3-3	5-1	4-3	3-3	4-2	2-4	4-2	1-5	1-5	6-0	4-2	42	39	.519
Detroit	2-4	....	1-5	3-4	4-3	2-4	4-3	2-4	5-1	4-2	3-3	4-2	4-2	2-4	40	41	.494
Boston	4-2	3-4	....	4-3	6-1	2-4	2-4	2-4	1-5	4-2	2-4	2-4	1-5	2-4	37	44	.457
Baltimore	2-5	2-4	1-5	....	4-3	3-4	3-3	3-3	2-4	2-4	3-3	4-2	3-3	4-2	36	45	.444
Cleveland	3-4	2-4	3-3	4-2	....	3-4	3-4	1-5	2-4	4-2	3-3	3-3	2-4	3-3	36	45	.444
Milwaukee	4-2	6-1	4-3	2-4	0-6	....	4-3	1-5	2-4	1-5	2-4	3-3	3-3	3-3	35	46	.432
New York	2-5	3-3	0-7	4-3	4-2	4-2	....	0-6	1-5	5-1	3-3	0-6	3-3	1-5	30	51	.370

WEST DIVISION

Club	Oak.	Chi.	Sea.	Cal.	Tex.	Min.	K.C.	Tor.	Det.	Bos.	Bal.	Cle.	Mil.	N.Y.	W.	L.	Pct.
Oakland	....	4-3	5-1	5-1	5-2	2-4	4-3	5-1	2-4	4-2	5-1	3-3	2-4	6-0	52	29	.642
Chicago	5-1	....	5-2	5-1	3-4	4-3	3-4	1-5	4-2	1-5	2-4	1-5	6-0	5-1	45	37	.556
Seattle	3-4	3-3	....	3-4	3-3	2-5	4-2	3-3	2-4	5-1	3-3	3-3	2-4		39	42	.481
California	3-4	4-3	1-5	....	4-3	3-3	4-2	2-4	2-4	3-3	4-2	3-3	3-3		38	43	.469
Texas	3-3	2-4	3-4	2-4	....	3-4	3-3	2-4	4-2	3-3	2-4	2-4	4-2	3-3	36	44	.450
Minnesota	2-5	3-3	3-4	1-6	1-5	....	1-5	3-3	4-2	3-3	3-3	1-5	5-1	3-3	33	48	.407
Kansas City	1-5	0-6	2-4	4-3	2-5	3-4	....	3-3	3-3	4-2	1-4	3-3	1-5	3-3	30	50	.375

1990 A.L. Pitching Against Each Club

BALTIMORE—76-85

Pitcher	Bos. W-L	Cal. W-L	Chi. W-L	Clev. W-L	Det. W-L	K.C. W-L	Milw. W-L	Minn. W-L	N.Y. W-L	Oak. W-L	Sea. W-L	Tex. W-L	Tor. W-L	Totals W-L
Aldrich	0-0	0-0	0-0	0-0	0-2	1-0	0-0	0-0	0-0	0-0	0-0	0-0	0-0	1-2
Ballard	0-2	0-2	0-0	0-1	0-0	0-1	1-0	0-0	0-0	0-2	0-0	0-1	1-0	2-11
Bautista	0-0	0-0	0-0	0-0	0-0	0-0	0-0	0-0	1-0	0-0	0-0	0-0	0-0	1-0
Harnisch	0-2	1-0	1-2	1-2	0-1	1-1	1-0	0-1	2-0	0-0	0-2	3-0	1-0	11-11
Hickey	0-0	0-0	0-0	0-0	0-0	0-0	0-0	0-0	0-0	0-1	0-0	0-0	0-0	1-3
Holton	0-0	1-0	0-1	0-1	0-0	0-0	0-1	0-0	1-0	0-0	0-0	0-0	0-0	2-3
Johnson	1-0	0-0	0-1	1-0	3-0	2-0	2-1	1-1	1-0	0-2	0-2	2-1	0-1	13-9
McDonald	0-2	1-0	1-0	1-0	1-0	0-0	0-1	0-0	0-1	1-1	1-0	0-0	1-0	8-5
Mesa	1-0	0-0	0-0	0-0	0-0	0-0	0-1	0-0	0-1	0-0	0-0	0-0	2-0	3-2
Milacki	0-1	0-0	0-1	1-0	1-1	0-0	0-0	2-2	1-0	0-0	0-0	0-1	0-1	5-8
Mitchell	1-1	1-0	2-0	0-0	0-1	2-0	0-1	0-0	0-0	0-2	0-0	0-1	0-0	6-6
Olson	0-1	0-1	0-0	1-1	1-0	0-0	1-0	0-1	0-0	0-0	0-0	2-0	1-1	6-5
Price	0-0	1-0	0-0	1-1	0-1	0-0	1-0	0-1	0-0	0-0	0-0	0-0	0-1	3-4
Schilling	0-0	0-0	0-0	0-0	0-0	1-0	0-0	0-0	0-0	0-0	0-0	0-0	0-1	1-2
Taylor	0-0	0-0	0-0	0-1	0-0	0-0	0-0	0-0	0-0	0-0	0-0	0-0	0-0	0-1
Telford	1-0	1-0	0-0	0-0	0-0	0-0	0-0	0-0	0-2	1-0	0-1	0-0	0-0	3-3
Tibbs	0-0	1-1	0-1	0-0	0-0	0-0	0-0	0-1	0-1	1-1	0-0	0-0	0-1	2-7
Weston	0-0	0-1	0-0	0-0	0-0	0-0	0-0	0-0	0-0	0-0	0-0	0-0	0-0	0-1
Williamson	0-0	0-0	2-0	0-0	0-0	0-1	1-0	3-0	0-0	1-0	1-1	0-0	0-0	8-2
Totals	4-9	7-5	6-6	6-7	6-7	8-3	7-6	6-6	6-7	4-8	3-9	8-4	5-8	76-85

No Decisions—Boone, Smith.

BOSTON—88-74

Pitcher	Balt. W-L	Cal. W-L	Chi. W-L	Clev. W-L	Det. W-L	K.C. W-L	Milw. W-L	Minn. W-L	N.Y. W-L	Oak. W-L	Sea. W-L	Tex. W-L	Tor. W-L	Totals W-L
Boddicker	4-0	1-2	1-0	1-0	1-1	1-1	1-3	0-0	2-0	1-0	1-0	2-1	1-0	17-8
Bolton	0-1	1-1	1-1	0-0	2-0	1-1	0-0	1-0	1-1	0-0	2-0	1-0	3-0	10-5
Clemens	0-1	3-0	2-0	3-0	2-0	1-1	2-0	1-1	1-0	1-3	1-0	0-0	2-0	21-6

BOSTON—Continued

Pitcher	Balt. W-L	Cal. W-L	Chi. W-L	Clev. W-L	Det. W-L	K.C. W-L	Mil. W-L	Minn. W-L	N.Y. W-L	Oak. W-L	Sea. W-L	Tex. W-L	Tor. W-L	Totals W-L
Gardner	1-0	0-0	0-0	1-1	0-1	0-0	0-1	0-0	0-0	0-0	0-0	0-1	0-2	1-1	3-7
Gray	1-0	0-0	0-0	0-0	0-0	0-0	0-0	0-1	0-0	0-0	1-0	0-2	0-0	2-4
Harris	3-1	1-0	0-1	0-1	3-1	0-1	1-0	0-1	2-0	1-2	1-1	0-0	1-0	13-9
Hesketh	0-0	0-0	0-1	0-0	0-0	0-0	0-0	0-0	0-0	0-0	0-1	0-0	0-2	0-4
Hetzel	0-0	0-0	0-0	0-0	0-0	0-0	0-1	0-2	0-0	0-1	1-0	0-0	0-0	1-4
Irvine	0-0	0-0	0-0	0-0	0-0	0-0	0-0	0-0	0-0	0-1	1-0	0-0	0-0	1-1
Kiecker	0-1	0-0	1-1	3-0	0-0	1-1	0-1	0-1	1-1	0-1	0-1	0-1	2-0	8-9
Lamp	0-0	0-2	0-1	0-1	0-1	0-0	0-0	2-0	0-0	0-0	0-0	0-0	1-0	3-5
Murphy	0-0	0-0	0-0	0-1	0-0	0-0	0-1	0-1	0-2	0-1	0-0	0-0	0-0	0-6
Reardon	0-0	0-0	1-0	0-0	0-0	0-0	0-2	0-0	0-0	2-0	1-0	0-0	1-0	5-3
Reed	0-0	0-0	0-0	1-0	0-0	0-0	0-0	0-0	0-0	0-0	0-0	1-0	0-0	2-1
Rochford	0-0	0-0	0-0	0-0	0-1	0-0	0-0	0-0	0-0	0-0	0-0	0-0	0-0	0-1
Smith	0-0	1-0	0-1	0-0	0-0	0-0	1-0	0-0	0-0	0-0	0-0	0-0	0-0	2-1
Totals	9-4	7-5	6-6	9-4	8-5	4-8	5-8	4-8	9-4	4-8	8-4	5-7	10-3	88-74

No Decisions—Andersen, Dopson, Heep, Leister.

CALIFORNIA—80-82

Pitcher	Balt. W-L	Bos. W-L	Chi. W-L	Clev. W-L	Det. W-L	K.C. W-L	Milw. W-L	Minn. W-L	N.Y. W-L	Oak. W-L	Sea. W-L	Tex. W-L	Tor. W-L	Totals W-L
Abbott	1-0	0-2	1-1	1-1	0-1	0-2	0-2	1-1	1-1	0-1	1-1	2-0	2-1	10-14
Bailes	0-0	0-0	0-0	0-0	1-0	0-0	0-0	0-0	0-0	0-0	0-0	0-0	1-0	2-0
Blyleven	1-0	0-1	0-0	2-0	1-1	2-0	1-0	0-2	0-0	0-1	0-1	1-0	0-1	8-7
Eichhorn	0-2	0-1	0-1	0-0	0-0	0-0	0-0	0-0	1-1	0-0	0-0	0-0	1-0	2-5
Fetters	0-0	0-0	0-0	0-0	0-0	0-0	1-0	0-0	0-0	0-0	0-1	0-0	0-0	1-1
Finley	2-0	2-0	1-1	3-0	1-2	2-2	1-0	3-0	0-1	0-1	2-1	0-1	1-0	18-9
Fraser	1-0	1-0	0-0	0-0	0-0	0-0	1-1	0-0	0-1	0-2	0-0	1-0	1-0	5-4
Grahe	0-1	0-0	1-1	0-0	0-2	0-0	0-0	1-0	0-0	1-0	0-0	0-0	0-0	3-4
Harvey	0-0	0-1	0-0	0-0	0-1	1-0	0-0	1-0	0-1	1-0	0-1	0-0	1-0	4-4
Langston	0-2	0-2	1-3	0-3	1-0	1-1	1-1	2-0	2-1	0-0	1-2	1-1	0-1	10-17
Lewis	0-0	0-0	0-0	0-0	0-0	0-0	0-0	0-0	0-0	0-0	1-0	0-0	0-0	1-1
McCaskill	0-1	2-0	1-1	1-1	1-0	1-0	1-0	1-0	2-1	0-2	2-2	0-2	0-2	12-11
McClure	0-0	0-0	0-0	0-0	0-0	0-0	0-0	0-0	1-0	0-0	1-0	0-0	0-0	2-0
Minton	0-0	0-0	0-0	0-0	0-0	0-0	1-1	0-0	0-0	0-0	0-0	0-0	0-0	1-1
Witt	0-1	0-0	0-0	0-0	0-0	0-0	0-0	0-1	0-0	0-1	0-0	0-0	0-0	0-3
Young	0-0	0-0	0-0	0-0	0-0	0-0	0-0	0-0	0-0	1-1	0-0	0-0	0-0	1-1
Totals	5-7	5-7	5-8	7-5	5-7	7-6	7-5	9-4	6-6	4-9	5-8	8-5	7-5	80-82

No Decisions—Clear, Corbett, Hill, Richardson.

CHICAGO—94-68

Pitcher	Balt. W-L	Bos. W-L	Cal. W-L	Clev. W-L	Det. W-L	K.C. W-L	Milw. W-L	Minn. W-L	N.Y. W-L	Oak. W-L	Sea. W-L	Tex. W-L	Tor. W-L	Totals W-L
Edwards	0-0	0-0	1-0	0-0	0-1	1-0	1-0	0-1	0-0	0-0	0-0	2-0	0-1	5-3
Fernandez	0-0	1-1	1-1	0-0	0-0	1-0	0-0	0-0	1-0	1-1	0-1	0-1	5-5
Hibbard	0-1	1-0	2-1	2-1	0-1	1-1	1-0	2-0	2-0	1-0	0-2	0-1	2-1	14-9
Jones	2-0	1-1	2-0	0-2	0-0	2-0	2-0	1-0	1-0	0-1	0-0	0-0	0-0	11-4
King	1-0	1-1	1-0	1-1	0-1	1-0	0-0	1-1	1-0	2-0	2-0	0-0	1-0	12-4
Kutzler	1-0	0-0	0-0	0-0	0-0	0-0	0-0	0-1	0-0	0-0	0-0	0-0	1-0	2-1
Long	0-0	0-0	0-0	0-1	0-0	0-0	0-0	0-0	0-0	0-0	0-0	0-0	0-0	0-1
McDowell	0-1	1-2	0-1	0-0	0-1	1-0	2-0	2-1	1-0	2-1	2-0	2-0	1-2	14-9
Pall	0-0	1-0	0-0	0-0	1-1	0-0	0-1	0-0	1-0	0-1	0-1	0-1	0-0	3-5
Patterson	0-0	0-0	0-0	0-0	1-1	0-0	0-0	0-0	1-0	0-0	0-0	0-0	0-0	2-1
Perez	1-1	0-0	1-1	1-2	2-1	1-1	1-0	0-1	1-2	1-2	2-0	2-2	0-1	13-14
Peterson	0-1	0-1	0-0	1-0	0-0	0-1	1-0	0-1	0-0	0-0	0-1	0-0	0-0	2-5
Radinsky	1-0	0-0	0-0	0-0	0-0	1-0	2-1	1-0	1-0	0-0	0-0	0-0	0-0	6-1
Rosenberg	0-0	0-0	0-0	0-0	0-0	0-0	0-0	0-0	0-0	0-0	1-0	0-0	0-0	1-0
Thigpen	0-2	0-0	0-1	0-0	1-0	0-1	0-0	0-0	1-0	1-0	0-0	1-1	0-1	4-6
Totals	6-6	6-6	8-5	5-7	5-7	9-4	10-2	7-6	10-2	8-5	8-5	7-6	5-7	94-68

No Decisions—Hillegas, Lyons.

CLEVELAND—77-85

Pitcher	Balt. W-L	Bos. W-L	Cal. W-L	Chi. W-L	Det. W-L	K.C. W-L	Milw. W-L	Minn. W-L	N.Y. W-L	Oak. W-L	Sea. W-L	Tex. W-L	Tor. W-L	Totals W-L
Bearse	0-0	0-0	0-0	0-1	0-0	0-0	0-0	0-0	0-0	0-0	0-0	0-0	0-1	0-2
Black	0-0	0-0	0-1	3-0	1-1	0-0	1-1	1-2	1-1	1-0	2-1	0-2	1-1	11-10
Candiotti	0-0	1-2	2-1	1-1	2-2	2-0	3-0	0-0	1-1	0-1	1-1	1-0	1-2	15-11
Farrell	0-1	0-2	0-1	1-0	0-0	0-1	1-0	1-0	0-0	0-0	1-0	0-0	0-0	4-5
Guante	0-0	0-0	1-0	0-0	0-0	0-1	0-0	0-0	0-1	1-0	0-0	0-1	0-0	2-3
Jones	3-0	0-3	0-0	1-0	0-0	0-0	1-0	0-0	0-0	0-1	0-0	0-1	0-0	5-5
Nagy	1-0	0-0	0-1	0-1	0-0	0-0	1-0	0-0	0-0	0-2	0-0	0-0	0-0	2-4
Nichols	0-0	0-0	0-0	0-1	0-0	0-0	0-0	0-0	0-0	0-1	0-0	0-0	0-1	0-3
Nipper	1-0	0-0	0-0	0-0	0-0	0-0	0-1	0-0	0-0	0-2	1-0	0-0	0-0	2-3
Olin	1-0	0-0	0-0	0-0	0-0	0-1	1-1	1-1	0-1	0-0	0-0	1-0	0-0	4-4
Orosco	0-1	0-0	0-1	1-0	0-0	0-0	0-0	1-0	1-1	0-0	2-1	0-0	0-0	5-4
Seanez	0-0	1-0	0-0	0-0	0-1	0-0	0-0	0-0	0-0	0-0	1-0	0-0	0-0	2-1

CLEVELAND—Continued

Pitcher	Balt. W-L	Bos. W-L	Cal. W-L	Chi. W-L	Det. W-L	K.C. W-L	Mil. W-L	Minn. W-L	N.Y. W-L	Oak. W-L	Sea. W-L	Tex. W-L	Tor. W-L	Totals W-L
Shaw	0-0	0-0	0-1	0-0	0-2	0-1	0-0	0-0	0-0	0-0	0-0	2-0	1-0	3-4
Swindell	1-1	1-0	2-0	0-1	1-1	2-0	0-0	2-1	1-2	2-1	0-0	0-0	0-2	12-9
E. Valdez	0-0	0-0	0-0	0-0	0-0	0-1	0-0	0-0	0-0	0-0	0-0	1-0	1-0	1-1
S. Valdez	0-2	1-1	0-0	0-0	0-1	2-0	1-0	1-0	0-0	0-2	0-0	1-0	0-0	6-6
Walker	0-0	0-1	0-1	0-0	1-0	0-1	0-0	0-1	1-1	0-0	0-0	0-1	0-0	2-6
Ward	0-1	0-0	0-0	0-0	0-0	0-0	0-1	0-0	0-0	0-0	0-0	1-0	0-1	1-3
Wickander	0-0	0-0	0-0	0-0	0-0	0-0	0-0	0-0	0-0	0-0	0-0	0-0	0-1	0-1
Totals	7-6	4-9	5-7	7-5	5-8	6-6	9-4	7-5	5-8	4-8	7-5	7-5	4-9	77-85

No Decisions—Gozzo, Kaiser.

DETROIT—79-83

Pitcher	Balt. W-L	Bos. W-L	Cal. W-L	Chi. W-L	Clev. W-L	K.C. W-L	Milw. W-L	Minn. W-L	N.Y. W-L	Oak. W-L	Sea. W-L	Tex. W-L	Tor. W-L	Totals W-L
Aldred	0-0	0-0	0-0	0-0	0-0	0-0	1-0	0-1	0-1	0-0	0-0	0-0	0-0	1-2
DuBois	0-0	0-0	0-1	1-0	1-1	0-1	0-0	0-0	0-0	0-0	0-0	1-0	0-2	3-5
Gibson	1-0	1-0	0-2	1-0	0-0	0-0	0-0	0-1	0-0	1-0	0-1	0-0	1-0	5-4
Gleaton	0-0	0-1	1-0	0-0	0-0	0-0	0-1	0-0	0-0	0-0	0-0	0-1	0-0	1-3
Henneman	1-1	0-0	0-0	1-2	1-0	0-1	0-0	0-1	0-0	1-0	3-0	1-0	0-1	8-6
Lugo	1-0	1-0	0-0	0-0	0-0	0-0	0-0	0-0	0-0	0-0	0-0	0-0	0-0	2-0
McCullers	0-0	0-0	0-0	1-0	0-0	0-0	0-0	0-0	0-0	0-0	0-0	0-0	0-0	1-0
Morris	1-1	0-2	3-1	0-2	2-1	2-1	0-3	1-2	3-0	1-1	2-0	0-2	0-2	15-18
Nosek	0-0	0-0	0-0	0-0	0-1	0-0	0-0	1-0	0-0	0-0	0-0	0-0	0-0	1-1
Nunez	0-0	0-0	0-0	2-0	0-0	1-0	0-0	0-0	0-1	0-0	0-0	0-0	0-0	3-1
Parker	0-0	0-0	0-0	0-0	0-0	0-0	0-0	1-0	1-0	0-1	0-0	0-0	0-1	2-2
Petry	1-0	2-0	1-0	0-0	1-1	1-2	1-2	0-0	0-1	0-2	0-1	2-0	1-0	10-9
Ritz	0-2	0-1	0-0	0-0	0-0	0-0	0-0	0-1	0-0	0-0	0-0	0-0	0-0	0-4
Robinson	1-1	1-2	1-0	0-1	0-0	1-1	0-1	1-0	0-0	2-0	0-1	1-1	2-1	10-9
Searcy	0-0	0-2	0-0	0-0	0-1	0-0	0-1	0-0	1-1	0-1	0-0	1-1	0-0	2-7
Tanana	1-1	0-0	0-1	1-0	1-0	0-1	1-1	0-0	2-1	1-0	1-2	0-1	0-0	9-8
Terrell	0-0	0-0	1-0	0-0	2-0	0-0	0-1	1-0	0-1	0-1	1-0	0-0	1-1	6-4
Totals	7-6	5-8	7-5	7-5	8-5	5-7	3-10	6-6	7-6	6-6	7-5	6-6	5-8	79-83

No Decisions—Kinzer, Schwabe, Wapnick.

KANSAS CITY—75-86

Pitcher	Balt. W-L	Bos. W-L	Cal. W-L	Chi. W-L	Clev. W-L	Det. W-L	Milw. W-L	Minn. W-L	N.Y. W-L	Oak. W-L	Sea. W-L	Tex. W-L	Tor. W-L	Totals W-L
Appier	0-0	1-0	1-0	1-1	1-1	1-0	1-0	0-0	2-0	1-3	1-1	1-1	0-1	12-8
Aquino	0-0	1-1	1-0	0-0	0-0	2-0	0-0	0-0	0-0	0-0	0-0	0-0	0-0	4-1
Baller	0-0	0-1	0-0	0-0	0-0	0-0	0-0	0-0	0-0	0-0	0-0	0-0	0-0	0-1
Campbell	0-0	0-0	0-0	0-0	0-0	0-0	0-0	0-0	0-0	0-0	1-0	0-0	0-0	1-0
Codiroli	0-0	0-0	0-0	0-0	0-0	0-0	0-0	0-0	0-0	0-0	0-0	0-1	0-0	0-1
Crawford	1-0	1-0	0-0	0-0	0-0	1-0	0-0	1-0	1-1	0-1	0-1	0-0	0-1	5-4
S. Davis	0-2	1-0	0-0	1-0	1-0	0-1	1-0	2-0	1-1	0-0	0-2	0-3	0-1	7-10
M. Davis	0-0	1-0	1-1	0-1	0-1	0-1	0-0	0-0	0-0	0-0	0-2	0-1	0-0	2-7
Dotson	0-0	0-0	0-1	0-2	0-0	0-0	0-1	0-0	0-0	0-0	0-0	0-0	0-0	0-4
Farr	0-2	1-0	2-0	1-2	1-0	2-0	0-0	1-0	1-1	0-1	2-0	1-1	1-0	13-7
Filson	0-1	0-0	0-0	0-1	0-0	0-0	0-1	0-0	0-1	0-0	0-0	0-0	0-0	0-4
Gordon	0-2	1-1	0-1	1-0	0-0	0-3	1-1	3-1	1-0	1-1	2-0	0-1	2-0	12-11
Gubicza	1-0	0-1	0-0	0-0	0-1	0-0	0-2	0-1	0-0	1-1	1-0	1-0	0-1	4-7
McGaffigan	1-0	0-0	1-0	0-1	1-1	0-0	0-1	0-0	0-0	0-0	0-0	1-0	0-0	4-3
M'tgomery	0-1	0-0	0-1	0-1	2-0	0-0	1-0	0-1	1-0	0-1	0-0	2-0	0-0	6-5
Saberhagen	0-0	1-0	0-3	0-0	0-0	1-0	0-2	0-2	1-0	1-1	0-0	0-0	1-1	5-9
Smith	0-0	0-0	0-0	0-0	0-1	0-0	0-0	0-0	0-0	0-0	0-0	0-0	0-0	0-1
Stottlemyre	0-0	0-0	0-0	0-0	0-0	0-0	0-0	0-0	0-0	0-0	0-0	0-0	0-1	0-1
Wagner	0-0	0-0	0-0	0-0	0-1	0-0	0-0	0-0	0-0	0-0	0-0	0-0	0-1	0-2
Totals	3-8	8-4	6-7	4-9	6-6	7-5	4-8	8-5	8-4	4-9	7-6	5-8	5-7	75-86

No Decisions—Encarnacion, Maldonado, McWilliams, Sanchez.

MILWAUKEE—74-88

Pitcher	Balt. W-L	Bos. W-L	Cal. W-L	Chi. W-L	Clev. W-L	Det. W-L	K.C. W-L	Minn. W-L	N.Y. W-L	Oak. W-L	Sea. W-L	Tex. W-L	Tor. W-L	Totals W-L
August	0-0	0-1	0-0	0-0	0-1	0-1	0-0	0-0	0-0	0-0	0-0	0-0	0-0	0-3
Bosio	0-0	0-1	0-1	0-0	0-1	1-1	1-0	0-0	0-1	1-1	0-1	1-1	0-1	4-9
Brown	0-1	0-0	0-0	0-0	0-0	0-0	0-0	0-0	0-0	0-0	0-0	1-0	0-0	1-1
Crim	0-0	1-0	0-0	0-0	0-0	1-0	0-0	0-1	0-1	0-0	1-1	0-1	0-1	3-5
Edens	0-0	1-0	1-1	0-1	2-0	0-0	0-0	0-1	0-1	0-0	0-0	0-1	0-0	4-5
Filer	0-0	1-0	0-0	0-1	0-0	0-0	1-0	0-0	0-0	0-2	0-0	0-0	0-0	2-3
Fossas	0-0	0-0	0-1	0-1	0-0	0-0	0-0	0-0	0-0	0-0	0-0	1-1	1-0	2-3
Higuera	1-1	2-1	1-1	0-0	0-2	1-0	0-1	0-1	1-1	0-2	1-0	2-0	2-0	11-10
Knudson	1-0	1-1	1-1	0-1	0-1	1-0	2-0	0-3	2-0	1-0	0-0	0-2	0-2	10-9
Krueger	0-2	0-0	0-0	0-1	0-0	2-1	0-0	0-1	1-0	0-2	1-0	0-1	2-0	6-8
Lee	0-0	0-0	0-0	0-0	0-0	0-0	0-0	0-0	1-0	0-0	0-0	0-0	0-0	1-0
Mirabella	0-1	0-0	1-0	1-0	0-0	2-0	0-0	0-0	0-0	0-0	0-1	0-0	0-0	4-2
Navarro	2-0	0-0	0-0	0-1	0-1	1-0	1-2	1-0	2-0	0-0	0-1	0-0	1-2	8-7

MILWAUKEE—Continued

Pitcher	Balt. W-L	Bos. W-L	Cal. W-L	Chi. W-L	Clev. W-L	Det. W-L	K.C. W-L	Minn. W-L	N.Y. W-L	Oak. W-L	Sea. W-L	Tex. W-L	Tor. W-L	Totals W-L
Plesac	0-1	1-1	0-0	1-1	1-0	0-0	0-1	0-1	0-1	0-0	0-1	0-0	0-0	3-7
Powell	0-0	0-0	0-0	0-1	0-1	0-0	0-1	0-0	0-1	0-0	0-0	0-0	0-0	0-4
Robinson	1-1	1-0	1-0	0-1	1-1	1-0	1-0	2-0	0-0	1-0	1-0	1-2	1-0	12-5
Sebra	1-0	0-0	0-0	0-0	0-1	0-0	0-0	0-0	0-1	0-0	0-0	0-0	0-0	1-2
Veres	0-0	0-0	0-1	0-1	0-0	0-0	0-0	0-0	0-0	0-0	0-0	0-1	0-0	0-3
Wegman	0-0	0-0	0-1	0-0	0-0	0-0	0-0	1-0	0-0	1-1	0-0	0-0	0-0	2-2
Totals	6-7	8-5	5-7	2-10	4-9	10-3	8-4	4-8	6-7	5-7	4-8	5-7	7-6	74-88

No Decisions—Capel, Elvira, Machado.

MINNESOTA—74-88

Pitcher	Balt. W-L	Bos. W-L	Cal. W-L	Chi. W-L	Clev. W-L	Det. W-L	K.C. W-L	Milw. W-L	N.Y. W-L	Oak. W-L	Sea. W-L	Tex. W-L	Tor. W-L	Totals W-L
Abbott	0-0	0-0	0-1	0-0	0-0	0-1	0-1	0-0	0-0	0-1	0-1	0-0	0-0	0-5
Aguilera	1-0	0-1	0-1	0-0	0-0	0-0	0-0	1-0	1-1	1-0	1-0	0-0	0-0	5-3
Anderson	1-2	0-1	1-2	1-2	1-1	0-2	0-1	0-1	1-0	1-2	0-2	0-0	1-2	7-18
Berenguer	1-1	1-1	0-0	0-1	1-0	0-0	0-0	1-0	1-0	1-1	1-0	1-1	0-0	8-5
Candelaria	0-0	2-0	0-0	1-0	0-1	2-0	0-0	1-0	0-0	0-0	0-0	0-1	1-1	7-3
Casian	0-0	0-0	0-0	0-0	0-0	0-0	0-1	0-0	0-0	0-0	1-0	1-0	0-0	2-1
Drummond	0-0	1-0	0-1	1-0	0-1	0-0	0-1	1-0	0-1	0-0	0-0	0-1	0-0	3-5
Erickson	0-1	0-1	0-0	0-0	1-0	2-0	1-1	1-0	0-0	1-0	0-0	2-0	0-0	8-4
Guthrie	1-0	0-0	0-0	3-0	1-0	0-1	0-2	1-1	1-0	0-2	0-1	0-1	0-1	7-9
Leach	0-1	0-0	0-0	0-1	0-0	1-0	0-0	0-1	0-0	0-0	1-0	0-1	0-1	2-5
Savage	0-0	0-0	0-0	0-0	0-1	0-0	0-0	0-0	0-0	0-0	0-1	0-0	0-0	0-2
Smith	1-0	2-0	0-1	0-1	1-1	0-1	0-0	0-1	0-3	1-1	0-0	0-0	0-1	5-10
Tapani	0-1	2-0	2-2	0-1	0-1	0-1	2-0	2-0	1-0	1-0	2-0	0-1	0-1	12-8
Wayne	0-0	0-0	0-0	0-0	0-0	0-0	1-0	0-1	0-0	0-0	0-0	0-0	0-0	1-1
West	1-0	0-0	1-1	0-1	0-1	1-0	1-1	0-0	1-0	0-0	0-2	1-2	1-1	7-9
Totals	6-6	8-4	4-9	6-7	5-7	6-6	5-8	8-4	6-6	6-7	6-7	5-8	3-9	74-88

No Decisions—Garces, Moses, Yett.

NEW YORK—67-95

Pitcher	Balt. W-L	Bos. W-L	Cal. W-L	Chi. W-L	Clev. W-L	Det. W-L	K.C. W-L	Milw. W-L	Minn. W-L	Oak. W-L	Sea. W-L	Tex. W-L	Tor. W-L	Totals W-L
Adkins	0-0	0-0	0-0	0-0	0-0	0-0	0-1	0-0	1-0	0-0	0-0	0-1	0-0	1-2
Cadaret	0-0	0-0	1-0	0-0	1-0	0-0	0-0	0-0	1-1	0-1	0-1	0-1	2-0	5-4
Cary	1-1	1-2	0-1	0-3	0-1	0-2	1-0	1-0	1-0	0-0	0-0	0-1	1-1	6-12
Eiland	1-0	0-0	0-0	0-0	0-0	0-1	0-0	1-0	0-0	0-0	0-0	0-0	0-0	2-1
Guetterman	0-0	1-0	1-1	0-2	1-0	1-0	0-1	3-0	1-0	0-0	2-0	1-2	0-1	11-7
Hawkins	1-0	0-1	1-0	0-2	2-0	0-1	0-2	0-0	0-1	0-3	0-1	0-1	1-0	5-12
Jones	1-0	0-0	0-0	0-0	0-0	0-0	0-1	0-1	0-0	0-0	0-0	0-0	0-0	1-2
LaPoint	1-1	0-1	2-2	1-0	0-0	1-1	0-1	0-0	1-2	0-1	1-0	0-0	0-1	7-10
Leary	1-1	0-2	0-2	0-1	1-1	2-0	0-2	0-2	2-1	0-3	3-0	0-2	0-2	9-19
Leiter	0-0	0-0	0-0	0-0	0-0	1-0	0-0	0-0	0-0	0-0	0-0	0-1	0-0	1-1
McCullers	0-0	0-0	0-0	0-0	0-0	0-0	1-0	0-0	0-0	0-0	0-0	0-0	0-0	1-0
Mills	0-2	0-0	0-0	0-1	0-0	0-1	0-0	0-0	0-0	0-0	0-0	0-0	1-1	1-5
Monteleone	0-0	0-0	0-0	0-0	0-1	0-0	0-0	0-0	0-0	0-0	0-0	0-0	0-0	0-1
Parker	0-0	0-0	1-0	0-0	0-0	0-0	0-0	0-0	0-0	0-1	0-0	0-0	0-0	1-1
Perez	0-0	0-0	0-0	0-0	0-1	0-0	0-0	0-0	0-0	0-0	0-1	1-0	0-0	1-2
Plunk	0-0	1-1	0-0	0-0	2-0	0-0	1-0	0-0	0-0	0-1	1-0	1-0	0-1	6-3
Righetti	0-0	0-0	0-0	0-0	0-0	0-0	0-0	1-0	0-0	0-0	0-0	0-0	0-0	1-1
Robinson	0-0	0-1	0-0	1-1	1-1	0-0	1-0	0-0	0-1	0-0	0-0	0-0	0-1	3-6
Witt	1-1	1-1	0-0	0-0	0-0	1-0	0-0	0-2	0-0	0-2	2-0	0-0	0-0	5-6
Totals	7-6	4-9	6-6	2-10	8-5	6-7	4-8	7-6	6-6	0-12	9-3	3-9	5-8	67-95

No Decisions—Habyan.

OAKLAND—103-59

Pitcher	Balt. W-L	Bos. W-L	Cal. W-L	Chi. W-L	Clev. W-L	Det. W-L	K.C. W-L	Milw. W-L	Min. W-L	N.Y. W-L	Sea. W-L	Tex. W-L	Tor. W-L	Totals W-L
Burns	0-0	0-0	0-1	0-0	0-0	0-1	0-0	0-0	0-0	0-0	0-0	2-0	1-1	3-3
Chitren	0-0	0-0	0-0	0-0	0-0	0-0	0-0	0-0	0-0	0-0	0-0	1-0	0-0	1-0
Eckersley	0-0	0-0	0-1	0-0	1-0	0-0	1-0	0-0	1-0	0-0	1-0	0-1	0-0	4-2
Harris	0-0	0-0	1-0	0-0	0-0	0-0	0-0	0-0	0-0	0-0	0-0	0-0	0-0	1-0
Honeycutt	0-0	0-0	0-0	0-0	0-1	0-0	0-0	0-0	0-1	1-0	1-0	0-0	0-0	2-2
Moore	2-1	0-1	0-1	1-3	1-1	0-1	1-1	2-1	0-2	2-0	0-1	2-1	2-1	13-15
Nelson	2-1	0-1	1-0	0-0	0-0	0-0	0-0	0-0	0-1	0-0	0-0	0-0	0-0	3-3
Norris	0-0	0-0	1-0	0-0	0-0	0-0	0-0	0-0	0-0	0-0	0-0	0-0	0-0	1-0
Sanderson	0-2	2-0	1-0	1-2	2-1	3-0	1-1	0-1	1-0	3-0	2-1	1-2	0-1	17-11
Stewart	1-0	4-0	1-1	1-3	2-0	0-2	2-1	2-2	3-1	2-0	3-0	0-0	1-1	22-11
Welch	3-0	0-1	3-0	2-0	2-0	3-1	3-0	1-1	2-1	1-2	2-0	2-0	2-0	27-6
Young	0-0	1-1	1-0	0-0	0-1	0-1	1-1	2-0	0-0	2-0	1-0	0-1	1-1	9-6
Totals	8-4	8-4	9-4	5-8	8-4	6-6	9-4	7-5	7-6	12-0	9-4	8-5	7-5	103-59

No Decisions—Bitker, Klink, Otto.

SEATTLE—77-85

Pitcher	Balt. W-L	Bos. W-L	Cal. W-L	Chi. W-L	Clev. W-L	Det. W-L	K.C. W-L	Milw. W-L	Minn. W-L	N.Y. W-L	Oak. W-L	Tex. W-L	Tor. W-L	Totals W-L
Bankhead	0-0	0-0	0-0	0-0	0-0	0-1	0-0	0-0	0-0	0-0	0-1	0-0	0-0	0-2
Clark	0-0	0-0	0-0	0-0	0-0	0-0	0-0	2-0	0-0	0-0	0-0	0-0	0-0	2-0
Comstock	1-0	0-0	0-1	0-0	0-0	1-1	1-0	2-0	0-1	0-1	0-0	1-0	1-0	7-4
DeLucia	0-0	0-0	0-0	0-1	0-0	0-1	0-0	0-0	0-0	0-0	0-0	1-0	0-0	1-2
Eave	0-0	0-1	0-1	0-0	0-0	0-0	0-0	0-0	0-0	0-0	0-1	0-0	0-0	0-3
Gardiner	0-0	0-0	0-0	0-0	0-0	0-0	0-0	0-0	0-0	0-0	0-1	0-1	0-0	0-2
Hanson	2-0	1-1	3-0	1-1	2-1	2-1	1-1	2-1	1-0	0-2	2-0	1-0	0-1	18-9
Harris	0-0	0-0	0-0	0-0	0-0	0-0	0-1	0-0	1-0	0-1	0-0	0-0	0-0	1-2
Holman	1-1	0-1	3-0	1-0	0-0	0-1	1-3	1-0	1-0	1-1	1-1	0-1	1-2	11-11
Jackson	1-2	0-2	0-0	0-0	0-0	0-1	1-0	0-1	1-0	0-0	0-0	1-1	1-0	5-7
Johnson	1-0	1-1	0-1	3-1	1-1	1-0	1-1	1-1	1-2	1-0	0-2	2-0	1-1	14-11
Knackert	0-0	0-0	1-0	0-1	0-0	0-0	0-0	0-0	0-0	0-0	0-0	0-0	0-0	1-1
Medvin	0-0	0-1	0-0	0-0	0-0	0-0	0-0	0-0	0-0	0-0	0-0	0-0	0-0	0-1
Reed	0-0	0-0	0-0	0-0	0-0	0-0	0-0	0-0	0-0	0-0	0-1	0-0	0-0	0-1
Schooler	0-0	0-1	0-0	0-0	1-1	0-0	0-0	0-0	0-1	0-0	0-1	0-0	0-0	1-4
Swan	0-0	0-0	0-0	0-0	0-0	0-0	1-0	1-1	0-0	0-1	0-0	0-0	0-1	2-3
Swift	1-0	1-0	1-0	0-0	1-0	0-0	0-0	0-1	1-0	0-1	1-0	0-1	0-1	6-4
Young	2-0	1-0	0-2	0-4	0-4	0-1	0-0	0-0	1-1	1-3	0-1	1-2	2-0	8-18
Totals	9-3	4-8	8-5	5-8	5-7	5-7	6-7	8-4	7-6	3-9	4-9	7-6	6-6	77-85

No Decisions—Burba, Lovelace, Melendez, Powell.

TEXAS—83-79

Pitcher	Balt. W-L	Bos. W-L	Cal. W-L	Chi. W-L	Clev. W-L	Det. W-L	K.C. W-L	Milw. W-L	Minn. W-L	N.Y. W-L	Oak. W-L	Sea. W-L	Tor. W-L	Totals W-L
Arnsberg	0-0	0-0	0-0	0-0	0-0	1-0	1-0	0-0	1-0	0-0	1-1	0-0	2-0	6-1
Barfield	0-0	1-0	0-2	1-0	0-0	0-0	0-0	0-1	1-0	0-0	0-0	1-0	0-0	4-3
Bohanon	0-0	0-0	0-0	0-0	0-1	0-1	0-0	0-0	0-0	0-0	0-1	0-0	0-0	0-3
Brown	0-3	1-1	2-0	0-0	1-2	1-1	1-2	1-0	1-1	2-0	0-0	1-0	1-0	12-10
Chiamparino	0-0	0-0	0-0	0-0	0-0	0-0	0-0	0-1	0-1	0-0	1-0	0-0	0-0	1-2
Hough	1-1	0-1	1-1	2-1	0-1	1-0	2-0	1-0	1-1	2-0	0-2	0-2	1-2	12-12
Jeffcoat	1-0	1-0	1-1	0-0	0-0	0-3	0-0	1-0	0-1	0-0	0-0	1-1	0-0	5-6
McMurtry	0-0	0-0	0-0	0-1	0-0	0-0	0-0	0-0	0-0	0-0	0-1	0-0	0-1	0-3
Mielke	0-0	0-1	0-0	0-0	0-0	0-0	0-1	0-0	0-1	0-0	0-0	0-0	0-0	0-3
Moyer	0-0	0-0	0-0	0-2	0-1	0-0	0-0	1-1	0-0	0-0	0-1	0-0	1-1	2-6
Rogers	0-1	2-1	1-0	2-0	1-0	0-0	1-1	1-1	0-0	2-0	0-0	0-2	0-0	10-6
Russell	0-1	0-1	0-0	0-0	0-1	0-1	1-0	0-0	0-0	0-1	0-0	0-0	0-0	1-5
Ryan	0-0	1-0	0-2	1-2	1-0	2-0	0-1	1-0	1-0	2-0	1-2	2-1	1-1	13-9
Witt	2-2	1-0	0-2	0-1	2-1	1-0	2-0	1-1	3-0	1-2	2-0	1-1	1-0	17-10
Totals	4-8	7-5	5-8	6-7	5-7	6-6	8-5	7-5	8-5	9-3	5-8	6-7	7-5	83-79

No Decisions—Alexander, Bitker, Hoover, Manon.

TORONTO—86-76

Pitcher	Balt. W-L	Bos. W-L	Cal. W-L	Chi. W-L	Clev. W-L	Det. W-L	K.C. W-L	Milw. W-L	Minn. W-L	N.Y. W-L	Oak. W-L	Sea. W-L	Tex. W-L	Totals W-L
Acker	0-0	0-0	0-0	0-0	2-0	0-0	0-0	0-1	0-0	0-2	0-0	1-1	1-0	4-4
Black	1-0	0-0	0-0	0-0	0-0	0-0	0-0	0-1	0-0	1-0	0-0	0-0	0-0	2-1
Blair	2-0	0-1	0-0	0-0	0-0	0-0	0-0	0-1	0-1	0-1	1-1	0-0	0-0	3-5
Candelaria	0-0	0-0	0-0	0-1	0-0	0-0	0-0	0-0	0-0	0-1	0-0	0-0	0-1	0-3
Cerutti	1-1	0-0	1-0	0-2	0-1	0-0	1-1	0-0	1-1	2-1	1-1	1-0	1-1	9-9
Flanagan	1-0	0-0	0-0	0-1	0-0	0-1	0-0	0-0	0-0	0-0	0-0	0-0	1-0	2-2
Gilles	0-0	0-0	0-0	0-0	0-0	0-0	0-0	1-0	0-0	0-0	0-0	0-0	0-0	1-0
Henke	1-1	1-1	0-2	0-0	0-0	0-0	0-0	0-0	0-0	0-0	0-0	0-0	0-0	2-4
Key	0-0	1-1	0-0	1-1	1-0	3-1	1-0	2-0	1-1	1-0	0-2	2-1	0-0	13-7
Stieb	1-1	1-0	1-1	2-0	2-1	0-0	2-0	2-1	3-0	0-0	2-1	0-0	2-1	18-6
Stottlemyre	1-0	0-3	1-1	2-0	3-1	1-2	1-3	0-1	2-0	2-0	0-1	0-3	0-2	13-17
Ward	0-0	0-2	0-3	1-0	0-0	1-1	0-1	0-0	0-0	0-0	0-0	0-1	0-0	2-8
Wells	0-1	0-2	1-0	0-0	0-0	3-0	1-0	1-2	2-0	1-0	1-0	0-0	0-1	11-6
Wills	0-1	0-0	1-0	1-0	1-1	0-0	1-0	0-0	0-0	1-0	0-1	1-0	0-1	6-4
Totals	8-5	3-10	5-7	7-5	9-4	8-5	7-5	6-7	9-3	8-5	5-7	6-6	5-7	86-76

No Decisions—Cummings, Kilgus, Leiter, Luecken, MacDonald.

OFFICIAL AMERICAN LEAGUE BATTING AVERAGES

(Compiled by the MLB-IBM Baseball Information Service)

CLUB BATTING

CLUB	AVG	G	AB	R	H	TB	2B	3B	HR	RBI	SH	SF	HP	BB	IBB	SO	SB	CS	GI DP	LOB	SHO	SLG	OBP
Boston	.272	162	5516	699	1502	2180	298	31	106	660	48	44	28	598	59	795	53	52	174	1233	16	.395	.344
Cleveland	.267	162	5485	732	1465	2143	266	41	100	675	54	61	29	458	33	836	107	52	122	1061	10	.391	.324
Kansas City	.267	161	5488	707	1465	2169	316	44	100	660	31	54	27	498	32	879	107	62	132	1123	9	.395	.328
Minnesota	.265	162	5499	666	1458	2117	281	39	100	625	40	49	53	445	32	749	96	53	148	1097	14	.385	.324
Toronto	.265	162	5589	767	1479	2343	263	50	167	729	18	62	28	526	35	970	111	52	125	1113	10	.419	.328
California	.260	162	5570	690	1448	2180	237	27	147	646	62	45	28	566	41	1000	69	51	142	1202	6	.391	.329
Seattle	.259	162	5474	640	1419	2043	251	26	107	610	58	48	40	596	45	749	105	51	140	1227	15	.373	.333
Texas	.259	162	5469	676	1416	2057	257	27	110	641	41	44	34	575	45	1054	115	48	142	1168	11	.376	.331
Detroit	.259	162	5479	750	1418	2239	241	32	172	714	54	41	34	634	44	952	82	57	139	1175	7	.409	.337
Chicago	.258	162	5402	682	1393	2050	251	44	106	637	75	47	36	575	50	903	140	90	112	1044	7	.379	.320
Milwaukee	.256	162	5503	732	1408	2111	247	36	128	680	59	71	33	519	46	821	164	72	101	1106	5	.384	.320
Oakland	.254	162	5433	733	1379	2124	209	22	164	693	60	48	46	651	38	992	141	54	122	1195	6	.391	.336
Baltimore	.245	161	5410	669	1328	2002	234	22	132	623	72	41	40	660	50	962	94	52	131	1230	7	.370	.330
New York	.241	162	5483	603	1322	2009	208	19	147	561	37	36	53	427	41	1027	119	45	114	1060	15	.366	.300
Totals	.259	1133	76800	9746	19900	29767	3559	460	1796	9154	683	697	509	7631	587	12689	1503	783	1844	16034	144	.388	.327

INDIVIDUAL BATTING

(Top Fifteen Qualifiers for Batting Championship—502 or More Plate Appearances)

(* Lefthanded Batter   †Switch-Hitter)

Player, Club	AVG	G	AB	R	H	TB	2B	3B	HR	RBI	SH	SF	HP	BB	IBB	SO	SB	CS	GI DP	SLG	OBP
Brett, George, Kansas City*	.329	142	544	82	179	280	45	7	14	87	0	7	0	56	14	63	9	2	18	.515	.387
Henderson, Rickey, Oakland	.325	136	489	119	159	282	33	3	28	61	2	2	4	97	2	60	65	10	13	.577	.439
Palmeiro, Rafael, Texas*	.319	154	598	72	191	280	35	6	14	89	2	8	3	40	6	59	3	3	24	.468	.361
Trammell, Alan, Detroit	.304	146	559	71	170	251	37	1	14	89	3	6	1	68	7	55	12	10	11	.449	.377
Boggs, Wade, Boston*	.302	155	619	89	187	259	44	5	6	63	0	6	5	87	3	68	0	1	14	.418	.386
Martinez, Edgar, Seattle	.302	144	487	71	147	211	27	2	11	49	0	3	2	74	19	62	1	4	13	.433	.397
Griffey, G. Kenneth Jr., Seattle*	.300	155	597	91	179	287	28	7	22	80	0	4	2	63	3	81	16	11	12	.481	.366
McGriff, Frederick, Toronto*	.300	153	557	91	167	295	21	1	35	88	0	4	4	94	12	108	5	3	7	.530	.400
James, D. Chris, Cleveland	.299	140	528	62	158	234	32	4	12	70	3	3	4	31	4	71	4	3	11	.443	.341
Puckett, Kirby, Minnesota	.298	146	551	82	164	246	40	3	12	80	1	3	3	57	11	73	5	7	15	.446	.365
Greenwell, Michael, Boston*	.297	159	610	71	181	265	30	6	14	73	0	3	3	65	4	43	8	4	19	.434	.367
Burks, Ellis, Boston	.296	152	588	89	174	286	33	8	21	89	2	2	1	48	4	82	9	8	18	.486	.349
Franco, Julio, Texas	.296	157	582	96	172	234	27	1	11	69	2	2	7	82	3	83	31	10	12	.402	.383
Harper, Brian, Minnesota	.294	134	479	61	141	207	42	3	6	54	0	4	3	19	2	27	3	2	20	.432	.328
Sheffield, Gary, Milwaukee	.294	125	487	67	143	205	30	1	10	67	4	9	3	44	1	41	25	10	11	.421	.350

DEPARTMENTAL LEADERS: G—Kelly, N.Y., 162; AB—Reynolds, Sea., 642; R—R. Henderson, Oak., 119; H—Palmeiro, Tex., 191; TB—Fielder, Det., 339; 2B—Reed, Bos., Brett, K.C., 45; 3B—Fernandez, Tor., 17; HR—Fielder, Det., 51; RBI—Fielder, Det., 132; SH—Gallego, Oak., B. Ripken, Balt., 17; SF—Parker, Milw., 14; HP—P. Bradley, Balt.-Chi., 11; BB—McGwire, Oak., 110; IBB—Boggs, Bos., 19; SO—Fielder, Det., 182; SB—R. Henderson, Oak., 65; CS—Johnson, Chi., 22; GIDP—Calderon, Chi., 26; Slg. Pct.—Fielder, Det., .592; OB. Pct.—R. Henderson, Oak., .439.

INDIVIDUAL BATTING
ALL PLAYERS LISTED ALPHABETICALLY
(*Lefthanded Batter   †Switch-Hitter)

Player, Club	AVG	G	AB	R	H	TB	2B	3B	HR	RBI	SH	SF	HP	BB	IBB	SO	SB	CS	GI DP	SLG	OBP
Afenir, Michael, Oakland	.143	14	16	0	2	2	0	0	0	2	0	0	0	0	0	6	0	0	0	.143	.133
Allred, Dale, Cleveland*	.188	4	16	2	3	7	1	0	1	2	0	0	0	2	0	3	0	0	0	.438	.278
Alomar, Santos, Cleveland	.290	132	445	60	129	186	26	2	9	66	0	6	2	25	2	46	4	1	10	.418	.326
Anderson, Brady, Baltimore*	.231	89	234	24	54	72	5	2	3	24	5	5	5	31	1	46	15	2	4	.308	.327
Anderson, Kent, California	.308	49	143	16	44	55	6	1	1	5	4	0	1	13	1	19	0	2	4	.385	.369
Azocar, Oscar, New York*	.248	65	214	24	53	76	5	0	2	19	0	1	1	2	0	15	7	2	4	.355	.257
Baerga, Carlos, Cleveland†	.260	108	312	46	81	123	17	2	7	47	1	5	4	16	2	57	0	3	17	.394	.300
Baines, Harold, Tex.-Oak.*	.284	135	415	52	118	183	15	1	16	65	0	7	0	67	10	80	0	0	17	.441	.378
Baker, Douglas, Minnesota†	.000	3	1	0	0	0	0	0	0	0	0	0	0	0	0	0	0	0	0	.000	.000
Balboni, Stephen, New York	.192	116	266	24	51	108	6	0	17	34	1	2	3	35	0	91	0	0	6	.406	.291
Barfield, Jesse, New York	.246	153	476	69	117	217	21	2	25	78	2	5	5	82	2	150	4	3	4	.456	.359
Barrett, Martin, Boston	.226	62	159	18	36	40	4	0	0	13	3	1	1	15	1	13	4	0	4	.252	.294
Bates, William, Milwaukee*	.103	14	29	6	3	4	1	0	0	2	2	0	1	4	0	7	3	2	0	.138	.206
Belcher, Kevin, Texas	.133	16	15	4	2	3	1	0	0	0	0	0	0	1	0	6	0	0	0	.200	.235
Bell, George, Toronto	.265	142	562	67	149	237	25	0	21	86	0	11	3	32	7	80	3	2	14	.422	.303
Bell, Juan, Baltimore†	.000	5	2	1	0	0	0	0	0	0	0	0	0	0	0	1	0	0	0	.000	.000
Belle, A. Jojuan, Cleveland†	.174	9	23	1	4	7	0	0	1	3	0	0	0	1	0	6	0	0	1	.304	.208
Bergman, David, Detroit*	.278	100	205	21	57	75	10	1	2	26	1	2	0	33	3	17	3	0	7	.366	.375
Berry, Sean, Kansas City	.217	8	23	2	5	8	0	0	1	4	0	0	0	2	0	5	0	0	0	.348	.280
Bichette, A. Dante, California	.255	109	349	40	89	151	15	1	15	53	4	2	3	16	1	79	5	2	9	.433	.292
Blankenship, Lance, Oakland	.191	86	136	18	26	29	3	0	0	10	6	0	3	20	0	23	3	1	6	.213	.295
Blowers, Michael, New York	.188	48	144	16	27	46	4	0	5	21	0	0	0	12	0	50	1	0	3	.319	.255
Boggs, Wade, Boston*	.302	155	619	89	187	259	44	5	6	63	0	6	1	87	19	68	0	1	14	.418	.386
Boone, Robert, Kansas City	.239	40	117	11	28	31	3	0	0	9	2	0	1	11	0	12	1	1	2	.265	.336
Borders, Patrick, Toronto	.286	125	346	36	99	172	24	2	15	49	2	3	0	18	2	57	0	0	17	.497	.319
Bordick, Michael, Oakland	.071	25	14	0	1	1	0	0	0	0	0	0	0	0	0	4	0	1	0	.071	.133
Bosley, Thaddis, Texas*	.138	30	29	3	4	7	0	0	1	3	0	0	0	4	1	7	1	0	1	.241	.242
Boston, Daryl, Chicago*	.000	5	1	0	0	0	0	0	0	0	0	0	0	0	0	0	0	0	0	.000	.000
Bradley, Phillip, Balt.-Chi.	.256	117	422	59	108	138	14	2	4	31	11	1	11	50	0	61	17	7	11	.327	.349
Bradley, Scott, Seattle*	.223	101	233	11	52	64	9	0	1	28	3	6	0	15	5	20	0	1	6	.275	.264
Braggs, Glenn, Milwaukee	.248	37	113	17	28	42	5	0	3	13	0	3	3	12	2	21	5	3	2	.372	.328
Brett, George, Kansas City*	.329	142	544	82	179	280	45	7	14	87	0	7	1	56	14	63	9	3	18	.515	.387
Briley, Greg, Seattle*	.246	125	337	40	83	120	18	2	5	29	2	4	1	37	0	48	16	4	6	.356	.319
Brock, Gregory, Milwaukee*	.248	123	367	42	91	135	23	0	7	50	2	3	0	43	9	45	4	2	6	.368	.324
Brookens, Thomas, Cleveland	.266	64	154	18	41	55	7	1	2	20	2	3	2	14	0	25	0	0	3	.357	.322
Brown, J. Kevin, Texas	.000	27	1	1	0	0	0	0	0	0	0	0	0	0	0	0	0	0	0	.000	.000
Brown, Marty, Baltimore	.200	9	15	0	3	3	0	0	0	0	0	0	0	1	0	7	0	0	1	.200	.250
Browne, Jerome, Cleveland†	.267	140	513	92	137	191	26	5	6	50	12	11	2	72	1	46	12	7	12	.372	.353
Brumley, A. Michael, Seattle†	.224	62	147	19	33	46	5	4	0	7	4	8	1	10	0	22	2	0	5	.313	.272
Brunansky, Thomas, Boston	.267	129	461	61	123	202	24	5	15	71	1	8	3	54	7	105	5	10	12	.438	.342
Buckner, William, Boston*	.186	22	43	4	8	11	3	0	0	3	0	1	0	3	2	2	0	0	1	.256	.234
Buechele, Steven, Texas	.215	91	251	30	54	85	10	0	7	30	2	1	2	27	1	63	1	2	5	.339	.294
Buhner, Jay, Seattle	.276	51	163	16	45	78	12	0	7	33	0	2	1	17	1	50	2	2	6	.479	.357
Burks, Ellis, Boston	.296	152	588	89	174	286	33	8	21	89	2	2	6	48	4	82	9	11	18	.486	.349
Bush, R. Randall, Minnesota*	.243	73	181	17	44	70	8	0	6	18	0	2	1	21	2	27	2	3	2	.387	.338
Calderon, Ivan, Chicago	.273	158	607	85	166	256	44	2	14	74	0	8	1	51	7	79	32	16	26	.422	.327

Player, Club	AVG	G	AB	R	H	TB	2B	3B	HR	RBI	SH	SF	HP	BB	IBB	SO	SB	CS	GIDP	SLG	OBP
Canale, George, Milwaukee *	.077	10	13	4	1	1	0	0	0	1	0	0	0	2	0	6	0	1	0	.154	.200
Canseco, Jose, Oakland	.274	131	481	83	132	261	14	2	37	101	0	5	5	72	8	158	19	10	9	.543	.371
Canseco, Osvaldo, Oakland	.105	9	19	2	2	3	1	0	0	1	0	0	0	1	0	10	0	0	0	.158	.150
Castillo, M. Carmelo, Minnesota	.219	64	137	11	30	34	4	0	0	12	1	1	1	3	1	23	0	1	1	.248	.239
Cerone, Richard, New York	.302	49	139	12	42	54	6	0	2	11	1	1	0	5	0	13	0	0	4	.388	.324
Coachman, Bobby, California	.311	16	45	3	14	17	3	0	0	5	0	0	2	1	0	7	0	0	1	.378	.354
Cochrane, David, Seattle†	.150	15	20	0	3	3	0	0	0	0	1	0	0	0	0	8	0	0	0	.150	.150
Cole, Alexander, Cleveland *	.300	63	227	43	68	81	5	4	0	13	0	0	1	28	0	38	40	9	2	.357	.379
Coles, Darnell, Sea.-Det.	.209	89	215	22	45	63	7	1	3	20	1	2	0	16	2	38	0	4	4	.293	.265
Conine, Jeffrey, Kansas City	.250	9	20	3	5	7	2	0	0	2	0	0	1	2	0	5	0	0	1	.350	.318
Coolbaugh, Scott, Texas	.200	67	180	21	36	48	6	0	2	13	4	1	0	15	0	47	1	1	2	.267	.264
Cooper, Scott, Boston *	.000	2	1	0	0	0	0	0	0	0	0	0	0	0	0	1	0	0	0	.000	.000
Cotto, Henry, Seattle	.259	127	355	40	92	124	14	3	4	33	6	3	4	22	2	52	21	3	13	.349	.307
Cuyler, Milton, Detroit	.255	19	51	8	13	18	3	1	0	8	2	1	2	5	0	10	1	2	1	.353	.316
Daugherty, John, Texas†	.300	125	310	63	93	135	20	0	6	47	0	3	4	22	10	49	0	0	4	.435	.347
Davis, Alvin, Seattle *	.283	140	494	63	140	212	21	2	17	68	0	9	4	85	4	68	2	2	9	.429	.387
Davis, Charles, California†	.265	113	412	58	109	164	17	1	12	58	0	3	0	61	6	89	7	2	14	.398	.357
Deer, Robert, Milwaukee	.209	134	440	57	92	190	15	1	27	69	0	3	6	64	0	147	2	3	10	.432	.313
Devereaux, Michael, Baltimore	.240	108	367	48	88	144	18	1	12	49	4	4	0	28	0	48	13	12	10	.392	.291
Diaz, Carlos, Toronto	.333	9	3	1	1	1	0	0	0	0	0	0	0	0	0	2	0	0	0	.333	.333
Diaz, Edgar, Milwaukee	.271	86	218	27	59	65	2	0	0	14	5	0	2	21	2	32	3	2	3	.298	.338
Disarcina, Gary, California	.140	18	57	8	8	11	1	2	0	0	1	0	0	3	0	10	0	0	3	.193	.183
Dorsett, Brian, New York	.143	14	35	8	5	7	2	0	0	0	0	0	0	1	0	4	1	0	3	.200	.189
Downing, Brian, California	.273	96	330	47	90	154	18	2	14	51	0	4	6	50	2	45	0	2	11	.467	.374
Ducey, Robert, Toronto *	.302	19	53	7	16	21	5	0	0	7	0	1	1	7	0	15	1	0	2	.396	.387
Dwyer, James, Minnesota *	.190	37	63	7	12	15	2	0	1	5	2	0	0	12	1	7	1	0	0	.238	.320
Eisenreich, James, Kansas City *	.280	142	496	61	139	197	29	7	5	51	0	4	2	42	2	51	12	14	7	.397	.335
Eppard, James, Toronto *	.200	6	3	0	1	1	0	0	0	0	0	0	0	0	0	2	1	0	2	.200	.333
Espinoza, Alvaro, New York	.224	150	438	31	98	120	12	3	2	20	11	2	5	16	0	54	2	2	13	.274	.258
Espy, Cecil, Texas†	.127	52	71	10	9	9	0	0	0	1	2	0	0	10	0	20	11	5	1	.127	.235
Evans, Dwight, Boston	.249	123	445	66	111	174	18	3	13	63	0	6	4	67	5	73	3	4	18	.391	.349
Felder, Michael, Milwaukee†	.274	121	237	65	65	85	7	7	3	27	8	5	0	22	0	17	20	9	0	.359	.330
Felix, Junior, Toronto†	.263	127	463	73	122	204	23	7	15	65	2	5	2	45	5	99	13	8	4	.441	.328
Fermin, Felix, Cleveland	.256	148	414	47	106	126	13	2	1	40	13	6	5	26	0	22	3	3	13	.304	.297
Fernandez, O. Antonio, Toronto†	.276	161	635	84	175	248	27	17	4	66	0	5	7	71	4	70	26	13	17	.391	.352
Fielder, Cecil, Detroit	.277	159	573	104	159	339	25	1	51	132	0	6	2	90	11	182	0	0	15	.592	.377
Finley, Steven, Baltimore *	.256	142	464	46	119	152	16	4	3	37	10	5	2	32	3	53	22	9	8	.328	.304
Fisk, Carlton, Chicago	.285	137	452	65	129	204	21	0	18	65	0	1	7	61	8	73	7	2	12	.451	.378
Fletcher, Scott, Chicago	.242	151	509	54	123	159	18	3	4	56	11	5	2	45	3	63	1	3	10	.312	.304
Franco, Julio, Texas	.296	157	582	96	172	234	27	1	11	69	0	2	1	82	3	83	31	10	12	.402	.383
Francona, Terry, Milwaukee *	.000	3	4	3	0	0	0	0	0	0	1	0	0	0	0	0	0	0	3	.000	.000
Fryman, Travis, Detroit	.297	66	232	32	69	109	11	1	9	27	0	2	3	17	1	51	3	3	3	.470	.348
Gaetti, Gary, Minnesota	.229	154	577	61	132	217	27	5	16	85	8	8	1	36	0	101	6	1	22	.376	.274
Gagne, Gregory, Minnesota	.235	138	388	38	91	140	22	3	7	38	17	2	1	24	1	76	8	8	5	.361	.280
Gallagher, David, Chi.-Balt.	.254	68	126	12	32	38	4	1	0	7	4	1	2	7	0	12	0	2	13	.302	.296
Gallego, Michael, Oakland	.206	140	323	36	80	106	13	2	3	34	0	4	4	29	1	50	5	5	10	.272	.277
Gantner, James, Milwaukee *	.263	88	323	36	85	103	8	5	0	25	6	0	2	5	0	19	18	3	3	.319	.328
Gedman, Richard, Boston *	.200	10	15	3	3	3	0	0	0	0	0	0	5	5	0	6	0	0	1	.200	.429
Geren, Robert, New York	.213	110	277	21	59	90	7	0	8	31	2	2	2	13	1	73	0	0	7	.325	.259

Player, Club	AVG	G	AB	R	H	TB	2B	3B	HR	RBI	SH	SF	HP	BB	IBB	SO	SB	CS	GI DP	SLG	OBP
Giles, Brian, Seattle	.232	45	95	15	22	40	6	0	4	11	0	0	0	15	0	24	1	1	1	.421	.336
Gladden, C. Daniel, Minnesota	.275	136	534	64	147	201	27	6	5	40	1	4	6	26	0	67	25	9	17	.376	.314
Gomez, Leonardo, Baltimore	.231	12	39	3	9	9	0	0	0	1	1	0	0	8	0	7	0	0	2	.231	.362
Gonzales, Rene, Baltimore	.214	67	103	13	22	30	3	1	1	12	6	1	2	8	0	14	1	0	3	.291	.296
Gonzalez, Juan, Texas	.289	25	90	11	26	47	7	1	4	12	0	1	0	2	0	18	0	1	2	.522	.316
Grebeck, Craig, Chicago	.168	59	119	7	20	28	3	1	1	9	3	3	2	2	0	24	0	0	2	.235	.227
Green, Gary, Texas	.216	62	88	10	19	22	3	0	0	8	4	1	0	6	0	18	1	0	2	.250	.263
Greenwell, Michael, Boston *	.297	159	610	71	181	265	30	6	14	73	0	3	4	65	12	43	8	11	19	.434	.367
Griffey, G. Kenneth Jr., Seattle *	.300	155	597	91	179	287	28	7	22	80	0	4	8	63	12	81	16	11	12	.481	.366
Griffey, G. Kenneth Sr., Seattle *	.377	21	77	13	29	40	2	0	3	18	0	0	1	10	2	3	0	0	2	.519	.443
Gruber, Kelly, Toronto	.274	150	592	92	162	303	36	6	31	118	0	13	0	48	8	94	14	2	14	.512	.330
Guillen, Oswaldo, Chicago *	.279	160	516	61	144	176	21	4	1	58	15	5	1	26	2	37	13	17	6	.341	.312
Hale, Walter, Minnesota *	.000	1	2	0	0	0	0	0	0	0	0	0	0	0	0	1	0	0	0	.000	.000
Hall, Melvin, New York *	.258	113	360	41	93	156	23	2	12	46	0	3	2	6	0	46	0	3	7	.433	.272
Hamilton, Darryl, Milwaukee *	.295	89	156	27	46	54	5	0	1	18	3	0	0	9	0	12	10	3	2	.346	.333
Harper, Brian, Minnesota	.294	134	479	61	141	207	42	3	6	54	0	4	7	19	2	27	3	1	20	.432	.328
Haselman, William, Texas	.154	7	13	0	2	2	0	0	0	3	1	0	0	1	0	5	0	0	0	.154	.214
Hassey, Ronald, Oakland *	.213	94	254	18	54	76	7	0	5	22	1	3	0	27	3	29	0	6	3	.299	.288
Heath, Michael, Detroit	.270	122	370	46	100	143	18	2	7	38	2	3	4	19	0	71	7	6	12	.386	.311
Heep, Daniel, Boston *	.174	41	69	3	12	15	1	1	0	8	0	1	1	7	0	14	0	0	0	.217	.256
Hemond, Scott, Oakland	.154	7	13	3	2	2	0	0	0	1	1	0	0	0	0	5	3	0	0	.154	.154
Henderson, David, Oakland	.271	127	450	65	122	210	28	0	20	63	1	2	4	40	1	105	3	0	5	.467	.331
Henderson, Rickey, Oakland	.325	136	489	119	159	282	33	3	28	61	2	3	1	97	2	60	65	10	13	.577	.439
Hernandez, Keith, Cleveland *	.200	43	130	7	26	31	2	0	1	8	0	1	0	14	3	17	0	0	2	.238	.283
Hill, Donald, California †	.264	103	352	36	93	124	18	2	3	32	6	0	1	29	1	27	1	3	10	.352	.319
Hill, Glenallen, Toronto	.231	84	260	47	60	113	11	3	12	32	0	0	7	18	0	62	8	3	5	.435	.281
Hoiles, Christopher, Baltimore	.190	23	63	7	12	18	3	0	1	6	1	0	0	5	1	12	0	0	5	.286	.250
Holman, Brian, Seattle	.000	28	2	0	0	0	0	0	0	0	1	0	0	0	0	0	0	0	0	.000	.000
Honeycutt, Frederick, Oakland *	.000	66	0	0	0	0	0	0	0	0	0	0	0	0	0	0	0	0	0	.000	.000
Horn, Samuel, Baltimore *	.248	79	246	30	61	116	13	0	14	45	0	2	0	32	1	62	0	0	8	.472	.332
Howard, Steven, Oakland	.231	21	52	5	12	16	4	0	0	1	0	0	1	4	0	17	3	0	0	.308	.286
Howell, Jack, California *	.228	105	316	35	72	117	19	1	8	33	1	0	2	46	5	61	3	0	3	.370	.326
Howitt, Dann, Oakland *	.136	14	22	3	3	5	0	1	0	1	0	0	1	3	0	12	0	0	0	.227	.240
Hrbek, Kent, Minnesota *	.287	143	492	61	141	233	26	0	22	79	0	8	7	69	8	45	5	5	17	.474	.377
Hulett, Timothy, Baltimore	.255	53	153	16	39	57	7	1	3	16	2	1	0	15	0	41	1	0	2	.373	.321
Huson, Jeffrey, Texas *	.240	145	396	57	95	111	12	2	0	28	7	3	0	46	0	54	12	4	8	.280	.320
Incaviglia, Peter, Texas	.233	153	529	59	123	222	27	0	24	85	0	4	2	45	5	146	3	4	18	.420	.302
Jackson, Vincent, Kansas City	.272	111	405	74	110	212	16	1	28	78	0	5	9	44	1	128	15	4	8	.523	.342
Jacoby, Brook, Cleveland	.293	155	553	77	162	236	24	4	14	75	2	6	2	63	5	58	1	9	20	.427	.365
James, D. Chris, Cleveland	.299	140	528	62	158	234	32	4	12	70	3	4	4	31	4	71	4	3	11	.443	.341
James, Dion, Cleveland †	.274	87	248	28	68	90	15	2	1	22	3	3	1	27	3	23	5	3	6	.363	.347
Javier, Stanley, Oakland †	.242	19	33	4	8	12	2	1	0	3	0	0	0	6	0	6	1	1	0	.364	.306
Jefferson, Stanley, Balt.-Clev.†	.231	59	117	22	27	41	8	0	2	10	2	0	2	10	0	26	5	0	0	.350	.295
Jeltz, L. Steven, Kansas City †	.155	74	116	11	18	22	2	1	0	10	4	0	1	17	0	21	1	3	3	.190	.275
Jennings, J. Douglas, Oakland *	.192	64	156	19	30	47	4	2	3	14	4	2	1	17	0	48	8	3	12	.301	.275
Johnson, K. Lance, Chicago *	.285	151	541	76	154	193	18	9	1	51	8	3	1	33	2	45	36	22	7	.357	.325
Jones, Tracy, Det.-Sea.	.260	75	204	23	53	81	8	1	6	24	2	1	5	9	0	25	8	2	8	.397	.307
Jose, D. Felix, Oakland †	.264	101	341	42	90	126	12	0	8	39	0	5	1	16	0	65	8	2	10	.370	.306
Joyner, Wallace, California *	.268	83	310	35	83	122	15	0	8	41	1	5	1	41	4	34	2	1	10	.394	.350

Player, Club	AVG	G	AB	R	H	TB	2B	3B	HR	RBI	SH	SF	HP	BB	IBB	SO	SB	CS	GI DP	SLG	OBP
Karkovice, Ronald, Chicago	.246	68	183	30	45	73	10	4	6	20	7	1	4	16	1	52	2	1	1	.399	.308
Kelly, Roberto, New York	.285	162	641	85	183	268	32	4	15	61	4	1	4	33	0	148	42	17	7	.418	.323
Kittle, Ronald, Chi.-Balt.	.231	105	338	33	78	148	16	0	18	46	0	1	4	26	2	91	0	0	6	.438	.293
Komminsk, Brad, Baltimore	.238	46	101	18	24	39	4	1	3	8	2	1	2	14	1	29	1	1	6	.386	.342
Kreuter, Chad, Texas	.045	22	22	2	1	2	1	0	0	2	1	0	0	1	0	9	0	0	0	.091	.130
Kunkel, Jeffrey, Texas	.170	99	200	17	34	56	11	1	3	17	5	1	2	8	0	66	2	1	2	.280	.221
Kutcher, Randy, Boston	.230	63	74	18	17	26	4	0	1	5	3	0	0	13	0	18	3	1	0	.351	.345
Lancellotti, Richard, Boston	.000	4	8	0	0	0	0	0	0	1	0	0	0	0	0	3	0	0	0	.000	.000
Lansford, Carney, Oakland	.268	134	507	58	136	162	15	1	3	50	2	4	6	45	4	50	16	3	7	.320	.333
Larkin, Eugene, Minnesota†	.269	119	401	46	108	157	26	1	5	42	5	4	5	42	2	55	5	3	10	.392	.343
Lawless, Thomas, Toronto	.083	15	12	1	1	1	0	0	0	1	1	0	0	0	0	1	3	1	0	.083	.083
Lee, Manny, Toronto†	.243	117	391	45	95	133	12	1	6	41	7	3	0	26	0	90	3	2	9	.340	.288
Leius, Scott, Minnesota	.240	14	25	4	6	10	1	0	1	4	0	0	0	2	0	2	0	0	1	.400	.296
Lemon, Chester, Detroit	.258	104	322	39	83	122	16	4	5	32	1	2	3	48	3	61	3	2	8	.379	.359
Leonard, Jeffrey, Seattle	.251	134	478	39	120	170	20	4	10	75	3	2	1	37	6	97	4	1	20	.356	.305
Lewis, Darren, Oakland	.229	25	35	4	8	8	0	1	0	1	0	0	1	7	0	4	2	3	2	.229	.372
Leyritz, James, New York	.257	92	303	28	78	108	13	1	5	25	4	1	0	27	1	51	0	0	11	.356	.331
Lindeman, James, Detroit	.219	12	32	5	7	14	1	0	2	8	0	0	1	2	0	13	0	0	0	.438	.265
Liriano, Nelson, Tor.-Minn.†	.234	103	355	46	83	116	12	9	1	28	4	2	3	38	0	44	8	7	8	.327	.308
Lusader, Scott, Detroit*	.241	45	87	13	21	29	2	0	2	16	1	3	0	12	2	8	1	1	1	.333	.324
Lyons, Stephen, Chicago*	.192	94	146	22	28	39	6	5	1	11	4	2	1	10	0	41	1	0	1	.267	.245
Maas, Kevin, New York*	.252	79	254	42	64	136	9	0	21	41	0	0	3	43	2	76	1	0	1	.535	.367
Macfarlane, Michael, Kansas City	.255	124	400	37	102	152	24	0	6	58	1	6	7	25	2	69	1	0	9	.380	.306
Mack, Shane, Minnesota	.326	125	313	50	102	144	10	4	8	44	6	0	5	29	1	69	13	4	7	.460	.392
Maldonado, Candido, Cleveland	.273	155	590	76	161	263	32	2	22	95	0	7	5	49	9	134	3	5	13	.446	.330
Manrique, R. Fred, Minnesota	.237	69	228	22	54	79	10	1	5	29	1	2	2	4	0	35	5	1	8	.346	.254
Manto, Jeffrey, Cleveland	.224	30	76	12	17	30	5	0	2	14	1	0	0	21	0	18	0	0	0	.395	.392
Marshall, Michael, Boston	.286	30	112	10	32	52	6	0	4	12	0	0	0	4	2	26	0	1	4	.464	.316
Martinez, Carlos, Chicago	.224	92	272	18	61	89	6	2	4	24	3	3	0	10	0	40	1	0	8	.327	.252
Martinez, Edgar, Seattle	.302	144	487	71	147	211	27	2	11	49	3	0	5	74	2	62	0	4	13	.433	.397
Martinez, Constantino, Seattle*	.221	24	68	4	15	19	4	0	0	5	3	0	0	5	0	9	1	0	0	.279	.308
Marzano, John, Boston	.241	32	83	8	20	24	4	0	0	6	0	1	3	9	0	10	0	0	0	.289	.281
Mattingly, Donald, New York*	.256	102	394	40	101	132	16	0	5	42	0	3	0	28	13	20	1	0	13	.335	.308
Mayne, Brett, Kansas City*	.231	5	13	2	3	3	0	0	0	1	2	0	0	3	0	3	0	0	0	.231	.375
McCray, Rodney, Chicago	.000	32	6	8	0	0	0	0	0	0	0	0	0	1	0	4	6	1	0	.000	.143
McGee, Willie, Oakland§	.274	29	113	23	31	38	3	2	0	15	1	0	0	10	0	18	3	6	4	.336	.333
McGriff, Frederick, Toronto*	.300	153	557	91	167	295	21	1	35	88	1	4	2	94	10	108	5	3	13	.530	.400
McGwire, Mark, Oakland	.235	156	523	87	123	256	16	0	39	108	0	9	7	110	12	116	2	0	13	.489	.370
McIntosh, Timothy, Milwaukee	.200	5	5	1	1	4	0	0	1	1	0	0	0	0	0	2	0	0	0	.800	.200
McKnight, Jefferson, Baltimore†	.150	29	60	6	9	11	2	0	0	4	1	0	0	5	0	17	0	0	1	.183	.200
McLemore, Mark, Cal.-Clev.†	.200	20	20	6	4	4	0	0	0	2	3	2	0	9	0	15	1	1	3	.200	.203
McRae, Brian, Kansas City†	.286	46	168	21	48	68	8	3	2	23	3	2	2	11	0	29	4	3	5	.405	.318
Melvin, Robert, Baltimore	.243	93	301	30	73	104	14	1	5	37	3	3	0	9	0	53	0	1	8	.346	.267
Meulens, Hensley, New York	.241	23	83	12	20	36	7	0	3	10	0	0	3	11	3	25	0	0	3	.434	.337
Milligan, Randy, Baltimore	.265	109	362	64	96	178	20	1	20	60	1	2	2	88	3	68	6	3	11	.492	.408
Molitor, Paul, Milwaukee	.285	103	418	64	119	194	27	6	12	45	1	1	1	37	4	51	18	3	7	.464	.343
Morman, Russell, Kansas City	.270	12	37	5	10	21	2	0	3	8	1	1	0	3	0	3	0	0	0	.568	.317
Moseby, Lloyd, Detroit*	.248	122	431	64	107	175	16	5	14	51	0	2	5	48	3	77	17	5	0	.406	.329
Moses, John, Minnesota†	.221	115	172	26	38	46	3	1	1	14	1	2	2	19	1	19	3	3	4	.267	.303

Player, Club	AVG	G	AB	R	H	TB	2B	3B	HR	RBI	SH	SF	HP	BB	IBB	SO	SB	CS	GI DP	SLG	OBP
Mulliniks, S. Rance, Toronto*	.289	57	97	11	28	38	4	0	2	16	0	1	0	22	2	19	2	1	2	.392	.417
Munoz, Pedro, Minnesota	.271	22	85	13	23	38	4	1	3	5	1	2	0	2	0	16	3	1	3	.341	.281
Myers, Gregory, Toronto*	.236	87	250	33	59	83	7	1	5	22	1	4	0	22	2	33	0	0	12	.332	.293
Naehring, Timothy, Boston	.271	24	85	10	23	35	6	0	2	12	0	0	0	8	0	15	0	1	2	.412	.333
Newman, Albert, Minnesota†	.242	144	388	43	94	108	14	1	0	30	8	2	0	33	1	34	13	6	7	.278	.304
Nixon, R. Donell, Baltimore	.250	8	20	1	5	7	2	0	0	2	0	0	0	1	0	7	5	2	0	.350	.286
Nokes, Matthew, Det.-N.Y.*	.248	136	351	33	87	131	9	1	11	40	1	1	6	24	6	47	1	0	11	.373	.306
O'Brien, Charles, Milwaukee	.186	46	145	11	27	38	9	1	0	11	8	0	2	11	1	26	0	0	3	.262	.253
O'Brien, Peter, Seattle*	.224	108	366	32	82	115	18	0	5	27	1	4	1	44	1	33	0	0	12	.314	.308
Olerud, John, Toronto*	.265	111	358	43	95	154	15	1	14	48	1	4	2	57	6	75	0	0	5	.430	.364
Orsulak, Joseph, Baltimore*	.269	124	413	49	111	164	14	3	11	57	4	1	1	46	9	48	6	8	7	.397	.343
Ortiz, Adalberto, Minnesota	.335	71	170	18	57	66	7	1	0	18	2	1	2	12	0	16	0	4	5	.388	.384
Ortiz, John, California	.190	31	84	8	16	24	5	0	1	6	4	0	1	5	0	31	2	2	2	.286	.244
Palacios, R. Rey, Kansas City	.232	41	56	8	13	22	3	0	2	9	2	0	0	5	0	24	0	3	0	.393	.295
Palmeiro, Rafael, Texas*	.319	154	598	72	191	280	35	6	14	89	0	8	3	40	6	59	3	2	24	.468	.361
Paredes, Johnny, Detroit	.125	6	8	1	1	1	0	0	0	0	0	0	0	1	0	1	0	0	0	.125	.222
Parker, David, Milwaukee*	.289	157	610	71	176	275	30	3	21	92	0	14	4	41	11	102	4	7	18	.451	.330
Parrish, Lance, California	.268	133	470	54	126	212	14	0	24	70	0	2	5	46	4	107	2	2	12	.451	.338
Pasqua, Daniel, Chicago*	.274	112	325	43	89	161	27	3	13	58	0	5	0	37	7	66	1	1	4	.495	.347
Pecota, William, Kansas City	.242	87	240	43	58	92	15	2	5	20	3	0	3	33	0	39	8	5	5	.383	.336
Pena, Antonio, Boston	.263	143	491	62	129	171	19	1	7	56	6	3	3	43	3	71	8	6	23	.348	.322
Perry, Gerald, Kansas City*	.254	133	465	57	118	168	22	2	8	57	2	5	3	39	4	56	17	4	14	.361	.313
Petralli, Eugene, Texas*	.255	133	325	28	83	98	13	1	0	21	0	3	3	50	3	49	0	2	12	.302	.357
Pettis, Gary, Texas†	.239	136	423	66	101	142	16	8	3	31	11	1	4	57	0	118	38	15	6	.336	.333
Phelps, Kenneth, Oak.-Clev.*	.150	56	120	10	18	23	2	0	1	6	0	0	0	22	3	21	0	0	4	.192	.280
Phillips, K. Anthony, Detroit†	.251	152	573	97	144	201	23	5	8	55	9	2	4	99	0	85	19	9	10	.351	.364
Plantier, Phillip, Boston*	.133	14	15	1	2	3	1	0	0	3	0	0	0	4	0	6	0	0	0	.200	.333
Polidor, Gustavo, California	.067	18	15	0	1	1	0	0	0	1	3	1	0	0	0	1	0	0	0	.067	.067
Polonia, Luis, N.Y.-Cal.*	.335	120	403	52	135	166	7	9	2	35	3	4	3	25	0	43	21	14	9	.412	.372
Puckett, Kirby, Minnesota	.298	146	551	82	164	246	40	3	12	80	0	6	3	57	11	73	5	0	15	.446	.365
Quinlan, Thomas, Toronto	.500	1	2	0	1	1	0	0	0	0	0	0	0	0	0	1	0	0	0	.500	.667
Quintana, Carlos, Boston	.287	149	512	56	147	196	28	0	7	67	5	6	0	52	7	74	1	2	19	.383	.354
Quirk, James, Oakland*	.281	56	121	12	34	50	5	1	3	26	1	3	1	14	1	34	0	0	1	.413	.353
Randolph, William, Oakland	.257	93	292	37	75	93	9	3	1	21	7	2	4	32	2	25	6	1	11	.318	.331
Ray, Johnny, California†	.277	105	404	47	112	150	23	0	5	43	3	3	0	19	4	44	4	3	10	.371	.308
Reed, Jody, Boston	.289	155	598	70	173	233	45	0	5	51	11	3	4	75	4	65	4	2	19	.390	.371
Reimer, Kevin, Texas*	.260	64	100	5	26	43	9	1	2	15	0	0	0	10	0	22	0	0	3	.430	.333
Reynolds, Harold, Seattle†	.252	160	642	100	162	223	36	5	5	55	5	6	4	81	3	52	31	16	9	.347	.336
Ripken, William, Baltimore	.291	129	406	48	118	157	28	1	3	38	17	1	3	28	2	43	5	2	7	.387	.342
Ripken, Calvin, Baltimore	.250	161	600	78	150	249	28	4	21	84	0	7	5	82	18	66	3	1	12	.415	.341
Rivera, Luis, Boston	.225	118	346	38	78	119	20	0	7	45	12	1	5	25	1	58	4	3	10	.344	.279
Robidoux, William, Boston*	.182	27	44	4	8	15	1	0	2	4	0	0	0	6	0	14	0	0	2	.341	.288
Romero, Edgardo, Detroit	.229	32	70	8	16	19	3	0	0	4	4	0	0	6	0	4	0	0	0	.271	.286
Romine, Kevin, Boston	.272	70	136	21	37	50	7	0	2	14	3	2	1	12	0	27	4	0	7	.368	.331
Rose, Robert, California	.385	7	13	5	5	8	1	1	0	2	1	0	0	2	0	1	0	0	0	.615	.467
Rowland, Richard, Detroit	.158	7	19	3	3	4	1	0	0	0	0	0	0	1	0	4	1	0	1	.211	.238
Russell, Jeffrey, Texas	.273	68	128	16	35	45	4	0	2	8	1	1	0	11	2	41	1	0	3	.352	.331
Salas, Mark, Detroit*	.232	74	164	18	38	68	9	0	9	24	1	1	1	21	2	28	0	0	3	.415	.323
Sanders, Deion, New York*	.158	57	133	24	21	36	2	2	3	9	1	0	0	13	0	27	8	2	2	.271	.236

Player, Club	AVG	G	AB	R	H	TB	2B	3B	HR	RBI	SH	SF	HP	BB	IBB	SO	SB	CS	GI DP	SLG	OBP
Santana, Rafael, Cleveland	.231	7	13	3	3	6			1	3	0	0	0	0	0	0	0	0	1	.462	.231
Sax, Stephen, New York	.260	155	615	70	160	200	24	2	4	42	6	6	4	49	3	46	43	9	13	.325	.316
Schaefer, Jeffrey, Seattle	.206	55	107	11	22	25	3	0	0	6	2	1	2	3	0	11	4	1	1	.234	.239
Schofield, Richard, California	.255	99	310	41	79	92	8	1	0	18	13	2	2	52	3	61	3	4	3	.297	.363
Schooler, Michael, Seattle	.000	49	1	0	0	0	0	0	0	0	0	0	0	0	0	0	0	0	0	.000	.000
Schroeder, A. William, California	.224	18	58	7	13	28	3	0	4	9	0	0	0	1	0	10	0	0	3	.483	.237
Schu, Richard, California*	.268	61	157	19	42	68	8	0	6	14	0	1	2	11	0	25	0	0	4	.433	.314
Schulz, Jeffrey, Kansas City*	.258	30	66	5	17	24	5	1	0	6	1	0	0	6	2	13	0	0	2	.364	.319
Segui, David, Baltimore†	.244	40	123	14	30	43	7	0	2	15	1	0	1	11	2	15	0	0	12	.350	.311
Seitzer, Kevin, Kansas City	.275	158	622	91	171	230	31	5	6	38	4	2	2	67	2	66	7	5	11	.370	.346
Sheets, Larry, Detroit*	.261	131	360	40	94	145	17	0	10	52	0	4	1	24	2	42	1	0	13	.403	.311
Sheffield, Gary, Milwaukee	.294	125	487	67	143	205	30	1	10	67	4	4	2	44	2	41	25	10	11	.421	.308
Shelby, John, Detroit†	.248	78	222	22	55	82	9	3	4	20	6	9	3	10	1	51	3	5	6	.369	.280
Shumpert, Terrance, Kansas City	.275	32	91	7	25	33	6	1	0	8	4	0	0	2	0	17	3	3	4	.363	.292
Sierra, Ruben, Texas†	.280	159	608	70	170	259	37	2	16	96	0	8	1	49	13	86	9	3	15	.426	.330
Sinatro, Matthew, Seattle	.300	30	50	7	15	16	1	0	0	4	3	0	0	4	0	10	1	0	2	.320	.352
Skinner, Joel, Cleveland	.252	49	139	16	35	47	4	1	2	16	4	1	0	7	0	44	0	0	3	.338	.288
Snyder, J. Cory, Cleveland	.233	123	438	46	102	177	27	3	14	55	0	6	2	21	3	118	1	4	11	.404	.268
Sojo, Luis, Toronto	.225	33	80	14	18	24	3	0	1	9	1	0	1	5	0	5	1	1	1	.300	.271
Sorrento, Paul, Minnesota*	.207	41	121	11	25	46	4	1	5	13	0	0	0	12	0	31	0	1	3	.380	.281
Sosa, Samuel, Chicago	.233	153	532	72	124	215	26	10	15	70	2	6	6	33	4	150	32	16	10	.404	.282
Spiers, William, Milwaukee*	.242	112	363	44	88	115	15	3	2	36	6	3	1	16	0	45	11	6	12	.317	.274
Springer, Steven, Cleveland	.167	4	12	1	2	2	0	0	0	1	1	0	0	0	0	6	0	0	0	.167	.154
Stanley, R. Michael, Texas	.249	103	189	21	47	63	8	1	2	19	6	1	4	30	2	25	1	1	4	.333	.350
Stark, Matthew, Chicago	.250	8	16	1	4	5	1	0	0	1	0	0	0	1	0	6	0	0	0	.313	.294
Steinbach, Terry, Oakland	.251	114	379	32	95	141	15	2	9	57	5	3	4	19	1	66	0	1	11	.372	.291
Stevens, D. Lee, California*	.214	67	248	28	53	84	10	0	7	32	4	7	1	22	3	75	1	0	8	.339	.275
Stillwell, Kurt, Kansas City†	.249	144	506	60	126	178	35	4	3	51	7	2	4	39	1	60	0	1	8	.352	.304
Stone, Jeffrey, Boston*	.500	10	3	0	0	0	0	0	0	0	0	0	0	0	0	1	0	0	0	.500	.500
Surhoff, William J., Milwaukee*	.276	135	474	55	131	178	21	2	6	59	7	7	1	41	0	37	18	7	8	.376	.331
Sveum, Dale, Milwaukee†	.197	48	117	15	23	33	7	0	1	12	1	1	2	12	0	30	1	1	2	.282	.278
Tabler, Patrick, Kansas City	.272	75	195	12	53	70	14	0	1	19	0	2	0	20	2	21	0	0	8	.359	.338
Tartabull, Danilo, Kansas City	.268	88	313	41	84	148	19	0	15	60	0	3	1	36	4	93	1	2	9	.473	.341
Tettleton, Mickey, Baltimore†	.223	135	444	68	99	169	21	2	15	51	0	4	5	106	7	160	2	4	7	.381	.376
Thomas, Frank, Chicago	.330	60	191	39	63	101	11	3	7	31	0	1	2	44	2	54	0	1	5	.529	.454
Thurman, Gary, Kansas City	.233	23	60	5	14	17	3	0	0	3	0	0	0	2	0	12	7	1	2	.283	.258
Tingley, Ronald, California	.000	5	3	0	0	0	0	0	0	1	0	0	0	0	0	1	0	0	0	.000	.250
Tolleson, J. Wayne, New York†	.149	73	74	12	11	14	3	0	0	4	2	0	0	6	0	21	0	0	1	.189	.210
Trammell, Alan, Detroit	.304	146	559	71	170	251	37	1	14	89	3	6	7	68	7	55	12	10	11	.449	.377
Valle, David, Seattle	.214	107	308	37	66	102	15	0	7	33	4	6	7	45	1	48	1	2	11	.331	.328
Vaughn, Gregory, Milwaukee	.220	120	382	51	84	165	26	2	17	61	7	1	6	33	0	91	7	4	11	.432	.280
Velarde, Randy, New York	.210	95	229	21	48	73	6	2	5	19	2	1	1	20	0	53	0	3	6	.319	.275
Venable, W. McKinley, California*	.259	93	189	26	49	76	9	3	4	21	7	2	1	24	2	31	5	1	9	.402	.340
Ventura, Robin, Chicago*	.249	150	493	48	123	157	17	1	5	54	13	3	3	55	3	53	1	5	10	.318	.324
Virgil, Osvaldo, Toronto	.000	3	5	0	0	0	0	0	0	0	0	0	0	0	0	3	0	0	0	.000	.000
Vizquel, Omar, Seattle†	.247	81	255	19	63	76	3	2	0	18	10	0	0	18	0	22	4	1	7	.298	.295
Walewander, James, New York†	.200	9	5	1	1	1	0	0	0	0	0	0	0	0	0	0	0	1	0	.200	.200
Walker, Gregory, Chi.-Balt.*	.154	16	39	2	6	6	0	0	0	2	0	2	1	3	0	11	0	1	2	.154	.233
Ward, Gary, Detroit	.256	106	309	32	79	121	11	1	9	46	2	2	1	30	0	50	2	0	12	.392	.322

Player, Club	AVG	G	AB	R	H	TB	2B	3B	HR	RBI	SH	SF	HP	BB	IBB	SO	SB	CS	GI DP	SLG	OBP
Ward, Turner, Cleveland†	.348	14	46	10	16	23	2	1	1	10	0	0	0	3	0	8	3	1	1	.500	.388
Washington, Claudell, Cal.-N.Y.*	.167	45	114	7	19	26	2	1	1	9	0	1	0	4	1	25	4	1	2	.228	.193
Webster, Leonard, Minnesota	.333	2	6	1	2	3	1	0	0	0	0	0	0	1	0	1	0	0	0	.500	.429
Webster, Mitchell, Cleveland†	.252	128	437	58	110	178	20	6	12	55	11	6	3	20	1	61	22	6	5	.407	.285
Weiss, Walter, Oakland†	.265	138	445	50	118	143	17	1	2	35	7	4	1	46	5	53	6	3	7	.321	.337
Whitaker, Louis, Detroit†	.237	132	472	75	112	192	22	1	18	60	0	5	0	74	5	71	8	6	10	.407	.338
White, Devon, California†	.217	125	443	57	96	152	17	3	11	44	1	3	3	44	5	116	21	6	6	.343	.290
White, Frank, Kansas City	.216	82	241	20	52	74	14	1	2	21	0	3	3	10	0	32	1	0	7	.307	.253
Whiten, Mark, Toronto†	.273	33	88	12	24	33	4	1	2	7	0	0	0	7	0	14	2	0	2	.375	.323
Willard, Gerald, Chicago*	.000	3	3	0	0	0	0	0	0	0	0	0	0	0	0	2	0	0	1	.000	.000
Williams, Kenneth, Det.-Tor.	.161	106	155	23	25	35	8	1	0	13	6	2	2	10	0	42	9	4	10	.226	.219
Wilson, William, Toronto†	.265	147	588	81	156	209	36	4	3	51	8	4	0	31	0	102	23	6	4	.355	.300
Wilson, Willie, Kansas City†	.290	115	307	49	89	114	13	3	2	42	1	3	2	30	1	57	24	6	17	.371	.354
Winfield, David, N.Y.-Cal.	.267	132	475	70	127	215	21	0	21	78	0	7	7	52	3	81	1	0	0	.453	.338
Witt, Robert, Texas	.000	35	0	1	0	0	0	0	0	0	0	0	0	0	0	0	0	0	0	.000	.000
Worthington, Craig, Baltimore	.226	133	425	46	96	137	17	0	8	44	0	8	3	63	2	96	1	2	13	.322	.328
Yount, Robin, Milwaukee	.247	158	587	98	145	223	17	5	17	77	4	8	6	78	6	89	15	8	7	.380	.337

AWARDED FIRST BASE ON CATCHER'S INTERFERENCE—Martinez, Sea. 2 (Heath, Macfarlane); Steinbach, Oak. 2 (Macfarlane, Petralli);   Daugherty, Tex. (Macfarlane); Kelly, N.Y. (Melvin); Macfarlane, K.C. (Surhoff).

PLAYERS WITH TWO OR MORE CLUBS

Player, Club	AVG	G	AB	R	H	TB	2B	3B	HR	RBI	SH	SF	HP	BB	IBB	SO	SB	CS	GI DP	SLG	OBP
Baines, Harold, Texas*	.290	103	321	41	93	144	10	1	13	44	0	3	0	47	9	63	0	1	13	.449	.377
Baines, Harold, Oakland*	.266	32	94	11	25	39	5	0	3	21	0	4	0	20	1	17	0	2	4	.415	.381
Bradley, Phillip, Baltimore	.270	72	289	39	78	101	9	1	4	26	6	1	7	30	2	35	10	4	9	.349	.352
Bradley, Phillip, Chicago	.226	45	133	20	30	37	5	1	0	5	5	0	4	20	3	26	7	3	2	.278	.344
Coles, Darnell, Seattle	.215	37	107	9	23	36	5	1	2	16	1	1	0	4	1	17	0	0	1	.336	.248
Coles, Darnell, Detroit	.204	52	108	13	22	27	2	1	1	4	1	1	1	12	1	21	0	1	3	.250	.281
Gallagher, David, Chicago	.280	45	75	5	21	26	3	1	0	5	5	0	3	3	0	9	1	0	0	.347	.316
Gallagher, David, Baltimore	.216	23	51	7	11	12	1	0	0	2	2	0	0	2	0	8	1	1	0	.235	.268
Jefferson, Stanley, Baltimore†	.000	10	19	1	0	0	0	0	0	0	0	0	0	2	0	8	8	4	0	.000	.095
Jefferson, Stanley, Cleveland†	.276	49	98	21	27	41	8	0	2	10	1	3	2	6	0	18	1	1	3	.418	.333
Jones, Tracy, Detroit	.229	50	118	15	27	45	4	1	4	9	1	0	3	8	0	13	8	1	4	.381	.283
Jones, Tracy, Seattle	.302	25	86	8	26	36	4	0	2	15	1	1	3	3	0	12	0	0	3	.419	.341
Kittle, Ronald, Chicago	.245	83	277	29	68	130	14	0	16	43	0	0	1	24	2	77	0	0	3	.469	.311
Kittle, Ronald, Baltimore	.164	22	61	7	10	18	2	0	2	3	1	1	1	2	0	14	0	0	0	.295	.203
Liriano, Nelson, Toronto†	.212	50	170	16	36	50	7	2	1	15	3	1	0	16	0	20	3	5	5	.294	.282
McLemore, Mark, California†	.254	53	185	30	47	66	5	7	0	13	3	1	0	22	0	24	5	2	1	.357	.332
McLemore, Mark, Cleveland†	.146	20	48	4	7	9	2	0	0	2	0	1	2	4	0	9	1	0	0	.188	.212
Nokes, Matthew, Detroit*	.167	8	12	2	2	2	0	0	0	2	0	0	2	0	0	6	0	0	0	.167	.167
Nokes, Matthew, New York*	.270	44	111	12	30	46	5	0	3	8	0	1	4	20	3	14	0	0	5	.414	.305
Phelps, Kenneth, Oakland*	.238	92	240	21	57	85	1	0	8	32	0	0	4	33	4	33	2	0	6	.354	.307
Phelps, Kenneth, Cleveland*	.186	32	59	6	11	16	2	0	2	6	0	0	0	12	1	10	2	2	3	.271	.319
Polonia, Luis, New York*	.115	24	61	4	7	7	0	0	0	0	0	0	0	10	0	11	1	0	1	.115	.239
Polonia, Luis, California*	.336	109	381	50	128	159	7	9	2	32	3	3	1	25	1	42	20	14	8	.417	.376

OFFICIAL AMERICAN LEAGUE DESIGNATED HITTING

Player, Club	AVG	G	AB	R	H	TB	2B	3B	HR	RBI	SH	SF	HP	BB	IBB	SO	SB	CS	GI DP	SLG	OBP
Walker, Gregory, Chicago*	.200	2	5	2	1	1	0	0	0	0	0	0	0	0	0	2	0	0	0	.200	.200
Walker, Gregory, Baltimore*	.147	14	34	3	5	5	0	0	0	2	0	0	1	3	0	9	1	0	1	.147	.237
Washington, Claudell, California*	.176	12	34	3	6	10	1	0	0	2	0	0	0	2	0	8	3	1	1	.294	.222
Washington, Claudell, New York*	.163	33	80	4	13	16	1	1	0	6	0	1	0	2	1	17	3	2	0	.200	.181
Williams, Kenneth, Detroit	.133	57	83	10	11	13	2	0	0	5	0	0	1	3	0	24	7	0	1	.157	.170
Williams, Kenneth, Toronto	.194	49	72	13	14	22	6	1	0	6	0	1	1	7	0	18	0	0	1	.306	.272
Winfield, David, New York	.213	20	61	7	13	22	3	0	2	6	0	1	1	4	0	13	0	1	2	.361	.269
Winfield, David, California	.275	112	414	63	114	193	18	2	19	72	1	1	4	48	3	68	0	1	15	.466	.348

CLUB DESIGNATED HITTING

Club	AVG	G	AB	R	H	TB	2B	3B	HR	RBI	SH	SF	HP	BB	IBB	SO	SB	CS	GI DP	SLG	OBP
Cleveland	.293	162	625	75	183	269	34	5	14	84	4	3	3	52	5	92	8	5	12	.430	.348
California	.285	162	617	89	176	280	35	3	21	87	0	7	6	88	5	96	6	5	20	.454	.376
Milwaukee	.274	162	634	79	174	274	31	3	21	96	1	17	5	49	11	109	6	11	20	.432	.323
Minnesota	.274	162	580	65	159	221	34	2	8	64	3	6	8	62	7	94	4	7	18	.381	.349
Kansas City	.268	161	624	74	167	254	43	1	14	85	0	8	8	54	6	99	15	5	9	.407	.325
Seattle	.250	162	608	68	152	246	25	0	23	99	2	12	3	72	9	102	3	5	18	.405	.330
Texas	.245	162	595	65	146	223	22	2	17	73	0	3	6	75	7	134	1	4	21	.375	.331
Oakland	.245	162	608	76	149	222	24	2	15	80	1	9	4	79	7	152	16	8	13	.365	.335
Boston	.244	162	602	82	147	228	24	3	17	77	1	7	6	80	7	113	5	5	20	.379	.331
Chicago	.242	162	616	79	149	271	32	2	28	92	4	9	4	65	7	130	9	4	15	.440	.316
Detroit	.235	162	614	75	144	224	31	2	15	74	0	4	4	54	8	103	3	7	20	.365	.296
New York	.228	162	619	66	141	239	21	1	25	79	1	7	7	49	9	123	4	4	12	.386	.290
Toronto	.220	162	604	68	133	211	28	4	14	68	1	11	8	69	9	132	4	4	14	.349	.298
Baltimore	.211	161	587	68	124	206	23	1	19	65	2	3	5	88	5	169	10	3	20	.351	.318
TOTALS	.251	1133	8533	1029	2144	3368	407	32	251	1123	19	106	67	936	102	1648	89	73	233	.395	.326

INDIVIDUAL DESIGNATED HITTING

Player, Club	AVG	G	AB	R	H	TB	2B	3B	HR	RBI	SH	SF	HP	BB	IBB	SO	SB	CS	GI DP	SLG	OBP
Parker, D, Mil*	.281	153	597	68	168	266	29	3	21	89	0	14	4	41	11	102	4	7	18	.446	.325
James, C, Cle.	.296	124	477	55	141	203	27	4	9	57	2	2	3	30	4	68	3	3	10	.426	.340
Evans, D, Bos.	.249	122	445	66	111	174	18	3	13	63	0	6	6	67	5	73	4	4	18	.391	.347
Baines, H, Tex-Oak*	.287	125	404	52	116	181	15	1	16	61	0	6	3	64	9	77	0	3	18	.448	.380
Downing, B, Cal.	.280	87	322	47	90	154	18	2	14	51	1	4	6	49	2	44	0	1	17	.478	.381
Olerud, J, Tor*	.258	90	302	34	78	124	14	0	12	38	0	4	3	44	8	66	0	2	5	.411	.350
Davis, A, Sea*	.272	87	301	39	82	134	16	0	10	52	0	6	2	57	8	46	0	2	6	.445	.387
Perry, G, KC*	.262	68	263	33	69	93	12	0	4	35	0	2	3	22	1	30	10	0	8	.354	.322
Kittle, R, Chi-Bal	.226	67	235	23	53	99	10	1	12	30	0	2	1	21	3	65	0	0	7	.421	.296
Davis, C, Cal*	.284	60	225	35	64	97	13	1	6	30	1	2	3	34	3	43	0	0	4	.431	.375
Horn, S, Bal*	.265	63	204	26	54	101	11	0	12	34	0	2	0	26	3	55	0	1	8	.495	.345
Pasqua, D, Chi*	.232	57	194	24	45	93	12	3	10	39	0	2	1	21	1	40	1	0	2	.479	.307
Leonard, J, Sea.	.245	48	192	17	47	74	6	0	7	34	0	5	1	7	1	38	2	1	8	.385	.268
Balboni, S, NY	.175	72	177	15	31	64	3	0	10	24	0	2	2	22	1	57	0	0	3	.362	.271

Player, Club	AVG	G	AB	R	H	TB	2B	3B	HR	RBI	SH	SF	HP	BB	IBB	SO	SB	CS	GIDP	SLG	OBP
Hall, M, NY*	.239	54	176	20	42	66	10	1	4	18	0	2	2	23	3	19	19	0	3	.375	.261
Canseco, J, Oak*	.233	43	159	23	37	60	5	0	6	25	1	2	1	18	2	59	9	3	4	.377	.315
Nokes, M, Det-NY*	.218	54	142	13	31	47	4	0	4	14	0	1	5	11	1	18	1	1	5	.331	.296
Larkin, G, Min†	.336	43	140	14	47	62	13	1	0	14	2	3	1	19	2	24	1	2	5	.443	.411
Bell, G, Tor.	.232	36	138	16	32	50	9	0	3	18	0	5	1	12	3	19	1	1	5	.362	.288
Tettleton, M, Bal†	.213	40	136	22	29	47	7	1	2	17	0	0	0	32	2	56	0	2	3	.346	.367
Sheets, L, Det*	.239	44	134	12	32	49	7	1	3	7	0	2	0	10	2	15	2	1	6	.366	.288
Brett, G, KC*	.292	32	120	18	35	60	9	0	4	18	0	3	0	9	0	18	1	0	3	.500	.333
Tartabull, D, KC	.271	32	118	15	32	53	7	1	1	16	0	2	0	15	2	30	2	0	4	.449	.348
Bergman, D, Det*	.322	51	115	15	37	49	9	0	0	19	0	1	1	17	1	13	0	0	3	.426	.403
Calderon, I, Chi	.304	27	112	20	34	59	7	0	6	15	0	1	0	6	1	7	4	2	5	.527	.336
Castillo, C, Min	.230	35	87	6	20	24	7	0	0	17	0	0	2	10	0	15	0	0	0	.276	.256
Bush, R, Min*	.231	29	78	6	18	24	3	0	1	3	0	0	0	4	0	17	0	1	0	.308	.333
Steinbach, T, Oak	.256	25	78	5	20	28	2	1	1	10	1	2	2	4	0	10	0	0	1	.359	.310
Maldonado, C, Cle	.333	20	75	11	25	44	5	0	4	18	0	0	0	9	0	5	1	3	2	.587	.405
Hrbek, K, Min*	.324	20	71	8	23	37	5	0	3	13	0	2	0	10	2	15	0	0	0	.521	.412
Daugherty, J, Tex†	.232	21	69	7	16	26	2	1	1	12	0	0	1	5	0	18	1	1	1	.377	.284
Sorrento, P, Min*	.194	23	67	8	13	24	3	0	2	9	1	1	0	5	0	8	0	0	3	.358	.257
Jones, T, Det-Sea	.197	25	66	8	13	26	1	0	4	6	0	0	3	1	0	6	0	0	3	.394	.243
Coles, D, Sea-Det	.188	31	64	7	12	14	2	0	0	2	0	1	0	7	0	21	0	3	0	.219	.264
Maas, K, NY*	.306	18	62	9	19	37	0	0	6	16	0	0	1	6	2	6	0	0	1	.597	.368
Polonia, L, NY-Cal*	.333	15	60	4	20	21	1	1	0	5	2	2	0	1	0	10	6	3	1	.350	.306
Phelps, K, Oak-Cle*	.140	21	57	5	8	9	1	0	0	6	0	0	1	14	1	22	0	1	0	.158	.258
Fielder, C, Det	.179	15	56	6	10	21	2	0	3	6	0	0	0	6	0	8	0	0	2	.375	.379
Henderson, R, Oak	.286	20	56	9	16	23	2	0	1	6	0	0	1	9	0	17	4	1	1	.411	.405
Hill, G, Tor	.196	14	56	8	11	16	1	2	0	9	0	0	0	4	0	13	0	1	0	.286	.250
Marshall, M, Bos	.339	23	52	6	19	35	4	0	4	3	0	0	0	1	0	6	0	0	2	.625	.362
Dwyer, J, Min*	.154	21	49	2	8	11	0	0	1	6	0	1	1	9	0	11	0	0	3	.212	.279
Reimer, K, Tex*	.224	15	49	5	11	17	3	0	1	4	0	0	0	4	0	5	0	0	2	.347	.296
Tabler, P, KC	.265	14	47	5	13	17	4	0	0	5	0	1	1	3	0	12	0	0	3	.347	.302
Fisk, C, Chi	.170	11	40	9	6	8	1	0	1	5	0	0	0	6	1	8	0	0	0	.255	.278
Harper, B, Min	.375	15	40	2	15	23	5	0	0	5	0	2	1	4	0	8	0	1	0	.575	.444
Hassey, R, Oak*	.200	13	39	5	8	12	1	0	1	5	0	0	0	3	0	9	0	0	0	.300	.244
Mattingly, D, NY*	.308	10	36	7	12	14	2	0	0	6	0	1	0	5	3	9	0	0	0	.359	.378
Winfield, D, NY-Cal	.278	10	35	6	10	23	2	0	3	2	0	0	1	5	0	11	2	2	2	.639	.357
Jackson, B, KC	.286	19	35	5	10	17	0	1	2	7	0	0	0	3	0	18	2	0	1	.486	.359
Russell, J, Tex	.171	12	34	3	6	7	1	0	0	2	0	0	1	6	0	8	0	0	2	.200	.293
Walker, G, Chi-Bal*	.147	9	34	6	5	5	0	0	0	1	0	0	0	2	0	9	0	0	2	.147	.216
Gonzalez, J, Tex	.182	10	33	3	6	11	2	0	1	7	0	1	0	0	0	9	0	0	2	.333	.206
Buhner, J, Sea	.219	10	32	6	7	18	1	0	3	3	0	0	0	4	0	7	0	0	0	.563	.316
Ward, G, Det	.250	13	32	4	8	10	1	0	0	4	0	0	0	3	0	12	2	0	1	.313	.314
Milligan, R, Bal	.226	9	31	4	7	7	0	0	0	7	0	1	0	4	1	11	1	0	0	.226	.314
Lindeman, J, Det.	.214	10	28	4	6	12	2	0	2	5	0	0	1	2	0	3	0	0	1	.429	.267
James, D, Cle*	.407	10	27	2	11	13	2	0	0	1	1	0	0	8	0	4	2	1	0	.481	.528
Stanley, M, Tex	.185	14	27	3	5	7	0	0	0	1	0	0	0	6	0	8	2	1	0	.259	.333
Mulliniks, R, Tor*	.192	10	26	3	5	6	1	0	0	2	1	0	0	2	0	7	0	0	1	.231	.316
Sierra, R, Tex†	.038	7	26	0	1	2	1	0	0	1	0	0	0	2	0	9	0	0	0	.077	.107
Bradley, P, Bal-Chi	.120	9	25	5	3	4	1	0	0	0	0	0	0	4	0	3	1	0	1	.160	.276
Wilson, M, Tor†	.160	6	25	3	4	7	3	0	0	1	1	0	0	2	0	3	1	0	1	.280	.241
Melvin, B, Bal.	.125	10	24	2	3	4	1	0	0	0	1	0	0	1	0	3	0	0	2	.167	.222
Thomas, F, Chi	.292	8	24	3	7	9	2	0	0	0	0	0	0	7	0	6	0	1	1	.375	.452

Player, Club	AVG	G	AB	R	H	TB	2B	3B	HR	RBI	SH	SF	HP	BB	IBB	SO	SB	CS	GI DP	SLG	OBP
Hoiles, C, Bal	.174	7	23	1	4	8	1	0	1	5	0	0	0	3	0	5	0	0	0	.348	.269
Randolph, W, Oak	.217	6	23	4	5	6	1	0	0	0	0	0	0	0	0	1	0	0	1	.261	.217
Macfarlane, M, KC	.227	5	22	1	5	10	2	0	1	4	0	0	0	1	0	2	0	0	0	.455	.261
McGriff, F, Tor*	.136	6	22	1	3	6	0	0	1	3	0	1	0	3	0	9	0	0	0	.273	.231
O'Brien, P, Sea*	.091	6	22	0	2	2	0	0	0	0	0	0	0	1	0	2	0	0	0	.091	.130
Palmeiro, R, Tex*	.091	6	22	0	2	2	0	0	0	2	0	1	0	3	0	3	0	0	1	.091	.200
Burks, E, Bos	.238	6	21	3	5	6	1	0	0	1	0	0	0	2	0	4	0	0	0	.286	.304
Jennings, J, Oak*	.238	8	21	1	5	9	2	0	0	1	0	0	0	3	0	6	0	0	0	.429	.333
Belle, J, Cle	.200	6	20	2	4	7	1	0	0	3	0	0	0	1	0	5	0	0	1	.350	.238
Brunansky, T, Bos	.100	7	20	1	2	2	0	0	0	2	0	0	0	5	0	6	0	0	0	.150	.269
Anderson, B, Bal*	.316	11	19	2	6	3	1	0	0	2	1	0	1	7	0	2	1	0	0	.316	.519
Howard, S, Oak	.211	7	19	3	4	6	2	0	0	0	0	0	0	1	0	10	0	0	0	.316	.250
Jose, F, Oak†	.316	7	19	4	6	6	0	0	0	5	0	1	0	1	0	2	2	0	0	.632	.350
Cerone, R, NY	.222	6	18	2	4	12	2	0	2	0	0	0	0	1	0	1	0	0	1	.278	.263
Henderson, D, Oak	.333	5	18	0	6	5	1	0	0	0	0	0	0	2	0	2	0	0	0	.389	.400
Lansford, C, Oak	.500	6	18	0	9	7	1	0	0	1	0	0	0	3	0	7	0	0	1	.556	.571
Bradley, S, Sea*	.118	6	17	0	2	10	1	0	2	1	0	0	0	1	0	2	0	0	1	.176	.167
Heep, D, Bos*	.176	6	17	2	3	3	0	0	0	1	0	0	0	0	0	3	0	0	0	.176	.176
Molitor, P, Mil	.118	4	17	0	2	3	1	0	0	2	0	0	0	3	0	5	0	0	0	.176	.250
Moseby, L, Det*	.235	4	17	1	4	8	1	0	1	3	0	0	0	0	0	4	1	0	0	.471	.263
Orsulak, J, Bal*	.125	5	16	0	2	2	1	0	0	0	0	0	0	2	0	0	0	0	0	.125	.222
Puckett, K, Min	.438	4	16	5	7	7	0	0	0	2	0	0	0	0	0	3	2	1	1	.438	.438
Dorsett, B, NY	.133	5	15	0	2	3	1	0	0	0	0	0	0	0	0	1	0	0	0	.200	.133
Phillips, T, Det†	.267	4	15	4	4	8	1	0	1	2	0	0	0	2	0	1	2	0	0	.533	.353
Stark, M, Chi	.267	6	15	1	4	5	1	0	0	3	0	0	0	1	0	5	0	0	2	.333	.313
Hulett, T, Bal	.143	6	14	0	2	8	0	0	2	3	0	0	0	3	0	3	0	0	0	.571	.294
Segui, D, Bal†	.071	8	14	1	1	1	0	0	0	1	1	0	0	1	0	3	0	0	1	.071	.188
Boggs, W, Bos*	.077	4	13	0	1	1	0	0	0	0	0	0	0	0	0	1	1	0	1	.077	.077
Trammell, A, Det	.308	3	13	4	4	5	1	0	0	4	0	1	0	0	0	0	0	0	0	.385	.286
Williams, K, Det-Tor	.077	15	13	0	1	1	0	0	0	2	0	0	1	2	0	5	4	1	0	.077	.235
Robidoux, B, Bos*	.167	4	12	0	2	2	0	0	0	0	0	0	1	1	0	5	0	0	0	.167	.286
Lemon, C, Det	.091	6	11	4	1	1	0	0	0	3	0	0	0	0	0	4	0	0	1	.091	.154
Vaughn, G, Mil	.091	8	11	1	1	2	1	0	0	1	0	0	0	4	0	3	0	0	0	.182	.333
Canseco, O, Oak	.111	4	9	1	1	1	0	0	0	0	0	0	0	1	0	4	0	0	1	.111	.200
Plantier, P, Bos*	.111	2	9	0	1	2	1	0	0	0	0	0	1	2	0	0	0	0	0	.222	.333
Griffey Jr., K, Sea*	.333	3	9	2	1	1	0	0	0	0	0	0	0	1	0	4	0	0	0	.111	.333
Haselman, B, Tex	.125	2	8	4	1	1	0	0	0	0	0	0	0	1	0	0	0	0	0	.125	.222
Martinez, E, Sea	.125	3	8	2	1	1	0	0	0	2	0	0	0	1	0	0	0	0	0	.125	.222
Moses, J, Min†	.500	10	8	0	4	4	0	0	0	1	0	0	0	0	0	0	1	0	0	.500	.556
Sojo, L, Tor	.125	3	8	0	1	5	0	0	1	1	0	0	0	1	0	3	0	0	0	.625	.500
Brown, M, Bal	.000	4	7	0	0	0	0	0	0	0	0	0	0	1	0	0	0	0	0	.125	.222
Eisenreich, J, KC*	.000	2	7	0	0	0	0	0	0	0	0	0	0	0	0	0	0	0	1	.000	.000
Franco, J, Tex	.143	3	7	1	1	2	1	0	0	2	0	0	0	4	0	1	1	0	0	.286	.125
Nixon, D, Bal	.286	3	7	0	2	2	0	0	0	1	0	0	0	1	0	1	3	0	1	.286	.455
Javier, S, Oak†	.167	2	6	1	1	1	0	0	0	0	0	0	0	2	0	3	1	1	0	.167	.375
Ortiz, J, Min	.167	3	6	0	1	1	0	0	0	2	0	0	0	1	0	1	0	0	0	.167	.167
Worthington, C, Bal	.000	2	6	0	0	0	0	0	0	0	0	0	0	2	0	3	0	0	0	.000	.375
Blankenship, L, Oak	.000	6	5	1	0	0	0	0	0	2	0	0	0	1	0	1	2	1	0	.000	.143
Blowers, M, NY	.400	2	5	2	2	5	0	0	1	0	0	0	0	0	0	3	0	0	0	1.000	.400
Coachman, P, Cal	.000	2	5	0	0	0	0	0	0	1	0	0	1	0	0	2	0	0	1	.000	.000
Heath, M, Det	.200	2	5	0	1	2	1	0	0	0	0	0	0	0	0	1	0	0	0	.400	.200

Player, Club	AVG	G	AB	R	H	TB	2B	3B	HR	RBI	SH	SF	HP	BB	IBB	SO	SB	CS	GIDP	SLG	OBP
Reed, J, Bos.	.400	1	5	0	2	2	0	0	0	0	0	0	0	0	0	0	0	0	0	.400	.400
Rowland, R, Det.	.200	2	5	2	1	1	0	0	0	0	0	0	0	1	0	1	0	0	0	.200	.333
Shelby, J, Det.	.400	5	5	1	2	2	0	0	0	0	0	0	0	0	0	0	0	0	0	.400	.400
Wilson, W, KC†	.400	1	5	1	2	2	0	0	0	0	0	0	0	0	0	0	1	0	0	.400	.400
Felix, J, Tor†	.250	1	4	1	1	1	0	0	0	0	0	0	0	0	0	2	0	0	0	.250	.250
Gladden, D, Min.	.000	2	4	2	0	0	0	0	0	1	0	0	0	1	0	1	0	0	0	.000	.200
Mack, S, Min.	.500	4	4	0	2	2	0	0	0	0	0	0	0	0	0	0	0	0	0	.500	.500
Martinez, C, Chi.	.000	3	4	0	0	0	0	0	0	2	0	0	0	1	0	2	0	0	0	.000	.200
Munoz, P, Min.	.000	1	4	0	0	0	0	0	0	0	0	0	0	0	0	0	0	0	0	.000	.000
Parrish, L, Cal.	.500	1	4	1	2	4	2	0	0	1	0	0	0	0	0	0	0	0	0	1.000	.500
Ray, J, Cal†	.250	1	4	1	1	1	0	0	0	0	0	0	0	0	0	0	0	0	1	.250	.250
Salas, M, Det*	.000	3	4	0	0	0	0	0	0	0	0	0	0	0	0	3	0	0	0	.000	.000
Springer, S, Cle.	.000	1	4	0	0	0	0	0	0	0	0	0	0	0	0	0	0	0	0	.000	.000
Virgil, O, Tor.	.333	1	3	2	1	1	0	0	0	2	0	0	0	0	0	2	0	0	0	.333	.333
Braggs, G, Mil.	.000	2	3	0	0	0	0	0	0	0	0	0	0	0	0	0	0	0	0	.000	.000
Briley, G, Sea*	.333	4	3	0	1	1	0	0	0	1	0	0	0	1	0	1	0	1	0	.333	.429
Cotto, H, Sea.	.667	3	3	0	2	3	1	0	0	0	0	0	0	0	0	0	1	0	0	1.000	.667
Devereaux, M, Bal.	.333	3	3	1	1	1	0	0	0	0	0	0	0	1	0	2	0	1	0	.333	.500
Gallagher, D, Chi-Bal.	.333	6	3	2	1	1	0	0	0	4	0	0	0	0	0	0	1	2	0	.333	.333
Hamilton, D, Mil*	.000	9	3	0	0	0	0	0	0	1	0	0	1	0	0	0	0	0	0	.000	.250
Incaviglia, P, Tex.	.333	3	3	0	1	2	1	0	0	1	0	0	0	0	0	2	0	0	1	.667	.333
Lawless, T, Tor.	.667	2	3	2	2	3	1	0	0	0	0	0	0	0	0	0	1	0	0	1.000	.667
Morman, R, KC.	.000	5	3	2	0	0	0	0	0	0	0	0	0	2	0	2	0	0	0	.000	.400
Romero, E, Det.	.333	1	3	0	1	1	0	0	0	2	0	0	0	0	0	0	0	0	0	.333	.333
Velarde, R, NY.	.667	3	3	2	2	3	1	0	0	2	0	0	0	0	0	1	0	0	1	1.000	.667
Yount, R, Mil.	.500	3	2	0	1	2	1	0	0	2	0	0	0	0	0	0	0	0	0	1.000	.500
Bosley, T, Tex*	.500	4	2	2	1	1	0	0	0	0	0	0	0	0	0	0	0	2	0	.500	.500
Liriano, N, Min†	.500	2	2	2	1	1	0	0	0	0	0	0	0	0	0	0	0	0	0	.500	.500
Lyons, S, Chi*	.000	3	2	0	0	0	0	0	0	0	0	0	0	0	0	2	0	0	0	.000	.000
McGee, W, Oak†	.500	1	2	0	1	1	0	0	0	0	1	0	0	0	0	1	0	0	0	.500	.500
McKnight, J, Bal†	.000	1	2	1	0	0	0	0	0	0	0	0	0	2	0	0	0	0	0	.000	.500
Pettis, G, Tex†	.000	2	2	0	0	0	0	0	0	0	0	0	0	2	0	0	1	0	0	.000	.500
Romine, K, Bos.	.000	1	2	0	0	0	0	0	0	0	0	0	0	0	0	0	0	0	0	.000	.000
Whiten, M, Tor†	.000	2	2	0	0	0	0	0	0	0	0	0	0	2	0	0	0	0	0	.000	.500
Afenir, M, Oak.	.000	1	1	0	0	0	0	0	0	0	0	0	0	0	0	1	0	0	0	.000	.000
Azocar, O, NY*	.000	1	1	0	0	0	0	0	0	0	0	0	0	0	0	0	0	0	0	.000	.000
Borders, P, Tor.	.000	1	1	0	0	0	0	0	0	0	0	0	0	0	0	0	0	0	0	.000	.000
Espy, C, Tex†	.000	4	1	0	0	0	0	0	0	0	0	0	0	0	0	1	0	0	0	.000	.000
Fryman, T, Det.	.000	1	1	0	0	0	0	0	0	0	0	0	0	0	0	0	0	0	0	.000	.000
Gallego, M, Oak.	.000	1	1	0	0	0	0	0	0	0	0	0	0	0	0	1	0	0	0	.000	.000
Geren, R, NY.	1.000	1	1	1	1	1	0	0	0	0	0	0	0	0	0	0	0	0	0	1.000	1.000
Gruber, K, Tor.	1.000	1	1	0	1	3	0	1	0	3	0	0	0	0	0	0	0	0	0	3.000	1.000
Hill, D, Cal†	.000	1	1	0	0	0	0	0	0	0	0	0	0	0	0	0	0	0	0	.000	.000
Honeycutt, R, Oak*	.000	6	1	3	0	0	0	0	0	0	0	0	0	0	0	0	2	0	0	.000	.000
Jefferson, S, Bal-Cle†	.000	3	1	1	0	0	0	0	0	0	0	0	0	0	0	0	0	0	0	.000	.000
Jeltz, S, KC†	.000	1	1	0	0	0	0	0	0	1	0	0	0	0	0	0	0	0	0	.000	.000
Karkovice, R, Chi.	1.000	2	1	0	1	1	0	0	0	0	0	0	0	0	0	0	0	0	0	1.000	1.000
Komminsk, B, Bal.	.000	1	1	0	0	0	0	0	0	0	0	0	0	0	0	1	0	1	0	.000	.000
Kutcher, R, Bos.	.000	5	1	3	0	0	0	0	0	0	0	0	0	1	0	1	0	0	0	.000	.500
Manrique, F, Min.	.000	1	1	0	0	0	0	0	0	0	0	0	0	0	0	0	0	0	0	.000	.000

Player, Club	AVG	G	AB	R	H	TB	2B	3B	HR	RBI	SH	SF	HP	BB	IBB	SO	SB	CS	GI DP	SLG	OBP
McGwire, M, Oak	.000	2	1	1	0	0	0	0	0	0	0	0	0	1	1	0	0	0	0	.000	.500
Schulz, J, KC*	.000	1	1	0	0	0	0	0	0	0	0	0	0	0	0	0	0	0	0	.000	.000
Stone, J, Bos*	1.000	2	1	0	1	1	0	0	0	1	0	0	0	0	0	0	0	0	0	1.000	1.000
Ward, T, Cle†	.000	1	1	1	0	0	0	0	0	0	0	0	0	0	0	0	0	0	0	.000	.000
Webster, M, Cle†	.000	3	1	0	0	0	0	0	0	1	0	0	0	1	0	1	0	0	0	.000	.500
Whitaker, L, Det*	.000	1	1	0	0	0	0	0	0	0	0	0	0	0	0	1	0	0	0	.000	.000
Barrett, M, Bos	.000	1	0	0	0	0	0	0	0	0	0	0	0	0	0	0	0	0	0	.000	.000
Boston, D, Chi*	.000	3	0	0	0	0	0	0	0	0	0	0	0	0	0	0	1	0	0	.000	.000
Brookens, T, Cle	.000	1	0	0	0	0	0	0	0	0	0	0	0	0	0	0	0	0	0	.000	.000
Canale, G, Mil*	.000	3	0	1	0	0	0	0	0	0	0	0	0	0	0	0	0	0	0	.000	1.000
Felder, M, Mil†	.000	1	0	0	0	0	0	0	0	0	0	0	0	1	0	0	1	0	0	.000	1.000
Finley, S, Bal*	.000	2	0	0	0	0	0	0	0	0	0	0	0	0	0	0	1	0	0	.000	.000
Johnson, L, Chi*	.000	1	0	0	0	0	0	0	0	0	1	0	0	0	0	0	0	0	0	.000	.000
Lewis, D, Oak	.000	2	0	0	0	0	0	0	0	0	0	0	0	0	0	0	0	0	0	.000	.000
McCray, R, Chi	.000	7	0	3	0	0	0	0	0	0	0	0	0	0	0	0	2	1	0	.000	.000
Pecota, B, KC	.000	2	0	0	0	0	0	0	0	0	0	0	0	1	0	0	0	0	0	.000	1.000
Quirk, J, Oak*	.000	1	0	0	0	0	0	0	0	0	0	0	0	0	0	0	0	0	0	.000	.000
Sanders, D, NY*	.000	4	0	1	0	0	0	0	0	0	0	0	0	1	0	0	1	1	0	.000	1.000
Shumpert, T, KC	.000	3	0	0	0	0	0	0	0	0	0	0	0	0	0	0	0	0	0	.000	.000
Tolleson, W, NY†	.000	5	0	1	0	0	0	0	0	0	0	0	0	0	0	0	0	0	0	.000	.000

DESIGNATED HITTERS WITH TWO OR MORE CLUBS

Player, Club	AVG	G	AB	R	H	TB	2B	3B	HR	RBI	SH	SF	HP	BB	IBB	SO	SB	CS	GI DP	SLG	OBP
Baines, H, Tex*	.296	95	311	41	92	143	10	1	13	42	0	3	0	44	8	60	0	1	13	.460	.380
Baines, H, Oak*	.258	30	93	11	24	38	5	0	3	19	0	3	0	20	1	17	0	2	4	.409	.379
Kittle, R, Chi	.242	54	190	20	46	87	8	0	11	28	0	1	2	20	1	55	0	0	1	.458	.319
Kittle, R, Bal	.156	13	45	3	7	12	2	0	1	2	0	0	1	1	0	10	0	0	3	.267	.191
Nokes, M, Det*	.217	24	60	7	13	22	3	0	2	5	0	1	1	1	0	8	0	0	3	.367	.238
Nokes, M, NY*	.220	30	82	6	18	25	1	0	2	9	0	0	4	10	1	10	1	1	3	.305	.333
Jones, T, Det	.156	20	45	5	7	17	1	0	3	3	0	0	2	1	0	5	0	1	2	.378	.208
Jones, T, Sea	.286	5	21	3	6	9	0	0	1	3	0	0	0	1	0	3	0	0	1	.429	.318
Coles, D, Sea	.000	1	1	0	0	0	0	0	0	0	0	0	0	0	0	0	0	0	0	.000	.000
Coles, D, Det	.190	30	63	7	12	14	2	0	0	2	0	1	0	7	0	6	0	3	2	.222	.268
Polonia, L, NY*	.333	4	15	3	5	5	0	0	0	3	1	0	0	0	0	1	0	0	0	.333	.313
Polonia, L, Cal*	.333	11	45	4	15	16	1	0	0	3	0	1	0	1	0	5	2	3	1	.356	.340
Phelps, K, Oak*	.158	15	38	1	6	7	1	0	0	4	0	1	0	11	1	7	0	0	1	.184	.340
Phelps, K, Cle*	.105	6	19	4	2	2	0	0	0	0	0	0	0	3	0	3	0	0	0	.105	.227
Winfield, D, NY	.240	7	25	3	6	15	3	0	2	3	0	1	1	1	0	6	0	0	1	.600	.259
Winfield, D, Cal	.364	3	11	3	4	8	1	0	1	2	0	0	0	4	0	3	0	0	1	.727	.533
Walker, D, Chi*	.000	1	2	0	0	0	0	0	0	0	0	0	0	0	0	1	0	0	0	.000	.000
Walker, G, Bal*	.156	11	32	2	5	5	0	0	0	2	0	0	1	2	0	7	1	0	2	.156	.229
Bradley, P, Bal	.000	2	3	1	0	0	0	0	0	0	0	0	0	1	0	1	0	0	0	.000	.250
Bradley, P, Chi	.136	7	22	4	3	4	0	0	0	2	0	0	0	3	0	2	1	1	1	.182	.240
Williams, K, Det	.000	6	1	2	0	0	0	0	0	0	1	0	0	1	0	1	1	1	0	.000	.500
Williams, K, Tor	.083	9	12	0	1	1	0	0	0	0	0	0	0	0	0	3	3	0	0	.083	.200
Gallagher, D, Chi	.333	4	3	1	1	1	0	0	0	0	0	0	0	0	0	0	1	1	0	.333	.333
Gallagher, D, Bal	.000	2	0	0	0	0	0	0	0	0	0	1	0	0	0	0	0	0	0	.000	.000
Jefferson, S, Bal†	.000	1	1	0	0	0	0	0	0	0	0	0	0	0	0	0	1	0	0	.000	.000
Jefferson, S, Cle†	.000	5	1	3	0	0	0	0	0	0	0	0	0	0	0	0	2	0	0	.000	.000

OFFICIAL AMERICAN LEAGUE FIELDING AVERAGES

CLUB FIELDING

Club	PCT	G	PO	A	E	TC	DP	TP	PB
Toronto	.986	162	4362	1720	86	6168	144	0	14
Oakland	.986	162	4368	1630	87	6085	152	0	14
Baltimore	.985	161	4306	1651	93	6050	151	1	5
Minnesota	.983	162	4307	1705	101	6113	161	2	11
Cleveland	.981	162	4282	1648	117	6047	146	0	14
Boston	.980	162	4326	1743	123	6192	154	0	7
Chicago	.980	162	4348	1706	124	6178	169	0	13
New York	.980	162	4334	1791	126	6251	164	0	27
Kansas City	.980	161	4262	1598	122	5982	161	0	13
Seattle	.979	162	4330	1730	130	6190	152	0	18
Detroit	.979	162	4291	1774	131	6196	178	0	15
Texas	.979	162	4334	1721	133	6188	161	0	35
California	.978	162	4362	1871	142	6375	186	0	15
Milwaukee	.976	162	4335	1737	149	6221	152	0	11
Totals	.981	1133	60547	24025	1664	86236	2231	3	212

INDIVIDUAL FIELDING

(*Throws Lefthanded)

FIRST BASEMEN

Leader, Club	PCT	G	PO	A	E	TC	DP
HRBEK, Min.	.997	120	1057	81	3	1141	100

Player, Club	PCT	G	PO	A	E	TC	DP
Balboni, N.Y.	.984	28	183	7	3	193	23
Bergman, Det. *	.995	27	203	13	1	217	19
Blankenship, Oak.	.000	1	0	0	0	0	0
Bradley, Sea.	1.000	1	2	0	0	2	0
Brett, K.C.	.993	102	865	66	7	938	89
Brock, Mil.	.995	115	885	63	5	953	89
Brookens, Cle.	1.000	2	3	1	0	4	1
Buckner, Bos. *	1.000	15	75	6	0	81	6
Bush, Min. *	1.000	6	12	2	0	14	1
Calderon, Chi.	1.000	2	1	0	0	1	0
Canale, N.Y.	1.000	6	32	4	0	36	1
Cochrane, Sea.	1.000	3	7	1	0	8	0
Coles, Det.	.955	4	18	3	1	22	1
Conine, K.C.	.977	9	39	4	1	44	7
Daugherty, Tex. *	.990	30	175	18	2	195	20
Davis, Sea.	.994	52	435	31	3	469	41
Deer, Mil.	.986	21	130	11	2	143	12
Fielder, Det.	.989	143	1190	111	14	1315	137
Francona, Mil. *	1.000	2	6	0	0	6	1
Gaetti, Min.	1.000	2	23	0	0	23	0
Harper, Min.	1.000	2	13	3	0	16	0
Hassey, Oak.	1.000	3	5	0	0	5	1
Heep, Bos. *	.963	5	23	3	1	27	1
Hernandez, Cle. *	.994	42	340	20	2	362	28
Hill, Cal.	1.000	3	23	2	0	25	5
Hoiles, Bal.	1.000	6	41	2	0	43	5
Horn, Bal. *	.970	10	58	6	2	66	7
Howell, Cal.	1.000	1	2	0	0	2	0
Howitt, Oak.	1.000	5	18	1	0	19	3
Hrbek, Min.	.997	120	1057	81	3	1141	100
Jacoby, Cle.	.997	78	584	28	2	614	61
James, Cle. *	.996	35	228	17	1	246	21
Jennings, Oak. *	1.000	4	28	0	0	28	5
Joyner, Cal. *	.995	83	727	62	4	793	78
Kittle, Chi.-Bal.	.989	30	176	6	2	184	19
Lancellotti, Bos. *	1.000	2	20	2	0	22	3
Lansford, Oak.	1.000	5	28	1	0	29	2
Larkin, Min.	.992	28	222	13	2	237	28
Lindeman, Det.	1.000	1	5	0	0	5	0
Lyons, Chi.	.991	61	206	19	2	227	26
Maas, N.Y. *	.983	57	486	35	9	530	45
Manto, Cle.	.990	25	179	18	2	199	18
Marshall, Bos.	1.000	8	42	7	0	49	5
C. Martinez, Chi.	.988	82	632	38	8	678	50
T. Martinez, Sea.	1.000	23	155	12	0	167	25

Player, Club	PCT	G	PO	A	E	TC	DP
Mattingly, N.Y. *	.997	89	800	78	3	881	81
McGriff, Tor. *	.996	147	1246	126	6	1378	119
McGwire, Oak.	.997	154	1329	95	5	1429	126
McKnight, Bal.	1.000	15	89	11	0	100	9
Melvin, Bal.	1.000	1	1	1	0	2	0
Milligan, Bal.	.990	98	846	87	9	942	94
Molitor, Mil.	.986	37	325	25	5	355	28
Morman, K.C.	1.000	3	19	3	0	22	1
Moses, Min. *	1.000	6	5	0	0	5	0
Mulliniks, Tor.	1.000	3	11	0	0	11	1
O'Brien, Sea. *	.995	97	850	76	5	931	68
Olerud, Tor. *	.986	18	133	10	2	145	10
Palacios, K.C.	1.000	7	8	0	0	8	1
Palmeiro, Tex. *	.995	146	1215	91	7	1313	123
Parker, Mil.	.960	3	24	0	1	25	4
Parrish, Cal.	1.000	4	34	2	0	36	6
Pecota, K.C.	1.000	4	19	1	0	20	2
Pena, Bos. *	1.000	1	2	0	0	2	0
Perry, K.C.	.986	51	394	40	6	440	41
Phelps, Oak.-Cle. *	.992	19	111	10	1	122	7
Quintana, Bos.	.987	148	1188	137	17	1342	116
Quirk, Oak.	1.000	8	13	0	0	13	0
Robidoux, Bos.	.981	11	49	4	1	54	4
Russell, Tex.	1.000	3	8	0	0	8	0
Schroeder, Cal.	1.000	3	26	3	0	29	0
Schu, Cal.	.989	15	85	4	1	90	7
Segui, Bal. *	.990	36	283	26	3	312	24
Sorrento, Min.	.992	15	118	7	1	126	14
Stanley, Tex.	1.000	6	14	1	0	15	2
Steinbach, Oak.	1.000	3	5	0	0	5	0
Stevens, Cal. *	.994	67	597	36	4	637	62
Sveum, Mil.	1.000	5	17	0	0	17	1
Tabler, K.C.	1.000	5	31	1	0	32	6
Tettleton, Bal.	.971	5	32	2	1	35	1
Thomas, Chi.	.989	51	428	26	5	459	53
Valle, Sea.	1.000	1	2	0	0	2	0
Ventura, Chi.	.000	1	0	0	0	0	0
Walker, Bal.	1.000	1	14	1	0	15	2
Ward, Det.	1.000	2	7	0	0	7	0
Webster, Cle. *	.895	3	15	2	2	19	2

TRIPLE PLAYS: Hrbek, Min. 2; Horn, Bal.

FIRST BASEMEN WITH TWO OR MORE CLUBS

Player, Club	PCT	G	PO	A	E	TC	DP
Kittle, Chi.	.987	25	150	5	2	157	18
Kittle, Bal.	1.000	5	26	1	0	27	1
Phelps, Oak. *	.964	5	24	3	1	28	3
Phelps, Cle. *	1.000	14	87	7	0	94	4

SECOND BASEMEN

Leader, Club	PCT	G	PO	A	E	TC	DP
LEE, Tor.	.993	112	259	286	4	549	65

Player, Club	PCT	G	PO	A	E	TC	DP
Anderson, Cal.	.955	5	10	11	1	22	2

SECOND BASEMEN—Continued

Player, Club	PCT	G	PO	A	E	TC	DP
Baerga, Cle.	.898	8	22	22	5	49	8
Baker, Min.	1.000	3	1	2	0	3	0
Barrett, Bos.	.992	60	90	147	2	239	27
Bates, Mil.	.962	14	18	33	2	53	6
Blankenship, Oak.	1.000	20	20	32	0	52	7
Bordick, Oak.	1.000	7	2	4	0	6	0
Brookens, Cle.	.989	21	40	48	1	89	14
Brown, Bal.	1.000	3	1	1	0	2	0
Browne, Cle.	.985	139	286	382	10	678	69
Brumley, Sea.	1.000	6	3	7	0	10	3
Buechele, Tex.	1.000	4	2	3	0	5	0
Cerone, N.Y.	1.000	1	2	0	0	2	0
Coachman, Cal.	.857	2	1	5	1	7	1
Diaz, Mil.	.945	15	23	29	3	55	7
Disarcina, Cal.	1.000	3	3	8	0	11	1
Espy, Tex.	.000	1	0	0	0	0	0
Felder, Mil.	1.000	1	2	0	0	2	0
Fermin, Cle.	1.000	1	1	2	0	3	0
Fletcher, Chi.	.988	151	305	436	9	750	115
Franco, Tex.	.975	152	310	444	19	773	101
Gallego, Oak.	.990	83	153	258	4	415	48
Gantner, Mil.	.982	80	164	220	7	391	54
Giles, Sea.	1.000	2	6	5	0	11	2
Gonzales, Bal.	.994	43	61	94	1	156	19
Grebeck, Chi.	1.000	6	6	12	0	18	2
Hale, Min.	1.000	1	2	6	0	8	2
Hemond, Oak.	.000	1	0	0	0	0	0
Hill, Cal.	.990	60	128	173	3	304	48
Hulett, Bal.	.986	16	27	45	1	73	11
Huson, Tex.	1.000	12	14	20	0	34	5
Jeltz, K.C.	.977	34	28	57	2	87	12
Kunkel, Tex.	1.000	13	12	18	0	30	3
Kutcher, Bos.	1.000	5	8	11	0	19	2
Lawless, Tor.	1.000	1	4	1	0	5	1
Lee, Tor.	.993	112	259	286	4	549	65
Liriano, Tor.-Mn.	.975	99	176	260	11	447	53
Lyons, Chi.	.951	15	29	29	3	61	6
Manrique, Min.	.974	67	104	155	7	266	40
McKnight, Bal.	1.000	5	8	8	0	16	1
McLemore, Cal-Cle	1.000	11	21	22	0	43	6
Molitor, Mil.	.988	60	136	190	4	330	36
Naehring, Bos.	.000	1	0	0	0	0	0
Newman, Min.	.993	89	118	173	2	293	48
Pankovits, Bos.	.000	2	0	0	0	0	0
Paredes, Det.	.917	4	4	7	1	12	2
Pecota, K.C.	.986	50	82	122	3	207	21
Petralli, Tex.	1.000	3	2	2	0	4	2
Phillips, Det.	.996	47	91	135	1	227	37
Polidor, Mil.	1.000	2	1	2	0	3	0
Puckett, Min.	.000	1	0	0	0	0	0
Randolph, Oak.	.982	84	148	240	7	395	62
Ray, Cal.	.987	100	241	295	7	543	82
Reed, Bos.	.990	119	215	374	6	595	82
Reynolds, Sea.	.978	160	330	499	19	848	110
Ripken, Bal.	.987	127	250	366	8	624	84
Rivera, Bos.	1.000	3	1	0	0	1	0
Rose, Cal.	1.000	4	1	2	0	3	0
Sax, N.Y.	.987	154	292	457	10	759	102
Schaefer, Sea.	1.000	3	1	1	0	2	1
Schu, Cal.	.750	1	3	3	2	8	0
Seitzer, K.C.	.974	10	18	19	1	38	5
Shumpert, K.C.	.977	27	56	74	3	133	15
Sojo, Tor.	.969	15	16	15	1	32	3
Sveum, Mil.	.981	16	22	30	1	53	6
Tolleson, N.Y.	1.000	13	14	14	0	28	4
Velarde, N.Y.	.833	3	0	5	1	6	1
Walewander, N.Y.	1.000	2	3	2	0	5	0
Whitaker, Det.	.991	130	286	372	6	664	98
White, K.C.	.978	79	142	218	8	368	51

TRIPLE PLAYS: Newman, Min. 2.

SECOND BASEMEN WITH TWO OR MORE CLUBS

Player, Club	PCT	G	PO	A	E	TC	DP
Liriano, Tor.	.983	49	93	132	4	229	26
Liriano, Min.	.968	50	83	128	7	218	27
McLemore, Cal.	1.000	8	14	15	0	29	3
McLemore, Cle.	1.000	3	7	7	0	14	3

THIRD BASEMEN

Leader, Club	PCT	G	PO	A	E	TC	DP
LANSFORD, Oak.	.970	126	100	194	9	303	22

Player, Club	PCT	G	PO	A	E	TC	DP
Anderson, Cal.	.944	16	12	39	3	54	3
Baerga, Cle.	.944	50	33	101	8	142	9
Barrett, Bos.	1.000	1	0	1	0	1	1
Berry, K.C.	.944	8	7	10	1	18	2
Blankenship, Oak.	.947	28	17	37	3	57	2
Blowers, N.Y.	.899	45	26	63	10	99	4
Boggs, Bos.	.946	152	108	241	20	369	18
Bordick, Oak.	1.000	10	2	3	0	5	0
Bradley, Sea.	1.000	5	3	6	0	9	0
Brett, K.C.	1.000	1	1	0	0	1	0
Brookens, Cle.	.923	35	9	51	5	65	4
Brown, Bal.	1.000	2	0	2	0	2	0
Brumley, Sea.	.750	3	1	5	2	8	0
Buechele, Tex.	.966	88	70	157	8	235	7
Coachman, Cal.	.958	9	5	18	1	24	3
Cochrane, Sea.	1.000	3	1	8	0	9	0
Coles, Sea.-Det.	.870	14	8	39	7	54	2
Coolbaugh, Tex.	.941	66	42	118	10	170	12
Diaz, Mil.	1.000	7	1	5	0	6	0
Felder, Mil.	1.000	1	0	1	0	1	0
Fryman, Det	.915	48	23	95	11	129	12
Gaetti, Min.	.959	151	102	318	18	438	36
Gallego, Oak.	.882	27	10	35	6	51	4
Gantner, Mil.	.920	9	3	20	2	25	2
Giles, Sea.	1.000	1	0	3	0	3	1
Gomez, Bal.	.886	12	11	20	4	35	2
Gonzales, Bal.	.929	16	3	10	1	14	1
Grebeck, Chi.	.987	35	17	58	1	76	3
Gruber, Tor.	.955	145	123	280	19	422	21
Harper, Min.	1.000	3	1	2	0	3	0
Hemond, Oak.	1.000	7	2	5	0	7	0
Hill, Cal.	.891	21	8	33	5	46	4
Howell, Cal.	.939	102	70	193	17	280	18
Howitt, Oak.	.000	1	0	0	0	0	0
Hrbek, Min.	1.000	1	0	2	0	2	0
Hulett, Bal.	.961	24	17	56	3	76	4
Huson, Tex.	.955	36	12	30	2	44	2
Jacoby, Cle.	.981	99	44	158	4	206	14
Jeltz, K.C.	1.000	3	1	1	0	2	0
Kunkel, Tex.	.950	15	10	28	2	40	3
Kutcher, Bos.	1.000	11	6	15	0	21	0
Lansford, Oak.	.970	126	100	194	9	303	22
Lawless, Tor.	.800	4	1	3	1	5	0
Leius, Min.	.000	1	0	0	0	0	0
Leyritz, N.Y.	.929	69	43	101	11	155	5
Lyons, Chi.	1.000	5	0	4	0	4	1
Manto, Cle.	1.000	5	6	6	0	12	0
Martinez, Sea.	.928	143	89	259	27	375	16
McLemore, Cle.	1.000	4	1	2	0	3	1
Molitor, Mil.	.900	2	2	7	1	10	1
Mulliniks, Tor.	.949	22	12	25	2	39	4
Naehring, Bos.	.923	5	3	9	1	13	1
Newman, Min.	.945	28	13	39	3	55	8
Palacios, K.C.	1.000	3	1	1	0	2	0
Pecota, K.C.	1.000	11	5	15	0	20	2
Petralli, Tex.	1.000	7	1	1	0	2	0
Phillips, Det.	.931	104	69	200	20	289	16
Polidor, Mil.	1.000	14	1	10	0	11	0
Puckett, Min.	1.000	1	0	0	0	0	0
Quinlan, Tor.	1.000	1	0	1	0	1	0
Quirk, K.C.	.833	8	4	1	1	6	1
Rivera, Bos.	.000	1	0	0	0	0	0
Romero, Det.	.982	27	15	41	1	57	9
Rose, Cal.	1.000	3	2	5	0	7	1
Russell, Tex.	.000	1	0	0	0	0	0
Salas, Det.	1.000	1	0	1	0	1	0
Schaefer, Sea.	.933	26	17	39	4	60	6
Schu, Cal.	.918	38	16	74	8	98	9
Seitzer, K.C.	.953	152	100	262	18	380	31

THIRD BASEMEN—Continued

Player, Club	PCT	G	PO	A	E	TC	DP
Sheffield, Mil.	.934	125	98	254	25	377	16
Sojo, Tor.	.875	4	2	5	1	8	1
Springer, Cle.	1.000	3	2	3	0	5	0
Stanley, Tex.	1.000	8	3	4	0	7	0
Surhoff, Mil.	.867	11	4	9	2	15	1
Sveum, Mil.	.918	22	17	28	4	49	2
Tabler, K.C.	.875	6	2	5	1	8	0
Tolleson, N.Y.	.000	3	0	0	0	0	0
Velarde, N.Y.	.945	74	43	128	10	181	11

Player, Club	PCT	G	PO	A	E	TC	DP
Ventura, Chi.	.939	147	116	268	25	409	32
Walewander, N.Y.	1.000	2	1	1	0	2	0
Worthington, Bal.	.945	131	90	218	18	326	28

TRIPLE PLAYS: Gaetti, Min. 2.

THIRD BASEMEN WITH TWO OR MORE CLUBS

Player, Club	PCT	G	PO	A	E	TC	DP
Coles, Sea.	.815	6	2	20	5	27	0
Coles, Det.	.926	8	6	19	2	27	2

SHORTSTOPS

Leader, Club	PCT	G	PO	A	E	TC	DP
C. RIPKEN, Balt.	.996	161	242	435	3	680	94

Player, Club	PCT	G	PO	A	E	TC	DP
Anderson, Cal.	.964	28	53	79	5	137	21
Baerga, Cle.	.942	48	24	41	4	69	10
Bell, Bal.	1.000	1	1	1	0	2	0
Bordick, Oak.	1.000	9	5	1	0	6	0
Brookens, Cle.	1.000	3	5	4	0	9	1
Brumley, Sea.	.983	47	58	111	3	172	23
Cochrane, Sea.	1.000	5	0	1	0	1	0
Diaz, Mil.	.950	65	101	163	14	278	36
Disarcina, Cal.	.940	14	14	49	4	67	8
Espinoza, N.Y.	.977	150	268	447	17	732	100
Fermin, Cle.	.975	147	213	421	16	650	81
Fernandez, Tor.	.989	161	297	480	9	786	93
Fryman, Det.	.961	17	24	50	3	77	9
Gaetti, Min.	1.000	2	0	1	0	1	0
Gagne, Min.	.976	135	184	377	14	575	62
Gallego, Oak.	.977	38	43	86	3	132	26
Giles, Sea.	.978	37	51	80	3	134	25
Gonzales, Bal.	1.000	9	4	10	0	14	3
Grebeck, Chi.	.953	16	13	28	2	43	5
Green, Tex.	.972	58	61	112	5	178	27
Guillen, Chi.	.977	159	252	474	17	743	100
Heath, Det.	1.000	1	1	0	0	1	0
Hill, Cal.	.965	24	35	47	3	85	7
Howell, Cal.	.875	1	4	3	1	8	0
Huson, Tex.	.960	119	157	254	17	428	69
Jeltz, K.C.	.969	23	23	39	2	64	9
Kunkel, Tex.	.958	67	77	126	9	212	28

Player, Club	PCT	G	PO	A	E	TC	DP
Lee, Tor.	1.000	9	6	15	0	21	1
Leius, Min.	1.000	12	20	25	0	45	10
Liriano, Min.	.000	1	0	0	0	0	0
Lyons, Chi.	1.000	1	0	1	0	1	0
McKnight, Bal.	1.000	1	1	1	0	2	1
McLemore, Cle.	.882	8	15	15	4	34	3
Naehring, Bos.	.918	19	33	57	8	98	12
Newman, Min.	.949	48	57	92	8	157	25
Pecota, K.C.	.981	21	44	57	2	103	19
Phillips, Det.	.978	11	12	33	1	46	9
Polidor, Mil.	1.000	2	0	1	0	1	0
Puckett, Min.	.000	1	0	0	0	0	0
Reed, Bos.	.944	50	63	104	10	177	21
C. Ripken, Bal.	.996	161	242	435	3	680	94
Rivera, Bos.	.965	112	186	310	18	514	69
Santana, Cle.	1.000	7	2	9	0	11	2
Schaefer, Sea.	.988	24	34	47	1	82	13
Schofield, Cal.	.966	99	170	318	17	505	77
Snyder, Cle.	.923	5	5	7	1	13	2
Sojo, Tor.	.842	5	6	10	3	19	3
Spiers, Mil.	.976	111	159	326	12	497	72
Stillwell, K.C.	.957	141	181	350	24	555	79
Sveum, Mil.	.889	5	3	5	1	9	1
Tolleson, N.Y.	.983	45	43	72	2	117	22
Trammell, Det.	.979	142	232	409	14	655	102
Velarde, N.Y.	.979	15	21	26	1	48	6
Vizquel, Sea.	.980	81	103	239	7	349	48
Walewander, N.Y.	1.000	1	0	2	0	2	0
Weiss, Oak.	.979	137	194	373	12	579	77

TRIPLE PLAY: C. Ripken, Bal.

OUTFIELDERS

Leader, Club	PCT	G	PO	A	E	TC	DP
EIS'REICH, KC	.996	138	261	6	1	268	3

Player, Club	PCT	G	PO	A	E	TC	DP
Allred, Cle. *	.833	4	5	0	1	6	0
Anderson, Bal. *	.987	63	149	3	2	154	1
Azocar, N.Y. *	.991	57	105	4	1	110	1
Baines, Oak. *	.833	2	5	0	1	6	0
Barfield, N.Y.	.973	151	305	16	9	330	3
Belcher, Tex.	1.000	9	12	0	0	12	0
Bell, Tor.	.979	106	226	4	5	235	1
Belle, Cle.	.000	1	0	0	0	0	0
Bergman, Det. *	.000	5	0	0	0	0	0
Bichette, Cal.	.965	105	183	12	7	202	5
Blankenship, Oak.	.935	28	29	0	2	31	0
Bosley, Tex. *	1.000	9	4	0	0	4	0
Boston, Chi. *	.000	1	0	0	0	0	0
Bradley, Bal.-Chi.	.982	108	219	4	4	227	0
Braggs, Mil.	.965	32	81	1	3	85	0
Brett, K.C.	1.000	9	14	1	0	15	0
Briley, Sea.	.989	107	177	4	2	183	1
Brumley, Sea.	1.000	1	0	1	0	1	0
Brunansky, Bos.	.982	121	267	7	5	279	1
Buhner, Sea.	.966	40	55	1	2	58	0
Burks, Bos.	.994	143	324	7	2	333	0
Bush, Min. *	1.000	32	52	1	0	53	0
Calderon, Chi.	.975	130	268	7	7	282	1
J. Canseco, Oak.	.995	88	182	7	1	190	2
O. Canseco, Oak.	1.000	2	3	0	0	3	0
Castillo, Min.	.923	21	24	0	2	26	0
Cole, Cle. *	.961	59	145	3	6	154	1
Coles, Sea.-Det.	.977	31	43	0	1	44	0
Cotto, Sea.	.990	118	194	4	2	200	1

Player, Club	PCT	G	PO	A	E	TC	DP
Cuyler, Det.	.976	17	38	2	1	41	0
Daugherty, Tex. *	.982	42	50	4	1	55	1
Davis, Cal.	.965	52	77	5	3	85	1
Deer, Mil.	.970	117	243	14	8	265	7
Devereaux, Bal.	.983	104	281	4	5	290	1
Ducey, Tor.	1.000	19	37	0	0	37	0
Dwyer, Min. *	1.000	2	2	0	0	2	0
Eisenreich, K.C. *	.996	138	261	6	1	268	3
Espy, Tex.	1.000	39	56	1	0	57	0
Felder, Mil.	.972	109	165	8	5	178	6
Felix, Tor.	.966	125	244	11	9	264	3
Finley, Cal. *	.977	133	298	4	7	309	1
Gagne, Min.	.000	1	0	0	0	0	0
Gallagher, Chi.-Bal.	.980	57	96	3	2	101	2
Gallego, Oak.	1.000	1	1	0	0	1	0
Gladden, Min.	.980	133	286	12	6	304	3
Gonzales, Bal.	.000	1	0	0	0	0	0
Gonzalez, Tex.	1.000	16	33	0	0	33	0
Greenwell, Bos.	.977	159	287	13	7	307	1
Griffey Jr, Sea. *	.980	151	330	8	7	345	1
Griffey Sr, Sea. *	.963	20	25	1	1	27	0
Gruber, Tor.	1.000	6	6	0	0	6	0
Hall, N.Y. *	.973	50	70	2	2	74	0
Hamilton, Mil.	.992	72	120	1	1	122	0
Heath, Det.	1.000	3	2	0	0	2	0
Heep, Bos. *	1.000	14	19	1	0	20	1
D. Henderson, Oak.	.988	116	319	5	4	328	1
R. Hend'son, Oak *	.983	118	289	5	5	299	0
Hill, Tor.	.983	60	115	4	2	121	0
Howard, Oak.	.933	14	14	0	1	15	0
Howitt, Oak.	1.000	11	16	0	0	16	0
Incaviglia, Tex.	.974	145	290	12	8	310	2

OUTFIELDERS—Continued

Player, Club	PCT	G	PO	A	E	TC	DP
Jackson, K.C.	.952	97	230	8	12	250	2
C. James, Cle.	1.000	14	25	1	0	26	0
D. James, Cle.*	.947	33	54	0	3	57	0
Javier, Oak.	1.000	13	19	0	0	19	0
Jefferson, Bal.-Cle.	.987	39	70	4	1	75	1
Jeltz, K.C.	1.000	13	6	1	0	7	0
Jennings, Oak.*	.984	45	62	1	1	64	0
Johnson, Chi.*	.973	148	353	5	10	368	3
Jones, Det.-Sea.	.973	45	68	3	2	73	0
Jose, Oak.	.977	92	212	5	5	222	1
Kelly, N.Y.	.988	160	420	5	5	430	2
Komminsk, Bal.	1.000	40	67	2	0	69	0
Kunkel, Tex.	1.000	5	2	0	0	2	0
Kutcher, Bos.	1.000	34	41	0	0	41	0
Larkin, Min.	1.000	47	77	5	0	82	1
Lawless, Tor.	1.000	2	6	0	0	6	0
Lemon, Det.	.973	96	209	7	6	222	1
Leonard, Sea.	.983	79	118	0	2	120	0
Lewis, Oak.	1.000	23	33	0	0	33	0
Leyritz, N.Y.	.955	14	19	2	1	22	0
Lindeman, Det.	.000	1	0	0	0	0	0
Lusader, Det.*	.982	42	53	1	1	55	0
Lyons, Chi.	1.000	7	9	0	0	9	0
Mack, Min.	.988	109	230	8	3	241	1
Maldonado, Cle.	.993	134	293	9	2	304	1
Marshall, Bos.	.929	8	13	0	1	14	0
Martinez, Chi.	.000	1	0	0	0	0	0
Mattingly, N.Y.*	.000	1	0	0	0	0	0
McCray, Chi.	1.000	13	8	0	0	8	0
McGee, Oak.	.986	28	72	1	1	74	1
McKnight, Bal.	1.000	8	8	0	0	8	0
McRae, K.C.	1.000	45	120	1	0	121	0
Meulens, N.Y.	.963	23	49	3	2	54	1
Morman, K.C.	1.000	8	8	1	0	9	0
Moseby, Det.	.983	116	288	9	5	302	5
Moses, Min.*	1.000	85	103	2	0	105	0
Munoz, Min.	.972	21	34	1	1	36	1
Newman, Min.	1.000	3	2	0	0	2	0
Nixon, Bal.	1.000	4	5	0	0	5	0
Nokes, N.Y.	1.000	2	1	0	0	1	0
O'Brien, Sea.*	1.000	6	2	0	0	2	0
Orsulak, Bal.*	.989	109	267	5	3	275	2
Palacios, K.C.	.000	1	0	0	0	0	0
Pasqua, Chi.*	.962	43	71	5	3	79	1
Pecota, K.C.	1.000	6	10	0	0	10	0
Pettis, Tex.	.993	128	285	10	2	297	4
Phillips, Det.	.889	8	8	0	1	9	0
Plantier, Bos.	.000	1	0	0	0	0	0
Polonia, Cal.*	.980	85	142	3	3	148	2
Puckett, Min.	.989	141	354	9	4	367	3
Quintana, Bos.	1.000	3	2	0	0	2	0
Quirk, Oak.	.000	1	0	0	0	0	0
Reimer, Tex.	.857	9	12	0	2	14	0
Romine, Bos.	.976	64	81	0	2	83	0
Russell, Tex.	1.000	6	5	0	0	5	0
Sanders, N.Y.*	.973	42	69	2	2	73	1
Schu, Cal.	.000	4	0	0	0	0	0
Schulz, K.C.	.943	22	33	0	2	35	0
Sheets, Det.	.981	79	98	7	2	107	1
Shelby, Det.	.973	68	138	5	4	147	3
Sierra, Tex.	.967	151	283	7	10	300	1
Snyder, Cle.	.975	120	224	11	6	241	2
Sojo, Tor.	1.000	5	10	1	0	11	0
Sosa, Chi.	.962	152	315	14	13	342	1
Tabler, K.C.	.986	42	68	4	1	73	1
Tartabull, K.C.	.965	52	81	1	3	85	0
Tettleton, Bal.	1.000	1	1	0	0	1	0
Thurman, K.C.	1.000	21	32	0	0	32	0
Vaughn, Mil.	.967	106	195	8	7	210	1
Velarde, N.Y.	1.000	5	6	0	0	6	0
Venable, Cal.	.975	77	112	3	3	118	1
G. Ward, Det.	.988	85	157	2	2	161	1
T. Ward, Cle.	.957	13	20	2	1	23	0
Wash'ton, Cal-NY*	1.000	30	61	3	0	64	0
Webster, Cal.*	.991	118	330	1	3	334	0
D. White, Cal.	.972	122	302	11	9	322	4
F. White, K.C.	.000	1	0	0	0	0	0
Whiten, Tor.	1.000	30	60	3	0	63	0
Williams, Det.-Tor.	1.000	77	103	5	0	108	2
M. Wilson, Tor.	.992	141	370	5	3	378	2
W. Wilson, Oak.	1.000	106	187	2	0	189	1
Winfield, N.Y.-Cal.	.989	120	177	7	2	186	1
Yount, Mil.	.991	157	422	3	4	429	0

OUTFIELDERS WITH TWO OR MORE CLUBS

Player, Club	PCT	G	PO	A	E	TC	DP
Bradley, Bal.	.987	70	149	3	2	154	0
Bradley, Chi.	.973	38	70	1	2	73	0
Coles, Sea.	.970	20	32	0	1	33	0
Coles, Det.	1.000	11	11	0	0	11	0
Gallagher, Chi.	.981	37	50	1	1	52	1
Gallagher, Bal.	.980	20	46	2	1	49	1
Jefferson, Bal.	1.000	5	9	0	0	9	0
Jefferson, Cle.	.985	34	61	4	1	66	1
Jones, Det.	.952	27	37	3	2	42	0
Jones, Sea.	1.000	18	31	0	0	31	0
Washington, Cal.*	1.000	9	19	1	0	20	0
Washington, N.Y.*	1.000	21	42	2	0	44	0
Williams, Det.	1.000	47	67	5	0	72	2
Williams, Tor.	1.000	30	36	0	0	36	0
Winfield, N.Y.	1.000	12	12	0	0	12	0
Winfield, Cal.	.989	108	165	7	2	174	1

CATCHERS

Leader, Club	PCT	G	PO	A	E	TC	DP	PB
VALLE, Sea.	.997	104	631	44	2	677	9	9

Player, Club	PCT	G	PO	A	E	TC	DP	PB
Afenir, Cal.	1.000	12	13	0	0	13	0	2
Alomar, Cle.	.981	129	686	46	14	746	6	11
Boone, K.C.	.985	40	243	19	4	266	0	4
Borders, Tor.	.993	115	515	46	4	565	6	6
Bradley, Sea.	.995	63	349	24	2	375	4	8
Cerone, N.Y.	.995	35	177	14	1	192	1	6
Cochrane, Sea.	.000	1	0	0	0	0	0	0
Diaz, Tor.	1.000	9	13	3	0	16	0	0
Dorsett, N.Y.	1.000	9	31	0	0	31	1	0
Fisk, Chi.	.994	116	660	63	4	727	10	11
Gedman, Bos.	.970	9	27	5	1	33	1	0
Geren, N.Y.	.993	107	487	55	4	546	5	10
Harper, Min.	.985	120	672	53	11	736	5	5
Haselman, Tex.	1.000	1	8	0	0	8	0	0
Hassey, Oak.	.997	59	307	18	1	326	2	5
Heath, Det.	.980	117	585	54	13	652	7	8
Hoiles, Bal.	1.000	7	21	4	0	25	1	0
Karkovice, Chi.	.994	64	296	31	2	329	4	2
Kreuter, Tex.	.977	20	39	4	1	44	0	1
Leyritz, N.Y.	.983	11	55	4	1	60	0	4
Macfarlane, KC	.991	112	660	23	6	689	9	7
Marzano, Bos.	1.000	32	153	14	0	167	3	1
Mayne, K.C.	.970	5	29	3	1	33	0	1
McIntosh, Mil.	.875	4	6	1	1	8	0	3
Melvin, Bal.	.997	76	364	25	1	390	2	1
Myers, Tor.	.993	87	411	30	3	444	4	8
Nokes, Det-NY	.993	65	236	34	2	272	6	8
O'Brien, Mil.	.992	46	217	24	2	243	5	3
Ortiz, Min.	1.000	68	247	25	0	272	6	6
Orton, Cal.	.987	31	139	15	2	156	1	1
Palacios, K.C.	.992	27	113	6	1	120	1	1
Parrish, Cal.	.993	131	760	88	6	854	15	12
Pena, Bos.	.995	142	864	74	5	943	13	6
Petralli, Tex.	.991	118	599	43	6	648	5	20
Quirk, Oak.	.977	37	151	17	4	172	3	1
Rowland, Det.	.967	5	29	0	1	30	0	0
Russell, Det.	.980	31	135	11	3	149	0	4
Salas, Det.	.988	57	227	22	3	252	3	6
Schroeder, Cal.	1.000	15	74	7	0	81	2	1
Sinatro, Sea.	.992	28	112	16	1	129	1	1
Skinner, Cle.	.996	49	222	16	1	239	3	3
Stanley, Tex.	.985	63	244	20	4	268	0	10
Steinbach, Oak.	.988	83	396	31	5	432	1	6
Surhoff, Mil.	.985	125	615	53	10	678	10	5
Tettleton, Bal.	.991	90	425	37	4	466	3	4

CATCHERS—Continued

Player, Club	PCT	G	PO	A	E	TC	DP	PB
Tingley, Cal.	1.000	5	12	0	0	12	0	1
Valle, Sea.	.997	104	631	44	2	677	9	9
Virgil, Tor.	1.000	2	1	0	0	1	0	0
Webster, Min.	1.000	2	9	0	0	9	0	0
Willard, Chi.	.000	1	0	0	0	0	0	0

CATCHERS WITH TWO OR MORE CLUBS

Player, Club	PCT	G	PO	A	E	TC	DP	PB
Nokes, Det.	.984	19	55	7	1	63	1	1
Nokes, N.Y.	.995	46	181	27	1	209	5	7

PITCHERS

Leader, Club	PCT	G	PO	A	E	TC	DP
WELCH, Oak.	1.000	35	20	31	0	51	2

Player, Club	PCT	G	PO	A	E	TC	DP
J. Abbott, Cal.*	.978	33	8	36	1	45	4
P. Abbott, Min.	.800	7	2	2	1	5	1
Acker, Tor.	1.000	59	5	19	0	24	0
Adkins, N.Y.*	1.000	5	0	3	0	3	0
Aguilera, Min.	1.000	56	2	4	0	6	0
Aldred, Det.*	1.000	4	0	2	0	2	0
Aldrich, Bal.	1.000	7	2	1	0	3	0
Alexander, Tex.	1.000	3	1	0	0	1	1
Andersen, Bos.	.667	15	2	0	1	3	0
Anderson, Min.*	1.000	31	7	37	0	44	2
Appier, K.C.	.923	32	15	21	3	39	3
Aquino, K.C.	1.000	20	4	10	0	14	2
Arnsberg, Tex.	1.000	53	5	11	0	16	2
August, Mil.	.750	5	1	2	1	4	0
Bailes, Cal.*	.923	27	2	10	1	13	0
Ballard, Bal.*	.969	44	11	20	1	32	0
Baller, K.C.	.000	3	0	0	0	0	0
Bankhead, Sea.	.000	4	0	0	0	0	0
Barfield, Tex.*	1.000	33	4	7	0	11	0
Bautista, Bal.	1.000	22	1	2	0	3	0
Bearse, Cle*	1.000	3	0	1	0	1	0
Berenguer, Min.	1.000	51	3	5	0	8	0
Bitker, Oak.-Tex.	1.000	6	1	2	0	3	1
Black, Cle.-Tor.*	.976	32	7	33	1	41	2
Blair, Tor.	1.000	27	3	6	0	9	0
Blyleven, Cal.	.964	23	3	24	1	28	0
Boddicker, Bos.	.966	34	29	27	2	58	6
Bohanon, Tex.*	1.000	11	1	10	0	11	2
Bolton, Bos.*	.962	21	4	21	1	26	1
Boone, Bal.*	1.000	4	0	2	0	2	0
Bosio, Mil.	.973	20	12	24	1	37	2
Brown, Tex.	.929	26	15	24	3	42	0
Brown, Mil.*	1.000	5	2	5	0	7	0
Burba, Sea.	.750	6	1	2	1	4	0
Burns, Oak.	1.000	43	2	7	0	9	1
Cadaret, N.Y.*	.971	54	7	27	1	35	1
Campbell, K.C.*	1.000	2	1	0	0	1	0
C'dlra, Mn-To.*	1.000	47	4	9	0	13	0
Candiotti, Cle.	.967	31	22	37	2	61	1
Capel, Mil.	.000	2	0	0	0	0	0
Cary, N.Y.*	.955	28	8	13	1	22	1
Casian, Min.*	1.000	5	0	3	0	3	1
Cerutti, Tor.*	1.000	30	11	18	0	29	2
Chia'parino, Tex.	1.000	6	3	1	0	4	0
Chitren, Oak.	1.000	8	1	2	0	3	0
Clark, Sea.*	1.000	12	1	3	0	4	1
Clear, Cal.	.000	4	0	0	0	0	0
Clemens, Bos.	.961	31	23	26	2	51	1
Codiroli, K.C.	1.000	6	1	0	0	1	0
Comstock, Sea.*	.929	60	2	11	1	14	0
Corbett, Cal.*	.000	4	0	0	0	0	0
Crawford, K.C.	1.000	46	8	13	0	21	0
Crim, Mil.	.957	67	10	12	1	23	1
Cummings, Cle.	1.000	6	1	1	0	2	0
M. Davis, K.C.*	.875	53	1	6	1	8	0
S. Davis, K.C.	.933	21	4	10	1	15	3
DeLucia, Sea.	.833	5	3	2	1	6	0
Dopson, Bos.	1.000	4	1	5	0	6	0
Dotson, K.C.	1.000	8	2	3	0	5	1
Drummond, Min.	.929	35	6	7	1	14	1
DuBois, Bal.*	.800	12	1	3	1	5	1
Eave, Sea.	1.000	8	1	5	0	6	1
Eckersley, Oak.	1.000	63	3	1	0	4	0
Edens, Mil.	.850	35	7	10	3	20	0
Edwards, Chi.*	.952	42	6	14	1	21	1
Eichhorn, Cal.	1.000	60	7	16	0	23	0
Eiland, N.Y.	1.000	5	1	3	0	4	0
Elvira, Mil.*	1.000	4	0	1	0	1	0
Encarnacion, KC.	1.000	4	1	0	0	1	0
Erickson, Min.	1.000	19	10	13	0	23	0
Farr, K.C.	.926	57	7	18	2	27	1
Farrell, Cle.	.909	17	8	12	2	22	1
Fernandez, Chi.	.882	13	3	12	2	17	0
Fetters, Cal.	.952	26	9	11	1	21	0
Filer, Mil.	1.000	7	1	1	0	2	0
Filson, K.C.*	1.000	8	2	3	0	5	0
Finley, Cal.*	.875	32	14	21	5	40	2
Flanagan, Tor.*	.857	5	0	6	1	7	0
Fossas, Mil.*	.625	32	1	4	3	8	0
Fraser, Cal.	1.000	45	2	6	0	8	0
Garces, Min.	1.000	5	0	1	0	1	0
Gardiner, Sea.	1.000	5	1	2	0	3	0
Gardner, Bos.	.938	34	8	7	1	16	1
Gibson, Det.*	1.000	61	9	11	0	20	1
Gilles, Tor.	1.000	2	0	1	0	1	0
Gleaton, Det.*	.923	57	1	11	1	13	0
Gordon, K.C.	.976	32	17	24	1	42	1
Gozzo, Cle.	.000	2	0	0	0	0	0
Grahe, Cal.	1.000	8	2	11	0	13	2
Gray, Bos.	1.000	41	2	5	0	7	1
Guante, Cle.	1.000	26	3	5	0	8	2
Gubicza, K.C.	.950	16	9	10	1	20	3
G'terman, NY*	.926	64	6	19	2	27	1
Guthrie, Min.*	.966	24	5	23	1	29	0
Habyan, N.Y.	1.000	6	2	0	0	2	0
Hanson, Sea.	.926	33	30	20	4	54	0
Harnisch, Bal.	.963	31	12	14	1	27	0
G. A. Harris, Bos	.937	34	23	36	4	63	1
G. W. Harris, Sea	1.000	25	4	2	0	6	1
R. Harris, Oak.	1.000	16	2	3	0	5	1
Harvey, Cal.	1.000	54	3	4	0	7	1
Hawkins, N.Y.	1.000	28	12	9	0	21	3
Heep, Bos.*	.000	1	0	0	0	0	0
Henke, Tor.	1.000	61	6	5	0	11	0
Henneman, Det.	.885	69	7	16	3	26	2
Hesketh, Bos.*	.750	12	0	3	1	4	0
Hetzel, Bos.	1.000	9	2	3	0	5	0
Hibbard, Chi.*	1.000	33	7	29	0	36	2
Hickey, Bal.*	1.000	37	1	4	0	5	0
Higuera, Mil.*	.926	27	7	18	2	27	2
Hill, Cal.	.000	1	0	0	0	0	0
Hillegas, Chi.	1.000	7	2	2	0	4	0
Holman, Sea.	.971	28	16	17	1	34	0
Holton, Bal.	.941	33	6	10	1	17	0
Honeycutt, Oak*	.938	63	0	15	1	16	0
Hoover, Tex.	.000	2	0	0	0	0	0
Hough, Tex.	.955	32	11	31	2	44	2
Irvine, Bos.	1.000	11	1	3	0	4	0
Jackson, Sea.	1.000	63	5	12	0	17	3
Jeffcoat, Tex.*	.933	44	4	10	1	15	3
D. Johnson, Bal.	.920	30	13	10	2	25	1
R. J'nson, Sea.*	.857	33	6	24	5	35	2
B. Jones, Chi.	1.000	65	4	19	0	23	1
D. Jones, Cle.	.818	66	0	9	2	11	0
J. Jones, N.Y.	.857	17	1	5	1	7	1
Kaiser, Cle.*	1.000	5	3	1	0	4	0
Key, Tor.*	.968	27	8	22	1	31	3
Kiecker, Bos.	.957	32	18	27	2	47	1
Kilgus, Tor.*	1.000	11	1	3	0	4	0
King, Chi.	1.000	25	8	15	0	23	1
Kinzer, Det.	.000	1	0	0	0	0	0
Klink, Oak.*	1.000	40	1	1	0	2	0
Knackert, Sea.	.800	24	4	4	2	10	0
Knudson, Mil.	.935	30	13	16	2	31	2
Krueger, Mil.*	1.000	30	2	17	0	19	2
Kutzler, Chi.	1.000	7	2	2	0	4	0
Lamp, Bos.	1.000	47	12	14	0	26	0

PITCHERS—Continued

Player, Club	PCT	G	PO	A	E	TC	DP
Langston, Cal.*	.942	33	7	42	3	52	0
LaPoint, N.Y.*	.935	28	6	23	2	31	3
Leach, Min.	.958	55	12	11	1	24	0
Leary, N.Y.	.926	31	14	36	4	54	4
Lee, Mil.*	1.000	11	1	1	0	2	0
Leister, Bos.	.000	2	0	0	0	0	0
A. Leiter, Tor.*	1.000	4	1	1	0	2	0
M. Leiter, N.Y.	1.000	8	0	8	0	8	1
Lewis, Cal.	1.000	2	0	1	0	1	0
Long, Chi.	1.000	4	1	2	0	3	0
Lovelace, Sea.*	.000	5	0	0	0	0	0
Luecken, Tor.	.000	1	0	0	0	0	0
Lugo, Det.	1.000	13	0	7	0	7	0
Lyons, Chi.	1.000	1	0	1	0	1	0
MacD'ald, Tor*	.000	4	0	0	0	0	0
Machado, Mil.	1.000	10	1	1	0	2	0
Maldonado, K.C.	.000	4	0	0	0	0	0
Manon, Tex.	1.000	1	2	0	0	2	0
McCaskill, Cal.	.941	29	19	29	3	51	2
McClure, Cal.*	1.000	11	0	1	0	1	0
McC'rs, NY-Det	1.000	20	4	2	0	6	0
McDonald, Bal.	.967	21	15	14	1	30	1
McDowell, Chi.	.974	33	17	20	1	38	3
McGaffigan, KC	.917	24	5	6	1	12	0
McMurtry, Tex.	1.000	23	1	8	0	9	3
McW'liams, KC*	1.000	13	0	3	0	3	0
Medvin, Sea.	.750	5	1	2	1	4	0
Melendez, Sea.	.000	3	0	0	0	0	0
Mesa, Bal.	.889	7	3	5	1	9	1
Mielke, Tex.	1.000	33	2	7	0	9	0
Milacki, Bal.	.974	27	21	16	1	38	2
Mills, N.Y.	.867	36	3	10	2	15	0
Minton, Cal.	1.000	11	0	3	0	3	0
Mirabella, Mil.*	.917	44	4	7	1	12	1
Mitchell, Bal.	.929	24	7	19	2	28	3
M'teleone, NY	1.000	5	1	1	0	2	0
M'tgomery, KC	1.000	73	3	13	0	16	0
Moore, Oak.	.981	33	22	31	1	54	1
Morris, Det.	.963	36	38	14	2	54	2
Moses, Min.*	.000	2	0	0	0	0	0
Moyer, Tex.*	1.000	33	6	14	0	20	2
Murphy, Bos.*	.917	68	4	7	1	12	2
Nagy, Cle.	.917	9	3	8	1	12	2
Navarro, Mil.	.967	32	10	19	1	30	2
Nelson, Oak.	.923	51	4	8	1	13	0
Nichols, Cle.	1.000	4	0	4	0	4	0
Nipper, Cle.	1.000	9	1	1	0	2	1
Norris, Oak.	1.000	14	3	3	0	6	0
Nosek, Det.	.000	3	0	0	0	0	0
Nunez, Det.	.923	42	7	5	1	13	1
Olin, Cle.	.900	50	3	24	3	30	1
Olson, Bal.	1.000	64	4	4	0	8	1
Orosco, Cle.*	.938	55	1	14	1	16	1
Otto, Oak.*	1.000	2	0	2	0	2	1
Pall, Chi.	1.000	56	1	11	0	12	2
Parker, NY-Det	1.000	29	5	10	0	15	1
Patterson, Chi.*	.933	43	2	12	1	15	0
M. Perez, Chi.	.960	35	4	20	1	25	0
P. Perez, N.Y.	.000	3	0	0	0	0	0
Peterson, Chi.	.917	20	4	7	1	12	0
Petry, Det.	1.000	32	19	23	0	42	2
Plesac, Mil.*	1.000	66	1	7	0	8	1
Plunk, N.Y.	.913	47	3	18	2	23	2
Powell, Sea-Mil*	1.000	11	2	9	0	11	0
Price, Bal.*	.818	50	1	8	2	11	0
Radinsky, Chi.*	1.000	62	7	4	0	11	0
Reardon, Bos.	.833	47	1	4	1	6	0
Reed, Sea.-Bos.	1.000	33	8	5	0	13	2
Richardson, Cal.	1.000	1	0	1	0	1	0
Righetti, N.Y.*	.800	53	3	1	1	5	0
Ritz, Det.	.857	4	2	4	1	7	0
JD Rob'son, NY	.903	54	5	23	3	31	1
JM Rob'son, Det	.906	27	14	15	3	32	1
R. Robinson, Mil.	1.000	22	17	17	0	34	0
Rochford, Bos.*	.000	2	0	0	0	0	0
Rogers, Tex.*	.931	69	5	22	2	29	1
Ro'nberg, Chi*	1.000	6	1	2	0	3	0
Russell, Tex.	.857	27	1	5	1	7	0
Ryan, Tex.	1.000	30	7	13	0	20	1
Sab'hagen, KC	.978	20	16	28	1	45	2
Sanchez, K.C.*	.667	11	1	1	1	3	0
Sanderson, Oak.	.935	34	11	18	2	31	2
Savage, Min.	1.000	17	0	4	0	4	0
Schilling, Bal.	1.000	35	1	4	0	5	0
Schooler, Sea.	.923	49	3	9	1	13	0
Schwabe, Det.	1.000	1	0	3	0	3	0
Seanez, Cle.	1.000	24	1	1	0	2	0
Searcy, Det.*	1.000	16	3	7	0	10	0
Sebra, Mil.	1.000	10	2	4	0	6	1
Shaw, Cle.	1.000	12	4	7	0	11	0
D. Smith, K.C.	.000	2	0	0	0	0	0
L. Smith, Bos.	1.000	11	0	2	0	2	0
M. Smith, Bal.	.000	2	0	0	0	0	0
R. Smith, Min.	.950	32	10	9	1	20	0
Stewart, Oak.	1.000	36	25	23	0	48	2
Stieb, Tor.	.941	33	24	40	4	68	3
M. St'lemyre, KC	1.000	13	1	5	0	6	0
T. St'lemyre, Tor	.979	33	17	30	1	48	5
Swan, Sea.*	1.000	11	3	7	0	10	0
Swift, Sea.	.939	55	10	21	2	33	1
Swindell, Cle.*	.966	34	8	20	1	29	1
Tanana, Det.*	1.000	34	9	27	0	36	0
Tapani, Min.	.971	28	14	20	1	35	1
Taylor, Bal.	.000	4	0	0	0	0	0
Telford, Bal.	1.000	8	3	5	0	8	0
Terrell, Det.	.917	13	3	8	1	12	1
Thigpen, Chi.	.947	77	10	8	1	19	2
Tibbs, Bal.	1.000	10	6	8	0	14	0
E. Valdez, Cle.*	.833	13	2	3	1	6	0
S. Valdez, Cle.	.905	24	8	11	2	21	1
Veres, Mil.	1.000	26	2	10	0	12	2
Wagner, K.C.	1.000	5	3	3	0	6	1
Walker, Cle.	1.000	18	4	9	0	13	1
Wapnick, Det.	.000	4	0	0	1	1	0
C. Ward, Cle.	1.000	22	3	3	0	6	0
D. Ward, Tor.	.964	73	9	18	1	28	0
Wayne, Min.*	1.000	38	1	4	0	5	1
Wegman, Mil.	.667	8	1	3	2	6	0
Welch, Oak.	1.000	35	20	31	0	51	2
Wells, Tor.*	1.000	43	7	32	0	39	1
West, Min.*	.905	29	3	16	2	21	2
Weston, Bal.	1.000	9	3	0	0	3	0
Wickander, Cl.*	1.000	10	0	1	0	1	0
Williamson, Bal.	.931	49	14	13	2	29	2
Wills, Tor.	1.000	44	9	10	0	19	2
B. Witt, Tex.	.878	33	18	18	5	41	2
M. Witt, Cal-NY	.964	26	9	18	1	28	1
Yett, Min.	.750	4	2	1	1	4	1
Cu. Young, Oak*	.969	26	6	25	1	32	3
Cl. Young, Cal*	.833	17	0	5	1	6	0
M. Young, Sea.*	.827	34	12	31	9	52	1

TRIPLE PLAY: Ballard, Bal.

PITCHERS WITH TWO OR MORE CLUBS

Player, Club	PCT	G	PO	A	E	TC	DP
Bitker, Oak.	1.000	1	0	1	0	1	1
Bitker, Tex.	1.000	5	1	1	0	2	0
Black, Cle.*	.971	29	7	27	1	35	2
Black, Tor.*	1.000	3	0	6	0	6	0
C'delaria, Min*	1.000	34	3	3	0	6	0
C'delaria, Tor*	1.000	13	1	6	0	7	0
McCullers, N.Y.	1.000	11	1	2	0	3	0
McCullers, Det.	1.000	9	3	0	0	3	0
Parker, N.Y.	1.000	5	0	2	0	2	0
Parker, Det.	1.000	24	5	8	0	13	1
Powell, Sea.*	.000	2	0	0	0	0	0
Powell, Mil.*	1.000	9	2	9	0	11	0
Reed, Sea.	1.000	4	2	1	0	3	1
Reed, Bos.	1.000	29	6	4	0	10	1
Witt, Cal.	1.000	10	2	4	0	6	1
Witt, N.Y.	.955	16	7	14	1	22	0

OFFICIAL AMERICAN LEAGUE PITCHING AVERAGES

CLUB PITCHING

CLUB	W-L	ERA	G	CG	SHO	SV	IP	H	R	TBF	ER	HR	SH	SF	HB	TBB	IBB	SO	WP	BK
Oakland	103-59	3.18	162	18	16	64	1456.0	1287	570	6020	514	123	40	50	27	494	19	831	50	7
Chicago	94-68	3.61	162	17	10	68	1449.1	1313	633	6073	581	106	52	46	39	548	27	914	35	11
Seattle	77-85	3.69	162	21	7	41	1443.1	1319	664	6165	592	120	48	50	41	606	55	1064	69	12
Boston	88-74	3.72	162	15	13	44	1442.0	1439	664	6174	596	92	47	46	45	519	47	997	63	6
California	80-82	3.79	162	21	13	42	1454.0	1482	706	6223	613	106	47	46	38	544	25	944	50	6
Texas	83-79	3.83	162	25	9	36	1444.2	1343	696	6181	615	113	37	57	44	623	39	997	61	6
Toronto	86-76	3.84	162	6	9	48	1454.0	1434	661	6092	620	143	48	38	37	445	44	892	43	5
Kansas City	75-86	3.93	161	18	8	33	1420.2	1449	709	6193	621	116	48	44	46	560	45	1006	59	5
Baltimore	76-85	4.04	161	10	5	43	1435.1	1445	698	6141	644	161	52	56	16	537	43	776	34	10
Milwaukee	74-88	4.08	162	23	13	42	1445.0	1558	760	6284	655	121	50	63	38	469	39	771	47	7
Minnesota	74-88	4.12	162	13	13	3	1435.2	1509	729	6140	658	134	47	46	27	489	40	872	55	5
New York	67-95	4.21	162	15	6	41	1444.2	1430	749	6227	676	144	60	48	26	618	40	909	83	6
Cleveland	77-85	4.26	162	12	10	47	1427.1	1491	737	6184	676	163	50	50	40	518	38	860	50	8
Detroit	79-83	4.39	162	15	12	45	1430.1	1401	754	6230	697	154	57	57	45	661	86	856	76	7
Totals	1133-1133	3.91	1133	229	144	637	20182.1	19900	9746	86327	8758	1796	683	697	509	7631	587	12689	775	101

NOTE—Totals for earned runs for several clubs do not agree with the composite totals for all pitchers for each respective club due to instances in which provisions of Section 10.18(i) of the Scoring Rules were applied. The following differences are to be noted: Baltimore pitchers add to 649, California pitchers add to 616, Chicago pitchers add to 582, Cleveland pitchers add to 677, Milwaukee pitchers add to 660, Minnesota pitchers add to 660, New York pitchers add to 679, Seattle pitchers add to 597.

PITCHERS' RECORDS
(Top Fifteen Qualifiers for Earned-Run Average Leadership—162 or More Innings)
(* Lefthanded Pitcher)

Pitcher, Club	W	L	ERA	G	GS	CG	SHO	GF	SV	IP	H	R	TBF	ER	HR	SH	SF	HB	BB	IBB	SO	WP	BK
Clemens, W. Roger, Boston	21	6	1.93	31	31	7	4	0	0	228.1	193	59	920	49	7	7	5	7	54	3	209	8	0
Finley, Charles, California *	18	9	2.40	32	32	7	2	0	0	236.0	210	77	962	63	17	12	3	5	81	1	177	9	0
Stewart, David, Oakland	22	11	2.56	36	36	11	4	0	0	267.0	226	84	1088	76	16	10	10	5	83	1	166	8	0
Appier, R. Kevin, Kansas City	12	8	2.76	32	24	3	1	1	0	185.2	179	67	784	57	13	5	9	6	54	2	127	6	1
Stieb, David, Toronto	18	6	2.93	33	33	2	2	0	0	208.2	179	73	861	68	11	6	3	10	64	0	125	5	0
Welch, Robert, Oakland	27	6	2.95	35	35	2	0	0	0	238.0	214	90	979	78	26	6	5	5	77	4	127	7	2
Wells, David, Toronto *	11	6	3.14	43	25	0	0	8	3	189.0	165	72	759	66	14	9	2	2	45	3	115	7	1
Hibbard, J. Gregory, Chicago *	14	9	3.16	33	33	3	1	0	0	211.0	202	80	871	74	11	8	10	6	55	6	92	10	2
Hanson, Erik, Seattle	18	9	3.24	33	33	5	0	0	0	236.0	205	88	964	85	15	3	6	2	68	2	211	10	1
McCaskill, Kirk, California	12	11	3.25	29	29	2	1	0	0	174.1	161	77	738	63	9	3	1	2	72	1	78	6	0
Boddicker, Michael, Boston	17	8	3.36	34	34	4	0	0	0	228.0	225	92	956	85	16	5	4	10	69	6	143	10	0
Witt, Robert, Texas	17	10	3.37	33	32	7	1	0	1	222.0	197	98	954	83	12	5	6	7	110	3	221	11	2
Ryan, L. Nolan, Texas	13	9	3.44	30	30	5	2	0	0	204.0	137	66	818	78	18	3	5	7	74	2	232	9	1
Young, Matthew, Seattle *	8	18	3.52	34	33	5	1	0	1	225.1	198	106	963	88	15	7	6	5	107	1	176	16	0
Black, Harry, Clev-Tor. *	13	11	3.57	32	31	5	2	0	2	206.2	181	86	857	82	19	6	7	6	61	1	106	6	1

DEPARTMENTAL LEADERS: W—Welch, Oak., 27; L—Leary, N.Y., 19; G—Thigpen, Chi., 77; GS—Stewart, Oak., Morris, Det., 36; CG—Stewart, Oak., Morris, Det., 11; ShO—Stewart, Oak., Clemens, Bos., 4; GF—Thigpen, Chi., 73; Sv—Thigpen, Chi., 57; IP—Stewart, Oak., 267.0; H—Abbott, Cal., 246; TBF—Stewart, Oak., 1088; R—Morris, Det., 144; ER—Morris, Det., 125; HR—Johnson, Balt., 30; SH—Finley, Cal., 12; SF—Hough, Tex., LaPoint, N.Y., Smith, Minn., 11; HB—Hough, Tex., 11; TBB—Johnson, Sea., 120; IBB—Morris, Det., 13; SO—Ryan, Tex., 232; WP—Leary, N.Y., 23; Bk.—Navarro, Milw., 5.

(ALL PITCHERS LISTED ALPHABETICALLY)

Pitcher, Club	W	L	ERA	G	GS	CG	SHO	GF	SV	IP	H	TBF	R	ER	HR	SH	SF	HB	BB	IBB	SO	WP	BK
Abbott, James, California *	10	14	4.51	33	33	4	1	0	0	211.2	246	925	116	106	16	9	6	5	72	6	105	4	3
Abbott, Paul, Minnesota	0	5	5.97	7	7	0	0	0	0	34.2	37	162	24	23	9	3	1	1	28	5	25	1	1
Acker, James, Toronto	4	4	3.83	59	0	0	0	19	0	91.2	103	403	49	39	9	3	3	0	30	5	54	4	1
Adkins, Steven, New York *	1	1	6.38	5	5	0	0	0	0	24.0	19	115	18	17	4	0	1	3	29	0	14	2	0
Aguilera, Richard, Minnesota *	5	3	2.76	56	0	0	0	54	32	65.1	55	268	27	20	5	0	2	4	19	6	61	3	0
Aldred, Scott, Detroit *	1	2	3.77	4	3	0	0	0	0	14.1	13	63	6	6	0	1	0	0	10	0	7	0	0
Aldrich, Jay, Baltimore	0	0	8.25	7	0	0	0	1	0	12.0	17	61	13	11	1	2	1	1	7	3	5	0	0
Alexander, Gerald, Texas	0	0	7.71	3	2	0	0	1	0	7.0	14	39	6	6	0	0	1	0	5	0	5	0	0
Andersen, Larry, Boston	0	0	1.23	15	0	0	0	4	0	22.0	18	86	3	3	0	0	1	1	3	1	25	0	1
Anderson, Allan, Minnesota *	7	18	4.53	31	31	5	1	0	0	188.2	214	797	106	95	20	4	8	5	39	2	82	2	0
Appier, R. Kevin, Kansas City	12	8	2.76	32	24	3	1	0	0	185.2	179	784	67	57	13	5	9	6	54	1	127	4	3
Aquino, Luis, Kansas City	4	1	3.16	20	3	0	0	3	0	68.1	59	287	25	24	6	2	6	4	27	2	28	6	1
Arnsberg, Bradley, Texas	6	1	2.15	53	0	0	0	20	5	62.2	56	277	20	15	4	2	2	2	33	1	44	3	1
August, Donald, Milwaukee	0	3	6.55	5	5	0	0	1	0	11.0	13	51	10	8	0	0	0	0	5	1	2	2	0
Bailes, Scott, California *	2	2	6.37	27	0	0	0	6	0	35.1	31	173	30	25	8	1	5	2	20	6	16	2	0
Ballard, Jeffrey, Baltimore *	2	11	4.93	44	17	0	0	6	0	133.1	152	578	79	73	16	5	2	3	42	6	50	1	1
Baller, Jay, Kansas City	0	0	15.43	3	0	0	0	2	0	2.1	4	14	4	4	1	0	0	0	2	1	1	0	0
Bankhead, M. Scott, Seattle	0	0	11.08	4	4	0	0	0	0	13.0	18	63	16	16	2	0	0	0	7	0	10	1	0
Barfield, John, Texas *	4	3	4.67	33	0	0	0	10	0	44.1	42	178	25	23	2	3	4	2	13	3	17	1	0
Bautista, Jose, Baltimore	1	0	4.05	22	3	0	0	9	0	26.2	28	112	15	12	4	1	1	2	7	0	15	2	0
Bearse, Kevin, Cleveland *	0	2	12.91	3	3	0	0	0	0	7.2	16	45	11	11	2	0	2	0	5	0	2	0	0
Berenguer, Juan, Minnesota	8	5	3.41	51	0	0	0	13	0	100.1	85	434	43	38	9	5	2	4	58	4	77	5	0
Bitker, Joseph, Oak.-Tex. *	0	0	2.25	6	0	0	0	5	0	12.0	8	48	3	3	0	0	7	1	4	1	8	0	0
Black, Harry, Clev.-Tor. *	13	11	3.57	32	31	5	2	0	0	206.2	181	857	86	82	19	6	4	5	61	1	106	6	1
Blair, William, Toronto	3	5	4.06	27	6	2	0	8	0	68.2	66	297	33	31	4	0	1	1	28	4	43	6	0
Blyleven, R. Aalbert, California	8	7	5.24	23	23	2	0	0	0	134.0	163	578	85	78	15	3	6	10	25	6	69	3	0
Boddicker, Michael, Boston	17	8	3.36	34	34	4	0	0	0	228.0	225	956	92	85	16	3	6	10	69	6	143	5	0
Bohanon, Brian, Texas *	0	3	6.62	11	6	0	0	1	0	34.0	40	158	30	25	6	0	3	2	18	3	15	1	0
Bolton, Thomas, Boston *	10	5	3.38	21	16	3	0	2	0	119.2	111	501	46	45	6	0	5	0	47	3	65	1	1
Boone, Daniel, Baltimore *	0	1	2.79	4	0	0	0	1	0	9.2	12	43	3	3	1	0	4	0	3	2	2	1	0
Bosio, Christopher, Milwaukee	4	9	4.00	20	20	4	1	0	0	132.2	131	557	67	59	15	4	4	3	38	1	76	7	0
Brown, J. Kevin, Texas	12	10	3.60	26	26	6	2	0	0	180.0	175	757	84	72	13	5	7	3	60	3	88	9	2
Brown, Kevin, Milwaukee *	1	1	2.57	5	3	0	0	1	0	21.0	18	87	7	6	1	1	2	1	12	1	12	2	0
Burba, David, Seattle	0	0	4.50	6	2	0	0	0	0	8.0	8	35	6	4	0	1	0	0	2	0	4	0	0
Burns, Todd, Oakland	3	3	2.97	43	2	0	0	9	3	78.2	78	337	28	26	8	5	3	1	32	4	43	0	0
Cadaret, Gregory, New York *	5	4	4.15	54	6	0	0	9	3	121.1	120	525	62	56	8	9	4	2	64	5	80	14	0
Campbell, Michael, Kansas City *	1	0	8.38	7	3	0	0	0	0	9.2	15	44	9	9	1	2	0	1	1	0	2	0	0
Candelaria, John, Minn.-Tor. *	7	6	3.95	47	3	0	0	15	5	79.2	87	345	36	35	11	2	6	6	20	5	63	5	3
Candiotti, Thomas, Cleveland	15	11	3.65	31	29	3	1	1	0	202.0	207	856	92	82	23	4	3	3	55	1	128	9	3
Capel, Michael, Milwaukee	0	0	135.00	2	0	0	0	1	0	0.1	6	9	6	5	0	0	0	1	1	0	1	0	0
Cary, Charles, New York *	6	2	4.19	28	27	2	0	0	0	156.2	155	661	77	73	21	3	5	4	55	1	134	11	2
Casian, Lawrence, Minnesota *	2	1	3.22	5	3	0	0	1	0	22.1	26	90	9	8	2	0	1	1	4	3	11	0	0
Cerutti, John, Toronto *	9	9	4.76	30	23	0	0	1	0	140.0	162	609	77	74	23	5	5	4	49	3	49	4	1
Chiamparino, Scott, Texas	1	2	2.63	6	6	0	0	0	0	37.2	36	160	14	11	1	1	5	1	12	0	19	5	0
Chitren, Stephen, Oakland	1	0	1.02	8	0	0	0	4	0	17.2	7	64	2	2	0	0	0	0	4	0	19	2	0
Clark, Bryan, Seattle *	2	0	3.27	12	4	0	0	1	0	11.0	9	48	4	4	0	0	0	2	10	0	6	1	0
Clear, Mark, California	0	0	5.87	4	0	0	0	2	0	7.2	5	38	7	5	0	2	2	2	9	0	6	1	0
Clemens, W. Roger, Boston	21	6	1.93	31	31	7	4	0	0	228.1	193	920	59	49	7	7	5	7	54	3	209	8	0

Pitcher, Club	W	L	ERA	G	GS	CG	SHO	GF	SV	IP	H	TBF	R	ER	HR	SH	SF	HB	BB	IBB	SO	WP	BK
Codiroli, Christopher, Kansas City	0	4	9.58	6	2	0	0	1	0	10.1	13	61	11	11	4	0	0	4	17	1	8	2	0
Comstock, Keith, Seattle*	7	4	2.89	60	0	0	0	19	2	56.0	40	228	22	18	1	5	0	0	26	5	50	2	1
Corbett, Sherman, California*	0	0	9.00	4	0	0	0	2	0	5.0	8	26	5	5	0	1	1	0	3	0	2	1	0
Crawford, Steve, Kansas City	5	4	4.16	46	0	0	0	14	1	80.0	79	341	38	37	7	5	2	3	23	3	54	0	1
Crim, Charles, Milwaukee	3	5	3.47	67	0	0	0	25	11	85.2	88	367	39	33	7	2	4	2	23	4	39	0	0
Cummings, Steven, Cleveland	0	2	5.11	6	2	0	0	2	0	12.1	22	58	7	7	4	0	0	1	5	0	4	0	0
Davis, George, Cleveland	2	7	5.11	53	3	0	0	28	6	68.2	71	334	43	39	9	4	3	2	52	3	73	6	1
Davis, Mark, Kansas City*	7	10	4.74	21	20	0	0	0	0	112.0	129	498	66	59	9	1	0	0	35	1	62	8	0
DeLucia, Richard, Seattle	1	0	2.00	5	4	1	0	0	0	36.0	30	144	9	8	2	2	1	0	9	0	20	0	0
Dopson, John, Boston	0	0	2.04	5	4	0	0	0	0	17.2	13	75	7	4	2	0	1	0	9	0	9	4	0
Dotson, Richard, Kansas City	3	4	8.48	8	7	0	0	1	0	28.2	43	139	29	27	3	4	1	2	14	1	9	0	0
Drummond, Timothy, Minnesota	0	5	4.35	35	4	0	0	14	1	91.0	104	399	46	44	8	5	4	5	36	1	49	4	0
DuBois, Brian, Baltimore*	3	5	5.09	12	11	0	0	0	0	58.1	70	255	37	33	5	2	4	1	22	1	34	5	0
Eave, Gary, Seattle	0	3	4.20	8	5	0	0	0	0	30.0	27	134	16	14	5	0	0	1	20	1	16	0	0
Eckersley, Dennis, Oakland	4	2	0.61	63	0	0	0	61	48	73.1	41	262	9	5	5	6	0	0	4	1	73	0	0
Edens, Thomas, Milwaukee	4	5	4.45	35	6	0	0	9	2	89.0	89	387	52	44	8	4	4	4	33	3	40	1	0
Edwards, Wayne, Chicago*	5	3	3.22	42	5	0	0	8	1	95.0	81	396	39	34	6	2	6	0	41	2	63	1	0
Eichhorn, Mark, California	2	5	3.08	60	0	0	0	40	13	84.2	98	374	36	29	2	2	4	4	23	0	69	0	0
Eiland, David, New York	2	1	3.56	5	5	0	0	0	0	30.1	31	127	14	12	2	0	0	0	5	0	16	0	0
Elvira, Narciso, Milwaukee*	0	0	5.40	4	0	0	0	2	0	5.0	14	25	3	3	1	0	0	0	4	0	6	1	0
Encarnacion, Luis, Kansas City	0	0	7.84	4	0	0	0	1	0	10.1	14	49	10	9	0	0	2	1	8	0	6	0	1
Erickson, Scott, Minnesota	8	4	2.87	19	17	1	0	0	0	113.0	108	485	49	36	9	5	2	5	51	4	53	3	0
Farr, Steven, Kansas City	13	7	1.98	57	0	0	0	20	1	127.0	99	515	32	28	6	10	5	1	48	9	94	3	0
Farrell, John, Cleveland	4	5	4.28	17	17	1	0	0	0	96.2	108	418	49	46	10	5	1	3	33	1	44	1	0
Fernandez, Alexander, Chicago	5	5	3.80	13	13	3	1	0	0	87.2	89	378	40	37	6	6	0	3	34	0	61	3	0
Fetters, Michael, California	1	1	4.12	26	2	0	0	10	1	67.2	77	291	33	31	9	4	2	1	20	0	35	2	0
Filer, Thomas, Milwaukee	2	3	6.14	7	4	0	0	1	0	22.0	26	99	17	15	2	2	1	3	9	0	8	3	1
Filson, W. Peter, Kansas City*	1	4	5.91	8	7	0	0	0	0	35.0	42	165	31	23	3	3	0	2	13	1	9	0	0
Finley, Charles, California*	18	9	2.40	32	32	7	2	0	0	236.0	210	962	77	63	17	3	3	2	81	3	177	9	0
Flanagan, Michael, Toronto*	2	2	5.31	5	5	0	0	0	0	20.1	28	94	14	12	3	1	2	1	8	3	5	0	0
Fossas, Tony, Milwaukee*	2	3	6.44	32	0	0	0	9	2	29.1	44	146	23	21	5	5	2	1	10	2	24	0	0
Fraser, William, California	5	3	3.08	45	0	0	0	20	2	76.0	69	315	29	26	4	2	1	2	24	3	32	1	0
Garces, Richard, Minnesota	0	0	1.59	5	0	0	0	3	0	5.2	4	24	2	1	0	0	0	0	4	0	1	0	1
Gardiner, Michael, Seattle	0	2	10.66	5	3	0	0	0	0	12.2	22	66	17	15	1	0	1	3	5	0	6	0	1
Gardner, Wesley, Boston	3	7	4.89	34	9	0	0	9	1	77.1	77	340	43	42	6	4	2	1	35	5	58	2	0
Gibson, Paul, Detroit*	5	4	3.05	61	0	0	0	17	3	97.1	99	422	36	33	10	4	5	1	44	0	56	1	0
Gilles, Thomas, Toronto	1	0	6.75	2	0	0	0	0	0	1.1	2	6	1	1	0	0	0	0	0	0	1	2	1
Gleaton, Jerry, Detroit*	1	3	2.94	57	0	0	0	34	13	82.2	62	325	27	27	5	2	4	3	25	2	56	1	1
Gordon, Thomas, Kansas City	12	11	3.73	32	32	6	1	0	0	195.1	192	858	99	81	17	8	2	3	99	1	175	11	0
Gozzo, Mauro, Cleveland	0	0	0.00	8	0	0	0	1	0	3.0	5	13	0	0	0	0	0	0	2	1	2	1	0
Grahe, Joseph, California	3	4	4.98	8	8	0	0	0	0	43.1	51	200	30	24	3	0	1	3	23	1	25	2	0
Gray, Jeffrey, Boston	2	3	4.44	41	0	0	0	28	9	50.2	53	217	27	25	10	3	1	1	15	3	50	1	1
Guante, Cecilio, Cleveland	2	7	5.01	26	0	0	0	6	0	46.2	38	197	26	26	5	1	2	1	18	4	30	2	1
Gubicza, Mark, Kansas City	4	7	4.50	16	16	2	0	0	0	94.0	80	409	48	47	6	5	4	4	38	4	71	2	1
Gutterman, A. Lee, New York*	11	7	3.39	64	0	0	0	21	2	93.0	101	376	37	35	8	6	3	1	26	7	48	2	1
Guthrie, Mark, Minnesota*	7	9	3.79	24	21	3	0	0	0	144.2	154	603	65	61	8	8	0	3	39	3	101	1	0
Habyan, John, New York	0	0	2.08	6	0	0	0	1	0	8.2	10	37	2	2	0	0	1	0	2	0	4	1	0
Hanson, Erik, Seattle	18	9	3.24	33	33	5	1	0	0	236.0	205	964	88	85	15	5	6	1	68	6	211	10	2
Harnisch, Peter, Baltimore	11	11	4.34	31	31	3	0	0	0	188.2	189	821	96	91	17	6	5	6	86	5	122	5	2
Harris, Greg A., Boston	13	9	4.00	34	30	1	0	3	0	184.1	186	803	90	82	13	8	9	6	77	7	117	8	2
Harris, T. Eugene, Seattle	1	2	4.74	25	0	0	0	12	0	38.0	31	176	25	20	5	0	2	1	30	5	43	2	0

Pitcher, Club	W	L	ERA	G	GS	CG	SHO	GF	SV	IP	H	TBF	R	ER	HR	SH	SF	HB	BB	IBB	SO	WP	BK
Harris, Reginald, Oakland	1	0	3.48	16	1	0	0	9	0	41.1	25	168	16	16	5	1	4	2	21	1	31	2	0
Harvey, Bryan, California	4	4	3.22	54	0	0	0	47	25	64.1	45	267	24	23	4	4	4	0	35	6	82	7	1
Hawkins, M. Andrew, New York	5	12	5.37	28	26	2	1	1	0	157.2	156	692	101	94	20	4	5	2	82	3	74	0	0
Heep, Daniel, Boston*	0	0	9.00	1	0	0	0	1	0	1.0	4	6	1	1	0	0	0	0	1	0	0	0	1
Henke, Thomas, Toronto	2	4	2.17	61	0	0	0	58	32	74.2	58	297	18	18	8	4	2	1	19	2	75	6	0
Henneman, Michael, Detroit	8	6	3.05	69	0	0	0	53	22	94.1	90	399	36	32	4	5	0	3	33	12	50	3	0
Hesketh, Joseph, Boston*	0	4	3.51	12	4	0	0	4	0	25.2	37	122	12	10	2	1	1	0	11	1	26	3	0
Hetzel, Eric, Boston	1	4	5.91	9	8	0	0	1	0	35.0	39	163	28	23	3	0	2	1	21	0	20	2	0
Hibbard, J. Gregory, Chicago*	14	9	3.16	33	33	3	1	0	0	211.0	202	871	80	74	11	8	10	6	55	2	92	1	1
Hickey, Kevin, Baltimore*	1	3	5.13	37	0	0	0	9	0	26.1	26	113	16	15	3	1	0	0	13	2	17	1	0
Higuera, Teodoro, Milwaukee*	11	10	3.76	27	27	4	1	0	0	170.0	167	720	80	71	16	8	4	3	50	2	129	0	0
Hill, Donald, California	0	0	0.00	1	0	0	0	1	0	1.0	1	4	1	0	0	0	0	0	0	0	1	0	0
Hillegas, Shawn, Chicago	0	0	0.79	7	0	0	0	3	0	11.1	4	43	1	1	0	1	1	0	5	0	5	0	0
Holman, Brian, Seattle	11	11	4.03	28	28	3	2	0	0	189.2	188	804	92	85	17	7	7	6	66	2	121	4	2
Holton, Brian, Baltimore	2	3	4.50	33	0	0	0	13	0	58.0	68	257	31	29	7	1	2	1	21	6	27	2	2
Honeycutt, Frederick, Oakland*	2	2	2.70	63	0	0	0	13	7	63.1	46	256	23	19	2	1	6	0	22	6	38	0	1
Hoover, John, Texas	0	2	11.57	2	2	0	0	1	0	4.2	8	26	6	6	0	1	0	1	3	0	3	0	0
Hough, Charles, Texas	12	12	4.07	32	32	5	2	0	0	218.2	190	950	108	99	24	2	11	11	119	0	114	4	1
Irvine, Daryl, Boston	1	2	4.67	11	0	0	0	6	0	17.1	15	75	10	9	0	2	1	1	11	3	9	1	0
Jackson, Michael, Seattle	5	7	4.54	63	0	0	0	11	3	77.1	64	338	42	39	8	8	3	2	44	10	69	9	2
Jeffcoat, J. Michael, Texas*	5	6	4.47	44	12	0	0	11	5	110.2	122	466	57	55	12	5	2	3	28	5	58	1	0
Johnson, David W., Baltimore	13	9	4.10	30	29	3	0	0	0	180.0	196	758	83	82	30	7	7	3	43	2	68	1	0
Johnson, Randall, Seattle*	14	11	3.65	33	33	5	2	0	0	219.2	174	944	103	89	26	7	6	5	120	2	194	4	2
Jones, Barry, Chicago	11	4	2.31	65	0	0	0	9	1	74.0	62	310	26	19	2	2	5	1	33	5	45	0	1
Jones, Douglas, Cleveland	5	5	2.56	66	0	0	0	64	43	84.1	66	331	27	24	5	7	2	2	22	4	55	0	0
Jones, James, New York	1	2	6.30	17	7	0	0	9	0	50.0	72	238	42	35	8	2	1	1	23	2	25	3	1
Kaiser, Jeffrey, Cleveland*	0	0	3.55	5	0	0	0	3	0	12.2	16	60	5	5	2	1	0	0	7	2	9	3	0
Key, James, Toronto*	13	7	4.25	27	27	0	0	0	0	154.2	169	641	79	73	20	5	6	6	22	2	88	3	0
Kiecker, Dana, Boston	8	9	3.97	32	25	2	0	3	0	152.0	145	636	74	67	7	1	3	9	54	2	93	3	1
Kilgus, Paul, Toronto*	0	2	6.06	11	0	0	0	4	0	16.1	19	74	11	11	2	6	1	0	7	1	7	0	0
King, Eric, Chicago	12	4	3.28	25	25	2	2	0	0	151.0	135	623	59	55	10	1	6	6	40	0	70	2	0
Kinzer, Matthew, Detroit	0	0	16.20	2	1	0	0	1	0	1.2	3	11	9	3	0	1	0	0	3	0	1	0	0
Klink, Joseph, Oakland*	0	0	2.04	40	0	0	0	19	1	39.2	34	165	9	9	1	0	0	2	18	8	19	0	0
Knackert, Brent, Seattle	1	1	6.51	24	0	0	0	6	0	37.1	50	186	28	27	5	3	2	3	21	2	28	3	0
Knudson, Mark, Milwaukee	10	9	4.12	30	27	4	0	0	0	168.1	187	719	84	77	14	8	3	3	40	6	56	3	0
Krueger, William, Milwaukee*	6	8	3.98	30	27	1	0	4	0	129.0	137	566	70	57	10	5	10	5	54	4	64	6	0
Kutzler, Jerry, Chicago	2	3	6.03	7	7	0	0	0	0	31.1	38	141	23	21	2	1	4	1	14	1	21	0	0
Lamp, Dennis, Boston	3	5	4.68	47	0	0	0	5	0	105.2	114	453	61	55	10	7	2	4	30	8	49	1	0
Langston, Mark, California*	10	17	4.40	33	33	5	1	0	0	223.0	215	950	120	109	13	6	6	5	104	8	195	5	0
LaPoint, David, New York*	7	10	4.11	28	27	2	1	0	0	157.2	180	694	84	72	11	8	11	1	57	3	67	8	0
Leach, Terry, Minnesota	2	5	3.20	55	0	0	0	29	2	81.2	84	344	31	29	2	7	4	2	21	10	46	4	0
Leary, Timothy, New York	9	19	4.11	31	31	6	2	0	0	208.0	202	881	105	95	18	7	1	7	78	1	138	8	0
Lee, Mark, Milwaukee*	0	0	2.11	11	0	0	0	5	0	21.1	20	85	5	5	0	1	1	0	4	3	14	1	0
Leister, John, Boston	0	0	4.76	2	1	0	0	1	0	5.2	7	29	5	3	0	1	0	2	4	0	3	0	0
Leiter, Alois, Toronto*	0	0	0.00	4	0	0	0	1	0	6.1	1	22	0	0	0	0	0	0	2	0	5	0	0
Leiter, Mark, New York*	1	1	6.84	8	3	0	0	1	0	26.1	33	119	21	20	5	2	0	2	9	1	21	1	0
Lewis, Scott, California	1	1	2.20	5	3	0	0	0	0	16.1	10	60	5	4	0	1	0	0	4	0	9	0	0
Long, William, Chicago	0	0	6.35	5	0	0	0	1	0	5.2	6	26	4	4	0	0	0	0	2	0	5	0	0
Lovelace, Vance, Seattle*	0	0	3.86	4	0	0	0	1	0	2.1	3	17	1	1	1	0	0	1	6	1	0	2	0
Luecken, Richard, Toronto	0	0	9.00	5	0	0	0	1	0	1.0	3	5	1	1	0	0	0	0	1	0	1	0	0
Lugo, Urbano, Detroit	2	0	7.03	13	1	0	0	4	0	24.1	30	116	19	19	9	4	0	3	13	1	12	2	0

Pitcher, Club	W	L	ERA	G	GS	CG	SHO	GF	SV	IP	H	TBF	R	ER	HR	SH	SF	HB	BB	IBB	SO	WP	BK
Lyons, Stephen, Chicago	0	0	4.50	1	0	0	0	1	0	2.0	2	9	1	1	0	0	0	0	4	0	0	1	0
MacDonald, Robert, Toronto*	0	0	0.00	4	0	0	0	1	0	2.1	0	8	0	0	0	0	0	0	2	2	2	0	0
Machado, Julio, Milwaukee	0	0	0.69	10	0	0	0	7	3	13.0	9	56	6	1	0	0	1	0	8	2	12	0	0
Maldonado, Carlos, Kansas City	0	0	9.00	4	0	0	0	1	0	6.0	9	31	6	6	0	0	1	0	3	1	9	1	0
Manon, Ramon, Texas	0	0	13.50	1	0	0	0	0	0	2.0	3	12	3	3	0	0	0	0	3	0	1	0	0
McCaskill, Kirk, California*	12	11	3.25	29	29	2	0	0	0	174.1	161	738	77	63	9	3	0	2	72	2	78	6	1
McClure, Robert, California*	0	1	6.43	11	0	0	0	1	0	7.0	7	30	6	5	0	0	1	0	7	1	6	1	1
McCullers, Lance, N.Y.-Det.	2	5	3.02	20	1	2	0	0	0	44.2	32	186	19	15	4	3	0	1	19	3	31	5	1
McDonald, L. Benard, Baltimore	8	9	2.43	21	15	1	2	14	0	118.2	88	472	36	32	9	1	5	5	35	0	65	5	0
McDowell, Jack, Chicago	14	9	3.82	33	33	4	0	0	0	205.0	189	866	93	87	20	2	5	7	77	1	165	7	2
McGaffigan, Andrew, Kansas City	4	3	3.09	24	11	0	0	2	2	78.2	75	336	40	27	6	0	2	2	28	1	49	3	0
McMurtry, J. Craig, Texas	0	3	4.32	23	3	0	0	6	1	41.2	43	188	25	20	4	0	2	1	30	0	14	1	0
McWilliams, Larry, Kansas City*	0	0	9.72	13	2	0	0	0	0	8.1	10	43	10	9	2	0	0	0	9	1	7	1	1
Medvin, Scott, Seattle	0	0	6.23	5	0	0	0	2	0	4.1	7	22	4	3	0	0	0	0	3	0	1	0	0
Melendez, Jose, Seattle	0	1	11.81	3	0	0	0	3	0	5.1	8	28	8	7	2	2	0	0	3	2	7	1	0
Mesa, Jose, Baltimore	3	2	3.86	7	7	0	0	0	0	46.2	37	202	20	20	2	2	2	1	27	5	24	2	1
Mielke, Gary, Texas	0	1	3.73	33	0	0	0	8	0	41.0	42	174	17	17	2	5	5	0	15	1	13	3	0
Milacki, Robert, Baltimore	5	8	4.46	27	24	1	1	0	0	135.1	143	594	73	67	18	4	1	5	61	6	60	1	1
Mills, Alan, New York	1	5	4.10	36	0	0	0	18	0	41.2	48	200	21	19	4	1	0	0	33	1	24	2	1
Minton, Gregory, California*	4	2	2.35	11	0	0	0	3	0	15.1	11	61	4	4	1	1	2	1	7	2	4	1	0
Mirabella, Paul, Milwaukee*	4	2	3.97	44	2	0	0	10	0	59.0	66	267	32	26	9	6	8	2	27	3	28	3	0
Mitchell, John, Baltimore	6	6	4.64	24	17	1	0	0	0	114.1	133	509	63	59	7	0	0	8	48	3	43	0	0
Monteleone, Richard, New York	0	1	6.14	5	0	0	0	2	0	7.1	8	31	5	5	0	2	2	0	2	0	8	3	0
Montgomery, Jeffrey, Kansas City	6	5	2.39	73	0	0	0	59	24	94.1	81	400	36	25	6	4	2	2	34	8	94	13	0
Moore, Michael, Oakland	13	15	4.65	33	33	3	0	0	0	199.1	204	862	113	103	14	4	7	5	84	13	73	16	2
Morris, John, Detroit*	15	18	4.51	36	36	11	3	0	0	249.2	231	1073	144	125	26	7	10	3	97	13	162	16	0
Moses, John, Minnesota*	0	0	13.50	2	0	0	0	2	0	2.0	5	13	3	3	0	0	0	1	2	0	0	0	0
Moyer, Jamie, Texas*	2	6	4.66	33	10	0	0	6	0	102.1	115	447	59	53	6	1	4	4	39	4	58	4	0
Murphy, Robert, Boston*	0	6	6.32	68	0	0	0	20	7	57.0	85	285	46	40	10	4	4	1	32	3	54	1	0
Nagy, Charles, Cleveland	2	4	5.91	9	8	0	0	1	0	45.2	58	208	31	30	7	1	5	1	21	1	26	6	0
Navarro, Jaime, Milwaukee	8	7	4.46	32	22	3	0	2	0	149.1	176	654	83	74	11	4	5	5	41	3	75	1	5
Nelson, W. Eugene, Oakland	3	3	1.57	51	2	1	0	17	5	74.2	55	291	14	13	5	5	0	4	17	1	38	5	0
Nichols, Rodney, Cleveland	0	3	7.88	9	5	3	0	0	1	16.0	24	79	14	14	5	1	5	2	6	0	6	0	0
Nipper, Albert, Cleveland	2	3	6.75	14	0	0	0	1	0	24.0	35	125	19	18	8	0	0	2	19	0	12	6	0
Norris, Michael, Oakland	1	0	3.00	3	2	0	0	0	0	27.0	24	113	10	9	0	2	1	2	9	0	16	3	2
Nosek, Randall, Detroit	0	1	7.71	3	0	0	0	0	0	7.0	7	35	6	6	1	0	1	0	9	1	3	1	0
Nunez, Edwin, Detroit	1	4	2.24	42	0	0	0	15	1	80.1	65	343	26	20	4	5	2	2	37	6	66	4	0
Olin, Steven, Cleveland	4	4	3.41	50	0	0	0	16	1	92.1	96	394	41	35	3	5	2	6	26	2	64	4	0
Olson, Gregg W., Baltimore	6	5	2.42	64	0	0	0	58	37	74.1	57	305	20	20	3	3	3	3	31	3	74	5	0
Orosco, Jesse, Cleveland*	5	4	3.90	55	0	0	0	28	2	64.2	58	289	35	28	9	1	0	0	38	7	55	1	0
Otto, David, Oakland*	0	0	7.71	2	0	0	0	2	0	2.1	3	13	7	2	2	5	2	3	3	0	2	0	0
Pall, Donn, Chicago	3	5	3.32	56	0	0	0	11	2	76.0	63	306	33	28	7	4	4	2	24	8	39	2	0
Parker, J. Clayton, N.Y.-Det.	2	3	3.58	29	3	3	0	8	0	73.0	64	308	33	29	11	3	3	1	32	6	40	4	0
Patterson, Kenneth, Chicago*	3	1	3.39	43	0	0	0	15	0	66.1	58	283	27	25	6	4	5	3	34	1	40	2	4
Perez, Melido, Chicago	13	14	4.61	35	35	3	3	0	0	197.0	177	833	111	101	14	0	6	2	86	1	161	8	0
Perez, Pascual, New York*	1	2	1.29	3	0	0	0	1	0	14.0	12	52	3	2	0	2	0	2	3	0	12	1	0
Peterson, Adam, Chicago	2	5	4.55	20	11	2	0	3	0	85.0	90	357	46	43	12	8	9	3	26	0	29	0	0
Petry, Daniel, Detroit	10	9	4.45	32	23	1	0	0	0	149.2	148	655	78	74	14	6	6	3	77	7	73	3	2
Plesac, Daniel, Milwaukee*	3	7	4.43	66	0	0	0	52	24	69.0	67	299	34	34	5	7	6	2	34	6	65	10	2
Plunk, Eric, New York	6	3	2.72	47	0	0	0	16	0	72.2	58	310	27	22	6	2	2	3	43	4	67	4	0
Powell, Dennis, Sea.-Milw.*	0	4	7.02	11	7	0	0	2	0	42.1	64	214	40	33	0	2	0	2	21	0	23	2	0

Pitcher, Club	W	L	ERA	G	GS	CG	SHO	GF	SV	IP	H	TBF	R	ER	HR	SH	SF	HB	BB	IBB	SO	WP	BK
Price, Joseph, Baltimore*	3	4	3.58	50	0	0	0	12	2	65.1	62	273	29	26	8	3	1	2	24	2	54	1	0
Radinsky, Scott, Chicago*	6	1	4.82	62	0	0	0	18	4	52.1	47	237	29	28	1	1	2	0	36	1	46	1	1
Reardon, Jeffrey, Boston..	5	3	3.16	47	0	0	0	37	21	51.1	63	210	19	18	5	2	1	1	19	4	33	2	0
Reed, Jerry, Sea.-Bos.	2	1	4.82	33	0	0	0	16	2	52.1	63	234	31	28	2	2	3	2	19	2	19	7	0
Richardson, Jeffrey, California	0	0	0.00	1	0	0	0	0	0	0.1	1	2	0	0	0	0	0	0	0	0	0	0	1
Righetti, David, New York*	1	1	3.57	53	0	0	0	47	36	53.0	48	235	24	21	8	1	1	6	26	2	43	3	0
Ritz, Kevin, Detroit	0	1	11.05	4	4	0	0	0	0	7.1	14	52	12	9	0	3	0	1	14	2	3	3	0
Robinson, Jeffrey D., New York	3	0	3.45	54	4	0	0	12	0	88.2	82	372	35	34	8	5	1	6	34	2	43	16	1
Robinson, Jeffrey M., Detroit	10	6	5.96	27	27	1	0	0	0	145.0	141	654	101	96	23	5	5	6	88	9	76	2	0
Robinson, Ronald, Milwaukee	12	5	2.91	22	22	7	1	0	0	148.1	158	627	60	48	5	3	7	6	37	1	57	5	0
Rochford, Michael, Boston*	0	1	18.00	2	1	0	0	0	0	4.0	10	25	10	8	1	1	1	0	4	0	0	1	0
Rogers, Kenneth, Texas*	10	6	3.13	69	3	0	0	46	15	97.2	93	428	40	34	6	6	4	2	42	5	74	5	2
Rosenberg, Steven, Chicago*	1	1	5.40	6	0	0	0	3	0	10.0	10	44	6	6	2	1	1	0	5	0	4	3	0
Russell, Jeffrey, Texas	1	5	4.26	27	0	0	0	22	10	25.1	23	111	15	12	1	7	0	5	16	5	16	3	0
Ryan, L. Nolan, Texas	13	9	3.44	30	30	5	2	0	0	204.0	137	818	86	78	18	0	5	7	74	2	232	9	1
Saberhagen, Bret, Kansas City	5	9	3.27	20	20	5	0	0	0	135.0	146	561	52	49	9	3	4	3	28	3	87	1	0
Sanchez, Israel, Kansas City*	0	0	8.38	11	1	0	0	3	0	9.2	10	47	9	9	1	0	1	0	3	0	5	0	0
Sanderson, Scott, Oakland	17	11	3.88	34	34	2	2	0	0	206.1	205	885	99	89	27	4	8	4	66	2	128	7	0
Savage, John, Minnesota	0	0	8.31	17	0	0	0	9	1	26.0	37	121	26	24	3	4	1	1	11	1	12	4	0
Schilling, Curt, Baltimore	1	2	2.54	35	0	0	0	16	3	46.0	38	191	13	13	3	1	4	0	19	0	32	1	0
Schooler, Michael, Seattle	1	4	2.25	49	0	0	0	45	30	56.0	47	229	18	14	5	2	2	4	16	5	45	5	0
Schwabe, Michael, Detroit	0	0	2.45	1	1	0	0	0	0	3.2	5	15	1	1	0	3	1	0	2	0	1	3	0
Seanez, Rudy, Cleveland	2	1	5.60	24	0	0	0	12	0	27.1	22	127	17	17	0	1	0	2	25	1	24	3	0
Searcy, W. Stephen, Detroit*	2	7	4.66	16	12	0	0	2	0	75.1	76	341	44	39	11	0	6	2	51	3	66	5	0
Sebra, Robert, Milwaukee	1	2	8.18	10	1	0	0	2	0	11.0	20	59	10	10	3	2	2	0	5	0	4	0	0
Shaw, Jeffrey, Cleveland	3	4	6.66	12	9	0	0	1	0	48.2	73	229	38	36	0	1	3	2	20	0	25	1	0
Smith, Daryl, Kansas City	2	1	4.05	2	1	0	0	0	0	6.2	5	27	4	3	2	1	0	0	9	2	6	3	0
Smith, Lee, Boston	2	1	1.88	11	0	0	0	8	4	14.1	13	64	4	3	0	0	0	1	1	0	17	0	0
Smith, Leroy, Minnesota	1	0	12.00	2	0	0	0	1	0	3.0	4	14	4	4	2	0	0	0	1	0	2	1	0
Smith, Michael A., Baltimore	5	10	4.81	32	23	0	0	1	0	153.1	191	671	91	82	20	2	11	5	47	1	87	10	1
Stewart, David, Oakland	22	11	2.56	36	36	11	2	0	0	267.0	226	1088	84	76	16	10	10	8	83	4	166	8	0
Stieb, David, Toronto	18	6	2.93	33	33	4	2	0	0	208.2	179	861	73	68	11	6	10	10	64	0	125	5	0
Stottlemyre, Melvin, Kansas City	0	1	4.88	13	2	0	0	3	0	31.1	35	138	20	17	3	3	0	0	12	1	14	0	0
Stottlemyre, Todd, Toronto	13	17	4.34	33	33	0	0	0	0	203.0	214	866	101	98	18	2	5	8	69	4	115	6	1
Swan, Russell, Seattle*	6	3	3.64	11	8	0	0	0	0	47.0	42	195	22	19	3	1	3	0	18	2	15	1	0
Swift, William, Seattle*	6	4	2.39	55	8	0	0	18	6	128.0	135	533	46	34	4	8	6	5	21	6	42	8	0
Swindell, F. Gregory, Cleveland*	12	9	4.40	34	34	3	0	0	0	214.2	245	912	110	105	27	1	8	7	47	1	135	8	3
Tanana, Frank, Detroit*	9	8	5.31	34	29	1	0	4	1	176.1	190	763	104	104	25	4	7	9	66	3	114	5	2
Tapani, Kevin, Minnesota	12	8	4.07	28	28	1	1	0	0	159.1	164	659	75	72	12	3	4	2	29	2	101	1	1
Taylor, Donald, Baltimore..	0	1	2.45	8	0	0	0	4	1	3.2	4	18	3	1	0	0	0	0	2	0	2	1	0
Telford, Anthony, Baltimore	0	3	4.95	8	8	0	0	0	0	36.1	43	168	22	20	4	4	2	1	19	1	20	1	0
Terrell, C. Walter, Detroit	6	4	4.54	13	12	0	0	0	0	75.1	86	333	39	38	8	8	1	0	24	3	30	2	0
Thigpen, Robert, Chicago	4	6	1.83	77	0	0	0	73	57	88.2	60	347	20	18	5	5	3	0	32	3	70	2	0
Tibbs, Jay, Baltimore	2	7	4.75	10	10	0	0	0	0	50.2	55	215	34	27	8	2	4	1	14	1	23	1	0
Valdez, Efrain, Cleveland*	1	0	3.04	13	0	0	0	4	0	23.2	20	104	10	8	2	2	1	0	14	2	13	3	0
Valdez, Sergio, Cleveland	0	6	4.75	24	13	0	0	0	0	102.1	109	440	62	54	17	4	3	1	35	3	63	3	0
Veres, Randolph, Milwaukee	0	0	3.67	26	0	0	0	12	1	41.2	38	175	17	17	5	2	2	2	16	1	16	3	1
Wagner, Hector, Kansas City	0	2	8.10	5	5	0	0	0	0	23.1	32	112	24	21	4	0	0	6	11	3	14	3	0
Walker, Michael, Cleveland	2	6	4.88	18	11	0	0	2	0	75.2	82	350	49	41	6	4	2	0	42	4	34	6	1
Wapnick, Steven, Detroit	0	3	6.43	4	0	0	0	1	0	7.0	8	37	5	5	0	0	0	2	10	0	6	0	0
Ward, R. Colby, Cleveland	1	3	4.25	22	0	0	0	7	1	36.0	31	158	17	17	3	4	2	1	21	4	23	6	0

Pitcher, Club	W	L	ERA	G	GS	CG	SHO	GF	SV	IP	H	TBF	R	ER	HR	SH	SF	HB	BB	IBB	SO	WP	BK
Ward, R. Duane, Toronto	2	8	3.45	73	0	0	0	39	11	127.2	101	508	51	49	9	6	2	1	42	10	112	5	0
Wayne, Gary, Minnesota*	1	1	4.19	38	0	0	0	12	0	38.2	38	166	19	18	5	1	2	1	13	1	28	4	0
Wegman, William, Milwaukee	2	2	4.85	8	5	1	0	1	0	29.2	37	132	21	16	6	6	5	1	6	1	20	2	0
Welch, Robert, Oakland	27	6	2.95	35	35	2	2	0	0	238.0	214	979	90	78	26	9	5	5	77	4	127	2	2
Wells, David, Toronto*	11	6	3.14	43	25	0	0	8	3	189.0	165	759	72	66	14	6	2	2	45	3	115	7	1
West, David, Minnesota*	7	9	5.10	29	27	2	0	0	0	146.1	142	646	88	83	21	6	4	0	78	1	92	4	1
Weston, Michael, Baltimore*	0	1	7.71	9	0	0	0	4	0	21.0	28	94	20	18	6	0	4	0	6	1	9	1	0
Wickander, Kevin, Cleveland*	0	1	3.65	10	0	0	0	3	0	12.1	14	53	6	5	0	0	0	1	4	2	10	1	0
Williamson, Mark, Baltimore	8	2	2.21	49	0	0	0	15	1	85.1	65	343	25	21	8	6	2	1	28	7	60	1	2
Wills, Frank, Toronto	6	4	4.73	44	4	0	0	6	1	99.0	101	422	54	52	13	2	7	1	38	3	72	1	0
Witt, Michael, Cal.-N.Y.	17	10	3.36	33	32	7	1	1	0	222.0	197	954	98	83	12	5	6	4	110	3	221	11	2
Witt, Robert, Texas	5	9	4.00	26	16	2	0	4	0	117.0	106	498	62	52	9	1	6	5	47	1	74	7	0
Yett, Richard, Minnesota	0	0	2.08	4	0	0	0	1	0	4.1	6	19	2	1	0	1	0	0	1	1	0	2	0
Young, Clifford, California*	9	6	4.85	26	21	0	0	0	0	124.1	124	527	70	67	17	4	2	4	53	1	56	3	0
Young, Curtis, Oakland*	1	1	3.52	17	0	0	0	5	0	30.2	40	137	14	12	2	2	4	2	7	1	19	1	0
Young, Matthew, Seattle*	8	18	3.51	34	33	7	0	0	0	225.1	198	963	106	88	15	7	7	6	107	7	176	16	0

PITCHERS WITH TWO OR MORE CLUBS IN 1990
(Listed Alphabetically, First Club on Top)

Pitcher, Club	W	L	ERA	G	GS	CG	SHO	GF	SV	IP	H	TBF	R	ER	HR	SH	SF	HB	BB	IBB	SO	WP	BK
Bitker, Joseph, Oakland	0	0	0.00	1	0	0	0	1	0	3.0	1	10	0	0	0	0	0	0	1	0	2	0	0
Bitker, Joseph, Texas	0	0	3.00	5	0	0	0	4	0	9.0	7	38	3	3	0	4	1	1	3	1	6	0	1
Black, Harry, Cleveland	11	10	3.53	29	29	5	2	0	0	191.0	171	796	79	75	17	4	5	4	58	1	103	6	0
Black, Harry, Toronto	2	1	4.02	3	1	0	0	1	0	15.2	10	61	7	7	2	2	2	1	3	0	3	0	0
Candelaria, John, Minnesota	7	3	3.39	34	2	0	0	10	4	58.1	55	239	23	22	9	2	3	3	9	3	44	3	0
Candelaria, John, Toronto*	0	3	5.48	13	2	0	0	5	1	21.1	32	106	13	13	2	0	1	2	11	3	19	2	0
McCullers, Lance, New York	1	0	3.60	11	0	0	0	7	1	15.0	14	65	8	6	2	0	1	0	6	1	11	3	0
McCullers, Lance, Detroit	1	1	2.73	9	1	0	0	7	0	29.2	18	121	11	9	2	3	2	0	13	1	20	1	0
Parker, J. Clayton, New York	1	1	4.50	5	2	0	0	0	0	22.0	19	91	11	11	5	0	0	0	7	1	20	3	0
Parker, J. Clayton, Detroit	2	2	3.18	24	1	0	0	7	0	51.0	45	217	18	18	6	6	2	1	25	5	20	0	0
Powell, Dennis, Seattle	0	0	9.00	2	0	0	0	1	0	3.0	5	17	3	3	0	0	0	1	2	0	0	0	0
Powell, Dennis, Milwaukee	0	4	6.86	9	7	0	0	1	0	39.1	59	197	37	30	3	3	2	2	19	1	23	2	0
Reed, Jerry, Seattle	0	1	4.91	4	0	0	0	1	0	7.1	8	31	4	4	1	1	0	0	3	2	2	7	1
Reed, Jerry, Boston	2	1	4.80	29	0	0	0	15	2	45.0	55	203	27	24	4	2	3	1	16	2	17	1	0
Witt, Michael, California	0	3	1.77	10	0	0	0	4	1	20.1	19	92	9	4	1	1	1	4	13	2	14	7	1
Witt, Michael, New York	5	6	4.47	16	16	2	1	0	0	96.2	87	406	53	48	8	0	5	4	34	2	60	6	0

NOTE—The following pitchers combined to pitch shutout games: Baltimore (2)—Milacki, Hickey and Holton; Harnisch and Olson; Boston (9)—Boddicker, Murphy and Reardon; Harris and Reardon; Harris and Gray; Gardner, Murphy and Reardon; Bolton and Reardon; Bolton, Kiecker and Murphy; Kiecker and Gray; Harris and Gray; Kiecker and Andersen; California (8)—Finley and Harvey 2; Finley and Eichhorn; Langston and Witt; Blyleven, Witt and Eichhorn; Finley and Bailes; McCaskill and Fraser; Grahe and Harvey; Cleveland (7)—Black and Jones 2, Swindell, Guante and Jones; Farrell and Orosco; Shaw, Orosco and Jones; Black, Guante and Jones; Candiotti and Jones; Chicago (4)—Hibbard and Thigpen; McDowell, Jones and Thigpen; Hibbard, Jones and Radinsky; McDowell, Patterson, Jones and Thigpen; Detroit (8)—Tanana, Henneman and Gleaton 2; Terrell and Gleaton 2; Tanana and Henneman; DuBois and McCullers; Robinson, Parker and Gleaton; Aldred and Nunez; Kansas City (3)—S. Davis, Montgomery and Farr; McGaffigan and Farr; Farr, Crawford and Montgomery; Milwaukee (6)—Higuera, Filer and Plesac; Filer, Fossas and Crim; Filer, Crim and Plesac; Krueger and Navarro; Knudson, Crim and Plesac; Brown, Crim and Plesac; Minnesota (9)—Tapani, Wayne, Leach and Aguilera; West and Candelaria; Drummond, Candelaria and Leach; Anderson, Berenger and Aguilera; Tapani and Candelaria; Anderson and Aguilera; Guthrie and Wayne; Anderson, Casian and Garces; Erickson, Wayne and Aguilera; New York (3)—Perez, Guetterman and Righetti; Leary and Guetterman; Hawkins and Righetti; Oakland (9)—Sanderson and Nelson 2; Welch, Honeycutt, Nelson and Eckersley; Stewart and Eckersley; Sanderson, Burns and Honeycutt; Young, Burns, Honeycutt and Nelson; Moore and Honeycutt; Stewart and Honeycutt; Welch and Chitren; Seattle (3)—Swift and Jackson; Swift, Harris and Comstock; Swan and Swift; Texas (4)—Brown and Rogers; Ryan, Arnsberg and Rogers; McMurtry, Barfield and Arnsberg; Chiamparino, Arnsberg, Rogers, Mielke and Jeffcoat; Toronto (7)—Stieb and Henke 2; Wells and Henke 2; Stieb, Ward and Henke; Key and Henke; Stottlemyre and Candelaria.

1990 CHAMPIONSHIP SERIES

Including

National League Review

National League Box Scores

National League Composite Box Score

American League Review

American League Box Scores

American League Composite Box Score

Reds Recall Roots, Beat Pirates

By TOM BARNIDGE

When a community that is steeped in baseball tradition goes 14 years between World Series visits, it clings dearly to the glorious moments of its past.

So, every time the Cincinnati Reds reported to Riverfront Stadium in the National League Championship Series against Pittsburgh, they were greeted by video scoreboard reminders of their championship ancestors from 1976, the juggernaut revered as the "Big Red Machine."

Johnny Bench, George Foster, Joe Morgan and Tony Perez would make triumphant appearances on the electronic screen and, just as they had in real life, sweep the New York Yankees in four games.

Whether these subconscious implants served to inspire the 1990 Reds as they eliminated the N.L. East champion Pittsburgh Pirates, four games to two, remains a matter for psychiatric debate. But one item is abundantly clear—the Reds of 1990 bear not the vaguest resemblance to their famous ancestors.

If the '76 Reds were lumberjacks with chain saws, this year's version features woodworkers with awls. If the Big Red Machine, which also won the World Series in 1975, was built of six-by-six timbers, the '90 Reds are interlocking mosaic tiles.

A highly polished defense, an extremely stingy bullpen and a roster so pliable that it produced a new lineup every day were the unlikely ingredients that the modern-day Reds used to beat the suddenly punchless Pirates.

So curious was the Reds' winning formula in the playoffs that although two of their players shared Most Valuable Player honors, neither was an everyday performer. Relievers Rob Dibble and Randy Myers, two-thirds of Cincinnati's ballyhooed "Nasty Boys" bullpen, accounted for saves in every game the champs won and were voted co-winners of the MVP award. Never before had a reliever won that honor in the N.L. playoffs, let alone two relievers sharing the honor.

So curious was the Reds' route to success that they employed six different lineups in six games. They used three batters in the No. 3 spot and pinch-hit for one of them, Paul O'Neill, who owned a .471 postseason average at the time. The pinch-hitter, Luis Quinones, made that move look divinely inspired when he singled home the decisive

With Cincinnati leading 2-1 in the ninth inning of Game 6, right fielder Glenn Braggs deprived the Pirates' Carmelo Martinez of a two-run homer to help the Reds clinch the N.L. pennant.

Cincinnati pitchers stymied Barry Bonds throughout the series. In fact, Pittsburgh's "big three" of Bonds, Bobby Bonilla and Andy Van Slyke hit a combined .200 with five RBIs.

run in the decisive game.

Not all of these happenings came as a surprise to the Reds, who did, after all, lead the N.L. West from the start of the season. Manager Lou Piniella, for instance, dismissed those who questioned removing a .471 batter from the game. With a cat-who-ate-the-canary-grin, Piniella explained: "I know my team."

Still, even the Reds recognized that they needed some helpful bounces and unlikely events to win a series that utilityman Todd Benzinger described after only three games as "crazy."

Asked to amplify on his remarks, Benzinger said, "Whatever you expect to hap-

pen doesn't."

The unexpected began with Game 1, when Reds ace Jose Rijo squandered a 3-0 lead at home and the Pirates' Bob Walk, a seven-game winner in the regular season, survived long enough to earn the victory.

The next excursion into the twilight zone featured Doug Drabek, the Pirates' 22-game winner and Cy Young Award winner, as a 2-1 loser in a game in which he surrendered a total of five hits. Pittsburgh Manager Jim Leyland was still lamenting that game when the series ended seven days later.

"That was the turning point," Leyland said. "We had a shot at (starting pitcher Tom) Browning in the first inning—he wasn't the Browning he usually is—and we let it get away." Left unsaid was the wasted performance of Drabek, the bulwark of the Pittsburgh staff.

That missed opportunity—runners on first and second, none out, with the Nos. 3-4-5 hitters coming to the plate—was eerily prophetic of a hitting drought that plagued the middle of the Pirates' order throughout the series.

Andy Van Slyke, Bobby Bonilla and Barry Bonds, a package worth 311 runs batted in during 162 regular-season games, had only 12 hits in 63 appearances (a .190 average) and collected a grand total of five RBIs. The Pirates watched chance after chance disappear—they left 41 runners on base— as they scored first only in Game 4. That 1-0 lead lasted only until the fourth inning.

"The thing that surprised me and disappointed me most about this series," Van Slyke said, "is that we didn't produce offensively the way we did all year long. It was a combination of their pitching and our not playing up to our capability. I'm as guilty as anyone."

Van Slyke was not alone in his puzzlement. Even Myers, unscored on in 5⅔ innings, had to shake his head.

"I was surprised that we were able to keep their big hitters off balance," he said. "They are a great hitting team."

Although teammates attempted to minimize the slumping "big boys"—"They had times during the season when they struggled, but other guys picked them up," Wally Backman said—the numbers told another story. In the six regular-season games the Pirates had won from the Reds, the "big boys" hit .368 with 19 RBIs. In the six games that the Pirates had lost to Cincinnati, the Nos. 3-4-5 hitters batted .200 with five RBIs.

The Pirates, as a team, batted only .194, an average that reflected the surprising ef-

Mariano Duncan's three-run homer in the fifth inning of Game 3 put the Reds up, 5-2, in a game they went on to win, 6-3.

Pittsburgh's Sid Bream is tagged out by Cincinnati's Jeff Reed after center fielder Billy Hatcher relayed a throw home in Game 4. Reds outfielders totaled four assists and no errors in the series.

fectiveness of Cincinnati's starters and the not-so-surprising effectiveness of the Reds' bullpen. "I didn't think their starters would dominate us the way they did," shortstop Jay Bell conceded.

"The way the game has been played in the last few years, you need a good bullpen," Piniella had explained. "We've got long men and closers and, basically, I can interchange them. It's a tremendous advantage when you're managing."

Say this for Piniella: He doesn't hesitate to utilize his advantage. The Nasty Boys—Dibble, Myers and Norm Charlton—appeared in four games each and permitted a total of six hits and one earned run in 15⅔ innings (an 0.57 earned-run average). Dibble, who wears the crazed glare of a man possessed, rang up 10 strikeouts in his five hitless innings. Charlton and Myers were only slightly more hittable.

The psychological effect of this late-inning trio was ever present in Pittsburgh's mind. Failure to grab a lead in the first six innings placed the Pirates' necks in a noose, and only once in six games did Pittsburgh own a lead at that point in a game.

"I sensed some frustration on their part," Benzinger said.

Although none of the games got out of hand—four of the six were one-run deci-

sions—Cincinnati seemed to wield the hammer throughout. What the Reds didn't do with their arms (2.38 ERA), they did with timely hitting and extraordinary defense. Plays made by the Reds' outfielders moved Pittsburgh's Backman to call them "the whole key to the series."

In Game 2, right fielder O'Neill launched a bull's-eye to third base after a fly by Bonds to nab the speedy Van Slyke, who had tagged up and was clearly amazed when he was gunned down.

In Game 4, center fielder Billy Hatcher nailed Sid Bream, who was trying to score from second on a single by Jose Lind. Later in the same game, when Bonilla drilled a shot to center and watched Hatcher bang off the wall in pursuit, he was cut down trying to stretch a double as left fielder Eric Davis, who had backed up the play, made a perfect throw to third base.

Bonilla called it "the play of the season." Reds General Manager Bob Quinn, who has spent more than 30 years in baseball, went further. He described it as "one of the best plays by one of the best players I've ever seen."

For the series, the Reds' outfielders had four assists and no errors (O'Neill also nabbed Bream trying to stretch a single in Game 1), which should have come as small surprise. During the season, the Reds' outfield led the N.L. in assists and fielding percentage.

"I keep waiting for their outfielders to make a throwing error," Van Slyke said with a sigh. "They're almost robotic out there."

By their normal standards, the Reds' bats were in a mild trance. Their .255 average in the series fell 10 points short of their league-leading .265 regular-season mark. Cleanup hitter Davis, still feeling the effects of a late-season shoulder injury, hit a particularly anemic .174, with two RBIs.

Against Pittsburgh, most of the telling blows came from unlikely sources at unexpected times. Hatcher, hitting in the No. 8 spot, delivered three hits, including a two-run homer, in Game 3. It was his first home run in five weeks.

In Game 4, Chris Sabo, who had only two hits in his previous 13 at-bats, provided a sacrifice fly and a two-run homer from the sixth spot in the order.

But the pennant-clinching victory in Game 6 may have provided the clearest insight into the success of the jigsaw-puzzle Reds, who have fitted everything neatly into place this season.

Utility infielder Ron Oester, who entered the game as part of a double switch when Charlton relieved starter Danny Jackson, singled in his only at-bat to open the seventh inning. With one out, he advanced to third on a base hit by Hatcher, who joined the Reds in the spring in a three-player deal with Pittsburgh. Then, switch-hitter Quinones, in his third plate appearance of the series, batted for O'Neill and sent home the decisive run with a single to right off hard-luck loser Zane Smith. In the top of the ninth, right fielder Glenn Braggs leaped above the wall to deprive the Pirates' Carmelo Martinez of a two-run homer and preserve the Reds' 2-1 victory.

Slumped over on a stool in front of his locker, the Pirates' Van Slyke summed up what had happened: "When the Reds needed something, they got it. When we needed it, we came up short."

It may not have been the way the Big Red Machine did things, but who was to deny that it worked?

GAME OF THURSDAY, OCTOBER 4
AT CINCINNATI

Pittsburgh	AB.	R.	H.	RBI.	PO.	A.
Backman, 3b	2	0	0	0	1	1
King, ph-3b	2	0	0	0	1	0
Bell, ss	3	0	0	0	0	3
Van Slyke, cf	4	0	1	1	1	1
Bonilla, rf	4	0	1	0	1	0
Bonds, lf	3	1	1	0	2	0
Bream, 1b	3	1	2	2	8	2
LaValliere, c	3	1	0	0	9	1

Pittsburgh	AB.	R.	H.	RBI.	PO.	A.
Lind, 2b	4	0	1	1	2	3
Walk, p	2	0	0	0	2	1
Redus, ph	1	1	1	0	0	0
Belinda, p	0	0	0	0	0	0
Reynolds, ph	1	0	0	0	0	0
Patterson, p	0	0	0	0	0	1
Power, p	0	0	0	0	0	0
Totals	32	4	7	4	27	13

Cincinnati	AB.	R.	H.	RBI.	PO.	A.
Larkin, ss	2	1	0	0	2	2
Hatcher, cf	3	0	0	0	2	0
Morris, 1b	3	1	1	1	4	1
Benzinger, ph	1	0	1	0	0	0
Davis, lf	3	1	1	1	3	0
O'Neill, rf	3	0	1	1	1	1
Oester, ph	1	0	0	0	0	0
Bates, pr	0	0	0	0	0	0
Sabo, 3b	4	0	1	0	1	1
Reed, c	3	0	0	0	12	0
Duncan, 2b	3	0	0	0	1	2
Rijo, p	2	0	0	0	0	0
Charlton, p	0	0	0	0	1	0
Winningham, ph	1	0	0	0	0	0
Dibble, p	0	0	0	0	0	0
Totals	29	3	5	3	27	7

Pittsburgh .... 0 0 1   2 0 0   1 0 0—4
Cincinnati .... 3 0 0   0 0 0   0 0 0—3

Pittsburgh	IP.	H.	R.	ER.	BB.	SO.
Walk (Winner)	6	4	3	3	2	5
Belinda	2	0	0	0	0	3
Patterson	⅓	1	0	0	1	0
Power (Save)	⅔	0	0	0	0	1

Cincinnati	IP.	H.	R.	ER.	BB.	SO.
Rijo	5⅓	4	3	3	3	8
Charlton (Loser)	2⅔	3	1	1	2	1
Dibble	1	0	0	0	0	3

Error—Bonilla. Double play—Cincinnati 1. Left on bases—Pittsburgh 6, Cincinnati 3. Two-base hits—Davis, O'Neill, Van Slyke. Three-base hit—Lind. Home run—Bream. Stolen bases—Larkin, Redus. Sacrifice hit—Hatcher. Umpires—Wendelstedt, McSherry, Runge, Rennert, Crawford and Davis. Time—2:51. Attendance—55,700.

GAME OF FRIDAY, OCTOBER 5
AT CINCINNATI

Pittsburgh	AB.	R.	H.	RBI.	PO.	A.
Redus, 1b	2	0	1	0	7	0
Bream, ph-1b	1	0	0	0	0	0
Bell, ss	3	0	2	0	1	3
Van Slyke, cf	4	0	1	0	3	0
Bonilla, rf-3b	4	0	1	0	0	2
Bonds, lf	4	0	0	0	2	0
King, 3b	0	0	0	0	0	0
Reynolds, rf	3	0	0	0	0	0
Slaught, c	2	0	0	0	5	0
Backman, ph	1	0	0	0	0	0
LaValliere, c	0	0	0	0	3	1
Lind, 2b	3	1	1	1	3	3
Drabek, p	3	0	0	0	0	3
Totals	30	1	6	1	24	12

Cincinnati	AB.	R.	H.	RBI.	PO.	A.
Larkin, ss	3	1	1	0	5	3
Winningham, cf	4	1	2	0	5	0
O'Neill, rf	4	0	2	2	3	1
Davis, lf	4	0	0	0	1	0
Morris, 1b	1	0	0	0	6	0
Sabo, 3b	3	0	0	0	1	0
Oliver, c	3	0	0	0	6	1
Duncan, 2b	3	0	0	0	0	1
Browning, p	2	0	0	0	0	1

Cincinnati	AB.	R.	H.	RBI.	PO.	A.
Dibble, p	1	0	0	0	0	0
Myers, p	0	0	0	0	0	0
Totals	28	2	5	2	27	7

Pittsburgh.............. 000 010 000—1
Cincinnati.............. 100 010 00x—2

Pittsburgh	IP.	H.	R.	ER.	BB.	SO.
Drabek (Loser)	8	5	2	2	2	8

Cincinnati	IP.	H.	R.	ER.	BB.	SO.
Browning (Winner)	6	6	1	1	3	3
Dibble	1⅓	0	0	0	1	2
Myers (Save)	1⅔	0	0	0	1	0

Error—None. Double play—Cincinnati 1. Left on bases—Pittsburgh 7, Cincinnati 5. Two-base hits—O'Neill, Winningham. Home run—Lind. Stolen bases—Larkin, O'Neill, Winningham. Hit by pitcher—By Drabek (Morris). Umpires—McSherry, Runge, Rennert, Crawford, Davis and Wendelstedt. Time—2:38. Attendance—54,456.

GAME OF MONDAY, OCTOBER 8
AT PITTSBURGH

Cincinnati	AB.	R.	H.	RBI.	PO.	A.
Larkin, ss	5	1	1	0	3	1
Duncan, 2b	5	1	3	4	1	1
Sabo, 3b	5	0	1	0	1	3
Davis, lf	4	0	0	0	3	0
Braggs, rf	4	0	1	0	1	0
Benzinger, 1b	4	0	1	0	7	0
Oliver, c	4	1	2	0	8	0
Bates, pr	0	1	0	0	0	0
Reed, c	0	0	0	0	3	0
Hatcher, cf	4	2	3	2	0	0
Jackson, p	1	0	0	0	0	1
Dibble, p	1	0	0	0	0	0
Charlton, ph	0	0	0	0	0	0
Morris, ph	1	0	1	0	0	0
Myers, p	0	0	0	0	0	0
Totals	38	6	13	6	27	6

Pittsburgh	AB.	R.	H.	RBI.	PO.	A.
King, 3b	5	0	1	0	0	2
Bell, ss	5	1	2	0	1	5
Van Slyke, cf	4	1	0	0	4	0
Bonilla, rf	4	0	1	1	0	0
Bonds, lf	3	1	1	0	2	0
Martinez, 1b	4	0	1	1	8	0
Slaught, c	2	0	1	0	8	0
Lind, 2b	4	0	1	0	4	3
Smith, p	2	0	0	0	0	0
Landrum, p	0	0	0	0	0	0
Redus, ph	1	0	0	0	0	0
Smiley, p	0	0	0	0	0	0
Reynolds, ph	1	0	0	0	0	0
Belinda, p	0	0	0	0	0	0
Totals	35	3	8	2	27	10

Cincinnati.............. 020 030 001—6
Pittsburgh.............. 000 200 010—3

Cincinnati	IP.	H.	R.	ER.	BB.	SO.
Jackson (Winner)	5⅓	7	2	2	3	4
Dibble	1⅔	0	0	0	0	3
Charlton	1	1	1	0	1	1
Myers (Save)	1	0	0	0	0	3

Pittsburgh	IP.	H.	R.	ER.	BB.	SO.
Smith (Loser)	5	8	5	5	0	5
Landrum	1	0	0	0	0	1
Smiley	2	2	0	0	0	0
Belinda	1	3	1	1	0	1

Error—Duncan. Double play—Pittsburgh 1. Left on bases—Cincinnati 6, Pittsburgh 9. Two-base hits—Slaught, Bell, Martinez, Hatcher, Lind. Home runs—Hatcher, Duncan. Sacrifice hit—

Jackson. Umpires—Runge, Rennert, Crawford, Davis, Wendelstedt and McSherry. Time—2:51. Attendance—45,611.

GAME OF TUESDAY, OCTOBER 9
AT PITTSBURGH

Cincinnati	AB.	R.	H.	RBI.	PO.	A.
Larkin, ss	5	0	0	0	5	1
Hatcher, cf	4	0	0	0	2	1
O'Neill, rf	4	1	3	1	2	0
Davis, lf	4	1	1	0	2	1
Morris, 1b	4	2	3	0	3	0
Sabo, 3b	3	1	2	3	2	0
Reed, c	3	0	0	0	8	1
Oliver, c	1	0	0	0	3	0
Duncan, 2b	3	0	1	0	0	2
Benzinger, ph	0	0	0	0	0	0
Oester, 2b	0	0	0	0	0	0
Rijo, p	3	0	0	0	0	0
Myers, p	0	0	0	0	0	0
Quinones, ph	0	0	0	0	1	0
Dibble, p	0	0	0	0	0	0
Totals	34	5	10	5	27	6

Pittsburgh	AB.	R.	H.	RBI.	PO.	A.
Backman, 3b	4	1	1	0	0	2
Bell, ss	4	1	1	1	0	6
Van Slyke, cf	4	1	1	1	1	0
Bonilla, rf	3	0	1	0	2	0
Bonds, lf	4	0	1	0	2	0
Bream, 1b	3	0	1	1	15	0
LaValliere, c	3	0	0	0	5	0
Lind, 2b	4	0	2	0	2	3
Walk, p	2	0	0	0	0	0
Reynolds, ph	0	0	0	0	0	0
Power, p	0	0	0	0	0	1
King, ph	1	0	0	0	0	0
Totals	32	3	8	3	27	12

Cincinnati.............. 000 200 201—5
Pittsburgh.............. 100 100 010—3

Cincinnati	IP.	H.	R.	ER.	BB.	SO.
Rijo (Winner)	7*	6	3	3	4	7
Myers	1	2	0	0	0	1
Dibble (Save)	1	0	0	0	0	2

Pittsburgh	IP.	H.	R.	ER.	BB.	SO.
Walk (Loser)	7	7	4	4	0	3
Power	2	3	1	1	1	2

*Pitched to one batter in eighth.

Error—Larkin. Double plays—Cincinnati 1, Pittsburgh 1. Left on bases—Cincinnati 5, Pittsburgh 6. Two-base hits—Backman, Bream, O'Neill, Bonilla, Morris. Home runs—O'Neill, Sabo, Bell. Stolen bases—Backman, Van Slyke, Bonds. Sacrifice flies—Sabo, Quinones. Umpires—Rennert, Crawford, Davis, Wendelstedt, McSherry and Runge. Time—3:00. Attendance—50,461.

GAME OF WEDNESDAY, OCTOBER 10
AT PITTSBURGH

Cincinnati	AB.	R.	H.	RBI.	PO.	A.
Larkin, ss	4	1	2	1	2	4
Winningham, cf	2	0	0	1	2	0
O'Neill, rf	4	0	1	0	2	0
Davis, lf	4	0	1	0	3	0
Morris, 1b	3	0	0	0	7	1
Sabo, 3b	3	0	1	0	1	1
Oliver, c	2	0	0	0	3	0
Oester, ph	1	0	0	0	0	0
Reed, c	1	0	0	0	1	0
Duncan, 2b	3	0	1	0	2	3
Browning, p	1	0	0	0	1	0

Cincinnati	AB.	R.	H.	RBI.	PO.	A.
Benzinger, ph	1	0	1	0	0	0
Mahler, p	0	0	0	0	0	0
Charlton, p	0	0	0	0	0	0
Quinones, ph	1	1	0	0	0	0
Scudder, p	0	0	0	0	0	0
Totals	30	2	7	2	24	9

Pittsburgh	AB.	R.	H.	RBI.	PO.	A.
Redus, 1b	3	0	0	0	9	0
Bream, 1b	1	0	1	0	3	1
Bell, ss	2	1	0	0	2	3
Van Slyke, cf	4	1	2	1	0	0
Bonilla, 3b	3	0	0	0	1	3
Bonds, lf	3	1	0	0	2	0
Reynolds, rf	4	0	2	0	2	0
Slaught, c	3	0	0	1	5	0
Lind, 2b	3	0	0	0	2	6
Drabek, p	3	0	1	0	1	3
Patterson, p	0	0	0	0	0	0
Totals	29	3	6	3	27	16

Cincinnati		1 0 0	0 0 0	0 1 0—2		
Pittsburgh		2 0 0	1 0 0	0 0 x—3		

Cincinnati	IP.	H.	R.	ER.	BB.	SO.
Browning (Loser)	5	3	3	3	3	2
Mahler	1⅔	2	0	0	0	0
Charlton	⅓	0	0	0	0	1
Scudder	1	1	0	0	0	1

Pittsburgh	IP.	H.	R.	ER.	BB.	SO.
Drabek (Winner)	8⅓	7	2	1	1	5
Patterson (Save)	⅔	0	0	0	1	0

Error—Drabek. Double plays—Pittsburgh 2. Left on bases—Cincinnati 5, Pittsburgh 7. Two-base hits—Larkin 2. Three-base hit—Van Slyke. Stolen bases—Bonds, Reynolds. Sacrifice hit—Morris. Sacrifice flies—Winningham, Slaught. Hit by pitcher—By Browning (Bell). Wild pitch—Drabek. Umpires—Crawford, Davis, Wendelstedt, McSherry, Runge and Rennert. Time—2:38. Attendance—48,221.

GAME OF FRIDAY, OCTOBER 12
AT CINCINNATI

Pittsburgh	AB.	R.	H.	RBI.	PO.	A.
King, 3b	2	0	0	0	0	2
Reynolds, ph-rf	1	0	0	0	0	0

Pittsburgh	AB.	R.	H.	RBI.	PO.	A.
Bell, ss	3	0	0	0	0	2
Van Slyke, cf	4	0	0	0	4	0
Bonilla, rf-3b	3	0	0	0	0	0
Bonds, lf	1	1	0	0	3	0
Martinez, 1b	4	0	1	1	7	1
Slaught, c	4	0	0	0	4	1
Lind, 2b	3	0	0	0	6	1
Power, p	1	0	0	0	0	0
Smith, p	1	0	0	0	0	1
Belinda, p	0	0	0	0	0	0
Redus, ph	1	0	0	0	0	0
Landrum, p	0	0	0	0	0	0
Totals	28	1	1	1	24	8

Cincinnati	AB.	R.	H.	RBI.	PO.	A.
Larkin, ss	4	1	2	0	4	4
Hatcher, cf	4	0	2	0	1	0
O'Neill, rf	2	0	1	0	1	0
Quinones, ph	1	0	1	1	0	0
Myers, p	0	0	0	0	0	0
Davis, lf	4	0	1	1	0	0
Sabo, 3b	4	0	0	0	1	2
Benzinger, 1b	3	0	0	0	10	0
Duncan, 2b	3	0	1	0	2	2
Charlton, p	0	0	0	0	0	0
Braggs, rf	1	0	0	0	1	0
Oliver, c	4	0	0	0	7	0
Jackson, p	2	0	0	0	0	1
Oester, 2b	1	1	1	0	0	1
Totals	33	2	9	2	27	10

Pittsburgh		0 0 0	0 1 0	0 0 0—1		
Cincinnati		1 0 0	0 0 0	1 0 x—2		

Pittsburgh	IP.	H.	R.	ER.	BB.	SO.
Power	2⅓	3	1	1	1	0
Smith (Loser)	4	6	1	1	1	3
Belinda	⅔	0	0	0	0	0
Landrum	1	0	0	0	0	0

Cincinnati	IP.	H.	R.	ER.	BB.	SO.
Jackson	6*	1	1	1	4	4
Charlton (Winner)	1	0	0	0	0	0
Myers (Save)	2	0	0	0	2	3

*Pitched to two batters in seventh.

Errors—Slaught, Bell, Reynolds. Left on bases—Pittsburgh 6, Cincinnati 9. Two-base hit—Martinez. Stolen bases—Larkin, Quinones. Umpires—Davis, Wendelstedt, McSherry, Runge, Rennert and Crawford. Time—2:57. Attendance—56,079.

CINCINNATI REDS' BATTING AND FIELDING AVERAGES

Player—Position	G.	AB.	R.	H.	TB.	2B.	3B.	HR.	RBI.	B.A.	PO.	A.	E.	F.A.
Quinones, ph	3	2	1	1	1	0	0	0	2	.500	0	0	0	.000
O'Neill, rf	5	17	1	8	14	3	0	1	4	.471	9	2	0	1.000
Morris, 1b-ph	5	12	3	5	6	1	0	0	1	.417	20	2	0	1.000
Hatcher, cf	4	15	2	5	9	1	0	1	2	.333	5	1	0	1.000
Benzinger, ph-1b	5	9	0	3	3	0	0	0	0	.333	17	0	0	1.000
Oester, ph-2b	4	3	1	1	1	0	0	0	0	.333	0	1	0	1.000
Duncan, 2b	6	20	1	6	9	0	0	1	4	.300	6	11	1	.944
Winningham, ph-cf	3	7	1	2	3	1	0	0	1	.286	7	0	0	1.000
Larkin, ss	6	23	5	6	8	2	0	0	1	.261	21	15	1	.973
Sabo, 3b	6	22	1	5	8	0	0	1	3	.227	7	7	0	1.000
Braggs, rf	2	5	0	1	1	0	0	0	0	.200	2	0	0	1.000
Davis, lf	6	23	2	4	5	1	0	0	2	.174	12	1	0	1.000
Oliver, c	5	14	1	2	2	0	0	0	0	.143	27	1	0	1.000
Bates, pr	2	0	1	0	0	0	0	0	0	.000	0	0	0	.000
Charlton, p	4	0	0	0	0	0	0	0	0	.000	1	0	0	1.000
Mahler, p	1	0	0	0	0	0	0	0	0	.000	0	0	0	.000
Myers, p	4	0	0	0	0	0	0	0	0	.000	0	0	0	.000
Scudder, p	1	0	0	0	0	0	0	0	0	.000	0	0	0	.000
Dibble, p	4	2	0	0	0	0	0	0	0	.000	0	0	0	.000
Browning, p	2	3	0	0	0	0	0	0	0	.000	1	1	0	1.000
Jackson, p	2	3	0	0	0	0	0	0	0	.000	0	2	0	1.000
Rijo, p	2	5	0	0	0	0	0	0	0	.000	0	0	0	.000
Reed, c	4	7	0	0	0	0	0	0	0	.000	24	1	0	1.000
Totals	6	192	20	49	70	9	0	4	20	.255	159	45	2	.990

PITTSBURGH PIRATES' BATTING AND FIELDING AVERAGES

Player—Position	G.	AB.	R.	H.	TB.	2B.	3B.	HR.	RBI.	B.A.	PO.	A.	E.	F.A.
Bream, 1b-ph	4	8	1	4	8	1	0	1	3	.500	26	3	0	1.000
Bell, ss	6	20	3	5	9	1	0	1	1	.250	4	22	1	.963
Martinez, 1b	2	8	0	2	4	2	0	0	2	.250	15	1	0	1.000
Redus, ph-1b	5	8	1	2	2	0	0	0	0	.250	16	0	0	1.000
Lind, 2b	6	21	1	5	11	1	1	1	2	.238	19	19	0	1.000
Van Slyke, cf	6	24	3	5	8	1	1	0	3	.208	13	1	0	1.000
Reynolds, ph-rf	6	10	0	2	2	0	0	0	0	.200	2	0	1	.667
Bonilla, rf-3b	6	21	0	4	5	1	0	0	1	.190	4	5	1	.900
Bonds, lf	6	18	4	3	3	0	0	0	1	.167	13	0	0	1.000
Drabek, p	2	6	0	1	1	0	0	0	0	.167	1	6	1	.875
Backman, 3b-ph	3	7	1	1	2	1	0	0	0	.143	1	3	0	1.000
King, ph-3b	5	10	0	1	1	0	0	0	0	.100	1	4	0	1.000
Slaught, c	4	11	0	1	2	1	0	0	1	.091	22	1	1	.958
Belinda, p	3	0	0	0	0	0	0	0	0	.000	0	0	0	.000
Landrum, p	2	0	0	0	0	0	0	0	0	.000	0	0	0	.000
Patterson, p	2	0	0	0	0	0	0	0	0	.000	0	1	0	1.000
Smiley, p	1	0	0	0	0	0	0	0	0	.000	0	0	0	.000
Power, p	3	1	0	0	0	0	0	0	0	.000	0	1	0	1.000
Smith, p	2	3	0	0	0	0	0	0	0	.000	0	1	0	1.000
Walk, p	2	4	0	0	0	0	0	0	0	.000	2	1	0	1.000
LaValliere, c	3	6	1	0	0	0	0	0	0	.000	17	2	0	1.000
Totals	6	186	15	36	58	9	2	3	14	.194	156	71	5	.978

CINCINNATI REDS' PITCHING RECORDS

Pitcher	G.	GS.	CG.	IP.	H.	R.	ER.	BB.	SO.	HB.	WP.	W.	L.	Pct.	ERA.
Myers	4	0	0	5⅔	2	0	0	3	7	0	0	0	0	.000	0.00
Dibble	4	0	0	5	0	0	0	1	10	0	0	0	0	.000	0.00
Mahler	1	0	0	1⅔	2	0	0	0	0	0	0	0	0	.000	0.00
Scudder	1	0	0	1	1	0	0	0	1	0	0	0	0	.000	0.00
Charlton	4	0	0	5	4	2	1	3	3	0	0	1	1	.500	1.80
Jackson	2	2	0	11⅓	8	3	3	7	8	0	0	1	0	1.000	2.38
Browning	2	2	0	11	9	4	4	6	5	1	0	1	1	.500	3.27
Rijo	2	2	0	12⅓	10	6	6	7	15	0	0	1	0	1.000	4.38
Totals	6	6	0	53	36	15	14	27	49	1	0	4	2	.667	2.38

No shutouts. Saves—Myers 3, Dibble.

PITTSBURGH PIRATES' PITCHING RECORDS

Pitcher	G.	GS.	CG.	IP.	H.	R.	ER.	BB.	SO.	HB.	WP.	W.	L.	Pct.	ERA.
Landrum	2	0	0	2	0	0	0	1	0	0	0	0	0	.000	0.00
Smiley	1	0	0	2	2	0	0	0	0	0	0	0	0	.000	0.00
Patterson	2	0	0	1	1	0	0	2	0	0	0	0	0	.000	0.00
Drabek	2	2	1	16⅓	12	4	3	3	13	1	1	1	1	.500	1.65
Belinda	3	0	0	3⅔	3	1	1	0	4	0	0	0	0	.000	2.45
Power	3	1	0	5	6	2	2	2	3	0	0	0	0	.000	3.60
Walk	2	2	0	13	11	7	7	2	8	0	0	1	1	.500	4.85
Smith	2	1	0	9	14	6	6	1	8	0	0	0	2	.000	6.00
Totals	6	6	1	52	49	20	19	10	37	1	1	2	4	.333	3.29

No shutouts. Saves—Power, Patterson.

COMPOSITE SCORE BY INNINGS

Cincinnati	6	2	0	2	4	0	3	1	2 — 20
Pittsburgh	3	0	1	6	2	0	1	2	0 — 15

Sacrifice hits—Hatcher, Jackson, Morris.
Sacrifice flies—Sabo, Quinones, Winningham, Slaught.
Stolen bases—Larkin 3, Bonds 2, Redus, O'Neill, Winningham, Backman, Van Slyke, Reynolds, Quinones.
Caught stealing—Bates, Redus, Winningham, Bonilla, Davis.
Double plays—Morris, Larkin and Charlton; O'Neill and Sabo; Bell, Lind and Martinez; Larkin and Morris; Lind and Bream; Lind, Bell and Bream; Bonilla, Lind and Bream.
Left on bases—Cincinnati 3, 5, 6, 5, 5, 9—33; Pittsburgh 6, 7, 9, 6, 7, 6—41.
Hit by pitcher—By Drabek (Morris), by Browning (Bell).
Passed balls—None.
Balks—None.
Time of games—First game, 2:51; second game, 2:38; third game, 2:51; fourth game, 3:00; fifth game, 2:38; sixth game, 2:57.
Attendance—First game, 55,700; second game, 54,456; third game, 45,611; fourth game, 50,461; fifth game, 48,221; sixth game, 56,079.
Umpires—Wendelstedt, McSherry, Runge, Rennert, Crawford and Davis.
Official scorers—Red Foley, BBWAA; Jack Lang, BBWAA; Evan Pattak, Pittsburgh official scorer; Glenn Sample, Cincinnati official scorer.

Oakland's 'System' Stifles Sox

By DAVE NIGHTINGALE

The theme for the 1990 American League Championship Series was suggested by Dave Duncan, pitching coach of the Oakland Athletics.

After Oakland's four-game sweep of the overmatched Boston Red Sox for its third straight A.L. pennant, Duncan said, "And now, let us talk about the guys who did things right, not the guys who did things wrong."

That means the tirade Boston pitcher Roger Clemens engaged in with home plate umpire Terry Cooney in Game 4 that led to Clemens' ejection should be overlooked. Truth be told, Clemens' ejection had little effect on the outcome of the championship series.

"Remember, we swept Boston in four games," Oakland pitcher Dave Stewart said. "To the real baseball fan, that's more important than any one game or one event."

The A's victory over Boston was accomplished primarily with pitching (the scores were 9-1, 4-1, 4-1 and 3-1) and with defense. "Bash Brothers" Jose Canseco and Mark McGwire batted .182 and .154, respectively, and the Oakland offense consisted of 34 singles, four doubles and a lot of legwork.

"Hey, we don't just 'bash,' we play baseball," A's second baseman Willie Randolph said. "We have the best defensive team I've ever seen. And our pitching? Well, that speaks for itself."

In the regular season, Oakland pitchers boasted a 3.18 earned-run average, nearly half a run better than anybody else in the league. In the A.L. championship series, the A's pitchers were even more impressive. They boasted a 1.00 ERA and held the Red Sox to a .183 batting average, 89 points under Boston's league-leading season mark.

The Red Sox had a .222 on-base percentage in the four postseason games. Only 13 percent of those Boston runners crossed home plate. The Red Sox had 22 opportunities to get a hit with runners in scoring position. They were successful once. Boston's Mike Greenwell and Carlos Quintana were a combined 0-for-27.

Had enough?

So, if pitching is the heart of the Oakland machine, then "The System" is the heart of the A's approach to pitching.

What exactly is The System? What is

Oakland first baseman Mark McGwire lifts relief pitcher Rick Honeycutt after the A's beat Boston to win the American League championship.

this monster that changed the Boston hitters from mashers to mashed potatoes and reduced Clemens to a blithering mass of 10- and 12-letter words in Game 4?

"I don't want this to sound corny but, basically, it has to do with creating the sense of team work," Duncan said. "It's making sure that everyone on our pitching staff knows his role and is willing to play that

Down three games to none, Boston's fate was sealed when Roger Clemens got ejected for arguing balls and strikes in the second inning of Game 4.

role for the benefit of the team as a whole—even though it might sometimes shortchange his individual numbers."

Free translation: Starting pitchers may leave a game for no apparent reason because the relievers are deemed stronger.

That's why Gene Nelson or Todd Burns is ready to take the mound in the seventh inning of any game that Bob Welch, Mike Moore or Scott Sanderson might start; the reason why lefthander Rick Honeycutt (or Joe Klink) is available for spot duty against selected lefthanded hitters.

The object is to take the lead into the ninth inning and toss the ball to Dennis Eckersley.

Much of the credit for the team's success is ascribed to relief ace Eckersley. Oakland Manager Tony La Russa calls him "the most valuable" of all the Oakland pitchers. Eckersley saved 48 games in 50 opportunities during the regular season.

"Our pitching staff thinks of itself as a team within a team," Duncan said. "And our bullpen thinks of itself as a team within a team that's, well, also within a team."

A classic example of The System at work was in Game 3 of the A.L. championship series, in which Moore started instead of Sanderson. On paper, it seemed that Sanderson should have been the starter. He had a 2-0 record against the Red Sox, including a shutout August 13. Meanwhile, the Red Sox had knocked out Moore in two innings the following night and he was a 2-0 loser in his only other 1990 appearance against Boston. Naturally, Moore started Game 3 in the playoffs. Why?

"Well, let's just say that after last year, we—Tony and I—knew what Moore was capable of doing in postseason competition and Sanderson has only been here this year so we didn't know what he could do," Duncan said.

There was more to it than that.

"Well, Moore has a power style of pitching and Sanderson has a control, finesse style," Duncan said, phrasing his words carefully. "It's easier for a power guy to get away with mistakes. If a finesse guy is perfect, he may be more difficult to beat, but he has less margin of error than a power guy."

Sanderson, who has been known to hang high, off-speed curves, had the fifth worst homers-to-innings-pitched ratio in the A.L. in 1990. He was more susceptible to a Boston offensive explosion than Moore. So, even if Moore had a rocky outing, the A's still thought he'd be able to keep them close.

What happened? Moore struggled early, but gave up only one run. The A's responded with four runs in the middle innings, and Nelson, Honeycutt and Eckersley closed out the game.

At this point, with Boston down, three games to none, Clemens thrust himself into the headlines. So, with Duncan's forgiveness, let's shift the story to "the guys who did things wrong."

The Game 4 faceoff between Clemens and Stewart was their fifth in 1990. It didn't last long.

Oakland already had a 1-0 lead in the bottom of the second when Clemens issued a two-out walk to Randolph to put two men on base. He then started a diatribe against Cooney.

The next scheduled batter was shortstop Mike Gallego. "I thought Roger was swearing at me," Gallego said with a straight face. He paused, laughed and then admitted: "But I couldn't understand why; it didn't make sense. So I stepped out of the batter's box."

That allowed the flow of Clemens' verbiage to proceed directly to Cooney's ears. Some 15 seconds later, Clemens was ejected.

"Dumb, dumb, dumb," Stewart declared. "Roger certainly has some idea of his importance to his ball club. There's no way he can let himself get thrown out in

With their bats relatively silenced, the A's used plays like this leaping grab by second baseman Willie Randolph to sweep the Red Sox.

that situation. But those 'magic words' that I heard him say were enough to get anyone tossed out of any game."

Afterward, Clemens, perhaps already back on his own little planet, said he could not recall the use of "magic words," nor could he recall making physical contact with at least two umpires exclusive of Cooney.

Oakland fans brought their brooms to the park for Game 4 in hopes of a sweep, and the A's obliged with a 3-1 win.

Fifteen minutes later, Gallego finally got to swing against reliever Tom Bolton, and he ripped the ball to the center field fence for a two-run double and a 3-0 Oakland lead.

After that, Stewart struggled but prevailed. "Stew didn't have his good fastball so he manufactured some pitches, turned his curveball over to get grounders," Duncan said. "That's why he's a winner, because he can find a way to beat you when he doesn't have his good stuff."

Many of those grounders went to Randolph, who started a ninth-inning double play that killed off Boston's last gasp. The A's clinched the four-game sweep with yet another ground ball.

Oakland seemed to have the series in control from the start. After the A's won the first two games of the best-of-seven series in Boston, Oakland figured its prey was ready for the taking.

"After winning the first two, we won't be coming back to Boston," Canseco said. Rickey Henderson added, "If they beat us

two out of three on our own field, then there's something wrong with us . . . which there isn't."

Oakland's first-game decision was right out of the textbook: Battle your opponent's best pitcher (Clemens) with your own best pitcher (Stewart); earn a basic standoff after seven innings; force your way into the lead with execution and some aggressiveness on the bases in the eighth inning and then blow the other team away with a seven-run ninth.

The second Oakland victory was similar and yet different, because the outgunned Red Sox fought the A's like rabid terriers. Boston matched Oakland defensively, but they couldn't match the A's offensively because of masterful pitching from starter Welch and Eckersley in the bullpen.

But even after Oakland took Game 3, Boston Manager Joe Morgan moaned about what he thought was an inordinate amount of Oakland luck. By the time it was over, Morgan gave the devils their due.

"Oakland isn't a dynasty yet, but it's as

good a team as I've seen in years," Morgan said. "Aw, hell, they're the best in the world."

La Russa said, "I'd have to agree with Joe on that last statement. I don't ever 'expect' anything from this team but I'm never surprised by anything it does. We look good on paper—and then we go out and do it on the field."

GAME OF SATURDAY, OCTOBER 6
AT BOSTON

Oakland	AB.	R.	H.	RBI.	PO.	A.
R. Henderson, lf	5	1	2	3	3	0
McGee, cf	4	1	0	0	1	0
Canseco, rf	2	1	1	1	5	0
Baines, dh	3	0	1	0	0	0
Blankenship, pr	0	1	0	0	0	0
Lansford, 3b	5	1	3	2	1	3
Steinbach, c	5	1	3	1	4	0
McGwire, 1b	3	1	0	0	8	0
Weiss, ss	3	2	0	0	1	2
Gallego, 2b	1	0	1	0	3	1
Quirk, ph	1	0	1	0	0	0
Randolph, pr-2b	2	0	1	1	1	1
Stewart, p	0	0	0	0	0	2
Eckersley, p	0	0	0	0	0	0
Totals	34	9	13	8	27	9

Boston	AB.	R.	H.	RBI.	PO.	A.
Reed, 2b-ss	3	0	0	0	5	3
Quintana, 1b	4	0	0	0	2	0
Boggs, 3b	4	1	1	1	1	1
Burks, cf	4	0	1	0	4	1
Greenwell, lf	4	0	0	0	2	0
Evans, dh	2	0	0	0	0	0
Brunansky, rf	3	0	1	0	7	0
Pena, c	3	0	0	0	3	2
Rivera, ss	2	0	1	0	3	0
Marshall, ph	1	0	1	0	0	0
Kutcher, pr	0	0	0	0	0	0
Barrett, 2b	0	0	0	0	0	0
Clemens, p	0	0	0	0	0	1
Andersen, p	0	0	0	0	0	0
Bolton, p	0	0	0	0	0	0
Gray, p	0	0	0	0	0	0
Lamp, p	0	0	0	0	0	0
Murphy, p	0	0	0	0	0	0
Totals	30	1	5	1	27	8

Oakland .... 000 000 117—9
Boston .... 000 100 000—1

Oakland	IP.	H.	R.	ER.	BB.	SO.
Stewart (Winner)	8	4	1	1	1	3
Eckersley	1	1	0	0	0	0

Boston	IP.	H.	R.	ER.	BB.	SO.
Clemens	6	4	0	0	4	4
Andersen (Loser)	1*	2	2	2	1	0
Bolton	1/3	0	0	0	0	0
Gray	2/3†	3	2	1	1	0
Lamp	1/3	2	4	4	2	0
Murphy	2/3	2	1	1	1	0

*Pitched to one batter in eighth.
†Pitched to two batters in ninth.

Error—Gray. Double plays—Oakland 1, Boston 1. Left on bases—Oakland 11, Boston 4. Two-base hits—Lansford, Burks. Home run—Boggs. Stolen bases—Canseco, R. Henderson, McGee. Sacrifice hits—Reed, Baines, McGee. Sacrifice flies—R. Henderson, Canseco. Wild pitch—Clemens. Passed ball—Pena. Umpires—Garcia, Hirschbeck, Evans, Cooney, Voltaggio and McCoy. Time—3:26. Attendance—35,192.

GAME OF SUNDAY, OCTOBER 7
AT BOSTON

Oakland	AB.	R.	H.	RBI.	PO.	A.
R. Henderson, lf	5	0	1	0	1	0
McGee, cf	5	2	2	0	1	0
Canseco, rf	3	1	1	0	3	0
Baines, dh	5	0	2	3	0	0
Blankenship, pr	0	0	0	0	0	0
McGwire, 1b	5	0	2	1	12	0
Lansford, 3b	5	0	3	0	1	2
Hassey, c	3	0	1	0	6	0
Weiss, ss	4	0	0	0	1	5
Randolph, 2b	0	0	0	0	0	0
Gallego, 2b-ss	3	1	1	0	2	4
Welch, p	0	0	0	0	0	3
Honeycutt, p	0	0	0	0	0	1
Eckersley, p	0	0	0	0	0	0
Totals	38	4	13	4	27	15

Boston	AB.	R.	H.	RBI.	PO.	A.
Reed, 2b-ss	4	0	1	0	3	3
Quintana, 1b	3	0	0	1	8	2
Boggs, 3b	4	0	2	0	0	1
Burks, cf	3	0	1	0	4	0
Greenwell, lf	3	0	0	0	0	0
Evans, dh	4	0	1	0	0	0
Brunansky, rf	3	0	0	0	3	0
Pena, c	4	0	0	0	5	0
Rivera, ss	2	1	1	0	2	7
Marshall, ph	1	0	0	0	0	0
Barrett, 2b	0	0	0	0	1	0
Heep, ph	1	0	0	0	0	0
Kiecker, p	0	0	0	0	0	0
Harris, p	0	0	0	0	0	0
Andersen, p	0	0	0	0	1	0
Reardon, p	0	0	0	0	0	0
Totals	32	1	6	1	27	13

Oakland .... 000 100 102—4
Boston .... 001 000 000—1

Oakland	IP.	H.	R.	ER.	BB.	SO.
Welch (Winner)	7 1/3	6	1	1	3	4
Honeycutt	1/3	0	0	0	0	0
Eckersley (Save)	1 1/3	0	0	0	0	2

Boston	IP.	H.	R.	ER.	BB.	SO.
Kiecker	5 2/3	6	1	1	1	2
Harris (Loser)	1/3*	3	1	1	0	0
Andersen	1†	1	0	0	1	1
Reardon	2	3	2	2	1	0

*Pitched to two batters in seventh.
†Pitched to one batter in eighth.

Error—Weiss. Double plays—Oakland 1, Boston 2. Left on bases—Oakland 12, Boston 8. Two-base hits—Evans, Rivera, McGee, Baines. Stolen bases—Burks, McGee. Sacrifice fly—Quintana. Hit by pitcher—By Kiecker (Gallego), by Reardon (Hassey). Umpires—Hirschbeck, Evans, Cooney, Voltaggio, McCoy and Garcia. Time—3:42. Attendance—35,070.

GAME OF TUESDAY, OCTOBER 9
AT OAKLAND

Boston	AB.	R.	H.	RBI.	PO.	A.
Reed, 2b-ss	4	0	0	0	2	3
Quintana, 1b	4	0	0	0	10	0
Boggs, 3b	4	0	2	0	1	3
Burks, cf	4	0	1	0	1	0
Greenwell, lf	3	1	0	0	1	0
Evans, dh	4	0	2	0	0	0
Brunansky, rf	3	0	0	1	1	0
Pena, c	4	0	3	0	7	2
Kutcher, pr	0	0	0	0	0	0

Boston	AB.	R.	H.	RBI.	PO.	A.
Rivera, ss	2	0	0	0	0	5
Marshall, ph	1	0	0	0	0	0
Barrett, 2b	0	0	0	0	1	0
Heep, ph	1	0	0	0	0	0
Boddicker, p	0	0	0	0	0	2
Totals	34	1	8	1	24	15

Oakland	AB.	R.	H.	RBI.	PO.	A.
R. Henderson, lf	4	0	1	0	3	0
Lansford, 3b	3	0	0	0	1	1
Canseco, rf	3	1	0	0	4	0
Baines, dh	3	2	1	0	0	0
McGwire, 1b	3	0	0	0	7	0
D. Henderson, cf	2	0	1	1	4	0
Steinbach, c	3	1	0	0	6	0
Randolph, 2b	4	0	2	2	1	0
Gallego, ss	3	0	1	0	1	2
Moore, p	0	0	0	0	0	0
Nelson, p	0	0	0	0	0	0
Honeycutt, p	0	0	0	0	0	0
Eckersley, p	0	0	0	0	0	0
Totals	28	4	6	3	27	7

Boston .... 0 1 0   0 0 0   0 0 0—1
Oakland .... 0 0 0   2 0 2   0 0 x—4

Boston	IP.	H.	R.	ER.	BB.	SO.
Boddicker (Loser)	8	6	4	2	3	7

Oakland	IP.	H.	R.	ER.	BB.	SO.
Moore (Winner)	6	4	1	1	1	5
Nelson	1⅔	3	0	0	0	0
Honeycutt	⅓	0	0	0	0	0
Eckersley (Save)	1	1	0	0	0	1

Errors—Boddicker, Rivera, Pena. Double play —Boston 1. Left on bases—Boston 8, Oakland 7. Two-base hit—Boggs. Stolen bases—Canseco, Baines, D. Henderson. Sacrifice hit—Lansford. Sacrifice flies—Brunansky, D. Henderson. Hit by pitcher—By Boddicker (McGwire, D. Henderson). Umpires—Evans, Cooney, Voltaggio, McCoy, Garcia and Hirschbeck. Time—2:47. Attendance—49,026.

GAME OF WEDNESDAY, OCTOBER 10 AT OAKLAND

Boston	AB.	R.	H.	RBI.	PO.	A.
Burks, cf	4	1	1	0	0	0
Reed, 2b	4	0	1	1	1	2

Boston	AB.	R.	H.	RBI.	PO.	A.
Boggs, 3b	4	0	2	0	4	5
Greenwell, lf	4	0	0	0	0	0
Pena, c	3	0	0	0	7	0
Evans, dh	3	0	0	0	0	0
Brunansky, rf	3	0	0	0	2	0
Quintana, 1b	2	0	0	0	9	0
Rivera, ss	3	0	0	0	1	4
Clemens, p	0	0	0	0	0	0
Bolton, p	0	0	0	0	0	0
Gray, p	0	0	0	0	0	0
Andersen, p	0	0	0	0	0	0
Totals	30	1	4	1	24	11

Oakland	AB.	R.	H.	RBI.	PO.	A.
R. Henderson, lf	3	0	1	0	3	0
D. Henderson, cf	4	0	0	0	3	0
Canseco, rf	3	0	0	0	2	0
Jennings, rf	1	0	0	0	0	0
Baines, dh	3	0	1	0	0	0
McGee, pr	0	0	0	0	0	0
Hassey, ph	0	0	0	0	0	0
Blankenship, pr	0	0	0	0	0	0
Lansford, 3b	3	1	1	0	0	5
Steinbach, c	3	0	2	0	1	0
McGwire, 1b	2	1	0	1	13	0
Randolph, 2b	2	1	0	0	3	4
Gallego, ss	3	0	1	2	2	2
Stewart, p	0	0	0	0	0	1
Honeycutt, p	0	0	0	0	0	0
Totals	27	3	6	3	27	12

Boston .... 0 0 0   0 0 0   0 0 1—1
Oakland .... 0 3 0   0 0 0   0 0 x—3

Boston	IP.	H.	R.	ER.	BB.	SO.
Clemens (Loser)	1⅔	3	3	3	1	0
Bolton	2⅔	2	0	0	2	3
Gray	2⅔	1	0	0	0	2
Andersen	1	0	0	0	1	2

Oakland	IP.	H.	R.	ER.	BB.	SO.
Stewart (Winner)	8*	4	1	1	1	1
Honeycutt (Save)	1	0	0	0	0	0

*Pitched to two batters in ninth.

Error—Greenwell. Double plays—Boston 2, Oakland 1. Left on bases—Boston 3, Oakland 5. Two-base hits—Gallego, Burks. Stolen bases—R. Henderson, Blankenship. Sacrifice hit—Lansford. Umpires—Cooney, Voltaggio, McCoy, Garcia, Hirschbeck and Evans. Time—3:02. Attendance—49,052.

OAKLAND ATHLETICS' BATTING AND FIELDING AVERAGES

Player—Position	G.	AB.	R.	H.	TB.	2B.	3B.	HR.	RBI.	B.A.	PO.	A.	E.	F.A.
Quirk, ph	1	1	0	1	1	0	0	0	0	1.000	0	0	0	.000
Steinbach, c	3	11	2	5	5	0	0	0	1	.455	11	0	0	1.000
Lansford, 3b	4	16	2	7	8	1	0	0	2	.438	3	11	0	1.000
Gallego, 2b-ss	4	10	1	4	5	1	0	0	2	.400	8	9	0	1.000
Randolph, pr-2b	4	8	1	3	3	0	0	0	3	.375	5	9	0	1.000
Baines, dh	4	14	2	5	6	1	0	0	3	.357	0	0	0	.000
Hassey, c-ph	2	3	0	1	1	0	0	0	0	.333	6	0	0	1.000
R. Henderson, lf	4	17	1	5	5	0	0	0	3	.294	10	0	0	1.000
McGee, cf-pr-dh	3	9	3	2	3	1	0	0	0	.222	2	0	0	1.000
Canseco, rf	4	11	3	2	2	0	0	0	1	.182	14	0	0	1.000
D. Henderson, cf	2	6	0	1	1	0	0	0	1	.167	7	0	0	1.000
McGwire, 1b	4	13	2	2	2	0	0	0	2	.154	40	0	0	1.000
Blankenship, pr	3	0	1	0	0	0	0	0	0	.000	0	0	0	.000
Eckersley, p	3	0	0	0	0	0	0	0	0	.000	0	1	0	1.000
Honeycutt, p	3	0	0	0	0	0	0	0	0	.000	0	0	0	.000
Moore, p	1	0	0	0	0	0	0	0	0	.000	0	0	0	.000
Nelson, p	1	0	0	0	0	0	0	0	0	.000	0	0	0	.000
Stewart, p	2	0	0	0	0	0	0	0	0	.000	0	3	0	1.000
Welch, p	1	0	0	0	0	0	0	0	0	.000	0	3	0	1.000
Jennings, rf	1	1	0	0	0	0	0	0	0	.000	0	0	0	.000
Weiss, ss	2	7	2	0	0	0	0	0	0	.000	2	7	1	.900
Totals	4	127	20	38	42	4	0	0	18	.299	108	43	1	.993

BOSTON RED SOX' BATTING AND FIELDING AVERAGES

Player—Position	G.	AB.	R.	H.	TB.	2B.	3B.	HR.	RBI.	B.A.	PO.	A.	E.	F.A.
Boggs, 3b	4	16	1	7	11	1	0	1	1	.438	6	10	0	1.000
Marshall, ph	3	3	0	1	1	0	0	0	0	.333	0	0	0	.000
Burks, cf	4	15	1	4	6	2	0	0	0	.267	9	1	0	1.000
Evans, dh	4	13	0	3	4	1	0	0	0	.231	0	0	0	.000
Rivera, ss	4	9	1	2	3	1	0	0	0	.222	6	16	1	.957
Pena, c	4	14	0	3	3	0	0	0	0	.214	22	4	1	.963
Reed, 2b-ss	4	15	0	2	2	0	0	0	1	.133	11	11	0	1.000
Brunansky, rf	4	12	0	1	1	0	0	0	1	.083	13	0	0	1.000
Andersen, p	3	0	0	0	0	0	0	0	0	.000	1	0	0	1.000
Barrett, 2b	3	0	0	0	0	0	0	0	0	.000	2	0	0	1.000
Boddicker, p	1	0	0	0	0	0	0	0	0	.000	0	2	1	.667
Bolton, p	2	0	0	0	0	0	0	0	0	.000	0	0	0	.000
Clemens, p	2	0	0	0	0	0	0	0	0	.000	0	1	0	1.000
Gray, p	2	0	0	0	0	0	0	0	0	.000	0	0	1	.000
Harris, p	1	0	0	0	0	0	0	0	0	.000	0	0	0	.000
Kiecker, p	1	0	0	0	0	0	0	0	0	.000	0	0	0	.000
Kutcher, pr	2	0	0	0	0	0	0	0	0	.000	0	0	0	.000
Lamp, p	1	0	0	0	0	0	0	0	0	.000	0	0	0	.000
Murphy, p	1	0	0	0	0	0	0	0	0	.000	0	0	0	.000
Reardon, p	1	0	0	0	0	0	0	0	0	.000	0	0	0	.000
Heep, ph	2	2	0	0	0	0	0	0	0	.000	0	0	0	.000
Quintana, 1b	4	13	0	0	0	0	0	0	1	.000	29	2	0	1.000
Greenwell, lf	4	14	1	0	0	0	0	0	0	.000	3	0	1	.750
Totals	4	126	4	23	31	5	0	1	4	.183	102	47	5	.968

OAKLAND ATHLETICS' PITCHING RECORDS

Pitcher	G.	GS.	CG.	IP.	H.	R.	ER.	BB.	SO.	HB.	WP.	W.	L.	Pct.	ERA.
Eckersley	3	0	0	3⅓	2	0	0	0	3	0	0	0	0	.000	0.00
Honeycutt	3	0	0	1⅔	0	0	0	0	0	0	0	0	0	.000	0.00
Nelson	1	0	0	1⅔	3	0	0	0	0	0	0	0	0	.000	0.00
Stewart	2	2	0	16	8	2	2	2	4	0	0	2	0	1.000	1.13
Welch	1	1	0	7⅓	6	1	1	3	4	0	0	1	0	1.000	1.23
Moore	1	1	0	6	4	1	1	1	5	0	0	1	0	1.000	1.50
Totals	4	4	0	36	23	4	4	6	16	0	0	4	0	1.000	1.00

No shutouts. Saves—Eckersley 2, Honeycutt.

BOSTON RED SOX' PITCHING RECORDS

Pitcher	G.	GS.	CG.	IP.	H.	R.	ER.	BB.	SO.	HB.	WP.	W.	L.	Pct.	ERA.
Bolton	2	0	0	3	2	0	0	2	3	0	0	0	0	.000	0.00
Kiecker	1	1	0	5⅔	6	1	1	1	2	1	0	0	0	.000	1.59
Boddicker	1	1	1	8	6	4	2	3	7	2	0	0	1	.000	2.25
Gray	2	0	0	3⅓	4	2	1	1	2	0	0	0	0	.000	2.70
Clemens	2	2	0	7⅔	7	3	3	5	4	0	1	0	1	.000	3.52
Andersen	3	0	0	3	3	2	2	3	3	0	0	0	1	.000	6.00
Reardon	1	0	0	2	3	2	2	1	0	1	0	0	0	.000	9.00
Murphy	1	0	0	⅔	2	1	1	1	0	0	0	0	0	.000	13.50
Harris	1	0	0	⅓	3	1	1	0	0	0	0	0	1	.000	27.00
Lamp	1	0	0	⅓	2	4	4	2	0	0	0	0	0	.000	108.00
Totals	4	4	1	34	38	20	17	19	21	4	1	0	4	.000	4.50

No shutouts or saves.

COMPOSITE SCORE BY INNINGS

Oakland	0	3	0	3	0	2	2	1	9 — 20
Boston	0	1	1	1	0	0	0	0	1 — 4

Sacrifice hits—Lansford 2, Reed, Baines, McGee.
Sacrifice flies—R. Henderson, Canseco, Quintana, Brunansky, D. Henderson.
Stolen bases—McGee 2, Canseco 2, R. Henderson 2, Burks, Baines, D. Henderson, Blankenship.
Caught stealing—Gallego, Steinbach, R. Henderson.
Double plays—Reed, Rivera and Quintana 2; Lansford, Gallego and McGwire; Reed and Rivera; Weiss, Gallego and McGwire; Quintana and Pena; Boggs, Reed and Quintana; Boggs and Quintana; Randolph and McGwire.
Left on bases—Oakland 11, 12, 7, 5—35; Boston 4, 8, 8, 3—23.
Hit by pitcher—By Boddicker 2 (McGwire, D. Henderson), by Kiecker (Gallego), by Reardon (Hassey).
Passed ball—Pena.
Balks—None.
Time of games—First game, 3:26; second game, 3:42; third game, 2:47; fourth game, 3:02.
Attendance—First game, 35,192; second game, 35,070; third game, 49,026; fourth game, 49,052.
Umpires—Garcia, Hirschbeck, Evans, Cooney, Voltaggio and McCoy.
Official scorers—Glenn Schwarz, San Francisco Examiner; Charlie Scoggins, Lowell (Mass.) Sun.

1990 WORLD SERIES

Including

Review of 1990 Series

Official Box Scores, Each Game

Official Composite Box Score

Cincinnati's shocking four-game sweep of the Athletics began with Eric Davis' two-run homer off Dave Stewart in the first inning of Game 1 (above) and ended with Reds Owner Marge Schott (below, left) and Manager Lou Piniella hoisting the championship trophy.

Little Red Machine Wrecks A's

By DAVE NIGHTINGALE

In many quarters, the 1990 World Series was billed with condescension as a match that had all the glitter of a confrontation between, say, the 1927 New York Yankees and, perhaps, the 1962 New York Mets.

But after Cincinnati and most valuable player-to-be Jose Rijo beat Oakland and pitching ace Dave Stewart, 7-0, in the opening game, one Reds' player reclined in front of his locker and put things in a new perspective.

"Well," he said, "so much for that '27 Yankees crap."

Four days later, it was official: The Reds are world champions, 14 years after their last title. And they prevailed just as the '76 Reds had done—in a four-game sweep.

The Reds won the second game over the A's, 5-4 in 10 innings, even though Oakland had started 27-game winner Bob Welch. They crushed Mike Moore, a 1989 World Series hero, 8-3 in the third game, then completed the sweep as Rijo outdueled Stewart, 2-1, in the finale.

Goodbye, Babe Ruth; hello, Rodney Dangerfield.

Two major questions dominated the aftermath of baseball's biggest postseason surprise since, well, the 1989 "Earthquake Series":

■ Were the Reds terribly underrated?

■ Were the A's terribly overrated?

The answers: "Probably" and "partially."

Before the four-game event, both casual and veteran observers might have taken a look at the Athletics' 306 regular-season victories over the last three years and the A's 17-5 postseason record in that span, and then leafed through their TV Guides for alternative programming.

But in starting their search, they failed to pay heed to the warnings of several baseball super scouts, the men who analyze such events for a living and who either do a good job of it or learn to love hamburger.

They didn't hear, for instance, the words of Philadelphia's Ray Shore, who noted: "The Reds can catch the ball, throw the ball and hit the ball. So, why shouldn't they give the A's some problems?"

Since Shore used to work for Cincinnati, some concluded that his analysis needed a dose of reality. Actually, it was perfect.

Among the reasons that many people failed to take the Reds' chances seriously

Mark McGwire and the rest of his teammates had their bats sawed off by Cincinnati pitchers, who limited the A's to a .207 average.

were these:

■ During the regular season, the Reds had to beat up only on a division, the National League West, in which the principal competition was either crippled by injuries (Los Angeles, San Francisco) or by constant dissension (San Diego).

■ Their players were young and inexperienced, unaccustomed to the strangling pressures of postseason play.

■ Their new manager, Lou Piniella, was untested, a probable bozo.

■ Their new general manager, Bob Quinn, couldn't deal himself a pair of deuces.

■ Their bullpen had a cute nickname (the Nasty Boys) but it had actually been weakened by the trade of John Franco to the Mets, a trade that was made ostensibly

Tony La Russa and his Oakland troops could do nothing to stem Cincinnati's tide in Game 3, watching the Reds take an 8-3 decision.

for one reason: to save Reds Owner Marge Schott a few bucks.

Here are the rebuttals, one at a time...

"I don't think our division was all that weak," Piniella said. "I think people had doubts about us because we only played .500 ball the last four months of the season. But we did have the fast start and we did go wire to wire and we were under intense scrutiny from Day One, which probably helped us a lot against Oakland."

Cincinnati pitching coach Stan Williams concurred. "Our young guys had to play pressure ball all year because we didn't make a habit of blowing out anybody. In fact, we spent most of the season 'eking' people out. I can't remember a lot of games when we scored seven or eight runs like we did in the Series. As a result, the players were relaxed when the Series rolled around. When it came to pressure, our guys thought that they'd already seen it all."

As for the so-called Piniella Factor, it was magnified by the manager's highly publicized base-throwing incident August 21 during a victory that snapped a five-game losing streak. Piniella, upset by a call at first base, argued with umpire Dutch Rennert and was ejected. Piniella yanked the base from its moorings, tossed it 30 feet toward second and then retrieved the bag and heaved it into right field. People wondered if it was Piniella who had snapped.

"I'll always regret that because it was a stupid thing to do," Piniella conceded. "But maybe it helped us because a lot of other managers thought I was on the verge of cracking up. They thought we were about one step from choking.

"I wouldn't have taken this job if I didn't think I could handle it. And I don't know how anybody could have judged me based on what I did with the Yankees. (He was hired and fired twice as manager in New York.) When you work for George (Steinbrenner), you may think you're managing, but..."

When it comes to dealing with legends, consider also that Piniella was selected to succeed Pete Rose to lead the Reds.

But, maybe that wasn't so tough after all. While Cincinnati had a 426-388 record under Rose, the club never qualified for anything except an Avis award—four run-

Joe Oliver celebrates after driving in the game-winning run in the tenth inning of Game 2, giving the Reds a two-games-to-none lead.

Chris Sabo provided the heroics in Game 3, blasting two home runs and tying a Series mark with 10 fielding chances in the Reds' 8-3 win.

ner-up finishes in five seasons.

"Last spring, when I took over the club, I saw I had a lot of talent, a team with speed, power, arms, defense and youth," Piniella said. "All I told my guys was this: 'You've played together four or five years and you're young and talented, but you haven't won anything. This year, it's your turn, it's your time.' "

It is certainly worth noting that few of the Reds players mentioned Rose once the Series was over. Third baseman Chris Sabo, who batted .563 in the four games, alluded to the fact that many of the players were still "Pete's boys." But back in April, it was Sabo who said, "Piniella taught me a lot more about hitting than Pete ever did. When I was in a slump, all Pete would do was tell me to grab a bat and get up there and swing."

As for Quinn, he was known in his days with the Yankees as a guy who'd get a deal in place but then couldn't pull the trigger.

With the Reds, Quinn damn near emptied an entire six-shooter.

He acquired Hal Morris from the Yankees, for pitcher Tim Leary. Morris hit .340 in the regular season and knocked in the run that closed the Series.

He sent pitcher Ron Robinson to Milwaukee for outfielder Glenn Braggs, and Braggs drove home the tying run in both the second and fourth games of the Series. Braggs also made a game-saving catch in the National League playoffs against Pittsburgh that may have been responsible for Cincinnati getting to face Oakland in the first place.

He acquired Billy Hatcher from Pittsburgh just hours before the start of the '90 season, and all Hatcher did was hit .276 in the regular season and then record a .750 mark in the Series, knocking—you guessed it—Babe Ruth (.625 in 1928) out of the history books.

Quinn picked up Billy Doran from Houston in late August to solidify the Reds' infield, and Doran batted .373 for Cincinnati down the stretch, at a time when the critics were waiting for the Reds to choke.

And he obtained lefthander Randy Myers (in that money-saving Franco deal with the Mets) to complete the team's bullpen chemistry.

Since Cincinnati hitters played bombs

Billy Hatcher's hot bat spelled trouble for the A's. He set World Series records with seven consecutive hits and a .750 batting average.

away in two Series games, and since the A's couldn't score after the third inning of any game, the Reds' bullpen was a major factor in only one of the four victories.

But the Nasty Boys were at least an ominous specter in every contest—as their 0.00 earned-run average attests.

As for the Athletics...

First, Jose Canseco was hurting—badly. And anyone with any degree of hindsight should have realized the A's had a big problem when Manager Tony La Russa said he was "satisfied" that Canseco had been able to collect—get this—a pair of walks in the first game.

A's pitching coach Dave Duncan rivaled Plato when it came to philosophy.

"I can accept what happened to us, but I'd have a better feeling if we had won at least a couple of games," Duncan said. "The beauty of the game of baseball is that you can get beat on any given day, no matter how good you are. The sport goes in cycles; there are changes nobody can control. You go through spells when everything you do works out. You get all the close calls; the broken-bat bloopers fall for hits and so forth. But when you're struggling, none of that happens for you. Instead, it happens for the other club."

It happened in the eighth inning of Game 4 when the Reds' Herm Winningham, acting on his own, bunted with two strikes for the hit that led to the game-winning, two-run rally against Stewart.

"A team of destiny bunts on an 0-and-2 count and beats it out," Reds first baseman Todd Benzinger declared.

A team of destiny also prevails with Winningham and Braggs on the field at gut-check time, after Hatcher (bruised hand) and clean-up hitter Eric Davis (bruised kidney) had been forced out of action.

The A's, however, are still a power to be reckoned with. Don't sell them short at this early date. "I'll personally guarantee we'll all be standing in this same clubhouse at this time next year," Stewart said.

But the A's are not immortal. Not yet.

In fact, La Russa, an annual manager of the year candidate, was quite mortal in Game 2 when his team had a 4-3 lead after seven innings, behind Welch, and lost. How many times had Welch made it through the eighth this season? Well, you could have kept your socks on and counted those games on your visible digits. And yet, La Russa allowed Welch to open the eighth—even with the best reliever in baseball (Dennis Eckersley) available in the bullpen.

What followed was ugly. Welch gave up the leadoff triple to Hatcher—La Russa

The 1990 World Series belonged to Cincinnati pitcher Jose Rijo, who beat Oakland twice en route to winning Most Valuable Player honors.

thought Canseco blew the catch—that led to the tying run.

Eckersley didn't get to pitch until the 10th inning that night. And he was touched for successive hits by Billy Bates, Sabo and Joe Oliver. Before the game, Bates' chief claim to fame was that he had outrun a cheetah on loan from the Cincinnati zoo during a Reds pregame promotion.

"I felt that in order for us to be classified as a special team, we had to win this Series," Oakland third baseman Carney Lansford said. "But if you drop two in three years (the A's also lost to the Los Angeles Dodgers in 1988), you can't be considered a great team yet."

La Russa, who finally benched Canseco in the fourth game, spoke of his "bad vibes" coming into the Series, about how he didn't think the team was peaking at the right time—even though it had just thoroughly embarrassed the Boston Red Sox in four straight games for the American League pennant.

Eckersley, in his intergalactic vernacular, said: "These guys (the Reds) were 'on

Led by Bob Welch, Oakland pitchers could not quiet the Reds' hitters, who batted .317 in the Series.

time,' Jack, and I don't think too many people could have beaten them."

Then Eck added, "They dominated us in every game. They crushed us twice and they beat us at our own game twice."

Oakland's "own game" is to never lose a one-run decision.

When Cincinnati had dynasty pretensions of its own, after 1975 and '76 world championships, the club was known as the Big Red Machine.

So, what do you call the current edition, a team that Sabo said "has no MVP, no Cy Young winner—it's just a team where everybody does his job"?

The Little Red Choo-Choo?

"I'll tell you what you can call us," shortstop Barry Larkin said. "You can call us world champions."

Game 1

At Cincinnati
October 16

Oakland (A.L.)	AB.	R.	H.	RBI.	PO.	A.
R. Henderson, lf	5	0	3	0	1	0
McGee, cf	5	0	1	0	3	0
Canseco, rf	2	0	0	0	2	0
McGwire, 1b	3	0	0	0	4	1
Lansford, 3b	4	0	2	0	1	1
Steinbach, c	4	0	1	0	5	1
Randolph, 2b	4	0	1	0	4	3
Gallego, ss	4	0	0	0	2	2

Oakland (A.L.)	AB.	R.	H.	RBI.	PO.	A.
Stewart, p	1	0	0	0	2	0
aJennings, ph	1	0	1	0	0	0
Burns, p	0	0	0	0	0	0
Nelson, p	0	0	0	0	0	0
bHassey, ph	1	0	0	0	0	0
Sanderson, p	0	0	0	0	0	0
Eckersley, p	0	0	0	0	0	0
dD. Henderson, ph	1	0	0	0	0	0
Totals	35	0	9	0	24	8

Cincinnati (N.L.)	AB.	R.	H.	RBI.	PO.	A.
Larkin, ss	4	1	0	0	1	5
Hatcher, cf	3	3	3	1	3	0
O'Neill, rf	2	1	0	1	6	0
Davis, lf	4	2	2	3	0	0
Morris, 1b	4	0	1	0	7	0
Sabo, 3b	3	0	1	2	0	1
Oliver, c	4	0	1	0	7	0
Duncan, 2b	3	0	1	0	3	3
Rijo, p	3	0	1	0	0	1
Dibble, p	0	0	0	0	0	0
cBenzinger, ph	1	0	0	0	0	0
Myers, p	0	0	0	0	0	0
Totals	31	7	10	7	27	10

Oakland	000	000	000—0			
Cincinnati	202	030	00x—7			

Oakland	IP.	H.	R.	ER.	BB.	SO.
Stewart (L)	4	3	4	3	4	3
Burns	⅔	4	3	3	1	0
Nelson	1⅓	2	0	0	1	0
Sanderson	1	1	0	0	0	0
Eckersley	1	0	0	0	0	1

Cincinnati	IP.	H.	R.	ER.	BB.	SO.
Rijo (W)	7	7	0	0	2	5
Dibble	1	1	0	0	1	0
Myers	1	1	0	0	0	2

Bases on balls—Off Stewart 4 (Duncan, Hatcher, Larkin, Sabo), off Burns 1 (O'Neill), off Nelson 1 (O'Neill), off Rijo 2 (Canseco 2), off Dibble 1 (McGwire).

Strikeouts—By Stewart 3 (Morris, O'Neill, Sabo), by Eckersley 1 (Duncan), by Rijo 5 (Canseco, Gallego, R. Henderson, Steinbach, Stewart), by Myers 2 (Gallego, D. Henderson).

aSingled for Stewart in fifth. bFlied out for Nelson in seventh. cFlied out for Dibble in eighth. dStruck out for Eckersley in ninth. Error—Gallego. Double plays—Oakland 2, Cincinnati 1. Left on bases—Oakland 11, Cincinnati 6. Two-base hits—R. Henderson 2, Hatcher 2. Home run—Davis. Stolen bases—McGee, Lansford. Wild pitch—Dibble. Umpires—Pulli, Roe, Quick, Hendry, Marsh and Barnett. Time—2:38. Attendance—55,830.

Game 2

At Cincinnati
October 17

Oakland (A.L.)	AB.	R.	H.	RBI.	PO.	A.
R. Henderson, lf	4	1	1	0	3	1
Lansford, 3b	4	0	1	0	0	6
Canseco, rf	5	1	1	2	2	0
McGwire, 1b	4	1	2	0	12	0
D. Henderson, cf	4	1	2	0	2	0
Steinbach, c	0	0	0	0	0	0
Randolph, 2b	4	0	0	0	5	0
Hassey, c	4	0	2	1	2	0
dBordick, pr-ss	0	0	0	0	0	1
Gallego, ss	4	0	1	1	2	3
eBaines, ph	1	0	0	0	0	0
Eckersley, p	0	0	0	0	0	0
Welch, p	3	0	0	0	0	2
Honeycutt, p	0	0	0	0	0	0
McGee, cf	0	0	0	0	0	0
Totals	37	4	10	4	28	13

Cincinnati (N.L.)	AB.	R.	H.	RBI.	PO.	A.
Larkin, ss	5	1	3	0	0	4
Hatcher, cf	4	2	4	1	4	0
O'Neill, rf	4	0	0	0	1	0
Davis, lf	5	0	0	1	2	0
Morris, 1b	3	0	0	0	11	1
cBraggs, ph	1	0	0	1	0	0
Dibble, p	0	0	0	0	0	0
fBates, ph	1	1	1	0	0	0
Sabo, 3b	5	0	3	0	0	3
Oliver, c	5	1	2	1	7	0
Duncan, 2b	3	0	0	0	4	4
Jackson, p	1	0	0	0	0	1
Scudder, p	0	0	0	0	0	0
aOester, ph	1	0	1	1	0	0
Armstrong, p	0	0	0	0	0	0
bWinningham, ph	1	0	0	0	0	0
Charlton, p	0	0	0	0	0	0
Benzinger, 1b	1	0	0	0	1	0
Totals	40	5	14	5	30	13

```
Oakland............... 1 0 3   0 0 0   0 0 0   0—4
Cincinnati........... 2 0 0   1 0 0   0 1 0   1—5
```
One out when winning run scored.

Oakland	IP.	H.	R.	ER.	BB.	SO.
Welch	7⅓	9	4	4	2	2
Honeycutt	1⅔	2	0	0	1	0
Eckersley (L)	⅓	3	1	1	0	0

Cincinnati	IP.	H.	R.	ER.	BB.	SO.
Jackson	2⅔	6	4	3	2	0
Scudder	1⅓	0	0	0	2	2
Armstrong	3	1	0	0	0	3
Charlton	1	1	0	0	0	0
Dibble (W)	2	2	0	0	0	2

Bases on balls—Off Welch 2 (Duncan, O'Neill), off Honeycutt 1 (Hatcher), off Jackson 2 (D. Henderson, Randolph), off Scudder 2 (R. Henderson, McGwire).
Strikeouts—By Welch 2 (Sabo, Jackson), by Scudder 2 (Welch, Canseco), by Armstrong 3 (Welch, Canseco, McGwire), by Dibble 2 (McGwire, Baines).
aSingled for Scudder in fourth. bLined out for Armstrong in seventh. cGrounded into RBI force-out for Morris in eighth. dRan for Hassey in tenth. eStruck out for Gallego in tenth. fSingled for Dibble in tenth. Errors—Jackson, Oliver, Hassey, McGwire. Double play—Cincinnati 1. Left on bases—Oakland 10, Cincinnati 10. Two-base hits—Larkin, Hatcher 2, Oliver. Three-base hit—Hatcher. Home run—Canseco. Stolen base—R. Henderson. Sacrifice hits—Lansford, Welch. Sacrifice fly—Hassey. Umpires—Roe, Quick, Hendry, Marsh, Barnett and Pulli. Time—3:31. Attendance—55,832.

Game 3

At Oakland
October 19

Cincinnati (N.L.)	AB.	R.	H.	RBI.	PO.	A.
Larkin, ss	5	0	2	1	0	3
Hatcher, cf	5	1	2	0	4	0
O'Neill, rf	3	1	1	0	2	0
Davis, lf	5	1	2	1	1	0
Morris, dh	4	0	0	1	0	0
Sabo, 3b	4	2	2	3	3	7
Benzinger, 1b	5	1	2	0	12	0
Oliver, c	5	1	2	1	5	0
Duncan, 2b	4	1	1	1	0	0
Browning, p	0	0	0	0	0	0
Dibble, p	0	0	0	0	0	0
Myers, p	0	0	0	0	0	0
Totals	40	8	14	8	27	10

Oakland (A.L.)	AB.	R.	H.	RBI.	PO.	A.
R. Henderson, lf	3	1	1	1	3	0
Lansford, 3b	3	0	0	0	0	5
Canseco, rf	4	0	0	0	0	0
D. Henderson, cf	4	1	1	0	2	0
Baines, dh	4	1	1	2	0	0
McGwire, 1b	4	0	1	0	15	0
Steinbach, c	4	0	0	0	3	0
Randolph, 2b	4	0	3	0	4	4
Gallego, ss	2	0	0	0	0	3
aMcGee, ph	1	0	0	0	0	0
Bordick, ss	0	0	0	0	0	1
bBlankenship, ph	1	0	0	0	0	0
Moore, p	0	0	0	0	0	0
Sanderson, p	0	0	0	0	0	0
Klink, p	0	0	0	0	0	0
Nelson, p	0	0	0	0	0	0
Burns, p	0	0	0	0	0	0
Young, p	0	0	0	0	0	0
Totals	34	3	7	3	27	13

```
Cincinnati........... 0 1 7   0 0 0   0 0 0—8
Oakland............... 0 2 1   0 0 0   0 0 0—3
```

Cincinnati	IP.	H.	R.	ER.	BB.	SO.
Browning (W)	6†	6	3	3	2	2
Dibble	1⅔	0	0	0	0	2
Myers	1⅓	1	0	0	0	1

Oakland	IP.	H.	R.	ER.	BB.	SO.
Moore (L)	2⅔	8	6	2	0	1
Sanderson	⅔	3	2	2	1	0
Klink	0*	0	0	0	1	0
Nelson	3⅔	1	0	0	1	0
Burns	1	1	0	0	1	0
Young	1	1	0	0	0	0

*Pitched to one batter in fourth.
†Pitched to one batter in seventh.

Bases on balls—Off Browning 2 (R. Henderson, Lansford), off Sanderson 1 (O'Neill), off Klink 1 (Morris), off Nelson 1 (Sabo), off Burns 1 (O'Neill).
Strikeouts—By Browning 2 (McGwire, Baines), by Dibble 2 (McGee, R. Henderson), by Myers 1 (Blankenship), by Moore 1 (Oliver).
aStruck out for Gallego in seventh. bStruck out for Bordick in ninth. Errors—McGwire. Double plays—Oakland 2. Left on bases—Cincinnati 9, Oakland 6. Two-base hits—D. Henderson, Oliver. Three-base hit—Larkin. Home runs—Sabo 2, Baines, R. Henderson. Stolen bases—Duncan, O'Neill, R. Henderson, Randolph. Wild pitches—Sanderson, Burns. Umpires—Quick, Hendry, Marsh, Froemming, Pulli and Roe. Time—3:01. Attendance—48,269.

Game 4

At Oakland
October 20

Cincinnati (N.L.)	AB.	R.	H.	RBI.	PO.	A.
Larkin, ss	3	1	1	0	0	2
Hatcher, cf	0	0	0	0	0	0
Winningham, cf	3	1	2	0	3	0
O'Neill, rf	3	0	0	0	2	0
Davis, lf	0	0	0	0	1	0
aBraggs, ph-lf	3	0	0	1	0	0
Morris, dh	3	0	0	1	0	0
Sabo, 3b	4	0	3	0	0	3
Benzinger, 1b	4	0	0	0	11	0
Oliver, c	4	0	1	0	8	1
Duncan, 2b	4	0	0	0	2	2
Rijo, p	0	0	0	0	0	1
Myers, p	0	0	0	0	0	0
Totals	31	2	7	2	27	9

Oakland (A.L.)	AB.	R.	H.	RBI.	PO.	A.
R. Henderson, lf	3	0	0	0	5	0
McGee, rf	4	1	1	0	2	0
D. Henderson, cf	4	0	0	0	3	0
Baines, dh	2	0	0	0	0	0

Oakland (A.L.)	AB.	R.	H.	RBI.	PO.	A.
cCanseco, ph	1	0	0	0	0	0
Lansford, 3b	4	0	1	1	0	2
Quirk, c	3	0	0	0	2	2
McGwire, 1b	3	0	0	0	11	0
Randolph, 2b	3	0	0	0	1	5
bGallego, ss	1	0	0	0	3	2
Hassey, ph	1	0	0	0	0	0
Bordick, ss	0	0	0	0	0	0
Stewart, p	0	0	0	0	0	1
Totals	29	1	2	1	27	12

Cincinnati .... 0 0 0 0 0 0 0 2 0—2
Oakland .... 1 0 0 0 0 0 0 0 0—1

Cincinnati	IP.	H.	R.	ER.	BB.	SO.
Rijo (W)	8⅓	2	1	1	3	9
Myers (S)	⅔	0	0	0	0	0

Oakland	IP.	H.	R.	ER.	BB.	SO.
Stewart (L)	9	7	2	1	2	2

Bases on balls—Off Rijo 3 (Baines, Gallego, R. Henderson), off Stewart 2 (Larkin, Braggs).

Strikeouts—By Rijo 9 (R. Henderson 2, McGee, D. Henderson 2, Quirk 2, McGwire, Gallego), by Stewart 2 (O'Neill, Duncan).

aFlied out for Davis in second. bGrounded out for Gallego in eighth. cGrounded out for Baines in ninth. Errors—Oliver, Stewart. Double play—Oakland 1. Left on bases—Cincinnati 7, Oakland 4. Two-base hits—McGee, Oliver, Sabo. Stolen bases—Gallego, R. Henderson. Sacrifice hit—O'Neill. Sacrifice fly—Morris. Hit by pitcher—By Stewart (Hatcher). Umpires—Hendry, Marsh, Froemming, Pulli, Roe and Quick. Time—2:48. Attendance—48,613.

CINCINNATI REDS' BATTING AND FIELDING AVERAGES

Player—Position	G.	AB.	R.	H.	TB.	2B.	3B.	HR.	RBI.	BB.	IBB.	SO.	B.A.	PO.	A.	E.	F.A.
Bates, ph	1	1	1	1	1	0	0	0	0	0	0	0	1.000	0	0	0	.000
Oester, ph	1	1	0	1	1	0	0	0	1	0	0	0	1.000	0	0	0	.000
Hatcher, cf	4	12	6	9	15	4	1	0	2	2	1	0	.750	11	0	0	1.000
Sabo, 3b	4	16	2	9	16	1	0	2	5	2	0	2	.563	3	14	0	1.000
Winningham, ph-cf	2	4	1	2	2	0	0	0	0	0	0	0	.500	3	0	0	1.000
Larkin, ss	4	17	3	6	9	1	1	0	1	2	0	0	.353	1	14	0	1.000
Oliver, c	4	18	2	6	9	3	0	0	2	0	0	1	.333	27	1	3	.903
Rijo, p	2	3	0	1	1	0	0	0	0	0	0	0	.333	0	2	0	1.000
Davis, lf	4	14	3	4	7	0	0	1	5	0	0	0	.286	4	0	0	1.000
Benzinger, ph-1b	4	11	1	2	2	0	0	0	0	0	0	0	.182	24	0	0	1.000
Duncan, 2b	4	14	1	2	2	0	0	0	1	2	0	2	.143	9	9	0	1.000
O'Neill, rf	4	12	2	1	1	0	0	0	1	5	0	2	.083	11	0	0	1.000
Morris, 1b-dh	4	14	0	1	1	0	0	0	2	1	0	1	.071	18	1	0	1.000
Armstrong, p	1	0	0	0	0	0	0	0	0	0	0	0	.000	0	0	0	.000
Browning, p	1	0	0	0	0	0	0	0	0	0	0	0	.000	0	0	0	.000
Charlton, p	1	0	0	0	0	0	0	0	0	0	0	0	.000	0	0	0	.000
Dibble, p	3	0	0	0	0	0	0	0	0	0	0	0	.000	0	0	0	.000
Myers, p	3	0	0	0	0	0	0	0	0	0	0	0	.000	0	0	0	.000
Scudder, p	1	0	0	0	0	0	0	0	0	0	0	0	.000	0	0	0	.000
Jackson, p	1	1	0	0	0	0	0	0	0	0	0	1	.000	0	1	1	.500
Braggs, ph-lf	2	4	0	0	0	0	0	0	2	1	0	0	.000	0	0	0	.000
Totals	4	142	22	45	67	9	2	3	22	15	1	9	.317	111	42	4	.975

Bates—Singled for Dibble in tenth inning of second game.
Benzinger—Flied out for Dibble in eighth inning of first game.
Braggs—Grounded into RBI force out for Morris in eighth inning of second game; flied out for Davis in second inning of fourth game.
Oester—Singled in one run for Scudder in fourth inning of second game.
Winningham—Lined out for Armstrong in seventh inning of second game.

OAKLAND ATHLETICS' BATTING AND FIELDING AVERAGES

Player—Position	G.	AB.	R.	H.	TB.	2B.	3B.	HR.	RBI.	BB.	IBB.	SO.	B.A.	PO.	A.	E.	F.A.
Jennings, ph	1	1	0	1	1	0	0	0	0	0	0	0	1.000	0	0	0	.000
R. Henderson, lf	4	15	2	5	10	2	0	1	1	3	0	4	.333	12	1	0	1.000
Hassey, ph-c	3	6	0	2	2	0	0	0	1	0	0	0	.333	2	0	1	.667
Lansford, 3b	4	15	0	4	4	0	0	0	1	1	0	0	.267	1	14	0	1.000
Randolph, 2b	4	15	0	4	4	0	0	0	0	1	0	0	.267	14	12	0	1.000
D. Henderson, ph-cf	4	13	2	3	4	1	0	0	0	1	0	3	.231	7	0	0	1.000
McGwire, 1b	4	14	1	3	3	0	0	0	0	2	0	4	.214	42	1	2	.956
McGee, cf-ph-rf	4	10	1	2	3	1	0	0	0	0	0	2	.200	5	0	0	1.000
Baines, ph-dh	3	7	1	1	4	0	0	1	2	1	1	2	.143	0	0	0	.000
Steinbach, c	3	8	0	1	1	0	0	0	0	0	0	1	.125	8	1	0	1.000
Gallego, ss	4	11	0	1	1	0	0	0	1	1	0	3	.091	7	10	1	.944
Canseco, rf-ph-dh	4	12	1	1	4	0	0	1	2	2	0	3	.083	4	0	0	1.000
Bordick, pr-ss	3	0	0	0	0	0	0	0	0	0	0	0	.000	0	2	0	1.000
Burns, p	2	0	0	0	0	0	0	0	0	0	0	0	.000	0	0	0	.000
Eckersley, p	2	0	0	0	0	0	0	0	0	0	0	0	.000	0	0	0	.000
Honeycutt, p	1	0	0	0	0	0	0	0	0	0	0	0	.000	0	0	0	.000
Klink, p	1	0	0	0	0	0	0	0	0	0	0	0	.000	0	0	0	.000
Moore, p	1	0	0	0	0	0	0	0	0	0	0	0	.000	0	0	0	.000
Nelson, p	2	0	0	0	0	0	0	0	0	0	0	0	.000	0	0	0	.000
Sanderson, p	2	0	0	0	0	0	0	0	0	0	0	0	.000	0	0	0	.000
Young, p	1	0	0	0	0	0	0	0	0	0	0	0	.000	0	0	0	.000
Blankenship, ph	1	1	0	0	0	0	0	0	0	0	0	1	.000	0	0	0	.000
Stewart, p	2	1	0	0	0	0	0	0	0	0	0	1	.000	2	1	1	.750
Quirk, c	1	3	0	0	0	0	0	0	0	0	0	2	.000	2	2	0	1.000
Welch, p	1	3	0	0	0	0	0	0	0	0	0	2	.000	2	2	0	1.000
Totals	4	135	8	28	41	4	0	3	8	12	1	28	.207	106	46	5	.968

Baines—Struck out for Gallego in tenth inning of second game.
Blankenship—Struck out for Bordick in ninth inning of third game.
Bordick—Ran for Hassey in tenth inning of second game.
Canseco—Grounded out for Baines in ninth inning of fourth game.
Hassey—Flied out for Nelson in seventh inning of first game; grounded out for Gallego in eighth inning of fourth game.
D. Henderson—Struck out for Eckersley in ninth inning of first game.
Jennings—Singled for Stewart in fifth inning of first game.
McGee—Struck out for Gallego in seventh inning of third game.

CINCINNATI REDS' PITCHING RECORDS

Pitcher	G.	GS.	CG.	IP.	H.	R.	ER.	HR.	BB.	IBB.	SO.	HB.	WP.	W.	L.	Pct.	ERA.
Dibble	3	0	0	4⅔	3	0	0	0	1	0	4	0	1	1	0	1.000	0.00
Armstrong	1	0	0	3	1	0	0	0	0	0	3	0	0	0	0	.000	0.00
Myers	3	0	0	3	2	0	0	0	0	0	3	0	0	0	0	.000	0.00
Scudder	1	0	0	1⅓	0	0	0	0	2	0	2	0	0	0	0	.000	0.00
Charlton	1	0	0	1	1	0	0	0	0	0	0	0	0	0	0	.000	0.00
Rijo	2	2	0	15⅓	9	1	1	0	5	1	14	0	0	2	0	1.000	0.59
Browning	1	1	0	6	6	3	3	2	2	0	2	0	0	1	0	1.000	4.50
Jackson	1	1	0	2⅔	6	4	3	1	2	0	0	0	0	0	0	.000	10.13
Totals	4	4	0	37	28	8	7	3	12	1	28	0	1	4	0	1.000	1.70

Shutout—Rijo, Dibble and Myers (combined). Save—Myers.

OAKLAND ATHLETICS' PITCHING RECORDS

Pitcher	G.	GS.	CG.	IP.	H.	R.	ER.	HR.	BB.	IBB.	SO.	HB.	WP.	W.	L.	Pct.	ERA.
Nelson	2	0	0	5	3	0	0	0	2	0	0	0	0	0	0	.000	0.00
Honeycutt	1	0	0	1⅔	2	0	0	0	1	1	0	0	0	0	0	.000	0.00
Young	1	0	0	1	1	0	0	0	0	0	0	0	0	0	0	.000	0.00
Klink	1	0	0	*0	0	0	0	0	1	0	0	0	0	0	0	.000	0.00
Stewart	2	2	1	13	10	6	4	1	6	0	5	1	0	0	2	.000	2.77
Welch	1	1	0	7⅓	9	4	4	0	2	0	2	0	0	0	0	.000	4.91
Moore	1	1	0	2⅔	8	6	2	2	0	0	1	0	0	0	1	.000	6.75
Eckersley	2	0	0	1⅓	3	1	1	0	0	0	1	0	0	0	1	.000	6.75
Sanderson	2	0	0	1⅔	4	2	2	0	1	0	0	0	1	0	0	.000	10.80
Burns	2	0	0	1⅔	5	3	3	0	2	0	0	0	1	0	0	.000	16.20
Totals	4	4	1	35⅓	45	22	†14	3	15	1	9	1	2	0	4	.000	3.57

*Pitched to one batter in fourth inning of Game 3.
†Individual earned runs do not add to team total because of rule 10.18 (i) being applied in Game 3. No shutouts or saves.

COMPOSITE SCORE BY INNINGS

Cincinnati	4	1	9	1	3	0	0	3	0	1 — 22
Oakland	2	2	4	0	0	0	0	0	0	0 — 8

Sacrifice hits—Lansford, Welch, O'Neill.
Sacrifice flies—Hassey, Morris.
Stolen bases—R. Henderson 3, McGee, Lansford, Duncan, O'Neill, Randolph, Gallego.
Caught stealing—Sabo, Hatcher.
Double plays—Gallego, Randolph and McGwire 2; Randolph and McGwire 2; Duncan, Larkin and Morris; Larkin, Duncan and Benzinger; Randolph, Gallego and McGwire.
Passed balls—None.
Hit by pitcher—By Stewart (Hatcher).
Balks—None.
Bases on balls—Off Rijo 5 (Canseco 2, Baines, Gallego, R. Henderson), off Browning 2 (R. Henderson, Lansford), off Jackson 2 (D. Henderson, Randolph), off Scudder 2 (R. Henderson, McGwire), off Dibble 1 (McGwire); off Stewart 6 (Larkin 2, Braggs, Duncan, Hatcher, Sabo), off Burns 2 (O'Neill 2), off Nelson 2 (O'Neill, Sabo), off Welch 2 (Duncan, O'Neill), off Honeycutt 1 (Hatcher), off Klink 1 (Morris), off Sanderson 1 (O'Neill).
Strikeouts—By Rijo 14 (R. Henderson 3, Gallego 2, D. Henderson 2, Quirk 2, Canseco, McGee, McGwire, Steinbach, Stewart); by Dibble 4 (Baines, R. Henderson, McGee, McGwire); by Armstrong 3 (Canseco, McGwire, Welch); by Myers 3 (Blankenship, Gallego, D. Henderson); by Browning 2 (Baines, McGwire); by Scudder 2 (Canseco, Welch); by Stewart 5 (O'Neill 2, Duncan, Morris, Sabo); by Welch 2 (Jackson, Sabo); by Eckersley 1 (Duncan); by Moore 1 (Oliver).
Left on bases—Oakland 11, 10, 6, 4—31; Cincinnati 6, 10, 9, 7—32.
Time of games—First game, 2:38; second game, 3:31; third game, 3:01; fourth game, 2:48.
Attendance—First game, 55,830; second game, 55,832; third game, 48,269; fourth game, 48,613.
Umpires—Pulli (N.L.), Roe (A.L.), Quick (N.L.), Hendry (A.L.), Marsh (N.L.), Barnett (A.L.) (Games 1 and 2), Froemming (N.L.) (Games 3 and 4).
Official scorers—John Hickey, Hayward (Calif.) Daily Review; Dave Nightingale, The Sporting News; Glenn Sample, Cincinnati official scorer; Gordon Verrell, Long Beach Press-Telegram.

1990 ALL-STAR GAME

Including

Review of 1990 Game

Official Box Score

Results of Previous Games

Julio Franco's seventh-inning double drove in the only two runs in the All-Star Game and earned him MVP honors as the A.L. prevailed, 2-0.

A.L. Pitchers Ration N.L. Two Hits

By DAVE SLOAN

In a year in which a record nine no-hitters were pitched, it should have surprised no one that a no-hitter was nearly thrown in baseball's mid-summer classic as well. Six American League pitchers combined to allow just two National League hits in the A.L.'s 2-0 victory in the 61st annual All-Star Game at Chicago's Wrigley Field on July 10.

The two hits were the fewest by either league since the series began in 1933. And both N.L. hits were singles, marking the third straight year in which N.L. batters were held without an extra-base hit. Not surprisingly, the N.L. lost all three games, the first time since 1946-49 that the A.L. had won three consecutive All-Star Games.

"I definitely think the pitchers have an advantage in the All-Star Game," said San Francisco's Kevin Mitchell, who led the majors with 47 home runs in 1989 and entered this game with a .312 average and 21 home runs. "Not only are you facing a guy who you've never seen before, but he knows that he's only going to have to be out there for an inning or two."

A.L. Manager Tony La Russa of Oakland used his pitching staff masterfully. He started with one of his own pitchers —righthander Bob Welch— and followed with Toronto's Dave Stieb and Kansas City's Bret Saberhagen, all of whom worked two nearly flawless innings. La Russa then used the White Sox' Bobby Thigpen and California's Chuck Finley for one inning each before going to his Oakland stopper, Dennis Eckersley, in the ninth.

Ironically, Saberhagen, the 1989 A.L. Cy Young Award winner and the only pitcher on the A.L. staff with a losing record (5-7), got the win.

A.L. hitters, however, were not much more productive than their N.L. counterparts. Cincinnati's Jack Armstrong, who became the first pitcher in nine years to start an All-Star Game in his first full major league season, struck out two and allowed only one hit in the first two innings. The A.L. had seven hits but only one of them—a double by Julio Franco of the Texas Rangers—was for extra bases. Franco's seventh-inning hit off Cincinnati's Rob Dibble drove home the game's only two runs and made him the game's Most Valuable Player.

Darryl Strawberry and his N.L. teammates registered just two hits, the fewest ever by either league.

"I knew (Dibble) was going to throw me a fastball because he'd been warming up about 30 minutes and I was stiff," said Franco, who delivered the game-deciding hit on Dibble's third pitch following a 68-minute rain delay. With Cleveland rookie Sandy Alomar Jr. at third base and California's Lance Parrish at first, Franco drove an 0-2 pitch into right field to break a scoreless tie.

"I waited inside all the time during the rain," Franco said. "I just decided to stretch and try to concentrate. Everybody said (Dibble) has a lot of body motion and throws hard. I was ready for him."

The lack of offense was probably due to the weather conditions. The batters had to contend with winds of 15 mph at game time, making it nearly impossible to hit a ball out of Wrigley Field's usually cozy confines.

"Not on a night like this," said Cubs second baseman Ryne Sandberg, who was asked before the game whether or not he would hit a homer in front of the home town fans. Sandberg, who won the home run derby in All-Star Game festivities the day before, came into the contest with 24

Bret Saberhagen earned the win after pitching nearly flawless in the fifth and sixth innings.

round-trippers in 334 at-bats.

Prior to the seventh inning, the closest either team came to scoring was the sixth inning, when Detroit's Cecil Fielder—the major leagues' leading home run hitter with 28—flied to center against San Francisco's Jeff Brantley with the bases loaded. The N.L., which had 16 batters retired in succession at one point, never really had a good scoring opportunity. Its only safeties were singles by the Giants' Will Clark in the first inning and the Phillies' Len Dykstra in the ninth. Just four N.L. players reached base all night.

"I spoke to them before the game and they were ready," San Francisco Giants and N.L. Manager Roger Craig said. "They just ran into great pitching. It's tough when you face pitching you've never seen before."

AMERICANS	AB.	R.	H.	RBI.	PO.	A.
R. Henderson, lf (A's) ..	3	0	0	0	2	0
Guillen, ss (White Sox)	2	0	0	0	0	2
Boggs, 3b (Red Sox)	2	0	2	0	0	4
eGruber, 3b (B. Jays) ..	1	0	0	0	0	1
Canseco, rf (A's)	4	0	0	0	1	0
C. Ripken, ss (Orioles) .	2	0	0	0	1	1
fBell, lf (Blue Jays)	2	0	0	0	2	0
Griffey, cf (Mariners) .	2	0	0	0	2	0
iPuckett, cf (Twins)	1	0	1	0	1	0
McGwire, 1b (A's)	2	0	0	0	7	0
gFielder, 1b (Tigers)	1	0	0	0	3	1
S. Alomar, c (Indians) .	3	1	2	0	3	0
Thigpen, p (White Sox)	0	0	0	0	1	0
jTrammell (Tigers)	1	0	0	0	0	0
Finley, p (Angels)	0	0	0	0	0	0
Eckersley, p (A's)	0	0	0	0	0	0
Sax, 2b (Yankees)	1	0	0	0	0	1
Saberhagen, p (Roy.)..	0	0	0	0	0	0
hParrish, c (Angels)	1	1	1	0	3	0
Welch, p (A's)	0	0	0	0	0	1
aJacoby (Indians)	1	0	0	0	0	0
Stieb, p (Blue Jays)	0	0	0	0	0	0
dJu. Franco, 2b (Ran.)	3	0	1	2	1	0
Totals	32	2	7	2	27	11

NATIONALS	AB.	R.	H.	RBI.	PO.	A.
Dykstra, cf (Phillies) ...	4	0	1	0	3	0
Sandberg, 2b (Cubs)	3	0	0	0	1	2
R. Alomar, 2b (Padres)	1	0	0	0	1	2
Clark, 1b (Giants)	3	0	1	0	6	0
Myers, p (Reds)	0	0	0	0	0	0
Jo. Franco, p (Mets)	0	0	0	0	0	0
lWilliams (Giants)	1	0	0	0	0	0
Mitchell, lf (Giants)	2	0	0	0	1	0
Viola, p (Mets)	0	0	0	0	0	0
Wallach, 3b (Expos)	2	0	0	0	0	0
Dawson, rf (Cubs)	2	0	0	0	1	0
Strawberry, rf (Mets) .	1	0	0	0	3	1
Sabo, 3b (Reds)	2	0	0	0	0	2
D. Smith, p (Astros)	0	0	0	0	0	0
Brantley, p (Giants)	0	0	0	0	0	0
Dibble, p (Reds)	0	0	0	0	0	0
Bonilla, 1b (Pirates)	1	0	0	0	1	0
Sioscia, c (Dodgers)	2	0	0	0	6	0
kGreg Olson, c (Bra.) ...	1	0	0	0	0	0
O. Smith, ss (Cards)	1	0	0	0	1	1
De. M'rtnz, p (Exp.)	0	0	0	0	0	0
Bonds, lf (Pirates)	1	0	0	0	2	0
Armstrong, p (Reds)	0	0	0	0	0	0
R. M'rtnz, p (Dodgers)	0	0	0	0	0	0
bGwynn (Padres)	0	0	0	0	0	0
cLarkin, ss (Reds)	0	0	0	0	1	2
Dunston, ss (Cubs)	2	0	0	0	0	0
Totals	29	0	2	0	27	10

Americans....................	0 0 0	0 0 0	2 0 0—2			
Nationals.....................	0 0 0	0 0 0	0 0 0—0			

AMERICANS	IP.	H.	R.	ER.	BB.	SO.
Welch (A's)	2	1	0	0	0	1
Stieb (Blue Jays)	2	0	0	0	1	1
Saberhagen (Royals) ..	2	0	0	0	0	1
Thigpen (White Sox) .	1	0	0	0	0	1
Finley (Angels)	1	0	0	0	1	1
Eckersley (A's)	1	1	0	0	0	1

NATIONALS	IP.	H.	R.	ER.	BB.	SO.
Armstrong (Reds)	2	1	0	0	0	2
R. M'rtnz (Dodgers)...	1	0	0	0	2	1
De. Martinez (Expos)	1	0	0	0	0	1
Viola (Mets)	1	1	0	0	0	0
D. Smith (Astros)	⅔	0	0	0	2	1
Brantley (Giants)	⅓*	2	2	2	0	0
Dibble (Reds)	1	1	0	0	1	0
Myers (Reds)	1	1	0	0	2	0
Jo. Franco (Mets)	1	0	0	0	0	0

*Pitched to two batters in seventh.

Winning Pitcher—Saberhagen. Losing Pitcher —Brantley. Save—Eckersley.

aGrounded out for Welch in third. bWalked for R. Martinez in third. cRan for Gwynn in third. dGrounded out for Stieb in fifth. eRan for Boggs in sixth. fStruck out for C. Ripken in sixth. gFlied out for McGwire in sixth. hSingled for Saberhagen in seventh. iSingled and went to third on two-base error for Griffey in eighth. jPopped out for Thigpen in eighth. kStruck out for Sioscia in eighth. lCalled out on strikes for John Franco in ninth. Error—Strawberry. Double plays—Sandberg, Larkin and Clark; Strawberry and Sioscia. Left on bases—Americans 10, Nationals 4. Two-base hit—Julio Franco. Stolen bases—Sax, Larkin, Gruber 2, Canseco. Bases on balls—Off Stieb 1 (Gwynn), off Finley 1 (Bonds), off R. Martinez 2 (Sax, Boggs), off D. Smith 2 (Canseco, Griffey), off Dibble 1 (Gruber), off Myers 2 (Fielder, Parrish). Strikeouts—By Welch 1 (Mitchell), by Stieb 1 (Dawson), by Saberhagen 1 (Sioscia), by

Thigpen 1 (Strawberry), by Finley 1 (Olson), by Eckersley 1 (Williams), by Armstrong 2 (Canseco, McGwire), by R. Martinez 1 (R. Henderson), by De. Martinez 1 (McGwire), by D. Smith 1 (Bell). Umpires—Montague (N.L) plate, Phillips (A.L.) first, Rippley (N.L.) second, Johnson (A.L.) third, DeMuth (N.L.) left field, Welke (A.L.) right field. Official scorers—Gordon Verrell (Long Beach Press-Telegram), Don Friske (Arlington Heights Ill. Daily Herald), Bob Rosenberg (White Sox official scorer). Time—2:53. Attendance—39,071.

Players listed on roster but not used: A.L.—Gregg Olson, Clemens, Jones, Parker, Johnson. N.L.—Heaton.

RESULTS OF PREVIOUS GAMES

1933—At Comiskey Park, Chicago, July 6. Americans 4, Nationals 2. Managers—Connie Mack, John McGraw. Winning pitcher—Lefty Gomez. Losing pitcher—Bill Hallahan. Attendance —47,595.

1934—At Polo Grounds, New York, July 10. Americans 9, Nationals 7. Managers—Joe Cronin, Bill Terry. Winning pitcher—Mel Harder. Losing pitcher—Van Mungo. Attendance—48,363.

1935—At Municipal Stadium, Cleveland, July 8. Americans 4, Nationals 1. Managers—Mickey Cochrane, Frankie Frisch. Winning pitcher—Lefty Gomez. Losing pitcher—Bill Walker. Attendance—69,831.

1936—At Braves Field, Boston, July 7. Nationals 4, Americans 3. Managers—Charlie Grimm, Joe McCarthy. Winning pitcher—Dizzy Dean. Losing pitcher—Lefty Gomez. Attendance—25,556.

1937—At Griffith Stadium, Washington, July 7. Americans 8, Nationals 3. Managers—Joe McCarthy, Bill Terry. Winning pitcher—Lefty Gomez. Losing pitcher—Dizzy Dean. Attendance—31,391.

1938—At Crosley Field, Cincinnati, July 6. Nationals 4, Americans 1. Managers—Bill Terry, Joe McCarthy. Winning pitcher—Johnny Vander Meer. Losing pitcher—Lefty Gomez. Attendance—27,067.

1939—At Yankee Stadium, New York, July 11. Americans 3, Nationals 1. Managers—Joe McCarthy, Gabby Hartnett. Winning pitcher—Tommy Bridges. Losing pitcher—Bill Lee. Attendance—62,892.

1940—At Sportsman's Park, St. Louis, July 9. Nationals 4, Americans 0. Managers—Bill McKechnie, Joe Cronin. Winning pitcher—Paul Derringer. Losing pitcher—Red Ruffing. Attendance—32,373.

1941—At Briggs Stadium, Detroit, July 8. Americans 7, Nationals 5. Managers—Del Baker, Bill McKechnie. Winning pitcher—Ed Smith. Losing pitcher—Claude Passeau. Attendance—54,674.

1942—At Polo Grounds, New York, July 6. Americans 3, Nationals 1. Managers—Joe Cronin, Leo Durocher. Winning pitcher—Spud Chandler. Losing pitcher—Mort Cooper. Attendance—34,178.

1943—At Shibe Park, Philadelphia, July 13 (night). Americans 5, Nationals 3. Managers—Joe McCarthy, Billy Southworth. Winning pitcher—Dutch Leonard. Losing pitcher—Mort Cooper. Attendance—31,938.

1944—At Forbes Field, Pittsburgh, July 11 (night). Nationals 7, Americans 1. Managers—Billy Southworth, Joe McCarthy. Winning pitcher—Ken Raffensberger. Losing pitcher—Tex Hughson. Attendance—29,589.

1945—No game played.

1946—At Fenway Park, Boston, July 9. Americans 12, Nationals 0. Managers—Steve O'Neill, Charlie Grimm. Winning pitcher—Bob Feller. Losing pitcher—Claude Passeau. Attendance—34,906.

1947—At Wrigley Field, Chicago, July 8. Americans 2, Nationals 1. Managers—Joe Cronin, Eddie Dyer. Winning pitcher—Frank Shea. Losing pitcher—Johnny Sain. Attendance—41,123.

1948—At Sportsman's Park, St. Louis, July 13. Americans 5, Nationals 2. Managers—Bucky Harris, Leo Durocher. Winning pitcher—Vic Raschi. Losing pitcher—Johnny Schmitz. Attendance—34,009.

1949—At Ebbets Field, Brooklyn, July 12. Americans 11, Nationals 7. Managers—Lou Boudreau, Billy Southworth. Winning pitcher—Virgil Trucks. Losing pitcher—Don Newcombe. Attendance—32,577.

1950—At Comiskey Park, Chicago, July 11. Nationals 4, Americans 3 (14 innings). Managers—Burt Shotton, Casey Stengel. Winning pitcher—Ewell Blackwell. Losing pitcher—Ted Gray. Attendance—46,127.

1951—At Briggs Stadium, Detroit, July 10. Nationals 8, Americans 3. Managers—Eddie Sawyer, Casey Stengel. Winning pitcher—Sal Maglie. Losing pitcher—Ed Lopat. Attendance—52,075.

1952—At Shibe Park, Philadelphia, July 8. Nationals 3, Americans 2 (five innings—rain). Managers—Leo Durocher, Casey Stengel. Winning pitcher—Bob Rush. Losing pitcher—Bob Lemon. Attendance—32,785.

1953—At Crosley Field, Cincinnati, July 14. Nationals 5, Americans 1. Managers—Chuck Dressen, Casey Stengel. Winning pitcher—Warren Spahn. Losing pitcher—Allie Reynolds. Attendance—30,846.

1954—At Municipal Stadium, Cleveland, July 13. Americans 11, Nationals 9. Managers—Casey Stengel, Walter Alston. Winning pitcher—Dean Stone. Losing pitcher—Gene Conley. Attendance—68,751.

1955—At Milwaukee County Stadium, Milwaukee, July 12. Nationals 6, Americans 5 (12 innings). Managers—Leo Durocher, Al Lopez. Winning pitcher—Gene Conley. Losing pitcher—Frank Sullivan. Attendance—45,643.

1956—At Griffith Stadium, Washington, July 10. Nationals 7, Americans 3. Managers—Walter Alston, Casey Stengel. Winning pitcher—Bob Friend. Losing pitcher—Billy Pierce. Attendance—28,843.

1957—At Busch Stadium, St. Louis, July 9. Americans 6, Nationals 5. Managers—Casey Stengel, Walter Alston. Winning pitcher—Jim Bunning. Losing pitcher—Curt Simmons. Attendance—30,693.

1958—At Memorial Stadium, Baltimore, July 8. Americans 4, Nationals 3. Managers—Casey Stengel, Fred Haney. Winning pitcher—Early Wynn. Losing pitcher—Bob Friend. Attendance—48,829.

1959 (first game)—At Forbes Field, Pittsburgh, July 7. Nationals 5, Americans 4. Managers—Fred Haney, Casey Stengel. Winning pitcher—Johnny Antonelli. Losing pitcher—Whitey Ford. Attendance—35,277.

1959 (second game)—At Memorial Coliseum, Los Angeles, August 3. Americans 5, Nationals 3. Managers—Casey Stengel, Fred Haney. Winning pitcher—Jerry Walker. Losing pitcher—Don Drysdale. Attendance—55,105.

1960 (first game)—At Municipal Stadium, Kansas City, July 11. Nationals 5, Americans 3. Managers—Walter Alston, Al Lopez. Winning pitcher—Bob Friend. Losing pitcher—Bill Monbouquette. Attendance—30,619.

1960 (second game)—At Yankee Stadium, New York, July 13. Nationals 6, Americans 0. Managers—Walter Alston, Al Lopez. Winning pitcher—Vernon Law. Losing pitcher—Whitey Ford. Attendance—38,362.

1961 (first game)—At Candlestick Park, San Francisco, July 11. Nationals 5, Americans 4 (10 innings). Managers—Danny Murtaugh, Paul Richards. Winning pitcher—Stu Miller. Losing pitcher—Hoyt Wilhelm. Attendance—44,115.

1961 (second game)—At Fenway Park, Boston, July 31. Americans 1, Nationals 1 (nine-inning tie, stopped by rain). Managers—Paul Richards, Danny Murtaugh. Attendance—31,851.

1962 (first game)—At District of Columbia Stadium, Washington, July 10. Nationals 3, Americans 1. Managers—Fred Hutchinson, Ralph Houk. Winning pitcher—Juan Marichal. Losing pitcher—Camilo Pascual. Attendance—45,480.

1962 (second game)—At Wrigley Field, Chicago, July 30. Americans 9, Nationals 4. Managers—Ralph Houk, Fred Hutchinson. Winning pitcher—Ray Herbert. Losing pitcher—Art Mahaffey. Attendance—38,359.

1963—At Municipal Stadium, Cleveland, July 9. Nationals 5, Americans 3. Managers—Alvin Dark, Ralph Houk. Winning pitcher—Larry Jackson. Losing pitcher—Jim Bunning. Attendance—44,160.

1964—At Shea Stadium, New York, July 7. Nationals 7, Americans 4. Managers—Walter Alston, Al Lopez. Winning pitcher—Juan Marichal. Losing pitcher—Dick Radatz. Attendance—50,850.

1965—At Metropolitan Stadium, Bloomington (Minnesota), July 13. Nationals 6, Americans 5. Managers—Gene Mauch, Al Lopez. Winning pitcher—Sandy Koufax. Losing pitcher—Sam McDowell. Attendance—46,706.

1966—At Busch Memorial Stadium, St Louis, July 12. Nationals 2, Americans 1 (10 innings). Managers—Walter Alston, Sam Mele. Winning pitcher—Gaylord Perry. Losing pitcher—Pete Richert. Attendance—49,936.

1967—At Anaheim Stadium, Anaheim (California), July 11. Nationals 2, Americans 1 (15 innings). Managers—Walter Alston, Hank Bauer. Winning pitcher—Don Drysdale. Losing pitcher—Jim Hunter. Attendance—46,309.

1968—At Astrodome, Houston, July 9 (night). Nationals 1, Americans 0. Managers—Red Schoendienst, Dick Williams. Winning pitcher—Don Drysdale. Losing pitcher—Luis Tiant. Attendance—48,321.

1969—At Robert F. Kennedy Memorial Stadium, Washington, July 23. Nationals 9, Americans 3. Managers—Red Schoendienst, Mayo Smith. Winning pitcher—Steve Carlton. Losing pitcher—Mel Stottlemyre. Attendance—45,259.

1970—At Riverfront Stadium, Cincinnati, July 14 (night). Nationals 5, Americans 4 (12 innings). Managers—Gil Hodges, Earl Weaver. Winning pitcher—Claude Osteen. Losing pitcher—Clyde Wright. Attendance—51,838.

1971—At Tiger Stadium, Detroit, July 13 (night). Americans 6, Nationals 4. Managers—Earl Weaver, George (Sparky) Anderson. Winning pitcher—Vida Blue. Losing pitcher—Dock Ellis. Attendance—53,559.

1972—At Atlanta Stadium, Atlanta, July 25 (night). Nationals 4, Americans 3 (10 innings). Managers—Danny Murtaugh, Earl Weaver. Winning pitcher—Tug McGraw. Losing pitcher—Dave McNally. Attendance—53,107.

1973—At Royals Stadium, Kansas City, July 24 (night). Nationals 7, Americans 1. Managers—George (Sparky) Anderson, Dick Williams. Winning pitcher—Rick Wise. Losing pitcher—Bert Blyleven. Attendance—40,849.

1974—At Three Rivers Stadium, Pittsburgh, July 23 (night). Nationals 7, Americans 2. Managers—Yogi Berra, Dick Williams. Winning pitcher

—Ken Brett. Losing pitcher—Luis Tiant. Attendance—50,706.

1975—At Milwaukee County Stadium, Milwaukee, July 15 (night). Nationals 6, Americans 3. Managers—Walter Alston, Alvin Dark. Winning pitcher—Jon Matlack. Losing pitcher—Jim Hunter. Attendance—51,480.

1976—At Veterans Stadium, Philadelphia, July 13 (night). Nationals 7, Americans 1. Managers—George (Sparky) Anderson, Darrell Johnson. Winning pitcher—Randy Jones. Losing pitcher—Mark Fidrych. Attendance—63,974.

1977—At Yankee Stadium, New York, July 19 (night). Nationals 7, Americans 5. Managers—Alfred (Billy) Martin, George (Sparky) Anderson. Winning pitcher—Don Sutton. Losing pitcher—Jim Palmer. Attendance—56,683.

1978—At San Diego Stadium, San Diego, July 11 (night). Nationals 7, Americans 3. Managers—Alfred (Billy) Martin, Thomas Lasorda. Winning pitcher—Bruce Sutter. Losing pitcher—Rich Gossage. Attendance—51,549.

1979—At Kingdome, Seattle, July 17. Nationals 7, Americans 6. Managers—Chuck Tanner, Bob Lemon. Winning pitcher—Bruce Sutter. Losing pitcher—Jim Kern. Attendance—58,905.

1980—At Dodger Stadium, Los Angeles, July 8. Nationals 4, Americans 2. Managers—Chuck Tanner, Earl Weaver. Winning pitcher—Jerry Reuss. Losing pitcher—Tommy John. Attendance—56,088.

1981—At Municipal Stadium, Cleveland, August 9 (night). Nationals 5, Americans 4. Managers—Dallas Green, Jim Frey. Winning pitcher—Vida Blue. Losing pitcher—Rollie Fingers. Attendance—72,086.

1982—At Olympic Stadium, Montreal, July 13 (night). Nationals 4, Americans 1. Managers—Thomas Lasorda, Alfred (Billy) Martin. Winning pitcher—Steve Rogers. Losing pitcher—Dennis Eckersley. Attendance—59,057.

1983—At Comiskey Park, Chicago, July 6 (night). Americans 13, Nationals 3. Managers—Harvey Kuenn, Dorrel (Whitey) Herzog. Winning pitcher—Dave Stieb. Losing pitcher—Mario Soto. Attendance—43,801.

1984—At Candlestick Park, San Francisco, July 10 (night). Nationals 3, Americans 1. Managers—Paul Owens, Joseph Altobelli. Winning pitcher—Charlie Lea. Losing pitcher—Dave Stieb. Attendance—57,756.

1985—At Metrodome, Minneapolis, July 16 (night). Nationals 6, Americans 1. Managers—Dick Williams, George (Sparky) Anderson. Winning pitcher—LaMarr Hoyt. Losing pitcher—Jack Morris. Attendance—54,960.

1986—At Astrodome, Houston, July 15 (night). Americans 3, Nationals 2. Managers—Dick Howser, Dorrel (Whitey) Herzog. Winning pitcher—Roger Clemens. Losing pitcher—Dwight Gooden. Attendance—45,774.

1987—At Oakland-Alameda County Coliseum, July 14 (night). Nationals 2, Americans 0 (13 innings). Managers—Dave Johnson, John McNamara. Winning pitcher—Lee Smith. Losing pitcher—Jay Howell. Attendance—49,671.

1988—At Riverfront Stadium, Cincinnati, July 12 (night). Americans 2, Nationals 1. Managers—Tom Kelly, Dorrel (Whitey) Herzog. Winning pitcher—Frank Viola. Losing pitcher—Dwight Gooden. Attendance—55,837.

1989—At Anaheim Stadium, Anaheim, Calif., July 11 (night). Americans 5, Nationals 3. Managers—Tony La Russa, Tommy Lasorda. Winning pitcher—Nolan Ryan. Losing pitcher—John Smoltz. Attendance—64,036.

BATTING, PITCHING

FEATURES

Including

No-Hit Pitching Performances

Low-Hit Pitching Performances

Top Strikeout Performances

Baseball's Top Firemen

Pitchers Winning 1-0 Games

Multi-Home Run Performances

Batters Hitting Grand Slams

Top One-Game Hitting Performances

Baseball's Top Pinch-Hitters

Top Performances in Debuts

Homers by Parks

Award Winners

Hall of Fame Electees

Hall of Famers List, Years Selected

Major League Draft

Pitchers Set No-hit Mark in '90

By DAVE SLOAN

If the 1990 baseball season were a Broadway play, it would have to be titled, "The Year of the No-hitter." A record nine no-hitters were thrown last year, surpassing the previous high of seven set in 1908 and matched in 1917. After a 1989 campaign in which no pitcher hurled a no-hit gem, major league pitchers went bonkers in that department last season.

Seven of the 1990 no-hitters were thrown in the American League, two in the National League, and each was noteworthy for its own particular reason.

● Two pitchers—California's Mark Langston and Mike Witt—combined to pitch the year's first no-hitter on April 11 at Anaheim Stadium against the Seattle Mariners. The game marked the California debut of Langston, who had signed a lucrative free-agent contract with the Angels the previous off-season, and came against the team with which he had began his professional career in 1981.

● On June 2 at Seattle, Mariners lefthander Randy Johnson pitched the year's second no-hitter in a 2-0 win over the Detroit Tigers. At 6-foot-10, Johnson is the tallest man ever to throw a no-hit game and, ironically, was one of the three pitchers traded by Montreal to Seattle in May 1989 for then free-agent-to-be Langston. It was the first no-hitter ever thrown by a Seattle pitcher.

● The record for the oldest player to throw a no-hitter was established just nine days later when 43-year-old Nolan Ryan of the Texas Rangers beat the world champion Oakland Athletics 6-0. It was the sixth no-hitter of Ryan's 24-year career, extending a major league record he already held.

● On June 29, Dave Stewart of the A's and Fernando Valenzuela of the Dodgers made baseball history by hurling no-hit gems against Toronto and St. Louis, respectively, just hours apart. It marked the first time in history that no-hitters were pitched in each league on the same day.

● On July 1, less than 48 hours after the Stewart-Valenzuela daily double, Andy Hawkins of the Yankees pitched eight no-hit innings against the Chicago White Sox only to lose the game, 4-0. Three errors in the eighth inning allowed four unearned runs to score and put Hawkins in the record books as only the second pitcher ever to lose a complete-game no-hitter.

● Eleven days later, Hawkins lost another no-hitter to Chicago, this time a six-inning, rain-shortened effort by White Sox righthander Melido Perez. Perez' older brother Pascual, a Yankees righthander, witnessed the feat from the New York dugout.

● On August 15 at Philadelphia, Phillies lefthander Terry Mulholland faced the minimum 27 batters in a 6-0, no-hit victory over the San Francisco Giants. The only baserunner against Mulholland came via a seventh-inning error by third baseman Charlie Hayes. Ironically, Mulholland and Hayes and the man who hit the ball—the Phillies' Rick Parker—were involved in a June 18, 1989, swap that saw relief ace Steve Bedrosian traded from the Phillies to the Giants.

● The season's ninth and final no-hitter was thrown by Toronto righthander Dave Stieb, who probably deserved the honor more than any other pitcher. Prior to his September 2 gem against the Cleveland Indians, Stieb had carried four other no-hit bids into the ninth inning in his career before yielding a hit. In his last two starts of 1988, Stieb came within one out of a no-hitter each time before giving up hits to Cleveland's Julio Franco and Baltimore's Jim Traber.

In 1990, however, the most heartwarming no-hit story belonged to Ryan; the most heart wrenching, to Hawkins.

Ryan, who struck out 14 batters in recording his 59th career shutout, was making only his second start after spending 15 days on the disabled list because of pain in his lower back. On June 6 at Arlington Stadium, Ryan was tagged for five runs in five innings in a 5-4 loss to the A's. That's part of the reason why his no-hitter against the same team less than one week later was so surprising and so sweet.

"It comes so late in my career that it makes it extra special," said Ryan, who previously had thrown no-hitters as a member of the California Angels and Houston Astros and is the only pitcher to perform the feat for three different teams. It was Ryan's first no-hit gem since a 6-0 victory for the Astros over the Los Angeles Dodgers on September 26, 1981.

What happened to Hawkins evoked memories of Harvey Haddix' 12-inning perfect game for Pittsburgh in 1959. Pitching for a Yankee team that had baseball's worst record (28-44) at the time, Hawkins retired the first 14 Chicago batters he

Within an 11-day span, the New York Yankees' Andy Hawkins lost two no-hitters to the Chicago White Sox. On July 1, he no-hit the White Sox but lost and July 12 he was the losing pitcher when Melido Perez hurled a six-inning, rain-shortened no-hitter.

faced. For most of the game, he and White Sox lefthander Greg Hibbard were locked in a scoreless tie.

But with two outs in the Chicago eighth, Sammy Sosa reached first base on an error by New York third baseman Mike Blowers. Hawkins then walked Ozzie Guillen and Lance Johnson to load the bases. The next batter, Robin Ventura, lifted a deep fly to left field that rookie Jim Leyritz—normally a third baseman—misplayed for a two-base error. Leyritz' miscue cleared the bases to give the Sox a 3-0 lead. Ivan Calderon then hit a fly to right field that Jesse Barfield lost in the sun. Ventura scored easily to give Chicago a 4-0 bulge.

"It's really tough to throw a no-hitter and get beat," said Hawkins, who joined Ken Johnson of the 1964 Houston Colt .45s as the only pitcher to lose a complete-game no-hitter.

"It's tough in the outfield, the wind's playing all kinds of tricks out there. . . . The guys are giving their best, we're all giving our best."

"I'm sorry he had to lose it," Johnson said when he was informed of Hawkins' fate. "Now we're a group of two."

A complete list of the 1990 no-hitters follows:

1990 No-Hitters

Date	Pitcher—Club—Opp.	Place	IP.	H.	R.	ER.	BB.	SO.	Result
April 11	Langston (7), Witt (2), Angels vs. Mariners	California	9	0	0	0	4	5	W 1-0
June 2	Johnson, Mariners vs. Tigers	Seattle	9	0	0	0	6	8	W 2-0
June 11	Ryan, Rangers vs. Athletics	Oakland	9	0	0	0	2	14	W 5-0
June 29	Stewart, Athletics vs. Blue Jays	Toronto	9	0	0	0	3	12	W 5-0
June 29	Valenzuela, Dodgers vs. Cardinals	Los Angeles	9	0	0	0	3	7	W 6-0
July 1	Hawkins, Yankees vs. White Sox	Chicago	8	0	4	0	5	3	L 0-4
July 12	Perez, White Sox vs. Yankees	New York	6	0	0	0	4	9	W 8-0
Aug. 15	Mulholland, Phillies vs. Giants	Philadelphia	9	0	0	0	0	8	W 6-0
Sept. 2	Stieb, Blue Jays vs. Indians	Cleveland	9	0	0	0	4	9	W 3-0

Drabek Paces Low-hit Parade

By DAVE SLOAN

The record nine no-hitters pitched in the major leagues last season garnered a lot of attention. But, with a break here or there, the no-hit total easily could have been 13 or 14.

There were 56 low-hit (one- and two-hit) games in the majors in 1990, 30 of them in the National League. All 26 teams were involved in at least one such game, with Philadelphia leading all clubs with nine. Baltimore, California, Minnesota and Toronto were the only teams that failed to pitch a low-hit game. The Chicago Cubs and Cleveland were never on the receiving end.

The Detroit Tigers led all teams with six low-hit performances, with Dan Petry and Jeff Robinson pitching two each. In addition, Greg Harris of Boston, Bruce Hurst of San Diego and San Francisco's Trevor Wilson pitched two low-hit games apiece. The individual leader, however, was Pittsburgh's Doug Drabek, who pitched three low-hit gems en route to winning the N.L. Cy Young Award.

Of the five pitchers who lost no-hit bids in the ninth inning in 1990, three of them lost their gems with two outs in the final frame. On April 20 at Oakland, Seattle righthander Brian Holman came within one out of pitching the 15th perfect game in baseball history before Oakland pinch-hitter Ken Phelps—a former Mariner —drilled Holman's first pitch over the right-field fence at Oakland-Alameda County Coliseum. On July 29 at San Francisco, Giants righthander Scott Garrelts held the Cincinnati Reds hitless until Paul O'Neill slapped Garrelts' first pitch to center field for a single. And less than a week later, on August 3, Drabek lost his no-hitter against Philadelphia when Sil Campusano drilled a 3-2 pitch to right-center for a hit.

In addition to Holman, Garrelts and Drabek, Atlanta's John Smoltz (on May 27 against the Phillies) and San Francisco's Wilson (on June 13 against San Diego) lost no-hit bids in the ninth inning.

The Phillies, who fell victim to Drabek twice, were on the receiving end of seven low-hit games, the most of any team.

The Rangers' Nolan Ryan and the Phillies' Terry Mulholland were the only pitchers to throw both a no-hitter and low-hitter in 1990. Ryan, who pitched a no-hitter against Oakland on June 11, tied Bob Fel-

Dan Petry hurled two low-hit games in 1990 as the Detroit Tigers led all teams with six low-hit efforts.

ler's record for career one-hitters when he hurled his 12th in a 1-0 victory over the Chicago White Sox on April 26. Mulholland, who faced the minimum 27 batters in his 6-0, no-hit victory over the Giants on August 15, retired 26 St. Louis Cardinals in succession in a September 25 game at Veterans Stadium. However, the Cards' leadoff batter—rookie Bernard Gilkey—hit a triple in the first inning and later scored the game's only run on a sacrifice fly in a 1-0 St. Louis win.

Mulholland, who also yielded a ninth-inning double to Gilkey, was one of only three pitchers to lose a low-hit game last year.

Thirteen of the 56 low-hit performances were one-hitters.

A complete list of one- and two-hit games for the 1990 season follows:

San Francisco's Trevor Wilson was one of three N.L. pitchers to toss at least two low-hit games last season.

AMERICAN LEAGUE

One-Hit Games

April 20—Holman, Seattle vs. Oakland, 6-1—Phelps, homer in ninth.

April 26—Ryan, Texas vs. Chicago, 1-0—Kittle, single in second.

June 7—Harris (eight innings) and Reardon (one inning), Boston vs. New York, 3-0—Barfield, single in fifth.

July 6—Morris, Detroit vs. Kansas City, 4-0—Stillwell, single in first.

July 7—Appier, Kansas City vs. Detroit, 4-0—Whitaker, single in first.

Two-Hit Games

April 22—Dopson (1⅓ innings), Lamp (4⅔ innings), Reardon (two innings) and L. Smith (three innings), Boston vs. Milwaukee 4-2—Vaughn, single in fifth; Yount, single in ninth.

April 27—Hibbard (eight innings), Radinsky (no innings) and Thigpen (one inning), Chicago vs. Toronto, 6-1—Hill, single in fifth; Felix, single in fifth.

May 6—Young (eight innings) and Eckersley (one inning), Oakland vs. Boston, 4-2—Pena, single in second; Boggs, double in third.

May 18—Saberhagen, Kansas City vs. New York, 4-1—Washington, single in second; Kelly, double in seventh.

May 20—S. Davis (7⅓ innings) and Montgomery (2⅔ innings), Kansas City vs. New York, 4-3—Kelly, single in first; Mattingly, homer in ninth.

May 23—King (six innings), Pall (two innings) and Thigpen (one inning), Chicago vs. Baltimore, 6-3—C. Ripken, single in fourth; Orsulak, homer in fourth.

June 6—Boddicker, Boston vs. New York, 4-1—Kelly, single in second; Nokes, single in second.

June 15—Petry (7⅓ innings), Gibson (⅔ inning), Nunez (1⅔ innings), and Gleaton (⅓ inning), Detroit vs. California, 2-1—Parrish, homer in second; White, double in second.

July 7—Black, Cleveland vs. Oakland, 1-0—R. Henderson, single in sixth; Lansford, single in sixth.

July 15—Bosio (five innings) and Navarro (three innings), Milwaukee vs. Oakland, 1-4—Jennings, double in first; Jose, homer in first.

July 18—Young, Seattle vs. Toronto, 5-2—Borders, double in fourth and single in sixth.

July 19—Robinson (eight innings), Parker (⅔ inning) and Gleaton (⅓ inning), Detroit vs. Boston, 1-0—Brunnansky, single in first; Greenwell, single in fourth.

July 21—Petry (eight innings) and Gibson (one inning), Detroit vs. Texas, 8-1—Daugherty, double in fifth; Incaviglia, single in second.

July 24—Robinson (eight innings) and Gleaton (one inning), Detroit vs. Baltimore, 8-2—Devereaux, homer in eighth; Anderson, homer in eighth.

Aug. 9—Leary (8⅓ innings) and Guetterman (⅔ inning), New York vs. Seattle, 1-0—Leonard, double in second; Reynolds, single in sixth.

Aug. 18—Witt, New York vs. Seattle, 6-0—Davis, singles in second and seventh.

Five pitchers lost no-hit bids in the ninth inning, including Seattle's Brian Holman.

Aug. 26—Harris (7⅔ innings) and Gray (1⅓ innings), Boston vs. Toronto, 1-0—McGriff, single in second; Myers, single in eighth.

Sept. 1—Swan (seven innings) and Swift (two innings), Seattle vs. Kansas City, 3-0—Pecota, single in seventh; Macfarlane, double in ninth.

Sept. 15—Welch (eight innings) and Eckersley (one inning), Oakland vs. Minnesota, 4-1—Gladden, single in third; Mack, single in fifth.

Sept. 16—Searcy (seven innings) and Gibson (two innings), Detroit vs. New York, 5-2—Barfield, single in first; Balboni, homer in seventh.

Sept. 21—Witt, Texas vs. Minnesota, 2-1—Munoz, single in second; Hrbek, single in sixth.

NATIONAL LEAGUE
One-Hit Games

June 13—Wilson, San Francisco vs. San Diego, 6-0—Pagliarulo, single in ninth.

July 21—Belcher, Los Angeles vs. Pittsburgh, 6-0—Bell, single in fourth.

July 29—Garrelts, San Francisco vs. Cincinnati, 4-0—O'Neill, single in ninth.

Aug. 3—Drabek, Pittsburgh vs. Philadelphia, 11-0—Campusano, single in ninth.

Aug. 17—Tewksbury, St. Louis vs. Houston, 5-0—Stubbs, double in eighth.

Sept. 5—Smith, Pittsburgh vs. New York, 1-0—Miller, single in first.

Sept. 16—Anderson (five innings), Ruskin (1⅔ innings), Burke (one inning) and Frey (1⅓ innings), Montreal vs. Pittsburgh, 4-1—Bell, double in first.

Sept. 20—Nabholz, Montreal vs. New York, 2-0—Herr, single in sixth.

Two-Hit Games

April 19—Martinez, Montreal vs. Philadelphia, 5-0—Daulton, double in eighth; Herr, single in ninth.

April 22—Fernandez, New York vs. Montreal, 5-0—Raines, singles in fourth and seventh.

April 26—Clancy (seven innings), Agosto (one inning) and Smith (one inning), Houston vs. Atlanta, 3-0—Murphy, single in second; Treadway, single in first.

April 26—Harkey (seven innings) and Williams (two innings), Chicago vs. San Diego, 3-1—Stephenson, homer in eighth; Roberts, double in eighth.

May 3—Glavine (seven innings), Kerfeld (one inning) and Boever (one inning), Atlanta vs. Montreal, 4-1—Nixon, single in third; Johnson, double in ninth.

May 14—Benes, San Diego vs. Philadelphia, 5-1—Daulton, single in fifth; Ford, single in fifth.

May 27—Smoltz, Atlanta vs. Philadelphia, 6-1—Dykstra, double in ninth; V. Hayes, single in ninth.

June 17—DeLeon (7⅓ innings) and DiPino (1⅔ innings), St. Louis vs. Montreal, 7-1—Owen, homer in first; Santovenia, single in fifth.

June 23—Gooden, New York vs. Philadelphia, 3-0—Kruk, double in fifth and single in seventh.

July 7—Hurst, San Diego vs. St. Louis, 3-1—Zeile, double in first; McGee, single in third.

July 20—Charlton (six innings) and Dibble (three innings), Cincinnati vs. Philadelphia, 5-1—C. Hayes, single in fifth; Hollins, homer in ninth.

July 24—Hurst, San Diego vs. Cincinnati, 10-0—Larkin, single in first; Morris, single in fourth.

July 24—Martinez, Los Angeles vs. San Francisco, 9-2—Butler, single in first; Mitchell, single in ninth.

July 27—Maddux (nine innings) and Long (one inning), Chicago vs. Montreal, 2-0—Grissom, singles in first and seventh.

July 29—Drabek, Pittsburgh vs. Philadelphia, 2-1—Daulton, homer in first; Dykstra, double in fifth.

July 30—Morgan, Los Angeles vs. Cincinnati, 4-1—Larkin, single in seventh; O'Neill, single in seventh.

Aug. 4—Wilson, San Francisco vs. Los Angeles, 2-1—Brooks, homer in fifth; Daniels, single in ninth.

Aug. 7—Neidlinger (7⅔ innings), Searage (no innings) and Crews (⅓ inning), Los Angeles vs. Cincinnati, 0-1—O'Neill, singles in fourth and sixth.

Aug. 7—DeJesus, Philadelphia vs. New York, 9-0—Boston, single in second; Strawberry, single in seventh.

Aug. 29—Drabek (six innings), Pittsburgh vs. Atlanta, 10-0—Gregg, single in second; Avery, single in third.

Sept. 17—Rijo, Cincinnati vs. San Francisco, 4-0—Bass, double in first and single in ninth.

Sept. 25—Mulholland, Philadelphia vs. St. Louis, 0-1—Gilkey, triple in first and Gilkey, double in ninth.

Pittsburgh, 4-1—Bell, double in first.

Mets' Foursome Fans Many Foes

By DAVE SLOAN

A second straight second-place finish in the National League East made 1990 a disappointing season for the New York Mets, the preseason favorite of many people to win the division title.

The runner-up Mets, however, did one thing better than any other team last year—strike out batters. New York pitchers combined to whiff 1,217 batters in 1990, just four shy of the major league record set by the 1969 Houston Astros.

David Cone (233 strikeouts), Dwight Gooden (223), Frank Viola (182) and Sid Fernandez (181) provided the Mets with a fearsome foursome for fanning the opposition.

Cone, who led the major leagues in strikeouts, also led all pitchers in 10-strikeout performances. Cone had nine such games, one more than perennial leader Nolan Ryan of the Texas Rangers. Ryan, who increased his career record total of 10-strikeout games to 207, paced the American League with 232 strikeouts.

Not surprisingly, the Mets led all clubs with 20 10-strikeout games as Cone, Gooden (six), Fernandez (four) and Viola (one) combined for that total. No other team had four pitchers perform the feat. The Texas Rangers led the A.L. with 15 such games. Ryan and Bobby Witt (seven) combined for the Rangers' total.

Overall, there were 92 such performances last season, with the feat being accomplished 47 times in the A.L. and 45 times in the N.L. All teams except Cleveland, Detroit, Minnesota, Toronto and Philadelphia had at least one 10-strikeout performance. A total of 36 pitchers did it at least once, and 10 pitchers had the distinction of being their club's lone 10-strikeout performer. Ironically, neither of the Cy Young Award winners, Oakland's Bob Welch or Pittsburgh's Doug Drabek, struck out 10 batters in one game.

Following is a list of all pitchers who recorded at least 10 strikeouts in a game in 1990, with the number of times the feat was

The New York Mets' David Cone led all pitchers with nine 10-strikeout performances.

accomplished:

AMERICAN LEAGUE: Baltimore (1)—Harnisch. Boston (4)—Clemens 3, Boddicker. California (6)—Langston 4, Finley 2. Chicago (3)—McDowell 2, Perez. Cleveland—None. Detroit—None. Kansas City (3)—Appier, Gubicza, Saberhagen. Milwaukee (1)—Higuera. Minnesota—None. New York (2)—Leary 2. Oakland (2)—Sanderson, Stewart. Seattle (10)—Johnson 5, Hanson 3, Young 2. Texas (15)—Ryan 8, Witt 7. Toronto—None.

NATIONAL LEAGUE: Atlanta (2)—Smoltz 2. Chicago (1)—Wilson. Cincinnati (4)—Rijo 4. Houston (2)—Darwin, Scott. Los Angeles (5)—Martinez 5. Montreal (5)—Gardner 4, Martinez. New York (20)—Cone 9, Gooden 6, Fernandez 4, Viola. Philadelphia—None. Pittsburgh (1)—Smith. St. Louis (3)—DeLeon 2, Magrane. San Diego (1)—Benes. San Francisco (1)—Garrelts.

1990 Games With 15 or More Strikeouts

Date	Pitcher—Club—Opp.	Place	IP.	H.	R.	ER.	BB.	SO.	Result
June 4—Martinez, Dodgers vs. Braves		Los Angeles	9	3	0	0	1	18	W 6-0
April 26—Ryan, Rangers vs. White Sox		Texas	9	1	0	0	2	16	W 1-0
May 11—Gooden, Mets vs. Dodgers		New York	7	9	3	3	1	15	W 9-4
June 8—Scott, Astros vs. Reds		Houston	10	3	1	1	1	15	W 3-1
Aug. 17—Ryan, Rangers vs. White Sox		Texas	10	3	0	0	0	15	W 1-0

Thigpen's Saves Mend White Sox

By DAVE SLOAN

The Chicago White Sox were baseball's most improved team in 1990, and the player most responsible for Chicago's 25-game resurgence over the previous year was relief ace Bobby Thigpen.

Thigpen, a former standout at Mississippi State, obliterated Dave Righetti's four-year-old major league record by saving 57 of Chicago's 94 victories last year. He tied Righetti's mark with his 46th save on September 1 and broke it two days later—exactly one month before the regular season ended.

Thigpen, who blew only eight save opportunities, kept the White Sox in contention for the American League Western Division title until the final week of the season. He finished fifth in the A.L. Most Valuable Player balloting, fourth in the Cy Young Award race and captured the league's Fireman of the Year Award as the best reliever.

With one point being awarded for each save or relief win, Thigpen finished the year with 61 points (57 saves and four wins), nine more than runner-up Dennis Eckersley of the Oakland Athletics (48 saves, four wins). Thigpen's 61 points were the most ever recorded in Fireman of the Year competition.

Not surprisingly, the White Sox (68) and Athletics (64) had more saves than any other major league teams last year.

Whereas the A.L. had a different pitcher win its Fireman Award for the fourth straight year, the National League winner was the New York Mets' John Franco, who also won the award in 1988 while playing for the Cincinnati Reds. Franco's 33 saves and five wins gave him 38 points, three more than second-place finisher Randy Myers of the world champion Reds. Ironically, Franco and Myers were the principals of a four-player trade between the Mets and Reds December 6, 1989.

Both reigning Firemen of the Year—Jeff Russell and Mark Davis—struggled last season. Russell saved 10 games for Texas but missed much of the year after undergoing elbow surgery in May. Davis, who won his 1989 Fireman honor while playing for San Diego, saved just six games for Kansas City after signing a lucrative free-agent contract the previous winter.

Following is a complete list of major league players who recorded saves or relief wins in 1990:

Bobby Thigpen

AMERICAN LEAGUE

Pitcher—Club	Saves	Relief Wins	Tot. Pts.
Thigpen, Chicago	57	4	61
Eckersley, Oakland	48	4	52
Jones, Cleveland	43	5	48
Olson, Baltimore	37	6	43
Aguilera, Minnesota	32	5	37
Righetti, New York	36	1	37
Henke, Toronto	32	2	34
Schooler, Seattle	30	1	31
Henneman, Detroit	22	8	30
Montgomery, Kansas City	24	6	30
Harvey, California	25	4	29
Plesac, Milwaukee	24	3	27
Reardon, Boston	21	5	26
Rogers, Texas	15	9	24
Eichhorn, California	13	2	15
Crim, Milwaukee	11	3	14
Gleaton, Detroit	13	1	14
Guetterman, New York	2	11	13
Ward, Toronto	11	2	13
Candelaria, Minn.-Tor.	5	7	12
Jones, Chicago	1	11	12
Arnsberg, Texas	5	6	11
Gray, Boston	9	2	11
Russell, Texas	10	1	11
Radinsky, Chicago	4	6	10
Comstock, Seattle	2	7	9
Farr, Kansas City	1	8	9
Honeycutt, Oakland	7	2	9
Nunez, Detroit	6	3	9
Swift, Seattle	6	3	9
Williamson, Baltimore	1	8	9
Berenguer, Minnesota	0	8	8
M. Davis, Kansas City	6	2	8
Gibson, Detroit	3	5	8
Jackson, Seattle	3	5	8
Nelson, Oakland	5	3	8
Cadaret, New York	3	4	7
Fraser, California	2	5	7
Jeffcoat, Texas	5	2	7
Murphy, Boston	7	0	7
Orosco, Cleveland	2	5	7
Crawford, Kansas City	1	5	6
Plunk, Oakland	0	6	6

Pitcher—Club	Saves	Relief Wins	Tot. Pts.	Pitcher—Club	Saves	Relief Wins	Tot. Pts.
Smith, Boston	4	2	6	Aldrich, Baltimore	1	1	2
Acker, Toronto	1	4	5	Aquino, Kansas City	0	2	2
Barfield, Texas	1	4	5	Bailes, California	0	2	2
Burns, Oakland	3	2	5	Bolton, Boston	0	2	2
Pall, Chicago	2	3	5	Clark, Seattle	0	2	2
Wills, Toronto	0	5	5	Fetters, California	1	1	2
Drummond, Minnesota	1	3	4	Fossas, Milwaukee	0	2	2
Edens, Milwaukee	2	2	4	Garces, Minnesota	2	0	2
Edwards, Chicago	2	2	4	Guante, Cleveland	0	2	2
Leach, Minnesota	2	2	4	Hickey, Baltimore	1	1	2
Mirabella, Milwaukee	0	4	4	Holton, Baltimore	0	2	2
Olin, Cleveland	1	3	4	Lugo, Detroit	0	2	2
Patterson, Chicago	2	2	4	McClure, California	0	2	2
Reed, Sea.-Bos.	2	2	4	McCullers, N.Y.-Det.	0	2	2
Schilling, Baltimore	3	1	4	McGaffigan, Kansas City	1	1	2
Wells, Toronto	3	1	4	Parker, N.Y.-Det.	0	2	2
Blair, Toronto	0	3	3	Petry, Detroit	0	2	2
Lamp, Boston	0	3	3	Seanez, Cleveland	0	2	2
Machado, Milwaukee	3	0	3	Ward, Cleveland	1	1	2
Price, Baltimore	0	3	3	Wayne, Minnesota	1	1	2

One save—Andersen, Boston; Klink, Oakland; Navarro, Milwaukee; Savage, Minnesota; Tapani, Minnesota; Veres, Milwaukee; Witt, Calif.-N.Y.

One relief win—Ballard, Baltimore; Bautista, Baltimore; Black, Clev.-Tor.; Casian, Minnesota; Cerutti, Toronto; Chitren, Oakland; Gardner, Boston; Gilles, Toronto; Guthrie, Minnesota; Harris, Seattle; Harris, Boston; Harris, Oakland; Irvine, Boston; Knackert, Seattle; Knudson, Milwaukee; Krueger, Milwaukee; Lee, Milwaukee; Mills, New York; Minton, California; Moyer, Texas; Norris, Oakland; Robinson, New York; Rosenberg, Chicago; Sebra, Milwaukee; E. Valdez, Cleveland; S. Valdez, Cleveland; Walker, Cleveland; Young, California.

NATIONAL LEAGUE

Pitcher—Club	Saves	Relief Wins	Tot. Pts.	Pitcher—Club	Saves	Relief Wins	Tot. Pts.
Franco, New York	33	5	38	Hesketh, Mon.-Atl.	5	1	6
Myers, Cincinnati	31	4	35	Parrett, Phil.-Atl.	2	4	6
Lefferts, San Diego	23	7	30	Thurmond, San Francisco	4	2	6
L. Smith, St. Louis	27	3	30	Grant, S.D.-Atl.	3	2	5
Smith, Houston	23	6	29	Kerfeld, Hou.-Atl.	2	3	5
McDowell, Philadelphia	22	6	28	Mahler, Cincinnati	4	1	5
Bedrosian, San Francisco	17	9	26	Ruskin, Pitt.-Mon.	2	3	5
Brantley, San Francisco	19	5	24	Castillo, Atlanta	1	3	4
Burke, Montreal	20	3	23	Cook, Phil.-L.A.	1	3	4
Howell, Los Angeles	16	5	21	Darwin, Houston	2	2	4
Landrum, Pittsburgh	13	7	20	Hartley, Los Angeles	1	3	4
Dibble, Cincinnati	11	8	19	Machado, New York	0	4	4
Assenmacher, Chicago	10	7	17	Oliveras, San Francisco	2	2	4
Boever, Atl.-Phil.	14	3	17	Rojas, Montreal	1	3	4
Frey, Montreal	9	8	17	Show, San Diego	1	3	4
Harris, San Diego	9	8	17	Terry, St. Louis	2	2	4
Williams, Chicago	16	1	17	Mohorcic, Montreal	2	1	3
Schmidt, Montreal	13	3	16	Ojeda, New York	0	3	3
Agosto, Houston	4	9	13	Palacios, Pittsburgh	3	0	3
Sampen, Montreal	2	11	13	Schiraldi, San Diego	1	2	3
Lancaster, Chicago	6	6	12	Whitehurst, New York	2	1	3
Andersen, Houston	6	5	11	Wilson, Chicago	1	2	3
Belinda, Pittsburgh	8	3	11	Bielecki, Chicago	1	1	2
Long, Chicago	5	6	11	Freeman, Phil.-Atl.	1	1	2
Mercker, Atlanta	7	4	11	Henry, Atlanta	0	2	2
Patterson, Pittsburgh	5	6	11	Hernandez, Houston	0	2	2
Akerfelds, Philadelphia	3	5	8	Horton, St. Louis	1	1	2
Charlton, Cincinnati	2	6	8	Innis, New York	1	1	2
Crews, Los Angeles	5	3	8	Luecken, Atlanta	1	1	2
DiPino, St. Louis	3	5	8	Meyer, Houston	1	1	2
Kipper, Pittsburgh	3	5	8	Niedenfuer, St. Louis	2	0	2
Pena, New York	5	3	8	Pavlas, Chicago	0	2	2
Power, Pittsburgh	7	1	8	Perez, St. Louis	1	1	2
Hall, Montreal	3	4	7	Pico, Chicago	2	0	2
Layana, Cincinnati	2	5	7	Rodriguez, San Diego	1	1	2
Aase, Los Angeles	3	3	6	Scudder, Cincinnati	0	2	2
Carman, Philadelphia	1	5	6	Stanton, Atlanta	2	0	2
Dayley, St. Louis	2	4	6	Walsh, Los Angeles	1	1	2
Gott, Los Angeles	3	3	6	Wetteland, Los Angeles	0	2	2

One save—Burkett, San Francisco; Clancy, Houston; Novoa, San Francisco; Reed, Pittsburgh; Reuschel, San Francisco; Tewksbury, St. Louis; Walk, Pittsburgh; Wilkins, Chicago.

One relief win—Birtsas, Cincinnati; Darling, New York; Dewey, San Francisco; Gross, Montreal; Hammaker, San Francisco; Huismann, Pittsburgh; Malone, Philadelphia; Nunez, Chicago; O'Neal, San Francisco; Osuna, Houston; Roesler, Pittsburgh; Ross, Pittsburgh; Schatzeder, Hou.-N.Y.; Searage, Los Angeles; Tibbs, Pittsburgh; Tudor, St. Louis; Vosberg, San Francisco; Wilson, San Francisco.

Twins Hit Hard by 1-0 Losses

By DAVE SLOAN

Just three years after capturing their first World Series championship, the Minnesota Twins fell upon hard times in 1990. Not only did they end up last in the American League Western Division, but their 29-game finish behind the Oakland Athletics was the farthest any major league team finished out of first place last season.

How bad did it get for the Twins last year? Well, they turned a record two triple plays July 17 against the Boston Red Sox but lost the game, 1-0. It was the first of four games Minnesota lost by that score in 1990, a figure equaled by the Mets, Yankees and Mariners. No team lost more 1-0 games.

Forty-three major league games ended in 1-0 scores last season, 30 in the A.L. and 13 in the National League. All clubs except the Braves, Giants and Orioles were involved in at least one such game, with the Rangers leading all clubs with eight. Texas won five 1-0 games, the most of any team, with reliever Kenny Rogers winning twice. Nolan Ryan, Kevin Brown and Bobby Witt also won 1-0 games for the Rangers.

Besides Russell, seven other pitchers won at least two 1-0 games, with St. Louis lefthander Joe Magrane leading the way with three. Magrane won on September 25 at Philadelphia despite the fact that Phillies lefthander Terry Mulholland retired 26 batters in a row after yielding a first-inning run.

Surprisingly, no pitcher lost more than one 1-0 game in 1990.

Home runs were the deciding factor in 10 such games, with the most dramatic being Paul O'Neill's two-out, ninth-inning blast on May 18 at Riverfront Stadium off Cardinals reliever Ken Dayley. O'Neill's homer gave the eventual World Series champion Reds their 24th victory in 32 games and a 7½-game lead over the Dodgers in the N.L. West.

On April 11, California's Mark Langston and Mike Witt combined to pitch a no-hitter in the A.L.'s first 1-0 game of the season.

The complete list of 1-0 games, including the winning and losing pitchers and the inning in which the run was scored, follows:

AMERICAN LEAGUE (30)

Date	Winner	Loser	Inning
APRIL—			
11	—*Langston, Cal.	*Hanson, Sea.	7
19	—*Swindell, Cle.	*Perez, N.Y.	6
25	—*Filer, Mil.	Saberhagen, K.C.	2
26	— Ryan, Tex.	*Perez, Chi.	5
29	—*Stewart, Oak.	*Clemens, Bos.	1
MAY—			
28	— Stieb, Tor.	Moore, Oak.	5
JUNE—			
4	—*Brown, Tex.	*McCaskill, Cal.	3
22	—*Bailes, Cal.	*Gibson, Det.	9
29	—*McDowell, Chi.	*Cary, N.Y.	2
JULY—			
6	—*Wells, Tor.	*Holman, Sea.	6
7	— Black, Cle.	*Young, Oak.	4
17	—*Bolton, Bos.	*Erickson, Minn.	5
19	—*Robinson, Det.	Harris, Bos.	6
27	—*Stieb, Tor.	*Hough, Tex.	3
27	—*Bolton, Bos.	Morris, Det.	4
AUGUST—			
1	— Stewart, Oak.	*Schooler, Sea.	11
9	—*Leary, N.Y.	Young, Sea.	2
14	—*Farr, K.C.	*Mielke, Tex.	9
17	— Finley, Cal.	Boddicker, Bos.	9
17†	— Rogers, Tex.	*Pall, Chi.	13
24	—*Knudson, Mil.	Leary, N.Y.	5
25	— Clemens, Bos.	*Wells, Tor.	7
26	— Witt, Tex.	*Leach, Minn.	9
26	—*Harris, Bos.	*Stottlemyre, Tor.	8
SEPTEMBER—			
2	—*Finley, Cal.	Fernandez, Chi.	5
10	—*Rogers, Tex.	*Guetterman, N.Y.	11
17	—*Farr, K.C.	*Casian, Minn.	6
19	—*Wayne, Minn.	*Montgomery, K.C.	11
30	—*Terrell, Det.	Guthrie, Minn.	2
OCTOBER—			
2	—*Brown, Mil.	*Rogers, Tex.	3

NATIONAL LEAGUE (13)

Date	Winner	Loser	Inning
APRIL—			
10	— Belcher, L.A.	*Show, S.D.	5
25	—*Frey, Mon.	*Smith, Hou.	9
27	—*Viola, N.Y.	*Portugal, Hou.	4
MAY—			
18	—*Charlton, Cin.	*Dayley, St.L.	9
JUNE—			
26	—*Ruskin, Pitt.	Ruffin, Phil.	8
JULY—			
18	— Scott, Hou.	*Pena, N.Y.	8
28	—*Magrane, St.L.	*Cone, N.Y.	7
AUGUST—			
7	—*Browning, Cin.	*Neidlinger, L.A.	8
29	—*Portugal, Hou.	*Sutcliffe, Chi.	2
SEPTEMBER—			
4	—*Magrane, St.L.	*Fernandez, N.Y.	4
5†	— Smith, Pitt.	*Franco, N.Y.	9
21	— Smith, Pitt.	*DeLeon, St.L.	7
25	—*Magrane, St.L.	Mulholland, Phil.	1

*Did not pitch complete game.
†First game of doubleheader.

Multi-HR Game Gives Fielder 51

By DAVE SLOAN

Ninety-five players hit two or more home runs in one game in 1990, but none did it with the flair or pressure that Detroit's Cecil Fielder faced on October 3.

Entering the Tigers' final game of the season at New York, Fielder had hit 49 home runs, and needed just one more to become the first major leaguer in 13 years and the 11th player in history to hit 50 in a season. But Fielder hadn't homered in Detroit's last five games, and the pressure to make baseball history on this day was squarely on his shoulders.

Then, as if it were choreographed for a Hollywood movie, Fielder delivered, hitting homers in the fourth and eighth innings to spur the Tigers to a 10-3 victory. It was the big first baseman's fifth multi-homer game of the year and helped him finish the year with the most homers since George Foster hit 52 for the 1977 Cincinnati Reds.

Overall, there were 163 multi-homer performances in the majors last year, 90 in the American League and 73 in the National. Fifty-three A.L. players performed the feat while 42 players did it in the N.L. Dave Winfield hit two homers for the Yankees on April 21 against Texas and had two more multi-homer games for the California Angels following his May 11 trade to the West Coast.

All 26 clubs had at least one player hit two homers in a game in 1990, with the A.L. champion Oakland Athletics leading all teams with 16 such performances. A's outfielder Jose Canseco led all players with seven multi-homer games and "Bash Brother" Mark McGwire had five. Not surprisingly, McGwire (39) and Canseco (37) finished second and third, respectively, behind Fielder in the A.L. home run derby.

Only four players—Canseco, McGwire, Rickey and Dave Henderson—contributed to the Oakland team total. Meanwhile, a major league-high eight players accounted for Atlanta's 13 multi-homer performances, tops among N.L. clubs. The Braves' Dave Justice, the N.L. Rookie of the Year, clubbed two homers in consecutive games against San Diego on August 7-8.

Two players managed multi-homer performances in the same game on eight occasions; three players did it in the same game three times. Fielder (three homers), teammate Chet Lemon and Toronto's Kelly

Jose Canseco's seven multi-homer games helped Oakland pace all teams with 16 such efforts.

Gruber all hit at least two homers in an 11-7 Blue Jays win on May 6; Ron Gant and Dale Murphy of the Braves and Pittsburgh's Bobby Bonilla did it in a 13-11 Atlanta victory on May 20, and three California players—Winfield, Dante Bichette and Brian Downing—each hit two homers in the Angels' 8-7 triumph over Toronto on July 14.

Boston's Ellis Burks became the 15th player in history to hit two homers in the same inning when he hit a pair in the fourth inning of the Red Sox' 12-4 victory over Cleveland on August 27.

Dave Winfield posted a multi-home run game with the New York Yankees in April and then two more with California after his trade in May.

Following is a list of players who had multi-homer games in '90 and the number of times:

AMERICAN LEAGUE: Baltimore (7)—Milligan 3, C. Ripken 2, Horn, Orsulak. Boston (6)—Brunansky 2, Burks 2, Evans, Greenwell. California (8)—Winfield 2, Bichette, Davis, Downing, Parrish, Schroeder, White. Chicago (4)—Kittle 3, Pasqua. Cleveland (2)—Maldonado, Snyder. Detroit (7)—Fielder 5, Lemon, Salas. Kansas City (3)—Jackson 2, Tartabull. Milwaukee (3)—Deer, Parker, Vaughn. Minnesota (4)—Puckett 2, Gaetti, Larkin. New York (8)—Balboni 2, Maas 2, Barfield, Blowers, Leyritz, Winfield. Oakland (16)—Canseco 7, McGwire 5, R. Henderson 3, D. Henderson 2. Seattle (6)—Leonard 2, Briley, Giles, Griffey, Jr., E. Martinez. Texas (4)—Incaviglia 2, Daugherty, Franco. Toronto (12)—Gruber 4, Bell 3, McGriff 3, Hill, Olerud.

NATIONAL LEAGUE: Atlanta (13)—Gant 3, Justice 3, Presley 2, Blauser, Lilliquist, Murphy, Olson, Treadway. Chicago (8)—Sandberg 4, Dawson 2, Dunston 2. Cincinnati (5)—O'Neill 2, Davis, Oliver, Sabo. Houston (4)—Davis 3, Stubbs. Los Angeles (10)—Daniels 3, Murray 3, Dempsey, Gibson, Gwynn, Samuel. Montreal (4)—Wallach 2, Galarraga, Martinez. New York (8)—McReynolds 4, Strawberry 2, Carreon, Sasser. Philadelphia (2)—Jones, Thon. Pittsburgh (9)—Bonds 3, Bonilla 3, Van Slyke 2, King. St. Louis (2)—Guerrero, Thompson. San Diego (1)—Je. Clark. San Francisco (7)—Williams 3, Clark 2, Mitchell 2.

A recap of the three-homer games:

1990 Three-Homer Games

Date	Player—Club—Opp.	Place	AB.	R.	H.	2B.	3B.	HR.	RBI.	Result
May 6	Fielder, Tigers vs. Blue Jays	Toronto	5	3	4	0	0	3	5	L 7-11
May 25	Mitchell, Giants vs. Pirates	Pittsburgh	5	3	3	0	0	3	5	W 9-8
May 26	Treadway, Braves vs. Phillies	Philadelphia	5	3	3	0	0	3	6	W 12-3
June 1	Davis, Astros vs. Giants	San Francisco	5	3	3	0	0	3	5	L 5-6*
June 6	Fielder, Tigers vs. Indians	Cleveland	3	3	3	0	0	3	5	W 6-4
June 9	Milligan, Orioles vs. Yankees	Baltimore	3	3	3	0	0	3	6	W 10-1
July 17	Jackson, Royals vs. Yankees	New York	3	3	3	0	0	3	7	W 10-7
Sept. 29	Brunansky, Red Sox vs. Blue Jays	Boston	4	3	3	0	0	3	5	W 7-5

*11 innings.

McGwire's '90 Slam Theatrical

By DAVE SLOAN

Mark McGwire of the Oakland Athletics is the first major leaguer to ever hit 30 or more home runs in his first four seasons. After clubbing a rookie record 49 round-trippers in 1987, McGwire has followed up by hitting 32, 33 and 39 the last three years, respectively. His record-setting 30th homer of 1990 was hit in dramatic fashion.

The A's and Boston Red Sox were tied, 2-2, in the bottom of the 10th inning on August 15 at the Oakland Coliseum. After the A's loaded the bases on two walks and an error, McGwire drilled the first pitch from Boston reliever Rob Murphy deep into the left-field stands for a grand slam. The 6-2 victory improved the A's record to 75-43, tops in the major leagues, and kept their lead over the Chicago White Sox at six games in the American League West.

McGwire's grand slam was one of 72 hit in the major leagues in 1990, one of 38 in the A.L. All clubs except for Houston and the New York Yankees hit at least one, with the Seattle Mariners leading all teams with six slams. Alvin Davis of the Mariners led all players with three slams, tying the Dodgers' Kal Daniels for individual honors.

Three other players—Pittsburgh's Bobby Bonilla, San Diego's Joe Carter and Detroit's Cecil Fielder—hit two slams last season.

On the debit side, all clubs except for San Diego and Cleveland gave up at least one slam in 1990. The Yankees and Cincinnati Reds gave up six slams apiece, with two Yankee pitchers—Tim Leary and Jeff Robinson—each giving up two. In addition to Leary and Robinson, seven other pitchers yielded two slams in 1990. In fact, Mets lefthander Frank Viola has given up two grand slams in each of the last two years.

The Mets and Pittsburgh Pirates led all N.L. teams with five slams each. Ironically, no Pittsburgh player hit a grand slam in either 1988 or '89 before four different Pirates connected in 1990. A major league-high five players hit slams for the Mets last season.

Three of the 1990 slams were of the inside-the-park variety, three were hit by pinch-hitters, three were hit in extra innings and two were hit in the same game. The most popular dates for grand slams in 1990 were May 22 and August 4. Three slams were hit on each of those days.

The complete list of grand slams, with

Alvin Davis helped Seattle hit a major league high six grand slams by belting a big-league best three slams in 1990.

the inning in which each was hit in parentheses, follows:

AMERICAN LEAGUE (38)

APRIL—

11	—Bell, Toronto vs. Brown, Texas	(3)

MAY—

5	—Harper, Minnesota vs. Plesac, Milwaukee	(8)
8	—Perry, Kansas City vs. Ryan, Texas	(1)
14	—Palacios, Kansas City vs. Reardon, Boston	(10)
17	—Giles, Seattle vs. Wills, Toronto	(5)
22	—J. Canseco, Oakland vs. Wills, Toronto	(6)
27	—Joyner, California vs. Fossas, Milwaukee	(7)

JUNE—

1	—Buhner, Seattle vs. Morris, Detroit	(1)
1	—Fielder, Detroit vs. Young, Seattle	(2)
17	—Parrish, California vs. McCullers, Detroit	(5)
20	—Steinbach, Oakland vs. McCullers, Detroit	(4)

JULY—

8	—Hamilton, Milwaukee vs. Eichhorn, California	(5)
13	—Bradley, Baltimore vs. Candelaria, Minnesota	(8)
15	—Jose, Oakland vs. Bosio, Milwaukee	(1)
17	—Davis, Seattle vs. Wells, Toronto	(6)
23	—Devereaux, Baltimore vs. Parker, Detroit	(3)
31	—Franco, Texas vs. Fossas, Milwaukee	(9)

Pittsburgh's Bobby Bonilla was one of five players to collect two or more grand slams last season.

AUGUST—
2 —Moseby, Detroit vs. Robinson, New York .... (6)
3 —Buechele, Texas vs. Acker, Toronto .... (7)
4 —Macfarlane, Kansas City vs. Harnisch, Balti. ..... (2)
4 —Snyder, Cleveland vs. Leary, New York .... (6)
10 —Webster, Cleveland vs. Searcy, Detroit .... (4)
14 —Polonia, California vs. Leary, New York .... (2)
14 —Hill, Toronto vs. Peterson, Chicago .... (7)
15 —McGwire, Oakland vs. Murphy, Boston .... (10)
30 —Karkovice, Chicago vs. West, Minnesota .... (4)
31 —Rivera, Boston vs. Robinson, New York .... (8)

SEPTEMBER—
1 —Greenwell, Boston vs. Cadaret, New York .... (5)
5 —Reynolds, Seattle vs. Hickey, Baltimore .... (9)
6 —Sierra, Texas vs. Codiroli, Kansas City .... (1)
11 —Fernandez, Toronto vs. Stottlemyre, K.C. .... (2)
14 —Horn, Baltimore vs. Ward, Toronto...................... (6)
18 —Davis, Seattle vs. Rogers, Texas .... (7)
23 —Fielder, Detroit vs. Moore, Oakland...................... (2)
23 —Gaetti, Minnesota vs. Hough, Texas..................... (1)
28 —Davis, Seattle vs. Rosenberg, Chicago................. (5)
29 —Gruber, Toronto vs. Lamp, Boston .... (9)

OCTOBER—
3 —Ward, Detroit vs. Adkins, New York .... (1)

NATIONAL LEAGUE (34)

APRIL—
17 —McClendon, Chicago vs. Fernandez, New York.. (5)
21 —Guerrero, St. Louis vs. Mulholland, Phila. .... (3)
23 —Carter, San Diego vs. Gunderson, San Francisco (1)
27 —Martinez, Philadelphia vs. Luecken, Atlanta ...... (8)

MAY—
2 —Thomas, Atlanta vs. Smith, Montreal.................... (3)
6 —Jordan, Philadelphia vs. Crews, Los Angeles ...... (7)

15 —Kennedy, San Francisco vs. Darling, New York (4)
18 —Templeton, San Diego vs. Viola, New York......... (2)
18 —Bonilla, Pittsburgh vs. Castillo, Atlanta .... (4)
19 —Daniels, Los Angeles vs. Carman, Philadelphia.. (4)
21 —McReynolds, New York vs. Morgan, L.A............. (3)
22 —Bonds, Pittsburgh vs. Schatzeder, Houston .... (3)
22 —Marshall, New York vs. Hartley, Los Angeles .... (6)

JUNE—
8 —Dunston, Chicago vs. Carman, Philadelphia....... (3)
12 —Olson, Atlanta vs. Jackson, Cincinnati .... (2)
13 —Johnson, New York vs. Lancaster, Chicago .... (9)

JULY—
15 —Wallach, Montreal vs. Avery, Atlanta................. (3)
16 —Davis, Cincinnati vs. Smith, Montreal................. (6)
17 —Williams, San Francisco vs. Smiley, Pittsburgh (6)
18 —Galarraga, Montreal vs. Myers, Cincinnati......... (9)
18 —King, Pittsburgh vs. Vosberg, San Francisco...... (8)
22 —Redus, Pittsburgh vs. Wells, Los Angeles........... (2)
23 —Thon, Philadelphia vs. Viola, New York .... (6)
29 —Sasser, New York vs. DeLeon, St. Louis.............. (5)

AUGUST—
4 —Carter, San Diego vs. Mahler, Cincinnati .... (11)
19 —Riles, San Francisco vs. Gooden, New York........ (6)
23 —Bonilla, Pittsburgh vs. Layana, Cincinnati........ (5)
29 —Gwynn, Los Angeles vs. Akerfelds, Philadelphia (6)
30 —Strawberry, New York vs. Oliveras, San Fran... (8)

SEPTEMBER—
4 —Daniels, Los Angeles vs. Portugal, Houston........ (2)
14 —Daniels, Los Angeles vs. Layana, Cincinnati....... (6)
19 —Santiago, San Diego vs. Holmes, Los Angeles.... (6)
25 —Justice, Atlanta vs. Charlton, Cincinnati .... (5)

OCTOBER—
1 —Raines, Montreal vs. DiPino, St. Louis .... (7)

Multi-Hit Games Spark Sandberg

By DAVE SLOAN

Although the Chicago Cubs last season failed to defend their 1989 National League Eastern Division title, no one could point an accusing finger at Ryne Sandberg. The Cubs' second baseman led the senior circuit in total bases (344), runs scored (116) and home runs (40), the latter making Sandberg the first N.L. second baseman since Rogers Hornsby in 1925 to lead the league in homers.

In addition, Sandberg drove in a career-high 100 runs and set a fielding record for second basemen with 123 consecutive errorless games.

Another category in which Sandberg led the N.L. was multi-hit (four or more) games. Sandberg had four hits in five games last season, one more than teammate Mark Grace and Philadelphia's Len Dykstra. The major league leader in multi-hit performances was Rafael Palmeiro of the Texas Rangers, who compiled six such games en route to finishing third with a .319 average in the American League batting race. Ironically, Palmeiro played three seasons with Sandberg and the Cubs before being traded to the Rangers following the 1988 season.

Palmeiro, who led the A.L. with 191 hits, had five hits in two different games, an achievement matched only by Minnesota's Kirby Puckett. Besides Palmeiro and Puckett, 11 other players had five-hit games in 1990, including Wally Backman's six hits in six at-bats for Pittsburgh in the Pirates' 9-4 victory at San Diego on April 27. Backman became the first major leaguer since Puckett on August 30, 1987, to have a six-hit game.

A.L. batting champion George Brett of the Kansas City Royals and Toronto's Fred McGriff finished behind Palmeiro in the A.L. with five multi-hit games last season. Brett also was the only player to hit for the cycle (single, double, triple and homer) in 1990. He did it in the Royals' 6-1 win at Toronto on July 25.

Overall, there were 274 multi-hit performances in the majors in 1990, 20 more than the year before. A.L. players accounted for 147 of that total and N.L. batsmen 127. All clubs had at least one player perform the feat, with four teams—Atlanta, San Diego, Baltimore and Boston—having nine different players with multi-hit games. Two second basemen—Bill Doran and Willie Randolph—had multi-hit games for two different clubs. Doran did it with both the Astros and Reds while Randolph had four-hit games with the Dodgers and A's.

The Baltimore Orioles led all clubs with 16 multi-hit performances while the Cincinnati Reds paced the N.L. with 15 such games.

Twenty-two players compiled hitting streaks of 15 or more games—12 in the A.L. and 10 in the N.L. The season's longest streak belonged to Minnesota's Brian Harper, who hit safely in 25 consecutive games between July 6 and August 4.

Besides Harper, the following players compiled hitting streaks of 15 or more games: 23 games—Len Dykstra, Phillies; 22 games—Willie McGee, Cardinals; 19 games—Paul Molitor, Brewers; 18 games—Mark Grace, Cubs; Barry Larkin, Reds; Darryl Strawberry, Mets; 17 games—Bobby Bonilla, Pirates; Kent Hrbek, Twins; Kevin Seitzer, Royals; 16 games—George Brett, Royals; Dion James, Indians; Gary Sheffield, Brewers; Matt Williams, Giants; 15 games—Vince Coleman, Cardinals; Andre Dawson, Cubs; Delino DeShields, Expos; Tony Fernandez, Blue Jays; Kelly Gruber, Blue Jays; Rafael Palmeiro, Rangers; Tony Pena, Red Sox; Ruben Sierra, Rangers.

The complete list of players with four or more hits in one game follows:

AMERICAN LEAGUE: Baltimore (16)—Bradley 3, Finley 3, Orsulak 3, Hulett 2, Anderson, Horn, McKnight, Milligan, Tettleton. Boston (12)—Greenwell 3, Quintana 2, Boggs, Brunansky, Burks, Marzano, Naehring, Pena, Reed. California (8)—Downing 3, Ray 2, Anderson, Bichette, Parrish. Chicago (8)—Calderon 3, Fisk, Fletcher, Guillen, Johnson, Karkovice. Cleveland (11)—Jacoby 4, C. James 2, Baerga, Browne, Cole, Jefferson, Snyder. Detroit (9)—Trammell 3, Bergman 2, Fielder 2, Heath, Phillips. Kansas City (12)—Brett 5, Seitzer 2, Eisenreich, McRae, Pecota, Perry, Stillwell. Milwaukee (8)—Molitor 2, Brock, Felder, Hamilton, Parker, Sheffield, Surhoff. Minnesota (9)—Puckett 3, Gaetti, Harper, Larkin, Manrique, Munoz, Ortiz. New York (4)—Kelly 2, Barfield, Sax. Oakland (13)—J. Canseco 3, D. Henderson 2, R. Henderson 2, Jose 2, Baines, Lansford, Randolph, Weiss. Seattle (9)—Griffey Jr. 3, E. Martinez 2, Reynolds 2, Buhner, Griffey Sr. Texas (15)—Palmeiro 6, Daugherty 4, Sierra 2, Franco, Gonzalez, Petralli. Toronto (13)—McGriff 5, Felix 2,

On five different occasions, Chicago's Ryne Sandberg collected four hits in a game to lead the N.L. in multi-hit performances.

Gruber 2, Bell, Borders, Fernandez, Myers.

NATIONAL LEAGUE: Atlanta (10)—Gant 2, Blauser, Gregg, Justice, Lemke, Murphy, Presley, L. Smith, Treadway. Chicago (11)—Sandberg 5, Grace 4, Dawson, Ramos. Cincinnati (15)—Hatcher 3, O'Neill 3, Davis 2, Larkin 2, Sabo 2, Braggs, Doran, Winningham. Houston (10)—Doran 2, Yelding 2, Biggio, Caminiti, Candaele, Ramirez, Stubbs, Wilson. Los Angeles (10)—Brooks 2, Javier 2, Scioscia 2, Daniels, Griffin, Randolph, Samuel. Montreal (7)—Wall- ach 3, DeShields, Da. Martinez, Nixon, Noboa. New York (10)—Magadan 3, McReynolds 3, Boston, Elster, Jefferies, Johnson. Philadelphia (10)—Dykstra 4, Herr 2, C. Hayes, Jordan, Morandini, Thon. Pittsburgh (11)—Backman 2, Bonds 2, Bonilla 2, Bream 2, LaValliere 2, Reynolds. St. Louis (11)—Coleman 2, Guerrero 2, Hudler 2, O. Smith 2, Lankford, McGee, Pendleton. San Diego (14)—Alomar 2, Cora 2, Gwynn 2, Roberts 2, Templeton 2, Carter, Je. Clark, Jackson, Santiago. San Francisco (8)—Butler 3, Carter, Leach, Parker, Uribe, Williams.

1990 5- & 6-Hit Games

The records of all players with five or more hits in a game follows:

Date	Player—Club—Opp.	Place	AB.	R.	H.	2B.	3B.	HR.	RBI.	Result
April 27	Backman, Pirates vs. Padres	A	6	1	6	1	0	0	2	W 9-4
May 14	Puckett, Twins vs. Athletics	H	5	1	5	2	0	0	1	W 6-2
May 19	Herr, Phillies vs. Dodgers (11 innings)	A	7	2	5	0	0	0	3	W 15-12
May 19	Brunansky, Red Sox vs. Twins	H	5	3	5	1	0	2	7	W 13-1
June 6	Puckett, Twins vs. Blue Jays	A	5	3	5	1	0	0	1	W 12-5
June 21	Seitzer, Royals vs. Twins	A	6	2	5	2	0	1	3	W 14-4
June 24	Eisenreich, Royals vs. Twins	A	5	1	5	1	0	0	2	W 11-2
June 26	Pendleton, Cardinals vs. Mets	H	6	2	5	1	0	0	2	L 6-8
June 30	Palmeiro, Rangers vs. Red Sox	A	5	0	5	2	0	0	0	W 6-5
July 7	Carter, Giants vs. Cubs	H	5	1	5	0	0	1	4	W 10-9
Aug. 6	Bonilla, Pirates vs. Phillies*	A	5	3	5	1	1	0	2	W 10-1
Aug. 18	Lemke, Braves vs. Cubs	A	6	1	5	1	0	0	2	W 17-6
Sept. 1	McGriff, Blue Jays vs. Indians	A	5	1	5	1	0	1	3	W 8-0
Sept. 17	Palmeiro, Rangers vs. Mariners	A	5	2	5	1	0	0	0	W 10-4
Sept. 24	Bell, Blue Jays vs. Brewers	A	5	1	5	2	0	0	2	W 9-5

*First game of doubleheader.

Gregg Delivers Best in a Pinch

Atlanta's Tommy Gregg was the most productive pinch-hitter in the major leagues last year, collecting 18 hits, 17 RBIs and four homers.

By DAVE SLOAN

Although his overall batting average last season was only .264, no major league player was more productive as a pinch-hitter in 1990 than Tommy Gregg of the Atlanta Braves. In 51 pinch at-bats, Gregg led both leagues with 18 hits, 17 runs batted in, 35 total bases and a .686 slugging percentage. In addition, his four pinch homers tied for the lead with San Francisco's Ernest Riles.

Gregg's pinch-hitting prowess enabled the Braves to finish the season with 62 pinch-hits, more than any club except San Francisco. The Giants led all teams with 67 hits, 10 home runs and 48 RBIs. It marked the second straight year in which San Francisco led the majors in total pinch hits.

The Giants' Dave Anderson led all players (with a minimum 10 at-bats) with a .462 pinch-hitting average. Anderson's average was 24 points higher than Minnesota's Shane Mack, who led the American League with a .438 mark. Mack's Twins led all clubs with a .281 team average.

Kevin Reimer of the Texas Rangers paced the A.L. with 12 pinch hits and 19 total bases. Cleveland rookie Carlos Baerga led the junior loop with nine RBIs and a .613 slugging percentage.

Three players—the Giants' Riles and Baltimore's Sam Horn and Phil Bradley—hit grand slams as pinch hitters in 1990. Riles and Horn each hit two pinch homers last season, as did Philadelphia's Dave Hollins (who hit three), the Yankees' Steve Balboni and Matt Nokes, the Mets' Tim Teufel, St. Louis' Rex Hudler and San Francisco's Bill Bathe.

Following is a list of all pinch-hitters with at least 10 at-bats in 1990:

NATIONAL LEAGUE PINCH-HITTING
Club Pinch-Hitting

Club	AB.	H.	HR.	RBI.	Pct.	Club	AB.	H.	HR.	RBI.	Pct.
San Francisco	262	67	10	48	.256	Philadelphia	246	52	4	29	.211
Atlanta	243	62	7	37	.255	San Diego	218	46	3	16	.211
Cincinnati	218	55	1	29	.252	Los Angeles	280	59	2	34	.211
St. Louis	204	50	2	23	.245	Houston	248	51	4	46	.206
Montreal	259	59	4	35	.228	Pittsburgh	222	45	3	18	.203
New York	249	54	4	37	.217	Totals	2886	651	45	377	.226
Chicago	237	51	1	25	.215						

Individual Pinch-Hitting
(10 or More At-Bats)

Player—Club	AB.	H.	HR.	RBI.	Pct.	Player—Club	AB.	H.	HR.	RBI.	Pct.
Anderson, S.F.	13	6	1	1	.462	Jackson, S.D.	18	4	1	1	.222
Kingery, S.F.	17	7	0	4	.412	Hollins, Phila.	37	8	3	5	.216
Magadan, N.Y.	22	9	0	4	.409	Martinez, Mon.	14	3	0	0	.214
Braggs, Cin.	10	4	0	2	.400	Nixon, Mon.	28	6	0	1	.214
Puhl, Hou.	20	8	0	8	.400	Shelby, L.A.	14	3	0	0	.214
Santovenia, Mon.	10	4	1	5	.400	Carter, S.F.	19	4	1	4	.211
Thomas, Atl.	10	4	0	0	.400	Parker, S.F.	19	4	0	3	.211
Wilson, St. L.	23	9	0	4	.391	Reynolds, Pitt.	38	8	0	7	.211
Kruk, Phila.	13	5	1	6	.385	Merced, Pitt.	24	5	0	0	.208
Wilkerson, Chi.	13	5	0	1	.385	McDowell, Atl.	34	7	0	0	.206
Sharperson, L.A.	19	7	0	3	.368	Backman, Pitt.	15	3	0	0	.200
Fitzgerald, Mon.	11	4	0	3	.364	Belliard, Pitt.	10	2	0	1	.200
Quinones, Cin.	36	13	1	9	.361	Daulton, Phila.	10	2	0	3	.200
Gregg, Atl.	51	18	4	17	.353	Gant, Atl.	10	2	0	1	.200
Leach, S.F.	20	7	0	3	.350	Pagliarulo, S.D.	15	3	1	2	.200
Lynn, S.D.	32	11	1	6	.344	Stephenson, S.D.	35	7	0	2	.200
Candaele, Hou.	30	10	1	6	.333	Wilson, Hou.	15	3	1	7	.200
Kennedy, S.F.	12	4	0	0	.333	Hudler, Mon.-St. L.	21	4	2	2	.190
Morris, Cin.	21	7	0	2	.333	Thompson, St. L.	21	4	0	3	.190
Trevino, Hs-NY-Cn.	22	7	1	8	.318	Abner, S.D.	27	5	0	2	.185
Slaught, Pitt.	16	5	1	5	.313	Bell, Atl.	11	2	0	0	.182
Vatcher, Phila.-Atl.	32	10	0	2	.313	Laga, S.F.	11	2	1	2	.182
Hatcher, L.A.	47	14	0	10	.298	Boston, N.Y.	17	3	0	1	.176
Cabrera, Atl.	21	6	1	2	.286	O'Malley, N.Y.	40	7	1	5	.175
Ja. Clark, S.D.	28	8	0	0	.286	Carreon, N.Y.	24	4	1	2	.167
Grissom, Mon.	21	6	0	3	.286	Villanueva, Chi.	18	3	1	3	.167
Jones, St. L.	14	4	0	0	.286	Griffey, Cin.	31	5	0	4	.161
Noboa, Mon.	35	10	0	4	.286	Redus, Pitt.	19	3	0	0	.158
Riles, S.F.	42	12	4	13	.286	Booker, Phila.	13	2	0	2	.154
Roomes, Cin.-Mon.	14	4	0	0	.286	Wynne, Chi.	26	4	0	5	.154
Teufel, N.Y.	29	8	2	8	.276	Bream, Pitt.	14	2	0	0	.143
Nichols, Hou.	11	3	0	5	.273	Gonzalez, L.A.	21	3	0	0	.143
Stubbs, Hou.	11	3	0	2	.273	Litton, S.F.	35	5	0	4	.143
Ready, Phila.	45	12	0	5	.267	Rohde, Hou.	22	3	0	2	.136
King, Pitt.	19	5	1	3	.263	Lemke, Atl.	15	2	0	2	.133
Smith, Atl.	19	5	0	4	.263	Oberkfell, Hou.	30	4	0	2	.133
Clark, Chi.	42	11	0	4	.262	Vizcaino, L.A.	15	2	0	0	.133
Varsho, Chi.	43	11	0	1	.256	Harris, L.A.	23	3	0	0	.130
Aldrete, Mon.	36	9	1	6	.250	Campusano, Phila.	16	2	0	2	.125
Javier, L.A.	20	5	0	4	.250	McClendon, Chi.-Pitt.	16	2	1	2	.125
Miller, N.Y.	16	4	0	1	.250	Ford, Phila.	17	2	0	0	.118
Winningham, Cin.	20	5	0	1	.250	Johnson, Mon.	34	4	1	5	.118
Collins, St. L.	25	6	0	1	.240	Ramos, Chi.	18	2	0	1	.111
Sasser, N.Y.	25	6	0	5	.240	Caminiti, Hou.	10	1	0	0	.100
Walling, St. L.	46	11	0	5	.239	Foley, Mon.	10	1	0	2	.100
Martinez, Phila.-Pitt.	17	4	0	2	.235	Anthony, Hou.	11	1	1	3	.091
Smith, Chi.	34	8	0	7	.235	Walker, Mon.	11	1	0	1	.091
Gwynn, L.A.	56	13	1	8	.232	Oester, Cin.	13	1	0	0	.077
Bathe, S.F.	39	9	2	11	.231	Dempsey, L.A.	16	1	0	1	.063
Hatcher, Cin.	13	3	0	1	.231	Benzinger, Cin.	15	0	0	1	.000
Cangelosi, Pitt.	36	8	0	0	.222	Meadows, Hou.-Phila.	16	0	0	0	.000

PINCH-HOMERS FOR 1990

NATIONAL LEAGUE: Atlanta (7)—Gregg 4, Blauser, Cabrera, Justice. Chicago (1)—Villanueva, Cincinnati (1)—Quinones. Houston (4)—Anthony, Candaele, Trevino, Wilson. Los Angeles (2)—Gwynn, Lyons. Montreal (4)—Aldrete, Goff, Johnson, Santovenia. New York (4)—Teufel 2, Carreon, O'Malley. Philadelphia (4)—Hollins 3, Kruk. Pittsburgh (3)—King, McClendon, Slaught. St. Louis (2)—Hudler 2. San Diego (2)—Jackson, Lynn, Pagliarulo. San Francisco (10)—Riles 4, Bathe 2, Anderson, Carter, Laga, Robinson.

AMERICAN LEAGUE: Baltimore (4)—Horn 2, Bradley, Hulett. Boston (1)—Burks. California (2)—Howell, Winfield. Chicago (1)—Kittle. Cleveland (3)—Baerga, James, Webster. Detroit (2)—Sheets, Shelby. Kansas City (1)—Jackson. Milwaukee—None. Minnesota (1)—Sorrento. New York (6)—Balboni 2, Nokes 2, Barfield, Hall. Oakland (2)—Phelps, Quirk. Seattle (1)—Griffey Jr. Texas (3)—Bosley, Incaviglia, Stanley. Toronto—None.

Texas' Kevin Reimer paced the A.L. with 12 pinch hits and 19 total bases in 1990.

AMERICAN LEAGUE PINCH-HITTING

Club Pinch-Hitting

	AB.	H.	HR.	RBI.	Pct.		AB.	H.	HR.	RBI.	Pct.
Minnesota	139	39	1	21	.281	Boston	79	17	1	20	.215
Cleveland	104	27	3	15	.260	New York	182	37	6	21	.203
Seattle	147	36	1	19	.245	Kansas City	96	19	1	13	.198
Oakland	154	37	2	26	.240	Detroit	202	39	2	29	.193
Baltimore	115	27	4	27	.235	Milwaukee	58	11	0	6	.190
Texas	250	55	3	41	.220	California	98	18	2	10	.184
Chicago	123	27	1	14	.220	Totals	1844	410	27	276	.222
Toronto	97	21	0	14	.216						

Individual Pinch-Hitting
(10 or More At-Bats)

Player—Club	AB.	H.	HR.	RBI.	Pct.	Player-Club	AB.	H.	HR.	RBI.	Pct.
Mack, Minn	16	7	0	3	.438	James, Clev	14	3	0	1	.214
Dwyer, Minn	15	6	0	3	.400	Orsulak, Balt.	14	3	0	2	.214
Mulliniks, Tor	22	8	0	7	.364	Petralli, Tex.	24	5	0	3	.208
Quirk, Oak.	11	4	1	4	.364	Balboni, N.Y.	40	8	2	5	.200
Ward, Det.	14	5	0	8	.357	Borders, Tor.	25	5	0	3	.200
Baerga, Clev.	31	11	1	9	.355	Gallagher, Chi.-Balt.	10	2	0	0	.200
Anderson, Balt.	18	6	0	4	.333	Hall, N.Y.	15	3	1	2	.200
Webster, Clev	12	4	1	1	.333	Komminsk, Balt.	10	2	0	2	.200
Polonia, N.Y.-Calif.	19	6	0	1	.316	Sheets, Balt.	21	4	1	5	.190
Baines, Tex.-Oak.	13	4	0	8	.308	Jones, Det.-Sea.	16	3	0	0	.188
Shelby, Det.	13	4	1	3	.308	Venable, Calif.	16	3	0	1	.188
Hassey, Oak.	20	6	0	2	.300	Bergman, Det.	33	6	0	5	.182
Martinez, Chi.	10	3	0	2	.300	Buckner, Bos.	11	2	0	2	.182
Reimer, Tex.	40	12	0	8	.300	Jose, Oak.	11	2	0	2	.182
Coles, Sea.-Det.	27	8	0	5	.296	Melvin, Balt.	11	2	0	0	.182
Bradley, Sea.	35	10	0	5	.286	Schu, Calif.	11	2	0	2	.182
Kittle, Chi.-Balt.	14	4	1	4	.286	Blankenship, Oak.	12	2	0	1	.167
Steinbach, Oak.	14	4	0	4	.286	Bush, Minn.	12	2	0	1	.167
Moses, Minn.	25	7	0	1	.280	Huson, Tex.	18	3	0	1	.167
Cotto, Sea.	29	8	0	1	.276	Newman, Minn.	12	2	0	1	.167
Javier, Oak.	11	3	0	0	.273	Bosley, Tex.	19	3	1	3	.158
Washington, Cal-NY.	11	3	0	0	.273	Incaviglia, Tex.	13	2	1	5	.154
Stanley, Tex.	27	7	1	7	.259	Cerone, N.Y.	14	2	0	0	.143
Tabler, K.C.	12	3	0	3	.250	Jennings, Oak.	14	2	0	1	.143
Johnson, Chi.	17	4	0	1	.235	Lyons, Chi.	21	3	0	0	.143
Nokes, Det.-N.Y.	34	8	2	8	.235	Salas, Det.	17	2	0	1	.118
Phelps, Oak.-Clev.	17	4	1	2	.235	Heep, Bos.	18	2	0	3	.111
Russell, Tex.	17	4	0	2	.235	Williams, Det.-Tor	18	2	0	0	.111
Barfield, N.Y.	13	3	1	3	.231	Schulz, K.C.	10	1	0	0	.100
Macfarlane, K.C.	13	3	0	4	.231	Robidoux, Bos.	11	1	0	1	.091
Castillo, Minn.	22	5	0	2	.227	Whitaker, Det.	11	1	0	0	.091
Daugherty, Tex.	45	10	0	7	.222	Finley, Balt.	12	0	0	0	.000
Briley, Sea.	18	4	0	1	.222	Perry, K.C.	12	0	0	1	.000
Pasqua, Chi.	18	4	0	2	.222						

A Dazzling Debut For DeShields

By DAVE SLOAN

Although he finished second to Atlanta's Dave Justice in balloting for National League Rookie of the Year, Montreal second baseman Delino DeShields put together a fine season of his own in 1990. And he got off to a roaring start in his first major league game.

DeShields, who turned down a basketball scholarship to Villanova in 1987 after the Expos selected him in the first round of that June's free-agent draft, smacked three singles and a double in a 6-5, 11-inning Montreal loss at St. Louis on April 9. His four hits in six at-bats tied the modern N.L. record for most hits by a player in his debut game.

DeShields finished the season with a .289 average, 28 doubles and 42 stolen bases despite being sidelined nearly a month by a broken finger.

DeShields was one of 171 players to make his major league debut in 1990, one of 84 in the N.L. Pitchers and non-pitchers split debut honors nearly evenly, with pitchers accounting for 86 of the debuts and non-pitchers 85.

Lefthander Chris Nabholz, a Montreal teammate of DeShields, had a nondescript debut on June 11, allowing five hits and two runs in five innings of work against Philadelphia. His rookie season, however, was anything but ordinary. After struggling to an 0-6 record and 4.83 earned-run average at Class AAA Indianapolis (American Association), Nabholz won his first six major league decisions after the Expos recalled him a second time on August 12.

Two pitchers had debut performances in 1990 they'd just as soon forget. On September 19 at Anaheim, Calif., Angels reliever Jeff Richardson surrendered a three-run triple to Detroit's Travis Fryman on his first pitch in the ninth inning of a 12-5 Tiger victory. One week earlier, Yankees starter Steve Adkins walked eight of the 11 batters he faced and was the losing pitcher in New York's 5-4 setback to Texas.

One Yankees player who had a successful rookie season was 25-year-old Kevin Maas, who set major league records for reaching the 10-, 13- and 15-homer plateaus in the fewest number of at-bats. Maas, who finished the year with 21 home runs in 254 at-bats, singled once in three at-bats as New York's designated hitter in his June 29 debut against the White Sox.

Outfielder Ozzie Canseco, the identical twin brother of Oakland slugger Jose, made his major league debut as a pinch-hitter in the Athletics' 5-2 victory over Cleveland in the second game of a July 18 doubleheader. However, Ozzie—a few minutes older than Jose—exhibited little of his younger brother's baseball prowess in two brief trials in the majors last season. He had only two hits in 19 at-bats with Oakland and spent most of 1990 with the A's Class AA Huntsville (Southern) farm team.

Dodgers shortstop Jose Offerman homered in his first big-league plate appearance in Los Angeles' 2-1 loss to Montreal on August 19. Ironically, Offerman did not homer in 535 plate appearances at Class AAA Albuquerque (Pacific Coast) before the Dodgers called him up the day before. Offerman, who hit safely in his first three plate appearances against Expos righthander Dennis Martinez, hit .326 and stole 60 bases at Albuquerque en route to winning The Sporting News' Minor League Player of the Year Award last year.

As usual, California led all 50 states in the number of players making their big-league debuts, with 40 players hailing from the nation's most populous state. Florida and Illinois tied for second with 10 players each while 20 states did not produce a single player.

Ten foreign countries produced at least one debuting major league player in 1990, with the Dominican Republic (11) leading the way.

An alphabetical list of the players who made their debuts in '90 follows:

Player	Pos.	Club	Date and Place of Birth	Debut
Abbott, Paul David	P	Minnesota	9-15-67—Van Nuys, Calif.	8-21
Adkins, Steven Thomas	P	New York A.L.	10-26-64—Chicago, Ill.	9-12
Aldred, Scott Phillip	P	Detroit	6-12-68—Flint, Mich.	9- 9
Alexander, Gerald Paul	P	Texas	3-26-68—Baton Rouge, La.	9- 9
Alou, Moises	PH	Montreal	7- 3-66—Atlanta, Ga.	9- 2
Anderson, Scott Richard	P	Montreal	8- 1-62—Corvallis, Ore.	8- 4
Avery, Steven Thomas	P	Atlanta	4-14-70—Trenton, Mich.	6-13
Azocar, Oscar Gregorio	PH	New York A.L.	2-21-65—Caracas, Ven.	7-17
Baerga, Carlos Obed	3B	Cleveland	11- 4-68—San Juan, P.R.	4-14
Baez, Kevin Richard	OF	New York N.L.	1-10-67—Brooklyn, N.Y.	9- 3
Baldwin, Jeffrey Allen	PH	Houston	9- 5-65—Milford, Del.	5-22

Player	Pos.	Club	Date and Place of Birth	Debut
Barnes, Brian Keith	P	Montreal	3-25-67—Roanoke Rapids, N.C.	9-14
Bearse, Kevin Gerard	P	Cleveland	11- 7-65—Jersey City, N.J.	4-15
Belcher, Kevin D.	OF	Texas	8- 8-67—Waco, Tex.	9- 3
Bell, Michael Allen	PR-1B	Atlanta	4-22-68—Lewiston, N.J.	5- 2
Berry, Sean Robert	3B	Kansas City	3-22-66—Santa Monica, Calif.	9-17
Bitker, Joseph Anthony	P	Oakland	2-12-64—Glendale, Calif.	7-31
Blair, William Allen	P	Toronto	12-18-65—Paintsville, Ky.	4-11
Bohanon, Brian Edward	P	Texas	8- 1-68—Denton, Tex.	4-10
Bordick, Michael Todd	2B	Oakland	7-21-65—Marquette, Mich.	4-11
Boskie, Shawn Kealoha	P	Chicago N.L.	3-28-67—Hawthorne, Nev.	5-20
Brewer, Rodney Lee	PH	St. Louis	2-24-66—Zellwood, Fla.	9- 5
Brown, Kevin Dewayne	P	New York N.L.	3- 5-66—Oroville, Calif.	7-27
Burba, David Allen	P	Seattle	7- 7-66—Dayton, O.	9- 8
Campbell, James Marcus	P	Kansas City	5-19-66—Santa Maria, Calif.	8-21
Canseco, Osvaldo Capas	PH	Oakland	7- 2-64—Havana, Cuba	7-18
Carr, Charles Lee Glenn Jr.	PH	New York N.L.	8-10-67—San Bernardino, Calif.	4-28
Casian, Lawrence Paul	P	Minnesota	10-28-65—Lynwood, Calif.	9- 9
Cedeno, Andujar	PH	Houston	8-21-69—La Romana, D.R.	9- 2
Chamberlain, Wesley Polk	PH	Philadelphia	4-13-66—Chicago, Ill.	8-31
Chiamparino, Scott Michael	P	Texas	8-22-66—San Mateo, Calif.	9- 5
Chitren, Stephen Vincent	P	Oakland	6- 8-67—Tokyo, Japan	9- 5
Coachman, Bobby Dean	3B	California	11-11-61—Cottonwood, Ala.	8-18
Cole, Alexander Jr.	OF	Cleveland	8-17-65—Fayetteville, N.C.	7-27
Conine, Jeffrey Guy	1B	Kansas City	6-27-66—Tacoma, Wash.	9-16
Cooper, Scott Kendrick	PH	Boston	10-13-67—St. Louis, Mo.	9- 5
Cuyler, Milton Jr.	OF	Detroit	10- 7-68—Macon, Ga.	9- 6
Decker, Steven M.	C	San Francisco	10-25-65—Rock Island, Ill.	9-18
DeLucia, Richard Anthony	P	Seattle	10- 7-64—Wyomissing, Pa.	9- 8
DeShields, Delino Lamont	OF	Montreal	1-15-69—Seaford, Del.	4- 9
Dewey, Mark Alan	P	San Francisco	1- 3-65—Grand Rapids, Mich.	8-24
Diaz, Carlos Francisco	C	Toronto	12-24-64—Elizabeth, N.J.	5- 8
Dickson, Lance Michael	P	Chicago N.L.	10-19-69—Fullerton, Calif.	8- 9
Elvira, Narciso	P	Milwaukee	10-29-67—Veracruz, Mexico	9- 9
Encarnacion, Luis Martin	P	Kansas City	10-20-63—Santo Domingo, D.R.	7-27
Erickson, Scott Gavin	P	Minnesota	2- 2-68—Long Beach, Calif.	6-25
Faries, Paul Tyrrell	2B	San Diego	2-20-65—Berkeley, Calif.	9- 6
Farmer, Howard Earl	P	Montreal	1-18-66—Gary, Ind.	7- 2
Fernandez, Alexander	P	Chicago A.L.	8-13-69—Miami Beach, Fla.	8- 2
Fryman, David Travis	SS	Detroit	4-25-69—Lexington, Ky.	7- 7
Garces, Richard Aron	P	Minnesota	5-18-71—Maracay, Aragua, Ven.	9-18
Garcia, Carlos Jesus	PH	Pittsburgh	10-15-67—Tachira, Ven.	9-20
Gardiner, Michael James	P	Seattle	10-19-65—Sarnia, Ontario, Canada	9- 8
Gilkey, Otis Bernard	OF	St. Louis	9-24-66—St. Louis, Mo.	9- 4
Gilles, Thomas Bradford	P	Toronto	7- 2-62—Peoria, Ill.	6- 7
Goff, Jerry Leroy	C	Montreal	4-12-64—San Rafael, Calif.	5-15
Gomez, Leonardo	3B	Baltimore	3- 2-67—Canovanas, P.R.	9-17
Gonzalez, Luis Emilio	PH	Houston	9- 3-67—Tampa, Fla.	9- 4
Grahe, Joseph Milton	P	California	6-14-67—West Palm Beach, Fla.	8- 4
Grebeck, Craig Allen	2B	Chicago A.L.	12-29-64—Cerritos, Calif.	4-13
Gross, Kip Lee	P	Cincinnati	8-24-64—Scottsbluff, Neb.	4-21
Gunderson, Eric Andrew	P	San Francisco	3-29-66—Portland, Ore.	4-11
Hammond, Christopher Andrew	P	Cincinnati	1-21-66—Atlanta, Ga.	7-16
Hansen, David Andrew	PH	Los Angeles	11-24-68—Long Beach, Calif.	9-16
Harris, Reginald Allen	P	Oakland	8-12-68—Waynesboro, Va.	7- 4
Haselman, William Joseph	PH	Texas	5-25-66—Long Branch, N.J.	9- 3
Hennis, Randall Philip	P	Houston	12-16-65—Clearlake, Calif.	9-17
Hernandez, Carlos Alberto	C	Los Angeles	5-24-67—Bolivar, Ven.	4-20
Hilton, Howard James	P	St. Louis	1- 3-64—Oxnard, Calif.	4- 9
Hollins, David Michaels	PH	Philadelphia	5-25-66—Buffalo, N.Y.	4-12
Holmes, Darren Lee	P	Los Angeles	4-25-66—Asheville, N.C.	9- 1
Hoover, John Nicklaus	P	Texas	11-22-62—Fresno, Calif.	5-23
Howard, Steven Bernard	DH-OF	Oakland	12- 7-63—Oakland, Calif.	6-16
Howard, Thomas Sylvester	OF	San Diego	12-11-64—Middletown, O.	7- 3
Hundley, Todd Randolph	C	New York N.L.	5-27-69—Martinsville, Va.	5-18
Irvine, Daryl Keith	P	Boston	11-15-64—Harrisonburg, Va.	4-28
Jelic, Christopher John	OF	New York N.L.	12-16-63—Bethlehem, Pa.	9-30
Kiecker, Dana Ervin	P	Boston	2-25-61—Sleepy Eye, Minn.	4-12
Knackert, Brent Bradley	P	Seattle	8- 1-69—Los Angeles, Calif.	4-10
Kremers, James Edward	C	Atlanta	10- 8-65—Little Rock, Ark.	6- 5
Kutzler, Jerry Scott	P	Chicago A.L.	3-25-65—Waukegan, Ill.	4-28
Lankford, Raymond Lewis	OF	St. Louis	6- 5-67—Modesto, Calif.	8-21
Layana, Timothy Joseph	P	Cincinnati	3- 2-64—Inglewood, Calif.	4- 9
Lee, Terry James	PH	Cincinnati	3-13-62—San Francisco, Calif.	9- 3
Leiter, Mark Edward	P	New York A.L.	4-13-63—Joliet, Ill.	7-24
Leius, Scott Thomas	SS	Minnesota	9-24-65—Yonkers, N.Y.	9- 4
Leonard, Mark David	PH	San Francisco	8-14-64—Mountain View, Calif.	7-21
Lewis, Darren Joel	OF	Oakland	8-28-67—Berkeley, Calif.	8-21
Lewis, Scott Allen	P	California	12- 5-65—Grants Pass, Ore.	9-25
Leyritz, James Joseph	PH-3B	New York A.L.	12-27-63—Lakewood, O.	6- 8
Liddell, David Alexander	PH-C	New York N.L.	6-15-66—Los Angeles, Calif.	6- 3

Player	Pos.	Club	Date and Place of Birth	Debut
Lopez, Luis A.	PH	Los Angeles	9- 1-64—Brooklyn, N.Y.	9-26
Maas, Kevin Christian	DH	New York A.L.	1-20-65—Castro Valley, Calif.	6-29
MacDonald, Robert Joseph	P	Toronto	4-27-65—East Orange, N.J.	9-23
Maldonado, Carlos Cesar	P	Kansas City	10-18-66—Chepo, Panama	9-16
Malloy, Robert William	P	Montreal	11-24-64—Garland, Tex.	6- 8
Malone, Charles Ray Jr.	P	Philadelphia	7- 8-65—Harrisburg, Ark.	9- 6
Manon, Ramon	P	Texas	1-20-68—Santo Domingo, D.R.	4-19
Manto, Jeffrey Paul	PH-1B	Cleveland	8-23-64—Bristol, Pa.	6- 7
Marak, Paul Patrick	P	Atlanta	8- 2-65—Lakenheath, England	9- 1
Martinez, Constantino	1B	Seattle	12- 7-67—Tampa, Fla.	8-20
May, Derrick Brant	OF	Chicago N.L.	7-14-68—Rochester, N.Y.	9- 6
Mayne, Brent Danem	C	Kansas City	4-19-68—Loma Linda, Calif.	9-18
McClellan, Paul William	P	San Francisco	2- 8-66—San Mateo, Calif.	9- 2
McCray, Rodney Duncan	OF	Chicago A.L.	9-13-63—Detroit, Mich.	4-30
McIntosh, Timothy Allen	C	Milwaukee	3-21-65—Crystal, Minn.	9- 3
McRae, Brian Wesley	OF	Kansas City	6-27-67—Bradenton, Fla.	8- 7
Melendez, Jose Luis	P	Seattle	9- 2-65—Naguabo, P.R.	9-11
Merced, Orlando Luis	PH	Pittsburgh	11- 2-66—San Juan, P.R.	6-27
Mills, Alan Bernard	P	New York A.L.	10-18-66—Lakeland, Fla.	6- 8
Minutelli, Gino Michael	P	Cincinnati	5-23-64—Wilmington, Del.	9-18
Morandini, Michael Robert	PH-2B	Philadelphia	4-22-66—Kittanning, Pa.	9- 1
Munoz, Pedro Javier	DH	Minnesota	9-19-68—Ponce, P.R.	9- 1
Nabholz, Christopher William	P	Montreal	1- 5-67—Harrisburg, Pa.	6-11
Naehring, Timothy James	2B	Boston	2- 1-67—Cincinnati, O.	7-15
Nagy, Charles Harrison	P	Cleveland	5- 5-67—Fairfield, Conn.	6-29
Neidlinger, James Llewellyn	P	Los Angeles	9-24-64—Vallejo, Calif.	8- 1
Novoa, Rafael Angel	P	San Francisco	10-26-67—New York, N.Y.	7-31
Offerman, Jose Antonio	SS	Los Angeles	11- 8-68—S.P. de Macoris, D.R.	8-19
Olivares, Omar	P	St. Louis	7- 6-67—Mayaguez, P.R.	8-18
Ortiz, Javier Victor	PH	Houston	1-22-63—Boston, Mass.	6-15
Osuna, Alfonso Jr.	P	Houston	8-10-65—Inglewood, Calif.	9- 2
Parker, Richard Allen	PH	San Francisco	3-20-63—Kansas City, Mo.	5- 4
Pavlas, David Lee	P	Chicago N.L.	8-12-62—Frankfurt, W. Germany	8-21
Pena, Geronimo	PH	St. Louis	3-29-67—Distrito Nacional, D.R.	9- 5
Perez, Michael Irvin	P	St. Louis	10-19-64—Yauco, P.R.	9- 5
Plantier, Phillip Alan	PH	Boston	1-27-69—Manchester, N.H.	8-21
Poole, James Richard	P	Los Angeles	4-28-66—Rochester, N.Y.	6-15
Quinlan, Thomas Raymond	3B	Toronto	3-27-68—St. Paul, Minn.	9- 4
Radinsky, Scott David	P	Chicago A.L.	3- 3-68—Glendale, Calif.	4- 9
Reed, Darren Douglas	PH	New York N.L.	10-16-65—Ventura, Calif.	5- 1
Rhodes, Karl Derrick	OF	Houston	8-21-68—Cincinnati, O.	8- 7
Richardson, Jeffrey Scott	P	California	8-29-63—Wichita, Kan.	9-19
Rodriguez, Richard Anthony	P	San Diego	3- 1-63—Los Angeles, Calif.	6-30
Rohde, David Grant	PH	Houston	5- 8-64—Los Altos, Calif.	4- 9
Rojas, Melquiades	P	Montreal	12-10-66—Haina, D.R.	8- 1
Rosario, Victor Manuel	SS	Atlanta	8-26-66—Hato Mayor d. R., D.R.	9- 6
Rowland, Richard Garnet	DH	Detroit	2-25-67—Cloverdale, Calif.	9- 7
Ruskin, Scott Drew	P	Pittsburgh	6- 8-63—Jacksonville, Fla.	4- 9
Sampen, William Albert	P	Montreal	1-18-63—Lincoln, Ill.	4-10
Santana, Andres Confesor	PR	San Francisco	3-19-68—S.P. de Macoris, D.R.	9-16
Segui, David Vincent	1B	Baltimore	7-19-66—Kansas City, Kan.	5- 8
Shaw, Jeffrey Lee	P	Cleveland	7- 7-66—Wash. Court House, O.	4-30
Sherrill, Timothy Shawn	P	St. Louis	9-10-65—Harrison, Ark.	8-14
Shumpert, Terrance Darnell	2B	Kansas City	8-16-66—Paducah, Ky.	5- 1
Simms, Michael Howard	PH	Houston	1-12-67—Orange, Calif.	9- 5
Smith, Daryl Clinton	P	Kansas City	7-29-60—Baltimore, Md.	9-18
Sojo, Luis	OF	Toronto	1- 3-66—Barquisimeto, Ven.	7-14
Springer, Steven Michael	3B	Cleveland	2-11-61—Long Beach, Calif.	5-22
Stephens, Carl Ray	C	St. Louis	9-22-62—Houston, Tex.	9-20
Stevens, DeWain Lee	1B	California	7-10-67—Kansas City, Mo.	7-16
Stottlemyre, Melvin Leon Jr.	P	Kansas City	12-28-63—Prosser, Wash.	7-17
Sutko, Glenn Edward	C	Cincinnati	5- 9-68—Atlanta, Ga.	10- 3
Telford, Anthony Charles	P	Baltimore	3- 6-66—San Jose, Calif.	8-19
Thomas, Frank Edward	1B	Chicago A.L.	5-27-68—Columbus, Ga.	8- 2
Tomlin, Randy Leon	P	Pittsburgh	6-14-66—Bainbridge, Md.	8- 6
Traxler, Brian Lee	PH-1B	Los Angeles	9-26-67—Waukegan, Ill.	4-24
Valdez, Efrain Antonio	P	Cleveland	6-11-66—Nizao de Bani, D.R.	8-13
Valdez, Rafael Emilio	P	San Diego	12-17-67—Nizao de Bani, D.R.	4-18
Valera, Julio E.	P	New York N.L.	10-13-68—San Sebastian, P.R.	9- 1
Vatcher, James Ernest	PH	Philadelphia	5-27-66—Santa Monica, Calif.	5-30
Villanueva, Hector	PH-1B	Chicago N.L.	10- 2-64—San Juan, P.R.	6- 1
Wagner, Hector Raul	P	Kansas City	11-26-68—Santo Domingo, D.R.	9-10
Walsh, David Peter	P	Los Angeles	9-25-60—Arlington, Mass.	8-13
Wapnick, Steven Lee	P	Detroit	9-25-65—Panorama, Calif.	4-14
Ward, Robert Colby	P	Cleveland	1- 2-64—Springville, Utah	7-27
Ward, Turner Max	OF	Cleveland	4-11-65—Orlando, Fla.	9-10
Wells, Terry	P	Los Angeles	9-10-63—Calumet City, Ill.	7- 3
Whiten, Mark Anthony	OF	Toronto	11-25-66—Pensacola, Fla.	7-12
York, Michael David	P	Pittsburgh	9- 6-64—Oak Park, Ill.	8-17
Young, Clifford Raphael	P	California	8- 2-64—Willis, Tex.	7-14

Homers by Parks for 1990

American League

	At Balt.	At Bos.	At Cal.	At Chi.	At Clev.	At Det.	At K.C.	At Mil.	At Min.	At N.Y.	At Oak.	At Sea.	At Tex.	At Tor.	Totals 1990	1989
Baltimore	74	1	3	4	6	6	6	5	6	5	2	2	4	8	132	129
Boston	4	61	5	3	10	4	2	2	1	3	1	5	3	2	106	108
California	6	1	89	5	3	4	5	8	2	5	5	4	4	6	147	145
Chicago	4	2	9	41	5	4	2	5	7	6	8	7	2	4	106	94
Cleveland	9	3	5	4	52	4	3	4	4	6	1	3	4	8	110	127
Detroit	2	2	2	8	8	92	5	10	6	11	3	5	7	11	172	116
Kansas City	5	1	3	2	3	6	42	3	3	8	8	6	4	6	100	101
Milwaukee	7	5	2	5	5	11	5	60	3	9	3	4	3	6	128	126
Minnesota	11	4	2	3	3	6	2	3	46	5	5	4	0	6	100	117
New York	8	5	3	7	6	5	3	4	12	64	2	4	14	10	147	130
Oakland	9	6	9	6	13	9	3	2	11	10	69	5	7	5	164	127
Seattle	6	3	5	2	6	4	3	4	6	4	4	49	5	6	107	134
Texas	3	3	5	1	7	4	2	4	3	2	5	3	64	4	110	122
Toronto	8	8	2	3	11	8	5	5	5	4	5	8	2	93	167	142
1990 Totals	156	105	144	94	138	167	88	119	115	142	121	109	123	175	1796	......
1989 Totals	126	122	148	94	107	151	64	123	128	152	116	135	138	114	......	1718

AT BALTIMORE (156): Baltimore (74)—Milligan 11, Orsulak 9, Horn 8, C. Ripken 8, Tettleton 8, Devereaux 6, Bradley 4, Komminsk 3, Melvin 3, Worthington 3, Hulett 2, B. Ripken 2, Anderson, Finley, Gonzales, Hoiles, Kittle, McKnight, Segui. **Boston (4)**—Boggs, Burks, Greenwell, Quintana. **California (6)**—Parrish 2, Bichette, Downing, Venable, White. **Chicago (4)**—Pasqua 2, Kittle, Ventura. **Cleveland (9)**—Baerga 3, Browne 2, Snyder 2, Alomar, Jacoby. **Detroit (2)**—Fielder, Whitaker. **Kansas City (5)**—Tartabull 2, Brett, Macfarlane, Wilson. **Milwaukee (7)**—Parker 2, Vaughn 2, Brock, Deer, Surhoff. **Minnesota (11)**—Hrbek 4, Puckett 2, Gaetti, Gladden, Manrique, Moses, Sorrento. **New York (8)**—Barfield 3, Nokes 2, Kelly, Maas, Velarde. **Oakland (9)**—McGwire 4, Jose 2, Canseco, R. Henderson, Weiss. **Seattle (6)**—Griffey Jr. 2, Reynolds 2, E. Martinez, Valle. **Texas (3)**—Palmeiro 2, Incaviglia. **Toronto (8)**—McGriff 2, Olerud 2, Bell, Borders, Gruber, Hill.

AT BOSTON (105): Baltimore (1)—Tettleton. **Boston (61)**—Brunansky 13, Burks 10, Evans 7, Greenwell 6, Rivera 4, Boggs 3, Marshall 3, Pena 3, Quintana 3, Reed 3, Naehring 2, Romine 2, Buckner, Robidoux. **California (1)**—Howell. **Chicago (2)**—Calderon, Fisk. **Cleveland (5)**—Allred, Alomar, Snyder. **Detroit (2)**—Fielder, Shelby. **Kansas City (1)**—Tabler. **Milwaukee (5)**—Deer, Parker, Sheffield, Vaughn, Yount. **Minnesota (4)**—Hrbek 2, Gaetti, Mack. **New York (5)**—Velarde 2, Espinoza, Hall, Kelly. **Oakland (6)**—McGwire 2, Hassey, R. Henderson, Jennings, Steinbach. **Seattle (3)**—Griffey Sr., E. Martinez, O'Brien. **Texas (3)**—Baines, Franco, Sierra. **Toronto (8)**—Gruber 3, Felix 2, McGriff 2, Olerud.

AT CALIFORNIA (144): Baltimore (3)—C. Ripken 3. **Boston (5)**—Brunansky 2, Burks, Greenwell, Pena. **California (89)**—Parrish 14, Winfield 13, Downing 11, Davis 10, Bichette 8, Joyner 5, Ray 5, White 5, Stevens 4, Howell 3, Schu 3, Venable 3, Polonia 2, Anderson, Rose, Schofield. **Chicago (9)**—Kittle 3, Fisk 2, Calderon, Karkovice, Sosa, Thomas. **Cleveland (5)**—Webster 2, Maldonado, Skinner, Snyder. **Detroit (2)**—Salas, Whitaker. **Kansas City (3)**—Brett, Jackson, Perry. **Milwaukee (2)**—Deer 2. **Minnesota (2)**—Hrbek, Leius. **New York (3)**—Barfield 2, Leyritz. **Oakland (9)**—Canseco 3, McGwire 2, Hassey, D. Henderson, R. Henderson, Lansford. **Seattle (5)**—Griffey Jr. 3, Griffey Sr., Valle. **Texas (3)**—Incaviglia 2, Palmeiro, Russell, Sierra. **Toronto (2)**—McGriff 2.

AT CHICAGO (94): Baltimore (4)—Milligan 2, Orsulak, Tettleton. **Boston (3)**—Burks, Greenwell, Kutcher. **California (5)**—Parrish 2, Bichette, Schu, Stevens. **Chicago (41)**—Sosa 10, Kittle 7, Calderon 6, Fisk 5, Pasqua 4, Martinez 2, Thomas 2, Ventura 2, Fletcher, Grebeck, Guillen. **Cleveland (4)**—Jacoby, C. James, Maldonado, Santana. **Detroit (8)**—Fielder 3, Whitaker 2, Bergman, Heath, Lusader. **Kansas City (2)**—Jackson, Perry. **Milwaukee (5)**—Brock, Deer, Felder, Sheffield, Yount. **Minnesota (3)**—Dwyer, Gaetti, Puckett. **New York (7)**—Barfield 2, Leyritz 2, Balboni, Hall, Kelly. **Oakland (6)**—D. Henderson 2, Gallego, R. Henderson, McGwire, Steinbach. **Seattle (2)**—Davis 2. **Texas (1)**—Baines. **Toronto (3)**—Bell, Hill, McGriff.

AT CLEVELAND (138): Baltimore (6)—Milligan 2, Tettleton 2, Devereaux, C. Ripken. **Boston (10)**—Burks 5, Boggs, Evans, Marshall, Reed, Rivera. **California (3)**—White 2, Joyner. **Chicago (5)**—Fisk 2, Karkovice, Martinez, Thomas. **Cleveland (52)**—Maldonado 12, Jacoby 10, C. James 6, Webster 6, Alomar 3, Baerga 3, Snyder 3, Belle, Fermin, Jefferson, Manto, Skinner. **Detroit (8)**—Fielder 4, Fryman, Jones, Trammell, Ward. **Kansas City (3)**—McRae, Morman, Perry. **Milwaukee (5)**—Sheffield 2, Deer, Vaughn, Yount. **Minnesota (3)**—Hrbek, Manrique, Puckett. **New York (6)**—Kelly 3, Azocar, Balboni, Sanders. **Oakland (13)**—Canseco 4, McGwire 4, R. Henderson 2, Hassey, Lansford, Quirk. **Seattle (6)**—Griffey Jr. 2, E. Martinez, Jones, Vizquel. **Texas (7)**—Baines 2, Sierra 2, Franco, Incaviglia, Palmeiro. **Toronto (11)**—McGriff 3, Felix 2, Hill 2, Bell, Fernandez, Gruber, Sojo.

AT DETROIT (167): Baltimore (6)—Devereaux 3, Anderson, Melvin, C. Ripken. **Boston (4)**—Greenwell, Pena, Reed, Rivera. **California (4)**—Parrish 2, White, Winfield. **Chicago (4)**—Fisk, Fletcher, Karkovice, Pasqua. **Cleveland (4)**—Jacoby, C. James, Maldonado, Snyder. **Detroit (92)**—Fielder 25, Trammell 9, Moseby 8, Salas 8, Whitaker 8, Sheets 7, Fryman 5, Phillips 4, Heath 3, Shelby 3, Jones 2, Lemon 2, Lindeman 2, Ward 2, Bergman, Coles, Lusader, Nokes. **Kansas City (2)**—Brett 2, Jackson 2, Perry, Tartabull. **Milwaukee (11)**—Deer 4, Yount 3, Braggs, Brock, Molitor, Sheffield, Vaughn. **Minnesota (6)**—Gaetti 3, Harper, Hrbek, Puckett. **New York (5)**—Balboni, Barfield, Blowers, Hall, Maas. **Oakland (9)**—Steinbach 3, R. Henderson 2, McGwire 2, Canseco, D. Henderson. **Seattle (4)**—Buhner 4. **Texas (4)**—Palmeiro, Reimer, Sierra, Stanley. **Toronto (8)**—McGriff 2, Wilson 2, Bell, Felix, Lee, Mulliniks.

AT KANSAS CITY (88): **Baltimore** (6)—Horn 3, Anderson, Hulett, Worthington. **Boston** (2)—Burks, Greenwell. **California** (5)—Winfield 2, Davis, Hill, Parrish. **Chicago** (2)—Fisk, Pasqua. **Cleveland** (3)—C. James, Jefferson, Ward. **Detroit** (5)—Phillips 2, Fielder, Nokes, Ward. **Kansas City** (42)—Jackson 12, Seitzer 5, Tartabull 5, Brett 3, Pecota 3, Perry 3, Stillwell 3, Eisenreich 2, White 2, Macfarlane, McRae, Palacios, Wilson. **Milwaukee** (5)—Deer 2, Sheffield, Vaughn, Yount. **Minnesota** (2)—Gladden, Hrbek. **New York** (3)—Geren, Maas, Nokes. **Oakland** (3)—Canseco, R. Henderson, McGwire. **Seattle** (3)—Davis, Griffey Jr., O'Brien. **Texas** (2)—Baines, Franco. **Toronto** (5)—McGriff 2, Bell, Borders, Fernandez.

AT MILWAUKEE (119): **Baltimore** (5)—Worthington 2, Devereaux, Kittle, Tettleton. **Boston** (2)—Evans, Quintana. **California** (8)—Downing 2, Howell 2, Parrish, Schroeder, Schu, Winfield. **Chicago** (5)—Calderon 3, Fisk, Sosa. **Cleveland** (4)—Brookens, Browne, Jacoby, Maldonado. **Detroit** (10)—Fielder 3, Fryman, Heath, Lemon, Moseby, Nokes, Phillips, Whitaker. **Kansas City** (3)—Brett 2, Macfarlane. **Milwaukee** (60)—Deer 11, Parker 9, Vaughn 9, Yount 8, Molitor 6, Surhoff 4, Brock 3, Sheffield 3, Spiers 2, Braggs, Felder, Hamilton, McIntosh, Sveum. **Minnesota** (3)—Bush, Harper, Sorrento. **New York** (4)—Barfield, Hall, Kelly, Velarde. **Oakland** (2)—R. Henderson, Steinbach. **Seattle** (4)—Briley, Davis, Griffey Jr., E. Martinez. **Texas** (4)—Baines, Franco, Incaviglia, Kunkel. **Toronto** (5)—Bell 2, Gruber, Myers, Whiten.

AT MINNESOTA (115): **Baltimore** (6)—Milligan 3, C. Ripken 2, Finley. **Boston** (1)—Evans. **California** (2)—Schroeder, Stevens. **Chicago** (7)—Calderon, Fisk, Karkovice, Kittle, Martinez, Pasqua, Thomas. **Cleveland** (4)—C. James, Maldonado, Snyder, Webster. **Detroit** (6)—Whitaker 2, Fielder, Moseby, Phillips, Ward. **Kansas City** (3)—Jackson, Seitzer, Tartabull. **Milwaukee** (3)—Braggs, Deer, Molitor. **Minnesota** (46)—Hrbek 8, Gaetti 7, Puckett 6, Larkin 5, Mack 5, Bush 4, Gagne 3, Manrique 3, Gladden 3, Sorrento 2, Harper. **New York** (12)—Balboni 4, Kelly 2, Azocar, Barfield, Espinoza, Geren, Hall, Sanders. **Oakland** (11)—Canseco 4, Jose 3, R. Henderson 2, McGwire 2. **Seattle** (6)—Buhner, Davis, Griffey Jr., E. Martinez, Reynolds, Vizquel. **Texas** (3)—Coolbaugh, Incaviglia, Reimer. **Toronto** (5)—McGriff 2, Borders, Felix, Hill.

AT NEW YORK (142): **Baltimore** (5)—C. Ripken 2, Tettleton 2, Milligan. **Boston** (3)—Burks 2, Greenwell. **California** (5)—Bichette, Joyner, Orton, Washington, White. **Chicago** (6)—Fisk, Johnson, Karkovice, Pasqua, Sosa, Ventura. **Cleveland** (6)—Snyder 2, C. James, D. James, Maldonado, Manto. **Detroit** (11)—Fielder 3, Fryman 2, Moseby 2, Ward 2, Heath, Sheets. **Kansas City** (8)—Jackson 3, Brett 2, Macfarlane, Palacios, Pecota. **Milwaukee** (9)—Deer 3, Parker 3, Brock, Felder, Sheffield. **Minnesota** (5)—Harper 2, Gagne, Hrbek, Puckett. **New York** (64)—Barfield 12, Maas 12, Balboni 8, Kelly 5, Geren 4, Mattingly 4, Azocar 3, Hall 3, Nokes 3, Sax 3, Meulens 2, Blowers, Cerone, Leyritz, Sanders, Velarde. **Oakland** (10)—R. Henderson 4, McGwire 3, Canseco 2, D. Henderson. **Seattle** (4)—E. Martinez 2, Leonard, Reynolds. **Texas** (2)—Buechele, Gonzalez. **Toronto** (4)—McGriff 2, Lee, Myers.

AT OAKLAND (121): **Baltimore** (2)—C. Ripken 2. **Boston** (1)—Evans. **California** (5)—Bichette, Hill, Howell, Stevens, Winfield. **Chicago** (8)—Fletcher 2, Pasqua 2, Calderon, Karkovice, Sosa, Thomas. **Cleveland** (1)—Maldonado. **Detroit** (3)—Fielder, Heath, Whitaker. **Kansas City** (8)—Tartabull 4, Eisenreich 2, Jackson 2. **Milwaukee** (3)—Deer, Parker, Vaughn. **Minnesota** (5)—Hrbek 2, Gagne, Gladden, Sorrento. **New York** (2)—Blowers, Maas. **Oakland** (69)—Canseco 18, McGwire 14, D. Henderson 11, R. Henderson 8, Baines 3, Jose 3, Steinbach 3, Hassey 2, Gallego, Jennings, Lansford, Phelps, Quirk, Randolph, Weiss. **Seattle** (4)—Griffey Jr. 2, Reynolds, Valle. **Texas** (5)—Franco 2, Daugherty, Kunkel, Russell. **Toronto** (5)—Bell, Borders, Felix, Gruber, Lee.

AT SEATTLE (109): **Baltimore** (2)—Horn, Worthington. **Boston** (5)—Evans, Greenwell, Pena, Quintana, Rivera. **California** (4)—Schroeder 2, Bichette, Howell. **Chicago** (7)—Fisk 2, Kittle, Pasqua, Sosa, Thomas, Ventura. **Cleveland** (3)—Alomar, Maldonado, Snyder. **Detroit** (5)—Fielder 2, Whitaker 2, Trammell. **Kansas City** (6)—Jackson 3, Tartabull 2, Pecota. **Milwaukee** (4)—Molitor 2, Parker, Yount. **Minnesota** (4)—Bush, Gaetti, Gagne, Harper. **New York** (4)—Barfield 2, Hall, Maas. **Oakland** (5)—McGwire 2, Gallego, D. Henderson, R. Henderson. **Seattle** (49)—Davis 12, Griffey Jr. 8, Leonard 7, Briley 4, E. Martinez 3, O'Brien 3, Buhner 2, Coles 2, Cotto 2, Giles 2, Bradley, Griffey Sr., Jones, Valle. **Texas** (2)—Incaviglia 2, Franco. **Toronto** (8)—McGriff 3, Bell, Borders, Felix, Gruber, Lee.

AT TEXAS (123): **Baltimore** (4)—Devereaux, Horn, Melvin, Orsulak. **Boston** (3)—Boggs, Pena, Quintana. **California** (4)—Bichette, Davis, Parrish, Schu. **Chicago** (2)—Fisk, Kittle. **Cleveland** (4)—Baerga, Browne, Snyder, Webster. **Detroit** (7)—Fielder 2, Jones, Moseby, Sheets, Trammell, Ward. **Kansas City** (4)—Jackson 2, Brett, Perry. **Milwaukee** (3)—Surhoff, Vaughn, Yount. **Minnesota**—None. **New York** (14)—Maas 3, Blowers 2, Hall 2, Winfield 2, Cerone, Geren, Kelly, Mattingly, Sax. **Oakland** (7)—D. Henderson 2, McGwire 2, Canseco, R. Henderson, Quirk. **Seattle** (5)—Valle 3, Griffey Jr. 2. **Texas** (64)—Incaviglia 15, Sierra 10, Palmeiro 9, Baines 6, Buechele 5, Daugherty 5, Franco 4, Gonzalez 3, Pettis 3, Bosley, Coolbaugh, Kunkel, Stanley. **Toronto** (2)—Bell, Wilson.

AT TORONTO (175): **Baltimore** (8)—C. Ripken 2, Finley, Horn, Milligan, B. Ripken, Segui, Worthington. **Boston** (2)—Evans, Greenwell. **California** (6)—Bichette, Hill, Joyner, Parrish, White, Winfield. **Chicago** (4)—Kittle 2, Calderon, Lyons. **Cleveland** (8)—Maldonado 2, Webster 2, Alomar, Hernandez, C. James, Snyder. **Detroit** (11)—Fielder 4, Lemon 2, Trammell 2, Moseby, Sheets, Ward. **Kansas City** (6)—Brett 2, Macfarlane 2, Eisenreich, Jackson. **Milwaukee** (6)—Parker 4, Molitor 2. **Minnesota** (6)—Gaetti 2, Mack 2, Gagne, Hrbek. **New York** (10)—Balboni 2, Nokes 2, Barfield, Geren, Hall, Leyritz, Maas, Meulens. **Oakland** (5)—Canseco 2, R. Henderson 2, D. Henderson. **Seattle** (6)—Cotto 2, Giles 2, Leonard 2. **Texas** (5)—Baines, Buechele, Incaviglia, Sierra. **Toronto** (93)—Gruber 23, McGriff 14, Bell 11, Borders 10, Olerud 11, Felix 7, Hill 7, Myers 3, Fernandez 2, Lee 2, Liriano, Mulliniks, Whiten.

National League

	At Atl.	At Chi.	At Cin.	At Hou.	At L.A.	At Mont.	At N.Y.	At Phi.	At Pitt.	At St.L.	At S.D.	At S.F.	Totals 1990	1989
Atlanta	85	6	11	2	8	8	5	9	6	4	8	10	162	128
Chicago	7	75	6	4	5	4	7	3	7	4	7	7	136	124
Cincinnati	8	4	70	5	6	4	5	7	6	0	7	3	125	128
Houston	5	8	6	35	8	4	3	4	3	4	7	7	94	97
Los Angeles	5	5	9	7	54	7	3	8	3	3	13	12	129	89
Montreal	9	8	7	4	6	48	4	3	6	5	8	6	114	100
New York	9	15	7	4	7	7	86	12	9	7	4	5	172	147
Philadelphia	4	4	4	5	3	7	7	47	7	7	4	4	103	123
Pittsburgh	5	14	8	3	5	7	7	9	59	5	8	8	138	95
St. Louis	2	4	0	3	2	5	2	5	2	43	2	3	73	73
San Diego	6	3	6	6	15	3	4	3	5	4	63	5	123	120
San Francisco	10	2	9	4	8	6	5	4	9	4	10	81	152	141
1990 Totals	155	148	143	82	127	110	138	114	122	90	141	151	1521	.....
1989 Totals	116	125	130	92	83	115	134	128	107	63	148	124	.....	1365

AT ATLANTA (155): Atlanta (85)—Justice 19, Gant 18, Presley 10, Murphy 8, Treadway 5, Cabrera 4, McDowell 4, Olson 4, Blauser 3, Gregg 2, Lilliquist 2, L. Smith 2, Whitt 2, Kremers, Thomas. Chicago (7)—Dawson 3, Grace, Salazar, Sandberg, D. Smith. Cincinnati (8)—Sabo 4, Braggs, Davis, Duncan, Hatcher. Houston (5)—Anthony, Biggio, Doran, Simms, Stubbs. Los Angeles (5)—Brooks 2, Daniels, Gibson, Gwynn. Montreal (9)—Fitzgerald 3, Wallach 3, Galarraga 2, Martinez. New York (9)—Elster 2, Johnson 2, Carreon, Magadan, Mercado, Sasser, Strawberry. Philadelphia (4)—Martinez 2, C. Hayes, Herr. Pittsburgh (5)—Bonilla 3, Backman, Bonds. St. Louis (2)—Hudler 2. San Diego (6)—Carter 2, Ja. Clark 2, Pagliarulo, Roberts. San Francisco (10)—Clark 3, Bass, Decker, Laga, Mitchell, Parker, Thompson, Williams.

AT CHICAGO (148): Atlanta (6)—Blauser 3, Gant, Gregg, Olson. Chicago (75)—Sandberg 25, Dawson 14, Dunston 7, Salazar 7, Grace 4, Clark 3, Dw. Smith 3, Ramos 2, Villanueva 2, Walton 2, Wynne 2, Berryhill, Dascenzo, Girardi, May. Cincinnati (4)—Davis, Hatcher, O'Neill, Sabo. Houston (8)—Davis 3, Stubbs 2, Caminiti, Rhodes, Wilson. Los Angeles (5)—Daniels 3, Samuel, Scioscia. Montreal (8)—Walker 3, Goff 2, Galarraga, Owen, Santovenia. New York (15)—McReynolds 3, Johnson 3, Boston 2, Carreon 2, Strawberry 2, Magadan, O'Malley. Philadelphia (4)—Jordan 2, C. Hayes, Murphy. Pittsburgh (14)—Bonds 4, Bonilla 4, Van Slyke 3, Bream, King, Slaught. St. Louis (4)—Guerrero, Jose, Olivares, Zeile. San Diego (3)—Ja. Clark, Santiago, Williams. San Francisco (2)—Williams 2.

AT CINCINNATI (143): Atlanta (11)—Gant 3, L. Smith 2, Justice, Mann, Murphy, Olson, Presley, Treadway. Chicago (6)—Grace 2, Sandberg 2, Dawson, Dunston. Cincinnati (70)—Sabo 15, Davis 13, O'Neill 10, Duncan 5, Benzinger 4, Braggs 4, Larkin 4, Morris 3, Oliver 3, Hatcher 2, Reed 2, Roomes 2, Doran, Griffey, Quinones. Houston (6)—Davis 2, Caminiti, Gullickson, Stubbs, Yelding. Los Angeles (9)—Daniels 3, Gibson, Griffin, Gwynn, Javier, Murray, Samuel. Montreal (7)—Galarraga 3, Fitzgerald, Martinez, Walker, Wallach. New York (7)—Strawberry 2, Boston, Carreon, Elster, Johnson, Teufel. Philadelphia (4)—Daulton, V. Hayes, Hollins, Kruk. Pittsburgh (8)—Bonilla 3, King 2, Bell, Bonds, Slaught. St. Louis—None. San Diego (6)—Carter 3, Ja. Clark, Pagliarulo, Santiago. San Francisco (9)—Clark 3, Mitchell 3, Williams 2, Thompson.

AT HOUSTON (82): Atlanta (2)—Blauser, Cabrera. Chicago (4)—Dawson 2, Clark, Sandberg. Cincinnati (5)—Duncan 2, Davis, Sabo, Winningham. Houston (35)—Stubbs 9, Anthony 5, Wilson 5, Davis 4, Doran 3, Biggio 2, Caminiti 2, Candaele, Ortiz, Ramirez, Trevino, Young. Los Angeles (7)—Scioscia 2, Brooks, Gibson, Javier, Murray, Randolph. Montreal (4)—Wallach 2, Galarraga, Martinez. New York (4)—Carreon, Elster, Jefferies, Johnson. Philadelphia (5)—Thon 3, Daulton, C. Hayes. Pittsburgh (3)—Bell, Bonds, King. St. Louis (3)—Hudler, McGee, O. Smith. San Diego (6)—Alomar, Carter, Ja. Clark, Lynn, Parent, Roberts. San Francisco (4)—Thompson 2, Riles, Robinson.

AT LOS ANGELES (127): Atlanta (8)—Justice 2, Blauser, Gant, Gregg, McDowell, Murphy, Presley. Chicago (5)—Dawson, Dunston, Salazar, Villanueva, Wynne. Cincinnati (6)—Davis 3, O'Neill 2, Sabo. Houston (8)—Candaele 2, Davis 2, Wilson 2, Anthony, Stubbs. Los Angeles (54)—Daniels 12, Murray 12, Brooks 9, Samuel 6, Scioscia 5, Dempsey 2, Gibson 2, Gonzalez 2, Javier, Offerman, Sharperson, Valenzuela. Montreal (6)—Raines 2, Aldrete, Goff, Gross, Wallach. New York (7)—McReynolds 3, Boston, Elster, Marshall, Strawberry. Philadelphia (3)—Cook, C. Hayes, Kruk. Pittsburgh (5)—Bonilla 2, Bonds, Bream, Van Slyke. St. Louis (2)—Guerrero 2. San Diego (15)—Je. Clark 3, Pagliarulo 3, Jackson 2, Lynn 2, Santiago 2, Carter, Parent, Roberts. San Francisco (8)—Mitchell 2, Williams 2, Carter, Clark, Decker, Leonard.

AT MONTREAL (110): Atlanta (8)—Presley 2, Thomas 2, Justice, Murphy, L. Smith, Treadway. Chicago (4)—Sandberg 2, Clark, Dw. Smith. Cincinnati (4)—Braggs, Oliver, O'Neill, Sabo. Houston (4)—Davis 2, Stubbs 2. Los Angeles (7)—Daniels 3, Harris, Murray, Scioscia, Sharperson. Montreal (48)—Walker 9, Wallach 9, Galarraga 6, Raines 6, Martinez 5, Santovenia 4, DeShields 3, Fitzgerald 2, Grissom 2, Owen 2. New York (7)—Boston 2, Jefferies, Johnson, Lyons, McReynolds, Strawberry, Teufel. Philadelphia (7)—Dykstra 2, Chamberlain, Daulton, V. Hayes, Kruk, Thon. Pittsburgh (7)—Bonds 4, Bream, Redus, Van Slyke. St. Louis (5)—Thompson 2, Gilkey, Lankford, B. Smith. San Diego (3)—Carter, Roberts, Templeton. San Francisco (6)—Mitchell 3, Thompson 2, Williams.

AT NEW YORK (138): Atlanta (5)—Gant, Murphy, Presley, L. Smith, Thomas. Chicago (7)—Sandberg 2, Dawson, Dunston, Grace, McClendon, Salazar. Cincinnati (5)—Davis 2, Oliver 2, Winningham. Houston (3)—Stubbs 2, Oberkfell. Los Angeles (3)—Brooks, Daniels, Sharperson. Montreal (4)—Galarraga, Raines, Walker, Wallach. New York (86)—Strawberry 24, Johnson 13, McReynolds 11, Jefferies 9, Boston 4, Marshall 4, Teufel 4, Sasser 3, Elster 2, Magadan 2, Mercado 2, Carreon, Gooden, Herr, Lyons, Miller, O'Malley, Reed, Tabler. Philadephia (7)—Daulton 2, Murphy 2, V. Hayes, Hollins, Martinez. Pittsburgh (7)—Bonilla 2, Van Slyke 2, Backman, Bell, Redus. St. Louis (2)—McGee, Zeile. San Diego (4)—Carter 2, Santiago, Stephenson. San Francisco (5)—Mitchell 2, Bass, Thompson, Williams.

AT PHILADELPHIA (114): Atlanta (9)—Treadway 3, Murphy 2, Presley 2, Gant, Olson. **Chicago (3)**—Sandberg, Villanueva, Wynne. **Cincinnati (7)**—Morris 3, Larkin 2, Duncan, Hatcher. **Houston (4)**—Anthony, Davis, Gedman, Stubbs. **Los Angeles (8)**—Brooks 3, Gwynn 2, Scioscia 2, Daniels. **Montreal (3)**—Fitzgerald, Galarraga, Walker. **New York (12)**—Jefferies 3, Magadan 2, Sasser 2, Strawberry 2, Boston, Marshall, McReynolds. **Philadelphia (47)**—V. Hayes 10, Dykstra 6, Daulton 5, Martinez 4, C. Hayes 3, Herr 3, Thon 3, Campusano 2, Hollins 2, Jones 2, Jordan 2, Kruk 2, Morandini, Murphy, Vatcher. **Pittsburgh (9)**—Bonds 2, Redus 2, Bonilla, Bream, LaValliere, McClendon, Van Slyke. **St. Louis (5)**—Zeile 3, Brunansky, Hudler. **San Diego (3)**—Alomar, Carter, Ja. Clark. **San Francisco (4)**—Bailey, Clark, Litton, Williams.

AT PITTSBURGH (122): Atlanta (6)—Justice 3, Cabrera, Murphy, Treadway. **Chicago (7)**—Dawson 2, Sandberg 2, Dunston, Grace, Villanueva. **Cincinnati (6)**—Oliver 2, Benzinger, Davis, Duncan, Sabo. **Houston (3)**—Doran, Stubbs, Wilson. **Los Angeles (3)**—Daniels, Murray, Samuel. **Montreal (6)**—Galarraga 2, Martinez 2, Fitzgerald, Grissom. **New York (9)**—Strawberry 3, Carreon 2, Teufel 2, Boston, Jelic. **Philadelphia (7)**—C. Hayes 3, Daulton 2, V. Hayes, Murphy. **Pittsburgh (59)**—Bonds 14, Bonilla 13, King 9, Bream 8, Van Slyke 6, LaValliere 2, Martinez 2, Redus 2, Bell, Lind, Slaught. **St. Louis (2)**—Coleman, Zeile. **San Diego (5)**—Gwynn 2, Carter, Ja. Clark, Williams. **San Francisco (9)**—Mitchell 4, Bass, Bathe, Clark, Uribe, Williams.

AT ST. LOUIS (90): Atlanta (4)—Gant 2, Justice, Thomas. **Chicago (4)**—Sandberg 3, Villanueva. **Cincinnati**—None. **Houston (4)**—Stubbs 2, Davidson, Ramirez. **Los Angeles (3)**—Murray, Samuel, Wetteland. **Montreal (5)**—Martinez, Owen, Santovenia, Walker, Wallach. **New York (7)**—Teufel 2, Boston, Carreon, Elster, Johnson, McReynolds. **Philadelphia (7)**—Chamberlain, V. Hayes, Hollins, Jones, Kruk, Murphy, Ready. **Pittsburgh (5)**—Bell, Bonds, Bonilla, Bream, Van Slyke. **St. Louis (43)**—Guerrero 8, Zeile 8, Pendleton 6, Coleman 5, Thompson 3, Hudler 2, Jose 2, Lankford 2, Pagnozzi 2, Jones, McGee, Oquendo, Stephens, Walling. **San Diego (4)**—Ja. Clark, Pagliarulo, Roberts, Templeton. **San Francisco (4)**—Mitchell 3, Clark.

AT SAN DIEGO (141): Atlanta (8)—Gant 2, McDowell 2, Murphy 2, L. Smith 2. **Chicago (7)**—Dunston 3, Dawson, Salazar, D. Smith, Villanueva. **Cincinnati (7)**—Davis 2, Larkin, Quinones, Reed, Sabo, Winningham. **Houston (7)**—Davis 3, Anthony, Doran, Stubbs, Wilson. **Los Angeles (13)**—Murray 4, Samuel 3, Brooks 2, Daniels, Gibson, Gwynn, Harris. **Montreal (8)**—Galarraga 2, Wallach 2, DeShields, Nixon, Owen, Walker. **New York (4)**—Elster, Johnson, McReynolds, Strawberry. **Philadelphia (4)**—V. Hayes, Jordan, Martinez, Murphy. **Pittsburgh (8)**—Bonds 3, Van Slyke 2, Bell, Bonilla, Slaught. **St. Louis (2)**—Guerrero, Hudler. **San Diego (63)**—Ja. Clark 16, Carter 12, Templeton 6, Santiago 5, Alomar 4, Roberts 4, Je. Clark 2, Gwynn 2, Lynn 2, Stephenson 2, Abner, Jackson, Lampkin, Pagliarulo, Parent, Schiraldi, Whitson, Williams. **San Francisco (10)**—Carter 2, Mitchell 2, Williams 2, Bass, Bathe, Clark, Parker.

AT SAN FRANCISCO (151): Atlanta (10)—Gant 3, Presley 2, Bell, Cabrera, Gregg, Justice, L. Smith. **Chicago (7)**—Dunston 3, Dawson 2, Salazar, Sandberg. **Cincinnati (3)**—O'Neill 2, Morris. **Houston (7)**—Davis 5, Anthony, Biggio. **Los Angeles (12)**—Murray 5, Brooks 2, Gibson 2, Daniels, Lyons, Scioscia. **Montreal (6)**—Walker 2, Fitzgerald, Galarraga, Johnson, Wallach. **New York (5)**—McReynolds 2, Carreon, Jefferies, O'Malley. **Philadelphia (4)**—Dykstra, V. Hayes, Kruk, Thon. **Pittsburgh (8)**—Bonilla 2, Bream 2, Bell, Bonds, Drabek, King. **St. Louis (3)**—Guerrero, Thompson, Zeile. **San Diego (5)**—Ja. Clark, Lynn, Santiago, Stephenson, Templeton. **San Francisco (81)**—Williams 20, Mitchell 15, Clark 8, Thompson 8, Riles 7, Carter 6, Bass 3, Butler 3, Benjamin 2, Kennedy 2, Leach 2, Anderson, Bathe, Decker, Laga, Robinson.

Major League Attendance for 1990

NATIONAL LEAGUE			AMERICAN LEAGUE		
	Home	Road		Home	Road
Atlanta	980,129	1,851,517	Baltimore	2,415,189	2,034,936
Chicago	2,243,791	2,160,568	Boston	2,528,986	2,398,442
Cincinnati	2,400,892	2,174,093	California	2,555,688	2,042,313
Houston	1,310,927	1,831,131	Chicago	2,002,357	2,205,062
Los Angeles	3,002,396	2,113,630	Cleveland	1,225,240	2,047,257
Montreal	1,373,087	1,941,918	Detroit	1,495,785	2,134,797
New York	2,732,745	2,349,021	Kansas City	2,244,956	2,073,923
Philadelphia	1,992,484	1,985,844	Milwaukee	1,752,900	2,181,099
Pittsburgh	2,049,908	2,033,535	Minnesota	1,751,584	2,003,575
St. Louis	2,573,225	1,908,633	New York	2,006,436	2,399,178
San Diego	1,856,396	1,911,315	Oakland	2,900,217	2,597,920
San Francisco	1,975,528	2,230,303	Seattle	1,509,727	2,193,421
			Texas	2,057,911	1,980,565
			Toronto	3,885,284	2,039,772
Total	24,491,508	24,491,508	Total	30,332,260	30,332,260

THE SPORTING NEWS AWARDS

THE SPORTING NEWS MVP AWARDS

	AMERICAN LEAGUE			NATIONAL LEAGUE		
Year	Player	Club	Points	Player	Club	Points
1929	Al Simmons, Philadelphia, of		40	No selection		
1930	Joseph Cronin, Washington, ss		52	William Terry, New York, 1b		47
1931	H. Louis Gehrig, New York, 1b		40	Charles Klein, Philadelphia, of		40
1932	James Foxx, Philadelphia, 1b		46	Charles Klein, Philadelphia, of		46
1933	James Foxx, Philadelphia, 1b		49	Carl Hubbell, New York, p		64
1934	H. Louis Gehrig, New York, 1b		51	Jerome Dean, St. Louis, p		57
1935	Henry Greenberg, Detroit, 1b		64	J. Floyd Vaughan, Pittsburgh, ss		42
1936	H. Louis Gehrig, New York, 1b		55	Carl Hubbell, New York, p		61
1937	Charles Gehringer, Detroit, 2b		78	Joseph Medwick, St. Louis, of		70
1938	James Foxx, Boston, 1b		304	Ernest Lombardi, Cincinnati, c		229
1939	Joseph DiMaggio, New York, of		280	William Walters, Cincinnati, p		303
1940	Henry Greenberg, Detroit, of		292	Frank McCormick, Cincinnati, 1b		274
1941	Joseph DiMaggio, New York, of		291	Adolph Camilli, Brooklyn, 1b		300
1942	Joseph Gordon, New York, 2b		270	Morton Cooper, St. Louis, p		263
1943	Spurgeon Chandler, New York, p		246	Stanley Musial, St. Louis, of		267
1944	Robert Doerr, Boston, 2b			Martin Marion, St. Louis, ss		
1945	Edward J. Mayo, Detroit, 2b			Thomas Holmes, Boston, of		

THE SPORTING NEWS PLAYER, PITCHER OF YEAR

AMERICAN LEAGUE

1948—Louis Boudreau, Cleveland, ss
    Robert Lemon, Cleveland, p
1949—Theodore Williams, Boston, of
    Ellis Kinder, Boston, p
1950—Philip Rizzuto, New York, ss
    Robert Lemon, Cleveland, p
1951—Ferris Fain, Philadelphia, 1b
    Robert Feller, Cleveland, p
1952—Luscious Easter, Cleveland, 1b
    Robert Shantz, Philadelphia, p
1953—Albert Rosen, Cleveland, 3b
    Erv (Bob) Porterfield, Washington, p
1954—Roberto Avila, Cleveland, 2b
    Robert Lemon, Cleveland, p
1955—Albert Kaline, Detroit, of
    Edward Ford, New York, p
1956—Mickey Mantle, New York, of
    W. William Pierce, Chicago, p
1957—Theodore Williams, Boston, of
    W. William Pierce, Chicago, p
1958—Jack Jensen, Boston, of
    Robert Turley, New York, p
1959—J. Nelson Fox, Chicago, 2b
    Early Wynn, Chicago, p
1960—Roger Maris, New York, of
    Charles Estrada, Baltimore, p
1961—Roger Maris, New York, of
    Edward Ford, New York, p
1962—Mickey Mantle, New York, of
    Richard Donovan, Cleveland, p
1963—Albert Kaline, Detroit, of
    Edward Ford, New York, p
1964—Brooks Robinson, Baltimore, 3b
    Dean Chance, Los Angeles, p
1965—Pedro (Tony) Oliva, Minnesota, of
    James Grant, Minnesota, p
1966—Frank Robinson, Baltimore, of
    James Kaat, Minnesota, p
1967—Carl Yastrzemski, Boston, of
    Jim Lonborg, Boston, p
1968—Ken Harrelson, Boston, of
    Denny McLain, Detroit, p
1969—Harmon Killebrew, Minnesota, 1b-3b
    Denny McLain, Detroit, p
1970—Harmon Killebrew, Minnesota, 3b
    Sam McDowell, Cleveland, p
1971—Pedro (Tony) Oliva, Minnesota, of
    Vida Blue, Oakland, p
1972—Richie Allen, Chicago, 1b
    Wilbur Wood, Chicago, p
1973—Reggie Jackson, Oakland, of
    Jim Palmer, Baltimore, p

NATIONAL LEAGUE

1948—Stanley Musial, St. Louis, of-1b
    John Sain, Boston, p
1949—Enos Slaughter, St. Louis, of
    Howard Pollet, St. Louis, p
1950—Ralph Kiner, Pittsburgh, of
    C. James Konstanty, Philadelphia, p
1951—Stanley Musial, St. Louis, of
    Elwin Roe, Brooklyn, p
1952—Henry Sauer, Chicago, of
    Robin Roberts, Philadelphia, p
1953—Roy Campanella, Brooklyn, c
    Warren Spahn, Milwaukee, p
1954—Willie Mays, New York, of
    John Antonelli, New York, p
1955—Edwin Snider, Brooklyn, of
    Robin Roberts, Philadelphia, p
1956—Henry Aaron, Milwaukee, of
    Donald Newcombe, Brooklyn, p
1957—Stanley Musial, St. Louis, 1b
    Warren Spahn, Milwaukee, p
1958—Ernest Banks, Chicago, ss
    Warren Spahn, Milwaukee, p
1959—Ernest Banks, Chicago, ss
    Samuel Jones, San Francisco, p
1960—Richard Groat, Pittsburgh, ss
    Vernon Law, Pittsburgh, p
1961—Frank Robinson, Cincinnati, of
    Warren Spahn, Milwaukee, p
1962—Maurice Wills, Los Angeles, ss
    Donald Drysdale, Los Angeles, p
1963—Henry Aaron, Milwaukee, of
    Sanford Koufax, Los Angeles, p
1964—Kenton Boyer, St. Louis, 3b
    Sanford Koufax, Los Angeles, p
1965—Willie Mays, San Francisco, of
    Sanford Koufax, Los Angeles, p
1966—Roberto Clemente, Pittsburgh, of
    Sanford Koufax, Los Angeles, p
1967—Orlando Cepeda, St. Louis, 1b
    Mike McCormick, San Francisco, p
1968—Pete Rose, Cincinnati, of
    Bob Gibson, St. Louis, p
1969—Willie McCovey, San Francisco, 1b
    Tom Seaver, New York, p
1970—Johnny Bench, Cincinnati, c
    Bob Gibson, St. Louis, p
1971—Joe Torre, St. Louis, 3b
    Ferguson Jenkins, Chicago, p
1972—Billy Williams, Chicago, of
    Steve Carlton, Philadelphia, p
1973—Bobby Bonds, San Francisco, of
    Ron Bryant, San Francisco, p

PLAYER, PITCHER OF YEAR—Continued

AMERICAN LEAGUE

1974—Jeff Burroughs, Texas, of
    Jim Hunter, Oakland, p
1975—Fred Lynn, Boston, of
    Jim Palmer, Baltimore, p
1976—Thurman Munson, New York, c
    Jim Palmer, Baltimore, p
1977—Rod Carew, Minnesota, 1b
    Nolan Ryan, California, p
1978—Jim Rice, Boston, of
    Ron Guidry, New York, p
1979—Don Baylor, California, of
    Mike Flanagan, Baltimore, p
1980—George Brett, Kansas City, 3b
    Steve Stone, Baltimore, p
1981—Tony Armas, Oakland, of
    Jack Morris, Detroit, p
1982—Robin Yount, Milwaukee, ss
    Dave Stieb, Toronto, p
1983—Cal Ripken, Baltimore, ss
    LaMarr Hoyt, Chicago, p
1984—Don Mattingly, New York, 1b
    Willie Hernandez, Detroit, p
1985—Don Mattingly, New York, 1b
    Bret Saberhagen, Kansas City, p
1986—Don Mattingly, New York, 1b
    Roger Clemens, Boston, p
1987—George Bell, Toronto, of
    Jimmy Key, Toronto, p
1988—Jose Canseco, Oakland, of
    Frank Viola, Minnesota, p
1989—Ruben Sierra, Texas, of
    Bret Saberhagen, Kansas City, p
1990—Cecil Fielder, Detroit, 1b
    Bob Welch, Oakland, p

NATIONAL LEAGUE

1974—Lou Brock, St. Louis, of
    Mike Marshall, Los Angeles, p
1975—Joe Morgan, Cincinnati, 2b
    Tom Seaver, New York, p
1976—George Foster, Cincinnati, of
    Randy Jones, San Diego, p
1977—George Foster, Cincinnati, of
    Steve Carlton, Philadelphia, p
1978—Dave Parker, Pittsburgh, of
    Vida Blue, San Francisco, p
1979—Keith Hernandez, St. Louis, 1b
    Joe Niekro, Houston, p
1980—Mike Schmidt, Philadelphia, 3b
    Steve Carlton, Philadelphia, p
1981—Andre Dawson, Montreal, of
    Fernando Valenzuela, Los Angeles, p
1982—Dale Murphy, Atlanta, of
    Steve Carlton, Philadelphia, p
1983—Dale Murphy, Atlanta, of
    John Denny, Philadelphia, p
1984—Ryne Sandberg, Chicago, 2b
    Rick Sutcliffe, Chicago, p
1985—Willie McGee, St. Louis, of
    Dwight Gooden, New York, p
1986—Mike Schmidt, Philadelphia, 3b
    Mike Scott, Houston, p
1987—Andre Dawson, Chicago, of
    Rick Sutcliffe, Chicago, p
1988—Andy Van Slyke, Pittsburgh, of
    Orel Hershiser, Los Angeles, p
1989—Kevin Mitchell, San Francisco, of
    Mark Davis, San Diego, p
1990—Barry Bonds, Pittsburgh, of
    Doug Drabek, Pittsburgh, p

FIREMAN (Relief Pitcher) OF THE YEAR

Year	Player Club	Player Club
1960	Mike Fornieles, Boston	Lindy McDaniel, St. Louis
1961	Luis Arroyo, New York	Stu Miller, San Francisco
1962	Dick Radatz, Boston	Roy Face, Pittsburgh
1963	Stu Miller, Baltimore	Lindy McDaniel, Chicago
1964	Dick Radatz, Boston	Al McBean, Pittsburgh
1965	Eddie Fisher, Chicago	Ted Abernathy, Chicago
1966	Jack Aker, Kansas City	Phil Regan, Los Angeles
1967	Minnie Rojas, California	Ted Abernathy, Cincinnati
1968	Wilbur Wood, Chicago	Phil Regan, L.A.-Chicago
1969	Ron Perranoski, Minnesota	Wayne Granger, Cincinnati
1970	Ron Perranoski, Minnesota	Wayne Granger, Cincinnati
1971	Ken Sanders, Milwaukee	Dave Giusti, Pittsburgh
1972	Sparky Lyle, New York	Clay Carroll, Cincinnati
1973	John Hiller, Detroit	Mike Marshall, Montreal
1974	Terry Forster, Chicago	Mike Marshall, Los Angeles
1975	Rich Gossage, Chicago	Al Hrabosky, St. Louis
1976	Bill Campbell, Minnesota	Rawly Eastwick, Cincinnati
1977	Bill Campbell, Boston	Rollie Fingers, San Diego
1978	Rich Gossage, New York	Rollie Fingers, San Diego
1979	Mike Marshall, Minnesota	Bruce Sutter, Chicago
	Jim Kern, Texas	
1980	Dan Quisenberry, Kansas City	Rollie Fingers, San Diego
		Tom Hume, Cincinnati
1981	Rollie Fingers, Milwaukee	Bruce Sutter, St. Louis
1982	Dan Quisenberry, Kansas City	Bruce Sutter, St. Louis
1983	Dan Quisenberry, Kansas City	Al Holland, Philadelphia
		Lee Smith, Chicago
1984	Dan Quisenberry, Kansas City	Bruce Sutter, St. Louis
1985	Dan Quisenberry, Kansas City	Jeff Reardon, Montreal
1986	Dave Righetti, New York	Todd Worrell, St. Louis
1987	Dave Righetti, New York	Steve Bedrosian, Philadelphia
	Jeff Reardon, Minnesota	
1988	Dennis Eckersley, Oakland	John Franco, Cincinnati
1989	Jeff Russell, Texas	Mark Davis, San Diego
1990	Bobby Thigpen, Chicago	John Franco, New York

THE SPORTING NEWS ROOKIE AWARDS

1946—Combined selection—Delmer Ennis, Philadelphia, N. L., of
1947—Combined selection—Jack Robinson, Brooklyn, 1b
1948—Combined selection—Richie Ashburn, Philadelphia, N. L., of

	AMERICAN LEAGUE		NATIONAL LEAGUE	
Year	Player	Club	Player	Club
1949—	Roy Sievers, St. Louis, of		Donald Newcombe, Brooklyn, p	
1950—	Combined selection—Edward Ford, New York, A. L., p			
1951—	Orestes Minoso, Chicago, of		Willie Mays, New York, of	
1952—	Clinton Courtney, St. Louis, c		Joseph Black, Brooklyn, p	
1953—	Harvey Kuenn, Detroit, ss		James Gilliam, Brooklyn, 2b	
1954—	Robert Grim, New York, p		Wallace Moon, St. Louis, of	
1955—	Herbert Score, Cleveland, p		William Virdon, St. Louis, of	
1956—	Luis Aparicio, Chicago, ss		Frank Robinson, Cincinnati, of	
1957—	Anthony Kubek, New York, inf-of		Edward Bouchee, Philadelphia, 1b	
	(No pitcher named)		Jack Sanford, Philadelphia, p	
1958—	Albert Pearson, Washington, of		Orlando Cepeda, San Francisco, 1b	
	Ryne Duren, New York, p		Carlton Willey, Milwaukee, p	
1959—	W. Robert Allison, Washington, of		Willie McCovey, San Francisco, 1b	
1960—	Ronald Hansen, Baltimore, ss		Frank Howard, Los Angeles, of	
1961—	Richard Howser, Kansas City, ss		Billy Williams, Chicago, of	
	Donald Schwall, Boston, p		Kenneth Hunt, Cincinnati, p	
1962—	Thomas Tresh, New York, of-ss		Kenneth Hubbs, Chicago, 2b	
1963—	Peter Ward, Chicago, 3b		Peter Rose, Cincinnati, 2b	
	Gary Peters, Chicago, p		Raymond Culp, Philadelphia, p	
1964—	Pedro (Tony) Oliva, Minnesota, of		Richard Allen, Philadelphia, 3b	
	Wallace Bunker, Baltimore, p		William McCool, Cincinnati, p	
1965—	Curtis Blefary, Baltimore, of		Joseph Morgan, Houston, 2b	
	Marcelino Lopez, California, p		Frank Linzy, San Francisco, p	
1966—	Tommie Agee, Chicago, of		Tommy Helms, Cincinnati, 3b	
	James Nash, Kansas City, p		Donald Sutton, Los Angeles, p	
1967—	Rod Carew, Minnesota, 2b		Lee May, Cincinnati, 1b	
	Tom Phoebus, Baltimore, p		Dick Hughes, St. Louis, p	
1968—	Del Unser, Washington, of		Johnny Bench, Cincinnati, c	
	Stan Bahnsen, New York, p		Jerry Koosman, New York, p	
1969—	Carlos May, Chicago, of		Coco Laboy, Montreal, 3b	
	Mike Nagy, Boston, p		Tom Griffin, Houston, p	
1970—	Roy Foster, Cleveland, of		Bernie Carbo, Cincinnati, of	
	Bert Blyleven, Minnesota, p		Carl Morton, Montreal, p	
1971—	Chris Chambliss, Cleveland, 1b		Earl Williams, Atlanta, c	
	Bill Parsons, Milwaukee, p		Reggie Cleveland, St. Louis, p	
1972—	Carlton Fisk, Boston, c		Dave Rader, San Francisco, c	
	Dick Tidrow, Cleveland, p		Jon Matlack, New York, p	
1973—	Al Bumbry, Baltimore, of		Gary Matthews, San Francisco, of	
	Steve Busby, Kansas City, p		Steve Rogers, Montreal, p	
1974—	Mike Hargrove, Texas, 1b		Greg Gross, Houston, of	
	Frank Tanana, California, p		John D'Acquisto, San Francisco, p	
1975—	Fred Lynn, Boston, of		Gary Carter, Montreal, of-c	
	Dennis Eckersley, Cleveland, p		John Montefusco, San Francisco, p	
1976—	Butch Wynegar, Minnesota, c		Larry Herndon, San Francisco, of	
	Mark Fidrych, Detroit, p		Butch Metzger, San Diego, p	
1977—	Mitchell Page, Oakland, of		Andre Dawson, Montreal, of	
	Dave Rozema, Detroit, p		Bob Owchinko, San Diego, p	
1978—	Paul Molitor, Milwaukee, 2b		Bob Horner, Atlanta, 3b	
	Rich Gale, Kansas City, p		Don Robinson, Pittsburgh, p	
1979—	Pat Putnam, Texas, 1b		Jeff Leonard, Houston, of	
	Mark Clear, California, p		Rick Sutcliffe, Los Angeles, p	
1980—	Joe Charboneau, Cleveland, of		Lonnie Smith, Philadelphia, of	
	Britt Burns, Chicago, p		Bill Gullickson, Montreal, p	
1981—	Rich Gedman, Boston, c		Tim Raines, Montreal, of	
	Dave Righetti, New York, p		Fernando Valenzuela, Los Angeles, p	
1982—	Cal Ripken, Baltimore, ss-3b		Johnny Ray, Pittsburgh, 2b	
	Ed Vande Berg, Seattle, p		Steve Bedrosian, Atlanta, p	
1983—	Ron Kittle, Chicago, of		Darryl Strawberry, New York, of	
	Mike Boddicker, Baltimore, p		Craig McMurtry, Atlanta, p	
1984—	Alvin Davis, Seattle, 1b		Juan Samuel, Philadelphia, 2b	
	Mark Langston, Seattle, p		Dwight Gooden, New York, p	
1985—	Ozzie Guillen, Chicago, ss		Vince Coleman, St. Louis, of	
	Teddy Higuera, Milwaukee, p		Tom Browning, Cincinnati, p	
1986—	Jose Canseco, Oakland, of		Robby Thompson, San Francisco, 2b	
	Mark Eichhorn, Toronto, p		Todd Worrell, St. Louis, p	
1987—	Mark McGwire, Oakland, 1b		Benito Santiago, San Diego, c	
	Mike Henneman, Detroit, p		Mike Dunne, Pittsburgh, p	
1988—	Walt Weiss, Oakland, ss		Mark Grace, Chicago, 1b	
	Bryan Harvey, California, p		Tim Belcher, Los Angeles, p	

THE SPORTING NEWS ROOKIE AWARDS—Continued

AMERICAN LEAGUE		NATIONAL LEAGUE	
Year	Player Club		Player Club
1989—	Craig Worthington, Baltimore, 3b		Jerome Walton, Chicago, of
	Tom Gordon, Kansas City, p		Andy Benes, San Diego, p
1990—	Sandy Alomar Jr., Cleveland, c		Dave Justice, Atlanta, of
	Kevin Appier, Kansas City, p		Mike Harkey, Chicago, p

MAJOR LEAGUE EXECUTIVE

Year	Executive Club	Year	Executive Club
1936—	Branch Rickey, St. Louis NL	1964—	Vaughan (Bing) Devine, St.L.NL
1937—	Edward Barrow, New York AL	1965—	Calvin Griffith, Minnesota AL
1938—	Warren Giles, Cincinnati NL	1966—	Lee MacPhail, Commissioner's
1939—	Larry MacPhail, Brooklyn NL		Office
1940—	W. O. Briggs, Sr., Detroit AL	1967—	Dick O'Connell, Boston AL
1941—	Edward Barrow, New York AL	1968—	James Campbell, Detroit AL
1942—	Branch Rickey, St. Louis NL	1969—	John Murphy, New York NL
1943—	Clark Griffith, Washington AL	1970—	Harry Dalton, Milwaukee AL
1944—	Wm. O. DeWitt, St. Louis AL	1971—	Cedric Tallis, Kansas City AL
1945—	Philip K. Wrigley, Chicago NL	1972—	Roland Hemond, Chicago AL
1946—	Thomas A. Yawkey, Boston AL	1973—	Bob Howsam, Cincinnati NL
1947—	Branch Rickey, Brooklyn NL	1974—	Gabe Paul, New York AL
1948—	Bill Veeck, Cleveland AL	1975—	Dick O'Connell, Boston AL
1949—	Robt. Carpenter, Phila'phia NL	1976—	Joe Burke, Kansas City AL
1950—	George Weiss, New York AL	1977—	Bill Veeck, Chicago AL
1951—	George Weiss, New York AL	1978—	Spec Richardson, San Fran. NL
1952—	George Weiss, New York AL	1979—	Hank Peters, Baltimore AL
1953—	Louis Perini, Milwaukee NL	1980—	Tal Smith, Houston NL
1954—	Horace Stoneham, N. York NL	1981—	John McHale, Montreal NL
1955—	Walter O'Malley, Brooklyn NL	1982—	Harry Dalton, Milwaukee AL
1956—	Gabe Paul, Cincinnati NL	1983—	Hank Peters, Baltimore AL
1957—	Frank Lane, St. Louis NL	1984—	Dallas Green, Chicago NL
1958—	Joe L. Brown, Pittsburgh NL	1985—	John Schuerholz, Kansas City AL
1959—	E. J. (Buzzie) Bavasi, L.A. NL	1986—	Frank Cashen, New York NL
1960—	George Weiss, New York AL	1987—	Al Rosen, San Francisco NL
1961—	Dan Topping, New York AL	1988—	Fred Claire, Los Angeles NL
1962—	Fred Haney, Los Angeles AL	1989—	Roland Hemond, Baltimore AL
1963—	Vaughan (Bing) Devine, St.L.NL	1990—	Bob Quinn, Cincinnati NL

MAJOR LEAGUE MANAGER

Year	Manager Club	Year	Manager Club
1936—	Joe McCarthy, New York AL	1967—	Dick Williams, Boston AL
1937—	Bill McKechnie, Boston NL	1968—	Mayo Smith, Detroit AL
1938—	Joe McCarthy, New York AL	1969—	Gil Hodges, New York NL
1939—	Leo Durocher, Brooklyn NL	1970—	Danny Murtaugh, Pittsb'gh NL
1940—	Bill McKechnie, Cincinnati NL	1971—	Charlie Fox, San Francisco NL
1941—	Billy Southworth, St. Louis NL	1972—	Chuck Tanner, Chicago AL
1942—	Billy Southworth, St. Louis NL	1973—	Gene Mauch, Montreal NL
1943—	Joe McCarthy, New York AL	1974—	Bill Virdon, New York AL
1944—	Luke Sewell, St. Louis AL	1975—	Darrell Johnson, Boston AL
1945—	Ossie Bluege, Washington AL	1976—	Danny Ozark, Philadelphia NL
1946—	Eddie Dyer, St. Louis NL	1977—	Earl Weaver, Baltimore AL
1947—	Bucky Harris, New York AL	1978—	George Bamberger, Milw'kee AL
1948—	Bill Meyer, Pittsburgh NL	1979—	Earl Weaver, Baltimore AL
1949—	Casey Stengel, New York AL	1980—	Bill Virdon, Houston NL
1950—	Red Rolfe, Detroit AL	1981—	Billy Martin, Oakland AL
1951—	Leo Durocher, New York NL	1982—	Whitey Herzog, St. Louis NL
1952—	Eddie Stanky, St. Louis NL	1983—	Tony LaRussa, Chicago AL
1953—	Casey Stengel, New York AL	1984—	Jim Frey, Chicago NL
1954—	Leo Durocher, New York NL	1985—	Bobby Cox, Toronto AL
1955—	Walter Alston, Brooklyn NL	1986—	John McNamara, Boston AL
1956—	Birdie Tebbetts, Cincinnati NL		Hal Lanier, Houston NL
1957—	Fred Hutchinson, St. Louis NL	1987—	Sparky Anderson, Detroit AL
1958—	Casey Stengel, New York AL		Buck Rodgers, Montreal NL
1959—	Walter Alston, Los Angeles NL	1988—	Tony LaRussa, Oakland AL
1960—	Danny Murtaugh, Pitts. NL		Tom Lasorda, Los Angeles NL (tie)
1961—	Ralph Houk, New York AL		Jim Leyland, Pittsburgh NL (tie)
1962—	Bill Rigney, Los Angeles AL	1989—	Frank Robinson, Baltimore AL
1963—	Walter Alston, Los Angeles NL		Don Zimmer, Chicago NL
1964—	Johnny Keane, St. Louis NL	1990—	Jeff Torborg, Chicago AL
1965—	Sam Mele, Minnesota AL		Jim Leyland, Pittsburgh NL
1966—	Hank Bauer, Baltimore AL		

MAJOR LEAGUE PLAYER

Year	Player	Club
1936	Carl Hubbell, New York NL	
1937	Johnny Allen, Cleveland AL	
1938	Johnny Vander Meer, Cinn. NL	
1939	Joe DiMaggio, New York AL	
1940	Bob Feller, Cleveland AL	
1941	Ted Williams, Boston AL	
1942	Ted Williams, Boston AL	
1943	Spud Chandler, New York AL	
1944	Marty Marion, St. Louis NL	
1945	Hal Newhouser, Detroit AL	
1946	Stan Musial, St. Louis NL	
1947	Ted Williams, Boston AL	
1948	Lou Boudreau, Cleveland AL	
1949	Ted Williams, Boston AL	
1950	Phil Rizzuto, New York AL	
1951	Stan Musial, St. Louis NL	
1952	Robin Roberts, Philadelphia NL	
1953	Al Rosen, Cleveland AL	
1954	Willie Mays, New York NL	
1955	Duke Snider, Brooklyn NL	
1956	Mickey Mantle, New York AL	
1957	Ted Williams, Boston AL	
1958	Bob Turley, New York AL	
1959	Early Wynn, Chicago AL	
1960	Bill Mazeroski, Pittsburgh NL	
1961	Roger Maris, New York AL	
1962	Maury Wills, Los Angeles NL	
	Don Drysdale, Los Angeles NL	
1963	Sandy Koufax, Los Angeles NL	
1964	Ken Boyer, St. Louis NL	
1965	Sandy Koufax, Los Angeles NL	
1966	Frank Robinson, Baltimore AL	
1967	Carl Yastrzemski, Boston AL	
1968	Denny McLain, Detroit AL	
1969	Willie McCovey, San Fran. NL	
1970	Johnny Bench, Cin. NL	
1971	Joe Torre, St. Louis NL	
1972	Billy Williams, Chicago NL	
1973	Reggie Jackson, Oakland AL	
1974	Lou Brock, St. Louis NL	
1975	Joe Morgan, Cincinnati NL	
1976	Joe Morgan, Cincinnati NL	
1977	Rod Carew, Minnesota AL	
1978	Ron Guidry, New York AL	
1979	Willie Stargell, Pittsburgh NL	
1980	George Brett, Kansas City AL	
1981	Fernando Valenzuela, Los Angeles NL	
1982	Robin Yount, Milwaukee AL	
1983	Cal Ripken, Baltimore AL	
1984	Ryne Sandberg, Chicago NL	
1985	Don Mattingly, New York AL	
1986	Roger Clemens, Boston AL	
1987	George Bell, Toronto AL	
1988	Orel Hershiser, Los Angeles NL	
1989	Kevin Mitchell, San Francisco NL	
1990	Barry Bonds, Pittsburgh NL	

MINOR LEAGUE EXECUTIVE (HIGHER CLASSIFICATIONS)
(Restricted to Class AAA Starting in 1963)

Year	Executive	Club
1936	Earl Mann, Atlanta, Southern	
1937	Robt. LaMotte, Savannah, Sally	
1938	Louis McKenna, St. Paul, A.A.	
1939	Bruce Dudley, Louisville, A.A.	
1940	Roy Hamey, Kansas City, A.A.	
1941	Emil Sick, Seattle, PCL	
1942	Bill Veeck, Milwaukee, A.A.	
1943	Clar. Rowland, Los Angeles, PCL	
1944	William Mulligan, Seattle, PCL	
1945	Bruce Dudley, Louisville, A.A.	
1946	Earl Mann, Atlanta, Southern	
1947	Wm. Purnhage, Waterloo, I.I.I.	
1948	Ed. Glennon, Bir'ham, Southern	
1949	Ted Sullivan, Indianapolis, A.A.	
1950	Cl. (Brick) Laws, Oakland, PCL	
1951	Robert Howsam, Denver, West.	
1952	Jack Cooke, Toronto, Int.	
1953	Richard Burnett, Dallas, Texas	
1954	Edward Stumpf, Indpls., A.A.	
1955	Dewey Soriano, Seattle, PCL	
1956	Robert Howsam, Denver, A.A.	
1957	John Stiglmeier, Buffalo, Int.	
1958	Ed. Glennon, Bir'ham, Southern	
1959	Ed. Leishman, Salt Lake, PCL	
1960	Ray Winder, Little Rock, Sou.	
1961	Elten Schiller, Omaha, A.A.	
1962	Geo. Sisler, Jr., Rochester, Int.	
1963	Lewis Matlin, Hawaii, PCL	
1964	Ed. Leishman, San Diego, PCL	
1965	Harold Cooper, Columbus, Int.	
1966	John Quinn, Jr., Hawaii, PCL	
1967	Hillman Lyons, Richmond, Int.	
1968	Gabe Paul, Jr., Tulsa, PCL	
1969	Bill Gardner, Louisville, Int.	
1970	Dick King, Wichita, A.A.	
1971	Carl Steinfeldt, Jr., Roch'ter, Int.	
1972	Don Labbruzzo, Evansville, A.A.	
1973	Merle Miller, Tucson, PCL	
1974	John Carbray, Sacramento, PCL	
1975	Stan Naccarato, Tacoma, PCL	
1976	Art Teece, Salt Lake City, PCL	
1977	George Sisler, Jr., Col'bus, Int.	
1978	Willie Sanchez, Albu'que, PCL	
1979	George Sisler, Jr., Col'bus, Int.	
1980	Jim Burris, Denver, A.A.	
1981	Pat McKernan, Albuquerque, PCL	
1982	A. Ray Smith, Louisville, A.A.	
1983	A. Ray Smith, Louisville, A.A.	
1984	Mike Tamburro, Pawtucket, Int.	
1985	Patty Cox Hampton, Okla City, A.A.	
1986	Bob Goughan, Rochester, Int.	
1987	Stu Kehoe, Vancouver PCL	
1988	Bob Rich, Buffalo, A.A.	
1989	Larry Schmittou, Nashville, A.A.	
1990	Greg Corns, Phoenix PCL	

MINOR LEAGUE EXECUTIVE (LOWER CLASSIFICATIONS)
(Separate Awards for Class AA and Class A Started in 1963; for Short Class A in 1988)

Year	Executive	Club
1950	H. Cooper, Hutch'son, West. A.	
1951	O. W. (Bill) Hayes, T'ple, B.S.	
1952	Hillman Lyons, Danville, MOV	
1953	Carl Roth, Peoria, III	
1954	James Meaghan, Cedar R., III	
1955	John Petrakis, Dubuque, MOV	
1956	Marvin Milkes, Fresno, Calif.	
1957	Richard Wagner, L'coln, West.	
1958	Gerald Waring, Macon, Sally	
1959	Clay Dennis, Des Moines, III	
1960	Hubert Kittle, Yakima, Northw.	
1961	David Steele, Fresno, California	
1962	John Quinn, Jr., S. Jose, Calif.	
1963	Hugh Finnerty, Tulsa, Texas	
	Ben Jewell, M. Valley, Pioneer	
1964	Glynn West, Birmingham, Sou.	
	Jas. Bayens, Rock Hill, W. Car.	
1965	Dick Butler, Dallas-Ft.W., Tex.	
	Ken. Blackman, Quad C., Midw.	
1966	Tom Fleming, Evansville, South.	
	Cappy Harada, Lodi, California	
1967	Robt. Quinn, Reading, East.	
	Pat Williams, Spar'burg, W. C.	
1968	Phil Howser, Charlotte, South.	
	Merle Miller, Burlington, Midw.	

MINOR LEAGUE EXECUTIVE (LOWER CLASSIFICATIONS) —Cont.

Year	Executive	Club
1969—	Charlie Blaney, Albuq., Texas	
	Bill Gorman, Visalia, Calif.	
1970—	Carl Sawatski, Arkansas, Texas	
	Bob Williams, Bakersfield, Calif.	
1971—	Miles Wolff, Savannah, Dixie A.	
	Ed Holtz, Appleton, Midwest	
1972—	John Begzos, S. Antonio, Texas	
	Bob Piccinini, Modesto, Calif.	
1973—	Dick Kravitz, Jacksonville, Sou.	
	Fritz Colschen, Clinton, Midw.	
1974—	Jim Paul, El Paso, Texas	
	Bing Russell, Portland, N'west	
1975—	Jim Paul, El Paso, Texas	
	Cordy Jensen, Eugene, N'west	
1976—	Woodrow Reid, Chat'ooga, Sou.	
	Don Buchheister, Ced. Rap., Mid.	
1977—	Jim Paul, El Paso, Texas	
	Harry Pells, Quad Cities, Midw.	
1978—	Larry Schmittou, Nashville, Sou.	
	Dave Hersh, Appleton, Midwest	
1979—	Bill Rigney Jr., Midland, Tex.	
	Tom Romenesko, G'sboro, W.C.	
1980—	Frances Crockett, C'lotte, Sou.	
	Tom Romenesko, G'sboro, W.C.	

Year	Executive	Club
1981—	Allie Prescott, Memphis, Southern	
	Dan Overstreet, Hagerstown, Caro.	
1982—	Art Clarkson, Birmingham, Sou.	
	Bob Carruesco, Stockton, Calif.	
1983—	Edward Kenney, New Britain, East.	
	Terry Reynolds, Vero Beach, Fla. St.	
1984—	Bruce Baldwin, Greenville, Sou.	
	Dave Tarrolly, Beloit, Midwest	
1985—	Ben Bernard, Albany-Colonie, Eastern	
	Pete Vonachen, Peoria, Midwest	
1986—	Bill Davidson, Midland, Texas	
	Rob Dlugozima, Durham, Carolina	
1987—	Joe Preseren, Tulsa, Texas	
	Skip Weisman, Greensboro, So. Atl.	
1988—	Bill Valentine, Arkansas, Texas	
	Dennis Bastien, Charleston, W.V., S. At.	
1989—	Chuck Domino, Reading, Eastern	
	John Baxter, South Bend, Midwest	
	Bill Pereira, Boise, Northwest	
1990—	Joe Preseren, Tulsa, Texas	
	Dan Chapman, Stockton, Calif.	
	Dave Baggott, Salt Lake City, Pion.	

MINOR LEAGUE MANAGER

Year	Manager	Club
1936—	Al Sothoron, Milwaukee, A.A.	
1937—	Jake Flowers, Salis'y, East. Sh.	
1938—	Paul Richards, Atlanta, South.	
1939—	Bill Meyer, Kansas City, A.A.	
1940—	Larry Gilbert, Nashville, South.	
1941—	Burt Shotton, Columbus, A.A.	
1942—	Eddie Dyer, Columbus, A.A.	
1943—	Nick Cullop, Columbus, A.A.	
1944—	Al Thomas, Baltimore, Int.	
1945—	Lefty O'Doul, San Fran., PCL	
1946—	Clay Hopper, Montreal, Int.	
1947—	Nick Cullop, Milwaukee, A.A.	
1948—	Casey Stengel, Oakland, PCL	
1949—	Fred Haney, Hollywood, PCL	
1950—	Rollie Hemsley, Columbus, A.A.	
1951—	Charlie Grimm, Milw., A.A.	
1952—	Luke Appling, Memphis, South.	
1953—	Bobby Bragan, Hollywood, PCL	
1954—	Kerby Farrell, Indpls., A.A.	
1955—	Bill Rigney, Minneapolis, A.A.	
1956—	Kerby Farrell, Indpls., A.A.	
1957—	Ben Geraghty, Wichita, A.A.	
1958—	Cal Ermer, Birmingham, South.	
1959—	Pete Reiser, Victoria, Texas	
1960—	Mel McGaha, Toronto, Int.	
1961—	Kerby Farrell, Buffalo, Int.	
1962—	Ben Geraghty, Jackson'le, Int.	
1963—	Rollie Hemsley, Indpls., Int.	

Year	Manager	Club
1964—	Harry Walker, Jacks'vle., Int.	
1965—	Grady Hatton, Okla. City, PCL	
1966—	Bob Lemon, Seattle, PCL	
1967—	Bob Skinner, San Diego, PCL	
1968—	Jack Tighe, Toledo, Int.	
1969—	Clyde McCullough, Tide., Int.	
1970—	Tom Lasorda, Spokane, PCL	
1971—	Del Rice, Salt Lake City, PCL	
1972—	Hank Bauer, Tidewater, Int.	
1973—	Joe Morgan, Charleston, Int.	
1974—	Joe Altobelli, Rochester, Int.	
1975—	Joe Frazier, Tidewater, Int.	
1976—	Vern Rapp, Denver, A.A.	
1977—	Tommy Thompson, Arkan., Tex.	
1978—	Les Moss, Evansville, A.A.	
1979—	Vern Benson, Syracuse, Int.	
1980—	Hal Lanier, Springfield, A.A.	
1981—	Del Crandall, Albuquerque, PCL	
1982—	George Scherger, Indianapolis, A.A.	
1983—	Bill Dancy, Reading, East.	
1984—	Bob Rodgers, Indianapolis, A.A.	
1985—	Jim Fregosi, Louisville, A.A.	
1986—	Joe Sparks, Indianapolis, A.A.	
1987—	Terry Collins, Albuquerque, PCL	
1988—	Joe Sparks, Indianapolis, A.A.	
1989—	Bob Bailor, Syracuse, Int.	
1990—	Sal Rende, Omaha, A.A.	

MINOR LEAGUE PLAYER

Year	Player	Club
1936—	Jn. Vander Meer, Durham, Pied.	
1937—	Charlie Keller, Newark, Int.	
1938—	Fred Hutchinson, Seattle, PCL	
1939—	Lou Novikoff, Tulsa-Los A'les.	
1940—	Phil Rizzuto, Kansas City, A.A.	
1941—	John Lindell, Newark, Int.	
1942—	Dick Barrett, Seattle, PCL	
1943—	Chet Covington, Scranton, East.	
1944—	Rip Collins, Albany, Eastern	
1945—	Gil Coan, Chattanooga, South.	
1946—	Sibby Sisti, Indianapolis, A.A.	
1947—	Hank Sauer, Syracuse, Int.	
1948—	Gene Woodling, S. F., PCL	
1949—	Orie Arntzen, Albany, Eastern	
1950—	Frank Saucier, San Ant'o, Tex.	
1951—	Gene Conley, Hartford, Eastern	
1952—	Bill Skowron, Kans. City, A.A.	

Year	Player	Club
1953—	Gene Conley, Toledo, A.A.	
1954—	Herb Score, Indianapolis, A.A.	
1955—	John Murff, Dallas, Texas	
1956—	Steve Bilko, Los Angeles, PCL	
1957—	Norm Siebern, Denver, A.A.	
1958—	Jim O'Toole, Nashville, South.	
1959—	Frank Howard, Victoria-Spok.	
1960—	Willie Davis, Spokane, PCL	
1961—	Howie Koplitz, Bir'ham, South.	
1962—	Bob Bailey, Columbus, Int.	
1963—	Don Buford, Indianapolis, Int.	
1964—	Mel Stottlemyre, Richm'd., Int.	
1965—	Joe Foy, Toronto, International	
1966—	Mike Epstein, Rochester, Int.	
1967—	Johnny Bench, Buffalo, Int.	
1968—	Merv Rettenmund, Roch'ter, Int.	
1969—	Danny Walton, Okla. City, A.A.	

MINOR LEAGUE PLAYER —Continued

Year	Player	Club
1970—Don Baylor, Rochester, Int.		
1971—Bobby Grich, Rochester, Int.		
1972—Tom Paciorek, Albuq'que, PCL		
1973—Steve Ontiveros, Phoenix, PCL		
1974—Jim Rice, Pawtucket, Int.		
1975—Hector Cruz, Tulsa, A.A.		
1976—Pat Putnam, Asheville, W. Car.		
1977—Ken Landreaux, S.L.C., PCL-El Paso, Tex.		
1978—Champ Summers, Indi'polis, A.A.		
1979—Mark Bomback, Vancouver, PCL		
1980—Tim Raines, Denver, A.A.		

Year	Player	Club
1981—Mike Marshall, Albuquerque, PCL		
1982—Ron Kittle, Edmonton, PCL		
1983—Kevin McReynolds, Las Vegas, PCL		
1984—Alan Knicely, Wichita, A.A.		
1985—Jose Canseco, Hunt., Sou.-Tac., PCL		
1986—Tim Pyznarski, Las Vegas, PCL		
1987—Randy Milligan, Tidewater, Int.		
1988—Sandy Alomar, Jr., Las Vegas, PCL (tie)		
Gary Sheffield, Denver, A.A. (tie)		
1989—Sandy Alomar, Jr., Las Vegas, PCL		
1990—Jose Offerman, Albuquerque, PCL		

Major League All-Star Teams

1925

Bottomley, St. Louis NL	1B
Hornsby, St. Louis NL	2B
Wright, Pittsburgh NL	SS
Traynor, Pittsburgh NL	3B
Cuyler, Pittsburgh NL	OF
Carey, Pittsburgh NL	OF
Goslin, Washington AL	OF
Cochrane, Philadelphia AL	C
Johnson, Washington AL	P
Rommel, Philadelphia AL	P
Vance, Brooklyn NL	P

1926

G. Burns, Cleve. AL
Hornsby, St. Louis NL
J. Sewell, Cleve. AL
Traynor, Pittsburgh NL
Goslin, Wash'ton AL
Mostil, Chicago AL
Ruth, New York AL
O'Farrell, St. Louis NL
Pennock, N. Y. AL
Uhle, Cleveland AL
Alexander, St. L. NL

1927

1B—Gehrig, N. Y. AL
2B—Hornsby, N. Y. NL
SS—Jackson, N. Y. NL
3B—Traynor, Pitts. NL
OF—Ruth, New York AL
OF—Simmons, Phila. AL
OF—P. Waner, Pitts. NL
C—Hartnett, Chicago NL
P—Root, Chicago NL
P—Lyons, Chicago AL

1928

Gehrig, New York AL	1B
Hornsby, Boston NL	2B
Jackson, New York NL	SS
Lindstrom, N. Y. NL	3B
Ruth, New York AL	OF
Manush, St. Louis AL	OF
P. Waner, Pittsburgh NL	OF
Cochrane, Philadelphia AL	C
Grove, Philadelphia AL	P
Hoyt, New York AL	P

1929

Foxx, Phila'phia AL
Hornsby, Chicago NL
Jackson, N. Y. NL
Traynor, Pittsb'gh NL
Simmons, Phila. AL
L. Wilson, Chi. NL
Ruth, New York AL
Cochrane, Phila. AL
Grove, Phila'phia AL
Grimes, Pittsburgh NL

1930

1B—Terry, New York NL
2B—Frisch, St. Louis NL
SS—Cronin, Wash'ton AL
3B—Lindstrom, N. Y. NL
OF—Simmons, Phila. AL
OF—L. Wilson, Chi. NL
OF—Ruth, New York AL
C—Cochrane, Phila AL
P—Grove, Phila'phia AL
P—W. Ferrell, Cleve. AL

1931

Gehrig, New York AL	1B
Frisch, St. Louis NL	2B
Cronin, Washington AL	SS
Traynor, Pittsburgh NL	3B
Simmons, Philadelphia AL	OF
Averill, Cleveland AL	OF
Ruth, New York AL	OF
Cochrane, Philadelphia AL	C
Grove, Philadelphia AL	P
Earnshaw, Philadelphia AL	P

1932

Foxx, Phila'phia AL
Lazzeri, N. Y. AL
Cronin, Wash'ton AL
Traynor, Pittsb'gh NL
O'Doul, Brooklyn NL
Averill, Cleveland AL
Klein, Philadelphia NL
Dickey, New York AL
Grove, Phila'phia AL
Warneke, Chicago NL

1933

1B—Foxx, Phila'phia AL
2B—Gehringer, Det. AL
SS—Cronin, Wash'ton AL
3B—Traynor, Pitts. NL
OF—Simmons, Chi. AL
OF—Berger, Boston NL
OF—Klein, Phila'phia NL
C—Dickey, N. Y. AL
P—Crowder, Wash. AL
P—Hubbell, N. Y. NL

1934

Gehrig, New York AL	1B
Gehringer, Detroit AL	2B
Cronin, Washington AL	SS
Higgins, Philadelphia AL	3B
Simmons, Chicago AL	OF
Averill, Cleveland AL	OF
Ott, New York NL	OF
Cochrane, Detroit AL	C
Gomez, New York AL	P
Rowe, Detroit AL	P
J. Dean, St. Louis NL	P

1935

Greenberg, Det. AL
Gehringer, Det. AL
Vaughan, Pitts. NL
J. Martin, St. L. NL
Medwick, St. L. NL
Cramer, Phila. AL
Ott, New York NL
Cochrane, Detroit AL
Hubbell, N. Y. NL
J. Dean, St. Louis NL

1936

1B—Gehrig, New York AL
2B—Gehringer, Det. AL
SS—Appling, Chicago AL
3B—Higgins, Phila. AL
OF—Medwick, St. L. NL
OF—Averill, Cleve. AL
OF—Ott, New York NL
C—Dickey, N. Y. AL
P—Hubbell, N. Y. NL
P—J. Dean, St. Louis NL

1937

Gehrig, New York AL	1B
Gehringer, Detroit AL	2B
Bartell, New York NL	SS
Rolfe, New York AL	3B
Medwick, St. Louis NL	OF
J. DiMaggio, New York AL	OF
P. Waner, Pittsburgh NL	OF
Hartnett, Chicago NL	C
Hubbell, New York NL	P
Ruffing, New York AL	P

1938

Foxx, Boston AL
Gehringer, Detroit AL
Cronin, Boston AL
Rolfe, New York AL
Medwick, St. Louis NL
J. DiMaggio, N. Y. AL
Ott, New York NL
Dickey, New York AL
Ruffing, New York AL
Gomez, New York AL
Vander Meer, Cin. NL

1939

1B—Foxx, Boston AL
2B—Gordon, N. Y. AL
SS—Cronin, Boston AL
3B—Rolfe, New York AL
OF—Medwick, St. L. NL
OF—J. DiMaggio, N. Y. AL
OF—Williams, Boston AL
C—Dickey, N. Y. AL
P—Ruffing, N. Y. AL
P—Feller, Cleveland AL
P—Walters, Cin. NL

1940

F. McCormick, Cin. NL	1B
Gordon, New York AL	2B
Appling, Chicago AL	SS
Hack, Chicago NL	3B
Greenberg, Detroit AL	OF
J. DiMaggio, New York AL	OF
Williams, Boston AL	OF
Danning, New York NL	C
Feller, Cleveland AL	P
Walters, Cincinnati NL	P
Derringer, Cincinnati NL	P

1941

Camilli, Brooklyn NL	
Gordon, N. Y. AL	
Travis, Wash'ton, AL	
Hack, Chicago NL	
Williams, Boston AL	
J. DiMaggio, N. Y. AL	
Reiser, Brooklyn NL	
Dickey, New York AL	
Feller, Cleveland AL	
Wyatt, Brooklyn NL	
Lee, Chicago NL	

1942

1B—Mize, New York NL	
2B—Gordon, N. Y. AL	
SS—Pesky, Boston AL	
3B—Hack, Chicago NL	
OF—Williams, Boston AL	
OF—J. DiMaggio, N. Y. AL	
OF—Slaughter, St. L. NL	
C—Owen, Brooklyn NL	
P—M. Cooper, St. L. NL	
P—Bonham, N. Y. AL	
P—Hughson, Boston AL	

1943

York, Detroit AL	1B
Herman, Brooklyn NL	2B
Appling, Chicago AL	SS
Johnson, New York AL	3B
Wakefield, Detroit AL	OF
Musial, St. Louis NL	OF
Nicholson, Chicago NL	OF
W. Cooper, St. Louis NL	C
Chandler, New York AL	P
M. Cooper, St. Louis NL	P
Sewell, Pittsburgh NL	P

1944

Sanders, St. Louis NL	
Doerr, Boston AL	
Marion, St. Louis NL	
Elliott, Pittsburgh NL	
Musial, St. Louis NL	
Wakefield, Detroit AL	
F. Walker, Brkn, NL	
W. Cooper, St. L. NL	
Newhouser, Det. AL	
M. Cooper, St. L. NL	
Trout, Detroit AL	

1945

1B—Cavarretta, Chi. NL	
2B—Stirnweiss, N. Y. AL	
SS—Marion, St. Louis NL	
3B—Kurowski, St. L. NL	
OF—Holmes, Boston NL	
OF—Pafko, Chicago NL	
OF—Rosen, Brooklyn NL	
C—Richards, Detroit AL	
P—Newhouser, Det. AL	
P—Ferriss, Boston AL	
P—Borowy, Chicago NL	

1946

Musial, St. Louis NL	1B
Doerr, Boston AL	2B
Pesky, Boston AL	SS
Kell, Detroit AL	3B
Williams, Boston AL	OF
D. DiMaggio, Boston AL	OF
Slaughter, St. Louis NL	OF
Robinson, New York AL	C
Newhouser, Detroit AL	P
Feller, Cleveland AL	P
Ferriss, Boston AL	P

1947

Mize, New York NL	
Gordon, Cleveland AL	
Boudreau, Cleve. AL	
Kell, Detroit AL	
Williams, Boston AL	
J. DiMaggio, N. Y. AL	
Kiner, Pittsburgh NL	
W. Cooper, N. Y. NL	
Blackwell, Cin. NL	
Feller, Cleveland AL	
Branca, Brooklyn NL	

1948

1B—Mize, New York NL	
2B—Gordon, Cleve. AL	
SS—Boudreau, Cleve. AL	
3B—Elliott, Boston NL	
OF—Williams, Boston AL	
OF—J. DiMaggio, N. Y. AL	
OF—Musial, St. Louis NL	
C—Tebbetts, Boston AL	
P—Sain, Boston NL	
P—Lemon, Cleveland AL	
P—Brecheen, St. L. NL	

1949

Henrich, New York AL	1B
Robinson, Brooklyn NL	2B
Rizzuto, New York AL	SS
Kell, Detroit AL	3B
Williams, Boston AL	OF
Musial, St. Louis NL	OF
Kiner, Pittsburgh NL	OF
Campanella, Brooklyn NL	C
Parnell, Boston AL	P
Kinder, Boston AL	P
Page, New York AL	P

1950

Dropo, Boston AL	
Robinson, Brkn. NL	
Rizzuto, New York AL	
Kell, Detroit AL	
Musial, St. Louis NL	
Kiner, Pittsburgh NL	
Doby, Cleveland AL	
Berra, New York AL	
Raschi, New York AL	
Lemon, Cleveland AL	
Konstanty, Phila. NL	

1951

1B—Fain, Phila. AL	
2B—Robinson, Brkn. NL	
SS—Rizzuto, N. Y. AL	
3B—Kell, Detroit AL	
OF—Musial, St. Louis NL	
OF—Williams, Boston AL	
OF—Kiner, Pittsburgh NL	
C—Campanella, Brkn. NL	
P—Maglie, N. Y. NL	
P—Roe, Brooklyn NL	
P—Reynolds, N. Y. AL	

1952

Fain, Philadelphia AL	1B
Robinson, Brooklyn NL	2B
Rizzuto, New York AL	SS
Kell, Boston AL	3B
Musial, St. Louis NL	OF
Sauer, Chicago NL	OF
Mantle, New York AL	OF
Berra, New York AL	C
Roberts, Philadelphia NL	P
Shantz, Philadelphia AL	P
Reynolds, New York AL	P

1953

Vernon, Wash'ton AL	
Schoendienst, St. L. NL	
Reese, Brooklyn NL	
Rosen, Cleveland AL	
Musial, St. Louis NL	
Snider, Brooklyn NL	
Furillo, Brooklyn NL	
Campanella, Brkn. NL	
Roberts, Phila'phia NL	
Spahn, Milwaukee NL	
Porterfield, Wash. AL	

1954

1B—Kluszewski, Cin. NL	
2B—Avila, Cleveland AL	
SS—Dark, New York NL	
3B—Rosen, Cleveland AL	
OF—Mays, New York NL	
OF—Musial, St. Louis NL	
OF—Snider, Brooklyn NL	
C—Berra, New York AL	
P—Lemon, Cleveland AL	
P—Antonelli, N. Y. NL	
P—Roberts, Phila. NL	

1955

Kluszewski, Cincinnati NL	1B
Fox, Chicago AL	2B
Banks, Chicago NL	SS
Mathews, Milwaukee NL	3B
Snider, Brooklyn NL	OF
Williams, Boston AL	OF
Kaline, Detroit AL	OF
Campanella, Brooklyn NL	C
Roberts, Philadelphia NL	P
Newcombe, Brooklyn NL	P
Ford, New York AL	P

1956

Kluszewski, Cin. NL	
Fox, Chicago AL	
Kuenn, Detroit AL	
Boyer, St. Louis NL	
Mantle, New York AL	
Aaron, Milwaukee NL	
Williams, Boston AL	
Berra, New York AL	
Newcombe, Brkn. NL	
Ford, New York AL	
Pierce, Chicago AL	

1957

1B—Musial, St. Louis NL	
2B—Scho'st, N.Y.-Mil. NL	
SS—McDougald, N. Y. AL	
3B—Mathews, Milw. NL	
OF—Mantle, N. Y. AL	
OF—Williams, Boston AL	
OF—Mays, New York NL	
C—Berra, New York AL	
P—Spahn, Milw. NL	
P—Pierce, Chicago NL	
P—Bunning, Detroit AL	

1958

Musial, St. Louis NL.................. 1B
Fox, Chicago AL........................ 2B
Banks, Chicago NL.................... SS
Thomas, Pittsburgh NL 3B
Williams, Boston AL .... OF
Mays, San Francisco NL .... OF
Aaron, Milwaukee NL .... OF
Crandall, Milwaukee NL C
Turley, New York AL .... P
Spahn, Milwaukee NL .... P
Friend, Pittsburgh NL.............. P

1959

Cepeda, San Fran. NL
Fox, Chicago AL
Banks, Chicago NL
Mathews, Milw. NL
Minoso, Cleveland AL
Mays, San Fran. NL
Aaron, Milwaukee NL
Lollar, Chicago AL
Wynn, Chicago AL
S. Jones, S. Fran. NL
Antonelli, S. Fran. NL

1960

1B—Skowron, N. Y. AL
2B—Mazeroski, Pitts. NL
SS—Banks, Chicago NL
3B—Mathews, Milw. NL
OF—Minoso, Chicago AL
OF—Mays, San Fran. NL
OF—Maris, New York AL
C—Crandall, Milw. NL
P—Law, Pittsburgh NL
P—Spahn, Milw. NL
P—Broglio, St. Louis NL

1961—National

1B—Orlando Cepeda, S.F.
2B—Frank Bolling, Milw.
SS—Maury Wills, L.A.
3B—Ken Boyer, St. Louis
OF—Willie Mays, S.F.
OF—Frank Robinson, Cin.
OF—Roberto Clemente, Pitts.
C—Smoky Burgess, Pitts.
P—Joey Jay, Cincinnati
P—Warren Spahn, Milw.

1961—American

1B—Norm Cash, Detroit
2B—Bobby Richardson, N.Y.
SS—Tony Kubek, N.Y.
3B—Brooks Robinson, Balt.
OF—Mickey Mantle, N.Y.
OF—Roger Maris, N.Y.
OF—Rocky Colavito, Detroit
C—Elston Howard, N.Y.
P—Whitey Ford, N.Y.
P—Frank Lary, Detroit

1962—National

1B—Orlando Cepeda, S.F.
2B—Bill Mazeroski, Pitts.
SS—Maury Wills, L.A.
3B—Ken Boyer, St. Louis
OF—Tommy Davis, L.A.
OF—Willie Mays, S.F.
OF—Frank Robinson, Cin.
C—Del Crandall, Milw.
P—Don Drysdale, L.A.
P—Bob Purkey, Cin.

1962—American

1B—Norm Siebern, K.C.
2B—Bobby Richardson, N.Y.
SS—Tom Tresh, N.Y.
3B—Brooks Robinson, Balt.
OF—Leon Wagner, L.A.
OF—Mickey Mantle, N.Y.
OF—Al Kaline, Detroit
C—Earl Battey, Minnesota
P—Ralph Terry, N.Y.
P—Dick Donovan, Cleve.

1963—National

1B—Bill White, St. Louis
2B—Jim Gilliam, L.A.
SS—Dick Groat, St. Louis
3B—Ken Boyer, St. Louis
OF—Tommy Davis, L.A.
OF—Willie Mays, S.F.
OF—Hank Aaron, Milw.
C—John Edwards, Cin.
P—Sandy Koufax, L.A.
P—Juan Marichal, S.F.

1963—American

1B—Joe Pepitone, N.Y.
2B—Bobby Richardson, N.Y.
SS—Luis Aparicio, Balt.
3B—Frank Malzone, Boston
OF—Carl Yastrzemski, Boston
OF—Albie Pearson, L.A.
OF—Al Kaline, Detroit
C—Elston Howard, N.Y.
P—Whitey Ford, N.Y.
P—Gary Peters, Chicago

1964—American

1B—Dick Stuart, Boston
2B—Bobby Richardson, N.Y.
SS—Jim Fregosi, L.A.
3B—Brooks Robinson, Balt.
OF—Harmon Killebrew, Minn.
OF—Mickey Mantle, N.Y.
OF—Tony Oliva, Minn.
C—Elston Howard, N.Y.
P—Dean Chance, L.A.
P—Gary Peters, Chicago

1964—National

1B—Bill White, St. Louis
2B—Ron Hunt, New York
SS—Dick Groat, St. Louis
3B—Ken Boyer, St. Louis
OF—Billy Williams, Chicago
OF—Willie Mays, San Fran.
OF—Roberto Clemente, Pitts.
C—Joe Torre, Milwaukee
P—Sandy Koufax, L.A.
P—Jim Bunning, Phila.

1965—American

1B—Fred Whitfield, Cleveland
2B—Bobby Richardson, N.Y.
SS—Zoilo Versalles, Minnesota
3B—Brooks Robinson, Balt.
OF—Carl Yastrzemski, Boston
OF—Jimmie Hall, Minnesota
OF—Tony Oliva, Minnesota
C—Earl Battey, Minnesota
P—Jim Grant, Minnesota
P—Mel Stottlemyre, N.Y.

1965—National

1B—Willie McCovey, S.F.
2B—Pete Rose, Cincinnati
SS—Maury Wills, Los Angeles
3B—Deron Johnson, Cincinnati
OF—Willie Stargell, Pitts.
OF—Willie Mays, San Fran.
OF—Hank Aaron, Milwaukee
C—Joe Torre, Milwaukee
P—Sandy Koufax, L.A.
P—Juan Marichal, S.F.

1966—American

1B—Boog Powell, Baltimore
2B—Bobby Richardson, N.Y.
SS—Luis Aparicio, Baltimore
3B—Brooks Robinson, Balt.
OF—Frank Robinson, Balt.
OF—Al Kaline, Detroit
OF—Tony Oliva, Minnesota
C—Paul Casanova, Wash.
P—Jim Kaat, Minnesota
P—Earl Wilson, Detroit

1966—National

1B—Felipe Alou, Atlanta
2B—Pete Rose, Cincinnati
SS—Gene Alley, Pittsburgh
3B—Ron Santo, Chicago
OF—Willie Stargell, Pittsburgh
OF—Willie Mays, San Fran.
OF—Roberto Clemente, Pitts.
C—Joe Torre, Atlanta
P—Sandy Koufax, L.A.
P—Juan Marichal, S.F.

1967—American

1B—Harmon Killebrew, Minn.
2B—Rod Carew, Minnesota
SS—Jim Fregosi, California
3B—Brooks Robinson, Balt.
OF—Carl Yastrzemski, Boston
OF—Al Kaline, Detroit
OF—Frank Robinson, Balt.
C—Bill Freehan, Detroit
P—Jim Lonborg, Boston
P—Earl Wilson, Detroit

1967—National

1B—Orlando Cepeda, St. Louis
2B—Bill Mazeroski, Pittsburgh
SS—Gene Alley, Pittsburgh
3B—Ron Santo, Chicago
OF—Hank Aaron, Atlanta
OF—Jim Wynn, Houston
OF—Roberto Clemente, Pitts.
C—Tim McCarver, St. Louis
P—Mike McCormick, S.F.
P—Ferguson Jenkins, Chi.

1968—American

1B—Boog Powell, Baltimore
2B—Rod Carew, Minnesota
SS—Luis Aparicio, Chicago
3B—Brooks Robinson, Balt.
OF—Ken Harrelson, Boston
OF—Willie Horton, Detroit
OF—Frank Howard, Wash.
C—Bill Freehan, Detroit
P—Dave McNally, Balt.
P—Denny McLain, Detroit

1968—National
1B—Willie McCovey, S.F.
2B—Tommy Helms, Cincinnati
SS—Don Kessinger, Chicago
3B—Ron Santo, Chicago
OF—Billy Williams, Chicago
OF—Curt Flood, St. Louis
OF—Pete Rose, Cincinnati
C—Johnny Bench, Cincinnati
P—Bob Gibson, St. Louis
P—Juan Marichal, S.F.

1969—American
1B—Boog Powell, Baltimore
2B—Rod Carew, Minnesota
SS—Rico Petrocelli, Boston
3B—Harmon Killebrew, Minn.
OF—Frank Howard, Wash.
OF—Paul Blair, Baltimore
OF—Reggie Jackson, Oak.
C—Bill Freehan, Detroit
RHP—Denny McLain, Detroit
LHP—Mike Cuellar, Baltimore

1969—National
1B—Willie McCovey, S.F.
2B—Glenn Beckert, Chicago
SS—Don Kessinger, Chicago
3B—Ron Santo, Chicago
OF—Cleon Jones, New York
OF—Matty Alou, Pittsburgh
OF—Hank Aaron, Atlanta
C—Johnny Bench, Cincinnati
RHP—Tom Seaver, New York
LHP—Steve Carlton, St. Louis

1970—American
1B—Boog Powell, Baltimore
2B—Dave Johnson, Baltimore
SS—Luis Aparicio, Chicago
3B—Harmon Killebrew, Minn.
OF—Frank Howard, Wash.
OF—Reggie Smith, Boston
OF—Tony Oliva, Minnesota
C—Ray Fosse, Cleveland
RHP—Jim Perry, Minnesota
LHP—Sam McDowell, Cleve.

1970—National
1B—Willie McCovey, S.F.
2B—Glenn Beckert, Chicago
SS—Don Kessinger, Chicago
3B—Tony Perez, Cincinnati
OF—Billy Williams, Chicago
OF—Bobby Tolan, Cincinnati
OF—Hank Aaron, Atlanta
C—Johnny Bench, Cincinnati
RHP—Bob Gibson, St. Louis
LHP—Jim Merritt, Cincinnati

1971—American
1B—Norm Cash, Detroit
2B—Cookie Rojas, K.C.
SS—Leo Cardenas, Minnesota
3B—Brooks Robinson, Balt.
OF—Merv Rettenmund, Balt.
OF—Bobby Murcer, N.Y.
OF—Tony Oliva, Minnesota
C—Bill Freehan, Detroit
RHP—Jim Palmer, Baltimore
LHP—Vida Blue, Oakland

1971—National
1B—Lee May, Cincinnati
2B—Glenn Beckett, Chicago
SS—Bud Harrelson, New York
3B—Joe Torre, St. Louis
OF—Willie Stargell, Pittsburgh
OF—Willie Davis, Los Angeles
OF—Hank Aaron, Atlanta
C—Manny Sanguillen, Pitts.
RHP—Ferguson Jenkins, Chi.
LHP—Steve Carlton, St. Louis

1972—American
1B—Dick Allen, Chicago
2B—Rod Carew, Minnesota
SS—Luis Aparicio, Boston
3B—Brooks Robinson, Balt.
OF—Joe Rudi, Oakland
OF—Bobby Murcer, N.Y.
OF—Richie Scheinblum, K.C.
C—Carlton Fisk, Boston
RHP—Gaylord Perry, Cleveland
LHP—Wilbur Wood, Chicago

1972—National
1B—Willie Stargell, Pittsburgh
2B—Joe Morgan, Cincinnati
SS—Chris Speier, San Fran.
3B—Ron Santo, Chicago
OF—Billy Williams, Chicago
OF—Cesar Cedeno, Houston
OF—Roberto Clemente, Pitts.
C—Johnny Bench, Cincinnati
RHP—Ferguson Jenkins, Chi.
LHP—Steve Carlton, Phila.

1973—American
1B—John Mayberry, K.C.
2B—Rod Carew, Minnesota
SS—Bert Campaneris, Oak.
3B—Sal Bando, Oakland
OF—Reggie Jackson, Oak.
OF—Amos Otis, Kansas City
OF—Bobby Murcer, N.Y.
C—Thurman Munson, N.Y.
RHP—Jim Palmer, Baltimore
LHP—Ken Holtzman, Oakland

1973—National
1B—Tony Perez, Cincinnati
2B—Dave Johnson, Atlanta
SS—Bill Russell, Los Angeles
3B—Darrell Evans, Atlanta
OF—Bobby Bonds, San Fran.
OF—Cesar Cedeno, Houston
OF—Pete Rose, Cincinnati
C—Johnny Bench, Cincinnati
RHP—Tom Seaver, New York
LHP—Ron Bryant, San Fran.

1974—American
1B—Dick Allen, Chicago
2B—Rod Carew, Minnesota
SS—Bert Campaneris, Oak.
3B—Sal Bando, Oakland
OF—Joe Rudi, Oakland
OF—Paul Blair, Baltimore
OF—Jeff Burroughs, Texas
C—Thurman Munson, N.Y.
DH—Tommy Davis, Baltimore
RHP—Jim Hunter, Oakland
LHP—Mike Cuellar, Baltimore

1974—National
1B—Steve Garvey, Los Angeles
2B—Joe Morgan, Cincinnati
SS—Dave Concepcion, Cin.
3B—Mike Schmidt, Phila.
OF—Lou Brock, St. Louis
OF—Jim Wynn, Los Angeles
OF—Richie Zisk, Pittsburgh
C—Johnny Bench, Cincinnati
RHP—Andy Messersmith, L.A.
LHP—Don Gullett, Cincinnati

1975—American
1B—John Mayberry, K.C.
2B—Rod Carew, Minnesota
SS—Toby Harrah, Texas
3B—Graig Nettles, New York
OF—Jim Rice, Boston
OF—Fred Lynn, Boston
OF—Reggie Jackson, Oakland
C—Thurman Munson, N.Y.
DH—Willie Horton, Detroit
RHP—Jim Palmer, Baltimore
LHP—Jim Kaat, Chicago

1975—National
1B—Steve Garvey, Los Ang.
2B—Joe Morgan, Cincinnati
SS—Larry Bowa, Philadelphia
3B—Bill Madlock, Chicago
OF—Greg Luzinski, Phila.
OF—Al Oliver, Pittsburgh
OF—Dave Parker, Pittsburgh
C—Johnny Bench, Cincinnati
RHP—Tom Seaver, New York
LHP—Randy Jones, San Diego

1976—American
1B—Chris Chambliss, N.Y.
2B—Bobby Grich, Baltimore
3B—George Brett, K.C.
SS—Mark Belanger, Balt.
OF—Joe Rudi, Oakland
OF—Mickey Rivers, N.Y.
OF—Reggie Jackson, Balt.
C—Thurman Munson, N.Y.
DH—Hal McRae, Kansas City
RHP—Jim Palmer, Baltimore
LHP—Frank Tanana, Calif.

1976—National
1B—Willie Montanez, S.F.-Atl.
2B—Joe Morgan, Cincinnati
3B—Mike Schmidt, Phila.
SS—Dave Concepcion, Cin.
OF—George Foster, Cincinnati
OF—Cesar Cedeno, Houston
OF—Ken Griffey, Cincinnati
C—Bob Boone, Philadelphia
RHP—Don Sutton, Los Angeles
LHP—Randy Jones, San Diego

1977—American
1B—Rod Carew, Minn.
2B—Willie Randolph, N.Y.
3B—Graig Nettles, N.Y.
SS—Rick Burleson, Boston
OF—Jim Rice, Boston
OF—Larry Hisle, Minn.
OF—Bobby Bonds, Calif.
C—Carlton Fisk, Boston
DH—Hal McRae, K.C.
RHP—Nolan Ryan, Calif.
LHP—Frank Tanana, Calif.

1977—National
1B—Steve Garvey, L.A.
2B—Joe Morgan, Cincinnati
3B—Mike Schmidt, Phila.
SS—Garry Templeton, St. L.
OF—George Foster, Cin.
OF—Dave Parker, Pitts.
OF—Greg Luzinski, Phila.
C—Ted Simmons, St. Louis
RHP—Rick Reuschel, Chicago
LHP—Steve Carlton, Phila.

1978—American
1B—Rod Carew, Minnesota
2B—Frank White, K.C.
3B—Graig Nettles, N.Y.
SS—Robin Yount, Milw.
OF—Jim Rice, Boston
OF—Larry Hisle, Milw.
OF—Fred Lynn, Boston
C—Jim Sundberg, Texas
DH—Rusty Staub, Detroit
RHP—Jim Palmer, Balt.
LHP—Ron Guidry, N.Y.

1978—National
1B—Steve Garvey, L.A.
2B—Dave Lopes, Los Angeles
3B—Pete Rose, Cincinnati
SS—Larry Bowa, Phila.
OF—George Foster, Cin.
OF—Dave Parker, Pitts.
OF—Jack Clark, San Fran.
C—Ted Simmons, St. Louis
RHP—Gaylord Perry, S.D.
LHP—Vida Blue, San Fran.

1979—American
1B—Cecil Cooper, Milw.
2B—Bobby Grich, Calif.
3B—George Brett, K.C.
SS—Roy Smalley, Minn.
OF—Jim Rice, Boston
OF—Fred Lynn, Boston
OF—Ken Singleton, Balt.
C—Darrell Porter, K.C.
DH—Don Baylor, Calif.
RHP—Jim Kern, Texas
LHP—Mike Flanagan, Balt.

1979—National
1B—Keith Hernandez, St. L.
2B—Dave Lopes, Los Angeles
3B—Mike Schmidt, Phila.
SS—Garry Templeton, St. L.
OF—Dave Kingman, Chicago
OF—Omar Moreno, Pittsburgh
OF—Dave Winfield, San Diego
C—Ted Simmons, St. Louis
RHP—Joe Niekro, Houston
LHP—Steve Carlton, Phila.

1980—American
1B—Cecil Cooper, Milw.
2B—Willie Randolph, N.Y.
3B—George Brett, K.C.
SS—Robin Yount, Milw.
OF—Ben Oglivie, Milw.
OF—Al Bumbry, Baltimore
OF—Reggie Jackson, N.Y.
DH—Reggie Jackson, N.Y.
C—Rick Cerone, N.Y.
RHP—Steve Stone, Balt.
LHP—Tommy John, N.Y.

1980—National
1B—Keith Hernandez, St. L.
2B—Manny Trillo, Phila.
3B—Mike Schmidt, Phila.
SS—Garry Templeton, St. L.
OF—Dusty Baker, L.A.
OF—Cesar Cedeno, Houston
OF—George Hendrick, St. L.
C—Gary Carter, Montreal
RHP—Jim Bibby, Pittsburgh
LHP—Steve Carlton, Phila.

1981—American
1B—Cecil Cooper, Milw.
2B—Bobby Grich, Calif.
3B—Buddy Bell, Texas
SS—Rick Burleson, Calif.
OF—Rickey Henderson, Oak.
OF—Dwayne Murphy, Oak.
OF—Tony Armas, Oak.
C—Jim Sundberg, Texas
DH—Richie Zisk, Seattle
RHP—Jack Morris, Detroit
LHP—Ron Guidry, N.Y.

1981—National
1B—Pete Rose, Phila.
2B—Manny Trillo, Phila.
3B—Mike Schmidt, Phila.
SS—Dave Concepcion, Cin.
OF—George Foster, Cin.
OF—Andre Dawson, Mon.
OF—Pedro Guerrero, L.A.
C—Gary Carter, Montreal
RHP—Tom Seaver, Cincinnati
LHP—Fernando Valenzuela, L.A.

1982—American
1B—Cecil Cooper, Milw.
2B—Damaso Garcia, Tor.
3B—Doug DeCinces, Calif.
SS—Robin Yount, Milw.
OF—Dave Winfield, N.Y.
OF—Gorman Thomas, Milw.
OF—Dwight Evans, Boston
C—Lance Parrish, Detroit
DH—Hal McRae, K.C.
RHP—Dave Stieb, Toronto
LHP—Geoff Zahn, Calif.

1982—National
1B—Al Oliver, Montreal
2B—Manny Trillo, Phila.
3B—Mike Schmidt, Phila.
SS—Ozzie Smith, St. Louis
OF—Lonnie Smith, St. Louis
OF—Dale Murphy, Atlanta
OF—Pedro Guerrero, L.A.
C—Gary Carter, Montreal
RHP—Steve Rogers, Montreal
LHP—Steve Carlton, Phila.

1983—American
1B—Eddie Murray, Balt.
2B—Lou Whitaker, Detroit
3B—Wade Boggs, Boston
SS—Cal Ripken, Balt.
OF—Jim Rice, Boston
OF—Dave Winfield, N.Y.
OF—Lloyd Moseby, Toronto
C—Carlton Fisk, Chicago
DH—Greg Luzinski, Chicago
RHP—LaMarr Hoyt, Chicago
LHP—Ron Guidry, New York

1983—National
1B—George Hendrick, St. L.
2B—Glenn Hubbard, Atlanta
3B—Mike Schmidt, Phila.
SS—Dickie Thon, Houston
OF—Dale Murphy, Atlanta
OF—Andre Dawson, Montreal
OF—Tim Raines, Montreal
C—Tony Pena, Pittsburgh
RHP—John Denny, Phila.
LHP—Larry McWilliams, Pitts.

1984—American
1B—Don Mattingly, N.Y.
2B—Lou Whitaker, Detroit
3B—Buddy Bell, Texas
SS—Cal Ripken, Baltimore
OF—Tony Armas, Boston
OF—Dwight Evans, Boston
OF—Dave Winfield, N.Y.
C—Lance Parrish, Detroit
DH—Dave Kingman, Oak.
RHP—Mike Boddicker, Balt.
LHP—Willie Hernandez, Det.

1984—National
1B—Keith Hernandez, N.Y.
2B—Ryne Sandberg, Chicago
3B—Mike Schmidt, Phila.
SS—Ozzie Smith, St. Louis
OF—Dale Murphy, Atlanta
OF—Jose Cruz, Houston
OF—Tony Gwynn, S.D.
C—Gary Carter, Montreal
RHP—Rick Sutcliffe, Chicago
LHP—Mark Thurmond, S.D.

1985—American
1B—Don Mattingly, N.Y.
2B—Damaso Garcia, Tor.
3B—Wade Boggs, Boston
SS—Cal Ripken, Balt.
OF—Rickey Henderson, N.Y.
OF—Harold Baines, Chicago
OF—Phil Bradley, Seattle
C—Carlton Fisk, Chicago
DH—Don Baylor, New York
RHP—Bret Saberhagen, K.C.
LHP—Ron Guidry, New York

1985—National
1B—Keith Hernandez, N.Y.
2B—Tom Herr, St. Louis
3B—Tim Wallach, Mon.
SS—Ozzie Smith, St. L.
OF—Dave Parker, Cin.
OF—Willie McGee, St. L.
OF—Dale Murphy, Atlanta
C—Gary Carter, N.Y.
RHP—Dwight Gooden, N.Y.
LHP—John Tudor, St. Louis

1986—American
1B—Don Mattingly, N.Y.
2B—Tony Bernazard, Cleve.
3B—Wade Boggs, Boston
SS—Tony Fernandez, Tor.
OF—Jim Rice, Boston
OF—George Bell, Toronto
OF—Kirby Puckett, Minn.
C—Rich Gedman, Boston
DH—Don Baylor, Boston
RHP—Roger Clemens, Boston
LHP—Teddy Higuera, Milw.

1986—National
1B—Keith Hernandez, N.Y.
2B—Steve Sax, L.A.
3B—Mike Schmidt, Phila.
SS—Ozzie Smith, St. Louis
OF—Tim Raines, Montreal
OF—Tony Gwynn, San Diego
OF—Dave Parker, Cincinnati
C—Gary Carter, New York
RHP—Mike Scott, Hou.
LHP—Fernando Valenzuela, L.A.

1987—American
1B—Don Mattingly, N.Y.
2B—Willie Randolph, N.Y.
3B—Wade Boggs, Boston
SS—Alan Trammell, Det.
OF—George Bell, Toronto
OF—Kirby Puckett, Minn.
OF—Dwight Evans, Bos.
C—Matt Nokes, Detroit
DH—Paul Molitor, Milw.
RHP—Roger Clemens, Bos.
LHP—Jimmy Key, Toronto

1987—National
1B—Jack Clark, St. Louis
2B—Juan Samuel, Philadelphia
3B—Tim Wallach, Montreal
SS—Ozzie Smith, St. Louis
OF—Andre Dawson, Chicago
OF—Tony Gwynn, San Diego
OF—Eric Davis, Cincinnati
C—Benito Santiago, S.D.
RHP—Rick Sutcliffe, Chicago
LHP—Zane Smith, Atlanta

1988—American
1B—George Brett, K.C.
2B—Johnny Ray, Calif.
3B—Wade Boggs, Boston
SS—Alan Trammell, Det.
OF—Kirby Puckett, Minn.
OF—Mike Greenwell, Bos.
OF—Jose Canseco, Oakland
C—Ernie Whitt, Toronto
DH—Harold Baines, Chi.
RHP—Dave Stewart, Oak.
LHP—Frank Viola, Minn.

1988—National
1B—Will Clark, S.F.
2B—Ryne Sandberg, Chi.
3B—Bobby Bonilla, Pitt.
SS—Barry Larkin, Cin.
OF—Darryl Strawberry, N.Y.
OF—Andy Van Slyke, Pitt.
OF—Kevin McReynolds, N.Y.
C—Mike LaValliere, Pitt.
RHP—Orel Hershiser, L.A.
LHP—Danny Jackson, Cin.

1989—American
1B—Fred McGriff, Tor.
2B—Julio Franco, Tex.
3B—Carney Lansford, Oak.
SS—Cal Ripken, Balt.
OF—Ruben Sierra, Tex.
OF—Kirby Puckett, Minn.
OF—Robin Yount, Milw.
C—Mickey Tettleton, Balt.
DH—Harold Baines, Chi.-Tex.
RHP—Bret Saberhagen, K.C.
LHP—Chuck Finley, Calif.

1989—National
1B—Will Clark, S.F.
2B—Ryne Sandberg, Chi.
3B—Howard Johnson, N.Y.
SS—Shawon Dunston, Chi.
OF—Tony Gwynn, San Diego
OF—Kevin Mitchell, S.F.
OF—Eric Davis, Cincinnati
C—Benito Santiago, S.D.
RHP—Mike Scott, Houston
LHP—Mark Davis, San Diego

1990—American
1B—Cecil Fielder, Det.
2B—Julio Franco, Tex.
3B—Kelly Gruber, Tor.
SS—Alan Trammell, Det.
OF—Rickey Henderson, Oak.
OF—Jose Canseco, Oak.
OF—Ellis Burks, Bos.
C—Carlton Fisk, Chi.
DH—Dave Parker, Milw.
RHP—Bob Welch, Oak.
LHP—Chuck Finley, Calif.

1990—National
1B—Eddie Murray, L.A.
2B—Ryne Sandberg, Chi.
3B—Matt Williams, S.F.
SS—Barry Larkin, Cin.
OF—Barry Bonds, Pitt.
OF—Bobby Bonilla, Pitt.
OF—Darryl Strawberry, N.Y.
C—Mike Scioscia, L.A.
RHP—Doug Drabek, Pitt.
LHP—Frank Viola, N.Y.

Gold Glove Fielding Teams

1957 Majors
P—Shantz, N.Y. AL
C—Lollar, Chicago AL
1B—Hodges, Brooklyn
2B—Fox, Chicago AL
3B—Malzone, Boston
SS—McMillan, Cin.
OF—Minoso, Chicago AL
OF—Mays, N.Y. NL
OF—Kaline, Detroit

1958 American
P—Shantz, New York
C—Lollar, Chicago
1B—Power, Cleveland
2B—Bolling, Detroit
3B—Malzone, Boston
SS—Aparicio, Chicago
OF—Siebern, New York
OF—Piersall, Boston
OF—Kaline, Detroit

1958 National
P—Haddix, Cincinnati
C—Crandall, Milwaukee
1B—Hodges, Los Angeles
2B—Mazeroski, Pitt.
3B—Boyer, St. Louis
SS—McMillan, Cin.
OF—Robinson, Cin.
OF—Mays, San Fran.
OF—Aaron, Milwaukee

1959 American
P—Shantz, New York
C—Lollar, Chicago
1B—Power, Cleveland
2B—Fox, Chicago
3B—Malzone, Boston
SS—Aparicio, Chicago
OF—Minoso, Cleveland
OF—Kaline, Detroit
OF—Jensen, Boston

1959 National
P—Haddix, Pittsburgh
C—Crandall, Milwaukee
1B—Hodges, Los Angeles
2B—Neal, Los Angeles
3B—Boyer, St. Louis
SS—McMillan, Cincinnati
OF—Brandt, San Fran.
OF—Mays, San Francisco
OF—Aaron, Milwaukee

1960 American
P—Shantz, New York
C—Battey, Washington
1B—Power, Cleveland
2B—Fox, Chicago
3B—Robinson, Baltimore
SS—Aparicio, Chicago
OF—Minoso, Chicago
OF—Landis, Chicago
OF—Maris, New York

1960 National
P—Haddix, Pittsburgh
C—Crandall, Milwaukee
1B—White, St. Louis
2B—Mazeroski, Pittsburgh
3B—Boyer, St. Louis
SS—Banks, Chicago
OF—Moon, Los Angeles
OF—Mays, San Francisco
OF—Aaron, Milwaukee

1961 American
P—Lary, Detroit
C—Battey, Chicago
1B—Power, Cleveland
2B—Richardson, N.Y.
3B—Robinson, Baltimore
SS—Aparicio, Chicago
OF—Kaline, Detroit
OF—Piersall, Cleveland
OF—Landis, Chicago

1961 National
P—Shantz, Pittsburgh
C—Roseboro, Los Angeles
1B—White, St. Louis
2B—Mazeroski, Pittsburgh
3B—Boyer, St. Louis
SS—Wills, Los Angeles
OF—Mays, San Francisco
OF—Clemente, Pittsburgh
OF—Pinson, Cincinnati

1962 American
P—Kaat, Minnesota
C—Battey, Minnesota
1B—Power, Minnesota
2B—Richardson, N.Y.
3B—Robinson, Baltimore
SS—Aparicio, Chicago
OF—Landis, Chicago
OF—Mantle, New York
OF—Kaline, Detroit

1962 National
P—Shantz, St. Louis
C—Crandall, Milwaukee
1B—White, St. Louis
2B—Hubbs, Chicago
3B—Davenport, S.F.
SS—Wills, Los Angeles
OF—Mays, San Francisco
OF—Clemente, Pittsburgh
OF—Virdon, Pittsburgh

1963 American
P—Kaat, Minnesota
C—Howard, New York
1B—Power, Minnesota
2B—Richardson, N.Y.
3B—Robinson, Baltimore
SS—Versalles, Minnesota
OF—Kaline, Detroit
OF—Yastrzemski, Boston
OF—Landis, Chicago

1963 National
P—Shantz, St. Louis
C—Edwards, Cincinnati
1B—White, St. Louis
2B—Mazeroski, Pittsburgh
3B—Boyer, St. Louis
SS—Wine, Philadelphia
OF—Mays, San Francisco
OF—Clemente, Pittsburgh
OF—Flood, St. Louis

1964 American
P—Kaat, Minnesota
C—Howard, New York
1B—Power, Los Angeles
2B—Richardson, N.Y.
3B—Robinson, Baltimore
SS—Aparicio, Baltimore
OF—Kaline, Detroit
OF—Landis, Chicago
OF—Davalillo, Cleveland

1964 National
P—Shantz, Philadelphia
C—Edwards, Cincinnati
1B—White, St. Louis
2B—Mazeroski, Pittsburgh
3B—Santo, Chicago
SS—Amaro, Philadelphia
OF—Mays, San Francisco
OF—Clemente, Pittsburgh
OF—Flood, St. Louis

1965 American
P—Kaat, Minnesota
C—Freehan, Detroit
1B—Pepitone, New York
2B—Richardson, N.Y.
3B—Robinson, Baltimore
SS—Versalles, Minnesota
OF—Kaline, Detroit
OF—Tresh, New York
OF—Yastrzemski, Boston

1965 National
P—Gibson, St. Louis
C—Torre, Atlanta
1B—White, St. Louis
2B—Mazeroski, Pittsburgh
3B—Santo, Chicago
SS—Cardenas, Cincinnati
OF—Mays, San Francisco
OF—Clemente, Pittsburgh
OF—Flood, St. Louis

1966 American
P—Kaat, Minnesota
C—Freehan, Detroit
1B—Pepitone, New York
2B—Knoop, California
3B—B. Robinson, Balt.
SS—Aparicio, Baltimore
OF—Kaline, Detroit
OF—Agee, Chicago
OF—Oliva, Minnesota

1966 National
P—Gibson, St. Louis
C—Roseboro, Los Angeles
1B—White, Philadelphia
2B—Mazeroski, Pittsburgh
3B—Santo, Chicago
SS—Alley, Pittsburgh
OF—Mays, San Francisco
OF—Flood, St. Louis
OF—Clemente, Pittsburgh

1967 American
P—Kaat, Minnesota
C—Freehan, Detroit
1B—Scott, Boston
2B—Knoop, California
3B—B. Robinson, Balt.
SS—Fregosi, California
OF—Yastrzemski, Boston
OF—Blair, Baltimore
OF—Kaline, Detroit

1967 National
P—Gibson, St. Louis
C—Hundley, Chicago
1B—Parker, Los Angeles
2B—Mazeroski, Pittsburgh
3B—Santo, Chicago
SS—Alley, Pittsburgh
OF—Clemente, Pittsburgh
OF—Flood, St. Louis
OF—Mays, San Francisco

1968 American
P—Kaat, Minnesota
C—Freehan, Detroit
1B—Scott, Boston
2B—Knoop, California
3B—B. Robinson, Balt.
SS—Aparicio, Chicago
OF—Stanley, Detroit
OF—Yastrzemski, Boston
OF—Smith, Boston

1968 National
P—Gibson, St. Louis
C—Bench, Cincinnati
1B—Parker, Los Angeles
2B—Beckert, Chicago
3B—Santo, Chicago
SS—Maxvill, St. Louis
OF—Mays, San Francisco
OF—Clemente, Pittsburgh
OF—Flood, St. Louis

1969 American
P—Kaat, Minnesota
C—Freehan, Detroit
1B—Pepitone, New York
2B—Johnson, Baltimore
3B—B. Robinson, Balt.
SS—Belanger, Baltimore
OF—Blair, Baltimore
OF—Stanley, Detroit
OF—Yastrzemski, Boston

1969 National
P—Gibson, St. Louis
C—Bench, Cincinnati
1B—Parker, Los Angeles
2B—Millan, Atlanta
3B—Boyer, Atlanta
SS—Kessinger, Chicago
OF—Clemente, Pittsburgh
OF—Flood, St. Louis
OF—Rose, Cincinnati

1970 American
P—Kaat, Minnesota
C—Fosse, Cleveland
1B—Spencer, California
2B—Johnson, Baltimore
3B—B. Robinson, Balt.
SS—Aparicio, Chicago
OF—Stanley, Detroit
OF—Blair, Baltimore
OF—Berry, Chicago

1970 National
P—Gibson, St. Louis
C—Bench, Cincinnati
1B—Parker, Los Angeles
2B—Helms, Cincinnati
3B—Rader, Houston
SS—Kessinger, Chicago
OF—Clemente, Pittsburgh
OF—Agee, New York
OF—Rose, Cincinnati

1971 American
P—Kaat, Minnesota
C—Fosse, Cleveland
1B—Scott, Boston
2B—Johnson, Baltimore
3B—B. Robinson, Balt.
SS—Belanger, Baltimore
OF—Blair, Baltimore
OF—Otis, Kansas City
OF—Yastrzemski, Boston

1971 National
P—Gibson, St. Louis
C—Bench, Cincinnati
1B—Parker, Los Angeles
2B—Helms, Cincinnati
3B—Rader, Houston
SS—Harrelson, New York
OF—Clemente, Pittsburgh
OF—Bonds, San Francisco
OF—Davis, Los Angeles

1972 American
P—Kaat, Minnesota
C—Fisk, Boston
1B—Scott, Milwaukee
2B—Griffin, Boston
3B—Robinson, Baltimore
SS—Brinkman, Detroit
OF—Blair, Baltimore
OF—Murcer, New York
OF—Berry, California

1972 National
P—Gibson, St. Louis
C—Bench, Cincinnati
1B—Parker, Los Angeles
2B—Millan, Atlanta
3B—Rader, Houston
SS—Bowa, Philadelphia
OF—Clemente, Pittsburgh
OF—Cedeno, Houston
OF—Davis, Los Angeles

1973 American
P—Kaat, Chicago
C—Munson, New York
1B—Scott, Milwaukee
2B—Grich, Baltimore
3B—Robinson, Baltimore
SS—Belanger, Baltimore
OF—Blair, Baltimore
OF—Otis, Kansas City
OF—Stanley, Detroit

1973 National
P—Gibson, St. Louis
C—Bench, Cincinnati
1B—Jorgensen, Montreal
2B—Morgan, Cincinnati
3B—Rader, Houston
SS—Metzger, Houston
OF—Bonds, San Francisco
OF—Cedeno, Houston
OF—Davis, Los Angeles

1974 American
P—Kaat, Chicago
C—Munson, New York
1B—Scott, Milwaukee
2B—Grich, Baltimore
3B—Robinson, Baltimore
SS—Belanger, Baltimore
OF—Blair, Baltimore
OF—Otis, Kansas City
OF—Rudi, Oakland

1974 National
P—Messersmith, L.A.
C—Bench, Cincinnati
1B—Garvey, Los Angeles
2B—Morgan, Cincinnati
3B—Rader, Houston
SS—Concepcion, Cincinnati
OF—Cedeno, Houston
OF—Geronimo, Cincinnati
OF—Bonds, San Francisco

1975 American
P—Kaat, Chicago
C—Munson, New York
1B—Scott, Milwaukee
2B—Grich, Baltimore
3B—Robinson, Baltimore
SS—Belanger, Baltimore
OF—Blair, Baltimore
OF—Rudi, Oakland
OF—Lynn, Boston

1975 National
P—Messersmith, L.A.
C—Bench, Cincinnati
1B—Garvey, Los Angeles
2B—Morgan, Cincinnati
3B—Reitz, St. Louis
SS—Concepcion, Cincinnati
OF—Cedeno, Houston
OF—Geronimo, Cincinnati
OF—Maddox, Philadelphia

1976 American
P—Palmer, Baltimore
C—Sundberg, Texas
1B—Scott, Milwaukee
2B—Grich, Baltimore
3B—Rodriguez, Detroit
SS—Belanger, Baltimore
OF—Rudi, Oakland
OF—Evans, Boston
OF—Manning, Cleveland

1976 National
P—Kaat, Philadelphia
C—Bench, Cincinnati
1B—Garvey, Los Angeles
2B—Morgan, Cincinnati
3B—Schmidt, Philadelphia
SS—Concepcion, Cincinnati
OF—Cedeno, Houston
OF—Geronimo, Cincinnati
OF—Maddox, Philadelphia

1977 American
P—Palmer, Baltimore
C—Sundberg, Texas
1B—Spencer, Chicago
2B—White, Kansas City
3B—Nettles, New York
SS—Belanger, Baltimore
OF—Beniquez, Texas
OF—Yastrzemski, Boston
OF—Cowens, Kansas City

1977 National
P—Kaat, Philadelphia
C—Bench, Cincinnati
1B—Garvey, Los Angeles
2B—Morgan, Cincinnati
3B—Schmidt, Philadelphia
SS—Concepcion, Cincinnati
OF—Geronimo, Cincinnati
OF—Maddox, Philadelphia
OF—Parker, Pittsburgh

1978 American
P—Palmer, Baltimore
C—Sundberg, Texas
1B—Chambliss, New York
2B—White, Kansas City
3B—Nettles, New York
SS—Belanger, Baltimore
OF—Lynn, Boston
OF—Evans, Boston
OF—Miller, California

1978 National
P—Niekro, Atlanta
C—Boone, Philadelphia
1B—Hernandez, St. Louis
2B—Lopes, Los Angeles
3B—Schmidt, Philadelphia
SS—Bowa, Philadelphia
OF—Maddox, Philadelphia
OF—Parker, Pittsburgh
OF—Valentine, Montreal

1979 American
P—Palmer, Baltimore
C—Sundberg, Texas
1B—Cooper, Milwaukee
2B—White, Kansas City
3B—Bell, Texas
SS—Burleson, Boston
OF—Evans, Boston
OF—Lezcano, Milwaukee
OF—Lynn, Boston

1979 National
P—Niekro, Atlanta
C—Boone, Philadelphia
1B—Hernandez, St. Louis
2B—Trillo, Philadelphia
3B—Schmidt, Philadelphia
SS—Concepcion, Cincinnati
OF—Maddox, Philadelphia
OF—Parker, Pittsburgh
OF—Winfield, San Diego

1980 American
P—Norris, Oakland
C—Sundberg, Texas
1B—Cooper, Milwaukee
2B—White, Kansas City
3B—Bell, Texas
SS—Trammell, Detroit
OF—Lynn, Boston
OF—Murphy, Oakland
OF—Wilson, Kansas City

1980 National
P—Niekro, Atlanta
C—Carter, Montreal
1B—Hernandez, St. Louis
2B—Flynn, New York
3B—Schmidt, Philadelphia
SS—Smith, San Diego
OF—Dawson, Montreal
OF—Maddox, Philadelphia
OF—Winfield, San Diego

1981 American
P—Norris, Oakland
C—Sundberg, Texas
1B—Squires, Chicago
2B—White, Kansas City
3B—Bell, Texas
SS—Trammell, Detroit
OF—Murphy, Oakland
OF—Evans, Boston
OF—Henderson, Oakland

1981 National
P—Carlton, Philadelphia
C—Carter, Montreal
1B—Hernandez, St. Louis
2B—Trillo, Philadelphia
3B—Schmidt, Philadelphia
SS—Smith, San Diego
OF—Dawson, Montreal
OF—Maddox, Philadelphia
OF—Baker, Los Angeles

1982 American
P—Guidry, New York
C—Boone, California
1B—Murray, Baltimore
2B—White, Kansas City
3B—Bell, Texas
SS—Yount, Milwaukee
OF—Evans, Boston
OF—Winfield, New York
OF—Murphy, Oakland

1982 National
P—Niekro, Atlanta
C—Carter, Montreal
1B—Hernandez, St. Louis
2B—Trillo, Philadelphia
3B—Schmidt, Philadelphia
SS—O. Smith, St. Louis
OF—Dawson, Montreal
OF—Murphy, Atlanta
OF—Maddox, Philadelphia

1983 American
P—Guidry, New York
C—Parrish, Detroit
1B—Murray, Baltimore
2B—Whitaker, Detroit
3B—Bell, Texas
SS—Trammell, Detroit
OF—Evans, Boston
OF—Winfield, New York
OF—Murphy, Oakland

1983 National
P—Niekro, Atlanta
C—Pena, Pittsburgh
1B—Hernandez, St.L.-N.Y.
2B—Sandberg, Chicago
3B—Schmidt, Philadelphia
SS—O. Smith, St. Louis
OF—Dawson, Montreal
OF—Murphy, Atlanta
OF—McGee, St. Louis

1984 American
P—Guidry, New York
C—Parrish, Detroit
1B—Murray, Baltimore
2B—Whitaker, Detroit
3B—Bell, Texas
SS—Trammell, Detroit
OF—Evans, Boston
OF—Winfield, New York
OF—Murphy, Oakland

1984 National
P—Andujar, St. Louis
C—Pena, Pittsburgh
1B—Hernandez, New York
2B—Sandberg, Chicago
3B—Schmidt, Philadelphia
SS—O. Smith, St. Louis
OF—Murphy, Atlanta
OF—Dernier, Chicago
OF—Dawson, Montreal

1985 American
P—Guidry, New York
C—Parrish, Detroit
1B—Mattingly, New York
2B—Whitaker, Detroit
3B—Brett, Kansas City
SS—Griffin, Oakland
OF—Pettis, California
OF—Winfield, New York
OF—Evans, Boston (tie)
 Murphy, Oakland (tie)

1985 National
P—Reuschel, Pittsburgh
C—Pena, Pittsburgh
1B—Hernandez, New York
2B—Sandberg, Chicago
3B—Wallach, Montreal
SS—O. Smith, St. Louis
OF—McGee, St. Louis
OF—Murphy, Atlanta
OF—Dawson, Montreal

1986 American
P—Guidry, New York
C—Boone, California
1B—Mattingly, New York
2B—White, Kansas City
3B—Gaetti, Minnesota
SS—Fernandez, Toronto
OF—Pettis, California
OF—Barfield, Toronto
OF—Puckett, Minnesota

1986 National
P—Valenzuela, Los Angeles
C—Davis, Chicago
1B—Hernandez, New York
2B—Sandberg, Chicago
3B—Schmidt, Philadelphia
SS—Smith, St. Louis
OF—Gwynn, San Diego
OF—Murphy, Atlanta
OF—McGee, St. Louis

1987 American
P—Langston, Seattle
C—Boone, California
1B—Mattingly, New York
2B—White, Kansas City
3B—Gaetti, Minnesota
SS—Fernandez, Toronto
OF—Barfield, Toronto
OF—Puckett, Minnesota
OF—Winfield, New York

1987 National
P—Reuschel, Pitt.-S.F.
C—LaValliere, Pittsburgh
1B—Hernandez, New York
2B—Sandberg, Chicago
3B—Pendleton, St. Louis
SS—Smith, St. Louis
OF—Davis, Cincinnati
OF—Gwynn, San Diego
OF—Dawson, Chicago

1988 American
P—Langston, Seattle
C—Boone, California
1B—Mattingly, New York
2B—Reynolds, Seattle
3B—Gaetti, Minnesota
SS—Fernandez, Toronto
OF—Puckett, Minnesota
OF—White, California
OF—Pettis, Detroit

1988 National
P—Hershiser, L.A.
C—Santiago, S.D.
1B—Hernandez, New York
2B—Sandberg, Chicago
3B—Wallach, Montreal
SS—Smith, St. Louis
OF—Van Slyke, Pitt.
OF—Davis, Cincinnati
OF—Dawson, Chicago

1989 American
P—Saberhagen, Kansas City
C—Boone, Kansas City
1B—Mattingly, New York
2B—Reynolds, Seattle
3B—Gaetti, Minnesota
SS—Fernandez, Toronto
OF—Puckett, Minnesota
OF—White, California
OF—Pettis, Detroit

1989 National
P—Darling, New York
C—Santiago, San Diego
1B—Galarraga, Montreal
2B—Sandberg, Chicago
3B—Pendleton, St. Louis
SS—Smith, St. Louis
OF—Van Slyke, Pittsburgh
OF—Gwynn, San Diego
OF—Davis, Cincinnati

1990 American
P—Boddicker, Boston
C—Alomar, Cleveland
1B—McGwire, Oakland
2B—Reynolds, Seattle
3B—Gruber, Toronto
SS—Guillen, Chicago
OF—Griffey Jr., Seattle
OF—Burks, Boston
OF—Pettis, Texas

1990 National
P—Maddux, Chicago
C—Santiago, San Diego
1B—Galarraga, Montreal
2B—Sandberg, Chicago
3B—Wallach, Montreal
SS—Smith, St. Louis
OF—Bonds, Pittsburgh
OF—Van Slyke, Pittsburgh
OF—Gwynn, San Diego

Silver Slugger Teams

1980 American
1B—Cecil Cooper, Milw.
2B—Willie Randolph, N.Y.
3B—George Brett, K.C.
SS—Robin Yount, Milw.
OF—Ben Oglivie, Milw.
OF—Al Oliver, Texas
OF—Willie Wilson, K.C.
 C—Lance Parrish, Detroit
DH—Reggie Jackson, N.Y.

1980 National
1B—Keith Hernandez, St.L.
2B—Manny Trillo, Phila.
3B—Mike Schmidt, Phila.
SS—Garry Templeton, St.L.
OF—Dusty Baker, Los Angeles
OF—Andre Dawson, Montreal
OF—George Hendrick, St.L.
 C—Ted Simmons, St. Louis
P—Bob Forsch, St. Louis

1981 American
1B—Cecil Cooper, Milw.
2B—Bobby Grich, Calif.
3B—Carney Lansford, Bos.
SS—Rick Burleson, Calif.
OF—Rickey Henderson, Oak.
OF—Dwight Evans, Boston
OF—Dave Winfield, N.Y.
 C—Carlton Fisk, Chicago
DH—Al Oliver, Texas

1981 National
1B—Pete Rose, Philadelphia
2B—Manny Trillo, Phila.
3B—Mike Schmidt, Phila.
SS—Dave Concepcion, Cin.
OF—Andre Dawson, Montreal
OF—George Foster, Cincinnati
OF—Dusty Baker, Los Angeles
  C—Gary Carter, Montreal
  P—Fernando Valenzuela, L.A.

1982 American
1B—Cecil Cooper, Milw.
2B—Damaso Garcia, Tor.
3B—Doug DeCinces, Calif.
SS—Robin Yount, Milw.
OF—Dave Winfield, N.Y.
OF—Willie Wilson, K.C.
OF—Reggie Jackson, Calif.
  C—Lance Parrish, Detroit
DH—Hal McRae, K.C.

1982 National
1B—Al Oliver, Montreal
2B—Joe Morgan, S.F.
3B—Mike Schmidt, Phila.
SS—Dave Concepcion, Cin.
OF—Dale Murphy, Atlanta
OF—Pedro Guerrero, L.A.
OF—Leon Durham, Chicago
  C—Gary Carter, Montreal
  P—Don Robinson, Pittsburgh

1983 American
1B—Eddie Murray, Balt.
2B—Lou Whitaker, Detroit
3B—Wade Boggs, Boston
SS—Cal Ripken, Baltimore
OF—Jim Rice, Boston
OF—Dave Winfield, N.Y.
OF—Lloyd Moseby, Toronto
  C—Lance Parrish, Detroit
DH—Don Baylor, New York

1983 National
1B—George Hendrick, St.L.
2B—Johnny Ray, Pittsburgh
3B—Mike Schmidt, Phila.
SS—Dickie Thon, Houston
OF—Andre Dawson, Montreal
OF—Dale Murphy, Atlanta
OF—Jose Cruz, Houston
  C—Terry Kennedy, San Diego
  P—Fernando Valenzuela, L.A.

1984 American
1B—Eddie Murray, Balt.
2B—Lou Whitaker, Detroit
3B—Buddy Bell, Texas
SS—Cal Ripken, Baltimore
OF—Tony Armas, Boston
OF—Jim Rice, Boston
OF—Dave Winfield, N.Y.
  C—Lance Parrish, Detroit
DH—Andre Thornton, Cleve.

1984 National
1B—Keith Hernandez, N.Y.
2B—Ryne Sandberg, Chicago
3B—Mike Schmidt, Phila.
SS—Garry Templeton, S.D.
OF—Dale Murphy, Atlanta
OF—Jose Cruz, Houston
OF—Tony Gwynn, San Diego
  C—Gary Carter, Montreal
  P—Rick Rhoden, Pittsburgh

1985 American
1B—Don Mattingly, N.Y.
2B—Lou Whitaker, Detroit
3B—George Brett, K.C.
SS—Cal Ripken, Baltimore
OF—Rickey Henderson, N.Y.
OF—Dave Winfield, N.Y.
OF—George Bell, Toronto
  C—Carlton Fisk, Chicago
DH—Don Baylor, New York

1985 National
1B—Jack Clark, St. Louis
2B—Ryne Sandberg, Chi.
3B—Tim Wallach, Montreal
SS—Hubie Brooks, Montreal
OF—Willie McGee, St. Louis
OF—Dale Murphy, Atlanta
OF—Dave Parker, Cincinnati
  C—Gary Carter, New York
  P—Rick Rhoden, Pittsburgh

1986 American
1B—Don Mattingly, N.Y.
2B—Frank White, K.C.
3B—Wade Boggs, Boston
SS—Cal Ripken, Baltimore
OF—George Bell, Toronto
OF—Kirby Puckett, Minn.
OF—Jesse Barfield, Toronto
  C—Lance Parrish, Detroit
DH—Don Baylor, Boston

1986 National
1B—Glenn Davis, Houston
2B—Steve Sax, L.A.
3B—Mike Schmidt, Phila.
SS—Hubie Brooks, Montreal
OF—Tony Gwynn, San Diego
OF—Tim Raines, Montreal
OF—Dave Parker, Cincinnati
  C—Gary Carter, New York
  P—Rick Rhoden, Pittsburgh

1987 American
1B—Don Mattingly, N.Y.
2B—Lou Whitaker, Det.
3B—Wade Boggs, Boston
SS—Alan Trammell, Det.
OF—George Bell, Toronto
OF—Dwight Evans, Boston
OF—Kirby Puckett, Minn.
  C—Matt Nokes, Detroit
DH—Paul Molitor, Milw.

1987 National
1B—Jack Clark, St. Louis
2B—Juan Samuel, Philadelphia
3B—Tim Wallach, Montreal
SS—Ozzie Smith, St. Louis
OF—Andre Dawson, Chicago
OF—Eric Davis, Cincinnati
OF—Tony Gwynn, San Diego
  C—Benito Santiago, S.D.
  P—Bob Forsch, St. Louis

1988 American
1B—George Brett, K.C.
2B—Julio Franco, Clev.
3B—Wade Boggs, Boston
SS—Alan Trammell, Det.
OF—Kirby Puckett, Minn.
OF—Jose Canseco, Oak.
OF—Mike Greenwell, Bos.
  C—Carlton Fisk, Chicago
DH—Paul Molitor, Milw.

1988 National
1B—Andres Galarraga, Mon.
2B—Ryne Sandberg, Chi.
3B—Bobby Bonilla, Pitt.
SS—Barry Larkin, Cin.
OF—Darryl Strawberry, N.Y.
OF—Andy Van Slyke, Pitt.
OF—Kirk Gibson, L.A.
  C—Benito Santiago, S.D.
  P—Tim Leary, L.A.

1989 American
1B—Fred McGriff, Tor.
2B—Julio Franco, Tex.
3B—Wade Boggs, Boston
SS—Cal Ripken, Balt.
OF—Kirby Puckett, Minn.
OF—Ruben Sierra, Tex.
OF—Robin Yount, Milw.
  C—Mickey Tettleton, Balt.
DH—H. Baines, Chi.-Tex.

1989 National
1B—Will Clark, S.F.
2B—Ryne Sandberg, Chi.
3B—Howard Johnson, N.Y.
SS—Barry Larkin, Cin.
OF—Kevin Mitchell, S.F.
OF—Tony Gwynn, S.D.
OF—Eric Davis, Cin.
  C—Craig Biggio, Hou.
  P—Don Robinson, S.F.

1990 American
1B—Cecil Fielder, Det.
2B—Julio Franco, Tex.
3B—Kelly Gruber, Tor.
SS—Alan Trammell, Det.
OF—Rickey Henderson, Oak.
OF—Jose Canseco, Oak.
OF—Ellis Burks, Bos.
  C—Lance Parrish, Calif.
DH—Dave Parker, Milw.

1990 National
1B—Eddie Murray, L.A.
2B—Ryne Sandberg, Chi.
3B—Matt Williams, S.F.
SS—Barry Larkin, Cin.
OF—Barry Bonds, Pitt.
OF—Bobby Bonilla, Pitt.
OF—Darryl Strawberry, N.Y.
  C—Benito Santiago, S.D.
  P—Don Robinson, S.F.

Baseball Writers' Association Awards
Most Valuable Player Citations

CHALMERS AWARD

AMERICAN LEAGUE			NATIONAL LEAGUE		
Year	Player Club	Points	Player Club		Points
1911—Tyrus Cobb, Detroit, of		64	Frank Schulte, Chicago, of		29
1912—Tristram Speaker, Boston, of		59	Lawrence Doyle, New York, 2b		48
1913—Walter Johnson, Washington, p		54	Jacob Daubert, Brooklyn, 1b		50
1914—Edward Collins, Philadelphia, 2b		63	John Evers, Boston, 2b		50

LEAGUE AWARDS

AMERICAN LEAGUE			NATIONAL LEAGUE		
Year	Player Club	Points	Player Club		Points
1922—George Sisler, St. Louis, 1b		59	No selection		
1923—George Ruth, New York, of		64	No selection		
1924—Walter Johnson, Washington, p		55	Arthur Vance, Brooklyn, p		74
1925—Roger Peckinpaugh, Washington, ss		45	Rogers Hornsby, St. Louis, 2b		73
1926—George Burns, Cleveland, 1b		63	Robert O'Farrell, St. Louis, c		79
1927—H. Louis Gehrig, New York, 1b		56	Paul Waner, Pittsburgh, of		72
1928—Gordon Cochrane, Philadelphia, c		53	James Bottomley, St. Louis, 1b		76
1929—No selection			Rogers Hornsby, Chicago, 2b		60

BASEBALL WRITERS' ASSOCIATION MVP AWARDS

AMERICAN LEAGUE			NATIONAL LEAGUE		
Year	Player Club	Points	Player Club		Points
1931—Robert Grove, Philadelphia, p		78	Frank Frisch, St. Louis, 2b		65
1932—James Foxx, Philadelphia, 1b		75	Charles Klein, Philadelphia, of		78
1933—James Foxx, Philadelphia, 1b		74	Carl Hubbell, New York, p		77
1934—Gordon Cochrane, Detroit, c		67	Jerome Dean, St. Louis, p		78
1935—Henry Greenberg, Detroit, 1b		*80	Charles Hartnett, Chicago, c		75
1936—H. Louis Gehrig, New York, 1b		73	Carl Hubbell, New York, p		60
1937—Charles Gehringer, Detroit, 2b		78	Joseph Medwick, St. Louis, of		70
1938—James Foxx, Boston, 1b		305	Ernest Lombardi, Cincinnati, c		229
1939—Joseph DiMaggio, New York, of		280	William Walters, Cincinnati, p		303
1940—Henry Greenberg, Detroit, of		292	Frank McCormick, Cincinnati, 1b		274
1941—Joseph DiMaggio, New York, of		291	Adolph Camilli, Brooklyn, 1b		300
1942—Joseph Gordon, New York, 2b		270	Morton Cooper, St. Louis, p		263
1943—Spurgeon Chandler, New York, p		246	Stanley Musial, St. Louis, of		267
1944—Harold Newhouser, Detroit, p		236	Martin Marion, St. Louis, ss		190
1945—Harold Newhouser, Detroit, p		236	Philip Cavarretta, Chicago, 1b		279
1946—Theodore Williams, Boston, of		224	Stanley Musial, St. Louis, 1b		319
1947—Joseph DiMaggio, New York, of		202	Robert Elliott, Boston, 3b		205
1948—Louis Boudreau, Cleveland, ss		324	Stanley Musial, St. Louis, of		303
1949—Theodore Williams, Boston, of		272	Jack Robinson, Brooklyn, 2b		264
1950—Philip Rizzuto, New York, ss		284	C. James Konstanty, Philadelphia, p		286
1951—Lawrence Berra, New York, c		184	Roy Campanella, Brooklyn, c		243
1952—Robert Shantz, Philadelphia, p		280	Henry Sauer, Chicago, of		226
1953—Albert Rosen, Cleveland, 3b		*336	Roy Campanella, Brooklyn, c		297
1954—Lawrence Berra, New York, c		230	Willie Mays, New York, of		283
1955—Lawrence Berra, New York, c		218	Roy Campanella, Brooklyn, c		226
1956—Mickey Mantle, New York, of		*336	Donald Newcombe, Brooklyn, p		223
1957—Mickey Mantle, New York, of		233	Henry Aaron, Milwaukee, of		239
1958—Jack Jensen, Boston, of		233	Ernest Banks, Chicago, ss		283
1959—J. Nelson Fox, Chicago, 2b		295	Ernest Banks, Chicago, ss		232½
1960—Roger Maris, New York, of		225	Richard Groat, Pittsburgh, ss		276
1961—Roger Maris, New York, of		202	Frank Robinson, Cincinnati, of		219
1962—Mickey Mantle, New York, of		234	Maurice Wills, Los Angeles, ss		209
1963—Elston Howard, New York, c		248	Sanford Koufax, Los Angeles, p		237
1964—Brooks Robinson, Baltimore, 3b		269	Kenton Boyer, St. Louis, 3b		243
1965—Zoilo Versalles, Minnesota, ss		275	Willie Mays, San Francisco, of		224
1966—Frank Robinson, Baltimore, of		*280	Roberto Clemente, Pittsburgh, of		218
1967—Carl Yastrzemski, Boston, of		275	Orlando Cepeda, St. Louis, 1b		*280
1968—Dennis McLain, Detroit, p		*280	Robert Gibson, St. Louis, p		242
1969—Harmon Killebrew, Minnesota, 1-3b		294	Willie McCovey, San Francisco, 1b		265
1970—John (Boog) Powell, Baltimore, 1b		234	Johnny Bench, Cincinnati, c		326
1971—Vida Blue, Oakland, p		268	Joseph Torre, St. Louis, 3b		318
1972—Richie Allen, Chicago, 1b		321	Johnny Bench, Cincinnati, c		263
1973—Reggie Jackson, Oakland, of		*336	Pete Rose, Cincinnati, of		274
1974—Jeff Burroughs, Texas, of		248	Steve Garvey, Los Angeles, 1b		270

BASEBALL WRITERS' ASSOCIATION MVP AWARDS—Cont.

AMERICAN LEAGUE				NATIONAL LEAGUE		
Year	Player	Club	Points	Player	Club	Points
1975—Fred Lynn, Boston, of.			326	Joe Morgan, Cincinnati, 2b		321½
1976—Thurman Munson, New York, c			304	Joe Morgan, Cincinnati, 2b		311
1977—Rod Carew, Minnesota, 1b			273	George Foster, Cincinnati, of		291
1978—Jim Rice, Boston, of			352	Dave Parker, Pittsburgh, of.		320
1979—Don Baylor, California, of			347	Willie Stargell, Pittsburgh, 1b		216
				Keith Hernandez, St. Louis, 1b		216
1980—George Brett, Kansas City, 3b			335	Mike Schmidt, Philadelphia, 3b		*336
1981—Rollie Fingers, Milwaukee, p			319	Mike Schmidt, Philadelphia, 3b		321
1982—Robin Yount, Milwaukee, ss			385	Dale Murphy, Atlanta, of.		283
1983—Cal Ripken, Baltimore, ss			322	Dale Murphy, Atlanta, of.		318
1984—Willie Hernandez, Detroit, p			306	Ryne Sandberg, Chicago, 2b		326
1985—Don Mattingly, New York, 1b			367	Willie McGee, St. Louis, of.		280
1986—Roger Clemens, Boston, p.			339	Mike Schmidt, Philadelphia, 3b		287
1987—George Bell, Toronto, of.			332	Andre Dawson, Chicago, of.		269
1988—Jose Canseco, Oakland, of			*392	Kirk Gibson, Los Angeles, of		272
1989—Robin Yount, Milwaukee, of.			256	Kevin Mitchell, San Francisco, of		314
1990—Rickey Henderson, Oakland, of			317	Barry Bonds, Pittsburgh, of		331

*Unanimous selection.

BASEBALL WRITERS' ASSOCIATION ROOKIE AWARDS

1947—Combined selection—Jack Robinson, Brooklyn, 1b.
1948—Combined selection—Alvin Dark, Boston, N. L., ss.

AMERICAN LEAGUE				NATIONAL LEAGUE		
Year	Player	Club	Votes	Player	Club	Votes
1949—Roy Sievers, St. Louis, of			10	Donald Newcombe, Brooklyn, p		21
1950—Walter Dropo, Boston, 1b			15	Samuel Jethroe, Boston, of		11
1951—Gilbert McDougald, New York, 3b			13	Willie Mays, New York, of		18
1952—Harry Byrd, Philadelphia, p			9	Joseph Black, Brooklyn, p		19
1953—Harvey Kuenn, Detroit, ss			23	James Gilliam, Brooklyn, 2b		11
1954—Robert Grim, New York, p			15	Wallace Moon, St. Louis, of		17
1955—Herbert Score, Cleveland, p			18	William Virdon, St. Louis, of.		15
1956—Luis Aparicio, Chicago, ss.			22	Frank Robinson, Cincinnati, of		*24
1957—Anthony Kubek, New York, inf-of			23	John Sanford, Philadelphia, p.		16
1958—Albert Pearson, Washington, of.			14	Orlando Cepeda, San Francisco, 1b		*†21
1959—W. Robert Allison, Washington, of			18	Willie McCovey, San Francisco, 1b		*24
1960—Ronald Hansen, Baltimore, ss.			22	Frank Howard, Los Angeles, of.		12
1961—Donald Schwall, Boston, p.			7	Billy Williams, Chicago, of.		10
1962—Thomas Tresh, New York, of-ss			13	Kenneth Hubbs, Chicago, 2b		19
1963—Gary Peters, Chicago, p			10	Peter Rose, Cincinnati, 2b		17
1964—Pedro (Tony) Oliva, Minnesota, of.			19	Richard Allen, Philadelphia, 3b		18
1965—Curtis Blefary, Baltimore, of			12	James Lefebvre, Los Angeles, 2b		13
1966—Tommie Agee, Chicago, of.			16	Tommy Helms, Cincinnati, 3b.		12
1967—Rod Carew, Minnesota, 2b			19	Tom Seaver, New York, p		11
1968—Stan Bahnsen, New York, p			17	Johnny Bench, Cincinnati, c		10½
1969—Lou Piniella, Kansas City, of			9	Ted Sizemore, Los Angeles, 2b		14
1970—Thurman Munson, New York, c			23	Carl Morton, Montreal, p.		11
1971—Chris Chambliss, Cleveland, 1b			11	Earl Williams, Atlanta, c		18
1972—Carlton Fisk, Boston, c.			*24	Jon Matlack, New York, p		19
1973—Al Bumbry, Baltimore, of			13½	Gary Matthews, San Francisco, of		11
1974—Mike Hargrove, Texas, 1b			16½	Bake McBride, St. Louis, of		16
1975—Fred Lynn, Boston, of.			23	John Montefusco, San Francisco, p		12
1976—Mark Fidrych, Detroit, p			22	Butch Metzger, San Diego, p		11
				Pat Zachry, Cincinnati, p		11
1977—Eddie Murray, Baltimore, dh-1b			12½	Andre Dawson, Montreal, of		10
1978—Lou Whitaker, Detroit, 2b.			21	Bob Horner, Atlanta, 3b		12½
1979—John Castino, Minnesota, 3b			7	Rick Sutcliffe, Los Angeles, p.		20
Alfredo Griffin, Toronto, ss.			7			
1980—Joe Charboneau, Cleveland, of			103	Steve Howe, Los Angeles, p		80
1981—Dave Righetti, New York, p			127	Fernando Valenzuela, Los Angeles, p		107
1982—Cal Ripken, Baltimore, ss-3b			132	Steve Sax, Los Angeles, 2b		63
1983—Ron Kittle, Chicago, of			104	Darryl Strawberry, New York, of		109
1984—Alvin Davis, Seattle, 1b			134	Dwight Gooden, New York, p		118
1985—Ozzie Guillen, Chicago, ss			101	Vince Coleman, St. Louis, of.		*120
1986—Jose Canseco, Oakland, of			110	Todd Worrell, St. Louis, p		118
1987—Mark McGwire, Oakland, 1b.			*140	Benito Santiago, San Diego, c		*120
1988—Walt Weiss, Oakland, ss.			103	Chris Sabo, Cincinnati, 3b.		79
1989—Gregg Olson, Baltimore, p.			136	Jerome Walton, Chicago, of		116
1990—Sandy Alomar Jr., Cleveland, c			*140	Dave Justice, Atlanta, of		118

*Unanimous selection. †Three writers did not vote.

BASEBALL WRITERS' ASSOCIATION MANAGER AWARDS

AMERICAN LEAGUE				NATIONAL LEAGUE		
Year	Player	Club	Points	Player	Club	Points
1983	Tony La Russa, Chicago		17	Tommy Lasorda, Los Angeles		10
1984	Sparky Anderson, Detroit		96	Jim Frey, Chicago		101
1985	Bobby Cox, Toronto		104	Whitey Herzog, St. Louis		86
1986	John McNamara, Boston		95	Hal Lanier, Houston		108
1987	Sparky Anderson, Detroit		90	Buck Rodgers, Montreal		92
1988	Tony La Russa, Oakland		103	Tommy Lasorda, Los Angeles		101
1989	Frank Robinson, Baltimore		125	Don Zimmer, Chicago		118
1990	Jeff Torborg, Chicago		128	Jim Leyland, Pittsburgh		99

CY YOUNG MEMORIAL AWARD

Year	Pitcher Club	Votes	Year	Pitcher Club	Votes
1956	Donald Newcombe, Brooklyn	10	1976	A. L.—Jim Palmer, Baltimore	108
1957	Warren Spahn, Milwaukee	15		N. L.—Randy Jones, San Diego	96
1958	Robert Turley, New York, A.L.	5	1977	A. L.—Sparky Lyle, New York	56½
1959	Early Wynn, Chicago, A.L.	13		N. L.—Steve Carlton, Philadelphia	*104
1960	Vernon Law, Pittsburgh	8	1978	A. L.—Ron Guidry, New York	*140
1961	Edward Ford, New York, A.L.	9		N. L.—Gaylord Perry, San Diego	116
1962	Don Drysdale, Los Angeles, N.L.	14	1979	A. L.—Mike Flanagan, Baltimore	136
1963	Sanford Koufax, Los Angeles, N.L.	*20		N. L.—Bruce Sutter, Chicago	72
1964	Dean Chance, Los Angeles, A.L.	17	1980	A. L.—Steve Stone, Baltimore	100
1965	Sanford Koufax, Los Angeles, N.L.	*20		N. L.—Steve Carlton, Philadelphia	118
1966	Sanford Koufax, Los Angeles, N.L.	*20	1981	A. L.—Rollie Fingers, Milwaukee	126
1967	Jim Lonborg, Boston	18		N. L.—Fernando Valenzuela, Los Ang.	70
	N. L.—M. McCormick, San Francisco	18	1982	A. L.—Pete Vuckovich, Milwaukee	87
1968	A. L.—Dennis McLain, Detroit	*20		N. L.—Steve Carlton, Philadelphia	112
	N. L.—Bob Gibson, St. Louis	*20	1983	A. L.—LaMarr Hoyt, Chicago	116
1969	A. L.—Dennis McLain, Detroit	10		N. L.—John Denny, Philadelphia	103
	Mike Cuellar, Baltimore	10	1984	A. L.—Willie Hernandez, Detroit	88
	N. L.—Tom Seaver, New York	23		N. L.—Rick Sutcliffe, Chicago	*120
1970	A. L.—Jim Perry, Minnesota	55	1985	A. L.—Bret Saberhagen, Kansas City	127
	N. L.—Bob Gibson, St. Louis	118		N. L.—Dwight Gooden, New York	*120
1971	A. L.—Vida Blue, Oakland	98	1986	A. L.—Roger Clemens, Boston	*140
	N. L.—Fergy Jenkins, Chicago	97		N. L.—Mike Scott, Houston	98
1972	A. L.—Gaylord Perry, Cleveland	64	1987	A. L.—Roger Clemens, Boston	124
	N. L.—Steve Carlton, Philadelphia	*120		N. L.—Steve Bedrosian, Philadelphia	57
1973	A. L.—Jim Palmer, Baltimore	88	1988	A. L.—Frank Viola, Minnesota	138
	N. L.—Tom Seaver, New York	71		N. L.—Orel Hershiser, Los Angeles	*120
1974	A. L.—Jim Hunter, Oakland	90	1989	A. L.—Bret Saberhagen, Kansas City	138
	N. L.—Mike Marshall, Los Angeles	96		N. L.—Mark Davis, San Diego	107
1975	A. L.—Jim Palmer, Baltimore	98	1990	A. L.—Bob Welch, Oakland	107
	N. L.—Tom Seaver, New York	98		N. L.—Doug Drabek, Pittsburgh	118

*Unanimous selection.

Carew Heads Hall of Fame Trio

By LARRY WIGGE

The crack of the bat could still be heard at Rod Carew's hitting school in Placentia, Calif., long after the seven-time American League batting champion had received the news that he had been voted to the Hall of Fame.

"When you're suddenly sitting there with a lot of the great hitters you've always been compared to, well, it's a great honor," said Carew, who was a landslide choice of 10-year members of the Baseball Writers Association of America with 401 of a possible 443 votes—90.5 percent. Only 13 other players have ever been elected with a higher percentage. Carew is only the 22nd player ever chosen to baseball's shrine in his first year of eligibility.

"When you get 3,000 hits, some of them have to be important," Carew said in answer to some of his critics, who point to his driving in 100 runs just once in his career. "I think people have looked at my career since I retired and maybe been surprised that there's more there than they thought."

Voters obviously saw more in the records of Gaylord Perry and Ferguson Jenkins than they had at first glance. The two veteran pitchers earned election to the Hall of Fame in 1991 on their third try.

Perry was named on 342 ballots, a 77.2 percentage, after falling 13 votes short in 1990. Meanwhile, Jenkins joined Ralph Kiner in being selected by the narrowest of margins—getting just one more vote (334 total) than the 75 percent that is required for election. He had been 37 votes short a year earlier.

Both pitchers had to overcome tarnished images before the Cooperstown doors opened to them. Perry admitted to throwing a spitball in his career, while Jenkins was arrested for allegedly carrying cocaine across the Canadian border in 1980. Those charges were later dropped.

It marked the first time since 1984 that three players (Luis Aparicio, Don Drysdale and Harmon Killebrew that year) were admitted to the Hall of Fame and only the third time it has happened in the 55-year history of the balloting.

Rollie Fingers finished fourth with 291 votes, 42 short of election. Jim Bunning, in his 15th and final year of balloting by the writers, had 282 votes.

Carew learned to hit a few short years after he was born on a train in the Panama Canal Zone in 1945. He moved with his family to New York when he was 17 and, one day after leaving high school, signed a contract with the Minnesota Twins. After three years in the minors, Carew won a spot as Minnesota's starting second baseman in 1967 and got his first major league hit off Baltimore's Dave McNally on opening day.

After hitting .292 in his rookie season and .273 in 1968, Carew hit .300 or better in 15 consecutive seasons, highlighted by a .388 average and the A.L. Most Valuable Player award in 1977. Only fellow Hall of Famers Ty Cobb, Stan Musial and Honus Wagner had more consecutive .300-plus seasons than Carew, who had a career batting average of .328 with 3,053 hits and four 200-hit seasons.

Carew, who won A.L. batting titles in 1969, 1972-75 and 1977-78, forced a deal to the California Angels for Ken Landreaux, Dave Engle, Brad Havens and Paul Hartzell in 1979 after he announced his intention of becoming a free agent after 12 seasons with the Twins.

In the first of his seven seasons with the Angels, Carew hit .318 and helped California to its first divisional title. Four years later, at the age of 38, he hit a club record .339.

Perry was 314-265 in 22 seasons with 3,534 strikeouts and is the only pitcher to win the Cy Young Award in each league. He won his 300th game at the age of 42 while pitching for Seattle in 1982.

Born in Williamston, N.C., Perry spent 10 seasons with San Francisco, sporting a 23-13 record in his best year with the Giants in 1970 when he won the National League Cy Young Award. He pitched a no-hitter against St. Louis on September 17, 1968.

After the 1971 season, the Giants sent Perry to Cleveland for Sam McDowell. He compiled a 24-16 record and a microscopic 1.92 earned-run average with the Indians in '72 to capture his second Cy Young honor. He won 21 games for Cleveland in 1974, one year before he was traded to Texas.

In 1978, Perry wound up in San Diego, where he authored his fourth 20-win season—going 21-6 at the age of 40. He returned to Texas and also pitched for the New York Yankees, Atlanta, Seattle and Kansas City before retiring after the 1983 season.

Jenkins, 284-226 with 3,192 strikeouts,

Rod Carew (above) won seven A.L. batting titles while Gaylord Perry (left) won 314 games en route to membership in Baseball's Hall of Fame.

was one of just five pitchers to win 100 games in each league and the only one ever to strike out more than 3,000 batters and walk fewer than 1,000 (he walked only 997 in 19 seasons).

The Chatham, Ontario, native was just 2-1 with the Philadelphia Phillies in 1965, his first season in the majors. Jenkins was traded to the Chicago Cubs in April 1966 along with Adolfo Phillips and John Hernstein for Bob Buhl and Larry Jackson and had a 6-8 record that season.

Working his way into the rotation with the Cubs, Jenkins posted six straight 20-win seasons. In that span, he was 20-13, 20-15, 21-15, 22-16, 24-13 and 20-12. His highest ERA over that period was 3.39 and he averaged almost 40 starts a year.

In 1968, he was 20-15 despite losing a major league record five 1-0 games.

After going 14-16 in 1973, Jenkins was traded to Texas for Bill Madlock and Vic Harris. With the Rangers in 1974, he was 25-12, the last of his seven 20-win seasons.

He wound up with Boston, Texas again and finished his career in a return engagement with the Cubs in 1982 and '83.

The complete 1991 Hall of Fame voting totals follow: Carew 401; Perry 342; Jenkins 334; Fingers 291; Bunning 282; Orlando Cepeda 192; Tony Oliva 160; Bill Mazeroski 142; Ron Santo 116; Harvey Kuenn 100; Jim Kaat 62; Maury Wills 61; Richie Allen 59; Ken Boyer 58; Joe Torre 41; Bobby Bonds 39; Minnie Minoso 38; Mickey Lolich 33; Luis Tiant 32; Vada Pinson 30; Thurman Munson and Rusty Staub 28 each; Curt Flood 23; Al Oliver 19; Sparky Lyle 15; Larry Bowa 11; Jerry Koosman 4; Jeff Burroughs, Mike Hargrove, Richie Hebner, Burt Hooton, Mike Jorgensen, John Lowenstein and Ellis Valentine 1 each.

Failing to receive a vote were Bob Bailor, Al Bumbry, Rich Dauer, Oscar Gamble, Larry Gura, Art Howe, Bruce Kison, Steve Rogers, John Wathan, Pat Zachry and Geoff Zahn.

Following is a complete list of those enshrined in the Hall of Fame prior to 1990 with the vote by which each enrollee was elected:

1936—Tyrus Cobb (222), John (Honus) Wagner (215), George (Babe) Ruth (215), Christy Mathewson (205), Walter Johnson (189), named by Baseball Writers' Association of America. Total ballots cast, 226.

1937—Napoleon Lajoie (168), Tristram Speaker (165), Denton (Cy) Young (153), named by the BBWAA. Total ballots cast, 201. George Wright, Morgan G. Bulkeley, Byron Bancroft Johnson, John J. McGraw, Cornelius McGillicuddy (Connie Mack), named by Centennial Commission.

1938—Grover C. Alexander (212), named by BBWAA. Total ballots, 262. Henry Chadwick, Alexander J. Cartwright, named by Centennial Commission.

1939—George Sisler (235), Edward Collins (213), William Keeler (207), Louis Gehrig, named by BBWAA (Gehrig by special election after retirement from game was announced). Total ballots cast, 274. Albert G. Spalding, Adrian C. Anson, Charles A. Comiskey, William (Buck) Ewing, Charles Radbourn, William A. (Candy) Cummings, named by committee of old-time players and writers.

1942—Rogers Hornsby (182), named by BBWAA. Total ballots cast, 233.

1944—Judge Kenesaw M. Landis, named by committee on old-timers.

1945—Hugh Duffy, Jimmy Collins, Hugh Jennings, Ed Delahanty, Fred Clarke, Mike Kelly, Wilbert Robinson, Jim O'Rourke, Dennis (Dan) Brouthers and Roger Bresnahan, named by committee on old-timers.

1946—Jesse Burkett, Frank Chance, Jack Chesbro, Johnny Evers, Clark Griffith, Tom McCarthy, Joe McGinnity, Eddie Plank, Joe Tinker, Rube Waddell and Ed Walsh, named by committee on old-timers.

1947—Carl Hubbell (140), Frank Frisch (136), Gordon (Mickey) Cochrane (128) and Robert (Lefty) Grove (123), named by BBWAA. Total ballots, 161.

1948—Herbert J. Pennock (94) and Harold (Pie) Traynor (93), named by BBWAA. Total ballots cast, 121.

1949—Charles Gehringer (159), named by BBWAA in runoff election. Total ballots cast, 187. Charles (Kid) Nichols and Mordecai (Three-Finger) Brown, named by committee on old timers.

1951—Mel Ott (197) and Jimmie Foxx (179), named by BBWAA. Total ballots cast, 226.

1952—Harry Heilmann (203) and Paul Waner (195), named by BBWAA. Total ballots cast, 234.

1953—Jerome (Dizzy) Dean (209) and Al Simmons (199), named by BBWAA. Total ballots cast, 264. Charles Albert (Chief) Bender, Roderick (Bobby) Wallace, William Klem, Tom Connolly, Edward G. Barrow and William Henry (Harry) Wright, named by the new Committee on Veterans.

1954—Walter (Rabbit) Maranville (209), William Dickey (202) and William Terry (195), named by BBWAA. Total ballots cast, 252.

1955—Joe DiMaggio (223), Ted Lyons (217), Arthur (Dazzy) Vance (205) and Charles (Gabby) Hartnett (195), named by BBWAA. Total ballots cast, 251. J. Franklin (Home Run) Baker and Ray Schalk, named by Committee on Veterans.

1956—Hank Greenberg (164) and Joe Cronin (152), named by BBWAA. Total ballots cast, 193.

1957—Joseph V. McCarthy and Sam Crawford, named by Committee on Veterans.

1959—Zachariah (Zack) Wheat, named by Committee on Veterans.

1961—Max Carey and William Hamilton, named by Committee on Veterans.

1962—Bob Feller (150) and Jackie Robinson (124), named by BBWAA. Total ballots cast, 160. Bill McKechnie and Edd Roush, named by Committee on Veterans.

1963—Eppa Rixey, Edgar (Sam) Rice, Elmer Flick and John Clarkson, named by Committee on Veterans.

1964—Luke Appling (189), named by BBWAA in runoff election. Total ballots cast, 225. Urban (Red) Faber, Burleigh Grimes, Tim Keefe, Heinie Manush, Miller Huggins and John Montgomery Ward, named by Committee on Veterans.

1965—James (Pud) Galvin, named by Committee on Veterans.

1966—Ted Williams (282), named by BBWAA. Total ballots cast, 302. Casey Stengel, named by Committee on Veterans.

1967—Charles (Red) Ruffing (266), named by BBWAA in runoff election. Total ballots cast, 306. Branch Rickey and Lloyd Waner, named by Committee on Veterans.

1968—Joseph (Ducky) Medwick (240), named by BBWAA. Total ballots cast, 283. Leon (Goose) Goslin and Hazen (Kiki) Cuyler, named by Committee on Veterans.

1969—Stan (The Man) Musial (317) and Roy Campanella (270), named by BBWAA. Total ballots cast, 340. Stan Coveleski and Waite Hoyt, named by Committee on Veterans.

1970—Lou Boudreau (232), named by BBWAA. Total ballots cast, 300. Earle Combs, Jesse Haines and Ford Frick, named by Committee on Veterans.

1971—Chick Hafey, Rube Marquard, Joe Kelley, Dave Bancroft, Harry Hooper, Jake Beckley and George Weiss, named by Committee on Veterans. Satchel Paige, named by Special Committee on Negro Leagues.

1972—Sandy Koufax (344), Yogi Berra (339) and Early Wynn (301), named by BBWAA. Total ballots cast, 396. Lefty Gomez, Will Harridge and Ross Youngs, named by Committee on Veterans. Josh Gibson and Walter (Buck) Leonard, named by Special Committee on Negro Leagues.

1973—Warren Spahn (316), named by BBWAA. Total ballots cast, 380. Roberto Clemente (393), in special election by BBWAA in which 424 ballots were cast. Billy Evans, George Kelly and Mickey Welch, named by Committee on Veterans. Monte Irvin, named by Special Committee on Negro Leagues.

1974—Mickey Mantle (322) and Whitey Ford (284), named by BBWAA. Total ballots cast, 365. Jim Bottomley, Sam Thompson and Jocko Conlan, named by Committee on Veterans. James (Cool Papa) Bell, named by Special Committee on Negro Leagues.

1975—Ralph Kiner (273), named by BBWAA. Total ballots cast, 362. Earl Averill,

Bucky Harris and Billy Herman, named by Committee on Veterans. William (Judy) Johnson, named by Special Committee on Negro Leagues.

1976—Robin Roberts (337) and Bob Lemon (305), named by BBWAA. Total ballots cast, 388. Roger Connor, Cal Hubbard and Fred Lindstrom, named by Committee on Veterans. Oscar Charleston, named by Special Committee on Negro Leagues.

1977—Ernie Banks (321), named by BBWAA. Total ballots cast, 383. Joe Sewell, Al Lopez and Amos Rusie, named by Committee on Veterans. Martin Dihigo and John Henry Lloyd, named by Special Committee on Negro Leagues.

1978—Eddie Mathews (301), named by BBWAA. Total ballots cast, 379. Larry MacPhail and Addie Joss, named by Committee on Veterans.

1979—Willie Mays (409), named by BBWAA. Total ballots cast, 432. Hack Wilson and Warren Giles, named by Committee on Veterans.

1980—Al Kaline (340) and Duke Snider (333), named by BBWAA. Total ballots cast, 385. Chuck Klein and Tom Yawkey, named by Committee on Veterans.

1981—Bob Gibson (337), named by BBWAA. Total ballots cast, 401. Johnny Mize and Rube Foster, named by Committee on Veterans.

1982—Henry Aaron (406) and Frank Robinson (370), named by BBWAA. Total ballots cast, 415. Albert B. (Happy) Chandler and Travis Jackson, named by Committee on Veterans.

1983—Brooks Robinson (344) and Juan Marichal (313), named by BBWAA. Total ballots cast, 374. George Kell and Walter Alston, named by Committee on Veterans.

1984—Luis Aparicio (341), Harmon Killebrew (335) and Don Drysdale (316), named by BBWAA. Total ballots cast, 403. Rick Ferrell and Pee Wee Reese, named by Committee on Veterans.

1985—Hoyt Wilhelm (331) and Lou Brock (315), named by BBWAA. Total ballots cast, 395. Enos Slaughter and Joseph (Arky) Vaughan, named by Committee on Veterans.

1986—Willie McCovey (346), named by BBWAA. Total ballots cast, 425. Bobby Doerr and Ernie Lombardi, named by Committee on Veterans.

1987—Billy Williams (354) and Jim (Catfish) Hunter (315), named by BBWAA. Total ballots cast, 413. Ray Dandridge, named by Committee on Veterans.

1988—Willie Stargell (352), named by BBWAA. Total ballots cast, 427.

1989—Johnny Bench (431) and Carl Yastrzemski (423), named by BBWAA. Total ballots cast, 447. Al Barlick and Albert (Red) Schoendienst, named by Committee on Veterans.

1990—Jim Palmer (411) and Joe Morgan (363), named by BBWAA. Total ballots cast, 444.

Pitchers Are The Pick in '90 Draft

By DAVE SLOAN

One year after major league clubs spent a record $900,000 for 18 players in the annual major league draft, the activity in the most recent draft—held December 3 in Chicago—was not quite so robust. Twelve players were selected in the 1990 draft, with the emphasis on pitching. Eight of the 12 players drafted were pitchers, including three of the first four selections.

The first pick, however, was an outfielder: Patrick Howell, a 22-year-old prospect who was drafted by the Minnesota Twins from the New York Mets' Class AAA Tidewater (International) farm team. Howell played the entire 1990 season at Class A Columbia, S.C., where he led the South Atlantic League with 79 stolen bases in 135 games and scored 98 runs while batting .264.

The Houston Astros used the second pick to take righthanded pitcher Dean Wilkins, one of only two draftees with any major league experience. Wilkins, who pitched in 18 games with the Cubs over the last two seasons, spent most of 1990 at Class AAA Iowa (American Association), where he compiled a 6-2 record and 3.70 earned-run average in 73 innings.

Besides Wilkins, the only other player with major league experience is outfielder Michael Huff, an Indians draftee who saw action in 12 games with the Dodgers in 1989. Huff played in Class AAA last year.

Ten clubs drafted at least one player, with the Expos and Athletics selecting two each. Nine teams had prospects taken from their minor league system, with the Phillies, Reds and Yankees losing two players each. Ironically, both players selected by Oakland came from the Cincinnati Reds' organization—the club that defeated the A's in four straight games in last fall's World Series.

It cost a major league club $50,000 to select a player, but the drafting team will get half that amount back if the prospect fails to make its season-opening roster.

Ten clubs did not draft or lose any players.

The 1990 draft choices in order of selection:

Twins—Outfielder Patrick Howell from Tidewater (International) of the Mets' organization.

Astros—Pitcher Dean Wilkins from Iowa (American Association) of the Cubs' organization.

Brewers—Pitcher Brandy Vann from Edmonton (Pacific Coast) of the Angels' organization.

Padres—Pitcher Frank Seminara from Columbus (International) of the Yankees' organization.

Expos—Outfielder Damon Riesgo from Scranton/Wilkes-Barre (International) of the Phillies' organization.

Indians—Outfielder Michael Huff from Albuquerque (Pacific Coast) of the Dodgers' organization.

Mets—Pitcher Doug Simons from Portland (Pacific Coast) of the Twins' organization.

Blue Jays—Pitcher Ricky Rhodes from Columbus (International) of the Yankees' organization.

White Sox—Pitcher Brian Harrison from Indianapolis (American Association) of the Expos' organization.

Athletics—Pitcher Joe Turek from Nashville (American Association) of the Reds' organization.

Expos—Pitcher Greg McCarthy from Scranton/Wilkes-Barre (International) of the Phillies' organization.

Athletics—Catcher Eddie Taubensee from Nashville (American Association) of the Reds' organization.

MAJOR LEAGUE TRANSACTIONS

NECROLOGY

Detroit Finds Thunder in The East

By DAVE SLOAN

After Cecil Fielder had hit 16 home runs through May 20, someone asked Detroit Tigers Manager Sparky Anderson to predict just how many homers his big first baseman would hit in 1990.

"He'll hit 30 for sure," Anderson said. "Anything more than that is up to him. When you start predicting more than 30 home runs for anyone, you're talking pretty big numbers. I don't go that far."

That was a gross understatement coming from Anderson, a man known for hyperbole. After all, this is the same person who once predicted stardom for players like Chris Pittaro, Mike Laga, Barbaro Garbey and Darnell Coles.

The Tiger manager was off the mark on Fielder, too, but in this instance happy about it. Fielder hit 51 home runs last year to become the first American League player to hit 50 since two Yankees—Roger Maris and Mickey Mantle—did so in 1961. He led the majors in home runs, runs batted in (132) and slugging percentage (.592).

Although Fielder's big season did not bring a pennant to the Motor City, it did pull the Tigers out of the A.L. Eastern Division basement. Detroit won 20 more games in 1990 than the year before, an improvement that coincided with Fielder's arrival.

Fielder hit 31 homers in parts of four seasons with the Toronto Blue Jays before spending the 1989 season in Japan. After hitting 38 homers in 384 at-bats for the Hanshin Tigers of the Japanese Central League, the 26-year-old Fielder leaped at the opportunity to play for the Detroit Tigers in 1990. He signed a two-year, $3 million contract with Detroit on January 15.

Although Fielder was last season's most prominent free-agent signee, there were other important ones. On January 31, the Pittsburgh Pirates signed veteran infielder Wally Backman, who spent the '89 season with Minnesota after nine seasons with the New York Mets. Although the Pirates envisioned Backman as a utility player, he spent much of the year as a part-time starter at third base and Pittsburgh's leadoff hitter.

Backman's presence took some of the pressure off third-base prospect Jeff King and enabled Manager Jim Leyland to move former leadoff man Barry Bonds down in the batting order. Bonds hit 33 homers,

When Seattle acquired Ken Griffey Sr. late in the 1990 season, he became the first player to play alongside his son on the same team, hitting .377 in 21 games.

drove in 114 runs and hit .301 en route to winning the National League's Most Valuable Player award. The Pirates, of course, won the N.L. East championship.

On March 30, the Philadelphia Phillies released Jeff Gray, a 26-year-old reliever who did not pitch in the majors in 1989 after making his big-league debut in five games with Cincinnati the year before. Gray, however, was not unemployed long. Eight days after his release, he signed a minor-league contract with Boston's Class AAA Pawtucket (International) affiliate. And when Red Sox closer Jeff Reardon was sidelined with a bad back in late July, Gray became the team's closer. He saved seven games in as many chances in August and September and finished the season with nine saves in 41 games to help the Red

Sox win the A.L. East flag.

Gray's performance eased the loss of veteran reliever Lee Smith, who was shipped by Boston to St. Louis for outfielder Tom Brunansky on May 4. Although the deal was second-guessed after Reardon's injury, Brunansky held up his end of the trade by hitting 15 homers with 71 RBIs in a Red Sox uniform. Particularly memorable was Brunansky's three-homer, five-RBI performance in a 7-5 win over Toronto on September 29 at Fenway Park. The victory gave the Red Sox a two-game lead over the Blue Jays in the A.L. East with four games left.

Another player who helped his club win a division title in 1990 was lefthanded pitcher Zane Smith, who was acquired by Pittsburgh from Montreal for three minor league players on August 8. (Ironically, Smith was the Expos' starting and losing pitcher in a 4-3, 12-inning loss to Pittsburgh that very night, a win that increased the Pirates' lead in the N.L. East to 2½ games over the Mets.)

Although Smith's recent past—a 1-13 record in 1989 and a 6-7 record and 3.23 earned-run average with Montreal in '90—did not seem to warrant a 3-for-1 trade, he was terrific for the Pirates in the stretch run. He posted a 6-2 record and 1.30 ERA in 10 starts, striking out 50 batters and walking nine.

The Oakland Athletics acquired three players who eventually became starters en route to winning their third straight A.L. pennant. On May 13, the A's picked up 16-year veteran second baseman Willie Randolph in a trade with Los Angeles. Outfielders Willie McGee and Harold Baines came over from St. Louis and Texas, respectively, on August 29. All three players contributed down the stretch and in the playoffs. Randolph and Baines hit .375 and .357, respectively, in Oakland's four-game sweep over Boston in the A.L. championship series.

Two veteran outfielders escaped last-place teams in 1990, although neither player's new team won a pennant, either.

On May 11, the Yankees bid adieu to Dave Winfield, whose 10-year career in New York was marked by numerous run-ins and legal squabbles with Owner George Steinbrenner. Winfield, who missed the entire 1989 season because of injury, averaged 25 homers and 102 RBIs in eight full years with the Yankees. But his personal success (eight All-Star Game appearances as a Yankee) never carried over to the team. The Yankees won just one division title during Winfield's tenure (1981) and the team went on to lose that year's World Series to the Dodgers in six games.

The other veteran outfielder to switch teams in 1990 was Atlanta's Dale Murphy, whose 17-year association with the Braves ended when he was traded to Philadelphia on August 3. Murphy won back-to-back MVP awards in 1982-83 and ranked in the top five among active players in hits, home runs and RBIs during the 1980s. Like Winfield, however, Murphy's teams never fared well in the standings. The Braves won the N.L. West flag in 1982 but never advanced to the World Series in Murphy's 14 major league seasons in Atlanta.

He missed out on playing on a World Series champion in 1990, but Ken Griffey Sr., did something no other major league player ever has: play alongside his son on the same team. Five days after the Cincinnati Reds gave the 40-year-old Griffey his outright release on August 24, the Seattle Mariners signed the 18-year veteran as a free agent.

Although 20-year-old Ken Griffey Jr., is Seattle's best player and the club knew that signing the elder Griffey would set a baseball precedent, the move proved to be more than just a publicity stunt. Griffey Sr. hit .377 in 21 games and provided veteran leadership to a young club that needed it. The Mariners were impressed enough to re-sign Griffey on December 17.

Two off-season deals completed late in 1990 stand out as noteworthy:

● In one of the biggest trades in recent years, the Toronto Blue Jays shipped first baseman/designated hitter Fred McGriff and shortstop Tony Fernandez to the San Diego Padres for outfielder Joe Carter and second baseman Roberto Alomar on December 5. The Blue Jays wanted to trade McGriff to make room for 22-year-old prospect John Olerud at first base while the Padres needed a first baseman with incumbent Jack Clark leaving the team via free agency. The Jays also wanted the power-hitting Carter, who hit 24 homers and drove in 115 runs while playing in every game for San Diego in 1990. Carter played just one season with the Padres after being traded by Cleveland to San Diego the previous off-season. The 28-year-old Fernandez is a three-time A.L. All-Star while the 22-year-old Alomar, the youngest of the four traded players, last season played in the first of what many observers feel will be many All-Star Games for him.

● On December 23, the Montreal Expos traded seven-time All-Star outfielder Tim Raines, minor league pitcher Jeff Carter and a player to be named to the Chicago

White Sox for outfielder Ivan Calderon and pitcher Barry Jones. The White Sox feel that the 31-year-old Raines will do for them what Rickey Henderson has done so well for the Oakland Athletics the past two years: be a dangerous leadoff man who has enough speed to scare the wits out of the opposition. The surprising White Sox, who won 94 games last season but still finished nine games behind Oakland in the A.L. West, figure Raines is a player who can help them gain ground on the A's. The Expos get more of a power threat in the 28-year-old Calderon, who hit 14 homers with 74 RBIs for Chicago in 1990. The key acquisition for Montreal, however, might be Jones, who posted an 11-4 record with a 2.31 ERA as a setup man last season. He played no small part in helping Bobby Thigpen set a major league record with 57 saves.

Following is a list of all player transactions for the 1990 calendar year:

January 4—Chunichi Dragons of Japanese Baseball League purchased infielder Vance Law from Cubs.

January 5—Rangers' organization re-signed pitcher Craig McMurtry, a free agent.

January 8—Twins re-signed outfielder Carmen Castillo, a free agent.

January 8—Braves' organization re-signed first baseman Darrell Evans, a free agent.

January 9—Red Sox signed pitcher Shane Rawley, a free agent formerly with the Twins.

January 9—Indians traded pitcher Scott Bailes to Angels for infielder Jeff Manto and pitcher Colin Charland.

January 10—Indians signed shortstop Rafael Santana, a free agent.

January 10—Orioles traded designated hitter Larry Sheets to Tigers for infielder Mike Brumley.

January 11—Reds signed catcher Dave Engle, a free agent.

January 12—Expos traded designated hitter Jim Dwyer to Twins for pitcher Jim Davins.

January 12—Orioles signed pitcher Joe Price, a free agent formerly with the Red Sox.

January 15—Tigers signed first baseman Cecil Fielder, a free agent formerly with the Blue Jays, and second baseman Ed Romero, a free agent formerly with the Brewers.

January 15—Pirates' Buffalo affiliate signed pitcher Stewart Cliburn and outfielder Mark Ryal, both free agents.

January 19—Giants signed catcher Gary Carter, a free agent.

January 22—Tigers' Toledo affiliate signed pitcher Dan Petry, a free agent formerly with the Angels.

January 22—Reds' Nashville affiliate signed third baseman Chris Brown, a free agent.

January 24—Braves traded pitcher Gary Eave and third baseman Ken Pennington to Mariners for third baseman Jim Presley; Mariners assigned Eave and Pennington to Calgary.

January 24—Expos released pitcher John Candelaria.

January 26—Dodgers signed pitcher Pat Perry, a free agent.

January 28—Giants signed pitcher Dan Quisenberry, a free agent.

January 29—Mariners released first baseman Jim Wilson.

January 30—Pirates' Buffalo affiliate re-signed catcher Dann Bilardello, a free agent.

January 31—Pirates signed second baseman Wally Backman, a free agent formerly with the Twins.

February 1—Astros signed pitcher Brian Fisher, a free agent.

February 1—Astros' Tucson affiliate signed pitcher Mark Thurmond, a free agent formerly with the Orioles.

February 2—Blue Jays' Syracuse affiliate signed catcher Ozzie Virgil, a free agent.

February 3—Angels released pitcher Greg Minton.

February 5—Angels' Edmonton affiliate signed infielder Rick Schu, a free agent.

February 15—Red Sox re-signed pitcher Greg A. Harris, a free agent.

February 15—Red Sox' Pawtucket affiliate signed first baseman Bill Buckner, a free agent formerly with the Royals.

February 15—Royals' Memphis affiliate signed outfielder Pat Sheridan, a free agent formerly with the Giants.

February 16—Cardinals' Louisville affiliate signed outfielder Dave Collins, a free agent formerly with the Reds.

February 17—Athletics' Tacoma affiliate signed pitcher Guillermo Hernandez, a free agent.

February 20—Dodgers' Albuquerque affiliate signed pitcher Don Aase, a free agent formerly with the Mets.

February 20—Orioles' Rochester affiliate signed first baseman Sam Horn, a free agent.

February 20—Indians' Colorado Springs affiliate signed pitcher Al Nipper, a free agent.

February 21—Angels re-signed pitcher Greg Minton, a free agent.

February 27—Padres traded pitcher Omar Olivares to Cardinals for outfielder Alex Cole and pitcher Steve Peters.

February 27—Mariners traded catcher Jerry Goff to Expos for pitcher Pat Pacillo.

February 28—Twins signed pitcher John Candelaria, a free agent.

March 7—Pirates' Buffalo affiliate signed pitcher Mark Huismann, a free agent.

March 9—Red Sox' New Britain affiliate signed pitcher Charlie Puleo, a free agent.

March 13—Giants' Phoenix affiliate signed pitcher Ed Vosberg, a free agent.

March 18—Braves traded outfielders Jeff Wetherby and Miguel Sabino to Indians for second baseman Tommy Hinzo.

March 27—Indians released catcher Andy Allanson.

March 29—Expos' Indianapolis affiliate signed pitcher Les Straker and catcher Dwight Lowry, both free agents.

March 29—Giants released outfielder Jim Weaver and catchers Wil Tejeda and Jose Pena.

March 30—Reds released infielder Chris Brown.

March 30—White Sox released pitcher Bill Dawley.

March 30—Phillies released pitcher Jeff Gray.

March 31—Royals released pitcher Mark Lee.

March 31—Cardinals' Louisville affiliate signed pitcher Steve Trout, a free agent.

March 31—Phillies traded shortstop Steve Jeltz to Royals for pitcher Jose DeJesus.

March 31—Phillies purchased pitcher Darrel Akerfelds from Rangers.

April 1—Dodgers traded first baseman/outfielder Franklin Stubbs to Astros for pitcher Terry Wells.

April 2—Yankees released pitcher Fred Toliver and infielder Damaso Garcia.

April 2—White Sox released pitcher John Davis.

April 2—Reds released catcher Dave Engle.

April 2—Red Sox released pitchers Shane Rawley, Rob Woodward and Steve Ellsworth.

April 2—Indians released shortstop Paul Zuvella, infielder Denny Gonzalez and pitcher Jeff Kaiser.

April 2—Royals released catcher Ed Hearn, pitcher Terry Leach and infielder Brad Wellman.

April 2—Royals traded pitcher Jerry Don Gleaton to Tigers for pitcher Greg Everson.

April 2—Rangers' Oklahoma City affiliate signed catcher Andy Allanson, a free agent.

April 2—Rangers traded pitcher Drew Hall to Expos for infielder Jeff Huson; Rangers assigned Huson to Oklahoma City.

April 3—Orioles released first baseman Francisco Melendez and infielder Mike Brumley.

April 3—Red Sox released pitcher Charlie Puleo.

April 3—Cubs released pitcher Greg Booker.

April 3—Royals released outfielder Pat Sheridan.

April 3—Phillies released pitcher Dickie Noles.

April 3—Pirates traded outfielder Billy Hatcher to Reds for pitcher Mike Roesler and infielder Jeff Richardson.

April 3—Mariners released pitcher Gene Walter.

April 3—White Sox' Vancouver affiliate released pitcher Jerry Reuss.

April 3—Astros released pitcher Roger Mason.

April 4—Astros released infielders Joel Youngblood and Luis Aguayo.

April 4—Pirates traded catcher Junior Ortiz and pitcher Orlando Lind to Twins for pitcher Mike Pomeranz; Pirates assigned Pomeranz to Salem and Twins assigned Lind to Portland.

April 4—Brewers released pitchers Bryan Clutterbuck and Juan Eichelberger.

April 4—Braves claimed catcher Phil Lombardi on waivers from Mets.

April 5—Braves released first baseman Darrell Evans.

April 5—Mariners claimed pitcher Brent Knackert on waivers from Mets.

April 5—Giants claimed outfielder Brad Komminsk on waivers from Indians.

April 5—Giants' Phoenix affiliate re-signed pitcher Bob Knepper, a free agent.

April 5—Expos traded pitcher Mike Campbell to White Sox for second baseman Rob Fletcher; White Sox assigned Campbell to Vancouver.

April 6—Mariners released pitcher Tom Niedenfuer.

April 6—Mariners signed infielder Mike Brumley.

April 6—Braves released catcher John Russell.

April 6—Phillies' Scranton/Wilkes-Barre affiliate signed pitcher Dickie Noles, a free agent.

April 6—Mariners granted outfielder Mike Kingery free agency.

April 7—Twins signed pitcher Terry Leach, a free agent.

April 7—Red Sox' Pawtucket affiliate signed pitcher Jeff Gray, a free agent.

April 7—Expos traded pitcher Andy McGaffigan to Giants for a player to be named; Expos acquired infielder Steve Hecht on June 26 and assigned him to Indianapolis.

April 8—Angels released pitcher Mike Smithson.

April 8—Tigers signed pitcher Urbano Lugo and catcher Mark Salas, both free agents.

April 8—Giants signed outfielder Rick Leach, a free agent.

April 8—Giants released outfielder Donell Nixon.

April 8—Brewers re-signed pitcher Paul Mirabella.

April 10—Cardinals' Louisville affiliate signed pitcher Tom Niedenfuer, a free agent.

April 10—Pirates traded catcher Joe Szekely to Blue Jays for outfielder Brian Morrison; Blue Jays assigned Morrison to Syracuse.

April 13—Rangers traded infielder Fred Manrique to Twins for pitcher Jeff Satzinger and cash; Rangers assigned Satzinger to Oklahoma City.

April 14—Giants' Phoenix affiliate signed outfielder Mike Kingery, a free agent.

April 16—Orioles' Rochester affiliate signed outfielder Donell Nixon, a free agent.

April 23—Cardinals traded pitcher John Costello to Expos for infielder Rex Hudler.

April 25—Indians released shortstop Rafael Santana.

April 25—Mariners released pitcher Jerry Reed.

April 25—Rangers released pitcher Craig McMurtry.

April 25—Giants released pitcher Andy McGaffigan.

April 26—Cubs' Iowa affiliate signed outfielder Pat Sheridan, a free agent.

April 27—Brewers released outfielder Terry Francona.

April 28—Angels traded outfielder Claudell Washington and pitcher Rich Monteleone to Yankees for outfielder Luis Polonia.

April 28—Astros traded pitcher Charley Kerfeld to Braves for outfielder Kevin Dean and a player to be named; Astros assigned Dean to Tucson. Astros acquired pitcher Lee Ellis Johnson on October 29.

April 30—Braves claimed pitcher Joe Hesketh on waivers from Expos.

April 30—White Sox traded pitcher Bill Long to Cubs for pitcher Frank Campos; White Sox assigned Campos to South Bend.

April 30—White Sox released first baseman Greg Walker.

April 30—Indians claimed pitcher Sergio Valdez on waivers from Braves.

April 30—Mets claimed outfielder Daryl Boston on waivers from White Sox.

April 30—Yankees reclaimed pitcher Ramon Manon from Rangers, who had selected him from Columbus in the 1989 major league draft; Yankees assigned him to Albany.

May 1—Mariners granted pitcher Dennis Powell free agency.

May 1—Expos reclaimed infielder Johnny Paredes from Tigers, who had selected him from

Indianapolis in the 1989 major league draft; Expos assigned him to Indianapolis.

May 1—Blue Jays reclaimed pitcher Steve Wapnick from Tigers, who had selected him from Syracuse in the 1989 major league draft; Blue Jays assigned him to Syracuse.

May 1—Astros traded pitcher Mark Thurmond to Giants for a player to be named; deal settled with cash.

May 2—Orioles claimed outfielder Brad Komminsk on waivers from Giants.

May 3—Red Sox signed pitcher Jerry Reed, a free agent.

May 4—Orioles' Rochester affiliate signed first baseman Greg Walker, a free agent.

May 4—Red Sox traded pitcher Lee Smith to Cardinals for outfielder Tom Brunansky.

May 7—Indians claimed outfielder Stan Jefferson on waivers from Orioles.

May 7—Rangers released catcher Andy Allanson.

May 8—Blue Jays released pitcher Mike Flanagan.

May 8—Rangers' Oklahoma City affiliate signed catcher John Russell, a free agent.

May 9—Rangers' Oklahoma City affiliate signed catcher Dave Engle, a free agent.

May 11—Yankees traded outfielder Dave Winfield to Angels for pitcher Mike Witt.

May 13—Dodgers traded second baseman Willie Randolph to Athletics for outfielder Stan Javier.

May 14—Royals released pitcher Larry McWilliams.

May 16—Braves released catcher Jody Davis.

May 23—Brewers' Stockton affiliate signed pitcher Mark Lee, a free agent.

May 24—Mariners traded pitcher Gary Eave to Giants for pitcher Russ Swan.

May 28—Astros released second baseman Steve Lombardozzi.

May 30—Twins traded pitcher Francisco Oliveras to Giants for a player to be named; Twins acquired pitcher Ed Gustafson on September 26 and assigned him to Visalia.

June 1—Twins released catcher Tim Laudner.

June 2—Dodgers released outfielder John Shelby.

June 2—Rangers released outfielder Thad Bosley.

June 4—Tigers traded catcher Matt Nokes to Yankees for pitchers Lance McCullers and Clay Parker.

June 5—Red Sox released first baseman Bill Buckner.

June 6—Angels released pitcher Mark Clear.

June 8—Red Sox traded catcher Rich Gedman to Astros for a player to be named; deal settled with cash.

June 9—Reds traded pitchers Ron Robinson and Bob Sebra to Brewers for outfielder Glenn Braggs and infielder Billy Bates; Brewers assigned Sebra to Denver and Reds assigned Bates to Nashville.

June 13—Tigers' Toledo affiliate signed outfielder John Shelby, a free agent.

June 13—Astros granted outfielder Louie Meadows free agency.

June 17—Indians purchased designated hitter Ken Phelps from Athletics.

June 18—Expos claimed outfielder Rolando Roomes on waivers from Reds.

June 18—Mariners traded outfielder Darnell Coles to Tigers for outfielder Tracy Jones.

June 18—Blue Jays claimed outfielder Kenny Williams on waivers from Tigers.

June 19—Mariners traded shortstop Mario Diaz to Mets for pitcher Brian Givens; Mariners assigned Givens to Calgary and Mets assigned Diaz to Tidewater.

June 21—Royals released pitcher Richard Dotson.

June 22—Twins released designated hitter Jim Dwyer.

June 25—Orioles traded pitcher Jay Tibbs to Pirates for a player to be named; Orioles acquired pitcher Dorn Taylor on September 5.

June 26—Giants released pitcher Bob Knepper.

June 30—Indians granted pitcher Doug Robertson free agency.

July 2—Cardinals' Louisville affiliate signed pitcher Ernie Camacho, a free agent.

July 3—Orioles released first baseman Greg Walker.

July 4—Phillies' Scranton/Wilkes-Barre affiliate signed outfielder Louie Meadows, a free agent.

July 7—Pirates' Buffalo affiliate signed pitcher Jerry Reuss, a free agent.

July 11—Padres traded outfielder Alex Cole to Indians for catcher Tom Lampkin.

July 12—Tigers released pitcher Matt Kinzer.

July 12—Braves traded pitcher Derek Lilliquist to Padres for pitcher Mark Grant.

July 12—Pirates purchased outfielder James Steels from Expos' Indianapolis affiliate and assigned him to Mexico City.

July 12—Pirates signed outfielder Ty Gainey, a free agent, and assigned him to Mexico City Reds.

July 15—Tigers released infielder Ed Romero.

July 15—Athletics released pitcher Mike Norris.

July 22—Mets traded pitcher Doug Sisk to Braves for pitcher Tony Valle; Mets assigned Valle to Columbia (S.C.).

July 22—Blue Jays released infielder Tom Lawless.

July 23—Braves traded pitcher Joe Boever to Phillies for pitcher Marvin Freeman; Braves assigned Freeman to Richmond.

July 23—Braves released pitcher Charlie Kerfeld.

July 24—Braves released pitcher Joe Hesketh.

July 24—Pirates released pitcher Walt Terrell.

July 25—Cardinals released pitcher Rick Horton.

July 27—Mets traded first baseman Mike Marshall to Red Sox for pitcher Greg Hansell, outfielder Ed Perozo and a player to be named; Mets acquired catcher Paul Williams on November 19.

July 27—Astros released catcher Alex Trevino.

July 27—Twins traded pitcher John Candelaria to Blue Jays for second baseman Nelson Liriano and outfielder Pedro Munoz.

July 28—Tigers signed pitcher Walt Terrell, a free agent.

July 30—Orioles traded outfielder Phil Bradley to White Sox for designated hitter/first baseman Ron Kittle.

July 31—Red Sox signed pitcher Joe Hesketh, a free agent.

August 1—Orioles claimed outfielder Dave Gallagher on waivers from White Sox.

August 3—Braves traded outfielder Dale Murphy and a player to be named to Phillies for pitcher Jeff Parrett and two players to be named; Phillies' Scranton/Wilkes-Barre affiliate acquired pitcher Tommy Greene on August 9, and Braves acquired outfielder Jim Vatcher on August 9 and shortstop Victor Rosario on September 4.

August 3—Mets signed catcher Alex Trevino, a free agent.

August 8—Expos traded pitcher Zane Smith to Pirates for pitcher Scott Ruskin, shortstop Willie Greene and a player to be named; Expos acquired outfielder Moises Alou on August 16.

August 11—Expos released first baseman Wallace Johnson.

August 12—Red Sox released pitcher Jerry Reed.

August 12—Indians released pitcher Cecilio Guante.

August 12—Giants released pitcher Atlee Hammaker.

August 17—Angels traded infielder Mark McLemore to Indians' Colorado Springs affiliate, completing deal in which Cleveland traded catcher Ron Tingley to Angels for a player to be named, September 6, 1989.

August 23—Red Sox' Pawtucket affiliate signed pitcher Cecilio Guante, a free agent.

August 24—Reds released outfielder Ken Griffey, Sr.

August 24—Padres signed pitcher Atlee Hammaker, a free agent.

August 28—Braves released pitcher Doug Sisk.

August 28—Astros released pitcher Brian Fisher.

August 29—Rangers traded outfielder/designated hitter Harold Baines to Athletics for two players to be named; Rangers acquired pitchers Joe Bitker and Scott Chiamparino on September 4.

August 29—Mariners signed outfielder Ken Griffey, Sr, a free agent.

August 29—Cardinals traded outfielder Willie McGee to Athletics for outfielder Felix Jose, third baseman Stan Royer and pitcher Daryl Green.

August 29—Orioles claimed pitcher Brian DuBois on waivers from Tigers.

August 30—Expos claimed catcher Orlando Mercado on waivers from Mets.

August 30—Phillies traded outfielder/first baseman Carmelo Martinez to Pirates for outfielders Wes Chamberlain and Julio Peguero and a player to be named; Phillies acquired outfielder Tony Longmire on September 28.

August 30—Royals traded first baseman/outfielder Pat Tabler to Mets for pitcher Archie Corbin.

August 30—Phillies traded second baseman Tom Herr to Mets for pitcher Rocky Elli and first baseman Nikco Riesgo; Phillies assigned Elli and Riesgo to Scranton/Wilkes-Barre.

August 30—Brewers traded catcher Charlie O'Brien and a player to be named to Mets for two players to be named; Brewers acquired pitchers Julio Machado and Kevin Brown on September 7 and Mets acquired pitcher Kevin Carmody on September 11.

August 30—Astros traded pitcher Larry Andersen to Red Sox for third baseman Jeff Bagwell.

August 30—Astros traded second baseman Bill Doran to Reds for three players to be named; Astros acquired catcher Terry McGriff and pitchers Keith Kaiser and Butch Henry on September 7.

September 3—Cubs traded pitcher Greg Kalle-

vig to Pirates for pitcher Randy Kramer.

September 4—Expos released pitcher Rich Thompson.

September 4—Expos claimed pitchers Kevin Bearse and Carl Keliipuleole on waivers from Indians.

September 4—Mets released catcher Barry Lyons.

September 7—Reds claimed catcher Alex Trevino on waivers from Mets.

September 7—Cubs traded outfielder Lloyd McClendon to Pirates for a player to be named; Cubs acquired pitcher Mike Pomeranz on September 28.

September 10—Astros traded pitcher Dan Schatzeder to Mets for pitcher Steve LaRose and infielder Nick Davis; Astros assigned LaRose to Tucson and Davis to Asheville.

September 13—Phillies traded pitcher Dennis Cook to Dodgers for catcher Darrin Fletcher.

September 15—White Sox re-signed designated hitter Jerry Hairston, a free agent.

September 16—Indians traded pitcher Bud Black to Blue Jays for pitcher Mauro Gozzo and two players to be named; Indians acquired pitcher Steve Cummings on September 21 and pitcher Alex Sanchez on September 24.

September 20—Orioles granted outfielder Donell Nixon free agency.

September 21—Dodgers signed catcher Barry Lyons, a free agent.

September 24—Blue Jays claimed pitcher Rick Luecken on waivers from Braves.

September 24—Braves claimed pitcher Nate Cromwell on waivers from Blue Jays.

September 24—Yankees released outfielder Deion Sanders.

September 27—Mariners released shortstop Mike Brumley.

September 30—Dodgers traded pitcher Mike Munoz to Tigers for pitcher Mike Wilkins.

October 1—Brewers released pitcher Bob Sebra.

October 3—Expos released infielder Johnny Paredes.

October 3—Phillies released second baseman Tommy Barrett.

October 3—Giants released pitcher Randy O'Neal.

October 4—Giants released catcher Bill Bathe.

October 4—Royals released pitchers Chris Codiroli and Pete Filson and catcher Rey Palacios.

October 4—Yankees released outfielder Claudell Washington.

October 4—Indians released pitcher Al Nipper.

October 4—Astros released pitcher Bill Gullickson.

October 4—White Sox released pinch-hitter Jerry Hairston.

October 5—Yankees released shortstop Wayne Tolleson.

October 10—Orioles released pitcher Dorn Taylor.

October 10—White Sox released pitcher Jose Segura.

October 11—Angels released catcher Bill Schroeder.

October 11—Cardinals released pitchers Stan Clarke and Ernie Camacho.

October 12—Mariners released outfielder Jeffrey Leonard.

October 15—Braves released catcher Ernie

Whitt.

October 16—Brewers released pitchers Tom Filer and Mike Birkbeck.

October 19—Brewers released pitcher Juan Nieves.

October 24—Giants released pitcher Jose Alvarez.

October 24—Blue Jays released infielder Jim Eppard.

October 25—Giants released first baseman Mike Laga.

October 25—Hanshin Tigers of Japanese Baseball League purchased infielder Tom O'Malley from Mets.

October 26—Red Sox released outfielder Dwight Evans.

October 26—Blue Jays released pitcher Rick Luecken.

October 26—Astros released pitcher Jose Cano.

October 30—Indians released outfielder Dion James.

November 1—Expos released pitcher Scott Anderson.

November 1—Hanshin Tigers purchased outfielder Marvell Wynne from Cubs.

November 6—Indians traded pitcher Alex Sanchez to Blue Jays for pitcher Willie Blair.

November 6—Braves traded pitcher Nate Cromwell to Blue Jays for pitcher Earl Sanders.

November 8—Dodgers signed outfielder Darryl Strawberry, a free agent formerly with the Mets.

November 9—Giants signed pitcher Bud Black, a free agent formerly with the Blue Jays.

November 9—Expos traded pitcher John Costello to Padres for pitcher Brian Harrison; Expos assigned Harrison to Indianapolis.

November 13—Mets released catcher Chris Jelic and outfielder Keith Hughes.

November 13—Braves released pitchers Marty Clary and Dwayne Henry.

November 13—Rangers released pitcher Jamie Moyer.

November 14—Yokohama Taiyo Whales of Japanese Baseball League signed outfielder R.J. Reynolds, a free agent formerly with the Pirates.

November 19—Yankees re-signed pitcher Tim Leary, a free agent.

November 19—Yankees released catcher Brian Dorsett.

November 20—Red Sox claimed pitcher Mike Miller on waivers from Mets.

November 20—Red Sox released outfielder Jeff Stone.

November 21—Royals signed pitcher Mike Boddicker, a free agent formerly with the Red Sox.

November 21—Cubs signed pitcher Danny Jackson, a free agent formerly with the Reds.

November 21—Reds re-signed pitcher Tom Browning, a free agent.

November 23—Tigers signed outfielder Rob Deer, a free agent formerly with the Brewers.

November 23—Padres claimed third baseman Tom Reddington on waivers from Braves.

November 26—Yankees signed pitcher Steve Farr, a free agent formerly with the Royals.

November 26—Blue Jays signed pitcher Ken Dayley, a free agent formerly with the Cardinals.

November 26—Tigers re-signed outfielder John Shelby, a free agent.

November 28—Athletics re-signed catcher Jamie Quirk, a free agent.

November 30—White Sox released catcher Jerry Willard.

December 1—Royals signed outfielder Kirk Gibson, a free agent formerly with the Dodgers.

December 2—Twins released pitcher Roy Smith.

December 2—Daiei Hawks of Japanese Baseball League purchased third baseman Eddie Williams from Padres.

December 2—Angels traded outfielder Devon White, pitcher Willie Fraser and a player to be named to Blue Jays for outfielder Junior Felix, infielder Luis Sojo and a player to be named; Blue Jays acquired pitcher Marcus Moore and Angels acquired catcher Ken Rivers on December 4.

December 3—Braves signed third baseman Terry Pendleton, a free agent formerly with the Cardinals.

December 3—Giants signed outfielder Willie McGee, a free agent formerly with the Athletics.

December 3—Orioles released pitcher Mike (Texas) Smith.

December 3—Tigers signed pitcher Bill Gullickson, a free agent.

December 3—Yankees traded outfielder Oscar Azocar to Padres for a player to be named.

December 3—Athletics signed outfielder Willie Wilson, a free agent formerly with the Royals.

December 3—Cubs released pitcher Kevin Coffman.

December 3—Dodgers signed pitcher Kevin Gross, a free agent formerly with the Expos.

December 3—Expos released pitcher Dale Mohorcic and outfielder Rolando Roomes.

December 3—Royals released outfielder Jeff Schulz.

December 4—Orioles traded outfielder Dave Gallagher to Angels for pitchers David Martinez and Mike Hook; Orioles assigned Hook to Rochester.

December 4—Royals signed pitcher Dan Schatzeder, a free agent formerly with the Mets.

December 4—Red Sox signed pitcher Matt Young, a free agent formerly with the Mariners.

December 4—Giants signed pitcher Dave Righetti, a free agent formerly with the Yankees.

December 4—Indians traded outfielder Cory Snyder and infielder Lindsay Foster to White Sox for pitchers Eric King and Shawn Hillegas.

December 4—Angels signed pitcher Ed Vosberg, a free agent.

December 4—Brewers signed pitcher Edwin Nunez, a free agent formerly with the Tigers.

December 4—Giants traded infielder Ernest Riles to Athletics for outfielder Darren Lewis and a player to be named later; Giants acquired pitcher Pedro Pena on December 17.

December 4—Blue Jays re-signed infielder Rance Mulliniks, a free agent.

December 4—Red Sox released first baseman Billy Jo Robidoux.

December 5—Giants traded pitcher Steve Bedrosian to Twins for pitcher Johnny Ard and a player to be named; Giants acquired pitcher Jimmy Williams on December 18.

December 5—Reds re-signed second baseman Bill Doran, a free agent.

December 5—Blue Jays signed designated hitter Pat Tabler, a free agent formerly with the Mets.

December 5—Tigers signed second baseman Tony Bernazard, a free agent.

December 5—Mets signed outfielder Vince Coleman, a free agent formerly with the Cardinals.

December 5—Brewers signed outfielder Franklin Stubbs, a free agent formerly with the Astros.

December 5—Blue Jays traded first baseman Fred McGriff and shortstop Tony Fernandez to Padres for outfielder Joe Carter and second baseman Roberto Alomar.

December 5—Braves signed first baseman Sid Bream, a free agent formerly with the Pirates.

December 5—Brewers re-signed pitcher Ted Higuera, a free agent.

December 5—Tigers released pitcher Mike Schwabe.

December 6—Cubs signed outfielder George Bell, a free agent formerly with the Blue Jays.

December 6—Royals re-signed pitcher Steve Crawford, a free agent.

December 6—Brewers released infielder Gus Polidor and pitcher Tony Fossas.

December 6—Pirates re-signed pitcher Zane Smith, a free agent.

December 6—Orioles signed outfielder Dwight Evans, a free agent.

December 7—Angels signed infielder Fred Manrique, a free agent.

December 8—Royals re-signed pitcher Andy McGaffigan, a free agent.

December 10—Athletics signed pitcher Eric Show, a free agent formerly with the Padres.

December 10—Athletics released pitcher Joe Law.

December 10—Pirates re-signed outfielder Gary Redus, a free agent.

December 10—Braves traded outfielder Dennis Hood to Mariners for pitcher Scott Taylor.

December 11—Athletics re-signed outfielder Dave Henderson, a free agent.

December 11—Reds released pitcher Tim Birtsas.

December 12—Angels signed pitcher Floyd Bannister, a free agent formerly with the Royals.

December 12—Rangers traded third baseman Scott Coolbaugh to Padres for catcher Mark Parent.

December 13—Cardinals signed first baseman Gerald Perry, a free agent formerly with the Royals.

December 13—Mets signed outfielder Terry Puhl, a free agent formerly with the Astros.

December 13—Dodgers released first baseman Luis Lopez.

December 13—Angels re-signed outfielder Max Venable, a free agent.

December 13—Indians released second baseman Mark McLemore.

December 14—Dodgers signed outfielder Brett Butler, a free agent formerly with the Giants.

December 14—Cardinals signed pitcher Juan Agosto, a free agent formerly with the Astros.

December 14—Reds signed pitcher Ted Power, a free agent formerly with the Pirates.

December 14—Red Sox released second baseman Marty Barrett.

December 14—Cubs traded infielder Greg Smith to Dodgers for infielder Jose Vizcaino.

December 14—Orioles traded pitcher Mickey Weston to Blue Jays for pitcher Paul Kilgus.

December 15—Red Sox signed first baseman Jack Clark, a free agent formerly with the Padres.

December 15—Athletics re-signed pitcher Bob Welch, a free agent.

December 15—Dodgers traded outfielder Hubie Brooks to Mets for pitchers Bob Ojeda and Greg Hansell.

December 15—Red Sox traded pitcher Wes Gardner to Padres for first baseman/outfielder Steve Hendricks and pitcher Brad Hoyer; Red Sox assigned Hendricks to New Britain and Hoyer to Lynchburg.

December 15—Dodgers released pitcher Ray Searage.

December 16—Dodgers re-signed infielder/outfielder Juan Samuel, a free agent.

December 17—Cubs signed pitcher Dave Smith, a free agent formerly with the Astros.

December 17—Cubs released pitcher Randy Kramer.

December 17—Mariners re-signed outfielder Ken Griffey, Sr., a free agent.

December 17—Phillies' Scranton/Wilkes-Barre affiliate signed pitcher Danny Cox, a free agent.

December 18—Cubs released pitcher Bill Long.

December 18—Twins re-signed outfielder Randy Bush, a free agent.

December 18—Braves signed shortstop Rafael Belliard, a free agent formerly with the Pirates.

December 19—Red Sox signed pitcher Danny Darwin, a free agent formerly with the Astros.

December 19—Pirates re-signed catcher Don Slaught, a free agent.

December 19—Red Sox re-signed outfielder Tom Brunansky, a free agent.

December 19—Tigers re-signed pitcher Dan Petry, a free agent.

December 19—Angels re-signed infielder Donnie Hill, a free agent.

December 19—Dodgers re-signed pitcher Fernando Valenzuela and infielder Mickey Hatcher, both free agents.

December 19—Mariners signed pitcher Bill Krueger, a free agent formerly with the Brewers.

December 19—Orioles re-signed catcher Mickey Tettleton, a free agent.

December 19—Athletics re-signed pitcher Scott Sanderson, a free agent.

December 20—Pirates claimed pitcher Rosario Rodriguez from Reds.

December 20—White Sox signed pitcher Charlie Hough, a free agent formerly with the Rangers.

December 20—Braves re-signed pitcher Charlie Leibrandt, a free agent.

December 20—Angels released second baseman Johnny Ray.

December 20—Yakult Swallows of Japanese Baseball League signed second baseman Johnny Ray, a free agent.

December 20—Brewers traded catcher Bert Heffernan to Dodgers for pitcher Darren Holmes.

December 21—Padres signed pitcher Larry Andersen, a free agent formerly with the Red Sox.

December 23—Expos traded outfielder Tim Raines, pitcher Jeff Carter and a player to be named to White Sox for outfielder Ivan Calderon and pitcher Barry Jones.

December 30—Dodgers traded pitcher Jim Poole and cash to Rangers for pitchers Steve Allen and David Lynch; Dodgers assigned Allen and Lynch to Albuquerque.

December 31—Yankees purchased pitcher Scott Sanderson from Athletics.

Conigliaro's Dream And Life Brief

By DAVE SLOAN

The dream of every red-blooded American boy is to grow up and play for his hometown team. Tony Conigliaro lived that dream for six years in the 1960s before tragedy cut the dream short. Conigliaro's life ended prematurely, too, when he died at age 45 from pneumonia and kidney failure in a Boston hospital on February 24.

Conigliaro, born at Revere, Mass., on January 7, 1945, broke into the major leagues as a 19-year-old outfielder with the Boston Red Sox in 1964. He hit 24 homers that season and clubbed an American League-leading 32 the following year. Conigliaro hit 28 home runs in 1966 and had 20 in Boston's first 95 games of the 1967 season before suffering an injury from which he never fully recovered.

In an August 18 game at Fenway Park, Conigliaro was struck flush in the face by a fastball that got away from California righthander Jack Hamilton. The pitch shattered Conigliaro's left cheekbone and permanently impaired his vision. The injury was so serious that it forced the Red Sox to put their star outfielder on the disabled list for the rest of the '67 season and the entire 1968 campaign. The disability prevented Conigliaro from playing in Boston's seven-game World Series loss to St. Louis in 1967.

After a brief, unsuccessful attempt to become a pitcher, Conigliaro wound up back in the Boston outfield in 1969. He hit 20 homers that year to capture A.L. Comeback Player of the Year honors. The following season, playing alongside younger brother Billy in the Red Sox outfield, Conigliaro hit a career-high 36 home runs and collected 116 runs batted in.

That 1970 season, however, is also when Conigliaro began to experience more trouble with his left eye, particularly with seeing the baseball in late-afternoon games. The Red Sox traded Conigliaro—then just 25 years old—to the California Angels on October 11, 1970.

After hitting just .222 in 74 games with the Angels in 1971, Conigliaro decided to retire. He attempted a comeback with Boston in 1975 but, after playing in only 21 games, gave up baseball for good to pursue a career in sports broadcasting.

Ironically, Conigliaro had just interviewed for a job with a Providence, R.I., television station on January 9, 1982, when he suffered a heart seizure—an attack that

Tony Conigliaro led the American League with 32 homers in 1965.

left him in a coma for three weeks and resulted in irreversible brain damage. Conigliaro, who never bettered his .290 rookie batting average in six subsequent major league seasons, required almost constant care the last eight years of his life.

The only member of baseball's Hall of Fame to die in 1990 was 91-year-old Joe Sewell, a standout infielder with the Cleveland Indians and New York Yankees in the 1920s and early '30s. Sewell, who was elected to the Hall of Fame by the Veterans Committee in 1977, died March 6 at Mobile, Ala.

Born October 9, 1898, at Titus, Ala., Sewell was the oldest of three brothers who played in the major leagues and the most successful. Whereas a tragedy prematurely ended Conigliaro's baseball career, the same type of tragedy helped spawn Sewell's.

Shortstop Ray Chapman of the Cleveland Indians was struck in the head by a pitch thrown by Yankees righthander Carl Mays on August 16, 1920. Chapman's death the following day forced the Indians—then in the midst of a tight pennant race—to scramble for a replacement. They eventually settled on the 21-year-old Sewell, who had played ball at the University of Alabama the previous spring. Cleveland purchased Sewell's rights from their New Orleans (Southern) farm club for $6,000 and also agreed to relinquish all claims to players it had optioned to New Orleans during the 1920 season.

Sewell reported to Cleveland on September 6 and hit .329 in the season's final 22 games to help the Indians win their first A.L. pennant. The Indians advanced to capture the World Series in seven games over Brooklyn, despite Sewell's .174 average.

Throughout the ensuing decade, he was a fixture in the Cleveland infield, first as a shortstop for eight seasons and later as a third baseman the last two. Sewell hit over .300 nine times for the Indians, including a career-high .353 in 1923.

After the Indians released him in January 1931, Sewell signed with the Yankees to play third base. He spent three seasons in New York, roomed with Lou Gehrig, and made it to his second World Series in 1932. He hit .333 in the Yankees' four-game sweep of the Chicago Cubs.

Over the course of his 14-year career, Sewell became the game's toughest player to strike out. He established four records in that regard that still stand: most consecutive games without striking out (115); fewest strikeouts in a season, 150 or more games (four in 1925 and 1929); fewest strikeouts in a career (113 in 7,132 at-bats) and most consecutive at-bats without a strikeout (437).

After his playing career ended in 1933, Sewell served as a Yankees coach for two seasons before later becoming a scout for the Indians and New York Mets. In 1964, 44 years after he left the school and at age 66, Sewell became the baseball coach at the University of Alabama. He served in that capacity for seven years, guiding the Crimson Tide to a 114-99 overall record and a Southeastern Conference title in 1968.

Another prominent player to die last year was outfielder Wally Moses, who played 17 seasons with three A.L. teams before later becoming a successful batting coach. He died October 10 at Vidalia, Ga., two days after his 80th birthday.

Moses' professional career began shortly after one of baseball's all-time greats, Ty Cobb, spotted the 20-year-old fellow Georgian playing in a sandlot game. Cobb was so impressed that he got Moses a contract to play for the Augusta, Ga., team in the Palmetto League in 1931. When that league folded in mid-season, Moses signed with the Elmira, N.Y., New York-Pennsylvania League club. He rode the bench until the team's general manager, Warren Giles (a future National League president), ordered his manager to play the youngster every day. Moses hit .248 in 40 games with Elmira that summer.

Moses spent the next three years in the minor leagues before breaking into the majors at age 24 with the Philadelphia A's in 1935. He hit .325 in his first 85 games that year but missed the rest of the season after breaking his left arm after crashing into an outfield wall on August 17. It was the first of seven straight seasons with the Athletics in which Moses hit better than .300.

After the last of those .300 seasons, 1941, A's Manager Connie Mack traded the outfielder to the Chicago White Sox. Moses toiled in Chicago for a little more than four years before being dealt to the Boston Red Sox midway through the 1946 season. He helped the Red Sox win the A.L. pennant that year and hit .417 in four World Series games against St. Louis. Moses spent the next two years in Boston before returning to the A's to conclude his playing career (1949-51).

His tenure as a major league batting coach included a stint with the Philadelphia Phillies (when pupil Richie Ashburn won N.L. batting titles in 1955 and '58) and the Yankees (when Roger Maris and Mickey Mantle combined to hit a record 115 homers in 1961).

An alphabetical list of baseball deaths in 1990 follows:

John Lawrence (Johnny) Antonelli, 74, an infielder with the St. Louis Cardinals and Philadelphia Phillies in the mid-1940s and a minor league manager, coach and scout, at Memphis on April 18; at age 19, was appointed player/manager of Lexington, the Cardinals' Kitty League outpost in 1935, thus beginning a steady rise through the organization; after eight games with St. Louis in 1944, he split the 1945 season with the Cards and Phillies, concluding his big-league career with a .252 average in 135 games; left baseball after managing in the Cotton States League in 1950, but returned in 1969 as interim skipper of the Mets'

Texas League affiliate in his native Memphis; named manager the next year, and went on to manage at Tidewater and Jackson, Miss., through 1976; was a Mets minor league instructor, coach and scout until 1989.

Robert Rudolph (Bobby) Balcena, 61, whose lack of size (5-7, 160 pounds) never hindered his hard hitting through 15 professional seasons, at San Pedro, Calif., on January 5; in only his second minor league tour, Balcena put together a 16-home run, 132-runs batted in campaign for Mexicali (Sunset League) in 1949, then a 21-homer season for San Antonio (Texas) in 1953; was called to the big leagues three years later for seven games and two at-bats with Cincinnati; twice led Texas League outfielders in fielding before concluding his career in 1962.

Lowell M. (Odie) Barnett, 74, a former minor league infielder and part-time baseball scout, at Muncie, Ind., on December 7; a shortstop and third baseman, he played in the minors from 1936 to 1940, mostly with Eau Claire, Wis., in the Northern League; later taught and coached in Muncie public schools until his appointment as high school athletic director.

Charles Henry (Red) Barrett, 75, a workmanlike righthander who led the National League in victories in 1945 and was credited with making the fewest number of pitches in a nine-inning game, at Wilson, N.C., on July 28; known for pinpoint control and constantly varying the speed of his pitches, he was nevertheless just a .500 pitcher (69-69) in parts of 11 big-league seasons; made his first major league appearance in 1937 with the Cincinnati Reds, who kept him buried in their system despite some eye-opening minor league seasons: 24-12 in '37, 16-3 in '38, 16-12 in '39, 20-16 in '41 and 20-12 in '42; sold to the Boston Braves in 1943, he finally spent a full season in the majors, fashioning a 3.18 earned-run average and 12-18 record for a sixth-place team; slipped to 9-16 in 1944, though he threw just 58 pitches (believed to be an all-time low) to shut out Cincinnati on August 10 in the quickest night game in major league history (1 hour, 15 minutes); was traded to St. Louis for Mort Cooper after a 2-3 start with Boston in '45, but wound up the season as the N.L. leader in victories (23), complete games (24) and innings pitched (285); was sold back to Boston after the 1946 season, ending his career there in 1949.

John Andrew (Johnny) Beazley, 70, who shot to stardom with the 1942 St. Louis Cardinals by winning 21 games and twice beating the Yankees in the World Series only to injure his arm in World War II, at Nashville, Tenn., on April 21; summoned to St. Louis after five seasons on the farm, he helped pitch the Cards to the '42 pennant with a 21-6 record and 2.13 earned-run average, then won a pair of complete-game decisions against New York in the Series; one month after winning the decisive fifth game, he was called to service in the South Pacific; three years later, he returned to the States with a lame arm—not because of combat, but due to frequent demands to pitch in service exhibition games; declined to undergo corrective surgery and was limited to a 7-5 record and one-inning stint in the Cards' 1946 Series victory over Boston; sold to the Red Sox in the off-season, he would pitch in only 13 more big-league games through 1949; later served on the Nashville City Council.

William Aloysius (Bill) Beckman, 82, a righthanded pitcher for the Philadelphia Athletics and St. Louis Cardinals from 1939 through 1942, at St. Louis on January 2; 12 years after signing his first contract out of St. Louis' Washington University in 1927, he joined Connie Mack's A's at the age of 31 in 1939; recorded a career-best 8-4 mark in the majors in 1940, but averaged 15 victories per year in the minors between 1929 and 1938; after

signing with the hometown Cardinals near the end of 1942, he won his only decision there to finish with 21-25 four-season totals; returned to the A's as a scout in 1947, remaining through the club's last season in Philadelphia (1954).

Clare Bertram, 71, a minor league pitcher who hurled three no-hitters in a two-season span, at Tulsa, Okla., on January 20; despite his no-hit prowess, Bertram never pitched in the majors, though he was transferred to the Chicago Cubs' roster near the end of the 1938 and '39 seasons; in 1937, he pitched no-hitters nine days apart with Pensacola of the Southeastern League, then fashioned a perfect game the following season with Moline in the Three-I circuit.

Fred Donald (Don) Bessent, 59, who won his first eight decisions as a rookie with the 1955 Brooklyn Dodgers and pitched in the first major league game played on the West Coast, at Jacksonville, Fla., on July 7; that he was able to pitch at all was testament to his resolve of spirit, for a severe back ailment left him nearly paralyzed at age 20 coming off 22-7 and 11-2 seasons in his first two minor league tours; a spinal-fusion operation proved successful but idled him for the '52 schedule, prompting the New York Yankees to leave their one-time prize prospect unprotected; claimed by Brooklyn in 1953, he was summoned to the Dodgers from their St. Paul affiliate on July 16, 1955, along with Roger Craig (from Montreal); the next day, the two rookies started and won both games of a doubleheader from Cincinnati; won two more games within a week and finished the season with an 8-1 record and 2.71 earned-run average; pitched in the World Series in 1955 and 1956, when he beat the Yankees in Game 2 after posting a 2.51 ERA during the season in relief; shoulder problems limited his effectiveness in 1957 and '58, but he pitched with Los Angeles in the first major league game on the West Coast, on April 15, 1958, in San Francisco; posted 14-7 big-league totals from 1955 through '58.

John Drew Betz, 72, part owner of the Philadelphia Phillies since 1981, at Philadelphia on October 6; one of five limited partners (along with his wife, Claire) in Bill Giles' ownership group that purchased the club in October 1981, Betz was a noted Quaker City philanthropist and businessman; his company was a leader in the treatment of industrial waste water and a frequent contributor to environmental projects.

Joseph Emil (Joe) Bowman, 80, the losing pitcher in the first night game ever played in the major leagues and later a minor league manager and scout, at Kansas City, Mo., on November 22; compiled a 77-96 career record pitching for six big-league teams between 1932 and 1945, but also played the outfield and third base when he broke into the minors in 1929; never lost his batting stroke, often being called upon as a pinch-hitter, and batted .344 (33-for-96) with Pittsburgh in 1939; on May 24, 1935, as a starting pitcher with the Philadelphia Phillies, he lost a 2-1 decision to Paul Derringer and Cincinnati in the first big-league game played under lights; after a 9-20 season in 1936, he moved on to the Pirates and Boston, posting a career-best 12-8 record for the Red Sox in 1944; concluded his major league career with the Reds in 1945, then managed in the minors for six seasons; Clete Boyer and Mike Boddicker were among the players he signed as a scout with the Kansas City A's, Cincinnati, Atlanta and Baltimore through 1987.

Chester (Chet) Brewer, 83, a hard-throwing righthander who plied his trade for more than a quarter-century in the old Negro leagues and the first black to manage in Organized Baseball in the United States, at Los Angeles on March 26; his smoke caught the eye of a traveling Kansas City

Monarchs "seasoning" club while he barnstormed with the Tennessee Rats as a teen-ager in the early 1920s; joined the Monarchs in 1925 and was a long-time roommate of Satchel Paige; in 1952, he made his debut in Organized Ball as player/manager of the Porterville entry in the Southwest International League; although his team folded before the end of its schedule, he gained distinction as the first black to manage a professional team in the United States; later was a scout with the Hollywood Stars, Pittsburgh Pirates and Major League Scouting Bureau.

Marshall Bridges, 59, a former Negro league star who pitched for four major league teams between 1959 and 1965, at Jackson, Miss., on September 3; became a student of baseball at age 11, quitting the fourth grade to become a clubhouse boy and groundskeeper's assistant at Jackson's League Park; a lefthanded pitcher, outfielder and first baseman for the Negro league Memphis Red Sox, he barnstormed during the winters against Roy Campanella's all-stars and was signed by the New York Giants' chain in 1953; played for eight minor league teams over the next seven seasons, leading the Western League with 18 wins and 213 strikeouts for Topeka in 1956 and the Pacific Coast League with 16 victories (co-leader) and 205 strikeouts at Sacramento in '58; made his big-league debut with the St. Louis Cardinals midway through '59, finishing 6-3 with 76 strikeouts in 76 innings; released to Cincinnati the following August, he tallied a 6-2 record and 2.37 earned-run average for the year but was dealt to the Yankees after spending most of 1961 in the minors; posted a career-high eight wins for New York in '62 and pitched in two World Series games; played with Washington in 1964-65, concluding his career with a 23-15 record.

Robert Murray (Bob) Brown, 79, a right-handed pitcher who won 14 games with the 1932 Boston Braves but managed only two more victories in the next four seasons due to an arm injury, at Pembroke, Mass., on August 17; signed out of Boston's Bingham High School by the Braves in 1930, he had just turned 21 when he made the club's opening-day roster out of training camp in 1932; armed with a hard, sharp-breaking curveball, he finished 14-7 for a second-division Braves team, making an immediate splash by twice out-dueling Brooklyn's Dazzy Vance within a month; seemingly on the brink of stardom, he developed a sore arm in spring training the following year; for four years, he bounced between Boston and the minors, sinking to 1-3 and 1-8 records in 1934 and '35, respectively; closed his career with a 16-21 mark.

Clarence Bruce, 65, a second baseman for the Homestead Grays when they won the next-to-last Negro league championship series in 1948, at Pittsburgh on January 23; a member of the Grays in 1947 and '48, he played a year in Canada before beginning a 35-year employment with the U.S. Postal Service; was honored at Pittsburgh's Three Rivers Stadium in September 1988 with other surviving members of the Grays on the 40th anniversary of their championship.

Thomas James (Tom) Caciavely, 65, an infielder in the St. Louis Browns' and Brooklyn Dodgers' organizations in the 1940s and owner of a St. Louis auto dealership for more than 20 years, at St. Louis on December 12; broke into the minor leagues in 1943, beginning a pro career that spanned eight seasons; operated a St. Louis Ford dealership, under the name Casavely, until retiring from the business in 1987.

Robert Ruliph Morgan (Bob) Carpenter Jr., 74, who in 1943 became the youngest club president in major league history at age 28 and presided over the Philadelphia Phillies until 1981, at Montchanin, Del., on July 8; a former football player at Duke, he became the Phils' president when his father, R.R.M. Carpenter Sr., vice president of the DuPont chemical firm, purchased the struggling franchise from William Cox for $400,000 in November 1943; before beginning a two-year hitch in World War II, he astutely hired Herb Pennock as general manager and began the buildup of a nearly depleted farm system; in 1950, the Whiz Kids won the club's first pennant in 35 years and Carpenter was named The Sporting News' Executive of the Year; actively ran the club's daily business until 1972, when he turned over the president's chair to his son, 32-year-old Ruly, and became chairman of the board; sold the team for $30.2 million to an investment group headed by Bill Giles in October 1981; born in Wilmington, Del., he brought professional basketball to the city as owner of the American Basketball League's Blue Bombers; a frequent athletics booster and trustee of the University of Delaware for 45 years, he was honored when the school broke ground in June on the $18 million Bob Carpenter/Sports Convocation Center.

Spurgeon Ferdinand (Spud) Chandler, 82, twice a 20-game winner and the 1943 American League Most Valuable Player when he set a standing New York Yankees record with a 1.64 earned-run average, at St. Petersburg, Fla., on January 9; a Yankee for all of his 11 big-league seasons, Chandler owned a 109-43 record and franchise-best .717 winning percentage upon his retirement in 1947; signed by the Yanks in 1932 after rising to notoriety at the University of Georgia as a pitcher and triple-threat tailback, he joined the club in '37 and finished 14-5 in his first full big-league season in 1938; overcame a tender elbow in 1939 and '40 to post 10-4 and 16-5 records leading up to his banner 1943 season; already 35 years old, he won 20 of 24 decisions, pitched a league-high 20 complete games, topped all hurlers with a 1.64 ERA and was voted the A.L. MVP; won the first and decisive fifth games in the Yanks' World Series victory over St. Louis, yielding one earned run in 18 innings; military service cut short the next two seasons, but he returned in 1946 to post a 20-8 record and 2.10 ERA; his arm problems became serious the next year, though he captured the A.L. ERA crown a second time with a 2.46 mark; released by New York after undergoing elbow surgery following the '47 World Series, he spent another four decades in the game, managing for the Yankees' farm in 1954-55, coaching for the Kansas City A's in 1957-58 and scouting for both clubs as well as Cleveland and Minnesota.

James B. Clegg, 81, a minor league umpire who worked more than 2,000 games between 1940 and 1955, at Calhoun, Ga., on January 26; his umpiring career took him to the South Atlantic, Middle Atlantic, Piedmont, Carolina and Texas leagues, the American Association and to Puerto Rico for winter baseball; later coached baseball and basketball at Centre College in Danville, Ky., and formed an umpiring association that provided arbiters for college games in northern Georgia.

Robert C. Clements, 75, a longtime associate of the late Branch Rickey and a farm director of the Pittsburgh Pirates, at Gastonia, N.C., on February 14; went to work for Rickey in 1936 in the St. Louis Cardinals' public relations department, then followed the renowned executive to the Brooklyn Dodgers and Pittsburgh; worked mostly as a scout, and in 1961 became the Pirates' farm director upon the sudden death of Branch Rickey Jr.; later scouted for the Seattle Pilots before concluding his baseball career as assistant director of the Major League Scouting Bureau.

Ralph O. Coleman Sr., 94, the winningest baseball coach in Oregon State University history in a career that spanned five decades, at Corvallis, Ore., on July 8; the Beavers' coach for 36 seasons, he compiled a 560-317 record and finished first in the Pacific-10 Conference's Northern Division in eight seasons; in 1952, the school made its only appearance in the College World Series under Coleman, who coached the Beavers from 1923 through 1931 and 1938 through 1966; in 1981, the home of the baseball Beavers was renamed Ralph Coleman Field.

Anthony Richard (Tony) Conigliaro, 45, a Boston Red Sox outfielder who became the baseball darling of his native New England only to have his glowing future darkened by tragedy, at Boston on February 24; a native of Revere, Mass., he realized his boyhood dream by joining the Red Sox in 1964 after less than one year of seasoning in the short-season New York-Pennsylvania League; at the tender age of 19, he slugged 24 home runs and batted a personal-best .290 in just 111 rookie games, then became the American League's youngest home run champion at 20, belting 32 homers in '65; following a 28-homer, 93-runs batted in campaign in '66, tragedy struck on August 18, 1967, when an errant fastball from California Angels righthander Jack Hamilton fractured his left cheekbone and left him legally blind in his left eye; was disabled the rest of 1967 and the entire 1968 season, but his vision miraculously returned and led to his 20-homer, 82-RBI comeback season of 1969; joined in the Boston outfield by brother Billy in 1970, he hung up the best numbers of his career with 36 homers and 116 RBIs; in a stunning postseason move, however, the Red Sox traded their hometown boy to California to acquire reliever Ken Tatum; his vision problems returned as the 1971 season unfolded, prompting his announced retirement in July; attempted a second comeback as a designated hitter with Boston in 1975, but called it quits after 21 games for a job as a television sportscaster; his life took another tragic turn on January 9, 1982, when he suffered a heart seizure after interviewing for the Red Sox's TV analyst job; lapsed into a coma for three weeks and suffered irreversible brain damage; required constant care thereafter, living with his parents (his father died of heart failure in 1987) and younger brother; died in a Boston hospital of pneumonia and kidney failure.

Larry Eugene Cox, 42, a major league catcher and coach and a minor league manager, of a heart attack while playing racquetball at Bellefontaine, O.; had just completed his second season as the Chicago Cubs' bullpen coach, a job he took after managing five seasons in the club's farm system; as a player, he spent parts of nine seasons in the majors with the Cubs, Philadelphia, Texas and Seattle; saw the most duty in 1979 and '80 as part of the Mariners' catching platoon; after retiring as a player in '82, he served one year as a minor league instructor before managing at Chicago's Quad City affiliate in 1983-84 and at Iowa of the American Association from 1985 through '87; posted a career .221 average in 348 big-league games.

Roger Maxwell (Doc) Cramer, 84, unsung hitter extraordinaire who rapped 2,705 hits in a career that spanned 20 American League seasons, at Manahawkin, N.J., on September 9; a line-drive hitting outfielder who met any pitcher's best challenge, he batted .300 or better eight times, struck out as many as 30 times only twice and is the lone A.L. player to twice collect six hits in six at-bats; saw his first big-league action in 1929 before cracking the Philadelphia Athletics' regular lineup in 1932 with a .336 average; led the league in at-bats the next three seasons, then was dealt in 1936 to Boston, where his range and hustle afield helped him lead A.L. outfielders in double plays and putouts in his first Fenway season; tied for the A.L. lead in hits in 1940, the last of his three 200-hit seasons, but spent the next year in Washington before joining Detroit in 1942; in all, topped the

league in at-bats seven times, a major league record, and fashioned a .296 career batting mark; at age 41 in 1947, his next-to-last season, he led all A.L. hitters in pinch hits; coached with the 1948 Tigers and 1951-53 Chicago White Sox before retiring from baseball.

Frank Angelo (Creepy) Crespi, 72, called "the best second baseman I ever teamed with" by former St. Louis Cardinals shortstop Marty Marion, at St. Louis on March 1; signed by the Cardinals off the St. Louis sandlots, he broke into the minors as an outfielder in 1937 but moved to shortstop after opening eyes with his nimble glove work and strong arm; nicknamed for his habit of inching toward the plate as the pitcher made his delivery; was summoned to St. Louis in 1941 after batting .301 with 80 runs batted in at Rochester (International League) in 1940; installed as the regular second baseman, he responded by leading the league in putouts and double plays at his position while batting .279; after a brief holdout and injury the following spring, he was bumped from the starting lineup but played in 93 games and made one World Series appearance as a pinch-runner; drafted into the Army the next spring, he suffered multiple leg fractures while playing with a service team in Fort Riley, Kan.; underwent numerous leg surgeries, but was unable to resume his big-league career; managed the Cardinals' Mount Vernon team in 1948 and scouted during the 1950s.

Frank Dascoli, 74, a colorful but controversial National League umpire with a quick temper and equally quick thumb, at Danielson, Conn., on August 11; was one of the league's most capable arbiters, but his 14 seasons on the job nevertheless were underscored by two separate controversies; promoted to the majors in July 1948 after umpiring in the Eastern Shore, Canadian-American and International leagues, Dascoli quickly developed a tough reputation by ejecting any player or manager who dared challenge his authority; in the eighth inning of a September 27, 1951, game between Boston and Brooklyn, he made a call that "made my career" but a decision that Brooklyn will never forget; with the fading Dodgers trying to cling to first place, his call on a bang-bang play at the plate allowed the Braves' Bob Addis to slide safely across with what proved to be the winning run; in the ensuing protest, he ejected Dodgers catcher Roy Campanella, who would have otherwise batted in the ninth inning with one out and the potential tying run on third base; the 4-3 loss shrank Brooklyn's lead to half a game over the New York Giants, who would win the pennant seven days later on Bobby Thomson's home run; in a fitting climax to his career, he took part in a heated on-the-air radio debate with longtime antagonist Solly Hemus, manager of the St. Louis Cardinals; when N.L. President Warren Giles banned the league's arbiters from appearing on all interview shows in the future, Dascoli lashed back in the newspapers, announcing he planned to retire at the end of the season due to "incompetent and spineless handling of umpires" by Giles; on August 10, 1961, he was dismissed by the league president.

Donald Davidson, 64, a short-statured man who became a giant baseball personality in various front-office roles for more than 40 years, at Houston on March 28; his growth stunted due to a childhood illness, he stood exactly 4 feet tall but made his presence felt everywhere with his quick wit and administrative competence; employed by the Braves for some 28 years, most of them as traveling secretary, he was the lone club employee to survive the moves from Boston to Milwaukee to Atlanta; received the Bill Slocum Award for long and meritorious service to baseball in 1971 and was named King of Baseball at the winter meetings in 1984, one year after undergoing surgery for throat cancer; in 1976, he joined the Houston Astros' front-office team, serving as special assistant to General Manager Bill Wood at the time of his death.

Margaret Holekamp DeWitt, 77, widow of former Cincinnati Reds president William O. DeWitt, at Cincinnati on February 23; a native of St. Louis, she married DeWitt in 1936 when he was general manager of the St. Louis Browns; after moving to Cincinnati in 1960, she attended 30 consecutive opening-day Reds games at Crosley Field and Riverfront Stadium.

Robert P. (Bobby) Dolan, 59, a minor league infielder in the 1950s, at Reno, Nev., on June 5; launched his pro baseball career in 1951 and led the Cotton States League with 14 triples a year later at Greenwood; played the following three seasons with Elmira of the Eastern League; posted his best season at Montreal of the International League in 1958, batting .270 in 135 games; completed his playing career in the American Association with St. Paul in 1959; became a real estate broker in Reno.

August J. (Augie) Donatelli, 75, a colorful National League umpire for 24 seasons and the driving force behind the formation of the Major League Umpires Association in 1964, at St. Petersburg, Fla., on May 24; played 14 games of minor league baseball as an infielder with Beaver Falls of the Pennsylvania State Association in 1938; served in World War II and spent 15 months as a German prisoner of war; returned to baseball as a Pioneer League umpire in 1946; advanced quickly to the South Atlantic League and then the International League, where he umpired from August 1947 through 1949; promoted to the N.L. umpiring staff for the 1950 season; gained a reputation for his fiery personality, quick thumb and the dramatic style in which he ejected players and managers and called signals; among his many memorable arguments was a 1952 New York Giants-St. Louis Cardinals game in which he ejected New York's Bob Elliott for arguing a called second strike and then thumbed out Elliott's replacement, Bobby Hofman, for complaining after taking strike three; in the famous "shoe polish" game of the 1957 World Series, he ruled that Milwaukee Braves pinch-hitter Nippy Jones was hit on the foot by a pitch after Jones showed him a smudge of shoe polish on the ball; the pinch-runner for Jones later scored the game-tying run in the bottom of the 10th inning and the Braves went on to win that fourth game and then to defeat the New York Yankees in seven games; lost his post as crew chief after organizing the umpires' union, although N.L. President Warren Giles denied that Donatelli's union activities were the reason; retired after working the 1973 World Series, his fifth fall classic to go along with four All-Star Games.

Henry J. (Dutch) Dotterer, 85, a minor league infielder and a scout for three major league organizations, at Syracuse, N.Y., on July 16; began a minor league career that spanned five years in 1929; playing career was halted by a spinal injury; became a scout for the Syracuse Chiefs of the International League in 1947 and later scouted for the Cincinnati Reds (1949-61), Cleveland Indians (1962-74) and New York Yankees (1977-85); father of Dutch Dotterer, a backup catcher for the Reds and Washington Senators from 1957 through '61.

Edward V. (Ed) Dunn, 67, a scout for the Minnesota Twins for 30 years, at Baltimore on March 15; played only 12 games of pro baseball, all with Amsterdam of the Canadian-American League in 1940; scouted for the Washington Senators in 1959 and '60; served the Twins as a scout from November 1960 until his death; signed right-hander Dave Boswell, an eight-year major league veteran, among others.

Nicholas R. (Nick) Etten, 76, a first baseman for three major league clubs in nine seasons who led the American League in home runs in 1944 and in runs batted in a year later, at Hinsdale, Ill., on October 18; played baseball for two years at Villanova College and then dropped out because of the Depression and signed a pro baseball contract; batted over .300 four times in six minor league seasons before getting a taste of the big leagues with the Philadelphia Athletics in 1938 and '39; his contract was sold to the Philadelphia Phillies in 1940, and he hit a career-high .311 with 14 homers and 79 RBIs with the Phils in 1941, his first of six consecutive full seasons in the majors; was traded to the New York Yankees before the 1943 season and proceeded to tally 107 RBIs for the pennant-winning Yanks; blasted 22 homers in 1944 and knocked in 111 runs in 1945, both league bests; was sold back to the Phillies in 1947, making his last 14 big-league appearances that season; finished his career in the minors after totaling 89 homers, 526 RBIs and a .277 average in 937 games in the big leagues.

Paul C. Frisz, 82, one of the founders of the Society for American Baseball Research and a former operator of the old Three-I League club in Terre Haute, Ind., of congestive heart failure at Terre Haute on January 2; was majority owner, president and general manager of the Terre Haute Huts in 1955 and '56; served as SABR vice president for two years; owned a large collection of baseball memorabilia.

Robert M. (Bob) Garbark, 80, a catcher with four major league teams in seven seasons between 1934 and 1945, at Meadville, Pa., on August 15; graduated from Allegheny College in Meadville in 1932 and launched a pro career in the Cleveland Indians' organization; batted over .300 for Toledo of the American Association in both 1934 and '35, getting brief trials with the Indians each year; was sold to the Chicago Cubs in September 1936; appeared in 48 games for the Cubs over the next three seasons; spent the next few years in the minors and out of baseball, coming out of retirement late in World War II to serve as a backup catcher with the Philadelphia Athletics in 1944 and the Boston Red Sox in 1945, when he batted .261 in 68 games; batted .248 in 145 big-league games overall; managed in the minors briefly in the early 1950s and then managed his alma mater's baseball team for 32 seasons; his younger brother, Mike Garbark, played 149 games for the New York Yankees in 1944 and '45.

George Goodale, 83, the California Angels' first publicity director and a front-office fixture with the club until he suffered a stroke in 1985, of cardiac arrest at Anaheim, Calif., on May 31; nicknamed "The Chief" because of his Cherokee Indian heritage; met Gene Autry, who later became the Angels' owner, in 1927 when the two were working in Tulsa, Okla., Goodale as a sportswriter for the Tulsa World, Autry as a telegraph operator; became Autry's first Hollywood publicist in 1935; worked as a publicist for the Los Angeles Angels of the Pacific Coast League after World War II; was one of the first front-office employees hired by Autry when the expansion Angels joined the American League in 1961; also served the club as director of special statistics and events.

Glen E. Gorbous, 59, an outfielder who played briefly with the Cincinnati Reds and Philadelphia Phillies but is best remembered for throwing a baseball farther than anyone in history, at Calgary, Alberta, on June 12; one of only four Alberta natives to reach the major leagues; a sandlot sensation in western Canada, he was signed by the Brooklyn Dodgers in 1948 because of his powerful right arm; played six years in the Dodgers' farm system, batting over .300 in four of those seasons, before being drafted by the Reds in November 1954; was traded to Philadelphia early in the 1955 season but spent the entire year in the majors, batting .244 with four home runs in 242 at-bats; managed only 18 more big-league appearances with the Phillies in 1956 and '57, finishing his big-league career with a .238 average in 115 games; carved a niche for himself in the Guinness Book of World Records on August 1, 1957, by throwing a baseball 445 feet, 10 inches, on the fly; used a six-step running start to heave the ball from the right-field corner to the left-field corner of Omaha Stadium, home of the American Association club that employed him that summer; retired from baseball two years later because of an arm injury.

Carmen P. Hill, 93, a screwballing righthander who won 22 games for the 1927 National League champion Pittsburgh Pirates, at Indianapolis on January 1; was the last surviving member of the '27 Pirates; spent much of his career prior to 1927 bouncing between Pittsburgh and the minor leagues (plus a brief stint with the New York Giants), winning nine games in just 34 big-league appearances from 1915 through 1926; after spending four years at Indianapolis of the American Association, he was reacquired by the Pirates late in the 1926 season; blossomed as Pittsburgh's big winner in 1927 but was granted only one World Series start, getting no decision in Game 4 as the New York Yankees completed a sweep; won 16 games for Pittsburgh in 1928 but only two over the next two seasons with the Pirates and the St. Louis Cardinals; returned to the minors in 1930 after compiling a 49-33 record with a 3.44 earned-run average in 10 big-league seasons.

Lawrence Curtis (Larry) Jackson, 59, a righthander who pitched effectively for 14 seasons in the National League without ever being a member of a championship team, of cancer at Boise, Idaho, on August 28; a workhorse from the start of his career in the St. Louis Cardinals' farm system, he pitched 300 innings, struck out 351 batters and went 28-4 for Fresno of the California League in 1952, his second pro season; advanced quickly through the ranks, reaching the majors in 1955; went 9-14 as a rookie but did not suffer another losing season during his eight years with the Cardinals; became a regular member of the St. Louis rotation in 1957 and kicked off a 12-year run in which he won at least 13 games every season and pitched less than 210 innings only once; led the National League in starts (38) and innings pitched (282) in 1960; was traded to the Chicago Cubs after the 1962 campaign; enjoyed his best season in 1964, when he posted an amazing 24-11 record with an eighth-place Cubs team; was traded again early in the 1966 season, going to Philadelphia in a multiplayer deal that sent future Hall of Famer Ferguson Jenkins to the Cubs; won 15 games for the Phillies and tied for the league lead with five shutouts in 1966; after winning 13 games, hurling 243⅔ innings and fashioning a 2.77 earned-run average in 1968, he retired from baseball at the age of 37; returned to his native Idaho, where he went to work as a lobbyist for a paper and pulp manufacturer; later started his own insurance business, served four terms in the Idaho House of Representatives, served as executive director of the Idaho Republican Party and campaigned unsuccessfully for the party's 1978 gubernatorial nomination; finished his major league career with a 194-183 record, a 3.40 ERA, 1,709 strikeouts and 149 complete games; pitched in four All-Star Games, winning one.

Charles (King Kong) Keller, 73, the left fielder in one of baseball's greatest outfields with New York Yankee teammates Joe DiMaggio and Tommy Henrich, of cancer near Frederick, Md., on May 23; earned his nickname for his brute strength and stocky build (5-foot-10, 185 pounds), which he parlayed into 760 runs batted in and 189 home runs over 13 major league seasons, despite being limited to less than 85 games in seven of those years; after playing two years at Newark, where he led the International League in hits and runs in both 1937 and 1938, the lefthanded batter was a rookie sensation with the '39 Yankees, batting .334 in 111 games and going 7-for-16 with three homers as the Yankees won the World Series; posted career highs of 33 homers and 122 RBIs in 1941, when the Yanks again won the fall classic; played in two more World Series (1942 and '43, the latter being another Yankee triumph), finishing with a .306 batting average and .611 slugging percentage in 19 World Series games; averaged 99 runs scored, 98 runs batted in and 24 homers per year while batting .294 from 1939 through '43; enlisted in the Merchant Marine in January 1944 and returned to the Yankees late in the '45 season; smacked 30 homers and drove in 101 runs in 1946, but missed most of the '47 season with a back injury; never regained his old form, hitting only 14 homers over the last five years of his career; was released by the Yankees in December 1949 and spent the next two years as a pinch-hitter and occasional outfielder with Detroit; was released by the Tigers after the '51 season and made two appearances with the Yankees late in 1952; batted .286 in 1,170 big-league games and played in three All-Star Games; retired to his native Maryland, where he developed a successful harness-horse breeding farm; brother of Hal Keller, a catcher with the Washington Senators in 1949, '50 and '52 who later became a major league executive.

William H. (Big Bill) Kelly, 90, a power-hitting first baseman who terrorized the International League in the mid-1920s before moving on to umpiring and managing in the minor leagues, at Syracuse, N.Y., on April 8; was signed to a pro contract by Philadelphia Athletics Manager Connie Mack in 1920 and appeared in nine games for the A's that year before launching an 11-year minor league playing career in 1921; played for Buffalo from 1922 through 1926, leading the International League in runs batted in three consecutive years (1924-26) with successive totals of 155, 125 and 151; led the circuit in home runs with 28 in 1924 and a league-record 44 in 1926; was sold to the Philadelphia Phillies in December 1927 and played 23 games for the National League club the following year; batted .179 in 84 at-bats during his two big-league stints; completed his playing career with Mobile of the Southern Association in 1931 but returned to baseball as an umpire in 1934, working in the New York-Pennsylvania League, Pacific Coast League, International League and American Association; began a managing career in the Chicago Cubs' organization in 1945 at Elizabethton of the Appalachian League; won pennants as manager of Davenport (Three-I) and Los Angeles (Pacific Coast) in 1946 and '47, respectively; executed an unusual move from Los Angeles to the Cubs' International League outpost in Springfield, Mass., after the 1950 season as he and Stan Hack swapped jobs; later became a scout for the Cubs, Phillies and New York Mets.

Barney Kremenko, 80, a sportswriter who covered the New York Giants and Mets and is credited with dubbing Willie Mays the "Say Hey Kid," at Mineola, N.Y., on January 20; worked for the old New York Journal-American, first covering the National Hockey League's Rangers and other events at Madison Square Garden in the 1940s before taking over the Giants' beat; claimed to have given Mays his famous moniker by addressing him "Say hey," explaining that the outfielder often responded to his questions by answering, "Say what?" or "Say that again"; campaigned for a replacement National League baseball team after the Giants moved to San Francisco following the 1957 season; began covering the Mets when they joined the senior circuit in 1962; later worked for the New York World Journal Tribune and then for the NHL's New York Islanders and the National Basketball Association's New Jersey Nets in a public relations capacity.

Willard A. (Bill) Lasley, 88, a righthander who had no record in two appearances with the St. Louis Browns in 1924, his only action in the major leagues, at Seattle on August 21; also pitched in the Pacific Coast League for Seattle and Mission as well as in Pacific Northwest semipro leagues.

Harry Arthur (Cookie) Lavagetto, 75, best remembered for his game-winning pinch-hit double that spoiled a no-hitter by the New York Yankees' Bill Bevens in the 1947 World Series and the first-ever manager of the Minnesota Twins, at Orinda, Calif., on August 10; a steady infielder who batted .269 in 10 big-league seasons, he acquired his nickname when signed as a semipro player by Oakland Oaks President V.A. (Cookie) Devincenzi, thus becoming "Cookie's boy"; batted .312 and knocked in 100 runs in his first Pacific Coast League season in 1933 and was signed by Pittsburgh, where he spent the 1934 through '36 seasons as a reserve; traded to Brooklyn before the 1937 campaign, he blossomed as a Dodger, batting .282 as a regular at second and third base; drove home more than 70 runs in four of his first five Brooklyn seasons, including a career-high 87 RBIs in 1939, when he set additional personal bests with 10 home runs and a .300 batting mark; after the '41 schedule, he was the first Dodger to join the service in World War II, spending two of his four years in the South Pacific; was relegated to a reserve role upon rejoining the club in 1946; the move ultimately paved the way for his finest hour, in Game 4 of the 1947 Brooklyn-New York World Series; came off the bench with two out in the ninth inning and the Yanks' Bill Bevens clinging to a no-hitter and a 2-1 lead to deliver a two-run pinch double that won the game for the Dodgers; released after the World Series, he returned to Oakland to play three more seasons, the last two under former Dodger Charlie Dressen; was a coach under Dressen with Brooklyn from 1951-53, with Oakland in 1954 and at Washington in 1955-56; when Dressen was fired as the Senators' manager early in 1957, he took over the club; the Senators finished last in '57, '58 and '59, but he managed the club to a fifth-place finish in 1960 and made the franchise move to Minnesota in 1961, becoming the Twins' first manager; was dismissed in June, but signed the next year as a coach and scout for the expansion New York Mets; joined the San Francisco coaching staff in 1964, remaining with the Giants until his retirement after the 1967 season.

Earl Mann, 84, celebrated owner of the old Atlanta Crackers of the Southern Association and a longtime advocate of independent operation of minor league clubs, at Palm Beach, Fla., on January 5; developed early reputation for business sense as a minor league operator in the Brooklyn and New York Yankee organizations; appointed president of the Crackers upon Wilbert Robinson's death in 1935, he was under the employ of Coca-Cola when the company took over the club in a mortgage foreclosure; purchased the club from Coke in 1949, beginning a long tenure that resulted in his building the Crackers into the most successful baseball operation in the South; noted for his successful promotions, he once booked the Jackie Robinson-era Dodgers into Atlanta for an exhibition despite threats from the Ku Klux Klan; was honored as The Sporting News' Minor League Executive of the Year in 1936 and 1946 as the Crackers shattered minor league attendance records; though his contemporaries never got behind his campaign for minor league independence, he was able to develop such players as Dutch Leonard, Billy Goodman, Connie Ryan and Johnny Rucker, whom he sold to major league clubs to generate capital; eventually signed a working agreement with the Boston Braves in 1950, then sold the club to Los Angeles after the 1959 season due to declining attendance and profits.

Everett (Ziggy) Marcell, 76, a catcher in the Negro leagues between 1942 and 1948 who played one season in the minors, at Los Angeles; a member of the Chicago American Giants and Newark Eagles during his Negro league career, he joined the Farnham, Que., club of the Provincial League for the 1950 season, batting .272 in 89 games; also played basketball briefly with the Harlem Globetrotters.

Philip Samuel (Phil) Masi, 73, a highly regarded defensive catcher who spent most of his 14 big-league seasons in a Boston Braves uniform and appeared in three All-Star Games, at Mount Prospect, Ill., on March 29; valued primarily for his receiving skills, it was hitting that vaulted him to the major leagues; between 1936 and 1938, his home run/runs batted in/ batting ledger read 10/61/.334, 31/11/.326 and 16/97/ .308 in the minor leagues; joined the Braves out of spring training in 1939 and served mostly as a backup to Al Lopez, Ray Berres and Ernie Lombardi through 1942; came of age in the mid-1940s, batting a career-best .304 in 1947 and appearing in the All-Star Game in 1946, 1947 and 1948; was the central figure in a controversial pickoff play in the 1948 World Series; entering the scoreless first game as a pinch-runner in the eighth inning, he appeared to be picked off second base by Cleveland's Bob Feller but was ruled safe over the strenuous objections of the Indians; one batter later, he ran home with the game's lone run, though Boston would lose the Series in six games; split the 1949 schedule in Boston and Pittsburgh, then was sold to the White Sox prior to the 1950 season; the native Chicagoan concluded his playing career with the Sox in 1952 with a career .264 batting average.

Marshall Reese (Mark) Mauldin, 75, who appeared in 10 games at third base with the 1934 Chicago White Sox and played another 10 years in the minor leagues, at Union City, Ga., on September 2; spent most of his playing career as an outfielder in the Southern Association, primarily with the old Atlanta Crackers; one year after breaking into pro ball with Atlanta in 1933, he was brought up to Chicago, where he collected 10 hits in 38 at-bats for a .263 average at age 19; was declared a free agent the following spring; back in the minors, he batted .337 for Longview in the West Dixie League in 1935 and .378 for Knoxville in the Southern Association in '36; scouted briefly for the Baltimore Orioles in the 1950s.

George Francis McNamara, 89, a minor league outfielder during the 1920s who netted three hits in 11 at-bats with the 1922 Washington Senators, at Hinsdale, Ill., on June 12; his minor league career included stops at Jersey City, Fort Smith and Waco following his three-game fling with Washington; after his playing days, he joined the Chicago Fire Department, rising to the rank of battalion chief; later worked as a mutuel manager at horse racing tracks in Illinois.

Richard A. (Dick) Meyer, 74, longtime member of the Anheuser-Busch brewery family and the St. Louis Cardinals' first general manager after the brewing giant purchased the club in 1953, at St. Louis on December 10; had risen from brewery messenger boy at age 19 to its vice president when appointed Cardinal general manager following the 1953 season; supervised front-office activities until 1957, when he returned to full-time duties at Anheuser-Busch; served as president of the brewery from 1971 to 1974.

Wilbert (Junior) Meyer, 64, a minor league manager and coach during the 1970s and 1980s, at Pompano Beach, Fla., on August 21; began his coaching career with the New York Mets' chain in 1972, coaching two years for their Pompano Beach affiliate; following a season with the Yankees' Fort Lauderdale club, he joined the Baltimore Orioles' organization in 1976; managed at the Orioles' Bluefield farm from 1977 through 1979 before moving to the Montreal Expos' system; managed at West Palm Beach in 1982 and '85.

Wallace (Wally) Moses Jr., 80, a swift, line-drive-hitting American League outfielder who batted over .300 in each of his first seven big-league seasons but never again reached the mark in 10 years thereafter, at Vidalia, Ga., on October 10, two days after his birthday; was signed to a minor league contract on the recommendation of Ty Cobb in 1931; joined the Philadelphia Athletics in 1935 and batted .325 until crashing into the outfield wall, breaking an arm, in August; installed as the A's starting right fielder the next spring, he strung together six more .300-plus campaigns, including a career-high .345 mark in his sophomore season; hit with extraordinary power the following year, driving in 86 runs and blasting 25 home runs; his next-best home run total was nine in 1940; was traded to the White Sox after the 1941 season, never to bat .300 again; had his moments with Chicago during the war years, setting a club record with 56 stolen bases and tying for the league lead with 12 triples in 1943 and rapping an A.L.-high 35 doubles in '45; the Boston Red Sox, looking for help that would ultimately enable them to win the 1946 pennant, acquired Moses for his defensive ability midway through that season; made the only World Series appearance of his career, batting .417 in four games; spent two more seasons in Boston as a part-time outfielder before returning to Philadelphia, where he retired after the '48 campaign with a career .291 average and 2,138 hits; after his playing days, he was a revered batting coach for a number of teams; was the Phillies' instructor when Richie Ashburn won N.L. batting titles in 1955 and '58, the Yankees' coach when Roger Maris and Mickey Mantle waged their home run duel in '61, the Cincinnati Reds' instructor when they ran away with the N.L. team batting title in 1959 despite finishing sixth in the standings and the batting coach for the 1968 World Series champion Detroit Tigers; voted into the Georgia Sports Hall of Fame in 1988.

Earl Eugene Naylor, 70, who pitched and played the outfield in the major leagues in the 1940s, at Winter Haven, Fla., on January 16; originally signed as a pitcher in 1937 by Fayetteville of the Arkansas-Missouri League, he achieved prospect status with a hitting stroke that netted five straight .300-plus seasons in the minors; playing the outfield, he belted 26 home runs with 100 runs batted in for Greenville of the Cotton States League in 1939; signed to a big-league contract in 1942 by the Philadelphia Phillies, he pitched in 20 games and played the field in 35 others; batted just .196 and posted a 6.12 earned-run average in four starts and 16 relief stints; after a .175 start in 1943, he was traded to the St. Louis Cardinals and assigned to their Rochester farm; returned to the majors for three games with Brooklyn in 1946; managed in the Dodger chain in the 1950s and for Mayaguez, Puerto Rico, in the winter leagues.

John Henry (Johnny) Neun, 89, a consummate baseball man who spent more than 65 years in the game as a player, manager, coach and scout, and one of only eight players in major league history to turn an unassisted triple play, at Baltimore on March 28; played first base for six seasons in the big leagues, with Detroit and the Boston Braves between 1925 and 1931, compiling a .288 average in

432 games; secured his place in the record book on May 31, 1927, when he executed the only unassisted triple play to end a game; playing first base for the Tigers, he snared a line drive by Cleveland's Homer Summa, tagged out Charlie Jamieson as he tried to return to first and won the race to second over the Indians' Glenn Myatt, who had dashed head-down to third; rare as the play is, an unaided triple play had been turned the previous day by Chicago Cubs shortstop Jimmy Cooney; later that season, he stole home twice (once in each game) in a July 13 doubleheader against Washington; released by Boston after the 1931 season, he was active as a player in the minors until 1937 but had already begun his managerial career in 1935 at Akron in the Middle Atlantic League; won four pennants in the New York Yankees' system before joining the big club as a coach in 1944; served as the Yanks' interim manager in 1946, then managed at Cincinnati in 1947, finishing fifth, and again for the Reds in 1948, when replaced by Bucky Walters in August; returned to the Yankees, beginning a long tenure as scouting supervisor and player development specialist until 1969, when he joined the Kansas City Royals to work with prospects at their Baseball Academy in Sarasota, Fla.; was a scout and instructor for California and Milwaukee into his 80s, finally retiring in 1989.

Paul (Pappy) Nohr, 86, longtime baseball coach who developed 10 future big leaguers at Cincinnati's Western Hills High School, at Cincinnati on April 9; coached at the school from its opening in 1928 until 1962, producing such talent as Pete Rose, Don Zimmer, Russ Nixon and Jim Frey—all future big-league managers—as well as Clyde Vollmer, Herm Wehmeier, Dick Drott, Art Mahaffey and Ed and Charlie Brinkman.

Joseph Leo (Joe) O'Rourke Jr., 85, a major league scout who pinch hit in three games for the 1929 Philadelphia Phillies, at Philadelphia on June 27; the son of scout Patsy O'Rourke, he signed with the Phillies' organization in 1927; after his brief stay in the majors, he played and managed in the Phillies' system another nine seasons; scouted for the Chicago White Sox, Philadelphia Athletics, Kansas City A's and Washington Senators until retiring in 1967.

Paul Franklin (Bill) Otis, 100, the oldest living former major leaguer up until his death, at Duluth, Minn., on December 15; would have turned 101 on Christmas Eve; was given a trial by the 1912 New York Yankees after batting .400 as a senior at Williams College in Massachusetts; played four games with New York between July 4 and 6 before being sent to Wilkes-Barre, Pa., for seasoning; fractured a once-broken ankle there while sliding into second and never played again; honored at a 1983 Yankee old-timer's game as oldest living former Yank.

Boyd Glenn Perry, 74, who appeared in 36 games for the Detroit Tigers at shortstop and second base in 1941, at Burlington, N.C., on June 29; attended Guilford College in Greensboro, N.C., before signing with the Tigers in 1936; was the regular shortstop with Detroit's 1938 Texas League championship team in Beaumont, batting .209 in 150 games; spent the 1939 season in the American Association with Toledo, returned to Beaumont in 1940 and then started the 1941 campaign with Detroit; was batting .181 as a reserve infielder in 36 games when he went on the disabled list with an injured throwing arm; returned to the minors in 1942 and retired before the 1943 season; was a nephew of pitcher Tom Zachary, a major leaguer from 1918 through 1936.

John Pezzullo, 78, who pitched in 42 games for the Philadelphia Phillies between 1935 and '36, of cancer at Dallas on May 16; was signed by the New York Giants in 1931 and assigned to Albany; posted

Hall of Famer Joe Sewell hit better than .300 nine times for the Cleveland Indians, including a career-high .353 in 1923.

a 16-4 record in 1934 for Richmond in the Piedmont League, but was released to Philadelphia after the season; registered a 3-5 mark in 41 appearances for the Phillies in 1935 and appeared in one game in 1936 before he was returned to Richmond; at Savannah in the South Atlantic League in 1937 he posted a 14-10 record; with the same team in 1938, the lefthander struck out 218 batters in 288 innings, pitched 19 complete games and compiled a 26-9 record; was acquired by the Boston Braves, but was assigned to Toronto, where he won only 11 of 23 decisions in 1939; pitched for Syracuse and Buffalo in the International League before ending his career after the 1942 season.

Raymond Poat, 72, a righthander who compiled a 22-30 record pitching for the Cleveland Indians, New York Giants and Pittsburgh Pirates in the 1940s, at Oak Lawn, Ill., on April 29; a standout at the University of Illinois, he signed with Cleveland in 1938 and compiled a 7-16 record in parts of three seasons (1942-44) with the Indians; released to Baltimore in 1946, Poat won 23 games in two seasons for the International League team before being released to the Giants late in the '47 season; won his first six decisions with New York in 1948, but developed a bone spur in his right arm and finished the season 11-10; was traded to the Pirates in June 1949, finishing the season 0-1; retired after several more years in the minors.

Nelson Potter, 78, a 19-game winner for the St. Louis Browns' only American League pennant-winning team in 1944 and who is believed to be the only man ever suspended for allegedly throwing a spitball, at Mount Morris, Ill., on September 30; was suspended for 10 days after being accused of doctoring the ball with a foreign substance (saliva) by umpire Cal Hubbard in a July 20, 1944, game against the New York Yankees in St. Louis; pitched in the 1944 World Series with the Browns and the 1948 Series with the Boston Braves; spent all or parts of 12 seasons in the majors and compiled a 92-97 career record; made his big-league debut with the St. Louis Cardinals in 1936, pitching in one game; returned to the minors later in the season and stayed there until the Philadelphia Athletics drafted him in 1938; recorded a 20-39 mark in 3½ years with the A's before finishing the 1941 season with a 2-1 record for the Boston Red Sox; was released to Louisville, where he spent 1942 season, finishing 18-8; was drafted by the Browns following the '42 campaign; spent a little more than five years in St. Louis and compiled a 57-43 mark; was sold back to the A's during the '48 season and went 2-2 before being released in June and signing with the Boston Braves; finished his career in 1949 with an 11-13 career mark in Boston.

John Ramsey, 62, longtime public-address announcer for the Los Angeles Dodgers and other sports teams in Southern California, of cardiac arrest due to complications from diabetes at Long Beach, Calif., on January 25; served as public-address announcer at Dodger games for 25 years, from their first season in Los Angeles in 1958 through 1982; periodically worked California Angels games; also worked University of Southern California football games and Los Angeles Rams, Kings and Lakers games for nearly two decades; was the public-address announcer for five Super Bowls, the Pro Bowl in years it was played in Los Angeles Memorial Coliseum and the 1984 Olympic basketball games.

Jim Rendel, 59, a baseball coach at Rose-Hulman Institute of Technology and Indiana State University, at Terre Haute, Ind., on April 29; compiled a 178-262 record from 1977 to 1989 at Rose-Hulman; began his collegiate coaching career at Indiana State, where he was 116-141 in nine seasons; coached soccer at Rose-Hulman for 10 years and was the school's intramural director before re-

signing in 1989.

James K. Romano, 63, a righthander who pitched in three games with the Brooklyn Dodgers in 1950, of cancer at Manhattan, N.Y., on September 12; was signed by the Dodgers following military service in World War II; was pitching for St. Paul in the American Association in 1950 when the Dodgers added him to their roster for the conclusion of a pennant battle with Philadelphia, earning no decisions in six innings; suffered an arm injury in spring training in 1951 and went 2-5 at St. Paul; retired after compiling a 4-5 record in 1952 for International League pennant winner Montreal.

Rolando Romero, 19, a righthander with the Texas Rangers' Class A affiliate in Gastonia, of a heart attack at Fayetteville, N.C., on May 14; signed with the Rangers as a free agent in 1987; pitched for Texas' rookie league team in Sarasota, Fla., in 1988, finishing 3-5; posted a 5-5 record at Gastonia in 1989 and was off to a 2-0 start with a 1.35 earned-run average in 1990.

Joe Sewell, 91, who began a Hall of Fame career as a replacement for the only player ever killed in a major league game, at Mobile, Ala., on March 6; began his 14-year career in the midst of a pennant race when the Cleveland Indians rushed him into the lineup shortly after shortstop Ray Chapman was fatally beaned by New York Yankees pitcher Carl Mays on August 16, 1920; the lefthander batted .329 in the final 22 games as the Indians won the American League pennant; hit .174 in the Indians' seven-game triumph over Brooklyn in the World Series; became the toughest man in baseball history to strike out, establishing four major league records; a career .312 hitter, he batted over .300 in nine of 11 seasons with the Indians, enjoying a career-high .353 average in 1923 along with 98 runs scored and 109 runs batted in; was acquired by the Yankees in 1931 to play third base; played in the 1932 World Series, batting .333 in a four-game sweep of the Chicago Cubs; retired after the 1933 season and became a Yankee coach in 1934 and '35 before returning to his native Alabama to set up a hardware store; was signed as a scout by the Indians in 1952; left the Indians' organization in 1962 and scouted for the New York Mets in 1963; a graduate of and former football and baseball player at the University of Alabama, he returned in 1964 as baseball coach; guided the Crimson Tide to the 1968 Southeastern Conference title, compiling a seven-year record of 114-99; was named to the Hall of Fame by the Veterans Committee in 1977; was the oldest of three brothers who all boasted major league experience; youngest brother Tommy's big-league career consisted of one pinch-hitting appearance with the Cubs in 1927; Luke spent 13 of his 20 years in the majors as a catcher with Cleveland, where he teamed with Joe from 1921 to 1930, and later managed the St. Louis Browns and Cincinnati Reds.

Charles L. Shoemaker, 50, who played in 28 games at second base with the Kansas City Athletics between 1961 and '64, of a self-inflicted gunshot wound at Mount Penn, Pa., on March 31; the University of Arizona graduate signed with Kansas City in 1961, appearing in seven games with the A's late that season; divided 1962 between Kansas City and Albuquerque, spent 1963 in military service and played 16 games with the A's in 1964; sported a career .258 average in the majors.

Abram Shorin, 91, the last survivor among four brothers who founded the Topps Co. Inc. to manufacture chewing gum and expanded the firm into the world's largest manufacturer of bubble gum and baseball cards, at Miami on May 28; established the gum-making company with brothers Joseph, Ira and Philip as the successor to a Brooklyn, N.Y., leaf tobacco business; began to include baseball cards in packages of bubble gum in 1951 after a nephew had made the suggestion to Shorin, a longtime Brooklyn Dodgers fan.

Lawrence (Paddy) Smith, 96, believed to be the oldest living former Boston Red Sox player, at New Rochelle, N.Y., on December 2; the catcher appeared in two games with the Red Sox in 1920; spent the rest of his career in the minor leagues playing for Bridgeport, Lewiston, Worcester, New Haven and Pittsfield.

George (Chips) Sobek, 70, who played professional baseball and basketball and spent 29 years as a scout in the Chicago White Sox and San Francisco Giants organizations, at Hammond, Ind., on April 9; played baseball and basketball at Notre Dame between 1940 and '42 before serving in the Navy in World War II; was a second baseman in the Chicago farm system in 1946, '48 and '49, serving as player/manager at Hot Springs and Superior; later managed Idaho Falls, Harlan and Eugene; also served as a scout for the White Sox (1959-'85) and Giants (1986-88); played with Indianapolis, Toledo and Hammond in the old National Basketball League and with the National Basketball Association's Sheboygan Redskins in the 1940s.

Tolia (Tony) Solaita, 43, the only native Samoan ever to play in the major leagues, shot to death near Tafuna, American Samoa, on February 10; apparently was killed in a dispute over land; had returned to his native islands five years before to work in the athletic division of the government's department of education; was introduced to baseball at age 8 when his family moved from American Samoa to Hawaii; moved to California three years later; signed his first pro contract in 1965 with the New York Yankees; a lefthanded-hitting first baseman, he led the Carolina League with 49 home runs and 122 runs batted in for High Point-Thomasville in 1968 and earned a one-game look-see with the Yankees; returned to the minors for the next five seasons, including one in the Pittsburgh Pirates' organization following a trade; was drafted from the Pirates' International League affiliate at Charleston by the Kansas City Royals in December 1973; backed up John Mayberry for the Royals until he was sold to the California Angels in July 1976, a year after he had batted .260 with 16 homers; had his busiest big-league season with the Angels in 1977, appearing in 116 games and smacking 14 homers; was relegated to reserve and pinch-hitting roles the next two seasons with the Angels, Montreal Expos and Toronto Blue Jays; became a free agent after the '79 season and went to Japan to play for the Nippon Ham Fighters from 1980 through '83; concluded his major league career with a .255 average, 50 homers and 203 RBIs in 525 games; returned to the South Pacific and served as head of the American Samoa Parks and Recreation Department.

Horace C. Stoneham, 86, who assumed control of the New York Giants in 1936, moved the club to San Francisco after the 1957 season and ended almost six decades of family ownership by selling the club in March 1976, at Scottsdale, Ariz., on January 7; became a Giants fan while attending games at the Polo Grounds with his father, Charles A. Stoneham, almost daily as a youngster; the elder Stoneham, a wealthy Wall Street stockbroker, bought the Giants in 1919 as a gift for his son; Horace worked in his father's copper mine on the West Coast before returning to work for the Giants in a variety of capacities, starting in the maintenance department and moving up; became the major leagues' youngest club owner (32) upon the death of his father in January 1936; established the Giants' minor league farm system, which Charles Stoneham had disdained in favor of buying veteran players; a true baseball man with no other

business interests, he enjoyed nothing more than talking baseball with friends for hours; grew attached to his players and hated to trade them; saw the Giants win National League pennants and then lose to the New York Yankees in the World Series in his first two years at the helm; enjoyed another pennant-winning season in 1951 and a world championship in 1954 before declining attendance and the decay of the Polo Grounds prompted him to move the club out of New York; selected San Francisco as the Giants' new home as he and Brooklyn Dodgers Owner Walter O'Malley brought major league baseball to the West Coast; housed his club in Seals Stadium for two years; saw his San Francisco teams draw well at first, particularly when new Candlestick Park opened in 1960 and when the Giants gave the Bay Area its first pennant in 1962; despite five straight second-place finishes to close out the '60s and an N.L. West crown in 1971, the Giants began to lag at the turnstiles when the Athletics moved from Kansas City to Oakland in 1968; once called "the link between baseball's sentimental past and its calculating present" by Milton Gross of the New York Post, he knew the game inside-out but not how to market it; failed to develop promotional campaigns to halt the attendance decline as the A's built a dynasty across the bay in the early '70s; was forced to deal some of his top players (Willie Mays, Willie McCovey and Bobby Bonds, among others) to meet the payroll as the Giants became coated in red ink; fell into disfavor with Bay Area fans and minority stockholders, who clamored for his resignation; sold the Giants to a group headed by Bob Lurie after the 1975 season; retired to Scottsdale and cut almost all ties to the Giants' organization.

Odie C. Strain Jr., 67, a shortstop in the New York Yankees' farm system in the 1940s, at Sinton, Tex., on March 22; son of a former minor league catcher and manager; went from the campus of Oklahoma A&M to Easton of the Eastern Shore League in 1940; rose through the Yankees' chain on the strength of his glove, not his bat; missed three years while serving in the Army Air Corps in World War II; resumed his career with the Yankees' American Association club in Kansas City in 1946; batted .213 in 125 games in 1947, his only full season in Kansas City; concluded his career with Enid of the Western Association in 1951.

Clinton C. (Clint) Thomas, 94, a star outfielder in the Negro leagues who played from 1921 through '38, at Charleston, W.Va., on December 3; called "the black Joe DiMaggio" by Hall of Famer Monte Irvin, Thomas was known for both his offensive and defensive prowess; batted around .300 over 17 seasons, according to incomplete records; spent most of his career with the Philadelphia Hilldales in the 1920s and the New York Black Yankees in the 1930s; later worked as chief messenger for the West Virginia state senate.

Fay W. (Scow) Thomas, 85, a righthander whose use of an alias got him into trouble at the beginning of a career that went nowhere in the major leagues but included a couple of glory years in the minors, at Chatsworth, Calif., on August 16; a baseball and football player at the University of Southern California, he and a friend decided to drive from the West Coast to Michigan in the summer of 1925; ran out of money in Ottumwa, Ia., where he decided to earn some cash by offering his services to the local Mississippi Valley League club; signed a pro contract as "P.J. Collins" because he had collegiate eligibility remaining; pitched and won the next day, with a scout for Oklahoma City of the Western League watching; the scout bought his contract from Ottumwa and told "Collins" to report to Oklahoma City; instead, Thomas and his friend cashed the paycheck from Ottumwa and resumed their journey; pitched for USC in 1926, then signed a pro contract (using his real name) with the New York Giants' organization; by July 1927 he was in New York, appearing in nine games for the Giants until he was discovered to be the same pitcher whose contract had been purchased by Oklahoma City two years before; was suspended for one year and ordered to return $2,500 to the Giants; starting with Oklahoma City late in 1928, he spent the next 15 years bouncing around the minors, making three more major league stops; pitched in 16 games for the Cleveland Indians in 1931, seven games for the Brooklyn Dodgers in 1932 and 49 games for the St. Louis Browns in 1935, when he posted a 7-15 record; compiled a 9-20 big-league record with a 4.95 earned-run average in 229 innings; enjoyed his greatest success with the Los Angeles Angels of the Pacific Coast League, going 20-14 in 1933 and 28-4 in 1934; retired from baseball in 1943.

Clifford E. (Earl) Torgeson, 66, a stylish first baseman who played in 1,668 major league games for five clubs from 1947 through '61, of leukemia at Everett, Wash., on November 8; spent two years in the minor leagues before entering military service in 1943; was wounded in France during World War II; played another year in the minors and then made his big-league debut in 1947, when he batted .281 with 16 home runs as the Boston Braves' regular first baseman; hit .253 for the Braves' National League pennant-winning club of 1948; was sidelined with a separated shoulder for most of the '49 campaign; returned to enjoy his two best seasons in 1950 and '51, batting a career-high .290 and scoring a league-leading 120 runs in '50 and producing 24 homers and 92 runs batted in, both career highs, the following year; was traded to the Philadelphia Phillies after slipping to .230 in 1952; was the Phils' starting first baseman for two years before being sold to the Detroit Tigers in June 1955; was sent to the Chicago White Sox as part of another midseason deal in 1957; was a member of the 1959 Go-Go Sox club that won the American League pennant; primarily a pinch-hitter by 1960, he was picked up by the New York Yankees after the White Sox released him in June 1961; stayed on as a coach during the Yanks' 1961 World Series triumph over Cincinnati after being released as a player in September; had a .265 average, 149 homers and 740 RBIs in his big-league career; returned to his native Snohomish, Wash., coming out of baseball retirement for one year to manage the Seattle Pilots' farm club at Newark of the New York-Pennsylvania League in 1969; served as a Snohomish County commissioner from 1972-76; served as the county's director for the development of emergency management for eight years until his death.

James R. (Junior) Walsh, 71, a righthander who had a 4-10 record in spot service with the Pittsburgh Pirates from 1946 through 1951, at Olyphant, Pa., on November 12; won his first 10 decisions as a pro with Oil City of the Pennsylvania State Association in 1941 and struck out 206 batters in 207 innings that season; spent three years in the Pirates' minor league organization before his career was interrupted by military service in 1944; returned to the diamond in 1946 and spent the next four years shuttling between Pittsburgh and the minors; posted a 15-4 record at the Pirates' American Association outpost in Indianapolis in 1949 before rejoining the Pirates late that season; spent the next two full seasons in Pittsburgh, pitching primarily out of the bullpen; totaled 193 innings and a 5.88 earned-run average in the big leagues; played for Hollywood and San Francisco of the Pacific Coast League from 1952 through '55; ended his pitching career with Buffalo of the International League in 1956.

Henry Levi (Johnny) Wertz, 89, a righthander who had a 15-21 record with the Boston Braves from 1926 through '29, at Newberry, S.C.,

on September 24; broke into baseball with Greenville of the South Atlantic Association in 1924; enjoyed his best major league season as a 1926 rookie with the Braves, going 11-9 with a 3.28 earned-run average; an arm injury in 1928 effectively ended his big-league career; tallied a 4.29 ERA in 378 innings in the majors; pitched for several minor league clubs from 1929 through '32, finishing at Knoxville of the Southern Association.

Merritt Willey, 66, the vice president of marketing for the Los Angeles Dodgers since 1972, of cancer at Glendale, Calif., on July 12; was a former vice president and general manager of radio station KWKW in Los Angeles; also worked as an executive in advertising and marketing prior to joining the Dodgers.

Jesse Williams, 76, a shortstop in the Negro leagues in the 1940s, at Kansas City, Mo., on February 27; played primarily with the Kansas City Monarchs from 1939 through '45 and again in 1947; a superb fielder and a contact-type hitter, he finished his career with the Indianapolis Clowns in 1949.

Nicholas J. (Mickey) Witek, 74, an infielder with the New York Giants who compiled a .277 average in 580 major league games in the 1940s, at Kingston, Pa., on August 24; was signed by the New York Yankees' organization in 1935 and established himself as a steady fielder and solid contact hitter in five minor league seasons; was named the International League's Most Valuable Player in 1939, when he hit .329 and knocked in 104 runs for Newark; was sold to the Giants after that season; was primarily a shortstop for the Giants in 1940 and spent most of the next season at Jersey City of the International League; became the Giants' regular second baseman, his natural position, in 1942; batted a career-high .314 for New York in 1943; missed the next two seasons while serving in the Coast Guard; returned to the Giants in 1946, but his next two seasons were shortened because of injuries; after spending the '48 campaign in the minors, he was reacquired by the Yankees and made one appearance with the American League club in 1949 before being sent to Newark; closed out his career in the Pacific Coast League with Seattle in 1950.

Richard L. Woodward, 86, a righthander who pitched in the minor leagues from 1925 through 1930, at Beech Grove, Ind., on May 26; pitched for Fort Smith of the Western Association in 1925 and Bloomington and Danville of the Three-I League in 1926; posted a 10-8 record with Haverhill of the New England League in 1927 but slipped to 3-17 the next year despite a 2.91 earned-run average with Haverhill and Portland (Me.); closed out his career in the New York-Pennsylvania League with Elmira.

John R. Wright Sr., 72, the first Negro league pitcher to sign an Organized Baseball contract in the modern era, at Jackson, Miss., on May 10; from 1937 until he entered the Navy in World War II, the righthander pitched for the Newark Eagles, Toledo Crawfords and Homestead Grays; starred for the Navy's first all-black team at the Great Lakes Naval Training Center and with a team at Floyd Bennett Naval Air Station; was signed by the Brooklyn Dodgers and assigned to Montreal of the International League after his Navy discharge early in 1946; was in uniform in the dugout when Jackie Robinson made his Organized Baseball debut in April 1946; made two relief appearances for Montreal early in the '46 season, then was assigned to the Dodgers' Class C team at Three Rivers, Que.; compiled a 12-8 record with a 4.15 earned-run average in 32 games with the Canadian-American League club; was released after the season and returned to pitch for the Grays through 1948.

LEAGUE AND CLUB INFORMATION

Including

Major League Directory

National League Directory

National League Team Directories

American League Directory

American League Team Directories

MAJOR LEAGUE BASEBALL

Office of the Commissioner
Commissioner—Francis T. Vincent, Jr.
Deputy Commissioner & Chief Operating Officer—Steven D. Greenberg
Officers and Directors
Director, Broadcasting & Baseball Information Systems—David Alworth
Controller—Thomas Duffy
Director, Special Events—David Dziedzic
Director, Security/Facility Management—Kevin Hallinan
Director, Public Relations—Richard Levin
Director, Baseball Operations—William Murray
General Counsel—Thomas J. Ostertag
Director, Broadcast Administration—Leslie Sullivan
Executive Director, Licensing Operations & President, MLBP—Rick White

Headquarters—350 Park Avenue, New York, N.Y. 10022
Telephone—371-7800 (area code 212)
Teletype—910-380-9482

National League

Organized 1876

WILLIAM D. WHITE
President and Treasurer

PHYLLIS B. COLLINS
Senior Vice-President & Secretary

KATY FEENEY
Vice-President of Media & Public Affairs

NANCY CROFTS
Assistant Secretary & Manager, Player Records

VALERIE DIETRICH
Executive Secretary

CATHY DAVIS
Administrative Assistant, Umpires

Headquarters—350 Park Avenue, New York, N. Y. 10022

Telephone—339-7700 (area code 212)

UMPIRES—Greg Bonin, Gerald Crawford, Gary Darling, Robert Davidson, Gerry Davis, Dana DeMuth, Bruce Froemming, Eric Gregg, Tom Hallion, H. Douglas Harvey, Mark Hirschbeck, Bill Hohn, Jerry Layne, Randall Marsh, John McSherry, Edward Montague, Frank Pulli, James Quick, Lawrence (Dutch) Rennert, Steve Rippley, Paul Runge, Terry Tata, Harry Wendelstedt, Joseph West, Charles Williams, Mike Winters.

OFFICIAL STATISTICIANS—Elias Sports Bureau, Inc., 500 5th Ave., Suite 2114, New York, N.Y. 10036. Telephone—(212) 869-1530.

ATLANTA BRAVES

Chairman of the Board—William C. Bartholomay

President—Stan Kasten
Senior V.P. & Asst. to President—Henry L. Aaron
Exec. Vice-President & General Manager—John Schuerholz
Vice-President & Special Asst. to the General Manager—John W. Mullen
Senior Vice-President, Administration & Finance—Charles S. Sanders
Director of Player Development & Scouting—Chuck LaMar
Asst. Vice-President & Special Asst. to the G.M.—Paul L. Snyder, Jr.
Assistant General Manager—Dean Taylor
Assistant Scouting Director—Scott Proefrock
Asst. Director of Player Development—Rod Gilbreath
Minor League Coordinator—Bobby Dews
V.P., Director of Marketing & Broadcasting—Wayne Long
Director of Team Travel & Equipment Manager—Bill Acree
Director of Public Relations—Jim Schultz
Director of Community Relations—Danny Goodwin
Director of Promotions—Miles McRea
Director of Ticket Sales—Jack Tyson
Director of Ticket Operations—Ed Newman
Assistant Director of Ticket Operations—Sam Willliams
Director of Advertising—Peter Diffin
Director of Merchandising—Robert A. Hope
Director of Stadium Operations & Security—Terri Brennan
Assistant Controller—Chip Moore
Public Relations Assistants—Glen Serra, Mike Ringering, Scott Sergent
Manager—Bobby Cox
Trainer—Dave Pursley
Assistant Trainer—Jeff Porter
Club Physician—Dr. David T. Watson
Associate Physicians—Dr. John Cantwell, Dr. Robert Crow
Club Orthopedist—Dr. Joe Chandler
Executive Offices—P.O. Box 4064, Atlanta, Ga. 30302
Telephone—522-7630 (area code 404)

SCOUTS—Mike Arbuckle, Ray Belanger, Sam Berry, Forrest (Smoky) Burgess, Joe Campise, Stu Cann, Joe Caputo, Bill Clark, Roy Clark, Harold Cronin, Bob Dunning, Rob English, Lou Fitzgerald, John Flannery, Ralph Garr, Pedro Gonzalez, John Hagemann, Ray Holton, Jim Johnson, Dean Jongewaard, Steve Jongewaard, Brian Kohlscheen, Robert Lucas, Robyn Lynch, Burney R. (Dickey) Martin, Red Murff, Ernie Pedersen, Jack Pierce, Rance Pless, Jorge Posada, Harry Postove, Jose Salado, Bill Serena, Fred Shaffer, Charles Smith, Ted Sparks, Andy Stewart, Tony Stiel, Bob Turzilli, Wesley Westrum, William R. Wight, Don Williams, H.F. (Red) Wooten.

PARK LOCATION—Atlanta-Fulton County Stadium, on Capitol Avenue at the junction of Interstate Highways 20, 75 and 85.

Seating capacity—52,007.

FIELD DIMENSIONS—Home plate to left field at foul line, 330 feet; to center field, 402 feet; to right field at foul line, 330 feet.

CHICAGO CUBS

Board of Directors—Stanton R. Cook, Chairman;
Thomas G. Ayers, Charles T. Brumback,
Donald C. Grenesko, Andrew J. McKenna, Walter E. Massey
President and Chief Executive Officer—Donald C. Grenesko
Executive Vice-President, Baseball Operations—Jim Frey
Vice-President, Business Operations—Mark McGuire
Vice-President, Scouting & Player Development—Dick Balderson
Director, Baseball Administration—Ned Colletti
Director, Finance & Information Systems—Keith Bode
Director, Human Resources—Wendy Lewis
Director, Marketing—John McDonough
Director, Media Relations—Sharon Pannozzo
Director, Minor League Operations—Bill Harford
Director, Stadium Operations—Tom Cooper
Director, Ticket Operations—Frank Maloney
Corporate Secretary—Stanley Gradowski
Corporate Counsel—Geoffrey A. Anderson
Special Player Consultants—Hugh Alexander, Scott Reid, Eddie Lyons
Traveling Secretary—Peter Durso
Assistant Director, Marketing—Conrad Kowal
Assistant Director, Scouting—Scott Nelson
Assistant Director, Stadium Operations—Paul Rathje
Assistant Director, Ticket Operations/Sales—Bill Galante
Assistant Director, Ticket Operations/Service—Joe Kirchen
Manager, Event Personnel and Security—Paul Gerlach
Manager, Cubs Care & Community Relations—Ellen Jensen
P.A. Announcer—Wayne Messmer
Team Photographer—Steve Green
Team Physician—John F. Marquardt, M.D.
Trainer—John Fierro
Equipment Manager—Yosh Kawano
Manager—Don Zimmer
Executive Offices—Wrigley Field, 1060 West Addison Street, Chicago, Ill. 60613
Telephone—404-2827 (area code 312)

SCOUTS—(Regional Supervisors)—Frank DeMoss, Doug Mapson, Earl Winn. (Latin American Coordinators)—Luis Rosa, Sandy Alomar, Sr. (Area Scouts)—Billy Blitzer, Jeff Brookens, Bill Capps, Billy Champion, Tom Davis, Frank DeMoss, Ed DiRamio, Bobby Gardner, John Gracio, Gene Handley, Elmore Hill, Joe Housey, Toney Howell, John (Spider) Jorgensen, Jeff Kahn, Gil Kubiski, Larry Maxie, Paul Provas, John Stockstill. (Part-Time Scouts)—Keith Bailey, Bob Beck, Claudio Brito, Jose Cassino, Morley Freitas, Ben Gonzalez, Jose Gonzalez, Jim Greenwald, John Hennessy, Carlos Hernandez, Diego Herrera, Vedie Himsl, Andres James, Rich Jeffries, Pat Kane, Bob Lofrano, Noe Maduro, Tony Malara, Jose Marcano, William Moore, Lee Phillips, Hector Rivera, Milton Rosario, Joe Sayers, Shawn Smith, Jose Trujillo, Juan Vicioso, Harry Von Suskil, Wally Walker, Larry Watts, Jim Willis.

PARK LOCATION—Wrigley Field, Addison Street, N. Clark Street, Waveland Avenue and Sheffield Avenue.

Seating capacity—38,710.

FIELD DIMENSIONS—Home plate to left field at foul line, 355 feet; to center field, 400 feet; to right field at foul line, 353 feet.

CINCINNATI REDS

General Partner—Marge Schott

President and Chief Executive Officer—Marge Schott
Executive Vice President—Stephen Schott
Vice-President & General Manager—Bob Quinn
Vice-President, Publicity—Jim Ferguson
Director, Player Development—Howie Bedell
Director, Scouting—Julian Mock
Special Player Consultant—Sheldon Bender
Controller—Timothy A. Sabo
Director, Stadium Operations—Tim O'Connell
Director, Ticket Department—Bill Stewart
Director, Season Ticket Sales—Pat McCaffrey
Director, Group Sales—Susan Toomey
Director, Marketing—Chip Baker
Director, Publicity—Jon Braude
Director, Speakers Bureau—Gordy Coleman
Traveling Secretary—Joel Pieper
Major League Scout—Jim Stewart
Coordinator, Scouting & Player Development—Brad Del Barba
Assistant Publicity Director—Joe Kelley
Assistant Ticket Director—John O'Brien
Admin. Asst., Player Development & Scouting—Jim Bowden
Chief Administrative Assistant—Joyce Pfarr
Administrative Assistant, Business—Ginny Kamp
Administrative Assistant, Scouting—Wilma Mann
Administrative Assistant, Player Development—Lois Schneider
Trainers—Larry Starr, Dan Wright
Field Superintendent—Tony Swain
Equipment Manager—Bernie Stowe
Manager—Lou Piniella
Executive Offices—100 Riverfront Stadium, Cincinnati, O. 45202
Telephone—421-4510 (area code 513)

SCOUTS—Johnny Almarez, Jeff Barton, Larry Barton, Jr., Ray Bellino, Gene Bennett, Jack Bowen, George Brill, Dave Calaway, Ray Corbett, Clay Daniel, Paul Faulk, Fred Ferreira, Les Houser, Eddie Kolo, Tom McDevitt, Julian Mock, Tom Severtson, Bob Szymkowski, Marion (Bo) Trumbo, Tom Wilson, Jeff Zimmerman. (Consultants)—Paul Campbell, Tony Robello.

PARK LOCATION—Riverfront Stadium, downtown Cincinnati, bounded by Pete Rose Way to the Ohio River and from Walnut Street to Broadway.

Seating capacity—52,952.

FIELD DIMENSIONS—Home plate to left field at foul line, 330 feet; to center field, 404 feet; to right field at foul line, 330 feet.

HOUSTON ASTROS

Board of Directors—Dr. John J. McMullen, Chairman. Owners—Dr. John J. McMullen, Mrs. James (Catherine) Blake, H.L. Brown, Jr., Mrs. Thomas E. (Mimi) Dompier, James A. Elkins, Jr., Alfred C. Glassell, Jr., Mrs. Stephen (Mary) Mochary, Mrs. R.E. (Bob) Smith Estate, Jack T. Trotter and Jacqueline, Peter and John McMullen, Jr.

General Manager—William J. Wood
Assistant General Manager—Bob Watson
Director of Minor League Operations—Fred Nelson
Director of Scouting—Dan O'Brien
Director of Public Relations—Rob Matwick
Director of Florida Operations—Pat O'Conner
Traveling Secretary—Barry Waters
Assistant to Dirs., Minor Leagues/Scouting—Lew Temple
Assistant Director of Public Relations—Chuck Pool
Assistant to General Manager—Tim Hellmuth
Admin. Asst., Minor Leagues/Scouting—David Rawnsley
Public Relations Assistant—Craig Sanders
Vice-President, Marketing—Ted Haracz
Director of Broadcasting—Jamie Hildreth
Director of Sales—Mike Levy
Director, Group Sales—Debra Fulmer
Director of Advertising Sales—Norm Miller
Director of Communications—Pam Gardner
Director, Community Services—Steve Wagman
Club Physicians—Dr. William Bryan, Dr. Michael Feltovich
Manager—Art Howe
Executive Offices—The Astrodome, P.O. Box 288
Houston, Tex. 77001
Telephone—799-9500 (area code 713)
HOUSTON SPORTS ASSOCIATION, INC.
President and Chief Operating Officer—Robert G. Harter
Executive Vice-President—Neal Gunn
Vice-President, Astrodome-Astrohall Stadium Corporation—John Elsner
Vice-President, Finance—Gary Brooks
Vice-President, Operations—W. Gary Keller
Vice-President, Public Affairs—Jim Weidler
General Counsel—Frank Rynd
Treasurer—Adam C. Richards
Controller—Robert McBurnett

SCOUTS—Jose Andrade, Jesus Aristimuno, Stan Benjamin, Bob Blair, Jack Bloomfield, Ralph Bratton, George Brophy, Ruben Cabrera, Rafael Cariel, Gerry Craft, Clark Crist, Jug DeFord, Doug Deutsch, Chuck Edmondson, Orlando Estevez, James Farrar, Charlie Fox, Steven Foucault, Ben Galante, Carl Greene, Howie Haak, Dick Hager, Sterling Housley, Dan Huston, Marc Johnson, Brian Keegan, Bill Kelso, Bob King, David Lakey, Julio Linares, Mike Maggart, Walt Matthews, Domingo Mercedes, Walter Millies, Tom Mooney, Carlos Muro, Hal Newhouser, Juan Oliveros, Shawn Pender, Ramon Perez, Joe Pittman, Andres Reiner, Adriano Rodriguez, Ross Sapp, Lynwood Stallings, Kevin Stein, Frankie Thon, Paul Weaver, Gene Wellman, Tom Wheeler.

PARK LOCATION—The Astrodome, Kirby and Interstate Loop 610

Seating capacity—54,816.

FIELD DIMENSIONS—Home plate to left field at foul line, 330 feet; to center field, 400 feet; to right field at foul line, 330 feet.

LOS ANGELES DODGERS

Board of Directors—Peter O'Malley, President; Harry M. Bardt;
Roland Seidler, Vice-President and Treasurer;
Mrs. Roland (Terry) Seidler, Secretary

President—Peter O'Malley
Executive Vice-President, Player Personnel—Fred Claire
Vice-President, Communications—Tom Hawkins
Vice-President, Finance—Bob Graziano
Vice-President, Marketing—Barry Stockhamer
Vice-President, Stadium Operations—Bob Smith
Vice-President, Ticket Operations—Walter Nash
Vice-President, Treasurer—Roland Seidler
Assistant to the President—Ike Ikuhara
Assistant Secretary & General Counsel—Santiago Fernandez
Director, Accounting and Finance—Bill Foltz
Director, Advertising and Special Events—Paul Kalil
Director, Broadcasting and Publications—Brent Shyer
Director, Community Relations—Don Newcombe
Community Relations—Roy Campanella
Director, Human Resources and Administration—Irene Tanji
Director, Data Processing—Mike Mularky
Director, Minor League Operations—Charlie Blaney
Director, Scouting—Terry Reynolds
Director, Publicity—Jay Lucas
Traveling Secretary—Bill DeLury
Manager—Tom Lasorda
Club Physicians—Dr. Frank W. Jobe, Dr. Michael F. Mellman, Dr. Herndon Harding
Executive Offices—Dodger Stadium, 1000 Elysian Park Avenue,
Los Angeles, Calif. 90012
Telephone—224-1500 (area code 213)

SCOUTS—Eleodoro Arias, Ralph Avila, Eddie Bane, Bill Barkley, Gil Bassetti,
Rick Birmingham, Bob Bishop, Gib Bodet, Flores Bolivar, Mike Brito, Joe Campbell,
Leonel Carrion, Jim Chapman, Bob Darwin, Eddie Fajardo, Lin Garrett, Ossie Al-
varez Gonzalez, Rafael Gonzalez, Michael Hankins, Dick Hanlon, Dennis Haren, Gail
Henley, Hank Jones, John Keenan, Gary LaRocque, Juan Lantigua, Don LeJohn,
Carl Loewenstine, Manuel Lunar, Teodoro Martinez, Teodoro Mata, Dale McReyn-
olds, Bob Miske, Tommy Mixon, Luis Angel Montalvo, Danny Montgomery, Victor
Nazario, Deni Pacini, Camilo Pasqual, Pablo Peguero, Cornelio Pena, Jose Pena,
Claude Pelletier, Bill Pleis, Silvano Quesada, Mark Sheehy, Jim Stoeckel, Dick Teed,
Glen Van Proyen, Corito Varona, Miguel Angel Villaran. Special Assignment Scouts
—Mel Didier, Phil Regan, Jerry Stephenson, Gary Sutherland.

PARK LOCATION—Dodger Stadium, 1000 Elysian Park Avenue.

Seating capacity—56,000.

FIELD DIMENSIONS—Home plate to left field at foul line, 330 feet; to center
field, 395 feet; to right field at foul line, 330 feet.

MONTREAL EXPOS

President & Chief Operating Officer—Claude R. Brochu
Vice-President, Baseball Operations—Bill Stoneman
Vice-President, Player Personnel & G.M.—David Dombrowski
Assistant General Manager—Dan Duquette
Director, Scouting—Gary Hughes
Director, Player Development—John Boles
Director, Team Travel—Erik Ostling
Asst. Dir., Scouting & Dir. of Latin American Operations—Frank Wren
Senior Consultant, Player Personnel—Whitey Lockman
Special Consultant, Baseball Operations—Jim Fanning
Special Consultant to V.P., Player Personnel—Angel Vazquez
Coordinator, Minor League Operations—Kent Qualls
G.M., West Palm Beach Operations—Rob Rabenecker
Vice-President, Marketing—Michel Lagace
Vice-President, Communications—Richard Morency
Vice-President, Business Operations—Gerry Trudeau
Controller—Raymond St. Pierre
Director, Ticket Department—Claude Delorme
Director, Media Services—Monique Giroux
Director, Media Relations—Richard Griffin
Director, Retailing—Catherine Goldner
Director, Ticket Sales—Ronald Martineau
Director, Stadium Operations—Monique Lacas
Director, Public Relations—Pierre Vidal
Manager—Buck Rodgers
Club Physician—Dr. Robert Brodrick
Club Orthopedist—Dr. Larry Coughlin
Mailing Address—P. O. Box 500, Station M, Montreal, Quebec,
Canada H1V 3P2
Telephone—253-3434 (area code 514)

SCOUTS—Jesus Alou, Edmundo Borrone, Emilio Carrusquel, Carl Cassell, Pepito Centeno, Ed Creech, Pat Daugherty, Richard DeHart, Brian Dermott, Manny Estrada, Jim Fleming, Orrin Freeman, Joseph Frisina, Eddie Haas, Rick Harig, Mercer Harris, Jack Henney, Herb Hippauf, Jim Holden, Bert Holt, Gary Hughes, Bob Johnson, Jack Jolly, Randy Kierce, Dick Lemay, Whitey Lockman, Bill MacKenzie, Rene Marchand, Gil Marrujo, Roy McMillan, Brian McRobie, Mike Murphy, Pat Murtaugh, Levy Ochoa, Bob Oldis, Cucho Rodriguez, Mark Servais, Larry Slusser, Keith Snider, Lynn Squires, Angel Vasquez, Ron Walters, Jeffrey Wren, Frank Wren, Fred Wright, Stan Zielinski, Greg Zunino.

PARK LOCATION—Olympic Stadium, 4549 Pierre de Coubertin St., Montreal, Quebec, Canada H1V 3N7.

Seating capacity—43,739.

FIELD DIMENSIONS—Home plate to left field at foul line, 325 feet; to center field, 404 feet; to right field at foul line, 325 feet.

NEW YORK METS

Chairman of the Board—Nelson Doubleday

President & Chief Executive Officer—Fred Wilpon
Directors—Nelson Doubleday, Fred Wilpon, J. Frank Cashen,
Saul Katz, Marvin Tepper
Special Consultant to the Board of Directors—Richard Cummins
Exec. Vice-President, G.M. & Chief Operating Officer—J. Frank Cashen
Executive Vice-President—Alan E. Harazin
Vice-President, Operations—Bob Mandt
Director of Baseball Operations—Gerald H. Hunsicker
Vice-President, Treasurer—Harold W. O'Shaughnessy
Vice-President, Marketing—James Ross
Vice-President, Broadcasting—Mike Ryan
Director of Public Relations—Jay Horwitz
Promotions Director—James Plummer
Executive Asst. to General Manager—Jean Coen
Director of Ticket Operations—Bill Iannicielo
Controller—Rick Iandoli
Traveling Secretary—Bob O'Hara
Director of Scouting—Roland Johnson
Stadium Manager—John McCarthy
Director of Amateur Baseball Relations—Tommy Holmes
Manager—Bud Harrelson
Club Physician—Dr. James C. Parkes II
Team Trainer—Steve Garland
Executive Offices—William A. Shea Stadium, Roosevelt
Avenue and 126th Street, Flushing, N.Y. 11368
Telephone—507-6387 (area code 718)

SCOUTS—Paul Baretta, Eric Broersma, Larry Chase, Phil Favia, Dick Gernert, Rob Guzik, Marty Harvat, Ken Houp, Reginald Jackson, Buddy Kerr, Craig Kornfeld, Joe Mason, Bob Minor, Harry Minor, Carlos Pascual, Jim Reeves, Paul Ricciarini, Junior Roman, Bob Rossi, Daraka Shaheed, Eddy Toledo, Terry Tripp, Bob Wellman, Jim Woodward.

PARK LOCATION—William A. Shea Stadium, Roosevelt Avenue and 126th Street, Flushing, N. Y. 11368.

Seating capacity—55,601.

FIELD DIMENSIONS—Home plate to left field at foul line, 338 feet; to center field, 410 feet; to right field at foul line, 338 feet.

PHILADELPHIA PHILLIES

President/General Partner—Bill Giles

Partners—Claire S. Betz, Estate of John Drew Betz,
Tri-Play Associates (Alexander K. Buck, J. Mahlon Buck Jr.,
William C. Buck); Fitz Eugene Dixon, Jr.; Mrs. Rochelle Levy
Executive Vice-President—David Montgomery
Vice-President, General Manager—Lee Thomas
Vice-President, Finance—Jerry Clothier
Vice-President, Public Relations—Larry Shenk
Director of Player Development—Del Unser
Director of Scouting—Jay Hankins
Secretary and Counsel—William Y. Webb
Player Personnel Administrator—Ed Wade
Assistant to President—Paul Owens
Director of Planning, Development & Super Boxes—Tom Hudson
Director of Promotions—Frank Sullivan
Manager, Advertising & Broadcasting—Jo-Anne Levy
Traveling Secretary—Eddie Ferenz
Director of Sales and Ticket Operations—Richard Deats
Director, Season Ticket Sales—Rory McNeil
Director of Community Relations—Regina Castellani
Director of Marketing—Dennis Mannion
Director of Stadium Operations—Mike DiMuzio
Director, Office Operations—Pat Cassidy
Controller—Mike Kent
Ticket Manager—Dan Goroff
Manager, Group Sales—Kathy Killian
Manager, Sales Operations—John Weber
Public Relations Assistants—Gene Dias, Leigh McDonald
Assistant Director of Community Relations—Karen Howard
Assistant Director of Promotions—Chris Legault
Business Manager, Minor Leagues—Bill Gargano
Club Physician—Dr. Phillip Marone
Club Trainer—Jeff Cooper
Strength and Flexibility Instructor—Gus Hoefling
Manager—Nick Leyva
Executive Offices—Philadelphia Veterans Stadium
Mailing Address—P.O. Box 7575, Philadelphia, Pa. 19101
Telephone—463-6000 (area code 215)

SCOUTS—(National Cross-Checkers)—Tony Roig and Randy Waddill. (Regional Cross-Checkers)—Jim Baumer, Ron King, Dick Lawlor and Bob Reasonover. (Special Assignment, Major Leagues)—Ray Shore. (Advance Scout, Major Leagues)—Hank King. (Special Assignment)—Eddie Bockman, Bing Devine and Larry Rojas. (Regular)—Oliver Bidwell, Jim Bierman, Wilfredo Calvino, Carlos Cuervo, Tom Ferguson, Bill Harper, Ken Hultzapple, Jerry Jordan, Jerry Lafferty, Terry Logan, Fred Mazuca, Cotton Nye, Arthur Parrack, Jack Pastore, Bob Poole, Larry Reasonover, Roy Tanner, Scott Trcka.

PARK LOCATION—Philadelphia Veterans Stadium, Broad Street and Pattison Avenue.

Seating capacity—62,382.

FIELD DIMENSIONS—Home plate to left field at foul line, 330 feet; to center field, 408 feet; to right field at foul line, 330 feet.

PITTSBURGH PIRATES

Board of Directors—Carl F. Barger, Joe L. Brown, Frank V. Cahouet, Richard M. Cyert, Douglas D. Danforth, Eugene Litman, John Marous, Sophie Masloff, John H. McConnell, Thomas H. O'Brien, Paul H. O'Neill, David M. Roderick, Vincent A. Sarni, Harvey M. Walken.

Chairman & Chief Executive Officer—Douglas D. Danforth
President—Carl F. Barger
Assistant to the President—Ken Wilson
Senior V.P. & G.M./Baseball Operations—Larry Doughty
Vice-President, Finance & Secretary—Kenneth C. Curcio
Vice-President, Administration & Operations—Richard L. Andersen
Vice-President, Public Relations—Richard J. Cerrone
Vice-President, Marketing—Steven N. Greenberg
Vice-President, Broadcasting & Advertising Sales—Dean Jordan
Assistant General Manager—Cam Bonifay
Asst. Vice-President, Finance—Patti Mistick
Traveling Secretary—Greg Johnson
Senior Dirs. of Sales & Marketing—Bob Derda, Mark Norelli
Director of Bradenton Baseball Operations—Jeff Podobnik
Director of Community Relations—Patty Paytas
Director of Community Services & Sales—Al Gordon
Director of Corporate Sales—Nellie Briles
Director of Diamond Club—Chris Cronin
Director of In-Game Entertainment—Mike Gordon
Director of Media Relations—Jim Lachimia
Director of Merchandising—Joe Billetdeaux
Director of Minor League Operations—Chet Montgomery
Director of Promotions—Kathy Guy
Director of Stadium Operations—Dennis DaPra
Director of Telemarketing—Phillip Trozzi
Director of Ticket Operations—Gary Remlinger
Asst. Director of Media Relations—Jim Trdinich
Asst. Director of Public Relations—Sally O'Leary
Asst., Baseball Operations—John Sirignano
Guest Relations & Food Service Coordinator—Elliot Falcione
Manager—Jim Leyland
Club Physician—Dr. Joseph Coroso
Team Orthopedist—Dr. Jack Failla
Trainers—Kent Biggerstaff, Dave Tumbas
Equipment Manager—John Hallahan
Executive Offices—Three Rivers Stadium, 600 Stadium Circle, Pittsburgh, Pa. 15212
Telephone—323-5000 (area code 412)

SCOUTS—(Coordinators)—Bart Braun, Jerry Gardner, Don Mitchell. (Supervisors)—Gene Baker, Joe L. Brown, Bill Bryk, Pablo Cruz, Larry D'Amato, Steve Demeter, Angel Figueroa, Steve Fleming, Jesse Flores, Dave Holliday, Leland Maddox, Rene Mons, Boyd Odom, Ed Roebuck, Paul Tinnell. (Major League)—Lenny Yochim. (Minor League)—Ken Parker.

PARK LOCATION—Three Rivers Stadium, 600 Stadium Circle.

Seating capacity—58,729.

FIELD DIMENSIONS—Home plate to left field at foul line, 335 feet; to center field, 400 feet; to right field at foul line, 335 feet.

ST. LOUIS CARDINALS

Chairman of the Board—August A. Busch, III

President & Chief Executive Officer—Fred L. Kuhlmann
Exec. Vice-President & Chief Operating Officer—Mark Sauer
Vice-President, Business Operations—Mark Gorris
Controller—Brad Wood
Vice-President, General Manager—Dal Maxvill
Manager—Joe Torre
Admin. Asst. to President & Chief Executive Officer—Jacqueline Hunter
Admin. Asst. to Exec. V.P. & Chief Operating Officer—Elaine Milo
Admin. Asst. to Vice-President, General Manager—Judy Carpenter Barada
Admin. Asst. to Vice-President, Business Operations—Bernadine Hogan
Vice-President, Marketing—Marty Hendin
Manager, Promotions—Nancy McElroy
Director of Player Development—Ted Simmons
Director of Scouting—Fred McAlister
Assistant Director of Scouting—Marty Maier
Asst. to Player Development & Scouting—Scott Smulczenski
Director of Public Relations—Jeff Wehling
Public Relations Manager—Brian Bartow
Director of Broadcasting & Market Development—Dan Farrell
Promotions Assistant—Joe Strohm
Director of Community Relations—Joe Cunningham
Director of Sales—Sue Ann McClaren
Manager, Community Relations—Ted Savage
Director of Tickets and Game Operations—Mike Bertani
Assistant Director of Tickets—Josephine Arnold
Manager, Human Resources—Marian Rhodes
Manager, Office Services—Kevin Wade
Director, Administration—Colin Allsop
Traveling Secretary—C.J. Cherre
Club Physician—Dr. Stan London
Executive Offices—Busch Stadium, 250 Stadium Plaza,
St. Louis, Mo. 63102
Telephone—421-3060 (area code 314)

SCOUTS—(Supervisors)—Jorge Aranzamendi, Jim Belz, Vern Benson, Jim Johnston, Marty Keough, Tom McCormack, Joe Morlan, Mel Nelson, Joe Rigoli, Mike Roberts, Hal Smith, Charles (Tim) Thompson, Rube Walker (special assignment). (Regulars)—James Brown, Roy Cromer, Roberto Diaz, Manuel Espinosa, Cecil Espy, Manuel Guerra, Juan Melo, Virgil Melvin, Charles Menzhuber, Ramon Ortiz, Joe Popek, Roger Smith, Kenneth Thomas.

PARK LOCATION—Busch Stadium, Broadway, Walnut Street, Stadium Plaza and Spruce Street.

Seating capacity—56,227.

FIELD DIMENSIONS—Home plate to left field at foul line, 330 feet; to center field, 414 feet; to right field at foul line, 330 feet.

SAN DIEGO PADRES

Chairman—Tom Werner

Vice Chairmen—Art Engle, Art Rivkin, Russell Goldsmith

Partners—Malin Burnham, Bruce Corwin, John Earhart, Jack Goodall, Keith Matson, Michael Monk, Leon Parma, Robert Payne, Peter Peckham, Ernest Rady, Scott Wolfe

President—Dick Freeman
Exec. V.P./Baseball Operations & General Manager—Joe McIlvaine
Vice-President, Business Operations—Bill Adams
Vice-President/Finance—Bob Wells
Vice-President/Public Relations—Andy Strasberg
Asst. Vice-President/General Manager—John Barr
Major League Scouts—Ken Bracey, Carmen Fusco
Director/Administrative Services—Lucy Freeman
Director/Broadcasting—Jim Winters
Director/Marketing—Tom Ryba
Director/Media Relations—Jim Ferguson
Director/Minor Leagues—Ed Lynch
Director/Publications—Jim Geschke
Director/Scouting—Randy Smith
Director/Stadium Operations—Doug Duennes
Director/Ticket Sales—Dave Gilmore
Traveling Secretary—John Mattei
Manager—Greg Riddoch
Club Physician—Scripps Clinic
Executive Offices—P. O. Box 2000, San Diego, Calif. 92112-2000
Telephone—283-7294 (area code 619)

SCOUTS—Pedro Avila, Mark Baca, Dave Bartosch, Billy Castell, Rich Chiles, Julio Coronado, Dave Freeland, Denny Galehouse, Ronquito Garcia, Andy Hancock, Al Hargesheimer, Jim Hicks, Cesar Jarquin, Randy Johnson, John Kosciak, Manny Lantigua, Bobby Malkmus, Abraham Martinez, Jim Miller, Darryl Milne, Damon Oppenheimer, Hosken Powell, Rolando Quintero, Earl Smith, Greg Smith, Scipio Spinks, Dale Sutherland, Kevin Towers, Jose Valentin, Hank Zacharias. (National Cross Checkers)—Ray Coley, Brian Granger, Brad Sloan.

PARK LOCATION—San Diego Jack Murphy Stadium, 9449 Friars Road.

Seating capacity—59,254.

FIELD DIMENSIONS—Home plate to left field at foul line, 327 feet; to center field, 405 feet; to right field at foul line, 327 feet.

SAN FRANCISCO GIANTS

Chairman—Bob Lurie

President & General Manager—Al Rosen
Executive Vice-President, Administration—Corey Busch
Vice-President, Baseball Operations—Bob Kennedy
Senior Vice-President—Pat Gallagher
V.P., Assistant General Manager—Ralph Nelson
Vice President, Scouting Operations—Bob Fontaine
Director of Player Development—Carlos Alfonso
Director of Minor Leagues—Tony Siegle
Director of Scouting—Dave Nahabedian
Director of Travel—Dirk Smith
Special Assistants to the President and G.M.—Willie Mays, Willie McCovey
Administrative Assistant—Florence Myers
Vice President, Public Relations—Duffy Jennings
Director of Media Relations—Matt Fischer
Director of Marketing—Mario Alioto
Director of Sales—Pennie Lundberg
Vice President, Stadium Operations—Jorge Costa
Director of Retail Operations—Bob Tolifson
Vice President, Ticket Operations—Arthur Schulze
Director of Ticket Operations—Judy Jones
Controller—Jeannie Hurley
Promotions Manager—Valerie McGuire
Director of Community Services—Dave Craig
Asst. Dir. of Media Relations—Robin Carr-Locke
Assistant Director of Stadium Operations—Gene Telucci
Staff Counsel—Michael Shapiro, Esq.
Asst. to the Dir. of Community Services—Mike Sadek
Community Representative—Vida Blue
Gov't Affairs, Broadcast Coordinator—Bob Hartzell
Producer, Broadcast Services—Jeff Kuiper
Manager—Roger Craig
Executive Offices—Candlestick Park, San Francisco, Calif. 94124
Telephone—468-3700 (area code 415)

SCOUTS—Harry Craft, Bob Cummings, Nino Escalera, Jim Fairey, George M. Genovese, Luis Gomez, Grady Hatton, Herman Hannah, Al Heist, Chuck Hensley, Elvio Jimenez, Mike Keenan, Richard Klaus, Andy Korenek, Tom Korenek, Alan Marr, Doug McMillan, Tony Michalak, Bob Miller, Rick Ragazzo, Mike Russell, Hank Sauer, John Shafer, Joe Strain, Todd Thomas, Gene Thompson, Mike Toomey, Jack Uhey, John Van Ornum, Tom Zimmer.

PARK LOCATION—Candlestick Point, Bayshore Freeway.

Seating capacity—58,000.

FIELD DIMENSIONS—Home plate to left field at foul line, 335 feet; to center field, 400 feet; to right field at foul line, 330 feet.

American League

Organized 1900

ROBERT W. BROWN, M.D.
President

JOHN E. FETZER, GENE AUTRY
Vice-Presidents

DICK WAGNER
Special Assistant to Baseball

MARTIN J. SPRINGSTEAD
Supervisor of Umpires

RICHARD BUTLER
Special Assistant to the President

PHYLLIS MERHIGE
Director of Public Relations

BRIAN SMALL
Assistant Director of Public Relations

TIM McCLEARY
Director, Waivers & Player Records

TESS BASTA
Administrator of Umpires/Travel

CAROLYN COEN
Administrative Assistant

Headquarters—350 Park Avenue, New York, N. Y. 10022

Telephone—339-7600 (area code 212)

ASSISTANT SUPERVISORS OF UMPIRES—Henry Soar, Jerry Neudecker.

UMPIRES—Lawrence Barnett, Joseph Brinkman, Alan Clark, Drew Coble, Terrance Cooney, Derryl Cousins, Donald Denkinger, James Evans, Dale Ford, Richard Garcia, Ted Hendry, John Hirschbeck, Mark Johnson, Jim Joyce, Kenneth Kaiser, Greg Kosc, Tim McClelland, Larry McCoy, James McKean, Durwood Merrill, Dan Morrison, Stephen Palermo, David Phillips, Rick Reed, Michael Reilly, John (Rocky) Roe, Dale Scott, John Shulock, Tim Tschida, Vic Voltaggio, Tim Welke, Larry Young.

OFFICIAL STATISTICIANS—Elias Sports Bureau, Inc., 500 5th Ave., Suite 2114, New York, N.Y. 10036. Telephone—(212) 869-1530.

BALTIMORE ORIOLES

Chairman—Eli S. Jacobs
President—Lawrence Lucchino

Exec. Vice-President & General Manager—Roland A. Hemond
Senior Vice-President/Asst. to the Chairman—Thomas A. Daffron
Vice-President, Finance—Joseph P. Hamper, Jr.
Vice-President, Administrative Personnel—Calvin Hill
Vice-President, Business Affairs—Robert R. Aylward
Vice-President/Sales—Louis I. Michaelson
Vice-President & Club Counsel—Lon Babby
Vice-President, Planning & Development—Janet Marie Smith
Vice-President—Sven Erik Holmes
Vice-President, Marketing—Martin B. Conway
Asst. G.M./Director of Player Personnel—R. Douglas Melvin
Acting Director of Scouting—Gary Nickels
Special Assistants to the Vice President—Gordon Goldsberry, Fred Uhlman Sr.
Controller—Aric Holsinger
Director of Publications—Robert W. Brown
Traveling Secretary—Philip E. Itzoe
Director of Public Relations—Richard L. Vaughn
Director of Stadium Services—Roy A. Sommerhof
Director of Research & Statistics—Eddie Epstein
Director of Orioles Productions—Charles A. Steinberg, DDS
Director of Sales Operations—Vince Dunbar
Director, Community Relations—Julia A. Wagner
Director, Computer Services—James L. Kline
Special Projects/Baseball Operations—Kenneth E. Nigro
Ticket Office Manager—Audrey Brown
Assistant Director of Public Relations—Bob Miller
Assistant Director of Marketing—Julie Dryer
Assistant Director of Sales Operations—Matt Dryer
Asst. Director, Player Development/Scouting—Roy H. Krasik
Assistant Director of Scouting—Fred Uhlman Jr.
Assistant Director of Community Relations—Stephanie Kelly
Assistant Ticket Office Managers—Joseph B. Codd, Denise C. Addicks
Manager—Frank Robinson
Club Physicians—Drs. Sheldon Goldgeier and Charles E. Silberstein
Trainers—Richie Bancells, Jamie Reed
Strength & Conditioning—Allan Johnson
Executive Offices—Memorial Stadium, Baltimore, Md. 21218
Telephone—243-9800 (area code 301)

SCOUTS—Rick Arnold, Carlos Bernhardt, Jesus Carmona, John Cox, Ray Crone, Jim Gilbert, Jesus Halabi, Jim Howard, Leo Labossiere, Mike Ledna, Ed Liberatore, Tim Luginbuhl, Miguel Machado, Lamar North, Camilo Nunez, Jim Pamlanye, Fred Peterson, Ed Sprague, Birdie Tebbetts, Mike Tullier, Logan White, Bennett Williams, Jerry Zimmerman.

PARK LOCATION—Memorial Stadium, 33rd Street, Ellerslie Avenue, 36th Street and Ednor Road.

Seating capacity—53,371.

FIELD DIMENSIONS—Home plate to left field at foul line, 309 feet; to center field, 405 feet; to right field at foul line, 309 feet.

BOSTON RED SOX

Owner
General Partner—JRY Corporation:
Majority Owner & Chairwoman of the Board—Jean R. Yawkey
President—John L. Harrington
Vice President & Treasurer—William B. Gutfarb

Owner
General Partner—Haywood C. Sullivan

Senior V.P. & General Manager—James (Lou) Gorman
Executive V.P. & Counsel—John F. Donovan, Jr.
Director of Community Relations & Personnel Admin.—Linda G. Ezell
V.P. & Chief Financial Officer—Robert C. Furbush
Vice President Baseball Development—Edward F. Kenney
Assistant General Manager—Elaine C. Weddington
Manager—Joseph M. Morgan
Director of Scouting—Edward M. Kasko
Director of Minor League Operations—Edward P. Kenney
Vice President Transportation—John J. Rogers
Traveling Secretary—Steven W. August
Special Assistant to the General Manager—John M. Pesky
Medical Director—Arthur M. Pappas, M.D.
Vice President Public Relations—Richard L. Bresciani
Vice President Broadcasting & Special Projects—James P. Healey
Director of Ticket Operations—Joseph P. Helyar
Vice President Stadium Operations—Joseph F. McDermott
Director of Facilities Management—Thomas L. Queenan, Jr.
Vice President Marketing—Lawrence C. Cancro
Director of Parking Facilities—Michael L. Silva
Director of Publicity—Josh S. Spofford
Director of Statistics—James A. Samia
Treasurer—John J. Reilly
Controller—Stanley H. Tran
Manager of Publications—Debra A. Matson
Superintendent of Grounds & Maintenance—Joseph Mooney
Manager of Advertising—Karla K. O'Hara
Executive Offices—4 Yawkey Way, Boston, Mass. 02215
Telephone—267-9440 (area code 617)

SCOUTS—Rafael Batista, Milton Bolling, Ray Boone, Sonny Bowers, Wayne Britton, Erwin Bryant, Luis Delgado, George Digby, Howard (Danny) Doyle, Bill Enos, Larry Flynn, Charles Koney, Jack Lee, Wilfrid (Lefty) Lefebvre, Don Lenhardt, Howard McCullough, Frank Malzone, Sam Mele, Willie Paffen, Phillip Rossi, Alex Scott, Edward Scott, Matt Sczesny, Joe Stephenson, Larry Thomas, Fay Thompson, Charlie Wagner, Luke Wrenn.

PARK LOCATION—Fenway Park, Yawkey Way, Lansdowne Street and Ipswich Street.

Seating capacity—34,142.

FIELD DIMENSIONS—Home plate to left field at foul line, 315 feet; to center field, 420 feet; to right field at foul line, 302 feet; average right-field distance, 382 feet.

CALIFORNIA ANGELS

President/Chairman of the Board—Gene Autry

Board of Directors—Gene Autry, Jackie Autry, Mike Port, Stanley B. Schneider,
John P. Singleton, Richard M. Brown, Peter V. Ueberroth
President & Chief Executive Officer—Richard M. Brown
Executive Vice-President & General Manager—Mike Port
Senior Vice-President, Baseball Operations—Dan O'Brien
Executive Vice-President—Jackie Autry
Senior Vice-President, Marketing—John Hays
Sr. Vice-President, Finance, Administration/Treasurer—James Wilson
Vice-President, Public Relations & Broadcasting—Tom Seeberg
Secretary & Legal Counsel—Richard M. Brown
Assistant to the General Manager—Preston Gomez
Director Minor League Operations—Bill Bavasi
Director Scouting—Bob Fontaine Jr.
Controller—Catherine Hellman
Admin. Assistant (Minor Leagues)—Jeff Parker
Admin. Assistant (National Association)—Cathy Carey
Admin. Assistant (Scouting)—Roberta Mazur
Traveling Secretary—Frank Sims
Director, Media Relations—Tim Mead
Director, Publications—John Sevano
Director, Community Relations—Darrell Miller
Director, Marketing—Bob Wagner
Asst. Director, Marketing—Jann Mueller
Director, Group Sales & Promotions—Lynn Biggs
Manager, Group Sales & Promotions—Marianne Zambrano
Director, Special Projects—Corky Lippert
Director, Stadium Operations—Kevin Uhlich
Director, Ticket Department—Carl Gordon
Medical Director—Dr. Robert Kerlan
Team Physician/Medicine—Dr. Jules Rasinski
Team Physician/Orthopedics—Dr. Lewis Yocum
Trainers—Rick Smith, Ned Bergert
Physical Therapist—Roger Williams
Manager—Doug Rader
Executive Offices—Anaheim Stadium, 2000 State College Blvd.,
Anaheim, Calif. 92806
Telephone—937-7200 (area code 714) or 625-1123 (area code 213)

SCOUTS—Ty Brown, Ted Brzenk, Joe Caro, Joe Carpenter, Loyd Christopher,
Ray Crone, Pompeyo Davalillo, Roger Ferguson, Bob Gardner, Red Gaskill, Rosey
Gilhousen, Jose Gomez, Dean Gruwell, Steve Gruwell, Bob Harrison, Fred Hatfield,
Davis Hodgson, Rick Ingalls, Nick Kamzic, Tim Kelly, Kris Kline, Tom Kotchman,
Tony LaCava, Jim McLaughlin, Bobby Myrick, Jon Neiderer, Tom Osowski, Eusebio
Perez, Vic Power, Paul Robinson, Cookie Rojas, Rich Schlenker, Brian York.

PARK LOCATION—Anaheim Stadium, 2000 State College Blvd.

Seating capacity—64,573.

FIELD DIMENSIONS—Home plate to left field at foul line, 333 feet; to center
field, 404 feet; to right field at foul line, 333 feet.

CHICAGO WHITE SOX

Chairman—Jerry M. Reinsdorf

Vice Chairman—Eddie M. Einhorn
Executive Vice-President—Howard C. Pizer
Senior Vice-President, Major League Operations—Ron Schueler
Senior Vice-President, Marketing & Broadcasting—Rob Gallas
Senior Vice-President, Baseball—Jack Gould
Vice-President, Finance—Timothy L. Buzard
Vice-President, Stadium Operations—Terry Savarise
V.P., Scouting & Minor League Operations—Larry Monroe
General Counsel—Allan B. Muchin
Secretary—Gerald Penner
Manager—Jeff Torborg
Director of Major League Operations—Dan Evans
Director of Scouting—Duane Shaffer
Director of Minor League Operations—Steve Noworyta
Special Assistants to Ron Schueler—Ed Brinkman, Ed Farmer, Bart Johnson
Asstistant to the Director of Scouting—Grace Guerrero Zwit
Traveling Secretary—Glen Rosenbaum
Major League Scouting & Video Analyst—Jeff Chaney
Major League Computer Scouting Analyst—Mike Maziarka
Trainers—Herm Schneider, Mark Anderson
Team Physicians—Drs. James Boscardin, Hugo Cuadros,
Bernard Feldman, David Orth, Scott Price
Controller—Bill Waters
Director of Marketing & Broadcasting—Mike Bucek
Director of Advertising & Promotions—Bob Grim
Director of Public Relations & Community Affairs—Doug Abel
Director of Park Operations—David Schaffer
Director of Purchasing—Don Esposito
Director of Ticket Administration—Millie Johnson
Director of Ticket Sales—Bob Voight
Ticket Manager—Bob Devoy
Director of Human Resources—Pam Storck
Director of Community Relations—Eric Ruden
Manager of Media Relations—Dana Noel
Manager of Publications & Fundraising—Barb Kozuh
Manager of Community Relations—Dan Fabian
Manager of Merchandising & Special Events—Sharon Sreniawaski
Executive Offices—Comiskey Park, 333 W. 35th Street, Chicago, Ill. 60616
Telephone—924-1000 (area code 312)

SCOUTS—(Major League)—Ed Brinkman, Ed Farmer, Bart Johnson. (Supervisors)—Mark Bernstein, Danny Monzon, Ed Pebley. (Regular)—Jose Bernhardt, Juan Ramon Bernhardt, Chuck Bizzell, Scott Cerny, Brian Collins, Alex Cosmidis, Marc Cuesta, Preston Douglas, Cal Emery, Jesse Flores, Rod Fridley, Warren Hughes, Miguel Ibarra, Joe Ingalls, Lou Laslo, Douglas Laumann, Reginald Lewis, Dario Lodigiani, Guy Mader, Jose Ortega, Ramon Ortis, David Owen, J.D. Patton, Gary Pellant, Orlando Pena, Michael Powers, Michael Rizzo, Elberto Rondon, Michael Sgobba, Bob Sloan, Michael Taylor, John Tumminia, Fermin Ubri, Henry Varlack, Bob Weinstein, Marti Wolever.

PARK LOCATION—Comiskey Park, 333 W. 35th Street, Chicago, Ill. 60616

Seating capacity—44,702.

FIELD DIMENSIONS—Home plate to left field at foul line, 347 feet; to center field, 400 feet; to right field at foul line, 347 feet.

CLEVELAND INDIANS

Board of Directors—Richard E. Jacobs, Chairman; David H. Jacobs, Vice-Chairman; Martin J. Cleary, Gary L. Bryenton

Chairman of the Board and Chief Executive Officer—Richard E. Jacobs
Vice-Chairman of the Board—David H. Jacobs
President and Chief Operating Officer—Hank Peters
Senior Vice President, Business—Dennis Lehman
Vice-President, Marketing—Jeff Overton
Vice-President, Finance—Gregg Olson
Vice President, Public Relations—Bob DiBiasio
Vice-President, Stadium Operations—Carl Hoerig
Vice-President—Martin J. Cleary
Manager—John McNamara
Director, Baseball Operations—John Hart
Director, Publications/Advertising Sales—Valerie Arcuri
Director, Merchandising/Licensing—Jayne Churchmack
Director, Ticket Services—Connie Minadeo
Director, Scouting—Mickey White
Director, Player Development—Dan O'Dowd
Director, Team Travel—Mike Seghi
Director, Promotions/Sales—Jon Starrett
Controller—Ken Stesanov
Assistant Director, Media Relations—Susie Gharrity
Assistant Director, Scouting—Jay Green
Administrator, Player Personnel—Wendy Hoppel
Manager, Media Relations—John Marohn
Manager, Promotions/Sales—Nadine Glinski
Manager, Community Relations—Glen Shumate
Manager, Box Office—Tom Sullivan
Manager, Operations—Kerry Wimsatt
Marketing Representative—Chris Previte
Account Executives, Ticket Sales—Scott Sterneckert, Devore Whitt
Speakers Bureau—Bob Feller
Indians Equipment & Clubhouse Manager—Cy Buynak
Medical Director—William T. Wilder, M.D.
Orthopedic Specialists—John Bergfeld, M.D., Tom Anderson, M.D.
Trainer—Jim Warfield
Assistant Trainer—Paul Spicuzza
Team Physicians—Drs. James R. Conforto, Godofredo Domingo,
K.V. Gopal, David Schultz, Chris Ruszkowski
Executive Offices—Cleveland Stadium, Cleveland, Ohio 44114
Telephone—861-1200 (area code 216)

SCOUTS—(National Crosschecker)—Tony DeMacio. (Supervisors)—Buzzy Keller, George Lauzerique, Jay Robertson. (Regulars)—Luis Aponte, Steve Avila, George Cecchetti, Tom Chandler, Ramon Conde, Tom Couston, Ed Crosby, Joe Delucca, Ken Duzich, Mark Germann, Dave Koblentz, Jerry LaPenta, Bill Lawlor, Alan Lewis, Winston Llenas, Buddy Mercado, Mark McKnight, Jim Richardson, Doug Takaragawa, Mark Weidemaier.

PARK LOCATION—Cleveland Stadium, Boudreau Blvd.

Seating capacity—74,483.

FIELD DIMENSIONS—Home plate to left field at foul line, 320 feet; to center field, 400 feet; to right field at foul line, 320 feet.

DETROIT TIGERS

Owner—Thomas S. Monaghan

Board of Directors
Thomas S. Monaghan, James A. Campbell, Douglas J. Dawson,
Glenn E. (Bo) Schembechler, George Kell, John E. Fetzer, George W. Griffith

Chairman & Chief Executive Officer—James A. Campbell
President & Chief Operating Officer—Glenn E. (Bo) Schembechler
Senior V.P., Finance—Alexander C. Callam
Senior Vice-President, Planning & Operations—William E. Haase
Senior V.P., Player Procurement & Development—Joseph A. McDonald
Senior V.P., Marketing, Radio & TV—Jeff Odenwald
V.P., Assistant to President—Alice Sloane
Vice President-Stadium Operations—Ralph E. Snyder
Vice President/Controller—Michael Wilson
Vice President-Media & Public Relations—Dan Ewald
Corporate Secretary—Douglas J. Dawson
Director of Radio & TV—Neal Fenkell
Director of Media & Public Relations—Greg Shea
Director, Ticket Operations—Ken Marchetti
Director, Minor League Administration—Dave Miller
Scouting Director—Jax Robertson
Director, Field Operations—Tom Petroff
Director, Marketing Services—Scott Nickle
Executive Secretary/Operations—Hazel McLane
Data Processing Manager—Richard Roy
Traveling Secretary—Bill Brown
Executive Consultant—Rick Ferrell
Manager, Promotions—Mike Pyle
Community Affairs Coordinator—Vince Desmond
Group Sales Coordinator—Irwin Cohen
Assistant Director of Stadium Operations—Frank Feneck
Assistant Director of Stadium Operations—Ed Goward
Trainers—Russ Miller, Pio DiSalvo
Manager—Sparky Anderson
Club Physicians—Clarence S. Livingood M.D., David Collon M.D., Louis Saco, M.D.
Executive Offices—Tiger Stadium, Detroit, Mich. 48216
Telephone—962-4000 (area code 313)

SCOUTS—Ruben Amaro, Wayne Blackburn, Charlie Gault, Mark Giegler, Jack Hays, Rich Henning, Joe Lewis, Dennis Lieberthal, Dave Littlefield, Jeff Malinoff, Stan Meek, John Mirabelli, Mark Monahan, Ramon Pena, Dee Phillips, Joe Robinson, Donny Rowland, Bill Schudlich, Steve Souchock, Mike Wallace, Clyde Weir, Dick Wiencek, Rob Wilfong, Dick Wilson, Gary York.

PARK LOCATION—Tiger Stadium, Michigan Avenue, Cochrane Avenue, Kaline Drive and Trumbull Avenue.

Seating capacity—52,416.

FIELD DIMENSIONS—Home plate to left field at foul line, 340 feet; to center field, 440 feet; to right field at foul line, 325 feet.

KANSAS CITY ROYALS

Board of Directors
Joe Burke, Charles Hughes, Ewing Kauffman,
Mrs. Ewing Kauffman, Earl Smith

Chairman of the Board (co-owner)—Ewing Kauffman
President—Joe Burke
Executive Vice-President and General Manager—Spencer (Herk) Robinson
Vice-President, Treasurer—Charles Hughes
Vice-President, Finance—Dale Rohr
Vice-President, Government & Consumer Affairs—Merle Wood
Vice-President, Public Relations—Dean Vogelaar
Vice-President, Marketing and Broadcasting—Dennis Cryder
Vice-President, Player Personnel—Joe Klein
Director of Scouting—Art Stewart
Assistant General Manager—Jay Hinrichs
Director of Stadium Operations—Tom Folk
Director of Season Ticket Sales—Joe Grigoli
Director of Group Sales/Lancer Coordinator—Chris Muehlbach
Director of Data Processing—Loretta Kratzberg
Director of Benefits & Compensation—Tom Pfannenstiel
Director of Accounting—Ken Willeke
Ticket Office Manager—Stacy Sherrow
Traveling Secretary—Dave Witty
Adm. Asst., Scouting & Player Development—Bob Hegman
Assistant Directors of Public Relations—Steve Fink, Kevin Henderson
Assistant Directors of Marketing—Mike Behymer, Laura Collins
Asst. Director of Stadium Operations—John Johnson
Accountant—Lisa Collins
Stadium Engineers—Duane Robinson, Chris Frank
Production Manager—Larry Magariel
Executive Secretary/Baseball—Peggy Mathews
Manager—John Wathan
Equipment Manager—Mike Wallace
Team Physician—Dr. Steve Joyce
Trainers—Nick Swartz, Steve Morrow
Executive Offices—Royals Stadium, Harry S Truman Sports Complex
Mailing Address—P. O. Box 419969, Kansas City, Mo. 64141
Telephone—921-2200 (area code 816)

SCOUTS—Allard Baird, Carl Blando, Gary Blaylock, Bob Carter, Floyd Chandler, Balos Davis, Tom Ferrick, Steve Flores, Ken Gonzales, Dave Herrera, Gary Johnson, Ken Kravec, Al Kubski, Tony Levato, Jeff McKay, Chuck McMichael, Jim Moran, Brian Murphy, Buck O'Neil, Wil Rutenschroer, Luis Silverio, Jerry Stephens, Terry Wetzel.

PARK LOCATION—Royals Stadium, Harry S Truman Sports Complex.

Seating capacity—40,625.

FIELD DIMENSIONS—Home plate to left field at foul line, 330 feet; to center field, 410 feet; to right field at foul line, 330 feet.

MILWAUKEE BREWERS

President, Chief Executive Officer—Allan H. (Bud) Selig

Executive Vice-President, General Manager—Harry Dalton
Vice-President, Marketing—Richard Hackett
Vice-President, Broadcast Operations—William Haig
Vice-President, Finance—Richard Hoffmann
Vice-President, Stadium Operations—Gabe Paul, Jr.
Director of Corporate Marketing—John Cordova
Asst. General Manager & Farm Director—Bruce Manno
Senior Advisor, Baseball Operations—Walter Shannon
Special Assistants to the General Manager—Dee Fondy, Sal Bando
General Counsel—Wendy Selig
Asst. General Counsel—Eugene (Pepi) Randolph
Traveling Secretary—Jimmy Bank
Scouting Coordinator—Dick Foster
V.P., International Baseball Oper.—Ray Poitevint
Dir. of Latin American Baseball Operations—Hiram Cuevas
Coord. of Player Development—Bob Humphreys
Asst. Dir., Spring Training Operations—Freddie Frederico
Director of Publicity—Tom Skibosh
Assistant Director of Stadium Operations and Advertising—Jack Hutchinson
Director of Electronic Systems—Terry Peterson
Director of Publications and Assistant Director of Publicity—Mario Ziino
Special Projects Manager—Jake Frego
Promotions Director—Tim Van Wagoner
Promotions Manager—Karen Brooks
Group Sales Director—Tim Trovato
Season Ticket Sales Director—Rich Fromstein
Ticket Office Manager—John Barnes
Director of Season Ticket Account Services—Alice Boettcher
Manager—Tom Trebelhorn
Club Physicians—Dr. Paul Jacobs, Dr. Dennis Sullivan
Trainers—John Adam, Al Price
Superintendent of Grounds and Maintenance—Gary Vandenberg
Equipment Manager—Tony Migliaccio
P.A. Announcer—Bob Betts
Executive Offices—Milwaukee Brewers Baseball Club
Milwaukee County Stadium, Milwaukee, Wis. 53214
Telephone—933-4114 (area code 414)

SCOUTS—Crosschecker/Special Assignments: Walter Youse. Special Assignment: Nelson Burbrink, Dave Garcia, Cal McLish, Danny Menendez, Ben Oglivie, Charlie Silvera, Paul Tretiak. Supervisors: Fred Been, Julio Blanco-Herrera, Ken Califano, Felix Delgado, Roland LeBlanc, Lee Sigman. Regulars: Al Bleser, Derek Bryant, Kevin Christman, Lou Cohenour, Ed Durkin, Al Geddes, Larry Keller, Harvey Kuenn, Jr., Terry Laschen, Steve McAllister, Jim McCray, Demie Mainieri, Ed Mathes, Steve Minor, Gus Mureo, Frank Pena, Ron Rizzi, Reuben Rodriguez, Art Schuerman, Harry Smith, Sam Suplizio, Tommy Thompson, Rip Tutor, Red Whitsett, David Young, George Zabala.

PARK LOCATION—Milwaukee County Stadium, 201 S. 46th Street off Bluemound Road.

Seating capacity—53,192.

FIELD DIMENSIONS—Home plate to left field at foul line, 315 feet; to center field, 402 feet; to right field at foul line, 315 feet.

MINNESOTA TWINS

Owner—Carl R. Pohlad

President—Jerry Bell
Chairman of Executive Committee—Howard Fox
Directors—Donald E. Benson, Paul R. Christen, James O. Pohlad, Robert C. Pohlad,
William M. Pohlad, Robert E. Woolley
Exec. Vice-President, Baseball Operations—Andy MacPhail
Vice-President, Player Personnel—Bob Gebhard
Vice-President, Consumer Affairs—Dave Moore
Director of Finance—Kevin Mather
Director of Minor Leagues—Jim Rantz
Director of Scouting—Terry Ryan
Director of Baseball Administration—Bill Smith
Director of Marketing—Laurel Prieb
Director of Media Relations—Tom Mee
Traveling Secretary—Remzi Kiratli
Manager—Tom Kelly
Club Physicians—Dr. Leonard J. Michienzi, Dr. John Steubs
Executive Offices—Hubert H. Humphrey Metrodome, 501 Chicago Ave. South,
Minneapolis, Minn. 55415
Telephone—375-1366 (area code 612)

SCOUTS—Floyd Baker, Vern Borning, Enrique Brito, Ellsworth Brown, Larry
Corrigan, Gene Deboer, Dan Durst, Cal Ermer, Marty Esposito, Vern Followell, Earl
Frishman, Angelo Giuliani, Bill Lohr, Kevin Malone, Kevin Murphy, Mike Radcliff,
Clair Rierson, Edwin Rodriguez, Mike Ruth, Cobby Saatzer, Jeff Schugel, Johnny
Sierra, Herb Stein, Ricky Taylor, Jerry Terrell, Steve Williams, John Wilson.

PARK LOCATION—Hubert H. Humphrey Metrodome, 501 Chicago Ave. South.

Seating capacity—55,883.

FIELD DIMENSIONS—Home plate to left field at foul line, 343 feet; to center
field, 408 feet; to right field at foul line, 327 feet.

NEW YORK YANKEES

Principal Owner—George M. Steinbrenner

Managing General Partner—Robert E. Nederlander
Limited Partners—Harold M. Bowman, Daniel M. Crown, James S. Crown, Lester Crown, Michael Friedman, Marvin Goldklang, Barry Halper, Harvey Leighton, Daniel McCarthy, Harry Nederlander, James Nederlander, William Rose Sr., Edward Rosenthal, Jack Satter, Joan Z. Steinbrenner, Charlotte Witkind, Richard Witkind

Exec. Vice-President & Chief Operating Officer—Leonard L. Kleinman
Vice President—Joseph Malloy
Senior Vice-President—Arthur Richman
Vice President & General Manager—Gene Michael
Vice President, Baseball Operations—George W. Bradley
Chief of Operations—John C. Lawn
Vice-President, Marketing—John C. Fugazy
Vice-President, Community Relations—Richard Kraft
Vice President—Ed Weaver
V.P., General Counsel & Secretary—David Sussman
Vice-President, Ticket Operations—Frank Swaine
Chief Controller—Harry Rabb
Vice President, Player Development & Scouting—Brian Sabean
Assistant General Manager—Bill Bergesch
Assistant to General Manager—Peter Jameson
Director of Minor League Operations—Mitch Lukevics
Coordinator of Scouting—Bill Livesey
Major League Administrator—Les Parker
Traveling Secretary—Tony Bartirome
Director of Stadium Operations—Timothy D. Hassett
Director of Customer Services—Joel S. White
Executive Director of Ticket Operations—Jeff Kline
Ticket Director—Ken Skrypek
Director of Group & Season Sales—Debbie Tymon
Director of Media Relations & Publicity—Jeff Idelson
Asst. Dir. of Media Relations & Publicity—Brian Walker
Assistant Directors of Public Relations—Ed Angelino, Keith Wiarda
Director of Publications—Tom Bannon
Director of Television & Video Production—Joe Violone
Team Physician—Dr. Stuart Hershon
Trainers—Gene Monahan, Steve Donohue
Manager—Carl (Stump) Merrill
Executive Offices—Yankee Stadium, Bronx, N.Y. 10451
Telephone—293-4300 (area code 212)

SCOUTS—(Major League)—Charles (Boots) Day, Brandy Davis, Ron Hansen, Dick Tidrow. (Special Assignments)—Lee Elder, Fred Goodman, Bill Haller, Jack Hubbard, Clyde King, Bob Lemon, Jack Lewellyn, Jim Naples. (Cross-checkers)—Dick Groch, Jack Gillis, Don Lindeberg, Bill Livesey, Stan Saleski. (Supervisors)—Mark Batchko, Hop Cassady, Joe DiCarlo, Walt Dixon, Carl Moesche, Greg Orr, Joe Robison, Rudy Santin, Bill Schmidt, Tim Schmidt, Ken Stauffer, Jeff Taylor, Paul Turco, Leon Wurth. (Associates)—Jack Carroll, Kermit Damont, Ray Griffin, Bruce King, Joe Ross, Chip Smith, Bob Stead.

PARK LOCATION—Yankee Stadium, E. 161st St. and River Ave., Bronx, N.Y. 10451.

Seating capacity—57,545.

FIELD DIMENSIONS—Home plate to left field at foul line, 312 feet; to center field, 410 feet; to right field at foul line, 310 feet.

OAKLAND ATHLETICS

Owner/Managing General Partner—Walter A. Haas, Jr.
President/Chief Operating Officer—Walter J. Haas
Vice-President, Baseball Operations—Sandy Alderson
Vice-President, Business Operations—Andy Dolich
Vice-President, Finance—Kathleen McCracken
Vice-President, Administration & Personnel—Raymond B. Krise Jr.
Assistant to the Exec. V.P., Baseball Matters—Bill Rigney
Director of Player Development—Karl Kuehl
Director of Scouting—Dick Bogard
Asst. Director of Scouting—Eric Kubota
Director of Baseball Administration—Walt Jocketty
Director of Latin American Scouting—Juan Marichal
Director of Team Travel—Mickey Morabito
Director of Baseball Information—Jay Alves
Asst. Director, Baseball Administration—Pamela Pitts
Admin. Assistant, Baseball Operations—Jennella Roark
Admin. Assistant, Baseball Relations—Doreen Alves
Director of Broadcasting—Tom Cordova
Director of Media Relations—Kathy Jacobson
Director of Community Affairs/Speakers Bureau—Dave Perron
Director of Stadium Operations—Kevin Kahn
Director of Publications—Rob Kelly
Director of Broadcast Operations—Bill King
Director of Business Administration—Alan Ledford
Director of Sales—John Kamperschroer
Director of Special Projects—Steve Page
Director of Season Tickets—Barbara Reilly
Director of Group Sales—Bettina Flores
Director of Outreach Activities—Sharon Jones
Director of Promotions—Sharon Kelly
Manager—Tony La Russa
Team Physician—Dr. Allan Pont
Team Orthopedist—Dr. Rick Bost
Trainers—Barry Weinberg, Larry Davis
Equipment Manager—Frank Ciensczyk
Visiting Clubhouse Manager—Steve Vucinich
Executive Offices—Oakland-Alameda County Coliseum,
P.O. Box 2220, Oakland, Calif. 94621
Telephone—638-4900 (area code 415)

SCOUTS—Tony Arias, Mark Conkin, Tim Corcoran, Grady Fuson, Bill Gayton, James Guinn, Mike Jones, John Kazanas, Billy Merkel, Bill Meyer, Marty Miller, Steve Nichols, J.P. Ricciardi, Dave Roberts, Jeff Scott, Kelly Smith, Mike Stafford, Pat Sullivan, Ron Vaughn, Craig Wallenbrock, Dave Wilder.

PARK LOCATION—Oakland-Alameda County Coliseum, Nimitz Freeway and Hegenberger Road.

Seating capacity—47,313.

FIELD DIMENSIONS—Home plate to left field at foul line, 330 feet; to center field, 400 feet; to right field at foul line, 330 feet.

SEATTLE MARINERS

Chairman—Jeff Smulyan

President—Gary Kaseff
Vice President, Baseball Operations—Woody Woodward
Vice President, Communications—Randy Adamack
Vice President, Finance & Administration—Brian Beggs
Vice President, Marketing—Stuart Layne
Vice President, Sales—John Thomas
V.P., Scouting & Player Development—Roger Jongewaard
Director of Baseball Administration—Lee Pelekoudas
Assistants to V.P., Baseball Operations—George Zuraw, Reggie Waller
Farm Director—Jim Beattie
Coordinator of Minor League Instruction—Jim Skaalen
Director of Team Travel—Craig Detwiler
Director of Community Relations—Joe Chard
Director of Corporate Sales—Greg Elliott
Director of Promotions—Carl Weinstein
Director of Public Relations—Dave Aust
Director of Stadium Operations—Jeff Klein
Director of Ticket Sales—J.C. Crouch
Controller—Denise Podosek
Assistant Director of Marketing—Kevin Martinez
Assistant Director of Public Relations—Pete Vanderwarker
Exec. Asst. to General Managing Partner—Janet Croft
Accounting Assistant—Shirley Shreve
Player Development & Scouting Assistant—Larry Beinfest
Public Relations Assistants—David Venneri, Molly Magan
Manager—Jim Lefebvre
Trainer—Rick Griffin
Home Clubhouse & Equipment Manager—Henry Genzale
Club Physicians—Dr. Larry Pedegana, Dr. Mitchel Storey
Club Dentist—Dr. Richard Leshgold
Head Groundskeeper—Wilbur Loo
P.A. Announcer—Tom Hutyler
Executive Offices—P.O. Box 4100
411 First Ave. S., Seattle, Washington 98104
Telephone—628-3555 (area code 206)

SCOUTS—(Special Assignment)—Bill Kearns. (Regulars)—Maximo Alvarez, Al Bundy, John Burden, Kendall Carter, Ken Compton, Edward D'Alessio, Miguel de la Cruz, Ramon De los Santos, Miguel Escobar, Mateo Fortunato, Matt Hall, Joe Henderson, Dan Jennings, Mark Jensen, Pete Jones, Dan Karaff, Bobby Lawrence, Gary McGraw, Ken Madeja, Jerry Marik, Omer Munoz, Glenn Murdock, Scott Nethery, Joe Nigro, Fran Oneta, Cliff Pastornicky, Myron Pines, Steve Pope, Phil Pote, John Ramey, Eddie Santiago, Louis Scheuermann, Ray Vince, Jack Webber, Bill Young, Phil Zelman.

PARK LOCATION—The Kingdome, 201 King Street, Seattle, Washington.

Seating capacity—57,748.

FIELD DIMENSIONS—Home plate to left field at foul line, 331 feet; to center field, 405 feet; to right field at foul line, 312 feet.

TEXAS RANGERS

General Partners—George W. Bush, Edward W. (Rusty) Rose
Partner, Ballpark Development—J. Thomas Schieffer

Vice President, General Manager—Thomas A. Grieve
Vice President, Business Operations—John F. McMichael
Vice President, Administration—Charles F. Wangner
Vice President, Public Relations—John Blake
General Counsel—Gerald W. Haddock
Assistant G.M., Player Personnel and Scouting—Sandy Johnson
Assistant General Manager—Wayne Krivsky
Director, Player Development—Marty Scott
Director, Sales, Broadcasting and Producer, Diamond Vision—Chuck Morgan
Director, Promotions and Director, Diamond Vision—Dave Fendrick
Director, Stadium Administration—Jay Miller
Director, Stadium Operations—Mat Stolley
Traveling Secretary—Dan Schimek
Controller—Steve McNeill
Manager, Ticket Operations—John Schriever
Manager, Group Sales—Rich Billings
Manager, Community Services—Taunee Paur
Manager, Telemarketing—Sean Doyle
Assistant Director, Public Relations—Larry Kelly
Assistant Manager, Ticket Operations—Ben Marthaler
Assistant, Special Projects—Bobby Bragan
Major League Scout/Special Assignments—John Young
General Manager, Charlotte County Operations—Ted Guthrie
Medical Director—Dr. Mike Mycoskie
Manager—Bobby Valentine
Field Superintendent—Jim Anglea
Assistant Field Superintendent—Brad Richards
Spring Training Director—John Welaj
Home Clubhouse and Equipment Manager—Joe Macko
Visiting Clubhouse Manager—Zack Minasian
Executive Offices—1250 Copeland Road, 11th Floor, Arlington, Tex. 76011
Arlington Stadium—1500 Copeland Road, Arlington, Tex. 76010
Mailing Address—P.O. Box 90111, Arlington, Tex. 76004
Telephone—273-5222 (area code 817)

SCOUTS—Hector Acevedo, Manuel Batista, Jim Benedict, Ray Blanco, Joe Branzell, Marco Cobos, Paddy Cottrell, Dick Coury, Antonio Cruz, Mike Daughtry, Amado Dinzey, Jim Dreyer, Bill Earnhart, Dick Egan, Doug Gassaway, Mike Grouse, Tim Hallgren, Calvin Koonce, Bryan Lambe, Robert Lavallee, Jim Lentine, Omar Minaya, Jose Offerman, Mike Piatnik, Bill Schmidt, Rick Schroeder, Don Shwery, Jim St. Laurent, Len Strelitz, Charles Taylor, Randy Taylor, Rudy Terrasas, Danilo Troncoso, Gorge Urribarri, Boris Villa.

PARK LOCATION—Arlington Stadium, 1500 Copeland Road, Arlington, Tex.

Seating capacity—43,508.

FIELD DIMENSIONS—Home plate to left field at foul line, 330 feet; to center field, 400 feet; to right field at foul line, 330 feet.

TORONTO BLUE JAYS

Board of Directors—John Craig Eaton, N. E. Hardy,
William Ferguson, G. W. Radford, P. N. T. Widdrington
Chairman & Chief Executive Officer—N. E. Hardy
President & Chief Operating Officer—Paul Beeston
Executive Vice-President, Baseball—Pat Gillick
Vice-Presidents, Baseball—Bob Mattick, Al LaMacchia
Vice-President, Business—Bob Nicholson
Special Asst. to Exec. V.P., Baseball—Al Widmar
Assistant General Manager—Gord Ash
Director, Public Relations—Howard Starkman
Director, Stadium & Ticket Operations—George Holm
Director, Marketing—Paul Markle
Director, Finance—Susan Quigley
Director, Scouting—Bob Engle
Director, International Scouting—Wayne Morgan
Director, Player Development—Mel Queen
Director, Canadian Scouting—Bob Prentice
Director, Minor League Business—Ken Carson
Administrator, Player Personnel—Bob Nelson
Assistant Director, Public Relations—Gary Oswald
Asst. Dir., Tickets & Box Office Manager—Randy Low
Assistant Director, Operations—Len Frejlich
Manager, Group Sales—Maureen Haffey
Manager, Team Travel—John Brioux
Manager, Promotions and Advertising—Rick Amos
Manager, Community Relations—Mark Edwards
Manager, Employee Compensation—Catherine Elwood
Manager, Information Systems—Hans Frauenlob
Manager, Ticket Vault—Paul Goodyear
Manager, Ticket Revenue—Mike Maunder
Managers, Ticket Mail Services—Allan Koyanagi, Doug Barr
Manager, Security—Fred Wootton
Manager, Event Personnel—Mario Coutinho
Systems Administrator—Mark Graham
Supervisor, Office & Game Services—Mick Bazinet
Trainers—Tommy Craig, Brent Andrews
Manager—Cito Gaston
Team Physician—Dr. Ron Taylor
Executive Offices—SkyDome, 300 Bremner Blvd., Gate #9
Toronto, Ontario M5V 3B3
Telephone—341-1000 (area code 416)

SCOUTS—David Blume, Chris Bourjos, Chris Buckley, Ellis Clary, John Cole, Ellis Dungan, Joe Ford, Epy Guerrero (Coordinator, Latin American Scouting & Player Development), Tim Hewes, Tom Hinkle, Jim Hughes, Moose Johnson (Special Assignment), Gordon Lakey (Special Assignment), Duane Larson, Ted Lekas, Ben McLure, Wayne Morgan, Andy Pienovi, Jorge Rivera, Mark Snipp, Jerry Sobeck, Neil Summers, Ron Tostenson, Ramon Webster, Don Welke, Tim Wilken (Special Assignment), Dave Yoakum (Advance).

PARK LOCATION—SkyDome, 300 Bremner Blvd. Between Lakeshore Boulevard and Front Street, east of Spadina Avenue.

Seating capacity—50,000.

FIELD DIMENSIONS—Home plate to left field at foul line, 330 feet; to center field, 400 feet; to right field at foul line, 330 feet.

OFFICIAL MINOR LEAGUE AVERAGES

Including

Official Averages of All Class AAA, Class AA, Class A and Rookie Leagues

Major League Farm Systems for '91

AMERICAN LEAGUE

BALTIMORE (6): AAA—Rochester. AA—Hagerstown. A—Frederick, Wausau. Rookie—Bluefield, Gulf Coast.

BOSTON (6): AAA—Pawtucket. AA—New Britain, Conn. A—Elmira, Lynchburg, Winter Haven. Rookie—Winter Haven.

CALIFORNIA (6): AAA—Edmonton. AA—Midland. A—Boise, Quad City, Palm Springs. Rookie—Mesa.

CHICAGO (6): AAA—Vancouver. AA—Birmingham. A—Sarasota, South Bend, Utica. Rookie—Gulf Coast.

CLEVELAND (7): AAA—Colorado Springs. AA—Canton-Akron. A—Columbus, Ga., Kinston, Reno, Watertown. Rookie—Burlington, N.C.

DETROIT (6): AAA—Toledo. AA—London, Ont. A—Lakeland, Fayetteville, Niagara Falls. Rookie—Bristol, Va.

KANSAS CITY (6): AAA—Omaha. AA—Memphis. A—Appleton, Baseball City, Fla., Eugene. Rookie—Boardwalk.

MILWAUKEE (6): AAA—Denver. AA—El Paso. A—Beloit, Stockton. Rookie—Helena, Peoria, Ariz.

MINNESOTA (6): AAA—Portland. AA—Orlando. A—Kenosha, Visalia. Rookie—Elizabethton, Gulf Coast.

NEW YORK (7): AAA—Columbus, O. AA—Albany-Colonie, N.Y. A—Fort Lauderdale, Greensboro, Oneonta, Prince William. Rookie—Sarasota.

OAKLAND (6): AAA—Tacoma. AA—Huntsville. A—Modesto, Madison, Southern Oregon. Rookie—Scottsdale.

SEATTLE (6): AAA—Calgary. AA—Jacksonville. A—Peninsula, San Bernardino, Bellingham. Rookie—Tempe.

TEXAS (6): AAA—Oklahoma City. AA—Tulsa. A—Port Charlotte, Gastonia. Rookie—Butte, Gulf Coast.

TORONTO (7): AAA—Syracuse. AA—Knoxville. A—Myrtle Beach, Dunedin, St. Catharines, Ont. Rookie—Gulf Coast, Medicine Hat, Santo Domingo.

NATIONAL LEAGUE

ATLANTA (7): AAA—Richmond. AA—Greenville. A—Durham, Sumter. Rookie—Bradenton, Idaho Falls, Pulaski.

CHICAGO (6): AAA—Iowa. AA—Charlotte. A—Geneva, Peoria, Ill., Winston-Salem. Rookie—Huntington.

CINCINNATI (6): AAA—Nashville. AA—Chattanooga. A—Cedar Rapids, Charleston, W. Va. Rookie—Billings, Princeton.

HOUSTON (7): AAA—Tucson. AA—Jackson. A—Asheville, Auburn, Burlington, Ia., Osceola, Fla. Rookie—Gulf Coast.

LOS ANGELES (7): AAA—Albuquerque. AA—San Antonio. A—Bakersfield, Salem, Ore., Vero Beach. Rookie—Great Falls, Gulf Coast.

MONTREAL (7): AAA—Indianapolis. AA—Harrisburg. A—Jamestown, Rockford, Sumter, West Palm Beach. Rookie—Bradenton.

NEW YORK (7): AAA—Tidewater. AA—Williamsport. A—Columbia, S.C., Pittsfield, Port St. Lucie. Rookie—Kingsport, Sarasota.

PHILADELPHIA (6): AAA—Scranton/Wilkes-Barre. AA—Reading. A—Batavia, Clearwater, Spartanburg. Rookie—Martinsville.

PITTSBURGH (6): AAA—Buffalo. AA—Columbus, Ga. A—Salem, Va., Augusta, Ga., Welland, Ont. Rookie—Bradenton.

ST. LOUIS (8): AAA—Louisville. AA—Arkansas. A—Hamilton, Ont., St. Petersburg, Savannah, Springfield, Ill. Rookie—Johnson City, Peoria, Ariz.

SAN DIEGO (7): AAA—Las Vegas. AA—Wichita. A—Charleston, S.C., High Desert, Spokane, Waterloo. Rookie—Scottsdale.

SAN FRANCISCO (5): AAA—Phoenix. AA—Shreveport. A—Clinton, San Jose. Rookie—Everett.

American Association

CLASS AAA

Leading Batter
MARK RYAL
Buffalo

League President
RANDY MOBLEY

Leading Pitcher
CHRIS HAMMOND
Nashville

CHAMPIONSHIP WINNERS IN PREVIOUS YEARS

1902—Indianapolis .... .683	1940—Kansas City .... .625	1963-1968—Did not operate.
1903—St. Paul .... .657	Louisville (4th)‡ .... .500	1969—Omaha .... .607
1904—St. Paul .... .646	1941—Columbus† .... .621	1970—Omaha* .... .529
1905—Columbus .... .658	Columbus (3rd)‡ .... .532	Denver .... .504
1906—Columbus .... .615	1942—Kansas City .... .549	1971—Indianapolis .... .604
1907—Columbus .... .584	Columbus (3rd)‡ .... .532	Denver* .... .521
1908—Indianapolis .... .601	1943—Milwaukee .... .596	1972—Wichita .... .621
1909—Louisville .... .554	Columbus (3rd)‡ .... .532	Evansville* .... .593
1910—Minneapolis .... .637	1944—Milwaukee .... .667	1973—Iowa .... .610
1911—Minneapolis .... .600	Louisville (3rd)‡ .... .574	Tulsa* .... .504
1912—Minneapolis .... .636	1945—Milwaukee .... .604	1974—Indianapolis .... .578
1913—Milwaukee .... .599	Louisville (3rd)‡ .... .545	Tulsa* .... .567
1914—Milwaukee .... .590	1946—Louisville† .... .601	1975—Evansville* .... .566
1915—Minneapolis .... .597	1947—Kansas City .... .608	Denver .... .596
1916—Louisville .... .605	Milwaukee (3rd)‡ .... .513	1976—Denver* .... .632
1917—Indianapolis .... .588	1948—Indianapolis .... .649	Omaha .... .574
1918—Kansas City .... .589	St. Paul (3rd)‡ .... .558	1977—Omaha .... .563
1919—St. Paul .... .610	1949—St. Paul .... .608	Denver* .... .522
1920—St. Paul .... .701	Indianapolis (2nd)‡ .... .604	1978—Indianapolis .... .578
1921—Louisville .... .583	1950—Minneapolis .... .584	Omaha* .... .489
1922—St. Paul .... .641	Columbus (3rd)‡ .... .549	1979—Evansville* .... .574
1923—Kansas City .... .675	1951—Milwaukee† .... .623	Oklahoma City .... .533
1924—St. Paul .... .578	1952—Milwaukee .... .656	1980—Denver .... .676
1925—Louisville .... .635	Kansas City (2nd)‡ .... .578	Springfield* .... .551
1926—Louisville .... .629	1953—Toledo .... .584	1981—Omaha .... .581
1927—Toledo .... .601	Kansas City (2nd)‡ .... .571	Denver* .... .559
1928—Indianapolis .... .593	1954—Indianapolis .... .625	1982—Indianapolis* .... .551
1929—Kansas City .... .665	Louisville (2nd)‡ .... .556	Omaha .... .518
1930—Louisville .... .608	1955—Minneapolis† .... .597	1983—Louisville .... .578
1931—St. Paul .... .623	1956—Indianapolis† .... .597	Denver‡ .... .545
1932—Minneapolis .... .595	1957—Wichita .... .604	1984—Denver .... .513
1933—Columbus* .... .604	Denver (2nd)‡ .... .584	Louisville‡ .... .510
Minneapolis .... .562	1958—Charleston .... .589	1985—Oklahoma City .... .556
1934—Minneapolis .... .570	Minneapolis (3rd)‡ .... .536	Louisville* .... .521
Columbus* .... .556	1959—Louisville§ .... .599	1986—Indianapolis* .... .563
1935—Minneapolis .... .591	Omaha§ .... .516	Denver .... .535
1936—Milwaukee† .... .584	Minneapolis (2nd)‡ .... .586	1987—Denver .... .564
1937—Columbus† .... .584	1960—Denver .... .571	Indianapolis‡ .... .536
1938—St. Paul .... .596	Louisville (2nd)‡ .... .556	1988—Indianapolis* .... .627
Kansas City (2nd)‡ .... .556	1961—Indianapolis .... .573	Omaha .... .570
1939—Kansas City .... .695	Louisville (2nd)‡ .... .533	1989—Indianapolis* .... .596
Louisville (4th)‡ .... .490	1962—Indianapolis .... .605	Omaha .... .507
	Louisville (4th)‡ .... .486	

*Won playoff (East vs. West). †Won championship and four-team playoff. ‡Won four-team playoff. §Respective Eastern and Western division winners.

STANDING OF CLUBS AT CLOSE OF SEASON, SEPTEMBER 4

EASTERN DIVISION

Club	W.	L.	T.	Pct.	G.B.
Nashville (Reds)	86	61	0	.585	....
Buffalo (Pirates)	85	62	0	.578	1
Louisville (Cardinals)	74	72	0	.507	11½
Indianapolis (Expos)	61	85	0	.418	24½

WESTERN DIVISION

Club	W.	L.	T.	Pct.	G.B.
Omaha (Royals)	86	60	0	.589	....
Iowa (Cubs)	72	74	0	.493	14
Denver (Brewers)	68	78	0	.466	18
Oklahoma City (Rangers)	58	87	0	.400	27½

COMPOSITE STANDING OF CLUBS AT CLOSE OF SEASON, SEPTEMBER 4

Club	Oma.	Nash.	Buf.	Lou.	Iowa	Den.	Ind.	O.C.	W.	L.	T.	Pct.	G.B.
Omaha (Royals)	...	6	4	8	13	9	6	12	86	60	0	.589	....
Nashville (Reds)	6	...	8	10	10	6	12	9	86	61	0	.585	½
Buffalo (Pirates)	8	11	...	9	6	6	13	8	85	62	0	.578	1½
Louisville (Cardinals)	4	8	9	...	7	3	14	7	74	72	0	.507	12
Iowa (Cubs)	5	2	6	5	...	12	5	13	72	74	0	.493	14
Denver (Brewers)	9	6	6	9	6	...	5	9	68	78	0	.466	18
Indianapolis (Expos)	6	6	5	4	7	7	...	8	61	85	0	.418	25
Oklahoma City (Rangers)	6	3	4	5	5	9	4	...	58	87	0	.400	27½

Major league affiliations in parentheses.

Iowa club represented Des Moines, Ia.

Playoffs—Omaha defeated Nashville, three games to two, to win league championship. Omaha defeated Rochester (International League), four games to one, to win Triple-A Alliance Championship.

Regular-Season Attendance—Buffalo, 1,156,661; Denver, 433,880; Indianapolis, 314,264; Iowa, 270,215; Louisville, 616,687; Nashville, 556,250; Oklahoma City, 282,773; Omaha, 341,129. Total, 3,971,859. Playoffs (5 games), 44,930. Alliance Playoffs (5 games), 24,621. AAA All-Star Game at Las Vegas, 10,323.

Managers—Buffalo, Terry Collins; Denver, Dave Machemer; Indianapolis, Tim Johnson; Iowa, Jim Essian; Louisville, Gaylen Pitts; Nashville, Pete Mackanin; Oklahoma City, Steve Smith; Omaha, Sal Rende.

All-Star Team—1B—Orlando Merced, Buffalo; 2B—Jeff Small, Iowa; 3B—Joe Redfield, Denver; SS—Paul Zuvella, Omaha; OF—Bernard Gilkey, Louisville; Juan Gonzalez, Oklahoma City; Ray Lankford, Louisville; C—Tim McIntosh, Denver; DH—Mark Ryal, Buffalo; RHP—Dorn Taylor, Buffalo; LHP—Chris Hammond, Nashville; Most Valuable Player—Juan Gonzalez, Oklahoma City; Most Valuable Pitcher—Chris Hammond, Nashville; Rookie of the Year—Juan Gonzalez, Oklahoma City; Manager of the Year—Sal Rende, Omaha.

(Compiled by Howe Sportsdata International, Boston, Mass.)

CLUB BATTING

Club	Pct.	G.	AB.	R.	OR.	H.	TB.	2B.	3B.	HR.	RBI.	SH.	SF.	HP.	BB.	Int. BB.	SO.	SB.	CS.	LOB.
Iowa	.272	146	4757	642	694	1294	1870	228	21	102	585	65	32	32	467	31	837	151	93	991
Denver	.271	146	4824	724	839	1309	2020	241	58	118	662	61	46	61	490	16	816	109	77	958
Omaha	.268	146	4769	678	555	1279	1872	190	56	97	606	49	58	54	511	24	973	170	77	1007
Nashville	.262	147	4888	628	553	1280	1852	242	33	88	579	67	45	49	448	33	776	130	62	1027
Buffalo	.260	147	4963	621	547	1289	1870	231	46	86	554	54	43	46	435	21	762	127	75	992
Indianapolis	.258	146	4810	573	596	1243	1732	217	34	68	509	50	40	38	403	23	863	140	74	957
Oklahoma City	.252	145	4915	639	747	1238	1886	264	48	96	575	24	41	29	499	9	978	116	61	1006
Louisville	.250	146	4615	564	591	1156	1614	202	47	54	502	61	45	49	519	35	707	123	88	965

INDIVIDUAL BATTING

(Leading Qualifiers for Batting Championship—394 or More Plate Appearances)

*Bats lefthanded.   †Switch-hitter.

Player and Club	Pct.	G.	AB.	R.	H.	TB.	2B.	3B.	HR.	RBI.	SH.	SF.	HP.	BB.	Int. BB.	SO.	SB.	CS.
Ryal, Mark, Buffalo*	.334	109	371	49	124	189	34	2	9	49	4	3	0	17	9	22	3	0
Thurman, Gary, Omaha	.331	98	381	65	126	156	14	8	0	26	6	2	4	31	1	68	39	15
Carter, Steven, Buffalo*	.303	120	426	62	129	196	19	12	8	45	2	0	9	25	3	61	10	10
Morman, Russell, Omaha	.298	121	436	67	130	201	14	9	13	81	0	5	3	51	2	78	21	5
May, Derrick, Iowa*	.296	119	459	55	136	189	27	1	8	69	1	6	0	23	4	50	5	6
Bierley, Brad, Iowa*	.296	133	436	71	129	209	28	2	16	71	7	3	5	66	3	71	9	7
Landrum, Cedric, Iowa*	.296	123	372	71	110	128	10	4	0	24	5	3	1	43	1	63	46	17
Gilkey, Bernard, Louisville	.295	132	499	83	147	198	26	8	3	46	1	1	2	75	3	49	45	33
Bates, William, 25 Den.-73 Nash.†	.293	98	362	51	106	127	15	3	0	34	5	3	0	29	2	28	15	8
Smith, Gregory, Iowa†	.291	105	398	54	116	152	19	1	5	44	4	1	2	37	1	57	26	14

Departmental Leaders: G—Barnes, Brewer, 144; AB—Barnes, 548; R—Redfield, 87; H—Barnes, 156; TB—J. Gonzalez, 252; 2B—Ryal, 34; 3B—Carter, 12; HR—J. Gonzalez, 29; RBI—J. Gonzalez, 101; SH—Olander, 9; SF—de los Santos, 12; HP—Pena, 18; BB—Gilkey, 75; IBB—Lankford, Ryal, 9; SO—R. Martinez, 129; SB—Landrum, 46; CS—Gilkey, 33.

(All Players—Listed Alphabetically)

Player and Club	Pct.	G.	AB.	R.	H.	TB.	2B.	3B.	HR.	RBI.	SH.	SF.	HP.	BB.	Int. BB.	SO.	SB.	CS.
Alba, Gibson, Louisville*	.083	10	12	0	1	1	0	0	0	0	1	0	0	0	0	7	0	0
Alexander, Gerald, Oklahoma City	.000	20	2	0	0	0	0	0	0	0	0	0	0	0	0	1	0	0
Alicea, Luis, Louisville†	.348	25	92	10	32	44	6	3	0	10	0	0	1	5	0	12	0	4
Allanson, Andrew, Oklahoma City	.100	13	40	3	4	4	0	0	0	4	1	0	0	6	0	7	0	0
Allen, Neil, Nashville	.000	12	0	0	0	0	0	0	0	1	0	1	0	0	0	0	0	0
Alou, Moises, 75 Buf.-15 Ind.	.264	90	326	44	86	118	5	6	5	37	2	5	2	33	0	50	13	7
Anderson, Scott, Indianapolis	.172	27	29	3	5	6	1	0	0	1	3	0	0	1	0	13	0	0
Arnold, Scott, Louisville	.000	14	7	0	0	0	0	0	0	0	0	0	0	0	0	4	0	0
Austin, Dominic, Louisville*	.000	8	8	0	0	0	0	0	0	1	0	0	1	0	1	0	0	2
Bafia, Robert, Iowa	.234	72	188	18	44	72	15	2	3	18	0	0	1	5	0	46	0	2
Bair, Douglas, Buffalo	.333	29	3	1	1	2	1	0	0	0	0	0	0	0	0	1	0	0
Banister, Jeffery, Buffalo	.320	12	25	3	8	13	2	0	1	3	0	1	0	3	1	5	0	0
Barnes, William, Nashville	.285	144	548	83	156	202	21	2	7	66	3	6	11	47	2	57	34	11
Bates, William, 25 Den.-73 Nash.†	.293	98	362	51	106	127	15	3	0	34	5	3	0	29	2	28	15	8
Beltre, Esteban, Indianapolis	.226	133	407	33	92	110	11	2	1	37	5	4	2	32	1	77	8	2
Benavides, Alfredo, Indianapolis	.211	77	266	30	56	75	7	3	2	20	4	1	3	12	3	50	3	1
Bennett, Chris, Indianapolis	.000	23	1	0	0	0	0	0	0	0	0	0	0	0	0	0	0	0
Berger, Michael, Oklahoma City	.236	83	267	32	63	105	15	6	5	21	1	2	1	35	0	64	2	1
Berryhill, Damon, Iowa†	.215	22	79	8	17	27	1	0	3	6	0	0	0	4	1	18	0	2
Bierley, Brad, Iowa*	.296	133	436	71	129	209	28	2	16	71	7	3	5	66	3	71	9	7
Bilardello, Dann, Buffalo	.286	52	154	19	44	69	8	1	5	26	2	2	3	7	2	20	0	0
Birkbeck, Michael, Denver	.182	26	11	2	2	5	0	0	1	2	1	0	1	3	0	1	0	0

Player and Club	Pct.	G.	AB.	R.	H.	TB.	2B.	3B.	HR.	RBI.	SH.	SF.	HP.	BB.	Int. BB.	SO.	SB.	CS.
Birtsas, Timothy, Nashville*	.000	8	5	0	0	0	0	0	0	0	0	0	0	0	0	1	0	0
Blankenship, Kevin, Iowa	.100	27	20	0	2	2	0	0	0	0	0	0	0	0	0	10	0	0
Boskie, Shawn, Iowa	.200	9	10	1	2	2	0	0	0	0	0	1	1	0	0	2	0	0
Brantley, Michael, Denver	.264	20	72	14	19	32	3	2	2	10	0	0	0	6	0	3	1	0
Braun, Randall, Indianapolis*	.221	23	68	3	15	22	4	0	1	8	1	0	0	4	0	11	0	0
Brewer, Rodney, Louisville*	.251	144	514	60	129	190	15	5	12	83	0	6	9	54	7	62	0	2
Brown, Keith, Nashville†	.214	39	14	1	3	3	0	0	0	0	0	0	0	1	0	5	0	0
Brumfield, Jacob, Omaha	.325	24	77	10	25	39	6	1	2	11	1	2	0	7	0	14	10	3
Bryant, Phillip, Oklahoma City	.000	14	0	0	0	0	0	0	0	0	1	0	0	0	0	0	0	0
Buechele, Steven, Oklahoma City	.143	6	21	1	3	6	0	0	1	1	0	0	0	2	0	4	0	0
Bullock, Eric, Indianapolis*	.281	107	434	62	122	164	19	7	3	32	0	2	2	32	4	43	40	19
Burdick, Kevin, Buffalo	.282	110	429	61	121	160	24	3	3	41	3	5	2	29	0	38	5	1
Burrell, Kevin, Omaha	.219	65	201	22	44	65	6	0	5	28	0	6	2	9	1	52	3	2
Canale, George, Denver*	.254	134	468	76	119	184	17	6	12	60	3	3	1	69	4	103	12	5
Cangelosi, John, Buffalo†	.348	24	89	17	31	37	2	2	0	7	0	0	1	12	0	8	15	4
Capra, Nick, Oklahoma City	.277	122	451	80	125	172	26	3	5	45	7	1	3	68	0	61	35	15
Carpenter, Cris, Louisville	.040	22	25	1	1	1	0	0	0	0	4	0	0	1	0	11	0	0
Carrillo, Matias, Denver*	.267	21	75	15	20	36	6	2	2	10	0	1	0	2	0	16	0	2
Carter, Steven, Buffalo*	.303	120	426	62	129	196	19	12	8	45	2	0	9	25	3	61	10	10
Casillas, Adam, Nashville*	.320	7	25	3	8	11	3	0	0	1	0	0	8	0	3	0	0	
Castaneda, Nick, Omaha*	.429	5	14	1	6	7	1	0	0	1	0	1	0	1	0	4	0	0
Castro, Jose, Indianapolis	.163	19	49	1	8	12	1	0	1	4	0	0	1	7	0	13	0	1
Chamberlain, Wesley, Nashville	.250	123	416	43	104	150	24	2	6	52	2	5	8	34	0	58	14	20
Chambers, Travis, Indianapolis*	.000	22	1	0	0	0	0	0	0	0	0	0	0	0	0	1	0	0
Clarke, Stanley, Louisville*	.107	32	28	0	3	4	1	0	0	0	3	0	0	0	0	14	0	0
Coffman, Kevin, Iowa	.250	9	12	2	3	5	2	0	0	0	1	0	0	1	0	6	1	0
Colvard, Ben, Nashville	.267	14	30	1	8	9	1	0	0	2	1	0	0	1	0	6	0	0
Cook, Jeffrey, Buffalo†	.220	53	141	19	31	42	4	2	1	13	2	1	0	8	0	23	14	3
Coolbaugh, Scott, Oklahoma City	.225	76	293	39	66	105	17	2	6	30	0	3	1	27	2	62	0	1
Cormier, Rheal, Louisville*	.000	4	3	0	0	0	0	0	0	0	0	0	0	1	0	1	0	0
Costello, John, Indianapolis	.000	22	1	0	0	0	0	0	0	0	0	0	0	0	0	0	0	0
Cox, Danny, Louisville	.000	4	1	0	0	0	0	0	0	0	0	0	0	0	0	1	0	0
Crosby, Todd, Louisville†	.294	97	255	37	75	95	8	0	4	24	3	0	0	37	2	32	3	2
Cucjen, Romulo, Indianapolis	.271	73	240	32	65	90	10	3	3	26	0	5	2	32	1	42	3	1
Damian, Leonard, Iowa	.000	23	4	0	0	0	0	0	0	0	2	0	0	0	0	0	0	0
Davins, James, Indianapolis	.000	41	2	0	0	0	0	0	0	0	1	0	0	0	0	0	0	0
DeFrancesco, Anthony, Nashville	.278	13	36	4	10	12	2	0	0	5	0	0	0	1	0	9	1	0
de los Santos, Luis, Omaha	.280	135	521	55	146	186	23	1	5	74	4	12	1	34	3	82	2	5
Dixon, Edward, Indianapolis	.091	57	11	0	1	1	0	0	0	0	1	0	0	0	0	9	0	0
Dodson, Patrick, Oklahoma City*	.217	23	69	4	15	20	2	0	1	2	0	0	9	0	13	0	0	
Engle, David, Oklahoma City	.241	16	54	6	13	24	6	1	1	7	0	0	6	0	6	0	0	
Escalera, Ruben, Denver*	.152	12	33	3	5	5	0	0	0	2	0	1	0	4	0	3	0	0
Espy, Cecil, Oklahoma City†	.270	34	126	15	34	46	4	1	2	20	1	4	1	15	0	29	7	4
Fariss, Monty, Oklahoma City	.302	62	225	30	68	98	12	3	4	31	0	2	0	34	0	48	1	1
Farmer, Howard, Indianapolis	.208	26	24	0	5	6	1	0	0	1	3	0	1	0	9	0	0	
Figueroa, Bienvenido, Louisville†	.240	128	396	41	95	117	18	2	0	39	7	2	3	24	2	37	5	1
Fireovid, Stephen, Indianapolis†	.148	30	27	2	4	5	1	0	0	3	3	0	0	0	4	0	0	
Fox, Michael, Louisville	.333	5	9	0	3	4	1	0	0	0	0	0	0	2	0	1	0	0
Francona, Terry, Louisville*	.263	86	285	29	75	108	9	3	6	30	0	4	1	12	2	23	1	1
Fulton, Edward, Louisville*	.240	36	100	9	24	39	5	2	2	14	1	3	0	8	1	16	2	0
Gainey, Telmanch, Buffalo*	.412	12	34	3	14	18	1	0	1	3	0	0	1	4	2	7	1	0
Gakeler, Daniel, Indianapolis	.136	22	22	1	3	4	1	0	0	1	1	0	0	0	10	0	0	
Gantner, James, Denver*	.364	6	22	1	8	9	1	0	0	1	0	0	0	2	0	1	1	0
Garber, Jeffrey, Omaha	.000	1	1	0	0	0	0	0	0	0	0	0	0	0	0	0	0	0
Garcia, Carlos, Buffalo	.264	63	197	23	52	77	10	0	5	18	1	2	2	16	2	41	7	4
Garcia, Leonardo, Nashville*	.287	129	435	62	125	192	33	8	6	39	8	4	1	33	5	44	11	4
Garcia, Miguel, Buffalo*	.000	9	2	0	0	0	0	0	0	0	0	0	0	0	0	0	0	0
Garman, Patrick, Oklahoma City	.236	19	55	3	13	19	1	1	1	6	0	0	7	0	22	0	0	
Gilkey, Bernard, Louisville	.295	132	499	83	147	198	26	8	3	46	1	1	2	75	3	49	45	33
Goff, Jerry, Indianapolis*	.287	39	143	23	41	70	10	2	5	26	0	0	24	3	33	3	1	
Gonzalez, Denio, Nashville	.397	52	184	36	73	105	8	0	8	36	3	2	2	37	3	33	3	1
Gonzalez, Juan, Oklahoma City	.258	128	496	78	128	252	29	4	29	101	0	8	1	32	2	109	2	2
Grater, Mark, Louisville	.000	24	1	0	0	0	0	0	0	0	0	0	0	0	0	1	0	0
Green, Gary, Oklahoma City	.234	55	167	19	39	62	11	0	4	25	2	2	0	22	0	43	1	2
Green, Otis, Indianapolis*	.274	76	197	34	54	75	12	3	1	16	5	1	1	18	0	34	5	3
Grissom, Marquis, Indianapolis	.182	5	22	3	4	10	0	0	2	3	0	0	0	0	5	1	0	
Gross, Kip, Nashville	.158	40	19	1	3	3	0	0	0	0	2	0	0	1	0	5	0	0
Guinn, Brian, Iowa†	.270	123	318	50	86	131	15	3	8	50	7	3	2	48	2	55	9	8
Hamelin, Robert, Omaha*	.232	90	271	31	63	102	11	2	8	30	1	2	4	62	5	78	2	2
Hammond, Christopher, Nash.*	.304	24	23	3	7	8	1	0	0	1	0	0	3	0	10	2	0	
Harrison, Phillip, Iowa†	.000	29	4	0	0	0	0	0	0	0	0	0	0	0	0	1	0	0
Hayward, Raymond, Oklahoma City*	.000	19	1	0	0	0	0	0	0	0	0	0	0	0	0	0	0	0
Hearron, Jeffrey, Iowa	.235	78	153	14	36	55	7	0	4	19	2	2	1	9	1	41	0	0
Hecht, Steven, Indianapolis*	.254	58	197	21	50	72	12	2	2	13	2	0	7	1	32	11	5	
Higgins, Mark, Denver	.283	107	361	55	102	173	21	1	16	65	3	5	6	32	3	68	1	5
Hill, Kenneth, Louisville	.133	12	15	2	2	3	1	0	0	1	4	0	0	0	0	3	0	0
Hill, Milton, Nashville	.000	48	4	0	0	0	0	0	0	0	0	0	0	0	0	0	0	0
Hinkle, Michael, Louisville	.179	31	28	4	5	6	1	0	0	3	4	1	0	1	0	4	0	0
Hinzo, Thomas, Omaha†	.243	35	111	16	27	34	5	1	0	9	1	1	2	0	22	6	2	
Hoover, John, 24 Ok City-4 Ind	.000	28	2	0	0	0	0	0	0	0	1	0	0	0	0	0	0	0
House, Bryan, Oklahoma City†	.277	126	513	79	142	184	26	8	0	36	2	2	4	37	0	70	30	13
Houston, Melvin, Indianapolis	.266	106	286	36	76	98	15	2	1	25	5	4	2	22	0	41	10	10
Huismann, Mark, Buffalo	.333	49	3	0	1	1	0	0	0	0	0	0	0	0	2	0	0	
Imes, Rodney, Nashville	.118	29	34	2	4	4	0	0	0	1	2	0	0	0	0	11	2	0
Jackson, Danny, Nashville*	.250	2	4	0	1	1	0	0	0	0	0	0	0	0	2	0	0	
Jefferson, Reginald, Nashville†	.270	37	126	24	34	64	11	2	5	23	0	1	0	14	1	30	1	0
Johnson, Wallace, Indianapolis†	.300	11	40	6	12	16	1	0	1	11	0	1	0	4	0	3	0	0
Jones, Christopher, Nashville	.261	134	436	53	114	173	23	3	10	52	5	1	2	23	3	86	12	8
Kallevig, Gregory, Iowa	.000	19	13	0	0	0	0	0	0	0	0	0	0	0	0	4	0	0
Kemp, Hubert, Buffalo*	.200	26	20	1	4	4	0	0	0	2	1	0	0	2	0	6	0	0
Kiefer, Steven, Buffalo	.233	84	275	30	64	108	18	1	8	33	2	2	5	24	1	76	2	1
Kmak, Joseph, Denver	.232	28	95	12	22	28	3	0	1	10	5	0	3	4	0	16	2	1

342

Player and Club	Pct.	G	AB	R	H	TB	2B	3B	HR	RBI	SH	SF	HP	BB	Int. BB	SO	SB	CS
Kraemer, Joseph, Iowa*	.176	20	17	1	3	3	0	0	0	0	2	0	0	0	0	5	0	2
Kramer, Randall, Buffalo	.200	18	10	0	2	2	0	0	0	1	0	1	0	0	0	4	0	0
Kreuter, Chad, Oklahoma City	.223	92	291	41	65	105	17	1	7	35	2	0	2	52	0	80	0	3
Kunkel, Jeffrey, Oklahoma City	.421	4	19	0	8	9	1	0	0	3	0	0	0	0	0	2	0	0
Lancaster, Lester, Iowa	.000	6	1	0	0	0	0	0	0	0	1	0	0	0	0	1	0	0
Landrum, Cedric, Iowa*	.296	123	372	71	110	128	10	4	0	24	5	3	1	43	1	63	46	17
Lane, Brian, Nashville	.193	48	161	17	31	57	8	0	6	20	1	4	3	18	0	48	3	1
Lankford, Raymond, Louisville*	.260	132	473	61	123	194	25	8	10	72	0	2	5	72	9	81	30	7
Leary, Robert, Indianapolis	.500	2	2	1	1	2	1	0	0	0	0	0	0	0	0	0	0	0
Lee, Terry, Nashville	.304	72	260	38	79	144	18	1	15	67	1	7	4	31	1	47	3	1
Little, Scott, Buffalo	.226	36	106	17	24	32	1	2	1	10	2	1	2	14	2	19	8	1
Lockhart, Keith, Nashville*	.260	126	431	48	112	172	25	4	9	63	1	4	5	51	3	74	8	7
Loggins, Michael, Omaha†	.250	73	208	25	52	76	10	4	2	31	7	5	0	20	1	39	10	8
Lombardozzi, Chris, Nashville*	.067	8	15	0	1	3	0	1	0	1	0	0	1	3	0	3	0	0
Lopez, Robert, Nashville*	.240	29	25	3	6	6	0	0	0	0	4	0	0	1	0	4	0	0
Lowry, Dwight, Indianapolis*	.310	73	187	23	58	72	6	1	2	25	0	4	0	19	0	34	0	3
Loy, Darren, Oklahoma City	.222	3	9	0	2	3	1	0	0	2	0	0	1	1	0	2	0	0
Mack, Quinn, Indianapolis*	.276	121	392	55	108	158	25	2	7	53	2	1	5	25	5	46	11	6
Maclin, Lonnie, Louisville*	.310	17	58	9	18	25	3	2	0	6	1	1	1	7	0	11	1	4
Mahler, Richard, Nashville	.000	1	2	0	0	0	0	0	0	0	0	0	0	0	0	2	0	0
Malloy, Robert, Nashville	.000	23	3	0	0	0	0	0	0	0	0	0	0	0	0	1	0	0
Marchok, Chris, Indianapolis*	.000	23	3	0	0	0	0	0	0	0	0	0	0	0	0	1	0	0
Marquez, Edwin, Indianapolis	.163	20	49	3	8	10	2	0	0	0	2	0	0	6	0	17	0	0
Martinez, Julian, Louisville	.213	94	267	34	57	80	17	0	2	23	2	3	2	38	1	51	1	5
Martinez, Reynaldo, Omaha*	.264	122	364	59	96	187	12	8	21	67	0	3	3	54	5	129	6	6
Mason, Roger, Buffalo	.111	29	9	0	1	1	0	0	0	0	0	0	0	0	0	4	0	0
Masters, David, Iowa	.000	9	3	0	0	0	0	0	0	0	0	0	0	0	0	2	0	0
Mathews, Gregory, Louisville	.250	4	4	0	1	1	0	0	0	2	0	0	0	0	0	2	0	0
Mattox, Frank, Denver†	.262	81	282	44	74	101	13	4	2	24	4	0	3	26	0	41	21	7
May, Derrick, Iowa*	.296	119	459	55	136	189	27	1	8	69	1	6	0	23	4	50	5	6
McClendon, Lloyd, Iowa	.286	25	91	14	26	34	2	0	2	10	0	1	2	8	1	19	3	1
McGriff, Terence, Nashville	.280	94	325	44	91	135	17	0	9	54	2	6	2	38	1	46	2	2
McIntosh, Timothy, Denver	.288	116	416	72	120	201	21	3	18	74	3	7	14	26	0	59	6	2
Meacham, Robert, Omaha	.225	114	329	50	74	106	13	5	3	35	8	5	10	49	0	84	9	4
Medvin, Scott, Buffalo	.000	13	3	0	0	0	0	0	0	0	1	0	0	0	0	1	0	0
Mendez, Jesus, Louisville*	.190	47	79	5	15	16	1	0	0	6	0	2	0	9	2	8	0	0
Merced, Orlando, Buffalo†	.262	101	378	52	99	150	12	6	9	55	1	1	0	46	3	63	14	5
Millay, Garrick, Oklahoma City	.257	104	327	39	84	113	16	2	3	42	1	5	8	38	0	53	4	4
Minutelli, Gino, Nashville*	.056	12	18	1	1	1	0	0	0	0	1	0	1	0	0	5	0	0
Mitchell, Charles, Nashville	.125	40	8	2	1	1	0	0	0	0	1	0	0	2	0	2	0	0
Mitchell, Joseph, Denver	.251	71	247	27	62	95	17	2	4	34	3	2	1	20	0	55	1	3
Monico, Mario, Denver*	.263	100	319	41	84	120	18	6	2	38	5	2	4	45	3	36	5	5
Moore, Robert, Nashville	.000	13	1	0	0	0	0	0	0	0	0	0	0	0	0	1	0	0
Moore, William, Denver	.288	120	416	74	120	212	30	4	18	68	2	3	5	56	0	77	6	4
Moreno, Armando, Buffalo	.273	92	286	39	78	130	20	1	10	30	5	3	1	47	0	43	2	4
Morman, Russell, Omaha	.298	121	436	67	130	201	14	9	13	81	0	5	3	51	2	78	21	5
Morris, Harold, Nashville*	.344	16	64	8	22	30	5	0	1	10	0	1	2	5	1	10	4	1
Motley, Darryl, 33 Nash.-67 O. C.	.266	100	350	42	93	124	18	2	3	38	3	1	2	31	0	67	8	2
Nabholz, Chris, Indianapolis*	.000	10	12	0	0	0	0	0	0	0	4	0	0	0	0	4	0	0
Nelson, Jerome, Nashville†	.220	51	132	19	29	39	3	2	1	8	5	0	0	9	0	17	6	4
Nichols, Scott, Louisville	.143	27	63	5	9	10	1	0	0	2	5	0	1	6	0	13	1	1
Noce, Paul, Nashville	.218	100	293	46	64	84	10	2	2	18	6	0	9	28	1	63	18	5
Nunez, Jose, Iowa	.071	17	14	0	1	1	0	0	0	0	2	0	0	0	0	5	0	0
Nunez, Mauricio, Louisville	.248	106	214	24	53	64	9	1	0	26	3	5	0	15	2	21	4	4
Olander, James, Denver	.288	74	233	33	67	96	12	4	3	36	9	6	4	20	1	47	2	6
Olivares, Omar, Louisville	.214	26	28	4	6	9	1	1	0	3	3	0	0	1	0	9	0	0
Osteen, David, Louisville	.118	13	17	0	2	3	1	0	0	1	2	0	0	0	0	3	0	0
Palacios, Rey, Omaha	.133	4	15	2	2	4	0	1	0	0	0	0	0	0	0	6	0	0
Palacios, Vicente, Buffalo	.194	28	36	2	7	7	0	0	0	6	4	0	0	0	0	7	0	0
Palmer, Dean, Oklahoma City	.218	88	316	33	69	130	17	4	12	39	0	3	4	20	0	106	1	1
Pappas, Erik, Iowa	.249	131	405	56	101	172	19	2	16	55	6	3	8	65	1	84	6	6
Paredes, John, Indianapolis	.261	94	322	46	84	102	7	1	3	17	6	2	6	42	1	38	20	6
Parker, Steve, 44 Iowa-6 Lou.*	.000	50	2	0	0	0	0	0	0	0	0	0	0	1	0	1	0	0
Pavlas, David, Iowa	.000	53	4	1	0	0	0	0	0	0	3	0	0	0	0	4	0	0
Pearson, Kevin, Nashville	.236	38	110	8	26	36	4	0	2	15	3	2	1	7	0	11	3	1
Pecota, William, Omaha	.302	29	116	30	35	53	6	0	4	13	0	1	3	17	1	17	11	1
Pena, Geronimo, Louisville†	.249	118	390	65	97	151	24	6	6	35	3	4	18	69	0	116	24	13
Pino, Rolando, Denver	.200	6	5	3	1	2	1	0	0	0	0	0	0	2	0	0	0	0
Polidor, Gustavo, Denver	.303	46	165	17	50	61	8	0	1	16	5	0	2	4	0	19	3	3
Prince, Thomas, Buffalo	.225	94	284	38	64	98	13	0	7	37	3	3	5	39	0	46	4	7
Pulliam, Harvey, Omaha	.268	123	436	72	117	193	18	5	16	72	2	4	3	49	0	82	9	3
Redfield, Joseph, Denver	.274	137	525	87	144	238	23	10	17	71	5	5	10	57	0	76	34	18
Reece, Thad, Omaha*	.232	64	190	25	44	56	3	3	1	14	3	1	3	14	0	16	6	6
Reed, Richard, Buffalo	.063	16	16	2	1	3	0	1	0	0	2	0	0	0	0	5	0	0
Reimer, Kevin, Oklahoma City*	.283	51	198	24	56	90	18	2	4	33	0	1	0	18	3	25	2	0
Renfroe, Cohen, Iowa†	.300	44	10	0	3	3	0	0	0	2	2	0	0	0	0	3	0	0
Reuss, Jerry, Buffalo*	.000	14	10	0	0	0	0	0	0	0	1	0	0	0	0	6	0	0
Reyes, Gilberto, Indianapolis	.233	89	309	22	72	115	14	1	9	45	0	6	2	24	2	79	2	3
Richardson, Jeffrey, Buffalo	.207	66	164	15	34	41	4	0	1	15	3	0	2	14	0	21	1	2
Rijo, Jose, Nashville	.000	1	3	0	0	0	0	0	0	0	0	0	0	0	0	0	0	0
Ritter, Reggie, Iowa*	.250	3	4	0	1	1	0	0	0	0	0	0	0	0	0	1	0	0
Rivera, German, Indianapolis	.287	125	446	67	128	193	25	5	10	59	0	4	6	41	2	75	1	1
Roesler, Michael, Buffalo	.000	24	1	0	0	0	0	0	0	0	0	0	0	0	0	0	0	0
Rojas, Melquiades, Indianapolis	.214	17	14	0	3	3	0	0	0	1	1	0	0	0	0	5	0	0
Roomes, Rolando, Indianapolis	.232	53	198	22	46	74	5	1	7	31	0	3	9	0	61	11	4	
Ross, Mark, Buffalo	.000	47	2	0	0	0	0	0	0	0	0	0	0	0	0	1	0	0
Rossy, Elam, Buffalo	.176	8	17	3	3	5	0	1	0	2	1	0	4	0	2	1	0	
Royer, Stanley, Louisville	.267	4	15	1	4	7	1	1	0	4	0	0	2	0	5	0	0	
Russell, John, Oklahoma City	.409	6	22	7	9	19	4	0	2	6	0	0	0	2	0	3	0	0
Ryal, Mark, Buffalo*	.334	109	371	49	124	189	34	2	9	49	4	3	0	17	9	22	3	0
Salazar, Argenis, Indianapolis	.208	15	53	2	11	14	3	0	0	0	0	0	0	4	0	7	0	0
Samuels, Roger, Buffalo*	.000	5	1	0	0	0	0	0	0	0	0	0	0	0	0	1	0	0

Player and Club	Pct.	G.	AB.	R.	H.	TB.	2B.	3B.	HR.	RBI.	SH.	SF.	HP.	BB.	Int. BB.	SO.	SB.	CS.
Santovenia, Nelson, Indianapolis	.318	11	44	3	14	19	2	0	1	10	0	1	1	0	7	0	0
Sauveur, Richard, Indianapolis*	.308	14	13	0	4	5	1	0	0	0	2	0	0	0	1	0	0
Schulz, Jeffrey, Omaha*	.299	69	231	35	69	99	16	1	4	27	1	3	1	16	4	46	2	0
Scott, Donald, Nashville†	.226	78	243	18	55	73	12	3	0	21	5	2	0	24	3	30	0	7
Scudder, Scott, Nashville	.300	11	10	1	3	4	1	0	0	2	0	0	0	0	0	2	0	0
Sebra, Robert, 23 Nash.-21 Den.	.000	44	1	0	0	0	0	0	0	0	0	0	0	0	0	0	0	0
Sheaffer, Danny, Buffalo	.243	55	144	23	35	48	7	0	2	19	1	1	1	11	1	14	4	1
Sheridan, Patrick, Iowa*	.329	23	70	16	23	38	3	0	4	10	0	0	0	11	1	18	2	2
Shields, Thomas, Buffalo	.247	123	380	42	94	126	20	3	2	30	6	3	2	21	1	72	12	7
Shines, Raymond, Buffalo†	.170	42	112	8	19	28	1	1	2	15	0	2	0	22	3	19	0	0
Shumpert, Terrance, Omaha	.255	39	153	24	39	59	6	4	2	12	4	1	3	14	0	28	18	0
Silver, Roy, Louisville†	.248	88	226	30	56	83	11	2	4	21	0	3	1	23	1	17	1	5
Slocumb, Heath, Iowa	.000	20	1	0	0	0	0	0	0	0	0	0	0	0	0	1	0	0
Small, Jeffrey, Iowa	.287	125	457	50	131	175	26	3	4	47	8	4	1	13	2	61	5	5
Smith, David, Denver	.275	94	295	35	81	114	6	6	5	38	6	4	1	24	0	34	3	6
Smith, Gregory, Iowa†	.291	105	398	54	116	152	19	1	5	44	4	1	2	37	1	57	26	14
Spehr, Timothy, Omaha	.225	102	307	42	69	101	10	2	6	34	6	2	10	41	0	88	5	5
Spiers, William, Denver*	.316	11	38	6	12	15	0	0	1	7	0	1	0	10	0	8	1	1
St. Laurent, James, Indianapolis*	.241	10	29	3	7	7	0	0	0	4	1	1	0	2	0	6	0	0
Steels, James, 71 Ind.-1 Buf.*	.266	72	248	37	66	97	15	2	4	22	2	2	4	26	2	41	10	5
Stephens, Carl Ray, Louisville	.221	98	294	20	65	84	8	1	3	27	9	1	4	27	3	74	0	1
Strange, Douglas, Iowa†	.305	82	269	31	82	116	17	1	5	35	3	1	1	28	2	42	6	3
Sullivan, Glenn, Iowa*	.103	28	68	5	7	10	3	0	0	8	2	0	1	4	0	10	2	0
Sutcliffe, Richard, Iowa*	.500	2	2	1	1	1	0	0	0	0	0	0	0	1	0	1	0	0
Sveum, Dale, Denver†	.289	57	218	25	63	90	17	2	2	26	2	0	0	20	3	49	1	2
Szekely, Joseph, Buffalo*	.000	2	4	1	0	0	0	0	0	0	0	0	0	1	0	0	0	0
Tanner, Bruce, Nashville*	.261	93	222	24	58	82	12	0	4	22	3	3	2	19	4	12	0	2
Tatis, Bernardo, Oklahoma City†	.189	55	175	23	33	50	4	2	3	17	2	3	0	18	1	36	11	5
Taylor, Donald, Buffalo	.125	31	40	2	5	5	0	0	0	5	1	1	0	1	0	6	0	0
Tewksbury, Robert, Louisville	.000	6	3	0	0	0	0	0	0	0	0	0	0	0	0	1	0	0
Thurman, Gary, Omaha	.331	98	381	65	126	156	14	8	0	26	6	2	4	31	1	68	39	15
Tibbs, Jay, Buffalo	.000	2	1	0	0	0	0	0	0	0	0	0	0	0	0	0	0	0
Tomlin, Randy, Buffalo*	.000	3	1	0	0	0	0	0	0	0	0	0	0	0	0	0	0	0
Torricelli, Timothy, Denver	.212	17	33	6	7	11	1	0	1	5	0	1	0	3	0	5	0	0
Trout, Steven, Louisville*	.500	4	2	0	1	1	0	0	0	0	0	0	0	1	0	0	0	0
Vanderwal, John, Indianapolis*	.296	51	135	16	40	52	6	0	2	14	0	0	0	13	0	28	0	1
Varsho, Gary, Iowa*	.301	63	229	35	69	99	9	0	7	33	0	2	3	25	2	35	18	7
Vasquez, Luis, Nashville	.118	21	17	3	2	3	1	0	0	0	0	0	0	0	0	4	0	0
Vierra, Joseph, Nashville*	.000	49	4	0	0	0	0	0	0	0	0	0	0	0	0	1	0	0
Villanueva, Hector, Iowa	.266	52	177	20	47	80	7	1	8	34	1	0	1	19	2	36	0	1
Walker, Cleotha, Iowa†	.360	32	114	30	41	68	7	1	6	19	1	0	1	25	5	17	9	3
Walters, Darryel, Denver	.244	100	287	45	70	124	16	4	10	45	0	3	4	36	2	77	5	4
Walton, Jerome, Iowa	.188	4	16	3	3	6	0	0	1	1	0	0	0	2	0	4	0	0
Washington, Ronald, Oklahoma City	.238	101	357	37	85	115	15	6	1	23	1	1	0	5	0	60	7	4
Wilkins, Dean, Iowa	.000	52	1	0	0	0	0	0	0	0	1	0	0	0	0	0	0	0
Williams, Reginald, Oklahoma City	.274	50	164	16	45	61	7	0	3	19	1	3	1	22	1	23	7	3
Wilson, Craig, Louisville	.279	57	204	30	57	76	9	2	2	23	5	6	1	28	0	15	5	3
Wilson, James, Indianapolis	.255	28	94	7	24	35	5	0	2	11	0	1	0	5	0	26	0	0
Wrona, Richard, Iowa	.226	58	146	16	33	43	4	0	2	15	3	0	1	10	1	35	0	2
Wrona, William, Iowa	.216	74	190	19	41	48	7	0	0	13	3	3	0	18	1	28	4	4
Xavier, Joseph, Denver*	.224	38	107	12	24	31	5	1	0	6	3	0	1	11	0	15	1	1
Yacopino, Edward, Buffalo†	.250	27	72	7	18	19	1	0	0	4	1	0	0	2	0	13	1	1
York, Michael, Buffalo	.103	29	29	1	3	4	1	0	0	2	1	1	0	0	0	7	0	0
Zuvella, Paul, Omaha	.283	111	407	47	115	148	16	1	5	41	6	2	3	38	1	39	11	10

The following pitchers, listed alphabetically by club, with games in parentheses, had no plate appearances, primarily through use of designated hitters:

BUFFALO—Belinda, Stanley (15); Dillard, Gordon (10); Hancock, Leland (1); Kipper, Robert (5); Minor, Blas (1); Neely, Jeffrey (6).

DENVER—August, Donald (22); Capel, Michael (41); Davis, John (6); Easley, Logan (46); Edens, Thomas (19); Filer, Thomas (9); Fossas, Anthony (25); George, Christopher (7); Gordon, Donald (5); Henry, Douglas (27); Horton, Ricky (5); Hunter, James (20); Lee, Mark (20); May, Scott (7); McGrath, Charles (12); Navarro, Jaime (6); Peterek, Jeffrey (9); Powell, Dennis (11); Puig, Edward (19); Robertson, Douglas (22); Sadler, Alan (12); Sebra, Robert (21); Thomas, Roy (7); Veres, Randolf (16); Watkins, Timothy (19); Wegman, William (3).

INDIANAPOLIS—Clay, Danny (19); Frey, Steven (2); Galvez, Balvino (3); Mohorcic, Dale (13); Olker, Joseph (1); Perez, Yorkis (9); Straker, Lester (3); Thompson, Richard (15).

IOWA—Bowden, Mark (11); Clay, Danny (6); Clear, Mark (2); Pico, Jeffrey (1); Rosario, David (21); Wilmet, Paul (25); Zarranz, Fernando (5).

LOUISVILLE—Camacho, Ernie (15); Heinkel, Donald (1); Hilton, Howard (56); Kisten, Dale (9); Niedenfuer, Thomas (5); Oyster, Jeffrey (2); Parker, Stephen (6); Perez, Michael (57); Potestio, Frank (2); Richardson, David (5); Sherrill, Timothy (52); Stone, Brian (3).

NASHVILLE—Lazor, Joseph (11); Powell, Ross (3); Rodriguez, Rosario (5).

OKLAHOMA CITY—Arnsberg, Bradley (14); Barfield, John (19); Bohanon, Brian (14); Bronkey, Jeffery (28); Castillo, Felipe (20); Cecena, Jose (9); Daniel, Clayton (5); Guzman, Jose (7); Hardy, John (54); Hoover, John (24); Lankard, Steven (12); Lynch, David (14); Mathews, Terry (12); McMurtry, Craig (6); Mielke, Gary (5); Miller, David (31); Petkovsek, Mark (28); Rosenthal, Wayne (42); Satzinger, Jeffrey (23); St. Claire, Randy (29).

OMAHA—Appier, Kevin (3); Baller, Jay (52); Campbell, James (4); Chadwick, Ray (42); Clark, Dera (17); Codiroli, Christopher (4); Crawford, Steven (4); Dozier, Thomas (4); Encarnacion, Luis (44); Everson, Gregory (33); Ferreira, Anthony (33); Filson, Peter (17); Johnston, Joel (2); LeMasters, James (30); Magnante, Michael (13); McGaffigan, Andrew (10); Moeller, Dennis (11); Smith, Daryl (11); Stottlemyre, Melvin (29); Tresemer, Michael (11); Walker, Hugh (1); Walter, Gene (20); Wilkinson, William (7).

GRAND SLAM HOME RUNS—Morman, Reyes, 2 each; Brewer, Canale, J. Gonzalez, Hearron, Jones, Lankford, Loggins, Merced, Pappas, Pulliam, Roomes, 1 each.

AWARDED FIRST BASE ON CATCHER'S INTERFERENCE—Steels 2 (Agostinelli, Graves); Barnes (Agostinelli); D. Smith (Berryhill).

CLUB FIELDING

Club	Pct.	G.	PO.	A.	E.	DP.	PB.	Club	Pct.	G.	PO.	A.	E.	DP.	PB.
Omaha	.979	146	3802	1523	113	149	9	Louisville	.972	146	3767	1488	150	139	16
Nashville	.975	147	3874	1639	142	150	17	Indianapolis	.969	146	3786	1562	170	114	28
Denver	.973	146	3786	1605	150	143	22	Oklahoma City	.966	145	3825	1594	191	139	13
Iowa	.972	146	3716	1590	151	151	17	Buffalo	.965	147	3966	1644	202	144	15

Triple Plays—Iowa, Oklahoma City.

INDIVIDUAL FIELDING

*Throws lefthanded.

FIRST BASEMEN

Player and Club	Pct.	G.	PO.	A.	E.	DP.
Bafia, Iowa	.977	25	124	3	3	20
Banister, Buffalo	.909	4	20	0	2	1
Barnes, Nashville	1.000	9	41	1	0	3
Berger, Oklahoma City	.984	33	286	24	5	31
Bierley, Iowa	.976	4	39	2	1	3
Bilardello, Buffalo	1.000	2	5	0	0	0
Braun, Indianapolis	.989	20	160	16	2	15
Brewer, Louisville*	.990	143	1153	126	13	118
Burrell, Omaha	1.000	2	9	1	0	0
CANALE, Denver	.991	118	1073	63	10	107
Casillas, Nashville*	1.000	5	61	2	0	4
Castaneda, Omaha	1.000	2	15	0	0	1
Coolbaugh, Oklahoma City	1.000	4	27	3	0	2
de los Santos, Omaha	1.000	29	187	16	0	26
Dodson, Oklahoma City*	.986	23	188	18	3	13
Engle, Oklahoma City	.982	11	99	8	2	13
Fariss, Oklahoma City	.964	3	27	0	1	1
Figueroa, Louisville	1.000	1	3	0	0	0
Francona, Louisville*	.973	6	33	3	1	1
Garman, Oklahoma City	.993	16	131	16	1	9
Goff, Indianapolis	1.000	1	13	1	0	0
Gonzalez, Nashville	.947	3	17	1	1	2
Green, Indianapolis*	.966	14	109	5	4	11
Guinn, Iowa	.991	40	307	27	3	30
Hamelin, Omaha*	.991	48	396	32	4	29
Hearron, Iowa	1.000	10	37	2	0	5
Higgins, Denver	.983	12	109	6	2	9
Jefferson, Nashville*	.988	35	314	20	4	30
Johnson, Indianapolis	.986	9	65	7	1	7
Kiefer, Buffalo	.984	17	114	13	2	8
Lee, Nashville	.992	68	592	47	5	62
Little, Buffalo	1.000	4	16	0	0	1
Lowry, Indianapolis	1.000	4	17	3	0	1
Marquez, Indianapolis	1.000	1	5	0	0	0
May, Iowa	1.000	1	10	1	0	1
McClendon, Iowa	.992	20	117	9	1	12
Mendez, Louisville*	1.000	8	28	2	0	1
Merced, Buffalo	.981	81	667	57	14	61
Millay, Oklahoma City	.966	22	158	12	6	14
Mitchell, Denver	.992	14	117	7	1	5
Morman, Omaha	.994	82	634	55	4	67
Noce, Nashville	1.000	10	45	4	0	4
Palmer, Oklahoma City	.978	22	165	15	4	21
Pappas, Iowa	.995	31	179	16	1	18
Prince, Buffalo	1.000	1	2	0	0	1
Redfield, Denver	.941	3	14	2	1	1
Reimer, Oklahoma City	.989	19	163	10	2	11
Richardson, Buffalo	1.000	1	0	1	0	0
Rivera, Indianapolis	.981	90	676	57	14	56
Ryal, Buffalo*	.989	42	323	34	4	33
Schulz, Omaha	1.000	1	7	0	0	0
Scott, Nashville	1.000	7	50	9	0	4
Sheaffer, Buffalo	.967	5	29	0	1	3
Shines, Buffalo	.994	22	156	11	1	15
Small, Iowa	1.000	1	1	0	0	0
Steels, Indianapolis*	1.000	9	52	2	0	3
Sullivan, Iowa*	.983	19	107	8	2	13
Sveum, Denver	1.000	10	79	4	0	6
Tanner, Nashville	.992	28	232	16	2	14
Varsho, Iowa	.992	19	113	9	1	13
Villanueva, Iowa	1.000	20	133	7	0	15
Washington, Oklahoma City	.981	10	46	5	1	3
Wilson, Indianapolis	.985	22	172	20	3	14
Wrona, Iowa	1.000	8	38	4	0	3

Triple Play—Millay.

SECOND BASEMEN

Player and Club	Pct.	G.	PO.	A.	E.	DP.
Bafia, Iowa	1.000	2	6	5	0	1
Bates, 23 Den.-65 Nash.	.983	88	167	240	7	53
Burdick, Buffalo	.967	104	213	283	17	63
Coolbaugh, Oklahoma City	1.000	3	3	7	0	1
Crosby, Louisville	.980	51	74	125	4	30
Cucjen, Indianapolis	1.000	12	24	37	0	5
Fariss, Oklahoma City	.939	8	22	24	3	3
Gantner, Denver	1.000	4	5	13	0	4
Guinn, Iowa	.960	20	44	52	4	12
Hecht, Indianapolis	.964	24	51	55	4	11
Hinzo, Omaha	.978	21	45	42	2	12
House, Oklahoma City	.971	118	244	353	18	76
Houston, Indianapolis	.974	32	68	81	4	20
Lockhart, Nashville	.989	55	101	168	3	26
Lombardozzi, Nashville	.875	3	2	5	1	1
Mattox, Denver	.970	76	104	216	10	39
Meacham, Omaha	.969	65	121	156	9	43
Moreno, Buffalo	.957	41	67	109	8	22
Noce, Nashville	.975	12	14	25	1	5
Pappas, Iowa	1.000	2	3	3	0	0
Paredes, Indianapolis	.973	92	179	248	12	37
Pearson, Nashville	.974	17	35	40	2	10
Pecota, Omaha	1.000	11	15	24	0	2
Pena, Louisville	.975	64	112	164	7	30
Pino, Denver	1.000	3	0	2	0	0
Polidor, Denver	1.000	15	37	45	0	13
Redfield, Denver	.976	10	15	26	1	8
Reece, Omaha	.981	23	38	65	2	14
Richardson, Buffalo	.958	13	19	27	2	5
Shields, Buffalo	1.000	1	3	1	0	1
Shumpert, Omaha	.960	39	72	95	7	17
SMALL, Iowa	.977	117	245	317	13	87
Smith, Denver	.500	2	1	0	1	0
Strange, Iowa	.933	4	2	12	1	4
Sveum, Denver	.895	3	8	9	2	2
Tanner, Nashville	1.000	10	15	22	0	8
Tatis, Oklahoma City	1.000	3	4	6	0	1
Torricelli, Denver	1.000	4	1	3	0	2
Washington, Oklahoma City	.963	19	43	62	4	16
Wilson, Louisville	.971	36	66	101	5	29
Wrona, Iowa	1.000	14	20	37	0	7
Xavier, Denver	.984	25	44	76	2	10

Triple Plays—Fariss, Small.

THIRD BASEMEN

Player and Club	Pct.	G.	PO.	A.	E.	DP.
Alicea, Louisville	.898	22	14	39	6	2
Bafia, Iowa	.937	37	23	36	4	5
Barnes, Nashville	1.000	3	2	5	0	1
Bierley, Iowa	.839	12	8	18	5	0
Buechele, Oklahoma City	1.000	6	4	15	0	1
Capra, Oklahoma City	1.000	2	1	1	0	0
Castro, Indianapolis	.943	15	7	26	2	1
Coolbaugh, Oklahoma City	.933	66	61	134	14	11
Crosby, Louisville	.600	9	3	3	4	2
Cucjen, Indianapolis	.909	51	34	86	12	11
de los Santos, Omaha	.929	91	55	155	16	14
Fariss, Oklahoma City	.750	3	2	7	3	1
Gantner, Denver	1.000	2	2	1	0	0
Garber, Omaha	1.000	1	1	0	0	0
Goff, Indianapolis	.864	10	8	11	3	1
Gonzalez, Nashville	.960	47	44	99	6	13
Guinn, Iowa	.896	26	9	34	5	4
Hearron, Iowa	1.000	2	4	4	0	0
Hecht, Indianapolis	.917	17	5	17	2	2
Higgins, Denver	.850	9	5	12	3	1
Hinzo, Omaha	.857	3	1	5	1	0
Houston, Indianapolis	.936	32	15	29	3	3
Kiefer, Buffalo	.943	60	40	126	10	11
Kunkel, Oklahoma City	1.000	1	1	0	0	0
Lane, Nashville	.960	46	36	83	5	9
Little, Buffalo	1.000	2	0	3	0	0
Lockhart, Nashville	.947	38	29	78	6	9
Lombardozzi, Nashville	1.000	5	0	12	0	2
Martinez, Louisville	.929	42	34	58	7	10
McClendon, Iowa	.857	3	3	3	1	0
Meacham, Omaha	1.000	9	6	16	0	4
Merced, Buffalo	.870	18	14	26	6	3
Mitchell, Denver	.846	12	10	12	4	1
Moreno, Buffalo	.863	17	12	32	7	1
Morman, Omaha	1.000	3	1	2	0	0
Nichols, Louisville	1.000	2	1	3	0	0
Noce, Nashville	1.000	3	1	2	0	0
Palacios, Omaha	.833	2	1	4	1	0
Palmer, Oklahoma City	.889	57	41	95	17	3
Pearson, Nashville	1.000	2	3	0	0	0
Pecota, Omaha	.976	17	8	32	1	2
Pena, Louisville	.873	56	41	97	20	12
Polidor, Denver	1.000	5	3	9	0	1
Redfield, Denver	.954	94	83	165	12	14
Reece, Omaha	.971	42	35	65	3	9
Richardson, Buffalo	1.000	2	2	2	0	1
Rivera, Indianapolis	.934	41	37	76	8	9
Royer, Louisville	1.000	4	0	7	0	0
Salazar, Indianapolis	.925	14	11	26	3	2
Shields, Buffalo	.918	71	41	116	14	15
Small, Iowa	1.000	1	0	2	0	1
Smith, Iowa	.933	7	5	9	1	2
Strange, Iowa	.925	79	54	132	15	16
Sveum, Denver	.927	31	24	65	7	6
Tanner, Nashville	.878	17	9	27	5	2
Tatis, Oklahoma City	.000	1	0	0	1	0

THIRD BASEMEN—Continued

Player and Club	Pct.	G.	PO.	A.	E.	DP.
Torricelli, Denver	1.000	4	1	2	0	0
Varsho, Iowa	.750	2	1	2	1	0
Washington, Oklahoma City	.861	13	8	23	5	2
Wilson, Louisville	.877	22	12	38	7	3
Wrona, Iowa	.667	6	0	2	1	0
Xavier, Denver	1.000	1	0	1	0	0

NOTE: No player qualified as fielding leader.

Triple Play—Strange.

SHORTSTOPS

Player and Club	Pct.	G.	PO.	A.	E.	DP.
Beltre, Indianapolis	.948	130	215	335	30	57
Benavides, Nashville	.954	76	134	200	16	38
Crosby, Louisville	1.000	1	1	0	0	0
Cucjen, Indianapolis	.981	17	28	25	1	5
Espy, Oklahoma City	1.000	1	4	3	0	1
Fariss, Oklahoma City	.932	45	87	120	15	32
FIGUEROA, Louisville	.977	123	222	330	13	75
Garcia, Buffalo	.936	61	106	170	19	37
Green, Oklahoma City	.961	53	101	145	10	36
Guinn, Iowa	1.000	7	2	7	0	1
Hecht, Indianapolis	1.000	1	1	3	0	0
Hinzo, Omaha	1.000	1	4	1	0	0
Houston, Indianapolis	.979	14	16	31	1	6
Kunkel, Oklahoma City	1.000	3	6	11	0	4
Martinez, Louisville	.947	40	39	87	7	17
Mattox, Denver	1.000	1	1	3	0	1
Meacham, Omaha	.964	38	62	71	5	14
Moreno, Buffalo	.667	2	2	4	3	1
Noce, Nashville	.929	58	68	167	18	32
Pearson, Nashville	.949	11	21	35	3	9
Pecota, Omaha	1.000	8	9	24	0	6
Pino, Denver	.833	2	2	3	1	2
Polidor, Denver	.944	26	43	58	6	17
Redfield, Denver	1.000	4	7	12	0	2
Richardson, Buffalo	.951	45	82	112	10	22
Rossy, Buffalo	.935	7	9	20	2	6
Salazar, Indianapolis	1.000	4	6	6	0	1
Shields, Buffalo	.938	45	83	143	15	32
Small, Iowa	.850	4	9	8	3	1
D. Smith, Denver	.983	89	149	264	7	55
G. Smith, Iowa	.963	96	150	294	17	65
Spiers, Denver	.957	11	22	23	2	6
Strange, Iowa	1.000	2	2	5	0	1
Sveum, Denver	.940	14	23	24	3	7
Tanner, Nashville	.889	7	13	11	3	3
Washington, Oklahoma City	.967	50	77	127	7	28
Wrona, Iowa	.942	50	92	134	14	35
Xavier, Denver	.947	11	15	21	2	6
Zuvella, Omaha	.971	107	184	314	15	78

OUTFIELDERS

Player and Club	Pct.	G.	PO.	A.	E.	DP.
Alou, 73 Buf.-14 Ind.	.963	87	196	12	8	7
Austin, Louisville	.750	3	3	0	1	0
Barnes, Nashville	.981	131	238	24	5	4
Bates, Denver	1.000	1	3	0	0	0
Berger, Oklahoma City	.889	6	7	1	1	0
BIERLEY, Iowa	.984	113	179	11	3	3
Brantley, Denver	1.000	20	37	1	0	0
Brumfield, Omaha	1.000	20	45	3	0	0
Bullock, Indianapolis*	.974	104	185	5	5	0
Cangelosi, Buffalo*	.980	22	49	0	1	0
Capra, Oklahoma City	.980	115	227	15	5	1
Carrillo, Denver*	.980	21	47	1	1	0
Carter, Buffalo	.983	114	222	9	4	1
Casillas, Nashville*	1.000	3	1	0	0	0
Chamberlain, Buffalo	.961	112	203	16	9	1
Colvard, Nashville	1.000	9	13	1	0	0
Cook, Buffalo	.964	46	76	5	3	1
Coolbaugh, Oklahoma City	.000	1	0	0	1	0
Escalera, Denver*	.963	12	24	2	1	1
Espy, Oklahoma City	.933	33	65	5	5	1
Francona, Louisville*	.990	63	93	3	1	0
Gainey, Buffalo	.905	8	19	0	2	0
Garcia, Nashville*	.968	119	235	10	8	5
Gilkey, Louisville	.958	132	236	18	11	4
Gonzalez, Oklahoma City	.966	107	220	7	8	4
Green, Indianapolis*	.987	43	75	2	1	1
Grissom, Indianapolis	1.000	5	16	0	0	0
Guinn, Iowa	.964	15	27	0	1	0
Hearron, Iowa	1.000	1	0	1	0	0
Hecht, Indianapolis	1.000	19	34	1	0	0
Higgins, Denver	.934	44	69	2	5	0
Hinzo, Omaha	.944	7	17	0	1	0
Houston, Indianapolis	1.000	30	62	0	0	0
Jones, Nashville	.966	121	209	17	8	6
Landrum, Iowa	.982	111	214	3	4	0
Lankford, Louisville*	.969	132	333	8	11	1
Little, Buffalo	.981	32	47	5	1	0
Lockhart, Nashville	1.000	34	43	2	0	0
Loggins, Omaha*	.992	65	127	4	1	2
Mack, Indianapolis*	.963	101	153	3	6	1
Maclin, Louisville*	.975	16	39	0	1	0
Marquez, Indianapolis	.917	6	11	0	1	0
J. Martinez, Louisville	1.000	5	7	0	0	0
R. Martinez, Omaha*	.976	118	228	18	6	3
May, Iowa	.952	103	149	9	8	1
McClendon, Iowa	1.000	2	1	0	0	0
McIntosh, Denver	.857	7	6	0	1	0
Mendez, Louisville*	1.000	20	25	0	0	0
Merced, Buffalo	1.000	3	8	0	0	0
Millay, Oklahoma City	.992	68	118	5	1	0
Monico, Denver*	.971	89	128	4	4	2
Moore, Denver*	.975	106	188	8	5	4
Moreno, Buffalo	1.000	13	23	2	0	0
Morman, Omaha	.970	21	30	2	1	0
Morris, Nashville*	.960	15	23	1	1	0
Motley, 19 Nash.-33 O.C.	1.000	52	82	2	0	0
Nelson, Nashville	.985	42	66	1	1	0
Noce, Nashville	1.000	7	10	1	0	1
Nunez, Louisville	.980	99	134	14	3	4
Olander, Denver	.982	74	163	2	3	1
Pappas, Denver	.968	44	53	7	2	2
Pulliam, Omaha	.980	103	188	12	4	2
Redfield, Denver	1.000	4	7	0	0	0
Reimer, Oklahoma City	1.000	7	7	1	0	0
Roomes, Indianapolis	.964	53	129	3	5	0
Ryal, Buffalo*	1.000	39	62	4	0	0
Schulz, Omaha	1.000	47	79	2	0	1
Sheaffer, Buffalo	.895	15	15	2	2	0
Sheridan, Iowa	1.000	22	32	0	0	0
Silver, Louisville	.979	25	45	1	1	1
St. Laurent, Indianapolis	1.000	5	8	0	0	0
Steels, Indianapolis*	.960	60	140	4	6	0
Sullivan, Iowa*	1.000	8	8	1	0	0
Tatis, Oklahoma City	.989	45	85	7	1	2
Thurman, Omaha	.966	92	163	6	6	0
Torricelli, Denver	1.000	2	2	0	0	0
Vanderwal, Indianapolis*	.963	29	48	4	2	0
Varsho, Iowa	.948	48	88	4	5	1
C. Walker, Iowa	.956	18	37	6	2	1
H. Walker, Omaha	1.000	1	1	0	0	0
Walters, Denver	.969	94	146	9	5	1
Walton, Iowa	1.000	4	6	1	0	0
Williams, Oklahoma City	.973	41	69	3	2	0
Yacopino, Buffalo*	.975	24	39	0	1	0

CATCHERS

Player and Club	Pct.	G.	PO.	A.	E.	DP.	PB.
Allanson, Oklahoma City	.978	13	79	12	2	1	0
Banister, Buffalo	.960	7	20	4	1	0	1
Berger, Oklahoma City	.977	38	191	20	5	4	8
Berryhill, Iowa	.985	18	115	13	2	2	3
Bilardello, Buffalo	.984	47	290	26	5	7	1
Burrell, Omaha	.979	53	286	34	7	3	4
DeFrancesco, Nashville	1.000	13	56	4	0	1	0
Fox, Louisville	1.000	5	18	1	0	1	0
Fulton, Louisville	.985	33	178	14	3	4	5
Goff, Indianapolis	.981	26	141	12	3	1	7
Hearron, Iowa	.988	22	78	7	1	1	6
Kmak, Denver	.968	27	160	20	6	3	4
Kreuter, Oklahoma City	.984	92	559	64	10	9	5
Lowry, Indianapolis	.985	30	114	15	2	1	5
Loy, Oklahoma City	1.000	3	16	0	0	0	0
Marquez, Indianapolis	.957	6	38	6	2	0	4
McClendon, Iowa	1.000	1	4	0	0	0	1
McGriff, Nashville	.986	88	564	59	9	11	8
McIntosh, Denver	.971	100	571	72	19	4	13
Mitchell, Denver	.961	20	103	20	5	2	5
Nichols, Louisville	1.000	26	145	6	0	1	5
Noce, Nashville	1.000	2	1	0	0	0	0
Palacios, Omaha	1.000	1	4	1	0	1	0
Pappas, Iowa	.997	66	354	43	1	2	4

CATCHERS—Continued

Player and Club	Pct.	G.	PO.	A.	E.	DP.	PB.
Prince, Buffalo	.985	88	459	62	8	12	11
Reyes, Indianapolis	.978	85	504	78	13	3	11
Russell, Oklahoma City	.969	5	30	1	1	0	0
Santovenia, Indianapolis	.979	6	40	7	1	1	1
Scott, Nashville	.983	56	306	46	6	10	8
Sheaffer, Buffalo	.984	23	119	8	2	0	2
Silver, Louisville	1.000	2	2	0	0	0	0
SPEHR, Omaha	.993	100	658	67	5	14	5
Stephens, Louisville	.987	98	552	55	8	7	6
Szekely, Buffalo	1.000	2	7	3	0	0	0
Torricelli, Denver	1.000	7	37	7	0	2	0
Villanueva, Iowa	1.000	22	130	20	0	5	5
Washington, Oklahoma City	.917	2	9	2	1	0	0
Wrona, Iowa	.981	46	273	33	6	4	3

PITCHERS

Player and Club	Pct.	G.	PO.	A.	E.	DP.
Alba, Louisville*	.833	9	1	4	1	0
Alexander, Oklahoma City	1.000	20	5	10	0	1
Allen, Nashville	1.000	12	2	6	0	0
Anderson, Indianapolis	1.000	27	14	22	0	1
Appier, Omaha	1.000	3	0	3	0	0
Arnold, Louisville	1.000	14	3	7	0	1
Arnsberg, Oklahoma City	.952	14	6	14	1	1
August, Denver	.944	22	4	13	1	1
Bair, Buffalo	1.000	29	5	5	0	1
Baller, Omaha	.929	52	3	10	1	2
Barfield, Oklahoma City*	1.000	19	6	15	0	0
Belinda, Buffalo	1.000	15	1	3	0	1
Bennett, Indianapolis	1.000	23	3	6	0	0
Bierley, Iowa	1.000	1	0	1	0	1
Birkbeck, Denver	.929	21	10	16	2	3
Birtsas, Nashville*	.571	8	1	3	3	1
BLANKENSHIP, Iowa	1.000	27	12	37	0	5
Bohanon, Oklahoma City*	1.000	14	0	5	0	0
Boskie, Iowa	1.000	8	5	13	0	2
Bowden, Iowa*	1.000	11	0	2	0	0
Bronkey, Oklahoma City	1.000	28	8	6	0	0
Brown, Nashville	.920	39	6	17	2	0
Bryant, Oklahoma City	.941	14	8	8	1	3
Camacho, Louisville	1.000	15	4	4	0	0
Campbell, Omaha*	1.000	4	0	4	0	0
Capel, Denver	.958	41	5	18	1	1
Carpenter, Louisville	.957	22	9	13	1	1
Castillo, Oklahoma City	1.000	20	2	3	0	1
Cecena, Oklahoma City	1.000	9	0	2	0	0
Chadwick, Omaha	.895	42	4	13	2	2
Chambers, Indianapolis	.800	22	0	4	1	0
Clark, Omaha	1.000	17	6	7	0	0
Clarke, Louisville*	1.000	32	6	18	0	1
Clay, 19 Ind.-6 Iowa	1.000	25	2	6	0	0
Clear, Iowa	1.000	2	0	1	0	0
Codiroli, Omaha	1.000	4	0	5	0	0
Coffman, Iowa	.818	9	3	6	2	1
Cormier, Louisville*	1.000	4	2	2	0	0
Costello, Indianapolis	1.000	22	2	4	0	1
Cox, Louisville	1.000	4	2	1	0	0
Crawford, Omaha	1.000	4	1	1	0	0
Damian, Iowa	1.000	23	4	6	0	0
Daniel, Oklahoma City*	1.000	5	0	1	0	0
Davins, Indianapolis	1.000	41	3	7	0	0
Davis, Denver	1.000	6	0	1	0	0
Dillard, Buffalo*	1.000	10	1	0	0	0
Dixon, Indianapolis	.970	57	13	19	1	1
Dozier, Omaha	1.000	4	0	2	0	0
Easley, Denver	.931	46	3	24	2	3
Edens, Denver	.909	19	2	8	1	3
Encarnacion, Omaha	.941	44	7	9	1	0
Everson, Omaha	1.000	33	5	17	0	1
Farmer, Indianapolis	.897	26	4	22	3	2
Ferreira, Omaha*	.943	33	7	26	2	5
Filer, Denver	1.000	9	4	13	0	0
Filson, Omaha*	1.000	17	6	27	0	3
FIREOVID, Indianapolis	1.000	29	9	40	0	2
Fossas, Denver*	1.000	25	3	7	0	0
Francona, Louisville*	1.000	5	0	1	0	0
Gakeler, Indianapolis	.852	22	7	16	4	1
Galvez, Indianapolis	1.000	3	1	0	0	0
Garcia, Buffalo*	1.000	9	0	4	0	0
George, Denver	1.000	7	1	1	0	0
Gordon, Denver	1.000	5	0	4	0	0
Grater, Louisville	.929	24	6	7	1	0
Gross, Nashville	.929	40	7	32	3	3
Guzman, Oklahoma City	.889	7	0	8	1	0
Hammond, Nashville*	.962	24	4	21	1	3
Hardy, Oklahoma City	.926	53	7	18	2	1
Harrison, Iowa*	.947	29	1	17	1	0
Hayward, Oklahoma City*	.867	18	4	22	4	1
Henry, Denver	1.000	27	3	12	0	1
K. Hill, Louisville	.923	12	10	14	2	2
M. Hill, Nashville	1.000	48	2	10	0	2
Hilton, Louisville	.929	56	4	9	1	1
Hinkle, Louisville	.968	29	32	29	2	3
Hoover, 24 O.C.-4 Ind.	1.000	28	12	20	0	3
Horton, Denver*	.833	5	0	5	1	0
Huismann, Buffalo	.895	49	7	10	2	2
Hunter, Denver	.960	20	3	21	1	4
Imes, Nashville	.953	29	8	33	2	1
Jackson, Nashville*	1.000	2	0	4	0	1
Kallevig, Iowa	.964	19	10	17	1	1
Kemp, Buffalo	.917	26	9	24	3	3
Kipper, Buffalo*	1.000	5	0	2	0	0
Kisten, Louisville	.800	9	1	3	1	0
Kraemer, Iowa*	.931	20	5	22	2	2
Kramer, Buffalo	1.000	18	7	11	0	2
Lancaster, Iowa	1.000	6	1	2	0	1
Lankard, Oklahoma City	1.000	12	2	5	0	1
Lazor, Nashville*	.500	11	1	0	1	0
Lee, Denver*	1.000	20	1	6	0	0
LeMasters, Omaha	.889	30	9	15	3	2
Lopez, Nashville	.880	28	9	13	3	1
Lynch, Oklahoma City*	1.000	14	1	4	0	0
Magnante, Omaha*	.960	13	5	19	1	1
Mahler, Nashville	1.000	1	1	5	0	1
Malloy, Indianapolis	1.000	23	1	5	0	0
Marchok, Indianapolis*	1.000	23	4	10	0	2
Martinez, Omaha*	1.000	1	1	0	0	0
Mason, Buffalo	1.000	29	6	10	0	0
Masters, Iowa	.875	9	2	5	1	0
G. Mathews, Louisville*	1.000	4	1	1	0	1
T. Mathews, Oklahoma City	.938	12	6	9	1	0
May, Denver	.833	7	3	2	1	0
McGaffigan, Omaha	1.000	10	2	3	0	0
McGrath, Denver	1.000	12	3	6	0	1
McMurtry, Oklahoma City	1.000	6	1	4	0	0
Medvin, Buffalo	.909	13	5	5	1	0
Mielke, Oklahoma City	.500	5	0	1	1	1
Miller, Oklahoma City	.828	31	6	18	5	2
Minor, Buffalo	1.000	1	0	2	0	0
Minutelli, Nashville*	.938	11	5	10	1	0
Mitchell, Nashville	1.000	40	5	19	0	2
Moeller, Omaha*	1.000	11	0	8	0	0
Mohorcic, Indianapolis	.833	13	1	4	1	0
Moore, Nashville	.667	13	0	2	1	0
Nabholz, Indianapolis*	.938	10	0	15	1	0
Navarro, Denver	1.000	6	0	7	0	1
Neely, Buffalo	1.000	6	0	2	0	0
Niedenfuer, Louisville	1.000	5	0	2	0	0
Nunez, Iowa	.917	16	8	14	2	2
Olivares, Louisville	.963	23	18	34	2	6
Osteen, Louisville	.923	13	9	3	1	0
Oyster, Louisville	1.000	2	1	0	0	0
Palacios, Buffalo	.875	28	9	19	4	2
Parker, 44 Iowa-6 Lou.*	.952	50	3	17	1	0
Pavlas, Iowa	.952	53	5	15	1	2
M. Perez, Louisville	.857	57	2	10	2	0
Y. Perez, Indianapolis*	1.000	9	0	2	0	0
Peterek, Denver	1.000	9	1	6	0	0
Petkovsek, Oklahoma City	.882	28	11	19	4	1
Pico, Louisville	1.000	1	0	0	0	0
Potestio, Louisville	1.000	2	0	2	0	0
Powell, Denver*	.905	11	1	18	2	1
Puig, Denver*	1.000	19	1	6	0	0
Reed, Buffalo	1.000	15	7	16	0	0
Renfroe, Iowa	.967	44	8	21	1	0
Reuss, Buffalo*	1.000	14	5	10	0	0
Richardson, Louisville*	1.000	5	0	1	0	0
Rijo, Nashville	1.000	1	1	0	0	0
Ritter, Iowa	.833	3	1	4	1	1
Robertson, Denver	1.000	21	0	1	0	0
Roesler, Buffalo	.833	24	1	4	1	0
Rojas, Indianapolis	.864	17	8	11	3	1
Rosario, Iowa*	.857	21	2	4	1	1
Rosenthal, Oklahoma City	1.000	42	4	7	0	0
Ross, Buffalo	1.000	47	8	17	0	0
Sadler, Denver	.947	12	6	12	1	0
Samuels, Buffalo*	1.000	5	0	1	0	0
Satzinger, Buffalo	.615	23	6	2	5	0
Sauveur, Indianapolis*	1.000	14	9	13	0	2
Scudder, Nashville	.875	11	3	4	1	0
Sebra, 23 Nash.-21 Den.	.857	44	3	3	1	0
Sherrill, Louisville*	1.000	52	2	8	0	0
Slocumb, Iowa	.800	20	0	4	1	0
Smith, Omaha	.923	11	2	10	1	1
St. Claire, Oklahoma City	.909	29	4	6	1	0
Stone, Louisville	1.000	3	1	0	0	0
Stottlemyre, Omaha	.917	29	6	5	1	1
Straker, Indianapolis	1.000	3	0	2	0	0
Sutcliffe, Iowa.	1.000	2	0	2	0	0

PITCHERS—Continued

Player and Club	Pct.	G.	PO.	A.	E.	DP.	Player and Club	Pct.	G.	PO.	A.	E.	DP.
Taylor, Buffalo	.915	31	28	26	5	0	Vierra, Nashville*	1.000	49	5	20	0	0
Tewksbury, Louisville	.800	6	4	4	2	1	Walter, Omaha*	1.000	20	6	12	0	1
Thomas, Denver	1.000	7	0	6	0	1	Watkins, Denver	1.000	18	3	6	0	0
Thompson, Indianapolis	1.000	15	4	8	0	0	Wegman, Denver	1.000	3	0	3	0	0
Tibbs, Buffalo	1.000	2	0	1	0	0	Wilkins, Iowa	.880	52	8	14	3	3
Tomlin, Buffalo*	1.000	3	1	1	0	0	Wilkinson, Omaha*	1.000	7	0	1	0	0
Tresemer, Omaha	1.000	11	0	2	0	1	Wilmet, Iowa	.889	25	3	5	1	0
Trout, Louisville*	1.000	4	1	3	0	0	York, Buffalo	.951	27	14	25	2	3
Vasquez, Nashville	.931	18	7	20	2	0	Zarranz, Iowa	1.000	5	0	2	0	0
Veres, Denver	1.000	16	3	17	0	1							

Triple Play—Hayward.

The following players did not have any fielding statistics at the positions indicated or appeared only as a designated hitter, pinch-hitter or pinch-runner: Bafia, of; Beltre, p; Brewer, p; Cucjen, 1b; Figueroa, p; Frey, p; Garman, 3b; Goff, 2b; Hancock, p; Hearron, p; Heinkel, p; Houston, p; Johnston, p; Leary, ph; Millay, ss, of; J. Mitchell, ss, of; Morman, 2b; Olker, p; Palmer, of; Pearson, of, p; Pino, of; R. Powell, p; J. Richardson, of, p; Rodriguez, p; David Smith, 3b; Strange, of; Tatis, ss; Washington, p; W. Wrona, c; Xavier, p; Zuvella, 3b.

CLUB PITCHING

Club	ERA.	G.	CG.	ShO.	Sv.	IP.	H.	R.	ER.	HR.	HB.	BB.	Int. BB.	SO.	WP.	Bk.
Buffalo	3.15	147	16	16	36	1322.0	1269	547	462	58	37	398	35	839	52	13
Nashville	3.23	147	22	17	34	1291.1	1146	553	463	93	30	498	16	879	49	32
Indianapolis	3.49	146	15	12	22	1262.0	1153	596	490	92	46	513	24	809	54	22
Omaha	3.50	146	11	14	48	1267.1	1223	555	493	88	48	517	18	899	64	32
Louisville	3.78	146	13	11	40	1255.2	1185	591	528	123	51	454	17	855	51	25
Iowa	4.34	146	10	5	33	1238.2	1309	694	598	111	51	570	61	900	70	15
Oklahoma City	4.40	145	10	5	25	1275.0	1432	747	623	82	57	477	23	838	80	29
Denver	5.16	146	10	7	41	1262.0	1460	839	723	99	43	493	24	866	66	24

PITCHERS' RECORDS

(Leading Qualifiers for Earned-Run Average Leadership—117 or More Innings)

*Throws lefthanded.

Pitcher—Club	W.	L.	Pct.	ERA.	G.	GS.	CG.	GF.	ShO.	Sv.	IP.	H.	R.	ER.	HR.	HB.	BB.	Int. BB.	SO.	WP.
Hammond, Nashville*	15	1	.938	2.17	24	24	5	0	3	0	149.0	118	43	36	7	5	63	1	149	9
Fireovid, Indianapolis	10	12	.455	2.63	29	26	4	1	2	0	171.0	163	70	50	10	3	34	0	84	6
Olivares, Louisville	10	11	.476	2.82	23	23	5	0	2	0	159.1	127	58	50	6	9	59	1	88	6
Taylor, Buffalo	14	6	.700	2.91	30	29	5	0	2	0	195.0	170	74	63	9	5	51	0	112	9
LeMasters, Omaha	11	10	.524	3.16	30	25	3	1	1	0	154.0	170	69	54	10	7	55	2	86	9
Gakeler, Indianapolis	5	5	.500	3.23	22	21	1	0	1	0	120.0	101	55	43	2	7	55	1	89	7
Hinkle, Louisville	8	7	.533	3.29	29	18	1	1	1	0	128.2	126	53	47	14	4	40	0	66	2
Anderson, Indianapolis	12	10	.545	3.31	27	25	6	2	2	0	182.0	166	74	67	16	0	61	2	116	6
Gross, Nashville	12	7	.632	3.33	40	11	2	11	1	3	127.0	113	54	47	6	7	47	3	62	6
Lopez, Nashville	7	10	.412	3.38	28	25	4	1	2	0	143.2	141	72	54	18	1	50	2	76	4

Departmental Leaders: G—Dixon, M. Perez, 57; W—Hammond, 15; L—Petkovsek, 14; Pct.—Hammond, .938; GS—Imes, Taylor, 29; CG—Anderson, 6; GF—M. Perez, 50; ShO—Hammond, 3; Sv.—M. Perez, 31; IP—Taylor, 195.0; H—Petkovsek, 187; R—Petkovsek, 103; ER—August, 93; HR—Clarke, Kallevig, 20; HB—Pavlas, 10; BB—Blankenship, York, 78; IBB—Renfroe, 7; SO—Hammond, 149; WP—Hayward, 12.

(All Pitchers—Listed Alphabetically)

Pitcher—Club	W.	L.	Pct.	ERA.	G.	GS.	CG.	GF.	ShO.	Sv.	IP.	H.	R.	ER.	HR.	HB.	BB.	Int. BB.	SO.	WP.
Alba, Louisville*	2	4	.333	5.09	9	9	1	0	1	0	40.2	36	25	23	5	2	21	0	41	2
Alexander, Oklahoma City	13	2	.867	4.10	20	20	2	0	1	0	118.2	126	58	54	6	3	45	0	94	5
Allen, Nashville	0	0	.000	6.60	12	0	0	2	0	1	15.0	22	12	11	3	1	6	0	10	0
Anderson, Indianapolis	12	10	.545	3.31	27	25	6	2	2	0	182.0	166	74	67	16	0	61	2	116	6
Appier, Omaha	2	0	1.000	1.50	3	3	0	0	0	0	18.0	15	3	3	0	1	3	0	17	0
Arnold, Louisville	1	3	.250	6.08	14	4	0	1	0	0	47.1	56	38	32	10	6	23	0	23	3
Arnsberg, Oklahoma City	0	4	.000	5.16	14	3	0	7	0	2	29.2	35	19	17	2	0	10	0	17	4
August, Denver	7	7	.500	6.75	22	22	3	0	1	0	124.0	164	98	93	17	5	27	1	67	1
Bair, Buffalo	4	2	.667	2.75	29	0	0	17	0	6	52.1	53	19	16	0	0	18	3	29	3
Baller, Omaha	3	6	.333	3.24	52	0	0	47	0	20	75.0	69	35	27	3	6	33	4	68	11
Barfield, Oklahoma City*	1	6	.143	3.53	19	3	0	2	0	1	43.1	44	21	17	3	1	21	3	25	0
Belinda, Buffalo	3	1	.750	1.90	15	0	0	10	0	5	23.2	20	8	5	1	1	8	1	25	0
Beltre, Indianapolis	0	0	.000	81.00	1	0	0	0	0	0	0.1	0	3	3	0	0	5	0	0	0
Bennett, Indianapolis	2	7	.222	4.89	23	0	0	13	0	3	35.0	36	24	19	6	1	24	1	15	2
Bierley, Iowa	0	0	.000	0.00	1	0	0	1	0	0	1.0	1	0	0	0	0	0	0	0	0
Birkbeck, Denver	3	8	.273	5.33	21	20	0	0	0	0	96.1	102	73	57	6	2	36	0	69	7
Birtsas, Nashville*	2	4	.333	4.37	8	5	2	2	2	0	35.0	33	21	17	0	0	16	1	34	3
Blankenship, Iowa	10	9	.526	3.42	27	27	1	0	0	0	163.0	175	79	62	9	8	78	3	101	2
Bohanon, Oklahoma City*	1	2	.333	3.66	14	4	0	4	0	1	32.0	35	16	13	0	0	8	0	22	2
Boskie, Iowa	4	2	.667	3.18	8	8	1	0	0	0	51.0	46	22	18	1	2	21	1	51	1
Bowden, Iowa*	0	0	.000	0.82	11	0	0	4	0	0	11.0	6	1	1	0	0	4	0	8	1
Brewer, Louisville*	0	0	.000	0.00	1	0	0	1	0	0	1.0	0	0	0	0	0	0	0	0	0
Bronkey, Oklahoma City	2	0	1.000	4.35	28	0	0	7	0	0	51.2	58	28	25	3	6	28	1	18	6
Brown, Nashville	7	8	.467	2.39	39	9	1	26	0	9	94.1	83	37	25	6	4	24	2	50	4
Bryant, Oklahoma City	4	5	.444	5.90	14	9	1	0	0	0	58.0	81	41	38	3	4	21	1	22	2
Camacho, Louisville	1	1	.500	4.41	15	0	0	4	0	2	16.1	16	10	8	0	0	7	0	15	2
Campbell, Omaha*	2	2	.500	1.32	4	4	1	0	1	0	27.1	25	4	4	0	1	10	0	19	0
Capel, Denver	4	3	.571	4.26	41	3	0	11	0	2	101.1	98	55	48	6	5	39	0	60	3
Carpenter, Louisville	10	8	.556	3.70	22	22	2	0	1	0	143.1	146	61	59	16	6	21	2	100	1
Castillo, Oklahoma City	1	3	.250	3.45	20	1	0	6	0	0	28.2	40	19	11	0	1	10	0	12	4
Cecena, Oklahoma City	0	0	.000	6.52	9	0	0	6	0	0	9.2	11	7	7	2	1	4	1	9	0
Chadwick, Omaha	7	11	.389	5.00	42	16	1	9	0	2	131.1	125	79	73	9	8	63	0	102	9
Chambers, Indianapolis	1	3	.250	4.55	22	1	0	10	0	1	27.2	25	18	14	0	2	20	3	33	2
Clark, Denver	8	3	.727	3.73	17	17	0	0	0	0	91.2	82	40	38	14	3	44	0	66	6
Clarke, Louisville*	10	9	.526	4.56	32	21	0	4	0	0	150.0	159	82	76	20	8	51	0	93	1
Clay, 19 Ind.-6 Iowa	2	2	.500	2.30	25	0	0	11	0	0	31.1	24	10	8	0	2	32	3	30	4
Clear, Iowa	0	0	.000	9.00	2	0	0	1	0	0	1.0	1	1	1	0	0	1	0	0	0
Codiroli, Omaha	1	1	.500	5.63	4	4	0	0	0	0	16.0	19	10	10	0	1	9	0	9	2

Pitcher—Club	W.	L.	Pct.	ERA.	G.	GS.	CG.	GF.	ShO.	Sv.	IP.	H.	R.	ER.	HR.	HB.	BB.	Int. BB.	SO.	WP.
Coffman, Iowa	2	5	.286	3.43	9	9	0	0	0	0	60.1	43	26	23	1	1	40	3	49	5
Cormier, Louisville*	1	1	.500	2.25	4	4	0	0	0	0	24.0	18	8	6	1	0	3	0	9	4
Costello, Indianapolis	0	3	.000	7.04	22	0	0	7	0	0	30.2	36	26	24	8	0	20	1	32	1
Cox, Louisville	0	3	.000	15.55	4	3	0	0	0	0	11.0	22	20	19	3	3	10	0	6	8
Crawford, Omaha	0	0	.000	0.00	4	0	0	0	0	0	6.0	2	0	0	0	1	2	0	11	1
Damian, Iowa	4	3	.571	4.38	23	5	0	6	0	0	51.1	59	30	25	6	2	20	5	26	2
Daniel, Oklahoma City*	0	0	.000	3.68	5	0	0	2	0	0	7.1	6	4	3	2	0	1	0	6	0
Davins, Indianapolis	3	6	.333	4.47	41	0	0	24	0	4	56.1	52	31	28	7	4	27	2	45	2
Davis, Denver	1	3	.250	12.46	6	0	0	4	0	1	4.1	4	7	6	0	0	8	2	3	2
Dillard, Buffalo*	1	0	1.000	0.00	10	1	0	2	0	1	11.1	10	1	0	0	2	1	0	7	0
Dixon, Indianapolis	6	7	.462	3.25	57	6	0	25	0	5	110.2	87	47	40	5	5	35	1	40	3
Dozier, Omaha	2	1	.667	5.63	4	2	0	0	0	0	16.0	14	11	10	3	0	10	0	7	0
Easley, Denver	3	1	.750	5.79	46	0	0	25	0	9	74.2	99	63	48	3	5	41	5	39	2
Edens, Denver	1	1	.500	5.40	19	0	0	9	0	4	36.2	32	23	22	3	0	22	0	26	3
Encarnacion, Omaha	6	5	.545	2.96	44	0	0	21	0	7	76.0	70	30	25	9	0	30	5	62	0
Everson, Omaha	4	0	1.000	2.35	33	0	0	12	0	2	61.1	48	18	16	1	1	30	3	29	2
Farmer, Indianapolis	7	9	.438	3.89	26	26	4	0	2	0	148.0	150	84	64	12	6	48	2	99	6
Ferreira, Omaha*	6	6	.500	3.78	33	17	1	8	0	1	138.0	143	61	58	9	9	52	0	79	8
Figueroa, Louisville	0	0	.000	9.00	1	0	0	1	0	0	1.0	2	1	1	1	0	0	0	0	0
Filer, Denver	3	5	.375	6.49	9	9	1	0	0	0	51.1	70	39	37	4	2	9	0	22	2
Filson, Denver	12	2	.857	2.78	17	17	1	0	0	0	107.0	107	41	33	7	2	31	1	66	3
Fireovid, Indianapolis	10	12	.455	2.63	29	26	4	1	2	0	171.0	163	70	50	10	3	34	0	84	6
Fossas, Denver*	5	2	.714	1.51	25	0	0	14	0	4	35.2	29	8	6	1	1	10	3	45	4
Francona, Louisville*	0	0	.000	1.17	5	0	0	5	0	0	7.2	4	1	1	1	0	2	0	6	1
Frey, Indianapolis*	0	0	.000	0.00	2	0	0	1	0	1	3.0	0	0	0	0	0	1	0	3	0
Gakeler, Indianapolis	5	5	.500	3.23	22	21	1	0	1	0	120.0	101	55	43	2	7	55	1	89	7
Galvez, Indianapolis	0	1	.000	10.29	3	2	0	0	0	0	7.0	11	8	8	2	0	8	0	5	1
Garcia, Buffalo*	0	2	.000	5.25	9	1	0	3	0	0	12.0	12	9	7	3	1	4	1	6	3
George, Denver	1	1	.500	18.56	7	0	0	1	0	0	5.1	17	11	11	1	0	4	0	4	1
Gordon, Denver	1	0	1.000	3.24	5	0	0	0	0	0	8.1	10	6	3	0	2	4	1	5	1
Grater, Louisville	0	2	.000	3.18	24	0	0	15	0	3	28.1	24	13	10	0	0	15	4	18	0
Gross, Nashville	12	7	.632	3.33	40	11	2	11	1	3	127.0	113	54	47	6	7	47	3	62	6
Guzman, Oklahoma City	0	3	.000	5.65	7	7	0	0	0	0	28.2	35	20	18	2	2	9	0	26	1
Hammond, Nashville*	15	1	.938	2.17	24	24	5	0	3	0	149.0	118	43	36	7	5	63	1	149	9
Hancock, Buffalo*	0	0	.000	0.00	1	0	0	0	0	0	0.0	0	0	0	0	0	1	0	0	0
Hardy, Oklahoma City	5	4	.556	2.34	53	0	0	24	0	4	88.1	81	29	23	4	5	25	6	78	2
Harrison, Iowa*	4	6	.400	4.77	29	10	0	9	0	1	66.0	61	42	35	8	3	43	1	58	2
Hayward, Oklahoma City*	9	7	.357	5.16	18	17	1	0	0	0	89.0	92	55	51	12	4	49	0	61	12
Hearron, Iowa	0	0	.000	13.50	2	0	0	2	0	0	2.0	3	3	3	1	0	1	0	0	1
Heinkel, Louisville	0	1	.000	10.38	1	1	0	0	0	0	4.1	3	5	5	1	1	0	2	0	0
Henry, Denver	2	3	.400	4.44	27	0	0	15	0	0	50.2	46	26	25	4	0	27	2	54	3
K. Hill, Louisville	6	1	.857	1.79	12	12	2	0	1	0	85.1	47	20	17	6	1	27	1	104	2
M. Hill, Nashville	4	4	.500	2.27	48	0	0	11	0	3	71.1	51	20	18	4	2	18	1	58	4
Hilton, Louisville	4	3	.571	3.60	56	1	0	20	0	0	80.0	73	40	32	8	1	34	1	55	4
Hinkle, Louisville	8	7	.533	3.29	29	18	1	1	1	0	128.2	126	53	47	14	4	40	0	66	2
Hoover, 24 O.C.-4 Ind.	4	5	.444	5.92	28	12	1	3	0	1	97.1	120	73	64	5	5	39	2	47	8
Horton, Denver*	3	1	.750	4.81	5	5	0	0	0	0	24.1	37	17	13	2	1	7	0	10	1
Houston, Indianapolis	0	0	.000	0.00	1	0	0	1	0	0	0.1	0	0	0	0	0	0	0	1	0
Huismann, Buffalo	6	2	.750	2.61	49	0	0	24	0	4	76.0	69	23	22	3	1	15	6	32	3
Hunter, Denver	6	8	.429	4.69	20	20	2	0	0	0	117.0	138	76	61	5	5	45	1	57	1
Imes, Nashville*	10	8	.556	3.71	29	29	3	0	1	0	169.2	175	82	70	15	3	68	1	97	4
Jackson, Nashville*	1	0	1.000	0.00	2	2	0	0	0	0	11.0	9	0	0	0	0	4	0	3	0
Johnston, Omaha	0	0	.000	0.00	2	0	0	0	0	0	3.0	1	0	0	0	0	1	0	3	0
Kallevig, Iowa	4	10	.286	5.67	19	16	0	0	0	0	93.2	118	73	59	20	5	36	3	35	1
Kemp, Buffalo	7	7	.500	3.42	26	21	1	2	0	0	134.1	134	66	51	12	7	27	0	80	4
Kipper, Buffalo*	0	0	.000	7.71	5	1	0	0	0	0	4.2	6	4	4	1	0	1	0	6	0
Kisten, Louisville	0	0	.000	6.75	9	0	0	3	0	0	13.1	15	10	10	2	0	8	2	10	1
Kraemer, Iowa*	7	6	.538	3.76	20	20	3	0	0	0	122.0	113	56	51	11	3	40	4	84	4
Kramer, Buffalo	6	1	.857	2.57	18	12	0	4	0	3	73.2	55	29	21	3	3	33	1	58	4
Lancaster, Iowa	0	1	.000	4.08	6	0	0	2	0	1	17.2	20	10	8	0	0	5	0	15	1
Lankard, Oklahoma City	0	1	.000	5.13	12	0	0	7	0	0	26.1	34	20	15	2	1	7	1	18	0
Lazor, Nashville*	0	1	.000	7.90	11	0	0	6	0	0	13.2	14	12	12	1	1	11	0	9	0
Lee, Denver*	3	1	.750	2.25	20	0	0	6	0	4	28.0	25	7	7	2	0	6	1	35	1
LeMasters, Omaha	11	10	.524	3.16	30	25	3	1	1	0	154.0	170	69	54	10	7	55	2	86	9
Lopez, Nashville	7	10	.412	3.38	28	25	4	1	2	0	143.2	141	72	54	18	1	50	2	76	4
Lynch, Oklahoma City*	0	4	.000	5.74	14	2	0	10	0	1	26.2	34	24	17	4	5	14	1	20	1
Magnante, Omaha*	2	5	.286	4.11	13	13	2	0	0	0	76.2	72	39	35	6	2	25	0	56	3
Mahler, Nashville	0	1	.000	2.45	1	1	0	0	0	0	7.1	6	2	2	1	0	3	0	5	2
Malloy, Indianapolis	2	2	.500	3.78	23	1	0	16	0	6	33.1	31	15	14	2	2	8	0	31	0
Marchok, Indianapolis*	1	2	.333	2.28	23	0	0	1	0	0	23.2	20	7	6	0	3	10	1	17	3
Martinez, Omaha*	0	0	.000	0.00	1	0	0	1	0	0	1.0	0	0	0	0	0	0	0	0	0
Mason, Buffalo	3	5	.375	2.10	29	2	0	6	0	3	77.0	78	21	18	2	1	25	4	45	2
Masters, Iowa	1	4	.200	12.30	9	8	0	0	0	0	26.1	42	36	36	5	1	32	2	22	7
G. Mathews, Louisville*	0	2	.000	9.22	4	4	0	0	0	0	13.2	18	15	14	2	2	12	0	6	1
T. Mathews, Oklahoma City	2	7	.222	3.69	12	11	1	0	1	0	70.2	81	39	29	4	3	15	0	36	2
May, Denver	1	1	.500	8.04	7	5	0	0	0	0	28.0	45	26	25	3	2	13	0	20	4
McGaffigan, Omaha	2	1	.667	3.71	10	0	0	3	0	0	17.0	22	7	7	0	1	5	0	17	0
McGrath, Denver	3	2	.600	6.07	12	4	0	2	0	0	46.0	57	32	31	5	2	17	1	30	3
McMurtry, Oklahoma City	1	1	.500	2.70	6	5	0	0	0	0	26.2	31	15	8	0	1	21	0	19	3
Medvin, Buffalo	2	2	.500	1.46	13	0	0	7	0	1	24.2	13	7	4	0	1	11	1	10	2
Mielke, Oklahoma City	0	0	.000	1.59	5	0	0	1	0	0	5.2	5	2	1	0	0	4	1	7	0
Millay, Oklahoma City	0	0	.000	18.00	1	0	0	1	0	0	1.0	2	2	2	0	0	1	0	0	0
Miller, Oklahoma City	7	9	.438	4.78	31	21	2	0	1	0	143.0	165	88	76	11	3	53	3	92	7
Minor, Buffalo	0	1	.000	3.38	1	0	0	0	0	0	2.2	2	1	1	0	0	2	0	2	0
Minutelli, Nashville*	5	2	.714	3.22	11	11	3	0	0	0	78.1	65	34	28	5	1	31	0	61	1
Mitchell, Nashville	6	3	.667	3.25	40	0	0	22	0	3	80.1	76	33	29	6	3	13	0	58	3
Moeller, Omaha*	5	2	.714	4.02	11	11	0	1	0	0	65.0	63	29	29	9	1	30	0	53	0
Mohorcic, Indianapolis	2	0	1.000	1.13	13	0	0	10	0	2	16.0	11	3	2	1	2	3	0	9	1
Moore, Nashville	1	1	.500	7.79	13	0	0	3	0	1	17.1	18	15	15	3	0	9	1	14	3
Nabholz, Indianapolis*	0	6	.000	4.83	10	10	0	0	0	0	63.1	66	38	34	7	1	28	0	44	3
Navarro, Denver	2	3	.400	4.20	6	6	1	0	0	0	40.2	41	27	19	1	0	14	0	28	2
Neely, Buffalo	1	0	1.000	4.15	6	0	0	6	0	1	8.2	5	4	4	1	0	4	1	5	0

Pitcher—Club	W.	L.	Pct.	ERA.	G.	GS.	CG.	GF.	ShO.	Sv.	IP.	H.	R.	ER.	HR.	HB.	BB.	Int. BB.	SO.	WP.
Niedenfuer, Louisville	0	0	.000	2.45	5	0	0	4	0	2	7.1	5	2	2	0	0	4	0	7	2
Nunez, Iowa	7	6	.538	3.94	16	16	4	0	1	0	107.1	105	51	47	13	0	32	1	109	11
Olivares, Louisville	10	11	.476	2.82	23	23	5	0	2	0	159.1	127	58	50	6	9	59	1	88	6
Olker, Indianapolis*	0	0	.000	0.00	1	0	0	0	0	0	1.0	0	0	0	0	0	1	0	0	0
Osteen, Louisville	5	2	.714	3.42	13	10	0	0	0	0	71.0	74	29	27	4	1	26	0	30	3
Oyster, Louisville	0	0	.000	4.50	2	0	0	1	0	0	2.0	2	1	1	1	0	2	0	1	0
Palacios, Buffalo	13	7	.650	3.43	28	28	5	0	2	0	183.2	173	77	70	8	1	53	2	137	9
Parker, 44 Iowa-6 Lou.*	1	2	.333	5.34	50	2	0	12	0	1	64.0	85	44	38	7	1	26	6	40	2
Pavlas, Iowa	8	3	.727	3.26	53	3	0	22	0	8	99.1	84	38	36	4	10	48	6	96	8
Pearson, Nashville	0	0	.000	9.00	1	0	0	1	0	0	1.0	0	1	1	0	0	3	0	1	0
M. Perez, Louisville	7	7	.500	4.28	57	0	0	50	0	31	67.1	64	34	32	9	2	33	4	69	3
Y. Perez, Indianapolis*	1	1	.500	2.31	9	0	0	2	0	0	11.2	8	5	3	1	0	6	0	8	0
Peterek, Denver	2	3	.400	6.82	9	6	0	2	0	0	34.1	43	29	26	2	1	15	1	23	2
Petkovsek, Oklahoma City	7	14	.333	5.25	28	28	2	0	1	0	151.0	187	103	88	9	4	42	1	81	8
Pico, Iowa	0	0	.000	5.79	1	1	0	0	0	0	4.2	7	3	3	1	0	0	0	1	0
Potestio, Louisville	0	1	.000	10.13	2	2	0	0	0	0	5.1	10	7	6	0	0	6	0	2	0
D. Powell, Denver*	4	4	.500	3.61	11	11	2	0	0	0	62.1	63	34	25	6	0	21	0	46	3
R. Powell, Nashville	0	0	.000	3.38	3	0	0	1	0	0	2.2	1	1	1	0	0	0	0	4	0
Puig, Denver*	2	0	1.000	3.38	19	0	0	9	0	0	26.2	35	12	10	3	3	9	0	24	0
Reed, Buffalo	7	4	.636	3.46	15	15	2	0	2	0	91.0	82	37	35	4	6	21	0	63	1
Renfroe, Iowa	7	3	.700	4.96	44	14	1	22	0	9	118.0	146	68	65	12	1	30	7	56	0
Reuss, Buffalo*	4	4	.500	3.52	14	9	0	2	0	1	61.1	73	25	24	1	0	12	1	29	2
D. Richardson, Louisville*	0	0	.000	1.69	5	0	0	2	0	0	5.1	1	1	1	0	1	0	0	2	0
J. Richardson, Buffalo	0	0	.000	4.50	2	0	0	2	0	0	2.0	5	1	1	0	0	0	0	0	0
Rijo, Nashville	0	0	.000	8.31	1	1	0	0	0	0	4.1	5	4	4	0	0	2	0	2	0
Ritter, Iowa	0	3	.000	9.00	3	3	0	0	0	0	11.0	22	15	11	2	0	5	2	5	2
Robertson, Denver	2	3	.400	4.44	21	0	0	12	0	0	26.1	27	18	13	2	1	21	1	20	1
Rodriguez, Nashville*	0	1	.000	10.38	5	0	0	1	0	0	4.1	4	5	5	1	0	3	0	1	0
Roesler, Buffalo	0	3	.000	4.29	24	0	0	7	0	0	42.0	50	25	20	2	1	17	6	19	3
Rojas, Indianapolis	2	4	.333	3.13	17	17	0	0	0	0	97.2	84	42	34	9	1	47	3	64	3
Rosario, Iowa*	2	3	.400	6.89	21	0	0	2	0	1	15.2	22	14	12	2	2	12	3	13	1
Rosenthal, Oklahoma City	3	4	.429	3.00	42	0	0	33	0	14	48.0	40	24	16	1	2	18	3	39	5
Ross, Buffalo	6	8	.429	2.02	47	0	0	36	0	11	71.1	73	23	16	1	2	12	6	36	0
Sadler, Denver	2	5	.286	5.50	12	12	1	0	0	0	52.1	54	33	32	5	3	23	0	26	3
Samuels, Buffalo*	0	0	.000	3.60	5	0	0	1	0	0	5.0	6	2	2	0	0	1	0	4	0
Satzinger, Oklahoma City	1	4	.200	5.13	23	4	0	7	0	0	47.1	51	28	27	3	4	27	0	23	4
Sauveur, Indianapolis*	2	2	.500	1.93	14	7	0	0	0	0	56.0	45	14	12	1	3	25	0	24	1
Scudder, Nashville	7	1	.875	2.34	11	11	1	0	0	0	80.2	53	27	21	1	0	32	0	60	0
Sebra, 23 Nash.-21 Den.	4	3	.571	3.27	44	2	0	36	0	20	63.1	61	26	23	3	0	24	2	69	2
Sherrill, Louisville	4	3	.571	2.49	52	0	0	20	0	2	61.1	49	17	17	4	1	21	2	57	4
Slocumb, Iowa	3	2	.600	2.00	20	0	0	10	0	1	27.0	16	10	6	1	2	18	2	21	3
Smith, Omaha	6	2	.750	3.09	11	10	0	0	0	0	64.0	59	25	22	4	2	32	0	56	3
St. Claire, Oklahoma City	1	2	.333	2.01	29	0	0	13	0	1	53.2	45	15	12	3	3	12	1	68	5
Stone, Louisville	1	0	1.000	6.23	3	0	0	0	0	0	4.1	4	4	3	0	1	8	0	3	1
Stottlemyre, Omaha	2	1	.667	1.51	29	0	0	19	0	13	41.2	26	9	7	0	0	11	1	33	1
Straker, Indianapolis	0	0	.000	0.00	3	1	0	1	0	0	6.2	1	2	0	0	2	3	0	7	0
Sutcliffe, Iowa	0	2	.000	7.82	2	2	0	0	0	0	12.2	18	13	11	2	0	7	0	12	0
Taylor, Buffalo	14	6	.700	2.91	30	29	5	0	2	0	195.0	170	74	63	9	5	51	0	112	9
Tewksbury, Louisville	3	2	.600	2.43	6	6	2	0	0	0	40.2	41	15	11	2	2	3	0	22	0
Thomas, Denver	2	1	.667	5.23	7	2	0	0	0	0	20.2	28	14	12	2	2	7	1	13	3
Thompson, Indianapolis	3	2	.600	5.47	15	1	0	8	0	0	24.2	31	16	15	3	1	10	3	14	3
Tibbs, Buffalo	0	0	.000	3.00	2	1	0	1	0	0	3.0	3	1	1	0	0	2	0	1	0
Tomlin, Buffalo*	0	0	.000	3.38	3	1	0	1	0	0	8.0	12	3	3	1	0	0	0	3	0
Tresemer, Omaha	1	1	.500	9.00	11	0	0	3	0	0	16.0	29	16	16	1	0	4	1	13	0
Trout, Louisville*	1	1	.500	5.68	4	4	0	0	0	0	19.0	24	12	12	3	1	9	0	12	0
Vasquez, Nashville	4	6	.400	3.64	18	18	1	0	1	0	99.0	85	46	40	10	2	59	1	54	2
Veres, Denver	1	6	.143	5.19	16	7	0	7	0	2	50.1	60	36	29	5	1	27	2	36	11
Vierra, Nashville*	3	3	.500	3.28	49	0	0	17	0	1	57.2	55	25	21	6	0	25	2	37	2
Walter, Omaha*	4	1	.800	3.20	20	7	1	9	1	3	59.0	52	24	21	2	1	32	1	43	6
Washington, Oklahoma City	0	0	.000	6.00	3	0	0	3	0	0	3.0	6	3	2	1	0	2	0	1	0
Watkins, Denver	1	3	.250	5.51	18	9	0	3	0	0	67.0	82	44	41	8	0	21	1	55	2
Wegman, Denver	1	0	1.000	3.29	3	3	0	0	0	0	13.2	10	5	5	0	0	7	0	14	0
Wilkins, Iowa	6	2	.750	3.70	52	2	0	33	0	11	73.0	75	37	30	4	6	38	5	61	10
Wilkinson, Omaha*	0	0	.000	7.11	7	0	0	2	0	0	6.1	10	5	5	1	1	5	0	4	0
Wilmet, Iowa	1	2	.333	4.09	25	2	0	7	0	0	44.0	47	23	20	4	4	23	3	38	5
Xavier, Denver	0	0	.000	9.00	1	0	0	1	0	0	1.0	2	1	1	0	0	0	0	0	0
York, Buffalo	8	7	.533	4.20	27	26	3	0	1	0	158.2	165	87	74	6	5	78	2	130	7
Zarranz, Iowa	1	0	1.000	6.75	5	0	0	1	0	0	6.2	5	6	5	0	0	10	3	3	1

BALKS—Chadwick, 10; Hayward, 8; Hammond, Lopez, 7 each; Alba, Moeller, York, 5 each; Clarke, Fireovid, Smith, Stottlemyre, Thomas, 4 each; Coffman, Cox, Gross, Hardy, Harrison, Hilton, Hinkle, Hoover, Lynch, Marchok, Moore, Sauveur, Scudder, 3 each; Baller, Barfield, Birkbeck, Capel, Davins, Easley, Farmer, M. Hill, Miller, Olivares, Palacios, Peterek, Thompson, Vasquez, Veres, Walter, Wilkins, Wilmet, 2 each; Alexander, Anderson, Arnsberg, August, Belinda, Beltre, Bennett, Bohanon, Brown, Bryant, Camacho, Campbell, Carpenter, Clark, Costello, Daniel, Dillard, Encarnacion, Everson, Filer, Guzman, Horton, Huismann, Kisten, Kraemer, Lazor, Lee, Magnante, Mason, G. Mathews, Mitchell, Navarro, Nunez, Pavlas, D. Powell, Renfroe, J. Richardson, Rijo, Robertson, Rodriguez, Rojas, Rosenthal, Ross, Sadler, Satzinger, Sebra, Straker, Sutcliffe, Tewksbury, Watkins, 1 each.

COMBINATION SHUTOUTS—Kramer-Bair 2, Kemp-Ross, Palacios-Belinda, Palacios-Roesler, Palacios-Tibbs, Reuss-Bair, Reuss-Mason, Taylor-Huismann, Buffalo; August-Edens-Easley, Birkbeck-Fossas, Filer-Sebra, Horton-Sebra, Peterek-Edens, Powell-McGrath, Denver; Fireovid-Mohorcic, Gakeler-Marchok, Galvez-Dixon-Davins, Sauveur-Dixon, Straker-Clay-Dixon-Davins, Indianapolis; Blankenship-Bowden-Renfroe, Coffman-Renfroe-Harrison-Pavlas, Kraemer-Pavlas, Renfroe-Harrison, Iowa; Hill-Hilton-Sherrill, Hilton-Arnold-Sherrill-Grater, Hinkle-Hilton-Sherrill-Perez, Olivares-Perez, Olivares-Sherrill-Hinkle-Perez, Louisville; Hammond-Sebra 2, Gross-Vierra, Jackson-Gross-Brown, Lopez-Sebra, Minutelli-Brown, Scudder-Vierra, Nashville; Alexander-St. Claire-Rosenthal, Oklahoma City; Filson-Stottlemyre 2, Campbell-Chadwick-Baller, Clark-Encarnacion, Codiroli-LeMasters-Baller, LeMasters-Stottlemyre, Magnante-LeMasters-Wilkinson, Smith-Everson, Smith-Everson-Baller-Encarnacion, Smith-Walter, Omaha.

NO-HIT GAME—Walter, Omaha, defeated Iowa, 3-0 (first game), July 13.

International League

CLASS AAA

**Leading Batter
JIM EPPARD
Syracuse**

**League President
HAROLD COOPER**

**Leading Pitcher
PAUL MARAK
Richmond**

CHAMPIONSHIP WINNERS IN PREVIOUS YEARS

1884—Trenton .520	1932—Newark .649	1962—Jacksonville .610
1885—Syracuse .584	1933—Newark .622	Atlanta (3rd)† .539
1886—Utica .646	Buffalo (4th)† .494	1963—Syracuse x .533
1887—Toronto .644	1934—Newark .608	Indianapolis‡ .562
1888—Syracuse .723	Toronto (3rd)† .559	1964—Jacksonville .589
1889—Detroit .649	1935—Montreal .597	Rochester (4th)† .532
1890—Detroit .617	Syracuse (2nd)† .565	1965—Columbus .582
1891—Buffalo (reg. season) .727	1936—Buffalo‡ .610	Toronto (3rd)† .556
Buffalo (supplem'l) .680	1937—Newark‡ .717	1966—Rochester .565
1892—Providence .615	1938—Newark‡ .684	Toronto (2nd-tied)† .558
Binghamton° .667	1939—Jersey City .582	1967—Richmond .574
1893—Erie .606	Rochester (2nd)† .556	Toledo (3rd)† .525
1894—Providence .696	1940—Rochester .611	1968—Toledo .565
1895—Springfield .687	Newark (2nd)† .594	Jacksonville (4th)† .514
1896—Providence .602	1941—Newark .649	1969—Tidewater .563
1897—Syracuse .632	Montreal (2nd)† .584	Syracuse (3rd)† .536
1898—Montreal .586	1942—Newark .601	1970—Syracuse‡ .600
1899—Rochester .624	Syracuse (3rd)† .513	1971—Rochester‡ .614
1900—Providence .616	1943—Toronto .625	1972—Louisville .563
1901—Rochester .642	Syracuse (3rd)† .536	Tidewater (3rd)† .545
1902—Toronto .669	1944—Baltimore‡ .553	1973—Charleston .586
1903—Jersey City .642	1945—Montreal .621	Pawtucket y† .534
1904—Buffalo .657	Newark (2nd)† .582	1974—Memphis .613
1905—Providence .638	1946—Montreal‡ .649	Rochester x‡ .611
1906—Buffalo .607	1947—Jersey City .610	1975—Tidewater‡ .610
1907—Toronto .619	Syracuse (3rd)† .575	1976—Rochester .638
1908—Baltimore .593	1948—Montreal‡ .614	Syracuse (2nd)† .590
1909—Rochester .596	1949—Buffalo .584	1977—Pawtucket .571
1910—Rochester .601	Montreal (3rd)† .545	Charleston (2nd)‡ .557
1911—Rochester .645	1950—Rochester .609	1978—Charleston .607
1912—Toronto .595	Baltimore (3rd)† .556	Richmond (4th)† .511
1913—Newark .625	1951—Montreal‡ .617	1979—Columbus‡ .612
1914—Providence .617	1952—Montreal .629	1980—Columbus‡ .593
1915—Buffalo .632	Rochester (3rd)† .619	1981—Columbus‡ .633
1916—Buffalo .586	1953—Rochester .630	1982—Richmond .590
1917—Toronto .604	Montreal (2nd)† .586	Tidewater (3rd)† .540
1918—Toronto .693	1954—Toronto .630	1983—Columbus .593
1919—Baltimore .671	Syracuse (4th)§ .510	Tidewater (4th)† .511
1920—Baltimore .719	1955—Montreal .617	1984—Columbus .590
1921—Baltimore .717	Rochester (4th)† .497	Pawtucket (4th)† .536
1922—Baltimore .689	1956—Toronto .566	1985—Syracuse .564
1923—Baltimore .677	Rochester (2nd)† .553	Tidewater (4th)† .540
1924—Baltimore .709	1957—Toronto .575	1986—Richmond‡ .571
1925—Baltimore .633	Buffalo (2nd)† .571	1987—Tidewater .579
1926—Toronto .657	1958—Montreal‡ .588	Columbus† .550
1927—Buffalo .667	1959—Buffalo .582	1988—Rochester z .546
1928—Rochester .549	Havana (3rd)† .523	Tidewater .546
1929—Rochester .613	1960—Toronto‡ .649	1989—Syracuse .572
1930—Rochester .629	1961—Columbus .597	Richmond z .555
1931—Rochester .601	Buffalo (3rd)† .559	

°Won split-season playoff. †Won four-team playoff. ‡Won championship and four-team playoff. §Defeated Havana in game to decide fourth place, then won four-team playoff. xLeague was divided into Northern, Southern divisions. yLeague divided into American, National divisions. z League divided into Eastern, Western divisions; won playoffs. (NOTE—Known as Eastern League in 1884, New York State League in 1885, International League in 1886-87, International Association in 1888, International League in 1889-90, Eastern Association in 1891, and Eastern League from 1892 until 1912.)

STANDING OF CLUBS AT CLOSE OF SEASON, SEPTEMBER 3

EASTERN DIVISION

Club	W.	L.	T.	Pct.	G.B.
Rochester (Orioles)	89	56	0	.614	....
Scranton-Wilkes Barre (Phillies)	68	78	0	.466	21½
Syracuse (Blue Jays)	62	83	0	.428	27
Pawtucket (Red Sox)	62	84	0	.425	27½

WESTERN DIVISION

Club	W.	L.	T.	Pct.	G.B.
Columbus (Yankees)	87	59	0	.596	....
Tidewater (Mets)	79	67	0	.541	8
Richmond (Braves)	71	74	0	.490	15½
Toledo (Tigers)	58	86	0	.403	28

COMPOSITE STANDING OF CLUBS AT CLOSE OF SEASON, SEPTEMBER 3

Club	Roc.	Col.	Tide.	Rich.	SWB	Syr.	Paw.	Tol.	W.	L.	T.	Pct.	G.B.
Rochester (Orioles)	....	7	8	7	11	11	13	9	89	56	0	.614	....
Columbus (Yankees)	5	....	7	10	8	8	10	11	87	59	0	.596	2½
Tidewater (Mets)	4	11	....	11	7	8	7	11	79	67	0	.541	10½
Richmond (Braves)	4	8	7	....	6	7	7	11	71	74	0	.490	18
Scranton-Wilkes Barre (Phillies)	7	4	5	6	....	7	9	7	68	78	0	.466	21½
Syracuse (Blue Jays)	7	4	4	5	11	....	8	5	62	83	0	.428	27
Pawtucket (Red Sox)	5	2	5	5	9	10	....	6	62	84	0	.425	27½
Toledo (Tigers)	3	7	7	7	5	6	6	....	58	86	0	.403	30½

Tidewater club represented Norfolk and Portsmouth, Va.

Major league affiliations in parentheses.

Playoffs—Rochester defeated Columbus, three games to two, to win league championship. Omaha (American Association) defeated Rochester, four games to one, to win Triple-A Alliance Championship.

Regular-Season Attendance—Columbus, 584,010; Pawtucket, 290,953; Richmond, 427,552; Rochester, 331,927; Scranton-Wilkes Barre, 545,844; Syracuse, 245,045; Tidewater, 159,009. Total—2,777,395. Playoffs (5 games)—12,605. Alliance Playoffs (5 games)—24,621. AAA All-Star Game at Las Vegas—10,323.

Managers—Columbus, Carl (Stump) Merrill (through June 5), Richard Down (June 7 through end of season); Pawtucket, Ed Nottle (through June 26), Johnny Pesky (June 27 through end of season); Richmond, Jim Beauchamp; Rochester, Greg Biagini; Scranton-Wilkes Barre, Bill Dancy; Syracuse, Bob Bailor; Tidewater, Steve Swisher; Toledo, John Wockenfuss (through April 28), Tom Gamboa (April 29 through end of season). Managerial records of teams with more than one manager: Columbus, Merrill 34-25, Down 53-34; Pawtucket, Nottle 30-43, Pesky, 32-41. Toledo, Wockenfuss 10-14, Gamboa, 48-72.

All-Star Team—1B—David Segui, Rochester; 2B—Luis Sojo, Syracuse; 3B—Leo Gomez, Rochester; SS—Tim Naehring, Pawtucket; OF—Hensley Meulens, Columbus; Phil Plantier, Pawtucket; Mark Whiten, Syracuse; C—Brian Dorsett, Columbus; DH—Chris Hoiles, Rochester; SP—Dave Eiland, Columbus; RP—Todd Frohwirth, Scranton-Wilkes Barre; Most Valuable Player—Hensley Meulens, Columbus; Most Valuable Pitcher—Dave Eiland, Columbus; Rookie of the Year—Phil Plantier, Pawtucket; Manager of the Year—Greg Biagini, Rochester.

(Compiled by Howe Sportsdata International, Boston, Mass.)

CLUB BATTING

Club	Pct.	G.	AB.	R.	OR.	H.	TB.	2B.	3B.	HR.	RBI.	SH.	SF.	HP.	BB.	Int. BB.	SO.	SB.	CS.	LOB.
Rochester	.273	145	4607	735	621	1259	1878	216	38	109	660	41	40	30	610	29	872	104	78	996
Syracuse	.261	145	4709	569	622	1230	1759	202	39	83	517	49	44	32	426	23	785	103	60	997
Columbus	.258	146	4695	710	524	1212	1866	249	33	113	632	35	47	54	656	30	871	173	57	1046
Tidewater	.256	146	4648	592	551	1191	1639	205	24	65	542	45	46	37	530	31	701	99	48	1036
Toledo	.254	144	4633	589	678	1178	1761	241	30	94	545	40	29	38	472	23	789	104	67	923
Scranton W.B.	.251	144	4628	580	641	1163	1689	184	36	90	553	57	41	32	525	22	936	96	47	992
Pawtucket	.249	146	4799	673	741	1194	1978	243	23	165	621	45	27	45	535	20	1066	87	53	982
Richmond	.245	145	4669	559	576	1143	1652	181	23	94	511	71	31	50	469	23	884	74	49	999

INDIVIDUAL BATTING

(Leading Qualifiers for Batting Championship—394 or More Plate Appearances)

*Bats lefthanded.   †Switch-hitter.

Player and Club	Pct.	G.	AB.	R.	H.	TB.	2B.	3B.	HR.	RBI.	SH.	SF.	HP.	BB.	Int. BB.	SO.	SB.	CS.
Eppard, James, Syracuse*	.310	133	461	72	143	179	18	3	4	48	6	4	2	47	1	49	5	7
Hughes, Keith, Tidewater*	.309	117	379	77	117	181	24	5	10	53	0	4	4	57	7	58	7	4
Torve, Kelvin, Tidewater*	.303	115	402	62	122	182	25	1	11	76	0	5	6	56	6	43	9	2
Vaughn, Maurice, Pawtucket*	.295	108	386	62	114	208	26	1	22	72	0	2	6	44	2	87	3	2
Azocar, Oscar, Columbus*	.291	94	374	49	109	154	20	5	5	52	4	7	2	9	2	26	8	8
Whiten, Mark, Syracuse†	.290	104	390	65	113	182	19	4	14	48	0	4	3	37	5	72	14	6
Meulens, Hensley, Columbus	.285	136	480	81	137	245	26	5	26	96	1	5	7	66	4	132	6	4
Stanicek, Stephen, Scranton W.B.	.282	127	425	52	120	173	23	0	10	76	0	6	4	58	1	65	2	2
Stone, Jeffrey, Pawtucket*	.280	112	393	51	110	164	28	1	8	41	4	1	2	31	4	84	25	4
Miller, Keith, Scranton W.B.†	.280	143	508	82	142	206	27	2	11	74	4	6	2	57	4	87	13	5

Departmental Leaders: G—K. Miller, Rosario, 143; AB—Sprague, 519; R—L. Gomez, 97; H—Eppard, 143; TB—Meulens, 245; 2B—Lovullo, 38; 3B—Morandini, 10; HR—Plantier, 33; RBI—L. Gomez, 97; SH—Pankovits, 11; SF—Sojo, 9; HP—Walewander, 11; BB—Walewander, 90; IBB—Hare, 9; SO—Plantier, 148; SB—Cuyler, 52; CS—Cuyler, 14.

(All Players—Listed Alphabetically)

Player and Club	Pct.	G.	AB.	R.	H.	TB.	2B.	3B.	HR.	RBI.	SH.	SF.	HP.	BB.	Int. BB.	SO.	SB.	CS.
Adduci, James, Scranton W.B.*	.244	121	353	30	86	117	11	1	6	40	3	3	1	17	5	89	2	3
Agostinelli, Salvatore, Scranton W.B.	.203	71	182	12	37	41	2	1	0	15	3	3	0	22	0	20	6	2
Alba, Gibson, Richmond*	.000	12	2	0	0	0	0	0	0	0	0	0	0	0	0	0	0	0
Allaire, Karl, Toledo*	.244	33	82	10	20	27	5	1	0	4	1	0	0	6	0	13	1	0
Alva, John, Richmond	.249	99	341	38	85	104	12	2	1	23	8	0	0	19	1	68	0	2
Alvarez, Jesus, Toledo*	.182	4	11	0	2	2	0	0	0	0	0	0	0	2	0	4	0	0
Avery, Steven, Richmond*	.200	13	15	1	3	6	0	0	1	5	1	0	0	0	0	6	0	0
Azocar, Oscar, Columbus*	.291	94	374	49	109	154	20	5	5	52	4	7	2	9	2	26	8	8
Barton, Shawn, Tidewater	.000	16	1	1	0	0	0	0	0	0	0	0	0	1	0	1	0	0
Bell, Derek, Syracuse	.261	109	402	57	105	149	13	5	7	56	0	6	3	23	1	75	21	7
Bell, Juan, Rochester†	.285	82	326	59	93	133	12	5	6	35	0	2	3	36	1	59	16	12
Bellino, Frank, Scranton W.B.*	.167	9	18	0	3	3	0	0	0	2	0	0	0	1	0	5	0	1
Berroa, Geronimo, Richmond	.269	135	499	56	134	191	17	2	12	80	0	4	7	34	1	89	4	2
Blowers, Michael, Columbus	.339	62	230	30	78	128	20	6	6	50	0	4	1	29	1	40	3	0
Bogar, Timothy, Tidewater	.162	33	117	10	19	21	2	0	0	4	4	0	1	8	0	22	1	1
Brower, Robert, Columbus	.230	66	204	41	47	60	5	1	2	27	1	3	0	30	1	38	34	6
Brown, Kevin, Rochester*	.167	27	18	1	3	5	0	1	0	2	0	0	0	0	6	0	0	0
Brown, Marty, Rochester	.242	67	211	32	51	82	8	4	5	25	2	1	1	21	1	47	5	2
Buonantony, Richard, Scranton W.B.	1.000	8	2	1	2	5	0	0	1	1	0	0	0	0	0	0	0	0
Cabrera, Francisco, Richmond	.227	35	132	12	30	56	3	1	7	20	0	2	1	7	0	23	2	0

Player and Club	Pct.	G.	AB.	R.	H.	TB.	2B.	3B.	HR.	RBI.	SH.	SF.	HP.	BB.	Int. BB.	SO.	SB.	CS.
Carr, Charles, Tidewater†	.259	20	81	13	21	28	5	1	0	8	0	2	0	4	0	12	6	4
Castillo, Antonio, Richmond°	.000	5	6	0	0	0	0	0	0	0	1	0	0	1	0	3	0	0
Cerone, Richard, Columbus	.091	4	11	0	1	1	0	0	0	1	0	0	0	2	0	1	0	0
Chance, Anthony, Rochester	.269	130	454	55	122	189	17	4	14	75	1	3	1	41	2	115	14	9
Childress, Rodney, Tidewater	.333	27	6	2	2	2	0	0	0	0	1	0	0	2	0	2	0	0
Clark, Phillip, Toledo	.227	75	207	15	47	69	14	1	2	22	6	2	4	14	0	35	1	1
Contreras, Joaquin, Rochester†	.250	61	208	32	52	71	10	3	1	29	6	2	2	28	1	38	6	7
Cooper, Scott, Pawtucket°	.266	124	433	56	115	170	17	1	12	44	4	3	7	39	3	75	2	0
Crabbe, Bruce, Richmond	.268	129	473	64	127	180	26	0	9	51	6	6	4	38	0	68	2	4
Cuevas, Angelo, Tidewater°	.255	20	47	6	12	14	2	0	0	3	0	1	0	4	0	4	0	0
Cuyler, Milton, Toledo†	.258	124	461	77	119	152	11	8	2	42	7	2	5	60	1	77	52	14
Datz, Jeffrey, Columbus	.238	28	63	4	15	19	4	0	0	10	0	1	1	5	1	9	0	0
Davis, Jody, Toledo	.125	3	8	1	1	1	0	0	0	0	0	0	0	0	0	0	0	0
DeButch, Michael, Tidewater	.239	82	238	36	57	69	7	1	1	15	2	0	2	38	1	37	12	4
DeCillis, Dean, Toledo	.286	31	77	8	22	26	4	0	0	9	0	1	1	8	0	7	0	1
DeJesus, Jose, Scranton W.B.	.200	10	5	0	1	1	0	0	0	1	1	0	0	0	0	2	0	0
DeLaCruz, Hector, Syracuse	.234	83	235	27	55	76	9	0	4	19	3	3	0	17	1	54	4	2
Denson, Andrew, Richmond	.231	90	295	25	68	95	4	1	7	29	0	3	9	26	2	57	0	0
Diaz, Alexis, Tidewater†	.256	124	437	55	112	134	15	2	1	36	7	4	1	30	4	39	23	13
Diaz, Carlos, Syracuse	.203	77	251	18	51	64	10	0	1	19	5	2	0	17	1	51	2	2
Diaz, Mario, Tidewater	.317	29	104	15	33	44	8	0	1	9	0	0	1	6	0	6	1	2
Dorsett, Brian, Columbus	.272	114	415	44	113	185	28	1	14	67	1	3	5	49	6	71	1	1
Dowell, Kenneth, Richmond	.200	36	80	7	16	20	2	1	0	7	0	0	2	17	0	13	0	1
Ducey, Robert, Syracuse°	.267	127	438	53	117	184	32	7	7	47	1	1	4	60	6	87	14	9
Dulin, Timothy, Rochester	.238	117	399	56	95	127	17	3	3	46	7	4	1	46	0	75	9	4
Dziadkowiec, Andrew, Syracuse°	.000	1	3	0	0	0	0	0	0	0	0	0	0	0	0	1	0	0
Eberle, Michael, Rochester	.233	19	43	1	10	10	0	0	0	4	1	0	0	1	0	13	0	1
Eppard, James, Syracuse°	.310	133	461	72	143	179	18	3	4	48	6	4	2	47	1	49	5	7
Escobar, Jose, Syracuse	.270	79	252	16	68	78	6	2	0	17	7	0	1	18	0	35	3	0
Fishel, John, Columbus	.200	93	185	20	37	57	11	0	3	21	2	5	0	39	1	36	6	2
Flaherty, John, Pawtucket	.227	99	317	35	72	102	18	0	4	32	2	2	2	24	0	43	1	1
Ford, Curtis, Scranton W.B.°	.222	56	194	28	43	69	5	3	5	12	1	1	1	23	0	39	14	6
Freeman, Lavell, Toledo°	.214	89	280	37	60	86	9	1	5	26	4	1	0	24	0	84	5	4
Freeman, Marvin, 7 SWB-7 Rich.	.250	14	4	0	1	1	0	0	0	0	2	0	0	0	0	2	0	0
Freiling, Howard, Tidewater°	.167	13	36	1	6	7	1	0	0	2	1	0	0	3	1	7	0	0
Frohwirth, Todd, Scranton W.B.	.000	67	4	0	0	0	0	0	0	0	1	0	0	0	0	3	0	0
Fryman, Travis, Toledo	.257	87	327	38	84	140	22	2	10	53	2	3	2	17	0	59	4	7
Gardner, Jeffrey, Tidewater°	.270	138	463	55	125	138	11	1	0	33	4	1	1	84	3	33	3	4
Garrison, Webster, Syracuse	.198	37	101	12	20	27	5	1	0	10	3	1	0	14	0	20	0	3
Gibbons, John Michael, Scranton W.B..	.223	78	202	29	45	75	8	2	6	30	2	1	4	33	1	66	2	0
Givens, Brian, Tidewater	.000	15	11	0	0	0	0	0	0	0	1	0	0	1	0	6	0	0
Gomez, Leonardo, Rochester	.277	131	430	97	119	231	26	4	26	97	0	7	6	89	4	89	2	2
Gomez, Patrick, Richmond°	.000	4	1	0	0	0	0	0	0	0	0	0	0	0	0	1	0	0
Gonzalez, Angel, Pawtucket	.185	66	173	27	32	43	6	1	1	12	3	2	2	22	0	25	1	2
Gonzalez, Denio, Tidewater	.274	65	212	27	58	82	13	1	3	29	0	1	2	37	1	37	1	1
Graves, Steven, Syracuse	.250	3	8	0	2	2	0	0	0	0	0	0	0	0	0	3	0	0
Green, Robert, Columbus	.000	1	2	0	0	0	0	0	0	0	0	0	0	0	0	0	0	0
Greene, Thomas, 19 Rich.-1 SWB	.125	20	16	0	2	2	0	0	0	1	3	0	0	0	0	6	0	0
Grimsley, Jason, Scranton W.B.	.059	22	17	1	1	1	0	0	0	1	2	0	0	1	0	8	0	0
Habyan, John, Columbus	.000	36	1	0	0	0	0	0	0	0	0	0	0	0	0	1	0	0
Hare, Shawn, Toledo°	.254	127	429	53	109	169	25	4	9	55	0	3	4	49	9	77	9	6
Harris, Walter, Rochester	.154	4	13	1	2	2	0	0	0	1	2	0	0	2	0	1	1	1
Heath, Kelly, Scranton W.B.	.237	80	236	33	56	90	7	3	7	33	3	3	2	33	0	47	3	3
Hernandez, Manuel, Tidewater	.105	27	19	0	2	2	0	0	0	0	1	0	0	0	0	6	0	0
Hinzo, Thomas, Richmond†	.224	17	49	9	11	17	0	0	2	5	0	0	2	5	0	12	1	1
Hithe, Victor, Rochester	.274	71	164	20	45	56	7	2	0	15	0	1	0	16	0	41	5	3
Hoiles, Christopher, Rochester	.348	74	247	52	86	162	20	1	18	56	1	1	1	44	4	47	4	2
Hood, Dennis, Richmond	.247	121	389	50	96	145	15	5	8	36	5	3	4	33	2	120	14	4
Horn, Samuel, Tidewater°	.414	17	58	16	24	54	3	0	9	26	0	0	0	9	1	13	0	1
Hughes, Keith, Tidewater°	.309	117	379	77	117	181	24	5	10	53	0	4	4	57	7	58	7	4
Hulett, Timothy, Rochester	.372	14	43	10	16	26	2	1	2	4	1	0	0	11	0	7	0	1
Hunter, Brian, Richmond	.197	43	137	13	27	46	4	0	5	16	1	1	0	18	0	37	2	1
Infante, Alexis, Richmond	.240	31	96	12	23	29	3	0	1	12	2	0	1	9	0	8	1	2
Infante, Kennedy, Scranton W.B.	.229	40	131	12	30	40	4	0	2	10	4	1	2	6	0	14	0	0
Innis, Jeffrey, Tidewater	.000	40	2	0	0	0	0	0	0	0	0	0	0	0	0	0	0	0
Jelic, Christopher, Tidewater	.306	92	265	39	81	116	21	1	4	49	3	8	2	48	1	52	2	1
Jones, LaBarry, Richmond°	.269	99	350	41	94	139	7	1	12	52	3	2	2	16	4	49	13	6
Jones, Ronald, Scranton W.B.°	.264	44	148	13	39	54	4	1	3	26	0	3	1	19	1	18	5	1
Jordan, Paul, Scranton W.B.	.279	27	104	8	29	36	1	0	2	11	0	1	1	5	0	18	0	0
Justice, David, Richmond°	.356	12	45	7	16	29	5	1	2	7	0	0	0	7	2	6	0	0
Kerfeld, Charles, Richmond	.000	15	2	0	0	0	0	0	0	0	1	0	0	0	0	1	0	0
Kiefer, Steven, Tidewater	.248	35	113	15	28	46	6	0	4	16	0	3	0	11	0	29	2	0
Knabenshue, Chris, Scranton W.B.	.237	128	375	61	89	161	16	1	18	61	4	4	2	76	3	107	11	7
Komminsk, Brad, Rochester	.291	28	79	7	23	28	2	0	1	8	1	2	1	10	2	16	0	3
Kremers, James, Richmond°	.232	63	190	25	44	70	8	0	6	24	0	1	1	35	1	47	1	0
Kutcher, Randy, Pawtucket	.316	35	136	18	43	56	8	1	1	14	0	1	0	14	1	19	2	2
Lancellotti, Richard, Pawtucket°	.223	127	430	63	96	173	15	1	20	61	4	2	3	61	4	105	1	2
Lara, Crucito, Tidewater†	.143	21	49	4	7	8	1	0	0	1	1	0	0	1	0	11	0	0
Laskey, William, Richmond	.000	49	4	1	0	0	0	0	0	0	1	0	0	1	0	4	0	0
Legg, Gregory, Scranton W.B.	.308	61	169	25	52	60	5	0	1	21	2	1	1	31	1	27	1	0
Leiper, Timothy, Toledo†	.293	74	249	26	73	95	14	1	2	34	1	2	0	27	1	21	2	1
Leyritz, James, Columbus	.289	59	204	36	59	96	11	1	8	32	2	1	3	37	1	33	4	2
Liddell, David, Tidewater	.212	73	189	16	40	51	5	0	2	15	6	0	2	21	1	50	0	0
Lilliquist, Derek, Richmond°	.333	8	6	0	2	2	0	0	0	0	0	0	0	0	0	1	0	0
Lindeman, James, Toledo	.227	109	374	48	85	162	17	2	12	50	1	3	6	26	2	83	2	3
Livingstone, Scott, Toledo°	.272	103	345	44	94	131	19	0	6	36	0	1	1	22	0	40	1	5
Lofton, Rodney, Rochester	.143	14	28	3	4	4	0	0	0	0	1	0	0	2	0	7	1	1
Lombardozzi, Stephen, Toledo	.248	62	210	31	52	87	11	3	6	23	5	0	1	19	1	30	1	0
Lovullo, Salvatore, Toledo†	.270	141	486	71	131	213	38	1	14	58	2	4	4	61	6	74	4	1
Lusader, Scott, Toledo°	.250	76	268	35	67	93	12	1	4	25	2	1	1	34	2	51	15	9
Lyden, Mitchell, Columbus	.224	41	147	18	33	62	8	0	7	20	0	1	4	7	0	34	0	0
Lyons, Barry, Tidewater	.171	57	164	8	28	33	5	0	0	17	0	1	2	16	1	25	0	0
Maas, Jason, Columbus°	.248	81	210	42	52	77	9	2	4	29	2	2	1	37	1	46	13	0

Player and Club	Pct.	G.	AB.	R.	H.	TB.	2B.	3B.	HR.	RBI.	SH.	SF.	HP.	BB.	Int. BB.	SO.	SB.	CS.
Maas, Kevin, Columbus°	.284	57	194	37	55	113	15	2	13	38	0	0	0	34	1	45	2	2
Machado, Julio, Tidewater	.000	16	1	0	0	0	0	0	0	0	0	0	0	0	0	0	0	0
Madrid, Alexander, Scranton W.B.	.000	16	7	0	0	0	0	0	0	0	1	0	0	2	0	4	0	0
Maldonado, Phillip, Richmond	.100	4	10	0	1	2	1	0	0	0	0	0	0	2	0	1	0	0
Malone, Charles, Scranton W.B.	.375	26	8	2	3	7	1	0	1	5	0	0	0	0	0	2	0	0
Mann, Kelly, Richmond	.202	63	203	18	41	63	13	0	3	20	3	1	4	16	1	36	1	0
Marak, Paul, Richmond	.167	32	18	3	3	3	0	0	0	0	1	0	0	3	0	6	0	0
Marshall, Michael, Pawtucket	.304	6	23	5	7	13	0	0	2	4	0	0	0	3	0	3	0	0
Marzano, John, Pawtucket	.320	26	75	16	24	36	4	1	2	8	0	0	0	11	0	9	6	3
Mauser, Timothy, Scranton W.B.	.154	16	13	1	2	2	0	0	0	0	1	0	0	3	0	5	0	0
McDougal, Julius, Pawtucket†	.246	105	362	45	89	133	13	2	9	47	3	2	2	46	0	68	9	5
McElroy, Charles, Scranton W.B.°	.333	57	3	0	1	1	0	0	0	0	0	0	0	0	0	0	0	0
McKnight, Jefferson, Rochester†	.280	100	339	56	95	143	21	3	7	45	4	6	0	41	3	59	7	5
Meadows, Louie, Scranton W.B.°_	.273	48	172	29	47	69	6	2	4	18	1	0	2	21	1	36	12	4
Mejia, Cesar, Tidewater	.143	19	14	1	2	2	0	0	0	0	1	0	0	0	0	3	0	0
Mercado, Orlando, Tidewater	.264	24	72	5	19	26	4	0	1	10	0	1	1	7	2	11	0	0
Mercker, Kent, Richmond°	.000	12	7	0	0	0	0	0	0	0	2	0	0	0	0	3	0	0
Meulens, Hensley, Columbus	.285	136	480	81	137	245	20	5	26	96	1	5	7	66	4	132	6	4
Michel, Domingo, Toledo	.269	110	327	35	88	131	14	4	7	51	1	3	4	46	0	59	4	9
Miller, Darrell, Rochester	.204	21	54	2	11	12	1	0	0	5	0	1	1	7	1	13	1	1
Miller, Keith, Scranton W.B.†	.280	143	508	82	142	206	27	2	11	74	4	6	2	57	4	87	13	5
Mizerock, John, Richmond°	.222	34	90	11	20	30	4	0	2	10	1	0	1	10	1	18	0	0
Monell, Johnny, Tidewater†	.182	13	33	3	6	6	0	0	0	4	0	0	0	2	0	5	1	0
Moore, Bradley, Scranton W.B.	.100	35	10	0	1	1	0	0	0	0	0	0	0	0	0	3	0	0
Morandini, Michael, Scranton W.B.°	.260	139	503	76	131	178	24	10	1	31	10	0	5	60	0	90	16	6
Morris, Richard, Richmond	.111	17	27	0	3	3	0	0	0	1	1	0	0	2	0	8	0	0
Munoz, Pedro, Syracuse	.319	86	317	41	101	150	22	3	7	56	1	3	1	24	3	64	16	7
Musselman, Jeffrey, Tidewater	.000	10	4	0	0	0	0	0	0	0	2	0	0	0	0	2	0	0
Myers, Gregory, Syracuse°	.182	3	11	0	2	3	1	0	0	2	0	1	0	1	0	1	0	0
Naehring, Timothy, Pawtucket	.269	82	290	45	78	141	16	1	15	47	2	3	3	37	2	56	0	1
Nezelek, Andrew, Richmond°	.200	25	10	0	2	3	1	0	0	1	1	0	0	0	0	2	0	0
Nielsen, Scott, Tidewater	.500	17	2	0	1	1	0	0	0	2	0	0	0	1	0	0	0	0
Nieto, Thomas, Scranton W.B.	.223	37	112	9	25	33	2	0	2	15	1	1	3	8	2	36	0	0
Nixon, Donell, Rochester	.247	85	291	54	72	89	3	4	2	26	3	1	1	42	0	55	21	5
Noles, Dickie, Scranton W.B.	.000	26	1	0	0	0	0	0	0	0	0	0	0	0	0	1	0	0
Olson, Gregory, Richmond	.000	3	7	0	0	0	0	0	0	0	0	0	0	0	0	0	0	0
Olwine, Edward, Richmond	.000	25	1	0	0	0	0	0	0	0	0	0	0	0	0	1	0	0
Ouellette, Philip, Toledo†	.245	99	274	30	67	105	12	1	8	33	5	1	4	40	1	40	1	3
Padget, Chris, Rochester°	.279	74	240	33	67	102	15	1	6	43	0	2	1	18	2	30	0	0
Pankovits, James, Pawtucket	.231	122	468	64	108	167	26	3	9	52	11	4	4	49	0	87	12	8
Pederson, Stuart, Syracuse°	.296	96	301	34	89	109	12	1	2	34	4	2	3	42	2	40	5	4
Pina, John, Pawtucket	.223	123	421	49	94	151	26	2	9	47	3	1	0	44	1	118	15	7
Plantier, Phillip, Pawtucket°	.253	123	430	83	109	236	22	3	33	79	3	3	9	62	3	148	1	8
Plummer, Dale, Tidewater	.000	17	2	0	0	0	0	0	0	0	0	0	0	0	0	1	0	0
Polley, Dale, Richmond	.125	36	8	1	1	1	0	0	0	0	0	0	2	0	0	3	0	0
Ramos, John, Columbus	.000	2	6	0	0	0	0	0	0	1	0	0	0	0	0	2	0	0
Rayford, Floyd, Scranton W.B.	.152	19	33	0	5	7	2	0	0	6	1	1	0	3	0	5	0	0
Reed, Darren, Tidewater	.265	104	359	58	95	179	21	6	17	74	0	4	6	51	4	62	16	4
Reynoso, Armando, Richmond	.000	4	3	0	0	0	0	0	0	0	1	0	0	0	0	1	0	0
Richards, Russell, Richmond°	.190	31	21	0	4	5	1	0	0	2	4	0	0	0	0	1	0	0
Ritchie, Wallace, Scranton W.B.°	.200	20	10	0	2	3	1	0	0	0	0	0	0	1	0	4	0	0
Rivers, Kenneth, Syracuse	.000	1	1	0	0	0	0	0	0	0	0	0	0	0	0	0	0	0
Robidoux, William, Pawtucket°	.204	22	54	5	11	21	1	0	3	7	1	0	0	9	0	16	0	0
Roca, Gilberto, Tidewater	.230	24	61	4	14	15	1	0	0	5	1	1	0	1	0	3	0	1
Rodriguez, Carlos, Columbus†	.273	71	220	31	60	72	12	0	0	16	2	2	2	30	2	8	3	1
Rosario, Victor, Scranton W.B.	.252	143	477	45	120	170	23	6	5	42	7	4	1	12	2	91	8	3
Rossy, Elam, Richmond	.232	107	380	58	88	113	13	0	4	32	7	2	3	69	1	43	13	6
Rowland, Richard, Toledo	.260	62	192	28	50	83	12	0	7	22	3	2	1	15	0	33	2	3
Runge, Paul, Syracuse	.233	119	391	45	91	126	11	3	6	31	8	2	2	59	1	67	3	5
Samuels, Roger, Syracuse°	1.000	35	2	1	2	2	0	0	0	1	0	0	0	1	0	0	0	0
Sanchez, Zoilo, Tidewater	.282	110	312	33	88	125	19	0	6	39	1	7	4	27	4	55	2	0
Sanders, Deion, Columbus°	.321	22	84	21	27	42	7	1	2	10	1	1	2	17	0	15	9	1
Sax, David, Columbus	.249	73	205	18	51	72	9	0	4	19	1	1	2	32	2	38	2	1
Scanlan, Robert, Scranton W.B.	.077	24	13	0	1	1	0	0	0	0	1	0	0	0	0	4	0	0
Schourek, Peter, Tidewater°	.000	2	4	0	0	0	0	0	0	0	0	0	0	0	0	2	0	0
Schunk, Jerry, Syracuse	.240	26	100	8	24	28	4	0	0	7	1	0	0	3	0	10	1	2
Segui, David, Rochester†	.336	86	307	55	103	137	28	0	2	51	0	5	0	45	4	28	5	4
Sepanek, Robert, Columbus°	.233	45	90	13	21	34	7	0	2	9	1	1	0	17	0	24	0	1
Service, Scott, Scranton W.B.	.400	45	5	0	2	2	0	0	0	0	0	0	0	0	0	2	0	0
Shamburg, Kenneth, Rochester	.333	2	6	1	2	2	0	0	0	0	0	0	0	0	0	1	0	0
Sharts, Stephen, Scranton W.B.°	.250	61	4	1	1	1	0	0	0	0	0	0	0	1	0	0	0	0
Shelby, John, Toledo†	.316	5	19	2	6	7	1	0	0	1	0	0	0	2	0	1	0	0
Shipley, Craig, Tidewater	.000	4	3	1	0	0	0	0	0	0	0	0	0	1	0	1	0	0
Sisk, Douglas, Tidewater	.000	8	2	0	0	0	0	0	0	0	0	0	0	0	0	0	0	0
Snider, Van, Columbus°	.235	127	409	61	96	167	26	0	15	49	1	2	2	35	4	118	7	7
Snyder, Brian, Richmond°	.000	46	2	0	0	0	0	0	0	0	0	0	0	0	0	1	0	0
Soff, Raymond, Tidewater	.000	31	11	0	0	0	0	0	0	0	2	0	0	0	0	3	0	0
Sojo, Luis, Syracuse	.296	75	297	39	88	124	12	3	6	25	3	9	1	14	0	23	10	2
Sparks, Donald, Columbus	.118	16	51	3	6	9	3	0	0	2	0	0	1	2	0	10	0	0
Sprague, Edward, Syracuse	.239	142	519	60	124	217	23	5	20	75	3	4	10	31	1	100	4	2
Stanicek, Peter, Rochester†	.174	28	86	13	15	18	3	0	0	6	1	0	1	12	0	12	0	1
Stanicek, Stephen, Scranton W.B.	.282	127	425	52	120	173	23	0	10	76	0	6	4	58	1	65	2	2
Stankiewicz, Andrew, Columbus	.229	135	446	68	102	127	14	4	1	48	7	4	10	71	1	63	25	8
Stone, Jeffrey, Pawtucket°	.280	112	393	51	110	164	28	1	8	41	4	1	2	31	4	84	25	4
Szekely, Joseph, Syracuse°	.174	50	155	17	27	49	3	2	5	16	4	1	1	10	0	20	1	2
Tackett, Jeffrey, Rochester	.239	108	306	37	73	99	8	3	4	33	3	0	7	47	0	50	4	8
Taylor, Dwight, Richmond°	.255	39	106	17	27	35	1	2	1	11	6	0	1	9	0	20	4	6
Taylor, William, Richmond†	.000	3	2	0	0	0	0	0	0	0	0	0	0	0	0	1	0	0
Thornton, Louis, Tidewater°	.227	109	379	42	86	115	9	4	4	38	3	2	2	10	2	51	13	7
Tomberlin, Andy, Richmond°	.304	80	283	36	86	123	19	3	4	31	4	2	1	39	7	43	11	4
Torve, Kelvin, Tidewater°	.303	115	402	62	122	182	25	1	11	76	0	5	6	56	6	43	9	2
Trautwein, David, Tidewater	.000	51	5	0	0	0	0	0	0	0	1	0	0	0	0	4	0	0
Tremblay, Gary, Pawtucket	.210	44	105	15	22	41	5	1	4	13	1	0	0	12	0	26	0	0

Player and Club	Pct.	G.	AB.	R.	H.	TB.	2B.	3B.	HR.	RBI.	SH.	SF.	HP.	BB.	Int. BB.	SO.	SB.	CS.
Tubbs, Gregory, Richmond	.217	11	23	3	5	5	0	0	0	1	1	0	0	11	0	6	0	2
Turner, Shane, Rochester°	.282	86	209	29	59	69	7	0	1	19	7	2	0	25	2	41	3	5
Turner, Matthew, Richmond	.000	22	1	0	0	0	0	0	0	0	0	0	0	0	0	0	0	0
Upshaw, Lee, Richmond°	.000	5	0	0	0	0	0	0	0	0	1	0	0	0	0	0	0	0
Valera, Julio, Tidewater	.158	24	19	1	3	3	0	0	0	2	1	1	0	2	0	6	0	0
Vatcher, James, Scranton W.B.	.254	55	181	30	46	81	12	4	5	22	1	2	0	32	1	33	1	4
Vaughn, Maurice, Pawtucket°	.295	108	386	62	114	208	26	1	22	72	0	2	6	44	2	87	3	2
Vesling, Donald, Toledo°	.000	35	1	0	0	0	0	0	0	0	0	0	0	0	0	0	0	0
Virgil, Osvaldo, Syracuse	.143	28	84	5	12	14	2	0	0	7	0	1	1	9	1	16	0	0
Wade, Scott, Pawtucket	.231	105	303	34	70	123	12	4	11	41	4	1	5	27	0	97	9	8
Walewander, James, Columbus†	.250	131	368	80	92	119	14	5	1	31	6	4	11	90	1	67	49	13
Walker, Gregory, Rochester°	.303	22	66	14	20	32	6	0	2	11	0	0	3	16	1	15	0	0
Wasinger, Mark, Columbus	.194	25	62	8	12	17	5	0	0	4	3	0	0	14	1	13	0	0
Whited, Edward, Richmond	.248	108	339	55	84	135	22	4	7	33	4	3	7	42	0	70	5	3
Whitehurst, Walter, Tidewater	.000	2	2	0	0	0	0	0	0	0	0	0	0	0	0	1	0	0
Whiten, Mark, Syracuse†	.290	104	390	65	113	182	19	4	14	48	0	4	3	37	5	72	14	6
Wiley, Craig, Toledo†	.167	3	6	0	1	2	1	0	0	1	0	0	0	0	0	1	0	0
Zeihen, Robert, Columbus°	.265	10	34	5	9	10	1	0	0	0	0	0	0	4	0	3	1	0

The following pitchers, listed alphabetically by club, with games in parentheses, had no plate appearances, primarily through use of designated hitters:

COLUMBUS—Adkins, Steven (27); Burns, Britt (1); Chapin, Darrin (6); Clayton, Royal (4); Davidson, Robert (40); Davis, Ronald (10); Eiland, David (29); Green, John (2); Holcomb, Scott (2); Jones, Jimmy (11); Leiter, Mark (30); McCullers, Lance (3); Mills, Alan (17); Mmahat, Kevin (20); Monteleone, Richard (38); Parker, Clayton (3); Pena, Hipolito (9); Smith, Michael (Miss.) (2); Smith, Willie (33); Taylor, Wade (15); Torres, Ricardo (21).

PAWTUCKET—Bast, Steven (25); Bolton, Thomas (4); Curry, Stephen (5); Dalton, Michael (49); Dopson, John (5); Gray, Jeffrey (21); Guante, Cecilio (2); Hetzel, Eric (19); Irvine, Daryl (42); Johnson, Joseph (29); Leister, John (19); Manzanillo, Josias (15); Owen, David (6); Plympton, Jeffrey (11); Rochford, Michael (9); Shikles, Larry (39); Stewart, Hector (40); Trautwein, John (51).

RICHMOND—Czarnik, Christopher (5); Henry, Dwayne (13); Luecken, Richard (8); Ziem, Stephen (7).

ROCHESTER—Aldrich, Jay (30); Bautista, Jose (27); Bell, Eric (27); Boone, Daniel (47); de la Rosa, Francisco (2); Hickey, Kevin (16); Holton, Brian (9); Jones, Michael (8); Kelley, Anthony (2); Linskey, Michael (19); McDonald, Benard (7); McKeon, Joel (24); Mesa, Jose (4); Mitchell, John (8); Mussina, Michael (2); Schilling, Curtis (15); Schwarz, Jeffrey (5); Smith, Michael (Tex.) (29); Stanhope, Chester (4); Tirado, Aristarco (8); Weston, Michael (29); Woodward, Robert (48).

SCRANTON WILKES-BARRE—Boudreaux, Eric (8); Greene, Thomas (1); Mulholland, Terence (1).

SYRACUSE—Blair, William (3); Blohm, Peter (4); Boucher, Denis (17); Buchanan, Robert (24); Cummings, Steven (16); Gilles, Thomas (43); Gozzo, Mauro (34); Jones, Christopher (10); Kilgus, Paul (20); Leiter, Alois (15); Linton, Douglas (26); Loynd, Michael (24); Lysander, Richard (10); MacDonald, Robert (9); Sanchez, Alex (22); Shea, John (40); Wapnick, Steven (11); Williams, Gregory (3); Wishnevski, Robert (9).

TIDEWATER—Glynn, Edward (1); Vasquez, Aguedo (3).

TOLEDO—Aldred, Scott (30); Burtt, Dennis (17); Cooper, David (7); DuBois, Brian (13); Hansen, Michael (15); Holman, Shawn (17); Kinzer, Matthew (15); Link, Robert (25); Lugo, Urbano (29); Nosek, Randall (22); Parker, Clayton (6); Ramos, Jose (31); Rightnowar, Ronald (28); Ritz, Kevin (20); Rivera, Lino (18); Schwabe, Michael (51); Searcy, Stephen (17); Stone, Eric (36).

GRAND SLAM HOME RUNS—Meulens, Stanicek, 2 each; Azocar, Berroa, Cooper, Cuyler, Dorsett, Gibbons, L. Gomez, D. Gonzalez, Hare, Heath, Horn, Michel, Ouellette, Pina, Plantier, Reed, Wade, Whiten, 1 each.

AWARDED FIRST BASE ON CATCHER'S INTERFERENCE—Livingstone 2 (Berger 2); Whited 2 (Agostinelli, Gibbons); Azocar (Mitchell); Lovullo (C. Diaz).

CLUB FIELDING

Club	Pct.	G.	PO.	A.	E.	DP.	PB.	Club	Pct.	G.	PO.	A.	E.	DP.	PB.
Columbus.................	.976	146	3767	1567	130	128	21	Rochester	.972	145	3643	1508	151	169	18
Scranton W.B.	.975	146	3692	1503	135	125	12	Syracuse	.970	145	3671	1513	160	144	10
Richmond	.974	145	3725	1556	139	130	21	Pawtucket	.968	146	3759	1519	174	137	9
Tidewater	.974	146	3693	1543	142	156	13	Toledo.........................	.968	144	3659	1541	174	141	12

Triple Plays—Rochester 2, Tidewater 2, Scranton-Wilkes Barre.

INDIVIDUAL FIELDING
FIRST BASEMEN

°Throws lefthanded.

Player and Club	Pct.	G.	PO.	A.	E.	DP.	Player and Club	Pct.	G.	PO.	A.	E.	DP.
Adduci, Scranton W.-B.°	.997	35	277	24	1	27	Lyden, Columbus	.991	38	326	18	3	33
Alvarez, Toledo	1.000	3	25	1	0	3	Lyons, Tidewater	.944	4	16	1	1	1
Azocar, Columbus°	.988	9	78	6	1	6	J. Maas, Columbus	.938	5	27	3	2	1
Blowers, Columbus..................	.972	4	33	2	1	2	K. Maas, Columbus°	.983	32	219	19	4	19
Brown, Rochester	.973	9	70	2	2	12	McKnight, Rochester	.988	12	75	5	1	8
Cabrera, Richmond	.986	31	257	24	4	15	Meulens, Columbus.................	.976	32	219	21	6	20
Chance, Rochester	1.000	1	1	0	0	0	Michel, Toledo	.971	52	422	17	13	38
Crabbe, Richmond	.980	27	172	20	4	20	Miller, Scranton W.-B.	1.000	2	15	1	0	2
DeLaCruz, Syracuse	.988	21	154	10	2	19	Mizerock, Richmond	1.000	1	6	0	0	0
Denson, Richmond	.993	81	684	38	5	71	Morris, Richmond....................	1.000	1	2	0	0	0
EPPARD, Syracuse°	.991	131	1010	93	10	100	Ouellette, Toledo	.970	7	30	2	1	2
Fishel, Columbus	1.000	7	43	4	0	4	Padget, Rochester	.984	30	229	17	4	24
Freiling, Tidewater	.989	10	89	5	1	4	Sax, Columbus	1.000	3	22	2	0	2
Gibbons, Scranton W.-B.	1.000	2	8	2	0	1	Segui, Rochester°	.996	85	703	62	3	90
Gomez, Rochester	1.000	1	12	1	0	0	Sepanek, Columbus°	.987	41	277	17	4	25
Hare, Toledo°	.967	4	27	2	1	5	Shamburg, Rochester	1.000	2	15	1	0	3
Hoiles, Rochester	.974	11	69	5	2	6	Sparks, Columbus	1.000	2	5	0	0	0
Horn, Rochester°	.933	4	27	1	2	3	Sprague, Syracuse	.955	9	62	2	3	5
Hughes, Tidewater°	.985	22	184	14	3	24	P. Stanicek, Rochester	1.000	5	31	1	0	2
Hunter, Tidewater°	.985	7	63	3	1	4	S. Stanicek, Scranton W.-B.	.988	92	746	64	10	66
Jelic, Tidewater	.992	18	116	8	1	15	Tackett, Rochester	1.000	1	2	0	0	1
Jordan, Scranton W.-B.	.996	25	225	8	1	16	Thornton, Richmond°	.977	5	38	4	1	3
Justice, Richmond°	.875	1	4	3	1	0	Tomberlin, Richmond°	.964	4	26	1	1	3
Kremers, Richmond	1.000	1	8	0	0	0	Torve, Tidewater	.983	100	812	75	15	98
Lancellotti, Pawtucket°	.991	50	429	34	4	39	Tremblay, Pawtucket...............	1.000	1	3	0	0	0
Legg, Scranton W.-B.	1.000	1	7	1	0	0	Vaughn, Pawtucket°	.988	99	828	60	11	77
Leiper, Toledo	.984	7	55	5	1	5	Virgil, Syracuse	1.000	2	14	3	0	1
Leyritz, Columbus	1.000	5	28	1	0	0	Walewander, Columbus	1.000	4	31	2	0	2
Lindeman, Toledo	.989	83	680	44	8	67	Walker, Rochester	.833	1	4	1	1	0
Lovullo, Toledo	.974	6	37	0	1	1	Whited, Richmond	.923	1	10	2	1	1

Triple Plays—Hoiles, Jelic, Jordan, Torve.

SECOND BASEMEN

Player and Club	Pct.	G.	PO.	A.	E.	DP.
Alva, Richmond	.989	71	144	204	4	48
Brown, Rochester	.964	8	13	14	1	4
Crabbe, Richmond	.965	27	50	59	4	14
DeButch, Tidewater	1.000	11	20	23	0	5
DeCillis, Toledo	.922	20	39	55	8	16
DeLaCruz, Syracuse	1.000	1	0	1	0	0
Diaz, Tidewater	.971	21	41	58	3	18
Dowell, Richmond	.979	23	38	57	2	10
Dulin, Rochester	.971	112	218	322	16	103
Escobar, Syracuse	.986	31	63	77	2	23
GARDNER, Tidewater	.988	119	301	330	7	85
Garrison, Syracuse	.915	30	55	64	11	15
Gonzalez, Pawtucket	.975	41	65	92	4	19
Heath, Scranton W.-B.	1.000	3	8	11	0	2
Hinzo, Richmond	.943	16	27	39	4	3
Hulett, Rochester	1.000	10	17	25	0	6
Infante, Richmond	.969	29	52	74	4	19
Legg, Scranton W.-B.	.969	8	15	16	1	3
Leyritz, Columbus	1.000	9	12	17	0	2
Lombardozzi, Toledo	.977	18	31	53	2	12
Lovullo, Toledo	.979	117	235	317	12	73
McDougal, Pawtucket	.955	46	89	121	10	30
McKnight, Rochester	1.000	2	3	2	0	1
Miller, Scranton W.-B.	1.000	1	0	2	0	0
Morandini, Scranton W.-B.	.984	136	271	419	11	89
Naehring, Pawtucket	1.000	4	2	10	0	2
Pankovits, Pawtucket	.970	65	143	146	9	35
Schunk, Syracuse	.982	24	47	62	2	13
Sojo, Syracuse	.970	67	129	194	10	53
Stanicek, Rochester	.955	6	9	12	1	3
Stankiewicz, Columbus	.994	73	138	201	2	41
Turner, Rochester	.973	18	37	34	2	12
Walewander, Columbus	.974	76	151	183	9	30
Wasinger, Columbus	1.000	6	8	14	0	4

Triple Plays—Gardner, Hulett, Morandini.

THIRD BASEMEN

Player and Club	Pct.	G.	PO.	A.	E.	DP.
Alva, Richmond	1.000	6	3	8	0	1
Blowers, Columbus	.944	50	31	87	7	6
Brown, Rochester	.910	31	16	45	6	2
Chance, Rochester	1.000	2	1	1	0	0
Cooper, Pawtucket	.938	121	94	240	22	22
Crabbe, Richmond	.950	45	20	93	6	14
DeButch, Tidewater	1.000	17	2	35	0	4
DeCillis, Toledo	.750	3	1	2	1	0
DeLaCruz, Syracuse	.882	6	4	11	2	1
Dowell, Richmond	1.000	3	4	4	0	2
Fishel, Columbus	1.000	1	1	1	0	0
Flaherty, Pawtucket	1.000	1	0	2	0	0
Gardner, Tidewater	.905	8	3	16	2	1
Gomez, Rochester	.934	119	80	203	20	26
A. Gonzalez, Pawtucket	.950	14	6	13	1	1
D. Gonzalez, Tidewater	.932	52	31	106	10	3
Heath, Scranton W.-B.	.891	39	26	56	10	4
Hulett, Rochester	1.000	2	3	4	0	0
Infante, Scranton W.-B.	.957	39	25	86	5	5
Jelic, Tidewater	.906	52	29	86	12	4
Kiefer, Tidewater	.922	20	20	39	5	8
Kutcher, Pawtucket	.938	4	4	11	1	2
Lara, Tidewater	1.000	6	1	7	0	2
Legg, Scranton W.-B.	.974	38	16	58	2	12
Leiper, Toledo	.887	28	21	65	11	6
Leyritz, Columbus	.896	52	25	78	12	10
Lindeman, Toledo	1.000	5	5	8	0	0
Livingstone, Toledo	.950	101	66	181	13	13
Lombardozzi, Toledo	1.000	1	0	1	0	0
Lovullo, Toledo	.896	20	8	35	5	4
Meulens, Columbus	.906	15	6	23	3	2
Miller, Scranton W.-B.	.935	43	23	63	6	4
Morris, Richmond	1.000	8	6	6	0	0
Naehring, Pawtucket	.915	13	14	29	4	2
Runge, Syracuse	.850	12	10	24	6	2
Schunk, Syracuse	1.000	1	3	1	0	0
Sparks, Columbus	.939	15	5	26	2	0
Sprague, Syracuse	.915	132	93	240	31	25
Stankiewicz, Columbus	1.000	1	0	1	0	0
Tackett, Rochester	1.000	2	1	1	0	0
Turner, Rochester	1.000	7	2	4	0	0
Vatcher, Scranton W.-B.	.926	12	6	19	2	2
Walewander, Columbus	.941	24	7	41	3	3
Wasinger, Columbus	.950	11	5	14	1	0
WHITED, Richmond	.959	100	73	182	11	17

Triple Play—Gomez.

SHORTSTOPS

Player and Club	Pct.	G.	PO.	A.	E.	DP.
Allaire, Toledo	.970	31	38	91	4	22
Alva, Richmond	.959	26	32	61	4	10
Bell, Rochester	.944	80	131	240	22	58
Bogar, Tidewater	.936	32	57	89	10	24
Brown, Rochester	.949	11	16	21	2	6
Cooper, Pawtucket	1.000	1	2	4	0	0
Crabbe, Richmond	.923	17	19	41	5	7
DeButch, Tidewater	.964	38	49	111	6	25
DeCillis, Toledo	1.000	1	2	2	0	1
A. Diaz, Tidewater	.929	19	23	42	5	9
M. Diaz, Tidewater	.956	28	38	92	6	23
Dowell, Richmond	.900	3	5	13	2	1
Escobar, Syracuse	.968	47	67	114	6	24
Fryman, Toledo	.940	86	128	277	26	62
Gardner, Tidewater	.938	14	21	39	4	13
Heath, Scranton W.-B.	1.000	5	4	5	0	0
Hulett, Rochester	.889	2	2	6	1	3
Kiefer, Tidewater	.971	13	26	41	2	8
Kutcher, Pawtucket	.959	31	53	86	6	20
Lara, Tidewater	1.000	11	11	29	0	8
Legg, Scranton W.-B.	1.000	3	2	5	0	1
Lofton, Rochester	.906	12	7	22	3	5
Lombardozzi, Toledo	.959	32	50	89	6	15
McDougal, Pawtucket	.901	51	82	146	25	37
McKnight, Rochester	.953	40	54	130	9	28
Naehring, Pawtucket	.963	66	110	201	12	33
Rodriguez, Columbus	.982	68	90	232	6	39
Rosario, Scranton W.-B.	.944	143	206	396	36	76
ROSSY, Richmond	.960	106	144	290	18	59
Runge, Syracuse	.977	96	127	299	10	58
Sojo, Syracuse	1.000	8	9	18	0	6
Stankiewicz, Columbus	.974	68	99	197	8	41
Turner, Rochester	.967	18	28	31	2	12
Walewander, Columbus	.892	20	27	56	10	10

Triple Plays—Bell, Bogar, DeButch, Rosario.

OUTFIELDERS

Player and Club	Pct.	G.	PO.	A.	E.	DP.
Adduci, Scranton W.-B.*	.914	48	51	2	5	0
Agostinelli, Scranton W.-B.	1.000	4	4	0	0	0
Azocar, Columbus*	.981	82	150	4	3	0
Bell, Syracuse	.979	104	220	9	5	0
Bellino, Scranton W.-B.	1.000	1	2	1	0	0
Berroa, Richmond	.968	89	200	10	7	3
Brower, Columbus	.979	45	90	2	2	0
Brown, Rochester	1.000	14	20	0	0	0
Carr, Tidewater	1.000	19	40	3	0	0
Chance, Rochester	.984	124	231	10	4	2
Clark, Toledo	1.000	15	19	0	0	0
Contreras, Rochester*	.959	54	113	5	5	0
Crabbe, Richmond	1.000	2	1	0	0	0
Cuevas, Tidewater*	1.000	11	18	0	0	0
Cuyler, Toledo	.977	124	290	4	7	2
DeButch, Tidewater	.833	4	5	0	1	0
DeLaCruz, Syracuse	.967	50	110	6	4	1
Diaz, Tidewater	.978	86	132	1	3	1
Ducey, Syracuse	.955	119	262	13	13	4
Fishel, Columbus	.989	79	83	5	1	1
Ford, Scranton W.-B.	.991	52	107	2	1	0
Freeman, Toledo*	.948	70	88	4	5	1
Garrison, Syracuse	1.000	1	1	0	0	0
Hare, Toledo*	.967	104	171	4	6	0
Harris, Rochester	1.000	4	7	0	0	0
Heath, Scranton W.-B.	1.000	16	26	2	0	1
Hithe, Rochester	1.000	64	93	2	0	1
Hood, Richmond	.974	114	294	10	8	2
Hughes, Tidewater*	.965	51	78	4	3	1
Hunter, Richmond*	.970	33	63	2	2	0
L. Jones, Richmond	.962	84	143	7	6	2
R. Jones, Scranton W.-B.	.979	28	46	1	1	1
Justice, Richmond*	.952	11	19	1	1	0
KNABENSHUE, Scr. W.-B.	.991	121	203	7	2	1
Komminsk, Rochester	.952	24	38	2	2	1
Lancellotti, Pawtucket*	1.000	17	32	2	0	1
Lara, Tidewater	1.000	1	1	0	0	0
Leiper, Toledo	1.000	32	63	2	0	1
Leyritz, Columbus	1.000	4	3	0	0	0
Lindeman, Toledo	1.000	21	24	1	0	0
Lusader, Toledo*	.973	73	140	5	4	1
Maas, Columbus	.988	50	81	3	1	0

OUTFIELDERS—Continued

Player and Club	Pct.	G.	PO.	A.	E.	DP.
Marshall, Pawtucket	1.000	3	1	0	0	0
McDougal, Pawtucket	1.000	2	1	0	0	0
McKnight, Rochester	.956	51	79	7	4	0
Meadows, Scranton W.-B.°	.990	46	99	3	1	1
Meulens, Columbus	.972	88	134	7	4	1
Michel, Toledo	.913	19	18	3	2	1
D. Miller, Rochester	1.000	14	18	6	0	3
K. Miller, Scranton W.-B.	.962	105	171	5	7	1
Monell, Tidewater	1.000	2	1	0	0	0
Munoz, Syracuse	.950	61	110	4	6	1
Nixon, Rochester	.974	73	145	2	4	0
Padget, Rochester	.971	22	32	1	1	0
Pankovits, Pawtucket	.969	53	124	2	4	0
Pederson, Syracuse°	.938	19	28	2	2	0
Pina, Pawtucket	.983	108	217	17	4	4
Plantier, Pawtucket	.948	113	245	8	14	2
Reed, Tidewater	.983	103	222	11	4	3
Runge, Syracuse	1.000	1	1	0	0	0
Sanchez, Tidewater	.966	79	137	7	5	1
Sanders, Columbus°	1.000	22	49	1	0	0
Segui, Rochester°	1.000	1	1	0	0	0
Shelby, Toledo	1.000	5	17	0	0	0
Snider, Columbus	.986	121	207	7	3	4
Stanicek, Scranton W.-B.	.968	14	28	2	1	0
Stone, Pawtucket	.979	88	182	7	4	3
Taylor, Richmond°	.983	28	54	4	1	1
Thornton, Tidewater	.966	98	166	7	6	2
Tomberlin, Richmond°	.982	77	154	8	3	0
Torve, Tidewater	1.000	18	27	2	0	0
Tubbs, Richmond	.944	10	17	0	1	0
Turner, Rochester	.962	36	50	1	2	0
Vatcher, Scranton W.-B.	1.000	43	82	5	0	0
Wade, Pawtucket	.969	72	150	6	5	3
Whiten, Syracuse	.966	92	158	14	6	2
Zeihen, Columbus°	.889	10	24	0	3	0

CATCHERS

Player and Club	Pct.	G.	PO.	A.	E.	DP.	PB.
Agostinelli, Scranton W.-B.	.976	62	334	26	9	1	3
Brown, Rochester	1.000	3	9	0	0	0	0
Cabrera, Richmond	1.000	1	12	1	0	0	1
Cerone, Columbus	.929	3	13	0	1	0	0
Clark, Toledo	.987	23	137	13	2	6	2
Datz, Columbus	.989	21	80	7	1	1	2
Davis, Toledo	1.000	3	20	0	0	0	1
Diaz, Syracuse	.983	77	421	37	8	5	7
Dorsett, Columbus	.982	86	548	37	11	6	13
Dziadkowiec, Syracuse	1.000	1	6	2	0	0	0
Eberle, Rochester	.986	19	63	6	1	0	2
Flaherty, Pawtucket	.983	98	509	57	10	4	5
Gibbons, Scranton W.-B.	.975	62	369	28	10	5	4
Graves, Tidewater	.846	2	9	2	2	1	2
Hoiles, Rochester	.986	35	199	8	3	2	2
Kremers, Richmond	.988	57	301	40	4	2	10
Leyritz, Columbus	.875	2	7	0	1	0	0
Liddell, Tidewater	.979	73	384	34	9	4	8
Lyons, Tidewater	.987	47	275	22	4	2	2
Maldonado, Richmond	1.000	4	23	2	0	0	1
Mann, Richmond	.983	63	353	49	7	7	8
Marzano, Pawtucket	1.000	21	100	12	0	2	2
Mercado, Tidewater	1.000	22	133	12	0	0	1
D. Miller, Rochester	1.000	3	12	3	0	0	3
K. Miller, Scranton W.-B.	1.000	1	2	0	0	0	0
Mizerock, Richmond	1.000	27	148	13	0	5	1
Myers, Syracuse	1.000	3	14	0	0	0	0
Nieto, Scranton W.-B.	1.000	35	189	15	0	1	5
Olson, Rochester	1.000	3	17	2	0	0	0
OUELLETTE, Toledo	.989	77	401	40	5	7	3
Ramos, Columbus	1.000	1	2	1	0	0	0
Rivers, Syracuse	1.000	1	1	0	0	0	0
Roca, Tidewater	1.000	23	116	9	0	0	0
Rowland, Toledo	.964	58	305	39	13	5	6
Sax, Columbus	.988	52	308	21	4	7	6
Sprague, Syracuse	.952	6	16	4	1	1	0
Szekely, Syracuse	.979	46	258	19	6	8	2
Tackett, Rochester	.981	103	570	62	12	11	11
Tremblay, Pawtucket	.974	43	198	26	6	3	2
Virgil, Syracuse	.986	20	133	11	2	1	1
Wiley, Toledo	1.000	3	13	1	0	0	0

PITCHERS

Player and Club	Pct.	G.	PO.	A.	E.	DP.
Adkins, Columbus°	.909	27	1	19	2	1
Alba, Richmond°	1.000	12	0	3	0	0
Aldred, Toledo°	.815	29	4	18	5	1
Aldrich, Rochester	.875	30	2	5	1	0
Avery, Richmond°	1.000	13	4	12	0	0
Barton, Tidewater°	.833	16	2	3	1	0
Bast, Pawtucket°	.975	25	7	32	1	1
Bautista, Rochester	1.000	27	14	12	0	2
Bell, Rochester°	1.000	27	11	34	0	3
Blair, Syracuse	1.000	3	2	2	0	0
Bolton, Pawtucket°	.667	4	1	1	1	0
Boone, Rochester°	.981	47	14	37	1	3
Boucher, Syracuse°	.964	17	5	22	1	0
Boudreaux, Scranton W.-B.	1.000	8	1	3	0	1
K. Brown, Tidewater°	.947	26	12	24	2	3
M. Brown, Rochester	1.000	1	0	1	0	0
Buchanan, Syracuse°	.923	24	2	10	1	1
Buonantony, Scranton W.-B.	1.000	8	0	2	0	0
Burns, Columbus°	1.000	1	1	2	0	0
Burtt, Toledo	.875	17	1	6	1	0
Castillo, Richmond°	1.000	5	2	2	0	0
Childress, Tidewater	1.000	27	6	8	0	1
Clayton, Columbus	1.000	4	0	1	0	0
Cooper, Toledo	1.000	7	0	1	0	0
Cummings, Syracuse	.800	16	5	7	3	1
Curry, Pawtucket	1.000	5	1	2	0	0
Czarnik, Richmond	1.000	5	1	1	0	0
Dalton, Pawtucket°	.783	49	5	13	5	2
Davidson, Columbus	.967	40	9	20	1	1
Davis, Columbus	1.000	10	1	3	0	1
DeButch, Tidewater	1.000	1	0	1	0	0
DeJesus, Scranton W.-B.	1.000	10	4	6	0	0
Dopson, Pawtucket	1.000	5	3	3	0	1
DuBois, Toledo°	.944	13	6	11	1	2
Eiland, Columbus	.983	28	17	40	1	6
Freeman, 7 SWB- 7 Rich.	1.000	14	8	6	0	0
Frohwirth, Scranton W.-B.	1.000	67	8	20	0	1
Gilles, Syracuse	.950	43	4	15	1	0
Givens, Tidewater°	.789	15	2	13	4	0
Gomez, Richmond°	1.000	4	0	1	0	0
Gozzo, Syracuse	.955	34	16	5	1	3
Gray, Pawtucket	1.000	21	2	4	0	0
Greene, 19 Rich.-1 SWB	1.000	20	9	17	0	0
Grimsley, Scranton W.-B.	.911	22	19	22	4	3
Habyan, Columbus	1.000	36	9	18	0	0
Hansen, Toledo	1.000	15	2	12	0	1
Henry, Richmond	1.000	13	0	3	0	0
Hernandez, Tidewater	.969	27	12	19	1	1
Hetzel, Pawtucket	.813	19	6	7	3	0
Hickey, Rochester°	1.000	16	2	5	0	0
Holman, Toledo	1.000	17	2	5	0	1
Holton, Rochester	1.000	9	1	0	0	0
Innis, Tidewater	1.000	40	1	10	0	0
Irvine, Pawtucket	.900	42	3	15	2	3
JOHNSON, Pawtucket	1.000	29	19	28	0	4
C. Jones, Syracuse	1.000	10	1	3	0	0
J. Jones, Columbus	1.000	11	4	17	0	2
M. Jones, Rochester°	1.000	8	1	1	0	0
Kelley, Rochester	.750	2	0	3	1	0
Kerfeld, Richmond	.750	15	4	2	2	0
Kilgus, Syracuse°	1.000	20	13	32	0	4
Kinzer, Toledo	.750	15	0	3	1	1
Laskey, Richmond	.864	5	14	3	1	
A. Leiter, Syracuse°	.900	15	1	8	1	1
M. Leiter, Columbus	.864	30	3	16	3	0
Lilliquist, Richmond°	1.000	5	1	0	0	1
Link, Toledo	.750	25	1	2	1	0
Linskey, Rochester°	.905	19	4	15	2	0
Linton, Syracuse	.955	26	13	29	2	1
Loynd, Syracuse	1.000	24	7	12	0	0
Luecken, Richmond	1.000	8	0	1	0	0
Lugo, Toledo	1.000	29	4	7	0	0
Lysander, Syracuse	1.000	10	3	2	0	1
MacDonald, Syracuse°	1.000	9	0	0	1	0
Machado, Tidewater	1.000	16	1	2	0	0
Madrid, Scranton W.-B.	.944	16	8	9	1	0
Malone, Scranton W.-B.	.889	26	4	4	1	0
Manzanillo, Pawtucket	.938	15	6	9	1	0
Marak, Richmond	.897	32	11	15	3	0
Mauser, Scranton W.-B.	1.000	16	10	10	0	4
McDonald, Rochester	.800	7	3	5	2	1
McElroy, Scranton W.-B.°	1.000	57	1	13	0	1
McKeon, Rochester°	1.000	24	3	4	0	0
Mejia, Tidewater	1.000	18	10	8	0	1
Mercer, Richmond°	.833	12	1	4	1	0
Mesa, Rochester	1.000	4	1	4	0	0
Mills, Columbus	1.000	17	4	4	0	1
Mitchell, Rochester	.778	8	2	5	2	1
Mmahat, Columbus°	.968	20	6	24	1	1

PITCHERS—Continued

Player and Club	Pct.	G.	PO.	A.	E.	DP.
Monteleone, Columbus	.923	38	4	8	1	0
Moore, Scranton W.-B.	.917	35	11	22	3	1
Mulholland, Scranton W.-B.*	1.000	1	0	1	0	0
Musselman, Tidewater*	.929	10	4	9	1	1
Mussina, Rochester	1.000	2	1	2	0	0
Nezelek, Richmond	.889	25	9	15	3	1
Nielsen, Tidewater	1.000	17	4	13	0	1
Noles, Scranton W.-B.	1.000	26	3	3	0	1
Nosek, Toledo	.905	22	8	11	2	0
Olwine, Richmond*	1.000	25	2	6	0	0
Owen, Pawtucket*	1.000	6	0	1	0	0
Parker, 3 Col.-6 Tol.	1.000	9	2	10	0	0
Pederson, Syracuse*	1.000	1	1	0	0	0
Pena, Columbus*	1.000	9	0	1	0	0
Plummer, Tidewater	1.000	17	3	3	0	0
Plympton, Pawtucket	.800	11	1	3	1	0
Polley, Richmond*	.911	36	6	35	4	1
Ramos, Toledo*	.900	31	2	7	1	0
Reynoso, Richmond	1.000	4	1	5	0	0
Richards, Richmond	.971	30	8	25	1	1
Rightnowar, Toledo	1.000	28	1	3	0	0
Ritchie, Scranton W.-B.*	.900	20	2	7	1	0
Ritz, Toledo	.926	20	5	20	2	4
Rivera, Toledo	1.000	18	1	2	0	0
Rochford, Pawtucket*	.923	9	4	8	1	0
Samuels, Scranton W.-B.	1.000	35	0	8	0	0
Sanchez, Syracuse	.938	22	5	10	1	1
Scanlan, Scranton W.-B.	.925	23	13	24	3	1
Schilling, Rochester	1.000	15	9	8	0	0
Schourek, Tidewater*	1.000	2	2	4	0	1
Schwabe, Toledo	.957	51	4	18	1	1

Player and Club	Pct.	G.	PO.	A.	E.	DP.
Schwarz, Rochester	1.000	5	1	0	0	0
Searcy, Toledo*	1.000	17	2	20	0	2
Service, Scranton W.-B.	1.000	45	5	9	0	1
Sharts, Scranton W.-B.*	1.000	61	7	11	0	0
Shea, Syracuse*	1.000	40	2	15	0	2
Shikles, Pawtucket	.967	39	7	22	1	0
Sisk, Tidewater	.875	8	1	6	1	1
M. Smith (Miss.), Columbus	1.000	2	0	1	0	0
M. Smith (Tex.), Rochester	.909	29	3	7	1	1
W. Smith, Columbus	1.000	33	4	4	0	0
Snyder, Richmond*	.941	46	4	12	1	2
Soff, Tidewater	.958	31	5	18	1	1
Stanhope, Rochester	1.000	4	1	2	0	0
Stewart, Pawtucket*	.900	40	4	5	1	0
Stone, Toledo	1.000	36	2	5	0	0
Wa. Taylor, Columbus	.923	14	7	17	2	0
Wi. Taylor, Richmond	1.000	2	0	1	0	0
Tirado, Rochester	1.000	8	3	2	0	0
Torres, Columbus	1.000	21	6	5	0	0
D. Trautwein, Tidewater	1.000	51	1	12	0	0
J. Trautwein, Pawtucket	.969	51	5	26	1	5
Turner, Richmond	1.000	22	3	3	0	0
Upshaw, Richmond*	1.000	5	0	4	0	0
Valera, Tidewater	1.000	24	9	13	0	0
Vesling, Toledo*	.935	35	6	23	2	0
Weston, Rochester	.964	29	7	20	1	1
Whitehurst, Tidewater	1.000	2	0	5	0	0
Williams, Rochester	1.000	3	0	1	0	0
Wishnevski, Syracuse	.909	9	5	5	1	0
Woodward, Rochester	.833	48	2	8	2	1
Ziem, Richmond	1.000	7	1	0	0	0

The following players did not have any fielding statistics at the positions indicated or appeared only as a designated hitter, pinch-hitter or pinch-runner: Blohm, p; Blowers, 2b; Cabrera, of; Chapin, p; DeLaCruz, p; DeLaRosa, p; M. Diaz, 3b; Escobar, 3b; Glynn, p; A. Gonzalez, ss; J. Green, p; R. Green, of; Guante, p; Holcomb, p; Jelic, c; Lancellotti, p; Lovullo, of; Marzano, 3b; McCullers, p; McDougal, 1b; Morandini, ss; Morris, of; Rayford, c; Robidoux, dh, ph; Schunk, ss; Shipley, ph, pr; P. Stanicek, p; S. Stanicek, p; Tackett, p; S. Turner, p; Vasquez, p; Wapnick, p.

CLUB PITCHING

Club	ERA.	G.	CG.	ShO.	Sv.	IP.	H.	R.	ER.	HR.	HB.	BB.	Int. BB.	SO.	WP.	Bk.
Columbus	3.28	146	31	16	38	1255.2	1129	524	458	66	25	465	13	935	54	11
Tidewater	3.42	146	21	15	44	1231.0	1186	551	468	69	41	446	20	880	63	18
Richmond	3.62	145	16	7	41	1241.2	1197	576	500	92	30	521	40	825	86	19
Rochester	3.89	145	20	9	36	1214.1	1206	621	525	110	38	431	6	820	68	18
Syracuse	3.94	145	25	14	26	1223.2	1165	622	536	108	42	559	22	785	56	19
Scranton Wilkes-Barre	4.10	146	8	5	39	1230.2	1096	641	560	96	54	575	29	862	61	14
Toledo	4.24	144	9	7	35	1219.2	1184	678	575	99	39	571	23	849	62	19
Pawtucket	4.65	146	20	4	31	1253.0	1318	741	648	136	44	507	38	775	63	23

PITCHERS RECORDS

(Leading Qualifiers for Earned-Run Average Leadership—117 or More Innings)

*Throws lefthanded.

Pitcher—Club	W.	L.	Pct.	ERA.	G.	GS.	CG.	GF.	ShO.	Sv.	IP.	H.	R.	ER.	HR.	HB.	BB.	Int. BB.	SO.	WP.
Marak, Richmond	9	8	.529	2.49	32	16	5	6	0	0	148.0	130	49	41	9	2	50	0	75	6
Boone, Rochester*	11	5	.688	2.60	47	9	3	24	1	8	121.0	96	44	35	8	1	30	0	65	7
Eiland, Columbus	16	5	.762	2.87	27	26	11	0	3	0	175.1	155	63	56	8	1	32	0	96	2
Adkins, Columbus*	15	7	.682	2.90	27	27	6	0	2	0	177.0	153	72	57	9	5	98	0	138	4
Kilgus, Syracuse*	6	8	.429	2.94	20	17	7	0	1	0	125.2	116	47	41	10	5	39	4	75	7
Valera, Tidewater	10	10	.500	3.02	24	24	9	0	2	0	158.0	146	66	53	12	5	39	3	133	7
Davidson, Columbus	5	8	.385	3.37	40	12	2	12	0	5	128.1	134	58	48	7	2	25	2	69	3
Linton, Syracuse	10	10	.500	3.40	26	26	8	0	3	0	177.1	174	77	67	14	8	67	3	113	4
Polley, Richmond*	4	7	.364	3.53	36	15	1	6	1	0	135.0	121	66	53	10	2	48	8	64	5
K. Brown, Tidewater*	10	6	.625	3.55	26	24	3	0	0	0	134.1	138	71	53	4	2	60	0	109	3

Departmental Leaders: G—Frohwirth, 67; W—Eiland, 16; L—Bast, 16; Pct.—Weston, .917; GS—Aldred, 29; CG—Eiland, 11; GF—Frohwirth, 52; ShO—Eiland, Linton, Wa. Taylor, 3; Sv.—Frohwirth, 21; IP—Linton, 177.1; H—Johnson, 213; R—Johnson, 107; ER—Johnson, 98; HR—Johnson, 24; HB—Johnson, 10; BB—Adkins, 98; IBB—Polley, 8; SO—Hernandez, 157; WP—Grimsley, 18.

(All Pitchers—Listed Alphabetically)

Pitcher—Club	W.	L.	Pct.	ERA.	G.	GS.	CG.	GF.	ShO.	Sv.	IP.	H.	R.	ER.	HR.	HB.	BB.	Int. BB.	SO.	WP.
Adkins, Columbus*	15	7	.682	2.90	27	27	6	0	2	0	177.0	153	72	57	9	5	98	0	138	4
Alba, Richmond*	1	3	.250	3.25	12	2	0	4	0	0	27.2	9	12	10	1	1	19	1	19	1
Aldred, Toledo*	6	15	.286	4.90	29	29	2	0	0	0	158.0	145	93	86	16	4	81	1	133	10
Aldrich, Rochester	4	1	.800	5.37	30	1	0	15	0	3	53.2	72	38	32	8	1	7	0	34	4
Avery, Richmond*	5	5	.500	3.39	13	13	3	0	0	0	82.1	85	35	31	7	2	21	0	69	5
Barton, Tidewater*	0	0	.000	5.82	16	0	0	4	0	0	21.2	27	17	14	1	1	10	0	23	1
Bast, Pawtucket*	7	16	.304	5.65	25	23	2	2	0	0	146.2	158	97	92	21	6	64	4	91	11
Bautista, Rochester	7	8	.467	4.06	27	13	3	4	0	2	108.2	115	51	49	10	4	15	0	50	3
Bell, Rochester*	9	6	.600	4.86	27	27	3	0	0	0	148.0	168	90	80	16	9	65	0	90	11
Blair, Syracuse	0	2	.000	4.74	3	3	1	0	0	0	19.0	20	13	10	1	0	8	1	6	0
Blohm, Syracuse	0	1	.000	7.20	4	0	0	2	0	0	5.0	5	7	4	1	0	3	0	4	0
Bolton, Pawtucket*	1	0	1.000	3.86	4	2	0	1	0	0	11.2	9	6	5	2	0	7	0	8	2
Boone, Rochester*	11	5	.688	2.60	47	9	3	24	1	8	121.0	96	44	35	8	1	30	0	65	7
Boucher, Syracuse*	8	5	.615	3.85	17	17	2	0	1	0	107.2	100	52	46	7	2	37	2	80	6
Boudreaux, Scranton W.-B.	1	2	.333	9.45	8	1	0	4	0	0	13.1	23	16	14	1	1	8	3	9	0
K. Brown, Tidewater*	10	6	.625	3.55	26	24	3	0	0	0	134.1	138	71	53	4	2	60	0	109	3
M. Brown, Rochester	0	0	.000	0.00	1	0	0	1	0	0	1.0	0	0	0	0	0	2	0	0	0
Buchanan, Syracuse*	5	3	.625	3.52	24	6	1	14	0	5	64.0	63	32	25	4	0	25	0	21	4
Buonantony, Scranton W.-B.	0	0	.000	5.40	8	0	0	2	0	0	11.2	11	8	7	0	1	11	2	10	0

Pitcher—Club	W.	L.	Pct.	ERA.	G.	GS.	CG.	GF.	ShO.	Sv.	IP.	H.	R.	ER.	HR.	HB.	BB.	Int. BB.	SO.	WP.
Burns, Columbus*	0	1	.000	12.00	1	1	0	0	0	0	3.0	5	4	4	1	0	3	0	3	0
Burtt, Toledo	2	6	.250	5.18	17	6	0	4	0	0	48.2	50	29	28	11	2	16	1	33	2
Castillo, Richmond*	3	1	.750	2.52	5	4	1	1	1	0	25.0	14	7	7	5	0	6	0	27	1
Chapin, Columbus	0	1	.000	7.27	6	0	5	0	2	2	8.2	10	8	7	0	0	6	0	8	1
Childress, Tidewater	7	5	.583	3.45	27	3	0	10	0	0	62.2	54	26	24	6	1	23	0	37	3
Clayton, Columbus	1	2	.333	3.81	4	4	0	0	0	0	26.0	33	12	11	1	0	7	0	15	1
Cooper, Toledo	1	1	.500	9.00	7	0	0	4	0	0	7.0	11	8	7	3	0	7	0	6	0
Cummings, Syracuse	5	3	.625	3.11	16	13	4	0	0	0	81.0	76	31	28	3	1	37	0	34	1
Curry, Pawtucket	0	1	.000	11.00	5	3	0	1	0	0	9.0	21	11	11	2	0	2	0	5	0
Czarnik, Richmond	0	1	.000	7.00	5	0	0	1	0	0	9.0	13	7	7	1	1	3	0	8	2
Dalton, Pawtucket*	7	4	.636	2.55	49	2	1	21	0	5	99.0	94	42	28	6	3	22	2	49	2
Davidson, Columbus	5	8	.385	3.37	40	12	2	12	0	5	128.1	134	58	48	7	2	25	2	69	3
Davis, Columbus	0	1	.000	4.76	10	0	0	3	0	1	11.1	6	6	6	2	1	6	1	6	0
DeButch, Tidewater	0	1	.000	16.20	1	0	0	1	0	0	1.2	3	3	3	1	0	1	1	2	0
DeJesus, Scranton W.-B.	1	4	.200	3.38	10	10	1	0	0	0	56.0	41	30	21	2	2	39	0	45	6
DeLaCruz, Syracuse	0	0	.000	9.00	1	0	0	1	0	0	1.0	3	7	1	2	0	3	0	1	0
DeLaRosa, Rochester	0	0	.000	0.00	2	0	0	1	0	0	0.2	0	0	0	0	0	1	0	1	0
Dopson, Pawtucket	2	1	.667	4.91	5	5	0	0	0	0	22.0	28	12	12	3	1	8	0	13	0
DuBois, Toledo*	5	4	.556	2.71	13	10	2	2	1	0	69.2	67	27	21	6	2	26	1	47	2
Eiland, Columbus	16	5	.762	2.87	27	26	11	0	3	0	175.1	155	63	56	8	1	32	0	96	2
Freeman, 7 SWB-7 Rich.	4	7	.364	4.84	14	14	1	0	1	0	74.1	72	43	40	8	1	41	0	56	4
Frohwirth, Scranton W.-B.	9	7	.563	3.04	67	0	0	52	0	21	83.0	76	34	28	3	8	32	3	56	0
Gilles, Syracuse	3	3	.500	2.02	43	0	0	25	0	5	71.1	58	21	16	6	2	21	2	44	4
Givens, Tidewater*	4	6	.400	4.12	15	15	0	0	0	0	83.0	99	45	38	9	2	39	0	53	9
Glynn, Tidewater*	0	0	.000	0.00	1	0	0	0	0	0	1.0	2	0	0	0	0	0	0	1	0
Gomez, Richmond*	1	1	.500	8.80	4	4	0	0	0	0	15.1	19	16	15	1	0	10	1	8	3
Gozzo, Syracuse	3	8	.273	3.58	34	10	0	19	0	7	98.0	87	46	39	5	3	44	3	62	3
Gray, Pawtucket	0	0	.000	3.41	21	0	0	8	0	1	31.2	20	14	12	4	1	7	1	35	3
Green, Columbus	0	0	.000	0.00	2	0	0	0	0	0	3.1	2	0	0	0	0	1	0	0	0
Greene, 19 Rich.-1 SWB.	5	8	.385	3.49	20	19	2	0	0	0	116.0	93	49	45	5	0	67	3	69	8
Grimsley, Scranton W.-B.	8	5	.615	3.93	22	22	0	0	0	0	128.1	111	68	56	7	4	78	1	99	18
Guante, Pawtucket	0	0	.000	0.00	2	0	0	1	0	0	5.0	1	0	0	0	0	2	1	4	0
Habyan, Columbus	7	7	.500	3.21	36	11	1	11	0	6	112.0	99	52	40	9	1	30	4	77	5
Hansen, Toledo	5	7	.417	4.76	15	13	1	0	0	0	75.2	89	47	40	5	2	24	0	52	5
Henry, Richmond	1	1	.500	2.33	13	0	0	6	0	2	27.0	12	7	7	1	1	16	1	36	1
Hernandez, Tidewater	12	11	.522	3.79	27	27	6	0	2	0	173.1	170	79	73	10	1	54	0	157	9
Hetzel, Pawtucket	6	5	.545	3.64	19	18	3	0	0	0	108.2	85	51	44	7	4	74	1	90	10
Hickey, Rochester	2	1	.667	5.79	16	0	0	8	0	3	23.1	31	15	15	2	0	7	1	28	1
Holcomb, Columbus*	0	0	.000	0.00	2	0	0	0	0	0	0.0	0	2	2	0	0	3	0	0	1
Holman, Toledo	2	1	.667	7.52	17	0	0	3	0	0	20.1	27	22	17	3	3	14	0	10	0
Holton, Rochester	1	4	.200	9.19	9	1	1	2	0	0	15.2	26	16	16	3	1	6	0	18	0
Innis, Tidewater	5	2	.714	1.71	40	0	0	33	0	19	52.2	34	11	10	1	3	17	5	42	0
Irvine, Pawtucket	2	5	.286	3.24	42	0	0	30	0	12	50.0	47	24	18	1	3	19	5	35	1
Johnson, Pawtucket	6	7	.462	5.16	29	27	2	2	0	1	171.0	213	107	98	24	10	35	3	70	7
C. Jones, Syracuse	0	0	.000	3.98	10	0	0	6	0	1	20.1	22	10	9	4	0	4	0	19	3
J. Jones, Columbus	5	2	.714	2.34	11	11	3	0	1	0	73.0	46	20	19	1	5	35	1	78	2
M. Jones, Rochester*	2	3	.400	6.00	8	5	0	2	0	0	30.0	36	23	20	6	0	14	0	27	1
Kelley, Rochester	1	0	1.000	5.14	2	1	0	0	0	0	7.0	7	4	4	1	0	6	0	2	0
Kerfeld, Richmond	2	0	1.000	3.38	15	1	0	6	0	0	21.1	22	10	8	0	0	16	3	24	2
Kilgus, Syracuse*	6	8	.429	2.94	20	17	7	0	1	0	125.2	116	47	41	10	5	39	4	75	6
Kinzer, Toledo	0	3	.000	2.50	15	0	0	13	0	8	18.0	15	7	5	1	2	8	0	25	1
Lancellotti, Pawtucket*	0	0	.000	27.00	1	0	0	1	0	0	1.0	3	3	3	1	0	0	0	0	0
Laskey, Richmond	6	4	.600	2.79	49	1	0	33	0	14	87.0	83	32	27	6	2	29	5	60	3
Leister, Pawtucket	2	10	.167	5.78	19	17	2	2	0	1	95.0	114	65	61	11	4	39	1	47	4
A. Leiter, Syracuse*	3	8	.273	4.62	15	14	1	1	1	0	78.0	59	43	40	4	5	68	0	69	5
M. Leiter, Columbus	9	4	.692	3.60	30	14	2	6	1	1	122.2	114	56	49	5	1	27	0	115	7
Lilliquist, Richmond*	4	0	1.000	2.57	5	5	1	0	0	0	35.0	31	11	10	3	0	11	0	24	0
Link, Toledo	1	1	.500	2.78	25	0	0	17	0	8	32.1	29	15	10	1	0	19	5	19	1
Linskey, Rochester*	7	9	.438	3.58	19	18	2	0	2	0	110.2	116	60	44	8	2	28	0	54	3
Linton, Syracuse	10	10	.500	3.40	26	26	8	0	3	0	177.1	174	77	67	14	8	67	3	113	4
Loynd, Syracuse	4	8	.333	3.68	24	8	0	7	0	1	85.2	68	39	35	7	6	34	1	65	3
Luecken, Richmond	1	1	.500	1.35	8	0	0	6	0	4	13.1	11	3	2	0	8	4	15	0
Lugo, Toledo	2	2	.500	3.93	29	6	1	10	0	1	66.1	56	30	29	7	4	27	1	43	1
Lysander, Syracuse	0	1	.000	6.92	10	0	0	7	0	0	13.0	18	10	10	2	0	7	0	8	2
MacDonald, Syracuse*	0	2	.000	5.40	9	0	0	5	0	2	8.1	4	5	5	1	0	9	0	6	0
Machado, Tidewater	0	1	.000	1.69	16	0	0	13	0	8	21.1	16	7	4	1	1	8	0	24	1
Madrid, Scranton Wilkes-Barre	3	8	.273	4.65	16	15	0	0	0	0	93.0	91	52	48	8	1	40	2	56	3
Malone, Scranton Wilkes-Barre	3	4	.571	6.39	26	11	0	3	0	0	76.0	47	57	54	9	7	78	0	79	8
Manzanillo, Pawtucket	4	7	.364	5.55	15	15	5	0	0	0	82.2	75	57	51	9	2	45	0	77	8
Marak, Richmond	9	8	.529	2.49	32	16	5	6	0	0	148.0	130	49	41	9	2	50	0	75	6
Mauser, Scranton Wilkes-Barre	5	7	.417	3.66	16	16	4	0	1	0	98.1	75	48	40	10	3	34	1	54	4
McCullers, Columbus	0	0	.000	0.00	3	0	0	1	0	0	3.0	0	0	0	0	0	2	0	2	1
McDonald, Rochester	3	3	.500	2.86	7	7	0	0	0	0	44.0	33	18	14	4	2	21	1	37	4
McElroy, Scranton W.-B.*	6	8	.429	2.72	57	1	0	26	0	7	76.0	62	24	23	6	5	34	4	78	3
McKeon, Rochester*	4	2	.667	4.68	24	1	1	10	0	3	42.1	45	25	22	2	3	17	1	35	5
Mejia, Tidewater	6	3	.667	4.96	18	15	0	2	0	0	81.2	87	53	45	6	4	42	0	40	6
Mercker, Richmond*	5	4	.556	3.55	12	10	0	1	0	1	58.1	60	30	23	1	1	27	1	69	5
Mesa, Rochester	1	2	.333	2.42	4	4	0	0	0	0	26.0	21	11	7	2	0	12	0	23	3
Mills, Columbus	3	3	.500	3.38	17	0	0	13	0	6	29.1	22	11	11	0	2	14	0	30	2
Mitchell, Rochester	5	0	1.000	1.57	8	7	3	0	2	0	46.0	39	9	8	3	1	9	0	15	0
Mmahat, Columbus*	11	5	.688	3.76	20	20	1	0	0	0	115.0	99	52	48	5	2	61	0	81	9
Monteleone, Columbus	4	4	.500	2.24	18	0	0	27	0	9	64.1	51	17	16	4	1	23	4	60	3
Moore, Scranton W.-B.	3	7	.300	3.72	35	12	1	5	0	0	101.2	97	48	42	8	4	28	3	45	2
Mulholland, Scranton W.-B.*	0	1	.000	3.00	1	1	0	0	0	0	6.0	9	4	2	0	0	2	0	2	0
Musselman, Tidewater*	4	3	.571	3.51	10	10	1	0	1	0	56.1	60	24	22	2	4	16	1	31	4
Mussina, Rochester	0	0	.000	1.35	2	2	0	0	0	0	13.1	8	2	2	2	0	4	0	15	0
Nezelek, Richmond	4	9	.308	5.13	25	14	2	3	0	0	80.2	101	52	46	7	7	26	1	39	12
Nielsen, Tidewater	1	4	.200	4.24	17	1	0	4	0	3	40.1	41	23	19	4	1	14	1	12	2
Noles, Scranton W.-B.	3	2	.600	3.35	26	0	0	17	0	6	37.2	31	15	14	1	2	14	2	18	1
Nosek, Toledo	5	8	.385	5.19	22	19	0	1	0	0	109.1	112	70	63	4	4	66	0	55	10
Olwine, Richmond*	3	1	.750	5.40	25	0	0	16	0	5	28.1	30	18	17	3	1	15	1	21	6
Owen, Pawtucket*	3	2	.600	4.71	6	6	2	0	0	0	42.0	40	23	22	4	1	19	0	26	0
Parker, 3 Col.-6 Tol.	2	5	.286	3.33	9	9	2	0	1	0	54.0	58	23	20	3	0	13	0	34	3

Pitcher—Club	W.	L.	Pct.	ERA.	G.	GS.	CG.	GF.	ShO.	Sv.	IP.	H.	R.	ER.	HR.	HB.	BB.	Int. BB.	SO.	WP.
Pederson, Syracuse*	0	0	.000	9.00	1	0	0	1	0	0	1.0	2	1	1	0	0	1	0	0	0
Pena, Columbus*	1	0	1.000	12.60	9	0	0	3	0	0	5.0	8	7	7	2	1	4	1	1	0
Plummer, Tidewater	2	2	.500	3.25	17	4	0	6	0	1	52.2	46	21	19	3	2	23	3	28	0
Plympton, Pawtucket	1	0	1.000	0.00	11	0	0	8	0	3	17.1	10	0	0	0	1	11	4	11	0
Polley, Richmond*	4	7	.364	3.53	36	15	1	6	1	0	135.0	121	66	53	10	2	48	8	64	5
Ramos, Toledo*	0	1	.000	4.22	31	0	0	9	0	1	32.0	40	19	15	3	0	14	3	16	2
Reynoso, Richmond	3	1	.750	2.25	4	3	0	0	0	0	24.0	26	7	6	3	0	7	0	15	0
Richards, Richmond	6	9	.400	4.55	30	26	0	0	0	0	140.1	159	83	71	12	3	73	5	56	12
Rightnowar, Toledo	4	5	.444	4.74	28	0	0	16	0	6	38.0	46	24	20	5	0	10	3	28	0
Ritchie, Scranton W.-B.*	4	3	.571	4.15	20	13	1	1	1	0	82.1	75	46	38	7	2	28	1	47	2
Ritz, Toledo	3	6	.333	5.22	20	18	0	1	0	0	89.2	93	68	52	5	9	59	3	57	6
Rivera, Toledo	0	3	.000	3.07	18	0	0	11	0	1	29.1	27	12	10	1	2	13	0	23	1
Rochford, Pawtucket*	3	3	.500	2.70	8	1	0	0	0	0	43.1	36	19	13	6	1	13	0	31	1
Samuels, Tidewater*	3	3	.500	2.83	35	1	0	18	0	2	41.1	39	15	13	2	5	13	3	29	4
Sanchez, Syracuse	5	9	.357	5.71	22	22	1	0	0	0	112.0	111	77	71	15	4	79	1	65	5
Scanlan, Scranton W.-B.	8	11	.421	4.85	23	23	1	0	0	0	130.0	128	79	70	11	7	59	3	74	3
Schilling, Rochester	4	4	.500	3.92	15	14	1	0	0	0	87.1	95	46	38	10	2	25	1	83	0
Schourek, Tidewater*	1	0	1.000	2.57	2	2	1	0	1	0	14.0	9	4	4	0	1	5	0	14	0
Schwabe, Toledo	6	5	.545	3.83	51	2	0	15	0	5	108.0	112	58	46	4	2	22	2	69	7
Schwarz, Rochester	0	0	.000	7.11	5	1	0	0	0	0	12.2	10	10	10	1	0	19	0	4	4
Searcy, Toledo*	10	5	.667	2.92	17	17	2	0	2	0	104.2	71	40	34	5	0	52	1	105	3
Service, Scranton W.-B.	5	4	.556	4.76	45	9	0	11	0	2	96.1	96	56	51	10	5	44	1	94	4
Sharts, Scranton W.-B.*	6	2	.750	2.99	61	4	0	15	0	3	96.1	76	33	32	8	1	25	3	58	4
Shea, Syracuse*	8	5	.615	3.64	40	0	0	26	0	3	81.2	83	45	33	9	4	40	4	58	6
Shikles, Pawtucket	8	12	.400	4.99	39	17	2	5	1	0	148.0	170	99	82	19	6	48	7	65	5
Sisk, Tidewater*	5	1	.833	2.81	8	6	0	1	0	0	41.2	39	16	13	1	1	10	0	20	0
M. Smith (Tex.), Rochester	9	6	.600	4.96	29	20	1	3	1	0	123.1	118	76	68	14	8	73	1	112	12
M. Smith (Miss.), Columbus	0	0	.000	0.00	2	0	0	1	0	0	3.2	5	1	0	0	1	0	4	0	0
W. Smith, Columbus	3	1	.750	6.23	33	0	0	21	0	7	34.2	38	24	24	3	0	29	0	47	6
Snyder, Richmond*	4	1	.800	2.48	46	0	0	28	0	12	58.0	54	19	16	2	4	20	4	49	2
Soff, Tidewater	6	4	.600	2.38	31	12	1	3	0	0	109.2	90	31	29	2	2	32	0	63	3
Stanhope, Rochester	1	0	1.000	4.09	4	0	0	3	0	0	11.0	7	5	5	1	0	4	0	5	1
Stanicek, Scranton W.-B.	0	0	.000	0.00	2	0	0	2	0	0	2.1	3	0	0	0	0	0	0	1	0
Stewart, Pawtucket*	4	4	.500	4.31	40	0	0	17	0	4	64.2	75	36	31	5	0	32	3	54	3
Stone, Toledo	2	4	.333	3.95	36	7	0	20	0	4	68.1	52	35	30	2	1	63	1	57	6
Tackett, Rochester	0	0	.000	0.00	2	0	0	2	0	0	2.0	1	0	0	0	0	0	0	4	0
Wa. Taylor, Columbus	6	4	.600	2.19	14	14	4	0	3	0	98.2	91	25	24	3	3	30	0	57	0
Wi. Taylor, Richmond	0	0	.000	0.00	2	0	0	0	0	0	2.2	4	0	0	0	0	0	0	0	0
Tirado, Rochester	1	0	1.000	7.43	8	0	0	3	0	1	13.1	13	11	11	1	1	8	0	6	0
Torres, Columbus	0	2	.000	4.46	21	3	0	12	0	1	42.1	37	24	21	5	0	21	0	34	3
D. Trautwein, Tidewater	1	5	.167	3.80	51	0	0	28	0	6	71.0	75	35	30	4	4	35	3	49	10
J. Trautwein, Pawtucket	6	7	.462	5.87	51	3	0	27	0	4	104.1	119	75	68	11	1	60	6	64	6
M. Turner, Richmond	2	3	.400	3.86	22	1	0	11	0	2	42.0	44	20	18	6	2	16	1	36	7
S. Turner, Richmond	0	0	.000	0.00	1	0	0	0	0	0	1.0	0	0	0	0	0	0	0	0	0
Upshaw, Richmond*	0	3	.000	6.17	5	5	0	0	0	0	23.1	35	19	16	5	0	8	1	16	4
Valera, Tidewater	10	10	.500	3.02	24	24	9	0	2	0	158.0	146	66	53	12	5	39	3	133	7
Vasquez, Tidewater	1	0	1.000	4.91	3	0	0	2	0	1	3.2	4	2	2	0	0	4	0	3	1
Vesling, Toledo*	3	6	.333	4.36	35	11	0	9	0	1	109.1	105	61	53	15	2	44	1	51	5
Wapnick, Syracuse	0	1	.000	5.06	11	1	0	6	0	2	16.0	16	9	9	2	1	6	0	19	1
Weston, Rochester	11	1	.917	1.98	29	12	2	13	0	6	109.1	93	36	24	3	0	22	0	58	3
Whitehurst, Tidewater	1	0	1.000	9.00	2	2	0	0	0	0	9.0	7	2	2	0	1	0	0	10	0
Williams, Syracuse	0	1	.000	10.00	3	0	0	0	0	0	9.0	15	10	10	1	0	4	0	8	1
Wishnevski, Syracuse	2	5	.286	6.66	9	8	0	0	0	0	48.2	65	40	36	6	0	23	1	28	2
Woodward, Rochester	6	1	.857	3.00	48	2	0	34	0	9	63.0	56	31	21	5	3	37	1	52	6
Ziem, Richmond	0	0	.000	3.60	7	0	0	1	0	1	10.0	13	4	4	1	1	5	0	7	0

BALKS—Bast, 12; A. Leiter, 6; Bautista, Searcy, Valera, 5 each; Aldred, Boone, DeJesus, Loynd, Ritz, 4 each; Dopson, Greene, Grimsley, Hernandez, Kilgus, Mmahat, Nezelek, Polley, Reynoso, Shea, Wa. Taylor, 3 each; Alba, K. Brown, Eiland, Freeman, Hetzel, Malone, Nosek, Owen, Plummer, Schilling, Michael Smith (Rochester), Vesling, Brown-Smith-Woodward, 2 each; Adkins, Aldrich, Bell, Burtt, Curry, Davidson, Gomez, Gozzo, Hansen, Holton, Innis, Irvine, Johnson, Linton, Lysander, Madrid, Marak, Mejia, Mercker, Moore, Nielsen, Noles, Sharts, Sisk, W. Smith, Soff, D. Trautwein, J. Trautwein, M. Turner, 1 each.

COMBINATION SHUTOUTS—Adkins-Mills, Clayton-Smith, Eiland-Torres, Jones-Davis-Torres, Leiter-Habyan, Mmahat-Torres, Columbus; Dopson-Dalton, Manzanillo-Trautwein, Rochford-Dalton-Gray-Irvine, Pawtucket; Avery-Laskey, Nezelek-Olwine, Richards-Laskey, Richmond; Bautista-Aldrich-Boone, Schilling-Boone, Woodward-Smith-Boone-M. Jones, Rochester; Malone-Sharts-McElroy-Frohwirth, Scanlan-Noles, Service-McElroy-Frohwirth, Scranton-Wilkes Barre; Boucher-Gilles 2, Boucher-Gozzo, Buchanan-Gozzo, Gozzo-Wapnick, Linton-Shea, Loynd-Jones, Sanchez-Shea-Wapnick, Syracuse; Brown-Machado 2, Brown-Childress-Innis, Brown-Plummer-Innis, Hernandez-Innis, Mejia-Innis, Musselman-Childress, Sisk-Machado, Sisk-Samuels-Machado, Tidewater; Aldred-Holman-Kinzer, Aldred-Stone, Ritz-Schwabe, Toledo.

NO-HIT GAMES—Ritchie, Scranton-Wilkes Barre, defeated Syracuse, 1-0 (eight innings, first game), May 25; Boone, Rochester, defeated Syracuse, 2-0 (second game), July 23.

Mexican League

CLASS AAA

CHAMPIONSHIP WINNERS IN PREVIOUS YEARS

1955—Mexico City Tigers* .... .539	1971—Jalisco§ .... .558	1981—Mexico City Reds .... .615
1956—Mexico City Reds .... .692	Saltillo .... .593	Reynosa .... .492
1957—Yucatan .... .567	1972—Saltillo .... .636	1982—Ciudad Juarez x .... .570
Mex. C. Reds (2nd)† .... .550	Cordoba§ .... .541	Mexico City Tigers .... .508
1958—Nuevo Laredo .... .625	1973—Saltillo .... .656	1983—Campeche z .... .614
1959—Poza Rica .... .575	Mexico City Reds x .... .590	Ciudad Juarez .... .535
Mex. C. Reds (3rd)† .... .507	1974—Jalisco .... .627	1984—Yucatan z .... .560
1960—Mexico City Tigers .... .538	Mexico City Reds x .... .551	Ciudad Juarez .... .509
1961—Veracruz .... .575	1975—Tampico x .... .541	1985—Mexico City Reds z .... .606
1962—Monterrey .... .592	Cordoba .... .649	Nuevo Laredo .... .5275
1963—Puebla .... .606	1976—Mexico City Reds x .... .543	1986—Puebla z .... .682
1964—Mexico City Reds .... .586	Union Laguna .... .547	Monclova .... .598
1965—Mexico City Tigers .... .590	1977—Mexico City Reds x .... .623	1987—Mexico City Reds z .... .605
1966—Mexico City Tigers‡ .... .614	Nuevo Laredo x .... .507	Monterrey .... .536
Mexico City Reds .... .571	1978—Aguascalientes x .... .589	1988—Mexico City Reds z .... .646
1967—Jalisco .... .607	Union Laguna .... .523	Nuevo Laredo .... .602
1968—Mexico City Reds .... .586	1979—Saltillo .... .704	1989—Nuevo Laredo z .... .621
1969—Reynosa .... .591	Puebla x .... .628	Yucatan .... .539
1970—Aguila§ .... .580	1980—No champion y	
Mexico City Reds .... .607		

*Defeated Nuevo Laredo, two games to none, in playoff for pennant. †Won four-team playoff. ‡Won split-season playoff. §League divided into Northern, Southern divisions; won two-team playoff. xLeague divided into Northern, Southern zones; sub-divided into Eastern, Western divisions, won eight-team playoff. yA players strike on July 1 forced the cancellation of the regular season and playoff schedule. zLeague divided into Northern, Southern zones; four clubs from each zone qualified for postseason play. Won final series for league championship.

STANDING OF CLUBS AT CLOSE OF SEASON
NORTHERN ZONE

Club	N.L.	U.L.	M.S.	Mva.	Sal.	M.I.	S.L.	M.T.	M.R.	Leo.	Cam.	Yuc.	Ags.	Tab.	W.	L.	T.	Pct.	G.B.
Nuevo Laredo	..	8	7	9	10	12	11	3	2	2	5	3	3	6	81	50	1	.618	....
Union Laguna	5	..	7	9	9	6	4	4	3	3	5	6	3	7	71	54	2	.568	7
Monterrey Sultans	7	7	..	4	8	12	9	3	2	5	5	2	4	70	62	0	.560	11½
Monclova	7	3	10	..	6	10	7	2	2	5	4	2	3	2	63	66	1	.488	17
Saltillo	4	9	6	8	..	8	10	2	1	2	3	3	6	64	68	0	.485	17½
Monterrey Industrials	2	5	4	4	6	..	12	2	3	2	3	2	3	1	49	82	1	.374	32
San Luis	3	7	5	7	4	2	..	2	1	2	2	2	2	3	42	87	2	.326	38

SOUTHERN ZONE

Club	N.L.	U.L.	M.S.	Mva.	Sal.	M.I.	S.L.	M.T.	M.R.	Leo.	Cam.	Yuc.	Ags.	Tab.	W.	L.	T.	Pct.	G.B.
Mexico City Tigers	3	2	3	4	4	4	8	..	11	8	5	7	8	6	73	50	1	.593	....
Mexico City Reds................	4	2	4	4	7	4	5	..	9	4	9	7	9	72	54	1	.571	2½
Leon	4	3	4	5	5	4	6	4	..	9	5	12	9	74	57	0	.565	3
Campeche	5	3	1	1	4	2	4	6	7	5	..	10	6	12	66	57	1	.537	7
Yucatan	3	1	5	4	3	4	4	6	4	9	6	..	8	8	65	64	2	.504	11
Aguascalientes	3	1	4	3	3	3	4	2	7	4	7	6	..	7	54	69	1	.439	19
Tabasco	0	3	2	4	4	5	4	7	5	2	5	6	..	52	76	3	.406	23½

Playoffs—Union Laguna defeated Monterrey Sultans, four games to two; Nuevo Laredo defeated Monclova, four games to three; Leon defeated Mexico City Reds, four games to one; Campeche defeated Mexico City Tigers, four games to two. Union Laguna defeated Nuevo Laredo, four games to two, in Northern Zone finals; Leon defeated Campeche, four games to two, in Southern Zone finals. Leon defeated Union Laguna, four games to one, in final series to capture league championship.

(Compiled by Ana Luisa Talarico, League Statistician, Mexico, D.F.)

CLUB BATTING

Club	Pct.	G.	AB.	R.	OR.	H.	TB.	2B.	3B.	HR.	RBI.	SH.	SF.	HP.	BB.	Int. BB.	SO.	SB.	CS.	LOB.
Mexico City Tigers ...	.298	123	3939	646	534	1172	1574	182	23	58	581	85	40	54	421	39	508	97	66	874
Leon	.296	131	4224	656	565	1249	1777	196	34	88	594	48	35	28	408	40	560	93	61	886
Aguascalientes	.295	124	3685	687	775	1087	1505	147	32	69	519	48	30	36	389	29	464	43	57	900
Mexico City Reds......	.291	127	3659	679	590	1063	1519	178	34	70	513	24	35	27	368	22	522	89	31	905
Saltillo	.290	124	4226	604	630	1227	1709	182	39	74	578	71	45	35	535	69	574	91	75	950
Union Laguna	.286	127	3821	626	559	1092	1543	187	27	70	492	64	33	38	406	45	537	38	33	892
Nuevo Laredo	.282	132	3987	631	482	1125	1574	129	25	90	531	47	24	32	492	51	510	72	55	963
Monterrey Sultans ...	.280	132	4100	591	547	1148	1634	197	32	75	512	68	28	32	486	39	607	100	70	963
Yucatan	.280	130	3643	616	534	1020	1516	168	20	96	501	43	26	31	458	46	628	41	30	984
Campeche	.279	124	4394	567	540	1225	1727	179	19	95	547	56	33	28	473	48	530	98	57	856
Monterrey Ind'als.....	.277	132	3342	504	690	926	1248	149	40	31	351	26	22	15	311	28	476	42	57	938
San Luis	.267	131	3539	542	767	945	1381	141	36	26	426	46	28	33	408	32	647	65	48	916
Monclova	.267	130	3981	586	589	1062	1431	164	35	45	463	83	43	28	469	38	682	79	55	952
Tabasco	.264	131	3700	433	566	976	1249	127	19	36	349	47	33	26	295	24	522	44	35	954

INDIVIDUAL BATTING
(Leading Qualifiers for Batting Championship—356 or More Plate Appearances)

*Bats lefthanded. †Switch-hitter.

Player and Club	Pct.	G.	AB.	R.	H.	TB.	2B.	3B.	HR.	RBI.	SH.	SF.	HP.	BB.	Int. BB.	SO.	SB.	CS.
Castaneda, Nick, Yucatan	.388	104	330	67	128	224	24	3	22	80	0	2	1	90	19	59	0	1
Mangham, Eric, Mexico City Tigers	.385	97	361	83	139	182	17	4	6	48	6	2	8	41	2	36	50	25
Davis, Trench, Saltillo	.380	127	498	84	189	245	33	4	5	50	2	5	1	56	9	32	20	16

Player and Club	Pct.	G.	AB.	R.	H.	TB.	2B.	3B.	HR.	RBI.	SH.	SF.	HP.	BB.	Int. BB.	SO.	SB.	CS.
Brown, Todd, Monclova	.374	101	348	78	130	218	24	4	19	76	0	8	2	52	10	55	19	4
Smith, Gregory, Saltillo	.372	121	452	73	168	244	19	3	17	102	0	6	0	46	15	38	32	19
Garbey, Barbaro, Mexico City Tigers	.362	120	423	63	153	214	23	1	12	90	1	7	5	46	12	48	1	1
Aikens, Willie, Leon	.358	130	419	83	150	247	32	1	21	106	0	8	2	101	20	61	0	2
Johnson, Roy, Campeche	.346	118	416	81	144	257	35	0	26	95	0	4	3	63	13	59	2	2
Stockstill, David, Union Laguna	.341	127	451	76	154	239	30	2	17	109	4	9	2	72	21	42	2	2
Sanchez, Alejandro, San Luis	.337	108	392	80	132	250	24	5	28	79	0	3	8	41	12	95	15	5

Departmental Leaders: G—Aguilera, Navarrete, Ge. Sanchez, 132; AB—R. Vizcarra, 525; R—Fernandez, 113; H—Davis, 189; TB—Johnson, 257; 2B—Johnson, 35; 3B—Blocker, Fernandez, 11; HR—Al. Sanchez, 28; RBI—Stockstill, 109; SH—Camacho, Wong, 19; SF—H. Estrada, Machiria, Stockstill, 9; HP—Abril, 11; BB—Castro, 112; IBB—Ortiz, 27; SO—R. Moreno, 109; SB—Cole, 56; CS—Mangham, 25.

(All Players—Listed Alphabetically)

Player and Club	Pct.	G.	AB.	R.	H.	TB.	2B.	3B.	HR.	RBI.	SH.	SF.	HP.	BB.	Int. BB.	SO.	SB.	CS.
Abrego, Jesus, Nuevo Laredo	.258	91	283	40	73	87	9	1	1	17	1	1	3	34	3	34	4	5
Abril, Ramon, Union Laguna	.292	119	411	65	120	135	13	1	0	28	18	4	11	27	1	19	10	3
Aganza, Ruben, Monclova	.154	9	13	1	2	2	0	0	0	1	0	0	0	0	0	1	0	0
Agramon, Antonio, Saltillo	.198	52	111	16	22	34	5	2	1	15	3	1	0	11	0	30	0	1
Aguilar, Enrique, Monterrey Sultans	.316	127	462	72	146	203	24	3	9	59	2	4	3	55	6	31	6	4
Aguilera, Antonio, Monterrey Sultans	.305	132	465	93	142	209	30	8	7	40	8	2	7	67	5	61	48	18
Aikens, Willie, Leon	.358	130	419	83	150	247	32	1	21	106	0	8	2	101	20	61	0	2
Almeida, Shamar, Saltillo	.000	2	3	0	0	0	0	0	0	0	0	0	0	0	0	2	0	0
Almodobar, Juan Francisco, Mon. Sul.	.222	62	126	15	28	41	7	0	2	11	3	0	0	17	1	22	1	4
Almodobar, Ricardo, M. C. Tigers	.258	116	314	42	81	97	12	2	0	36	14	2	2	26	0	35	8	11
Alvarez, Hector, Mexico City Tigers	.279	123	441	57	123	150	20	2	1	52	10	1	7	30	3	46	10	9
Alvarez, Heriberto, Yucatan	.295	111	349	49	103	150	12	7	7	43	10	2	6	22	1	52	3	4
Alvarez, Juan Carlos, Yucatan	.093	31	75	3	7	9	0	1	0	4	2	1	1	3	0	28	0	0
Alyea, Brant, Tabasco	.364	11	44	6	16	23	2	1	1	7	0	0	0	4	1	9	0	0
Amador, Arturo, Nuevo Laredo	.323	13	31	4	10	11	1	0	0	4	0	0	1	0	0	7	1	1
Aparicio, Miguel A., Yucatan	.000	10	15	0	0	0	0	0	0	1	0	0	0	0	0	4	0	1
Arce, Francisco Javier, Saltillo	.279	109	348	40	97	140	19	3	6	51	3	4	5	52	7	51	2	4
Arevalo, Guadalupe, Aguascalientes	.261	27	46	7	12	15	1	1	0	8	0	2	1	2	1	6	1	1
Arias, Everardo, Mexico City Tigers	.263	33	19	9	5	6	1	0	0	3	1	0	0	1	0	4	2	1
Arredondo, Luis, Monclova	.270	29	37	5	10	12	2	0	0	1	0	0	0	3	0	10	1	1
Arzate, Martin, Leon	.232	91	237	35	55	61	6	0	0	14	6	2	0	27	0	27	3	1
Avila, Ruben, Union Laguna	.260	99	277	36	72	100	9	2	5	29	6	1	1	32	2	69	2	1
Avina, Reyes, Leon	.375	44	40	13	15	20	5	0	0	4	0	0	0	6	1	12	1	1
Baca, Manuel, Aguascalientes	.270	108	378	51	102	152	12	1	12	61	2	2	4	29	3	58	2	5
Banuelos, Fidel, Union Laguna	.312	41	77	15	24	37	3	2	2	9	2	0	1	11	1	20	0	1
Barajas, Mario, Yucatan	.236	81	225	29	53	71	12	3	0	14	5	1	1	24	0	49	6	4
Barranca, German, Monclova	.400	2	5	0	2	2	0	0	0	0	0	0	0	0	0	0	1	0
Barrera, Jesus Antonio, Campeche	.228	80	237	30	54	67	7	3	0	16	5	0	0	24	0	16	5	3
Barrera, Nelson, Mexico City Reds	.278	124	464	61	129	219	26	2	20	82	0	5	6	35	9	64	6	1
Bellazetin, Jose Juan, M. C. Tigers	.304	93	293	61	89	122	20	2	3	37	5	3	3	73	9	22	5	5
Beltran, Gerardo, Mexico City Reds	.409	16	22	4	9	13	1	0	1	4	0	0	2	0	5	0	0	0
Beristain, Gregorio, Mon. Sultans	.038	38	26	6	1	1	0	0	0	0	0	0	0	4	0	7	0	0
Blocker, Terry, Leon	.310	121	451	77	140	198	21	11	5	74	1	4	0	34	3	48	21	6
Bobadilla, Manuel, Saltillo	.250	58	144	24	36	49	3	2	2	19	1	1	1	23	4	16	2	1
Bocardo, Manuel, Monclova	.212	22	33	2	7	12	2	0	1	6	1	0	1	6	2	3	0	0
Brown, Darrell, Monterrey Industrials	.322	45	180	30	58	69	8	0	1	12	3	1	0	13	0	12	9	7
Brown, Todd, Monclova	.374	101	348	78	130	219	24	4	19	76	0	8	2	52	10	55	19	4
Buenrostro, Jose Luis, Leon	.174	26	23	4	4	6	0	1	0	4	0	0	0	1	0	7	0	0
Burke, Norberto, Yucatan	.248	124	423	51	105	177	19	1	17	82	0	3	2	41	1	52	2	3
Bustamante, Miguel Angel, M. C. T.	.213	82	122	24	26	28	2	0	0	10	7	0	0	27	0	32	5	1
Camacho, Adulfo, Mexico City Tigers	.291	103	313	65	91	122	16	3	3	53	19	3	8	65	1	57	7	2
Camargo, Alonso, Mexico City Reds	.265	40	113	14	30	41	6	1	1	12	0	1	1	9	1	23	0	2
Cangas, Rosendo, Mexico City Reds	.161	23	31	2	5	7	2	0	0	1	1	0	0	2	0	5	0	0
Cano, Guadalupe, Tabasco	.283	23	60	7	17	20	3	0	0	11	0	1	0	7	0	9	0	1
Cantu, Gerardo, Saltillo	.175	22	40	2	7	8	1	0	0	2	1	0	1	4	0	14	0	0
Cartaya, Joel, Tabasco	.261	26	88	11	23	27	2	1	0	6	1	1	3	5	0	6	2	1
Castaneda, Nick, Yucatan	.388	104	330	67	128	224	24	3	22	80	0	2	1	90	19	59	0	1
Castaneda, Rafael, Mexico City Tigers	.158	53	38	6	6	6	0	0	0	1	0	0	0	5	0	7	1	0
Castelan, Miguel Angel, Mon. Ind.	.269	116	391	35	105	126	12	3	1	32	2	3	0	22	3	56	17	15
Castillo, Raul, Tabasco	.253	54	150	21	38	51	6	2	1	10	4	0	1	9	0	30	3	2
Castro, Eddie, Saltillo	.308	124	399	93	123	224	24	1	25	91	1	2	7	112	11	91	5	5
Cavia, Jesus, San Luis	.286	8	7	1	2	2	0	0	0	1	0	0	0	1	0	3	0	0
Cazarin, Manuel, Leon	.329	117	423	51	139	191	25	0	9	73	6	6	3	23	2	46	7	4
Cepeda, Alejandro, Monclova	.179	54	106	12	19	21	2	0	0	5	3	0	1	6	0	10	0	0
Cervera, Francisco, Nuevo Laredo	.143	19	14	3	2	4	2	0	0	2	0	0	0	2	0	6	1	0
Chavez, Guadalupe, Leon	.000	1	1	0	0	0	0	0	0	0	0	0	0	0	0	0	0	0
Chavez, Heriberto, Tabasco	.167	30	18	2	3	4	1	0	0	0	1	0	0	2	0	3	0	1
Clayton, Leonardo, Monclova	.224	124	361	48	81	120	14	2	7	41	3	7	1	66	5	70	8	5
Cole, Mike, Campeche	.336	123	452	91	152	171	15	2	0	34	6	3	8	64	4	34	56	20
Contreras, Cuitlahuac, Union Laguna	.176	62	91	8	16	26	7	0	1	12	0	0	1	8	2	24	0	1
Cosey, Donald Ray, Tabasco	.190	30	100	4	19	23	4	0	0	12	0	1	0	5	2	14	2	0
Cruz, Fernando, Union Laguna	.221	72	181	20	40	64	6	0	6	23	1	3	2	25	0	31	1	2
Cruz, Luis Alfonso, Union Laguna	.293	127	475	62	139	219	29	3	15	76	1	2	7	25	7	61	3	3
Daut, Manuel, Monclova	.261	91	238	31	62	84	11	1	3	28	5	2	3	20	1	66	6	3
Davis, Trench, Saltillo	.380	127	498	84	189	245	33	4	5	50	2	5	1	56	9	32	20	16
DeLeon, Luis, Mexico City Tigers	1.000	1	1	0	1	1	0	0	0	0	0	0	0	0	0	0	0	0
Delgado, Tomas, Monterrey Sultans	.296	71	186	30	55	79	10	1	4	29	1	2	1	18	0	34	0	2
DeLosSantos, Carlos E. Tabasco	.183	75	142	12	26	30	4	0	0	9	5	2	3	21	1	21	1	2
Diaz, Luis Fernando, Nuevo Laredo	.311	104	367	61	114	157	13	6	6	46	5	3	2	46	5	70	9	8
Dominguez, David, San Luis	.272	126	445	60	121	170	21	2	8	63	2	2	0	46	2	75	2	2
Douglas, Arthur, Tabasco	.220	30	109	10	24	36	3	0	3	7	0	1	0	10	0	28	6	4
Elizondo, Fernando, Aguascalientes	.323	110	415	63	134	166	18	1	4	56	8	2	1	38	1	30	4	7
Espinoza, Antonio, San Luis	.284	99	296	39	84	117	11	2	6	37	7	2	3	28	0	62	10	12
Esquer, Ramon, Leon	.292	127	438	86	128	166	12	10	2	36	11	4	4	51	0	58	23	7
Estrada, Francisco, Leon	.193	23	57	3	11	12	1	0	0	4	1	1	1	3	0	5	0	0
Estrada, Hector, Mexico City Reds	.296	110	409	47	121	173	18	2	10	69	0	9	4	8	1	64	4	2
Estrada, Roberto, Tabasco	.287	116	422	58	121	148	15	3	2	37	6	1	4	29	0	51	10	4

Player and Club	Pct.	G.	AB.	R.	H.	TB.	2B.	3B.	HR.	RBI.	SH.	SF.	HP.	BB.	Int. BB.	SO.	SB.	CS.
Felice, Jason, Union Laguna	.268	40	123	15	33	55	7	0	5	18	1	0	0	24	0	27	1	2
Fernandez, Daniel, Mexico City Reds	.328	123	445	113	146	201	24	11	3	61	8	3	2	87	2	56	43	6
Flores, Jose Humberto, San Luis	.246	20	57	4	14	16	2	0	0	1	3	0	0	6	0	13	0	3
Gainey, Ty, Mexico City Reds	.400	36	135	22	54	99	14	2	9	53	0	1	0	14	0	33	3	2
Garbey, Barbaro, Mexico City Tigers	.362	120	423	63	153	214	23	1	12	90	1	7	5	46	12	48	1	1
Garcia, Carlos M., San Luis	.213	56	178	31	38	53	6	0	3	14	2	1	2	30	0	30	1	1
Garcia, Cornelio, Yucatan	.290	40	145	32	42	53	5	0	2	19	2	1	1	29	1	33	9	3
Garcia, Jorge Luis, Mon. Industrials	.000	1	1	0	0	0	0	0	0	0	0	0	0	0	0	0	0	0
Garcia, Jose Luis, Monterrey Ind.	.256	86	227	34	58	88	10	4	4	20	2	0	6	40	0	51	2	4
Garcia, Juan Manuel, Aguascalientes	.296	94	243	40	72	90	7	4	1	30	6	1	4	39	7	13	8	9
Garcia, Martin, San Luis	.264	107	314	28	83	108	12	5	1	32	6	4	2	39	1	48	3	3
Garibay, Roberto, San Luis	.091	15	11	1	1	1	0	0	0	0	0	0	0	0	0	4	0	0
Garza, Adolfo, Monclova	.233	66	176	16	41	63	8	1	4	28	3	1	3	32	6	33	0	1
Garza, Gerardo, Nuevo Laredo	.234	113	376	26	88	103	10	1	1	34	7	0	1	19	0	32	5	6
Garzon, Eliseo, Mexico City Reds	.259	33	81	11	21	40	8	1	3	15	0	1	0	7	2	24	0	0
Garzon, Felix, Campeche	.265	64	204	16	54	67	7	0	2	21	2	2	2	16	1	28	0	1
Gassos, Genaro, Tabasco	.332	79	184	20	61	69	6	1	0	16	2	5	1	17	4	25	2	1
Gastelum, Carlos, Mexico City Reds	.293	74	188	22	55	63	8	0	0	17	3	1	1	14	0	25	0	0
Gomez, Alejandro, Aguascalientes	.260	93	277	22	72	80	8	0	0	20	10	2	2	13	0	27	2	9
Gonzalez, Jesus, Tabasco	.247	122	465	38	115	137	16	0	2	31	2	6	0	26	2	28	1	1
Gonzalez, Juan, Saltillo	.147	20	34	8	5	7	0	1	0	4	0	1	0	5	0	3	0	0
Gonzalez, Mario A., Yucatan	.214	60	159	21	34	41	4	0	1	8	2	2	0	10	1	49	5	0
Gonzalez, Noe, Leon	.229	101	340	27	78	99	9	0	4	31	3	1	3	27	1	56	3	3
Gonzalez, Orlando, Aguascalientes	.167	11	36	5	6	9	3	0	0	2	0	0	0	3	1	4	0	0
Gonzalez, Pedro, Yucatan	.163	66	104	16	17	24	4	0	1	8	0	1	3	14	0	25	1	1
Green, David, Tabasco	.322	110	385	59	124	197	20	1	17	67	0	4	2	51	9	54	6	1
Griffin, Dave, Monclova	.316	17	57	9	18	23	2	0	1	9	0	1	1	9	0	9	1	0
Guerrero, Francisco, Union Laguna	.293	119	443	95	130	172	21	6	3	39	12	2	4	73	2	59	11	7
Guerrero, Francisco N., Mont. Sultans	.000	1	2	0	0	0	0	0	0	0	0	0	0	0	0	0	0	0
Guerrero, Jamie, Monterrey Sultans	.220	87	209	34	46	66	6	1	4	16	8	1	1	23	0	60	6	8
Guerrero, Leobardo, Leon	.306	57	124	12	38	43	2	0	1	7	2	0	1	10	1	18	2	3
Gutierrez, Andres, San Luis	.118	41	17	9	2	2	0	0	0	0	0	0	0	3	0	5	4	2
Gutierrez, Arnoldo, Union Laguna	.253	68	91	9	23	31	6	1	0	5	1	0	2	7	0	29	0	1
Gutierrez, Felipe, Campeche	.266	116	399	42	106	153	18	1	9	50	11	3	2	17	2	44	1	6
Gutierrez, Jose Luis, Leon	.288	92	271	40	78	93	10	1	1	21	7	0	6	24	0	40	8	7
Guzman, Marco Antonio, Campeche	.304	117	404	52	123	170	16	5	7	54	5	2	2	39	1	34	1	1
Hernandez, Leo, Campeche	.291	124	437	66	127	220	17	2	24	88	0	8	1	57	9	40	4	2
Hernandez, Miguel, Monterrey Sultans	.276	104	261	37	72	87	4	4	1	24	5	0	5	40	0	29	9	7
Hernandez, Rodolfo, Mont. Sultans	.282	115	383	41	108	154	21	2	7	62	1	4	5	51	5	45	1	5
Herrera, Isidro, Campeche	.248	38	113	17	28	35	4	0	1	9	1	1	0	18	0	12	4	3
Herrera, Rene, Campeche	.176	36	74	12	13	13	0	0	0	3	0	0	0	4	0	5	1	0
Herrera, Ricardo, Campeche	.238	100	349	62	83	102	15	2	0	23	6	1	1	47	0	41	21	9
Hurtado, Hector, Leon	.172	15	29	3	5	5	0	0	0	1	1	0	0	0	0	9	0	0
Ibarra, Jose A., Monterrey Sultans	.231	39	39	9	9	12	0	0	1	1	2	0	0	8	0	15	1	1
Iturbe, Pedro A., Saltillo	.149	36	47	10	7	9	2	0	0	1	2	0	0	5	1	13	0	1
Jarrell, Joe, Monterrey Sultans	.242	18	66	12	16	25	3	0	2	4	0	0	0	7	0	14	2	2
Jimenez, Eduardo, Aguascalientes	.320	81	272	62	87	147	13	4	13	54	0	1	5	58	3	56	5	3
Jimenez, Jose A., Mont. Industrials	.279	28	61	5	17	20	3	0	0	5	2	1	0	2	0	20	1	1
Jimenez, Leopoldo, Campeche	.268	83	250	33	67	90	14	0	3	31	5	4	1	24	1	41	0	0
Johnson, Roy, Campeche	.346	118	416	81	144	257	35	0	26	95	0	4	3	63	13	59	2	2
Kinnard, Kenneth, San Luis	.262	12	42	7	11	15	1	0	1	6	1	1	1	3	1	11	4	1
Lavagnino, J. Ernesto, San Luis	.273	34	66	10	18	23	2	0	1	3	1	0	0	4	0	13	0	0
Leal, Jose Guadalupe, Mont. Sultans	.271	111	332	25	90	124	14	4	4	51	7	6	1	25	4	48	3	6
Leyva, German, Monclova	.279	124	448	74	125	150	11	7	0	47	13	6	0	60	2	38	11	10
Lizarraga, Alejandro, Leon	.236	45	165	18	39	54	6	0	3	15	1	1	1	4	0	14	2	0
Lopez, Gonzalo, Monclova	.184	42	49	11	9	10	1	0	0	1	1	0	1	12	0	9	0	2
Lopez, Jesus Manuel, San Luis	.189	17	37	5	7	10	3	0	0	1	3	0	0	5	0	11	0	0
Lopez, Salvador, San Luis	.233	29	73	11	17	20	1	1	0	3	1	0	1	11	0	7	4	0
Loredo, Jorge Luis, Mont. Industrials	.067	13	15	1	1	1	0	0	0	1	0	0	0	4	0	3	0	0
Luna, Jose Luis, Saltillo	.249	122	333	31	83	98	9	3	0	34	14	1	1	27	0	21	4	1
Machiria, Pablo, Mexico City Tigers	.293	114	423	68	124	184	17	5	11	83	6	9	7	28	2	44	1	3
Magana, Gabriel, Yucatan	.129	38	62	12	8	8	0	0	0	3	2	0	1	7	0	17	0	0
Mangham, Eric, Mexico City Tigers	.385	97	361	83	139	182	17	4	6	48	6	2	8	41	2	36	50	25
Marquez, Saul, Aguascalientes	.000	4	5	0	0	0	0	0	0	0	0	0	0	0	0	2	0	0
Marte, Alejandro, Tabasco	.320	28	103	16	33	40	3	2	0	7	2	1	2	9	0	11	8	4
Martinez, Grimaldo, Monclova	.268	117	351	57	94	117	18	1	1	33	16	2	3	43	0	46	13	7
Martinez, Raul, Mexico City Tigers	.271	89	273	30	74	93	14	1	1	31	2	1	3	23	2	42	1	1
Mena, Evaristo, Monclova	.188	38	80	10	15	20	5	0	0	11	0	1	0	13	0	20	0	0
Mendoza, Luis Alonso, Mont. Indus.	.000	1	1	0	0	0	0	0	0	0	0	0	0	0	0	1	0	0
Mendoza, Mario, Monterrey Sultans	.243	81	247	20	60	75	6	0	3	18	7	2	1	22	0	23	1	3
Mercado, Felipe, San Luis	.230	33	61	9	14	15	1	0	0	2	1	0	0	4	0	7	0	0
Mere, Pedro, Nuevo Laredo	.277	106	375	58	104	158	9	0	15	64	0	0	5	48	3	65	4	6
Meza, Alfredo, Monterrey Industrials	.189	36	95	5	18	23	3	1	0	11	0	1	1	2	0	26	0	0
Miller, Eddie, Aguascalientes	.304	39	148	28	45	75	4	4	6	23	0	1	4	8	0	30	9	2
Monell, John, San Luis	.311	49	183	27	57	85	10	0	6	17	1	0	0	14	2	18	15	5
Monroy, Victor Hugo, Union Laguna	.258	36	89	7	23	28	5	0	0	6	1	0	0	4	0	20	1	0
Mora, Andres, Nuevo Laredo	.306	121	422	54	129	198	19	1	16	68	0	4	5	53	8	57	2	1
Morales, Florentino, San Luis	.328	48	174	28	57	77	12	4	0	8	2	0	1	18	1	24	10	6
Morales, Manuel, San Luis	.203	55	153	16	31	38	3	2	0	6	4	2	3	13	0	11	0	4
Moreno, Leonardo, Mexico City Tigers	.230	62	100	9	23	26	3	0	0	3	1	0	0	4	1	17	0	2
Moreno, Roberto, Monclova	.262	126	413	51	108	130	16	3	0	33	11	3	3	25	0	109	3	5
Morfin, Jorge, Campeche	.000	17	4	1	0	0	0	0	0	0	0	0	0	0	0	1	0	0
Morones, Martin, Mexico City Tigers	.307	118	368	78	113	162	14	7	7	39	5	2	5	45	1	51	13	6
Munoz, Noe, Monterrey Industrials	.302	24	43	5	13	16	3	0	0	7	0	0	0	7	0	8	0	0
Navarrete, Juan, Mont. Industrials	.325	132	504	71	164	205	24	4	3	55	6	5	1	38	5	15	9	12
Navarro, Ruben, Campeche	.266	85	274	23	73	90	6	4	1	26	3	3	2	21	1	41	1	2
Noris, Rogelio, Mexico City Reds	.190	20	21	4	4	6	2	0	0	2	0	0	0	2	0	5	1	1
Ontiveros, Juan, Tabasco	.000	1	0	1	0	0	0	0	0	0	0	0	0	0	0	0	0	0
Ortiz, Alejandro, Nuevo Laredo	.307	129	423	87	130	231	20	0	27	104	0	6	5	102	27	61	9	6
Osuna, Hector Manuel, Aguascalientes	.233	57	129	17	30	34	2	1	0	10	4	0	0	11	0	20	1	0
Pacho, Juan Jose, Yucatan	.284	126	450	58	128	150	16	3	0	29	9	2	1	25	1	46	9	5
Pardo, Victor Manuel, Saltillo	.273	10	22	1	6	9	1	1	0	1	0	0	0	0	0	3	0	0

Player and Club	Pct.	G.	AB.	R.	H.	TB.	2B.	3B.	HR.	RBI.	SH.	SF.	HP.	BB.	Int. BB.	SO.	SB.	CS.
Paris, Kelly, Mexico City Reds	.326	27	95	17	31	53	10	0	4	20	0	1	0	16	0	21	0	0
Payton, Eric, Tabasco	.254	51	181	20	46	64	7	1	3	23	1	2	1	18	6	31	2	4
Peralta, Amado, San Luis	.218	121	349	53	76	123	13	2	10	48	4	5	4	84	10	83	1	1
Perez, Jose Luis, Saltillo	.176	41	85	8	15	22	1	0	2	6	0	1	1	15	2	24	0	1
Pena, Luis Alberto, Campeche	.262	123	412	60	108	176	17	0	17	61	3	1	2	48	14	56	1	5
Perez, Tovar Raul, Mont. Industrials	.310	19	58	7	18	22	4	0	0	6	0	0	1	6	0	10	1	2
Plascencia, Obed, Nuevo Laredo	.310	39	113	14	35	44	3	0	2	13	1	0	0	6	0	13	1	4
Ponce, Hector, Campeche	.228	76	149	19	34	44	4	0	2	15	6	0	0	3	0	24	1	0
Quintero, Guadalupe, Aguascalientes	.265	47	113	17	30	34	4	0	0	11	4	1	2	21	0	14	1	1
Quiroz, Jose Julian, Mont. Industrials	.255	98	278	32	71	110	19	4	4	36	2	3	2	58	5	61	2	1
Rabb, John, Union Laguna	.257	56	187	32	48	86	11	0	9	36	0	2	2	31	2	47	11	2
Ramirez, Efren, Aguascalientes	.235	42	98	19	23	36	3	2	2	14	1	0	2	9	0	23	1	2
Ramirez, Enrique, Nuevo Laredo	.272	129	449	61	122	147	8	7	1	37	7	5	0	39	0	31	13	8
Ramirez, Gustavo, Monclova	.277	111	364	34	101	132	19	3	2	53	7	2	8	26	4	31	1	5
Ramos, Enrique, Monterrey Sultans	.000	14	13	2	0	0	0	0	0	0	0	0	0	1	0	9	0	0
Reid, Jessie, Mexico City Reds	.379	27	95	22	36	64	5	1	7	28	0	3	1	22	2	18	1	0
Reyes, Genaro, San Luis	.204	59	137	11	28	33	3	1	0	7	6	3	6	13	0	34	0	2
Reyes, Juan, Monterrey Sultans	.309	115	408	59	126	209	27	1	18	86	4	1	4	28	10	108	5	2
Reyna, Luis, Saltillo	.303	80	300	46	91	148	17	5	10	41	0	2	7	25	3	49	13	5
Rios, Jose Luis, Union Laguna	1.000	1	1	0	1	1	0	0	0	0	0	0	0	0	0	0	0	0
Rivera, Eleazar, San Luis	.263	102	316	30	83	106	7	2	4	37	5	2	3	24	0	69	2	2
Rivera, Jose Luis, Union Laguna	.303	10	33	7	10	13	0	0	1	3	0	0	1	3	2	9	0	0
Roca, Gilberto, Monterrey Industrials	.333	26	99	12	33	38	3	1	0	13	0	0	1	4	0	8	2	2
Rodriguez, Cecilio, Nuevo Laredo	.297	83	236	21	70	79	9	0	0	27	6	0	1	37	0	24	0	1
Rodriguez, Genaro, Mexico City Tigers	.271	73	214	25	58	83	10	0	5	39	2	3	2	17	1	33	1	1
Rodriguez, Guillermo, M. C. Tigers	.289	117	433	75	125	195	21	2	15	65	5	8	5	25	6	67	5	2
Rodriguez, Gustavo, Monclova	.223	60	139	19	31	45	6	1	2	18	2	3	0	13	0	35	2	1
Rodriguez, Jose Luis, Saltillo	.194	43	62	3	12	16	1	0	1	7	0	3	0	7	2	17	0	1
Rodriguez, Juan Francisco, Mont. Sul.	.292	124	424	73	124	166	22	4	4	55	15	3	2	69	3	21	12	4
Romero, Marco Antonio, N. Laredo	.293	125	434	82	127	178	11	5	10	57	8	4	4	55	4	56	16	2
Rosales, Arturo, Tabasco	.218	88	284	24	62	87	14	1	3	37	3	3	3	17	3	57	4	3
Ruiz, Demetrio, Tabasco	.230	90	265	19	61	75	4	2	2	20	4	1	2	13	0	13	1	1
Ruiz, Juan De Dios, Union Laguna	.100	14	10	3	1	1	0	0	0	1	0	0	0	1	0	6	0	0
Saenz, Ricardo, Saltillo	.272	110	356	47	97	150	16	5	9	54	7	7	2	40	6	61	7	7
Saiz, Herminio, Union Laguna	.289	123	356	61	103	140	18	2	5	46	7	5	5	31	2	51	3	4
Salinas, Luis, Campeche	.263	67	190	22	50	62	3	0	3	19	2	1	4	27	2	48	0	2
Samaniego, Manuel, Mont. Industrials	.235	96	310	25	73	90	7	2	2	39	1	1	2	13	2	34	2	4
Sanchez, Alejandro, San Luis	.337	108	392	80	132	250	24	5	28	79	0	3	8	41	12	95	15	5
Sanchez, Andres, Tabasco	.246	122	378	32	93	117	9	6	1	27	3	4	1	37	0	70	3	4
Sanchez, Armando, Mexico City Reds	.250	26	100	21	25	35	5	1	1	16	1	0	1	13	0	2	1	1
Sanchez, Gerardo, Nuevo Laredo	.261	132	464	69	121	177	15	4	11	58	12	1	5	51	1	54	7	7
Sanchez, Gilberto, Yucatan	.000	5	0	1	0	0	0	0	0	0	0	0	0	1	0	0	0	0
Sandoval, Jose Luis, Mexico City Reds	.252	122	408	55	103	147	19	5	5	36	3	0	0	37	0	80	9	4
Sconiers, Daryl, Mont. Industrials	.218	41	133	14	29	42	5	1	2	16	0	1	1	22	2	27	0	2
See, Larry, Monterrey Sultans	.297	86	300	40	89	140	17	2	10	49	2	1	0	36	5	35	7	5
Serna, Joel, Tabasco	.264	91	276	21	73	88	4	1	3	24	4	1	2	23	3	45	0	1
Serratos, Miguel, Aguascalientes	.287	98	317	35	91	128	16	3	5	43	3	2	1	19	1	47	1	0
Shepherd, Ron, Leon	.318	108	400	75	127	208	22	4	17	72	1	3	0	32	2	72	5	2
Shines, Anthony, Mexico City Reds	.276	78	268	51	74	107	15	0	6	49	0	6	1	55	5	28	6	3
Smith, Gregory, Saltillo	.372	121	452	73	168	244	19	3	17	102	0	6	0	46	15	38	32	19
Solis, Daniel, Tabasco	.000	2	6	0	0	0	0	0	0	0	0	0	0	0	0	1	0	0
Sommers, Jesus, Union Laguna	.277	84	285	34	79	111	14	0	6	43	0	5	1	38	6	29	1	0
Soto, Carlos, San Luis	.282	92	308	32	87	139	10	0	14	62	1	3	0	33	4	44	2	1
St. Laurent, Jim, Tabasco	.186	13	43	3	8	10	2	0	0	4	1	0	1	4	1	11	0	0
Steels, James, Mexico City Reds	.372	23	86	22	32	39	5	1	0	14	0	2	3	13	0	6	3	2
Stockstill, David, Union Laguna	.341	127	451	76	154	239	30	2	17	109	4	9	2	72	21	42	2	2
Tellez, Alonso, Monterrey Industrials	.312	128	475	75	148	239	29	10	14	78	1	3	2	41	10	66	3	8
Threadgill, George, Monclova	.339	30	109	23	37	46	3	3	0	18	1	1	5	18	1	27	0	3
Tillman, Kelly, Monterrey Sultans	.344	74	244	48	84	136	9	5	11	40	0	2	1	45	7	46	19	5
Tiquet, Lazaro, Tabasco	.301	127	462	43	139	167	18	2	2	41	13	3	7	28	0	74	5	9
Tirado, Federico, Mexico City Tigers	.301	75	193	27	58	69	6	1	1	30	6	1	4	10	0	23	0	2
Tirado, Victor, Yucatan	.257	66	167	11	43	46	3	0	0	6	4	0	3	7	0	20	0	1
Torres, Eduardo, Saltillo	.232	113	353	59	82	124	16	4	6	43	2	2	8	64	9	73	8	6
Torres, Guillermo, Saltillo	.267	40	45	3	12	13	1	0	0	0	1	0	0	3	0	11	0	0
Torres, Raymundo, Saltillo	.222	103	334	52	74	156	22	0	20	63	2	6	4	59	12	83	1	0
Tubbs, Greg, Mexico City Reds	.315	57	213	37	67	102	5	9	4	33	3	2	0	36	2	45	11	5
Uzcanga, Ali, Monterrey Industrials	.265	105	339	32	90	105	13	1	0	20	5	2	0	28	0	48	1	6
Valdez, Baltazar, Yucatan	.300	127	453	60	136	222	20	0	22	87	2	3	3	47	6	52	1	4
Valdez, Francisco, Monterrey Sultans	.184	53	87	13	16	22	4	1	0	1	1	0	1	6	0	23	0	1
Valdez, Jesus, Aguascalientes	.257	73	148	28	38	54	2	4	2	18	0	3	0	5	0	20	4	5
Valdez, Jose Luis, Nuevo Laredo	1.000	1	1	0	1	1	0	0	0	0	0	0	0	0	0	0	0	0
Valdez, Julio Alberto, Aguascalientes	.258	68	124	11	32	38	6	0	0	8	3	0	1	11	4	18	0	2
Valdivia, Arturo, Campeche	.281	16	32	7	9	10	1	0	0	2	1	0	0	1	0	6	0	1
Valencia, Carlos, Aguascalientes	.320	101	344	69	110	149	18	6	3	48	4	4	5	44	0	35	3	6
Valenzuela, Armando, Aguascalientes	.284	122	423	47	120	142	14	4	0	51	15	5	5	25	1	46	4	6
Valenzuela, Eduardo, Saltillo	.500	4	4	0	2	2	0	0	0	0	0	0	0	1	0	1	0	0
Valenzuela, Horacio, San Luis	.271	123	447	52	121	196	23	2	16	83	0	2	2	32	7	78	4	7
Valenzuela, Jose Luis, Aguascalientes	.000	18	3	3	0	0	0	0	0	0	0	0	0	2	0	3	0	0
Valenzuela, Leonardo, Monclova	.315	117	419	55	132	180	18	6	6	54	10	6	0	50	7	67	8	6
Valle, Guadalupe, Monterrey Sultans	.273	65	132	12	36	46	5	1	1	10	2	2	1	16	0	36	0	0
Valverde, Aaron, San Luis	.224	53	143	9	32	40	6	1	0	10	4	1	1	13	0	26	0	2
Valverde, Raul, Union Laguna	.293	113	382	64	112	155	15	8	4	39	6	2	1	22	1	41	3	4
Vargas, Hediberto, Aguascalientes	.332	105	370	81	123	219	19	1	25	92	0	7	5	65	6	76	1	4
Vargas, Rogelio, Mont. Industrials	.080	31	25	6	2	2	0	0	0	2	1	0	0	9	0	12	0	1
Vazquez, Rodolfo, Mexico City Tigers	.000	2	0	0	0	0	0	0	0	0	0	0	0	0	0	0	0	0
Vega, Ramon, Aguascalientes	.267	25	45	4	12	13	1	0	0	0	0	0	0	3	0	5	0	0
Vela, Francisco Javier, Campeche	.000	2	2	0	0	0	0	0	0	0	0	0	0	0	0	0	0	0
Verdugo, Vincente, Mexico City Reds	.283	121	452	58	128	154	13	2	3	37	3	2	1	25	1	24	2	3
Villaescusa, Fernando, Aguascalientes	.325	92	366	46	119	150	17	4	2	43	3	3	3	22	3	16	9	3
Villagomez, David, Mexico City Reds	.228	66	189	18	43	54	5	0	2	24	1	2	3	15	0	34	0	0
Villalobos, Juan Enrique, Leon	.429	6	7	0	3	4	1	0	0	2	0	1	0	1	0	1	0	0
Villela, Carlos, Monterrey Industrials	.296	125	466	54	138	182	21	10	1	30	4	2	1	32	1	54	5	3

Player and Club	Pct.	G.	AB.	R.	H.	TB.	2B.	3B.	HR.	RBI.	SH.	SF.	HP.	BB.	Int. BB.	SO.	SB.	CS.
Vizcarra, Marco Antonio, U. Laguna ...	.291	50	79	15	23	30	4	0	1	9	4	0	0	6	0	9	0	2
Vizcarra, Roberto, Leon	.305	131	525	89	160	232	28	4	12	64	9	4	6	37	3	23	16	18
Vizcarra, Sergio, San Luis	.233	44	146	15	34	43	5	2	0	8	7	0	0	13	0	13	1	2
Walker, Bernie, Nuevo Laredo	.301	69	246	49	74	108	12	5	4	18	2	0	4	49	2	62	33	4
Washington, Randy, Monclova	.256	38	125	25	32	50	6	0	4	25	0	1	1	23	1	30	2	0
Wong, Julian, Saltillo	.306	125	470	78	144	173	17	6	0	47	19	6	3	39	2	29	7	6
Wright, George, Yucatan	.322	127	459	96	148	232	31	4	15	73	3	1	3	68	4	63	4	3
Yuriar, Jesus, Monclova	.237	64	215	21	51	63	5	2	1	20	6	2	0	25	0	55	5	0
Zambrano, Rosario, Monclova	.224	81	237	24	53	65	4	4	0	14	3	0	3	23	3	28	2	5
Zamudio, Aurelio, Tabasco	.000	1	0	0	0	0	0	0	0	0	0	0	0	0	0	0	0	0
Zulueta, Felix, Yucatan	.265	60	147	15	39	53	8	0	2	21	2	1	1	14	0	31	0	1
Zuniga, Armando, San Luis	.229	18	35	4	8	10	2	0	0	3	1	1	0	7	0	10	0	0

The following pitchers, listed alphabetically by club, with games in parentheses, had no plate appearances, primarily through use of designated hitters:

AGUASCALIENTES—Acosta, Martin (31); Cardenas, Benito (16); Carranza, Javier (26); Chambers, Travis (9); Delgadillo, Gustavo (10); Delgado, Tomas (2); Espinoza, Salvador (14); Gonzalez, Juan (1); Granillo, Carlos (29); Lara, Eddie (22); Lopez, Juan (28); Medina, Gilberto (7); Montano, Francisco (21); Puerto, Carlos (10); Quinonez, Enrique (30); Sanchez, Geraldo (7); Soto, Alvaro (37); Urrea, Leonel (31); Valenzuela, Adan (7); Vargas, Ignacio (12).

CAMPECHE—Dominguez, Herminio (22); Garcia, Rene (24); Guzman, Gelacio (20); Huerta, Luis Enrique (27); Moreno, Juan deDios (21); Onofre, Francisco (17); Pulido, Antonio (42); Raygoza, Martin (27); Toledo, Mario (8); Valdez, Rodolfo (29); Velazquez, Ildefonso (27); Velez, Alberto (27); Zavaleta, Marcelino (30).

LEON—Duarte, Adolfo (5); Hernandez, Julio (14); Orozco, Jaime (27); Orozco, Pedro (3); Purata, Julio (28); Sanchez, Martin (49); Sinohui, David (32); Soto, Fernando (27); Velazquez, Israel (23); Villanueva, Luis (25); Villegas, Ramon (27).

MEXICO CITY REDS—Alvarez, Juan Carlos (27); Barojas, Salome (35); Barron, Avelino (30); Felix, Antonio (18); Leyva, Filiberto (14); Luevano, Juan (20); Martinez, Ramon (28); Mendez, Luis Fernando (25); Moreno, Leobardo (13); Osuna, Ricardo (18); Pulido, Alfonso (19); Tejeda, Felix (6); Williams, Roger (18); Zamorano, Gabriel (1).

MEXICO CITY TIGERS—Ek, Roberto (27); Garcia, Juan (32); Grajales, Norberto (13); Herrera, Calixto (45); Jimenez, Isaac (15); Lopez, Emigdio (26); Moreno, Angel (23); Ordaz, Reynaldo (15); Rios, Jesus (24); Rodriguez, Raul (24); Valenzuela, Saul (15).

MONCLOVA—Arias, Daniel (35); Browning, Mike (25); Campos, Jorge (20); Cano, Ezequiel (12); Cook, Glenn (4); Cosio, Mario Alberto (27); Escamilla, Sergio (26); Garcia, Rogelio (16); Lopez, Raul (22); Murillo, Felipe (26); Normand, Guy (21); Quiroz, Emanuel (21); Rodriguez, Ignacio (27); Vazquez, Florentino (31); Vejar, Maximino (1).

MONTERREY INDUSTRIALS—Chavarin, Jose Angel (17); Diaz, Octavio (8); Dobbi, Reginald (4); Guajardo, Octavio (11); Mack, Tony (4); Morrow, Ben (32); Orozco, Octavio (4); Pena, Ramon Arturo (24); Quiroz, Aaron (11); Serafin, Hector (28); Soto, Ernesto (10); Torres, Guadalupe (18); Valdez, Armando (37); Velazquez, Ernesto (33); Velazquez, Luis A. (19); Villegas, Jose Angel (33).

MONTERREY SULTANS—Acosta, Aaron (20); Alicea, Miguel (49); Garcia, Horacio (29); Garza, Alejandro (19); Gonzalez, Arturo (22); Navarro, Adolfo (23); Ortiz, Gregorio (23); Osuna, Roberto (22); Perez, Joaquin (35); Pruneda, Armando (9); Serna, Ramon (1); Straker, Lester (15); Tejeda, Juan (38); Villarreal, Antonio (17).

NUEVO LAREDO—Alvarez, Juan Jesus (24); Barraza, Ernesto (27); Castillo, Luis Trinidad (14); Couch, Enrique (25); Grovom, Carl (14); Leslie, Reggie (2); Moore, Robert (4); Moreno, Jesus (26); Ochoa, Porfirio (47); Rodgers, Darrel (12); Romo, Manuel (11); Solis, Jesus (8); Tinoco, Ruben (30); Tirado, Sebastian (14).

SALTILLO—Aguilar, Miguel (25); Alvarez, Martin (32); Castellanos, Humberto (34); Mendez, Martin (10); Miranda, Julio Cesar (51); Munoz, Miguel (26); Padilla, Raymundo (13); Reynoso, Armando (27); Rodriguez, Mario A. (31); Sanchez, Hector (26); Solis, Ricardo (22); Velez, Luis Alberto (14).

SAN LUIS—Cabrales, Gabriel (26); Castaneda, Aurelio (48); Castro, Rodrigo (29); Cazares, Juan (24); Contreras, Benjamin (3); Guzman, Benjamin (12); Kinnunen, Mike (13); Lazorko, Jack (5); Lizarraga, Hugo (27); Lopez, Hector (12); Lopez, Jose Ramon (32); Lunar, Luis (39); Meagher, Tom (5); Morales, Isidro (29); Moya, Ramon (19); Raygoza, Jose Ramon (12); Reyes, Jesus Manuel (11); Rosales, Arturo (1); Sandoval, Carlos (7); Soto, Ramon Eugenio (7); Veliz, A. Francisco (22).

TABASCO—Camarena, Martin (25); Cruz, Jesus (31); Dimas, Rodolfo (3); Enriquez, Martin (54); Garcia, Zenon (5); Jimenez, German (14); Ledon, Juan Carlos (3); Marcos, C. Jose (13); Martinez, Victor (2); Romero, Juan (10); Salas, Ernesto (9); Saldana, Edgardo (25); Sanchez, Felipe (2); Sombra, Francisco (32); Sosa, Mario (23); Torres, Martin (4); Ulin, Miguel Angel (11).

UNION LAGUNA—Castaneda, Maximiliano (29); Cervantes, Lauro (26); Diaz, Garcia Cesar (9); Esquivias, Ruben (4); Flores, Jesus A. (34); Hernandez, Encarnacion (30); Hernandez, Martin (14); Palafox, Juan Manuel (25); Perry, Jeff (46); Pimentel, Roberto (3); Quintero, Victor Hugo (3); Renteria, Hilario (25); Rincon, Ricardo (19); Torres, Sotero (7).

YUCATAN—Acosta, Cervantes Martin (8); Antunez, Martin (33); Beltran, Eleazar (21); Colorado, Salvador (31); Dozier, Tom (25); Duarte, Florentino (11); Esquer, Mercedes (20); Garibay, Roberto (26); Ibarra, Carlos (23); Jaime, G. Ismael (46); Retes, Lorenzo (24); Urias, Rosario (6).

GRAND SLAM HOME RUNS—L.A. Cruz, J. Reyes, R. Torres, 2 each; Aguilar, Avila, Baca, N. Barrera, N. Castaneda, Dominguez, F. Guerrero, R. Hernandez, E. Jimenez, Ortiz, Peralta, Ge. Rodriguez, Ju. F. Rodriguez, Ge. Sanchez, Soto, Stockstill, Tellez, H. Valenzuela, H. Vargas, M.A. Vizcarra, Washington, Wright, 1 each.

AWARDED FIRST BASE ON CATCHER'S INTERFERENCE—Arce (Monroy); Leyva (G. Garza); Luna (R. Martinez); Steels (R. Martinez); R. Torres (R. Martinez).

CLUB FIELDING

Club	Pct.	G.	PO.	A.	E.	DP.	PB.	Club	Pct.	G.	PO.	A.	E.	DP.	PB.
Yucatan	.974	130	3110	1381	121	132	20	Mexico City Reds	.966	127	2646	1492	144	146	10
Leon	.972	131	3066	1562	132	120	11	Monclova	.966	130	3166	1466	163	148	12
Mexico City Tigers	.972	123	3068	1380	128	118	22	Nuevo Laredo	.965	124	3012	1443	161	117	20
Union Laguna	.971	127	3080	1418	132	153	7	Aguascalientes	.965	124	3115	1377	165	123	9
Tabasco	.971	131	3094	1450	138	119	19	Saltillo	.964	132	3250	1473	177	122	15
Campeche	.970	124	3127	1497	142	117	21	Monterrey Sultans	.964	132	3380	1311	176	135	29
Monterrey Industrials	.969	132	3113	1333	142	132	33	San Luis	.962	131	2835	1473	170	133	30

Triple Play—Mexico City Tigers.

INDIVIDUAL FIELDING
FIRST BASEMEN

Player and Club	Pct.	G.	PO.	A.	E.	DP.	Player and Club	Pct.	G.	PO.	A.	E.	DP.
A. Garza, Monclova	1.000	12	102	4	0	8	Quiroz, Monterrey Industrials	.997	38	292	22	1	28
Ibarra, Monterrey Sultans	1.000	23	71	4	0	6	B. Valdez, Yucatan	.996	86	739	58	3	89
Co. Garcia, Yucatan	1.000	17	165	7	0	14	Avila, Union Laguna	.996	31	227	11	1	35
L. Hernandez, Campeche	1.000	11	86	3	0	5	See, Monterrey Sultans	.994	25	160	6	1	17
Villaescusa, Aguascalientes	1.000	10	69	3	0	6	A. Valverde, San Luis	.993	42	273	15	2	42
Villagomez, Monterrey Inds.	1.000	29	185	7	0	20	Gui. Rodriguez, M. C. Tigers	.992	116	982	51	8	101
J.L. Perez, Saltillo	1.000	12	95	2	0	9	Soto, San Luis	.992	16	107	11	1	7
F. Garzon, Campeche	.997	39	305	22	1	31	N. Castaneda, Yucatan	.992	12	113	5	1	10

FIRST BASEMEN—Continued

Player and Club	Pct.	G.	PO.	A.	E.	DP.
Sconiers, Monterrey Industrials	.991	41	328	14	3	41
Paris, Mexico City Reds	.991	23	217	5	2	28
Alyea, Tabasco	.991	11	105	3	1	10
Green, Tabasco	.991	85	813	40	8	70
Shines, Mexico City Reds	.989	76	688	42	8	68
Mora, Monterrey Industrials	.989	11	80	10	1	7
H. Valenzuela, Leon	.989	104	921	47	11	84
R. Valverde, Union Laguna	.988	53	393	29	5	48
Camargo, Mexico City Reds	.988	32	230	13	3	26
J. Reyes, Monterrey Sultans	.987	18	140	12	2	18
Sommers, Union Laguna	.987	54	441	14	6	45
Clayton, Monclova	.986	121	887	58	13	107
Rosales, Tabasco	.986	47	376	32	6	38
Romero, Nuevo Laredo	.985	121	1065	77	17	99
Roca, Monterrey Industrials	.985	15	124	10	2	11
H. Vargas, Aguascalientes	.982	38	308	23	6	27
Peralta, San Luis	.982	30	254	17	5	35
R. Hernandez, Mon. Sultans	.981	89	637	30	13	70
Cepeda, Monclova	.981	12	50	1	1	5
Gassos, Tabasco	.980	14	95	2	2	10
Burke, Yucatan	.979	18	132	11	3	11
Castro, Saltillo	.979	95	875	53	20	101
Smith, Saltillo	.979	77	640	46	15	54
Pena, Campeche	.977	78	644	46	16	70
O. Gonzalez, Aguascalientes	.968	10	88	2	3	8
Aikens, Leon	.965	21	185	10	7	15
Lavagnino, San Luis	.964	13	51	3	2	1
Reyna, Saltillo	.952	15	132	8	7	14

(Fewer Than Ten Games)

Player and Club	Pct.	G.	PO.	A.	E.	DP.
J.L. Gutierrez, Leon	1.000	3	17	0	0	1
Navarro, Campeche	1.000	1	3	0	0	0
J. Jimenez, Mon. Industrials	1.000	2	6	0	0	0
Jose L. Garcia, Mon. Ind.	1.000	6	29	2	0	7
H. Estrada, Mexico City Reds	1.000	1	6	0	0	1
N. Barrera, Mexico City Reds	1.000	4	26	3	0	4
L. Valenzuela, Monclova	1.000	1	3	0	0	0
Mena, Monclova	1.000	6	36	3	0	2
Zulueta, Yucatan	1.000	3	14	1	0	3
E. Rivera, San Luis	1.000	1	5	0	0	0
L.A. Cruz, Union Laguna	1.000	6	32	4	0	6
Je. Valdez, Aguascalientes	1.000	1	3	0	0	1
Arce, Saltillo	1.000	8	25	1	0	0
Steels, Mexico City Reds	1.000	1	8	0	0	2
E. Jimenez, Aguascalientes	1.000	1	4	0	0	0
Aganza, Monclova	1.000	1	1	2	0	2
Leal, Monterrey Sultans	1.000	7	28	1	0	3
Diaz, Nuevo Laredo	1.000	8	52	3	0	3
Tellez, Monterrey Industrials	1.000	4	8	0	0	2
Ar. Gutierrez, Union Laguna	1.000	1	5	0	0	0
Davis, Saltillo	1.000	1	4	0	0	1
Bobadilla, Saltillo	1.000	1	6	1	0	1
Almeida, Saltillo	1.000	1	4	0	0	1
Iturbe, Saltillo	1.000	1	1	0	0	0
Samaniego, Mon. Industrials	1.000	1	7	0	0	0
An. Gutierrez, San Luis	1.000	1	1	0	0	0
Cosey, Tabasco	.985	8	63	3	1	9
Griffin, Monclova	.985	7	57	7	1	7
Ge. Rodriguez, M. C. Tigers	.981	7	49	2	1	4
Dominguez, San Luis	.980	6	44	4	1	4
Valle, Monterrey Sultans	.971	9	31	3	1	2
Serna, Tabasco	.952	5	36	4	2	5
C. Rodriguez, Nuevo Laredo	.950	6	33	5	2	2
Gainey, Mexico City Reds	.909	1	10	0	1	2
J.M. Garcia, Aguascalientes	.909	4	9	1	1	0
Salinas, Nuevo Laredo	.900	1	9	0	1	0
Monroy, Union Laguna	.500	1	1	0	1	0
Jorge L. Garcia, Mon. Ind.	.000	1	0	0	0	0
Buenrostro, Leon	.000	1	0	0	1	0

Triple Play—Gui. Rodriguez.

SECOND BASEMEN

Player and Club	Pct.	G.	PO.	A.	E.	DP.
L. Guerrero, Leon	1.000	14	18	20	0	3
An. Sanchez, Tabasco	1.000	11	20	15	0	5
M. Morales, Saltillo	1.000	10	16	23	0	4
M.A. Vizcarra, Union Laguna	1.000	20	36	35	0	14
Zuniga, San Luis	1.000	11	22	18	0	7
Magana, Yucatan	.989	26	43	51	1	17
Abril, Union Laguna	.987	46	105	127	3	22
Elizondo, Aguascalientes	.984	116	266	338	10	94
Camacho, Mexico City Tigers	.984	99	247	295	9	60
Je. Gonzalez, Tabasco	.982	123	273	371	12	70
Verdugo, Mexico City Reds	.981	83	191	229	8	70
Mere, Nuevo Laredo	.981	105	272	286	11	71
M. Garcia, San Luis	.979	30	76	65	3	15
Flores, San Luis	.979	19	48	46	2	10
Bustamante, Mexico City Tigers	.979	40	68	70	3	16
J.F. Rodriguez, Mon. Sultans	.978	124	285	301	13	87
J.A. Barrera, Campeche	.978	71	180	170	8	49
Ri. Herrera, Campeche	.977	89	201	232	10	60
Barajas, Yucatan	.976	75	163	166	8	39
Leyva, Monclova	.976	26	44	38	2	13
Villela, Monterrey Industrials	.975	126	287	343	16	80
Esquer, Leon	.974	128	302	380	18	94
Villaescusa, Aguascalientes	.972	80	192	220	12	57
Ca. Garcia, San Luis	.970	38	81	114	6	30
Ar. Sanchez, Mexico City Reds	.966	26	65	79	5	24
L.A. Valdez, Monterrey Sultans	.966	28	35	50	3	10
Sandoval, Mexico City Reds	.964	19	36	71	4	17
C. Rodriguez, Nuevo Laredo	.959	28	56	84	6	16
Wong, Saltillo	.955	123	257	339	28	74
F. Morales, San Luis	.955	50	105	126	11	40
G. Martinez, Monclova	.952	116	267	313	29	77
Re. Herrera, Campeche	.950	22	53	43	5	6
Avina, Leon	.947	14	5	13	1	2
N. Barrera, Mexico City Reds	.942	18	19	30	3	7

(Fewer Than Ten Games)

Player and Club	Pct.	G.	PO.	A.	E.	DP.
Beristain, Monterrey Sultans	1.000	2	5	0	0	0
Cangas, Mexico City Reds	1.000	1	2	1	0	1
Ju. Gonzalez, Saltillo	1.000	4	3	7	0	3
M. Mendoza, Monterrey Sultans	1.000	2	2	7	0	3
Ge. Sanchez, Nuevo Laredo	1.000	2	4	4	0	0
G. Lopez, Monclova	1.000	6	8	6	0	3
Arce, Saltillo	1.000	1	2	0	0	0
F.N. Guerrero, Mon. Sultans	1.000	1	1	0	0	0
J. Guerrero, Monterrey Sultans	1.000	1	2	2	0	0
H. Chavez, Tabasco	1.000	9	6	4	0	1
An. Gutierrez, San Luis	1.000	1	1	0	0	0
Mercado, San Luis	1.000	3	3	2	0	1
Navarrete, Mon. Industrials	.960	8	14	10	1	4
Contreras, Union Laguna	.960	7	13	11	1	2
Pardo, Saltillo	.958	8	12	11	1	4
Arevalo, Aguascalientes	.947	8	9	9	1	4
Gus. Rodriguez, Monclova	.833	3	2	3	1	0
Burke, Yucatan	.714	5	3	2	2	1
Banuelos, Union Laguna	.000	1	0	0	0	0
Villela, Monterrey Industrials	.000	0	0	0	0	0
Serna, Tabasco	.000	1	0	0	0	0

Triple Play—Camacho.

THIRD BASEMEN

Player and Club	Pct.	G.	PO.	A.	E.	DP.
Cazarin, Leon	1.000	10	10	15	0	1
Avina, Leon	1.000	13	12	16	0	2
M. Mendoza, Monterrey Sultans	1.000	11	8	15	0	2
L. Jimenez, Campeche	.957	20	14	30	2	2
Burke, Yucatan	.953	50	39	103	7	14
J.F. Almodobar, Mon. Sultans	.947	39	23	48	4	5
Arevalo, Aguascalientes	.944	13	7	27	2	0
Valencia, Aguascalientes	.943	11	8	25	2	2
Serna, Tabasco	.943	72	38	126	10	8
L. Hernandez, Yucatan	.942	113	89	205	18	18
N. Barrera, Mexico City Reds	.940	117	100	200	19	17
Ortiz, Nuevo Laredo	.939	129	89	263	23	20
Cepeda, Monclova	.935	22	8	21	2	2
Garbey, Mexico City Tigers	.928	116	80	179	20	20
Leyva, Monclova	.927	104	97	195	23	20
N. Gonzalez, Leon	.925	100	51	182	19	14

THIRD BASEMEN—Continued

Player and Club	Pct.	G.	PO.	A.	E.	DP.
Peralta, San Luis	.924	92	81	174	21	15
Contreras, Union Laguna	.923	13	1	11	1	1
Navarrete, Mon. Industrials	.919	126	89	184	24	20
M. Garcia, San Luis	.918	21	17	28	4	5
An. Sanchez, Tabasco	.916	72	46	107	14	12
Arce, Saltillo	.914	101	60	183	23	14
Mercado, San Luis	.912	13	16	15	3	1
R. Castaneda, M. C. Tigers	.911	45	15	26	4	0
Aguilar, Monterrey Sultans	.911	125	122	247	36	33
L.A. Valdez, Monterrey Sultans	.909	13	5	15	2	3
Saiz, Union Laguna	.904	124	83	218	32	27
Ca. Garcia, San Luis	.898	16	22	31	6	9
Valle, Monterrey Sultans	.897	26	14	47	7	10
L. Guerrero, Leon	.894	25	10	32	5	3
Camacho, Mexico City Tigers	.889	14	3	5	1	0
Serratos, Aguascalientes	.883	92	72	191	35	18
Cangas, Mexico City Reds	.875	16	5	16	3	3
Bobadilla, Saltillo	.862	40	18	57	12	2
Gus. Rodriguez, Monclova	.838	21	10	21	6	1
See, Monterrey Sultans	.833	20	17	28	9	1

(Fewer Than Ten Games)

Player and Club	Pct.	G.	PO.	A.	E.	DP
Solis, Tabasco	1.000	2	1	3	0	0
Gastelum, Mexico City Reds	1.000	2	1	1	0	0
Noris, Mexico City Reds	1.000	1	0	1	0	0
Shines, Mexico City Reds	1.000	3	0	3	0	0
Cazarin, Leon	1.000	1	1	1	0	0
J. Ruiz, Union Laguna	1.000	4	1	1	0	0
Beristain, Monterrey Sultans	1.000	5	0	4	0	0
Vazquez, Mexico City Tigers	1.000	3	2	1	0	0
Re. Herrera, Campeche	1.000	1	0	1	0	0
E. Torres, Saltillo	1.000	2	2	6	0	0
Elizondo, Aguascalientes	1.000	6	4	14	0	0
Aganza, Monclova	1.000	2	0	4	0	0
Castillo, Tabasco	1.000	1	1	0	0	0
H. Chavez, Tabasco	1.000	2	1	0	0	0
C. Rodriguez, Nuevo Laredo	1.000	3	0	1	0	0
Cervera, Nuevo Laredo	1.000	2	0	1	0	0
Cano, Tabasco	.958	9	5	18	1	2
Meza, Monterrey Industrials	.913	9	7	14	2	1
Sandoval, Mexico City Reds	.909	4	6	4	1	0
Marquez, Aguascalientes	.900	4	2	7	1	0
Jarrell, Monterrey Sultans	.895	8	6	11	2	2
Ju. Gonzalez, Aguascalientes	.800	2	2	2	1	0
M.A. Vizcarra, Union Laguna	.800	1	2	2	1	0
T.R. Perez, Monterrey Sultans	.750	1	0	3	1	0
Romero, Nuevo Laredo	.750	2	0	3	1	0
Paris, Mexico City Reds	.667	3	1	1	1	0
Zuniga, San Luis	.500	5	2	3	5	1
An. Gutierrez, San Luis	.000	1	0	0	0	0
G. Lopez, Monclova	.000	2	0	0	0	0
Ge. Sanchez, Nuevo Laredo	.000	3	0	0	1	0
Loredo, Monterrey Industrials	.000	2	0	0	0	0
Peralta, San Luis	.000	1	0	0	0	0

SHORTSTOPS

Player and Club	Pct.	G.	PO.	A.	E.	DP.
C. Rodriguez, Nuevo Laredo	1.000	14	29	47	0	9
Pacho, Yucatan	.978	127	219	416	14	80
Elizondo, Aguascalientes	.967	64	116	232	12	45
F. Guerrero, Union Laguna	.965	119	266	421	25	101
M. Garcia, San Luis	.964	60	118	180	11	40
R. Vizcarra, Leon	.957	131	213	381	27	77
G. Lopez, Monclova	.955	12	8	13	1	4
R. Almodobar, M.C. Tigers	.954	113	155	318	23	44
Ju. Gonzalez, Saltillo	.953	10	11	30	2	3
M. Morales, San Luis	.953	35	65	96	8	22
A. Valenzuela, Saltillo	.953	121	226	417	32	80
DeLosSantos, Tabasco	.951	73	93	158	13	31
M. Mendoza, Monterrey Sultans	.948	69	103	169	15	43
Sandoval, Mexico City Reds	.947	91	149	294	25	64
Uzcanga, Monterrey Industrials	.946	101	181	272	26	58
En. Ramirez, Nuevo Laredo	.944	126	181	345	31	57
R. Moreno, Monclova	.944	126	201	358	33	83
Verdugo, Mexico City Reds	.944	50	82	152	14	36
F. Gutierrez, Campeche	.943	116	184	358	33	71
Gomez, Monterrey Industrials	.942	103	140	252	24	57
M.A. Vizcarra, Union Laguna	.941	13	17	31	3	5
S. Vizcarra, San Luis	.940	44	56	116	11	18
An. Sanchez, Tabasco	.939	54	71	128	13	27
Bustamante, Mexico City Tigers	.928	36	29	61	7	13
Cano, Tabasco	.922	11	21	26	4	5
J. Guerrero, Monterrey Sultans	.918	84	125	189	28	37
Loredo, Monterrey Industrials	.917	10	14	8	2	1
Cartaya, Tabasco	.909	17	25	55	8	3
H. Chavez, Tabasco	.906	13	13	16	3	4
Beristain, Monterrey Sultans	.846	12	2	9	2	2

(Fewer Than Ten Games)

Player and Club	Pct.	G.	PO.	A.	E.	DP.
Esquer, Leon	1.000	6	4	6	0	0
Re. Herrera, Campeche	1.000	5	6	6	0	2
A. Valverde, San Luis	1.000	1	1	0	0	0
Magana, Yucatan	1.000	5	4	4	0	0
Wong, Saltillo	1.000	5	8	11	0	2
Bobadilla, Satillo	1.000	2	1	0	0	0
L.A. Valdez, Aguascalientes	1.000	1	1	1	0	0
Ca. Garcia, San Luis	1.000	1	3	0	0	1
Gus. Rodriguez, Monclova	1.000	1	1	3	0	0
Ri. Herrera, Yucatan	.929	8	9	17	2	0
L. Jimenez, Campeche	.921	7	9	26	3	7
Cervera, Nuevo Laredo	.875	1	2	5	1	0
Zuniga, San Luis	.833	2	0	5	1	1
Arias, Mexico City Tigers	.786	7	3	8	3	2
An. Gutierrez, San Luis	.750	7	4	5	3	2
Barajas, Yucatan	.333	3	1	0	2	1
Villaescusa, Aguascalientes	.000	1	0	0	1	0
Arevalo, Aguascalientes	.000	1	0	0	0	0

OUTFIELDERS

Player and Club	Pct.	G.	PO.	A.	E.	DP.
J.L. Valenzuela, Aguascalientes	1.000	12	5	0	0	0
Miller, Aguascalientes	1.000	10	16	0	0	0
Ar. Gutierrez, Union Laguna	1.000	54	45	1	0	0
R. Vargas, Mont. Industrials	1.000	13	7	1	0	0
Reid, Mexico City Reds	1.000	10	10	0	0	0
Villagomez, Mont. Industrials	1.000	13	8	1	0	0
Bellazetin, Mexico City Tigers	1.000	42	50	3	0	0
R. Valverde, Union Laguna	1.000	23	35	3	0	2
L. Moreno, Mexico City Tigers	1.000	27	37	1	0	1
Plascencia, Nuevo Laredo	1.000	36	57	2	0	1
Steels, Mexico City Reds	1.000	24	58	3	0	1
Ramos, Monterrey Sultans	1.000	12	10	0	0	0
Amador, Nuevo Laredo	1.000	11	16	2	0	1
J.L. Perez, Saltillo	1.000	16	13	1	0	0
Iturbe, Saltillo	1.000	25	27	0	0	0
Cole, Campeche	.994	123	309	21	2	7
R. Torres, Yucatan	.991	100	199	12	2	1
R. Estrada, Campeche	.990	111	184	14	2	2
J.M. Garcia, Aguascalientes	.989	60	86	8	1	0
Yuriar, Monclova	.989	57	90	2	1	0
Zulueta, Yucatan	.987	41	71	4	1	0
Fernandez, Mexico City Reds	.987	122	288	11	4	2
Aguilera, Monterrey Sultans	.986	132	279	9	4	2
Arzate, Leon	.986	89	134	7	2	1
Hec. Alvarez, Mexico City Tigers	.986	122	262	14	4	3
Blocker, San Luis	.985	118	249	8	4	3
Tellez, Monterrey Industrials	.984	124	295	12	5	3
Monell, San Luis	.983	47	115	4	2	2
Shepherd, Leon	.983	107	214	12	4	3
S. Lopez, Nuevo Laredo	.982	26	53	3	1	1
Lizarraga, San Luis	.982	38	52	4	1	0
T. Brown, Monclova	.982	94	212	7	4	4
Co. Garcia, Yucatan	.981	24	49	2	1	1
Saenz, Saltillo	.980	102	182	16	4	3
Threadgill, Monclova	.980	27	46	3	1	1
Tiquet, Tabasco	.980	127	224	16	5	2
Castelan, Monterrey Industrials	.979	114	223	13	5	5
Tillman, Monterrey Sultans	.979	73	132	5	3	0
Espinoza, San Luis	.978	89	168	6	4	1
Dominguez, San Luis	.978	94	162	12	4	2
Felice, Union Laguna	.977	38	41	2	1	0
Ponce, Campeche	.977	70	76	8	2	1
Wright, Yucatan	.977	126	242	8	6	0
Diaz, Nuevo Laredo	.975	96	151	7	4	0
Stockstill, Nuevo Laredo	.974	121	205	16	6	0
Castro, Saltillo	.973	24	32	4	1	0
Walker, Nuevo Laredo	.973	68	136	7	4	2
Johnson, Campeche	.973	100	172	6	5	2

OUTFIELDERS

Player and Club	Pct.	G.	PO.	A.	E.	DP.
D. Brown, Monterrey Industrials	.972	44	65	5	2	1
Leal, Monterrey Sultans	.972	101	135	4	4	0
Marte, Tabasco	.972	27	67	2	2	1
Gutierrez, Leon	.971	84	127	9	4	1
Rosales, Tabasco	.971	18	33	1	1	0
Machiria, Mexico City Tigers	.971	114	187	11	6	2
Mangham, Mexico City Tigers	.969	77	120	6	4	1
L. Valenzuela, Monclova	.968	116	243	32	9	2
Rabb, Union Laguna	.967	48	87	1	3	0
Washington, Monclova	.967	28	52	6	2	0
Je. Valdez, Aguascalientes	.966	49	53	4	2	0
I. Herrera, Mont. Industrials	.966	36	55	2	2	0
Delgado, Monterrey Sultans	.966	52	80	5	3	1
Quiroz, Monterrey Industrials	.966	46	79	5	3	1
T.R. Perez, Monterrey Sultans	.966	17	27	1	1	1
Zambrano, Monclova	.966	70	80	4	3	2
Ge. Sanchez, Nuevo Laredo	.965	130	190	3	7	1
L.A. Cruz, Union Laguna	.965	115	212	8	8	1
P. Gonzalez, Yucatan	.963	45	48	4	2	0
E. Torres, Saltillo	.961	111	179	16	8	1
Morones, Mexico City Reds	.960	115	184	7	8	0
Tubbs, Mexico City Reds	.957	57	103	8	5	0
Valencia, Aguascalientes	.957	86	148	6	7	1
Payton, Tabasco	.956	46	104	4	5	1
Baca, Aguascalientes	.953	105	194	7	10	0
Cepeda, Monclova	.952	13	19	1	1	0
Al. Sanchez, San Luis	.952	105	214	22	12	5
Davis, Saltillo	.951	126	264	10	14	2
Navarro, Campeche	.951	60	93	4	5	0
Kinnard, San Luis	.950	12	18	1	1	0
Her. Alvarez, Yucatan	.948	91	123	4	7	0
Arredondo, Monclova	.947	18	17	1	1	0
Agramon, Saltillo	.944	37	33	1	2	0
Abrego, Nuevo Laredo	.937	53	68	6	5	1
E. Jimenez, Aguascalientes	.935	81	135	10	10	1
J. F. Almodobar, Mont. Sultans	.929	24	12	1	1	0
Jose L. Garcia, Mont. Indus.	.926	44	62	1	5	0
Douglas, Tabasco	.925	29	60	2	5	0
Mercado, San Luis	.923	13	11	1	1	0
Noris, Mexico City Reds	.917	11	11	0	1	0
L. Jimenez, Campeche	.917	45	64	2	6	0
Mena, Monclova	.917	11	11	0	1	0
Jarrell, Monterrey Sultans	.913	13	20	1	2	0
See, Monterrey Sultans	.907	52	71	7	8	1
Banuelos, Union Laguna	.902	33	35	2	4	0
Buenrostro, Leon	.889	12	6	2	1	0
Garibay, San Luis	.889	12	7	1	1	0

(Fewer Than Ten Games)

Player and Club	Pct.	G.	PO.	A.	E.	DP.
L. Guerrero, Leon	1.000	5	8	0	0	0
N. Castaneda, Yucatan	1.000	6	8	0	0	0
Reyna, Saltillo	1.000	2	2	0	0	0
G. Lopez, Monclova	1.000	8	5	0	0	0
Sandoval, Mexico City Reds	1.000	7	9	0	0	0
V. Tirado, Yucatan	1.000	1	2	0	0	0
M.A. Gonzalez, Mont. Sultans	1.000	7	3	0	0	0
Ibarra, Monterrey Sultans	1.000	3	1	0	0	0
An. Sanchez, Tabasco	1.000	4	4	0	0	0
A. Valverde, San Luis	1.000	1	1	0	0	0
F. Garzon, Campeche	1.000	1	1	0	0	0
Clayton, Monclova	1.000	4	9	1	0	0
Jose L. Rodriguez, Saltillo	1.000	6	3	0	0	0
Beristain, Monterrey Sultans	1.000	1	0	0	0	0
Cazarin, Leon	1.000	1	5	0	0	0
Gus. Rodriguez, Monclova	1.000	4	5	0	0	0
Lavagnino, San Luis	1.000	8	7	0	0	0
Cosey, Tabasco	1.000	5	5	0	0	0
St. Laurent, Tabasco	1.000	1	4	0	0	0
D. Ruiz, Tabasco	1.000	2	1	0	0	0
Gassos, Tabasco	1.000	1	2	0	0	0
J. Jimenez, Mont. Industrials	1.000	6	6	0	0	0
Smith, Saltillo	1.000	5	5	0	0	0
J.L. Rivera, Union Laguna	.923	9	10	2	1	1
Beltran, Mexico City Reds	.800	5	4	0	1	0
Pena, Campeche	.800	5	7	1	2	0
B. Valdez, Yucatan	.750	2	1	0	1	0
Bocardo, Monclova	.000	1	0	0	1	0

CATCHERS

Player and Club	Pct.	G.	PO.	A.	E.	DP.	PB.
F. Estrada, Leon	1.000	23	100	11	0	0	1
G. Torres, Saltillo	1.000	38	85	6	0	1	5
D. Ruiz, Tabasco	.996	89	399	56	2	6	5
J.C. Alvarez, Yucatan	.992	32	120	11	1	0	3
H. Estrada, Mexico City Reds	.990	66	282	25	3	3	6
B. Valdez, Yucatan	.989	20	81	11	1	0	3
Guzman, Campeche	.988	117	559	83	8	15	18
Vega, Aguascalientes	.988	24	69	10	1	1	1
Gastelum, Mexico City Reds	.987	71	266	40	4	5	3
Avila, Union Laguna	.986	62	252	40	4	5	2
M. Hernandez, Mon. Sul.	.985	108	567	80	10	7	20
F. Tirado, Mexico City Tigers	.985	68	287	36	5	4	9
Roca, Monterrey Industrials	.984	11	54	6	1	1	2
Osuna, Aguascalientes	.984	55	152	28	3	3	5
Castillo, Tabasco	.983	50	201	27	4	2	10
Ef. Ramirez, Aguascalientes	.983	42	157	13	3	3	2
Luna, Saltillo	.982	122	587	84	12	11	8
F. Valdez, Monterrey Sultans	.982	47	142	21	3	1	5
G. Ramirez, Monclova	.981	86	459	64	10	15	7
F. Cruz, Union Laguna	.980	70	293	50	7	6	3
J.M. Lopez, San Luis	.980	12	43	6	1	1	2
G. Garza, Nuevo Laredo	.980	111	656	73	15	5	16
Daut, Monclova	.979	56	239	40	6	6	8
Samaniego, Mon. Ind.	.978	78	400	45	10	5	21
E. Rivera, San Luis	.977	97	387	77	11	6	20
Hurtado, Leon	.974	15	36	2	1	1	2
Abrego, Union Laredo	.974	24	137	11	4	4	4
V. Tirado, Yucatan	.973	64	228	23	7	2	4
R. Martinez, M.C. Tigers	.973	77	385	41	12	4	12
E. Reyes, Mon. Ind.	.973	39	191	22	6	4	4
Cantu, Saltillo	.972	14	33	2	1	2	0
Meza, Monterrey Industrials	.970	26	108	20	4	0	9
Cazarin, Leon	.969	107	512	88	19	9	4
M.A. Gonzalez, Mon. Sul.	.968	46	186	25	7	4	9
Quintero, Aguascalientes	.966	45	195	29	8	2	1
Monroy, Union Laguna	.966	15	50	6	2	2	1
Valdivia, Campeche	.964	13	50	4	2	1	2
E. Garzon, Mexico City Reds	.943	14	43	7	3	0	0
Munoz, Monterrey Industrials	.923	15	42	6	4	1	2

(Fewer Than Ten Games)

Player and Club	Pct.	G.	PO.	A.	E.	DP.	PB.
Villalobos, Leon	1.000	1	4	2	0	0	1
Gassos, Tabasco	1.000	8	21	4	0	0	1
Aparicio, Yucatan	1.000	9	26	1	0	1	3
Bocardo, Monclova	1.000	8	13	1	0	0	0
E. Valenzuela, Saltillo	1.000	4	10	0	0	0	1
See, Monterrey Sultans	1.000	7	21	3	0	1	1
Amador, Nuevo Laredo	1.000	1	2	0	0	0	0
Jose L. Garcia, Mon. Ind.	1.000	1	2	0	0	0	0
Cavia, San Luis	.933	9	14	0	1	0	1
Zulueta, Yucatan	.500	2	1	0	1	0	1

PITCHERS

Player and Club	Pct.	G.	PO.	A.	E.	DP.
Granillo, Aguascalientes	1.000	29	1	4	0	0
A. Soto, Aguascalientes	1.000	37	2	12	0	0
Delgadillo, Aguascalientes	1.000	10	0	12	0	0
Quinonez, Aguascalientes	1.000	30	8	22	0	0
Espinoza, Monclova	1.000	14	0	1	0	0
Cardenas, Aguascalientes	1.000	16	2	3	0	0
J.R. Raygoza, San Luis	1.000	12	1	3	0	0
Villanueva, Leon	1.000	25	0	3	0	0
M. Sanchez, Leon	1.000	49	2	16	0	0
J. Orozco, Leon	1.000	27	19	45	0	6
Sinohui, Leon	1.000	33	3	25	0	0
J. Hernandez, Leon	1.000	14	0	7	0	0
Ju. Moreno, Campeche	1.000	21	4	3	0	0
G. Guzman, Campeche	1.000	19	0	3	0	0
An. Pulido, Campeche	1.000	41	1	5	0	0
Camarena, Tabasco	1.000	25	10	14	0	1
C. Ibarra, Yucatan	1.000	24	5	12	0	2
Jaime Granillo, Yucatan	1.000	46	3	3	0	1
Onofre, Campeche	1.000	17	1	2	0	0
Vargas, Aguascalientes	1.000	12	0	2	0	1
Jonas Lopez, Aguascalientes	1.000	28	2	9	0	1
M. Acosta, Aguascalientes	1.000	31	8	20	0	0

PITCHERS—Continued

Player and Club	Pct.	G.	PO.	A.	E.	DP.
F. Duarte, Yucatan	1.000	11	0	3	0	0
Ju. Garcia, Mexico City Tigers	1.000	32	7	14	0	0
Je. Rios, Mexico City Tigers	1.000	24	10	23	0	1
Ordaz, Mexico City Tigers	1.000	15	2	3	0	0
E. Lopez, Mexico City Tigers	1.000	25	3	11	0	2
M. Alvarez, Saltillo	1.000	32	4	16	0	0
Aguilar, Saltillo	1.000	25	4	23	0	2
DeLeon, Mexico City Tigers	1.000	39	5	6	0	0
Munoz, Saltillo	1.000	26	7	34	0	1
Rincon, Union Laguna	1.000	19	2	2	0	0
Sombra, Tabasco	1.000	32	1	14	0	1
Flores, Union Laguna	1.000	34	4	10	0	0
E. Hernandez, Union Laguna	1.000	30	6	25	0	1
R. Lopez, Monclova	1.000	22	5	4	0	0
Campos, Monclova	1.000	20	1	2	0	0
E. Quiroz, Monclova	1.000	20	1	1	0	0
Murillo, Monclova	1.000	26	4	13	0	3
Vazquez, Monclova	1.000	31	5	10	0	1
Cano, Monclova	1.000	12	3	9	0	1
Escamilla, Monclova	1.000	26	1	6	0	0
I. Rodriguez, Monclova	1.000	27	2	16	0	1
Normand, Monclova	1.000	21	10	16	0	1
Alicea, Monterrey Sultans	1.000	49	2	9	0	0
Moya, San Luis	1.000	19	3	11	0	3
Lizarraga, San Luis	1.000	27	6	15	0	2
Villarreal, Monterrey Sultans	1.000	17	0	3	0	0
Cazares, San Luis	1.000	24	1	5	0	0
Morrow, Monterrey Industrials	1.000	32	12	19	0	1
Chavarin, Monterrey Industrials	1.000	10	2	0	0	0
Al. Pulido, Mexico City Tigers	1.000	19	4	17	0	4
Luevano, Mexico City Reds	1.000	20	6	8	0	2
Barron, Mexico City Reds	1.000	30	0	6	0	0
L. Moreno, Mexico City Reds	1.000	13	0	4	0	1
Barojas, Mexico City Reds	1.000	34	6	17	0	1
J.C. Alvarez, Mexico City Reds	1.000	27	1	12	0	1
Felix, Mexico City Reds	1.000	18	3	10	0	1
Ulin, Tabasco	1.000	11	1	1	0	0
G. Jimenez, Tabasco	1.000	14	2	20	0	0
G. Torres, Monterrey Industrials	1.000	16	2	5	0	1
J.A. Villegas, Mont. Industrials	1.000	33	6	19	0	3
Jose L. Rios, Union Laguna	1.000	17	3	3	0	0
Morales, San Luis	1.000	29	2	10	0	0
Puerto, Aguascalientes	1.000	10	0	3	0	0
Grajales, Mexico City Tigers	1.000	13	2	5	0	0
Marcos, Tabasco	1.000	13	2	13	0	2
Grovom, Nuevo Laredo	1.000	14	0	5	0	0
Browning, Monclova	1.000	25	8	11	0	4
Rodgers, Union Laredo	1.000	12	1	5	0	0
M. Mendez, Saltillo	1.000	10	3	2	0	0
Padilla, Saltillo	1.000	13	2	1	0	0
H. Sanchez, Saltillo	1.000	26	4	12	0	1
H. Lopez, San Luis	1.000	12	1	1	0	0
Urrea, Aguascalientes	1.000	31	0	10	0	0
Carranza, Aguascalientes	1.000	26	10	15	0	2
Romero, Tabasco	1.000	10	0	1	0	1
Guajardo, Monterrey Industrials	1.000	11	2	2	0	0
Purata, Leon	.980	28	5	43	1	2
A. Gonzalez, Monterrey Sultans	.974	22	7	31	1	3
Esquer, Yucatan	.974	20	7	30	1	1
R. Rodriguez, M.C. Tigers	.972	24	8	27	1	1
R. Solis, Saltillo	.969	22	3	28	1	1
Garza, Monterrey Sultans	.967	20	7	22	1	2
Zamudio, Tabasco	.967	24	5	24	1	1
Palafox, Union Laguna	.967	25	3	26	1	2
Straker, Monterrey Sultans	.964	15	9	18	1	0
Dominguez, Campeche	.964	22	6	21	1	3
R. Castro, San Luis	.960	29	4	20	1	1
Montano, Aguascalientes	.960	21	8	16	1	1
A. Castaneda, San Luis	.960	48	4	20	1	0
Navarro, Monterrey Sultans	.958	23	7	16	1	0
Retes, Yucatan	.957	24	7	15	1	1
L.F. Mendez, Mexico City Reds	.957	25	9	35	2	3
Herrera, Mexico City Tigers	.955	44	3	18	1	1
Perez, Monterrey Sultans	.955	35	4	17	1	0
Il. Velazquez, Campeche	.952	26	4	16	1	0
J.L. Valdez, Nuevo Laredo	.950	28	1	18	1	2
Ochoa, Nuevo Laredo	.950	47	2	17	1	1
R. Valdez, Campeche	.950	30	3	16	1	1
Couch, Nuevo Laredo	.949	25	15	22	2	3
Castillo, Nuevo Laredo	.947	14	8	10	1	1
L. Velazquez, Mont. Industrials	.947	20	4	14	1	2
Cervantes, Union Laguna	.946	26	11	24	2	2
A. Valdez, Monterrey Industrials	.945	37	7	45	3	3
Cabrales, San Luis	.944	26	5	12	1	1
Jorge L. Garcia, Mont. Indus.	.944	27	6	28	2	3
Jose R. Lopez, San Luis	.941	32	2	14	1	1
Veliz, San Luis	.941	22	4	28	2	0
A. Moreno, Mexico City Tigers	.940	23	14	33	3	7
M. Raygoza, Campeche	.939	27	15	47	4	4
M. Hernandez, Union Laguna	.938	14	3	12	1	1
R. Villegas, Nuevo Laredo	.938	27	3	12	1	0
Tinoco, Nuevo Laredo	.933	30	2	12	1	0
Ro. Osuna, Monterrey Sultans	.933	22	6	22	2	2
Kinnunen, San Luis	.933	13	3	11	1	0
Dozier, Yucatan	.933	25	7	21	2	2
Reynoso, Saltillo	.932	27	12	29	3	2
R. Martinez, Mexico City Reds	.929	28	4	22	2	0
Ortiz, Monterrey Sultans	.929	23	1	12	1	1
Colorado, Yucatan	.927	31	11	27	3	1
Chavez, Leon	.926	20	7	18	2	0
Je. Moreno, Nuevo Laredo	.925	26	11	26	3	4
Renteria, Union Laguna	.923	25	4	20	2	0
Sosa, Tabasco	.921	23	5	30	3	3
Huerta, Campeche	.920	27	8	15	2	2
J.J. Alvarez, Nuevo Laredo	.917	24	4	18	2	2
Ontiveros, Union Laguna	.917	40	2	9	1	0
Lunar, San Luis	.917	39	0	11	1	0
Garibay, Yucatan	.917	26	7	15	2	0
J. Tejeda, Monterrey Sultans	.909	38	2	8	1	1
E. Velazquez, Mont. Industrials	.900	33	2	7	1	1
Castellanos, Saltillo	.900	34	6	12	2	1
Miranda, Saltillo	.900	51	5	13	2	0
Serafin, Monterrey Industrials	.900	28	1	17	2	3
Pena, Monterrey Industrials	.900	22	1	8	1	1
F. Soto, Leon	.897	27	7	19	3	1
E. Beltran, Yucatan	.895	21	4	13	2	1
A. Acosta, Monterrey Sultans	.895	20	3	14	2	0
Ek, Mexico City Tigers	.895	27	3	14	2	1
Saldana, Tabasco	.893	25	12	38	6	3
I. Jimenez, Mexico City Tigers	.889	15	2	23	3	1
Ri. Osuna, Mexico City Reds	.885	18	7	16	3	1
Cosio, Monclova	.882	27	0	15	2	1
Enriquez, Tabasco	.875	54	5	16	3	1
Tirado, Nuevo Laredo	.875	14	1	6	1	0
Williams, Mexico City Reds	.857	18	9	15	4	1
Re. Gonzalez, Campeche	.852	24	4	19	4	1
H. Garcia, Monclova	.846	29	3	8	2	0
Barraza, Nuevo Laredo	.837	27	13	23	7	1
B. Guzman, San Luis	.833	12	0	5	1	0
Reyes, San Luis	.833	11	0	5	1	0
M. Castaneda, Union Laguna	.833	29	2	8	2	1
Perry, Union Laguna	.818	46	0	9	2	1
Antunez, Yucatan	.818	33	5	13	4	1
Lara, Aguascalientes	.800	22	3	9	3	0
A.A. Velez, Campeche	.800	28	1	3	1	0
Zavaleta, Campeche	.800	28	3	1	1	1
A. Quiroz, Monterrey Industrials	.800	10	3	1	1	0
M. Rodriguez, Saltillo	.800	31	2	14	4	1
Arias, Monclova	.786	35	4	7	3	0
Ro. Garcia, Monclova	.750	16	1	2	1	0
J. Cruz, Tabasco	.750	30	1	5	2	0
Is. Velazquez, Leon	.750	23	1	5	2	0
Leyva, Mexico City Reds	.500	14	0	1	1	0

(Fewer Than Ten Games)

Player and Club	Pct.	G.	PO.	A.	E.	DP.
A. Valenzuela, Aguascalientes	1.000	7	0	2	0	0
A. Duarte, Leon	1.000	5	0	1	0	0
P. Orozco, Leon	1.000	3	0	1	0	0
Salas, Tabasco	1.000	8	2	3	0	0
Z. Garcia, Tabasco	1.000	6	0	2	0	0
Delgado, Aguascalientes	1.000	1	0	1	0	0
Pruneda, Aguascalientes	1.000	9	0	4	0	1
F. Tejeda, Mexico City Reds	1.000	6	0	1	0	0
J.J. Quiroz, Mont. Industrials	1.000	2	0	1	0	0
J. Solis, Nuevo Laredo	1.000	8	2	6	0	2
Quintero, Union Laguna	1.000	3	1	2	0	0
Urias, Yucatan	1.000	6	0	1	0	0
Dimas, Tabasco	1.000	3	1	0	0	0
Lazorko, San Luis	1.000	5	0	2	0	0
G. Beltran, Mexico City Reds	1.000	3	0	2	0	0
Chambers, Aguascalientes	1.000	9	2	5	0	1
G. Sanchez, Aguascalientes	1.000	7	5	4	0	0
V. Martinez, Tabasco	1.000	2	0	1	0	0
A. Sanchez, Tabasco	1.000	1	1	0	0	0
Leslie, Nuevo Laredo	1.000	2	1	0	0	0
O. Orozco, Mont. Industrials	1.000	3	0	1	0	0
O. Diaz, Monterrey Industrials	1.000	7	0	1	0	0
Mack, Monterrey Industrials	1.000	4	3	1	0	0
Cook, Monclova	1.000	4	1	4	0	0
G.C. Diaz, Union Laguna	1.000	9	2	3	0	0
Ramirez, Saltillo	1.000	9	1	3	0	1
S. Valenzuela, M.C. Tigers	.889	7	3	5	1	0
M. Torres, Tabasco	.800	4	0	4	1	0
Meagher, San Luis	.750	5	1	2	1	0
Toledo, Campeche	.500	8	0	1	1	0

CLUB PITCHING

Club	ERA.	G.	CG.	ShO.	Sv.	IP.	H.	R.	ER.	HR.	HB.	BB.	Int. BB.	SO.	WP.	Bk.
Nuevo Laredo	3.48	132	36	15	23	1004.0	885	482	388	74	25	447	28	614	54	4
Yucatan	3.66	130	48	12	8	1036.2	1072	534	422	79	31	364	29	527	55	5
Monterrey Sultans	3.67	132	25	9	24	1126.2	1135	547	460	63	34	474	31	709	70	4
Leon	3.84	131	46	10	25	1022.0	1126	565	436	70	22	333	13	576	50	1
Monclova	3.85	130	26	7	24	1055.1	1100	589	452	57	43	522	41	644	56	2
Tabasco	3.87	131	27	13	21	1031.1	1095	566	443	62	28	312	39	531	54	6
Union Laguna	3.92	127	31	13	33	1026.2	1136	559	447	66	24	420	41	541	54	3
Mexico City Tigers	3.94	123	23	8	29	1022.2	1117	534	448	77	42	427	49	622	47	3
Saltillo	4.20	132	29	10	22	1083.1	1221	630	505	65	38	415	52	656	52	6
Campeche	4.27	124	31	11	28	1042.1	1135	540	494	69	22	450	44	588	47	5
Mexico City Reds	4.28	127	23	8	33	882.0	950	590	419	68	27	349	17	457	53	2
Monterrey Industrials	4.65	132	22	6	21	1037.2	1217	690	536	69	37	442	47	595	51	7
San Luis	5.27	131	13	3	11	945.0	1185	767	553	73	38	500	78	453	81	5
Aguascalientes	5.69	124	23	4	22	1038.1	282	775	657	93	52	509	50	548	61	4

PITCHERS' RECORDS
(Leading Qualifiers for Earned-Run Average Leadership — 106 or More Innings)

*Throws lefthanded.

Pitcher—Club	W.	L.	Pct.	ERA.	G.	GS.	CG.	GF.	ShO.	Sv.	IP.	H.	R.	ER.	HR.	HB.	BB.	Int. BB.	SO.	WP.
Normand, Monclova	14	4	.778	2.08	21	21	7	0	3	0	142.2	114	42	33	2	2	64	1	107	5
Barraza, Nuevo Laredo	6	6	.500	2.46	27	15	4	12	1	2	117.0	102	44	32	1	3	83	4	63	10
Navarro, Monterrey Sultans	9	5	.643	2.57	23	23	3	0	0	0	133.1	137	53	38	6	7	41	2	98	5
Reynoso, Saltillo	20	3	.870	2.60	27	27	12	0	5	0	200.2	174	61	58	7	10	73	7	170	14
A. Gonzalez, Mont. Sultans	14	5	.737	2.61	22	21	9	1	3	0	165.2	156	58	48	8	3	30	5	114	3
Dozier, Yucatan	15	7	.682	2.66	25	25	12	0	3	0	189.1	165	62	56	10	2	60	2	120	8
Cervantes, Union Laguna	17	6	.739	2.71	26	26	9	0	3	0	169.2	180	72	51	9	3	58	8	86	3
J.J. Alvarez, Nuevo Laredo	9	7	.563	2.76	24	22	2	2	0	0	133.2	122	60	41	5	2	81	2	70	7
A. Moreno, M. C. Tigers	10	5	.667	2.81	23	23	7	0	1	0	150.2	160	61	47	8	3	49	5	107	4
Retes, Yucatan	6	5	.545	2.82	24	11	9	13	2	1	108.1	95	41	34	6	1	48	4	40	6

Departmental Leaders: G—Enriquez, 54; W—Reynoso, 20; L—Jo. L. Garcia, Munoz, 15; Pct.—Castillo, .900; GS—J. Orozco, Reynoso, F. Soto, 27; CG—Orozco, 21; GF—Enriquez, 54; ShO—Je. Moreno, 6; Sv.—Perry, 27; IP—J. Orozco, 214.1; H—J. Orozco, 224; R—Munoz, 107; ER—Serafin, 84; HR—Je. Rios, 21; HB—Quinonez, 14; BB—Carranza, 92; IBB—A. Castaneda, 12; SO—Reynoso, 170; WP—Couch, 17.

(All Pitchers—Listed Alphabetically)

Pitcher—Club	W.	L.	Pct.	ERA.	G.	GS.	CG.	GF.	ShO.	Sv.	IP.	H.	R.	ER.	HR.	HB.	BB.	Int. BB.	SO.	WP.
A. Acosta, Mont. Sultans	4	7	.364	4.37	20	12	2	8	1	0	82.1	97	57	40	7	0	36	2	40	6
C.M. Acosta, Yucatan	0	0	.000	4.58	8	0	0	8	0	0	17.2	19	9	9	3	3	10	1	10	6
M. Acosta, Aguascalientes	7	7	.500	5.46	31	17	2	14	0	1	118.2	130	83	72	12	1	66	3	63	6
Aguilar, Saltillo	5	8	.385	4.47	25	22	2	3	0	0	108.2	122	66	54	7	2	45	3	66	4
Alicea, Monterrey Sultans	10	4	.714	2.34	49	0	0	48	0	21	73.0	51	21	19	5	0	19	3	56	2
J.C. Alvarez, M.C. Reds	4	0	1.000	5.06	27	0	0	27	0	2	48.0	55	33	27	3	0	30	4	16	5
J.J. Alvarez, Nuevo Laredo	9	7	.563	2.76	24	22	2	2	0	0	133.2	122	60	41	5	2	81	2	70	7
M. Alvarez, Saltillo	0	6	.000	4.58	32	13	0	19	0	1	76.2	75	46	39	2	3	48	3	54	6
Antunez, Yucatan	7	7	.500	3.61	33	10	2	23	0	3	87.1	81	41	35	6	0	46	4	50	6
Arias, Monclova	4	8	.333	3.84	35	7	2	28	0	6	84.1	94	50	36	5	2	52	6	46	10
Barojas, Mexico City Reds	6	2	.750	1.23	35	0	0	35	0	23	65.2	58	16	9	4	0	26	5	53	4
Barraza, Nuevo Laredo	6	6	.500	2.46	27	15	4	12	1	2	117.0	102	44	32	1	3	83	4	63	10
Barron, Mexico City Reds	1	4	.200	7.71	30	0	0	30	0	4	49.0	73	45	42	2	4	23	3	29	2
E. Beltran, Aguascalientes	1	7	.125	4.93	21	9	2	12	0	0	76.2	90	45	42	10	4	20	1	25	4
G. Beltran, M. City Reds	1	0	1.000	0.00	3	0	0	3	0	0	4.2	3	0	0	0	0	3	0	2	0
Browning, Monclova	7	4	.636	2.10	25	0	0	25	0	10	55.2	50	17	13	1	0	17	5	37	1
Cabrales, San Luis	5	4	.556	4.28	26	13	4	13	1	0	94.2	115	55	45	10	3	33	7	30	6
Camarena, Tabasco	7	9	.438	3.32	25	24	8	1	4	0	154.1	157	66	57	10	2	42	5	62	8
Campos, Monclova	0	0	.000	2.40	20	0	0	20	0	0	15.0	23	7	4	0	1	11	1	4	0
Cano, Monclova	5	4	.556	2.42	12	12	5	0	1	0	74.1	68	29	20	3	4	19	4	64	1
Cardenas, Aguascalientes	0	2	.000	10.25	16	2	0	14	0	0	26.1	46	35	30	4	1	14	1	10	1
Carranza, Aguascalientes	8	11	.421	4.19	26	26	7	0	2	0	150.1	158	85	70	11	8	92	4	100	5
A. Castaneda, San Luis	2	3	.400	5.36	48	2	0	46	0	2	100.2	128	77	60	6	5	57	12	48	9
M. Castaneda, Union Laguna	4	2	.667	4.97	29	2	0	27	0	1	58.0	72	43	32	2	2	26	4	22	4
Castellanos, Saltillo	6	7	.462	3.64	34	10	3	24	1	1	116.1	126	56	47	6	5	53	7	72	5
Castillo, Nuevo Laredo	9	1	.900	2.47	14	14	1	0	1	0	94.2	76	32	26	8	2	35	0	55	2
E. Castro, Saltillo	0	0	.000	0.00	1	0	0	1	0	0	0.1	1	0	0	0	0	1	0	0	1
R. Castro, San Luis	3	9	.250	5.98	29	14	1	15	0	0	99.1	134	77	66	2	3	53	8	51	8
Cazares, San Luis	0	1	.000	4.86	24	0	0	24	0	0	37.0	42	22	20	3	3	18	3	24	4
Cazarin, Leon	0	0	.000	0.00	1	0	0	1	0	0	1.0	0	0	0	0	0	0	0	2	0
Cervantes, Union Laguna	17	6	.739	2.71	26	26	9	0	3	0	169.2	180	72	51	9	3	58	8	86	3
Chambers, Aguascalientes	1	2	.333	5.79	9	0	0	9	0	4	14.0	19	9	9	2	1	5	2	11	2
Chavarin, Mont. Industrials	1	1	.500	3.46	17	1	0	16	0	0	52.0	57	24	20	7	0	22	0	17	1
Chavez, Leon	5	5	.500	4.25	20	20	2	0	1	0	101.2	121	63	48	11	2	37	2	47	6
Colorado, Leon	14	10	.583	3.49	31	23	10	8	0	2	173.0	205	79	67	13	4	23	7	66	1
Contreras, San Luis	0	0	.000	16.20	3	0	0	3	0	0	3.1	6	6	6	0	1	5	0	0	1
Cook, Monclova	0	3	.000	3.25	4	4	0	0	0	0	27.2	27	13	10	3	1	11	1	19	0
Cosio, Monclova	8	9	.471	4.10	27	25	6	2	1	0	145.0	157	79	66	6	5	79	3	66	5
Couch, Nuevo Laredo	14	8	.636	3.83	25	25	11	0	3	0	166.2	143	78	71	15	4	74	4	121	17
J. Cruz, Tabasco	1	2	.333	6.75	31	0	0	31	0	3	25.1	38	21	19	3	0	15	2	9	4
L.A. Cruz, Union Laguna	0	0	.000	0.00	1	0	0	1	0	0	0.1	0	0	0	0	0	0	0	0	0
DeLeon, Mexico City Tigers	4	4	.500	1.94	40	0	0	40	0	22	60.1	55	16	13	4	5	19	5	69	2
Delgadillo, Aguascalientes	2	4	.333	8.06	10	9	0	1	0	0	41.1	71	41	37	7	1	14	0	7	2
Delgado, Aguascalientes	0	0	.000	11.57	2	0	0	2	0	0	2.1	7	4	3	1	0	1	0	0	0
G.C. Diaz, Union Laguna	1	1	.500	5.54	9	0	0	9	0	1	13.0	15	9	8	2	0	8	3	8	1
O. Diaz, Mon. Industrials	0	0	.000	6.91	8	0	0	8	0	0	14.1	18	13	11	1	0	10	0	6	2
Dimas, Tabasco	0	1	.000	10.80	3	0	0	3	0	0	1.2	3	2	2	0	1	0	0	0	0
Dobbi, Mont. Industrials	0	2	.000	8.25	4	4	0	0	0	0	12.0	23	16	11	1	1	10	0	2	0
Dominguez, Campeche	12	5	.706	3.66	22	22	4	0	1	0	135.1	124	58	55	5	0	52	5	95	7
Dozier, Yucatan	15	7	.682	2.66	25	25	12	0	3	0	189.1	165	62	56	10	2	60	2	120	8
A. Duarte, Leon	1	0	1.000	3.72	5	0	0	5	0	0	9.2	6	4	4	0	0	3	0	4	0
F. Duarte, Yucatan	1	0	1.000	5.53	11	0	0	11	0	0	27.2	34	17	17	3	3	9	1	7	3

(All Players—Listed Alphabetically)

Pitcher—Club	W.	L.	Pct.	ERA.	G.	GS.	CG.	GF.	ShO.	Sv.	IP.	H.	R.	ER.	HR.	HB.	BB.	Int. BB.	SO.	WP.
Ek, Mexico City Tigers	7	2	.778	4.43	27	7	2	20	0	1	83.1	82	45	41	7	3	48	6	51	7
Enriquez, Tabasco	8	3	.727	1.10	54	0	0	54	0	15	89.2	66	18	11	1	6	34	8	74	4
Escamilla, Monclova	0	2	.000	3.93	26	0	0	26	0	6	52.2	63	28	23	2	2	18	2	22	0
Espinoza, Aguascalientes	0	1	.000	4.05	14	1	0	13	0	1	20.0	20	10	9	0	1	13	0	9	3
Esquer, Yucatan	8	4	.667	3.18	20	19	5	1	0	0	141.1	126	56	50	16	4	36	1	113	3
Esquivias, Union Laguna	0	0	.000	16.62	4	0	0	4	0	0	4.1	11	11	8	0	0	3	0	3	1
Felix, Mexico City Reds	5	2	.714	3.57	18	6	2	12	1	2	70.2	62	34	28	3	4	38	0	52	6
Flores, Union Laguna	5	6	.455	3.77	34	5	0	29	0	3	74.0	80	33	31	1	1	43	0	33	5
H. Garcia, Mon. Sultans	2	1	.667	4.50	29	4	0	25	0	0	66.0	69	42	33	3	6	46	2	41	9
Jo. L. Garcia, Mon. Industrials	12	15	.444	4.53	27	26	9	1	2	0	163.0	205	91	82	10	7	49	6	71	6
Ju. Garcia, Mexico City Tigers	10	2	.883	3.87	32	7	1	25	1	2	90.2	99	43	39	6	3	40	7	55	7
Re. Garcia, Campeche	6	8	.429	4.40	24	15	1	9	1	0	102.1	123	62	50	7	2	55	5	56	10
Ro. Garcia, Monclova	1	2	.333	7.48	16	0	0	16	0	1	27.2	36	27	23	4	4	12	4	14	0
Z. Garcia, Tabasco	0	2	.000	7.59	5	1	0	4	0	0	10.2	19	12	9	0	1	9	0	2	3
Garibay, Yucatan	7	10	.412	4.53	26	14	5	12	1	0	87.1	93	55	44	4	3	52	2	53	6
Garza, Mont. Sultans	9	8	.529	3.27	19	15	1	4	0	0	107.1	99	48	39	5	6	40	1	76	10
A. Gonzalez, Mon. Sultans	14	5	.737	2.61	22	21	9	1	3	0	165.2	156	58	48	8	3	30	5	114	3
J. Gonzalez, Aguascalientes	0	0	.000	16.20	1	0	0	1	0	0	1.2	1	3	3	1	0	3	0	1	0
Grajales, M.C. Tigers	0	3	.000	7.39	13	6	0	7	0	0	28.0	53	26	23	1	0	15	1	14	1
Granillo, Aguascalientes	2	5	.286	8.16	29	5	0	24	0	4	46.1	69	43	42	5	2	19	1	39	4
Grovom, Nuevo Laredo	2	0	1.000	4.01	14	4	1	10	1	1	33.2	28	15	15	1	1	17	0	38	1
Guajardo, Mon. Industrials	0	2	.000	4.88	11	1	0	10	0	0	24.0	17	14	13	2	4	14	1	7	3
B. Guzman, San Luis	2	3	.400	4.80	12	6	1	6	0	0	54.1	64	31	29	8	2	19	1	23	3
G. Guzman, Campeche	3	3	.500	4.01	20	2	0	18	0	1	24.2	27	14	11	1	0	18	2	11	2
E. Hernandez, Union Laguna	11	8	.579	3.97	30	26	3	4	1	1	152.0	176	86	67	9	6	65	5	62	6
J. Hernandez, Leon	2	1	.667	6.48	14	0	0	14	0	0	25.0	31	20	18	3	1	17	0	19	4
M. Hernandez, Union Laguna	4	4	.500	4.38	14	12	2	2	2	0	72.0	92	43	35	6	0	37	1	26	3
Herrera, Mex. City Tigers	8	6	.571	3.08	45	1	0	44	0	3	84.2	73	36	29	5	2	48	6	47	8
Huerta, Campeche	10	9	.526	3.01	27	24	7	3	4	1	146.1	154	70	49	7	1	54	8	82	3
C. Ibarra, Yucatan	3	9	.250	5.25	23	16	3	7	1	0	97.2	132	73	57	8	6	31	2	33	8
J.A. Ibarra, Mon. Sultans	0	0	.000	0.00	1	0	0	1	0	0	0.1	1	0	0	0	0	0	0	0	0
Jaime Granillo, Yucatan	4	2	.667	3.84	46	0	0	46	0	3	58.2	61	33	25	3	0	36	5	21	7
G. Jimenez, Tabasco	5	7	.417	2.73	14	14	5	0	1	0	99.0	84	39	30	2	1	22	0	62	1
I. Jimenez, M.C. Tigers	4	6	.400	4.97	15	15	2	0	0	0	70.2	87	52	39	4	4	42	4	34	4
L. Jimenez, Campeche	0	0	.000	0.00	1	0	0	1	0	0	1.0	1	0	0	0	0	0	0	0	0
Kinnunen, San Luis	2	7	.222	4.66	13	11	3	2	1	1	77.1	77	45	40	5	1	36	3	53	3
Lara, Aguascalientes	4	9	.308	6.13	22	18	2	4	1	1	101.1	137	77	69	7	4	58	6	53	7
Lazorko, San Luis	0	0	.000	3.14	5	1	0	4	0	3	14.1	15	7	5	0	1	4	0	11	0
Ledon, Tabasco	0	0	.000	15.43	3	0	0	3	0	0	2.1	7	4	4	0	1	4	2	0	0
Leslie, Nuevo Laredo	0	0	.000	0.00	2	1	0	1	0	0	2.1	2	0	0	1	0	6	0	1	3
Leyva, Mexico City Reds	1	1	.667	5.65	14	0	0	14	0	0	14.1	14	11	9	1	0	8	1	6	1
Lizarraga, San Luis	6	11	.353	4.35	27	18	1	9	0	0	120.0	148	69	58	10	5	51	4	46	6
E. Lopez, M.C. Tigers	7	6	.538	4.43	26	14	4	12	1	1	101.2	118	59	50	11	5	30	5	58	5
H. Lopez, San Luis	0	0	.000	10.61	12	0	0	12	0	0	9.1	14	11	11	1	0	10	0	5	1
Jonas Lopez, Aguascalientes	2	1	.667	5.43	28	1	1	27	1	0	61.1	76	43	37	3	5	17	5	15	2
Jose Lopez, San Luis	2	10	.167	7.15	32	16	0	16	0	0	90.2	132	86	72	6	4	65	12	41	9
R. Lopez, Monclova	3	9	.250	5.38	22	22	2	0	0	0	110.1	138	86	66	13	2	41	1	80	7
Luevano, Mexico City Reds	2	6	.250	3.78	20	7	3	13	2	2	69.0	65	33	29	4	3	25	0	38	3
Lunar, San Luis	7	8	.467	3.90	39	2	2	37	0	7	62.1	50	33	27	2	3	62	12	57	16
Mack, Mon. Industrials	0	2	.000	6.86	4	4	1	0	0	0	19.2	29	19	15	2	0	6	1	15	1
Marcos, Tabasco	3	4	.429	4.33	13	4	0	9	0	0	35.1	43	19	17	2	3	7	3	15	1
R. Martinez, Mex. City Reds	11	10	.524	5.08	28	24	6	4	1	0	141.2	153	86	80	17	6	63	0	71	10
V. Martinez, Tabasco	0	0	.000	189.00	2	0	0	2	0	0	0.1	5	7	7	1	0	3	0	1	0
Meagher, San Luis	1	2	.333	6.30	5	5	0	0	0	0	20.0	22	20	14	1	0	17	1	16	4
Medina, Aguascalientes	0	0	.000	15.75	7	0	0	7	0	0	8.0	22	20	14	1	1	5	0	4	0
L.F. Mendez, Mex. City Reds	16	5	.762	3.04	25	25	5	0	1	0	166.0	172	67	56	7	5	42	4	86	9
M. Mendez, Saltillo	0	1	.000	5.47	10	1	0	9	0	0	24.2	27	15	15	2	2	3	0	17	3
Miranda, Saltillo	9	10	.474	4.38	51	0	0	50	0	16	72.0	72	45	35	5	5	43	10	70	6
Montano, Aguascalientes	4	14	.222	4.48	21	21	6	0	0	0	126.2	143	78	63	11	5	50	6	58	4
Moore, Nuevo Laredo	0	2	.000	9.45	4	0	0	4	0	1	6.2	10	7	7	1	0	3	0	6	0
Morales, San Luis	2	2	.500	5.12	29	0	0	29	0	1	51.0	54	32	29	3	1	26	3	33	9
A. Moreno, Mex. City Tigers	10	5	.667	2.81	23	23	7	0	1	0	150.2	160	61	47	8	3	49	5	107	4
Je. Moreno, Nuevo Laredo	16	7	.696	3.29	26	26	15	0	6	0	191.2	155	72	70	19	7	43	3	132	6
Ju. Moreno, Campeche	0	0	.000	3.65	21	0	0	21	0	0	37.0	41	19	15	0	2	18	1	13	3
L. Moreno, Mex. City Reds	0	1	.000	9.00	13	1	0	12	0	0	15.0	20	15	15	1	0	14	0	10	3
Morfin, Campeche	0	0	.000	36.00	1	0	0	1	0	0	1.0	4	4	4	0	0	1	0	1	0
Morrow, Mon. Industrials	8	9	.471	3.79	32	18	4	14	0	6	145.0	137	76	61	7	0	45	3	136	2
Moya, San Luis	4	11	.267	7.05	19	16	2	3	0	0	75.1	120	59	59	9	2	33	5	21	2
Murillo, Monclova	8	5	.615	3.50	26	8	0	18	0	1	92.2	98	50	36	5	3	40	3	26	6
Munoz, Saltillo	9	15	.375	4.14	26	26	6	0	0	0	165.1	214	107	76	8	3	33	4	54	4
Navarro, Mon. Sultans	9	5	.643	2.57	23	23	3	0	0	0	133.1	137	53	38	6	7	41	2	98	5
Normand, Monclova	14	4	.778	2.08	21	21	7	0	3	0	142.2	114	42	33	2	2	64	1	107	5
Ochoa, Nuevo Laredo	8	7	.533	2.84	47	0	0	47	0	11	76.0	66	36	24	0	1	21	4	45	2
Onofre, Campeche	1	0	1.000	6.60	17	0	0	17	0	0	30.0	35	23	22	3	1	17	2	11	3
Ontiveros, Tabasco	1	4	.200	4.32	41	2	0	39	0	3	75.0	71	40	36	3	1	22	3	40	6
Ordaz, Mexico City Tigers	1	2	.333	6.69	13	1	0	14	0	0	35.0	52	29	26	2	2	14	3	7	0
J. Orozco, Leon	17	8	.680	2.98	27	27	21	0	3	0	214.1	224	78	71	14	3	29	2	93	3
O. Orozco, Mon. Industrials	0	0	.000	7.94	4	0	0	4	0	0	5.2	8	5	5	0	0	2	1	0	0
P. Orozco, Leon	0	0	.000	15.88	3	0	0	3	0	0	5.2	13	11	10	0	0	4	1	3	0
Ortiz, Monterrey Sultans	4	8	.333	6.21	23	14	1	9	0	0	79.2	96	77	55	8	3	87	1	52	10
Ri. Osuna, Mexico City Reds	7	6	.538	4.03	18	17	5	1	0	0	114.0	118	60	51	8	3	43	0	61	4
Ro. Osuna, Mon. Sultans	11	6	.647	2.92	22	21	4	1	0	0	138.2	109	54	45	10	0	31	1	107	4
Padilla, Saltillo	0	0	.000	7.33	13	0	0	13	0	1	23.1	35	22	19	2	2	10	1	8	2
Palafox, Union Laguna	7	11	.389	4.52	25	23	6	2	2	1	125.1	128	69	63	8	5	47	6	48	4
Pena, Mon. Industrials	2	2	.500	3.58	24	0	0	24	0	7	37.2	42	17	15	3	0	8	4	29	3
Perez, Monterrey Sultans	4	10	.286	4.27	35	12	2	23	1	0	92.2	92	54	44	4	5	53	5	35	9
Perry, Union Laguna	6	6	.500	2.99	46	5	1	41	0	27	99.1	85	39	33	5	2	42	4	117	12
Pimentel, Union Laguna	1	0	1.000	9.00	3	0	0	3	0	0	8.0	19	9	8	1	0	4	1	3	2
Pruneda, Monterrey Sultans	0	2	.000	4.63	9	3	0	6	0	0	23.1	27	18	12	1	0	21	1	6	3
Puerto, Aguascalientes	0	1	.000	9.28	10	1	0	9	0	2	10.2	21	11	11	0	1	3	1	4	0
Al. Pulido, Mex. C. Reds	6	4	.600	5.18	19	19	2	0	0	0	106.0	132	66	61	16	0	30	0	24	5

Pitcher—Club	W.	L.	Pct.	ERA.	G.	GS.	CG.	GF.	ShO.	Sv.	IP.	H.	R.	ER.	HR.	HB.	BB.	Int. BB.	SO.	WP.
An. Pulido, Campeche	3	4	.429	2.06	42	0	0	42	0	25	56.2	43	13	13	2	1	17	2	40	0
Purata, Leon	11	9	.550	3.47	28	27	7	1	1	0	174.0	182	90	67	8	2	76	2	131	15
Quinonez, Aguascalientes	11	8	.579	5.36	30	20	5	10	0	0	137.2	156	90	82	11	14	71	6	81	8
Quintero, Union Laguna	0	0	.000	5.06	3	0	0	3	0	0	5.1	6	3	3	1	0	1	0	2	1
A. Quiroz, Mont. Industrials	1	2	.333	4.50	11	2	0	9	0	0	28.0	31	17	14	3	1	19	0	25	0
E. Quiroz, Monclova	0	0	.000	4.03	21	1	0	20	0	0	51.1	54	29	23	4	3	29	2	24	2
J.J. Quiroz, Mon. Industrials	0	0	.000	8.31	3	0	0	3	0	0	4.1	12	4	4	0	0	0	0	3	1
J.R. Raygoza, San Luis	2	3	.400	6.67	12	3	1	9	0	0	27.0	31	21	20	2	1	16	2	10	2
M. Raygoza, Campeche	13	8	.619	2.90	27	24	11	3	3	1	189.1	180	76	61	6	0	59	6	109	4
Renteria, Union Laguna	11	8	.579	3.60	25	24	9	1	3	0	170.0	183	74	68	15	1	42	10	90	6
Retes, Yucatan	6	5	.545	2.82	24	11	9	13	2	1	108.1	95	41	34	6	5	48	4	40	6
Reyes, San Luis	0	0	.000	6.56	11	0	0	11	0	0	23.1	42	20	17	1	1	3	2	14	1
Reynoso, Saltillo	20	3	.870	2.60	27	27	12	0	5	0	200.2	174	61	58	7	10	73	7	170	14
Rincon, Union Laguna	3	0	1.000	3.78	19	4	0	15	0	0	47.2	53	22	20	6	4	32	0	29	2
Je. Rios, Mexico City Tigers	9	10	.474	4.42	24	24	2	0	0	0	148.2	157	83	73	21	5	54	2	89	1
Jo. L. Rios, Union Laguna	2	1	.667	6.15	17	3	1	14	0	0	41.0	51	33	28	3	0	20	2	20	5
Rodgers, Nuevo Laredo	4	1	.800	3.33	12	12	1	0	0	0	67.2	63	35	25	7	1	19	1	67	7
I. Rodriguez, Monclova	7	12	.368	5.32	27	26	3	1	0	0	115.0	125	78	68	8	11	82	1	95	11
M.A. Rodriguez, Saltillo	3	7	.300	6.34	31	12	1	19	0	2	103.2	149	88	73	12	4	48	6	61	4
R. Rodriguez, M.C. Tigers	10	2	.833	3.71	24	21	5	3	0	0	133.1	136	66	55	8	6	54	4	71	8
Romero, Tabasco	1	1	.500	5.56	10	2	0	8	0	0	22.2	32	18	14	0	0	13	0	16	0
Romo, Nuevo Laredo	0	0	.000	3.18	11	0	0	10	0	0	5.2	4	3	2	1	2	8	0	3	2
Rosales, San Luis	0	0	.000	0.00	1	0	0	1	0	0	1.1	0	0	0	0	0	1	0	0	0
Salas, Tabasco	0	0	.000	6.43	9	0	0	4	0	0	14.0	21	13	10	2	1	3	1	8	1
Saldana, Tabasco	10	12	.455	4.36	25	24	4	1	3	0	138.1	161	74	67	11	5	82	5	67	12
A. Sanchez, Tabasco	0	0	.000	3.00	1	0	0	1	0	0	3.0	5	1	1	0	0	0	0	3	0
F. Sanchez, Tabasco	0	1	.000	15.00	2	1	0	1	0	0	3.0	9	6	5	1	1	0	0	1	0
G. Sanchez, Aguascalientes	2	1	.667	7.56	7	4	0	3	0	0	25.0	34	25	21	4	0	8	1	11	2
H. Sanchez, Saltillo	2	4	.333	4.83	26	2	1	24	0	0	63.1	84	41	34	11	1	26	7	21	1
M. Sanchez, Leon	1	4	.200	3.12	49	0	0	49	0	18	49.0	58	20	17	3	2	22	1	34	9
Sandoval, San Luis	0	2	.000	6.35	7	2	0	5	0	0	11.1	14	9	8	3	0	5	1	5	2
Serafin, Mont. Industrials	7	12	.368	5.55	28	26	1	2	0	0	136.1	190	104	84	12	4	53	9	69	6
Serna, Monterrey Sultans	0	0	.000	0.00	1	0	0	1	0	0	0.1	1	0	0	0	0	0	0	0	0
Sinohui, Leon	10	9	.526	4.88	32	13	6	19	0	5	134.2	151	76	73	12	4	56	1	71	7
J. Solis, Nuevo Laredo	3	1	.750	14.17	8	5	2	3	0	0	33.2	35	65	53	4	1	12	0	15	0
R. Solis, Saltillo	9	7	.563	3.82	22	19	4	3	1	1	127.1	141	62	54	3	1	31	4	62	2
Sombra, Tabasco	3	5	.375	4.52	32	11	1	21	0	0	77.2	97	46	39	4	3	29	3	34	6
Sosa, Tabasco	6	13	.316	3.68	23	22	7	1	1	0	141.2	157	74	58	10	5	63	2	68	3
A. Soto, Aguascalientes	4	3	.571	6.83	37	1	0	35	0	6	54.0	76	52	41	5	3	24	7	27	4
E. Soto, Mont. Industrial	1	1	.500	6.41	10	2	0	8	0	0	19.2	31	15	14	2	2	9	0	7	0
F. Soto, Leon	11	8	.579	4.31	27	27	9	0	0	0	173.1	210	87	83	9	4	48	3	95	3
R.E. Soto, San Luis	0	0	.000	12.96	7	0	0	7	0	0	8.1	14	12	12	1	1	5	1	3	1
Stockstill, Union Laguna	0	0	.000	27.00	1	0	0	1	0	0	0.1	2	1	1	0	0	1	0	0	1
Straker, Mont. Sultans	6	6	.500	4.52	15	15	3	0	0	0	97.2	118	60	49	3	0	40	2	52	5
F. Tejeda, Mex. City Reds	1	2	.333	6.00	6	3	0	3	0	0	18.0	25	14	12	2	0	4	0	9	1
J. Tejeda, Mont. Sultans	0	2	.000	5.65	38	1	0	37	0	1	43.0	54	28	27	2	2	20	4	18	1
Tinoco, Nuevo Laredo	6	2	.750	3.50	30	0	0	30	0	7	43.2	34	20	17	5	1	18	3	22	2
Tirado, Nuevo Laredo	1	0	1.000	2.92	14	4	1	10	0	0	37.0	36	16	12	3	1	25	0	20	3
Toledo, Campeche	0	0	.000	7.71	8	0	0	7	0	0	9.1	12	9	8	0	0	10	0	8	0
G. Torres, Mont. Industrials	0	2	.000	11.52	18	2	0	16	0	0	25.0	45	37	32	2	0	25	3	15	5
M. Torres, Tabasco	0	3	.000	9.00	4	4	0	0	0	0	22.0	36	24	22	1	1	13	1	15	3
S. Torres, Union Laguna	0	0	.000	6.23	7	0	0	7	0	0	4.1	8	4	3	0	1	3	0	1	1
Ulin, Tabasco	0	0	.000	6.75	11	0	0	11	0	0	16.0	22	13	12	3	0	12	2	10	1
Urias, Yucatan	0	0	.000	4.26	6	0	0	6	0	0	6.1	9	3	3	0	0	2	0	1	0
Urrea, Aguascalientes	3	5	.375	5.37	31	0	0	31	0	3	63.2	75	51	38	8	3	35	7	38	5
A. Valdez, Mont. Indus	11	12	.478	3.04	37	19	5	18	0	4	171.2	164	70	58	8	8	65	10	120	9
J.L. Valdez, Nuevo Laredo	2	5	.286	2.45	27	1	0	26	0	2	69.2	71	23	19	3	0	25	8	37	3
R. Valdez, Campeche	3	12	.200	7.60	29	16	1	13	0	0	81.2	111	83	69	8	7	59	6	44	3
A. Valenzuela, Aguascalientes	1	1	.500	5.23	7	2	0	5	0	0	20.2	28	13	12	0	2	8	0	10	2
S. Valenzuela, M.C.Tigers	2	2	.500	3.24	15	4	0	11	0	0	41.2	48	16	15	1	4	14	1	23	0
Vargas, Aguascalientes	0	0	.000	6.20	12	0	0	12	0	0	20.1	23	17	14	3	0	12	0	12	4
Vazquez, Monclova	6	4	.600	4.03	31	4	1	27	0	0	87.0	79	49	39	4	4	64	6	58	3
Vejar, Monclova	0	0	.000	10.80	1	0	0	1	0	0	1.2	1	3	2	0	0	4	1	1	0
E. Velazquez, Mont. Indus	0	3	.000	5.02	33	1	1	32	0	0	75.1	89	54	42	3	2	37	2	29	7
Il. Velazquez, Campeche	11	10	.524	4.38	27	26	7	1	1	0	148.0	171	86	72	17	5	45	3	73	3
Is. Velazquez, Leon	3	5	.375	4.65	23	3	1	20	1	2	40.2	43	27	21	3	2	16	1	30	1
L.A. Velazquez, Mont. Ind	4	8	.333	4.99	19	19	0	0	0	0	79.1	93	54	44	6	0	56	3	34	3
A.A. Velez, Campeche	1	1	.500	9.20	27	3	0	24	0	0	30.1	46	33	31	4	1	19	0	18	5
L.A. Velez, Saltillo	0	0	.000	9.00	4	0	0	4	0	0	1.0	1	1	1	0	0	1	0	1	0
Veliz, San Luis	6	9	.400	4.55	22	20	1	2	1	1	114.2	149	75	58	8	6	56	7	58	5
Villanueva, Leon	2	1	.667	5.25	25	0	0	25	0	0	12.0	12	10	7	3	0	7	0	10	1
Villarreal, Mont. Sultans	1	1	.500	4.18	17	0	0	17	0	0	23.2	29	13	11	1	2	10	2	14	3
J.A. Villegas, Mont. Ind.	5	8	.385	5.46	33	8	2	25	1	4	92.1	112	72	56	6	9	49	6	56	5
R. Villegas, Leon	6	2	.750	2.77	27	1	0	26	0	0	87.2	88	36	27	4	2	22	1	42	1
Williams, Mex. City Reds	9	6	.600	3.89	18	18	6	0	0	0	122.2	124	60	53	6	2	47	0	58	6
Zamorano, Mex. City Reds	0	0	.000	......	1	0	0	1	0	0	......	1	0	0	0	0	1	0	0	0
Zamudio, Tabasco	8	10	.444	4.20	24	24	2	0	2	0	150.0	148	80	70	11	1	68	6	69	8
Zavaleta, Campeche	3	3	.500	6.66	30	1	0	29	0	0	51.1	68	42	38	9	2	27	4	28	4

BALKS—Cook, 4; Raygoza, E. Velazquez, L. Velazquez, 3 each; Enriquez, Quinonez, Reynoso, I. Rodriguez, H. Sanchez, Straker, 2 each; Aguilar, J.J. Alvarez, Barraza, E. Beltran, M. Castaneda, R. Castro, Cazares, Cervantes, Couch, O. Diaz, Dominguez, Dozier, Ek, Espinoza, H. Garcia, Garibay, B. Guzman, E. Hernandez, J. Hernandez, Herrera, Huerta, Ibarra, I. Jimenez, Lara, Luevano, R. Martinez, Ochoa, Ontiveros, O. Orozco, Retes, Saldana, Sandoval, R. Solis, Sosa, E. Soto, J. Tejeda, Zamudio, 1 each.

COMBINATION SHUTOUTS—R. Valdez-Re. Garcia, Campeche; Chavez-Villanueva-M. Sanchez, Purata-M. Sanchez, L.A. Velazquez-M. Sanchez, L.A. Velazquez-Villanueva, Leon; R. Martinez-Barojas 2, Ri. Osuna-Barojas, Mexico City Reds; Ju. Garcia-DeLeon, Grajales-E. Lopez, A. Moreno-DeLeon, Je. Rios-DeLeon, R. Rodriguez-DeLeon, Mexico City Tigers; Normand-Browning 2, Monclova; E. Soto-J.A. Villegas, A. Valdez-Pena, L.A. Velazquez-Pena, Monterrey Industrials; Navarro-J. Tejeda-Alicea, Navarro-Alicea, Ro. Osuna-Villarreal-Alicea, Perez-Alicea, Monterrey Sultans; Barraza-Ochoa, Castillo-Ochoa, Castillo-Romo-Tinoco, Nuevo Laredo; Aguilar-Miranda, R. Solis-Miranda, Saltillo; G. Jimenez-Ontiveros, Saldana-J. Cruz-Enriquez, Tabasco; E. Hernandez-Perry, Renteria-Perry, Union Laguna; Antunez-Jaime Granillo, Colorado-C. Ibarra, Dozier-Antunez, Dozier-Garibay, Esquer-Jaime Granillo, Yucatan.

NO-HIT GAMES—Is. Velazquez, Leon, defeated Mexico City Tigers, 5-0 (seven innings), July 4; Reynoso, Saltillo, defeated Monterrey Industrials, 1-0 (seven innings), July 20; Cervantes, Union Laguna, defeated Monterrey Industrials, 4-0, August 4.

Pacific Coast League

CLASS AAA

Leading Batter
LUIS LOPEZ
Albuquerque

League President
BILL CUTLER

Leading Pitcher
MIKE COOK
Portland

CHAMPIONSHIP WINNERS IN PREVIOUS YEARS

1903—Los Angeles .... .630	1936—Portland‡ .... .549	1968—Tulsa a .... .642
1904—Tacoma .... .589	1937—Sacramento............. .573	Spokane............. .586
Tacoma§............. .571	San Diego (3rd)†............. .545	1969—Tacoma a .... .589
Los Angeles§............. .571	1938—Los Angeles .... .590	Eugene............. .603
1905—Tacoma .... .583	Sacramento (3rd)†............. .537	1970—Spokane a............. .644
Los Angeles° .... .604	1939—Seattle............. .589	Hawaii............. .671
1906—Portland............. .657	Sacramento (4th)†............. .500	1971—Salt Lake City............. .534
1907—Los Angeles .... .608	1940—Seattle‡............. .629	Tacoma............. .545
1908—Los Angeles .... .585	1941—Seattle‡............. .598	1972—Albuquerque .... .622
1909—San Francisco .... .623	1942—Sacramento............. .590	Eugene............. .534
1910—Portland............. .567	Seattle (3rd)†............. .539	1973—Tucson............. .583
1911—Portland............. .589	1943—Los Angeles .... .710	Spokane............. .563
1912—Oakland............. .591	S. Francisco (2nd)†............. .574	1974—Spokane a............. .549
1913—Portland............. .559	1944—Los Angeles .... .586	Albuquerque .... .535
1914—Portland............. .574	S. Francisco (3rd)†............. .509	1975—Salt Lake City............. .556
1915—San Francisco .... .570	1945—Portland............. .622	Hawaii a .... .611
1916—Los Angeles .... .601	S. Francisco (4th)†............. .525	1976—Salt Lake City............. .625
1917—San Francisco .... .561	1946—San Francisco‡............. .628	Hawaii a............. .531
1918—Vernon............. .569	1947—Los Angeles††............. .567	1977—Phoenix a............. .579
Los Angeles (2nd) x............. .548	1948—Oakland‡............. .606	Hawaii............. .541
1919—Vernon............. .613	1949—Hollywood‡............. .583	1978—Tacoma b............. .584
1920—Vernon............. .556	1950—Oakland............. .590	Albuquerque b............. .557
1921—Los Angeles .... .574	1951—Seattle‡............. .593	1979—Albuquerque .... .581
1922—San Francisco .... .638	1952—Hollywood .... .606	Salt Lake City c............. .541
1923—San Francisco .... .617	1953—Hollywood .... .589	1980—Albuquerque° .... .578
1924—Seattle............. .545	1954—San Diego y .... .604	Hawaii............. .539
1925—San Francisco .... .643	1955—Seattle............. .552	1981—Albuquerque° .... .712
1926—Los Angeles .... .599	1956—Los Angeles .... .637	Tacoma............. .561
1927—Oakland............. .615	1957—San Francisco .... .601	1982—Albuquerque° .... .594
1928—San Francisco° .... .630	1958—Phoenix .... .578	Spokane............. .545
Sacramento§§............. .626	1959—Salt Lake City............. .552	1983—Albuquerque° .... .594
San Francisco§§............. .626	1960—Spokane............. .601	Portland°............. .528
1929—Mission .... .643	1961—Tacoma .... .630	1984—Albuquerque .... .621
Hollywood° .... .592	1962—San Diego .... .604	Edmonton°............. .486
1930—Hollywood .... .576	1963—Spokane............. .620	1985—Vancouver° .... .552
Hollywood° .... .650	Oklahoma City a............. .632	Phoenix............. .563
1931—Hollywood .... .626	1964—Arkansas............. .609	1986—Vancouver .... .616
San Francisco° .... .608	San Diego a............. .576	Las Vegas°............. .563
1932—Portland............. .587	1965—Oklahoma City a .... .628	1987—Calgary............. .596
1933—Los Angeles .... .610	Portland............. .547	Albuquerque° .... .542
1934—Los Angeles z .... .786	1966—Seattle a .... .561	1988—Vancouver............. .599
Los Angeles z .... .689	Tulsa............. .578	Las Vegas°............. .529
1935—Los Angeles .... .648	1967—San Diego a .... .574	1989—Albuquerque............. .563
San Francisco° .... .608	Spokane............. .541	Vancouver° .... .514

STANDING OF CLUBS AT CLOSE OF FIRST HALF, JUNE 21

NORTHERN DIVISION

Club	W.	L.	T.	Pct.	G.B.
Tacoma (Athletics)	43	27	0	.614	....
Vancouver (White Sox)	42	27	0	.609	½
Calgary (Mariners)	37	35	0	.514	7
Edmonton (Angels)	31	38	0	.449	11½
Portland (Twins)	23	47	0	.329	20

SOUTHERN DIVISION

Club	W.	L.	T.	Pct.	G.B.
Albuquerque (Dodgers)	46	25	0	.648	....
Colorado Springs (Indians)	37	34	0	.521	9
Phoenix (Giants)	35	33	0	.515	9½
Tucson (Astros)	29	43	0	.403	17½
Las Vegas (Padres)	29	43	0	.403	17½

STANDING OF CLUBS AT CLOSE OF SECOND HALF, SEPTEMBER 3

NORTHERN DIVISION

Club	W.	L.	T.	Pct.	G.B.
Edmonton (Angels)	47	25	0	.653	....
Portland (Twins)	33	36	0	.478	12½
Vancouver (White Sox)	32	40	0	.444	15
Tacoma (Athletics)	32	40	0	.444	15
Calgary (Mariners)	29	42	0	.408	17½

SOUTHERN DIVISION

Club	W.	L.	T.	Pct.	G.B.
Albuquerque (Dodgers)	45	26	0	.634	....
Tucson (Astros)	42	28	0	.600	2½
Colorado Springs (Indians)	39	33	0	.542	6½
Las Vegas (Padres)	29	43	0	.403	16½
Phoenix (Giants)	28	43	0	.394	17

COMPOSITE STANDING OF CLUBS AT CLOSE OF SEASON, SEPTEMBER 3

Club	Alb.	Edm.	C.S.	Tac.	Van.	Tuc.	Cal.	Phoe.	Port.	L.V.	W.	L.	T.	Pct.	G.B.
Albuquerque (Dodgers)	....	10	9	8	7	10	12	10	12	13	91	51	0	.641	....
Edmonton (Angels)	6	....	9	9	7	10	9	10	10	8	78	63	0	.553	12½
Colorado Springs (Indians)	7	7	....	9	8	8	8	11	10	10	76	67	0	.531	15½
Tacoma (Athletics)	7	7	7	....	11	10	8	9	6	10	75	67	0	.528	16
Vancouver (White Sox)	9	9	7	5	....	7	9	10	10	8	74	67	0	.525	16½
Tucson (Astros)	6	6	8	6	9	....	8	8	9	11	71	71	0	.500	20
Calgary (Mariners)	4	7	8	8	7	7	....	9	8	8	66	77	0	.462	25½
Phoenix (Giants)	6	3	8	6	6	8	7	....	9	10	63	76	0	.453	26½
Portland (Twins)	3	6	5	10	4	6	8	6	....	8	56	83	0	.403	33½
Las Vegas (Padres)	3	8	6	6	8	5	8	5	8	....	58	86	0	.403	34

Major league affiliations in parentheses.

Playoffs—Albuquerque defeated Colorado Springs, three games to two; Edmonton defeated Tacoma, three games to two; Albuquerque defeated Edmonton, three games to none, to win league championship.

Regular-Season Attendance—Albuquerque, 324,046; Calgary, 312,416; Colorado Springs, 201,642; Edmonton, 229,307; Las Vegas, 312,522; Phoenix, 248,660; Portland, 150,054; Tacoma, 309,210; Tucson, 238,629; Vancouver, 281,540. Total, 2,608,026. Playoffs (13 games)—35,429. AAA All-Star Game at Las Vegas—10,323.

Managers—Albuquerque, Kevin Kennedy; Calgary, Tom Jones; Colorado Springs, Bobby Molinaro (through June 21), Charlie Manuel (June 22 through end of season); Edmonton, Max Oliveras; Las Vegas, Pat Kelly; Phoenix, Duane Espy; Portland, Phil Roof; Tacoma, Brad Fischer; Tucson, Bob Skinner; Vancouver, Marv Foley. Managerial records of teams with more than one manager: Colorado Springs, Molinaro 37-34, Manuel, 39-33.

All-Star Team—1B—Tino Martinez, Calgary; 2B—Todd Haney, Calgary; 3B—Dave Hansen, Albuquerque; SS—Jose Offerman, Albuquerque; OF—Mark Leonard, Phoenix; Mike Huff, Albuquerque; Butch Davis, Albuquerque; C—Jerry Willard, Vancouver; DH—Tom Dodd, Calgary; RHP—Scott Chiamparino, Tacoma; LHP—Grady Hall, Vancouver; RP—Joe Bitker, Tacoma; Most Valuable Player, Jose Offerman, Albuquerque; Manager of the Year—Kevin Kennedy, Albuquerque.

(Compiled by Howe Sportsdata International, Boston, Mass.)

CLUB BATTING

Club	Pct.	G.	AB.	R.	OR.	H.	TB.	2B.	3B.	HR.	RBI.	SH.	SF.	HP.	BB.	Int. BB.	SO.	SB.	CS.	LOB.
Albuquerque	.307	142	4692	813	658	1441	2000	244	51	71	733	41	71	35	572	38	614	195	82	1043
Colorado Springs	.292	143	4689	832	758	1369	2070	272	45	113	766	30	58	33	633	19	764	124	76	1007
Tucson	.281	142	4755	768	779	1335	1954	263	58	80	700	55	54	37	571	35	835	103	67	1036
Calgary	.279	143	4698	737	803	1312	1925	242	40	97	677	50	50	30	508	26	749	122	71	958
Las Vegas	.279	144	4872	753	876	1357	2025	234	49	112	683	55	56	38	623	30	913	157	65	1118
Edmonton	.277	141	4779	738	652	1324	1988	274	48	98	679	43	45	41	584	28	847	124	75	1056
Phoenix	.272	139	4659	671	731	1267	1883	229	60	89	605	17	37	51	537	29	883	115	86	1022
Tacoma	.265	142	4628	695	661	1228	1827	248	42	89	634	48	43	46	541	21	890	124	58	1006
Vancouver	.260	141	4574	661	628	1189	1729	223	43	77	588	46	41	39	573	30	756	127	84	998
Portland	.254	139	4514	591	713	1148	1770	241	33	105	532	26	42	32	499	18	811	83	60	936

INDIVIDUAL BATTING

(Leading Qualifiers for Batting Championship—389 or More Plate Appearances)

*Bats lefthanded.   †Switch-hitter.

Player and Club	Pct.	G.	AB.	R.	H.	TB.	2B.	3B.	HR.	RBI.	SH.	SF.	HP.	BB.	Int. BB.	SO.	SB.	CS.
Lopez, Luis, Albuquerque	.353	128	448	65	158	218	23	2	11	81	0	2	4	47	4	49	3	3
Davis, Wallace, Albuquerque	.342	124	480	87	164	243	31	9	10	85	0	11	4	24	5	53	25	14
Haney, Todd, Calgary	.339	108	419	81	142	172	15	6	1	36	6	0	4	37	1	38	16	11
Leonard, Mark, Phoenix*	.333	109	390	76	130	213	22	2	19	82	0	4	4	76	1	81	6	3
Howard, Thomas, Las Vegas†	.328	89	341	58	112	169	26	8	5	51	4	4	0	44	5	63	27	5
Offerman, Jose, Albuquerque†	.326	117	454	104	148	186	16	11	0	56	4	4	2	71	2	81	60	19
Huff, Michael, Albuquerque	.325	138	474	99	154	225	28	11	7	84	6	10	3	82	5	68	27	13
Cockrell, Alan, 6 Port.-113 C.S.	.323	119	375	77	121	206	24	5	17	71	0	3	3	50	2	73	6	3
Powell, Alonzo, Portland	.322	107	376	56	121	176	25	3	8	62	0	3	4	40	1	79	23	11
Martinez, Constantino, Calgary*	.320	128	453	83	145	226	28	1	17	93	2	8	3	74	11	37	8	5

Departmental Leaders: G—Huff, 138; AB—Faries, 552; R—Faries, 109; H—Faries, 172; TB—W. Davis, 243; 2B—Amaral, 39; 3B—K. Ward, 14; HR—Brito, 25; RBI—Dodd, 114; SH—Castillo, McGuire, 11; SF—W. Davis, 11; HP—K. Ward, 14; BB—Hansen, 90; IBB—Martinez, Stevens, 11; SO—Simms, 135; SB—Offerman, 60; CS—Cole, Offerman, 19.

(All Players—Listed Alphabetically)

Player and Club	Pct.	G.	AB.	R.	H.	TB.	2B.	3B.	HR.	RBI.	SH.	SF.	HP.	BB.	Int. BB.	SO.	SB.	CS.
Afenir, Troy, Tacoma	.249	88	289	44	72	135	14	2	15	47	4	1	1	30	0	81	1	1
Aguayo, Luis, Edmonton	.286	23	77	12	22	37	7	1	2	14	0	1	3	6	0	7	1	2
Aldrich, Jay, Phoenix	.000	8	1	0	0	0	0	0	0	0	0	0	0	0	0	0	0	0
Alfonzo, Edgar, Edmonton*	.182	4	11	1	2	2	0	0	0	1	0	0	0	0	0	1	0	0
Allaire, Karl, Edmonton*	.254	44	122	16	31	41	6	2	0	14	4	1	0	16	1	18	3	2
Allred, LeBeau, Colorado Springs*	.278	115	378	79	105	179	23	6	13	74	2	7	4	60	1	54	6	3
Amaral, Richard, Vancouver	.301	130	462	87	139	200	39	5	4	56	9	4	4	88	3	68	20	14

Player and Club	Pct.	G.	AB.	R.	H.	TB.	2B.	3B.	HR.	RBI.	SH.	SF.	HP.	BB.	Int. BB.	SO.	SB.	CS.
Amaro, Ruben, Edmonton†	.289	82	318	53	92	124	15	4	3	32	5	3	7	40	2	43	32	14
Anderson, Kent, Edmonton	.271	18	59	10	16	24	6	1	0	7	2	0	2	8	0	8	1	1
Anthony, Eric, Tucson°	.286	40	161	28	46	78	10	2	6	26	0	3	1	17	0	41	8	3
Arndt, Larry, Tacoma	.251	121	438	59	110	143	17	5	2	59	6	4	3	38	1	87	16	5
Baerga, Carlos, Colorado Springs†	.380	12	50	11	19	26	2	1	1	11	0	0	0	5	2	4	1	0
Bailey, Mark, Phoenix†	.223	57	175	19	39	64	4	0	7	28	0	2	0	28	2	31	2	0
Baine, Thomas, Portland	.241	26	83	11	20	29	3	0	2	7	0	2	1	13	1	11	2	0
Baker, Douglas, Portland†	.216	91	301	46	65	93	15	2	3	18	4	1	2	41	1	61	6	8
Baldwin, Jeffrey, Tucson°	.135	19	37	4	5	6	1	0	0	5	0	0	0	7	2	11	0	0
Bass, Kevin, Phoenix†	.242	8	33	2	8	10	2	0	0	4	0	0	0	0	0	4	1	1
Basso, Michael, Las Vegas	.193	50	150	5	29	37	5	0	1	12	1	2	0	16	1	20	1	1
Bathe, William, Phoenix	.286	18	56	9	16	24	5	0	1	9	0	0	0	6	0	7	0	0
Bean, William, Albuquerque°	.295	129	427	85	126	183	26	5	7	67	1	4	6	69	2	63	16	8
Beauchamp, Kash, Phoenix	.281	55	121	12	34	45	4	2	1	15	0	1	1	7	1	21	2	3
Beck, Rodney, Phoenix	.083	12	12	1	1	1	0	0	0	0	0	0	0	0	0	3	0	0
Belle, Albert, Colorado Springs	.344	24	96	16	33	53	3	1	5	19	0	0	0	5	0	16	4	3
Benjamin, Michael, Phoenix	.251	118	419	61	105	155	21	7	5	39	2	5	5	25	3	89	13	7
Bittiger, Jeffrey, Albuquerque	.238	28	21	2	5	6	1	0	0	6	1	0	0	1	0	2	0	0
Blankenship, Lance, Tacoma	.258	24	93	18	24	36	7	1	1	9	0	0	1	14	0	16	7	3
Bones, Ricardo, Las Vegas	.000	5	2	0	0	0	0	0	0	0	0	0	0	0	0	0	0	0
Bonilla, George, Phoenix°	.000	36	1	0	0	0	0	0	0	0	0	0	0	0	0	0	0	0
Booker, Gregory, Phoenix	.000	49	2	0	0	0	0	0	0	0	0	0	0	0	0	0	0	0
Bordick, Michael, Tacoma	.227	111	348	49	79	103	16	1	2	30	7	2	3	46	0	40	3	0
Bowen, Ryan, Tucson	1.000	11	1	1	1	2	1	0	0	0	0	0	0	0	0	0	0	0
Brady, Brian, Phoenix°	.254	102	303	36	77	103	11	3	3	32	0	2	4	48	1	68	3	8
Brantley, Michael, Calgary	.233	29	103	17	24	30	3	0	1	8	1	0	0	8	1	12	3	0
Brennan, William, Tucson	.250	41	12	3	3	4	1	0	0	0	0	0	0	2	0	5	0	0
Brito, Bernardo, Portland	.282	113	376	48	106	213	26	3	25	79	2	4	2	27	3	102	1	4
Brosius, Scott, Tacoma	.143	3	7	2	1	3	0	1	0	0	0	0	0	1	0	3	0	0
Brown, Adam, Albuquerque	.364	5	11	2	4	4	0	0	0	1	0	0	0	1	0	1	0	0
Brown, Todd, Tucson	.400	8	20	2	8	8	0	0	0	2	0	0	1	1	0	1	0	0
Bruett, Joseph, Portland°	.235	10	34	8	8	10	2	0	0	3	0	1	0	11	0	4	2	1
Brumley, Michael, Calgary†	.321	8	28	4	9	10	1	0	0	1	0	0	0	1	1	3	3	0
Brundage, David, Calgary°	.304	92	309	63	94	131	22	3	3	48	2	5	0	60	0	60	8	3
Buhner, Jay, Calgary	.206	13	34	6	7	14	1	0	2	5	0	1	0	7	0	11	0	0
Bush, Randall, Portland°	.222	3	9	2	2	4	2	0	0	1	0	0	0	3	1	1	0	0
Camacho, Ernie, Phoenix	.000	13	1	0	0	0	0	0	0	0	0	0	0	0	0	1	0	0
Campbell, Darrin, Vancouver°	.143	2	7	0	1	1	0	0	0	0	0	0	0	0	0	1	0	0
Candaele, Casey, Tucson†	.214	7	28	2	6	7	1	0	0	2	1	0	1	3	1	2	1	2
Cano, Joselito, Tucson	.125	10	8	0	1	1	0	0	0	0	0	0	0	0	0	1	0	0
Carter, Jeffrey, Phoenix†	.292	121	435	80	127	172	21	9	2	63	2	2	5	63	1	81	28	11
Casey, Timothy, Tacoma°	.189	48	106	15	20	33	5	1	2	7	0	1	0	17	3	35	0	0
Castillo, Juan, Colorado Springs†	.284	113	345	56	98	117	8	4	1	33	11	0	0	42	0	56	16	9
Christopher, Michael, Albuquerque	.000	54	3	0	0	0	0	0	0	0	1	0	0	0	0	1	0	0
Clancy, James, Tucson	.000	10	4	0	0	0	0	0	0	0	0	0	0	0	0	1	0	0
Clark, Jerald, Las Vegas	.304	40	161	30	49	100	7	4	12	32	0	2	0	5	0	35	2	0
Clark, Terry, Tucson	.100	32	20	2	2	3	1	0	0	1	2	0	0	0	0	1	0	0
Clements, Patrick, Las Vegas	.000	26	8	0	0	0	0	0	0	0	2	0	0	1	0	1	0	0
Close, Casey, Calgary	.270	128	463	71	125	199	30	4	12	69	3	1	5	34	3	76	15	6
Coachman, Dean, Edmonton	.291	111	419	78	122	156	15	2	5	51	2	5	6	74	1	49	27	4
Cochrane, David, Calgary†	.275	69	262	43	72	118	14	4	8	36	0	2	1	23	1	62	2	0
Cockrell, Alan, 6 Port.-113 C.S.	.323	119	375	77	121	206	24	5	17	71	0	3	3	50	2	73	6	3
Colbert, Craig, Phoenix	.280	111	400	41	112	162	22	2	8	47	1	2	3	31	3	80	4	5
Cole, Alexander, 90 L.V.-14 C.S.°	.308	104	390	71	120	137	9	4	0	31	8	2	1	55	1	69	38	19
Colombino, Carlo, Tucson	.252	81	290	31	73	98	7	3	4	40	1	2	0	10	2	35	3	7
Conley, Gregory, Las Vegas	.333	2	6	1	2	2	0	0	0	1	0	0	0	1	0	2	0	0
Cook, Michael, Portland	.000	20	1	0	0	0	0	0	0	0	0	0	0	0	0	0	0	0
Cora, Jose, Las Vegas†	.351	51	211	41	74	105	13	9	0	24	1	4	4	29	2	16	15	7
Cron, Christopher, Edmonton	.287	104	401	54	115	197	31	0	17	75	1	5	5	28	1	92	7	5
Dalena, Peter, 56 Van.-43 Port.°	.254	99	355	39	90	123	19	4	2	42	1	5	1	30	4	42	2	5
Davidson, Mark, Tucson	.335	56	182	35	61	94	13	1	6	46	2	6	3	22	2	35	5	1
Davis, Douglas, Edmonton	.247	53	162	18	40	58	12	0	2	23	0	1	1	25	1	31	0	4
Davis, John, Las Vegas	.111	18	9	0	1	1	0	0	0	1	0	0	0	0	0	2	0	0
Davis, Mark, Edmonton	.368	35	133	30	49	96	10	5	9	34	2	2	0	17	0	23	7	8
Davis, Steven, Albuquerque°	.111	31	9	0	1	1	0	0	0	2	3	0	0	0	0	1	0	0
Davis, Wallace, Albuquerque	.342	124	480	87	164	243	31	9	10	85	0	11	4	24	5	53	25	14
Dean, Kevin, Tucson	.257	13	35	5	9	10	1	0	0	5	0	1	0	4	0	12	0	2
DeAngelis, Steven, Edmonton°	.299	61	224	34	67	91	8	2	4	30	0	1	0	16	1	39	3	2
DeLima, Rafael, Portland°	.202	61	188	23	38	51	6	2	1	19	1	3	1	18	0	18	6	3
Dewey, Mark, Phoenix	.000	19	1	0	0	0	0	0	0	0	0	0	0	0	0	0	0	0
Diaz, Mario, Calgary	.333	32	105	10	35	45	5	1	1	19	0	1	1	0	0	8	0	1
Dietrick, Patrick, Tacoma	.200	13	30	3	6	8	2	0	0	1	0	0	3	0	0	10	0	1
DiMascio, Daniel, Calgary	.357	14	42	4	15	20	3	1	0	2	0	0	2	4	0	7	0	1
Disarcina, Gary, Edmonton	.212	97	330	46	70	98	12	2	4	37	5	2	4	25	0	46	5	3
Dodd, Thomas, Calgary	.281	135	501	71	141	226	31	3	16	114	1	8	1	42	1	101	6	5
Downs, Kelly, Phoenix	.000	1	1	0	0	0	0	0	0	0	0	0	0	0	0	0	0	0
Dunne, Michael, Las Vegas°	.000	4	2	0	0	0	0	0	0	0	1	0	0	0	0	1	0	0
Eave, Gary, 1 Cal.-10 Phoe.	.200	11	5	2	1	1	0	0	0	0	1	0	0	0	0	1	0	0
Eichhorn, David, Tucson†	.000	28	1	0	0	0	0	0	0	0	0	0	0	0	0	0	0	0
Faries, Paul, Las Vegas	.312	137	552	109	172	222	29	3	5	64	7	1	6	75	1	60	48	15
Fields, Bruce, Tacoma°	.280	87	336	46	94	122	18	2	2	34	1	1	1	36	3	62	8	2
Fisher, Brian, Tucson	.200	30	10	1	2	2	0	0	0	1	0	0	1	0	0	5	0	0
Fletcher, Darrin, Albuquerque°	.291	105	350	58	102	166	23	1	13	65	3	6	5	40	6	37	1	1
Fox, Eric, Tacoma†	.276	62	221	37	61	86	9	2	4	34	5	2	0	20	0	34	8	8
Fulton, Gregory, Calgary†	.291	22	55	11	16	21	5	0	0	4	0	0	0	7	0	6	0	0
Gainey, Telmando, Colorado Springs°..	.237	19	38	7	9	15	3	0	1	8	0	0	1	0	6	1	8	0
Gaither, Horace, Vancouver°	.000	1	3	0	0	0	0	0	0	0	0	0	0	0	0	1	0	0
Garbey, Barbaro, Albuquerque	.000	1	4	0	0	0	0	0	0	0	0	0	0	0	0	0	0	0
Gerhart, Kenneth, Colorado Springs	.000	4	7	1	0	0	0	0	0	0	0	0	0	1	0	4	0	0
Gibson, Kirk, Albuquerque°	.429	5	14	6	6	11	2	0	1	4	0	0	0	4	2	3	1	0
Gieseke, Mark, Las Vegas†	.227	5	22	2	5	6	1	0	0	3	0	0	0	2	0	2	0	0
Giles, Brian, Calgary	.262	38	122	28	32	55	8	0	5	19	0	1	1	23	2	33	5	3

Player and Club	Pct.	G.	AB.	R.	H.	TB.	2B.	3B.	HR.	RBI.	SH.	SF.	HP.	BB.	Int. BB.	SO.	SB.	CS.
Gilmore, Terrance, Las Vegas	.071	48	14	1	1	1	0	0	0	2	3	0	0	1	0	5	0	0
Grebeck, Craig, Vancouver	.195	12	41	8	8	11	0	0	1	3	0	0	0	6	0	7	1	0
Green, Otis, Phoenix°	.273	8	22	4	6	8	2	0	0	0	0	1	1	0	0	7	0	1
Grunhard, Daniel, Edmonton°	.301	126	462	69	139	192	27	4	6	58	1	2	2	59	3	78	7	9
Gunderson, Eric, Phoenix	.308	16	13	1	4	6	2	0	0	1	2	0	0	0	0	4	0	0
Hale, Walter, Portland°	.280	130	479	71	134	171	24	2	3	40	7	7	1	68	3	57	6	6
Haney, Todd, Calgary	.339	108	419	81	142	172	15	6	1	36	6	0	4	37	1	38	16	11
Hansen, David, Albuquerque°	.316	135	487	90	154	213	20	3	11	92	0	9	3	90	4	54	9	4
Harris, Russell, Tucson†	.294	44	126	24	37	50	7	3	0	8	5	0	2	7	0	19	2	3
Hartsock, Jeffrey, Albuquerque	.200	11	10	0	2	2	0	0	0	1	0	0	0	1	0	4	0	0
Hearn, Edward, Colorado Springs	.288	17	52	7	15	21	3	0	1	8	0	0	0	0	0	6	0	0
Hemond, Scott, Tacoma	.243	72	218	32	53	88	11	0	8	35	3	3	1	24	3	52	10	5
Henley, Daniel, Albuquerque	.305	87	243	40	74	92	12	0	2	31	4	8	3	24	1	35	4	3
Hennis, Randall, Tucson	.111	29	18	0	2	2	0	0	0	1	1	0	0	0	0	8	0	0
Heredia, Gilbert, Phoenix	.000	30	15	0	0	0	0	0	0	0	0	0	0	0	0	3	0	0
Hernandez, Carlos, Albuquerque	.315	52	143	11	45	55	8	1	0	16	0	3	1	8	1	25	2	2
Hickerson, Bryan, Phoenix°	.000	12	1	0	0	0	0	0	0	0	0	0	0	1	0	1	0	0
Higgins, Kevin, Las Vegas°	.269	9	26	4	7	10	1	1	0	3	0	1	1	4	0	3	0	0
Hill, Orsino, Vancouver°	.284	106	366	61	104	163	20	3	11	60	0	4	4	55	7	86	5	4
Hillemann, Charles, Las Vegas	.243	91	300	36	73	99	11	3	3	25	7	0	6	23	2	63	3	6
Hinshaw, George, Phoenix	.272	90	294	29	80	117	11	4	6	49	0	3	2	18	1	57	2	2
Hoffman, Glenn, Albuquerque	.302	24	63	7	19	24	3	1	0	10	1	1	0	2	1	9	1	1
Holmes, Darren, Albuquerque	.400	56	5	2	2	2	0	0	0	0	0	0	0	0	0	1	0	0
Howard, Steven, Tacoma	.270	97	330	55	89	145	18	4	10	45	1	3	8	42	1	100	17	5
Howard, Thomas, Las Vegas†	.328	89	341	58	112	169	26	8	5	51	4	4	0	44	5	63	27	5
Howell, Jack, Edmonton°	.333	20	75	14	25	40	7	1	2	15	0	1	0	7	0	13	3	0
Howitt, Dann, Tacoma°	.265	118	437	58	116	181	30	1	11	69	0	4	2	38	3	95	4	4
Hubbard, Trent, Tucson†	.222	12	27	5	6	12	2	2	0	2	0	0	3	0	6	1	1	
Huff, Michael, Albuquerque	.325	138	474	99	154	225	28	11	7	84	6	10	3	82	5	68	27	13
Humphreys, Michael, Las Vegas	.238	12	42	7	10	17	1	0	2	6	2	0	1	4	0	11	1	0
Ilsley, Blaise, Tucson°	.714	23	7	3	5	5	0	0	0	3	0	0	0	0	0	1	0	0
Jacas, David, Portland	.231	112	350	57	81	128	18	4	7	26	2	3	5	30	1	60	18	8
Jackson, Charles, Phoenix	.289	74	273	47	79	105	18	4	0	26	1	0	3	33	0	28	3	7
Jackson, Darrin, Las Vegas	.276	29	98	14	27	46	4	0	5	15	0	2	0	9	0	21	3	0
Jefferson, Stanley, Colorado Springs†	.345	33	119	27	41	65	9	3	3	17	0	1	0	20	1	22	8	6
Jennings, Douglas, Tacoma°	.346	60	208	32	72	111	19	1	6	30	1	3	2	31	4	36	4	2
Johnson, Erik, Phoenix	.000	2	3	0	0	0	0	0	0	0	0	0	0	1	0	1	0	0
Johnson, Wallace, Tacoma†	.333	6	18	5	6	9	1	1	0	2	0	0	0	3	0	1	0	0
Jorgensen, Terry, Portland	.259	123	440	43	114	178	28	3	10	50	1	4	0	44	2	83	0	4
Jurak, Edward, Calgary	.255	114	353	47	90	132	17	2	7	52	0	4	2	54	0	56	5	8
Kellner, Frank, Tucson†	.300	19	60	13	18	19	1	0	0	7	2	0	0	15	0	6	1	0
Kile, Darryl, Tucson	.071	29	14	0	1	1	0	0	0	0	2	0	0	0	0	6	0	0
Kingery, Michael, Phoenix°	.240	35	100	12	24	40	9	2	1	16	0	3	1	18	2	15	2	4
Kirby, Wayne, Albuquerque°	.278	119	342	56	95	119	14	5	0	30	4	3	3	28	1	36	29	7
Knapp, Michael, Edmonton	.205	12	39	3	8	10	0	1	0	4	0	0	0	4	0	6	0	0
Laga, Michael, Phoenix°	.298	89	309	63	92	182	18	3	22	71	0	5	10	42	9	62	0	6
Lampkin, Thomas, 69 C.S.-1 L.V.°	.224	70	201	32	45	65	7	5	1	18	0	1	2	19	0	20	7	2
Lanoux, Carol, Portland°	.187	28	75	5	14	22	5	0	1	10	2	0	0	11	2	7	0	0
Laudner, Timothy, Portland	.000	9	29	2	0	0	0	0	0	0	0	0	0	3	0	9	0	0
Lawton, Marcus, Vancouver†	.252	122	417	48	105	151	22	9	2	43	10	1	0	36	3	50	16	12
Leius, Scott, Portland	.229	103	353	34	81	110	13	5	2	23	4	0	0	35	0	66	5	3
Leonard, Mark, Phoenix°	.333	109	390	76	130	213	22	2	19	82	0	4	4	76	1	81	6	3
LeVasseur, Thomas, Las Vegas	.218	90	257	35	56	87	10	3	5	37	3	7	1	36	2	37	7	4
Lewis, Darren, Tacoma	.291	60	247	32	72	87	5	2	2	26	4	2	1	16	0	35	16	6
Lewis, James, Las Vegas	.000	59	4	0	0	0	0	0	0	0	0	0	0	0	0	3	0	0
Lewis, Mark, Colorado Springs	.306	34	124	16	38	51	8	1	1	21	1	1	0	9	0	13	2	3
Litton, Gregory, Phoenix	.273	6	22	3	6	7	1	0	0	4	0	1	0	2	0	7	0	0
Lopez, Luis, Albuquerque	.353	128	448	65	158	218	23	2	11	81	0	2	4	47	4	49	3	3
Lynch, Joseph, Las Vegas	.000	58	7	2	0	0	0	0	0	0	1	0	0	1	0	1	0	0
Madden, Morris, Albuquerque°	.200	31	5	1	1	2	1	0	0	0	2	0	0	0	0	3	0	0
Maddux, Michael, Albuquerque°	.000	20	8	0	0	0	0	0	0	0	0	0	0	2	0	1	0	0
Magallanes, Everardo, C. S.°	.308	125	377	60	116	142	17	3	1	63	5	6	1	43	0	49	3	2
Magrann, Thomas, Colorado Springs	.276	88	228	36	63	85	16	0	2	39	3	3	2	33	1	30	1	4
Mangham, Eric, Albuquerque	.111	6	9	1	1	1	0	0	0	0	0	0	0	0	0	6	0	0
Manrique, Fred, Portland	1.000	1	1	0	1	1	0	0	0	1	0	0	0	0	0	0	0	1
Manto, Jeffrey, Colorado Springs	.297	96	316	73	94	177	27	1	18	82	1	3	9	78	2	65	10	3
Manwaring, Kirt, Phoenix	.235	74	247	20	58	81	10	2	3	14	0	3	24	1	34	0	3	
Manzanillo, Ravelo, Vancouver°	1.000	39	1	0	1	2	1	0	0	0	0	0	0	0	0	0	0	0
Marquez, Edwin, Tucson	.339	18	56	12	19	28	2	2	1	10	1	1	0	6	0	7	1	1
Martin, Norberto, Vancouver†	.266	130	508	77	135	172	20	4	3	45	8	6	5	27	0	63	10	7
Martinez, Constantino, Calgary	.320	128	453	83	145	226	28	1	17	93	2	8	3	74	11	37	8	5
Mayberry, Gregory, Albuquerque°	.000	32	5	0	0	0	0	0	0	0	0	0	0	0	0	1	0	0
Maysey, Matthew, Las Vegas	.118	26	17	0	2	2	0	0	0	0	1	0	1	0	0	7	0	0
McCament, Randall, Phoenix	.000	46	3	0	0	0	0	0	0	0	0	0	0	0	0	3	0	0
McClellan, Paul, Phoenix	.250	29	20	0	5	6	1	0	0	3	0	2	0	0	0	3	1	0
McCollom, James, Edmonton	.292	6	24	6	7	10	1	1	0	3	0	0	0	3	0	3	0	0
McConnell, Walter, Albuquerque°	.204	34	49	5	10	12	2	0	0	5	0	0	1	6	0	20	0	1
McCray, Rodney, Vancouver	.226	19	53	7	12	20	4	2	0	6	1	0	2	10	0	20	4	3
McGinnis, Russell, Tacoma	.248	110	359	57	89	149	19	1	13	77	1	7	6	75	2	70	2	1
McGuire, William, Calgary	.229	118	358	47	82	119	12	2	7	46	11	5	1	33	0	69	2	1
McLemore, Mark, 9 Edm.-14 C.S.†	.269	23	93	15	25	32	4	0	1	10	0	0	0	17	0	18	5	3
McNamara, James, Phoenix°	.450	6	20	2	9	9	0	0	0	1	0	0	0	3	0	4	0	0
McPhail, Marlin, Vancouver	.288	109	386	50	111	168	23	5	8	60	5	6	3	35	0	59	6	6
Mead, Timber, Phoenix	.000	22	0	0	0	0	0	0	0	0	1	0	0	0	0	0	0	0
Meadows, Michael, Tucson°	.298	25	84	16	25	43	3	3	3	18	1	2	0	18	3	8	6	1
Medina, Luis, Colorado Springs	.272	94	320	58	87	156	15	0	18	53	0	3	3	33	0	68	7	3
Meier, Kevin, Phoenix	.143	13	7	0	1	1	0	0	0	1	1	0	0	0	0	1	0	0
Melendez, Francisco, C. S.°	.294	34	102	15	30	50	6	1	4	18	1	3	2	12	1	14	0	0
Mercedes, Henry, Tacoma	.194	12	31	3	6	7	1	0	0	2	2	0	0	3	0	7	0	1
Meyer, Brian, Tucson	.000	64	1	0	0	0	0	0	0	0	0	0	0	0	0	0	0	0
Mikulik, Joseph, Tucson	.331	62	175	31	58	76	11	2	1	29	1	2	1	13	2	17	3	4
Miller, Darrell, Calgary	.297	59	172	25	51	69	5	2	3	26	2	0	5	11	1	31	4	4

Player and Club	Pct.	G.	AB.	R.	H.	TB.	2B.	3B.	HR.	RBI.	SH.	SF.	HP.	BB.	Int. BB.	SO.	SB.	CS.
Morales, Richard, Calgary	.000	2	7	0	0	0	0	0	0	0	0	0	1	0	0	1	0	0
Mota, Jose, Las Vegas†	.300	92	247	44	74	98	4	4	4	21	3	1	3	42	2	35	2	1
Munoz, Michael, Albuquerque°	1.000	49	1	0	1	1	0	0	0	0	1	0	0	0	0	0	0	0
Munoz, Pedro, Portland	.318	30	110	19	35	54	4	0	5	21	0	0	4	15	1	18	8	4
Murphy, Daniel, Las Vegas	.250	27	4	1	1	1	0	0	0	0	0	0	0	0	0	3	0	0
Murray, Stephen, Calgary†	.292	22	65	8	19	20	1	0	0	6	0	1	0	5	1	15	3	1
Naveda, Edgar, Portland	.231	78	255	28	59	82	11	3	2	28	0	3	1	32	0	19	2	3
Neel, Troy, Colorado Springs°	.281	98	288	39	81	114	15	0	6	50	0	4	2	43	1	52	5	4
Neidlinger, James, Albuquerque†	.150	20	20	3	3	4	1	0	0	2	3	0	0	2	0	3	0	1
Nelson, James, Portland	.253	76	217	25	55	76	9	0	4	24	3	3	1	15	0	31	0	3
Nelson, Robert, Las Vegas°	.264	112	390	56	103	183	18	1	20	90	0	6	1	68	3	129	1	0
Newson, Warren, Las Vegas°	.304	123	404	80	123	188	20	3	13	58	1	4	0	83	3	110	13	5
Nichols, Carl, Tucson	.253	58	170	24	43	66	11	0	4	33	2	1	2	30	7	39	1	0
Nichols, Howard, Edmonton	.118	5	17	0	2	3	1	0	0	1	0	0	0	3	0	4	0	0
Nichols, Rodney, Colorado Springs	.000	23	1	0	0	0	0	0	0	0	0	0	0	0	0	1	0	0
Nolte, Eric, Las Vegas°	.000	33	5	0	0	0	0	0	0	0	2	0	0	0	0	3	0	0
O'Neal, Randall, Phoenix	.000	7	4	0	0	0	0	0	0	0	1	0	0	0	0	1	0	0
Offerman, Jose, Albuquerque†	.326	117	454	104	148	186	16	11	0	56	4	4	2	71	2	81	60	19
Ohnoutka, Brian, 10 L.V.-2 Edm.	.000	12	1	0	0	0	0	0	0	0	0	0	0	0	0	0	0	0
Olander, James, Tucson	.235	33	98	12	23	38	8	2	1	12	1	0	1	14	1	24	0	3
Ortiz, Javier, Tucson	.352	49	179	36	63	98	16	2	5	39	0	3	1	22	1	36	2	3
Ortiz, Joseph, Tucson	.250	7	12	1	3	3	0	0	0	3	1	0	0	0	2	0	0	0
Orton, John, Edmonton	.241	50	174	29	42	68	8	0	6	26	1	1	0	19	1	63	4	2
Owens, Mark, Phoenix°	.143	11	21	4	3	3	0	0	0	1	0	0	0	2	0	7	0	0
Pacillo, Patrick, Calgary	.000	33	1	0	0	0	0	0	0	1	0	1	0	0	0	0	0	0
Parker, Richard, Phoenix	.335	44	173	38	58	76	7	4	1	18	0	0	2	22	0	25	18	10
Parks, Derek, Portland	.177	76	231	27	41	84	8	1	11	27	0	1	8	18	0	56	0	0
Pedrique, Alfredo, Tacoma	.261	123	380	54	99	119	16	2	0	46	8	6	3	49	0	37	3	4
Penigar, Charles Lee, Vancouver†	.211	90	289	40	61	107	16	6	6	46	1	1	2	41	0	74	13	10
Perezchica, Antonio, Phoenix	.268	105	392	55	105	166	22	6	9	49	0	4	7	34	3	76	8	5
Peters, Reed, Edmonton	.232	51	181	16	42	59	9	1	2	22	2	2	1	19	1	29	2	4
Peters, Steven, Las Vegas°	.000	47	2	0	0	0	0	0	0	0	0	0	0	0	0	1	0	0
Pledger, Kinnis, Vancouver°	.000	1	1	0	0	0	0	0	0	0	0	0	0	0	0	0	0	0
Powell, Alonzo, Portland	.322	107	376	56	121	176	25	3	8	62	0	3	4	40	1	79	23	11
Renteria, Edinson, Tucson†	.291	35	110	15	32	37	2	0	1	12	3	2	2	7	0	14	2	2
Reynolds, Ronn, Las Vegas	.255	81	247	35	63	107	17	0	9	41	1	2	3	25	1	62	0	1
Rhodes, Karl, Tucson°	.275	107	385	68	106	161	24	11	3	59	3	5	0	47	2	75	24	4
Ritchie, Gregory, Phoenix°	.237	105	342	53	81	117	13	10	1	28	1	1	1	50	1	74	23	9
Roberts, Peter, Las Vegas°	.000	12	2	0	0	0	0	0	0	0	1	0	0	0	0	0	0	0
Rodriguez, Ricardo, Phoenix	.000	14	0	0	0	0	0	0	0	0	0	1	0	0	0	0	0	0
Rodriguez, Richard, Las Vegas°	.286	27	7	2	2	2	0	0	0	1	0	0	0	1	0	3	0	0
Rodriguez, Victor, Portland	.282	12	39	4	11	15	1	0	1	2	0	0	2	0	0	5	0	0
Rohde, David, Tucson†	.353	47	170	42	60	74	10	2	0	20	1	0	1	40	0	20	5	2
Rood, Nelson, Edmonton	.077	18	26	4	2	2	0	0	0	1	0	0	0	6	0	5	0	1
Rose, Robert, Edmonton	.283	134	502	84	142	216	27	10	9	68	7	6	4	56	0	83	6	2
Sambo, Ramon, Vancouver†	.250	102	324	46	81	90	3	3	0	31	3	1	0	54	3	59	30	10
Sanchez, Pedro, Vancouver†	.183	73	202	29	37	48	5	3	0	15	3	1	1	20	1	45	13	2
Santiago, Benito, Las Vegas	.300	6	20	5	6	11	2	0	1	8	0	1	0	3	0	1	0	0
Schaefer, Jeffrey, Edmonton	.241	49	170	24	41	54	9	2	0	19	9	2	0	18	0	15	8	7
Schofield, Richard, Edmonton	.389	5	18	4	7	11	1	0	1	4	0	0	0	3	0	4	0	0
Schu, Richard, Edmonton	.300	18	60	8	18	28	7	0	1	8	0	2	1	6	0	3	0	0
Sconiers, Daryl, Edmonton°	.333	2	6	1	2	3	1	0	0	2	0	0	0	2	0	1	0	0
Scott, Richard, Tacoma	.308	21	26	2	8	10	2	0	0	3	0	0	0	3	0	5	0	0
Servais, Scott, Tucson	.218	89	303	37	66	98	11	3	5	37	3	4	4	18	1	61	0	0
Sherman, Darrell, Las Vegas°	.000	4	12	1	0	0	0	0	0	0	1	0	0	1	0	2	1	0
Shockey, Scott, Tacoma°	.279	13	43	1	12	18	4	1	0	7	1	0	0	0	0	7	0	0
Sierra, Ulises, Las Vegas	.000	15	1	0	0	0	0	0	0	0	0	0	0	0	0	1	0	0
Simms, Michael, Tucson	.273	124	421	75	115	198	34	5	13	72	1	8	8	74	3	135	3	6
Sinatro, Matthew, Calgary	.300	9	20	1	6	9	0	0	1	2	1	0	0	2	0	3	0	0
Siwa, Joseph, Portland	.190	6	21	1	4	5	1	0	0	0	0	0	0	0	0	5	0	0
Skurla, John, 1 Phoe.-2 Edm.°	.229	43	144	20	33	53	7	2	3	21	3	2	1	15	1	28	0	2
Smajstrla, Craig, Tucson†	.313	124	473	86	148	187	25	4	2	42	5	2	4	58	1	36	8	7
Smith, Keith, Vancouver†	.236	85	259	36	61	71	7	0	1	24	7	1	0	28	0	39	4	2
Smithberg, Roger, Las Vegas	.000	13	3	0	0	0	0	0	0	0	2	0	0	0	0	2	0	0
Sorrento, Paul, Portland°	.302	102	354	59	107	193	27	1	19	72	0	5	1	64	2	95	3	0
Spilman, Harry, Tucson°	.268	77	190	11	51	78	13	1	4	42	1	5	0	16	2	27	0	1
Springer, Steven, 73 C.S.-22 L.V.	.272	95	324	46	88	148	26	5	8	52	1	10	0	24	1	67	6	4
Stevens, Lee, Edmonton°	.293	90	338	57	99	182	31	2	16	66	0	3	1	55	11	83	1	2
Strange, Douglas, Tucson†	.224	37	98	7	22	25	3	0	0	7	2	0	0	8	0	23	0	0
Sullivan, Marc, Colorado Springs	.313	12	32	4	10	16	3	0	1	7	0	0	0	4	0	6	0	0
Swain, Robert, Colorado Springs	.244	18	41	5	10	15	3	1	0	3	0	1	0	4	0	9	0	1
Swan, Russell, 6 Phoe.-5 Cal.°	.429	11	7	1	3	5	2	0	0	0	0	0	0	0	0	1	0	0
Taylor, Dwight, Colorado Springs°	.179	13	28	3	5	10	2	0	1	1	0	0	0	2	0	3	1	2
Tingley, Ronald, Edmonton	.267	54	172	27	46	74	9	2	5	23	1	2	2	21	0	39	1	1
Tolentino, Jose, Tucson°	.308	116	377	69	116	217	32	3	21	78	2	4	5	48	2	44	0	1
Trafton, Todd, Vancouver	.188	42	117	10	22	30	2	0	2	15	0	3	1	18	0	27	4	1
Traxler, Brian, Albuquerque°	.277	98	318	43	88	132	23	0	7	53	2	7	0	39	1	39	4	0
Tunnell, Lee, Tucson	.143	34	7	1	1	1	0	0	0	0	2	0	0	0	0	3	0	0
Turang, Brian, Calgary	.222	3	9	1	2	2	0	0	0	1	0	0	0	2	0	4	0	0
Valdez, Rafael, Las Vegas	.176	20	17	2	3	3	0	0	0	0	0	0	0	1	0	1	0	0
Vice, Darryl, Tacoma†	.400	7	10	3	4	5	1	0	0	1	0	0	0	7	0	2	1	0
Vizcaino, Jose, Albuquerque†	.279	81	276	46	77	97	10	2	2	38	3	0	3	30	3	33	13	6
Vizquel, Omar, Calgary†	.233	48	150	18	35	45	6	2	0	8	9	2	2	13	0	10	4	3
Vosberg, Edward, Phoenix°	1.000	24	1	0	1	1	0	0	0	0	0	0	0	0	0	0	0	0
Wakamatsu, Donald, Vancouver	.262	62	187	20	49	59	10	0	0	13	1	1	7	13	7	35	2	2
Walsh, David, Albuquerque°	.000	47	2	0	0	0	0	0	0	0	0	0	0	0	0	0	0	0
Walters, Daniel, Las Vegas	.255	53	184	19	47	65	9	0	3	26	0	3	0	13	0	24	0	0
Ward, Kevin, Tacoma	.297	123	421	83	125	213	30	14	10	60	4	4	14	44	1	72	24	10
Ward, Turner, Colorado Springs†	.299	133	495	89	148	208	24	9	6	65	5	9	4	72	1	70	22	15
Wasinger, Mark, Edmonton	.277	68	195	31	54	69	10	1	1	30	4	4	1	38	2	28	9	2
Weaver, James, Calgary°	.257	120	354	43	91	141	23	3	7	42	2	7	0	41	3	69	20	8
Weber, Weston, 35 Tac.-4 Port.	1.000	39	1	0	1	2	1	0	0	3	0	0	0	0	0	0	0	0

Player and Club	Pct.	G.	AB.	R.	H.	TB.	2B.	3B.	HR.	RBI.	SH.	SF.	HP.	BB.	Int. BB.	SO.	SB.	CS.
Webster, Casey, Colorado Springs........	.218	27	78	12	17	24	7	0	0	12	0	1	1	15	0	13	3	2
Wells, Terry, Albuquerque*	.000	24	10	0	0	0	0	0	0	0	1	0	0	1	0	6	0	0
Wetherby, Jeffrey, Colorado Springs*.	.313	96	268	48	84	122	23	0	5	42	1	3	1	41	2	51	6	4
Wetteland, John, Albuquerque.............	1.000	8	1	0	1	1	0	0	0	1	0	0	0	0	0	0	0	0
White, Devon, Edmonton†	.364	14	55	9	20	32	4	4	0	6	0	0	0	7	2	12	4	2
Willard, Gerald, Vancouver*	.279	121	380	66	106	187	21	0	20	76	0	5	2	85	7	60	2	4
Williams, Dana, Vancouver	.196	32	107	16	21	30	6	0	1	4	0	0	2	6	0	14	2	1
Williams, Edward, Las Vegas	.316	93	348	59	110	194	29	2	17	75	0	8	8	42	3	47	0	0
Williams, Ted, Calgary†	.266	43	143	30	38	67	3	4	6	20	1	1	1	8	0	22	9	4
Wilson, Trevor, Phoenix*	.200	12	10	0	2	3	1	0	0	3	1	0	1	0	0	3	0	1
Witmeyer, Ronald, Tacoma*	.290	10	31	5	9	14	2	0	1	7	0	0	1	0	0	3	0	0
Woodson, Tracy, Vancouver	.267	131	480	70	128	211	22	5	17	81	0	5	6	50	2	70	6	4
Young, Gerald, Tucson†	.333	49	183	37	61	76	7	4	0	24	2	2	0	40	1	18	14	11
Yurtin, Jeffrey, Las Vegas*	.260	102	334	39	87	125	15	4	5	49	1	4	2	39	4	52	1	4

The following pitchers, listed alphabetically by club, with games in parentheses, had no plate appearances, primarily through use of designated hitters:

ALBUQUERQUE—DeLeon, Luis (1); Fischer, Jeffrey (3); Hartley, Michael (3); Scott, Timothy (17); Springer, Dennis (2).

CALGARY—Bankhead, Scott (2); Blasucci, Anthony (15); Burba, David (31); Clark, Bryan (18); DeLucia, Richard (5); Eave, Gary (1); Givens, Brian (2); Harris, Eugene (6); Helton, Keith (60); Lazorko, Jack (31); Lovelace, Vance (56); Medvin, Scott (43); Melendez, Jose (45); Rice, Patrick (15); Shaw, Theodore (27); Swan, Russell (5); Taylor, Terry (25); Vande Berg, Edward (10); Walker, Michael A. (25).

COLORADO SPRINGS—Bearse, Kevin (25); Browning, Michael (5); Collins, Allen (1); Curtis, Michael (19); Edwards, Jeffrey (4); Kaiser, Jeffrey (25); Lambert, Reese (5); McMichael, Gregory (12); Nipper, Albert (17); Olin, Steven (14); Robertson, Douglas (31); Scott, Charles (3); Seanez, Rudy (12); Shaw, Jeffrey (17); Sisk, Douglas (8); Skalski, Joseph (21); Valdez, Efrain (46); Valdez, Sergio (7); Walker, Michael C. (18); Ward, Colby (43); Willis, Carl (41).

EDMONTON—Abbott, Kyle (19); Bailes, Scott (9); Beasley, Scott (9); Beasley, Christopher (28); Bockus, Randy (2); Buckels, Gary (53); Burcham, Timothy (27); Clear, Mark (12); Corbett, Sherman (47); Erb, Michael (16); Fetters, Michael (5); Fraser, William (3); Grahe, Joseph (5); Heathcock, Jeffrey (8); Lewis, Scott (27); Meeks, Timothy (4); Montalvo, Rafael (48); Monteleone, Richard (5); Ohnoutka, Brian (2); Richardson, Jeffrey (38); Tolliver, Freddie (14); Trudeau, Kevin (22); Young, Clifford (30).

LAS VEGAS—Quinzer, Paul (5); Raczka, Michael (4).

PHOENIX—Bordi, Richard (4); Burkett, John (3); Knepper, Robert (4).

PORTLAND—Abbott, Paul (23); Bangston, Patrick (29); Casian, Lawrence (37); Delkus, Peter (65); Dyer, Michael (2); Guthrie, Mark (9); Johnson, Gregory (15); Lind, Orlando (7); Mason, Michael (3); Oliveras, Francisco (11); Pittman, Park (28); Redding, Michael (1); Savage, John (16); Scott, Charles (29); Wayne, Gary (22); Weber, Weston (4); Williams, Jimmy (51); Yett, Richard (22).

TACOMA—Allison, Dana (2); Ariola, Anthony (6); Bitker, Joseph (48); Chiamparino, Scott (26); Chitren, Stephen (1); Corsi, James (5); Lambert, Reese (31); Law, Joseph (17); Leiper, David (6); McCoy, Timothy (8); Miller, Russell (4); Norris, Michael (3); Otto, David (2); Raczka, chael (42); Shaver, Jeffrey (19); Slusarski, Joseph (9); Strebeck, Richard (3); Veres, David (32); Walton, Bruce (46); Wojna, Edward (24); Young, Raymond (28).

TUCSON—Browning, Michael (3); Buchanan, Robert (9); Heredia, Hector (34); Normand, Guy (4); Reuss, Jerry (5); St. Claire, Randy (23); Thurmond, Mark (9); Walter, Gene (3).

VANCOUVER—Alvarez, Wilson (17); Campbell, Michael (21); Cedeno, Vinicio (4); Davino, Michael (1); Drees, Thomas (17); Garcia, Ramon (1); Hall, Gardner (28); Hernandez, Roberto (11); Hillegas, Shawn (36); Kutzler, Jerry (19); Menendez, Antonio (24); Pawlowski, John (30); Peterson, Adam (6); Rosenberg, Steven (40); Scheid, Richard (20); Segura, Jose (40); Stephens, Ronald (3).

GRAND SLAM HOME RUNS—Cron, R. Nelson, 3 each; Skurla, Willard, 2 each; Afenir, Anthony, J. Clark, Dalena, Diaz, Hansen, Hemond, Howitt, Huff, Laga, Leius, MacPhail, Martinez, P. Munoz, Neel, Ja. Ortiz, Powell, Rose, Santiago, K. Ward, 1 each.

AWARDED FIRST BASE ON CATCHER'S INTERFERENCE—Rohde 2 (Fletcher, Reynolds); Yurtin 2 (Lampkin, Parks); Brady (D. Davis); D. Davis (Manwaring); Nichols (Willard); T. Ward (Reynolds).

CLUB FIELDING

Club	Pct.	G.	PO.	A.	E.	DP.	PB.	Club	Pct.	G.	PO.	A.	E.	DP.	PB.
Vancouver.....................	.974	141	3628	1447	133	135	29	Portland	.971	139	3553	1460	152	147	25
Phoenix........................	.973	143	3594	1581	142	140	21	Edmonton	.970	141	3721	1631	164	161	13
Calgary........................	.972	143	3621	1525	149	142	17	Albuquerque	.968	142	3604	1514	167	140	11
Las Vegas.....................	.971	144	3736	1556	158	155	20	Colorado Springs	.965	143	3620	1552	190	122	20
Tacoma........................	.971	142	3617	1557	154	155	18	Tucson	.964	142	3666	1552	195	138	13

Triple Plays—Albuquerque, Colorado Springs, Tacoma.

INDIVIDUAL FIELDING

*Throws lefthanded.

FIRST BASEMEN

Player and Club	Pct.	G.	PO.	A.	E.	DP.	Player and Club	Pct.	G.	PO.	A.	E.	DP.
Aguayo, Edmonton	1.000	7	62	3	0	2	Jurak, Calgary............................	1.000	1	5	0	0	0
Amaral, Vancouver	1.000	2	11	0	0	0	Knapp, Edmonton	1.000	3	14	1	0	1
Amaro, Edmonton	1.000	2	1	0	0	0	Laga, Phoenix*	.996	88	760	64	3	67
Arndt, Tacoma	.977	21	122	4	3	9	Lopez, Albuquerque	.989	57	443	25	5	43
Bailey, Phoenix	1.000	13	107	8	0	12	Manto, Colorado Springs	.994	47	294	27	2	26
Baine, Portland	.968	4	25	5	1	3	MARTINEZ, Calgary	.991	125	1051	98	10	117
Baker, Portland	1.000	2	14	0	0	0	McCollom, Edmonton	1.000	2	19	3	0	1
Basso, Las Vegas	1.000	2	20	2	0	2	McConnell, Albuquerque	1.000	1	2	0	0	1
Bean, Albuquerque*	1.000	3	3	0	0	1	McGinnis, Tacoma	.992	41	353	31	3	41
Brady, Phoenix*	.983	33	251	30	5	30	McPhail, Vancouver	1.000	11	90	2	0	11
Brundage, Calgary*	1.000	7	51	5	0	3	Medina, Colorado Springs*	.969	5	29	2	1	4
Clark, Las Vegas	.991	28	210	9	2	28	Melendez, Colorado Springs*	.989	34	256	19	3	26
Cockrell, Colorado Springs	1.000	4	12	2	0	1	Naveda, Portland	.988	9	76	8	1	14
Colbert, Phoenix	1.000	5	36	4	0	3	Neel, Colorado Springs	.988	62	518	55	7	41
Cron, Edmonton	.994	91	839	57	5	102	J. Nelson, Portland	.976	5	40	0	1	5
Dalena, 51 Van.-26 Port.	.987	77	620	39	9	67	R. Nelson, Las Vegas*	.988	89	764	59	10	77
Davis, Edmonton	1.000	5	41	2	0	2	C. Nichols, Tucson	1.000	1	8	1	0	0
Dean, Tucson	1.000	1	4	0	0	0	H. Nichols, Edmonton	1.000	2	11	1	0	0
Dodd, Calgary	1.000	12	87	6	0	5	Powell, Portland	1.000	7	51	5	0	5
Fulton, Calgary	1.000	2	21	1	0	4	Reynolds, Las Vegas	1.000	6	41	0	0	7
Gieseke, Las Vegas*	1.000	1	13	0	0	0	Rodriguez, Portland....................	.973	5	30	6	1	3
Henley, Albuquerque	1.000	1	3	0	0	0	Schu, Edmonton	.988	9	76	6	1	7
Hinshaw, Phoenix	.983	11	100	13	2	14	Sconiers, Edmonton*	1.000	2	18	0	0	1
Howell, Edmonton......................	1.000	1	11	1	0	1	Scott, Tacoma	1.000	1	4	0	0	0
Howitt, Tacoma..........................	.990	66	549	49	6	64	Shockey, Tacoma*	.989	12	85	7	1	8
Jennings, Tacoma*	.941	10	43	5	3	10	Simms, Tucson	.983	117	1010	74	19	96
Johnson, Tacoma	1.000	2	20	0	0	1	Skurla, Edmonton*	1.000	1	6	0	0	1

FIRST BASEMEN—Continued

Player and Club	Pct.	G.	PO.	A.	E.	DP.
Sorrento, Portland	.984	86	678	52	12	77
Spilman, Tucson	1.000	3	25	0	0	3
Stevens, Edmonton°	.988	21	160	6	2	16
Tolentino, Tucson°	.989	34	243	18	3	17
Trafton, Vancouver	.992	32	237	21	2	23
Traxler, Albuquerque°	.989	91	730	47	9	81
Walters, Las Vegas	1.000	1	1	0	0	0
Ward, Tacoma	.947	3	17	1	1	1
Wasinger, Edmonton	1.000	13	89	7	0	10
Wetherby, Colorado Springs°	.978	20	125	9	3	10
Willard, Vancouver	1.000	1	1	0	0	0
Williams, Las Vegas	1.000	8	56	3	0	3
Witmeyer, Tacoma°	.976	9	81	2	2	9
Woodson, Vancouver	.998	54	421	33	1	40
Yurtin, Las Vegas	1.000	24	188	19	0	12

Triple Plays—Lopez, Medina.

SECOND BASEMEN

Player and Club	Pct.	G.	PO.	A.	E.	DP.
Aguayo, Edmonton	.984	17	20	42	1	9
Allaire, Edmonton	1.000	4	6	16	0	3
Amaral, Vancouver	1.000	19	41	37	0	10
Anderson, Edmonton	.982	8	25	29	1	8
Arndt, Tacoma	1.000	8	14	19	0	5
Baker, Portland	1.000	13	22	37	0	4
Blankenship, Tacoma	.976	19	30	52	2	12
Bordick, Tacoma	1.000	7	11	13	0	3
Brosius, Tacoma	1.000	2	3	5	0	0
Candaele, Tucson	.974	7	14	24	1	6
Carter, Phoenix	.962	58	115	163	11	35
Castillo, Colorado Springs	.971	62	103	133	7	29
Coachman, Edmonton	1.000	14	24	43	0	8
Cochrane, Calgary	.952	12	13	27	2	4
Cora, Las Vegas	.983	20	51	65	2	14
Diaz, Calgary	.958	4	11	12	1	6
Faries, Las Vegas	.968	117	250	363	20	80
Giles, Tucson	1.000	5	4	8	0	2
Grebeck, Vancouver	1.000	1	1	0	0	0
HALE, Portland	.982	127	311	356	12	101
Haney, Calgary	.971	106	206	292	15	69
Harris, Tucson	1.000	3	2	3	0	0
Hemond, Tacoma	.982	63	101	165	5	39
Henley, Albuquerque	.959	71	145	206	15	48
Hoffman, Albuquerque	1.000	3	1	3	0	0
Hubbard, Tucson	.923	6	14	22	3	8
Huff, Albuquerque	.977	8	17	25	1	5
Johnson, Phoenix	1.000	1	3	0	0	0
Jorgensen, Portland	.500	1	0	1	1	0
Jurak, Calgary	.912	10	19	12	3	5
Lampkin, Colorado Springs	.909	4	5	5	1	0
Lawton, Vancouver	1.000	1	4	4	0	4
Leius, Portland	1.000	1	1	0	0	0
Litton, Phoenix	.778	1	1	6	2	2
Magallanes, Colorado Springs	.959	30	64	99	7	18
Martin, Vancouver	.973	126	283	324	17	73
McLemore, 7 Edm.-9 C.S.	.968	16	37	53	3	15
Mota, Las Vegas	.962	5	6	19	1	2
Murray, Calgary	.911	16	24	27	5	3
Naveda, Portland	1.000	3	2	4	0	0
Offerman, Albuquerque	1.000	1	0	1	0	0
Parker, Phoenix	1.000	2	1	0	0	0
Pedrique, Tacoma	.974	48	87	138	6	36
Perezchica, Phoenix	.962	86	176	260	17	66
Renteria, Tucson	1.000	8	12	25	0	6
Rohde, Tucson	.970	29	51	77	4	12
Rood, Edmonton	.909	4	5	5	1	0
Rose, Edmonton	.962	100	205	333	21	86
Sanchez, Tucson	.947	6	9	9	1	1
Scott, Tacoma	1.000	14	8	23	0	3
Smajstrla, Tucson	.972	99	192	267	13	56
Springer, 52 C.S.-2 L.V.	.966	54	105	149	9	32
Swain, Colorado Springs	.920	7	8	15	2	2
Turang, Calgary	.909	3	5	5	1	1
Vice, Tacoma	.900	5	4	5	1	2
Vizcaino, Albuquerque	.967	71	123	196	11	60
Ward, Colorado Springs	1.000	1	0	2	0	0
Wasinger, Edmonton	1.000	1	1	1	0	1

Triple Plays—Henley, Pedrique.

THIRD BASEMEN

Player and Club	Pct.	G.	PO.	A.	E.	DP.
Aguayo, Edmonton	1.000	2	1	1	0	0
Amaral, Vancouver	.948	21	8	47	3	1
Anderson, Edmonton	.962	7	4	21	1	1
Arndt, Tacoma	.908	99	50	176	23	19
Baerga, Colorado Springs	.925	12	18	31	4	1
Baker, Portland	.967	17	12	17	1	1
Basso, Las Vegas	1.000	1	1	3	0	0
Bean, Albuquerque°	1.000	1	1	1	0	0
Blankenship, Tacoma	1.000	2	1	5	0	0
Campbell, Vancouver	1.000	2	2	3	0	0
Carter, Phoenix	1.000	17	10	23	0	2
Castillo, Colorado Springs	.960	20	11	37	2	4
Coachman, Edmonton	.907	41	30	77	11	4
Cochrane, Calgary	.855	22	15	38	9	5
Colbert, Phoenix	.930	66	61	126	14	14
Colombino, Tucson	.953	76	58	143	10	21
Cron, Edmonton	.946	11	8	27	2	5
Dalena, Portland	.800	2	1	3	1	0
Davis, Edmonton	1.000	1	1	1	0	0
Diaz, Calgary	.978	25	13	32	1	5
Faries, Las Vegas	1.000	6	2	5	0	0
Fulton, Calgary	1.000	12	6	16	0	0
Grebeck, Vancouver	1.000	3	1	3	0	1
Hale, Portland	1.000	1	0	1	0	0
HANSEN, Albuquerque	.926	131	69	254	26	25
Harris, Tucson	1.000	1	2	0	0	0
Hemond, Tacoma	.875	6	1	6	1	1
Henley, Albuquerque	.900	3	1	8	1	2
Howell, Edmonton	.977	13	11	32	1	1
Howitt, Tacoma	.969	19	7	24	1	3
Hubbard, Tucson	1.000	3	3	0	0	1
Jackson, Phoenix	.882	42	22	68	12	8
Jorgensen, Portland	.900	122	102	203	34	18
Jurak, Calgary	.944	80	56	129	11	11
Litton, Phoenix	1.000	1	0	1	0	0
Lopez, Albuquerque	.500	2	0	2	2	1
Magallanes, Colorado Springs	1.000	3	2	9	0	0
Manto, Colorado Springs	.949	61	46	104	8	7
Marquez, Tucson	.800	1	2	2	1	0
McConnell, Albuquerque	.917	9	2	20	2	5
McLemore, Colorado Springs	.875	4	2	5	1	0
McPhail, Vancouver	.917	53	42	91	12	15
Miller, Calgary	.842	15	6	26	6	1
Mota, Las Vegas	.944	9	5	12	1	1
Naveda, Portland	1.000	1	0	1	0	0
Neel, Colorado Springs	1.000	1	1	0	0	0
Nelson, Portland	.833	3	1	4	1	0
Nichols, Edmonton	1.000	3	2	1	0	0
Ortiz, Tucson	1.000	1	0	1	0	0
Parker, Phoenix	.970	24	16	48	2	5
Pedrique, Tacoma	.953	38	20	61	4	5
Perezchica, Phoenix	1.000	1	1	2	0	0
Renteria, Tucson	.875	15	9	19	4	2
Rood, Edmonton	.667	1	1	1	1	0
Rose, Edmonton	.938	29	18	42	4	4
Schaefer, Calgary	.933	11	6	22	2	2
Schu, Edmonton	.950	7	5	14	1	1
Simms, Tucson	1.000	1	2	1	0	0
Smajstrla, Tucson	.859	25	29	32	10	4
Springer, 25 C.S.-12 L.V.	.934	37	26	73	7	6
Strange, Calgary	.859	34	9	46	9	5
Swain, Colorado Springs	.737	9	2	12	5	2
Wasinger, Edmonton	.970	41	19	78	3	13
Webster, Colorado Springs	.882	27	13	47	8	5
Williams, Las Vegas	.908	77	50	118	17	11
Woodson, Vancouver	.923	68	49	130	15	15
Yurtin, Las Vegas	.926	43	28	85	9	8

Triple Plays—Arndt, Hansen.

SHORTSTOPS

Player and Club	Pct.	G.	PO.	A.	E.	DP.
Alfonzo, Edmonton	1.000	4	6	4	0	2
Allaire, Edmonton	.914	33	36	92	12	22
Amaral, Vancouver	.955	56	76	176	12	33
Anderson, Edmonton	.875	3	2	5	1	0
Arndt, Tacoma	1.000	2	0	2	0	0
Baker, Portland	.980	43	68	126	4	34
Benjamin, Phoenix	.962	117	216	386	24	81
BORDICK, Tacoma	.972	106	199	353	16	82
Brumley, Calgary	.947	8	13	23	2	7
Castillo, Colorado Springs	.925	32	32	66	8	9
Cochrane, Calgary	.980	15	18	32	1	10
Colbert, Phoenix	.920	8	9	14	2	4
Colombino, Tucson	1.000	1	1	5	0	0
Cora, Las Vegas	.929	31	74	83	12	24
Diaz, Calgary	1.000	5	11	17	0	6
Disarcina, Edmonton	.950	96	165	289	24	68

SHORTSTOPS—Continued

Player and Club	Pct.	G.	PO.	A.	E.	DP.	Player and Club	Pct.	G.	PO.	A.	E.	DP.
Faries, Las Vegas	.938	13	25	50	5	10	Murray, Calgary	.969	8	11	20	1	1
Gaither, Vancouver	.600	1	2	1	2	1	Naveda, Portland	1.000	2	0	1	0	0
Giles, Calgary	.955	32	49	98	7	18	Offerman, Albuquerque	.937	115	174	360	36	74
Grebeck, Vancouver	.980	9	26	23	1	2	Pedrique, Tacoma	.964	42	58	101	6	25
Hale, Calgary	.857	1	1	5	1	2	Perezchica, Phoenix	.944	18	22	63	5	8
Hansen, Albuquerque	1.000	1	0	1	0	1	Renteria, Tucson	.847	11	15	35	9	4
Harris, Tucson	.955	37	49	120	8	22	Rohde, Tucson	.966	24	25	60	3	8
Hemond, Tacoma	.700	2	4	3	3	2	Rood, Edmonton	1.000	2	1	9	0	1
Hoffman, Albuquerque	.986	19	29	44	1	9	Rose, Edmonton	1.000	2	2	1	0	1
Jorgensen, Portland	1.000	1	2	2	0	0	Sanchez, Tucson	.924	64	91	175	22	28
Jurak, Calgary	.800	2	2	2	1	0	Schaefer, Calgary	.970	37	75	117	6	32
Kellner, Tucson	.923	18	30	54	7	20	Schofield, Edmonton	.952	5	6	14	1	6
Leius, Portland	.964	101	154	323	18	67	Smith, Vancouver	.964	82	133	237	14	50
LeVasseur, Las Vegas	.966	77	111	232	12	55	Springer, Las Vegas	1.000	2	1	1	0	0
Lewis, Colorado Springs	.925	34	52	84	11	23	Strange, Tucson	1.000	2	0	1	0	0
Magallanes, Colorado Springs	.938	93	141	251	26	48	Vizcaino, Albuquerque	.944	16	18	33	3	6
McLemore, 3 Edm.-1 C.S.	.917	4	8	14	2	4	Vizquel, Calgary	.972	47	70	142	6	27
Mota, Las Vegas	.967	30	35	81	4	15	Wasinger, Edmonton	.947	4	8	10	1	3
							Yurtin, Las Vegas	1.000	2	4	6	0	1

Triple Plays—Castillo, Hoffman.

OUTFIELDERS

Player and Club	Pct.	G.	PO.	A.	E.	DP.	Player and Club	Pct.	G.	PO.	A.	E.	DP.
Allaire, Edmonton	1.000	4	6	0	0	0	Jacas, Portland	.974	108	207	16	6	5
Allred, Colorado Springs°	.951	109	203	12	11	2	C. Jackson, Phoenix	.987	33	72	4	1	2
Amaral, Vancouver	1.000	7	18	0	0	0	D. Jackson, Phoenix	1.000	29	61	4	0	3
Amaro, Edmonton	.988	80	159	4	2	0	Jefferson, Colorado Springs	1.000	33	69	6	0	0
Anthony, Tucson°	.958	40	84	7	4	2	Jennings, Tacoma°	.976	44	80	2	2	0
Arndt, Tacoma	1.000	2	2	0	0	0	Johnson, Tacoma	1.000	1	1	0	0	0
Baine, Portland	.955	14	20	1	1	1	Jurak, Calgary	1.000	20	25	2	0	0
Baker, Portland	1.000	18	25	4	0	0	Kingery, Phoenix°	.985	31	61	4	1	2
Baldwin, Tucson°	.909	12	18	2	2	1	Kirby, Albuquerque	.956	103	185	11	9	2
Bass, Phoenix	1.000	6	5	2	0	1	LAWTON, Vancouver	.992	118	260	2	2	0
Bean, Albuquerque°	.965	123	205	13	8	3	Leonard, Phoenix	.992	72	120	3	1	0
Beauchamp, Phoenix	.962	41	73	2	3	1	Lewis, Tacoma	.986	60	132	9	2	3
Belle, Colorado Springs	.939	23	31	0	2	0	Litton, Phoenix	1.000	4	5	0	0	0
Blankenship, Tacoma	1.000	3	8	0	0	0	Mangham, Albuquerque	.800	5	3	1	1	0
Brady, Phoenix°	.990	57	98	2	1	0	Manzanillo, Vancouver°	1.000	1	2	0	0	0
Brantley, Calgary	.963	28	52	0	2	0	McCray, Vancouver	.964	19	50	4	2	1
Brito, Portland	.952	31	40	0	2	0	McPhail, Vancouver	.949	26	54	2	3	0
Brown, Tucson	1.000	5	2	0	0	0	Meadows, Tucson°	.958	18	23	0	1	0
Bruett, Portland°	1.000	10	20	0	0	0	Mikulik, Tucson	.990	52	96	4	1	2
Brundage, Calgary°	.985	82	192	7	3	1	Miller, Calgary	1.000	18	21	0	0	0
Buhner, Calgary	1.000	6	14	1	0	1	Mota, Las Vegas	.917	14	18	4	2	1
Carter, Phoenix	.941	47	79	1	5	0	Munoz, Portland	.945	29	51	1	3	0
Casey, Tacoma°	1.000	14	17	0	0	0	Naveda, Portland	.990	64	91	8	1	2
Clark, Las Vegas	1.000	18	26	1	0	0	Neel, Colorado Springs	1.000	5	4	0	0	0
Close, Calgary	.971	127	224	12	7	1	Newson, Las Vegas°	.938	96	146	4	10	0
Coachman, Edmonton	1.000	14	18	2	0	0	Nichols, Tucson	.875	7	6	1	1	0
Cochrane, Calgary	.957	21	41	3	2	1	Olander, Tucson	.972	27	65	5	2	2
Cockrell, 6 Port.-76 C.S.°	.967	82	112	7	4	1	Ortiz, Tucson	.981	44	98	4	2	0
Cole, 86 L.V.-14 C.S.°	.954	100	181	6	9	1	Pacillo, Calgary	1.000	1	1	0	0	0
Davidson, Tucson	.990	45	98	4	1	1	Parker, Phoenix	1.000	19	40	3	0	1
M. Davis, Edmonton	.951	35	56	2	3	0	Penigar, Vancouver	.916	56	96	2	9	1
W. Davis, Albuquerque	.985	92	131	4	2	1	Peters, Edmonton	.981	51	98	6	2	0
Dean, Tucson	.926	10	25	0	2	0	Powell, Portland	.972	98	203	5	6	0
DeAngelis, Edmonton°	.938	25	27	3	2	0	Rhodes, Tucson°	.967	103	214	20	8	2
DeLima, Portland°	.978	59	84	7	2	3	Ritchie, Phoenix°	.972	99	242	3	7	0
Dietrick, Tacoma	.955	11	19	2	1	0	Rood, Edmonton	1.000	1	5	0	0	0
DiMascio, Calgary	1.000	1	2	0	0	0	Sambo, Vancouver	.975	89	148	8	4	0
Fields, Tacoma	.976	39	76	6	2	0	Schaefer, Calgary	1.000	3	5	0	0	0
Fox, Tacoma°	.964	60	130	3	5	0	Schu, Edmonton	1.000	2	2	0	0	0
Fulton, Colorado Springs	1.000	5	1	0	0	0	Sherman, Las Vegas°	1.000	4	5	1	0	1
Gainey, Colorado Springs	1.000	10	16	0	0	0	Shockey, Tacoma°	1.000	1	2	0	0	0
Gerhart, Colorado Springs	1.000	4	4	0	0	0	Simms, Tucson	1.000	1	1	0	0	0
Gibson, Albuquerque°	.667	3	2	0	1	0	Skurla, 1 Phoe.-40 Edm.°	.988	41	74	5	1	1
Gieseke, Las Vegas°	.800	4	4	0	1	0	Sorrento, Portland	.944	8	17	0	1	0
Green, Phoenix°	1.000	5	16	1	0	0	Springer, Las Vegas	1.000	2	2	0	0	0
Grunhard, Edmonton°	.952	111	199	17	11	3	Stevens, Edmonton°	.970	70	124	4	4	1
Hansen, Albuquerque	1.000	1	2	0	0	0	Taylor, Colorado Springs°	1.000	10	21	0	0	0
Harris, Tucson	1.000	1	1	1	0	0	Tolentino, Tucson°	.958	47	66	2	3	1
Henley, Albuquerque	1.000	2	2	0	0	0	K. Ward, Tacoma	.935	103	152	6	11	4
Hill, Vancouver	.974	95	221	8	6	2	T. Ward, Colorado Springs	.971	130	292	5	9	1
Hillemann, Las Vegas	.982	88	211	8	4	2	Wasinger, Edmonton	1.000	3	6	0	0	0
Hinshaw, Phoenix	.976	42	81	2	2	1	Weaver, Calgary°	.956	114	183	14	9	2
S. Howard, Tacoma	.962	70	124	4	5	0	Wetherby, Colorado Springs°	.953	63	97	4	5	0
T. Howard, Las Vegas	.988	80	159	6	2	0	White, Edmonton	.914	14	31	1	3	0
Howitt, Tacoma	.930	40	52	1	4	1	D. Williams, Vancouver	.983	31	58	1	1	0
Huff, Albuquerque	.986	130	268	4	4	0	T. Williams, Calgary	.982	43	105	4	2	0
Humphreys, Las Vegas	1.000	12	19	5	0	1	Young, Tucson	.952	48	112	8	6	3
							Yurtin, Las Vegas	.978	27	40	4	1	0

Triple Play—Fox.

CATCHERS

Player and Club	Pct.	G.	PO.	A.	E.	DP.	PB.	Player and Club	Pct.	G.	PO.	A.	E.	DP.	PB.
Afenir, Tacoma	.987	75	457	60	7	4	11	Davis, Edmonton	.981	43	233	29	5	4	4
Bailey, Phoenix	.985	34	119	15	2	2	1	DiMascio, Calgary	1.000	4	20	4	0	0	0
Basso, Phoenix	.970	44	256	32	9	7	8	Fletcher, Albuquerque	.9898	103	715	64	8	3	3
Brown, Albuquerque	1.000	3	11	0	0	0	0	Hearn, Colorado Springs	.955	15	59	4	3	0	3
Cochrane, Calgary	1.000	4	17	1	0	0	1	Hemond, Tacoma	.921	8	32	3	3	0	0
Colbert, Phoenix	.990	38	175	22	2	2	9	Hernandez, Albuquerque	.967	41	207	31	8	6	5
Conley, Las Vegas	1.000	1	5	2	0	0	0	Higgins, Las Vegas	.966	8	53	4	2	0	1

CATCHERS—Continued

Player and Club	Pct.	G.	PO.	A.	E.	DP.	PB.
Hubbard, Tucson	1.000	1	3	0	0	0	0
Knapp, Edmonton	.947	10	53	1	3	0	1
Lampkin, 58 C.S.-1 L.V.	.969	59	310	31	11	4	8
Laudner, Portland	.909	5	29	1	3	0	1
LeVasseur, Las Vegas	1.000	1	1	1	0	0	0
Lopez, Albuquerque	1.000	14	51	6	0	1	3
Magrann, Colorado Springs....	.980	80	385	63	9	5	8
MANWARING, Phoenix..........	.9900	73	352	45	4	4	10
Marquez, Tucson	.955	13	71	13	4	4	0
McGinnis, Tacoma	.986	64	334	30	5	1	7
McGuire, Calgary	.977	117	650	81	17	9	12
McNamara, Phoenix	1.000	6	24	6	0	0	0
Mercedes, Tacoma	1.000	9	46	4	0	0	0
Miller, Calgary	1.000	22	90	13	0	0	4
Morales, Calgary	1.000	2	9	1	0	0	0
Nelson, Portland	.982	67	338	37	7	8	16
Nichols, Tucson	.981	46	228	34	5	4	5
Ortiz, Tucson	.875	5	13	1	2	0	0
Orton, Edmonton	.978	48	277	36	7	5	5
Owens, Phoenix	1.000	4	11	3	0	0	1
Parks, Portland	.976	74	488	45	13	5	7
Reynolds, Las Vegas	.982	58	297	26	6	6	5
Santiago, Las Vegas	1.000	5	25	5	0	1	1
Servais, Tucson	.983	87	453	63	9	9	8
Sinatro, Calgary	1.000	8	33	1	0	0	0
Siwa, Portland	.976	6	38	3	1	0	1
Sullivan, Colorado Springs	1.000	12	45	6	0	2	1
Tingley, Edmonton	.976	48	284	35	8	2	3
Wakamatsu, Vancouver	.994	59	285	33	2	4	11
Walters, Las Vegas	.993	47	246	28	2	7	5
Willard, Vancouver	.981	96	549	74	12	7	18

Triple Play—Afenir.

PITCHERS

Player and Club	Pct.	G.	PO.	A.	E.	DP.
Abbott, Portland	.950	23	7	12	1	0
Aldrich, Phoenix	1.000	8	1	2	0	1
Alvarez, Vancouver*	1.000	17	4	14	0	2
Ariola, Tacoma*	.714	6	1	4	2	0
Bailes, Edmonton*	1.000	9	0	2	0	0
Bangtson, Portland	1.000	29	4	13	0	1
Bearse, Colorado Springs*	1.000	25	7	22	0	2
Beasley, Edmonton	.930	28	19	34	4	3
Beck, Phoenix	.846	12	4	7	2	1
Bitker, Tacoma	1.000	48	10	8	0	2
Bittiger, Albuquerque	.941	28	11	21	2	0
Blasucci, Calgary*	1.000	15	2	4	0	0
Bockus, Edmonton	1.000	2	0	1	0	0
Bones, Las Vegas	.857	5	3	3	1	1
Bonilla, Phoenix*	1.000	36	4	3	0	1
Booker, Phoenix	1.000	49	7	10	0	2
Bordi, Phoenix	.500	4	1	0	1	0
Bowen, Tucson	1.000	10	1	5	0	1
Brennan, Tucson	.852	41	9	14	4	0
Browning, 3 Tuc.-5 C.S.	1.000	8	0	1	0	0
Brundage, Calgary*	1.000	2	1	0	0	0
Buchanan, Tucson*	1.000	9	0	4	0	0
Buckels, Edmonton	1.000	53	3	7	0	2
Burba, Calgary	1.000	31	9	11	0	2
Burcham, Edmonton	.917	27	13	20	3	0
Burkett, Phoenix	.875	3	4	3	1	1
Camacho, Phoenix	1.000	12	0	3	0	0
Campbell, Vancouver	1.000	21	0	5	0	0
Cano, Tucson	1.000	10	1	9	0	1
Casian, Portland*	.977	37	6	37	1	1
Chiamparino, Tacoma	.848	26	5	23	5	3
Christopher, Albuquerque	.923	54	2	10	1	1
Clancy, Tucson	.900	10	6	3	1	0
B. Clark, Calgary*	1.000	18	5	16	0	2
T. Clark, Tucson	.978	29	14	30	1	2
Clear, Edmonton	1.000	12	0	1	0	0
Clements, Las Vegas*	.967	26	7	22	1	1
Cook, Portland	.960	19	8	16	1	2
Corbett, Edmonton*	1.000	47	5	11	0	2
Curtis, Colorado Springs*	.800	19	4	8	3	1
J. Davis, Las Vegas	.889	18	0	8	1	1
S. Davis, Albuquerque*	.944	31	6	11	1	0
Delkus, Portland	.952	65	7	13	1	2
DeLucia, Calgary.	1.000	5	2	3	0	0
Dewey, Phoenix	1.000	19	2	2	0	0
Downs, Phoenix	.000	1	0	0	1	0
Drees, Las Vegas*	1.000	17	3	17	0	0
Dyer, Portland	.000	2	0	0	1	0
Dunne, Las Vegas	1.000	4	0	9	0	0
Edwards, Colorado Springs*	1.000	4	2	2	0	0
Eave, 1 Cal.-10 Phoe.	1.000	11	2	4	0	0
Eichhorn, Tucson	1.000	28	4	8	0	1
Erb, Edmonton	.938	16	3	12	1	2
Fetters, Edmonton	1.000	5	3	3	0	0
Fisher, Tucson	.864	30	4	15	3	0
Fox, Tacoma*	.000	2	0	0	0	0
Fraser, Edmonton	.667	3	1	1	1	0
Gilmore, Las Vegas	.929	42	8	18	2	1
Givens, Calgary*	1.000	2	0	1	0	0
Grahe, Edmonton	1.000	5	1	8	0	1
Gunderson, Phoenix*	.900	16	2	16	2	1
Guthrie, Portland*	.909	9	1	9	1	0
Hall, Vancouver*	.959	28	12	35	2	0
Harris, Vancouver	1.000	6	0	2	0	0
Hartsock, Albuquerque	1.000	11	2	5	0	0
Heathcock, Edmonton	.857	8	1	5	1	0
Helton, Calgary*	1.000	60	4	10	0	1
Hennis, Tucson	.971	28	11	22	1	3
Heredia, Phoenix	.981	29	18	35	1	4
Heredia, Tucson	1.000	34	6	6	0	0
Hernandez, Vancouver	.800	11	5	7	3	0
Hickerson, Phoenix*	1.000	12	4	0	0	0
Hillegas, Vancouver	1.000	36	3	8	0	0
Holmes, Albuquerque	.909	56	4	6	1	1
Ilsley, Tucson*	.923	20	4	8	1	1
Johnson, Portland	1.000	15	0	1	0	0
Kaiser, Colorado Springs*	.952	25	6	14	1	1
Kile, Tucson	.957	26	4	18	1	3
Knepper, Phoenix*	1.000	4	1	4	0	0
Kutzler, Vancouver	.933	19	5	9	1	0
Lambert, 31 Tac.-5 C.S.*	.909	36	0	10	1	0
Law, Tacoma	.875	17	3	11	2	2
Lazorko, Calgary	.923	31	12	24	3	3
Leiper, Tacoma*	1.000	6	1	3	0	0
J. Lewis, Las Vegas	.909	59	3	7	1	1
S. Lewis, Edmonton	.971	27	14	19	1	4
Lind, Portland	1.000	7	1	4	0	0
Lovelace, Calgary*	1.000	56	4	14	0	0
Lynch, Las Vegas	1.000	58	0	7	0	1
Madden, Albuquerque*	.895	31	1	16	2	1
Maddux, Albuquerque	.941	20	5	11	1	1
Manzanillo, Vancouver*	1.000	38	5	10	0	1
Mason, Portland*	.500	3	1	0	1	0
Mayberry, Albuquerque	1.000	32	6	13	0	0
Maysey, Las Vegas	.926	26	7	18	2	3
McCament, Phoenix	1.000	46	5	14	0	2
McCLELLAN, Phoenix	1.000	29	25	21	0	3
McCoy, Tacoma*	1.000	8	2	2	0	0
McMichael, Colorado Springs	1.000	12	6	7	0	0
Mead, Phoenix	.938	22	3	12	1	0
Medvin, Calgary	1.000	43	4	3	0	0
Meeks, Edmonton	1.000	4	0	2	0	0
Meier, Phoenix	.938	13	7	8	1	0
Melendez, Calgary	.909	45	6	14	2	2
Menendez, Vancouver	1.000	24	6	5	0	0
Meyer, Tucson	1.000	64	6	7	0	0
Miller, Tacoma	1.000	4	1	0	0	1
Montalvo, Edmonton	1.000	48	9	15	0	0
Monteleone, Edmonton	1.000	5	0	1	0	0
Munoz, Albuquerque*	.885	49	8	15	3	2
Murphy, Las Vegas	.750	27	4	5	3	1
Neidlinger, Albuquerque	.962	20	10	15	1	3
Nichols, Colorado Springs	1.000	22	6	11	0	0
Nipper, Colorado Springs	1.000	17	5	13	0	2
Nolte, Las Vegas*	.968	33	8	22	1	0
Normand, Tucson*	1.000	4	0	3	0	1
Norris, Tacoma	1.000	3	2	2	0	0
O'Neal, Phoenix	1.000	7	2	2	0	0
Ohnoutka, 10 L.V.-2 Edm.	.889	12	3	5	1	0
Olin, Colorado Springs	.857	14	1	5	1	0
Oliveras, Portland	1.000	11	4	3	0	0
Otto, Tacoma*	1.000	2	1	1	0	0
Pacillo, Calgary	.800	32	7	13	5	0
Pawlowski, Vancouver	1.000	30	4	13	0	1
Penigar, Vancouver	1.000	1	0	1	0	1
Peters, Las Vegas*	1.000	47	3	4	0	0
Peterson, Vancouver	1.000	6	2	4	0	0
Pittman, Portland	.900	28	6	3	1	0
Raczka, 4 L.V.-42 Tac.	.963	46	3	23	1	1
Reuss, Tucson	1.000	5	1	0	0	0
Rice, Calgary	.900	15	5	4	1	1
Richardson, Edmonton	.750	38	3	6	3	0
Roberts, Las Vegas	1.000	12	2	4	0	0
Robertson, Colorado Springs	1.000	31	2	3	0	0
Ricardo Rodriguez, Phoenix	1.000	14	4	12	0	1
Richard Rodriguez, Las Vegas*	1.000	27	6	8	0	1
Rosenberg, Vancouver*	.882	40	2	13	2	1
Savage, Portland	1.000	16	0	3	0	0
Scheid, Vancouver*	1.000	20	2	5	0	2
C. Scott, 3 C.S.-29 Port.	.968	32	12	18	1	1
R. Scott, Tacoma	.000	1	0	0	0	0
T. Scott, Albuquerque	1.000	17	1	0	0	0

PITCHERS—Continued

Player and Club	Pct.	G.	PO.	A.	E.	DP.	Player and Club	Pct.	G.	PO.	A.	E.	DP.
Seanez, Colorado Springs	.667	12	0	2	1	0	S. Valdez, Colorado Springs	.909	7	3	7	1	2
Segura, Vancouver	1.000	40	5	7	0	0	Vande Berg, Calgary*	.800	10	0	4	1	0
Shaver, Tacoma	1.000	19	6	11	0	1	Veres, Tacoma	.913	32	7	14	2	0
J. Shaw, Colorado Springs	.941	17	3	13	1	1	Vosberg, Phoenix*	.941	24	5	11	1	1
T. Shaw, Calgary	.903	23	12	16	3	1	M.A. Walker, Calgary	.967	25	9	20	1	1
Sierra, Las Vegas	1.000	15	2	2	0	0	M.C. Walker, Colorado Springs	.913	18	9	12	2	1
Sisk, Colorado Springs	1.000	8	1	0	0	0	Walsh, Albuquerque*	1.000	47	1	11	0	2
Skalski, Colorado Springs	.905	21	10	9	2	1	Walter, Tucson*	1.000	3	1	0	0	0
Slusarski, Tacoma	.917	9	3	8	1	2	Walton, Tacoma	.833	46	3	12	3	1
Smithberg, Las Vegas	.889	13	1	7	1	0	Ward, Colorado Springs	1.000	43	6	6	0	0
Springer, Albuquerque	1.000	2	0	1	0	1	Wayne, Portland*	1.000	22	4	3	0	0
St. Claire, Tucson	.900	23	2	7	1	0	Weber, 35 Tac.-4 Port.	.947	39	9	9	1	3
Stephens, Vancouver	1.000	3	0	1	0	1	Wells, Albuquerque*	.900	24	3	15	2	0
Swan, 6 Phoe.-5 Cal.*	1.000	11	5	9	0	1	Wetteland, Albuquerque	1.000	8	1	4	0	0
Taylor, Calgary	.933	25	4	10	1	1	Williams, Portland*	.909	51	6	14	2	3
Thurmond, Tucson*	1.000	9	0	1	0	0	Willis, Colorado Springs	1.000	41	12	26	0	3
Tolliver, Edmonton	1.000	13	2	10	0	3	Wilson, Phoenix*	.864	11	8	11	3	1
Trudeau, Edmonton	1.000	22	5	9	0	1	Wojna, Tacoma	1.000	24	13	20	0	0
Tunnell, Tucson	.875	33	6	8	2	1	Yett, Portland	.926	22	14	11	2	4
E. Valdez, Colorado Springs*	.957	46	3	19	1	3	C. Young, Edmonton*	1.000	30	3	9	0	2
R. Valdez, Las Vegas	.909	17	1	9	1	1	R. Young, Tacoma	.943	28	11	22	2	4
							Yurtin, Las Vegas	1.000	4	0	1	0	0

Triple Play—Kaiser.

The following players did not have any fielding statistics at the positions indicated or appeared only as a designated hitter, pinch-hitter or pinch-runner: K. Abbott, p; Allison, p; Baker, p; Bankhead, p; Bathe, dh, ph; Bush, of; Castillo, p; Cedeno, p; Chitren, p; Cockrell, p; Collins, p; Corsi, p; Dalena, p; Davino, p; DeLeon, p; Fischer, p; Fox, 1b; Gainey, p; Garbey, dh; Garcia, p; Gilmore, of; Hartley, p; E. Johnson, 3b; Lanoux, dh, ph; Lopez, ss; Manrique, ph; Martinez, 3b; McPhail, p; D. Miller, 2b; S. Murray, p; Naveda, p; Nelson, p; Pedrique, 1b; Pledger, ph; Quinzer, p; Redding, p; Ritchie, p; V. Rodriguez, 3b; R. Scott, ss, p; T. Shaw, of; Skurla, p; Strebeck, p; Tolliver, of; Traxler, p.

CLUB PITCHING

Club	ERA.	G.	CG.	ShO.	Sv.	IP.	H.	R.	ER.	HR.	HB.	BB.	Int. BB.	SO.	WP.	Bk.
Edmonton	3.97	141	17	4	41	1240.1	1338	652	547	92	41	481	31	802	44	5
Vancouver	4.03	141	20	8	31	1209.1	1157	628	542	74	41	575	9	807	40	14
Albuquerque	4.25	142	13	7	45	1201.1	1211	638	567	102	18	544	28	966	72	11
Tacoma	4.27	142	10	11	42	1205.2	1184	661	572	80	34	607	23	833	58	31
Portland	4.55	139	10	6	25	1184.1	1227	713	599	94	32	610	14	849	49	16
Phoenix	4.67	139	10	5	33	1198.0	1367	731	621	89	28	497	26	667	50	25
Colorado Springs	4.76	143	19	9	38	1206.2	1347	758	638	106	47	526	32	789	77	14
Tucson	5.00	142	13	3	34	1222.0	1378	779	679	73	50	589	44	727	69	26
Calgary	5.31	143	9	4	34	1207.0	1310	803	712	110	54	589	28	772	65	10
Las Vegas	5.51	144	10	5	28	1215.1	1451	876	763	111	37	623	39	850	71	18

PITCHERS' RECORDS
(Leading Qualifiers for Earned-Run Average Leadership—115 or More Innings)

*Throws lefthanded.

Pitcher—Club	W.	L.	Pct.	ERA.	G.	GS.	CG.	GF.	ShO.	Sv.	IP.	H.	R.	ER.	HR.	HB.	BB.	Int. BB.	SO.	WP.
Cook, Portland	6	8	.429	3.20	19	19	2	0	1	0	115.1	105	54	41	8	5	59	0	63	4
Chiampino, Tacoma	13	9	.591	3.28	26	26	4	0	2	0	173.0	174	79	63	10	5	72	1	110	9
T. Clark, Tucson	11	4	.733	3.54	29	22	3	2	1	1	155.0	172	73	61	9	8	41	2	80	3
Melendez, Calgary	11	4	.733	3.90	45	10	1	14	0	2	124.2	119	61	54	11	6	44	2	95	2
S. Lewis, Edmonton	13	11	.542	3.90	27	27	6	0	0	0	177.2	198	90	77	16	7	35	1	124	2
Wojna, Tacoma	10	5	.667	3.99	24	23	3	0	1	0	142.0	121	71	63	4	5	55	1	99	9
G. Heredia, Phoenix	9	7	.563	4.10	29	19	0	2	0	1	147.0	159	81	67	7	3	37	0	75	4
Bittiger, Albuquerque	15	6	.714	4.15	28	26	2	2	0	0	154.0	162	78	71	15	2	62	3	125	9
R. Young, Tacoma	14	7	.667	4.20	28	27	1	0	1	0	165.0	155	87	77	8	4	105	1	137	9
Hall, Vancouver*	13	8	.619	4.24	28	28	4	0	0	0	184.2	185	100	87	14	6	89	0	106	9

Departmental Leaders: G—Delkus, 65; W—Bittiger, 15; L—McClellan, 16; Pct.—Holmes, .857; GS—Hall, Hennis, 28; CG—Bearse, S. Lewis, 6; GF—Meyer, 45; ShO—Bearse, Chiamparino, Nichols, Peterson, 2; Sv.—Bitker, 26; IP—Hall, 184.2; H—Beasley, 201; R—Nolte, 130; ER—Nolte, 117; HR—C. Scott, 23; HB—Beasley, 16; BB—R. Young, 105; IBB—Helton, Lynch, Meyer, E. Valdez, 8; SO—R. Young, 137; WP—Wells, 17.

(All Pitchers—Listed Alphabetically)

Pitcher—Club	W.	L.	Pct.	ERA.	G.	GS.	CG.	GF.	ShO.	Sv.	IP.	H.	R.	ER.	HR.	HB.	BB.	Int. BB.	SO.	WP.
K. Abbott, Edmonton*	1	0	1.000	14.81	3	3	0	0	0	0	10.1	26	18	17	4	0	4	0	14	4
P. Abbott, Portland	5	14	.263	4.56	23	23	4	0	1	0	128.1	110	75	65	9	1	82	0	129	8
Aldrich, Phoenix	0	0	.000	4.32	8	1	0	4	0	0	16.2	19	8	8	2	0	9	2
Allison, Tacoma*	0	0	.000	0.00	2	0	0	1	0	0	1.1	1	0	0	0	0	1	0	2	0
Alvarez, Vancouver*	7	7	.500	6.00	17	15	1	0	0	0	75.0	91	54	50	7	4	51	0	35	1
Ariola, Tacoma*	0	1	.000	5.51	6	2	0	1	0	0	16.1	24	14	10	1	1	2	0	6	0
Bailes, Edmonton*	0	1	.000	6.00	9	3	0	1	0	0	18.0	21	13	12	3	0	8	0	12	0
Baker, Portland	0	0	.000	0.00	1	0	0	0	0	0	1.0	1	0	0	0	0	0	0	0	0
Bangtson, Portland	6	7·	.462	5.55	29	12	0	6	0	1	105.1	130	76	65	11	5	53	1	64	6
Bankhead, Calgary	0	1	.000	6.43	2	2	0	0	0	0	7.0	9	6	5	1	0	3	0	7	0
Bearse, Colorado Springs*	11	9	.550	5.00	25	24	6	0	2	0	145.2	170	92	81	17	8	49	1	79	12
Beasley, Edmonton	12	9	.571	4.49	28	27	5	0	0	0	176.1	201	107	88	15	16	70	5	108	5
Beck, Phoenix	4	7	.364	4.93	12	12	2	0	0	0	76.2	100	51	42	8	1	18	1	43	6
Bitker, Tacoma	2	3	.400	3.20	48	0	0	43	0	26	56.1	51	22	20	6	0	20	0	52	2
Bittiger, Albuquerque	15	6	.714	4.15	28	26	2	2	0	0	154.0	162	78	71	15	2	62	3	125	9
Blasucci, Calgary*	1	2	.333	4.80	15	0	0	5	0	1	30.0	25	17	16	6	0	16	0	33	0
Bockus, Edmonton	0	0	.000	0.00	2	0	0	1	0	1	3.2	3	0	0	0	0	2	0	2	0
Bones, Las Vegas	2	1	.667	3.47	5	5	0	0	0	0	36.1	45	17	14	2	1	10	0	25	1
Bonilla, Phoenix*	2	1	.667	5.09	36	0	0	9	0	0	40.2	38	24	23	3	1	19	2	26	4
Booker, Phoenix	2	4	.333	4.58	49	0	0	28	0	10	72.2	83	46	37	3	2	36	3	29	7
Bordi, Phoenix	0	0	.000	3.86	4	0	0	1	0	0	9.1	10	5	4	0	2	0	4	1
Bowen, Tucson	1	3	.250	9.35	10	7	0	0	0	0	34.2	41	36	36	5	0	38	1	29	0
Brennan, Tucson	8	7	.533	4.73	41	8	2	5	0	0	110.1	104	68	58	5	10	89	3	88	10
Browning, 3 Tuc.-5 C.S.	1	1	.500	2.63	8	0	0	4	0	0	13.2	9	4	4	0	0	8	0
Brundage, Calgary*	0	0	.000	13.50	2	0	0	2	0	0	2.2	4	4	4	1	0	3	0	5	1

Pitcher—Club	W.	L.	Pct.	ERA.	G.	GS.	CG.	GF.	ShO.	Sv.	IP.	H.	R.	ER.	HR.	HB.	BB.	Int. BB.	SO.	WP.
Buchanan, Tucson°	0	0	.000	5.54	9	0	0	3	0	1	13.0	13	8	8	2	1	9	0	8	1
Buckels, Edmonton	2	7	.222	4.57	53	0	0	29	0	10	67.0	66	38	34	8	0	32	7	61	3
Burba, Calgary	10	6	.625	4.67	31	18	1	8	0	2	113.2	124	64	59	11	2	45	0	47	5
Burcham, Edmonton	9	10	.474	4.57	27	26	3	1	0	0	157.2	182	94	80	5	3	69	1	97	10
Burkett, Phoenix	2	1	.667	2.74	3	3	2	0	1	0	23.0	18	8	7	2	0	3	0	9	0
Camacho, Phoenix	1	0	1.000	1.80	13	0	0	11	0	4	15.0	12	4	3	0	0	11	1	17	0
Campbell, Vancouver	4	5	.444	5.83	21	8	0	5	0	0	66.1	76	45	43	6	1	30	1	50	0
Cano, Tucson	2	5	.286	7.09	10	10	1	0	0	0	45.2	61	43	36	4	4	24	1	19	5
Casian, Portland°	9	9	.500	4.48	37	23	1	4	0	0	156.2	171	90	78	14	3	59	5	89	2
Castillo, Colorado Springs	0	0	.000	13.50	1	0	0	1	0	0	2.0	3	3	3	1	0	4	0	0	0
Cedeno, Vancouver	0	1	.000	3.38	4	0	0	3	0	0	8.0	5	3	3	0	0	7	0	8	0
Chiamparino, Tacoma	13	9	.591	3.28	26	26	4	0	2	0	173.0	174	79	63	10	5	72	1	110	9
Chitren, Tacoma	0	0	.000	0.00	1	0	0	1	0	0	0.2	1	0	0	0	0	0	0	2	0
Christopher, Albuquerque	6	1	.857	1.97	54	0	0	25	0	8	68.2	62	20	15	3	2	23	3	47	0
Clancy, Tucson°	3	2	.600	2.98	10	5	0	0	0	0	42.1	48	17	14	1	2	9	2	34	0
B. Clark, Calgary°	4	3	.571	3.95	18	10	0	1	0	0	57.0	55	40	25	5	3	29	1	27	6
T. Clark, Tucson	11	4	.733	3.54	29	22	3	2	1	1	155.0	172	73	61	9	8	41	2	80	3
Clear, Edmonton	1	0	1.000	3.07	12	0	0	6	0	2	14.2	14	5	5	1	1	8	0	21	1
Clements, Las Vegas°	4	3	.571	6.05	26	13	1	5	0	0	86.1	106	68	58	7	0	34	3	57	0
Cockrell, Colorado Springs	0	0	.000	0.00	1	0	0	1	0	0	1.0	1	0	0	0	0	1	0	0	0
Collins, Colorado Springs	0	0	.000	0.00	1	0	0	1	0	0	1.2	0	0	0	0	0	0	0	1	0
Cook, Portland	6	8	.429	3.20	19	19	2	0	1	0	115.1	105	54	41	8	5	59	0	63	4
Corbett, Edmonton°	3	1	.750	3.50	47	1	0	18	0	5	69.1	64	31	27	2	2	25	2	44	7
Corsi, Tacoma	0	0	.000	1.50	5	0	0	2	0	0	6.0	9	2	1	0	0	1	0	3	2
Curtis, Colorado Springs°	2	2	.500	4.55	19	6	0	7	0	1	55.1	66	33	28	6	0	17	0	33	3
Dalena, 1 Van.-1 Port.	0	0	.000	9.00	2	0	0	2	0	0	2.0	4	2	2	0	0	1	0	1	0
Davino, Vancouver	0	0	.000	0.00	1	0	0	0	0	0	1.0	1	0	0	0	0	1	0	1	0
J. Davis, Las Vegas	2	4	.333	4.34	18	11	1	6	0	1	74.2	68	40	36	3	8	43	0	68	8
S. Davis, Albuquerque°	7	8	.467	4.31	31	18	2	5	0	0	129.1	145	81	62	14	0	44	2	76	4
DeLeon, Albuquerque	0	0	.000	13.50	1	0	0	0	0	0	1.1	4	2	2	0	1	2	0	1	0
Delkus, Portland	5	3	.625	4.18	65	0	0	31	0	4	90.1	109	48	42	7	2	21	0	35	1
DeLucia, Calgary	2	2	.500	3.62	5	5	1	0	0	0	32.1	30	17	13	2	2	12	0	23	3
Dewey, Phoenix	2	3	.400	2.67	19	0	0	17	0	8	30.1	26	14	9	2	2	10	2	27	1
Downs, Phoenix	0	0	.000	1.80	1	1	0	0	0	0	5.0	5	3	1	1	0	0	0	4	0
Drees, Vancouver°	8	5	.615	3.98	17	16	4	0	1	0	97.1	94	49	43	3	4	51	0	63	1
Dunne, Las Vegas	1	2	.333	3.21	4	4	1	0	1	0	28.0	20	12	10	2	1	10	1	12	0
Dyer, Portland	0	1	.000	34.71	2	2	0	0	0	0	2.1	6	10	9	1	0	9	0	0	0
Eave, 1 Cal.-10 Phoe.	3	3	.500	7.82	11	11	0	0	0	0	50.2	63	47	44	7	3	40	0	27	2
Edwards, Colorado Springs°	1	1	.500	5.00	4	4	0	0	0	0	18.0	25	11	10	0	1	11	0	16	1
Eichhorn, Tucson	2	4	.333	3.38	28	0	0	9	0	3	48.0	55	24	18	2	1	16	4	13	2
Erb, Edmonton	4	4	.500	4.26	16	14	0	0	0	0	82.1	90	46	39	8	4	60	3	45	3
Fetters, Edmonton	1	1	.500	0.99	5	5	1	0	1	0	27.1	22	9	3	0	1	13	0	26	2
Fischer, Albuquerque	0	0	.000	6.00	3	0	0	2	0	0	3.0	3	2	2	1	0	1	0	4	0
Fisher, Tucson	8	8	.500	6.80	30	13	0	15	0	0	87.1	113	72	66	7	3	36	4	47	1
Fox, Tacoma°	0	0	.000	0.00	2	0	0	2	0	0	3.0	2	2	0	0	1	2	0	1	1
Fraser, Edmonton	1	0	1.000	3.14	3	3	0	0	0	0	14.1	11	8	5	1	0	6	1	12	2
Gainey, Colorado Springs	0	0	.000	0.00	1	0	0	1	0	0	0.1	0	0	0	0	0	0	0	1	0
Garcia, Vancouver	0	0	.000	0.00	1	0	0	1	0	0	1.0	2	0	0	0	0	0	0	0	0
Gilmore, Las Vegas	13	7	.650	5.13	42	18	3	20	1	6	154.1	182	96	88	16	3	41	4	122	6
Givens, Calgary°	0	1	.000	12.71	2	2	0	0	0	0	5.2	7	8	8	1	0	8	0	4	1
Grahe, Edmonton	3	0	1.000	1.35	5	5	2	0	0	0	40.0	35	10	6	4	0	11	0	21	0
Gunderson, Phoenix°	5	7	.417	8.23	16	16	0	0	0	0	82.0	137	87	75	11	3	46	1	41	4
Guthrie, Portland°	1	3	.250	2.98	9	8	1	1	0	0	42.1	47	19	14	1	2	12	0	39	0
Hall, Vancouver°	13	8	.619	4.24	28	28	4	0	0	0	184.2	185	100	87	14	6	89	0	106	9
Harris, Calgary	3	0	1.000	2.35	6	0	0	6	0	2	7.2	7	2	2	0	0	4	0	9	2
Hartley, Albuquerque	0	0	.000	0.00	3	0	0	2	0	0	3.0	3	0	0	0	0	2	0	3	0
Hartsock, Albuquerque	3	3	.500	6.22	11	10	0	0	0	0	46.1	62	38	32	5	0	30	1	33	4
Heathcock, Edmonton	1	3	.250	7.52	8	4	0	1	0	0	26.1	42	23	22	3	1	6	1	11	0
Helton, Calgary°	6	7	.462	5.80	60	1	0	23	0	6	80.2	88	59	52	10	4	51	8	68	4
Hennis, Tucson	10	8	.556	4.41	28	28	3	0	1	0	159.1	153	87	78	6	3	92	3	101	10
G. Heredia, Phoenix	9	7	.563	4.10	29	19	0	2	0	1	147.0	159	81	67	7	3	37	0	75	4
H. Heredia, Tucson	2	2	.500	5.27	34	0	0	15	0	3	56.1	66	36	33	1	1	21	4	47	3
Hernandez, Vancouver	3	5	.375	2.84	11	11	3	0	1	0	79.1	73	33	25	4	2	26	0	49	3
Hickerson, Phoenix°	0	4	.000	5.50	12	4	0	3	0	0	34.1	48	25	21	2	0	16	2	26	0
Hillegas, Vancouver	5	3	.625	1.74	36	0	0	23	0	9	67.1	49	22	13	4	1	15	0	52	2
Holmes, Albuquerque	12	2	.857	3.11	56	0	0	30	0	13	92.2	78	34	32	3	4	39	2	99	5
Ilsley, Tucson°	2	1	.667	6.46	20	6	1	4	0	2	62.2	87	50	45	4	3	24	0	39	8
Johnson, Portland	3	0	1.000	4.50	15	0	0	4	0	1	26.0	27	20	13	3	1	14	1	24	3
Kaiser, Colorado Springs°	2	2	.500	2.93	25	0	0	11	0	3	43.0	36	16	14	3	2	22	2	46	5
Kile, Tucson	5	10	.333	6.64	26	23	1	1	0	0	123.1	147	97	91	16	5	68	1	77	13
Knepper, Phoenix°	1	2	.333	3.65	4	4	0	0	0	0	24.2	21	14	10	1	1	9	1	13	0
Kutzler, Vancouver	5	7	.417	4.20	19	19	2	0	0	0	113.2	124	64	53	8	6	34	0	73	2
Lambert, 31 Tac.-5 C.S.	3	3	.500	6.12	36	0	0	14	0	0	57.1	71	40	39	2	1	30	1	35	5
Law, Tacoma	2	5	.286	6.16	17	11	0	3	0	1	61.1	66	43	42	6	0	42	3	46	3
Lazorko, Calgary	4	8	.333	5.18	31	13	1	4	0	2	114.2	129	74	66	14	9	43	3	79	2
Leiper, Tacoma°	0	1	.000	5.82	6	0	0	4	0	2	17.0	19	12	11	1	0	9	3	8	0
J. Lewis, Las Vegas	5	6	.455	4.55	59	1	0	18	0	5	93.0	109	60	47	6	2	46	3	54	7
S. Lewis, Edmonton	13	11	.542	3.90	27	27	6	0	0	0	177.2	198	90	77	16	7	35	1	124	2
Lind, Portland	0	3	.000	5.06	7	0	0	0	0	0	16.0	18	9	9	1	0	9	1	14	1
Lovelace, Calgary°	5	5	.500	3.47	56	0	0	29	0	6	70.0	64	33	27	0	2	44	0	40	2
Lynch, Las Vegas	5	8	.385	5.22	58	0	0	23	0	2	88.0	121	59	51	9	2	31	8	44	6
Madden, Albuquerque°	6	4	.600	4.78	31	13	1	4	1	0	92.1	86	55	49	5	1	68	5	99	12
Maddux, Albuquerque	8	5	.615	4.25	20	19	2	0	0	0	108.0	122	59	51	8	4	32	2	85	7
Manzanillo, Vancouver°	7	3	.700	3.61	38	6	0	18	0	4	92.1	74	41	37	2	3	60	1	64	3
Mason, Portland°	0	0	.000	0.00	3	0	0	0	0	0	3.0	4	2	0	0	0	3	0	1	0
Mayberry, Albuquerque	4	7	.364	5.66	32	12	0	2	0	0	95.1	106	69	60	10	2	36	0	76	4
Maysey, Las Vegas	6	10	.375	5.62	26	25	1	1	0	0	137.2	155	97	86	10	5	88	5	72	12
McCament, Phoenix	3	3	.500	3.79	46	0	0	21	0	6	78.1	99	40	33	4	2	32	5	32	3
McClellan, Phoenix	7	16	.304	5.17	28	27	1	0	0	0	172.1	192	112	99	17	5	78	3	102	7
McCoy, Tacoma°	0	0	.000	8.46	8	5	0	0	0	0	22.1	26	24	21	2	0	18	0	8	2
McMichael, Colorado Springs	2	3	.400	5.80	12	12	1	0	1	0	59.0	72	45	38	5	0	30	0	34	6
McPhail, Vancouver	0	0	.000	0.00	1	0	0	0	0	0	1.0	1	0	0	0	0	0	0	0	0

Pitcher—Club	W.	L.	Pct.	ERA.	G.	GS.	CG.	GF.	ShO.	Sv.	IP.	H.	R.	ER.	HR.	HB.	BB.	Int. BB.	SO.	WP.
Mead, Phoenix	0	2	.000	5.23	22	3	0	11	0	1	41.1	49	26	24	2	1	14	0	19	0
Medvin, Calgary	1	3	.250	4.97	43	0	0	31	0	11	50.2	47	30	28	5	4	24	6	31	5
Meeks, Edmonton	0	1	.000	12.27	4	0	0	3	0	0	3.2	12	7	5	1	0	2	1	4	0
Meier, Phoenix	5	3	.625	4.35	13	13	0	0	0	0	68.1	82	41	33	9	2	21	0	25	0
Melendez, Calgary	11	4	.733	3.90	45	10	1	14	0	2	124.2	119	61	54	11	6	44	2	95	2
Menendez, Vancouver	2	5	.286	3.72	24	9	2	2	1	0	72.2	63	34	30	6	6	28	1	48	1
Meyer, Tucson	5	7	.417	2.97	64	0	0	45	0	15	100.0	91	43	33	3	7	38	8	54	2
Miller, Tacoma	0	1	.000	8.31	4	1	0	2	0	0	8.2	7	8	8	1	0	12	0	3	1
Montalvo, Edmonton	1	5	.167	2.74	48	0	0	21	0	9	85.1	76	33	26	3	1	22	4	42	2
Monteleone, Edmonton	1	0	1.000	1.93	5	1	0	1	0	1	14.0	7	3	3	1	0	4	0	9	0
Munoz, Albuquerque°	4	1	.800	4.25	49	0	0	14	0	6	59.1	65	33	28	8	0	19	3	40	3
Murphy, Las Vegas	4	7	.364	5.81	27	10	1	10	0	3	69.2	74	54	45	5	0	56	2	60	2
Murray, Calgary	0	0	.000	0.00	1	0	0	1	0	0	1.0	3	0	0	0	0	0	0	1	0
Naveda, Portland	0	0	.000	18.00	1	0	0	1	0	0	1.0	1	2	2	1	0	1	0	0	0
Neidlinger, Albuquerque	8	5	.615	4.29	20	18	4	2	1	0	119.2	129	70	57	13	1	34	3	81	2
Nelson, Portland	0	0	.000	6.75	3	0	0	2	0	0	4.0	3	3	3	0	0	5	0	2	0
Nichols, Colorado Springs	12	9	.571	5.13	22	22	4	0	2	0	133.1	160	84	76	12	11	48	3	74	3
Nipper, Colorado Springs	5	5	.500	4.74	17	16	1	1	0	1	89.1	80	53	47	6	5	56	0	47	5
Nolte, Las Vegas°	2	11	.154	8.58	33	18	1	4	0	0	122.2	187	130	117	15	1	49	4	79	8
Normand, Tucson°	2	0	1.000	7.71	4	0	0	3	0	0	4.2	3	4	4	0	0	5	1	1	1
Norris, Tacoma	0	1	.000	3.72	3	2	0	1	0	0	9.2	7	4	4	0	1	2	0	5	0
O'Neal, Phoenix	5	0	1.000	2.97	7	6	2	1	1	0	39.1	34	14	13	2	1	8	0	25	2
Ohnoutka, 10 L.V.-2 Edm.	1	4	.200	4.96	12	3	0	2	0	1	32.2	41	21	18	4	2	15	1	20	2
Olin, Colorado Springs	3	1	.750	0.66	14	0	0	8	0	2	27.1	18	9	2	0	1	15	2	30	0
Oliveras, Portland	3	4	.429	2.90	11	6	1	1	0	1	62.0	44	23	20	2	3	22	0	56	1
Otto, Tacoma°	0	0	.000	4.50	2	0	0	0	0	0	2.0	3	1	1	0	0	1	0	2	1
Pacillo, Calgary	5	4	.556	5.20	32	13	0	3	0	0	90.0	91	65	52	5	6	64	3	66	2
Pawlowski, Vancouver	7	7	.500	4.76	30	14	1	7	0	2	117.1	125	68	62	10	2	64	1	67	7
Penigar, Vancouver	0	0	.000	3.86	1	0	0	0	0	0	2.1	5	2	1	0	0	0	0	0	0
Peters, Las Vegas°	0	2	.000	7.52	47	0	0	22	0	2	40.2	49	35	34	7	1	39	6	32	2
Peterson, Vancouver	4	1	.800	2.09	6	6	3	0	2	0	43.0	26	11	10	3	1	15	0	30	0
Pittman, Portland	0	1	.000	6.99	28	0	0	20	0	6	28.1	28	24	22	2	2	34	0	22	5
Quinzer, Las Vegas	0	0	.000	3.24	5	0	0	0	0	0	8.1	8	3	3	1	0	2	0	5	1
Raczka, 4 L.V.-42 Tac.°	7	5	.583	4.28	46	2	0	18	0	2	67.1	59	37	32	5	3	44	3	61	3
Redding, Portland	0	1	.000	11.57	1	1	0	0	0	0	2.1	6	4	3	0	0	1	0	1	0
Reuss, Tucson°	0	0	.000	15.19	5	0	0	1	0	0	5.1	18	14	9	0	1	2	1	3	0
Rice, Calgary	1	1	.500	6.35	15	2	0	2	0	2	28.1	34	21	20	2	1	13	2	27	4
Richardson, Edmonton	5	0	1.000	1.86	38	0	0	26	0	10	48.1	46	17	10	1	0	27	1	31	0
Ritchie, Phoenix°	0	0	.000	0.00	1	0	0	1	0	0	1.0	0	0	0	0	0	2	0	0	0
Roberts, Las Vegas°	1	3	.250	5.40	12	4	1	1	0	0	36.2	40	24	22	1	1	14	1	29	1
Robertson, Colorado Springs	1	2	.333	5.76	31	0	0	25	0	12	29.2	33	21	19	1	0	35	2	28	5
Ricardo Rodriguez, Phoenix	4	2	.667	4.75	14	4	1	4	0	0	41.2	36	24	22	3	0	22	0	21	2
Richard Rodriguez, Las Vegas° ..	3	4	.429	3.51	27	2	0	13	0	8	59.0	50	24	23	5	1	22	1	46	3
Rosenberg, Vancouver°	6	5	.545	3.57	40	7	0	21	0	8	88.1	66	43	35	5	4	44	3	74	2
Savage, Portland	1	2	.333	1.31	16	0	0	12	0	3	20.2	17	8	3	0	2	11	3	25	0
Scheid, Vancouver°	2	2	.500	3.20	20	2	0	10	0	0	39.1	37	19	14	2	0	24	1	38	2
C. Scott, 3 C.S.-29 Port.	7	11	.389	4.59	32	21	0	4	0	1	157.0	170	87	80	23	2	66	1	130	2
R. Scott, Tacoma	0	0	.000	0.00	1	0	0	1	0	0	1.0	2	0	0	0	0	0	0	0	0
T. Scott, Albuquerque	1	2	.667	4.20	17	0	0	8	0	3	15.0	14	9	7	1	0	14	2	15	0
Seanez, Colorado Springs	1	4	.200	6.75	12	0	0	10	0	1	12.0	15	10	9	2	0	10	0	7	3
Segura, Vancouver	1	3	.250	5.10	40	0	0	27	0	8	54.2	49	34	31	0	1	35	1	47	6
Shaver, Tacoma	0	4	.000	5.76	19	6	0	5	0	2	45.1	54	33	29	5	2	26	1	42	1
J. Shaw, Colorado Springs	10	3	.769	4.29	17	16	4	0	0	0	98.2	98	54	47	7	3	52	0	55	5
T. Shaw, Calgary	6	9	.400	5.62	23	23	2	0	0	0	129.2	141	86	81	11	5	56	2	50	9
Sierra, Las Vegas	2	1	.667	5.59	15	0	0	5	0	0	19.1	25	12	12	3	2	10	0	16	1
Sisk, Colorado Springs	1	0	1.000	7.04	8	0	0	2	0	0	7.2	8	6	6	0	0	5	0	7	0
Skalski, Colorado Springs	5	7	.417	5.73	21	17	1	1	0	0	99.0	129	76	63	14	2	21	2	81	9
Skurla, Edmonton°	0	0	.000	0.00	1	0	0	1	0	0	0.1	2	0	0	0	1	0	0	1	0
Slusarski, Tacoma	4	2	.667	3.40	9	9	0	0	0	0	55.2	54	24	21	3	2	22	0	37	1
Smithberg, Las Vegas	2	7	.222	6.95	13	13	0	0	0	0	66.0	91	63	51	8	6	39	0	30	6
Springer, Albuquerque	0	0	.000	5.68	2	2	0	0	0	0	6.1	10	4	4	1	2	7	0	2	0
St. Claire, Tacoma	4	3	.571	5.46	23	0	0	16	0	0	31.1	45	22	19	3	1	21	5	16	6
Stephens, Vancouver	0	0	.000	7.36	3	0	0	2	0	0	3.2	9	4	3	0	0	0	1	1	0
Strebeck, Tacoma	0	0	.000	0.00	3	0	0	2	0	0	2.2	3	0	0	0	2	1	0	0	1
Swan, 6 Phoe.- 5 Cal.°	3	6	.333	4.45	11	11	0	0	0	0	56.2	69	35	28	1	2	27	0	35	4
Taylor, Calgary	0	7	.000	9.97	25	14	0	4	0	0	71.1	96	84	79	7	5	61	1	71	6
Thurmond, Tucson°	0	0	.000	3.27	9	0	0	2	0	1	11.0	11	4	4	0	0	1	0	6	0
Tolliver, Edmonton	8	2	.800	3.99	13	12	0	0	0	0	67.2	71	34	30	9	3	28	0	45	1
Traxler, Albuquerque°	0	0	.000	0.00	1	0	0	1	0	0	1.0	0	0	0	0	0	1	0	1	1
Trudeau, Edmonton	5	2	.714	4.12	22	8	0	1	0	1	74.1	87	41	34	4	0	34	3	35	1
Tunnell, Tucson	6	7	.462	4.78	33	20	2	6	0	2	124.1	144	76	66	5	0	48	4	59	4
E. Valdez, Colorado Springs°	4	2	.667	3.81	46	1	0	17	0	6	75.2	72	38	32	6	4	30	8	52	4
R. Valdez, Las Vegas	4	7	.364	4.92	17	17	0	0	0	0	86.0	82	58	47	6	2	65	0	79	4
S. Valdez, Colorado Springs	4	3	.571	5.19	7	7	2	0	1	0	43.1	55	29	25	7	1	13	0	33	4
Vande Berg, Calgary°	1	0	1.000	8.27	10	0	0	1	0	0	16.1	29	17	15	0	0	8	0	10	1
Veres, Tacoma	11	8	.579	4.69	32	23	2	2	0	1	151.2	136	90	79	13	3	88	1	88	7
Vosberg, Phoenix°	1	3	.250	2.65	24	0	0	16	0	3	34.0	36	14	10	2	1	16	3	28	3
M.A. Walker, Calgary	5	11	.313	5.35	25	24	3	0	0	0	144.2	176	92	86	16	3	45	0	64	7
M.C. Walker, Colorado Springs ...	2	7	.222	5.58	18	12	0	2	0	1	79.0	96	62	49	6	7	36	5	50	6
Walsh, Albuquerque°	6	0	1.000	2.61	47	0	0	28	0	12	62.0	50	21	18	2	0	31	1	66	4
Walter, Tucson°	0	0	.000	0.00	3	0	0	1	0	0	3.0	4	3	0	0	0	3	1	4	0
Walton, Tacoma	5	5	.500	3.11	46	5	0	21	0	7	98.1	103	42	34	12	2	23	5	67	1
Ward, Colorado Springs	4	3	.571	2.00	43	0	0	28	0	9	63.0	45	23	14	2	0	30	3	56	2
Wayne, Portland°	2	4	.333	3.41	22	0	0	13	0	5	31.2	29	14	12	1	0	13	1	30	3
Weber, 35 Tac.-4 Port.	5	2	.714	5.42	39	3	0	19	0	1	73.0	79	54	44	4	5	48	2	42	3
Wells, Albuquerque°	8	6	.571	4.62	24	19	1	2	1	1	115.0	83	64	59	6	0	87	0	86	17
Wetteland, Albuquerque	2	2	.500	5.59	8	5	1	2	0	0	29.0	27	19	18	5	0	13	0	26	0
Williams, Portland°	4	6	.400	5.04	51	3	0	27	0	3	84.0	73	64	47	4	3	74	2	62	7
Willis, Colorado Springs	5	3	.625	6.39	41	6	0	5	0	2	98.2	136	80	70	9	1	32	3	42	3
Wilson, Phoenix°	5	5	.500	3.82	11	10	2	0	1	0	66.0	63	31	28	2	0	44	2	45	1
Wojna, Tacoma	10	5	.667	3.99	24	23	3	0	1	0	142.0	121	71	63	4	5	55	1	99	5
Yett, Portland	4	6	.400	6.17	22	20	1	1	1	0	100.2	117	72	69	7	1	60	1	58	6

Pitcher—Club	W.	L.	Pct.	ERA.	G.	GS.	CG.	GF.	ShO.	Sv.	IP.	H.	R.	ER.	HR.	HB.	BB.	Int. BB.	SO.	WP.
C. Young, Edmonton*	7	4	.636	2.42	30	0	0	14	0	4	52.0	45	15	14	1	1	10	1	30	0
R. Young, Tacoma	14	7	.667	4.20	28	27	1	0	1	0	165.0	155	87	77	8	4	105	1	137	9
Yurtin, Las Vegas	0	1	.000	6.75	4	0	0	4	0	0	4.0	4	3	3	1	0	4	0	1	0

BALKS—R. Young, 16; Nolte, 7; McClelland, 6; P. Abbott, T. Clark, Walton, 5 each; Booker, Cano, Eichhorn, Fisher, Kile, 4 each; Burba, Knepper, Manzanillo, Pawlowski, Robertson, Scheid, R. Valdez, Walsh, Wilson, 3 each; Alvarez, Bangtson, Casian, Clements, Gunderson, Hartsock, Hennis, Holmes, Lazorko, Madden, McCoy, Nichols, C. Scott, T. Shaw, Skalski, E. Valdez, Veres, C. Young, 2 each; Bailes, Bearse, Brennan, Browning, Camacho, Chiamparino, Clancy, B. Clark, Curtis, Delkus, Eave, Fetters, Guthrie, Hall, Heathcock, G. Heredia, H. Heredia, Hickerson, Hillegas, Kaiser, Kutzler, Lambert, Law, Mayberry, Maysey, McCament, Melendez, Munoz, Murphy, Oliveras, Peters, Roberts, Richard Rodriguez, Shaver, Slusarski, Smithberg, Swan, S. Valdez, Vande Berg, Vosberg, Wayne, Williams, Wojna, 1 each.

COMBINATION SHUTOUTS—Bittiger-Walsh, Madden-Holmes, Mayberry-Scott-Walsh, Wells-Christopher, Albuquerque; Burba-Lovelace-Rice, Burba-Melendez-Lovelace, Lazorko-Melendez, Swan-Burba, Calgary; Curtis-Kaiser, Nipper-Willis, Shaw-Willis-Valdez-Robertson, Colorado Springs; Burcham-Corbett, Erb-Richardson-Buckels, Lewis-Clear-Buckels, Edmonton; Maysey-Lewis-Davis, Valdez-Lewis, Valdez-Rodriguez-Murphy, Las Vegas; Gunderson-Camacho, McClelland-Dewey, Phoenix; Bangtson-Wayne, Cook-Scott, Scott-Delkus, Portland; Chiamparino-Raczka, Chiamparino-Veres, Law-Walton, Veres-Bitker, Veres-Walton, Wojna-Ariola-Bitker, Young-Bitker, Tacoma; Hennis-Browning, Tucson; Alvarez-Hillegas, Drees-Rosenberg-Segura, Hall-Hillegas, Vancouver.

NO-HIT GAME—Dunne, Las Vegas, defeated Portland, 2-0, May 6.

Eastern League

CLASS AA

Leading Batter
LUIS MERCEDES
Hagerstown

League President
CHARLES ESHBACH

Leading Pitcher
MIKE GARDINER
Williamsport

CHAMPIONSHIP WINNERS IN PREVIOUS YEARS

1923—Williamsport .... .661	1949—Albany.............................. .664	1972—West Haven b........................ .600
1924—Williamsport .... .654	Binghamton (4th)‡.............. .500	Three Rivers .... .559
1925—York§ .... .583	1950—Wilkes-Barre‡ .... .652	1973—Reading b .... .551
Williamsport§ .... .583	1951—Wilkes-Barre .... .612	Pittsfield............................... .551
1926—Scranton .... .627	Scranton (2nd)† .... .562	1974—Thetford Mines (2nd)c .... .536
1927—Harrisburg .... .630	1952—Albany.............................. .603	Pittsfield (2nd)..................... .496
1928—Harrisburg .... .603	Binghamton (2nd)‡ .... .562	1975—Reading.............................. .613
1929—Binghamton .... .597	1953—Reading.............................. .682	Bristol° .... .587
1930—Wilkes-Barre .... .572	Binghamton (2nd)‡ .... .636	1976—Three Rivers .... .601
1931—Harrisburg .... .597	1954—Wilkes-Barre....................... .576	West Haven d........................ .576
1932—Wilkes-Barre........................ .561	Albany (3rd)‡........................ .540	1977—West Haven e .... .623
1933—Binghamton .... .690	1955—Reading.............................. .613	Three Rivers .... .551
1934—Binghamton .... .694	Allentown (2nd)‡ .... .565	1978—Reading.............................. .642
Williamsport° .... .603	1956—Schenectady† .... .609	Bristol° .... .580
1935—Scranton .... .657	1957—Binghamton.......................... .607	1979—West Haven f .... .597
Binghamton° .... .580	Reading (3rd)‡...................... .529	1980—Holyoke° .... .561
1936—Scranton° .... .609	1958—Lancaster x.......................... .568	Waterbury.............................. .540
Elmira .... .629	Binghamton (6th)‡.............. .493	1981—Glens Falls .... .615
1937—Elmira† .... .622	1959—Springfield†........................ .607	Bristol° .... .577
1938—Binghamton .... .622	1960—Williamsport y.................... .551	1982—West Haven° .... .614
Elmira (3rd)‡........................ .522	Springfield (3rd)y................ .496	Lynn .... .590
1939—Scranton† .... .571	1961—Springfield.......................... .612	1983—Lynn .... .554
1940—Scranton .... .568	1962—Williamsport........................ .593	New Britain‡.......................... .518
Binghamton (2nd)‡ .... .554	Elmira (2nd)‡........................ .514	1984—Waterbury .... .543
1941—Wilkes-Barre........................ .630	1963—Charleston.......................... .593	Vermont‡ .... .536
Elmira (3rd)‡........................ .514	1964—Elmira .... .586	1985—Albany................................ .540
1942—Albany.............................. .600	1965—Pittsfield.......................... .607	Vermont‡ .... .514
Scranton (2nd)‡ .... .593	1966—Elmira .... .633	1986—Reading.............................. .566
1943—Scranton .... .630	1967—Binghamton z .... .586	Vermont‡ .... .554
Elmira (2nd)‡........................ .568	Elmira .... .532	1987—Pittsfield............................ .630
1944—Hartford .... .723	1968—Pittsfield.......................... .604	Harrisburg‡ .... .550
Binghamton (4th)‡.............. .474	Reading (2nd)‡...................... .579	1988—Glens Falls .... .584
1945—Utica .... .615	1969—York.................................... .640	Albany‡................................ .522
Albany (3rd)‡........................ .564	1970—Waterbury a........................ .560	1989—Albany‡................................ .657
1946—Scranton† .... .691	Reading a .... .553	Harrisburg.............................. .522
1947—Utica† .... .652	1971—Three Rivers .... .569	
1948—Scranton† .... .636	Elmira b................................ .561	

°Won split-season playoff. †Won championship and four-team playoff. ‡Won four-team playoff. §Tied for pennant, York winning playoff. xLeague was divided into Northern, Southern divisions and played a split season; Lancaster over-all season leader. yPlayoff finals canceled after one game because of rain with Williamsport and Springfield declared playoff co-champions. zLeague was divided into Eastern, Western divisions; Binghamton won playoff. aTied for pennant, Waterbury winning playoff. bLeague was divided into American, National divisions; won playoff. cLeague was divided into American and National divisions; won four-team playoff. dLeague was divided into Northern, Southern divisions, won playoff. eLeague was divided into New England and Canadian-American divisions; won playoff. fWon both halves of split season (no playoffs). (NOTE—Known as New York-Pennsylvania League prior to 1938.)

STANDING OF CLUBS AT CLOSE OF SEASON, SEPTEMBER 2

Club	Alb.	Lon.	C.A.	N.B.	Har.	Hag.	Wpt.	Read.	W.	L.	T.	Pct.	G.B.
Albany (Yankees)	....	12	11	12	11	10	15	8	79	60	0	.568	....
London (Tigers)	8	....	8	11	10	12	12	15	76	63	0	.547	3
Canton-Akron (Indians)	9	12	....	8	12	12	11	12	76	64	0	.543	3½
New Britain (Red Sox)	8	9	12	....	8	10	12	13	72	67	0	.518	7
Harrisburg (Pirates)	9	10	8	12	....	10	12	8	69	69	0	.500	9½
Hagerstown (Orioles)	10	7	8	9	10	....	9	14	67	71	0	.486	11½
Williamsport (Mariners)	5	8	9	8	8	11	....	12	61	79	0	.436	18½
Reading (Phillies)	11	5	8	7	10	6	8	....	55	82	0	.401	23

London club represented London, Ontario, Can.

Major league affiliations in parentheses.

Playoffs—New Britain defeated Albany, three games to two; London defeated Canton-Akron, three games to two; London defeated New Britain, three games to none, to win league championship.

Regular-Season Attendance—Albany, 203,423; Canton-Akron, 204,193; Hagerstown, 167,725; Harrisburg, 223,033; London, 167,694; New Britain, 123,017; Reading, 204,240; Williamsport, 76,779. Totals—1,370,104. Playoffs (13 games)—22,296. All-Star Game—4,023.

Managers—Albany, Rick Down (through June 5), Dan Radison (June 6 through end of season); Canton-Akron, Ken Bolek; Hagerstown, Jerry Narron; Harrisburg, Marc Bombard; London, Chris Chambliss; New Britain, Butch Hobson; Reading, Don McCormack; Williamsport, Rich Morales. Managerial record of team with more than one manager: Albany, Down (24-21), Radison (55-39).

All-Star Team—1B—Rico Brogna, London; 2B—Pat Kelly, Albany; 3B—Jeff Bagwell, New Britain; SS—Mark Lewis, Canton-Akron; OF—Scott Meadows, Hagerstown; OF—Luis Mercedes, Hagerstown; OF—Bernie Williams, Albany; C—Mitch Lyden, Albany; DH—Jeff Grotewold, Reading; RHP—Mike Gardiner, Williamsport; LHP—Randy Tomlin, Harrisburg; Relief Pitcher—Darrin Chapin, Albany; Most Valuable Player—Jeff Bagwell, New Britain; Pitcher of the Year—Mike Gardiner, Williamsport; Manager of the Year—Chris Chambliss, London.

(Compiled by Howe Sportsdata International, Boston, Mass.)

CLUB BATTING

Club	Pct.	G.	AB.	R.	OR.	H.	TB.	2B.	3B.	HR.	RBI.	SH.	SF.	HP.	BB.	Int. BB.	SO.	SB.	CS.	LOB.
Hagerstown	.267	138	4504	566	513	1202	1612	188	33	52	520	40	58	44	450	24	776	144	72	983
Albany	.262	139	4449	620	533	1166	1711	233	30	84	563	22	44	56	486	19	836	117	71	968
Harrisburg	.258	138	4539	531	526	1169	1528	182	30	39	470	21	26	34	366	17	746	110	59	937
London	.251	139	4550	549	528	1144	1581	174	25	71	493	40	34	37	432	26	755	89	38	948
Canton-Akron	.245	140	4459	556	546	1091	1543	185	30	69	497	38	54	36	437	28	787	108	66	887
New Britain	.241	139	4433	506	519	1068	1446	219	33	31	455	74	47	32	523	31	752	52	49	1024
Williamsport	.236	140	4472	467	526	1057	1414	174	21	47	413	29	44	38	380	16	810	104	49	893
Reading	.235	137	4299	474	578	1012	1457	188	13	77	428	46	23	40	360	13	859	82	49	839

INDIVIDUAL BATTING

(Leading Qualifiers for Batting Championship—378 or More Plate Appearances)

*Bats lefthanded.   †Switch-hitter.

Player and Club	Pct.	G.	AB.	R.	H.	TB.	2B.	3B.	HR.	RBI.	SH.	SF.	HP.	BB.	Int. BB.	SO.	SB.	CS.
Mercedes, Luis, Hagerstown	.334	108	416	71	139	168	12	4	3	37	6	2	6	34	2	70	38	14
Bagwell, Jeffrey, New Britain	.333	136	481	63	160	220	34	7	4	61	3	6	6	73	12	57	5	7
Austin, Dominic, Hagerstown	.307	97	375	53	115	137	10	6	0	34	5	4	0	31	2	30	22	11
Twardoski, Michael, New Britain*	.293	127	413	72	121	164	34	3	1	46	7	2	0	95	4	46	4	3
Meadows, Scott, Hagerstown	.293	138	495	60	145	198	29	3	6	75	2	7	9	66	5	70	9	11
Yacopino, Edward, Harrisburg†	.290	96	362	39	105	144	19	4	4	49	0	2	3	26	1	57	5	3
Wehner, John, Harrisburg	.288	138	511	71	147	188	27	1	4	62	4	6	4	40	4	51	24	11
Williams, Bernabe, Albany†	.281	134	466	91	131	193	28	5	8	54	1	2	4	98	6	97	39	18
Peguero, Julio, Reading†	.277	107	423	40	117	152	14	9	1	28	0	2	0	31	1	54	8	12
Batiste, Kimothy, Reading	.276	125	486	57	134	174	14	4	6	33	5	2	2	13	1	73	28	14

Departmental Leaders: G—Meadows, Wehner, 138; AB—Wehner, 511; R—B. Williams, 91; H—Bagwell, 160; TB—Bagwell, 220; 2B—Bagwell, Twardoski, 34; 3B—Peguero, 9; HR—Brogna, 21; RBI—Brogna, G. Sparks, 77; SH—Milstein, 12; SF—Voigt, 11; HP—DeJardin, Waller, 10; BB—B. Williams, 98; IBB—Bagwell, 12; SO—G. Sparks, 119; SB—B. Williams, 39; CS—B. Williams, 18.

(All Players—Listed Alphabetically)

Player and Club	Pct.	G.	AB.	R.	H.	TB.	2B.	3B.	HR.	RBI.	SH.	SF.	HP.	BB.	Int. BB.	SO.	SB.	CS.
Adams, Steven, Harrisburg	.000	26	1	0	0	0	0	0	0	0	0	0	0	0	0	0	0	0
Agostinelli, Salvatore, Reading	.000	5	9	0	0	0	0	0	0	0	0	0	0	0	0	2	0	0
Aldrich, Thomas, London	.136	9	22	4	3	5	2	0	0	4	0	1	0	5	0	6	0	0
Alexander, Gary, Reading	.255	129	428	73	109	195	29	0	19	60	1	2	6	74	0	99	1	1
Alfredson, Thomas, Williamsport	.235	35	119	15	28	46	3	3	3	12	1	1	2	13	0	18	0	1
Allison, James, Canton-Akron*	.187	50	123	4	23	28	3	1	0	10	0	1	0	10	0	25	4	1
Alou, Moises, Harrisburg	.295	36	132	19	39	64	12	2	3	22	0	1	1	16	3	21	7	4
Alvarez, Jesus, London*	.200	60	180	23	36	49	4	0	3	20	0	2	4	41	3	21	1	0
Anderson, Brady, Hagerstown*	.382	9	34	8	13	20	0	2	1	5	1	0	0	5	1	5	2	1
Austin, Dominic, Hagerstown	.307	97	375	53	115	137	10	6	0	34	5	4	0	31	2	30	22	11
Bagwell, Jeffrey, New Britain	.333	136	481	63	160	220	34	7	4	61	3	6	6	73	12	57	5	7
Balthazar, Doyle, London	.282	36	117	15	33	48	3	3	2	19	2	1	0	13	1	21	0	0
Banister, Jeffery, Harrisburg	.269	101	368	43	99	142	13	0	10	57	0	5	3	23	0	71	2	0
Barbara, Daniel, Williamsport	.400	2	5	0	2	2	0	0	0	0	0	0	0	1	0	3	2	0
Barczi, Scott, Harrisburg	.197	86	264	35	52	61	7	1	0	17	1	0	8	35	0	53	1	5
Batiste, Kimothy, Reading	.276	125	486	57	134	174	14	4	6	33	5	2	2	13	1	73	28	14
Baxter, James, London	.237	13	38	6	9	13	1	0	1	4	3	0	0	5	0	5	0	0
Belle, Albert, Canton-Akron	.250	9	32	4	8	9	1	0	0	3	1	0	0	3	1	7	0	0
Bellino, Frank, Reading*	.258	115	403	46	104	152	23	2	7	57	1	2	3	39	3	77	0	1
Berlin, Randolph, Hagerstown	.118	6	17	2	2	2	0	0	0	1	0	0	0	1	0	7	1	0
Bettendorf, David, Hagerstown*	.211	23	71	5	15	27	1	1	3	10	0	2	0	8	1	12	0	0
Beyeler, Arnold, London	.247	103	388	48	96	105	5	2	0	26	7	2	4	33	1	57	5	5
Blackwell, Barry, Canton-Akron	.266	23	64	7	17	24	4	0	1	7	0	0	1	5	0	16	0	0
Bowie, James, Williamsport*	.274	128	446	45	122	155	18	0	5	48	1	3	3	51	6	47	0	2
Brogna, Rico, London*	.262	137	488	70	128	218	21	3	21	77	3	5	3	50	8	100	1	2
Brown, Don, Hagerstown	.173	28	52	3	9	9	0	0	0	1	2	0	0	9	0	16	2	1
Brumfield, Harvey, Reading*	.119	14	59	3	7	10	1	1	0	0	0	0	0	2	0	16	2	1
Brundage, David, Williamsport*	.333	31	99	19	33	40	4	0	1	9	1	0	0	31	0	13	9	2
Buford, Don, Hagerstown†	.196	50	163	28	32	41	4	1	1	6	0	0	1	18	0	25	12	4
Byrd, James, New Britain	.200	2	5	1	1	2	1	0	0	0	0	0	0	0	0	1	0	0
Cabrera, Basilio, London	.231	78	308	31	71	95	9	3	3	25	5	3	5	14	0	66	15	6

Player and Club	Pct.	G.	AB.	R.	H.	TB.	2B.	3B.	HR.	RBI.	SH.	SF.	HP.	BB.	Int. BB.	SO.	SB.	CS.
Calvert, Christopher, Reading	.067	7	15	2	1	2	1	0	0	1	0	0	0	0	0	3	1	2
Clark, Isaiah, Williamsport	.254	80	279	29	71	87	13	0	1	28	4	4	2	8	0	28	12	3
Cook, Jeffrey, Harrisburg†	.186	13	43	5	8	8	0	0	0	1	0	0	0	5	0	4	3	0
Crowley, Terrence, Harrisburg†	.253	123	471	54	119	153	18	2	4	52	3	1	0	33	4	54	7	4
DeCillis, Dean, London	.280	72	264	27	74	104	19	1	3	29	1	4	0	17	0	21	5	0
Degifico, Vincent, New Britain°	.249	120	377	46	94	127	18	3	3	54	3	5	4	62	6	72	2	1
DeJardin, Robert, Albany†	.263	103	388	52	102	126	21	0	1	27	8	5	10	43	0	75	12	8
Delgado, Alexander, New Britain	.056	7	18	3	1	2	1	0	0	0	0	0	0	2	0	5	0	0
Devereaux, Michael, Hagerstown	.250	4	20	4	5	8	3	0	0	3	0	0	0	0	0	1	0	1
Dickerson, Bobby, Albany	.220	58	182	20	40	55	8	2	1	17	2	2	1	7	0	29	0	0
Eberle, Michael, Hagerstown	.250	39	124	10	31	42	8	0	1	10	0	0	1	8	0	36	0	0
Edge, Gregory, Harrisburg†	.214	50	187	18	40	43	3	0	0	13	4	1	0	22	0	10	2	2
Epley, Daren, Canton-Akron°	.261	119	403	50	105	146	21	1	6	37	6	5	1	39	4	63	6	5
Faulkner, Craig, Hagerstown	.249	104	370	36	92	125	18	0	5	44	0	5	5	22	1	75	0	3
Ferretti, Samuel, Canton-Akron	.258	129	434	58	112	132	15	1	1	43	6	2	4	35	1	51	10	7
Figueroa, Fernando, Williamsport°	.000	40	1	1	0	0	0	0	0	0	0	0	0	0	0	1	0	0
Fitzgerald, Michael, Reading	.236	53	174	17	41	72	7	0	8	20	1	1	1	6	2	47	0	1
Foley, Martin, Reading	.146	53	144	12	21	24	3	0	0	9	0	0	2	14	0	31	3	2
Foster, Lindsay, Canton-Akron†	.244	13	41	7	10	10	0	0	0	4	0	2	0	0	0	7	1	1
Francois, Manuel, Canton-Akron†	.175	62	143	20	25	39	8	0	2	12	6	1	0	18	0	35	3	5
Frazier, Louis, London†	.219	81	242	29	53	59	4	1	0	15	1	1	0	27	0	52	20	3
Galindo, Luis, London	.225	108	374	36	84	97	6	2	1	28	5	1	2	40	0	44	0	0
Garcia, Carlos, Harrisburg	.277	65	242	36	67	97	11	2	5	25	1	1	3	16	0	36	12	1
Gonzalez, Ruben, Williamsport	.190	7	21	0	4	5	1	0	0	4	0	0	0	6	0	5	0	0
Green, Stephen, London	.238	47	143	18	34	45	6	1	1	15	2	0	1	13	0	33	0	2
Grotewold, Jeffrey, Reading°	.269	127	412	56	111	191	33	1	15	72	2	4	1	62	5	83	2	2
Gutierrez, Ricardo, Hagerstown	.234	20	64	4	15	17	0	1	0	6	1	1	0	3	0	8	2	0
Hailey, Freddie, Albany	.261	31	92	7	24	34	7	0	1	14	0	0	0	7	1	14	0	2
Haney, Todd, Williamsport	.500	1	2	0	1	2	1	0	0	0	0	0	0	1	0	0	0	0
Hansen, Michael, London	.500	13	2	1	1	2	1	0	0	0	0	0	0	0	0	1	0	0
Harris, Robert, Harrisburg	.226	79	239	28	54	66	6	0	2	18	1	1	5	13	0	60	12	6
Harris, Walter, Hagerstown	.167	8	24	0	4	4	0	0	0	2	0	1	0	5	0	5	0	0
Hayden, Paris, Hagerstown	.233	47	129	16	30	41	5	0	2	8	0	1	1	6	0	30	1	0
Hearn, Edward, Canton-Akron	.270	29	89	14	24	34	4	0	2	11	0	1	1	5	0	16	0	1
Hithe, Victor, Hagerstown	.270	27	100	24	27	39	4	1	2	11	0	0	0	19	0	25	11	5
Holyfield, Vince, Reading	.201	97	323	36	65	105	11	1	9	28	3	3	1	21	0	96	17	4
Hooper, Jeffrey, Williamsport	.217	78	249	20	54	86	11	0	7	36	2	3	2	12	0	67	0	1
Horn, Samuel, Hagerstown°	.261	7	23	2	6	11	2	0	1	3	0	0	0	6	1	5	0	1
Housie, Wayne, New Britain†	.274	30	113	13	31	48	8	3	1	12	5	0	1	6	0	33	7	2
Howard, Christopher, Williamsport	.237	118	401	48	95	131	19	1	5	49	4	4	3	37	1	91	3	1
Hurst, Joseph, London	.257	44	152	26	39	63	10	1	4	13	2	1	2	20	1	46	6	3
Huyler, Michael, Harrisburg	.246	36	114	14	28	33	5	0	0	5	1	0	1	4	0	18	1	1
Infante, Kennedy, Reading	.248	36	125	8	31	41	4	0	2	6	3	0	1	4	0	15	1	0
Ingram, Riccardo, London	.255	92	271	27	69	83	10	2	0	26	1	0	4	27	1	49	3	1
Jackson, Leverne, Canton-Akron	.234	104	346	32	81	112	12	2	5	46	2	9	5	33	1	65	6	6
Jewett, Trent, Harrisburg	.156	15	45	4	7	7	0	0	0	3	1	0	0	4	0	22	0	0
Kelly, Michael, New Britain	.256	123	430	40	110	139	17	3	2	46	9	5	2	41	0	62	1	4
Kelly, Patrick, Albany	.270	126	418	67	113	168	19	6	8	44	5	4	6	37	1	79	32	14
Kesselmark, Joseph, Canton-Akron°	.114	27	79	9	9	10	1	0	0	3	0	0	0	11	1	6	1	0
King, Bryan, Williamsport	.188	54	144	14	27	32	3	1	0	4	6	0	0	22	0	18	7	5
Kirkpatrick, Stephen, Reading°	.243	107	346	51	84	92	8	0	0	19	10	1	2	42	0	43	12	7
Kosco, Andrew, Williamsport°	.195	96	267	19	52	66	11	0	1	25	0	0	0	23	5	58	1	0
Latmore, Robert, Canton-Akron	.259	132	479	52	124	174	19	2	9	64	1	7	4	21	3	80	7	4
Leiper, Timothy, London†	.301	48	166	30	50	63	7	0	2	20	3	2	1	26	1	14	8	2
Lennon, Patrick, Williamsport	.293	49	167	24	49	78	6	4	5	22	0	3	2	10	0	37	10	4
Letterio, Shane, Williamsport	.251	120	450	42	113	143	18	3	2	34	2	6	1	31	1	69	3	3
Lewis, Mark, Canton-Akron	.272	102	390	55	106	161	19	3	10	60	2	5	4	23	3	49	8	7
Liebert, Allen, Canton-Akron°	.243	114	362	32	88	134	17	1	9	45	2	7	2	39	5	89	1	0
Lindsey, Douglas, Reading	.173	107	323	16	56	70	11	0	1	32	6	3	1	26	1	78	2	1
Livesey, Jeffrey, Albany	.158	9	19	0	3	3	0	0	0	1	0	0	0	1	0	7	0	0
Lofton, Rodney, Hagerstown	.272	89	294	35	80	91	7	2	0	34	10	2	2	23	0	50	24	4
Longmire, Anthony, Harrisburg†	.297	24	91	9	27	36	6	0	1	13	0	1	0	7	0	11	5	1
Lozinski, Anthony, Reading	.087	10	23	0	2	3	1	0	0	0	1	0	0	0	0	8	0	1
Lundblade, Frederick, Hagerstown	.259	18	58	9	15	24	3	0	2	8	0	1	0	10	1	10	1	1
Lyden, Mitchell, Albany	.296	85	311	55	92	167	22	1	17	63	0	4	9	24	1	67	1	0
Marigny, Ronald, London	.251	72	255	28	64	79	10	1	1	19	1	3	3	19	0	30	3	2
Marsh, Thomas, Reading	.258	41	132	13	34	45	6	1	1	10	4	1	3	8	0	27	5	0
Masse, William, Albany	.188	31	96	12	18	28	1	0	3	8	0	1	1	22	0	20	0	1
McDonald, Michael, Williamsport°	.239	124	452	46	108	148	19	3	5	34	0	3	3	30	1	92	5	6
McDougal, Julius, New Britain†	.200	12	40	3	8	14	1	1	1	5	0	0	0	0	0	10	1	0
Meadows, Scott, Hagerstown	.293	138	495	60	145	198	29	3	6	75	2	7	9	66	5	70	9	11
Melendez, Francisco, Canton-Akron°..	.244	41	131	13	32	42	2	2	1	16	0	2	3	15	2	22	0	2
Mercedes, Luis, Hagerstown	.334	108	416	71	139	168	12	4	3	37	6	2	6	34	2	70	38	14
Merchant, Mark, Williamsport†	.179	44	156	16	28	33	5	0	0	10	0	2	1	14	2	36	7	2
Merejo, Domingo, Harrisburg	.231	36	117	11	27	31	4	0	0	6	0	0	1	5	0	28	2	2
Milstien, David, New Britain	.215	115	376	31	81	93	12	0	0	24	12	4	1	23	1	44	6	3
Mota, Carlos, Canton-Akron	.048	8	21	1	1	2	1	0	0	1	0	0	0	1	0	4	0	0
Muratti, Rafael, Reading	.115	9	26	2	3	3	0	0	0	1	0	0	0	5	0	6	0	0
Orsag, James, Canton-Akron°	.260	65	181	26	47	80	10	1	7	28	0	4	4	27	2	57	12	3
Osborne, Jeffrey, Harrisburg°	.241	84	266	28	64	86	15	2	1	34	0	1	1	27	3	52	0	1
Paris, Juan, New Britain	.212	74	179	29	38	49	6	1	1	12	3	2	0	11	0	27	2	3
Peguero, Julio, 104 Har.-3 Read.†	.277	107	423	40	117	152	14	9	1	28	0	2	0	31	1	54	8	12
Pegues, Steven, London	.271	126	483	48	131	187	22	5	8	63	3	4	3	12	1	59	17	8
Pennington, Kenneth, Williamsport	.260	134	461	59	120	163	14	4	7	51	1	5	7	43	0	66	8	5
Pennye, Darwin, Harrisburg	.156	11	32	2	5	7	2	0	0	0	1	0	1	4	0	10	2	1
Perez, Julio, London	.232	63	194	20	45	56	6	1	1	23	2	2	0	7	0	27	3	2
Phillips, Vincent, Albany°	.241	117	402	49	97	133	20	5	2	46	1	6	6	36	1	67	6	5
Posey, John, Reading	.300	5	10	0	3	3	0	0	0	1	0	0	0	0	0	1	0	0
Pratt, Todd, New Britain	.231	70	195	15	45	67	14	1	2	22	3	2	0	18	0	56	0	1
Ramos, John, Albany	.314	84	287	38	90	124	20	1	4	46	0	5	3	36	0	39	1	0
Ramos, Kenneth, Canton-Akron°	.329	19	73	12	24	30	2	2	0	11	0	1	0	8	0	10	2	1
Randle, Randy, New Britain	.214	111	384	62	82	104	8	4	2	24	7	4	1	47	1	86	10	10

Player and Club	Pct.	G.	AB.	R.	H.	TB.	2B.	3B.	HR.	RBI.	SH.	SF.	HP.	BB.	Int. BB.	SO.	SB.	CS.
Razook, Mark, Williamsport	.171	88	258	19	44	60	10	0	2	15	3	4	2	22	0	65	2	3
Robbins, Douglas, Hagerstown	.242	102	322	43	78	104	16	2	2	38	5	7	9	56	1	51	2	4
Robertson, Roderick, Reading†	.206	51	189	16	39	45	3	0	1	12	2	2	3	6	0	26	7	9
Rodriguez, Carlos, Albany	.280	18	75	10	21	25	4	0	0	7	0	0	1	2	0	2	1	1
Rowland, Richard, London	.286	47	161	22	46	80	10	0	8	30	0	1	3	20	3	33	1	1
Sabino, Miguel, Canton-Akron⊕	.270	65	230	37	62	80	2	5	2	19	3	1	1	22	0	41	10	7
Scarsone, Steven, Reading	.265	74	245	26	65	88	12	1	3	23	4	0	1	14	0	63	0	0
Shamburg, Kenneth, Hagerstown	.276	72	272	29	75	110	19	5	2	42	0	6	1	18	2	37	2	1
Silvestri, David, Albany	.286	2	7	0	2	2	0	0	0	2	0	0	0	0	0	1	0	0
Simonds, Daniel, Hagerstown	.206	11	34	2	7	8	1	0	0	1	0	0	1	0	4	0	1	1
Skeels, Andrew, Albany⊕	.270	75	215	18	58	68	7	0	1	21	2	2	0	23	4	29	1	1
Smith, Jackson, Williamsport	.190	67	174	14	33	46	7	0	2	14	4	5	2	11	0	37	1	0
Sparks, Donald, Albany	.266	112	418	48	111	153	20	5	4	52	0	5	4	33	2	70	3	4
Sparks, Gregory, Albany⊕	.246	129	455	66	112	195	24	1	19	77	1	3	5	42	1	119	0	2
Stanicek, Peter, Hagerstown†	.241	33	112	10	27	29	0	1	0	6	1	0	0	21	3	17	2	2
Swain, Robert, Canton-Akron	.239	79	222	24	53	76	13	2	2	21	5	3	0	31	1	41	3	3
Tatis, Bernardo, Canton-Akron†	.272	69	272	53	74	115	16	5	5	33	2	0	2	27	1	46	25	10
Tatum, James, Canton-Akron	.179	30	106	6	19	31	6	0	2	11	0	2	1	6	1	19	1	0
Toale, John, London⊕	.257	108	354	44	91	140	16	0	11	48	0	2	2	34	5	71	1	0
Tubbs, Gregory, Harrisburg	.282	54	213	35	60	85	6	5	3	21	1	1	0	23	0	35	8	1
Turgeon, David, Albany	.179	12	28	1	5	6	1	0	0	1	0	0	0	2	0	4	0	1
Turner, Shane, Hagerstown⊕	.237	10	38	5	9	10	1	0	0	1	0	0	0	0	0	10	1	0
Twardoski, Michael, New Britain⊕	.293	127	413	72	121	164	34	3	1	46	7	2	0	95	4	46	4	3
Valentin, John, New Britain	.218	94	312	20	68	94	18	1	2	31	11	3	0	25	1	46	1	2
Vizcaino, Reyes, Harrisburg	.254	84	236	20	60	70	8	1	0	23	1	1	3	27	1	73	6	2
Voigt, John, Harrisburg	.256	126	418	55	107	173	26	2	12	70	6	11	5	59	1	97	5	3
Waller, Casey, Reading†	.242	67	236	24	57	81	11	2	3	24	1	2	10	15	1	32	1	1
Webster, Casey, Canton-Akron	.153	27	85	12	13	20	2	1	1	3	3	0	1	17	0	13	0	0
Wedge, Eric, New Britain	.227	103	339	36	77	107	13	1	5	47	0	5	2	50	2	54	1	3
Wehner, John, Harrisburg	.288	138	511	71	147	188	27	1	4	62	4	6	4	40	4	51	24	11
Weidie, Stuart, New Britain†	.174	76	219	22	38	61	6	4	3	20	3	2	7	29	2	66	2	1
Wiley, Craig, London†	.225	49	142	16	32	46	8	0	2	12	1	1	0	16	1	26	3	3
Williams, Bernabe, Albany†	.281	134	466	91	131	193	28	5	8	54	1	2	4	98	6	97	39	18
Williams, Cary, Reading	.246	49	179	16	44	60	10	0	2	18	2	0	3	7	0	32	0	3
Williams, Gerald, Albany	.250	96	324	54	81	141	17	2	13	58	1	3	2	35	1	74	18	8
Williams, Ted, Williamsport†	.227	81	321	37	73	91	11	2	1	18	0	1	8	14	0	59	34	11
Wilson, Craig, New Britain	.165	37	91	5	15	23	2	0	2	10	2	0	2	5	0	22	0	1
Wine, Robert, Canton-Akron	.206	19	63	3	13	18	2	0	1	6	0	0	0	6	1	15	2	0
Yacopino, Edward, Harrisburg†	.290	96	362	39	105	144	19	4	4	49	0	2	3	26	1	57	5	3
Young, Delwyn, Canton-Akron†	.250	49	176	23	44	68	10	1	4	23	1	3	0	13	1	38	7	4
Zambrano, Roberto, Canton-Akron	.257	115	393	53	101	142	14	3	7	44	0	5	6	43	3	52	6	3
Zeihen, Robert, Albany⊕	.248	92	266	32	66	90	14	2	2	25	1	2	4	38	1	43	3	6
Zupcic, Robert, New Britain	.213	132	461	45	98	132	26	1	2	41	6	7	6	36	2	65	10	8

The following pitchers, listed alphabetically by club, with games in parentheses, had no plate appearances, primarily through use of designated hitters:

ALBANY—Bond, Daven (35); Chapin, Darrin (43); Clayton, Royal (21); Cook, Andrew (24); Draper, Michael (8); Garcia, Victor (16); Gogolewski, Douglas (5); Holcomb, Scott (6); Howard, Christian (2); Johnson, Jeffrey (9); Kamieniecki, Scott (22); Manon, Ramon (9); Newell, Thomas (22); Popplewell, Thomas (14); Rub, Jerry (22); Smith, Michael (10); Smith, Willie (9); Stanford, Donald (56); Taylor, Wade (12); Torres, Ricardo (9).

CANTON-AKRON—Borgatti, Michael (9); Bowden, Mark (2); Bruske, James (33); Collins, Allen (37); Curtis, Michael (13); Dipoto, Gerald (3); Egloff, Bruce (34); Farrell, John (2); Fassero, Jeffrey (61); Ferlenda, Gregory (9); Heinkel, Donald (5); Keliipuleole, Carl (27); Kramer, Thomas (12); McMichael, Gregory (13); Mutis, Jeffrey (26); Nagy, Charles (23); Roscoe, Gregory (20); Seanez, Rudy (15); Soper, Michael (16); Spagnola, Glenn (4); Taylor, Dwight (1); Walker, Michael C. (1).

HAGERSTOWN—Borgatti, Michael (19); Burdick, Stacey (20); Cavers, Michael (32); Culkar, Steven (2); de la Rosa, Francisco (23); Jones, Stacy (19); Kinzer, Matthew (3); Linskey, Michael (8); McDonald, Benard (3); McKeon, Joel (22); Mesa, Jose (15); Miller, David (24); Mussina, Michael (7); Myers, Chris (21); Peraza, Oswaldo (2); Rhodes, Arthur (12); Sander, Michael (38); Telford, Anthony (14); Thorpe, Paul (46).

HARRISBURG—Ausanio, Joseph (43); Czajkowski, James (9); Garcia, Miguel (22); Hancock, Leland (20); Miller, Paul (5); Minor, Blas (38); Murphy, Peter (28); Neely, Jeffrey (41); Richardson, Keith (8); Roesler, Michael (10); Tomlin, Randy (19); Tracy, James (25); Webb, Benjamin (28).

LONDON—DeSilva, John (14); Haas, David (27); Holman, Shawn (28); Jones, Michael (25); Kiely, John (46); Knudsen, Kurt (15); Lumley, Michael (15); Meacham, Russell (26); O'Neill, Daniel (2); Ramos, Jose (16); Richards, David (45); Rightnowar, Ronald (23); Wilkins, Michael (25); Williams, Kenneth (22).

NEW BRITAIN—Carista, Michael (17); Conroy, Brian (1); Davis, Freddie (23); Fischer, Thomas (27); Florence, Donald (34); Kuzniar, Paul (3); Livernois, Derek (15); Manzanillo, Josias (12); Morton, Kevin (26); O'Neill, Daniel (33); Owen, David (20); Plympton, Jeffrey (37); Quantrill, Paul (22); Sanders, Alan (6); Stewart, Hector (7); Taylor, Scott (5); Walters, David (43).

READING—Ashby, Andrew (23); Ayrault, Robert (44); Backs, Jason (1); Borland, Toby (14); Boudreaux, Eric (35); Brantley, Clifford (17); Buonantony, Richard (9); Carreno, Amalio (25); Christopher, Frederick (6); Holdridge, David (24); Magee, Warren (19); Mauser, Timothy (8); McLarnan, John (13); Moore, Bradley (1); Ontiveros, Steven (2); Shelton, Michael (5); Sims, Mark (54); Stevens, Matthew (25); Wilson, Gary (33).

WILLIAMSPORT—Balabon, Richard (13); Blasucci, Anthony (28); Blueberg, James (25); DeLucia, Richard (18); Evers, Troy (28); Gardiner, Michael (26); Goff, Michael (2); Hancock, Leland (7); Hensley, Charles (15); Jones, Dennis (4); Nelson, Jeffrey (10); Newlin, James (20); Rice, Patrick (25); Ridenour, Dana (45); Rojas, Ricardo (43); Wooden, Mark (10).

GRAND SLAM HOME RUNS—Brogna, 2; Banister, Latmore, Lewis, McDougal, Meadows, Orsag, G. Sparks, Voigt, Wedge, Wehner, B. Williams, G. Williams, 1 each.

AWARDED FIRST BASE ON CATCHER'S INTERFERENCE—Hooper 2 (Eberle, Pratt); Epley (Toale); R. Harris (Toale); Hayden (Banister); Twardoski (Mota).

CLUB FIELDING

Club	Pct.	G.	PO.	A.	E.	DP.	PB.	Club	Pct.	G.	PO.	A.	E.	DP.	PB.
Albany	.972	139	3495	1514	145	159	10	London	.968	139	3605	1496	170	134	27
Williamsport	.971	140	3580	1450	152	120	18	Hagerstown	.966	138	3548	1324	173	133	14
New Britain	.970	139	3580	1476	157	132	12	Harrisburg	.966	138	3527	1485	178	125	22
Canton-Akron	.968	140	3603	1558	172	148	15	Reading	.965	137	3416	1395	174	118	15

Triple Plays—Albany, Reading.

INDIVIDUAL FIELDING

*Throws lefthanded.

FIRST BASEMEN

Player and Club	Pct.	G.	PO.	A.	E.	DP.	Player and Club	Pct.	G.	PO.	A.	E.	DP.
Aldrich, London	1.000	3	30	1	0	3	Latmore, Hagerstown	1.000	1	7	0	0	0
Alexander, Reading	.990	62	465	34	5	41	Lindsey, Reading	1.000	1	5	0	0	1
Alvarez, London	1.000	1	4	0	0	0	Lundblade, Hagerstown	.988	9	71	9	1	6
Balthazar, London	1.000	1	9	1	0	1	Lyden, Albany	.988	18	152	7	2	22
Banister, Harrisburg	.992	37	335	23	3	29	Meadows, Hagerstown	.981	13	92	14	2	10
Bettendorf, Hagerstown	1.000	1	3	0	0	0	Melendez, Canton-Akron*	1.000	14	112	10	0	11
Bowie, Williamsport*	.990	126	1066	76	11	98	Orsag, Canton-Akron	1.000	11	91	7	0	6
Brogna, London*	.990	135	1155	93	13	117	Osborne, Harrisburg	.982	41	348	26	7	25
Brundage, Williamsport*	1.000	2	21	2	0	2	Pennington, Williamsport	.968	6	28	2	1	2
Clark, Williamsport	.979	5	44	2	1	3	Pratt, New Britain	.983	10	50	7	1	5
DeCillis, London	1.000	3	19	2	0	2	Robbins, Hagerstown	.988	19	152	10	2	18
Degifico, New Britain	.989	28	164	19	2	15	Shamburg, Hagerstown	.986	58	455	33	7	47
Dickerson, Albany	.969	3	31	0	1	4	Sparks, Albany*	.991	123	1093	65	10	114
EPLEY, Canton-Akron*	.994	114	1040	75	7	114	Tatis, Canton-Akron	1.000	1	6	0	0	1
Faulkner, Hagerstown	.992	42	326	29	3	38	Tatum, Canton-Akron	.967	6	28	1	1	4
Fitzgerald, Reading	.987	26	213	16	3	21	Toale, London	1.000	1	8	0	0	1
Gonzalez, Williamsport	1.000	7	59	0	0	6	Twardoski, New Britain*	.990	116	938	69	10	100
Grotewold, Reading	.988	55	454	48	6	40	Vizcaino, Harrisburg	.978	72	575	38	14	57

Triple Plays—Fitzgerald, Sparks.

SECOND BASEMEN

Player and Club	Pct.	G.	PO.	A.	E.	DP.	Player and Club	Pct.	G.	PO.	A.	E.	DP.
Austin, Hagerstown	.956	77	165	179	16	47	Kelly, Albany	.970	126	266	381	20	97
Beyeler, London	.968	103	200	277	16	58	King, Williamsport	1.000	2	8	7	0	2
Buford, Hagerstown	.971	42	89	110	6	29	Latmore, Hagerstown	1.000	1	3	1	0	0
Byrd, New Britain	1.000	2	5	4	0	2	LETTERIO, Williamsport	.980	120	256	282	11	62
Crowley, Harrisburg	.979	92	188	227	9	56	Marigny, London	.973	27	59	85	4	17
Dickerson, Albany	.933	14	33	37	5	6	Milstien, New Britain	.970	114	234	309	17	82
Edge, Harrisburg	.977	15	39	45	2	9	Perez, Harrisburg	.982	36	76	86	3	26
Ferretti, Canton-Akron	.973	36	64	113	5	22	Randle, New Britain	.963	35	54	75	5	15
Foley, Reading	.959	32	55	63	5	14	Razook, Williamsport	.990	20	37	58	1	12
Francois, Canton-Akron	.935	54	95	135	16	38	Robertson, Reading	.971	45	85	113	6	25
Frazier, London	.929	15	28	37	5	6	Scarsone, Reading	.981	66	128	176	6	36
Haney, Williamsport	1.000	1	1	1	0	1	Stanicek, Hagerstown	1.000	21	45	42	0	7
							Swain, Canton-Akron	.966	69	122	166	10	37

Triple Play—Kelly.

THIRD BASEMEN

Player and Club	Pct.	G.	PO.	A.	E.	DP.	Player and Club	Pct.	G.	PO.	A.	E.	DP.
Alexander, Reading	.875	27	20	50	10	6	Lennon, Williamsport	.879	16	13	38	7	4
Alvarez, London	.881	56	39	101	19	6	Marigny, London	.943	48	23	76	6	6
Austin, Hagerstown	1.000	3	1	5	0	0	Pennington, Williamsport	.910	84	57	146	20	12
Bagwell, New Britain	.914	133	93	267	34	30	Ramos, Albany	1.000	1	1	1	0	0
Berlin, Hagerstown	1.000	2	1	3	0	0	Randle, New Britain	.864	8	4	15	3	0
Beyeler, London	1.000	1	1	4	0	1	Razook, Williamsport	1.000	20	18	41	0	5
Clark, Williamsport	.936	29	14	59	5	3	Shamburg, Hagerstown	.912	16	12	19	3	2
DeCillis, London	.867	8	5	8	2	0	Skeels, Albany	.750	2	0	3	1	0
Dickerson, Albany	.946	20	8	45	3	6	SPARKS, Albany	.933	111	68	226	21	23
Edge, Harrisburg	1.000	3	1	9	0	2	Swain, Canton-Akron	.833	11	4	11	3	0
Faulkner, Hagerstown	.750	3	2	1	1	0	Tatis, Canton-Akron	.900	22	13	41	6	1
Ferretti, Canton-Akron	.937	64	36	156	13	16	Tatum, Canton-Akron	.878	28	29	50	11	13
Foley, Reading	.909	14	6	14	2	3	Turgeon, Albany	.880	11	1	21	3	1
Frazier, London	.750	1	1	5	2	1	Waller, Reading	.910	64	51	110	16	18
Galindo, London	.880	24	16	28	6	4	Webster, Canton-Akron	.899	27	14	57	8	8
Infante, Reading	.933	36	31	67	7	6	Wehner, Harrisburg	.895	135	109	317	50	40
Latmore, Hagerstown	.889	119	78	209	36	23	Wiley, London	1.000	2	2	2	0	0
Leiper, London	1.000	10	9	17	0	3							

SHORTSTOPS

Player and Club	Pct.	G.	PO.	A.	E.	DP.	Player and Club	Pct.	G.	PO.	A.	E.	DP.
Austin, Hagerstown	.931	6	8	19	2	2	Latmore, Hagerstown	.927	14	22	29	4	7
Batiste, Reading	.936	125	182	333	35	57	Lewis, Canton-Akron	.934	98	152	286	31	65
Berlin, Hagerstown	.900	3	3	6	1	1	Lofton, Hagerstown	.937	88	142	244	26	56
Clark, Williamsport	.889	4	6	10	2	2	McDougal, New Britain	.894	10	9	33	5	8
DeCillis, London	.934	51	85	142	16	28	Perez, Harrisburg	1.000	8	11	30	0	9
DeJARDIN, Albany	.963	103	168	323	19	81	Randle, New Britain	.937	35	48	85	9	13
Delgado, New Britain	.875	7	4	10	2	2	Razook, Williamsport	.958	41	39	76	5	16
Dickerson, Albany	.945	19	31	55	5	10	Robertson, Reading	.960	6	6	18	1	4
Edge, Harrisburg	.947	32	49	77	7	14	Rodriguez, Albany	.964	18	23	58	3	10
Ferretti, Canton-Akron	.931	33	41	108	11	16	Scarsone, Reading	.956	11	13	30	2	6
Foster, Canton-Akron	.899	13	18	44	7	9	Silvestri, Albany	.889	2	3	5	1	2
Frazier, London	.923	7	12	24	3	5	Smith, Williamsport	.945	67	96	164	15	32
Galindo, London	.945	84	133	266	23	62	Sparks, Albany	1.000	1	2	1	0	1
Garcia, Harrisburg	.957	65	101	209	14	37	Tatis, Canton-Akron	.800	4	3	1	1	1
Gutierrez, Hagerstown	.944	20	31	36	4	7	Turner, Hagerstown	.961	10	18	31	2	10
Huyler, Harrisburg	.917	36	49	105	14	11	Valentin, New Britain	.951	94	139	266	21	60
King, Williamsport	.948	51	86	150	13	28							

Triple Plays—Batiste, Dickerson.

OUTFIELDERS

Player and Club	Pct.	G.	PO.	A.	E.	DP.	Player and Club	Pct.	G.	PO.	A.	E.	DP.
Alexander, Reading	.944	28	43	8	3	4	Brumfield, Reading*	1.000	14	35	2	0	1
Alfredson, Williamsport	1.000	34	65	3	0	0	Brundage, Williamsport*	.981	27	52	1	1	0
Allison, Canton-Akron*	.970	40	63	1	2	0	Buford, Hagerstown	1.000	1	1	0	0	0
Alou, Harrisburg	.990	36	93	2	1	0	Cabrera, London	.971	75	130	6	4	2
Anderson, Hagerstown*	1.000	4	8	1	0	0	Calvert, Reading	.800	5	8	0	2	0
Austin, Hagerstown	1.000	1	2	0	0	0	Clark, Williamsport	.955	48	80	5	4	0
Bellino, Reading	.942	91	138	7	9	0	Cook, Harrisburg	.889	13	15	1	2	0
Brown, Hagerstown	.952	22	37	3	2	0	Devereaux, Hagerstown	.929	4	13	0	1	0

OUTFIELDERS—Continued

Player and Club	Pct.	G.	PO.	A.	E.	DP.
Ferretti, Canton-Akron	1.000	3	3	0	0	0
Figueroa, Williamsport°	1.000	1	2	0	0	0
Frazier, London	.944	44	82	2	5	0
Green, London	.987	42	74	1	1	0
Grotewold, Reading	1.000	1	2	0	0	0
Hailey, Albany	.882	15	14	1	2	0
R. Harris, Harrisburg	.965	66	107	4	4	0
W. Harris, Hagerstown	1.000	7	13	0	0	0
Hayden, Hagerstown	.961	45	94	4	4	1
Hithe, Hagerstown	.986	27	66	2	1	1
Holyfield, Reading	.965	83	186	5	7	0
Housie, New Britain	.989	30	83	4	1	2
Hurst, London°	.990	43	97	1	1	0
Ingram, London	.967	72	108	8	4	2
Jackson, Canton-Akron	.975	90	185	7	5	1
Kelly, New Britain	.983	121	222	16	4	3
Kesselmark, Canton-Akron°	1.000	26	32	2	0	1
Kirkpatrick, Reading	.967	101	201	7	7	1
Kosco, Williamsport	.978	57	86	5	2	1
Leiper, London	.936	37	72	1	5	0
Lennon, Williamsport	.944	26	49	2	3	2
Longmire, Harrisburg	.962	22	46	4	2	1
Marsh, Reading	.970	41	93	3	3	0
Masse, Harrisburg	.968	19	27	3	1	1
McDONALD, Williamsport	.989	121	249	13	3	2
McDougal, New Britain	1.000	1	2	0	0	0
Meadows, Hagerstown	.964	126	205	10	8	0
Mercedes, Hagerstown	.947	71	157	5	9	1
Merchant, Williamsport	1.000	33	48	0	0	0
Merejo, Harrisburg°	.952	33	56	3	3	0
Muratti, Reading	.950	8	17	2	1	1
Orsag, Canton-Akron	.940	22	46	1	3	0
Paris, New Britain	.976	65	114	10	3	2
Peguero, Harrisburg	.984	97	239	4	4	1
Pegues, London	.965	122	244	7	9	2
Pennye, Harrisburg	1.000	11	17	1	0	0
Phillips, Albany°	.971	110	166	1	5	1
Ramos, Canton-Akron°	.981	19	53	0	1	0
Randle, New Britain	.941	21	45	3	3	1
Razook, Williamsport	.955	14	21	0	1	0
Sabino, Canton-Akron°	1.000	63	110	5	0	1
Stanicek, Hagerstown	.667	1	2	0	1	0
Tatis, Canton-Akron	.974	48	106	5	3	2
Toale, London	1.000	1	1	0	0	0
Tubbs, Harrisburg	.981	51	102	3	2	1
Twardoski, New Britain°	1.000	5	13	0	0	0
Voigt, Hagerstown	.978	126	249	12	6	1
Weidie, New Britain	.989	72	173	7	2	2
B. Williams, Albany	.987	131	288	15	4	4
C. Williams, Reading	.974	49	107	4	3	3
G. Williams, Albany	.969	96	210	6	7	1
T. Williams, Williamsport	.979	81	177	8	4	3
Yacopino, Harrisburg°	.969	95	181	6	6	2
Young, Canton-Akron	.979	26	46	1	1	0
Zambrano, Canton-Akron	.983	109	173	3	3	0
Zeihen, Albany°	.962	53	97	3	4	3
Zupcic, New Britain	.987	130	286	10	4	2

CATCHERS

Player and Club	Pct.	G.	PO.	A.	E.	DP.	PB.
Agostinelli, Reading	1.000	5	15	1	0	0	0
Balthazar, London	.984	30	173	17	3	0	5
Banister, Harrisburg	.976	40	179	24	5	1	5
Barbara, Williamsport	1.000	2	11	1	0	0	0
Barczi, Harrisburg	.980	86	471	61	11	3	16
Baxter, London	1.000	12	70	3	0	0	1
Blackwell, Canton-Akron	.973	13	70	2	2	1	1
Eberle, Hagerstown	.995	35	186	15	1	2	4
Faulkner, Hagerstown	.992	50	331	34	3	7	4
Grotewold, Reading	.970	26	123	6	4	0	3
Hearn, Canton-Akron	.988	26	145	14	2	0	3
Hooper, Williamsport	.987	27	139	11	2	1	4
Howard, Williamsport	.976	114	680	84	19	6	14
Jewett, Harrisburg	.971	14	63	5	2	2	1
LIEBERT, Canton-Akron	.994	81	451	52	3	4	5
Lindsey, Reading	.988	105	569	70	8	7	10
Livesey, Albany	1.000	6	27	0	0	0	0
Lozinski, Reading	.964	10	51	3	2	0	2
Lyden, Albany	.993	46	255	15	2	2	3
Mota, Canton-Akron	.950	7	36	2	2	0	2
Posey, Reading	.938	5	14	1	1	1	0
Pratt, New Britain	.976	21	116	8	3	2	4
Ramos, Albany	.984	48	229	20	4	5	2
Robbins, Hagerstown	.994	54	317	30	2	2	5
Rowland, London	.988	39	231	24	3	5	5
Simonds, Hagerstown	.984	11	55	6	1	2	1
Skeels, Albany	.986	53	247	29	4	6	5
Toale, London	.958	23	121	16	6	2	8
Wedge, New Britain	.986	103	583	62	9	8	7
Wiley, London	.993	44	271	30	2	1	8
Wilson, New Britain	.987	30	139	13	2	1	1
Wine, Canton-Akron	.979	19	126	15	3	1	4

PITCHERS

Player and Club	Pct.	G.	PO.	A.	E.	DP.
Adams, Harrisburg	.971	26	15	19	1	1
Ashby, Reading	.936	23	19	25	3	2
Ausanio, Harrisburg	1.000	43	0	4	0	0
Ayrault, Reading	1.000	44	5	11	0	0
Backs, Reading	1.000	1	0	1	0	0
Balabon, Williamsport	.923	13	7	17	2	2
Blasucci, Williamsport°	1.000	28	0	7	0	0
Blueberg, Williamsport	.789	25	8	22	8	2
Bond, Albany	.895	35	5	12	2	0
Borgatti, 19 Hager.-9 C.A.	.923	28	3	9	1	1
Borland, Reading	1.000	14	2	6	0	0
Boudreaux, Reading	1.000	35	7	20	0	2
Bowden, Canton-Akron°	1.000	2	0	1	0	1
Brantley, Reading	.944	17	6	11	1	0
Bruske, Canton-Akron	.944	32	9	25	2	2
Buonantony, Reading	.750	9	1	2	1	0
Burdick, Hagerstown	.895	20	8	9	2	1
Carista, New Britain	1.000	17	3	5	0	1
Carreno, Reading	.897	25	10	16	3	1
Cavers, Hagerstown°	.913	32	5	16	2	1
Chapin, Albany	1.000	43	0	8	0	1
Christopher, Reading°	1.000	6	3	1	0	1
Clayton, Albany	.977	21	9	33	1	6
Collins, Canton-Akron	.789	37	6	9	4	1
Conroy, New Britain	1.000	1	0	1	0	0
Cook, Albany	.979	24	12	35	1	4
Culkar, Hagerstown	1.000	2	1	1	0	0
Curtis, Canton-Akron°	.917	13	1	10	1	1
Czajkowski, Harrisburg	1.000	9	0	4	0	0
Davis, New Britain	.909	23	4	6	1	3
DeLaRosa, Hagerstown	.950	23	5	14	1	0
DeLucia, Williamsport	1.000	18	12	20	0	1
DeSilva, London	.923	14	4	8	1	0
Dipoto, Canton-Akron	.750	3	2	1	1	0
Draper, Albany	1.000	8	3	10	0	0
Egloff, Canton-Akron	1.000	34	3	6	0	2
Evers, Williamsport	.939	28	7	24	2	2
Fassero, Canton-Akron°	1.000	61	7	12	0	2
Ferlenda, Canton-Akron	1.000	9	2	0	0	0
Figueroa, Williamsport°	.889	37	5	19	3	0
Fischer, New Britain°	.931	27	9	18	2	1
Florence, New Britain	.947	34	4	14	1	0
M. Garcia, Harrisburg°	.952	21	7	33	2	1
V. Garcia, Albany°	1.000	16	0	12	0	0
Gardiner, Williamsport	.975	26	13	26	1	2
Gogolewski, Albany	.500	5	1	0	1	0
Haas, London	.950	27	15	23	2	1
Hancock, 7 Will.-20 Harris.°	.936	27	15	29	3	2
Hansen, Albany	.909	13	12	8	2	1
Heinkel, Canton-Akron	.833	5	3	2	1	0
Hensley, Williamsport°	1.000	15	2	5	0	0
Holdridge, Reading	.909	24	11	9	2	1
Holman, London	1.000	28	7	2	0	0
Johnson, Albany°	.929	9	3	10	1	1
D. Jones, Williamsport°	1.000	4	0	1	0	0
M. Jones, London	.921	25	12	23	3	2
S. Jones, Hagerstown	.857	19	3	3	1	0
Kamieniecki, Albany	.944	22	12	22	2	3
Keliipuleole, Canton-Akron	1.000	27	5	14	0	1
Kiely, London	.969	46	6	25	1	3
Kinzer, Hagerstown	1.000	3	0	1	0	0
Kirkpatrick, Reading	1.000	2	0	1	0	0
Knudsen, London	1.000	15	0	1	0	0
Kramer, Canton-Akron	1.000	12	9	15	0	1
Latmore, Hagerstown	1.000	1	0	1	0	0
Linskey, Hagerstown°	1.000	8	5	6	0	0
Livernois, New Britain	.929	15	4	9	1	1
Lumley, London	.857	15	2	4	1	1
Magee, Reading	.857	19	3	9	2	0
Manon, Albany	.818	9	1	8	2	1
Manzanillo, New Britain	.950	12	8	11	1	0
Mauser, Reading	.769	8	8	2	3	0
McDonald, Hagerstown	.667	3	0	2	1	0
McKeon, Hagerstown°	.889	22	3	5	1	0
McLarnan, Reading	.833	13	0	5	1	2
McMichael, Canton-Akron	1.000	13	1	4	0	1
Meacham, London	.983	26	15	43	1	2
Mesa, Hagerstown	1.000	15	7	14	0	1

PITCHERS—Continued

Player and Club	Pct.	G.	PO.	A.	E.	DP.
D. Miller, Hagerstown	1.000	24	3	14	0	1
P. Miller, Harrisburg	1.000	5	3	4	0	1
Minor, Harrisburg	.913	38	6	15	2	1
Moore, Reading	1.000	1	0	2	0	0
Morton, New Britain*	.933	26	8	20	2	0
Murphy, Harrisburg	1.000	28	5	14	0	1
Mussina, Hagerstown	1.000	7	1	4	0	0
MUTIS, Canton-Akron*	1.000	26	14	40	0	4
Myers, Hagerstown*	.958	21	8	15	1	1
Nagy, Canton-Akron	.978	23	20	24	1	2
Neely, Harrisburg	.900	41	3	6	1	0
Nelson, Williamsport	1.000	10	1	5	0	1
Newell, Albany	.867	22	2	11	2	2
Newlin, Williamsport	.929	20	3	10	1	2
O'Neill, 2 Lon.-33 N.B.*	1.000	35	4	1	0	0
Owen, New Britain*	.936	20	7	37	3	1
Peraza, Hagerstown	1.000	2	3	3	0	0
Plympton, New Britain	.818	37	3	6	2	0
Popplewell, Albany	.857	14	2	4	1	1
Quantrill, New Britain	.978	22	6	38	1	0
Ramos, London*	1.000	16	3	22	0	1
Rhodes, Hagerstown*	.800	12	2	10	3	2
Rice, Williamsport	1.000	25	3	10	0	1
Richards, London*	1.000	45	3	7	0	0
Richardson, Harrisburg	.800	8	2	6	2	0
Ridenour, Williamsport	.933	45	3	11	1	1
Rightnowar, London	1.000	23	4	9	0	3
Roesler, Harrisburg	1.000	10	1	4	0	0
Rojas, Williamsport	.952	43	4	16	1	2
Roscoe, Canton-Akron	.913	20	5	16	2	2
Rub, Albany*	.571	22	0	4	3	0
Sander, Hagerstown	.929	38	14	12	2	3
Sanders, New Britain	1.000	6	0	2	0	0
Seanez, Canton-Akron	1.000	15	0	1	0	0
Shelton, Reading	.800	5	1	3	1	0
Sims, Reading*	.949	54	7	30	2	5
Smith, Albany	.750	10	1	2	1	0
Soper, Canton-Akron	1.000	16	3	5	0	1
Spagnola, Canton-Akron	1.000	4	0	1	0	0
Stanford, Albany	.857	56	1	5	1	0
Stevens, Reading	.933	25	3	11	1	0
Stewart, New Britain*	1.000	7	0	3	0	1
S. Taylor, New Britain*	.800	5	0	4	1	1
W. Taylor, Albany	1.000	12	3	14	0	1
Telford, Hagerstown	1.000	14	8	16	0	1
Thorpe, Hagerstown	.897	46	7	19	3	1
Tomlin, Harrisburg*	.966	19	11	17	1	0
Torres, Albany	1.000	9	0	3	0	0
Tracy, Harrisburg	1.000	25	6	17	0	2
Walters, New Britain	.857	43	3	9	2	0
Webb, Harrisburg	.850	28	7	10	3	1
Wilkins, London	1.000	25	8	31	0	3
Williams, London*	.917	22	1	10	1	0
Wilson, Reading	1.000	33	14	39	0	2
Wooden, Williamsport	1.000	10	0	3	0	0

Triple Play—Carreno.

The following players did not have any fielding statistics at the positions indicated or appeared only as a designated hitter, pinch-hitter or pinch-runner: Allison, p; Belle, dh; DeCillis, of; Farrell, p; Foley, p; Francois, of; Goff, p; Holcomb, p; Horn, dh; Christian Howard, p; King, of; Kuzniar, p; Muratti, p; Ontiveros, p; W. Smith, p; D. Taylor, pr; Walker, p.

CLUB PITCHING

Club	ERA.	G.	CG.	ShO.	Sv.	IP.	H.	R.	ER.	HR.	HB.	BB.	Int. BB.	SO.	WP.	Bk.
Hagerstown	3.17	138	13	14	38	1182.2	1088	513	416	51	41	435	15	867	41	13
New Britain	3.17	139	19	16	38	1193.1	1133	519	420	44	47	390	26	809	54	19
Harrisburg	3.20	138	22	13	33	1175.2	1091	526	418	68	46	390	32	710	38	10
London	3.26	139	24	17	33	1201.2	1125	528	435	69	42	431	19	840	54	10
Williamsport	3.30	140	17	8	26	1193.1	1137	526	437	65	34	366	15	785	58	11
Canton-Akron	3.33	140	26	13	32	1201.0	1145	546	444	55	40	435	23	818	48	14
Albany	3.48	139	19	13	36	1165.0	1068	533	451	57	27	534	20	731	47	23
Reading	3.73	137	12	11	33	1138.2	1122	578	472	61	40	453	24	761	66	10

PITCHERS' RECORDS

(Leading Qualifiers for Earned-Run Average Leadership—112 or More Innings)

*Throws lefthanded.

Pitcher—Club	W.	L.	Pct.	ERA.	G.	GS.	CG.	GF.	ShO.	Sv.	IP.	H.	R.	ER.	HR.	HB.	BB.	Int. BB.	SO.	WP.
Gardiner, Williamsport	12	8	.600	1.90	26	26	5	0	1	0	179.2	136	47	38	8	1	29	1	149	4
DeLaRosa, Hagerstown	9	5	.643	2.06	23	20	2	2	0	0	131.0	97	42	30	5	4	51	0	105	1
DeLucia, Williamsport	6	6	.500	2.11	18	18	2	0	1	0	115.0	92	30	27	7	2	30	2	76	1
Tomlin, Harrisburg*	9	6	.600	2.28	19	18	4	1	3	0	126.1	101	43	32	3	6	34	6	92	2
Wilkins, London	13	5	.722	2.42	25	25	6	0	3	0	174.2	156	57	47	12	5	47	1	91	1
Wilson, Reading	7	12	.368	2.44	33	21	3	10	0	2	151.0	140	64	41	7	8	39	1	70	7
Nagy, Canton-Akron	13	8	.619	2.52	23	23	9	0	0	0	175.0	132	62	49	9	6	39	0	99	3
Owen, New Britain*	7	9	.438	2.93	20	20	4	0	0	0	132.0	123	54	43	0	5	48	2	88	2
Haas, London	13	8	.619	2.99	27	27	3	0	1	0	177.2	151	64	59	10	10	74	1	116	14
Tracy, Harrisburg	14	8	.636	3.00	25	23	5	1	2	1	153.0	143	63	51	8	8	37	0	106	9

Departmental Leaders: G—Fassero, 61; W—Meacham, 15; L—Morton, 14; Pct.—Telford, .833; GS—Haas, 27; CG—Meacham, Nagy, 9; GF—Chapin, 40; ShO—Meacham, Mutis, Tomlin, Wilkins, 3; Sv.—Chapin, 21; IP—Gardiner, 179.2; H—Mutis, 178; R—Fischer, 89; ER—Fischer, 76; HR—Clayton, Holdridge, Webb, 13; HB—Morton, 14; BB—Holdridge, 79; IBB—Neely, 10; SO—Gardiner, 149; WP—Ridenour, 15.

(All Pitchers—Listed Alphabetically)

Pitcher—Club	W.	L.	Pct.	ERA.	G.	GS.	CG.	GF.	ShO.	Sv.	IP.	H.	R.	ER.	HR.	HB.	BB.	Int. BB.	SO.	WP.
Adams, Harrisburg	7	8	.467	3.84	26	21	5	4	0	2	138.1	151	67	59	8	11	39	0	40	0
Allison, Canton-Akron*	0	0	.000	0.00	1	0	0	1	0	1	1.0	0	0	0	0	0	3	0	0	0
Ashby, Reading	10	7	.588	3.42	23	23	4	0	1	0	139.2	134	65	53	3	4	48	0	94	10
Ausanio, Harrisburg	3	2	.600	1.83	43	0	0	38	0	15	54.0	36	15	11	2	2	16	4	50	4
Ayrault, Reading	4	6	.400	2.30	44	9	0	29	0	10	109.1	77	33	28	4	2	34	1	84	2
Backs, Reading	1	0	1.000	1.50	1	1	0	0	0	0	6.0	6	1	1	0	1	3	0	5	0
Balabon, Williamsport	3	4	.429	3.27	13	13	1	0	0	0	77.0	76	35	28	5	2	18	0	62	9
Blasucci, Williamsport*	2	0	1.000	3.60	28	0	0	19	0	3	35.0	26	16	14	2	1	14	0	34	1
Blueberg, Williamsport	9	11	.450	3.83	25	25	4	0	0	0	152.2	161	81	65	12	7	42	0	82	8
Bond, Albany	6	2	.750	2.76	35	2	0	12	0	0	65.1	71	27	20	1	0	20	3	41	3
Borgatti, 19 Hager.-9 C.A.	1	4	.200	4.65	28	0	0	16	0	0	62.0	86	40	32	1	4	26	3	33	1
Borland, Reading	4	1	.800	1.44	14	0	0	5	0	0	25.0	16	4	4	1	1	11	1	26	2
Boudreaux, Reading	3	4	.429	4.13	35	5	0	16	0	0	85.0	111	52	39	3	2	29	5	43	2
Bowden, Canton-Akron*	0	1	.000	3.38	2	0	0	0	0	0	2.2	4	2	1	1	0	1	0	0	0
Brantley, Reading	4	9	.308	4.55	17	17	0	0	0	0	87.0	93	51	44	4	3	39	0	69	4
Bruske, Canton-Akron	9	3	.750	3.28	32	13	3	6	2	0	118.0	118	53	43	6	4	42	2	62	5
Buonantony, Reading	1	2	.333	7.24	9	0	0	2	0	0	13.2	13	11	11	1	0	12	1	10	1
Burdick, Hagerstown	8	9	.471	3.93	20	16	2	3	1	0	91.2	81	48	40	2	4	43	0	81	3
Carista, New Britain	3	1	.750	5.60	17	1	0	5	0	0	35.1	43	24	22	4	4	12	1	21	2
Carreno, Harrisburg	4	13	.235	3.66	25	23	3	1	1	1	128.0	137	62	52	5	5	47	4	86	8
Cavers, Hagerstown*	2	10	.167	5.64	32	12	0	8	0	1	97.1	110	69	61	9	3	44	1	63	5
Chapin, Albany	3	2	.600	2.73	43	0	0	40	0	21	52.2	43	20	16	2	1	21	1	61	4
Christopher, Reading*	0	0	.000	3.27	6	0	0	2	0	1	11.0	11	4	4	0	0	2	0	10	1

Pitcher—Club	W.	L.	Pct.	ERA.	G.	GS.	CG.	GF.	ShO.	Sv.	IP.	H.	R.	ER.	HR.	HB.	BB.	Int. BB.	SO.	WP.
Clayton, Albany	10	9	.526	3.18	21	21	6	0	2	0	141.2	149	58	50	13	1	43	4	68	2
Collins, Canton-Akron	2	5	.286	4.25	37	3	0	12	0	2	72.0	70	51	34	4	5	39	2	46	2
Conroy, New Britain	0	1	.000	6.00	1	1	0	0	0	0	6.0	7	4	4	1	0	1	1	3	0
Cook, Albany	12	8	.600	3.45	24	24	5	0	0	0	156.2	146	69	60	12	4	52	2	53	5
Culkar, Hagerstown	0	0	.000	6.35	2	0	0	1	0	1	5.2	8	4	4	0	0	5	0	2	0
Curtis, Canton-Akron*	5	4	.556	2.95	13	13	1	0	0	0	79.1	72	34	26	4	3	23	1	73	7
Czajkowski, Harrisburg	0	0	.000	4.30	9	0	0	4	0	0	14.2	17	7	7	1	1	6	0	6	1
Davis, New Britain	0	0	.000	2.08	23	0	0	15	0	4	34.2	30	8	8	1	2	6	0	21	1
DeLaRosa, Hagerstown	9	5	.643	2.06	23	20	2	2	0	0	131.0	97	42	30	5	4	51	0	105	1
DeLucia, Williamsport	6	6	.500	2.11	18	18	2	0	1	0	115.0	92	30	27	7	2	30	2	76	1
DeSilva, London	5	6	.455	3.84	14	14	1	0	1	0	89.0	87	47	38	4	2	27	0	76	3
Dipoto, Canton-Akron	1	0	1.000	2.57	3	2	0	0	0	0	14.0	11	5	4	0	2	4	0	12	1
Draper, Albany	2	2	.500	6.44	8	8	0	0	0	0	43.1	51	34	31	4	2	19	0	15	0
Egloff, Canton-Akron	3	2	.600	1.98	34	0	0	24	0	15	54.2	44	16	12	5	3	15	1	53	4
Evers, Williamsport	4	12	.250	3.69	28	23	4	0	1	0	156.0	152	74	64	6	10	48	0	66	6
Farrell, Canton-Akron	1	1	.500	7.20	2	2	0	0	0	0	10.0	13	8	8	1	1	2	0	5	1
Fassero, Canton-Akron*	5	4	.556	2.80	61	0	0	30	0	6	64.1	66	24	20	5	1	24	6	61	2
Ferlenda, Canton-Akron	1	0	1.000	7.15	9	0	0	5	0	1	11.1	17	12	9	1	0	5	0	7	0
Figueroa, Williamsport*	2	10	.167	3.96	37	4	0	15	0	4	61.1	65	34	27	5	2	21	0	32	2
Fischer, New Britain	13	10	.565	4.19	27	26	3	0	0	0	163.1	166	89	76	7	5	64	4	116	11
Florence, New Britain*	6	4	.600	3.50	34	4	0	12	0	1	79.2	85	37	31	3	1	26	3	39	4
M. Garcia, Harrisburg*	8	10	.444	3.98	21	20	0	0	0	0	131.0	143	76	58	6	7	38	1	52	5
V. Garcia, Albany*	3	4	.429	2.12	16	9	1	2	0	1	72.1	49	26	17	6	2	39	0	42	4
Gardiner, Williamsport	12	8	.600	1.90	26	26	5	0	1	0	179.2	136	47	38	8	1	29	1	149	4
Goff, Williamsport	0	0	.000	2.45	2	0	0	0	0	0	3.2	3	1	1	0	0	1	0	5	0
Gogolewski, Albany	1	3	.250	13.81	5	5	0	0	0	0	14.1	17	24	22	1	1	19	0	21	3
Haas, London	13	8	.619	2.99	27	27	3	0	1	0	177.2	151	64	59	10	10	74	1	116	14
Hancock, 7 Will.-20 Harris.*	9	9	.500	3.22	27	26	3	0	1	0	164.2	145	71	59	6	1	77	2	92	9
Hansen, London	5	6	.455	2.17	13	13	3	0	1	0	91.1	80	32	22	7	5	16	2	63	1
Heinkel, Canton-Akron	1	1	.500	2.25	5	4	0	0	0	0	28.0	21	8	7	1	1	14	0	15	1
Hensley, Williamsport*	0	2	.000	3.63	15	0	0	6	0	0	22.1	20	12	9	2	2	13	0	16	2
Holcomb, Albany*	0	0	.000	14.09	6	0	0	4	0	0	7.2	10	14	12	0	1	15	0	9	2
Holdridge, Reading	8	12	.400	4.58	24	24	1	0	0	0	127.2	114	74	65	13	6	79	0	78	8
Holman, Albany	0	3	.000	6.10	28	0	0	14	0	8	31.0	35	26	21	2	5	15	0	26	1
Howard, Albany*	0	0	.000	14.40	2	0	0	1	0	0	5.0	9	8	8	0	0	7	0	2	0
Johnson, Albany*	4	3	.571	1.63	9	9	3	0	1	0	60.2	44	14	11	0	2	15	0	41	1
D. Jones, Williamsport*	1	1	.500	9.90	4	1	0	1	0	0	10.0	11	11	11	1	0	11	0	6	1
M. Jones, London	7	9	.438	3.57	25	21	1	1	0	0	126.0	140	72	50	5	1	39	3	81	10
S. Jones, Hagerstown	1	6	.143	5.13	19	0	0	11	0	2	40.1	46	27	23	1	1	11	1	41	2
Kamieniecki, Albany	10	9	.526	3.20	22	21	3	1	1	0	132.0	113	55	47	5	0	61	2	99	4
Keiiipuleole, Canton-Akron	5	9	.357	4.22	27	19	0	7	0	1	106.2	113	56	50	4	5	60	1	59	5
Kiely, London	3	0	1.000	1.76	46	0	0	25	0	12	76.2	62	17	15	2	2	42	6	52	2
Kinzer, Hagerstown	0	1	.000	0.00	3	0	0	3	0	1	3.2	0	1	0	0	2	2	1	3	0
Kirkpatrick, Reading	0	0	.000	9.00	2	0	0	1	0	0	5.0	10	5	5	1	0	5	0	2	0
Knudsen, London	2	1	.667	2.08	15	0	0	8	0	1	26.0	15	6	6	1	2	11	0	26	2
Kramer, Canton-Akron	6	3	.667	3.00	12	10	2	0	0	0	72.0	67	25	24	3	0	14	1	46	1
Kuzniar, New Britain	0	0	.000	0.00	3	0	0	0	0	0	3.1	3	1	0	0	0	3	0	3	0
Latmore, Hagerstown	0	0	.000	0.00	1	0	0	1	0	0	1.0	1	0	0	0	0	0	0	0	0
Linskey, Hagerstown*	7	1	.875	1.47	8	7	0	0	0	0	55.0	40	16	9	0	1	14	0	40	1
Livernois, New Britain	9	2	.818	1.98	15	14	1	0	1	0	95.2	80	24	21	3	3	31	1	67	5
Lumley, London	0	2	.000	6.42	15	2	0	5	0	0	33.2	38	33	24	2	2	27	0	28	3
Magee, Reading	2	3	.400	5.36	19	2	0	8	0	0	45.1	46	30	27	1	2	34	2	36	4
Manon, Albany	1	2	.333	5.96	9	3	0	3	0	0	25.2	24	19	17	1	2	29	0	21	3
Manzanillo, New Britain	4	4	.500	3.41	12	12	2	0	1	0	74.0	66	34	28	3	2	37	1	51	7
Mauser, Reading	3	4	.429	3.30	8	8	1	0	0	0	46.1	35	20	17	2	3	15	0	40	4
McDonald, Hagerstown	0	1	.000	6.55	3	0	0	0	0	0	11.0	11	8	8	1	1	3	0	15	0
McKeon, Hagerstown*	1	0	1.000	2.10	22	0	0	14	0	7	34.1	31	10	8	2	1	11	1	29	2
McLarnan, Reading	0	2	.000	6.64	13	0	0	5	0	2	20.1	18	16	15	2	0	8	1	15	2
McMichael, Canton-Akron	2	3	.400	3.35	13	4	0	4	0	0	40.1	39	17	15	3	1	17	1	19	3
Meacham, London	15	9	.625	3.13	26	26	9	0	3	0	178.0	161	70	62	11	4	36	0	123	5
Mesa, Hagerstown	5	5	.500	3.42	15	15	3	0	1	0	79.0	77	35	30	4	1	30	0	72	2
D. Miller, Hagerstown	4	5	.444	2.81	24	7	0	10	0	7	83.1	80	34	26	3	7	22	0	37	1
P. Miller, Harrisburg	2	1	.667	2.19	5	2	0	1	0	0	37.0	27	9	9	1	2	10	0	11	0
Minor, Harrisburg	6	4	.600	3.06	38	6	0	23	0	5	94.0	81	41	32	5	0	29	7	98	3
Moore, Reading	1	0	1.000	0.00	1	0	0	0	0	0	6.0	2	0	0	0	1	0	0	4	0
Morton, New Britain*	8	14	.364	3.81	26	26	7	0	2	0	163.0	151	86	69	6	14	48	0	131	6
Muratti, Reading	0	0	.000	18.00	1	0	0	1	0	0	3.0	8	6	6	0	0	0	0	1	0
Murphy, Harrisburg	3	2	.600	2.86	28	3	0	11	0	1	63.0	63	29	20	4	1	20	1	35	1
Mussina, Hagerstown	3	0	1.000	1.49	7	7	2	0	1	0	42.1	34	10	7	1	0	7	0	40	3
Mutis, Canton-Akron*	11	10	.524	3.16	26	26	7	0	3	0	165.0	178	73	58	6	3	44	2	94	5
Myers, Hagerstown*	6	11	.353	3.44	21	21	1	0	0	0	110.0	108	53	42	8	2	56	0	74	5
Nagy, Canton-Akron	13	8	.619	2.52	23	23	9	0	0	0	175.0	132	62	49	9	6	39	0	99	3
Neely, Harrisburg	4	4	.500	1.78	40	0	0	29	0	9	65.2	49	22	13	5	1	18	10	62	1
Nelson, Williamsport	1	4	.200	6.44	10	10	0	0	0	0	43.1	65	35	31	2	2	18	1	14	2
Newell, Albany	4	4	.500	4.79	22	0	0	5	0	0	62.0	54	42	33	0	2	53	0	34	6
Newlin, Williamsport	1	1	.500	3.49	20	0	0	12	0	0	38.2	45	22	15	2	2	15	0	23	0
O'Neill, 2 Lon.-33 N.B.*	7	0	1.000	0.72	35	0	0	28	0	11	62.2	36	7	5	1	0	13	0	49	0
Ontiveros, Reading	0	2	.000	9.00	2	0	0	0	0	0	6.0	7	6	6	0	2	2	0	8	0
Owen, New Britain*	7	9	.438	2.93	20	20	4	0	0	0	132.0	123	54	43	0	5	48	2	88	2
Peraza, Hagerstown	0	0	.000	1.93	2	2	0	0	0	0	14.0	3	3	3	1	0	3	1	4	0
Plympton, New Britain.	3	4	.429	2.67	37	0	0	30	0	13	64.0	62	31	19	1	1	16	5	55	0
Popplewell, Albany	8	2	.800	4.08	14	12	0	0	0	0	64.0	56	31	29	4	3	36	0	34	2
Quantrill, New Britain	7	11	.389	3.53	22	22	1	0	1	0	132.2	148	65	52	3	4	23	2	53	3
Ramos, London*	5	2	.714	3.12	16	6	1	3	1	0	52.0	50	21	18	1	0	19	0	25	0
Rhodes, Hagerstown*	3	4	.429	3.73	12	12	0	0	0	0	72.1	62	32	30	3	0	39	0	60	5
Rice, Williamsport	4	4	.500	3.98	25	8	0	4	0	0	72.1	77	36	32	4	1	24	1	58	5
Richards, London*	6	6	.500	4.28	45	0	0	36	0	1	54.2	61	27	26	5	1	35	5	74	5
Richardson, Harrisburg.	0	6	.000	5.11	8	8	0	0	0	0	37.0	40	25	21	5	1	21	0	22	0
Ridenour, Williamsport	4	7	.364	2.86	45	2	1	29	1	6	78.2	75	31	25	2	1	41	7	70	15
Rightnowar, London	2	2	.500	3.25	23	0	0	18	0	4	44.1	40	20	16	4	2	9	0	33	1
Roesler, Harrisburg	2	1	.667	4.56	10	0	0	1	0	0	23.2	29	14	12	3	0	6	1	11	0
Rojas, Williamsport	8	6	.571	3.39	43	3	0	28	0	11	85.0	83	37	32	5	0	16	1	57	1

Pitcher—Club	W.	L.	Pct.	ERA	G.	GS.	CG.	GF.	ShO.	Sv.	IP.	H.	R.	ER.	HR.	HB.	BB.	Int. BB.	SO.	WP.
Roscoe, Canton-Akron	6	7	.462	3.78	20	20	4	0	1	0	119.0	115	63	50	1	2	41	2	106	6
Rub, Albany°	3	0	1.000	4.45	22	0	0	11	0	0	32.1	43	21	16	2	1	31	4	37	2
Sander, Hagerstown	5	6	.455	2.48	38	2	0	24	0	7	101.2	99	42	28	5	5	27	5	55	3
Sanders, New Britain	2	1	.667	2.55	6	6	0	0	0	0	35.1	31	12	10	3	1	11	0	30	2
Seanez, Canton-Akron	1	0	1.000	2.16	15	0	0	11	0	5	16.2	9	4	4	0	1	12	0	27	0
Shelton, Reading	0	1	.000	13.94	5	1	0	1	0	0	10.1	22	17	16	2	0	9	0	5	4
Sims, Reading°	0	1	.000	3.41	54	0	0	32	0	13	68.2	79	32	26	7	1	16	2	41	3
M. Smith, Albany	0	1	.000	2.91	10	1	0	3	0	0	21.2	24	7	7	0	1	10	0	16	2
W. Smith, Albany	1	1	.500	0.00	9	0	0	9	0	4	8.2	6	1	0	0	0	5	1	12	1
Soper, Canton-Akron	2	1	.667	3.92	16	0	0	9	0	1	20.2	16	10	9	1	0	14	1	20	1
Spagnola, Canton-Akron	1	0	1.000	5.87	4	0	0	1	0	0	7.2	4	5	5	0	0	5	2	2	0
Stanford, Albany	4	2	.667	2.15	56	1	0	26	0	10	88.0	68	21	21	2	1	24	2	65	1
Stevens, Reading	3	3	.500	2.84	25	0	0	12	0	4	44.1	43	23	14	5	0	20	6	34	4
Stewart, New Britain°	1	2	.333	1.42	7	0	0	4	0	1	12.2	11	5	2	1	1	3	0	7	2
S. Taylor, New Britain°	0	2	.000	1.65	5	5	1	0	0	0	27.1	23	8	5	0	1	13	1	27	1
W. Taylor, Albany	6	4	.600	2.88	12	12	1	0	0	0	84.1	71	30	27	3	2	18	0	44	2
Telford, Hagerstown	10	2	.833	1.97	14	13	3	1	1	0	96.0	80	26	21	3	3	25	1	73	4
Thorpe, Hagerstown	3	2	.600	4.05	46	1	0	35	0	12	66.2	66	31	30	2	4	29	2	49	4
Tomlin, Harrisburg°	9	6	.600	2.28	19	18	4	1	3	0	126.1	101	43	32	3	6	34	6	92	2
Torres, Albany	1	2	.333	2.36	9	3	0	3	0	0	26.2	20	12	7	1	1	17	1	16	0
Tracy, Harrisburg	14	8	.636	3.00	25	23	5	1	2	1	153.0	143	63	51	8	8	37	0	106	9
Walker, Canton-Akron	1	0	1.000	0.00	1	1	0	0	0	0	7.0	4	0	0	0	0	4	0	3	0
Walters, New Britain	2	2	.500	3.13	43	2	0	26	0	8	74.2	72	32	26	3	3	38	5	50	8
Webb, Harrisburg	5	10	.333	3.59	28	15	3	4	0	0	120.1	105	64	48	13	5	59	1	60	4
Wilkins, London	13	5	.722	2.42	25	25	6	0	3	0	174.2	156	57	47	12	5	47	1	91	1
Williams, London°	0	4	.000	6.18	22	5	0	5	0	0	43.2	45	34	30	3	1	31	1	24	6
Wilson, Reading	7	12	.368	2.44	33	21	3	10	0	2	151.0	140	64	41	7	8	39	1	70	7
Wooden, Williamsport	1	1	.500	2.30	10	0	0	9	0	2	15.2	11	4	4	0	1	5	1	8	0

BALKS—Roscoe, Stanford, 6 each; Morton, Owen, 5 each; Cook, Hancock, Hansen, 4 each; Burdick, Clayton, Manzanillo, Nagy, Newlin, 3 each; Ashby, Ayrault, Cavers, M. Garcia, Linskey, Magee, Plympton, Quantrill, Ridenour, M. Smith, W. Taylor, Thorpe, Wilkins, 2 each; Blasucci, Bond, Borgatti, Brantley, Carista, DeLaRosa, Draper, Egloff, Figueroa, Fischer, V. Garcia, Gardiner, Gogolewski, Haas, Heinkel, Hensley, M. Jones, Kamieniecki, Keliipuleole, Knudsen, McDonald, McLarnan, Meacham, Minor, Mussina, Mutis, Richardson, Rojas, Shelton, Sims, W. Smith, Spagnola, Tomlin, Tracy, Wooden, 1 each.

COMBINATION SHUTOUTS—Kamieniecki-Stanford-Chapin 2, Popplewell-Chapin 2, Cook-Chapin, Cook-Torres-Smith, Garcia-Chapin, Johnson-Rub, Popplewell-Bond-Stanford-Chapin, Albany; Bruske-Fassero-Soper, Farrell-Collins-Fassero, Heinkel-Fassero, Keliipuleole-Fassero-Egloff, Kramer-Egloff, Kramer-Fassero, Walker-Fassero, Canton-Akron; Burdick-Sander 2, DeLaRosa-Miller 2, Burdick-McKeon, DeLaRosa-Cavers, Linskey-Thorpe, Miller-Jones, Mussina-Thorpe, Telford-Thorpe, Hagerstown; Hancock-Ausanio 2, Hancock-Tracy, Tomlin-Ausanio, Tracy-Adams, Webb-Neely, Harrisburg; Haas-Holman, Haas-Kiely, Hansen-Knudsen-Holman, M. Jones-Richards, Meacham-Williams-Kiely, Ramos-Holman, Wilkins-Rightnowar, London; Fischer-Davis, Fischer-Florence-O'Neill, Fischer-Walters, Livernois-O'Neill, Livernois-Walters, Manzanillo-O'Neill, Morton-Walters, Owen-Florence-Walters, Quantrill-Florence-Plympton, Sanders-Davis, Taylor-O'Neill, New Britain; Ashby-Stevens-Ayrault, Ayrault-Christopher, Ayrault-Sims, Boudreaux-Stevens-Ayrault, Brantley-Sims-Ayrault, Carreno-Stevens, Mauser-McLarnan-Sims, Mauser-Wilson, Moore-Ayrault, Reading; Gardiner-Rojas 2, Blueberg-Ridenour, Gardiner-Blasucci, Williamsport.

NO-HIT GAME—Morton, New Britain, defeated Reading, 1-0 (first game, perfect game), August 25.

Southern League

CLASS AA

Leading Batter
ADAM CASILLAS
Chattanooga

League President
JIMMY BRAGAN

Leading Pitcher
JEFF CARTER
Jacksonville

CHAMPIONSHIP WINNERS IN PREVIOUS YEARS

1904—Macon	.598	
1905—Macon	.625	
1906—Savannah	.637	
1907—Charleston	.620	
1908—Jacksonville	.694	
1909—Chattanooga*	.738	
Augusta	.702	
1910—Columbus	.588	
1911—Columbus*	.681	
Columbia	.710	
1912—Jacksonville*	.679	
Columbus	.632	
1913—Savannah	.754	
Savannah	.593	
1914—Savannah*	.667	
Albany	.650	
1915—Macon	.588	
Columbus*	.686	
1916—Augusta*	.617	
Columbia	.631	
1917—Charleston	.741	
Columbia*	.667	
1918—Did not operate.		
1919—Columbia	.585	
1920—Columbia	.633	
1921—Columbia	.642	
1922—Charleston	.625	
1923—Charlotte*	.653	
Macon	.580	
1924—Augusta	.612	
1925—Spartanburg	.620	
1926—Greenville	.662	
1927—Greenville	.622	
1928—Asheville	.664	
1929—Asheville*	.605	
Knoxville*	.634	
1930—Greenville*	.620	
Macon	.643	
1931-35—Did not operate.		
1936—Jacksonville*	.652	
Columbus*	.650	
1937—Columbus	.572	
Savannah (3rd)†	.565	
1938—Savannah	.574	
Macon (2nd)†	.570	

1939—Columbus	.601	
Augusta (2nd)†	.597	
1940—Savannah	.627	
Columbus (2nd)†	.583	
1941—Macon	.643	
Columbia (2nd)†	.636	
1942—Charleston	.620	
Macon (2nd)†	.585	
1943-45—Did not operate.		
1946—Columbus	.568	
Augusta (4th)†	.547	
1947—Columbus	.575	
Savannah (2nd)†	.563	
1948—Charleston	.572	
Greenville (3rd)†	.549	
1949—Macon‡	.623	
1950—Macon‡	.588	
1951—Montgomery	.607	
1952—Columbia	.649	
Montgomery (3rd)†	.558	
1953—Jacksonville	.679	
Savannah (2nd)†	.571	
1954—Jacksonville	.593	
Savannah (2nd)†	.571	
1955—Columbia	.636	
Augusta (3rd)†	.543	
1956—Jacksonville‡	.621	
1957—Augusta	.636	
Charlotte (2nd)†	.562	
1958—Augusta	.550	
Macon (3rd)†	.500	
1959—Knoxville	.557	
Gastonia (4th)†	.504	
1960—Columbia	.597	
Savannah (3rd)†	.561	
1961—Asheville	.635	
1962—Savannah	.662	
Macon (3rd)†	.576	
1963—Augusta*	.661	
Lynchburg	.662	
1964—Lynchburg	.579	
1965—Columbus	.572	
1966—Mobile	.629	

1967—Birmingham	.604	
1968—Asheville	.614	
1969—Charlotte	.579	
1970—Columbus	.569	
1971—Did not operate as league—clubs were members of Dixie Association.		
1972—Asheville	.583	
Montgomery§	.561	
1973—Montgomery§	.580	
Jacksonville	.559	
1974—Jacksonville	.565	
Knoxville§	.533	
1975—Orlando	.587	
Montgomery§	.545	
1976—Montgomery x	.591	
Orlando	.540	
1977—Montgomery x	.628	
Jacksonville	.522	
1978—Knoxville x	.611	
Savannah	.500	
1979—Columbus	.587	
Nashville x	.576	
1980—Memphis	.576	
Charlotte x	.500	
1981—Nashville	.566	
Orlando x	.556	
1982—Jacksonville	.576	
Nashville x	.535	
1983—Birmingham x	.628	
Jacksonville	.531	
1984—Charlotte x	.510	
Knoxville	.483	
1985—Charlotte	.545	
Huntsville x	.542	
1986—Huntsville	.553	
Columbus x	.500	
1987—Charlotte	.586	
Birmingham x	.476	
1988—Greenville	.604	
Chattanooga x	.566	
1989—Birmingham x	.615	
Greenville	.504	

*Won split-season playoff. †Won four-club playoff. ‡Won championship and four-club playoff. §League was divided into Eastern and Western divisions; won playoff. xLeague was divided into Eastern and Western divisions and played split season; won playoff.

STANDING OF CLUBS AT CLOSE OF FIRST HALF, JUNE 19

EASTERN DIVISION

Club	W.	L.	T.	Pct.	G.B.
Orlando (Twins)	42	30	0	.583	....
Jacksonville (Expos)	38	33	0	.535	3½
Columbus (Astros)	33	39	0	.458	9
Charlotte (Cubs)	32	40	0	.444	10
Greenville (Braves)	28	44	0	.389	14

WESTERN DIVISION

Club	W.	L.	T.	Pct.	G.B.
Memphis (Royals)	44	28	0	.611	....
Huntsville (Athletics)	41	31	0	.569	3
Birmingham (White Sox)	37	34	1	.521	6½
Chattanooga (Reds)	35	36	0	.493	8½
Knoxville (Blue Jays)	28	43	1	.394	15½

STANDING OF CLUBS AT CLOSE OF SECOND HALF, SEPTEMBER 1

EASTERN DIVISION

Club	W.	L.	T.	Pct.	G.B.
Jacksonville (Expos)	46	27	0	.630	....
Orlando (Twins)	43	29	0	.597	2½
Columbus (Astros)	34	38	0	.472	11½
Charlotte (Cubs)	33	39	0	.458	12½
Greenville (Braves)	29	43	0	.403	16½

WESTERN DIVISION

Club	W.	L.	T.	Pct.	G.B.
Birmingham (White Sox)	40	33	0	.548	....
Knoxville (Blue Jays)	39	34	0	.534	1
Huntsville (Athletics)	38	34	0	.528	1½
Chattanooga (Reds)	31	42	0	.425	9
Memphis (Royals)	29	43	0	.403	10½

COMPOSITE STANDING OF CLUBS AT CLOSE OF SECOND HALF, SEPTEMBER 1

Club	Orl.	Jax.	Hunt.	Birm.	Mem.	Knox.	Col.	Chat.	Char.	Grn.	W.	L.	T.	Pct.	G.B.
Orlando (Twins)	....	10	10	5	9	7	11	11	11	11	85	59	0	.590	....
Jacksonville (Expos)	6	....	11	8	8	9	8	10	14	10	84	60	0	.583	1
Huntsville (Athletics)	6	5	....	11	9	10	10	11	8	9	79	65	0	.549	6
Birmingham (White Sox)	11	8	5	....	8	11	9	9	8	8	77	67	1	.535	8
Memphis (Royals)	7	8	7	8	....	9	8	8	9	9	73	71	0	.507	12
Knoxville (Blue Jays)	9	7	6	5	7	....	8	9	9	7	67	77	1	.465	18
Columbus (Astros)	5	8	6	7	8	8	....	6	8	11	67	77	0	.465	18
Chattanooga (Reds)	5	6	5	7	8	7	10	....	7	11	66	78	0	.458	19
Charlotte (Cubs)	5	2	8	8	7	7	8	9	....	11	65	79	0	.451	20
Greenville (Braves)	5	6	7	8	7	9	5	5	5	....	57	87	0	.396	28

Major league affiliations in parentheses.

Playoffs—Memphis defeated Birmingham, three games to one; Orlando defeated Jacksonville, three games to one; Memphis defeated Orlando, three games to two, to win league championship.

Regular-Season Attendance—Birmingham, 256,227; Charlotte, 271,502; Chattanooga, 135,825; Columbus, 94,265; Greenville, 204,929; Huntsville, 228,821; Jacksonville, 244,494; Knoxville, 82,676; Memphis, 193,758; Orlando, 147,070. Total, 1,859,567. Playoffs (13 games)—21,335. All-Star Game—5,918.

Managers—Birmingham, Ken Berry; Charlotte, Tommy Helms (through August 3), Jay Loviglio (August 4 through end of season); Chattanooga, Jim Tracy; Columbus, Rick Sweet; Greenville, Buddy Bailey; Huntsville, Jeff Newman; Jacksonville, Jerry Manuel; Knoxville, John Stearns; Memphis, Jeff Cox; Orlando, Ron Gardenhire. Managerial record of team with more than one manager: Charlotte, Helms (50-65), Loviglio (15-14).

All-Star Team—1B—Jeff Conine, Memphis; 2B—William Suero, Knoxville; 3B—Sean Berry, Memphis; SS—Eddie Zosky, Knoxville; OF—Terrel Hansen, Jacksonville; Adam Casillas, Chattanooga; Brian McRae, Memphis; Bobby Moore, Memphis; C—Greg Colbrunn, Jacksonville; DH—Matt Stark, Birmingham; RHP—Scott Erickson, Orlando; LHP—Brian Barnes, Jacksonville; Relief Pitcher—Steve Chitren, Huntsville; Outstanding Pitcher— Brian Barnes, Jacksonville; Most Valuable Player—Jeff Conine, Memphis; Manager of the Year—(tie) Ron Gardenhire, Orlando; Jerry Manuel, Jacksonville.

(Compiled by Howe Sportsdata International, Boston, Mass.)

CLUB BATTING

Club	Pct.	G.	AB.	R.	OR.	H.	TB.	2B.	3B.	HR.	RBI.	SH.	SF.	HP.	BB.	Int. BB.	SO.	SB.	CS.	LOB.
Birmingham	.271	145	4767	771	717	1292	1896	251	37	93	703	44	52	44	675	25	923	144	92	1095
Memphis	.266	144	4750	721	625	1264	1785	207	46	74	634	71	56	31	603	15	740	165	67	1056
Knoxville	.260	144	4751	615	673	1234	1834	212	44	100	551	63	35	44	436	24	944	148	107	961
Chattanooga	.257	144	4711	642	705	1210	1745	236	34	77	563	59	37	35	590	25	828	94	52	1085
Orlando	.254	144	4678	685	582	1189	1688	218	31	73	613	36	38	62	635	25	762	129	61	1083
Huntsville	.252	144	4746	678	681	1197	1792	216	23	111	607	71	36	42	592	26	876	87	50	1053
Columbus	.251	144	4712	645	676	1181	1803	188	43	116	583	55	48	50	535	29	1095	179	73	997
Jacksonville	.249	144	4792	665	557	1195	1808	227	34	106	601	47	45	77	515	29	947	113	65	1040
Greenville	.237	144	4710	575	722	1118	1592	189	21	81	508	43	36	41	570	29	896	103	78	1048
Charlotte	.234	144	4624	583	642	1080	1642	201	20	107	515	56	42	71	475	19	823	109	64	941

INDIVIDUAL BATTING

(Leading Qualifiers for Batting Championship—389 or More Plate Appearances)

*Bats lefthanded.   †Switch-hitter.

Player and Club	Pct.	G.	AB.	R.	H.	TB.	2B.	3B.	HR.	RBI.	SH.	SF.	HP.	BB.	Int. BB.	SO.	SB.	CS.
Casillas, Adam, Chattanooga*	.336	123	378	56	127	165	27	1	3	64	2	8	0	76	3	29	2	3
Thomas, Frank, Birmingham	.323	109	353	85	114	205	27	5	18	71	0	4	5	112	2	74	7	5
Conine, Jeffrey, Memphis	.320	137	487	89	156	254	37	8	15	95	0	4	1	94	6	88	21	6
Stark, Matthew, Birmingham	.309	129	453	69	140	208	26	0	14	109	1	12	7	85	5	52	3	4
Cole, Stewart, Memphis	.308	113	357	61	110	135	18	2	1	49	4	3	5	55	2	55	20	6
Moore, Robert, Memphis	.303	112	422	93	128	166	20	6	2	36	8	4	2	56	0	32	27	7
Colbrunn, Gregory, Jacksonville	.301	125	458	57	138	208	29	1	13	76	3	6	6	38	4	78	1	2
Brosius, Scott, Huntsville	.296	142	547	94	162	274	39	2	23	88	7	9	1	81	2	81	12	3
Magallanes, William, Birmingham	.292	123	459	72	134	212	24	3	16	65	2	1	6	41	4	139	10	5
Berry, Sean, Memphis	.292	135	487	73	142	217	25	4	14	77	7	5	5	44	1	89	19	9

Department Leaders: G—Bernhardt, Brosius, Rodgers, 142; AB—Bernhardt, 574; R—J. Brown, 104; H—Brosius, 162; TB—Brosius, 274; 2B—Brosius, 39; 3B—Cedeno, 11; HR—Gonzalez, Hansen, 24; RBI—Stark, 109; SH—Rodgers, 14; SF—Gonzalez, Stark, 12; HP—Crockett, 32; BB—Thomas, 112; IBB—A. Brown, Gonzalez, 9; SO—Quinlan, 157; SB—Rodgers, 41; CS—Suero, 22.

(All Players—Listed Alphabetically)

Player and Club	Pct.	G.	AB.	R.	H.	TB.	2B.	3B.	HR.	RBI.	SH.	SF.	HP.	BB.	Int. BB.	SO.	SB.	CS.
Acta, Manuel, Columbus	.239	41	109	15	26	33	4	0	1	10	1	0	1	5	0	24	0	1
Alborano, Peter, Memphis*	.255	81	259	33	66	82	8	1	2	35	3	2	0	32	1	31	0	0
Alfredson, Thomas, Birmingham	.255	51	157	23	40	61	9	0	4	28	1	4	2	23	2	47	1	3
Allen, Harold, Columbus*	.158	23	19	1	3	4	1	0	0	0	2	0	0	0	0	11	0	0

Player and Club	Pct.	G.	AB.	R.	H.	TB.	2B.	3B.	HR.	RBI.	SH.	SF.	HP.	BB.	Int. BB.	SO.	SB.	CS.
Alva, John, Greenville	.161	15	62	6	10	12	2	0	0	5	1	1	0	3	0	6	0	0
Ansley, Willie, Columbus	.255	120	415	69	106	156	9	7	9	37	2	1	1	54	2	121	33	8
Anthony, Eric, Columbus*	.167	4	12	2	2	5	0	0	1	3	0	0	0	3	0	4	0	0
Arias, Alejandro, Charlotte	.246	119	419	55	103	137	16	3	4	38	9	3	2	42	0	53	12	5
Bafia, Robert, Charlotte	.253	28	91	13	23	38	6	0	3	12	0	1	0	6	0	13	2	3
Baldwin, Jeffrey, Columbus*	.316	77	250	43	79	113	11	1	7	37	0	4	3	33	4	36	0	1
Banning, Douglas, Chattanooga	.069	33	29	6	2	2	0	0	0	0	4	0	0	3	0	5	0	0
Barberie, Bret, Jacksonville†	.260	133	431	71	112	157	18	3	7	56	4	5	11	86	5	64	20	7
Barnes, Brian, Jacksonville*	.050	29	20	0	1	2	1	0	0	1	2	0	0	3	0	7	0	0
Batiste, Kevin, Greenville†	.235	98	340	44	80	108	14	1	4	31	1	1	4	40	1	94	14	18
Bauer, Peter, Columbus	.000	34	2	0	0	0	0	0	0	0	0	0	0	0	0	1	0	0
Bell, Leonard, Charlotte	.155	32	84	7	13	22	4	1	1	6	0	0	0	5	0	32	1	0
Bell, Michael, Greenville*	.291	106	405	50	118	164	24	2	6	42	4	2	5	41	6	63	10	4
Benavides, Alfredo, Chattanooga	.259	55	197	20	51	66	10	1	1	28	3	2	2	11	0	25	4	2
Bennett, Christopher, Jacksonville	.000	37	3	0	0	0	0	0	0	0	0	0	0	0	0	3	0	0
Bernhardt, Cesar, Birmingham	.279	142	574	96	160	222	26	9	6	82	3	7	3	46	0	53	30	15
Berry, Sean, Memphis	.292	135	487	73	142	217	25	4	14	77	7	5	5	44	1	89	19	9
Boltz, Brian, Greenville*	.056	28	18	1	1	1	0	0	0	0	3	0	0	1	0	7	0	0
Borrelli, Dean, Huntsville	.179	27	78	7	14	23	4	1	1	3	1	1	1	5	0	20	0	0
Bottenfield, Kent, Jacksonville†	.120	29	25	2	3	6	0	0	1	6	3	0	0	1	0	11	0	0
Bowen, Ryan, Columbus	.000	19	13	1	0	0	0	0	0	1	2	1	0	0	0	5	0	0
Branson, Jeffery, Chattanooga*	.210	63	233	19	49	66	9	1	2	29	1	2	0	13	2	48	3	1
Brito, Jorge, Huntsville	.268	57	164	17	44	58	6	1	2	20	3	1	3	30	1	49	0	1
Brito, Mario, Jacksonville	.267	18	15	3	4	4	0	0	0	1	2	0	0	1	0	6	0	0
Brosius, Scott, Huntsville	.296	142	547	94	162	274	39	2	23	88	7	9	1	81	2	81	12	3
Brown, Anthony, Huntsville*	.290	127	445	74	129	190	29	1	10	60	2	2	5	67	9	96	4	3
Brown, Jarvis, Orlando	.260	135	527	104	137	215	22	7	14	57	5	2	9	80	1	79	33	19
Brown, Kurt, Birmingham	.269	82	253	38	68	88	8	0	4	43	4	2	1	19	0	47	8	4
Browning, Michael, Columbus	.000	16	2	0	0	0	0	0	0	0	0	0	0	0	0	0	0	0
Bruno, Joseph, Chattanooga	.000	21	6	0	0	0	0	0	0	0	0	0	0	0	0	3	0	0
Bryant, Scott, Chattanooga	.313	44	131	23	41	75	10	3	6	30	0	0	2	22	0	28	1	1
Buccheri, James, Huntsville	.209	84	278	39	58	62	2	1	0	22	7	1	3	40	0	38	15	6
Bullinger, James, Charlotte	.143	11	7	2	1	1	0	0	0	0	1	0	1	1	0	3	0	0
Busby, LeWayne, Birmingham	.262	102	386	46	101	142	27	4	2	43	6	2	0	37	0	91	16	11
Caceres, Edgar, Birmingham†	.262	62	214	31	56	63	5	1	0	17	3	1	1	15	0	26	7	4
Campbell, Darrin, Birmingham	.182	3	11	0	2	2	0	0	0	0	0	0	1	1	0	3	0	0
Canan, Richard, Charlotte	.233	123	404	38	94	135	17	3	6	40	2	3	4	26	0	83	9	9
Cano, Joselito, Columbus	.000	7	1	0	0	0	0	0	0	0	0	0	0	0	0	1	0	0
Canseco, Osvaldo, Huntsville	.225	97	325	50	73	154	21	0	20	67	2	2	7	47	2	103	2	2
Carcione, Thomas, Huntsville	.194	24	62	6	12	14	0	1	0	9	3	0	0	13	0	12	1	3
Carter, Dennis, Greenville	.075	14	40	3	3	7	1	0	1	5	0	2	1	3	0	13	0	0
Carter, Jeffrey, Jacksonville	.071	52	14	1	1	1	0	0	0	0	2	0	0	2	0	4	0	0
Casarotti, Richard, Greenville†	.226	113	367	39	83	112	10	2	5	42	5	4	2	32	4	74	3	3
Casey, Timothy, Greenville*	.175	37	80	9	14	24	1	0	3	9	0	0	2	15	0	28	1	0
Casillas, Adam, Chattanooga*	.336	123	378	56	127	165	27	1	3	64	2	8	0	76	3	29	2	3
Castilla, Vinicio, Greenville	.235	46	170	20	40	59	5	1	4	16	0	1	2	13	0	23	4	4
Castillo, Frank, Charlotte	.100	18	10	0	1	1	0	0	0	0	3	0	0	1	0	5	0	0
Cedeno, Andujar, Columbus	.240	132	495	57	119	219	21	11	19	64	7	5	6	33	1	135	6	10
Champion, Brian, Greenville	.265	34	102	10	27	35	5	0	1	7	0	0	1	18	1	12	2	0
Cianfrocco, Angelo, Jacksonville	.219	62	196	18	43	68	10	0	5	29	0	3	2	12	1	45	0	1
Coffman, Kevin, Charlotte	.129	24	31	5	4	13	0	0	3	3	1	0	0	3	0	9	0	0
Colbrunn, Gregory, Jacksonville	.301	125	458	57	138	208	29	1	13	76	3	6	6	38	4	78	1	2
Cole, Stewart, Memphis	.308	113	357	61	110	135	18	2	1	49	4	3	3	55	2	55	20	6
Colvard, Ben, Chattanooga	.288	97	326	49	94	164	25	3	13	56	4	2	2	25	2	69	5	5
Conine, Jeffrey, Memphis	.320	137	487	89	156	254	37	8	15	95	0	8	1	94	6	88	21	6
Coomer, Ronald, Huntsville	.222	66	194	22	43	59	7	0	3	27	4	3	1	21	1	40	3	1
Cooper, Gary, Columbus	.263	54	160	29	42	73	7	0	8	30	0	1	1	30	0	30	1	2
Cordero, Wilfredo, Jacksonville	.234	131	444	63	104	151	18	4	7	40	3	1	5	56	0	122	9	4
Costello, Fred, Columbus	.000	35	4	0	0	0	0	0	0	0	0	1	0	0	0	3	0	0
Credeur, Todd, Columbus*	.000	11	0	1	0	0	0	0	0	0	0	0	0	0	0	0	0	0
Crockett, Russell, Charlotte	.243	133	403	65	98	138	18	2	6	34	8	3	32	44	5	50	19	9
Czarnik, Christopher, Greenville	.125	21	8	0	1	1	0	0	0	1	1	0	0	0	0	0	0	0
Damian, Leonard, Charlotte	.000	7	1	0	0	0	0	0	0	0	0	0	0	0	0	1	0	0
Davis, Glenn, Columbus	.297	12	37	3	11	14	0	0	1	8	0	0	1	2	0	9	1	0
Deak, Brian, Greenville	.218	66	188	24	41	63	13	0	3	26	2	3	4	43	1	47	2	2
Dean, Kevin, 22 Green.-22 Col.	.246	44	130	14	32	46	12	1	0	14	0	2	1	35	1	34	6	2
DeFrancesco, Anthony, Chattanooga	.253	70	217	24	55	73	8	2	2	15	2	2	0	15	3	53	1	0
DelRosario, Maximo, Greenville	.000	63	4	1	0	0	0	0	0	0	0	0	0	0	0	1	0	0
Dickson, Lance, Charlotte	.400	3	5	1	2	2	0	0	0	0	0	0	0	0	0	1	0	0
Dodd, William, Chattanooga	.000	32	2	0	0	0	0	0	0	0	0	0	0	0	0	1	0	0
Duffy, Darrin, Charlotte	.241	108	319	48	77	106	18	1	3	23	6	3	2	50	1	62	4	3
Dunbar, Thomas, Memphis*	.203	95	290	44	59	87	7	3	5	42	2	3	0	33	0	31	9	2
Dziadkowiec, Andrew, Knoxville*	.221	38	122	7	27	30	3	0	0	12	3	1	4	11	1	20	2	4
Eccles, John, Orlando	.185	62	178	16	33	48	9	0	2	10	3	1	3	24	1	66	0	2
Eusebio, Antonio, Columbus	.283	92	318	36	90	120	18	0	4	37	1	1	4	21	0	80	6	2
Faulk, James, Jacksonville*	.258	52	190	40	49	60	3	1	2	12	3	0	0	38	0	39	19	12
Finley, Brian, Chattanooga*	.192	116	343	46	66	80	8	3	0	25	5	0	4	71	4	46	9	14
Forney, Jeffrey, Chattanooga	.278	122	356	57	99	161	29	3	9	44	0	2	3	76	1	86	10	5
Fulton, Gregory, Jacksonville†	.278	11	36	4	10	14	1	0	1	4	1	0	0	4	0	4	0	0
Gaither, Horace, Birmingham*	.121	16	33	5	4	4	0	0	0	2	0	0	1	4	0	9	0	1
Galvez, Balvino, Jacksonville	1.000	1	1	1	1	3	0	1	0	2	0	0	0	0	0	0	0	0
Garcia, Cornelio, Birmingham*	.343	25	67	9	23	29	6	0	0	6	1	0	1	12	0	16	3	1
Garcia, Victor, Charlotte	.212	63	198	23	42	77	11	0	8	38	0	4	4	19	1	30	1	3
Gilbert, Shawn, Orlando	.254	123	433	68	110	144	18	2	4	44	4	3	5	61	0	69	31	9
Gomez, Patrick, Greenville*	.000	23	14	0	0	0	0	0	0	0	1	0	0	2	0	7	0	0
Gonzalez, Luis, Columbus*	.265	138	495	86	131	245	30	6	24	89	1	12	6	54	9	100	27	9
Grayum, Richard, Charlotte*	.237	113	316	38	75	113	8	0	10	35	0	4	4	31	1	64	6	0
Griffin, Tyrone, Charlotte†	.209	78	249	34	52	87	9	1	8	27	1	1	3	57	1	55	7	4
Grovom, Carl, Chattanooga*	.000	9	1	0	0	0	0	0	0	0	0	0	0	0	0	0	0	0
Hall, Lamar, Greenville	.214	32	103	11	22	27	5	0	0	7	2	0	0	4	0	17	3	2
Hall, Todd, Birmingham*	.000	33	1	0	0	0	0	0	0	0	0	0	0	0	0	0	0	0
Hannon, Phillip, Charlotte†	.205	98	190	22	39	53	4	2	2	18	6	1	0	22	0	47	13	7

Player and Club	Pct.	G.	AB.	R.	H.	TB.	2B.	3B.	HR.	RBI.	SH.	SF.	HP.	BB.	Int. BB.	SO.	SB.	CS.
Hansen, Terrel, Jacksonville	.260	123	420	72	109	211	26	2	24	83	1	3	24	43	3	88	3	4
Harris, Russell, Columbus†	.245	64	208	42	51	62	5	3	0	19	0	2	1	49	2	29	8	2
Harrison, Phillip, Charlotte°	.250	9	4	1	1	1	0	0	0	1	1	0	0	0	0	0	0	0
Hartgraves, Dean, Columbus	.176	33	17	2	3	3	0	0	0	1	0	0	0	0	0	6	0	0
Hayden, Alan, Chattanooga°	.266	93	241	40	64	79	9	3	0	15	6	3	1	21	0	27	24	7
Henry, Floyd, Chattanooga°	.091	24	22	2	2	2	0	0	0	0	1	0	0	7	0	8	0	0
Hernandez, Cesar, Jacksonville	.239	118	393	58	94	159	21	7	10	50	1	6	7	18	3	75	17	11
Hinzo, Thomas, 26 Green.-20 Mem.†	.223	46	121	15	27	39	3	3	1	14	4	1	3	14	0	21	6	4
Howard, David, Memphis†	.250	116	384	41	96	129	10	4	5	44	10	6	1	39	0	74	15	4
Hubbard, Trent, Columbus†	.251	95	335	39	84	118	14	4	4	35	8	2	3	37	0	51	17	8
Hunter, Bertram, Columbus†	.233	133	443	56	103	150	12	4	9	39	6	2	2	65	5	137	36	11
Hunter, Brian, Greenville	.241	88	320	45	77	134	13	1	14	55	0	4	3	43	1	62	3	4
Ilsley, Blaise, Columbus°	.667	13	9	0	6	6	0	0	0	2	0	0	0	2	0	0	0	0
Jeffery, Scott, Chattanooga	.000	33	14	0	0	0	0	0	0	0	2	0	0	1	0	5	0	0
Jenkins, Bernard, Columbus	.228	51	162	19	37	62	6	2	5	20	2	1	1	20	0	45	6	3
Jeter, Shawn, Knoxville°	.273	131	461	66	126	167	25	2	4	43	6	7	2	39	5	95	25	14
Johnson, Lee, Greenville	.000	9	4	0	0	0	0	0	0	0	0	0	0	0	0	0	0	0
Johnson, Lloyd, Greenville	.000	29	15	1	0	0	0	0	0	0	1	0	0	2	0	8	0	0
Jones, Alfornia, Greenville	.000	5	2	0	0	0	0	0	0	0	0	0	0	1	0	2	0	0
Jose, Manuel, Greenville†	.234	68	239	25	56	83	6	3	5	22	4	0	1	17	0	46	13	10
Juden, Jeffrey, Columbus	.143	11	7	0	1	1	0	0	0	0	0	0	0	0	0	2	0	0
Kaiser, Keith, Chattanooga†	.143	34	28	1	4	8	2	1	0	1	0	1	0	4	0	15	0	0
Kallevig, Gregory, Charlotte	.000	15	1	0	0	0	0	0	0	0	0	0	0	0	0	1	0	0
Kating, James, Huntsville	.227	72	220	37	50	71	11	2	2	20	3	2	1	31	0	34	1	1
Kazmierczak, William, Charlotte†	.200	22	10	3	2	2	0	0	0	1	3	0	0	0	0	1	0	0
Kilner, John, Greenville°	.000	28	0	0	0	0	0	0	0	0	1	0	0	0	0	0	0	0
Knoblauch, Charles, Orlando	.289	118	432	74	125	166	23	6	2	53	2	3	9	63	0	31	23	7
Knorr, Randy, Knoxville	.276	116	392	51	108	161	12	1	13	64	4	6	2	31	2	83	0	3
Kosco, Bryn, Jacksonville†	.248	33	113	7	28	36	8	0	0	15	2	1	0	11	2	23	0	0
Koslofski, Kevin, Memphis°	.213	118	367	52	78	108	11	5	3	32	7	3	2	54	1	89	12	7
Kowitz, Brian, Greenville°	.132	20	68	4	9	9	0	0	0	4	1	0	0	8	1	10	1	0
Kuld, Peter, Huntsville	.220	57	168	23	37	68	8	1	7	23	4	0	3	14	3	57	2	3
Ladnier, Deric, Memphis†	.143	2	7	0	1	2	1	0	0	1	0	0	0	1	0	2	0	0
Lane, Brian, Chattanooga	.239	79	293	41	70	105	13	2	6	51	1	4	0	37	0	73	2	2
Laureano, Francisco, Memphis	.241	108	320	44	77	107	14	2	4	36	6	6	4	57	1	51	7	9
Lazor, Joseph, Chattanooga	.000	31	8	0	0	0	0	0	0	0	5	0	0	2	0	1	0	0
Lee, Derek, Birmingham°	.255	126	411	68	105	153	21	3	7	75	3	5	6	71	5	93	14	10
Lee, Terry, Chattanooga	.327	43	156	25	51	85	8	1	8	20	1	2	2	20	1	27	4	1
Leibrandt, Charles, Greenville	.000	2	2	0	0	0	0	0	0	0	0	0	0	0	0	0	0	0
Lewis, Darren, Huntsville	.296	71	284	52	84	110	11	3	3	23	0	3	7	36	3	28	21	7
Lombardozzi, Stephen, Columbus	.200	6	20	1	4	7	0	0	1	2	0	0	0	0	0	2	1	0
Lonigro, Gregory, Chattanooga	.256	106	347	40	89	129	22	0	6	38	5	3	6	25	2	29	5	3
Lopez, Marcos, Charlotte	.231	15	13	1	3	3	0	0	0	2	1	0	0	0	0	4	0	0
Magallanes, William, Birmingham	.292	123	459	72	134	212	24	3	16	65	2	1	6	41	4	139	10	5
Makarewicz, Scott, Columbus	.235	28	85	5	20	27	1	0	2	11	0	2	1	11	2	13	0	1
Maksudian, Michael, Knoxville°	.287	121	422	51	121	177	22	5	8	55	0	1	2	50	6	66	6	4
Maldonado, Phillip, Greenville	.182	8	22	2	4	5	1	0	0	1	0	0	3	2	1	2	0	0
Malloy, Robert, Jacksonville	.000	8	9	0	0	0	0	0	0	1	0	0	0	0	0	3	0	0
Maloney, Richard, Greenville	.205	59	161	26	33	37	2	1	0	16	2	0	0	33	1	14	1	3
Mann, Kelly, Greenville	.316	50	155	25	49	83	13	0	7	27	1	1	0	32	1	22	6	3
Marchok, Christopher, Jacksonville°	.000	25	1	0	0	0	0	0	0	0	0	0	0	0	0	1	0	0
Marquez, Edwin, Jacksonville	.122	17	49	5	6	7	1	0	0	4	0	0	3	0	19	0	0
Martin, Albert, Greenville°	.242	133	455	64	110	168	17	4	11	50	1	3	3	43	4	101	20	8
Martinez, Domingo, Knoxville	.257	128	463	53	119	196	20	3	17	66	1	2	5	51	1	81	2	4
Marzan, Jose, Orlando	.230	77	200	22	46	54	5	0	1	16	2	3	3	35	2	27	0	1
Masters, David, Jacksonville	.143	20	7	1	1	1	0	0	0	1	0	0	0	0	0	3	0	0
Matos, Francisco, Huntsville	.228	45	180	18	41	50	3	3	0	12	2	1	1	9	1	18	7	4
Mayne, Brent, Memphis°	.267	115	412	48	110	138	16	3	2	61	7	8	2	52	1	51	5	2
McCray, Rodney, Birmingham	.197	60	188	36	37	46	2	2	1	16	6	2	5	36	0	42	25	10
McRae, Brian, Memphis†	.268	116	470	78	126	192	24	6	10	64	14	1	3	44	1	65	21	10
Merullo, Matthew, Birmingham°	.291	102	378	57	110	162	26	1	8	50	3	2	3	34	6	49	2	4
Mikulik, Joseph, Columbus	.258	46	120	17	31	50	3	2	4	20	1	1	0	16	1	22	8	1
Minutelli, Gino, Chattanooga°	.071	17	14	1	1	1	0	0	0	0	2	0	0	0	0	5	0	0
Mizerock, John, Greenville°	.250	2	4	1	1	2	1	0	0	0	0	0	0	1	0	1	0	0
Monzon, Jose, Knoxville	.333	1	3	1	1	1	0	0	0	0	0	0	0	0	0	0	0	0
Moore, Robert, Memphis	.303	112	422	93	128	166	20	6	2	36	8	4	2	56	0	32	27	7
Morgan, Kenneth, Orlando°	.247	136	462	54	114	188	21	7	13	82	2	6	3	59	7	85	11	8
Morris, Richard, Greenville	.242	75	198	29	48	59	9	1	0	19	0	1	0	36	0	30	1	4
Morrison, Brian, Knoxville	.000	1	1	0	0	0	0	0	0	0	0	0	0	0	0	0	0	0
Moscrey, Michael, Chattanooga	.000	41	4	0	0	0	0	0	0	0	1	0	0	0	0	2	0	0
Mota, Andres, Columbus	.286	111	413	59	118	174	21	1	11	62	9	6	10	28	2	81	17	7
Mount, Charles, Charlotte	.211	41	19	0	4	4	0	0	0	0	3	0	0	1	0	9	0	0
Mullino, Ray, Charlotte	.000	39	5	0	0	0	0	0	0	0	0	0	0	1	0	2	0	0
Munoz, Omer, Jacksonville	.254	70	197	19	50	58	5	0	1	18	1	1	2	5	0	18	3	0
Nabholz, Christopher, Jacksonville°.	.133	11	15	0	2	2	0	0	0	0	1	0	0	0	0	5	0	0
Natal, Robert, Jacksonville	.246	62	171	23	42	72	7	1	7	25	1	2	5	14	2	42	0	1
Naveda, Edgar, Orlando	.347	28	98	10	34	44	7	0	1	19	0	1	0	12	1	8	0	0
Nelson, Jerome, Chattanooga†	.282	69	252	46	71	104	10	4	5	29	1	1	2	40	2	27	14	4
Nunez, Bernardino, Knoxville	.233	105	313	30	73	100	11	5	2	39	6	2	1	16	1	67	10	9
Nyssen, Daniel, Columbus	.218	18	55	4	12	20	5	0	1	6	1	0	0	4	0	10	1	2
Ocasio, Javier, Birmingham	.000	2	6	0	0	0	0	0	0	0	0	0	0	0	0	2	1	0
Olmeda, Jose, Greenville†	.125	2	8	1	1	1	0	0	0	1	0	0	0	1	0	3	0	0
Olmstead, Reed, Orlando°	.266	102	335	43	89	130	11	3	8	65	0	3	3	33	0	64	0	0
Ortiz, Joseph, Columbus	.152	42	112	13	17	27	2	1	2	11	2	4	2	9	1	29	0	2
Ortiz, Raymond, Orlando°	.257	71	265	41	68	111	16	0	9	49	0	4	6	27	1	57	1	0
Osuna, Alfonso, Columbus	.333	60	3	1	1	1	0	0	0	0	0	0	0	0	0	0	0	0
Pearson, Kevin, Chattanooga	.317	60	227	31	72	103	12	2	5	29	2	2	0	14	0	21	0	0
Pedre, Jorge, Memphis	.258	99	360	55	93	136	14	1	9	54	0	7	6	27	1	47	6	1
Penn, Trevor, Jacksonville°	.222	104	316	43	70	108	11	3	7	34	2	3	7	39	6	60	7	2
Perez, Yorkis, Jacksonville°	.000	28	3	0	0	0	0	0	0	0	0	0	0	0	0	3	0	0
Piatt, Douglas, Jacksonville°	.000	35	1	0	0	0	0	0	0	0	0	0	0	0	0	0	0	0
Pino, Rolando, Greenville	.207	12	29	0	6	9	3	0	0	2	0	0	0	6	0	4	0	1

Player and Club	Pct.	G.	AB.	R.	H.	TB.	2B.	3B.	HR.	RBI.	SH.	SF.	HP.	BB.	Int. BB.	SO.	SB.	CS.
Plumb, David, Greenville	.192	68	177	17	34	45	5	0	2	14	0	1	0	12	0	35	0	1
Ponte, Edward, Columbus	.000	18	0	1	0	0	0	0	0	0	1	0	0	1	0	0	0	0
Posey, John, Charlotte	.194	26	72	5	14	21	1	0	2	11	1	0	3	4	0	6	2	0
Powell, Ross, Chattanooga°	.130	29	23	2	3	3	0	0	0	3	3	0	3	0	0	5	0	0
Quinlan, Thomas, Knoxville	.258	141	481	70	124	205	24	6	15	51	7	1	14	49	2	157	8	9
Ralston, Robert, Huntsville	.147	36	109	5	16	17	1	0	0	5	9	0	1	5	0	11	1	2
Randle, Michael, Orlando°	.234	102	342	56	80	102	10	3	2	36	4	0	10	31	1	46	16	4
Reboulet, Jeffery, Orlando	.230	97	287	43	66	88	12	2	2	28	5	4	2	57	1	37	10	5
Redington, Thomas, Greenville	.252	124	409	55	103	154	13	1	12	52	1	4	4	63	3	69	2	1
Reese, Kyle, Memphis	.103	16	29	1	3	4	1	0	0	1	0	0	0	0	0	15	0	0
Renteria, Edinson, Columbus	.257	62	179	22	46	58	10	1	0	19	3	1	2	21	0	27	6	2
Resetar, Gary, Orlando°	.278	95	299	41	83	112	15	1	4	44	5	2	2	41	3	42	0	0
Reynolds, Shane, Columbus	.107	30	28	2	3	3	0	0	0	0	0	0	1	1	0	17	0	0
Richardson, Allen, Orlando°	.250	1	4	0	1	1	0	0	0	1	0	0	0	0	0	2	0	1
Rivera, Bienvenido, Greenville	.250	13	8	0	2	2	0	0	0	1	0	1	0	0	0	1	0	0
Rivera, Hector, Jacksonville	.000	18	13	0	0	0	0	0	0	2	2	0	1	0	4	0	0	0
Rivera, Pablo, Charlotte	.136	36	81	7	11	16	3	1	0	7	1	0	0	6	1	12	1	1
Roberson, Kevin, Charlotte†	.244	31	119	14	29	54	6	2	5	16	1	2	0	8	0	25	2	0
Robinson, Brett, Charlotte†	.222	21	9	0	2	3	1	0	0	2	1	0	0	0	0	2	0	0
Robinson, Marteese, Huntsville	.265	104	366	43	97	132	13	2	6	50	1	3	2	34	0	66	5	4
Rodgers, Paul, Knoxville	.228	142	482	64	110	145	15	4	4	35	14	3	3	49	1	84	41	16
Rodriguez, Boi, Jacksonville°	.281	105	367	50	103	162	22	5	9	58	7	7	2	45	0	81	2	0
Rodriguez, Rosario, Chattanooga	.000	36	3	0	0	0	0	0	0	0	1	0	0	0	0	1	0	0
Rosario, David, Charlotte°	.000	28	1	0	0	0	0	0	0	0	0	0	0	0	0	0	0	0
Rosario, Melvin, Chattanooga	.207	66	179	19	37	55	6	0	4	22	1	1	1	23	2	44	1	1
Rossy, Elam, Greenville	.190	5	21	4	4	5	1	0	0	0	0	0	0	1	0	2	0	2
Roth, Gregory, Birmingham°	.196	57	179	34	35	51	8	1	2	16	1	2	0	41	0	40	4	2
Royer, Stanley, Huntsville	.258	137	527	69	136	213	29	3	14	89	8	4	3	43	0	113	4	1
Santana, Miguel, Jacksonville†	.221	92	303	56	67	80	4	3	1	10	4	0	0	27	0	35	21	15
Satzinger, Jeffrey, Greenville	.000	29	0	0	0	0	0	0	0	0	1	0	0	0	0	0	0	0
Schunk, Jerry, Knoxville	.288	85	274	32	79	103	13	1	3	31	14	3	3	9	0	25	8	7
Scott, Gary, Charlotte	.308	35	143	21	44	65	9	0	4	17	0	3	0	7	1	17	3	4
Sellner, Scott, Chattanooga	.267	129	446	71	119	151	20	3	2	49	6	2	9	65	1	69	7	2
Sepanek, Robert, Chattanooga°	.230	17	61	11	14	24	1	0	3	8	0	1	0	8	1	10	1	0
Sheehan, John, Columbus	.000	8	2	0	0	0	0	0	0	0	0	0	0	0	0	1	0	0
Simmons, Nelson, Huntsville†	.256	123	453	70	116	182	19	1	15	55	4	4	1	62	4	64	0	3
Simon, Richard, Columbus	.000	49	5	2	0	0	0	0	0	0	2	0	1	3	0	3	0	0
Slocumb, Heath, Charlotte	.000	43	1	0	0	0	0	0	0	0	0	0	0	0	0	0	0	0
Smith, Edward, Birmingham	.247	72	247	22	61	84	14	3	1	23	3	4	0	22	0	49	2	1
Snover, Daniel, Greenville	.294	15	34	4	10	13	3	0	0	4	1	0	0	2	0	3	1	0
Sodders, Michael, Charlotte	.000	15	14	1	0	0	0	0	0	0	0	0	0	1	0	4	0	0
Sossamon, Timothy, Jacksonville	.500	7	2	0	1	1	0	0	0	0	0	0	0	0	0	0	0	0
Stairs, Matthew, Jacksonville	.254	79	280	26	71	97	17	0	3	34	0	5	3	22	1	43	5	3
Stark, Matthew, Birmingham	.309	129	453	69	140	208	26	0	14	109	1	12	7	85	5	52	3	4
Stefero, John, Charlotte°	.190	57	126	9	24	34	5	1	1	15	0	0	2	10	0	28	0	0
Stephens, Ronald, Birmingham	.000	39	2	0	0	0	0	0	0	0	0	0	0	0	0	1	0	0
Strauss, Julio, Charlotte	.000	24	1	0	0	0	0	0	0	0	0	0	0	1	0	0	0	0
Stroud, Derek, Charlotte°	.000	12	3	0	0	0	0	0	0	0	0	0	0	2	0	1	0	0
Suero, William, Knoxville	.263	133	483	80	127	218	29	7	16	60	6	2	7	78	3	78	40	22
Sullivan, Glenn, Charlotte°	.254	100	335	50	85	122	20	1	5	34	6	4	4	35	1	27	7	7
Sutko, Glenn, Chattanooga	.167	53	174	12	29	44	7	1	2	11	0	0	1	8	1	66	1	1
Tafoya, Dennis, Columbus	.000	31	3	0	0	0	0	0	0	0	0	0	0	0	0	3	0	0
Taylor, Matthew, Knoxville	.133	12	15	2	2	2	0	0	0	2	1	0	0	2	0	6	1	1
Tedder, Scott, Birmingham°	.333	2	3	1	1	1	0	0	0	0	0	0	0	2	0	1	0	0
Thomas, Frank, Birmingham	.323	109	353	85	114	205	27	5	18	71	0	4	5	112	2	74	7	5
Tomberlin, Andy, Greenville°	.311	60	196	31	61	84	9	1	4	25	4	1	5	20	0	35	9	4
Trafton, Todd, Birmingham	.259	35	116	21	30	52	5	1	5	25	5	3	0	18	0	28	0	3
Trice, Walter, Columbus°	.000	33	21	0	0	0	0	0	0	0	3	0	0	0	0	10	0	0
Turner, Matthew, Greenville	.000	40	3	0	0	0	0	0	0	0	0	0	0	0	0	2	0	0
Upshaw, Lee, Greenville°	.188	22	16	1	3	3	0	0	0	0	4	0	1	0	5	0	0	0
Valdez, Frank, Orlando	.233	111	361	44	84	111	18	0	3	38	4	3	7	44	2	92	4	5
Vanderwal, John, Jacksonville°	.303	77	277	45	84	139	25	3	8	40	0	2	3	39	2	46	6	3
Waggoner, Aubrey, Birmingham°	.257	81	276	57	71	111	17	4	5	32	2	1	2	56	1	60	11	9
Wainhouse, David, Jacksonville°	.056	17	18	0	1	1	0	0	0	1	0	0	0	0	0	11	0	0
Walker, Cleotha, Charlotte†	.265	88	310	49	82	135	15	1	12	45	0	5	0	44	1	72	10	3
Webster, Leonard, Orlando	.262	126	455	69	119	174	31	0	8	71	0	3	0	68	5	57	0	0
Weems, Danny, Greenville	.167	24	6	1	1	1	0	0	0	0	1	0	0	0	0	3	0	0
Wendell, Steven, Greenville°	.143	37	7	0	1	1	0	0	0	0	0	0	0	0	0	2	0	0
Whitt, Ernest, Greenville°	.333	4	12	1	4	5	1	0	0	2	0	0	0	2	0	1	0	0
Wilkins, Richard, Charlotte°	.227	127	449	48	102	173	18	1	17	71	1	3	5	43	5	95	4	5
Williams, Dana, Charlotte	.294	50	180	23	53	86	12	0	7	19	0	2	5	4	1	8	6	1
Wilson, Michael, Huntsville	.220	83	255	34	56	67	9	1	0	16	11	0	0	39	0	30	9	6
Winston, Darrin, Jacksonville	.000	47	2	0	0	0	0	0	0	0	0	0	0	0	0	1	0	0
Witmeyer, Ronald, Huntsville°	.319	27	91	18	29	48	4	0	5	18	0	0	2	15	0	16	0	0
Wohlers, Mark, Greenville	.000	14	1	0	0	0	0	0	0	0	0	0	0	0	0	1	0	0
Wright, George, Memphis†	.216	18	51	6	11	17	0	0	2	5	1	0	1	11	0	11	0	1
Xavier, Joseph, Greenville°	.238	64	189	11	45	54	6	0	1	17	0	3	1	16	0	39	3	2
Yan, Julian, Knoxville	.244	113	389	55	95	164	18	3	15	48	0	4	6	25	1	108	2	1
Zarranz, Fernando, Charlotte	.000	51	1	0	0	0	0	0	0	0	0	0	0	0	0	1	0	0
Zosky, Edward, Knoxville	.271	115	450	53	122	165	20	7	3	45	6	3	5	26	1	73	3	13

The following pitchers, listed alphabetically by club, with games in parentheses, had no plate appearances, primarily through use of designated hitters:

BIRMINGHAM—Alvarez, Wilson (7); Cedeno, Vinicio (21); Cortes, Argenis (8); DeLaCruz, Carlos (13); Drahman, Brian (50); Fernandez, Alexander (4); Groom, Wedsel (20); Hasler, Curtis (23); Hernandez, Roberto (17); Hudek, John (42); Kennedy, Bo (30); Perschke, Gregory (4); Resnikoff, Robert (14); Reynolds, David (33); Scheid, Richard (25); Ventura, Jose (1).

CHARLOTTE—Davis, Braz (4); Rodriguez, Gabriel (3).

CHATTANOOGA—Foster, Stephen (50); Watson, Steven (1).

COLUMBUS—Bond, Daven (27); Eichhorn, David (10); Normand, Guy (3); Reuss, Jerry (10).

GREENVILLE—Barton, Shawn (15); Diez, Scott (11); Smith, Peter (2); Stanton, Michael (4); Stockam, Douglas (34); Watson, Preston (11).

HUNTSVILLE—Allison, Dana (35); Berg, Richard (33); Briscoe, John (3); Chavez, Samuel (18); Chitren, Stephen (48); Eskew, Daniel (25); Garcia, Apolinar (7); Green, Daryl (13); Grott, Matthew (10); Guzman, Dionini (16); Harris, Ray (12); Harris, Reginald (5); Kracl, Darin (12); MacLeod, Kevin (6); McCoy, Timothy (6); Schock, William (29); Slusarski, Joseph (17); Stancel, Mark (46); Strebeck, Richard (12); Veilleux, Brian (11); Wernig, Patrick (19).

JACKSONVILLE—Davins, James (3); Haney, Christopher (1); Lewis, Richie (11); Peters, Timothy (2); Schmidt, David (3).

KNOXVILLE—Blohm, Peter (30); Cromwell, Nathaniel (27); Guzman, Juan (37); Hall, Darren (28); Hentgen, Patrick (28); Horsman, Vincent (8); Jones, Christopher (35); Jones, Dennis (11); MacDonald, Robert (37); Rauth, Christopher (8); Rogers, James (31); Sanders, Earl (37); Timlin, Michael (17); Williams, Gregory (42); Wishnevski, Robert (20).

MEMPHIS—Campbell, James (40); Centala, Scott (25); Codiroli, Christopher (4); Cole, Victor (46); Cruz, Andres (28); Everson, Gregory (24); Hudson, James (4); Johnston, Joel (4); LeBlanc, Richard (30); Maldonado, Carlos (55); McCormack, Brian (28); Moeller, Dennis (14); Nelson, Douglas (6); Parnell, Mark (17); Pierce, Edward (1); Sanchez, Israel (15); Schaefer, Christopher (1); Smith, Daryl (21); Vaughn, Randall (4); Wagner, Hector (40).

ORLANDO—Ard, John (29); Banks, Willie (28); Erickson, Scott (15); Garces, Richard (15); Hull, Jeffrey (1); Johnson, Gregory (43); Lind, Orlando (25); Meyer, Basil (55); Muh, Steven (9); Neagle, Dennis (17); Redding, Michael (34); Simons, Douglas (29); Stowell, Steven (60); Wassenaar, Robert (52).

GRAND SLAM HOME RUNS—V. Garcia, McRae, Olmstead, 2 each; Batiste, M. Bell, Berry, Bottenfield, A. Brown, Bryant, Conine, Hansen, Magallanes, Nelson, R. Ortiz, Pedre, Posey, Rodgers, Roth, Waggoner, Walker, Wilkins, Witmeyer, Yan, 1 each.

AWARDED FIRST BASE ON CATCHER'S INTERFERENCE—M. Bell 4 (Colbrunn, Dziadkowiec, Merullo, J. Ortiz); Walker 3 (Webster 2, Colbrunn); Mota 2 (Colbrunn, Merullo); Barberie (Wilkins); Berry (Wilkins); Casillas (Hubbard); Dziadkowiec (Merullo); Hansen (Knorr); D. Lee (Wilkins); M. Robinson (Colbrunn); Suero (Wilkins).

CLUB FIELDING

Club	Pct.	G.	PO.	A.	E.	DP.	PB.	Club	Pct.	G.	PO.	A.	E.	DP.	PB.
Chattanooga	.972	144	3678	1434	145	127	15	Memphis	.965	144	3739	1504	188	135	16
Greenville	.968	144	3739	1677	179	148	10	Huntsville	.964	144	3781	1537	196	135	14
Orlando	.968	144	3718	1531	173	117	14	Charlotte	.962	144	3729	1551	207	139	21
Knoxville	.966	144	3759	1470	182	131	19	Birmingham	.958	145	3726	1555	229	132	18
Jacksonville	.965	144	3805	1513	191	116	14	Columbus	.958	144	3753	1533	234	135	27

Triple Plays—Chattanooga, Knoxville.

INDIVIDUAL FIELDING

*Throws lefthanded.

FIRST BASEMEN

Player and Club	Pct.	G.	PO.	A.	E.	DP.	Player and Club	Pct.	G.	PO.	A.	E.	DP.
Bafia, Charlotte	.989	10	85	4	1	9	Marzan, Orlando	.988	65	447	46	6	37
Baldwin, Columbus*	.969	4	30	1	1	3	Merullo, Birmingham	.950	15	106	7	6	12
L. Bell, Charlotte	1.000	28	193	9	0	14	Mikulik, Columbus	1.000	1	9	0	0	0
M. BELL, Greenville*	.993	104	981	85	8	100	Morris, Greenville	1.000	1	12	2	0	2
Canan, Charlotte	.958	5	20	3	1	4	Munoz, Jacksonville	1.000	4	12	2	0	2
Casillas, Chattanooga*	.985	60	433	34	7	48	Olmstead, Orlando*	.988	98	817	55	11	67
Champion, Greenville	.996	30	237	13	1	22	Ortiz, Columbus	1.000	5	34	3	0	4
Cianfrocco, Jacksonville	.992	29	221	23	2	11	Pearson, Chattanooga	.988	24	148	10	2	14
Conine, Memphis	.983	134	1164	95	22	108	Pedre, Memphis	.973	4	31	5	1	2
Coomer, Huntsville	.977	20	154	13	4	20	Penn, Jacksonville*	.992	76	560	43	5	57
Cooper, Columbus	.969	9	57	5	2	7	Plumb, Greenville	1.000	1	8	1	0	4
Davis, Columbus	.966	12	79	7	3	6	Reboulet, Orlando	1.000	1	3	0	0	0
DeFrancesco, Chattanooga	.971	6	34	0	1	1	Reese, Memphis	1.000	1	2	0	0	1
Dunbar, Memphis*	.987	11	70	5	1	5	Resetar, Orlando	1.000	1	1	0	0	0
Fulton, Jacksonville	1.000	5	38	4	0	3	Robinson, Huntsville	.986	100	914	41	14	83
Garcia, Charlotte	.995	23	180	12	1	15	Rodriguez, Jacksonville	.979	34	261	18	6	24
Gonzalez, Columbus	.987	124	1026	63	14	95	Rosario, Chattanooga	1.000	4	19	1	0	4
Hansen, Jacksonville	.971	16	123	9	4	11	Sepanek, Chattanooga*	.986	16	130	7	2	14
Be. Hunter, Columbus	.941	7	45	3	3	7	Smith, Birmingham	.982	6	54	2	1	6
Br. Hunter, Greenville	.984	7	54	6	1	5	Stark, Birmingham	1.000	1	2	0	0	0
Kating, Huntsville	1.000	7	41	4	0	2	Stefero, Columbus	1.000	6	31	3	0	2
Lee, Chattanooga	.984	42	331	27	6	34	Sullivan, Charlotte*	.991	90	762	50	7	73
Maksudian, Knoxville	1.000	2	10	1	0	0	Sutko, Chattanooga	.944	2	17	0	1	2
Maldonado, Greenville	.977	4	40	3	1	5	Thomas, Birmingham	.987	109	954	77	14	86
Maloney, Greenville	1.000	2	6	0	0	2	Trafton, Birmingham	.988	21	155	8	2	13
Marquez, Jacksonville	1.000	7	39	3	0	1	Witmeyer, Huntsville*	.987	25	220	15	3	18
Martinez, Knoxville	.995	83	681	61	4	67	Yan, Knoxville	.984	65	494	46	9	49

Triple Plays—Martinez, Sepanek.

SECOND BASEMEN

Player and Club	Pct.	G.	PO.	A.	E.	DP.	Player and Club	Pct.	G.	PO.	A.	E.	DP.
Acta, Columbus	.917	2	2	9	1	1	Marzan, Orlando	1.000	1	1	0	0	0
BARBERIE, Jacksonville	.977	131	263	322	14	74	Morris, Greenville	1.000	10	26	25	0	5
Bernhardt, Birmingham	.961	140	277	371	26	93	Mota, Columbus	.958	106	247	256	22	58
Branson, Chattanooga	.962	46	95	108	8	31	Munoz, Jacksonville	.951	20	44	34	4	11
Brosius, Huntsville	.977	42	99	111	5	31	Naveda, Columbus	1.000	3	6	3	0	1
Buccheri, Huntsville	.951	50	94	118	11	22	Ocasio, Birmingham	1.000	1	1	1	0	0
Caceres, Birmingham	.920	4	11	12	2	4	Pearson, Chattanooga	1.000	1	6	2	0	1
Casarotti, Greenville	.981	89	181	280	9	54	Ralston, Huntsville	.974	36	75	111	5	25
Cole, Memphis	.957	34	55	77	6	15	Reboulet, Orlando	1.000	29	60	86	0	19
Coomer, Huntsville	.963	27	40	64	4	8	Renteria, Columbus	1.000	4	4	10	0	2
Crockett, Charlotte	.958	103	186	273	20	53	Robinson, Huntsville	1.000	1	2	0	0	0
Duffy, Charlotte	.968	58	148	157	10	49	Schunk, Knoxville	1.000	13	26	33	0	9
Hinzo, 7 Green.-8 Mem.	.984	15	21	40	1	7	Sellner, Chattanooga	.971	66	143	126	8	31
Howard, Memphis	1.000	5	7	12	0	2	Snover, Greenville	.957	5	9	13	1	4
Hubbard, Columbus	.977	35	85	87	4	24	Stairs, Jacksonville	1.000	4	5	7	0	1
Knoblauch, Orlando	.966	116	275	300	20	68	Suero, Birmingham	.963	130	259	333	23	67
Laureano, Memphis	.964	108	193	286	18	66	Taylor, Knoxville	.964	5	11	16	1	2
Lombardozzi, Columbus	.778	2	3	4	2	1	Walker, Charlotte	.889	4	2	6	1	1
Lonigro, Chattanooga	.984	43	82	101	3	21	Xavier, Greenville	.939	38	74	95	11	28
Maloney, Greenville	.969	7	11	20	1	4							

Triple Plays—Sellner, Suero.

THIRD BASEMEN

Player and Club	Pct.	G.	PO.	A.	E.	DP.
Acta, Columbus	.864	34	19	57	12	10
Alfredson, Birmingham	.500	3	0	2	2	0
Berry, Memphis	.922	134	79	238	27	20
Brosius, Huntsville	1.000	1	0	1	0	0
Brown, Birmingham	.833	6	1	4	1	0
Caceres, Birmingham	.968	21	14	47	2	4
Canan, Charlotte	.854	66	60	122	31	11
Cianfrocco, Jacksonville	.918	17	16	29	4	2
Cole, Memphis	.852	15	8	15	4	1
Coomer, Huntsville	.906	16	6	23	3	1
Cooper, Columbus	.923	6	3	9	1	2
DeFrancesco, Chattanooga	1.000	1	2	1	0	0
Duffy, Charlotte	.957	11	7	15	1	1
Fulton, Jacksonville	1.000	4	5	8	0	2
Gaither, Birmingham	.867	6	4	9	2	0
Gonzalez, Columbus	.809	16	13	25	9	0
Griffin, Charlotte	.833	37	29	61	18	10
Hall, Greenville	1.000	1	1	5	0	0
Harris, Columbus	.900	60	31	122	17	14
Hinzo, Greenville	1.000	1	2	0	0	0
Hubbard, Columbus	.889	9	6	18	3	0
Kosco, Jacksonville	.919	28	18	61	7	2
Lane, Chattanooga	.958	79	71	157	10	20
Lonigro, Chattanooga	1.000	12	5	27	0	2
Maksudian, Knoxville	.900	4	3	6	1	0
Maloney, Greenville	.864	14	7	12	3	0
Marzan, Orlando	.778	4	1	6	2	0
Morris, Greenville	.941	26	18	46	4	2
Mota, Columbus	1.000	1	0	2	0	1
Munoz, Jacksonville	1.000	28	13	42	0	2
Naveda, Orlando	.952	12	5	15	1	3
Ortiz, Columbus	1.000	1	2	1	0	0
Quinlan, Knoxville	.920	139	103	252	31	19
Reboulet, Orlando	.913	28	21	74	9	4
REDINGTON, Greenville	.946	112	60	258	18	18
Renteria, Columbus	.926	38	30	82	9	5
Robinson, Huntsville	.714	2	0	5	2	0
Rodriguez, Jacksonville	.899	37	21	77	11	7
Roth, Birmingham	.871	52	20	102	18	8
Royer, Huntsville	.902	130	80	269	38	28
Schunk, Knoxville	.846	4	4	7	2	1
Scott, Charlotte	.941	34	25	102	8	13
Sellner, Chattanooga	.908	59	41	116	16	18
Smith, Birmingham	.930	67	49	136	14	13
Stairs, Jacksonville	.864	51	37	90	20	3
Valdez, Orlando	.879	107	53	201	35	15
Xavier, Greenville	1.000	1	1	0	0	0

Triple Play—Lane.

SHORTSTOPS

Player and Club	Pct.	G.	PO.	A.	E.	DP.
Acta, Columbus	1.000	3	4	12	0	2
Alfredson, Birmingham	.625	5	5	10	9	2
Alva, Greenville	.945	15	24	45	4	9
Arias, Charlotte	.915	116	171	284	42	68
Benavides, Chattanooga	.971	55	76	157	7	28
Branson, Chattanooga	.933	18	27	43	5	9
Brosius, Huntsville	.928	100	154	307	36	60
Buccheri, Huntsville	1.000	1	1	0	0	0
Busby, Birmingham	.925	101	180	288	38	65
Caceres, Birmingham	.964	38	49	111	6	22
Canan, Charlotte	1.000	4	0	9	0	1
Castilla, Greenville	.971	46	71	167	7	39
Cedeno, Columbus	.911	129	167	354	51	66
Cole, Memphis	.941	43	48	96	9	22
Cordero, Jacksonville	.928	130	179	349	41	71
Duffy, Charlotte	.935	35	47	82	9	10
Gaither, Birmingham	1.000	6	5	14	0	3
Gilbert, Orlando	.927	122	157	361	41	57
Hall, Greenville	.892	31	45	87	16	17
Hinzo, 10 Green.-1 Mem.	.926	11	20	30	4	5
Howard, Memphis	.939	113	187	309	32	76
Lombardozzi, Columbus	1.000	2	1	6	0	0
Lonigro, Chattanooga	.951	47	54	120	9	15
Maloney, Greenville	.943	31	40	75	7	19
Matos, Huntsville	.900	45	53	146	22	29
Munoz, Jacksonville	.939	19	27	50	5	12
Olmeda, Greenville	1.000	2	2	1	0	1
Pearson, Chattanooga	.933	33	49	76	9	15
Pino, Greenville	.872	11	17	24	6	8
Quinlan, Knoxville	1.000	3	3	7	0	0
Reboulet, Orlando	.974	27	43	70	3	15
Renteria, Columbus	.881	14	24	28	7	12
Rossy, Greenville	.941	5	9	23	2	4
Roth, Birmingham	.769	3	3	7	3	1
Royer, Huntsville	1.000	1	1	1	0	0
Schunk, Knoxville	.939	33	46	77	8	11
Stairs, Jacksonville	1.000	4	6	9	0	0
Xavier, Greenville	.913	4	10	11	2	5
ZOSKY, Knoxville	.941	115	196	295	31	80

Triple Play—Zosky.

OUTFIELDERS

Player and Club	Pct.	G.	PO.	A.	E.	DP.
Alborano, Memphis*	.958	50	66	2	3	1
Alfredson, Birmingham	.959	38	67	3	3	0
Ansley, Columbus	.949	108	198	7	11	2
Anthony, Columbus*	1.000	2	3	0	0	0
Baldwin, Columbus*	.982	67	105	4	2	1
Batiste, Greenville	.952	89	172	7	9	0
A. Brown, Huntsville	.987	75	143	6	2	1
J. Brown, Orlando	.970	135	316	12	10	4
K. Brown, Birmingham	.750	3	1	2	1	0
Bryant, Chattanooga	.974	36	70	6	2	0
Buccheri, Huntsville	.979	35	91	3	2	1
Canan, Charlotte	.985	43	60	7	1	2
Canseco, Huntsville	.953	93	157	5	8	2
Carter, Greenville	1.000	13	20	0	0	0
Casey, Columbus*	.913	16	21	0	2	0
Casillas, Chattanooga*	1.000	25	51	1	0	0
Cianfrocco, Jacksonville	.900	6	7	2	1	0
Cole, Memphis	1.000	3	3	0	0	0
Colvard, Chattanooga	.961	82	142	6	6	2
Cooper, Columbus	1.000	9	15	1	0	0
Crockett, Charlotte	.987	41	75	2	1	0
Dean, 21 Col.-21 Green.	.938	42	70	5	5	1
Dunbar, Memphis*	.976	53	78	4	2	1
Faulk, Jacksonville*	.959	51	91	2	4	0
Finley, Chattanooga*	.989	110	256	6	3	1
Forney, Chattanooga	.948	89	158	5	9	0
Fulton, Jacksonville	1.000	2	2	1	0	0
C. Garcia, Birmingham*	.935	17	28	1	2	0
V. Garcia, Charlotte	1.000	28	26	3	0	1
Grayum, Charlotte	.967	96	144	3	5	0
Griffin, Charlotte	.980	28	47	3	1	0
Hannon, Charlotte	.984	85	123	4	2	0
Hansen, Jacksonville	.971	99	166	3	5	0
Hayden, Chattanooga*	.979	69	128	9	3	1
Hernandez, Jacksonville	.986	107	203	14	3	0
Hinzo, Memphis	1.000	6	3	2	0	2
Hubbard, Columbus	.987	34	71	5	1	2
Be. Hunter, Columbus	.973	122	241	10	7	4
Br. Hunter, Greenville	.955	81	135	13	7	1
Jenkins, Columbus	.958	49	66	3	3	1
Jeter, Knoxville	.962	129	290	11	12	1
Jose, Greenville	.918	57	117	6	11	1
Kating, Huntsville	1.000	60	116	3	0	1
Koslofski, Memphis	.975	115	221	16	6	1
Kowitz, Greenville*	1.000	20	40	1	0	0
Lee, Birmingham	.960	119	188	6	8	0
Lewis, Huntsville	1.000	71	186	6	0	2
Magallanes, Birmingham	.972	121	270	9	8	0
Maksudian, Knoxville	.974	70	106	8	3	2
Marquez, Jacksonville	.750	7	3	0	1	0
Martin, Greenville*	.967	111	200	8	7	0
Marzan, Birmingham	1.000	4	5	2	0	0
McCray, Birmingham	.976	59	156	8	4	2
McRae, Memphis	.975	115	265	8	7	2
Mikulik, Columbus	.929	28	38	1	3	0
MOORE, Memphis	.996	106	224	6	1	2
Morgan, Orlando*	.992	133	226	12	2	1
Morris, Greenville	.958	18	20	3	1	1
Naveda, Orlando	.923	16	23	1	2	0
Nelson, Chattanooga	.984	67	174	7	3	4
Nunez, Columbus	.969	101	151	7	5	3
Nyssen, Columbus	.950	11	18	1	1	0
Ortiz, Orlando	.955	58	100	6	5	1
Penn, Jacksonville*	.968	20	29	1	1	0
Randle, Orlando*	.985	97	189	10	3	2
Reboulet, Orlando	.800	4	4	0	1	0
Rivera, Charlotte	.980	29	45	4	1	0
Roberson, Charlotte	1.000	31	63	1	0	0
Rodgers, Knoxville	.974	139	330	11	9	1
Rodriguez, Jacksonville	1.000	7	6	0	0	0
Royer, Huntsville	1.000	5	7	1	0	0
Santana, Jacksonville	.993	81	144	7	1	0
Schunk, Knoxville	.949	28	37	0	2	0
Simmons, Huntsville	.968	36	56	4	2	0
Stairs, Jacksonville	.935	18	28	1	2	0
Sullivan, Charlotte*	1.000	5	3	0	0	0
Tedder, Birmingham*	1.000	1	1	0	0	0
Tomberlin, Greenville*	.971	55	95	4	3	1
Trafton, Birmingham	.969	13	27	4	1	2
Vanderwal, Jacksonville*	.991	71	106	4	1	0
Waggoner, Birmingham	.971	80	164	3	5	0
Walker, Charlotte	.973	68	105	4	3	0
Williams, Charlotte	.953	46	79	3	4	0
Wilson, Huntsville	.979	77	178	5	4	2
Wright, Memphis	.964	15	27	0	1	0

CATCHERS

Player and Club	Pct.	G.	PO.	A.	E.	DP.	PB.	Player and Club	Pct.	G.	PO.	A.	E.	DP.	PB.
Borrelli, Huntsville	.987	27	142	14	2	0	3	Mayne, Memphis	.983	92	591	61	11	10	4
Brito, Huntsville	1.000	56	307	36	0	3	4	Merullo, Birmingham	.965	85	455	44	18	4	11
Brown, Birmingham	.981	64	341	30	7	4	5	Mizerock, Greenville	1.000	1	8	0	0	0	1
Campbell, Birmingham	.960	3	22	2	1	0	1	Monzon, Knoxville	1.000	1	9	1	0	0	1
Carcione, Huntsville	.991	24	96	12	1	0	3	Natal, Jacksonville	.975	58	344	46	10	4	7
Colbrunn, Jacksonville	.981	98	698	58	15	4	7	Ortiz, Columbus	.964	32	159	30	7	0	7
Deak, Greenville	.985	61	353	45	6	4	4	Pedre, Memphis	.960	49	270	38	13	3	11
DeFrancesco, Chattanooga	.993	53	265	37	2	6	3	Plumb, Greenville	.982	44	204	19	4	1	2
Dziadkowiec, Knoxville	.988	38	226	25	3	4	2	Posey, Charlotte	1.000	22	117	13	0	2	4
Eccles, Orlando	.980	17	87	11	2	1	2	Reese, Memphis	.962	14	45	5	2	0	1
EUSEBIO, Columbus	.994	86	558	69	4	5	14	Resetar, Orlando	.994	30	160	12	1	0	6
Hubbard, Columbus	.952	11	54	6	3	1	3	Rosario, Chattanooga	.984	56	275	30	5	1	7
Knorr, Knoxville	.978	96	599	72	15	5	14	Stark, Birmingham	1.000	5	4	0	0	0	1
Kuld, Huntsville	.974	54	307	34	9	4	4	Stefero, Charlotte	.979	16	87	7	2	1	2
Makarewicz, Columbus	.990	28	174	17	2	0	3	Sutko, Chattanooga	.992	50	334	33	3	3	5
Maksudian, Knoxville	.973	17	97	12	3	1	2	Trafton, Jacksonville	.958	4	22	1	1	0	0
Maldonado, Greenville	1.000	4	23	1	0	0	0	Webster, Orlando	.987	101	629	70	9	6	6
Mann, Greenville	.983	41	249	38	5	4	3	Whitt, Greenville	1.000	4	14	1	0	0	0
Marquez, Jacksonville	1.000	1	5	0	0	0	0	Wilkins, Charlotte	.984	118	740	103	14	11	15

PITCHERS

Player and Club	Pct.	G.	PO.	A.	E.	DP.	Player and Club	Pct.	G.	PO.	A.	E.	DP.
Allen, Columbus*	.906	22	5	24	3	1	Horsman, Knoxville*	1.000	8	1	4	0	0
Allison, Huntsville*	1.000	35	2	8	0	0	Hudek, Birmingham	.958	42	8	15	1	1
Alvarez, Birmingham*	1.000	7	1	3	0	0	Hudson, Memphis	1.000	4	0	2	0	0
ARD, Orlando	1.000	29	15	31	0	1	Ilsley, Columbus*	.917	12	4	18	2	0
Banks, Orlando	.897	28	11	15	3	0	Jeffery, Chattanooga	.895	31	4	13	2	0
Banning, Chattanooga	.980	31	18	30	1	4	G. Johnson, Orlando	.800	43	0	4	1	0
Barnes, Jacksonville	.923	29	8	40	4	3	Le. Johnson, Greenville	.875	9	3	4	1	1
Barton, Greenville*	.800	15	2	2	1	0	Ll. Johnson, Greenville*	1.000	28	12	31	0	4
Bauer, Columbus	.875	34	3	4	1	1	Johnston, Memphis	1.000	4	0	3	0	0
Bennett, Jacksonville	1.000	37	6	8	0	0	A. Jones, Jacksonville	.714	5	2	3	2	1
Berg, Huntsville	.818	33	3	6	2	0	C. Jones, Knoxville	.706	35	4	8	5	2
Blohm, Knoxville	1.000	30	10	17	0	0	D. Jones, Knoxville*	.800	11	1	3	1	0
Boltz, Greenville*	.950	28	9	29	2	2	Juden, Columbus	.857	11	2	4	1	0
Bond, Columbus	.889	27	1	7	1	1	Kaiser, Chattanooga	.962	33	7	18	1	1
Bottenfield, Jacksonville	.970	29	12	20	1	2	Kallevig, Charlotte	1.000	15	1	10	0	0
Bowen, Columbus	.917	18	3	8	1	1	Kazmierczak, Charlotte	.909	18	3	17	2	0
Brito, Jacksonville	.909	18	8	22	3	2	Kennedy, Birmingham	.878	30	10	33	6	2
Brown, Huntsville	1.000	4	0	1	0	1	Kilner, Greenville*	1.000	28	2	3	0	0
Browning, Columbus	.909	16	3	7	1	3	Kracl, Huntsville	.700	12	4	3	3	1
Bruno, Chattanooga	1.000	20	3	2	0	0	Lazor, Chattanooga*	.944	31	3	14	1	1
Bullinger, Charlotte	1.000	9	8	7	0	0	LeBlanc, Memphis	.938	30	14	16	2	1
Campbell, Memphis*	1.000	40	7	14	0	2	Leibrandt, Greenville*	1.000	2	0	3	0	1
Cano, Columbus	1.000	7	0	2	0	0	Lewis, Jacksonville	1.000	11	0	2	0	0
Carter, Jacksonville	.857	52	7	17	4	0	Lind, Orlando	1.000	25	6	10	0	0
Castillo, Charlotte	.917	18	5	17	2	0	Lopez, Charlotte	.923	15	7	17	2	0
Cedeno, Birmingham	.857	20	4	2	1	1	MacDonald, Knoxville*	.962	37	5	20	1	4
Centala, Memphis	.882	25	13	17	4	6	MacLeod, Huntsville*	1.000	6	1	5	0	0
Chavez, Huntsville*	.846	18	4	7	2	1	Maldonado, Memphis	1.000	55	4	8	0	1
Chitren, Huntsville	1.000	48	3	7	0	0	Malloy, Jacksonville	1.000	8	3	8	0	0
Codiroli, Memphis	1.000	4	0	3	0	0	Marchok, Jacksonville	1.000	25	2	6	0	0
Coffman, Charlotte	.960	14	7	17	1	0	Martinez, Knoxville	1.000	3	0	1	0	1
Cole, Memphis	.926	46	3	22	2	1	Masters, Jacksonville	.714	20	2	3	2	0
Cortes, Birmingham	1.000	8	1	1	0	0	McCormack, Memphis	1.000	28	5	12	0	1
Costello, Columbus	1.000	35	3	5	0	1	McCoy, Huntsville*	1.000	6	0	2	0	0
Credeur, Columbus*	.800	11	0	4	1	0	Meyer, Orlando	1.000	55	7	9	0	0
Cromwell, Knoxville*	.889	27	5	11	2	0	Minutelli, Chattanooga*	.964	17	9	18	1	2
Cruz, Memphis	.896	28	16	27	5	1	Moeller, Memphis*	.875	14	3	11	2	0
Czarnik, Greenville	.889	21	9	7	2	0	Moscrey, Chattanooga*	.714	41	1	9	4	1
Damian, Charlotte	1.000	7	0	4	0	0	Mount, Charlotte	.857	40	4	14	3	3
DeLaCruz, Birmingham	.923	13	7	17	2	0	Muh, Orlando*	.929	9	3	10	1	0
DelRosario, Greenville	1.000	60	14	28	0	2	Mullino, Charlotte	.897	39	5	21	3	2
Dickson, Charlotte*	1.000	3	0	2	0	0	Nabholz, Jacksonville*	.929	11	5	8	1	0
Dodd, Chattanooga	1.000	32	1	10	0	0	Neagle, Orlando*	1.000	17	4	23	0	2
Drahman, Birmingham	.935	50	9	20	2	0	Nelson, Memphis	1.000	6	3	5	0	0
Dunbar, Memphis*	1.000	3	1	0	0	0	Osuna, Columbus*	1.000	60	5	12	0	1
Eichhorn, Columbus	1.000	10	0	3	0	0	Parnell, Memphis	.500	17	0	2	2	0
Erickson, Orlando	1.000	15	8	15	0	2	Perez, Jacksonville	.778	28	3	4	2	0
Eskew, Huntsville	.964	25	7	20	1	2	Perschke, Birmingham	.875	4	1	6	1	0
Everson, Memphis	.900	24	1	17	2	1	Peters, Jacksonville	1.000	2	1	0	0	0
Fernandez, Birmingham	.750	4	2	4	2	0	Piatt, Columbus	1.000	35	4	7	0	1
Foster, Chattanooga	.947	50	5	13	1	3	Ponte, Columbus	.900	18	4	5	1	1
Galvez, Jacksonville	1.000	1	0	2	0	0	Powell, Chattanooga*	.950	29	3	16	1	0
Garces, Orlando	1.000	15	0	2	0	0	Rauth, Knoxville	1.000	8	0	2	0	0
Garcia, Huntsville	1.000	7	2	8	0	1	Reboulet, Knoxville	1.000	1	0	1	0	0
Gomez, Greenville*	.962	23	7	18	1	2	Redding, Orlando	.917	34	5	6	1	0
Green, Huntsville	.833	13	1	4	1	0	Resnikoff, Birmingham*	.667	14	0	2	1	0
Groom, Birmingham*	.970	20	5	27	1	2	Reuss, Charlotte*	.889	10	3	5	1	0
Grovom, Chattanooga*	1.000	9	1	4	0	0	D. Reynolds, Birmingham	.926	31	6	19	2	4
D. Guzman, Huntsville*	1.000	16	1	14	0	0	S. Reynolds, Columbus	.951	29	12	27	2	1
J. Guzman, Knoxville	.962	37	9	16	1	2	B. Rivera, Greenville	.786	13	7	4	3	1
D. Hall, Knoxville	.900	28	3	6	1	1	H. Rivera, Jacksonville	1.000	18	12	12	0	2
T. Hall, Birmingham*	1.000	33	6	10	0	1	Robinson, Charlotte	.792	21	5	14	5	2
Haney, Jacksonville	1.000	1	1	1	0	0	G. Rodriguez, Charlotte*	1.000	3	0	1	0	0
Ra. Harris, Huntsville*	.960	12	6	18	1	2	R. Rodriguez, Chattanooga*	.864	36	2	17	3	2
Re. Harris, Huntsville	.333	5	1	1	4	0	Rogers, Knoxville	.868	31	11	22	5	2
Harrison, Charlotte*	.882	9	0	15	2	1	Rosario, Charlotte*	.875	28	2	5	1	0
Hartgraves, Columbus*	.958	33	4	19	1	1	Sanchez, Memphis*	1.000	15	3	6	0	0
Hasler, Birmingham	.951	23	15	24	2	2	Sanders, Knoxville	1.000	37	5	18	0	2
Henry, Chattanooga*	1.000	24	5	17	0	1	Satzinger, Greenville	1.000	29	2	3	0	0
Hentgen, Knoxville	1.000	28	7	9	0	2	Schaefer, Memphis	1.000	1	0	1	0	0
Hernandez, Birmingham	1.000	17	7	23	0	0	Scheid, Birmingham*	1.000	25	0	7	0	1

PITCHERS—Continued

Player and Club	Pct.	G.	PO.	A.	E.	DP.
Schmidt, Jacksonville	1.000	3	0	2	0	0
Schock, Huntsville	.930	29	13	27	3	1
Sheehan, Columbus	1.000	8	3	2	0	1
Simon, Columbus	.944	49	4	13	1	0
Simons, Orlando*	.942	29	20	29	3	1
Slocumb, Charlotte	.938	43	3	12	1	1
Slusarski, Huntsville	1.000	17	3	17	0	0
Smith, Memphis	.882	21	7	8	2	1
Sodders, Charlotte*	1.000	15	9	16	0	2
Sossamon, Jacksonville	1.000	7	2	1	0	0
Stancel, Huntsville	1.000	46	5	15	0	1
Stanton, Greenville*	1.000	4	0	1	0	0
Stephens, Birmingham	.903	39	9	19	3	1
Stockam, Greenville*	.750	34	1	2	1	0
Stowell, Orlando*	.900	60	0	9	1	0
Strauss, Charlotte	1.000	24	0	5	0	0
Strebeck, Huntsville	1.000	12	1	1	0	0
Stroud, Charlotte*	1.000	12	1	2	0	0
Tafoya, Columbus	.938	31	2	13	1	0
Timlin, Knoxville	1.000	17	2	8	0	0
Trice, Columbus*	.867	33	9	30	6	2
Turner, Greenville	.571	40	0	4	3	0
Upshaw, Greenville*	.952	22	7	13	1	2
Veilleux, Huntsville	1.000	11	1	2	0	0
Ventura, Birmingham	1.000	1	0	1	0	0
Wagner, Memphis	.975	40	9	30	1	3
Wainhouse, Jacksonville	.792	17	3	16	5	0
Wassenaar, Orlando	1.000	52	10	14	0	2
Watson, Greenville	1.000	11	2	6	0	1
Weems, Greenville	.917	24	5	6	1	0
Wendell, Greenville	.952	36	3	17	1	1
Wernig, Huntsville*	.889	19	3	13	2	4
Williams, Knoxville	.912	42	6	25	3	0
Winston, Jacksonville*	1.000	47	4	12	0	1
Wishnevski, Knoxville	.966	20	9	19	1	0
Wohlers, Greenville	1.000	14	1	1	0	0
Zarranz, Charlotte	.938	51	8	7	1	2

The following players did not have any fielding statistics at the positions indicated or appeared only as a designated hitter, pinch-hitter or pinch-runner: Banning, of; Briscoe, p; K. Brown, p; Casillas, p; Cedeno, of; Conine, 3b; Coomer, p; Davins, p; B. Davis, p; Diez, p; Duffy, p; Finley, p; Grott, p; Hull, p; Ladnier, dh; Martinez, 3b; Morrison, ph; Mota, of; Normand, p; Ocasio, of; Pierce, p; Reese, p; Schunk, p; P. Smith, p; Richardson, dh; Taylor, of; Tedder, 1b; Tomberlin, p; Vaughn, p; S. Watson, p.

CLUB PITCHING

Club	ERA.	G.	CG.	ShO.	Sv.	IP.	H.	R.	ER.	HR.	HB.	BB.	Int. BB.	SO.	WP.	Bk.
Jacksonville	3.17	144	13	15	47	1268.1	1058	557	447	82	44	544	24	1000	56	13
Orlando	3.35	144	17	8	47	1239.1	1114	582	461	81	45	501	16	860	67	16
Memphis	3.67	144	11	7	37	1246.1	1172	625	508	108	47	555	7	872	55	16
Charlotte	3.73	144	14	9	35	1243.0	1208	642	515	107	54	567	42	909	70	9
Columbus	3.86	144	13	13	31	1251.0	1248	676	536	96	47	546	21	916	85	25
Huntsville	3.96	144	10	4	47	1260.1	1229	681	554	101	63	514	15	852	77	12
Knoxville	4.15	145	10	12	36	1253.0	1143	673	578	83	36	675	30	928	106	30
Birmingham	4.18	145	8	5	37	1242.0	1239	717	577	85	63	550	23	811	83	17
Greenville	4.35	144	5	10	36	1246.1	1316	722	603	93	53	575	25	836	90	31
Chattanooga	4.55	144	20	4	37	1226.0	1233	705	620	102	55	599	37	850	85	36

PITCHERS' RECORDS
(Leading Qualifiers for Earned-Run Average Leadership—115 or More Innings)

Pitcher—Club	W.	L.	Pct.	ERA.	G.	GS.	CG.	GF.	ShO.	Sv.	IP.	H.	R.	ER.	HR.	HB.	BB.	Int. BB.	SO.	WP.
Carter, Jacksonville	8	3	.727	1.84	52	7	2	30	1	15	117.1	90	36	24	4	1	33	1	76	3
Wagner, Memphis	12	4	.750	2.03	40	11	1	8	1	1	133.1	114	37	30	7	2	41	0	63	3
Neagle, Orlando*	12	3	.800	2.45	17	17	4	0	1	0	121.1	94	40	33	11	5	31	0	94	2
Simons, Orlando*	15	12	.556	2.54	29	28	5	0	0	0	188.0	160	76	53	13	6	43	2	109	7
Barnes, Jacksonville*	13	7	.650	2.77	29	28	3	0	1	0	201.1	144	78	62	12	9	87	2	213	8
Hentgen, Knoxville	9	5	.643	3.05	28	26	0	0	0	0	153.1	121	57	52	10	3	68	0	142	8
Williams, Knoxville	7	9	.438	3.14	42	12	0	19	0	5	126.0	111	55	44	7	2	39	3	74	6
Brito, Jacksonville	9	7	.563	3.19	18	18	1	0	0	0	115.2	100	57	41	6	3	34	1	49	4
Schock, Huntsville	11	7	.611	3.22	29	28	2	0	0	0	178.2	165	84	64	13	10	57	2	100	12
Centala, Memphis	11	8	.579	3.22	25	25	1	0	0	0	142.1	131	57	51	12	8	66	0	116	5

Departmental Leaders: G—DelRosario, Osuna, Stowell, 60; W—Simons, 15; L—Cromwell, Powell, 14; Pct.—Eskew, .824; GS—Kennedy, Rogers, 30; CG—LeBlanc, Powell, 6; GF—Maldonado, 48; ShO—Blohm, Ilsley, 3; Sv.—Chitren, 27; IP—Barnes, 201.1; H—Banning, S. Reynolds, 181; R—Kaiser, 122; ER—Kaiser, 109; HR—Kaiser, LeBlanc, 21; HB—Kaiser, 12; BB—Kaiser, 109; IBB—Mount, 9; SO—Barnes, 213; WP—J. Guzman, 21.

(All Pitchers—Listed Alphabetically)

Pitcher—Club	W.	L.	Pct.	ERA.	G.	GS.	CG.	GF.	ShO.	Sv.	IP.	H.	R.	ER.	HR.	HB.	BB.	Int. BB.	SO.	WP.
Allen, Columbus*	7	9	.438	3.71	22	22	0	0	0	0	114.0	98	59	47	8	3	70	0	78	15
Allison, Huntsville*	7	1	.875	2.39	35	0	0	14	0	2	52.2	52	14	14	2	0	6	3	38	1
Alvarez, Birmingham*	5	1	.833	4.27	7	7	1	0	0	0	46.1	44	24	22	4	0	25	0	36	2
Ard, Orlando	12	9	.571	3.79	29	29	4	0	2	0	180.1	167	90	76	11	7	85	0	101	8
Banks, Orlando	7	9	.438	3.93	28	28	1	0	0	0	162.2	161	93	71	15	7	98	0	114	6
Banning, Chattanooga	9	10	.474	4.48	31	26	1	1	1	0	164.2	181	96	82	13	8	56	2	77	10
Barnes, Jacksonville*	13	7	.650	2.77	29	28	3	0	1	0	201.1	144	78	62	12	9	87	2	213	8
Barton, Greenville*	1	0	1.000	8.10	15	0	0	11	0	1	16.2	24	15	15	2	1	9	1	8	0
Bauer, Orlando	0	4	.000	2.52	34	0	0	15	0	3	50.0	37	15	14	3	1	21	1	42	4
Bennett, Jacksonville	3	4	.429	3.24	37	0	0	24	0	9	50.0	45	23	18	2	2	13	6	45	0
Berg, Huntsville	3	3	.500	3.93	33	0	0	22	0	4	50.1	51	27	22	4	5	31	0	21	3
Blohm, Knoxville	5	5	.500	4.50	30	12	3	9	3	2	108.0	101	58	54	9	3	37	3	53	5
Boltz, Greenville*	9	10	.474	3.78	28	28	0	0	0	0	159.1	157	81	67	8	2	55	0	98	10
Bond, Columbus	0	3	.000	6.40	27	0	0	15	0	0	32.1	44	25	23	3	3	19	1	21	4
Bottenfield, Jacksonville	12	10	.545	3.41	29	28	2	0	1	0	169.0	158	72	64	14	11	67	1	121	7
Bowen, Columbus	8	4	.667	3.74	18	18	2	0	2	0	113.0	103	59	47	7	0	49	0	109	5
Briscoe, Huntsville	0	0	.000	13.50	3	0	0	0	0	0	4.2	7	7	7	1	0	7	0	7	1
Brito, Jacksonville	9	7	.563	3.19	18	18	1	0	0	0	115.2	100	57	41	6	3	34	1	49	4
A. Brown, Huntsville	0	0	.000	14.40	4	0	0	4	0	0	5.0	7	8	8	1	0	7	0	3	1
K. Brown, Birmingham	0	0	.000	6.00	2	0	0	2	0	0	3.0	2	2	2	1	0	2	0	0	0
Browning, Columbus	3	3	.500	2.59	16	0	0	10	0	4	24.1	22	10	7	3	1	3	1	14	2
Bruno, Chattanooga	1	1	.500	5.93	20	0	0	6	0	1	27.1	25	18	18	1	3	19	1	19	1
Bullinger, Greenville*	3	4	.429	5.11	9	9	0	0	0	0	44.0	42	30	25	7	3	18	0	33	3
Campbell, Memphis*	5	5	.500	2.44	40	12	0	8	0	0	99.2	78	38	27	7	4	32	0	79	1
Cano, Columbus	1	0	1.000	0.63	7	5	0	1	0	0	14.1	11	3	1	0	1	8	1	12	0
Carter, Jacksonville	8	3	.727	1.84	52	7	2	30	1	15	117.1	90	36	24	4	1	33	1	76	3
Casillas, Chattanooga*	0	0	.000	4.50	2	0	0	2	0	0	2.0	2	1	1	0	0	0	0	3	0
Castillo, Huntsville	6	6	.500	3.88	18	18	4	0	1	0	111.1	113	54	48	8	2	27	4	112	5
Cedeno, Birmingham	2	1	.667	3.13	20	2	0	8	0	1	37.1	40	17	13	1	7	17	0	26	3
Centala, Memphis	11	8	.579	3.22	25	25	1	0	0	0	142.1	131	57	51	12	8	66	0	116	5
Chavez, Huntsville*	4	4	.500	6.70	18	5	0	3	0	0	47.0	58	38	35	5	12	61	0	34	1
Chitren, Huntsville	2	4	.333	1.68	48	0	0	39	0	27	53.2	32	18	10	4	3	22	1	61	2
Codiroli, Memphis	1	1	.500	8.10	4	3	0	0	0	0	13.1	16	12	12	3	0	10	0	13	4

Pitcher—Club	W.	L.	Pct.	ERA.	G.	GS.	CG.	GF.	ShO.	Sv.	IP.	H.	R.	ER.	HR.	HB.	BB.	Int. BB.	SO.	WP.
Coffman, Charlotte	7	3	.700	2.03	14	14	5	0	0	0	93.0	77	28	21	10	0	54	0	84	14
Cole, Memphis	3	8	.273	4.35	46	6	0	15	0	4	107.2	91	61	52	6	3	70	2	102	2
Coomer, Huntsville	0	0	.000	9.00	1	0	0	1	0	0	2.0	3	2	2	0	0	0	0	2	0
Cortes, Birmingham	0	0	.000	6.55	8	0	0	3	0	0	11.0	13	8	8	0	1	10	0	9	2
Costello, Columbus	0	5	.000	4.17	35	5	0	20	0	7	45.1	54	31	21	4	1	23	3	39	6
Credeur, Columbus°	1	1	.500	3.52	11	3	0	3	0	0	23.0	17	21	9	0	0	20	0	16	2
Cromwell, Knoxville°	5	14	.263	5.56	27	23	2	2	0	0	121.1	119	85	75	11	4	91	2	79	8
Cruz, Memphis	8	12	.400	3.67	28	28	3	0	1	0	162.0	173	90	66	16	5	47	0	76	5
Czarnik, Greenville	4	4	.500	2.98	21	4	0	7	0	1	57.1	53	28	19	4	4	27	2	31	0
Damian, Charlotte	1	2	.333	6.11	7	1	0	3	0	0	17.2	24	12	12	4	2	3	0	12	1
Davis, Jacksonville	0	0	.000	4.50	3	0	0	2	0	0	6.0	2	4	3	0	0	3	0	7	0
Davis, Charlotte	1	2	.333	9.28	4	3	0	1	0	0	10.2	16	13	11	1	0	14	1	3	3
DeLaCruz, Birmingham	1	7	.125	7.55	13	12	1	1	0	0	53.2	64	55	45	7	2	36	0	30	4
DelRosario, Greenville	7	7	.500	4.05	60	2	0	12	0	1	115.2	128	71	52	4	5	43	5	67	5
Dickson, Charlotte°	2	1	.667	0.38	3	3	1	0	1	0	23.2	13	1	1	0	0	3	0	28	2
Diez, Greenville°	0	0	.000	2.89	11	0	0	2	0	0	9.1	10	3	3	0	0	6	0	7	1
Dodd, Chattanooga	3	0	1.000	2.85	32	0	0	11	0	2	47.1	35	16	15	5	2	24	3	27	6
Drahman, Birmingham	6	4	.600	4.08	50	1	0	31	0	17	90.1	90	50	41	6	3	24	2	72	12
Duffy, Charlotte	0	0	.000	0.00	3	0	0	3	0	0	3.2	2	1	0	0	0	1	0	2	0
Dunbar, Memphis°	0	0	.000	3.00	3	0	0	3	0	0	3.0	1	1	1	1	0	5	0	2	0
Eichhorn, Columbus	3	1	.750	0.57	10	0	0	6	0	1	15.2	14	3	1	1	1	2	0	3	3
Erickson, Orlando	8	3	.727	3.03	15	15	3	0	1	0	101.0	75	38	34	3	5	24	0	69	4
Eskew, Huntsville	14	3	.824	3.34	25	25	0	0	0	0	148.1	133	62	55	8	8	60	1	128	14
Everson, Memphis	3	3	.500	2.43	24	0	0	10	0	2	40.2	33	14	11	1	4	13	2	28	2
Fernandez, Birmingham	3	0	1.000	1.08	4	4	0	0	0	0	25.0	20	7	3	0	0	6	0	27	0
Finley, Chattanooga°	0	0	.000	31.50	2	0	0	2	0	0	2.0	5	7	7	0	1	5	0	0	1
Foster, Chattanooga	5	10	.333	5.34	50	0	0	42	0	20	59.0	69	38	35	6	4	33	4	52	3
Galvez, Jacksonville	0	0	.000	6.75	1	1	0	0	0	0	4.0	6	4	3	1	0	1	0	3	0
Garces, Orlando	2	1	.667	2.08	15	0	0	14	0	8	17.1	17	4	4	0	0	14	2	22	2
Garcia, Huntsville	5	1	.833	3.50	7	7	2	0	0	0	54.0	45	24	21	6	2	18	0	29	3
Gomez, Greenville°	6	8	.429	4.49	23	21	0	1	0	0	124.1	126	75	62	9	2	71	1	94	16
Green, Huntsville	1	0	1.000	6.41	13	0	0	5	0	2	26.2	31	20	19	2	1	12	0	23	0
Groom, Birmingham°	6	8	.429	5.07	20	20	0	0	0	0	115.1	135	81	65	10	2	48	1	66	6
Grott, Huntsville°	0	0	.000	2.87	10	0	0	6	0	1	15.2	8	5	5	1	0	10	0	12	0
Grovom, Chattanooga°	1	3	.250	10.35	9	4	0	2	0	0	20.0	28	23	23	2	1	13	0	15	4
D. Guzman, Huntsville°	5	6	.455	3.58	16	16	0	0	0	0	105.2	89	52	42	9	7	54	1	63	6
J. Guzman, Knoxville	11	9	.550	4.24	37	21	2	7	0	1	157.0	145	84	74	10	3	80	5	138	21
D. Hall, Knoxville	3	5	.375	4.86	28	0	0	13	0	1	33.1	29	23	18	6	1	33	6	28	7
T. Hall, Birmingham°	3	1	.750	4.19	33	2	0	14	0	0	68.2	62	35	32	2	10	36	0	43	7
Haney, Jacksonville°	1	0	1.000	0.00	1	1	0	0	0	0	6.0	6	0	0	0	0	3	0	6	0
Ra. Harris, Huntsville°	4	4	.500	4.31	12	12	1	0	0	0	71.0	75	47	34	7	0	25	0	44	2
Re. Harris, Huntsville	0	2	.000	3.03	5	1	0	0	0	0	29.2	26	12	10	3	4	16	0	34	4
Harrison, Charlotte°	5	3	.625	3.48	9	9	0	0	0	0	54.1	49	25	21	4	2	31	2	41	2
Hartgraves, Columbus°	8	8	.500	4.70	33	14	0	6	0	0	99.2	108	66	52	8	3	48	1	64	6
Hasler, Birmingham	9	6	.600	3.27	23	19	1	2	0	0	123.2	118	61	45	12	8	33	1	58	5
Henry, Chattanooga°	8	8	.500	4.21	24	22	2	0	0	0	143.1	151	74	67	15	3	58	0	95	12
Hentgen, Knoxville	9	5	.643	3.05	28	26	0	0	0	0	153.1	121	57	52	10	3	68	0	142	8
Hernandez, Birmingham	8	5	.615	3.67	17	17	1	0	0	0	108.0	103	57	44	6	6	43	2	62	3
Horsman, Knoxville°	2	1	.667	4.63	8	0	0	2	0	0	11.2	11	7	6	1	0	5	2	10	1
Hudek, Birmingham	6	6	.500	4.58	42	10	0	23	0	4	92.1	84	59	47	9	6	52	3	67	5
Hudson, Memphis	1	3	.250	6.48	4	4	0	0	0	0	16.2	23	15	12	1	2	10	0	5	1
Hull, Orlando	0	0	.000	27.00	1	0	0	0	0	0	0.1	1	2	1	0	0	1	0	1	0
Ilsley, Columbus°	6	4	.600	1.94	12	12	3	0	3	0	83.2	70	26	18	5	3	13	1	70	1
Jeffery, Chattanooga	3	6	.333	4.10	31	9	3	5	1	0	90.0	91	48	41	9	5	34	7	70	1
G. Johnson, Orlando	3	3	.500	2.93	43	0	0	37	0	19	43.0	39	21	14	2	3	15	1	42	2
Le. Johnson, Greenville	0	4	.000	3.31	9	5	0	3	0	0	35.1	38	21	13	3	0	18	1	24	1
Ll. Johnson, Greenville°	5	10	.333	4.11	28	24	3	1	2	1	149.0	159	75	68	17	1	43	1	59	3
Johnston, Memphis	0	0	.000	6.75	4	3	0	1	0	0	6.2	5	9	5	1	0	16	0	6	3
A. Jones, Jacksonville	1	3	.250	4.79	5	3	0	0	0	0	20.2	30	18	11	1	0	6	0	12	2
C. Jones, Knoxville	4	4	.500	5.33	35	0	0	11	0	0	72.2	78	49	43	4	3	38	2	50	4
D. Jones, Knoxville°	0	1	.000	6.66	11	4	0	2	0	1	24.1	14	22	18	1	2	35	0	33	5
Juden, Columbus	1	3	.250	5.37	11	11	0	0	0	0	52.0	55	36	31	2	4	42	2	40	9
Kaiser, Chattanooga	9	11	.450	5.74	33	28	1	1	1	0	171.0	166	122	109	21	12	109	3	123	13
Kallevig, Charlotte	2	2	.500	3.54	15	0	0	4	0	1	28.0	23	12	11	1	2	9	1	14	0
Kazmierczak, Charlotte	6	9	.400	4.37	18	16	1	2	0	0	90.2	89	58	44	8	5	46	1	66	6
Kennedy, Birmingham	11	12	.478	4.73	30	30	3	0	0	0	175.0	175	118	92	12	3	89	1	121	19
Kilner, Greenville°	0	3	.000	2.75	28	0	0	23	0	15	36.0	24	11	11	1	1	28	3	28	0
Kracl, Huntsville	4	6	.400	7.12	12	10	1	0	0	0	54.1	72	50	43	6	2	26	0	31	1
Lazor, Chattanooga°	6	5	.545	3.53	31	8	1	8	0	2	91.2	71	39	36	3	1	55	3	80	4
LeBlanc, Memphis	12	10	.545	3.81	30	29	6	0	1	0	181.2	175	95	77	21	9	70	0	94	3
Leibrandt, Greenville°	1	0	1.000	0.00	2	2	0	0	0	0	13.0	5	4	0	0	0	5	0	12	1
Lewis, Jacksonville	0	0	.000	1.26	11	0	0	8	0	5	14.1	7	2	2	0	0	5	0	14	3
Lind, Orlando	6	4	.600	4.41	25	13	0	9	0	4	87.2	88	47	43	2	4	39	0	82	9
Lopez, Charlotte	1	7	.125	4.18	15	11	0	2	0	0	84.0	97	47	39	4	4	17	2	46	2
MacDonald, Knoxville°	1	2	.333	1.89	36	0	0	29	0	15	57.0	37	17	12	2	0	29	4	54	3
MacLeod, Huntsville°	0	2	.000	5.14	6	3	0	0	0	0	21.0	27	17	12	0	0	11	0	9	2
Maldonado, Memphis	4	5	.444	2.91	55	0	0	48	0	20	77.1	61	29	25	5	1	37	0	77	5
Malloy, Jacksonville	4	1	.800	3.32	8	5	1	1	0	0	43.1	34	17	16	4	2	16	0	25	0
Marchok, Jacksonville°	0	2	.000	2.86	25	0	0	7	0	3	28.1	26	12	9	1	2	16	3	27	3
Martinez, Knoxville	0	0	.000	3.00	3	0	0	3	0	0	3.0	5	1	1	1	0	0	0	3	0
Masters, Jacksonville	0	2	.000	3.46	20	4	0	8	0	0	41.2	28	22	16	2	1	44	2	49	5
McCormack, Memphis	1	1	.500	6.10	28	7	0	9	0	2	62.0	74	48	42	10	2	41	2	46	2
McCoy, Huntsville°	1	1	.500	2.70	6	1	0	1	0	0	13.1	18	8	4	0	0	4	1	17	4
Meyer, Orlando	4	4	.500	4.33	55	0	0	20	0	3	70.2	66	46	34	6	1	40	5	58	7
Minutelli, Chattanooga°	9	5	.643	3.99	17	17	3	0	1	0	108.1	106	52	48	9	2	46	1	75	5
Moeller, Memphis°	7	6	.538	6.25	14	14	0	0	0	0	67.2	79	55	47	11	2	30	1	42	3
Moscrey, Chattanooga°	2	3	.400	5.62	41	0	0	21	0	5	72.2	72	47	36	3	0	40	3	41	6
Mount, Charlotte	11	9	.550	4.15	40	20	2	8	0	0	154.0	154	97	71	12	7	93	9	77	6
Muh, Orlando°	2	1	.667	4.04	9	8	0	0	0	0	42.1	47	21	19	2	1	21	0	23	1
Mullino, Charlotte	3	4	.429	4.52	39	7	0	8	0	1	95.2	98	63	48	12	5	35	5	70	5
Nabholz, Jacksonville°	7	2	.778	3.03	11	11	0	0	0	0	74.1	62	28	25	6	0	27	0	77	6
Neagle, Orlando°	12	3	.800	2.45	17	17	4	0	1	0	121.1	94	40	33	11	5	31	0	94	2
Nelson, Memphis	1	1	.500	2.93	6	1	0	3	0	0	15.1	16	5	5	0	1	3	0	8	0

Pitcher—Club	W.	L.	Pct.	ERA.	G.	GS.	CG.	GF.	ShO.	Sv.	IP.	H.	R.	ER.	HR.	HB.	BB.	Int. BB.	SO.	WP.
Normand, Columbus*	0	0	.000	2.70	3	0	0	1	0	0	3.1	3	1	1	0	0	3	0	4	0
Osuna, Columbus*	7	5	.583	3.38	60	0	0	26	0	6	69.1	57	30	26	4	3	33	2	82	4
Parnell, Memphis	1	1	.500	3.72	17	0	0	8	0	1	29.0	24	13	12	2	2	17	0	28	2
Perez, Jacksonville*	2	2	.500	6.00	28	2	0	8	0	1	42.0	36	34	28	5	1	34	2	39	4
Perschke, Birmingham	3	1	.750	2.60	4	4	1	0	0	0	27.2	20	9	8	3	3	6	0	18	1
Peters, Jacksonville	0	0	.000	4.50	2	0	0	0	0	0	2.0	3	1	1	0	0	2	0	1	0
Piatt, Jacksonville	5	1	.833	2.20	35	0	0	22	0	6	49.0	30	17	12	1	3	29	2	51	1
Pierce, Memphis*	0	0	.000	0.00	1	0	0	0	0	0	1.0	0	0	0	0	1	0	1	0	0
Ponte, Columbus	1	2	.333	3.00	18	0	0	3	0	0	33.0	32	14	11	2	1	17	1	30	2
Powell, Chattanooga*	8	14	.364	3.55	29	27	6	1	1	0	185.0	172	89	73	10	6	57	5	132	11
Rauth, Knoxville	0	1	.000	6.75	8	0	0	1	0	0	17.1	23	16	13	2	1	13	0	16	2
Reboulet, Orlando	0	0	.000	0.00	1	0	0	1	0	0	1.0	0	0	0	0	0	0	0	0	0
Redding, Orlando	5	2	.714	2.81	34	5	0	9	0	1	73.2	60	32	23	7	1	37	0	44	9
Reese, Memphis	0	0	.000	9.00	1	0	0	0	0	0	2.0	3	2	2	0	2	3	0	1	0
Resnikoff, Birmingham*	1	0	1.000	7.91	14	0	0	7	0	0	19.1	24	17	17	2	2	11	2	16	1
Reuss, Columbus*	1	0	1.000	1.66	10	0	0	3	0	0	21.2	23	4	4	1	1	4	0	11	0
D. Reynolds, Birmingham	4	4	.500	3.09	31	1	0	13	0	5	75.2	80	29	26	4	3	28	1	48	1
S. Reynolds, Columbus	9	10	.474	4.81	29	27	2	1	1	0	155.1	181	104	83	14	5	70	1	92	6
B. Rivera, Greenville	1	4	.200	6.58	13	13	0	0	0	0	52.0	68	40	38	6	3	26	0	32	10
H. Rivera, Jacksonville	6	6	.500	3.60	18	18	2	0	0	0	105.0	93	46	42	10	1	44	0	60	1
Robinson, Charlotte	5	6	.455	3.99	21	13	0	6	0	0	94.2	111	47	42	8	4	36	1	56	7
G. Rodriguez, Charlotte*	0	1	.000	13.50	3	0	0	1	0	0	2.2	4	8	4	0	0	5	2	0	0
R. Rodriguez, Chattanooga*	2	2	.500	4.36	36	2	1	22	0	7	53.2	52	29	26	5	6	48	5	39	7
Rogers, Knoxville	9	12	.429	4.47	31	30	2	0	1	0	173.1	179	98	86	8	6	104	1	113	12
Rosario, Charlotte*	1	1	.500	2.55	28	0	0	10	0	4	35.1	26	12	10	1	2	19	2	42	1
Sanchez, Memphis*	1	2	.333	3.10	15	0	0	13	0	6	29.0	21	11	10	3	0	8	0	32	3
Sanders, Knoxville	4	4	.500	4.75	37	0	0	17	0	2	60.2	63	41	32	4	3	57	7	39	14
Satzinger, Greenville	1	2	.333	4.02	29	0	0	14	0	1	40.1	32	20	18	4	6	22	2	45	5
Schaefer, Memphis	0	0	.000	0.00	1	1	0	0	0	0	3.1	2	0	0	0	0	3	0	1	0
Scheid, Birmingham*	2	1	.667	2.22	25	0	0	13	0	4	44.2	37	17	11	0	1	21	4	37	4
Schmidt, Jacksonville	0	1	.000	4.50	3	2	0	0	0	0	6.0	3	3	3	1	1	0	0	4	0
Schock, Huntsville	11	7	.611	3.22	29	28	2	0	0	0	178.2	165	84	64	13	10	57	2	100	12
Schunk, Knoxville	0	0	.000	0.00	2	0	0	2	0	0	2.1	3	0	0	0	0	0	0	1	0
Sheehan, Columbus	0	1	.000	4.50	8	4	0	1	0	0	22.0	23	12	11	2	2	16	0	18	2
Simon, Columbus	5	2	.714	3.32	49	1	0	12	0	2	86.2	88	41	32	8	3	34	2	59	5
Simons, Orlando*	15	12	.556	2.54	29	28	5	0	0	0	188.0	160	76	53	13	6	43	2	109	7
Slocumb, Charlotte	3	1	.750	2.15	43	0	0	37	0	12	50.1	50	20	12	0	3	32	5	37	4
Slusarski, Huntsville	6	8	.429	4.47	17	17	2	0	0	0	108.2	114	65	54	9	3	35	0	75	5
D. Smith, Memphis	2	1	.667	3.17	21	0	0	5	0	1	48.1	46	27	17	1	0	23	0	48	10
P. Smith, Greenville	0	0	.000	0.00	2	2	0	0	0	0	3.1	1	0	0	0	0	1	0	1	0
Sodders, Charlotte*	1	9	.100	4.64	15	14	0	1	0	0	85.1	89	50	44	12	2	46	1	57	1
Sossamon, Jacksonville	0	0	.000	3.95	7	0	0	1	0	1	13.2	19	8	6	2	0	5	0	17	0
Stancel, Huntsville	5	8	.385	4.39	46	4	0	24	0	7	96.1	102	59	47	6	8	47	5	51	10
Stanton, Greenville	0	1	.000	1.59	4	4	0	0	0	0	5.2	7	1	1	1	0	3	0	4	0
Stephens, Birmingham	7	10	.412	3.65	39	16	0	20	0	7	123.1	122	65	50	6	6	61	6	74	7
Stockam, Greenville*	1	4	.200	5.21	34	0	0	9	0	2	46.2	59	29	27	4	2	21	2	33	5
Stowell, Orlando*	1	3	.250	4.39	60	0	0	20	0	6	53.1	54	33	26	2	2	33	4	36	7
Strauss, Charlotte	2	1	.667	3.45	24	0	0	14	0	2	44.1	39	21	17	3	4	21	6	44	4
Strebeck, Huntsville	1	1	.500	5.02	12	0	0	7	0	2	14.1	13	8	8	2	1	6	0	7	0
Stroud, Charlotte*	2	5	.286	3.58	12	6	1	4	1	2	37.2	28	19	15	4	0	26	0	32	2
Tafoya, Columbus	0	5	.000	6.75	31	0	0	11	0	2	40.0	55	36	30	4	2	18	2	21	5
Timlin, Knoxville	1	2	.333	1.73	17	0	0	15	0	8	26.0	20	6	5	0	1	7	1	21	0
Tomberlin, Greenville*	0	0	.000	0.00	1	0	0	0	0	0	1.0	1	0	0	0	0	1	0	0	0
Trice, Columbus*	6	7	.462	4.02	33	22	2	1	0	0	152.1	153	80	68	17	9	33	2	91	4
Turner, Greenville	6	4	.600	2.66	40	0	0	26	0	4	67.2	59	24	20	6	3	29	2	60	4
Upshaw, Greenville*	6	12	.333	4.42	22	21	1	0	0	0	128.1	148	77	63	6	6	58	0	75	13
Vaughn, Memphis	0	0	.000	12.46	4	0	0	2	0	0	4.1	6	6	6	0	0	9	0	4	1
Veilleux, Huntsville*	1	0	1.000	3.27	11	0	0	4	0	1	11.0	13	4	4	1	0	3	0	4	0
Ventura, Birmingham	0	0	.000	32.40	1	0	0	0	0	0	1.2	6	6	6	0	0	2	0	1	1
Wagner, Memphis	12	4	.750	2.03	40	11	1	8	1	1	133.1	114	37	30	7	2	41	0	63	3
Wainhouse, Jacksonville	7	7	.500	4.33	17	16	2	0	0	0	95.2	97	59	46	7	7	47	2	59	2
Wassenaar, Orlando	8	5	.615	2.98	52	1	0	17	0	6	96.2	85	39	32	7	3	20	2	65	3
P. Watson, Greenville	3	1	.750	8.44	11	0	0	2	0	0	16.0	25	17	15	1	3	11	0	8	1
S. Watson, Chattanooga	0	0	.000	9.00	1	0	0	0	0	0	3.0	7	6	3	0	1	2	0	2	1
Weems, Greenville	3	2	.600	6.75	24	5	0	3	0	0	62.2	73	53	47	12	2	37	3	43	6
Wendell, Greenville	4	9	.308	5.74	36	13	1	13	1	2	91.0	105	70	58	5	11	48	2	85	8
Wernig, Huntsville*	5	4	.556	3.27	19	11	2	3	1	1	96.1	86	50	35	12	7	36	0	59	5
Williams, Knoxville	7	9	.438	3.14	42	12	0	19	0	5	126.0	111	55	44	7	2	39	3	74	6
Winston, Jacksonville	6	2	.750	2.14	47	0	0	20	0	7	63.0	38	16	15	3	0	28	2	45	5
Wishnevski, Knoxville	5	6	.667	3.83	20	17	1	3	1	0	105.2	84	54	45	7	4	39	0	74	10
Wohlers, Greenville	0	1	.000	4.02	14	0	0	11	0	0	15.2	14	7	7	0	1	14	0	20	1
Zarranz, Charlotte	0	2	.000	2.09	51	0	0	26	0	13	82.0	64	24	19	6	1	31	2	51	2

BALKS—Minutelli, 13; Gomez, 12; J. Guzman, 8; Boltz, Stowell, Trice, 7 each; S. Reynolds, 6; Banning, 5; Cromwell, Cruz, Rogers, Williams, 4 each; Allen, Bennett, Eskew, Finley, Ra. Harris, Hentgen, Kaiser, Masters, R. Rodriguez, Scheid, Wishnevski, 3 each; Alvarez, Ard, Bottenfield, Campbell, Centala, Cole, Costello, Foster, Groom, Grovom, D. Guzman, T. Hall, Henry, Ll. Johnson, Juden, Moeller, Mullino, Powell, Redding, Robinson, Simon, Turner, Wendell, 2 each; Banks, Barnes, Berg, Bowen, Bullinger, Carter, Castillo, Czarnik, DeLaCruz, DelRosario, Diez, Drahman, Erickson, Garcia, D. Hall, Hernandez, C. Jones, D. Jones, Kennedy, Kilner, LeBlanc, Lind, Lopez, Marchok, McCormack, McCoy, Moscrey, Mount, Nabholz, Nelson, Osuna, Rauth, D. Reynolds, H. Rivera, R. Rodriguez, Sanchez, Satzinger, Schock, Sheehan, Stephens, Upshaw, Wassenaar, 1 each.

COMBINATION SHUTOUTS—Fernandez-Stephens, Hasler-Cedeno-Hudek, Hasler-Scheid-Hudek, Hernandez-Stephens, Stephens-Reynolds, Birmingham; Castillo-Mullino-Rosario-Slocumb, Coffman-Slocumb, Harrison-Mount-Slocumb, Harrison-Zarranz, Kazmierczak-Zarranz, Robinson-Mullino, Charlotte; Allen-Bauer-Osuna, Allen-Osuna-Bond, Allen-Tafoya-Bond, Cano-Trice-Bauer-Costello, Ilsley-Simon, Reynolds-Bond-Reuss-Browning, Sheehan-Browning-Osuna, Columbus; Boltz-Czarnik, Boltz-Weems-Kilner, Boltz-Wendell-Kilner, Czarnik-Satzinger-Diez-Wohlers, Gomez-Czarnik, Upshaw-Czarnik, Wendell-Turner, Greenville; Eskew-Chitren, Schock-Chitren, Slusarski-Allison-Stancel, Huntsville; Bottenfield-Winston 2, Bottenfield-Marchok-Carter, Bottenfield-Sossamon, Bottenfield-Winston-Masters, Brito-Wendell, Malloy-Carter-Bennett, Rivera-Winston-Wainhouse-Masters, Schmidt-Barnes-Bennett-Winston, Wainhouse-Bennett, Wainhouse-Carter, Wainhouse-Piatt, Jacksonville; Guzman-Timlin 2, Hentgen-Jones 2, Guzman-MacDonald, Hentgen-Hall-Williams, Hentgen-MacDonald, Knoxville; Campbell-Wagner-Cole-Maldonado, Centala-Campbell-Wagner, Cruz-Cole-Maldonado, Wagner-McCormack-Parnell, Memphis; Banks-Meyer-Redding-Johnson, Lind-Wassenaar-Stowell-Garces, Redding-Wassenaar-Garces, Simons-Stowell-Meyer, Orlando.

NO-HIT GAMES—Wishnevski, Knoxville, defeated Charlotte, 3-0 (first game), June 4; Bottenfield, Jacksonville, defeated Orlando, 1-0, June 17; Castillo, Charlotte, defeated Huntsville, 4-0 (first game), July 13; Blohm, Knoxville, defeated Greenville, 2-0 (six innings), August 9; Ard, Orlando, defeated Chattanooga, 2-0 (first game), August 30.

Texts League

CLASS AA

**Leading Batter
ERIC KARROS
San Antonio**

**League President
CARL SAWATSKI**

**Leading Pitcher
ANTHONY YOUNG
Jackson**

CHAMPIONSHIP WINNERS IN PREVIOUS YEARS

Year	Team	Avg
1888	Dallas	.671
1889	Houston	.551
1890	Galveston	.705
1892	Houston	.741
	Houston	.613
1895	Dallas	.754
	Fort Worth°	.750
1896	Fort Worth	.757
	Houston°	.679
	Galveston	.548
1897	San Antonio†	.657
	Galveston†	.717
1898	League disbanded.	
1899	Galveston	.632
	Galveston	.762
1900-01	Did not operate.	
1902	Corsicana	.866
	Corsicana	.682
1903	Paris-Waco	.615
	Dallas°	.648
1904	Corsicana°	.615
	Fort Worth	.800
1905	Fort Worth	.545
1906	Fort Worth	.677
	Cleburne x	.609
1907	Austin	.629
1908	San Antonio	.664
1909	Houston	.601
1910	Dallas†	.586
	Houston†	.586
1911	Austin	.575
1912	Houston	.626
1913	Houston†	.620
1914	Houston†	.671
	Waco†	.671
1915	Waco	.592
1916	Waco	.587
1917	Dallas	.600
1918	Dallas	.584
1919	Shreveport°	.677
	Fort Worth	.651
1920	Fort Worth	.703
	Fort Worth	.750
1921	Fort Worth	.691
	Fort Worth	.662
1922	Fort Worth	.694
	Fort Worth	.711
1923	Fort Worth	.632
1924	Fort Worth	.689
	Fort Worth	.763
1925	Fort Worth	.711
	Fort Worth y	.653
1926	Dallas	.574
1927	Wichita Falls	.654

Year	Team	Avg
1928	Houston°	.679
	Wichita Falls	.731
1929	Dallas°	.588
	Wichita Falls	.620
1930	Wichita Falls	.697
	Fort Worth°	.632
1931	Houston a	.625
	Houston	.734
1932	Beaumont°	.640
	Dallas	.727
1933	Houston	.623
	San Antonio (4th)§	.523
1934	Galveston‡	.579
1935	Oklahoma City‡	.590
1936	Dallas	.604
	Tulsa (3rd)§	.519
1937	Oklahoma City	.635
	Fort Worth (3rd)§	.535
1938	Beaumont	.635
1939	Houston	.606
	Fort Worth (4th)§	.540
1940	Houston‡	.652
1941	Houston	.673
	Dallas (4th)§	.519
1942	Beaumont	.605
	Shreveport (2nd)§	.576
1943-44-45	Did not operate.	
1946	Fort Worth	.656
	Dallas (2nd)§	.591
1947	Houston‡	.623
1948	Fort Worth‡	.601
1949	Fort Worth	.649
	Tulsa (2nd)§	.584
1950	Beaumont	.595
	San Antonio (4th)§	.513
1951	Houston‡	.619
1952	Dallas	.571
	Shreveport (3rd)§	.522
1953	Dallas‡	.571
1954	Shreveport	.559
	Houston (2nd)§	.553
1955	Dallas	.581
	Shreveport (3rd)§	.540
1956	Houston‡	.623
1957	Dallas	.662
	Houston (2nd)§	.630
1958	Fort Worth	.582
	Cor. Christi (3rd)§	.507
1959	Victoria	.589
	Austin (2nd)§	.548
1960	Rio Grande Valley	.590
	Tulsa (3rd)	.528
1961	Amarillo	.643
	San Antonio (3rd)§	.532

Year	Team	Avg
1962	El Paso	.571
	Tulsa (2nd)§	.550
1963	San Antonio	.564
	Tulsa (3rd)§	.529
1964	San Antonio‡	.607
1965	Tulsa	.574
	Albuquerque b	.550
1966	Arkansas	.579
1967	Albuquerque	.557
1968	Arkansas	.586
	El Paso b	.562
1969	Amarillo	.593
	Memphis b	.504
1970	Albuquerque a	.615
	Memphis	.507
1971	Did not operate as league—clubs were members of Dixie Association.	
1972	Alexandria	.600
	El Paso b	.557
1973	San Antonio	.590
	Memphis b	.558
1974	Victoria b	.581
	El Paso	.555
1975	Lafayette c	.558
	Midland c	.604
1976	Amarillo b	.600
	Shreveport	.515
1977	El Paso	.600
	Arkansas d	.485
1978	El Paso d	.593
	Jackson	.567
1979	Arkansas d	.571
	Midland	.563
1980	Arkansas d	.596
	San Antonio	.544
1981	San Antonio	.571
	Jackson d	.507
1982	El Paso	.559
	Tulsa d	.515
1983	Jackson	.507
	Beaumont d	.500
1984	Beaumont	.654
	Jackson d	.610
1985	El Paso	.632
	Jackson d	.537
1986	El Paso d	.630
	Jackson	.533
1987	Wichita d	.515
	Jackson	.515
1988	El Paso	.552
	Tulsa d	.522
1989	Arkansas b	.585
	Wichita	.537

°Won split-season playoff. †No playoff for title. ‡Finished first and won four-club playoff. §Won four-club playoff. xTitle to Cleburne by default. yTied with Dallas in second half and won playoff for championship. zFort Worth disbanded. aTied with Beaumont at end of first half and won title in best-of-five series played as part of second half schedule. bLeague divided into Eastern, Western divisions; won two-team playoff. cLeague divided into Eastern, Western divisions; declared co-champions when playoffs were not completed. dLeague divided into Eastern and Western divisions and played split-season; won playoffs. NOTE—Championship awarded to winner of four-team playoff, 1933-51; first-place team and playoff winner co-champions, 1952-64.

STANDING OF CLUBS AT CLOSE OF FIRST HALF, JUNE 19

EASTERN DIVISION						WESTERN DIVISION					
Club	W.	L.	T.	Pct.	G.B.	Club	W.	L.	T.	Pct.	G.B.
Shreveport (Giants)	34	31	0	.523	....	El Paso (Brewers)	39	29	0	.574	....
Jackson (Mets)	35	32	0	.522	....	Wichita (Padres)	37	29	1	.561	1
Tulsa (Rangers)	34	32	0	.515	½	San Antonio (Dodgers)	35	31	0	.530	3
Arkansas (Cardinals)	27	40	0	.403	8	Midland (Angels)	25	42	1	.373	13½

STANDING OF CLUBS AT CLOSE OF SECOND HALF, SEPTEMBER 1

EASTERN DIVISION						WESTERN DIVISION					
Club	W.	L.	T.	Pct.	G.B.	Club	W.	L.	T.	Pct.	G.B.
Jackson (Mets)	38	30	0	.559	....	San Antonio (Dodgers)	43	25	0	.632	....
Tulsa (Rangers)	34	36	0	.486	5	El Paso (Brewers)	38	29	0	.567	4½
Shreveport (Giants)	31	37	0	.456	7	Midland (Angels)	31	38	0	.449	12½
Arkansas (Cardinals)	29	40	0	.420	9½	Wichita (Padres)	30	39	0	.435	13½

COMPOSITE STANDING OF CLUBS AT CLOSE OF SEASON, SEPTEMBER 1

Club	S.A	El P	Jax.	Tul.	Wich.	Shrv.	Mid.	Ark.	W.	L.	T.	Pct.	G.B.
San Antonio (Dodgers)	...	19	6	7	18	4	17	7	78	56	0	.582	....
El Paso (Brewers)	13	...	8	4	18	7	19	8	77	58	0	.570	1½
Jackson (Mets)	4	2	...	18	6	16	7	20	73	62	0	.541	5½
Tulsa (Rangers)	3	6	14	...	6	14	7	18	68	68	0	.500	11
Wichita (Padres)	14	14	3	4	...	7	21	4	67	68	1	.496	11½
Shreveport (Giants)	4	2	16	18	3	...	5	17	65	68	0	.489	12½
Midland (Angels)	15	13	3	3	11	5	...	6	56	80	1	.412	23
Arkansas (Cardinals)	3	2	12	14	6	15	4	...	56	80	0	.412	23

Arkansas club represented Little Rock, Ark.

Major league affiliations in parentheses.

Playoffs—San Antonio defeated El Paso, two games to one; Shreveport defeated Jackson, two games to none; Shreveport defeated San Antonio, four games to two, to win league championship.

Regular-Season Attendance—Arkansas, 256,074; El Paso, 201,068; Jackson, 124,142; Midland, 168,742; San Antonio, 180,931; Shreveport, 204,872; Tulsa, 226,461; Wichita, 218,109. Total—1,580,399. Playoffs (11 games)—23,611. All-Star Game at Tulsa—4,291.

Managers—Arkansas, Dave Bialas; El Paso, Dave Huppert; Jackson, Clint Hurdle; Midland, Eddie Rodriguez; San Antonio, John Shoemaker; Shreveport, Bill Evers; Tulsa, Tommy Thompson; Wichita, Steve Lubratich.

All-Star Team—1B—Eric Karros, San Antonio; 2B—Dean Kelley, Wichita; 3B—Steve Finken, San Antonio; SS—Charlie Montoya, El Paso; C—Steve Decker, Shreveport; Bill Haselman, Tulsa; OF—Henry Rodriguez, San Antonio; Tom Goodwin, San Antonio; Mike Humphreys, Wichita; DH—Jesus Alfaro, El Paso; P—Anthony Young, Jackson; Pete Schourek, Jackson; Terry Bross, Jackson; Mike James, San Antonio; Ricky Bones, Wichita; Most Valuable Player—Henry Rodriguez, San Antonio; Pitcher of the Year—Anthony Young, Jackson; Manager of the Year—Clint Hurdle, Jackson.

(Compiled by Howe Sportsdata International, Boston, Mass.)

CLUB BATTING

Club	Pct.	G.	AB.	R.	OR.	H.	TB.	2B.	3B.	HR.	RBI.	SH.	SF.	HP.	BB.	Int. BB.	SO.	SB.	CS.	LOB.
Midland	.281	137	4793	709	827	1346	1987	231	43	108	639	33	34	53	443	27	797	144	74	1009
San Antonio	.277	134	4579	668	544	1267	1826	213	41	88	612	60	50	41	467	41	789	153	73	973
Tulsa	.275	136	4487	624	620	1232	1839	217	51	96	576	42	20	40	423	23	903	121	76	934
Wichita	.274	136	4604	683	684	1262	1827	225	29	94	624	30	40	34	491	29	746	186	68	989
El Paso	.272	135	4622	653	613	1259	1726	199	41	62	574	36	44	27	530	21	757	132	60	1029
Shreveport	.253	133	4352	538	496	1099	1587	182	39	76	479	64	28	35	417	26	778	128	83	883
Jackson	.251	135	4366	555	499	1094	1544	204	42	54	480	56	52	32	518	39	920	173	98	917
Arkansas	.245	136	4247	503	650	1042	1477	202	40	51	444	46	39	36	473	28	842	120	78	920

INDIVIDUAL BATTING

(Leading Qualifiers for Batting Championship—367 or More Plate Appearances)

*Bats lefthanded. †Switch-hitter.

Player and Club	Pct.	G.	AB.	R.	H.	TB.	2B.	3B.	HR.	RBI.	SH.	SF.	HP.	BB.	Int. BB.	SO.	SB.	CS.
Karros, Eric, San Antonio	.352	131	509	91	179	282	45	2	18	78	1	6	6	57	5	79	8	9
Haselman, William, Tulsa	.319	120	430	68	137	234	39	2	18	80	2	3	6	44	1	96	3	7
Rohrmeier, Daniel, Tulsa	.305	119	453	76	138	206	24	7	10	62	1	4	0	37	0	51	14	12
Brooks, Jerome, San Antonio	.302	106	391	52	118	165	20	0	9	58	1	5	4	26	4	39	5	8
Alfaro, Jesus, El Paso	.301	129	485	80	146	231	29	4	16	88	1	5	1	68	3	81	0	0
Maurer, Robert, Tulsa*	.300	104	367	55	110	212	31	4	21	78	0	2	6	54	6	112	4	2
Lee, Wiley, Midland*	.297	102	377	70	112	163	15	6	8	38	7	2	2	27	3	65	45	8
David, Gregory, Wichita*	.296	112	402	55	119	189	29	1	13	59	3	3	1	38	4	91	3	3
Belcher, Kevin, Tulsa	.293	110	423	66	124	189	18	7	11	43	0	1	5	55	3	88	29	6
Decker, Steven, Shreveport	.293	110	403	52	118	187	22	1	15	80	0	7	3	39	1	64	3	7

Departmental Leaders: G—Karros, E. Wood, 131; AB—Dixon, 535; R—Humphreys, 92; H—Karros, 179; TB—Karros, 282; 2B—Karros, 45; 3B—E. Wood, 11; HR—Rodriguez, 28; RBI—Rodriguez, 109; SH—F. Burgos, J. Cooper, 13; SF—Rodriguez, 14; HP—Amaro, L. Martinez, 9; BB—Donnels, 111; IBB—Cuevas, 10; SO—J. Cooper, 136; SB—Goodwin, 60; CS—W. Taylor, 29.

(All Players—Listed Alphabetically)

Player and Club	Pct.	G.	AB.	R.	H.	TB.	2B.	3B.	HR.	RBI.	SH.	SF.	HP.	BB.	Int. BB.	SO.	SB.	CS.
Abreu, Franklin, Arkansas	.273	11	22	1	6	8	2	0	0	1	0	0	0	3	0	4	0	0
Aguayo, Luis, Midland	.317	50	186	28	59	99	10	0	10	35	0	1	6	20	0	31	5	2
Aldrete, Richard, Shreveport*	.228	123	434	43	99	130	21	2	2	46	3	8	1	37	1	56	7	4
Alfaro, Jesus, El Paso	.301	129	485	80	146	231	29	4	16	88	1	5	1	68	3	81	0	0
Alfonzo, Edgar, Midland	.298	37	121	20	36	45	4	1	1	9	1	1	2	8	0	18	1	0
Alicea, Luis, Arkansas†	.286	14	49	11	14	19	3	1	0	4	0	0	1	7	0	8	2	2
Allen, Steven, Tulsa	.000	54	1	0	0	0	0	0	0	0	0	0	0	0	0	0	0	0
Alleyne, Isaac, Arkansas*	.000	20	3	0	0	0	0	0	0	0	0	0	0	1	0	1	0	0
Alyea, Brant, Tulsa	.150	6	20	1	3	5	2	0	0	2	0	0	0	0	0	6	0	0
Amaro, Ruben, Midland†	.357	57	224	50	80	119	15	6	4	38	2	2	9	29	1	23	10	8
Arnold, Scott, Arkansas	.000	4	3	0	0	0	0	0	0	0	0	0	0	0	0	1	0	0
Ashley, Shon, El Paso	.261	122	429	53	112	174	23	3	11	67	0	6	5	55	3	91	6	1
Austin, James, El Paso	.000	38	1	0	0	0	0	0	0	0	0	0	0	0	0	1	0	0

Player and Club	Pct.	G.	AB.	R.	H.	TB.	2B.	3B.	HR.	RBI.	SH.	SF.	HP.	BB.	Int. BB.	SO.	SB.	CS.
Aylward, James, Midland	.263	69	274	36	72	101	13	2	4	27	0	1	3	17	2	23	1	6
Baez, Kevin, Jackson	.233	106	326	29	76	93	11	0	2	29	11	2	2	38	4	44	3	4
Barns, Jeffrey, Midland	.287	58	178	17	51	64	7	0	2	24	1	1	1	7	1	18	3	2
Beauchamp, Kash, Shreveport	.319	38	141	15	45	71	11	0	5	18	1	1	2	8	0	16	7	3
Beck, Rodney, Shreveport	.130	14	23	2	3	3	0	0	0	3	2	0	0	4	0	4	1	0
Belcher, Kevin, Tulsa	.293	110	423	66	124	189	18	7	11	43	0	1	5	55	3	88	29	16
Bones, Ricardo, Wichita	.143	21	21	3	3	4	1	0	0	0	1	0	0	3	0	5	0	1
Bournigal, Rafael, San Antonio	.211	69	194	20	41	49	4	2	0	14	7	2	0	8	0	25	2	1
Brocail, Douglas, Wichita*	.333	18	9	7	3	4	1	0	0	3	0	0	0	0	2	2	0	
Brooks, Jerome, San Antonio	.302	106	391	52	118	165	20	0	9	58	1	5	4	26	4	39	5	8
Bross, Terrence, Jackson	.000	58	5	0	0	0	0	0	0	0	0	0	0	0	0	3	0	0
Brown, Adam, San Antonio	.300	43	120	13	36	53	9	1	2	21	2	1	1	11	4	27	1	0
Brown, Don, Jackson	.138	15	29	3	4	4	0	0	0	1	2	0	0	4	0	13	4	0
Bumgarner, Jeffrey, Jackson	.000	3	2	0	0	0	0	0	0	0	0	0	0	0	0	1	0	0
Burgos, Francisco, Tulsa†	.257	126	470	60	121	167	17	7	5	41	13	2	0	18	4	48	9	5
Burgos, John, Arkansas*	.000	6	8	0	0	0	0	0	0	0	0	1	0	1	0	1	0	0
Bustillos, Albert, San Antonio	1.000	5	1	0	1	1	0	0	0	0	0	0	0	0	0	0	0	0
Campbell, Kevin, San Antonio	.000	49	5	0	0	0	0	0	0	0	0	0	0	0	0	2	0	0
Carmona, Gregorio, Arkansas†	.232	114	319	29	74	83	3	3	0	20	5	0	0	74	5	82	20	13
Carr, Charles, Jackson†	.258	93	361	60	93	139	19	9	3	24	3	2	2	43	2	77	48	15
Carr, Ernest, San Antonio*	.260	72	146	13	38	51	5	1	2	21	0	1	0	15	2	23	0	1
Carter, Edward, Arkansas*	.188	10	16	0	3	4	1	0	0	2	0	1	0	1	0	3	0	0
Carter, Larry, Shreveport	.000	5	5	1	0	0	0	0	0	0	1	0	1	0	0	2	0	0
Castillo, Braulio, San Antonio	.228	75	241	34	55	81	11	3	3	24	0	1	2	14	2	72	11	6
Cerny, Scott, Midland	.250	116	440	58	110	130	12	1	2	50	5	3	4	43	1	41	5	4
Chavez, Rafael, Wichita	.333	46	3	0	1	1	0	0	0	1	0	0	0	0	0	0	0	0
Christian, Ricardo, Arkansas	.235	111	336	55	79	106	18	3	1	20	4	2	2	23	0	92	34	17
Cinnella, Douglas, Arkansas	.111	40	18	0	2	3	1	0	0	0	3	0	0	1	0	5	0	0
Cisarik, Brian, Wichita*	.267	118	434	84	116	137	13	1	2	37	2	4	2	71	2	63	45	10
Clark, Mark, Arkansas	.182	19	22	1	4	4	0	0	0	2	3	0	0	2	0	10	0	0
Coleman, Dale, San Antonio	.000	14	2	0	0	0	0	0	0	0	0	0	0	0	0	1	0	0
Colon, Cristobal, Tulsa†	.244	65	234	24	57	77	9	1	3	29	3	2	1	5	1	37	6	4
Connolly, Stephen, Shreveport*	.000	50	2	0	0	0	0	0	0	0	2	0	0	0	0	0	0	0
Cooper, Craig, El Paso	.282	130	493	73	139	212	34	3	11	63	1	4	0	61	2	89	1	1
Cooper, James, Shreveport	.231	126	471	56	109	156	17	6	6	30	13	0	7	17	4	136	25	17
Cormier, Rheal, Arkansas*	.091	22	22	2	2	2	0	0	0	2	4	0	0	3	0	5	0	0
Cuevas, Angelo, Jackson*	.234	77	222	32	52	76	11	2	3	24	3	2	2	42	10	29	3	5
David, Gregory, Wichita*	.296	112	402	55	119	189	29	1	13	59	3	3	1	38	4	91	3	3
Davis, Douglas, Midland	.304	42	148	22	45	72	8	5	3	18	0	1	2	9	0	32	1	1
Davis, Kevin, Midland	.264	59	201	28	53	82	7	2	6	26	4	1	0	14	0	45	8	5
Davis, Mark, Midland	.266	92	353	66	94	148	16	1	12	41	3	3	6	48	2	96	16	8
Davis, Steven, Jackson*	.215	81	228	26	49	74	11	4	2	18	0	3	2	19	0	79	11	9
DeAngelis, Steven, Midland*	.336	56	217	37	73	128	24	2	9	53	0	6	2	23	5	31	3	2
Decker, Steven, Shreveport	.293	116	403	52	118	187	22	1	15	80	0	7	3	39	1	64	3	7
Dellicarri, Joseph, Jackson	.275	49	120	18	33	49	7	3	1	9	1	0	1	15	0	35	2	3
Dewey, Mark, Shreveport	.000	33	1	0	0	0	0	0	0	0	1	0	0	1	0	0	0	0
Dewey, Todd, Wichita†	.269	10	26	2	7	9	2	0	0	2	0	0	0	3	0	4	0	0
Diez, Scott, Jackson*	.000	1	1	0	0	0	0	0	0	0	0	0	0	0	0	1	0	0
DiMichele, Frank, 34 Mid.-12 Wich.	.000	46	1	0	0	0	0	0	0	0	0	0	0	0	0	0	0	0
Dixon, Andrew, El Paso*	.286	127	535	81	153	200	17	6	6	61	3	2	2	40	1	80	53	28
Donnels, Chris, Jackson*	.272	130	419	66	114	174	24	0	12	63	5	7	1	111	5	80	10	8
Doran, Mark, Midland	.286	38	147	25	42	63	7	1	4	14	0	1	1	20	3	25	4	4
Dostal, Bruce, San Antonio*	.260	53	127	16	33	44	3	4	0	16	4	1	3	18	2	29	10	9
Douma, Todd, Jackson*	.500	1	2	0	1	1	0	0	0	0	0	0	0	0	0	1	0	0
Dozier, William, Jackson	.324	29	102	20	33	58	5	7	2	23	0	6	0	16	0	28	3	1
Ealy, Thomas, Shreveport	.257	103	276	25	71	102	9	2	6	23	1	1	1	28	0	60	2	2
Edge, Gregory, El Paso†	.180	57	167	17	30	30	0	0	0	12	2	1	0	12	0	9	8	2
Elli, Rocky, Jackson*	.133	17	15	0	2	2	0	0	0	2	0	0	0	1	0	4	0	0
Elliot, Terrill, Arkansas	.000	2	1	0	0	0	0	0	0	0	0	0	0	0	0	0	0	0
Ericks, John, Arkansas	1.000	4	3	1	3	4	1	0	0	2	0	0	0	0	0	0	0	0
Escalera, Ruben, El Paso*	.281	112	402	54	113	146	15	6	2	56	3	4	4	46	2	73	6	5
Estes, Joel, Shreveport*	.000	9	1	0	0	0	0	0	0	0	0	0	0	0	0	0	0	0
Fanning, Steven, Arkansas	.225	126	404	50	91	134	23	4	4	34	0	2	5	59	3	91	0	2
Fariss, Monty, Tulsa	.299	71	244	45	73	121	15	6	7	34	1	0	1	36	0	60	8	5
Fernandez, Joey, Arkansas*	.269	123	402	62	108	176	22	2	14	63	0	4	2	59	7	55	8	2
Fernandez, Jose, Arkansas*	.169	55	177	13	30	49	5	1	4	25	2	4	1	14	0	65	0	0
Finken, Steven, San Antonio	.284	120	395	68	112	182	25	3	13	66	4	3	2	82	2	98	22	5
Fitzgerald, Michael, Arkansas	.240	41	129	13	31	47	4	0	4	16	0	1	1	12	0	32	0	0
Flora, Kevin, Midland	.228	71	232	35	53	95	17	5	5	32	3	1	0	23	0	54	11	5
Freiling, Howard, Jackson*	.264	74	197	21	52	71	7	3	2	29	1	4	1	25	2	37	1	1
Fulton, Edward, Arkansas*	.264	48	148	24	39	59	9	1	3	25	0	4	3	19	2	26	0	0
Garman, Patrick, Tulsa	.360	7	25	5	9	16	2	1	1	4	0	0	1	0	4	0	0	
Garner, Darrin, Tulsa	.250	107	348	50	87	103	7	3	1	24	9	0	7	62	2	71	20	9
Gideon, Ronnie, Jackson*	.333	9	3	1	1	1	0	0	0	0	0	0	1	0	2	0	0	
Gonzalez, Javier, Jackson	.175	45	137	16	24	40	4	0	4	15	3	2	0	13	1	43	0	1
Goodwin, Thomas, San Antonio*	.278	102	428	76	119	142	15	4	0	28	8	3	1	38	2	72	60	11
Grater, Mark, Arkansas	.000	29	0	0	0	0	0	0	0	0	1	0	0	0	0	0	0	0
Graves, Steven, Jackson	.167	4	12	0	2	3	1	0	0	3	0	0	0	0	0	0	0	0
Green, David, Tulsa	.286	16	49	4	14	16	2	0	0	8	0	1	1	4	1	10	0	0
Guerrero, Epifano, El Paso*	.248	118	452	45	112	149	21	5	2	45	4	6	1	32	3	48	6	9
Guerrero, Juan, Shreveport	.241	118	390	55	94	165	21	1	16	47	2	2	5	26	0	74	4	7
Gunderson, Eric, Shreveport	.273	8	11	1	3	5	2	0	0	5	0	0	0	0	0	3	0	0
Hall, Andrew, Midland	.107	7	28	2	3	6	0	0	1	0	0	1	0	0	12	0	0	
Hall, Joseph, Arkansas	.271	115	399	44	108	141	13	4	4	44	2	6	3	35	4	41	21	12
Ham, Michael, Shreveport	.205	19	39	3	8	9	1	0	0	2	0	0	3	0	13	1	0	
Hannahs, Mitchell, El Paso	.331	37	121	20	40	55	9	0	2	24	3	1	1	16	1	14	4	0
Hansen, Todd, Wichita*	.000	27	6	0	0	0	0	0	0	0	0	0	0	0	0	4	0	0
Harris, Donald, Tulsa	.160	64	213	16	34	44	5	1	1	15	3	0	3	7	0	69	7	3
Hartmann, Reid, Jackson†	.200	8	20	4	4	8	1	0	1	0	0	0	2	0	6	1	0	
Hartsock, Jeffrey, San Antonio	.000	16	13	0	0	0	0	0	0	0	1	0	0	0	0	4	0	0
Haselman, William, Tulsa	.319	120	430	68	137	234	39	2	18	80	2	3	6	44	1	96	3	7
Hecht, Steven, Shreveport*	.300	64	200	37	60	92	12	7	2	27	0	1	1	13	3	15	12	5
Heffernan, Bertram, El Paso*	.279	110	390	49	109	134	18	2	1	42	7	3	1	60	4	68	6	3

Player and Club	Pct.	G.	AB.	R.	H.	TB.	2B.	3B.	HR.	RBI.	SH.	SF.	HP.	BB.	Int. BB.	SO.	SB.	CS.
Hernandez, Jeremy, Wichita	.200	28	25	5	5	9	1	0	1	3	2	0	0	0	0	7	0	0
Hernandez, Manuel, Jackson	.333	1	3	1	1	1	0	0	0	2	0	0	0	0	0	1	0	0
Hernandez, Rodolfo, Jackson	.242	123	443	63	107	131	14	5	0	30	7	4	3	41	3	61	32	16
Hickerson, Bryan, Shreveport°	.000	27	7	0	0	0	0	0	0	0	0	0	0	0	0	3	0	0
Higgins, Kevin, Wichita°	.358	52	187	24	67	79	7	1	1	23	1	4	1	16	3	8	5	0
Hillemann, Charles, Wichita	.296	19	71	16	21	35	3	1	3	12	0	0	2	14	1	16	7	0
Hillman, Eric, Jackson°	.313	15	16	0	5	5	0	0	0	0	1	0	0	0	0	4	0	0
Hoffman, Richard, Arkansas°	.000	4	2	0	0	0	0	0	0	0	2	0	0	0	0	1	0	0
Holsman, Richard, Wichita°	.000	46	4	1	0	0	0	0	0	0	0	0	0	1	0	3	0	0
Hostetler, Thomas, Shreveport	.125	23	16	0	2	2	0	0	0	0	3	0	0	0	0	8	0	0
Howie, Mark, Midland	.291	113	453	55	132	172	22	0	6	58	0	9	3	30	3	42	4	6
Humphreys, Michael, Wichita	.276	116	421	92	116	196	21	4	17	79	2	4	5	67	4	79	38	9
Hundley, Todd, Jackson†	.265	81	279	27	74	93	12	2	1	35	0	3	1	34	3	44	5	3
Iavarone, Gregory, Tulsa	.267	32	90	10	24	29	5	0	0	9	2	0	0	14	0	28	2	0
James, Michael, San Antonio	.115	27	26	1	3	3	0	0	0	2	2	0	0	2	0	17	0	0
Jimenez, Alejandro, Jackson°	.280	123	421	50	118	173	33	2	6	61	0	6	3	37	3	72	4	6
Johnson, Erik, Shreveport	.222	91	270	35	60	69	6	0	1	15	3	0	3	22	3	38	6	6
Jones, James, Shreveport†	.241	19	29	1	7	8	1	0	0	1	1	0	2	7	1	4	2	0
Jordan, Brian, Arkansas	.160	16	50	4	8	9	1	0	0	0	0	0	1	0	0	11	0	0
Kappesser, Brian, El Paso	.222	14	36	3	8	8	0	0	0	2	1	1	0	1	0	7	0	0
Karros, Eric, San Antonio	.352	131	509	91	179	282	45	2	18	78	1	6	6	57	5	79	8	9
Kelley, Dean, Wichita°	.271	124	468	71	127	191	24	5	10	59	3	3	3	34	3	54	9	5
Kisten, Dale, Arkansas	.000	45	2	0	0	0	0	0	0	0	0	0	0	0	0	0	0	0
Kline, Douglas, Jackson	.091	31	22	0	2	2	0	0	0	3	2	0	0	0	0	13	0	0
Kmak, Joseph, El Paso	.284	35	109	8	31	44	3	2	2	11	3	2	2	7	0	22	0	0
Knapp, Michael, Midland	.259	57	193	16	50	64	8	0	2	21	0	1	0	16	0	29	1	1
Lara, Crucito, Jackson†	.196	61	163	11	32	37	2	0	1	10	0	1	9	0	45	1	1
LaRose, Steven, Jackson†	.000	19	2	0	0	0	0	0	0	0	0	0	0	0	0	1	0	0
Lee, Wiley, Midland°	.297	102	377	70	112	163	15	6	8	38	7	2	2	27	3	65	45	8
Lepley, John, Arkansas°	.333	59	3	0	1	1	0	0	0	0	0	0	0	0	0	5	0	0
Lienhard, Stephen, Shreveport	.273	48	11	1	3	3	0	0	0	0	2	0	0	0	0	5	0	0
Lombardozzi, Christopher, El Paso°	.250	34	100	15	25	31	1	1	1	7	1	1	0	11	0	16	1	0
Loubier, Stephen, Wichita	.000	15	3	0	0	0	0	0	0	0	0	0	0	1	0	0	0	0
Lutticken, Robert, Wichita	.250	49	152	14	38	55	5	0	4	20	1	1	2	10	1	27	2	0
Lynch, David, Tulsa	.000	22	1	0	0	0	0	0	0	0	0	0	0	0	0	0	0	0
Maclin, Lonnie, Arkansas°	.311	74	264	32	82	112	14	5	2	25	5	2	0	19	1	35	11	7
Majer, Steffen, Arkansas	.000	3	2	0	0	0	0	0	0	0	0	0	0	0	0	2	0	0
Martinez, Luis, San Antonio	.277	109	383	60	106	130	12	0	4	37	5	1	9	37	2	46	4	7
Martinez, Pedro, Wichita°	.238	24	21	0	5	5	0	0	0	1	1	0	0	2	0	5	0	0
Mathews, Gregory, Arkansas	.000	1	2	0	0	0	0	0	0	0	0	0	0	0	0	1	0	0
Mathews, Terry, Tulsa°	.000	15	2	0	0	0	0	0	0	0	0	0	0	0	0	2	0	0
Mattox, Frank, El Paso†	.244	12	41	5	10	16	1	1	1	6	0	0	0	11	0	4	2	3
Maurer, Robert, Tulsa	.300	104	367	55	110	212	31	4	21	78	0	2	6	54	6	112	4	2
McAndrew, James, San Antonio	.286	12	7	0	2	2	0	0	0	1	3	0	0	0	0	3	0	0
McDaniel, Terrence, Jackson	.286	67	234	34	67	100	14	2	5	37	0	3	7	31	3	70	19	9
McNamara, James, Shreveport°	.241	28	79	2	19	26	7	0	0	13	0	0	7	0	9	0	1
McWilliam, Timothy, Wichita	.284	112	401	54	114	148	17	1	5	63	3	5	5	35	0	42	8	2
Mead, Timber, Shreveport	.000	16	2	0	0	0	0	0	0	0	0	0	0	0	0	1	0	0
Meier, Kevin, Shreveport	.261	14	23	2	6	6	0	0	0	2	2	0	0	2	0	3	0	0
Melvin, Scott, Arkansas	.273	74	154	17	42	53	11	0	0	17	1	1	2	23	1	20	0	3
Milchin, Michael, Arkansas°	.259	19	27	2	7	11	4	0	0	9	2	0	0	6	0	2	0	0
Miller, Michael, Jackson	.259	22	27	2	7	8	1	0	0	2	4	0	0	0	0	12	0	0
Monell, Johnny, Midland°	.262	32	126	12	33	49	5	1	3	19	0	0	1	11	1	15	5	3
Montoyo, Carlos, El Paso	.289	94	322	71	93	123	15	3	3	44	1	2	8	72	1	43	9	0
Morrisette, James, Jackson	.220	16	50	3	11	15	1	0	1	6	0	0	2	3	0	14	2	1
Navarro, Norberto, Jackson	.182	3	11	0	2	3	1	0	0	1	0	0	0	2	0	2	0	1
Nelson, Richard, Shreveport	.176	17	34	4	6	11	2	0	1	2	1	0	0	4	1	9	0	1
Nichols, Scott, Arkansas	.157	43	108	7	17	17	0	0	0	10	0	2	0	19	0	33	1	0
Nichols, Howard, Midland	.330	57	224	38	74	122	10	1	12	44	0	3	3	25	4	42	0	2
Nivens, Toby, Jackson	.250	18	12	2	3	6	0	0	1	2	1	0	0	0	0	4	0	0
Novoa, Rafael, Shreveport°	.000	11	10	0	0	0	0	0	0	0	1	0	0	0	0	2	0	0
Opperman, Daniel, San Antonio	.250	28	24	3	6	9	0	0	1	4	4	0	0	1	0	5	0	0
Osteen, David, Arkansas	.000	14	11	0	0	0	0	0	0	0	2	0	0	0	0	3	0	0
Owens, Mark, Shreveport°	.216	55	125	5	27	37	4	0	2	13	3	0	0	25	0	28	2	0
Ozuna, Gabriel, Arkansas	.000	54	2	0	0	0	0	0	0	0	0	0	0	0	0	2	0	0
Palmer, Dean, Tulsa	.292	7	24	4	7	18	0	1	3	9	0	0	1	4	1	10	0	1
Patterson, David, Shreveport	.286	126	423	52	121	158	18	5	3	54	3	5	1	58	6	69	5	3
Peltier, Daniel, Tulsa°	.279	117	448	66	125	186	20	4	11	57	1	2	6	40	2	67	10	6
Pena, James, Shreveport°	.094	25	32	2	3	3	0	0	0	1	2	0	0	1	0	8	0	0
Perez, Vladimir, Jackson	.200	26	5	1	1	1	0	0	0	0	0	0	0	0	0	3	0	0
Peters, Reed, Midland	.280	69	236	41	66	100	8	4	6	34	3	1	2	32	1	24	14	4
Picota, Lenin, Arkansas	.115	28	26	1	3	5	2	0	0	2	5	1	0	0	0	8	0	0
Pierson, Lawrence, Arkansas	.000	21	5	0	0	0	0	0	0	0	2	0	0	0	0	3	0	0
Pitz, Michael, San Antonio	.025	26	8	1	1	1	0	0	0	1	0	0	0	0	0	2	0	0
Poole, James, San Antonio°	.000	54	1	0	0	0	0	0	0	0	0	0	0	0	0	0	0	0
Postier, Paul, Tulsa	.236	89	301	27	71	81	8	1	0	33	4	2	0	12	1	55	2	0
Pye, Edward, San Antonio	.248	119	455	67	113	151	18	7	2	44	3	5	6	45	1	68	19	7
Quinzer, Paul, El Paso°	.000	31	3	0	0	0	0	0	0	0	0	0	0	1	0	1	0	0
Redman, Timothy, Arkansas	.304	9	23	0	7	9	2	0	0	4	0	0	2	0	3	0	0
Reed, Steven, Shreveport	.000	45	1	0	0	0	0	0	0	0	1	0	0	0	0	0	0	0
Remlinger, Michael, Shreveport°	.115	25	26	0	3	3	0	0	0	0	3	0	0	3	0	7	0	0
Repoz, Craig, Wichita	.213	59	141	23	30	51	9	0	4	15	1	1	5	26	0	40	3	2
Rice, Lance, San Antonio	.241	79	245	25	59	74	11	2	0	35	3	4	1	24	3	47	3	1
Roberts, Peter, Wichita°	.000	18	11	0	0	0	0	0	0	0	0	0	0	1	0	3	0	0
Roca, Gilberto, Jackson	.267	8	30	4	8	9	1	0	0	3	0	0	1	0	5	0	0
Rodriguez, Henry, San Antonio°	.291	129	495	82	144	268	22	9	28	109	1	14	2	61	9	66	5	4
Rohrmeier, Daniel, Tulsa	.305	119	453	76	138	206	24	7	10	62	1	4	0	37	0	51	14	12
Rojas, Homar, San Antonio	.282	82	241	29	68	97	10	2	5	36	2	3	3	24	2	34	0	3
Roseboro, Jaime, Jackson	.275	93	349	53	96	140	19	2	7	44	1	8	4	24	3	46	23	14
Ross, Michael, Arkansas	.251	128	435	55	109	172	35	2	8	56	2	6	7	41	1	93	1	1
Sager, Anthony, Wichita	.100	26	20	0	2	2	0	0	0	0	2	0	0	3	0	1	0	0
Salmon, Timothy, Midland	.268	27	97	17	26	40	3	1	3	16	0	1	1	18	0	38	1	0
Santana, Andres, Shreveport†	.292	92	336	50	98	111	5	4	0	24	7	1	1	31	0	41	32	18

Player and Club	Pct.	G.	AB.	R.	H.	TB.	2B.	3B.	HR.	RBI.	SH.	SF.	HP.	BB.	Int. BB.	SO.	SB.	CS.
Schourek, Peter, Jackson°	.182	19	22	2	4	6	2	0	0	0	2	0	0	1	0	6	0	0
Sconiers, Daryl, Midland°	.323	8	31	7	10	14	1	0	1	5	0	0	0	5	0	6	1	0
Scott, Timothy, San Antonio	.500	30	2	0	1	1	0	0	0	0	0	0	0	0	0	0	0	0
Scruggs, Anthony, Tulsa	.344	53	195	28	67	96	5	6	4	37	3	1	2	14	1	50	4	5
Shinall, Zakary, San Antonio	.000	20	11	0	0	0	0	0	0	0	1	0	0	0	0	7	0	0
Skeete, Rafel, El Paso°	.278	109	367	57	102	119	6	4	1	28	6	3	1	19	0	72	28	8
Skurla, John, Midland°	.268	32	127	17	34	58	9	3	3	16	0	0	0	9	0	34	3	3
Springer, Dennis, San Antonio	.235	24	17	0	4	4	0	0	0	1	4	0	0	0	0	4	0	0
Staton, David, Wichita	.305	45	164	26	50	79	11	0	6	31	0	1	1	22	0	36	0	0
Stone, Brian, Arkansas	.111	7	9	1	1	1	0	0	0	0	1	0	0	0	0	5	0	0
Strijek, Randy, Shreveport	.111	17	27	2	3	3	0	0	0	0	1	0	0	1	0	13	0	0
Sturdivant, David, Midland°	.218	32	101	6	22	30	5	0	1	9	2	0	0	5	0	26	1	0
Taylor, Terry, Midland°	.125	4	16	0	2	4	2	0	0	4	0	0	0	1	0	8	0	0
Taylor, William, Wichita+	.266	102	414	57	110	154	18	7	4	31	3	0	3	37	2	78	51	29
Terrill, James, San Antonio°	.500	3	2	1	1	2	1	0	0	1	0	0	0	0	0	1	0	0
Thoutsis, Paul, Arkansas°	.282	101	266	25	75	115	15	5	5	37	0	3	1	12	2	37	0	1
Threadgill, George, Tulsa	.208	41	149	19	31	39	8	0	0	11	0	0	1	16	0	39	3	1
Valdez, Amilcar, San Antonio	.220	18	41	5	9	10	1	0	0	3	0	0	0	1	0	11	0	0
Valentin, Jose, Wichita+	.278	11	36	4	10	12	2	0	0	2	1	0	0	5	0	7	2	1
Vanzytveld, Jeffrey, San Antonio°	.000	8	1	0	0	0	0	0	0	0	0	0	0	0	0	0	0	0
Vargas, Jose, Arkansas	.000	15	1	0	0	0	0	0	0	0	0	0	0	0	0	0	0	0
Vasquez, Aguedo, Jackson	.000	53	5	0	0	0	0	0	0	0	1	0	0	0	0	3	0	0
Velasquez, Guillermo, Wichita°	.271	105	377	48	102	163	21	2	12	72	0	4	1	35	5	66	0	1
Villanueva, Juan, Wichita	.240	105	359	43	86	113	11	2	4	38	0	5	1	22	2	63	4	2
Wagner, Daniel, Midland	.196	19	56	4	11	15	2	1	0	6	2	0	0	2	0	17	1	0
Wallace, Timothy, Wichita+	.317	77	224	29	71	99	17	4	1	31	4	3	1	23	0	23	7	3
Walters, Daniel, Wichita	.296	58	199	25	59	92	12	0	7	40	0	2	1	21	2	21	0	0
Webster, Casey, El Paso	.209	50	172	22	36	54	7	1	3	18	0	3	1	19	1	39	2	0
Weese, Dean, Arkansas	.000	29	2	0	0	0	0	0	0	0	0	0	0	0	0	1	0	0
Westbrooks, Elanis, Shreveport	.208	31	48	11	10	11	1	0	0	0	0	0	0	6	1	11	2	1
White, Charlie, Arkansas	.251	118	390	53	98	136	14	9	2	26	2	1	4	41	2	65	22	18
White, Michael, San Antonio°	.391	13	46	10	18	24	1	1	1	14	0	0	1	3	1	3	1	1
Wood, Brian, Wichita°	.000	44	1	0	0	0	0	0	0	0	0	0	0	0	0	1	0	0
Wood, Edward, Shreveport°	.265	131	456	81	121	216	22	11	17	72	4	2	7	74	5	76	17	8
Wray, James, San Antonio	.000	45	2	1	0	0	0	0	0	0	2	0	0	0	0	2	0	0
Young, Anthony, Jackson	.303	23	33	4	10	13	1	1	0	4	3	0	0	0	0	13	0	0
Zayas, Carlos, Midland	.429	2	7	2	3	4	1	0	0	1	0	0	0	1	0	2	0	0
Zinter, Alan, Jackson+	.200	6	20	2	4	5	1	0	0	1	0	0	0	3	0	11	1	0

The following pitchers, listed alphabetically by club, with games in parentheses, had no plate appearances, primarily through use of designated hitters:

ARKANSAS—Cox, Danny (1); Smith, Kenneth (3).

EL PASO—Chapman, Mark (42); Eldred, Calvin (19); Elvira, Narciso (4); Fleming, Keith (18); Fortugno, Timothy (12); Freeland, Dean (26); Garces, Robinson (28); George, Christopher (39); Henry, Douglas (15); Hunter, James (9); Ignasiak, Michael (15); May, Scott (22); McGrath, Charles (13); Miglio, John (8); Monson, Steven (22); Puig, Edward (19); Sparks, Steven (7); Watkins, Timothy (5).

JACKSON—Plummer, Dale (4).

MIDLAND—Abbott, Kyle (24); Acosta, Jose (2); Bockus, Randy (7); Butcher, Michael (35); Carter, Glenn (20); Cliburn, Stewart (5); DiMichele, Frank (34); Erb, Michael (6); Grahe, Joseph (18); Hamilton, Carlton (20); Holzemer, Mark (15); Hook, Michael (7); Martinez, David (34); Meeks, Timothy (35); Merejo, Luis (29); Merriman, Brett (2); Minton, Gregory (4); Moore, Robert (20); Trudeau, Kevin (19); Vann, Brandy (32); Vidmar, Donald (11); Zappelli, Mark (35).

SAN ANTONIO—Hershiser, Gordon (3); Marquez, Isidro (13).

SHREVEPORT—Bonilla, George (9); Potestio, Frank (12).

TULSA—Bryant, Phillip (19); Castillo, Felipe (20); Compres, Fidel (6); Cunningham, Everett (17); Guzman, Jose (1); Hoover, John (4); Hurst, Jonathan (8); Hvizda, James (32); McCray, Eric (25); Nen, Robb (7); Pavlik, Roger (16); Reed, Robert (5); Rockman, Marvin (24); Rosenthal, Wayne (12); Shaw, Cedric (14); Shiflett, Christian (13); Smith, Daniel (7); Taylor, Michael (33); Thomas, Mitchell (8).

GRAND SLAM HOME RUNS—Humphreys, Rodriguez, Walters, 2 each; Aldrete, Ashley, Beauchamp, Brooks, A. Brown, Cuevas, David, DeAngelis, Fanning, Joey Fernandez, Jose Fernandez, Finken, Harris, Haselman, Knapp, Patterson, Peters, Rojas, Thoutsis, Villanueva, Webster, E. Wood, 1 each.

AWARDED FIRST BASE ON CATCHER'S INTERFERENCE—Brooks (A. Hall); F. Burgos (Hundley); Carmona (Haselman); Dostal (Knapp); Monell (Rojas); Sturdivant (Haselman).

CLUB FIELDING

Club	Pct.	G.	PO.	A.	E.	DP.	PB.	Club	Pct.	G.	PO.	A.	E.	DP.	PB.
El Paso	.972	135	3595	1553	147	137	16	Shreveport	.967	133	3473	1392	165	95	15
San Antonio	.970	134	3589	1501	156	150	14	Wichita	.967	136	3534	1488	172	117	22
Jackson	.969	135	3563	1491	162	130	18	Midland	.964	137	3605	1619	196	158	28
Tulsa	.969	136	3465	1565	163	145	27	Arkansas	.960	136	3379	1504	203	117	20

Triple Plays—Arkansas, Midland, San Antonio.

INDIVIDUAL FIELDING

°Throws lefthanded.

FIRST BASEMEN

Player and Club	Pct.	G.	PO.	A.	E.	DP.	Player and Club	Pct.	G.	PO.	A.	E.	DP.
Aldrete, Shreveport°	.990	98	744	84	8	61	Hall, Arkansas	1.000	2	22	2	0	2
Alfaro, El Paso	.988	9	77	8	1	4	Haselman, Tulsa	1.000	7	39	1	0	2
Aylward, Midland	.970	3	30	2	1	4	Howie, Midland	.991	111	1067	83	10	121
Barns, Midland	1.000	5	37	3	0	2	Jimenez, Jackson°	.988	111	984	64	13	93
Brown, San Antonio	1.000	1	5	0	0	2	Jones, Shreveport	1.000	1	7	0	0	0
Cisarik, Wichita°	1.000	32	238	27	0	15	KARROS, San Antonio	.994	131	1223	106	8	129
Cooper, El Paso	.986	126	1190	76	18	108	Lara, Jackson	.818	1	8	1	2	1
David, Wichita	1.000	8	42	5	0	3	Lutticken, Wichita	1.000	1	2	0	0	1
Davis, Midland	1.000	1	2	0	0	0	Mathews, Tulsa	1.000	1	2	1	0	0
Dellicarri, Jackson	.963	3	25	1	1	4	Maurer, Tulsa°	.989	99	939	72	11	108
Donnels, Jackson	.947	2	16	2	1	4	Melvin, Arkansas	1.000	21	125	10	0	12
Escalera, El Paso°	1.000	4	19	0	0	4	Nelson, Shreveport	.969	5	30	1	1	1
Fernandez, Arkansas	.991	101	900	64	9	71	Nichols, Midland	.975	9	68	10	2	5
Fitzgerald, Arkansas	.984	21	174	15	3	15	Owens, Shreveport	.941	3	15	1	1	1
Freiling, Jackson°	.988	28	237	15	3	14	Patterson, Shreveport	.987	40	284	21	4	20
Green, Tulsa	1.000	2	14	2	0	1	Postier, Tulsa	1.000	32	260	23	0	21

FIRST BASEMEN—Continued

Player and Club	Pct.	G.	PO.	A.	E.	DP.	Player and Club	Pct.	G.	PO.	A.	E.	DP.
Rohrmeier, Tulsa	1.000	1	1	1	0	0	Sturdivant, Midland	1.000	1	12	2	0	2
Sconiers, Midland*	1.000	8	73	3	0	8	Thoutsis, Arkansas	1.000	7	43	4	0	6
Skurla, Midland*	1.000	1	7	0	0	1	Valdez, San Antonio	1.000	5	26	1	0	3
Staton, Wichita	.989	37	326	27	4	25	Velasquez, Wichita	.980	72	631	50	14	57

Triple Plays—Barns, Fernandez, Karros.

SECOND BASEMEN

Player and Club	Pct.	G.	PO.	A.	E.	DP.	Player and Club	Pct.	G.	PO.	A.	E.	DP.
Aguayo, Midland	.951	8	13	26	2	7	Hannahs, El Paso	.915	35	78	95	16	25
Alfonzo, Midland	.966	11	16	41	2	5	Hecht, Shreveport	.978	13	17	27	1	2
Alicea, Midland	.935	14	24	34	4	9	HERNANDEZ, Jackson	.980	123	259	369	13	80
Allen, Tulsa	1.000	1	0	2	0	0	Johnson, Shreveport	1.000	21	31	48	0	10
Bournigal, San Antonio	.961	20	35	39	3	14	Jones, Shreveport	1.000	4	7	6	0	2
Burgos, Tulsa	.966	35	67	105	6	24	Kelley, Wichita	.974	119	238	327	15	74
Cerny, Midland	.971	110	216	384	18	86	Lara, Jackson	.957	15	20	25	2	7
Dellicarri, Jackson	1.000	15	11	20	0	4	Lombardozzi, El Paso	1.000	12	12	34	0	4
Edge, El Paso	.978	11	19	25	1	3	Mattox, El Paso	1.000	12	20	32	0	5
Fanning, Arkansas	.966	97	181	277	16	53	Melvin, Arkansas	.943	8	9	24	2	1
Finken, San Antonio	1.000	4	6	10	0	3	Pye, San Antonio	.963	117	216	375	23	80
Flora, Midland	.955	10	16	26	2	4	Ross, Arkansas	.955	26	43	64	5	19
Garner, Tulsa	.972	106	201	317	15	68	Skeete, El Paso*	1.000	1	2	4	0	2
E. Guerrero, El Paso	.992	71	130	220	3	53	Villanueva, Wichita	.941	3	5	11	1	0
J. Guerrero, Shreveport	.964	110	210	268	18	51	Wallace, Wichita	.957	18	35	53	4	16

Triple Play—Bournigal.

THIRD BASEMEN

Player and Club	Pct.	G.	PO.	A.	E.	DP.	Player and Club	Pct.	G.	PO.	A.	E.	DP.
Abreu, Arkansas	1.000	2	0	1	0	0	Hecht, Shreveport	.813	17	11	15	6	2
Aguayo, Midland	.867	30	20	52	11	4	Howie, Midland	1.000	2	1	5	0	2
Alfaro, El Paso	1.000	34	11	76	0	7	Johnson, Shreveport	.926	24	4	46	4	2
Alfonzo, Midland	.714	5	1	4	2	1	Jones, Shreveport	.923	7	1	11	1	0
Aylward, Midland	.944	64	50	136	11	8	Lara, Jackson	.900	3	3	6	1	2
Barns, Midland	.800	4	1	7	2	1	Lombardozzi, El Paso	1.000	6	2	5	0	0
Bournigal, San Antonio	1.000	1	0	1	0	0	Melvin, Arkansas	.960	27	14	34	2	7
Burgos, Tulsa	.944	83	53	151	12	13	Morrisette, Jackson	.667	7	5	9	7	3
Carr, San Antonio	.964	30	18	36	2	4	Nichols, Midland	.920	26	16	30	4	3
Cerny, Midland	1.000	4	9	5	0	0	Owens, Shreveport	.919	17	9	25	3	4
David, Wichita	.886	103	54	180	30	9	Palmer, Tulsa	.833	7	9	6	3	0
Davis, Midland	.750	3	1	5	2	1	PATTERSON, Shreveport	.930	91	57	141	15	16
Dellicarri, Jackson	.800	6	6	6	3	0	Postier, Tulsa	.985	46	32	97	2	13
Donnels, Jackson	.912	123	79	242	31	24	Repoz, Wichita	.922	34	18	65	7	3
Edge, El Paso	.947	14	8	28	2	6	Ross, Arkansas	.925	106	72	173	20	13
Fanning, Arkansas	1.000	4	0	10	0	3	Staton, Wichita	1.000	5	0	8	0	0
Finken, San Antonio	.913	113	77	215	28	23	Strijek, Shreveport	1.000	1	0	0	0	0
Garman, Tulsa	.889	6	3	13	2	0	Taylor, Midland	.938	4	7	8	1	1
Guerrero, El Paso	.912	46	37	87	12	12	Villanueva, Wichita	.600	4	1	2	2	0
Hall, Arkansas	.923	19	8	28	3	2	Webster, El Paso	.918	48	39	96	12	10
Haselman, Tulsa	1.000	2	1	2	0	0							

Triple Play—Nichols.

SHORTSTOPS

Player and Club	Pct.	G.	PO.	A.	E.	DP.	Player and Club	Pct.	G.	PO.	A.	E.	DP.
Abreu, Arkansas	.885	6	4	19	3	2	J. Guerrero, Shreveport	.933	3	4	10	1	1
Aguayo, Midland	.875	1	2	5	1	1	Hartmann, Jackson	.800	1	1	3	1	1
Alfaro, El Paso	.991	27	33	76	1	15	Hecht, Shreveport	1.000	1	1	1	0	1
Alfonzo, Midland	.909	9	12	18	3	7	Johnson, Shreveport	.934	47	59	112	12	20
Baez, Jackson	.953	105	184	301	24	54	Jones, Shreveport	1.000	1	0	0	0	0
Barns, Midland	.902	22	35	39	8	13	Lara, Jackson	.977	26	43	83	3	19
Bournigal, San Antonio	.964	43	64	96	6	23	Lombardozzi, El Paso	.889	4	7	9	2	2
Carmona, Arkansas	.887	112	110	321	55	61	Martinez, San Antonio	.950	105	177	283	24	68
Colon, Tulsa	.917	65	108	192	27	60	MONTOYO, El Paso	.963	91	131	256	15	50
Davis, Midland	.923	57	92	173	22	47	Navarro, Jackson	.882	3	4	11	2	3
Dellicarri, Jackson	.958	10	17	29	2	7	Pye, San Antonio	1.000	2	0	4	0	1
Edge, El Paso	.947	20	32	57	5	11	Santana, Shreveport	.911	89	131	207	33	31
Fanning, Arkansas	.947	27	44	63	6	11	Strijek, Shreveport	.900	9	8	10	2	4
Fariss, Midland	.932	71	141	190	24	39	Valentin, Wichita	.959	11	14	33	2	4
Flora, Midland	.918	59	82	187	24	42	Villanueva, Wichita	.932	93	145	254	29	62
E. Guerrero, El Paso	1.000	1	2	4	0	1	Wallace, Wichita	.935	41	52	121	12	18

Triple Play—Carmona.

OUTFIELDERS

Player and Club	Pct.	G.	PO.	A.	E.	DP.	Player and Club	Pct.	G.	PO.	A.	E.	DP.
Aldrete, Shreveport*	.966	18	27	1	1	0	S. Davis, Jackson	.966	67	111	4	4	2
Alfonzo, Midland	1.000	3	2	0	0	0	DeAngelis, Midland*	.844	33	36	2	7	0
Amaro, Midland	1.000	57	97	8	0	0	Dixon, El Paso*	.966	104	196	5	7	2
Ashley, El Paso	.980	96	185	14	4	3	Doran, Midland	.990	38	94	4	1	2
Barns, Midland	1.000	5	4	0	0	0	Dostal, San Antonio*	.978	36	43	1	1	0
Beauchamp, Shreveport	.974	38	72	2	2	0	Dozier, Jackson	1.000	29	44	4	0	0
Belcher, Tulsa	.959	69	107	9	5	2	Ealy, Shreveport	.935	69	96	4	7	0
Brooks, San Antonio	.982	90	153	8	3	5	Edge, El Paso	.938	11	13	2	1	0
Brown, Jackson	1.000	12	14	0	0	0	Escalera, El Paso*	.981	104	198	8	4	2
Carr, Jackson	.967	92	226	12	8	1	Fernandez, Arkansas	1.000	1	2	0	0	0
Carter, Arkansas*	1.000	4	3	1	0	0	Finken, San Antonio	1.000	5	7	0	0	0
Castillo, San Antonio	.943	60	125	7	8	1	GOODWIN, San Antonio	.989	102	264	7	3	2
Christian, Arkansas	.943	95	127	6	8	0	Green, Tulsa	1.000	6	9	0	0	0
Cisarik, Wichita*	.993	81	137	4	1	0	Hall, Arkansas	.928	97	145	10	12	2
Cooper, Shreveport	.978	125	337	11	8	2	Harris, Tulsa	.942	64	123	6	8	1
Cuevas, Jackson*	.979	56	92	0	2	0	Hartmann, Jackson	1.000	5	6	0	0	0
M. Davis, Midland	.990	90	194	8	2	1	Haselman, Tulsa	1.000	7	6	0	0	0

OUTFIELDERS—Continued

Player and Club	Pct.	G.	PO.	A.	E.	DP.
Hecht, Shreveport	.942	33	49	0	3	0
Hillemann, Wichita	.958	19	44	2	2	0
Humphreys, Wichita	.983	113	277	8	5	3
Jordan, Arkansas	.933	15	28	0	2	0
Kelley, Wichita	1.000	2	5	0	0	0
Lara, Jackson	1.000	9	5	1	0	0
Lee, Midland	.985	44	62	5	1	1
Lombardozzi, El Paso	1.000	2	2	0	0	0
Maclin, Arkansas*	.959	72	111	5	5	0
McDaniel, Jackson	.971	66	129	3	4	1
McWilliam, Wichita	.988	102	162	8	2	1
Monell, Midland	.981	23	49	3	1	1
Montoyo, El Paso	1.000	1	1	0	0	0
Morrisette, Jackson	.938	8	14	1	1	0
Nelson, Shreveport	.909	6	10	0	1	0
Nichols, Arkansas	1.000	5	4	0	0	0
Peltier, Tulsa*	.958	110	173	9	8	3
Peters, Midland	.985	64	120	9	2	2
Postier, Tulsa	1.000	10	22	0	0	0
Repoz, Wichita	.962	14	25	0	1	0
Rodriguez, San Antonio*	.958	126	223	5	10	0
Rohrmeier, Tulsa	.979	60	92	3	2	0
Roseboro, Jackson	.971	92	163	3	5	0
Salmon, Midland	.950	27	51	6	3	1
Scruggs, Tulsa	.991	53	112	2	1	0
Skeete, El Paso*	.949	105	221	3	12	0
Skurla, Midland*	.985	30	63	1	1	1
Taylor, Wichita	.963	92	169	13	7	4
Thoutsis, Arkansas	.960	54	67	5	3	2
Threadgill, Tulsa	.977	38	42	1	1	1
Wagner, Midland	1.000	12	25	1	0	1
Westbrooks, Shreveport	1.000	24	24	2	0	1
White, Arkansas	.945	103	198	9	12	2
Wood, Shreveport*	.977	128	247	8	6	0

Triple Plays—Hall, Monell.

CATCHERS

Player and Club	Pct.	G.	PO.	A.	E.	DP.	PB.
Barns, Midland	.988	14	82	2	1	1	8
Davis, Midland	.979	42	242	44	6	4	5
Decker, Shreveport	.986	97	650	71	10	8	9
Dewey, Wichita	.926	7	45	5	4	0	0
Fernandez, Arkansas	.992	55	349	40	3	4	8
Fulton, Arkansas	.984	46	270	35	5	2	9
Gonzalez, Jackson	.992	44	216	29	2	8	2
Graves, Jackson	.968	3	25	5	1	0	0
A. Hall, Midland	.941	7	41	7	3	2	1
J. Hall, Arkansas	1.000	1	4	0	0	0	0
Ham, Shreveport	.983	13	49	10	1	1	3
Hannahs, El Paso	.889	1	7	1	1	0	0
Haselman, Tulsa	.975	109	676	90	20	6	20
HEFFERNAN, El Paso	.990	100	587	87	7	11	8
Higgins, San Antonio	.977	41	236	21	6	1	11
Hundley, Jackson	.984	79	474	63	9	9	12
Iavarone, Tulsa	.971	32	153	14	5	2	7
Kappesser, El Paso	.963	14	70	8	3	0	1
Kmak, El Paso	.991	31	194	28	2	3	7
Knapp, Midland	.971	54	333	33	11	1	9
Lutticken, Wichita	.970	41	272	22	9	3	6
McNamara, Shreveport	.984	22	110	13	2	2	1
Nichols, Arkansas	.977	37	186	25	5	3	2
Owens, Shreveport	1.000	14	81	16	0	2	2
Redman, Arkansas	1.000	8	27	5	0	0	1
Rice, San Antonio	.990	79	407	70	5	8	6
Roca, Jackson	1.000	7	40	5	0	1	3
Rojas, San Antonio	.983	71	423	48	8	5	8
Sturdivant, Midland	.993	29	135	17	1	2	4
Walters, Wichita	.991	51	276	41	3	5	5
Zayas, Midland	1.000	2	17	1	0	0	1
Zinter, Jackson	1.000	6	31	2	0	1	1

Triple Play—Davis.

PITCHERS

Player and Club	Pct.	G.	PO.	A.	E.	DP.
Abbott, Midland*	.972	24	10	25	1	1
Abreu, Arkansas	1.000	2	0	1	0	0
Acosta, Midland*	1.000	2	0	2	0	0
Allen, Tulsa	1.000	54	3	22	0	0
Alleyne, Arkansas*	.800	20	1	7	2	0
Arnold, Arkansas	1.000	4	2	4	0	0
Austin, El Paso	1.000	38	2	18	0	1
Beck, Shreveport	1.000	14	15	13	0	0
Bockus, Midland	.833	7	3	2	1	0
Bones, Wichita	.978	21	13	31	1	0
Brocail, Wichita	1.000	12	5	10	0	1
Bross, Jackson	1.000	58	4	7	0	0
Bryant, Tulsa	.958	19	6	17	1	0
Bumgarner, Jackson	1.000	3	1	3	0	0
Burgos, Arkansas*	1.000	6	0	6	0	0
Bustillos, San Antonio	1.000	5	1	3	0	0
Butcher, Midland	.765	35	4	9	4	1
Campbell, San Antonio	1.000	49	4	13	0	1
G. Carter, Midland	.952	20	7	13	1	1
L. Carter, Shreveport	1.000	5	1	4	0	0
Castillo, Tulsa	1.000	20	3	10	0	0
Chapman, El Paso	.864	42	6	13	3	1
Chavez, Wichita	.964	46	10	17	1	1
Cinnella, Jackson	.968	40	13	17	1	2
Clark, Arkansas	.957	19	6	16	1	1
Cliburn, Midland	1.000	5	0	1	0	0
Coleman, San Antonio	.889	14	2	6	1	0
Compres, Tulsa	1.000	6	1	1	0	0
Connolly, Shreveport*	1.000	50	5	6	0	0
Cormier, Arkansas*	1.000	22	12	29	0	1
Cunningham, Tulsa	.882	17	6	9	2	1
Dewey, Shreveport	.833	33	1	9	2	1
Diez, Jackson*	1.000	1	0	1	0	0
DiMichele, 34 Mid.-12 Wich.*	.923	46	2	10	1	0
Eldred, El Paso	1.000	19	7	18	0	4
Elli, Jackson*	.938	17	4	11	1	1
Elvira, El Paso*	.833	4	2	3	1	0
Erb, Midland	.714	6	3	2	2	1
Ericks, Arkansas	.750	4	0	3	1	0
Estes, Shreveport*	.909	9	0	8	0	1
Fleming, El Paso	.909	18	4	6	1	1
Fortugno, El Paso*	1.000	12	1	6	0	0
Freeland, El Paso	.950	26	12	45	3	3
Garces, Arkansas	1.000	28	2	5	0	0
George, El Paso	.867	39	3	10	2	0
Gideon, Jackson*	1.000	9	1	1	0	0
Grahe, Midland	.959	18	11	36	2	3
Grater, Arkansas	.933	29	0	14	1	0
Gunderson, Shreveport*	1.000	8	3	13	0	1
Guzman, Tulsa	1.000	1	0	2	0	0
Ham, Shreveport	.000	1	0	0	1	0
Hamilton, Midland*	.960	20	4	20	1	2
Hansen, Wichita*	1.000	27	8	9	0	2
Hartsock, San Antonio	.906	16	5	24	3	2
Henry, El Paso	1.000	15	3	5	0	0
Hernandez, Wichita	.955	26	17	25	2	2
Hershiser, San Antonio	1.000	3	0	1	0	0
Hickerson, Shreveport*	.933	27	5	9	1	0
Hillman, Jackson*	.909	15	2	8	1	0
Hoffman, Arkansas	.917	4	7	4	1	0
Holsman, Wichita*	1.000	46	2	5	0	0
Holzemer, Midland	.958	15	4	19	1	0
Hook, Midland*	1.000	7	1	2	0	0
Hoover, Tulsa	1.000	4	1	3	0	0
Hostetler, Shreveport	.953	23	14	27	2	1
Hunter, El Paso	1.000	9	5	9	0	0
Hurst, Tulsa	1.000	8	2	4	0	0
Hvizda, Tulsa	1.000	32	3	5	0	0
Ignasiak, El Paso	.935	15	4	25	2	1
James, San Antonio	.960	26	9	15	1	2
Kisten, Arkansas	.947	45	7	11	1	2
Kline, Jackson	.880	31	8	14	3	1
Lara, Jackson	1.000	4	1	0	0	0
LaRose, Jackson	.900	19	2	7	1	2
Lepley, Arkansas*	.931	59	8	19	2	2
Lienhard, Shreveport	.953	48	8	33	2	3
Loubier, Wichita	1.000	15	1	6	0	0
Lynch, Tulsa*	1.000	21	6	21	0	4
Majer, Arkansas	.800	3	2	2	1	0
Marquez, San Antonio	.857	13	2	4	1	1
D. Martinez, Midland	.778	34	2	12	4	0
P. Martinez, Wichita*	.893	24	2	23	3	1
G. Mathews, Arkansas*	1.000	1	0	2	0	0
T. Mathews, Tulsa	1.000	14	10	16	0	1
May, El Paso	.923	22	5	7	1	1
McAndrew, San Antonio	1.000	12	6	4	0	0
McCray, Tulsa*	.952	25	10	30	2	2
McGrath, El Paso	.765	13	4	9	4	1
Mead, Shreveport	1.000	16	1	4	0	0
Meeks, Shreveport	1.000	35	3	9	0	2
Meier, Shreveport	.955	14	6	15	1	1
Merejo, Jackson	.786	29	4	7	3	1
Miglio, El Paso*	1.000	8	0	2	0	0
Milchin, Arkansas*	.952	17	5	15	1	0
Miller, Jackson	.952	22	3	17	1	0
Minton, Midland	1.000	4	1	5	0	0
Monson, El Paso	.950	22	6	13	1	1
Moore, Midland	1.000	20	5	11	0	2
Nen, Tulsa	1.000	7	0	3	0	0
Nivens, Jackson	.966	18	8	20	1	0

PITCHERS—Continued

Player and Club	Pct.	G.	PO.	A.	E.	DP.
Novoa, Shreveport*	1.000	11	8	9	0	0
Opperman, San Antonio	.914	27	10	22	3	3
Osteen, Arkansas	.950	13	6	13	1	0
Ozuna, Arkansas	.885	54	4	19	3	1
Pavlik, Tulsa	1.000	16	10	15	0	2
Pena, Shreveport*	.962	25	8	17	1	1
Perez, Jackson	.923	26	4	8	1	0
Picota, Arkansas	.895	26	12	22	4	2
Pierson, Arkansas	1.000	21	5	16	0	0
Pitz, San Antonio	.909	26	11	19	3	1
Poole, San Antonio*	.857	54	3	9	2	0
Postier, Tulsa	1.000	5	1	0	0	0
Potestio, Shreveport	1.000	12	2	3	0	0
Puig, El Paso*	1.000	19	1	5	0	0
Quinzer, Wichita	.733	31	1	10	4	1
R. Reed, Tulsa	.857	5	1	5	1	0
S. Reed, Shreveport	.955	45	5	16	1	2
Remlinger, Shreveport*	.932	25	7	34	3	3
Roberts, Wichita*	1.000	18	7	19	0	0
Rockman, Tulsa	1.000	24	1	11	0	1
Rosenthal, Tulsa	1.000	12	1	3	0	0
SAGER, Wichita	1.000	26	14	29	0	2
Schourek, Jackson*	.882	19	5	10	2	0
Scott, San Antonio	1.000	30	4	6	0	0
Shaw, Tulsa*	.963	14	5	21	1	0
Shiflett, Tulsa	1.000	13	2	7	0	1
Shinall, San Antonio	.941	20	12	20	2	1
D. Smith, Tulsa*	1.000	7	1	9	0	0
K. Smith, Arkansas	1.000	3	0	1	0	0
Sparks, El Paso	1.000	7	4	6	0	1
Springer, San Antonio	.851	24	19	21	7	2
Stone, Arkansas	1.000	7	4	6	0	0
Taylor, Tulsa	.906	33	3	26	3	3
Terrill, San Antonio*	1.000	3	3	3	0	0
Thomas, Tulsa	.952	8	4	16	1	0
Trudeau, Midland	1.000	19	3	8	0	2
Vann, Midland	.833	32	3	7	2	2
Vanzytveld, San Antonio	.900	8	1	8	1	0
Vargas, Arkansas	1.000	15	2	4	0	0
Vasquez, Jackson	1.000	53	4	14	0	1
Vidmar, Midland	.857	11	2	4	1	0
Watkins, El Paso	1.000	5	1	4	0	0
Weese, Arkansas	.889	29	2	6	1	0
Wood, Wichita	.947	44	4	14	1	1
Wray, San Antonio*	1.000	45	5	11	0	0
Young, Jackson	.900	23	11	34	5	4
Zappelli, Midland	.778	35	1	13	4	1

Triple Play—Zappelli.

The following players did not have any fielding statistics at the positions indicated or appeared only as a designated hitter, pinch-hitter or pinch-runner: Abreu, of; Alyea, dh, ph; Barns, p; Bonilla, p; A. Brown, c; E. Carr, of, p; Cox, p; David, of; DeAngelis, p; Donnels, 2b; Douma, p; Edge, p; Elliot, of; Escalera, p; M. Hernandez, p; Hundley, 3b; Kelley, ss; Lynch, of; Merriman, p; Plummer, p; Postier, 2b; Thoutsis, p; M. White, of.

CLUB PITCHING

Club	ERA.	G.	CG.	ShO.	Sv.	IP.	H.	R.	ER.	HR.	HB.	BB.	Int. BB.	SO.	WP.	Bk.
Jackson	3.15	135	10	16	42	1187.2	1082	499	416	72	43	396	32	748	56	15
Shreveport	3.16	133	11	12	31	1157.2	1125	496	406	64	28	388	32	869	61	10
San Antonio	3.30	134	10	7	40	1196.1	1104	544	438	75	34	479	30	815	58	13
El Paso	3.99	135	8	4	43	1198.1	1254	613	531	82	30	483	41	837	78	20
Tulsa	4.11	136	12	6	35	1155.0	1136	620	527	62	49	592	27	820	108	19
Arkansas	4.22	136	19	12	27	1126.1	1168	650	528	74	33	454	38	817	78	15
Wichita	4.48	136	10	4	28	1178.0	1276	684	586	108	40	414	10	794	72	11
Midland	5.33	137	5	3	24	1201.2	1456	827	711	92	41	556	24	832	91	33

PITCHERS' RECORDS

(Leading Qualifiers for Earned-Run Average Leadership—109 or More Innings)

*Throws lefthanded.

Pitcher—Club	W.	L.	Pct.	ERA.	G.	GS.	CG.	GF.	ShO.	Sv.	IP.	H.	R.	ER.	HR.	HB.	BB.	Int. BB.	SO.	WP.
Young, Jackson	15	3	.833	1.65	23	23	3	0	1	0	158.0	116	38	29	3	3	52	5	95	7
Cinnella, Jackson	6	3	.667	2.27	40	8	0	9	0	2	111.0	105	33	28	1	5	41	6	69	4
Lienhard, Shreveport	5	7	.417	2.50	48	6	1	17	0	5	115.0	108	42	32	7	0	35	6	68	4
Miller, Jackson	7	7	.500	2.91	22	21	3	0	1	0	139.0	113	54	45	14	8	32	1	95	6
Hostetler, Shreveport	5	8	.385	3.04	23	22	1	1	0	0	130.1	120	55	44	5	3	40	3	112	5
Schourek, Jackson*	11	4	.733	3.04	19	19	1	0	0	0	124.1	109	53	42	8	8	39	2	94	5
Springer, San Antonio	8	6	.571	3.31	24	24	3	0	0	0	163.1	147	76	60	8	1	73	0	77	7
James, San Antonio	11	4	.733	3.32	26	26	3	0	0	0	157.0	144	73	58	14	9	78	1	97	10
Opperman, San Antonio	12	8	.600	3.41	27	27	3	0	0	0	155.2	153	75	59	16	7	62	2	96	7
Bones, Wichita	6	4	.600	3.48	21	21	2	0	1	0	137.0	138	66	53	15	5	45	0	96	6

Departmental Leaders: G—Lepley, 59; W—Young, 15; L—Cormier, Sager, 12; Pct.—Young, .833; GS—Opperman, 27; CG—Clark, 5; GF—Bross, 48; ShO—Osteen, 3; Sv.—Bross, 28; IP—Springer, 163.1; H—Sager, 200; R—Sager, 105; ER—Sager, 94; HR—J. Hernandez, 18; HB—Taylor, 10; BB—McCray, 82; IBB—George, 7; SO—Hostetler, 112; WP—Freeland, 20.

(All Pitchers—Listed Alphabetically)

Pitcher—Club	W.	L.	Pct.	ERA.	G.	GS.	CG.	GF.	ShO.	Sv.	IP.	H.	R.	ER.	HR.	HB.	BB.	Int. BB.	SO.	WP.
Abbott, Midland*	6	9	.400	4.14	24	24	2	0	0	0	128.1	124	75	59	8	8	73	0	91	6
Abreu, Arkansas	0	1	.000	13.50	2	0	0	2	0	0	1.1	3	2	2	1	0	2	1	0	0
Acosta, Midland*	1	0	1.000	1.50	2	2	0	0	0	0	12.0	15	4	2	0	0	4	0	6	0
Allen, Tulsa	8	4	.667	3.83	54	0	0	23	0	5	89.1	97	43	38	4	7	42	6	84	8
Alleyne, Arkansas*	1	4	.200	5.86	20	7	0	2	0	0	50.2	61	42	33	4	1	33	3	43	6
Arnold, Arkansas	1	0	1.000	2.63	4	4	0	0	0	0	24.0	21	11	7	0	2	7	1	15	0
Austin, El Paso	11	3	.786	2.44	38	3	0	24	0	6	92.1	91	36	25	5	1	26	4	77	8
Barns, Midland	0	0	.000	2.70	4	0	0	4	0	0	3.1	4	2	1	0	0	0	0	2	0
Beck, Shreveport	10	3	.769	2.23	14	14	2	0	1	0	93.0	85	26	23	4	1	17	1	71	7
Bockus, Midland	2	0	1.000	2.08	7	4	0	1	0	0	30.1	27	9	7	2	1	7	0	8	1
Bones, Wichita	6	4	.600	3.48	21	21	2	0	1	0	137.0	138	66	53	15	5	45	0	96	6
Bonilla, Shreveport*	0	1	.000	4.00	9	0	0	2	0	0	9.0	12	4	4	2	0	2	0	12	1
Brocail, Wichita	2	2	.500	4.33	12	9	0	1	0	0	52.0	53	30	25	7	2	24	0	27	4
Bross, Wichita	3	4	.429	2.64	58	0	0	48	0	28	71.2	46	21	21	4	2	40	5	51	4
Bryant, Tulsa	6	4	.600	3.38	19	7	1	7	1	1	69.1	75	35	26	6	3	17	2	36	5
Bumgarner, Jackson	0	2	.000	4.50	3	0	0	2	0	0	8.0	11	5	4	0	0	2	0	4	0
Burgos, Arkansas*	2	3	.400	2.77	6	6	1	0	1	0	39.0	37	13	12	1	3	10	1	15	0
Bustillos, San Antonio	0	1	.000	6.48	5	0	0	1	0	1	8.1	8	6	6	0	0	5	0	6	1
Butcher, Midland	3	7	.300	6.21	35	8	0	6	0	0	87.0	109	68	60	7	3	55	2	84	3
Campbell, San Antonio	2	6	.250	2.33	49	0	0	29	0	8	81.0	67	29	21	1	1	25	6	84	7
Carr, San Antonio	0	0	.000	36.00	1	0	0	1	0	0	1.0	3	5	4	1	0	1	0	1	0
G. Carter, Midland	3	8	.273	5.87	20	20	1	0	0	0	102.2	132	84	67	9	1	46	0	66	4
L. Carter, Shreveport	1	0	1.000	3.50	5	4	0	0	0	0	18.0	15	7	7	3	1	4	0	12	1
Castillo, Tulsa	6	1	.857	2.35	20	0	0	6	0	1	46.0	41	13	12	2	3	26	1	39	7
Chapman, El Paso	3	4	.429	3.92	42	1	0	19	0	3	87.1	87	42	38	4	4	42	5	76	6
Chavez, Wichita	6	5	.545	4.18	46	1	0	36	0	1	84.0	85	46	39	4	3	16	1	47	8

Pitcher—Club	W.	L.	Pct.	ERA.	G.	GS.	CG.	GF.	ShO.	Sv.	IP.	H.	R.	ER.	HR.	HB.	BB.	Int. BB.	SO.	WP.
Cinnella, Jackson	6	3	.667	2.27	40	8	0	9	0	2	111.0	105	33	28	1	5	41	6	69	4
Clark, Arkansas	5	11	.313	3.82	19	19	5	0	0	0	115.1	111	56	49	11	0	37	2	87	6
Cliburn, Midland	0	0	.000	1.80	5	0	0	3	0	1	10.0	10	2	2	1	0	4	0	5	0
Coleman, San Antonio	1	1	.500	3.90	14	0	0	6	0	3	27.2	30	14	12	1	2	8	0	16	1
Compres, Tulsa	0	1	.000	6.10	6	0	0	3	0	0	10.1	12	10	7	0	0	11	1	9	2
Connolly, Shreveport°	2	5	.286	3.19	50	0	0	18	0	2	59.1	61	24	21	6	0	20	6	50	5
Cormier, Arkansas°	5	12	.294	5.04	22	21	3	1	1	0	121.1	133	81	68	9	5	30	2	102	6
Cox, Arkansas	1	0	1.000	1.29	1	1	1	0	0	0	7.0	3	1	1	0	0	1	0	3	0
Cunningham, Tulsa	7	2	.778	4.35	17	12	1	1	0	0	78.2	75	42	38	6	3	49	1	47	8
DeAngelis, Midland°	0	0	.000	18.00	2	0	0	2	0	0	3.0	5	6	6	0	0	5	0	1	0
Dewey, Shreveport	1	5	.167	1.88	33	0	0	32	0	13	38.1	37	11	8	1	1	10	2	23	1
Diez, Jackson°	0	0	.000	13.50	1	0	0	0	0	0	2.2	4	4	4	2	0	1	0	0	0
DiMichele, 34 Mid.-12 Wich.°	4	5	.444	6.27	46	1	0	12	0	2	66.0	95	60	46	9	4	34	1	60	12
Douma, Jackson°	0	0	.000	3.00	1	1	0	0	0	0	6.0	3	2	2	0	0	3	0	5	0
Edge, El Paso	0	0	.000	18.00	1	0	0	1	0	0	1.0	4	2	2	0	0	0	0	1	0
Eldred, El Paso	5	4	.556	4.49	19	19	0	0	0	0	110.1	126	61	55	9	2	47	0	93	4
Elli, Jackson°	3	6	.333	4.54	17	15	1	1	0	0	75.1	74	43	38	8	4	34	1	52	5
Elvira, El Paso°	0	2	.000	4.50	4	4	0	0	0	0	18.0	17	11	9	4	0	6	0	12	0
Erb, Midland	1	1	.500	5.17	6	6	0	0	0	0	31.1	39	20	18	2	0	24	0	25	8
Ericks, Arkansas	1	2	.333	9.39	4	4	1	0	1	0	15.1	17	19	16	2	1	19	0	19	3
Escalera, El Paso°	0	0	.000	0.00	1	0	0	1	0	0	1.0	1	0	0	0	0	1	0	0	0
Estes, Shreveport°	0	0	.000	5.79	9	0	0	4	0	0	14.0	20	10	9	0	1	5	0	9	2
Fleming, El Paso	3	1	.750	7.03	18	0	0	5	0	0	32.0	42	30	25	3	1	14	2	21	3
Fortugno, El Paso°	2	3	.400	3.14	12	2	0	4	0	2	28.2	23	12	10	0	1	22	2	24	4
Freeland, El Paso	10	8	.556	4.01	26	26	2	0	1	0	157.0	145	74	70	8	2	74	2	94	20
Garces, El Paso°	2	4	.333	3.56	28	0	0	9	0	1	55.2	47	24	22	5	2	22	5	52	4
George, El Paso	8	3	.727	1.78	39	0	0	30	0	13	55.2	41	16	11	1	3	20	7	38	8
Gideon, Jackson°	0	0	.000	7.47	9	0	0	2	0	0	15.2	19	14	13	2	1	6	0	10	2
Grahe, Midland	7	5	.583	5.29	18	18	1	0	0	0	119.0	145	75	70	10	4	34	1	58	11
Grater, Arkansas	2	0	1.000	2.86	29	0	0	22	0	17	44.0	31	18	14	1	4	18	0	43	6
Gunderson, Shreveport°	2	2	.500	3.25	8	8	1	0	1	0	52.2	51	24	19	7	2	17	1	44	1
Guzman, Tulsa	0	0	.000	6.00	1	1	0	0	0	0	3.0	3	2	2	0	0	0	0	2	0
Ham, Shreveport	0	0	.000	36.00	1	0	0	0	0	0	1.0	4	5	4	0	0	3	0	2	0
Hamilton, Midland°	3	8	.273	7.39	20	20	0	0	0	0	91.1	116	82	75	5	4	56	0	62	6
Hansen, Wichita°	6	3	.667	4.67	27	8	0	6	0	0	94.1	103	49	49	12	2	37	0	52	5
Hartsock, San Antonio	6	4	.600	3.93	16	16	0	0	0	0	94.0	88	42	41	2	2	42	2	68	4
Henry, El Paso	1	0	1.000	2.93	15	0	0	12	0	9	30.2	31	13	10	1	0	11	0	25	0
J. Hernandez, Wichita	7	6	.538	4.53	26	26	1	0	0	0	155.0	163	92	78	18	7	50	0	101	6
M. Hernandez, Jackson	1	0	1.000	3.00	1	1	0	0	0	0	6.0	6	2	2	0	0	1	0	1	0
Hershiser, San Antonio	0	0	.000	1.13	3	0	0	0	0	0	8.0	5	1	1	0	0	2	0	7	1
Hickerson, Shreveport°	3	6	.333	4.23	27	6	0	7	0	1	66.0	71	37	31	2	1	26	2	63	2
Hillman, Jackson°	6	5	.545	3.93	15	15	0	0	0	0	89.1	92	42	39	3	4	30	2	61	7
Hoffman, Arkansas	0	2	.000	3.66	4	4	0	0	0	0	19.2	21	13	8	1	1	12	0	16	2
Holsman, Wichita°	7	6	.538	4.20	46	0	0	38	0	6	70.2	81	39	33	3	3	30	2	85	9
Holzemer, Midland	1	7	.125	5.26	15	15	1	0	0	0	77.0	92	55	45	10	6	41	0	54	6
Hook, Midland°	0	1	.000	9.35	7	0	0	3	0	0	8.2	9	9	9	0	1	7	1	10	2
Hoover, Tulsa	2	1	.667	3.42	4	4	0	0	0	0	23.2	29	12	9	0	0	11	2	18	3
Hostetler, Shreveport	5	8	.385	3.04	23	22	1	1	0	0	130.1	120	55	44	5	3	40	3	112	5
Hunter, El Paso	6	3	.667	3.92	9	9	2	0	0	0	62.0	64	31	27	9	1	15	0	37	1
Hurst, Tulsa	0	2	.000	9.47	8	3	0	2	0	0	25.2	29	30	27	4	0	17	1	23	1
Hvizda, Tulsa	1	3	.250	3.77	32	0	0	23	0	9	43.0	50	20	18	5	1	11	1	24	2
Ignasiak, El Paso	6	3	.667	4.35	15	15	1	0	0	0	82.2	96	45	40	5	1	34	1	39	4
James, San Antonio	11	4	.733	3.32	26	26	3	0	0	0	157.0	144	73	58	14	9	78	1	97	10
Kisten, Arkansas	2	3	.400	3.25	45	0	0	21	0	3	52.2	46	29	19	2	1	21	3	40	9
Kline, Jackson	6	8	.429	3.94	31	14	1	7	0	1	109.2	119	55	48	9	1	31	0	79	5
Lara, Jackson	0	0	.000	3.60	4	0	0	4	0	0	5.0	3	2	2	0	1	0	1	1	1
LaRose, Jackson	1	3	.250	3.90	19	0	0	8	0	1	27.2	36	20	12	2	4	15	4	18	3
Lepley, Arkansas°	4	6	.400	2.62	59	0	0	27	0	4	79.0	70	36	23	3	1	36	4	61	5
Lienhard, Shreveport	5	7	.417	2.50	48	6	1	17	0	5	115.0	108	42	32	7	0	35	6	68	4
Loubier, Wichita	1	4	.200	6.68	15	3	0	3	0	0	33.2	42	36	25	4	4	18	0	20	12
Lynch, Tulsa°	4	4	.500	3.81	21	6	0	10	0	5	59.0	60	25	25	5	3	21	1	37	2
Majer, Arkansas	0	2	.000	10.22	3	3	0	0	0	0	12.1	19	15	14	4	0	8	1	4	2
Marquez, San Antonio	3	1	.750	4.86	13	0	0	7	0	0	16.2	20	10	9	0	0	8	0	15	1
D. Martinez, Midland	6	6	.500	5.17	34	0	0	11	0	0	71.1	95	47	41	5	4	30	5	74	6
P. Martinez, Wichita°	6	10	.375	4.80	24	23	2	0	0	0	129.1	139	83	69	15	3	70	2	88	4
G. Mathews, Arkansas°	0	1	.000	2.57	1	1	0	0	0	0	7.0	4	2	2	0	1	0	0	4	0
T. Mathews, Tulsa	5	7	.417	4.27	14	14	4	0	2	0	86.1	88	50	41	1	2	36	2	48	9
May, El Paso	6	4	.600	3.79	22	13	2	3	0	0	99.2	113	48	42	7	1	38	3	85	4
McAndrew, San Antonio	7	3	.700	1.93	12	12	0	0	0	0	79.1	68	28	17	2	4	32	2	50	1
McCray, Tulsa°	8	7	.533	4.21	25	25	1	0	0	0	141.0	142	79	66	9	2	82	2	98	16
McGrath, El Paso	3	3	.500	3.48	13	12	1	0	0	0	77.2	89	39	30	4	3	27	5	32	3
Mead, Shreveport	2	2	.500	2.25	16	0	0	8	0	2	28.0	19	9	7	1	1	6	1	23	0
Meeks, Midland	7	4	.636	4.74	35	6	0	23	0	6	74.0	86	40	39	6	1	28	3	53	7
Meier, Shreveport	5	4	.545	3.08	14	14	1	0	1	0	87.2	91	32	30	2	1	21	1	61	3
Merejo, Midland	1	3	.250	7.13	29	0	0	9	0	1	48.0	66	44	38	4	0	20	1	27	2
Merriman, Midland	1	0	1.000	2.25	2	0	0	1	0	0	4.0	7	1	1	0	0	0	0	1	0
Miglio, El Paso°	2	0	1.000	4.02	8	0	0	2	0	0	15.2	16	8	7	1	2	6	0	10	2
Milchin, Arkansas°	6	8	.429	4.31	17	17	4	0	2	0	102.1	103	62	49	8	1	47	3	75	6
Miller, Jackson	7	7	.500	2.91	22	21	3	0	1	0	139.0	113	54	45	14	8	32	1	95	6
Minton, Midland	0	0	.000	0.00	4	0	0	0	0	0	5.2	3	0	0	0	1	0	0	1	0
Monson, El Paso	6	9	.400	6.33	22	20	0	0	0	0	108.0	125	87	76	11	4	49	3	61	4
Moore, Midland	4	1	.800	4.95	20	1	0	5	0	0	56.1	55	31	31	7	1	18	1	40	7
Nen, Tulsa	0	5	.000	5.06	7	7	0	0	0	0	26.2	23	20	15	1	0	21	0	21	3
Nivens, Jackson	6	8	.429	3.86	18	18	1	0	0	0	102.2	115	54	44	10	0	19	2	36	5
Novoa, Shreveport°	5	4	.556	2.64	11	10	2	1	1	0	71.2	60	21	21	3	3	25	0	65	4
Opperman, San Antonio	12	8	.600	3.41	27	27	3	0	0	0	155.2	153	75	59	16	7	62	2	96	7
Osteen, Arkansas	5	5	.500	3.01	13	13	4	0	3	0	83.2	77	32	28	4	3	21	3	51	5
Ozuna, Arkansas	3	2	.600	3.30	54	0	0	15	0	0	71.0	82	36	26	2	2	26	5	61	5
Pavlik, Tulsa	6	5	.545	2.33	16	16	2	0	1	0	100.1	66	29	26	4	5	71	2	91	7
Pena, Shreveport°	10	7	.588	3.69	25	24	1	0	0	0	139.0	138	70	57	9	2	57	2	101	8
Perez, Jackson	2	1	.667	2.20	26	0	0	5	0	0	49.0	42	16	12	2	1	19	1	33	1
Picota, Arkansas	10	8	.556	4.57	26	24	0	0	0	0	138.0	159	84	70	8	4	57	3	71	6

Pitcher—Club	W.	L.	Pct.	ERA.	G.	GS.	CG.	GF.	ShO.	Sv.	IP.	H.	R.	ER.	HR.	HB.	BB.	Int. BB.	SO.	WP.
Pierson, Arkansas	3	4	.429	5.48	21	6	0	3	0	0	47.2	68	30	29	3	1	12	2	21	2
Pitz, San Antonio	4	4	.500	4.12	26	9	1	4	0	0	87.1	82	45	40	11	1	16	5	56	3
Plummer, Jackson	1	1	.500	2.00	4	0	0	2	0	0	9.0	5	2	2	1	0	3	1	3	0
Poole, San Antonio*	6	7	.462	2.40	54	0	0	35	0	16	63.2	55	31	17	3	2	27	5	77	6
Postier, Tulsa	0	0	.000	1.35	5	0	0	5	0	0	6.2	4	1	1	0	1	2	0	2	1
Potestio, Shreveport	1	1	.500	5.06	12	0	0	4	0	0	26.2	31	17	15	1	1	8	0	19	1
Puig, El Paso*	1	0	1.000	1.14	19	0	0	16	0	8	23.2	18	3	3	1	1	11	2	24	1
Quinzer, Wichita	2	4	.333	4.56	31	2	0	8	0	2	73.0	75	42	37	10	2	24	2	43	0
R. Reed, Tulsa	2	1	.667	2.79	5	5	1	0	0	0	29.0	31	12	9	2	1	11	0	14	4
S. Reed, Shreveport	3	1	.750	1.64	45	0	0	28	0	8	60.1	53	20	11	2	2	20	6	59	0
Remlinger, Shreveport*	9	11	.450	3.90	25	25	2	0	1	0	147.2	149	82	64	9	8	72	1	75	16
Roberts, Wichita*	9	6	.600	3.76	18	16	3	0	0	0	103.0	107	49	43	7	2	27	0	63	7
Rockman, Tulsa	1	2	.333	3.79	24	0	0	14	0	4	38.0	46	20	16	1	3	13	1	23	5
Rosenthal, Tulsa	2	2	.500	2.40	12	0	0	10	0	4	15.0	9	6	4	1	0	9	1	18	3
Sager, Wichita	11	12	.478	5.48	26	26	2	0	1	0	154.1	200	105	94	7	3	29	1	79	3
Schourek, Jackson*	11	4	.733	3.04	19	19	1	0	0	0	124.1	109	53	42	8	8	39	2	94	5
Scott, San Antonio	3	3	.500	2.85	30	0	0	20	0	7	47.1	35	17	15	5	1	14	0	52	0
Shaw, Tulsa*	4	5	.444	6.86	14	12	0	2	0	0	63.0	72	51	48	2	3	44	1	41	4
Shiflett, Tulsa	0	1	.000	3.00	13	0	0	8	0	4	27.0	24	12	9	0	1	9	1	26	2
Shinall, San Antonio	6	3	.667	3.55	20	15	0	3	0	0	91.1	93	44	36	2	1	41	1	43	6
D. Smith, Tulsa*	3	2	.600	3.76	7	7	0	0	0	0	38.1	27	16	16	2	0	16	0	32	0
K. Smith, Arkansas	0	0	.000	10.80	3	0	0	0	0	0	3.1	7	4	4	1	0	1	1	2	0
Sparks, El Paso	1	2	.333	6.53	7	6	0	1	0	0	30.1	43	24	22	4	1	15	0	17	2
Springer, San Antonio	8	6	.571	3.31	24	24	3	0	0	0	163.1	147	76	60	8	1	73	0	77	7
Stone, Arkansas	1	1	.500	3.90	7	6	0	1	0	0	27.2	22	14	12	0	2	23	0	27	4
Taylor, Tulsa	1	6	.143	5.79	33	9	2	10	0	2	98.0	108	69	63	5	10	47	1	59	10
Terrill, San Antonio*	1	1	.500	3.52	3	3	0	0	0	0	15.1	15	8	6	1	0	2	0	5	0
Thomas, Tulsa	2	3	.400	3.35	8	8	0	0	0	0	37.2	25	23	14	2	1	26	0	28	6
Thoutsis, Arkansas	0	0	.000	9.00	3	0	0	3	0	0	3.0	3	4	3	0	0	2	0	2	0
Trudeau, Midland	2	2	.500	5.26	19	2	0	7	0	1	53.0	68	35	31	4	0	12	2	29	2
Vann, Midland	2	5	.286	4.13	32	0	0	25	0	7	52.1	59	26	24	3	1	27	4	43	5
Vanzytveld, San Antonio	0	1	.000	1.66	8	2	0	2	0	1	21.2	16	6	4	0	1	13	1	9	2
Vargas, Arkansas	1	4	.200	6.75	15	0	0	10	0	3	21.1	27	18	16	3	1	13	3	21	1
Vasquez, Jackson	5	7	.417	3.36	53	0	0	37	0	10	77.2	64	39	29	3	1	27	2	41	1
Vidmar, Midland	1	6	.143	7.51	11	11	0	0	0	0	44.1	67	45	37	2	0	18	0	20	4
Watkins, El Paso	1	2	.333	2.17	5	5	0	0	0	0	29.0	35	7	7	0	0	3	0	19	0
Weese, Arkansas	1	3	.250	5.22	29	0	0	10	0	0	39.2	43	28	23	4	0	17	0	34	4
Wood, Wichita	2	4	.333	2.73	44	0	0	32	0	11	69.1	61	26	21	3	2	32	3	70	2
Wray, San Antonio*	8	3	.727	3.71	45	0	0	16	0	4	77.2	75	34	32	8	2	30	5	56	1
Young, Jackson	15	3	.833	1.65	23	23	3	0	1	0	158.0	116	38	29	3	3	52	5	95	7
Zappelli, Midland	3	4	.429	4.40	35	0	0	22	0	6	45.0	57	28	22	1	4	14	3	35	5

BALKS—Meeks, 7; Moore, 5; Bones, Bross, Hamilton, Monson, Opperman, Shaw, 4 each; Abbott, G. Carter, Elli, Freeland, Hostetler, Ignasiak, Picota, Sager, 3 each; Bockus, Chapman, Cunningham, DiMichele, Hartsock, Henry, Hickerson, Hillman, Lepley, Lynch, D. Martinez, Miglio, Pavlik, Pena, Terrill, 2 each; Bryant, Burgos, Bustillos, Butcher, Campbell, Castillo, Chavez, Clark, Cormier, Eldred, Ericks, Garces, George, Grahe, Hansen, J. Hernandez, Hook, Hoover, Kisten, Kline, LaRose, Lienhard, G. Mathews, McCray, McGrath, Merejo, Milchin, Miller, Nivens, Ozuna, Potestio, S. Reed, Rockman, Rosenthal, Schourek, Shinall, D. Smith, Springer, Taylor, Thomas, Thoutsis, Weese, Wood, Wray, Young, Zappelli, 1 each.

COMBINATION SHUTOUTS—Arnold-Lepley, Burgos-Grater, Cormier-Ozuna, Pierson-Grater, Arkansas; Eldred-Austin, Hunter-Austin-Garces, Ignasiak-Austin, El Paso; Cinnella-Kline, Elli-Cinnella-Bross, Elli-Vasquez-Bross, Kline-Perez, Miller-Bross, Miller-Cinnella, Nivens-Bross, Nivens-Bross-LaRose, Schourek-Bross, Schourek-Cinnella-Bross, Young-Bross, Young-Cinnella-Bross, Young-LaRose-Bross, Young-Vasquez-Bross, Jackson; Bockus-Moore-Cliburn, Butcher-Moore-Martinez, Grahe-Meeks, Midland; Hartsock-Campbell, Hartsock-Poole-Marquez-Wray, Hartsock-Scott, James-Poole, Shinall-Campbell-Poole, Springer-Poole, Vanzytveld-Scott, San Antonio; Beck-Bonilla-Lienhard, Beck-Lienhard, Beck-Reed, Meier-Dewey, Novoa-Pena-Connolly-Mead, Pena-Connolly, Pena-Dewey, Shreveport; Hoover-Allen, McCray-Hvizda, Tulsa; Bones-Wood, Sager-Holsman, Wichita.

NO-HIT GAMES—None.

California League

CLASS A

CHAMPIONSHIP WINNERS IN PREVIOUS YEARS

1914—Fresno	.571	1961—Reno	.743	1976—Salinas	.650
1915—Modesto	.857	Reno	.643	Reno§	.547
1916-40—Did not operate.		1962—San José§	.686	1977—Salinas	.564
1941—Fresno	.643	Reno	.587	Lodi§	.579
S. Barbara (2nd)*	.597	1963—Modesto	.589	1978—Visalia§	.698
1942—Santa Barbara†	.642	Stockton§	.687	Lodi	.607
1943-44-45—Did not operate.		1964—Fresno	.638	1979—San José§	.636
1946—Stockton‡	.600	Fresno	.600	Reno	.525
1947—Stockton‡	.679	1965—San Jose	.586	1980—Stockton§	.638
1948—Fresno	.607	Stockton§	.614	Visalia	.507
S. Barbara (3rd)*	.529	1966—Modesto	.577	1981—Visalia	.621
1949—Bakersfield	.612	Modesto	.671	Lodi§	.521
San Jose (4th)*	.543	1967—San José§	.676	1982—Modesto§	.671
1950—Ventura	.607	Modesto	.586	Visalia	.586
Modesto (2nd)*	.586	1968—San Jose	.629	1983—Visalia	.621
1951—Santa Barbara‡	.599	Fresno§	.623	Redwood§	.529
1952—Fresno‡	.629	1969—Stockton§	.600	1984—Modesto§	.597
1953—San Jose‡	.664	Visalia	.614	Bakersfield	.486
1954—Modesto‡	.623	1970—Bakersfield	.667	1985—Fresno§	.575
1955—Stockton	.733	Bakersfield	.671	Stockton	.566
Fresno§	.718	1971—Visalia§	.583	1986—Palm Springs	.613
1956—Fresno‡	.650	Fresno	.500	Stockton§	.585
1957—Visalia x	.622	1972—Modesto§	.547	1987—Fresno§	.559
Salinas (4th)*	.504	Bakersfield	.629	Reno	.535
1958—Fresno*	.639	1973—Lodi§	.657	1988—Stockton	.657
Bakersfield	.672	Bakersfield	.571	Riverside§	.599
1959—Bakersfield	.592	1974—Fresno§	.607	1989—Stockton	.627
Modesto§	.643	San Jose	.579	Bakersfield§	.577
1960—Reno	.614	1975—Reno	.614		
Reno	.657	Reno	.614		

*Won four-club playoff. †League disbanded June 28. ‡Won championship and four-club playoff. §Won split-season playoff. xWon both halves of split-season.

STANDING OF CLUBS AT CLOSE OF FIRST HALF, JUNE 17

NORTHERN DIVISION

Club	W.	L.	T.	Pct.	G.B.
Stockton (Brewers)	47	23	0	.671	....
Reno (Independent)	33	35	0	.485	13
San Jose (Giants)	33	38	0	.465	14½
Modesto (Athletics)	28	42	0	.400	19
Salinas (Independent)	22	47	0	.319	24½

SOUTHERN DIVISION

Club	W.	L.	T.	Pct.	G.B.
Visalia (Twins)	48	22	0	.686	....
Bakersfield (Dodgers)	40	31	0	.563	8½
San Bernardino (Mariners)	39	32	0	.549	9½
Riverside (Padres)	35	36	0	.493	13½
Palm Springs (Angels)	26	45	0	.366	22½

STANDING OF CLUBS AT CLOSE OF SECOND HALF, AUGUST 29

NORTHERN DIVISION

Club	W.	L.	T.	Pct.	G.B.
San Jose (Giants)	41	30	0	.577	....
Reno (Independent)	38	33	0	.535	3
Stockton (Brewers)	35	36	0	.493	6
Modesto (Athletics)	31	40	0	.437	10
Salinas (Independent)	25	46	0	.352	16

SOUTHERN DIVISION

Club	W.	L.	T.	Pct.	G.B.
Visalia (Twins)	42	29	0	.592	....
Bakersfield (Dodgers)	40	31	0	.563	2
San Bernardino (Mariners)	38	33	0	.535	4
Palm Springs (Angels)	36	35	0	.507	6
Riverside (Padres)	29	42	0	.408	13

COMPOSITE STANDING OF CLUBS AT CLOSE OF SEASON, AUGUST 29

Club	Vis.	Sto.	Bak.	S.B.	S.J.	Reno	Riv.	P.S.	Mod.	Sal.	W.	L.	T.	Pct.	G.B.
Visalia (Twins)	....	8	8	10	10	8	12	16	8	10	90	51	0	.638	....
Stockton (Brewers)	4	....	4	7	12	14	6	8	15	12	82	59	0	.582	8
Bakersfield (Dodgers)	14	8	....	9	5	8	12	10	7	7	80	62	0	.563	10½
San Bernardino (Mariners)	10	5	10	....	7	6	12	12	8	7	77	65	0	.542	13½
San Jose (Giants)	2	5	7	6	....	13	7	8	8	14	74	68	0	.521	16½
Reno (Independent)	3	6	4	6	7	....	10	7	14	14	71	68	0	.511	18
Riverside (Padres)	7	6	9	9	5	3	....	11	6	8	64	78	0	.451	26½
Palm Springs (Angels)	5	4	10	9	4	5	9	....	6	10	62	80	0	.437	28½
Modesto (Athletics)	4	5	5	4	12	6	6	6	....	11	59	82	0	.418	31
Salinas (Independent)	2	5	5	5	6	5	4	2	10	....	47	93	0	.336	42½

Major league affiliations in parentheses.

Playoffs—Stockton defeated San Jose, three games to one; Bakersfield defeated Visalia, three games to two; Stockton defeated Bakersfield, three games to two, to win league championship.

Regular-Season Attendance—Bakersfield, 142,280; Modesto, 62,089; Palm Springs, 76,462; Reno, 87,048; Riverside, 82,420; Salinas, 33,465; San Bernardino, 190,890; San Jose, 108,478; Stockton, 85,436; Visalia, 78,212. Total, 946,780. Playoffs (14 games)—25,126. All-Star Game at San Bernardino—2,688.

Managers—Bakersfield, Tom Beyers; Modesto, Ted Kubiak; Palm Springs, Nate Oliver; Reno, Mike Brown; Riverside, Bruce Bochy; Salinas, Hide Koga; San Bernardino, Keith Bodie; San Jose, Tom Spencer; Stockton, Chris Bando; Visalia, Scott Ullger.

All-Star Team—1B—Bo Dodson, Stockton; 2B—John Patterson, San Jose; 3B—Frank Bolick, San Bernardino-Stockton; SS—Royce Clayton, San Jose; OF—Darrell Sherman, Riverside; Tom Eiterman, Reno; J.T. Bruett, Visalia; C—Bryan Baar, Bakersfield; DH—Brett Magnusson, Bakersfield; P—Dan Rambo, San Jose; Rich Garces, Visalia; George Tsamis, Visalia; Jason Brosnan, Bakersfield; Jamie McAndrew, Bakersfield; Chris Johnson, Stockton; Most Valuable Player—Frank Bolick, San Bernardino-Stockton; Pitcher of the Year—Dan Rambo, San Jose; Rookie of the Year—Dave Staton, Riverside; Scott Ullger, Visalia.

(Compiled by Howe Sportsdata International, Boston, Mass.)

CLUB BATTING

Club	Pct.	G.	AB.	R.	OR.	H.	TB.	2B.	3B.	HR.	RBI.	SH.	SF.	HP.	BB.	Int. BB.	SO.	SB.	CS.	LOB.
Reno	.282	139	4716	816	795	1330	1923	208	47	97	704	34	53		566	30	884	120	86	1004
Visalia	.279	141	4776	724	568	1331	1831	209	39	71	631	31	38	57	596	25	821	126	62	1147
San Bernardino	.276	142	4829	803	746	1333	1965	212	33	118	690	32	42	76	548	25	1030	202	110	999
Bakersfield	.263	142	4774	730	661	1256	1878	241	30	107	647	23	41	50	522	26	1011	191	81	1008
San Jose	.262	142	4788	766	688	1254	1743	177	48	72	676	47	58	87	606	17	976	159	95	1096
Riverside	.254	142	4619	608	709	1172	1586	172	40	54	536	34	37	47	573	27	955	205	103	1006
Palm Springs	.251	142	4715	609	705	1185	1585	196	42	40	524	35	29	53	466	13	1098	110	77	958
Modesto	.250	141	4696	625	684	1172	1705	203	27	92	545	50	35	48	536	15	1036	140	105	1026
Stockton	.247	141	4409	691	611	1087	1547	169	45	67	587	43	53	56	604	15	953	182	117	905
Salinas	.243	140	4535	565	770	1103	1510	163	32	60	481	71	28	35	525	22	1019	152	107	953

INDIVIDUAL BATTING

(Leading Qualifiers for Batting Championship—383 or More Plate Appearances)

°Bats lefthanded.   †Switch-hitter.

Player and Club	Pct.	G.	AB.	R.	H.	TB.	2B.	3B.	HR.	RBI.	SH.	SF.	HP.	BB.	Int. BB.	SO.	SB.	CS.
Eiterman, Thomas, Reno	.331	121	471	92	156	208	19	6	7	73	4	3	9	55	4	73	6	7
Bolick, Frank, 50 Stock.-78 S.B.†	.324	128	441	100	143	240	33	5	18	102	0	13	4	91	7	86	8	9
Harper, Milton, Reno°	.317	91	322	69	102	189	23	2	20	73	1	6	4	62	4	58	0	0
Magnusson, Brett, Bakersfield	.311	121	434	92	135	242	34	2	23	85	1	1	10	73	5	104	5	4
Buckley, Troy, Visalia	.307	117	404	69	124	171	24	4	5	64	2	5	11	43	2	58	5	2
Bruett, Joseph, Visalia°	.307	123	437	86	134	158	15	3	1	33	8	3	4	101	4	60	50	21
Chimelis, Joel, 85 Reno-46 Mod.	.303	131	531	87	161	219	26	10	4	70	6	3	3	49	4	56	30	15
Patterson, John, San Jose†	.302	131	530	91	160	207	23	6	4	66	5	6	9	46	2	74	29	17
DeJardin, Bradford, Reno°	.297	114	387	66	115	152	17	1	6	54	4	7	2	38	5	89	15	9
Turang, Brian, San Bernardino	.296	132	487	86	144	215	25	5	12	67	6	4	7	69	0	98	25	16

Departmental Leaders: G—Five players tied with 139; AB—Howard, 551; R—Listach, 116; H—Chimelis, 161; TB—Magnusson, 242; 2B—Magnusson, 34; 3B—Raley, 14; HR—Whitfield, 24; RBI—Bolick, 102; SH—Yanagida, 22; SF—Bolick, Jackson, 13; HP—Davenport, 16; BB—Listach, 105; IBB—Keitges, 12; SO—S. Hosey, 139; SB—Maynard, 80; CS—Maynard, 15.

(All Players—Listed Alphabetically)

Player and Club	Pct.	G.	AB.	R.	H.	TB.	2B.	3B.	HR.	RBI.	SH.	SF.	HP.	BB.	Int. BB.	SO.	SB.	CS.
Alegre, Paul, Salinas°	.130	14	23	1	3	7	1	0	1	4	0	0	0	1	0	13	0	1
Alfonzo, Edgar, Palm Springs	.276	57	203	44	56	70	4	2	2	12	5	2	0	30	0	37	5	4
Allanson, Andrew, Salinas	.291	36	127	21	37	54	6	1	3	19	0	2	2	19	0	22	6	5
Arguelles, Fernando, San Bernardino ...	.249	82	257	28	64	80	7	0	3	32	6	1	5	36	1	60	5	5
Ashley, Billy, Bakersfield	.218	99	331	48	72	114	13	1	9	40	3	1	3	25	1	135	17	3
Ayala, Adan, Riverside	.228	44	114	8	26	33	5	1	0	16	0	2	2	21	1	34	3	3
Aylward, James, Palm Springs	.347	59	219	38	76	104	14	1	4	31	0	1	3	22	1	16	2	2
Baar, Bryan, Bakersfield	.285	111	389	53	111	196	23	1	20	71	2	5	4	34	4	114	1	2
Barbara, Donald, Palm Springs°	.291	66	220	22	64	84	8	0	4	39	1	3	2	24	0	27	1	0
Barker, Timothy, Bakersfield	.271	125	443	83	120	178	22	6	8	63	4	4	5	71	1	117	33	14
Barton, Shawn, 16 Reno-88 Sal.	.275	104	338	41	93	113	11	3	1	37	8	4	1	34	2	30	12	7
Bass, Kevin, San Jose†	.364	6	22	2	8	9	1	0	0	4	0	0	1	0	0	1	1	0
Beals, Bryan, Bakersfield°	.125	13	24	3	3	4	1	0	0	0	0	0	0	3	0	6	5	2
Beard, Garrett, Bakersfield	.200	5	15	2	3	7	2	1	0	3	0	0	0	1	0	2	0	0
Beeler, Robert, Salinas	.200	15	45	1	9	10	1	0	0	4	0	0	0	1	0	5	0	0
Bethea, Stephen, Riverside†	.171	104	315	38	54	69	9	3	0	21	0	1	1	57	0	105	13	0
Bigham, Scott, Riverside	.244	117	409	46	100	119	13	3	0	37	9	4	6	38	1	68	13	4
Blackwell, Barry, Reno	.286	32	98	18	28	55	6	0	7	20	1	3	4	8	0	23	0	1
Bolick, Frank, 50 Stock.-78 S.B.†	.324	128	441	100	143	240	33	5	18	102	0	13	4	91	7	86	8	9
Booker, Eric, Modesto	.320	8	25	4	8	9	1	0	0	5	2	0	0	1	0	5	2	0
Borrelli, Dean, Modesto	.230	52	148	22	34	48	9	1	1	11	1	0	6	25	0	25	0	2
Brady, Patrick, San Jose	.212	54	151	22	32	42	5	1	1	17	2	2	0	24	0	32	2	2
Brauning, Jeff, San Jose	.278	99	331	63	92	115	8	3	3	45	11	4	7	34	0	38	17	8
Bruett, Joseph, Visalia°	.307	123	437	86	134	158	15	3	1	33	8	3	4	101	4	60	50	21
Buccheri, James, Modesto	.280	36	125	27	35	41	4	1	0	7	2	0	2	25	0	16	15	9
Buckley, Troy, Visalia	.307	117	404	69	124	171	24	4	5	64	2	5	11	43	2	58	5	2
Butcher, Arthur, Stockton°	.125	3	8	1	1	1	0	0	0	0	0	0	1	0	0	4	1	1
Cala, Craig, San Jose	.227	48	88	12	20	25	5	0	0	9	0	1	2	7	0	30	0	1
Capellan, Carlos, Visalia	.284	105	415	54	118	138	13	2	1	50	3	3	4	13	0	33	9	7
Carcione, Thomas, Modesto	.231	66	195	22	45	65	5	0	5	25	5	0	0	29	1	47	0	4
Carey, Frank, San Jose°	.282	27	85	21	24	29	3	1	0	11	1	1	2	15	0	25	2	0
Carlson, William, Salinas	.261	139	487	72	127	192	21	4	12	59	0	3	9	73	5	97	15	11
Carmody, Kevin, Stockton°	.000	51	1	0	0	0	0	0	0	0	0	0	0	0	0	0	0	0
Carr, Terence, Palm Springs	.151	52	159	23	24	30	2	2	0	12	0	2	5	24	0	48	4	3
Cassels, Christopher, Stockton	.284	93	299	42	85	133	17	2	9	50	0	6	7	27	0	64	0	1
Cedeno, Ramon, Visalia	.281	91	313	44	88	138	20	6	6	45	1	4	1	13	2	71	1	2
Charbonnet, Mark, Reno°	.074	9	27	1	2	2	0	0	0	1	0	0	0	0	0	5	0	0
Chimelis, Joel, 85 Reno-46 Mod.	.303	131	531	87	161	219	26	10	4	70	6	3	3	49	4	56	30	15
Christopherson, Eric, San Jose	.174	7	23	4	4	4	0	0	0	1	0	0	0	3	0	6	0	0
Clark, Isaiah, San Bernardino	.323	62	251	51	81	136	15	2	12	45	1	3	4	19	0	20	4	3
Clayton, Royce, San Jose	.267	123	460	80	123	179	15	10	7	71	0	4	4	68	3	98	33	15
Cohen, John, Visalia°	.302	49	169	20	51	67	10	0	2	27	1	2	1	8	0	35	0	1
Conte, Michael, Modesto	.243	73	268	31	65	99	14	1	6	37	1	2	1	35	0	50	6	8
Correia, Ronald, Modesto	.244	87	246	27	60	72	6	3	0	16	5	1	4	22	0	41	4	6
Craig, Rodney, Salinas†	.000	6	14	1	0	0	0	0	0	0	1	0	0	5	0	2	2	2
Crowe, Ronald, San Jose	.333	19	57	11	19	20	1	0	0	12	1	1	1	8	0	7	0	0
Davenport, Adell, San Jose	.251	132	495	76	124	205	20	5	17	66	2	3	16	46	3	108	3	6
Davis, Kevin, Palm Springs	.254	30	126	11	32	38	6	0	0	16	0	2	0	6	0	32	5	3
Davis, Michael, San Jose°	.088	9	34	2	3	3	0	0	0	1	0	1	0	7	2	7	0	1
Deiley, Louis, Salinas	.205	32	83	12	17	23	0	0	2	8	3	0	1	10	0	21	0	1
DeJardin, Bradford, Reno°	.297	114	387	66	115	152	17	1	6	54	4	7	2	38	5	89	15	9
Delpozo, Roberto, San Bernardino	.252	76	214	29	54	67	8	1	1	17	2	1	1	30	0	63	7	4
Deutsch, Jim, Bakersfield°	.255	120	415	62	106	156	20	0	10	74	0	7	6	73	6	77	3	1
Deville, Daniel, Riverside	.000	42	1	0	0	0	0	0	0	0	0	0	0	0	0	1	0	0
Dewey, Todd, Riverside†	.300	26	80	12	24	32	6	1	0	6	0	0	0	14	1	19	2	1
Diaz, Remigio, Stockton	.216	84	231	25	50	53	3	0	0	28	11	2	1	24	0	37	3	4

Player and Club	Pct.	G.	AB.	R.	H.	TB.	2B.	3B.	HR.	RBI.	SH.	SF.	HP.	BB.	Int. BB.	SO.	SB.	CS.
Diaz, Stephen, Stockton	.000	12	13	0	0	0	0	0	0	0	0	0	0	1	0	7	0	0
Dodson, Bryan, Stockton*	.273	120	363	70	99	141	16	4	6	46	1	1	3	73	2	103	1	1
Dombrowski, Robert, Riverside	.208	85	259	20	54	73	10	3	1	33	5	3	2	17	0	57	6	4
Dominguez, Frank, Palm Springs	.251	56	199	16	50	67	15	1	0	19	3	2	2	10	0	32	1	1
Donahue, Timothy, Reno†	.264	103	352	68	93	130	16	3	5	45	3	2	3	50	1	69	19	12
Doran, Mark, Palm Springs	.364	15	55	16	20	33	4	0	3	10	0	1	0	10	0	11	3	1
Dunn, Stephen, Palm Springs*	.500	29	2	0	1	1	0	0	0	0	0	0	0	0	0	1	0	0
Durham, Leon, Salinas*	.228	36	114	20	26	57	5	1	8	26	0	1	0	19	2	25	0	1
Easley, Michael, Reno*	.263	124	438	86	115	159	16	5	6	46	4	7	5	90	3	69	10	9
Edmonds, James, Palm Springs*	.293	91	314	36	92	131	18	6	3	56	1	2	2	27	3	75	5	2
Eiterman, Thomas, Reno	.331	121	471	92	156	208	19	6	7	73	4	3	9	55	4	73	6	7
Esquer, David, 29 P.S.-19 Stock.	.213	48	141	16	30	32	2	0	0	16	2	0	1	16	0	25	4	4
Estes, Joel, San Jose*	.000	33	1	0	0	0	0	0	0	0	0	0	0	0	0	1	0	0
Evans, David, San Bernardino	.000	27	1	0	0	0	0	0	0	0	0	0	0	0	0	1	0	0
Farmer, Reginald, Riverside*	.255	118	411	54	105	151	15	8	5	42	4	4	1	47	3	113	25	24
Fernandez, Daniel, San Jose	.263	36	76	19	20	25	2	0	1	14	3	2	0	13	0	21	0	1
Ferran, Alexander, Reno*	.208	46	125	14	26	32	4	1	0	8	2	2	3	18	1	28	2	1
Finn, John, Stockton	.207	95	290	48	60	67	4	0	1	23	6	6	1	52	0	50	29	15
Firova, Daniel, Reno	.262	57	183	17	48	59	7	2	0	21	2	0	1	14	0	34	3	2
Fitzgerald, David, Stockton	.000	35	1	0	0	0	0	0	0	0	0	0	0	0	0	1	0	0
Foley, James, San Jose†	.500	27	2	0	1	1	0	0	0	0	0	0	0	0	0	1	0	0
Forrester, Gary, Bakersfield	.153	48	111	9	17	25	5	0	1	12	3	0	1	8	0	25	1	2
Fraticelli, Carl, Visalia†	.111	11	18	0	2	2	0	0	0	0	0	0	0	2	0	5	0	0
Garcia, Jose, Visalia†	.274	137	486	68	133	200	29	4	10	71	0	4	7	56	1	68	10	5
Garcia, Santiago, Reno	.194	14	36	6	7	9	2	0	0	2	0	0	0	1	0	8	0	0
Gieseke, Mark, Riverside†	.270	128	482	59	130	172	26	2	4	60	1	4	3	51	6	93	5	3
Gonzalez, Ruben, San Bernardino	.336	44	140	27	47	69	5	1	5	26	0	2	2	27	2	24	1	1
Goodwin, Thomas, Bakersfield*	.291	32	134	24	39	49	6	2	0	13	1	0	0	11	0	22	22	4
Griffin, Mark, Bakersfield*	.275	106	429	77	118	149	14	4	3	32	2	4	0	39	1	70	33	18
Guerrero, Miguel, Stockton	.250	105	320	36	80	98	5	5	1	36	6	1	3	24	1	54	14	10
Hahn, Brent, Salinas*	.221	123	348	30	77	87	8	1	0	33	5	2	1	36	0	58	4	7
Hailey, Freddie, Stockton	.176	33	74	5	13	14	1	0	0	2	0	1	1	18	0	13	2	5
Ham, Michael, San Jose	.500	5	8	2	4	5	1	0	0	0	0	0	0	0	0	1	0	0
Harper, Milton, Reno*	.317	91	322	69	102	189	23	2	20	73	1	6	4	62	4	58	0	0
Harris, Vincent, Riverside†	.282	69	245	44	69	75	4	1	0	21	2	1	1	35	1	35	40	9
Haslock, Christopher, Riverside	1.000	44	1	0	1	1	0	0	0	0	0	0	0	0	0	0	0	0
Hendley, Brett, Modesto*	.184	67	201	26	37	65	8	1	6	27	0	0	0	37	1	68	3	3
Hendricks, Steven, Riverside	.289	128	484	59	140	214	27	7	11	90	0	5	6	32	1	77	10	5
Hernandez, Carlos, Modesto†	.143	15	42	5	6	7	1	0	0	3	0	0	0	5	0	17	1	1
Higgins, Kevin, Riverside*	.301	49	176	27	53	66	5	1	2	18	2	1	2	27	3	15	0	1
Hoffman, John, San Bernardino	.114	13	35	2	4	4	0	0	0	2	2	1	0	2	0	11	0	0
Hosey, Dwayne, Modesto†	.294	113	453	77	133	212	21	5	16	61	8	2	8	50	5	70	30	23
Hosey, Steven, San Jose	.232	139	479	85	111	184	13	6	16	78	1	4	5	71	2	139	16	17
House, Michael, Visalia	.266	88	308	47	82	120	8	0	10	42	0	2	5	38	4	83	1	0
Housie, Wayne, Salinas†	.270	92	367	51	99	146	20	6	5	49	5	3	4	22	1	72	27	11
Howard, Matthew, Bakersfield	.261	137	551	75	144	175	22	3	1	54	4	6	13	37	1	39	47	10
Jackson, Kenneth, Stockton	.231	84	273	37	63	102	18	3	5	55	4	13	6	17	2	65	8	6
Jaha, John, Stockton	.262	26	84	12	22	39	5	0	4	19	0	0	2	18	0	25	0	0
Jaster, Scott, Salinas	.264	59	212	23	56	83	10	1	5	29	3	2	0	22	1	38	3	4
Johnson, Christopher, Stockton	.000	24	1	0	0	0	0	0	0	0	0	0	0	0	0	1	0	0
Johnson, Dodd, Reno	.330	29	103	27	34	52	5	2	3	21	2	1	2	19	0	18	0	1
Jones, James, San Jose†	.224	53	156	20	35	44	3	3	0	14	4	4	1	24	0	48	6	1
Jones, Robert, San Bernardino	.312	82	308	55	96	153	13	1	14	59	0	1	2	34	1	77	7	5
Jose, Manuel, Salinas†	.304	48	207	39	63	86	8	3	3	25	1	0	0	17	3	54	19	11
Kappesser, Robert, Stockton	.184	63	147	17	27	31	2	1	0	12	2	1	2	15	0	39	2	6
Keitges, Jeffrey, San Bernardino*	.276	124	420	53	116	169	26	0	9	60	0	4	9	39	12	85	3	1
Kelso, Jeffrey, Palm Springs	.167	14	42	4	7	8	1	0	0	2	0	0	0	2	0	25	1	1
Kennedy, Michael, Modesto	.119	14	42	1	5	5	0	0	0	1	2	1	0	4	0	15	0	2
Kingwood, Tyrone, San Bernardino	.310	26	84	18	26	44	6	0	4	14	1	0	1	8	0	14	3	2
Kipila, Jeffrey, Palm Springs	.241	72	253	29	61	92	12	5	3	30	0	2	2	34	2	75	6	4
Kohno, Takayuki, Salinas	1.000	2	1	1	1	1	0	0	0	1	0	0	0	0	0	0	0	0
Kvasnicka, Jay, Visalia*	.232	114	384	63	89	137	18	6	6	43	3	2	2	56	5	83	32	10
Lachmann, Thomas, Reno	.533	6	15	5	8	12	1	0	1	9	0	0	1	4	0	2	0	1
Landphere, Edward, Salinas	.172	18	58	2	10	13	0	0	1	6	0	1	0	10	0	19	0	0
Ledinsky, Raymond, Palm Springs	.267	55	180	20	48	62	3	1	3	29	1	1	2	11	1	37	2	3
Lennon, Patrick, San Bernardino	.288	44	163	29	47	81	6	2	8	30	0	1	0	15	1	51	6	0
Lewis, Alan, Bakersfield*	.304	96	329	56	100	146	20	4	6	49	0	5	0	43	3	42	4	3
Lewis, Daniel, San Jose*	.292	116	415	58	121	192	23	4	14	93	2	10	10	61	1	78	7	5
Listach, Patrick, Stockton†	.272	139	503	116	137	176	21	6	2	39	3	1	6	105	2	122	78	28
Lofthus, Kevin, Modesto	.200	23	80	6	16	23	4	0	1	10	0	0	1	5	0	34	1	1
Logan, Todd, Stockton	.287	108	352	60	101	159	18	2	12	62	0	6	2	72	3	70	2	2
Lopez, Luis, Riverside†	.370	14	46	5	17	25	3	1	1	4	1	0	0	3	2	3	4	2
Lott, Billy, Bakersfield	.203	38	133	11	27	36	1	1	2	14	1	1	1	6	0	46	3	2
Love, Sylvester, Stockton*	.183	46	131	21	24	42	7	4	1	15	1	1	1	21	1	32	8	4
Magallanes, Robert, San Bernardino	.187	56	193	26	36	49	4	0	3	21	1	1	4	24	1	52	1	3
Magnusson, Brett, Bakersfield*	.311	121	434	92	135	242	34	2	23	85	1	1	10	73	5	104	5	4
Manahan, Anthony, San Bernardino	.318	51	198	46	63	98	10	2	7	30	1	3	2	24	0	35	8	1
Mannion, Gregory, Salinas*	.227	7	22	2	5	5	0	0	0	0	0	0	0	3	0	8	0	0
Masteller, Dan, Visalia*	.281	135	473	71	133	175	20	5	4	73	4	3	9	81	0	76	2	5
Matos, Francisco, Modesto	.274	83	321	46	88	105	12	1	1	20	7	2	5	15	0	65	26	5
Maynard, Ellerton, San Bernardino	.236	127	488	92	115	148	10	7	3	25	2	0	14	63	0	116	80	32
McCreary, Robert, Visalia†	.284	139	503	72	143	166	12	4	1	45	5	3	8	58	1	88	8	6
McDonald, Chad, Reno	.353	34	119	21	42	55	7	0	2	29	0	2	0	22	1	24	0	3
McGee, Anthony, Riverside	.209	80	235	23	49	56	7	0	0	30	2	1	1	29	0	61	0	1
McLemore, Mark, Palm Springs†	.273	6	22	3	6	6	0	0	0	3	0	0	0	1	0	3	2	2
McMurray, Brock, Bakersfield	.290	66	238	41	69	114	20	2	7	35	0	1	0	28	0	58	3	3
McNamara, James, San Jose*	.203	53	158	20	32	41	2	2	1	22	1	1	1	18	0	30	0	4
Merchant, Mark, San Bernardino†	.314	29	102	22	32	47	3	0	4	19	0	0	0	20	0	34	8	2
Meredith, Steven, Salinas	.237	15	38	3	9	9	0	0	0	2	1	0	0	5	0	9	2	2
Messerly, Michael, Modesto	.241	113	353	49	85	121	22	1	4	33	4	3	7	53	2	86	3	4
Meury, William, Riverside	.173	49	150	16	26	31	2	0	1	8	2	1	7	13	0	38	1	3
Meyers, Paul, San Jose	.000	10	1	1	0	0	0	0	0	0	0	0	0	0	0	0	1	0

Player and Club	Pct.	G.	AB.	R.	H.	TB.	2B.	3B.	HR.	RBI.	SH.	SF.	HP.	BB.	Int. BB.	SO.	SB.	CS.
Milene, Jeffrey, Visalia	.109	22	46	5	5	6	1	0	0	1	0	0	0	6	0	19	0	0
Miller, Roger, San Jose	.571	3	7	1	4	4	0	0	0	2	0	0	0	1	0	0	0	0
Morales, Richard, San Bernardino	.232	34	82	6	19	23	4	0	0	12	4	3	4	3	0	14	0	2
Morrow, Christian, Bakersfield°	.240	95	325	37	78	114	17	2	5	40	1	3	2	20	3	53	8	6
Mota, Carlos, Reno	.276	85	275	42	76	103	14	2	3	32	4	2	1	19	0	50	14	5
Munoz, Jose, Bakersfield†	.179	14	39	3	7	8	1	0	0	6	0	0	0	6	0	7	2	1
Musolino, Michael, Palm Springs°	.140	20	43	4	6	7	1	0	0	3	0	0	0	8	0	8	0	1
Nalls, Gary, Reno	.214	72	192	26	41	57	7	0	3	25	2	1	1	23	1	43	7	1
Nava, Lipso, San Bernardino	.174	7	23	1	4	5	1	0	0	1	1	0	2	0	0	9	0	0
Nelson, Richard, Palm Springs	.224	40	143	17	32	59	7	1	6	22	2	1	1	11	1	52	1	2
Nes Smith, John, San Jose	.000	1	1	0	0	0	0	0	0	0	0	0	0	0	0	1	0	0
Nichols, Howard, Palm Springs	.373	21	75	17	28	37	6	0	1	11	0	1	5	8	0	17	0	0
Nilsson, David, Stockton°	.290	107	359	70	104	153	22	3	7	47	0	4	0	43	3	36	6	5
Nishijima, Takayuki, Salinas°	.269	31	78	15	21	29	4	2	0	7	2	0	0	14	0	30	4	2
O'Donnell, Stephen, Bakersfield	.243	68	230	32	56	97	12	1	9	36	0	1	3	25	0	59	4	4
O'Leary, Troy, Stockton°	.500	2	6	1	3	4	1	0	0	0	0	0	0	2	1	1	0	0
Oberdank, Jeffrey, Palm Springs	.236	116	428	56	101	128	17	5	0	42	5	4	13	29	0	66	12	9
Ohtsuka, Yoshiki, Salinas	.225	60	178	12	40	48	5	0	1	12	2	0	1	20	2	40	1	2
Ortiz, Joseph, Modesto	.333	7	6	0	2	2	0	0	0	0	0	0	0	0	0	4	2	0
Ortiz, Raymond, Visalia°	.315	62	235	43	74	130	15	1	13	53	0	1	1	26	3	47	1	0
Palma, Brian, Salinas°	.313	55	166	24	52	69	7	2	2	18	0	1	2	22	1	34	7	4
Paquette, Craig, Modesto	.238	130	495	65	118	194	23	4	15	59	0	4	3	47	1	123	8	5
Parker, Richard, Palm Springs	.176	71	199	21	35	54	6	5	1	16	2	1	0	13	0	58	3	1
Parry, Robert, Modesto	.252	80	282	38	71	113	14	2	8	42	2	3	3	32	0	46	3	4
Partrick, David, Palm Springs	.169	44	154	14	26	37	5	3	0	5	1	0	0	3	0	72	8	1
Patterson, John, San Jose†	.302	131	530	91	160	207	23	6	4	66	5	6	9	46	2	74	29	17
Paul, Corey, Salinas°	.226	89	230	34	52	76	8	2	4	28	5	2	3	42	0	83	10	9
Peguero, Jeremias, Salinas	.175	45	154	9	27	33	3	0	1	11	1	1	0	9	0	31	4	5
Perea, Michael, Salinas	.139	18	36	3	5	5	0	0	0	2	1	0	0	0	0	12	0	0
Perez, Beban, Palm Springs°	.298	76	228	30	68	81	9	2	0	27	4	1	5	16	0	55	1	6
Phillips, Charles, Palm Springs°	.198	46	162	14	32	41	4	1	1	15	1	1	1	10	1	58	3	1
Pirkl, Gregory, San Bernardino	.295	58	207	37	61	86	10	0	5	28	0	1	3	13	0	34	3	0
Pough, Clyde, Reno	.151	16	53	1	8	10	0	1	0	2	0	0	0	6	1	18	0	1
Raabe, Brian, Visalia	.246	42	138	11	34	41	3	2	0	17	1	0	1	10	0	9	5	1
Raley, Timothy, Stockton°	.256	124	399	54	102	172	12	14	10	71	0	6	2	51	1	71	6	7
Ramirez, Fausto, Palm Springs†	.224	51	156	20	35	43	4	2	0	14	3	0	1	10	0	24	4	4
Renfroe, Randal, Palm Springs	.164	28	55	9	9	15	0	0	2	7	1	1	1	5	0	13	2	0
Romero, Charles, Palm Springs†	.220	29	100	6	22	24	2	0	0	3	0	0	1	6	0	25	3	1
Rowe, Peter, Salinas	.000	1	1	0	0	0	0	0	0	0	0	0	0	0	0	0	0	0
Salmon, Timothy, Palm Springs	.288	36	118	19	34	46	6	0	2	21	0	0	4	21	0	44	11	1
Sarbaugh, Michael, Reno	.291	121	454	78	132	186	22	7	6	67	1	5	12	46	1	76	14	13
Sass, James, Stockton	.235	111	281	41	66	76	8	1	0	27	5	0	6	41	1	79	15	14
Schroeder, William, Palm Springs	.333	6	12	2	4	5	1	0	0	1	0	0	1	0	3	0	0	0
Seda, Israel, San Bernardino	.300	3	10	1	3	4	1	0	0	2	0	0	0	0	0	1	0	0
Segui, Daniel, Visalia	.211	33	95	11	20	23	3	0	0	5	3	0	1	13	0	16	0	0
Shaw, Kerry, San Jose†	.223	83	211	25	47	55	8	0	0	22	4	3	1	36	0	38	5	3
Shepperd, Richard, Palm Springs	.162	26	68	8	11	11	0	0	0	2	0	0	0	8	0	13	2	1
Sherman, Darrell, Riverside°	.290	131	483	97	140	158	10	4	0	35	6	2	12	89	2	51	74	26
Shevlin, James, Salinas	.167	19	54	4	9	9	0	0	0	2	1	1	0	12	0	7	0	0
Shockey, Scott, Modesto°	.325	51	200	32	65	105	13	0	9	50	0	6	2	13	2	48	1	0
Smiley, Rueben, San Jose°	.266	135	455	78	121	149	9	5	3	48	7	4	10	40	0	105	25	7
Smith, David, San Bernardino	.269	54	119	14	32	43	4	2	1	11	3	0	4	4	0	33	3	3
Smith, Gregory, Riverside	.221	117	393	44	87	136	14	4	9	51	0	4	1	48	1	107	5	7
Stargell, Timothy, San Bernardino	.262	136	545	84	143	222	22	3	17	96	1	7	6	29	1	93	20	15
Staton, David, Riverside	.290	92	335	56	97	175	16	1	20	64	0	4	2	52	5	78	4	1
Stiner, Rick, Stockton	.159	58	126	10	20	26	1	1	1	14	2	1	3	15	0	48	0	0
Sturdivant, David, Palm Springs°	.207	30	87	8	18	19	1	0	0	5	1	0	1	14	0	18	0	0
Swain, Robert, Reno	.077	4	13	1	1	1	0	0	0	1	0	0	0	1	0	5	0	0
Tashiro, Hiroyuki, Salinas	.125	24	48	3	6	8	2	0	0	2	0	0	1	4	0	26	0	0
Tatum, James, Stockton	.262	70	260	41	68	120	16	0	12	59	0	4	8	13	0	49	4	5
Taylor, Terry, Palm Springs°	.293	124	434	66	127	175	26	5	4	53	3	1	1	69	2	109	10	14
Teel, Garett, Bakersfield	.208	42	101	13	21	28	1	0	2	6	1	1	1	10	0	17	0	1
Thomas, Keith, Modesto†	.223	62	215	24	48	67	7	0	4	21	1	2	1	14	0	65	16	10
Thompson, Sean, Salinas†	.157	62	115	14	18	18	0	0	0	5	0	1	0	11	0	31	2	2
Tucker, Eddie, San Jose	.280	123	439	59	123	170	28	2	5	71	2	6	13	71	4	69	9	3
Turang, Brian, San Bernardino	.296	132	487	86	144	215	25	5	12	67	6	4	7	69	0	98	25	16
Valdez, Amilcar, Bakersfield	.291	30	103	9	30	40	7	0	1	14	0	1	1	9	1	18	0	1
Vannaman, Timothy, Modesto	.200	57	190	18	38	46	5	0	1	19	3	1	1	18	0	52	7	5
Vargas, Trinidad, Stockton	.000	5	15	0	0	0	0	0	0	0	0	0	0	1	0	7	0	0
Vice, Darryl, Modesto†	.277	59	202	25	56	70	3	1	3	25	1	3	1	26	0	40	1	3
Vizquel, Omar, San Bernardino†	.250	6	28	5	7	7	0	0	0	3	0	0	3	0	1	1	1	2
Waggoner, James, Modesto°	.163	35	86	13	14	17	3	0	0	5	2	0	2	21	1	25	1	1
Wallace, Timothy, Palm Springs†	.233	35	116	18	27	34	7	0	0	4	0	1	1	17	1	12	11	7
West, Hassen, Salinas†	.111	7	9	1	1	1	0	0	0	0	0	0	1	2	0	4	0	0
Westbrooks, Elanis, San Jose	.252	48	103	14	26	35	7	1	0	9	1	1	4	13	0	18	3	4
Whitfield, Kenneth, Reno	.281	112	437	82	123	224	21	4	24	90	0	7	2	36	2	108	7	8
Williams, Ray, San Bernardino	.239	78	197	30	47	61	8	3	0	24	1	1	4	33	0	51	14	7
Witmeyer, Ronald, Modesto°	.234	92	333	38	78	132	14	5	10	45	1	4	1	41	2	74	0	4
Wong, Kaha, Reno	.294	83	238	36	70	89	9	2	2	36	1	3	3	20	1	44	3	2
Yamanouchi, Kenichi, Salinas°	.204	118	338	36	69	107	15	4	5	31	7	0	3	34	4	125	2	4
Yanagita, Shikato, Salinas	.270	139	463	65	125	154	21	1	2	45	22	3	5	61	2	83	13	8
Young, Delwyn, Salinas†	.248	45	153	20	38	56	4	1	4	16	1	0	1	14	0	35	16	5
Young, Selwyn, Salinas†	.238	20	63	7	15	18	3	0	0	1	3	0	0	6	0	7	1	3
Zayas, Carlos, Palm Springs	.242	20	62	7	15	24	6	0	1	7	1	0	0	3	1	15	0	0

The following pitchers, listed alphabetically by club, with games in parentheses, had no plate appearances, primarily through use of designated hitters:

BAKERSFIELD—Aase, Donald (6); Astacio, Pedro (10); Bishop, Craig (5); Braase, John (29); Brosnan, Jason (26); Coleman, Dale (39); Crane, Richard (33); Delahoya, Javier (9); Frame, Michael (31); Gott, James (7); Helmick, Anthony (34); Humber, Frank (57); Jones, Keith (9); Knapp, John (12); McAndrew, James (14); Mesa, Baltazar (5); Parisotto, Barry (13); Perry, Patrick (3); Potthoff, Michael (7); Robinson, Napoleon (45); Sampson, Michael (12); Searage, Raymond (10); Tapia, Jose (13); Tatis, Fausto (18).

MODESTO—Allison, Dana (10); Briscoe, John (29); Chavez, Samuel (9); Erwin, Scott (25); Garcia, Apolinar (20); Green, Daryl (6); Grott, Matthew (12); Guzman, Dionini (13); Hill, Fredrick (2); Lardizabal, Ruben (26); Lawson, James (23); Leiper, David (3); Love, William (37); McCoy, Timothy (11); Miller, Richard (10); Patrick, Bronswell (14); Peck, Steven (30); Pena, Pedro (12); Phoenix, Steven (6); Rose, Scott (6); Shaver, Jeffrey (1); Smith, Todd (41); Strebeck, Richard (14); Taylor, William (22); Zancanaro, David (4).

PALM SPRINGS—Acosta, Jose (29); Archibald, Daniel (9); Cliburn, Stewart (16); Cobb, Marvin (32); Fritz, John (31); Hillman, Stewart (4); James, Todd (12); Loubier, Stephen (9); Martinez, David (12); McClure, Robert (2); Meeks, Timothy (6); Merejo, Luis (25); Merriman, Brett (24); Neal, David (10); Search, Michael (25); Shull, Michael (15); Tolliver, Freddie (7); Vann, Brandy (28); Vidmar, Donald (17); Warrecker, William (37); Zappelli, Mark (21).

RENO—Alexander, Charles (1); Anderson, David (27); Bickler, David (1); Caraballo, Felix (17); Chavez, Samuel (1); Clark, Garry (23); Cole, Christopher (14); Dwyer, Vincent (5); Green, Daryl (20); Guthrie, Joseph (5); Hurst, James (25); Langley, Wesley (42); Ortiz, Angel (16); Palmer, David (3); Paxton, Gregory (6); Pettiford, Cecil (24); Powers, Tad (54); Rauth, Christopher (14); Shepherd, Keith (5); Soper, Michael (43); Wertz, William (17); Whitney, Jeffrey (17).

RIVERSIDE—Beckett, Robert (3); Bryand, Renay (47); Davis, Richard (29); Estrada, Jay (13); Harrison, Brian (37); Knox, Kerry (27); Lane, Heath (32); Lifgren, Kelly (27); Marx, William (2); Reed, William (4); Reichle, Darrin (6); Sierra, Ulises (38); Smithberg, Roger (3); Thomas, Royal (27).

SALINAS—Arola, Bruce (18); Carrasco, Carlos (26); Emoto, Kouichi (54); Gardey, Rodolfo (3); Howe, Steven (10); Leslie, Reginald (19); Maye, Stephen (30); Murakami, Seiichi (25); Myers, Michael (30); Ohtsuka, Kenichi (31); Page, Gregory (11); Reilley, John (19); Sasaki, Shigeki (35); Stewart, John (11); Tanoue, Keisaburo (10); Uchiyama, Kenichi (37); Velasquez, Raymond (6).

SAN BERNARDINO—Bennett, James (4); Cummings, John (7); DeLucia, Richard (5); Felix, Nicholas (37); Fleming, David (12); Furcal, Manuel (35); Goff, Michael (3); Green, Derek (5); Jones, Calvin (53); McDonald, David (9); Newlin, James (36); Pitcher, Scott (36); Salkeld, Roger (25); Sheehan, John (22); Taylor, Scott (34); Wiggs, Johnny (64); Woodson, Walter (27).

SAN JOSE—Brock, Don (9); Dour, Brian (25); Downs, Kelly (1); Fye, Christopher (43); Gustafson, Edward (2); Hancock, Christopher (1); Herring, Vincent (35); Johnson, Dominick (25); LaCoss, Michael (1); Mead, Timber (2); Myers, James (60); O'Neal, Randall (9); Oliveras, Francisco (1); Potestio, Frank (6); Rambo, Daniel (26); Robinson, Don (2); Rogers, Kevin (28); Sharko, Gary (44); Taylor, Robert (13); Vuz, John (5).

STOCKTON—Cangemi, James (62); Carter, Larry (1); Czajkowski, James (2); DeLaRosa, Domingo (2); Eldred, Calvin (7); Enriquez, Martin (8); Guilbe, Victor (4); Hamilton, Scott (38); Henry, Douglas (4); Ignasiak, Michael (6); Kiefer, Mark (11); Krippner, Curt (2); Lee, Mark (5); McGrath, Charles (1); Miranda, Angel (52); Perez, Leonardo (6); Sandoval, Guillermo (34); Schwarz, Jeffrey (19); Sparks, Steven (21); Uribe, Juan (31).

VISALIA—Aspray, Michael (19); Best, Jayson (4); Fine, Thomas (3); Garces, Richard (47); Krol, David (28); Lipson, Marc (17); Mahomes, Patrick (28); Muh, Steven (12); Neagle, Dennis (10); Newman, Alan (5); Russo, Pasquale (17); Swanson, Chad (39); Trombley, Michael (27); Tsamis, George (26); White, Frederick (37); Wiese, Phillip (20).

GRAND SLAM HOME RUNS—D. Hosey, 3; Clayton, 2; Ashley, Barker, Bolick, Carcione, Cassels, Clark, Conte, Durham, Farmer, S. Hosey, House, Jaha, R. Jones, Lott, Magnusson, Manahan, Nilsson, O'Donnell, R. Ortiz, Sarbaugh, Shockey, Stargell, Turang, 1 each.

AWARDED FIRST BASE ON CATCHER'S INTERFERENCE—Oberdank 3 (Borrelli, Carcione, Pirkl); Bigham (Teel); Clayton (Parker); Dewey (Kennedy); Griffin (Parker); Hahn (Borrelli); R. Jones (Parker); McGee (Arguelles); Stiner (Borrelli); Shockey (Nilsson); Yamanouchi (Mota).

CLUB FIELDING

Club	Pct.	G.	PO.	A.	E.	DP.	PB.	Club	Pct.	G.	PO.	A.	E.	DP.	PB.
Bakersfield	.969	142	3705	1549	167	155	43	Palm Springs	.960	142	3699	1675	224	158	38
Stockton	.968	141	3608	1467	169	115	21	San Bernardino	.958	142	3747	1539	231	113	44
Visalia	.968	141	3685	1505	174	126	25	San Jose	.958	142	3737	1577	233	112	33
Riverside	.962	143	3677	1511	204	105	32	Reno	.957	139	3606	1553	234	156	34
Modesto	.960	141	3682	1511	215	109	35	Salinas	.949	140	3606	1316	264	119	29

Triple Play—Modesto.

INDIVIDUAL FIELDING

*Throws lefthanded.

FIRST BASEMEN

Player and Club	Pct.	G.	PO.	A.	E.	DP.	Player and Club	Pct.	G.	PO.	A.	E.	DP.
Alegre, Salinas	1.000	1	1	0	0	0	Kipila, Palm Springs	.971	8	63	5	2	8
Aylward, Palm Springs	1.000	12	102	6	0	13	Ledinsky, Palm Springs	1.000	1	4	0	0	0
Barbara, Palm Springs*	.988	62	547	40	7	73	Lewis, San Jose*	.983	7	56	2	1	3
Bolick, Stockton	1.000	7	44	3	0	8	Magnuson, Bakersfield	.984	10	59	3	1	5
Buckley, Visalia	.958	5	42	4	2	7	Masteller, Visalia*	.984	135	1119	95	20	100
Carlson, Salinas	.990	75	533	46	6	45	McNamara, San Jose	1.000	5	36	1	0	6
Cassels, Stockton	.991	16	108	7	1	8	Merchant, San Bernardino	1.000	1	9	0	0	0
Clark, San Bernardino	1.000	7	43	2	0	7	Messerly, Modesto	.988	20	148	16	2	12
Cohen, Visalia	1.000	2	8	0	0	1	Morales, San Bernardino	1.000	2	2	0	0	0
Crowe, San Jose	1.000	4	12	0	0	2	Nichols, Palm Springs	.972	17	128	10	4	14
Davenport, San Jose	.978	119	1016	72	25	74	Nilsson, Stockton	.979	7	44	2	1	8
Deiley, Salinas	.833	1	5	0	1	0	O'Donnell, Bakersfield	.948	9	69	4	4	7
DeJardin, Salinas	1.000	1	1	0	0	0	J. Ortiz, Modesto	1.000	1	13	0	0	0
Deutsch, Bakersfield*	.988	116	1028	78	14	119	R. Ortiz, Visalia	1.000	1	2	0	0	0
Diaz, Stockton	1.000	1	5	0	0	1	Palma, Salinas	.963	4	24	2	1	4
DODSON, Stockton*	.992	105	788	66	7	63	Phillips, Palm Springs*	.967	46	436	26	16	41
Durham, Salinas*	.982	15	106	6	2	9	Renfroe, Palm Springs	1.000	1	1	0	0	0
Easley, Reno	.984	90	810	50	14	79	Sass, Stockton	1.000	1	5	0	0	0
Esquer, 4 P.S.-5 Stock.	.989	9	79	7	1	7	Shaw, San Jose	.986	28	133	11	2	11
Firova, Reno	1.000	6	33	4	0	2	Shockey, Modesto*	.981	28	243	14	5	17
Gieseke, Riverside*	.988	58	466	30	6	31	Smith, Riverside*	.970	11	88	8	3	4
Gonzalez, San Bernardino	1.000	28	218	12	0	19	Stargell, San Bernardino	.949	11	74	1	4	6
Harper, Reno*	.991	48	405	47	4	56	Staton, Riverside	.983	13	110	7	2	2
Hendley, Modesto	1.000	16	113	7	0	10	Tashiro, Salinas	.875	3	7	0	1	1
Hendricks, Riverside	.989	67	569	38	7	55	Tatum, Stockton	.992	14	117	14	1	13
Higgins, Riverside	1.000	1	7	0	0	0	Valdez, Bakersfield	1.000	14	103	9	0	10
House, Visalia*	.955	3	21	0	1	6	Witmeyer, Modesto*	.989	81	709	43	8	56
Kappesser, Stockton	1.000	1	0	1	0	0	Wong, Reno	.944	3	16	1	1	1
Keitges, San Bernardino	.984	107	950	67	17	72	Yamanouchi, Salinas*	.957	55	386	16	18	42
Kelso, Palm Springs	1.000	1	9	0	0	0							

SECOND BASEMEN

Player and Club	Pct.	G.	PO.	A.	E.	DP.	Player and Club	Pct.	G.	PO.	A.	E.	DP.
Alfonzo, Palm Springs	1.000	3	6	7	0	0	Capellan, Visalia	.957	92	171	229	18	55
Barton, 4 Reno-77 Sal.	.968	81	159	199	12	42	Carey, San Jose	.931	8	8	19	2	3
Beals, Bakersfield	1.000	6	5	6	0	2	Correia, Stockton	.960	35	74	96	7	20
Bethea, Riverside	.950	10	15	23	2	2	Crowe, San Jose	1.000	1	0	2	0	1
Bigham, Riverside	.950	117	227	305	28	64	Davis, Palm Springs	1.000	1	3	3	0	1
Brauning, San Jose	.948	13	26	29	3	6	Diaz, Stockton	1.000	1	3	0	0	0
Buccheri, Modesto	.977	30	65	106	4	19	Dombrowski, Riverside	.951	24	58	59	6	5

SECOND BASEMEN—Continued

Player and Club	Pct.	G.	PO.	A.	E.	DP.
Donahue, Reno	.952	100	211	283	25	66
Easley, Reno	.945	22	43	61	6	13
Esquer, 5 P.S.-6 Stock.	.939	11	11	20	2	4
Finn, Stockton	.919	9	15	19	3	3
Forrester, Bakersfield	.917	5	6	5	1	2
Fraticelli, Visalia	.952	9	10	10	1	3
J. Garcia, Visalia	.929	16	34	44	6	10
S. Garcia, Reno	.833	6	4	6	2	2
Guerrero, Stockton	.957	16	14	31	2	4
Hahn, Salinas	.944	5	7	10	1	3
Hernandez, Modesto	.898	12	22	22	5	2
Housie, Salinas	1.000	3	2	0	0	1
HOWARD, Bakersfield	.991	137	253	432	6	107
Jones, San Jose	.939	6	14	17	2	2
Kappesser, Stockton	1.000	1	1	1	0	1
Listach, Stockton	.969	122	276	326	19	62
Magallanes, San Bernardino	1.000	1	1	1	0	1
McLemore, Palm Springs	1.000	6	20	22	0	8
Munoz, Bakersfield	1.000	1	1	2	0	1
Oberdank, Palm Springs	.977	29	71	100	4	24
Patterson, San Jose	.956	126	247	322	26	65
Peguero, Salinas	1.000	4	3	2	0	0
Raabe, Visalia	.990	42	98	98	2	22
Ramirez, Palm Springs	1.000	2	0	2	0	0
Sarbaugh, Reno	.985	15	27	38	1	10
Stargell, San Bernardino	.944	52	102	150	15	35
Swain, Reno	1.000	3	9	10	0	1
Taylor, Palm Springs	.965	107	227	321	20	84
Thompson, Salinas	.933	17	25	17	3	2
Turang, San Bernardino	.974	99	181	300	13	47
Vice, Modesto	.958	59	129	168	13	34
Waggoner, Modesto	.975	16	28	51	2	9
Yanagita, Salinas	.946	47	90	102	11	17
Young, Salinas	.900	9	8	10	2	3

Triple Play—Vice.

THIRD BASEMEN

Player and Club	Pct.	G.	PO.	A.	E.	DP.
Alfonzo, Palm Springs	1.000	7	5	14	0	3
Aylward, Palm Springs	.942	50	25	89	7	5
Barton, Salinas	1.000	4	0	5	0	1
Beals, Bakersfield	1.000	3	1	1	0	0
Beard, Bakersfield	1.000	2	1	0	0	0
Bethea, Riverside	.865	16	7	25	5	1
Bolick, 41 Stock.-78 S.B.	.932	119	70	206	20	13
Brady, San Jose	1.000	3	0	2	0	0
Brauning, San Jose	.917	56	28	94	11	6
Buckley, Visalia	1.000	1	1	2	0	0
Carey, San Jose	.879	16	10	19	4	2
Carlson, Salinas	.850	18	11	23	6	3
Cassels, Stockton	.824	10	5	9	3	2
Clark, San Bernardino	.874	34	27	56	12	4
Conte, Modesto	.917	3	3	8	1	1
Correia, Modesto	.920	27	26	55	7	9
Crowe, San Jose	.931	13	8	19	2	1
Dombrowski, Riverside	.911	56	38	95	13	9
Dominguez, Palm Springs	1.000	5	3	4	0	0
Easley, Reno	.750	3	1	5	2	1
Esquer, 5 P.S.-3 Stock.	.900	8	6	3	1	1
Finn, Stockton	.909	7	3	17	2	3
Forrester, Bakersfield	.875	5	3	4	1	1
Garcia, Visalia	.920	122	74	236	27	24
Guerrero, Stockton	.925	37	17	57	6	7
Hahn, Salinas	.885	89	44	117	21	12
Hendricks, Riverside	1.000	8	9	5	0	1
Johnson, Reno	1.000	1	0	3	0	0
Jones, San Jose	.923	40	33	75	9	3
Kipila, Palm Springs	.847	62	46	131	32	10
Lennon, San Bernardino	.887	25	17	38	7	3
Lewis, Bakersfield	.941	76	60	131	12	14
McDonald, Reno	.922	34	26	68	8	10
Munoz, Bakersfield	.970	12	6	26	1	1
Nichols, Palm Springs	.909	4	2	8	1	0
Nilsson, Stockton	.889	5	5	11	2	1
O'Donnell, Bakersfield	.928	55	29	100	10	14
Oberdank, Palm Springs	.957	15	10	34	2	1
PAQUETTE, Modesto	.922	112	88	218	26	19
Peguero, Salinas	1.000	3	2	6	0	0
Pough, Reno	.947	16	9	27	2	1
Ramirez, Palm Springs	.500	2	0	1	1	0
. Sarbaugh, Reno	.932	66	64	142	15	17
Segui, Visalia	.920	27	11	35	4	2
Shaw, San Jose	.851	37	19	55	13	5
Shevlin, Salinas	.831	19	18	31	10	5
Stargell, San Bernardino	.862	14	5	20	4	3
Staton, Riverside	.946	75	39	155	11	2
Tashiro, Salinas	.640	17	7	9	9	0
Tatum, Stockton	.958	55	43	94	6	9
Taylor, Palm Springs	.947	7	4	14	1	1
Thompson, Salinas	.778	11	5	2	2	0
Waggoner, Modesto	.778	7	3	4	2	1
Wong, Reno	.919	27	16	52	6	8
Young, Reno	1.000	5	2	6	0	1

Triple Play—Correia.

SHORTSTOPS

Player and Club	Pct.	G.	PO.	A.	E.	DP.
Alfonzo, Palm Springs	.800	2	0	4	1	0
BARKER, Bakersfield	.946	120	192	372	32	84
Barton, 10 Reno-12 Sal.	.893	22	31	44	9	10
Bethea, Riverside	.908	79	124	232	36	44
Brauning, San Jose	.871	25	38	50	13	12
Capellan, Visalia	1.000	6	6	7	0	2
Carey, San Jose	1.000	3	0	4	0	1
Chimelis, 84 Reno-46 Mod.	.909	130	180	349	53	64
Clark, San Bernardino	.898	12	10	34	5	5
Clayton, San Jose	.938	117	202	358	37	64
Correia, Modesto	.903	8	13	15	3	5
Crowe, San Jose	1.000	1	1	1	0	1
Davis, Palm Springs	.928	28	46	108	12	22
Diaz, Stockton	.969	80	142	205	11	31
Dombrowski, Riverside	.833	6	5	5	2	0
Esquer, 5 P.S.-7 Stock.	.905	12	12	26	4	5
Forrester, Bakersfield	.915	27	36	61	9	19
Garcia, Reno	.778	8	11	17	8	2
Guerrero, Stockton	.930	58	65	134	15	23
Hahn, Salinas	1.000	3	6	10	0	2
Hernandez, Modesto	1.000	3	3	1	0	1
Jones, San Jose	.909	8	9	11	2	2
Lewis, Bakersfield	1.000	2	2	5	0	1
Listach, Stockton	.957	11	16	29	2	4
Lopez, Riverside	.903	14	18	38	6	6
Magallanes, San Bernardino	.921	54	56	155	18	28
Manahan, San Bernardino	.916	49	83	147	21	28
Matos, Modesto	.919	81	95	223	28	36
McCreary, Visalia	.940	139	198	378	37	75
Meury, Riverside	.949	49	64	141	11	24
Nava, San Bernardino	.917	5	8	14	2	3
Oberdank, Palm Springs	.955	40	65	128	9	39
Peguero, Salinas	.905	38	48	85	14	14
Ramirez, Palm Springs	.950	45	65	145	11	34
Sarbaugh, Reno	.954	40	80	106	9	33
Seda, San Bernardino	1.000	3	0	6	0	1
Shaw, San Jose	.750	1	0	3	1	1
Stargell, San Bernardino	.878	17	21	51	10	7
Swain, Reno	.800	1	1	3	1	1
Turang, San Bernardino	1.000	1	2	2	0	0
Vargas, Stockton	.935	5	14	15	2	8
Vizquel, San Bernardino	.914	6	11	21	3	6
Waggoner, Modesto	.922	14	18	29	4	5
Wallace, Palm Springs	.936	33	52	110	11	21
Yanagita, Salinas	.926	91	171	239	33	48

OUTFIELDERS

Player and Club	Pct.	G.	PO.	A.	E.	DP.
Alegre, San Jose	.800	9	6	2	2	0
Ashley, Bakersfield	.926	83	122	3	10	0
Bass, San Jose	1.000	4	3	0	0	0
Bethea, Riverside	1.000	1	3	0	0	0
Booker, Modesto	.913	8	21	0	2	0
Brady, San Jose	.965	45	74	8	3	1
Brauning, San Jose	1.000	6	4	1	0	0
Bruett, Visalia*	.986	122	268	13	4	1
Bucceri, Modesto	.900	7	7	2	1	0
Butcher, Stockton*	1.000	1	3	1	0	0
Cala, San Jose	.950	21	18	1	1	0
Capellan, Visalia	1.000	15	29	4	0	1
Carlson, Salinas	.857	10	16	2	3	0
Carr, Palm Springs	.974	46	73	3	2	1
Cassels, Stockton	.950	38	54	3	3	1
Cedeno, Visalia	.934	78	91	8	7	0
Charbonnet, Reno*	.952	9	20	0	1	0
Clark, San Bernardino	.957	9	21	1	1	1
Cohen, Visalia*	.984	42	60	1	1	1
Conte, Modesto	.981	70	150	7	3	3
Correia, Modesto	.929	10	12	1	1	0
Craig, Salinas	.667	5	4	0	2	0
Crowe, San Jose	1.000	3	7	1	0	0
Davis, San Jose*	.750	6	6	0	2	0

OUTFIELDERS—Continued

Player and Club	Pct.	G.	PO.	A.	E.	DP.
DeJardin, Reno*	.962	107	172	4	7	2
Delpozo, San Bernardino	.890	64	78	3	10	0
Dewey, Riverside	1.000	2	1	0	0	0
Doran, Palm Springs	.969	15	31	0	1	0
Easley, Reno	.875	6	7	0	1	0
Edmonds, Palm Springs*	.954	88	199	9	10	0
Eiterman, Reno	.945	98	141	15	9	3
Farmer, Riverside	.946	114	226	21	14	6
Ferran, Reno*	.946	40	65	5	4	4
Finn, Stockton	.981	82	150	2	3	0
Firova, Reno	1.000	2	0	1	0	0
Forrester, Bakersfield	1.000	3	1	1	0	0
Garcia, Visalia	.833	3	5	0	1	0
Gieseke, Riverside*	.950	66	90	6	5	0
Goodwin, Bakersfield	1.000	30	55	2	0	0
Griffin, Bakersfield	.968	106	198	11	7	3
Hahn, Salinas	1.000	2	4	0	0	0
Hailey, Stockton	.949	27	36	1	2	0
Harris, Riverside	.964	65	104	3	4	0
Hendley, Modesto	1.000	4	9	0	0	0
D. Hosey, Modesto	.961	105	210	13	9	0
S. Hosey, San Jose	.969	135	239	11	8	3
House, Visalia*	.966	44	55	2	2	1
Housie, Salinas	.981	90	247	12	5	5
Jackson, Stockton	.987	80	139	9	2	3
Jaster, Salinas	.923	59	101	7	9	0
Johnson, Reno	.921	28	54	4	5	3
Jones, San Bernardino	.953	75	97	5	5	0
Jose, Salinas	.970	46	92	4	3	0
Kappesser, Stockton	1.000	3	3	0	0	0
Kelso, Palm Springs	1.000	3	5	2	0	1
Kingwood, San Bernardino	.925	24	35	2	3	0
Kipila, Palm Springs	1.000	1	1	0	0	0
KVASNICKA, Visalia*	.989	109	174	6	2	1
Landphere, Salinas	.939	18	30	1	2	0
Ledinsky, Palm Springs	.975	51	73	5	2	0
Lennon, San Bernardino	1.000	11	12	2	0	0
Lewis, San Jose*	.929	75	113	5	9	0
Listach, Stockton	.875	17	27	1	4	1
Lott, Bakersfield	.981	36	52	1	1	0
Love, Stockton*	.917	34	32	1	3	0
Magnusson, Bakersfield	.966	43	84	2	3	0
Mannion, Salinas*	1.000	6	10	1	0	0
Maynard, San Bernardino	.942	125	207	4	13	2
McMurray, Bakersfield	.964	53	103	3	4	0
Merchant, San Bernardino	.800	14	4	0	1	0
Meredith, Salinas	.939	14	30	1	2	1
Messerly, Modesto	.921	76	113	4	10	1
Morales, San Bernardino	1.000	7	8	0	0	0
Morrow, Bakersfield*	.940	88	103	6	7	0
Nalls, Reno	.935	64	124	6	9	2
Nelson, Palm Springs	.968	32	58	3	2	1
Nichols, Palm Springs	1.000	3	2	0	0	0
Nishijima, Salinas*	.930	26	52	1	4	0
O'Leary, Salinas	.750	2	3	0	1	0
Oberdank, Palm Springs	.921	38	64	6	6	0
Ortiz, Visalia	.951	44	55	3	3	0
Palma, Salinas	.980	24	47	2	1	1
Parry, Modesto	1.000	44	61	1	0	0
Partrick, Palm Springs	.947	44	83	6	5	0
Paul, Salinas*	.910	72	122	9	13	1
Perez, Palm Springs*	.981	59	98	8	2	1
Raley, Stockton	.924	88	105	5	9	1
Romero, Stockton	.961	25	45	4	2	0
Salmon, Palm Springs	.985	35	63	3	1	0
Sass, Stockton	.974	104	144	3	4	0
Shaw, San Jose	1.000	7	3	0	0	0
Shepperd, Palm Springs	1.000	21	17	2	0	0
Sherman, Riverside*	.966	130	303	14	11	4
Shockey, Modesto*	.889	13	15	1	2	0
Smiley, San Jose	.947	134	241	9	14	1
D. Smith, San Bernardino	.906	44	42	6	5	1
G. Smith, Riverside*	.978	65	87	3	2	0
Stargell, San Bernardino	.949	36	51	5	3	0
Thomas, Modesto	.943	49	98	2	6	0
Thompson, Salinas	.833	20	20	0	4	0
Tucker, San Jose	1.000	4	4	0	0	0
Turang, San Bernardino	.983	38	56	2	1	1
Vannaman, Modesto	.969	56	87	7	3	3
West, Salinas	.833	4	5	0	1	0
Westbrooks, San Jose	1.000	46	41	1	0	0
Whitfield, Reno	.963	62	102	3	4	1
Williams, San Bernardino	.962	27	23	2	1	1
Wong, Reno	.857	28	22	2	4	0
D. Young, Salinas	.970	43	91	7	3	3
S. Young, Salinas	.944	9	17	0	1	0

CATCHERS

Player and Club	Pct.	G.	PO.	A.	E.	DP.	PB.
Allanson, Salinas	.992	36	223	28	2	6	7
Arguelles, San Bernardino	.987	81	609	54	9	1	23
Ayala, Riverside	.987	27	140	9	2	2	8
Baar, Bakersfield	.979	103	741	98	18	4	29
Beard, Bakersfield	.962	3	23	2	1	0	1
Beeler, Salinas	.982	15	94	13	2	1	5
Blackwell, Reno	.969	27	164	22	6	3	3
Borrelli, Modesto	.971	51	326	48	11	1	14
BUCKLEY, Visalia	.991	77	577	49	6	9	9
Carcione, Modesto	.982	62	391	52	8	2	10
Christopherson, San Jose	.977	7	42	1	1	0	2
Deiley, Salinas	.965	28	173	19	7	2	2
Dewey, Riverside	1.000	14	80	10	0	1	1
Diaz, Stockton	.960	8	23	1	1	0	0
Dominguez, Palm Springs	.959	18	102	16	5	0	5
Fernandez, San Jose	.972	36	154	18	5	2	3
Firova, Reno	.994	46	282	61	2	8	13
Gieseke, Riverside*	1.000	1	3	0	0	0	0
Hahn, Salinas	.991	26	94	12	1	1	3
Ham, San Jose	.913	5	17	4	2	1	0
Hendley, Modesto	.976	28	148	14	4	1	8
Higgins, Riverside	.994	47	292	42	2	1	16
Hoffman, San Bernardino	.990	13	95	7	1	1	3
Kappesser, Stockton	.984	58	329	40	6	1	8
Kennedy, Modesto	.973	13	100	9	3	1	3
Lachmann, Reno	.973	6	34	2	1	0	3
Logan, Visalia	.979	65	456	57	11	4	13
Magnusson, Bakersfield	1.000	13	75	10	0	0	2
McGee, Riverside	.992	70	431	42	4	6	7
McNamara, San Jose	.991	31	200	31	2	1	8
Milene, Visalia	1.000	14	61	7	0	0	3
Miller, San Jose	1.000	3	11	2	0	0	0
Morales, San Bernardino	.960	22	152	15	7	1	10
Mota, Reno	.982	73	429	57	9	7	15
Musolino, Palm Springs	1.000	10	38	3	0	0	4
Nilsson, Stockton	.986	86	551	73	9	3	7
Ohtsuka, Salinas	.983	48	307	36	6	6	6
Ortiz, Salinas	1.000	4	11	5	0	0	0
Palma, Salinas	.968	3	30	0	1	0	2
Parker, Palm Springs	.964	68	288	38	12	1	15
Perea, Salinas	.985	16	57	7	1	1	4
Pirkl, San Bernardino	.976	43	325	40	9	0	8
Renfroe, Palm Springs	.983	25	108	11	2	0	5
Schroeder, Palm Springs	1.000	6	18	4	0	0	0
Stiner, Stockton	.978	29	119	13	3	1	6
Sturdivant, Palm Springs	.989	28	162	14	2	2	5
Teel, Bakersfield	.970	39	204	22	7	1	11
Thompson, Salinas	1.000	1	1	0	0	0	0
Tucker, San Jose	.984	84	595	88	11	7	20
Valdez, Bakersfield	1.000	1	9	0	0	0	0
Zayas, Palm Springs	.981	19	89	17	2	0	4

Triple Play—Borrelli.

PITCHERS

Player and Club	Pct.	G.	PO.	A.	E.	DP.
Aase, Bakersfield	1.000	6	1	1	0	0
Acosta, Palm Springs*	1.000	29	7	23	0	1
Alexander, Reno*	1.000	1	0	2	0	0
Allison, Modesto*	1.000	10	0	1	0	0
Anderson, Reno	1.000	27	3	12	0	1
Archibald, Palm Springs	.667	9	2	0	1	0
Arola, Salinas	1.000	18	2	3	0	0
Aspray, Visalia	1.000	19	2	9	0	1
Astacio, Bakersfield	.867	10	6	7	2	1
Barton, Reno	.750	3	0	3	1	0
Beckett, Riverside*	.833	3	1	4	1	0
Bennett, San Bernardino*	1.000	4	0	2	0	0
Best, Visalia	1.000	4	2	0	0	0
Bishop, Bakersfield*	1.000	5	0	1	0	0
Braase, Bakersfield	.917	29	4	7	1	0
Briscoe, Modesto	.850	29	3	14	3	1
Brock, San Jose	1.000	9	1	5	0	0
Brosnan, Bakersfield*	.905	26	1	18	2	1
Bryand, Riverside*	.933	47	7	21	2	0
Cangemi, Stockton	.933	62	9	19	2	2
Caraballo, Reno	1.000	17	0	2	0	0
Carmody, Riverside*	.923	49	5	19	2	2
Carrasco, Salinas	.800	26	3	21	6	0
Carter, Stockton	1.000	1	1	0	0	0
Chavez, 1 Reno-9 Mod.*	.857	10	2	10	2	1
Clark, Reno	.917	23	6	16	2	2
Cliburn, Palm Springs	1.000	16	4	8	0	0
Cobb, Palm Springs	.556	32	3	2	4	0
Cole, Reno	.958	14	8	15	1	0
Coleman, Bakersfield	1.000	39	4	7	0	1

PITCHERS—Continued

Player and Club	Pct.	G.	PO.	A.	E.	DP.
Crane, Bakersfield*	.875	33	2	12	2	0
Cummings, San Bernardino*	.875	7	2	5	1	0
Czajkowski, Stockton	1.000	2	0	1	0	0
Davis, Riverside	.939	26	10	36	3	1
Delahoya, Bakersfield	1.000	9	3	4	0	0
DeLucia, San Bernardino	1.000	5	0	4	0	0
Deville, Riverside	.875	42	6	1	1	0
Dour, San Jose	.979	25	6	41	1	4
Downs, San Jose	.667	1	0	2	1	1
Dunn, Palm Springs*	.950	28	7	12	1	0
Dwyer, Reno*	.667	5	0	2	1	0
Eldred, Stockton	.875	7	3	4	1	0
Emoto, Salinas*	.950	54	5	14	1	2
Enriquez, Stockton	1.000	8	1	2	0	0
Erwin, Modesto	.929	25	6	7	1	0
Estes, San Jose*	1.000	33	1	8	0	0
Estrada, Stockton	1.000	13	0	5	0	0
Evans, San Bernardino	.846	26	5	17	4	0
Felix, San Bernardino*	.917	37	3	8	1	0
Fine, Visalia	1.000	3	0	1	0	0
Fitzgerald, Stockton	.897	34	7	19	3	0
Fleming, San Bernardino*	1.000	12	4	15	0	1
Foley, San Jose	.889	27	7	9	2	0
Frame, Bakersfield	1.000	31	2	8	0	0
Fritz, Palm Springs	1.000	31	8	9	0	0
Furcal, San Bernardino*	.944	35	6	11	1	0
Fye, San Jose*	.875	43	7	21	4	4
Garces, Visalia	.778	47	1	6	2	1
Garcia, Modesto	.923	20	9	15	2	0
Gardey, Salinas	.500	3	1	0	1	0
Goff, San Bernardino	1.000	3	0	1	0	0
Gott, Bakersfield	1.000	7	0	2	0	0
Da. Green, 20 Reno-6 Mod.	1.000	26	3	10	0	1
De. Green, San Bernardino	.000	5	0	0	1	0
Grott, Modesto*	1.000	12	1	1	0	0
Guilbe, Stockton	1.000	4	2	0	0	0
Gustafson, San Jose	1.000	2	0	2	0	0
Guthrie, Reno	.500	5	1	0	1	0
Guzman, Modesto*	.875	13	4	10	2	0
Hamilton, Stockton	1.000	38	7	9	0	2
Hancock, San Jose*	1.000	1	1	4	0	0
Harrison, Riverside*	.400	37	0	2	3	0
Haslock, Riverside	.957	43	6	16	1	0
Helmick, Bakersfield	1.000	34	8	13	0	1
Herring, San Jose*	.952	35	3	17	1	0
Hill, Modesto	1.000	2	1	1	0	1
Hillman, Palm Springs	1.000	4	0	1	0	0
Howe, Salinas*	1.000	10	0	4	0	0
Humber, Bakersfield*	.929	57	3	10	1	1
Hurst, Reno*	.808	25	5	16	5	3
Ignasiak, Stockton	1.000	6	1	4	0	0
James, Palm Springs*	1.000	12	3	15	0	0
Jaster, Salinas	1.000	1	0	1	0	0
C. Johnson, Stockton	.964	23	12	15	1	0
D. Johnson, San Jose	.938	25	9	21	2	2
C. Jones, San Bernardino	.769	53	3	7	3	0
K. Jones, Bakersfield	1.000	9	8	7	0	1
Kiefer, Stockton	1.000	11	9	15	0	0
Knapp, Bakersfield	1.000	12	7	11	0	2
Knox, Riverside*	.941	27	8	24	2	0
Krol, Visalia	1.000	28	5	11	0	0
LaCoss, San Jose	.000	1	0	0	1	0
Lane, Riverside	.962	32	7	18	1	2
Langley, Reno*	.923	42	5	7	1	1
Lardizabal, Modesto	.880	26	7	15	3	0
Lawson, Modesto	1.000	23	3	9	0	0
Lee, Stockton*	1.000	5	0	5	0	0
Leslie, Salinas	.833	19	3	7	2	1
Lewis, Bakersfield	1.000	3	1	0	0	0
Lifgren, Riverside	.929	27	15	24	3	4
Lipson, Visalia	.875	17	3	4	1	0
Loubier, Palm Springs	1.000	9	1	2	0	0
Love, Modesto*	.900	37	3	15	2	1
Mahomes, Visalia	.941	28	11	21	2	2
Martinez, Palm Springs	.750	12	2	4	2	0
Marx, Riverside	1.000	2	1	2	0	0
Maye, Salinas	.854	30	8	27	6	3
McAndrew, Bakersfield	.826	14	6	13	4	2
McCoy, Modesto	.833	11	2	3	1	0
McDonald, San Bernardino*	1.000	9	0	1	0	0
McGrath, Stockton	1.000	1	0	1	0	0
Mead, San Jose	1.000	2	0	1	0	0
Merejo, Palm Springs	.929	25	7	6	1	0
Merriman, Palm Springs	.903	24	9	19	3	1
Mesa, Bakersfield	1.000	5	2	1	0	0
Meyers, San Jose*	.923	9	3	9	1	1
Miller, Modesto*	1.000	10	2	2	0	0
Miranda, Stockton*	.950	52	8	11	1	1
Muh, Visalia*	.833	12	4	6	2	0
Murakami, Salinas	.923	25	1	11	1	0
J. Myers, San Jose	.938	60	6	24	2	1
M. Myers, Salinas	1.000	30	6	13	0	2
Neagle, Visalia*	.889	10	0	8	1	0
Neal, Palm Springs*	1.000	10	0	3	0	0
Newlin, San Bernardino	.800	36	1	3	1	0
Newman, Visalia*	1.000	5	1	2	0	0
Ohtsuka, Salinas*	.871	31	3	24	4	0
Oliveras, San Jose	1.000	1	0	1	0	0
Ortiz, Reno*	1.000	16	1	13	0	0
Page, Salinas	1.000	11	0	2	0	0
Palmer, Reno	1.000	3	1	3	0	1
Pardo, Palm Springs	.727	25	10	14	9	1
Parisotto, Bakersfield	1.000	13	4	8	0	1
Patrick, Modesto	.917	14	6	5	1	2
Paxton, Reno*	.714	6	2	3	2	0
Peck, Modesto	.833	30	1	9	2	1
Pena, Modesto	.833	12	5	10	3	1
Perez, Stockton	1.000	6	2	4	0	0
Pettiford, Reno	.962	24	22	28	2	2
Phoenix, Modesto	1.000	6	5	4	0	0
Pitcher, San Bernardino	.765	36	6	7	4	0
Potthoff, Bakersfield	.000	7	0	0	1	0
Powers, Reno	.897	54	9	26	4	1
Rambo, San Jose	.969	26	10	21	1	1
Rauth, Reno	1.000	14	7	8	0	0
Reed, Riverside*	1.000	4	1	2	0	0
Reichle, Riverside	1.000	6	0	1	0	0
Reilley, Salinas	.852	19	3	20	4	0
Robinson, San Bernardino	.900	45	8	10	2	1
Rogers, San Jose*	.848	28	6	22	5	1
Rose, Modesto	1.000	6	2	0	0	0
Russo, Visalia	.833	17	1	4	1	1
Salkeld, San Bernardino	.962	25	4	21	1	1
Sampson, Bakersfield	.889	12	4	4	1	0
Sandoval, Stockton	1.000	34	8	10	0	0
Sasaki, Stockton	.917	34	7	26	3	4
Schwarz, Stockton	.833	19	2	8	2	1
Searage, Bakersfield*	1.000	10	2	1	0	0
Search, Palm Springs*	.889	24	2	6	1	3
Sharko, San Jose	1.000	44	3	18	0	1
Shaver, Modesto	1.000	1	1	3	0	1
Sheehan, San Bernardino	1.000	22	2	1	0	0
Shepherd, Reno	.857	5	0	6	1	0
Shull, Palm Springs	1.000	15	3	6	0	1
Sierra, Riverside	.889	38	2	6	1	1
Smith, San Bernardino	.889	41	3	5	1	0
Smithberg, Riverside	.750	3	0	3	1	1
Soper, Reno	1.000	43	3	10	0	0
Sparks, Stockton	.878	19	8	28	5	5
Stewart, Salinas	1.000	11	2	4	0	0
Strebeck, Modesto	1.000	14	0	3	0	0
Swanson, Visalia	.920	39	5	18	2	1
Tanoue, Salinas	1.000	10	2	2	0	0
Tapia, Bakersfield	.857	13	4	2	1	0
Tatis, Stockton	.750	18	1	2	1	0
R. Taylor, San Jose	1.000	13	4	2	0	0
S. Taylor, San Bernardino	.920	34	10	13	2	2
W. Taylor, Modesto	1.000	22	1	4	0	0
Thomas, Riverside	.929	27	9	30	3	2
Tolliver, Palm Springs	1.000	7	0	4	0	0
Trombley, Visalia	.938	27	12	18	2	1
Tsamis, Visalia	.963	26	5	72	3	4
Uchiyama, Salinas	.722	37	3	10	5	0
Uribe, San Bernardino	1.000	31	1	2	0	0
Vann, Palm Springs	1.000	28	1	4	0	0
Velasquez, Salinas	1.000	6	1	3	0	0
Vidmar, Palm Springs	.960	17	12	12	1	0
Vuz, San Jose	.800	5	2	2	1	0
Warrecker, Palm Springs*	.818	17	1	8	2	0
Wertz, Reno	1.000	17	5	4	0	0
White, Reno	.813	37	3	10	3	0
Whitney, Reno	1.000	17	7	6	0	1
WIESE, Visalia*	1.000	20	4	27	0	4
Wiggs, San Bernardino	.938	64	7	38	3	0
Woodson, San Bernardino	.947	27	14	22	2	2
Zancanaro, Modesto*	1.000	4	0	3	0	0
Zappelli, Palm Springs	1.000	21	2	1	0	0

The following players did not have any fielding statistics at the positions indicated or appeared only as a designated hitter, pinch-hitter or pinch-runner: Arguelles, of; Beals, of; Bethea, p; Bickler, p; Brady, 1b; Capellan, 3b, p; Carmody, of; Cassels, 2b, p; I. Clark, p; Correia, p; DeLaRosa, p; Dodson, of; Dunn, of; Esquer, of; Firova, p; Forrester, p; Gonzalez, of; Henry, p; Housie, 3b; Humber, p; Jaha, dh, ph; Kelso, p; Kohno, 3b; Krippner, p; Leiper, p; A. Lewis, 2b; Lofthus, dh, ph; Magallanes, 3b; McClure, p; McCreary, p; McMurray, 1b; Meeks, p; Morales, 3b; Munoz, of; J. Myers, of; Nesmith, ph; Nilsson, 2b, of; Nishijima, 1b, an; O'Neal, p; Parker, of, p; Perry, p; Potestio, p; D. Robinson, p; Rowe, ph; Search, of; Tashiro, 2b; Tatum, p; Teel, 3b; Westbrooks, 2b; Wiggs, p; Yamanouchi, of.

CLUB PITCHING

Club	ERA.	G.	CG.	ShO.	Sv.	IP.	H.	R.	ER.	HR.	HB.	BB.	Int. BB.	SO.	WP.	Bk.
Visalia	3.36	141	16	20	49	1228.1	1112	568	459	68	43	530	10	1101	82	10
Bakersfield	3.87	142	4	8	46	1235.0	1225	661	531	72	61	600	29	1043	85	16
Stockton	3.88	141	13	13	47	1202.2	1148	611	518	68	79	512	17	1013	58	12
San Jose	3.89	142	8	8	36	1245.2	1135	688	539	59	59	571	26	999	100	11
Modesto	3.97	141	6	4	34	1227.1	1150	684	542	101	45	610	18	940	112	20
Riverside	4.12	142	7	5	35	1225.2	1358	709	561	81	45	459	35	904	76	14
San Bernardino	4.18	142	15	7	36	1249.0	1210	746	580	86	63	667	19	1198	77	20
Palm Springs	4.22	142	7	3	29	1233.0	1266	705	578	62	63	525	27	761	79	11
Salinas	4.63	140	28	3	19	1202.0	1321	770	618	88	54	498	17	944	112	25
Reno	4.71	139	13	6	34	1202.0	1298	795	629	93	53	570	17	880	97	21

PITCHERS' RECORDS
(Leading Qualifiers for Earned-Run Average Leadership—114 or More Innings)

*Throws lefthanded.

Pitcher—Club	W.	L.	Pct.	ERA.	G.	GS.	CG.	GF.	ShO.	Sv.	IP.	H.	R.	ER.	HR.	HB.	BB.	Int. BB.	SO.	WP.
Rambo, San Jose	12	2	.857	2.19	26	17	2	3	1	1	143.2	104	47	35	8	4	42	1	142	3
Tsamis, Visalia*	17	4	.810	2.21	26	26	4	0	3	0	183.2	168	62	45	4	4	61	0	145	7
Wiese, Visalia*	10	4	.714	2.52	20	19	2	0	1	0	118.0	109	43	33	5	2	44	1	95	3
C. Johnson, Stockton	13	6	.684	2.98	23	23	1	0	0	0	142.0	121	56	47	7	9	54	1	112	4
Davis, Riverside	10	9	.526	3.04	26	26	0	0	0	0	162.2	175	72	55	6	5	44	2	122	10
Woodson, San Bernardino	8	6	.571	3.10	27	23	1	1	1	0	136.2	111	62	47	2	12	83	1	131	8
Brosnan, Bakersfield*	12	4	.750	3.11	26	25	0	0	0	0	136.0	113	63	47	4	7	91	1	157	7
Mahomes, Visalia	11	11	.500	3.30	28	28	5	0	1	0	185.1	136	77	68	14	4	118	1	178	19
Salkeld, San Bernardino	11	5	.688	3.40	25	25	2	0	0	0	153.1	140	77	58	3	3	83	0	167	9
Trombley, Visalia	14	6	.700	3.43	27	25	3	1	1	0	176.0	163	79	67	12	11	50	0	164	8

Departmental Leaders: G—Wiggs, 64; W—Tsamis, 17; L—Carrasco, Lifgren, Maye, Sasaki, 14; Pct.—Rambo, .857; GS—Mahomes, 28; CG—Maye, 14; GF—J. Myers, 50; ShO—Tsamis, 3; Sv.—Garces, 28; IP—Mahomes, Maye, 185.1; H—Thomas, 209; R—Carrasco, 112; ER—Carrasco, 89; HR—Hurst, 19; HB—Woodson, 12; IBB—Emoto, 8; SO—Rogers, 186; WP—Fye, 22.

(All Pitchers—Listed Alphabetically)

Pitcher—Club	W.	L.	Pct.	ERA.	G.	GS.	CG.	GF.	ShO.	Sv.	IP.	H.	R.	ER.	HR.	HB.	BB.	Int. BB.	SO.	WP.
Aase, Bakersfield	0	0	.000	1.00	6	6	0	0	0	0	9.0	6	1	1	0	0	2	0	4	0
Acosta, Palm Springs*	10	10	.500	4.40	29	26	2	1	0	0	159.2	182	97	78	7	2	40	1	93	9
Alexander, Reno*	0	1	.000	11.57	1	1	0	0	0	0	4.2	5	6	6	0	0	6	0	5	4
Allison, Modesto*	0	0	.000	2.33	10	0	0	8	0	4	19.1	13	9	5	0	0	3	0	19	0
Anderson, Reno	4	1	.800	3.90	27	4	0	10	0	0	57.2	60	30	25	4	4	25	1	56	0
Archibald, Palm Springs	1	1	.500	4.80	9	0	0	2	0	0	15.0	18	8	8	1	1	4	0	7	2
Arola, Salinas	2	0	1.000	3.05	18	2	0	5	0	0	38.1	33	20	13	2	1	15	0	17	1
Aspray, Visalia	2	2	.500	3.46	19	0	0	11	0	3	41.2	41	20	16	4	0	8	0	30	0
Astacio, Bakersfield	5	2	.714	2.77	10	7	1	0	0	0	52.0	46	22	16	3	3	15	1	34	2
Barton, 3 Reno-0 Sal.	1	0	1.000	1.29	3	0	0	2	0	0	7.0	7	2	1	0	0	2	1	2	0
Beckett, Riverside*	2	1	.667	7.02	3	3	0	0	0	0	16.2	18	13	13	0	0	11	0	11	1
Bennett, San Bernardino*	0	0	.000	1.69	4	0	0	0	0	0	5.1	6	2	1	0	0	1	0	2	0
Best, Visalia	1	1	.500	5.87	4	3	0	1	0	0	15.1	16	14	10	2	0	16	0	13	2
Bethea, Riverside	0	0	.000	0.00	1	0	0	1	0	0	1.0	2	0	0	0	0	0	0	0	0
Bickler, Reno*	0	0	.000	9.00	1	0	0	1	0	0	1.0	1	1	1	0	0	2	0	1	1
Bishop, Bakersfield*	0	1	.000	9.00	5	1	0	1	0	0	7.0	9	10	7	0	0	9	1	6	1
Braase, Bakersfield	3	3	.500	4.84	29	1	0	10	0	2	67.0	83	44	36	6	4	17	1	58	4
Briscoe, Modesto	3	6	.333	4.59	29	12	1	12	0	4	86.1	72	50	44	12	2	52	0	66	7
Brock, San Jose	0	2	.000	6.23	9	1	0	3	0	0	17.1	19	13	12	0	0	11	0	11	0
Brosnan, Bakersfield*	12	4	.750	3.11	26	25	0	0	0	0	136.0	113	63	47	4	7	91	1	157	7
Bryand, Riverside*	7	2	.778	5.30	47	6	0	14	0	0	88.1	128	66	52	9	1	31	4	68	4
Cangemi, Stockton	3	7	.300	3.01	62	1	0	25	0	6	98.2	86	41	33	4	3	52	3	102	5
Capellan, Visalia	0	0	.000	0.00	1	0	0	1	0	0	1.0	1	0	0	0	0	0	0	1	0
Caraballo, Reno	2	0	1.000	9.68	17	4	0	6	0	0	30.2	45	35	33	6	0	20	1	22	2
Carmody, Stockton*	5	3	.625	5.16	49	0	0	18	0	1	83.2	90	60	48	4	7	35	2	58	3
Carrasco, Salinas	5	14	.263	5.22	26	25	4	0	0	0	153.1	174	112	89	16	3	66	0	107	13
Carter, Stockton	0	0	.000	15.00	1	1	0	0	0	0	3.0	5	5	5	1	1	2	0	2	0
Cassels, Stockton	0	0	.000	9.00	1	0	0	1	0	0	1.0	1	1	1	1	0	0	0	0	0
Chavez, 1 Reno-9 Mod.*	5	2	.714	3.94	10	10	1	0	0	0	59.1	61	30	26	4	1	23	0	48	1
G. Clark, Reno	6	2	.750	4.87	23	11	3	6	0	0	92.1	97	57	50	10	1	24	1	55	8
I. Clark, San Bernardino	0	0	.000	4.50	1	0	0	1	0	0	2.0	1	1	1	0	1	3	0	5	1
Cliburn, Palm Springs	2	1	.667	4.07	16	0	0	11	0	6	24.1	29	11	11	0	0	5	2	23	1
Cobb, Palm Springs	4	1	.800	4.75	32	0	0	15	0	2	47.1	50	30	25	0	2	31	1	31	6
Cole, Reno	5	5	.500	3.72	14	12	3	0	0	0	84.2	90	51	35	5	6	27	0	49	2
Coleman, Bakersfield	1	6	.143	4.61	39	0	0	31	0	16	54.2	50	33	28	3	2	26	4	52	1
Correia, Modesto	0	1	.000	0.00	1	0	0	1	0	0	1.0	1	4	0	0	1	3	0	0	0
Crane, Bakersfield	3	3	.500	3.42	33	8	0	8	0	1	92.0	99	43	35	4	4	42	2	75	7
Cummings, San Bernardino*	2	4	.333	4.20	7	7	1	0	0	0	40.2	47	27	19	3	0	20	0	30	3
Czajkowski, Stockton	0	0	.000	0.00	2	0	0	1	0	1	2.2	1	0	0	0	0	2	0	2	0
Davis, Riverside	10	9	.526	3.04	26	26	0	0	0	0	162.2	175	72	55	6	5	44	2	122	10
Delahoya, Bakersfield	4	1	.800	5.95	9	7	0	0	0	0	39.1	50	30	26	5	1	24	0	37	6
DeLaRosa, Stockton	0	0	.000	9.00	2	0	0	2	0	0	2.0	1	2	2	0	0	3	0	2	1
DeLucia, San Bernardino	4	1	.800	2.05	5	5	1	0	0	0	30.2	19	9	7	4	4	3	0	35	1
Deville, Riverside	3	2	.600	4.67	42	1	0	17	0	2	81.0	89	49	42	9	3	32	1	74	5
Dour, San Jose	6	6	.500	4.03	25	24	1	0	1	0	127.1	133	85	57	5	11	41	1	77	8
Downs, San Jose	1	0	1.000	1.80	1	1	0	0	0	0	5.0	5	2	1	0	1	0	0	3	0
Dunn, Palm Springs*	4	4	.500	5.28	28	7	0	4	0	0	90.1	112	62	53	4	5	35	2	49	7
Dwyer, Reno*	0	0	.000	4.05	5	0	0	2	0	0	6.2	10	5	3	0	1	2	0	5	1
Eldred, Stockton	4	2	.667	1.62	7	7	3	0	1	0	50.0	31	12	9	2	3	19	0	75	2
Emoto, Salinas*	7	4	.636	3.07	54	0	0	36	0	6	82.0	81	36	28	3	4	38	8	72	5
Enriquez, Stockton	1	0	1.000	3.24	8	0	0	1	0	0	8.1	10	3	3	2	0	6	0	9	0
Erwin, Modesto	6	11	.353	4.32	25	25	2	0	0	0	131.1	122	89	63	10	2	78	0	128	15
Estes, San Jose*	2	2	.500	2.60	33	0	0	18	0	4	52.0	53	20	15	0	4	8	2	42	0
Estrada, Riverside	0	1	.000	2.70	13	0	0	8	0	0	16.2	11	5	5	0	1	12	2	12	1
Evans, San Bernardino	14	9	.609	4.18	26	26	4	0	0	0	155.0	135	83	72	9	7	74	0	143	10
Felix, San Bernardino*	0	3	.000	6.68	37	2	0	10	0	0	66.0	78	58	49	6	6	42	0	67	10
Fine, Visalia	0	0	.000	5.06	3	0	0	1	0	0	5.1	3	3	3	0	1	6	0	4	0
Firova, Reno	2	0	1.000	0.00	4	1	0	3	0	0	9.1	4	0	0	0	1	6	0	6	2
Fitzgerald, Stockton*	10	10	.500	6.02	34	24	1	1	0	0	128.2	146	102	86	10	11	56	4	87	11

Pitcher—Club	W.	L.	Pct.	ERA.	G.	GS.	CG.	GF.	ShO.	Sv.	IP.	H.	R.	ER.	HR.	HB.	BB.	Int. BB.	SO.	WP.
Fleming, San Bernardino*	7	3	.700	2.60	12	12	4	0	0	0	79.2	64	29	23	0	1	30	1	77	1
Foley, San Jose	4	5	.444	4.82	27	12	0	9	0	2	93.1	88	54	50	6	8	61	3	85	7
Forrester, Bakersfield	0	0	.000	18.00	2	0	0	2	0	0	2.0	5	4	4	0	0	2	0	2	0
Frame, Bakersfield	1	3	.250	4.50	31	1	0	13	0	4	46.0	47	27	23	2	4	30	5	26	10
Fritz, Palm Springs	8	7	.533	4.19	31	21	1	2	1	0	131.0	131	80	61	13	5	75	3	64	13
Furcal, San Bernardino*	7	8	.467	4.65	35	14	1	4	0	2	108.1	106	75	56	18	0	41	0	98	3
Fye, San Jose*	7	11	.389	5.47	43	15	1	14	1	0	126.2	120	90	77	2	3	75	6	84	22
Garces, Visalia	2	2	.500	1.81	47	0	0	42	0	28	54.2	33	14	11	2	1	16	0	75	6
Garcia, Modesto	3	11	.214	3.59	20	20	1	0	0	0	123.0	113	63	49	13	4	41	0	96	8
Gardey, Salinas	0	0	.000	2.70	3	0	0	0	0	0	6.2	6	2	2	0	2	3	0	6	1
Goff, San Bernardino	0	1	.000	1.93	3	0	0	0	0	0	4.2	6	2	1	0	1	2	0	4	0
Gott, Bakersfield	0	0	.000	2.77	7	3	0	1	0	0	13.0	13	5	4	0	1	4	0	16	2
Da. Green, 20 Reno- 6 Mod.	3	2	.600	3.06	26	2	0	14	0	2	50.0	47	24	17	2	1	23	3	49	2
De. Green, San Bernardino	0	0	.000	12.60	5	0	0	2	0	0	10.0	16	17	14	2	1	12	0	11	0
Grott, Modesto*	2	0	1.000	2.04	12	0	0	8	0	4	17.2	10	7	4	0	0	14	1	28	4
Guilbe, Stockton	0	0	.000	11.25	4	0	0	2	0	0	4.0	10	7	5	0	0	4	0	2	0
Gustafson, San Jose	0	0	.000	0.00	2	0	0	0	0	0	3.0	2	0	0	0	0	4	0	4	0
Guthrie, Reno	0	1	.000	4.26	5	0	0	1	0	0	6.1	6	7	3	0	0	4	0	6	0
Guzman, Modesto*	7	4	.636	1.91	13	13	1	0	1	0	84.2	67	25	18	3	4	23	2	58	2
Hamilton, Stockton	4	4	.500	3.51	38	9	0	4	0	0	84.2	88	42	33	9	2	38	1	73	7
Hancock, San Jose*	0	0	.000	1.17	1	1	0	0	0	0	7.2	7	1	1	0	0	4	0	7	0
Harrison, Riverside*	5	2	.714	1.19	37	0	0	35	0	18	45.1	31	9	6	0	1	20	3	55	2
Haslock, Riverside	2	4	.333	4.91	43	1	0	23	0	3	80.2	75	47	44	6	9	38	5	86	4
Helmick, Bakersfield	6	6	.500	3.73	34	9	0	9	0	4	113.1	110	56	47	8	7	51	1	110	6
Henry, Stockton	1	0	1.000	1.13	4	0	0	3	0	1	8.0	4	1	1	0	2	3	0	13	1
Herring, San Jose*	2	4	.333	3.41	35	0	0	15	0	2	71.1	61	34	27	5	2	42	2	63	12
Hill, Modesto	0	0	.000	10.80	2	0	0	1	0	0	1.2	4	2	2	0	1	2	0	1	0
Hillman, Palm Springs	0	1	.000	13.06	4	1	0	1	0	0	10.1	15	15	15	2	0	2	0	5	0
Howe, Salinas*	0	1	.000	2.12	10	6	0	2	0	0	17.0	19	8	4	0	1	5	0	14	2
Humber, Bakersfield*	6	5	.545	3.47	57	0	0	38	0	13	70.0	68	30	27	6	4	32	7	44	2
Hurst, Reno*	4	11	.267	5.47	25	21	1	1	0	1	131.2	165	102	80	19	4	68	0	90	8
Ignasiak, Stockton	3	1	.750	3.94	6	6	1	0	1	0	32.0	18	14	14	3	2	17	0	23	2
James, Palm Springs*	3	3	.500	4.37	12	12	1	0	0	0	70.0	63	36	34	3	6	38	0	44	3
Jaster, Salinas	0	0	.000	9.00	1	0	0	1	0	0	2.0	3	2	2	0	0	3	0	0	0
C. Johnson, Stockton	13	6	.684	2.98	23	23	1	0	0	0	142.0	121	56	47	7	9	54	1	112	4
D. Johnson, San Jose	5	8	.385	5.40	25	19	2	2	0	0	100.0	89	72	60	8	6	72	0	61	10
C. Jones, San Bernardino	5	3	.625	2.96	53	0	0	27	0	8	67.0	43	32	22	4	4	54	2	94	6
K. Jones, Bakersfield	3	3	.500	3.48	9	8	0	0	0	0	44.0	33	20	17	1	1	23	0	38	0
Kelso, Palm Springs	0	0	.000	4.50	1	0	0	1	0	0	2.0	2	1	1	0	0	2	0	1	1
Kiefer, Stockton	5	2	.714	3.30	11	10	0	1	0	0	60.0	65	23	22	5	8	17	0	37	3
Knapp, Bakersfield	8	2	.800	5.15	12	11	1	0	0	0	71.2	93	45	41	7	2	18	0	36	4
Knox, Riverside*	11	12	.478	3.66	27	27	3	0	1	0	179.2	188	97	73	14	3	49	2	111	8
Krippner, Stockton	0	1	.000	22.50	2	0	0	0	0	0	2.0	5	5	5	1	2	1	0	1	0
Krol, Visalia	4	3	.571	5.94	28	10	0	9	0	1	66.2	71	48	44	6	5	42	0	42	6
LaCoss, San Jose	1	0	1.000	1.50	1	1	0	0	0	0	6.0	5	1	1	1	0	0	0	6	0
Lane, Riverside	5	7	.417	4.93	32	11	0	11	0	1	100.1	117	72	55	7	6	58	7	55	9
Langley, Reno*	6	1	.857	4.46	42	0	0	13	0	2	76.2	83	43	38	3	1	57	1	84	6
Lardizabal, Modesto	3	10	.231	4.36	26	18	0	2	0	0	130.0	138	76	63	12	4	52	0	70	8
Lawson, Modesto	3	5	.375	4.61	23	2	0	8	0	2	52.2	40	33	27	4	2	39	2	39	13
Lee, Stockton*	1	0	1.000	2.35	5	0	0	2	0	1	7.2	5	2	2	0	0	3	0	7	0
Leiper, Modesto*	1	0	1.000	0.00	3	1	0	0	0	0	9.0	2	1	0	0	1	1	0	6	0
Leslie, Salinas	5	3	.625	3.89	19	2	0	11	0	2	34.2	39	18	15	1	1	24	0	28	5
Lewis, Bakersfield	0	0	.000	4.50	3	0	0	0	0	0	4.0	4	2	2	1	0	0	0	4	0
Lifgren, Riverside	6	14	.300	4.55	27	27	3	0	0	0	164.1	195	107	83	13	9	68	1	113	13
Lipson, Visalia	1	0	1.000	1.64	17	0	0	14	0	12	22.0	21	5	4	0	0	6	0	15	1
Loubier, Palm Springs	0	1	.000	5.40	9	1	0	3	0	0	16.2	14	10	10	0	2	13	1	14	5
Love, Modesto*	1	1	.500	4.90	37	2	0	14	0	2	68.0	71	46	37	5	7	50	1	60	17
Mahomes, Visalia	11	11	.500	3.30	28	28	5	0	1	0	185.1	136	77	68	14	4	118	1	178	19
Martinez, Palm Springs	0	6	.000	4.72	12	9	0	1	0	0	55.1	59	32	29	2	6	16	0	37	3
Marx, Riverside	0	1	.000	7.00	2	2	0	0	0	0	9.0	8	7	7	0	2	6	0	2	1
Maye, Salinas	10	14	.417	3.74	30	27	14	1	2	0	185.1	195	102	77	13	11	66	0	114	7
McAndrew, Bakersfield	10	3	.769	2.27	14	14	1	0	1	0	95.0	88	31	24	2	5	29	1	82	6
McClure, Palm Springs*	0	0	.000	0.00	2	1	0	0	0	0	3.0	0	0	0	0	0	1	0	6	0
McCoy, Modesto*	1	1	.500	1.74	11	1	0	9	0	0	20.2	9	4	4	0	0	9	1	23	4
McCreary, Visalia	0	0	.000	0.00	1	0	0	1	0	0	1.0	1	0	0	0	0	0	0	0	0
McDonald, San Bernardino*	0	0	.000	5.27	9	0	0	5	0	0	13.2	18	13	8	0	0	9	0	10	1
McGrath, Stockton	0	0	.000	2.25	1	1	0	0	0	0	4.0	3	1	1	0	1	1	0	3	0
Mead, San Jose	1	0	1.000	0.00	2	1	0	0	0	0	10.1	8	1	0	0	1	5	0	9	0
Meeks, Palm Springs	1	0	1.000	0.00	6	0	0	4	0	1	10.1	5	0	0	0	2	2	0	12	0
Merejo, Palm Springs	5	3	.625	2.54	25	0	0	14	0	4	39.0	37	11	11	0	1	12	2	18	1
Merriman, Palm Springs	3	10	.231	3.75	24	16	0	0	0	0	100.2	106	60	42	8	9	55	1	53	6
Mesa, Bakersfield	0	1	.000	9.49	5	2	0	0	0	0	12.1	12	15	13	2	0	12	1	6	0
Meyers, San Jose*	2	3	.400	4.78	8	8	0	0	0	0	37.2	36	26	20	2	5	22	0	20	5
Miller, Modesto*	2	3	.400	3.24	10	1	0	3	0	1	25.0	22	13	9	1	2	11	0	20	0
Miranda, Stockton*	9	4	.692	2.66	52	9	2	40	1	24	108.1	75	37	32	7	2	49	1	138	2
Muh, Visalia*	5	3	.625	3.96	12	12	2	0	2	0	84.0	80	40	37	6	1	38	0	54	5
Murakami, Salinas	3	5	.375	4.54	25	8	1	11	0	0	83.1	77	48	42	8	3	33	0	69	8
J. Myers, San Jose	5	8	.385	3.21	60	0	0	50	0	25	84.0	80	44	30	2	2	34	6	61	3
M. Myers, Salinas	3	7	.300	3.77	30	5	1	6	0	3	71.2	83	42	30	3	1	18	2	61	9
Neagle, Visalia*	8	0	1.000	1.43	10	10	0	0	0	0	63.0	39	13	10	2	0	16	0	92	0
Neal, Visalia	2	1	.667	5.27	10	3	0	0	0	0	27.1	24	18	16	3	2	21	1	22	3
Newlin, San Bernardino	1	5	.167	3.60	36	0	0	28	0	12	45.0	35	24	18	2	4	21	5	56	3
Newman, Visalia*	3	1	.750	2.23	5	5	0	0	0	0	36.1	29	15	9	0	1	22	0	42	1
Nishijima, Salinas*	0	0	.000	5.40	1	0	0	1	0	0	1.2	1	2	1	0	1	1	0	1	0
O'Neal, San Jose	0	0	.000	3.00	1	1	0	0	0	0	3.0	4	1	1	0	0	2	0	2	0
Ohtsuka, Salinas*	5	10	.333	4.82	31	23	4	2	0	1	151.1	188	94	81	9	5	44	1	121	6
Oliveras, San Jose	0	0	.000	2.45	1	1	0	0	0	0	3.2	4	2	1	0	0	1	0	3	0
Ortiz, Reno*	7	6	.538	4.27	16	16	0	0	0	0	90.2	108	67	43	9	2	52	0	68	8
Page, Salinas	0	2	.000	7.31	11	0	0	3	0	0	16.0	30	18	13	2	1	6	0	11	2
Palmer, Reno	1	0	1.000	3.38	3	3	0	0	0	0	10.2	8	4	4	0	1	8	0	10	0
Pardo, Palm Springs	9	10	.474	4.16	25	24	1	0	0	0	138.1	137	77	64	7	10	57	2	78	2
Parisotto, Bakersfield	3	4	.429	3.93	13	8	1	0	0	0	52.2	59	41	23	4	3	28	2	42	4

Pitcher—Club	W.	L.	Pct.	ERA.	G.	GS.	CG.	GF.	ShO.	Sv.	IP.	H.	R.	ER.	HR.	HB.	BB.	Int. BB.	SO.	WP.
Parker, Palm Springs	0	0	.000	11.57	1	0	0	0	0	0	2.1	5	4	3	0	0	1	0	1	0
Patrick, Modesto	3	7	.300	5.18	14	14	0	0	0	0	74.2	92	58	43	10	4	32	0	37	5
Paxton, Reno	2	3	.400	7.56	6	6	0	0	0	0	25.0	33	25	21	2	4	10	0	22	1
Peck, Modesto	4	2	.667	4.14	30	2	0	10	0	3	58.2	58	29	27	6	2	28	3	46	5
Pena, Modesto	3	7	.300	3.75	12	12	0	0	0	0	72.0	66	37	30	3	2	37	0	43	5
Perez, Stockton	1	1	.500	3.97	6	5	0	0	0	0	22.2	24	11	10	1	0	5	0	23	0
Perry, Bakersfield°	0	0	.000	3.60	3	3	0	0	0	0	5.0	3	3	2	0	0	1	0	7	1
Pettiford, Reno	12	9	.571	4.75	24	24	2	0	0	0	142.0	151	91	75	8	3	62	1	87	5
Phoenix, Modesto	4	1	.800	4.58	6	6	0	0	0	0	37.1	43	21	19	2	2	10	0	23	3
Pitcher, San Bernardino	3	1	.750	5.04	36	7	0	14	0	3	75.0	82	55	42	6	7	47	3	66	3
Potestio, San Jose	3	0	1.000	4.55	6	4	0	1	0	0	29.2	24	18	15	3	0	14	0	21	1
Potthoff, Bakersfield	0	0	.000	3.00	7	2	0	2	0	1	15.0	17	6	5	1	1	10	1	15	1
Powers, Reno	5	6	.455	3.88	54	0	0	27	0	8	106.2	114	59	46	3	8	41	7	82	7
Rambo, San Jose	12	2	.857	2.19	26	17	2	3	1	1	143.2	104	47	35	8	4	42	1	142	3
Rauth, Reno	2	7	.222	6.12	14	12	2	1	0	0	75.0	101	58	51	5	7	34	0	40	11
Reed, Riverside°	0	2	.000	3.57	4	2	0	0	0	0	17.2	18	10	7	1	1	16	0	10	2
Reichle, Riverside	0	2	.000	6.19	6	6	0	0	0	0	16.0	19	13	11	1	0	13	0	15	1
Reilley, Salinas	1	8	.111	5.09	19	14	1	1	0	0	81.1	66	57	46	4	6	55	0	90	20
D. Robinson, San Jose	1	0	1.000	3.86	2	2	0	0	0	0	7.0	6	3	3	1	1	1	0	8	0
N. Robinson, Bakersfield	7	4	.636	3.11	45	4	0	12	0	4	101.1	94	47	35	4	3	48	0	81	11
Rogers, San Jose°	14	5	.737	3.61	28	26	1	1	1	0	172.0	143	86	69	9	11	68	1	186	19
Rose, Modesto	0	0	.000	1.29	6	0	0	3	0	1	14.0	14	5	2	0	0	6	1	10	2
Russo, Visalia	0	3	.000	5.59	17	0	0	11	0	0	29.0	34	29	18	1	7	22	4	26	5
Salkeld, San Bernardino	11	5	.688	3.40	25	25	2	0	0	0	153.1	140	77	58	3	3	83	0	167	9
Sampson, Bakersfield	3	4	.429	4.96	12	10	0	0	0	0	52.2	46	36	29	4	2	45	1	37	3
Sandoval, Stockton	8	5	.615	4.08	34	16	0	5	0	0	123.2	131	63	56	4	6	54	4	79	2
Sasaki, Salinas	3	14	.176	6.02	34	16	2	6	0	0	122.2	140	98	82	11	9	75	4	86	16
Schwarz, Stockton	3	3	.500	4.79	19	8	0	3	0	2	56.1	59	36	30	1	9	36	0	59	5
Searage, Bakersfield°	1	2	.333	3.21	10	5	0	1	0	0	14.0	8	5	5	1	1	8	0	17	0
Search, Palm Springs°	1	0	1.000	4.13	24	0	0	9	0	0	28.1	38	21	13	2	2	21	3	13	2
Sharko, San Jose	6	5	.545	3.38	44	3	0	9	0	0	96.0	97	49	35	1	1	36	2	60	6
Shaver, Modesto	0	1	.000	9.00	1	1	0	0	0	0	4.0	7	5	4	1	0	3	0	1	1
Sheehan, San Bernardino	0	2	.000	6.19	22	0	0	11	0	2	36.1	43	32	25	4	2	25	2	19	2
Shepherd, Reno	1	4	.200	5.40	5	5	0	0	0	0	25.0	22	25	15	1	2	18	0	16	6
Shull, Palm Springs	0	6	.000	6.99	15	3	0	3	0	0	28.1	33	32	22	4	2	14	1	26	2
Sierra, Riverside	3	4	.429	2.14	38	0	0	26	0	11	67.1	63	32	16	3	0	17	5	71	5
Smith, Modesto	2	5	.286	4.43	41	0	0	26	0	4	65.0	62	40	32	6	2	48	3	65	10
Smithberg, Riverside	1	2	.333	4.15	3	3	0	0	0	0	13.0	12	7	6	1	0	2	0	5	0
Soper, Reno	2	3	.400	1.81	43	0	0	39	0	21	44.2	24	11	9	4	2	17	2	46	4
Sparks, Stockton	10	7	.588	3.69	19	19	5	0	1	0	129.1	136	63	53	4	8	31	0	77	7
Stewart, Salinas°	0	1	.000	3.86	11	0	0	3	0	0	16.1	20	9	7	2	1	5	1	22	1
Strebeck, Modesto	2	1	.667	3.05	14	0	0	12	0	4	20.2	12	7	7	3	1	10	2	13	0
Swanson, Visalia	6	7	.462	4.99	39	0	0	18	0	3	79.1	90	55	44	5	3	37	4	68	11
Tanoue, Salinas	0	0	.000	4.58	10	1	0	6	0	0	17.2	19	9	9	0	1	3	0	8	1
Tapia, Bakersfield	1	2	.333	3.93	13	6	0	2	0	0	34.1	31	21	15	3	1	17	0	21	5
Tatis, Bakersfield	3	3	.500	5.97	18	1	0	5	0	1	31.2	38	21	21	1	5	16	0	36	2
Tatum, Stockton	0	0	.000	0.00	1	0	0	1	0	0	1.0	1	1	0	0	0	0	0	1	0
R. Taylor, San Jose	3	2	.600	7.08	13	0	0	9	0	2	20.1	24	19	16	1	1	15	2	18	1
S. Taylor, San Bernardino	8	8	.500	5.41	34	21	1	3	0	1	126.1	148	100	76	17	7	69	0	86	10
W. Taylor, Modesto	4	1	.800	3.51	22	0	0	14	0	2	33.1	29	15	13	3	0	19	1	29	3
Thomas, Riverside	9	13	.409	4.72	27	27	1	0	0	0	166.0	209	103	87	11	4	49	3	93	10
Tolliver, Palm Springs	0	1	.000	2.87	7	1	0	3	0	0	15.2	15	5	5	1	1	6	2	5	1
Trombley, Visalia	14	6	.700	3.43	27	25	3	1	1	0	176.0	163	79	67	12	11	50	0	164	8
Tsamis, Visalia°	17	4	.810	2.21	26	26	4	0	3	0	183.2	168	62	45	4	4	61	0	145	7
Uchiyama, Salinas	3	10	.231	5.92	37	11	1	13	0	6	111.0	141	88	73	13	2	32	1	111	9
Uribe, Stockton	1	3	.250	4.62	31	2	0	19	0	11	39.0	32	23	20	2	3	24	0	28	1
Vann, Palm Springs	1	0	1.000	2.05	28	0	0	22	0	8	26.1	17	8	6	0	0	12	0	29	2
Velasquez, Salinas	0	0	.000	3.72	6	0	0	4	0	1	9.2	6	5	4	0	2	6	0	7	4
Vidmar, Palm Springs	5	10	.333	3.43	17	17	2	0	0	0	112.2	105	51	43	8	7	29	1	60	2
Vuz, San Jose	0	4	.000	4.08	5	5	1	0	0	0	28.2	23	20	13	2	1	19	0	26	3
Warrecker, Palm Springs°	3	3	.500	3.49	37	0	0	20	0	2	56.2	52	29	22	3	0	24	2	45	2
Wertz, Reno	1	3	.250	6.60	17	9	0	1	0	0	61.1	61	58	45	6	5	52	0	52	12
White, Visalia	6	4	.600	5.45	37	3	0	15	0	1	66.0	77	51	40	5	3	28	0	57	8
Whitney, Reno	4	3	.571	4.54	17	7	2	3	1	1	67.1	65	40	34	8	1	15	0	31	6
Wiese, Visalia°	10	4	.714	2.52	20	19	2	0	1	0	118.0	109	43	33	5	2	44	1	95	3
Wiggs, San Bernardino°	7	6	.538	3.95	64	0	0	21	0	8	93.1	112	48	41	6	3	48	5	97	6
Woodson, San Bernardino	8	6	.571	3.10	27	23	1	1	0	0	136.2	111	62	47	2	12	83	1	131	8
Zancanaro, Modesto°	1	2	.333	6.23	4	2	0	0	0	0	13.0	13	9	9	1	0	14	0	7	0
Zappelli, Palm Springs	0	1	.000	2.45	21	0	0	19	0	6	22.0	17	7	6	0	0	9	1	25	4

BALKS—Anderson, 7; Sasaki, 6; Fleming, Garcia, Murakami, 5 each; Davis, Furcal, Knox, Love, McAndrew, Rogers, 4 each; Maye, Paxton, Shull, Velasquez, 3 each; Brosnan, Carrasco, Coleman, Deville, Fitzgerald, Howe, Hurst, Lane, Langley, Lardizabal, Neagle, Newlin, Pena, Powers, Rambo, Salkeld, Sharko, Smith, Uchiyama, White, Wiggs, Woodson, 2 each; Acosta, Allison, Arola, Aspray, Astacio, Barton, Beckett, Bishop, Braase, Carmody, G. Clark, Cole, Eldred, Felix, Fritz, Gott, De. Green, Guilbe, Guzman, Helmick, Herring, Ignasiak, C. Johnson, K. Jones, Kiefer, Lawson, Leslie, Mahomes, McClure, McCoy, Meeks, Miranda, J. Myers, Neal, Patrick, Pettiford, Potthoff, Schwarz, Shepherd, Smithberg, Sparks, Tatis, S. Taylor, Trombley, Tsamis, Uribe, Vann, Vidmar, Vuz, Warrecker, Wiese, 1 each.

COMBINATION SHUTOUTS—Astacio-Coleman, Astacio-Robinson-Humber, Brosnan-Robinson, Brosnan-Tatis, Gott-Delahoya-Crane, Knapp-Humber-Searage, McAndrew-Robinson, Bakersfield; Chavez-Smith, Garcia-Lardizabal-Taylor, Leiper-Smith, Modesto; James-Loubier, Merriman-Warrecker-Zappelli, Palm Springs; Clark-Anderson-Langley-Soper, Firova-Langley, Palmer-Powers, Pettiford-Hurst, Rauth-Soper, Reno; Davis-Harrison, Davis-Haslock, Davis-Sierra, Lane-Sierra, Riverside; Reilley-Sasaki-Emoto, Salinas; DeLucia-Pitcher, Evans-Jones, Evans-Wiggs, Furcal-Jones-Newlin, Furcal-Felix, Salkeld-Wiggs-Jones, San Bernardino; Eldred-Hamilton-Uribe, Fitzgerald-Miranda, Hamilton-Cangemi-Carmody, Johnson-Carmody, Johnson-Hamilton-Uribe, Johnson-Uribe, Kiefer-Enriquez-Miranda, Miranda-Cangemi, Sandoval-Miranda, Stockton; Krol-Garces 2, Trombley-Garces 2, Krol-Trombley-Lipson, Mahomes-Aspray-Garces, Muh-Aspray, Neagle-Fine, Neagle-White-Aspray, Neagle-White-Garces, Trombley-Aspray-Garces, Wiese-White, Visalia.

NO-HIT GAME—Ignasiak-Henry, Stockton, defeated San Jose, 6-3 (first game), April 15.

Carolina League

CLASS A

CHAMPIONSHIP WINNERS IN PREVIOUS YEARS

1945—Danville	.681	1963—Kinston§	.538	1975—Rocky Mount	.667
1946—Greensboro	.599	Greensboro§	.590	Rocky Mount	.614
Raleigh (2nd)†	.563	Wilson (2nd)†	.535	1976—Winston-Salem	.618
1947—Burlington	.613	1964—Kinston§	.572	Winston-Salem	.551
Raleigh (3rd)†	.574	Winston-Salem§†	.590	1977—Lynchburg	.591
1948—Raleigh	.592	1965—Peninsula§	.597	Peninsula‡	.556
Martinsville (2nd)†	.570	Durham§	.580	1978—Peninsula	.696
1949—Danville	.601	Tidewater†	.528	Lynchburg‡	.614
Burlington (4th)†	.500	1966—Kinston§	.547	1979—Winston-Salem a	.607
1950—Winston-Salem°	.693	Winston-Salem§	.586	1980—Peninsula‡	.714
1951—Durham	.600	Rocky Mount†	.533	Durham	.600
Wins-Salem (2nd)†	.583	1967—Durham x (West.)	.536	1981—Peninsula	.522
1952—Raleigh	.581	Raleigh (East.)	.542	Hagerstown‡	.507
Reidsville (4th)†	.536	1968—Salem (West.)	.607	1982—Alexandria‡	.597
1953—Raleigh	.593	Ral-Dur (East.)	.597	Durham	.588
Danville (2nd)†	.572	HP-Thom. y (W.)	.493	1983—Lynchburg‡	.691
1954—Fayetteville°	.628	1969—Rocky M (East.)	.569	Winston-Salem	.529
1955—HP-Thomasville	.580	Salem (West.)	.542	1984—Lynchburg‡	.645
Danville (2nd)†	.533	Ral-Dur z (East.)	.560	Durham	.486
1956—HP-Thomasville	.591	1970—Winston-Salem‡	.586	1985—Lynchburg	.679
Fayetteville (4th)†	.523	Burlington	.597	Winston-Salem‡	.417
1957—Durham	.632	1971—Peninsula‡	.647	1986—Hagerstown	.655
HP-Thomasville	.622	Kinston	.623	Winston-Salem‡	.594
1958—Danville	.576	1972—Salem‡	.657	1987—Salem‡	.576
Burlington (4th)†	.511	Burlington	.632	Kinston	.536
1959—Raleigh	.600	1973—Lynchburg§	.588	1988—Kinston‡	.629
Wilson (2nd)†	.550	Winston-Salem‡	.557	Lynchburg	.486
1960—Greensboro‡	.636	1974—Salem	.671	1989—Durham	.609
Burlington	.586	Salem	.582	Prince William‡	.522
1961—Wilson	.594				
1962—Durham	.636				
Wilson	.600				
Kinston (2nd)†	.593				

°Won championship and four-club playoff. †Won four-club playoff. ‡Won split-season playoff. §League was divided into Eastern, Western divisions. xWon eight-club, two-division playoff. yWon eight-club, two-division playoff against Raleigh-Durham. zWon eight-club, two-division playoff against Burlington. aWon both halves of split-season (no playoffs).

STANDING OF CLUBS AT CLOSE OF FIRST HALF, JUNE 21

NORTHERN DIVISION

Club	W.	L.	T.	Pct.	G.B.
Frederick (Orioles)	39	31	0	.557	......
Prince William (Yankees)	33	37	0	.471	6
Lynchburg (Red Sox)	33	37	0	.471	6
Salem (Pirates)	25	45	0	.357	14

SOUTHERN DIVISION

Club	W.	L.	T.	Pct.	G.B.
Kinston (Indians)	46	24	0	.657	......
Winston-Salem (Cubs)	45	25	0	.643	1
Durham (Braves)	37	33	0	.529	9
Peninsula (Mariners)	22	48	0	.314	24

STANDING OF CLUBS AT CLOSE OF SECOND HALF, SEPTEMBER 2

NORTHERN DIVISION

Club	W.	L.	T.	Pct.	G.B.
Frederick (Orioles)	35	31	0	.530	......
Prince William (Yankees)	31	38	0	.449	5½
Salem (Pirates)	30	39	0	.435	6½
Lynchburg (Red Sox)	25	43	0	.368	11

SOUTHERN DIVISION

Club	W.	L.	T.	Pct.	G.B.
Kinston (Indians)	42	23	0	.646	......
Winston-Salem (Cubs)	41	29	0	.586	3½
Peninsula (Mariners)	35	35	0	.500	9½
Durham (Braves)	34	35	0	.493	10

COMPOSITE STANDING OF CLUBS AT CLOSE OF SEASON, SEPTEMBER 2

Club	Kin.	W.S.	Fre.	Dur.	P.W.	Lyn.	Pen.	Sal.	W.	L.	T.	Pct.	G.B.
Kinston (Indians)	...	12	12	10	12	12	14	16	88	47	0	.652	......
Winston-Salem (Cubs)	8	...	13	12	15	14	12	12	86	54	0	.614	4½
Frederick (Orioles)	5	7	...	12	14	9	13	14	74	62	0	.544	14½
Durham (Braves)	9	8	8	...	9	10	14	13	71	68	0	.511	19
Prince William (Yankees)	8	5	6	11	...	12	12	10	64	75	0	.460	26
Lynchburg (Red Sox)	7	6	10	10	8	...	9	8	58	80	0	.420	31½
Peninsula (Mariners)	6	8	7	6	8	11	...	11	57	83	0	.407	33½
Salem (Pirates)	4	8	6	7	9	12	9	...	55	84	0	.396	35

Peninsula club represented Hampton, Va.

Major league affiliations in parentheses.

Playoffs—Frederick defeated Kinston, three games to two, to win league championship.

Regular-Season Attendance—Durham, 300,499; Frederick, 277,802; Kinston, 106,219; Lynchburg, 92,607; Peninsula, 70,647; Prince William, 210,262; Salem, 126,121; Winston-Salem, 102,558. Total, 1,286,715. Playoffs (5 games)—11,448. All-Star Game—5,947.

Managers—Durham, Grady Little; Frederick, Wally Moon; Kinston, Brian Graham; Lynchburg, Gary Allenson; Peninsula, Jim Nettles; Prince William, Gary Denbo; Salem, Stan Cliburn; Winston-Salem, Brad Mills.

All-Star Team—1B—J.T. Snow, Prince William; 2B—Rouglas Odor, Kinston; 3B—Rick Gutierrez, Frederick; SS—Gary Scott, Winston-Salem; OF—Greg Blosser, Lynchburg; Keith Mitchell, Durham; Ken Ramos, Kinston; C—Armando Romero, Salem; DH—Doug Welch, Winston-Salem; Starting Pitcher—Frank Seminara, Prince William; Relief Pitcher—Mike Gardella, Prince William; Most Valuable Player—Gary Scott, Winston-Salem; Pitcher of the Year—Frank Seminara, Prince William; Manager of the Year—Wally Moon, Frederick.

(Compiled by Howe Sportsdata International, Boston, Mass.)

CLUB BATTING

Club	Pct.	G.	AB.	R.	OR.	H.	TB.	2B.	3B.	HR.	RBI.	SH.	SF.	HP.	BB.	Int. BB.	SO.	SB.	CS.	LOB.
Kinston	.270	135	4527	697	509	1222	1701	198	40	67	610	45	49	43	522	21	914	171	80	982
Frederick	.268	136	4553	612	517	1221	1660	225	32	50	543	58	31	50	440	22	801	93	70	993
Winston-Salem	.260	140	4692	674	540	1219	1726	194	32	83	606	58	43	58	538	33	888	147	51	1063
Salem	.255	140	4695	633	801	1199	1792	205	47	98	583	41	53	50	524	24	1054	114	58	1042
Durham	.254	139	4672	605	622	1189	1701	212	33	78	530	32	53	34	523	24	764	138	82	1005
Prince William	.246	139	4544	554	533	1119	1595	222	37	60	507	29	36	43	447	8	916	114	59	963
Peninsula	.234	140	4497	507	631	1051	1397	149	22	51	453	26	35	77	468	9	967	142	57	975
Lynchburg	.232	138	4538	549	678	1052	1555	176	27	91	483	28	29	47	524	16	1198	99	50	986

INDIVIDUAL BATTING

(Leading Qualifiers for Batting Championship—378 or More Plate Appearances)

*Bats lefthanded.   †Switch-hitter.

Player and Club	Pct.	G.	AB.	R.	H.	TB.	2B.	3B.	HR.	RBI.	SH.	SF.	HP.	BB.	Int. BB.	SO.	SB.	CS.
Ramos, Kenneth, Kinston*	.345	96	339	71	117	145	16	6	0	31	5	2	1	48	4	34	18	14
Welch, Douglas, Winston-Salem	.320	107	363	58	116	175	20	3	11	68	1	8	3	29	3	65	1	2
Holland, Timothy, Frederick	.302	115	424	63	128	186	26	4	8	68	4	2	4	38	0	75	6	4
Levis, Jesse, Kinston*	.296	107	382	63	113	158	18	3	7	64	1	6	5	64	1	42	4	1
Scott, Gary, Winston-Salem	.295	102	380	63	112	170	22	0	12	70	5	6	14	29	4	66	17	3
Mitchell, Keith, Durham	.294	129	456	81	134	182	24	3	6	48	1	7	4	92	2	48	18	17
Cole, Robert, Durham	.293	118	389	64	114	139	11	4	2	40	5	3	5	27	2	52	24	14
Romero, Armando, Salem†	.291	124	460	62	134	222	31	3	17	90	2	4	5	55	3	68	0	2
Schreiber, Bruce, Salem	.290	134	552	71	160	206	24	5	4	48	5	7	9	33	2	109	6	4
Pennye, Darwin, Salem	.284	104	405	51	115	180	27	4	10	52	4	5	1	23	1	74	15	6

Departmental Leaders: G—Snow, 138; AB—Schreiber, 552; R—Sims, 91; H—Schreiber, 160; TB—Romero, 222; 2B—Davis, 37; 3B—Gomez, Hines, 8; HR—Blosser, 18; RBI—Romero, 90; SH—Beasley, 12; SF—Costo, Welch, 8; HP—Campanis, 18; BB—Sims, 111; IBB—Jensen, 8; SO—Whitehead, 164; SB—Ramsey, 43; CS—Gilbert, 20.

(All Players—Listed Alphabetically)

Player and Club	Pct.	G.	AB.	R.	H.	TB.	2B.	3B.	HR.	RBI.	SH.	SF.	HP.	BB.	Int. BB.	SO.	SB.	CS.
Adames, Juan, Winston-Salem	.167	36	54	5	9	12	1	1	0	4	0	0	0	6	0	10	1	0
Alicea, Edwin, Durham†	.278	113	370	55	103	170	28	0	13	49	6	4	4	68	3	79	14	8
Allison, James, Kinston*	.281	49	171	34	48	73	6	2	5	25	1	2	0	20	4	34	5	3
Anderson, Brady, Frederick*	.429	2	7	2	3	4	1	0	0	3	0	0	0	1	0	1	0	0
Antigua, Felix, Salem	.194	30	108	9	21	23	2	0	0	7	0	3	0	7	0	16	0	0
Ausmus, Bradley, Prince William	.236	107	364	46	86	102	12	2	0	27	3	0	3	32	0	73	2	8
Bailey, Lash, Peninsula†	.211	102	342	40	72	103	10	0	7	33	3	3	12	43	2	100	3	4
Bailey, Robert, Salem*	.181	74	227	28	41	54	6	2	1	19	6	4	2	25	0	71	12	4
Barbara, Daniel, Peninsula	.279	79	247	27	69	75	6	0	0	17	3	4	2	37	0	62	3	2
Bautista, Ramon, Kinston	.235	84	260	40	61	75	12	1	0	20	3	0	2	25	0	81	12	7
Beasley, Anthony, Frederick	.251	124	399	57	100	129	14	6	1	31	12	2	7	30	1	68	10	9
Bell, Leonard, Winston-Salem	.250	51	176	20	44	72	12	2	4	27	1	4	4	17	1	55	2	1
Berthel, Daniel, Frederick	.267	110	363	58	97	128	18	2	3	35	2	2	6	33	1	61	8	5
Blackwell, Juan, Prince William	.241	27	79	10	19	21	2	0	0	6	2	1	0	1	0	24	2	1
Blair, Paul, Winston-Salem*	.278	118	425	48	118	138	11	3	1	36	8	3	2	53	2	62	11	5
Blosser, Gregory, Lynchburg*	.282	119	447	63	126	205	23	1	18	62	0	1	1	55	3	99	5	4
Boone, Bret, Peninsula	.267	74	255	42	68	109	13	2	8	38	0	0	1	47	0	57	5	2
Brakebill, Mark, Peninsula	.178	50	157	15	28	36	6	1	0	13	1	1	5	8	0	53	1	0
Brewington, Michael, Salem*	.237	21	76	11	18	30	4	1	2	12	0	1	2	10	0	14	0	1
Bridges, Jason, Prince William	.210	58	157	16	33	44	9	1	0	10	3	1	0	8	1	28	4	1
Brust, David, Durham*	.175	86	228	18	40	67	6	0	7	23	0	2	2	15	1	49	1	0
Byrd, James, Lynchburg	.225	131	511	59	115	161	20	1	8	45	1	4	15	38	0	139	24	11
Campanis, James, Peninsula	.250	112	364	47	91	155	22	0	14	60	0	7	18	40	1	76	3	3
Campbell, Donovan, Durham*	.219	108	338	44	74	117	15	5	6	37	0	5	2	47	1	61	21	6
Caraballo, Nelson, Salem	.000	1	1	0	0	0	0	0	0	0	0	0	0	0	0	0	0	0
Castellano, Pedro, Winston-Salem	.197	19	66	6	13	16	0	0	1	8	2	0	2	10	0	11	1	0
Castleberry, Kevin, Durham*	.242	119	372	59	90	137	18	4	7	27	3	2	2	23	1	64	15	4
Champion, Brian, Durham	.263	94	334	36	88	126	18	1	6	55	2	6	1	34	0	58	4	3
Cole, Robert, Durham	.293	118	389	64	114	139	11	4	2	40	5	3	5	27	2	52	24	14
Costo, Timothy, Kinston	.316	56	206	34	65	92	13	1	4	42	0	8	6	23	0	47	4	0
Craig, Dale, Winston-Salem	.181	56	127	15	23	30	1	0	2	9	4	0	2	17	1	34	1	0
Cuevas, Johnny, Durham	.255	66	192	12	49	56	5	1	0	16	3	4	1	8	0	30	0	1
Davis, Russell, Prince William	.249	137	510	55	127	218	37	3	16	71	0	6	5	37	1	136	3	1
Deak, Brian, Durham	.188	43	133	14	25	39	3	1	3	16	1	0	3	23	2	41	2	0
DeJardin, Bradford, Kinston*	.000	3	0	0	0	0	0	0	0	0	0	0	0	1	0	0	0	0
Devereaux, Michael, Frederick	.500	2	8	3	4	7	0	0	1	3	0	0	0	1	0	2	1	0
Dewey, Todd, Durham†	.167	7	18	1	3	5	2	0	0	0	0	0	0	4	0	2	0	1
Dorante, Luis, Lynchburg	.213	14	47	7	10	14	2	1	0	3	0	0	1	8	0	11	1	0
Duncan, Calvin, Salem	.500	37	2	1	1	4	0	0	1	3	0	0	0	0	0	0	0	0
Eiterman, Thomas, Kinston	.364	2	11	1	4	7	0	0	1	4	0	0	0	2	0	0	0	0
Erhardt, Herbert, Prince William	.210	43	105	5	22	31	3	0	2	12	1	0	2	11	0	26	0	0
Estep, Christopher, Salem	.214	110	350	52	75	143	13	2	17	53	2	4	2	58	2	126	9	8
Falkner, Richard, Kinston	.242	61	157	13	38	54	5	1	3	15	2	1	2	20	1	34	0	0
Flaherty, John, Lynchburg	.000	1	4	0	0	0	0	0	0	0	0	0	0	0	0	1	0	0
Foster, Lindsay, Kinston†	.280	91	329	46	92	104	10	1	0	28	6	3	0	23	0	46	35	8
Fowler, John, Frederick†	.077	7	13	1	1	2	1	0	0	1	0	0	2	0	0	7	0	0
Garcia, Marcos, Peninsula	.000	36	1	0	0	0	0	0	0	0	0	0	0	0	0	0	0	0
Gilbert, Roy, Frederick†	.253	125	471	81	119	157	26	3	2	48	2	2	7	55	1	56	22	20
Gilmore, Matthew, Kinston	.143	9	28	2	4	4	0	0	0	0	0	0	0	2	0	11	1	1
Gomez, Fabio, Kinston	.247	121	430	72	106	164	18	8	8	52	4	4	53	0	91	13	8
Greene, William, Salem*	.183	17	60	9	11	23	1	1	3	9	0	1	1	7	1	18	0	1
Griffin, Tyrone, Winston-Salem†	.217	33	120	18	26	39	8	1	1	10	0	0	1	28	2	39	8	2
Gutierrez, Ricardo, Frederick	.275	112	425	54	117	144	16	4	1	46	9	3	6	38	0	59	12	6
Hanks, Christopher, Lynchburg	.286	56	161	20	46	69	14	0	3	16	1	0	3	9	0	38	4	2
Harms, Thomas, Frederick	.100	3	10	0	1	1	0	0	0	0	0	0	0	2	0	6	0	0
Harring, Kenneth, Durham	.211	96	251	19	53	71	13	1	1	20	3	4	0	12	0	34	3	1
Hayden, Paris, Frederick	.296	22	54	7	16	19	1	1	0	5	0	0	0	3	0	12	1	0
Hedge, Patrick, Frederick	.227	67	172	22	39	51	3	0	3	12	3	0	2	14	0	45	4	1

Player and Club	Pct.	G.	AB.	R.	H.	TB.	2B.	3B.	HR.	RBI.	SH.	SF.	HP.	BB.	Int. BB.	SO.	SB.	CS.
Hernandez, Enrique, Prince William	.250	107	360	39	90	132	20	2	6	47	1	1	2	40	0	88	0	0
Hildreth, Bradley, Frederick	.091	5	11	1	1	2	1	0	0	1	0	0	0	0	0	4	0	0
Hines, Timothy, Salem*	.279	106	380	44	106	172	17	8	11	55	0	4	8	28	2	72	3	4
Holland, Timothy, Frederick	.302	115	424	63	128	186	26	4	8	68	4	2	4	38	0	75	6	4
Holley, Robert, Peninsula	.258	85	306	35	79	120	15	1	8	43	1	5	1	33	0	46	4	0
Holmes, William, Salem*	.000	6	11	0	0	0	0	0	0	0	0	0	0	0	0	3	0	0
Horowitz, Edward, Frederick	.315	55	149	18	47	62	9	0	2	19	0	1	0	13	1	34	1	2
Howell, David, Prince William*	.220	104	337	36	74	97	12	1	3	24	1	0	4	59	1	63	1	4
Huyler, Michael, Salem	.296	67	247	23	73	92	9	2	2	30	2	3	1	10	0	40	6	1
Jensen, John, Winston-Salem*	.246	126	403	59	99	160	17	4	12	67	2	4	5	77	8	96	4	4
Johnson, Brian, Kinston	.242	80	269	30	65	111	17	1	9	43	3	3	6	23	1	83	5	4
Kessinger, Keith, Frederick	.152	64	145	18	22	26	4	0	0	8	5	0	3	20	0	36	0	0
King, Bryan, Peninsula	.231	70	260	37	60	72	6	3	0	28	3	1	0	32	0	31	13	6
Kingwood, Tyrone, Frederick	.335	90	334	47	112	154	21	0	7	52	0	3	2	20	2	48	13	4
Klesko, Ryan, Durham*	.274	77	292	40	80	119	16	1	7	47	0	6	2	32	4	53	10	5
Knoblauh, Jay, Prince William	.221	38	131	17	29	41	6	0	2	9	0	0	1	10	0	23	5	1
Lane, Nolan, Kinston	.253	123	435	66	110	165	21	5	8	73	6	6	5	36	2	105	25	15
Leach, Christopher, Lynchburg*	.194	97	279	36	54	71	3	1	4	22	4	5	1	55	2	87	3	2
Lehman, Michael, Frederick	.260	105	346	37	90	129	20	2	5	42	4	4	4	44	5	69	7	6
Levis, Jesse, Kinston*	.296	107	382	63	113	158	18	3	7	64	1	6	5	64	1	42	4	1
Lewis, Theodore, Frederick	.325	22	80	12	26	39	4	3	1	11	0	0	2	11	1	11	5	0
Lofton, Rodney, Frederick	.556	2	9	1	5	6	1	0	0	2	0	0	0	1	0	1	2	0
Longuil, Richard, Durham	.000	12	1	0	0	0	0	0	0	0	0	0	0	0	0	1	0	0
Luis, Joseph, Lynchburg*	.169	26	65	4	11	12	1	0	0	7	1	0	0	4	0	15	0	0
Maldonado, Phillip, Durham	.215	48	130	7	28	31	3	0	0	11	2	0	3	8	1	19	1	2
Maloney, Richard, Durham	.300	47	160	23	48	65	7	2	2	12	3	0	0	19	0	18	2	5
Malzone, John, Lynchburg*	.257	65	187	18	48	60	4	1	2	15	1	0	1	27	0	63	3	1
Manahan, Austin, Salem	.279	41	154	22	43	65	6	2	4	24	1	1	1	11	0	51	8	1
McNabb, Glen, Salem	.267	49	146	21	39	44	5	0	0	13	1	1	3	19	1	21	3	2
Merejo, Domingo, Salem*	.283	82	290	37	82	133	12	6	9	56	3	6	1	23	5	50	11	3
Miller, William, Kinston*	.167	19	42	3	7	8	1	0	0	7	1	1	0	8	2	6	0	1
Mitchell, Keith, Durham	.294	129	456	81	134	182	24	3	6	48	1	7	4	92	2	48	18	17
Mondile, Steven, Frederick	.000	32	1	0	0	0	0	0	0	0	0	0	0	0	0	1	0	0
Monegro, Miguel, Lynchburg	.262	69	183	18	48	58	10	0	0	18	3	1	2	13	0	43	0	1
Moore, Timothy, Winston-Salem	.200	4	5	0	1	1	0	0	0	0	0	0	0	0	0	2	0	0
Mordecai, Michael, Durham†	.280	72	271	42	76	110	11	7	3	36	2	2	2	42	2	45	10	6
Morrison, Brian, Salem	.183	18	60	4	11	13	2	0	0	3	0	1	0	5	0	25	1	1
Murphy, James, Winston-Salem	.246	23	69	7	17	24	2	1	1	11	2	0	0	1	0	17	2	1
Obando, Sherman, Prince William	.267	121	439	67	117	183	24	6	10	67	0	6	11	42	1	85	5	3
Odor, Rouglas, Kinston	.261	114	445	64	116	145	21	1	2	42	11	2	2	42	2	99	30	10
Orsag, James, Kinston*	.296	47	169	39	50	76	7	2	5	34	0	4	2	24	0	45	7	0
Oster, Paul, Prince William†	.239	96	327	39	78	111	13	4	4	34	2	2	0	17	0	53	3	7
Paulino, Elvin, Winston-Salem*	.262	109	409	69	107	176	23	2	14	63	1	2	1	49	4	66	5	3
Pennye, Darwin, Salem	.284	104	405	51	115	180	27	4	10	52	4	5	1	23	1	74	15	6
Perez, Eduardo, Durham	.237	31	93	9	22	32	1	0	3	10	0	1	1	10	0	12	0	0
Perozo, Ender, Lynchburg	.230	73	222	12	51	78	10	4	3	26	3	2	3	17	0	68	4	0
Pezzoni, Ronald, Peninsula	.267	109	408	47	109	138	15	4	2	42	2	2	1	23	0	59	26	6
Pilkinton, Lemuel, Peninsula	.239	114	394	37	94	124	13	4	3	43	1	1	4	54	1	104	3	3
Posey, John, Winston-Salem	.254	27	71	10	18	21	3	0	0	4	1	0	1	17	1	4	0	1
Powers, Scott, Lynchburg	.238	122	433	54	103	126	13	2	2	36	6	3	3	59	0	99	7	8
Raasch, Glen, Peninsula	.000	5	12	1	0	0	0	0	0	0	0	0	0	2	0	7	0	0
Raisanen, Keith, Salem	.120	19	50	7	6	8	2	0	0	3	0	0	0	10	0	22	0	0
Ramos, Kenneth, Kinston*	.345	96	339	71	117	145	16	6	0	31	5	2	1	48	4	34	18	14
Ramsey, Fernando, Winston-Salem	.255	124	428	52	109	144	12	4	5	48	9	2	3	19	0	50	43	7
Reynolds, Douglas, Frederick	.246	55	126	14	31	45	5	0	3	13	0	1	0	18	1	44	0	0
Ricci, Charles, Frederick	.000	27	2	0	0	0	0	0	0	0	0	0	0	0	0	1	0	0
Richardson, Michael, Frederick*	.234	110	334	33	78	102	13	1	3	33	7	1	0	29	5	66	0	3
Riddle, David, Frederick	.000	25	2	0	0	0	0	0	0	0	0	0	0	0	0	1	0	0
Rivers, Mickey, Lynchburg†	.216	113	408	42	88	124	13	7	3	39	3	2	3	8	1	102	22	7
Roberson, Kevin, Winston-Salem†	.268	85	313	49	84	128	23	3	5	45	1	2	3	25	0	70	7	3
Roble, Josman, Durham*	.236	32	89	10	21	35	5	0	3	14	0	1	0	9	0	18	0	0
Robles, Jorge, Peninsula†	.252	98	345	34	87	98	9	1	0	27	4	1	3	38	0	23	18	9
Rodriguez, Andres, Prince William	.241	33	79	9	19	21	2	0	0	7	5	1	0	2	0	19	2	1
Rodriguez, Roman, Salem	.183	24	82	6	15	19	4	0	0	7	3	0	0	6	0	17	0	1
Romero, Armando, Salem†	.291	124	460	62	134	222	31	3	17	90	2	4	5	55	3	68	0	2
Rose, Peter, Frederick*	.232	97	323	32	75	96	14	2	1	41	7	5	1	26	0	33	0	3
Ross, Sean, Durham*	.272	21	81	9	22	32	4	0	2	13	0	0	3	15	4	0	0
Saetre, Damon, Peninsula*	.216	110	352	36	76	91	8	2	1	32	2	6	6	42	5	66	8	2
Sanders, Tracy, Kinston*	.438	10	32	6	14	23	3	3	0	9	0	0	0	7	0	6	1	1
Santana, Ruben, Peninsula	.213	26	80	3	17	18	1	0	0	5	0	0	1	1	0	22	6	1
Sarbaugh, Michael, Kinston	.375	2	8	2	3	6	0	0	1	3	0	0	1	2	0	1	0	0
Schreiber, Bruce, Salem	.290	134	552	71	160	206	24	5	4	48	5	7	9	33	2	109	6	4
Scott, Gary, Winston-Salem	.295	102	380	63	112	170	22	0	12	70	5	6	14	29	4	66	17	3
Shamburg, Kenneth, Frederick	.321	66	243	35	78	123	20	2	7	54	0	3	3	31	4	38	1	6
Shelton, Benjamin, Salem	.206	109	320	44	66	110	10	2	10	36	4	4	8	55	0	116	1	2
Silvestri, David, Prince William	.258	131	465	74	120	179	30	7	5	56	5	6	7	70	0	90	37	13
Simonds, Daniel, Winston-Salem	.156	27	64	5	10	10	0	0	0	2	2	0	1	4	0	4	0	1
Sims, Gregory, Salem	.245	128	466	91	114	157	16	6	5	46	6	3	4	111	5	104	31	16
Smith, Tracy, Winston-Salem	.243	68	144	19	35	45	5	1	1	21	4	3	1	11	1	33	7	2
Snover, Daniel, Durham	.215	23	65	11	14	21	4	0	1	6	0	1	0	3	0	3	0	1
Snow, Jack, Prince William†	.256	138	520	57	133	184	25	1	8	72	0	7	5	46	3	65	2	0
Spencer, John, Lynchburg	.250	7	16	4	4	6	2	0	0	4	0	0	1	2	0	4	0	0
Stiegele, Robert, Lynchburg	.217	10	23	2	5	7	2	0	0	0	0	0	1	4	0	3	0	0
Tatum, Willie, Lynchburg†	.223	93	319	38	71	116	16	1	9	35	2	1	5	38	2	69	14	5
Tavarez, Jesus, Peninsula	.237	108	379	39	90	102	10	1	0	32	2	2	0	20	0	79	40	12
Taylor, Scott, Winston-Salem	.276	63	203	25	56	64	8	0	0	25	3	1	3	18	0	23	0	1
Tepper, Marc, Kinston*	.276	108	373	54	103	139	17	2	5	55	1	2	2	33	3	56	5	3
Thomas, Delvin, Peninsula	.194	84	258	28	50	71	7	1	4	19	2	0	6	14	0	81	3	2
Thomas, Kelvin, Peninsula*	.194	104	278	32	54	77	7	2	4	20	1	2	16	26	0	78	4	4
Thome, James, Kinston*	.308	33	117	19	36	54	4	1	4	16	0	1	1	24	0	26	4	1
Todd, Theron, Durham*	.255	126	408	49	104	146	18	3	6	50	0	5	2	53	5	62	9	9
Trusky, Kenneth, Salem*	.304	43	148	24	45	59	10	2	0	9	0	1	2	21	2	20	7	0

Player and Club	Pct.	G.	AB.	R.	H.	TB.	2B.	3B.	HR.	RBI.	SH.	SF.	HP.	BB.	Int. BB.	SO.	SB.	CS.
Verdugo, Armando, Kinston	.154	20	52	4	8	12	1	0	1	7	0	0	0	7	0	16	1	0
Viera, John, Prince William*	.243	68	235	33	57	83	6	4	4	26	1	3	2	36	1	59	27	5
Wallin, Leslie, Lynchburg*	.234	114	389	56	91	155	17	1	15	50	1	3	4	48	7	95	1	0
Wearing, Melvin, Frederick	.329	22	79	13	26	41	5	2	2	14	0	2	0	9	0	19	0	1
Weeks, Thomas, Prince William*	.211	9	19	0	4	5	1	0	0	3	0	0	0	1	0	3	0	1
Weidie, Stuart, Lynchburg†	.146	26	96	10	14	18	1	0	1	7	0	1	0	14	0	32	1	1
Welch, Douglas, Winston-Salem	.320	107	363	58	116	175	20	3	11	68	1	8	3	29	3	65	1	2
White, William, Winston-Salem	.269	134	505	85	136	170	15	2	5	54	9	3	9	70	3	108	25	8
Whitehead, Christopher, Lynchburg	.210	117	377	50	79	119	13	3	7	33	1	1	0	71	1	164	7	7
Williams, Daniel, Kinston	.176	28	68	8	12	16	1	0	1	10	0	3	1	10	0	13	0	0
Williams, Edward, Winston-Salem*	.234	114	367	61	86	131	11	5	8	34	3	2	6	58	3	73	12	7
Williams, Flavio, Salem	.230	47	100	16	23	35	4	1	2	8	2	0	0	7	0	17	1	1
Williams, Landon, Peninsula	.119	23	59	6	7	8	1	0	0	1	1	0	1	8	0	23	2	1
Williams, Paul, Lynchburg	.236	113	394	58	93	163	14	4	16	64	1	4	4	58	0	69	3	1
Wright, William, Durham	1.000	50	1	0	1	1	0	0	0	0	1	0	0	0	0	0	0	0
Zambrano, Eduardo, Kinston	.245	63	204	26	50	70	7	2	3	30	1	2	1	29	1	36	1	3
Zazueta, Mauricio, Prince William	.266	122	417	51	111	143	20	6	0	36	5	3	2	28	0	81	21	13

The following pitchers, listed alphabetically by club, with games in parentheses, had no plate appearances, primarily through use of designated hitters:

DURHAM—Borbon, Pedro (11); Byerly, Rodney (26); Cummings, Brian (14); Czarnik, Christopher (17); Diez, Scott (20); Hailey, Roger (11); Johnson, Lee (37); Karasinski, David (24); Mathews, Edward (6); Minchey, Nathan (25); Nied, David (10); Richey, Rodney (42); Rivera, Bienvenido (16); Smith, Chad (4); Taylor, William (5); Tilmon, Patton (38); Vazquez, Marcos (12); Watson, Preston (34); Weems, Danny (6); Wendell, Steven (6).

FREDERICK—Brooks, Brian (7); Bumgarner, Jeffrey (17); Deutsch, Michael (23); Jones, Stacy (15); Kerr, Zachary (26); Leinen, Patrick (14); O'Donoghue, John (1); Oquist, Michael (25); Peraza, Oswaldo (7); Rhodes, Arthur (13); Schullstrom, Erik (2); Slomkowski, Richard (26); Stephan, Todd (42); Telford, Anthony (8); Williams, Jeffrey (16).

KINSTON—Borgatti, Michael (7); Bryant, Shawn (2); Cole, Christopher (7); Dipoto, Gerald (24); Ellis, Timothy (9); Ferlenda, Gregory (46); Gonzales, Michael (14); Gonzales, Todd (19); Howard, Christian (8); Kiser, Garland (55); Kovach, Ty (18); Kramer, Thomas (16); Leskanic, Curtis (14); Morgan, Scott (12); Munoz, Oscar (9); Neill, Scott (41); Oliveras, David (4); Person, Robert (4); Peters, Timothy (12); Pinder, Christopher (29); Poehl, Michael (4); Vespe, William (18).

LYNCHBURG—Abril, Odie (2); Brown, Paul (27); Conroy, Brian (26); Davis, Freddie (35); Estrada, Peter (25); Landry, Howard (28); Powers, Terry (11); Pratts, Alberto (29); Ryan, Kenneth (28); Scott, Rennie (57); Stange, Timothy (33); Taylor, Scott (13); Uhrhan, Kevin (29).

PENINSULA—Balabon, Richard (14); Czarkowski, Mark (21); Darwin, Jeffery (26); Duke, Kyle (14); Gordon, Anthony (25); Gutierrez, James (28); King, Kevin (7); Lodgek, Scott (12); Loe, Darin (46); Mullins, Ronald (35); Nelson, Jeffrey (18); Poissant, Rodney (26); Rivas, Oscar (34); Rivera, Randy (17).

PRINCE WILLIAM—Canestro, Arthur (29); Draper, Michael (5); Gardella, Michael (62); Gilbert, Brent (13); Greer, Kenneth (1); Hartzog, Cullen (18); Marris, Mark (7); Martel, Edward (25); Moody, James (54); Nielsen, Gerald (26); Polak, Richard (44); Prybylinski, Bruce (9); Ralph, Curtis (43); Seminara, Frank (25); Wiley, James (22).

SALEM—Bird, David (8); Buckholz, Steven (32); Czajkowski, James (18); Deller, Thomas (16); Fansler, Stanley (10); Felix, Antonio (8); Honeywell, Brent (22); Latham, John (8); McDowell, Timothy (32); Miller, Paul (22); Murphy, Peter (3); Neely, Jeffrey (6); Pomeranz, Michael (35); Richardson, Keith (9); Schlopy, Clifford (16); Underwood, Robert (10); Wagner, Paul (11); Wakefield, Timothy (28); Williams, Roger (10); Zimmerman, Michael (19).

WINSTON-SALEM—Bullinger, James (14); Caballero, Eduardo (9); Davis, Braz (16); DiBartolomeo, Stephen (41); Eddings, Jay (29); Gardner, John (34); Jaques, Eric (2); Jones, Shannon (18); Kazmierczak, William (9); Lopez, Marcos (15); Massicotte, Jeffrey (6); Melvin, William (30); Rasp, Ronnie (4); Robinson, Brett (2); Salles, John (25); Sodders, Michael (12); Strauss, Julio (25); Stroud, Derek (34); Taylor, Aaron (2); Willis, Travis (2).

GRAND SLAM HOME RUNS—Lane, 2; Allison, Boone, Campbell, Gilbert, Hedge, Hines, Merejo, Obando, Odor, Pennye, Roberson, Scott, Snow, Welch, P. Williams, 1 each.

AWARDED FIRST BASE ON CATCHER'S INTERFERENCE—Gilbert 5 (Hernandez 2, Barbara, Brust, Hines); Blosser (Simonds); Jensen (Campanis); Richardson (P. Williams).

CLUB FIELDING

Club	Pct.	G.	PO.	A.	E.	DP.	PB.	Club	Pct.	G.	PO.	A.	E.	DP.	PB.
Prince William	.973	139	3564	1519	139	135	15	Lynchburg	.963	138	3603	1447	195	112	24
Winston-Salem	.966	140	3704	1508	181	129	19	Peninsula	.961	140	3593	1488	208	136	21
Frederick	.966	136	3540	1392	176	111	17	Salem	.960	139	3645	1574	216	123	23
Kinston	.964	135	3570	1479	186	125	20	Durham	.959	139	3701	1534	223	132	23

Triple Play—Frederick.

INDIVIDUAL FIELDING

*Throws lefthanded.

FIRST BASEMEN

Player and Club	Pct.	G.	PO.	A.	E.	DP.	Player and Club	Pct.	G.	PO.	A.	E.	DP.
Bailey, Peninsula	.982	72	618	42	12	64	Perez, Durham	1.000	2	9	1	0	1
Bell, Winston-Salem	.988	35	310	30	4	30	Pilkinton, Peninsula	.989	63	509	33	6	50
Brewington, Salem*	1.000	7	55	4	0	4	Raisanen, Salem	1.000	3	40	2	0	4
Brust, Durham	1.000	3	19	0	0	0	Reynolds, Frederick	1.000	1	3	0	0	0
Campbell, Durham*	1.000	2	4	1	0	0	Richardson, Frederick*	.987	103	797	30	11	71
Champion, Durham	.991	55	504	25	5	38	Roble, Durham*	.977	19	165	3	4	20
Costo, Kinston	.997	32	267	19	1	25	Saetre, Peninsula*	1.000	4	22	1	0	2
DeJardin, Kinston*	1.000	2	2	0	0	0	Shamburg, Frederick	.987	20	140	17	2	11
Erhardt, Prince William	1.000	3	18	3	0	2	Shelton, Salem*	.982	107	923	55	18	78
Foster, Kinston	1.000	8	43	2	0	7	Smith, Winston-Salem	1.000	5	21	1	0	3
Hanks, Lynchburg	1.000	5	40	1	0	2	Snow, Prince William*	.9908	136	1208	78	12	120
Hines, Salem	.988	35	294	30	4	20	Tatum, Lynchburg	.981	45	288	29	6	33
Holland, Frederick	1.000	13	61	7	0	7	Taylor, Winston-Salem	1.000	1	1	0	0	0
Holmes, Salem*	1.000	2	18	0	0	2	Tepper, Salem*	.979	71	567	38	13	57
Howell, Prince William*	1.000	2	2	0	0	0	Thomas, Peninsula	1.000	4	13	0	0	3
Kingwood, Frederick	.867	2	11	2	2	0	WALLIN, Lynchburg*	.9912	101	844	64	8	61
Klesko, Durham*	.976	58	490	34	13	49	Wearing, Frederick	.982	22	155	5	3	14
Maldonado, Durham	.980	13	92	4	2	9	Weeks, Prince William	1.000	2	17	0	0	1
Orsag, Kinston	.992	26	243	18	2	14	Williams, Kinston	.971	9	62	4	2	7
Paulino, Winston-Salem	.983	106	885	77	17	83							

Triple Play—Wearing.

SECOND BASEMEN

Player and Club	Pct.	G.	PO.	A.	E.	DP.
Adames, Winston-Salem	.943	18	17	33	3	8
Alicea, Durham	.934	14	23	48	5	7
Bailey, Salem	.940	41	76	113	12	22
Bautista, Kinston	.975	77	135	220	9	47
Beasley, Frederick	.958	123	224	392	27	56
Blackwell, Prince William	.921	19	24	46	6	9
BLAIR, Winston-Salem	.987	117	246	356	8	67
Boone, Peninsula	.951	70	154	216	19	49
Castleberry, Durham	.960	104	197	257	19	64
Cole, Durham	1.000	1	4	3	0	2
Foster, Kinston	1.000	1	1	3	0	1
Harring, Durham	.983	41	71	106	3	22
Hildreth, Frederick	1.000	2	1	4	0	1
Kessinger, Frederick	.985	21	24	43	1	9
Lehman, Frederick	1.000	1	1	0	0	0
McNabb, Salem	.946	48	80	129	12	25
Monegro, Lynchburg	.946	46	70	106	10	20
Moore, Winston-Salem	1.000	3	1	5	0	0
Odor, Kinston	.985	66	137	186	5	37
Powers, Lynchburg	.962	104	192	285	19	52
Robles, Peninsula	.981	11	22	29	1	8
Rodriguez, Prince William	.961	22	41	58	4	12
Santana, Peninsula	1.000	8	10	13	0	6
Sarbaugh, Kinston	1.000	1	2	4	0	1
Schreiber, Salem	.955	39	58	133	9	20
Smith, Winston-Salem	.939	10	13	18	2	4
Snover, Durham	1.000	4	9	14	0	3
Stiegele, Frederick	.880	7	9	13	3	3
Thomas, Peninsula	.945	41	79	111	11	22
White, Winston-Salem	.891	11	18	23	5	5
F. Williams, Salem	.964	29	36	44	3	9
L. Williams, Peninsula	.955	15	21	42	3	5
Zazueta, Prince William	.960	106	200	308	21	60

Triple Play—Kessinger.

THIRD BASEMEN

Player and Club	Pct.	G.	PO.	A.	E.	DP.
Adames, Winston-Salem	1.000	8	5	6	0	0
Alicea, Durham	.892	67	34	115	18	13
Bell, Winston-Salem	.857	11	5	13	3	1
Brakebill, Peninsula	.907	44	32	65	10	7
Brust, Durham	.841	51	18	77	18	5
Castellano, Winston-Salem	.962	19	14	37	2	2
Champion, Durham	.778	4	2	5	2	1
Davis, Prince William	.929	131	68	244	24	18
Dewey, Durham	.750	3	1	5	2	0
Foster, Kinston	.976	15	19	22	1	2
Gilmore, Kinston	1.000	1	0	2	0	0
Gomez, Kinston	.863	87	57	164	35	14
Harring, Durham	.902	37	15	40	6	4
Hildreth, Frederick	.667	3	0	2	1	0
Hines, Salem	1.000	1	0	1	0	0
Holland, Frederick	.903	43	25	68	10	6
Holley, Peninsula	.920	9	7	16	2	3
Kessinger, Frederick	.913	14	3	18	2	0
King, Peninsula	1.000	3	6	7	0	1
Lehman, Frederick	1.000	6	2	3	0	0
Lewis, Frederick	.667	1	1	1	1	0
Malzone, Lynchburg	.952	43	22	58	4	5
Manahan, Salem	.882	41	30	82	15	8
Monegro, Lynchburg	.846	15	4	18	4	3
Odor, Kinston	.667	1	1	1	1	0
Pilkinton, Peninsula	.871	35	24	57	12	4
Powers, Lynchburg	.909	12	8	22	3	3
Robles, Peninsula	.971	46	33	69	3	4
Rose, Frederick	.934	93	51	120	12	8
Sarbaugh, Kinston	1.000	1	3	2	0	1
SCHREIBER, Salem	.938	94	61	198	17	16
Scott, Winston-Salem	.895	101	63	184	29	11
Shamburg, Frederick	1.000	9	1	17	0	1
Smith, Winston-Salem	.925	12	11	26	3	1
Snover, Durham	.846	13	6	16	4	1
Stiegele, Frederick	.500	4	0	1	1	1
Thomas, Peninsula	.818	9	6	12	4	0
Thome, Kinston	.905	33	10	66	8	5
Weidie, Lynchburg	1.000	2	2	3	0	0
Whitehead, Lynchburg	.941	79	49	144	12	8
Williams, Salem	.714	7	3	7	4	1
Zazueta, Prince William	.913	10	5	16	2	0

Triple Play—Rose.

SHORTSTOPS

Player and Club	Pct.	G.	PO.	A.	E.	DP.
Alicea, Durham	.844	7	10	17	5	2
Bailey, Salem	.904	32	40	92	14	16
Blair, Winston-Salem	1.000	2	1	5	0	0
Byrd, Lynchburg	.928	130	223	348	44	76
Castleberry, Durham	.894	10	14	28	5	2
Costo, Kinston	.861	19	31	56	14	9
Foster, Kinston	.925	65	96	176	22	39
Gilmore, Kinston	.789	7	5	10	4	1
Greene, Salem	.970	17	22	43	2	7
Gutierrez, Frederick	.948	110	192	286	26	57
Harring, Durham	.800	10	11	29	10	4
Hildreth, Frederick	1.000	1	0	1	0	0
Holley, Peninsula	.924	32	51	107	13	22
Huyler, Salem	.949	67	123	215	18	46
Kessinger, Frederick	.913	31	42	74	11	15
King, Peninsula	.953	66	122	200	16	50
Maloney, Durham	.964	47	58	127	7	24
Mordecai, Durham	.920	71	111	221	29	38
Odor, Kinston	.961	52	74	173	10	37
Powers, Lynchburg	.946	12	8	27	2	3
Robles, Peninsula	.937	34	61	88	10	13
A. Rodriguez, Prince William	.821	8	7	16	5	4
R. Rodriguez, Salem	.924	24	32	65	8	9
Santana, Peninsula	.931	19	29	52	6	9
Schreiber, Salem	1.000	2	1	2	0	1
SILVESTRI, Prince William	.965	130	218	382	22	96
Smith, Winston-Salem	.895	23	26	51	9	18
Snover, Durham	.667	1	0	2	1	1
White, Winston-Salem	.926	125	184	307	39	76
Williams, Salem	.636	7	3	4	4	2
Zazueta, Prince William	1.000	11	7	22	0	2

OUTFIELDERS

Player and Club	Pct.	G.	PO.	A.	E.	DP.
Alicea, Durham	1.000	17	17	0	0	0
Allison, Kinston*	.986	40	61	7	1	3
Anderson, Frederick*	1.000	1	1	0	0	0
Berthel, Frederick	.976	109	151	11	4	2
Blosser, Lynchburg*	.927	98	171	8	14	3
Brewington, Salem*	1.000	8	6	0	0	0
Bridges, Prince William	.972	52	67	2	2	0
Campbell, Durham*	.945	92	164	7	10	0
Cole, Durham	.955	105	146	2	7	1
Devereaux, Frederick	1.000	2	4	2	0	0
Eiterman, Kinston	1.000	1	1	0	0	0
Estep, Salem	.914	98	149	11	15	3
Falkner, Kinston	.978	54	80	7	2	3
Foster, Kinston	1.000	9	7	3	0	0
Gilbert, Frederick	.972	123	271	9	8	2
Gomez, Kinston	.918	31	59	8	6	0
Griffin, Winston-Salem	.958	32	42	4	2	0
Harms, Frederick	1.000	3	5	0	0	0
Harring, Durham	1.000	1	3	1	0	0
Hayden, Frederick	.966	22	25	3	1	0
Hedge, Frederick	.956	58	84	3	4	0
Holland, Frederick	.918	50	64	3	6	0
Holley, Peninsula	.967	49	84	3	3	0
Holmes, Salem*	.000	1	0	0	1	0
Howell, Prince William*	.960	96	180	12	8	1
Jensen, Winston-Salem	.955	121	200	12	10	1
Kingwood, Frederick	.973	80	134	10	4	3
Knoblauh, Prince William	.978	31	42	2	1	0
Lane, Frederick	.957	123	199	3	9	1
Leach, Lynchburg*	.970	94	155	7	5	0
Merejo, Salem*	.873	56	97	6	15	1
Miller, Kinston*	.875	13	6	1	1	0
Mitchell, Durham	.981	124	256	9	5	4
Morrison, Salem	1.000	5	7	1	0	0
Murphy, Winston-Salem	.957	18	22	0	1	0
Obando, Prince William	.958	113	156	4	7	0
Orsag, Kinston	1.000	1	2	0	0	0
Oster, Prince William*	.989	90	171	9	2	4
Pennye, Salem	.975	103	192	7	5	2
Perozo, Lynchburg	.937	71	83	6	6	0
Pezzoni, Peninsula	.984	97	181	4	3	0
Pilkinton, Peninsula	1.000	3	6	0	0	0
Ramos, Kinston*	.982	92	163	5	3	2
Ramsey, Winston-Salem	.980	123	293	7	6	1
Reynolds, Frederick	1.000	3	1	0	0	0
Rivers, Lynchburg	.957	113	301	10	14	3
Roberson, Winston-Salem	.959	82	136	4	6	1
Ross, Durham*	1.000	1	1	0	0	0
SAETRE, Peninsula*	1.000	96	172	8	0	1
Sanders, Kinston	1.000	9	20	0	0	0
Sims, Salem	.980	126	289	10	6	1
Spencer, Lynchburg	1.000	5	6	0	0	0

OUTFIELDERS—Continued

Player and Club	Pct.	G.	PO.	A.	E.	DP.	Player and Club	Pct.	G.	PO.	A.	E.	DP.
Tavarez, Peninsula	.964	104	228	12	9	4	Viera, Prince William*	.959	56	89	4	4	2
Tepper, Kinston*	1.000	7	14	0	0	0	Weidie, Lynchburg	1.000	24	52	4	0	0
D. Thomas, Peninsula	.962	18	23	2	1	0	Welch, Winston-Salem	1.000	6	8	0	0	0
K. Thomas, Peninsula*	.924	80	147	10	13	1	Whitehead, Lynchburg	.930	34	65	1	5	0
Todd, Durham*	.979	113	183	8	4	0	Williams, Winston-Salem*	.982	67	106	3	2	1
Trusky, Salem	1.000	36	53	3	0	1	Zambrano, Kinston	.967	62	108	8	4	1

CATCHERS

Player and Club	Pct.	G.	PO.	A.	E.	DP.	PB.	Player and Club	Pct.	G.	PO.	A.	E.	DP.	PB.
Antigua, Salem	.980	19	136	10	3	0	5	Johnson, Kinston	.990	60	482	32	5	0	10
AUSMUS, Prince William	.993	97	662	84	5	4	10	Lehman, Frederick	.990	91	649	54	7	6	10
Barbara, Peninsula	.961	43	211	12	9	2	5	Levis, Kinston	.991	74	517	63	5	10	10
Brust, Durham	.919	13	51	6	5	0	6	Luis, Lynchburg	.953	25	124	17	7	0	1
Campanis, Peninsula	.980	101	604	87	14	8	14	Maldonado, Durham	.979	22	129	8	3	1	5
Caraballo, Salem	1.000	1	1	0	0	0	0	Perez, Durham	.986	25	188	16	3	1	1
Craig, Winston-Salem	.987	52	284	30	4	1	7	Pilkinton, Peninsula	.944	5	31	3	2	0	2
Cuevas, Durham	.990	59	349	36	4	2	7	Posey, Winston-Salem	.984	27	162	17	3	3	6
Deak, Durham	.990	39	266	39	3	2	4	Raasch, Peninsula	.889	3	22	2	3	0	0
Dewey, Durham	1.000	4	18	4	0	0	0	Reynolds, Frederick	.975	26	109	6	3	0	2
Dorante, Lynchburg	.975	13	109	10	3	1	1	Romero, Salem	.989	91	565	60	7	8	18
Erhardt, Prince William	1.000	9	46	5	0	0	0	Simonds, Winston-Salem	.982	26	148	12	3	0	0
Flaherty, Lynchburg	1.000	1	3	2	0	0	0	Taylor, Winston-Salem	.986	63	388	46	6	5	6
Hanks, Lynchburg	.957	5	22	0	1	0	0	Verdugo, Kinston	1.000	1	1	0	0	0	0
Hernandez, Prince William	.993	37	256	35	2	1	5	Welch, Winston-Salem	1.000	3	8	0	0	0	0
Hines, Salem	.977	33	185	26	5	3	0	D. Williams, Kinston	1.000	10	33	2	0	0	0
Horowitz, Frederick	.975	43	246	22	7	5	5	P. Williams, Lynchburg	.982	105	668	83	14	11	22

PITCHERS

Player and Club	Pct.	G.	PO.	A.	E.	DP.	Player and Club	Pct.	G.	PO.	A.	E.	DP.
Abril, Lynchburg	1.000	2	0	1	0	0	Leskanic, Kinston	1.000	14	5	6	0	1
Balabon, Peninsula	.885	14	4	19	3	2	Lodgek, Peninsula	.800	12	0	4	1	0
Bird, Salem*	.667	8	0	2	1	0	Loe, Peninsula	1.000	46	3	11	0	0
Borbon, Durham	.882	11	3	12	2	1	Longuil, Durham	1.000	12	0	6	0	0
Borgatti, Kinston	1.000	7	1	1	0	0	Lopez, Winston-Salem	.909	15	8	22	3	2
Brooks, Frederick*	.667	3	0	2	1	1	Marris, Prince William	.833	7	1	4	1	1
Brown, Lynchburg*	.952	27	6	14	1	2	Martel, Prince William	.972	25	11	24	1	4
Buckholz, Salem	.855	32	10	37	8	2	Massicotte, Winston-Salem	1.000	6	2	0	0	0
Bullinger, Winston-Salem	.964	14	6	21	1	0	Mathews, Durham	1.000	6	1	0	0	0
Bumgarner, Frederick	.778	17	5	9	4	0	McDowell, Salem	.920	32	7	16	2	1
Byerly, Durham*	.667	26	0	2	1	0	Melvin, Winston-Salem	.970	30	10	22	1	3
Caballero, Winston-Salem	1.000	9	4	4	0	0	Miller, Salem	.957	22	10	35	2	3
CANESTRO, Prince William*	1.000	29	6	20	0	1	Minchey, Durham	.895	25	8	26	4	3
Cole, Kinston	1.000	7	2	9	0	0	Mondile, Frederick	.900	32	3	15	2	0
Conroy, Lynchburg	.927	26	13	25	3	1	Moody, Prince William	.944	54	5	12	1	0
Cummings, Durham	1.000	14	3	8	0	2	Morgan, Kinston	1.000	12	2	3	0	0
Czajkowski, Salem	1.000	18	2	3	0	0	Mullins, Peninsula	.929	35	2	11	1	0
Czarkowski, Peninsula*	.921	21	8	27	3	1	Munoz, Kinston	1.000	9	5	7	0	0
Czarnik, Durham	1.000	17	3	17	0	1	Murphy, Salem	1.000	3	3	2	0	0
Darwin, Peninsula	.905	25	15	23	4	1	Neely, Kinston	1.000	6	0	3	0	0
B. Davis, Winston-Salem	.926	26	6	19	2	1	Neill, Kinston	.920	41	1	22	2	0
F. Davis, Lynchburg	1.000	35	6	12	0	3	Nelson, Peninsula	1.000	18	6	8	0	0
Deller, Salem	1.000	16	2	6	0	0	Nied, Durham	.947	10	5	13	1	0
Deutsch, Frederick	1.000	23	4	8	0	0	Nielsen, Prince William*	1.000	26	4	19	0	0
DiBartolomeo, Winston-Salem	.900	41	5	13	2	3	O'Donoghue, Frederick*	1.000	1	0	1	0	0
Diez, Durham*	1.000	20	2	6	0	0	Oliveras, Kinston	1.000	4	1	1	0	0
DiPoto, Kinston	.840	24	8	13	4	1	Oquist, Frederick	.929	25	10	16	2	1
Draper, Prince William	1.000	5	5	3	0	0	Peraza, Frederick	1.000	7	4	6	0	2
Duke, Peninsula*	1.000	14	2	6	0	0	Person, Kinston	1.000	4	0	2	0	1
Duncan, Salem	.962	37	0	25	1	3	Peters, Kinston	.800	12	1	3	1	0
Eddings, Winston-Salem	1.000	29	5	6	0	1	Pinder, Kinston*	.900	29	5	13	2	1
Ellis, Kinston*	.429	9	0	3	4	0	Poehl, Kinston	1.000	4	2	2	0	0
Estrada, Lynchburg	.929	25	14	25	3	3	Poissant, Peninsula	.833	26	3	7	2	1
Fansler, Salem	1.000	10	1	5	0	0	Polak, Prince William	1.000	44	11	14	0	1
Felix, Salem	.600	8	0	3	2	0	Pomeranz, Salem*	1.000	35	2	11	0	0
Ferlenda, Kinston	.875	46	4	3	1	1	Powers, Peninsula	1.000	11	4	14	0	2
Garcia, Peninsula	.955	36	6	15	1	0	Pratts, Lynchburg	1.000	29	6	7	0	0
Gardella, Prince William*	1.000	62	2	15	0	1	Prybylinski, Prince William	1.000	9	1	1	0	0
Gardner, Winston-Salem	1.000	34	8	9	0	2	Ralph, Prince William	1.000	43	4	17	0	0
Gilbert, Prince William	1.000	13	2	3	0	0	Rasp, Winston-Salem	1.000	4	1	0	0	0
M. Gonzales, Kinston	1.000	14	2	6	0	1	Rhodes, Frederick*	.778	13	1	6	2	1
T. Gonzales, Kinston*	.913	19	5	16	2	0	Ricci, Frederick	1.000	27	1	20	0	0
Gordon, Peninsula	.750	25	0	6	2	1	Richardson, Salem	1.000	9	4	6	0	1
Gutierrez, Peninsula	.974	28	13	24	1	1	Richey, Durham	.818	42	4	5	2	0
Hailey, Durham*	.909	11	1	9	1	2	Riddle, Frederick	.733	25	2	9	4	2
Hartzog, Prince William	1.000	18	7	11	0	1	Rivas, Peninsula*	.786	34	1	10	3	1
Honeywell, Salem*	1.000	22	2	7	0	1	B. Rivera, Durham	1.000	16	5	17	0	1
Jaques, Winston-Salem*	1.000	2	2	0	0	0	R. Rivera, Peninsula	.889	17	1	7	1	1
Johnson, Durham	.889	29	1	15	2	0	Ryan, Lynchburg	.946	28	9	26	2	0
Sh. Jones, Winston-Salem	.944	18	3	14	1	0	Salles, Winston-Salem	.980	25	12	38	1	1
St. Jones, Frederick	.833	15	3	2	1	0	Schlopy, Salem*	1.000	16	3	5	0	0
Karasinski, Durham*	1.000	24	2	5	0	1	Schullstrom, Frederick	1.000	2	1	1	0	0
Kazmierczak, Winston-Salem	.938	8	4	11	1	1	Scott, Lynchburg	1.000	57	6	19	0	0
Kerr, Frederick	.968	26	3	27	1	1	Seminara, Prince William	.904	25	15	32	5	6
King, Peninsula*	.889	7	1	7	1	0	Slomkowski, Frederick	.833	26	2	3	1	1
Kiser, Kinston*	.955	55	5	16	1	1	C. Smith, Durham*	1.000	4	0	1	0	0
Kovach, Kinston	.900	18	7	20	3	0	T. Smith, Winston-Salem	1.000	3	0	1	0	0
Kramer, Kinston	.864	16	4	15	3	1	Sodders, Winston-Salem*	1.000	12	7	13	0	0
Landry, Lynchburg*	.886	28	11	20	4	1	Stange, Lynchburg	1.000	33	6	8	0	1
Latham, Salem*	1.000	8	3	8	0	0	Stephan, Frederick	1.000	42	2	12	0	1
Leinen, Frederick*	1.000	14	3	20	0	2	Strauss, Winston-Salem	1.000	25	1	2	0	0

PITCHERS—Continued

Player and Club	Pct.	G.	PO.	A.	E.	DP.	Player and Club	Pct.	G.	PO.	A.	E.	DP.
Stroud, Winston-Salem*	.800	34	2	6	2	0	Watson, Durham	.857	34	6	18	4	0
Taylor, Lynchburg*	.947	13	3	15	1	0	Weems, Durham	1.000	6	2	2	0	0
Telford, Frederick	.933	8	8	6	1	0	Wendell, Durham	.800	6	5	3	2	1
Tilmon, Durham	.957	38	2	20	1	2	Whitehead, Lynchburg	1.000	2	0	1	0	0
Uhrhan, Lynchburg	1.000	29	10	7	0	0	Wiley, Prince William	.833	22	6	14	4	2
Underwood, Salem*	.909	10	2	8	1	0	J. Williams, Frederick	1.000	16	1	2	0	1
Vazquez, Durham	1.000	12	4	17	0	0	R. Williams, Salem	1.000	10	1	0	0	0
Vespe, Kinston	1.000	18	2	13	0	0	Wright, Durham	.960	50	6	18	1	0
Wagner, Salem	.857	11	0	6	1	0	Zimmerman, Salem	1.000	19	2	4	0	1
Wakefield, Salem	.978	28	16	29	1	2							

The following players did not have any fielding statistics at the positions indicated or appeared only as a designated hitter, pinch-hitter or pinch-runner: Adames, of; Barbara, p; Blair, 3b; Brakebill, of; Bryant, p; Castellano, of; Estep, 2b; Fowler, ph, dh; Greer, p; Holland, 2b, ss; Howard, p; B. Johnson, 1b; Lofton, dh; Maldonado, p; Malzone, p; W. Miller, p; Pilkinton, p; Raasch, of; M. Richardson, of; B. Robinson, p; Simonds, p; T. Smith, of, c; A. Taylor, p; W. Taylor, p; Tepper, p; Todd, p; Whitehead, ss; L. Williams, 3b; p. Williams, of; Willis, p.

CLUB PITCHING

Club	ERA.	G.	CG.	ShO.	Sv.	IP.	H.	R.	ER.	HR.	HB.	BB.	Int. BB.	SO.	WP.	Bk.
Kinston	3.04	135	9	11	43	1190.0	1033	509	402	52	51	481	10	1011	81	30
Frederick	3.13	136	17	16	27	1180.0	1068	517	410	59	41	449	23	981	53	12
Winston-Salem	3.24	140	21	10	44	1234.2	1166	540	445	62	43	483	23	960	67	21
Prince William	3.42	139	9	15	34	1188.0	1108	533	451	53	51	497	15	963	69	18
Durham	3.65	139	9	9	36	1233.2	1158	622	500	84	57	500	30	995	91	21
Peninsula	3.79	140	13	9	29	1197.2	1193	631	504	63	30	495	10	847	81	26
Lynchburg	4.26	138	14	11	30	1201.0	1236	678	568	82	47	489	13	885	87	16
Salem	4.80	139	15	8	25	1215.0	1310	801	648	123	82	592	33	860	110	21

PITCHERS' RECORDS

(Leading Qualifiers for Earned-Run Average Leadership—112 or More Innings)

*Throws lefthanded.

Pitcher—Club	W.	L.	Pct.	ERA.	G.	GS.	CG.	GF.	ShO.	Sv.	IP.	H.	R.	ER.	HR.	HB.	BB.	Int. BB.	SO.	WP.
Seminara, Prince William	16	8	.667	1.90	25	25	4	0	2	0	170.1	136	51	36	5	10	52	1	132	12
Czarkowski, Peninsula*	8	6	.571	2.32	21	16	3	1	0	0	116.1	128	50	30	4	3	34	1	40	3
Watson, Durham	10	6	.625	2.42	34	16	2	7	1	3	137.1	101	51	37	4	5	60	1	122	14
P. Miller, Salem	8	6	.571	2.45	22	22	5	0	1	0	150.2	145	58	41	6	7	33	1	83	5
Kovach, Kinston	12	3	.800	2.56	18	18	2	0	1	0	123.0	78	46	35	4	8	53	0	90	6
Salles, Winston-Salem	14	5	.737	2.58	25	25	4	0	1	0	171.0	160	59	49	7	7	48	1	100	6
Oquist, Frederick	9	8	.529	2.81	25	25	3	0	1	0	166.1	134	64	52	11	4	48	3	170	9
Kerr, Frederick	14	7	.667	2.94	26	26	5	0	2	0	177.2	160	64	58	12	5	56	0	129	5
Estrada, Lynchburg	7	7	.500	3.05	25	25	2	0	1	0	153.1	153	71	52	5	4	55	0	88	9
Wright, Durham	6	7	.462	3.16	50	1	0	22	0	8	116.2	101	46	41	8	2	34	8	100	6

Departmental Leaders: G—Gardella, 62; W—Seminara, 16; L—Darwin, Ryan, Wakefield, 14; Pct.—Kovach, Stephan, .800; GS—Gutierrez, Ryan, Wakefield, 28; CG—Conroy, 8; GF—Gardella, 57; ShO—Conroy, 4; Sv.—Gardella, 30; IP—Wakefield, 190.1; H—Wakefield, 187; R—Buckholz, 110; ER—Wakefield, 100; HR—Wakefield, 24; HB—Buckholz, 13; BB—Wakefield, 85; IBB—Wright, 8; SO—Oquist, 170; WP—Pomeranz, 24.

(All Pitchers—Listed Alphabetically)

Pitcher—Club	W.	L.	Pct.	ERA.	G.	GS.	CG.	GF.	ShO.	Sv.	IP.	H.	R.	ER.	HR.	HB.	BB.	Int. BB.	SO.	WP.
Abril, Lynchburg	0	1	.000	7.36	2	0	0	0	0	0	3.2	9	4	3	0	0	1	0	3	1
Balabon, Peninsula	7	4	.636	2.65	14	14	4	0	1	0	102.0	73	35	30	9	0	24	0	107	3
Barbara, Peninsula	0	0	.000	0.00	2	0	0	1	0	0	4.0	0	1	0	0	0	3	0	2	0
Bird, Salem*	3	1	.750	2.93	8	0	0	6	0	0	15.1	13	9	5	1	2	10	1	27	1
Borbon, Durham	4	5	.444	5.43	11	11	0	0	0	0	61.1	73	40	37	8	2	16	0	37	2
Borgatti, Kinston	1	1	.500	6.75	7	0	0	3	0	0	13.1	16	11	10	1	1	7	1	13	0
Brooks, Frederick*	0	0	.000	12.46	3	0	0	1	0	0	4.1	5	9	6	1	0	8	0	7	0
Brown, Lynchburg*	4	7	.364	5.17	27	11	0	7	0	1	92.1	96	64	53	6	4	56	1	77	4
Bryant, Kinston*	1	1	.500	5.19	2	2	0	0	0	0	8.2	10	6	5	0	0	7	0	13	1
Buckholz, Salem	8	10	.444	6.01	32	22	3	4	0	0	137.2	168	110	92	15	13	75	0	64	18
Bullinger, Winston-Salem	7	6	.538	3.70	14	13	3	0	0	0	90.0	81	43	37	5	7	46	0	85	6
Bumgarner, Frederick	6	6	.500	3.09	17	15	1	1	0	0	96.0	101	42	33	2	0	47	2	67	5
Byerly, Durham*	2	2	.500	3.33	26	0	0	11	0	1	27.0	29	16	10	1	1	8	1	18	0
Caballero, Winston-Salem	4	3	.571	3.28	9	9	0	0	0	0	49.1	49	25	18	0	0	15	0	29	3
Canestro, Prince William*	7	7	.500	4.34	29	10	0	10	0	0	83.0	85	47	40	10	2	33	2	46	7
Cole, Kinston	1	3	.250	5.00	7	6	0	0	0	0	36.0	53	26	20	5	0	15	0	23	3
Conroy, Lynchburg	10	12	.455	3.53	26	26	8	0	4	0	186.1	160	84	73	13	7	51	0	147	11
Cummings, Durham	2	5	.286	5.40	14	13	1	0	0	0	63.1	69	42	38	5	4	27	1	50	1
Czajkowski, Salem	1	1	.500	2.57	18	0	0	17	0	6	28.0	17	10	8	3	3	11	3	26	1
Czarkowski, Peninsula*	8	6	.571	2.32	21	16	3	1	0	0	116.1	128	50	30	4	3	34	1	40	3
Czarnik, Durham	5	1	.833	1.15	17	5	0	6	0	2	54.2	33	11	7	2	3	17	1	39	5
Darwin, Peninsula	8	14	.364	4.01	25	25	1	0	0	0	150.1	153	86	67	12	4	57	0	89	6
B. Davis, Winston-Salem	9	9	.500	3.91	26	18	3	5	1	1	126.2	118	71	55	5	5	46	0	109	11
F. Davis, Lynchburg	3	2	.600	2.70	35	0	0	32	0	15	46.2	43	17	14	1	2	11	2	29	3
Deller, Salem	1	2	.333	4.43	16	0	0	8	0	3	22.1	26	17	11	0	1	18	1	19	1
Deutsch, Frederick	4	0	1.000	4.39	23	4	1	5	0	0	67.2	75	39	33	8	1	32	1	42	4
DiBartolomeo, Winston-Salem	5	4	.556	3.50	41	4	2	21	1	12	108.0	101	54	42	7	2	48	5	73	4
Diez, Durham*	2	1	.667	5.34	20	0	0	5	0	2	30.1	36	20	18	2	2	16	0	17	5
Dipoto, Kinston	11	4	.733	3.78	24	24	1	0	0	0	145.1	129	75	61	6	10	77	1	143	12
Draper, Prince William	0	2	.000	6.35	5	4	1	0	0	0	22.2	31	20	16	2	2	9	0	8	4
Duke, Peninsula*	0	8	.000	7.79	14	12	0	2	0	0	54.1	78	54	47	3	1	36	0	36	4
Duncan, Peninsula	6	4	.600	5.21	37	3	2	17	0	1	84.2	105	61	49	5	4	48	3	95	9
Eddings, Winston-Salem	2	3	.400	3.89	29	0	0	24	0	12	41.2	38	19	18	3	2	8	4	34	1
Ellis, Kinston*	1	1	.500	3.20	9	2	0	4	0	0	19.2	21	14	7	1	0	12	0	7	1
Estrada, Lynchburg	7	7	.500	3.05	25	25	2	0	1	0	153.1	153	71	52	5	4	55	0	88	9
Fansler, Salem	0	5	.000	4.26	10	10	0	0	0	0	50.2	44	29	24	5	9	23	0	35	0
Felix, Salem	0	3	.000	7.54	8	3	0	0	0	0	22.2	21	19	19	7	4	19	1	17	4
Ferlenda, Kinston	0	2	.000	1.22	46	0	0	43	0	23	51.2	23	10	7	0	1	18	1	60	4
Garcia, Peninsula	3	7	.300	4.31	36	7	0	11	0	1	100.1	113	54	48	4	4	45	2	89	6
Gardella, Prince William*	4	3	.571	2.01	62	0	0	57	0	30	71.2	61	18	16	0	1	31	3	86	7

Pitcher—Club	W.	L.	Pct.	ERA.	G.	GS.	CG.	GF.	ShO.	Sv.	IP.	H.	R.	ER.	HR.	HB.	BB.	Int. BB.	SO.	WP.
Gardner, Winston-Salem	5	4	.556	3.53	34	2	0	19	0	5	86.2	70	40	34	5	5	55	5	97	6
Gilbert, Prince William	0	1	.000	3.49	13	1	0	7	0	0	28.1	29	12	11	1	1	10	0	22	2
M. Gonzales, Kinston	1	0	1.000	4.06	14	0	0	9	0	1	31.0	37	18	14	3	1	15	1	11	3
T. Gonzales, Kinston*	11	4	.733	3.14	19	17	0	0	0	0	91.2	81	41	32	3	7	35	0	61	6
Gordon, Peninsula*	0	3	.000	5.02	25	3	0	12	0	0	43.0	40	37	24	0	2	48	0	45	10
Greer, Prince William	1	0	1.000	2.35	1	1	0	0	0	0	7.2	7	2	2	0	0	2	0	7	0
Gutierrez, Peninsula	11	13	.458	3.44	28	28	4	0	2	0	186.0	171	82	71	9	6	41	0	95	6
Hailey, Durham*	3	5	.375	5.11	11	11	1	0	0	0	56.1	57	40	32	5	3	26	1	48	1
Hartzog, Prince William	5	6	.455	3.75	18	18	1	0	0	0	105.2	101	48	44	2	2	57	0	100	4
Honeywell, Salem*	2	2	.500	6.65	22	0	0	8	0	0	43.1	60	39	32	7	3	23	2	21	3
Howard, Kinston*	1	1	.500	2.45	8	0	0	3	0	0	14.2	21	5	4	0	2	6	0	16	0
Jaques, Winston-Salem*	0	0	.000	3.86	2	0	0	0	0	0	2.1	5	1	1	0	0	1	0	0	0
Johnson, Durham	4	4	.500	3.59	29	8	0	9	0	3	85.1	71	38	34	4	5	47	4	73	6
Sh. Jones, Winston-Salem	7	5	.583	3.22	18	17	1	1	0	0	100.2	99	44	36	7	1	28	1	107	12
St. Jones, Frederick	1	2	.333	3.38	15	0	0	11	0	2	26.2	31	13	10	0	1	7	1	24	1
Karasinski, Durham*	2	1	.667	5.23	24	1	0	10	0	4	31.0	40	25	18	1	2	8	0	24	4
Kazmierczak, Winston-Salem	3	4	.429	3.25	8	8	0	0	0	0	52.2	68	20	19	4	2	26	0	32	2
Kerr, Frederick	14	7	.667	2.94	26	26	5	0	2	0	177.2	160	64	58	12	5	56	0	129	5
King, Peninsula*	4	2	.667	4.46	7	7	0	0	0	0	36.1	42	23	18	2	0	13	0	20	2
Kiser, Kinston*	5	3	.625	1.71	55	0	0	24	0	9	94.2	81	25	18	3	3	27	1	82	5
Kovach, Kinston	12	3	.800	2.56	18	18	2	0	1	0	123.0	78	46	35	4	8	53	0	90	6
Kramer, Kinston	7	4	.636	2.85	16	16	2	0	1	0	98.0	82	34	31	5	2	29	0	96	2
Landry, Lynchburg*	7	8	.467	5.00	28	20	0	6	0	1	122.1	146	76	68	10	1	49	0	84	9
Latham, Salem*	1	4	.200	6.46	8	8	0	0	0	0	39.0	51	39	28	3	4	24	0	25	6
Leinen, Frederick*	6	6	.500	3.00	14	14	0	0	0	0	87.0	81	36	29	2	2	37	0	45	3
Leskanic, Kinston	6	5	.545	3.68	14	14	2	0	0	0	73.1	61	34	30	6	2	30	1	71	10
Lodgek, Peninsula	1	6	.143	4.44	12	8	0	1	0	0	46.2	54	26	23	0	4	21	0	27	5
Loe, Peninsula	4	5	.444	3.25	46	3	0	22	0	5	88.2	81	33	32	3	0	39	1	76	4
Longuil, Durham	2	2	.500	3.27	11	0	0	3	0	0	22.0	21	12	8	1	1	15	1	15	1
Lopez, Winston-Salem	8	3	.727	2.54	15	15	4	0	1	0	109.2	110	40	31	3	1	18	0	66	4
Maldonado, Durham	0	0	.000	0.00	1	0	0	0	0	0	0.2	1	0	0	0	0	0	0	0	0
Malzone, Lynchburg	0	0	.000	4.50	1	0	0	1	0	0	2.0	4	1	1	0	0	1	0	1	0
Marris, Prince William	0	1	.000	6.38	7	5	0	0	0	0	24.0	26	21	17	1	2	8	0	13	5
Martel, Prince William	8	13	.381	4.08	25	25	2	0	0	0	143.1	134	77	65	8	6	65	0	95	2
Massicotte, Winston-Salem	1	0	1.000	3.38	6	0	0	3	0	0	8.0	8	5	3	1	2	4	1	7	1
Mathews, Durham	1	0	1.000	11.37	6	0	0	2	0	1	6.1	11	10	8	1	0	2	0	7	0
McDowell, Salem	6	9	.400	3.82	32	11	0	11	0	2	113.0	114	62	48	9	5	56	6	90	8
Melvin, Winston-Salem	8	3	.727	3.41	30	14	1	7	1	0	118.2	107	51	45	5	2	71	1	88	6
P. Miller, Salem	8	6	.571	2.45	22	22	5	0	1	0	150.2	145	58	41	6	7	33	1	83	5
W. Miller, Kinston*	0	0	.000	0.00	1	0	0	1	0	0	1.0	1	0	0	0	0	1	0	2	0
Minchey, Durham	4	11	.267	3.79	25	24	2	0	2	0	133.0	143	75	56	11	5	46	0	100	13
Mondile, Frederick	5	4	.556	3.53	32	1	0	17	0	3	66.1	69	35	26	3	5	26	2	27	3
Moody, Prince William	3	2	.600	2.35	54	0	0	30	0	3	88.0	67	25	23	1	2	31	4	103	4
Morgan, Kinston	1	1	.500	1.32	12	1	0	2	0	1	34.0	21	7	5	0	2	16	0	37	5
Mullins, Peninsula	2	5	.286	5.57	35	3	0	15	0	1	74.1	84	61	46	8	2	53	2	66	16
Munoz, Kinston	7	0	1.000	2.39	9	9	2	0	1	0	64.0	43	18	17	6	1	18	0	55	3
Murphy, Salem	2	2	.500	5.59	3	3	0	0	0	0	19.1	22	15	12	3	1	8	1	12	1
Neely, Salem	0	1	.000	2.45	6	0	0	6	0	2	7.1	5	2	2	0	0	3	2	11	1
Neill, Kinston	8	3	.727	2.74	41	0	0	15	0	0	82.0	80	34	25	5	6	27	4	67	9
Nelson, Peninsula	2	2	.500	3.15	18	7	1	8	1	6	60.0	47	21	21	5	1	25	1	49	2
Nied, Durham	1	1	.500	3.83	10	10	0	0	0	0	42.1	38	19	18	3	1	14	0	27	4
Nielsen, Prince William*	7	12	.368	3.92	26	26	1	0	1	0	151.2	149	76	66	9	11	79	1	119	9
O'Donoghue, Frederick*	0	1	.000	4.50	1	1	0	0	0	0	4.0	5	2	2	0	0	0	0	3	0
Oliveras, Kinston	1	0	1.000	5.40	4	4	0	0	0	0	15.0	11	13	9	0	0	17	0	17	3
Oquist, Frederick	9	8	.529	2.81	25	25	3	0	1	0	166.1	134	64	52	11	4	48	3	170	9
Peraza, Frederick	2	0	.000	3.33	7	7	0	0	0	0	24.1	19	14	9	0	1	12	1	28	3
Person, Kinston	1	0	1.000	2.70	4	3	0	1	0	0	16.2	17	6	5	0	0	9	0	7	0
Peters, Kinston	2	1	.667	1.96	12	0	0	3	0	1	23.0	19	7	5	0	2	7	0	27	2
Pilkinton, Peninsula	0	0	.000	0.00	1	0	0	0	0	0	1.0	1	0	0	0	0	0	0	0	0
Pinder, Kinston*	7	4	.636	3.29	29	13	0	9	0	3	98.1	104	50	36	1	1	28	0	68	1
Poehl, Kinston	0	1	.000	7.50	4	4	0	0	0	0	12.0	11	10	10	1	1	6	0	7	1
Poissant, Peninsula	1	2	.333	1.47	26	0	0	23	0	9	30.2	24	10	5	1	2	18	0	27	8
Polak, Prince William	3	6	.333	2.69	44	1	0	7	0	1	77.0	75	30	23	4	3	25	0	61	2
Pomeranz, Salem*	3	7	.300	6.90	35	3	0	17	0	1	58.2	68	58	45	4	2	54	5	43	24
Powers, Lynchburg	7	0	.000	4.45	11	10	0	0	0	0	54.2	60	40	27	4	2	28	0	27	3
Pratts, Lynchburg	6	1	.857	6.64	29	0	0	6	0	0	62.1	73	54	46	8	3	34	1	23	4
Prybylinski, Prince William	1	2	.333	3.92	9	1	0	3	0	0	20.2	17	9	9	2	0	4	0	20	1
Ralph, Frederick	4	3	.571	3.15	43	0	0	16	0	0	80.0	69	30	28	3	5	40	3	75	5
Rasp, Winston-Salem	0	0	.000	12.27	4	0	0	1	0	0	3.2	8	5	5	0	1	1	0	3	0
Rhodes, Frederick*	4	6	.400	2.12	13	13	4	0	0	0	80.2	62	25	19	6	1	21	0	103	3
Ricci, Frederick	7	12	.368	4.41	26	18	2	5	1	0	122.1	126	79	60	8	6	47	3	94	8
Richardson, Salem	3	3	.500	3.82	9	9	3	0	1	0	66.0	64	34	28	7	0	19	0	50	4
Richey, Durham	7	1	.875	2.75	42	0	0	34	0	10	59.0	46	21	18	3	3	39	5	72	2
Riddle, Frederick	2	3	.400	2.34	25	1	0	15	0	1	50.0	45	19	13	0	1	26	4	28	1
Rivas, Peninsula*	1	3	.250	4.46	34	0	0	22	0	5	42.1	50	33	21	3	1	13	2	42	3
B. Rivera, Durham	5	3	.625	3.60	16	13	1	3	1	1	75.0	69	41	30	7	5	33	1	64	4
R. Rivera, Peninsula	5	3	.625	3.23	17	7	0	8	0	2	61.1	54	25	22	0	0	25	1	37	3
Robinson, Winston-Salem	0	1	.000	1.04	2	1	1	1	0	0	8.2	8	1	1	0	0	1	1	5	1
Ryan, Lynchburg	6	14	.300	5.13	28	28	3	0	1	0	161.1	182	104	92	10	6	82	0	109	19
Salles, Winston-Salem	14	5	.737	2.58	25	25	4	0	1	0	171.0	160	59	49	7	7	48	1	100	6
Schlopy, Salem*	1	4	.200	4.07	16	6	0	3	0	0	48.2	55	31	22	2	7	18	0	25	3
Schullstrom, Frederick	2	0	1.000	3.46	2	2	0	0	0	0	13.0	9	5	5	0	1	6	0	8	0
Scott, Lynchburg	6	8	.429	3.87	57	0	0	38	0	11	90.2	93	44	39	9	3	29	5	90	6
Seminara, Prince William	16	8	.667	1.90	25	25	4	0	2	0	170.1	136	51	36	5	10	52	1	132	12
Simonds, Winston-Salem	0	0	.000	0.00	1	0	0	1	0	0	1.0	0	0	0	0	1	0	0	0	0
Slomkowski, Frederick	0	0	.000	6.00	26	0	0	18	0	3	33.0	41	22	22	3	5	16	1	24	2
C. Smith, Durham*	0	2	.000	3.86	4	3	0	1	0	0	18.2	17	10	8	1	1	5	0	8	1
T. Smith, Winston-Salem	0	0	.000	0.00	3	0	0	3	0	0	5.0	1	0	0	0	1	0	0	1	0
Sodders, Winston-Salem*	7	1	.875	2.06	12	12	2	0	1	0	74.1	57	20	17	3	0	25	0	43	2
Stange, Lynchburg	0	3	.000	5.97	33	0	0	24	0	1	57.1	62	40	38	8	6	23	0	31	3
Stephan, Frederick	8	2	.800	1.32	42	1	0	33	0	17	82.0	47	17	12	0	2	32	4	102	1
Strauss, Winston-Salem	1	1	.500	1.93	25	0	0	19	0	11	28.0	24	8	6	2	2	6	0	25	0

Pitcher—Club	W.	L.	Pct.	ERA.	G.	GS.	CG.	GF.	ShO.	Sv.	IP.	H.	R.	ER.	HR.	HB.	BB.	Int. BB.	SO.	WP.
Stroud, Winston-Salem*	5	1	.833	3.35	34	0	0	12	0	3	40.1	37	18	15	2	2	26	4	47	2
A. Taylor, Winston-Salem.........	0	0	.000	6.75	2	0	0	2	0	0	4.0	4	4	3	1	0	5	0	5	0
S. Taylor, Lynchburg*	5	6	.455	2.73	13	13	1	0	0	0	89.0	76	36	27	2	2	30	2	120	7
W. Taylor, Durham	0	0	.000	3.24	5	0	0	3	0	0	8.1	8	3	3	0	0	1	1	10	0
Telford, Frederick	4	2	.667	1.68	8	8	1	0	0	0	53.2	35	15	10	1	4	11	1	49	4
Tepper, Kinston*	0	0	.000	4.50	1	0	0	0	0	0	2.0	2	1	1	0	0	2	0	2	0
Tilmon, Durham	6	5	.545	3.90	38	7	0	10	0	1	101.2	105	54	44	7	4	37	3	104	14
Todd, Durham*	0	0	.000	0.00	1	0	0	1	0	0	1.0	0	0	0	0	0	0	0	0	0
Uhrhan, Lynchburg................	4	4	.500	4.21	29	5	0	8	0	1	77.0	77	45	36	5	6	38	2	53	8
Underwood, Salem*	1	4	.200	6.80	10	7	0	1	0	0	41.0	52	38	31	10	2	24	0	26	2
Vazquez, Durham	4	2	.667	3.79	12	11	1	0	0	0	57.0	60	33	24	6	5	29	1	28	6
Vespe, Kinston	3	5	.375	3.29	18	2	0	9	0	4	41.0	31	18	15	2	1	19	0	36	4
Wagner, Salem	0	1	.000	5.00	11	4	0	3	0	2	36.0	39	22	20	7	0	17	1	28	3
Wakefield, Salem................	10	14	.417	4.73	28	28	2	0	0	0	190.1	187	109	100	24	10	85	2	127	11
Watson, Durham................	10	6	.625	2.42	34	16	2	7	1	3	137.1	101	51	37	4	5	60	1	122	14
Weems, Durham................	0	1	.000	4.05	6	0	0	3	0	0	6.2	5	5	3	1	1	5	0	6	0
Wendell, Durham................	1	3	.250	1.86	6	5	1	0	0	0	38.2	24	10	8	3	2	15	1	26	2
Whitehead, Lynchburg................	0	0	.000	4.50	2	0	0	2	0	0	2.0	2	1	1	1	1	1	0	3	0
Wiley, Prince William	5	9	.357	4.34	22	22	0	0	0	0	114.0	121	67	55	5	4	51	1	76	5
J. Williams, Frederick	2	1	.667	4.68	16	0	0	13	0	1	25.0	23	17	13	2	2	17	0	31	1
R. Williams, Salem	0	0	.000	8.59	10	0	0	7	0	0	14.2	24	18	14	4	0	8	1	12	2
Willis, Winston-Salem	0	1	.000	20.77	2	2	0	0	0	0	4.1	13	12	10	2	2	3	0	2	0
Wright, Durham	6	7	.462	3.16	50	1	0	22	0	8	116.2	101	46	41	8	2	34	8	100	6
Zimmerman, Salem	1	1	.500	5.96	19	0	0	13	0	8	25.2	28	19	17	1	5	16	3	24	3

BALKS—Darwin, 9; Leskanic, 8; Conroy, 6; Johnson, Salles, 5 each; Polak, 4; Balabon, Buckholz, Deller, Dipoto, Garcia, King, Martel, McDowell, Melvin, Morgan, Pinder, Slomkowski, S. Taylor, Vespe, Watson, Wiley, 3 each; Bryant, Canestro, Eddings, Estrada, Hailey, Howard, Sh. Jones, Latham, Mathews, P. Miller, Minchey, Mullins, Nielsen, Peraza, Peters, Poissant, Pomeranz, B. Rivera, Seminara, Willis, Zimmerman, 2 each; Borbon, Borgatti, Brown, Bullinger, Bumgarner, B. Davis, Diez, Duncan, Fansler, Gardner, T. Gonzales, Gutierrez, Hartzog, Honeywell, St. Jones, Kazmierczak, Kerr, Kramer, Leinen, Lodgek, Loe, Longuil, Lopez, Mondile, Oquist, Poehl, Powers, Pratts, Ralph, Rhodes, R. Rivera, Ryan, T. Smith, Stroud, W. Taylor, Uhrhan, R. Williams, Wright, 1 each.

COMBINATION SHUTOUTS—Cummings-Tilmon-Karasinski, Czarnik-Wright, Rivera-Watson-Tilmon-Wright, Vazquez-Richey, Watson-Diez, Durham; Kerr-Stephan 2, Leinen-Stephan 2, Bumgarner-Riddle, Bumgarner-Stephan, Kerr-Williams, Leinen-Slomkowski-Stephan, Oquist-Jones, Rhodes-Jones, Telford-Bumgarner, Telford-Stephan-Slomkowski, Frederick; Dipoto-Ferlenda, Dipoto-Vespe, Kovach-Ferlenda, Kovach-Kiser-Ferlenda, Kramer-Vespe, Leskanic-Gonzales-Pinder, Leskanic-Kiser, Leskanic-Neill, Kinston; Taylor-Davis 2, Estrada-Pratts-Landry, Estrada-Scott, Landry-Scott, Lynchburg; Darwin-Poissant, Darwin-Rivas, Garcia-Czarkowski-Poissant, Gutierrez-Nelson, Rivera-Rivas, Peninsula; Seminara-Gardella 3, Canestro-Ralph-Moody, Hartzog-Polak-Gardella, Hartzog-Ralph-Polak, Nielsen-Polak-Gardella, Nielsen-Prybylinski, Nielsen-Ralph-Polak-Moody, Seminara-Polak-Gardella, Wiley-Gardella, Wiley-Polak-Gardella, Prince William; Miller-Czajkowski 3, McDowell-Buckholz-Zimmerman, Wakefield-Czajkowski, Wakefield-Neely, Salem; Melvin-Gardner, Salles-Melvin-Gardner, Salles-Stroud-Eddings, Sodders-Eddings, Winston-Salem.

NO-HIT GAMES—Czarnik, Durham, lost to Winston-Salem, 3-2 (14 innings), May 24; Balabon, Peninsula, defeated Frederick, 4-0 (first game), June 16.

Florida State League

CLASS A

CHAMPIONSHIP WINNERS IN PREVIOUS YEARS

1919—Sanford* .605	1952—DeLand x .704	1971—Miami b .667
Orlando* .703	Palatka (3rd)‡ .569	Daytona Beach .586
1920—Tampa .654	1953—Daytona Beach† .657	1972—Miami c .562
Tampa .722	DeLand .703	Daytona Beach .606
1921—Orlando .635	1954—Jacksonville Beach .629	1973—St. Petersburg d .575
1922—St. Petersburg .503	Lakeland† .594	West Palm Beach .580
St. Petersburg .618	1955—Orlando .671	1974—West Palm Beach d .598
1923—Orlando .667	Orlando .643	Fort Lauderdale .626
Orlando .678	1956—Cocoa .614	1975—St. Petersburg d .652
1924—Lakeland .695	Cocoa .671	Miami .581
Lakeland .683	1957—Palatka .629	1976—Tampa .559
1925—St. Petersburg .667	Tampa† .681	Lakeland d .536
Tampa† .696	1958—St. Petersburg .732	1977—Lakeland .616
1926—Sanford .647	St. Petersburg .681	West Palm Beach .583
Sanford .623	1959—Tampa .591	1978—Lakeland .565
1927—Orlando† .600	St. Petersburg† .612	Miami§ .539
Miami .661	1960—Lakeland .731	1979—Fort Lauderdale .643
1928-35—Did not operate.	Palatka† .614	Winter Haven e .577
1936—Gainesville .542	1961—Tampa† .710	1980—Daytona Beach .628
St. Augustine (4th)† .492	Sarasota .696	Fort Lauderdale d .606
1937—Gainesville§ .616	1962—Sarasota .689	1981—Fort Myers .554
1938—Leesburg .626	Fort Lauderdale† .623	Daytona Beach f .504
Gainesville (2nd)‡ .615	1963—Sarasota .645	1982—Fort Lauderdale f .621
1939—Sanford§ .787	Sarasota .667	Tampa .546
1940—Daytona Beach .619	1964—Fort Lauderdale† .629	1983—Daytona Beach .634
Orlando (4th)‡ .507	St. Petersburg .594	Vero Beach f .515
1941—St. Augustine .659	1965—Fort Lauderdale .627	1984—Tampa .532
Leesburg (4th)‡ .488	Fort Lauderdale .634	Fort Lauderdale f .521
1942-45—Did not operate.	1966—Leesburg† .781	1985—Fort Myers g .590
1946—Orlando§ .681	St. Petersburg .700	Fort Lauderdale .550
1947—St. Augustine .625	1967—St. Petersburg y .691	1986—St. Petersburg g .647
Gainesville (2nd)‡ .584	Orlando .638	West Palm Beach .593
1948—Orlando .643	1968—Miami .613	1987—Fort Lauderdale g .616
Daytona Beach (2nd)‡ .616	Orlando z .579	Osceola .576
1949—Gainesville .635	1969—Miami a .606	1988—Osceola .606
St. Augustine (3rd)‡ .556	Orlando .606	St. Lucie h .532
1950—Orlando .629	1970—Miami b .662	1989—Port Charlotte h .540
DeLand (3rd)‡ .590	St. Petersburg .600	St. Petersburg .540
1951—DeLand§ .643		

*Split-season playoff abandoned after each team won three games. †Won split-season playoff. ‡Won four-club playoff. §Won championship and four-club playoff. xWon both halves of split season. yLeague divided into Eastern and Western divisions with split season. St. Petersburg and Orlando won both halves of split season; St. Petersburg won playoff. zLeague divided into Eastern and Western divisions. Miami won regular-season pennant on basis of highest won-lost percentage. Orlando won four-club playoff involving first two teams in each division. aLeague divided into Southern and Central divisions. Miami won playoff between division leaders. (NOTE—Pennant awarded to playoff winner in 1936.) bLeague divided into Eastern and Western divisions. Miami won regular-season pennant on basis of highest won-loss percentage, and also won four-club playoff involving first two teams in each division. cLeague divided into Eastern and Western divisions. Won four-club playoff involving first two teams in each division. dLeague divided into Northern and Southern divisions. Won four-club playoff involving first two teams in each division. eLeague divided into Northern and Southern divisions. Same two clubs won both halves; won playoffs. fWon split-season playoff. gLeague divided into Western, Central and Southern divisions. Won four-club playoff. hLeague divided into Eastern, Western and Central divisions; played split-season. Won six-club playoff.

STANDING OF CLUBS AT CLOSE OF FIRST HALF, JUNE 15

EAST DIVISION						WEST DIVISION					
Club	W.	L.	T.	Pct.	G.B.	Club	W.	L.	T.	Pct.	G.B.
West Palm Beach (Expos)	49	19	0	.721	......	Dunedin (Blue Jays)	53	14	0	.791	......
Vero Beach (Dodgers)	41	27	0	.603	8	Charlotte (Rangers)	44	24	0	.647	9½
St. Lucie (Mets)	39	29	0	.574	10	St. Petersburg (Cardinals)	30	35	0	.462	22
Fort Lauderdale (Yankees)	33	36	0	.478	16½	Sarasota (White Sox)	27	42	0	.391	27
Miami (Independent)	15	54	0	.217	34½	Clearwater (Phillies)	23	46	0	.333	31

CENTRAL DIVISION

Club	W.	L.	T.	Pct.	G.B.
Lakeland (Tigers)	44	24	0	.647	......
Osceola (Astros)	36	34	0	.514	9
Baseball City (Royals)	29	41	0	.414	16
Winter Haven (Red Sox)	16	54	0	.229	29

STANDING OF CLUBS AT CLOSE OF SECOND HALF, AUGUST 30

EAST DIVISION						WEST DIVISION					
Club	W.	L.	T.	Pct.	G.B.	Club	W.	L.	T.	Pct.	G.B.
West Palm Beach (Expos)	43	21	0	.672	......	Charlotte (Rangers)	41	29	0	.586	......
Vero Beach (Dodgers)	38	29	1	.567	6½	Sarasota (White Sox)	36	33	0	.522	4½
St. Lucie (Mets)	37	29	0	.561	7	Dunedin (Blue Jays)	31	38	0	.449	9½
Miami (Independent)	29	39	0	.426	16	St. Petersburg (Cardinals)	30	39	0	.435	10½
Fort Lauderdale (Yankees)	29	39	0	.426	16	Clearwater (Phillies)	27	41	0	.397	13

CENTRAL DIVISION

Club	W.	L.	T.	Pct.	G.B.
Lakeland (Tigers)	39	25	1	.609	......
Osceola (Astros)	36	32	0	.529	5
Baseball City (Royals)	31	37	0	.456	10
Winter Haven (Red Sox)	24	40	0	.375	15

COMPOSITE STANDING OF CLUBS AT CLOSE OF SEASON, AUGUST 30

Club	WPB	Lak.	Dun.	Char.	V.B.	StL	Osc.	Sar.	Ft.L	St.P	B.C.	Clw	Mia.	W.H.	W.	L.	T.	Pct.	G.B.
West Palm Beach (Expos)	....	4	1	6	12	10	5	6	14	7	5	6	12	4	92	40	0	.697	....
Lakeland (Tigers)	3	....	3	2	1	3	8	7	4	7	16	7	6	16	83	49	1	.629	9
Dunedin (Blue Jays)	6	5	....	10	3	5	3	8	5	7	5	11	8	8	84	52	0	.618	10
Charlotte (Rangers)	2	5	7	....	4	5	5	12	4	11	4	12	6	8	85	53	0	.616	10
Vero Beach (Dodgers)	5	6	4	4	....	7	4	6	9	4	4	7	13	6	79	56	1	.585	14½
St. Lucie (Mets)	7	2	1	3	11	....	6	5	10	3	5	5	13	5	76	58	0	.567	17
Osceola (Astros)	3	12	5	3	4	2	....	1	5	6	14	2	2	13	72	66	0	.522	23
Sarasota (White Sox)	2	0	9	4	2	3	7	....	4	10	5	8	3	6	63	75	0	.457	32
Fort Lauderdale (Yankees)	4	4	3	3	7	6	2	4	....	3	4	6	11	5	62	75	0	.453	32½
St. Petersburg (Cardinals)	0	0	5	7	3	4	2	8	4	....	3	11	5	4	60	74	0	.448	33
Baseball City (Royals)	3	4	3	4	2	3	6	3	4	5	....	6	5	12	60	78	0	.435	35
Clearwater (Phillies)	1	1	7	5	1	3	5	9	2	4	2	....	5	5	50	87	0	.365	44½
Miami (Independent)	4	2	0	2	4	4	6	4	7	3	3	3	....	2	44	93	0	.321	50½
Winter Haven (Red Sox)	0	4	0	0	2	3	7	2	3	4	8	3	4	....	40	94	0	.299	53

Charlotte played home games in Port Charlotte, Fla.

Osceola played home games in Kissimmee, Fla.

Major league affiliations in parentheses.

Playoffs—Charlotte defeated Dunedin, two games to none; Vero Beach defeated St. Lucie, two games to one; West Palm Beach defeated Lakeland, two games to one; Vero Beach defeated Charlotte, two games to one; Vero Beach defeated West Palm Beach, two games to one, to win league championship.

Regular-Season Attendance—Baseball City, 18,884; Charlotte, 122,478; Clearwater, 91,040; Dunedin, 65,348; Fort Lauderdale, 34,826; Lakeland, 57,967; Miami, 43,580; Osceola, 46,421; St. Lucie, 65,597; St. Petersburg, 190,146; Sarasota, 51,775; Vero Beach, 94,832; West Palm Beach, 83,673; Winter Haven, 23,008. Total-989,575. Playoffs (14 games)-10,346. All-Star Game-2,396.

Managers—Baseball City, Brian Poldberg; Charlotte, Bobby Jones; Clearwater, Lee Elia; Dunedin, Dennis Holmberg; Fort Lauderdale, Mike Hart; Lakeland, John Lipon; Miami, Mike Easler (through August 13), Freddi Gonzalez (August 14 through end of season); Osceola, Sal Butera; St. Lucie, Tim Blackwell; St. Petersburg, Joe Pettini; Sarasota, Tony Franklin; Vero Beach, Joe Alvarez; West Palm Beach, Felipe Alou; Winter Haven, Dave Holt. Managerial records of teams with more than one manager: Miami, Easler (34-83), Gonzalez (10-10).

All-Star Team—1B—Nikco Riesgo, St. Lucie; 2B—Jeff Kent, Dunedin; 3B—Fred Samson, Charlotte; SS—Keith Kimberlin, Lakeland; LF—D.J. Dozier, St. Lucie; CF—Kenny Lofton, Osceola; RF—Jacob Brumfield, Baseball City; C—Ivan Rodriguez, Charlotte; Jason Townley, Dunedin; DH—Greg O'Halloran, Dunedin; RHP—John Johnstone, St. Lucie; Ramon Taveras, Vero Beach; LHP—Anthony Ward, Dunedin; Chris Pollack, West Palm Beach; Rel—Barry Manuel, Charlotte; Larry Stanford, Fort Lauderdale; Most Valuable Player—Nikco Riesgo, St. Lucie; Manager of the Year—Felipe Alou, West Palm Beach.

(Compiled by Howe Sportsdata International, Boston, Mass.)

CLUB BATTING

Club	Pct.	G.	AB.	R.	OR.	H.	TB.	2B.	3B.	HR.	RBI.	SH.	SF.	HP.	BB.	Int. BB.	SO.	SB.	CS.	LOB.
Vero Beach	.266	136	4406	673	532	1173	1634	219	31	60	589	44	48	69	522	30	746	307	81	954
Dunedin	.256	136	4548	639	511	1163	1734	203	46	92	560	39	37	30	454	26	966	111	57	910
Charlotte	.252	138	4480	581	404	1130	1507	183	52	30	500	57	41	31	539	28	855	127	76	1009
Lakeland	.252	133	4239	559	406	1067	1424	162	45	35	482	67	43	32	485	23	757	123	48	923
West Palm Beach	.251	132	4359	597	428	1096	1460	168	44	36	514	69	25	43	509	39	764	172	76	988
St. Lucie	.250	134	4253	641	531	1063	1480	154	43	59	571	43	42	55	533	23	8100	273	96	876
Osceola	.246	138	4496	603	576	1106	1475	151	55	36	509	60	45	62	587	20	942	207	68	1020
Fort Lauderdale	.246	137	4387	537	654	1078	1492	199	37	47	471	25	43	46	490	30	866	150	69	941
Baseball City	.243	138	4437	542	675	1079	1375	148	35	26	461	39	36	46	434	20	820	234	79	917
Sarasota	.241	138	4488	536	575	1080	1407	155	38	32	442	59	33	56	561	31	912	145	97	1025
St. Petersburg	.239	134	4366	515	527	1044	1377	164	38	31	446	16	39	54	512	28	774	120	108	906
Clearwater	.235	137	4419	476	595	1037	1366	161	45	26	416	48	38	54	422	13	775	111	54	974
Miami.....................	.227	137	4349	401	703	987	1299	163	25	33	376	61	16	46	505	26	1038	157	74	991
Winter Haven	.222	134	4367	439	658	970	1294	156	33	34	367	56	20	42	432	19	1016	169	60	920

INDIVIDUAL BATTING

(Leading Qualifiers for Batting Championship—378 or More Plate Appearances)

*Bats lefthanded.   †Switch-hitter.

Player and Club	Pct.	G.	AB.	R.	H.	TB.	2B.	3B.	HR.	RBI.	SH.	SF.	HP.	BB.	Int. BB.	SO.	SB.	CS.
Brumfield, Jacob, Baseball City	.336	109	372	66	125	155	24	3	0	40	2	2	2	60	6	44	47	10
Lofton, Kenneth, Osceola*	.331	124	481	98	159	190	15	5	2	35	8	3	3	61	2	77	62	16
Vargas, Hector, Fort Lauderdale	.308	117	429	48	132	170	20	9	0	61	4	11	3	30	1	68	22	11
Riesgo, Nikco, St. Lucie.....................	.298	131	456	93	136	219	35	3	14	94	0	5	8	74	10	77	46	14
Barron, Anthony, Vero Beach	.297	111	344	58	102	147	21	3	6	60	2	5	7	30	1	82	42	7
Massarelli, John, Osceola	.295	120	396	55	117	137	8	3	2	50	5	7	2	41	4	73	54	6
Munoz, Jose, Vero Beach†	.295	113	397	57	117	147	18	3	2	47	8	4	2	34	3	43	28	8
Townley, Jason, Dunedin	.292	119	397	58	116	173	22	1	11	63	5	3	3	41	0	82	1	2
Ocasio, Javier, Sarasota	.292	127	497	65	145	167	13	3	1	45	10	1	12	55	1	67	45	27
Zinter, Alan, St. Lucie†	.291	98	333	63	97	149	19	6	7	63	0	6	1	54	1	70	8	1

Departmental Leaders: G—Madsen, Woodruff, 135; AB—de la Rosa, 519; R—E. Young, 101; H—Lofton, 159; TB—Riesgo, 219; 2B—Riesgo, 35; 3B—Madsen, 11; HR—Giannelli, 18; RBI—Riesgo, 94; SH—Kimberlin, 21; SF—Vargas, 11; HP—Beams, Ocasio, 12; BB—Pledger, 94; IBB—Peters, 11; SO—Pledger, Watkins, 134; SB—E. Young, 76; CS—Ocasio, 27.

(All Players—Listed Alphabetically)

Player and Club	Pct.	G.	AB.	R.	H.	TB.	2B.	3B.	HR.	RBI.	SH.	SF.	HP.	BB.	Int. BB.	SO.	SB.	CS.
Abreu, Franklin, St. Petersburg...........	.276	86	293	30	81	95	10	2	0	27	2	3	3	21	1	49	6	7
Acta, Manuel, Osceola	.206	44	126	12	26	29	3	0	0	2	0	0	1	15	0	17	2	0
Adams, Brian, Clearwater	.179	23	67	3	12	14	2	0	0	8	0	0	1	0	0	6	0	0
Albright, Eric, Lakeland......................	.202	70	203	34	41	53	9	0	1	23	3	2	41	0	42	4	2
Aldrich, Thomas, Lakeland...................	.266	92	305	26	81	107	23	0	1	37	1	3	1	47	0	63	3	1
Alegre, Paul, Miami*	.250	3	4	0	1	2	1	0	0	0	0	0	1	1	3	0	0
Alicea, Luis, St. Petersburg†	.232	29	95	14	22	31	1	4	0	12	0	1	5	20	2	14	9	2
Alvarez, Clemente, Sarasota	.160	37	119	9	19	28	4	1	1	9	2	0	0	8	0	24	0	0
Alvarez, Jorge, Vero Beach.................	.289	124	454	56	131	163	19	5	1	48	3	2	9	31	0	58	31	12
Andrews, Jay, Baseball City†	.278	21	79	5	22	25	1	1	0	5	1	0	1	3	0	17	4	2
Anglero, Jose, 28 B.C.-38 Lake..........	.244	66	176	24	43	54	3	4	0	15	4	2	12	0	19	11	2
Angotti, Donald, Osceola	.143	24	35	2	5	7	2	0	0	1	0	1	0	5	0	17	0	0
Balthazar, Doyle, Lakeland	.259	43	147	17	38	52	5	3	1	20	1	1	0	9	0	25	3	0
Bargman, Todd, Miami*	.067	5	15	1	1	1	0	0	0	2	0	0	1	0	9	0	0

Player and Club	Pct.	G.	AB.	R.	H.	TB.	2B.	3B.	HR.	RBI.	SH.	SF.	HP.	BB.	Int. BB.	SO.	SB.	CS.
Barnwell, Richard, Fort Lauderdale	.274	71	274	54	75	112	15	5	4	20	0	1	4	32	1	62	24	11
Barragan, Jaime, Clearwater°	.209	13	43	6	9	12	3	0	0	3	0	0	0	10	0	4	0	0
Barron, Anthony, Vero Beach	.297	111	344	58	102	147	21	3	6	60	2	5	7	30	1	82	42	7
Beacom, Christopher, Dunedin°	.227	84	238	26	54	82	14	4	2	24	6	1	1	17	0	52	0	0
Beall, Michael, Baseball City°	.201	64	204	20	41	51	5	1	1	24	2	2	2	31	1	26	0	2
Beams, Michael, Osceola	.253	126	419	62	106	162	21	4	9	50	3	5	12	62	0	96	15	7
Beard, Garrett, Vero Beach	.250	6	16	1	4	5	1	0	0	3	0	0	0	2	0	2	0	0
Beaulac, Joseph, Miami°	.158	17	38	3	6	6	0	0	0	2	1	0	0	9	1	13	0	0
Belbru, Juan, St. Petersburg	.000	4	5	1	0	0	0	0	0	1	0	1	0	1	0	0	0	0
Bethea, Scott, Winter Haven†	.429	5	14	0	6	6	0	0	0	1	1	0	1	2	0	2	0	0
Bible, Michael, Miami	.231	14	26	1	6	6	0	0	0	1	0	0	1	2	0	9	1	0
Boddie, Eric, Vero Beach	.236	80	144	21	34	42	3	1	1	15	2	0	4	22	1	38	3	3
Boddie, Rodney, W. Palm Beach†	.266	90	334	49	89	109	12	4	0	41	5	4	1	35	2	50	14	9
Boyce, Thomas, Miami†	.206	53	136	15	28	47	5	1	4	9	2	0	1	20	2	36	3	4
Bradbury, Miah, Miami	.210	50	157	10	33	44	8	0	1	12	0	1	5	16	0	25	0	2
Bridges-Clements, Anthony, B. C.	.257	63	214	32	55	63	3	1	1	14	4	2	0	20	0	40	11	3
Brown, Dana, Clearwater	.256	96	363	55	93	112	9	5	0	28	3	4	5	40	2	47	30	7
Brown, Don, St. Lucie	.148	22	61	13	9	10	1	0	0	4	1	2	0	18	0	17	9	2
Brown, Todd, Fort Lauderdale°	.247	56	146	10	36	44	8	0	0	16	0	2	0	22	1	32	3	1
Brumfield, Jacob, Baseball City	.336	109	372	66	125	155	24	3	0	40	2	2	2	60	6	44	47	10
Burnett, Joe, Miami	.179	12	28	3	5	5	0	0	0	1	0	0	0	5	0	12	2	2
Burnitz, Jeromy, St. Lucie°	.156	11	32	6	5	6	1	0	0	3	0	0	4	7	0	12	1	0
Busby, LeWayne, Sarasota	.186	23	70	11	13	16	3	0	0	6	0	0	1	6	0	7	2	2
Butterfield, Christian, St. Lucie†	.197	118	386	50	76	108	10	5	4	36	7	2	4	64	5	128	21	9
Campbell, Darrin, Sarasota	.235	93	319	26	75	99	10	1	4	37	2	4	2	26	4	67	4	4
Carey, Paul, Miami°	.327	49	153	23	50	73	5	3	4	20	0	1	2	43	1	39	4	3
Carroll, Kevin, St. Lucie	.000	6	7	1	0	0	0	0	0	1	0	1	1	1	0	4	0	1
Carter, Edward, St. Petersburg°	.230	47	135	17	31	37	6	0	0	13	2	0	0	15	2	15	6	4
Castillo, Alberto, St. Lucie	.364	3	11	4	4	7	0	0	1	3	0	0	0	1	0	1	0	0
Cedeno, Domingo, Dunedin†	.221	124	493	64	109	162	12	10	7	61	4	8	2	48	2	127	10	6
Chasey, Mark, Sarasota°	.263	116	400	56	105	144	18	6	3	52	5	1	11	64	1	111	8	2
Chick, Bruce, Winter Haven	.227	37	128	10	29	31	2	0	0	4	0	0	0	11	0	23	4	2
Cole, Mark, Lakeland	.230	105	369	43	85	103	10	4	0	33	6	3	4	31	4	63	10	2
Coleman, Kenneth, Sarasota†	.249	65	225	23	56	67	6	1	1	22	7	3	2	14	0	30	14	8
Collier, Anthony, Vero Beach°	.276	115	380	58	105	140	21	1	4	59	1	4	7	57	5	74	14	11
Collins, Sean, Baseball City	.238	85	256	36	61	76	8	2	1	30	2	1	1	40	0	40	31	4
Colon, Felix, Winter Haven	.196	89	275	21	54	90	14	2	6	25	1	0	3	38	0	80	1	3
Cooper, Gary, Osceola	.154	8	26	4	4	8	4	0	0	2	0	1	1	3	0	3	0	0
Cornelius, Brian, Lakeland°	.238	34	122	17	29	41	5	2	1	15	0	0	1	6	0	15	1	0
Cortes, Hernan, Fort Lauderdale°	.303	84	277	46	84	112	21	2	1	25	2	2	0	51	2	51	1	1
Crespo, Michael, Charlotte†	.135	23	52	3	7	9	0	1	0	3	3	0	0	5	0	14	0	0
Cromer, Roy, St. Petersburg	.216	121	408	53	88	125	12	5	5	38	3	5	5	46	0	78	7	12
Cronk, Douglas, Charlotte°	.186	106	322	30	60	103	15	8	4	47	1	10	0	57	3	91	0	1
Cruz, Bernardo, Sarasota	.314	12	35	7	11	13	0	1	0	0	0	0	4	4	0	4	1	1
Cruz, Ivan, Lakeland°	.285	118	414	61	118	178	23	2	11	73	2	4	5	49	3	71	8	1
Cruz, Ruben, Osceola°	.000	1	1	0	0	0	0	0	0	0	0	0	0	0	0	0	0	0
Cummings, Brian, Clearwater°	.243	103	341	21	83	107	11	2	3	32	0	4	6	21	4	34	6	3
D'Alexander, Gregory, Miami	.218	63	220	17	48	56	8	0	0	24	4	2	1	20	0	43	2	3
Davis, Brian, St. Lucie	.176	5	17	2	3	3	0	0	0	2	0	0	0	2	0	4	1	0
Dean, Kevin, Osceola	.223	28	94	13	21	30	2	2	1	22	0	3	1	21	0	32	9	1
de la Rosa, Juan, Dunedin	.257	131	529	57	136	201	19	8	10	76	0	7	3	19	2	98	9	3
DeLeon, Huascar, Baseball City	.206	12	34	2	7	10	3	0	0	4	0	0	1	3	1	10	0	0
Delgado, Alexander, Winter Haven	.224	89	303	37	68	84	9	2	1	25	6	3	2	37	0	36	10	4
Dellicarri, Joseph, St. Lucie	.206	40	126	16	26	31	1	2	0	13	0	3	3	17	0	34	5	2
DeLoach, Bobby, St. Petersburg	.238	123	466	54	111	176	24	7	9	58	0	3	10	23	4	98	9	7
Devereaux, Todd, Fort Lauderdale°	.237	102	346	36	82	104	17	1	1	33	0	1	5	42	5	53	6	6
Dixon, Colin, Winter Haven	.246	117	414	35	102	124	19	0	1	39	1	3	9	31	1	64	4	1
Dostal, Bruce, Vero Beach°	.302	58	192	43	58	89	9	2	6	29	1	1	2	24	1	20	31	5
Douglas, Arthur, Charlotte	.286	3	7	0	2	2	0	0	0	0	0	0	1	0	0	3	1	0
Dozier, William, St. Lucie	.297	93	317	56	94	150	11	3	13	57	0	3	1	45	0	76	33	5
Dukes, Willie, Winter Haven	.186	24	70	6	13	18	5	0	0	8	1	0	0	8	1	30	1	0
Dullom, Kirk, Fort Lauderdale	.172	76	204	16	35	51	8	1	2	24	0	0	1	33	2	46	1	1
Durkin, Martin, Miami°	.256	109	360	52	92	135	16	6	5	29	3	1	4	36	5	83	20	6
Dyer, Linton, Baseball City	.196	42	92	15	18	19	1	0	0	6	1	2	1	19	0	27	4	0
Ebel, Dino, Vero Beach	.167	96	198	26	33	39	6	0	0	12	6	1	1	14	0	33	5	1
Ehrhard, Rodney, Fort Lauderdale	.197	78	254	27	50	76	7	2	5	18	3	2	1	30	1	68	7	0
Erhardt, Herbert, Fort Lauderdale°	.250	36	116	8	29	39	4	0	2	12	1	2	1	16	4	20	0	0
Fagnant, Ray, Winter Haven	.179	47	95	7	17	23	4	1	0	11	2	0	2	5	0	23	1	0
Faulk, James, W. Palm Beach°	.315	70	254	52	80	107	12	3	3	31	1	0	2	30	3	47	33	4
Federico, Joseph, St. Petersburg°	.162	31	99	6	16	18	2	0	0	9	0	0	1	10	0	24	0	0
Ferguson, James, St. Petersburg	.333	6	3	2	1	1	0	0	0	0	0	0	0	2	0	1	0	1
Fernandez, Jose, St. Petersburg°	.254	42	138	12	35	48	10	0	1	19	0	0	0	34	2	39	0	1
Fielitz, William, St. Petersburg	.077	7	13	0	1	1	0	0	0	0	0	0	0	1	0	5	0	0
Fiore, Michael, St. Petersburg	.271	118	436	57	118	161	24	2	5	56	1	7	4	53	3	36	19	13
Fletcher, Robert, W. Palm Beach°	.260	103	393	59	102	132	15	6	1	32	7	0	4	32	3	42	22	6
Foster, Bryan, Osceola	.218	35	110	15	24	25	1	0	0	4	4	0	0	11	0	34	2	0
Foster, Kevin, W. Palm Beach	.167	3	6	0	1	3	0	1	0	2	0	0	0	1	0	2	0	0
Fox, Blane, Winter Haven°	.222	65	212	23	47	66	6	5	1	17	2	2	3	18	2	30	10	2
Friedman, Jason, Winter Haven	.160	50	163	12	26	34	5	0	1	11	2	0	6	16	1	26	1	0
Frye, Jeffrey, Charlotte	.272	131	503	77	137	167	16	7	0	50	7	4	2	80	5	66	29	6
Fulton, Gregory, W. Palm Beach†	.260	44	169	27	44	75	10	6	3	39	0	3	1	11	1	25	3	0
Gaither, Horace, Sarasota°	.179	75	240	16	43	51	6	1	0	14	6	1	2	7	0	42	3	5
Galle, Michael, Lakeland	.095	9	21	2	2	2	0	0	0	4	1	2	0	2	0	5	0	0
Garber, Jeffrey, Baseball City	.215	129	446	53	96	130	12	2	6	46	4	6	8	53	0	96	17	4
Garcia, Librado, Miami	.177	30	79	8	14	19	0	1	1	5	1	2	0	5	0	24	4	1
Garczyk, Edward, Miami	.184	38	76	13	14	14	0	0	0	2	4	1	3	9	0	20	5	2
Garibaldo, Christobal, Baseball City	.205	93	303	27	62	74	8	2	0	20	4	1	4	16	1	33	4	6
Giannelli, Raymond, Dunedin°	.288	118	416	64	120	194	18	1	18	57	1	3	1	66	7	56	5	8
Gillette, Michael, Lakeland	.143	23	63	10	9	14	2	0	1	8	3	0	0	9	0	24	1	0
Giordano, Marc, Miami°	.224	122	343	31	77	93	10	0	2	38	3	0	5	71	6	94	8	6
Gomez, Pierre, Miami†	.000	7	4	2	0	0	0	0	0	0	0	0	0	2	0	4	0	0
Gonzalez, Clifford, Sarasota°	.239	109	348	35	83	108	10	3	3	40	4	6	1	40	4	44	7	8

Player and Club	Pct.	G.	AB.	R.	H.	TB.	2B.	3B.	HR.	RBI.	SH.	SF.	HP.	BB.	Int. BB.	SO.	SB.	CS.
Gonzalez, David, Baseball City	.206	20	68	8	14	17	3	0	0	4	1	0	0	4	0	16	6	4
Gonzalez, Eduardo, W. Palm Beach	.084	32	83	8	7	13	3	0	1	5	0	0	1	10	2	23	0	2
Gonzalez, Freddy, Vero Beach	.299	106	335	49	100	168	17	6	13	51	1	7	6	27	1	85	28	5
Gonzalez, Pedro, Vero Beach	.217	90	198	31	43	61	12	0	2	21	5	3	11	42	2	40	2	2
Goodale, Jeffrey, Lakeland	.244	107	308	40	75	100	14	4	1	31	2	4	6	49	4	76	4	6
Gorman, Dirk, Vero Beach°	.167	6	6	0	1	1	0	0	0	1	0	0	0	1	0	1	0	0
Grace, Michael, W. Palm Beach	.143	5	14	0	2	2	0	0	0	1	1	0	0	3	0	1	0	0
Graham, Gregory, Winter Haven†	.051	15	39	0	2	2	0	0	0	1	1	0	0	2	0	16	0	0
Graham, Steven, St. Petersburg°	.257	80	276	27	71	88	11	3	0	26	0	2	2	20	2	41	10	3
Graves, Steven, St. Lucie	.213	42	122	11	26	34	3	1	1	15	2	0	1	8	0	32	1	0
Gregory, Bradford, Miami	.000	17	1	0	0	0	0	0	0	0	0	0	0	0	0	0	0	0
Grier, Antron, St. Petersburg†	.244	98	352	37	86	98	8	2	0	26	3	4	5	27	2	66	15	21
Griesser, Grant, Baseball City	.248	44	129	10	32	38	3	0	1	9	0	1	6	14	2	24	2	1
Griffin, Mark, Vero Beach°	.189	31	106	12	20	24	2	1	0	6	0	0	0	11	0	14	16	3
Gutierrez, Joaquin, Miami	.220	121	381	39	84	106	15	2	1	35	13	1	1	40	2	63	8	6
Hall, Lamar, Miami	.294	39	143	15	42	52	6	2	0	14	4	0	1	8	1	24	8	5
Hargis, Daniel, W. Palm Beach	.226	13	31	1	7	10	3	0	0	2	1	0	0	1	0	11	1	1
Hartmann, Reid, St. Lucie†	.227	31	97	10	22	27	2	0	1	10	2	1	2	12	0	23	1	2
Hayes, Von, Clearwater°	.167	2	6	0	1	2	1	0	0	0	0	0	0	2	1	1	0	0
Hays, Daren, Charlotte°	.226	70	186	19	42	58	5	1	3	27	2	0	0	20	1	34	2	4
Henderson, David, Osceola	.184	86	250	43	46	59	7	0	2	23	5	3	7	39	1	63	10	5
Henderson, Derek, St. Lucie	.207	59	184	16	38	44	2	2	0	26	3	5	5	15	0	34	7	5
Hernandez, Henry, St. Petersburg°	.157	41	121	6	19	21	2	0	0	7	1	1	4	25	3	36	5	2
Hernandez, Jose, Charlotte	.255	121	388	43	99	130	14	7	1	44	11	2	4	50	4	122	11	8
Hodge, Timothy, Dunedin°	.244	91	291	30	71	98	14	2	3	30	3	2	1	37	1	90	5	5
Holley, Robert, Baseball City	.205	27	88	16	18	32	5	0	3	14	1	1	1	15	0	20	1	1
Hornacek, Jay, Sarasota	.143	17	35	1	5	9	1	0	1	2	1	0	0	5	0	8	0	0
Hudson, Lance, Miami†	.189	27	95	11	18	27	4	1	1	11	2	0	0	13	1	19	7	3
Hulse, Jeffery, Clearwater	.221	69	213	20	47	65	10	4	0	14	1	1	2	28	0	56	0	1
Hurst, Joseph, Lakeland	.301	75	286	38	86	138	12	5	10	47	1	5	1	25	3	50	19	6
Indriago, Juan, Baseball City†	.135	19	37	8	5	7	0	1	0	1	0	0	0	11	0	12	1	3
Infante, Kennedy, Clearwater	.293	42	157	21	46	67	11	2	2	22	1	1	3	8	0	11	1	1
Irish, Jeffrey, Dunedin	.200	10	15	2	3	3	0	0	0	1	0	0	0	4	0	5	0	0
Jenkins, Garrett, Winter Haven	.244	63	209	32	51	65	10	2	0	13	3	1	0	28	2	69	40	7
Jordan, Brian, St. Petersburg	.167	9	30	3	5	7	0	1	0	1	0	0	0	2	0	11	0	2
Kellner, Frank, Osceola†	.247	109	369	43	91	114	9	7	0	34	9	3	1	65	2	65	14	7
Kelly, Jimy, St. Lucie	.250	30	104	12	26	30	4	0	0	6	1	1	1	10	0	23	3	2
Kent, Jeffrey, Dunedin	.277	132	447	72	124	208	32	2	16	60	3	3	6	53	5	98	17	7
Kidd, Dennis, Miami°	.246	102	349	36	86	106	10	5	0	25	4	1	5	26	3	92	25	6
Kimberlin, Keith, Lakeland†	.260	122	419	56	109	135	16	5	0	35	21	1	1	54	4	68	16	3
Kindred, Vincent, St. Petersburg°	.181	55	155	18	28	35	5	1	0	11	0	1	3	17	1	30	3	4
Knoblauh, Jay, Fort Lauderdale	.288	96	361	54	104	150	18	2	8	48	1	0	5	30	0	59	26	6
Koenig, Gary, Baseball City	.229	89	275	23	63	74	11	0	0	22	2	0	5	14	1	68	0	3
Lake, Kenneth, W. Palm Beach	.245	103	306	39	75	116	8	6	7	52	2	1	6	35	4	76	8	9
Laker, Timothy, W. Palm Beach	.000	2	3	0	0	0	0	0	0	0	0	0	0	0	0	1	0	0
Lamphere, Lawrence, Osceola†	.186	74	167	28	31	38	7	0	0	22	6	2	5	30	0	35	11	7
Landrum, Terry, Miami	.152	26	66	4	10	12	2	0	0	2	0	0	1	1	0	12	0	3
Lansing, Michael, Miami	.242	61	207	20	50	65	5	2	2	11	3	0	1	29	0	35	15	5
Law, Travis, Charlotte	.198	58	182	21	36	47	5	3	0	9	0	0	1	24	0	31	7	6
Lewis, Alan, Vero Beach°	.354	15	48	6	17	20	3	0	0	8	0	0	0	8	2	2	0	0
Lewis, Mica, Osceola	.195	43	118	15	23	35	3	3	1	12	0	1	0	23	0	42	6	1
Livesey, Jeffrey, Fort Lauderdale	.176	45	148	11	26	44	6	0	4	15	2	1	2	15	0	55	0	3
Lofton, Kenneth, Osceola°	.331	124	481	98	159	190	15	5	2	35	8	3	3	61	2	77	62	16
Long, Kevin, Baseball City°	.282	85	308	53	87	120	17	5	2	33	7	2	0	32	0	28	22	6
Losa, William, Charlotte	.264	22	53	7	14	17	3	0	0	9	0	0	2	9	0	15	0	2
Lozinski, Anthony, Clearwater	.246	36	122	11	30	32	2	0	0	10	2	1	1	12	0	25	0	0
Lukachyk, Robert, Sarasota°	.243	118	428	56	104	157	23	9	4	36	4	4	2	31	4	88	17	8
Maclin, Lonnie, St. Petersburg	.387	31	119	18	46	64	6	3	2	17	0	1	0	11	0	12	6	2
Madsen, Lance, Osceola	.244	135	488	62	119	182	23	11	6	62	3	2	6	59	1	131	7	5
Makarewicz, Scott, Osceola	.277	94	343	35	95	123	12	2	4	49	8	3	4	21	0	62	0	1
Marabell, Scott, Vero Beach	.265	89	226	38	60	107	19	2	8	42	2	4	9	22	1	56	5	2
Marigny, Ronald, Lakeland	.251	55	203	26	51	63	5	2	1	18	5	0	2	25	2	22	6	7
Martin, Christopher, W. Palm Beach	.279	59	222	31	62	90	17	1	3	31	1	2	1	27	6	37	7	5
Martin, Darryl, Lakeland	.246	110	354	48	87	120	8	8	3	41	4	7	3	36	0	63	19	5
Martinez, Luis, St. Petersburg†	.311	19	74	14	23	30	3	2	0	9	0	0	3	2	1	6	3	2
Mason, Robert, W. Palm Beach	.148	26	61	5	9	9	0	0	0	5	3	0	1	3	0	20	0	0
Massarelli, John, Osceola	.295	120	396	55	117	137	8	3	2	50	5	7	2	41	4	73	54	6
Masse, William, Fort Lauderdale	.274	68	230	42	63	96	15	0	6	33	0	5	6	33	2	28	9	0
Matilla, Pedro, Winter Haven	.193	118	353	28	68	89	12	0	3	34	11	2	3	42	0	77	1	1
May, Lee, St. Lucie†	.253	124	447	70	113	142	17	6	0	35	7	2	7	46	2	122	52	18
Mayo, Todd, W. Palm Beach°	.261	108	375	54	98	106	6	1	0	28	6	0	6	52	3	39	9	13
McBride, Loy, St. Lucie	.249	81	297	43	74	104	11	8	1	37	3	3	2	27	0	60	30	11
McCoy, Homer, Charlotte	.231	45	160	19	37	55	11	0	3	18	0	0	1	23	0	35	0	0
McDevitt, Terrance, Clearwater°	.189	53	111	10	21	26	2	0	1	13	1	2	1	16	0	25	1	1
McGough, Gregory, Sarasota°	.190	9	21	2	4	5	1	0	0	1	0	0	2	2	1	5	0	0
McKinley, Timothy, Miami	.149	26	47	4	7	9	2	0	0	2	0	0	0	13	0	13	0	0
McNeely, Jeffrey, Winter Haven	.161	16	62	4	10	10	0	0	0	3	0	0	0	3	0	19	7	1
Mello, John, W. Palm Beach	.212	87	312	39	66	104	16	2	6	43	4	4	3	29	3	64	8	3
Michael, Steven, Winter Haven	.211	102	318	41	67	108	10	2	9	43	1	4	5	30	1	110	4	3
Miller, Scott, Dunedin	.214	17	42	2	9	9	0	0	0	5	0	0	0	2	0	7	0	0
Miller, William, Miami	.169	73	183	17	31	52	9	0	4	10	4	0	3	12	0	73	2	1
Millette, Joe, Clearwater	.183	108	295	31	54	59	5	0	0	18	7	6	7	29	0	53	4	4
Monzon, Jose, Dunedin	.303	30	76	11	23	30	5	1	0	7	1	0	1	10	0	19	1	0
Moore, Barton, Winter Haven	.205	82	185	18	38	43	3	1	0	10	4	1	0	27	0	46	35	6
Moore, Sean, Winter Haven	.255	123	431	46	110	155	19	7	4	33	1	0	3	32	3	99	17	7
Morris, Angel, Miami	.255	37	110	10	28	38	7	0	1	17	0	0	0	14	0	18	2	0
Morris, Roderick, Charlotte°	.255	120	436	66	111	136	11	4	2	45	8	4	2	42	3	66	18	10
Morrisette, James, St. Lucie	.268	89	313	53	84	123	13	1	8	48	2	4	9	33	1	78	16	6
Morrison, James, Winter Haven	.238	75	227	26	54	71	3	4	2	16	6	0	3	41	5	68	15	6
Moser, Ricky, Baseball City	.146	12	41	3	6	6	0	0	0	3	0	0	0	3	0	15	0	0
Munoz, Jose, Vero Beach†	.295	113	397	57	117	147	18	3	2	47	8	4	2	34	3	43	28	0
Munoz, Luis, Winter Haven	.129	32	70	6	9	12	3	0	0	5	1	0	1	4	1	18	0	0

Player and Club	Pct.	G.	AB.	R.	H.	TB.	2B.	3B.	HR.	RBI.	SH.	SF.	HP.	BB.	Int. BB.	SO.	SB.	CS.
Nelloms, Sylvester, Fort Lauderdale* ..	.236	120	407	44	96	128	16	5	2	47	1	4	3	46	7	88	14	10
Niethammer, Darren, Charlotte	.276	72	214	31	59	64	5	0	0	20	1	1	1	28	2	24	3	4
Noriega, Reynaldo, Fort Lauderdale† ..	.226	84	305	52	69	103	17	4	3	28	6	4	2	35	1	85	7	6
Norris, William, Winter Haven*	.189	28	95	8	18	20	2	0	0	11	0	1	0	9	1	21	0	0
Nyssen, Daniel, Osceola	.233	112	417	48	97	147	13	8	7	66	4	9	9	44	3	61	6	3
O'Halloran, Gregory, Dunedin*	.284	121	465	70	132	199	26	4	11	75	1	3	3	37	7	70	2	3
Ocasio, Javier, Sarasota	.292	127	497	65	145	167	13	3	1	45	10	1	12	55	1	67	45	27
Olah, Robert, St. Lucie	.257	84	288	29	74	99	10	0	5	45	3	3	3	19	2	54	1	1
Oller, Jeffrey, Charlotte*	.275	104	327	37	90	112	17	1	1	39	3	2	0	43	3	67	3	2
Ortiz, Joseph, Osceola	.146	19	48	3	7	9	2	0	0	4	0	0	3	3	0	9	0	0
Paulsen, Troy, Clearwater	.198	54	167	11	33	36	3	0	0	9	0	1	0	16	0	21	1	1
Payton, Raymond, Sarasota	.260	95	285	26	74	105	14	1	5	38	4	3	3	32	2	68	1	2
Peel, Jack, Charlotte	.229	87	271	43	62	104	14	2	8	40	0	3	5	20	2	43	4	1
Perozo, Ender, St. Lucie	.500	1	2	1	1	2	1	0	0	0	0	0	0	0	0	1	0	0
Peters, Rex, Vero Beach†	.267	129	408	65	109	155	19	0	9	72	3	6	3	88	11	50	15	3
Piazza, Michael, Vero Beach	.250	88	272	27	68	106	20	0	6	45	0	1	1	11	0	68	0	1
Pimentel, Edward, Fort Lauderdale	.192	115	355	36	68	83	10	1	1	18	2	1	11	30	1	57	10	6
Pledger, Kinnis, Sarasota*	.248	131	460	72	114	149	18	4	3	40	6	3	8	94	3	134	26	14
Prager, Howard, Osceola*	.248	99	331	44	82	104	11	4	1	45	3	2	2	61	5	49	2	4
Provence, Todd, Dunedin	.197	19	61	10	12	20	3	1	1	6	3	0	2	3	0	22	2	0
Raffo, Thomas, Miami	.258	67	225	16	58	80	13	0	3	30	0	3	5	24	1	46	1	2
Raley, Daniel, Lakeland*	.226	10	31	1	7	8	1	0	0	3	0	1	0	3	0	6	0	1
Redman, Timothy, St. Petersburg	.242	79	236	21	57	65	4	2	0	22	3	2	1	23	0	44	4	4
Reed, Toncie, Osceola	.191	89	277	21	53	76	8	6	1	26	2	0	5	25	2	76	7	5
Reimink, Robert, Lakeland†	.222	112	388	52	86	106	8	3	2	41	7	5	2	47	0	80	6	5
Riesgo, Nikco, St. Lucie	.298	131	456	93	136	219	35	3	14	94	0	5	8	74	10	77	46	14
Rigsby, Timothy, Miami	.232	54	164	19	38	46	6	1	0	14	5	0	1	14	0	43	4	4
Robertson, Roderick, Clearwater†	.216	58	204	17	44	59	7	1	2	21	5	2	2	18	1	30	8	3
Robinson, Darryl, Baseball City	.262	115	409	38	107	128	9	3	2	65	4	8	1	17	2	33	7	1
Rodriguez, Abimael, W. Palm Beach	.111	4	9	0	1	1	0	0	0	1	1	0	0	4	0	2	0	0
Rodriguez, Ivan, Charlotte	.287	109	408	48	117	154	17	7	2	55	1	4	7	12	2	50	1	0
Rosado, Edwin, Clearwater†	.171	63	170	14	29	36	3	2	0	14	6	0	2	10	2	30	2	0
Roth, Gregory, Sarasota*	.210	62	186	33	39	53	7	2	1	17	1	0	0	56	2	53	1	0
Sable, Luke, Charlotte	.267	67	206	24	55	70	5	5	0	23	1	1	0	23	0	30	18	7
Samson, Frederick, Charlotte	.286	104	350	60	100	138	21	1	5	38	6	4	2	51	3	68	12	8
Sanchez, John, W. Palm Beach*	.143	2	7	1	1	1	0	0	0	0	0	0	0	0	0	1	0	0
Santangelo, Frank, W. Palm Beach†	.277	116	394	63	109	132	19	2	0	38	18	2	5	51	2	49	22	7
Sardinha, Eduardo, Miami	.176	13	34	2	6	6	0	0	0	1	0	0	0	1	0	8	1	0
Saunders, Douglas, St. Lucie	.225	115	408	52	92	111	8	4	1	43	7	2	2	43	0	96	24	10
Scarsone, Steven, Clearwater	.275	59	211	20	58	86	9	5	3	23	5	1	4	19	1	57	3	4
Schreiner, John, Baseball City	.161	8	31	2	5	8	0	0	1	3	0	0	1	0		8	0	0
Sellick, John, St. Petersburg	.197	110	370	49	73	124	20	2	9	44	0	3	6	59	4	105	7	4
Shelton, Harry, Miami*	.254	107	346	34	88	103	15	0	0	26	3	0	0	24	1	68	26	7
Shireman, Jeffrey, St. Petersburg†	.255	123	415	61	106	118	10	1	0	37	0	5	1	87	0	34	11	13
Siddall, Joseph, W. Palm Beach*	.223	106	349	29	78	92	12	1	0	32	10	2	1	20	0	55	6	7
Singley, Joseph, 17 Mia.-27 Sara.	.178	44	118	7	21	29	5	0	1	6	3	2	1	0	0	35	1	1
Smith, Edward, Sarasota	.192	63	239	22	46	74	10	3	4	23	1	3	7	11	1	61	0	3
Smith, Chad, Miami†	.000	22	1	0	0	0	0	0	0	0	0	0	0	0	0	0	0	0
Smith, Joel, W. Palm Beach†	.203	52	177	18	36	48	4	1	2	20	1	0	3	14	1	58	14	2
Spann, Emmanuel, Lakeland	.194	23	72	11	14	19	3	1	0	3	0	1	0	11	1	22	1	0
Stairs, Matthew, W. Palm Beach	.339	55	183	30	62	86	9	3	3	30	0	2	5	41	4	19	15	2
Sullivan, Carl, Sarasota*	.207	34	116	7	24	27	3	0	0	10	1	0	2	8	2	24	3	3
Swain, Thayer, Charlotte	.245	105	322	44	79	106	19	4	0	25	4	4	1	42	0	73	15	13
Taveras, Marcos, Dunedin	.258	41	62	16	16	26	2	1	2	6	1	0	1	7	0	15	2	1
Taylor, David, Miami	.154	9	13	0	2	2	0	0	0	0	0	0	1	2	0	7	1	1
Taylor, Michael, Dunedin	.237	69	169	29	40	47	7	0	0	14	5	2	0	32	0	37	8	6
Tedder, Scott, Sarasota*	.283	121	381	65	108	118	6	2	0	47	2	3	0	90	6	46	13	9
Teel, Garett, Vero Beach	.000	8	14	1	0	0	0	0	0	0	1	0	1	0	6	0	4	0	0
Tejada, Alejandro, Sarasota	.083	5	12	0	1	1	0	0	0	0	1	0	0	0	0	5	0	1
Tenhunfeld, Joseph, Clearwater	.191	74	204	22	39	52	9	2	0	13	2	1	2	11	0	69	1	0
Terris, Adam, W. Palm Beach*	.250	108	352	53	88	119	14	1	5	48	3	3	0	56	2	60	0	5
Thomas, Orlando, St. Petersburg	.250	23	48	4	12	17	3	1	0	5	1	0	3	10	0	19	0	2
Thompson, Ryan, Dunedin	.231	117	438	56	101	144	15	5	6	37	3	4	2	20	1	100	18	5
Threadgill, George, Charlotte	.238	20	63	5	15	23	3	1	1	9	0	2	2	9	0	13	2	2
Townley, Jason, Dunedin	.292	119	397	58	116	173	22	1	11	63	5	3	3	41	0	82	1	2
Tresh, Michael, Lakeland†	.268	122	471	69	126	156	16	4	2	49	7	5	3	37	2	59	19	7
Trevino, Antonio, Clearwater	.258	133	465	60	120	162	20	5	4	62	2	7	10	65	1	85	2	5
Trujillo, Jose, St. Petersburg	.177	28	79	11	14	17	3	0	0	8	0	0	1	2	0	12	0	2
Turgeon, David, Fort Lauderdale	.211	98	331	28	70	86	13	0	1	30	3	5	0	29	1	42	1	2
Urbon, Joseph, Clearwater*	.257	60	191	21	49	61	8	2	0	16	2	1	0	19	1	35	2	2
Vargas, Hector, Fort Lauderdale	.308	117	429	48	132	170	20	9	0	61	4	11	3	30	1	68	22	11
Varni, Patrick, Miami	.129	50	93	11	12	20	5	0	1	9	2	1	1	16	0	27	3	0
Ventress, Leroy, Clearwater†	.193	39	140	24	27	29	2	0	0	9	2	1	0	26	0	30	12	5
Villalobos, Gary, Winter Haven	.271	88	291	33	79	99	14	3	0	19	9	1	1	9	1	53	5	10
Walker, Hugh, Baseball City*	.244	128	463	51	113	152	15	6	4	54	0	4	5	32	5	107	28	17
Waller, Casey, Clearwater†	.284	59	208	29	59	105	14	4	8	31	0	1	6	18	0	31	4	1
Watkins, Darren, Baseball City	.250	120	448	53	112	146	18	5	2	48	4	3	7	31	1	134	40	11
Weimerskirch, Michael, W. P. Beach	.282	22	71	13	20	23	3	0	0	4	0	1	2	8	1	11	1	0
Weinheimer, Wayne, Miami	.204	71	206	17	42	61	8	1	3	22	1	1	4	22	1	67	3	0
Williams, Cary, Clearwater*	.261	63	245	20	64	85	12	3	1	21	2	1	7	7	0	33	2	2
Williams, Fred, W. Palm Beach	.232	82	254	26	59	82	5	6	2	29	5	1	1	46	2	72	9	1
Williams, Gerald, Fort Lauderdale	.289	50	204	25	59	94	4	5	7	43	0	2	2	16	1	52	19	5
Williams, Reginald, Charlotte	.267	7	30	4	8	10	2	0	0	2	0	0	1	0		10	1	2
Wismer, Michael, Vero Beach*	.198	61	187	19	37	43	6	0	0	15	4	3	1	21	1	36	9	2
Witherspoon, Richard, Winter Haven	.179	34	106	16	19	29	2	1	2	6	0	0	3	16	0	34	7	1
Woodruff, Patrick, Clearwater	.240	135	496	60	119	159	18	8	2	49	7	3	1	46	0	92	32	14
Wright, Donald, Baseball City	.250	20	48	7	12	21	1	1	2	11	0	0	0	9	0	11	1	1
Young, Derrick, St. Lucie	.257	79	245	40	63	81	5	2	3	30	5	1	1	37	2	54	14	8
Young, Eric, Vero Beach	.287	127	460	101	132	175	23	7	2	50	5	4	6	69	1	35	76	16
Young, Mark, Dunedin	.237	117	409	72	97	138	14	6	5	38	3	1	4	58	1	88	31	11
Zambrano, Jose, Winter Haven	.270	88	307	30	83	115	14	3	4	32	4	0	3	23	0	72	6	4
Zinter, Alan, St. Lucie†	.291	98	333	63	97	149	19	6	7	63	0	6	1	54	1	70	8	1

The following pitchers, listed alphabetically by club, with games in parentheses, had no plate appearances, primarily through use of designated hitters:

BASEBALL CITY—Alicano, Alberto (20); Berumen, Andres (9); Brucato, Robert (4); Chrisman, James (2); Drohan, William (7); Dunn, William (19); Harvey, Gregory (7); Harwell, David (13); Hoeme, Steven (33); Hopper, Bradley (30); Hudson, James (16); Johnston, Joel (31); Magee, Byron (32); McCormick, John (11); Nelson, Douglas (1); Otto, Steven (24); Parnell, Mark (36); Pichardo, Hipolito (11); Pierce, Benjamin (18); Pierce, Edward (37); Sanchez, Israel (7); Shaw, Kevin (10); Vaughn, Randall (21); Webster, Michael (7).

CHARLOTTE—Alexander, Gerald (7); Arner, Michael (12); Brown, Robert (40); Cecena, Jose (20); Compres, Fidel (22); Cunningham, Everett (11); Gore, Bryan (23); Guzman, Jose (2); Hurst, Jonathan (6); Hvizda, James (13); MacNeil, Timothy (7); Nen, Robb (11); Pavlik, Roger (11); Perez, David (14); Reitzel, Michael (13); Romero, Brian (12); Rowley, Stephen (5); Russell, Jeffrey (1); Shaw, Cedric (11); Spencer, Kyle (43); Stafford, Timothy (1).

CLEARWATER—Backs, Jason (15); Borland, Toby (44); Brantley, Clifford (8); Carter, Andrew (26); Christopher, Fredrick (32); Dell, Timothy (17); Elam, Todd (32); Fletcher, Paul (20); Fynan, Kevin (9); Gunderson, Gregory (10); Langley, Wesley (9); Lindsey, Darrell (26); Madrid, Alexander (5); Martin, John (1); McCarthy, Gregory (42); Ontiveros, Steven (3); Patterson, Jeffrey (11); Randall, Mark (16); Stevens, Matthew (10); Sullivan, Michael (13); Tabaka, Jeffrey (8); Wells, Robert (6); Wiegandt, Scott (33).

DUNEDIN—Aylmer, Robert (8); Blohm, Peter (2); Boucher, Denis (9); Brown, Timothy (36); Cross, Jesse (28); DePastino, Richard (22); Horsman, Vincent (28); Jordan, Ricardo (13); Key, James (3); Leiter, Alois (6); Martin, Gregg (12); Rudolph, Blaine (35); Silverstein, Allan (45); Timlin, Michael (42); Trlicek, Richard (26); Ward, Anthony (27); Weathers, David (27).

FORT LAUDERDALE—Brubaker, Franklin (40); Burns, Britt (4); Draper, Michael (14); Garcia, Victor (20); Gietzen, Peter (23); Gogolewski, Douglas (16); Green, John (5); Green, Kenneth (38); Johnson, Jeffrey (17); Malone, Todd (8); Manon, Ramon (11); Marris, Mark (27); Newell, Thomas (7); Ohlms, Mark (21); Perez, Pascual (1); Popplewell, Thomas (15); Rub, Jerry (15); Seiler, Keith (8); Smith, Shad (1); Stanford, Lawrence (57); Tucker, Stephen (21).

LAKELAND—Alcantara, Francisco (2); Berrios, Hector (21); Cook, Ronald (43); Debrand, Genaro (1); DeSilva, John (14); Doherty, John (30); Ettles, Mark (45); Ferm, Edward (18); Gohr, Gregory (25); Hursey, Darrin (25); Knudsen, Kurt (14); Krumm, Todd (25); Lira, Felipe (1); Lumley, Michael (13); Marshall, Randy (13); Rivera, Lino (36); Torres, Leonardo (12); Willis, Marty (34).

MIAMI—Alexander, David (16); Boyle, Robert (4); Cakora, Matthew (45); Czarnetzki, Michael (1); Daniel, Clayton (16); Delgado, Timothy (4); Ericson, Michael (25); Kelley, Anthony (30); Kerfut, George (45); Lugo, Angel (22); MacNeil, Timothy (10); Magria, Javier (19); Michno, Thomas (31); Olson, Daniel (1); Pascual, Jorge (37); Ponder, Kevin (17); Reitzel, Michael (13); Rogers, Thomas (14); Sauveur, Richard (11); Williams, Kenneth (13).

OSCEOLA—Bauer, Peter (24); Black, Scott (13); Dovey, Troy (6); Dunnum, Rick (51); Griffiths, Brian (28); Hyson, Cole (26); Jones, Todd (27); Juden, Jeffrey (15); Luckham, Kenneth (27); Mallicoat, Robbin (3); Ponte, Edward (32); Rambo, Matthew (25); Rodriguez, Gabriel (51); Tafoya, Dennis (22); Windes, Rodney (44).

ST. LUCIE—Brady, Michael R. (38); Corbin, Archie (20); Furmanik, Daniel (22); Hansell, Gregory (6); Harriger, Dennis (27); Hill, Christopher (27); Hillman, Eric (4); Johnson, Paul (22); Johnstone, John (25); LaRose, Steven (17); Mejia, Cesar (2); Newton, Stephen (31); Perez, Vladimir (19); Reich, Andrew (2); Rogers, Bryan (29); Schourek, Peter (5); Telgheder, David (14).

ST. PETERSBURG—Burgos, John (19); Clark, Mark (10); Duvall, Bradley (1); Ericks, John (4); Green, Donald (35); Grimes, David (58); Hitt, Daniel (27); Hoffman, Richard (23); Keller, Clyde (15); Lata, Timothy (8); Majer, Steffen (14); Meamber, Timothy (6); Milchin, Michael (11); Pacheco, Albert (5); Plemel, Lee (10); Richardson, David (47); Satterfield, Cory (17); Shackle, Richard (8); Smith, Kenneth (17); Tolbert, Mark (5); Vargas, Jose (38); Weese, Dean (20); Wiseman, Dennis (17).

SARASOTA—Dabney, Frederick (24); Davino, Michael (46); Fernandez, Alexander (2); Forrester, Thomas (20); Galvan, Michael (39); Garcia, Ramon (26); Gennings, Brian (8); Keyser, Brian (38); King, Eric (2); Merigliano, Frank (21); Middaugh, Scott (22); Perschke, Gregory (42); Resnikoff, Robert (45); Smith, Roosevelt (4); Ventura, Jose (25); Wickman, Robert (2).

VERO BEACH—Astacio, Pedro (8); Bene, William (17); Biberdorf, Cameron (48); Brady, Michael K. (9); Bustillos, Albert (22); Calhoun, Raymond (31); Delahoya, Javier (4); Enno, Clayton (29); Fischer, Jeffrey (5); Fletcher, Randel (2); Knapp, John (26); Nina, Robin (7); Patrick, Tim (4); Perez, Pedro (15); Taveras, Ramon (26); Terrill, James (23); Treadwell, Jody (16); Vanzytveld, Jeffrey (17); Wengert, William (22).

WEST PALM BEACH—Ciaglo, Paul (1); Collins, Stacey (16); Cornelius, Jonathan (11); Davis, Bret (43); Freed, Daniel (26); Kerrigan, Robert (5); Lewis, Richie (10); Logan, Joseph (6); Piatt, Douglas (21); Pollack, Christopher (24); Reyes, Rafael (16); Shehan, Brian (2); Sommer, David (29); Thoden, John (13); Tuss, Jeffrey (29); Wainhouse, David (12); Wenrick, John (21); Young, Bryan (39).

WINTER HAVEN—Allen, Tracy (18); Burgo, Dale (4); Crouch, Matthew (3); Davis, Freddie (3); Delgado, Richard (12); Dennison, James (8); Hansell, Gregory (21); Hoy, Peter (52); Kane, Thomas (34); Kite, Daniel (15); Miller, Todd (1); Mosley, Anthony (29); Painter, Gary (4); Quantrill, Paul (7); Richardson, Ronnie (34); Riley, Edward (31); Rush, Andrew (30); Sanders, Alan (31); Thompson, Michael (15).

GRAND SLAM HOME RUNS—Cedeno, Riesgo, 2 each; C. Alvarez, Collier, Cornelius, Cronk, de la Rosa, Payton, Peel, Reed, Robinson, Sellick, Walker, Woodruff, 1 each.

AWARDED FIRST BASE ON CATCHER'S INTERFERENCE—Kidd 5 (P. Gonzalez, Koenig, O'Halloran, I. Rodriguez, Zinter); Devereaux 3 (Marabell, Mason, Zinter); Ventress 2 (I. Rodriguez, Townley); Ebel (Balthazar); Friedman (Koenig); S. Graham (Matilla); Da. Henderson (Dyer); Jenkins (Makarewicz); Knoblauh (Albright); Lake (Erhardt); Martinez (I. Rodriguez); McGough (Monzon); Peel (C. Alvarez); Scarsone (Campbell).

CLUB FIELDING

Club	Pct.	G.	PO.	A.	E.	DP.	PB.	Club	Pct.	G.	PO.	A.	E.	DP.	PB.
Charlotte	.970	138	3604	1463	155	94	20	Baseball City	.964	138	3507	1385	183	108	42
West Palm Beach	.970	132	3497	1419	152	110	12	Miami	.963	137	3470	1391	187	112	10
Lakeland	.969	133	3429	1391	155	106	20	Sarasota	.963	138	3623	1314	190	109	29
Dunedin	.968	136	3610	1571	170	126	18	Clearwater	.962	137	3481	1442	197	123	21
Vero Beach	.965	136	3492	1500	180	112	18	Fort Lauderdale	.960	137	3500	1428	203	113	26
St. Petersburg	.964	134	3553	1389	182	108	22	Osceola	.958	138	3639	1504	227	108	21
St. Lucie	.964	134	3435	1480	183	117	20	Winter Haven	.956	134	3486	1325	223	98	19

Triple Plays—Miami 2, Dunedin, Fort Lauderdale, St. Lucie, St. Petersburg, Sarasota.

INDIVIDUAL FIELDING

*Throws lefthanded.

FIRST BASEMEN

Player and Club	Pct.	G.	PO.	A.	E.	DP.	Player and Club	Pct.	G.	PO.	A.	E.	DP.
Abreu, St. Petersburg	1.000	2	1	0	0	0	Cortes, Fort Lauderdale*	.986	54	450	28	7	37
Acta, Osceola	.968	33	205	10	7	18	Cronk, Charlotte*	.989	101	815	49	10	60
Aldrich, Lakeland	.981	26	198	13	4	14	Cruz, Lakeland*	.989	106	938	44	11	75
Anglero, Baseball City	1.000	1	2	0	0	0	Cummings, Clearwater*	.983	52	425	26	8	37
Angotti, Osceola	1.000	9	45	1	0	0	Dellicarri, St. Lucie	1.000	1	3	0	0	0
Bargman, Miami	.917	2	11	0	1	1	Devereaux, Fort Lauderdale*	.992	44	374	19	3	24
Barragan, Clearwater*	.985	13	127	5	2	9	Dixon, Winter Haven	.954	12	77	6	4	12
Beacom, Dunedin	.990	65	560	29	6	46	Durkin, Miami	1.000	3	2	0	0	0
Beall, Baseball City*	.987	44	341	28	5	39	Erhardt, Fort Lauderdale	1.000	8	59	4	0	6
Beard, Vero Beach	1.000	4	22	4	0	4	Federico, St. Petersburg*	.979	26	226	8	5	18
Beaulac, Miami*	1.000	15	95	4	0	11	Fiore, St. Petersburg	1.000	8	53	1	0	4
Bible, Miami	1.000	1	2	0	0	0	Fox, Winter Haven*	1.000	4	26	0	0	3
Boyce, Miami	1.000	10	66	8	0	4	Friedman, Winter Haven	.972	40	328	22	10	30
Brown, Fort Lauderdale	1.000	9	63	2	0	5	Fulton, West Palm Beach	1.000	18	144	6	0	15
Carey, Miami	.889	2	7	1	1	0	Giannelli, Dunedin	.989	79	691	45	8	69
Chasey, Sarasota*	.981	112	847	54	17	69	Giordano, Miami*	1.000	21	131	9	0	9
Colon, Winter Haven	.993	18	130	7	1	6	E. Gonzalez, West Palm Beach...	.987	11	70	4	1	7

FIRST BASEMEN—Continued

Player and Club	Pct.	G.	PO.	A.	E.	DP.	Player and Club	Pct.	G.	PO.	A.	E.	DP.
F. Gonzalez, Vero Beach	.988	21	157	12	2	18	Peters, Vero Beach*	.992	116	956	87	8	75
P. Gonzalez, Vero Beach	1.000	2	6	0	0	0	Piazza, Vero Beach	.967	10	54	4	2	4
Griesser, Baseball City	1.000	8	63	5	0	4	Prager, Osceola*	.982	89	799	39	15	61
Hernandez, St. Petersburg*	.969	28	236	17	8	14	Provence, Dunedin	.938	1	14	1	1	0
Holley, Baseball City	1.000	2	15	0	0	2	Raffo, Miami*	.991	66	500	51	5	46
Hornacek, Sarasota	1.000	2	11	2	0	1	Raley, Lakeland	.944	3	16	1	1	2
Infante, Clearwater	.957	3	21	1	1	3	Reimink, Lakeland	1.000	1	3	0	0	0
Lake, West Palm Beach	1.000	1	7	2	0	0	Riesgo, St. Lucie	.983	89	781	50	14	73
Long, Baseball City*	.974	14	102	9	3	7	Robinson, Baseball City	.993	72	529	48	4	36
Martin, Lakeland	1.000	1	2	1	0	1	Rosado, Clearwater	1.000	1	15	2	0	0
Massarelli, Osceola	.942	10	76	5	5	8	Schreiner, Baseball City	.987	8	71	6	1	9
McKinley, Miami	1.000	1	1	0	0	0	Sellick, St. Petersburg	.983	81	686	53	13	55
Mello, West Palm Beach	1.000	15	94	6	0	8	Singley, Miami	1.000	1	4	0	0	1
Michael, Winter Haven	.975	68	502	34	14	34	Smith, Sarasota	1.000	7	40	5	0	4
Miller, Miami	1.000	4	14	0	0	1	Tedder, Sarasota*	.988	24	163	8	2	18
Morrisette, St. Lucie	1.000	1	1	0	0	0	Tenhunfeld, Clearwater	1.000	2	5	0	0	0
Moser, Baseball City	.833	1	5	0	1	0	TERRIS, West Palm Beach*	.993	101	836	51	6	72
Niethammer, Charlotte	.991	52	395	27	4	23	Trevino, Clearwater	.993	69	538	40	4	59
Olah, St. Lucie	.991	53	412	35	4	29	Turgeon, Fort Lauderdale	.985	33	240	23	4	25
Ortiz, Osceola	.985	19	116	12	2	11	Weinheimer, Miami	.987	38	277	20	4	27
Peel, Charlotte	.900	1	8	1	1	1	Young, Dunedin	.875	1	5	2	1	0

Triple Plays—Beacom, Hernandez, Raffo, Riesgo, Turgeon.

SECOND BASEMEN

Player and Club	Pct.	G.	PO.	A.	E.	DP.	Player and Club	Pct.	G.	PO.	A.	E.	DP.
Abreu, St. Petersburg	.813	3	6	7	3	1	McDevitt, Clearwater	.918	19	18	38	5	4
Alicea, St. Petersburg	1.000	11	20	23	0	8	Mello, West Palm Beach	1.000	21	56	55	0	15
Alvarez, Vero Beach	.975	69	112	206	8	36	Miller, Dunedin	1.000	8	8	20	0	1
Anglero, Baseball City	1.000	3	1	4	0	0	Millette, Clearwater	1.000	3	4	7	0	1
Bridges-Clements, Baseball City	.976	33	72	89	4	22	Moore, Winter Haven	.964	70	167	159	12	24
Busby, Sarasota	1.000	2	4	8	0	1	Moser, Baseball City	.800	2	2	2	1	1
Butterfield, St. Lucie	.900	5	10	17	3	4	J. Munoz, Vero Beach	.917	4	5	6	1	0
Cole, Lakeland	.962	86	167	233	16	42	L. Munoz, Winter Haven	1.000	9	8	9	0	4
Coleman, Sarasota	.945	54	118	123	14	29	Noriega, Fort Lauderdale	.952	78	158	215	19	44
Collins, Baseball City	.964	70	136	184	12	34	Ocasio, Sarasota	.960	79	164	194	15	39
Colon, Winter Haven	.860	15	16	27	7	5	Paulsen, Clearwater	.955	41	90	100	9	22
Delgado, Winter Haven	1.000	9	17	26	0	5	Pimentel, Fort Lauderdale	.957	62	115	153	12	31
Dellicarri, St. Lucie	.833	2	1	4	1	0	Reimink, Lakeland	.964	43	82	105	7	25
Durkin, Miami	.883	21	45	38	11	13	Rigsby, Miami	.936	29	48	55	7	15
Fletcher, West Palm Beach	.957	84	164	214	17	43	Robertson, Clearwater	.964	26	43	64	4	13
FRYE, Charlotte	.979	129	252	350	13	61	Roth, Sarasota	.857	5	7	11	3	5
Gaither, Sarasota	.500	1	0	1	1	0	Sable, Charlotte	.979	11	22	25	1	5
Garber, Baseball City	.931	30	42	66	8	14	Santangelo, West Palm Beach	.981	14	24	29	1	3
Garczyk, Miami	.968	34	63	59	4	11	Sardinha, Miami	.917	3	6	5	1	1
Garibaldo, Baseball City	1.000	1	1	1	0	0	Saunders, St. Lucie	.975	115	233	349	15	75
Gomez, Miami	.833	2	2	3	1	0	Scarsone, Clearwater	.953	59	116	147	13	35
Graham, Winter Haven	1.000	3	6	6	0	1	Shireman, St. Petersburg	.965	104	156	255	15	41
Gutierrez, Miami	.970	46	73	120	6	23	Taylor, Dunedin	1.000	10	13	19	0	5
Hartmann, St. Lucie	.959	16	30	41	3	12	Tejada, Sarasota	.750	1	1	2	1	0
Henderson, Osceola	.948	42	76	108	10	19	Tresh, Lakeland	.930	9	17	23	3	8
Indriago, Baseball City	.973	15	16	20	1	3	Trujillo, St. Petersburg	.991	24	36	72	1	17
Kellner, Osceola	.956	26	52	78	6	13	Varni, Miami	.946	27	37	51	5	7
Kent, Dunedin	.978	128	261	404	15	83	Villalobos, Winter Haven	.971	48	85	113	6	17
Lamphere, Osceola	.961	41	74	121	8	28	Williams, West Palm Beach	.958	27	54	61	5	18
Lewis, Osceola	.948	36	74	110	10	14	E. Young, Vero Beach	.936	74	135	216	24	33
							M. Young, Dunedin	1.000	1	1	0	0	0

Triple Plays—Kent, Noriega, Ocasio, Saunders.

THIRD BASEMEN

Player and Club	Pct.	G.	PO.	A.	E.	DP.	Player and Club	Pct.	G.	PO.	A.	E.	DP.
Abreu, St. Petersburg	.901	73	47	126	19	7	Hartmann, St. Lucie	.944	7	7	10	1	3
Acta, Osceola	1.000	6	3	11	0	0	Holley, Baseball City	.833	3	2	3	1	0
C. Alvarez, Sarasota	.667	1	1	1	1	0	Indriago, Baseball City	.500	3	0	1	1	0
J. Alvarez, Vero Beach	.919	17	7	27	3	2	Infante, Clearwater	.902	19	14	32	5	6
Anglero, 11 B.C.-21 Lake.	.911	32	18	54	7	3	Kellner, Osceola	1.000	2	0	1	0	0
Beacom, Dunedin	.972	14	6	29	1	3	Lamphere, Osceola	.875	6	2	5	1	0
Boyce, Miami	.857	6	3	9	2	2	Lewis, Vero Beach	.950	13	9	29	2	4
Brown, Fort Lauderdale	.846	18	9	24	6	1	Lukachyk, Sarasota	.844	13	9	18	5	1
Busby, Sarasota	.900	4	2	7	1	0	MADSEN, Osceola	.870	130	115	265	57	16
Butterfield, St. Lucie	.904	89	54	173	24	13	Marigny, Lakeland	.933	49	28	83	8	9
Campbell, Sarasota	1.000	2	2	1	0	0	McDevitt, Clearwater	1.000	3	3	3	0	0
Coleman, Sarasota	.917	7	4	7	1	0	Mello, West Palm Beach	.889	48	40	80	15	9
Colon, Winter Haven	.889	23	13	27	5	5	Moore, Winter Haven	1.000	3	1	4	0	0
D'Alexander, Miami	.894	60	47	113	19	8	Morrisette, St. Lucie	.888	37	26	77	13	9
Delgado, Winter Haven	.875	11	11	17	4	2	Moser, Baseball City	.833	9	6	9	3	1
Dixon, Winter Haven	.880	80	58	118	24	5	J. Munoz, Vero Beach	.873	57	31	79	16	3
Dullom, Fort Lauderdale	.853	38	30	63	16	5	L. Munoz, Winter Haven	.750	5	3	3	2	1
Durkin, Miami	.735	11	7	18	9	2	Norris, Winter Haven	.887	24	12	43	7	5
Dyer, Baseball City	.750	2	1	5	2	0	Oller, Charlotte	.852	50	24	68	16	7
Ferguson, St. Petersburg	1.000	6	2	6	0	1	Paulsen, Clearwater	.000	1	0	0	1	0
Fiore, St. Petersburg	.897	58	35	96	15	6	Pimentel, Fort Lauderdale	.889	51	31	73	13	7
Fletcher, West Palm Beach	.854	19	15	20	6	2	Provence, Dunedin	.870	12	6	14	3	0
Foster, West Palm Beach	1.000	2	2	1	0	0	Reimink, Lakeland	.952	65	41	97	7	9
Fulton, West Palm Beach	.954	25	25	37	3	2	Riesgo, St. Lucie	1.000	1	2	6	0	0
Gaither, Sarasota	.778	11	7	7	4	1	Rigsby, Miami	.880	10	2	20	3	2
Galle, Vero Beach	.875	9	3	11	2	0	Robinson, Baseball City	.925	38	31	68	8	6
Garber, Baseball City	.929	85	60	124	14	14	Rosado, Clearwater	1.000	1	1	0	0	0
Giannelli, Dunedin	.950	36	20	75	5	5	Roth, Sarasota	.925	52	30	81	9	9
Gonzalez, Vero Beach	.750	3	1	5	2	0	Sable, Charlotte	.946	22	16	37	3	2
Grace, West Palm Beach	.909	5	4	6	1	1	Samson, Charlotte	.921	72	43	154	17	9
Hall, Miami	.916	37	29	58	8	7	Santangelo, West Palm Beach	.815	9	6	16	5	4

THIRD BASEMEN—Continued

Player and Club	Pct.	G.	PO.	A.	E.	DP.	Player and Club	Pct.	G.	PO.	A.	E.	DP.
Sardinha, Miami	.960	11	6	18	1	1	Tresh, Lakeland	.926	7	4	21	2	1
Shireman, St. Petersburg	.933	15	8	20	2	2	Trevino, Clearwater	.898	60	41	100	16	6
Smith, Sarasota	.894	59	51	92	17	11	Turgeon, Fort Lauderdale	.939	43	26	81	7	5
Stairs, West Palm Beach	.906	38	24	72	10	5	Varni, Miami	.893	21	12	13	3	1
Taylor, Dunedin	.935	50	22	79	7	13	Waller, Clearwater	.918	58	43	126	15	9
Teel, Vero Beach	1.000	1	0	1	0	0	Wismer, Vero Beach	.921	54	37	80	10	10
Tejada, Sarasota	.889	3	3	5	1	0	Young, Dunedin	.912	51	22	81	10	7

Triple Play—Pimentel.

SHORTSTOPS

Player and Club	Pct.	G.	PO.	A.	E.	DP.	Player and Club	Pct.	G.	PO.	A.	E.	DP.
Abreu, St. Petersburg	.925	10	14	35	4	5	Kelly, St. Lucie	.922	27	32	98	11	16
Acta, Osceola	.800	1	1	3	1	1	Kimberlin, Lakeland	.944	118	195	360	33	61
Alvarez, Vero Beach	.917	21	39	38	7	10	Lamphere, Osceola	1.000	1	1	0	0	0
Anglero, 9 B.C.-4 Lake	.829	13	12	50	8	10	Lansing, Miami	.964	61	104	166	10	31
Bethea, Winter Haven	.944	5	6	11	1	1	Marigny, Lakeland	1.000	7	9	20	0	3
Bridges-Clements, Baseball City	.889	9	16	32	6	5	Martin, West Palm Beach	.951	59	96	178	14	29
Busby, Sarasota	.942	17	19	46	4	9	McDevitt, Clearwater	.848	20	15	24	7	2
Butterfield, St. Lucie	.907	8	18	21	4	1	Mello, West Palm Beach	.909	3	4	6	1	0
Cedeno, Dunedin	.943	124	215	382	36	74	Miller, Dunedin	.909	7	6	24	3	4
Colon, Winter Haven	.925	12	12	25	3	3	Millette, Clearwater	.940	102	171	316	31	64
Cromer, St. Petersburg	.944	120	202	334	32	65	Morrisette, St. Lucie	1.000	1	2	0	0	0
Cruz, Sarasota	.875	12	16	26	6	2	J. Munoz, Vero Beach	.956	64	85	174	12	30
Delgado, Winter Haven	.932	70	135	210	25	43	L. Munoz, Winter Haven	.938	17	28	32	4	7
Dellicarri, St. Lucie	.927	37	56	122	14	35	Noriega, Fort Lauderdale	.939	9	13	18	2	4
Dixon, Winter Haven	1.000	2	0	1	0	0	Ocasio, Sarasota	.957	47	71	127	9	17
Ebel, Vero Beach	.946	90	112	186	17	41	Rigsby, Miami	.892	11	17	16	4	3
Foster, Osceola	.884	35	40	89	17	14	Robertson, Clearwater	.906	33	52	93	15	24
Gaither, Sarasota	.940	64	104	161	17	29	Rodriguez, West Palm Beach	1.000	4	5	8	0	1
Garber, Baseball City	.919	19	29	39	6	5	Roth, Sarasota	.962	5	9	16	1	5
Garibaldo, Baseball City	.943	92	133	263	24	42	Sable, Charlotte	.914	8	11	21	3	5
Gomez, Miami	.667	2	0	2	1	1	Samson, Charlotte	.936	11	14	30	3	4
Gonzalez, Baseball City	.948	15	25	48	4	7	Santangelo, West Palm Beach	.935	54	77	154	16	24
Graham, Winter Haven	.880	10	8	14	3	2	Shireman, St. Petersburg	1.000	6	6	14	0	3
Gutierrez, Miami	.929	69	102	161	20	34	Stairs, West Palm Beach	.889	19	16	40	7	14
Hall, Miami	1.000	6	7	5	0	2	Taylor, Dunedin	.973	8	11	25	1	9
Hartmann, St. Lucie	1.000	7	10	9	0	2	Tejada, Sarasota	1.000	1	1	3	0	1
Da. Henderson, Osceola	.888	38	49	101	19	13	Tresh, Lakeland	.946	9	13	22	2	4
De. Henderson, St. Lucie	.941	58	73	152	14	26	Turgeon, Fort Lauderdale	.885	24	28	64	12	5
HERNANDEZ, Charlotte	.959	119	192	372	24	52	Vargas, Fort Lauderdale	.931	109	207	343	41	63
Kellner, Osceola	.959	76	109	245	15	44	Villalobos, Winter Haven	.929	41	59	98	12	14

Triple Plays—Lansing 2, Cromer, Gaither, De. Henderson.

OUTFIELDERS

Player and Club	Pct.	G.	PO.	A.	E.	DP.	Player and Club	Pct.	G.	PO.	A.	E.	DP.
Alegre, Miami	.667	2	2	0	1	0	Hayes, Clearwater	1.000	1	3	0	0	0
Andrews, Baseball City	.978	20	42	2	1	1	Hays, Charlotte	.975	59	73	5	2	1
Barnwell, Fort Lauderdale	.972	70	138	3	4	0	Hernandez, Charlotte	.000	1	0	0	0	0
Barron, Vero Beach	.981	101	144	9	3	2	Hodge, Dunedin	.956	89	126	4	6	0
Beams, Osceola	.960	124	180	12	8	1	Hudson, Miami	.956	26	61	4	3	0
Belbru, St. Petersburg	1.000	3	2	0	0	0	Hurst, Lakeland*	.974	74	143	5	4	1
Bible, Miami	.929	7	13	0	1	0	Jenkins, Winter Haven	.980	59	139	5	3	2
E. Boddie, Vero Beach	.991	75	107	1	1	0	Jordan, St. Petersburg	1.000	8	23	0	0	0
R. Boddie, West Palm Beach	.994	85	156	11	1	0	Kidd, Miami*	.973	99	210	9	6	2
Boyce, Miami	1.000	16	22	1	0	0	Kindred, St. Petersburg	.986	40	71	0	1	0
Da. Brown, Clearwater*	.967	95	192	12	7	0	Knoblauh, Fort Lauderdale	.968	92	171	12	6	2
Do. Brown, St. Lucie	.945	21	48	4	3	1	LAKE, West Palm Beach	.995	101	180	8	1	1
Brumfield, Baseball City	.962	89	186	17	8	3	Lamphere, Osceola	1.000	4	6	1	0	0
Burnett, Miami	1.000	10	19	2	0	0	Landrum, Miami	.970	21	30	2	1	1
Burnitz, St. Lucie	1.000	10	18	1	0	0	Law, Charlotte	.991	57	106	3	1	0
Carey, Miami	.972	36	63	6	2	1	Lofton, Osceola*	.974	123	246	13	7	2
Carter, St. Petersburg*	.955	38	62	2	3	0	Long, Baseball City*	.979	55	88	4	2	0
Chick, Winter Haven	.966	36	83	3	3	1	Lukachyk, Sarasota	.982	98	214	7	4	0
Collier, Vero Beach*	.974	93	143	6	4	2	Maclin, St. Petersburg*	.944	31	65	3	4	1
Collins, Baseball City	.952	11	19	1	1	0	Marabell, Vero Beach	.991	66	105	7	1	1
Colon, Winter Haven	1.000	3	2	0	0	0	Martin, Lakeland	.966	109	184	13	7	0
Cooper, Osceola	1.000	1	5	0	0	0	Martinez, St. Petersburg	1.000	4	5	1	0	0
Cornelius, Lakeland	.962	32	48	2	2	0	Massarelli, Osceola	.800	3	4	0	1	0
Cortes, Fort Lauderdale*	1.000	10	11	1	0	0	Masse, Fort Lauderdale	.985	64	123	10	2	1
Davis, St. Lucie	1.000	4	8	1	0	0	May, St. Lucie	.978	119	250	12	6	5
de la Rosa, Dunedin	.976	129	230	9	6	2	Mayo, West Palm Beach*	.984	104	238	13	4	0
DeLoach, St. Petersburg	.949	105	218	6	12	2	McBride, St. Lucie	.977	75	124	5	3	2
Devereaux, Fort Lauderdale*	1.000	24	38	2	0	0	McCoy, Charlotte	.941	24	32	0	2	0
Dostal, Vero Beach*	1.000	56	112	3	0	1	McNeely, West Palm Beach	.978	16	41	3	1	0
Douglas, Charlotte	1.000	3	3	0	0	0	Mello, West Palm Beach	.900	9	8	1	1	0
Dozier, St. Lucie	.984	71	116	6	2	1	Miller, Miami	.917	8	10	1	1	0
Dukes, Winter Haven	.939	18	31	0	2	0	Moore, Winter Haven	.969	102	215	4	7	2
Durkin, Miami	.977	44	80	6	2	0	Morris, Charlotte*	.977	116	203	10	5	2
Dyer, Baseball City	1.000	4	6	0	0	0	Morrisette, St. Lucie	.979	49	85	8	2	0
Faulk, West Palm Beach*	.957	53	107	3	5	0	Morrison, Winter Haven	.951	64	128	9	7	1
Fiore, St. Petersburg	.955	35	57	6	3	2	Nelloms, Fort Lauderdale	.965	105	159	6	6	0
Fox, Winter Haven*	1.000	17	31	1	0	0	Nyssen, Osceola	.990	107	200	6	2	3
Garcia, Miami	.936	26	40	4	3	0	Payton, Sarasota	.947	36	53	1	3	1
Giordano, Miami*	1.000	48	64	7	0	1	Peel, Charlotte	.982	58	100	7	2	0
C. Gonzalez, Sarasota	.972	74	163	12	5	5	Pledger, Sarasota	.983	125	330	10	6	2
F. Gonzalez, Vero Beach	.959	57	64	7	3	0	Provence, Dunedin	1.000	5	12	0	0	0
Goodale, Lakeland	.988	103	163	5	2	2	Reed, Osceola*	.991	73	109	7	1	1
Gorman, Vero Beach*	1.000	6	2	0	0	0	Riesgo, St. Lucie	1.000	1	2	0	0	0
Graham, St. Petersburg*	.982	70	158	6	3	2	Santangelo, West Palm Beach	1.000	25	44	3	0	0
Grier, St. Petersburg	.978	94	212	15	5	4	Shelton, Miami	.960	98	133	11	6	3
Griffin, Vero Beach	.969	31	60	2	2	0	Smith, West Palm Beach	1.000	31	55	2	0	1

OUTFIELDERS—Continued

Player and Club	Pct.	G.	PO.	A.	E.	DP.	Player and Club	Pct.	G.	PO.	A.	E.	DP.
Spann, Lakeland	1.000	21	32	4	0	0	Watkins, Baseball City	.983	116	275	6	5	3
Sullivan, Sarasota	.951	28	55	3	3	0	Weimerskirch, W. Palm Beach	.935	20	28	1	2	0
Swain, Charlotte	.990	105	198	4	2	1	Weinheimer, Miami	1.000	16	16	0	0	0
Taveras, Dunedin	1.000	30	29	2	0	0	C. Williams, Clearwater	.981	62	144	9	3	2
Tedder, Sarasota*	.979	80	128	11	3	2	G. Williams, Fort Lauderdale	.975	50	115	1	3	0
Tenhunfeld, Clearwater	.911	41	40	1	4	0	R. Williams, Charlotte	1.000	7	15	0	0	0
Thompson, Dunedin	.972	116	237	7	7	0	Witherspoon, Winter Haven	.938	31	74	2	5	0
Threadgill, Charlotte	1.000	20	38	0	0	0	Woodruff, Clearwater	.958	133	238	14	11	4
Tresh, Lakeland	.983	77	109	6	2	0	Wright, Baseball City	.897	15	25	1	3	0
Trevino, Clearwater	1.000	1	1	0	0	0	D. Young, St. Lucie	.991	64	109	7	1	1
Urbon, Clearwater*	.973	56	107	3	3	0	E. Young, Vero Beach	.958	11	21	2	1	0
Ventress, Clearwater	.988	38	82	1	1	0	M. Young, Dunedin	.966	59	80	4	3	1
Walker, Baseball City	.948	116	178	4	10	1	Zambrano, Winter Haven	.960	77	156	11	7	1

Triple Play—Carey.

CATCHERS

Player and Club	Pct.	G.	PO.	A.	E.	DP.	PB.	Player and Club	Pct.	G.	PO.	A.	E.	DP.	PB.
Adams, Clearwater	.982	23	150	15	3	1	5	Koenig, Baseball City	.976	81	474	55	13	5	24
Albright, Lakeland	.976	70	479	48	13	3	7	Laker, West Palm Beach	1.000	2	2	0	0	0	0
Alvarez, Sarasota	.980	34	220	29	5	2	5	Livesey, Fort Lauderdale	.988	45	287	37	4	2	4
Angotti, Osceola	1.000	11	32	2	0	0	2	Losa, Charlotte	.940	13	68	10	5	0	1
Balthazar, Lakeland	.981	43	333	30	7	3	8	Lozinski, Clearwater	.986	32	196	16	3	0	5
Beard, Vero Beach	1.000	2	11	1	0	0	0	Makarewicz, Osceola	.978	76	544	71	14	8	8
Bradbury, Lakeland	.987	43	275	36	4	1	1	Marabell, Vero Beach	.900	8	7	2	1	1	0
Butterfield, St. Lucie	.989	13	77	9	1	0	0	Mason, West Palm Beach	.987	25	132	16	2	0	2
Campbell, Sarasota	.977	82	536	49	14	8	16	Massarelli, Osceola	.978	67	406	41	10	2	11
Carroll, St. Lucie	.950	6	18	1	1	0	2	Matilla, Winter Haven	.978	117	666	98	17	4	25
Castillo, St. Lucie	1.000	3	16	2	0	0	2	McGough, Sarasota	.976	8	37	4	1	0	1
Crespo, Charlotte	.971	22	123	12	4	0	4	McKinley, Miami	.984	23	116	11	2	1	0
DeLeon, Baseball City	.988	12	67	18	1	0	6	Miller, Miami	.970	46	257	33	9	5	4
Dyer, Baseball City	.966	28	155	14	6	0	7	Monzon, Dunedin	.964	18	77	4	3	1	0
Ehrhard, Fort Lauderdale	.985	75	476	48	8	1	21	Morris, Miami	.995	33	189	26	1	3	3
Erhardt, Fort Lauderdale	.952	20	110	10	6	2	2	Niethammer, Charlotte	1.000	14	69	7	0	0	2
Fagnant, Winter Haven	.976	43	153	10	4	1	6	O'Halloran, Dunedin	.965	35	250	28	10	0	5
Fernandez, St. Petersburg	.985	42	300	32	5	3	8	Piazza, Vero Beach	.967	73	374	34	14	3	6
Fielitz, St. Petersburg	1.000	7	17	0	0	0	0	Redman, St. Petersburg	.986	79	447	50	7	6	11
Gillette, Lakeland	.970	22	139	22	5	3	5	Rodriguez, Charlotte	.983	104	727	101	14	4	13
E. Gonzalez, W. Palm Beach	1.000	1	3	0	0	0	0	Rosado, Clearwater	.972	43	248	28	8	5	5
P. Gonzalez, Vero Beach	.983	87	451	71	9	4	12	Sanchez, West Palm Beach	.938	2	12	3	1	1	0
Graves, St. Lucie	.981	41	239	23	5	0	3	SIDDALL, West Palm Beach	.991	106	644	105	7	7	9
Griesser, Baseball City	.995	33	193	13	1	3	5	Singley, 12 Mia.-18 Sara.	.981	30	195	13	4	1	8
Hargis, West Palm Beach	.972	13	64	6	2	0	1	Teel, Vero Beach	.926	7	21	4	2	0	0
Hornacek, Sarasota	1.000	3	18	1	0	1	0	Thomas, St. Petersburg	.976	23	108	13	3	2	3
Hulse, Clearwater	.988	49	276	40	4	3	6	Townley, Dunedin	.981	90	619	70	13	6	13
Irish, Dunedin	.933	10	28	0	2	0	0	Zinter, St. Lucie	.981	85	500	54	11	5	13

PITCHERS

Player and Club	Pct.	G.	PO.	A.	E.	DP.	Player and Club	Pct.	G.	PO.	A.	E.	DP.
D. Alexander, Miami	1.000	16	1	5	0	0	Daniel, Miami*	.941	15	3	13	1	0
G. Alexander, Charlotte	1.000	7	1	7	0	0	Davino, Sarasota	.952	46	3	17	1	2
Alicano, Baseball City*	.846	20	5	6	2	0	B. Davis, West Palm Beach	.895	43	6	11	2	0
Allen, Winter Haven	.750	18	1	5	2	1	F. Davis, Winter Haven	.500	3	0	1	1	0
Arner, Charlotte	.917	12	3	8	1	0	Delahoya, Vero Beach	1.000	4	0	3	0	0
Astacio, Vero Beach	.833	8	4	6	2	0	Delgado, Winter Haven	1.000	12	0	1	0	0
Aylmer, Dunedin*	.909	8	3	7	1	0	Dell, Clearwater	1.000	17	1	14	0	0
Backs, Clearwater	.875	15	6	8	2	0	Dennison, Winter Haven*	1.000	8	1	0	0	0
Bauer, Osceola	1.000	24	0	3	0	0	DePastino, Dunedin	.850	22	3	14	3	0
Beall, Baseball City*	1.000	1	1	0	0	1	DeSilva, Lakeland	1.000	14	2	14	0	1
Bene, Vero Beach	.750	17	1	11	4	2	Doherty, Lakeland	1.000	30	5	6	0	1
Berrios, Lakeland*	.923	21	1	11	1	0	Dovey, Osceola	1.000	6	0	1	0	0
Berumen, Baseball City	.800	9	3	5	2	0	Draper, Fort Lauderdale	.935	14	7	22	2	1
Biberdorf, Vero Beach	1.000	48	5	7	0	0	Drohan, Baseball City	1.000	7	0	4	0	1
Black, Osceola	1.000	13	2	5	0	1	Dunn, Baseball City	.933	19	5	9	1	0
Borland, Clearwater	1.000	44	3	16	0	1	Dunnum, Osceola	.850	51	5	12	3	0
Boucher, Dunedin*	.962	9	2	23	1	0	Duvall, St. Petersburg	1.000	1	0	1	0	0
Boyce, Miami	1.000	1	0	1	0	0	Elam, Clearwater	.786	32	4	7	3	0
Boyle, Miami	1.000	4	0	1	0	0	Enno, Vero Beach*	1.000	29	3	9	0	1
M.K. Brady, Vero Beach*	1.000	9	1	2	0	0	Ericks, St. Petersburg	1.000	4	0	3	0	0
M.R. Brady, St. Lucie	.714	38	5	5	4	0	Ericson, Miami	.923	25	5	7	1	0
Brantley, Clearwater	1.000	8	3	7	0	0	Ettles, Lakeland	.923	45	4	8	1	1
R. Brown, Charlotte	.903	40	5	23	3	1	Ferm, Lakeland	.824	18	2	12	3	0
T. Brown, Dunedin	.857	36	3	9	2	1	Fernandez, Sarasota	1.000	2	2	0	0	0
Brubaker, Fort Lauderdale	.952	40	3	17	1	0	Fischer, Vero Beach	.857	5	2	4	1	0
Brucato, Baseball City	1.000	4	0	2	0	0	P. Fletcher, Clearwater	1.000	20	5	14	0	2
Burgo, Winter Haven	.833	4	1	4	1	0	R. Fletcher, Vero Beach*	1.000	32	0	3	0	0
Burgos, St. Petersburg*	.909	19	6	14	2	2	Forrester, Sarasota*	1.000	20	1	5	0	0
Bustillos, Vero Beach	.907	22	14	25	4	3	Freed, West Palm Beach	.925	26	10	39	4	3
Cakora, Miami*	1.000	45	4	16	0	4	Furmanik, St. Lucie	.895	22	4	13	2	1
Calhoun, Vero Beach	1.000	31	4	19	0	1	Fynan, Clearwater	1.000	9	0	4	0	0
Carter, Clearwater*	.882	26	3	12	2	0	Galvan, Sarasota*	.909	39	2	8	1	1
Cecena, Clearwater	1.000	20	0	3	0	0	R. Garcia, Sarasota	1.000	26	11	17	0	1
Christopher, Clearwater*	1.000	32	4	10	0	1	V. Garcia, Fort Lauderdale*	1.000	20	0	13	0	0
Clark, St. Petersburg	.727	10	6	2	3	0	Gennings, Sarasota	1.000	8	2	2	0	0
Collins, West Palm Beach	1.000	16	1	11	0	2	Gietzen, Fort Lauderdale*	1.000	23	3	6	0	0
Compres, Charlotte	.833	22	7	8	3	0	Gogolewski, Fort Lauderdale	.864	16	7	12	3	1
Cook, Lakeland*	1.000	43	4	14	0	0	Gohr, Lakeland	1.000	25	7	26	0	2
Corbin, St. Lucie	.828	20	7	17	5	0	Gore, Charlotte*	.867	23	2	11	2	0
Cornelius, West Palm Beach	1.000	11	6	13	0	0	D. Green, St. Petersburg*	1.000	35	0	11	0	0
Cross, Dunedin	.952	28	2	18	1	3	J. Green, Fort Lauderdale	1.000	5	0	1	0	0
Cunningham, Charlotte	1.000	11	4	10	0	0	Greer, Fort Lauderdale	.875	38	3	11	2	1
Dabney, Sarasota*	.905	24	4	15	2	1	Gregory, Miami	.905	16	6	13	2	4

PITCHERS—Continued

Player and Club	Pct.	G.	PO.	A.	E.	DP.
Griffiths, Osceola	1.000	28	9	10	0	0
Grimes, St. Petersburg	1.000	58	2	17	0	1
Gunderson, Clearwater	1.000	10	1	2	0	0
Hansell, 21 W.H.-6 St.L.	.949	27	22	15	2	2
Harriger, St. Lucie	.960	27	2	22	1	2
Harvey, Baseball City	1.000	7	2	4	0	0
Harwell, Baseball City	1.000	13	0	2	0	0
Hill, St. Lucie*	.895	27	6	28	4	1
Hillman, St. Lucie*	1.000	4	1	6	0	0
Hitt, St. Petersburg*	.846	27	3	8	2	1
Hoeme, Baseball City	1.000	33	2	2	0	0
Hoffman, St. Petersburg	.947	23	13	23	2	1
HOPPER, Baseball City	1.000	30	15	25	0	3
Horsman, Dunedin*	1.000	28	4	7	0	0
Hoy, Winter Haven	.913	52	7	35	4	3
Hudson, Baseball City	1.000	16	3	13	0	0
Hursey, Lakeland*	1.000	25	9	17	0	1
Hurst, Charlotte	1.000	6	1	1	0	0
Hvizda, Charlotte	1.000	13	4	3	0	0
Hyson, Osceola	1.000	26	11	9	0	0
J. Johnson, Fort Lauderdale*	1.000	17	6	18	0	3
P. Johnson, St. Lucie	1.000	22	1	6	0	0
Johnston, Baseball City	.923	31	6	6	1	2
Johnstone, St. Lucie	.929	25	13	39	4	0
Jones, Osceola	.897	27	9	17	3	0
Jordan, Dunedin*	1.000	13	3	2	0	0
Juden, Osceola	1.000	15	1	10	0	0
Kane, Winter Haven	.786	34	4	7	3	1
Keller, St. Petersburg	.833	15	2	3	1	0
Kelley, Miami	.971	30	9	24	1	1
Kerfut, Miami	.943	45	13	20	2	1
Kerrigan, West Palm Beach	1.000	51	0	7	0	1
Key, Dunedin*	1.000	3	3	0	0	0
Keyser, Sarasota	.951	38	9	30	2	2
King, Sarasota	1.000	2	1	1	0	0
Kite, Winter Haven	.714	15	3	7	4	0
Knapp, Vero Beach	.882	18	6	9	2	1
Knudsen, Lakeland	1.000	14	6	6	0	0
Krumm, Lakeland	.977	25	10	33	1	4
LaRose, St. Lucie	.800	17	1	3	1	1
Lata, St. Petersburg	.875	8	3	4	1	0
Leiter, Dunedin*	1.000	6	0	6	0	0
Lewis, West Palm Beach	.800	10	2	2	1	0
Lindsey, Clearwater	.973	26	10	26	1	2
Logan, West Palm Beach	1.000	6	0	3	0	0
Luckham, Osceola	.950	27	12	26	2	0
Lugo, Miami	1.000	19	5	10	0	1
Lumley, Lakeland	.789	13	6	9	4	1
MacNeil, 10 Mia.-7 Char.	.867	17	3	10	2	0
Madrid, Clearwater	.667	5	1	1	1	0
Magee, Baseball City*	.909	32	0	10	1	0
Magria, Miami	1.000	19	0	1	0	1
Majer, St. Petersburg	.875	14	3	4	1	1
Mallicoat, Osceola*	1.000	3	0	1	0	1
Malone, Fort Lauderdale*	.857	8	0	6	1	0
Manon, Fort Lauderdale	.750	11	1	5	2	0
Manuel, Charlotte	1.000	57	1	7	0	1
Marris, Fort Lauderdale	.750	27	5	10	5	0
Marshall, Lakeland*	1.000	13	4	11	0	0
Martin, Dunedin	1.000	12	1	2	0	0
McCarthy, Clearwater*	1.000	42	5	17	0	1
McCormick, Baseball City*	.500	11	1	1	2	0
Mejia, St. Lucie	1.000	2	4	0	0	0
Merigliano, Sarasota	.955	21	8	13	1	0
Michno, Miami	.933	31	9	19	2	4
Middaugh, Sarasota	.923	22	5	7	1	1
Milchin, St. Petersburg*	1.000	11	2	10	0	1
Miller, Winter Haven	1.000	1	0	1	0	0
Mosley, Winter Haven*	1.000	29	1	5	0	0
Nelson, Baseball City	1.000	1	0	1	0	0
Nen, Charlotte	.857	11	7	5	2	0
Newell, Fort Lauderdale	1.000	7	3	9	0	0
Newton, St. Lucie	1.000	31	2	1	0	0
Niethammer, Charlotte	.000	2	0	0	0	0
Nina, Vero Beach*	1.000	7	1	0	0	0
Ohlms, Fort Lauderdale	.971	21	14	20	1	3
Olson, Miami	1.000	1	1	0	0	0
Ontiveros, Clearwater	1.000	3	1	0	0	0
Otto, Baseball City	1.000	24	5	17	0	3
Pacheco, St. Petersburg	.750	5	0	3	1	0
Painter, Winter Haven	.750	4	0	3	1	0
Parnell, Baseball City	1.000	36	3	1	0	0
Pascual, Miami	.818	37	4	14	4	0
Patrick, Vero Beach*	1.000	4	2	1	0	0

Player and Club	Pct.	G.	PO.	A.	E.	DP.
Patterson, Clearwater	1.000	11	3	8	0	0
Pavlik, Charlotte	1.000	11	5	8	0	1
D. Perez, Charlotte	.952	14	4	16	1	3
Pe. Perez, Vero Beach	1.000	15	3	2	0	0
V. Perez, St. Lucie	.900	19	4	5	1	1
Perschke, Sarasota	.958	42	8	15	1	0
Piatt, West Palm Beach	1.000	21	2	3	0	0
Pichardo, Baseball City	.875	11	3	4	1	0
B. Pierce, Baseball City*	1.000	18	6	1	0	0
E. Pierce, Baseball City*	.933	37	7	7	1	1
Plemel, St. Petersburg	1.000	10	5	13	0	1
Pollack, West Palm Beach*	.917	24	2	31	3	2
Ponder, Miami	1.000	15	2	6	0	0
Ponte, Osceola	.882	32	9	6	2	0
Popplewell, Fort Lauderdale	.947	15	6	12	1	0
Quantrill, Winter Haven	.938	7	4	11	1	0
Rambo, Osceola*	.950	25	3	16	1	1
Randall, Clearwater	.750	16	1	2	1	0
Reitzel, 13 Mia.-13 Char.*	.969	26	6	25	1	0
Resnikoff, Sarasota*	.867	45	1	12	2	1
Reyes, West Palm Beach	.769	16	2	8	3	1
D. Richardson, St. Petersburg*	1.000	47	2	15	0	0
R. Richardson, Winter Haven	.833	34	3	12	3	0
Riley, Winter Haven*	.929	31	3	23	2	2
Rivera, Lakeland	1.000	36	3	8	0	0
Rodriguez, Osceola	1.000	51	5	15	0	2
B. Rogers, St. Lucie	1.000	29	14	17	0	0
T. Rogers, Miami*	.882	14	2	13	2	1
Romero, Charlotte*	.870	12	3	17	3	0
Rowley, Charlotte	.875	5	2	5	1	0
Rub, Fort Lauderdale*	1.000	15	1	5	0	0
Rudolph, Dunedin	.857	35	2	10	2	1
Rush, Winter Haven	1.000	30	6	15	0	0
Sanchez, Baseball City*	.929	7	1	1	0	0
Sanders, Winter Haven	1.000	31	6	15	0	0
Satterfield, St. Petersburg	.929	17	5	8	1	1
Sauveur, Miami*	1.000	11	6	9	0	1
Schourek, St. Lucie*	1.000	5	0	3	0	0
Seiler, Fort Lauderdale*	1.000	8	1	2	0	0
Shackle, St. Petersburg	.889	8	2	6	1	0
C. Shaw, Charlotte*	.880	11	2	20	3	1
K. Shaw, Baseball City	1.000	10	1	5	0	0
Silverstein, Dunedin	.962	45	4	21	1	1
C. Smith, Miami*	.667	22	1	1	1	0
K. Smith, St. Petersburg	1.000	17	6	8	0	1
R. Smith, Sarasota	1.000	4	0	2	0	0
Sommer, West Palm Beach	1.000	29	7	15	0	0
Spencer, Charlotte	.750	43	0	6	2	1
Stanford, Fort Lauderdale	.867	57	7	6	2	1
Stevens, Clearwater	.750	10	1	2	1	0
Sullivan, Clearwater	1.000	13	2	0	0	0
Tabaka, Clearwater*	.818	8	0	9	2	1
Tafoya, Osceola	1.000	22	1	7	0	0
TAVERAS, Vero Beach	1.000	26	19	21	0	1
Telgheder, St. Lucie	.850	14	3	14	3	1
Terrill, Vero Beach*	.885	23	12	34	6	3
Thoden, West Palm Beach	.933	13	3	11	1	0
Thompson, Winter Haven	.938	15	4	11	1	0
Timlin, Dunedin	.938	42	3	12	1	1
Tolbert, St. Petersburg	.333	5	0	1	2	0
Torres, Lakeland	.500	12	0	1	1	0
Treadwell, Vero Beach	.944	16	7	10	1	1
Trlicek, Dunedin	.938	26	15	30	3	0
Tucker, Fort Lauderdale*	.882	21	2	13	2	1
Tuss, West Palm Beach	1.000	29	4	7	0	1
Vanzytveld, Vero Beach	.889	17	7	9	2	1
Vargas, St. Petersburg	.950	38	4	15	1	0
Vaughn, Baseball City	.867	21	13	13	4	0
Ventura, Sarasota	.917	25	7	26	3	3
Wainhouse, West Palm Beach	.813	12	4	9	3	1
Ward, Dunedin*	.879	27	3	26	4	2
Weathers, Dunedin	.902	27	10	27	4	2
Webster, Baseball City*	1.000	7	0	3	0	0
Weese, St. Petersburg	.800	20	1	3	1	0
Wells, Clearwater	1.000	6	1	2	0	0
Wengert, Vero Beach	.947	22	8	10	1	1
Wenrick, West Palm Beach	.900	21	1	8	1	2
Wickman, Sarasota	1.000	2	1	4	0	1
Wiegandt, Clearwater*	.962	33	7	18	1	2
Williams, Miami*	1.000	13	1	7	0	0
Willis, Lakeland	.941	34	9	7	1	1
Windes, Osceola*	1.000	44	3	9	0	0
Wiseman, St. Petersburg	1.000	17	9	16	0	0
Young, West Palm Beach	1.000	39	11	21	0	0

Triple Plays—Horsman, Resnikoff.

The following players did not have any fielding statistics at the positions indicated or appeared only as a designated hitter, pinch-hitter or pinch-runner: Abreu, p; Acta, 2b; Alcantara, p; C. Alvarez, of; Anglero, p; Bible, c; Blohm, p; Bridges-Clements, of; Burns, p; Butterfield, of; Chasey, ss, of; Chrisman, p; Ciaglo, p; Crouch, p; R. Cruz, ph; Czarnetzki, of; Dean, dh; Debrand, c; T. Delgado, p; Devereaux, p; Ebel, 3b, p; Erhardt, 3b; Friedman, of; Gillette, of; Giordano, p; E. Gonzalez, of; Gutierrez, p; Guzman, p; Infante, 2b; Koenig, p; Langley, p; Lira, p; J. Martin, p; Meamber, p; Michael, 3b; S. Miller, 3b; Niethammer, of, p; Peel, p; P. Perez, p; Perozo, p; Reich, p; Reimink, of; Rosado, of; Russell, p; Samson, 2b; Sellick, p; Shehan, p; Shelton, 2b; S. Smith, p; Stafford, p; D. Taylor, of; Tedder, p; Turgeon, of; F. Williams, of; K. Williams, 2b; Zambrano, 1b.

CLUB PITCHING

Club	ERA.	G.	CG.	ShO.	Sv.	IP.	H.	R.	ER.	HR.	HB.	BB.	Int. BB.	SO.	WP.	Bk.
Charlotte	2.35	138	10	20	51	1201.1	860	404	314	39	32	492	15	982	53	22
Lakeland	2.51	133	9	21	40	1143.0	983	406	319	26	46	388	12	932	60	29
West Palm Beach	2.63	132	5	17	59	1165.2	1055	428	341	29	46	423	18	840	57	18
Dunedin	3.16	136	5	15	41	1203.1	1037	511	423	34	65	482	24	966	103	43
St. Lucie	3.30	134	25	8	33	1145.0	1063	531	420	42	44	421	11	808	71	12
Osceola	3.32	138	6	7	33	1213.0	1047	576	447	32	61	586	26	947	96	31
St. Petersburg	3.35	134	10	11	30	1184.1	1107	527	441	42	24	439	59	842	60	24
Sarasota	3.41	138	12	9	33	1207.2	1135	575	458	36	50	460	24	898	65	48
Vero Beach	3.43	136	15	16	36	1164.0	1048	532	444	45	34	525	54	859	80	16
Clearwater	3.58	137	13	4	26	1160.1	1085	595	462	57	60	536	19	830	82	19
Winter Haven	4.07	134	10	9	23	1162.0	1129	658	525	43	43	530	7	777	74	30
Fort Lauderdale	4.10	137	12	3	39	1166.2	1177	654	532	48	39	491	15	851	114	30
Baseball City	4.29	138	4	3	37	1169.0	1146	675	557	43	52	606	3	837	106	22
Miami	4.51	137	16	7	18	1156.2	1201	703	579	61	70	606	64	862	73	54

PITCHERS' RECORDS

(Leading Qualifiers for Earned-Run Average Leadership—112 or More Innings)

*Throws lefthanded.

Pitcher—Club	W.	L.	Pct.	ERA.	G.	GS.	CG.	GF.	ShO.	Sv.	IP.	H.	R.	ER.	HR.	HB.	BB.	Int. BB.	SO.	WP.
R. Brown, Charlotte	8	5	.615	1.90	40	4	0	19	0	4	118.2	73	33	25	2	2	40	2	102	4
Freed, West Palm Beach	12	8	.600	2.00	26	25	1	0	0	0	171.0	188	63	38	4	6	32	0	98	8
Pollack, West Palm Beach*	13	2	.867	2.05	24	24	0	0	0	0	140.1	111	38	32	1	1	62	0	91	10
Compres, Charlotte	9	2	.818	2.24	22	16	2	2	0	1	116.2	89	38	29	0	3	43	0	69	8
Johnstone, St. Lucie	15	6	.714	2.24	25	25	9	0	3	0	172.2	145	53	43	3	5	60	1	120	16
Sanders, Winter Haven	7	7	.500	2.30	31	11	3	8	2	0	113.1	95	37	29	3	3	35	1	113	3
Sommer, West Palm Beach	11	4	.733	2.37	29	19	1	2	1	0	133.0	89	43	35	3	7	64	1	126	6
Krumm, Lakeland	7	9	.438	2.41	25	24	6	1	4	1	145.2	135	48	39	7	7	49	0	112	5
Terrill, Vero Beach*	12	4	.750	2.53	23	21	1	0	1	0	131.2	117	44	37	7	1	35	2	80	4
Gohr, Lakeland	13	5	.722	2.62	25	25	0	0	0	0	137.2	125	52	40	0	5	50	0	90	11

Departmental Leaders: G—Grimes, 58; W—Johnstone, 15; L—Carter, R. Garcia, Hansell, 14; Pct.—Juden, .909; GS—Hansell, Jones, Luckham, Weathers, 27; CG—Johnstone, 9; GF—Manuel, 56; ShO—Krumm, 4; Sv.—Manuel, 36; IP—Ward, 181.1; H—Freed, 188; R—Griffiths, Luckham, 88; ER—Dabney, 74; HR—R. Garcia, 10; HB—Silverstein, 17; BB—Jones, 109; IBB—Grimes, 13; SO—Ward, 137; WP—Bene, 23.

(All Pitchers—Listed Alphabetically)

Pitcher—Club	W.	L.	Pct.	ERA.	G.	GS.	CG.	GF.	ShO.	Sv.	IP.	H.	R.	ER.	HR.	HB.	BB.	Int. BB.	SO.	WP.
Abreu, St. Petersburg	0	0	.000	0.00	2	0	0	2	0	0	2.0	0	0	0	0	0	0	0	3	0
Alcantara, Lakeland*	0	0	.000	0.00	2	0	0	2	0	0	2.0	1	0	0	0	0	0	0	0	0
D. Alexander, Miami	0	2	.000	6.29	16	0	0	6	0	0	24.1	25	19	17	3	2	15	4	17	1
G. Alexander, Charlotte	6	1	.857	0.63	7	7	0	0	0	0	42.2	24	7	3	0	1	14	0	39	2
Alicano, Baseball City*	3	3	.500	4.13	20	0	0	9	0	1	48.0	51	27	22	3	1	21	1	28	8
Allen, Winter Haven	0	2	.000	6.00	18	0	0	5	0	1	36.0	35	29	24	0	0	28	2	31	4
Anglero, Lakeland	0	0	.000	4.50	2	0	0	2	0	0	2.0	1	1	1	0	0	2	0	1	0
Arner, Charlotte	3	3	.500	2.97	12	12	0	0	0	0	78.2	56	26	26	6	1	17	0	72	0
Astacio, Vero Beach	1	5	.167	6.32	8	8	0	0	0	0	47.0	54	39	33	3	1	23	0	41	4
Aylmer, Dunedin*	1	1	.500	1.69	8	0	0	3	0	0	16.0	14	6	3	1	2	4	2	8	1
Backs, Clearwater	5	7	.417	3.75	15	15	4	0	2	0	96.0	80	46	40	3	4	40	0	62	5
Bauer, Osceola	4	1	.800	1.55	24	0	0	22	0	10	29.0	18	6	5	0	1	11	3	32	0
Beall, Baseball City*	0	0	.000	9.00	1	0	0	1	0	0	1.0	2	1	1	0	0	2	0	0	0
Bene, Vero Beach	1	10	.091	6.99	17	14	0	2	0	0	56.2	49	55	44	3	6	96	0	34	23
Berrios, Lakeland*	2	2	.500	1.80	21	0	0	4	0	0	45.0	36	14	9	1	2	14	1	42	6
Berumen, Baseball City	3	5	.375	4.30	9	9	1	0	1	0	44.0	30	27	21	0	4	28	0	35	2
Biberdorf, Vero Beach	6	4	.600	2.00	48	0	0	43	0	25	67.1	51	17	15	1	0	20	6	87	2
Black, Osceola	1	0	1.000	3.48	13	0	0	6	0	0	20.2	21	8	8	2	1	10	0	9	1
Blohm, Dunedin	1	0	1.000	1.29	2	0	0	2	0	1	7.0	5	1	1	0	0	0	0	6	0
Borland, Clearwater	1	2	.333	2.26	44	0	0	23	0	5	59.2	44	21	15	1	3	35	4	44	6
Boucher, Dunedin*	7	0	1.000	0.75	9	9	2	0	2	0	60.0	45	8	5	1	2	8	0	62	4
Boyce, Miami	0	0	.000	0.00	1	0	0	0	0	0	2.0	1	0	0	0	0	3	0	0	0
Boyle, Miami	0	0	1.000	14.29	4	0	0	1	0	0	5.2	14	10	9	0	1	4	1	0	1
M.K. Brady, Vero Beach*	0	0	.000	2.65	9	0	0	4	0	1	17.0	11	6	5	0	0	8	1	13	1
M.R. Brady, St. Lucie	2	4	.333	4.67	38	0	0	24	0	8	44.1	45	28	23	0	0	33	4	42	3
Brantley, Clearwater	1	4	.200	2.94	8	8	2	0	0	0	49.0	44	20	16	3	1	17	0	37	5
R. Brown, Charlotte	8	5	.615	1.90	40	4	0	19	0	4	118.2	73	33	25	2	2	40	2	102	4
T. Brown, Dunedin	2	3	.400	4.43	36	0	0	19	0	1	67.0	76	41	33	3	5	18	3	55	7
Brubaker, Fort Lauderdale	4	5	.444	5.74	40	1	0	12	0	2	78.1	103	61	50	1	3	47	3	35	13
Brucato, Baseball City*	0	0	1.000	14.54	4	0	0	2	0	0	4.1	8	7	7	1	1	3	1	2	0
Burgo, Winter Haven	3	1	.750	1.33	4	4	1	0	0	0	27.0	18	6	4	0	0	7	0	12	0
Burgos, St. Petersburg*	4	4	.636	3.11	19	14	0	1	0	0	92.2	77	37	32	5	1	36	1	67	3
Burns, Fort Lauderdale*	1	2	.333	10.80	4	3	1	1	0	0	10.0	16	14	12	0	0	7	0	3	0
Bustillos, Vero Beach	11	5	.688	3.04	22	20	2	0	1	0	136.0	131	50	46	3	0	45	5	89	6
Cakora, Miami*	1	3	.250	3.56	45	3	1	20	0	2	73.1	78	36	29	5	5	30	3	48	4
Calhoun, Vero Beach	7	1	.875	2.81	31	0	0	14	0	2	57.2	51	20	18	0	3	23	5	34	4
Carter, Clearwater*	4	14	.222	4.88	26	26	2	0	0	0	131.0	121	82	71	8	9	69	2	90	10
Cecena, Charlotte	3	2	.600	2.03	20	0	0	10	0	0	31.0	24	7	7	3	0	13	0	35	4
Chrisman, Baseball City	0	0	.000	4.50	2	0	0	2	0	0	4.0	4	2	2	1	0	1	0	4	0
Christopher, Clearwater*	1	3	.250	5.68	32	1	0	7	0	2	52.1	54	35	33	3	4	40	2	56	3
Ciaglo, West Palm Beach*	0	0	.000	18.00	1	0	0	0	0	0	1.0	2	2	2	0	1	1	0	2	0
Clark, St. Petersburg	3	2	.600	3.05	10	10	1	0	1	0	62.0	63	33	21	3	1	14	0	58	3
Collins, West Palm Beach	3	0	1.000	2.35	16	8	0	2	0	0	57.1	53	20	15	1	2	17	0	33	2
Compres, Charlotte	9	2	.818	2.24	22	16	2	2	0	1	116.2	89	38	29	0	3	43	0	69	8
Cook, Lakeland*	2	2	.500	1.90	43	2	0	17	0	5	75.2	56	21	16	1	3	30	2	59	0
Corbin, St. Lucie	7	8	.467	2.97	20	18	3	2	0	0	118.0	97	47	39	2	7	59	0	105	10
Cornelius, West Palm Beach	2	3	.400	3.38	11	11	0	0	0	0	56.0	54	25	21	1	5	25	0	47	3
Cross, Dunedin	13	7	.650	3.29	28	18	0	2	0	0	139.1	100	54	51	3	6	70	2	126	16
Crouch, Winter Haven	0	0	.000	4.50	3	3	0	0	0	0	6.0	3	3	3	0	2	2	0	8	0
Cunningham, Charlotte	6	3	.667	2.15	11	11	2	0	0	0	75.1	50	25	18	5	2	28	0	57	3
Dabney, Sarasota*	6	7	.462	5.27	24	21	1	0	0	0	126.1	146	81	74	8	6	57	1	77	6
Daniel, Miami*	6	5	.545	2.65	15	10	4	0	1	0	74.2	68	24	22	3	4	13	1	44	0
Davino, Sarasota	8	9	.471	3.91	46	13	1	22	1	6	124.1	128	63	54	2	4	55	5	101	8
B. Davis, West Palm Beach	4	0	1.000	3.29	43	0	0	17	0	11	65.2	57	25	24	1	0	25	5	49	2

Pitcher—Club	W.	L.	Pct.	ERA.	G.	GS.	CG.	GF.	ShO.	Sv.	IP.	H.	R.	ER.	HR.	HB.	BB.	Int. BB.	SO.	WP.
F. Davis, Winter Haven	1	0	1.000	1.08	3	0	0	2	0	0	8.1	6	1	1	0	0	1	0	8	0
Delahoya, Vero Beach	1	2	.333	5.57	4	4	0	0	0	0	21.0	14	14	13	0	1	20	2	22	0
R. Delgado, Winter Haven	0	1	.000	4.67	12	0	0	6	0	0	17.1	28	17	9	0	3	10	0	11	1
T. Delgado, Miami	0	1	.000	5.59	4	2	0	1	0	0	9.2	13	6	6	1	0	5	0	4	3
Dell, Clearwater	2	6	.250	5.46	16	9	0	1	0	0	56.0	68	41	34	4	3	18	0	41	9
Dennison, Winter Haven°	0	0	.000	12.19	8	0	0	5	0	0	10.1	18	16	14	1	1	7	0	5	1
DePastino, Dunedin	6	3	.667	5.02	22	14	0	2	0	0	84.1	85	54	47	9	5	57	0	72	11
DeSilva, Lakeland	8	1	.889	1.48	14	14	0	0	0	0	91.0	54	18	15	4	4	25	0	113	3
Devereaux, Fort Lauderdale°	0	0	.000	12.00	3	0	0	3	0	0	3.0	5	4	4	2	0	1	0	0	0
Doherty, Lakeland	5	1	.833	1.10	30	0	0	20	0	10	41.0	33	7	5	1	1	5	2	23	0
Dovey, Osceola	0	0	.000	5.23	6	0	0	0	0	0	10.1	13	6	6	0	0	8	0	7	2
Draper, Fort Lauderdale	9	1	.900	2.25	14	14	1	0	1	0	96.0	80	30	24	1	3	22	0	52	5
Drohan, Baseball City	1	5	.167	8.54	7	7	0	0	0	0	32.2	48	38	31	1	2	22	0	16	6
Dunn, Baseball City	4	3	.571	3.86	19	7	0	3	0	0	67.2	43	36	29	3	2	44	0	55	5
Dunnum, Osceola	5	1	.833	2.80	51	2	0	19	0	5	112.2	83	45	35	3	1	44	2	113	12
Duvall, St. Petersburg	0	0	.000	1.80	1	1	0	0	0	0	5.0	5	2	1	0	1	1	0	0	0
Ebel, Vero Beach	0	0	.000	0.00	1	0	0	1	0	0	2.0	2	0	0	0	0	1	0	0	0
Elam, Clearwater	2	4	.333	3.12	32	7	1	11	0	1	80.2	64	37	28	7	5	49	0	61	13
Enno, Vero Beach°	1	2	.333	2.68	29	3	0	7	0	2	50.1	49	20	15	2	3	26	8	29	0
Ericks, St. Petersburg	2	1	.667	1.57	4	4	0	0	0	0	23.0	16	5	4	0	0	6	0	25	1
Ericson, Miami	2	2	.500	4.00	25	1	0	9	0	1	36.0	33	16	16	2	4	19	6	27	2
Ettles, Lakeland	5	5	.500	3.31	45	0	0	21	0	3	68.0	63	34	25	1	6	16	1	62	4
Ferm, Lakeland	6	7	.462	4.46	18	18	0	0	0	0	80.2	80	57	40	0	6	58	0	60	12
Fernandez, Sarasota	1	1	.500	1.84	2	2	0	0	0	0	14.2	8	4	3	0	0	3	0	23	0
Fischer, Vero Beach	1	2	.333	4.09	5	5	1	0	0	0	22.0	24	10	10	1	2	1	0	18	0
P. Fletcher, Clearwater	5	8	.385	3.38	20	18	2	1	0	1	117.1	104	56	44	3	13	49	0	104	7
R. Fletcher, Vero Beach°	1	2	.333	5.19	32	0	0	14	0	3	34.2	40	25	20	1	1	21	2	26	10
Forrester, Sarasota°	0	1	.000	2.95	20	0	0	6	0	0	21.1	11	8	7	0	1	11	0	14	1
Freed, West Palm Beach	12	8	.600	2.00	26	25	1	0	0	0	171.0	188	63	38	4	6	32	0	98	8
Furmanik, St. Lucie	6	6	.500	4.21	22	9	0	7	0	2	72.2	71	43	34	8	6	30	0	45	3
Fynan, Clearwater	0	2	.000	4.26	9	0	0	1	0	0	12.2	16	7	6	0	2	1	0	9	1
Galvan, Sarasota°	2	2	.500	3.19	39	0	0	14	0	5	73.1	67	33	26	1	2	33	3	62	7
R. Garcia, Sarasota	9	14	.391	3.95	26	26	1	0	0	0	157.1	155	84	69	10	12	45	1	130	4
V. Garcia, Fort Lauderdale°	1	4	.200	2.36	20	3	0	8	0	1	49.2	45	16	13	0	0	22	0	56	6
Gennings, Sarasota	0	0	.000	7.90	8	0	0	4	0	0	13.2	15	15	12	2	2	10	0	5	1
Gietzen, Fort Lauderdale°	0	2	.000	6.80	23	4	0	5	0	0	47.2	62	49	36	0	6	32	0	37	14
Giordano, Miami°	0	0	.000	9.00	1	0	0	0	0	0	1.0	1	3	1	0	0	2	0	0	0
Gogolewski, Fort Lauderdale	5	9	.357	4.67	16	16	2	0	0	0	88.2	87	58	46	7	4	50	0	88	9
Gohr, Lakeland	13	5	.722	2.62	25	25	0	0	0	0	137.2	125	52	40	0	5	50	0	90	11
Gore, Charlotte°	9	4	.692	2.19	23	15	0	2	0	0	111.0	82	36	27	5	2	29	1	60	3
D. Green, St. Petersburg°	2	2	.500	2.79	35	1	0	7	0	0	58.0	52	19	18	0	8	38	5	43	2
J. Green, Fort Lauderdale	1	0	1.000	1.04	5	0	0	4	0	1	8.2	7	3	1	0	0	4	1	2	0
Greer, Fort Lauderdale	4	9	.308	5.44	38	5	0	11	0	1	89.1	115	64	54	5	7	33	2	55	3
Gregory, Miami	4	7	.364	4.12	16	13	1	2	0	0	78.2	96	52	36	3	5	24	2	57	5
Griffiths, Osceola	5	10	.333	4.81	28	23	0	3	0	0	129.0	129	88	69	3	9	75	1	79	21
Grimes, St. Petersburg	2	6	.250	2.28	58	0	0	24	0	2	83.0	60	25	21	1	0	25	13	58	2
Gunderson, Clearwater	1	0	1.000	7.80	10	0	0	8	0	0	15.0	26	14	13	1	2	8	1	7	1
Gutierrez, Miami	0	0	.000	4.50	3	0	0	2	0	0	2.0	1	1	1	0	1	3	0	1	0
Guzman, Charlotte	0	1	.000	2.16	2	2	0	0	0	0	8.1	10	3	2	0	0	4	0	7	0
Hansell, 21 W.H.-6 St. L.	9	14	.391	3.40	27	27	2	0	1	0	153.1	129	85	58	8	12	79	0	95	7
Harriger, St. Lucie	5	3	.625	3.52	27	7	1	9	0	2	71.2	73	36	28	0	1	20	0	47	2
Harvey, Baseball City	5	1	.833	2.04	7	7	0	0	0	0	39.2	27	14	9	1	3	19	0	29	3
Harwell, Baseball City	1	2	.333	7.04	13	1	0	5	0	0	15.1	15	16	12	1	2	29	0	14	2
Hill, St. Lucie°	9	8	.529	3.19	27	25	2	2	0	1	149.2	149	77	53	4	3	69	0	82	8
Hillman, St. Lucie°	2	0	1.000	0.67	4	3	0	0	0	0	27.0	15	2	2	0	1	8	0	23	3
Hitt, St. Petersburg	1	3	.250	3.51	27	0	0	9	0	0	41.0	44	19	16	0	0	18	5	16	0
Hoeme, Baseball City	2	2	.500	3.30	33	1	0	7	0	0	60.0	49	28	22	2	5	40	0	51	13
Hoffman, St. Petersburg	6	8	.429	3.61	23	19	2	3	1	0	119.2	122	58	48	0	4	47	2	60	11
Hopper, Baseball City	10	10	.500	4.13	30	18	0	4	0	2	137.1	138	71	63	4	7	55	1	72	10
Horsman, Dunedin°	4	7	.364	3.24	28	0	0	14	0	1	50.0	53	21	18	0	1	15	2	41	2
Hoy, Winter Haven	2	10	.167	3.56	52	3	0	30	0	7	108.2	110	54	43	3	3	30	1	48	5
Hudson, Baseball City	9	5	.643	3.16	16	15	0	1	0	0	102.2	105	43	36	5	3	22	1	50	1
Hursey, Lakeland°	5	5	.500	3.12	25	13	0	5	0	1	89.1	101	41	31	1	0	26	1	59	3
Hurst, Charlotte	0	1	.000	2.19	6	0	0	3	0	0	12.1	8	3	3	1	0	5	1	8	0
Hvizda, Charlotte	3	0	1.000	1.57	13	0	0	8	0	4	28.2	18	5	5	0	0	8	2	18	0
Hyson, Osceola	6	12	.333	4.01	26	26	0	0	0	0	141.1	130	76	63	5	14	70	0	92	10
J. Johnson, Fort Lauderdale°	6	8	.429	3.65	17	17	1	0	0	0	103.2	101	55	42	2	3	25	0	84	5
P. Johnson, St. Lucie	0	1	.000	5.60	22	0	0	10	0	0	35.1	46	29	22	6	3	10	0	20	3
Johnston, Baseball City	2	4	.333	4.88	31	7	1	18	0	7	55.1	36	37	30	2	3	49	0	60	6
Johnstone, St. Lucie	15	6	.714	2.24	25	25	9	0	3	0	172.2	145	53	43	3	5	60	1	120	16
Jones, Osceola	12	10	.545	3.51	27	27	1	0	0	0	151.1	124	81	59	2	3	109	1	106	16
Jordan, Dunedin°	0	2	.000	2.38	13	2	0	4	0	0	22.2	15	9	6	0	1	19	3	16	1
Juden, Osceola	10	1	.909	2.27	15	15	2	0	0	0	91.0	72	37	23	2	5	42	0	85	7
Kane, Winter Haven	2	5	.286	3.72	34	0	0	22	0	5	67.2	58	32	28	1	5	27	2	65	7
Keller, St. Petersburg	1	0	1.000	3.78	15	0	0	12	0	6	16.2	16	11	7	3	0	3	0	16	1
Kelley, Miami	2	5	.385	4.58	30	19	0	6	0	0	131.2	145	81	67	9	5	58	7	90	3
Kerfut, Miami	8	6	.571	3.82	45	13	2	12	2	1	125.0	107	60	53	4	4	68	8	93	8
Kerrigan, West Palm Beach	10	2	.833	3.46	51	0	0	33	0	11	83.1	79	33	32	4	2	23	7	70	3
Key, Dunedin°	2	0	1.000	2.50	3	3	0	0	0	0	18.0	21	7	5	0	0	3	0	14	1
Keyser, Sarasota	6	7	.462	3.66	38	10	2	13	1	2	115.2	107	54	47	5	1	40	1	83	6
King, Sarasota	1	0	1.000	2.25	2	2	0	0	0	0	8.0	8	4	2	0	0	2	0	5	1
Kite, Winter Haven	1	10	.091	7.57	15	14	0	0	0	0	52.1	49	53	44	4	2	60	0	45	10
Knapp, Vero Beach	3	5	.375	3.31	18	9	1	3	0	1	73.1	64	37	27	6	4	25	7	48	5
Knudsen, Lakeland	5	0	1.000	2.28	14	8	0	5	0	3	67.0	42	18	17	2	0	22	0	70	5
Koenig, Baseball City	0	0	.000	9.00	1	0	0	1	0	0	1.0	2	1	1	0	0	1	0	1	0
Krumm, Lakeland	7	9	.438	2.41	25	24	6	1	4	1	145.2	135	48	39	7	7	49	0	112	5
Langley, Clearwater°	0	0	.000	2.25	9	0	0	2	0	0	12.0	11	9	3	1	0	9	0	9	1
LaRose, St. Lucie	1	1	.500	3.57	17	0	0	16	0	7	17.2	16	9	7	1	2	10	3	13	1
Lata, St. Petersburg	1	5	.167	4.97	8	8	3	0	0	0	50.2	52	30	28	8	0	22	4	27	7
Leiter, Dunedin°	0	0	.000	2.63	6	6	0	0	0	0	24.0	18	8	7	1	0	12	0	14	2
Lewis, West Palm Beach	0	1	.000	3.00	10	0	0	6	0	2	15.0	12	8	5	0	0	11	0	14	1
Lindsey, Clearwater	10	9	.526	3.43	26	26	1	0	1	0	154.2	166	76	59	8	6	53	1	73	5

Pitcher—Club	W.	L.	Pct.	ERA.	G.	GS.	CG.	GF.	ShO.	Sv.	IP.	H.	R.	ER.	HR.	HB.	BB.	Int. BB.	SO.	WP.
Lira, Lakeland	0	0	.000	5.40	1	0	0	0	0	0	1.2	3	1	1	0	0	3	0	4	0
Logan, West Palm Beach	1	0	1.000	1.88	6	1	0	1	0	0	14.1	13	5	3	0	1	5	0	10	2
Luckham, Osceola	6	12	.333	4.14	27	27	1	0	0	0	150.0	158	88	69	5	10	90	2	89	11
Lugo, Miami	0	6	.000	6.99	19	6	1	2	0	0	47.2	58	42	37	3	4	30	5	14	5
Lumley, Lakeland	5	4	.556	2.38	13	9	1	2	0	2	64.1	56	22	17	0	4	22	1	47	2
MacNeil, 10 Mia.-7 Char.	1	4	.200	6.00	17	6	0	4	0	0	48.0	53	39	32	4	3	30	2	40	1
Madrid, Clearwater	1	1	.500	0.95	5	2	1	0	0	0	19.0	15	3	2	1	0	7	2	16	0
Magee, Baseball City*	2	5	.286	6.24	32	4	0	8	0	1	62.0	71	50	43	2	1	52	0	25	6
Magria, Javier, Miami	1	1	.500	9.79	19	0	0	9	0	2	26.2	29	30	29	2	5	28	1	34	4
Majer, St. Petersburg	2	3	.400	1.52	14	8	0	1	0	0	59.1	47	11	10	2	3	20	3	45	1
Mallicoat, Osceola*	0	0	.000	0.00	3	3	0	0	0	0	12.0	8	2	0	0	0	9	0	10	1
Malone, Fort Lauderdale*	0	5	.000	5.45	8	7	1	1	0	0	36.1	46	26	22	1	1	29	2	29	8
Manon, Fort Lauderdale	2	3	.400	5.86	11	5	0	2	0	0	35.1	39	26	23	2	1	23	0	40	7
Manuel, Charlotte	1	5	.167	2.88	57	0	0	56	0	36	56.1	39	23	18	2	3	30	2	60	1
Marris, Fort Lauderdale	5	7	.417	5.36	27	11	0	6	0	1	87.1	93	57	52	4	2	59	1	43	7
Marshall, Lakeland*	7	2	.778	3.25	13	13	2	0	2	0	72.0	71	29	26	3	1	14	1	40	3
G. Martin, Dunedin	2	1	.667	3.77	12	0	0	11	0	6	14.1	10	7	6	0	2	11	2	16	4
J. Martin, Clearwater	0	0	.000	0.00	1	0	1	0	0	0	1.0	1	0	0	0	0	0	0	1	0
McCarthy, Clearwater*	1	3	.250	3.47	42	1	0	19	0	5	59.2	47	33	23	4	1	38	1	67	5
McCormick, Baseball City*	1	4	.200	7.00	11	3	0	3	0	1	36.0	52	35	28	0	1	25	0	33	7
Meamber, St. Petersburg	0	2	.000	5.87	6	0	0	3	0	0	7.2	11	8	5	1	0	1	1	10	0
Mejia, St. Lucie	1	1	.500	10.61	2	2	0	0	0	0	9.1	13	12	11	2	2	3	0	4	0
Merigliano, Sarasota	3	11	.214	3.76	21	21	1	0	0	0	122.0	130	64	51	3	4	44	2	85	11
Michno, Miami	5	9	.357	2.83	31	10	3	12	1	2	101.2	79	37	32	3	4	58	8	78	6
Middaugh, Sarasota	4	3	.571	1.54	22	4	2	9	0	1	70.0	46	17	12	1	0	26	1	46	2
Milchin, St. Petersburg*	6	1	.857	2.77	11	11	1	0	1	0	68.1	57	25	21	1	1	20	0	66	4
Miller, Winter Haven	0	1	.000	11.25	1	1	0	0	0	0	4.0	7	5	5	1	0	3	0	2	1
Mosley, Winter Haven*	1	4	.200	6.16	29	1	0	15	0	1	61.1	73	50	42	1	0	38	0	49	0
Nelson, Baseball City	0	0	.000	4.50	1	1	0	0	0	0	2.0	3	1	1	0	0	0	0	2	0
Nen, Charlotte	1	4	.200	3.69	11	11	1	0	0	0	53.2	44	28	22	1	0	36	0	38	6
Newell, Fort Lauderdale	0	3	.000	5.67	7	7	0	0	0	0	33.1	32	22	21	2	0	19	0	22	5
Newton, St. Lucie	2	1	.667	5.19	31	1	0	18	0	1	67.2	77	44	39	8	1	34	1	48	8
Niethammer, Charlotte	0	1	.000	16.20	2	1	0	1	0	0	3.1	6	6	6	1	0	2	0	1	1
Nina, Vero Beach*	0	0	.000	7.20	7	0	4	0	0	0	10.0	12	8	8	1	0	5	0	4	1
Ohlms, Fort Lauderdale	8	8	.500	3.43	21	19	1	1	0	0	115.1	103	57	44	9	1	15	0	104	8
Olson, Miami	0	1	.000	15.00	1	1	0	0	0	0	3.0	7	7	5	0	0	5	0	1	1
Ontiveros, Clearwater	0	0	.000	2.35	3	3	0	0	0	0	7.2	4	2	2	0	0	3	0	2	0
Otto, Baseball City	5	6	.455	3.83	24	16	2	2	0	1	105.2	119	52	45	4	1	25	0	60	9
Pacheco, St. Petersburg	0	3	.000	11.81	5	4	0	0	0	0	10.2	14	20	14	1	0	22	0	4	2
Painter, Winter Haven	1	3	.250	3.80	4	4	0	0	0	0	21.1	17	9	9	1	0	12	0	15	5
Parnell, Baseball City	2	2	.500	1.86	36	0	0	34	0	17	38.2	24	9	8	2	3	15	2	40	2
Pascual, Miami	2	10	.167	4.76	37	12	0	17	0	6	98.1	102	67	52	5	6	63	2	84	10
Patrick, Vero Beach*	0	3	.000	6.23	4	4	0	0	0	0	21.2	29	18	15	1	0	10	1	11	3
Patterson, Clearwater	3	6	.333	2.96	11	11	0	0	0	0	67.0	63	34	22	2	2	22	0	28	1
Pavlik, Charlotte	5	3	.625	2.44	11	11	1	0	0	0	66.1	50	21	18	1	5	40	2	76	6
Peel, Charlotte	0	0	.000	9.00	1	0	0	1	0	0	1.0	1	1	1	0	0	1	0	0	0
D. Perez, Charlotte	6	4	.600	3.35	14	14	0	0	0	0	83.1	63	35	31	3	3	28	0	83	2
Pa. Perez, Fort Lauderdale	0	0	.000	6.00	1	1	0	0	0	0	3.0	3	2	2	1	0	1	0	1	0
Pe. Perez, Vero Beach*	1	1	.500	6.75	15	0	0	9	0	1	30.2	42	33	23	2	0	26	3	29	0
V. Perez, St. Lucie	2	2	.500	3.44	19	0	0	14	0	5	36.2	34	15	14	2	1	20	2	41	1
Perschke, Sarasota	7	3	.700	1.21	42	10	2	23	0	9	111.1	83	32	15	3	4	29	3	107	5
Piatt, West Palm Beach	4	1	.800	0.99	21	0	0	13	0	9	27.1	12	6	3	0	1	16	0	41	2
Pichardo, Baseball City*	1	6	.143	3.80	11	10	0	0	0	0	45.0	47	28	19	1	1	25	0	40	4
B. Pierce, Baseball City*	1	1	.500	5.19	18	2	0	7	0	2	34.2	33	25	20	1	4	23	2	38	5
E. Pierce, Baseball City*	3	1	.750	3.24	37	0	0	22	0	5	50.0	49	21	18	3	0	32	0	53	7
Plemel, St. Petersburg	3	3	.500	3.02	10	9	1	0	1	0	62.2	66	25	21	3	0	10	0	42	3
Pollack, West Palm Beach*	13	2	.867	2.05	24	24	0	0	0	0	140.1	111	38	32	1	1	62	0	91	10
Ponder, Miami	4	2	.667	3.89	15	7	0	6	0	2	44.0	57	30	19	1	2	9	3	44	1
Ponte, Osceola	1	3	.250	2.83	32	0	0	16	0	4	57.1	36	23	18	1	4	28	4	67	3
Popplewell, Fort Lauderdale	5	5	.545	2.23	15	15	3	0	1	0	101.0	82	38	25	2	1	23	0	59	4
Quantrill, Winter Haven	2	5	.286	4.14	7	7	1	0	0	0	45.2	46	24	21	3	0	6	0	14	3
Rambo, Osceola*	5	8	.385	3.09	25	15	2	4	1	0	105.0	97	50	36	3	6	38	3	91	5
Randall, Clearwater	2	3	.400	8.31	16	0	0	12	0	3	17.1	19	17	16	2	0	9	2	10	1
Reich, St. Lucie	0	0	.000	20.25	2	0	0	1	0	0	2.2	8	6	6	0	0	2	0	1	0
Reitzel, 13 Mia.-13 Char.*	5	9	.357	3.80	26	15	1	6	0	3	104.1	111	61	44	7	3	45	3	64	5
Resnikoff, Sarasota*	4	6	.400	2.26	45	0	0	31	0	10	59.2	44	19	15	1	1	17	5	59	4
Reyes, West Palm Beach	4	5	.444	4.74	16	10	0	4	0	1	57.0	58	32	30	4	2	32	2	47	5
D. Richardson, St. Petersburg*	4	1	.800	2.11	47	0	0	15	0	1	64.0	38	18	15	3	0	13	5	51	2
R. Richardson, Winter Haven	0	0	.000	4.34	34	6	0	22	0	7	83.0	87	48	40	3	2	42	1	51	7
Riley, Winter Haven*	4	9	.308	3.11	31	24	0	4	0	0	159.0	152	79	55	5	1	64	0	106	5
Rivera, Lakeland	1	0	1.000	0.41	36	0	0	33	0	14	44.0	31	3	2	1	3	12	0	38	2
Rodriguez, Osceola	12	5	.706	1.68	51	0	0	32	0	10	91.0	57	21	17	4	4	25	5	89	5
B. Rogers, St. Lucie	9	8	.529	3.09	29	19	5	6	0	4	148.2	127	66	51	3	4	26	0	96	7
T. Rogers, Miami*	2	5	.286	2.63	14	10	2	1	1	1	72.0	57	26	21	3	3	49	1	64	4
Romero, Charlotte*	7	2	.778	1.70	12	12	2	0	0	0	74.1	45	19	14	0	2	24	0	72	4
Rowley, Charlotte	0	4	.000	5.32	5	5	0	0	0	0	23.2	19	16	14	0	1	21	1	7	3
Rub, Fort Lauderdale*	1	1	.500	6.23	15	0	0	6	0	2	21.2	26	15	15	4	1	10	1	16	1
Rudolph, Dunedin	3	0	1.000	3.11	35	5	0	12	0	4	81.0	71	37	28	4	0	45	2	62	8
Rush, Winter Haven	5	12	.294	4.08	30	23	2	4	0	2	154.1	139	86	70	7	10	58	0	88	10
Russell, Charlotte	0	1	.000	0.00	1	0	0	0	0	0	0.0	1	1	1	0	0	0	0	0	0
Sanchez, Baseball City*	1	1	.500	1.08	7	1	0	2	0	0	16.2	18	8	2	0	1	1	0	17	0
Sanders, Winter Haven	7	7	.500	2.30	31	11	3	8	2	0	113.1	95	37	29	3	3	35	1	113	3
Satterfield, St. Petersburg	1	8	.111	6.12	17	10	0	0	0	0	60.1	70	45	41	3	1	22	4	38	3
Sauveur, Miami*	0	4	.000	3.32	11	6	1	2	0	0	40.2	41	16	15	2	4	17	0	34	0
Schourek, St. Lucie	4	1	.800	0.97	5	5	2	0	2	0	37.0	29	4	4	1	2	8	0	28	0
Seiler, Fort Lauderdale*	0	0	.000	0.56	8	0	0	4	0	0	16.0	13	1	1	0	0	6	3	15	2
Shackle, St. Petersburg	3	4	.429	2.40	8	8	1	0	0	0	45.0	41	19	12	1	2	15	0	30	3
C. Shaw, Charlotte*	5	3	.625	1.59	11	11	1	0	0	0	68.0	48	18	12	3	1	27	0	69	3
K. Shaw, Baseball City	0	0	.000	5.70	10	0	0	8	0	0	30.0	32	20	19	1	0	14	0	6	4
Shehan, West Palm Beach*	0	0	.000	3.00	2	0	0	1	0	0	3.0	2	2	1	0	0	0	0	2	0
Silverstein, Dunedin	7	5	.583	2.26	45	0	0	22	0	6	75.2	52	28	19	0	17	34	6	70	3
C. Smith, Miami*	1	7	.125	7.02	22	5	0	6	0	1	41.0	58	42	32	4	4	30	1	34	7

Pitcher—Club	W.	L.	Pct.	ERA.	G.	GS.	CG.	GF.	ShO.	Sv.	IP.	H.	R.	ER.	HR.	HB.	BB.	Int. BB.	SO.	WP.
K. Smith, St. Petersburg	0	3	.000	6.75	17	5	0	5	0	0	37.1	50	28	28	1	0	20	3	21	1
R. Smith, Sarasota	0	2	.000	4.05	4	2	0	2	0	0	13.1	16	10	6	0	0	13	1	7	2
S. Smith, Fort Lauderdale	0	0	.000	0.00	1	0	0	1	0	0	2.2	2	0	0	0	0	2	0	1	0
Sommer, West Palm Beach	11	4	.733	2.37	29	19	1	2	1	0	133.0	89	43	35	3	7	64	1	126	6
Spencer, Charlotte	8	2	.800	1.63	43	0	0	20	0	3	83.0	50	28	15	3	5	52	3	78	2
Stafford, Charlotte	1	0	1.000	1.50	1	1	0	0	0	0	6.0	4	1	1	0	0	3	0	3	0
Stanford, Fort Lauderdale	3	1	.750	1.31	57	0	0	53	0	29	61.2	40	15	9	1	0	18	2	60	7
Stevens, Clearwater	1	1	.500	0.75	10	0	0	8	0	1	12.0	4	1	1	1	0	4	1	11	0
Sullivan, Clearwater	2	1	.667	1.23	13	0	0	11	0	3	14.2	8	2	2	0	1	4	0	16	1
Tabaka, Clearwater*	5	2	.714	3.03	8	5	0	1	0	0	35.2	39	17	12	1	0	18	0	23	2
Tafoya, Osceola	1	3	.250	4.91	22	0	0	11	0	2	44.0	53	27	24	1	2	8	3	24	2
Taveras, Vero Beach	13	7	.650	3.11	26	26	5	0	2	0	165.0	143	67	57	5	6	65	4	116	7
Tedder, Sarasota*	0	0	.000	9.00	1	0	0	1	0	0	1.0	1	1	1	0	0	2	0	1	0
Telgheder, St. Lucie	9	4	.692	3.00	14	14	3	0	0	0	96.0	84	38	32	3	3	14	0	77	3
Terrill, Vero Beach*	12	4	.750	2.53	23	21	1	0	1	0	131.2	117	44	37	7	1	35	2	80	4
Thoden, West Palm Beach	3	5	.375	3.30	13	10	1	2	0	1	71.0	73	31	26	2	6	14	0	40	2
Thompson, Winter Haven	4	6	.400	4.82	15	12	1	1	0	0	71.0	93	46	38	2	2	36	0	27	8
Timlin, Dunedin	7	2	.778	1.43	42	0	0	40	0	22	50.1	36	11	8	0	1	16	2	46	3
Tolbert, St. Petersburg	2	3	.400	6.85	5	5	0	0	0	0	23.2	30	21	18	1	6	12	0	14	2
Torres, Lakeland	2	0	1.000	2.60	12	0	0	5	0	0	17.1	15	7	5	3	0	10	2	16	0
Treadwell, Vero Beach	9	1	.900	1.79	16	8	2	5	1	1	80.1	59	17	16	2	1	22	6	80	2
Trlicek, Dunedin	5	8	.385	3.73	26	26	0	0	0	0	154.1	128	74	64	2	6	72	0	125	22
Tucker, Fort Lauderdale*	6	2	.750	4.15	21	9	2	7	0	2	78.0	77	41	36	4	6	43	0	49	10
Tuss, West Palm Beach	6	3	.667	2.11	29	0	0	13	0	1	47.0	34	16	11	1	5	25	2	28	3
Vanzytveld, Vero Beach	6	1	.857	1.38	17	7	3	9	2	0	65.0	40	12	10	2	1	17	1	51	4
Vargas, St. Petersburg	4	6	.400	3.35	38	0	0	26	0	12	53.2	51	24	20	2	2	25	8	46	6
Vaughn, Baseball City	3	6	.333	4.08	21	21	0	0	0	0	121.1	124	65	55	3	7	48	0	91	6
Ventura, Sarasota	12	8	.600	3.39	25	25	2	0	1	0	162.0	153	79	61	5	13	69	1	85	8
Wainhouse, West Palm Beach	6	3	.667	2.11	12	12	2	0	1	0	76.2	68	28	18	1	5	34	0	58	2
Ward, Dunedin*	14	6	.700	2.83	27	26	1	0	0	0	181.1	150	63	57	8	8	39	0	137	8
Weathers, Dunedin	10	7	.588	3.70	27	27	2	0	0	0	158.0	158	82	65	2	9	59	0	96	10
Webster, Baseball City*	1	1	.500	8.36	7	0	0	3	0	0	14.0	16	13	13	2	0	10	0	15	0
Weese, St. Petersburg	2	2	.500	2.52	20	0	0	16	0	9	25.0	17	7	7	0	0	13	2	27	1
Wells, Clearwater	0	2	.000	4.91	6	1	0	2	0	1	14.2	17	9	8	0	1	6	1	11	0
Wengert, Vero Beach	5	1	.833	3.86	22	7	0	6	0	0	74.2	66	40	32	5	4	36	1	47	4
Wenrick, West Palm Beach	4	1	.800	3.62	21	0	0	8	0	4	37.1	40	16	15	3	0	8	0	22	0
Wickman, Sarasota	0	1	.000	1.98	2	2	0	0	0	0	13.2	17	7	3	0	0	4	0	8	0
Wiegandt, Clearwater*	4	8	.333	2.63	33	4	0	16	0	4	75.1	70	33	22	4	3	37	2	52	6
Williams, Miami*	0	3	.000	7.03	13	3	1	2	0	0	24.1	24	22	19	0	2	25	4	18	3
Willis, Lakeland	10	6	.625	2.65	34	7	0	7	0	1	98.2	80	33	29	1	4	30	1	96	4
Windes, Osceola*	4	0	1.000	1.98	44	0	0	19	0	2	68.1	48	18	15	1	1	19	2	54	0
Wiseman, St. Petersburg	9	3	.750	2.63	17	17	1	0	0	0	113.0	108	37	33	3	2	36	3	75	2
Young, West Palm Beach	8	3	.727	2.47	39	12	0	25	0	19	109.1	106	36	30	3	2	27	1	62	6

BALKS—T. Rogers, 14; R. Garcia, 13; Riley, Weathers, 9 each; Perschke, 8; Gregory, Luckham, 7 each; Cross, Dabney, Gohr, Trlicek, 6 each; Astacio, Ericson, Hoy, Jordan, Pascual, Reitzel, Silverstein, Stanford, 5 each; Arner, T. Brown, B. Davis, Doherty, Draper, Ferm, Gogolewski, Gore, Hansell, Juden, Lata, Merigliano, Romero, 4 each; Black, Burgos, Collins, Cornelius, Davino, Dunn, Dunnum, Greer, Griffiths, Hudson, Jones, Kelley, Kerfut, Keyser, Krumm, Middaugh, Newton, Rudolph, Sauveur, Terrill, Treadwell, Tucker, Wainhouse, Ward, Wiegandt, 3 each; Boyle, R. Brown, Burns, Drohan, Ettles, P. Fletcher, Hitt, Hoeme, Hursey, Hvizda, J. Johnson, Johnstone, Knudsen, Lugo, Magee, McCarthy, Milchin, Mosley, Ohlms, Patterson, Pichardo, E. Pierce, Ponte, Rambo, Randall, Resnikoff, R. Richardson, Sanders, Shackle, Sommer, Thompson, Tolbert, Ventura, Willis, 2 each; Allen, Anglero, Backs, Bauer, Bene, Berumen, Borland, M.K. Brady, Cakora, Calhoun, Carter, Clark, Compres, Cunningham, Daniel, T. Delgado, Dell, DeSilva, Elam, Ericks, Fernandez, Furmanik, Galvan, Gietzen, Grimes, Harriger, Hill, Hopper, P. Johnson, Johnston, Kane, Kerrigan, King, Leiter, Lindsey, Magrin, Majer, Mallicoat, Manon, G. Martin, McCormick, Michno, Miller, Ontiveros, Otto, Pacheco, Painter, Parnell, Patrick, Pavlik, D. Perez, P. Perez, V. Perez, Plemel, Pollack, Popplewell, D. Richardson, Rivera, B. Rogers, Rowley, Satterfield, Seiler, C. Shaw, Tabaka, Taveras, Tedder, Thoden, Torres, Weese, Windes, 1 each.

COMBINATION SHUTOUTS—Hopper-Pierce-Parnell, Johnston-Dunn-Parnell, Baseball City; Compres-Manuel 2, Gore-Manuel 2, Alexander-Compres-Spencer, Alexander-Spencer-Manuel, Arner-Manuel, Cunningham-Brown-Manuel, Cunningham-Hvizda-Compres, Cunningham-Manuel, Gore-Brown-Manuel, Gore-Spencer, Pavlik-Brown-Spencer, Pavlik-Spencer-Manuel, Perez-Cecena, Perez-Cecena-Manuel, Romero-Brown, Romero-Cecena-Manuel, Shaw-Manuel, Shaw-Reitzel, Charlotte; Carter-Borland-Sullivan, Clearwater; Boucher-Rudolph, Boucher-Silverstein-Timlin, Cross-Horsman, Cross-Martin, Cross-Timlin, Leiter-Cross-Timlin, Trlicek-Cross-Timlin, Trlicek-Silverstein, Ward-DePastino, Ward-Silverstein, Weathers-Horsman, Weathers-Rudolph-Aylmer, Weathers-Timlin, Dunedin; Popplewell-Rub-Stanford, Fort Lauderdale; DeSilva-Cook-Willis, DeSilva-Doherty, DeSilva-Ettles-Rivera, DeSilva-Willis-Rivera, Ferm-Willis-Rivera, Gohr-Cook, Gohr-Cook-Rivera, Hursey-Berrios-Willis-Ettles, Hursey-Ettles-Cook, Hursey-Knudsen, Hursey-Lumley, Krumm-Cook, Krumm-Knudsen, Marshall-Willis-Ettles-Alcantara, Willis-Doherty, Lakeland; Kerfut-Pascual-Michno, Ponder-Magria, Rogers-Cakora, Miami; Hyson-Windes, Jones-Rodriguez, Jones-Rodriguez-Rambo-Dunnum, Juden-Dovey-Bauer, Luckham-Rodriguez-Windes-Bauer, Mallicoat-Rodriguez, Osceola; Corbin-Furmanik-Johnson-Newton, Corbin-Harriger, Hillman-Brady, St. Lucie; Burgos-Green-Hitt, Burgos-Grimes-Richardson, Majer-Grimes-Richardson-Weese, Milchin-Weese, Shackle-Grimes-Vargas, Wiseman-Richardson, Wiseman-Richardson-Hitt, St. Petersburg; Dabney-Perschke, Perschke-Davino, Perschke-Forrester-Middaugh, Ventura-Middaugh, Ventura-Resnikoff, Wickman-Forrester-Davino, Sarasota; Bustillos-Calhoun, Bustillos-Enno-Biberdorf; Taveras-Fletcher, Terrill-Biberdorf, Terrill-Brady-Biberdorf, Terrill-Calhoun, Terrill-Perez, Treadwell-Brady, Bustillos-Calhoun-Biberdorf, Vero Beach; Freed-Kerrigan 2, Pollack-Kerrigan 2, Collins-Young, Cornelius-Freed-Young, Cornelius-Sommer-Piatt-Kerrigan, Pollack-Davis, Pollack-Young, Reyes-Thoden, Sommer-Kerrigan, Sommer-Young, Young-Davis, Young-Piatt, Young-Wenrick-Tuss, West Palm Beach; Burgo-Mosley, Hansell-Richardson, Kite-Bush, Kite-Sanders-Kane, Riley-Kane, Sanders-Hoy, Winter Haven.

NO-HIT GAMES—Daniel, Miami, defeated Fort Lauderdale, 7-0 (second game), June 12; Draper, Fort Lauderdale, defeated St. Petersburg, 6-0, July 21.

Midwest League

CLASS A

CHAMPIONSHIP WINNERS IN PREVIOUS YEARS

1947—Belleville .667	1963—Clinton .710	1977—Waterloo .580
Belleville .672	Clinton .629	Burlington a .511
1948—West Frankfort* .708	1964—Clinton .667	1978—Appleton a .708
1949—Centralia .627	Fox Cities z .667	Burlington .500
Paducah (4th)† .454	1965—Burlington .667	1979—Waterloo .600
1950—Centralia‡ .675	Burlington .677	Quad Cities a .579
1951—Paris§ .700	1966—Fox Cities z .689	1980—Waterloo a .610
Danville (4th)† .432	Cedar Rapids .762	Quad Cities .532
1952—Danville x .685	1967—Wisconsin Rapids .685	1981—Wausau a .636
Decatur (3rd)† .584	Appleton z .587	Quad Cities .570
1953—Decatur* .576	1968—Decatur .656	1982—Madison .626
1954—Decatur .587	Quad Cities z .648	Appleton b .579
Danville (2nd)‡ .528	1969—Appleton .648	1983—Springfield .635
1955—Dubuque* .587	Appleton .690	Springfield .576
1956—Paris y .656	1970—Quincy z .691	1984—Appleton c .640
Dubuque .603	Quad Cities .581	Springfield .504
1957—Decatur y .683	1971—Appleton .642	1985—Kenosha b .568
Clinton .623	Quad Cities a .548	Peoria .536
1958—Michigan City .623	1972—Appleton .598	1986—Springfield .621
Waterloo z .613	Danville a .584	Waterloo b .557
1959—Waterloo .613	1973—Wisconsin Rapids a .562	1987—Springfield .671
Waterloo .613	Danville .537	Kenosha b .586
1960—Waterloo .629	1974—Appleton .593	1988—Cedar Rapids a .621
Waterloo .677	Danville a .517	Kenosha .579
1961—Waterloo .613	1975—Waterloo a .727	1989—South Bend a .644
Quincy z .594	Quad Cities .624	Springfield .541
1962—Dubuque z .667	1976—Waterloo a .600	
Waterloo .625	Cedar Rapids .595	

*Won championship and four-club playoff. †Won four-club playoff. ‡Playoff finals canceled because of bad weather. §Won both halves of split-season. xWon first half of split-season and tied Paris for second-half title. yWon first-half title and four-team playoff. zWon split-season playoff. aLeague divided into Northern and Southern divisions and played split-season. Playoff winner. bLeague divided into Northern, Central and Southern divisions. Playoff winner. cLeague divided into Northern, Central and Southern divisions; regular-season and playoff winner. (NOTE—Known as Illinois State League in 1947-48 and Mississippi-Ohio Valley League from 1949 through 1955.)

STANDING OF CLUBS AT CLOSE OF FIRST HALF, JUNE 16

NORTHERN DIVISION

Club	W.	L.	T.	Pct.	G.B.
Madison (Athletics)	40	28	0	.588	....
South Bend (White Sox)	35	31	0	.530	4
Beloit (Brewers)	35	32	0	.522	4½
Rockford (Expos)	34	34	0	.500	6
Kenosha (Twins)	29	39	0	.426	11
Appleton (Royals)	26	37	0	.413	11½
Wausau (Orioles)	23	45	0	.338	17

SOUTHERN DIVISION

Club	W.	L.	T.	Pct.	G.B.
Cedar Rapids (Reds)	45	21	0	.682	....
Burlington (Braves)	43	26	0	.623	3½
Clinton (Giants)	40	25	0	.615	4½
Quad City (Angels)	36	34	0	.514	11
Springfield (Cardinals)	32	38	0	.457	15
Peoria (Cubs)	27	41	0	.397	19
Waterloo (Padres)	26	40	0	.394	19

STANDING OF CLUBS AT CLOSE OF SECOND HALF, AUGUST 29

NORTHERN DIVISION

Club	W.	L.	T.	Pct.	G.B.
South Bend (White Sox)	42	26	0	.618	....
Beloit (Brewers)	37	31	0	.544	5
Appleton (Royals)	36	34	0	.514	7
Madison (Athletics)	34	33	0	.507	7½
Kenosha (Twins)	32	38	0	.457	11
Wausau (Orioles)	26	42	0	.382	16
Rockford (Expos)	22	46	0	.324	20

SOUTHERN DIVISION

Club	W.	L.	T.	Pct.	G.B.
Quad City (Angels)	45	25	0	.643	....
Cedar Rapids (Reds)	43	25	0	.632	1
Clinton (Giants)	36	33	0	.522	8½
Burlington (Braves)	35	33	0	.515	9
Waterloo (Padres)	34	36	0	.486	11
Springfield (Cardinals)	31	38	0	.449	13½
Peoria (Cubs)	28	41	0	.406	16½

COMPOSITE STANDING OF CLUBS AT CLOSE OF SEASON, AUGUST 29

Club	C.R.	Q.C.	S.B.	Bur.	Cln.	Mad.	Bel.	App.	Spr.	Ken.	Wat.	Roc.	Peo.	Wau.	W.	L.	T.	Pct.	G.B.
Cedar Rapids (Reds)	...	7	6	8	8	5	6	4	8	4	11	5	12	4	88	46	0	.657	....
Quad City (Angels)	7	....	4	7	3	5	4	5	10	4	8	5	11	8	81	59	0	.579	10
South Bend (White Sox)	2	4	....	4	4	10	10	5	6	9	3	9	4	7	77	57	0	.575	11
Burlington (Braves)	5	7	4	....	8	3	3	5	11	6	7	5	8	6	78	59	0	.569	11½
Clinton (Giants)	4	11	4	6	....	5	2	3	7	6	11	5	7	5	76	58	0	.567	12
Madison (Athletics)	3	3	4	5	2	....	6	8	5	10	5	6	5	12	74	61	0	.548	14½
Beloit (Brewers)	1	4	4	4	6	5	....	9	7	9	3	8	3	9	72	63	0	.533	16½
Appleton (Royals)	2	3	7	3	4	6	5	....	3	6	2	7	6	8	62	71	0	.466	25½
Springfield (Cardinals)	6	4	2	3	7	3	1	5	....	4	9	4	10	5	63	76	0	.453	27½
Kenosha (Twins)	4	4	4	2	4	5	8	4	4	....	10	3	7	6	61	77	0	.442	29
Waterloo (Padres)	3	6	4	7	2	3	5	5	5	4	....	4	7	5	60	76	0	.441	29
Rockford (Expos)	3	3	5	2	2	7	6	6	4	4	4	....	2	8	56	80	0	.412	33
Peoria (Cubs)	2	3	4	6	7	3	5	2	3	4	7	6	....	3	55	82	0	.401	34½
Wausau (Orioles)	4	0	5	2	3	2	5	6	3	7	2	6	4	....	49	87	0	.360	40

Quad City's home games played in Davenport, Ia.

Major league affiliations in parentheses.

Playoffs—Quad City defeated Cedar Rapids, two games to none; South Bend defeated Madison, two games to none; Quad City defeated South Bend, three games to one, to win league championship.

Regular-Season Attendance—Appleton, 84,396; Beloit, 95,876; Burlington, 81,230; Cedar Rapids, 121,340; Clinton, 75,325; Kenosha, 53,373; Madison, 82,490; Peoria, 195,671; Quad City, 204,889; Rockford, 140,864; South Bend, 212,485; Springfield, 161,271; Waterloo, 82,451; Wausau, 56,434. Total-1,648,095. Playoffs-22,335. All-Star Game-6,873.

Managers—Appleton, Joe Breeden; Beloit, Bob Derksen; Burlington, Jim Saul; Cedar Rapids, Dave Miley; Clinton, Jack Mull; Kenosha, Steve Liddle; Madison, Casey Parsons; Peoria, Greg Mahlberg; Quad City, Don Long; Rockford, Mike Quade; South Bend, Rick Patterson; Springfield, Keith Champion; Waterloo, Bryan Little; Wausau, Mike Young.

All-Star Team—1B—Rich Tunison, Appleton; 2B—Chad Curtis, Quad City; 3B—John Byington, Beloit; SS—Damion Easley, Quad City; OF—Reggie Sanders, Cedar Rapids; Troy O'Leary, Beloit; Scott Bryant, Cedar Rapids; C—Eddie Taubensee, Cedar Rapids; DH—Fred Cooley, Madison; LHP—Alan Newman, Kenosha; RHP—Darin Kracl, Madison; LH Reliever—Mike Hock, Quad City; RH Reliever—Clyde Keller, Springfield; Most Valuable Player—Reggie Sanders, Cedar Rapids; Prospect of the Year—Reggie Sanders, Cedar Rapids; Manager of the Year—Don Long, Quad City.

(Compiled by Howe Sportsdata International, Boston, Mass.)

CLUB BATTING

Club	Pct.	G.	AB.	R.	OR.	H.	TB.	2B.	3B.	HR.	RBI.	SH.	SF.	HP.	BB.	Int. BB.	SO.	SB.	CS.	LOB.
South Bend	.262	134	4235	611	568	1109	1534	195	40	50	509	79	38	48	483	24	946	154	127	866
Cedar Rapids	.251	134	4293	574	430	1079	1604	199	22	94	504	33	40	22	522	23	825	141	86	961
Quad City	.250	140	4376	660	525	1093	1601	208	18	88	570	42	37	82	553	20	956	171	76	958
Burlington	.249	137	4454	646	570	1110	1602	185	35	79	555	39	33	45	528	17	863	122	76	957
Beloit	.246	135	4253	595	563	1046	1500	202	18	72	520	53	35	38	492	16	999	128	110	852
Peoria	.245	137	4509	532	595	1105	1554	200	39	57	464	53	23	48	412	15	943	91	60	969
Clinton	.239	134	4291	563	452	1027	1417	165	33	53	491	57	39	59	493	21	813	194	80	957
Waterloo	.235	136	4317	533	559	1014	1392	181	28	47	468	39	39	46	515	23	1050	141	80	916
Madison	.235	135	4311	602	567	1012	1480	166	28	82	506	37	46	40	529	25	1151	144	69	916
Appleton	.235	133	4225	564	557	994	1343	162	38	37	477	39	32	58	509	15	929	173	89	901
Springfield	.234	139	4519	549	668	1059	1447	177	20	57	476	42	34	40	545	16	1031	70	54	1010
Kenosha	.230	138	4329	521	545	997	1392	174	22	59	452	53	37	82	489	15	1055	194	92	925
Wausau	.227	136	4313	461	723	981	1369	148	24	64	397	45	26	46	451	8	883	113	64	906
Rockford	.226	136	4339	525	614	982	1363	187	34	42	444	26	33	46	523	13	1063	122	67	956

INDIVIDUAL BATTING
(Leading Qualifiers for Batting Championship—378 or More Plate Appearances)

*Bats lefthanded.   †Switch-hitter.

Player and Club	Pct.	G.	AB.	R.	H.	TB.	2B.	3B.	HR.	RBI.	SH.	SF.	HP.	BB.	Int. BB.	SO.	SB.	CS.
Cepicky, Scott, South Bend*	.312	128	462	65	144	205	30	5	7	77	6	6	3	55	7	72	12	12
Curtis, Chad, Quad City	.307	135	492	87	151	223	28	1	14	65	4	3	12	57	3	78	64	22
McCoy, Brent, Burlington†	.304	125	461	80	140	180	23	1	5	71	4	9	6	58	3	75	17	3
Tunison, Richard, Appleton†	.300	129	490	69	147	204	21	6	8	86	0	6	6	39	4	115	32	16
O'Leary, Troy, Beloit*	.298	118	436	73	130	179	29	1	6	62	6	3	0	41	2	90	12	12
Dunn, Steven, Kenosha*	.297	130	478	48	142	203	29	1	10	72	1	6	6	49	8	105	13	6
Caraballo, Ramon, Burlington†	.290	102	390	83	113	180	18	14	7	55	2	2	7	49	2	68	41	20
James, Joseph, Clinton*	.289	125	450	58	130	217	25	4	18	76	0	3	6	34	4	67	3	1
Grace, Michael, Rockford	.287	107	366	41	105	138	20	2	3	42	2	2	3	44	0	56	7	2
Sanders, Reginald, Cedar Rapids	.285	127	466	89	133	213	21	4	17	63	2	1	4	59	2	97	40	15

Departmental Leaders: G—Gardner, 137; AB—Curtis, 492; R—Moore, 93; H—Curtis, 151; TB—Curtis, 223; 2B—Franco, 33; 3B—R. Caraballo, 14; HR—Cooley, 22; RBI—Byington, 89; SH—Washington, 12; SF—Beck, Eatinger, McCoy, 9; HP—Morris, 18; BB—Moore, 111; IBB—Dunn, 8; SO—Tinsley, 175; SB—McFarlin, 73; CS—Noland, 24.

(All Players—Listed Alphabetically)

Player and Club	Pct.	G.	AB.	R.	H.	TB.	2B.	3B.	HR.	RBI.	SH.	SF.	HP.	BB.	Int. BB.	SO.	SB.	CS.
Abbott, Kurt, Madison	.232	104	362	38	84	102	18	0	0	28	5	4	5	47	1	74	21	9
Adames, Juan, Peoria	.091	8	22	2	2	2	0	0	0	1	1	0	0	2	0	3	2	1
Ahrens, Kelly, Clinton	.178	21	45	4	8	9	1	0	0	3	1	0	0	4	0	16	1	0
Alexander, Manuel, Wausau	.178	44	152	16	27	32	3	1	0	11	1	3	1	12	1	41	8	3
Allen, Richard, Cedar Rapids	.233	121	390	47	91	136	19	1	8	46	3	5	5	37	1	65	7	8
Alvarez, Clemente, South Bend	.236	48	127	14	30	41	5	0	2	12	5	2	1	20	0	38	2	1
Andujar, Juan, Springfield†	.213	105	366	32	78	104	13	2	3	30	9	0	1	23	1	109	10	4
Apolinario, Oswaldo, Burlington	.211	42	133	16	28	32	2	1	0	7	2	0	0	6	0	32	6	4
Armas, Marco, Madison	.238	75	260	32	62	96	13	0	7	33	1	3	2	10	0	80	3	5
Asencio, Matires, Wausau	.111	19	36	1	4	4	0	0	0	2	0	0	0	3	0	12	0	1
Baldwin, Anthony, Burlington	.212	84	264	41	56	89	7	1	8	40	1	1	1	52	3	60	9	10
Bautista, Hector, Wausau*	.223	32	94	11	21	37	5	1	3	13	0	0	1	8	0	13	0	1
Beck, Wynn, Madison*	.264	102	330	41	87	126	13	1	8	51	2	9	1	46	3	66	0	1
Beeler, Robert, Cedar Rapids	.274	79	277	28	76	107	10	0	7	42	1	3	1	28	0	58	3	3
Bell, David, Springfield	.143	55	84	11	12	15	3	0	0	4	0	0	1	9	0	31	1	1
Bellinger, Clayton, Clinton	.217	109	383	52	83	138	17	4	10	48	5	3	7	27	0	102	13	6
Benitez, Christian, Wausau	.229	75	205	16	47	52	2	0	1	6	1	0	0	20	0	33	9	3
Berlin, Randolph, Springfield	.234	51	128	15	30	36	6	0	0	9	3	1	1	13	0	34	1	2
Berryhill, Damon, Peoria†	.385	7	26	10	10	21	2	0	3	8	0	0	1	3	1	6	0	1
Billingsley, Rodney, Waterloo	.043	18	23	1	1	1	0	0	0	2	0	0	0	2	0	10	0	0
Billmeyer, Michael, Quad City*	.269	77	234	30	63	92	14	0	5	33	3	4	0	28	2	36	1	0
Blanks, Daryl, Burlington*	.203	48	133	8	27	34	2	1	1	11	1	2	1	11	0	20	1	1
Bonner, Jeffry, Clinton*	.214	78	196	30	42	56	10	2	0	20	3	3	1	27	2	34	13	6
Borgogno, Matthew, Clinton*	.120	10	25	0	3	3	0	0	0	0	0	0	0	3	0	7	1	0
Brady, Patrick, Clinton	.224	49	156	23	35	49	6	1	2	20	0	0	2	23	1	25	2	4
Branson, Jeffery, Cedar Rapids*	.251	62	239	37	60	99	13	4	6	24	0	2	0	24	3	44	11	3
Bryant, Scott, Cedar Rapids	.264	67	212	40	56	114	10	3	14	48	0	3	1	50	5	47	6	4
Buford, Damon, Wausau†	.300	41	160	31	48	62	7	2	1	14	1	2	4	21	1	32	15	4
Bushing, Christopher, Rockford	.000	46	1	0	0	0	0	0	0	0	0	0	0	0	0	1	0	0
Butcher, Arthur, Beloit*	.258	75	213	21	55	86	14	1	5	33	1	2	0	7	1	42	10	1
Byington, John, Beloit	.263	127	438	75	115	191	23	1	17	89	2	7	8	49	2	68	2	4
Cairo, Sergio, Wausau	.240	111	333	31	80	105	8	4	3	29	2	3	3	25	0	49	12	1
Campa, Eric, Madison	.255	29	102	11	26	27	1	0	0	8	0	1	1	4	0	19	0	1
Campas, Michael, Springfield†	.242	121	392	52	95	134	15	0	8	46	5	3	3	62	1	95	1	4
Cancel, Daniel, Peoria	.164	40	110	11	18	19	1	0	0	5	1	0	2	13	0	38	4	1
Caraballo, Edgardo, Appleton	.214	123	406	37	87	125	14	3	6	50	0	7	12	39	0	62	6	5
Caraballo, Ramon, Burlington†	.290	102	390	83	113	180	18	14	7	55	2	2	7	49	2	68	41	20
Carey, Frank, Clinton*	.296	66	213	31	63	80	5	3	2	32	3	1	4	28	1	54	8	1

Player and Club	Pct.	G.	AB.	R.	H.	TB.	2B.	3B.	HR.	RBI.	SH.	SF.	HP.	BB.	Int. BB.	SO.	SB.	CS.
Carter, Edward, Springfield*	.233	7	30	4	7	9	0	1	0	2	0	0	0	1	0	5	2	0
Castellano, Pedro, Peoria	.276	117	417	61	115	156	27	4	2	44	3	4	3	63	2	73	7	1
Cepicky, Scott, South Bend*	.312	128	462	65	144	205	30	5	7	77	6	6	3	55	7	72	12	12
Charpia, Reed, Beloit	.000	4	2	0	0	0	0	0	0	0	0	0	0	1	0	0	1	0
Clark, Jeffrey, Burlington*	.257	96	288	47	74	82	4	2	0	27	2	1	0	51	2	38	9	7
Clark, Timothy, Beloit*	.260	67	219	27	57	84	13	1	4	44	2	3	3	31	1	45	3	4
Clemens, Troy, Springfield*	.272	105	316	37	86	112	16	2	2	40	5	3	5	30	1	44	0	5
Cole, George, Appleton	.232	34	112	16	26	32	2	2	0	10	0	1	1	5	0	14	3	3
Cole, Marvin, Peoria	.250	60	236	25	59	73	9	1	1	20	3	0	4	14	0	10	2	5
Collins, Sean, Appleton	.226	22	53	9	12	15	0	0	1	4	1	1	0	15	0	12	11	2
Colon, David, Waterloo	.216	85	268	23	58	84	18	1	2	32	6	3	1	33	0	61	3	4
Conley, Gregory, Waterloo	.209	82	239	20	50	60	7	0	1	12	0	1	5	17	0	90	2	1
Conte, Michael, Madison	.173	55	173	24	30	46	2	1	4	16	3	1	1	21	1	38	4	3
Cooley, Fred, Madison	.259	101	363	50	94	180	18	1	22	66	0	2	4	29	7	112	1	2
Cordova, Martin, Kenosha	.216	81	269	35	58	96	7	5	7	25	0	1	5	28	0	73	6	3
Cornell, Daren, Beloit	.204	39	108	12	22	26	4	0	0	14	2	2	1	8	0	40	0	2
Cramer, William, Rockford	.158	66	183	15	29	37	8	0	0	12	0	4	2	17	0	40	0	2
Crowe, Ronald, Clinton	.280	101	332	56	93	142	20	4	7	42	1	6	3	36	1	50	6	4
Cudjo, Lavell, Cedar Rapids	.127	30	79	10	10	13	3	0	0	2	3	0	1	15	0	21	2	4
Cunningham, Earl, Peoria	.216	78	269	24	58	82	9	0	5	26	0	3	6	13	0	108	2	2
Curtis, Chad, Quad City	.307	135	492	87	151	223	28	1	14	65	4	3	12	57	3	78	64	22
Darter, Keith, Appleton*	.244	46	131	9	32	39	5	1	0	7	5	0	3	11	0	21	4	3
Dattola, Kevin, Madison†	.324	25	102	12	33	40	0	2	1	9	0	0	2	7	0	10	11	4
David, Gregory, Waterloo*	.000	1	1	0	0	0	0	0	0	0	0	0	0	1	0	0	0	0
Davis, Allen, Wausau*	.164	28	61	5	10	14	2	1	0	1	0	0	1	3	0	26	1	1
Davis, Courtney, Clinton	.210	38	119	11	25	35	1	0	3	15	2	2	0	16	0	45	13	4
Davison, Scotty, Rockford	.215	127	441	52	95	125	13	7	1	48	6	4	3	60	1	115	22	9
de la Nuez, Rexford, Kenosha	.245	72	253	35	62	97	16	2	5	35	1	1	6	42	1	49	20	10
DeLaRosa, Cesar, Quad City†	.236	23	72	7	17	20	3	0	0	6	5	0	0	3	0	18	1	0
Delarwelle, Chris, Kenosha	.298	66	252	31	75	104	15	1	4	45	1	7	1	21	0	24	6	3
Devares, Cesar, Wausau	.199	56	171	7	34	49	4	1	3	19	2	0	0	7	0	28	2	3
Diggs, Antonio, Beloit†	.000	2	4	0	0	0	0	0	0	0	0	0	0	0	0	0	0	0
DiMarco, Steven, Wausau*	.138	18	65	4	9	13	1	0	1	3	1	0	1	5	0	15	2	1
Dombrowski, Robert, Cedar Rapids	.095	10	21	4	2	2	0	0	0	1	0	0	4	0	7	0	0	
Doyle, Thomas, Waterloo*	.220	120	413	37	91	116	14	1	3	36	0	1	3	27	1	80	1	3
Dunn, Steven, Kenosha*	.297	130	478	48	142	203	29	1	10	72	1	6	6	49	8	105	13	6
Easley, Damion, Quad City	.274	103	365	59	100	155	19	3	10	56	1	2	8	41	0	60	25	8
Eatinger, Michael, South Bend	.264	129	477	63	126	176	29	3	5	57	6	9	3	36	2	63	16	7
Ebright, Christopher, Peoria*	.234	107	338	41	79	133	15	3	11	41	2	1	1	41	4	67	2	3
Edwards, Todd, Beloit*	.303	21	66	5	20	22	2	0	0	4	2	1	0	11	0	20	4	6
Elder, Isaac, Rockford†	.227	89	216	43	49	70	13	1	2	15	4	0	6	34	1	71	21	7
Ellis, Jason, Burlington	.000	1	2	0	0	0	0	0	0	0	0	0	0	0	0	2	0	0
Ellis, Paul, Springfield*	.235	50	183	18	43	63	5	0	5	25	0	0	2	26	1	34	0	1
Erdman, Bradley, Peoria	.193	37	119	9	23	26	3	0	0	4	1	0	1	12	0	42	0	0
Esquer, David, Beloit	.305	19	59	8	18	19	1	0	0	3	3	0	1	4	0	9	2	2
Federico, Joseph, Springfield*	.242	90	293	44	71	118	19	2	8	37	0	2	0	39	2	82	2	0
Fielitz, William, Springfield	.174	13	23	1	4	5	1	0	0	0	0	0	0	6	0	8	0	1
Forrester, Thomas, South Bend*	.529	23	17	2	9	11	0	1	0	7	0	0	0	4	1	1	0	1
Fowler, John, Wausau†	.224	70	223	25	50	83	16	1	5	25	4	1	0	16	0	53	6	1
Francisco, Rene, Peoria	.237	75	228	29	54	65	5	3	0	19	5	3	2	21	0	49	4	2
Franco, Matthew, Peoria*	.282	123	443	52	125	180	33	2	6	65	1	2	1	43	2	39	4	4
Fuller, Paul, Wausau	.234	55	175	21	41	56	9	0	2	26	3	3	0	26	1	30	3	0
Gantner, James, Beloit*	.379	9	29	10	11	18	1	0	2	6	0	0	7	1	2	1		
Garcia, Francisco, Appleton	.111	7	18	2	2	2	0	0	0	0	0	0	0	7	0	7	1	1
Garcia, Librado, Beloit	.136	42	81	10	11	19	0	1	2	10	1	0	2	5	0	37	2	2
Gardner, Glen, Burlington*	.260	137	489	64	127	185	30	2	8	61	1	3	3	60	4	47	3	5
Garibaldo, Christobal, Appleton	.125	7	16	1	2	2	0	0	0	2	0	0	0	2	0	4	0	1
Gay, Jeffrey, Quad City*	.241	81	278	26	67	101	16	0	6	34	2	1	1	13	0	47	0	0
Gentile, Randy, Kenosha*	.209	80	258	28	54	87	12	0	7	34	0	1	6	22	0	84	3	1
Gerald, Edward, Appleton	.216	45	125	22	27	33	4	1	0	6	2	0	0	17	0	45	4	1
Gilcrist, John, Appleton	.252	129	472	82	119	168	16	9	5	60	4	6	5	44	0	78	24	13
Gill, Steven, Waterloo*	.264	56	197	24	52	64	5	2	1	19	4	2	5	22	1	34	3	3
Gillis, Timothy, Burlington	.256	131	464	66	119	187	28	2	12	61	3	1	8	41	0	98	4	3
Gillum, Kenneth, Cedar Rapids*	.375	4	16	3	6	7	1	0	0	2	0	0	1	0	3	0	0	
Glenn, Leon, Beloit*	.193	65	202	19	39	64	4	3	5	29	2	0	0	20	1	93	10	6
Godin, Steven, Wausau	.248	48	145	14	36	51	6	0	3	13	3	0	0	18	0	32	4	2
Gonzales, Lawrence, Quad City	.307	99	309	44	95	137	16	1	8	75	2	2	8	36	1	56	2	1
Grace, Michael, Rockford	.287	107	366	41	105	138	20	2	3	42	2	2	3	44	0	56	7	2
Grahovac, Michael, Clinton	.147	33	102	8	15	20	5	0	0	3	5	0	0	5	0	33	1	0
Greene, William, Rockford*	.400	11	35	4	14	17	3	0	0	2	0	0	0	7	0	7	2	1
Griesser, Grant, Appleton	.236	35	89	9	21	28	4	0	1	12	0	1	1	13	0	18	1	1
Gross, Deryk, Kenosha	.204	59	167	22	34	42	5	0	1	17	2	1	0	14	0	47	10	6
Gustafson, Edward, Clinton	.000	40	1	0	0	0	0	0	0	0	0	0	0	0	0	1	0	0
Hairston, John, South Bend†	.238	98	252	48	60	95	15	4	4	33	8	0	4	33	1	100	8	10
Harper, Gregory, Burlington	.000	9	16	0	0	0	0	0	0	1	1	0	0	1	0	8	0	0
Harris, Keith, South Bend	.209	15	43	4	9	15	0	3	0	4	0	0	0	3	0	14	3	2
Haugen, Troy, Beloit†	.226	109	363	48	82	101	15	2	0	26	8	4	0	78	1	93	9	17
Henry, Scott, Madison*	.239	46	134	21	32	43	6	1	1	15	0	5	0	32	1	22	0	3
Hernandez, Arned, Appleton	.159	44	113	19	18	23	2	0	1	7	1	0	7	5	0	35	4	6
Hernandez, Henry, Springfield*	.234	41	128	14	30	48	3	0	5	26	1	3	0	14	0	29	0	0
Herrera, Ezequiel, Springfield	.265	123	490	56	130	152	14	4	0	42	5	0	3	35	0	99	11	10
Hicks, Aman, Wausau*	.208	99	289	36	60	79	11	4	0	12	6	3	3	29	1	60	12	7
Hildreth, Bradley, Wausau	.239	87	268	23	64	83	7	0	4	18	5	1	2	24	0	36	4	4
Hirtensteiner, Richard, Quad City*	.220	87	259	36	57	81	12	0	4	24	7	5	7	26	2	78	10	3
Hoerner, Troy, Kenosha	.148	25	88	7	13	23	4	0	2	3	0	0	2	6	0	39	1	0
Holbert, Ray, Waterloo	.204	133	411	51	84	105	10	1	3	39	9	1	4	51	0	117	16	16
Hollis, Jackson, Cedar Rapids*	.309	49	149	21	46	68	10	0	4	19	4	2	0	21	1	33	6	2
Hudson, Deryk, Rockford	.207	111	376	38	78	102	12	0	4	41	2	4	6	41	0	96	1	5
Ingram, Jeffrey, South Bend	.286	61	168	22	48	67	3	2	4	22	2	1	1	15	0	32	3	4
James, Joseph, Clinton	.289	125	450	58	130	217	25	4	18	76	0	3	6	34	4	67	3	1
Javier, Vicente, Cedar Rapids†	.193	62	135	14	26	36	3	2	1	15	2	0	0	13	0	33	1	2
Jeffery, Scott, Cedar Rapids	.000	9	3	0	0	0	0	0	0	1	0	0	0	1	0	0	0	0

Player and Club	Pct.	G.	AB.	R.	H.	TB.	2B.	3B.	HR.	RBI.	SH.	SF.	HP.	BB.	Int. BB.	SO.	SB.	CS.
Johnson, Randall, Clinton	.222	32	81	12	18	24	4	1	0	10	2	0	2	27	0	22	3	5
Jones, Eugene, Cedar Rapids	.251	59	215	41	54	74	12	1	2	23	1	4	0	33	1	39	14	5
Jones, Robert, Quad City†	.236	108	351	40	83	127	20	0	8	47	0	2	3	37	3	94	6	8
Kapano, Corey, Quad City	.244	106	352	57	86	133	18	1	9	51	0	2	5	48	0	89	4	4
Kasper, Kevin, Clinton	.210	102	314	43	66	77	8	0	1	25	8	0	8	50	2	54	21	11
Kaub, Keith, Rockford	.200	42	130	9	26	38	3	0	3	13	1	2	1	5	0	44	0	1
Keating, Michael, Springfield	.136	10	22	1	3	4	1	0	0	0	0	0	0	0	0	7	0	0
Kessinger, Keith, Wausau	.216	37	134	17	29	37	8	0	0	9	0	0	3	6	0	23	1	1
Kindred, Vincent, Springfield	.280	38	125	22	35	52	6	1	3	20	0	1	1	21	0	31	7	1
King, David, Appleton	.266	90	316	34	84	131	23	0	8	64	0	1	5	22	2	72	1	1
Knabenshue, Jeffrey, Beloit	.177	23	62	8	11	13	0	1	0	6	2	0	1	7	1	16	2	5
Kobza, Gregory, South Bend°	.268	97	284	37	76	115	18	3	5	51	2	3	3	58	2	83	3	3
Kraft, Michael, Springfield°	.241	109	349	34	84	113	16	2	3	36	3	6	1	50	1	78	1	3
Krause, Ronald, Rockford°	.215	115	344	53	74	90	9	2	1	28	1	2	5	84	2	96	12	8
Kremblas, Frank, Cedar Rapids	.252	92	266	18	67	95	13	0	5	26	4	3	1	23	0	54	2	8
Kroeger, John, South Bend°	.250	9	16	0	4	5	1	0	0	2	0	0	0	3	0	5	0	1
Krumback, Mark, Cedar Rapids†	.236	122	440	59	104	131	14	2	3	29	6	2	2	64	1	73	17	14
Kuhn, Chadwick, Madison°	.250	22	4	0	1	2	1	0	0	0	0	0	0	0	0	2	0	0
Laker, Timothy, Rockford	.221	120	425	46	94	139	18	3	7	57	1	8	1	32	1	83	7	2
Lamitola, Michael, Wausau	.180	42	122	11	22	25	1	1	0	6	7	0	3	5	0	21	1	4
Landinez, Carlos, Springfield	.120	60	133	22	16	22	3	0	1	7	2	1	5	12	0	39	5	2
Langiotti, Freddie, Springfield	.219	98	306	31	67	88	9	0	4	34	4	5	1	47	0	50	0	5
Leary, Robert, Rockford	.243	34	70	9	17	23	3	0	1	7	2	0	2	10	0	15	1	1
Lee, Keith, Wausau°	.079	16	38	0	3	3	0	0	0	0	0	0	0	1	0	10	0	1
Lewis, Mica, Kenosha	.227	64	238	33	54	77	9	1	4	14	3	0	2	25	1	73	20	6
Lewis, Theodore, Wausau	.285	115	404	60	115	167	24	2	8	45	1	1	5	46	0	64	10	5
Lloyd, Michael, Kenosha	.266	83	267	41	71	78	4	0	1	26	7	4	3	36	0	50	28	6
Lombardozzi, Christopher, C. R.°	.272	47	169	11	46	57	6	1	1	25	0	2	0	18	0	20	8	3
Lopez, Javier, Burlington	.265	116	422	48	112	168	17	3	11	55	4	0	5	14	2	84	0	2
Lydy, Scott, Madison	.190	54	174	33	33	55	6	2	4	19	0	2	1	25	1	62	7	5
Malinowski, Christopher, Rockford	.258	21	66	4	17	23	2	2	0	7	0	1	0	5	0	8	2	2
Marrero, Oreste, Beloit°	.275	119	400	59	110	185	25	1	16	55	0	1	0	45	3	107	8	4
Marrero, Vilato, Beloit	.271	87	255	37	69	99	13	1	5	24	1	3	2	24	1	34	3	5
Martin, Steven, Waterloo	.251	122	398	64	100	156	21	4	9	48	0	2	1	57	4	118	31	4
Martinez, Luis, Springfield†	.267	105	382	58	102	152	12	4	10	54	0	7	2	40	7	50	7	4
Martinez, Ramon, Quad City	.225	105	306	47	69	106	10	0	9	40	4	6	9	58	1	82	4	7
Marze, Dickey, Burlington	.204	86	221	32	45	67	6	2	4	22	3	1	4	27	0	75	11	1
Mathiot, Michael, Kenosha	.184	48	158	22	29	42	10	0	1	15	5	1	5	19	0	47	3	4
McCormick, Glenn, Madison	.163	19	49	6	8	10	2	0	0	5	1	1	1	11	0	17	0	1
McCoy, Brent, Burlington†	.304	125	461	80	140	180	23	1	5	71	4	9	6	58	3	75	17	3
McFarlin, Jason, Clinton°	.227	129	475	68	108	127	9	5	0	31	7	1	9	48	2	79	73	18
Meares, Patrick, Kenosha	.239	52	197	26	47	73	10	2	4	22	2	1	4	25	2	45	2	1
Mercedes, Henry, Madison	.227	90	282	29	64	90	13	2	3	37	6	2	1	30	0	100	6	0
Milene, Jeffrey, Kenosha	.000	2	1	0	0	0	0	0	0	0	0	0	0	0	0	1	0	0
Miller, Brent, Wausau°	.301	19	83	9	25	35	7	0	1	8	1	1	1	2	0	18	2	0
Miller, Roger, Clinton	.257	111	319	31	82	104	11	1	3	41	8	3	1	28	3	30	1	3
Minnis, William, Quad City	.333	3	9	2	3	4	1	0	0	2	0	1	0	0	0	3	0	0
Miranda, Giovanni, Appleton	.227	55	141	15	32	37	1	2	0	7	1	0	3	16	0	26	8	4
Molitor, Paul, Beloit	.500	1	4	1	2	5	0	0	1	1	0	0	0	0	0	0	0	0
Moore, Kerwin, Appleton†	.222	128	451	93	100	137	17	7	2	36	6	1	3	111	3	139	57	20
Morris, Steven, Kenosha†	.235	105	349	59	82	101	13	3	0	29	7	4	18	65	0	74	41	19
Morrison, Brian, Burlington	.242	69	240	29	58	116	14	1	14	50	1	3	1	26	1	76	0	1
Mota, William, Kenosha†	.181	80	265	20	48	60	8	2	0	20	1	4	1	18	2	39	0	2
Mulvaney, Michael, Cedar Rapids	.259	101	367	42	95	146	27	0	8	47	1	4	0	26	3	43	5	5
Mundy, Richard, Peoria	.236	43	123	16	29	42	8	1	1	11	1	0	0	14	0	32	0	2
Murphy, James, Peoria	.260	58	200	31	52	66	8	0	2	16	1	0	3	20	0	49	8	5
Nichols, Brian, Cedar Rapids	.286	7	14	3	4	5	1	0	0	3	0	0	0	1	0	4	0	0
Nicosia, Steven, Wausau	.141	31	71	3	10	10	0	0	0	2	1	0	0	6	0	20	2	1
Noland, James, Waterloo°	.246	125	456	75	112	156	20	6	4	51	4	6	1	71	3	84	48	24
Nunez, Alejandro, Kenosha†	.197	117	365	42	72	78	4	1	0	21	11	1	2	32	0	105	20	11
O'Leary, Troy, Beloit°	.298	118	436	73	130	179	29	1	6	62	6	3	0	41	2	90	12	12
Olmeda, Jose, Burlington°	.259	27	112	6	29	32	3	0	0	7	0	1	0	8	0	17	1	1
Ortegon, Ronnie, Quad City°	.224	134	442	73	99	133	17	4	3	49	7	2	11	68	2	87	9	3
Osinski, Glenn, Madison	.249	54	213	32	53	74	13	1	2	26	1	3	4	16	1	49	9	4
Owens, Jay, Kenosha	.236	66	216	31	51	79	9	2	5	30	1	1	13	39	0	59	15	7
Palyan, Vincent, Clinton	.262	95	290	42	76	87	7	2	0	35	3	4	5	41	1	35	12	10
Parry, Robert, Madison	.125	2	8	3	1	1	0	0	0	0	0	0	0	3	0	3	0	0
Pattin, Jon, Clinton°	.135	46	111	6	15	18	3	0	0	10	1	0	1	14	0	27	1	0
Paynter, William, Peoria	.115	19	52	2	6	7	1	0	0	2	1	0	0	1	0	13	0	0
Peek, Timothy, Madison	.000	41	3	0	0	0	0	0	0	0	0	0	0	0	0	1	0	0
Pichardo, Francisco, Kenosha	.188	45	133	10	25	32	2	1	1	9	4	2	2	12	0	38	3	4
Plemmons, Ronald, South Bend°	.263	129	438	89	115	167	21	5	7	51	9	1	2	86	5	71	22	20
Ramirez, John, Rockford	.259	119	432	56	112	149	21	5	2	51	5	1	8	53	3	58	6	6
Ramos, Jorge, South Bend	.165	51	121	19	20	27	2	1	1	9	3	1	5	10	0	34	5	2
Ramsey, Jeffrey, Rockford°	.159	48	132	10	21	25	2	1	0	3	0	0	1	9	0	52	1	1
Reis, Paulo, Burlington	.227	111	379	67	86	105	8	4	1	40	8	6	6	81	0	60	11	12
Reynoso, Henry, Beloit†	.223	94	260	37	58	68	6	2	0	13	5	0	1	21	0	64	27	13
Ricker, Troy, Rockford	.195	55	185	24	36	54	7	1	3	11	0	0	4	19	2	60	11	4
Ritter, Darren, Burlington	.000	25	1	0	0	0	0	0	0	0	0	0	0	0	0	0	0	0
Rittman, Alvin, Springfield	.175	81	183	23	32	48	8	1	2	16	1	1	9	21	1	62	1	4
Robertson, William, Beloit	.220	38	118	14	26	36	7	0	1	8	1	0	0	20	0	26	3	5
Robinson, Jimmy, Peoria	.224	26	67	4	15	18	3	0	0	8	2	1	0	8	0	8	0	1
Rodriguez, Buenaventura, Rockford°	.212	95	231	33	49	75	13	2	3	23	2	2	1	20	0	76	8	3
Rodriguez, Edgal, Quad City	.242	118	388	49	94	132	17	3	5	49	1	5	2	43	4	80	6	6
Rolen, Steven, Clinton	.237	77	257	31	61	90	14	3	3	36	3	5	4	20	1	51	6	3
Roskom, Bryan, Kenosha	.191	28	89	6	17	25	2	0	2	4	0	0	1	8	0	21	2	0
Roso, James, Wausau	.242	97	298	24	72	93	9	0	4	30	0	2	8	29	0	62	1	3
Rupp, Robert, Waterloo	.249	105	358	30	89	125	18	0	6	51	1	8	13	33	2	120	2	0
Rush, Edward, Cedar Rapids	.267	57	172	23	46	51	5	0	0	10	4	3	1	25	1	22	1	2
Russell, Frederick, Appleton†	.264	122	401	48	106	142	22	4	2	45	6	3	5	46	3	103	12	6
Ryan, Colin, Appleton	.165	86	242	27	40	47	7	0	0	18	1	2	1	36	0	68	2	1
Sanchez, Osvaldo, Waterloo°	.266	122	448	62	119	194	23	5	14	67	2	4	3	52	2	112	13	5

Player and Club	Pct.	G.	AB.	R.	H.	TB.	2B.	3B.	HR.	RBI.	SH.	SF.	HP.	BB.	Int. BB.	SO.	SB.	CS.
Sanders, Reginald, Cedar Rapids	.285	127	466	89	133	213	21	4	17	63	2	1	4	59	2	97	40	15
Savinon, Odalis, Springfield	.169	55	136	12	23	25	2	0	0	8	0	0	2	13	0	39	2	2
Schiel, Robert, 29 Ken.-38 C.R.	.179	67	195	20	35	50	6	0	3	12	1	0	3	20	0	58	4	1
Schmidt, Keith, Wausau°	.153	32	85	7	13	25	1	1	3	12	1	1	2	8	0	37	1	0
Shingledecker, Gary, Wausau	.243	24	74	10	18	27	4	1	1	6	2	1	1	8	0	4	0	0
Shockey, Scott, Madison°	.261	71	253	45	66	116	16	2	10	43	2	4	5	26	3	60	2	4
Simmons, Enoch, Madison	.184	117	359	47	66	87	10	1	3	29	5	2	4	47	0	98	17	6
Simmons, Randolph, Burlington°	.230	106	361	50	83	130	21	1	8	42	3	3	2	32	0	79	9	6
Simonds, Daniel, Peoria	.318	19	66	8	21	26	5	0	0	4	2	0	1	3	0	7	1	0
Singley, Joseph, South Bend	.262	24	61	9	16	23	2	1	1	4	1	0	1	5	0	19	1	1
Siwa, Joseph, Kenosha	.246	67	211	17	52	76	13	1	3	25	6	2	3	17	1	54	0	3
Smith, Woodrow, Peoria	.230	89	318	31	73	112	15	6	4	40	0	4	5	10	1	73	2	2
Smith, Charles, Rockford°	.223	81	251	38	56	87	13	3	4	38	0	0	2	39	2	64	16	6
Smith, Robert, Beloit	.270	96	318	57	86	123	21	2	4	44	2	4	11	39	0	61	8	7
Snyder, Randall, Beloit	.201	101	319	43	64	93	17	0	4	29	7	2	2	30	2	71	7	2
Solseth, David, Appleton°	.212	94	273	22	58	86	15	2	3	35	0	2	5	38	3	31	1	1
Specyalski, Brian, Quad City†	.067	6	15	1	1	2	1	0	0	0	0	0	1	4	0	2	0	0
St. Peter, William, Peoria	.250	121	448	52	112	179	23	4	12	56	5	2	7	41	0	107	6	6
Stevens, Scott, South Bend	.000	50	2	0	0	0	0	0	0	0	0	0	0	0	0	1	0	0
Stillwell, Rod, Appleton†	.213	92	240	31	51	58	5	1	0	16	6	1	2	27	0	47	1	4
Sullivan, Carl, South Bend	.276	62	210	29	58	87	13	2	4	35	5	3	4	19	0	46	5	6
Sutko, Glenn, Cedar Rapids	.300	4	10	0	3	3	0	0	0	0	0	0	1	0	0	2	0	0
Swail, Steven, Burlington	.147	33	75	9	11	13	2	0	0	3	2	0	1	10	0	24	0	0
Tamarez, Carlos, Madison†	.146	17	41	6	6	7	1	0	0	3	1	0	1	5	0	21	0	0
Tatarian, Dean, South Bend	.295	38	112	19	33	38	3	1	0	10	1	2	2	16	0	31	9	2
Taubensee, Edward, Cedar Rapids°	.259	122	417	57	108	179	21	1	16	62	1	4	4	51	5	98	11	4
Tejada, Alejandro, South Bend	.175	23	57	6	10	11	1	0	0	2	3	0	0	5	0	12	8	2
Tejada, Eugenio, South Bend	.243	83	243	28	59	70	7	2	0	17	7	1	1	10	2	44	4	5
Terzarial, Anthony, Cedar Rapids	.190	44	116	15	22	37	6	3	1	11	0	2	0	18	0	33	4	3
Teter, Craig, South Bend	.262	27	61	4	16	19	3	0	0	8	1	0	0	1	0	24	2	1
Thomas, John, Springfield°	.250	39	152	19	38	52	11	0	1	12	0	0	0	10	0	36	3	3
Thomas, Keith, Madison†	.211	44	142	21	30	44	3	1	3	20	1	2	0	10	0	42	12	1
Thomas, Orlando, Springfield	.140	19	43	2	6	6	0	0	0	2	0	0	0	16	0	17	1	1
Thompson, Kourtney, Springfield	.182	6	22	1	4	6	2	0	0	1	0	0	0	3	0	9	1	1
Threadgill, Henry, Quad City°	.216	75	204	34	44	57	3	2	2	20	1	1	7	29	2	49	15	7
Threadgill, Christopher, Quad City	.167	44	108	17	18	28	2	1	2	7	3	0	4	22	0	35	0	1
Tinsley, Lee, Madison†	.251	132	482	88	121	195	14	12	12	59	3	2	5	78	7	175	44	11
Toole, Matthew, Waterloo	.207	71	174	13	36	46	6	2	0	11	5	0	2	10	0	42	1	2
Torres, Paul, Peoria	.244	36	123	18	30	51	4	1	5	18	1	0	2	13	0	33	1	1
Tredway, Edward, Madison	.211	42	90	9	19	21	2	0	0	8	2	1	0	3	0	21	1	0
Trujillo, Jose, Springfield	.270	75	233	39	63	83	12	1	2	25	4	1	3	54	1	43	14	2
Tunison, Richard, Appleton†	.300	129	490	69	147	204	21	6	8	86	0	6	6	39	4	115	32	16
Tyler, Brad, Wausau°	.232	57	190	31	44	60	4	3	2	24	1	2	2	44	2	45	11	4
Vazquez, Pedro, Appleton†	.211	66	128	17	27	31	4	0	0	9	6	0	1	18	0	28	0	0
Verstandig, Mark, Waterloo°	.207	81	188	34	39	52	6	2	1	12	2	1	0	57	4	32	0	2
Vice, Darryl, Madison†	.235	65	196	28	46	53	7	0	0	12	3	0	2	39	0	45	1	4
Vollmer, Gustavo, Clinton	.230	67	200	25	46	66	9	1	3	23	2	3	2	35	2	25	2	1
Waggoner, James, Madison°	.246	39	114	16	28	34	3	0	1	8	1	1	0	26	0	18	4	3
Walbeck, Matthew, Peoria†	.227	25	66	2	15	16	1	0	0	5	2	0	2	5	0	7	1	0
Walker, Dennis, South Bend	.210	125	410	53	86	118	14	3	4	44	10	5	9	28	2	119	20	14
Washington, Kraig, Peoria	.249	98	366	39	91	106	9	3	0	26	12	1	5	28	1	34	15	12
Wearing, Melvin, Wausau	.256	105	336	45	86	149	9	0	18	56	0	2	4	72	2	101	6	7
Weaver, Trent, Madison	.293	22	75	10	22	31	4	1	1	11	0	1	0	14	0	16	1	2
Weber, Peter, Clinton°	.271	31	107	17	29	42	6	2	1	15	1	2	1	17	0	26	7	1
Weinheimer, Wayne, Peoria	.292	8	24	3	7	9	2	0	0	2	0	0	0	3	0	8	0	0
Whalen, Shawn, Waterloo°	.234	93	273	24	64	83	9	2	2	33	1	3	2	23	3	46	2	2
Wheatcroft, Robert, Wausau	.000	28	1	0	0	0	0	0	0	0	0	0	0	0	0	1	0	0
White, Darrin, Beloit°	.166	82	217	23	36	42	4	1	0	12	4	2	3	37	0	65	11	2
Williams, Jerrone, Peoria†	.248	124	448	62	111	165	17	11	5	43	9	2	2	39	4	137	30	12
Williams, Kent, Quad City†	.000	1	3	1	0	0	0	0	0	0	0	0	0	1	0	2	0	0
Williams, Reginald, Quad City†	.243	58	189	50	46	70	11	2	3	12	2	1	4	39	0	60	24	6
Witkowski, Matthew, Waterloo	.253	128	470	75	119	150	24	2	1	55	5	7	6	59	3	104	19	14
Wolak, Jerome, South Bend	.278	121	352	48	98	118	17	0	1	28	4	2	6	37	1	68	11	15
Woods, Tyrone, Rockford	.242	123	455	50	110	171	27	5	8	46	0	3	1	45	1	121	5	7
Wrona, David, Beloit†	.300	24	80	7	24	27	3	0	0	8	2	1	3	7	0	17	2	5
Young, Donald, Appleton†	.167	6	18	2	3	3	0	0	0	0	0	0	1	5	0	5	3	1
Young, Jason, Clinton	.252	37	115	15	29	33	4	0	0	6	1	1	5	10	1	31	7	2
Zaksek, John, South Bend°	.286	93	322	52	92	126	11	4	5	38	5	2	3	39	1	69	20	18
Zaun, Gregory, Wausau†	.130	37	100	3	13	18	0	1	1	7	2	0	1	7	0	17	0	0
Zeller, William, Burlington	.667	5	3	0	2	2	0	0	0	1	0	0	0	1	0	0	0	0

The following pitchers, listed alphabetically by club, With games in parentheses, had no plate appearances, primarily through use of designated hitters:

APPLETON—Ahern, Brian (12); Baez, Francisco (10); Baldwin, Kirk (9); Chrisman, James (11); Conner, John (30); Gross, John (13); Hoeme, Steven (7); Jacobs, Develon (25); Jirschele, Michael (2); Karchner, Matthew (27); Lindsey, Donald (21); Milton, Herbert (22); Schaefer, Christopher (13); Shifflett, Steven (57); Smith, James (35); Talbert, Louis (24); Walter, Gene (2); Wiley, Warren (57).

BELOIT—Andrzejewski, Joseph (24); Archer, Kurt (11); Bosio, Christopher (1); Carter, Larry (21); Correa, Ramser (5); Crim, Charles (1); Czajkowski, James (21); DeLaRosa, Domingo (8); Drake, Samuel (13); Elvira, Narciso (8); Fleming, Keith (31); Fortugno, Timothy (31); Garces, Robinson (15); Kimball, Scott (22); Krueger, William (1); Landry, Gregory (8); McGraw, Thomas (12); Miller, Patrick (4); Muscat, Scott (20); Nieves, Juan (7); Snyder, Bret (31); Vancho, Robert (32); Wegman, William (1); Wheeler, Bradley (3).

BURLINGTON—Borbon, Pedro (14); Bruck, Thomas (19); Byerly, Rodney (14); Calderone, Jeffrey (46); DeLeon, Roberto (26); Grove, Scott (20); Kelly, Kevin (34); Murray, Matthew (26); Nied, David (10); Reis, David (44); Roy, Walter (34); Slomkowski, Richard (5); Valle, Anthony (12); Vazquez, Marcos (15).

CEDAR RAPIDS—Anderson, Michael (23); Ayala, Robert (18); Borcherding, Mark (21); Economy, Scott (4); Garcia, Victoriano (49); Grovom, Carl (8); Hester, Steven (1); King, Douglas (32); Leslie, Reginald (6); Manon, Ramon (19); Marsh, Quinn (2); McAuliffe, David (41); McCarthy, Steven (8); Risley, William (22); Rodgers, Darrell (9); Sanford, Meredith (25); Spradlin, Jerry (5); Turek, Joseph (25).

CLINTON—Aleys, Maximo (26); Brummett, Gregory (6); Callahan, Stephen (41); Ebert, Scott (10); Flanagan, Daniel (25); Foley, James (7); Hancock, Christopher (18); Hanselman, Carl (25); Hernandez, Marino (15); Hillman, Stewart (17); Huisman, Richard (14); Huslig, James (12); Novoa, Rafael (15); Rapp, Patrick (27); Taylor, Stuart (31); Whatley, Fred (4).

KENOSHA—Best, Jayson (19); Diaz, Sandy (14); Harrington, Jody (22); Hoppe, Dennis (4); Krol, David (5); Lindaman, Chad (16); Lipson, Marc (47); Misuraca, Michael (26); Musselwhite, Darren (42); Nedin, Timothy (27); Newman, Alan (22); Pulido, Carlos (56); Robles, Scott (34);

Swope, Mark (16); Thelen, Jeffrey (28).

MADISON—Brimhall, Bradley (11); Cormier, Russell (8); DeLeon, Gerbacio (15); Gibbs, James (18); Grott, Matthew (22); Gulledge, Hugh (19); Kracl, Darin (14); Latter, David (43); Lawson, James (7); Martinez, Reynaldo (6); Mejia, Leandro (20); Mohler, Michael (42); Osteen, Gavin (27); Patrick, Bronswell (13); Peck, Steven (5); Pena, Pedro (14); Sudbury, Craig (7); Taylor, William (19); Van Poppel, Todd (3).

PEORIA—Bradford, Troy (8); Campos, Frank (1); Dickson, Lance (5); Doss, Jason (18); Duenas, Anthony (1); Eddings, Jay (8); Gelb, Jac (23); Gomez, Henrique (30); Hirsch, Jeffrey (10); Hollins, Jessie (5); Jaques, Eric (52); Lutz, Christopher (25); Mann, Thomas (9); Mullino, Ray (6); Rasp, Ronnie (26); Swartzbaugh, David (29); Sweeney, James (35); Willis, Travis (31); Young, Mark (24).

QUAD CITY—Adams, David (12); Archibald, Daniel (1); Bennett, Erik (18); Castillo, Roberto (17); Craven, Britt (15); Haffner, Leslie (45); Helm, Wayne (4); Heredia, Julian (5); Hillman, Stewart (7); Hook, Michael (30); King, Steven (31); Marchese, John (35); Martin, Justin (8); Martinez, Filiberto (26); Montoya, Norman (4); Moore, Marcus (27); Neal, David (14); Refnes, Todd (9); Vegely, Bruce (37).

ROCKFORD—Archibald, Daniel (13); Batista, Miguel (3); Bochtler, Douglas (25); Eddy, James (34); Haney, Christopher (8); Howze, Benjamin (19); Kilgo, Raymond (45); Logan, Joseph (18); Martinez, Martin (27); Regira, Gary (28); Sullivan, Brian (13); Thoden, John (12); Whitehead, Steven (23); Wilkinson, Brian (42).

SOUTH BEND—Bolton, Rodney (7); Brutcher, Lenny (22); Campos, Frank (12); Gennings, Brian (11); Gorman, David (7); Johnson, Earnie (27); Long, Richard (27); Matznick, Daniel (26); Mitchener, Michael (34); Mongiello, Michael (38); Ruffin, Johnny (24); Schrenk, Steven (20); Thoma, Scott (7); Vanderwel, William (9); Van Winkle, David (29); Wickman, Robert (9).

SPRINGFIELD—Botkin, Alan (6); Cimorelli, Frank (41); Corona, John (54); Cox, Danny (1); Eversgerd, Bryan (20); Gewecke, Stephen (38); Gorton, Christopher (59); Hensley, Michael (5); Infante, Thomas (50); Keller, Clyde (44); Lata, Timothy (19); Meamber, Timothy (26); Smith, Mark (8); Spiller, Derron (3); Tolbert, Mark (6); Weber, Ronald (30); Wiseman, Dennis (10).

WATERLOO—Embry, Todd (29); Florie, Bryce (14); Galindez, Luis (26); Hart, Jeffrey (48); Hays, Robert (12); Hoyer, Bradley (51); Lebron, Jose (26); Lewis, Anthony (47); McKeon, Brian (28); Morton, Ronald (44); Reed, William (23); Sanders, Scott (7).

WAUSAU—Anderson, Matthew (18); Boothby, John (25); Dedrick, James (3); Hale, Deshane (12); Heiden, Shawn (19); Leinen, Patrick (13); Marett, John (14); Martin, Thomas (9); Medina, Victor (16); Mercedes, Juan (6); Moore, Daryl (36); Paveloff, David (28); Pennington, Brad (32); Riddle, David (19); Schullstrom, Erik (5); Smith, Richard (6); Taylor, Thomas (23); Teixeira, Joseph (7); Unrein, Todd (23); Williams, Steven (26); Yaughn, Kip (10).

GRAND SLAM HOME RUNS—H. Hernandez, James, 2 each; Baldwin, E. Caraballo, Crowe, Davison, Gilcrist, Glenn, Lopez, L. Martinez, E. Rodriguez, Sanders, R. Simmons, J. Williams, 1 each.

AWARDED FIRST BASE ON CATCHER'S INTERFERENCE—Clemens 2 (Paynter 2); Byington (Swail); Gonzales (Alvarez); Noland (Devares); Palyan (Mercedes); Ramirez (Henry); Reis (Mercedes); Snyder (Billmeyer); Washington (P. Ellis).

CLUB FIELDING

Club	Pct.	G.	PO.	A.	E.	DP.	PB.	Club	Pct.	G.	PO.	A.	E.	DP.	PB.
Waterloo	.971	136	3484	1565	152	132	28	Springfield	.960	139	3616	1566	216	128	28
Appleton	.968	133	3396	1394	160	120	26	Burlington	.959	137	3523	1557	215	148	34
Cedar Rapids	.967	134	3431	1259	158	91	22	Madison	.959	135	3466	1373	209	86	27
Kenosha	.966	134	3518	1526	178	111	27	Rockford	.958	136	3453	1502	219	109	30
Clinton	.962	134	3445	1285	185	89	26	Beloit	.954	135	3433	1285	226	102	34
Peoria	.962	137	3505	1360	193	89	26	Wausau	.954	136	3458	1303	230	105	43
South Bend	.962	134	3437	1384	193	110	45	Quad City	.954	140	3506	1366	236	96	28

Triple Plays—Kenosha 2, Springfield, Wausau.

INDIVIDUAL FIELDING

*Throws lefthanded.

FIRST BASEMEN

Player and Club	Pct.	G.	PO.	A.	E.	DP.	Player and Club	Pct.	G.	PO.	A.	E.	DP.
Alvarez, South Bend	1.000	2	5	0	0	0	Kaub, Rockford	.983	41	318	24	6	25
Armas, Madison	.974	25	175	14	5	13	King, Appleton	1.000	10	73	1	0	9
Beeler, Cedar Rapids	.990	25	192	10	2	14	Kobza, South Bend	.984	34	222	31	4	26
Berlin, Springfield	1.000	7	31	4	0	3	Kraft, Springfield	1.000	3	18	1	0	4
Brady, Clinton	1.000	3	14	3	0	2	Kremblas, Cedar Rapids	.942	7	56	9	4	6
Bryant, Cedar Rapids	1.000	6	33	1	0	5	Krumback, Cedar Rapids	1.000	1	1	0	0	0
Campas, Springfield	.968	7	54	7	2	5	Leary, Rockford	1.000	3	6	1	0	0
Cepicky, South Bend	.987	99	857	74	12	62	Lombardozzi, Cedar Rapids	1.000	2	19	0	0	0
Conley, Waterloo	1.000	5	13	3	0	2	O. Marrero, Beloit*	.990	86	650	30	7	56
Cooley, Madison	.990	60	462	30	5	25	V. Marrero, Beloit	1.000	2	9	0	0	0
Cramer, Rockford	.977	36	256	38	7	19	L. Martinez, Springfield	1.000	11	81	9	0	7
Crowe, Clinton	.984	26	172	13	3	15	R. Martinez, Quad City	.972	5	32	3	1	4
Delarwelle, Kenosha	1.000	4	25	4	0	2	Marze, Burlington	.800	2	4	0	1	0
Doyle, Waterloo*	.988	92	809	60	11	72	McCormick, Madison	1.000	6	50	3	0	4
Dunn, Kenosha*	.9919	130	1125	97	10	92	B. Miller, Wausau	.977	19	153	17	4	8
Eatinger, South Bend	1.000	2	1	0	0	1	R. Miller, Clinton	.833	1	4	1	1	0
Ebright, Peoria*	1.000	5	14	2	0	0	Mota, Kenosha	1.000	1	6	0	0	0
Edwards, Beloit*	1.000	2	15	2	0	1	Mulvaney, Cedar Rapids	.983	96	717	39	13	53
Ellis, Springfield	1.000	6	35	5	0	1	Mundy, Peoria	.973	10	68	5	2	5
Federico, Springfield*	.994	87	716	62	5	62	Ortegon, Quad City*	.9920	134	1007	104	9	73
Fowler, Wausau	.978	13	85	4	2	11	Pattin, Clinton	.994	27	143	13	1	12
Franco, Peoria	.984	101	804	60	14	55	Peek, Madison	1.000	1	7	1	0	2
Gardner, Burlington	.978	137	1289	98	31	125	Rodriguez, Rockford*	1.000	11	20	2	0	3
Gay, Quad City	.962	4	23	2	1	2	Roskom, Kenosha	.938	2	14	1	1	1
Gentile, Kenosha	.900	2	7	2	1	0	Roso, Wausau	.984	8	57	5	1	2
Gillis, Burlington	1.000	2	4	0	0	0	Rupp, Waterloo	.984	46	401	23	7	33
Glenn, Beloit	.975	51	362	23	10	28	Shockey, Madison*	.985	47	369	24	6	27
Gonzales, Quad City	.923	2	12	0	1	3	Siwa, Kenosha	1.000	1	3	0	0	0
Grace, Rockford	1.000	19	140	15	0	12	Smith, Rockford*	.952	2	20	0	1	1
Hairston, South Bend	1.000	4	17	1	0	1	Snyder, Beloit	1.000	2	3	0	0	1
Henry, Madison	.984	11	54	6	1	2	Solseth, Appleton	.973	7	35	1	1	4
Hernandez, Springfield*	.995	40	341	24	2	27	Torres, Peoria	.991	24	212	13	2	9
Hudson, Rockford	.969	46	375	38	13	37	TUNISON, Appleton	.9922	120	1098	52	9	94
Ingram, South Bend	1.000	1	8	0	0	2	Wearing, Wausau	.972	99	716	58	22	67
James, Clinton	.986	96	673	46	10	48	Weinheimer, Peoria	1.000	7	57	3	0	2
Jones, Cedar Rapids	1.000	1	5	1	0	1	Whalen, Waterloo*	.968	4	29	1	1	5

Triple Plays—Dunn 2, Federico, Wearing.

SECOND BASEMEN

Player and Club	Pct.	G.	PO.	A.	E.	DP.	Player and Club	Pct.	G.	PO.	A.	E.	DP.
Abbott, Madison	.947	13	20	34	3	6	Borgogno, Clinton	1.000	9	11	19	0	3
Adames, Peoria	.939	8	12	19	2	3	Campa, Madison	.970	6	8	24	1	1
Apolinario, Burlington	.926	30	50	63	9	15	Campas, Springfield	.938	25	31	60	6	9
Asencio, Wausau	.889	9	7	9	2	2	Caraballo, Burlington	.933	4	7	7	1	2
Benitez, Wausau	.922	63	100	135	20	21	Carey, Clinton	.955	62	105	130	11	26

SECOND BASEMEN—Continued

Player and Club	Pct.	G.	PO.	A.	E.	DP.	Player and Club	Pct.	G.	PO.	A.	E.	DP.
Cole, Peoria	.952	60	113	162	14	26	Miranda, Appleton	.974	45	62	90	4	14
Collins, Appleton	.977	19	20	22	1	7	Olmeda, Burlington	.942	12	25	40	4	12
Crowe, Clinton	1.000	2	2	3	0	1	Osinski, Madison	.939	48	68	131	13	21
Curtis, Quad City	.943	86	147	219	22	31	Ramirez, Rockford	.938	25	46	59	7	11
DeLaRosa, Quad City	.912	13	17	14	3	4	Reis, Burlington	.960	98	187	347	22	71
Dombrowski, Cedar Rapids	.946	9	10	25	2	4	Reynoso, Beloit	.911	80	132	165	29	25
Eatinger, South Bend	.965	128	231	344	21	62	Rittman, Springfield	.967	19	26	33	2	8
Gantner, Beloit	.750	3	2	1	1	0	Schiel, Cedar Rapids	.955	36	73	75	7	21
Haugen, Beloit	.935	66	114	144	18	35	Shingledecker, Wausau	1.000	1	1	2	0	0
Hildreth, Wausau	.981	14	23	28	1	6	Smith, Peoria	.946	20	30	40	4	6
Javier, Cedar Rapids	.980	40	43	56	2	7	Specyalski, Quad City	1.000	1	3	3	0	2
Kasper, Clinton	.938	39	71	79	10	19	Stillwell, Appleton	1.000	39	69	94	1	25
Kessinger, Wausau	.913	12	20	22	4	8	Tamarez, Madison	1.000	3	3	0	0	0
Krause, Rockford	.977	111	191	279	11	54	Tatarian, South Bend	1.000	4	9	8	0	2
Kremblas, Cedar Rapids	.941	38	62	65	8	10	A. Tejada, South Bend	1.000	1	1	0	0	0
Lamitola, Wausau	.950	37	62	70	7	19	E. Tejada, South Bend	1.000	3	4	0	0	1
Landinez, Springfield	.920	37	56	93	13	11	Threadgill, Quad City	.964	42	76	84	6	13
Lewis, Kenosha	.973	53	101	156	7	29	Toole, Waterloo	1.000	12	22	31	0	10
Lloyd, Kenosha	.984	55	98	147	4	36	Trujillo, Springfield	.967	75	144	236	13	55
Lombardozzi, Cedar Rapids	.957	37	54	80	6	14	Tyler, Wausau	.988	21	33	52	1	9
Malinowski, Rockford	.909	5	3	17	2	0	Vazquez, Appleton	.982	62	91	128	4	28
Marrero, Beloit	1.000	3	8	1	0	1	Vice, Madison	.977	65	127	170	7	30
Martinez, Quad City	1.000	4	2	3	0	0	Waggoner, Madison	1.000	3	6	4	0	0
Mathiot, Kenosha	.978	37	59	76	3	11	Washington, Peoria	.944	50	73	112	11	18
Meares, Kenosha	1.000	1	2	2	0	0	WITKOWSKI, Waterloo	.980	127	295	379	14	85
Mercedes, Madison	.857	2	3	3	1	0	Wolak, South Bend	.923	7	4	8	1	1
Minnis, Quad City	1.000	1	2	1	0	0	Young, Clinton	.955	35	63	85	7	18

Triple Plays—Benitez, Lloyd, Mathiot.

THIRD BASEMEN

Player and Club	Pct.	G.	PO.	A.	E.	DP.	Player and Club	Pct.	G.	PO.	A.	E.	DP.
Abbott, Madison	.905	10	5	14	2	1	Langiotti, Springfield	.885	6	8	15	3	1
ALLEN, Cedar Rapids	.955	120	85	230	15	11	Leary, Rockford	1.000	1	1	0	0	0
Armas, Madison	.868	36	20	46	10	2	M. Lewis, Kenosha	.875	1	2	5	1	0
Bellinger, Clinton	1.000	1	2	1	0	0	T. Lewis, Wausau	.838	70	45	120	32	13
Berlin, Springfield	.911	22	8	43	5	5	Lloyd, Kenosha	.964	19	13	41	2	3
Byington, Beloit	.883	87	69	127	26	12	Lombardozzi, Cedar Rapids	.900	7	3	6	1	0
Campa, Madison	.846	11	6	5	2	0	Malinowski, Rockford	.800	11	8	20	7	0
Campas, Springfield	.910	91	74	179	25	21	Marrero, Beloit	.876	47	42	92	19	5
Caraballo, Appleton	.896	123	80	230	36	20	Martin, Waterloo	.907	110	71	202	28	17
Carey, Clinton	1.000	2	0	3	0	0	Martinez, Quad City	.922	51	40	79	10	8
Castellano, Peoria	.951	106	77	194	14	15	McCormick, Madison	1.000	6	2	7	0	1
Charpia, Beloit	.750	1	1	2	1	0	McCoy, Burlington	.917	10	7	15	2	3
Colon, Waterloo	1.000	4	6	6	0	0	Meares, Kenosha	.887	51	33	92	16	12
Conte, Madison	.920	30	22	47	6	4	Mercedes, Madison	1.000	3	1	2	0	3
Cooley, Madison	.867	4	5	8	2	1	Osinski, Madison	.900	5	2	7	1	0
Crowe, Clinton	.862	52	25	81	17	8	Ramirez, Rockford	.800	4	4	4	2	0
David, Waterloo	1.000	1	1	2	0	0	Ramos, South Bend	.833	10	5	15	4	0
Davison, Rockford	.857	3	2	4	1	1	Reynoso, Beloit	1.000	2	1	0	0	0
DeLaRosa, Quad City	.824	6	4	10	3	1	Rittman, Springfield	.878	41	20	59	11	4
Devares, Wausau	.500	1	0	1	1	0	Rolen, Clinton	.921	73	47	116	14	10
DiMarco, Wausau	.847	18	18	32	9	3	Schiel, 7 Ken.-2 C.R.	.909	9	6	14	2	1
Fowler, Wausau	.643	7	5	4	5	0	Shingledecker, Wausau	.900	23	14	31	5	1
Franco, Peoria	.840	9	6	15	4	0	Smith, Peoria	.805	12	11	22	8	1
Gentile, Kenosha	.905	63	43	119	17	10	Snyder, Beloit	.900	7	3	15	2	1
Gillis, Burlington	.921	128	95	233	28	23	Specyalski, Quad City	.909	4	6	4	1	0
Grace, Rockford	.929	74	67	128	15	10	St. Peter, Peoria	1.000	2	2	6	0	0
Haugen, Beloit	.889	3	2	6	1	1	Stillwell, Appleton	.907	14	9	30	4	1
Henry, Madison	.927	21	11	40	4	1	Tatarian, South Bend	.923	8	1	11	1	1
Hildreth, Wausau	.907	14	9	30	4	3	Threadgill, Quad City	.857	4	2	4	1	0
Hudson, Rockford	.852	48	46	75	21	8	Toole, Waterloo	.960	28	15	57	3	5
Johnson, Clinton	1.000	3	2	1	0	0	Tredway, Madison	.667	1	1	1	1	0
Kapano, Quad City	.853	86	70	139	36	14	Tyler, Wausau	1.000	2	3	1	0	0
Kasper, Clinton	.895	15	10	7	2	0	Waggoner, Madison	.864	23	15	36	8	5
Kessinger, Wausau	.947	12	5	13	1	2	Walker, South Bend	.890	120	104	196	37	17
Kobza, South Bend	.000	1	0	0	1	0	Washington, Peoria	.865	12	8	24	5	1
Krumback, Cedar Rapids	.828	13	11	13	5	1							

SHORTSTOPS

Player and Club	Pct.	G.	PO.	A.	E.	DP.	Player and Club	Pct.	G.	PO.	A.	E.	DP.
Abbott, Madison	.915	81	155	220	35	35	Garibaldo, Appleton	.958	6	8	15	1	5
Alexander, Wausau	.938	41	66	99	11	20	Grace, Rockford	.889	10	13	35	6	6
Andujar, Springfield	.893	103	133	250	46	48	Greene, Rockford	.927	10	14	37	4	5
Apolinario, Burlington	.000	1	0	0	1	0	Haugen, Beloit	.926	44	57	106	13	20
Asencio, Wausau	.870	11	7	13	3	3	Hildreth, Wausau	.935	57	87	130	15	30
Bellinger, Clinton	.927	90	142	228	29	45	Holbert, Waterloo	.952	133	233	378	31	75
Berlin, Springfield	.930	17	14	39	4	4	Javier, Cedar Rapids	.892	21	29	37	8	7
Branson, Cedar Rapids	.973	61	96	152	7	35	Kasper, Clinton	.890	49	65	97	20	15
Byington, Beloit	.885	20	18	28	6	3	Keating, Springfield	.875	10	8	13	3	3
Campa, Madison	.829	11	19	15	7	1	Kessinger, Wausau	.909	21	19	41	6	3
Campas, Springfield	1.000	1	0	1	0	0	Krause, Rockford	1.000	1	1	2	0	1
Caraballo, Burlington	.923	93	139	280	35	63	Landinez, Springfield	.833	13	14	31	9	12
Castellano, Peoria	.921	8	16	19	3	4	Lewis, Kenosha	1.000	10	16	21	0	7
Cornell, Beloit	.905	39	52	82	14	12	Lloyd, Kenosha	.500	1	1	1	1	0
Crowe, Clinton	1.000	1	1	0	0	0	Marrero, Beloit	.800	1	2	2	1	0
Davison, Rockford	.948	120	180	309	27	68	Martinez, Quad City	.946	44	57	102	9	12
DeLaRosa, Quad City	.875	3	3	4	1	2	McCoy, Burlington	.924	29	43	78	10	23
Easley, Quad City	.893	99	136	206	41	36	Minnis, Quad City	1.000	2	6	3	0	0
Eatinger, South Bend	1.000	1	1	0	0	0	Nunez, Kenosha	.918	116	189	283	42	60
Esquer, Beloit	.930	19	28	38	5	7	Olmeda, Burlington	.946	15	18	35	3	6

SHORTSTOPS—Continued

Player and Club	Pct.	G.	PO.	A.	E.	DP.	Player and Club	Pct.	G.	PO.	A.	E.	DP.
Ramos, South Bend	.905	38	45	79	13	13	A. Tejada, South Bend	.862	22	27	54	13	9
Rittman, Springfield	.981	12	12	39	1	8	E. Tejada, South Bend	.932	73	107	169	20	39
Rush, Cedar Rapids	.937	57	99	140	16	22	Toole, Waterloo	.867	8	3	10	2	1
Russell, Appleton	.947	120	186	334	29	71	Tyler, Wausau	.956	24	40	69	5	13
Schiel, Kenosha	.864	15	23	34	9	5	Waggoner, Madison	.887	14	21	34	7	6
ST. PETER, Peoria	.958	119	182	300	21	50	Washington, Peoria	.886	12	20	19	5	3
Stillwell, Appleton	.937	17	24	35	4	8	Weaver, Madison	.967	22	38	50	3	8
Tamarez, Madison	.906	14	23	35	6	9	Wrona, Beloit	.938	24	40	65	7	19
Tatarian, South Bend	.958	20	23	46	3	11							

Triple Plays—Andujar, Kessinger.

OUTFIELDERS

Player and Club	Pct.	G.	PO.	A.	E.	DP.	Player and Club	Pct.	G.	PO.	A.	E.	DP.
Armas, Madison	.902	16	32	5	4	0	Laker, Rockford	1.000	1	1	0	0	0
Baldwin, Burlington	.964	75	101	7	4	1	Lee, Wausau*	.882	16	14	1	2	0
Bautista, Wausau*	.927	31	48	3	4	1	Lydy, Madison	.957	50	85	3	4	1
Bell, Springfield	.786	34	21	1	6	1	Malinowski, Rockford	1.000	5	2	0	0	0
Billingsley, Waterloo	1.000	2	3	0	0	0	Martinez, Springfield	.960	82	112	8	5	1
Blanks, Burlington*	.938	41	39	6	3	1	Marze, Burlington	.965	75	106	3	4	1
Bonner, Clinton	.983	73	110	4	2	0	Mathiot, Kenosha	.938	10	15	0	1	1
Brady, Clinton	.966	32	52	4	2	0	McFarlin, Clinton*	.955	127	249	5	12	2
Bryant, Cedar Rapids	.969	58	87	7	3	3	Mercedes, Madison	1.000	1	0	1	0	0
Buford, Wausau	.978	39	89	2	2	0	Moore, Appleton	.957	128	257	11	12	2
Butcher, Beloit*	.975	62	77	0	2	0	Morris, Kenosha	.994	89	173	5	1	1
Cairo, Wausau	.941	105	170	7	11	1	Morrison, Burlington	.882	55	57	3	8	0
Cancel, Peoria	.948	36	52	3	3	0	Murphy, Peoria	.947	55	86	4	5	2
Carter, Springfield*	.957	7	22	0	1	0	Nicosia, Wausau	.897	27	26	0	3	0
J. CLARK, Burlington	.984	94	168	11	3	1	Noland, Waterloo	.956	124	211	6	10	1
T. Clark, Beloit	.966	62	103	9	4	0	O'Leary, Beloit*	.961	113	184	14	8	4
Cole, Appleton	.957	30	42	3	2	0	Owens, Kenosha	.972	62	102	3	3	0
Collins, Appleton	1.000	1	1	0	0	0	Palyan, Clinton	.960	84	133	10	6	2
Colon, Waterloo	.980	66	93	5	2	2	Parry, Madison	1.000	2	2	0	0	0
Conte, Madison	1.000	23	32	2	0	1	Pichardo, Kenosha	.958	45	67	1	3	0
Cordova, Kenosha	.948	65	87	5	5	1	Plemmons, South Bend	.965	122	205	18	8	4
Crowe, Clinton	1.000	17	19	2	0	0	Ramsey, Rockford	.976	32	36	4	1	0
Cudjo, Cedar Rapids	1.000	24	31	1	0	0	Reynoso, Beloit	1.000	2	3	0	0	0
Cunningham, Peoria	.943	77	107	8	7	3	Ricker, Rockford	1.000	54	96	9	0	2
Curtis, Quad City	.947	33	69	2	4	0	Robertson, Beloit	.952	37	53	6	3	2
Darter, Appleton*	.974	32	33	4	1	0	B. Rodriguez, Rockford*	.955	80	120	8	6	2
Dattola, Madison	.979	24	45	2	1	1	E. Rodriguez, Quad City	.909	115	152	18	17	4
A. Davis, Wausau	.944	24	31	3	2	2	Roskom, Kenosha	.927	25	33	5	3	2
C. Davis, Clinton	.938	29	44	1	3	0	Roso, Wausau	.946	39	52	1	3	0
Davison, Rockford	1.000	5	4	0	0	0	Sanchez, Waterloo*	.947	117	198	18	12	4
de la Nuez, Kenosha	.980	38	49	1	1	1	Sanders, Cedar Rapids	.962	127	241	10	10	4
Diggs, Beloit	.500	2	1	0	1	0	Savino, Springfield	.977	54	83	3	2	1
Doyle, Waterloo*	.917	9	10	1	1	0	Schiel, Kenosha	1.000	3	6	0	0	0
Ebright, Peoria*	.908	58	69	0	7	0	Schmidt, Wausau	.944	26	33	1	2	0
Edwards, Beloit*	.833	8	5	0	1	0	Shockey, Madison*	.968	26	29	1	1	0
Elder, Rockford*	.972	77	135	6	4	1	E. Simmons, Madison	.971	113	225	7	7	2
Fowler, Wausau	1.000	14	13	0	0	0	R. Simmons, Burlington*	.977	105	161	7	4	3
Francisco, Peoria	.953	63	98	3	5	1	C. Smith, Rockford*	.917	71	105	6	10	0
F. Garcia, Appleton	1.000	6	6	0	0	0	R. Smith, Beloit	.966	96	156	13	6	2
L. Garcia, Beloit	.893	24	24	1	3	0	Stillwell, Appleton	1.000	10	11	0	0	1
Gentile, Kenosha	.957	15	20	2	1	2	Sullivan, South Bend	.975	62	108	8	3	2
Gerald, Appleton	.955	42	62	2	3	1	Tejada, South Bend	1.000	5	4	0	0	0
Gilcrist, Appleton	.964	127	199	15	8	2	Terzarial, Cedar Rapids	1.000	28	37	1	0	0
Gill, Waterloo*	.979	55	128	10	3	1	Teter, South Bend	1.000	12	2	3	0	1
Gillum, Cedar Rapids	1.000	4	8	0	0	0	J. Thomas, Springfield	.979	38	89	6	2	0
Glenn, Beloit	1.000	1	1	0	0	0	K. Thomas, Madison	.920	39	66	3	6	1
Godin, Wausau	.972	48	90	15	3	6	C. Threadgill, Quad City	.952	42	58	2	3	0
Gross, Kenosha	.982	56	102	6	2	2	H. Threadgill, Quad City	1.000	6	11	2	0	1
Hairston, South Bend	.950	47	72	4	4	1	Thompson, Springfield	1.000	5	10	0	0	0
Harris, South Bend	1.000	14	19	0	0	0	Tinsley, Madison	.966	129	302	7	11	2
Hernandez, Appleton	.930	41	62	4	5	0	Toole, Waterloo	1.000	10	23	1	0	1
Herrera, Springfield	.963	122	239	24	10	7	Tredway, Madison	1.000	1	2	0	0	0
Hicks, Wausau	.954	91	157	9	8	3	Tyler, Wausau	1.000	4	1	0	0	0
Hirtensteiner, Quad City*	.977	82	119	6	3	2	Vollmer, Clinton	.943	30	32	1	2	0
Hoerner, Kenosha	.944	25	33	1	2	0	Washington, Peoria	.957	15	21	1	1	0
Hollis, Cedar Rapids	.911	29	40	1	4	1	Weber, Clinton*	.962	29	47	3	2	0
Johnson, Clinton	.943	27	33	0	2	0	Whalen, Waterloo*	1.000	49	68	3	0	0
E. Jones, Cedar Rapids	.989	49	88	2	1	0	White, Beloit	1.000	10	8	1	0	0
R. Jones, Quad City	.949	104	137	12	8	2	J. Williams, Peoria	.968	123	262	7	9	2
Kindred, Springfield	1.000	38	79	3	0	0	K. Williams, Quad City	1.000	1	1	0	0	0
Knabenshue, Beloit	.955	21	21	0	1	0	R. Williams, Quad City	.991	56	110	6	1	0
Kraft, Springfield	.956	85	129	1	6	0	Wolak, South Bend	.983	103	168	8	3	0
Kremblas, Cedar Rapids	.900	6	8	1	1	0	Woods, Rockford	.962	122	166	13	7	0
Krumback, Cedar Rapids	.970	100	181	12	6	1	Young, Appleton	.833	6	5	0	1	0
							Zaksek, South Bend*	.981	84	153	5	3	2

Triple Play—Pichardo.

CATCHERS

Player and Club	Pct.	G.	PO.	A.	E.	DP.	PB.	Player and Club	Pct.	G.	PO.	A.	E.	DP.	PB.
Ahrens, Clinton	.978	21	117	16	3	0	6	Cramer, Rockford	1.000	13	53	5	0	0	5
Alvarez, South Bend	.989	48	318	47	4	7	6	Devares, Wausau	.980	46	320	30	7	5	18
Beck, Madison	.984	21	111	12	2	1	5	Ellis, Springfield	.971	32	183	18	6	1	7
Beeler, Cedar Rapids	.980	22	137	13	3	0	5	Erdman, Peoria	.989	37	244	28	3	3	5
Berryhill, Peoria	.988	7	75	4	1	0	0	Fielitz, Springfield	.979	11	44	2	1	0	3
Billingsley, Waterloo	1.000	8	13	7	0	0	0	Fuller, Wausau	.980	27	184	14	4	2	6
Billmeyer, Quad City	.982	61	440	40	9	6	15	Gay, Quad City	.976	35	260	29	7	0	4
Clemens, Springfield	1.000	6	15	2	0	0	0	Gonzales, Quad City	.994	63	422	46	3	6	9
Conley, Waterloo	.983	78	403	51	8	9	17	Grahovac, Clinton	.987	27	143	13	2	0	7

CATCHERS—Continued

Player and Club	Pct.	G.	PO.	A.	E.	DP.	PB.
Griesser, Appleton	1.000	34	176	17	0	0	5
Harper, Burlington	.979	9	41	5	1	1	0
Henry, Madison	.991	18	92	15	1	0	6
Ingram, South Bend	.987	38	203	19	3	2	8
Kobza, South Bend	.982	48	258	22	5	4	20
Kremblas, Cedar Rapids	.977	12	79	6	2	0	2
Kroeger, South Bend	1.000	6	29	3	0	0	1
Laker, Rockford	.981	117	801	125	18	9	23
Langiotti, Springfield	.992	90	569	56	5	8	8
Leary, Rockford	.975	15	104	11	3	1	2
Lopez, Burlington	.986	111	724	79	11	11	31
Marrero, Beloit	.983	12	53	4	1	0	2
Martinez, Springfield	.955	3	20	1	1	0	0
Mercedes, Madison	.988	87	551	104	8	6	13
Milene, Kenosha	1.000	2	2	0	0	0	0
MILLER, Clinton	.996	109	809	102	4	8	11
Mota, Kenosha	.977	78	495	68	13	5	21
Mundy, Peoria	.964	27	173	16	7	2	8
Nichols, Cedar Rapids	1.000	4	28	1	0	0	1
Owens, Kenosha	.947	5	31	5	2	0	2
Pattin, Clinton	.980	10	44	5	1	1	2
Paynter, Peoria	.968	17	106	15	4	0	4
Robinson, Peoria	.979	26	163	25	4	2	1
Roso, Wausau	.997	43	310	29	1	2	11
Ryan, Appleton	.981	86	560	67	12	4	17
Simonds, Peoria	.970	16	119	9	4	2	5
Singley, South Bend	.974	23	138	11	4	0	10
Siwa, Kenosha	.989	65	454	74	6	6	4
Snyder, Beloit	.990	84	669	87	8	10	19
Solseth, Appleton	1.000	39	180	20	0	3	4
Sutko, Cedar Rapids	1.000	3	21	2	0	0	0
Swail, Burlington	.979	32	170	13	4	2	3
Taubensee, Cedar Rapids	.982	101	795	94	16	9	16
Thomas, Springfield	.989	19	84	9	1	0	5
Tredway, Madison	.980	32	133	17	3	0	3
Verstandig, Waterloo	.980	74	370	73	9	6	11
Walbeck, Peoria	.987	25	137	16	2	1	3
White, Beloit	.989	57	410	61	5	3	13
Zaun, Wausau	.990	35	270	26	3	2	8
Zeller, Burlington	1.000	3	6	1	0	0	0

PITCHERS

Player and Club	Pct.	G.	PO.	A.	E.	DP.
Adams, Quad City	.938	12	1	14	1	1
Ahern, Appleton	.950	12	3	16	1	1
Aleys, Clinton*	1.000	25	4	15	0	0
Ma. Anderson, Wausau*	1.000	18	3	5	0	1
Mi. Anderson, Cedar Rapids	.909	23	11	19	3	0
Andrzejewski, Beloit	.813	24	1	12	3	0
Archer, Beloit	.833	11	0	5	1	0
Archibald, 13 Rock.-1 Q.C.	1.000	14	1	5	0	0
Ayala, Cedar Rapids	.889	18	2	6	1	0
Baez, Appleton*	.923	10	2	10	1	0
Baldwin, Appleton*	1.000	9	0	2	0	2
Batista, Rockford	1.000	3	1	1	0	0
Bennett, Quad City	.921	18	11	24	3	1
Best, Kenosha	.950	19	4	15	1	0
Bochtler, Rockford	.857	25	9	27	6	3
Bolton, South Bend	.818	7	2	7	2	0
Boothby, Wausau	.929	25	6	7	1	1
Borbon, Burlington	.929	14	3	23	2	2
Borcherding, Cedar Rapids	.947	21	0	18	1	3
Botkin, Springfield*	1.000	6	1	4	0	0
Bradford, Peoria	.900	8	3	6	1	1
Brimhall, Madison	.750	11	1	5	2	0
Bruck, Burlington	.903	19	4	24	3	2
Brummett, Clinton	.909	6	1	9	1	1
Brutcher, South Bend	.893	22	10	15	3	1
Bushing, Rockford	.871	46	11	16	4	2
Byerly, Burlington*	1.000	14	3	2	0	0
Calderone, Burlington	.947	46	1	17	1	1
Callahan, Clinton*	1.000	41	3	6	0	0
Campos, 1 Peo.-12 S.B.	.857	13	1	5	1	0
Carter, Quad City	.962	21	4	21	1	3
Castillo, Quad City	.875	17	7	14	3	1
Chrisman, Appleton	.800	11	2	2	1	0
Cimorelli, Springfield	.929	41	17	22	3	1
Conner, Appleton	1.000	30	4	20	0	0
Cormier, Madison	1.000	8	2	10	0	0
Corona, Springfield*	.973	54	9	27	1	3
Correa, Beloit	.500	5	1	0	1	0
Cox, Springfield	1.000	1	1	0	0	0
Craven, Quad City	.778	15	5	9	4	1
Crim, Beloit	1.000	1	1	0	0	0
Czajkowski, Beloit	.875	21	1	6	1	1
Dedrick, Wausau	.857	3	3	3	1	0
DeLaRosa, Beloit	.750	8	1	5	2	0
G. DeLeon, Madison	.846	15	3	8	2	0
R. DeLeon, Burlington*	1.000	26	2	6	0	0
Diaz, Kenosha	.923	14	3	9	1	1
Dickson, Peoria*	.857	5	1	5	1	0
Doss, Peoria	.944	18	9	8	1	0
Drake, Beloit	.818	13	5	4	2	0
Duenas, Peoria*	1.000	1	0	1	0	0
Ebert, Clinton	.833	10	0	5	1	0
Eddings, Peoria	1.000	8	3	5	0	0
Eddy, Rockford	.938	34	12	33	3	1
Elvira, Beloit*	1.000	8	3	8	0	0
Embry, Waterloo	.933	29	4	10	1	1
Eversgerd, Springfield*	.921	20	11	24	3	2
Flanagan, Clinton	1.000	25	4	14	0	0
Fleming, Beloit	1.000	31	5	9	0	1
Florie, Waterloo	.900	14	3	15	2	1
Foley, Clinton	1.000	7	1	3	0	0
Forrester, South Bend*	.500	13	0	1	1	0
Fortugno, Beloit*	.500	31	0	3	3	0
Galindez, Waterloo*	.973	26	5	31	1	1
Garces, Beloit*	1.000	15	2	2	0	0
Garcia, Cedar Rapids	1.000	49	2	6	0	0
Gelb, Peoria	1.000	23	4	7	0	1
Gennings, South Bend	1.000	11	1	2	0	0
Gewecke, Springfield*	.909	38	7	23	3	1
Gibbs, Madison	.667	18	1	1	1	0
Gomez, Peoria	.963	30	8	18	1	2
Gorman, South Bend	.889	7	1	7	1	1
Gorton, Springfield	.857	59	5	13	3	1
Gross, Appleton	.917	13	1	10	1	1
Grott, Madison*	1.000	22	1	4	0	1
Grove, Burlington	.969	20	8	23	1	3
Grovom, Springfield*	1.000	8	2	7	0	0
Gulledge, Madison	.957	19	9	13	1	1
Gustafson, Clinton	.958	40	4	19	1	1
Haffner, Quad City	.903	45	4	24	3	3
Hale, Wausau*	.900	12	2	7	1	0
Hancock, Clinton*	.800	18	2	18	5	0
Haney, Rockford*	.944	8	6	11	1	1
Hanselman, Clinton	.778	25	6	15	6	0
Harrington, Kenosha*	.857	22	2	4	1	0
Hart, Waterloo	.913	46	4	17	2	3
Hays, Waterloo	1.000	12	0	3	0	0
Heiden, Wausau	1.000	19	2	5	0	0
Helm, Quad City	1.000	4	0	2	0	0
Hensley, Springfield	.875	5	1	6	1	1
Hernandez, Clinton*	1.000	15	0	5	0	1
Hester, Cedar Rapids	1.000	1	0	3	0	0
Hillman, 17 Clint.-7 Q.C.	1.000	24	5	12	0	0
Hirsch, Peoria	1.000	10	0	6	0	0
Hoeme, Appleton	1.000	7	0	1	0	0
Hook, Quad City*	.818	30	1	8	2	0
Hoppe, Kenosha	.857	4	1	5	1	0
Howze, Rockford	.846	19	6	5	2	0
Hoyer, Waterloo*	1.000	51	3	9	0	0
Huisman, Clinton	1.000	14	4	14	0	1
Huslig, Clinton	.818	12	4	5	2	2
Infante, Springfield	1.000	50	5	9	0	1
Jacobs, Appleton	.900	25	5	13	2	1
Jaques, Peoria*	.882	52	4	11	2	0
Jeffery, Cedar Rapids	1.000	9	2	16	0	0
Johnson, South Bend*	.938	27	2	13	1	2
Karchner, Appleton	.870	27	0	20	3	3
Keller, Springfield	1.000	44	4	12	0	1
Kelly, Burlington*	.600	34	1	8	6	0
Kilgo, Rockford*	1.000	45	7	24	0	0
Kimball, Beloit	.857	22	8	22	5	2
D. King, Cedar Rapids*	1.000	32	4	12	0	1
S. King, Quad City	.952	31	17	23	2	3
Kracl, Springfield	.938	14	4	26	2	1
Kremblas, Cedar Rapids	1.000	1	0	1	0	0
Krol, Kenosha	1.000	5	2	4	0	0
Krueger, Beloit*	1.000	1	0	1	0	0
Kuhn, Madison*	1.000	21	2	14	0	1
Landry, Beloit	.857	8	4	8	2	1
Lata, Springfield	.912	19	13	18	3	2
Latter, Madison	.889	43	8	8	2	0
Lawson, Madison	1.000	7	1	3	0	0
Lebron, Waterloo	.982	26	13	41	1	6
Leinen, Wausau*	.905	13	3	16	2	2
Lewis, Waterloo	1.000	47	3	18	0	3
Lindaman, Kenosha	1.000	16	2	6	0	0
Lindsey, Appleton*	1.000	21	2	8	0	0
Lipson, Peoria	.935	47	9	20	2	6
Lloyd, Kenosha	.000	3	0	0	1	0
Logan, Rockford	.971	18	12	22	1	1
Long, South Bend*	1.000	27	1	10	0	0
Lutz, Peoria	.925	25	8	29	3	0
Mann, Peoria	1.000	9	2	4	0	0
Manon, Cedar Rapids	1.000	19	2	4	0	0
Marchese, Quad City	1.000	35	3	8	0	2
Marrero, Beloit	1.000	3	0	1	0	0

PITCHERS—Continued

Player and Club	Pct.	G.	PO.	A.	E.	DP.
Marsh, Cedar Rapids	1.000	2	0	1	0	0
J. Martin, Quad City	1.000	8	1	4	0	0
T. Martin, Wausau*	.882	9	4	11	2	0
F. Martinez, Quad City*	.864	26	5	33	6	1
M. Martinez, Rockford	.865	27	24	21	7	1
R. Martinez, Madison	1.000	6	0	3	0	0
Matznick, South Bend	.879	26	8	21	4	0
McAuliffe, Cedar Rapids	1.000	41	3	4	0	1
McCarthy, Cedar Rapids*	1.000	8	0	3	0	0
McGraw, Beloit*	1.000	12	2	19	0	0
McKeon, Waterloo	.976	28	10	31	1	1
Meamber, Springfield	1.000	26	8	17	0	0
Medina, Wausau	1.000	16	2	3	0	0
Mejia, Madison	1.000	20	1	8	0	0
Mercedes, Wausau*	1.000	6	1	0	0	0
Milton, Appleton	.875	22	4	24	4	3
Misuraca, Kenosha	.969	26	12	51	2	0
Mitchener, South Bend	.920	34	4	19	2	2
Mohler, Madison*	1.000	42	4	10	0	1
MONGIELLO, South Bend	1.000	38	6	30	0	2
Montoya, Quad City*	1.000	4	0	3	0	0
D. Moore, Wausau*	.917	36	2	9	1	0
M. Moore, Quad City	.833	27	20	20	8	0
Morton, Waterloo	.975	44	11	28	1	1
Mullino, Peoria	1.000	6	0	4	0	0
Murray, Burlington	.898	26	18	26	5	1
Muscat, Beloit	.941	20	2	14	1	0
Musselwhite, Kenosha	1.000	42	12	18	0	3
Neal, Quad City	.733	14	1	10	4	1
Nedin, Kenosha*	.947	27	11	25	2	0
Newman, Kenosha*	.911	22	2	49	5	1
Nied, Burlington	.938	10	3	12	1	3
Nieves, Beloit*	1.000	7	3	4	0	0
Novoa, Clinton*	.963	15	6	20	1	2
Osteen, Madison*	.882	27	6	24	4	1
Patrick, Madison	.913	13	7	14	2	1
Paveloff, Wausau	.923	28	3	9	1	0
Peck, Madison	.800	5	1	3	1	1
Peek, Madison	.800	39	2	10	3	0
Pena, Madison	.842	14	6	10	3	1
Pennington, Wausau*	.864	32	9	10	3	2
Pulido, Kenosha*	.923	56	2	10	1	0
Rapp, Clinton..	.979	27	16	30	1	1
Rasp, Peoria	.786	26	3	8	3	1
Reed, Waterloo*	.972	23	7	28	1	2
Refnes, Quad City	1.000	9	2	4	0	1
Regira, Rockford	.929	28	4	9	1	0
Reis, Burlington	1.000	44	8	9	0	1
Riddle, Wausau	1.000	19	3	10	0	0
Risley, Cedar Rapids	.943	22	13	20	2	2
Ritter, Burlington	.953	25	9	32	2	2
Robles, Kenosha	.870	34	7	13	3	0
Rodgers, Cedar Rapids	.938	9	7	8	1	2
Roskom, Kenosha	1.000	1	2	0	0	0
Roy, Burlington	.929	34	7	19	2	2
Ruffin, South Bend	.885	24	11	12	3	0
Sanders, Waterloo	1.000	7	3	7	0	0
Sanford, Cedar Rapids	.944	25	4	13	1	0
Schaefer, Appleton	.966	13	6	22	1	1
Schrenk, South Bend	.951	20	13	26	2	2
Schullstrom, Wausau	1.000	5	1	2	0	0
Shifflett, Appleton	.929	57	1	25	2	1
Slomkowski, Burlington	1.000	5	1	1	0	0
J. Smith, Appleton	.864	35	9	10	3	2
M. Smith, Springfield	1.000	8	1	9	0	0
Snyder, Beloit	.938	30	6	9	1	2
Spiller, Springfield*	1.000	3	0	1	0	0
Spradlin, Cedar Rapids	.667	5	0	2	1	0
Stevens, South Bend	.893	50	10	15	3	2
Sudbury, Madison	1.000	7	1	6	0	0
Sullivan, Rockford*	.833	13	0	5	1	0
Swartzbaugh, Peoria	.951	29	23	35	3	3
Sweeney, Peoria	1.000	35	1	12	0	1
Swope, Kenosha	1.000	16	6	14	0	3
Talbert, Appleton	.947	24	5	13	1	0
R. Taylor, Clinton	.833	31	2	3	1	0
T. Taylor, Wausau	.900	23	4	14	2	1
W. Taylor, Madison	1.000	19	1	1	0	1
Teixeira, Wausau	1.000	7	1	4	0	0
Thelen, Kenosha	1.000	28	7	17	0	1
Thoden, Rockford	.900	12	11	16	3	3
Thoma, South Bend	1.000	7	0	1	0	0
Tolbert, Springfield	.909	6	5	5	1	0
Turek, Cedar Rapids	.857	25	10	20	5	0
Unrein, Wausau*	1.000	23	3	6	0	0
Valle, Burlington	.923	12	3	9	1	0
Van Poppel, Madison	.500	3	0	2	2	0
Vancho, Beloit	1.000	32	6	7	0	0
Vanderwel, South Bend	1.000	9	4	5	0	0
Van Winkle, South Bend	.900	29	6	3	1	0
Vazquez, Burlington	.929	15	11	15	2	1
Vegely, Quad City*	1.000	37	3	16	0	2
Walter, Appleton*	1.000	2	0	1	0	0
Weber, Springfield*	.966	29	3	25	1	0
Whatley, Clinton	1.000	4	0	2	0	0
Wheatcroft, Wausau	1.000	27	11	24	0	0
Whitehead, Rockford	.714	23	10	15	10	1
Wickman, South Bend	.895	9	9	8	2	1
Wiley, Appleton	.923	57	3	21	2	1
Wilkinson, Rockford	.960	42	5	19	1	1
Williams, Wausau*	1.000	26	10	24	0	3
Willis, Peoria	.919	31	16	41	5	3
Wiseman, Springfield	.941	10	2	14	1	1
Yaughn, Wausau	1.000	10	2	4	0	0
Young, Peoria	.800	24	2	6	2	0

Triple Play—Corona.

The following players did not have any fielding statistics at the positions indicated or appeared only as a designated hitter, pinch-hitter or pinch-runner: Apolinario, 3b; Beck, 1b; Beeler, 3b; Berlin, p; Bosio, p; Cairo, 3b; Charpia, 2b; Clemens, ss; Cole, c; Conte, p; Cooley, 2b; Cornell, p; Eatinger, 3b; Economy, p; Ellis, dh; Gonzales, 3b; D. Gross, p; Hairston, c; Henry, p; Heredia, p; Hildreth, of; Hollins, p; Hollis, 1b; Hudson, of; Jirschele, p; R. Johnson, 2b; Knabenshue, p; Krause, 1b; Lamitola, 3b; Langiotti, 1b; Leary, 2b; Leslie, p; Marett, p; Marze, 3b; P. Miller, p; Molitor, dh; Ramos, 2b; Reis, 3b; Rittman, of; Sanchez, 1b; Shingledecker, ss; R. Smith, p; R. Snyder, p; Specyalski, ss; Stillwell, p; Trujillo, p; Verstandig, p; Vice, p; Waggoner, p; Walker, 2b; Wegman, p; Wheeler, p.

CLUB PITCHING

Club	ERA.	G.	CG.	ShO.	Sv.	IP.	H.	R.	ER.	HR.	HB.	BB.	Int. BB.	SO.	WP.	Bk.
Cedar Rapids	2.66	134	26	18	48	1143.2	917	403	338	74	38	418	29	1035	79	7
Clinton	2.77	134	12	17	38	1148.1	904	452	354	45	52	529	13	1108	81	37
Quad City	2.90	140	21	17	33	1168.2	1026	525	377	52	46	550	12	1049	69	45
Beloit	3.09	135	10	9	38	1144.1	1015	563	393	49	60	533	19	1109	84	34
Kenosha	3.27	138	15	14	33	1172.2	1034	545	426	68	62	503	25	995	67	32
South Bend	3.32	134	15	14	40	1145.2	984	568	422	36	59	588	17	927	76	31
Madison	3.33	135	13	14	30	1155.1	1027	567	427	64	25	507	9	871	65	31
Burlington	3.34	137	27	14	27	1174.1	1113	570	436	58	31	444	14	903	86	18
Appleton	3.65	133	6	14	33	1132.0	1034	557	459	46	70	505	13	916	90	34
Waterloo	3.65	136	15	15	29	1161.1	1049	569	471	87	55	479	23	766	83	14
Peoria	3.69	137	22	10	24	1168.1	1079	595	479	65	56	410	16	987	78	36
Rockford	3.68	136	9	6	33	1151.0	1103	614	471	47	49	523	18	932	83	26
Springfield	3.93	139	9	10	39	1205.1	1217	668	526	79	45	451	26	877	76	33
Wausau	4.37	136	9	4	26	1152.2	1106	723	560	111	42	604	17	1032	94	40

PITCHERS' RECORDS

(Leading Qualifiers for Earned-Run Average Leadership—112 or More Innings)

*Throws lefthanded.

Pitcher—Club	W.	L.	Pct.	ERA.	G.	GS.	CG.	GF.	ShO.	Sv.	IP.	H.	R.	ER.	HR.	HB.	BB.	Int. BB.	SO.	WP.
Newman, Kenosha*	10	4	.714	1.64	22	22	5	0	1	0	154.0	95	41	28	2	6	78	2	158	10
Turek, Cedar Rapids	13	6	.684	2.34	25	25	4	0	1	0	169.1	131	54	44	8	2	61	4	154	7
Carter, Beloit	7	9	.438	2.54	21	19	3	0	1	0	127.2	118	50	36	3	6	41	1	78	4
F. Martinez, Quad City*	12	7	.632	2.57	26	26	7	0	3	0	171.1	128	66	49	6	9	79	1	195	7
Rapp, Clinton	14	10	.583	2.64	27	26	4	1	0	0	167.1	132	60	49	2	7	79	2	132	8
McKeon, Waterloo	11	11	.500	2.70	28	25	7	0	5	0	180.0	152	66	54	12	8	34	4	141	8

Pitcher—Club	W.	L.	Pct.	ERA.	G.	GS.	CG.	GF.	ShO.	Sv.	IP.	H.	R.	ER.	HR.	HB.	BB.	Int. BB.	SO.	WP.
S. King, Quad City	9	9	.500	2.70	31	20	3	3	1	0	160.0	139	64	48	3	8	69	1	162	7
Sanford, Cedar Rapids	13	4	.765	2.74	25	25	2	0	1	0	157.2	112	50	48	15	4	55	1	180	8
Brutcher, South Bend	11	4	.733	2.74	22	22	4	0	1	0	128.0	87	49	39	2	11	77	0	118	4
Galindez, Waterloo*	10	7	.588	2.78	26	26	2	0	1	0	148.2	122	61	46	10	9	75	0	99	10

Departmental Leaders: G—Gorton, 59; W—M. Moore, 16; L—Lebron, Whitehead, 14; Pct.—Kracl, Logan, .833; GS—Gomez, Swartzbaugh, 29; CG—F. Martinez, McKeon, Risley, 7; GF—Wiley, 44; ShO—McKeon, 5; Sv.—Keller, McAuliffe, 26; IP—McKeon, 180.0; H—Lebron, 177; R—Gomez, 92; ER—Gomez, 79; HR—Lebron, 17; HB—Willis, 14; BB—Pennington, 121; IBB—Cimorelli, 7; SO—F. Martinez, 195; WP—Andrzejewski, Conner, 20.

(All Pitchers—Listed Alphabetically)

Pitcher—Club	W.	L.	Pct.	ERA.	G.	GS.	CG.	GF.	ShO.	Sv.	IP.	H.	R.	ER.	HR.	HB.	BB.	Int. BB.	SO.	WP.
Adams, Quad City	3	5	.375	4.97	12	10	1	1	0	0	50.2	59	36	28	5	0	22	0	41	5
Ahern, Appleton	2	9	.182	5.12	12	11	1	0	0	0	63.1	85	46	36	5	7	22	0	38	6
Aleys, Clinton*	2	3	.400	3.77	25	4	0	11	0	3	59.2	52	30	25	2	0	37	1	49	5
Ma. Anderson, Wausau*	1	3	.250	4.43	18	2	0	7	0	0	42.2	49	31	21	5	4	24	1	39	3
Mi. Anderson, Cedar Rapids	10	5	.667	3.38	23	23	2	0	0	0	138.1	134	67	52	6	5	62	0	101	10
Andrzejewski, Beloit	6	9	.400	5.61	24	19	1	2	0	0	78.2	57	67	49	5	7	97	0	81	20
Archer, Beloit	5	0	1.000	1.53	11	0	0	3	0	0	29.1	24	11	5	1	1	9	1	27	2
Archibald, 13 Rock.-1 Q.C.	0	0	.000	3.52	14	0	0	6	0	0	23.0	21	12	9	1	1	11	2	11	2
Ayala, Cedar Rapids	3	2	.600	3.38	18	7	3	3	1	1	53.1	40	24	20	6	4	18	0	59	6
Baez, Appleton*	1	7	.125	5.44	10	10	0	0	0	0	46.1	56	40	28	1	1	25	0	28	7
Baldwin, Appleton*	0	1	.000	3.07	9	0	0	5	0	0	14.2	14	7	5	1	2	13	0	14	0
Batista, Rockford	0	1	.000	8.76	3	2	0	0	0	0	12.1	16	13	12	2	4	5	0	7	3
Bennett, Quad City	7	7	.500	2.99	18	18	3	0	1	0	108.1	91	48	36	10	4	37	0	100	2
Berlin, Springfield	0	0	.000	45.00	1	0	0	1	0	0	1.0	2	5	5	0	1	3	0	1	0
Best, Kenosha	8	6	.571	3.56	19	19	1	0	0	0	93.2	67	45	37	10	5	59	0	98	6
Bochtler, Rockford	9	12	.429	3.50	25	25	1	0	1	0	139.0	142	82	54	3	8	54	2	109	6
Bolton, South Bend	5	1	.833	1.94	7	7	3	0	1	0	51.0	34	14	11	0	1	12	1	50	1
Boothby, Wausau	3	1	.750	6.75	25	0	0	19	0	0	45.1	48	39	34	4	5	36	1	30	10
Borbon, Burlington	11	3	.786	1.47	14	14	6	0	2	0	97.2	73	25	16	3	3	23	0	76	4
Borcherding, Cedar Rapids	6	3	.667	1.45	21	9	1	6	0	3	74.2	59	24	12	5	4	20	2	49	7
Bosio, Beloit	0	0	.000	3.00	1	1	0	0	0	0	3.0	4	2	1	0	0	1	0	2	0
Botkin, Springfield*	0	4	.000	6.17	6	5	0	1	0	0	23.1	27	23	16	3	1	12	1	20	2
Bradford, Peoria	2	6	.250	4.47	8	8	1	0	0	0	52.1	51	30	26	2	1	19	0	35	6
Brimhall, Madison	0	1	.000	8.06	11	3	0	5	0	0	22.1	29	23	20	2	2	20	0	18	5
Bruck, Burlington	9	6	.600	4.15	19	18	1	0	0	0	104.0	89	65	48	9	4	66	1	81	9
Brummett, Clinton	2	2	.500	3.51	6	4	0	0	0	0	25.2	18	14	10	0	3	9	0	22	1
Brutcher, South Bend	11	4	.733	2.74	22	22	4	0	1	0	128.0	87	49	39	2	11	77	0	118	4
Bushing, Rockford	3	6	.333	3.28	46	0	0	32	0	12	79.2	62	38	29	5	2	38	5	99	3
Byerly, Burlington*	0	1	.000	1.93	14	0	0	8	0	0	9.1	5	3	2	0	1	3	0	8	0
Calderone, Burlington	4	7	.364	3.38	46	0	0	22	0	3	82.2	74	42	31	4	3	38	4	75	7
Callahan, Clinton*	2	4	.333	2.25	41	0	0	21	0	2	64.0	52	25	16	2	3	25	1	47	4
Campos, 1 Peo.-12 S.B.	1	0	1.000	9.39	13	1	0	8	0	1	15.1	19	17	16	2	0	16	0	13	4
Carter, Beloit	7	9	.438	2.54	21	19	3	0	1	0	127.2	118	50	36	3	6	41	1	78	4
Castillo, Quad City	3	6	.333	2.40	17	11	2	1	1	0	82.2	75	31	22	3	2	28	0	50	2
Chrisman, Appleton	3	1	.750	6.16	11	0	0	5	0	0	19.0	24	14	13	1	1	12	2	16	1
Cimorelli, Springfield	4	8	.333	4.56	41	15	1	6	0	0	120.1	125	80	61	9	7	41	7	86	8
Conner, Appleton	5	8	.385	4.21	30	12	0	8	0	0	113.1	115	59	53	1	5	52	0	70	20
Conte, Madison	0	0	.000	0.00	1	0	0	1	0	0	1.0	0	0	0	0	0	0	0	0	1
Cormier, Madison	3	0	1.000	2.06	8	8	2	0	2	0	52.1	34	17	12	3	2	17	0	38	1
Cornell, Beloit	0	0	.000	0.00	1	0	0	1	0	0	2.0	0	0	0	0	0	2	0	0	0
Corona, Springfield*	5	1	.833	3.71	54	0	0	16	0	1	68.0	68	36	28	6	2	29	4	58	7
Correa, Beloit	3	0	1.000	2.19	4	4	0	0	0	0	24.2	24	8	6	1	0	9	0	30	1
Cox, Springfield	0	0	.000	0.00	1	1	0	0	0	0	5.0	1	0	0	0	0	0	0	3	0
Craven, Quad City	2	1	.667	2.90	15	6	1	2	1	0	59.0	56	33	19	3	3	18	0	43	4
Crim, Beloit	0	0	.000	4.50	1	1	0	0	0	0	2.0	3	2	1	0	0	0	0	0	1
Czajkowski, Beloit	2	0	1.000	1.65	21	0	0	21	0	11	27.1	16	7	5	1	3	8	4	37	0
Dedrick, Wausau	0	1	.000	2.70	3	1	0	1	0	0	10.0	6	4	3	0	0	4	0	8	0
DeLaRosa, Beloit	1	1	.500	3.98	8	0	0	1	0	0	20.1	28	16	9	1	3	11	0	17	1
G. DeLeon, Madison	4	6	.400	4.78	15	15	0	0	0	0	81.0	108	64	43	7	2	26	0	46	2
R. DeLeon, Burlington*	3	1	.750	2.45	26	0	0	17	0	1	29.1	31	9	8	0	0	11	0	16	0
Diaz, Kenosha	1	5	.167	4.86	14	7	0	5	0	0	46.1	47	30	25	5	4	27	0	35	3
Dickson, Peoria*	3	1	.750	1.51	5	5	1	0	0	0	35.2	22	9	6	1	0	11	0	54	2
Doss, Peoria	2	6	.250	4.64	18	13	1	2	0	0	77.2	77	47	40	3	1	37	0	71	12
Drake, Beloit	2	4	.333	5.40	13	13	0	0	0	0	57.0	60	44	34	4	2	38	1	63	5
Duenas, Peoria*	0	0	.000	9.00	1	0	0	1	0	0	1.0	1	1	1	1	0	0	0	0	0
Ebert, Clinton	1	2	.333	5.92	10	5	0	5	0	0	24.1	19	20	16	1	3	37	0	14	12
Economy, Cedar Rapids	0	0	.000	3.68	4	0	0	2	0	0	7.1	9	3	3	0	0	4	0	14	1
Eddings, Beloit	0	3	.000	5.25	8	0	0	5	0	1	12.0	23	8	7	0	0	7	0	7	0
Eddy, Rockford	7	7	.500	3.48	34	8	0	14	0	4	113.2	119	52	44	6	10	38	3	80	10
Elvira, Beloit*	3	2	.600	2.35	8	7	0	1	0	1	38.1	37	16	10	1	0	9	0	45	2
Embry, Waterloo	0	5	.000	7.25	29	8	0	10	0	4	63.1	68	56	51	9	1	56	3	40	8
Eversgerd, Springfield*	6	8	.429	4.14	20	15	2	2	0	0	104.1	123	60	48	6	4	26	1	55	2
Flanagan, Clinton	0	2	.000	2.86	25	0	0	11	0	3	34.2	33	12	11	2	5	10	2	25	1
Fleming, Beloit	6	2	.750	1.95	31	1	0	25	0	8	73.2	60	23	16	3	2	17	1	85	2
Florie, Waterloo	4	5	.444	4.39	14	14	1	0	0	0	65.2	60	37	32	3	8	37	0	38	6
Foley, Clinton	1	0	1.000	3.77	7	0	0	2	0	0	14.1	12	8	6	0	1	10	0	13	1
Forrester, South Bend*	0	0	.000	4.66	13	0	0	7	0	5	9.2	7	6	5	0	1	13	1	8	2
Fortugno, Beloit*	8	4	.667	1.56	31	0	0	29	0	7	63.1	38	16	11	1	0	38	3	106	4
Galindez, Waterloo*	10	7	.588	2.78	26	26	2	0	1	0	148.2	122	61	46	10	9	75	0	99	10
Garces, Beloit*	3	2	.600	2.65	15	1	0	7	0	2	37.1	29	11	11	3	4	12	1	57	3
Garcia, Cedar Rapids	8	3	.727	1.52	49	0	0	26	0	15	71.0	36	15	12	6	0	18	5	106	4
Gelb, Peoria	2	6	.250	5.14	23	5	0	7	0	0	63.0	60	41	36	4	7	26	1	56	3
Gennings, South Bend	1	1	.500	3.77	11	0	0	8	0	4	14.1	13	13	6	0	0	11	2	7	1
Gewecke, Springfield*	3	5	.375	3.61	38	13	0	6	0	0	104.2	103	52	42	3	4	38	2	79	10
Gibbs, Madison	2	0	1.000	4.05	18	0	0	14	0	7	20.0	16	10	9	0	0	20	0	24	1
Gomez, Peoria	7	12	.368	4.06	30	29	2	0	1	0	175.1	165	92	79	15	9	55	4	138	3
Gorman, South Bend	1	1	.500	1.88	7	0	0	1	0	0	14.1	14	5	3	2	0	6	1	8	4
Gorton, Springfield	5	7	.417	1.18	59	0	0	27	0	12	76.1	65	23	10	3	0	30	4	83	6
D. Gross, Kenosha	0	0	.000	0.00	1	0	0	1	0	0	2.0	2	0	0	0	0	0	0	1	0
J. Gross, Appleton	3	4	.429	3.36	13	13	0	0	0	0	67.0	61	28	25	3	4	22	1	65	5

Pitcher—Club	W.	L.	Pct.	ERA.	G.	GS.	CG.	GF.	ShO.	Sv.	IP.	H.	R.	ER.	HR.	HB.	BB.	Int. BB.	SO.	WP.
Grott, Madison*	2	0	1.000	0.36	22	0	0	19	0	12	25.0	15	5	1	0	0	14	1	36	1
Grove, Burlington	5	6	.455	3.40	20	18	2	1	1	1	108.2	112	53	41	3	3	29	0	68	3
Grovom, Cedar Rapids*	4	1	.800	3.94	8	4	0	1	0	0	32.0	32	14	14	1	0	16	2	29	3
Gulledge, Madison	3	6	.333	3.74	19	13	1	1	0	0	79.1	78	38	33	6	1	36	0	54	4
Gustafson, Clinton	7	1	.875	1.81	40	1	0	29	0	12	84.1	50	23	17	1	4	32	5	123	6
Haffner, Quad City	5	1	.833	2.33	45	0	0	36	0	10	58.0	46	18	15	0	0	21	1	27	4
Hale, Wausau*	3	4	.429	4.79	12	9	1	0	1	0	56.1	47	34	30	5	3	39	0	57	8
Hancock, Clinton*	11	3	.786	2.28	18	17	2	0	1	0	110.2	78	33	28	4	3	43	0	123	5
Haney, Rockford*	2	4	.333	2.21	8	8	3	0	0	0	53.0	40	15	13	1	1	6	0	45	0
Hanselman, Clinton	9	10	.474	3.23	25	24	2	0	1	0	145.0	120	71	52	12	7	75	1	128	15
Harrington, Kenosha*	3	4	.429	1.74	22	1	0	5	0	1	46.2	26	13	9	0	4	29	1	36	9
Hart, Waterloo	3	4	.429	2.63	46	0	0	25	0	5	65.0	57	24	19	4	1	26	1	49	8
Hays, Waterloo	0	1	.000	4.03	12	0	0	2	0	0	22.1	23	11	10	0	1	12	0	17	4
Heiden, Wausau	2	4	.333	5.02	19	2	0	15	0	6	28.2	29	17	16	3	0	27	1	37	1
Helm, Quad City	1	1	.500	4.00	4	1	0	0	0	0	9.0	8	6	4	0	1	8	0	8	1
Henry, Madison	0	0	.000	4.50	1	0	0	1	0	0	2.0	4	1	1	0	0	1	0	3	0
Hensley, Springfield	2	1	.667	5.48	5	4	0	0	0	0	21.1	21	14	13	0	0	12	0	15	0
Heredia, Quad City	0	0	.000	3.86	5	0	0	3	0	0	7.0	5	6	3	0	0	6	0	10	0
Hernandez, Clinton*	1	2	.333	4.17	15	1	0	8	0	0	36.2	33	19	17	3	2	25	1	27	5
Hester, Cedar Rapids	0	1	.000	1.50	1	1	0	0	0	0	6.0	9	4	1	0	0	0	0	3	0
Hillman, 17 Clint.-7 Q.C.	2	6	.250	3.38	24	11	1	6	0	1	90.2	88	45	34	4	8	34	1	69	6
Hirsch, Peoria	0	3	.000	3.97	10	0	0	7	0	1	11.1	11	6	5	0	3	5	0	11	3
Hoeme, Appleton	1	1	.500	3.86	7	0	0	2	0	0	11.2	10	5	5	0	2	8	0	15	2
Hollins, Peoria	0	0	.000	5.59	5	0	0	1	0	0	9.2	12	9	6	2	1	5	0	8	1
Hook, Quad City*	6	3	.667	1.89	30	0	0	22	0	7	38.0	18	10	8	0	1	22	1	66	4
Hoppe, Kenosha	1	3	.250	4.10	4	4	1	0	0	0	26.1	29	14	12	1	1	8	1	12	2
Howze, Rockford	2	7	.222	6.28	19	14	0	1	0	0	71.2	83	58	50	10	4	48	0	31	7
Hoyer, Waterloo*	7	4	.636	2.28	51	1	0	22	0	6	90.2	58	26	23	6	2	40	6	61	6
Huisman, Clinton	6	5	.545	2.05	14	13	0	0	0	0	79.0	56	19	18	2	0	33	0	103	5
Huslig, Clinton	4	4	.500	2.55	12	12	0	0	0	0	74.0	51	24	21	3	0	34	0	62	4
Infante, Springfield	3	5	.375	5.35	50	0	0	26	0	0	72.1	94	59	43	6	3	32	3	41	4
Jacobs, Appleton	7	6	.538	3.47	25	18	2	3	2	1	127.0	117	59	49	10	6	46	0	105	8
Jaques, Peoria*	6	6	.500	3.33	52	0	0	32	0	12	67.2	57	36	25	3	1	18	2	73	10
Jeffery, Cedar Rapids	6	1	.857	1.38	9	9	0	0	3	0	71.2	45	15	11	5	3	11	2	56	1
Jirschele, Appleton	0	0	.000	2.25	2	0	0	2	0	0	4.0	3	1	1	0	0	2	0	3	2
Johnson, South Bend*	5	3	.625	2.09	27	0	0	11	0	3	60.1	50	20	14	2	3	23	1	52	3
Karchner, Appleton	2	7	.222	4.82	27	11	1	5	0	0	71.0	70	42	38	3	6	31	2	58	4
Keller, Springfield	3	3	.500	1.87	44	0	0	42	0	26	53.0	30	13	11	3	6	15	1	58	3
Kelly, Burlington*	3	1	.750	4.65	34	7	0	5	0	1	79.1	85	60	41	5	2	55	1	74	15
Kilgo, Rockford*	4	4	.500	2.23	45	0	0	31	0	9	88.2	62	26	22	2	3	20	1	85	6
Kimball, Beloit	5	8	.385	2.88	22	18	4	2	2	2	128.0	134	65	41	4	4	46	2	79	2
D. King, Cedar Rapids	3	6	.333	3.71	32	0	0	15	0	2	51.0	49	31	21	2	5	23	6	45	1
S. King, Quad City	9	9	.500	2.70	31	20	3	3	1	0	160.0	139	64	48	3	8	69	1	162	7
Knabenshue, Beloit	0	0	.000	27.00	1	0	0	1	0	0	1.0	2	4	3	0	0	3	0	0	0
Kracl, Madison	10	2	.833	1.98	14	14	4	0	0	0	100.0	73	39	22	4	1	37	0	58	7
Kremblas, Cedar Rapids	0	0	.000	0.00	1	0	0	1	0	0	1.0	1	0	0	0	0	0	0	0	0
Krol, Kenosha	0	2	.000	1.84	5	0	0	2	0	0	14.2	9	4	3	0	1	2	0	15	0
Krueger, Beloit*	1	0	1.000	1.50	1	1	0	0	0	0	6.0	4	1	1	0	1	2	0	4	0
Kuhn, Madison*	5	4	.556	3.18	21	7	0	4	0	0	65.0	60	30	23	5	1	26	0	37	4
Landry, Beloit	3	2	.600	2.68	8	8	0	0	0	0	40.1	35	18	12	1	1	27	0	29	8
Lata, Springfield	10	5	.667	3.55	19	19	1	0	0	0	124.1	122	68	49	11	2	36	0	75	12
Latter, Madison	6	8	.429	2.53	43	1	0	16	0	1	78.1	52	29	22	2	1	34	2	77	4
Lawson, Madison	0	0	.000	19.85	7	0	0	3	0	0	11.1	29	28	25	1	0	9	0	8	3
Lebron, Waterloo	7	14	.333	4.18	26	26	3	0	1	0	163.2	177	89	76	17	4	61	4	93	10
Leinen, Wausau*	3	9	.250	3.54	13	13	3	0	0	0	81.1	73	42	32	6	2	25	0	73	4
Leslie, Cedar Rapids*	0	0	.000	4.26	6	0	0	4	0	0	6.1	6	3	3	0	4	0	7	1	
Lewis, Waterloo	2	4	.333	4.98	47	0	0	36	0	12	65.0	71	46	36	3	9	22	2	36	7
Lindaman, Kenosha	1	2	.333	3.10	16	0	0	10	0	1	20.1	17	8	7	0	2	11	3	19	0
Lindsey, Appleton*	2	2	.500	7.47	21	3	0	6	0	0	37.1	53	38	31	4	2	27	0	31	1
Lipson, Kenosha	1	4	.200	2.53	47	0	0	37	0	20	53.1	38	19	15	5	1	17	5	34	1
Lloyd, Kenosha	0	0	.000	0.00	3	0	0	2	0	0	3.0	2	2	0	0	0	2	0	5	0
Logan, Rockford	10	2	.833	2.63	18	15	2	1	2	0	89.0	83	36	26	5	4	36	0	67	3
Long, South Bend*	1	5	.167	4.35	27	7	0	7	0	0	70.1	75	41	34	4	7	36	2	56	5
Lutz, Peoria	12	9	.571	2.90	25	25	6	0	3	0	167.1	132	62	54	12	4	45	2	168	1
Mann, Peoria	1	0	1.000	1.65	9	1	0	6	0	1	16.1	19	3	3	1	1	7	1	11	0
Manon, Cedar Rapids	5	6	.455	4.54	19	0	0	8	0	1	39.2	43	21	20	7	0	7	2	14	0
Marchese, Quad City	3	1	.750	1.98	35	0	0	25	0	12	50.0	38	15	11	2	3	32	4	40	3
Marett, Wausau	1	0	1.000	5.88	14	0	0	7	0	0	26.0	40	27	17	3	0	8	0	14	3
Marrero, Beloit*	0	0	.000	3.27	3	0	0	2	0	0	11.0	11	4	4	0	1	4	0	3	0
Marsh, Cedar Rapids	0	0	.000	0.00	2	0	0	2	0	0	2.1	2	0	0	0	1	0	0	5	1
J. Martin, Quad City	2	0	1.000	0.73	8	0	0	6	0	1	12.1	9	3	1	0	7	0	15	1	
T. Martin, Wausau	2	3	.400	2.48	9	9	0	0	0	0	40.0	31	25	11	1	5	27	0	45	4
F. Martinez, Quad City*	12	7	.632	2.57	26	26	7	0	3	0	171.1	128	66	49	5	9	79	1	195	7
M. Martinez, Rockford	8	11	.421	4.65	27	26	1	0	0	0	133.2	151	86	69	1	11	63	1	91	14
R. Martinez, Madison	0	0	.000	4.70	6	0	0	2	0	0	7.2	11	4	4	0	0	4	0	6	3
Matznick, South Bend	10	7	.588	3.48	26	25	0	0	0	0	121.2	100	58	47	2	2	82	0	127	6
McAuliffe, Cedar Rapids	6	1	.857	1.97	41	0	0	39	0	26	50.1	34	13	11	2	1	25	2	40	6
McCarthy, Cedar Rapids*	0	1	.000	0.75	8	0	0	3	0	0	12.0	8	6	1	2	0	6	1	11	2
McGraw, Beloit*	7	3	.700	1.93	12	12	1	0	1	0	70.0	49	33	15	1	2	34	0	61	4
McKeon, Waterloo	11	11	.500	2.70	28	25	7	0	5	0	180.0	152	66	54	12	8	34	4	141	8
Meamber, Springfield	5	11	.313	5.59	26	18	1	1	0	0	112.2	143	84	70	11	5	39	0	83	8
Medina, Wausau	0	2	.000	3.38	16	0	0	7	0	2	18.2	16	8	7	4	0	6	1	16	1
Mejia, Madison	6	2	.750	1.92	20	5	0	3	0	0	65.2	52	19	14	4	1	21	2	42	0
Mercedes, Wausau*	0	2	.000	4.64	6	4	0	1	0	0	21.1	22	16	11	4	0	14	0	16	1
Miller, Beloit	0	2	.000	5.66	4	3	0	1	0	0	20.2	26	15	13	2	1	7	1	20	1
Milton, Appleton	4	5	.444	3.13	22	22	0	0	0	0	112.0	75	47	39	5	8	84	0	80	16
Misuraca, Kenosha	9	9	.500	3.33	26	26	1	0	0	0	167.1	164	81	62	6	12	57	1	116	6
Mitchener, South Bend	6	6	.500	4.40	34	8	0	9	0	1	86.0	82	50	42	4	9	51	1	40	8
Mohler, Madison*	1	1	.500	3.41	42	2	0	10	0	1	63.1	56	34	24	2	2	32	0	72	4
Mongiello, South Bend	6	6	.500	3.30	38	15	3	21	1	13	106.1	98	55	39	2	2	54	4	89	5
Montoya, Quad City*	3	1	.750	3.14	4	4	1	0	0	0	28.2	30	12	10	0	0	6	0	13	0
D. Moore, Wausau*	4	6	.400	2.47	36	0	0	27	0	12	54.2	41	26	15	3	1	17	1	72	4

Pitcher—Club	W.	L.	Pct.	ERA.	G.	GS.	CG.	GF.	ShO.	Sv.	IP.	H.	R.	ER.	HR.	HB.	BB.	Int. BB.	SO.	WP.
M. Moore, Quad City	16	5	.762	3.31	27	27	2	0	1	0	160.1	150	83	59	6	3	106	0	160	13
Morton, Waterloo	8	11	.421	3.45	44	8	1	21	0	2	125.1	114	54	48	12	4	16	1	89	7
Mullino, Peoria	0	0	.000	4.15	6	0	0	4	0	1	8.2	10	5	4	1	0	4	0	9	0
Murray, Burlington	11	7	.611	3.26	26	26	6	0	3	0	163.0	139	72	59	9	3	61	0	134	10
Muscat, Beloit	4	6	.400	3.89	20	10	1	1	0	0	76.1	65	46	33	5	6	44	0	51	8
Musselwhite, Kenosha	6	5	.545	3.13	42	1	0	17	0	3	72.0	64	31	25	6	2	15	0	63	0
Neal, Quad City*	2	6	.250	5.43	14	10	0	4	0	0	53.0	66	46	32	9	1	36	2	34	6
Nedin, Kenosha*	3	13	.188	3.39	27	22	3	1	2	0	140.2	131	74	53	6	8	63	1	144	9
Newman, Kenosha*	10	4	.714	1.64	22	22	5	0	1	0	154.0	95	41	28	2	6	78	2	158	10
Nied, Burlington	5	3	.625	2.25	10	9	1	1	1	0	64.0	55	21	16	2	1	10	0	66	3
Nieves, Beloit*	2	3	.400	3.99	7	7	0	0	0	0	29.1	29	17	13	1	1	6	0	22	4
Novoa, Clinton*	9	2	.818	2.40	15	14	3	0	1	0	97.2	73	32	26	6	4	30	0	113	2
Osteen, Madison*	10	10	.500	3.10	27	27	1	0	1	0	154.0	126	69	53	6	3	80	0	120	10
Patrick, Madison	3	7	.300	3.60	13	12	3	0	0	0	80.0	88	44	32	6	1	19	0	40	3
Paveloff, Wausau	2	3	.400	2.98	28	1	0	11	0	1	57.1	51	29	19	4	1	20	2	44	2
Peck, Madison	2	2	.500	5.24	5	4	0	1	0	0	22.1	24	15	13	3	1	9	1	14	0
Peek, Madison	5	3	.625	2.70	39	0	0	30	0	7	56.2	41	19	17	4	1	10	2	70	0
Pena, Madison	5	4	.556	2.68	14	14	2	0	1	0	84.0	63	31	25	4	3	41	0	48	9
Pennington, Wausau*	4	9	.308	5.18	32	18	1	7	0	0	106.0	81	89	61	12	4	121	1	142	10
Pulido, Kenosha*	5	5	.500	2.34	56	0	0	29	0	6	61.2	55	21	16	2	4	36	3	70	3
Rapp, Clinton	14	10	.583	2.64	27	26	4	1	0	0	167.1	132	60	49	2	7	79	2	132	8
Rasp, Peoria	2	2	.500	3.77	26	0	0	20	0	3	43.0	49	26	18	1	0	15	1	30	9
Reed, Waterloo*	6	8	.429	3.75	23	21	1	0	0	0	129.2	100	66	54	7	7	76	2	70	9
Refnes, Quad City	3	1	.750	2.41	9	5	1	0	1	0	33.2	43	16	9	0	4	15	0	22	4
Regira, Rockford	0	4	.000	4.23	28	3	0	12	0	0	61.2	53	39	29	1	1	54	0	62	5
Reis, Burlington	5	7	.417	3.38	44	0	0	37	0	17	66.2	62	33	25	0	3	34	6	45	6
Riddle, Wausau	3	1	.750	3.21	19	0	0	10	0	4	47.2	42	18	17	6	0	12	1	35	1
Risley, Cedar Rapids	8	9	.471	2.81	22	22	7	0	1	0	137.2	99	51	43	8	7	68	1	123	13
Ritter, Burlington	6	10	.375	3.78	25	25	6	0	2	0	157.1	172	80	66	10	3	53	1	108	10
Robles, Kenosha	3	5	.375	4.75	34	8	0	7	0	1	89.0	105	57	47	9	4	27	3	70	5
Rodgers, Cedar Rapids	3	2	.600	3.42	9	9	1	0	1	0	50.0	55	27	19	0	3	13	0	37	5
Roskom, Kenosha	1	0	1.000	0.00	1	1	0	0	0	0	6.0	3	0	0	0	0	3	0	3	0
Roy, Burlington	7	0	1.000	2.60	34	0	0	15	0	4	69.1	74	26	20	4	2	11	0	62	2
Ruffin, South Bend	7	6	.538	4.17	24	24	0	0	0	0	123.0	117	86	57	7	3	82	0	92	17
Sanders, Waterloo	2	2	.500	4.86	7	7	0	0	0	0	37.0	43	21	20	2	1	21	0	29	0
Sanford, Cedar Rapids	13	4	.765	2.74	25	25	2	0	1	0	157.2	112	50	48	15	4	55	1	180	8
Schaefer, Appleton	6	2	.750	1.71	13	12	1	0	1	0	79.0	63	18	15	2	8	18	0	68	1
Schrenk, South Bend	7	6	.538	2.95	20	14	2	2	1	0	103.2	79	44	34	7	11	25	0	92	7
Schullstrom, Wausau	0	2	.000	4.66	5	5	0	0	0	0	19.1	20	12	10	3	0	7	0	21	0
Shifflett, Appleton	6	5	.545	2.94	57	0	0	34	0	10	82.2	67	35	27	3	3	28	4	40	1
Slomkowski, Burlington	1	0	1.000	4.76	5	0	0	2	0	0	11.1	9	7	6	1	2	8	0	7	0
J. Smith, Appleton	1	1	.500	3.16	35	0	0	11	0	4	68.1	47	30	24	0	4	37	0	85	9
M. Smith, Springfield	4	2	.667	3.96	8	8	0	0	0	0	52.1	50	25	23	6	4	15	1	34	0
R. Smith, Wausau*	1	0	1.000	15.26	6	0	0	3	0	0	7.2	16	18	13	4	0	9	1	6	3
B. Snyder, Beloit	1	4	.200	3.32	30	7	0	9	0	3	81.1	78	45	30	6	8	38	2	86	5
R. Snyder, Beloit	1	0	1.000	0.00	1	1	0	1	0	0	4.0	2	0	0	0	0	3	0	6	0
Spiller, Springfield*	0	2	.000	12.27	3	3	0	0	0	0	11.0	20	16	15	3	0	9	0	3	1
Spradlin, Cedar Rapids	0	1	.000	3.00	5	0	0	0	0	0	12.0	13	8	4	1	0	5	1	6	0
Stevens, South Bend	6	8	.429	2.47	50	0	0	25	0	12	102.0	82	45	28	1	3	31	4	81	7
Stillwell, Appleton	0	0	.000	9.00	1	0	0	1	0	0	1.0	1	1	1	0	0	0	0	0	1
Sudbury, Madison	4	2	.667	4.62	7	6	0	0	0	0	37.0	32	23	19	2	0	29	0	18	2
Sullivan, Rockford*	2	0	1.000	2.31	13	0	0	7	0	2	23.1	16	7	6	1	1	6	0	20	0
Swartzbaugh, Peoria	8	11	.421	3.82	29	29	5	0	2	0	169.2	147	88	72	11	7	89	1	128	10
Sweeney, Peoria	0	3	.000	3.52	35	0	0	12	0	2	61.1	62	36	24	1	6	19	3	54	4
Swope, Kenosha	6	1	.857	4.58	16	10	1	2	1	0	70.2	69	41	36	6	4	30	1	52	6
Talbert, Appleton	11	6	.647	3.50	24	19	1	1	0	0	123.1	107	55	48	6	4	55	1	110	4
R. Taylor, Clinton	5	2	.714	1.53	31	0	0	30	0	17	35.1	29	13	6	2	4	16	0	42	2
T. Taylor, Waterloo	3	11	.214	5.27	23	20	1	1	1	0	111.0	103	74	65	11	5	62	0	78	8
W. Taylor, Madison	1	2	.333	3.26	19	1	0	9	0	2	30.1	27	12	11	2	2	11	1	23	2
Teixeira, Wausau	1	0	1.000	9.53	7	0	0	1	0	0	11.1	22	15	12	0	1	4	3	7	1
Thelen, Kenosha	3	9	.250	4.80	28	17	3	4	0	0	105.0	111	64	56	10	4	39	4	64	7
Thoden, Rockford	4	3	.571	2.28	12	12	1	0	0	0	75.0	71	33	19	3	1	14	2	73	3
Thoma, South Bend	1	0	1.000	6.35	7	0	0	4	0	0	5.2	6	4	4	0	0	6	0	9	0
Tolbert, Springfield	4	1	.800	3.24	6	5	1	0	1	0	33.1	40	13	12	1	1	9	0	21	1
Trujillo, Springfield	0	0	.000	9.00	1	0	0	1	0	0	1.0	1	1	1	0	1	0	0	0	1
Turek, Cedar Rapids	13	6	.684	2.34	25	25	4	0	1	0	169.1	131	54	44	8	2	61	4	154	7
Unrein, Wausau*	1	1	.500	2.03	23	1	0	6	0	0	31.0	30	12	7	2	1	15	1	24	7
Valle, Burlington	2	2	.500	4.06	12	7	0	1	0	0	44.1	44	24	20	6	0	22	1	42	9
Van Poppel, Madison	2	1	.667	3.95	3	3	0	0	0	0	13.2	8	11	6	0	1	10	0	17	0
Vancho, Beloit	2	2	.500	2.99	32	2	0	17	0	4	84.1	71	35	28	4	8	26	2	108	5
Vanderwel, South Bend	0	0	.000	3.00	9	1	0	3	0	0	12.0	9	7	4	0	3	15	0	9	3
Van Winkle, South Bend	2	1	.667	5.18	29	1	0	13	0	1	57.1	62	36	33	2	2	34	0	27	3
Vazquez, Burlington	6	5	.545	3.81	15	13	5	1	0	0	87.1	89	50	37	2	1	20	0	41	8
Vegely, Quad City*	3	4	.429	2.28	37	1	0	13	0	3	71.0	59	26	18	4	3	30	1	56	4
Verstandig, Waterloo	0	0	.000	3.60	5	0	0	5	0	0	5.0	4	2	2	2	0	3	0	4	0
Vice, Madison	0	0	.000	0.00	2	0	0	2	0	0	2.0	1	0	0	0	0	0	0	1	0
Waggoner, Madison	0	0	.000	0.00	1	0	0	1	0	0	1.0	1	0	0	0	0	0	0	0	0
Walter, Appleton*	1	0	1.000	1.00	2	2	0	0	0	0	9.0	3	1	1	0	0	1	0	8	1
Weber, Springfield*	5	10	.333	3.47	29	23	1	1	0	0	158.0	133	71	61	5	2	88	2	121	10
Wegman, Beloit	0	0	.000	0.00	1	1	0	0	0	0	2.0	1	0	0	0	0	1	0	2	0
Whatley, Clinton	1	1	.500	3.66	4	3	0	0	0	0	19.2	14	10	8	1	1	8	0	22	1
Wheatcroft, Wausau	6	12	.333	3.91	27	22	3	1	0	0	152.0	149	78	66	15	4	50	1	115	8
Wheeler, Beloit*	0	0	.000	10.13	3	0	0	1	0	0	5.1	8	7	6	0	0	4	0	8	2
Whitehead, Rockford	2	14	.125	5.47	23	22	1	0	0	0	110.1	117	87	67	5	5	81	0	77	13
Wickman, South Bend	7	2	.778	1.38	9	9	3	0	0	0	65.1	50	16	10	1	1	16	0	50	0
Wiley, Rockford	7	6	.538	2.30	57	0	0	44	0	18	86.0	63	31	21	1	7	22	3	82	1
Wilkinson, Rockford	3	5	.375	2.77	42	1	0	24	0	6	78.0	67	30	24	1	4	49	2	76	8
Williams, Wausau*	7	9	.438	4.25	26	19	0	3	1	0	133.1	144	77	63	11	3	48	2	106	8
Willis, Peoria	10	11	.476	3.26	31	22	6	4	3	0	163.0	152	78	59	6	14	41	1	93	9
Wiseman, Springfield	4	3	.571	2.71	10	10	2	0	1	0	63.0	49	25	19	3	2	16	0	41	1
Yaughn, Wausau	2	4	.333	5.29	10	10	0	0	0	0	51.0	46	32	30	5	3	29	0	47	2
Young, Peoria	0	3	.000	3.31	24	0	0	14	0	3	32.2	29	16	12	1	1	11	0	40	2

BALKS—Infante, S. King, 10 each; M. Moore, Muscat, Wheatcroft, 9 each; Misuraca, Mongiello, 8 each; Aleys, 7; Castillo, Drake, Gorton, Pena, Weber, Willis, 6 each; Bochtler, Boothby, Flanagan, Gewecke, Hale, Jaques, Milton, Sweeney, Talbert, Thoden, 5 each; Adams, Ahern, Bennett, Cormier, Dickson, Huisman, Lutz, McGraw, Osteen, Pulido, Reis, Ruffin, M. Smith, Swartzbaugh, Vancho, 4 each; Brummett, Brutcher, Calderone, Conner, Dedrick, G. DeLeon, Eddy, Florie, Gorman, Gustafson, Hanselman, Jacobs, Johnson, M. Martinez, Medina, Musselwhite, Nedin, Rapp, Risley, T. Taylor, Wickman, Wiley, Wilkinson, 3 each; Best, Carter, Diaz, Doss, Heredia, Hook, Hoyer, Huslig, Kilgo, Kimball, Kracl, Latter, Lindsey, Lipson, McKeon, Newman, Novoa, Regira, Sanders, Schaefer, Schullstrom, J. Smith, Sudbury, Thelen, Tolbert, Valle, Vazquez, Vegely, Whatley, Wheeler, Yaughn, 2 each; Ma. Anderson, Archer, Bolton, Borbon, Borcherding, Bosio, Bradford, Bruck, Callahan, Campos, Chrisman, DeLaRosa, R. DeLeon, Forrester, Galindez, Gibbs, Gomez, J. Gross, Grott, Gulledge, Haffner, Hancock, Harrington, Heiden, Helm, Hillman, Hirsch, Hoeme, Hoppe, Howze, Karchner, Kelly, Kuhn, Lebron, Leinen, Lewis, Logan, Long, Marchese, Marrero, F. Martinez, Matznick, McCarthy, Mejia, Mitchener, Mohler, Montoya, Morton, Murray, Neal, Paveloff, Peek, Pennington, Rasp, Reed, Riddle, Ritter, Robles, Roy, Sanford, Schrenk, Shifflett, B. Snyder, Stevens, Swope, W. Taylor, Turek, Unrein, Whitehead, Williams, Young, 1 each.

COMBINATION SHUTOUTS—Gross-Wiley 2, Schaefer-Wiley 2, Conner-Smith, Jacobs-Karchner-Wiley, Schaefer-Jacobs, Schaefer-Karchner-Shifflett-Wiley, Talbert-Baldwin, Talbert-Karchner-Baldwin, Talbert-Wiley, Appleton; Carter-Czajkowski, Carter-Fortugno, Garces-Czajkowski, McGraw-Snyder-Garces, Nieves-Fleming, Beloit; Borbon-Calderone, Borbon-Valle, Grove-Reis, Murray-Kelly-Reis, Nied-Ries, Burlington; Anderson-Ayala-Garcia-McAuliffe, Anderson-Garcia, Anderson-Garcia-McAuliffe, Borcherding-Garcia-McAuliffe, Rodgers-Garcia, Sanford-Garcia, Turek-Borcherding, Turek-Garcia, Turek-Garcia-McAuliffe, Turek-Leslie, Cedar Rapids; Hanselman-Callahan 2, Huisman-Gustafson 2, Ebert-Callahan, Hancock-Callahan-Taylor, Hancock-Gustafson-Taylor, Hancock-Taylor, Huisman-Callahan-Gustafson, Huisman-Flanagan, Huslig-Flanagan, Rapp-Callahan-Gustafson, Rapp-Flanagan-Gustafson, Rapp-Novoa-Taylor, Clinton; Best-Harrington, Best-Musselwhite-Lipson, Best-Thelen, Misuraca-Harrington-Lipson, Misuraca-Lipson, Newman-Lipson, Newman-Lipson-Diaz, Newman-Musselwhite-Lipson, Roskom-Pulido, Thelen-Musselwhite-Pulido, Kenosha; Gulledge-Sudbury-Gibbs, Gulledge-Taylor, Kracl-Grott, Mejia-Gibbs, Mejia-Kuhn-Taylor, Osteen-Grott, Osteen-Latter-Grott, Osteen-Peek-Gibbs, Peck-Latter-Grott, Pena-Mohler-Peck, Madison; Lutz-Jaques, Swartzbaugh-Jaques, Peoria; Castillo-Marchese, King-Hook, King-Vegely, Martinez-Hillman-Haffner-Marchese, Martinez-Hook, Moore-Haffner, Moore-Neal, Quad City; Bochtler-Bushing-Wilkinson, Bochtler-Wilkinson, Thoden-Bushing, Rockford; Brutcher-Campos, Brutcher-Forrester, Brutcher-Long, Brutcher-Stevens, Matznick-Mitchener, Matznick-Mitchener-Forrester, Matznick-Mongiello, Matznick-Stevens, Matznick-Van Winkle-Mongiello, Wickman-Mongiello, South Bend; Cimorelli-Corona-Gorton, Cimorelli-Keller, Eversgerd-Cimorelli-Corona-Gorton, Gewecke-Corona, Hensley-Corona-Gorton-Keller, Smith-Gorton, Weber-Keller, Wiseman-Keller, Springfield; Galindez-Hart-Lewis 2, Galindez-Hart, Galindez-Hoyer-Lewis, Galindez-Lewis, Hoyer-Hart, Lebron-Hart, Lebron-Lewis, Waterloo; Pennington-Riddle, Williams-Moore, Wausau.

NO-HIT GAMES—Conner-Smith, Appleton, defeated Wausau, 8-0, July 26; Nedin, Kenosha, defeated Burlington, 1-0 (first game), August 21.

NY-Pennsylvania League

CLASS A

CHAMPIONSHIP WINNERS IN PREVIOUS YEARS

1939—Olean*	.631	1959—Wellsville†	.635	1977—Oneonta y	.671
1940—Olean*	.625	1960—Erie	.643	Batavia	.600
1941—Jamestown	.618	Wellsville (2nd)†	.535	1978—Oneonta	.729
Bradford (2nd)†	.549	1961—Geneva	.616	Geneva z	.718
1942—Jamestown*	.672	Olean (4th)†	.512	1979—Geneva	.725
1943—Lockport	.591	1962—Jamestown	.580	Oneonta z	.618
Wellsville (3rd)†	.532	Auburn (3rd)†	.521	1980—Oneonta y	.662
1944—Lockport	.608	1963—Auburn	.585	Geneva	.649
Jamestown (2nd)†	.565	Batavia (3rd)†	.485	1981—Oneonta y	.658
1945—Batavia*	.677	1964—Auburn§	.622	Jamestown	.649
1946—Jamestown‡	.672	1965—Binghamton	.677	1982—Oneonta	.566
Batavia‡	.672	Binghamton	.607	Niagara Falls y	.553
1947—Jamestown*	.690	1966—Auburn x	.620	1983—Utica y	.649
1948—Lockport*	.603	Binghamton	.646	Newark	.649
1949—Bradford*	.635	1967—Auburn	.667	1984—Newark	.622
1950—Hornell	.653	1968—Auburn	.645	Little Falls y	.587
Olean (2nd)†	.568	Oneonta (2nd)*	.558	1985—Oneonta*	.705
1951—Olean	.622	1969—Oneonta	.662	Auburn	.603
Hornell (3rd)†	.568	1970—Auburn	.623	1986—Oneonta	.766
1952—Hamilton	.659	1971—Oneonta	.662	St. Catharines z	.632
Jamestown (2nd)†	.643	1972—Niagara Falls	.686	1987—Geneva y	.632
1953—Jamestown*	.704	1973—Auburn	.667	Watertown	.579
1954—Corning*	.621	1974—Oneonta	.768	1988—Oneonta y	.632
1955—Hamilton*	.656	1975—Newark	.688	Jamestown	.618
1956—Wellsville*	.617	Newark	.714	1989—Pittsfield	.697
1957—Wellsville	.632	1976—Elmira	.727	Jamestown y	.579
Erie (2nd)†	.598	Elmira	.703		
1958—Wellsville	.556				
Geneva (2nd)†	.548				

*Won championship and four-club playoff. †Won four-club playoff. ‡Jamestown and Batavia declared co-champions; Batavia defeated Jamestown in final of four-club playoff. §Won championship and two-club playoff. xWon split-season playoff. yLeague divided into Eastern and Western Divisions; won playoff. zLeague divided into Wrigley and Yawkey Divisions; won playoff. (NOTE—Known as Pennsylvania-Ontario-New York League from 1939 through 1956.)

STANDING OF CLUBS AT CLOSE OF SEASON, SEPTEMBER 3

McNAMARA DIVISION

EASTERN DIVISION

Club	W.	L.	T.	Pct.	G.B.
Oneonta (Yankees)	52	26	0	.667	......
Watertown (Indians)	43	34	1	.558	8½
Pittsfield (Mets)	43	34	0	.558	8½
Utica (White Sox)	31	47	0	.397	21

WESTERN DIVISION

Club	W.	L.	T.	Pct.	G.B.
Geneva (Cubs)	51	26	0	.662	......
Batavia (Phillies)	41	35	0	.539	9½
Elmira (Red Sox)	32	45	0	.416	19
Auburn (Astros)	31	46	1	.403	20

STEDLER DIVISION

Club	W.	L.	T.	Pct.	G.B.
Erie (Cardinals)	44	33	1	.571	......
Jamestown (Expos)	41	36	0	.532	3
Welland (Pirates)	36	42	0	.462	8½
Niagara Falls (Tigers)	35	42	0	.455	9
Hamilton (Cardinals)	30	46	1	.395	13½
St. Catharines (Blue Jays)	29	47	0	.382	14½

COMPOSITE STANDING OF CLUBS AT CLOSE OF SEASON, SEPTEMBER 3

Club	Ont.	Gen.	Eri.	Wat.	Pit.	Bat.	Jam.	Wel.	N.F.	Elm.	Aub.	Uti.	Ham.	St.C.	W.	L.	T.	Pct.	G.B.
Oneonta (Yankees)	...	3	3	5	4	3	3	3	6	3	6	7	3	3	52	26	0	.667	......
Geneva (Cubs)	3	...	0	3	4	5	4	3	6	6	6	4	4	3	51	26	0	.662	½
Erie (Independent)	1	4	...	3	3	3	4	5	5	3	2	1	4	6	44	33	1	.571	7½
Watertown (Indians)	5	3	1	...	3	7	2	2	3	1	3	5	6	2	43	34	1	.558	8½
Pittsfield (Mets)	6	2	1	3	...	4	2	2	4	5	3	8	3	0	43	34	0	.558	8½
Batavia (Phillies)	3	4	1	4	2	...	0	2	3	6	9	2	2	3	41	35	0	.539	10
Jamestown (Expos)	1	0	6	2	2	4	...	4	4	0	1	4	6	7	41	36	0	.532	10½
Welland (Pirates)	1	1	4	1	2	2	5	...	5	1	2	3	5	4	36	42	0	.462	16
Niagara Falls (Tigers)	1	1	4	3	0	1	4	5	...	2	1	1	5	7	35	42	0	.455	16½
Elmira (Red Sox)	0	4	1	3	1	3	4	3	2	...	7	1	1	2	32	45	0	.416	19½
Auburn (Astros)	0	4	1	1	3	1	3	2	3	3	...	4	3	3	31	46	1	.403	20½
Utica (White Sox)	3	0	3	4	2	4	0	1	3	5	2	...	1	3	31	47	0	.397	21
Hamilton (Cardinals)	1	0	5	0	1	2	3	4	4	3	1	3	...	3	30	46	1	.395	21
St. Catharines (Blue Jays)	1	0	3	2	3	1	2	5	2	2	1	1	6	...	29	47	0	.382	22

Major league affiliations in parentheses.

Playoffs—Erie defeated Jamestown, two games to none; Oneonta defeated Geneva, two games to none; Oneonta defeated Erie, two games to one, to win league championship.

Regular-Season Attendance—Auburn, 45,475; Batavia, 39,257; Elmira, 66,204; Erie, 61,606; Geneva, 35,032; Hamilton, 74,744; Jamestown, 35,364; Niagara Falls, 56,157; Oneonta, 58,742; Pittsfield, 101,110; St. Catharines, 29,742; Utica, 52,074; Watertown, 51,992; Welland, 37,331. Totals—744,830. Playoffs (7 games)—5,922.

Managers—Auburn, Ricky Peters; Batavia, Dave Cash (through July 9), Tony Scott (July 11), Ramon Aviles (July 12 through end of season); Elmira, Mike Verdi; Erie, Mal Fichman; Geneva, Bill Hayes; Hamilton, Luis Melendez; Jamestown, Don Werner; Niagara Falls, Aurelio Rodriguez;

Oneonta, Trey Hillman; Pittsfield, Jim Eschen; St. Catharines, Doug Ault; Utica, Tommy Thompson; Watertown, Jim Gabella; Welland, Jack Lind. Managerial records of teams with more than one manager: Batavia, Cash (12-11), Scott (1-0), Aviles (28-24).

All-Star Team—1B—Mike Brown, Welland; 2B—Kevin Jordan, Oneonta; 3B—Mike Songini, Erie; SS—Andy Postema, Erie; OF—Robbie Katzaroff, Jamestown; Jeff McNeely, Elmira; Jalal Leach, Oneonta; Scott Bullet, Welland; C—Carlos Delgado, St. Catharines; Rob Fitzpatrick, Jamestown; RHP—Jessie Hollins, Geneva; Sam Militello, Oneonta; LHP—Kirt Ojala, Oneonta; Alan Botkin, Hamilton; DH—Andrew Hartung, Geneva; Rookie of the Year—Robbie Katzaroff, Jamestown; Manager of the Year—Trey Hillman, Oneonta.

(Compiled by Howe Sportsdata International, Boston, Mass.)

CLUB BATTING

Club	Pct.	G.	AB.	R.	OR.	H.	TB.	2B.	3B.	HR.	RBI.	SH.	SF.	HP.	BB.	Int. BB.	SO.	SB.	CS.	LOB.
Erie	.265	78	2547	435	373	676	1042	117	21	69	377	47	29	37	352	12	521	37	28	612
Pittsfield	.260	77	2474	379	346	643	879	95	30	27	287	25	31	37	356	15	504	129	61	588
Oneonta	.259	78	2440	363	266	632	825	85	24	20	295	21	18	25	355	8	501	165	72	564
Geneva	.257	77	2487	421	283	638	943	121	17	50	362	37	17	45	382	11	564	73	36	615
Jamestown	.251	77	2519	320	319	633	883	104	22	34	252	16	18	34	279	21	570	107	44	591
Welland	.248	78	2500	366	375	634	860	104	16	30	307	18	18	29	292	20	569	138	59	532
Auburn	.246	78	2553	345	452	629	864	106	21	29	281	37	26	28	263	17	652	129	45	550
Watertown	.244	78	2590	369	303	632	892	102	31	32	303	12	22	23	311	13	570	113	62	550
Batavia	.240	76	2467	369	328	592	878	102	20	48	310	25	18	32	341	10	602	118	53	538
St. Catharines	.234	76	2359	254	317	552	754	80	10	34	220	37	20	22	285	8	600	74	66	545
Elmira	.229	77	2442	315	379	560	739	74	18	23	253	48	25	37	287	8	582	133	62	525
Utica	.226	78	2487	313	372	561	725	80	15	18	248	29	14	22	338	9	700	128	73	546
Hamilton	.223	77	2478	287	330	552	765	80	5	41	236	13	23	21	252	7	596	71	52	499
Niagara Falls	.213	77	2365	295	388	504	695	82	8	31	231	17	10	41	333	15	571	94	57	528

INDIVIDUAL BATTING

(Leading Qualifiers for Batting Championship—211 or More Plate Appearances)

*Bats lefthanded.   †Switch-hitter.

Player and Club	Pct.	G.	AB.	R.	H.	TB.	2B.	3B.	HR.	RBI.	SH.	SF.	HP.	BB.	Int. BB.	SO.	SB.	CS.
Katzaroff, Robert, Jamestown*	.364	74	294	57	107	139	15	7	1	20	1	0	5	29	4	18	34	13
Postema, Andrew, Erie	.345	75	261	53	90	121	18	2	3	39	6	0	6	37	0	33	0	1
Jordan, Kevin, Oneonta	.333	73	276	47	92	131	13	7	4	54	0	1	5	23	0	31	19	6
Bartung, Andrew, Geneva	.331	74	263	48	87	143	19	2	11	70	1	3	6	43	3	55	1	1
Songini, Michael, Erie*	.321	78	280	61	90	130	12	2	8	51	8	2	6	39	4	29	2	1
Barry, Jeffrey, Jamestown†	.315	51	197	30	62	82	6	1	4	23	2	0	0	17	2	25	25	5
McNeely, Jeffrey, Elmira	.313	73	246	41	77	109	4	5	6	37	8	2	3	40	5	60	39	10
Lambert, Layne, Auburn*	.303	66	218	33	66	95	9	4	4	37	1	3	1	30	6	50	4	3
Bullett, Scott, Welland†	.302	74	255	46	77	105	11	4	3	33	1	0	2	13	2	50	30	6
Burnitz, Jeromy, Pittsfield*	.301	51	173	37	52	86	6	5	6	22	0	4	3	45	6	39	12	5

Departmental Leaders: G—Songini, 78; AB—Katzaroff, 294; R—Songini, 61; H—Katzaroff, 107; TB—Hartung, 143; 2B—Torres, 24; 3B—K. Jordan, Katzaroff, 7; HR—Ryan, 16; RBI—Hartung, 70; SH—Heckel, 10; SF—McClinton, 6; HP—Torres, 10; BB—Ryan, 66; IBB—Burnitz, Lambert, Rogers, 6; SO—Mobley, 91; SB—McNeely, 39; CS—S. Scott, 19.

(All Players—Listed Alphabetically)

Player and Club	Pct.	G.	AB.	R.	H.	TB.	2B.	3B.	HR.	RBI.	SH.	SF.	HP.	BB.	Int. BB.	SO.	SB.	CS.
Alesio, Christopher, Hamilton	.217	39	83	5	18	20	2	0	0	10	0	1	1	3	0	7	2	3
Allison, Thomas, Pittsfield†	.250	59	160	35	40	51	4	2	1	15	5	2	4	25	0	31	10	4
Alvarez, David, Elmira*	.195	37	77	4	15	23	5	0	1	11	0	0	0	6	0	16	1	0
Ambrosio, Joseph, St. Catharines	.245	68	216	23	53	69	12	2	0	22	5	3	2	43	0	51	7	4
Arrendondo, Joseph, Pittsfield	.276	58	170	21	47	60	9	2	0	12	1	2	2	17	0	21	2	6
Ball, Jeffrey, Auburn	.289	70	263	40	76	111	18	1	5	38	3	5	4	22	1	35	20	5
Barry, Jeffrey, Jamestown†	.315	51	197	30	62	82	6	1	4	23	2	0	0	17	2	25	25	5
Beasley, Andrew, Hamilton*	.175	16	57	4	10	15	2	0	1	9	0	0	0	2	0	16	0	0
Belbru, Juan, Hamilton	.267	72	251	40	67	110	9	2	10	34	1	4	6	29	0	61	10	7
Benitez, Luis, Geneva	.167	2	6	0	1	1	0	0	0	0	0	0	0	0	0	1	0	0
Berni, Denny, Elmira†	.207	45	140	12	29	41	6	0	2	22	1	3	1	15	0	36	1	1
Biasucci, Joseph, Geneva	.298	51	168	29	50	74	8	2	4	29	3	1	2	16	0	43	4	1
Bieser, Steven, Batavia†	.231	54	160	36	37	50	11	1	0	12	2	2	1	26	1	28	13	2
Blackwell, Juan, Oneonta	.263	5	19	1	5	6	1	0	0	2	0	0	1	0	0	7	2	1
Boyce, Joseph, Erie*	.183	68	186	31	34	53	4	0	5	28	1	4	3	42	1	41	5	0
Bradish, Michael, Utica	.240	59	183	20	44	54	7	0	1	18	1	2	1	21	1	32	2	0
Bradshaw, Terry, Watertown*	.234	68	235	37	55	71	5	1	3	13	2	1	1	24	1	60	15	3
Brown, Anthony, Welland*	.247	59	182	26	45	57	6	3	0	20	3	1	0	27	1	40	6	4
Brown, Michael, Welland*	.292	65	192	23	56	69	7	0	2	31	0	1	1	22	4	35	5	3
Brown, Randy, Elmira	.236	74	212	27	50	57	4	0	1	8	9	0	4	17	0	47	18	5
Buhe, Timothy, Pittsfield	.262	66	206	39	54	75	11	2	2	36	6	2	6	35	0	33	12	2
Bullett, Scott, Welland†	.302	74	255	46	77	105	11	4	3	33	1	0	2	13	2	50	30	6
Burnitz, Jeromy, Pittsfield*	.301	51	173	37	52	86	6	5	6	22	0	4	3	45	6	39	12	5
Caines, Arturo, Niagara Falls	.203	49	148	19	30	42	9	0	1	13	1	1	0	18	1	42	3	2
Campusano, Genaro, Welland	.212	45	118	17	25	58	6	0	9	30	0	3	2	18	2	55	0	0
Canate, Emisael, Watertown	.261	57	199	28	52	67	5	2	2	25	1	0	3	10	0	43	9	4
Cancel, Victor, Geneva	.286	67	203	38	58	69	7	2	0	23	1	0	4	48	1	47	13	6
Carlton, Andrew, St. Catharines	.248	71	254	26	63	94	11	1	6	24	2	1	2	25	1	72	4	2
Carvajal, Jovino, Oneonta†	.287	52	171	19	49	54	3	1	0	18	3	0	0	37	15	11	15	11
Castillo, Alberto, Pittsfield	.219	58	187	19	41	63	8	1	4	24	1	2	5	26	1	35	3	3
Cerny, Mark, Erie*	.200	2	5	0	1	1	0	0	0	0	0	0	0	0	0	3	0	0
Charbonnet, Mark, Watertown*	.254	61	224	21	57	79	4	3	4	32	3	0	2	9	1	56	10	7
Ciesla, Theodore, Jamestown	.239	62	222	28	53	74	9	0	4	25	1	1	1	25	1	48	5	2
Cofer, Brian, Watertown	.333	13	6	3	2	3	1	0	0	0	0	0	0	0	0	1	1	1
Coffey, Stephen, Geneva	.191	67	209	21	40	48	4	2	0	21	9	2	0	24	0	58	8	4
Cook, Stanley, Erie*	.255	70	212	29	54	96	9	6	7	40	0	3	1	23	0	37	7	1
Cooper, Gary, Hamilton	.180	65	211	19	38	56	6	4	0	16	0	1	1	22	2	59	3	1
Cotton, John, Watertown*	.210	73	286	53	60	83	9	4	2	21	2	2	2	40	2	71	24	7
Coughlin, Kevin, Utica*	.274	68	215	37	59	71	9	0	1	16	3	2	0	27	2	41	17	8
Cruz, Ismael, Batavia†	.252	45	139	17	35	38	1	1	0	12	3	0	1	19	0	23	6	7
Curtis, John, Welland	.290	47	124	26	36	54	8	2	2	18	2	0	1	17	0	24	7	6
Daniels, Gary, Erie*	.258	41	124	23	32	44	4	0	0	14	4	0	2	25	0	24	5	2
Dauphin, Philip, Geneva*	.236	73	233	47	55	101	8	1	12	47	8	3	7	51	1	45	8	6
Davis, Michael, Watertown*	.252	59	210	21	53	74	6	3	3	23	0	4	2	17	2	39	3	0

Player and Club	Pct.	G.	AB.	R.	H.	TB.	2B.	3B.	HR.	RBI.	SH.	SF.	HP.	BB.	Int. BB.	SO.	SB.	CS.
Davis, Nicky, Pittsfield*	.263	73	247	34	65	98	11	2	6	48	0	1	4	35	3	67	10	8
Davis, Timothy, Elmira	.236	59	161	16	38	49	9	1	0	16	2	3	5	16	0	18	7	6
Debrand, Genaro, Niagara Falls	.143	17	49	7	7	11	2	1	0	3	3	0	1	3	0	8	0	0
Delgado, Carlos, St. Catharines*	.281	67	228	30	64	95	13	0	6	39	1	4	5	35	2	65	2	8
Deller, Robert, Oneonta*	.243	54	169	33	41	53	7	1	1	22	1	1	1	42	0	33	16	4
De los Santos, Alberto, Welland	.375	5	8	1	3	5	0	1	0	1	0	0	0	0	0	0	0	0
Delpiano, Marc, Auburn	.250	13	20	2	5	5	0	0	0	3	0	0	2	2	0	7	0	0
Demetre, Douglas, Oneonta	.204	20	49	5	10	15	2	0	1	12	0	0	0	15	0	15	0	1
Demus, Joseph, Elmira†	.244	51	119	13	29	32	3	0	0	7	2	0	0	9	0	31	2	4
DeRicco, John, Geneva*	.240	63	196	40	47	67	9	1	3	27	4	0	1	44	3	39	2	4
Diaz, German, Geneva*	.254	61	209	39	53	77	11	2	3	19	1	0	2	36	0	44	6	3
Dukes, Willie, Elmira	.213	63	178	24	38	58	3	1	5	25	2	2	7	25	0	67	12	10
Dunn, Brian, Pittsfield	.301	31	83	8	25	36	6	1	1	7	0	1	1	10	1	10	3	1
Echols, Tracy, Erie*	.263	40	137	20	36	50	5	0	3	14	1	1	1	17	2	29	4	6
Edge, Timothy, Welland	.215	63	149	6	32	40	5	0	1	12	0	1	2	19	1	27	4	3
Eenhoorn, Robert, Oneonta	.268	57	220	30	59	80	9	3	2	18	2	2	1	18	0	29	11	4
Eldridge, Rodney, Hamilton	.255	55	200	22	51	71	8	0	4	24	0	2	4	10	0	38	3	0
Ellis, Paul, Hamilton*	.310	15	58	8	18	31	4	0	3	18	0	2	0	6	3	13	0	0
Erdman, Bradley, Geneva	.225	34	111	12	25	29	4	0	0	15	3	0	1	11	0	31	2	0
Fayne, Jeffrey, Hamilton*	.250	58	176	20	44	67	5	0	6	26	2	1	0	20	0	45	1	4
Feliz, Janeiro, Welland	.165	48	85	13	14	20	2	2	0	4	3	0	1	7	0	33	6	1
Fiacco, Charles, Geneva†	.251	60	223	41	56	80	8	2	4	25	1	1	5	36	1	39	5	4
Fidler, Andrew, Pittsfield	.000	10	2	0	0	0	0	0	0	0	0	0	0	0	0	1	0	0
Fitzpatrick, Robert, Jamestown	.268	62	209	23	56	88	14	0	6	34	0	1	0	28	2	53	1	0
Flores, Jose, Auburn	.183	42	109	13	20	22	2	0	0	6	7	0	0	18	0	16	3	3
Floyd, Daniel, Erie	.249	65	185	24	46	72	9	1	5	27	4	3	2	26	0	50	0	0
Friedland, Michael, Jamestown	.226	66	226	22	51	75	8	2	4	28	0	5	3	29	1	77	7	4
Friedman, Jason, Elmira	.239	67	213	25	51	61	10	0	0	23	0	2	2	26	1	28	3	4
Gallardo, Luis, Oneonta	.284	40	141	27	40	61	7	1	4	25	0	5	2	9	0	34	1	0
Garcia, Manuel, Utica	.211	29	76	12	16	25	2	2	1	6	0	0	0	9	0	27	4	1
Giles, Brian, Watertown*	.289	70	246	44	71	93	15	2	1	23	0	1	0	48	2	23	11	3
Gilmore, Anthony, Auburn	.217	33	106	9	23	31	8	0	0	7	1	1	0	6	0	23	3	1
Gonzalez, Richard, Hamilton	.255	40	137	13	35	40	2	0	1	7	2	1	1	11	0	17	4	2
Gorman, David, Utica	.000	18	4	0	0	0	0	0	0	0	0	0	0	0	0	1	0	0
Graham, Timothy, Elmira*	.203	70	212	25	43	54	5	3	0	22	5	2	1	19	0	64	7	8
Grant, Lawrence, Elmira	.271	76	262	41	71	102	9	2	6	33	7	4	4	30	0	69	11	5
Green, Thomas, Welland	.278	16	36	3	10	12	2	0	0	4	0	0	0	3	0	7	3	2
Grisham, Wesley, Welland	.265	46	147	16	39	49	7	0	1	20	2	1	6	8	0	24	3	0
Gumbs, Lincoln, Auburn	.182	15	33	3	6	6	0	0	0	0	0	0	0	5	0	11	1	2
Guzik, Robert, Pittsfield	.192	67	208	26	40	58	5	5	1	17	3	3	3	16	0	68	4	4
Hamm, Stacy, Watertown	.259	21	54	16	14	15	1	0	0	6	0	0	0	10	1	20	2	3
Hanel, Marcus, Welland	.153	40	98	5	15	17	2	0	0	8	0	0	1	5	2	26	1	2
Hankins, Michael, Oneonta†	.271	50	166	20	45	49	4	0	0	18	1	0	2	30	1	27	11	4
Hargis, Daniel, Jamestown	.164	47	159	11	26	36	7	0	1	10	3	0	3	16	3	44	2	0
Harmes, Kristopher, St. Catharines*.	.500	3	10	1	5	5	0	0	0	1	0	1	0	0	0	2	0	1
Hartung, Andrew, Geneva	.331	74	263	48	87	143	19	2	11	70	1	3	6	45	3	55	1	1
Hartwig, Robert, Batavia†	.331	50	157	26	52	62	6	2	0	12	0	1	4	26	0	17	14	4
Hatcher, Christopher, Auburn	.247	72	259	37	64	101	10	0	9	45	0	5	5	27	4	86	8	2
Heckel, Walter, St. Catharines*	.204	73	196	30	40	42	2	0	0	10	10	0	2	33	0	64	7	7
Hirsch, Christopher, Jamestown	.278	25	72	9	20	23	3	0	0	6	0	1	3	10	0	14	0	1
Holland, Michael, Erie	.194	24	36	7	7	11	1	0	1	3	1	0	0	1	0	14	2	2
Horne, Tyrone, Jamestown*	.304	7	23	1	7	11	2	1	0	5	0	0	0	4	0	5	3	0
Hudik, Matthew, St. Catharines	.148	18	27	4	4	6	2	0	0	1	0	1	0	2	0	2	2	1
Huff, Bradford, Geneva	.279	39	122	22	34	42	8	0	0	14	0	1	1	7	0	20	4	1
Hurlbutt, Robert, Auburn	.176	42	131	6	23	32	3	0	2	18	0	1	0	5	0	53	1	0
Ingram, Jeffrey, Utica	.228	29	92	5	21	26	3	1	0	10	0	0	1	1	0	25	2	1
Irish, Jeffrey, St. Catharines	.135	16	37	2	5	5	0	0	0	0	1	0	0	8	0	11	1	0
Jackson, Jeffrey, Batavia	.198	63	227	30	45	71	11	3	3	22	3	0	4	30	1	80	12	11
Johnson, Benjamin, Welland	.256	40	90	6	23	31	5	0	1	15	0	0	2	8	0	24	0	1
Johnson, Mark, Welland*	.375	5	8	2	3	4	1	0	0	2	0	0	0	2	0	0	0	0
Jones, Maurice, Auburn	.200	30	50	9	10	20	0	0	2	6	1	0	1	5	0	24	3	2
Jones, Thomas, Batavia	.000	20	2	0	0	0	0	0	0	0	0	0	0	0	0	2	0	0
Jordan, Adrian, Niagara Falls*	.213	31	89	13	19	23	2	1	0	5	1	0	0	12	1	14	2	2
Jordan, Kevin, Oneonta	.333	73	276	47	92	131	13	7	4	54	0	1	5	23	0	31	19	6
Judson, Erik, Batavia	.258	55	178	29	46	71	13	2	3	23	1	1	6	23	2	57	8	5
Katzaroff, Robert, Jamestown*	.364	74	294	57	107	139	15	7	1	20	1	0	5	29	4	18	34	13
Kemper, Robbie, Erie*	.234	62	175	30	41	77	9	0	9	23	4	3	6	15	1	36	0	1
Kimbler, Douglas, Niagara Falls	.192	59	177	21	34	52	10	1	2	18	1	1	3	26	1	42	11	5
King, Jason, Pittsfield†	.245	51	143	27	35	39	2	1	0	9	2	2	2	30	0	17	3	2
Kinyoun, Travis, Pittsfield†	.263	16	38	6	10	15	2	0	1	8	1	0	1	3	0	6	2	0
Kirt, Timothy, Niagara Falls	.213	63	169	20	36	42	3	0	1	12	1	0	2	23	0	28	4	5
Kluss, Dennis, Watertown	.237	40	118	11	28	37	5	2	0	12	0	0	2	5	0	29	5	4
Lambert, Layne, Auburn*	.303	66	218	33	66	95	9	4	4	37	1	3	1	30	6	50	4	3
Lammon, John, Elmira	.186	30	70	8	13	19	3	0	1	11	2	1	0	6	0	12	2	0
Lantrip, Richard, Oneonta	.183	70	230	31	42	64	5	4	3	33	2	3	4	48	1	81	7	8
Leach, Jalal, Oneonta*	.288	69	257	41	74	89	7	1	2	18	4	0	0	37	3	52	33	13
Limoncelli, Jeffrey, Elmira	.218	69	197	23	43	47	2	1	0	11	2	1	5	35	1	34	2	3
Lohry, Adin, Oneonta*	.197	44	137	14	27	32	1	2	0	14	3	2	1	20	1	28	5	5
Long, Steven, Jamestown	1.000	22	1	1	1	1	0	0	0	0	0	0	0	0	0	0	0	0
Lora, Jose, Elmira	.212	67	184	35	39	49	2	4	0	13	2	1	2	20	0	44	22	3
Lorms, John, Watertown†	.178	32	73	10	13	17	2	1	0	4	1	1	2	29	1	21	3	1
Lowe, Christopher, Hamilton	.188	9	16	2	3	3	0	0	0	1	0	1	0	2	0	9	0	2
MacArthur, Mark, Hamilton	.131	47	137	19	18	34	3	0	3	8	1	1	0	18	0	49	4	2
MacMillan, Darrell, Erie	.261	38	115	12	30	42	4	1	2	17	1	2	0	10	1	15	0	0
Malave, Jose, Elmira	.138	13	29	4	4	5	1	0	0	3	0	1	0	2	0	12	1	0
Marabella, Antonio, Jamestown*	.300	3	10	2	3	4	1	0	0	1	0	0	0	1	0	0	0	0
Marquez, Edgar, St. Catharines	.176	36	102	6	18	27	3	0	2	7	2	1	0	10	0	39	4	0
Martin, Todd, Utica	.157	43	121	11	19	20	1	0	0	11	0	0	0	13	0	39	4	5
Martin, Jon, Welland	.181	44	94	11	17	29	3	0	3	12	1	1	1	14	0	27	6	0
Martinez, Ramon, Welland	.232	48	151	26	35	40	3	1	0	15	1	2	0	7	0	38	19	6
Mastropietro, David, Niagara Falls	.187	32	107	14	20	33	1	0	4	7	1	0	3	19	2	38	6	3
Matos, Domingo, Jamestown	.203	47	153	13	31	48	3	1	4	18	0	4	7	0	41	0	4

Player and Club	Pct.	G.	AB.	R.	H.	TB.	2B.	3B.	HR.	RBI.	SH.	SF.	HP.	BB.	Int. BB.	SO.	SB.	CS.
Mauro, Michael, Niagara Falls	.000	11	11	0	0	0	0	0	0	0	0	0	0	0	0	4	0	0
McClinton, Timothy, Pittsfield	.284	73	257	35	73	90	8	3	1	36	1	6	1	37	2	57	18	6
McCumiskey, Stephen, Auburn	.143	18	28	4	4	5	1	0	0	3	1	1	1	3	0	10	0	0
McNamara, Dennis, Niagara Falls	.222	10	36	6	8	10	0	1	0	3	0	0	2	3	0	6	2	2
McNeely, Jeffrey, Elmira	.313	73	246	41	77	109	4	5	6	37	8	2	3	40	5	60	39	10
Medina, Ricardo, Geneva	.222	41	90	11	20	31	5	0	2	8	1	1	0	15	0	10	4	1
Mendenhall, Kirk, Niagara Falls	.249	63	217	28	54	63	9	0	0	15	2	1	4	36	0	29	16	7
Minnifield, Wallace, Pittsfield	.260	19	50	3	13	15	2	0	0	1	0	0	0	3	0	13	1	3
Mitchell, Thomas, Erie	.239	70	230	48	55	107	17	1	11	38	2	1	2	54	1	70	3	2
Mobley, Anton, St. Catharines†	.184	66	212	26	39	68	4	2	7	25	1	3	5	27	0	91	4	5
Moccia, Mario, Niagara Falls	.143	10	28	2	4	5	1	0	0	1	0	0		1	1	8	0	0
Montalvo, Robert, St. Catharines	.183	38	115	11	21	23	2	0	0	5	1	1	1	21	1	16	1	2
Montgomery, Raymond, Auburn	.233	61	193	19	45	55	8	1	0	13	4	1	1	23	0	32	12	5
Monzon, Daniel, Utica	.243	64	214	36	52	75	14	0	3	27	3	2	1	39	0	44	14	7
Morgan, Gary, Batavia	.182	15	33	4	6	6	0	0	0	2	0	1	1	5	0	3	3	2
Morris, Aaron, Watertown*	.266	21	64	6	17	27	3	2	1	10	2	0	0	7	1	21	0	0
Mota, Rafael, Auburn	.258	69	248	39	64	93	12	4	3	19	3	2	2	26	2	74	12	1
Murray, Glenn, Jamestown	.224	53	165	20	37	56	8	4	1	14	0	0	3	21	0	43	12	3
Neitzel, Roderick, Batavia*	.266	62	218	40	58	68	7	0	1	27	5	3	4	36	1	37	17	6
Nuneviller, Thomas, Batavia	.232	71	259	36	60	97	10	0	9	31	0	3	3	30	1	45	15	4
Nunez, Rogelio, Utica†	.267	35	90	11	24	32	1	2	1	11	1	2	0	5	2	24	5	2
Nyman, Gerald, Jamestown	.151	33	93	10	14	15	1	0	0	4	0	0	1	6	0	28	2	2
O'Neal, Kelley, Niagara Falls*	.240	53	192	28	46	63	6	1	3	11	1	0	1	17	0	33	9	6
Ochoa, Rafael, Utica	.192	61	167	18	32	37	5	0	0	17	4	0	1	20	0	71	12	7
Osik, Keith, Welland	.278	29	97	13	27	34	4	0	1	20	1	3	2	11	1	12	2	6
Owens, Michael, Batavia*	.264	61	220	37	58	112	12	3	12	49	0	1	4	19	2	75	9	0
Paynter, William, Geneva	.224	29	76	8	17	23	3	0	1	6	2	0	3	4	0	27	0	1
Pena, Porfirio, Utica	.170	15	47	3	8	16	2	0	2	9	0	1	0	2	0	16	0	0
Perez, Eulogio, Batavia	.187	37	91	7	17	21	1	0	1	9	2	0	0	6	0	34	3	0
Perez, Ozzie, Hamilton	.184	61	179	25	33	45	6	0	2	14	1	3	2	36	1	41	7	6
Perez, Joseph, Watertown*	.238	63	231	27	55	82	9	3	4	27	0	2	2	19	0	47	9	3
Perez, Robert, St. Catharines	.261	52	207	21	54	83	10	2	5	25	0	0	2	8	1	34	7	5
Perkins, Ronald, Utica	.130	19	46	3	6	7	1	0	0	2	0	0	2	10	0	17	0	0
Perozo, Ender, Pittsfield	.342	32	111	15	38	52	6	1	2	18	0	3	2	16	1	19	4	5
Peterson, Robert, Welland	.283	22	53	7	15	23	5	0	1	10	0	0	0	10	1	17	2	0
Pimentel, Wander, Hamilton	.188	69	192	15	36	43	7	0	0	12	2	1	1	15	0	32	3	6
Plantenburg, Erik, Elmira†	.000	16	1	0	0	0	0	0	0	0	0	0	0	0	0	0	0	0
Polewski, Stephen, Welland†	.317	37	63	13	20	21	1	0	0	4	3	0	0	10	0	10	2	6
Postema, Andrew, Erie	.345	75	261	53	90	121	18	2	3	39	6	0	6	37	0	33	0	1
Pough, Clyde, Watertown	.253	76	285	47	72	116	15	1	9	48	0	4	2	40	0	71	21	5
Querecuto, Juan, St. Catharines	.200	9	20	0	4	5	1	0	0	2	1	0	0	2	0	4	0	1
Radachowsky, Gregg, Niagara Falls	.192	45	99	15	19	32	4	0	3	12	3	0	6	24	0	26	5	2
Randazzo, Michael, Utica*	.250	24	56	6	14	15	1	0	0	4	0	1		4	0	4	3	2
Reimsnyder, Brian, Erie*	.000	8	5	0	0	0	0	0	0	0	1	0	0	0		5	0	2
Ridenour, Ryan, Batavia	.235	32	85	5	20	30	5	1	1	9	1	1	0	9	0	18	1	1
Rodriguez, Abimael, Jamestown	.189	65	190	27	36	39	3	0	0	13	5	4	0	34	0	52	2	2
Rodriguez, Ahmed, Hamilton†	.216	56	190	17	41	46	5	0	0	9	1	1	0	17	0	59	8	10
Rodriguez, Ruben, Erie	.267	63	243	48	65	83	6	3	2	18	4	3	2	24	0	54	10	7
Roebuck, Joseph, Erie	.310	61	174	32	54	95	12	1	9	45	2	4	3	19	2	53	0	0
Rogers, Daniel, Niagara Falls*	.204	71	226	29	46	85	9	0	10	38	0	2	6	42	6	86	8	4
Rojas, Wilberto, St. Catharines	.231	63	212	21	49	65	2	1	4	19	2	2	0	20	2	57	1	4
Roman, Vincent, Auburn	.269	64	193	42	52	71	6	5	1	15	6	1	2	14	0	40	27	7
Romano, Scott, Oneonta	.242	57	178	30	43	58	8	2	1	19	2	2	6	30	1	38	18	3
Ronan, Marcus, Hamilton*	.228	56	167	14	38	47	6	0	1	15	0	3	1	15	0	37	1	2
Ronca, Joseph, Welland	.214	63	140	21	30	35	2	0	1	4	0	0		8	1	26	15	5
Rudolph, Mason, Pittsfield	.192	8	26	4	5	7	2	0	0	0	1	0	0	2	0	6	0	0
Ryan, Sean, Batavia†	.273	73	231	54	63	124	11	1	16	53	0	3	6	66	1	52	5	2
Sadler, Richard, Niagara Falls	.251	62	207	21	52	60	8	0	0	25	0	2	2	22	0	51	2	3
Saltzgaber, Brian, Niagara Falls	.225	53	178	23	40	54	6	1	2	20	1	1	3	31	0	24	17	9
Samples, Todd, Jamestown	.246	59	183	22	45	62	6	4	1	13	2	1	4	13	0	48	13	7
Sanders, Adam, Utica	.164	50	122	12	20	26	6	0	0	4	2	0	1	18	0	46	6	2
Sanderson, Shaun, Erie	.128	25	39	2	5	9	1	0	1	4	1	1	0	2	0	4	0	1
Savage, James, Watertown	.241	55	162	22	39	49	6	2	0	15	6	1	0	22	1	19	3	6
Sawkiw, Warren, Niagara Falls†	.400	7	20	7	8	11	1	1	0	4	0	0	0	5	2	3	2	0
Schaefer, Cory, Welland	.279	23	61	15	17	19	2	0	0	7	1	0	1	11	0	12	7	1
Schulte, John, Welland*	.216	63	171	24	37	45	6	1	0	7	0	0	0	41	3	46	10	5
Sciortino, Michael, Pittsfield*	.286	31	7	0	2	2	0	0	0	0	0	0	0	0	0	4	0	0
Scott, Philip, Pittsfield	.246	24	61	7	15	17	2	0	0	4	3	0	1	9	0	9	2	5
Scott, Shawn, St. Catharines†	.284	75	278	29	79	96	10	2	1	14	8	3	2	30	1	53	31	19
Shelton, Todd, Watertown*	.083	14	12	2	1	1	0	0	0	1	0	0	0	2	0	3	2	0
Smith, Bryan, Auburn	.211	62	199	27	42	49	5	1	0	15	5	1	2	29	1	58	9	4
Smith, Lance, Auburn	.291	16	55	9	16	24	5	0	1	6	0	1	1	5	0	15	2	0
Smith, Mark, Hamilton	.333	8	3	0	1	1	0	0	0	0	0	0	0	1	0	0	0	0
Smith, Timothy, Elmira	.000	24	2	1	0	0	0	0	0	0	0	0	0	0	0	2	0	0
Smith, William, Batavia†	.186	30	70	5	13	17	2	1	0	6	0	1	0	7	0	29	2	2
Solimine, Joseph, Utica	.200	53	140	12	28	40	7	1	1	20	3	4	1	18	0	48	3	4
Songini, Michael, Erie*	.321	78	280	61	90	130	12	2	8	51	8	2	6	39	4	29	2	1
Sparrow, Christopher, Utica	.281	53	153	17	43	66	7	2	4	22	0	0	4	19	0	39	1	1
Stacey, Albert, Erie*	.309	47	55	3	17	18	1	0	0	6	3	1	1	5	0	11	1	1
Stinnett, Kelly, Watertown	.240	60	192	29	46	66	10	2	2	21	2	2	4	40	2	43	3	7
Strange, Keith, Utica	.277	68	206	28	57	81	8	2	4	34	1	0	3	52	1	49	5	3
Strickland, Dedrick, Oneonta†	.245	59	200	37	49	62	5	1	2	18	2	1	1	39	0	41	20	9
Tagliaferri, Eugene, Niagara Falls*	.177	74	243	24	43	61	4	0	4	26	0	3	5	24	1	88	4	4
Tatarian, Dean, Utica	.262	18	65	11	17	23	0	0	2	8	0	0	1	8	1	16	5	1
Tena, Paulino, Watertown	.245	73	277	36	68	102	12	5	4	37	0	5	0	19	0	67	9	10
Teter, Craig, Utica	.138	35	94	8	13	18	2	0	1	6	1	0	1	6	0	45	3	3
Tewell, Terrance, Batavia	.193	33	109	11	21	29	3	1	1	12	1	2	1	9	0	38	2	1
Thomas, John, Hamilton*	.271	33	118	20	32	49	8	0	3	14	0	2	1	15	0	30	3	3
Thomas, Michael, Pittsfield*	.000	28	1	0	0	0	0	0	0	0	0	0	0	0	0	4	0	0
Thompson, Fletcher, Auburn*	.286	59	199	35	57	71	8	3	0	21	5	2	6	37	3	45	19	9
Thornton, Eric, Pittsfield*	.226	52	115	20	26	34	4	2	0	6	1	1		4	0	16	11	3
Tollison, David, St. Catharines	.214	42	154	14	33	45	6	0	2	14	0	0	0	13	0	25	2	3

Player and Club	Pct.	G.	AB.	R.	H.	TB.	2B.	3B.	HR.	RBI.	SH.	SF.	HP.	BB.	Int. BB.	SO.	SB.	CS.
Torres, Paul, Geneva	.266	77	271	46	72	128	24	1	10	45	2	5	10	39	2	72	9	3
Tsitouris, Marc, Jamestown°	.246	46	142	20	35	56	7	1	4	17	2	4	5	15	5	29	0	0
Turco, Frank, Erie	.217	29	83	12	18	32	5	0	3	9	2	1	1	8	0	16	1	0
Turner, Brian, Oneonta°	.247	69	227	28	56	71	13	1	0	24	1	1	2	36	1	48	7	3
Turvey, Joseph, Hamilton°	.206	27	68	7	14	16	2	0	0	6	1	0	1	7	0	22	1	1
Valencia, Gilbert, Batavia°	.177	26	79	7	14	17	1	1	0	7	1	0	1	6	0	29	5	0
Valrie, Kerry, Utica	.188	42	149	14	28	34	4	1	0	10	1	0	1	8	1	46	12	6
Varni, Patrick, Erie	.500	3	2	0	1	1	0	0	0	0	0	0	0	0	0	0	0	0
Vazquez, Edgardo, Pittsfield	.000	19	1	1	0	0	0	0	0	0	0	0	0	0	0	1	0	0
Veit, Stephen, Auburn	.225	67	249	18	56	73	11	0	2	29	0	2	0	6	0	73	5	1
Voutour, James, Niagara Falls°	.191	20	47	6	9	14	2	0	1	2	0	0	0	6	0	15	2	1
Walker, Peter, Pittsfield	1.000	16	1	0	1	1	0	0	0	0	0	0	0	0	0	0	0	0
Wardwell, Shea, Elmira	.146	54	137	16	20	27	2	1	1	11	6	3	3	21	1	42	5	3
Washington, Kyle, Pittsfield	.267	63	225	42	60	79	7	3	2	23	0	2	1	44	1	53	32	4
Weinberg, Michael, Niagara Falls	.238	40	122	12	29	34	5	0	0	16	2	1	3	10	0	26	1	2
Welch, Kenneth, Watertown	.204	40	113	15	23	30	5	1	0	17	2	1	2	12	1	15	1	2
White, Clinton, Geneva	.208	35	106	19	22	29	3	2	0	12	1	0	3	6	0	33	7	1
Williams, Barry, Utica†	.209	59	129	19	27	32	3	1	0	8	1	0	3	32	1	41	16	12
Wilson, Brandon, Utica	.248	53	165	31	41	43	2	0	0	14	3	2	0	28	0	45	14	6
Wilson, Bryan, Geneva	1.000	1	1	0	1	1	0	0	0	1	0	0	0	0	0	0	0	0
Wilson, Thomas, Pittsfield	.500	21	2	0	1	1	0	0	0	0	0	0	0	0	0	1	0	0
Wilstead, Randon, Jamestown°	.272	56	180	24	49	74	11	1	4	21	0	0	2	25	3	44	1	1
Yorro, Jacinto, St. Catharines°	.231	28	91	10	21	26	2	0	1	12	3	0	1	8	0	14	1	4
Young, Brian, Elmira	.000	17	2	0	0	0	0	0	0	0	0	0	0	0	0	2	0	0
Young, Kevin, Welland	.244	72	238	46	58	93	16	2	5	30	0	5	7	31	2	36	10	2

The following pitchers, listed alphabetically by club, with games in parentheses, had no plate appearances, primarily through use of designated hitters:

AUBURN—Allen, David (14); Barreiro, Efrain (20); Brown, Duane (6); Hampton, Mark (13); Hurta, Robert (15); Irwin, Michael (22); Ketchen, Douglas (19); Martinez, Juan (1); Powers, Steve (16); Reed, Dennis (25); Rinaldi, Kevin (7); Scott, Tyrone (15); Stiteler, Mark (3); Wall, Jason (12); Williams, Brian (3); Wilson, David (23).

BATAVIA—Baur, Albert (13); Gray, Elliott (11); Hill, Eric (10); Hurst, Charles (14); Ingram, John (12); Lovdal, Stewart (19); McGovern, Steven (14); Montgomery, Michael (21); Parris, Steven (14); Ross, David (26); Slaughter, Garland (7); Williams, Michael (27).

ELMIRA—Davis, Christopher (15); Dennison, James (15); Finnvold, Gar (15); Konopki, Mark (4); Locker, John (20); Mitchelson, Mark (10); Ring, David (15); Santamaria, Silverio (28); Santiago, Cedric (15).

ERIE—Currie, Brian (18); Golden, Brian (20); Golmont, Van (14); Jockish, Michael (29); Larson, Michael (10); Lomeli, Michael (15); Marte, Roberto (5); McCutcheon, Gregory (10); Mikkelsen, Lincoln (14); Rizza, Gerard (18); Santana, Ernesto (6); Tafoya, Rodney (3); Thomas, Timothy (1); Voit, David (41); Woide, Steven (15); Wurm, Garry (35).

GENEVA—Bradford, Troy (7); Cheetham, Sean (2); Correa, Amilcar (21); Delgado, Timothy (17); Dickson, Lance (3); Doss, Jason (9); Gelb, Jac (23); Godfrey, Tyson (1); Hollins, Jessie (17); Kessler, Gregory (18); Kirk, Charles (14); Parker, Timothy (12); Porcelli, Joseph (31); Rodriguez, Gabriel (15); Smalls, Roberto (10); Stanley, Karl (7); Young, Michael (1).

HAMILTON—Arias, Jose (10); Bailey, Ray (17); Betances, Marcos (18); Boss, David (11); Botkin, Alan (13); Fusco, Thomas (24); MacLeod, Kevin (29); Newby, Michael (24); Osborne, Donovan (4); Rupkey, Richard (17); Salvior, Troy (29); Sells, George (6); Tolbert, Mark (1); Urbani, Thomas (5).

JAMESTOWN—Aucoin, Derek (8); Baxter, Robert (13); Brewer, William (11); Diaz, Rafael (24); Grewal, Ranbir (19); Haney, Christopher (6); Kotch, Darrin (18); Mathile, Michael (14); Moya, Felix (14); Norris, Joseph (13); Polasek, John (25); Ricker, Troy (20); Turner, Brandon (3); Wessel, Troy (3).

NIAGARA FALLS—Alcantara, Francisco (24); Coppeta, Gregory (14); Drell, Thomas (14); Fazekas, Robert (14); Keon, Kevin (21); Leimeister, Eric (4); Marcero, Douglas (2); Nelson, Brian (12); Pierce, Benjamin (3); Pinto, Gustavo (18); Rightnowar, Ronald (1); Rodriguez, Eddy (3); Schubert, Brian (6); Shea, Kurt (6); Thigpen, Arthur (8); Turri, Shawn (6); Undorf, Robert (22); Warren, Brian (12); Wolf, Steven (6).

ONEONTA—Dunbar, Matthew (19); Faw, Bryan (1); Frazier, Ronald (13); Hodges, Darren (14); Malone, Todd (9); Militello, Sam (13); Morphy, Patrick (25); Ojala, Kirt (14); Perez, Cesar (28); Perry, Stevie (20); Quirico, Rafael (14); Siberz, Gregory (35).

PITTSFIELD—Castillo, Juan (16); Coffee, Kenneth (7); Douma, Todd (15); Freitas, Michael (5); Parker, Jarrod (4); Scheffler, James (27); Thomas, Steven (19).

ST. CATHARINES—Aylmer, Robert (12); Brow, Scott (9); Burrell, Scott (7); Filter, Russell (19); Flener, Gregory (14); Ganote, Joseph (18); Karsay, Stefan (5); Kower, Frank (15); Mandia, Samuel (8); Marcon, David (16); Menhart, Paul (8); Nellenbach, Rodney (5); Rhea, Allen (16); Singer, Thomas (13); Steed, Ricky (14); Taylor, Michael (14); Watson, Matthew (16).

UTICA—Altaffer, Todd (13); Bolton, Rodney (6); Campos, Frank (21); Caridad, Rolando (14); Dinuzzo, Jeffrey (18); Dorsey, Lee (2); Fruge, Christopher (25); Hoey, Andrew (12); Hotz, Todd (27); Hulme, Patrick (4); Jenkins, Jonathan (14); Santana, Ernesto (5); Smith, John (16); Tolar, Kevin (15).

WATERTOWN—Allen, Chad (15); Bryant, Shawn (10); Ellis, Timothy (2); Elston, Cary (1); Gonzales, Michael (7); Kallevig, Dane (15); Langdon, Timothy (9); Mlicki, David (7); Morgan, Scott (4); Munoz, Oscar (2); Person, Robert (5); Rivera, Roberto (14); Ryan, Robert (27); Shepherd, Keith (24); Wertz, William (14); Woodfin, Olonzo (5).

WELLAND—Carlson, Lynn (16); Cooke, Stephen (11); Futrell, Mark (16); Lyle, Jeffrey (30); Miller, Kurt (14); Mooney, Troy (2); Pacheco, Alexander (13); Redmond, Andre (15); Robertson, Richard (16); Roeder, Steven (18); Shouse, Brian (17); Simpson, Shelton (18); Tellers, David (20); Way, Ronald (9); White, Richard (9); Zimmerman, Michael (9).

GRAND SLAM HOME RUNS—Belbru, Campusano, Canate, Dauphin, Dukes, Ellis, Fiacco, M. Jones, Lantrip, Owens, Pena, Pough, Roebuck, Rogers, Ryan, Tena, Yorro, 1 each.

AWARDED FIRST BASE ON CATCHER'S INTERFERENCE—Cook (L. Smith); Cruz (Stinnett); DeRicco (Castillo); Romano (Stinnett).

CLUB FIELDING

Club	Pct.	G.	PO.	A.	E.	DP.	PB.	Club	Pct.	G.	PO.	A.	E.	DP.	PB.
Oneonta	.964	78	1970	755	101	63	34	Niagara Falls	.952	77	1927	800	139	60	23
Jamestown	.958	77	1968	852	123	74	18	Welland	.952	78	2014	733	140	53	23
St. Catharines	.958	76	1900	759	117	68	20	Pittsfield	.951	77	1971	834	143	48	22
Geneva	.956	77	1978	745	124	53	16	Watertown	.949	78	2054	860	155	55	28
Batavia	.956	76	1987	899	132	66	14	Utica	.948	78	2006	900	159	67	20
Hamilton	.956	77	1972	763	127	53	8	Erie	.947	78	1980	792	156	66	14
Elmira	.953	77	1976	830	138	59	27	Auburn	.947	78	1985	800	157	68	28

Triple Plays—Batavia, Erie.

INDIVIDUAL FIELDING

*Throws lefthanded.

FIRST BASEMEN

Player and Club	Pct.	G.	PO.	A.	E.	DP.
Alvarez, Elmira	.993	22	137	5	1	11
Arrendondo, Pittsfield	.990	14	96	7	1	5
Beasley, Hamilton	1.000	5	49	3	0	3
Berni, Elmira	.981	14	96	8	2	5
Bradish, Utica	.985	47	356	34	6	32
Brown, Welland*	.974	62	427	16	12	36
Campusano, Welland	1.000	1	2	0	0	0
Carlton, St. Catharines	.968	18	141	8	5	11
Castillo, Pittsfield	1.000	1	6	0	0	1
Cofer, Watertown	1.000	1	1	0	0	0
Cooper, Hamilton	.980	17	134	15	3	10
Coughlin, Utica*	.955	9	38	4	2	6
M. Davis, Watertown*	.976	46	366	33	10	31
N. Davis, Pittsfield	.985	68	568	33	9	38
T. Davis, Elmira	1.000	1	2	0	0	0
DeRicco, Geneva	.982	58	408	26	8	26
Edge, Welland	.917	4	8	3	1	1
Eldridge, Hamilton	.982	53	409	27	8	28
Fitzpatrick, Jamestown	1.000	1	0	0	0	0
FRIEDMAN, Elmira	.998	52	420	29	1	32
Gallardo, Oneonta	.957	3	20	2	1	4
Grant, Elmira	1.000	1	1	0	0	0
Hartung, Geneva	1.000	3	17	1	0	2
Johnson, Welland*	1.000	2	2	1	0	0
Kemper, Erie*	.980	43	322	17	7	36
Kluss, Watertown	1.000	2	12	1	0	0
Lantrip, Oneonta	.983	7	58	1	1	3
J. Martin, Welland	.976	31	153	7	4	8
T. Martin, Utica	1.000	1	1	0	0	0
Mauro, Niagara Falls	1.000	1	3	0	0	2
Medina, Geneva	.980	28	186	13	4	15
Mitchell, Erie	.976	24	148	13	4	5
Moccia, Niagara Falls	.974	6	36	2	1	2
Montgomery, Auburn	.975	32	188	11	5	24
Morris, Watertown*	1.000	13	103	6	0	3
Nunez, Utica	1.000	1	2	0	0	0
Nyman, Jamestown	1.000	1	1	0	0	0
Osik, Welland	1.000	3	15	0	0	2
Owens, Batavia*	.975	44	447	18	12	41
Roebuck, Erie	1.000	2	7	1	0	1
Rogers, Niagara Falls*	.976	68	597	20	15	43
Rojas, St. Catharines	.984	60	454	32	8	50
Ronan, Hamilton	.972	7	34	1	1	3
Ryan, Batavia	.988	33	321	14	4	21
Sadler, Niagara Falls	.987	7	72	3	1	6
Sciortino, Pittsfield*	1.000	10	14	1	0	0
Smith, Hamilton	1.000	1	5	0	0	1
Solimine, Utica	1.000	4	12	3	0	1
Sparrow, Utica	.977	37	271	22	7	19
Stacey, Erie*	.978	47	171	6	4	13
Stinnett, Watertown	1.000	1	1	0	0	0
Strange, Utica	1.000	2	15	1	0	0
Tsitouris, Jamestown	.989	33	255	19	3	22
Turner, Oneonta*	.988	68	523	50	7	47
Veit, Auburn	.982	59	456	26	9	35
Washington, Pittsfield	1.000	1	1	0	0	0
Welch, Watertown	.995	28	208	7	1	14
Wilstead, Jamestown*	.983	51	433	27	8	43

Triple Plays—Ryan, Stacey.

SECOND BASEMEN

Player and Club	Pct.	G.	PO.	A.	E.	DP.
Allison, Pittsfield	.954	42	72	94	8	18
Ambrosio, St. Catharines	1.000	1	2	1	0	0
Benitez, Geneva	1.000	2	4	6	0	0
Biasucci, Geneva	.963	39	67	91	6	14
Boyce, Erie	.929	61	114	134	19	30
Brown, Elmira	1.000	1	2	2	0	1
Buhe, Pittsfield	.955	44	62	86	7	16
Ciesla, Jamestown	.971	60	104	163	8	36
Cofer, Watertown	1.000	2	4	5	0	2
Cotton, Watertown	.929	73	144	194	26	39
Cruz, Batavia	.948	35	63	102	9	21
Davis, Elmira	.937	35	41	78	8	12
Delpiano, Auburn	.957	11	10	12	1	1
Diaz, Geneva	1.000	3	4	5	0	1
Feliz, Welland	.902	27	19	27	5	7
Fiacco, Geneva	.956	42	59	94	7	16
Flores, Auburn	1.000	1	4	3	0	3
Friedland, Jamestown	.930	16	34	46	6	10
Gumbs, Auburn	1.000	1	0	1	0	0
Hankins, Oneonta	.962	14	15	36	2	6
HECKEL, St. Catharines	.973	71	157	170	9	47
Holland, Erie	.862	10	10	15	4	0
Hudik, St. Catharines	.814	14	16	19	8	3
Johnson, Welland	.857	6	2	4	1	0
Jordan, Oneonta	.973	65	131	158	8	36
Judson, Batavia	1.000	1	1	1	0	0
Katzaroff, Jamestown	.800	1	1	7	2	1
Kirt, Niagara Falls	1.000	1	1	0	0	0
Kluss, Watertown	.955	5	7	14	1	1
Lambert, Auburn	.900	19	24	39	7	8
Limoncelli, Elmira	.951	57	100	134	12	27
MacArthur, Hamilton	.894	16	25	34	7	5
Marabella, Jamestown	1.000	3	6	8	0	2
Mauro, Niagara Falls	1.000	1	0	1	0	0
Mendenhall, Niagara Falls	.976	29	44	79	3	14
Monzon, Utica	.939	62	125	185	20	35
Neitzel, Batavia	.967	45	102	129	8	22
O'Neal, Niagara Falls	.964	47	86	129	8	25
Osik, Welland	1.000	3	7	9	0	2
E. Perez, Batavia	.917	3	4	7	1	1
O. Perez, Hamilton	.971	24	45	54	3	9
Polewski, Welland	.899	30	19	43	7	2
Querecuto, St. Catharines	1.000	1	1	1	0	0
Rodriguez, Hamilton	.938	44	78	87	11	11
Sanders, Utica	.903	14	32	33	7	7
Sanderson, Erie	1.000	3	1	1	0	1
Sawkiw, Niagara Falls	.900	3	3	6	1	0
Schulte, Welland	.940	56	80	91	11	20
Scott, Pittsfield	1.000	5	8	16	0	0
Strickland, Oneonta	1.000	2	4	3	0	2
Tatarian, Utica	1.000	1	0	1	0	0
Thompson, Auburn	.919	57	126	135	23	31
Turco, Erie	.925	23	44	42	7	14
Williams, Utica	1.000	1	3	0	0	0
Wilson, Utica	1.000	4	4	10	0	0

Triple Play—Neitzel.

THIRD BASEMEN

Player and Club	Pct.	G.	PO.	A.	E.	DP.
Allison, Pittsfield	.875	6	4	3	1	0
Arrendondo, Pittsfield	.925	40	21	65	7	6
Ball, Auburn	.898	69	48	119	19	10
Berni, Elmira	1.000	1	0	1	0	0
Biasucci, Geneva	1.000	1	0	1	0	0
Bieser, Batavia	.833	4	0	5	1	1
Blackwell, Oneonta	.857	3	3	3	1	2
Bradish, Utica	1.000	3	4	2	0	0
Brown, Elmira	1.000	1	0	1	0	0
Carlton, St. Catharines	.914	33	14	50	6	2
Cooper, Hamilton	.883	43	22	69	12	2
Coughlin, Utica*	1.000	1	0	1	0	0
Cruz, Batavia	.897	9	11	15	3	0
Davis, Elmira	.833	3	1	4	1	0
Delpiano, Auburn	1.000	2	1	5	0	0
Diaz, Geneva	.835	50	35	66	20	6
Edge, Welland	.500	2	1	0	1	0
Fiacco, Geneva	.935	18	14	15	2	1
Friedland, Jamestown	.907	37	29	68	10	9
GRANT, Elmira	.921	69	57	117	15	11
Gumbs, Auburn	.833	3	0	5	1	0
Hankins, Oneonta	.841	17	7	30	7	4
Hartung, Geneva	.863	16	12	32	7	4
Ingram, Utica	.750	2	1	2	1	0
Johnson, Welland	1.000	4	1	0	0	0
Judson, Batavia	.886	50	35	97	17	11
Kimbler, Niagara Falls	1.000	5	4	7	0	0
Kluss, Watertown	.500	3	0	1	1	0
Lambert, Auburn	.882	9	3	12	2	1
Lantrip, Oneonta	.892	60	47	85	16	11
Limoncelli, Elmira	.952	11	3	17	1	2
MacArthur, Hamilton	.619	10	6	7	8	1
Martin, Utica	.933	14	9	19	2	1
Matos, Jamestown	.843	47	38	80	22	15
Mauro, Niagara Falls	1.000	4	0	2	0	0
McClinton, Pittsfield	.825	49	27	77	22	5
Mitchell, Erie	.859	31	12	43	9	11
Monzon, Utica	.667	1	1	1	1	0
Neizel, Batavia	.960	19	11	37	2	1
Osik, Welland	.958	11	6	17	1	0
Perez, Hamilton	.935	37	42	59	7	4
Pough, Watertown	.888	75	51	170	28	15
Querecuto, St. Catharines	.750	3	1	5	2	0
Rodriguez, Hamilton	1.000	1	1	3	0	0
Sadler, Niagara Falls	.848	11	4	24	5	0
Sanders, Utica	.880	15	7	15	3	2
Sanderson, Erie	1.000	1	0	3	0	1
Solimine, Utica	1.000	1	1	0	0	0
Songini, Erie	.842	51	38	116	29	5
Strange, Utica	.873	37	34	62	14	2
Tagliaferri, Niagara Falls	.887	64	38	96	17	2
Tatarian, Utica	.907	18	17	32	5	4

SHORTSTOPS—Continued

Player and Club	Pct.	G.	PO.	A.	E.	DP.
Tollison, St. Catharines	.825	41	30	55	18	4
Wardwell, Elmira	.889	4	4	4	1	1
Triple Play—Cruz.						
Welch, Watertown	.800	3	3	5	2	1
Wilson, Utica	.500	1	0	1	1	0
Young, Welland	.883	72	79	118	26	6

SHORTSTOPS

Player and Club	Pct.	G.	PO.	A.	E.	DP.
Allison, Pittsfield	.923	13	7	17	2	3
Ambrosio, St. Catharines	.929	40	64	106	13	28
Arrendondo, Pittsfield	.500	1	0	1	1	0
Biasucci, Geneva	.974	12	14	23	1	3
Blackwell, Oneonta	.857	1	2	4	1	1
Boyce, Erie	1.000	2	2	3	0	1
Brown, Elmira	.892	69	91	174	32	27
Buhe, Pittsfield	.875	13	16	33	7	3
Ciesla, Jamestown	.667	1	1	1	1	1
Cofer, Watertown	.000	1	0	0	1	0
Coffey, Geneva	.935	67	85	173	18	35
Davis, Elmira	.857	18	20	40	10	8
Delpiano, Auburn	1.000	1	1	0	0	0
Diaz, Geneva	.600	5	2	4	4	0
EENHOORN, Oneonta	.960	57	83	135	9	29
Feliz, Welland	.957	19	17	27	2	6
Flores, Auburn	.944	39	55	96	9	20
Friedland, Jamestown	.917	18	18	26	4	6
Grant, Elmira	.800	2	0	4	1	0
Gumbs, Auburn	.800	8	7	21	7	5
Hankins, Oneonta	.986	18	21	47	1	6
Holland, Erie	.800	6	2	6	2	2
Johnson, Welland	.917	34	33	44	7	9
Judson, Batavia	1.000	1	0	1	0	0
Kimbler, Niagara Falls	.932	46	74	159	17	26
King, Pittsfield	.894	51	76	110	22	16
Triple Play—Postema.						
Kluss, Watertown	1.000	1	0	1	0	0
Lambert, Auburn	.901	41	42	85	14	16
Lantrip, Oneonta	.875	3	1	6	1	1
MacArthur, Hamilton	.733	9	4	7	4	1
Martin, Utica	.973	20	30	41	2	7
Martinez, Welland	.876	43	69	87	22	18
Mauro, Niagara Falls	.500	3	1	2	1	1
Mendenhall, Niagara Falls	.927	34	48	92	11	22
Montalvo, St. Catharines	.958	38	56	128	8	23
Osik, Welland	.857	2	3	3	1	1
E. Perez, Batavia	.897	33	39	100	16	22
O. Perez, Hamilton	1.000	2	1	2	0	0
Pimentel, Hamilton	.905	69	90	168	27	28
Postema, Erie	.920	74	100	177	24	40
Querecuto, St. Catharines	.000	1	0	0	1	0
Ab. Rodriguez, Jamestown	.921	65	74	148	19	29
Ah. Rodriguez, Hamilton	.918	12	17	28	4	6
Sanders, Utica	.923	21	36	48	7	12
Savage, Batavia	.920	53	67	162	20	26
Schulte, Welland	.000	1	0	0	1	0
Scott, Pittsfield	.942	19	29	52	5	9
Tatarian, Utica	1.000	1	1	2	0	2
Tena, Watertown	.909	73	112	187	30	28
Turco, Erie	.923	3	5	7	1	1
Welch, Watertown	.941	6	9	7	1	1
Brandon Wilson, Utica	.895	44	75	122	23	30
Bryan Wilson, Geneva	1.000	1	0	3	0	0

OUTFIELDERS

Player and Club	Pct.	G.	PO.	A.	E.	DP.
Alesio, Hamilton	.969	22	28	3	1	2
Barry, Jamestown	.950	48	88	8	5	2
Belbru, Hamilton	.966	65	135	5	5	4
Bieser, Batavia	1.000	45	83	2	0	0
Bradish, Utica	.950	13	19	0	1	0
Bradshaw, Hamilton	.982	65	106	1	2	0
A. Brown, Welland	.970	50	55	10	2	1
R. Brown, Elmira	1.000	1	1	0	0	0
Buhe, Pittsfield	1.000	5	10	1	0	0
Bullett, Welland*	.958	69	110	5	5	0
Burnitz, Pittsfield	1.000	44	79	2	0	0
Caines, Niagara Falls	.913	31	40	2	4	1
Canate, Watertown	.961	56	120	3	5	1
Cancel, Geneva	.918	65	85	5	8	0
Carvajal, Oneonta	.949	50	70	4	4	1
Castillo, Pittsfield	1.000	3	1	0	0	0
Cerny, Erie*	1.000	2	2	0	0	0
Charbonnet, Watertown*	.918	53	54	2	5	0
Cook, Erie*	.939	66	102	6	7	0
Coughlin, Utica*	.974	59	108	4	3	0
Curtis, Welland	1.000	43	36	0	0	0
Daniels, Erie*	.945	28	47	5	3	1
Dauphin, Geneva*	.969	71	118	5	4	0
Deller, Oneonta*	.945	40	50	2	3	0
Dukes, Elmira	.939	22	31	0	2	0
Dunn, Pittsfield	.000	1	0	0	1	0
Echols, Erie*	1.000	36	55	2	0	0
Edge, Welland	1.000	1	3	0	0	0
Fayne, Hamilton	.981	32	48	4	1	1
Fiacco, Geneva	1.000	2	3	0	0	0
Friedman, Elmira	1.000	6	4	0	0	0
Garcia, Utica	.867	14	12	1	2	1
Giles, Watertown*	.991	58	108	8	1	0
Gonzalez, Hamilton	.966	32	56	1	2	1
GRAHAM, Elmira	1.000	69	135	2	0	0
Grant, Elmira	1.000	3	1	1	0	0
Green, Welland	1.000	11	19	0	0	0
Grisham, Welland	.941	34	45	3	3	0
Guzik, Pittsfield	.953	60	79	3	4	0
Hamm, Watertown	.833	16	18	2	4	0
Hankins, Oneonta	1.000	1	1	0	0	0
Hartwig, Batavia	1.000	41	53	1	0	0
Hatcher, Auburn	.931	50	62	5	5	2
Horne, Jamestown	1.000	1	1	0	0	0
Huff, Geneva	1.000	1	1	0	0	0
Jackson, Batavia	.943	63	126	6	8	0
M. Jones, Auburn	.917	21	22	0	2	0
T. Jones, Batavia	1.000	1	0	1	0	0
Jordan, Niagara Falls*	.871	28	26	1	4	0
Katzaroff, Jamestown	.993	69	127	11	1	2
Kirt, Niagara Falls	.972	62	98	8	3	1
Kluss, Watertown	1.000	21	20	1	0	0
Leach, Oneonta*	.974	66	107	4	3	0
Lora, Elmira	.937	51	71	3	5	1
Triple Play—Jackson.						
Lowe, Hamilton	1.000	5	9	0	0	0
MacArthur, Hamilton	1.000	3	2	0	0	0
Malave, Elmira	.800	5	4	0	1	0
Marquez, St. Catharines	.960	23	21	3	1	2
Mastropietro, Niagara Falls	.914	29	32	0	3	0
McClinton, Pittsfield	.960	19	23	1	1	0
McNamara, Niagara Falls	.941	10	16	0	1	0
McNeely, Elmira	.950	71	124	8	7	2
Medina, Geneva	1.000	6	2	0	0	0
Minnifield, Pittsfield	.950	15	18	1	1	0
Mitchell, Erie	1.000	12	15	0	0	0
Mobley, St. Catharines	.964	63	75	5	3	1
Montgomery, Auburn	.952	34	57	3	3	1
Monzon, Utica	1.000	1	1	0	0	0
Morgan, Batavia	.750	6	6	0	2	0
Mota, Auburn	.974	62	110	4	3	2
Murray, Jamestown	.915	49	48	6	5	0
Nuneviller, Batavia	.932	67	92	4	7	1
Nyman, Jamestown	.920	25	22	1	2	0
Ochoa, Utica	.926	54	84	3	7	0
J. Perez, Watertown*	.947	42	64	7	4	0
R. Perez, St. Catharines	.988	51	80	5	1	0
Perozo, Pittsfield	.933	17	25	3	2	1
Querecuto, St. Catharines	.800	2	4	0	1	0
Randazzo, Utica*	1.000	19	20	1	0	0
Reimsnyder, Erie*	1.000	1	1	0	0	0
Rodriguez, Erie	.940	61	76	3	5	0
Roebuck, Erie	.930	54	63	3	5	2
Roman, Auburn	.893	29	24	1	3	0
Romano, Oneonta	.982	42	53	3	1	1
Ronca, Welland	.948	50	52	3	3	0
Rudolph, Pittsfield	1.000	3	7	0	0	0
Saltzgaber, Niagara Falls	.949	50	69	5	4	2
Samples, Jamestown	.953	53	73	8	4	3
Sawkiw, Niagara Falls	1.000	1	3	0	0	0
Schaefer, Welland	.979	22	42	4	1	2
Scott, St. Catharines	.971	75	122	12	4	1
Smith, Auburn	.944	56	114	4	7	0
Strickland, Oneonta	.898	40	51	2	6	0
Tagliaferri, Niagara Falls	.882	11	15	0	2	0
Teter, Utica	.946	30	33	2	2	0
Thomas, Hamilton	.952	27	39	1	2	0
Thornton, Pittsfield	.917	35	44	0	4	0
Torres, Geneva	.932	77	116	7	9	2
Turner, Oneonta*	1.000	1	0	0	0	0
Valencia, Batavia*	.974	23	35	3	1	0
Valrie, Utica	.984	40	58	4	1	0
Wardwell, Elmira	.963	42	74	4	3	1
Washington, Pittsfield	.882	58	79	3	11	0
Weinberg, Niagara Falls	1.000	27	42	1	0	0
White, Geneva	.933	26	27	1	2	0
Williams, Utica	.955	43	59	5	3	0
Yorro, St. Catharines*	.970	21	31	1	1	0

CATCHERS

Player and Club	Pct.	G.	PO.	A.	E.	DP.	PB.	Player and Club	Pct.	G.	PO.	A.	E.	DP.	PB.
Bailey, Hamilton	1.000	1	2	0	0	0	0	Lohry, Oneonta	.982	44	341	37	7	3	18
Beasley, Hamilton	.986	8	61	8	1	0	0	Lorms, Watertown	.982	31	241	39	5	1	17
Berni, Elmira	.979	17	83	12	2	1	5	MacMillan, Erie	.983	15	108	9	2	0	1
Castillo, Pittsfield	.980	55	371	61	9	1	17	Marquez, St. Catharines	1.000	2	7	1	0	0	0
Debrand, Niagara Falls	.973	17	129	15	4	1	0	McCumiskey, Auburn	.952	17	72	7	4	1	4
Delgado, St. Catharines	.987	60	471	62	7	6	17	Nunez, Utica	.981	27	177	33	4	3	5
Demetre, Oneonta	.988	12	81	3	1	0	2	Osik, Welland	1.000	5	28	0	0	0	2
Demus, Elmira	.970	49	235	27	8	3	5	Paynter, Geneva	.995	27	207	7	1	0	1
Dukes, Elmira	.941	12	51	13	4	2	8	Pena, Batavia	.964	13	71	10	3	0	3
Dunn, Pittsfield	1.000	20	76	18	0	0	2	Perkins, Utica	.958	9	41	5	2	0	2
Edge, Welland	.979	45	272	49	7	0	5	Peterson, Welland	.974	14	100	13	3	1	4
Ellis, Hamilton	1.000	3	26	4	0	0	0	Radachowsky, Niagara Falls ..	.968	42	221	24	8	1	8
Erdman, Geneva	.991	34	304	31	3	2	9	Ridenour, Batavia	.979	20	123	16	3	2	5
Fitzpatrick, Jamestown	.973	31	214	37	7	2	9	Ronan, Hamilton	.979	49	323	42	8	3	6
FLOYD, Erie	.990	62	430	50	5	1	13	Rudolph, Pittsfield	.909	5	25	5	3	1	1
Gallardo, Oneonta	.989	28	256	21	3	2	14	Sadler, Niagara Falls	.978	23	168	12	4	0	11
Gilmore, Auburn	.974	33	252	46	8	4	8	Sanderson, Erie	.973	15	66	5	2	1	0
Grant, Elmira	.971	7	29	4	1	2	3	Shelton, Watertown	1.000	3	16	3	0	0	2
Hanel, Welland	.987	40	277	37	4	4	12	L. Smith, Auburn	.983	15	93	26	2	1	2
Hargis, Jamestown	.975	30	238	38	7	2	5	W. Smith, Batavia	.986	29	121	22	2	0	4
Harmes, St. Catharines	.964	3	25	2	1	0	1	Solimine, Utica	1.000	26	141	29	0	0	10
Hirsch, Jamestown	1.000	19	125	20	0	2	4	Stinnett, Watertown	.956	47	347	48	18	4	9
Huff, Geneva	.990	28	175	16	2	1	6	Strange, Utica	.964	5	26	1	1	0	1
Hurlbutt, Auburn	.969	29	192	27	7	0	14	Tewell, Watertown	.988	29	145	24	2	0	2
Ingram, Utica	.950	21	101	13	6	1	2	Turvey, Hamilton	.981	27	139	14	3	2	2
Irish, St. Catharines	.915	15	93	4	9	2	2	Voutour, Niagara Falls	1.000	7	22	2	0	0	4
Kinyoun, Pittsfield	.990	14	95	9	1	0	2	Welch, Watertown	1.000	1	1	0	0	0	0
Lammon, Elmira	.980	22	123	23	3	0	6								

PITCHERS

Player and Club	Pct.	G.	PO.	A.	E.	DP.	Player and Club	Pct.	G.	PO.	A.	E.	DP.
Alcantara, Niagara Falls*	.889	24	2	6	1	0	Golden, Erie	.875	20	3	4	1	0
Alesio, Hamilton	1.000	3	2	0	0	0	Golmont, Erie	.875	14	4	10	2	0
C. Allen, Watertown	.967	15	10	19	1	0	Gonzales, Watertown	1.000	7	0	2	0	0
D. Allen, Auburn	1.000	14	0	1	0	0	Gorman, Utica	.886	17	10	29	5	1
Altaffer, Utica*	.846	13	2	9	2	1	Graham, Elmira	1.000	1	1	0	0	0
Alvarez, Elmira	1.000	4	1	2	0	0	Gray, Batavia	.818	11	3	6	2	0
Arias, Hamilton	.778	10	1	6	2	0	Grewal, Jamestown	1.000	19	0	6	0	0
Aucoin, Jamestown	1.000	8	4	7	0	1	Hampton, Auburn	.818	13	3	6	2	0
Aylmer, St. Catharines*	1.000	12	2	2	0	0	Haney, Jamestown*	1.000	6	0	9	0	1
Bailey, Hamilton	1.000	16	7	13	0	0	Hill, Batavia	.909	10	0	10	1	2
Barreiro, Auburn	.824	20	2	12	3	2	Hodges, Oneonta	.864	14	9	10	3	0
Baur, Batavia	1.000	13	0	5	0	0	Hoey, Utica	1.000	12	1	3	0	0
BAXTER, Jamestown*	1.000	13	5	18	0	2	Hollins, Geneva	.833	17	6	14	4	1
Betances, Hamilton	1.000	18	3	18	0	2	Hotz, Utica*	.833	27	1	14	3	2
Bolton, Utica	.944	6	6	11	1	1	Hulme, Utica	1.000	4	0	1	0	0
Boss, Hamilton	.923	11	2	10	1	0	Hurst, Batavia	.882	14	8	7	2	1
Botkin, Hamilton*	.933	13	2	12	1	1	Hurta, Auburn*	.875	15	0	7	1	1
Bradford, Geneva	1.000	7	1	5	0	1	Ingram, Batavia*	1.000	12	3	5	0	0
Brewer, Jamestown*	1.000	11	2	4	0	1	Irwin, Auburn	1.000	22	3	11	0	0
Brow, St. Catharines	1.000	9	1	7	0	1	Jenkins, Utica	.909	14	2	8	1	0
Brown, Auburn	.778	6	3	4	2	0	Jockish, Erie*	1.000	29	0	4	0	1
Bryant, Watertown*	.944	10	7	10	1	1	Jones, Batavia	.941	19	2	14	1	2
Burrell, St. Catharines	.857	7	2	4	1	0	Jordan, Niagara Falls*	1.000	1	0	1	0	0
Campos, Utica	.905	19	7	12	2	2	Kallevig, Watertown	.800	15	7	9	4	0
Caridad, Utica	.861	14	9	22	5	2	Karsay, St. Catharines	.857	5	2	4	1	0
Carlson, Welland	1.000	16	4	7	0	1	Keon, Niagara Falls	.643	21	5	4	5	0
Castillo, Pittsfield	.882	16	2	13	2	1	Kessler, Geneva	.889	18	2	14	2	0
Cheetham, Geneva	1.000	2	0	1	0	0	Ketchen, Auburn	.947	19	3	15	1	1
Cofer, Watertown	1.000	8	1	5	0	1	Kirk, Geneva	.933	14	2	12	1	1
Coffee, Pittsfield	1.000	6	1	4	0	0	Konopki, Elmira	1.000	4	0	1	0	1
Coffey, Geneva	1.000	1	1	0	0	0	Kotch, Jamestown*	.960	18	5	19	1	0
Cooke, Welland*	.857	11	3	3	1	1	Kower, St. Catharines	1.000	15	2	10	0	3
Coppeta, Niagara Falls*	1.000	14	4	16	0	0	Langdon, Watertown*	1.000	9	1	13	0	0
Correa, Geneva	1.000	21	2	7	0	0	Larson, Erie	.800	10	2	2	1	0
Currie, Erie*	.957	18	5	17	1	0	Leimeister, Niagara Falls	1.000	4	1	0	0	0
Davis, Elmira	.900	15	3	6	1	0	Locker, Elmira	.818	20	3	6	2	0
Delgado, Geneva	.857	17	3	9	2	1	Lomeli, Erie	.962	15	8	17	1	4
Dennison, Elmira*	.964	15	2	25	1	1	Long, Jamestown	.857	22	4	8	2	0
Diaz, Jamestown	1.000	24	2	6	0	1	Lovdal, Batavia	1.000	19	1	9	0	0
Dickson, Geneva*	1.000	3	0	5	0	0	Lyle, Welland	.938	30	6	9	1	0
Dinuzzo, Utica	.750	18	4	2	2	0	MacLeod, Hamilton*	1.000	29	2	4	0	0
Dorsey, Utica	1.000	2	0	1	0	0	Malone, Oneonta*	1.000	9	1	4	0	0
Doss, Geneva	.750	9	2	7	3	0	Mandia, St. Catharines	1.000	8	1	3	0	0
Douma, Pittsfield*	.906	15	5	24	3	1	Marcero, Niagara Falls*	1.000	2	0	3	0	0
Drell, Niagara Falls	.920	14	5	18	2	2	Marcon, St. Catharines*	1.000	16	1	7	0	0
Dukes, Elmira	1.000	2	1	2	0	0	Mathile, Jamestown	.944	14	1	16	1	1
Dunbar, Oneonta*	.692	19	3	6	4	0	McCutcheon, Erie	1.000	10	5	4	0	0
Ellis, Watertown*	1.000	2	1	2	0	0	McGovern, Batavia	1.000	14	2	11	0	0
Faw, Oneonta	1.000	1	0	3	0	0	Menhart, St. Catharines	.917	8	3	8	1	0
Fazekas, Niagara Falls	.833	14	3	12	3	0	Mikkelsen, Erie	.895	14	3	14	2	2
Fidler, Pittsfield*	.857	10	3	9	2	1	Militello, Oneonta	1.000	13	3	10	0	0
Filter, St. Catharines	1.000	19	2	2	0	1	Miller, Welland	.909	14	1	9	1	0
Finnvold, Elmira	.762	15	6	10	5	1	Mitchelson, Elmira*	1.000	10	2	12	0	2
Flener, St. Catharines*	.929	14	4	9	1	0	Mlicki, Watertown	1.000	7	2	4	0	0
Frazier, Oneonta	.786	13	8	14	6	2	Montgomery, Batavia	.727	21	0	8	3	1
Freitas, Pittsfield	1.000	5	1	1	0	0	Mooney, Welland	1.000	2	0	4	0	1
Fruge, Utica	.800	25	2	2	1	0	Morgan, Watertown	1.000	4	1	0	0	0
Fusco, Hamilton*	1.000	24	2	9	0	0	Morphy, Oneonta	1.000	25	4	12	0	0
Futrell, Welland	.818	16	0	9	2	0	Moya, Jamestown	.958	14	9	14	1	2
Ganote, St. Catharines	1.000	18	1	2	0	0	Munoz, Watertown	.667	2	0	2	1	0
Gelb, Geneva	.875	23	1	6	1	0	Nellenbach, St. Catharines	.000	5	0	0	1	0

PITCHERS—Continued

Player and Club	Pct.	G.	PO.	A.	E.	DP.	Player and Club	Pct.	G.	PO.	A.	E.	DP.
Nelson, Niagara Falls	1.000	12	1	3	0	0	Shea, Niagara Falls	.714	6	1	4	2	0
Newby, Hamilton	.900	24	4	5	1	1	Shepherd, Watertown	.909	24	1	9	1	0
Norris, Jamestown	.833	13	2	8	2	2	Shouse, Welland*	.950	17	7	12	1	1
Ojala, Oneonta*	.920	14	5	18	2	0	Siberz, Oneonta	1.000	35	3	6	0	0
Osborne, Hamilton*	1.000	4	6	3	0	1	Simpson, Welland	1.000	18	4	3	0	1
Pacheco, Welland	1.000	13	2	8	0	1	Singer, St. Catharines*	.857	13	1	5	1	0
J. Parker, Pittsfield	1.000	4	1	0	0	0	Slaughter, Batavia	1.000	7	1	7	0	0
T. Parker, Geneva	.926	12	7	18	2	2	Smalls, Geneva	1.000	10	3	8	0	0
Parris, Batavia	.967	14	8	21	1	0	J. Smith, Utica	.968	16	6	24	1	0
Perez, Oneonta	1.000	28	1	3	0	1	M. Smith, Hamilton	1.000	7	0	5	0	0
Perry, Oneonta*	1.000	20	1	10	0	2	T. Smith, Elmira	1.000	23	5	14	0	0
Person, Watertown	1.000	5	1	1	0	0	Stanley, Geneva	1.000	7	0	2	0	0
Pierce, Niagara Falls*	.500	3	0	1	1	0	Steed, St. Catharines	.833	14	5	10	3	1
Pinto, Niagara Falls	.818	18	1	8	2	2	Stiteler, Auburn*	1.000	3	0	1	0	0
Plantenburg, Elmira*	.889	16	0	8	1	0	Tafoya, Erie*	1.000	3	0	2	0	0
Polasek, Jamestown*	.900	25	1	8	1	0	Taylor, St. Catharines*	.818	14	3	6	2	1
Porcelli, Geneva*	.846	31	2	9	2	0	Tellers, Welland	.889	20	0	8	1	1
Powers, Auburn*	.938	16	4	11	1	2	Thigpen, Niagara Falls	1.000	8	0	3	0	1
Quirico, Oneonta*	.906	14	6	23	3	0	M. Thomas, Pittsfield*	1.000	28	2	7	0	0
Redmond, Welland	.941	15	4	12	1	2	S. Thomas, Pittsfield	.895	19	4	13	2	0
Reed, Auburn	.714	25	0	10	4	0	Tolar, Utica*	.864	15	2	17	3	0
Reimsnyder, Erie*	1.000	1	0	1	0	0	Tolbert, Hamilton	1.000	1	0	1	0	0
Rhea, St. Catharines*	1.000	16	4	9	0	0	Turner, Jamestown	1.000	3	1	1	0	1
Ricker, Jamestown	.875	17	1	6	1	1	Turri, Niagara Falls	.500	6	1	0	1	0
Rightnowar, Niagara Falls	1.000	1	0	2	0	1	Undorf, Niagara Falls	.933	22	4	10	1	2
Rinaldi, Auburn*	1.000	7	0	1	0	0	Urbani, Hamilton*	1.000	5	2	6	0	0
Ring, Elmira	.600	15	1	2	2	0	Vazquez, Pittsfield	.943	18	6	27	2	0
Rivera, Watertown*	1.000	14	6	16	0	1	Voit, Erie	.960	41	5	19	1	0
Rizza, Erie	.857	18	1	5	1	1	Walker, Pittsfield	1.000	16	5	12	0	0
Robertson, Welland*	.929	16	0	13	1	1	Wall, Auburn*	1.000	12	0	1	0	0
Rodriguez, Geneva*	.800	15	1	3	1	2	Warren, Niagara Falls	.846	12	5	6	2	0
Roeder, Welland	1.000	18	0	8	0	3	Watson, St. Catharines	1.000	16	1	1	0	0
Roman, Auburn	1.000	2	0	1	0	0	Way, Welland*	1.000	9	0	1	0	1
Ross, Batavia*	1.000	26	1	6	0	0	Wertz, Watertown	.923	14	4	8	1	1
Rupkey, Hamilton	1.000	17	2	15	0	0	White, Welland	.857	9	1	5	1	1
Ryan, Watertown*	.889	27	1	7	1	0	B. Williams, Auburn	.750	3	1	2	1	0
Salvior, Hamilton	.818	29	1	8	2	0	M. Williams, Batavia	.938	27	2	13	1	1
Santamaria, Elmira	.923	28	5	7	1	0	D. Wilson, Auburn	1.000	22	2	10	0	0
Santana, 5 Uti.-6 Erie	.833	11	0	5	1	0	T. Wilson, Pittsfield	.769	21	0	10	3	0
Santiago, Elmira*	.833	15	2	8	2	0	Woide, Erie*	.700	15	3	11	6	0
Scheffler, Pittsfield	1.000	27	2	7	0	1	Wolf, Niagara Falls	.833	6	1	4	1	0
Schubert, Niagara Falls	1.000	6	1	8	0	0	Woodfin, Watertown*	.818	5	1	8	2	0
Sciortino, Pittsfield*	1.000	16	0	5	0	0	Wurm, Erie	1.000	35	0	12	0	1
Scott, Auburn*	.938	15	1	14	1	1	Young, Elmira	.882	16	3	12	2	0
Sells, Hamilton*	1.000	6	0	1	0	1	Zimmerman, Welland	1.000	9	0	1	0	0

Triple Play—Slaughter.

The following players did not have any fielding statistics at the positions indicated or appeared only as a designated hitter, pinch-hitter or pinch-runner: Arrendondo, of; Boyce, 3b; Campusano, c; Cofer, of; Cook, p; Cooper, p; N. Davis, of; T. Davis, of; p; DeLosSantos, of; DeRicco, 3b; Dukes, 2b, 3b; Elston, p; Flores, 3b; Friedman, p; Godfrey, p; Hankins, p; Holland, of; M. Jones, p; Kirt, p; Kluss, p; Lora, p; MacMillan, 1b; Marte, p; J. Martinez, p; McClinton, 1b; Medina, p; Ochoa, 1b; Owens, p; O. Perez, p; Polewski, 3b; Radachowski, of; A. Rodriguez, 2b; E. Rodriguez; Saltzgaber, 2b; Schulte, of; Songini, 2b; Sparrow, of; M. Thomas, of; T. Thomas, pr; Turco, of; Varni, 2b; Wardwell, p; Wessel, p; B. Young, of; M. Young, p.

CLUB PITCHING

Club	ERA.	G.	CG.	ShO.	Sv.	IP.	H.	R.	ER.	HR.	HB.	BB.	Int. BB.	SO.	WP.	Bk.
Oneonta	2.62	78	8	9	19	656.2	541	266	191	21	19	306	6	669	54	22
Geneva	2.88	77	6	10	25	659.1	550	283	211	34	28	299	8	677	76	19
Watertown	2.97	78	8	6	20	684.2	608	303	226	30	26	275	8	593	50	13
Jamestown	3.09	77	9	3	19	656.0	605	319	225	28	24	307	7	580	45	14
Batavia	3.38	76	6	7	24	662.1	615	328	249	51	17	211	16	452	57	19
St. Catharines	3.52	76	1	3	17	633.1	577	317	248	40	29	292	7	584	53	19
Welland	3.63	78	2	4	17	671.1	584	375	271	45	45	425	20	670	67	14
Pittsfield	3.63	77	8	9	15	657.0	604	346	265	22	18	329	14	573	49	14
Utica	3.65	77	8	4	10	668.2	617	372	271	23	53	365	14	484	51	18
Hamilton	3.67	77	7	7	22	657.1	607	330	268	35	27	309	18	538	63	7
Erie	3.75	78	7	1	23	660.0	639	373	275	57	34	257	18	620	48	14
Elmira	3.88	77	16	3	13	658.2	617	379	284	28	30	296	6	515	78	28
Niagara Falls	4.34	77	8	9	19	642.1	627	388	310	30	28	315	24	533	50	16
Auburn	4.68	78	3	2	12	661.2	647	452	344	42	55	440	8	614	77	20

PITCHERS' RECORDS

(Leading Qualifiers for Earned-Run Average Leadership—62 or More Innings)

*Throws lefthanded.

Pitcher—Club	W.	L.	Pct.	ERA.	G.	GS.	CG.	GF.	ShO.	Sv.	IP.	H.	R.	ER.	HR.	HB.	BB.	Int. BB.	SO.	WP.
Ryan, Watertown*	5	3	.625	0.73	27	0	0	23	0	9	62.0	47	11	5	0	1	20	6	69	4
Militello, Oneonta	8	2	.800	1.22	13	13	3	0	3	0	88.2	53	14	12	2	1	24	0	119	0
T. Parker, Geneva	6	0	1.000	1.53	12	12	1	0	1	0	76.2	61	22	13	2	1	28	1	81	10
Botkin, Hamilton*	7	4	.636	1.55	13	13	4	0	3	0	87.0	65	26	15	1	1	26	0	68	12
Hodges, Oneonta	6	3	.667	1.67	14	14	1	0	0	0	86.0	81	30	16	1	2	24	0	85	4
Douma, Pittsfield*	5	4	.556	2.14	15	11	2	1	1	0	84.0	60	25	20	1	1	26	2	84	6
Ojala, Oneonta*	7	2	.778	2.16	14	14	1	0	0	0	79.0	75	28	19	2	3	43	0	87	1
Warren, Niagara Falls	2	6	.250	2.17	12	10	1	2	0	0	62.1	53	26	15	3	4	15	0	62	2
Mikkelsen, Erie	7	5	.583	2.34	14	14	2	0	0	0	88.1	69	36	23	2	7	36	2	83	7
Vazquez, Pittsfield	10	2	.833	2.41	18	14	3	1	2	0	100.2	81	36	27	3	3	23	1	49	2

Departmental Leaders: G—Voit, 41; W—Hollins, Vazquez, Wertz, 10; L—Caridad, Castillo, Gorman, 8; Pct.—Parris, .875; GS—Hollins, 16; CG—Finnvold, 5; GF—Siberz, Wurm, 33; ShO—Botkin, 3; Sv.—Wurm, 19; IP—Vazquez, Wertz, 100.2; H—J. Smith, 100; R—Caridad, 61; ER—Caridad, Fazekas, Scott, 44; HR—Pacheco, 11; HB—Irwin, 16; BB—Scott, 63; IBB—Voit, 7; SO—Militello, 119; WP—Hollins, 21.

(All Pitchers—Listed Alphabetically)

Pitcher—Club	W.	L.	Pct.	ERA.	G.	GS.	CG.	GF.	ShO.	Sv.	IP.	H.	R.	ER.	HR.	HB.	BB.	Int. BB.	SO.	WP.
Alcantara, Niagara Falls°	0	1	.000	1.70	24	0	0	17	0	10	47.2	34	14	9	3	1	18	4	57	4
Alesio, Hamilton	0	0	.000	6.00	3	0	0	3	0	1	6.0	3	4	4	0	0	4	0	2	2
C. Allen, Watertown	7	6	.538	3.48	15	15	1	0	0	0	93.0	90	49	36	2	5	30	0	62	4
D. Allen, Auburn	0	1	.000	4.02	14	0	0	11	0	3	15.2	16	8	7	2	1	2	1	19	1
Altaffer, Utica°	0	2	.000	6.26	13	2	0	4	0	1	23.0	25	27	16	1	2	15	0	24	7
Alvarez, Elmira	0	0	.000	9.00	4	0	0	3	0	0	4.0	2	7	4	0	1	6	0	1	1
Arias, Hamilton	2	3	.400	3.95	10	9	0	0	0	0	54.2	58	32	24	2	2	25	0	39	10
Aucoin, Jamestown	1	3	.250	4.46	8	8	1	0	0	0	36.1	28	20	18	3	1	18	0	27	6
Aylmer, St. Catharines°	1	2	.333	3.68	12	0	0	9	0	2	14.2	18	9	6	0	0	4	0	11	2
Bailey, Hamilton	4	6	.400	3.98	16	15	1	1	0	1	83.2	91	46	37	6	4	45	2	48	7
Barreiro, Auburn	2	4	.333	2.44	20	8	0	7	0	1	66.1	50	38	18	4	10	39	0	51	6
Baur, Batavia	4	0	1.000	2.28	13	0	0	9	0	5	23.2	15	7	6	1	0	7	2	23	1
Baxter, Jamestown°	5	4	.556	3.87	13	13	2	0	0	0	74.1	85	44	32	4	0	25	1	67	4
Betances, Hamilton	4	7	.364	3.70	18	12	2	2	0	0	82.2	71	43	34	6	6	31	3	60	4
Bolton, Utica	5	1	.833	0.41	6	6	1	0	1	0	44.0	27	4	2	0	3	11	0	45	0
Boss, Hamilton	1	5	.167	4.84	11	5	0	0	0	0	35.1	39	22	19	3	2	14	2	27	6
Botkin, Hamilton°	7	4	.636	1.55	13	13	4	0	3	0	87.0	65	26	15	1	1	26	0	68	12
Bradford, Geneva	5	0	1.000	1.79	7	7	1	0	0	0	45.1	27	9	9	2	0	14	0	54	1
Brewer, Jamestown°	2	2	.500	2.93	11	2	0	4	0	1	27.2	23	10	9	0	0	13	0	37	2
Brow, St. Catharines	3	1	.750	2.27	9	7	0	0	0	0	39.2	34	18	10	2	2	11	0	39	4
Brown, Auburn	2	2	.500	3.00	6	6	0	0	0	0	36.0	29	17	12	6	1	15	0	22	1
Bryant, Watertown°	6	3	.667	2.77	10	10	2	0	0	0	61.2	49	24	19	3	3	23	1	56	8
Burrell, St. Catharines	1	4	.200	5.86	7	7	0	0	0	0	27.2	29	20	18	4	1	15	0	24	2
Campos, Utica	3	1	.750	3.00	19	6	1	9	0	0	60.0	41	27	20	0	2	47	1	37	3
Caridad, Utica	4	8	.333	4.43	14	14	1	0	0	0	89.1	91	61	44	3	7	40	2	62	7
Carlson, Welland	4	1	.800	4.02	16	8	0	1	0	0	53.2	32	27	24	4	2	52	1	55	8
Castillo, Pittsfield	5	8	.385	4.73	16	14	0	0	0	0	70.1	64	52	37	0	2	58	2	65	13
Cheetham, Geneva	1	1	.500	8.64	2	2	0	0	0	0	8.1	8	9	8	2	3	4	0	7	1
Cofer, Watertown	0	1	.000	9.82	8	0	0	4	0	0	14.2	15	16	16	1	0	21	0	12	6
Coffee, Pittsfield	2	0	1.000	3.57	6	1	1	2	0	0	22.2	21	12	9	1	0	9	0	17	2
Coffey, Geneva	0	0	.000	18.00	1	0	0	1	0	0	1.0	2	5	2	2	0	2	0	0	1
Cook, Erie°	0	0	.000	12.00	1	0	0	0	0	0	3.0	7	5	4	1	0	1	0	2	2
Cooke, Welland°	2	3	.400	2.35	11	11	0	0	0	0	46.0	36	21	12	2	2	17	0	43	6
Cooper, Hamilton	0	0	.000	0.00	1	0	0	0	0	0	0.1	1	0	0	0	0	0	0	0	0
Coppeta, Niagara Falls°	5	7	.417	3.21	14	14	2	0	0	0	73.0	61	34	26	4	1	34	0	44	1
Correa, Geneva	5	3	.625	2.05	21	1	0	5	0	1	52.2	29	18	12	0	5	31	1	58	12
Currie, Erie°	6	3	.667	4.06	18	11	0	2	0	0	68.2	78	41	31	6	2	19	2	66	5
C. Davis, Elmira	1	3	.250	5.14	15	9	0	3	0	1	56.0	59	35	32	4	1	25	1	41	6
T. Davis, Elmira	0	0	.000	0.00	1	0	0	0	0	0	1.0	0	0	0	0	0	1	0	1	1
Delgado, Geneva	1	1	.500	2.80	17	2	0	7	0	4	45.0	43	19	14	1	1	14	2	37	2
Dennison, Elmira°	7	4	.636	3.11	15	14	4	0	1	0	92.2	73	43	32	5	1	37	0	72	13
Diaz, Jamestown	4	3	.571	3.02	24	4	0	14	0	4	41.2	33	18	14	2	2	15	2	39	2
Dickson, Geneva°	2	1	.667	0.53	3	3	0	0	0	0	17.0	5	1	1	1	0	4	0	29	0
Dinuzzo, Utica	1	3	.250	5.35	18	3	0	10	0	0	33.2	54	25	20	1	3	15	2	28	1
Dorsey, Utica	0	0	.000	81.00	2	0	0	0	0	0	0.2	2	6	6	0	0	7	0	0	0
Doss, Jamestown	3	3	.500	3.27	9	8	1	0	1	0	44.0	36	19	16	3	1	23	0	39	4
Douma, Pittsfield°	5	4	.556	2.14	15	11	2	1	1	0	84.0	60	25	20	1	1	26	2	84	6
Drell, Niagara Falls	2	7	.222	4.01	14	14	3	0	1	0	83.0	87	44	37	3	5	24	3	53	2
Dukes, Elmira	0	0	.000	3.00	2	0	0	2	0	0	3.0	3	1	1	0	0	2	0	1	1
Dunbar, Oneonta°	1	4	.200	4.15	19	2	0	8	0	0	30.1	32	23	14	1	1	24	2	24	5
Ellis, Watertown°	0	1	.000	10.38	2	1	0	0	0	0	4.1	8	5	5	0	1	6	0	3	1
Elston, Watertown	0	0	.000	40.50	1	0	0	0	0	0	0.2	3	3	3	0	0	1	0	1	1
Faw, Oneonta	0	0	.000	9.00	1	0	0	0	0	0	3.0	6	3	3	0	0	2	0	0	0
Fazekas, Niagara Falls	6	6	.500	5.55	14	14	1	0	0	0	71.1	79	53	44	7	1	27	0	58	5
Fidler, Pittsfield°	1	2	.333	5.17	10	9	1	0	1	0	47.0	50	35	27	1	2	37	0	38	2
Filter, St. Catharines	0	2	.000	4.50	19	0	0	12	0	2	22.0	28	13	11	1	0	7	0	21	0
Finnvold, Elmira	5	5	.500	3.13	15	15	5	0	1	0	95.0	91	43	33	1	5	22	0	89	6
Flener, St. Catharines°	4	3	.571	3.36	14	7	0	3	0	1	61.2	45	29	23	4	1	33	0	46	4
Frazier, Oneonta	6	2	.750	2.46	13	13	0	0	0	0	80.1	67	32	22	4	2	33	0	67	4
Freitas, Pittsfield	1	0	1.000	3.86	5	0	0	1	0	0	9.1	7	4	4	0	0	4	0	8	0
Friedman, Elmira	0	0	.000	0.00	1	0	0	0	0	0	1.0	1	0	0	0	0	1	0	2	1
Fruge, Utica	2	4	.333	3.21	25	0	0	17	0	5	33.2	20	13	12	2	3	29	3	33	3
Fusco, Hamilton°	4	0	1.000	2.98	24	2	0	10	0	1	45.1	27	16	15	0	2	43	1	44	1
Futrell, Welland	2	4	.333	1.67	16	0	0	9	0	3	37.2	37	19	7	1	4	15	2	32	3
Ganote, St. Catharines	3	0	1.000	2.73	18	0	0	12	0	4	29.2	26	9	9	0	3	7	0	33	2
Gelb, Geneva	2	1	.667	3.56	23	0	0	18	0	9	30.1	28	15	12	2	4	19	0	43	0
Godfrey, Geneva	1	0	1.000	0.00	1	0	0	0	0	0	3.0	2	0	0	0	0	2	1	3	1
Golden, Erie	1	2	.333	7.39	20	1	0	7	0	1	28.0	29	27	23	4	1	17	0	37	4
Golmont, Erie	7	4	.636	3.14	14	14	1	0	1	0	80.1	68	36	28	8	3	35	2	58	4
Gonzales, Watertown	0	0	.000	0.00	7	0	0	5	0	2	14.2	8	2	0	0	0	6	0	17	1
Gorman, Utica	4	8	.333	3.29	17	10	1	6	0	1	79.1	62	39	29	5	7	41	2	47	3
Graham, Elmira	0	0	.000	0.00	1	0	0	1	0	0	2.0	1	0	0	0	0	1	0	0	0
Gray, Batavia	5	3	.625	2.89	11	11	2	0	1	0	65.1	67	29	21	1	0	13	0	46	8
Grewal, Jamestown	0	3	.000	2.72	19	1	0	7	0	3	36.1	28	15	11	1	1	22	1	30	7
Hampton, Auburn	3	5	.375	6.93	13	13	1	0	0	0	50.2	51	46	39	8	9	43	2	27	10
Haney, Jamestown°	3	0	1.000	0.96	6	5	0	0	1	0	28.0	17	3	3	1	4	10	0	26	0
Hankins, Oneonta	1	0	1.000	0.00	3	0	0	2	0	0	3.0	1	0	0	0	0	1	0	3	0
Hill, Batavia	2	4	.333	4.02	10	8	2	1	0	0	53.2	49	27	24	9	0	10	0	34	5
Hodges, Oneonta	6	3	.667	1.67	14	14	1	0	0	0	86.0	81	30	16	1	2	24	0	85	4
Hoey, Utica	1	1	.500	4.13	12	1	0	5	0	1	24.0	25	13	11	3	2	13	2	15	1
Hollins, Geneva	10	3	.769	2.77	17	16	1	1	0	0	97.1	87	49	30	5	3	49	1	115	21
Hotz, Utica	0	4	.000	6.55	27	1	0	13	0	2	34.1	33	28	25	2	5	23	1	25	6
Hulme, Utica	0	0	.000	5.40	4	0	0	2	0	0	3.1	4	4	2	0	1	7	0	4	2
Hurst, Batavia	4	3	.571	2.84	14	14	1	0	1	0	82.1	81	38	26	4	0	23	1	54	5
Hurta, Auburn°	1	4	.200	4.31	15	5	0	9	0	4	31.1	21	19	15	1	4	29	0	41	4
Ingram, Batavia°	0	1	.000	2.18	12	0	0	7	0	3	20.2	15	6	5	1	0	9	2	21	3
Irwin, Auburn	1	6	.143	8.46	22	1	0	11	0	0	44.2	48	48	42	1	16	43	1	28	10
Jenkins, Utica	2	3	.400	3.04	14	6	2	2	0	0	50.1	42	20	17	3	4	21	0	44	4
Jockish, Erie°	3	2	.600	3.38	29	0	0	5	0	1	21.1	12	10	8	1	2	21	2	24	0
M. Jones, Auburn	0	0	.000	27.00	3	0	0	2	0	0	2.1	4	8	7	0	0	7	0	4	1
T. Jones, Batavia	2	4	.333	4.92	19	6	0	6	0	0	60.1	71	48	33	8	2	26	0	31	9

Pitcher—Club	W.	L.	Pct.	ERA	G.	GS.	CG.	GF.	ShO.	Sv.	IP.	H.	R.	ER.	HR.	HB.	BB.	Int. BB.	SO.	WP.
Jordan, Niagara Falls*	0	0	.000	63.00	1	0	0	0	0	0	1.0	8	7	7	0	0	2	0	0	0
Kallevig, Watertown	2	4	.333	3.06	15	5	1	8	0	3	61.2	65	30	21	3	3	16	0	46	1
Karsay, St. Catharines	1	1	.500	0.79	5	5	0	0	0	0	22.2	11	4	2	0	0	12	0	25	0
Keon, Niagara Falls	4	3	.571	6.47	21	2	0	11	0	3	48.2	55	39	35	2	6	27	3	37	6
Kessler, Geneva	2	4	.333	2.74	18	8	0	4	0	0	62.1	60	27	19	5	3	18	0	38	3
Ketchen, Auburn	6	5	.545	3.40	19	12	1	2	0	0	92.2	81	43	35	4	4	40	2	76	8
Kirk, Geneva	4	2	.667	3.44	14	7	2	7	1	3	55.0	48	24	21	3	2	10	1	48	4
Kirt, Niagara Falls	0	0	.000	0.00	2	0	0	2	0	0	2.2	2	0	0	0	0	2	0	2	0
Kluss, Watertown	0	0	.000	0.00	1	0	0	1	0	1	1.0	1	0	0	0	0	1	0	1	0
Konopki, Elmira	0	0	.000	5.40	4	0	0	1	0	0	3.1	8	2	2	0	0	1	0	5	0
Kotch, Jamestown*	5	1	.833	2.14	18	2	1	5	0	0	54.2	42	20	13	1	3	20	0	53	2
Kower, St. Catharines	0	1	.000	2.84	15	0	0	7	0	2	31.2	38	14	10	1	3	11	1	17	3
Langdon, Watertown*	1	4	.200	2.92	9	9	0	0	0	0	49.1	49	24	16	3	1	19	0	46	1
Larson, Erie	1	2	.333	14.81	10	0	0	2	0	0	10.1	23	26	17	3	3	8	0	5	1
Leimeister, Niagara Falls	0	1	.000	1.17	4	0	0	3	0	1	7.2	4	2	1	0	0	3	1	12	0
Locker, Elmira	3	4	.429	6.03	20	4	0	8	0	0	37.1	30	30	25	2	9	37	0	22	6
Lomeli, Erie	5	3	.625	3.70	15	12	0	0	0	0	73.0	81	37	30	5	3	17	1	49	6
Long, Jamestown	4	2	.667	1.37	22	0	0	11	0	2	39.1	26	15	6	1	3	24	0	35	2
Lora, Elmira	0	0	.000	9.00	2	0	0	0	0	0	1.0	2	1	1	0	0	2	0	0	0
Lovdal, Batavia	2	4	.333	3.59	19	3	0	7	0	0	47.2	37	24	19	8	3	20	2	26	6
Lyle, Welland	4	4	.500	4.18	30	3	1	15	0	2	64.2	63	39	30	6	7	25	3	44	7
MacLeod, Hamilton*	1	1	.500	1.47	29	0	0	13	0	3	43.0	24	8	7	1	1	27	2	44	3
Malone, Oneonta*	3	0	1.000	2.28	9	3	2	2	1	0	27.2	15	9	7	1	1	14	0	36	3
Mandia, St. Catharines	1	1	.500	2.70	8	0	0	7	0	2	16.2	12	6	5	0	2	8	1	25	0
Marcero, Niagara Falls*	0	0	.000	7.36	2	2	0	0	0	0	7.1	8	7	6	2	1	7	0	3	0
Marcon, St. Catharines*	3	5	.375	3.61	16	4	0	5	0	2	52.1	53	27	21	7	2	12	0	44	1
Marte, Erie	0	0	.000	1.69	5	1	0	1	0	0	10.2	7	3	2	0	0	7	0	7	0
Martinez, Auburn	0	0	.000	5.40	1	0	0	0	0	0	1.2	1	2	1	0	0	2	0	1	2
Mathile, Jamestown	2	6	.250	2.50	14	14	1	0	0	0	90.0	95	40	25	4	1	28	1	54	1
McCutcheon, Erie	1	0	1.000	3.27	10	6	0	0	0	0	33.0	40	24	12	4	0	8	0	38	1
McGovern, Batavia	4	4	.500	5.02	14	11	1	1	1	0	61.0	76	41	34	8	0	14	0	31	3
Medina, Geneva	0	0	.000	4.50	1	0	0	1	0	0	2.0	1	1	1	0	0	0	0	3	0
Menhart, St. Catharines	0	5	.000	4.05	8	8	0	0	0	0	40.0	34	27	18	2	5	19	0	38	6
Mikkelsen, Erie	7	5	.583	2.34	14	14	2	0	0	0	88.1	69	36	23	2	7	36	2	83	7
Militello, Oneonta	8	2	.800	1.22	13	13	3	0	2	0	88.2	53	14	12	2	1	24	0	119	0
Miller, Welland	3	2	.600	3.29	14	12	0	0	0	0	65.2	59	39	24	3	1	37	0	62	5
Mitchelson, Elmira*	3	3	.500	3.86	10	8	2	2	0	0	49.0	49	31	21	3	1	23	0	31	2
Mlicki, Watertown	3	0	1.000	3.38	7	4	0	3	0	0	32.0	33	15	12	3	0	11	0	28	2
Montgomery, Batavia	4	5	.444	5.56	21	3	0	5	0	1	45.1	45	33	28	7	3	22	2	31	3
Mooney, Welland	0	1	.000	5.40	2	2	0	0	0	0	8.1	7	6	5	0	1	5	0	7	2
Morgan, Watertown	0	0	.000	0.00	4	0	0	4	0	2	8.2	3	2	0	0	0	4	0	9	1
Morphy, Oneonta	3	5	.375	3.02	25	2	0	5	0	0	59.2	56	32	20	3	3	26	1	56	12
Moya, Jamestown	6	2	.750	2.54	14	14	3	0	1	0	88.2	83	32	25	4	2	26	0	78	0
Munoz, Watertown	1	1	.500	1.69	2	2	0	0	0	0	10.2	8	2	2	1	0	3	0	9	1
Nellenbach, St. Catharines	0	0	.000	3.52	5	0	0	4	0	1	7.2	8	4	3	0	0	0	0	10	0
Nelson, Niagara Falls	0	0	.000	14.58	12	0	0	2	0	0	16.2	16	30	27	0	3	34	0	9	13
Newby, Hamilton	3	1	.750	2.73	24	0	0	9	0	2	33.0	27	12	10	4	1	8	2	32	4
Norris, Jamestown	3	7	.300	5.20	13	13	1	0	0	0	62.1	63	48	36	2	4	43	0	72	9
Ojala, Oneonta*	7	2	.778	2.16	14	14	1	0	0	0	79.0	75	28	19	2	3	43	0	87	1
Osborne, Hamilton*	0	2	.000	3.60	4	4	0	0	0	0	20.0	21	8	8	0	0	5	1	14	1
Owens, Auburn*	1	0	1.000	0.00	1	0	0	1	0	0	1.0	0	0	0	0	0	1	0	3	0
Pacheco, Welland	2	6	.250	5.58	13	13	0	0	0	0	61.1	55	42	38	11	5	49	2	67	3
J. Parker, Pittsfield	0	1	.000	1.80	4	1	0	0	0	0	5.0	5	7	1	1	1	5	0	4	0
T. Parker, Geneva	6	0	1.000	1.53	12	12	1	0	1	0	76.2	61	22	13	2	1	28	1	81	10
Parris, Batavia	7	1	.875	2.64	14	14	0	0	0	0	81.2	70	34	24	1	3	22	2	50	7
C. Perez, Oneonta	2	2	.500	3.14	28	0	0	15	0	2	28.2	21	12	10	3	0	17	0	33	4
O. Perez, Hamilton	0	0	.000	0.00	1	0	0	1	0	0	1.0	0	0	0	0	0	2	0	1	0
Perry, Oneonta*	6	1	.857	4.64	20	3	0	5	0	1	42.2	38	29	22	0	1	38	1	42	6
Person, Watertown	1	0	1.000	1.10	5	2	0	2	0	0	16.1	8	2	2	0	0	7	0	19	0
Pierce, Niagara Falls*	0	0	.000	2.79	3	0	0	0	0	0	9.2	8	4	3	0	2	5	1	8	0
Pinto, Niagara Falls	2	3	.400	4.11	18	4	0	8	0	1	46.0	48	28	21	1	0	26	1	35	3
Plantenburg, Elmira*	2	3	.400	4.02	16	5	0	4	0	1	40.1	44	26	18	2	0	19	0	36	4
Polasek, Jamestown*	2	3	.400	1.89	25	0	0	16	0	8	33.1	35	17	7	2	2	16	1	35	1
Porcelli, Geneva*	3	2	.600	4.57	31	2	0	9	0	1	45.1	46	29	23	1	3	35	1	47	9
Powers, Auburn*	0	5	.000	6.06	16	5	0	3	0	0	49.0	63	44	33	4	2	28	1	51	5
Quirico, Oneonta*	6	3	.667	3.21	14	14	1	0	0	0	87.0	69	38	31	2	4	39	0	69	9
Redmond, Welland	1	1	.500	5.00	15	8	0	2	0	0	45.0	37	32	25	1	4	60	0	46	14
Reed, Auburn	6	4	.600	4.52	25	0	0	14	0	0	67.2	78	42	34	5	2	49	1	83	8
Reimsnyder, Erie*	0	0	.000	4.15	1	0	0	1	0	0	4.1	4	2	2	0	1	0	3	1
Rhea, St. Catharines*	2	4	.333	3.22	16	4	0	5	0	0	44.2	49	18	16	4	1	13	0	42	3
Ricker, Jamestown	3	0	1.000	4.11	17	1	0	9	0	0	35.0	31	24	16	1	1	39	0	21	3
Rightnowar, Niagara Falls	1	0	1.000	0.00	1	1	0	0	0	0	7.0	4	1	0	0	1	0	9	0
Rinaldi, Auburn*	1	1	.500	6.23	7	0	0	3	0	0	13.0	13	12	9	0	0	12	0	15	1
Ring, Elmira	0	6	.000	7.24	15	2	1	8	0	2	27.1	23	28	22	2	1	17	0	28	4
Rivera, Watertown*	4	4	.500	3.60	14	13	2	0	1	0	85.0	85	43	34	9	1	10	0	63	2
Rizza, Erie	0	1	.000	6.38	18	1	0	5	0	0	24.0	30	22	17	3	2	15	1	14	6
Robertson, Welland*	3	4	.429	3.08	16	13	0	0	0	0	64.1	51	34	22	4	1	55	2	80	6
E. Rodriguez, Niagara Falls*	0	0	.000	3.68	3	0	0	0	0	0	7.1	3	3	3	1	0	3	0	7	0
G. Rodriguez, Geneva*	1	1	.500	0.38	15	0	0	15	0	7	24.0	11	2	1	0	1	8	0	21	2
Roeder, Welland	1	3	.250	5.74	18	1	0	5	0	0	31.1	32	33	20	3	9	38	1	25	4
Roman, Auburn	0	0	.000	18.00	2	0	0	1	0	0	3.0	8	7	6	2	2	0	0	0
Ross, Batavia*	3	1	.750	2.20	26	3	0	9	0	3	49.0	30	17	12	2	4	25	1	49	6
Rupkey, Hamilton	1	2	.333	7.82	17	1	0	4	0	0	38.0	57	38	33	1	4	19	2	19	1
Ryan, Watertown*	5	3	.625	0.73	27	0	0	23	0	9	62.0	47	11	5	0	1	20	6	69	4
Salvior, Hamilton	0	0	.000	2.72	29	1	0	24	0	14	39.2	38	16	12	1	0	13	2	50	5
Santamaria, Elmira	1	5	.167	3.97	28	2	0	6	0	3	59.0	53	33	26	3	1	33	3	41	18
Santana, 5 Utica-6 Erie	0	1	.000	3.98	11	0	0	3	0	0	20.1	24	16	9	2	1	17	0	14	4
Santiago, Elmira*	1	1	.500	4.93	15	5	1	4	0	0	34.2	43	27	19	1	7	12	0	33	3
Scheffler, Pittsfield	4	2	.667	2.16	27	0	0	24	0	9	41.2	27	13	10	1	1	22	4	32	3
Schubert, Niagara Falls	3	1	.750	3.48	6	6	0	0	0	0	31.0	35	14	12	1	1	7	2	25	2
Sciortino, Pittsfield*	0	0	.000	8.20	16	0	0	10	0	1	26.1	45	34	24	2	0	20	1	22	5
Scott, Auburn*	5	5	.500	4.52	15	15	0	0	0	0	87.2	93	59	44	3	2	63	0	78	8

Pitcher—Club	W.	L.	Pct.	ERA.	G.	GS.	CG.	GF.	ShO.	Sv.	IP.	H.	R.	ER.	HR.	HB.	BB.	Int. BB.	SO.	WP.
Sells, Hamilton*	1	3	.250	5.40	6	5	0	0	0	0	25.0	17	16	15	0	1	19	0	37	5
Shea, Niagara Falls	0	4	.000	12.79	6	2	0	0	0	0	19.0	33	33	27	1	0	24	1	14	3
Shepherd, Watertown	3	3	.500	2.48	24	0	0	19	0	3	54.1	41	22	15	1	4	29	1	55	9
Shouse, Welland*	4	3	.571	5.22	17	1	0	7	0	2	39.2	50	27	23	2	3	7	0	39	1
Siberz, Oneonta	3	2	.600	3.32	35	0	0	33	0	16	40.2	27	16	15	2	1	22	2	48	6
Simpson, Welland	2	3	.400	2.77	18	1	0	8	0	1	48.2	44	19	15	3	1	27	3	37	2
Singer, St. Catharines*	2	3	.400	4.66	13	4	0	4	0	1	38.2	38	24	20	2	2	23	0	44	1
Slaughter, Batavia	1	2	.333	1.90	7	3	0	3	0	0	23.2	20	7	5	1	1	6	0	11	0
Smalls, Geneva	4	4	.500	4.85	10	9	0	0	0	0	39.0	38	25	21	2	1	26	0	42	4
J. Smith, Utica	5	5	.500	3.12	16	14	2	1	0	0	92.1	100	55	32	1	9	29	0	44	3
M. Smith, Hamilton	2	4	.333	4.05	7	5	0	2	0	0	33.1	33	15	15	5	0	13	0	34	1
T. Smith, Elmira	4	6	.400	3.68	23	2	2	16	0	5	66.0	62	33	27	0	2	25	1	52	5
Stanley, Geneva	1	0	1.000	7.20	7	0	0	2	0	0	10.0	14	9	8	2	0	12	0	10	2
Steed, St. Catharines	3	6	.333	3.07	14	14	0	0	0	0	73.1	58	32	25	4	2	39	2	72	10
Stiteler, Auburn*	0	1	.000	14.21	3	2	0	0	0	0	6.1	10	11	10	1	0	8	0	4	0
Tafoya, Erie*	1	2	.333	12.34	3	3	0	0	0	0	11.2	21	20	16	5	1	5	0	8	0
Taylor, St. Catharines*	4	6	.400	3.88	14	14	1	0	0	0	72.0	66	35	31	5	4	49	2	54	6
Tellers, Welland	4	2	.667	1.36	20	0	0	16	0	5	39.2	23	9	6	2	1	7	0	53	1
Thigpen, Niagara Falls	1	1	.500	7.36	8	1	0	2	0	0	18.1	25	19	15	1	1	13	1	11	4
M. Thomas, Pittsfield*	3	3	.500	2.67	28	3	0	13	0	3	64.0	51	23	19	3	3	29	2	80	6
S. Thomas, Pittsfield	3	1	.750	4.78	19	8	0	7	0	1	52.2	62	37	28	2	1	30	0	53	7
Tolar, Utica*	4	6	.400	3.29	15	15	1	0	0	0	90.1	80	44	33	2	4	61	1	69	9
Tolbert, Hamilton	0	0	.000	6.00	1	0	0	1	0	0	3.0	2	2	2	1	0	0	0	2	0
Turner, Jamestown	0	0	.000	6.75	3	0	0	1	0	0	5.1	11	7	4	1	0	3	1	4	1
Turri, Niagara Falls	0	1	.000	4.66	6	1	0	5	0	0	9.2	8	6	5	0	0	7	0	10	1
Undorf, Niagara Falls	4	1	.800	3.35	22	0	0	17	0	4	40.1	34	19	15	1	2	22	5	38	1
Urbani, Hamilton*	0	4	.000	6.15	5	5	0	0	0	0	26.1	33	26	18	4	3	15	1	17	1
Vazquez, Pittsfield	10	2	.833	2.41	18	14	3	1	2	0	100.2	81	36	27	3	3	23	1	49	2
Voit, Erie	5	6	.455	1.97	41	0	0	12	0	3	59.1	40	20	13	1	3	31	7	87	3
Walker, Pittsfield	5	7	.417	4.16	16	13	1	1	0	0	80.0	74	43	37	1	3	46	0	73	1
Wall, Auburn*	0	1	.000	5.23	12	0	0	6	0	2	10.1	10	8	6	0	1	9	0	10	3
Wardwell, Elmira	0	0	.000	3.00	1	0	0	0	0	0	3.0	2	1	1	0	0	3	0	1	0
Warren, Niagara Falls	2	6	.250	2.17	12	10	1	2	0	0	62.1	53	26	15	3	4	15	0	62	2
Watson, St. Catharines	1	3	.250	4.70	16	2	0	7	0	0	38.1	30	28	20	4	1	29	1	39	9
Way, Welland*	1	1	.500	3.38	9	0	0	5	0	2	13.1	12	5	5	0	1	8	4	15	0
Wertz, Watertown	10	2	.833	2.86	14	14	2	0	0	0	100.2	81	39	32	3	4	48	0	92	6
Wessel, Jamestown	1	0	1.000	18.00	3	0	0	0	0	0	3.0	5	6	6	1	0	5	0	2	4
White, Welland	1	4	.200	3.26	9	5	1	1	0	0	38.2	39	19	14	3	2	14	2	43	4
B. Williams, Auburn	0	0	.000	4.05	3	3	0	0	0	0	6.2	6	5	3	0	1	6	0	7	1
M. Williams, Batavia	2	3	.400	2.30	27	0	0	21	0	11	47.0	39	17	12	0	1	13	4	42	1
D. Wilson, Auburn	4	2	.667	2.70	22	8	1	6	0	2	76.2	65	35	23	1	2	43	0	97	8
T. Wilson, Pittsfield	4	4	.500	3.71	21	3	0	8	0	1	53.1	57	25	22	6	1	20	2	48	2
Woide, Erie*	5	3	.625	3.10	15	15	4	0	0	0	93.0	88	44	32	10	3	13	0	90	4
Wolf, Niagara Falls	5	0	1.000	0.55	6	6	0	0	0	0	32.2	22	5	2	0	0	14	2	39	3
Woodfin, Watertown*	0	2	.000	5.14	5	3	0	1	0	0	14.0	14	14	8	1	3	20	0	5	2
Wurm, Erie	2	0	1.000	2.20	35	0	0	33	0	19	41.0	29	10	10	0	4	12	1	42	2
B. Young, Elmira	5	5	.500	2.49	16	11	1	3	0	1	83.0	71	38	23	4	1	29	1	59	8
M. Young, Geneva	0	0	.000	0.00	1	0	0	1	0	0	1.0	1	0	0	0	0	0	0	2	0
Zimmerman, Welland	0	0	.000	0.68	9	0	0	7	0	2	13.1	7	4	1	0	1	9	0	22	1

BALKS—Quirico, 9; Caridad, C. Davis, S. Thomas, B. Young, 6 each; Finnvold, Frazier, T. Jones, Mitchelson, Norris, Schubert, 5 each; C. Allen, Bryant, Hollins, Mikkelsen, Stiteler, 4 each; Aylmer, Fazekas, Flener, Golden, Gray, Hotz, Ingram, Irwin, Karsay, Long, Morphy, Parris, Porcelli, 3 each; Castillo, Currie, Drell, Filter, Freitas, Ganote, Gorman, Hampton, Jenkins, Ketchen, Kirk, Langdon, Lomeli, Lyle, Marcon, McGovern, Menhart, Militello, Moya, Ojala, Osborne, T. Parker, Reed, Robertson, Shouse, T. Smith, Stanley, Tellers, Wall, Wolf, 2 each; Alesio, Alvarez, Bailey, Betances, Bradford, Brewer, Brown, Carlson, Coffee, Cook, Cooke, Coppeta, Correa, Delgado, Dennison, Dinuzzo, Douma, Dunbar, Fidler, Fruge, Gelb, Haney, Hoey, Hurst, Kallevig, Kessler, Miller, Montgomery, Munoz, Nelson, Newby, Pacheco, Pierce, Pinto, Plantenburg, Polasek, Powers, Rhea, Ricker, Rizza, Rupkey, Sciortino, Scott, Shepherd, Simpson, Smalls, J. Smith, Steed, Tafoya, Tolar, Wardwell, B. Williams, M. Williams, D. Wilson, Zimmerman, 1 each.

COMBINATION SHUTOUTS—Ketchen-Reed-Hurta, Wilson-Wall, Auburn; Gray-Williams, Hill-Ingram, Hurst-Montgomery, Parris-Baur, Batavia; Plantenberg-Smith, Elmira; Bradford-Rodriguez 2, Dickson-Rodriguez 2, Hollins-Kirk, Smalls-Gelb, Smalls-Young, Geneva; Arias-Bailey, Bailey-Salvoir, Bailey-Sells-Salvoir, Osborne-Fusco-Betances, Hamilton; Diaz-Kotch, Moya-Ricker, Jamestown; Coppeta-Alcantara 2, Schubert-Keon, Schubert-Pinto, Warren-Alcantara, Warren-Keon, Wolf-Alcantara, Wolf-Undorf, Niagara Falls; Frazier-Perez, Hodges-Perez-Siberz, Militello-Malone-Perez, Ojala-Dunbar-Siberz, Ojala-Morphy, Quirico-Perez-Siberz, Oneonta; Castillo-Thomas, Castillo-Vazquez-Scheffler, Douma-Thomas, Walker-Scheffler, Walker-Sciortino-Wilson, Pittsfield; Burrell-Ganote, Steed-Rhea-Marcon, Taylor-Ganote, St. Catharines; Campos-Gorman, Jenkins-Campos, Tolar-Campos, Utica; Allen-Kallevig, Allen-Ryan, Langdon-Person, Munoz-Ryan, Wertz-Morgan, Watertown; Cooke-Lyle-White-Tellers, Miller-Shouse-Futrell, Robertson-Carlson-Tellers, Robertson-Tellers, Welland.

NO-HIT GAME—Turri-Undorf, Niagara Falls, defeated Elmira, 6-1 (seven innings), August 29.

Northwest League

CLASS A

CHAMPIONSHIP WINNERS IN PREVIOUS YEARS

1901—Portland .675	1948—Spokane .614	1971—Tri-City a .625
1902—Butte .608	1949—Yakima .660	Bend .538
1903—Butte .578	Vancouver (2nd)† .615	1972—Lewiston a .675
1904—Boise .625	1950—Yakima .613	Walla Walla .513
1905—Vancouver .586	1951—Spokane .655	1973—Walla Walla b .638
Everett* .667	1952—Victoria .631	Portland .563
1906—Tacoma .600	1953—Salem .635	1974—Bellingham .619
1907—Aberdeen .625	Spokane* .590	Eugene c .571
1908—Vancouver .578	1954—Vancouver* .636	1975—Portland .545
1909—Seattle .653	Lewiston .629	Eugene d .684
1910—Spokane .596	1955—Salem .646	1976—Portland .556
1911—Vancouver .628	Eugene* .639	Walla Walla d .639
1912—Seattle .600	1956—Yakima .691	1977—Bellingham e .618
1913—Vancouver .600	Yakima .619	Portland .667
1914—Vancouver .632	1957—Eugene .576	1978—Grays Harbor f .671
1915—Seattle .564	Wenatchee* .647	Eugene .514
1916—Spokane .622	1958—Lewiston .621	1979—Central Oregon d .606
1917—Great Falls .592	Yakima* .594	Walla Walla .571
1918—Seattle .588	1959—Salem .623	1980—Bellingham g .643
1919—Seattle .590	Yakima* .563	Eugene g .529
1920—Victoria .600	1960—Yakima .638	1981—Medford d .600
1921—Yakima .710	Yakima .562	Bellingham .557
Yakima† .660	1961—Lewiston* .621	1982—Medford .757
1922—Calgary† .600	Yakima .600	Salem d .486
1923-36—Did not operate.	1962—Wenatchee* .574	1983—Medford h .735
1937—Wenatchee .603	Tri-City .580	Bellingham .588
Tacoma* .627	1963—Lewiston .594	1984—Tri-Cities h .622
1938—Yakima .583	Yakima* .613	Medford .608
Bellingham (2nd)† .511	1964—Eugene .636	1985—Everett h .541
1939—Wenatchee .601	Yakima* .611	Eugene .541
Tacoma (2nd)† .533	1965—Lewiston .667	1986—Bellingham h .608
1940—Spokane .587	Tri-City* .681	Eugene .608
Tacoma (4th)† .500	1966—Tri-City .679	1987—Spokane c .711
1941—Spokane .669	1967—Medford .607	Everett .653
1942—Vancouver .594	1968—Tri-City .600	1988—Southern Oregon .605
1943-45—Did not operate.	1969—Rogue Valley .633	Spokane d .553
1946—Wenatchee .622	1970—Lewiston a .538	1989—Southern Oregon .600
1947—Vancouver .566	Coos Bay-No. Bend .563	Spokane d .547

*Won split-season playoff. †Won four-club playoff. §League disbanded June 18. aLeague divided into Northern and Southern divisions, declared champion under league rules. bLeague divided into Eastern and Western divisions, declared champion under league rules. cLeague divided into Eastern and Western divisions; won two-team playoff. dLeague divided into Northern and Southern divisions; won two-team playoff. eLeague divided into Affiliate and Independent divisions; won two-team playoff. fDeclared league champion after winning one-game playoff. Balance of playoff canceled due to rain and wet grounds. gDeclared co-champion after winning one game. Balance of playoff canceled due to rain and wet grounds. hLeague divided into Washington and Oregon divisions; won two-team playoff. (NOTE—Known as Pacific Northwest League 1901-02, Pacific National League 1903-04, Northwestern League 1905-18, Pacific Coast International League 1919-22 and Western International League 1937-54.)

STANDING OF CLUBS AT CLOSE OF SEASON, SEPTEMBER 3

NORTHERN DIVISION

Club	W.	L.	T.	Pct.	G.B.
Spokane (Padres)	49	27	0	.645	......
Yakima (Dodgers)	36	40	0	.474	13
Everett (Giants)	35	41	0	.461	14
Bellingham (Mariners)	32	44	0	.421	17

SOUTHERN DIVISION

Club	W.	L.	T.	Pct.	G.B.
Boise (Angels)	53	23	0	.697	......
Southern Oregon (Athletics)	40	36	0	.526	13
Eugene (Royals)	30	46	0	.395	23
Bend (Independent)	29	47	0	.382	24

COMPOSITE STANDING OF CLUBS AT CLOSE OF SEASON, SEPTEMBER 3

Club	Boi.	Spo.	S.O.	Yak.	Ev.	Bel.	Eug.	Bend	W.	L.	T.	Pct.	G.B.
Boise (Angels)	...	5	7	6	8	6	9	12	53	23	0	.697	......
Spokane (Padres)	5	...	9	9	7	5	6	8	49	27	0	.645	4
Southern Oregon (Athletics)	3	1	...	7	6	5	10	8	40	36	0	.526	13
Yakima (Dodgers)	4	7	3	...	4	8	5	5	36	40	0	.474	17
Everett (Giants)	2	3	4	6	...	9	6	5	35	41	0	.461	18
Bellingham (Mariners)	4	5	5	2	7	...	4	5	32	44	0	.421	21
Eugene (Royals)	1	4	6	5	4	6	...	4	30	46	0	.395	23
Bend (Independent)	4	2	2	5	5	5	6	...	29	47	0	.382	24

Southern Oregon played home games in Medford and Cline Falls.

Major league affiliations in parentheses.

Playoffs—Spokane defeated Boise, two games to one, to win league championship.

Regular-Season Attendance—Bellingham, 52,461; Bend, 40,849; Boise, 124,270; Eugene, 128,831; Everett, 74,577; Southern Oregon, 69,247; Spokane, 129,999; Yakima, 71,892. Total—692,126. Playoffs (3 games)—11,375.

Managers—Bellingham, P.J. Carey; Bend, Mike Bubalo; Boise, Tom Kotchman; Eugene, Paul Kirsch; Everett, Deron McCue; Southern Oregon, Grady Fuson; Spokane, Gene Glynn; Yakima, Jerry Royster.

All-Star Team—1B—Jay Gainer, Spokane; 2B—Giovanni Miranda, Eugene; 3B—Mike Galle, Yakima; SS—Kevin Farlow, Spokane; OF—Matt Mieske, Spokane; Eric Booker, Southern Oregon; Mark Dalesandro, Boise; C—Eric Helfand, Southern Oregon; DH—Brian Stephens, Bellingham; LHP—Hilly Hathaway, Boise; RHP—Randy Powers, Boise; Most Valuable Player—Matt Mieske, Spokane; Manager of the Year—Gene Glynn, Spokane.

476

(Compiled by Howe Sportsdata International, Boston, Mass.)

CLUB BATTING

Club	Pct.	G.	AB.	R.	OR.	H.	TB.	2B.	3B.	HR.	RBI.	SH.	SF.	HP.	BB.	Int. BB.	SO.	SB.	CS.	LOB.
Yakima	.263	76	2608	398	403	687	941	124	20	30	336	26	36	23	274	10	494	111	56	532
Southern Oregon	.259	76	2612	391	325	676	889	99	15	28	328	19	23	56	333	5	674	94	52	602
Spokane	.255	76	2627	394	360	669	930	107	17	40	325	15	25	30	338	9	694	106	53	600
Boise	.250	76	2540	425	250	634	901	86	17	49	358	36	21	25	405	8	646	70	30	611
Bend	.240	76	2545	348	460	610	803	84	11	29	268	14	17	26	305	3	649	183	79	534
Everett	.238	76	2563	349	369	611	855	121	9	35	283	17	18	39	326	7	597	105	40	604
Bellingham	.224	76	2562	273	342	574	828	100	11	44	238	21	6	25	236	16	675	76	49	515
Eugene	.224	76	2501	303	372	559	779	79	15	37	240	30	16	34	265	4	673	98	43	506

INDIVIDUAL BATTING
(Leading Qualifiers for Batting Championship—205 or More Plate Appearances)

*Bats lefthanded.   †Switch-hitter.

Player and Club	Pct.	G.	AB.	R.	H.	TB.	2B.	3B.	HR.	RBI.	SH.	SF.	HP.	BB.	Int. BB.	SO.	SB.	CS.
Gainer, Jonathan, Spokane*	.356	74	281	41	100	151	21	0	10	54	1	4	5	31	3	49	4	4
Mieske, Matthew, Spokane	.340	76	291	59	99	155	20	0	12	63	1	6	6	45	3	43	26	12
Dalesandro, Mark, Boise	.335	55	224	35	75	107	10	2	6	44	0	1	1	18	2	42	6	1
Galle, Michael, Yakima	.317	65	224	43	71	108	21	2	4	42	0	2	0	53	5	42	3	3
Booker, Eric, Southern Oregon	.305	53	187	38	57	81	12	0	4	33	1	3	4	43	1	44	14	7
Hiatt, Philip, Eugene	.294	73	289	33	85	119	18	5	2	44	1	4	1	17	1	70	15	4
Reid, Derek, Everett	.288	62	215	35	62	94	15	1	5	40	4	3	3	20	2	49	21	3
Helfand, Eric, Southern Oregon*	.285	57	207	29	59	77	12	0	2	39	0	1	7	20	1	49	4	1
Grebeck, Brian, Boise	.282	58	202	45	57	74	10	2	1	33	5	2	1	64	1	57	1	4
Lanfranco, Luis, Southern Oregon	.278	69	245	37	68	88	10	2	2	28	4	0	1	25	1	74	6	3

Departmental Leaders: G—Mieske, 76; AB—Mieske, 291; R—Mieske, 59; H—Gainer, 100; TB—Mieske, 155; 2B—Gainer, Galle, 21;
3B—Gash, 6; HR—Mieske, 12; RBI—Mieske, 63; SH—Forbes, 8; SF—Beard, 9; HP—C. Hart, 11; BB—Grebeck, 64; IBB—Galle, 5;
SO—Partrick, 91; SB—Sammonds, 45; CS—Frias, 14.

(All Players—Listed Alphabetically)

Player and Club	Pct.	G.	AB.	R.	H.	TB.	2B.	3B.	HR.	RBI.	SH.	SF.	HP.	BB.	Int. BB.	SO.	SB.	CS.
Adams, David, Spokane*	.218	46	156	23	34	44	5	1	1	20	1	2	2	31	2	38	3	1
Ahrens, Kelly, Bend	.231	43	121	16	28	53	7	0	6	13	1	0	4	17	0	55	4	1
Alimena, Charles, Everett*	.057	14	35	2	2	2	0	0	0	0	0	0	1	4	0	6	1	0
Alvarez, Javier, Eugene	.186	45	129	17	24	36	3	0	3	6	0	1	7	26	0	36	7	1
Anderson, Garret, Boise*	.253	25	83	11	21	29	3	1	1	8	0	1	0	4	0	18	0	1
Avent, Steven, Bend	.235	45	153	21	36	43	4	0	1	15	2	1	0	5	0	38	5	3
Beard, Garrett, Yakima	.272	60	232	29	63	93	13	1	5	39	2	9	4	17	2	30	6	6
Bish, Brenden, Spokane	.249	65	225	28	56	62	4	1	0	23	3	1	2	20	0	42	12	5
Bohringer, Helmut, Yakima	.327	21	49	9	16	22	2	2	0	10	0	2	1	6	0	6	1	1
Booker, Eric, Southern Oregon	.305	53	187	38	57	81	12	0	4	33	1	3	4	43	1	44	14	7
Borgogno, Matthew, Everett*	.217	31	106	11	23	26	3	0	0	10	2	1	2	12	0	18	5	1
Brooks, Raymond, Eugene	.103	10	29	4	3	8	2	0	1	2	0	0	0	7	0	8	0	0
Brummer, Jeffrey, Yakima*	.270	70	274	46	74	101	10	4	3	32	2	6	0	36	0	61	33	7
Bruno, Julio, Spokane	.251	68	251	36	63	80	7	2	2	22	0	0	2	25	1	78	7	5
Burroughs, Kenneth, Yakima	.000	13	1	0	0	0	0	0	0	0	0	0	0	0	0	1	0	0
Cabrera, Juan, Southern Oregon	.308	8	26	1	8	8	0	0	0	1	0	0	0	4	0	2	3	0
Campa, Eric, Southern Oregon	.237	14	38	4	9	10	1	0	0	5	0	0	2	2	0	10	2	2
Carballo, Julio, Eugene	.216	53	148	18	32	43	3	1	2	11	5	0	1	24	0	25	4	9
Cardenas, Daniel, Yakima	.254	19	71	14	18	32	6	1	2	14	0	1	0	7	0	23	1	1
Chevalier, Boanerge, Bend†	.210	58	195	24	41	51	6	2	0	13	0	1	0	16	0	37	16	10
Christopherson, Eric, Everett	.265	48	162	20	43	56	8	1	1	22	1	2	0	31	1	29	7	2
Clifford, Jeffrey, Southern Oregon	.000	20	1	0	0	0	0	0	0	0	0	0	0	0	0	0	0	0
Dakin, Brian, Everett	.243	35	107	14	26	36	4	0	2	15	2	1	3	16	0	23	1	3
Dalesandro, Mark, Boise	.335	55	224	35	75	107	10	2	6	44	0	1	1	18	2	42	6	1
Dattola, Kevin, Southern Oregon†	.270	41	148	33	40	51	9	1	0	13	3	2	2	36	0	33	16	6
Davis, Courtney, Everett	.091	4	11	4	1	1	0	0	0	1	0	0	0	3	0	7	0	0
Davis, Matthew, Everett†	.270	39	141	23	38	59	9	0	4	18	0	0	4	14	0	21	8	3
Doffek, Scott, Yakima*	.257	61	202	23	52	79	7	4	4	30	1	3	4	11	0	14	1	6
Ebanks, Weddison, Eugene	.188	8	16	2	3	3	0	0	0	2	0	0	1	0	0	5	0	0
Elliott, James, Spokane	.186	35	113	13	21	33	3	0	3	11	0	2	2	14	0	54	1	0
Farlow, Kevin, Spokane	.243	68	267	39	65	90	10	3	3	31	1	4	2	32	0	67	11	6
Forbes, Patrick, Boise	.249	43	169	29	42	53	9	1	0	20	8	1	0	23	1	22	11	4
Fowler, Yale, Yakima	.232	35	82	6	19	22	3	0	0	11	0	2	1	5	0	30	0	0
Frias, Pedro, Bend	.264	68	231	29	61	70	5	2	0	16	3	1	2	15	0	51	25	14
Gainer, Jonathan, Spokane*	.356	74	281	41	100	151	21	0	10	54	1	4	5	31	3	49	4	4
Galle, Michael, Yakima	.317	65	224	43	71	108	21	2	4	42	0	2	0	53	5	42	3	3
Garcia, Francisco, Eugene	.238	53	189	22	45	53	6	1	0	12	3	0	2	7	0	43	7	2
Garrett, Clifton, Boise*	.203	53	148	28	30	33	1	1	0	7	6	1	3	42	0	27	15	3
Gash, Darius, Spokane†	.236	64	254	47	60	85	7	6	2	27	2	0	2	37	0	71	20	9
Gil, Daniel, Boise	.309	51	152	27	47	74	12	0	5	34	0	3	3	25	1	43	0	2
Gonzalez, Paul, Spokane*	.250	1	4	0	1	2	1	0	0	0	0	0	0	1	0	1	0	0
Grahovac, Michael, Bend	.423	7	26	5	11	14	3	0	0	1	0	0	0	3	0	2	0	1
Grebeck, Brian, Boise	.282	58	202	45	57	74	10	2	1	33	5	2	1	64	1	57	1	4
Guanchez, Harry, Eugene	.263	66	194	13	51	77	8	0	6	35	0	4	5	14	0	51	0	1
Haber, David, Eugene	.199	56	161	12	32	36	2	1	0	14	6	0	2	18	0	44	11	3
Harrel, Donald, Eugene	.223	55	184	17	41	65	8	2	4	25	1	1	2	12	0	57	2	0
Hart, Christopher, Southern Oregon	.264	67	239	50	63	99	14	2	6	32	1	3	11	37	0	86	15	3
Hart, Shelby, Everett	.203	54	182	12	37	42	5	0	0	17	0	2	4	18	0	35	3	0
Hawks, Lawrence, Spokane	.213	31	89	12	19	26	5	1	0	14	1	3	1	21	0	24	0	0
Helfand, Eric, Southern Oregon*	.285	57	207	29	59	77	12	0	2	39	0	1	7	20	1	49	4	1
Helms, Michael, 9 Ever.-23 Bend	.159	32	82	6	13	14	1	0	0	7	1	0	0	12	0	31	7	2
Henry, Scott, Southern Oregon*	.294	6	17	4	5	6	1	0	0	2	0	0	1	3	0	4	1	0
Hernandez, Carlos, Southern Oregon†	.282	16	39	4	11	12	1	0	0	3	0	1	0	6	0	10	3	4
Hiatt, Philip, Eugene	.294	73	289	33	85	119	18	5	2	44	1	4	1	17	1	70	15	4
Hoffman, John, Bellingham	.250	4	12	1	3	3	0	0	0	1	0	0	0	0	0	4	0	0
Horan, Michael, Bend	.125	4	8	1	1	3	0	1	0	2	1	0	0	3	0	3	0	0
Hunt, Shannon, Bend	.141	38	92	9	13	21	2	0	2	7	2	1	1	15	0	46	2	1
Hunter, Gregory, Bellingham*	.213	56	183	21	39	51	5	2	1	13	3	0	0	22	3	36	2	6
Hyde, Mickey, Bend	.265	68	260	35	69	98	9	1	6	40	1	3	0	19	0	53	13	4
Hyzdu, Adam, Everett	.245	69	253	31	62	98	16	1	6	34	0	5	2	28	1	78	2	4

Player and Club	Pct.	G.	AB.	R.	H.	TB.	2B.	3B.	HR.	RBI.	SH.	SF.	HP.	BB.	Int. BB.	SO.	SB.	CS.
Jackson, John, Everett*	.304	26	92	26	28	37	2	2	1	7	1	1	4	27	0	11	14	4
Jennings, Lance, Eugene	.185	31	92	8	17	34	3	1	4	9	2	1	0	6	0	21	0	0
Jensen, Marcus, Everett†	.170	51	171	21	29	38	3	0	2	12	0	0	5	24	0	60	0	1
Johnson, Darron, Eugene	.171	42	117	9	20	32	6	0	2	14	0	0	3	8	0	40	0	2
Jones, Heath, Everett	.000	6	18	1	0	0	0	0	0	0	0	0	0	2	0	8	0	0
Klavitter, Clayton, Bellingham	.173	22	52	4	9	11	2	0	0	1	0	0	0	6	0	15	0	0
Kliafas, Stephen, Yakima	.186	39	118	8	22	27	2	0	1	12	1	0	0	8	0	19	4	4
Kluge, Matthew, Bellingham†	.242	34	99	9	24	31	7	0	0	7	1	1	0	3	0	34	2	0
Kotchman, Randy, Boise†	.244	56	164	30	40	49	7	1	0	24	2	0	0	34	0	35	6	2
Kounas, Anthony, Bellingham	.231	19	65	9	15	22	4	0	1	11	0	0	1	8	0	13	1	0
Krokroskia, Sean, Bend	.248	37	109	21	27	35	4	2	0	15	0	1	1	29	0	33	15	3
Lanfranco, Luis, Southern Oregon	.278	69	245	37	68	88	10	2	2	28	4	0	1	25	1	74	6	3
Lasher, Matthew, Boise	.143	9	21	3	3	7	1	0	1	4	0	0	0	5	0	3	0	0
Ledinsky, Raymond, Boise	.250	1	4	0	1	1	0	0	0	1	0	0	0	0	0	1	0	0
Lott, Billy, Yakima	.275	65	240	37	66	95	13	2	4	38	0	4	3	10	0	62	4	0
Lyons, Mario, Bend†	.179	46	123	19	22	32	5	1	1	10	1	1	0	19	0	45	14	6
Magallanes, Robert, Bellingham	.191	46	157	14	30	36	3	0	1	12	1	0	1	18	1	31	1	0
Markiewicz, Brandon, Boise	.000	1	1	0	0	0	0	0	0	0	0	0	0	0	0	1	0	0
Martinez, Manuel, Southern Oregon	.246	66	244	36	60	71	5	0	2	17	1	0	5	16	0	59	6	4
McCormick, Glenn, Bend	.239	72	251	37	60	77	6	1	3	24	1	2	2	39	0	67	2	4
McKoy, Keith, Spokane*	.242	64	236	39	57	72	8	2	1	24	2	0	0	16	0	59	18	5
McNair, Frederick, Bellingham†	.205	50	176	16	36	53	8	0	3	17	1	0	3	15	1	55	7	3
Mercado, Rafael, Southern Oregon	.164	49	140	13	23	27	4	0	0	14	1	0	3	11	0	44	3	3
Mesa, Audy, 35 Bend-28 Ever.	.251	63	239	27	60	80	8	0	4	35	0	2	2	13	1	55	9	5
Meury, William, Spokane	.111	5	18	1	2	2	0	0	0	2	0	1	1	0	0	5	0	0
Mieske, Matthew, Spokane	.340	76	291	59	99	155	20	0	12	63	1	6	6	45	3	43	26	12
Miller, Barry, Everett*	.265	38	136	19	36	54	12	0	2	15	0	0	0	13	1	25	1	1
Mintz, Stephen, Yakima*	.283	39	53	11	15	22	4	0	1	3	0	0	1	7	0	16	2	0
Miranda, Giovanni, Eugene	.338	42	145	30	49	52	3	0	0	15	3	2	1	15	0	30	16	6
Moser, Ricky, Eugene	.209	31	86	13	18	25	0	2	1	9	1	0	0	18	1	37	3	3
Muhlethaler, Michael, S. Oregon	.256	62	211	34	54	78	8	2	4	31	1	1	4	22	0	48	1	2
Nava, Lipso, Bellingham	.251	46	171	11	43	55	12	0	0	15	3	0	2	15	2	31	2	2
Nes Smith, John, Everett	.235	14	34	6	8	16	2	0	2	3	1	0	1	9	0	15	0	1
Nichols, Robert, Bellingham	.225	57	209	22	47	69	13	0	3	23	2	2	7	12	0	59	0	0
Olson, Kurt, Yakima*	.259	53	170	25	44	61	8	0	3	23	1	0	1	20	0	39	2	7
Ordway, Jeffrey, Spokane	.218	39	101	19	22	27	3	1	0	4	0	0	0	11	0	35	2	2
Ortiz, Hector, Yakima	.272	52	173	16	47	52	3	1	0	12	1	0	1	5	1	15	1	1
Osinski, Glenn, Southern Oregon	.200	6	30	1	6	7	1	0	0	3	0	0	1	0	0	9	1	0
Ostermeyer, William, Spokane	.221	46	145	16	32	56	6	0	6	18	1	1	3	19	0	52	0	0
Partrick, David, Boise	.226	66	239	25	54	89	6	1	9	35	4	1	1	17	0	91	0	1
Pearce, Jeffrey, Spokane*	.162	21	74	5	12	14	2	0	0	2	0	0	0	8	0	38	0	1
Percival, Troy, Boise	.203	29	79	12	16	16	0	0	0	5	1	0	2	19	0	25	0	0
Perez, Jose, Yakima†	.282	22	71	14	20	24	4	0	0	5	6	1	2	7	0	11	2	2
Phillips, Charles, Boise*	.194	70	237	30	46	82	6	0	10	34	1	2	0	20	0	78	1	2
Picketts, William, Southern Oregon†	.250	68	252	30	63	73	8	1	0	41	5	5	4	44	0	39	5	8
Raasch, Glen, Bellingham	.190	47	163	16	31	53	4	0	6	13	2	0	1	5	0	56	0	1
Reid, Derek, Everett	.288	62	215	35	62	94	15	1	5	40	4	3	3	20	2	49	21	3
Reid, Gregory, Southern Oregon†	.333	3	3	0	1	1	0	0	0	0	0	0	0	1	0	0	0	0
Reyes, Amner, Bend	.236	57	199	28	47	56	3	0	2	27	1	2	7	22	0	24	11	3
Rijo, Rafael, Yakima	.260	51	200	30	52	66	9	1	1	13	5	2	3	12	0	32	23	5
Ringgold, Keith, Everett	.239	22	46	10	11	12	1	0	0	2	0	0	1	6	0	14	3	1
Roa, Pedro, Bend	.156	11	32	4	5	5	0	0	0	2	0	0	3	0	0	13	2	1
Rolls, David, Eugene	.281	45	128	24	36	56	5	0	5	13	1	2	6	21	0	27	1	1
Romay, Guillermo, Bellingham	.235	55	179	26	42	79	10	3	7	24	2	1	1	26	2	66	2	5
Salazar, Carlos, Southern Oregon	.273	57	165	14	45	57	7	1	1	19	0	5	4	18	0	44	1	2
Sambel, Arnold, Eugene	.143	8	28	1	4	4	0	0	0	1	0	0	0	4	0	7	0	0
Sammons, Lee, Bend	.261	69	253	49	66	76	5	1	1	20	0	2	1	46	1	50	45	11
Santana, Jose, Boise*	.267	58	180	34	48	55	1	3	0	32	2	1	2	33	2	35	13	3
Santana, Ruben, Bellingham	.252	47	155	22	39	58	3	2	4	13	0	1	6	18	2	39	10	9
Sena, Sean, Yakima	.227	32	75	11	17	25	5	0	1	11	2	1	0	5	0	17	0	0
Shepperd, Richard, Boise	.300	16	40	9	12	14	2	0	0	2	0	0	0	7	0	8	1	0
Shields, Douglas, Eugene	.192	71	250	38	48	67	8	1	3	15	3	0	2	24	1	62	13	7
Showalter, John, Boise	.267	58	187	26	50	81	5	1	8	35	1	2	5	22	0	33	1	2
Siebert, Steven, Spokane	.182	4	11	2	2	2	0	0	0	2	0	0	0	2	0	2	0	1
Sievers, Jason, Everett	.160	17	50	2	8	9	1	0	0	5	0	0	0	8	0	15	0	0
Slater, Vernon, Eugene*	.190	53	137	15	26	41	1	1	4	9	2	0	1	19	1	62	9	2
Specyalski, Brian, Boise†	.250	25	68	18	17	24	2	1	1	8	3	1	2	17	0	10	8	2
Spires, Tony, Everett	.244	65	213	27	52	63	8	0	1	9	4	0	3	20	2	39	5	4
Staydohar, David, Boise	.284	53	169	31	48	77	7	2	6	18	0	0	3	13	0	51	4	3
Stephens, Brian, Bellingham*	.273	59	231	23	63	96	10	1	7	31	0	0	2	14	3	55	6	1
Stewart, Brady, Eugene	.165	34	85	15	14	16	2	0	0	2	2	0	0	10	0	16	6	0
Strong, Shannon, Eugene*	.117	38	94	12	11	12	1	0	0	2	0	1	1	14	0	32	4	2
Tamarez, Carlos, 2 Bend-58 S.O.†	.220	60	200	23	44	52	0	4	0	17	2	1	4	15	0	54	7	2
Tejero, Fausto, Boise	.216	39	74	14	16	18	2	0	0	7	2	3	2	23	1	23	1	0
Terrell, James, Bellingham	.223	51	184	18	41	54	4	0	3	16	3	0	0	11	0	38	6	4
Tredway, Edward, Southern Oregon	.250	22	60	7	15	18	0	0	1	7	0	0	0	1	0	15	4	1
Troncoso, Nolberto, Yakima	.250	66	228	51	57	73	9	2	1	32	3	2	0	40	2	40	22	6
Twitty, Douglas, Bend	.240	57	192	17	46	60	8	0	2	22	0	0	5	24	1	38	14	10
Twitty, Sean, Bellingham	.225	67	253	30	57	86	9	1	6	22	0	0	0	31	2	72	24	7
Vandebrake, Kevin, Yakima†	.167	5	12	1	2	2	0	0	0	2	1	0	0	1	0	4	0	0
Varnell, Daniel, 4 Ever.-35 Bend*	.298	39	104	10	31	48	11	0	2	15	0	1	2	16	0	34	2	0
Vega, Julio, Everett†	.147	35	109	12	16	17	1	0	0	3	1	0	0	13	0	46	0	0
Ward, Ricky, Everett	.262	39	149	25	39	55	11	1	1	22	1	1	3	17	0	28	7	6
Weber, Peter, Everett*	.316	40	158	27	50	81	15	2	4	24	0	0	0	22	0	33	20	5
West, James, Spokane	.216	42	111	14	24	29	5	0	0	6	2	1	2	25	0	36	2	2
White, Craig, Yakima*	.241	52	133	23	32	37	5	0	0	7	1	1	2	24	0	32	6	7
Wilder, William, Bellingham	.152	37	125	13	19	32	3	2	2	10	0	0	1	10	0	37	8	5
Wilkerson, William, Bellingham*	.243	47	148	18	36	39	3	0	0	10	3	1	0	21	0	34	5	6
Williams, Kent, Boise†	.056	5	18	4	1	1	0	0	0	2	0	0	1	4	0	7	2	0
Williams, Joseph, Boise	.123	41	81	14	10	17	2	1	1	5	1	0	0	15	0	36	0	0
Young, Ernest, Southern Oregon	.280	50	168	34	47	75	6	2	6	23	0	1	3	29	2	53	4	4
Young, Jason, Everett	.262	13	42	10	11	24	2	1	3	8	0	1	2	8	0	8	2	1

The following pitchers, listed alphabetically by club, with games in parentheses, had no plate appearances, primarily through use of designated hitters:

BELLINGHAM—Adam, David (19); Callistro, Robert (22); Converse, James (12); Cummings, John (6); Duke, Kyle (12); Fitzer, Douglas (25); Green, Derek (7); King, Kevin (6); Lodding, Richard (13); Magill, James (15); McDonald, David (8); Rivera, Randy (3); Schanz, Scott (7); Tegtmeier, Douglas (17); Williams, Tyler (17); Yianacopolus, Kevin (23); Youngblood, Todd (17).

BEND—Blankenship, Robert (27); Boker, Michael (12); Gibbs, James (4); Henrikson, Daniel (7); Hill, Fredrick (6); Klonoski, Jason (26); Miller, Russell (9); Minder, Troy (9); Nielson, Kenneth (2); Pena, Antonio (8); Potter, Lon (12); Reyes, Jose (21); Ross, Gary (16); Russell, Todd (15); Sims, Jon (3); Wagner, Darrell (21); Wanke, Chuck (6).

BOISE—Ball, Jeffrey (13); Cobb, Marvin (2); Craven, Britt (6); Edenfield, Kenneth (31); Gamez, Robert (14); Hathaway, Hillard (15); Helm, Wayne (19); James, Todd (1); Lachemann, Bret (2); Leftwich, Phillip (15); McCray, Todd (17); Musset, Jose (1); Pakele, Louis (5); Powers, Randall (15); Scott, Darryl (27); Search, Michael (16); Stenz, Daniel (18); Swingle, Paul (14).

EUGENE—Baez, Francisco (11); Davis, Scott (17); Franceschi, Sean (24); Frederick, Charles (22); Gill, Stephen (13); Gutierrez, Rafael (22); Harris, Douglas (15); Hierholzer, David (32); Holman, Bradley (17); Long, William (16); Myers, Rodney (6); Peters, Douglas (15); Pineda, Gabriel (20); Pollard, Damon (14); Rea, Shayne (9).

EVERETT—Ayres, Lenny (22); Boker, Michael (7); Carlson, Daniel (17); Ebert, Scott (5); Flanagan, Daniel (4); Gould, Frank (17); Henrikson, Daniel (8); Huffman, Rodney (21); Huisman, Richard (1); Huslig, James (2); McGehee, George (15); McLeod, Brian (22); Myers, Michael (15); Peltzer, Kurt (18); Rosselli, Joseph (15); Whatley, Fred (8); Yockey, Mark (23).

SOUTHERN OREGON—Brimhall, Bradley (16); Connolly, Craig (21); Craft, Mark (17); Dillon, James (9); Dressendorfer, Kirk (7); Garland, Chaon (11); Johns, Douglas (6); Myers, Eric (24); Peters, Donald (11); Revenig, Todd (24); Scharff, Anthony (4); Shaw, Curtis (17); Sudbury, Craig (7); Tripp, David (16); Van Poppel, Todd (5); Vizzini, Daniel (16); Zancanaro, Daniel (10).

SPOKANE—Bensching, Bruce (32); Bradley, Michael (15); Devore, Paul (10); Fredrickson, Scott (26); Garside, Russell (17); Hays, Robert (10); Mortensen, Anthony (18); Painter, Lance (23); Perez, Tirson (1); Sanders, Scott (3); Silcox, Russell (16); Thibault, Ryan (22); Waldron, Joseph (21).

YAKIMA—Astacio, Pedro (3); Bishop, Craig (15); Branconier, Paul (18); Cantres, Jorge (24); Delahoya, Javier (14); Freeman, Scott (14); Kelly, Joseph (17); Madsen, Erik (13); Mimbs, Michael (13); O'Connor, Benjamin (21); Patrick, Tim (11); Perez, Pedro (24); Sampson, Michael (3); Tatis, Fausto (13).

GRAND SLAM HOME RUNS—Gainer, 2; Galle, Hyde, Johnson, Mieske, Partrick, 1 each.

AWARDED FIRST BASE ON CATCHER'S INTERFERENCE—Nichols 3 (Rolls 2, Harrel); Hawks 2 (Gil, Jennings); Fowler (Harrel); Hyzdu (Beard); McKoy (Percival); Miller (Percival); Olson (Rolls); Vega (Grahovac).

CLUB FIELDING

Club	Pct.	G.	PO.	A.	E.	DP.	PB.	Club	Pct.	G.	PO.	A.	E.	DP.	PB.
Bellingham	.960	76	2040	816	119	59	20	Eugene	.954	76	2023	858	139	74	23
Spokane	.959	76	2070	801	122	64	22	Southern Oregon	.951	76	2051	764	144	57	20
Everett	.959	76	2007	746	119	63	25	Yakima	.948	76	2035	790	155	57	27
Boise	.958	76	2036	815	124	56	14	Bend	.945	76	2002	842	165	76	18

Triple Play—Yakima.

INDIVIDUAL FIELDING

°Throws lefthanded.

FIRST BASEMEN

Player and Club	Pct.	G.	PO.	A.	E.	DP.	Player and Club	Pct.	G.	PO.	A.	E.	DP.
Adams, Spokane	.984	8	60	0	1	4	Jones, Everett	1.000	5	40	1	0	0
Ahrens, Bend	.500	1	1	0	1	0	Klavitter, Bellingham	1.000	6	49	3	0	1
Alimena, Everett°	.987	13	74	2	1	8	Kounas, Bellingham	1.000	16	127	16	0	9
Beard, Yakima	.978	6	41	3	1	4	McCormick, Bend	.987	65	557	29	8	59
Bohringer, Yakima	1.000	1	1	0	0	0	Mercado, Southern Oregon	.986	40	270	15	4	27
Dakin, Everett	1.000	2	4	0	0	1	Miller, Everett°	.989	37	263	8	3	30
Dalesandro, Boise	1.000	1	3	1	0	2	Muhlethaler, Southern Oregon	.983	32	213	18	4	15
Fowler, Yakima	1.000	3	10	0	0	0	Nichols, Bellingham	.987	48	422	29	6	37
Gainer, Bend	.989	71	610	40	7	53	Olson, Everett°	.971	37	283	19	9	19
GUANCHEZ, Eugene	.998	62	477	28	1	43	Ostermeyer, Spokane	1.000	1	1	1	0	0
Harrel, Eugene	.980	10	90	6	2	7	Phillips, Boise°	.988	68	641	42	8	34
Hart, Everett	.996	29	231	10	1	21	Salazar, Southern Oregon	.969	19	117	9	4	10
Hawks, Spokane	1.000	1	1	0	0	0	Santana, Boise°	.963	13	98	6	4	11
Henry, Southern Oregon	1.000	1	10	0	0	1	Showalter, Boise	1.000	3	26	0	0	2
Hunt, Bend	.969	14	88	6	3	9	Troncoso, Yakima	.981	45	292	20	6	22
Hunter, Bellingham	.990	9	91	8	1	8	Twitty, Bend	1.000	3	14	1	0	0
Johnson, Eugene	.985	19	127	8	2	11	Varnell, 1 Ever.-1 Bend	1.000	2	2	0	0	0

Triple Play—Olson.

SECOND BASEMEN

Player and Club	Pct.	G.	PO.	A.	E.	DP.	Player and Club	Pct.	G.	PO.	A.	E.	DP.
Adams, Spokane	1.000	1	2	0	0	0	Mesa, 31 Bend-27 Ever.	.958	58	105	147	11	34
Alvarez, Eugene	.950	35	77	95	9	20	Miranda, Eugene	.978	35	78	96	4	18
BISH, Spokane	.974	61	111	150	7	34	Ordway, Spokane	.967	17	31	56	3	9
Bohringer, Yakima	1.000	2	2	4	0	1	Osinski, Southern Oregon	1.000	5	6	14	0	2
Borgogno, Everett	.957	24	50	62	5	17	Picketts, Southern Oregon	.959	48	106	103	9	23
Cabrera, Southern Oregon	1.000	1	4	4	0	0	Reyes, Bend	1.000	1	0	2	0	0
Campa, Southern Oregon	.824	6	10	4	3	0	Roa, Bend	.967	9	12	17	1	4
Carballo, Eugene	.917	1	5	6	1	3	Santana, Bellingham	.956	38	77	96	8	22
Chevalier, Bend	.976	22	32	49	2	11	Sena, Yakima	.938	21	24	36	4	3
Dakin, Everett	1.000	5	10	5	0	1	Siebert, Spokane	.700	2	2	5	3	0
Davis, Everett	1.000	7	15	16	0	5	Specyalski, Boise	.958	7	7	16	1	2
Doffek, Yakima	.927	56	112	117	18	29	Spires, Everett	1.000	1	5	2	0	2
Forbes, Boise	.962	41	93	109	8	24	Stewart, Eugene	.875	10	17	18	5	8
Grebeck, Boise	.950	25	39	56	5	8	Tamarez, Southern Oregon	.870	5	6	14	3	2
Haber, Eugene	1.000	3	4	3	0	1	Vandebrake, Yakima	1.000	4	8	4	0	2
Helms, 8 Ever.-22 Bend	.903	30	61	70	14	16	White, Yakima	.905	5	6	13	2	0
Hernandez, Southern Oregon	1.000	5	6	5	0	1	Wilkerson, Bellingham	.960	45	83	111	8	19
Lanfranco, Southern Oregon	.912	15	23	39	6	5	Williams, Boise	.667	2	0	2	1	0
Lasher, Boise	.971	8	10	23	1	4	Young, Everett	.938	11	25	36	4	7

THIRD BASEMEN

Player and Club	Pct.	G.	PO.	A.	E.	DP.	Player and Club	Pct.	G.	PO.	A.	E.	DP.
Adams, Spokane	.833	4	4	6	2	0	Dakin, Everett	.842	25	15	33	9	2
Beard, Yakima	.750	5	4	2	2	0	Dalesandro, Boise	.852	12	3	20	4	3
Bohringer, Yakima	.810	11	5	12	4	1	Davis, Everett	.714	4	1	9	4	0
Borgogno, Everett	.714	3	0	5	2	1	GALLE, Yakima	.931	60	40	121	12	12
Bruno, Spokane	.879	68	38	122	22	10	Gonzalez, Spokane	.667	1	1	1	1	0
Campa, Southern Oregon	.882	5	4	11	2	2	Hart, Everett	.000	4	0	0	1	0
Chevalier, Bend	.763	16	10	19	9	3	Hiatt, Eugene	.920	63	39	145	16	18

THIRD BASEMEN — Continued

Player and Club	Pct.	G.	PO.	A.	E.	DP.
Hunt, Bend	.842	6	12	4	3	1
Hunter, Bellingham	.918	27	18	49	6	2
Klavitter, Bellingham	.750	2	0	3	1	0
Kotchman, Boise	.878	50	27	103	18	4
Lanfranco, Southern Oregon	.889	48	35	93	16	10
Magallanes, Bellingham	.892	34	19	64	10	2
McCormick, Bend	.941	7	3	13	1	0
McNair, Bellingham	.769	4	3	7	3	1
Moser, Eugene	.886	16	6	33	5	5
Muhlethaler, Southern Oregon	.600	7	0	6	4	0
Nichols, Bellingham	.929	8	6	20	2	3
Ordway, Spokane	.933	6	3	11	1	1
Picketts, Southern Oregon	.778	8	7	7	4	1
Reyes, Bend	.878	54	45	106	21	8
Salazar, Southern Oregon	.934	17	14	43	4	3
Santana, Bellingham	.850	7	4	13	3	2
Showalter, Boise	1.000	2	0	1	0	0
Specyalski, Boise	1.000	2	2	3	0	0
Spires, Everett	.916	47	25	84	10	7
White, Yakima	.955	9	8	13	1	2
Williams, Boise	.882	27	10	35	6	4
Young, Everett	1.000	1	0	3	0	0

SHORTSTOPS

Player and Club	Pct.	G.	PO.	A.	E.	DP.
Alvarez, Eugene	.837	12	10	26	7	2
Borgogno, Everett	.923	4	4	8	1	3
Cabrera, Southern Oregon	.926	7	5	20	2	2
Campa, Southern Oregon	1.000	1	2	1	0	0
Carballo, Eugene	.899	52	69	118	21	21
Chevalier, Bend	.929	20	27	51	6	16
Davis, Everett	.912	25	30	74	10	13
Farlow, Spokane	.904	68	68	187	27	37
Frias, Bend	.882	61	96	195	39	42
Grebeck, Boise	.918	34	36	110	13	17
Hernandez, Southern Oregon	.843	11	18	25	8	5
Hiatt, Eugene	1.000	3	2	6	0	3
Hunter, Bellingham	.957	20	23	44	3	10
Kliafas, Yakima	.907	38	51	85	14	15
Magallanes, Bellingham	.981	13	16	36	1	7
Meury, Spokane	1.000	5	9	13	0	2
Nava, Bellingham	.940	46	59	113	11	20
Ordway, Spokane	.923	6	10	14	2	3
Osinski, Southern Oregon	.833	2	5	5	2	1
Perez, Yakima	.899	22	38	51	10	7
Picketts, Southern Oregon	.935	10	7	22	2	1
Sena, Yakima	.857	3	2	4	1	0
Showalter, Boise	.931	45	52	109	12	13
Specyalski, Boise	1.000	2	4	8	0	2
Spires, Everett	.957	14	25	41	3	14
Stewart, Eugene	.860	20	23	57	13	8
TAMAREZ, 2 Bend-53 S.O.	.918	55	68	145	19	22
Ward, Eugene	.899	38	49	102	17	19
White, Yakima	.868	25	32	80	17	18

Triple Plays—Perez.

OUTFIELDERS

Player and Club	Pct.	G.	PO.	A.	E.	DP.
Adams, Spokane	.969	22	28	3	1	0
Anderson, Boise*	.950	24	38	0	2	0
Booker, Southern Oregon	1.000	32	52	4	0	1
Brummer, Yakima*	.957	68	110	2	5	0
Cardenas, Yakima	1.000	10	16	1	0	0
Dalesandro, Boise	.943	42	31	2	2	0
Dattola, Southern Oregon	.957	40	66	0	3	0
Davis, Everett	.667	3	2	0	1	0
Ebanks, Eugene	.750	7	9	0	3	0
Fowler, Yakima	.906	21	29	0	3	0
Garcia, Eugene	.926	51	67	8	6	3
Garrett, Boise*	.930	51	50	3	4	1
Gash, Spokane	.974	62	104	8	3	3
Haber, Eugene	.957	51	63	4	3	1
C. Hart, Southern Oregon	.923	54	79	5	7	1
S. Hart, Everett	.929	19	25	1	2	0
Hawks, Spokane	1.000	2	3	0	0	0
Horan, Bend	1.000	4	1	0	0	0
Hyde, Bend	.967	61	113	6	4	1
Hyzdu, Everett	.963	68	128	2	5	1
Jackson, Everett*	.944	26	50	1	3	0
Kounas, Bellingham	.500	1	0	1	1	0
Krokroskia, Bend	.955	29	41	1	2	0
Lott, Yakima	.904	63	97	7	11	0
Lyons, Bend	.980	33	40	9	1	2
Martinez, Southern Oregon	.957	63	124	9	6	3
McKoy, Spokane	.933	53	92	5	7	0
Mercado, Southern Oregon	1.000	8	5	0	0	0
Mieske, Spokane	.953	72	134	7	7	0
Ordway, Spokane	1.000	4	2	0	0	0
Ostermeyer, Spokane	1.000	12	7	1	0	0
PARTRICK, Boise	.991	66	104	10	1	2
Pearce, Spokane*	.957	15	20	2	1	1
Phillips, Boise*	1.000	1	1	0	0	0
Picketts, Southern Oregon	.667	8	4	0	2	0
Reid, Everett	.939	43	57	5	4	0
Rijo, Yakima	.983	50	110	5	2	3
Ringgold, Everett	.900	18	16	2	2	0
Rolls, Eugene	1.000	3	3	0	0	0
Romay, Bellingham	.982	48	106	4	2	0
Sambel, Eugene	1.000	7	11	1	0	0
Sammons, Bend	.950	56	108	5	6	3
Santana, Boise*	1.000	2	1	1	0	1
Shepperd, Boise	1.000	11	13	0	0	0
Shields, Eugene	.949	70	125	5	7	3
Slater, Eugene*	.891	42	48	1	6	0
Specyalski, Boise	.800	10	12	0	3	0
Staydohar, Boise	.902	35	42	4	5	0
Stephens, Bellingham	.931	48	76	5	6	0
Strong, Boise	1.000	31	31	4	0	0
Terrell, Bellingham	.984	48	50	10	1	2
Troncoso, Yakima	.878	26	33	3	5	0
D. Twitty, Bend	.943	41	63	3	4	0
S. Twitty, Bend	.942	57	76	5	5	1
Varnell, 2 Ever.-23 Bend	.902	25	36	1	4	0
Vega, Everett	.882	27	26	4	4	0
Weber, Everett*	.990	40	97	2	1	0
White, Yakima	.909	8	10	0	1	0
Wilder, Bellingham	.973	34	70	2	2	0
Williams, Boise	1.000	5	2	0	0	0
Young, Southern Oregon	.971	41	62	5	2	0

CATCHERS

Player and Club	Pct.	G.	PO.	A.	E.	DP.	PB.
Adams, Spokane	1.000	1	3	0	0	0	0
Ahrens, Bend	.986	39	234	49	4	3	4
Avent, Bend	.958	41	285	34	14	2	11
Beard, Yakima	.974	29	208	16	6	3	13
Brooks, Eugene	.970	10	89	8	3	0	4
CHRISTOPHERSON, Everett	.991	38	299	34	3	3	9
Elliott, Spokane	.990	25	181	20	2	0	8
Gil, Boise	.991	27	197	17	2	1	5
Grahovac, Bend	.962	6	47	4	2	1	3
Harrel, Eugene	.982	21	138	25	3	4	10
Hawks, Spokane	.973	21	160	18	5	3	8
Helfand, Southern Oregon	.988	49	383	33	5	2	13
Henry, Southern Oregon	1.000	5	43	3	0	0	1
Hoffman, Bellingham	1.000	4	1	0	0	1	0
Jennings, Eugene	.977	28	191	22	5	0	3
Jensen, Everett	.986	25	191	27	3	0	9
Klavitter, Bellingham	1.000	5	10	0	0	0	2
Kluge, Bellingham	.967	34	213	19	8	0	10
Kounas, Bellingham	1.000	1	11	1	0	0	0
Mintz, Boise	.964	8	48	5	2	1	6
Nes Smith, Everett	.986	8	67	5	1	0	3
Ortiz, Yakima	.985	52	392	62	7	5	8
Percival, Boise	.980	28	215	25	5	2	5
Raasch, Bellingham	.988	44	366	45	5	2	8
Rolls, Eugene	.982	31	185	38	4	5	6
Salazar, Southern Oregon	.993	19	123	10	1	2	5
Sievers, Bellingham	.983	16	112	5	2	0	4
Tejero, Boise	.985	39	243	22	4	0	4
Tredway, Southern Oregon	.993	20	145	7	1	0	1
West, Spokane	.984	42	347	20	6	2	6

PITCHERS

Player and Club	Pct.	G.	PO.	A.	E.	DP.
Adam, Bellingham	.929	19	4	9	1	3
Astacio, Yakima	.857	3	4	2	1	0
Ayres, Everett	1.000	22	0	6	0	0
Baez, Eugene*	1.000	11	1	6	0	0
Ball, Boise	1.000	13	0	1	0	0
Bensching, Spokane	.900	32	3	6	1	0
Bishop, Yakima*	1.000	15	3	1	0	0
Blankenship, Bend	.889	27	2	6	1	1
Boker, 7 Ever.-12 Bend	.667	19	1	1	1	0
Bradley, Spokane	.900	15	6	12	2	0
Branconier, Yakima	.889	18	2	6	1	0
Brimhall, Southern Oregon	.667	16	3	3	3	0
Burroughs, Yakima	1.000	12	1	3	0	0
Callistro, Bellingham	.500	22	2	2	4	0
Cantres, Yakima	1.000	24	1	5	0	0
Carlson, Everett	1.000	17	2	3	0	0
Clifford, Southern Oregon	.700	20	1	6	3	0
Connolly, Southern Oregon	1.000	21	2	13	0	2

PITCHERS—Continued

Player and Club	Pct.	G.	PO.	A.	E.	DP.
Converse, Bellingham	.867	12	4	9	2	0
Craft, Southern Oregon	.714	17	2	3	2	0
Craven, Boise	1.000	6	1	2	0	0
Cummings, Bellingham*	.900	6	2	7	1	2
Davis, Eugene	.833	17	2	3	1	0
Delahoya, Yakima	.786	14	1	10	3	1
Devore, Spokane	.889	10	3	5	1	0
Dillon, Southern Oregon	1.000	9	4	4	0	0
Dressendorfer, S. Oregon	1.000	7	1	1	0	0
Duke, Bellingham*	.909	12	3	7	1	0
Ebert, Everett	1.000	5	0	5	0	1
Edenfield, Boise	.867	31	2	11	2	0
Fitzer, Bellingham*	.714	25	0	5	2	0
Franceschi, Eugene*	.889	24	1	7	1	0
Frederick, Eugene	.625	22	2	3	3	0
Fredrickson, Spokane	.833	26	3	7	2	0
Freeman, Yakima	.864	14	1	18	3	1
Gamez, Boise*	.889	14	0	8	1	1
Garland, Southern Oregon	.750	11	2	10	4	0
Garside, Spokane*	.905	17	4	15	2	1
Gibbs, Bend	1.000	4	0	2	0	0
Gill, Eugene	1.000	13	0	1	0	0
Gould, Everett*	.833	17	1	4	1	0
Green, Bellingham	.909	7	1	9	1	1
Gutierrez, Eugene	.875	22	2	5	1	1
Harris, Eugene	.952	15	5	15	1	2
Hathaway, Boise*	.800	15	2	10	3	0
Hays, Spokane	1.000	10	1	5	0	1
Helm, Boise	.625	19	2	3	3	0
Henrikson, 7 Bend-8 Ever.*	.900	15	0	9	1	0
Hierholzer, Eugene	1.000	32	1	7	0	0
Hill, Bend	1.000	6	1	1	0	1
Holman, Eugene	1.000	17	4	3	0	0
Huffman, Everett	1.000	21	0	7	0	1
Huslig, Everett	.667	2	0	2	1	0
Johns, Southern Oregon*	1.000	6	0	2	0	0
Kelly, Yakima*	.625	17	1	4	3	1
King, Bellingham	1.000	6	1	5	0	0
Klonoski, Bend*	.889	26	2	14	2	0
Lachemann, Boise	1.000	2	0	2	0	0
Leftwich, Boise	.950	15	8	11	1	1
Lodding, Bellingham	.905	13	8	11	2	1
Long, Eugene*	1.000	16	3	9	0	0
Madsen, Yakima	.750	13	0	3	1	0
Magill, Bellingham	.742	15	7	16	8	0
McCray, Boise	1.000	17	3	2	0	0
McDonald, Bellingham*	1.000	8	1	2	0	0
McGehee, Everett	.929	15	2	11	1	1
McLeod, Everett	1.000	22	2	8	0	1
Miller, Bend	1.000	9	4	4	0	0
Mimbs, Yakima*	1.000	12	3	11	0	2
Minder, Bend	1.000	9	3	6	0	2
Mintz, Yakima	1.000	20	1	3	0	0
Mortensen, Spokane*	.833	18	1	9	2	0
E. Myers, Southern Oregon	.750	24	0	6	2	1
M. Myers, Everett*	.909	15	1	9	1	0
R. Myers, Eugene	.818	6	4	5	2	1
O'Connor, Yakima*	1.000	21	1	4	0	0
Painter, Spokane*	.947	23	2	16	1	2
Pakele, Boise	.933	15	7	7	1	0
Patrick, Yakima*	1.000	11	0	4	0	0
Peltzer, Everett*	1.000	18	3	8	0	0
Pena, Bend	.700	8	1	6	3	0
Perez, Yakima	1.000	24	2	9	0	1
P. Peters, Southern Oregon	.727	11	4	4	3	0
T. Peters, Eugene	1.000	15	3	7	0	1
Pineda, Eugene	1.000	20	7	10	0	1
Pollard, Eugene	.810	14	3	14	4	1
Potter, Bend	.500	12	1	0	1	0
Powers, Boise	.929	15	10	16	2	0
Rea, Eugene	1.000	9	1	2	0	0
Revenig, Southern Oregon	.875	24	3	4	1	0
Reyes, Bend	1.000	21	0	10	0	0
Rivera, Bellingham	1.000	3	1	2	0	0
Ross, Bend	.960	16	6	18	1	1
Rosselli, Everett*	.909	15	2	8	1	1
Russell, Bend	.800	15	1	3	1	1
Sampson, Yakima	1.000	3	2	2	0	0
Sanders, Spokane	1.000	3	1	3	0	1
Schanz, Bellingham	1.000	7	2	0	0	0
Scharff, Southern Oregon	1.000	4	0	3	0	0
Scott, Boise	1.000	27	0	6	0	0
Search, Boise*	.600	16	0	3	2	0
Shaw, Southern Oregon*	.905	17	3	16	2	0
Silcox, Spokane	.926	16	10	15	2	1
Stenz, Boise*	1.000	18	0	2	0	0
Sudbury, Southern Oregon	.769	7	2	8	3	3
Swingle, Boise	1.000	14	1	1	0	0
TATIS, Yakima	1.000	13	3	16	0	1
Tegtmeier, Bellingham	.857	17	0	6	1	0
Thibault, Spokane*	.923	22	2	10	1	0
Tripp, Southern Oregon	1.000	16	2	3	0	0
Van Poppel, Southern Oregon	1.000	5	1	0	0	0
Vizzini, Southern Oregon*	.750	16	1	2	1	0
Wagner, Bend*	.882	21	1	14	2	1
Waldron, Spokane*	1.000	21	2	8	0	0
Wanke, Bend*	1.000	6	1	1	0	0
Williams, Bellingham	1.000	17	2	4	0	1
Yianacopolus, Bellingham*	.875	23	4	10	2	0
Yockey, Everett*	1.000	23	1	5	0	0
Youngblood, Bellingham	.800	17	2	2	1	0
Zancanaro, Southern Oregon*	.750	10	0	3	1	0

The following players did not have any fielding statistics at the positions indicated or appeared only as a designated hitter, pinch-hitter or pinch-runner: Bish, ss; Cobb, p; Flanagan, p; Frias, 3b; Gil, of; Hawks, p; Huisman, p; Hunt, of; James, p; Kotchman, of; Lanfranco, 1b, ss; Ledinsky, of; Markiewicz, ph; Martinez, p; McKoy, 2b; Musset, p; Nielson, p; Olson, p; T. Perez, p; G. Reid, ph, dh; Shepperd, 3b; Sims, p; Specyalski, 1b; Whatley, p.

CLUB PITCHING

Club	ERA.	G.	CG.	ShO.	Sv.	IP.	H.	R.	ER.	HR.	HB.	BB.	Int. BB.	SO.	WP.	Bk.
Boise	2.43	76	4	10	21	678.2	570	250	183	26	21	225	15	664	38	16
Southern Oregon	3.32	76	1	8	15	683.2	586	325	252	31	21	293	15	677	53	28
Eugene	3.62	76	2	2	15	674.1	636	372	271	38	51	306	4	595	70	25
Bellingham	3.67	76	6	4	9	680.0	577	342	277	31	31	353	3	624	62	21
Spokane	3.86	76	2	4	30	690.0	646	360	296	36	32	290	2	691	46	16
Yakima	3.91	76	2	17	678.1	642	403	295	30	38	335	15	638	51	14
Everett	4.13	76	4	3	13	669.0	662	369	307	48	33	305	3	664	66	17
Bend	4.60	76	1	2	18	667.1	701	460	341	52	31	375	5	549	68	12

PITCHERS' RECORDS

(Leading Qualifiers for Earned-Run Average Leadership—61 or More Innings)

*Throws lefthanded.

Pitcher—Club	W.	L.	Pct.	ERA.	G.	GS.	CG.	GF.	ShO.	Sv.	IP.	H.	R.	ER.	HR.	HB.	BB.	Int. BB.	SO.	WP.
Adam, Bellingham	4	4	.500	1.43	19	7	4	7	1	1	69.1	40	13	11	0	4	22	1	76	6
Hathaway, Boise*	8	2	.800	1.47	15	15	0	0	0	0	86.0	56	18	14	1	2	25	0	113	7
Painter, Spokane*	7	3	.700	1.51	23	1	0	10	0	3	71.2	45	18	12	4	2	15	0	104	3
Doug Peters, Eugene	7	2	.778	1.73	15	14	0	0	0	0	83.0	76	23	16	2	4	20	0	74	10
Leftwich, Boise	8	2	.800	1.86	15	15	0	0	0	0	92.0	88	36	19	0	1	22	1	81	3
Powers, Boise	7	3	.700	2.56	15	15	4	0	3	0	102.0	87	40	29	5	1	19	0	76	1
Pakele, Boise	5	3	.625	2.78	15	13	0	0	0	0	74.1	76	28	23	2	3	7	0	52	1
Henrikson, 7 Bend-8 Ever.*	10	3	.769	3.08	15	15	1	0	0	0	102.1	103	43	35	5	4	39	0	77	6
Pollard, Eugene	3	3	.500	3.34	14	14	1	0	0	0	70.0	46	35	26	4	6	42	0	77	7
Bradley, Spokane	7	2	.778	3.44	15	15	0	0	0	0	89.0	68	37	34	7	5	43	0	91	1

Departmental Leaders: G—Bensching, Hierholzer, 32; W—Henrikson, 10; L—McGehee, 8; Pct.—Bensching, .889; GS—Garside, 17; CG—Adam, Powers, 4; GF—Hierholzer, 26; ShO—Powers, 3; Sv.—Blankenship, 12; IP—Henrikson, 102.1; H—Garside, 111; R—Ross, 62; ER—Ross, 53; HR—Ross, 11; HB—Delahoya, Freeman, Silcox, 7; BB—Magill, 52; IBB—E. Myers, 7; SO—Hathaway, 113; WP—McGehee, 16.

(All Pitchers—Listed Alphabetically)

Pitcher—Club	W.	L.	Pct.	ERA.	G.	GS.	CG.	GF.	ShO.	Sv.	IP.	H.	R.	ER.	HR.	HB.	BB.	Int. BB.	SO.	WP.
Adam, Bellingham	4	4	.500	1.43	19	7	4	7	1	1	69.1	40	13	11	0	4	22	1	76	6
Astacio, Yakima	2	0	1.000	1.74	3	3	0	0	0	0	20.2	9	8	4	0	2	4	0	22	3
Ayres, Everett	3	3	.500	1.73	22	0	0	18	0	4	36.1	25	10	7	1	3	24	1	42	5
Baez, Eugene*	0	3	.000	3.40	11	8	0	1	0	0	39.2	38	22	15	3	0	25	0	32	4

Pitcher—Club	W.	L.	Pct.	ERA.	G.	GS.	CG.	GF.	ShO.	Sv.	IP.	H.	R.	ER.	HR.	HB.	BB.	Int. BB.	SO.	WP.
Ball, Boise	2	0	1.000	5.02	13	0	0	7	0	0	14.1	17	11	8	3	1	6	2	12	2
Bensching, Spokane	8	1	.889	1.54	32	0	0	25	0	10	58.1	45	14	10	2	2	14	1	78	7
Bishop, Yakima*	0	2	.000	4.08	15	0	0	3	0	0	17.2	18	11	8	1	1	15	3	18	2
Blankenship, Bend	2	4	.333	1.36	27	0	0	25	0	12	46.1	41	11	7	3	3	11	2	54	6
Boker, 7 Ever.-12 Bend	1	2	.333	5.50	19	0	0	9	0	0	34.1	35	25	21	0	5	27	0	33	7
Bradley, Spokane	7	2	.778	3.44	15	15	2	0	0	0	89.0	68	37	34	7	5	43	0	91	1
Branconier, Yakima	1	4	.200	5.28	18	6	0	2	0	1	61.1	85	44	36	4	3	16	1	35	3
Brimhall, Southern Oregon	2	6	.250	5.10	16	16	0	0	0	0	67.0	74	49	38	4	0	44	0	64	10
Burroughs, Yakima	0	1	.000	9.64	12	0	0	4	0	0	14.0	10	18	15	1	3	25	0	17	9
Callistro, Bellingham	2	2	.500	5.55	22	0	0	10	0	2	35.2	35	28	22	3	6	34	1	35	3
Cantres, Yakima	3	2	.600	3.89	24	0	0	13	0	3	41.2	29	20	18	2	3	19	1	34	2
Carlson, Everett	2	6	.250	5.34	17	11	0	3	0	0	62.1	60	42	37	5	1	33	1	77	9
Clifford, Southern Oregon	2	1	.667	3.93	20	0	0	9	0	0	50.1	42	30	22	5	2	26	1	52	5
Cobb, Boise	0	0	.000	0.00	2	0	0	1	0	0	4.0	3	0	0	0	0	1	0	6	0
Connolly, Southern Oregon	6	3	.667	3.33	21	1	0	9	0	2	46.0	40	19	17	1	2	20	2	45	3
Converse, Bellingham	2	4	.333	3.92	12	12	0	0	0	0	66.2	50	31	29	1	2	32	0	75	2
Craft, Southern Oregon	3	3	.500	4.19	17	1	0	2	0	0	34.1	33	20	16	1	3	20	1	24	4
Craven, Boise	1	0	1.000	3.77	6	0	0	0	0	0	14.1	14	6	6	1	1	6	0	9	3
Cummings, Bellingham*	1	1	.500	2.12	6	6	0	0	0	0	34.0	25	11	8	1	0	9	0	39	2
Davis, Eugene	3	2	.600	7.07	17	0	0	5	0	0	28.0	34	24	22	1	2	16	0	22	2
Delahoya, Yakima	3	5	.375	4.46	14	14	0	0	0	0	70.2	65	52	35	2	7	39	2	71	9
Devore, Spokane	1	3	.250	3.07	10	5	0	1	0	1	44.0	33	16	15	1	0	20	0	34	1
Dillon, Southern Oregon	4	1	.800	1.54	9	7	1	0	1	0	35.0	25	9	6	1	0	5	0	31	0
Dressendorfer, Southern Oregon	0	1	.000	2.33	7	4	0	0	0	0	19.1	18	7	5	0	1	2	0	22	1
Duke, Bellingham*	4	5	.444	3.71	12	11	0	0	0	0	60.2	57	30	25	1	1	46	0	40	3
Ebert, Everett	1	1	.500	5.68	5	5	1	0	0	0	25.1	25	19	16	1	2	23	0	21	5
Edenfield, Boise	8	4	.667	1.65	31	0	0	24	0	9	54.2	38	15	10	1	4	17	4	57	2
Fitzer, Bellingham*	5	1	.833	2.70	25	0	0	21	0	3	43.1	24	15	13	3	0	21	0	62	0
Flanagan, Everett	0	0	.000	0.00	4	0	0	3	0	2	2.2	2	1	0	0	0	0	0	2	0
Franceschi, Eugene*	0	4	.000	4.05	24	0	0	11	0	2	33.1	31	21	15	4	4	20	1	38	10
Frederick, Eugene	1	6	.143	3.67	22	0	0	7	0	0	34.1	33	26	14	1	2	19	1	26	4
Fredrickson, Spokane	3	3	.500	3.28	26	1	0	15	0	8	46.2	35	22	17	3	2	18	1	61	6
Freeman, Yakima	2	7	.222	4.00	14	14	1	0	0	0	83.1	94	58	37	4	7	28	1	44	11
Gamez, Boise*	3	0	1.000	2.91	14	7	0	0	0	0	46.1	42	19	15	3	2	15	2	38	5
Garland, Southern Oregon	4	3	.571	3.08	11	9	0	0	0	0	49.2	40	21	17	3	1	15	0	42	5
Garside, Spokane*	8	3	.727	5.66	17	17	0	0	0	0	82.2	111	60	52	4	1	22	0	57	3
Gibbs, Bend	0	0	.000	0.00	4	0	0	3	0	2	11.0	1	0	0	0	1	3	0	18	0
Gill, Eugene	0	1	.000	4.39	13	0	0	6	0	3	26.2	28	13	13	4	4	6	0	27	2
Gould, Everett*	0	1	.000	3.60	17	0	0	10	0	0	30.0	31	19	12	2	1	9	0	36	0
Green, Bellingham	1	3	.250	2.17	7	7	0	0	0	0	37.1	24	19	9	2	0	19	0	34	3
Gutierrez, Eugene	2	2	.500	3.71	22	1	0	6	0	0	43.2	39	24	18	1	4	20	0	44	5
Harris, Eugene	4	5	.444	4.41	15	15	0	0	0	0	69.1	74	46	34	5	4	28	0	46	6
Hathaway, Boise*	8	2	.800	1.47	15	15	0	0	0	0	86.0	56	18	14	1	2	25	0	113	7
Hawks, Spokane	0	0	.000	7.71	2	0	0	2	0	0	2.1	5	2	2	0	0	0	0	2	0
Hays, Spokane	2	0	1.000	4.15	10	2	0	1	0	0	30.1	26	18	14	0	4	14	0	30	3
Helm, Boise	3	1	.750	2.21	19	3	0	1	0	0	40.2	31	13	10	2	3	24	0	48	1
Henrikson, 7 Bend-8 Ever.*	10	3	.769	3.08	15	15	1	0	0	0	102.1	103	43	35	5	4	39	0	77	6
Hierholzer, Eugene	4	5	.444	2.23	32	0	0	26	0	9	40.1	36	16	10	2	6	17	1	39	6
Hill, Bend	0	0	.000	2.38	6	0	0	3	0	0	11.1	12	3	3	0	0	5	0	12	1
Holman, Eugene	0	3	.000	4.78	17	4	0	3	0	0	43.1	43	28	23	3	4	17	0	31	4
Huffman, Everett	1	0	1.000	3.66	21	0	0	10	0	2	39.1	41	20	16	1	3	12	0	30	3
Huisman, Everett	0	0	.000	4.50	1	0	0	0	0	0	2.0	3	1	1	0	0	2	0	2	1
Huslig, Everett	0	1	.000	4.50	2	1	0	0	0	0	8.0	9	8	4	1	0	4	0	9	0
James, Boise*	0	1	.000	13.50	1	1	0	0	0	0	3.1	8	5	5	0	0	3	0	3	0
Johns, Southern Oregon*	0	2	.000	5.73	6	2	0	4	0	1	11.0	13	9	7	0	0	11	1	9	2
Kelly, Yakima*	2	2	.500	4.56	17	0	0	7	0	1	23.2	29	16	12	1	1	15	0	25	0
King, Bellingham*	3	2	.600	4.78	6	6	0	0	0	0	32.0	37	18	17	3	0	10	0	27	1
Klonoski, Bend*	7	4	.636	2.81	26	1	0	15	0	2	48.0	42	21	15	3	1	12	1	61	5
Lachemann, Boise	0	1	.000	1.50	2	0	0	1	0	0	6.0	4	1	1	0	0	3	0	3	2
Leftwich, Boise	8	2	.800	1.86	15	15	0	0	0	0	92.0	88	36	19	0	1	22	1	81	3
Lodding, Bellingham	1	5	.167	5.21	13	11	0	2	0	0	57.0	58	42	33	3	5	42	1	47	14
Long, Eugene*	2	4	.333	3.66	16	10	0	4	0	1	64.0	68	32	26	5	6	17	1	58	1
Madsen, Yakima	1	0	1.000	3.38	13	1	0	4	0	1	24.0	17	15	9	2	0	22	1	23	1
Magill, Bellingham	4	7	.364	4.18	15	15	2	0	1	0	84.0	72	48	39	5	5	52	0	49	11
Martinez, Southern Oregon	0	0	.000	45.00	1	0	0	1	0	0	1.0	5	5	5	0	0	2	0	0	0
McCray, Boise	1	1	.500	3.65	17	7	0	3	0	0	37.0	27	24	15	2	2	31	1	38	2
McDonald, Bellingham*	1	0	1.000	1.13	8	0	0	1	0	0	16.0	11	5	2	1	0	8	0	12	0
McGehee, Everett	4	8	.333	4.76	15	14	1	0	0	0	73.2	74	47	39	6	4	38	0	86	16
McLeod, Everett	2	5	.286	4.56	22	2	0	7	0	2	49.1	33	28	25	6	6	29	0	43	4
Miller, Bend	1	6	.143	7.88	9	9	0	0	0	0	40.0	52	51	35	5	2	37	0	18	3
Mimbs, Yakima*	4	3	.571	3.88	12	12	0	0	0	0	67.1	58	36	29	5	3	39	0	72	1
Minder, Bend	0	1	.000	4.24	9	6	0	1	0	0	40.1	40	23	19	4	1	30	1	29	5
Mintz, Yakima	2	3	.400	2.42	20	0	0	12	0	3	26.0	21	9	7	1	1	16	1	38	2
Mortensen, Spokane*	4	2	.667	3.77	18	6	0	8	0	4	59.2	54	29	25	5	1	18	0	49	4
Musset, Boise	0	0	.000	0.00	1	0	0	1	0	0	0.2	0	0	0	0	0	1	0	0	0
E. Myers, Southern Oregon	1	2	.333	2.93	24	0	0	14	0	5	43.0	39	16	14	0	3	12	7	44	1
M. Myers, Everett*	4	5	.444	3.90	15	14	1	0	0	0	85.1	91	43	37	9	5	30	0	73	7
R. Myers, Eugene	0	2	.000	1.19	6	4	0	0	0	0	22.2	19	9	3	2	0	13	0	17	1
Nielson, Bend	1	1	.500	4.70	2	0	0	2	0	0	7.2	8	4	4	0	0	5	1	7	0
O'Connor, Yakima*	2	2	.500	2.25	21	0	0	9	0	2	36.0	24	11	9	1	3	18	1	38	2
Olson, Yakima*	0	0	.000	0.00	1	0	0	0	0	0	1.0	1	0	0	0	0	0	0	1	0
Painter, Spokane*	7	3	.700	1.51	23	1	0	10	0	3	71.2	45	18	12	4	2	15	0	104	3
Pakele, Boise	5	3	.625	2.78	15	13	0	0	0	0	74.1	76	28	23	2	3	7	0	52	1
Patrick, Boise*	5	2	.714	3.09	11	10	0	1	0	0	58.1	56	34	20	2	0	26	0	66	2
Peltzer, Everett*	3	1	.750	4.31	18	5	0	4	0	0	48.0	58	30	23	2	0	23	1	39	5
Pena, Bend	2	2	.500	2.77	8	6	0	2	0	0	39.0	32	20	12	3	1	17	0	23	4
P. Perez, Yakima	6	3	.667	2.34	24	0	0	18	0	6	42.1	24	14	11	2	2	18	4	47	1
T. Perez, Spokane	0	0	.000	6.75	1	0	0	0	0	0	2.2	5	2	2	1	0	0	0	2	0
Don Peters, Southern Oregon	1	1	.500	0.76	11	7	0	3	0	0	35.2	20	7	3	0	0	17	0	34	5
Doug Peters, Eugene	7	2	.778	1.73	15	14	1	0	0	0	83.0	76	23	16	2	4	20	0	74	10
Pineda, Eugene	2	0	1.000	3.57	20	0	0	4	0	0	45.1	39	29	18	0	3	24	0	43	5
Pollard, Eugene	3	3	.500	3.34	14	14	1	0	0	0	70.0	46	35	26	4	6	42	0	77	7

Pitcher—Club	W.	L.	Pct.	ERA.	G.	GS.	CG.	GF.	ShO.	Sv.	IP.	H.	R.	ER.	HR.	HB.	BB.	Int. BB.	SO.	WP.
Potter, Bend	0	0	.000	8.39	12	0	0	5	0	0	34.1	53	47	32	2	2	31	0	27	9
Powers, Boise	7	3	.700	2.56	15	15	4	0	3	0	102.0	87	40	29	5	1	19	0	76	1
Rea, Eugene	2	4	.333	5.28	9	6	0	1	0	0	30.2	32	24	18	1	2	22	0	21	3
Revenig, Southern Oregon	3	2	.600	0.81	24	0	0	14	0	6	44.2	33	13	4	2	0	9	2	46	1
Reyes, Bend	3	7	.300	3.67	23	5	1	1	0	0	76.0	80	41	31	9	3	23	0	64	5
Rivera, Bellingham	0	0	.000	0.00	3	0	0	1	0	1	5.2	2	0	0	0	0	1	0	6	0
Ross, Bend	5	7	.417	5.61	16	16	0	0	0	0	85.0	93	62	53	11	3	44	0	42	4
Rosselli, Everett*	4	4	.500	4.71	15	15	0	0	0	0	78.1	87	47	41	10	0	29	0	90	4
Russell, Bend	1	4	.200	6.02	15	13	0	1	0	0	64.1	78	57	43	3	4	45	0	34	4
Sampson, Yakima	2	0	1.000	4.50	3	3	0	0	0	0	16.0	14	12	8	1	1	11	0	11	0
Sanders, Spokane	2	1	.667	0.95	3	3	0	0	0	0	19.0	12	3	2	0	2	5	0	21	0
Schanz, Bellingham	1	0	1.000	4.50	7	1	0	3	0	0	8.0	7	4	4	0	0	3	0	3	0
Scharff, Southern Oregon	0	0	.000	12.54	4	2	0	0	0	0	9.1	13	16	13	1	0	14	0	12	1
Scott, Boise	2	1	.667	1.34	27	0	0	11	0	6	53.2	41	11	8	3	0	20	1	57	5
Search, Boise*	4	2	.667	2.04	16	0	0	5	0	0	17.2	14	6	4	0	0	8	2	21	2
Shaw, Southern Oregon*	4	6	.400	3.53	17	9	0	3	0	0	66.1	53	28	26	4	3	30	0	74	5
Silcox, Spokane	3	1	.750	6.43	16	16	0	0	0	0	71.1	79	58	51	3	7	43	0	61	6
Sims, Bend	0	0	.000	2.70	3	0	0	2	0	1	3.1	2	2	1	0	0	1	0	2	0
Stenz, Boise*	1	1	.500	7.50	18	0	0	6	0	0	18.0	19	16	15	3	1	13	1	25	2
Sudbury, Southern Oregon	2	2	.500	2.91	7	5	0	0	0	0	34.0	26	13	11	1	0	13	0	29	1
Swingle, Boise	0	1	.000	0.66	14	0	0	12	0	6	13.2	5	1	1	0	4	1	25	0
Tatis, Yakima	1	4	.200	4.48	13	13	1	0	1	0	74.1	88	45	37	1	1	24	0	76	3
Tegtmeier, Bellingham	1	1	.500	2.21	17	0	0	3	0	0	36.2	35	9	9	1	0	10	0	30	1
Thibault, Spokane*	3	4	.429	3.84	22	9	0	8	0	4	65.2	67	36	28	4	3	38	0	58	7
Tripp, Southern Oregon	3	2	.600	4.28	16	0	0	4	0	0	40.0	39	26	19	3	1	15	1	34	5
Van Poppel, Southern Oregon	1	1	.500	1.13	5	5	0	0	0	0	24.0	10	5	3	1	2	9	0	32	0
Vizzini, Southern Oregon*	1	0	1.000	2.20	16	0	0	12	0	1	28.2	19	10	7	1	2	16	0	41	1
Wagner, Bend*	2	6	.250	5.31	21	7	0	9	0	1	62.2	64	52	37	4	4	45	0	69	10
Waldron, Spokane*	1	4	.200	6.17	21	1	0	4	0	0	46.2	61	45	32	2	3	40	0	43	5
Wanke, Bend*	0	3	.000	4.88	6	6	0	0	0	0	27.2	27	22	15	2	2	26	0	25	5
Whatley, Everett	0	1	.000	4.11	8	0	0	0	0	0	15.1	16	8	7	0	0	8	0	15	1
Williams, Bellingham	0	1	.000	4.55	17	0	0	5	0	2	31.2	29	18	16	1	2	9	0	23	2
Yianacopolus, Bellingham*	2	5	.286	4.46	23	0	0	11	0	0	36.1	37	22	18	5	1	18	0	42	0
Yockey, Everett*	5	2	.714	3.86	23	1	0	14	0	3	46.2	45	22	20	2	3	15	0	53	0
Youngblood, Bellingham	0	0	.000	7.71	17	0	0	6	0	0	25.2	34	29	22	1	5	17	0	24	14
Zancanaro, Southern Oregon*	3	0	1.000	3.86	10	8	0	0	0	0	44.1	44	22	19	2	1	13	0	42	3

BALKS—Converse, 9; Craft, Gutierrez, 6 each; Carlson, Hathaway, Long, McGehee, Yockey, 5 each; Fredrickson, Pakele, Zancanaro, 4 each; Branconier, Cummings, Freeman, E. Myers, Painter, 3 each; Ball, Bensching, Boker, Davis, Devore, Gill, Green, Harris, Holman, Johns, Kelly, Leftwich, Mimbs, Minder, Pena, Powers, Revenig, Scharff, Tegtmeier, Tripp, Waldron, 2 each; Adam, Ayres, Bishop, Connolly, Dillon, Frederick, Garland, Helm, Henrikson, Huffman, King, Klonoski, Lodding, Martinez, McDonald, Miller, Mintz, R. Myers, Patrick, Doug Peters, Pineda, Pollard, Potter, Rea, Sanders, Shaw, Silcox, Sudbury, Tatis, Thibault, Vizzini, Wagner, Wanke, Williams, 1 each.

COMBINATION SHUTOUTS—Duke-Tegtmeier-Yianacopolus, Green-Youngblood-Adam, Bellingham; Ross-Reyes-Blankenship, Russell-Klonoski-Blankenship, Bend; Gamez-Helm-Stenz-Ball, Gamez-Scott-Swingle, Hathaway-Helm-Scott, Hathaway-McCray-Search, Hathaway-Scott, Hathaway-Search-Swingle, Powers-Search-Swingle, Boise; Harris-Hierholzer, Myers-Long, Eugene; Carlson-Huffman, Henrikson-Yockey, McGehee-Ayres, Everett; Brimhall-Connolly-Revenig, Brimhall-Shaw-Myers, Dillon-Clifford-Tripp, Garland-Dressendorfer-Peters, Peters-Tripp-Myers, Sudbury-Revenig, Van Poppel-Craft-Myers, Southern Oregon; Sanders-Bensching 2, Mortensen-Waldron, Silcox-Bensching, Spokane; Astacio-Kelly, Yakima.

NO-HIT GAMES—None.

South Atlantic League

CLASS A

CHAMPIONSHIP WINNERS IN PREVIOUS YEARS

1948—Lincolnton* .627	1967—Spartanburg .730	1979—Greenwood‡ .565
1949—Newton-Conover .667	Spartanburg .567	Spartanburg .525
Ruth'ford Co. (2nd)† .627	1968—Spartanburg .597	1980—Greensboro .590
1950—Newton-Conover .627	Greenwood‡ .597	Charleston .561
Lenoir (2nd)† .626	1969—Greenwood‡ .587	1981—Greensboro‡ .695
1951—Morganton .645	Shelby .565	Greenwood .549
Shelby (2nd)† .604	1970—Greenville .576	1982—Greensboro‡ .681
1952—Lincolnton .649	Greenville .619	Florence .546
Shelby (2nd)† .645	1971—Greenwood .631	1983—Columbia .620
1953-59—League inactive.	Greenwood .759	Gastonia‡ .587
1960—Lexington .707	1972—Spartanburg‡ .788	1984—Charleston .549
Salisbury (2nd)† .650	Greenville .652	Asheville‡ .510
1961—Salisbury .627	1973—Spartanburg‡ .646	1985—Florence‡ .599
Shelby (4th)† .481	Gastonia .619	Greensboro .540
1962—Statesville .563	1974—Gastonia .606	1986—Columbia‡ .682
Statesville .700	Gastonia .672	Asheville .643
1963—Greenville† .576	1975—Spartanburg .543	1987—Asheville .655
Salisbury .631	Spartanburg .614	Myrtle Beach‡ .597
1964—Rock Hill .672	1976—Asheville .544	1988—Charleston (S.C.) .616
Salisbury‡ .631	Greenwood‡ .600	Spartanburg‡ .500
1965—Salisbury .641	1977—Greenwood .557	1989—Gastonia .657
Rock Hill‡ .603	Gastonia‡ .590	Augusta‡ .535
1966—Spartanburg .682	1978—Greenwood .614	
Spartanburg .767	Greenwood .565	

*Won championship and four-club playoff. †Won four-club playoff. ‡Won split-season playoff. (NOTE—Known as Western Carolina League from 1948 through 1962 and known as Western Carolinas League through 1979.)

STANDING OF CLUBS AT CLOSE OF FIRST HALF, JUNE 16

NORTHERN DIVISION

Club	W.	L.	T.	Pct.	G.B.
Fayetteville (Tigers)	46	26	0	.639	....
Gastonia (Rangers)	44	28	0	.611	2
Spartanburg (Phillies)	37	34	0	.521	8½
Charleston (WVa.)(Reds)	30	41	0	.423	15½
Greensboro (Yankees)	29	43	0	.403	17
Asheville (Astros)	28	43	0	.394	17½

SOUTHERN DIVISION

Club	W.	L.	T.	Pct.	G.B.
Columbia (Mets)	46	26	0	.639	....
Augusta (Pirates)	41	30	0	.577	4½
Myrtle Beach (Blue Jays)	39	31	0	.557	6
Sumter (Braves)	38	34	0	.528	8
Savannah (Cardinals)	30	41	0	.423	15½
Charleston (SC)(Padres)	20	51	0	.282	25½

STANDING OF CLUBS AT CLOSE OF SECOND HALF, AUGUST 30

NORTHERN DIVISION

Club	W.	L.	T.	Pct.	G.B.
Charleston (WVa.)(Reds)	47	25	0	.653	....
Gastonia (Rangers)	38	33	0	.535	8½
Asheville (Astros)	38	34	0	.528	9
Fayetteville (Tigers)	36	35	0	.507	10½
Greensboro (Yankees)	30	42	0	.417	17
Spartanburg (Phillies)	26	44	0	.371	20

SOUTHERN DIVISION

Club	W.	L.	T.	Pct.	G.B.
Savannah (Cardinals)	43	27	0	.614	....
Myrtle Beach (Blue Jays)	38	32	0	.543	5
Columbia (Mets)	37	34	0	.521	6½
Sumter (Braves)	35	35	0	.500	8
Augusta (Pirates)	32	40	0	.444	12
Charleston (SC)(Padres)	26	45	0	.366	17½

COMPOSITE STANDING OF CLUBS AT CLOSE OF SEASON, AUGUST 30

Club	Col.	Gas.	Fay.	M.B.	CWV	Sav.	Sum.	Aug.	Ash.	Spar.	Gbr.	ChSC	W.	L.	T.	Pct.	G.B.
Columbia (Mets)	....	3	5	9	6	9	7	11	4	8	8	13	83	60	0	.580	....
Gastonia (Rangers)	7	....	10	5	7	7	5	7	9	9	11	5	82	61	0	.573	1
Fayetteville (Tigers)	5	10	....	5	7	5	7	6	10	10	12	5	82	61	0	.573	1
Myrtle Beach (Blue Jays)	6	4	5	....	4	10	12	7	4	6	6	13	77	63	0	.550	4½
Charleston (WVa.)(Reds)	4	9	9	5	....	4	6	4	6	10	15	5	77	66	0	.538	6
Savannah (Cardinals)	7	3	5	6	6	....	7	9	8	4	4	13	73	68	0	.518	9
Sumter (Braves)	9	5	2	8	4	8	....	8	8	5	4	12	73	69	0	.514	9½
Augusta (Pirates)	9	3	4	9	6	7	8	....	5	5	10	13	73	70	0	.510	10
Asheville (Astros)	6	7	6	5	10	2	2	2	....	10	8	8	66	77	0	.462	17
Spartanburg (Phillies)	2	7	6	4	6	5	5	5	10	....	8	5	63	78	0	.447	19
Greensboro (Yankees)	2	5	4	4	5	3	6	6	8	8	....	7	59	85	0	.410	24½
Charleston (SC)(Padres)	3	5	5	3	5	4	4	6	2	4	3	....	46	96	0	.324	36½

Playoffs—Charleston (WV) defeated Fayetteville, two games to none; Savannah defeated Columbia, two games to none; Charleston (WV) defeated Savannah, three games to none, to win league championship.

Regular-Season Attendance—Asheville, 101,193; Augusta, 125,105; Charleston (SC), 76,133; Charleston (WV), 152,359; Columbia, 99,385; Fayetteville, 95,040; Gastonia, 48,767; Greensboro, 153,232; Myrtle Beach, 71,598; Savannah, 94,686; Spartanburg, 45,104; Sumter, 37,412. Total—1,100,014. Playoffs (7 games)—11,386. All-Star Game—3,089.

Managers—Asheville, Frank Cacciatore; Augusta, Lee Driggers; Charleston (SC), Jack Krol; Charleston (WV), Jim Lett; Columbia, Bill Stein; Fayetteville, Gene Roof; Gastonia, Orlando Gomez; Greensboro, Brian Butterfield; Myrtle Beach, Mike Fischlin; Savannah, Rick Colbert; Spartanburg, Mel Roberts; Sumter, Ned Yost.

All-Star Team—1B—Ryan Klesko, Sumter; 2B—David Hajek, Asheville; 3B—Tim Howard, Columbia; SS—Tito Navarro, Columbia; OF—Pat Howell, Columbia; OF—Scott Pose, Charleston (WV); OF—Tony Scruggs, Gastonia; C—Brook Fordyce, Columbia; DH—Mike Burton, Gastonia; RHP— Tim Pugh, Charleston (WV); LHP—Randy Marshall, Fayetteville; Manager of the Year—Bill Stein, Columbia; Most Valuable Player—Tim Howard, Columbia; Most Outstanding Pitcher—Randy Marshall, Fayetteville; Most Outstanding Major League Prospect—Ryan Klesko, Sumter.

(Compiled by Howe Sportsdata International, Boston, Mass.)

CLUB BATTING

Club	Pct.	G.	AB.	R.	OR.	H.	TB.	2B.	3B.	HR.	RBI.	SH.	SF.	HP.	BB.	Int. BB.	SO.	SB.	CS.	LOB.
Columbia	.277	143	4916	732	603	1362	1858	211	42	67	608	28	46	37	431	20	908	248	85	1008
Augusta	.263	143	4835	683	663	1272	1682	174	52	44	597	22	48	35	596	27	948	134	73	1118
Asheville	.260	143	4665	638	699	1215	1686	218	32	63	564	27	39	62	481	23	960	207	95	963
Charleston (W.Va.)..	.252	143	4600	657	528	1157	1511	200	32	30	560	54	42	56	629	25	772	157	65	1084
Gastonia	.245	143	4661	627	511	1143	1659	212	23	86	536	55	38	51	512	17	954	152	91	1001
Myrtle Beach	.244	140	4545	610	548	1109	1636	190	23	97	529	37	32	61	478	13	1024	89	51	948
Sumter	.240	142	4603	607	529	1106	1579	186	40	69	493	51	51	57	579	22	894	147	82	1050
Fayetteville	.234	143	4584	601	552	1072	1429	153	36	44	497	41	43	45	582	26	921	80	54	1013
Spartanburg	.232	141	4664	530	573	1084	1429	155	32	42	449	37	26	44	477	21	905	74	41	1016
Greensboro	.227	144	4657	547	670	1058	1459	180	28	55	437	39	25	45	566	23	1077	166	86	997
Savannah	.227	141	4577	552	619	1038	1437	164	23	63	442	36	34	56	462	23	898	169	99	900
Charleston (S.C.)	.223	142	4601	473	762	1026	1376	156	31	44	416	27	30	62	459	10	958	102	59	1024

INDIVIDUAL BATTING
(Leading Qualifiers for Batting Championship—389 or More Plate Appearances)

*Bats lefthanded.   †Switch-hitter.

Player and Club	Pct.	G.	AB.	R.	H.	TB.	2B.	3B.	HR.	RBI.	SH.	SF.	HP.	BB.	Int. BB.	SO.	SB.	CS.
Howard, Timothy, Columbia†	.323	128	505	80	163	233	18	11	10	89	1	9	0	46	7	44	30	10
Fordyce, Brook, Columbia	.315	104	372	45	117	178	29	1	10	54	1	2	0	39	0	42	4	1
Navarro, Norberto, Columbia	.314	136	497	86	156	189	25	4	0	54	7	7	2	69	1	55	50	14
Hajek, David, Asheville	.313	135	498	86	156	202	28	0	6	60	6	10	2	61	1	50	43	24
Miller, Orlando, Asheville	.313	121	438	60	137	190	29	6	4	62	2	4	10	25	2	52	12	5
Manahan, Austin, Augusta	.302	94	378	59	114	167	12	10	7	52	2	4	4	46	2	105	26	14
Rivers, Kenneth, Myrtle Beach	.299	100	358	51	107	165	18	2	12	67	0	5	14	31	2	61	1	2
Pose, Scott, Charleston (W. Va.)*	.298	135	480	106	143	166	13	5	0	46	5	6	7	114	8	56	49	21
Ratliff, Daryl, Augusta	.295	122	417	70	123	149	11	6	1	55	1	0	0	67	2	62	24	7
Nieves, Melvin, Sumter†	.283	126	459	60	130	195	24	7	9	59	1	9	9	53	4	125	10	6

Departmental Leaders: G—Jimenez, 143; AB—Howell, 573; R—Pose, 106; H—T. Howard, 163; TB—T. Howard, 233; 2B—M. Burton, 35; 3B—Cornelius, T. Howard, 11; HR—Brannon, 18; RBI—T. Howard, 89; SH—Ortega, 20; SF—Hajek, 10; HP—Ferguson, 18; BB—Pose, 114; IBB—Pose, 8; SO—M. Thomas, 150; SB—Howell, 79; CS—Hajek, 24.

(All Players—Listed Alphabetically)

Player and Club	Pct.	G.	AB.	R.	H.	TB.	2B.	3B.	HR.	RBI.	SH.	SF.	HP.	BB.	Int. BB.	SO.	SB.	CS.
Abare, William, Myrtle Beach*	.251	118	391	49	98	147	19	0	10	44	2	3	1	59	0	121	1	2
Adams, Brian, Spartanburg	.220	40	118	9	26	36	8	1	0	9	1	2	3	13	1	22	0	1
Anderson, Tony, Sumter	.000	7	20	0	0	0	0	0	0	0	0	0	0	2	0	5	0	0
Antigua, Felix, Augusta	.286	78	290	36	83	100	14	0	1	41	0	5	3	18	1	21	0	0
Arland, Mark, Charleston (W.Va.)	.125	13	24	2	3	4	1	0	0	2	0	1	0	3	0	11	2	0
Arredondo, Roberto, Char. (S.C.)*	.249	136	490	50	122	161	19	4	4	48	3	2	5	24	0	87	2	3
Aude, Richard, Augusta	.234	128	475	48	111	154	23	1	6	61	0	4	7	41	1	133	4	1
Bailey, Robert, Augusta†	.237	36	131	26	31	40	3	3	0	10	2	1	2	18	0	37	15	6
Banton, Scott, Savannah	.229	106	306	45	70	87	11	0	2	23	2	2	2	49	1	53	14	7
Barton, Jeffery, Charleston (S.C.)*	.230	84	304	27	70	96	10	2	4	39	0	4	4	28	1	39	1	4
Baxter, David, Charleston (W.Va.)†	.133	9	15	2	2	2	0	0	0	0	0	0	0	2	0	3	1	0
Beanblossom, Bradley, Savannah	.240	60	208	28	50	72	10	0	4	27	2	2	3	17	1	20	12	3
Beasley, Andrew, Savannah*	.180	32	89	7	16	19	3	0	0	9	1	2	0	9	0	26	0	1
Beck, Brian, Charleston (S.C.)*	.231	127	436	39	101	160	20	3	11	50	2	1	4	33	2	111	2	1
Bennett, Albert, Spartanburg	.345	16	58	8	20	31	6	1	1	6	1	0	3	1	0	16	2	0
Berry, Mark, Charleston (W.Va.)	.286	14	35	7	10	14	4	0	0	5	0	0	0	7	0	2	0	0
Berry, Perry, Asheville	.223	61	202	26	45	64	11	1	2	19	0	3	3	26	0	44	4	4
Beuerlein, Edward, Asheville	.299	54	187	21	56	69	11	1	0	25	0	0	3	11	0	47	1	5
Brannon, Clifford, Savannah	.247	132	445	70	110	185	21	0	18	65	6	6	2	51	4	109	7	5
Bream, Scott, Charleston (S.C.)	.071	4	14	2	1	1	0	0	0	0	1	0	0	4	0	7	1	0
Brewington, Michael, Augusta*	.310	60	213	33	66	89	8	6	1	36	1	1	1	37	2	51	12	7
Broderick, Sean, Greensboro	.126	31	87	5	11	15	1	0	1	4	0	1	4	0	0	23	0	0
Brooks, Eric, Myrtle Beach	.263	68	213	26	56	73	8	0	3	23	1	1	2	44	1	34	1	1
Brooks, Monte, Charleston (S.C.)	.249	113	414	55	103	131	20	4	0	38	4	4	3	48	0	81	30	14
Brown, Dana, Spartanburg	.291	34	134	27	39	47	6	1	0	15	1	2	1	22	0	18	10	2
Bruno, John, Charleston (S.C.)	.227	19	75	11	17	20	1	1	0	5	1	1	0	1	0	21	0	0
Buhe, Timothy, Columbia	.385	8	13	1	5	6	1	0	0	1	0	0	0	3	0	2	0	0
Burton, Christopher, Sumter*	.167	6	18	3	3	4	1	0	0	0	0	0	0	1	0	3	1	0
Burton, Michael, Gastonia	.272	135	486	75	132	222	35	2	17	80	1	7	4	59	1	79	3	5
Bustamante, Rafael, Char. (W.Va.)	.255	89	318	40	81	95	10	2	0	38	1	3	0	42	0	52	3	3
Caines, Arturo, Fayetteville	.217	59	189	29	41	65	12	0	4	30	0	1	1	20	1	48	4	2
Calder, Joseph, Augusta	.000	1	0	0	0	0	0	0	0	1	0	1	0	0	0	0	0	0
Calzado, Lorenzo, Savannah	.239	109	331	34	79	109	8	2	6	38	0	2	2	32	3	74	4	2
Cameron, Stanton, Columbia	.298	87	302	57	90	156	19	1	15	57	0	7	4	52	1	68	3	2
Carr, Terence, Charleston (W.Va.)	.247	54	186	28	46	60	7	2	1	21	4	2	3	18	0	38	5	2
Carroll, Kevin, Columbia	.145	31	83	7	12	18	3	0	1	6	0	0	1	10	0	26	0	0
Castilla, Vinicio, Sumter	.268	93	339	47	91	137	15	2	9	53	1	5	8	28	1	54	2	5
Castillo, Alberto, Columbia	.233	30	103	8	24	37	4	3	1	14	2	2	0	10	0	21	1	1
Churchill, Timothy, Spartanburg	.252	93	337	38	85	105	10	2	2	49	1	6	1	21	0	33	0	0
Clinton, James, Gastonia	.202	60	124	13	25	32	5	1	0	7	4	0	1	13	0	34	3	7
Coleman, Paul, Savannah	.209	104	340	33	71	109	12	4	6	35	2	1	10	23	0	66	9	8
Coleman, Rico, Charleston (S.C.)	.175	107	303	27	53	66	10	0	1	14	1	2	10	24	0	66	9	4
Colon, Cristobal, Gastonia†	.321	38	140	23	45	67	2	4	4	16	4	0	1	4	1	24	7	1
Cornelius, Brian, Fayetteville*	.305	94	331	51	101	151	16	11	4	58	7	2	0	33	1	40	3	1
Cox, Darron, Charleston (W.Va.)	.253	103	367	53	93	113	11	3	1	44	3	7	7	40	1	75	14	3
Curley, Timothy, Augusta*	.230	64	213	28	49	71	9	2	3	25	0	3	1	38	1	41	3	1
Curnow, Robert, Charleston (S.C.)	.196	63	194	11	38	45	4	0	1	13	1	2	2	16	0	35	1	1
Current, Matthew, Spartanburg*	.211	68	194	20	41	46	2	0	1	14	2	1	2	28	1	30	0	0
Curtis, Craig, Asheville*	.228	119	360	65	82	146	7	3	17	51	2	5	3	75	6	91	33	8
Dallas, Gershon, Asheville	.278	124	468	48	130	161	20	1	3	55	3	3	8	19	2	75	17	8
Davis, Brian, Columbia	.273	111	388	60	106	136	13	4	3	32	0	1	8	19	1	101	27	11
Davis, Nicky, Columbia*	.176	10	34	6	6	8	2	0	0	2	0	1	0	1	0	19	1	0
DeCareau, Thomas, Charleston (S.C.).	.125	10	24	2	3	5	0	1	0	6	0	0	0	6	1	13	0	0
DeLosSantos, Alberto, Augusta	.348	52	207	26	72	88	8	4	0	26	0	2	1	7	0	23	3	1

Player and Club	Pct.	G.	AB.	R.	H.	TB.	2B.	3B.	HR.	RBI.	SH.	SF.	HP.	BB.	Int. BB.	SO.	SB.	CS.
Diaz, Alberto, Columbia	.270	106	363	40	98	115	10	2	1	32	2	3	14	0	47	17	11
Diaz, Serafin, Charleston (S.C.)*	.230	113	404	40	93	122	15	1	4	42	0	2	4	53	2	64	1	2
Duran, Ignacio, Savannah	.209	127	412	42	86	110	14	2	2	31	2	3	4	24	0	95	10	7
Eklund, Troy, Gastonia	.236	98	305	41	72	101	11	0	6	32	6	1	6	28	0	47	8	8
Encarnacion, Juan, Asheville	.202	104	341	32	69	108	12	3	7	44	2	1	3	24	0	108	9	6
Escobar, John, Spartanburg	.232	126	466	42	108	130	10	3	2	31	3	0	1	37	1	76	9	3
Estevez, Carlos, Spartanburg*	.243	53	189	21	46	80	11	1	7	27	0	1	3	20	2	53	0	0
Ferguson, James, Savannah	.217	113	300	46	65	81	11	1	1	14	2	0	18	63	0	39	11	7
Fielitz, William, Savannah	.063	5	16	1	1	3	0	1	0	2	0	0	2	0	7	0	0
Fordyce, Brook, Columbia	.315	104	372	45	117	178	29	1	10	54	1	2	0	39	0	42	4	1
Fox, Andrew, Greensboro*	.218	134	455	68	99	153	19	4	9	55	1	2	4	92	5	132	26	5
Fuller, Jon, Charleston (W.Va.)	.241	67	224	34	54	83	12	1	5	33	8	2	6	34	1	38	1	0
Garland, Timothy, Greensboro	.213	77	258	25	55	66	6	1	1	12	0	1	5	21	0	73	15	4
Gill, Christopher, Charleston (W.Va.)	.251	126	462	69	116	138	22	0	0	40	9	4	11	53	1	51	16	8
Gillette, Michael, Fayetteville	.161	62	199	16	32	36	4	0	0	10	2	1	3	30	1	47	4	4
Gilliam, Sean, Greensboro	.200	131	476	42	95	153	25	3	9	45	0	4	5	18	2	132	11	10
Gillum, Kenneth, Charleston (W.Va.)*	.234	18	64	10	15	24	4	1	1	5	0	0	1	8	0	18	2	0
Giovanola, Edward, Sumter*	.244	35	119	20	29	33	4	0	0	8	3	0	0	34	0	17	8	6
Gonzalez, Paul, Charleston (S.C.)*	.242	69	231	30	56	102	7	3	11	32	2	2	3	37	0	62	0	0
Green, Thomas, Augusta	.223	38	121	18	27	35	1	2	1	13	1	3	2	15	0	28	5	1
Greene, William, Augusta*	.258	86	291	59	75	128	12	4	11	47	1	5	3	61	3	58	7	5
Gryskevich, Larry, Savannah*	.240	100	329	22	79	115	15	0	7	32	0	3	2	16	3	75	5	6
Hajek, David, Asheville	.313	135	498	86	156	202	28	0	6	60	6	10	2	61	1	50	43	24
Hall, Christopher, Fayetteville	.000	2	6	1	0	0	0	0	0	0	0	0	0	1	0	3	1	0
Hall, Lamar, Sumter	.000	1	1	0	0	0	0	0	0	0	0	0	0	0	0	0	0	0
Haller, James, Greensboro*	.000	52	0	0	0	0	0	0	0	0	1	0	0	0	0	0	0	0
Hamburg, Charles, Spartanburg	.194	35	98	10	19	26	7	0	0	7	1	0	2	23	0	24	0	0
Hardgrove, Thomas, Spartanburg*	.205	92	308	27	63	93	13	1	5	47	0	4	2	50	3	87	0	0
Harris, Donald, Gastonia	.208	58	221	27	46	65	10	0	3	13	4	0	2	14	0	63	15	8
Harris, James, Columbia	.282	122	451	60	127	159	23	3	1	64	1	6	2	33	0	54	4	3
Hartmann, Reid, Columbia†	.215	39	107	16	23	34	6	1	1	9	0	1	2	13	0	28	2	3
Heath, Lee, Sumter†	.207	126	455	59	94	119	9	5	2	25	11	1	6	39	1	112	35	22
Henderson, Lee, Charleston (S.C.)	.210	87	305	22	64	72	8	0	0	18	1	2	4	22	1	71	3	1
Hernandez, Thomas, Gastonia	.200	17	35	2	7	7	0	0	0	3	0	1	0	2	0	9	0	0
Hill, Lewellyn, Greensboro†	.196	83	270	28	53	82	11	0	6	25	2	3	9	41	1	83	19	3
Hoffman, Hunter, Fayetteville*	.130	9	23	4	3	6	0	0	1	1	0	0	0	4	1	10	0	0
Hoffman, Trevor, Charleston (W.Va.)	.212	103	278	41	59	77	10	1	2	23	4	0	2	38	0	53	3	3
Hoffner, Jamie, Columbia*	.298	86	309	42	92	109	14	0	1	37	1	2	2	13	3	46	3	2
Holifield, Rickey, Myrtle Beach*	.201	99	279	37	56	78	9	2	3	18	1	0	6	28	0	88	13	8
Hollis, Jackson, Charleston (W.Va.)*	.221	49	140	13	31	34	3	0	0	17	0	0	0	19	2	29	3	2
Holmes, William, Augusta*	.291	40	134	13	39	53	8	0	2	30	2	3	1	14	3	11	0	0
Holtzclaw, Shawn, Myrtle Beach*	.252	133	476	63	120	192	28	1	14	72	1	4	3	52	4	123	1	1
Holum, Brett, Asheville*	.221	33	77	8	17	19	2	0	0	1	1	1	1	4	1	18	0	1
Houston, Tyler, Sumter*	.210	117	442	58	93	152	14	3	13	56	2	7	2	49	1	101	6	2
Howard, David, Augusta†	.192	27	78	16	15	25	4	0	2	8	0	0	0	19	1	24	0	1
Howard, Ronald, Fayetteville†	.210	121	362	56	76	100	16	1	2	31	3	3	0	65	1	70	19	7
Howard, Timothy, Columbia†	.323	128	505	80	163	233	18	11	10	89	1	9	0	46	7	44	30	10
Howell, Patrick, Columbia†	.264	135	573	98	151	179	15	5	1	37	10	3	7	22	2	111	79	11
Hunter, Brian, Asheville	.250	127	444	84	111	137	14	6	0	16	1	1	8	60	1	72	45	13
Jaime, Juan, Myrtle Beach	.197	66	203	14	40	58	4	1	4	21	2	4	3	14	0	34	1	0
Jarvis, John, Greensboro*	.247	60	170	20	42	63	6	3	3	18	2	1	2	7	0	50	1	1
Jimenez, Ramon, Greensboro*	.279	143	537	73	150	223	29	7	10	75	2	4	2	64	6	109	23	11
Johnson, Brian, Greensboro	.238	137	496	58	118	154	15	0	7	51	2	4	4	57	4	65	4	6
Johnson, Deron, Augusta	.179	30	78	11	14	22	2	0	2	14	0	3	1	13	2	21	1	2
Johnson, Luther, Asheville*	.253	110	344	44	87	142	21	5	8	61	2	0	1	48	5	92	12	7
Johnson, Mark, Augusta*	.250	43	144	12	36	43	7	0	0	19	0	2	0	24	2	18	4	2
Jones, Eugene, Charleston (W.Va.)	.253	71	261	36	66	99	19	4	2	46	1	8	1	32	0	41	19	1
Jones, Kevin, Charleston (W.Va.)†	.083	6	12	2	1	2	1	0	0	1	0	0	3	0	7	0	0
Keating, David, Fayetteville	.212	25	66	6	14	22	2	3	0	7	2	1	1	4	0	18	1	0
Keating, Michael, Savannah	.125	42	88	8	11	12	1	0	0	4	2	0	1	12	0	20	2	4
Kelly, Patrick, Sumter	.222	121	437	57	97	116	12	2	1	44	9	6	8	61	0	65	23	8
Klesko, Ryan, Sumter*	.368	63	231	41	85	132	15	1	10	38	0	5	1	31	5	30	13	1
Kupsey, John, Sumter	.216	68	213	22	46	67	9	0	4	20	1	1	7	25	1	60	2	4
Lewis, Anthony, Savannah*	.254	128	465	55	118	172	22	4	8	49	2	1	1	24	6	79	10	13
Lewis, Joseph, Gastonia*	.235	32	81	7	19	23	2	1	0	9	1	0	0	6	1	15	2	0
Linares, Antonio, Spartanburg	.268	72	276	27	74	93	13	3	0	37	0	3	1	11	1	38	5	2
Lopez, Alfred, Sumter	.224	53	152	19	34	44	7	0	1	13	1	2	4	40	0	37	0	0
Lopez, Pedro, Charleston (S.C.)	.198	32	101	9	20	22	2	0	0	5	0	2	4	7	0	18	0	1
Lowery, Josh, Spartanburg	.213	59	207	17	44	61	5	3	2	16	1	0	3	20	0	34	2	1
Lucin, Anthony, Asheville	.198	34	91	13	18	37	4	0	5	9	0	0	1	8	0	34	0	2
Maldonado, Carlos, Fayetteville†	.137	43	117	10	16	16	0	0	0	5	1	1	0	5	0	29	0	0
Manahan, Austin, Augusta	.302	94	378	59	114	167	12	10	7	52	2	4	4	46	2	105	26	14
Marsh, Thomas, Spartanburg	.280	24	75	14	21	37	2	1	4	15	0	0	3	8	1	21	5	2
Marshall, Randolph, Gastonia*	.249	122	433	53	108	172	24	2	12	62	1	1	2	57	6	78	6	7
Martin, Eugene, Sumter	.232	79	271	45	63	94	13	6	2	19	0	3	30	0	61	7	8
Martinez, Nicio, Savannah†	.189	61	106	13	20	27	4	0	1	7	0	0	0	9	0	38	1	2
Martinez, Pablo, Charleston (S.C.)†	.221	136	453	51	100	124	12	6	0	33	7	2	4	41	0	104	16	11
Mateo, Jose, Charleston (S.C.)†	.161	20	62	6	10	13	0	0	1	1	2	0	1	5	0	19	1	1
McClinton, Timothy, Columbia	.204	54	147	20	30	38	3	1	1	19	2	2	3	19	1	38	7	2
McCoy, Homer, Gastonia	.338	24	80	13	27	45	6	0	4	11	0	2	0	12	1	12	1	1
McCray, Justin, Asheville	.287	61	178	16	51	65	6	0	2	25	1	2	2	7	0	47	4	1
McKeon, Kasey, Fayetteville†	.183	104	290	28	53	63	5	1	1	18	1	1	2	30	1	73	2	0
McNamara, Dennis, Fayetteville	.230	48	161	17	37	42	3	1	0	11	1	0	4	19	0	24	1	0
Mendez, Miguel, Sumter	.111	3	9	2	1	1	0	0	0	1	0	0	0	2	0	3	1	0
Mengel, Bradley, Myrtle Beach	.273	115	403	50	110	144	17	1	5	47	5	3	8	36	0	80	4	2
Mercedes, Hector, Myrtle Beach†	.196	98	326	37	64	87	11	0	4	24	3	3	0	14	1	77	7	3
Micheu, Tony, Gastonia	.219	71	192	20	42	68	9	1	5	20	3	1	5	17	1	50	3	1
Miller, Orlando, Asheville	.313	121	438	60	137	190	29	6	4	62	2	4	10	25	2	52	12	5
Miller, Scott, Myrtle Beach	.249	96	313	41	78	108	18	0	4	32	11	3	3	44	0	44	5	4
Mobley, Anton, Myrtle Beach	.181	52	177	20	32	51	1	0	6	13	0	0	4	11	0	78	1	0
Montalvo, Robert, Myrtle Beach	.200	45	125	15	25	26	1	0	0	11	3	1	1	9	0	14	2	2
Morrow, Timmie, Gastonia	.206	105	378	55	78	113	10	2	7	34	6	3	4	33	0	99	19	15

Player and Club	Pct.	G.	AB.	R.	H.	TB.	2B.	3B.	HR.	RBI.	SH.	SF.	HP.	BB.	Int. BB.	SO.	SB.	CS.
Navarro, Norberto, Columbia	.314	136	497	86	156	189	25	4	0	54	7	7	2	69	1	55	50	14
Newkirk, Craig, Gastonia	.268	135	467	73	125	163	23	0	5	46	6	5	5	63	0	81	16	9
Nichols, Brian, Charleston (W.Va.)	.181	21	72	7	13	15	2	0	0	11	0	1	2	10	0	11	0	0
Nieves, Melvin, Sumter†	.283	126	459	60	130	195	24	7	9	59	1	9	9	53	4	125	10	6
Nixon, Jason, Augusta	.077	6	13	3	1	2	1	0	0	0	0	0	0	4	0	6	0	0
Noreen, Keith, Sumter	.234	16	47	5	11	15	4	0	0	6	1	0	1	10	1	11	2	0
Ochs, Anthony, Savannah	.248	102	331	43	82	107	10	3	3	36	5	3	3	42	2	65	13	8
Oliva, Jose, Gastonia	.209	120	387	43	81	138	25	1	10	52	3	8	4	26	0	104	9	3
Olmeda, Jose, Sumter†	.253	103	367	60	93	140	14	6	7	40	4	4	2	55	2	49	17	9
Ortega, Eduardo, Spartanburg°	.237	130	518	61	123	136	9	2	0	30	20	2	2	43	1	61	11	16
Ozuna, Mateo, Savannah	.236	121	449	65	106	124	8	2	2	29	4	5	5	37	1	42	66	21
Parese, Billy, Myrtle Beach	.237	121	439	67	104	145	16	5	5	47	5	1	4	60	1	73	16	7
Parsons, William, Charleston (S.C.)°	.174	56	195	21	34	41	5	1	0	11	0	1	3	31	0	25	3	1
Pedersen, Donald, Fayetteville°	.200	15	30	4	6	6	0	0	0	2	0	0	0	6	0	10	0	0
Pemberton, Rudy, Fayetteville	.278	127	454	59	126	168	14	5	6	61	1	9	12	42	1	91	12	9
Pennyfeather, William, Augusta	.262	122	465	69	122	156	14	4	4	48	3	3	3	23	0	85	21	12
Perez, Eduardo, Sumter	.179	41	123	11	22	40	7	1	3	17	3	1	2	14	0	18	0	0
Perez, Eulogio, Spartanburg	.187	22	75	6	14	19	3	1	0	3	1	0	1	7	0	24	0	1
Perez, Robert, Myrtle Beach	.292	21	72	8	21	26	2	0	1	10	0	1	2	3	0	9	2	1
Perozo, Daniel, Charleston (W.Va.)	.279	106	337	39	94	121	11	2	4	43	8	2	5	29	0	69	17	11
Pesavento, Patrick, Fayetteville°	.280	132	457	82	128	142	10	2	0	35	8	2	8	84	5	49	12	15
Peterson, Robert, Augusta	.159	23	69	8	11	14	1	1	0	6	1	0	0	11	0	20	0	0
Pineda, Jorge, Asheville	.198	37	106	13	21	34	3	2	2	9	1	0	1	11	0	25	2	2
Pose, Scott, Charleston (W.Va.)°	.298	135	480	106	143	166	13	5	0	46	5	6	7	114	8	56	49	21
Powell, Kenneth, Gastonia	.233	103	322	31	75	97	8	4	2	37	1	4	6	37	1	83	17	10
Pride, Curtis, Columbia°	.267	53	191	38	51	81	4	4	6	25	0	1	0	21	3	45	11	8
Provence, Todd, Myrtle Beach	.236	98	330	55	78	127	15	2	10	38	1	1	4	43	1	117	12	6
Pueschner, Craig, Charleston (S.C.)	.241	94	344	41	83	116	11	2	6	41	0	2	6	43	2	77	29	14
Quijada, Edward, Asheville	.228	119	356	43	81	107	16	2	2	36	1	2	10	59	3	84	5	1
Ratliff, Daryl, Augusta	.295	122	417	70	123	149	11	6	1	55	1	0	0	67	2	62	24	7
Rendina, Michael, Fayetteville°	.255	137	475	59	121	183	23	3	11	77	0	4	3	76	7	90	4	4
Rhodes, Michael, Greensboro	.213	31	89	12	19	28	4	1	1	16	0	3	1	16	0	21	3	2
Riggs, Kevin, Charleston (W.Va.)°	.250	2	4	0	1	1	0	0	0	1	0	0	0	0	0	1	0	1
Rivers, Kenneth, Myrtle Beach	.299	100	358	51	107	165	18	2	12	67	0	5	14	31	2	61	1	2
Roa, Hector, Sumter	.217	24	92	5	20	26	4	1	0	7	1	0	0	4	1	12	1	1
Robertson, Jason, Greensboro°	.250	133	496	71	124	174	22	5	6	44	4	1	2	67	2	110	21	13
Roble, Josman, Sumter°	.246	71	236	31	58	89	12	2	5	35	1	7	2	27	3	46	3	0
Rodriguez, Andres, Greensboro	.241	56	216	22	52	56	2	1	0	14	6	0	0	11	1	36	6	8
Rodriguez, Hector, Augusta	.263	30	114	10	30	37	2	1	1	13	0	0	1	5	0	24	0	1
Rodriguez, Roman, Augusta	.275	99	364	38	100	126	14	3	2	37	2	1	0	27	2	61	3	4
Romano, Scott, Greensboro	.201	58	189	17	38	46	8	0	0	11	4	0	3	23	0	43	12	5
Rush, Edward, Charleston (W.Va.)	.214	68	229	29	49	62	10	0	1	26	2	2	1	30	0	22	1	1
Sanchez, Daniel, Greensboro	.218	49	142	11	31	33	2	0	0	9	1	0	1	14	0	32	4	1
Santa Cruz, Nick, Spartanburg	.233	12	30	2	7	7	0	0	0	3	0	0	0	3	0	10	0	0
Santana, Jose, Asheville†	.243	31	70	6	17	19	2	0	0	5	0	0	2	10	1	16	2	1
Santoya, Cristobal, Sumter	.212	20	66	5	14	15	1	0	0	4	4	0	1	6	0	9	1	0
Sawkiw, Warren, Fayetteville†	.257	59	210	31	54	63	6	0	1	18	2	4	1	30	1	35	4	1
Scott, Kevin, Asheville	.274	129	460	66	126	174	29	2	5	79	4	7	5	37	2	93	17	6
Scott, Philip, Columbia	.224	21	58	6	13	13	0	0	0	6	1	0	0	8	0	11	0	3
Scruggs, Anthony, Gastonia	.307	75	274	50	84	124	16	0	8	48	1	1	7	26	1	57	20	3
Sellers, Rick, Fayetteville	.230	130	430	49	99	141	13	4	7	57	1	8	2	61	2	102	5	3
Seymour, Winston, Augusta°	.182	12	33	5	6	8	2	0	0	3	1	0	0	8	2	8	0	0
Shannon, Daniel, Spartanburg°	.156	58	167	15	26	37	5	0	2	14	1	0	0	19	1	47	1	2
Sims, Daniel, Sumter°	.185	58	151	15	28	38	8	1	0	11	3	0	0	31	0	19	6	5
Sirak, Kenneth, Spartanburg°	.213	53	164	20	35	44	5	2	0	13	0	1	0	20	1	40	0	1
Smith, Thomas, Greensboro	.209	24	67	7	14	17	3	0	0	5	1	0	7	7	0	20	2	1
Sondrini, Joseph, Augusta	.203	28	79	14	16	20	2	1	0	4	1	1	0	7	0	17	0	1
Spivey, James, Savannah	.000	6	9	0	0	0	0	0	0	0	0	0	0	0	0	3	0	0
Tagliaferri, Eugene, Fayetteville	.212	58	179	24	38	60	8	1	4	18	1	1	2	22	1	74	0	2
Tahan, Kevin, Savannah	.222	106	302	36	67	95	11	4	3	40	5	4	1	44	2	66	5	4
Tarasco, Anthony, Sumter°	.265	107	355	42	94	122	13	3	3	37	5	3	1	37	2	57	9	5
Taylor, Samuel, Spartanburg°	.308	75	289	46	89	127	13	5	5	36	0	1	3	24	4	30	10	3
Thomas, Corey, Spartanburg	.234	92	321	53	75	102	10	1	5	26	4	1	7	48	0	82	11	2
Thomas, Mark, Columbia	.233	110	420	65	98	169	22	2	15	70	0	1	2	39	1	150	9	3
Torres, Freddy, Fayetteville	.204	106	304	42	62	71	3	3	0	29	6	3	4	21	0	32	2	1
Torres, Jessie, Augusta	.243	51	148	20	36	42	6	0	0	14	2	1	3	33	0	39	0	1
Trusky, Kenneth, Augusta°	.272	79	294	52	80	95	9	3	0	28	1	3	2	52	3	35	5	6
Turco, Frank, Gastonia	.125	5	8	2	1	1	0	0	0	0	0	0	0	1	0	1	0	0
Turner, Brian, Greensboro°	.203	37	118	14	24	31	5	1	0	5	1	0	0	16	0	29	3	2
Turvey, Joseph, Savannah°	.137	27	51	4	7	10	3	0	0	1	0	1	0	2	8	21	0	1
Ufret, Ricardo, Augusta†	.174	33	86	7	15	18	1	1	0	6	1	1	0	8	0	20	1	0
Urbon, Joseph, Spartanburg°	.258	63	233	30	60	83	8	3	3	23	0	1	1	20	2	34	7	5
Valencia, Gilbert, Spartanburg°	.155	37	116	17	18	19	1	0	0	4	0	0	0	19	0	28	0	0
Valentin, Edwin, Asheville†	.244	15	45	7	11	12	1	0	0	7	1	0	1	4	0	12	1	1
Van Scoyoc, Aaron, Greensboro†	.222	108	347	47	77	93	11	1	1	23	6	1	2	60	0	62	3	6
Velez, Noel, Charleston (W.Va.)	.300	54	180	15	40	53	8	1	1	12	1	0	4	17	1	44	3	2
Vondran, Steven, Charleston (W.Va.)	.269	75	275	30	74	100	19	2	1	47	0	4	1	29	2	37	1	2
Walker, Bernard, Char. (W.Va.)°	.324	51	170	39	55	97	9	6	7	39	2	0	1	45	2	52	16	2
Walker, Duane, Fayetteville	.224	72	214	26	48	66	13	1	1	19	5	1	2	15	2	54	6	5
Walker, Lawrence, Greensboro	.230	79	244	27	56	72	11	1	1	25	6	1	4	48	2	57	11	8
Wardlow, Joseph, Gastonia°	.245	122	396	48	97	116	12	2	1	42	9	4	1	75	3	51	9	11
Watson, Todd, Charleston (W.Va.)°	.235	105	353	39	83	106	15	1	2	44	3	4	3	43	7	45	2	2
Weaver, Trent, Charleston (S.C.)	.232	75	250	28	58	79	12	3	1	26	2	1	5	36	1	58	3	1
Welch, Daniel, Spartanburg	.175	86	291	20	51	70	8	1	3	24	0	1	5	22	0	97	1	0
Wilson, Bradley, Fayetteville°	.195	29	87	7	17	28	5	0	2	10	0	1	0	14	1	22	0	0
Wilson, Daniel, Charleston (W.Va.)	.248	32	113	16	28	45	9	1	2	17	1	1	0	13	0	17	0	0
Wilson, Nigel, Myrtle Beach°	.273	110	440	77	120	209	23	9	16	62	2	6	30	3	71	22	12	
Winford, Barry, Gastonia	.238	96	332	51	79	105	14	3	2	24	5	0	3	39	1	67	14	3
Wright, Benny, Charleston (W.Va.)	.000	2	1	0	0	0	0	0	0	0	0	0	0	0	0	0	0	0

The following pitchers, listed alphabetically by club, with games in parentheses, had no plate appearances, primarily through use of designated hitters:

ASHEVILLE—August, Samuel (5); Brown, Duane (3); Dovey, Troy (33); Gardner, Christopher (23); Gonzales, Benjamin (53); Gutierrez,

Anthony (41); McDowell, Michael (41); Munoz, Julio (9); Perez, Francisco (36); Rinaldi, Kevin (7); Rivas, Limbert (33); Rosario, Eliezel (30); Small, Mark (34); Wall, Donnell (28); Wheeler, Kenneth (21).

AUGUSTA—Arvesen, Scott (28); Bird, David (44); Dooley, Marvin (4); Fajardo, Hector (7); Futrell, Mark (3); Honeywell, Brent (13); Latham, John (28); Martinez, Ramon (35); Masters, Wayne (38); Mooney, Troy (10); Parkinson, Eric (31); Redmond, Andre (4); Rychel, Kevin (28); Santiago, Delvy (31); Underwood, Robert (10); Wagner, Paul (35); Watson, David (23); Way, Ronald (24).

CHARLESTON (S.C.)—Banks, Lance (48); Bennett, James (23); Cunningham, Troy (40); Ellis, Timothy (3); Embry, Todd (2); Garside, Russell (2); Guzman, Pedro (29); Johnson, William (25); Marx, William (32); Murdock, Joseph (5); Pickett, Dan (7); Santiago, Rafael (27); Thompson, Charles (26); Thompson, William (11); Worrell, Timothy (20); Zinter, Edward (45).

CHARLESTON (W.Va.)—Ayala, Robert (21); Borcherding, Mark (6); Cecil, Timothy (29); Culberson, Calvin (14); Doty, Sean (19); Duff, Scott (3); Hook, Christopher (30); Jackson, Danny (1); King, Douglas (11); Malley, Michael (7); McCarthy, Steven (29); Nieves, Ernesto (20); Plemmons, Scott (18); Pugh, Timothy (27); Ray, John (30); Satre, Jason (24); Spradlin, Jerry (43); Wilburn, Ema (23).

COLUMBIA—Butler, Christopher (15); Dorn, Chris (27); Emm, Arthur (39); Freitas, Michael (13); Furmanik, Daniel (8); Gasser, Steven (5); Johnson, Paul (16); Langbehn, Gregory (26); McCann, Joseph (25); Parker, Jarrod (4); Reich, Andrew (26); Richmond, Ryan (22); Sample, Deron (46); Telgheder, David (14); Valle, Anthony (11); Vasquez, Julian (25); Vitko, Joseph (16).

FAYETTEVILLE—Braley, Jeffrey (57); Doherty, John (7); Ferm, Edward (3); Garcia, Michael (28); Gonzales, Francisco (25); Guzman, Jose (26); Herrmann, Timothy (7); Ingram, Linty (33); Koller, Michael (9); Leimeister, Eric (26); Link, Robert (6); Marshall, Randy (14); Neidlinger, Joseph (18); Pierce, Benjamin (7); Pinto, Gustavo (16); Raley, Daniel (2); Rodriguez, Eddy (7); Rountree, Brian (6); Seibert, Malcolm (7); Shea, Kurt (17); Stefany, Marino (40); Stokes, Randall (1); Torres, Leonardo (30); Wolf, Steven (8).

GASTONIA—Arner, Michael (14); Asche, Scott (34); Bickhardt, Eric (50); Buckley, Travis (27); Eischen, Joseph (17); Evans, Brian (57); Franklin, Jay (28); Graves, John (33); Holcomb, Louis (15); Hurst, Jonathan (15); McGraw, Frank (1); Oliver, Darren (1); Phillips, Brad (12); Randle, Carl (29); Reed, Robert (8); Romero, Brian (15); Romero, Ronaldo (11); Rowley, Stephen (13); Stafford, Timothy (4); Steiner, Brian (21); Wells, Timothy (10).

GREENSBORO—Batchelor, Richard (27); Hitchcock, Sterling (27); Hoffman, Jeffrey (47); Hutton, Mark (21); Johnston, Daniel (46); Juarbe, Kenneth (16); Malone, Todd (17); Mauldin, James (13); Munoz, Roberto (25); Perez, Cesar (13); Quirico, Rafael (13); Rhodes, Ricky (27); Smith, Shad (16); Springer, Russell (10); Tucker, Stephen (11).

MYRTLE BEACH—Bicknell, Greg (34); Blumberg, Robert (25); Bradley, Eric (46); Brown, Daren (25); Hutson, Scott (13); Kizziah, Daren (35); Kulina, Kenneth (28); Lloyd, Graeme (19); Mandia, Samuel (9); Martin, Gregg (37); Menhart, Paul (5); Nowak, Richard (5); Ogliaruso, Michael (26); Olivares, Jose (8); Small, Aaron (27); Wanish, John (35).

SAVANNAH—Arias, Jose (20); Baker, Ernie (70); Betances, Marcos (7); Cassidy, David (18); Dixon, Steven (64); Duvall, Bradley (7); Espinal, William (46); Faccio, Luis (29); Fletcher, Dennis (66); Gaston, Russell (31); Green, Donald (12); Hurst, William (7); Nielsen, Kevin (7); Osborne, Donovan (6); Pacheco, Albert (22); Sells, George (4); Shackle, Richard (17); Tolbert, Mark (29).

SPARTANBURG—Backs, Jason (11); Baur, Albert (12); Bratlien, Erik (23); Elliott, Donald (20); Fletcher, Paul (9); Gaddy, Robert (30); Goedhart, Darrell (29); Goergen, Todd (19); Gray, Elliott (3); Gunderson, Gregory (38); Kent, Troy (18); Limbach, Chris (42); Randall, Mark (32); Stevens, Matthew (14); Sullivan, Michael (7); Wells, Robert (20); Wiegandt, Scott (10).

SUMTER—Brown, Terrance (23); Burlingame, Dennis (12); Cronin, Jeffrey (6); Cummings, Brian (7); Gabriele, Michael (11); Gasser, Steven (6); Haeberle, Kevin (23); Hailey, Roger (17); Jewett, Karl (27); Karasinski, David (23); Lemon, Donald (4); Mathews, Edward (4); Newman, Thomas (8); Schafer, William (39); Shiflett, Matthew (15); Sottile, Shaun (40); Steinmetz, Robert (25); Strange, Donald (46); Thomas, Ronald (16); Weems, Danny (10); Wohlers, Mark (37).

GRAND SLAM HOME RUNS—Arredondo, M. Thomas, 2 each; Abare, Barton, Beanblossom, Cameron, Castilla, Churchill, Fox, Gilliam, Gonzalez, Hardgrove, Morrow, Quijada, Rendina, Rivers, Taylor, N. Wilson, 1 each.

AWARDED FIRST BASE ON CATCHER'S INTERFERENCE—D. Walker 5 (L. Walker 2, B. Johnson, J. Lewis, Winford); R. Coleman 4 (Curnow, Houston, B. Johnson, L. Walker); Beck 3 (Hamburg, Houston, B. Johnson); P. Coleman 3 (K. Scott 2, P. Lopez); P. Lopez 3 (Jaime 2, B. Johnson); Marshall 2 (E. Brooks, Ochs); Pueschner 2 (Antigua, Castillo); Rendina 2 (E. Brooks, Lucin); Arredondo (Castillo); Calzado (Houston); Cornelius (Current); Cox (Fordyce); Curnow (Hamburg); Encarnacion (Sellers); Heath (Sellers); Houston (Winford); L. Johnson (Cox); McCoy (K. Scott); Robles (Winford); Velez (E. Brooks); Winford (Sellers).

CLUB FIELDING

Club	Pct.	G.	PO.	A.	E.	DP.	PB.	Club	Pct.	G.	PO.	A.	E.	DP.	PB.
Charleston (W.Va.)	.966	143	3660	1585	186	120	26	Savannah	.958	141	3721	1512	228	130	28
Fayetteville	.965	143	3711	1560	190	137	33	Columbia	.957	143	3754	1636	240	134	38
Sumter	.962	142	3693	1682	214	141	34	Greensboro	.956	144	3762	1623	249	120	39
Gastonia	.960	143	3724	1557	218	163	37	Asheville	.954	143	3659	1642	256	156	52
Myrtle Beach	.959	140	3617	1450	214	123	31	Charleston (S.C.)	.954	142	3624	1591	253	110	39
Spartanburg	.959	141	3676	1575	222	114	36	Augusta	.952	143	3736	1457	260	126	48

Triple Play—Gastonia.

INDIVIDUAL FIELDING

*Throws lefthanded.

FIRST BASEMEN

Player and Club	Pct.	G.	PO.	A.	E.	DP.	Player and Club	Pct.	G.	PO.	A.	E.	DP.
Abare, Myrtle Beach*	.979	113	926	56	21	86	D. Howard, Augusta	1.000	7	36	2	0	3
Arredondo, Charleston (S.C.)*	.986	129	1153	92	18	84	R. Howard, Fayetteville	1.000	2	3	0	0	0
Aude, Augusta	.985	59	490	26	8	35	Jimenez, Greensboro*	.986	140	1235	116	19	105
Beck, Charleston (S.C.)*	.981	11	101	4	2	8	B. Johnson, Greensboro	1.000	3	19	1	0	1
M. Berry, Charleston (W.Va.)	.989	14	87	7	1	6	D. Johnson, Augusta	.982	15	102	7	2	10
P. Berry, Asheville	1.000	1	2	0	0	0	L. Johnson, Asheville*	.923	7	46	2	4	7
Beuerlein, Asheville	1.000	6	40	1	0	3	M. Johnson, Augusta*	.981	32	240	18	5	28
Brewington, Augusta*	.993	16	128	5	1	14	Klesko, Sumter*	.978	63	575	43	14	61
Brooks, Charleston (S.C.)	1.000	2	21	1	0	0	Kupsey, Sumter	.983	6	58	0	1	6
Burton, Gastonia	.9922	96	829	56	7	98	Marshall, Gastonia	.989	48	408	30	5	43
Bustamante, Char. (W.Va.)	1.000	1	3	1	0	0	McCray, Asheville	.985	15	129	4	2	19
Calzado, Savannah	.971	52	371	38	12	34	McKeon, Fayetteville	1.000	9	73	1	0	8
Cameron, Columbia	1.000	1	2	0	0	0	Mengel, Myrtle Beach	1.000	2	5	0	0	1
Churchill, Spartanburg	.992	67	583	34	5	53	Navarro, Columbia	1.000	1	12	0	0	0
Clinton, Gastonia	1.000	1	4	0	0	1	Pedersen, Fayetteville*	1.000	1	1	0	0	0
Curnow, Charleston (S.C.)	.900	3	16	2	2	4	Perez, Sumter	1.000	8	61	7	0	10
Curtis, Asheville*	.988	113	1001	59	13	105	Provence, Myrtle Beach	.993	33	258	26	2	22
Davis, Columbia	.983	7	51	7	1	4	RENDINA, Fayetteville*	.9923	134	1216	78	10	118
Diaz, Charleston (S.C.)	.917	1	11	0	1	4	Rhodes, Greensboro	.955	4	40	2	2	2
Estevez, Columbia	.992	13	123	9	1	8	Roble, Sumter*	.985	68	675	36	11	50
Gryskevich, Savannah*	.990	88	707	63	8	72	Rodriguez, Augusta	1.000	1	9	0	0	1
Hardgrove, Spartanburg	.989	64	569	47	7	39	Scott, Asheville	.967	12	107	9	4	5
Harris, Columbia	.991	99	854	78	8	75	Sellers, Fayetteville	.933	4	27	1	2	0
Hartmann, Columbia	1.000	2	15	0	0	1	Seymour, Augusta*	.968	12	88	4	3	6
Hernandez, Gastonia	1.000	3	17	0	0	2	Sims, Sumter*	1.000	1	1	1	0	0
Hoffner, Columbia	.995	41	336	37	2	32	Tahan, Savannah	.973	22	134	11	4	10
Holmes, Augusta*	.984	17	118	9	2	12	Thomas, Columbia	1.000	2	4	0	0	1
Holum, Asheville	1.000	2	6	1	0	1	Vondran, Charleston (W.Va.)	.994	36	287	30	2	16
							Watson, Charleston (W.Va.)	.987	103	888	77	13	82

Triple Play—Marshall.

SECOND BASEMEN

Player and Club	Pct.	G.	PO.	A.	E.	DP.	Player and Club	Pct.	G.	PO.	A.	E.	DP.
Bailey, Augusta	.954	14	22	40	3	5	Miller, Myrtle Beach	.970	17	30	34	2	4
Berry, Asheville	.930	53	90	162	19	38	Montalvo, Myrtle Beach	.959	9	19	28	2	7
Broderick, Greensboro	.930	15	19	47	5	6	Newkirk, Gastonia	.930	25	40	53	7	19
Brooks, Charleston (S.C.)	.952	4	7	13	1	2	Oliva, Gastonia	1.000	1	0	1	0	0
Buhe, Columbia	.800	3	2	2	1	1	Olmeda, Sumter	.967	98	190	303	17	65
Bustamante, Char. (W.Va.)	.968	25	34	57	3	11	Ortega, Spartanburg	.963	130	224	375	23	78
Clinton, Gastonia	.949	10	13	24	2	3	Ozuna, Savannah	.943	112	218	309	32	63
DeLosSantos, Augusta	.667	1	2	2	2	0	Parese, Myrtle Beach	.967	118	211	317	18	70
Diaz, Columbia	.933	105	224	305	38	59	Parsons, Charleston (S.C.)	.940	56	136	148	18	26
Escobar, Spartanburg	.920	11	21	25	4	0	Riggs, Charleston (W.Va.)	.750	1	0	3	1	0
Ferguson, Savannah	.961	26	50	48	4	11	A. Rodriguez, Greensboro	1.000	3	7	17	0	3
GILL, Charleston (W.Va.)	.975	122	254	383	16	78	R. Rodriguez, Augusta	.920	40	71	101	15	19
Giovanola, Sumter	.984	35	61	125	3	27	Romano, Greensboro	.942	51	93	119	13	24
Greene, Augusta	1.000	1	3	1	0	0	Sanchez, Greensboro	.933	29	50	76	9	11
Hajek, Asheville	.973	74	157	244	11	63	Santa Cruz, Spartanburg	1.000	2	0	4	0	1
Hartmann, Columbia	.957	7	13	9	1	2	Sawkiw, Fayetteville	.978	19	35	56	2	8
Holum, Asheville	.889	3	3	5	1	0	Scott, Columbia	.957	6	8	14	1	5
R. Howard, Fayetteville	.964	113	216	340	21	65	Smith, Greensboro	.941	21	48	63	7	15
T. Howard, Columbia	.981	32	63	90	3	19	Sondrini, Augusta	.945	25	53	67	7	16
Kelly, Sumter	.985	16	24	43	1	11	Thomas, Spartanburg	.833	2	2	3	1	0
Maldonado, Fayetteville	.985	18	30	37	1	7	Torres, Fayetteville	.958	10	11	12	1	2
Manahan, Augusta	.943	46	92	106	12	29	Ufret, Augusta	.887	27	51	59	14	11
N. Martinez, Savannah	.941	25	38	42	5	11	Valentin, Asheville	.917	15	19	36	5	7
P. Martinez, Charleston (S.C.)	.943	62	115	201	19	38	Van Scoyoc, Greensboro	.974	35	81	110	5	20
Mateo, Charleston (S.C.)	.943	20	31	52	5	6	Wardlow, Gastonia	.955	118	207	345	26	86
McCray, Asheville	.977	13	15	28	1	6	Weaver, Charleston (S.C.)	1.000	7	7	7	0	1

Triple Play—Wardlow.

THIRD BASEMEN

Player and Club	Pct.	G.	PO.	A.	E.	DP.	Player and Club	Pct.	G.	PO.	A.	E.	DP.
Aude, Augusta	.847	45	32	84	21	9	Maldonado, Fayetteville	.921	19	9	26	3	1
Broderick, Greensboro	1.000	4	3	1	0	0	Manahan, Augusta	.852	48	28	87	20	8
Brooks, Charleston (S.C.)	.947	31	30	77	6	6	Martinez, Charleston (S.C.)	1.000	2	0	8	0	0
Bruno, Charleston (S.C.)	.738	16	9	22	11	2	McClinton, Columbia	.838	28	13	49	12	3
Buhe, Columbia	.000	1	0	0	1	0	McCray, Asheville	.800	13	6	14	5	1
Bustamante, Char. (W.Va.)	.934	34	17	40	4	5	McKeon, Fayetteville	.864	23	14	37	8	3
Clinton, Gastonia	.800	7	2	6	2	1	Mendez, Sumter	1.000	2	1	5	0	1
Colon, Gastonia	1.000	1	0	3	0	0	Mengel, Myrtle Beach	.912	103	76	183	25	11
Curnow, Charleston (S.C.)	.000	1	0	0	1	0	Miller, Myrtle Beach	.917	39	36	75	10	11
Davis, Columbia	1.000	1	0	1	0	1	Montalvo, Myrtle Beach	.500	4	0	1	1	0
DeLosSantos, Augusta	.970	9	11	21	1	1	NEWKIRK, Gastonia	.945	116	91	203	17	26
Diaz, Charleston (S.C.)	.813	28	15	59	17	3	Noreen, Sumter	.786	5	3	8	3	1
Duran, Savannah	.902	127	129	239	40	22	Ochs, Savannah	1.000	1	0	2	0	0
Escobar, Spartanburg	.919	103	68	215	25	14	Oliva, Gastonia	.926	34	24	51	6	3
Ferguson, Savannah	.951	29	14	44	3	5	Provence, Myrtle Beach	1.000	1	1	7	0	0
Fox, Greensboro	.880	133	93	238	45	21	H. Rodriguez, Augusta	.917	29	17	38	5	5
Gonzalez, Charleston (S.C.)	.910	68	51	131	18	7	R. Rodriguez, Augusta	.947	15	7	29	2	2
Hajek, Asheville	.864	22	15	36	8	5	Romano, Greensboro	.789	6	4	11	4	0
Hall, Fayetteville	1.000	2	0	4	0	0	Santa Cruz, Spartanburg	.938	10	2	13	1	2
Harris, Columbia	.860	15	6	31	6	0	K. Scott, Asheville	1.000	2	2	2	0	0
Hartmann, Columbia	.930	18	6	34	3	3	P. Scott, Columbia	1.000	3	1	4	0	0
Hoffman, Charleston (W.Va.)	.925	41	13	49	5	2	Sirak, Spartanburg	.892	32	19	55	9	6
Holum, Asheville	1.000	5	0	2	0	0	Tagliaferri, Fayetteville	.862	54	22	97	19	8
R. Howard, Fayetteville	.857	1	3	3	1	0	Torres, Fayetteville	.916	70	31	110	13	9
T. Howard, Columbia	.893	87	55	162	26	16	Ufret, Augusta	.333	1	1	0	2	0
Johnson, Greensboro	.846	5	2	9	2	1	Velez, Charleston (W.Va.)	.859	46	39	71	18	6
Jones, Charleston (W.Va.)	1.000	4	1	5	0	0	Vondran, Charleston (W.Va.)	.850	41	30	61	16	7
Kelly, Sumter	.920	95	54	212	23	19							
Kupsey, Sumter	.861	48	26	92	19	7							

SHORTSTOPS

Player and Club	Pct.	G.	PO.	A.	E.	DP.	Player and Club	Pct.	G.	PO.	A.	E.	DP.
Bailey, Augusta	.951	22	25	73	5	17	O. Miller, Asheville	.922	111	208	348	47	93
Beanblossom, Savannah	.934	59	76	138	15	30	S. Miller, Myrtle Beach	.908	20	35	44	8	12
Bream, Charleston (S.C.)	.714	4	4	11	6	2	Montalvo, Myrtle Beach	.952	33	40	79	6	16
Broderick, Greensboro	.960	6	11	13	1	4	Navarro, Columbia	.942	134	212	440	40	74
Buhe, Columbia	.700	2	2	5	3	1	Oliva, Gastonia	.907	86	139	232	38	62
Bustamante, Char. (W.Va.)	.958	20	18	51	3	9	Olmeda, Sumter	1.000	9	11	16	0	4
Castilla, Sumter	.952	93	139	320	23	60	Perez, Spartanburg	.920	22	36	67	9	12
Clinton, Gastonia	.953	34	57	84	7	27	PESAVENTO, Fayetteville	.952	126	187	386	29	77
Colon, Gastonia	.900	37	50	76	14	25	Roa, Sumter	.906	24	34	91	13	12
Escobar, Spartanburg	.965	15	30	52	3	13	A. Rodriguez, Greensboro	.924	53	73	171	20	35
Ferguson, Savannah	.946	55	86	141	13	20	H. Rodriguez, Augusta	1.000	1	2	1	0	1
Greene, Augusta	.904	81	114	208	34	39	R. Rodriguez, Augusta	.910	47	84	128	21	22
Hajek, Asheville	.911	32	50	93	14	14	Rush, Charleston (W.Va.)	.948	67	108	221	18	38
Hartmann, Columbia	.828	7	9	15	5	2	Sanchez, Greensboro	.919	22	19	49	6	11
Hoffman, Charleston (W.Va.)	.913	62	101	160	25	36	Santoya, Sumter	.894	20	31	62	11	13
Howard, Columbia	1.000	1	2	1	0	0	Scott, Columbia	.891	11	17	24	5	7
Keating, Savannah	.918	40	50	85	12	20	Sirak, Spartanburg	.926	14	26	49	6	10
Lowery, Spartanburg	.863	57	90	161	40	26	Thomas, Spartanburg	.864	37	57	95	24	18
N. Martinez, Savannah	.906	23	21	27	5	9	Torres, Fayetteville	.925	28	39	72	9	12
P. Martinez, Charleston (S.C.)	.935	74	123	279	28	33	Turco, Gastonia	.909	2	6	4	1	2
McCray, Asheville	.857	1	3	3	3	2	Van Scoyoc, Greensboro	.934	72	108	218	23	33
Mengel, Myrtle Beach	1.000	2	0	2	0	1	Weaver, Charleston (S.C.)	.948	65	130	199	18	39
Mercedes, Myrtle Beach	.932	97	169	273	32	58	Wright, Charleston (W.Va.)	.000	2	0	0	1	0

Triple Play—Clinton.

OUTFIELDERS

Player and Club	Pct.	G.	PO.	A.	E.	DP.
Arland, Charleston (W.Va.)	1.000	9	15	0	0	0
Banton, Savannah	.981	96	146	11	3	3
Barton, Charleston (S.C.)	1.000	78	154	7	0	1
Baxter, Charleston (W.Va.)	1.000	6	6	1	0	0
Beck, Charleston (S.C.)*	.956	100	166	6	8	0
Bennett, Spartanburg	.971	14	31	2	1	2
Brannon, Savannah	.962	116	189	14	8	2
Brewington, Augusta*	1.000	21	29	5	0	1
Broderick, Greensboro	1.000	6	6	1	0	0
Brooks, Charleston (S.C.)	.977	76	161	9	4	2
Brown, Spartanburg*	.961	32	48	1	2	0
C. Burton, Sumter	1.000	3	3	0	0	0
M. Burton, Gastonia	1.000	6	10	0	0	0
Caines, Fayetteville	.952	53	96	3	5	1
Calzado, Savannah	1.000	6	7	2	0	1
Cameron, Columbia	.970	55	92	5	3	2
Carr, Charleston (W.Va.)	.970	53	93	5	3	0
Clinton, Gastonia	1.000	5	2	0	0	0
P. Coleman, Savannah	.974	104	213	8	6	1
R. Coleman, Charleston (S.C.)	.959	97	158	5	7	2
Cornelius, Fayetteville	.965	93	157	8	6	2
Curley, Augusta*	.971	59	92	7	3	2
Curnow, Charleston (S.C.)	1.000	1	7	0	0	0
Dallas, Asheville	.912	116	176	10	18	1
Davis, Columbia	.980	95	183	15	4	2
DeCareau, Charleston (S.C.)	1.000	9	17	0	0	0
DeLosSantos, Augusta	1.000	9	10	0	0	0
Eklund, Gastonia	.979	95	132	5	3	1
Encarnacion, Asheville	.948	92	135	11	8	2
Garland, Greensboro	.971	63	94	5	3	1
Gillette, Fayetteville	1.000	2	1	0	0	0
Gilliam, Greensboro	.937	124	172	7	12	1
Gillum, Charleston (W.Va.)	1.000	15	19	5	0	0
Green, Augusta	.973	38	71	1	2	0
Harris, Gastonia	.957	58	104	6	5	1
Hartman, Columbia	.900	6	9	0	1	0
Heath, Sumter	.960	124	232	11	10	1
Hill, Greensboro	.960	67	116	4	5	0
Hoffman, Fayetteville	.000	1	0	0	1	0
Holifield, Myrtle Beach*	.945	89	171	2	10	0
Hollis, Charleston (W.Va.)	.897	26	32	3	4	0
Holtzclaw, Myrtle Beach*	.953	117	191	13	10	3
Howard, Columbia	.750	4	6	0	2	0
Howell, Columbia	.955	131	303	16	15	3
Hunter, Asheville	.955	124	219	13	11	3
D. Johnson, Augusta	.750	8	6	0	2	0
L. Johnson, Asheville*	.931	79	125	10	10	0
Jones, Charleston (W.Va.)	.989	54	88	5	1	0
Keating, Fayetteville*	.980	25	47	2	1	1
Lewis, Savannah*	.942	118	169	10	11	2
Linares, Spartanburg	.946	69	98	8	6	1
Martin, Sumter	.981	67	100	5	2	1
McClinton, Columbia	1.000	14	10	0	0	0
McCoy, Gastonia	1.000	16	15	0	0	0
McCray, Asheville	1.000	1	2	0	0	0
McKeon, Fayetteville	.939	21	31	0	2	0
McNamara, Fayetteville	.978	47	79	9	2	2
Mengel, Myrtle Beach	.955	10	18	3	1	0
Mobley, Myrtle Beach	.943	45	61	5	4	1
Morrow, Gastonia	.966	104	189	8	7	3
Nieves, Columbia	.955	123	227	7	11	2
Ochs, Savannah	1.000	4	4	0	0	0
Pedersen, Fayetteville*	1.000	3	1	0	0	0
Pemberton, Fayetteville	.953	112	192	12	10	4
Pennyfeather, Augusta	.960	118	275	16	12	6
Perez, Myrtle Beach	.976	21	40	1	1	0
Perozo, Charleston (W.Va.)	.972	106	205	7	6	1
Pineda, Columbia	.962	21	22	3	1	1
POSE, Charleston (W.Va.)	.987	128	210	17	3	3
Powell, Gastonia	.926	97	106	6	9	1
Pride, Columbia	.874	39	72	4	11	1
Provence, Myrtle Beach	.990	58	99	3	1	0
Pueschner, Charleston (S.C.)	.987	92	219	9	3	3
Ratliff, Augusta	.963	122	218	13	9	0
Rhodes, Greensboro	.918	19	42	3	4	0
Robertson, Greensboro*	.952	128	234	4	12	0
Santana, Asheville*	.968	24	30	0	1	0
Sawkiw, Fayetteville	.982	35	51	3	1	0
Scott, Asheville	1.000	1	1	0	0	0
Scruggs, Gastonia	.959	74	118	0	5	0
Shannon, Spartanburg	.963	40	50	2	2	1
Sims, Sumter*	.955	19	20	1	1	0
Tagliaferri, Fayetteville	1.000	1	1	0	0	0
Tahan, Savannah	.944	19	34	0	2	0
Tarasco, Sumter	.954	106	173	14	9	5
Taylor, Spartanburg*	.964	73	127	6	5	1
C. Thomas, Spartanburg	.971	48	99	3	3	0
M. Thomas, Columbia	.962	103	162	13	7	1
Trusky, Augusta	.957	71	105	5	5	1
Turner, Greensboro*	.984	36	60	2	1	0
Urbon, Spartanburg*	.939	60	121	3	8	0
Valencia, Spartanburg*	1.000	23	25	0	0	0
B. Walker, Charleston (W.Va.)	.979	48	88	4	2	0
D. Walker, Fayetteville	.981	71	152	3	3	0
Wardlow, Gastonia	1.000	1	2	0	0	0
Welch, Spartanburg	.956	79	123	6	6	2
Wilson, Myrtle Beach*	.931	97	127	7	10	0

CATCHERS

Player and Club	Pct.	G.	PO.	A.	E.	DP.	PB.
Adams, Spartanburg	.994	40	282	45	2	1	6
Antigua, Savannah	.987	76	537	59	8	5	21
Beasley, Savannah	.982	32	204	18	4	0	6
Beuerlein, Asheville	.985	29	171	30	3	1	14
Brooks, Myrtle Beach	.982	60	394	48	8	2	6
Carroll, Columbia	.962	30	136	15	6	2	4
Castillo, Columbia	.977	26	187	22	5	3	4
Cox, Charleston (W.Va.)	.983	80	486	89	10	5	12
Curnow, Charleston (S.C.)	.963	49	223	14	9	0	14
Current, Spartanburg	.986	68	488	70	8	5	11
Estevez, Savannah	.800	1	4	0	1	0	3
Ferguson, Savannah	1.000	1	2	1	0	0	2
Fielitz, Savannah	.977	5	40	3	1	0	2
Fordyce, Columbia	.977	97	574	63	15	7	30
Fuller, Charleston (W.Va.)	.995	25	179	23	1	4	7
Gillette, Fayetteville	.982	55	333	47	7	3	17
Hamburg, Spartanburg	.982	35	206	18	4	3	7
Henderson, Charleston (S.C.)	.975	77	376	52	11	2	17
Hernandez, Gastonia	1.000	4	20	1	0	0	2
Hoffman, Fayetteville	1.000	1	3	0	0	0	0
Holum, Asheville	1.000	6	14	2	0	0	1
Houston, Sumter	.968	84	498	55	18	5	27
Jaime, Myrtle Beach	.981	53	371	39	8	5	16
Jarvis, Greensboro	.973	10	33	3	1	1	2
Johnson, Greensboro	.987	101	752	81	11	2	28
Keating, Savannah	1.000	1	3	0	0	0	1
Lewis, Gastonia	.984	12	56	6	1	1	2
A. Lopez, Sumter	.975	31	169	23	5	1	5
P. Lopez, Charleston (S.C.)	.942	22	109	21	8	2	8
Lucin, Asheville	.959	28	147	18	7	1	9
Marsh, Spartanburg	1.000	10	46	6	0	0	9
McKeon, Fayetteville	.962	16	87	14	4	2	6
Micheu, Gastonia	.989	55	393	49	5	9	7
Nichols, Charleston (W.Va.)	.989	14	69	19	1	1	6
Nixon, Augusta	.976	5	35	6	1	2	3
Ochs, Savannah	.981	93	583	53	12	9	15
Perez, Sumter	.989	34	254	25	3	4	2
Peterson, Augusta	.988	23	147	17	2	3	10
Rivers, Myrtle Beach	.983	36	260	24	5	3	9
SCOTT, Asheville	.988	106	564	69	8	6	28
Sellers, Fayetteville	.981	72	420	34	9	1	8
Spivey, Savannah	.950	6	18	1	1	0	0
Torres, Augusta	.980	51	319	30	7	5	14
Turvey, Savannah	.985	23	120	11	2	0	2
Walker, Greensboro	.965	40	253	26	10	0	9
B. Wilson, Fayetteville	.960	10	68	4	3	1	2
D. Wilson, Char. (W.Va.)	.995	28	190	24	1	2	1
Winford, Gastonia	.983	89	619	78	12	4	26

PITCHERS

Player and Club	Pct.	G.	PO.	A.	E.	DP.
Arias, Savannah	.667	20	3	5	4	0
Arner, Gastonia	.909	14	3	7	1	0
Arvesen, Gastonia	.857	28	6	24	5	0
Asche, Gastonia*	.944	34	9	8	1	1
August, Asheville	1.000	5	2	4	0	0
Ayala, Charleston (W.Va.)	.765	21	5	8	4	1
Backs, Spartanburg	1.000	11	2	4	0	0
Baker, Savannah	.857	70	7	17	4	1
Banks, Charleston (S.C.)	1.000	48	2	17	0	2
Batchelor, Greensboro	.875	27	4	10	2	1
Baur, Spartanburg	1.000	12	0	9	0	0
Bennett, Charleston (S.C.)*	.846	23	10	23	6	1
Betances, Savannah	.800	7	2	2	1	0
Bickhardt, Gastonia	.933	50	7	7	1	2
Bicknell, Myrtle Beach	.905	34	4	15	2	0
Bird, Augusta*	.909	44	2	8	1	0
Blumberg, Myrtle Beach*	.926	25	3	22	2	1
Borcherding, Char. (W.Va.)	1.000	6	1	2	0	0
Bradley, Myrtle Beach	1.000	46	5	8	0	1
Braley, Fayetteville	.963	57	8	18	1	2
Brannon, Savannah	1.000	6	0	1	0	0
Bratlien, Spartanburg	.962	23	5	20	1	2
Da. Brown, Myrtle Beach	.938	25	13	17	2	2
Du. Brown, Asheville	1.000	3	1	1	0	1
T. Brown, Sumter	.923	23	10	26	3	3
Buckley, Gastonia	.872	27	5	36	6	1

PITCHERS—Continued

Player and Club	Pct.	G.	PO.	A.	E.	DP.
Burlingame, Sumter	1.000	12	1	4	0	1
Burton, Gastonia	1.000	2	0	1	0	0
Butler, Columbia	1.000	15	3	4	0	1
CASSIDY, Savannah*	1.000	18	15	35	0	3
Cecil, Charleston (W.Va.)	.912	29	11	20	3	1
Cronin, Sumter	1.000	6	1	5	0	0
Culberson, Charleston (W.Va.)	.941	14	10	6	1	1
Cummings, Sumter	1.000	7	0	1	0	0
Cunningham, Charleston (S.C.)	.857	40	13	17	5	0
Dixon, Savannah*	.923	64	8	16	2	2
Doherty, Fayetteville	1.000	7	1	1	0	0
Dooley, Augusta	1.000	4	0	2	0	0
Dorn, Columbia	.906	27	14	15	3	2
Doty, Charleston (W.Va.)	.941	19	8	8	1	1
Dovey, Asheville	.900	33	3	6	1	0
Duvall, Savannah	.727	7	4	4	3	0
Eischen, Gastonia*	.700	17	2	12	6	0
Elliott, Spartanburg	.905	20	7	12	2	2
Ellis, Charleston (S.C.)*	1.000	3	3	2	0	0
Emm, Columbia	.952	39	5	15	1	1
Espinal, Savannah	1.000	46	4	11	0	1
Evans, Gastonia	1.000	57	1	11	0	1
Faccio, Savannah	.939	29	5	26	2	3
Fajardo, Augusta	.667	7	1	3	2	1
Ferm, Fayetteville	1.000	3	2	1	0	1
D. Fletcher, Savannah	.938	66	8	7	1	1
P. Fletcher, Spartanburg	1.000	9	1	10	0	0
Franklin, Gastonia	.893	28	9	16	3	1
Freitas, Columbia	.950	13	7	12	1	1
Furmanik, Columbia	.952	8	7	13	1	1
Futrell, Augusta	1.000	3	0	2	0	0
Gabriele, Sumter	.000	11	0	0	1	0
Gaddy, Spartanburg*	.969	30	6	25	1	0
Garcia, Fayetteville	.903	28	11	17	3	1
Gardner, Asheville	.938	23	8	22	2	2
Garside, Charleston (S.C.)*	1.000	2	1	1	0	0
Gasser, 5 Col.-6 Sum.	.800	11	3	1	1	0
Gaston, Savannah	.885	31	6	17	3	1
Goedhart, Spartanburg	.933	29	10	18	2	0
Goergen, Spartanburg	1.000	19	10	8	0	0
B. Gonzales, Asheville	.933	53	2	12	1	2
F. Gonzales, Fayetteville*	1.000	25	8	16	0	4
Graves, Gastonia	.667	33	3	3	3	0
Gray, Spartanburg	1.000	3	1	8	0	0
Green, Savannah*	1.000	12	2	2	0	1
Gunderson, Spartanburg	.914	38	7	25	3	1
Gutierrez, Asheville*	.920	41	3	20	2	0
J. Guzman, Fayetteville	.857	26	3	9	2	0
P. Guzman, Charleston (S.C.)	.765	28	5	8	4	2
Haeberle, Sumter	.920	23	10	13	2	0
Hailey, Sumter*	.952	17	6	14	1	1
Haller, Greensboro*	.952	52	7	13	1	1
Herrmann, Fayetteville	.857	7	2	4	1	0
Hitchcock, Greensboro*	.936	27	10	34	3	1
Hoffman, Greensboro*	.973	47	10	26	1	1
Holcomb, Gastonia*	1.000	15	1	2	0	0
Honeywell, Augusta*	1.000	13	0	4	0	0
Hook, Charleston (W.Va.)	.950	30	7	12	1	1
J. Hurst, Gastonia	.929	15	1	12	1	0
W. Hurst, Savannah	1.000	7	3	7	0	1
Hutson, Myrtle Beach	1.000	13	2	5	0	0
Hutton, Greensboro	.750	21	5	10	5	0
Ingram, Fayetteville	.879	33	8	21	4	0
Jackson, Charleston (W.Va.)*	1.000	1	0	1	0	0
Jewett, Sumter	.909	27	3	17	2	4
P. Johnson, Columbia	1.000	16	3	3	0	1
W. Johnson, Charleston (S.C.)	.867	25	4	9	2	1
Johnston, Greensboro	.946	46	9	26	2	1
Juarbe, Greensboro*	.857	16	2	4	1	0
Karasinski, Sumter*	1.000	23	3	5	0	1
Kent, Spartanburg	1.000	18	6	10	0	0
King, Charleston (W.Va.)*	.667	11	1	1	1	0
Kizziah, Myrtle Beach	.854	35	11	24	6	4
Koller, Fayetteville	.867	9	3	10	2	0
Kulina, Myrtle Beach*	.923	28	1	11	1	1
Langbehn, Columbia*	.980	26	14	34	1	2
Latham, Fayetteville*	.923	28	2	10	1	4
Leimeister, Fayetteville	1.000	26	1	3	0	0
Lemon, Sumter	1.000	4	1	3	0	1
Limbach, Spartanburg*	.938	42	2	13	1	0
Lloyd, Myrtle Beach*	.944	19	5	12	1	0
Malley, Charleston (W.Va.)*	.571	7	2	2	3	1
Malone, Greensboro*	1.000	17	4	6	0	0
Mandia, Myrtle Beach	.900	9	0	2	0	0
Marshall, Fayetteville*	1.000	14	5	18	0	1
Martin, Myrtle Beach	1.000	37	2	3	0	0
Martinez, Augusta	1.000	35	4	12	0	1
Marx, Charleston (S.C.)	.913	32	5	16	2	1
Masters, Augusta	1.000	37	8	10	0	1
Mathews, Sumter	1.000	4	1	2	0	0
Mauldin, Greensboro	1.000	13	2	3	0	0
McCann, Columbia	.971	25	16	18	1	5
McCarthy, Charleston (W.Va.)*	1.000	29	4	3	0	0

Player and Club	Pct.	G.	PO.	A.	E.	DP.
McDowell, Asheville	1.000	41	4	13	0	0
Menhart, Myrtle Beach	.750	5	2	1	1	0
Mooney, Augusta	.938	10	3	12	1	0
J. Munoz, Asheville	1.000	9	7	7	0	0
R. Munoz, Greensboro	.933	25	13	29	3	2
Murdock, Charleston (S.C.)*	.667	5	2	0	1	0
Neidinger, Fayetteville	1.000	18	10	15	0	1
Newman, Sumter	.800	8	0	4	1	1
Nielsen, Savannah*	.667	7	1	1	1	0
Nieves, Charleston (W.Va.)	.923	20	3	9	1	0
Nowak, Myrtle Beach	1.000	5	3	5	0	0
Ogliaruso, Myrtle Beach	.860	26	12	25	6	2
Olivares, Myrtle Beach*	.333	8	0	1	2	0
Oliver, Gastonia*	1.000	1	0	1	0	0
Osborne, Savannah*	.938	6	2	13	1	0
Pacheco, Savannah	.923	22	13	11	2	0
Parker, Columbia	1.000	4	2	0	0	0
Parkinson, Augusta	.897	31	8	18	3	2
C. Perez, Greensboro	.600	13	1	2	2	1
F. Perez, Asheville	.941	36	0	16	1	0
Phillips, Gastonia	1.000	12	1	2	0	0
Pickett, Charleston (S.C.)*	1.000	7	0	4	0	0
Pierce, Fayetteville*	.833	7	2	3	1	1
Pinto, Fayetteville	.833	16	1	4	1	1
Plemmons, Charleston (W.Va.)	.857	18	2	16	3	0
Pugh, Charleston (W.Va.)	.893	27	13	37	6	2
Quirico, Greensboro*	.810	13	4	13	4	1
Randall, Spartanburg	1.000	32	8	9	0	1
Randle, Gastonia	.929	29	10	42	4	4
Ray, Charleston (W.Va.)	.963	30	9	17	1	1
Redmond, Augusta	1.000	4	0	1	0	0
Reed, Gastonia	1.000	8	2	12	0	0
Reich, Columbia	.929	26	11	15	2	3
Rhodes, Greensboro	.902	27	11	26	4	0
Richmond, Columbia	.789	22	3	12	4	0
Rinaldi, Asheville*	1.000	7	0	4	0	1
Rivas, Asheville	1.000	33	2	3	0	0
B. Romero, Gastonia*	.853	15	4	25	5	2
R. Romero, Gastonia	.750	11	3	0	1	0
Rosario, Asheville*	.898	30	11	33	5	0
Rountree, Fayetteville	1.000	6	0	2	0	0
Rowley, Gastonia	.810	13	2	15	4	2
Rychel, Augusta	.833	27	9	16	5	1
Sample, Columbia	.889	46	5	3	1	0
D. Santiago, Augusta	.897	31	9	17	3	1
R. Santiago, Charleston (S.C.)*	.943	25	5	28	2	0
Satre, Charleston (W.Va.)	.920	24	16	7	2	1
Schafer, Sumter	.905	39	5	14	2	0
Seibert, Fayetteville*	1.000	7	0	2	0	0
Sells, Savannah*	.857	4	2	4	1	1
Shackle, Savannah	1.000	17	5	6	0	0
Shea, Fayetteville	1.000	17	0	4	0	0
Shiflett, Sumter	1.000	15	1	3	0	0
A. Small, Myrtle Beach	.879	27	12	17	4	1
M. Small, Asheville	.765	34	5	8	4	0
Smith, Greensboro	1.000	16	6	10	0	0
Sottile, Sumter	.962	40	8	17	1	4
Spradlin, Charleston (W.Va.)	1.000	43	6	11	0	1
Springer, Greensboro	.923	10	5	7	1	0
Stafford, Gastonia	1.000	4	3	5	0	1
Stefany, Fayetteville	1.000	40	6	8	0	2
Steiner, Gastonia*	.833	21	4	6	2	1
Steinmetz, Sumter	.950	25	7	12	1	0
Stevens, Spartanburg	.714	14	0	5	2	0
Strange, Sumter	.938	46	5	10	1	0
Sullivan, Spartanburg	1.000	22	2	5	0	0
Telgheder, Columbia	1.000	14	9	14	0	2
Thomas, Sumter*	1.000	16	5	12	0	1
C. Thompson, Charleston (S.C.)	.854	26	16	19	6	2
W. Thompson, Charleston (S.C.)	.500	11	0	1	1	0
Tolbert, Savannah	1.000	29	5	8	0	1
Torres, Fayetteville	1.000	30	0	5	0	0
Tucker, Greensboro*	1.000	11	2	7	0	0
Underwood, Augusta*	1.000	10	3	7	0	0
Valle, Columbia	1.000	11	1	1	0	0
Vasquez, Columbia	1.000	25	3	3	0	0
Vitko, Columbia	1.000	16	9	13	0	3
Wagner, Augusta	1.000	35	3	14	0	0
Wall, Asheville	.931	28	7	20	2	2
Wanish, Myrtle Beach	.889	35	4	12	2	2
Watson, Augusta*	.913	23	5	16	2	1
Way, Augusta*	.900	24	3	6	1	0
Weems, Sumter	1.000	16	1	5	0	0
R. Wells, Spartanburg	.871	20	9	18	4	1
T. Wells, Gastonia	.889	10	1	7	1	2
Wheeler, Asheville	.944	21	11	23	2	1
Wiegandt, Spartanburg*	1.000	10	2	2	0	0
Wilburn, Charleston (W.Va.)	.900	23	2	7	1	0
Wohlers, Sumter	1.000	37	3	9	0	1
Wolf, Fayetteville	.750	8	4	2	2	1
Worrell, Charleston (S.C.)	.900	20	7	11	2	1
Zinter, Charleston (S.C.)	.875	45	1	6	1	1

The following players did not have any fielding statistics at the positions indicated or appeared only as a designated hitter, pinch-hitter or pinch-runner: Anderson, dh, ph; Beanblossom, 3b; Broderick, p; M. Brooks, c, p; M. Burton, 3b; Calder, ph; Cox, 1b; Curnow, p; B. Davis, p; Dixon, of; Duff, p; Embry, p; Fordyce, of; Gryskevich, p; L. Hall, ss; J. Harris, ss, p; Jarvis, of, p; L. Johnson, p; M. Johnson, p; Keating, 2b, p; Link, p; P. Lopez, 3b, of; Lowery, 3b; Manahan, ss; Randolph Marshall, of; N. Martinez, 3b, of; McCray, p; McGraw, p; Micheu, 1b, of; S. Miller, of; Raley, p; Rendina, of; E. Rodriguez, p; R. Rodriguez, p; Romano, of; Shannon, p; Stokes, p; Turner, 1b.

CLUB PITCHING

Club	ERA.	G.	CG.	ShO.	Sv.	IP.	H.	R.	ER.	HR.	HB.	BB.	Int. BB.	SO.	WP.	Bk.
Gastonia	2.83	143	9	16	41	1241.1	1053	511	390	45	53	573	23	1085	77	11
Sumter	3.04	142	15	13	35	1231.0	1086	529	416	66	54	443	25	890	76	24
Myrtle Beach	3.12	140	6	8	48	1205.2	1115	548	418	56	27	483	23	1031	92	15
Charleston (W.Va.)	3.14	143	19	10	37	1220.0	1057	528	425	43	46	526	28	912	77	18
Columbia	3.25	143	25	14	36	1251.1	1216	603	452	51	46	449	10	858	93	14
Fayetteville	3.27	143	15	14	39	1237.0	1111	552	449	57	39	472	28	886	68	15
Spartanburg	3.28	141	8	7	30	1225.1	1126	573	447	60	42	430	3	1024	79	20
Savannah	3.42	141	6	4	37	1240.1	1113	619	471	65	78	578	25	927	100	20
Greensboro	3.52	144	7	12	25	1254.0	1081	670	491	51	53	564	22	1051	100	29
Augusta	3.70	143	7	9	34	1245.1	1233	663	512	67	50	576	21	1006	92	23
Asheville	3.98	143	15	11	34	1219.2	1156	699	540	82	69	642	26	867	116	18
Charleston (S.C.)	4.34	142	17	6	26	1208.0	1295	762	582	61	54	516	16	682	109	17

PITCHERS' RECORDS

(Leading Qualifiers for Earned-Run Average Leadership—115 or More Innings)

*Throws lefthanded.

Pitcher—Club	W.	L.	Pct.	ERA.	G.	GS.	CG.	GF.	ShO.	Sv.	IP.	H.	R.	ER.	HR.	HB.	BB.	Int. BB.	SO.	WP.
Hoffman, Greensboro	8	3	.727	1.47	47	1	0	21	0	1	116.0	86	43	19	3	2	40	3	93	9
Pugh, Charleston (W.Va.)	15	6	.714	1.93	27	27	8	0	2	0	177.1	142	58	38	5	7	56	0	153	10
Hailey, Sumter*	10	1	.909	2.02	17	17	4	0	2	0	120.1	66	31	27	3	6	46	2	126	2
Blumberg, Myrtle Beach*	13	4	.765	2.16	25	23	1	0	0	0	129.1	101	43	31	4	0	68	0	128	14
Ogliaruso, Myrtle Beach	14	9	.609	2.52	26	26	2	0	1	0	164.1	132	57	46	4	4	61	2	158	14
Garcia, Fayetteville	12	8	.600	2.55	28	28	6	0	2	0	180.1	152	69	51	7	6	41	0	113	3
Gardner, Asheville	5	10	.333	2.62	23	23	3	0	1	0	134.0	102	57	39	6	7	69	2	81	8
A. Small, Myrtle Beach	9	9	.500	2.80	27	27	1	0	0	0	147.2	150	72	46	6	4	56	2	96	16
Dorn, Columbia	9	11	.450	2.81	27	19	6	2	3	1	144.0	140	67	45	2	5	49	1	69	2
Buckley, Gastonia	12	6	.667	2.84	27	26	3	0	0	0	161.2	149	66	51	10	4	61	0	149	7

Departmental Leaders: G—Baker, 70; W—Pugh, 15; L—C. Thompson, 17; Pct.—Marshall, 1.000; GS—Faccio, 29; CG—Pugh, 8; GF—Braley, 51; ShO—Hitchcock, 5; Sv.—Braley, 27; IP—Garcia, 180.1; H—Cunningham, 188; R—C. Thompson, 110; ER—W. Johnson, 79; HR—Wall, 18; HB—Faccio, 18; BB—Randle, 105; IBB—B. Gonzales, 9; SO—Hitchcock, 171; WP—Gasser, 27.

(All Pitchers—Listed Alphabetically)

Pitcher—Club	W.	L.	Pct.	ERA.	G.	GS.	CG.	GF.	ShO.	Sv.	IP.	H.	R.	ER.	HR.	HB.	BB.	Int. BB.	SO.	WP.
Arias, Savannah	1	5	.167	6.34	20	11	0	4	0	0	59.2	59	50	42	2	6	58	2	41	7
Arner, Gastonia	8	2	.800	2.03	14	14	1	0	0	0	88.2	74	25	20	3	2	16	1	86	4
Arvesen, Augusta	8	11	.421	4.32	28	28	2	0	1	0	158.1	186	89	76	6	2	54	0	102	4
Asche, Gastonia*	3	1	.750	3.59	34	1	0	12	0	2	57.2	55	28	23	1	2	24	2	60	6
August, Asheville	3	0	1.000	2.25	5	4	0	0	0	0	20.0	17	6	5	0	1	6	0	17	1
Ayala, Charleston (W.Va.)	6	1	.857	2.43	21	4	2	8	1	2	74.0	48	23	20	2	3	21	1	73	0
Backs, Spartanburg	3	2	.600	6.43	11	1	0	4	0	0	21.0	15	18	15	1	5	18	0	18	1
Baker, Savannah	6	3	.667	2.03	70	0	0	23	0	1	93.0	76	34	21	5	4	21	1	59	3
Banks, Charleston (S.C.)	7	1	.875	2.82	48	0	0	26	0	2	99.0	92	45	31	1	1	43	3	43	6
Batchelor, Greensboro	2	2	.500	1.58	27	0	0	18	0	8	51.1	39	15	9	1	0	14	1	38	2
Baur, Spartanburg	1	3	.250	2.77	12	0	0	10	0	1	26.0	27	13	8	3	1	8	0	15	3
Bennett, Charleston (S.C.)*	5	15	.250	3.06	23	23	6	0	1	0	150.0	172	75	51	2	8	27	3	75	6
Betances, Savannah	0	4	.000	5.79	7	5	0	1	0	0	23.1	31	21	15	5	1	18	0	15	4
Bickhardt, Gastonia	8	6	.571	3.14	50	0	0	16	0	4	80.1	67	34	28	4	2	35	2	82	3
Bicknell, Myrtle Beach	5	4	.556	3.65	34	15	0	5	0	0	120.2	118	63	49	8	2	45	3	89	12
Bird, Augusta*	4	4	.500	2.09	44	5	0	35	0	15	86.0	72	24	20	3	0	35	3	114	6
Blumberg, Myrtle Beach*	13	4	.765	2.16	25	23	1	0	0	0	129.1	101	43	31	4	0	68	0	128	14
Borcherding, Charleston (W.Va.)	0	4	.000	5.02	6	0	0	1	0	0	14.1	16	12	8	2	2	10	1	5	0
Bradley, Myrtle Beach	2	4	.333	3.31	46	0	0	34	0	8	73.1	80	34	27	6	1	19	2	77	1
Braley, Fayetteville	9	3	.750	1.87	57	0	0	51	0	27	86.2	69	25	18	0	1	43	7	69	4
Brannon, Savannah	0	0	.000	2.84	6	0	0	5	0	0	6.1	5	2	2	0	0	5	0	7	0
Bratlien, Spartanburg	5	7	.417	3.77	23	11	2	4	0	0	100.1	102	45	42	7	6	19	1	66	0
Broderick, Greensboro	0	0	.000	0.00	2	0	0	2	0	0	1.2	0	0	0	0	0	1	0	1	0
Brooks, Charleston (S.C.)	0	0	.000	0.00	2	0	0	2	0	0	2.0	0	0	0	0	0	2	0	2	0
Da. Brown, Myrtle Beach	11	7	.611	4.11	25	25	0	0	0	0	142.1	155	81	65	8	3	51	1	120	8
Du. Brown, Asheville	0	1	.000	7.82	3	2	0	0	0	0	12.2	17	13	11	4	0	7	0	8	1
T. Brown, Sumter	5	7	.417	3.49	23	22	3	0	0	0	136.2	149	71	53	9	4	43	2	69	10
Buckley, Gastonia	12	6	.667	2.84	27	26	3	0	0	0	161.2	149	66	51	10	4	61	0	149	7
Burlingame, Sumter	1	3	.250	2.27	12	12	0	0	0	0	35.2	36	14	9	2	1	6	0	20	0
Burton, Gastonia	0	0	.000	11.57	2	0	0	2	0	0	4.2	11	6	6	0	1	4	0	1	0
Butler, Columbia	7	2	.778	2.70	15	11	1	1	1	0	80.0	75	33	24	3	1	29	0	50	5
Cassidy, Savannah	9	5	.643	1.94	18	17	3	0	1	0	111.1	99	32	24	3	4	24	0	56	3
Cecil, Charleston (W.Va.)	7	5	.583	3.76	29	17	1	5	1	0	115.0	121	59	48	3	3	45	2	67	6
Cronin, Sumter	2	1	.667	2.27	6	6	1	0	1	0	39.2	36	13	10	3	0	12	0	14	1
Culberson, Charleston (W.Va.)	5	5	.500	3.08	14	14	0	0	0	0	79.0	62	32	27	4	2	32	1	57	8
Cummings, Sumter	1	0	1.000	4.00	7	0	0	5	0	1	9.0	10	4	4	1	0	4	0	6	2
Cunningham, Charleston (S.C.)	4	11	.267	4.33	40	15	2	13	0	1	151.2	188	92	73	11	7	55	3	77	7
Curnow, Charleston (S.C.)	0	0	.000	4.50	4	0	0	4	0	0	6.0	7	3	3	0	0	2	0	4	2
Davis, Columbia	0	0	.000	4.50	1	0	0	0	0	0	2.0	2	1	1	0	0	3	0	2	0
Dixon, Savannah*	7	3	.700	1.94	64	0	0	21	0	8	83.2	59	34	18	1	4	38	5	93	4
Doherty, Fayetteville	1	0	1.000	5.79	4	0	0	3	0	1	9.1	17	12	6	0	1	1	0	6	1
Dooley, Augusta	0	0	.000	2.70	4	0	0	1	0	0	3.1	6	8	1	1	1	3	0	2	1
Dorn, Columbia	9	11	.450	2.81	27	19	6	2	3	1	144.0	140	67	45	2	5	49	1	69	2
Doty, Charleston (W.Va.)	3	1	.750	0.82	19	0	0	12	0	4	43.2	23	6	4	0	0	22	1	30	2
Dovey, Asheville	9	7	.563	4.18	33	15	1	8	0	2	112.0	94	65	52	6	6	75	0	100	12
Duff, Charleston (W.Va.)*	1	0	1.000	1.42	3	0	0	0	0	0	6.1	5	1	1	0	0	5	0	5	1
Duvall, Savannah	2	3	.400	2.13	7	7	0	0	0	0	38.0	32	19	9	1	2	19	1	23	2
Eischen, Gastonia*	3	7	.300	2.70	17	14	0	0	0	0	73.1	51	36	22	0	3	40	0	69	9
Elliott, Spartanburg	4	8	.333	3.50	20	20	0	0	0	0	105.1	101	52	41	6	2	46	0	109	7

Pitcher—Club	W.	L.	Pct.	ERA.	G.	GS.	CG.	GF.	ShO.	Sv.	IP.	H.	R.	ER.	HR.	HB.	BB.	Int. BB.	SO.	WP.
Ellis, Charleston (S.C.)*	1	2	.333	7.90	3	3	0	0	0	0	13.2	16	12	12	1	0	12	0	3	3
Embry, Charleston (S.C.)	1	0	1.000	1.38	2	2	1	0	1	0	13.0	8	2	2	0	0	7	0	15	0
Emm, Columbia	4	4	.500	4.95	39	2	0	16	0	1	72.2	86	54	40	3	2	33	3	47	9
Espinal, Savannah	7	2	.778	2.63	46	0	0	25	0	13	61.2	50	22	18	1	7	27	3	48	1
Evans, Gastonia	3	3	.500	1.09	57	0	0	41	0	17	74.1	57	13	9	4	0	26	3	60	4
Faccio, Savannah	8	11	.421	3.88	29	29	1	0	0	0	164.2	153	95	71	10	18	84	3	169	19
Fajardo, Augusta	2	2	.500	3.86	7	7	0	0	0	0	39.2	41	18	17	1	2	15	0	28	0
Ferm, Fayetteville	0	3	.000	4.02	3	3	0	0	0	0	15.2	17	7	7	0	1	11	0	13	0
D. Fletcher, Savannah	3	6	.333	3.49	66	0	0	39	0	15	80.0	76	36	31	6	0	32	3	74	3
P. Fletcher, Spartanburg	2	4	.333	3.28	9	9	1	0	0	0	49.1	46	24	18	3	2	18	0	53	7
Franklin, Gastonia	4	7	.364	3.10	28	12	0	7	0	1	93.0	92	50	32	3	3	47	2	64	4
Freitas, Columbia	5	2	.714	2.44	13	9	0	2	0	0	70.0	60	27	19	5	2	14	0	47	5
Furmanik, Columbia	3	3	.500	2.48	8	8	1	0	1	0	54.1	50	20	15	0	3	10	0	27	1
Futrell, Augusta	0	1	.000	2.25	3	0	0	1	0	0	4.0	5	2	1	0	0	3	0	1	1
Gabriele, Sumter	0	0	.000	8.16	11	0	0	5	0	0	14.1	24	18	13	0	0	11	1	8	1
Gaddy, Spartanburg*	9	7	.563	3.33	30	19	0	2	0	2	140.1	107	65	52	12	4	67	0	143	8
Garcia, Fayetteville	12	8	.600	2.55	28	28	6	0	2	0	180.1	152	69	51	7	6	41	0	113	3
Gardner, Asheville	5	10	.333	2.62	23	23	3	0	1	0	134.0	102	57	39	6	7	69	2	81	8
Garside, Charleston (S.C.)*	0	2	.000	11.25	2	2	0	0	0	0	8.0	15	10	10	4	0	0	0	5	0
Gasser, 5 Col.-6 Sum.	0	3	.000	11.25	11	6	0	3	0	0	24.0	13	31	30	1	0	55	0	23	27
Gaston, Savannah	3	10	.231	4.61	31	17	0	6	0	0	121.0	100	74	62	9	2	86	3	88	15
Goedhart, Spartanburg	8	10	.444	4.43	29	28	1	0	0	0	150.1	162	96	74	7	5	62	0	92	13
Goergen, Spartanburg	7	8	.467	3.30	19	18	0	0	0	0	103.2	117	49	38	4	4	12	0	73	3
B. Gonzales, Asheville	3	4	.429	2.35	53	0	0	43	0	18	72.2	50	25	19	5	8	46	9	66	4
F. Gonzales, Fayetteville*	10	6	.625	3.02	25	25	0	0	0	0	143.0	123	54	48	2	4	66	0	101	9
Graves, Gastonia	3	5	.375	2.01	33	0	0	26	0	13	44.2	34	17	10	1	1	20	3	53	3
Gray, Spartanburg	1	1	.500	1.23	3	3	1	0	0	0	22.0	16	6	3	0	1	2	0	22	0
Green, Savannah*	1	0	1.000	1.46	12	0	0	3	0	0	12.1	13	3	2	0	0	2	0	11	2
Gryskevich, Savannah*	0	0	.000	16.88	3	0	0	2	0	0	2.2	3	5	5	1	0	5	0	1	2
Gunderson, Spartanburg	0	1	.000	2.06	38	0	0	25	0	3	70.0	53	21	16	2	5	18	0	58	2
Gutierrez, Asheville*	7	7	.500	4.62	41	12	0	12	0	0	101.1	91	66	52	3	5	74	3	88	21
J. Guzman, Fayetteville	3	3	.500	6.30	26	6	0	7	0	0	64.1	75	50	45	7	4	33	3	32	11
P. Guzman, Charleston (S.C.)	1	1	.500	4.10	28	2	0	13	0	1	74.2	86	45	34	3	1	29	0	38	5
Haeberle, Sumter	8	10	.444	3.02	23	21	2	0	0	0	131.1	119	57	44	6	7	48	3	73	7
Hailey, Sumter*	10	1	.909	2.02	17	17	4	0	2	0	120.1	66	31	27	3	6	46	2	126	2
Haller, Greensboro*	2	6	.250	2.99	52	0	0	46	0	14	72.1	66	31	24	3	1	28	5	58	8
Harris, Columbia	0	0	.000	0.00	2	0	0	2	0	0	2.1	2	0	0	1	1	0	2	0	1
Herrmann, Fayetteville	0	4	.000	6.75	7	7	0	0	0	0	29.1	34	24	22	3	0	10	0	18	1
Hitchcock, Greensboro*	12	12	.500	2.91	27	27	6	0	5	0	173.1	122	68	56	7	8	60	1	171	6
Hoffman, Greensboro	8	3	.727	1.47	47	1	0	21	0	1	116.0	86	43	19	3	2	40	3	93	9
Holcomb, Gastonia	1	1	.500	4.33	15	1	0	6	0	0	27.0	31	16	13	0	1	18	0	16	4
Honeywell, Augusta*	4	1	.800	1.15	13	0	0	13	0	4	15.2	9	4	2	0	0	8	1	8	0
Hook, Charleston (W.Va.)	6	5	.545	4.07	30	16	0	3	0	0	119.1	117	65	54	3	8	62	4	87	19
J. Hurst, Gastonia	8	1	.889	2.64	15	7	0	3	0	1	61.1	48	21	18	2	4	19	0	49	3
W. Hurst, Savannah	2	1	.667	3.41	7	7	0	0	0	0	31.2	22	17	12	0	1	27	1	14	3
Hutson, Myrtle Beach	0	2	.000	4.85	13	1	0	4	0	2	26.0	21	15	14	2	2	13	2	25	3
Hutton, Greensboro	1	10	.091	6.31	21	19	0	1	0	0	81.1	77	78	57	2	7	62	0	72	14
Ingram, Savannah	8	7	.533	3.97	32	21	2	3	2	0	143.0	141	75	63	8	5	50	7	101	4
Jackson, Charleston (W.Va.)*	0	0	.000	6.00	1	1	0	0	0	0	3.0	2	2	2	0	0	1	0	2	0
Jarvis, Greensboro	0	0	.000	27.00	1	0	0	1	0	0	0.2	2	2	2	0	0	3	0	0	3
Jewett, Sumter	6	5	.545	2.40	27	12	2	3	1	0	108.2	89	43	29	5	5	39	2	72	6
L. Johnson, Asheville*	0	0	.000	6.75	1	0	0	0	0	0	1.1	1	1	1	0	0	2	0	1	1
M. Johnson, Augusta*	0	0	.000	3.86	1	0	0	1	0	0	2.1	3	1	1	0	0	0	0	1	0
P. Johnson, Columbia	1	1	.500	2.88	16	0	0	8	0	1	25.0	39	13	8	1	1	7	1	19	2
W. Johnson, Charleston (S.C.)	3	14	.176	6.81	25	20	1	2	1	0	104.1	113	102	79	12	10	90	0	84	20
Johnston, Greensboro	5	5	.500	2.51	46	0	0	17	0	0	100.1	80	44	28	2	6	32	6	66	5
Juarbe, Greensboro*	2	3	.400	4.34	16	3	0	6	0	0	37.1	40	28	18	3	1	17	1	33	1
Karasinski, Sumter*	1	3	.250	2.05	23	0	0	10	0	0	26.1	27	9	6	0	0	12	0	21	2
Keating, Savannah	0	0	.000	13.50	1	0	0	1	0	0	1.1	3	2	2	0	0	0	0	0	0
Kent, Spartanburg	2	6	.250	3.01	18	12	1	5	0	1	83.2	75	41	28	4	0	30	0	75	11
King, Charleston (W.Va.)*	0	1	.000	5.06	11	0	0	9	0	1	10.2	12	6	6	1	2	5	0	10	0
Kizziah, Myrtle Beach	6	6	.500	3.47	35	6	1	12	0	4	98.2	103	56	38	3	7	35	1	48	5
Koller, Fayetteville	2	2	.500	3.06	9	9	0	0	0	0	47.0	38	20	16	1	6	20	1	33	3
Kulina, Myrtle Beach*	3	3	.500	4.60	28	0	0	14	0	3	47.0	50	30	24	3	1	20	2	40	4
Langbehn, Columbia*	13	11	.542	3.31	26	25	7	1	2	0	174.0	165	84	64	6	5	59	1	132	9
Latham, Augusta*	3	2	.600	4.39	28	6	0	13	0	2	65.2	64	42	32	2	9	55	6	61	14
Leimeister, Fayetteville	1	1	.500	3.54	26	0	0	10	0	1	40.2	35	17	16	2	0	16	0	38	2
Lemon, Sumter	1	2	.333	6.33	4	4	0	0	0	0	21.1	29	20	15	2	0	5	0	3	2
Limbach, Spartanburg*	7	4	.636	2.37	42	0	0	26	0	4	87.1	72	29	23	2	0	33	2	91	10
Link, Fayetteville	1	0	1.000	1.04	6	0	0	5	0	3	8.2	4	2	1	1	0	3	1	12	2
Lloyd, Myrtle Beach*	5	2	.714	2.72	19	6	0	8	0	6	49.2	51	20	15	3	0	16	1	42	1
Malley, Charleston (W.Va.)*	1	0	1.000	2.74	7	3	0	2	0	0	23.0	12	10	7	1	0	16	0	19	2
Malone, Greensboro*	4	3	.571	4.86	17	6	0	3	0	1	46.1	45	32	25	1	0	26	0	44	7
Mandia, Myrtle Beach	0	1	.000	0.64	9	0	0	8	0	4	14.0	6	1	1	0	0	4	1	16	1
Marshall, Fayetteville*	13	0	1.000	1.33	14	14	5	0	3	0	101.2	64	17	15	3	0	9	1	81	0
Martin, Myrtle Beach	2	4	.333	2.39	37	0	0	31	0	16	49.0	22	16	13	1	2	34	2	71	0
Martinez, Augusta	3	2	.600	5.26	35	2	0	8	0	0	77.0	103	56	45	10	4	34	1	40	2
Marx, Charleston (S.C.)	3	4	.429	3.48	32	2	0	17	0	4	75.0	71	38	29	4	4	28	1	34	6
Masters, Augusta	2	1	.667	3.18	37	0	0	20	0	5	68.0	62	34	24	6	1	24	0	55	3
Mathews, Sumter	1	0	1.000	0.00	4	0	0	3	0	0	5.0	3	0	0	0	0	1	0	4	0
Mauldin, Greensboro	2	2	.500	4.56	13	0	0	6	0	0	23.2	23	14	12	3	4	11	1	23	2
McCann, Columbia	13	5	.722	3.29	25	23	1	1	0	0	142.1	149	64	52	10	3	38	0	83	8
McCarthy, Charleston (W.Va.)*	2	3	.400	2.61	29	0	0	21	0	10	38.0	32	14	11	0	1	21	4	31	1
McCray, Asheville	0	0	.000	9.00	1	0	0	1	0	0	3.0	3	3	3	1	0	1	0	2	1
McDowell, Asheville	4	3	.571	5.13	41	0	0	7	0	1	86.0	84	64	49	5	11	79	0	60	12
McGraw, Gastonia*	0	0	.000	5.40	1	1	0	0	0	0	5.0	6	3	3	0	0	2	0	1	0
Menhart, Myrtle Beach	3	0	1.000	0.59	5	4	1	1	0	0	30.2	18	5	2	0	2	5	0	18	1
Mooney, Augusta	3	3	.500	4.64	10	8	0	0	0	0	42.2	40	27	22	3	1	30	0	18	5
J. Munoz, Asheville	3	2	.600	2.35	9	9	0	0	0	0	38.1	31	15	10	0	2	17	0	16	3
R. Munoz, Greensboro	5	12	.294	3.73	25	24	0	0	0	0	132.2	133	70	55	4	5	58	1	100	4
Murdock, Charleston (S.C.)*	0	1	.000	6.10	5	0	0	4	0	1	10.1	13	10	7	0	0	4	0	4	1
Neidinger, Fayetteville	4	8	.333	4.47	18	18	2	0	1	0	104.2	117	60	52	4	1	24	0	43	4

Pitcher—Club	W.	L.	Pct.	ERA.	G.	GS.	CG.	GF.	ShO.	Sv.	IP.	H.	R.	ER.	HR.	HB.	BB.	Int. BB.	SO.	WP.
Newman, Sumter	0	0	.000	1.64	8	0	0	3	0	0	11.0	9	2	2	0	0	4	0	11	2
Nielsen, Savannah°	1	4	.200	7.36	7	6	0	1	0	0	22.0	34	23	18	1	4	12	0	20	3
Nieves, Charleston (W.Va.)	1	3	.250	3.60	20	0	0	11	0	2	25.0	19	14	10	3	3	16	3	21	1
Nowak, Myrtle Beach	1	2	.333	2.33	5	5	0	0	0	0	27.0	17	8	7	0	1	12	0	29	4
Ogliaruso, Myrtle Beach	14	9	.609	2.52	26	26	2	0	1	0	164.1	132	57	46	4	4	61	2	158	14
Olivares, Myrtle Beach°	0	1	.000	3.86	8	0	0	0	0	0	11.2	13	6	5	1	0	7	2	5	0
Oliver, Gastonia°	0	0	.000	13.50	1	1	0	0	0	0	2.0	1	3	3	0	0	4	0	2	0
Osborne, Savannah°	2	2	.500	2.61	6	6	1	0	0	0	41.1	40	20	12	2	3	7	0	28	2
Pacheco, Savannah	8	6	.571	3.90	22	18	0	2	0	0	99.1	86	47	43	2	7	53	1	45	16
Parker, Columbia	0	0	.000	13.50	4	1	0	0	0	0	10.0	20	21	15	4	1	7	0	5	1
Parkinson, Augusta	6	13	.316	4.50	31	26	0	2	0	0	138.0	139	93	69	11	7	78	4	127	9
C. Perez, Greensboro	0	0	.000	3.15	13	0	0	7	0	0	20.0	18	13	7	0	1	12	0	27	6
F. Perez, Asheville	6	4	.600	5.35	36	8	1	9	1	1	99.1	115	81	59	6	4	46	3	77	9
Phillips, Gastonia	0	1	.000	6.85	12	1	0	4	0	0	22.1	24	18	17	1	2	11	2	18	1
Pickett, Charleston (S.C.)°	1	0	1.000	3.72	7	0	0	1	0	0	19.1	22	14	8	0	0	13	0	9	1
Pierce, Fayetteville°	1	3	.250	4.40	7	1	0	2	0	1	14.1	14	7	7	0	1	10	1	13	3
Pinto, Fayetteville	0	0	.000	3.15	16	0	0	10	0	0	20.0	14	9	7	2	0	12	0	17	0
Plemmons, Charleston (W.Va.)	6	6	.500	3.48	18	18	1	0	0	0	108.2	90	50	42	2	2	50	0	92	5
Pugh, Charleston (W.Va.)	15	6	.714	1.93	27	27	8	0	2	0	177.1	142	58	38	5	7	56	0	153	10
Quirico, Greensboro°	2	6	.250	5.00	13	13	1	0	0	0	72.0	74	60	40	4	3	30	0	52	5
Raley, Fayetteville	0	0	.000	0.00	2	0	0	2	0	0	1.1	0	0	0	0	0	1	0	1	1
Randall, Spartanburg	2	3	.400	2.44	32	1	0	19	0	7	66.1	55	26	18	1	1	21	0	60	3
Randle, Gastonia	8	9	.471	4.19	29	27	2	0	2	0	148.1	113	79	69	7	13	105	3	121	11
Ray, Charleston (W.Va.)	14	7	.667	2.93	30	20	3	4	2	0	153.2	147	60	50	6	2	48	4	81	2
Redmond, Augusta	0	2	.000	13.50	4	0	0	0	0	0	4.2	6	9	7	1	0	5	0	3	0
Reed, Gastonia	3	1	.750	0.00	8	5	1	2	1	1	38.0	16	1	0	0	2	9	0	26	1
Reich, Columbia	3	6	.333	4.07	26	10	0	10	0	3	84.0	93	55	38	1	13	35	1	47	5
Rhodes, Greensboro	7	10	.412	3.73	27	27	0	0	0	0	154.1	121	75	64	8	5	95	0	147	17
Richmond, Columbia	1	5	.167	4.96	22	7	0	4	0	2	65.1	79	50	36	1	3	29	0	34	3
Rinaldi, Asheville°	0	0	.000	7.62	7	0	0	2	0	0	13.0	20	14	11	2	0	7	0	7	3
Rivas, Asheville	2	3	.400	2.79	33	0	0	25	0	5	42.0	39	14	13	1	2	20	2	30	8
E. Rodriguez, Fayetteville°	1	1	.500	3.38	7	2	0	3	0	0	18.2	14	7	7	3	0	14	0	22	0
R. Rodriguez, Augusta	0	0	.000	0.00	1	0	0	1	0	0	1.0	0	0	0	0	0	3	0	0	0
B. Romero, Gastonia°	9	2	.818	1.48	15	15	1	0	0	0	91.0	74	17	15	2	2	35	0	87	3
R. Romero, Gastonia	2	1	.667	2.45	11	2	0	2	0	0	22.0	17	13	6	2	3	14	0	21	2
Rosario, Asheville°	8	15	.348	3.50	30	26	4	2	1	0	174.2	173	95	68	14	2	49	1	94	7
Rountree, Fayetteville	0	1	.000	13.50	6	0	0	1	0	0	4.2	9	10	7	1	5	0	3	1	
Rowley, Gastonia	6	3	.667	2.55	13	13	1	0	0	0	81.1	66	36	23	2	4	46	1	78	8
Rychel, Augusta	10	4	.714	4.12	27	23	0	0	0	0	129.0	127	79	59	3	8	87	0	105	26
Sample, Columbia	6	2	.750	1.99	46	2	0	37	0	18	81.1	48	20	18	6	1	46	3	84	8
D. Santiago, Augusta	9	10	.474	3.42	31	19	3	5	2	2	144.2	137	69	55	11	7	37	2	101	5
R. Santiago, Charleston (S.C.)°	8	15	.348	3.68	25	23	3	1	0	0	146.2	143	82	60	11	8	50	0	94	11
Satre, Charleston (W.Va.)	6	12	.333	4.73	24	22	3	0	1	0	116.0	99	70	61	8	3	75	1	105	16
Schafer, Sumter	4	6	.400	3.09	39	1	0	15	0	1	87.1	59	36	30	8	5	39	6	69	5
Seibert, Fayetteville°	0	0	.000	3.60	7	0	0	3	0	0	10.0	9	4	4	1	0	5	0	5	1
Sells, Savannah°	2	0	1.000	1.11	4	4	0	0	0	0	24.1	14	4	3	0	0	17	0	17	3
Shackle, Savannah	8	2	.800	2.71	17	11	1	0	0	0	86.1	81	35	26	10	1	14	0	70	2
Shannon, Spartanburg	1	1	.500	21.60	4	0	0	4	0	0	3.1	9	8	8	0	1	7	0	0	0
Shea, Fayetteville	1	3	.250	4.08	17	1	0	7	0	0	28.2	24	18	13	4	1	22	2	24	6
Shiflett, Sumter	0	2	.000	8.10	15	1	0	5	0	0	26.2	29	26	24	4	1	16	0	21	3
A. Small, Myrtle Beach	9	9	.500	2.80	27	27	1	0	0	0	147.2	150	72	46	6	4	56	2	96	16
M. Small, Asheville	3	4	.429	4.15	34	0	0	16	0	6	52.0	54	36	24	2	4	37	5	34	9
Smith, Greensboro	4	7	.364	3.60	16	13	0	1	0	0	85.0	69	41	34	5	6	32	3	54	8
Sottile, Sumter	8	7	.533	2.49	40	4	0	16	0	4	101.1	94	36	28	6	4	23	1	71	4
Spradlin, Charleston (W.Va.)	3	4	.429	2.54	43	1	1	34	0	17	74.1	74	23	21	1	2	17	5	39	3
Springer, Greensboro	2	3	.400	3.67	10	10	0	0	0	0	56.1	51	33	23	3	1	31	0	51	3
Stafford, Gastonia	0	3	.000	3.96	4	3	0	0	0	0	25.0	27	14	11	2	3	8	1	12	2
Stefany, Fayetteville	6	5	.545	2.01	40	0	0	13	0	1	62.2	42	25	14	2	2	29	4	48	4
Steiner, Gastonia°	0	0	.000	1.38	21	0	0	3	0	0	26.0	25	6	4	0	1	17	1	23	0
Steinmetz, Sumter	11	8	.579	3.42	25	24	2	0	1	0	144.2	148	67	55	11	7	34	3	105	5
Stevens, Spartanburg	0	2	.000	2.17	14	0	0	8	0	2	29.0	24	12	7	1	0	10	0	31	2
Stokes, Fayetteville	0	0	.000	0.00	1	0	0	0	0	0	3.0	1	0	0	0	0	2	0	2	0
Strange, Sumter	4	1	.800	0.66	46	0	0	41	0	24	54.1	34	6	4	0	3	12	3	53	2
Sullivan, Spartanburg	4	3	.571	4.50	22	0	0	18	0	8	36.0	39	19	18	1	0	17	0	28	5
Telgheder, Columbia	9	3	.750	1.54	14	13	5	1	1	0	99.1	79	22	17	2	0	10	0	81	0
Thomas, Sumter°	4	4	.500	3.97	16	11	1	3	0	0	68.0	79	37	30	5	3	22	1	29	5
C. Thompson, Charleston (S.C.)	4	17	.190	4.73	26	26	1	0	0	0	148.1	166	110	78	6	6	58	2	56	11
W. Thompson, Charleston (S.C.)	0	3	.000	17.00	11	5	0	1	0	0	18.0	20	40	34	0	6	46	0	6	18
Tolbert, Savannah	3	1	.750	4.13	29	3	0	2	0	0	76.1	77	44	35	6	14	29	2	48	1
Torres, Fayetteville	5	1	.833	2.04	30	1	0	8	0	3	61.2	57	16	14	2	4	24	1	60	5
Tucker, Greensboro°	1	1	.500	5.52	11	1	0	8	0	1	29.1	37	23	18	2	3	12	0	21	0
Underwood, Augusta°	3	1	.750	3.12	10	10	0	0	0	0	57.2	45	23	20	1	0	23	0	52	1
Valle, Columbia	0	0	.000	6.98	11	0	0	4	0	0	19.1	27	15	15	2	1	11	0	13	6
Vasquez, Columbia	1	4	.200	2.17	25	0	0	24	0	9	29.0	28	15	7	1	3	17	0	37	4
Vitko, Columbia	8	1	.889	2.49	16	12	4	2	2	1	90.1	70	29	25	3	1	30	0	72	12
Wagner, Augusta	7	7	.500	2.75	35	1	0	20	0	4	72.0	71	30	22	3	2	30	3	71	7
Wall, Asheville	6	8	.429	5.18	28	22	1	3	0	1	132.0	149	87	76	18	9	47	1	111	10
Wanish, Myrtle Beach	3	5	.375	4.24	35	2	0	17	0	5	74.1	78	41	35	6	0	37	2	69	8
Watson, Augusta°	4	4	.500	2.30	23	8	2	6	1	1	86.0	76	31	22	1	4	31	0	75	6
Way, Augusta°	5	2	.714	3.08	24	0	0	10	0	1	49.2	41	24	17	4	2	21	1	42	2
Weems, Sumter	1	2	.333	2.41	10	0	0	3	0	0	18.2	10	8	5	0	4	12	1	14	3
R. Wells, Spartanburg	5	8	.385	2.87	20	19	2	0	0	0	113.0	94	47	36	6	5	40	0	73	4
T. Wells, Gastonia	1	2	.333	5.27	10	0	0	10	0	2	13.2	15	9	8	1	0	12	2	7	2
Wheeler, Asheville	7	9	.438	3.45	21	20	5	0	3	0	125.1	116	57	48	9	8	60	0	76	7
Wiegandt, Spartanburg°	2	0	1.000	0.98	10	0	0	8	0	2	18.1	12	2	2	0	0	2	0	17	0
Wilburn, Charleston (W.Va.)	1	3	.250	3.49	23	0	0	14	0	1	38.2	36	23	15	2	6	24	1	35	1
Wohlers, Sumter	5	4	.556	1.88	37	2	0	16	0	5	52.2	27	13	11	1	4	20	0	85	0
Wolf, Fayetteville	4	2	.667	3.82	8	7	0	0	0	0	37.2	41	24	16	4	1	21	0	32	3
Worrell, Charleston (S.C.)	5	8	.385	4.64	20	19	4	0	0	0	110.2	120	65	57	6	1	28	2	68	9
Zinter, Charleston (S.C.)	3	2	.600	2.20	45	0	0	40	0	17	57.1	43	17	14	0	2	23	2	65	3

BALKS—Quirico, 10; Parkinson, 7; R. Munoz, Rychel, Steinmetz, 6 each; Arias, Arner, Rivas, A. Small, Sottile, 5 each; Bicknell, Pacheco, Plemmons, 4 each; Culberson, Gardner, Gasser, Goedhart, Ingram, Juarbe, Masters, Osborne, Pickett, Reich, Satre, W. Thompson, Wheeler, Wilburn, 3 each; Bennett, Da. Brown, T. Brown, Doherty, Espinal, Gaddy, Gunderson, Gutierrez, Haeberle, Hailey, Herrmann, Hitchcock, Hoffman, W. Hurst, Jewett, W. Johnson, Kent, Martin, Randall, Ray, Richmond, Rinaldi, Stefany, Sullivan, Underwood, Vasquez, Wohlers, Wolf, 2 each; Arvesen, Backs, Baker, Banks, Baur, Betances, Bickhardt, Bird, Blumberg, Bratlien, Burlingame, Cassidy, Cecil, Cunningham, Curnow, Dorn, Elliott, Fajardo, P. Fletcher, Furmanik, F. Gonzales, Graves, Gray, J. Guzman, P. Guzman, Haller, Holcomb, Hook, Hutton, Johnston, Latham, Lloyd, Mauldin, McDowell, Oliver, F. Perez, Pierce, Randle, Rosario, Rowley, Sample, D. Santiago, R. Santiago, Seibert, Spradlin, Springer, Stevens, Telgheder, Tolbert, Tucker, Vitko, Weems, Worrell, Zinter, 1 each.

COMBINATION SHUTOUTS—Gardner-Gonzales, McDowell-Small, Munoz-Dovey, Wall-Gonzales, Wall-Rivas-Gonzales, Bird-Wagner-Masters, Parkinson-Bird, Rychel-Santiago, Rychel-Way-Watson, Watson-Latham, Augusta; Bennett-Zinter, Santiago-Marx, Worrell-Cunningham-Zinter, Culberson-Spradlin, Pugh-Spradlin, Satre-Wilburn-Nieves, Charleston (W.Va.); Dorn-Richmond, Furmanik-Emm, McCann-Sample, Reich-Sample, Columbia; Garcia-Braley, Garcia-Stefany-Seibert, Gonzales-Braley, Gonzales-Leimeister, Marshall-Stefany-Pinto, Marshall-Torres-Braley, Fayetteville; Arner-Hurst, Arner-Franklin, Asche-Wells, Buckley-Franklin, Eischen-Bickhardt, Hurst-Reed, Randle-Asche, Randle-Franklin-Asche, Randle-Hurst-R. Romero-Graves, Reed-Evans, B. Romero-Evans, B. Romero-Graves, B. Romero-Hurst-R. Romero, Gastonia; Hitchcock-Hoffman, Munoz-Batchelor, Munoz-Dovey, Rhodes-Hoffman-Batchelor, Rhodes-Johnston, Smith-Batchelor, Springer-Hoffman-Batchelor, Springer-Johnston, Greensboro; Blumberg-Lloyd-Bradley, Blumberg-Martin-Bradley, Brown-Bicknell-Bradley, Brown-Bradley-Martin, Ogliaruso-Bradley-Mandia, Ogliaruso-Mandia, Ogliaruso-Olivares-Bradley, Myrtle Beach; Pacheco-Baker-Dixon-Espinal, Pacheco-Fletcher, Shackle-Dixon-Espinal, Savannah; Elliott-Sullivan, Fletcher-Stevens-Limbach, Gaddy-Gunderson, Goedhart-Stevens, Goergen-Gunderson, Goergen-Wiegandt, Wells-Limbach, Spartanburg; Hailey-Strange 2, Steinmetz-Wohlers 2, Haeberle-Schafer, Haeberle-Strange, Sottile-Karasinski, Steinmetz-Sottile, Sumter.

NO-HIT GAMES—Randle, Gastonia, defeated Greensboro, 4-0, May 19; Ingram, Fayetteville, defeated Charleston (W.Va.), 7-0 (first game), June 5; Jewett, Sumter, defeated Spartanburg, 1-0, July 6; Hitchcock, Greensboro, defeated Sumter, 1-0, July 16.

Appalachian League

SUMMER CLASS A CLASSIFICATION

CHAMPIONSHIP WINNERS IN PREVIOUS YEARS

1921—Greenville .608	1951—Kingsport‡ .659	1973—Kingsport .757
Johnson City° .627	1952—Johnson City .595	1974—Bristol a .754
1922—Bristol .557	Welch (3rd)† .509	Bluefield .536
1923—Knoxville .635	1953—Welch° .705	1975—Marion .515
1924—Knoxville° .642	Johnson City .672	Johnson City a .603
Bristol .607	1954—Bluefield‡ .619	1976—Johnson City a .714
1925—Greenville .667	1955—Salem°° .689	Bluefield .600
1926-36—Did not operate.	1956—Did not operate.	1977—Kingsport .623
1937—Elizabethton .559	1957—Bluefield .701	1978—Elizabethton .594
Pennington Gap° .580	1958—Johnson City .662	1979—Paintsville .800
1938—Elizabethton .664	1959—Morristown .603	1980—Paintsville .657
Greenville (3rd)† .571	1960—Wytheville .614	1981—Paintsville .657
1939—Elizabethton‡ .597	1961—Middlesboro .591	1982—Bluefield a .681
1940—Johnson City§ .726	1962—Bluefield .671	Johnson City .478
Elizabethton .750	1963—Bluefield .652	1983—Paintsville .653
1941—Johnson City .614	1964—Johnson City .662	1984—Elizabethton b .580
Elizabethton° .661	1965—Salem .614	Pulaski .536
1942—Bristol .667	1966—Marion .623	1985—Bristol c .638
Bristol x .660	1967—Bluefield .627	1986—Johnson City .667
1943—Bristol .755	1968—Marion .583	Pulaski b .621
Bristol y .617	1969—Pulaski a .576	1987—Burlington b .729
1944—Kingsport‡ .575	Johnson City .544	Johnson City .609
1945—Kingsport‡ .670	1970—Bluefield .638	1988—Kingsport b .644
1946—New River‡ .675	1971—Bluefield a .609	Burlington .529
1947—Pulaski .648	Kingsport .559	1989—Elizabethton b .691
New River (3rd)† .516	1972—Bristol a .588	Pulaski .618
1948—Pulaski‡ .680	Covington .586	
1949—Bluefield‡ .721		
1950—Bluefield .600		
Bluefield z .745		

°Won split-season playoff. †Won four-team playoff. ‡Won championship and four-team playoff. §Johnson City, first-half winner, won playoff involving six clubs. xWon both halves and defeated second-place Elizabethton in playoff. yWon both halves, but Erwin won four-team playoff. zWon both halves, but Bristol won two-club playoff. °°Salem and Johnson City declared playoff co-champions when weather forced cancellation of final series. aLeague was divided into Northern, Southern divisions; declared league champion, based on highest won-lost percentage. bLeague was divided into Northern, Southern divisions; won playoff for league championship. cBristol declared league champion based on regular-season record.

STANDING OF CLUBS AT CLOSE OF SEASON, AUGUST 31

Club	Eliz.	Hun.	Kng.	Blu.	Pul.	Bur.	Prn.	J.C.	Mar.	Bri.	W.	L.	T.	Pct.	G.B.
Elizabethton (Twins)	...	5	6	5	7	6	4	6	7	5	51	16	0	.761	....
Huntington (Cubs)	0	...	4	5	4	5	4	6	6	6	40	29	0	.580	12
Kingsport (Mets)	2	4	...	4	4	5	6	5	7	4	41	31	0	.569	12½
Bluefield (Orioles)	3	3	4	...	4	5	5	5	3	7	38	32	0	.543	14½
Pulaski (Braves)	1	4	4	5	...	4	5	4	4	6	37	35	0	.514	16½
Burlington (Indians)	2	3	3	4	4	...	4	5	6	5	35	37	0	.486	18½
Princeton (Independent)	3	4	2	1	3	4	...	5	5	4	31	36	0	.463	20
Johnson City (Cardinals)	1	2	3	4	3	2	2	...	5	5	28	42	0	.400	24½
Martinsville (Phillies)	1	2	1	5	4	2	3	3	...	4	25	44	0	.362	27
Bristol (Tigers)	3	2	4	1	2	3	3	3	1	...	22	46	0	.324	29½

Major league affiliations in parentheses.

Playoffs—No playoffs scheduled.

Regular-Season Attendance—Bluefield, 33,354; Bristol, 26,026; Burlington, 66,330; Elizabethton, 17,013; Huntington, 66,042; Johnson City, 24,163; Kingsport, 37,363; Martinsville, 69,182; Princeton, 26,620; Pulaski, 17,673. Total—383,766.

Managers—Bluefield, Gus Gil; Bristol, Ken Cunningham; Burlington, Dave Keller; Elizabethton, Ray Smith; Huntington, Steve Roadcap; Johnson City, Mark DeJohn; Kingsport, Jim Thrift; Martinsville, Rollie Dearmas; Princeton, Eli Grba; Pulaski, Randy Ingle.

All-Star Team—1B—Pat Dando, Pulaski; 2B—Jeff Borgese, Martinsville; 3B—Jose Viera, Huntington; SS—Aaron Ledesma, Kingsport; OF—Tracy Sanders, Burlington; OF—Brian Kowitz, Pulaski; OF—Rich Becker, Elizabethton; C—Greg Zaun, Bluefield; RHP—Brad Hassinger, Princeton; LHP—Roger Dixon, Elizabethton; Relief Pitcher—Tom Benson, Elizabethton; Player of the Year—Paul Russo, Elizabethton; Manager of the Year—Ray Smith, Elizabethton.

(Compiled by Howe Sportsdata International, Boston, Mass.)

CLUB BATTING

Club	Pct.	G.	AB.	R.	OR.	H.	TB.	2B.	3B.	HR.	RBI.	SH.	SF.	HP.	BB.	Int. BB.	SO.	SB.	CS.	LOB.
Kingsport	.270	72	2429	370	307	655	953	115	12	53	312	11	25	30	206	9	521	132	65	460
Pulaski	.264	72	2458	361	334	649	930	112	23	41	274	23	20	25	273	14	457	88	53	547
Elizabethton	.262	67	2248	423	268	590	884	87	12	61	357	11	22	38	315	11	517	79	26	502
Bluefield	.259	70	2316	344	344	599	868	111	10	46	283	12	16	26	230	4	502	59	50	465
Huntington	.244	69	2217	308	288	540	781	103	6	42	252	15	16	39	263	9	465	58	40	487
Burlington	.234	72	2418	337	325	567	823	96	11	46	276	14	19	32	296	6	550	120	48	533
Martinsville	.230	69	2344	280	341	540	767	97	14	34	232	8	16	24	199	5	599	42	20	478
Princeton	.230	67	2238	299	321	515	746	88	19	35	244	10	21	25	240	5	530	82	42	471
Johnson City	.223	70	2269	301	371	505	706	78	12	33	232	13	11	14	301	1	564	98	49	488
Bristol	.211	68	2216	224	340	468	642	68	11	28	191	20	6	27	205	9	578	37	29	449

INDIVIDUAL BATTING
(Leading Qualifiers for Batting Championship—194 or More Plate Appearances)

*Bats lefthanded.   †Switch-hitter.

Player and Club	Pct.	G.	AB.	R.	H.	TB.	2B.	3B.	HR.	RBI.	SH.	SF.	HP.	BB.	Int. BB.	SO.	SB.	CS.
Dando, Patrick, Pulaski*	.360	69	253	46	91	144	19	2	10	38	2	4	1	25	5	32	8	8
Russo, Paul, Elizabethton	.335	62	221	58	74	156	14	3	22	67	0	2	1	39	5	56	4	1
Garcia, Omar, Kingsport	.333	67	246	42	82	119	15	2	6	36	0	2	0	24	1	25	12	9
Ledesma, Aaron, Kingsport	.333	66	243	50	81	109	11	1	5	38	1	3	8	30	2	28	27	7
Sandy, Timothy, Kingsport*	.331	49	163	31	54	75	6	3	3	14	0	1	2	32	0	16	9	9
Viera, Jose, Huntington	.331	65	245	34	81	129	22	1	8	37	0	3	1	18	2	30	4	1
Gavin, Thomas, Elizabethton	.329	59	222	43	73	100	13	1	4	42	1	4	8	27	0	49	5	2
Kowitz, Brian, Pulaski*	.324	43	182	40	59	98	13	1	8	19	2	2	1	16	2	16	13	7
Millan, Bernardo, Kingsport†	.311	57	183	14	57	64	5	1	0	20	2	2	1	12	1	17	2	2
Lockett, Ron, Princeton*	.310	63	229	32	71	111	12	5	6	34	1	0	2	15	2	51	11	9

Departmental Leaders: G—Huskey, 72; AB—Huskey, 279; R—Russo, 58; H—Dando, 91; TB—Russo, 156; 2B—Viera, 22; 3B—Edwards, 6; HR—Russo, 22; RBI—Russo, 67; SH—Fermin, 9; SF—Meyer, 7; HP—Postiff, 13; BB—Becker, 53; IBB—Dando, Russo, 5; SO—Alder, Bradford, 75; SB—Donald, 44; CS—Donald, 15.

(All Players—Listed Alphabetically)

Player and Club	Pct.	G.	AB.	R.	H.	TB.	2B.	3B.	HR.	RBI.	SH.	SF.	HP.	BB.	Int. BB.	SO.	SB.	CS.
Alder, James, Bristol	.188	63	224	29	42	89	9	1	12	33	0	1	3	24	0	75	1	2
Alstead, Jason, Bluefield*	.251	56	203	35	51	63	3	0	3	16	2	0	0	27	0	44	13	5
Andujar, Hector, Burlington	.200	10	30	1	6	6	0	0	0	0	0	0	0	2	0	4	1	0
Asencio, Matires, Bluefield	.000	12	17	0	0	0	0	0	0	0	1	0	1	3	0	11	0	0
Aversa, Joseph, Johnson City†	.156	41	90	10	14	15	1	0	0	8	0	0	1	10	0	18	2	1
Ball, Harrison, Johnson City*	.200	66	225	43	45	71	7	2	5	26	2	1	1	37	0	54	8	9
Bark, Brian, Pulaski*	.000	6	1	0	0	0	0	0	0	0	0	0	0	0	0	1	0	0
Bautista, Daniel, Bristol	.274	27	95	9	26	35	3	0	2	12	1	0	0	8	1	21	2	3
Becker, Richard, Elizabethton†	.289	56	194	54	56	81	5	1	6	24	5	0	3	53	0	54	18	2
Bell, David, Burlington	.167	12	42	4	7	10	1	1	0	2	0	1	1	2	0	5	2	1
Bell, Derek, Bluefield†	.222	24	45	6	10	15	2	0	1	6	0	0	2	8	0	10	1	0
Bennett, Gary, Martinsville	.269	16	52	3	14	18	2	1	0	10	0	1	0	4	0	15	0	1
Biasucci, Joseph, Huntington	.188	6	16	2	3	4	1	0	0	1	0	0	0	2	0	3	0	0
Blakeman, Todd, Elizabethton*	.233	49	180	27	42	68	11	0	5	34	1	1	2	13	1	39	0	1
Borgese, Jeff, Martinsville	.300	61	223	36	67	90	13	2	2	28	1	1	4	37	0	25	2	2
Bradford, Vincent, Bristol	.100	52	110	12	11	13	2	0	0	1	0	0	7	17	0	75	0	2
Brede, Brent, Elizabethton*	.245	46	143	39	35	40	5	0	0	14	0	1	0	30	0	30	14	0
Brito, Luis, Princeton†	.242	27	95	15	23	25	2	0	0	4	1	0	2	2	0	11	4	2
Brohm, Jeffrey, Burlington	.213	34	136	25	29	43	8	0	2	12	0	1	1	15	0	38	10	3
Brown, Matthew, Elizabethton	.233	28	90	11	21	25	1	0	1	11	0	0	0	8	0	13	0	1
Bruno, Paul, Elizabethton	.184	28	103	15	19	34	3	0	4	22	0	4	1	14	0	32	0	1
Bryant, Patrick, Burlington	.100	17	50	3	5	8	0	0	1	2	0	0	7	0	0	23	5	1
Burguillos, Robert, Bluefield	.150	18	20	1	3	3	0	0	0	1	0	0	0	1	0	2	0	1
Carmona, William, Martinsville	.225	43	151	15	34	51	8	0	3	17	0	0	3	4	0	52	1	0
Carpenter, Kevin, Johnson City	.135	23	52	2	7	8	1	0	0	1	0	0	1	9	0	20	1	0
Carson, Paul, Martinsville	.167	10	30	3	5	8	0	0	1	5	0	0	0	6	0	10	0	0
Cheek, Patrick, Princeton	.235	62	221	32	52	63	5	0	2	23	3	1	2	23	0	37	3	6
Clark, Anthony, Bristol†	.164	25	73	2	12	17	2	0	1	8	0	0	1	6	0	28	0	0
Craig, Morris, Huntington*	.310	48	155	22	48	62	11	0	1	14	0	0	0	16	0	26	8	2
Crump, James, Pulaski	.175	43	137	16	24	42	9	0	3	15	2	3	1	18	0	34	2	1
Cruz, Daniel, Bristol	.241	62	191	17	46	51	3	1	0	16	2	0	1	17	0	27	6	1
Dando, Patrick, Pulaski*	.360	69	253	46	91	144	19	2	10	38	2	4	1	25	5	32	8	8
Davis, Allen, Bluefield	.224	50	152	28	34	43	3	0	2	11	2	0	2	24	0	47	3	2
Davis, Darwin, Kingsport	.000	1	4	0	0	0	0	0	0	0	0	0	0	0	0	3	0	0
Davis, Gerrod, Kingsport*	.230	68	261	39	60	82	7	0	5	28	1	4	1	8	1	37	20	10
Davis, Jerry, Johnson City	.112	39	116	9	13	19	6	0	0	5	1	0	0	6	0	39	0	1
Debrand, Genaro, Bristol	.230	32	113	11	26	36	3	2	1	10	0	1	1	4	0	14	1	0
Delgado, Pablo, Huntington	.204	46	108	8	22	28	3	0	1	6	2	1	2	18	1	22	0	4
Dempsey, John, Johnson City*	.249	52	173	16	43	49	4	1	0	15	1	1	1	24	0	30	1	0
DiMarco, Steven, Bluefield*	.273	43	150	18	41	56	13	1	0	18	0	0	0	15	1	23	1	0
Donald, Tremayne, Johnson City†	.187	63	230	37	43	51	6	1	0	10	2	0	2	44	0	50	44	15
DuBose, Brian, Bristol*	.251	67	223	31	56	82	8	0	6	21	0	1	3	24	2	53	5	3
Ealy, Tracey, Johnson City†	.276	57	214	33	59	73	8	0	2	18	1	3	1	27	0	58	17	6
Edwards, Johnny, Princeton	.192	64	229	39	44	63	4	6	1	20	1	2	1	30	0	66	27	7
Ellsworth, Ben, Johnson City†	.183	41	115	10	21	25	2	1	0	10	1	2	1	8	0	22	0	2
Ewing, Brian, Elizabethton	.148	8	27	2	4	4	0	0	0	0	0	0	0	4	0	8	2	1
Farmer, Michael, Martinsville†	.268	55	194	33	52	103	11	5	10	34	1	2	1	13	1	56	11	2
Fermin, Carlos, Bristol	.222	67	203	22	45	57	4	4	0	15	9	1	2	21	0	36	7	3
Fernandez, Rolando, Huntington*	.252	47	111	16	28	50	10	0	4	20	0	1	27	3	0	21	4	2
Flores, Miguel, Burlington	.250	57	208	33	52	71	8	1	3	25	0	2	2	20	0	18	22	7
Flowers, Douglas, Bluefield*	.269	39	104	13	28	39	5	0	2	12	0	0	3	8	0	25	1	2
Ford, Calvin, Huntington	.184	55	141	13	26	33	4	0	1	10	2	1	2	12	0	38	5	4
Foster, Lamar, Martinsville*	.214	66	234	24	50	82	12	1	6	36	1	0	5	30	0	52	0	0
Franklin, Micah, Kingsport†	.259	39	158	29	41	78	10	3	7	25	0	2	1	8	0	44	5	2
French, Deron, Johnson City	.241	51	162	18	39	49	7	0	1	14	0	0	0	13	0	46	17	4
Fully, Edwards, Kingsport	.278	66	237	29	66	86	18	1	0	35	0	2	3	16	0	57	17	5
Fults, Nathan, Pulaski	.263	14	38	3	10	14	4	0	0	8	0	0	0	7	0	15	2	0
Gabbani, Michael, Huntington	.275	50	178	25	49	73	7	1	5	18	2	0	0	17	0	36	2	2
Garces, Jesus, Princeton	.149	49	161	18	24	27	1	1	0	10	0	1	1	12	0	34	7	3
Garcia, Omar, Kingsport	.333	67	246	42	82	119	15	2	6	36	0	2	0	24	1	25	12	9
Gardner, Willie, Huntington	.298	52	168	18	50	68	7	1	3	27	0	1	1	8	0	50	2	5
Gavin, Thomas, Elizabethton	.329	59	222	43	73	100	13	1	4	42	1	4	8	27	0	49	5	2
Gilmore, Matthew, Burlington	.230	40	148	30	34	42	5	0	1	16	1	1	5	14	0	26	3	0
Gonzalez, Wallace, Pulaski	.263	47	156	17	41	66	10	3	3	27	0	1	3	9	1	37	0	3
Gordian, Carlos, Bluefield	.125	8	8	2	1	1	0	0	0	1	0	0	0	0	0	2	0	0
Graffagnino, Anthony, Pulaski	.206	42	131	23	27	34	5	1	0	11	1	1	2	26	0	17	6	4
Graham, Gordon, Bluefield*	.281	24	64	10	18	28	2	1	2	8	2	0	1	3	0	26	2	2
Grissom, Antonio, Martinsville	.176	5	17	1	3	4	1	0	0	0	0	0	1	2	0	3	0	1
Gumpf, John, Elizabethton	.236	51	191	31	45	77	9	1	7	20	0	1	7	12	0	71	4	1
Gunn, Jeffrey, Princeton	.154	37	117	11	18	20	2	0	0	6	0	0	4	0	0	38	1	3
Haeger, Gregoty, Bristol*	.158	34	38	3	6	6	0	0	0	5	0	0	4	0	0	10	0	0
Hall, Christopher, Bristol	.202	54	183	14	37	49	9	0	1	16	1	1	2	14	0	48	1	0

Player and Club	Pct.	G.	AB.	R.	H.	TB.	2B.	3B.	HR.	RBI.	SH.	SF.	HP.	BB.	Int. BB.	SO.	SB.	CS.
Hammond, David, Princeton*	.000	21	1	0	0	0	0	0	0	0	0	0	0	0	0	1	0	0
Hardtke, Jason, Burlington†	.268	39	142	18	38	57	7	0	4	16	0	0	2	23	0	19	11	1
Hays, Kevin, Johnson City	.200	6	15	1	3	3	0	0	0	0	0	0	0	3	0	4	0	0
Hedley, Darren, Martinsville	.200	41	125	14	25	32	7	0	0	8	1	0	0	30	0	48	1	1
Helms, Tommy, Huntington	.211	27	71	9	15	18	3	0	0	3	1	0	0	6	0	15	0	2
Hence, Samuel, Burlington	.216	35	125	11	27	42	6	0	3	11	0	1	0	5	0	31	4	5
Henderson, Pedro, Burlington	.221	43	140	22	31	49	7	1	3	18	1	1	0	18	0	46	5	4
Hernandez, Luis, Bristol	.203	54	182	21	37	44	5	1	0	11	4	0	2	13	1	46	7	2
Hines, Maurice, Martinsville*	.191	15	47	3	9	11	2	0	0	0	0	0	0	2	0	10	0	0
Hocking, Dennis, Elizabethton†	.294	54	201	45	59	87	6	2	6	30	1	2	6	40	1	26	14	4
Hodge, Roy, Bluefield	.229	26	48	4	11	11	0	0	0	3	1	0	3	0	8	0	0
Holbert, Aaron, Johnson City	.172	54	174	27	30	39	4	1	1	18	1	1	3	24	1	31	4	5
Hollins, Steven, Princeton	.265	54	204	27	54	81	17	2	2	28	0	6	1	24	0	24	8	3
Hughes, Troy, Pulaski	.269	46	145	22	39	51	7	1	1	17	2	1	0	16	0	39	5	1
Huskey, Robert, Kingsport	.269	72	279	39	75	130	13	0	14	53	0	5	2	24	1	74	7	3
Jenkins, Anthony, Johnson City	.167	16	48	5	8	16	2	0	2	4	1	0	0	6	0	21	0	0
Jimenez, Roberto, Burlington	.241	40	137	12	33	42	7	1	0	10	0	2	2	10	0	29	2	1
Jiminez, Vincent, Pulaski	.245	29	98	11	24	35	4	2	1	5	0	0	2	15	0	22	1	4
Johnson, Anthony, Pulaski	.223	42	121	20	27	39	4	1	2	13	2	1	3	17	0	25	5	0
Johnson, Marcel, Kingsport	.220	35	100	6	22	31	4	1	1	9	0	1	0	9	1	30	1	2
Jordan, Adrian, Bristol*	.102	16	49	7	5	6	1	0	0	1	1	0	0	8	1	9	1	0
Jordan, Timothy, Johnson City*	.276	61	199	25	55	72	5	0	4	23	2	2	1	15	0	52	4	3
Keating, David, Bristol	.160	7	25	1	4	6	2	0	0	3	0	0	1	0	0	8	1	1
Kinyoun, Travis, Kingsport†	.000	5	17	0	0	0	0	0	0	0	0	0	0	1	0	6	1	0
Kowitz, Brian, Pulaski*	.324	43	182	40	59	98	13	1	8	19	2	2	1	16	2	16	13	7
Larregui, Edgardo, Huntington	.186	34	102	13	19	28	3	0	2	16	2	3	0	7	0	12	3	1
Larson, Danny, Martinsville*	.226	19	62	4	14	20	6	0	0	8	0	0	1	1	0	17	0	0
Ledesma, Aaron, Kingsport	.333	66	243	50	81	109	11	1	5	38	1	3	8	30	2	28	27	7
Lieberthal, Michael, Martinsville	.228	49	184	26	42	63	9	0	4	22	0	2	11	0	40	2	0
Little, Michael, Huntington	.221	38	104	17	23	49	5	0	7	16	0	1	0	20	1	32	0	0
Llanos, Aurelio, Princeton†	.221	47	154	18	34	54	8	0	4	17	0	3	5	9	0	51	12	2
Lockett, Ron, Princeton*	.310	63	229	32	71	111	12	5	6	34	1	0	2	15	2	51	11	9
Martinez, John, Burlington†	.263	41	156	14	41	49	5	0	1	18	6	2	1	9	0	24	0	4
Mathis, Wayne, Kingsport*	.160	34	81	15	13	16	3	0	0	2	0	0	6	6	0	19	11	3
Mathis, Monte, Pulaski	.333	12	30	6	10	12	2	0	0	0	0	0	0	1	0	4	0	1
Mauro, Michael, Bristol	.157	18	51	6	8	9	1	0	0	3	0	0	0	5	0	14	1	2
McCall, Roderick, Burlington*	.163	31	92	8	15	23	5	0	1	11	0	2	2	10	0	43	0	1
McClain, Scott, Bluefield	.196	40	107	20	21	35	2	0	4	15	0	4	2	22	0	35	2	3
Medina, Facaner, Martinsville	.245	50	208	22	51	66	3	3	2	10	2	0	1	10	1	62	8	6
Medina, Patricio, Martinsville†	.203	47	192	18	39	41	2	0	0	6	1	1	0	8	1	41	5	3
Merrill, Lawrence, Johnson City*	.083	5	12	0	1	1	0	0	0	0	0	0	0	2	0	5	0	0
Meyer, Richard, Martinsville	.242	65	240	32	58	78	11	0	3	23	0	7	1	18	0	66	2	2
Millan, Bernardo, Kingsport†	.311	57	183	14	57	64	5	1	0	20	2	2	1	12	1	17	2	2
Millares, Jose, Bluefield	.273	48	176	25	48	69	12	0	3	25	0	1	0	10	1	28	6	6
Miller, Brent, Bluefield*	.325	32	117	21	38	80	10	1	10	28	1	2	0	7	0	22	0	0
Miller, Damian, Elizabethton	.222	14	45	7	10	14	1	0	1	6	0	0	9	0	3	1	0
Miller, Kevin, Bristol	.269	61	212	21	57	78	6	0	5	22	0	1	2	20	2	45	1	1
Monastero, Frank, Burlington	.151	21	53	6	8	9	1	0	0	6	2	1	2	4	0	6	1	1
Mongero, Trent, Pulaski†	.222	44	144	17	32	41	2	2	1	9	3	0	3	14	0	35	4	4
Montero, Cesar, Burlington	.313	14	16	1	5	7	2	0	0	1	0	0	0	2	0	6	0	2
Moore, Devren, Kingsport	.223	44	139	21	31	54	11	0	4	14	1	1	3	12	1	65	11	6
Moore, Timothy, Huntington	.281	54	178	28	50	68	10	1	2	17	2	0	5	27	0	22	5	4
Morse, Matthew, Elizabethton†	.251	63	235	34	59	83	9	3	3	29	1	4	2	26	4	31	8	8
Murphy, Micah, Huntington*	.200	47	130	21	26	35	3	0	2	15	0	1	1	17	1	24	1	1
Murphy, Michael, Martinsville†	.097	9	31	4	3	3	0	0	0	1	0	0	0	7	0	17	1	2
Ortiz, Ramon, Burlington	.200	9	20	0	4	4	0	0	0	2	0	0	1	2	0	3	1	0
Page, Sean, Johnson City	.244	49	160	26	39	67	8	1	6	18	0	1	29	0	47	0	1
Paredes, German, Bluefield	.266	60	218	24	58	88	12	0	6	30	0	1	0	6	1	41	2	2
Pascual, Jorge, Martinsville	.233	37	159	21	37	49	5	2	1	13	0	2	1	4	0	20	2	0
Pena, Porfirio, Martinsville	.161	14	56	6	9	10	1	0	0	4	0	1	0	1	1	22	0	0
Peppers, Devin, Elizabethton	.143	17	42	5	6	6	0	0	0	2	0	0	7	0	28	0	1
Pfeffer, Kurt, Elizabethton	.281	29	96	16	27	40	5	1	2	21	0	1	5	13	0	30	0	0
Philyaw, Delvic, Burlington	.114	17	44	2	5	5	0	0	0	1	0	0	1	5	0	22	3	1
Pichardo, Francisco, Elizabethton	.229	33	105	16	24	27	3	0	0	15	2	1	0	9	0	18	6	3
Pinckes, Michael, Burlington	.233	54	163	18	38	55	7	2	2	20	1	2	0	38	1	46	1	2
Postiff, James, Huntington	.246	56	171	32	42	58	7	0	3	23	1	2	13	27	1	37	10	3
Pullins, Jimmie, Pulaski	.179	11	28	2	5	5	0	0	0	3	0	0	2	0	6	1	0
Ramirez, Daniel, Bluefield	.289	57	211	36	61	79	12	0	2	22	1	1	9	22	0	23	9	8
Reinisch, Paul, Burlington†	1.000	15	1	0	1	2	1	0	0	1	0	0	0	0	0	0	0	0
Roa, Hector, Pulaski†	.348	21	92	23	32	48	3	2	3	14	1	0	1	5	1	17	7	0
Roberts, Keith, Bristol†	.170	42	88	7	15	20	3	1	0	2	0	0	2	9	0	37	2	6
Rodriguez, Armando, Pulaski*	.277	46	137	21	38	56	8	2	2	19	1	3	2	21	0	29	5	2
Rodriguez, Beto, Johnson City*	.288	68	229	33	66	110	16	2	8	50	1	1	1	41	0	50	0	2
Rosario, Francisco, Martinsville†	.184	21	76	11	14	19	2	0	1	2	1	0	4	8	1	27	6	1
Rudison, Karl, Pulaski	.218	47	133	20	29	39	4	3	0	12	2	2	1	24	2	25	6	2
Rudolph, Mason, Kingsport	.175	48	154	26	27	53	5	0	7	21	2	2	1	8	0	65	0	2
Ruiz, Estuar, Bluefield†	.206	22	34	4	7	8	1	0	0	0	3	0	0	5	0	14	1	0
Rusk, Troy, Princeton*	.242	59	194	31	47	48	7	2	10	33	0	1	3	52	2	66	0	1
Russo, Paul, Elizabethton	.335	62	221	58	74	156	10	3	22	67	0	2	1	39	5	56	4	1
Saa, Humberto, Huntington	.156	27	45	6	7	8	1	0	0	4	0	1	0	8	0	7	0	1
Sanders, Tracy, Burlington*	.281	51	178	38	50	94	12	1	10	34	0	1	2	33	0	36	10	3
Sandy, Timothy, Kingsport*	.331	49	163	31	54	75	6	3	3	14	0	1	2	32	0	16	9	9
Schmidt, Keith, Bluefield*	.278	55	169	24	47	78	12	2	5	24	0	1	4	17	0	62	5	6
Sehorn, Jason, Huntington	.184	49	125	21	23	31	3	1	1	10	3	1	4	8	0	52	9	1
Shirley, Michael, Burlington	.196	32	112	14	22	32	1	0	3	9	1	0	1	8	1	33	3	1
Silvers, Chadwick, Princeton	.234	47	167	18	39	47	6	1	0	8	1	0	0	7	1	26	4	1
Smith, Robert, Burlington	.158	8	19	2	3	3	0	0	0	0	0	0	1	5	0	11	1	0
Smith, Terrell, Princeton†	.100	5	10	0	1	1	0	0	0	0	0	0	0	2	0	7	1	0
Sosa, Jose, Princeton	.156	14	32	0	5	6	1	0	0	3	0	1	0	2	0	18	0	0
Soto, Rafael, Huntington	.085	42	59	10	5	6	1	0	0	2	1	0	2	11	0	15	4	3
Spaan, Anthony, Elizabethton	.205	24	73	11	15	17	2	0	0	5	0	1	1	5	0	18	3	0
Spivey, James, Johnson City	.345	23	55	6	19	38	1	3	4	12	0	0	0	3	0	17	0	0

498

Player and Club	Pct.	G.	AB.	R.	H.	TB.	2B.	3B.	HR.	RBI.	SH.	SF.	HP.	BB.	Int. BB.	SO.	SB.	CS.
Sprick, Scott, Bluefield*	.241	62	220	27	53	86	15	3	4	33	0	3	2	18	0	51	4	4
Steele, Steven, Kingsport	.500	2	4	0	2	2	0	0	0	1	0	0	0	0	0	1	0	0
Steffens, Mark, Princeton*	.248	35	121	14	30	44	6	1	2	10	0	2	1	6	0	21	3	1
Tejada, Francisco, Princeton	.238	52	172	24	41	62	7	1	4	29	1	3	2	27	0	49	0	3
Tewell, Terrance, Martinsville	.222	17	63	4	14	19	2	0	1	5	0	1	0	3	0	16	1	0
Thomas, Michael, Bluefield	.203	24	69	9	14	16	2	0	0	9	0	1	0	8	0	13	4	1
Thomas, Timothy, Burlington	.196	15	56	5	11	12	1	0	0	3	0	0	1	4	1	8	3	0
Thome, James, Burlington*	.373	34	118	31	44	89	7	1	12	34	0	0	4	27	3	18	6	3
Torres, Ramon, Burlington*	.270	43	137	22	37	44	5	1	0	13	2	3	1	26	0	31	17	4
Toth, David, Pulaski	.268	26	82	9	22	22	0	0	0	10	1	2	1	11	0	12	2	0
Ubina, Samuel, Bristol	.256	39	78	9	20	25	3	1	0	8	2	0	0	6	0	10	0	3
Vargas, Julio, Princeton	.244	43	131	20	32	54	10	0	4	17	1	0	5	26	0	30	1	1
Veras, Quilvio, Kingsport†	.383	24	94	21	36	45	6	0	1	14	1	0	1	13	1	14	9	5
Viera, John, Huntington	.331	65	245	34	81	129	22	1	8	37	0	3	1	18	2	30	4	1
Virgilio, George, Pulaski†	.259	58	220	35	57	79	9	2	3	21	3	0	1	27	2	18	7	4
Walker, John, Pulaski*	.212	39	132	12	28	43	3	0	4	11	0	0	1	8	0	28	5	4
Wallgren, Charles, Elizabethton	.263	23	80	9	21	25	4	0	0	7	0	0	2	6	0	11	0	0
Whitmore, Darrell, Burlington*	.241	30	112	18	27	34	3	2	0	13	0	1	2	9	0	30	9	5
Williams, Charles, Kingsport	.121	24	66	8	8	9	1	0	0	2	3	0	1	3	0	20	0	0
Williams, Juan, Pulaski*	.273	58	198	18	54	62	6	1	0	22	1	0	2	11	1	45	9	8
Wilson, Bradley, Bristol*	.182	24	77	2	14	17	3	0	0	3	0	0	0	5	1	22	1	0
Wolff, James, Huntington	.191	31	94	11	18	26	0	1	2	11	0	1	7	12	0	17	1	2
Zaun, Gregory, Bluefield†	.299	61	184	29	55	70	5	2	2	21	0	1	1	23	1	15	5	8

The following pitchers, listed alphabetically by club, with games in parentheses, had no plate appearances, primarily through use of designated hitters:

BLUEFIELD—Anderson, Matthew (12); Benge, James (4); Chouinard, Robert (10); Egleston, Michael (11); Hays, Gregory (14); Hebb, Michael (15); Heiden, Shawn (1); Marquez, Ihosvany (13); Medina, Victor (9); Mercedes, Juan (15); O'Connell, Shawn (18); O'Donoghue, John (10); Tippitt, Bradley (15); Wiley, Michael (11); Williams, Jeffrey (9).

BRISTOL—Guilfoyle, Michael (16); Henry, James (10); Lima, Jose (14); Lira, Felipe (13); Maietta, Ronald (6); Nelson, Brian (5); Riker, Robert (19); Rodriguez, Eddy (13); Salazar, Luis (7); Stokes, Randall (21); Warren, Brian (1); Withem, Shannon (14).

BURLINGTON—Baker, Samuel (24); Brown, Clarence (13); Bryant, Shawn (2); Elston, Cary (12); Embree, Alan (15); Gajkowski, Stephen (14); Johnson, Carl (27); McElfish, Shawn (19); McLochlin, Michael (14); Mlicki, David (8); Tillman, Tommy (30); Walden, Alan (15); Wechsberg, Von (5).

ELIZABETHTON—Benson, Thomas (30); Bethancourt, Jose (13); Bigham, David (29); Diaz, Sandy (13); Dixon, Roger (14); Fritz, Scott (3); Henry, Jon (14); Persing, Timothy (11); Ritchie, Todd (11); Taylor, Steve (10).

HUNTINGTON—Camarena, Miguel (13); Cheetham, Sean (13); Gardner, Scott (13); Godfrey, Tyson (13); Hawblitzel, Ryan (14); Kennedy, Daniel (1); Kirk, Charles (10); Mann, Thomas (10); Perez, Leopoldo (20); Ramirez, Nelson (3); Sanchez, Adrian (13); Stanley, Karl (9); Stevens, David (14); Taylor, Aaron (26).

JOHNSON CITY—Alberro, Hector (5); Baker, Scott (32); Brumley, Duff (12); Gonzalez, Cecilio (13); Hurst, William (2); Kelly, John (25); Lopez, Jose (14); McGarity, Jeremy (12); Norris, David (24); Rodriguez, Manuel (19); Ruyak, Craig (24); Speek, Frank (27); Urbani, Thomas (9).

KINGSPORT—Anaya, Michael (3); Benson, Nathaniel (13); Bristow, Richard (26); Carpentier, Robert (22); Carrasco, Hector (3); Engle, Thomas (14); Lehnerz, Michael (3); Lindsay, Darian (15); Martinez, Reynaldo (20); Polanco, Nicholas (22); Rees, Robert (14); Van Rynbach, Caspar (12); Wegmann, Thomas (14).

MARTINSVILLE—Agado, David (14); Anderson, Chad (13); Badacour, Bruce (12); Cooper, Darren (15); Croak, David (1); Domecq, Raymond (26); Freeman, Peter (20); Higgins, William (23); Kamerschen, Robert (20); Lance, Gary (1); Munoz, Jarrod (14); Wheeler, Winston (21).

PRINCETON—Adamson, Joel (12); Blazier, Ronald (14); Edwards, Samuel (9); Garcia, Mario (15); Hassinger, Brad (13); Manicchia, Bryan (22); Perez, Leopoldo (2); Repoz, Jeffrey (5); Snyder, Christopher (14); Stohr, William (16); Villarreal, Juan (7); Whisenant, Matthew (9).

PULASKI—Bryan, Russell (9); Chiles, Barry (17); Dunlap, Travis (17); Ford, Stewart (15); Grebe, Brett (5); Mack, Raymond (17); Morrison, Keith (13); Owens, Lawrence (4); Place, Michael (22); Roa, Joseph (14); Shepherd, Michael (18); Werland, Henry (14); Williams, David (14).

GRAND SLAM HOME RUNS—Alder, Blakeman, Franklin, Gabbini, Hocking, Hughes, Postiff, B. Rodriguez, Schmidt, Walker, 1 each.

AWARDED FIRST BASE ON CATCHER'S INTERFERENCE—Ball (Zaun); Lockett (Dempsey); Philyaw (Zaun).

CLUB FIELDING

Club	Pct.	G.	PO.	A.	E.	DP.	PB.	Club	Pct.	G.	PO.	A.	E.	DP.	PB.
Bristol	.956	68	1770	702	115	51	13	Kingsport	.951	72	1889	796	137	49	25
Princeton	.953	67	1757	796	125	72	25	Bluefield	.944	70	1808	664	146	44	20
Elizabethton	.953	67	1764	758	125	60	10	Burlington	.944	72	1911	884	166	68	20
Martinsville	.953	69	1802	746	127	52	11	Huntington	.943	69	1759	646	146	56	8
Pulaski	.952	72	1896	794	137	58	30	Johnson City	.941	70	1798	754	161	58	21

Triple Play—Kingsport.

INDIVIDUAL FIELDING

*Throws lefthanded.

FIRST BASEMEN

Player and Club	Pct.	G.	PO.	A.	E.	DP.	Player and Club	Pct.	G.	PO.	A.	E.	DP.
Alder, Bristol	.973	11	68	4	2	6	Johnson, Kingsport	1.000	10	40	5	0	4
Blakeman, Elizabethton	.978	34	288	24	7	27	Lockett, Princeton*	.988	63	548	53	7	62
Burguillos, Bluefield	.981	17	52	1	1	1	McCall, Burlington	.952	31	286	12	15	16
Carpenter, Johnson City	1.000	1	10	1	0	1	Meyer, Martinsville	.971	3	29	4	1	0
Crump, Pulaski	1.000	1	10	0	0	7	Millan, Kingsport	1.000	2	17	1	0	0
Dando, Pulaski*	.974	63	523	42	15	44	Miller, Bluefield	.974	28	216	7	6	20
Davis, Kingsport*	1.000	1	4	0	0	1	Murphy, Huntington*	.979	39	259	18	6	27
DiMarco, Bluefield	.963	3	23	3	1	1	Page, Johnson City	1.000	6	37	1	0	2
DuBose, Bristol	.983	51	363	31	7	29	Pinckes, Burlington	.985	37	314	16	5	35
Flowers, Bluefield	.983	24	163	7	3	11	Postiff, Huntington	.976	36	231	11	6	20
Foster, Martinsville	.983	65	548	37	10	43	Rodriguez, Johnson City*	.978	65	596	40	14	49
Gabbani, Huntington	1.000	3	12	3	0	0	Rusk, Princeton	1.000	3	27	4	0	1
GARCIA, Kingsport	.989	67	625	33	7	40	Russo, Elizabethton	.987	34	274	32	4	26
Gonzalez, Pulaski	1.000	6	44	5	0	1	Sprick, Bluefield	.958	3	23	0	1	3
Graham, Bluefield*	.973	14	105	2	3	4	Steffens, Princeton*	.974	5	36	2	1	3
Gumpf, Elizabethton	1.000	5	20	1	0	0	Tewell, Martinsville	.962	3	20	5	1	1
Haeger, Bristol*	1.000	2	2	0	0	1	Thomas, Burlington	.953	15	133	8	7	9
Hall, Bristol	.984	7	59	4	1	6	Ubina, Bristol	1.000	8	52	9	0	2
Hughes, Pulaski	1.000	1	5	1	0	0	Wilson, Bristol	1.000	2	9	1	0	0

Triple Play—Johnson.

SECOND BASEMEN

Player and Club	Pct.	G.	PO.	A.	E.	DP.	Player and Club	Pct.	G.	PO.	A.	E.	DP.
Andujar, Burlington	.909	3	7	3	1	2	F. Medina, Martinsville	1.000	1	0	1	0	1
Ball, Johnson City	.966	56	110	148	9	30	P. Medina, Martinsville	1.000	1	1	6	0	0
Biasucci, Huntington	.909	3	6	4	1	2	Millan, Kingsport	.925	13	21	41	5	4
Borgese, Martinsville	.928	39	52	90	11	14	Millares, Bluefield	.915	36	61	100	15	13
Cheek, Princeton	.953	21	40	61	5	12	Monastero, Burlington	.944	14	22	29	3	5
Craig, Huntington	.949	44	90	113	11	30	Mongero, Pulaski	.938	12	18	42	4	10
Donald, Johnson City	.968	14	20	41	2	6	Montero, Huntington	.714	9	2	3	2	1
Ellsworth, Johnson City	.871	8	8	19	4	2	Moore, Huntington	.966	10	14	14	1	5
Fermin, Bristol	1.000	1	1	1	0	1	MORSE, Elizabethton	.971	62	125	172	9	34
Flores, Burlington	.949	51	117	143	14	35	Pascual, Martinsville	.951	30	55	99	8	18
Foster, Martinsville	1.000	1	1	0	0	0	Pichardo, Elizabethton	.800	1	0	4	1	0
Franklin, Kingsport	.929	37	72	98	13	23	Pinckes, Burlington	.957	7	4	18	1	3
Garces, Princeton	.973	15	25	48	2	10	Ramirez, Bluefield	.935	26	40	46	6	14
Hall, Bristol	.930	22	28	52	6	11	Ruiz, Bluefield	.896	19	15	28	5	2
Helms, Huntington	.969	25	26	37	2	3	Saa, Huntington	1.000	2	1	1	0	0
Hernandez, Bristol	.951	47	70	105	9	17	Smith, Burlington	.952	8	22	18	2	4
Hocking, Elizabethton	.955	5	8	13	1	5	Soto, Huntington	.667	1	1	1	1	0
Hollins, Princeton	.951	38	89	126	11	28	Spaan, Elizabethton	1.000	1	0	1	0	0
Mathis, Pulaski	1.000	10	8	21	0	3	Ubina, Bristol	1.000	2	0	1	0	0
Mauro, Bristol	.938	8	15	15	2	2	Veras, Kingsport	.944	24	55	79	8	11
							Virgilio, Pulaski	.954	56	90	158	12	29

Triple Play—Franklin.

THIRD BASEMEN

Player and Club	Pct.	G.	PO.	A.	E.	DP.	Player and Club	Pct.	G.	PO.	A.	E.	DP.
Alder, Bristol	.845	46	32	66	18	7	Mathis, Pulaski	1.000	2	0	3	0	0
Andujar, Burlington	.875	3	2	5	1	0	Mauro, Bristol	.333	2	0	1	2	0
Aversa, Johnson City	.917	31	13	53	6	3	McClain, Bluefield	.901	33	27	46	8	1
Ball, Johnson City	.765	10	7	19	8	1	Merrill, Johnson City	.846	5	1	10	2	0
Bell, Burlington	.921	12	8	27	3	1	MEYER, Martinsville	.925	62	48	113	13	7
Borgese, Martinsville	1.000	9	5	14	0	3	Millan, Kingsport	.882	5	4	11	2	2
Cheek, Princeton	.892	43	27	56	10	3	Millares, Bluefield	.800	6	2	6	2	1
Craig, Huntington	1.000	3	0	1	0	0	Monastero, Burlington	.667	3	0	8	4	0
Crump, Pulaski	.961	30	14	60	3	3	Mongero, Pulaski	.786	14	6	16	6	0
DiMarco, Bluefield	.922	35	33	74	9	7	Montero, Huntington	1.000	1	1	0	0	0
Donald, Johnson City	.667	2	1	3	2	0	Page, Johnson City	.837	22	13	23	7	1
DuBose, Bristol	1.000	1	1	0	0	0	Pinckes, Burlington	.947	14	10	26	2	0
Ellsworth, Johnson City	.795	21	8	23	8	4	Postiff, Huntington	.900	4	5	4	1	0
Flores, Burlington	1.000	6	3	17	0	2	Rudison, Pulaski	.862	35	24	51	12	2
Garcia, Kingsport	1.000	2	0	2	0	1	Russo, Elizabethton	.762	8	2	14	5	0
Gavin, Elizabethton	.850	57	35	90	22	11	Saa, Huntington	.889	7	3	5	1	1
Gilmore, Burlington	.778	4	0	7	2	0	Smith, Burlington	1.000	1	1	0	0	0
Gordian, Bluefield	1.000	1	1	1	0	0	Soto, Huntington	1.000	5	0	1	0	0
Hall, Bristol	.907	24	12	37	5	2	Tejada, Princeton	.830	23	8	31	8	3
Hocking, Elizabethton	1.000	3	0	6	0	0	Thome, Burlington	.907	33	28	79	11	6
Hollins, Princeton	.813	7	4	9	3	0	Ubina, Bristol	1.000	1	2	0	0	0
Huskey, Kingsport	.899	67	45	150	22	11	Viera, Huntington	.897	64	43	88	15	10
Martinez, Burlington	.833	7	1	9	2	3	Zaun, Bluefield	1.000	1	1	2	0	0

SHORTSTOPS

Player and Club	Pct.	G.	PO.	A.	E.	DP.	Player and Club	Pct.	G.	PO.	A.	E.	DP.
Andujar, Burlington	.933	5	2	12	1	1	Mauro, Bristol	1.000	6	1	6	0	0
Asencio, Bluefield	.750	11	8	7	5	2	Medina, Martinsville	.927	46	75	129	16	27
Aversa, Johnson City	.950	9	10	28	2	4	Millan, Kingsport	.967	13	19	39	2	7
Biasucci, Huntington	.600	1	2	1	2	0	Monastero, Burlington	1.000	3	0	3	0	0
Borgese, Martinsville	.714	2	3	2	2	2	Mongero, Pulaski	.915	14	26	39	6	11
Brito, Princeton	.863	27	39	62	16	19	Moore, Huntington	.866	46	56	73	20	10
Ellsworth, Johnson City	.891	15	21	36	7	4	Morse, Elizabethton	1.000	1	1	1	0	0
FERMIN, Bristol	.941	66	121	164	18	34	Pinckes, Burlington	1.000	2	1	5	0	0
Flores, Burlington	1.000	2	3	6	0	1	Ramirez, Bluefield	.878	31	46	83	18	11
Garces, Princeton	.905	37	52	91	15	20	Roa, Pulaski	.925	21	41	57	8	15
Gilmore, Burlington	.880	35	28	97	17	24	Rosario, Martinsville	.848	21	34	55	16	11
Graffagnino, Pulaski	.873	39	60	105	24	13	Rudison, Pulaski	1.000	2	3	3	0	0
Hall, Bristol	1.000	2	2	2	0	0	Ruiz, Bluefield	.667	2	2	0	1	0
Hardtke, Burlington	.945	33	36	118	9	13	Saa, Huntington	.968	18	12	18	1	3
Hernandez, Bristol	.800	3	3	1	1	1	Smith, Princeton	1.000	1	1	4	0	1
Hocking, Elizabethton	.923	48	69	160	19	22	Soto, Huntington	.869	34	33	60	14	13
Holbert, Johnson City	.881	51	87	136	30	27	Spaan, Elizabethton	.871	22	31	57	13	18
Hollins, Princeton	.889	14	22	42	8	11	Sprick, Bluefield	.913	38	45	101	14	16
Ledesma, Kingsport	.912	61	78	170	24	22	Zaun, Bluefield	1.000	1	0	1	0	0

Triple Play—Millan.

OUTFIELDERS

Player and Club	Pct.	G.	PO.	A.	E.	DP.	Player and Club	Pct.	G.	PO.	A.	E.	DP.
ALSTEAD, Bluefield	.977	52	81	5	2	0	DuBose, Bristol	.889	16	14	2	2	1
Bautista, Bristol	1.000	27	43	2	0	0	Ealy, Johnson City	.969	23	30	1	1	0
Becker, Elizabethton*	.908	55	87	2	9	1	Edwards, Princeton	.970	64	157	6	5	1
Bradford, Bristol	.905	40	54	3	6	0	Ewing, Elizabethton	.833	7	9	1	2	0
Brede, Elizabethton*	.971	44	63	3	2	1	Farmer, Martinsville*	.959	55	85	8	4	2
Brohm, Burlington	.941	24	45	3	3	1	Fernandez, Huntington*	.867	13	11	2	2	2
Bryant, Burlington	.773	14	16	1	5	0	Ford, Huntington	.962	55	69	7	3	0
Carmona, Martinsville	.948	39	53	2	3	0	French, Johnson City	.925	42	46	3	4	0
Carpenter, Johnson City	1.000	6	7	1	0	0	Fully, Kingsport	.921	63	89	4	8	0
Carson, Martinsville	.917	9	11	0	1	0	Fults, Pulaski	.933	14	11	3	1	0
Clark, Bristol	1.000	18	23	3	0	0	Gardner, Huntington	.878	51	62	3	9	0
Cruz, Bristol	.945	58	76	10	5	1	Grissom, Martinsville	.667	3	0	2	1	0
A. Davis, Bristol	.918	39	53	3	5	0	Gumpf, Elizabethton	.968	45	86	5	3	0
G. Davis, Kingsport*	.953	66	111	10	6	1	Gunn, Princeton	.925	34	46	3	4	1
J. Davis, Johnson City	.897	29	48	4	6	1	Hedley, Martinsville	.950	40	52	5	3	0
Delgado, Huntington	.931	45	63	4	5	1	Hence, Burlington	.897	25	49	3	6	0
Donald, Johnson City	.914	42	48	5	5	1	Henderson, Burlington	.929	33	49	3	4	1

OUTFIELDERS—Continued

Player and Club	Pct.	G.	PO.	A.	E.	DP.	Player and Club	Pct.	G.	PO.	A.	E.	DP.
Hines, Martinsville*	.923	7	11	1	1	0	Peppers, Elizabethton	.889	12	8	0	1	0
Hodge, Bluefield	.958	19	23	0	1	0	Pfeffer, Elizabethton	1.000	20	28	2	0	0
Hughes, Pulaski	.960	44	65	7	3	1	Philyaw, Burlington	.933	12	14	0	1	0
Jenkins, Johnson City	.846	11	10	1	2	0	Pichardo, Elizabethton	.949	31	69	5	4	1
Johnson, Pulaski	.917	42	54	1	5	0	Pullins, Pulaski	1.000	3	6	0	0	0
A. Jordan, Bristol*	1.000	15	28	3	0	0	Roberts, Bristol*	.905	31	36	2	4	1
T. Jordan, Johnson City	.907	51	90	7	10	0	Rodriguez, Pulaski*	.938	15	14	1	1	0
Keating, Bristol*	.833	5	5	0	1	0	Sanders, Burlington	.959	42	63	7	3	2
Kowitz, Pulaski*	.919	42	66	2	6	0	Sandy, Kingsport	.987	44	73	1	1	1
Larregui, Huntington	.978	33	44	1	1	1	Schmidt, Bluefield	.938	49	71	5	5	2
Larson, Martinsville*	1.000	14	19	1	0	0	Sehorn, Huntington	.944	46	82	3	5	0
Little, Huntington	.857	7	6	0	1	0	Shirley, Burlington	.952	29	40	0	2	0
Llanos, Princeton	.947	44	68	4	4	2	Silvers, Princeton	.897	46	60	1	7	0
Mathis, Kingsport	.943	26	29	4	2	1	Sosa, Princeton	.727	9	8	0	3	0
Medina, Martinsville	.915	44	81	5	8	0	Steffens, Princeton*	.974	23	35	3	1	1
Miller, Bristol	.963	39	49	3	2	0	Thomas, Bluefield	.964	20	26	1	1	0
Moore, Kingsport	.906	31	58	0	6	0	Torres, Burlington*	.921	26	35	0	3	0
Murphy, Martinsville	.900	9	9	0	1	0	Walker, Pulaski	.967	29	29	0	1	0
Ortiz, Burlington	.667	7	2	0	1	0	Whitmore, Burlington	.879	23	28	1	4	1
Page, Johnson City	1.000	23	28	3	0	0	Williams, Pulaski	.973	57	69	4	2	0
Paredes, Bluefield	.925	56	108	3	9	0							

CATCHERS

Player and Club	Pct.	G.	PO.	A.	E.	DP.	PB.	Player and Club	Pct.	G.	PO.	A.	E.	DP.	PB.
Bell, Bluefield	.969	18	79	14	3	1	2	Pena, Martinsville	.939	7	51	11	4	1	2
Bennett, Martinsville	.965	11	80	3	3	0	1	Pinckes, Burlington	1.000	1	1	0	0	0	0
Brown, Elizabethton	.972	26	150	26	5	1	3	Postiff, Huntington	1.000	9	33	1	0	0	1
Bruno, Elizabethton	1.000	12	95	9	0	0	1	Rudolph, Kingsport	.984	48	317	41	6	3	12
Carpenter, Johnson City	.985	12	58	7	1	1	3	Rusk, Princeton	.970	32	169	26	6	2	11
Debrand, Bristol	.973	30	230	27	7	2	3	Russo, Elizabethton	1.000	2	14	1	0	1	0
Dempsey, Johnson City	.970	49	323	32	11	2	11	Spivey, Johnson City	.940	14	87	7	6	0	5
Gabbani, Huntington	.983	44	374	40	7	4	5	Steele, Kingsport	.800	2	4	0	1	0	0
Gonzalez, Pulaski	.975	31	229	42	7	1	15	Tejada, Princeton	1.000	13	59	17	0	0	4
Gordian, Bluefield	.931	7	25	2	2	0	6	Tewell, Martinsville	1.000	3	22	1	0	0	0
Hays, Johnson City	1.000	5	37	3	0	0	2	Toth, Pulaski	.992	24	216	26	2	4	8
R. Jimenez, Burlington	.970	40	250	46	9	6	10	Ubina, Bristol	.986	21	129	14	2	1	5
V. Jimenez, Pulaski	.968	18	140	9	5	0	7	Vargas, Princeton	.986	26	197	22	3	0	10
Kennedy, Huntington	1.000	1	2	0	0	0	0	Wallgren, Elizabethton	.994	21	149	17	1	1	2
Kinyoun, Kingsport	1.000	5	41	3	0	1	1	Williams, Kingsport	.953	24	147	16	8	0	12
LIEBERTHAL, Martinsville	.990	49	421	52	5	3	8	Wilson, Bristol	.992	16	101	20	1	3	5
Martinez, Burlington	.983	36	250	35	5	2	10	Wolff, Huntington	.971	24	180	22	6	1	2
D. Miller, Elizabethton	.982	12	102	6	2	1	4	Zaun, Bluefield	.980	58	460	31	10	2	12
K. Miller, Bristol	.985	18	110	19	2	3	0								

PITCHERS

Player and Club	Pct.	G.	PO.	A.	E.	DP.	Player and Club	Pct.	G.	PO.	A.	E.	DP.
Adamson, Princeton*	.944	12	3	14	1	0	Godfrey, Huntington	.947	13	5	13	1	1
Agado, Martinsville	.789	14	6	9	4	0	Gonzalez, Johnson City	1.000	13	9	7	0	2
Alberro, Johnson City	1.000	5	0	1	0	0	Grebe, Pulaski	.857	5	2	4	1	1
Anaya, Kingsport	1.000	3	1	1	0	0	Guilfoyle, Bristol*	1.000	16	0	7	0	0
C. Anderson, Martinsville	.938	13	4	11	1	0	Haeger, Bristol*	.917	24	1	10	1	1
M. Anderson, Bluefield*	.850	12	3	14	3	1	Hammond, Princeton*	1.000	21	3	13	0	1
Badacour, Martinsville	.947	12	5	13	1	0	Hassinger, Princeton	.969	13	8	23	1	5
Sa. Baker, Burlington	.875	24	2	5	1	0	Hawblitzel, Huntington	.824	14	3	11	3	0
Sc. Baker, Johnson City*	.929	32	2	11	1	2	Hays, Bluefield	1.000	14	0	6	0	0
Bark, Pulaski*	.875	5	1	6	1	0	Hebb, Bluefield	1.000	15	5	15	0	0
N. Benson, Kingsport	.833	13	3	7	2	0	Heiden, Bluefield	.500	1	0	1	1	0
T. Benson, Elizabethton	1.000	30	5	11	0	0	Ja. Henry, Bristol*	.857	10	1	11	2	0
Bethancourt, Elizabethton	.867	13	5	8	2	0	Jo. Henry, Elizabethton	.938	14	4	11	1	0
Bigham, Elizabethton*	.941	29	2	14	1	0	Higgins, Martinsville*	1.000	23	5	5	0	0
Blazier, Princeton	.889	14	2	14	2	1	Hurst, Johnson City	1.000	2	1	1	0	0
Bristow, Kingsport	.909	26	3	7	1	0	Johnson, Burlington	1.000	27	4	9	0	0
Brown, Burlington	.840	13	5	16	4	0	Kamerschen, Martinsville	.833	20	2	3	1	1
Brumley, Johnson City	.929	12	4	9	1	0	Kelly, Johnson City	.889	25	1	7	1	0
Bryan, Pulaski*	1.000	9	0	3	0	0	Kirk, Huntington	.800	10	2	2	1	0
Bryant, Burlington*	.667	2	0	2	1	0	Lehnerz, Kingsport	1.000	3	0	1	0	0
Camarena, Huntington	.800	13	2	6	2	0	Lima, Bristol	1.000	14	7	16	0	0
Carpentier, Kingsport	1.000	22	6	12	0	0	Lindsay, Kingsport*	.900	15	2	7	1	1
Cheetham, Huntington	.955	12	6	15	1	3	Lira, Bristol	.864	13	6	13	3	0
Chiles, Pulaski	.947	17	10	8	1	0	Lopez, Johnson City	.828	14	3	21	5	1
Chouinard, Bluefield	.923	10	3	9	1	0	Mack, Pulaski	.625	17	2	3	3	0
Cooper, Martinsville	.789	15	5	10	4	1	Maietta, Bristol	.800	6	2	2	1	0
Croak, Martinsville	.000	1	0	0	1	0	Manicchia, Princeton	1.000	22	6	9	0	1
Cruz, Bristol	.000	7	0	0	0	0	Mann, Huntington	.875	10	3	4	1	0
Davis, Johnson City	1.000	1	1	0	0	0	Marquez, Bluefield	.700	13	1	6	3	0
Diaz, Elizabethton	.783	13	7	11	5	0	Martinez, Kingsport	1.000	20	3	0	0	0
Dixon, Elizabethton*	.941	13	4	12	1	0	McElfish, Burlington*	.933	19	3	11	1	1
Domecq, Martinsville	.933	26	3	11	1	0	McGarity, Johnson City	.950	12	7	12	1	1
Dunlap, Pulaski	.933	17	8	6	1	0	McLochlin, Burlington	.882	14	7	8	2	1
Edwards, Princeton	1.000	9	2	3	0	1	Medina, Martinsville	1.000	9	1	1	0	0
Egleston, Bluefield	1.000	11	0	4	0	0	Mercedes, Bluefield*	.875	15	0	7	1	0
Elston, Burlington	.875	12	1	6	1	0	Mlicki, Burlington	.667	8	1	3	2	1
Embree, Burlington*	1.000	15	4	16	0	1	Morrison, Bluefield	1.000	13	9	5	0	0
Engle, Kingsport	.813	14	3	10	3	1	Munoz, Martinsville*	.933	14	1	27	2	1
Ford, Pulaski*	1.000	15	2	3	0	0	Nelson, Bristol	1.000	5	0	2	0	0
Freeman, Martinsville	1.000	20	1	4	0	0	Norris, Johnson City*	.714	24	1	4	2	0
Fritz, Elizabethton	.500	3	0	1	1	0	O'Connell, Princeton	1.000	18	1	2	0	0
Gajkowski, Burlington	.882	14	3	12	2	0	O'Donoghue, Bluefield*	.923	10	2	10	1	1
Garcia, Princeton	1.000	15	4	4	0	1	Owens, Pulaski*	.667	4	2	0	1	0
Gardner, Huntington	.769	13	3	7	3	0	Perez, Huntington	.933	20	3	11	1	1

PITCHERS—Continued

Player and Club	Pct.	G.	PO.	A.	E.	DP.
Persing, Elizabethton	.926	14	13	12	2	3
Place, Pulaski	1.000	22	5	9	0	1
Polanco, Kingsport	.667	22	2	2	2	0
Ramirez, Huntington*	1.000	3	0	1	0	0
Rees, Kingsport	.903	14	9	19	3	1
Reinisch, Bristol	.857	15	3	3	1	0
Repoz, Princeton	1.000	4	2	4	0	0
Riker, Bristol	.875	19	3	4	1	0
Ritchie, Elizabethton	.935	11	9	20	2	3
ROA, Pulaski	1.000	14	8	23	0	2
E. Rodriguez, Bristol*	1.000	13	1	5	0	1
M. Rodriguez, Johnson City	1.000	19	3	4	0	0
Ruyak, Johnson City	1.000	24	4	9	0	1
Salazar, Bristol	.667	7	0	2	1	0
Sanchez, Huntington	.846	13	5	17	4	0
Shepherd, Pulaski	.818	18	5	4	2	2
Snyder, Princeton*	.938	14	5	25	2	0
Speek, Johnson City	.917	27	4	7	1	0
Stanley, Huntington	1.000	9	1	1	0	0
Stevens, Huntington	.909	14	3	7	1	0
Stohr, Princeton*	1.000	16	5	14	0	0
Stokes, Bristol	1.000	21	1	6	0	1
A. Taylor, Huntington	.706	26	0	12	5	0
S. Taylor, Elizabethton	1.000	10	2	6	0	0
Tillman, Burlington*	.917	30	1	10	1	1
Tippitt, Bluefield	1.000	15	2	1	0	0
Ubina, Bristol	1.000	6	0	2	0	0
Urbani, Johnson City*	.833	9	4	6	2	0
Van Rynbach, Kingsport	.765	12	3	10	4	0
Villarreal, Princeton	1.000	7	0	1	0	0
Walden, Burlington	.840	15	6	15	4	0
Warren, Bristol	.500	1	0	1	1	0
Wechsberg, Burlington	.909	5	4	6	1	1
Wegmann, Kingsport	1.000	14	5	12	0	0
Werland, Pulaski*	.917	14	2	9	1	1
Wheeler, Martinsville	1.000	21	4	7	0	1
Whisenant, Princeton*	1.000	9	0	1	0	0
Wiley, Bluefield*	1.000	11	1	9	0	2
Williams, Pulaski	.870	14	11	9	3	0
Withem, Bristol	1.000	14	7	8	0	0

The following players do not have any fielding statistics at the positions indicated or appeared only as a designated hitter, pinch-hitter or pinch-runner: Alder, p; Aversa, p; Bark, of; Benge, p; Bradford, 3b; Carrasco, p; Crump, p; Cruz, 3b; D. Davis, dh; Debrand, 3b; DiMarco, p; Haeger, of; Hall, p; K. Hays, p; Hardtke, 2b; Helms, 1b; Hernandez, 3b; Hodge, p; Lance, p; McClain, of, p; Paredes, 3b; D. Ramirez, p; Ruiz, p; Silvers, 3b; Spivey, 3b; Sprick, 3b; J. Williams, p; Zaun, p.

CLUB PITCHING

Club	ERA.	G.	CG.	ShO.	Sv.	IP.	H.	R.	ER.	HR.	HB.	BB.	Int. BB.	SO.	WP.	Bk.
Elizabethton	3.00	67	8	4	22	588.0	494	268	196	47	32	241	5	506	31	17
Huntington	3.30	69	6	6	18	586.1	517	288	215	37	34	246	0	577	43	14
Burlington	3.33	72	3	3	20	637.0	615	325	236	25	32	262	7	499	55	17
Kingsport	3.36	72	16	7	16	629.2	547	307	235	53	24	252	7	487	74	17
Pulaski	3.63	72	7	4	13	632.0	551	334	255	34	30	277	11	604	74	30
Princeton	3.67	67	12	4	13	585.2	561	321	239	41	25	253	16	410	48	21
Bluefield	3.81	70	13	6	11	602.2	592	344	255	48	24	222	1	550	45	20
Martinsville	4.00	69	11	3	10	600.2	584	341	267	53	26	264	3	583	53	17
Johnson City	4.14	70	2	2	14	599.1	588	371	276	35	21	249	10	487	38	24
Bristol	4.24	68	3	4	11	590.0	579	340	278	46	32	262	13	580	64	25

PITCHERS' RECORDS
(Leading Qualifiers for Earned-Run Average Leadership—58 or More Innings)

*Throws lefthanded.

Pitcher—Club	W.	L.	Pct.	ERA.	G.	GS.	CG.	GF.	ShO.	Sv.	IP.	H.	R.	ER.	HR.	HB.	BB.	Int. BB.	SO.	WP.
Carpenter, Kingsport	6	1	.857	1.76	22	8	2	6	1	1	82.0	53	24	16	5	5	30	0	56	5
Ritchie, Elizabethton	5	2	.714	1.94	11	11	1	0	0	0	65.0	45	22	14	5	6	24	0	49	2
Hassinger, Princeton	7	4	.636	2.18	13	13	5	0	1	0	91.0	66	30	22	6	6	20	1	48	4
Cheetham, Huntington	4	2	.667	2.38	12	12	0	0	0	0	68.0	55	27	18	6	6	27	0	76	4
Lira, Bristol	5	5	.500	2.41	13	10	2	2	1	1	78.1	70	26	21	4	3	16	1	71	4
Snyder, Princeton*	5	5	.500	2.48	14	13	4	0	1	0	98.0	103	40	27	6	3	23	2	48	3
M. Anderson, Bluefield*	6	4	.600	2.60	12	12	2	0	0	0	83.0	72	29	24	6	0	21	0	88	4
Embree, Burlington*	4	4	.500	2.64	15	15	0	0	0	0	81.2	87	36	24	3	0	30	0	58	5
Wegmann, Kingsport	5	4	.556	2.67	14	12	4	1	2	0	84.1	53	34	25	8	1	30	0	103	10
Munoz, Martinsville*	6	7	.462	2.75	14	14	3	0	2	0	95.0	70	35	29	12	1	48	0	126	12

Departmental Leaders: G—Sc. Baker, 32; W—Godfrey, 9; L—Withem, 9; Pct.—Carpenter, .857; GS—Embree, Walden, 15; CG—Rees, 7; GF—T. Benson, 28; ShO—Munoz, O'Donoghue, Wegmann, Wiley, 2; Sv.—T. Benson, Johnson, 14; IP—Rees, 101.2; H—Snyder, 103; R—Sanchez, 60; ER—Sanchez, 45; HR—Munoz, 12; HB—Dunlap, 10; BB—Dixon, Munoz, 48; IBB—Five pitchers tied with 4; SO—Munoz, 126; WP—Five pitchers tied with 12.

(All Pitchers—Listed Alphabetically)

Pitcher—Club	W.	L.	Pct.	ERA.	G.	GS.	CG.	GF.	ShO.	Sv.	IP.	H.	R.	ER.	HR.	HB.	BB.	Int. BB.	SO.	WP.
Adamson, Princeton*	2	5	.286	3.88	12	8	1	3	0	1	48.2	56	27	21	2	3	12	1	40	6
Agado, Martinsville	2	5	.286	3.98	14	14	1	0	0	0	81.1	80	43	36	7	2	46	0	64	3
Alberto, Johnson City	2	0	1.000	5.06	5	0	0	0	0	0	5.1	3	3	3	0	0	3	0	3	0
Alder, Bristol	1	0	1.000	0.00	1	0	0	1	0	0	2.0	0	0	0	0	1	0	1	1	1
Anaya, Kingsport	0	0	.000	0.00	3	1	0	0	0	0	7.0	3	1	0	0	0	3	0	11	0
C. Anderson, Martinsville	1	6	.143	4.97	13	13	1	0	0	0	70.2	77	50	39	4	3	21	0	52	6
M. Anderson, Bluefield*	6	4	.600	2.60	12	12	2	0	0	0	83.0	72	29	24	6	0	21	0	88	4
Aversa, Johnson City	0	0	.000	18.00	2	0	0	2	0	0	2.0	4	4	4	0	1	0	2	1	1
Badacour, Martinsville	3	6	.333	3.53	12	12	2	0	0	0	74.0	65	37	29	6	1	20	0	53	2
Sa. Baker, Burlington	2	3	.400	4.10	24	0	17	0	5	41.2	47	29	19	1	3	17	0	29	6
Sc. Baker, Johnson City*	4	2	.667	2.28	32	0	0	7	0	0	51.1	44	21	13	2	0	29	1	65	6
Bark, Pulaski*	2	2	.500	2.66	5	5	0	0	0	0	23.2	17	19	7	3	1	13	0	33	2
Benge, Bluefield	0	1	.000	12.54	4	2	0	1	0	0	9.1	11	14	13	0	1	8	0	6	2
N. Benson, Kingsport	6	4	.600	3.38	13	10	1	2	0	1	61.1	56	42	23	5	2	37	0	33	7
T. Benson, Elizabethton	6	2	.750	1.70	30	0	28	0	14	47.2	32	10	9	0	1	15	2	39	1
Bethancourt, Elizabethton	4	2	.667	3.65	13	4	1	5	0	2	49.1	34	27	20	6	3	19	0	40	2
Bigham, Elizabethton*	6	2	.750	4.15	29	0	18	0	5	56.1	50	35	26	5	3	35	2	66	7
Blazier, Princeton	3	5	.375	4.46	14	13	1	1	0	0	78.2	77	46	39	10	1	29	1	45	3
Bristow, Kingsport	3	3	.500	2.92	26	0	22	0	8	37.0	36	13	12	2	1	16	3	26	8
Brown, Burlington	3	4	.429	5.75	13	12	0	0	0	0	67.1	76	45	43	6	4	30	0	53	10
Brumley, Johnson City	2	6	.250	6.14	12	12	0	0	0	0	55.2	62	48	38	4	3	29	0	43	2
Bryan, Pulaski*	0	2	.000	1.83	9	1	0	4	0	0	19.2	18	10	4	1	1	12	2	19	6
Bryant, Burlington*	1	0	1.000	0.84	2	2	0	0	0	0	10.2	5	2	1	0	0	6	0	17	2
Camarena, Huntington	0	0	.000	3.18	13	0	0	6	0	2	28.1	27	16	10	3	0	14	0	21	5
Carpenter, Kingsport	6	1	.857	1.76	22	8	2	6	1	1	82.0	53	24	16	5	5	30	0	56	5
Carrasco, Kingsport	0	0	.000	4.05	3	1	0	0	0	0	6.2	8	3	3	1	0	5	2		
Cheetham, Huntington	4	2	.667	2.38	12	12	0	0	0	0	68.0	55	27	18	6	6	27	0	76	4
Chiles, Pulaski	4	2	.667	3.99	17	6	1	4	0	3	56.1	46	36	25	8	1	26	0	44	11

Pitcher—Club	W.	L.	Pct.	ERA.	G.	GS.	CG.	GF.	ShO.	Sv.	IP.	H.	R.	ER.	HR.	HB.	BB.	Int. BB.	SO.	WP.
Chouinard, Bluefield	2	5	.286	3.70	10	10	2	0	1	0	56.0	61	34	23	10	1	14	0	30	2
Cooper, Martinsville	1	6	.143	5.08	15	12	3	2	0	0	67.1	76	50	38	9	1	39	0	50	9
Croak, Martinsville	0	1	.000	12.00	1	1	0	0	0	0	3.0	3	4	4	1	0	3	0	3	0
Crump, Pulaski	0	0	.000	27.00	1	0	0	1	0	0	1.0	6	4	3	0	0	0	0	0	0
Cruz, Bristol	0	0	.000	9.28	7	0	0	4	0	0	10.2	15	12	11	0	1	5	0	6	2
Davis, Johnson City	0	0	.000	0.00	1	0	0	0	0	0	0.0	0	3	3	0	0	3	0	0	0
Diaz, Elizabethton	4	2	.667	3.07	13	12	1	0	0	0	70.1	67	40	24	4	3	32	0	61	4
DiMarco, Bluefield	0	0	.000	0.00	2	0	0	2	0	1	1.0	0	0	0	0	0	0	0	0	0
Dixon, Elizabethton*	7	2	.778	2.79	13	13	1	0	1	0	84.0	66	34	26	6	2	48	0	57	7
Domecq, Martinsville	5	2	.714	2.18	26	0	0	23	0	8	33.0	21	9	8	0	5	17	1	40	2
Dunlap, Pulaski	1	3	.250	3.83	17	4	0	6	0	2	51.2	34	26	22	2	10	30	0	60	12
Edwards, Princeton	0	2	.000	9.75	9	0	0	7	0	0	12.0	17	13	13	0	0	11	4	8	5
Egleston, Bluefield	1	0	1.000	4.43	11	0	0	4	0	1	22.1	25	12	11	3	2	3	0	15	3
Elston, Burlington	0	5	.000	5.35	12	5	0	5	0	0	35.1	40	28	21	1	3	30	0	34	8
Embree, Burlington*	4	4	.500	2.64	15	15	0	0	0	0	81.2	87	36	24	3	0	30	0	58	5
Engle, Kingsport	6	3	.667	3.26	14	12	1	0	0	0	77.1	68	35	28	9	4	31	0	75	7
Ford, Pulaski*	0	1	.000	6.20	15	0	0	9	0	0	20.1	18	17	14	1	1	16	0	11	5
Freeman, Martinsville	0	1	.000	4.35	20	0	0	5	0	0	39.1	47	24	19	4	4	17	0	53	4
Fritz, Elizabethton	0	0	.000	6.75	3	0	0	1	0	0	5.1	6	4	4	1	0	5	0	2	0
Gajkowski, Burlington	2	6	.250	4.10	14	10	1	1	0	0	63.2	74	34	29	0	3	23	0	44	0
Garcia, Princeton	3	2	.600	5.40	15	1	0	8	0	1	35.0	40	23	21	5	2	26	4	34	6
Gardner, Huntington	3	2	.600	1.87	13	4	0	5	0	2	43.1	36	16	9	1	2	20	0	52	5
Godfrey, Huntington	9	2	.818	3.29	13	13	2	0	0	0	82.0	76	34	30	4	3	31	0	57	6
Gonzalez, Johnson City	2	7	.222	4.18	13	13	0	0	0	0	71.0	74	41	33	4	4	20	0	52	1
Grebe, Pulaski	2	2	.500	3.77	5	5	0	0	0	0	28.2	27	16	12	1	0	13	0	24	4
Guilfoyle, Bristol*	4	6	.400	3.06	16	7	0	3	0	1	64.2	54	35	22	6	1	25	0	80	4
Haeger, Bristol*	0	2	.000	5.15	24	2	0	14	0	3	36.2	37	25	21	3	2	24	1	51	9
Hall, Bristol	0	0	.000	0.00	1	0	0	1	0	0	1.0	0	0	0	0	0	0	0	0	0
Hammond, Princeton*	3	5	.375	3.06	21	1	0	7	0	1	47.0	43	33	16	1	1	28	2	35	3
Hassinger, Princeton	7	4	.636	2.18	13	13	5	0	1	0	91.0	66	30	22	6	6	20	1	48	4
Hawblitzel, Huntington	6	5	.545	3.93	14	14	2	0	1	0	75.2	72	38	33	8	6	25	0	71	2
G. Hays, Bluefield	2	1	.667	3.42	14	0	0	13	0	3	23.2	20	11	9	1	2	6	0	21	2
K. Hays, Johnson City	0	0	.000	0.00	1	0	0	1	0	0	2.0	2	0	0	0	0	2	0	1	0
Hebb, Bluefield	6	7	.462	3.54	15	14	3	0	0	0	89.0	89	53	35	5	2	26	0	80	6
Heiden, Bluefield	1	0	1.000	7.20	1	1	0	0	0	0	5.0	5	4	4	1	1	3	0	2	2
Ja. Henry, Bristol*	1	3	.250	4.10	10	10	0	0	0	0	41.2	39	26	19	3	0	28	0	38	6
Jo. Henry, Elizabethton	7	2	.778	3.61	14	13	1	1	0	0	87.1	81	40	35	11	7	28	0	89	1
Higgins, Martinsville*	5	3	.625	2.93	23	0	0	12	0	2	40.0	41	21	13	1	4	11	1	40	0
Hodge, Bluefield	0	0	.000	27.00	1	0	0	0	0	0	0.2	2	2	2	0	0	1	0	1	0
Hurst, Johnson City	0	0	.000	1.69	2	2	0	0	0	0	10.2	5	2	2	0	0	6	0	12	0
Johnson, Burlington	2	1	.667	1.08	27	0	0	24	0	14	50.0	35	8	6	0	2	28	4	46	5
Kamerschen, Martinsville	1	3	.250	5.33	20	2	1	2	0	0	50.2	56	39	30	7	3	23	1	47	12
Kelly, Johnson City	1	2	.333	0.79	25	0	0	22	0	13	34.1	22	7	3	1	2	12	3	41	1
Kirk, Huntington	2	1	.667	2.84	10	0	0	10	0	1	12.2	10	5	4	0	1	1	0	9	1
Lance, Martinsville	0	1	.000	54.00	1	1	0	0	0	0	0.1	0	2	2	0	0	1	0	1	0
Lehnerz, Kingsport	0	2	.000	32.40	3	2	0	0	0	0	3.1	4	12	12	0	2	16	0	2	8
Lima, Bristol	3	8	.273	5.02	14	12	1	2	0	1	75.1	89	49	42	9	3	22	3	64	4
Lindsay, Kingsport*	3	2	.600	2.08	15	0	0	7	0	1	21.2	15	5	5	0	0	7	1	14	0
Lira, Bristol	5	5	.500	2.41	13	10	2	2	1	1	78.1	70	26	21	4	3	16	1	71	4
Lopez, Johnson City	5	5	.500	2.76	14	14	1	0	0	0	81.2	86	40	25	3	2	24	1	43	1
Mack, Pulaski	1	2	.333	2.05	17	0	0	11	0	4	22.0	11	7	5	0	1	12	4	34	0
Maietta, Bristol	0	3	.000	3.82	6	6	0	0	0	0	30.2	30	13	13	1	3	11	0	28	3
Manicchia, Princeton	2	1	.667	2.16	22	0	0	15	0	8	50.0	33	22	12	2	0	21	0	46	4
Mann, Huntington	1	0	1.000	2.29	10	0	0	2	0	0	19.2	12	10	5	1	1	8	0	20	2
Marquez, Kingsport	3	3	.500	3.20	13	9	1	1	0	1	56.1	51	30	20	0	2	38	0	40	7
Martinez, Kingsport	0	3	.000	7.41	20	1	0	12	0	0	34.0	43	33	28	8	1	22	3	26	5
McClain, Bluefield	0	0	.000	9.00	1	0	0	0	0	0	1.0	1	1	1	1	0	0	0	0	0
McElfish, Burlington*	2	1	.667	2.53	19	0	0	8	0	1	42.2	46	21	12	2	3	19	0	27	5
McGarity, Johnson City	0	8	.000	5.17	12	12	1	0	0	0	62.2	60	49	36	4	3	26	0	47	6
McLochlin, Burlington	2	3	.400	3.11	14	7	0	0	0	0	55.0	47	28	19	2	2	18	0	42	1
Medina, Bluefield	0	0	.000	1.88	9	0	0	6	0	1	14.1	10	5	3	1	1	0	0	14	2
Mercedes, Bluefield*	3	2	.600	6.08	15	5	0	1	0	0	37.0	42	40	25	2	3	38	0	30	5
Mlicki, Burlington	3	1	.750	3.50	8	1	0	2	0	0	18.0	16	11	7	1	1	6	0	17	0
Morrison, Pulaski	6	6	.500	4.10	13	13	2	0	0	0	79.0	77	46	36	4	1	37	0	79	6
Munoz, Martinsville*	6	7	.462	2.75	14	14	3	0	2	0	95.0	70	35	29	12	1	48	0	126	12
Nelson, Bristol	0	1	.000	13.06	5	1	0	0	0	0	10.1	7	16	15	0	2	25	0	8	4
Norris, Johnson City*	2	2	.500	4.50	24	5	0	5	0	1	52.0	49	28	26	3	1	29	0	48	4
O'Connell, Bluefield	1	1	.500	8.16	18	0	0	8	0	1	32.0	45	38	29	4	2	23	1	28	3
O'Donoghue, Bluefield*	4	2	.667	2.01	10	6	2	3	2	0	49.1	50	13	11	2	1	10	0	67	2
Owens, Pulaski*	1	1	.500	7.11	4	2	0	1	0	0	12.2	18	13	10	0	1	7	1	9	1
Perez, 2 Prin.-20 Hunt.	5	1	.833	1.90	22	1	0	10	0	3	52.0	36	12	11	2	5	11	0	72	5
Persing, Elizabethton	8	2	.800	2.93	14	14	3	0	0	0	95.1	81	47	31	5	7	30	1	81	7
Place, Pulaski	4	3	.571	2.61	22	1	0	15	0	3	48.1	41	20	14	2	3	17	3	38	1
Polanco, Kingsport	2	2	.500	3.93	22	2	0	6	0	1	52.2	50	27	23	4	3	11	0	42	6
D. Ramirez, Bluefield	0	0	.000	0.00	1	0	0	1	0	0	2.0	0	0	0	0	0	2	0	1	0
N. Ramirez, Huntington*	0	0	.000	9.53	3	0	0	1	0	0	5.2	7	6	6	1	0	4	0	7	1
Rees, Kingsport	6	6	.500	2.92	14	14	7	0	1	0	101.2	102	46	33	8	5	26	0	59	5
Reinisch, Bristol	2	1	.667	1.52	15	0	0	10	0	1	23.2	24	6	4	1	1	5	0	26	1
Repoz, Princeton	2	0	1.000	3.54	4	4	0	0	0	0	20.1	23	9	8	1	3	10	0	7	1
Riker, Bristol	2	5	.286	6.12	19	5	0	4	0	0	60.1	68	46	41	9	6	21	3	60	2
Ritchie, Elizabethton	5	2	.714	1.94	11	11	1	0	0	0	65.0	45	22	14	5	6	24	0	49	2
Roa, Pulaski	4	2	.667	2.97	14	11	3	1	0	0	75.2	55	29	25	3	2	26	0	49	2
E. Rodriguez, Bristol*	0	3	.000	4.60	13	1	0	3	0	0	31.1	32	22	16	5	1	10	0	45	2
M. Rodriguez, Johnson City	2	1	.667	7.83	19	3	0	8	0	0	46.0	64	44	40	8	2	17	0	27	4
Ruiz, Bluefield	0	0	.000	54.00	1	0	0	0	0	0	0.1	1	2	2	1	0	3	0	0	1
Ruyak, Johnson City*	1	4	.200	5.49	24	1	0	9	0	1	41.0	47	37	25	3	1	21	2	30	8
Salazar, Bristol	0	0	.000	1.93	7	0	0	4	0	1	9.1	7	4	2	2	1	9	0	7	1
Sanchez, Huntington	2	5	.300	5.35	13	13	2	0	0	0	75.2	89	60	45	4	4	34	0	55	1
Shepherd, Pulaski	2	5	.286	4.02	18	1	0	11	0	1	40.1	42	20	18	4	1	19	1	35	4
Snyder, Princeton*	5	5	.500	2.48	14	13	4	0	1	0	98.0	103	40	27	6	3	23	2	48	3
Speek, Johnson City	3	2	.600	1.78	27	0	0	14	0	1	35.1	23	9	7	1	2	12	3	33	0
Stanley, Huntington	1	1	.500	2.19	9	1	0	4	0	0	24.2	17	7	6	1	0	14	0	35	3

Pitcher—Club	W.	L.	Pct.	ERA.	G.	GS.	CG.	GF.	ShO.	Sv.	IP.	H.	R.	ER.	HR.	HB.	BB.	Int. BB.	SO.	WP.
Stevens, Huntington	2	4	.333	4.61	13	11	0	1	0	0	56.2	48	44	29	3	7	47	0	55	6
Stohr, Princeton°	4	7	.364	4.30	16	12	1	4	0	1	75.1	77	45	36	5	1	42	1	59	4
Stokes, Bristol	1	0	1.000	2.13	21	0	0	13	0	3	38.0	25	10	9	1	2	18	4	43	5
A. Taylor, Huntington	4	4	.500	1.84	26	0	0	25	0	11	44.0	32	13	9	3	1	10	0	50	3
S. Taylor, Elizabethton	4	0	1.000	2.30	10	0	0	6	0	1	27.1	32	9	7	4	0	5	0	22	0
Tillman, Burlington°	7	2	.778	2.89	30	0	0	12	0	0	53.0	51	24	17	3	1	12	3	47	2
Tippitt, Bluefield	3	3	.500	3.65	15	2	1	8	0	3	49.1	40	23	20	6	1	11	0	61	2
Ubina, Bristol	0	0	.000	4.50	6	0	0	5	0	0	10.0	8	6	5	0	1	5	0	4	1
Urbani, Johnson City°	4	3	.571	3.35	9	9	0	0	0	0	48.1	43	35	18	2	1	15	0	40	4
Van Rynbach, Kingsport	4	1	.800	4.01	12	9	1	0	0	0	60.2	56	32	27	3	0	22	0	35	11
Villarreal, Princeton	0	0	.000	3.55	7	0	0	7	0	0	12.2	10	6	5	0	0	11	0	12	2
Walden, Burlington	5	6	.455	2.89	15	15	1	0	1	0	93.1	67	45	30	4	7	33	0	72	9
Warren, Bristol	0	0	.000	2.25	1	1	0	0	0	0	4.0	4	1	1	0	0	2	0	0	0
Wechsberg, Burlington	2	1	.667	2.92	5	5	1	0	0	0	24.2	24	14	8	2	3	10	0	13	2
Wegmann, Kingsport	5	4	.556	2.67	14	12	4	1	2	0	84.1	53	34	25	8	1	30	0	103	10
Werland, Pulaski°	5	2	.714	2.94	14	10	0	1	0	0	64.1	48	27	21	0	0	26	0	98	12
Wheeler, Martinsville	1	3	.250	4.61	21	0	0	14	0	0	46.0	48	27	21	2	1	18	0	54	3
Whisenant, Princeton°	0	0	.000	11.40	9	2	0	2	0	0	15.0	16	27	19	3	3	20	0	25	7
Wiley, Bluefield°	5	2	.714	3.84	11	9	2	0	2	0	58.2	59	30	25	5	4	9	0	51	1
D. Williams, Pulaski	5	2	.714	3.97	14	13	1	1	0	0	88.1	93	44	39	5	7	23	0	71	8
J. Williams, Bluefield	2	0	1.000	1.59	9	0	0	9	0	0	11.1	7	3	2	0	1	5	0	14	1
Withem, Bristol	3	9	.250	5.23	14	13	0	1	0	0	62.0	70	43	36	2	5	35	1	48	12
Zaun, Bluefield	0	0	.000	0.00	1	0	0	0	0	0	1.0	1	0	0	0	0	1	0	1	0

BALKS—Ja. Henry, 9; Morrison, Stevens, 8 each; Adamson, Wegmann, 7 each; Werland, 6; Mack, McGarity, 5 each; Embree, Hebb, Jo. Henry, Wechsberg, 4 each; Agado, Sc. Baker, Benge, Bethancourt, Chouinard, Dixon, Freeman, Guilfoyle, Hammond, Kelly, Lopez, Manicchia, Perez, Ritchie, Ruyak, Wheeler, D. Williams, 3 each; C. Anderson, Bigham, Brown, Carpentier, Chiles, Cooper, Domecq, Garcia, Gonzalez, Hassinger, Lindsay, Lira, Marquez, Martinez, Persing, Place, Riker, Roa, Snyder, Speek, Van Rynbach, Walden, Wiley, Withem, 2 each; M. Anderson, Aversa, Badacour, Blazier, Bristow, Brumley, Bryan, Cheetham, Ford, Gajkowski, Gardner, Haeger, G. Hays, Johnson, Lance, Lima, Maietta, Mann, McElfish, McLochlin, Medina, Mercedes, Nelson, O'Connell, O'Donoghue, Rees, Reinisch, M. Rodriguez, Tillman, Ubina, Villarreal, Warren, 1 each.

COMBINATION SHUTOUTS—Anderson-Marquez, Bluefield; Guilfoyle-Salazar, Henry-Riker-Salazar, Lira-Stokes, Bristol; Embree-Baker-Johnson, Embree-Johnson, Burlington; Henry-Benson 2, Henry-Bigham, Elizabethton; Cheetham-Perez, Gardner-Perez, Hawblitzel-Mann-Taylor, Hawblitzel-Perez-Taylor, Sanchez-Perez-Taylor, Huntington; McGarity-Speek-Kelly, Norris-Baker, Johnson City; Benson-Bristow, Carpentier-Van Rynbach-Bristow, Van Rynbach-Polanco, Kingsport; Munoz-Kamerschen-Domecq, Martinsville; Blazier-Hassinger, Hassinger-Adamson, Princeton; Roa-Mack, Werland-Dunlap, Werland-Place-Mack, Pulaski.

NO-HIT GAME—Wegmann, Kingsport, defeated Pulaski, 7-0 (first game, perfect game), July 31.

Arizona League

SUMMER CLASS A CLASSIFICATION

CHAMPIONSHIP WINNERS IN PREVIOUS YEARS

1988—Peoria Brewers .... .690   1989—Peoria Brewers .... .732

STANDING OF CLUBS AT CLOSE OF SEASON, AUGUST 31

Club	Brew.	Mar.	Car.	Ath.	Pad.	Ang.	W.	L.	T.	Pct.	G.B.
Brewers	...	9	5	4	7	11	36	17	0	.679	.....
Mariners	2	...	7	10	7	6	32	21	1	.604	4
Cardinals	5	2	...	5	10	6	28	24	1	.538	7½
Athletics	6	2	5	...	6	7	26	27	0	.491	10
Padres	3	4	2	4	...	6	19	35	0	.352	17½
Angels	1	4	5	4	5	...	19	36	0	.345	18

Games played in Mesa, Peoria, Scottsdale and Tempe.

Club names are major league affiliations.

Playoffs—No playoffs scheduled.

Regular-Season Attendance—No total official attendance figures reported.

Managers—Angels, Bill Lachemann; Athletics, Gary Jones; Brewers, Alex Taveras; Cardinals, Larry Milbourne; Mariners, Dave Myers; Padres, Jaime Moreno.

All-Star Team—1B—Marc Newfield, Mariners; 2B—Julian Salazar, Brewers; Carlos Polanco, Angels; 3B—Jon Halland, Mariners; SS—Israel Seda, Mariners; OF—Orlando Barrios, Brewers; Jose Velez, Cardinals; Tony Pritchett, Athletics; C—Don Prybylinski, Cardinals; DH—Paul Brannon, Mariners; Jonas Hamlin, Cardinals; LHP—Derron Spiller, Cardinals; RHP—Phil Angelos, Brewers; LHRP—Bill Kostich, Mariners; RHRP—Victor Rojas, Angels; Most Valuable Player—Marc Newfield, Mariners; Manager of the Year—Jaime Moreno, Padres; Bill Lachemann, Angels.

(Compiled by Howe Sportsdata International, Boston, Mass.)

CLUB BATTING

Club	Pct.	G.	AB.	R.	OR.	H.	TB.	2B.	3B.	HR.	RBI.	SH.	SF.	HP.	BB.	Int. BB.	SO.	SB.	CS.	LOB.
Mariners	.277	54	1955	354	280	542	756	85	33	21	276	9	17	26	246	4	370	43	36	445
Brewers	.267	53	1844	334	238	492	663	60	36	13	254	10	22	27	220	4	329	64	42	402
Angels	.262	55	1876	281	351	491	613	52	26	6	222	7	25	34	248	4	399	52	22	460
Cardinals	.259	53	1862	312	277	483	644	60	25	17	244	5	15	25	220	6	301	46	26	419
Athletics	.256	53	1855	292	309	474	641	74	21	17	232	5	15	27	213	7	477	77	29	405
Padres	.214	54	1773	261	379	379	499	66	12	10	183	12	7	29	250	6	463	117	45	383

INDIVIDUAL BATTING
(Leading Qualifiers for Batting Championship—151 or More Plate Appearances)

*Bats lefthanded.   †Switch-hitter.

Player and Club	Pct.	G.	AB.	R.	H.	TB.	2B.	3B.	HR.	RBI.	SH.	SF.	HP.	BB.	Int. BB.	SO.	SB.	CS.
Boudreau, Thomas, Mariners	.378	36	135	27	51	75	8	2	4	29	0	2	3	19	0	34	1	2
Johnson, Wayne, Angels	.366	39	131	33	48	56	3	1	1	13	0	1	3	32	0	23	19	5
Hamlin, Jonas, Cardinals	.344	53	221	45	76	122	11	4	9	39	0	1	1	13	1	30	0	2
Stela, Jose, Angels	.331	48	169	25	56	73	9	4	0	23	2	4	4	16	1	17	2	3
Prybylinski, Donald, Cardinals	.325	45	154	32	50	68	13	1	1	28	0	2	2	26	1	16	2	0
Velez, Jose, Cardinals*	.317	46	183	26	58	77	7	6	0	29	1	2	2	8	0	12	5	2
Barrios, Orlando, Brewers	.313	42	166	34	52	71	5	4	2	22	0	0	4	14	0	14	10	5
Newfield, Marc, Mariners	.313	51	192	34	60	95	13	2	6	38	0	2	2	25	2	20	4	4
Polanco, Carlos, Angels	.301	42	136	28	41	49	2	0	2	21	0	0	1	26	0	18	8	3
Spears, Brian, Brewers	.300	52	210	33	63	91	9	2	5	45	1	6	5	11	1	21	2	3

Departmental Leaders: G—Hamlin, 53; AB—Hamlin, 221; R—Hamlin, 45; H—Hamlin, 76; TB—Hamlin, 122; 2B—Newfield, Prybylinski, Vasquez, 13; 3B—Pritchett, 6; HR—Hamlin, 9; RBI—Spears, 45; SH—Salazar, Vasquez, 4; SF—J.A. Cabrera, Spears, 6; HP—Bobo, 7; BB—Singleton, 43; IBB—Mowry, 4; SO—Hust, 60; SB—Pritchett, 20; CS—Shannon, 13.

(All Players—Listed Alphabetically)

Player and Club	Pct.	G.	AB.	R.	H.	TB.	2B.	3B.	HR.	RBI.	SH.	SF.	HP.	BB.	Int. BB.	SO.	SB.	CS.
Abercrombie, John, Padres	.288	43	156	35	45	78	10	1	7	23	0	0	5	20	0	23	10	2
Acosta, Jose, Athletics	.455	15	11	3	5	10	1	2	0	2	0	0	0	0	0	3	0	0
Alcaraz, Vladimiro, Angels	.228	17	57	10	13	15	2	0	0	10	0	0	3	10	0	14	0	0
Anderson, Garret, Angels*	.213	32	127	5	27	29	2	0	0	14	0	3	2	2	0	24	3	0
Anthony, Mark, Padres*	.161	27	87	14	14	14	0	0	0	5	0	0	2	11	0	31	10	1
Aracena, Luinis, Athletics	.293	49	164	27	48	59	9	1	0	21	0	0	4	29	1	45	11	5
Aversa, Joseph, Cardinals†	.235	9	34	5	8	9	1	0	0	4	0	0	1	8	0	8	2	3
Baber, Larue, Brewers	.180	31	128	23	23	29	4	1	0	7	0	0	2	11	0	27	8	4
Baez, Hector, Angels	.167	2	6	2	1	1	0	0	0	0	0	0	0	1	0	1	0	0
Bailey, Reginald, Athletics	.148	43	135	11	20	28	2	0	2	17	0	1	2	4	0	29	0	1
Barlow, Clemmon, Mariners	.245	37	102	23	25	44	8	4	1	16	2	4	4	13	0	37	2	2
Barrios, Orlando, Brewers	.313	42	166	34	52	71	5	4	2	22	0	0	4	14	0	14	10	5
Benjamin, Robert, Brewers*	.296	26	81	19	24	39	3	6	0	14	0	0	0	19	0	19	3	3
Bertucci, Joseph, Angels	.180	31	100	12	18	20	0	1	0	6	0	1	1	17	1	32	1	1
Bobo, Elgin, Angels	.297	42	145	20	43	59	6	5	0	19	0	2	7	18	1	30	2	1
Boudreau, Thomas, Mariners	.378	36	135	27	51	75	8	2	4	29	0	2	3	19	0	34	1	2
Brannon, Paul, Brewers	.278	25	97	11	27	41	5	3	1	15	0	1	1	4	0	16	3	1
Brito, Francisco, Angels	.300	4	20	2	6	7	1	0	0	1	0	0	1	0	0	2	0	0
Buldier, Nelson, Angels	.333	1	3	0	1	1	0	0	0	0	0	0	0	0	0	0	0	0
Bullock, Corey, Padres	.169	48	148	19	25	32	7	0	0	9	0	1	3	27	1	44	6	1
Cabrera, Juan A., Brewers	.255	44	165	27	42	57	6	3	1	26	1	6	0	10	0	27	7	2
Cabrera, Juan C., Athletics†	.254	18	67	7	17	20	1	1	0	8	1	0	0	4	0	14	3	1
Candelario, Francisco, Mariners	.212	24	66	4	14	16	2	0	0	5	1	0	0	2	0	26	0	1
Carion, German, Padres†	.179	13	39	2	7	7	0	0	0	2	1	0	0	4	0	8	0	3
Carlsen, Robert, Athletics*	.367	36	120	34	44	56	9	0	1	20	1	1	1	23	1	14	9	1
Carpenter, Kevin, Cardinals	.182	10	33	4	6	6	0	0	0	4	1	0	1	2	0	5	0	0

Player and Club	Pct.	G.	AB.	R.	H.	TB.	2B.	3B.	HR.	RBI.	SH.	SF.	HP.	BB.	Int. BB.	SO.	SB.	CS.
Colon, Hector, Cardinals†	.174	23	46	6	8	8	0	0	0	6	1	0	2	19	0	8	3	4
Cruz, Juan, Padres	.214	46	159	18	34	44	8	1	0	16	0	1	1	9	0	53	8	4
Davenport, Jimmy, Cardinals	.183	40	115	16	21	33	3	3	1	14	0	1	4	15	0	39	5	0
DeCareau, Thomas, Padres	.262	29	103	16	27	35	8	0	0	13	0	1	3	17	0	31	5	1
Diaz, Stephen, Brewers	.148	25	81	8	12	17	2	0	1	11	1	0	3	7	0	18	0	1
Dionicio, Eurben, Athletics	.167	37	108	16	18	26	2	0	2	11	0	1	2	13	0	41	2	0
Dudek, Steven, Cardinals*	.304	31	125	19	38	44	4	1	0	12	0	2	0	4	1	19	3	3
Duncan, Jeffrey, Athletics*	.250	42	152	30	38	60	12	2	2	27	0	5	1	25	0	45	5	3
Enriquez, Luis, Brewers†	.231	43	169	30	39	60	10	4	1	19	1	1	1	19	0	37	5	2
Fermaint, Michael, Mariners	.299	33	117	26	35	41	4	1	0	8	0	0	1	28	0	18	3	4
Fernandez, Julio, Mariners*	.303	38	109	24	33	46	3	5	0	12	0	3	1	20	0	23	4	1
Flores, Carlos, Brewers	.257	23	70	9	18	20	0	1	0	12	0	1	2	9	0	9	1	3
Francisco, Vicente, Athletics†	.246	43	175	23	43	50	3	2	0	14	2	1	1	6	0	42	5	1
Fuentes, Nelson, Athletics	.205	16	44	5	9	13	1	0	1	6	0	0	2	0	0	11	0	0
Gale, William, Cardinals	.239	40	155	29	37	52	8	2	1	21	0	2	2	22	0	21	3	3
Gonzalez, Richard, Cardinals	.226	8	31	3	7	7	0	0	0	0	0	0	0	3	1	0	1	0
Guzik, Brian, Angels	.242	18	62	11	15	22	2	1	1	9	1	1	2	8	0	18	2	0
Halland, Steven, Athletics	.296	38	159	28	47	77	6	6	4	33	1	3	0	12	0	35	3	4
Hamlin, Jonas, Cardinals	.344	53	221	45	76	122	11	4	9	39	0	1	1	13	1	30	0	2
Hood, Randall, Brewers	.231	4	13	2	3	3	0	0	0	1	0	1	1	2	0	4	0	0
House, Kenneth, Angels	.246	42	130	17	32	47	5	5	0	20	1	2	3	28	0	31	4	0
Hust, Gary, Athletics	.200	44	150	13	30	38	1	2	1	9	0	0	4	11	0	60	3	2
Irwin, Ryan, Brewers*	.271	23	70	13	19	20	1	0	0	8	0	0	1	8	0	12	1	1
Johnson, John, Mariners	.277	13	47	9	13	15	2	0	0	5	1	0	0	4	0	7	0	0
Johnson, Wayne, Angels	.366	39	131	33	48	56	3	1	1	13	0	1	3	32	0	23	19	5
Jorge, Genaro, Angels*	.200	18	50	5	10	11	1	0	0	6	0	0	0	12	0	12	0	2
Joyce, James, Padres	.161	30	93	4	15	17	2	0	0	6	0	1	1	9	0	17	1	2
Keathley, Donald, Athletics	.254	45	130	17	33	41	2	0	2	10	0	0	3	19	2	36	0	3
Keating, Michael, Cardinals	.180	30	89	16	16	20	1	0	1	8	0	1	2	12	0	16	1	1
Kennedy, Michael, Athletics	.227	13	44	1	10	14	1	0	1	7	0	2	1	2	0	5	0	1
Klavitter, Clayton, Mariners	.289	10	38	3	11	18	4	0	1	7	0	0	0	1	0	7	0	0
Landinez, Carlos, Cardinals	.260	29	104	30	27	42	5	2	2	14	0	0	4	29	0	12	16	2
Lawson, David, Mariners*	.170	34	112	22	19	23	2	1	0	15	1	0	0	23	0	24	5	0
List, Paul, Mariners	.292	15	48	7	14	26	3	3	1	9	0	0	1	12	1	6	1	2
Lowman, Sydney, Cardinals*	.301	20	73	9	22	23	1	0	0	6	0	0	1	4	0	16	0	0
Lozano, Jose, Mariners†	.255	22	51	6	13	14	1	0	0	6	0	0	2	7	0	11	0	1
Lydy, Scott, Athletics	.340	18	50	8	17	29	6	0	2	11	0	0	0	10	0	14	0	0
Markiewicz, Brandon, Angels	.162	31	99	14	16	18	2	0	0	4	0	0	1	10	0	22	1	0
Mateo, Jose, Padres†	.000	5	1	0	0	0	0	0	0	0	0	0	0	0	0	0	0	0
Matos, Alberto, Padres	.135	32	104	14	14	20	2	2	0	8	2	0	2	11	0	48	8	1
McDavid, Darnell, Padres*	.146	13	41	4	6	10	0	2	0	1	1	0	0	6	1	5	3	1
Meek, Darryl, Cardinals*	.186	43	113	20	21	29	3	1	1	18	0	0	1	26	0	37	1	1
Mercado, Rafael, Athletics	.286	5	21	4	6	6	0	0	0	6	0	0	0	2	0	6	1	0
Meza, Lorenzo, Cardinals*	.245	51	204	29	50	56	1	1	1	22	1	0	1	5	2	19	0	3
Minnis, William, Angels	.269	24	78	16	21	30	4	1	1	8	1	2	1	7	0	18	2	1
Molina, Islay, Athletics	.339	39	127	20	43	59	12	2	0	18	1	3	2	9	1	22	5	0
Moncion, Pedro, Mariners	.253	31	99	23	25	29	2	1	0	9	0	0	1	19	0	15	0	3
Moriso, Pablo, Athletics	.000	1	1	0	0	0	0	0	0	0	0	0	0	0	0	1	0	0
Mowry, David, Padres*	.239	50	180	25	43	52	6	0	1	28	0	1	1	38	4	34	9	5
Newfield, Marc, Mariners	.313	51	192	34	60	95	13	2	6	38	0	2	2	25	2	20	4	4
Oliver, Felix, Angels	.300	3	10	1	3	3	0	0	0	0	0	0	0	0	0	4	0	0
Olofson, Christopher, Athletics	.231	24	52	10	12	12	0	0	0	2	0	0	0	4	0	17	5	0
Osuna, Julio, Angels*	.370	16	46	9	17	22	1	2	0	8	0	1	0	5	0	6	0	0
Perez, Tirson, Padres	.000	17	0	1	0	0	0	0	0	0	0	0	0	1	0	0	0	0
Peterson, Andrew, Angels	.276	7	29	4	8	9	1	0	0	3	1	0	0	1	0	6	1	0
Pineiro, Michael, Angels	.333	28	69	11	23	27	2	1	0	9	1	0	1	3	0	10	0	2
Polanco, Carlos, Angels	.301	42	136	28	41	49	2	0	2	21	0	0	1	26	0	18	8	3
Powell, L.V., Mariners	.214	18	42	10	9	10	1	0	0	5	0	0	5	2	0	10	2	1
Pritchett, Anthony, Athletics†	.274	51	197	44	54	87	6	9	3	35	0	1	6	32	2	42	20	7
Prybylinski, Donald, Cardinals	.325	45	154	32	50	68	13	1	1	28	0	2	2	26	1	16	2	0
Ramos, Martin, Mariners	.261	22	69	13	18	29	3	1	2	14	0	1	0	9	0	21	2	1
Reid, Gregory, Athletics†	.252	34	107	19	27	33	6	0	0	8	0	0	1	18	0	30	8	4
Rios, Christopher, Angels	.400	14	45	9	18	25	1	3	0	11	0	2	1	8	0	2	1	0
Robertson, Tommy, Mariners*	.254	38	130	25	33	41	4	2	0	16	1	0	0	8	0	19	1	2
Rodriguez, Francisco, Brewers	.276	31	98	16	27	38	1	5	0	14	0	3	1	11	0	28	2	1
Rodriguez, Pascual, Angels	.250	4	4	1	1	1	0	0	0	0	0	0	0	2	0	0	0	0
Rolfes, Michael, Brewers*	.000	16	1	0	0	0	0	0	0	0	0	0	0	0	0	0	0	0
Salazar, Julian, Brewers	.288	47	156	29	45	56	6	1	1	18	4	0	5	23	0	30	7	4
Seda, Israel, Mariners	.266	31	124	21	33	43	5	1	1	19	1	1	2	13	0	13	7	4
Shannon, Samuel, Padres	.244	39	127	23	31	37	2	2	0	9	0	1	2	26	0	30	19	13
Siebert, Steven, Padres	.154	28	91	15	14	18	1	0	1	8	0	1	5	14	0	28	6	3
Sierra, Domingo, Angels	.268	23	71	8	19	22	1	1	0	7	0	1	1	4	0	15	2	0
Sigloch, Steven, Angels	.235	27	68	16	16	27	2	3	1	12	1	2	1	11	1	12	3	0
Simmons, Mark, Angels	.194	29	103	14	20	21	1	0	0	11	0	0	0	15	0	27	3	3
Singleton, Duane, Brewers*	.238	45	126	30	30	41	6	1	1	12	1	1	1	43	0	37	7	9
Spears, Brian, Brewers	.300	52	210	33	63	91	9	2	5	45	1	6	5	11	1	21	2	3
Stela, Jose, Angels	.331	48	169	25	56	73	9	4	0	23	2	4	4	16	1	17	2	3
Stephens, Reginald, Padres†	.231	35	117	20	27	32	1	2	0	12	2	0	2	23	0	26	10	5
Stowell, James, Angels	.225	19	71	11	16	24	3	1	1	12	0	3	1	12	0	17	1	0
Tallent, Ronald, Angels	.161	33	112	12	18	21	3	0	0	7	0	2	1	10	1	47	0	1
Tatum, John, Brewers	.280	21	75	10	21	23	0	1	0	10	0	0	7	1	0	16	0	1
Thurston, Jerry, Padres	.228	43	149	23	34	42	6	1	0	16	2	0	0	16	0	38	6	1
Tomso, Matthew, Cardinals	.000	29	3	0	0	0	0	0	0	0	0	0	0	0	0	2	0	0
Ugueto, Jesus, Cardinals	.179	34	112	13	20	25	1	2	0	14	1	4	0	11	0	31	2	2
Valentin, Jose, Mariners	.288	28	104	25	30	34	4	0	0	8	1	1	0	12	0	11	4	4
Valverde, Osvaldo, Mariners	.262	21	65	6	17	21	4	0	0	6	0	1	3	2	0	10	1	0
Vargas, Trinidad, Brewers	.339	36	127	30	43	53	4	3	0	20	0	1	0	15	1	13	5	3
Vargas, Victor, Cardinals	.269	18	67	10	18	23	1	2	0	5	0	0	1	13	0	10	2	0
Vasquez, Pedro, Padres	.242	49	178	28	43	61	13	1	1	27	4	0	2	18	0	47	16	1
Velez, Jose, Cardinals*	.317	46	183	26	58	77	7	6	0	29	1	2	2	8	0	12	5	2
Walker, James, Brewers	.375	9	40	5	15	18	1	1	0	3	0	0	0	0	0	5	3	0
Walles, Todd, Mariners	.306	19	49	7	15	18	1	1	0	1	0	0	0	11	1	7	0	0
Watson, Ronald, Angels*	.000	21	3	0	0	0	0	0	0	0	0	0	0	1	0	1	0	0

The following pitchers, listed alphabetically by club, with games in parentheses, had no plate appearances, primarily through use of designated hitters:

ANGELS—Heredia, Julian (5); Heusman, Theron (10); Kelso, Jeffrey (17); Lachemann, Bret (14); Lyke, Jim (13); Martinez, Eric (14); Martinez, Francisco (17); Montoya, Norman (10); Musset, Jose (13); Refnes, Todd (3); Rice, David (12); Rojas, Victor (23); Severino, Blas (7); Silverio, Victor (13).

ATHLETICS—Floyd, Tony (13); Fults, Anthony (4); Gechter, Anthony (10); Hill, Fredrick (9); Hokuf, Kenneth (20); Johns, Douglas (8); Lara, Nelson (15); Lynch, Jeffrey (5); McCarty, Scott (10); Miller, Richard (7); Morillo, Santiago (13); Newson, Michael (3); Orr, Daniel (2); Phoenix, Steven (6); Rose, Scott (9); Scharff, Anthony (14); Sturtze, Tanyon (14).

BREWERS—Angelos, Phillip (9); Blair, Donald (6); Boze, Marshall (15); Bumgarner, Wesley (11); Coffey, Michael (13); Gamez, Francisco (11); Griego, Orlando (20); Kiefer, Mark (1); Lynch, Michael (13); McCreadie, Brant (7); McCutchen, James (13); Nichols, Douglas (7); Stone, Bradley (8); White, David (2).

CARDINALS—Anderson, Paul (5); Avram, Brian (19); Davis, Jeffery (6); Eaton, Dann (8); Glover, Gregory (7); Jolley, Michael (28); Kinney, Thomas (25); Marchesi, James (17); Nielsen, Kevin (7); Petersen, Andy (15); Spiller, Derron (9).

MARINERS—Gargagliano, Dion (1); Hampton, Michael (14); Hartman, Kelly (7); Kostich, William (23); Neugent, Jimmy (14); Pena, Antonio (5); Perkins, Paul (13); Polanco, Giovanni (8); Roberts, Timothy (13); Russell, Richard (19); Urso, Salvatore (20); Wallace, Stafford (12); Whitney, Michael (16); Wiley, Charles (15).

PADRES—Beckett, Robert (10); Brown, Jeffrey (17); Davila, Jose (16); Devore, Paul (7); Ellis, Timothy (8); Eubanks, Craig (19); Huber, Jeffrey (9); Ivie, Thomas (13); Martin, Paul (19); Narcisse, Tyrone (7); O'Neill, Kevin (15); Ploeger, Timothy (16).

GRAND SLAM HOME RUNS—Duncan, Landinez, 1 each.

AWARDED FIRST BASE ON CATCHER'S INTERFERENCE—Prybylinski 2 (Joyce, Lozano); P. Rodriguez (F. Rodriguez).

CLUB FIELDING

Club	Pct.	G.	PO.	A.	E.	DP.	PB.	Club	Pct.	G.	PO.	A.	E.	DP.	PB.
Brewers	.961	53	1412	569	81	47	9	Padres	.938	54	1398	584	132	27	16
Cardinals	.960	53	1404	581	83	50	9	Angels	.935	55	1428	621	142	51	11
Mariners	.956	54	1471	584	95	43	24	Athletics	.935	53	1421	607	141	46	25

Triple Play—Padres.

INDIVIDUAL FIELDING

*Throws lefthanded.

FIRST BASEMEN

Player and Club	Pct.	G.	PO.	A.	E.	DP.	Player and Club	Pct.	G.	PO.	A.	E.	DP.
Abercrombie, Padres	.923	1	12	0	1	0	Lydy, Athletics	1.000	4	6	1	0	0
Alcaraz, Angels	1.000	5	43	1	0	3	Mercado, Athletics	1.000	5	50	5	0	4
Bailey, Athletics	.948	18	139	6	8	8	Molina, Athletics	1.000	1	1	0	0	0
Benjamin, Brewers	1.000	1	3	0	0	0	Moriso, Athletics	1.000	1	2	0	0	0
Bobo, Angels	.989	10	84	7	1	11	Mowry, Padres*	.980	50	461	23	10	26
Boudreau, Mariners	1.000	2	7	0	0	0	Newfield, Mariners	.986	42	348	13	5	35
Brannon, Mariners	.917	2	11	0	1	0	Rodriguez, Brewers	1.000	1	4	0	0	0
Dudek, Cardinals*	1.000	1	7	0	0	0	Sierra, Angels	1.000	1	3	0	0	0
Hamlin, Cardinals	.990	53	493	19	5	45	Sigloch, Brewers	1.000	1	1	0	0	0
House, Angels	.955	16	117	11	6	15	SPEARS, Brewers	.998	52	508	22	1	44
Joyce, Padres	1.000	2	4	0	0	0	Tallent, Angels	.978	28	259	14	6	15
Keathley, Athletics	.982	39	312	17	6	32	Thurston, Padres	.966	3	26	2	1	0
Lozano, Mariners	1.000	3	4	0	0	0	Valverde, Mariners	.962	6	48	3	2	2
							Walles, Mariners	.961	10	72	1	3	4

Triple Play—Mowry.

SECOND BASEMEN

Player and Club	Pct.	G.	PO.	A.	E.	DP.	Player and Club	Pct.	G.	PO.	A.	E.	DP.
Brito, Angels	.947	4	8	10	1	3	Moncion, Mariners	.909	2	4	6	1	2
Cabrera, Athletics	.900	7	9	18	3	2	Polanco, Mariners	.936	35	61	100	11	22
Carion, Padres	.853	12	13	16	5	3	Pritchett, Athletics	.890	26	48	57	13	11
Carlsen, Athletics	.953	25	56	67	6	16	Rodriguez, Brewers	1.000	1	1	0	0	0
Colon, Cardinals	.941	14	24	24	3	4	SALAZAR, Brewers	.987	44	96	139	3	35
Davenport, Cardinals	1.000	1	3	1	0	0	Shannon, Padres	.955	28	50	77	6	10
Fermaint, Mariners	.941	31	65	78	9	13	Siebert, Padres	.891	13	24	33	7	1
Francisco, Athletics	1.000	1	1	1	0	0	Sierra, Angels	.935	11	19	24	3	5
Gale, Cardinals	1.000	1	6	2	0	1	Sigloch, Brewers	.938	8	13	17	2	1
Halland, Mariners	1.000	2	4	5	0	0	Stephens, Padres	.860	9	13	24	6	4
Hood, Brewers	.500	1	0	1	1	0	Tatum, Brewers	1.000	1	1	0	0	0
Keating, Cardinals	1.000	3	6	10	0	2	Valentin, Mariners	.950	23	51	63	6	12
Landinez, Cardinals	.964	24	55	53	4	15	T. Vargas, Brewers	.895	4	8	9	2	1
Minnis, Angels	1.000	16	31	44	0	9	V. Vargas, Cardinals	.967	14	42	45	3	14

THIRD BASEMEN

Player and Club	Pct.	G.	PO.	A.	E.	DP.	Player and Club	Pct.	G.	PO.	A.	E.	DP.
Abercrombie, Padres	1.000	1	0	3	0	0	Keathley, Athletics	.800	1	0	4	1	0
Alcaraz, Angels	.600	2	1	2	2	0	Keating, Cardinals	.933	7	6	8	1	2
Aversa, Cardinals	.800	2	0	4	1	0	Meza, Cardinals	.907	50	38	108	15	11
Bertucci, Angels	.853	24	14	50	11	2	Perez, Padres	1.000	1	1	0	0	0
Bullock, Padres	.905	46	31	93	13	2	Peterson, Angels	.909	6	4	16	2	2
JUAN A. CABRERA, Brewers	.910	42	35	97	13	11	Shannon, Padres	.926	9	9	16	2	0
Juan C. Cabrera, Athletics	1.000	3	2	11	0	0	Siebert, Padres	.714	3	2	3	2	0
Carlsen, Athletics	.750	8	4	14	6	1	Sierra, Angels	.900	4	3	6	1	2
Dionicio, Athletics	.818	4	2	7	2	0	Simmons, Angels	.906	25	6	42	5	2
Duncan, Athletics	.856	42	25	88	19	5	Tatum, Brewers	.750	11	4	26	10	3
Halland, Mariners	.913	32	16	78	9	6	Valverde, Mariners	.765	13	11	15	8	2
Hood, Brewers	1.000	1	0	2	0	0	Vargas, Cardinals	1.000	1	1	1	0	0
Johnson, Mariners	.917	13	10	23	3	3							

SHORTSTOPS

Player and Club	Pct.	G.	PO.	A.	E.	DP.	Player and Club	Pct.	G.	PO.	A.	E.	DP.
Acosta, Athletics	.941	3	7	9	1	0	Markiewicz, Angels	.806	29	32	76	26	20
Aversa, Cardinals	1.000	7	7	19	0	3	Mateo, Padres	.000	1	0	0	1	0
Cabrera, Athletics	.935	8	7	22	2	4	Meza, Cardinals	1.000	1	2	3	0	1
Carlsen, Athletics	.833	2	1	4	1	1	Moncion, Mariners	.919	28	32	93	11	10
Flores, Brewers	.855	20	16	43	10	9	Salazar, Mariners	.929	3	4	9	1	2
FRANCISCO, Athletics	.887	42	56	148	26	23	Seda, Mariners	.902	27	39	80	13	18
Guzik, Angels	.827	13	19	24	9	4	Siebert, Padres	.806	9	20	7	2	2
Hood, Brewers	.917	2	4	7	1	2	Ugueto, Cardinals	.930	32	38	94	10	16
Johnson, Angels	.883	20	34	57	12	14	Vargas, Brewers	.920	31	25	79	9	16
Keating, Cardinals	.895	18	14	37	6	10	Vasquez, Padres	.849	48	66	153	39	19
							Watson, Angels	.750	1	1	2	1	0

Triple Play—Vasquez.

OUTFIELDERS

Player and Club	Pct.	G.	PO.	A.	E.	DP.	Player and Club	Pct.	G.	PO.	A.	E.	DP.
Abercrombie, Padres	.962	40	69	7	3	0	Lawson, Mariners*	1.000	30	46	1	0	0
Anderson, Angels*	.965	32	53	2	2	1	List, Mariners	.941	14	16	0	1	0
Anthony, Padres	1.000	15	18	2	0	0	Lowman, Cardinals	1.000	2	4	0	0	0
Aracena, Athletics	.957	46	63	3	3	0	Mateo, Padres	1.000	1	1	0	0	0
Baber, Brewers	.953	30	60	1	3	0	Matos, Padres	1.000	29	41	4	0	0
Baez, Angels	.667	2	1	1	1	0	McDavid, Padres	.970	13	30	2	1	0
Bailey, Athletics	.885	15	23	0	3	0	Meek, Cardinals	.875	30	29	6	5	1
Barlow, Mariners	.983	35	54	4	1	0	Minnis, Angels	.714	4	5	0	2	0
Barrios, Brewers	.895	22	34	0	4	0	Newfield, Mariners	1.000	6	10	0	0	0
Benjamin, Brewers	1.000	22	24	1	0	0	Oliver, Angels	.750	3	3	0	1	0
Bertucci, Angels	1.000	4	5	0	0	0	Olofson, Athletics	1.000	13	14	0	0	0
Bobo, Angels	.952	17	19	1	1	0	Pineiro, Angels	.667	6	2	0	1	0
Boudreau, Brewers	.974	22	35	3	1	0	Polanco, Angels	.875	4	6	1	1	0
Carpenter, Cardinals	.857	7	6	0	1	0	Powell, Mariners	.500	1	1	0	1	0
Colon, Cardinals	1.000	1	1	0	0	0	Pritchett, Athletics	.875	26	41	1	6	0
Cruz, Padres	.947	45	104	4	6	0	Prybylinski, Cardinals	1.000	1	0	1	0	0
Davenport, Cardinals	.909	24	37	3	4	1	Ramos, Mariners	1.000	21	28	0	0	0
DeCareau, Padres	.976	25	37	3	1	1	Reid, Athletics	.889	5	7	1	1	1
Dionicio, Athletics	.930	29	52	1	4	0	Rios, Angels	.941	13	16	0	1	0
Dudek, Cardinals*	.923	20	32	4	3	1	Robertson, Mariners	.929	26	25	1	2	0
ENRIQUEZ, Brewers	.979	43	87	7	2	0	Sierra, Angels	.750	5	3	0	1	0
Fernandez, Mariners*	.905	33	55	2	6	0	Sigloch, Brewers	1.000	12	14	0	0	0
Gale, Cardinals	.942	37	64	1	4	0	Simmons, Angels	.667	4	2	0	1	0
Gonzalez, Cardinals	.938	8	14	1	1	0	Singleton, Brewers	.961	41	67	6	3	2
Guzik, Angels	.800	1	2	2	1	0	Stela, Angels	.889	13	16	0	2	0
House, Angels	1.000	19	27	1	0	1	Stephens, Padres	.900	5	9	0	1	0
Hust, Athletics	.945	42	50	2	3	0	Stowell, Athletics*	1.000	19	37	2	0	0
Johnson, Angels	.952	19	39	1	2	0	Sturtze, Athletics	1.000	2	1	0	0	0
Jorge, Angels*	.909	18	30	0	3	0	Velez, Cardinals*	.944	45	83	1	5	0
Keating, Cardinals	1.000	2	2	0	0	0	Walker, Brewers	1.000	8	10	0	0	0

CATCHERS

Player and Club	Pct.	G.	PO.	A.	E.	DP.	PB.	Player and Club	Pct.	G.	PO.	A.	E.	DP.	PB.
Bertucci, Angels	1.000	2	7	0	0	0	0	Klavitter, Mariners	.989	11	82	6	1	0	6
Bobo, Angels	.959	13	81	12	4	2	3	Lowman, Cardinals	.984	11	52	9	1	1	2
Brannon, Mariners	1.000	15	111	4	0	1	6	Lozano, Mariners	.993	20	129	10	1	1	5
Buldier, Angels	1.000	1	3	2	0	0	0	Molina, Athletics	.979	37	260	17	6	1	10
Candelario, Mariners	.993	24	134	6	1	0	6	Osuna, Angels	.942	15	89	9	6	1	3
Carpenter, Cardinals	1.000	3	13	2	0	0	1	Pineiro, Angels	1.000	16	49	8	0	1	2
Diaz, Brewers	.990	25	185	23	2	1	4	PRYBYLINSKI, Cardinals	.984	45	311	59	6	1	6
Fuentes, Athletics	.969	13	83	10	3	1	11	Rodriguez, Brewers	.951	14	56	2	3	0	3
Irwin, Brewers	.993	22	127	14	1	0	2	Stela, Angels	.988	26	136	25	2	0	2
Joyce, Padres	.960	20	109	10	5	0	2	Tallent, Angels	1.000	3	23	4	0	1	1
Keathley, Athletics	.889	4	7	1	1	0	2	Thurston, Padres	.981	35	239	25	5	0	14
Kennedy, Athletics	1.000	10	66	12	0	0	2	Valverde, Mariners	1.000	1	2	0	0	0	0

Triple Play—Joyce.

PITCHERS

Player and Club	Pct.	G.	PO.	A.	E.	DP.	Player and Club	Pct.	G.	PO.	A.	E.	DP.
Acosta, Athletics	.813	12	7	19	6	2	Martin, Padres	.900	19	2	7	1	0
Anderson, Cardinals	1.000	5	2	5	0	0	E. Martinez, Angels	1.000	14	2	0	0	0
Angelos, Brewers	.909	9	2	8	1	0	F. Martinez, Angels	1.000	17	6	6	0	0
Avram, Cardinals	1.000	19	0	7	0	0	McCarty, Athletics*	.929	10	1	12	1	0
Beckett, Padres*	.875	10	1	6	1	1	McCreadie, Brewers	1.000	7	1	0	0	0
Blair, Brewers	.750	6	2	1	1	0	McCutchen, Brewers	.571	13	1	3	3	0
Boze, Brewers	1.000	15	1	1	0	0	Miller, Athletics*	1.000	7	2	2	0	1
Brown, Padres*	.900	17	5	4	1	0	Montoya, Angels*	1.000	10	4	6	0	0
BUMGARNER, Brewers	1.000	11	3	12	0	0	Morillo, Athletics*	.875	13	0	7	1	1
Coffey, Brewers	1.000	13	3	3	0	0	Musset, Angels	1.000	13	5	7	0	0
Davila, Padres	1.000	16	1	6	0	0	Narcisse, Padres	1.000	7	0	1	0	0
Davis, Cardinals*	1.000	6	0	1	0	0	Nichols, Brewers	.833	7	0	5	1	0
Devore, Padres	.833	7	3	2	1	0	Nielsen, Cardinals*	.923	7	1	11	1	0
Eaton, Cardinals	1.000	8	0	1	0	0	Neugent, Mariners*	.800	14	0	4	1	1
Ellis, Padres*	1.000	8	0	1	0	0	O'Neill, Padres*	1.000	15	1	9	0	0
Eubanks, Padres	.857	19	1	5	1	1	Pena, Mariners	1.000	5	1	1	0	0
Floyd, Athletics	.750	13	0	3	1	0	Perez, Padres	1.000	16	1	5	0	0
Fults, Athletics*	1.000	4	0	1	0	0	Perkins, Mariners	.958	13	3	20	1	0
Gamez, Brewers	1.000	11	3	7	0	1	Petersen, Cardinals	.857	15	4	8	2	0
Gechter, Athletics	1.000	10	0	3	0	0	Phoenix, Athletics	.833	6	1	4	1	0
Glover, Cardinals	1.000	7	0	3	0	0	Ploeger, Padres	.667	16	1	5	3	0
Griego, Brewers	1.000	20	0	5	0	0	Refnes, Angels	1.000	3	1	1	0	0
Hampton, Mariners*	.964	14	7	20	1	3	Rice, Angels	.750	12	0	3	1	0
Hartman, Mariners*	1.000	7	0	1	0	0	Roberts, Mariners*	1.000	13	2	1	0	0
Heredia, Angels	.700	5	1	6	3	0	Rojas, Angels	.667	23	0	2	1	1
Heusman, Angels*	1.000	10	1	6	0	0	Rolfes, Brewers*	1.000	16	3	3	0	0
Hill, Athletics	.333	9	0	1	2	0	Rose, Athletics	1.000	9	2	3	0	2
Hokuf, Athletics	.800	20	1	3	1	1	Russell, Mariners	.800	19	3	9	3	1
Huber, Padres*	.857	9	3	9	2	0	Scharff, Athletics	1.000	14	4	3	0	0
Ivie, Padres*	1.000	13	1	4	0	0	Severino, Angels	.667	7	0	2	1	0
Johns, Athletics*	.789	8	2	13	4	1	Silverio, Angels	.714	13	3	7	4	0
Jolley, Cardinals	.909	28	1	9	1	0	Spiller, Cardinals*	1.000	9	1	8	0	1
Kelso, Angels	.900	16	2	7	1	0	Stone, Brewers	1.000	8	1	4	0	0
Kinney, Cardinals*	1.000	25	2	6	0	0	Sturtze, Athletics	1.000	12	4	3	0	0
Kostich, Mariners*	.875	23	0	7	1	0	Tomso, Cardinals	1.000	29	0	3	0	0
Lachemann, Angels	.800	14	4	4	2	0	Urso, Mariners*	.917	20	0	11	1	0
Lara, Cardinals*	1.000	15	1	3	0	1	Wallace, Mariners	1.000	12	0	2	0	0
Lyke, Angels*	1.000	13	1	4	0	0	Watson, Angels	1.000	20	5	3	0	0
J. Lynch, Padres	1.000	5	1	0	0	0	White, Mariners	.000	2	0	0	1	0
M. Lynch, Brewers	.850	13	5	12	3	1	Whitney, Mariners	.857	16	3	3	1	0
Marchesi, Cardinals	.875	17	3	4	1	0	Wiley, Mariners	1.000	15	2	10	0	0

Triple Play—Ploeger.

The following players did not have any fielding statistics at the positions indicated or appeared only as a designated hitter, pinch-hitter or pinch-runner: Abercrombie, c; Bullock, p; Juan A. Cabrera, ss; Colon, ss; Flores, 3b; Gargagliano, p; Joyce, 3b; Kiefer, p; Landinez, 1b, 3b; Markiewicz, 3b; Moncion, 3b; Mowry, p; Newson, p; Olofson, 1b; Orr, p; C. Polanco, 3b; G. Polanco, p; Powell, 1b; P. Rodriguez, of.

CLUB PITCHING

Club	ERA.	G.	CG.	ShO.	Sv.	IP.	H.	R.	ER.	HR.	HB.	BB.	Int. BB.	SO.	WP.	Bk.
Brewers	3.44	53	7	3	14	470.2	434	238	180	15	26	184	1	369	29	22
Mariners	3.73	54	0	2	10	490.1	442	280	203	8	38	261	5	459	26	26
Athletics	3.93	53	1	3	6	473.2	472	309	207	14	21	232	3	415	36	18
Cardinals	4.17	53	3	3	8	468.0	501	277	217	17	16	200	9	371	16	21
Angels	4.61	55	1	1	6	476.0	472	351	244	6	37	281	3	382	53	21
Padres	5.33	54	0	1	5	466.0	540	379	276	24	30	239	10	343	34	36

PITCHERS' RECORDS

(Leading Qualifiers for Earned-Run Average Leadership—45 or More Innings)

*Throws lefthanded.

Pitcher—Club	W.	L.	Pct.	ERA.	G.	GS.	CG.	GF.	ShO.	Sv.	IP.	H.	R.	ER.	HR.	HB.	BB.	Int. BB.	SO.	WP.
Kostich, Mariners*	3	1	.750	0.40	23	0	0	18	0	6	45.1	28	7	2	1	1	6	1	39	0
Montoya, Angels*	3	3	.500	2.11	10	6	1	2	0	1	47.0	49	20	11	1	1	7	0	28	0
Spiller, Cardinals*	4	2	.667	2.34	9	9	1	0	0	0	57.2	46	18	15	1	0	15	0	46	0
Angelos, Brewers	7	1	.875	2.49	9	7	4	1	1	0	65.0	51	26	18	1	1	9	0	45	3
Hampton, Mariners*	7	2	.778	2.66	14	13	0	0	0	0	64.1	52	32	19	0	4	40	0	59	10
Gamez, Brewers	2	3	.400	2.66	11	7	1	1	0	0	50.2	42	21	15	5	3	20	0	31	0
M. Lynch, Brewers	4	2	.667	2.85	13	13	1	0	1	0	75.2	66	31	24	2	7	31	0	69	9
Urso, Mariners*	3	2	.600	3.02	20	0	0	6	0	1	50.2	36	25	17	3	6	23	1	63	5
Russell, Mariners	5	1	.833	3.60	19	5	0	3	0	0	55.0	51	33	22	1	6	26	1	51	1
Jolley, Cardinals	1	0	1.000	3.70	28	0	0	4	0	0	48.2	55	24	20	0	3	22	1	37	0

Departmental Leaders: G—Tomso, 29; W—Angelos, Hampton, 7; L—Brown, Musset, 7; Pct.—Angelos, .875; GS—Hampton, M. Lynch, Musset, Perkins, 13; CG—Angelos, 4; GF—Rojas, 21; ShO—Angelos, Blair, M. Lynch, 1; Sv.—Kinney, 7; IP—M. Lynch, 75.2; H—Petersen, 83; R—Kelso, Musset, Perkins, 54; ER—Musset, 42; HR—Gamez, Ivie, Marchesi, 5; HB—Davila, M. Lynch, 7; BB—Beckett, 45; IBB—Kinney, 4; SO—M. Lynch, 69; WP—Hampton, 10.

(All Pitchers—Listed Alphabetically)

Pitcher—Club	W.	L.	Pct.	ERA.	G.	GS.	CG.	GF.	ShO.	Sv.	IP.	H.	R.	ER.	HR.	HB.	BB.	Int. BB.	SO.	WP.
Acosta, Athletics	5	5	.500	3.92	12	12	0	0	0	0	62.0	71	45	27	3	2	20	0	27	4
Anderson, Cardinals	0	0	.000	1.29	5	1	0	1	0	0	14.0	10	2	2	1	1	3	0	15	0
Angelos, Brewers	7	1	.875	2.49	9	7	4	1	1	0	65.0	51	26	18	1	1	9	0	45	3
Avram, Cardinals	2	0	1.000	5.10	19	3	0	1	0	0	42.1	57	34	24	2	2	26	0	24	1
Beckett, Padres*	2	5	.286	4.38	10	10	0	0	0	0	49.1	40	28	24	1	2	45	0	54	8
Blair, Brewers	4	1	.800	0.91	6	6	1	0	1	0	39.2	24	5	4	0	0	6	0	46	0
Boze, Brewers	1	0	1.000	7.84	15	0	0	5	0	3	20.2	27	22	18	0	3	13	1	17	3
Brown, Padres*	1	7	.125	5.40	17	7	0	6	0	1	65.0	76	53	39	4	2	15	3	66	0
Bullock, Padres	0	0	.000	0.00	2	0	0	2	0	0	2.0	2	0	0	0	0	0	0	1	0
Bumgarner, Brewers	6	3	.667	4.89	11	11	0	0	0	0	57.0	54	38	31	2	2	24	0	27	4
Coffey, Brewers	0	1	.000	4.71	13	0	0	4	0	1	21.0	25	16	11	0	0	13	0	17	0
Davila, Padres	2	3	.400	6.14	16	5	0	4	0	0	44.0	55	46	30	2	7	21	0	24	3
Davis, Cardinals*	1	0	1.000	10.97	6	1	0	2	0	0	10.2	11	14	13	2	1	15	1	4	1
Devore, Padres	3	2	.600	6.84	7	2	0	4	0	1	25.0	37	24	19	0	2	10	0	22	1
Eaton, Cardinals	5	2	.714	5.45	8	7	0	0	0	0	36.1	39	24	22	1	0	15	0	42	1
Ellis, Padres*	0	0	.000	6.43	8	0	0	2	0	0	14.0	18	14	10	0	0	8	0	7	0
Eubanks, Padres	5	4	.556	4.13	19	9	0	9	0	1	52.1	49	34	24	2	3	32	2	37	5
Floyd, Athletics	2	0	1.000	2.25	13	0	0	0	0	0	32.0	28	10	8	1	0	8	0	35	2
Fults, Athletics*	1	1	.500	6.35	4	1	0	0	0	0	5.2	5	5	4	0	1	10	0	6	0
Gamez, Brewers	2	3	.400	2.66	11	7	1	1	0	0	50.2	42	21	15	5	3	20	0	31	0
Gargagliano, Mariners*	0	0	.000	0.00	1	0	0	0	0	0	1.0	0	1	0	0	2	0	1	0	0
Gechter, Athletics	0	0	.000	1.42	10	0	0	1	0	0	19.0	13	8	3	0	3	9	0	14	1
Glover, Cardinals	3	2	.600	5.67	7	7	0	0	0	0	27.0	27	24	17	1	3	17	0	31	3
Griego, Brewers	2	2	.500	3.00	20	0	0	14	0	3	27.0	30	13	9	0	2	8	0	14	2
Hampton, Mariners*	7	2	.778	2.66	14	13	0	0	0	0	64.1	52	32	19	0	4	40	0	59	10
Hartman, Mariners*	0	2	.000	7.90	7	2	0	2	0	0	13.2	22	14	12	1	1	12	0	15	1
Heredia, Angels	2	2	.500	3.81	5	5	0	0	0	0	26.0	25	14	11	1	0	10	0	18	0
Heusman, Angels*	1	2	.333	1.06	10	1	0	7	0	0	17.0	8	6	2	0	1	16	0	18	7
Hill, Athletics	1	1	.500	2.70	9	0	0	7	0	2	13.1	15	7	4	0	0	7	0	14	0
Hokuf, Athletics	3	4	.429	5.40	20	0	0	14	0	0	36.2	43	33	22	0	1	26	2	36	1
Huber, Padres*	1	4	.200	3.53	9	7	0	1	0	1	35.2	32	19	14	0	1	15	0	21	2
Ivie, Padres*	3	0	1.000	3.38	13	4	0	4	0	0	34.2	39	17	13	5	2	11	1	24	1
Johns, Athletics*	3	1	.750	1.84	8	7	1	1	0	0	44.0	36	17	9	1	0	9	0	38	2
Jolley, Cardinals	1	0	1.000	3.70	28	0	0	4	0	0	48.2	55	24	20	0	3	22	1	37	0
Kelso, Angels	2	4	.333	8.93	16	8	0	0	0	0	41.1	51	54	41	1	4	42	1	42	4
Kiefer, Brewers	0	0	.000	3.38	1	1	0	0	0	0	2.2	3	1	1	0	1	1	0	2	0
Kinney, Cardinals*	4	1	.800	3.26	25	1	0	19	0	7	38.2	42	14	14	1	0	14	4	19	1
Kostich, Mariners*	3	1	.750	0.40	23	0	0	18	0	6	45.1	28	7	2	1	1	6	1	39	0
Lachemann, Angels	2	1	.667	4.40	14	2	0	2	0	0	28.2	32	22	14	0	2	13	0	36	3
Lara, Athletics*	0	1	.000	5.09	15	0	0	8	0	0	17.2	24	17	10	0	1	10	0	12	2
Lyke, Angels*	1	0	1.000	7.33	13	0	0	6	0	0	23.1	38	32	19	1	3	16	0	9	2
J. Lynch, Athletics	0	1	.000	11.05	5	2	0	1	0	0	7.1	5	10	9	0	1	15	0	6	1
M. Lynch, Brewers	4	2	.667	2.85	13	13	1	0	1	0	75.2	66	31	24	2	7	31	0	69	9
Marchesi, Cardinals	3	5	.375	4.86	17	6	0	2	0	0	46.1	50	33	25	5	3	16	0	23	4
Martin, Padres	1	1	.500	9.10	19	0	0	6	0	0	29.2	41	36	30	2	5	21	1	23	3
E. Martinez, Angels	0	3	.000	4.56	14	1	0	4	0	0	23.2	29	19	12	0	1	10	0	22	6
F. Martinez, Angels	3	2	.600	6.27	17	3	0	0	0	0	33.0	31	40	23	0	3	32	0	29	8
McCarty, Athletics*	0	5	.000	4.24	10	9	0	0	0	0	51.0	52	35	24	1	1	32	0	59	6
McCreadie, Brewers	0	0	.000	6.55	7	0	0	4	0	1	11.0	11	10	8	0	1	11	0	17	0
McCutchen, Brewers	4	3	.571	3.06	13	3	0	5	0	0	35.1	29	13	12	2	2	19	0	28	2
Miller, Angels	4	0	1.000	3.38	7	2	0	2	0	0	29.1	22	11	11	2	1	12	0	28	1
Montoya, Angels*	3	3	.500	2.11	10	6	1	2	0	1	47.0	49	20	11	1	1	7	0	28	0
Morillo, Athletics*	1	1	.500	4.30	13	3	0	6	0	0	29.1	37	20	14	0	1	15	1	27	2
Mowry, Padres*	0	0	.000	0.00	1	0	0	0	0	0	0.2	1	0	0	0	0	0	0	0	0
Musset, Angels	2	7	.222	6.03	18	13	0	0	0	0	62.2	63	54	42	2	4	41	1	49	7
Narcisse, Padres	0	0	.000	5.06	7	1	0	0	0	0	10.2	13	11	6	0	2	6	0	5	0
Newson, Athletics	0	0	.000	5.40	3	0	0	0	0	0	3.1	2	2	2	0	1	3	0	1	0

Pitcher—Club	W.	L.	Pct.	ERA.	G.	GS.	CG.	GF.	ShO.	Sv.	IP.	H.	R.	ER.	HR.	HB.	BB.	Int. BB.	SO.	WP.
Nichols, Brewers	3	0	1.000	3.70	7	3	0	2	0	1	24.1	25	17	10	2	0	12	0	29	1
Nielsen, Cardinals*	2	3	.400	1.91	7	7	2	0	0	0	42.1	43	20	9	0	0	17	0	41	2
Nuegent, Mariners*	1	0	1.000	2.04	14	0	0	5	0	1	17.2	14	8	4	0	2	13	0	23	1
O'Neill, Padres*	1	3	.250	4.82	15	4	0	3	0	0	37.1	37	23	20	3	1	14	0	16	2
Orr, Athletics	0	0	.000	38.57	2	0	0	0	0	0	2.1	1	10	10	1	3	9	0	3	0
Pena, Mariners	2	1	.667	2.88	5	5	0	0	0	0	25.0	17	9	8	0	2	13	0	24	0
Perez, Padres	0	3	.000	5.81	16	1	0	7	0	0	31.0	44	29	20	4	2	16	2	18	1
Perkins, Mariners	5	4	.556	5.20	13	13	0	0	0	0	71.0	74	54	41	0	3	31	0	62	2
Petersen, Cardinals	3	5	.375	4.83	15	11	0	1	0	0	69.0	83	49	37	1	2	26	1	45	2
Phoenix, Athletics	3	1	.750	1.45	6	6	0	0	0	0	31.0	25	14	5	0	1	4	0	31	0
Ploeger, Padres	0	3	.000	7.01	16	4	0	3	0	0	34.2	56	45	27	1	1	25	1	24	5
Polanco, Mariners	0	3	.000	8.68	8	4	0	0	0	0	18.2	38	25	18	1	1	16	0	17	1
Refnes, Angels	0	1	.000	4.20	3	3	0	0	0	0	15.0	19	7	7	0	2	3	0	15	1
Rice, Angels	0	1	.000	3.00	12	1	0	1	0	0	24.0	26	12	8	0	4	14	1	14	1
Roberts, Mariners*	1	1	.500	8.59	13	1	0	2	0	0	22.0	25	21	21	0	3	18	1	8	1
Rojas, Angels	0	0	.000	3.16	23	0	0	21	0	5	25.2	12	14	9	0	6	20	0	30	4
Rolfes, Brewers*	1	1	.500	5.40	16	0	0	6	0	2	18.1	20	13	11	1	4	12	0	17	2
Rose, Athletics	0	0	.000	2.34	9	1	0	4	0	2	18.1	12	5	3	0	0	3	0	21	1
Russell, Mariners	5	1	.833	3.60	19	5	0	3	0	0	55.0	51	33	22	1	6	26	1	51	1
Scharff, Athletics	1	1	.500	5.01	14	0	0	6	0	2	23.1	26	19	13	2	0	13	0	27	8
Severino, Angels	0	2	.000	2.30	7	5	0	1	0	0	31.1	24	13	8	0	0	14	0	32	0
Silverio, Angels	2	4	.333	5.08	13	7	0	2	0	0	44.1	39	30	25	0	3	29	0	29	3
Spiller, Cardinals*	4	2	.667	2.34	9	9	1	0	0	0	57.2	46	18	15	1	0	15	0	46	0
Stone, Brewers	2	0	1.000	3.50	8	0	0	4	0	1	18.0	25	10	7	0	0	1	0	8	2
Sturtze, Athletics	2	5	.286	5.44	12	10	0	1	0	0	48.0	55	41	29	3	4	27	0	30	5
Tomso, Cardinals	0	4	.000	4.89	29	0	0	20	0	1	35.0	38	21	19	2	1	18	2	44	1
Urso, Mariners*	3	2	.600	3.02	20	0	0	6	0	1	50.2	36	25	17	3	6	23	1	63	5
Wallace, Mariners	0	1	.000	0.86	12	0	0	8	0	1	21.0	9	2	2	0	1	14	1	11	0
Watson, Angels	2	3	.400	3.27	20	0	0	8	0	0	33.0	26	14	12	0	1	14	0	21	2
White, Brewers	0	0	.000	2.08	2	0	0	0	0	0	4.1	2	2	1	0	0	4	0	2	1
Whitney, Mariners	0	1	.000	3.05	16	0	0	7	0	1	20.2	18	12	7	0	5	13	0	18	2
Wiley, Mariners	5	2	.714	4.20	15	11	0	3	0	0	64.1	58	37	30	1	3	34	0	68	2

BALKS—Davila, 9; Gamez, Petersen, 7 each; Brown, Hampton, Pena, 6 each; Devore, Nichols, Rojas, 5 each; Eubanks, Kinney, Lyke, Roberts, Scharff, 4 each; Beckett, Coffey, Eaton, Morillo, O'Neill, Silverio, Whitney, Wiley, 3 each; Huber, Kostich, Lachemann, Miller, Narcisse, Newson, Nielsen, Phoenix, Ploeger, Sturtze, Watson, White, 2 each; Angelos, Avram, Gechter, Glover, Griego, Heredia, Hokuf, Kelso, J. Lynch, M. Lynch, Marchesi, McCreadie, Musset, Polanco, Refnes, Russell, Severino, Spiller, Stone, Tomso, 1 each.

COMBINATION SHUTOUTS—Lachemann-Watson, Angels; Acosta-Rose, Morillo-Floyd-Fults-Lynch, Sturtze-Gechter-Scharff, Athletics; Avram-Jolley-Tomso, Eaton-Jolley-Avram, Spiller-Marchesi-Tomso, Cardinals; Hampton-Wallace-Hartman, Hampton-Whitney-Kostich, Mariners; Eubanks-Ellis-Brown, Padres.

NO-HIT GAMES—None.

Gulf Coast League

SUMMER CLASS A CLASSIFICATION

CHAMPIONSHIP WINNERS IN PREVIOUS YEARS

1964—Sarasota Braves .610	1975—Texas .774	1985—Yankees d .705
1965—Bradenton Astros .632	1976—Texas .704	Rangers .532
1966—New York A.L. .667	1977—Chicago-A.L. .731	1986—Reds .548
1967—Kansas City .614	1978—Texas .600	Dodgers b .541
1968—Oakland .650	1979—Houston .635	1987—Dodgers b .683
1969—Montreal .585	1980—Kansas City-Blue .635	Royals .635
1970—Chicago A.L. .600	1981—Kansas City-Gold .688	1988—Yankees b .714
1971—Kansas City .755	1982—New York-A.L. .667	Royals .619
1972—Chicago N.L. a .651	1983—Texas .645	1989—Yankees c .651
Kansas City a .651	Los Angeles b .617	Dodgers .635
1973—Texas .732	1984—White Sox .651	
1974—Chicago N.L. .702	Rangers b .571	

(Note—Known as Sarasota Rookie League in 1964 and Florida Rookie League in 1965.) aDeclared co-champions; no playoff. bLeague divided into Northern and Southern divisions; won one-game playoff for league championship. cLeague divided into Northern and Southern divisions; won best-of-three playoff for league championship. dYankees declared champion based on winning percentage when one-game playoff against Rangers was rained out.

STANDING OF CLUBS AT CLOSE OF SEASON, AUGUST 31

NORTHERN DIVISION

Club	W.	L.	T.	Pct.	G.B.
Dodgers	38	25	1	.603	......
Reds	36	27	1	.571	2
Red Sox	34	29	0	.540	4
Astros	33	30	1	.524	5
Royals	25	38	1	.397	13
Indians	23	40	0	.365	15

SOUTHERN DIVISION

Club	W.	L.	T.	Pct.	G.B.
Expos	40	23	0	.635	......
Rangers	36	27	1	.571	4
Braves	33	29	0	.532	6½
Yankees	32	30	0	.516	7½
Twins	32	30	1	.516	7½
Mets	29	30	1	.492	9
Pirates	25	37	1	.403	14½
White Sox	21	42	0	.333	19

COMPOSITE STANDING OF CLUBS AT CLOSE OF SEASON, AUGUST 31

Club	Exp.	Dod.	Rds.	Rng.	RS	Brv.	Ast.	Yan.	Twi.	Met.	Pir.	Roy.	Ind.	WS	W.	L.	T.	Pct.	G.B.
Expos	...	0	0	5	0	6	0	4	4	9	5	0	0	7	40	23	0	.635	......
Dodgers	0	...	0	7	0	6	0	6	0	0	0	11	8	0	38	25	1	.603	2
Reds	0	5	...	0	6	0	7	0	0	0	0	9	9	0	36	27	1	.571	4
Rangers	4	0	0	...	0	6	0	5	4	4	5	0	0	8	36	27	1	.571	4
Red Sox	0	6	7	0	...	0	7	0	0	0	0	6	8	0	34	29	0	.540	6
Braves	3	0	0	3	0	...	0	6	5	4	5	0	0	7	33	29	0	.532	6½
Astros	0	7	6	0	6	0	...	0	0	0	0	7	7	0	33	30	1	.524	7
Yankees	5	0	0	4	0	3	0	...	7	3	5	0	0	5	32	30	0	.516	7½
Twins	5	0	0	5	0	4	0	2	...	3	7	0	0	6	32	30	1	.516	7½
Mets	0	0	0	5	0	4	0	5	5	...	5	0	0	5	29	30	1	.492	9
Pirates	4	0	0	4	0	4	0	4	2	3	...	0	0	4	25	37	1	.403	14½
Royals	0	2	4	0	6	0	5	0	0	0	0	...	8	0	25	38	1	.397	15
Indians	0	5	3	0	5	0	5	0	0	0	0	5	...	0	23	40	0	.365	17
White Sox	2	0	0	1	0	2	0	4	3	4	5	0	0	...	21	42	0	.333	19

Games played in Bradenton and Sarasota, Fla.

Club names are major league affiliations.

Playoffs—Dodgers defeated Expos, two games to none, to win league championship.

Regular-Season Attendance—No official attendance figures reported.

Managers—Astros, Julio Linares; Braves, Jim Procopio; Dodgers, Ivan DeJesus; Expos, Gomer Hodge; Indians, Dean Treanor; Mets, John Tamargo; Pirates, Julio Garcia; Rangers, Chino Cadahia; Reds, Sam Mejias; Red Sox, Felix Maldonado; Royals, Carlos Tosca; Twins, Joel Lepel; White Sox, Mike Gellinger; Yankees, Glenn Sherlock.

All-Star Team—1B—Peter Laake, Rangers; 2B—Claudio Ozario, Expos; 3B—David Lowery, Rangers; SS—Tom Nevers, Astros; OF —Rondell White, Expos; Raul Robinson, Braves; Domingo Mota, Dodgers; C—Jose Valdez, Dodgers; Starting Pitcher—John Roper, Reds; Relief Pitcher—Tony Bouton, Rangers; Manager of the Year—Sam Mejias, Reds.

(Compiled by Howe Sportsdata International, Boston, Mass.)

CLUB BATTING

Club	Pct.	G.	AB.	R.	OR.	H.	TB.	2B.	3B.	HR.	RBI.	SH.	SF.	HP.	BB.	Int. BB.	SO.	SB.	CS.	LOB.
Astros	.273	64	2095	336	275	571	745	91	28	9	280	9	19	28	288	7	314	133	68	453
Dodgers	.265	64	2051	312	257	544	674	78	14	8	265	13	22	29	290	6	397	87	66	453
Expos	.250	63	2038	319	218	509	681	74	19	20	246	8	17	44	192	3	427	71	37	409
Red Sox	.248	63	2121	341	311	527	667	80	18	8	263	18	20	22	305	5	380	40	37	462
Braves	.246	62	2001	267	287	493	637	65	14	17	217	35	20	22	179	7	409	89	46	394
Rangers	.240	64	2052	263	229	492	615	69	18	6	211	5	12	26	200	6	358	118	49	417
Reds	.238	64	2110	293	278	503	692	83	14	26	246	24	18	28	237	8	382	121	42	447
Twins	.234	63	2108	295	320	493	670	63	33	16	217	8	21	21	190	1	570	118	37	403
Pirates	.233	64	2055	280	280	479	600	68	13	9	189	6	15	27	141	0	425	58	45	403
Royals	.232	64	2003	241	291	465	604	78	17	9	181	19	20	36	249	6	430	104	47	439
Yankees	.223	62	1980	251	221	442	573	60	19	11	190	14	14	31	229	3	468	80	36	435
Indians	.219	63	1933	224	353	423	524	56	9	9	191	8	17	42	336	4	390	96	51	455
Mets	.219	60	1881	225	226	411	566	54	25	17	170	11	17	24	201	4	475	90	34	388
White Sox	.203	63	1942	216	285	394	513	64	14	9	163	13	17	31	217	4	500	122	72	350

INDIVIDUAL BATTING

(Leading Qualifiers for Batting Championship—170 or More Plate Appearances)

*Bats lefthanded.   †Switch-hitter.

Player and Club	Pct.	G.	AB.	R.	H.	TB.	2B.	3B.	HR.	RBI.	SH.	SF.	HP.	BB.	Int. BB.	SO.	SB.	CS.
Houk, Thomas, Twins	.344	46	157	25	54	83	10	5	3	37	1	5	2	22	0	18	3	5
Mota, Domingo, Dodgers	.343	61	213	46	73	92	12	2	1	34	2	1	8	36	3	19	23	15
Laake, Peter, Rangers*	.324	64	213	36	69	91	15	2	1	37	0	1	6	39	0	38	2	3
Schmidt, David, Red Sox†	.322	50	180	44	58	82	8	8	0	28	0	1	0	37	0	36	3	1
Valdez, Jose, Dodgers	.320	59	206	31	66	86	15	1	1	43	0	3	5	22	0	29	1	2
Cummings, Midre, Twins†	.316	47	177	28	56	82	3	4	5	28	0	4	2	13	1	32	14	7
Williams, Leroy, Dodgers	.313	58	198	25	62	70	8	0	0	25	0	2	1	26	2	26	5	8
Hennessey, Scott, Royals	.313	48	160	21	50	59	7	1	0	14	0	1	3	21	0	18	6	4
Lowery, David, Rangers†	.300	62	240	41	72	80	8	0	0	18	0	0	4	27	1	14	40	13
White, Rondall, Expos	.299	57	221	33	66	96	7	4	5	34	0	0	5	17	0	33	10	7

Departmental Leaders: G—Laake, 64; AB—Arias, 248; R—Arias, Mota, 46; H—Mota, 73; TB—R. White, 96; 2B—Laake, Valdez, 15; 3B—Schmidt, 8; HR—Dismuke, 7; RBI—Valdez, 43; SH—Arias, 7; SF—Houk, S. Thomas, 5; HP—Mota, Rappoli, Robertson, 8; BB—R. Powell, 42; IBB—Dismuke, 5; SO—Meyer, 62; SB—Lowery, 40; CS—Mota, 15.

(All Players—Listed Alphabetically)

Player and Club	Pct.	G.	AB.	R.	H.	TB.	2B.	3B.	HR.	RBI.	SH.	SF.	HP.	BB.	Int. BB.	SO.	SB.	CS.
Abel, Jackie, Twins	.000	23	1	0	0	0	0	0	0	0	0	0	0	0	0	1	0	0
Allison, Thomas, Mets†	.000	1	4	0	0	0	0	0	0	0	0	0	0	0	0	1	0	0
Anderson, Tony, Braves	.273	24	77	7	21	28	1	0	2	13	0	1	0	2	0	12	1	1
Andrews, Shane, Expos	.242	56	190	31	46	64	7	1	3	24	1	1	3	29	0	46	11	4
Andrews, Jay, Royals†	.277	33	112	15	31	53	4	3	4	21	0	1	4	15	3	24	6	2
Andujar, Hector, Indians	.252	38	119	13	30	34	4	0	0	12	0	0	2	23	0	14	6	5
Andujar, Robert, White Sox	.214	36	117	15	25	34	4	1	1	9	1	0	1	10	0	38	11	6
Anthony, Alexander, Braves	.065	17	31	3	2	5	0	0	1	3	1	0	0	5	0	15	1	1
Antoine, Junior, Rangers†	.212	17	52	3	11	12	1	0	0	4	0	0	2	1	0	16	1	0
Arace, Pasquale, Pirates*	.212	36	99	10	21	24	3	0	0	10	1	1	1	4	0	15	7	0
Archer, Carl, Braves	.222	27	45	3	10	13	3	0	0	4	0	0	1	5	0	6	1	1
Arendt, James, Braves	.000	3	4	0	0	0	0	0	0	0	0	0	0	0	0	2	0	0
Arias, Amadoz, Reds†	.254	61	248	46	63	80	8	3	1	27	7	0	0	21	0	37	25	6
Ashford, Jerry, Indians*	.163	16	43	2	7	7	0	0	0	5	0	0	1	5	0	5	0	1
Aubin, Kevin, Reds	.154	5	13	1	2	2	0	0	0	1	0	1	2	0	0	4	0	0
Awkard, Herman, Red Sox	.263	8	19	4	5	7	2	0	0	1	0	0	1	0	0	5	1	1
Ayrault, Joseph, Braves	.276	30	87	8	24	30	2	2	0	12	2	0	1	9	0	15	1	0
Basey, Marsalis, Astros	.000	1	5	0	0	0	0	0	0	0	0	0	0	0	0	0	0	0
Bell, David, Indians	.261	30	111	18	29	36	5	1	0	13	0	1	4	10	1	8	1	1
Benitez, Yamil, Expos	.229	22	83	6	19	23	1	0	1	5	0	0	8	0	0	18	0	0
Bennington, Jeffrey, Astros	.296	31	71	13	21	31	8	1	0	12	1	2	4	4	0	10	1	0
Berni, Denny, Red Sox†	.258	24	93	11	24	29	5	0	0	11	1	1	0	12	0	11	0	0
Bethea, Scott, Red Sox†	.236	43	161	24	38	42	4	0	0	8	1	1	2	31	0	21	6	3
Blanco, Henry, Dodgers	.219	60	178	23	39	50	8	0	1	19	0	4	1	26	0	41	7	2
Blanco, Pedro, Twins†	.202	34	104	11	21	23	0	1	0	5	0	0	1	8	0	27	10	3
Borrero, Ricky, Red Sox	.211	34	109	13	23	32	6	0	1	10	0	1	0	16	1	28	0	3
Brown, Alvin, Twins	.286	36	112	18	32	40	2	3	0	15	0	2	1	12	0	45	6	2
Brown, Jimmy, Dodgers†	.204	28	49	9	10	10	0	0	0	8	1	1	0	13	0	12	3	2
Bryant, Patrick, Indians	.196	17	51	3	10	12	2	0	0	3	0	1	4	8	0	18	2	0
Burris, Pierre, Reds†	.242	52	194	27	47	52	5	0	0	10	3	0	1	20	0	30	21	5
Burton, Darren, Royals	.207	15	58	10	12	14	0	1	0	2	1	2	0	4	0	17	6	0
Cabral, Irene, Reds*	.230	48	126	21	29	30	1	0	0	9	6	0	1	21	0	34	5	4
Cabrera, Miguel, Astros	.246	20	57	8	14	16	2	0	0	7	0	0	0	4	1	15	3	1
Calder, Joseph, Pirates	.237	57	211	17	50	69	9	2	2	34	0	4	0	12	0	50	6	0
Callari, Raimondo, Expos	.257	35	113	28	29	36	4	0	1	11	1	1	2	16	1	10	6	2
Capriotti, Joseph, Pirates*	.234	33	77	6	18	19	1	0	0	7	0	0	0	9	0	8	2	4
Caridad, Ronald, Twins	.167	10	18	2	3	4	1	0	0	0	0	0	0	0	0	3	0	0
Carrera, Mahaly, Indians†	.147	26	75	3	11	13	2	0	0	9	2	3	2	11	0	14	1	1
Carroll, Donald, Dodgers*	.333	21	3	0	1	1	0	0	0	0	0	0	0	0	0	0	1	0
Cartagena, Ivan, Reds	.152	32	99	11	15	21	3	0	1	5	0	0	0	3	0	18	2	2
Casanova, Raul, Mets	.077	23	65	4	5	5	0	0	0	1	0	0	4	0	0	16	0	1
Cerda, Jose, Royals	.118	16	34	3	4	5	1	0	0	0	0	0	0	2	0	7	1	2
Cerone, Richard, Yankees	.143	3	7	0	1	1	0	0	0	0	1	0	0	1	0	1	0	0
Chambers, Mark, Braves	.258	30	66	15	17	17	0	0	0	2	1	0	4	0	0	13	12	3
Chavez, Raul, Astros	.323	48	155	23	50	60	8	1	0	23	2	1	2	7	0	12	5	2
Chick, Bruce, Red Sox	.323	24	93	12	30	42	5	2	1	23	0	2	0	12	0	11	4	2
Christopherson, Gary, Astros	.273	53	187	24	51	69	12	0	2	31	0	4	2	24	0	12	4	4
Cintron, Miguel, Pirates†	.133	34	113	10	15	18	1	1	0	6	0	1	2	7	0	20	3	3
Clow, Craig, Expos*	.281	46	153	14	43	56	6	2	1	22	0	1	3	12	1	35	3	1
Coachman, James, White Sox	.218	57	193	20	42	54	9	0	1	12	0	1	6	21	0	43	10	9
Cofer, Brian, Indians	.750	8	4	1	3	4	1	0	0	0	0	0	0	0	0	1	0	0
Colon, Angel, Pirates	.228	39	101	6	23	26	3	0	0	10	1	0	1	2	0	13	2	0
Colon, Felix, Red Sox	.278	29	108	22	30	44	11	0	1	22	0	2	2	16	1	21	0	0
Conger, Jeffrey, Pirates*	.183	46	120	19	22	27	3	1	0	6	1	0	1	17	0	52	4	2
Cooper, Timothy, Yankees	.268	53	179	27	48	69	9	3	2	22	1	1	6	27	0	39	7	3
Correa, Miguel, Braves	.231	33	108	19	25	31	6	0	0	10	4	2	0	6	1	20	11	4
Couvertier, Edwin, Indians†	.169	31	89	8	15	19	1	0	1	12	0	0	1	16	0	8	1	2
Crespo, Michael, Rangers†	.429	5	14	3	6	11	1	2	0	5	0	0	2	0	0	2	0	0
Crimmins, John, Red Sox	.258	31	97	16	25	38	1	3	2	13	3	1	0	13	1	18	0	1
Cruz, Ruben, Astros*	.255	39	141	12	36	47	5	3	0	13	1	0	2	11	0	2	3	6
Cumberbatch, Abdiel, Yankees†	.197	45	122	13	24	28	1	0	1	4	1	0	2	21	0	39	12	3
Cummings, Midre, Twins†	.316	47	177	28	56	82	3	4	5	28	0	4	2	13	1	32	14	7
Daubach, Brian, Mets*	.270	45	152	26	41	60	8	4	1	19	0	3	2	22	0	41	2	1
Davis, Darwin, Mets	.309	30	94	10	29	44	5	2	2	13	2	1	2	10	0	16	4	3
Davis, Bradley, Pirates*	.212	35	66	4	14	16	2	0	0	5	0	0	1	8	0	12	2	1
Day, George, Royals	.291	57	196	27	57	64	5	1	0	19	3	3	4	23	0	24	12	7
DeKneef, Michael, Red Sox	.249	47	189	25	47	56	7	1	0	17	7	1	1	20	0	25	8	8
Delgado, Richard, Red Sox	.000	25	4	0	0	0	0	0	0	0	0	0	0	0	0	2	0	0
Demerson, Timothy, Yankees	.223	42	139	15	31	44	8	1	1	14	1	0	2	12	0	19	9	3
Diaz, Andres, Dodgers	.267	60	191	27	51	68	6	4	1	30	3	1	5	28	0	23	12	8
Diggs, Corey, Astros	.275	29	80	16	22	29	3	2	0	10	0	0	1	14	0	10	5	3
Dismuke, James, Reds*	.355	39	124	22	44	81	8	4	7	28	0	2	5	28	5	8	3	3

Player and Club	Pct.	G.	AB.	R.	H.	TB.	2B.	3B.	HR.	RBI.	SH.	SF.	HP.	BB.	Int. BB.	SO.	SB.	CS.
Dorante, Luis, Red Sox	.333	5	9	2	3	3	0	0	0	2	0	0	0	2	0	1	0	1
Douglas, Arthur, Rangers	.500	2	4	0	2	2	0	0	0	0	0	0	0	0	0	2	0	0
Duncan, Enrique, Reds	.217	15	46	6	10	12	2	0	0	5	0	0	3	2	0	13	5	3
Durham, Ray, White Sox†	.276	35	116	18	32	41	3	3	0	13	0	1	4	15	0	36	23	9
Ebanks, Weddison, Royals	.207	11	29	4	6	6	0	0	0	5	0	0	2	3	0	9	3	1
Eberly, Ryan, Yankees†	.179	17	39	2	7	8	1	0	0	0	0	0	0	3	0	10	1	1
Ellis, Jason, Braves	.286	4	7	0	2	2	0	0	0	1	0	0	0	1	0	1	0	0
Evangelista, George, Rangers	.219	32	105	13	23	28	3	1	0	9	0	1	2	7	0	21	1	1
Evans, Glenn, Twins†	.175	41	126	13	22	26	2	1	0	7	1	3	0	12	0	35	2	3
Everett, Carl, Yankees†	.259	48	185	28	48	69	8	5	1	14	2	1	6	15	0	38	15	2
Felix, Nathaniel, Yankees	.226	42	133	19	30	32	0	1	0	11	7	1	2	21	0	22	7	3
Feno, Quinn, Red Sox	.169	26	71	10	12	12	0	0	0	8	2	0	1	9	0	16	0	4
Fernandez, Manuel, Twins	.000	2	1	0	0	0	0	0	0	0	0	0	0	0	0	1	0	0
Ferran, Alexander, Indians°	.125	15	8	1	1	1	0	0	0	1	0	0	1	3	0	3	1	0
Figga, Michael, Yankees	.285	40	123	19	35	44	1	1	2	18	0	1	1	17	2	33	4	2
Fimbres, Javier, Twins	.246	48	142	20	35	48	10	0	1	11	1	1	4	24	0	18	1	3
Flinn, Geoffrey, Rangers°	.207	20	58	5	12	18	1	1	1	7	0	1	0	9	1	13	0	1
Fowler, Jake, Red Sox	.178	41	146	20	26	34	5	0	1	10	0	0	2	11	0	24	0	0
Gallego, Christopher, Pirates	.238	38	105	11	25	31	6	0	0	9	0	1	1	7	0	7	2	3
Garcia, Adrian, Braves	.240	18	50	2	12	15	3	0	0	5	0	1	0	2	1	9	3	0
Garcia, Francisco, Royals	.481	7	27	5	13	15	2	0	0	7	0	0	1	4	0	1	0	2
Garcia, Guillermo, Mets	.184	42	136	9	25	30	1	2	0	6	2	1	1	7	1	34	1	0
Garcia, Manuel, White Sox	.240	7	25	2	6	12	1	1	1	5	0	0	0	3	0	2	0	0
Garr, Ralph, Braves°	.265	21	34	7	9	9	0	0	0	1	0	0	0	5	0	8	1	1
Gerald, Edward, Royals	.216	15	51	8	11	19	1	2	1	5	0	0	1	6	0	15	5	0
Gianni, Gaetano, Reds	.250	2	4	1	1	1	0	0	0	0	0	0	0	0	0	0	0	0
Gibralter, Stephan, Reds	.259	52	174	26	45	74	11	3	4	27	3	1	3	23	1	30	9	3
Giegling, Matthew, Reds°	.286	53	189	21	54	76	11	1	3	37	0	2	2	14	0	20	1	1
Gilligan, Lawrence, White Sox	.158	19	57	3	9	12	3	0	0	7	3	3	1	6	0	10	0	3
Gonzales, Melvin, Red Sox	1.000	14	1	0	1	1	0	0	0	0	0	0	0	0	0	0	0	0
Gonzalez, Efrain, Rangers	.135	33	89	9	12	13	1	0	0	11	0	0	0	4	0	17	2	1
Gorman, Dirk, Dodgers°	.212	27	52	8	11	16	0	1	1	2	1	0	0	6	0	12	3	2
Graham, Derick, Reds	.168	44	125	20	21	23	2	0	0	7	0	2	2	20	0	28	10	4
Graham, Gregory, Red Sox†	.226	26	93	16	21	23	2	0	0	11	1	2	1	21	0	13	1	1
Graves, Randall, Dodgers	.284	57	190	38	54	72	10	4	0	28	3	3	1	40	0	42	5	4
Green-Shornock, Timothy, W. S.°	.225	44	138	10	31	41	2	4	0	17	0	1	0	14	3	21	10	4
Guerra, Pete, Indians	.262	38	107	8	28	34	6	0	0	10	1	1	0	13	0	15	1	2
Guzman, Eduardo, Red Sox	.195	13	41	5	8	9	1	0	0	4	0	0	0	4	0	6	1	0
Guzman, Ramon, White Sox	.119	36	101	8	12	15	3	0	0	6	0	0	2	9	0	33	4	3
Hamm, Stacy, Indians	.357	5	14	6	5	5	0	0	0	1	0	0	0	5	0	5	4	1
Hammond, Gregory, Reds	.200	42	130	12	26	32	6	0	0	6	3	0	7	20	1	20	6	1
Hardge, Michael, Expos	.222	53	176	33	39	47	5	0	1	13	0	2	2	15	0	43	6	2
Harley, Alquertin, Astros†	.321	35	109	19	35	43	6	1	0	12	0	0	2	23	1	11	17	2
Harris, Adolfo, Yankees	.236	39	127	11	30	40	3	2	1	22	0	3	2	7	0	35	0	2
Haughney, Trevor, Rangers°	.214	48	140	18	30	35	5	0	0	12	1	0	0	19	1	37	14	4
Hawkins, Craig, Twins†	.217	37	129	16	28	35	3	2	0	8	1	0	1	4	0	35	9	2
Hayes, Allen, Twins	.145	27	76	8	11	18	3	2	0	9	1	0	3	6	0	47	1	0
Hennessey, Scott, Royals	.313	48	160	21	50	59	7	1	0	14	0	1	3	21	0	18	6	4
Hernandez, Keith, Indians°	.455	5	11	3	5	9	1	0	1	2	0	0	0	1	0	2	0	0
Hernandez, Rafael, Mets	.198	28	86	6	17	18	1	0	0	5	1	0	0	7	0	21	4	0
Hernandez, Ramon, Reds	.222	60	221	22	49	73	10	1	4	29	0	3	0	12	0	47	4	3
Hinson, Dean, Pirates	.177	36	79	7	14	16	2	0	0	9	0	0	2	4	0	15	0	1
Hodge, Lee, Rangers	.264	54	193	27	51	69	11	2	1	25	1	1	5	6	0	19	14	7
Hoerner, Troy, Twins	.278	40	126	22	35	56	4	4	3	21	0	2	2	11	0	44	2	0
Hoffman, Robert, Dodgers	.208	13	24	3	5	5	0	0	0	2	0	0	0	4	0	7	1	0
Holland, Sidney, Rangers	.213	53	174	20	37	54	3	4	2	24	1	2	0	22	0	35	14	4
Houk, Thomas, Twins	.344	46	157	25	54	83	10	5	3	37	1	5	2	22	0	18	3	5
House, Mitchell, Pirates	.284	55	201	25	57	80	13	2	2	20	0	1	4	16	0	39	4	9
Hurford, Jeffery, Braves	.182	21	55	6	10	10	0	0	0	3	3	1	0	3	0	17	3	2
Indriago, Juan, Royals†	.161	41	124	16	20	22	2	0	0	9	3	1	4	24	0	19	11	4
Isava, Jesus, Royals†	.202	31	84	4	17	25	4	2	0	11	0	1	2	6	1	21	2	2
Jabalera, Miguel, Royals	.123	25	57	4	7	9	2	0	0	0	2	0	0	5	0	10	0	2
Jackson, Muzzy, White Sox°	.227	33	88	11	20	22	2	0	0	5	0	1	2	15	0	24	1	2
James, Gregory, White Sox	.146	41	103	11	15	17	2	0	0	4	0	1	2	9	0	33	7	5
Jarad, Samir, Astros	.000	1	3	0	0	0	0	0	0	0	0	0	0	0	0	1	0	0
Jennings, Lance, Royals	.292	15	48	4	14	18	4	0	0	5	0	0	1	4	0	12	0	4
Jester, Brian, Braves	.277	43	119	23	33	49	8	1	2	16	1	4	3	23	1	25	2	3
Jones, Brian, Expos†	.127	36	102	16	13	14	1	0	0	5	3	0	0	9	0	36	3	5
Jones, Lance, Rangers°	.247	29	97	14	24	27	3	0	0	6	0	0	0	8	0	20	11	1
Jones, Larry, Braves†	.229	44	140	20	32	38	1	1	1	18	2	2	6	14	1	25	5	3
King, Karl, Twins	.120	33	75	7	9	12	3	0	0	5	0	0	0	6	0	16	0	1
Kliafas, Stephen, Dodgers	.342	20	79	9	27	34	7	0	0	17	1	1	1	3	0	5	2	1
Laake, Peter, Rangers°	.324	64	213	36	69	91	15	2	1	37	0	1	6	39	0	38	2	3
Lachmann, Thomas, Indians	.333	5	18	1	6	8	2	0	0	4	0	0	0	1	0	1	0	0
Lanfranco, Lepido, Astros	.217	26	69	6	15	17	2	0	0	7	0	0	0	10	0	16	3	0
Leavell, Barry, Pirates	.245	39	106	15	26	32	4	1	0	7	0	0	1	3	0	25	1	2
Ledee, Ricardo, Yankees°	.108	19	37	5	4	6	2	0	0	1	0	0	0	6	0	18	2	0
Lemke, Mark, Braves†	.364	4	11	2	4	7	0	0	1	5	0	1	0	1	0	3	0	0
Leon, Johnny, Braves	.294	54	204	40	60	75	10	1	1	25	0	2	2	22	1	20	4	5
Lindsay, Jon, Rangers°	.134	21	67	2	9	10	1	0	0	2	0	1	0	12	0	12	0	1
Lowery, David, Rangers†	.300	62	240	41	72	80	8	0	0	18	0	0	4	27	1	14	40	13
Loyola, Juan, Reds	.086	29	70	3	6	10	1	0	0	5	0	0	0	10	0	24	0	1
Luciano, Suliban, Mets	.181	46	160	19	29	43	2	0	4	13	0	1	3	10	0	35	3	0
Macu, Andres, Dodgers°	.274	38	117	20	32	41	1	1	2	16	0	1	2	11	0	37	4	5
Maldonado, Albert, Dodgers°	.000	17	1	0	0	0	0	0	0	0	0	0	0	0	0	0	0	0
Malinowski, Christopher, Expos	.295	26	78	16	23	28	3	1	0	14	1	2	5	8	0	12	3	3
Marin, Jose, Red Sox	.226	15	31	3	7	8	1	0	0	4	1	0	0	1	0	8	0	1
Marks, Lansing, Braves	.230	42	152	19	35	44	6	0	1	19	0	2	2	8	0	22	3	1
Martinez, Javier, Pirates†	.150	18	20	2	3	3	0	0	0	1	0	0	0	1	0	6	0	0
Martinez, Ramon, Pirates	.362	15	58	8	21	25	2	1	0	5	0	2	0	3	0	6	2	5
Mathis, Cory, Braves	.212	19	33	5	7	9	2	0	0	1	0	0	2	0	0	10	0	1
Matouzas, Jeffrey, Yankees	.146	29	82	9	12	15	0	0	1	9	0	1	3	15	0	34	1	3

Player and Club	Pct.	G.	AB.	R.	H.	TB.	2B.	3B.	HR.	RBI.	SH.	SF.	HP.	BB.	Int. BB.	SO.	SB.	CS.
Mays, Terrance, Royals	.125	45	104	20	13	15	2	0	0	7	1	0	0	20	0	33	11	3
McCall, Roderick, Indians°	.278	10	36	5	10	12	2	0	0	6	0	0	0	5	1	10	0	0
McGough, Gregory, White Sox°	.181	28	72	13	13	18	2	0	1	6	0	0	5	8	1	24	3	2
McKeel, Walter, Red Sox	.250	13	44	2	11	14	3	0	0	6	0	1	0	3	0	8	0	2
McLin, Joseph, Pirates	.189	31	95	17	18	26	3	1	1	8	0	0	1	13	0	26	1	0
McMullan, Christopher, Rangers	.246	24	57	6	14	14	0	0	0	2	1	0	2	11	0	8	0	1
Melendez, Luis, Royals	.252	37	111	9	28	31	3	0	0	9	0	1	2	5	0	23	3	0
Mendez, Miguel, Braves	.180	15	50	6	9	10	1	0	0	0	1	0	1	8	0	14	1	0
Meyer, Paul, Mets	.215	46	177	18	38	56	7	4	1	20	0	2	3	12	0	62	4	1
Minter, Larry, Indians°	.203	26	69	6	14	17	3	0	0	5	0	0	0	4	0	19	1	2
Mitchell, Antonio, Pirates†	.294	44	102	18	30	47	4	2	3	13	0	0	1	7	0	21	3	3
Mitchell, Timothy, Red Sox°	.000	3	7	0	0	0	0	0	0	0	0	0	0	0	0	3	0	0
Mompres, Danilo, Mets	.193	50	187	26	36	50	4	2	2	19	3	1	3	13	0	47	9	2
Monastero, Frank, Indians	.300	22	70	9	21	23	2	0	0	13	0	0	2	16	0	11	2	2
Montero, Sixto, Astros†	.262	36	126	21	33	42	6	0	1	16	0	0	2	13	0	20	1	1
Moore, Doyle, Braves	.182	7	11	0	2	2	0	0	0	1	0	0	0	0	0	0	0	0
Moore, Timothy, Twins†	.260	27	77	19	20	37	2	3	3	15	0	1	1	13	0	24	7	3
Moreno, Juan, Mets	.208	32	77	7	16	21	3	1	0	5	0	1	5	15	1	31	4	2
Morgan, James, Indians	.180	41	133	20	24	28	4	0	0	10	1	3	4	22	0	38	13	5
Morillo, Cesar, Royals†	.270	55	185	21	50	63	6	2	1	17	3	0	2	22	0	45	7	4
Morris, Aaron, Indians°	.354	27	96	14	34	53	5	1	4	17	0	3	0	10	0	22	2	1
Mota, Domingo, Dodgers	.343	61	213	46	73	92	12	2	1	34	2	1	8	36	3	19	23	15
Moye, Wayne, White Sox°	.218	27	78	11	17	22	5	0	0	3	0	0	1	2	0	16	5	5
Munoz, Jesus, Reds	.333	2	3	0	1	1	0	0	0	1	0	0	0	0	0	0	0	0
Murphy, James, Indians°	.353	22	68	9	24	32	4	2	0	9	0	0	0	14	1	19	1	1
Nevers, Thomas, Astros	.238	50	185	23	44	70	10	5	2	32	0	3	3	27	0	38	13	4
Newhouse, Andre, Royals	.200	20	40	7	8	11	3	0	0	2	0	0	1	12	0	15	0	2
Nixon, Jason, Pirates	.222	32	63	6	14	17	1	1	0	5	1	2	2	4	0	11	3	1
Norman, Kenneth, Twins†	.252	44	131	22	33	46	6	2	1	9	1	1	2	9	0	47	24	2
Norris, William, Red Sox°	.309	28	97	20	30	37	7	0	0	13	0	1	1	20	0	13	2	0
Nurre, Peter, Dodgers	.238	29	63	11	15	15	0	0	0	0	1	0	1	8	0	12	3	3
O'Neil, Barry, Indians	.200	6	15	1	3	4	1	0	0	3	0	0	1	2	0	0	0	0
Ogden, Jamie, Twins°	.198	28	101	11	20	25	1	2	0	5	0	0	0	7	0	41	2	0
Owen, Tommy, Braves	.217	10	23	1	5	6	1	0	0	2	0	0	3	0	11	0	0	
Ozario, Claudio, Expos	.294	54	204	43	60	92	9	4	5	30	1	2	4	17	0	51	9	4
Pacheco, Gaspar, Expos	.190	27	79	2	15	20	3	1	0	9	0	0	0	4	0	9	2	0
Pages, Javier, Expos	.221	34	104	14	23	37	8	0	2	17	0	4	2	11	0	27	0	3
Parra, Franklin, Rangers†	.259	37	116	11	30	34	2	1	0	9	0	1	1	4	0	28	8	3
Patrizi, Michael, Mets	.178	30	90	7	16	19	3	0	0	7	0	1	0	7	0	34	6	1
Paulino, Dario, Braves	.216	31	97	13	21	29	3	1	1	11	0	1	1	2	0	18	4	3
Peppers, Cedrick, Pirates°	.194	48	139	7	27	28	1	0	0	6	1	1	1	8	0	27	5	4
Perez, Francisco, Dodgers°	.067	7	15	0	1	1	0	0	0	0	0	0	0	0	0	6	0	0
Perez, Jose, Dodgers†	.217	26	60	12	13	14	1	0	0	5	0	0	1	15	0	7	3	4
Perez, Juan, Pirates	.250	5	12	4	3	4	1	0	0	1	0	0	2	0	2	0	1	
Perez, Pablo, Royals°	.192	53	151	22	29	42	7	3	0	9	0	2	1	32	1	35	6	1
Perna, Robert, Reds†	.290	46	169	29	49	63	6	1	2	31	0	2	0	25	0	22	18	3
Person, Robert, Indians	.087	24	46	6	4	4	0	0	0	3	0	0	0	10	0	12	1	1
Petagine, Roberto, Astros°	.289	55	187	35	54	73	5	4	2	24	1	2	2	26	2	23	9	7
Phillips, Thomas, Expos†	.176	15	51	7	9	12	3	0	0	7	0	0	0	6	0	16	1	1
Philyaw, Delvic, Indians	.259	25	81	15	21	26	3	1	0	3	2	0	2	14	0	17	15	2
Pickering, Norbert, Astros	.383	16	47	9	18	24	4	1	0	9	1	0	1	3	0	8	2	1
Pinkney, Alton, Dodgers°	.167	35	90	7	15	19	2	1	0	7	0	0	2	10	0	22	2	4
Poe, Charles, White Sox	.177	46	147	13	26	33	3	2	0	15	0	4	4	16	0	38	11	4
Portu, Richard, Twins	.168	37	101	10	17	24	3	2	0	8	0	1	0	10	0	37	0	2
Powell, Corey, Expos	.181	33	83	6	15	21	3	0	1	10	0	0	2	3	0	21	0	0
Powell, Ricky, Indians°	.214	31	70	19	15	18	3	0	0	8	1	1	4	42	0	16	14	6
Prater, Steven, Twins	.000	1	1	0	0	0	0	0	0	0	0	0	0	0	0	0	0	0
Puchales, Javier, Dodgers°	.200	29	55	7	11	11	0	0	0	4	0	0	0	7	0	20	4	2
Quillin, Ty, Mets°	.134	34	119	10	16	18	2	0	0	5	0	0	1	12	0	23	1	1
Ramirez, Francisco, Twins	.160	27	81	7	13	14	1	0	0	8	1	0	0	4	0	19	1	0
Ramirez, Victor, Indians	.172	18	58	6	10	10	0	0	0	2	0	0	0	11	0	10	2	4
Rappoli, Paul, Red Sox°	.284	53	162	31	46	53	4	0	1	22	1	3	8	34	0	16	4	4
Reyes, Glen, Astros†	.313	20	48	6	15	17	0	1	0	7	0	0	1	5	0	7	5	6
Richison, David, Astros	.186	25	43	10	8	8	0	0	0	8	0	1	1	6	0	7	7	0
Rivera, David, Twins	.252	40	127	29	32	39	5	1	0	8	0	0	0	13	0	35	25	3
Rivera, Melvin, Braves	.220	24	50	8	11	12	1	0	0	7	3	1	1	9	0	21	3	1
Roa, Hector, Braves†	.209	13	43	7	9	13	1	0	1	2	0	0	1	5	1	5	4	0
Robertson, Stanley, Expos	.224	48	161	25	36	47	5	3	0	18	1	2	8	5	0	32	10	1
Robinson, Don, Braves°	.195	41	118	13	23	30	3	2	0	15	5	0	1	13	0	36	5	1
Robinson, Raul, Braves	.385	42	135	24	52	72	6	1	4	22	3	1	0	11	0	19	11	4
Robledo, Nilson, White Sox	.190	35	105	10	20	35	3	0	4	11	1	1	1	5	0	34	4	3
Rodriguez, Hector, Pirates	.241	17	58	9	14	20	1	1	1	6	0	0	1	3	0	10	0	1
Romero, Richard, Indians	.111	40	126	12	14	17	1	1	0	3	0	0	1	17	0	26	9	3
Ross, Sean, Braves†	.385	6	26	6	10	20	1	3	1	3	0	0	2	0	0	3	5	0
Rumsey, Darrell, Twins	.176	39	136	15	24	28	2	1	0	8	0	0	1	11	0	25	8	1
Sabino, Guillermo, Astros°	.179	10	28	3	5	7	0	1	0	2	1	0	0	6	0	7	4	3
Salcedo, Edwin, Yankees	.152	16	33	0	5	9	2	1	0	2	0	0	1	1	0	16	1	0
Sanchez, Daniel, Yankees	.186	14	43	5	8	10	2	0	0	2	0	0	0	1	0	12	0	2
Sanchez, Perry, Expos°	.255	15	51	11	13	14	1	0	0	7	0	1	2	8	0	5	1	1
Santana, Raul, Expos	.200	5	20	3	4	5	1	0	0	1	0	0	0	0	0	4	0	0
Santoya, Cristobal, Braves	.410	31	122	21	50	59	7	1	0	12	1	0	1	5	0	8	10	9
Schaefer, Cory, Pirates°	.273	26	55	6	15	15	0	0	0	4	0	1	1	5	0	19	3	0
Schmidt, David, Red Sox†	.322	50	180	44	58	82	8	8	0	28	0	1	0	37	0	36	3	1
Schreiner, John, Royals	.361	24	83	11	30	51	10	1	3	20	1	3	0	10	0	16	9	1
Schultz, Robert, Indians°	.264	31	87	9	23	26	3	0	0	8	1	0	6	14	0	18	5	4
Schwartz, Brian, Indians	.140	24	57	5	8	8	0	0	0	4	0	0	3	14	0	13	0	1
Seefried, Tate, Yankees°	.157	52	178	15	28	31	3	0	0	20	0	1	2	22	0	53	2	1
Sheppard, Donald, White Sox	.179	46	151	15	27	35	6	1	0	6	1	0	0	12	0	40	12	6
Shirley, Michael, Indians°	.080	7	25	1	2	4	0	1	0	4	0	1	1	4	0	10	2	1
Sly, Kian, Braves°	.185	17	27	3	5	7	2	0	0	3	0	0	2	7	0	7	0	0
Smith, Thomas, Yankees°	.258	9	31	5	8	12	2	1	0	4	1	1	0	2	0	8	0	1
Smith, Demond, Mets†	.261	46	153	19	40	56	9	2	1	7	1	2	0	20	0	34	17	6
Smith, Frank, Dodgers	.222	50	162	18	36	42	3	0	1	17	0	1	1	24	1	47	6	1

Player and Club	Pct.	G.	AB.	R.	H.	TB.	2B.	3B.	HR.	RBI.	SH.	SF.	HP.	BB.	Int. BB.	SO.	SB.	CS.
Smith, Lance, Astros	.271	23	70	12	19	24	2	0	1	9	0	0	2	13	0	6	1	5
Smith, Robert, Indians	.333	20	57	11	19	21	2	0	0	7	0	0	3	20	0	11	2	2
Smith, Thomas, Royals†	.142	39	134	11	19	25	4	1	0	4	0	1	4	11	0	49	7	4
Sondrini, Joseph, Pirates	.358	24	53	9	19	21	2	0	0	10	0	0	2	4	0	12	4	1
Soto, Emirson, Red Sox	.254	39	126	19	32	36	2	1	0	16	0	1	2	13	1	17	3	1
Spencer, Michael, Yankees	.184	42	147	20	27	31	4	0	0	7	0	1	1	20	0	23	11	2
Steele, Steven, Mets	.311	15	45	6	14	14	0	0	0	3	0	0	0	5	0	8	1	3
Stewart, Andrew, Royals	.192	21	52	5	10	14	4	0	0	1	3	0	3	9	1	13	3	0
Story, Jonathan, White Sox	.282	44	149	25	42	54	7	1	1	22	2	2	2	15	0	40	6	4
Strickland, Chad, Royals	.221	50	163	14	36	43	7	0	0	12	2	4	0	11	0	24	6	2
Sued, Jose, Indians	.229	11	35	0	8	9	1	0	0	2	0	0	0	2	0	8	0	1
Sweeney, Robert, Dodgers	.125	21	32	1	4	4	0	0	0	2	0	1	0	4	0	16	0	0
Swinton, Jermaine, Astros	.320	39	122	29	39	50	8	0	1	12	0	0	2	27	2	34	15	3
Tackett, Timothy, Red Sox	.056	6	18	3	1	2	1	0	0	3	0	0	0	2	0	5	0	0
Taylor, Jonathon, White Sox	.143	18	35	2	5	5	0	0	0	0	1	0	4	0	10	1	0
Texidor, Jose, Rangers	.232	50	168	29	39	53	5	3	1	19	0	1	1	20	1	23	3	3
Thomas, Steven, Reds	.236	49	174	25	41	61	9	1	3	18	2	5	2	18	1	47	12	3
Thomas, Timothy, Indians	.239	19	71	10	17	25	2	0	2	9	0	2	0	2	0	23	6	0
Tolliver, Jerome, Mets	.272	55	184	26	50	78	5	4	5	37	0	1	1	30	2	36	16	5
Tooch, Charles, Pirates	.246	43	122	14	30	36	6	0	0	7	1	1	2	6	0	31	3	4
Trevino, Gerald, Braves°	.180	23	61	7	11	13	2	0	0	5	1	0	0	12	0	15	1	3
Turco, Frank, Rangers	.300	5	10	1	3	4	1	0	0	1	0	0	0	1	0	2	0	1
Turrentine, Richard, Yankees	.211	50	171	18	36	49	4	3	1	15	1	1	0	17	0	48	4	4
Valdez, Jose, Dodgers	.320	59	206	31	66	86	15	1	1	43	0	3	5	22	0	29	1	2
Valette, Ramon, Twins	.257	34	109	12	28	30	2	0	0	10	1	0	1	3	0	20	3	1
Vandebrake, Kevin, Dodgers†	.247	24	73	17	18	23	5	0	0	6	1	2	1	7	0	14	2	3
Vandemark, John, Astros°	.217	9	23	2	5	6	1	0	0	4	0	1	0	8	0	4	1	0
Vann, Troy, Red Sox	.192	8	26	7	5	6	1	0	0	2	0	0	3	0	8	0	0
Veras, Quilvio, Mets†	.296	30	98	26	29	41	3	3	1	5	2	1	2	19	0	16	16	8
Vivas, Domingo, Reds	.000	23	1	0	0	0	0	0	0	0	0	0	0	0	0	0	0	0
Vogel, Michael, White Sox†	.175	43	103	13	18	23	5	0	0	7	1	1	0	31	0	26	5	6
Waldenberger, David, Braves†	.188	35	112	10	21	27	4	1	0	8	2	1	2	8	0	22	5	1
Wallace, David, Astros	.270	50	159	33	43	54	3	4	0	24	2	3	0	28	0	21	23	14
Walling, Kevin, Braves°	.196	38	107	9	21	30	1	1	2	13	1	2	0	11	2	27	1	2
Weimerskirch, Michael, Expos	.317	30	101	22	32	37	3	1	0	10	0	1	6	8	0	15	5	2
White, Jimmy, Astros°	.244	52	180	32	44	58	6	4	0	18	0	2	1	29	1	50	11	7
White, Rondall, Expos	.299	57	221	33	66	96	7	4	5	34	0	0	5	17	0	33	10	7
Whitehurst, Todd, Indians	.273	7	11	1	3	5	0	1	0	2	0	0	1	7	2	4	0	1
Williams, Charles, Mets	.182	5	11	0	2	3	1	0	0	1	0	1	1	0	0	4	1	0
Williams, Clifford, Rangers	.219	28	64	8	14	16	2	0	0	7	0	1	1	8	0	15	3	2
Williams, Leroy, Dodgers	.313	58	198	25	62	70	8	0	0	25	0	2	1	26	2	26	5	8
Williams, Terrell, Mets†	.186	18	43	6	8	10	0	1	0	4	0	1	0	7	0	16	1	0
Wilson, Brandon, White Sox	.268	11	41	4	11	12	1	0	0	5	1	1	0	4	0	5	1	0
Wilson, Dewayne, Indians°	.164	43	140	25	23	32	0	3	1	10	0	1	1	25	0	28	5	1
Wiseman, Gregory, Rangers°	.212	34	99	8	21	30	5	2	0	10	1	1	0	8	2	24	2	2
Witherspoon, Richard, Red Sox	.200	11	40	5	8	8	0	0	0	2	0	1	3	0	11	1	0
Woodall, Kevin, Rangers	.141	30	92	9	13	14	1	0	0	3	0	1	2	3	0	12	3	1
Younker, Jason, Red Sox	.231	47	156	27	36	49	4	3	1	27	1	1	1	25	1	53	6	5
Zarate, Vincent, White Sox	.187	42	123	12	23	28	3	1	0	10	2	0	0	18	0	27	6	0

The following pitchers, listed alphabetically by club, with games in parentheses, had no plate appearances, primarily through use of designated hitters:

ASTROS—August, Samuel (7); Bennett, Brian (22); Black, Scott (9); Boatman, Steve (13); Brown, Duane (4); Bullard, Scott (4); Correa, Jorge (9); DeLaCruz, Juan (18); Farmer, Gordon (3); Hampton, Mark (1); Hernandez, Javier (15); Kemp, Douglas (3); Locke, Roger (3); Mallicoat, Robbin (7); Navarro, Luis (13); Nieves, Fionel (10); Nix, David (13); Prats, Mario (20); Quaid, Jon (12); Rinaldi, Kevin (13); Vejar, Max (13).

BRAVES—Bridges, Bradford (11); Bryan, Russell (6); Creamer, Gerald (6); Cronin, Jeffrey (7); Garcia, Franklin (7); Honeycutt, Ronald (13); Kempfer, Jason (13); Koller, Jerome (13); Ledwik, Shannon (12); Lemon, Donald (2); Petit, Ricardo (6); Potts, Michael (23); Rutter, Samuel (16); Smith, Michael (7); Spires, Stuart (8); Vasquez, Julio (13).

DODGERS—Botts, Jacob (15); Broyles, Jason (11); Castro, Nelson (10); Cruz, Jose (17); Daniel, Anthony (17); Davis, Gregory (17); Farnsworth, Ross (12); Matthews, Thomas (11); Parra, Jose (10); Racobaldo, Michael (16).

EXPOS—Alvarez, Cesar (11); Ashley, Duane (10); Batista, Miguel (9); Clelland, Richard (12); Conley, Matthew (10); Foster, Kevin (4); Ortega, Oscar (20); Pacheco, Alexander (6); Perez, Carlos (13); Renko, Steve (2); Shehan, Brian (16); Vanryn, Benjamin (10); White, Gabriel (11); Whitman, Ryan (14); Wicks, Raymond (18).

INDIANS—Crawford, Carlos (10); Day, Kenneth (19); Fleet, Joseph (12); Hasenzahl, Kirk (20); Hernandez, Fernando (11); Langdon, Timothy (6); Morgan, Scott (6); Rosado, Jose (3); Sawyer, Richard (22); Sides, Craig (3); Sweeney, Mark (10); Winiarski, Ronald (13).

METS—Belmonte, Pedro (18); Corbell, Eric (17); Hernandez, Hermes (7); Langan, Richard (12); Lehnmer, Michael (3); Lindsay, Darian (6); Manfred, James (14); Martinez, Jose (13); Ramirez, Hector (11); Schorr, Bradley (12); Seymour, Steven (9); Smith, Ottis (13); Wegmann, Thomas (2); Williams, Scott (15).

PIRATES—Arias, Alexander (17); Bradley, David (10); Coombs, Glenn (12); Fajardo, Hector (5); French, Timothy (14); Gobel, Donnie (18); Goytia, Victor (12); Hunter, Troy (13); Mejia, Juan (1); Pike, David (8); Ramirez, Robert (11); Shade, Derek (4); Sosa, Juan R. (16); Sparks, Shane (16); Way, Ronald (12); White, Richard (7).

RANGERS—Ayala, Jason (18); Berthau, Terrell (12); Bouton, Anthony (26); Cain, Timothy (16); DeVaughan, Todd (15); Devereaux, Brandon (1); Duval, Avery (6); Gibson, David (43); Henson, Michael (4); Holcomb, Louis (2); Johnson, Johnny (15); Kunz, Richard (9); Madrigal, Victor (12); McGough, Keith (3); Oliver, Darren (3); Phillips, Brad (3); Quero, Juan (13); Rhoades, Troy (3); Stafford, Timothy (8); Watson, Andy (10).

REDS—Balentine, Bryant (12); Brothers, John (17); Diaz, Rafael (13); Fenton, Richard (10); Garcia, Fermin (21); Griffen, Leonard (11); Langford, Richard (15); McClain, Charles (12); Roper, John (13); Tobin, Daniel (13); Wiggins, James (14); Wyatt, Charles (11).

RED SOX—Allen, Tracy (7); Anacki, Paul (12); Brown, Ernest (10); Burgo, Dale (5); Centeno, Luis (16); Curry, Stephen (3); Kite, Daniel (4); Konopki, Mark (1); LeMaster, Matthew (9); Maloney, Ryan (17); Miller, Todd (3); Mitchelson, Mark (5); Mosley, Anthony (2); Niemeyer, Bryan (14); Painter, Gary (5); Powers, Terry (3); Sosa, Juan (12).

ROYALS—Baaske, Keith (15); Berumen, Andres (5); Brea, Julio (6); Budnick, Alan (18); Chrisman, James (8); Foster, Clinton (9); Fyock, Wade (11); Henn, Jonathan (4); Jacobs, John (11); Lee, Anthony (12); Lee, Thomas (14); Miceli, Daniel (27); Perez, Dario (10); Stewart, Reginald (13); Toth, Robert (7); West, Eric (16).

TWINS—Asp, Brian (13); Berson, Candido (5); Correa, Jose (14); Fritz, Scott (8); Hoppe, Dennis (9); Juarbe, Victor (23); Landis, Kipp (19); Lindaman, Chad (10); Mieses, Melanio (25); Roskom, Bryan (10); Taylor, Kerry (14).

WHITE SOX—Altaffer, Todd (6); Baldwin, James (9); Bere, Jason (16); Borowski, Joseph (12); Cortes, Argenis (6); Culberson, Donald (3); DeLaCruz, Carlos (3); Dinuzzo, Jeffrey (3); Dorsey, Lee (1); Fernandez, Alexander (2); Fritz, Gregory (12); Hoey, Andrew (9); Hulme, Patrick (10); Jean, Domingo (13); Locklear, Dean (14); Marshall, Terrance (14); McGraw, Walter (10); Micucci, Ronald (4); Middaugh, Scott (2); Perigny, Donald (7); Ruiz, Jorge (7); Smith, Roosevelt (7); Vanderwel, William (2); Wickman, Robert (2).

YANKEES—Dunbar, Matthew (3); Faw, Bryan (12); Gilbert, Brent (10); Hayes, James (11); Hines, Richard (11); Kindall, Scott (4); Laviano, Frank (17); Rivera, Mariano (22); Rumer, Timothy (12); Santaella, Alexis (14); Santiago, Sandi (23); Seiler, Keith (16); Smith, Michael (6); Springer, Russell (6); Thibert, John (13).

GRAND SLAM HOME RUNS—Cummings, Giegling, Mompres, 1 each.

AWARDED FIRST BASE ON CATCHER'S INTERFERENCE—Leavell 2 (McGraw, Vogel); Arace (Anderson); Dismuke (Valdez); Giegling (Lanfranco); Graves (L. Smith); Rafael Hernandez (Robledo); Macu (Strickland); McKeel (Guerra); Petagine (Strickland); Robertson (Robledo); Schultz (L. Smith).

CLUB FIELDING

Club	Pct.	G.	PO.	A.	E.	DP.	PB.	Club	Pct.	G.	PO.	A.	E.	DP.	PB.
Rangers	.963	64	1630	711	89	45	20	Mets	.950	60	1526	621	112	46	18
Dodgers	.962	64	1653	749	94	67	22	Pirates	.949	63	1592	680	122	43	14
Red Sox	.960	63	1691	827	104	60	13	Indians	.947	63	1618	678	128	52	24
Royals	.954	64	1635	747	115	55	23	Braves	.942	62	1601	696	141	45	26
Astros	.954	64	1654	812	120	66	29	Twins	.942	63	1651	694	144	54	22
Expos	.953	63	1598	693	114	50	13	Yankees	.939	62	1584	667	146	49	23
Reds	.951	64	1692	731	126	64	11	White Sox	.930	63	1624	648	170	36	17

Triple Play—Expos.

INDIVIDUAL FIELDING
FIRST BASEMEN

*Throws lefthanded.

Player and Club	Pct.	G.	PO.	A.	E.	DP.	Player and Club	Pct.	G.	PO.	A.	E.	DP.
Anderson, Braves	.933	3	14	0	1	4	Malinowski, Expos	1.000	4	20	1	0	1
Berni, Red Sox	.988	15	150	10	2	11	McCall, Indians	.989	10	85	6	1	7
Brown, Twins	1.000	2	10	0	0	0	McGough, White Sox	.974	7	37	1	1	4
Cabrera, Astros	1.000	1	2	0	0	0	McLin, Pirates	.985	21	191	12	3	16
Calder, Pirates	.971	44	378	21	12	22	Melendez, Royals	1.000	1	9	0	0	0
Cartagena, Reds	.963	21	148	8	6	19	Meyer, Mets	.977	29	247	13	6	21
Christopherson, Astros	1.000	1	15	0	0	4	Mitchell, Red Sox*	1.000	2	7	0	0	1
Clow, Expos	.986	43	322	22	5	22	Morris, Indians*	.980	23	188	9	4	23
Coachman, White Sox	1.000	1	5	1	0	1	Ogden, Twins*	.978	25	199	19	5	19
Colon, Red Sox	.996	22	205	17	1	21	Pacheco, Expos	.972	22	172	4	5	19
Daubach, Mets	.976	31	274	16	7	20	Perez, Royals*	.981	52	429	41	9	43
Diaz, Dodgers	.989	54	425	30	5	45	PETAGINE, Astros*	.990	54	473	36	5	46
Dismuke, Reds	.987	30	278	22	4	29	Phillips, Expos	.905	2	18	1	2	0
Fimbres, Twins	.990	35	271	24	3	11	Pickering, Astros	.976	7	36	4	1	4
Fowler, Red Sox*	.990	29	287	17	3	24	Ramirez, Twins	1.000	1	2	0	0	0
Giegling, Reds	.994	19	152	12	1	10	Richison, Astros	1.000	8	76	1	0	8
Green-Shornock, White Sox*	.972	40	334	8	10	18	Rivera, Braves	.500	1	1	1	2	0
Harris, Yankees	1.000	4	15	1	0	1	Sanchez, Expos	1.000	1	8	1	0	1
Hernandez, Indians*	1.000	2	10	1	0	1	Schreiner, Royals	.979	15	135	8	3	6
Hoerner, Twins	1.000	1	6	0	0	1	Seefried, Yankees	.987	49	418	30	6	34
Houk, Twins	.983	10	49	8	1	7	Thomas, Indians	.993	15	141	4	1	7
Jackson, White Sox	.974	25	179	12	5	11	Valdez, Dodgers	.962	8	47	3	2	4
Jester, Braves	.975	38	300	16	8	16	Vandemark, Astros*	1.000	3	20	3	0	0
Jones, Expos	1.000	1	2	0	0	0	Walling, Braves	.980	32	231	16	5	20
Laake, Rangers*	.986	64	600	37	9	39	Williams, Dodgers	.976	15	112	8	3	7
Leon, Expos	.971	12	96	6	3	8	Wilson, Indians	.974	16	139	11	4	10
Macu, Dodgers*	.857	2	5	1	1	1	Wiseman, Rangers*	1.000	1	2	0	0	0

Triple Play—Malinowski.

SECOND BASEMEN

Player and Club	Pct.	G.	PO.	A.	E.	DP.	Player and Club	Pct.	G.	PO.	A.	E.	DP.
Allison, Mets	1.000	1	3	2	0	0	Lemke, Braves	1.000	3	4	6	0	1
Andujar, White Sox	.867	11	5	21	4	3	Malinowski, Expos	1.000	2	3	5	0	1
Arias, Reds	.948	58	116	158	15	36	Martinez, Pirates	1.000	12	6	10	0	2
Basey, Astros	1.000	1	1	7	0	1	Mompres, Mets	1.000	1	1	2	0	0
Blanco, Twins	1.000	1	0	1	0	0	Monastero, Indians	.971	8	10	23	1	1
Brown, Dodgers	.969	26	37	58	3	14	Morillo, Royals	1.000	1	1	4	0	0
Callari, Expos	.978	12	21	24	1	3	Mota, Dodgers	.977	11	17	25	1	6
Carrera, Indians	.922	23	38	56	8	10	Ozario, Expos	.917	48	83	115	18	16
Chavez, Astros	.940	21	33	46	5	10	Paulino, Braves	.950	24	30	46	4	7
Cofer, Indians	1.000	1	3	3	0	0	Quillin, Mets	1.000	1	4	0	0	0
Colon, Pirates	.926	11	23	27	4	5	Reyes, Astros	.957	17	28	38	3	10
Day, Royals	.959	47	109	149	11	32	Richison, Astros	.833	3	2	3	1	1
DeKneef, Red Sox	.981	18	36	68	2	13	Rivera, Twins	.959	26	57	60	5	11
Diggs, Astros	.978	29	55	78	3	19	Roa, Braves	1.000	8	21	17	0	3
Duncan, Reds	.963	5	12	14	1	3	Romero, Indians	.955	14	32	32	3	4
Durham, White Sox	.910	31	56	75	13	16	Sabino, Astros	.942	10	22	27	3	8
Eberly, Yankees	.936	14	19	25	3	5	D. Sanchez, Yankees	.875	6	9	5	2	1
Evangelista, Rangers	.944	23	41	43	5	7	P. Sanchez, Expos	1.000	1	3	2	0	0
Evans, Twins	1.000	1	0	1	0	0	Santoya, Braves	.957	19	45	45	4	6
Felix, Yankees	.921	38	63	101	14	19	Schmidt, Red Sox	.955	46	92	165	12	31
Fernandez, Twins	1.000	1	1	0	0	0	R. Smith, Indians	.947	20	39	51	5	9
Gallego, Pirates	.970	37	38	91	4	14	T. Smith, Yankees	.923	9	15	21	3	3
Garcia, Mets	.981	33	83	76	3	20	Sondrini, Pirates	.921	23	18	40	5	3
Gilligan, White Sox	.907	9	18	21	4	5	Thomas, Reds	1.000	3	2	6	0	1
Graves, Dodgers	.921	19	33	37	6	8	Tooch, Pirates	.909	7	8	12	2	0
Guzman, Red Sox	1.000	1	1	1	0	1	Trevino, Braves	.956	23	28	37	3	11
Hardge, Expos	1.000	4	10	9	0	4	Turrentine, Yankees	.870	6	7	13	3	1
Hawkins, Twins	.886	33	64	76	18	20	Vandebrake, Dodgers	.972	24	58	46	3	21
HODGE, Rangers	.970	44	71	92	5	22	Veras, Mets	.976	28	45	76	3	13
Houk, Twins	.964	9	13	14	1	4	B. Wilson, White Sox	1.000	2	0	7	0	0
Indriago, Royals	.978	15	45	42	2	5	D. Wilson, Indians	.875	1	5	2	1	0
Jabalera, Royals	.938	3	6	9	1	1	Zarate, White Sox	.929	7	14	12	2	3
James, White Sox	.838	11	9	22	6	0							

THIRD BASEMEN

Player and Club	Pct.	G.	PO.	A.	E.	DP.
Andrews, Expos	.896	51	42	105	17	5
Ashford, Indians	1.000	4	2	2	0	0
Bell, Indians	.919	27	29	50	7	6
Bethea, Red Sox	.875	18	17	39	8	1
Blanco, Dodgers	.941	60	48	129	11	12
Callari, Expos	.944	5	4	13	1	1
Caridad, Twins	.625	2	3	2	3	0
Carrera, Indians	.818	4	2	7	2	0
Cartagena, Reds	.750	1	0	3	1	0
Cerda, Royals	.786	14	6	16	6	1
Chavez, Astros	1.000	1	1	0	0	0
Christopherson, Astros	.864	29	13	63	12	5
Cintron, Pirates	.943	32	32	67	6	7
Coachman, White Sox	.865	56	36	111	23	6
Colon, Red Sox	.929	3	2	11	1	0
Cooper, Yankees	.874	46	37	102	20	10
Davis, Mets	.803	27	20	33	13	5
Day, Royals	.950	9	8	11	1	0
DeKneef, Red Sox	.667	1	1	1	1	0
Eberly, Yankees	1.000	2	1	2	0	0
Evangelista, Rangers	1.000	4	1	3	0	0
Evans, Twins	.865	34	24	59	13	5
Garcia, Mets	.760	10	4	15	6	1
D. Graham, Reds	.875	4	1	6	1	0
G. Graham, Red Sox	.909	12	11	29	4	1
Graves, Dodgers	1.000	1	0	3	0	1
Guzman, Red Sox	.750	2	1	5	2	0
Hernandez, Mets	.890	25	19	54	9	4
Houk, Twins	.946	25	26	61	5	8
House, Pirates	.860	17	17	20	6	1
Indriago, Royals	.905	20	20	37	6	1
Jabalera, Royals	.944	7	7	10	1	2
Lemke, Braves	.857	1	1	5	1	1
Leon, Yankees	.841	17	8	29	7	2
LOWERY, Rangers	.955	62	47	142	9	17
Malinowski, Expos	.864	8	5	14	3	4
Marks, Braves	.824	23	16	40	12	1
Mendez, Braves	.846	12	4	29	6	2
Meyer, Mets	.000	1	0	0	2	0
Monastero, Indians	.818	14	7	20	6	3
Montero, Astros	.894	35	29	81	13	6
Norris, Red Sox	.967	28	21	67	3	7
Nurre, Dodgers	1.000	1	0	3	0	0
Ozario, Expos	.500	1	0	1	1	0
Perna, Reds	.857	20	17	31	8	4
Richison, Astros	.778	4	4	3	2	0
D. Rivera, Twins	.810	8	7	10	4	2
M. Rivera, Braves	1.000	4	1	3	0	0
Rodriguez, Pirates	.833	16	8	27	7	2
Schreiner, Royals	.929	9	3	23	2	1
Smith, Royals	.920	8	10	13	2	0
Stewart, Royals	1.000	7	3	8	0	0
Story, White Sox	.875	7	6	15	3	1
Thomas, Reds	.917	41	41	81	11	11
Waldenberger, Braves	.854	31	31	57	15	2
Whitehurst, Indians	.000	1	0	0	1	0
Williams, Dodgers	.778	9	9	5	4	4
Wilson, Indians	.806	19	21	29	12	6

SHORTSTOPS

Player and Club	Pct.	G.	PO.	A.	E.	DP.
Andujar, Indians	.886	38	47	100	19	13
Bethea, Red Sox	.917	23	34	66	9	13
Blanco, Twins	.914	34	60	88	14	12
Callari, Expos	.927	17	22	54	6	9
Caridad, Twins	1.000	1	1	2	0	1
Chavez, Astros	.964	25	33	73	4	14
Cintron, Pirates	1.000	2	1	5	0	1
Colon, Pirates	.786	27	30	36	18	6
Cooper, Yankees	.833	6	7	18	5	2
DeKneef, Red Sox	.935	23	57	88	10	17
Durham, White Sox	.882	3	5	10	2	0
Evans, Twins	.909	2	6	4	1	0
Felix, Yankees	.778	2	5	2	2	1
Gallego, Pirates	1.000	1	0	2	0	1
Gilligan, White Sox	.811	10	11	19	7	2
D. Graham, Reds	.889	9	11	13	3	1
G. Graham, Red Sox	.862	11	18	32	8	8
Graves, Dodgers	.970	27	42	56	3	15
Hardge, Expos	.912	49	90	138	22	17
Raf. Hernandez, Mets	.900	2	3	6	1	1
Ram. Hernandez, Reds	.925	57	105	166	22	34
Houk, Twins	.909	3	4	6	1	2
Indriago, Royals	.958	5	8	15	1	1
Jabalera, Royals	.857	13	16	26	7	3
Jones, Braves	.919	44	64	140	18	16
Kliafas, Dodgers	.970	20	28	68	3	14
Leon, Yankees	.800	4	3	5	2	0
Marin, Red Sox	.935	11	15	28	3	5
Martinez, Pirates	.922	15	19	40	5	1
MOMPRES, Mets	.943	46	72	142	13	21
Monastero, Indians	1.000	1	0	3	0	0
Morillo, Royals	.911	50	73	151	22	28
Mota, Dodgers	1.000	1	1	1	0	1
Nevers, Astros	.913	41	87	134	21	32
Parra, Rangers	.893	35	54	88	17	14
Paulino, Braves	.767	8	11	22	10	6
Perez, Dodgers	.946	25	29	77	6	15
Richison, Astros	1.000	1	0	1	0	0
Roa, Braves	.880	4	8	14	3	2
Rodriguez, Pirates	1.000	1	3	3	0	1
Romero, Indians	.935	26	48	82	9	15
Sanchez, Yankees	.783	9	6	12	5	2
Santoya, Braves	.882	13	23	37	8	9
Story, White Sox	.884	36	60	92	20	13
Tooch, Pirates	.880	37	37	80	16	15
Turco, Rangers	1.000	3	1	1	0	0
Turrentine, Yankees	.886	46	61	142	26	26
Valette, Twins	.916	33	44	87	12	14
Whitehurst, Indians	.900	2	5	4	1	2
L. Williams, Dodgers	1.000	1	0	1	0	0
T. Williams, Mets	.852	14	14	32	8	4
Wilson, Rangers	.872	10	15	26	6	4
Woodall, Rangers	.933	30	41	71	8	9
Zarate, White Sox	.938	7	7	23	2	4

Triple Play—Hardge.

OUTFIELDERS

Player and Club	Pct.	G.	PO.	A.	E.	DP.
Andrews, Royals	.935	18	27	2	2	1
Andujar, White Sox	.971	23	32	2	1	0
Anthony, Braves	1.000	13	16	0	0	0
Antoine, Rangers	.969	17	28	3	1	0
Arace, Pirates	.970	35	32	0	1	0
Archer, Braves	.500	1	1	0	1	0
Awkard, Red Sox	.800	8	4	0	1	0
Benitez, Expos	.976	22	38	2	1	1
Brown, Twins	.750	7	7	2	3	0
Bryant, Indians	.963	13	25	1	1	0
Burris, Reds	.951	49	74	3	4	0
Burton, Royals	.970	15	31	1	1	1
Cabral, Reds°	.979	45	85	7	2	1
Cabrera, Astros	1.000	12	21	0	0	0
Capriotti, Pirates°	.929	31	23	3	2	0
Chambers, Braves	.880	22	18	4	3	1
Chick, Red Sox	.984	23	58	5	1	0
Conger, Pirates°	.957	46	86	3	4	0
Correa, Braves	.949	33	55	1	3	0
Couvertier, Indians	.971	27	32	1	1	1
Cruz, Astros	.980	34	46	3	1	1
Cumberbatch, Yankees	.954	44	59	3	3	2
Cummings, Twins	.926	45	73	2	6	0
Demerson, Yankees	.943	37	31	2	2	0
Diaz, Dodgers	1.000	14	14	1	0	0
Douglas, Rangers	1.000	1	1	0	0	0
Duncan, Reds	.875	7	14	0	2	0
Ebanks, Royals	1.000	10	14	2	0	0
Evans, Twins	1.000	4	3	0	0	0
Everett, Yankees	.932	46	64	5	5	1
Feno, Red Sox	.958	26	45	1	2	0
Ferran, Indians°	1.000	2	2	0	0	0
F. Garcia, Royals	1.000	7	7	0	0	0
M. Garcia, White Sox	1.000	4	1	1	0	0
Garr, Braves°	.944	13	16	1	1	0
Gerald, Royals	.929	15	24	2	2	0
Gibralter, Reds	.948	51	100	9	6	1
Gonzalez, Rangers	.968	31	27	3	1	1
Gorman, Dodgers°	.970	27	32	0	1	0
Graham, Reds	.950	22	38	0	2	0
Graves, Dodgers	.895	13	17	0	2	0
Green-Shornock, White Sox°	1.000	2	3	1	0	0
Guzman, White Sox	.868	35	44	2	7	1
Hamm, Indians	1.000	4	7	0	0	0
Harley, Astros	.944	35	49	2	3	0
Harris, Yankees	.957	18	19	3	1	1
Haughney, Rangers	.961	46	69	4	3	2
Hawkins, Twins	1.000	1	1	0	0	0
Hayes, Twins	.941	16	16	0	1	0
Hennessey, Royals	.988	44	79	5	1	3
Hernandez, Mets	1.000	1	1	0	0	0
Hoerner, Twins	1.000	16	19	1	0	1
Holland, Rangers	.944	24	16	1	1	0
Hurford, Braves°	1.000	19	25	1	0	0
James, White Sox	.943	27	32	1	2	0
B. Jones, Expos	.958	34	66	3	3	0

OUTFIELDERS—Continued

Player and Club	Pct.	G.	PO.	A.	E.	DP.
L. Jones, Rangers°	1.000	18	25	4	0	0
Leavell, Pirates	.964	39	47	6	2	2
Ledee, Yankees°	1.000	15	18	1	0	0
Loyola, Reds	.920	19	23	0	2	0
Luciano, Mets	.932	46	52	3	4	1
Macu, Dodgers°	.984	35	58	3	1	0
Malinowski, Expos	1.000	3	3	0	0	0
Mathis, Braves	1.000	14	16	0	0	0
Mays, Royals	.968	36	59	1	2	0
Melendez, Royals	.979	32	44	2	1	1
Minter, Indians	.952	12	19	1	1	0
Mitchell, Pirates	1.000	43	43	2	0	0
D. Moore, Braves	1.000	7	9	1	0	0
T. Moore, Twins°	.946	23	33	2	2	0
Moreno, Mets	.940	31	43	4	3	0
Morgan, Indians	.974	39	75	1	2	0
Mota, Dodgers	.968	33	56	5	2	2
Moye, White Sox°	.974	20	33	5	1	0
Murphy, Expos	1.000	10	14	2	0	1
Newhouse, Royals	.833	15	13	2	3	0
Norman, Twins	.956	39	59	6	3	1
O'Neil, Indians	1.000	3	4	1	0	0
Peppers, Pirates°	.905	47	55	2	6	0
F. Perez, Dodgers°	1.000	6	5	0	0	0
J. Perez, Pirates	1.000	5	7	1	0	1
Perna, Reds	.971	19	30	3	1	1
Person, Indians	1.000	9	9	1	0	1
Petagine, Astros°	1.000	1	1	0	0	0
Philyaw, Indians	.952	21	39	1	2	0
Pinkney, Dodgers	.895	25	33	1	4	0
Poe, White Sox	1.000	27	41	3	0	0
Portu, Twins	.978	28	42	3	1	0
Powell, Indians°	.981	23	50	1	1	0
Puchales, Dodgers°	1.000	29	25	0	0	0
Quillin, Mets	.956	30	41	2	2	0
Ramirez, Indians	.969	17	29	2	1	0
Rappoli, Red Sox	.982	53	102	5	2	0
Rivera, Braves	.974	14	36	2	1	0
Robertson, Expos	.966	45	77	7	3	2
D. Robinson, Braves	.935	36	56	2	4	0
R. Robinson, Braves	.972	41	64	5	2	1
Ross, Braves°	1.000	1	4	0	0	0
Rumsey, Twins	.970	33	59	5	2	2
Sanchez, Expos	1.000	1	1	0	0	0
Schaefer, Pirates	.968	26	25	5	1	1
Schultz, Indians	.977	27	41	1	1	0
Sheppard, White Sox	.944	43	63	4	4	0
Shirley, Indians	.909	7	9	1	1	0
Sly, Braves	1.000	13	4	0	0	0
D. Smith, Braves	.969	35	60	2	2	0
F. Smith, Dodgers	.961	42	72	1	3	1
T. Smith, Royals	.920	20	20	3	2	0
Soto, Red Sox	1.000	33	49	8	0	1
Spencer, Yankees	.965	41	79	3	3	0
Sweeney, Dodgers	1.000	2	1	0	0	0
Swinton, Astros	.953	35	33	8	2	1
Texidor, Rangers	.961	48	64	9	3	1
TOLLIVER, Mets	1.000	48	69	2	0	0
Vann, Red Sox	.929	8	12	1	1	0
Vogel, White Sox	1.000	4	2	0	0	0
Wallace, Astros	.955	48	60	3	3	1
Weimerskirch, Expos	.974	27	35	3	1	1
J. White, Astros	.976	47	71	9	2	1
R. White, Expos	.973	52	71	1	2	0
Williams, Dodgers	1.000	18	19	2	0	1
Wiseman, Rangers°	.973	29	33	3	1	0
Witherspoon, Red Sox	.944	10	16	1	1	1
Younker, Red Sox	.978	47	85	3	2	0
Zarate, White Sox	.947	24	34	2	2	1

CATCHERS

Player and Club	Pct.	G.	PO.	A.	E.	DP.	PB.
Anderson, Braves	.970	15	86	11	3	0	3
Ashford, Indians	.981	9	45	6	1	0	4
Aubin, Reds	1.000	3	17	0	0	0	1
Ayrault, Braves	.986	30	182	30	3	1	7
Bennington, Astros	.984	31	164	20	3	0	9
Berni, Red Sox	.963	4	24	2	1	0	0
Borrero, Red Sox	.951	34	156	18	9	0	6
Brown, Twins	.964	21	93	15	4	2	7
Casanova, Mets	.953	23	141	20	8	3	9
Cerone, Yankees	1.000	2	11	1	0	0	1
Crespo, Rangers	.951	5	35	4	2	1	1
Crimmins, Red Sox	.974	16	65	9	2	0	1
DAVIS, Pirates	.993	35	121	21	1	1	2
Ellis, Braves	1.000	4	15	1	0	0	0
Figga, Yankees	.976	37	270	19	7	2	10
Fimbres, Twins	.974	7	31	6	1	0	2
Garcia, Braves	.974	18	87	25	3	1	14
Gianni, Reds	.750	2	3	0	1	0	1
Giegling, Reds	.984	26	161	25	3	2	0
Guerra, Indians	.972	35	179	30	6	2	12
Hammond, Reds	.973	40	230	56	8	4	8
Hinson, Pirates	.976	35	146	20	4	1	3
Hoffman, Dodgers	.943	11	47	3	3	0	3
Isava, Royals	.970	17	73	24	3	1	5
Jennings, Royals	.987	13	67	10	1	0	2
King, Twins	.969	28	136	18	5	1	3
Lachmann, Indians	1.000	2	5	0	0	0	0
Lanfranco, Astros	.973	26	117	29	4	1	13
Lindsay, Rangers	.983	21	142	29	3	2	2
Matouzas, Yankees	.981	25	190	22	4	2	7
McGough, White Sox	.988	11	66	16	1	0	3
McKeel, Red Sox	.959	9	42	5	2	0	4
McMullan, Rangers	1.000	24	151	21	0	0	7
Munoz, Reds	1.000	2	6	1	0	0	1
Nixon, Pirates	.977	32	151	22	4	0	9
Nurre, Dodgers	.975	24	110	7	3	0	3
Owen, Braves	.949	10	51	5	3	1	2
Pacheco, Expos	.967	4	26	3	1	0	1
Pages, Expos	.992	34	220	23	2	1	7
Patrizi, Mets	.957	28	193	27	10	0	8
Phillips, Expos	.963	13	94	10	4	1	1
Prater, Twins	1.000	1	3	0	0	0	0
Ramirez, Twins	.971	25	185	18	6	3	10
Robledo, White Sox	.965	32	248	26	10	1	3
Salcedo, Yankees	.935	10	41	2	3	0	5
Sanchez, Expos	.986	9	59	11	1	0	3
Santana, Expos	.974	5	37	0	1	0	1
Schultz, Indians	1.000	1	3	1	0	0	0
Schwartz, Indians	.993	24	113	25	1	2	4
Smith, Astros	.960	23	132	34	7	0	7
Soto, Red Sox	1.000	6	11	3	0	0	1
Steele, Mets	.963	13	71	7	3	0	0
Stewart, Royals	1.000	4	13	6	0	1	1
Strickland, Royals	.979	42	232	54	6	1	15
Sued, Indians	.964	8	50	4	2	0	4
Sweeney, Dodgers	1.000	18	66	12	0	0	7
Tackett, Red Sox	1.000	6	34	3	0	1	1
Taylor, White Sox	.987	16	68	10	1	0	1
Valdez, Dodgers	.979	34	179	56	5	3	9
Vogel, White Sox	.973	27	134	12	4	1	10
Ch. Williams, Mets	.972	5	34	1	1	0	1
Cl. Williams, Rangers	.967	27	150	28	6	2	10

PITCHERS

Player and Club	Pct.	G.	PO.	A.	E.	DP.
Abel, Twins	.786	23	3	8	3	0
Allen, Red Sox	1.000	7	1	5	0	0
Altaffer, White Sox°	.500	6	0	1	1	0
Alvarez, Expos	.938	11	3	12	1	0
Anacki, Red Sox	1.000	12	0	3	0	0
Archer, Braves	1.000	14	0	3	0	1
Arias, Pirates°	1.000	17	2	7	0	0
Ashley, Expos	1.000	10	0	2	0	0
Asp, Twins	1.000	13	8	6	0	0
August, Astros	1.000	7	2	6	0	0
Ayala, Rangers	.571	18	1	3	3	0
Baaske, Twins	.750	15	0	3	1	0
Baldwin, White Sox	.846	9	2	9	2	0
Balentine, Reds°	.867	12	1	12	2	0
Batista, Expos	.944	9	3	14	1	0
Belmonte, Mets	.889	18	2	6	1	1
Bennett, Astros	.750	22	2	4	2	1
Bere, White Sox	.625	16	2	3	3	0
Berson, Twins°	.000	5	0	0	1	0
Berthau, Rangers	1.000	12	5	7	0	0
Berumen, Royals	.833	5	2	3	1	0
Black, Astros	1.000	9	0	2	0	0
Boatman, Astros	.882	13	4	11	2	1
Borowski, White Sox	.818	12	2	7	2	1
Botts, Dodgers	.667	15	0	8	4	0
Bouton, Rangers	1.000	26	0	8	0	1
Bradley, Pirates	.941	10	4	12	1	1
Brea, Royals°	.500	6	0	1	1	0
Bridges, Braves	1.000	11	0	3	0	0
Brothers, Royals	.800	17	1	3	1	0
D. Brown, Astros	.667	4	0	2	1	0
E. Brown, Astros	1.000	10	0	1	0	0
Broyles, Dodgers	.727	11	0	8	3	0
Bryan, Braves°	1.000	6	2	2	0	0
Budnick, Royals	1.000	18	6	2	0	1
Bullard, Astros	1.000	4	2	2	0	0
Burgo, Red Sox	.846	5	4	7	2	0
Cain, Rangers	.750	16	2	7	3	0
Caridad, Twins	1.000	5	0	1	0	0
Carroll, Dodgers°	1.000	18	1	11	0	0

PITCHERS—Continued

Player and Club	Pct.	G.	PO.	A.	E.	DP.
Castro, Dodgers	1.000	10	3	21	0	1
Centeno, Red Sox	.692	16	1	8	4	0
Chrisman, Royals	1.000	8	1	8	0	1
Clelland, Expos	.867	12	3	10	2	3
Cofer, Indians	.929	7	4	9	1	0
Conley, Expos	.833	10	1	4	1	1
Coombs, Pirates	.818	12	5	4	2	1
Corbell, Mets	1.000	17	0	5	0	0
Jorge Correa, Astros	.667	9	1	5	3	0
Jose Correa, Twins	.857	14	1	11	2	0
Cortes, White Sox	1.000	6	0	3	0	0
Crawford, Indians	.786	10	1	10	3	1
Creamer, Braves*	.500	6	0	1	1	0
Cronin, Braves	1.000	7	2	8	0	1
Cruz, Dodgers	.700	17	2	5	3	0
Culberson, White Sox	1.000	3	0	1	0	0
Curry, Red Sox	1.000	3	1	0	0	0
Daniel, Dodgers*	.800	17	1	3	1	1
Davis, Dodgers	.769	17	3	7	3	0
Day, Indians	.867	19	2	11	2	0
C. DeLaCruz, White Sox	1.000	3	1	0	0	0
J. DeLaCruz, Astros	.889	18	3	5	1	0
Delgado, Red Sox	.889	25	5	11	2	0
DeVaughan, Rangers	1.000	15	1	8	0	0
Diaz, Reds*	.833	13	0	10	2	0
Dinuzzo, White Sox	.000	3	0	0	1	0
Dunbar, Yankees*	1.000	3	0	3	0	0
Duval, Rangers	1.000	6	0	2	0	0
Fajardo, Pirates	1.000	5	1	6	0	0
Farmer, Astros	1.000	3	2	1	0	0
Farnsworth, Dodgers*	.882	12	4	11	2	1
Faw, Yankees	.880	12	2	20	3	0
Fenton, Reds	1.000	10	1	4	0	0
Fernandez, White Sox	1.000	2	3	0	0	0
Ferran, Indians*	.500	12	1	1	2	1
Fleet, Indians	.900	12	3	6	1	1
C. Foster, Royals	.500	9	1	0	1	0
K. Foster, Expos	1.000	4	0	5	0	0
French, Pirates	1.000	14	6	7	0	0
G. Fritz, White Sox*	.833	12	1	4	1	0
S. Fritz, Twins	1.000	8	2	7	0	1
Fyock, Royals	.824	11	7	7	3	0
Fe. Garcia, Reds	.867	21	2	11	2	0
Fr. Garcia, Braves	.875	7	3	4	1	0
Giberti, Rangers*	.903	13	1	27	3	0
Gilbert, Yankees	1.000	10	3	0	0	0
Gobel, Pirates*	1.000	18	5	4	0	0
Gonzales, Red Sox	.963	14	3	23	1	1
Goytia, Pirates	1.000	11	1	1	0	0
Griffin, Reds	.929	11	4	9	1	1
Hampton, Astros	1.000	1	0	3	0	0
Hasenzahl, Indians*	1.000	20	3	13	0	0
A. Hayes, Twins	.500	3	0	1	1	0
J. Hayes, Yankees	.500	11	1	0	1	0
Henn, Royals	.846	13	3	8	2	1
Henson, Rangers	.667	4	1	1	1	0
F. Hernandez, Indians	.842	11	3	13	3	0
H. Hernandez, Mets	1.000	7	1	3	0	0
J. Hernandez, Astros	1.000	15	2	5	0	0
Hines, Yankees*	.667	11	0	6	3	0
Hoey, White Sox	1.000	9	1	2	0	0
Holcomb, Rangers*	1.000	2	0	1	0	0
Honeycutt, Braves*	.700	13	2	5	3	0
Hooper, Pirates	.957	13	2	20	1	2
Hoppe, Twins	.750	9	4	8	4	0
Houk, Twins	1.000	2	0	1	0	0
Hulme, White Sox	.857	10	2	4	1	0
Hunter, Pirates	.818	9	2	7	2	1
Jean, White Sox	.731	13	4	15	7	0
Johnson, Rangers	.833	15	0	5	1	0
Juarbe, Twins	.846	23	8	3	2	1
Kempfer, Braves	.750	16	2	7	3	0
Kindall, Yankees*	1.000	4	0	3	0	0
King, Twins	1.000	1	0	3	0	0
Kite, Red Sox	1.000	4	0	1	0	0
Koller, Braves	.900	13	3	6	1	0
Kunz, Rangers*	1.000	9	2	4	0	1
Landis, Twins	.875	19	5	9	2	0
Langan, Mets	1.000	12	3	3	0	0
Langdon, Indians*	.714	6	1	4	2	0
Langford, Reds	.909	15	3	7	1	1
Laviano, Yankees	.889	17	2	6	1	1
Ledwik, Braves	.900	22	3	6	1	0
A. Lee, Royals	.857	12	5	7	2	2
T. Lee, Royals	.900	14	1	8	1	0
LeMaster, Red Sox	.667	9	1	1	1	0
Lemon, Braves	1.000	2	0	4	0	0
Lindaman, Twins	.714	10	2	3	2	1
Lindsay, Mets*	1.000	6	1	2	0	0
Locke, Astros	1.000	3	0	2	0	1
Locklear, White Sox*	.875	14	2	5	1	1
Madrigal, Rangers	1.000	12	0	5	0	0
Maldonado, Dodgers*	1.000	17	1	7	0	0
Mallicoat, Astros*	.778	7	1	6	2	1
Maloney, Red Sox*	1.000	17	2	18	0	1
Manfred, Mets	.923	14	6	6	1	0
Marshall, White Sox*	.857	14	0	6	1	0
Martinez, Mets	.966	13	7	21	1	0
Matthews, Dodgers*	1.000	11	5	11	0	2
McClain, Reds	.852	12	6	17	4	3
McGough, Rangers	.933	13	3	11	1	1
McGraw, White Sox	.750	10	0	9	3	0
Miceli, Royals	.846	27	3	8	2	0
Micucci, White Sox	.667	4	0	2	1	1
Middaugh, White Sox	1.000	2	0	1	0	1
Mieses, Twins	.824	25	6	8	3	1
Miller, Red Sox	1.000	3	1	6	0	0
Mitchelson, Red Sox*	.889	5	0	8	1	0
Morgan, Indians	1.000	6	2	5	0	0
Mosley, Red Sox*	1.000	2	0	2	0	0
Navarro, Astros	.875	13	2	12	2	0
Niemeyer, Red Sox	1.000	14	9	9	0	1
Nieves, Astros	.765	10	4	9	4	1
Nix, Astros*	.818	13	1	8	2	1
Oliver, Rangers*	1.000	3	0	3	0	0
Ortega, Expos*	.889	20	2	6	1	1
Pacheco, Expos	1.000	6	0	2	0	0
Painter, Red Sox	1.000	5	2	3	0	1
Parra, Dodgers	.846	10	4	7	2	0
C. Perez, Expos*	.923	13	4	8	1	0
D. Perez, Astros	.857	10	2	4	1	0
Perigny, White Sox	1.000	7	2	1	0	0
Person, Indians	1.000	8	1	1	0	0
Petit, Braves	1.000	6	1	0	0	0
Phillips, Rangers	.500	3	1	0	1	0
Pike, Pirates	.750	8	3	0	1	0
Potts, Braves*	.667	23	2	4	3	0
Powell, Expos	.909	10	8	22	3	3
Powers, Red Sox	1.000	3	0	5	0	0
Prats, Astros*	.833	20	1	4	1	0
Quaid, Astros*	1.000	12	1	10	0	0
QUERO, Rangers*	1.000	13	8	26	0	1
Racobaldo, Dodgers	.909	16	4	6	1	0
H. Ramirez, Mets	.800	11	1	7	2	0
R. Ramirez, Pirates*	.846	11	1	10	2	2
Renko, Expos	1.000	2	0	1	0	0
Rhoades, Rangers	.833	8	1	4	1	1
Rinaldi, Astros*	.750	13	0	6	2	0
Rivera, Yankees	1.000	22	5	5	0	0
Roper, Reds	.875	13	1	13	2	2
Rosado, Indians	1.000	3	1	2	0	0
Roskom, Twins	.947	10	5	13	1	0
Ruiz, White Sox	.750	7	1	2	1	0
Rumer, Yankees*	.842	12	3	13	3	0
Rutter, Braves	.909	16	2	8	1	0
Santaella, Yankees	.714	14	1	4	2	0
Santiago, Yankees	.833	23	7	7	2	1
Sawyer, Indians	.818	22	3	6	2	0
Schorr, Mets	.923	12	2	10	1	0
Seiler, Yankees*	1.000	16	2	4	0	0
Seymour, Mets	.900	9	3	6	1	0
Shade, Pirates	1.000	4	1	0	0	0
Shehan, Expos*	.875	16	2	5	1	0
Sides, Indians	.667	3	0	4	2	0
M.D. Smith, Braves*	1.000	7	1	2	0	0
M.S. Smith, Yankees	.750	6	1	2	1	1
O. Smith, Mets*	1.000	13	5	10	0	2
R. Smith, White Sox	.786	7	1	10	3	0
Juan Sosa, Red Sox	1.000	12	3	8	0	0
Juan R. Sosa, Pirates	1.000	16	4	5	0	0
Sparks, Pirates	1.000	16	7	9	0	3
Spires, Braves	1.000	8	1	3	0	0
Springer, Yankees	1.000	4	0	4	0	0
Stafford, Rangers	.857	8	3	3	1	0
Stewart, Royals	.800	13	1	3	1	0
M. Sweeney, Indians	.750	10	4	8	4	1
R. Sweeney, Dodgers	1.000	2	0	2	0	1
Taylor, Twins	.824	14	0	14	3	1
Thibert, Yankees	.955	13	9	12	1	2
Tobin, Reds	.813	13	5	8	3	1
Toth, Royals	1.000	7	5	4	0	0
Vanderwel, White Sox	.667	2	1	1	1	0
Vanryn, Expos*	.714	10	1	4	2	0
Vasquez, Braves	1.000	13	3	10	0	1
Vejar, Astros	1.000	13	2	3	0	1
Vivas, Reds	.833	23	0	5	1	0
Watson, Rangers	1.000	10	2	0	0	0
Way, Pirates*	1.000	12	1	4	0	0
West, Royals	.917	16	7	4	1	0
G. White, Expos*	1.000	11	0	13	0	1
R. White, Pirates	1.000	7	2	6	0	0
Whitman, Expos	1.000	14	1	4	0	0
Wickman, White Sox	1.000	2	1	1	0	0
Wicks, Expos	.917	18	4	7	1	0
Wiggins, Reds	.846	14	4	7	2	1
Williams, Mets	.889	15	1	7	1	0
Winiarski, Indians	1.000	13	2	12	0	0
Wyatt, Reds	.500	11	0	1	1	0

The following players did not have any fielding statistics at the positions indicated or appeared only as a designated hitter, pinch-hitter or pinch-runner: Arendt, of; Carroll, of; G. Day, 1b; Devereaux, p; Dorante, dh, ph; Dorsey, p; Evangelista, ss; Flinn, ph, dh; M. Garcia, 3b; Gilligan, 3b; Guerra, 2b; Harris, 3b; R. Hernandez, of, p; Hoffman, 3b; House, c; Jacobs, p; Jarad, dh; Kemp, p; Konopki, p; Lehnerz, p; Marin, 3b; Mejia, p; T. Moore, p; J. Morgan, p; F. Parra, 1b; F. Ramirez, p; Romero, 3b; P. Sanchez, 3b; Wegmann, p; D. Wilson, p.

CLUB PITCHING

Club	ERA.	G.	CG.	ShO.	Sv.	IP.	H.	R.	ER.	HR.	HB.	BB.	Int. BB.	SO.	WP.	Bk.
Yankees	2.44	62	4	8	13	528.0	388	221	143	6	25	193	2	505	50	21
Mets	2.58	60	8	6	14	508.2	427	226	146	10	22	156	4	432	43	27
Expos	2.89	63	1	6	14	532.2	457	218	171	12	20	185	4	421	35	21
Rangers	2.92	64	2	8	26	543.1	491	229	176	21	33	154	4	484	40	26
White Sox	3.04	63	1	4	14	541.1	471	285	183	11	25	189	5	514	45	27
Braves	3.15	62	7	2	14	533.2	470	287	187	17	23	231	3	415	63	37
Dodgers	3.36	64	3	5	17	551.0	501	257	206	7	27	247	2	413	35	14
Pirates	3.44	63	3	5	11	530.2	491	280	203	7	47	209	4	425	31	31
Reds	3.54	64	1	5	22	564.0	503	278	222	9	25	284	7	402	50	17
Astros	3.61	64	2	5	6	551.1	445	275	221	10	56	300	3	413	55	22
Twins	3.66	63	5	3	19	550.1	518	320	224	21	32	232	4	436	59	40
Royals	3.67	64	0	3	13	545.0	496	291	222	7	31	320	16	360	48	14
Red Sox	3.98	63	8	5	11	563.2	562	311	249	15	15	258	5	315	50	16
Indians	4.21	63	6	0	10	539.1	526	353	252	21	31	296	3	390	61	35

PITCHERS' RECORDS

(Leading Qualifiers for Earned-Run Average Leadership—50 or More Innings)

*Throws lefthanded.

Pitcher—Club	W.	L.	Pct.	ERA.	G.	GS.	CG.	GF.	ShO.	Sv.	IP.	H.	R.	ER.	HR.	HB.	BB.	Int. BB.	SO.	WP.
Rivera, Yankees	5	1	.833	0.17	22	1	1	12	1	1	52.0	17	3	1	0	2	7	0	58	2
Roper, Reds	7	2	.778	0.97	13	13	0	0	0	0	74.0	41	10	8	1	3	31	0	76	2
O. Smith, Mets*	6	5	.545	1.36	13	13	3	0	1	0	79.1	53	21	12	1	4	28	0	89	6
Martinez, Mets	8	3	.727	1.57	13	13	4	0	2	0	92.0	68	27	16	1	1	9	0	90	4
Rumer, Yankees*	6	3	.667	1.70	12	12	2	0	0	0	74.0	34	23	14	1	3	21	0	88	4
Griffen, Reds	4	2	.667	1.71	11	8	1	2	1	1	58.0	44	15	11	0	5	9	0	38	0
Vanryn, Expos*	5	3	.625	1.74	10	9	0	0	0	0	51.2	44	13	10	0	2	15	0	56	0
Fe. Garcia, Reds	4	0	1.000	1.76	21	0	0	10	0	2	51.0	44	12	10	1	2	18	0	25	2
Hines, Yankees*	5	2	.714	1.77	11	9	0	0	0	0	61.0	44	18	12	0	2	19	0	73	9
D. Perez, Royals	2	4	.333	1.95	10	10	0	0	0	0	50.2	43	20	11	0	1	11	0	37	4

Departmental Leaders: G—Miceli, 27; W—Gonzales, 9; L—Borowski, Coombs, 8; Pct.—Maloney, 1.000; GS—Several pitchers tied with 13; CG—Gonzales, Martinez, 4; GF—Bouton, 26; ShO—Martinez, 2; Sv.—Bouton, 17; IP—Martinez, 92.0; H—Gonzales, 88; R—Borowski, 47; ER—Borowski, 38; HR—Giberti, Winiarski, 5; HB—Crawford, Nieves, Nix, 8; BB—Abel, 63; IBB—Miceli, 5; SO—Martinez, 90; WP—Rutter, Tobin, 12.

(All Pitchers—Listed Alphabetically)

Pitcher—Club	W.	L.	Pct.	ERA.	G.	GS.	CG.	GF.	ShO.	Sv.	IP.	H.	R.	ER.	HR.	HB.	BB.	Int. BB.	SO.	WP.
Abel, Twins	3	2	.600	2.74	29	9	0	9	0	1	69.0	49	35	21	0	1	63	0	61	11
Allen, Red Sox	0	3	.000	8.47	7	2	0	3	0	2	17.0	23	17	16	1	0	11	0	14	3
Altaffer, White Sox*	1	0	1.000	3.09	6	0	0	4	0	2	11.2	10	7	4	0	1	3	0	14	1
Alvarez, Expos	5	2	.714	2.60	11	10	0	0	0	0	52.0	42	17	15	0	1	16	0	47	1
Anacki, Red Sox	0	1	.000	6.75	12	4	0	1	0	0	22.2	32	20	17	0	1	13	0	20	2
Archer, Braves	2	2	.500	2.57	14	3	0	5	0	1	28.0	24	13	8	2	0	15	0	32	3
Arias, Pirates*	3	1	.750	2.30	17	0	0	11	0	0	27.1	21	9	7	0	2	12	0	26	1
Ashley, Expos	2	1	.667	1.17	10	0	0	0	0	0	23.0	13	4	3	0	1	9	1	28	3
Asp, Twins	4	3	.571	4.62	13	8	1	2	0	2	50.2	57	32	26	4	7	21	0	41	5
August, Astros	4	2	.667	1.53	7	7	0	0	0	0	29.1	25	10	5	1	0	2	0	22	1
Ayala, Rangers	2	5	.286	6.82	18	0	0	7	0	2	31.2	34	27	24	4	2	21	2	29	7
Baaske, Royals	1	2	.333	4.63	15	0	0	12	0	5	23.1	22	12	12	0	2	16	0	13	1
Baldwin, White Sox	1	6	.143	4.10	9	7	0	1	0	0	37.1	32	29	17	1	0	18	0	32	6
Balentine, Reds*	2	3	.400	5.03	12	10	0	0	0	0	48.1	48	33	27	3	1	33	0	44	7
Batista, Expos	4	3	.571	2.06	9	6	0	1	0	0	39.1	33	16	9	0	1	17	0	21	1
Belmonte, Mets	3	2	.600	2.68	18	3	0	5	0	1	43.2	36	23	13	0	2	17	0	27	4
Bennett, Astros	2	1	.667	4.58	22	0	0	6	0	0	37.1	39	23	19	0	2	26	0	22	5
Bere, White Sox	0	4	.000	2.37	16	2	0	6	0	1	38.0	26	19	10	1	1	19	0	41	1
Berson, Twins*	0	0	.000	8.53	5	0	0	1	0	0	6.1	9	8	6	0	1	3	0	5	4
Berthau, Rangers	4	1	.800	2.33	12	4	0	0	0	0	38.2	38	12	10	1	0	7	0	24	0
Berumen, Royals	0	2	.000	2.38	5	4	0	1	0	1	22.2	24	9	6	0	0	8	1	18	0
Black, Astros	0	0	.000	1.50	9	0	0	0	0	0	12.0	11	3	2	0	1	4	0	8	2
Boatman, Astros	3	4	.429	3.12	13	10	1	1	1	0	57.2	36	23	20	0	7	39	1	50	6
Borowski, White Sox	2	8	.200	5.58	12	11	0	0	0	0	61.1	74	47	38	3	2	25	0	67	2
Botts, Dodgers	5	5	.500	4.60	15	7	0	5	0	1	43.0	35	26	22	1	6	33	0	50	4
Bouton, Rangers	4	1	.800	0.94	26	0	0	26	0	17	28.2	19	6	3	1	4	9	0	45	5
Bradley, Pirates	3	5	.375	3.73	10	9	0	0	0	0	50.2	56	30	21	0	5	12	0	29	3
Brea, Royals*	0	1	.000	1.32	6	0	0	6	0	0	13.2	9	5	2	0	1	1	0	9	0
Bridges, Braves	1	1	.500	4.08	11	0	0	6	0	0	17.2	23	16	8	0	1	11	0	12	7
Brothers, Reds	1	3	.250	5.55	17	1	0	7	0	3	35.2	40	28	22	0	0	16	0	37	4
D. Brown, Astros	1	2	.333	6.43	4	3	0	0	0	0	14.0	18	10	10	0	1	6	0	12	2
E. Brown, Red Sox	0	1	.000	8.05	10	1	0	3	0	0	19.0	21	20	17	0	1	23	0	18	5
Broyles, Dodgers	4	2	.667	2.58	11	11	0	0	0	0	59.1	50	29	17	0	3	40	0	38	5
Bryan, Braves*	0	0	.000	3.60	6	3	0	1	0	0	20.0	17	12	8	0	1	10	0	14	3
Budnick, Royals	1	5	.167	5.59	18	5	0	6	0	1	37.0	50	34	23	2	4	23	0	12	6
Bullard, Astros	2	1	.667	1.64	4	3	0	0	0	0	11.0	5	3	2	0	0	1	0	6	2
Burgo, Red Sox	2	1	.667	1.55	5	5	1	0	0	0	29.0	22	7	5	0	0	9	1	18	0
Cain, Rangers	0	3	.000	3.75	16	1	0	4	0	1	36.0	27	22	15	1	5	5	0	37	2
Caridad, Twins	0	0	.000	7.71	5	1	0	1	0	0	7.0	5	6	6	0	1	8	0	2	1
Carroll, Dodgers*	2	1	.667	4.11	18	4	0	8	0	1	46.0	43	26	21	0	4	19	1	23	3
Castro, Dodgers	3	1	.750	4.25	10	10	0	0	0	0	55.0	65	30	26	2	0	7	0	35	1
Centeno, Red Sox	2	2	.500	6.10	16	1	0	6	0	1	41.1	52	35	28	4	2	23	1	21	6
Chrisman, Royals	2	0	1.000	3.86	6	0	0	5	0	1	16.1	14	8	7	0	0	8	1	10	0
Clelland, Expos	2	6	.250	4.50	12	12	0	0	0	0	58.0	51	39	29	0	1	36	0	45	7
Cofer, Indians	1	1	.500	0.96	7	1	2	2	0	0	28.0	10	6	3	0	2	13	0	21	3
Conley, Expos	1	2	.333	4.15	10	3	0	2	0	0	17.1	18	12	8	1	0	16	0	13	3
Coombs, Pirates	1	8	.111	5.02	12	11	1	0	0	0	52.0	66	39	29	2	3	20	0	47	4
Corbell, Mets	1	3	.250	2.02	17	3	0	11	0	4	35.2	35	15	8	0	1	10	0	19	2

Pitcher—Club	W.	L.	Pct.	ERA.	G.	GS	CG	GF	ShO	Sv.	IP.	H.	R.	ER.	HR	HB	BB.	Int. BB.	SO.	WP.
Jorge Correa, Astros	1	3	.250	6.12	9	8	0	0	0	0	32.1	25	26	22	2	4	23	0	26	7
Jose Correa, Twins	4	5	.444	4.55	14	8	1	0	0	0	59.1	55	37	30	4	6	13	0	47	3
Cortes, White Sox	0	0	.000	0.64	6	1	0	1	0	1	14.0	12	2	1	0	1	3	0	17	0
Crawford, Indians	2	3	.400	4.36	10	9	0	0	0	0	53.2	68	43	26	0	8	25	0	39	6
Creamer, Braves*	1	1	.500	3.86	6	1	0	0	0	0	14.0	14	11	6	1	0	6	0	12	2
Cronin, Braves	4	0	1.000	2.13	7	5	1	0	1	0	38.0	25	14	9	1	1	6	0	28	0
Cruz, Dodgers	0	4	.000	4.79	17	1	0	6	0	0	41.1	45	24	22	0	2	33	0	35	4
Culberson, White Sox	0	1	.000	1.59	3	0	0	0	0	0	5.2	6	6	1	0	0	0	0	7	1
Curry, Red Sox	1	2	.333	2.57	3	3	0	0	0	0	14.0	11	5	4	2	0	2	0	12	0
Daniel, Dodgers*	2	1	.667	2.86	17	2	0	14	0	6	28.1	16	11	9	0	0	18	0	21	1
Davis, Dodgers	2	2	.500	2.88	17	1	0	9	0	3	40.2	29	16	13	0	2	23	1	28	1
Day, Indians	1	3	.250	3.55	19	1	0	7	0	1	50.2	56	31	20	2	1	17	2	32	1
C. DeLaCruz, White Sox	0	0	.000	0.00	3	2	0	0	0	0	8.0	7	0	0	0	1	0	0	9	0
J. DeLaCruz, Astros	4	1	.800	2.15	18	0	0	17	0	0	29.1	21	8	7	1	1	5	1	14	0
Delgado, Red Sox	4	5	.444	3.59	25	0	0	23	0	6	52.2	54	25	21	0	0	14	3	30	2
DeVaughan, Rangers	2	1	.667	1.27	15	1	0	6	0	3	28.1	23	7	4	0	1	14	1	26	3
Devereaux, Rangers*	0	0	.000	16.20	1	0	0	0	0	0	1.2	5	3	3	0	0	0	0	3	0
Diaz, Reds*	4	1	.800	5.95	13	4	0	3	0	1	39.1	44	29	26	1	1	23	1	32	7
Dinuzzo, White Sox	0	0	.000	0.00	3	0	0	2	0	1	5.0	0	0	0	0	0	1	0	9	1
Dorsey, White Sox	0	0	.000	0.00	1	0	0	0	0	0	1.0	1	1	0	0	1	0	0	1	0
Dunbar, Yankees*	0	0	.000	3.00	3	0	0	2	0	1	6.0	4	2	2	0	2	3	0	7	0
Duval, Rangers	1	0	1.000	5.65	6	2	0	0	0	0	14.1	24	12	9	1	0	1	0	13	2
Fajardo, Pirates	1	1	.500	3.86	5	4	0	0	0	0	21.0	23	10	9	0	3	8	0	17	1
Farmer, Astros	1	0	1.000	0.00	3	3	0	0	0	0	12.0	5	0	0	0	1	1	0	19	0
Farnsworth, Dodgers*	3	2	.600	2.60	12	7	1	2	0	1	52.0	33	18	15	2	2	22	0	49	3
Faw, Yankees	7	5	.583	2.13	12	12	1	0	1	0	80.1	56	27	19	1	3	16	0	66	2
Fenton, Reds	1	2	.333	12.86	10	1	0	6	0	1	14.0	24	20	20	1	2	9	1	4	0
Fernandez, White Sox	1	0	1.000	3.60	2	2	0	0	0	0	10.0	11	4	4	0	2	1	0	16	1
Ferran, Indians*	0	4	.000	11.22	12	5	0	4	0	0	21.2	25	34	27	3	3	27	0	22	6
Fleet, Indians	1	6	.143	6.65	12	7	1	2	0	0	44.2	46	38	33	2	0	44	0	31	11
C. Foster, Royals	0	1	.000	8.35	9	3	0	1	0	0	18.1	18	18	17	1	1	20	0	11	4
K. Foster, Expos	2	0	1.000	5.06	4	0	0	1	0	0	10.2	9	6	6	0	1	6	0	11	0
French, Pirates	1	6	.143	4.40	14	8	0	1	0	0	47.0	40	29	23	1	7	26	1	42	7
G. Fritz, White Sox*	0	1	.000	3.80	12	0	0	8	0	1	23.2	32	14	10	0	1	4	2	17	2
S. Fritz, Twins	2	2	.500	3.44	8	6	1	1	0	0	36.2	26	18	14	2	2	17	0	31	3
Fyock, Royals	1	2	.333	2.45	11	10	0	1	0	0	55.0	49	24	15	0	3	30	0	27	4
Fe. Garcia, Reds	4	0	1.000	1.76	21	0	0	10	0	2	51.0	44	12	10	1	2	18	0	25	2
Fr. Garcia, Braves	0	2	.000	4.24	7	2	0	1	0	0	17.0	17	8	8	1	0	4	0	6	1
Giberti, Rangers*	4	5	.444	2.66	13	12	0	0	0	0	64.1	59	29	19	5	2	16	0	60	4
Gilbert, Yankees	0	2	.000	3.50	10	1	0	3	0	2	18.0	15	9	7	0	0	5	0	16	3
Gobel, Pirates*	1	2	.333	4.05	18	1	0	11	0	3	33.1	29	21	15	0	3	16	0	43	3
Gonzales, Red Sox	9	1	.900	3.04	14	12	4	0	0	0	91.2	88	45	31	3	0	22	0	42	4
Goytia, Pirates	1	1	.500	4.76	11	0	0	7	0	0	17.0	23	12	9	0	2	12	0	5	2
Griffen, Reds	4	2	.667	1.71	11	8	1	2	1	1	58.0	44	15	11	0	5	9	0	38	0
Hampton, Astros	0	0	.000	0.00	1	1	0	0	0	0	6.0	4	0	0	0	0	2	0	2	0
Hasenzahl, Indians*	2	3	.400	5.23	20	3	0	7	0	0	53.1	63	40	31	1	4	34	0	38	7
A. Hayes, Twins	0	0	.000	6.00	3	0	0	1	0	0	6.0	9	7	4	0	0	9	0	5	0
J. Hayes, Yankees	2	0	1.000	4.15	11	0	0	7	0	1	13.0	3	9	6	1	1	19	0	24	6
Henn, Royals	2	1	.667	4.91	13	0	0	7	0	0	18.1	18	12	10	0	0	17	3	13	3
Henson, Rangers	0	1	.000	3.86	4	4	0	0	0	0	11.2	9	6	5	1	0	7	0	8	1
F. Hernandez, Indians	4	4	.500	4.00	11	2	0	0	0	0	69.2	61	36	31	3	1	30	0	43	2
H. Hernandez, Mets	0	0	.000	7.45	7	1	0	3	0	0	9.2	18	12	8	0	0	7	0	5	4
J. Hernandez, Astros	0	3	.000	3.49	15	0	0	10	0	2	28.1	27	13	11	0	2	10	0	21	3
R. Hernandez, Reds	0	0	.000	0.00	1	0	0	1	0	0	0.1	0	0	0	0	0	0	0	0	0
Hines, Yankees*	5	2	.714	1.77	11	9	0	0	0	0	61.0	44	18	12	0	2	19	0	73	9
Hoey, White Sox	2	1	.667	0.45	9	0	0	4	0	1	20.0	7	5	1	0	2	5	0	17	1
Holcomb, Rangers*	1	0	1.000	5.40	2	0	0	0	0	0	3.1	4	2	2	0	0	1	0	3	1
Honeycutt, Braves*	3	4	.429	2.25	13	10	0	0	0	0	52.0	32	23	13	0	4	43	0	42	7
Hooper, Pirates	3	5	.375	2.71	13	13	0	1	0	0	66.1	56	29	20	0	7	22	0	67	4
Hoppe, Twins	4	1	.800	2.76	9	7	1	0	0	0	49.0	51	23	15	3	2	9	0	28	2
Houk, Twins	0	0	.000	9.00	2	0	0	2	0	0	2.0	4	2	2	0	0	0	0	0	1
Hulme, White Sox	1	1	.500	2.25	10	0	0	8	0	1	20.0	17	8	5	0	0	8	2	18	0
Hunter, Pirates	0	2	.000	2.06	9	5	0	3	0	2	35.0	17	13	8	0	5	14	0	30	0
Jacobs, Royals	1	1	.500	1.77	11	0	0	0	0	0	20.1	20	11	4	0	0	16	2	19	1
Jean, White Sox	2	5	.286	2.29	13	13	1	0	0	0	78.2	55	32	20	1	6	16	0	65	10
Johnson, Rangers	1	1	.500	2.82	15	0	0	6	0	0	22.1	25	8	7	1	2	10	1	27	1
Juarbe, Twins	2	4	.333	4.50	23	0	0	12	0	4	48.0	51	31	24	3	1	13	1	52	6
Kemp, Astros	0	0	.000	2.45	3	0	0	1	0	0	3.2	1	2	1	0	0	3	0	3	1
Kempfer, Braves	4	0	1.000	3.27	16	3	0	5	0	0	41.1	34	19	15	0	1	18	0	28	4
Kindall, Yankees*	0	1	.000	5.68	4	0	0	3	0	0	6.1	8	4	4	0	0	1	0	6	1
King, Twins	0	0	.000	4.50	1	0	0	0	0	0	2.0	5	2	1	0	0	0	0	3	0
Kite, Red Sox	0	1	.000	12.27	4	0	0	0	0	0	3.2	5	5	5	0	0	13	0	3	2
Koller, Braves	4	3	.571	2.12	13	8	1	1	1	0	51.0	45	24	12	0	4	13	2	45	4
Konopki, Red Sox	0	0	.000	9.00	1	0	0	0	0	0	1.0	2	1	1	0	0	1	0	1	0
Kunz, Rangers*	2	2	.500	2.86	9	2	0	0	0	0	22.0	17	10	7	0	1	9	0	20	1
Landis, Twins	4	3	.571	3.17	18	1	0	7	0	0	48.1	47	22	17	2	0	8	1	23	3
Langan, Mets	2	2	.500	4.44	12	1	0	3	0	0	26.1	24	17	13	2	2	12	0	26	7
Langdon, Indians*	3	2	.600	0.61	6	4	0	1	0	0	29.1	21	10	2	0	1	12	0	20	3
Langford, Reds	3	3	.500	2.35	15	0	0	8	0	1	30.2	27	10	8	0	2	17	1	27	2
Laviano, Yankees	0	3	.000	4.61	17	1	0	4	0	0	27.1	36	21	14	1	0	17	0	14	3
Ledwik, Braves	1	1	.500	1.72	22	0	0	14	0	8	31.1	26	14	6	0	1	4	0	19	0
A. Lee, Royals	4	3	.571	4.47	12	12	0	0	0	0	54.1	57	29	27	1	4	36	1	36	2
T. Lee, Royals	3	3	.500	2.90	14	6	0	6	0	0	49.2	43	25	16	0	3	34	0	37	5
Lehnerz, Mets	0	0	.000	0.00	3	0	0	0	0	0	0.0	0	1	0	0	1	2	0	0	1
LeMaster, Red Sox	0	0	.000	11.05	9	1	0	7	0	0	14.2	19	20	18	1	3	10	0	7	1
Lemon, Braves	1	0	1.000	2.25	2	1	0	1	0	0	12.0	14	5	3	0	0	1	0	13	0
Lindaman, Twins	2	1	.667	4.50	10	1	0	3	0	1	18.0	18	10	9	0	0	8	1	8	2
Lindsay, Mets*	0	1	.000	2.89	6	0	0	6	0	1	9.1	7	4	3	2	0	2	0	11	1
Locke, Astros	0	0	.000	11.57	3	0	0	1	0	0	2.1	4	3	3	0	0	3	0	1	0
Locklear, White Sox*	0	2	.000	4.07	14	0	0	10	0	1	24.1	25	17	11	1	1	7	0	29	3
Madrigal, Rangers	3	1	.750	2.11	12	9	0	1	0	0	47.0	40	13	11	0	2	10	0	43	0
Maldonado, Dodgers*	6	1	.857	3.71	17	0	0	10	0	3	34.0	43	17	14	0	6	6	0	31	0

Pitcher—Club	W.	L.	Pct.	ERA.	G.	GS.	CG.	GF.	ShO.	Sv.	IP.	H.	R.	ER.	HR.	HB.	BB.	Int. BB.	SO.	WP.
Mallicoat, Astros*	0	1	.000	4.96	7	4	0	0	0	0	16.1	15	15	9	0	3	15	0	21	4
Maloney, Red Sox*	7	0	1.000	2.26	17	8	0	6	0	2	63.2	52	20	16	1	2	35	0	28	7
Manfred, Mets	1	3	.250	3.18	14	3	0	7	0	3	39.2	31	16	14	2	2	17	3	28	5
Marshall, White Sox*	2	1	.667	3.50	14	5	0	5	0	1	43.2	36	20	17	2	0	13	1	33	4
Martinez, Mets	8	3	.727	1.57	13	13	4	0	2	0	92.0	68	27	16	1	1	9	0	90	4
Matthews, Dodgers*	5	3	.625	3.69	11	11	1	0	0	0	63.1	69	31	26	1	2	20	0	35	5
McClain, Reds	4	2	.667	2.76	12	12	0	0	0	0	65.1	44	27	20	1	3	38	1	57	6
McGough, Rangers	4	2	.667	2.73	13	11	1	0	1	0	59.1	44	20	18	1	6	17	0	48	3
McGraw, White Sox	4	6	.400	3.44	10	10	0	0	0	0	49.2	49	32	19	0	5	21	0	33	5
Mejia, Pirates	0	0	.000	67.50	1	0	0	0	0	0	0.2	1	5	5	0	1	4	0	0	0
Miceli, Royals	3	4	.429	3.91	27	0	0	13	0	4	53.0	45	27	23	0	2	29	5	48	4
Micucci, White Sox	0	1	.000	5.14	4	0	1	0	0	0	7.0	5	4	4	0	1	10	0	4	0
Middaugh, White Sox	0	0	.000	2.25	2	0	0	1	0	0	4.0	3	1	1	0	0	1	0	5	1
Mieses, Twins	0	5	.000	3.58	25	3	0	17	0	11	37.2	38	28	15	1	3	13	1	24	6
Miller, Red Sox	2	0	1.000	0.64	3	2	0	1	0	0	14.0	6	1	1	0	0	5	0	10	1
Mitchelson, Red Sox*	2	2	.500	3.92	5	1	0	1	0	0	20.2	19	10	9	2	1	6	0	15	1
Moore, Twins*	0	0	.000	0.00	1	0	0	1	0	0	1.0	0	0	0	0	0	0	0	0	0
J. Morgan, Indians	0	0	.000	0.00	1	0	0	1	0	0	1.0	1	0	0	0	0	2	0	2	1
S. Morgan, Indians	2	0	1.000	0.69	6	0	0	6	0	1	13.0	5	1	1	0	1	7	0	10	1
Mosley, Red Sox*	0	0	.000	0.00	2	0	0	1	0	0	4.0	1	0	0	0	0	1	0	4	0
Navarro, Astros*	3	6	.333	4.72	13	11	1	0	1	0	55.1	49	34	29	2	7	42	0	31	1
Niemeyer, Red Sox	3	3	.500	3.56	14	7	2	2	0	0	65.2	64	32	26	0	2	31	0	20	4
Nieves, Astros	2	3	.400	5.52	10	7	0	2	0	1	31.0	26	23	19	1	8	23	0	18	7
Nix, Astros*	2	1	.667	2.90	13	4	0	2	0	1	40.1	31	18	13	1	8	27	0	30	6
Oliver, Rangers*	0	0	.000	0.00	3	3	0	0	0	0	6.0	1	1	0	0	1	1	0	7	1
Ortega, Expos*	3	1	.750	2.63	20	0	0	13	0	3	37.2	34	12	11	4	2	10	0	21	5
Pacheco, Expos	1	0	1.000	5.19	6	0	0	0	0	0	8.2	11	7	5	0	0	4	0	5	2
Painter, Red Sox	2	0	1.000	1.38	5	5	1	0	0	0	32.2	23	8	5	0	1	9	0	27	1
Parra, Dodgers	5	3	.625	2.67	10	10	1	0	0	0	57.1	50	22	17	1	1	18	0	50	1
C. Perez, Expos*	3	1	.750	2.52	13	2	0	6	0	2	35.2	24	14	10	0	1	15	0	38	1
D. Perez, Royals	2	4	.333	1.95	10	10	0	0	0	0	50.2	43	20	11	0	1	11	0	37	4
Perigny, White Sox	1	1	.500	0.54	7	1	0	5	0	3	16.2	9	1	1	0	0	6	0	19	0
Person, Indians	0	2	.000	7.36	8	0	0	7	0	2	7.1	10	7	6	0	0	4	1	8	1
Petit, Braves	0	0	.000	6.48	6	0	0	2	0	0	8.1	6	9	6	0	1	12	0	6	1
Phillips, Rangers	0	0	.000	0.00	3	0	0	2	0	1	6.0	6	0	0	0	0	1	0	6	0
Pike, Pirates	0	1	.000	6.17	8	0	0	3	0	1	11.2	12	10	8	0	2	7	0	12	0
Potts, Braves*	5	2	.714	3.46	23	1	0	17	0	4	39.0	30	23	15	2	1	25	1	39	6
Powell, Expos	3	1	.750	4.30	10	9	0	0	0	0	52.1	49	30	25	3	4	14	0	28	3
Powers, Red Sox	0	1	.000	2.77	3	3	0	0	0	0	13.0	10	5	4	0	0	3	0	10	0
Prats, Astros*	2	0	1.000	3.16	20	1	0	10	0	2	42.2	32	17	15	0	4	19	1	48	4
Quaid, Astros*	3	1	.750	2.28	12	1	0	2	0	0	27.2	17	8	7	1	2	17	0	17	0
Quero, Rangers*	5	1	.833	2.12	13	11	1	0	1	0	63.2	59	18	15	4	4	8	0	54	2
Racobaldo, Dodgers	1	0	1.000	1.26	16	0	0	5	0	2	28.2	22	7	4	0	5	8	0	18	2
F. Ramirez, Twins	0	1	.000	18.00	1	0	0	0	0	0	1.0	4	3	2	0	1	0	0	0	0
H. Ramirez, Mets	3	5	.375	4.26	11	8	1	1	0	0	50.2	54	34	24	2	4	21	1	43	7
R. Ramirez, Pirates*	2	1	.667	0.53	11	3	0	0	0	0	33.2	20	4	2	1	1	18	0	27	1
Renko, Expos	1	0	1.000	1.80	2	1	0	1	0	0	5.0	6	1	1	0	0	1	0	5	0
Rhoades, Rangers	1	0	1.000	4.30	8	1	0	4	0	1	14.2	18	12	7	0	1	4	0	4	2
Rinaldi, Astros*	3	0	1.000	2.38	13	1	0	3	0	0	41.2	29	17	11	1	0	15	0	29	2
Rivera, Yankees	5	1	.833	0.17	22	1	1	12	1	1	52.0	17	3	1	0	2	7	0	58	2
Roper, Reds	7	2	.778	0.97	13	13	0	0	0	0	74.0	41	10	8	1	3	31	0	76	2
Rosado, Indians	0	1	.000	6.48	3	2	0	0	0	0	8.1	15	11	6	0	0	5	0	2	3
Roskom, Twins	4	2	.667	1.39	10	6	0	0	0	0	45.1	33	19	7	0	3	14	0	46	7
Ruiz, White Sox	1	0	1.000	1.42	7	0	0	4	0	1	12.2	19	7	2	1	0	5	0	10	0
Rumer, Yankees*	6	3	.667	1.70	12	12	2	0	0	0	74.0	34	23	14	1	3	21	0	88	4
Rutter, Braves	3	4	.429	3.59	16	6	1	2	0	0	57.2	54	29	23	4	4	17	0	49	12
Santaella, Yankees	3	2	.600	3.35	14	5	0	3	0	0	37.2	30	19	14	1	4	23	0	39	4
Santiago, Yankees	1	1	.500	1.82	23	0	0	12	0	4	39.2	38	13	8	0	3	7	0	27	2
Sawyer, Indians	3	1	.750	2.87	22	0	0	14	0	5	37.2	32	16	12	1	3	10	0	30	1
Schorr, Mets	2	3	.400	2.97	12	8	0	4	0	3	57.2	44	23	19	0	2	7	0	47	2
Seiler, Yankees*	2	1	.667	2.18	16	0	0	12	0	4	20.2	18	5	5	1	0	3	2	23	1
Seymour, Mets	3	1	.750	1.91	9	6	0	1	0	0	33.0	34	19	7	0	2	13	0	27	2
Shade, Pirates	0	0	.000	7.50	4	0	0	2	0	0	6.0	7	7	5	0	0	6	0	4	1
Shehan, Expos*	1	1	.500	1.52	16	1	0	10	0	3	29.2	27	9	5	0	1	12	0	25	3
Sides, Indians	0	1	.000	9.45	3	3	0	0	0	0	6.2	7	7	7	0	1	11	0	3	4
M.D. Smith, Braves*	0	0	.000	3.38	7	0	0	3	0	0	13.1	8	5	5	1	1	6	0	12	2
M.S. Smith, Yankees	0	2	.000	5.09	6	6	0	0	0	0	23.0	22	21	13	0	1	18	0	12	5
O. Smith, Mets*	6	5	.545	1.36	13	13	3	0	1	0	79.1	53	21	12	1	4	28	0	89	6
R. Smith, White Sox	1	3	.250	3.50	7	7	0	0	0	0	36.0	26	23	14	1	1	20	0	35	3
Juan Sosa, Red Sox	0	4	.000	5.19	12	8	0	1	0	0	43.1	60	35	25	1	2	27	0	15	5
Juan R. Sosa, Pirates	2	2	.500	4.82	16	1	0	5	0	0	37.1	42	27	20	2	3	13	1	15	2
Sparks, Pirates	3	1	.750	3.51	16	2	0	5	0	1	41.0	39	18	16	1	0	14	2	19	0
Spires, Braves	1	4	.200	3.76	8	5	0	1	0	0	26.1	36	26	11	1	0	9	0	11	0
Springer, Yankees	0	2	.000	1.20	4	4	0	0	0	0	15.0	10	6	2	0	0	4	0	17	1
Stafford, Rangers	2	1	.667	2.25	8	3	0	1	0	1	28.0	20	8	7	0	0	6	0	16	0
Stewart, Royals	1	3	.250	6.98	13	0	0	5	0	0	19.1	13	18	15	0	3	21	3	14	4
M. Sweeney, Indians	2	6	.250	3.15	10	10	1	0	0	0	60.0	45	34	21	4	2	36	0	50	4
R. Sweeney, Dodgers	0	0	.000	0.00	2	0	0	2	0	0	2.0	1	0	0	0	0	0	0	0	0
Taylor, Twins	3	1	.750	3.57	14	13	1	1	1	0	63.0	57	37	25	2	4	33	0	59	5
Thibert, Yankees	1	5	.167	4.67	13	11	0	0	0	0	54.0	53	41	28	1	4	30	0	35	7
Tobin, Reds	3	3	.500	4.11	13	13	0	0	0	0	57.0	54	38	26	0	2	36	1	26	12
Toth, Royals	2	2	.500	1.66	7	7	0	0	0	0	38.0	34	8	7	1	2	4	0	22	3
Vanderwel, White Sox*	0	1	.000	0.00	2	0	0	2	0	0	2.0	2	2	0	0	0	1	0	2	1
Vanryn, Expos*	5	3	.625	1.74	10	9	0	0	0	0	51.2	44	13	10	0	2	15	0	56	0
Vasquez, Braves	3	5	.375	4.19	13	13	3	0	0	0	66.2	65	36	31	3	3	31	0	47	11
Vejar, Astros	0	1	.000	6.86	13	0	0	1	0	0	21.0	25	19	16	0	4	11	0	13	2
Vivas, Reds	0	5	.000	3.29	23	0	0	20	0	12	38.1	41	17	14	1	1	8	2	18	2
Watson, Rangers	0	2	.000	5.74	10	0	0	5	0	0	15.2	19	13	10	1	2	7	0	11	5
Way, Pirates	1	0	1.000	1.80	12	0	0	12	0	4	15.0	13	6	3	0	1	1	0	15	0
Wegmann, Mets	0	0	.000	0.00	2	0	0	2	0	0	2.0	0	0	0	0	0	0	0	4	0
West, Royals	2	4	.333	4.42	16	7	0	3	0	0	55.0	37	31	27	2	5	46	0	34	7
G. White, Expos*	4	2	.667	3.14	11	11	1	0	0	0	57.1	50	21	20	3	3	12	0	41	5

Pitcher—Club	W.	L.	Pct.	ERA.	G.	GS.	CG.	GF.	ShO.	Sv.	IP.	H.	R.	ER.	HR.	HB.	BB.	Int. BB.	SO.	WP.
R. White, Pirates	3	1	.750	0.76	7	6	0	0	0	0	35.2	26	11	3	0	2	4	0	27	2
Whitman, Expos	1	0	1.000	1.17	14	0	0	13	0	3	23.0	14	3	3	0	1	0	0	23	0
Wickman, White Sox	2	0	1.000	2.45	2	2	0	0	0	0	11.0	7	4	3	0	0	1	0	15	2
Wicks, Expos	2	0	1.000	3.16	18	0	0	15	0	3	31.1	32	14	11	1	1	2	1	14	1
Wiggins, Reds	2	0	1.000	2.56	14	0	0	4	0	1	31.2	26	13	9	0	1	21	0	8	1
Williams, Mets	0	2	.000	2.73	15	1	0	9	0	1	29.2	23	15	9	0	1	11	0	16	3
Wilson, Indians	0	0	.000	0.00	1	0	0	1	0	0	3.2	2	0	0	0	0	0	0	4	0
Winiarski, Indians	2	3	.400	4.62	13	6	1	5	0	1	50.2	59	39	26	5	4	19	0	35	5
Wyatt, Reds	1	1	.500	9.30	11	2	0	2	0	0	20.1	26	26	21	0	2	25	0	10	2

BALKS—Hooper, 11; Koller, 8; Cronin, F. Hernandez, Juarbe, Landis, Petit, 7 each; Giberti, McGraw, Nieves, Pike, Sawyer, 6 each; Castro, Conley, Langford, Laviano, O. Smith, 5 each; Abel, Centeno, Clelland, Corbell, Crawford, Ferran, Gonzales, Honeycutt, Taylor, Thibert, 4 each; Baldwin, Boatman, Day, S. Fritz, A. Hayes, Johnson, Langan, Langdon, A. Lee, Lindaman, Locklear, Niemeyer, D. Perez, Rumer, Rutter, Sparks, Tobin, Wickman, Wicks, Williams, 3 each; Altaffer, Ashley, Balentine, Belmonte, Borowski, Botts, E. Brown, Bullard, Cain, Coombs, Jose Correa, Daniel, J. DeLaCruz, Fernandez, Fleet, French, Griffen, J. Hernandez, Hines, Jacobs, Jean, Kunz, Maldonado, Manfred, Martinez, McGough, Mitchelson, S. Morgan, Quero, H. Ramirez, Renko, Rinaldi, Roskom, Schorr, Seiler, M. Sweeney, Watson, R. White, Wiggins, 2 each; Asp, Ayala, Baaske, Batista, Bennett, Bere, Berson, Berthau, Black, Bouton, Brea, Bridges, Bryan, Budnick, Burgo, Caridad, Jorge Correa, Cortes, Creamer, Davis, Dunbar, Fajardo, Farnsworth, C. Foster, Fyock, Fr. Garcia, Hasenzahl, Henson, Holcomb, Hoppe, Houk, Hunter, Kindall, Ledwik, T. Lee, Lemon, Lindsay, Madrigal, Mallicoat, McClain, Ortega, Pacheco, Parra, Powell, R. Ramirez, Rosado, Ruiz, Santiago, M.D. Smith, M.S. Smith, R. Smith, Sosa (Pirates), Spires, Springer, Stafford, Vejar, Vivas, Way, Wegmann, G. White, Wyatt, 1 each.

COMBINATION SHUTOUTS—Correa-Bennett-DeLaCruz, Farmer-Nieves, Mallicoat-Navarro-Bennett-Hernandez, Astros; Broyles-Daniel, Broyles-Maldonado, Farnsworth-Davis, Farnsworth-Davis-Daniel, Parra-Daniel, Dodgers; Alvarez-Foster, Alvarez-Whitman, Batista-Conley, Clelland-Powell-Shehan, Perez-Whitman, Vanryn-Shehan, Expos; Belmonte-Manfred, Seymour-Manfred, Smith-Shaw, Mets; Hooper-Sosa-Arias, Ramirez-French-Arias-Way, Ramirez-Sparks-Way, White-Ramirez-Way, Pirates; Giberti-DeVaughan-Bouton, McGough-Ayala, McGough-Cain, McGough-Stafford-Bouton, Oliver-Berthau-Bouton, Quero-Stafford, Rangers; Roper-Garcia 2, Griffen-Brothers-Wyatt-Fenton, Griffen-Fenton, Reds; Anacki-Centeno-Mosley-Maloney, Burgo-Allen, Curry-Niemeyer-Delgado, Gonzales-Delgado, Maloney-Delgado, Red Sox; West-Miceli 2, Lee-Berumen, Royals; Fritz-Landis, Roskom-Juarbe, Twins; McGraw-Hoey, McGraw-Micucci, Smith-Marshall, Wickman-Bere-Locklear, White Sox; Faw-Rivera, Hines-Rivera, Hines-Santiago, Rumer-Rivera-Seiler, Rumer-Santiago-Seiler, Santaella-Gilbert-Seiler, Yankees.

NO-HIT GAMES—Smith, Mets, defeated Twins, 1-0, July 24; Rivera, Yankees, defeated Pirates, 3-0 (first game), August 31.

Pioneer League

SUMMER CLASS A CLASSIFICATION

CHAMPIONSHIP WINNERS IN PREVIOUS YEARS

1939—Twin Falls*	.581	1956—Boise	.561	1975—Great Falls	.577
1940—Salt Lake City	.608	1957—Salt Lake City	.650	1976—Great Falls	.577
Ogden (4th)*	.492	Billings†	.582	1977—Lethbridge	.629
1941—Boise	.623	1958—Great Falls	.582	1978—Billings x	.735
Ogden (2nd)*	.598	Boise†	.615	1979—Helena	.623
1942—Pocatello†	.690	1959—Boise	.633	Lethbridge y	.559
Boise	.683	Billings (2nd)*	.523	1980—Lethbridge y	.743
1943-44-45—Did not operate.		1960—Boise†	.686	Billings	.629
1946—Twin Falls‡	.585	Idaho Falls	.650	1981—Calgary	.657
Salt Lake City†	.585	1961—Boise	.638	Butte y	.557
1947—Salt Lake City	.618	Great Falls*	.571	1982—Medicine Hat y	.629
Twin Falls†	.600	1962—Boise§	.565	Idaho Falls	.600
1948—Pocatello	.611	Billings†	.706	1983—Billings y	.614
Twin Falls (2nd)*	.595	1963—Idaho Falls	.702	Calgary	.600
1949—Twin Falls	.624	Magic Valley†	.643	1984—Billings	.691
Pocatello (3rd)*	.595	1964—Treasure Valley	.615	Helena y	.647
1950—Pocatello	.635	1965—Treasure Valley	.530	1985—Great Falls	.771
Billings (3rd)*	.571	1966—Ogden	.591	Salt Lake City y	.657
1951—Salt Lake City	.618	1967—Ogden	.621	1986—Salt Lake City z	.643
Great Falls (3rd)*	.559	1968—Ogden	.609	Great Falls	.571
1952—Pocatello	.595	1969—Ogden	.620	1987—Salt Lake City z	.700
Idaho Falls (2nd)*	.573	1970—Idaho Falls	.629	Helena	.657
1953—Ogden	.679	1971—Great Falls	.643	1988—Great Falls z	.754
Salt Lake C. (4th)*	.527	1972—Billings	.694	Butte	.629
1954—Salt Lake City	.595	1973—Billings	.629	1989—Great Falls z	.791
Great Falls (4th)*	.530	1974—Idaho Falls	.569	Butte	.621
1955—Boise	.588				
Magic Valley (4th)*	.489				

*Won four-club playoff. †Won split-season playoff. ‡Ended first half in tie with Salt Lake City and won one-game playoff. §Ended first half in tie with Billings and Great Falls and won playoff. xBillings (first place) defeated Idaho Falls (second place) in First Place-Second Place playoff. yLeague divided into Northern and Southern divisions; won two-club playoff. zWon two-club playoff.

STANDING OF CLUBS AT CLOSE OF SEASON, AUGUST 31

NORTHERN DIVISION

Club	W.	L.	T.	Pct.	G.B.
Great Falls (Dodgers)	48	20	0	.706	....
Helena (Brewers)	37	28	0	.569	9½
Billings (Reds)	32	34	0	.485	15
Medicine Hat (Blue Jays)	20	46	0	.303	27

SOUTHERN DIVISION

Club	W.	L.	T.	Pct.	G.B.
Salt Lake City (Independent)	42	26	0	.618	....
Idaho Falls (Braves)	39	30	0	.557	4
Butte (Rangers)	37	30	0	.552	4½
Gate City (Independent)	15	55	0	.214	28

COMPOSITE STANDING OF CLUBS AT CLOSE OF SEASON, AUGUST 31

Club	GF.	SLC.	Hel.	IF.	But.	Bil.	MH.	GC.	W.	L.	T.	Pct.	G.B.
Great Falls (Dodgers)	...	4	7	6	3	7	14	7	48	20	0	.706	....
Salt Lake City (Independent)	3	...	5	8	6	3	4	13	42	26	0	.618	6
Helena (Brewers)	5	2	...	2	4	9	11	4	37	28	0	.569	9½
Idaho Falls (Braves)	1	6	5	...	9	3	3	12	39	31	0	.557	10
Butte (Rangers)	4	6	3	5	...	6	2	11	37	30	0	.552	10½
Billings (Reds)	7	4	4	4	0	...	8	5	32	34	0	.485	15
Medicine Hat (Blue Jays)	0	3	1	4	5	4	...	3	20	46	0	.303	27
Gate City (Independent)	0	1	3	1	3	2	4	...	15	55	0	.214	34

Gate City's home games played in Pocatello, Ida.

Major league affiliations in parentheses.

Playoffs—Great Falls defeated Salt Lake City, three games to none, to win league championship.

Regular-Season Attendance—Billings, 94,245; Butte, 30,116; Gate City, 20,926; Great Falls, 72,609; Helena, 40,524; Idaho Falls, 77,942; Medicine Hat, 13,350; Salt Lake City, 192,366. Total, 542,078. Playoffs (3 games)-6,695.

Managers—Billings, Dave Keller; Butte, Bump Wills; Gate City, Ed Creech; Great Falls, Joe Vavra; Helena, Gary Calhoun; Idaho Falls, Steve Curry; Medicine Hat, Garth Iorg; Salt Lake City, Nick Belmonte.

All-Star Team—1B—Mike Busch, Great Falls; 2B—Vince Castaldo, Helena; 3B—Tom Duffin, Salt Lake City; SS—Chris Brittain, Idaho Falls; OF— David Hulse, Butte; K.C. Gillum, Billings; Raul Mondesi, Great Falls; C—Todd Guggiana, Butte; DH—Kevin McMullan, Salt Lake City; P—William Ambos, Salt Lake City; RP—Michael Ferry, Billings; Manager of the Year—Steve Curry, Idaho Falls.

(Compiled by Howe Sportsdata International, Boston, Mass.)

CLUB BATTING

Club	Pct.	G.	AB.	R.	OR.	H.	TB.	2B.	3B.	HR.	RBI.	SH.	SF.	HP.	BB.	Int. BB.	SO.	SB.	CS.	LOB.
Butte	.313	67	2355	437	384	738	1015	112	27	37	391	6	26	23	286	6	361	95	42	533
Great Falls	.288	68	2401	435	257	692	1011	112	36	45	379	22	27	35	276	8	451	106	43	540
Salt Lake City	.285	68	2357	447	354	671	927	105	29	31	384	27	25	45	328	11	429	79	52	544
Billings	.280	66	2290	391	380	642	902	96	16	44	347	22	22	26	280	9	490	81	42	505
Idaho Falls	.277	70	2399	395	376	665	936	115	21	38	335	12	23	32	316	5	527	106	47	581
Helena	.268	65	2210	365	325	593	858	108	17	41	311	15	23	36	279	4	446	100	36	494
Gate City	.251	70	2306	279	510	579	792	96	21	25	244	19	19	20	246	6	566	84	39	515
Medicine Hat	.239	66	2244	264	427	536	745	92	21	25	224	8	8	21	213	7	485	82	37	464

INDIVIDUAL BATTING
(Leading Qualifiers for Batting Championship—189 or More Plate Appearances)

*Bats lefthanded.   †Switch-hitter.

Player and Club	Pct.	G.	AB.	R.	H.	TB.	2B.	3B.	HR.	RBI.	SH.	SF.	HP.	BB.	Int. BB.	SO.	SB.	CS.
Hulse, David, Butte*	.358	64	257	54	92	114	12	2	2	36	2	0	2	25	1	30	24	6
Gillum, Kenneth, Billings*	.356	57	225	50	80	115	14	3	5	43	0	1	4	20	1	45	13	2
Shave, Jonathan, Butte	.352	64	250	41	88	109	9	3	2	42	2	4	3	25	0	27	21	8
Guggiana, Todd, Butte*	.351	66	248	50	87	132	23	5	4	52	0	4	3	26	1	22	6	3
Bargas, Robert, Salt Lake City†	.348	58	221	44	77	92	5	2	2	36	3	0	4	20	2	30	6	5
Greer, Thurman, Butte*	.345	62	226	48	78	132	12	6	10	50	0	2	1	41	2	23	9	6
Ingram, Garey, Great Falls	.343	56	198	43	68	102	12	8	2	21	0	1	3	22	0	37	10	6
Castaldo, Vincent, Helena*	.335	62	236	54	79	127	20	2	8	47	3	2	4	29	1	36	10	5
Moberg, Michael, Salt Lake City	.331	68	269	64	89	119	12	3	4	38	3	2	4	41	0	38	12	8
Quinones, Eliezer, Billings	.330	54	215	38	71	99	8	1	6	46	0	5	1	17	0	27	10	4

Departmental Leaders: G—Karcher, Moberg, 68; AB—Moberg, 269; R—Moberg, 64; H—Hulse, 92; TB—Busch, 134; 2B—Guggiana, 23; 3B—Ingram, 8; HR—Busch, 13; RBI—T. Carter, 58; SH—Urcioli, 9; SF—Karcher, 8; HP—Several players tied with 6; BB—Brittain, 63; IBB—McMullen, 4; SO—Santiago, 76; SB—Burton, 34; CS—Burton, 10.

(All Players—Listed Alphabetically)

Player and Club	Pct.	G.	AB.	R.	H.	TB.	2B.	3B.	HR.	RBI.	SH.	SF.	HP.	BB.	Int. BB.	SO.	SB.	CS.
Adams, Gary, Gate City*	.263	65	217	26	57	97	7	3	9	31	2	3	1	16	1	58	5	3
Andrews, Daniel, Great Falls*	.276	41	98	12	27	28	1	0	0	9	0	0	0	8	1	12	1	1
Asai, Itsuki, Gate City*	.253	58	162	26	41	62	7	4	2	21	1	2	0	26	1	32	10	4
Atwater, Tyrone, Gate City*	.245	59	192	28	47	59	7	1	1	16	1	1	2	25	1	52	7	5
Baber, Larue, Helena	.150	23	80	7	12	16	1	0	1	3	1	1	0	7	0	28	2	3
Bargas, Robert, Salt Lake City†	.348	58	221	44	77	92	5	2	2	36	3	0	4	20	2	30	6	5
Battle, Howard, Medicine Hat	.266	61	233	25	62	96	17	1	5	32	0	0	2	15	2	38	5	2
Beaulac, Joseph, Salt Lake City*	.080	13	25	2	2	2	0	0	0	1	0	1	0	3	1	10	0	1
Beck, Robert, Helena	.250	32	100	11	25	41	6	2	2	14	0	3	1	6	0	21	2	1
Benjamin, Robert, Helena*	.311	20	61	14	19	31	4	1	2	10	0	0	0	20	0	20	6	0
Bielski, Richard, Salt Lake City	.285	46	137	23	39	64	8	4	3	27	3	3	6	21	0	44	0	3
Biggers, Brian, Salt Lake City	.296	38	98	19	29	33	2	1	0	11	1	1	1	9	0	18	1	0
Blackwell, Eric, Great Falls*	.313	60	163	33	51	80	7	5	4	31	1	1	1	36	3	40	12	5
Blevins, Gregory, Butte*	.237	41	118	17	28	44	7	0	3	20	0	2	1	10	0	28	0	2
Bohringer, Helmut, Great Falls	.238	10	21	7	5	5	0	0	0	4	0	1	0	6	0	1	1	1
Bourgeois, Jerry, Idaho Falls*	.000	5	1	0	0	0	0	0	0	0	0	0	0	0	0	0	0	0
Bowers, Brent, Medicine Hat*	.274	60	212	30	58	80	7	3	3	27	1	0	1	30	0	35	19	9
Briggs, Kenneth, Salt Lake City†	.227	35	88	15	20	37	6	1	3	17	0	1	1	14	0	22	2	2
Brittain, Grant, Idaho Falls*	.274	67	226	48	62	97	14	3	5	48	0	1	3	63	1	61	6	3
Burnett, Joe, Salt Lake City	.200	27	45	9	9	9	0	0	0	5	1	1	1	15	0	16	7	4
Burroughs, Eric, Billings*	.300	41	150	27	45	59	6	1	2	21	1	3	0	8	0	34	9	4
Burton, Christopher, Idaho Falls*	.305	66	256	47	78	101	13	2	2	29	0	2	2	30	1	43	34	10
Busch, Michael, Great Falls	.327	61	220	48	72	134	19	2	13	40	0	3	3	38	1	49	3	2
Carter, Michael, Helena	.307	61	241	45	74	91	11	3	0	30	2	5	6	16	0	20	22	7
Carter, Timothy, Helena	.279	63	233	40	65	116	15	0	12	58	0	2	6	32	1	56	3	1
Castaldo, Vincent, Helena*	.335	62	236	54	79	127	20	2	8	47	3	2	4	29	1	36	10	5
Castellanos, Miguel, Butte	.273	60	216	33	59	77	4	1	4	32	1	6	5	20	0	29	4	3
Chiyomaru, Akihiko, Gate City	.245	50	151	16	37	56	5	1	4	26	2	1	1	7	0	38	2	0
Choate, Mark, Medicine Hat	.234	62	214	30	50	65	7	1	2	22	2	1	7	33	0	51	11	2
Chumbley, Steven, Idaho Falls	.000	10	9	3	0	0	0	0	0	0	0	0	0	1	0	4	0	0
Coble, Antony, Helena	.240	32	121	10	29	46	6	1	3	16	0	2	0	6	0	29	2	0
Columbano, Jeffery, Idaho Falls*	.406	17	32	6	13	15	2	0	0	3	0	0	0	1	0	1	0	0
Coolbaugh, Michael, Medicine Hat	.190	58	211	21	40	55	9	0	2	16	1	2	1	13	0	47	3	2
Couture, Michael, Helena	.217	42	120	27	26	41	4	1	3	17	1	0	5	25	0	39	7	1
Crump, Gerald, Medicine Hat*	.000	1	5	0	0	0	0	0	0	0	0	0	0	0	0	0	0	0
Czarnetzki, Michael, Salt Lake City	.185	17	27	4	5	6	1	0	0	4	0	0	1	2	1	3	0	0
Daniels, Lee, Medicine Hat	.168	31	95	3	16	19	3	0	0	9	0	1	2	7	1	39	4	2
Diggs, Antonio, Helena†	.256	42	129	18	33	38	5	0	0	13	1	2	2	11	0	19	10	5
Dipino, Paul, Idaho Falls†	.222	4	9	0	2	2	0	0	0	0	0	0	0	1	0	2	0	0
Doyle, James, Salt Lake City	.203	40	128	28	26	32	3	0	1	17	0	2	3	22	0	12	12	2
Drabinski, Marek, Idaho Falls	.265	52	151	19	40	46	6	0	0	14	1	1	2	21	0	24	0	2
Duffin, Thomas, Salt Lake City	.306	65	245	56	75	111	16	4	4	48	2	4	6	33	3	34	11	3
Edwards, Todd, Helena*	.352	35	108	20	38	47	7	1	0	17	0	1	1	20	1	12	5	3
Farrish, Keoki, Great Falls	.252	61	202	24	51	63	7	1	1	26	1	1	1	18	0	41	5	2
Filotei, Robert, Billings	.197	57	183	33	36	46	3	2	1	18	3	2	3	35	0	36	5	5
Fister, Corbett, Idaho Falls	.208	38	106	19	22	31	6	0	1	13	1	1	2	19	0	17	2	2
Flores, Juan, Helena	.287	33	108	15	31	36	5	0	0	11	0	1	4	10	0	14	3	1
Frauenhoffer, Michael, Great Falls	.231	41	108	16	25	29	2	1	0	12	2	3	1	12	0	23	4	1
Fults, Nathan, Idaho Falls	.065	13	31	2	2	2	0	0	0	1	0	0	0	2	0	12	0	0
Garcia, Anastacio, Medicine Hat	.188	18	48	3	9	12	3	0	0	3	0	0	1	5	0	12	0	0
Garczyk, Edward, Salt Lake City	.214	12	28	6	6	7	1	0	0	3	0	0	0	6	0	14	0	0
Gillum, Kenneth, Billings*	.356	57	225	50	80	115	14	3	5	43	0	1	4	20	1	45	13	2
Giovanola, Edward, Idaho Falls*	.388	25	98	25	38	44	6	0	0	13	2	1	0	17	0	9	6	2
Glenn, Leon, Helena*	.235	42	153	19	36	58	6	2	4	26	1	1	1	29	1	41	12	3
Gordon, Keith, Billings	.234	49	154	21	36	46	5	1	1	14	2	1	3	24	1	51	6	4
Gray, Daniel, Great Falls	.267	38	120	22	32	50	3	3	3	13	1	0	2	14	0	22	2	0
Greer, Thurman, Butte*	.345	62	226	48	78	132	12	6	10	50	0	2	1	41	2	23	9	6
Gress, Loren, Idaho Falls	.330	53	197	26	65	91	10	2	4	33	0	2	1	13	1	53	1	2
Griffin, Timothy, Great Falls	.322	40	143	26	46	66	11	0	3	25	0	4	3	10	2	33	2	1
Guggiana, Todd, Butte*	.351	66	248	50	87	132	23	5	4	52	0	4	3	26	1	22	6	3
Hammargren, Roy, Billings*	.296	57	189	36	56	95	12	0	9	45	1	1	2	36	1	68	5	3
Harmes, Kristopher, Medicine Hat*	.261	50	165	18	43	56	8	1	1	18	0	0	1	24	1	21	2	4
Harris, Freeman, Salt Lake City	.244	39	90	8	22	31	5	2	0	15	0	2	2	14	0	23	2	3
Heilgeist, James, Helena*	.097	33	93	2	9	10	1	0	0	6	0	0	2	4	0	47	0	3
Hines, Keith, Medicine Hat	.262	38	126	15	33	52	7	3	2	14	2	0	1	14	1	41	4	2
Hood, Randall, Helena	.315	48	178	43	56	84	11	4	3	20	3	0	5	37	0	30	7	3
Horne, Tyrone, Gate City*	.282	56	202	26	57	75	11	2	1	13	2	2	2	24	1	62	23	8
Hulse, David, Butte*	.358	64	257	54	92	114	12	2	2	36	2	0	2	25	1	30	24	6
Hyers, Timothy, Medicine Hat*	.219	61	224	29	49	66	7	2	2	19	1	2	0	29	1	22	4	1
Ingram, Garey, Great Falls	.343	56	198	43	68	102	12	8	2	21	0	1	3	22	0	37	10	6
Jones, Kevin, Billings†	.278	46	162	24	45	68	8	0	5	22	3	2	1	9	0	36	2	1
Karcher, Richard, Idaho Falls*	.304	68	247	34	75	116	15	4	6	45	0	8	0	26	1	43	8	2

Player and Club	Pct.	G.	AB.	R.	H.	TB.	2B.	3B.	HR.	RBI.	SH.	SF.	HP.	BB.	Int. BB.	SO.	SB.	CS.
Keighley, Steven, Salt Lake City	.261	34	92	23	24	33	4	1	1	16	1	0	4	33	0	17	1	0
Kelly, Brian, Salt Lake City	.280	28	82	14	23	34	4	2	1	12	1	0	3	11	0	11	3	3
Kidd, Dennis, Salt Lake City°	.343	8	35	6	12	19	2	1	1	3	0	0	1	0	0	7	1	3
Loeb, Marc, Medicine Hat	.302	29	96	15	29	40	5	0	2	12	1	1	0	13	0	28	2	1
Lucky, Keith, Idaho Falls	.240	13	25	4	6	14	2	0	2	6	0	0	0	3	0	4	0	1
Lund, Edward, Great Falls	.162	31	68	11	11	19	3	1	1	8	1	2	2	4	0	8	1	1
Marabella, Antonio, Gate City°	.252	59	206	18	52	61	9	0	0	32	2	3	0	25	2	23	2	1
Markulike, Joseph, Idaho Falls	.132	23	38	6	5	5	0	0	0	0	0	0	0	7	0	5	2	0
Martin, Dillard, Salt Lake City	.286	19	84	13	24	31	5	1	0	13	0	0	1	9	0	16	2	2
Matachun, Paul, Butte°	.282	57	174	30	49	62	6	2	1	27	1	1	0	28	1	17	6	0
Matos, Malvin, Butte	.222	50	158	27	35	55	2	3	4	27	0	0	3	12	0	49	6	4
Maurer, Ronald, Great Falls	.270	62	237	43	64	90	8	0	6	43	5	4	6	28	0	38	5	2
McMillan, Stuart, Idaho Falls	.274	66	241	40	66	107	10	5	7	51	0	2	6	26	0	63	22	8
McMullen, Kevin, Salt Lake City	.303	60	234	44	71	123	14	4	10	56	0	1	1	30	4	56	2	1
Mercado, Brian, Butte	.324	52	148	29	48	70	9	2	3	26	0	1	4	35	1	32	0	1
Meyers, Don, Great Falls	.326	38	92	14	30	40	5	1	1	23	1	1	2	11	0	25	0	1
Moberg, Michael, Salt Lake City	.331	68	269	64	89	119	12	3	4	38	3	2	4	41	0	38	12	8
Mondesi, Raul, Great Falls	.303	44	175	35	53	95	10	4	8	31	0	1	2	11	1	30	30	7
Montes, Daniel, Salt Lake City†	.235	31	81	10	19	23	4	0	0	12	1	0	1	7	0	12	5	4
Moseley, Scott, Helena†	.143	3	7	2	1	1	0	0	0	1	0	0	0	1	0	1	0	0
Mouton, Brian, Butte	.294	55	194	34	57	76	11	1	2	33	0	3	0	28	0	34	5	5
Murray, Keith, Butte°	.615	7	13	7	8	12	4	0	0	5	0	0	0	2	0	2	3	0
Nettnin, Rodney, Salt Lake City°	.000	14	0	1	0	0	0	0	0	0	0	0	0	1	0	0	0	0
Nichols, Brian, Billings	.279	42	140	12	39	48	9	0	0	19	4	1	2	8	0	20	2	5
Noce, Doug, Gate City	.251	56	183	24	46	60	12	1	0	16	2	3	1	32	0	35	1	1
Norris, Michael, Helena°	.179	32	67	8	12	13	1	0	0	1	0	0	1	6	0	17	3	1
O'Connor, Kevin, Idaho Falls°	.234	12	47	6	11	16	2	0	1	4	0	0	0	0	0	5	4	0
Orr, Geoffrey, Idaho Falls	.289	67	242	44	70	106	13	1	7	39	0	4	4	33	0	54	11	7
Ortega, Hector, Gate City	.283	65	244	34	69	88	6	5	1	17	0	2	1	22	0	60	20	6
Owens, Tommy, Idaho Falls	.091	6	11	1	1	1	0	0	0	0	0	0	1	2	0	7	0	1
Penn, Shannon, Butte	.325	60	197	38	64	72	4	2	0	18	0	2	1	15	0	35	9	4
Perez, Junior, Great Falls	.267	41	90	15	24	30	4	1	0	19	0	0	2	4	0	10	0	1
Perez, Victor, Billings	.143	24	49	7	7	7	0	0	0	0	0	2	0	1	0	24	2	0
Perna, Robert, Billings†	.333	14	48	12	16	21	2	0	1	8	0	0	0	9	0	3	3	1
Phillips, Thomas, Gate City†	.311	25	74	7	23	30	5	1	0	6	1	0	0	5	0	20	1	0
Posey, Martin, Butte°	.321	46	109	21	35	49	8	0	2	18	0	1	0	18	0	23	0	0
Powell, Gordon, Helena	.217	45	152	17	33	46	4	0	3	18	0	3	0	8	0	41	5	2
Pullins, Jimmie, Idaho Falls	.304	37	92	12	28	38	3	2	1	13	2	0	3	13	1	20	2	4
Quinones, Eliezer, Billings	.330	54	215	38	71	99	8	1	6	46	0	5	1	17	0	27	10	4
Rambadt, Charles, Helena	.107	15	28	4	3	4	1	0	0	1	0	0	0	10	0	7	0	0
Ramharter, Stephen, Butte°	.000	23	1	0	0	0	0	0	0	0	0	0	0	0	0	0	0	0
Reams, Ronald, Medicine Hat	.243	48	206	28	50	73	10	2	3	15	0	0	1	5	1	30	12	4
Reimsnyder, Brian, Salt Lake City°	.200	10	20	1	4	5	1	0	0	1	1	0	0	4	0	8	0	0
Reyes, Victor, Butte	.217	23	46	7	10	11	1	0	0	5	0	0	1	0	0	10	2	0
Riggs, Kevin, Billings°	.318	57	192	49	61	77	9	2	1	21	0	0	2	50	2	24	16	3
Rivera, Hector, Gate City	.095	10	21	1	2	3	1	0	0	0	0	0	0	1	0	13	0	0
Roberts, Lonell, Medicine Hat†	.212	38	118	14	25	27	2	0	0	8	0	0	6	0	0	29	8	1
Sanchez, Perry, Gate City°	.292	24	89	9	26	32	3	0	1	9	0	0	2	8	0	5	1	1
Santiago, Angelo, Gate City	.241	60	191	35	46	70	7	1	5	26	0	0	6	37	0	76	3	2
Satoh, Hiroyuki, Gate City	.267	60	206	22	55	74	12	2	1	23	6	2	2	14	0	36	6	3
Schifman, James, Salt Lake City	.464	8	28	8	13	15	0	1	0	6	0	0	2	3	0	3	2	1
Septimo, Felix, Medicine Hat	.219	43	155	15	34	55	5	2	4	17	0	1	4	10	0	62	4	1
Shave, Jonathan, Butte	.352	64	250	41	88	109	9	3	2	42	2	4	3	25	0	27	21	8
Simmerson, Peter, Gate City	.160	24	75	5	12	15	3	0	0	2	0	0	2	2	0	9	3	2
Smith, Ira, Great Falls	.261	50	142	31	37	53	7	3	1	28	2	3	2	25	0	33	8	6
Stofsky, Wayne, Salt Lake City	.310	21	87	19	27	32	5	0	0	8	1	2	0	4	0	13	1	2
Surane, John, Idaho Falls	.288	61	212	33	61	79	8	2	2	21	4	1	6	31	0	54	5	1
Sweeney, Michael, Idaho Falls	.147	26	68	9	10	12	2	0	0	2	0	1	3	0	0	34	1	1
Tavarez, Hector, Medicine Hat†	.279	39	136	18	38	49	7	2	0	12	0	0	0	9	0	28	4	6
Urcioli, John, Salt Lake City	.258	63	213	30	55	69	7	2	1	35	9	5	4	25	0	35	5	4
Vasquez, Chris, Billings°	.286	54	182	25	52	80	9	2	5	34	2	2	2	14	0	29	4	5
Velez, Noel, Billings	.284	44	169	27	48	69	5	2	4	21	1	2	1	12	0	32	5	2
Walker, James, Helena	.143	3	7	0	1	1	0	0	0	0	0	0	0	0	0	3	0	0
Watts, Burgess, Great Falls	.267	51	176	26	47	64	9	1	2	22	2	2	2	14	0	24	3	1
Webb, Lonnie, Great Falls	.331	40	148	29	49	63	4	5	0	17	4	0	2	15	0	26	19	5
Wentz, Leonard, Billings	.500	6	12	3	6	7	1	0	0	4	2	0	0	5	0	4	1	1
Wheat, Christopher, Helena	.247	31	81	11	20	21	1	0	0	8	3	0	0	6	0	12	1	0
Wheeler, David, Billings	.137	38	117	10	16	24	2	0	2	15	1	1	3	15	0	32	1	1
Wilburn, Ema, 7 G.C.-13 Bil.†	.296	20	27	2	8	9	1	0	0	2	0	0	1	2	1	3	0	1
Wilson, Todd, Billings°	.263	22	76	15	20	32	2	2	2	14	0	1	0	10	3	22	1	0
Wood, John, Idaho Falls	.182	32	55	11	10	13	3	0	0	0	0	0	1	4	0	11	2	1
Zeller, William, Idaho Falls	.000	3	5	0	0	0	0	0	0	0	0	0	0	0	0	1	0	0

The following pitchers, listed alphabetically by club, with games in parentheses, had no plate appearances, primarily through use of designated hitters:

BILLINGS—Berry, James (19); Doty, Sean (8); Duff, Scott (13); Edwards, Ryan (20); Ferry, Michael (27); Fry, Brian (22); Keim, Christopher (12); Luebbers, Larry (13); Margheim, Gregory (14); Nieves, Ernesto (20); Robinson, Scott (12); Stewart, Carl (14); Tatar, Kevin (13).

BUTTE—Burrows, Terry (14); Busha, Rodney (15); Cardona, Jose (23); Dreyer, Steven (8); Erickson, Scott (16); Gies, Christopher (15); Goetz, Barry (4); Patterson, Daniel (13); Scheetz, Brian (15); Smith, Daniel (5); St. Pe, Irving (15); Surico, Stephen (7); Washington, Tyrone (13); Watson, Andy (4); Wells, Timothy (16); Whiteside, Matthew (18).

GATE CITY—Carter, David (26); Casey, Keith (7); Emerick, Christopher (13); Espinoza, Carlos (24); Fier, Michael (13); Foster, Kevin (10); Frederiksen, Kelly (20); Hutto, Paul (26); Maema, Takashi (20); Martinez, William (24); Mizusawa, Hideki (17); Renko, Steve (11); Wilburn, Ema (7).

GREAT FALLS—Baumann, David (13); Daspit, James (14); Dejarld, John (22); Hamilton, Kenneth (13); Jacinto, Larry (17); Kerr, Jason (19); Martinez, Pedro (14); Mimbs, Mark (14); Mimbs, Michael (3); O'Connor, Benjamin (1); Piotrowicz, Brian (22); Stryker, Edward (21); Tipton, Gordon (24); Walden, Ronnie (4).

HELENA—Angelos, Phillip (9); Archer, Kurt (10); Brakeley, William (6); Hooper, Michael (5); Kellogg, Geoffrey (15); McDonald, Kevin (9); Miller, Patrick (8); Mobley, Joseph (6); Patton, Eric (17); Pruitt, Donald (13); Rupp, Mark (13); Souza, Brian (19); Stephens, Mark (14); Wilson, Timothy (13); Zimbauer, Jason (12).

IDAHO FALLS—Bates, William (21); Carter, Eric (18); Creamer, Gerald (1); Dare, Brian (15); Dease, Don'l (13); Gabriele, Michael (4); Halliday, Allen (15); Hodges, Steven (25); Hoog, Michael (29); Kooiman, William (15); Langston, Keith (5); Lemon, Donald (11); Mack, Raymond (2); Newman, Thomas (7); Rizzo, Thomas (14); Rohrwild, Shawn (24); Ryder, Scott (14).

MEDICINE HAT—Adams, Morgan (13); Burley, Travis (12); Darley, Ned (9); Duey, Kyle (15); Fletcher, David (3); Garcia, Raphael (13); Gilligan, John (18); Hotchkiss, Thomas (20); Kistaitis, Dale (12); Miller, Scott (19); Orman, Richard (19); Perez, Jose (11); Reese, Jason (17); Spoljaric, Paul (15); Wilcox, Gregory (13).

SALT LAKE CITY—Alexander, David (15); Ambos, William (14); Boone, Gary (20); Gerstein, Ronald (2); Hagy, Jeffrey (16); Jobes, Tracy (13); Jurado, Pat (13); Mirabella, Gennaro (14); Sawaia, Joseph (2); Steinkamp, Michael (13); Sweet, Pat (4); White, Andrew (18); Whitworth, Kenneth (13).

GRAND SLAM HOME RUNS—Bargas, Blackwell, Castaldo, Chiyomaru, Couture, Guggiana, Hammargren, Karcher, Mercado, Meyers, Wilson, 1 each.

AWARDED FIRST BASE ON CATCHER'S INTERFERENCE—T. Carter (J. Perez); Frauenhoffer (Hammargren); Kidd (Owens); Nichols (Guggiana); Velez (Guggiana).

CLUB FIELDING

Club	Pct.	G.	PO.	A.	E.	DP.	PB.	Club	Pct.	G.	PO.	A.	E.	DP.	PB.
Great Falls	.963	68	1827	732	98	67	8	Butte	.953	67	1728	731	120	53	13
Idaho Falls	.961	70	1825	767	106	73	18	Gate City	.947	70	1763	749	141	61	10
Helena	.956	65	1725	710	111	58	16	Billings	.944	66	1739	720	146	58	16
Salt Lake City	.956	68	1819	851	122	73	7	Medicine Hat	.943	66	1718	743	150	55	29

Triple Play—Helena.

INDIVIDUAL FIELDING

*Throws lefthanded.

FIRST BASEMEN

Player and Club	Pct.	G.	PO.	A.	E.	DP.	Player and Club	Pct.	G.	PO.	A.	E.	DP.
Asai, Gate City*	1.000	3	16	0	0	2	Hyers, Medicine Hat*	.981	61	516	38	11	44
Bargas, Salt Lake City	.983	48	420	36	8	38	Jones, Billings	.973	7	30	6	1	5
Beaulac, Salt Lake City*	1.000	6	30	4	0	1	Karcher, Idaho Falls*	.981	36	293	14	6	33
Bielski, Salt Lake City	.986	9	67	4	1	6	Kelly, Salt Lake City	1.000	1	3	0	0	0
Biggers, Salt Lake City	1.000	1	2	0	0	0	Markulike, Idaho Falls	.958	7	21	2	1	1
BUSCH, Great Falls	.992	60	481	47	4	56	Meyers, Great Falls	.979	15	86	6	2	7
Carter, Helena	.985	42	377	28	6	32	Mouton, Butte	.983	51	432	26	8	31
Castellanos, Butte	.989	22	171	11	2	16	Nichols, Billings	.980	6	43	6	1	4
Chiyomaru, Gate City	1.000	5	22	1	0	1	Ortega, Gate City	1.000	10	72	10	0	5
Columbano, Idaho Falls	1.000	1	2	1	0	0	J. Perez, Great Falls	1.000	5	12	0	0	1
Crump, Medicine Hat*	1.000	1	12	0	0	0	V. Perez, Billings	.889	4	7	1	1	0
Edwards, Helena*	1.000	2	5	0	0	1	Phillips, Gate City	1.000	2	3	1	0	0
Filotei, Billings	1.000	2	0	1	0	0	Posey, Butte	1.000	2	4	1	0	0
Glenn, Billings	.991	24	207	13	2	17	Sanchez, Gate City	1.000	5	41	10	0	5
Gress, Idaho Falls	.991	37	302	15	3	33	Santiago, Gate City	.982	53	406	29	8	41
Hammargren, Billings*	.974	28	245	14	7	19	Vasquez, Billings	1.000	1	1	0	0	1
Harmes, Medicine Hat	.984	7	54	7	1	4	Velez, Billings	1.000	2	1	0	0	0
Harris, Salt Lake City	1.000	19	160	4	0	17	Wheeler, Billings	.989	12	85	6	1	6
							Wilson, Billings*	.978	21	173	9	4	16

Triple Play—Carter.

SECOND BASEMEN

Player and Club	Pct.	G.	PO.	A.	E.	DP.	Player and Club	Pct.	G.	PO.	A.	E.	DP.
Atwater, Gate City	.916	33	60	71	12	10	Guggiana, Butte	1.000	2	1	3	0	0
Biggers, Salt Lake City	.967	26	53	65	4	13	Horne, Gate City	1.000	2	0	2	0	0
Bohringer, Great Falls	.926	6	13	12	2	1	Jones, Billings	1.000	1	4	5	0	1
Brittain, Idaho Falls	1.000	3	5	3	0	0	Marabella, Gate City	.978	20	44	47	2	10
CASTALDO, Helena	.964	52	108	136	9	31	Matachun, Butte	1.000	16	27	34	0	4
Chiyomaru, Gate City	.933	9	13	15	2	5	Montes, Salt Lake City	.948	29	43	85	7	9
Choate, Medicine Hat	.964	51	98	142	9	25	Moseley, Helena	.667	2	1	3	2	1
Chumbley, Idaho Falls	1.000	2	2	2	0	0	Penn, Butte	.940	55	110	154	17	28
Coolbaugh, Medicine Hat	.933	17	25	45	5	7	Reams, Medicine Hat	1.000	1	3	0	0	0
Diggs, Helena	.913	10	17	25	4	6	Reyes, Gate City	1.000	1	3	0	0	0
Doyle, Salt Lake City	.971	18	35	64	3	15	Riggs, Billings	.944	50	100	135	14	23
Filotei, Billings	.909	18	36	44	8	6	Simmerson, Gate City	.915	19	28	37	6	12
Frauenhoffer, Great Falls	.959	18	31	39	3	12	Surane, Idaho Falls	.961	50	95	176	11	36
Garczyk, Salt Lake City	.914	11	19	34	5	11	Tavares, Medicine Hat	1.000	1	3	3	0	2
Giovanola, Idaho Falls	.981	22	32	72	2	19	Webb, Great Falls	.930	38	73	86	12	20
Griffin, Great Falls	.920	14	32	37	6	10	Wentz, Billings	1.000	1	2	7	0	1
							Wheat, Helena	.955	9	9	12	1	2

Triple Play—Castaldo.

THIRD BASEMEN

Player and Club	Pct.	G.	PO.	A.	E.	DP.	Player and Club	Pct.	G.	PO.	A.	E.	DP.
Bargas, Salt Lake City	1.000	2	1	4	0	0	Jones, Billings	.903	28	17	48	7	3
Battle, Medicine Hat	.775	52	25	92	34	2	Lucky, Idaho Falls	1.000	4	1	0	0	0
Bohringer, Great Falls	.857	4	1	5	1	0	Marabella, Gate City	.881	32	28	68	13	3
Briggs, Salt Lake City	1.000	1	1	1	0	0	Markulike, Idaho Falls	.882	13	7	8	2	1
Burnett, Salt Lake City	1.000	1	1	0	0	0	Matachun, Butte	.950	34	16	60	4	4
Castaldo, Helena	.857	12	5	13	3	0	Maurer, Great Falls	1.000	1	0	2	0	0
Castellanos, Butte	.917	20	16	28	4	1	Meyers, Great Falls	.840	18	5	16	4	2
Chiyomaru, Gate City	.888	32	24	47	9	7	Orr, Idaho Falls	.913	63	53	94	14	10
Coolbaugh, Medicine Hat	.762	8	3	13	5	1	Ortega, Gate City	.875	15	15	27	6	4
Diggs, Helena	.667	2	3	1	2	0	Powell, Helena	.882	41	44	83	17	3
Dipino, Idaho Falls	1.000	1	0	1	0	0	Reams, Medicine Hat	.879	9	10	19	4	0
Doyle, Salt Lake City	1.000	5	4	9	0	1	Sanchez, Gate City	.800	2	0	4	1	1
Duffin, Salt Lake City	.883	65	34	140	23	12	Surane, Idaho Falls	.857	2	1	5	1	0
Filotei, Billings	.838	14	13	18	6	3	Velez, Billings	.890	30	15	50	8	1
Griffin, Great Falls	.762	9	5	11	5	4	WATTS, Great Falls	.930	50	26	81	8	4
Guggiana, Butte	.852	27	20	49	12	4	Wheat, Helena	.917	14	4	18	2	0
Hood, Helena	.714	3	2	3	2	2							

SHORTSTOPS

Player and Club	Pct.	G.	PO.	A.	E.	DP.	Player and Club	Pct.	G.	PO.	A.	E.	DP.
Atwater, Gate City	.794	7	13	14	7	1	Choate, Medicine Hat	.914	11	18	46	6	8
Biggers, Salt Lake City	.943	11	12	21	2	10	Chumbley, Idaho Falls	1.000	2	3	4	0	1
BRITTAIN, Idaho Falls	.954	66	134	177	15	52	Coolbaugh, Medicine Hat	.847	25	49	78	23	12
Carter, Helena	.906	60	97	174	28	31	Filotei, Billings	.907	25	34	64	10	19
Chiyomaru, Gate City	.824	5	2	12	3	0	Frauenhoffer, Great Falls	.938	11	12	33	3	5

SHORTSTOPS—Continued

Player and Club	Pct.	G.	PO.	A.	E.	DP.	Player and Club	Pct.	G.	PO.	A.	E.	DP.
Gordon, Billings	.906	48	79	134	22	27	Riggs, Billings	1.000	1	1	1	0	0
Hood, Helena	.875	2	3	4	1	1	Satoh, Gate City	.933	59	93	172	19	34
Lucky, Idaho Falls	1.000	4	2	3	0	0	Shave, Butte	.925	63	112	159	22	35
Matachun, Butte	.951	8	14	25	2	0	Simmerson, Gate City	.750	5	3	3	2	0
Maurer, Great Falls	.937	60	92	191	19	43	Tavares, Medicine Hat	.904	37	60	91	16	18
Orr, Idaho Falls	.919	7	16	18	3	1	Urcioli, Salt Lake City	.927	63	106	211	25	39
							Wheat, Helena	.875	9	9	19	4	1

Triple Play—Carter.

OUTFIELDERS

Player and Club	Pct.	G.	PO.	A.	E.	DP.	Player and Club	Pct.	G.	PO.	A.	E.	DP.
Adams, Gate City*	.937	55	70	4	5	0	Martin, Salt Lake City	.919	19	32	2	3	1
Andrews, Great Falls	.970	37	31	1	1	0	Matos, Butte	.966	48	53	3	2	0
Asai, Gate City*	.990	50	94	4	1	1	McMillan, Idaho Falls	.934	61	82	3	6	1
Atwater, Gate City	1.000	2	4	0	0	0	Mercado, Butte	1.000	6	6	0	0	0
Baber, Helena	.909	23	28	2	3	0	Moberg, Salt Lake City	.951	68	131	6	7	1
Benjamin, Helena	1.000	20	24	1	0	0	Mondesi, Great Falls	.986	43	65	4	1	1
Bielski, Salt Lake City	.982	34	50	5	1	2	Mouton, Butte	1.000	2	3	0	0	0
Blackwell, Great Falls	.925	57	72	2	6	0	Murray, Butte	1.000	3	2	0	0	0
BOWERS, Medicine Hat	.992	60	117	7	1	3	Noce, Gate City	1.000	9	18	2	0	0
Burnett, Salt Lake City	.885	24	23	0	3	0	Norris, Helena	.938	25	28	2	2	2
Burroughs, Billings*	.949	30	54	2	3	0	O'Connor, Idaho Falls	1.000	12	15	1	0	0
Burton, Idaho Falls	.969	65	120	3	4	0	Ortega, Gate City	.935	46	82	5	6	0
Castellanos, Butte	.966	22	26	2	1	0	Perez, Billings	1.000	9	8	1	0	0
Coble, Helena	1.000	11	17	3	0	1	Perna, Billings	1.000	8	15	1	0	0
Couture, Helena	.940	41	42	5	3	1	Posey, Butte	.944	15	17	0	1	0
Czarnetzki, Salt Lake City	1.000	11	9	0	0	0	Pullins, Idaho Falls	.949	35	55	1	3	1
Daniels, Medicine Hat	.867	28	37	2	6	0	Quinones, Billings	.928	46	73	4	6	0
Diggs, Helena	.964	24	48	5	2	0	Reams, Medicine Hat	.983	32	56	3	1	1
Doyle, Salt Lake City	1.000	16	20	3	0	0	Reimsnyder, Salt Lake City*	.600	5	2	1	2	0
Edwards, Helena*	.962	30	47	4	2	1	Rivera, Gate City	.857	7	12	0	2	0
Farrish, Great Falls	.983	60	111	4	2	1	Roberts, Medicine Hat	.975	31	35	4	1	1
Filotei, Billings	1.000	2	3	0	0	0	Sanchez, Gate City	1.000	2	2	0	0	0
Fister, Idaho Falls	.907	32	36	3	4	0	Santiago, Gate City	.857	5	5	1	1	0
Fults, Idaho Falls	1.000	10	11	0	0	0	Schifman, Gate City	1.000	7	8	0	0	0
Gillum, Billings	.935	51	91	10	7	5	Septimo, Medicine Hat	.961	37	48	1	2	0
Greer, Butte*	.918	60	84	5	8	1	Smith, Great Falls	.950	49	57	0	3	0
Guggiana, Butte	1.000	6	4	0	0	0	Stofsky, Salt Lake City	.974	20	37	1	1	0
Heilgeist, Gate City	.947	27	34	2	2	1	Sweeney, Idaho Falls	.944	20	17	0	1	0
Hines, Medicine Hat	.909	23	26	4	3	0	Vasquez, Billings	.956	51	106	2	5	0
Hood, Helena	.961	41	71	2	3	1	Velez, Billings	.909	7	10	1	1	0
Horne, Gate City	.944	35	64	3	4	1	Walker, Helena	1.000	3	1	0	0	0
Hulse, Butte*	.947	60	102	5	6	1	Webb, Great Falls	1.000	2	2	0	0	0
Kelly, Salt Lake City	.933	21	27	1	2	0	Wheeler, Billings	1.000	3	4	0	0	0
Kidd, Salt Lake City*	1.000	8	13	0	0	0	Wilburn, Billings	1.000	5	7	0	0	0

CATCHERS

Player and Club	Pct.	G.	PO.	A.	E.	DP.	PB.	Player and Club	Pct.	G.	PO.	A.	E.	DP.	PB.
Beck, Helena	1.000	31	200	30	0	4	9	Lund, Great Falls	.993	26	130	8	1	1	2
Blevins, Butte	.991	34	193	23	2	2	5	McMullen, Salt Lake City	.971	15	93	8	3	2	5
Briggs, Salt Lake City	.981	33	136	18	3	2	1	Meyers, Great Falls	1.000	1	2	0	0	0	0
Columbano, Idaho Falls	.975	12	35	4	1	0	1	Nichols, Billings	.978	36	198	27	5	4	5
Drabinski, Idaho Falls	.975	52	304	42	9	3	11	Noce, Gate City	.979	39	278	42	7	5	5
Flores, Helena	.981	33	223	29	5	5	4	Owens, Idaho Falls	.949	6	31	6	2	0	2
Garcia, Medicine Hat	1.000	15	74	5	0	1	8	Perez, Great Falls	.986	32	198	16	3	3	3
GRAY, Great Falls	.989	36	236	26	3	1	3	Phillips, Gate City	.975	18	103	15	3	1	2
Guggiana, Butte	.983	38	211	25	4	0	7	Rambadt, Helena	.987	15	67	9	1	0	3
Hammargren, Billings*	.965	20	123	13	5	0	5	Reyes, Butte	.973	18	61	10	2	0	1
Harmes, Medicine Hat	.979	36	256	24	6	1	10	Sanchez, Gate City	.958	13	78	14	4	0	3
Harris, Salt Lake City	1.000	3	7	1	0	0	0	Wheeler, Billings	.942	20	117	13	8	0	4
Hines, Medicine Hat	1.000	2	7	1	0	0	3	Wilburn, Billings	.875	1	14	0	2	0	2
Keighley, Salt Lake City	.978	33	190	30	5	3	1	Wood, Idaho Falls	.978	30	112	20	3	0	4
Loeb, Medicine Hat	.994	21	144	23	1	1	8	Zeller, Idaho Falls	1.000	2	7	1	0	0	0

PITCHERS

Player and Club	Pct.	G.	PO.	A.	E.	DP.	Player and Club	Pct.	G.	PO.	A.	E.	DP.
Adams, Medicine Hat	1.000	13	0	1	0	0	Duff, Billings*	.923	13	0	12	1	1
Alexander, Salt Lake City	.875	15	2	5	1	1	Edwards, Billings	.800	20	3	1	1	0
AMBOS, Salt Lake City	1.000	14	14	15	0	3	Emerick, Gate City	.625	12	3	2	3	0
Angelos, Helena	.800	9	2	2	1	0	Erickson, Butte*	.750	16	0	3	1	0
Archer, Helena	1.000	10	1	1	0	0	Espinoza, Gate City	1.000	24	3	1	0	0
Asai, Gate City*	1.000	1	0	1	0	0	Ferry, Billings	1.000	27	1	4	0	0
Bates, Idaho Falls	1.000	21	0	5	0	0	Fier, Gate City*	.750	13	1	8	3	0
Baumann, Great Falls	.857	13	5	13	3	1	Fletcher, Medicine Hat	1.000	3	1	0	0	0
Berry, Billings	1.000	19	5	8	0	0	Foster, Gate City	1.000	10	5	6	0	0
Boone, Salt Lake City*	.625	20	2	3	3	0	Frederiksen, Gate City	.947	20	4	14	1	3
Bourgeois, Idaho Falls	1.000	4	1	0	0	0	Fry, Billings*	.857	22	2	4	1	0
Brakeley, Helena*	1.000	6	1	1	0	0	Gabriele, Idaho Falls	.667	4	1	3	2	1
Burley, Medicine Hat	.889	12	1	7	1	0	Garcia, Medicine Hat	1.000	13	5	14	0	1
Burrows, Butte*	.706	14	2	10	5	1	Gies, Butte	.967	15	9	20	1	0
Busha, Butte	.909	15	1	9	1	2	Gilligan, Medicine Hat	.957	18	5	17	1	0
Carmona, Butte	.941	23	4	12	1	1	Goetz, Butte*	1.000	4	3	0	0	0
D. Carter, Gate City	.727	26	3	5	3	0	Hagy, Salt Lake City	1.000	16	1	4	0	0
E. Carter, Idaho Falls	.833	18	2	3	1	1	Halliday, Idaho Falls*	.667	15	0	2	1	0
Dare, Idaho Falls*	.955	15	4	17	1	0	Hamilton, Great Falls	.947	13	7	11	1	3
Darley, Medicine Hat	.750	9	1	2	1	0	Hodges, Idaho Falls	.857	25	0	6	1	0
Daspit, Great Falls	1.000	14	8	9	0	4	Hoog, Idaho Falls*	.909	29	3	7	1	1
Dease, Idaho Falls	1.000	13	2	6	0	0	Hooper, Helena	1.000	5	1	3	0	0
Dejarld, Great Falls	.818	22	3	6	2	0	Hotchkiss, Medicine Hat	.875	20	3	11	2	2
Doty, Billings	.714	8	2	3	2	0	Hutto, Gate City	.895	26	5	12	2	1
Dreyer, Butte	.846	8	4	7	2	0	Jacinto, Great Falls	1.000	17	4	4	0	0
Duey, Medicine Hat	.800	15	7	9	4	0	Jobes, Salt Lake City	.857	13	4	2	1	0

PITCHERS—Continued

Player and Club	Pct.	G.	PO.	A.	E.	DP.	Player and Club	Pct.	G.	PO.	A.	E.	DP.
Jurado, Salt Lake City	.778	13	3	4	2	0	Reese, Medicine Hat	1.000	17	1	1	0	0
Keim, Billings*	1.000	12	0	1	0	0	Renko, Gate City	.952	11	4	16	1	0
Kellogg, Helena	1.000	15	4	4	0	1	Rizzo, Idaho Falls	.625	14	1	4	3	0
Kerr, Great Falls*	1.000	19	4	3	0	1	Robinson, Billings	.857	12	1	11	2	0
Kistaitis, Medicine Hat*	.947	12	5	13	1	0	Rohrwild, Idaho Falls	1.000	24	0	3	0	0
Kooiman, Idaho Falls	1.000	15	1	1	0	0	Rupp, Helena	.667	13	0	2	1	0
Langston, Idaho Falls	1.000	5	1	3	0	0	Ryder, Idaho Falls	.938	14	5	10	1	2
Lemon, Idaho Falls	.900	11	6	12	2	2	Scheetz, Butte	.714	12	1	4	2	0
Luebbers, Billings	.913	13	5	16	2	4	Smith, Butte*	.909	5	2	8	1	0
Mack, Idaho Falls	1.000	2	0	1	0	1	Souza, Helena	.929	19	1	12	1	0
Maema, Gate City*	1.000	19	3	5	0	1	Spoljaric, Medicine Hat*	.882	15	4	11	2	1
Margheim, Billings*	1.000	14	1	18	0	1	St. Pe, Butte	.667	15	0	2	1	0
P. Martinez, Great Falls	.947	14	6	12	1	1	Steinkamp, Salt Lake City	.955	13	6	15	1	0
W. Martinez, Gate City	.833	24	3	7	2	2	Stephens, Helena*	.909	14	4	6	1	1
McDonald, Helena	1.000	9	2	8	0	1	Stewart, Billings	.923	14	8	4	1	2
P. Miller, Helena	1.000	8	3	3	0	0	Stryker, Great Falls	1.000	21	5	7	0	1
S. Miller, Medicine Hat	.750	19	4	2	2	0	Surico, Butte*	.667	7	1	1	1	0
Ma. Mimbs, Great Falls*	.964	14	6	21	1	1	Sweet, Salt Lake City*	.750	4	1	2	1	0
Mi. Mimbs, Great Falls*	1.000	3	0	1	0	1	Tatar, Billings	.857	13	0	6	1	0
Mirabella, Salt Lake City	.875	14	2	12	2	2	Tipton, Great Falls	.929	24	5	8	1	0
Mizusawa, Gate City	1.000	17	1	6	0	1	Walden, Great Falls*	1.000	4	1	5	0	0
Mobley, Helena*	1.000	6	2	2	0	1	Washington, Butte	.895	13	7	10	2	0
Nettnin, Salt Lake City*	.897	13	9	17	3	1	Watson, Butte	.667	4	0	2	1	0
Newman, Idaho Falls	.818	7	4	5	2	0	Wells, Butte	1.000	16	0	4	0	0
Nieves, Billings	.769	20	1	9	3	3	White, Salt Lake City	1.000	18	1	5	0	0
Orman, Medicine Hat*	1.000	19	1	4	0	0	Whiteside, Butte	.875	18	4	10	2	3
Patterson, Butte	1.000	13	2	4	0	0	Whitworth, Salt Lake City	1.000	13	5	9	0	1
Patton, Helena	.923	17	6	6	1	0	Wilburn, 7 G.C.-1 Bill.	.875	8	1	6	1	0
Perez, Medicine Hat	1.000	11	1	2	0	1	Wilcox, Medicine Hat	.800	13	3	1	1	0
Piotrowicz, Great Falls	1.000	22	0	5	0	1	Wilson, Helena	1.000	13	5	6	0	0
Pruitt, Helena	1.000	13	2	16	0	0	Zimbauer, Helena	.900	12	4	14	2	0
Ramharter, Butte*	.600	22	0	3	2	0							

The following players did not have any fielding statistics at the positions indicated or appeared only as a designated hitter, pinch-hitter or pinch-runner: Beaulac, of; Casey, p; Chiyomaru, p; Creamer, p; Frauenhoffer, 3b, of; Garczyk, 1b; Gerstein, p; Guggiana, p; Ingram, dh, ph, pr; Karcher, of; Lund, 1b; Markulike, ss; Meyers, of; Montes, of; B. O'Connor, p; Perna, 3b; Reyes, of; Riggs, of; Santiago, p; Sawaia, p; Simmerson, p; Watts, 2b; Wentz, ss, of.

CLUB PITCHING

Club	ERA.	G.	CG.	ShO.	Sv.	IP.	H.	R.	ER.	HR.	HB.	BB.	Int. BB.	SO.	WP.	Bk.
Great Falls	3.07	68	0	4	20	609.0	554	257	208	25	36	261	4	559	28	9
Salt Lake City	4.04	68	9	2	20	606.1	689	354	272	32	28	209	4	417	52	20
Helena	4.27	65	4	2	13	575.0	622	325	273	45	18	251	13	477	38	9
Idaho Falls	4.50	70	4	5	18	608.1	653	376	304	28	26	301	10	477	41	21
Billings	4.55	66	2	2	16	579.2	589	380	293	29	30	294	5	450	80	18
Butte	4.78	67	8	1	15	576.0	614	384	306	35	28	282	2	461	43	15
Medicine Hat	5.12	66	1	2	9	572.2	623	427	326	50	30	348	1	465	69	19
Gate City	6.22	70	3	0	7	587.2	772	510	406	42	42	278	17	449	90	9

PITCHERS' RECORDS
(Leading Qualifiers for Earned-Run Average Leadership—56 or More Innings)

*Throws lefthanded.

Pitcher—Club	W.	L.	Pct.	ERA.	G.	GS.	CG.	GF.	ShO.	Sv.	IP.	H.	R.	ER.	HR.	HB.	BB.	Int. BB.	SO.	WP.
Ambos, Salt Lake City	7	3	.700	2.57	14	12	3	2	0	0	87.2	89	33	25	3	3	21	0	47	5
Dease, Idaho Falls	4	2	.667	2.91	13	13	0	0	0	0	58.2	58	25	19	1	5	29	0	55	2
Baumann, Great Falls	7	3	.700	3.03	13	11	0	0	0	0	68.1	66	25	23	3	2	26	0	49	4
Nettnin, Salt Lake City*	4	4	.500	3.23	13	12	3	0	0	0	75.1	75	38	27	1	3	29	0	47	3
Ma. Mimbs, Great Falls*	7	4	.636	3.23	14	14	0	0	0	0	78.0	69	32	28	3	1	29	0	94	4
Whitworth, Salt Lake City	7	2	.778	3.32	13	12	1	1	0	1	76.0	77	31	28	2	3	32	0	54	5
Whiteside, Butte	4	4	.500	3.45	18	5	0	5	0	2	57.1	57	33	22	4	9	25	0	45	4
P. Martinez, Great Falls	8	3	.727	3.62	14	14	0	0	0	0	77.0	74	39	31	5	8	40	1	82	6
Hamilton, Great Falls	4	2	.667	3.63	13	13	0	0	0	0	67.0	76	34	27	4	8	28	1	37	1
Zimbauer, Helena	3	6	.333	3.67	12	12	0	0	0	0	73.2	70	38	30	6	4	27	1	64	0

Departmental Leaders: G—Hoog, 29; W—Ryder, 9; L—Fier, Maema, 8; Pct.—Patton, .875; GS—Several pitchers tied with 14; CG—Gies, 5; GF—Ferry, 24; ShO—Lemon, Luebbers, P. Miller, 1; Sv.—Ferry, 11; IP—Mirabella, 89.1; H—Pruitt, 102; R—Pruitt, 54; ER—Margheim, Pruitt, 45; HR—Pruitt, 8; HB—Whiteside, 9; BB—Patton, 55; IBB—Souza, 5; SO—Ma. Mimbs, 94; WP—Stewart, 15.

(All Pitchers—Listed Alphabetically)

Pitcher—Club	W.	L.	Pct.	ERA.	G.	GS.	CG.	GF.	ShO.	Sv.	IP.	H.	R.	ER.	HR.	HB.	BB.	Int. BB.	SO.	WP.
Adams, Medicine Hat	0	1	.000	8.49	13	2	0	3	0	0	23.1	37	26	22	3	0	21	0	17	6
Alexander, Salt Lake City	3	0	1.000	4.67	15	0	0	10	0	1	34.2	48	30	18	7	2	7	0	13	2
Ambos, Salt Lake City	7	3	.700	2.57	14	12	3	2	0	0	87.2	89	33	25	3	3	21	0	47	5
Angelos, Helena	6	0	1.000	1.29	9	0	0	7	0	1	28.0	12	7	4	0	0	14	0	23	2
Archer, Helena	0	2	.000	3.66	10	0	0	9	0	3	19.2	19	9	8	0	2	3	2	23	0
Asai, Gate City*	0	0	.000	9.00	1	0	0	0	0	0	1.0	3	1	1	0	0	0	0	1	0
Bates, Idaho Falls	2	4	.333	5.44	21	7	0	6	0	1	49.2	52	36	30	3	0	20	0	62	1
Baumann, Great Falls	7	3	.700	3.03	13	11	0	0	0	0	68.1	66	25	23	3	2	26	0	49	4
Berry, Billings	1	2	.333	4.84	19	0	0	5	0	2	35.1	40	22	19	2	2	23	0	38	11
Boone, Salt Lake City*	2	3	.400	5.40	20	0	0	9	0	4	28.1	34	22	17	1	1	13	3	26	1
Bourgeois, Idaho Falls	0	0	.000	9.39	4	0	0	2	0	0	7.2	10	9	8	1	0	10	0	7	2
Brakeley, Helena*	0	0	.000	4.91	6	6	0	0	0	0	18.1	17	11	10	2	0	15	0	23	2
Burley, Medicine Hat	3	4	.429	6.69	12	7	0	0	0	0	36.1	34	32	27	2	3	37	0	23	3
Burrows, Butte*	3	6	.333	4.02	14	11	1	1	0	0	62.2	56	35	28	1	0	35	0	64	6
Busha, Butte	2	1	.667	5.44	15	5	1	2	0	0	41.1	44	35	25	2	1	30	0	32	5
Cardona, Butte	6	3	.667	1.99	23	0	0	13	0	4	40.2	29	10	9	2	1	16	0	31	3
D. Carter, Butte	2	2	.500	6.15	26	0	0	13	0	4	45.1	65	45	31	3	4	23	4	27	7
E. Carter, Idaho Falls	2	1	.667	7.94	18	0	0	8	0	0	22.2	27	22	20	3	0	21	2	14	5
Casey, Gate City	0	0	.000	15.68	7	0	0	2	0	0	10.1	26	23	18	2	2	9	2	4	0
Chiyomaru, Gate City	0	0	.000	0.00	2	0	0	0	0	0	1.2	2	0	0	0	0	1	0	2	0

Pitcher—Club	W.	L.	Pct.	ERA.	G.	GS.	CG.	GF.	ShO.	Sv.	IP.	H.	R.	ER.	HR.	HB.	BB.	Int. BB.	SO.	WP.
Creamer, Idaho Falls*	0	0	.000	18.00	1	0	0	0	0	0	1.0	1	2	2	0	0	4	0	2	2
Dare, Idaho Falls*	3	6	.333	4.05	15	13	1	0	0	0	80.0	85	49	36	5	2	24	0	36	5
Darley, Medicine Hat	0	4	.000	4.71	9	8	0	0	0	0	28.2	29	24	15	2	3	26	0	13	5
Daspit, Great Falls	5	2	.714	4.06	14	9	0	1	0	0	51.0	45	26	23	0	5	30	0	40	1
Dease, Idaho Falls	4	2	.667	2.91	13	13	0	0	0	0	58.2	58	25	19	1	5	29	0	55	2
Dejarld, Great Falls	3	1	.750	1.64	22	0	0	11	0	4	49.1	35	10	9	1	1	20	1	56	2
Doty, Billings	1	1	.500	4.24	8	0	0	3	0	0	17.0	8	9	8	0	1	8	0	24	0
Dreyer, Butte	1	1	.500	4.54	8	8	0	0	0	0	35.2	32	21	18	2	0	10	0	29	1
Duey, Medicine Hat	4	6	.400	3.86	15	11	0	1	0	0	72.1	72	38	31	4	4	34	0	54	8
Duff, Billings*	2	2	.500	3.58	13	0	0	6	0	1	27.2	23	12	11	0	2	13	1	32	3
Edwards, Billings	0	1	.000	5.55	20	0	0	5	0	0	35.2	50	33	22	3	2	21	1	21	1
Emerick, Gate City	2	5	.286	5.37	12	12	0	0	0	0	52.0	62	38	31	4	1	20	0	42	14
Erickson, Butte*	0	0	.000	5.31	16	1	0	1	0	0	20.1	17	13	12	1	3	23	0	24	1
Espinoza, Gate City	1	2	.333	6.70	24	3	0	8	0	1	49.2	70	41	37	1	2	17	1	40	1
Ferry, Billings	2	5	.286	2.84	27	0	0	24	0	11	31.2	29	13	10	3	1	12	1	29	6
Fier, Gate City*	0	8	.000	6.51	13	13	0	0	0	0	55.1	64	48	40	4	1	32	1	43	9
Fletcher, Medicine Hat	0	0	.000	14.73	3	0	0	2	0	0	3.2	8	6	6	1	0	4	0	1	1
Foster, Gate City	1	7	.125	4.58	10	10	0	0	0	0	55.0	43	42	28	3	6	34	0	52	10
Frederiksen, Gate City	1	7	.125	5.43	20	5	0	10	0	3	56.1	78	48	34	2	3	30	4	37	8
Fry, Billings*	3	2	.600	6.00	22	0	0	12	0	1	21.0	23	16	14	1	2	22	1	19	8
Gabriele, Idaho Falls	1	1	.500	7.84	4	1	0	0	0	0	10.1	16	12	9	1	0	6	0	8	1
Garcia, Medicine Hat	3	5	.375	5.05	13	8	0	2	0	1	57.0	68	44	32	6	5	32	0	37	6
Gerstein, Salt Lake City*	0	1	.000	14.54	2	1	0	0	0	0	4.1	7	7	7	1	0	5	0	3	0
Gies, Butte	6	2	.750	3.77	15	14	5	0	0	0	88.1	86	40	37	7	1	27	0	64	3
Gilligan, Medicine Hat	1	6	.143	2.75	18	2	1	5	0	1	55.2	58	28	17	4	2	10	1	43	3
Goetz, Butte*	0	1	.000	1.59	4	0	0	2	0	1	5.2	2	1	1	0	1	3	0	2	0
Guggiana, Butte	0	0	.000	0.00	1	0	0	1	0	0	0.1	1	0	0	0	0	0	0	0	0
Hagy, Salt Lake City*	0	1	.000	4.91	16	1	0	11	0	0	29.1	32	20	16	3	1	9	0	20	4
Halliday, Idaho Falls*	1	0	1.000	7.43	15	1	0	5	0	0	13.1	22	13	11	3	1	11	0	10	3
Hamilton, Great Falls	4	2	.667	3.63	13	13	0	0	0	0	67.0	76	34	27	4	8	28	1	37	1
Hodges, Idaho Falls	4	3	.571	3.56	25	0	0	12	0	2	43.0	35	20	17	2	2	23	1	45	0
Hoog, Idaho Falls*	4	1	.800	3.86	29	0	0	7	0	5	42.0	47	19	18	1	2	21	0	38	0
Hooper, Helena	0	1	.000	4.22	5	5	0	0	0	0	21.1	29	12	10	2	0	8	0	15	3
Hotchkiss, Medicine Hat	1	2	.333	4.91	20	0	0	6	0	0	36.2	42	24	20	1	2	23	0	29	8
Hutto, Gate City	0	1	.000	7.49	26	0	0	7	0	0	45.2	78	50	38	4	2	20	2	24	10
Jacinto, Great Falls	0	0	.000	4.29	17	0	0	13	0	0	21.0	27	12	10	0	4	7	0	15	1
Jobes, Salt Lake City	1	1	.500	6.95	13	3	0	4	0	1	33.2	56	36	26	3	2	15	0	20	3
Jurado, Salt Lake City	3	1	.750	0.83	13	0	0	10	0	7	32.2	24	7	3	0	0	7	1	28	1
Keim, Billings*	0	0	.000	1.00	12	0	0	3	0	0	18.0	12	10	2	0	1	13	0	20	4
Kellogg, Helena	2	1	.667	2.17	15	2	0	8	0	2	37.1	35	12	9	1	1	18	1	36	2
Kerr, Great Falls*	1	1	.500	3.57	19	1	0	4	0	1	35.1	32	21	14	4	1	27	0	40	1
Kistaitis, Medicine Hat*	1	4	.200	4.50	12	10	0	0	0	0	52.0	44	37	26	4	3	29	0	54	4
Kooiman, Idaho Falls	0	1	.000	6.35	15	0	0	4	0	0	22.2	28	18	16	2	1	14	2	21	2
Langston, Idaho Falls	0	1	.000	3.09	5	1	0	1	0	0	11.2	10	6	4	0	2	5	0	5	1
Lemon, Idaho Falls	6	2	.750	4.46	11	11	2	0	1	0	70.2	78	38	35	3	1	17	1	36	2
Luebbers, Billings	5	4	.556	4.48	13	13	1	0	1	0	72.1	74	46	36	3	6	31	0	48	7
Mack, Idaho Falls	0	0	.000	2.25	2	0	0	1	0	0	4.0	3	1	1	0	1	2	0	4	1
Maema, Gate City*	1	8	.111	7.16	19	9	0	7	0	0	49.0	71	43	39	5	6	24	0	47	8
Margheim, Billings*	6	7	.462	5.55	14	14	1	0	0	0	73.0	86	53	45	4	0	33	0	45	6
P. Martinez, Great Falls	8	3	.727	3.62	14	14	0	0	0	0	77.0	74	39	31	5	8	40	1	82	6
W. Martinez, Gate City	2	7	.222	7.90	24	3	0	8	0	2	49.0	70	47	43	3	6	21	2	37	12
McDonald, Helena	3	2	.600	4.70	9	8	0	0	0	0	46.0	62	27	24	3	1	21	0	37	4
P. Miller, Helena	3	3	.500	3.75	8	8	2	0	1	0	48.0	55	24	20	2	0	9	0	42	1
S. Miller, Medicine Hat	0	0	.000	1.19	19	0	0	17	0	5	22.2	18	12	3	0	0	13	0	19	1
Ma. Mimbs, Great Falls*	7	4	.636	3.23	14	14	0	0	0	0	78.0	69	32	28	3	1	29	0	94	4
Mi. Mimbs, Great Falls*	0	0	.000	4.05	3	0	0	0	0	0	6.2	4	5	3	0	2	5	0	7	0
Mirabella, Salt Lake City	7	5	.583	3.93	14	14	2	0	0	0	89.1	98	47	39	3	5	34	0	90	8
Mizusawa, Gate City	2	3	.400	7.44	17	5	1	6	0	0	42.1	68	42	35	7	4	15	0	10	1
Mobley, Helena*	0	0	.000	15.00	6	0	0	3	0	0	9.0	19	15	15	2	0	2	0	8	0
Nettnin, Salt Lake City*	4	4	.500	3.23	13	12	3	0	0	0	75.1	75	38	27	1	3	29	0	47	3
Newman, Idaho Falls	1	3	.250	4.25	7	7	0	0	0	0	29.2	34	21	14	0	3	14	1	16	5
Nieves, Billings	2	0	1.000	4.20	20	0	0	5	0	1	40.2	48	27	19	4	2	18	0	22	7
O'Connor, Great Falls*	0	1	.000	8.10	1	1	0	0	0	0	3.1	7	4	3	0	0	4	0	4	0
Orman, Medicine Hat*	1	2	.333	8.42	19	0	0	7	0	1	25.2	39	28	24	7	1	16	0	24	4
Patterson, Butte	0	3	.000	6.35	13	3	0	2	0	1	28.1	36	23	20	3	1	14	1	18	3
Patton, Helena	7	1	.875	5.37	17	2	0	4	0	0	57.0	50	39	34	5	6	55	2	37	7
Perez, Medicine Hat	0	3	.000	10.74	11	4	0	4	0	0	31.0	47	44	37	5	3	15	0	21	6
Piotrowicz, Great Falls	2	1	.667	1.74	22	0	0	14	0	7	41.1	29	15	8	3	0	8	0	41	1
Pruitt, Helena	5	4	.556	5.60	13	13	1	0	0	0	72.1	102	54	45	8	4	16	0	52	5
Ramharter, Butte*	2	1	.667	6.52	22	0	0	9	0	1	19.1	24	19	14	1	2	15	0	19	1
Reese, Medicine Hat	1	0	1.000	6.48	17	0	0	10	0	0	25.0	31	19	18	2	0	26	0	19	8
Renko, Gate City	3	4	.429	3.92	11	10	2	0	0	0	59.2	56	32	26	4	2	23	1	68	6
Rizzo, Idaho Falls	1	1	.500	6.49	14	2	0	3	0	0	26.1	36	23	19	0	1	18	0	16	6
Robinson, Billings	4	3	.571	5.37	12	12	0	0	0	0	58.2	63	53	35	2	1	35	1	38	7
Rohrwild, Idaho Falls	1	0	1.000	2.65	24	0	0	17	0	10	37.1	26	12	11	1	0	23	3	43	2
Rupp, Helena	0	2	.000	3.70	13	0	0	5	0	1	24.1	30	15	10	3	0	11	2	18	6
Ryder, Idaho Falls	9	5	.643	4.29	14	14	1	0	0	0	77.2	81	50	37	2	5	39	0	59	1
Santiago, Gate City	0	0	.000	36.00	1	0	0	1	0	0	1.0	3	4	4	0	0	3	0	2	1
Sawaia, Salt Lake City	0	0	.000	40.50	2	0	0	1	0	0	1.1	7	6	6	1	0	0	0	1	0
Scheetz, Butte	1	2	.333	5.96	12	1	0	3	0	0	22.2	38	26	15	1	0	14	0	14	1
Simmerson, Gate City	0	0	.000	0.00	1	0	0	1	0	0	0.1	1	0	0	0	0	0	0	0	0
Smith, Butte*	2	0	1.000	3.65	5	5	0	0	0	0	24.2	23	10	10	3	2	6	0	27	3
Souza, Butte	3	4	.429	5.36	19	4	0	14	0	4	45.1	50	30	27	6	0	29	5	39	2
Spoljaric, Medicine Hat*	3	7	.300	4.34	15	13	0	2	0	1	66.1	57	43	32	6	0	35	0	62	3
St. Pe, Butte	3	0	1.000	11.30	15	1	0	3	0	0	28.2	57	48	36	3	3	15	0	24	2
Steinkamp, Salt Lake City	6	4	.600	4.54	13	12	0	0	0	0	69.1	89	46	35	5	4	19	0	29	12
Stephens, Helena*	3	2	.600	3.48	14	5	1	6	0	1	44.0	40	20	17	3	0	16	0	41	1
Stewart, Billings	3	4	.429	4.15	14	14	0	0	0	0	73.2	51	41	34	4	5	47	0	64	15
Stryker, Great Falls	2	1	.667	4.39	21	1	0	7	0	1	41.0	46	20	20	1	2	13	0	31	2
Surico, Butte*	0	1	.000	6.75	7	0	0	2	0	0	10.2	6	13	8	1	2	14	0	9	2
Sweet, Salt Lake City*	1	0	1.000	3.38	4	0	0	1	0	0	8.0	6	3	3	0	1	5	0	4	1
Tatar, Billings	3	3	.500	4.64	13	13	0	0	0	0	73.2	82	45	38	3	5	17	0	48	5
Tipton, Great Falls	6	1	.857	1.50	24	0	0	18	0	7	48.0	35	10	8	1	2	17	1	43	1

Pitcher—Club	W.	L.	Pct.	ERA.	G.	GS.	CG.	GF.	ShO.	Sv.	IP.	H.	R.	ER.	HR.	HB.	BB.	Int. BB.	SO.	WP.
Walden, Great Falls*	3	0	1.000	0.42	4	4	0	0	0	0	21.2	9	4	1	0	0	11	0	20	4
Washington, Butte	7	2	.778	4.82	13	13	1	0	0	0	65.1	79	38	35	3	2	24	0	45	6
Watson, Butte	0	0	.000	24.30	4	0	0	1	0	0	3.1	6	9	9	1	0	5	0	1	1
Wells, Butte	0	3	.000	3.05	16	0	0	14	0	6	20.2	21	10	7	0	0	6	1	13	1
White, Salt Lake City	1	1	.500	5.45	18	1	0	11	0	6	36.1	47	28	22	2	3	13	0	35	7
Whiteside, Butte	4	4	.500	3.45	18	5	0	5	0	2	57.1	57	33	22	4	9	25	0	45	4
Whitworth, Salt Lake City	7	2	.778	3.32	13	12	1	1	0	1	76.0	77	31	28	2	3	32	0	54	5
Wilburn, 7 G.C.-1 Bill.	0	1	.000	3.52	8	0	0	3	0	1	15.1	12	6	6	0	3	7	0	15	4
Wilcox, Medicine Hat	2	2	.500	4.21	13	1	0	4	0	0	36.1	39	22	17	3	4	27	0	49	3
Wilson, Helena	2	0	1.000	2.93	13	0	0	5	0	1	30.2	32	12	10	2	0	7	0	19	3
Zimbauer, Helena	3	6	.333	3.67	12	12	0	0	0	0	73.2	70	38	30	6	4	27	1	64	0

BALKS—Tatar, 7; Pruitt, Whiteside, 6 each; Dease, Hagy, 5 each; Boone, Burley, Edwards, Ryder, 4 each; Hotchkiss, Ma. Mimbs, Mirabella, Newman, Spoljaric, Steinkamp, Washington, 3 each; Berry, Burrows, Ferry, Garcia, Hodges, Jobes, Maema, W. Martinez, Orman, 2 each; Adams, Ambos, Archer, Baumann, Brakeley, D. Carter, E. Carter, Casey, Dare, Fry, Gies, Hutto, Jacinto, Jurado, Kellogg, Kistaitis, Kooiman, Langston, Lemon, Luebbers, P. Martinez, S. Miller, Mi. Mimbs, Mizusawa, Nieves, Patterson, Perez, Piotrowicz, Reese, Renko, Rizzo, Rohrwild, Smith, Surico, Tipton, Whitworth, 1 each.

COMBINATION SHUTOUTS—Robinson-Duff-Ferry, Billings; Gies-Cardona-Patterson-Wells, Butte; Hamilton-Jacinto, Hamilton-Kerr, Mimbs-Dejarld, Walden-Baumann-Piotrowicz, Great Falls; Miller-Archer, Helena; Dare-Hodges-Rohrwild, Dease-Rohrwild, Newman-Hodges-Hoog-Rohrwild, Ryder-Hoog, Idaho Falls; Duey-Orman-Miller, Garcia-Miller, Medicine Hat; Ambos-White, Whitworth-Alexander, Salt Lake City.

NO-HIT GAME—Ryder, Idaho Falls, defeated Medicine Hat, 2-1, August 5.

Index to Minor League Clubs, Cities

1991 N.L. EAST DIVISION SLATE . . .

EAST

1991	AT CHICAGO	AT MONTREAL	AT NEW YORK	AT PHILADELPHIA	AT PITTSBURGH	AT ST. LOUIS
CHICAGO........		May 31* June 1*, **2** Aug. 19*, 20*, 21* Sept. 20*, 21*, **22**	May 21*, 22*, 23* Aug. 2*, 3*, **4**, 5* Sept. 18*, 19*	May 17*, 18*, **19*** Aug. 6*, 7*, 8 Sept. 30* Oct. 1*, 2*	April 18*, 19*, 20*, **21** June 25*, 26*, 27* Sept. 16*, 17*	April 22*, 23*, 24* July 5*, 6*, **7*** Sept. 27*, 28, **29**
MONTREAL	May 24, 25, **26** Aug. 13*, 14, 15 Sept. 13, 14, **15**		April 11*, 12*, 13, **14** June 25*, 26*, 27 Sept. 9*, 10	May 27*, 28*, **29*** Aug. 9*, 10*, **11**, 12* Sept. 11*, 12*	April 8*, 9*, 10 July 5*, 6*, **7** Oct. 4*, 5*, **6**	April 26*, 27*, **28** Aug. 6*, 7*, 8* Sept. 23*, 24*, 25*
NEW YORK	May 27, 28*, 29 Aug. 9, 10, **11***, 12 Sept. 11, 12	April 19*, 20, **21*** July 1, 2*, 3*, **4** Sept. 16*, 17*		April 23*, 24*, 25* July 5*, 6*, **7** Oct. 4*, 5, **6**	April 15*, 16*, 17* Aug. 16*, 17*, **18** Sept. 30* Oct. 1*, 2*	May 31* June 1*, **2** Aug. 13*, 14*, 15* Sept. 13*, 14*, **15**
PHILADELPHIA	April 15*, 16, 17 Aug. 16, 17, **18** Sept. 23*, 24*, 25	May 21*, 22*, 23 Aug. 1*, 2*, 3*, **4** Sept. 18*, 19*	April 8, 9, 10* June 28*, 29*, **30** Sept. 27*, 28, **29**		May 24*, 25*, **26** Aug. 13*, 14*, 15* Sept. 20*, 21*, **22**	April 18*, 19*, 20*, **21** June 25*, 26*, 27* Sept. 9*, 10*
PITTSBURGH..	April 12, 13, **14** July 1*, 2, 3, 4 Sept. 9, 10*	April 23*, 24*, 25* June 28*, 29*, **30** Sept. 27*, 28*, **29**	April 26*, 27, **28** Aug. 6*, 7*, 8 Sept. 24*, 25*, 26*	May 31* June 1*, **2** Aug. 20*, 21*, 22 Sept. 13*, 14*, **15**		May 27*, 28*, **29*** Aug. 1*, 2*, 3*, **4** Sept. 11*, 12*
ST. LOUIS	April 9, 10, 11 June 28, 29, **30** Oct. 4, 5, **6**	April 15, 16*, 17* Aug. 16*, 17*, **18** Sept. 30* Oct. 1*, 2*	May 24*, 25, **26** Aug. 20*, 21*, 22* Sept. 20*, 21, **22**	April 12*, 13, **14** July 1*, 2*, 3*, 4* Sept. 16*, 17*	May 21*, 22*, 23* Aug. 9*, 10*, **11**, 12* Sept. 18*, 19*	
ATLANTA.......	May 13*, 14*, 15 July 26, 27, **28**	June 14*, 15*, **16** Sept. 2, 3*, 4*	June 11*, 12*, 13* Sept. 6*, 7, **8**	June 17*, 18*, 19 Aug. 30*, 31* Sept. 1	May 10*, 11*, **12** July 22*, 23*, 24*	April 29*, 30* May 1 July 19*, 20*, **21**
CINCINNATI ...	May 10, 11, **12** July 23*, 24, 25	June 11*, 12*, 13* Sept. 6*, 7*, **8**	June 17*, 18*, 19* Aug. 23*, 24, **25***	June 14*, 15*, **16** Sept. 2*, 3*, 4*	May 6*, 7*, 8* July 19*, 20*, **21***	May 13*, 14*, 15 July 26*, 27*, **28**
HOUSTON.......	April 30* May 1 July 11*, 12, 13, **14**	June 17*, 18*, 19* Aug. 30*, 31* Sept. 1	June 14*, 15*, **16** Sept. 2, 3*, 4*	June 20*, 21*, 22*, **23** Aug. 28*, 29*	May 3*, 4*, **5** July 15*, 16*, 17*	May 17*, 18*, **19** July 22*, 23*, 24*
LOS ANGELES	June 7, 8, **9**, 10* Aug. 26*, 27	April 30* May 1* July 11*, 12*, 13*, **14**	May 7*, 8* July 18*, 19*, 20, **21**	May 3*, 4*, **5** July 15*, 16*, 17	June 11*, 12*, 13 Sept. 6*, 7*, **8**	June 4*, 5*, 6* Aug. 23*, 24*, **25**
SAN DIEGO.....	June 4*, 5, 6 Aug. 23, 24, **25**	May 3*, 4, **5** July 15*, 16*, 17*	April 30* May 1* July 11*, 12*, 13*, **14**	April 26*, 27*, **28**, 29* July 30*, 31*	June 7*, 8*, **9**, 10* Aug. 26*, 27	June 21*, 22*, **23**, 24* Aug. 28*, 29*
SAN FRAN......	June 11, 12, 13 Sept. 6, 7, **8**	May 6*, 7*, **8*** July 19*, 20*, **21**	May 3*, 4, **5** July 15*, 16*, 17	April 30* May 1* July 11*, 12*, 13*, **14**	June 4*, 5*, 6* Aug. 23*, 24*, **25**	June 7*, 8*, **9**, 10 Aug. 26*, 27*
1991	81 HOME DATES 16 NIGHTS	81 HOME DATES 63 NIGHTS	81 HOME DATES 53 NIGHTS	81 HOME DATES 63 NIGHTS	81 HOME DATES 66 NIGHTS	81 HOME DATES 62 NIGHTS

*NIGHT GAME
NIGHT GAME: Any game starting after 5:00 p.m.
HEAVY BLACK FIGURES DENOTE SUNDAY

AND COMPLETE WEST SCHEDULES

1991	WEST					
	AT ATLANTA	AT CINCINNATI	AT HOUSTON	AT LOS ANGELES	AT SAN DIEGO	AT SAN FRANCISCO
CHICAGO........	May 3*, 4*, **5** July 15*, 16*, 17*	April 25*, 26*, 27, **28** July 30*, 31*	May 6*, 7*, 8* July 19*, 20*, **21**	June 17*, 18*, 19* Aug. 30*, 31* Sept. **1**	June 14*, 15, **16** Sept. 2*, 3*, 4*	June 20*, 21*, 22, **23** Aug. 28*, 29
MONTREAL	June 7*, 8*, **9**, 10* Aug. 26*, 27*	June 20*, 21*, 22*, **23** Aug. 28*, 29*	June 4*, 5*, 6* Aug. 23*, 24*, **25**	May 13*, 14*, 15* July 26*, 27*, **28**	May 10*, 11*, **12** July 23*, 24*, 25	May 16*, 17*, 18, **19** July 29*, 30
NEW YORK	June 20*, 21*, 22*, **23** Aug. 28*, 29*	June 4*, 5*, 6* Aug. 30*, 31* Sept. **1**	June 7*, 8*, **9**, 10* Aug. 26*, 27*	May 17*, 18, **19** July 29*, 30*, 31*	May 13*, 14*, 15 July 26*, 27*, **28**	May 10*, 11, **12** July 23*, 24*, 25
PHILADELPHIA	June 4*, 5*, 6* Aug. 23*, 24*, **25**	June 7*, 8*, **9**, 10 Aug. 26*, 27*	June 11*, 12*, 13 Sept. 6*, 7*, **8**	May 10*, 11*, **12** July 23*, 24*, 25*	May 7*, 8*, 9 July 19*, 20*, **21**	May 13*, 14*, 15 July 26*, 27, **28**
PITTSBURGH..	May 17*, 18*, **19** July 29*, 30*, 31*	April 30* May 1* July 11*, 12*, 13*, **14**	May 14*, 15*, 16* July 26*, 27*, **28**	June 20*, 21*, 22, **23** Aug. 28*, 29*	June 17*, 18*, 19* Aug. 30*, 31* Sept. 1*	June 14*, 15, **16*** Sept. 2, 3*, 4
ST. LOUIS	May 7*, 8* July 11*, 12*, 13*, **14**	May 3*, 4*, **5** July 15*, 16*, 17*	May 10*, 11*, **12*** July 29*, 30*, 31*	June 14*, 15*, **16** Sept. 2*, 3*, 4*	June 11*, 12*, 13 Sept. 5, 6*, 7*	June 17*, 18*, 19 Aug. 30*, 31 Sept. 1
ATLANTA.......		April 12*, 13, **14** Aug. 20*, 21*, 22* Sept. 30* Oct. 1*, 2*	April 26*, 27*, **28** June 25*, 26*, 27* Sept. 27*, 28*, **29**	April 22*, 23*, 24* July 5*, 6*, **7** Sept. 20*, 21*, **22**	May 27*, 28*, 29* Aug. 15, 16*, 17*, **18** Sept. 18*, 19*	May 30*, 31* June 1, **2** Aug. 12*, 13*, 14 Sept. 16*, 17*
CINCINNATI ...	April 19*, 20*, **21** July 2*, 3*, 4* Sept. 24*, 25*, 26*		April 22*, 23*, 24* July 5*, 6*, **7** Sept. 20*, 21*, **22**	May 30*, 31* June 1*, **2** Aug. 12*, 13*, 14* Sept. 16*, 17*	April 15*, 16*, 17* Aug. 9*, 10*, **11** Oct. 4*, 5*, **6**	May 27*, 28*, 29 Aug. 15*, 16*, 17, **18** Sept. 18*, 19
HOUSTON.......	April 15*, 16*, 17* Aug. 9*, 10*, **11** Oct. 4*, 5*, **6**	April 8*, 10*, 11* June 28*, 29*, **30** Sept. 13*, 14*, **15**		May 27*, 28*, 29* Aug. 15*, 16*, 17*, **18** Sept. 18*, 19	May 30, 31* June 1*, **2** Aug. 12*, 13*, 14* Sept. 16*, 17*	April 19*, 20, **21** July 2*, 3*, 4* Sept. 30* Oct. 1*, 2
LOS ANGELES	April 9*, 10*, 11 June 28*, 29*, **30*** Sept. 13*, 14*, **15**	May 24*, 25, **26** Aug. 5*, 6*, 7*, 8 Sept. 9*, 10*	May 20*, 21*, 22*, 23* Aug. 2*, 3*, **4** Sept. 11*, 12*		April 18, 19*, 20*, **21** July 2*, 3*, 4* Sept. 24*, 25*	April 15*, 16*, 17 Aug. 9*, 10, **11** Oct. 4*, 5, **6**
SAN DIEGO.....	May 20*, 21*, 22*, 23* Aug. 2*, 3*, **4** Sept. 11*, 12*	May 17*, 18*, **19** June 25*, 26*, 27 Sept. 27*, 28*, **29**	May 24*, 25*, **26** Aug. 5*, 6*, 7*, 8* Sept. 9*, 10*	April 12, 13*, **14** Aug. 19*, 20*, 21 Sept. 30* Oct.1*, 2*		April 22*, 23*, 24 July 5*, 6, **7** Sept. 13*, 14, **15**
SAN FRAN......	May 24*, 25*, **26** Aug. 5*, 6*, 7*, 8* Sept. 9*, 10*	May 21*, 22*, 23* Aug. 1*, 2*, 3*, **4*** Sept. 11*, 12	April 12*, 13*, **14** Aug. 20*, 21*, 22 Sept. 23*, 24*, 25*	April 25*, 26*, 27*, **28** Aug. 25*, 26* Sept. 27*, 28, **29***	April 9*, 10*, 11 June 28*, 29*, **30** Sept. 20*, 21, **22**	
1991	81 HOME DATES 68 NIGHTS	81 HOME DATES 61 NIGHTS	81 HOME DATES 67 NIGHTS	81 HOME DATES 63 NIGHTS	81 HOME DATES 59 NIGHTS	81 HOME DATES 43 NIGHTS

JULY 9—ALL-STAR GAME AT SKYDOME IN TORONTO
JULY 22—HALL OF FAME GAME AT COOPERSTOWN, N.Y. (Minnesota Twins vs. San Francisco Giants)

1991 A.L. EAST DIVISION SLATE . . .

1991	EAST						
	AT MILWAUKEE	AT DETROIT	AT CLEVELAND	AT TORONTO	AT BALTIMORE	AT NEW YORK	AT BOSTON
MILWAUKEE...		June 25*, 26*, 27* Sept. 20*, 21*, 22	July 4*, 5*, 6*, 7 Oct. 1*, 2*, 3*	April 11*, 12*, 13, 14 Aug. 20*, 21*, 22*	April 26*, 27*, 28 Aug. 5*, 6*, 7*, 8*	May 31* June 1, 2 Sept. 16*, 17*, 18*	May 20*, 21*, 22* Oct. 4*, 5, 6
DETROIT.........	May 27, 28*, 29 Sept. 12*, 13*, 14*, 15		May 31* June 1, 2, 3* Sept. 17*, 18*	April 25*, 26*, 27, 28 Aug. 6*, 7*, 8*	July 1*, 2*, 3* Oct. 4*, 5, 6	April 22*, 23*, 24* Aug. 9*, 10*, 11	July 4*, 5*, 6, 7 Oct. 1*, 2*, 3*
CLEVELAND ...	May 23*, 24*, 25, 26* Sept. 10*, 11*	June 28*, 29, 30 Sept. 23*, 24*, 25*, 26*		June 21*, 22, 23, 24 July 31* Aug. 1	May 27*, 28*, 29* Sept. 12*, 13*, 14*, 15	July 1*, 2*, 3* Oct. 4*, 5, 6	April 11 13, 14, 15 Aug. 19*, 20*, 21*
TORONTO	April 19*, 20, 21 Aug. 13*, 14*, 15	April 15*, 16*, 17 Aug. 16*, 17*, 18	June 11*, 12*, 13* Sept. 5*, 6*, 7, 8		June 6*, 7*, 8*, 9* Aug. 26*, 27*, 28*	June 3*, 4*, 5* Aug. 29*, 30*, 31 Sept. 1	April 22*, 23*, 24* Aug. 2, 3, 4
BALTIMORE....	April 15, 17*, 18 Aug. 16*, 17*, 18	May 20*, 21*, 22* Sept. 27*, 28, 29, 30	June 25*, 26*, 27* Sept. 20*, 21, 22	June 14*, 15, 16 Sept. 2, 3*, 4*		July 4, 5*, 6, 7 Oct. 1*, 2*, 3*	May 30*, 31* June 1, 2 Sept. 16*, 17*, 18*
NEW YORK	June 28*, 29*, 30 Sept. 23*, 24*, 25*, 26*	April 8, 10, 11 Aug. 2*, 3*, 4, 5*	May 20*, 21*, 22* Sept. 27*, 28*, 29, 30*	June 18*, 19*, 20* Aug. 23*, 24, 25	May 24*, 25*, 26 Sept. 9*, 10*, 11*		June 25*, 26*, 27* Sept. 20*, 21, 22
BOSTON	July 1*, 2*, 3* Sept. 27, 28, 29, 30*	May 23*, 24*, 25, 26 Sept. 10*, 11*	April 19*, 20, 21 Aug. 13*, 14*, 15*	April 8, 9*, 10* Aug. 9*, 10, 11, 12*	June 28*, 29, 30 Sept. 23*, 24*, 25*	May 27*, 28*, 29* Sept. 12*, 13*, 14, 15*	
SEATTLE........	June 20*, 21*, 22*, 23 July 17*, 18	June 4*, 5*, 6 Aug. 23*, 24, 25	May 14*, 15*, 16* July 26*, 27, 28	June 28*, 29, 30 July 1 Sept. 10*, 11*	April 29*, 30* May 1* July 19*, 20*, 21	May 17*, 18, 19 July 23*, 24*, 25	June 18*, 19* Sept. 5*, 6*, 7, 8
OAKLAND	June 14*, 15*, 16, 17* Sept. 3*, 4*	June 18*, 19* Sept. 5*, 6*, 7*, 8	May 17*, 18 19 July 23*, 24*, 25*	May 28*, 29*, 30* Sept. 13*, 14, 15	May 14*, 15*, 16* July 26*, 27*, 28	May 10*, 11, 12, 13* July 29*, 30*	June 20*, 21*, 22, 23 July 31* Aug. 1*
CALIFORNIA...	June 18*, 19 Aug. 30*, 31* Sept. 1, 2	June 20*, 21*, 22*, 23* July 31* Aug. 1	May 10*, 11, 12, 13* July 29*, 30*	May 31* June 1, 2 Sept. 30* Oct. 1*, 2*	May 17*, 18*, 19 July 23*, 24*, 25*	May 14*, 15*, 16* July 26*, 27, 28	June 14*, 15, 16, 17* Sept. 3*, 4*
TEXAS	April 23*, 24*, 25 Aug. 2*, 3*, 4	May 3*, 4*, 5 July 15*, 16*, 17	April 16, 18* Aug. 16(Tn), 17*, 18	May 7*, 8* July 11*, 12*, 13, 14*	April 19*, 20, 21 Aug. 13*, 14*, 15*	June 7*, 8*, 9 Aug. 26*, 27*, 28*	May 9*, 10*, 11, 12 July 29*, 30
KANSAS CITY	May 10*, 11*, 12 July 30*, 31* Aug. 1	May 7*, 8 July 11*, 12*, 13, 14	April 22*, 23*, 24* Aug. 2*, 3*, 4	May 13*, 14*, 15* July 26*, 27, 28	June 11*, 12*, 13* Sept. 6*, 7*, 8	April 19*, 20, 21 Aug. 13*, 14*, 15	April 16, 17, 18 Aug. 16*, 17, 18
MINNESOTA...	May 2*, 3*, 4, 5 July 15*, 16*	May 17*, 18, 19 July 23*, 24*, 25*	June 14*, 15*, 16 Aug. 26*, 27*, 28*	July 2*, 3*, 4 Sept. 27, 28, 29	June 17*, 18*, 19 Aug. 23*, 24, 25	June 21*, 22*, 23, 24* July 31* Aug. 1	May 7*, 8* July 18*, 19*, 20, 21
CHICAGO........	April 30* May 1 July 11*, 12*, 13*, 14	April 12*, 13, 14 Aug. 13*, 14*, 15*	June 4*, 5*, 6* Aug. 23*, 24, 25*	May 9*, 10*, 11, 12 July 29*, 30*	April 8 10* Aug. 9*, 10*, 11, 12*	April 15*, 16*, 17 Aug. 16*, 17*, 18	May 13*, 14*, 15* July 26*, 27, 28
1991	81 HOME DATES 54 NIGHTS	81 HOME DATES 55 NIGHTS	80 HOME DATES 61 NIGHTS	81 HOME DATES 50 NIGHTS	81 HOME DATES 62 NIGHTS	81 HOME DATES 53 NIGHTS	81 HOME DATES 50 NIGHTS

*NIGHT GAME
NIGHT GAME: Any game starting after 5:00 p.m.
HEAVY BLACK FIGURES DENOTE SUNDAY

AND COMPLETE WEST SCHEDULES

WEST

1991	AT SEATTLE	AT OAKLAND	AT CALIFORNIA	AT TEXAS	AT KANSAS CITY	AT MINNESOTA	AT CHICAGO
MILWAUKEE...	June 7*, 8*, **9** Aug. 26*, 27*, 28*	June 4*, 5*, 6 Aug. 23*, 24, **25**	June 10*, 11*, 12 Sept. 6*, 7*, **8**	April 8*, 10* Aug. 9*, 10*, **11**, 12*	May 17*, 18*, **19** July 23*, 24*, 25*	May 14*, 15*, 16 July 26*, 27*, **28**	May 7*, 8* July 19*, 20*, **21**, 22*
DETROIT.........	June 13*, 14*, 15*, **16** Sept. 2, 3*	June 10*, 11*, 12 Aug. 30*, 31 Sept. 1	June 7*, 8*, **9** Aug. 26*, 27*, 28	May 13*, 14*, 15* July 26*, 27*, **28***	April 29*, 30* May 1* July 19*, 20, **21**	May 9*, 10*, 11*, **12** July 29*, 30	April 18, 20, **21** Aug. 19*, 20*, 21*
CLEVELAND ...	May 7*, 8* July 11*, 12*, 13*, **14**	May 3*, 4, **5** July 15*, 16*, 17	April 30* May 1* July 18*, 19*, 20*, **21**	April 26*, 27*, **28** Aug. 5*, 6*, 7*	April 8, 9*, 10 Aug. 9*, 10*, **11**	June 7*, 8*, **9**, 10* Sept. 2, 4*	June 18*, 19* Aug. 29*, 30*, 31* Sept. **1**
TORONTO	July 5*, 6*, **7** Sept. 16*, 17*, 18*	May 20*, 21*, 22 Sept. 20*, 21, **22**	May 24*, 25, **26** Sept. 23*, 24*, 25	April 30* May 1* July 18*, 19*, 20*, **21***	May 2*, 3*, 4*, **5** July 15*, 16*	June 25*, 26*, 27 Oct. 4*, 5*, **6**	May 17*, 18*, **19** July 23*, 24*, 25
BALTIMORE....	May 10*, 11*, **12*** July 29*, 30*, 31*	May 7*, 8 July 11*, 12*, 13, **14**	May 3*, 4*, **5**, 6* July 15*, 16*	April 12*, 13*, **14** Aug. 19*, 20*, 21*	June 20*, 21*, 22*, **23** July 17*, 18*	June 3*, 4*, 5* Aug. 30*, 31* Sept. **1**	April 22*, 23*, 24* Aug. 2*, 3*, **4**
NEW YORK	May 3*, 4*, **5**, 6* July 15*, 16	April 30* May 1 July 18*, 19*, 20*, **21**	May 7*, 8* July 11*, 12*, 13*, **14**	June 14*, 15*, **16*** Sept. 2, 3*, 4*	April 12*, 13, **14** Aug. 19*, 20*, 21*	June 11*, 12*, 13* Sept. 6*, 7*, **8**	April 26*, 27*, **28** Aug. 6*, 7*, 8
BOSTON	June 10*, 11*, 12 Aug. 30*, 31* Sept. **1**	June 7*, 8, **9** Aug. 26*, 27*, 28	June 4*, 5*, 6* Aug. 23*, 24*, **25**	May 17*, 18*, **19** July 22*, 23*, 24*	April 26*, 27, **28*** Aug. 5*, 6*, 7*	April 30* May 1* July 11*, 12*, 13*, **14**	May 3*, 4*, **5** July 15*, 16*, 17*
SEATTLE........		April 12*, 13, **14** August 5*, 6*, 7	April 22*, 23*, 24 Aug. 2*, 3*, **4**	May 30*, 31* June 1*, **2*** Sept. 30* Oct. 1*, 2*	May 20*, 21*, 22* Sept. 13*, 14*, **15**	April 25*, 26*, 27, **28** Aug. 20*, 21*, 22	June 24*, 25*, 26*, 27 Sept. 27*, 28*, **29**
OAKLAND	April 19*, 20*, **21** Aug. 12*, 13*, 14*, 15		April 15*, 16*, 17*, 18* Aug. 9*, 10*, **11**	July 2*, 3*, 4* Oct. 4*, 5*, **6**	July 5*, 6*, **7** Sept. 30* Oct. 1*, 2*	April 22*, 23*, 24 Aug. 16*, 17*, **18*** , 19*	May 31* June 1*, **2***, 3* Sept. 17*, 18*
CALIFORNIA ...	April 9*, 10*, 11 Aug. 16*, 17*, **18**, 19*	April 26*, 27*, **28** Aug. 20*, 21*, 22		July 5*, 6*, **7*** Sept. 17*, 18*, 19*	June 24*, 25*, 26* Sept. 26*, 27*, 28*, **29**	April 12*, 13*, **14** Aug. 12*, 13*, 14*, 15*	May 28*, 29*, 30 Sept. 20*, 21*, **22**
TEXAS	May 24*, 25*, **26** Sept. 23*, 24*, 25	June 25*, 26*, 27 Sept. 26*, 27*, 28, **29**	June 28*, 29*, **30** July 1* Sept. 9*, 10*, 11*		June 4*, 5*, 6 Aug. 22*, 23*, 24*, **25**	May 21*, 22*, 23 Sept. 20*, 21*, **22**	June 20*, 21*, 22*, **23** July 31* Aug. 1*
KANSAS CITY	May 27*, 28*, 29 Sept. 19*, 20*, 21*, **22**	June 28*, 29, **30** July 1* Sept. 23*, 24*, 25	July 2*, 3*, 4* Oct. 4*, 5*, **6**	June 17*, 18*, 19* Aug. 30*, 31* Sept. **1**		May 24*, 25*, **26** Sept. 16*, 17*, 18	June 14*, 15*, **16** Sept. 2*, 3*, 4*, 5
MINNESOTA ...	April 15*, 16*, 17* Aug. 9*, 10*, **11**	April 9*, 10*, 11 Aug. 2*, 3, **4**	April 19*, 20*, **21** Aug. 5*, 6*, 7	May 27*, 28*, 29* Sept. 12*, 13*, 14*, **15**	May 30*, 31* June 1*, **2** Sept. 9*, 10*, 11*		July 5*, 6*, **7** Sept. 30* Oct. 1*, 2*, 3
CHICAGO.........	July 2*, 3*, 4 Oct. 4*, 5*, **6**	May 23*, 24*, 25, **26** Sept. 9*, 10*, 11	May 20*, 21*, 22* Sept. 12*, 13*, 14, **15**	June 10*, 11*, 12*, 13* Sept. 6*, 7*, **8**	June 7*, 8*, **9** Aug. 26*, 27*, 28*	June 28*, 29*, **30** July 1* Sept. 24*, 25*	
1991	81 HOME DATES 59 NIGHTS	81 HOME DATES 42 NIGHTS	81 HOME DATES 61 NIGHTS	81 HOME DATES 73 NIGHTS	81 HOME DATES 63 NIGHTS	81 HOME DATES 60 NIGHTS	81 HOME DATES 60 NIGHTS

JULY 9—ALL-STAR GAME AT SKYDOME IN TORONTO
JULY 22—HALL OF FAME GAME AT COOPERSTOWN, N.Y. (Minnesota Twins vs. San Francisco Giants)

Index to Contents

AMERICAN LEAGUE

NATIONAL LEAGUE

1990 Game Scores

1990 Game Scores

NATIONAL ASSOCIATION (MINOR LEAGUE) AVERAGES